Directory of
Publishing Opportunities

Bibliographical reference works
published by Marquis Academic Media

Annual Register of Grant Support
Consumer Protection Directory
Directory of Registered Federal and State Lobbyists
Environmental Protection Directory
NASA Factbook
NSF Factbook
Standard Education Almanac
Yearbook of Adult and Continuing Education
Yearbook of Equal Educational Opportunity
Yearbook of Higher Education
Yearbook of Special Education
Worldwide Directory of Computer Companies
Worldwide Directory of Federal Libraries

Directory of Publishing Opportunities

Third edition

Marquis Academic Media
Marquis Who's Who, Inc.
200 East Ohio Street
Chicago, Illinois 60611

Copyright 1975 by Marquis Who's Who, Incorporated. All rights reserved.
No part of this publication may be reproduced, stored in a retrieval system,
or transmitted, in any form or by any means, electronic, mechanical,
photocopying, recording, or otherwise, without the prior written permission
of the publisher, except in a magazine or newspaper article referring
to a specific entry.

Library of Congress Card Number 75-12146
International Standard Book Number 0-8379-2301-8

Distributed in the United Kingdom by
George Prior Associated Publishers
Rugby Chambers, 2 Rugby Street
London WC1N 3QU

Manufactured in the United States of America

Contents

Introduction : ix

Key to information : x

Key to abbreviations : xii

General : 3

Humanities : 23
Humanities (general) : 25
Creative and performing arts : 40
Language and linguistics : 59
Library : 74
Literature : 94
Philosophy : 127
Poetry and contemporary literature : 135
Religion and theology : 149

Interdisciplinary and area studies : 173
Interdisciplinary : 175
African studies : 181
Asian and Pacific studies : 183
European studies : 186
Latin American studies : 191
Middle Eastern studies : 193
North American studies : 195

Social sciences : 201
Social sciences (general) : 203
Accounting : 212
Business and economics : 215
Finance and banking : 234
Labor : 237
Management and personnel : 240
Public relations and advertising : 244

Communications : 247
Communications (general) : 249
Audio-visual : 253
Film : 254
Journalism : 257
Radio and television : 259
Speech : 262

Education : 265

Geography : 323

History : 329

Law and public administration : 353

Military : 389

Political science : 395

Psychology and mental health : 407

Social welfare : 445

Sociology and anthropology : 459

Women's studies : 475

Science and technology : 481
Science and technology (general) : 483
Archaeology : 495
Architecture : 497

Earth sciences : 501
Earth sciences (general) : 503
Geology : 509
Mining and mineralogy : 512
Marine sciences : 515

Engineering and allied sciences : 519

Environment and conservation : 551

Life sciences : 571
Life sciences (general) : 573
Agrology and agriculture : 576
Biology : 580
Botany and horticulture : 595
Zoology : 603

Physical sciences : 617
Physical sciences (general) : 619
Aeronautics and astronautics : 626
Astronomy : 629
Chemistry : 631
Physics : 649
Nuclear sciences : 661

Mathematics : 665
Mathematics (general) : 667
Computer sciences : 677

Medicine and medical sciences : 685
Medicine (general) : 687
Dentistry : 752
Nursing : 758
Surgery : 762
Veterinary : 764

Trades, manufacturing and industry : 769

Indexes : 793
Periodical index : 795
Subject index : 814
Publisher and sponsoring organization index : 824
Editorial staff index : 836

Introduction

Academic and professional journals expand constantly in number and topic. This proliferation, combined with the pressure to communicate rapidly in a continually changing and growing professional environment, requires of writers a knowledge of current publishing opportunities available to them. In an attempt to serve this need, the third edition of the *Directory of Publishing Opportunities* includes more than 2,600 specialized and professional journals, about 800 of which appear for the first time with this edition. Indexes of professional journals, new serials listings, bibliographies of specialized publications, and many other sources have yielded titles for inclusion, some familiar, many issued for the first time within the last year.

The third edition of the *Directory* has been completely reorganized to expedite the user's search for his own specialty. Entries have been arranged alphabetically within sixty-nine specific fields of interest. Institutional or professional "Proceedings" and "Journals" are filed by organization name. Only those periodicals are included that represent real publishing opportunities and accept submissions in English; exceptions are a few French-Canadian journals published entirely in French. Not listed are abstracting service publications, periodicals that are direct translations from a foreign journal, or periodicals prepared by an in-house staff. General interest publications have been avoided. Listed are those with special interests aimed at a limited section of the public, trade journals, professional magazines, technical journals, and publications produced by business firms, unions, or associations.

Editors or publishers of these journals completed data questionnaires requesting such relevant information as manuscript requirements, author payment, and copyright data, as well as an editorial description of the journal, languages of publication, and circulation. Nearly forty categories of information may be contained in each entry, depending both on the character of the periodical and the data supplied by the editor or publisher. An explanation of each together with pertinent related data is contained in the Key to Information in the *Directory*.

Each journal appears in the chapter that reflects its predominant subject matter and is cross-indexed under other topics to which it pertains. The user is urged to refer frequently to the Subject Index to locate periodicals published in his field. The Periodical Title Index lists all publications in the *Directory* alphabetically by principal element, with no inversion for titles that include a proper name. The Publisher and Sponsoring Organization Index alphabetically lists societies, professional groups, publishing houses, or organizations that sponsor or publish the periodicals included. Departments or research organizations that are part of a university or college will most often be found under the university or college name. Finally, in the Editorial Staff Index all editors cited in the entries appear alphabetically by last name. All references in the indexes are to entry numbers, not pages.

Marquis Academic Media, a division of Marquis Who's Who, Inc., constantly strives to provide the academic and professional communities with the most comprehensive and up-to-date information on the continually expanding range of journals and new titles opening in specialized and scholarly fields. The staff of Marquis Academic Media urges the users of this edition to inform us of corrections or additions to existing entries, periodicals not included, and suggestions for improvement of future editions.

Key to Information

1. Title of periodical, appearing in boldface in each case.
2. The subtitle or foreign language title, if any.
3. Publisher's or sponsor's address or, when not listed under item 13, the editorial address.
4. Publisher's or sponsor's telephone number or, when not listed under item 13, the editorial telephone number.
5. Previous title or titles, in the case of a name change or a merger.
6. Year in which the periodical or its direct predecessors were established.
7. Subscription data
    a. Frequency of issue.
    b. Average paid circulation. Domestic, foreign, institutional or individual rates are sometimes indicated. The word "Controlled" appears after figures that represent the total free or exchange circulation.
    c. Cost of an annual subscription, usually expressed in the currency of the country of publication. Foreign, institutional, student membership, or Pan-American Postal Union rates are occasionally supplied.
    d. The name of the professional group, organization, or society that publishes or sponsors the periodical.
    e. Managing Editor, included when this name differs from that to whom the manuscript should be submitted.
8. Editorial interest
    a. A brief description of the contents or editorial purposes of the periodical.
    b. The number of manuscripts published in an average issue.
    c. The audience to whom the periodical is directed.
    d. Languages in which manuscripts are accepted.
9. Manuscript information
    a. Specific subject areas covered by the periodical, including any topical, geographical, or chronological limitations.
10. Manuscript requirements
    a. Specific style requirements preferred for preparation of the manuscript, or reference where they may be obtained. Abbreviations or acronyms used may be found in the Key to Abbreviations.
    b. Preferred length of manuscript.
    c. Number of copies to be submitted. Unless otherwise specified, the first copy of a manuscript should always be a typed original and any additional copies should be good machine copies.
    d. Abstract requirements.
11. Author information and reprints
    a. Payment for the manuscript's publication, by whom—the journal, author, or neither—and in what amount, based on printed not manuscript length, per word, per page, or per article, or the number of reprints or issues offered as compensation.
    b. Simultaneous submission to other journals, whether permitted or not and, if so, the requirements for notification or limitations on submission.

    c. Manuscript rights, whether the periodical holds exclusive rights to the publication of the manuscript between the time that it is accepted and the time that it is actually published.
    d. Copyright information. The copyright law is currently before Congress for revision. However, references used in the *Directory* specify the copyright arrangement normally made by the editor or publisher: whether held by author or by publication; whether the publication holds all rights and the author forfeits any future use of the material in its present form; if First Serial Rights, in which the publication has first right to publish the material and the author all subsequent rights; if Second Serial Rights, when the periodical is granted permission to use previously published material; if Simultaneous Rights, which allows simultaneous publication.
    e. Reprint availability.
    f. Additional manuscript information.
12. Disposition of manuscript
    a. Necessity for a query letter.
    b. Acknowledgement of manuscript's receipt by the periodical.
    c. Average length of time required for a decision to accept or reject the manuscript. If no reply has been received by the maximum date, a follow-up inquiry may be sent.
    d. Average length of time after acceptance before publication.
    e. Disposition of rejected manuscripts.
    f. Criticism of rejected manuscripts, whether or not it is done and, if so, any attendant stipulations.
13. Submission of manuscript
    a. Individual to whom it should be directed.
    b. Individual's title.
    c. Address, if other than that given in item 3.
    d. Telephone number, if other than that given in item 4.
15. Special stipulations, if applicable.

* An asterisk following the periodical title indicates that no updated information was returned by the editor or publisher. Entries are included as they appeared in the last edition.

Key to Abbreviations

Style requirements abbreviations

AA	*American Antiquity,* Society for American Archaeology; consult issues for style.
AAA	American Anthropological Association, *American Anthropologist;* consult issues for style.
ACS	American Chemical Society, *Handbook for Authors of Papers in the Journals of the American Chemical Society,* Washington, 1967.
AER	*American Economic Review;* consult issues for style.
AGU	American Geophysical Union; journal format.
AHR	*American Historical Review;* consult issues for style.
AIBS	American Institute of Biological Sciences, *Style Manual for Biological Journals,* 3rd edition, Washington, 1973.
AJS	*American Journal of Sociology;* consult issues for style.
AMA	American Medical Association, Division of Scientific Publications, *Style Book and Editorial Manual.*
AMS	American Mathematical Society, *Manual for Authors of Mathematical Papers,* 1973.
ANSI	American National Standards Institute, *American National Standard Abbreviations for use on Drawings and in Text,* New York, 1972, (Y1.1-1972).
AP	Associated Press, *AP Style Book,* New York, 1970.
APA	American Psychological Association, *Publication Manual,* Washington, 1974.
ASA	American Sociological Association; journal format.
ASCE	American Society of Civil Engineers, *Author's Guide,* 1973.
ASMT	American Society of Medical Technologists, *Handbook for Authors.*
ASR	*American Sociological Review;* consult current issue.
AVMA	American Veterinary Medical Association; journal format.
BA	*Biological Abstracts* style for footnote and bibliography citations.
CA	*Chemical Abstracts* style for footnote and bibliography citations.
Chicago	University of Chicago Press, *A Manual of Style for Authors,* 12th ed., Chicago, 1969.
GPO	U. S. Government Printing Office, *Style Manual,* Washington, 1973.
HLRA	Harvard Law Review Association, *A Uniform System of Citation; Forms of Citation and Abbreviation,* 11th edition, Cambridge, Mass., 1967. (Also known as "Harvard Blue Book" or "White Book.")
IEEE	Institute of Electrical and Electronic Engineers, *IEEE Spectrum;* consult latest issue.
IM	*Index Medicus* style for footnote and bibliography citations.
JAH	*Journal of American History;* consult issues for style.
LSA	Linguistic Society of America; journal format.
MLA	Modern Language Association of America, *The MLA Style Sheet,* compiled by William Riley Parker, 2nd edition, New York, 1970.

NEA	National Education Association of the United States, *NEA Style Manual for Writers and Editors,* Washington, 1974.
NYT	*New York Times, Style Book for Writers and Editors,* New York, 1962.
Skillin	Skillin, Marjorie, *Words Into Type: A Guide in the Preparation of Manuscripts for Writers, Editors, Proofreaders and Printers,* 3rd edition, New York, 1974.
Strunk	Strunk and White, *The Elements of Style,* Macmillan, New York, 1962.
Turabian	Turabian, Kate, *Manual for Writers of Term Papers, Theses and Dissertations,* 3rd edition rev., University of Chicago Press, Chicago, 1973.
UPI	United Press International.
USGS	U. S. Geological Survey, *Suggestions to Authors of the Reports of the United States Geological Survey,* 5th edition, Washington, 1958.
Webster 3	*Webster's Third New International Dictionary: The Great Library of the English Language,* G. & C. Merriam Co., 1971.
Westminster	Westminster Press, *Style Rules: A Manual for Use in Editing Publications for the Westminster Press,* Board of Christian Education of the Presbyterian Church in the U. S., revised edition, Philadelphia, 1964.

Other abbreviations

Dfl.	Dutch guilders
DM	German marks (West Germany)
I£	Israeli pounds
£	Pounds sterling
R.	rand (South Africa)
Rs.	rupees (India)
Sfr.	Swiss francs
SI Units	International System of Units
$	dollars (United States)
$A	dollars (Australia)
PUAS	Pan American Postal Union

General

General

ABERDEEN UNIVERSITY REVIEW [1]
Department of Mathematics
Kings College, High Street
Aberdeen AB9 20B, Scotland
0224-40241 ext. 317

First published in 1913

SUBSCRIPTION DATA
Issues and rates: Published semi-annually.
  Average paid circulation: 1450; 120 controlled
  Annual rate(s): £1.50
Publisher or Sponsor: Aberdeen University Alumnus Association
Managing Editor: Eric E. Morrison

EDITORIAL DESCRIPTION
  Contains articles of literary and general interest.

MANUSCRIPT INFORMATION
Manuscript requirements: See latest issue for style requirements.
  Preferred length: 3000-5000 words
  Number of copies to be submitted: One
Author information and reprints: Payment: None.
  Is simultaneous submission of article to other journals permitted: No
  Exclusive manuscript rights between acceptance and publication: Yes
  Copyright: Held by publication.
  Reprints: Available, 12 free; further offprints available on payment, prior request necessary.
Disposition of manuscript:
  Receipt of manuscript acknowledged: Yes
  Decision to publish in: One month
  Accepted manuscript published in: 12-18 months
  Rejected manuscript returned: Yes, if self-addressed, stamped envelope is sent with manuscript.
  Rejected manuscript criticized: No
Submit to:
  Eric Elmslie Morrison
  Editor
  (See address above)

THE AMERICAN RATIONALIST [2]
P. O. Box 994
St. Louis, Missouri 63188

First published in 1953

SUBSCRIPTION DATA
Issues and rates: Published bi-monthly.
  Average paid circulation: 700
  Annual rate(s): $4.50; Foreign $4.50
Managing Editor: Arthur Stahl

EDITORIAL DESCRIPTION
  A general magazine on philosophical and religious subjects.
Articles per average issue: 8
Audience: Liberal religious, freethinkers, humanists, rationalists, those uncommitted to any authoritarian philosophy or religion.
  Manuscripts accepted in English

MANUSCRIPT INFORMATION
Subject field(s): Philosophy, ethics, science, use of reason past and present, freedom of religion, separation of church and state, religious influence on personal and national problems, criticism of superstition, myths and dogmas.
Manuscript requirements: No specific style guide.
  Preferred length: 1,300 to 4,000 words
  Number of copies to be submitted: 1
  Abstract: Not necessary.
Author information and reprints: Payment: Reprints only. 10 issues
  Is simultaneous submission of article to other journals permitted: Permitted.
  Exclusive manuscript rights between acceptance and publication: No
  Copyright: No copyright arrangements
  Reprints: Available at cost.
Disposition of manuscript:
  Query letter: Not necessary.
  Receipt of manuscript acknowledged: No
  Decision to publish in: 1 month
  Accepted manuscript published in: 6 months
  Rejected manuscript returned: Yes, if return postage is supplied by author.
  Rejected manuscript criticized: No
Submit to:
  Arthur Stahl
  Managing Editor
  (See address above)

THE AMERICAN SCHOLAR [3]
1811 Q Street, N.W.
Washington, D.C. 20009
(202) 265-3808

First published in 1932

SUBSCRIPTION DATA
Issues and rates: Published quarterly.
  Average paid circulation: 45,000
  Annual rate(s): $6.50
Publisher or Sponsor: The United Chapters of Phi Beta Kappa
Managing Editor: Joseph Epstein

EDITORIAL DESCRIPTION
  A general publication directed toward the intelligent reader; contains book reviews and commentary on arts and letters. On occasion an issue is given to a single subject.
Articles per average issue: 10
Audience: The intelligent layman
  Manuscripts accepted in English

MANUSCRIPT INFORMATION
Subject field(s): Science, the arts, religion, politics, literature, national and foreign affairs
Manuscript requirements: See latest issue for style requirements.
  Preferred length: 3,500 to 4,000 words; typewritten, double-spaced
  Number of copies to be submitted: One
  Abstract: Not necessary.
Author information and reprints: Payment: By publication to author. $250 per article.
  Is simultaneous submission of article to other journals permitted: No
  Exclusive manuscript rights between acceptance and publication: No
  Copyright: Held by publication.
  Reprints: Available
Additional information: A small amount of poetry is also published.
Disposition of manuscript:
  Query letter: Not necessary.
  Receipt of manuscript acknowledged: Yes
  Decision to publish in: 2-4 weeks
  Accepted manuscript published in: 2 months
  Rejected manuscript returned: Yes
  Rejected manuscript criticized: No
Submit to:
  Editor
  (See address above)

THE ATLANTIC MONTHLY [4]
Subscription Processing Center
Box 1857
Greenwich, Connecticut 06830

First published in 1857

SUBSCRIPTION DATA
Issues and rates: Published monthly.
  Average paid circulation: 334,932
  Annual rate(s): $11.50; Foreign $13.50
Managing Editor: Michael C. Janeway

EDITORIAL DESCRIPTION
  A magazine of literature and public affairs, the arts and other antic pursuits, which assumes on the part of its readers a modest sophistication in literary and political matters, and a willingness to be challenged by tendentious and sometimes conflicting points of view
Articles per average issue: 15-20
Audience: College educated, broad cultural interests, concerned with public affairs
  Manuscripts accepted in English

MANUSCRIPT INFORMATION
Subject field(s): Art, biography, economics, education, history, humanities, journalism, literary and political reviews, literature, music, political science, music, psychology, sociology
Manuscript requirements: See latest issue for style requirements.
  Preferred length: 2,000-6,000 words
  Number of copies to be submitted: 1
  Abstract: Not necessary.

Author information and reprints: Payment:
By publication to author. $100.00 per
page.
Is simultaneous submission of article to
other journals permitted: Permitted, but
not encouraged.
Exclusive manuscript rights between
acceptance and publication: Yes
Copyright: Held by publication. will
assign to author upon request
Reprints: Available at no cost. Limited
Available at cost.
Disposition of manuscript:
Query letter: Not necessary, but
advisable.
Receipt of manuscript acknowledged: Yes
Decision to publish in: 4-8 weeks
Accepted manuscript published in:
Immediate to several months
Rejected manuscript returned: Yes, if
return postage is supplied by author.
Rejected manuscript criticized:
Sometimes
Submit to:
Robert Manning
Editor-in-Chief
Eight Arlington Street
Boston, Massachusetts 02116
(617) 536-9500

AZTLÁN [5]

Chicano Journal of the Social Sciences and
the Arts
Chicano Studies Center, UCLA
Campbell Hall, 405 Hilgard Avenue
Los Angeles, California 90024
(213) 825-2642

First published in 1970

SUBSCRIPTION DATA

Issues and rates: Published semi-annually.
Average paid circulation: 5,000; 2,500
controlled
Annual rate(s): $7.00; Pan-Am $8.00;
Foreign $9.00; Institutions $10.00
Publisher or Sponsor: Chicano Studies
Center, UCLA

EDITORIAL DESCRIPTION

Focuses scholarly discussion and analysis
on Chicano matters as they relate to the
group and to the total American society;
to serve as an authoritative and credible
information source for the general public,
as well as a publishing outlet and a
meaningful classroom aid for teachers at
all educational levels
Articles per average issue: 8-10
Manuscripts accepted in English, Spanish

MANUSCRIPT INFORMATION

Subject field(s): The arts and social sciences
as they relate to the Chicano experience
Manuscript requirements: Style sheet sent
on request.
Preferred length: 30-40 pages
Number of copies to be submitted: 1
Abstract: Not necessary.
Author information and reprints: Payment:
None.
Is simultaneous submission of article to
other journals permitted: Permitted.

Exclusive manuscript rights between
acceptance and publication: No
Copyright: Held by author.
Reprints: Available at cost.
Disposition of manuscript:
Query letter: Necessary.
Receipt of manuscript acknowledged: Yes
Decision to publish in: 4 months
Accepted manuscript published in: 1 year
Rejected manuscript returned: Yes, with
return postage paid by publication.
Rejected manuscript criticized: Yes
Submit to:
Reynaldo Macéas
Managing Editor
(See address above)

BALL STATE UNIVERSITY
FORUM [6]

Ball State University
Muncie, Indiana 47306
(317) 285-6197

Previously entitled *Ball State Teachers
College Forum*

First published in 1960

SUBSCRIPTION DATA

Issues and rates: Published quarterly.
Average paid circulation: 500; 700
controlled
Annual rate(s): $5.00
Publisher or Sponsor: Ball State University
Managing Editor: Gertrude Kane

EDITORIAL DESCRIPTION

Contains criticism (literary, historical),
poetry, short fiction, drama.
Articles per average issue: 25
Audience: General
Manuscripts accepted in English only

MANUSCRIPT INFORMATION

Subject field(s): Literature, history, creative
arts
Manuscript requirements: MLA
Preferred length: 400-2,000 words
Number of copies to be submitted: Two;
poetry: six, short stories, 7
Author information and reprints: Payment:
Reprints only. offprints
Is simultaneous submission of article to
other journals permitted: Discouraged
Exclusive manuscript rights between
acceptance and publication: Yes
Copyright: Held by publication.
Reprints: Available, cost varies
Disposition of manuscript:
Query letter: No
Receipt of manuscript acknowledged: Yes
Decision to publish in: 3 months
Accepted manuscript published in: 18
months
Rejected manuscript returned: Yes, if
return postage is supplied by author.
Rejected manuscript criticized:
Sometimes
Submit to:
Editor
(See address above)

BLACK TIMES [7]

Voices of the National Community
Box 1024
Palo Alto, California 94303
(415) 326-4875

First published in 1971

SUBSCRIPTION DATA

Issues and rates: Published monthly.
Average paid circulation: 25,000
Annual rate(s): $10.00; Foreign $11.00
Managing Editor: Eric L. Bakalinsky

EDITORIAL DESCRIPTION

Provides a celebration of Black America
for all; aimed at creating awareness of
developments in the Black community
Articles per average issue: 5
Audience: General
Manuscripts accepted in English

MANUSCRIPT INFORMATION

Subject field(s): National and international
news bearing on Black America;
individual and group efforts and
achievements in the community, book
reviews, history, poetry, short stories
Manuscript requirements: Style sheet sent
on request. Cost: $1.00
Preferred length: None
Number of copies to be submitted: 1
Abstract: Not necessary
Author information and reprints: Payment:
Reprints only. 40
Is simultaneous submission of article to
other journals permitted: Permitted.
Exclusive manuscript rights between
acceptance and publication: No
Copyright: Held by publication.
Re-assigned to author after publication.
Reprints: Available at cost.
Disposition of manuscript:
Query letter: Not necessary.
Receipt of manuscript acknowledged: No
Decision to publish in: 2 weeks
Accepted manuscript published in: 1-2
months
Rejected manuscript returned: Yes, if
return postage is supplied by author.
Rejected manuscript criticized:
Sometimes
Submit to:
Sally Forth;
Harry Justice
Non-fiction Editors
(See address above)

BOOK FORUM [8]

An International Transdisciplinary Review
Box 126
Rhinecliff, New York 12574

First published in 1974

SUBSCRIPTION DATA

Issues and rates: Published quarterly.
Average paid circulation: 2,500
Annual rate(s): $10.00; Institutions
$20.00

General

EDITORIAL DESCRIPTION
A lively, intellectual journal providing comprehensive reviews and essay-reviews of the important books of interdisciplinary interest published on both sides of the Atlantic.
Articles per average issue: 15-20
Audience: Academic, professional
Manuscripts accepted in English

MANUSCRIPT INFORMATION
Subject field(s): Ranges a broad spectrum of disciplines
Manuscript requirements: MLA
Preferred length: None
Number of copies to be submitted: 1
Author information and reprints: Payment: Reprints only. 6 issues
Is simultaneous submission of article to other journals permitted: Permitted, but not encouraged.
Exclusive manuscript rights between acceptance and publication: Yes
Copyright: Depends on individual circumstances
Reprints: Available at cost.
Additional information: Clearly written, jargon-free; believes that good writing and rigorous intellectual standards are not incompatible.
Disposition of manuscript:
Query letter: Not necessary, but advisable.
Receipt of manuscript acknowledged: Yes
Decision to publish in: 3 weeks
Accepted manuscript published in: 3-6 months
Rejected manuscript returned: Yes, if return postage is supplied by author.
Rejected manuscript criticized: Reasons for rejections only
Submit to:
Marshall Hayes
Editorial Offices
38 East 76th Street
New York, New York 10021
(212) TR 6-6117

SPECIAL STIPULATIONS
The Editor will assign reviews on the basis of queries received.

BOSTON UNIVERSITY JOURNAL [9]
Office of Scholarly Publications
775 Commonwealth Avenue, Room 338, West Tower
Boston, Massachusetts 02215
353-4106

Previously entitled *Boston University Graduate Journal*

First published in 1969

SUBSCRIPTION DATA
Issues and rates: Published three times per year.
Annual rate(s): $6.00; Institutions $9.00; Foreign individuals $7.00; Foreign institutions $10.00

Publisher or Sponsor: Boston University

EDITORIAL DESCRIPTION
A review of literary criticism, social and political commentary, translations, poetry, and art
Articles per average issue: 4 articles; 4 groups of poems
Audience: Educated laymen, academic
Manuscripts accepted in English, French, German

MANUSCRIPT INFORMATION
Subject field(s): All fields, as long as the article is devoid of jargon and intelligible to the educated layman; article should be lively and of general interest
Manuscript requirements: No specific style guide.
Preferred length: 20-25 pages
Number of copies to be submitted: 1
Abstract: Not necessary.
Author information and reprints: Payment: By publication to author. $10.00-$25.00 minimum per page.
Is simultaneous submission of article to other journals permitted: Not permitted.
Exclusive manuscript rights between acceptance and publication: Yes
Copyright: Held by publication.
Reprints: Available at cost.
Disposition of manuscript:
Query letter: Not necessary.
Receipt of manuscript acknowledged: Yes
Decision to publish in: 1 month
Accepted manuscript published in: 1-6 months
Rejected manuscript returned: Yes, if return postage is supplied by author.
Rejected manuscript criticized: No
Submit to:
Paul Kurt Ackermann;
Ruth R. Lepson
Editor and Assistant Editor
Room 333, West Tower
775 Commonwealth Avenue
Boston, Massachusetts 02215
(617) 353-2699

THE CANADIAN FORUM [10]
56 Esplanade Street East
Toronto, Ontario M5E 1A8, Canada
(416) 364-2431

First published in 1920

SUBSCRIPTION DATA
Issues and rates: Published monthly.
Average paid circulation: 7,400
Annual rate(s): Foreign $10.00; Individuals $7.00; Institutions $10.00; Students $5.00 (all Can.)
Managing Editor: Michael S. Cross

EDITORIAL DESCRIPTION
An independent journal of opinion and the arts, aimed at an intellectual audience.
Articles per average issue: 8-10
Audience: Academic, general
Manuscripts accepted in English, French

MANUSCRIPT INFORMATION
Subject field(s): Any topic in political, economic or cultural affairs, primarily interested in Canada
Manuscript requirements: See latest issue for style requirements.
Preferred length: 2,000-3,000 words
Number of copies to be submitted: 2
Abstract: Not necessary.
Author information and reprints: Payment: Reprints only. 5 copies of issue
Is simultaneous submission of article to other journals permitted: Not permitted.
Exclusive manuscript rights between acceptance and publication: Yes
Copyright:
Annual rate(s): Reprint royalties divided equally with author.
Reprints: Not available.
Disposition of manuscript:
Query letter: Not necessary.
Receipt of manuscript acknowledged: Yes
Decision to publish in: 1 month
Accepted manuscript published in: Varies
Rejected manuscript returned: Yes, if return postage is supplied by author.
Rejected manuscript criticized: Yes
Submit to:
Michael Cross
Managing Editor
(See address above)

CANADIAN HOME ECONOMICS JOURNAL [11]
Canadian Home Economics Association, National Office
151 Slater Street
Ottawa, Ontario K1P 5H3, Canada
(613) 232-9791

SUBSCRIPTION DATA
Issues and rates: Published quarterly.
Annual rate(s): $8.00
Publisher or Sponsor: Canadian Home Economics Association

EDITORIAL DESCRIPTION
Acts as a link for professional home economists to communicate new trends, programs, happenings, provicial activities across Canada
Articles per average issue: 3-4
Audience: Professional, academic
Manuscripts accepted in English, French

MANUSCRIPT INFORMATION
Subject field(s): Foods, textiles, consumer trends and studies, family life education, human ecology, metric conversion, etc.
Manuscript requirements: See latest issue for style requirements. Style sheet sent on request.
Preferred length: None
Number of copies to be submitted: 1
Abstract: Not necessary.
Author information and reprints: Payment: None.
Is simultaneous submission of article to other journals permitted: Permitted with permission of journal
Exclusive manuscript rights between acceptance and publication: No
Copyright: Held by publication.

Reprints: Available at cost.
Additional information: Double-spaced typescript with author's name, title, bibliography, etc.
Disposition of manuscript:
 Query letter: Not necessary.
 Receipt of manuscript acknowledged: Yes
 Decision to publish in: 1 month
 Accepted manuscript published in: 3-6 months
 Rejected manuscript returned: Yes, with return postage paid by publication.
 Rejected manuscript criticized: No
Submit to:
 Jane C. Hope
 Editor
 Consumer's Company
 19 Toronto Street
 Toronto, Ontario, M5C 2E8, Canada
 (416) 492-5250

COAST MAGAZINE [12]
291 South La Cienega Boulevard
Suite 205
Beverly Hills, California 90211
(213) 655-9775

Previously entitled *FM and Fine Arts Guide*

SUBSCRIPTION DATA
Issues and rates: Published monthly.
 Average paid circulation: 85,000
 Annual rate(s): $6.89
Managing Editor: Evelyn Renold

EDITORIAL DESCRIPTION
 Contains coverage of society, culture, politics, and the arts in the American West and especially in California.
Articles per average issue: 15
 Manuscripts accepted in English

MANUSCRIPT INFORMATION
Manuscript requirements: See latest issue for style requirements.
 Preferred length: 800-4000 words
 Number of copies to be submitted: One
 Abstract: Not necessary.
Author information and reprints: Payment: By publication to author. Payment varies.
 Is simultaneous submission of article to other journals permitted: Permitted, but not preferred
 Exclusive manuscript rights between acceptance and publication: Yes
 Copyright: Held by author.
 Reprints: Not available.
Disposition of manuscript:
 Receipt of manuscript acknowledged: No
 Decision to publish in: 3-6 weeks
 Accepted manuscript published in: 1-3 months
 Rejected manuscript returned: Yes
 Rejected manuscript criticized: No
Submit to:
 Colman Andrews
 Editor
 (See address above)

THE COLORADO QUARTERLY [13]
Hellems 134, University of Colorado
Boulder, Colorado 80302
(303) 492-6660

SUBSCRIPTION DATA
Issues and rates: Published quarterly.
 Average paid circulation: 650; 150 controlled
 Annual rate(s): $4.00, Foreign $5.00
Publisher or Sponsor: University of Colorado
Managing Editor: Claudine Seever

EDITORIAL DESCRIPTION
 Non-technical journal of general and regional interest designed to promote more effective communication between specialists in all academic fields and the public. Includes fiction and poetry.
Articles per average issue: 6 articles; 2 stories; 10 poems
Audience: General reader

MANUSCRIPT INFORMATION
Subject field(s): No specific fields, general interest publication.
Manuscript requirements: Chicago
 Preferred length: 4,000-6,000 words; 12-20 pages
 Number of copies to be submitted: One
 Abstract: Not necessary.
Author information and reprints: Payment: Reprints only. Four copies of the issue
 Is simultaneous submission of article to other journals permitted: Not permitted.
 Copyright: Held by publication.
 Reprints: Available at cost
Disposition of manuscript:
 Query letter: No
 Receipt of manuscript acknowledged: No
 Decision to publish in: 2-3 weeks
 Accepted manuscript published in: Six to nine months for an article or story; a year or longer for poetry.
 Rejected manuscript returned: Yes, if self-addressed, stamped envelope is sent with manuscript.
 Rejected manuscript criticized: No
Submit to:
 Paul Carter
 Editor
 (See address above)

THE COLUMBIA FORUM [14]
612 West 114th Street
New York, New York 10025
(212) 280-4032

Previously entitled *The Columbia University Forum*

First published in 1957

SUBSCRIPTION DATA
Issues and rates: Published quarterly.
 Average paid circulation: 10,000
 Annual rate(s): $7.50, Students $5.00, Foreign $8.00

Publisher or Sponsor: Columbia University
Managing Editor: Mia Leo

EDITORIAL DESCRIPTION
 A general national magazine, treating the arts, history, education, law, social criticism, broadly interpretative social science (all non-fiction); poetry and satire.
Articles per average issue: 9-10 articles; 3 poems
Audience: General adult audience
 Manuscripts accepted in English

MANUSCRIPT INFORMATION
Subject field(s): Social sciences, humanities, poetry, satire
Manuscript requirements: No specific style guide.
 Preferred length: 1500-5500 words; 6-25 pages
 Number of copies to be submitted: One
 Abstract: No
Author information and reprints: Payment: By publication to author. $250 per article. $75 per poem.
 Is simultaneous submission of article to other journals permitted: Yes
 Exclusive manuscript rights between acceptance and publication: Yes
 Copyright: Held by publication.
 Reprints: Not available.
Additional information: 5 magazines given to author; 10 magazines sent to individuals of the author's choosing; additional magazines available at variable cost.
Disposition of manuscript:
 Query letter: No
 Receipt of manuscript acknowledged: No
 Decision to publish in: 3-6 months
 Accepted manuscript published in: 3-4 months
 Rejected manuscript returned: Yes, if return postage is supplied by author.
 Rejected manuscript criticized: Sometimes
Submit to:
 Erik Wensberg
 Editor
 (See address above)

SPECIAL STIPULATIONS
 Avoid use of footnotes wherever possible.

CONSUMERS DIGEST [15]
6316 North Lincoln Avenue
Chicago, Illinois 60659
(312) 588-3020

SUBSCRIPTION DATA
Issues and rates: Published bi-monthly.
 Average paid circulation: 225,000
 Annual rate(s): $4.00, Foreign $5.00

EDITORIAL DESCRIPTION
 Contains articles on consumer education in products and services, advises best buys, low discount prices, where to buy. Unbiased conclusions give consumer true facts; no advertising accepted.
Articles per average issue: 8
Audience: General

Manuscripts accepted in English

MANUSCRIPT INFORMATION

Subject field(s): All consumer products, health, education, insurance, finance, travel, food, consumer services, repair, law for layman, investments
Manuscript requirements: See latest issue for style requirements.
  Preferred length: 1500-2500 words
  Number of copies to be submitted: One
  Abstract: No
Author information and reprints: Payment: By publication to author. $.05- $.075 per word.
  Is simultaneous submission of article to other journals permitted: No
  Exclusive manuscript rights between acceptance and publication: Yes
  Copyright: Held by publication.
  Reprints: Available, no cost
Disposition of manuscript:
  Query letter: Yes
  Receipt of manuscript acknowledged: No
  Decision to publish in: 30 to 60 days
  Accepted manuscript published in: Up to 6 months
  Rejected manuscript returned: Yes, if self-addressed, stamped envelope is sent with manuscript.
  Rejected manuscript criticized: No
Submit to:
  Arthur Darack
  Editor
  (See address above)

THE CRESSET [16]
A Review of Literature, the Arts, and Public Affairs
Valparaiso University
Valparaiso, Indiana 46383
(219) 462-5111, ext. 398

SUBSCRIPTION DATA

Issues and rates: 10 issues per year
  Average paid circulation: 625; 5,800 controlled
  Annual rate(s): $3.00
Publisher or Sponsor: Valparaiso University
Managing Editor: Kenneth F. Korby

EDITORIAL DESCRIPTION

  Contains review materials as described in the sub-title, including issues and items pertinent to Christian concerns; to serve educated men and women who do not use abstract, conceptual language in their everyday work.
Articles per average issue: 8
Audience: Educated laymen
  Manuscripts accepted in English

MANUSCRIPT INFORMATION

Subject field(s): Religious, ethical issues; education and university; literary studies; political, economic issues; law and justice; healing (medicine, mental health, etc); film and theater reviews; poetry
Manuscript requirements: Chicago
  Preferred length: 2,000-4,000 words; 10-15 pages
  Number of copies to be submitted: Two
  Abstract: No

Author information and reprints: Payment: By publication to author. $5.00 per page.
  Is simultaneous submission of article to other journals permitted: Permitted, but the editor must be informed.
  Exclusive manuscript rights between acceptance and publication: No
  Copyright: Held by publication.
  Reprints: Available at no cost. 10 copies
Additional information: Prefer an educational curriculum vitae and present work of the author with the manuscript, especially in the first contact.
Disposition of manuscript:
  Query letter: Not necessary.
  Receipt of manuscript acknowledged: Yes
  Decision to publish in: 1 month
  Accepted manuscript published in: 3 months
  Rejected manuscript returned: Yes, if return postage is supplied by author.
  Rejected manuscript criticized: No
Submit to:
  Kenneth F. Korby
  Editor
  (See address above)

THE CRISIS [17]
1790 Broadway
New York, New York 10019
(212) 245-2100

First published in 1910

SUBSCRIPTION DATA

Issues and rates: Published monthly.
  Average paid circulation: 100,000
  Annual rate(s): $3.50; Foreign $4.00
Publisher or Sponsor: National Association for the Advancement of Colored People

EDITORIAL DESCRIPTION

  Publishes articles for persons interested in civil rights, the problems and achievements of black people and other minorities, and in the status of race relations in the U. S. and abroad
Articles per average issue: 5-6
Audience: Black leadership across the nation, membership
  Manuscripts accepted in English

MANUSCRIPT INFORMATION

Subject field(s): Editorial and feature articles deal with such aspects of the racial issue as politics, education, employment, housing, health and cultural developments, literature, poetry and drama, music and the graphic arts
Manuscript requirements: No specific style guide.
  Preferred length: 2,500-3,000 words
  Number of copies to be submitted: 1
  Abstract: Not necessary.
Author information and reprints: Payment: Reprints only. 6
  Is simultaneous submission of article to other journals permitted: Not permitted.
  Exclusive manuscript rights between acceptance and publication: Yes
  Copyright: Held by publication.
  Reprints: Available at cost.

Disposition of manuscript:
  Query letter: Not necessary.
  Receipt of manuscript acknowledged: Yes
  Decision to publish in: 3-4 weeks
  Accepted manuscript published in: 3 months
  Rejected manuscript returned: Yes, if return postage is supplied by author.
  Rejected manuscript criticized: No
Submit to:
  Warren Marr, II
  Editor
  (See address above)

THE DALHOUSIE REVIEW [18]
Dalhousie University Press, Ltd.
Killam Library 4413
Halifax, Nova Scotia B3H 4H8, Canada
(902) 424-2541

First published in 1921

SUBSCRIPTION DATA

Issues and rates: Published quarterly.
  Average paid circulation: 1,100 controlled
  Annual rate(s): $6.00

EDITORIAL DESCRIPTION

  A general scholarly review.
Articles per average issue: 14-15
Audience: Academic
  Manuscripts accepted in English

MANUSCRIPT INFORMATION

Subject field(s): All subjects considered
Manuscript requirements: No specific style guide.
  Preferred length: 5,000 words prose; 300 in verse
  Number of copies to be submitted: 2
  Abstract: Not necessary.
Author information and reprints: Payment: By publication to author. A small honorarium
  Reprints: Available at no cost. 25
Disposition of manuscript:
  Query letter: Not necessary.
  Receipt of manuscript acknowledged: Yes
  Decision to publish in: Varies
  Accepted manuscript published in: 3-4 months
  Rejected manuscript returned: Yes, if return postage is supplied by author.
  Rejected manuscript criticized: Sometimes
Submit to:
  Dr. Allan R. Bevan
  Editor
  (See address above)

EL GRITO [19]
Quinto Sol Publications, Inc.
P.O. Box 9275
Berkeley, California 94709
549-1171

First published in 1967

SUBSCRIPTION DATA
Issues and rates: Published quarterly.
    Average paid circulation: 6,000
    Annual rate(s): $7.00, Foreign $8.00
Managing Editor: Octavio I. Romano-V.;
Andres Ybarra

EDITORIAL DESCRIPTION
    A forum of Mexican-American thought.
Contents include fiction, poetry, social
research and commentary.
Articles per average issue: Varies
Audience: General
    Manuscripts accepted in Spanish, English

MANUSCRIPT INFORMATION
Subject field(s): Contributions in both
written and graphic form: academic
papers, book reviews, short stories,
poetry, satire, drawings, photographs
Manuscript requirements: See latest issue for
style requirements.
    Preferred length: None
    Number of copies to be submitted: 1
    Abstract: No
Author information and reprints: Payment:
Prorated per page
    Exclusive manuscript rights between
acceptance and publication: Yes
    Copyright: Held by publication.
    Reprints: Not available.
Submit to:
    Editors
    (See address above)

FIFTH ESTATE [20]
4403 2nd Street
Detroit, Michigan 48201
(313) 831-6800

First published in 1965

SUBSCRIPTION DATA
Issues and rates: Published bi-weekly.
    Average paid circulation: 14,500
    Annual rate(s): $10.00, Foreign $9.00

EDITORIAL DESCRIPTION
    Contents include local and international
news and analyses from a socialistic
standpoint; alternative, advocacy
journalism; also related cultural and
other features.

MANUSCRIPT INFORMATION
Manuscript requirements: Style sheet sent
on request.
    Preferred length: 3 to 4 pages
Author information and reprints: Payment:
None.
    Is simultaneous submission of article to
other journals permitted: Yes
    Exclusive manuscript rights between
acceptance and publication: Yes
    Copyright: Held by publication.
    Reprints: Available, cost is negotiable
Disposition of manuscript:
    Query letter: Not necessary.
    Receipt of manuscript acknowledged: Yes
    Decision to publish in: One to two weeks
    Accepted manuscript published in: One
to two weeks

    Rejected manuscript returned: Yes
    Rejected manuscript criticized: No
Submit to:
    W. Rowe
    Managing Editor
    (See address above)

FOCUS/MIDWEST [21]
P.O. Box 3086
St. Louis, Missouri 63130
(314) 991-1698

First published in 1961

SUBSCRIPTION DATA
Issues and rates: Published bi-monthly.
    Average paid circulation: 8,000
    Annual rate(s): $5, Foreign $7
Managing Editor: Charles L. Klotzer

EDITORIAL DESCRIPTION
    Presents political, social, cultural and
literary issues on the local, regional and
national scene of direct interest to the
reader in the Mid West.
    Manuscripts accepted in English only

MANUSCRIPT INFORMATION
Subject field(s): Political, social issues, urban
affairs, civil rights and liberties, poems
Manuscript requirements: See latest issue for
style requirements.
    Preferred length: 1,000 to 6,000 words
    Preferred length: One
Author information and reprints: Payment:
By publication to author.
    Is simultaneous submission of article to
other journals permitted: No
    Exclusive manuscript rights between
acceptance and publication: Yes
    Copyright: Held by publication.
    Reprints: Available
Disposition of manuscript:
    Query letter: Not necessary, but
advisable.
    Receipt of manuscript acknowledged: No
    Decision to publish in: 4-6 weeks
    Rejected manuscript returned: Yes
    Rejected manuscript criticized: No
Submit to:
    Charles L. Klotzer
    Editor and Publisher
    (See address above)

THE FREEMAN [22]
Ideas on Liberty
Foundation for Economic Education
30 South Broadway
Irvington-on-Hudson, New York 10533
(914) 941-7230

First published in 1950

SUBSCRIPTION DATA
Issues and rates: Published monthly.
    Average paid circulation: 20,000; 30,000
controlled
    Annual rate(s): $5.00; Pan-Am $5.00;
Institutions $5.00

Publisher or Sponsor: Foundation for
Economic Education
Managing Editor: Paul L. Poirot

EDITORIAL DESCRIPTION
    Articles on the principles and practices of
private property, voluntary exchange, free
market, limited government
Articles per average issue: 8
    Manuscripts accepted in English

MANUSCRIPT INFORMATION
Manuscript requirements: No specific style
guide.
    Preferred length: 2,000 to 3,000 words
    Number of copies to be submitted: 1
    Abstract: Not necessary.
Author information and reprints: Payment:
By publication to author. $5.00 per word.
    Is simultaneous submission of article to
other journals permitted: Permitted, but
not encouraged.
    Exclusive manuscript rights between
acceptance and publication: Yes
    Copyright: Held by publication.
    Reprints: Available at cost.
Disposition of manuscript:
    Query letter: Not necessary.
    Receipt of manuscript acknowledged: Yes
    Decision to publish in: 1 week
    Accepted manuscript published in: 3
months
    Rejected manuscript returned: Yes, if
return postage is supplied by author.
    Rejected manuscript criticized: Reasons
for rejections only
Submit to:
    Paul L. Poirot
    Managing Editor
    (See address above)

THE FUTURIST [23]
A Journal of Forecasts, Trends and Ideas
About the Future
P. O. Box 30369
Bethesda Branch
Washington, D.C. 20014
(301) 656-8274

First published in 1967

SUBSCRIPTION DATA
Issues and rates: Published bi-monthly.
    Average paid circulation: 16,000; 500
controlled $12.00; Foreign $12.00;
Institutions $75; Students $12.00;
Members $12.00; Foreign individuals
$12.00; Foreign institutions $75
Publisher or Sponsor: The World Future
Society
Managing Editor: Sally W. Cornish

EDITORIAL DESCRIPTION
    A journal publishing the viewpoints of
varied specialists regarding the future of
areas from art to urban planning.
Articles by leading scientists, government
officials, business leaders and others
describe possible developments in such
fields as technology, family living, values,
government, and human relations.
Articles per average issue: 4

General   11

Audience: Generally well-educated scientists, government officials, educators, businessmen.
Manuscripts accepted in English

MANUSCRIPT INFORMATION
Subject field(s): All subjects are covered, but the manuscript must focus on the Future of that subject: The Future of art, the Future of urban planning, etc.
Manuscript requirements: Style sheet sent on request.
  Preferred length: 2,000-5,000 words
  Number of copies to be submitted: Two
  Abstract: Not necessary.
Author information and reprints: Payment: Reprints only. 10
  Is simultaneous submission of article to other journals permitted: Permitted.
  Exclusive manuscript rights between acceptance and publication: No
  Copyright: Held by the World Future Society
  Reprints: Available at cost.
Disposition of manuscript:
  Query letter: Not necessary, but advisable.
  Receipt of manuscript acknowledged: Yes
  Decision to publish in: 6 months
  Accepted manuscript published in: 6 months to 1 year
  Rejected manuscript returned: Yes, with return postage paid by publication.
  Rejected manuscript criticized: Sometimes
Submit to:
  Edward S. Cornish
  Editor
  (See address above)

HISTORIC PRESERVATION [24]
National Trust for Historic Preservation
740-748 Jackson Place, N. W.
Washington, D. C. 20006
(202) 382-3304

First published in 1949

SUBSCRIPTION DATA
Issues and rates: Published quarterly.
  Average paid circulation: 64,000
  Annual rate(s): Members $15.00
Publisher or Sponsor: National Trust for Historic Preservation
Managing Editor: Wendy J. Adler

EDITORIAL DESCRIPTION
Publishes informative features of permanent general interest regarding historic preservation and related subjects
Articles per average issue: 7
Audience: Professional, general, membership
Manuscripts accepted in English

MANUSCRIPT INFORMATION
Subject field(s): Emphasis is on the preservation of sites, buildings, objects, districts and structures significant in American history and culture
Manuscript requirements: Style sheet sent on request. Chicago
  Preferred length: 1,000-2,500 words
  Number of copies to be submitted: 1
  Abstract: Not necessary.
Author information and reprints: Payment: Honorarium, if available
  Is simultaneous submission of article to other journals permitted: Not permitted.
  Exclusive manuscript rights between acceptance and publication: Yes
  Copyright: Not copyrighted
  Reprints: Not available.
Additional information: No footnotes.
Disposition of manuscript:
  Query letter: Not necessary, but advisable.
  Receipt of manuscript acknowledged: Yes
  Decision to publish in: 1 month
  Accepted manuscript published in: 6 months
  Rejected manuscript returned: Yes, with return postage paid by publication.
  Rejected manuscript criticized: Reasons for rejections only
Submit to:
  Terry B. Morton
  Director-Editor
  (See address above)
  (202) 382-3287

HORIZON MAGAZINE [25]
1221 Avenue of the Americas
New York, New York 10020
(212) 997-4501

SUBSCRIPTION DATA
Issues and rates: Published quarterly.
  Average paid circulation: 106,000
  Annual rate(s): $26.00

EDITORIAL DESCRIPTION
A magazine of history and the arts.
Articles per average issue: 15-16
Manuscripts accepted in English

MANUSCRIPT INFORMATION
Manuscript requirements: See latest issue for style requirements.
  Preferred length: Major articles: 4500-5000 words; short articles: 1500-2000 words
  Number of copies to be submitted: One
Author information and reprints: Payment: By publication to author. On acceptance.
  Copyright: Held by publication.
  Reprints: Not available.
Disposition of manuscript:
  Receipt of manuscript acknowledged: No
  Decision to publish in: 4-6 weeks
  Accepted manuscript published in: Varies
  Rejected manuscript returned: Yes
  Rejected manuscript criticized: No
Submit to:
  Shirley Tomkievicz
  Editor
  (See address above)

IDEAS MAGAZINE [26]
Jewish Society of America, Inc.
28-13 Steinway Street
Long Island City, New York 11103
(212) 932-8555

First published in 1968

SUBSCRIPTION DATA
Issues and rates: Published three times per year.
  Annual rate(s): $6.00; Foreign $12.00
Managing Editor: Jack Ross

EDITORIAL DESCRIPTION
Contains articles on social and political issues of interest to the Jewish community; reflects a wide variety of thoughtful and responsible conservative views.
Articles per average issue: 20-25
Audience: Jewish opinion makers: religious, academic, journalistic, organizational
Manuscripts accepted in English

MANUSCRIPT INFORMATION
Subject field(s): Contemporary Jewish thought
Manuscript requirements: No specific style guide.
  Preferred length: None
  Number of copies to be submitted: 1
  Abstract: Not necessary.
Author information and reprints: Payment: None.
  Is simultaneous submission of article to other journals permitted: Not permitted.
  Exclusive manuscript rights between acceptance and publication: Yes
  Copyright: Held by publication.
  Reprints: Available at cost.
Disposition of manuscript:
  Query letter: Not necessary, but advisable.
  Receipt of manuscript acknowledged: No
  Rejected manuscript returned: Yes, if return postage is supplied by author.
  Rejected manuscript criticized: No
Submit to:
  Michael S. Kogan
  Editor
  181 Longhill Road
  Building 2, No. 3
  Little Falls, New Jersey 07424

THE INTERCOLLEGIATE REVIEW [27]
A Journal of Scholarship and Opinion
14 South Bryn Mawr Avenue
Bryn Mawr, Pennsylvania 19010
(215) LA 5-7501

First published in 1965

SUBSCRIPTION DATA
Issues and rates: Published quarterly.
  Average paid circulation: 1,000; 30,000 controlled
  Annual rate(s): $5.00; Foreign $5.00; Individuals $5.00; Institutions $4.00; Students Free
Publisher or Sponsor: The Intercollegiate Studies Institute
Managing Editor: Robert A. Schadler

EDITORIAL DESCRIPTION
An interdisciplinary journal of scholarship and opinion covering the fields of history, literary and social

criticism, economics, political science, international relations and philosophy. The Review presents a variety of scholarly conservative perspectives in support of traditional social and educational values and a free market approach in economics.
Articles per average issue: Seven
Audience: College faculty and students
Manuscripts accepted in English

MANUSCRIPT INFORMATION
Subject field(s): Literature, history, economics, international politics, political philosophy, sociology, and education.
Manuscript requirements: See latest issue for style requirements.
　Preferred length: 10-25 pages
　Number of copies to be submitted: one
　Abstract: Not necessary.
Author information and reprints: Payment: $75.00 per article. By publication to author.
　Is simultaneous submission of article to other journals permitted: Permitted, but not encouraged.
　Exclusive manuscript rights between acceptance and publication: Yes
　Copyright: Held by publication.
　Reprints: Available at no cost. Up to 200
Additional information: Careful examination of publication before submission of articles is highly desirable.
Disposition of manuscript:
　Query letter: Not necessary, but advisable.
　Receipt of manuscript acknowledged: Yes
　Decision to publish in: 3-4 months
　Accepted manuscript published in: 3-4 months
　Rejected manuscript returned: Yes, if return postage is supplied by author.
　Rejected manuscript criticized: Sometimes
Submit to:
　Robert A. Schadler
　Editor
　(See address above)

JOURNAL OF CONSUMER AFFAIRS [28]
American Council on Consumer Interests
Stanley Hall, University of Missouri
Columbia, Missouri 65201

First published in 1967

SUBSCRIPTION DATA
Issues and rates: Published semi-annually.
　Average paid circulation: 3,000
　Annual rate(s): $10.00; Foreign $10.00
Publisher or Sponsor: American Council on Consumer Interests
Managing Editor: Joseph N. Uhl

EDITORIAL DESCRIPTION
Articles on consumer economics, consumer behavior, consumer policy and consumer education related to the consumer interest
Articles per average issue: 6-8
Audience: Educators, researchers, government policy makers, business

Manuscripts accepted in English

MANUSCRIPT INFORMATION
Manuscript requirements: See latest issue for style requirements.
　Preferred length: As required
　Number of copies to be submitted: 3
　Abstract: Yes.
Author information and reprints: Payment: None.
　Is simultaneous submission of article to other journals permitted: Permitted.
　Exclusive manuscript rights between acceptance and publication: No
　Copyright: Held by publication.
　Reprints: Available at cost.
Disposition of manuscript:
　Query letter: Not necessary.
　Receipt of manuscript acknowledged: Yes
　Decision to publish in: 3-5 months
　Accepted manuscript published in: 3-5 months
　Rejected manuscript returned: Yes, with return postage paid by publication.
　Rejected manuscript criticized: Reasons for rejections only
Submit to:
　Joseph N. Uhl
　Editor
　647 Krannert Building
　Purdue University
　West Lafayette, Indiana 47906

LIBERATION [29]
339 Lafayette Street
New York, New York 10012
(212) 674-0050

SUBSCRIPTION DATA
Issues and rates: Published monthly.
　Average paid circulation: 8000
　Annual rate(s): $7.00, Institutions $15.00

EDITORIAL DESCRIPTION
Publishes from a radical viewpoint criticism and analysis of socio-political trends. Includes articles on international affairs, the labor movement, history, psychology, etc.
Articles per average issue: 6
Audience: Intellectually open and radical
Manuscripts accepted in English

MANUSCRIPT INFORMATION
Subject field(s): American society, revolutionary movements, women's liberation, gay liberation, the Third World, radical psychology, education, economics, culture, politics, ecology, American working class
Manuscript requirements: No specific style guide.
　Preferred length: Not to exceed 25 pages
　Number of copies to be submitted: One
　Abstract: Not necessary.
Author information and reprints: Payment: None. 10 complimentary copies of issue, and one year's free subscription
　Is simultaneous submission of article to other journals permitted: No
　Exclusive manuscript rights between acceptance and publication: Yes
　Copyright: Held by publication.

　Reprints: Available at no cost.
Disposition of manuscript:
　Receipt of manuscript acknowledged: No
　Decision to publish in: 2 months
　Accepted manuscript published in: Varies
　Rejected manuscript returned: Yes, if self-addressed, stamped envelope is sent with manuscript.
　Rejected manuscript criticized: Sometimes
Submit to:
　Editor
　(See address above)

THE LIBERTARIAN FORUM [30]
Box 341, Madison Square Station
New York, New York 10010

SUBSCRIPTION DATA
Issues and rates: Published monthly.
　Average paid circulation: 500; 600 controlled
　Annual rate(s): $8.00

EDITORIAL DESCRIPTION
A monthly analysis of current political, social, intellectual and cultural events from a libertarian, anarcho-capitalist viewpoint with strong anti-militarist, anti-imperialist and pro-civil libertarian bias.
Articles per average issue: 4
Audience: General
Manuscripts accepted in English

MANUSCRIPT INFORMATION
Subject field(s): Political analysis, American history, natural law theory, free market operations, U.S. foreign policy, rationalist philosophy, statism, social psychology, anarchism
Manuscript requirements: No specific style guide.
　Preferred length: 1500-2000 words or less; 20 pages
　Number of copies to be submitted: One
Author information and reprints: Payment: None.
　Is simultaneous submission of article to other journals permitted: Yes
　Exclusive manuscript rights between acceptance and publication: No
　Copyright: Held by author.
　Reprints: Available; no cost
Disposition of manuscript:
　Receipt of manuscript acknowledged: Yes
　Decision to publish in: 6 weeks
　Accepted manuscript published in: 3 months
　Rejected manuscript returned: Yes, if return postage is supplied by author.
　Rejected manuscript criticized: No
Submit to:
　Murray N. Rothbard
　Editor
　(See address above)

MEANJIN QUARTERLY [31]
A Review of Arts and Letters
University of Melbourne
Parkville, Victoria 3052, Australia
345-1844

Previously entitled *Meanjin*

First published in 1940

SUBSCRIPTION DATA
Issues and rates: Published quarterly.
  Average paid circulation: 3500 controlled
  Annual rate(s): $10.00
Publisher or Sponsor: University of Melbourne

EDITORIAL DESCRIPTION
  Publishes imaginative writings, literary and art criticism.
Articles per average issue: 18 essays; 6 poems
Audience: Academic, writers
  Manuscripts accepted in English

MANUSCRIPT INFORMATION
Subject field(s): Poetry, short stories, articles and essays on literary and art subjects, also on socio-political problems, international relations.
Manuscript requirements: MLA
  Preferred length: 3000-4000 words
  Number of copies to be submitted: One
  Abstract: No
Author information and reprints: Payment: Upwards of $30.00 per article.
  Is simultaneous submission of article to other journals permitted: No
  Exclusive manuscript rights between acceptance and publication: Yes
  Copyright: Held by author.
  Reprints: Available at cost
Disposition of manuscript:
  Query letter:
  Receipt of manuscript acknowledged: Yes
  Decision to publish in: 2 months
  Accepted manuscript published in: 3-6 months
  Rejected manuscript returned: Yes, if self-addressed, stamped envelope is sent with manuscript.
  Rejected manuscript criticized: No
Submit to:
  Editor
  (See address above)

MEDIA & CONSUMER [32]
P. O. Box 111
Uxbridge, Massachusetts 01569
(203) 972-0441

First published in 1972

SUBSCRIPTION DATA
Issues and rates: Published monthly.
  Average paid circulation: 12,200
  Annual rate(s): $12.00; Foreign $15.00; Students $6.00
Publisher or Sponsor: Media & Consumer Foundation

EDITORIAL DESCRIPTION
  Endeavors to cover the latest consumer problems and their relation to the media.
Articles per average issue: 3-4
Audience: Consumers, journalists, educators, students, business, public relations
  Manuscripts accepted in English

MANUSCRIPT INFORMATION
Subject field(s): Consumer activism, media coverage of consumer problems, advertiser pressure on media
Manuscript requirements: No specific style guide.
  Preferred length: 250-1,500 words
  Number of copies to be submitted: 1
  Abstract: Not necessary.
Author information and reprints: Payment: By publication to author. $25.00-$50.00 per article.
  Is simultaneous submission of article to other journals permitted: Not permitted.
  Exclusive manuscript rights between acceptance and publication: Yes
  Copyright: Held by publication. Then assigned to author.
  Reprints: Not available.
Disposition of manuscript:
  Query letter: Not necessary, but advisable.
  Receipt of manuscript acknowledged: No
  Decision to publish in: 3 weeks
  Accepted manuscript published in: 2-3 months
  Rejected manuscript returned: Yes, if return postage is supplied by author.
  Rejected manuscript criticized: Reasons for rejections only
Submit to:
  Francis X. Pollock
  Editor
  P. O. Box 850
  Norwalk, Connecticut 06852
  (203) 972-0441

MICHIGAN QUARTERLY REVIEW [33]
3032 Rackham Building
University of Michigan
Ann Arbor, Michigan 48104
(313) 764-9265

Previously entitled *Michigan Alumnus Quarterly Review*

First published in 1962

SUBSCRIPTION DATA
Issues and rates: Published quarterly.
  Average paid circulation: 3000
Publisher or Sponsor: University of Michigan
Managing Editor: Paula Weiland

EDITORIAL DESCRIPTION
  Publication has a literary emphasis with general essays, poems, fiction, reviews.
Articles per average issue: 15-20
Audience: Professional, academic
  Manuscripts accepted in English

MANUSCRIPT INFORMATION
Subject field(s): Literary essays, poetry, fiction, general essays
Manuscript requirements: No specific style guide.
  Preferred length: 3000-5000 words
  Number of copies to be submitted: One
  Abstract: No
Author information and reprints: Payment: By publication to author. $.025 per word. $.50-$1.00 per line for poetry, and 3 copies of issue
  Is simultaneous submission of article to other journals permitted: No
  Exclusive manuscript rights between acceptance and publication: Yes
  Copyright: Held by publication.
  Reprints: Available at printer's cost
Disposition of manuscript:
  Query letter: No
  Receipt of manuscript acknowledged: No
  Decision to publish in: 4-6 weeks
  Accepted manuscript published in: 1 year
  Rejected manuscript returned: Yes, if self-addressed, stamped envelope is sent with manuscript.
  Rejected manuscript criticized: No
Submit to:
  Editor
  (See address above)

MIDSTREAM MAGAZINE [34]
A Monthly Jewish Review
515 Park Avenue
New York, New York 10022
(212) 752-0600 ext. 261

First published in 1955

SUBSCRIPTION DATA
Issues and rates: Published monthly.
  Average paid circulation: 10,000
  Annual rate(s): $7.00
Publisher or Sponsor: Theodor Herzl Foundation

EDITORIAL DESCRIPTION
  A monthly review of the political scene here and in Israel; the arts; current events; fiction; book reviews.
Articles per average issue: 12
Audience: General and academic
  Manuscripts accepted in English only

MANUSCRIPT INFORMATION
Subject field(s): Of general Jewish interest; politics, arts, fiction, book reviews.
Manuscript requirements: See latest issue for style requirements.
  Preferred length: 5000-10,000 words
  Number of copies to be submitted: One
  Abstract: Not necessary.
Author information and reprints: Payment: By publication to author. $.06 per word.
  Is simultaneous submission of article to other journals permitted: No
  Exclusive manuscript rights between acceptance and publication: Yes
  Copyright: Held by publication.
  Reprints: Available, up to 30 free
Disposition of manuscript:
  Query letter: Not necessary.

Receipt of manuscript acknowledged: No
Decision to publish in: 1 week to 10 days
Accepted manuscript published in: 1-2 months
Rejected manuscript returned: Yes, if self-addressed, stamped envelope is sent with manuscript.
Rejected manuscript criticized: No
Submit to:
Editor
(See address above)

THE NATIONAL HUMANE REVIEW [35]
P.O. Box 1266
Denver, Colorado 80201
(303) 771-1300

First published in 1913

SUBSCRIPTION DATA
Issues and rates: Published monthly.
Average paid circulation: 15,000
Annual rate(s): $2.75
Publisher or Sponsor: The American Humane Association
Managing Editor: Eileen F. Schoen

EDITORIAL DESCRIPTION
Publicizes the activities of the American Humane Association; reports on trends and accomplishments of or in the humane movement; to illustrate how kindness achieves more positive results than brutality.
Articles per average issue: 5-6
Audience: General
Manuscripts accepted in English

MANUSCRIPT INFORMATION
Subject field(s): Animal-human relationships, conservation
Manuscript requirements: Style sheet sent on request.
Preferred length: 2000 words
Number of copies to be submitted: One
Abstract: No
Author information and reprints: Payment: By publication to author. $.015 per word.
Is simultaneous submission of article to other journals permitted: No
Exclusive manuscript rights between acceptance and publication: Yes
Copyright: Held by publication.
Reprints: Not available.
Additional information: All authors planning to submit material should first study recent issues.
Disposition of manuscript:
Query letter: No
Receipt of manuscript acknowledged: No
Decision to publish in: One week to three months
Accepted manuscript published in: 3-4 months
Rejected manuscript returned: Yes, if self-addressed, stamped envelope is sent with manuscript.
Rejected manuscript criticized: No
Submit to:
Eileen F. Schoen
Editor
(See address above)

NATIONAL REVIEW [36]
150 East 35th Street
New York, New York 10016
(212) 679-7330

First published in 1955

SUBSCRIPTION DATA
Issues and rates: Published bi-weekly.
Average paid circulation: 120,000
Annual rate(s): $15.00; Foreign $18.00
Managing Editor: Priscilla L. Buckley

EDITORIAL DESCRIPTION
Publishes conservative-oriented political, social and economic analysis, with an occasional article that is historical in bias; book review section and an arts section
Articles per average issue: 3-6
Audience: General
Manuscripts accepted in English (French, Spanish)

MANUSCRIPT INFORMATION
Subject field(s): Politics, economics, social analysis, books, arts; preference for articles that are not strictly local in interest, and prefer topical to historical articles.
Manuscript requirements: No specific style guide.
Preferred length: 900-3,500 words
Number of copies to be submitted: 1
Abstract: Not necessary.
Author information and reprints: Payment: By publication to author. $0.075 per word.
Is simultaneous submission of article to other journals permitted: Not permitted.
Exclusive manuscript rights between acceptance and publication: Yes
Copyright: Held by publication.
Reprints: Available at cost.
Disposition of manuscript:
Query letter: Not necessary.
Receipt of manuscript acknowledged: Yes
Decision to publish in: 3 weeks
Accepted manuscript published in: Varies
Rejected manuscript returned: Yes, if return postage is supplied by author.
Rejected manuscript criticized: Reasons for rejections only
Submit to:
Daniel Oliver
Articles Editor
(See address above)

NEGRO HERITAGE [37]
11372 Links Drive
Reston, Virginia 22090
(703) 471-1108

First published in 1961

SUBSCRIPTION DATA
Issues and rates: Published bi-monthly.
Annual rate(s): $6.00, Foreign $7.00
Managing Editor: Sylvestre C. Watkins, Sr.

EDITORIAL DESCRIPTION
Contains informative articles, facts, biographical sketches, African food recipes, book lists, etc., profusely illustrated.
Audience: General
Manuscripts accepted in English only

MANUSCRIPT INFORMATION
Subject field(s): Seeks to inform about the achievements of Negro Americans.
Manuscript requirements: See latest issue for style requirements.
Preferred length: 10-20 pages
Number of copies to be submitted: One
Author information and reprints: Payment: None.
Is simultaneous submission of article to other journals permitted: Yes
Exclusive manuscript rights between acceptance and publication: Yes
Copyright: Held by publication.
Reprints: Available, cost to be arranged
Additional information: Require photos (with credits) for reproduction with rights previously cleared.
Disposition of manuscript:
Receipt of manuscript acknowledged: No
Decision to publish in: Sixty days
Accepted manuscript published in: Depends upon schedule
Rejected manuscript returned: Yes, if self-addressed, stamped envelope is sent with manuscript.
Rejected manuscript criticized: No
Submit to:
Sylvestre C. Watkins, Sr.
Editor and Publisher
(See address above)

NEW HUMANIST [38]
Journal of the Rationalist Press Association
88 Islington High Street
London N18EL, England
01-226-7251

Previously entitled *Humanist; Literary Guide*

SUBSCRIPTION DATA
Issues and rates: Published monthly.
Average paid circulation: 5,000; 1,000 controlled
Annual rate(s): £2.25, Foreign $6.75
Publisher or Sponsor: The Rationalist Press Association

EDITORIAL DESCRIPTION
Contains articles on social and personal affairs, science, politics, economics, religion, ethics.
Articles per average issue: 12 plus reviews and notes
Audience: General
Manuscripts accepted in English

MANUSCRIPT INFORMATION
Subject field(s): Humanism, rationalism, secularism, free thought, religion, ideas

Manuscript requirements: See latest issue for style requirements.
Preferred length: 2,000 words
Number of copies to be submitted: One
Abstract: No
Author information and reprints: Payment: By publication to author. £10 per 1000 words published
Is simultaneous submission of article to other journals permitted: Yes, outside the United Kingdom only.
Exclusive manuscript rights between acceptance and publication: Yes
Copyright: Held by publication.
Reprints: Available
Additional information: Typewritten, double-spaced, one side of paper only
Disposition of manuscript:
Query letter: Adivsable
Receipt of manuscript acknowledged: Yes
Decision to publish in: 1 week
Accepted manuscript published in: 3 weeks to 3 months
Rejected manuscript returned: Yes, if return postage is supplied by author.
Rejected manuscript criticized: No
Submit to:
Nicholas Walter
Editor
(See address above)

THE NEW LEADER [39]
212 Fifth Avenue
New York, New York 10010
(212) 889-6316

Previously entitled *New York Call* until 1924

SUBSCRIPTION DATA
Issues and rates: Published bi-weekly.
Average paid circulation: 23,000
Annual rate(s): $12.00, Foreign $14.00
Publisher or Sponsor: American Labor Conference on International Affairs, Inc.
Managing Editor: Myron Kolatch

EDITORIAL DESCRIPTION
An independent, liberal, democratic forum covering all facets of domestic and international affairs, literature and the arts.
Articles per average issue: 15
Audience: Those interested in political, cultural matters; professionals in foreign affairs
Manuscripts accepted in English

MANUSCRIPT INFORMATION
Subject field(s): Foreign policy, domestic policy, urban affairs, education, environment, local politics, international politics, international conflicts, literary criticism, book reviews
Manuscript requirements: See latest issue for style requirements.
Preferred length: 1,500-3,000 words
Number of copies to be submitted: One
Abstract: Not necessary.
Author information and reprints: Payment: None.
Is simultaneous submission of article to other journals permitted: No

Exclusive manuscript rights between acceptance and publication: Yes
Copyright: Held by publication.
Reprints: Available, cost depends on quantity
Additional information: Manuscripts must be double-spaced originals.
Disposition of manuscript:
Query letter: Not necessary.
Receipt of manuscript acknowledged: No
Decision to publish in: 4-6 weeks
Accepted manuscript published in: Depends on timeliness
Rejected manuscript returned: Yes, if self-addressed, stamped envelope is sent with manuscript.
Rejected manuscript criticized: No
Submit to:
Editor
(See address above)

NEW STATESMAN [40]
10 Great Turnstile
London WC1V 7HJ, England
01-405 8471

First published in 1913

SUBSCRIPTION DATA
Issues and rates: Published weekly.
Average paid circulation: 53,000
Annual rate(s): Foreign $30.00
Managing Editor: Anthony Howard

EDITORIAL DESCRIPTION
Contains articles on politics, current affairs, literature and arts.
Articles per average issue: 30
Audience: Political, literary
Manuscripts accepted in English only

MANUSCRIPT INFORMATION
Subject field(s): Politics, environment, literature, arts
Manuscript requirements: Chicago
Preferred length: 1200 words
Number of copies to be submitted: Two
Abstract: Yes.
Author information and reprints: Payment: By publication to author. £20 per article
Is simultaneous submission of article to other journals permitted: No
Exclusive manuscript rights between acceptance and publication: Yes
Copyright: Held by publication, then returned to author
Reprints: One free voucher copy of issue in which article appears. Further copies at normal price.
Disposition of manuscript:
Query letter: Necessary.
Receipt of manuscript acknowledged: Yes
Decision to publish in: Three weeks
Accepted manuscript published in: Up to one year
Rejected manuscript returned: Yes
Rejected manuscript criticized: No
Submit to:
Anthony Howard
Editor
(See address above)

NORTHWEST PASSAGE [41]
Box 105, South Bellingham
Bellingham, Washington 98225
(206) 733-9672

First published in 1968

SUBSCRIPTION DATA
Issues and rates: Published semi-monthly.
Average paid circulation: 3,000
Annual rate(s): $6.00, Foreign $7.50

EDITORIAL DESCRIPTION
Contains articles on ecology, politics, alternative living, gardening, the arts. Slanted towards alternative culture and ways to make that life both decent, cheap, and political.
Articles per average issue: 15
Audience: General
Manuscripts accepted in English

MANUSCRIPT INFORMATION
Manuscript requirements: See latest issue for style requirements.
Preferred length: 5 pages
Number of copies to be submitted: Two
Author information and reprints: Payment: None.
Is simultaneous submission of article to other journals permitted: Yes
Exclusive manuscript rights between acceptance and publication: No
Copyright: Not copyrighted
Reprints: Available
Additional information: No sexist themes or wording.
Disposition of manuscript:
Query letter: No
Receipt of manuscript acknowledged: No
Decision to publish in: 4 weeks
Accepted manuscript published in: 4-8 weeks
Rejected manuscript returned: Yes, if self-addressed, stamped envelope is sent with manuscript.
Rejected manuscript criticized: Sometimes
Submit to:
Editor
(See address above)

THE OCCASIONAL REVIEW [42]
A Journal of Contemporary Thought in the Arts, Humanities & Social Sciences
11722 Sorrento Valley Road
San Diego, California 92121
(714) 755-9761

First published in 1974

SUBSCRIPTION DATA
Issues and rates: Published semi-annually.
Average paid circulation: 5,000
Annual rate(s): $5.00; Institutions $4.00
Publisher or Sponsor: World Research, Inc.
Managing Editor: Karl M. Keating

EDITORIAL DESCRIPTION
Covers economics, literature, political science, philosophy, history, sociology,

psychology, cultural criticism; articles are scholarly, as distinguished from popular.
Articles per average issue: 10
Audience: College professors, students
Manuscripts accepted in English only

MANUSCRIPT INFORMATION

Subject field(s): Economics, literature, political science, philosophy, history, sociology, psychology, cultural criticism; no particular chronological or geographical limitations.
Manuscript requirements: No specific style guide.
  Preferred length: Under 7,000 words; 28 pages
  Number of copies to be submitted: 1
  Abstract: Not necessary.
Author information and reprints: Payment: By publication to author. $25 to $150.00 per article.
  Is simultaneous submission of article to other journals permitted: Not permitted.
  Exclusive manuscript rights between acceptance and publication: Yes
  Copyright: Held by publication.
  Reprints: Not available.
Disposition of manuscript:
  Query letter: Not necessary.
  Receipt of manuscript acknowledged: No
  Decision to publish in: 6 weeks
  Accepted manuscript published in: 4 months
  Rejected manuscript returned: Yes, with return postage paid by publication.
  Rejected manuscript criticized: Reasons for rejections only
Submit to:
  Karl M. Keating
  Editor
  (See address above)

PEOPLE'S WORLD [43]

1819 Tenth Street
Berkeley, California 94710
(415) 848-1373

First published in 1938

SUBSCRIPTION DATA

Issues and rates: Published weekly.
  Average paid circulation: 10,000
  Annual rate(s): $7.00, Students $5.00
Managing Editor: Conn Halinan

EDITORIAL DESCRIPTION

Contains foreign and domestic news; union and organizing coverage; mass movements; peace, political prisoners, economic cutbacks, liberation, Marxist analysis of news and events and people in struggle.
Audience: Oppressed people, national minorities, students
Manuscripts accepted in English, Spanish, French

MANUSCRIPT INFORMATION

Subject field(s): Mass movements, international, book reviews, cultural news, sports, labor
Manuscript requirements: Style sheet sent on request. Chicago
  Preferred length: 750-1000 words; 3-8 pages
  Number of copies to be submitted: Two
  Abstract: Not necessary.
Author information and reprints: Payment: None.
  Is simultaneous submission of article to other journals permitted: Permitted.
  Exclusive manuscript rights between acceptance and publication: No
  Reprints: Available
Disposition of manuscript:
  Query letter: Not necessary.
  Receipt of manuscript acknowledged: Yes
  Decision to publish in: 2-3 weeks
  Accepted manuscript published in: Varies
  Rejected manuscript returned: Yes, if self-addressed, stamped envelope is sent with manuscript.
  Rejected manuscript criticized: Yes
Submit to:
  Carl Bloice
  Executive Editor
  (See address above)

PRESENT TENSE [44]

The Magazine of World Jewish Affairs
165 East 56th Street
New York, New York 10022
(212) 751-4000 ext. 211

First published in 1973

SUBSCRIPTION DATA

Issues and rates: Published quarterly.
  Average paid circulation: 15,000
  Annual rate(s): $6.00; Foreign $8.00
Publisher or Sponsor: The American Jewish Committee
Managing Editor: Murray Polner

EDITORIAL DESCRIPTION

Serious journalism and reportage expressing a wide diversity of opinion on the situation of Jews around the world, the special problems of Israel, and the relationships among the Jewish community and those issues which affect Jewish life and institutions.
Articles per average issue: 15
Audience: A literate, educated readership concerned with Jewish life everywhere.
Manuscripts accepted in English

MANUSCRIPT INFORMATION

Subject field(s): Politics, economics, memoirs, social and communal issues worldwide.
Manuscript requirements: See latest issue for style requirements. Style sheet sent on request.
  Preferred length: 3,000 to 4,000 words; 15 to 20 pages
  Number of copies to be submitted: Two
  Abstract: Not necessary.
Author information and reprints: Payment: By publication to author. $150.00-$250.00 per article.
  Is simultaneous submission of article to other journals permitted: Not permitted.
  Exclusive manuscript rights between acceptance and publication: Yes
  Copyright: Held by publisher but transferred to authors at their request.
  Reprints: Not available.
Additional information: Prospective authors should write query letters to the editor and see the latest issue of the periodical.
Disposition of manuscript:
  Query letter: Necessary.
  Receipt of manuscript acknowledged: Yes
  Decision to publish in: 4 weeks
  Accepted manuscript published in: 3-6 months
  Rejected manuscript returned: Yes, if return postage is supplied by author.
  Rejected manuscript criticized: No
Submit to:
  Murray Polner
  Editor
  (See address above)

QUEEN'S QUARTERLY [45]

A Canadian Review
Queen's University
Kingston, Ontario, Canada
(613) 547-2608

First published in 1893

SUBSCRIPTION DATA

Issues and rates: Published quarterly.
  Average paid circulation: 1700; 2,100 controlled
  Annual rate(s): $8.00
Publisher or Sponsor: Queen's University
Managing Editor: Kerry McSweeney

EDITORIAL DESCRIPTION

Publishes articles on literature and the arts, politics, foreign affairs, history, science; some poetry and fiction; review articles. Addresses a general readership but popular material is not published.
Articles per average issue: 15
Manuscripts accepted in English

MANUSCRIPT INFORMATION

Manuscript requirements: MLA. See latest issue for style requirements.
  Preferred length: Up to 20 pages
  Number of copies to be submitted: Two
  Abstract: Not necessary.
Author information and reprints: Payment: By publication to author. $3.00 per page.
  Is simultaneous submission of article to other journals permitted: No
  Exclusive manuscript rights between acceptance and publication: Yes
  Copyright: Held by author.
  Reprints: Available
Additional information: In some subject areas preference is given to Canadian authors.
Disposition of manuscript:
  Query letter: Not necessary, but advisable.
  Receipt of manuscript acknowledged: No
  Decision to publish in: 3 weeks
  Accepted manuscript published in: Up to one year

General

Rejected manuscript returned: Yes, if self-addressed, stamped envelope is sent with manuscript.
Rejected manuscript criticized: Sometimes
Submit to:
Kerry McSweeney
Editor
(See address above)

RACE TODAY [46]
74 Shakespeare Road
London SE24, England
(01)737-2268

SUBSCRIPTION DATA
Issues and rates: Published monthly.
Average paid circulation: 5,000
Annual rate(s): £2.60; Foreign $10.00
Publisher or Sponsor: Towards Racial Justice

EDITORIAL DESCRIPTION
Publishes material on race relations both in Britain and abroad. Active and campaigning magazine dedicated to fighting racial injustice.

MANUSCRIPT INFORMATION
Subject field(s): Racial discrimination, police affairs, education, housing, jobs and employment, politics and politicians, community action, cultural matters
Manuscript requirements: No specific style guide.
Preferred length: 4,000 words maximum
Number of copies to be submitted: One
Author information and reprints: Payment: By publication to author.
Is simultaneous submission of article to other journals permitted: No
Exclusive manuscript rights between acceptance and publication: Yes
Copyright: Held by publication.
Reprints: Not available.
Disposition of manuscript:
Receipt of manuscript acknowledged: Yes
Decision to publish in: One month
Accepted manuscript published in: One month
Rejected manuscript returned: Yes
Rejected manuscript criticized: No
Submit to:
Darlus Howe
Editor
(See address above)

RE: ARTES LIBERALES [47]
School of Liberal Arts
Stephen F. Austin State University
Nacogdoches, Texas 75961
(713) 569-2101

Previously entitled *RE: Arts & Letters*

SUBSCRIPTION DATA
Issues and rates: Published semi-annually.
Average paid circulation: 1,000 controlled
Annual rate(s): $3.00, Foreign $4.00
Publisher or Sponsor: Stephen F. Austin State University, School of Liberal Arts
Managing Editor: Edwin W. Gaston, Jr.

EDITORIAL DESCRIPTION
Contains articles on anthropology, geography, history, languages, literature, philosophy, political science, psychology, religion, sociology; fiction and poetry.
Articles per average issue: 10-20
Audience: Academic and general
Manuscripts accepted in English

MANUSCRIPT INFORMATION
Manuscript requirements: MLA
Preferred length: 1000-10,000 words; 5-50 pages
Number of copies to be submitted: One
Abstract: Not necessary.
Author information and reprints: Payment: None. 3 copies of journal
Is simultaneous submission of article to other journals permitted: No
Exclusive manuscript rights between acceptance and publication: Yes
Copyright: Held by author.
Reprints: Not available.
Disposition of manuscript:
Query letter: Not necessary.
Receipt of manuscript acknowledged: Yes
Decision to publish in: 3 months
Accepted manuscript published in: 3-6 months
Rejected manuscript returned: Yes, if self-addressed, stamped envelope is sent with manuscript.
Rejected manuscript criticized: Yes
Submit to:
Edwin W. Gaston, Jr.
Editor
(See address above)

RENAISSANCE REVIEW [48]
A Radically Biblical Campus Critique
Box 5252
Stanford, California 94305
(415) 328-6826

First published in 1969

SUBSCRIPTION DATA
Issues and rates: Published monthly.
Average paid circulation: 300; 2700 controlled
Annual rate(s): Institutions $10.00
Publisher or Sponsor: Center for Christian Studies

EDITORIAL DESCRIPTION
Composed of 3 quarterlies, a different one each month, the point of view is Biblical Christian; the word-revelation of God is normative for all scientific and analytical activity.
Articles per average issue: 3-4
Audience: Secular university community
Manuscripts accepted in English only

MANUSCRIPT INFORMATION
Subject field(s): Popular arts, music, TV-movies, the media, issues in science, issues in education, social trends, political theory, the future, student opinion
Manuscript requirements: Chicago
Preferred length: 600-1000 words; 3-6 pages
Number of copies to be submitted: One
Author information and reprints: Payment: None.
Is simultaneous submission of article to other journals permitted: Simultaneous submission is permitted only to those having non-academic circulation.
Exclusive manuscript rights between acceptance and publication: Yes
Copyright: Not copyrighted
Reprints: Available, cost on request
Additional information: Articles are accepted on basis of how widespread interest in the subject is believed to be, and how they enhance that interest.
Disposition of manuscript:
Query letter: Not necessary, but advisable.
Receipt of manuscript acknowledged: Yes
Decision to publish in: 2 weeks
Accepted manuscript published in: 3 months
Rejected manuscript returned: Yes
Rejected manuscript criticized: Yes
Submit to:
Jon R. Kennedy
Editor
(See address above)

SPECIAL STIPULATIONS
Although basic perspective is radical (biblical) Christian, publication is interested in movements in other religions or philosophies which are similar.

RENDEZVOUS [49]
Journal of Arts and Letters
P. O. Box 8113
Idaho State University
Pocatello, Idaho 83201

First published in 1966

SUBSCRIPTION DATA
Issues and rates: Published semi-annually.
Annual rate(s): $2.50 for all
Managing Editor: Waller E Wigginton

EDITORIAL DESCRIPTION
Dedicated to the encouragement of innovative, speculative work both within and without the traditional disciplines; articles and essays in the areas of education, public affairs, art, humanities, and the sciences
Articles per average issue: 10
Audience: General
Manuscripts accepted in English

MANUSCRIPT INFORMATION
Subject field(s): Education, the arts, government, history, philosophy, sociology, speech and drama, economics, and architecture
Manuscript requirements: MLA
Preferred length: 20 pages maximum
Number of copies to be submitted: 1
Abstract: Not necessary.

Author information and reprints: Payment: None.
　Is simultaneous submission of article to other journals permitted: Permitted.
　Exclusive manuscript rights between acceptance and publication: Yes
　Copyright: Held by publication.
　Reprints: Not available.
Disposition of manuscript:
　Query letter: Not necessary.
　Receipt of manuscript acknowledged: Yes
　Decision to publish in: 6 weeks
　Rejected manuscript returned: Yes, if return postage is supplied by author.
　Rejected manuscript criticized: Sometimes
Submit to:
　Waller Wigginton
　Editor-in-Chief
　(See address above)

SALMAGUNDI [50]
A Quarterly of Humanities and Social Sciences
Skidmore College
Saratoga Springs, New York 12866
(518) 584-5000

First published in 1965
　Average paid circulation: 1,200
　Annual rate(s): $6.00; Institutions $9.00
Managing Editor: Peggy A. O'Higgins

EDITORIAL DESCRIPTION
　Publishes articles in a broad area of interest: cultural history, philosophy, sociology, literary criticism, poems, plays, stories, political commentary, art, art criticism, film, interviews, all of high quality
Articles per average issue: 6
Audience: Those seriously interested in ideas.
　Manuscripts accepted in English

MANUSCRIPT INFORMATION
Manuscript requirements: See latest issue for style requirements.
　Preferred length: 6,000-7,500 words
　Number of copies to be submitted: 1
　Abstract: Not necessary.
Author information and reprints: Payment: By publication to author. Varies
　Is simultaneous submission of article to other journals permitted: Permitted.
　Exclusive manuscript rights between acceptance and publication: Yes
　Copyright: Held by publication.
　Reprints: Available at no cost. 6
Disposition of manuscript:
　Query letter: Not necessary.
　Receipt of manuscript acknowledged: No
　Decision to publish in: 3-6 months
　Accepted manuscript published in: 18 months
　Rejected manuscript returned: Yes, if return postage is supplied by author.
　Rejected manuscript criticized: Sometimes
Submit to:
　Robert Boyers
　Editor
　(See address above)

SAN JOSÉ STUDIES [51]
San José University
San José, California 95192
(408) 277-2819

First published in 1975

SUBSCRIPTION DATA
Issues and rates: Published three times per year.
　Annual rate(s): $8.00; Foreign $10.00; Institutions $15.00; Foreign institutions $15.00
Publisher or Sponsor: San José State University
Managing Editor: Dirk Wassenaar

EDITORIAL DESCRIPTION
　An intellectual journal offering an eclectic forum for critical, creative, and informative writing in the broad areas of the arts, humanities, sciences, and the social sciences. Each issue also contains short stories and some poetry.
Articles per average issue: 10
Audience: General
　Manuscripts accepted in English

MANUSCRIPT INFORMATION
Subject field(s): There is some special interest in the Northern California region, but not exclusively; book reviews of regional fiction and poetry
Manuscript requirements: MLA, but open to any recognized style
　Preferred length: 5,000 words 20-25 pages
　Number of copies to be submitted: Original and 1 copy
　Abstract: Not necessary.
Author information and reprints: Payment: Reprints only. 2 copies of the issue
　Is simultaneous submission of article to other journals permitted: Not permitted.
　Exclusive manuscript rights between acceptance and publication: Yes
　Copyright: Held by San José State University. Author retains rights for future re-use.
　Reprints: Not available.
Additional information: Everything typewritten, double-spaced on standard white bond paper. Only previously unpublished work will be considered.
Disposition of manuscript:
　Query letter: Not necessary.
　Receipt of manuscript acknowledged: Yes
　Decision to publish in: 3 months
　Accepted manuscript published in: 3 months
　Rejected manuscript returned: Yes, if return postage is supplied by author.
　Rejected manuscript criticized: Sometimes
Submit to:
　Arlene N. Okerlund
　Editor
　(See address above)

SCIENCE AND SOCIETY [52]
Room 4331
445 West 59th Street
New York, New York 10019
(212) 477-1021

First published in 1936

SUBSCRIPTION DATA
Issues and rates: Published quarterly.
　Average paid circulation: 2,600; 200 controlled
　Annual rate(s): Individuals $8.00, Institutions $11.00, Foreign individuals $9.00, Foreign institutions $12.00

EDITORIAL DESCRIPTION
　An independent journal of Marxist scholarship in all academic fields.
Articles per average issue: 4-6
Audience: Academic community
　Manuscripts accepted in English

MANUSCRIPT INFORMATION
Subject field(s): History, philosophy, arts, applied science, sociology, psychology, economics, political science
Manuscript requirements: No specific style guide.
　Preferred length: Articles: 5,000-10,000 words; Reviews: 1,500 words
　Number of copies to be submitted: Three
　Abstract: Not necessary.
Author information and reprints: Payment: None.
　Is simultaneous submission of article to other journals permitted: No
　Exclusive manuscript rights between acceptance and publication: No
　Copyright: Held by publication.
　Reprints: Available, $50 per 100
Disposition of manuscript:
　Query letter: Not necessary.
　Receipt of manuscript acknowledged: Yes
　Decision to publish in: 2 months
　Accepted manuscript published in: 4 months
　Rejected manuscript returned: Yes, if self-addressed, stamped envelope is sent with manuscript.
　Rejected manuscript criticized: Sometimes
Submit to:
　Editorial Board
　(See address above)

SECOND CITY POLITICAL AND LITERARY REVIEW [53]
1155 West Webster
Chicago, Illinois 60614
(312) 549-8760

Previously entitled *Second City*

SUBSCRIPTION DATA
Issues and rates: Published monthly.
　Average paid circulation: 3,000-5,000
　Annual rate(s): $3.50, Foreign $5.00

Author information and reprints: Payment: None.
　Is simultaneous submission of article to other journals permitted: Permitted.
　Exclusive manuscript rights between acceptance and publication: Yes
　Copyright: Held by publication.
　Reprints: Not available.
Disposition of manuscript:
　Query letter: Not necessary.
　Receipt of manuscript acknowledged: Yes
　Decision to publish in: 6 weeks
　Rejected manuscript returned: Yes, if return postage is supplied by author.
　Rejected manuscript criticized: Sometimes
Submit to:
　Waller Wigginton
　Editor-in-Chief
　(See address above)

SALMAGUNDI [50]
A Quarterly of Humanities and Social Sciences
Skidmore College
Saratoga Springs, New York 12866
(518) 584-5000

First published in 1965
　Average paid circulation: 1,200
　Annual rate(s): $6.00; Institutions $9.00
Managing Editor: Peggy A. O'Higgins

EDITORIAL DESCRIPTION
Publishes articles in a broad area of interest: cultural history, philosophy, sociology, literary criticism, poems, plays, stories, political commentary, art, art criticism, film, interviews, all of high quality
Articles per average issue: 6
Audience: Those seriously interested in ideas.
　Manuscripts accepted in English

MANUSCRIPT INFORMATION
Manuscript requirements: See latest issue for style requirements.
　Preferred length: 6,000-7,500 words
　Number of copies to be submitted: 1
　Abstract: Not necessary.
Author information and reprints: Payment: By publication to author. Varies
　Is simultaneous submission of article to other journals permitted: Permitted.
　Exclusive manuscript rights between acceptance and publication: Yes
　Copyright: Held by publication.
　Reprints: Available at no cost. 6
Disposition of manuscript:
　Query letter: Not necessary.
　Receipt of manuscript acknowledged: No
　Decision to publish in: 3-6 months
　Accepted manuscript published in: 18 months
　Rejected manuscript returned: Yes, if return postage is supplied by author.
　Rejected manuscript criticized: Sometimes
Submit to:
　Robert Boyers
　Editor
　(See address above)

SAN JOSÉ STUDIES [51]
San José University
San José, California 95192
(408) 277-2819

First published in 1975

SUBSCRIPTION DATA
Issues and rates: Published three times per year.
　Annual rate(s): $8.00; Foreign $10.00; Institutions $15.00; Foreign institutions $15.00
Publisher or Sponsor: San José State University
Managing Editor: Dirk Wassenaar

EDITORIAL DESCRIPTION
An intellectual journal offering an eclectic forum for critical, creative, and informative writing in the broad areas of the arts, humanities, sciences, and the social sciences. Each issue also contains short stories and some poetry.
Articles per average issue: 10
Audience: General
　Manuscripts accepted in English

MANUSCRIPT INFORMATION
Subject field(s): There is some special interest in the Northern California region, but not exclusively; book reviews of regional fiction and poetry
Manuscript requirements: MLA, but open to any recognized style
　Preferred length: 5,000 words 20-25 pages
　Number of copies to be submitted: Original and 1 copy
　Abstract: Not necessary.
Author information and reprints: Payment: Reprints only. 2 copies of the issue
　Is simultaneous submission of article to other journals permitted: Not permitted.
　Exclusive manuscript rights between acceptance and publication: Yes
　Copyright: Held by San José State University. Author retains rights for future re-use.
　Reprints: Not available.
Additional information: Everything typewritten, double-spaced on standard white bond paper. Only previously unpublished work will be considered.
Disposition of manuscript:
　Query letter: Not necessary.
　Receipt of manuscript acknowledged: Yes
　Decision to publish in: 3 months
　Accepted manuscript published in: 3 months
　Rejected manuscript returned: Yes, if return postage is supplied by author.
　Rejected manuscript criticized: Sometimes
Submit to:
　Arlene N. Okerlund
　Editor
　(See address above)

SCIENCE AND SOCIETY [52]
Room 4331
445 West 59th Street
New York, New York 10019
(212) 477-1021

First published in 1936

SUBSCRIPTION DATA
Issues and rates: Published quarterly.
　Average paid circulation: 2,600; 200 controlled
　Annual rate(s): Individuals $8.00, Institutions $11.00, Foreign individuals $9.00, Foreign institutions $12.00

EDITORIAL DESCRIPTION
An independent journal of Marxist scholarship in all academic fields.
Articles per average issue: 4-6
Audience: Academic community
　Manuscripts accepted in English

MANUSCRIPT INFORMATION
Subject field(s): History, philosophy, arts, applied science, sociology, psychology, economics, political science
Manuscript requirements: No specific style guide.
　Preferred length: Articles: 5,000-10,000 words; Reviews: 1,500 words
　Number of copies to be submitted: Three
　Abstract: Not necessary.
Author information and reprints: Payment: None.
　Is simultaneous submission of article to other journals permitted: No
　Exclusive manuscript rights between acceptance and publication: No
　Copyright: Held by publication.
　Reprints: Available, $50 per 100
Disposition of manuscript:
　Query letter: Not necessary.
　Receipt of manuscript acknowledged: Yes
　Decision to publish in: 2 months
　Accepted manuscript published in: 4 months
　Rejected manuscript returned: Yes, if self-addressed, stamped envelope is sent with manuscript.
　Rejected manuscript criticized: Sometimes
Submit to:
　Editorial Board
　(See address above)

SECOND CITY POLITICAL AND LITERARY REVIEW [53]
1155 West Webster
Chicago, Illinois 60614
(312) 549-8760

Previously entitled *Second City*

SUBSCRIPTION DATA
Issues and rates: Published monthly.
　Average paid circulation: 3,000-5,000
　Annual rate(s): $3.50, Foreign $5.00

General

Rejected manuscript returned: Yes, if self-addressed, stamped envelope is sent with manuscript.
Rejected manuscript criticized: Sometimes
Submit to:
Kerry McSweeney
Editor
(See address above)

RACE TODAY [46]
74 Shakespeare Road
London SE24, England
(01)737-2268

SUBSCRIPTION DATA
Issues and rates: Published monthly.
Average paid circulation: 5,000
Annual rate(s): £2.60; Foreign $10.00
Publisher or Sponsor: Towards Racial Justice

EDITORIAL DESCRIPTION
Publishes material on race relations both in Britain and abroad. Active and campaigning magazine dedicated to fighting racial injustice.

MANUSCRIPT INFORMATION
Subject field(s): Racial discrimination, police affairs, education, housing, jobs and employment, politics and politicians, community action, cultural matters
Manuscript requirements: No specific style guide.
Preferred length: 4,000 words maximum
Number of copies to be submitted: One
Author information and reprints: Payment: By publication to author.
Is simultaneous submission of article to other journals permitted: No
Exclusive manuscript rights between acceptance and publication: Yes
Copyright: Held by publication.
Reprints: Not available.
Disposition of manuscript:
Receipt of manuscript acknowledged: Yes
Decision to publish in: One month
Accepted manuscript published in: One month
Rejected manuscript returned: Yes
Rejected manuscript criticized: No
Submit to:
Darlus Howe
Editor
(See address above)

RE: ARTES LIBERALES [47]
School of Liberal Arts
Stephen F. Austin State University
Nacogdoches, Texas 75961
(713) 569-2101

Previously entitled *RE: Arts & Letters*

SUBSCRIPTION DATA
Issues and rates: Published semi-annually.
Average paid circulation: 1,000 controlled
Annual rate(s): $3.00, Foreign $4.00
Publisher or Sponsor: Stephen F. Austin State University, School of Liberal Arts
Managing Editor: Edwin W. Gaston, Jr.

EDITORIAL DESCRIPTION
Contains articles on anthropology, geography, history, languages, literature, philosophy, political science, psychology, religion, sociology; fiction and poetry.
Articles per average issue: 10-20
Audience: Academic and general
Manuscripts accepted in English

MANUSCRIPT INFORMATION
Manuscript requirements: MLA
Preferred length: 1000-10,000 words; 5-50 pages
Number of copies to be submitted: One
Abstract: Not necessary.
Author information and reprints: Payment: None. 3 copies of journal
Is simultaneous submission of article to other journals permitted: No
Exclusive manuscript rights between acceptance and publication: Yes
Copyright: Held by author.
Reprints: Not available.
Disposition of manuscript:
Query letter: Not necessary.
Receipt of manuscript acknowledged: Yes
Decision to publish in: 3 months
Accepted manuscript published in: 3-6 months
Rejected manuscript returned: Yes, if self-addressed, stamped envelope is sent with manuscript.
Rejected manuscript criticized: Yes
Submit to:
Edwin W. Gaston, Jr.
Editor
(See address above)

RENAISSANCE REVIEW [48]
A Radically Biblical Campus Critique
Box 5252
Stanford, California 94305
(415) 328-6826

First published in 1969

SUBSCRIPTION DATA
Issues and rates: Published monthly.
Average paid circulation: 300; 2700 controlled
Annual rate(s): Institutions $10.00
Publisher or Sponsor: Center for Christian Studies

EDITORIAL DESCRIPTION
Composed of 3 quarterlies, a different one each month, the point of view is Biblical Christian; the word-revelation of God is normative for all scientific and analytical activity.
Articles per average issue: 3-4
Audience: Secular university community
Manuscripts accepted in English only

MANUSCRIPT INFORMATION
Subject field(s): Popular arts, music, TV-movies, the media, issues in science, issues in education, social trends, political theory, the future, student opinion
Manuscript requirements: Chicago
Preferred length: 600-1000 words; 3-6 pages
Number of copies to be submitted: One
Author information and reprints: Payment: None.
Is simultaneous submission of article to other journals permitted: Simultaneous submission is permitted only to those having non-academic circulation.
Exclusive manuscript rights between acceptance and publication: Yes
Copyright: Not copyrighted
Reprints: Available, cost on request
Additional information: Articles are accepted on basis of how widespread interest in the subject is believed to be, and how they enhance that interest.
Disposition of manuscript:
Query letter: Not necessary, but advisable.
Receipt of manuscript acknowledged: Yes
Decision to publish in: 2 weeks
Accepted manuscript published in: 3 months
Rejected manuscript returned: Yes
Rejected manuscript criticized: Yes
Submit to:
Jon R. Kennedy
Editor
(See address above)

SPECIAL STIPULATIONS
Although basic perspective is radical (biblical) Christian, publication is interested in movements in other religions or philosophies which are similar.

RENDEZVOUS [49]
Journal of Arts and Letters
P. O. Box 8113
Idaho State University
Pocatello, Idaho 83201

First published in 1966

SUBSCRIPTION DATA
Issues and rates: Published semi-annually.
Annual rate(s): $2.50 for all
Managing Editor: Waller E Wigginton

EDITORIAL DESCRIPTION
Dedicated to the encouragement of innovative, speculative work both within and without the traditional disciplines; articles and essays in the areas of education, public affairs, art, humanities, and the sciences
Articles per average issue: 10
Audience: General
Manuscripts accepted in English

MANUSCRIPT INFORMATION
Subject field(s): Education, the arts, government, history, philosophy, sociology, speech and drama, economics, and architecture
Manuscript requirements: MLA
Preferred length: 20 pages maximum
Number of copies to be submitted: 1
Abstract: Not necessary.

Publisher or Sponsor: Guild Cooperative Fellowship
Managing Editor: Robbyelee Terry

EDITORIAL DESCRIPTION
Contains news, feature articles, poetry, reviews of books, plays, records, theatre. Point of view is Marxist.
Articles per average issue: 12
Manuscripts accepted in English

MANUSCRIPT INFORMATION
Subject field(s): Muckraking, Chicago news, political analysis, book reviews, poetry, theater reviews, movie reviews, record reviews
Manuscript requirements: See latest issue for style requirements.
Preferred length: None
Number of copies to be submitted: One
Abstract: Not necessary.
Author information and reprints: Payment: None.
Is simultaneous submission of article to other journals permitted: No
Exclusive manuscript rights between acceptance and publication: Yes
Copyright: Held by author.
Reprints: Not available.
Disposition of manuscript:
Query letter: Not necessary.
Receipt of manuscript acknowledged: Yes
Decision to publish in: 2-3 weeks
Accepted manuscript published in: 1-2 months
Rejected manuscript returned: Yes, if self-addressed, stamped envelope is sent with manuscript.
Rejected manuscript criticized: No
Submit to:
Robbyelee Terry
Editor
(See address above)

SNOWY EGRET [54]
Exploring the Cultural Aspects of Natural History
205 South Ninth Street
Williamsburg, Kentucky 40769
(606)-549-0850

First published in 1922

SUBSCRIPTION DATA
Issues and rates: Published semi-annually.
Average paid circulation: 150; 150 controlled
Annual rate(s): $1.50

EDITORIAL DESCRIPTION
Contains articles, essays, reviews, criticism, poetry, fiction, related to natural history, especially living organisms in relation to man.
Articles per average issue: 15
Manuscripts accepted in English

MANUSCRIPT INFORMATION
Subject field(s): Man and natural history, birds and other living things, literary natural history, nature in music, ecology, conservation, nature painters, biographies of naturalists
Manuscript requirements: See latest issue for style requirements.
Preferred length: 2000-5000 words
Number of copies to be submitted: One
Abstract:
Author information and reprints: Payment: By publication to author. $2.00 per page.
Is simultaneous submission of article to other journals permitted: No
Exclusive manuscript rights between acceptance and publication: Yes
Copyright: Held by publication.
Reprints: Available at cost.
Disposition of manuscript:
Query letter:
Receipt of manuscript acknowledged: No
Decision to publish in: 1 month
Accepted manuscript published in: 1 year
Rejected manuscript returned: Yes, if self-addressed, stamped envelope is sent with manuscript.
Rejected manuscript criticized: No
Submit to:
Humphrey A. Olsen
Editor
(See address above)

Submit poetry to:
Alan Seaburg
17 Usher Road
West Medford, Massachusetts 02155

Submit fiction to:
William T. Hamilton
Department of English
Otterbein College
Westerville, Ohio 43081

THE SOUTH ATLANTIC QUARTERLY [55]
Duke University Press
Box 6697, College Station
Durham, North Carolina 27708
(919) 864-2173

First published in 1902

SUBSCRIPTION DATA
Issues and rates: Published quarterly.
Average paid circulation: 1,200
Annual rate(s): $7.00; Institutions $10.00
Managing Editor: Oliver W. Ferguson

EDITORIAL DESCRIPTION
A scholarly periodical in the area of the general humanities, social sciences and issues of current interest
Articles per average issue: 10
Audience: Academic general
Manuscripts accepted in English

MANUSCRIPT INFORMATION
Subject field(s): Humanities, social sciences, current affairs, familiar essays.
Manuscript requirements: See latest issue for style requirements.
Preferred length: 4,500 words maximum
Number of copies to be submitted: 1
Abstract: Not necessary.

Author information and reprints: Payment: None.
Is simultaneous submission of article to other journals permitted: Permitted.
Exclusive manuscript rights between acceptance and publication: Yes
Copyright: Held by publication.
Reprints: Available at cost.
Disposition of manuscript:
Query letter: Not necessary.
Receipt of manuscript acknowledged: No
Decision to publish in: 4-6 weeks
Accepted manuscript published in: 12-18 months
Rejected manuscript returned: Yes, if return postage is supplied by author.
Rejected manuscript criticized: Sometimes
Submit to:
Editor
(See address above)

SOUTHERN HUMANITIES REVIEW [56]
9090 Haley Center
Auburn University
Auburn, Alabama 36830
(205) 826-4606

First published in 1967

SUBSCRIPTION DATA
Issues and rates: Published quarterly.
Average paid circulation: 500
Annual rate(s): $6.00, Foreign $7.00
Publisher or Sponsor: Auburn University
Managing Editor: David K. Jeffrey

EDITORIAL DESCRIPTION
Contains non-fiction prose articles dealing with varied problems and/or interests in the humanities —literary, philosophical, historical, theological, aesthetic, etc.; short fiction and poems, plus assorted book reviews in humanities areas.
Articles per average issue: 10
Audience: Humanists
Manuscripts accepted in English

MANUSCRIPT INFORMATION
Subject field(s): Literary criticism, history, philosophy, religion, poetry, fiction, fine arts, educational problems, social problems, political theory, environmental problems
Manuscript requirements: MLA
Preferred length: 3000-3500 words; 10-15 pages
Number of copies to be submitted: One
Abstract: Not necessary.
Author information and reprints: Payment: Reprints only. 2 copies of issue, 10-15 offprints
Is simultaneous submission of article to other journals permitted: No
Exclusive manuscript rights between acceptance and publication: Yes
Copyright: Held by publication, but transferred to author upon request if re-publication in book form is indicated.
Reprints: Available, page rate set by printer

Additional information: Manuscripts of all articles must be clearly typed and double-spaced throughout on standard size sheets. Documentary notes may be placed at end of article.
Disposition of manuscript:
Query letter: Not necessary.
Receipt of manuscript acknowledged: Yes
Decision to publish in: 3-5 months
Accepted manuscript published in: 6 months
Rejected manuscript returned: Yes, if return postage is supplied by author.
Rejected manuscript criticized: Sometimes
Submit to:
Eugene Current-Garcia;
Norman A. Brittin
Co-Editors
(See address above)

SOUTHWEST REVIEW [57]
Southern Methodist University Press
Dallas, Texas 75275
(214) 692-2263

Previously entitled *Texas Review* (1915-1924)

First published in 1915

SUBSCRIPTION DATA
Issues and rates: Published quarterly.
Average paid circulation: 1,100; 1,400 controlled
Annual rate(s): $5.00; Foreign $5.75
Publisher or Sponsor: Southern Methodist University
Managing Editor: Margaret L. Hartley

EDITORIAL DESCRIPTION
Contents include articles of literary criticism, the arts, social and economic and political problems, history, short stories, poems, book reviews. Point of view is eclectic; strives for excellence both in material and in writing.
Articles per average issue: 25
Audience: College graduates
Manuscripts accepted in English only

MANUSCRIPT INFORMATION
Subject field(s): Modern American literature, social problems, the arts, southwestern regional, history, folklore
Manuscript requirements: Chicago
Preferred length: 3,000-5,000 words
Number of copies to be submitted: One
Abstract: Only required for articles in literary criticism
Author information and reprints: Payment: By publication to author. $.05 per word; $5.00 per poem.
Is simultaneous submission of article to other journals permitted: No
Exclusive manuscript rights between acceptance and publication: Yes
Copyright: Held by Southern Methodist University Press
Reprints: Available; cost quoted on publication
Disposition of manuscript:
Query letter: Not necessary.
Receipt of manuscript acknowledged: Yes
Decision to publish in: Three months maximum
Rejected manuscript returned: Yes
Rejected manuscript criticized: No
Submit to:
Margaret L. Hartley
Editor
(See address above)

SPECIALIA [58]
A Multi-Disciplinary Journal
P. O. Box 2662
Carbondale, Illinois 62901
(618) 549-3914

First published in 1969

SUBSCRIPTION DATA
Issues and rates: Irregular
Average paid circulation: 250; 25 controlled
Annual rate(s): $60.00; Institutions $60.00; Foreign institutions $60.00 all for 10 issues
Publisher or Sponsor: Professional Productivity Associates
Managing Editor: Charles Ekker

EDITORIAL DESCRIPTION
To provide significant information in fields which require publishing support. Each issue is centered around a theme with which every article deals.
Articles per average issue: 8-12
Audience: Interested persons who may be benefited by the contents of any given issue.
Manuscripts accepted in Any language, with summaries in principal languages

MANUSCRIPT INFORMATION
Subject field(s): Any multi-disciplinary field which does not have publishing access and for which a team of authors can be brought together to complete one volume.
Manuscript requirements: See latest issue for style requirements.
Preferred length: 160 pages maximum
Number of copies to be submitted: 1
Abstract: Not necessary.
Author information and reprints: Payment: Reprints only. 10
Exclusive manuscript rights between acceptance and publication: No
Copyright: Held by author.
Reprints: Available at cost. 5 cents per page
Additional information: Each issue is assembled by a team which is responsible for unity of topics, meeting mechanical requirements, and helping with distribution.
Disposition of manuscript:
Query letter: Necessary.
Receipt of manuscript acknowledged: Yes
Decision to publish in: 6 weeks
Accepted manuscript published in: 6-24 months
Rejected manuscript returned: Yes, if return postage is supplied by author.
Rejected manuscript criticized: Sometimes
Submit to:
Albert W. Bork;
Charles Ekker
Editors
(See address above)

SPECIAL STIPULATIONS
All manuscripts must be sensible and intellectually honest, subject-specific, and non-polemic.

SURVIVE [59]
The American Journal of Civil Defense
P. O. Box 910
Starke, Florida 32091
(904) 964-5305

First published in 1968

SUBSCRIPTION DATA
Issues and rates: Published bi-monthly.
Average paid circulation: 2,000; 3,000 controlled
Annual rate(s): $5.00
Publisher or Sponsor: Association for Community-Wide Protection from Nuclear Attack
Managing Editor: Walter Murphey

EDITORIAL DESCRIPTION
Contains articles on civil defense, natural disaster, conservation, related fields.
Articles per average issue: 5
Audience: Political and civic leaders, public safety officials, civil defense personnel, general public
Manuscripts accepted in English, French, German

MANUSCRIPT INFORMATION
Subject field(s): Civil defense, disaster control, safety, national defense
Manuscript requirements: See latest issue for style requirements.
Preferred length: 1500 words
Number of copies to be submitted: One
Author information and reprints: Payment: None.
Is simultaneous submission of article to other journals permitted: No
Exclusive manuscript rights between acceptance and publication: Yes
Copyright: Held by publication.
Reprints: Available at printer's cost
Additional information: Manuscripts should be typewritten, double-spaced, on letter-size paper.
Disposition of manuscript:
Query letter: Not necessary, but advisable.
Receipt of manuscript acknowledged: Yes
Decision to publish in: 1 month
Accepted manuscript published in: 2-4 months
Rejected manuscript returned: Yes
Rejected manuscript criticized: Yes
Submit to:
Editor
(See address above)

TALL WINDOWS [60]
1515 West 10th Street
Topeka, Kansas 66604
(913) 235-2307

First published in 1971

SUBSCRIPTION DATA
Issues and rates: Published quarterly.
  Average paid circulation: 500; 2,000 controlled
  Annual rate(s): $5.00 for all
Publisher or Sponsor: Topeka Public Library

EDITORIAL DESCRIPTION
An open forum: no boundaries, only limitations; interests are catholic, probing, scrutinizing, commenting on what is of substance from any angle, height, any depth.
Articles per average issue: 15-20
Audience: A mixed literary, cultural, library audience
  Manuscripts accepted in any language

MANUSCRIPT INFORMATION
Subject field(s): All
Manuscript requirements: See latest issue for style requirements. Style sheet sent on request.
  Preferred length: None
  Number of copies to be submitted: 1
  Abstract: Not necessary.
Author information and reprints: Payment: Reprints only. 5
  Is simultaneous submission of article to other journals permitted: Not permitted.
  Exclusive manuscript rights between acceptance and publication: Yes
  Copyright: First serial rights only
  Reprints: Not available.
Additional information: Everything typewritten, double-spaced
Disposition of manuscript:
  Query letter: Not necessary.
  Receipt of manuscript acknowledged: No
  Decision to publish in: Up to 3 months
  Accepted manuscript published in: 6 months
  Rejected manuscript returned: Yes, if return postage is supplied by author.
  Rejected manuscript criticized: Sometimes
Submit to:
  Tod W. Hawks
  Editor
  (See address above)

THOUGHT [61]
A Review of Culture and Ideas
Fordham University Press
Bronx, New York 10458
(212) 933-2233

First published in 1924

SUBSCRIPTION DATA
Issues and rates: Published quarterly.
  Average paid circulation: 1,500
  Annual rate(s): $10.00

EDITORIAL DESCRIPTION
Contains articles on topics of permanent value and contemporary interest in every field of learning and culture, particularly literature, theology, philosophy, history, sociology, education, political philosophy, and the more humanistic aspects of the sciences.
Articles per average issue: 10
Audience: Literary, academic
  Manuscripts accepted in English

MANUSCRIPT INFORMATION
Manuscript requirements: Chicago or MLA
  Preferred length: 4,000 to 10,000 words
  Number of copies to be submitted: One
Author information and reprints: Payment: Reprints only. 25 offprints
  Is simultaneous submission of article to other journals permitted: No
  Exclusive manuscript rights between acceptance and publication: No
  Copyright: Held by publisher
  Reprints: Not available.
Additional information: Typed on hard white paper, double spaced, footnotes kept to a minimum in number and length.
Disposition of manuscript:
  Query letter: Necessary.
  Receipt of manuscript acknowledged: Yes
  Decision to publish in: One month
  Accepted manuscript published in: One year
  Rejected manuscript returned: Yes, if self-addressed, stamped envelope is sent with manuscript.
  Rejected manuscript criticized: No
Submit to:
  Joseph Eugene O'Neill
  Editor
  (See address above)

TULSA [62]
616 South Boston Avenue
Tulsa, Oklahoma 74119
(918) 585-1202 ext. 55

First published in 1959

SUBSCRIPTION DATA
Issues and rates: Published monthly.
  Average paid circulation: 5000; 500 controlled
  Annual rate(s): $7.50
Publisher or Sponsor: Metropolitan Tulsa Chamber of Commerce
Managing Editor: Larry Silvey

EDITORIAL DESCRIPTION
Contains articles on community issues such as livability, economy, social issues.
Articles per average issue: 6
Audience: Business leadership
  Manuscripts accepted in English only

MANUSCRIPT INFORMATION
Subject field(s): Topics related to the Tulsa area
Manuscript requirements: See latest issue for style requirements.
  Preferred length: 1500-2500 words
  Number of copies to be submitted: One
Author information and reprints: Payment: By publication to author. $50-$75 per article.
  Is simultaneous submission of article to other journals permitted: Yes, if out of Tulsa area of circulation
  Exclusive manuscript rights between acceptance and publication: No
  Copyright: Held by publication.
  Reprints: Not available.
Disposition of manuscript:
  Query letter: Not necessary.
  Receipt of manuscript acknowledged: Yes
  Decision to publish in: 2 weeks
  Accepted manuscript published in: 2-4 months
  Rejected manuscript returned: Yes
  Rejected manuscript criticized: No
Submit to:
  Larry Silvey
  Editor
  (See address above)

UNDERSTANDING [63]
P.O. Box 206
Merlin, Oregon 97532
(503) 476-4011

SUBSCRIPTION DATA
Issues and rates: Ten issues yearly
  Average paid circulation: 500; 200 controlled
  Annual rate(s): $2.50
Managing Editor: Daniel W. Fry

EDITORIAL DESCRIPTION
Contains articles on the understanding of man and the many worlds in which he lives.

MANUSCRIPT INFORMATION
Subject field(s): Philosophy, understanding, metaphysics, science, education, etc.
Manuscript requirements: See latest issue for style requirements.
  Preferred length: No more than 1000 words
  Number of copies to be submitted: One
Author information and reprints: Payment: By publication to author. $.01 per word.
  Is simultaneous submission of article to other journals permitted: Preferably not
  Exclusive manuscript rights between acceptance and publication: Yes
  Copyright: Held by author.
  Reprints: Not available.
Disposition of manuscript:
  Receipt of manuscript acknowledged: Yes
  Decision to publish in: One month
  Accepted manuscript published in: 6-8 months
  Rejected manuscript returned: Yes, if self-addressed, stamped envelope is sent with manuscript.
  Rejected manuscript criticized: No
Submit to:
  Editor
  (See address above)
  (503) 476-3792

UNIVERSITY OF PORTLAND REVIEW [64]

5000 North Willamette Boulevard
Portland, Oregon 97203
(503) 283-7144

First published in 1948

SUBSCRIPTION DATA
Issues and rates: Published semi-annually.
  Average paid circulation: 400; 600 controlled
  Annual rate(s): $1.00
Managing Editor: Thompson M. Faller

EDITORIAL DESCRIPTION
  Contains articles, short stories, poetry, book reviews. Seeks academically sound articles which bring the content of particular disciplines to bear on the problems of contemporary society and culture.
Articles per average issue: 4-8
Audience: College educated layman
  Manuscripts accepted in English

MANUSCRIPT INFORMATION
Manuscript requirements: No specific style guide.
  Preferred length: None
  Number of copies to be submitted: One
  Abstract: Not necessary.
Author information and reprints: Payment: None. 5 copies of article.
  Is simultaneous submission of article to other journals permitted: No
  Exclusive manuscript rights between acceptance and publication: Yes
  Copyright: Held by publication.
  Reprints: Available, $.50 each
Additional information: With regard to fiction, only that which makes a significant statement about the contemporary scene will be accepted.
Disposition of manuscript:
  Query letter: Not necessary.
  Receipt of manuscript acknowledged: No
  Decision to publish in: 2 months
  Accepted manuscript published in: One year
  Rejected manuscript returned: Yes, if self-addressed, stamped envelope is sent with manuscript.
  Rejected manuscript criticized: Yes
Submit to:
  Thompson M. Faller
  Editor
  (See address above)

SPECIAL STIPULATIONS
  The primary concern is communication appeal to the reader through engaging his interest in articles of substance.

UNIVERSITY OF WINDSOR REVIEW [65]

University of Windsor
Sunset Avenue
Windsor, Ontario N9B 3P4, Canada
(519) 253-4232

First published in 1965

SUBSCRIPTION DATA
Issues and rates: Published semi annually.
  Annual rate(s): $2.50 plus postage
Publisher or Sponsor: University of Windsor
Managing Editor: Eugene J. McNamara

EDITORIAL DESCRIPTION
  Devoted to the arts, social sciences and sciences. A limited amount of short fiction and poetry is also published.
Articles per average issue: 4 articles; 2 poems; 10 poems
Audience: Literate, general
  Manuscripts accepted in English, French

MANUSCRIPT INFORMATION
Manuscript requirements: MLA
  Preferred length: 3,000-2,500 words; 10-20 pages
  Number of copies to be submitted: 1
  Abstract: Not necessary.
Author information and reprints: Payment: Reprints only. 20 offprints and 2 copies of issue
  Is simultaneous submission of article to other journals permitted: Not permitted.
  Exclusive manuscript rights between acceptance and publication: Yes
  Copyright: First serial rights only
Disposition of manuscript:
  Query letter: Not necessary, but advisable.
  Receipt of manuscript acknowledged: No
  Decision to publish in: 2 months
  Accepted manuscript published in: 1 year
  Rejected manuscript returned: Yes, if return postage is supplied by author.
  Rejected manuscript criticized: No
Submit to:
  Eugene J. McNamara
  Editor
  (See address above)

THE VIRGINIA QUARTERLY REVIEW [66]

University of Virginia
One West Range
Charlottesville, Virginia 22903
(804) 924-3124

First published in 1925

SUBSCRIPTION DATA
Issues and rates: Published quarterly.
  Average paid circulation: 4,000
  Annual rate(s): $7.00, Foreign $8.00

EDITORIAL DESCRIPTION
  Publishes articles in a wide range of fields: literary, historical, political; short stories; poetry; book reviews: long essay discussions and brief critiques.

MANUSCRIPT INFORMATION
Manuscript requirements: See latest issue for style requirements.
  Preferred length: 3,000 to 7,000 words
  Number of copies to be submitted: One
Author information and reprints: Payment; $5.00 per printed page of 350 words upon publication.
  Is simultaneous submission of article to other journals permitted: No
  Exclusive manuscript rights between acceptance and publication: Yes
  Copyright: Held by publication.
  Reprints: Available to author, at printer's charges
Additional information: No footnotes.
Disposition of manuscript:
  Query letter: Not necessary.
  Receipt of manuscript acknowledged: No
  Decision to publish in: Two to eight weeks
  Decision to publish in: Three to nine months
  Rejected manuscript returned: Yes, if return postage is supplied by author.
  Rejected manuscript criticized: No
Submit to:
  Charlotte Kohler
  Editor
  (See address above)

Humanities

Humanities (general)

THE ACADEMIC REVIEWER [67]
14 South Bryn Mawr Avenue
Bryn Mawr, Pennsylvania 19010
(215) LA 5-7501

First published in 1967

SUBSCRIPTION DATA

Issues and rates: Published semi-annually.
Average paid circulation: 30,000 controlled
Publisher or Sponsor: The Intercollegiate Studies Institute

EDITORIAL DESCRIPTION

Contains short reviews of books as well as articles in the social sciences and humanities, with particular emphasis on works with a conservative and free market perspective
Articles per average issue: 20
Audience: Academic
Manuscripts accepted in English

MANUSCRIPT INFORMATION

Subject field(s): Philosophy, political science, international relations, history, economics, literary and social criticism
Manuscript requirements: No specific style guide.
Preferred length: 3-4 pages
Number of copies to be submitted: 1
Abstract: Not necessary.
Author information and reprints: Payment: None.
Is simultaneous submission of article to other journals permitted: Not permitted.
Exclusive manuscript rights between acceptance and publication: Yes
Copyright: Held by publication.
Reprints: Available at no cost.
Disposition of manuscript:
Query letter: Necessary.
Receipt of manuscript acknowledged: No
Decision to publish in: 3 months
Accepted manuscript published in: 2 months
Rejected manuscript returned: Yes, if return postage is supplied by author.
Rejected manuscript criticized: No
Submit to:
Robert A. Schadler
Editor
(See address above)

AMERICAN NOTES & QUERIES [68]
31 Alden Road
New Haven, Connecticut 06515
(203) 389-0678

First published in 1962

SUBSCRIPTION DATA

Issues and rates: Monthly except July and August
Average paid circulation: 1000
Annual rate(s): $6.50
Managing Editor: Marian Neal Ash

EDITORIAL DESCRIPTION

Contains brief notes of scholarly interest, especially historical, bibliographical and biographical in all fields: literature, history, folklore, lexicography, discovery and exploration, history of science, etc.
Articles per average issue: 6
Audience: Academic, antiquarian
Manuscripts accepted in English only

MANUSCRIPT INFORMATION

Manuscript requirements: MLA
Preferred length: Notes: up to 2000 words; Queries: brief
Number of copies to be submitted: One
Author information and reprints: Payment: None. Four copies of issue
Is simultaneous submission of article to other journals permitted: No
Exclusive manuscript rights between acceptance and publication: Yes
Copyright: None
Reprints: Not available.
Additional information: Place footnotes on separate pages following text.
Disposition of manuscript:
Query letter: No
Receipt of manuscript acknowledged: No
Decision to publish in: One month
Accepted manuscript published in: 3-5 years
Rejected manuscript returned: Yes, if self-addressed, stamped envelope is sent with manuscript.
Rejected manuscript criticized: No
Submit to:
Lee Ash
Editor
(See address above)

AMERICAN PHILOLOGICAL ASSOCIATION TRANSACTIONS AND PROCEEDINGS* [69]
Case Western Reserve University Press
Frank Adgate Quail Building
Cleveland, Ohio 44106
(216) 368-3770

SUBSCRIPTION DATA

Issues and rates: Published annually.
Average paid circulation: 2700
Annual rate(s): $15.00
Publisher or Sponsor: The American Philological Association, Inc.
Managing Editor: J. Bateman

EDITORIAL DESCRIPTION

Contains articles on classical languages and literatures, ancient history, philosophy and related fields.

MANUSCRIPT INFORMATION

Subject field(s): Greek and Latin literature, ancient history, classical philology, medieval Latin, neo-Latin
Manuscript requirements: See latest issue for style requirements.
Preferred length: 15-20 pages
Number of copies to be submitted: One
Author information and reprints: Payment: None.
Is simultaneous submission of article to other journals permitted: No
Exclusive manuscript rights between acceptance and publication: Yes
Copyright: Held by publication.
Reprints: Available
Disposition of manuscript:
Receipt of manuscript acknowledged: Yes
Decision to publish in: 2 months
Accepted manuscript published in: 12-14 months
Rejected manuscript returned: Yes
Rejected manuscript criticized: No
Submit to:
Editor of Publications
(See address above)

ANNUALE MEDIAEVALE [70]
Humanities Press, Inc.
Atlantic Highlands, New Jersey 07716

SUBSCRIPTION DATA

Issues and rates: Published annually.
Annual rate(s): $10.00
Managing Editor: Herbert H. Petit

EDITORIAL DESCRIPTION

Contains papers on medieval literature, medieval history, middle English language, old French, Anglo-Norman language.

MANUSCRIPT INFORMATION

Manuscript requirements: MLA
Author information and reprints: Payment: None.
Exclusive manuscript rights between acceptance and publication: Yes
Copyright: Held by publication.
Reprints: Available at cost
Disposition of manuscript:
Receipt of manuscript acknowledged: Yes
Decision to publish in: Two months
Accepted manuscript published in: One year
Rejected manuscript returned: Yes
Rejected manuscript criticized: Yes
Submit to:
Herbert H. Petit
Editor
Duquesne University
Pittsburgh, Pennsylvania 15219
(412) 434-6441

ARIEL [71]

A Review of Arts and Letters in Israel
c/o Yuval Tal
P.O.B. 2160
Jerusalem, Israel 91020
(02) 528191

First published in 1962

SUBSCRIPTION DATA

Issues and rates: Published quarterly.
  Annual rate(s): 32.00 Israeli lirat;
  Foreign $8.00
Publisher or Sponsor: Israeli Ministry for
  Foreign Affairs, Cultural and Scientific
  Relations Division

EDITORIAL DESCRIPTION

  Contains translations of Hebrew prose
  and poetry; articles reflecting the cultural
  life of Israel: theater, art, music, dance,
  archaeology, Judaic research, ethnology,
  architecture, education, etc.
Articles per average issue: 7-8
Audience: Literary, academic
  Manuscripts accepted in English, French,
  Spanish, German, Hebrew

MANUSCRIPT INFORMATION

Manuscript requirements: See latest issue for
  style requirements.
  Preferred length: 5,000 words maximum
  Number of copies to be submitted: Two
  Abstract: No
Author information and reprints: Payment:
  By publication to author. $8.00 per page.
  Is simultaneous submission of article to
  other journals permitted: No, unless
  agreed upon in advance.
  Exclusive manuscript rights between
  acceptance and publication: Yes
  Copyright: Held by publication.
  Reprints: Available, 50 free
Disposition of manuscript:
  Query letter: Yes
  Receipt of manuscript acknowledged: Yes
  Decision to publish in: 1-2 months
  Accepted manuscript published in: 3-6
  months
  Rejected manuscript returned: Yes
  Rejected manuscript criticized: No
Submit to:
  Yael Lotan
  Editor
  (See address above)

SPECIAL STIPULATIONS

  Articles usually received only on
  commission.

ARION [72]

A Journal of Humanities and the Classics
Boston University
270 Bay State Road
Boston, Massachusetts 02215
(617) 353-4025

First published in 1962

SUBSCRIPTION DATA

Issues and rates: Published quarterly.
  Average paid circulation: 900
  Annual rate(s): Individuals $10.00;
  Institutions $15.00
Publisher or Sponsor: Boston University,
  Department of University Professors
Managing Editor: Morris Fry

EDITORIAL DESCRIPTION

  Contains literary criticism of the Greek
  and Latin classical writers and later
  writers in the classical tradition. Special
  interest in translation from classical
  writers.
Articles per average issue: 7
Audience: Literary

MANUSCRIPT INFORMATION

Subject field(s): Greek literature, Latin
  literature, translation, literary theory,
  reform of professions
Manuscript requirements: Chicago;
  typewritten, double-spaced
  Preferred length: 10-20 pages
  Number of copies to be submitted: One
  Abstract: Not necessary.
Author information and reprints: Payment:
  None.
  Is simultaneous submission of article to
  other journals permitted: No
  Exclusive manuscript rights between
  acceptance and publication: Yes
  Copyright: Held by Trustees of Boston
  University
  Reprints: Available, cost varies
Disposition of manuscript:
  Query letter: Necessary.
  Receipt of manuscript acknowledged: Yes
  Decision to publish in: 6-12 months
  Accepted manuscript published in: 1-2
  years
  Rejected manuscript returned: Yes, if
  self-addressed, stamped envelope is sent
  with manuscript.
  Rejected manuscript criticized: No
Submit to:
  Morris Fry
  Managing Editor
  (See address above)

SPECIAL STIPULATIONS

  Interested in reviews of important books
  in the field of classical literature.

ARTS IN SOCIETY [73]

University of Wisconsin-Extension
Lowell Hall, 610 Langdon Street
Madison, Wisconsin 53706
(608) 262-0646

First published in 1958

SUBSCRIPTION DATA

Issues and rates: Published three times per
  year.
  Average paid circulation: 5,000
  Annual rate(s): $7.50, Foreign $8.50
Publisher or Sponsor: University of
  Wisconsin
Managing Editor: D. Jean Collins

EDITORIAL DESCRIPTION

  Exists to discuss, interpret, and illustrate
  the various functions of the arts in
  contemporary civilization. Its purpose is
  to present the insights of experience,
  research and theory in support of
  educational and organizational efforts to
  enhance the position of the arts in
  America.
Articles per average issue: 10
Audience: Scholars and laymen interested in
  the arts
  Manuscripts accepted in Any language

MANUSCRIPT INFORMATION

Subject field(s): Art, aesthetics, theatre,
  dance, film
Manuscript requirements: MLA
  Preferred length: 1500-3500 words
  Number of copies to be submitted: One
  Abstract: Not necessary.
Author information and reprints: Payment:
  By publication to author. Honorarium.
  Is simultaneous submission of article to
  other journals permitted: Yes
  Exclusive manuscript rights between
  acceptance and publication: Yes
  Copyright: Held by publication.
  Reprints: Available at cost
Disposition of manuscript:
  Query letter: Not necessary, but
  advisable.
  Receipt of manuscript acknowledged: Yes
  Decision to publish in: 6 weeks
  Accepted manuscript published in: 3
  months
  Rejected manuscript returned: Yes, if
  self-addressed, stamped envelope is sent
  with manuscript.
  Rejected manuscript criticized: No
Submit to:
  Edward L. Kamarck
  Editor
  (See address above)

BERKSHIRE REVIEW [74]

P. O. Box 633
Williams College
Williamstown, Massachusetts 01267
(413) 597-2377

First published in 1965

SUBSCRIPTION DATA

Issues and rates: Published semi-annually.
  Average paid circulation: 100; 1500
  controlled
  Annual rate(s): $1.00
Publisher or Sponsor: Williams College
Managing Editor: S. Lane Faison

EDITORIAL DESCRIPTION

  Contains articles, poems, stories,
  review-essays.
Articles per average issue: 4 to 5
Audience: Graduates, trustees, and friends
  of the college.
  Manuscripts accepted in English

MANUSCRIPT INFORMATION

Subject field(s): Arts and letters, history and
  politics, philosophy, regional interest,
  poems
Manuscript requirements: See latest issue for
  style requirements.
  Preferred length: 3000-5000 words
  (typewritten double-spaced)

Humanities (general)

Number of copies to be submitted: One
Abstract: Not necessary.
Author information and reprints: Payment: By publication to author. $50- $75 per article. $25 for poems.
Is simultaneous submission of article to other journals permitted: Yes
Exclusive manuscript rights between acceptance and publication: Yes
Copyright: Held by publication.
Reprints: Available at no cost. 5 copies available to authors free.
Disposition of manuscript:
Query letter: Not necessary.
Receipt of manuscript acknowledged: Yes
Decision to publish in: 1 month
Accepted manuscript published in: Varies
Rejected manuscript returned: Yes, if return postage is supplied by author.
Rejected manuscript criticized: No
Submit to:
Editor
(See address above)

BLACKWOOD'S MAGAZINE [75]
32 Thistle Street
Edinburgh EH2 IHA, Scotland
(031) 225-3411

First published in 1817

SUBSCRIPTION DATA
Issues and rates: Published monthly.
Average paid circulation: 11,500
Annual rate(s): $11.50
Managing Editor: Douglas Blackwood

EDITORIAL DESCRIPTION
Contains articles on history, biography, travel; short stories, poems.
Articles per average issue: 8
Audience: The intelligent general reader
Manuscripts accepted in English

MANUSCRIPT INFORMATION
Subject field(s): Emphasis is on quality and originality of experience and research.
Manuscript requirements: See latest issue for style requirements.
Preferred length: 3000-9000 words
Number of copies to be submitted: One
Abstract: No
Author information and reprints: Payment: By publication to author. £8 per thousand words for the first 3,000; £4 per thousand thereafter.
Is simultaneous submission of article to other journals permitted: Not permitted.
Exclusive manuscript rights between acceptance and publication: Yes
Copyright: Held by author.
Reprints: Available at cost.
Additional information: Contributors are asked to study the magazine before submitting material. All submissions must be accompanied by return postage.
Disposition of manuscript:
Query letter: No
Receipt of manuscript acknowledged: Yes
Decision to publish in: Immediate
Accepted manuscript published in: Next issue

Rejected manuscript returned: Yes
Rejected manuscript criticized: Sometimes
Submit to:
Douglas Blackwood
Editor
(See address above)

THE BRITISH JOURNAL OF AESTHETICS [76]
Oxford University Press
Press Road
Neasden London NW10 0DD England

First published in 1960

SUBSCRIPTION DATA
Issues and rates: Published quarterly.
Annual rate(s): £6.00; Foreign $17.00
Publisher or Sponsor: The British Society of Aesthetics

EDITORIAL DESCRIPTION
Contains articles on aesthetics, theory of art, from philosophical, sociological, psychological, scientific, historical, critical or educational standpoint.
Articles per average issue: 6
Manuscripts accepted in English

MANUSCRIPT INFORMATION
Subject field(s): Aesthetics and theory of art
Manuscript requirements: See latest issue for style requirements.
Preferred length: 5000 to 9000 words
Number of copies to be submitted: One
Author information and reprints: Payment: None.
Is simultaneous submission of article to other journals permitted: No
Exclusive manuscript rights between acceptance and publication: Yes
Copyright: Held by The Society
Reprints: Available, 20 free
Disposition of manuscript:
Query letter: No
Receipt of manuscript acknowledged: Yes
Decision to publish in: Varies
Accepted manuscript published in: Up to one year
Rejected manuscript returned: Yes, if return postage is supplied by author.
Rejected manuscript criticized: No
Submit to:
H. Osborne
90A St. John's Wood High Street
London NW8, England

THE CENTENNIAL REVIEW [77]
Michigan State University
110 Morrill Hall
East Lansing, Michigan 48824
(517) 355-1905

First published in 1957

SUBSCRIPTION DATA
Issues and rates: Published quarterly.
Average paid circulation: 1000

Annual rate(s): $3.00
Managing Editor: Margaret Blackman

MANUSCRIPT INFORMATION
Subject field(s): Humanities, sciences
Manuscript requirements: Style sheet sent on request.
Preferred length: 5000-6000 words; 25 pages
Number of copies to be submitted: Two
Abstract: Not necessary.
Author information and reprints: Payment: None.
Is simultaneous submission of article to other journals permitted: No
Exclusive manuscript rights between acceptance and publication: Yes
Copyright: Held by either author or publication.
Reprints: Not available.
Disposition of manuscript:
Receipt of manuscript acknowledged: Yes
Decision to publish in: Three months
Accepted manuscript published in: Varies, usually within a year
Rejected manuscript returned: Yes
Rejected manuscript criticized: Sometimes
Submit to:
C. David Mead
Editor
(See address above)

CLASSICAL PHILOLOGY
University of Chicago Press [78]
5801 Ellis Avenue
Chicago, Illinois 60637
(312) 753-3347

SUBSCRIPTION DATA
Issues and rates: Published quarterly.
Average paid circulation: 1400
Annual rate(s): $8.00, Foreign $9.00

EDITORIAL DESCRIPTION
Contains research in Latin and Greek, including language, literature, history, life of classical antiquity.

MANUSCRIPT INFORMATION
Subject field(s): literary analysis, history, textual criticism and lexicography
Manuscript requirements: Chicago; also see publication
Number of copies to be submitted: One
Author information and reprints: Payment: None.
Is simultaneous submission of article to other journals permitted: No
Exclusive manuscript rights between acceptance and publication: Yes
Copyright: Held by publication.
Reprints: Available
Additional information: Manuscripts should be double-spaced (footnotes also) on stout paper with ample margins.
Disposition of manuscript:
Receipt of manuscript acknowledged: Yes
Decision to publish in: 4 weeks
Accepted manuscript published in: 12-18 months
Rejected manuscript returned: Yes
Rejected manuscript criticized: Yes

Submit to:
　Editor
　(See address above)

THE CLASSICAL WORLD [79]
325 Smith Hall
University of Delaware
Newark, Delaware 19711
(302) 738-2373

First published in 1907

SUBSCRIPTION DATA

Issues and rates: 7 times per year
　Average paid circulation: 3,000; 3,200 controlled
　Annual rate(s): $8.00; Institutions $8.00; Students $6.25; Members $7.50
Publisher or Sponsor: The Classical Association of the Atlantic States

EDITORIAL DESCRIPTION
　Contains articles and notes of a general and a scholarly nature; bibliographical surveys of ancient authors and genres; book reviews, etc. dealing with the general field of classical studies
Articles per average issue: 3
Audience: Classicists
　Manuscripts accepted in English (Latin)

MANUSCRIPT INFORMATION

Subject field(s): Greco-Roman antiquity and its aftermath; methodology of teaching classical subjects
Manuscript requirements: TAPA format
　Preferred length: 20 pages maximum
　Number of copies to be submitted: 1
　Abstract: Not necessary.
Author information and reprints: Payment: None.
　Is simultaneous submission of article to other journals permitted: Not permitted.
　Exclusive manuscript rights between acceptance and publication: Yes
　Copyright: Held by the Association
　Reprints: Available at no cost. 10 Available at cost.
Additional information: Manuscripts must be typewritten, double-spaced, with wide margins, notes at the end. Greek inclusions must be transliterated.
Disposition of manuscript:
　Query letter: Not necessary.
　Receipt of manuscript acknowledged: Yes
　Decision to publish in: 60 days
　Accepted manuscript published in: 18-24 months
　Rejected manuscript returned: Yes, with return postage paid by publication.
　Rejected manuscript criticized: Yes
Submit to:
　Walter Donlan
　Editor
　Department of Classics, 120 Carnegie
　The Pennsylvania State University
　University Park, Pennsylvania 16801
　(814) 865-8851

COMPARATIVE STUDIES IN SOCIETY AND HISTORY [80]
Cambridge University Press
32 East 57th Street
New York, New York 10022

EDITORIAL DESCRIPTION
　A forum for the presentation and discussion of new research into problems of change and stability that recur in human societies through time or in the contemporary world as well as setting a working alliance between specialists in all branches of the social sciences and humanities.
　Manuscripts accepted in English

MANUSCRIPT INFORMATION

Manuscript requirements: See latest issue for style requirements. Style sheet sent on request.
　Preferred length: As required
　Number of copies to be submitted: 2
　Abstract: Yes.
Author information and reprints: Payment: Reprints only. 50 offprints
　Is simultaneous submission of article to other journals permitted: Not permitted.
　Exclusive manuscript rights between acceptance and publication: Yes
　Copyright: Held by publication.
　Reprints: Available at cost.
Disposition of manuscript:
　Query letter: Not necessary, but advisable.
　Receipt of manuscript acknowledged: Yes
　Rejected manuscript returned: Yes, if return postage is supplied by author.
　Rejected manuscript criticized: Sometimes
Submit to:
　The Editors
　Department of History
　University of Michigan
　Ann Arbor, Michigan 48104

THE DALHOUSIE REVIEW [81]
Dalhousie University
Killam Library
Halifax, Nova Scotia, Canada
424-2541

First published in 1921

SUBSCRIPTION DATA

Issues and rates: Published quarterly.
　Average paid circulation: 900; 1100 controlled
　Annual rate(s): $6.00
Publisher or Sponsor: Dalhousie University
Managing Editor: A. R. Bevan

EDITORIAL DESCRIPTION
　Contains articles, poems, occasionally fiction, book reviews.
Articles per average issue: 12
Audience: University population

MANUSCRIPT INFORMATION

Subject field(s): Literature, history, politics, philosophy, aesthetics, poems, fiction
Manuscript requirements: See latest issue for style requirements.
　Preferred length: 5000 words maximum
　Number of copies to be submitted: One
Author information and reprints: Payment: By publication to author. $1.00 per page. Honorarium. $3.00 for poetry
　Is simultaneous submission of article to other journals permitted: No
　Exclusive manuscript rights between acceptance and publication: Yes
　Copyright: Held by publication.
　Reprints: Available at time of publication
Disposition of manuscript:
　Query letter: Not necessary.
　Receipt of manuscript acknowledged: Yes
　Decision to publish in: Two months
　Accepted manuscript published in: 1 year or more
　Rejected manuscript returned: Yes, if return postage is supplied by author.
　Rejected manuscript criticized: If requested
Submit to:
　Allan R. Bevan
　(See address above)

DURHAM UNIVERSITY JOURNAL [82]
43 North Bailey
Durham, Great Britain
4466

First published in 1876

SUBSCRIPTION DATA

Issues and rates: Published three times per year.
　Average paid circulation: 800
　Annual rate(s): £1.15
Publisher or Sponsor: University of Durham
Managing Editor: M. E. James

EDITORIAL DESCRIPTION
　A general scholarly publication.

MANUSCRIPT INFORMATION

Subject field(s): Literature, history, philosophy, theology, sociology, political thought
Manuscript requirements: No specific style guide.
　Preferred length: 9000 words
　Number of copies to be submitted: One
　Abstract: Not necessary.
Author information and reprints: Payment: Reprints only. 25 offprints
　Is simultaneous submission of article to other journals permitted: No
　Exclusive manuscript rights between acceptance and publication: Yes
　Copyright: Held by University of Durham
　Reprints: Available at cost. Current price
Disposition of manuscript:
　Query letter: Not necessary.
　Receipt of manuscript acknowledged: Yes
　Decision to publish in: 3-4 months
　Accepted manuscript published in: One year
　Rejected manuscript returned: Yes
　Rejected manuscript criticized: No

Humanities (general)

Submit to:
The Editor
(See address above)

EIGHTEENTH-CENTURY STUDIES [83]
An Interdisciplinary Journal
English Department
University of California
Davis, California 95616
(916) 752-2249

First published in 1967

SUBSCRIPTION DATA
Issues and rates: Published quarterly.
 Average paid circulation: 2,500
 Annual rate(s): Individuals $9; Institutions $12; Foreign $10
Publisher or Sponsor: American Society for Eighteenth-Century Studies
Managing Editor: Robert H. Hopkins

EDITORIAL DESCRIPTION
A general magazine which explores literature, art, painting, music and intellectual history. Contributions must have some bearing on the eighteenth century. Preference will be given to articles of potential value to students in more than one discipline. Will not publish highly technical and specialized articles on narrowly limited subjects in a single field, nor popular essays designed for the general reader.
Articles per average issue: 5-7
Audience: Academic, general
Manuscripts accepted in English only

MANUSCRIPT INFORMATION
Subject field(s): Literature, history, philosophy, art, architecture, drama, music, politics, criticism
Manuscript requirements: MLA
 Preferred length: Under 6,500 words
 Number of copies to be submitted: Two
 Abstract: Yes
Author information and reprints: Payment: None.
 Is simultaneous submission of article to other journals permitted: No
 Exclusive manuscript rights between acceptance and publication: Yes
 Copyright: Held by publication.
 Reprints: Available; 25 free, additional at cost
Additional information: Manuscripts should be double-spaced, with footnotes collected on separate pages at the end.
Disposition of manuscript:
 Query letter: No
 Receipt of manuscript acknowledged: Yes
 Decision to publish in: 4 months
 Accepted manuscript published in: 6-24 months
 Rejected manuscript returned: Yes, if return postage is supplied by author.
 Rejected manuscript criticized: Yes
Submit to:
The Editors
(See address above)

ENGLISH STUDIES IN AFRICA [84]
A Journal of the Humanities
Witwatersrand University Press
Jan Smuts Avenue
Johannesburg, South Africa
724-1311 ext. 794

First published in 1958

SUBSCRIPTION DATA
Issues and rates: Published bi-monthly.
 Average paid circulation: 500
 Annual rate(s): R 5.00
Publisher or Sponsor: Witwatersrand University
Managing Editor: B. D. Cheadle

EDITORIAL DESCRIPTION
Contains articles on English studies and on the humanities.
Articles per average issue: 6
Manuscripts accepted in English

MANUSCRIPT INFORMATION
Subject field(s): English humanities
Manuscript requirements: Oxford English Dictionary and Oxford University Press Style.
 Preferred length: 2,500 words (typewritten, double-spaced)
 Number of copies to be submitted: One
 Abstract: Yes.
Author information and reprints: Payment: None.
 Is simultaneous submission of article to other journals permitted: No
 Exclusive manuscript rights between acceptance and publication: Yes
 Copyright: Held by publication.
 Reprints: Available at no cost.
Disposition of manuscript:
 Query letter: Not necessary.
 Receipt of manuscript acknowledged: Yes
 Decision to publish in: 3 months
 Accepted manuscript published in: 6 months
 Rejected manuscript returned: Yes
 Rejected manuscript criticized: No
Submit to:
Mrs. N. H. Wilson
Publications Officer
(See address above)

FOUR QUARTERS [85]
La Salle College
Philadelphia, Pennsylvania 19141
(215) 848-8300 ext. 337

First published in 1951-52

SUBSCRIPTION DATA
Issues and rates: Published quarterly.
 Average paid circulation: 500
 Annual rate(s): $3.00
Publisher or Sponsor: La Salle College
Managing Editor: John J. Keenan

EDITORIAL DESCRIPTION
Primarily a literary quarterly publishing short stories, poetry, and articles on literary criticism. Also open to articles on the arts, politics, or social questions if the articles are well-written and of interest to the intelligent reader.
Articles per average issue: 12
Audience: Intelligent readers with literary interests
Manuscripts accepted in English

MANUSCRIPT INFORMATION
Subject field(s): Literature, the arts, politics, history, social sciences
Manuscript requirements: MLA
 Preferred length: 2000 to 5000 words
 Number of copies to be submitted: One
 Rejected manuscript returned: No
Author information and reprints: Payment: By publication to author. $25 per article. 3 to 5 copies sent free to author on publication.
 Is simultaneous submission of article to other journals permitted: Strongly discouraged
 Exclusive manuscript rights between acceptance and publication: Yes
 Copyright: Held by publication. Assigned to author on request
 Reprints: Not available.
Additional information: Author should keep carbon or Xerox; cannot be responsible for manuscripts lost or strayed in the mails.
Disposition of manuscript:
 Query letter: No
 Receipt of manuscript acknowledged: No
 Decision to publish in: 6 weeks
 Accepted manuscript published in: 3-12 months
 Rejected manuscript returned: Yes, if self-addressed, stamped envelope is sent with manuscript.
 Rejected manuscript criticized: No
Submit to:
John J. Keenan
Editor
(See address above)

SPECIAL STIPULATIONS
Not interested in highly specialized articles or re-hashed dissertation chapters. Welcome lively and informal essays on a particular author or work.

GESTA [86]
International Center for Medieval Art
The Cloisters, Fort Tryon Park
New York, New York 10040
(212) WA 3-3700

First published in 1963

SUBSCRIPTION DATA
Issues and rates: Published semi-annually.
 Average paid circulation: 550
Publisher or Sponsor: International Center of Medieval Art
Managing Editor: Linda Seidel

EDITORIAL DESCRIPTION
To publish new research on the art and architecture of western Europe and of Byzantium during the Middle Ages, including the early Christian period; to

develope a corpus of selected types of medieval objects in American collections
Articles per average issue: 5
Audience: Art and architectural historians, medievalists
Manuscripts accepted in English (Western European languages considered)

MANUSCRIPT INFORMATION

Subject field(s): Medieval art and civilization, with special emphasis on the painting, sculpture, music, literature, architecture and civilization; the period circa 325 A.D. to 1500 A.D.
Manuscript requirements: See latest issue for style requirements. *Art Bulletin*
Preferred length: 20-25 pages
Number of copies to be submitted: 1
Abstract: Yes. An abstract, in English, for articles written in languages other than English.
Author information and reprints: Payment: None.
Is simultaneous submission of article to other journals permitted: Not permitted.
Exclusive manuscript rights between acceptance and publication: Yes
Copyright: None
Reprints: Available at no cost. 12
Additional information: The author must provide his own high-quality glossy photographs.
Disposition of manuscript:
Query letter: Not necessary.
Receipt of manuscript acknowledged: Yes
Decision to publish in: 2-3 months
Accepted manuscript published in: 6 months
Rejected manuscript returned: Yes, with return postage paid by publication.
Rejected manuscript criticized: Yes
Submit to:
Linda Seidel
Editor
Fogg Art Museum
Cambridge, Massachusetts 02138

GREEN RIVER REVIEW [87]
Box 56
University Center, Michigan 48710

First published in 1968

SUBSCRIPTION DATA

Issues and rates: Published semi-annually.
Average paid circulation: 500
Annual rate(s): $4.00; Foreign $4.50
Managing Editor: Raymond Tyner

EDITORIAL DESCRIPTION

Contains critical essays on literary figures, history of ideas, music, art.
Articles per average issue: 20
Audience: People with literary interest, particularly, poetry.
Manuscripts accepted in English

MANUSCRIPT INFORMATION

Subject field(s): Short fiction, poetry, critical essays book reviews.
Manuscript requirements: None
Preferred length: 1000-3000 words
Number of copies to be submitted: One
Abstract: Not necessary.
Author information and reprints: Payment: None. Copies of periodical.
Is simultaneous submission of article to other journals permitted: Not permitted.
Copyright: Held by publication.
Reprints: Not available.
Disposition of manuscript:
Query letter: Not necessary.
Receipt of manuscript acknowledged: Yes, if return postage is supplied by author.
Decision to publish in: 1-2 months
Accepted manuscript published in: 6-12 months
Rejected manuscript returned: Yes
Rejected manuscript criticized: Sometimes
Submit to:
The Editors
(See address above)

HESPERIA [88]
Journal of the American School of Classical Studies at Athens
Care Institute for Advanced Study
Princeton, New Jersey 08540
(609) 924-4400 ext. 498

First published in 1931

SUBSCRIPTION DATA

Issues and rates: Published quarterly.
Average paid circulation: 880
Annual rate(s): $15.00; Foreign $16.00
Managing Editor: Dr. Marian H. McAllister
Articles per average issue: 6
Audience: Scholars in Classical Studies, (Greek Archaeology, History and Literature)
Manuscripts accepted in English

MANUSCRIPT INFORMATION

Subject field(s): Subjects usually limited to field of Ancient Greek Civilization
Manuscript requirements: Style sheet sent on request.
Preferred length: 15-30 pages
Number of copies to be submitted: 1
Abstract: Not necessary.
Author information and reprints: Payment: None.
Is simultaneous submission of article to other journals permitted: Permitted, but not encouraged.
Exclusive manuscript rights between acceptance and publication: Yes
Reprints: Available at cost. 25 Free
Disposition of manuscript:
Query letter: Not necessary, but advisable.
Receipt of manuscript acknowledged: Yes
Decision to publish in: Up to 6 months
Accepted manuscript published in: 1 1/2 years
Rejected manuscript returned: Yes, with return postage paid by publication.
Rejected manuscript criticized: Sometimes
Submit to:
Dr. Marian H. McAllister
Editor of Publications
(See address above)

SPECIAL STIPULATIONS

Manuscripts must be by staff or alumni of the American School of Classical Studies at Athens, or be concerned with material from the excavations sponsored by the school.

THE HUMANIST [89]
923 Kensington Avenue
Buffalo, New York 14215
(716) 837-0306

First published in 1941

SUBSCRIPTION DATA

Issues and rates: Published bi-monthly.
Average paid circulation: 27,800
Annual rate(s): $9.00, Foreign $10.50
Publisher or Sponsor: American Humanist Association;
American Ethical Union
Managing Editor: Paul Kurtz

EDITORIAL DESCRIPTION

Deals with ethical and humanist issues on the frontier of social concern.
Articles per average issue: 6 to 8
Audience: The educated
Manuscripts accepted in English

MANUSCRIPT INFORMATION

Subject field(s): Social sciences, behavioral sciences, ethics, philosophy, religion
Manuscript requirements: None
Preferred length: 2000-3000 words; 10 pages
Number of copies to be submitted: Three
Abstract: Yes.
Author information and reprints: Payment: By publication to author. Payment depends on article.
Is simultaneous submission of article to other journals permitted: No
Exclusive manuscript rights between acceptance and publication: Yes
Copyright: Held by publication.
Reprints: Not available.
Disposition of manuscript:
Query letter: Not necessary, but advisable.
Receipt of manuscript acknowledged: Yes
Decision to publish in: 2 months
Accepted manuscript published in: 6 months
Rejected manuscript returned: Yes
Rejected manuscript criticized: No
Submit to:
Paul Kurtz
Editor
(See address above)

Humanities (general) 31

HUMANITIES ASSOCIATION REVIEW [90]
La Revue de l'Association des Humanites
Mrs. S. J. Wynne-Edwards
Queen's University, Department of English
Kingston, Ontario, Canada

Previously entitled *Humanities Association Bulletin*

First published in 1951

SUBSCRIPTION DATA
Issues and rates: Published quarterly.
  Annual rate(s): $5.00, Institutions $7.50
Publisher or Sponsor: The Humanities Association of Canada
Managing Editor: Phillip W. Rogers

EDITORIAL DESCRIPTION
  Presents articles of general and special interest in all branches of the humanities; especially interested in articles that are interdisciplinary
Articles per average issue: 5
Audience: Professional, academic
  Manuscripts accepted in English, French

MANUSCRIPT INFORMATION
Manuscript requirements: MLA
  Preferred length: 5,000 words
  Number of copies to be submitted: 1
  Abstract: Yes.
Author information and reprints: Payment: Reprints only. 10 offprints
  Is simultaneous submission of article to other journals permitted: Not permitted.
  Exclusive manuscript rights between acceptance and publication: Yes
  Copyright: Held by author.
  Reprints: Not available.
Disposition of manuscript:
  Query letter: Not necessary.
  Receipt of manuscript acknowledged: Yes
  Decision to publish in: 3-6 months
  Accepted manuscript published in: 6-12 months
  Rejected manuscript returned: Yes, if return postage is supplied by author.
  Rejected manuscript criticized: Yes
Submit to:
  Phillip W. Rogers
  Editor
  John Watson Hall
  Queen's University
  Kingston, Ontario, Canada

INTERNATIONAL JOURNAL OF SYMBOLOGY [91]
Department of Psychology
Georgia State University
Atlanta, Georgia 30303
(404) 658-2856

First published in 1967

SUBSCRIPTION DATA
Issues and rates: Published three times per year.
  Average paid circulation: 400
  Annual rate(s): Institutions $20.00; Foreign $21.00
Publisher or Sponsor: International Society for the Study of Symbols
Managing Editor: I. H. Craddick

EDITORIAL DESCRIPTION
  Contains articles on all areas of symbology: psychology, philosophy, art, literature, psycholinguistics, and religion.
Articles per average issue: 5-6
Audience: Anyone with an interest in symbols.
  Manuscripts accepted in English

MANUSCRIPT INFORMATION
Manuscript requirements: See latest issue for style requirements.
  Preferred length: 10 pages
  Number of copies to be submitted: Two
  Abstract: Yes
Author information and reprints: Payment: Reprints only. 50 free issues
  Is simultaneous submission of article to other journals permitted: No
  Exclusive manuscript rights between acceptance and publication: No
  Copyright: Held by publication.
  Reprints: Not available.
Disposition of manuscript:
  Query letter: No
  Receipt of manuscript acknowledged: Yes
  Decision to publish in: 2 months
  Accepted manuscript published in: 6 months
  Rejected manuscript returned: Yes
  Rejected manuscript criticized: Yes
Submit to:
  Ray A. Craddick
  Co-Editor
  (See address above)

JOURNAL OF THE HISTORY OF IDEAS [92]
Devoted to Cultural and Intellectual History
750 Humanities Bldg.
Temple University
Philadelphia, Pennsylvania 19122
(215) 787-8591

First published in 1940

SUBSCRIPTION DATA
Issues and rates: Published quarterly.
  Average paid circulation: 3600; 4100 controlled
  Annual rate(s): Individuals $10.00, Institutions $12.75, Foreign $1.00 additional
Managing Editor: Edward Rosen

EDITORIAL DESCRIPTION
  Contains interdisciplinary discussions of the histories of influential ideas, since antiquity, that affected the growth of the arts, sciences, philosophy; and the results of researches into the unknown.
Articles per average issue: 12
Audience: Scholars
  Manuscripts accepted in English

MANUSCRIPT INFORMATION
Subject field(s): Interrelations of ideas in philosophy and literature, sciences and literature, arts and science, philosophy and social thought.
Manuscript requirements: Chicago
  Preferred length: Under 10,000 words including footnotes
  Number of copies to be submitted: One
  Abstract: Not necessary.
Author information and reprints: Payment: None. Only authors of solicited review articles are paid.
  Is simultaneous submission of article to other journals permitted: Yes
  Exclusive manuscript rights between acceptance and publication: Yes
  Copyright: Held by publication.
  Reprints: Available at cost.
Additional information: Manuscript should be typewritten, double-spaced; footnotes, also typewritten, double-spaced, must be submitted separately on pages numbered consecutively.
Disposition of manuscript:
  Query letter: Not necessary.
  Receipt of manuscript acknowledged: Yes
  Decision to publish in: Two to three months
  Accepted manuscript published in: 18-30 months
  Rejected manuscript returned: Yes, if return postage is supplied by author.
  Rejected manuscript criticized: Sometimes
Submit to:
  Philip P. Wiener
  Executive Editor
  (See address above)

SPECIAL STIPULATIONS
  Foreign languages may be quoted or given only briefly. Greek, Latin, Russian, Oriental languages must be transliterated and translated into English.

JOURNAL OF ROMAN STUDIES [93]
31-34 Gordon Square
London W.C.I., England
01-387-8157

First published in 1911

SUBSCRIPTION DATA
Issues and rates: Published annually.
  Average paid circulation: 2800
  Annual rate(s): £4.50
Publisher or Sponsor: Society for the Promotion of Roman Studies

EDITORIAL DESCRIPTION
  Publishes articles on Roman history and antiquities, literature and archaeology.
Articles per average issue: 10-20
Audience: Professional
  Manuscripts accepted in English, French

MANUSCRIPT INFORMATION
Manuscript requirements: See latest issue for style requirements.
  Preferred length: Not to exceed 16,000 words

Number of copies to be submitted: One
Abstract: No
Author information and reprints: Payment: None.
Is simultaneous submission of article to other journals permitted: No
Exclusive manuscript rights between acceptance and publication: Yes
Copyright: Held by publication.
Reprints: Available at cost
Additional information: Typewritten, double-spaced, on one side only.
Disposition of manuscript:
Query letter: No
Receipt of manuscript acknowledged: Yes
Decision to publish in: 2-3 months
Accepted manuscript published in: Within a year
Rejected manuscript returned: Yes
Rejected manuscript criticized: No
Submit to:
Fergus Graham;
Burtholme Millar
(See address above)

LANGUAGE AND STYLE [94]
An International Journal
Department of English
Southern Illinois University
Carbondale, Illinois 62901
(618) 453-5321 ext. 233

First published in 1968

SUBSCRIPTION DATA
Issues and rates: Published quarterly.
Average paid circulation: 300; 250 controlled
Annual rate(s): $7.50, Foreign $8.50

EDITORIAL DESCRIPTION
Contains articles, scholarly and critical, on specific and general aspects of style in all its manifestations, in all the arts and society.
Articles per average issue: 7
Audience: Critics and scholars of style
Manuscripts accepted in English, French, German

MANUSCRIPT INFORMATION
Subject field(s): Linguistics, literature, music, cinema, painting and architecture, sociology, psychology, etc.
Manuscript requirements: MLA
Preferred length: 2000-10,000 words; 6-30 pages
Number of copies to be submitted: Two
Abstract: Yes
Author information and reprints: Payment: None.
Is simultaneous submission of article to other journals permitted: Yes
Exclusive manuscript rights between acceptance and publication: No
Copyright: Held by publication.
Reprints: Available
Disposition of manuscript:
Query letter: No
Receipt of manuscript acknowledged: Yes
Decision to publish in: 6 weeks
Accepted manuscript published in: 1-2 years
Rejected manuscript returned: Yes
Rejected manuscript criticized: Yes
Submit to:
Edmund L. Epstein
Editor
(See address above)

LEEDS PHILOSOPHICAL AND LITERARY SOCIETY PROCEEDINGS [95]
Central Museum, Calverly Street
Leeds, England

First published in 1925

SUBSCRIPTION DATA
Issues and rates: Irregular
Average paid circulation: 650; 500 controlled
Publisher or Sponsor: Leeds Philosophical and Literary Society
Managing Editor: J. Taylor

EDITORIAL DESCRIPTION
Contains articles in literary and historical fields.
Articles per average issue: Varies
Audience: Academic
Manuscripts accepted in English

MANUSCRIPT INFORMATION
Manuscript requirements: See latest issue for style requirements.
Author information and reprints: Payment: None.
Is simultaneous submission of article to other journals permitted: No
Exclusive manuscript rights between acceptance and publication: Yes
Copyright: Held by publication.
Reprints: Available
Disposition of manuscript:
Query letter: Yes
Receipt of manuscript acknowledged: Yes
Decision to publish in: Varies
Accepted manuscript published in: Six months
Rejected manuscript returned: Yes, if return postage is supplied by author.
Rejected manuscript criticized: Sometimes
Submit to:
John Taylor
Editor
School of History
University of Leeds
Leeds, England

MANUSCRIPTA [96]
Saint Louis University
Pius XII Memorial Library
3655 West Pine Boulevard
St. Louis, Missouri 63108
(314) 535-3300 ext. 397

SUBSCRIPTION DATA
Issues and rates: Published three times per year.
Average paid circulation: Not available.
Annual rate(s): $5.00, Foreign $5.50
Managing Editor: Lowrie J. Daly

EDITORIAL DESCRIPTION
Contains historical and literary studies based on manuscripts.

MANUSCRIPT INFORMATION
Manuscript requirements: MLA
Preferred length: Articles: 3000-5000; Notes: 1500 words
Number of copies to be submitted: Two
Author information and reprints: Payment: None.
Is simultaneous submission of article to other journals permitted: No
Reprints: Available, 20 copies free
Disposition of manuscript:
Decision to publish in: 2 weeks
Accepted manuscript published in: One year
Rejected manuscript returned: Yes, if return postage is supplied by author.
Rejected manuscript criticized: Yes
Submit to:
Lowrie J. Daly
Editor
(See address above)

MANUSCRIPTS [97]
Manuscript Society
154 Wells Avenue
Newton, Massachusetts 02159

First published in 1947

SUBSCRIPTION DATA
Issues and rates: Published quarterly.
Average paid circulation: 1,150
Annual rate(s): Institutions $20.00; Students $4.00; Members $10.00; Foreign individuals $10.00; Foreign institutions $20.00
Publisher or Sponsor: The Manuscript Society
Managing Editor: Paul V. Lutz

EDITORIAL DESCRIPTION
Articles deal with some aspect of manuscripts: collection, perservation, use in research, origin or people connected therewith, methods of illustration, etc.
Articles per average issue: 9
Manuscripts accepted in English

MANUSCRIPT INFORMATION
Subject field(s): History and literature as connected with manuscripts
Manuscript requirements: See latest issue for style requirements.
Preferred length: 2,000 to 5,000 words
Number of copies to be submitted: 2
Abstract: Not necessary.
Author information and reprints: Payment: Reprints only. 5
Is simultaneous submission of article to other journals permitted: Not permitted.
Exclusive manuscript rights between acceptance and publication: Yes
Copyright: Held by publication but will accommodate author's wishes
Reprints: Available at cost.

Disposition of manuscript:
  Query letter: Not necessary.
  Receipt of manuscript acknowledged: Yes
  Decision to publish in: 4 to 6 weeks
  Accepted manuscript published in: 3 to 5 months
  Rejected manuscript returned: Yes, if return postage is supplied by author.
  Rejected manuscript criticized: Sometimes
Submit to:
  Paul V. Lutz
  Editor
  1023 Amherst Street
  Tyler, Texas 75704
  (214) 593-9243

THE MARKHAM REVIEW [98]
Horrmann Library
Wagner College
Staten Island, New York 10301
(212) 390-3000

First published in 1968

SUBSCRIPTION DATA
Issues and rates: Published three times per year.
  Average paid circulation: 2000 controlled
Publisher or Sponsor: Wagner College, Horrmann Library

EDITORIAL DESCRIPTION
  Contains articles on literary, social, and political figures in America of the period 1865-1940.
Articles per average issue: 5
Audience: Scholars
  Manuscripts accepted in English

MANUSCRIPT INFORMATION
Subject field(s): Literature, politics, society, philosophy, book reviews
Manuscript requirements: MLA
  Preferred length: Less than 6000 words
  Number of copies to be submitted: Two
  Abstract: No
Author information and reprints: Payment: 24 copies of issue
  Is simultaneous submission of article to other journals permitted: No
  Exclusive manuscript rights between acceptance and publication: No
  Copyright: Held by author.
  Reprints: Not available.
Additional information: Typewritten, double-spaced, with footnotes at end
Disposition of manuscript:
  Query letter: No
  Receipt of manuscript acknowledged: Yes
  Decision to publish in: 4 weeks
  Accepted manuscript published in: 6-12 months
  Rejected manuscript returned: Yes, if self-addressed, stamped envelope is sent with manuscript.
  Rejected manuscript criticized: Yes
Submit to:
  Joseph W. Slade
  Editor
  (See address above)

MEDIEVALIA ET HUMANISTICA [99]
Studies in Medieval and Renaissance Culture
P. O. Box 13348
North Texas Station
Denton, Texas 76203
(817) 788-2101

Previously entitled *An American Journal for the Middle Ages and Renaissance*

First published in 1943

SUBSCRIPTION DATA
Issues and rates: Published annually.
  Average paid circulation: 2,000
  Annual rate(s): $11.95
Publisher or Sponsor: Modern Language Association; North Texas State University
Managing Editor: Julie S. Davis

EDITORIAL DESCRIPTION
  Publishes significant scholarship, criticism, and reviews in all areas of medieval and renaissance culture; encourages the individual scholar to examine the relationship of his discipline to other disciplines and to relate his study in a theoretical or practical way to its cultural and historical context
Articles per average issue: 17
Audience: Academic, intelligent general reader
  Manuscripts accepted in English

MANUSCRIPT INFORMATION
Subject field(s): All areas of medieval and renaissance culture: literature, art, history, law, philosophy, music, science, social and economic institutions
Manuscript requirements: MLA
  Preferred length: 20 pages maximum
  Number of copies to be submitted: 1 original
  Abstract: Yes.
Author information and reprints: Payment: Reprints only. 25 free offprints
  Is simultaneous submission of article to other journals permitted: Not permitted.
  Exclusive manuscript rights between acceptance and publication: Yes
  Copyright: Held by publication.
Additional information: Consult the editorial note published in each volume as well as the quality and style of the articles published.
Disposition of manuscript:
  Query letter: Not necessary, but advisable.
  Receipt of manuscript acknowledged: Yes
  Decision to publish in: 2-3 months
  Accepted manuscript published in: 9 months
  Rejected manuscript returned: Yes, if return postage is supplied by author.
  Rejected manuscript criticized: Sometimes
Submit to:
  Prof. Paul Clogan
  Editor
  (See address above)

THE MIDWEST QUARTERLY [100]
A Journal of Contemporary Thought
Kansas State College of Pittsburg
Pittsburg, Kansas 66762
(316) 231-7000 ext. 378

First published in 1959

SUBSCRIPTION DATA
Issues and rates: Published quarterly.
  Average paid circulation: 1000
  Annual rate(s): $2.50
Publisher or Sponsor: Kansas State College of Pittsburg
Managing Editor: Rebecca Patterson

EDITORIAL DESCRIPTION
  To discover and publish scholarly articles dealing with a broad range of subjects of current interest; particularly discussions of an analytical and speculative nature rather than heavily documented research studies.
Articles per average issue: 6 articles; 12 poems
Audience: Academic
  Manuscripts accepted in English

MANUSCRIPT INFORMATION
Subject field(s): Literary criticism, political science, art, music, history, sociology, the humanities in general
Manuscript requirements: MLA
  Preferred length: Under 5000 words
  Number of copies to be submitted: One
  Abstract: Not necessary.
Author information and reprints: Payment: None.
  Is simultaneous submission of article to other journals permitted: No
  Exclusive manuscript rights between acceptance and publication: Yes
  Copyright: Held by publication, but transferred upon request after publication.
  Reprints: Available, $.50 each
Additional information: Prefer a minimal documentation within parentheses in text, supplemented if necessary by select bibliography, in preference to footnotes.
Disposition of manuscript:
  Query letter: Not necessary.
  Receipt of manuscript acknowledged: Yes
  Decision to publish in: 2 months
  Accepted manuscript published in: 6-9 months
  Rejected manuscript returned: Yes, if return postage is supplied by author.
  Rejected manuscript criticized: Sometimes
Submit to:
  Rebecca Patterson
  Editor
  (See address above)

NAMES [101]
Journal of the American Name Society
The State University College
Potsdam, New York 13676
(315) 268-2742

SUBSCRIPTION DATA
Issues and rates: Published quarterly.
  Average paid circulation: 975
  Annual rate(s): Individuals $15.00;
  Institutions $15.00
Publisher or Sponsor: American Name
  Society
Managing Editor: Conrad M. Rothrauff

EDITORIAL DESCRIPTION
  Contains articles on etymology, origin, meaning and application of names (personal, place, scientific, commercial) in all disciplines, genealogies excluded. Articles must be scholarly and investigative in nature.
Articles per average issue: 5
Audience: Academic
  Manuscripts accepted in any language

MANUSCRIPT INFORMATION
Subject field(s): Onomatology, philology, linguistics, behaviorial sciences, literature, history, physical sciences, aesthetics, social sciences, arts
Manuscript requirements: MLA
  Preferred length: None
  Number of copies to be submitted: One
  Abstract: Yes
Author information and reprints: Payment: None.
  Is simultaneous submission of article to other journals permitted: No
  Exclusive manuscript rights between acceptance and publication: Yes
  Copyright: Held by author.
  Reprints: Available, 25 free
Additional information: Footnotes must be at end, but will be printed at page-bottom; manuscript must be typewritten and double-spaced.
Disposition of manuscript:
  Query letter: No
  Receipt of manuscript acknowledged: Yes
  Decision to publish in: Six weeks
  Accepted manuscript published in: One year or more
  Rejected manuscript returned: Yes
  Rejected manuscript criticized: Yes
Submit to:
  Conrad M. Rothrauff
  Editor
  (See address above)
  (315)268-3754

SPECIAL STIPULATIONS
  Preference is given to members of the American Name Society. Book reviews are solicited.

NEW ORLEANS REVIEW [102]
Loyola University
New Orleans, Louisiana 70118
(504) 866-5471 ext. 431

First published in 1968

SUBSCRIPTION DATA
Issues and rates: Published quarterly.
  Average paid circulation: 500; 1,000 controlled
  Annual rate(s): $6.00
Publisher or Sponsor: Loyola University, New Orleans
Managing Editor: Tom Bell

EDITORIAL DESCRIPTION
  Contains fiction, articles, poetry, interviews, reviews, photography and art work.
Articles per average issue: 50
Audience: Educated individuals who are interested in literature and culture.
  Manuscripts accepted in English

MANUSCRIPT INFORMATION
Subject field(s): Literature, science, popular culture, history, art, political science
Manuscript requirements: See latest issue for style requirements.
  Preferred length: 12-24 pages
  Number of copies to be submitted: One
  Abstract: Not necessary.
Author information and reprints: Payment: By publication to author. $50.00 per article. $10.00 per poem
  Is simultaneous submission of article to other journals permitted: Not permitted.
  Exclusive manuscript rights between acceptance and publication: Yes
  Copyright: Held by publication.
  Reprints: Available, $5.00 per 25
Disposition of manuscript:
  Query letter: Not necessary.
  Receipt of manuscript acknowledged: Yes
  Decision to publish in: 2-8 weeks
  Accepted manuscript published in: 3 to 12 months
  Rejected manuscript returned: Yes, if return postage is supplied by author.
  Rejected manuscript criticized: No
Submit to:
  Marcus Smith
  Editor
  (See address above)

THE NEW RENAISSANCE [103]
A Magazine of Ideas & Opinions, Emphasizing Literature & the Arts
9 Heath Road
Arlington, Massachusetts 02174

First published in 1968

SUBSCRIPTION DATA
Issues and rates: Published semi-annually.
  Average paid circulation: 400-800
  Annual rate(s): $5.50; Foreign $6.50; Individuals $5.50; Foreign individuals $6.50; Foreign institutions $6.50
Managing Editor: Louise T. Reynolds

EDITORIAL DESCRIPTION
  To offer readers a wide range of subject matter & of styles; interested in political, sociological, artistic subjects that would appeal to the serious & informed reader but that would not appeal to the scholar; general point of view is that of a classicist.
Articles per average issue: 2-6
Audience: The well-read person with artistic sensibilities.
  Manuscripts accepted in English

MANUSCRIPT INFORMATION
Subject field(s): Political—national, international, local; sociological but not highly specialized as to view and/or language; artistic, literary, theatre, visual arts, artists, cinema, music (classical & jazz); other if applicable to contemporary scene in a universal way).
Manuscript requirements: No specific style guide.
  Preferred length: Up to 35 pages
  Number of copies to be submitted: One
  Abstract: Not necessary
Author information and reprints: Payment: By publication to author. $15.00-$50.00 per article.
  Is simultaneous submission of article to other journals permitted: Not permitted.
  Exclusive manuscript rights between acceptance and publication: Yes
  Copyright: Held by publication. all rights.
Additional information: Non-fiction should be an opinion piece, interestingly developed with style and some grace, or a well-researched article with documentation where necessary.
Disposition of manuscript:
  Query letter: Necessary.
  Receipt of manuscript acknowledged: No
  Decision to publish in: 10-16 weeks
  Accepted manuscript published in: 1 year
  Rejected manuscript returned: Yes, if return postage is supplied by author.
  Rejected manuscript criticized: Sometimes
Submit to:
  Louise T. Reynolds
  Editor
  (See address above)

THE NEWBERRY LIBRARY BULLETIN [104]
60 West Walton Street
Chicago, Illinois 60610
(312) 943-9090 ext. 256

First published in 1944

SUBSCRIPTION DATA
Issues and rates: Irregular
  Average paid circulation: 2,400 controlled
Publisher or Sponsor: The Newberry Library
Managing Editor: James M. Wells

EDITORIAL DESCRIPTION
  Contains articles, bibliographies, etc. drawn from research in the library's collections or reflecting its holdings.
Articles per average issue: 6

MANUSCRIPT INFORMATION
Subject field(s): History and literature, English, American, and European; Spanish and Portuguese colonial history to independence; history of printing and musicology
Manuscript requirements: Chicago
  Preferred length: 1,000-3,000 words
  Number of copies to be submitted: One

Author information and reprints: Payment:
None. Complimentary copies
Is simultaneous submission of article to
other journals permitted: Yes
Exclusive manuscript rights between
acceptance and publication: No
Copyright: Held by publication.
Reprints: Not available.
Disposition of manuscript:
Receipt of manuscript acknowledged: Yes
Decision to publish in: 6-12 months
Accepted manuscript published in: 12
months or more
Rejected manuscript returned: Yes
Rejected manuscript criticized: No
Submit to:
James M. Wells
Editor
(See address above)

NOTTINGHAM MEDIAEVAL STUDIES [105]

The University
Nottingham, NGY 2RD, England
0602 56101 ext. 2476

First published in 1957

SUBSCRIPTION DATA
Issues and rates: Published annually.
Average paid circulation: 500
Publisher or Sponsor: The University of
Nottingham
Annual rate(s): $5.00; Individuals $5.00

EDITORIAL DESCRIPTION
Contains articles on literature, language,
history, painting, music, economics, etc.
of the Middle Ages.
Articles per average issue: 4-5
Audience: Academic
Manuscripts accepted in English

MANUSCRIPT INFORMATION
Manuscript requirements: See latest issue for
style requirements.
Preferred length: 10,000 words; 20 pages
Number of copies to be submitted: One
Abstract: No
Author information and reprints: Payment:
None.
Is simultaneous submission of article to
other journals permitted: Yes
Exclusive manuscript rights between
acceptance and publication: Yes
Copyright: Held by publication.
Reprints: Available, 50 free
Disposition of manuscript:
Query letter: No
Receipt of manuscript acknowledged: Yes
Decision to publish in: 2-3 months
Accepted manuscript published in: 6
months
Rejected manuscript returned: Yes
Rejected manuscript criticized: No
Submit to:
Lewis Thorpe
Editor
(See address above)

OPINION [106]

A Journal of Thought
Post Office Box 1319
Dodge City, Kansas 67801
(312) 761-5645

First published in 1959

SUBSCRIPTION DATA
Issues and rates: Published monthly.
Average paid circulation: 5,000
controlled
Annual rate(s): $5.00
Managing Editor: Sue Meyer

EDITORIAL DESCRIPTION
Publishes provocative "think" articles
relating to philosophy, sociology and
theology; current essays projecting
thoughts on events of the day.
Articles per average issue: 5
Audience: Professional
Manuscripts accepted in English only

MANUSCRIPT INFORMATION
Subject field(s): Sociology, philosophy,
theology
Manuscript requirements: No specific style
guide.
Preferred length: 2500 words; 9-10 pages
Number of copies to be submitted: One
Abstract: Yes.
Author information and reprints: Payment:
Copies of issue
Is simultaneous submission of article to
other journals permitted: Yes
Exclusive manuscript rights between
acceptance and publication: Yes
Copyright: Not copyrighted
Reprints: Available, cost varies
Disposition of manuscript:
Query letter: Not necessary.
Receipt of manuscript acknowledged: No
Decision to publish in: 2-3 weeks
Accepted manuscript published in: Varies
Rejected manuscript returned: Yes, if
return postage is supplied by author.
Rejected manuscript criticized: Yes
Submit to:
S. Meyer
Associate Editor
(See address above)

SPECIAL STIPULATIONS
Articles must be clear and camera-ready.

PROGRESSIVE WORLD [107]

377 Vernon Street
Oakland, California 94610
(805) 644-3678

First published in 1925

SUBSCRIPTION DATA
Issues and rates: Published monthly.
Average paid circulation: 1,000; 75
controlled
Annual rate(s): $14.50; Foreign $6.00
Managing Editor: Sydney A. Zucker

EDITORIAL DESCRIPTION
Humanist freethought
Articles per average issue: 10
Audience: Freethinkers
Manuscripts accepted in English

MANUSCRIPT INFORMATION
Subject field(s): Humanities, social sciences,
sciences, politics
Manuscript requirements: No specific style
guide.
Preferred length: Under 1600 words
Number of copies to be submitted: One
Abstract: Not necessary.
Author information and reprints: Payment:
None. Reprints only. 12
Is simultaneous submission of article to
other journals permitted: Permitted.
Exclusive manuscript rights between
acceptance and publication: No
Copyright: Held by author.
Reprints: Available at cost.
Disposition of manuscript:
Query letter: Not necessary.
Receipt of manuscript acknowledged: Yes
Decision to publish in: One week
Accepted manuscript published in: Three
months
Rejected manuscript returned: Yes, if
return postage is supplied by author.
Rejected manuscript criticized: Reasons
for rejections only
Submit to:
Sydney A. Zucker
Editor
65 Victor Herbert Drive
Ventura, California 93003
(805) 644-3678

RENAISSANCE QUARTERLY [108]

1161 Amsterdam Avenue
New York, New York 10027
(212) 280-2318

Previously entitled *Renaissance News*

First published in 1948

SUBSCRIPTION DATA
Issues and rates: Published quarterly.
Average paid circulation: 3250
Annual rate(s): Individuals $12.50,
Institutions $16.00
Publisher or Sponsor: Renaissance Society of
America
Managing Editor: Elizabeth Story Donno

EDITORIAL DESCRIPTION
Publishes articles and reviews of books
on all aspects of history and culture of
the Renaissance period 1399-1660.
Articles per average issue: 3-4 articles, 30
reviews
Audience: Scholars
Manuscripts accepted in English

MANUSCRIPT INFORMATION
Subject field(s): All areas of Renaissance life
and culture: literature, history, art,
music, philosophy, religion, science
Manuscript requirements: MLA
Preferred length: No more than 20 pages
for short articles

Number of copies to be submitted: One
Abstract: No
Author information and reprints: Payment: None.
Is simultaneous submission of article to other journals permitted: No
Exclusive manuscript rights between acceptance and publication: Yes
Copyright: Held by publication.
Reprints: Available at cost, depending on length of article. Double-spaced typescript throughout; notes at end.
Disposition of manuscript:
Query letter: No
Receipt of manuscript acknowledged: Yes
Decision to publish in: 1-2 months
Accepted manuscript published in: 1 year
Rejected manuscript returned: Yes, if return postage is supplied by author.
Rejected manuscript criticized: Yes
Submit to:
The Editors
(See address above)

RESEARCH STUDIES [109]
Washington State University
Pullman, Washington 99163
(509) 335-3518

First published in 1929

SUBSCRIPTION DATA
Issues and rates: Published quarterly.
Average paid circulation: 900
Annual rate(s): $4.00
Managing Editor: Henry Grosshans

EDITORIAL DESCRIPTION
Contains scholarly articles, commentaries, and reviews of contemporary literary, historical, social, and cultural subjects. Emphasis upon speculative material that incorporates scholarship and critical insight.
Articles per average issue: 9
Audience: Scholars
Manuscripts accepted in English

MANUSCRIPT INFORMATION
Subject field(s): Literature, history, social comment, philosophy, sociology, anthropology, theory of science
Manuscript requirements: See latest issue for style requirements.
Preferred length: 3000-5000 words; 12-20 pages
Number of copies to be submitted: One
Abstract: Not necessary.
Author information and reprints: Payment: None.
Is simultaneous submission of article to other journals permitted: No
Exclusive manuscript rights between acceptance and publication: No
Copyright: Not copyrighted
Reprints: Available, $10 per 25 reprints
Disposition of manuscript:
Query letter: Not necessary.
Receipt of manuscript acknowledged: Yes
Decision to publish in: 2-4 weeks
Accepted manuscript published in: 3-6 months
Rejected manuscript returned: Yes

Rejected manuscript criticized: Yes
Submit to:
Henry Grosshans
Editor
(See address above)

SATURDAY REVIEW [110]
P. O. Box 2045
Rock Island, Illinois 61201

First published in 1924

SUBSCRIPTION DATA
Issues and rates: Published bi-weekly.
Average paid circulation: 558,040
Annual rate(s): $12.00; Pan-Am $14.00; Foreign $14.00; Students $10.00
Managing Editor: Peter Young

EDITORIAL DESCRIPTION
A review of ideas, the arts, and the human condition; cultural subjects plus advance comment on issues and ideas.
Audience: An educated, literate, individualistic general audience
Manuscripts accepted in English

MANUSCRIPT INFORMATION
Subject field(s): Almost any cultural issue or idea.
Manuscript requirements: See latest issue for style requirements. Chicago
Preferred length: 1,000 to 3,000 words
Abstract: Not necessary.
Author information and reprints: Payment: By publication to author. $150 to $200 per page.
Is simultaneous submission of article to other journals permitted: Not permitted.
Exclusive manuscript rights between acceptance and publication: Yes
Copyright: First serial rights only
Reprints: Not available.
Disposition of manuscript:
Query letter: Not necessary, but advisable.
Receipt of manuscript acknowledged: No
Accepted manuscript published in: 1-2 months
Rejected manuscript returned: Yes, if return postage is supplied by author.
Rejected manuscript criticized: Reasons for rejections only
Submit to:
Peter Young
Managing Editor
488 Madison Avenue
New York, New York 10022
(212) 751-7900

SEVENTEENTH-CENTURY NEWS [111]
(Including Neo-Latin News)
Department of English, Burrowes Building
The Pennsylvania State University
University Park, Pennsylvania 16802
(814) 865-1824

Previously entitled *Seventeenth-Century Newsletter*

First published in 1941

SUBSCRIPTION DATA
Issues and rates: Published quarterly.
Average paid circulation: 1,050; 150 controlled
Annual rate(s): $2.00
Managing Editor: Harrison T. Meserole

EDITORIAL DESCRIPTION
Contains reviews, review-articles, and short original essays on all aspects of seventeenth-century literature, history, art, music, and culture; abstracts of recently published articles and monographs in these fields.
Articles per average issue: 25-30
Audience: Academic
Manuscripts accepted in English, French, German, Italian

MANUSCRIPT INFORMATION
Subject field(s): Literature, history, art, music, bibliography
Manuscript requirements: MLA
Preferred length: 1,500 words
Number of copies to be submitted: Two
Abstract: Yes
Author information and reprints: Payment: None. Ten copies of issue free to authors.
Is simultaneous submission of article to other journals permitted: No
Exclusive manuscript rights between acceptance and publication: Yes
Copyright: Held by author.
Reprints: Not available.
Additional information: Typewritten, double spaced, on one side of standard sized paper.
Disposition of manuscript:
Query letter: No
Receipt of manuscript acknowledged: Yes
Decision to publish in: 4-6 weeks
Accepted manuscript published in: 6-14 months
Rejected manuscript returned: Yes, if return postage is supplied by author.
Rejected manuscript criticized: Yes
Submit to:
Harrison T. Meserole
(See address above)

THE SIXTEENTH CENTURY JOURNAL [112]
Center for Reformation Research
6477 San Bonita Avenue
St. Louis, Missouri 63105
(314) 727-6655

First published in 1969

SUBSCRIPTION DATA
Issues and rates: Published semi-annually.
Average paid circulation: 800; 200 controlled
Annual rate(s): $8.00; Foreign $15.00; Institutions $12.50; Students $8.00

Humanities (general)

Publisher or Sponsor: The Sixteenth Century Studies Conference; Center for Reformation Research, Central Renaissance Conference
Managing Editor: Robert V. Schnucker

EDITORIAL DESCRIPTION
Contains articles of high academic quality devoted to man's activities during the sixteenth century
Articles per average issue: 6-7
Audience: Students and instructors in Renaissance and Reformation
Manuscripts accepted in English

MANUSCRIPT INFORMATION
Subject field(s): History, literature, theology, religion, economics demography, philosophy, science from 1450-1650 in Europe, the Near East, Russia, Africa and the Far East
Manuscript requirements: Chicago
Preferred length: None
Number of copies to be submitted: 2
Abstract: Not necessary.
Author information and reprints: Payment: Reprints only. 25 free reprints
Is simultaneous submission of article to other journals permitted: Permitted, but not encouraged.
Exclusive manuscript rights between acceptance and publication: Yes
Copyright: Held by publication.
Reprints: Available at cost.
Disposition of manuscript:
Query letter: Not necessary.
Receipt of manuscript acknowledged: Yes
Decision to publish in: Under 6 weeks
Accepted manuscript published in: 6 months
Rejected manuscript criticized: Sometimes
Submit to:
Robert A. Kolb
Associate Editor
(See address above)

SOUNDINGS [113]
An Interdisciplinary Journal
P.O. Box 6309, Station B
Nashville, Tennessee 37235
(615) 322-2776

Previously entitled *The Christian Scholar*

First published in 1968

SUBSCRIPTION DATA
Issues and rates: Published quarterly.
Average paid circulation: 1,650; 50 controlled
Annual rate(s): $9.00, Foreign $10.00
Publisher or Sponsor: The Society for Religion in Higher Education; Vanderbilt University
Managing Editor: Sallie TeSelle

EDITORIAL DESCRIPTION
Publishes articles in all fields (literature, social sciences, history, philosophy, religion, higher education, etc.).
Audience: Professionals in higher education
Manuscripts accepted in English

MANUSCRIPT INFORMATION
Manuscript requirements: MLA
Preferred length: 6000-8000 words; 20-25 pages
Number of copies to be submitted: One
Abstract: Not necessary.
Author information and reprints: Payment: Reprints only. 10 free copies of issue.
Is simultaneous submission of article to other journals permitted: No
Exclusive manuscript rights between acceptance and publication: Yes
Copyright: Held by publication.
Reprints: Offprints available
Disposition of manuscript:
Query letter: Not necessary.
Receipt of manuscript acknowledged: Yes
Decision to publish in: One month
Accepted manuscript published in: 3-6 months
Rejected manuscript returned: Yes, if return postage is supplied by author.
Rejected manuscript criticized: Sometimes
Submit to:
Sallie TeSelle
Editor
(See address above)

STUDIES IN THE HUMANITIES [114]
111-B Leonard Hall
Indiana University of Pennsylvania
Indiana, Pennsylvania 15701
(412) 357-2262

First published in 1969

SUBSCRIPTION DATA
Issues and rates: Published semi-annually.
Average paid circulation: 134
Annual rate(s): $3.00
Managing Editor: John R. Freund

EDITORIAL DESCRIPTION
Publishes articles concerned with literature, philosophy, films and language.
Articles per average issue: 8-10
Audience: Scholars in the humanities
Manuscripts accepted in English

MANUSCRIPT INFORMATION
Subject field(s): Literature, philosophy, films, language
Manuscript requirements: MLA
Preferred length: 4000 words; 16 pages maximum
Number of copies to be submitted: One
Author information and reprints: Payment: Reprints only. 3 issues
Is simultaneous submission of article to other journals permitted: No
Exclusive manuscript rights between acceptance and publication: Yes
Copyright: Held by Indiana University of Pennsylvania
Reprints: Available by special arrangement; at cost
Disposition of manuscript:
Query letter: Not necessary.
Receipt of manuscript acknowledged: Yes
Decision to publish in: 3 months
Accepted manuscript published in: 6-9 months
Rejected manuscript returned: Yes, if self-addressed, stamped envelope is sent with manuscript.
Rejected manuscript criticized: No
Submit to:
John R. Freund
Editor
(See address above)

STUDIES IN ROMANTICISM [115]
236 Bay State Road
Boston, Massachusetts 02215
(617) 353-2505

First published in 1951

SUBSCRIPTION DATA
Issues and rates: Published quarterly.
Average paid circulation: 1,300
Annual rate(s): $9.50; Institutions $12.50
Publisher or Sponsor: Boston University
Managing Editor: C.F. Stone, III

EDITORIAL DESCRIPTION
Contains articles on literature, music, art, philosophy, history of the Romantic Period.
Articles per average issue: 5
Audience: Professional scholars and critics
Manuscripts accepted in English only

MANUSCRIPT INFORMATION
Subject field(s): Literature, music, art, general culture
Manuscript requirements: MLA
Preferred length: 5,000-7,500 words; 20-30 pages
Number of copies to be submitted: One original
Abstract: Yes.
Author information and reprints: Payment: None.
Is simultaneous submission of article to other journals permitted: No
Exclusive manuscript rights between acceptance and publication: No
Copyright: Held by publication.
Reprints: Available, cost varies
Disposition of manuscript:
Query letter: Not necessary.
Receipt of manuscript acknowledged: Yes
Decision to publish in: 2 months
Accepted manuscript published in: 12 months
Rejected manuscript returned: Yes
Rejected manuscript criticized: Yes
Submit to:
Charles F. Stone, III
Editor
(See address above)

STUDIES IN THE TWENTIETH CENTURY [116]

A Scholarly and Critical Journal
PO Box 12
Troy, New York, 12181

SUBSCRIPTION DATA

Issues and rates: Published semi-annually.
  Average paid circulation: 300
  Annual rate(s): $4.00
Managing Editor: Stephen Goode

EDITORIAL DESCRIPTION

Contains articles on the philosophies of the art and literary movements of the 20th century.
Articles per average issue: 5-6
Audience: College, research librarians
  Manuscripts accepted in English, French, German, Spanish

MANUSCRIPT INFORMATION

Subject field(s): Literature, art
Manuscript requirements: MLA
  Number of copies to be submitted: One
  Abstract: No
Author information and reprints: Payment: 3 issues plus 25 offprints
  Is simultaneous submission of article to other journals permitted: Yes
  Exclusive manuscript rights between acceptance and publication: Yes
  Copyright: Held by author.
Disposition of manuscript:
  Query letter: No
  Receipt of manuscript acknowledged: No
  Decision to publish in: 2 weeks
  Accepted manuscript published in: One year or more
  Rejected manuscript returned: Yes, if return postage is supplied by author.
  Rejected manuscript criticized: No
Submit to:
  Stephen Goode
  Editor
  (See address above)

THE TEILHARD REVIEW [117]

The Teilhard Centre, St. Mark's Chambers
Kennington Park Road
London SE11 4PW, England
(01) 582-9510

First published in 1966

SUBSCRIPTION DATA

Issues and rates: Published three times per year.
  Annual rate(s): £1.50; Foreign £1.50
Publisher or Sponsor: The Teilhard Centre for the Future of Man

EDITORIAL DESCRIPTION

This is an international journal of integrative studies concerned with the future of humanity increasingly responsible for its own evolution.
Articles per average issue: 5 full length plus shorter ones
Audience: General, academic
  Manuscripts accepted in English

MANUSCRIPT INFORMATION

Subject field(s): Interdisciplinary studies in the light of evolutionary thought, and especially those derived from the thinking of Pierre Teilhard de Chardin, the French scientist and priest
Manuscript requirements: See latest issue for style requirements. Style sheet sent on request.
  Preferred length: 1,500-6,000 words
  Number of copies to be submitted: 1
  Abstract: Not necessary.
Author information and reprints: Payment: Reprints only. 1-10 depending on length
  Is simultaneous submission of article to other journals permitted: Not permitted.
  Exclusive manuscript rights between acceptance and publication: Yes
  Copyright: Held by publication.
  Reprints: Available at cost.
Disposition of manuscript:
  Query letter: Not necessary, but advisable.
  Receipt of manuscript acknowledged: Yes
  Decision to publish in: 2-3 months
  Accepted manuscript published in: 6-12 months
  Rejected manuscript returned: Yes, if return postage is supplied by author.
  Rejected manuscript criticized: No
Submit to:
  Dr. John D. Newson
  Editor
  Christ Church College
  Canterbury, Kent CT1 1QU, England

TELOS [118]

A Journal of Revolutionary Theory
Sociology Department
Washington University
St. Louis, Missouri 63130
(314) 863-0100 ext. 4383

First published in 1968

SUBSCRIPTION DATA

Issues and rates: Published quarterly.
  Average paid circulation: 1,800
  Annual rate(s): $8.00, Foreign $8.80
Managing Editor: Patricia Tummons

EDITORIAL DESCRIPTION

Contains scholarly articles on radical topics. Point of view is neo-Marxist.
Articles per average issue: 10
Audience: Radical Scholars and activists interested in developing a theory adequate to their praxis
  Manuscripts accepted in English

MANUSCRIPT INFORMATION

Subject field(s): Social sciences, philosophy, literary criticism, political science, economics
Manuscript requirements: See latest issue for style requirements.
  Preferred length: Under 100 pages
  Number of copies to be submitted: Two
  Abstract: Yes. Should be a brief one paragraph summary of the author's argument and conclusions.
Author information and reprints: Payment: Reprints only. 50 reprints
  Is simultaneous submission of article to other journals permitted: No
  Exclusive manuscript rights between acceptance and publication: Yes
  Copyright: Held by publication.
  Reprints: Available at no cost
Disposition of manuscript:
  Query letter: Not necessary.
  Receipt of manuscript acknowledged: Yes
  Decision to publish in: 3 months
  Accepted manuscript published in: 5 months
  Rejected manuscript returned: Yes
  Rejected manuscript criticized: Occasionally
Submit to:
  Editor
  (See address above)

THE TEXAS QUARTERLY [119]

Box 7517, University Station
Austin, Texas 78712
(512) 471-1458

First published in 1958

SUBSCRIPTION DATA

Issues and rates: Published quarterly.
  Average paid circulation: 2000
  Annual rate(s): $4.00, Foreign $5.00
Publisher or Sponsor: The University of Texas at Houston
Managing Editor: Thomas M. Cranfill; Miguel González-Gerth

EDITORIAL DESCRIPTION

Contains poetry and essays on the humanities.
  Manuscripts accepted in English, Spanish, Portuguese (with translations)

MANUSCRIPT INFORMATION

Subject field(s): Scholarly works on humor, poetry, adventure, history
Manuscript requirements: Chicago
  Preferred length: 6000 words maximum
  Number of copies to be submitted: One
  Abstract: Not necessary.
Author information and reprints: Payment: Reprints only. Copies and reprints
  Is simultaneous submission of article to other journals permitted: No
  Copyright: Held by publication.
  Reprints: Available
Additional information: Prefer manuscripts to be typewritten, double-spaced with no footnotes.
Disposition of manuscript:
  Query letter: Not necessary.
  Receipt of manuscript acknowledged: No
  Decision to publish in: 4-6 weeks
  Accepted manuscript published in: 6 months
  Rejected manuscript returned: Yes, if self-addressed, stamped envelope is sent with manuscript.
  Rejected manuscript criticized: Sometimes
Submit to:
  Editors

(See address above)
(512) 471-1833

TRADITIO [120]
Studies in Ancient and Medieval History, Thought and Religion
Fordham University Press
University Box L
Bronx, New York 10458
(212) 933-2233

First published in 1943

SUBSCRIPTION DATA
Average paid circulation: 1,000
Annual rate(s): $20.00
Publisher or Sponsor: Fordham University
Managing Editor: H. G. Fletcher

EDITORIAL DESCRIPTION
Publishes critical text and magisterial studies of classical and medieval works; history, philosophy, literature, palaeography; general manuscript studies; bibliography; medieval jurisprudence
Articles per average issue: 15
Audience: Classical and medieval scholars
Manuscripts accepted in all major western languages

MANUSCRIPT INFORMATION
Subject field(s): Up to but not including the Italian Renaissance
Manuscript requirements: Style sheet sent on request. Specialized
Preferred length: As required
Number of copies to be submitted: 1
Abstract: Not necessary.
Author information and reprints: Payment: Reprints only. 25 free offprints
Is simultaneous submission of article to other journals permitted: Not permitted.
Exclusive manuscript rights between acceptance and publication: Yes
Copyright: Held by author.
Reprints: Available at no cost. In lots of 25
Disposition of manuscript:
Query letter: Not necessary, but advisable.
Receipt of manuscript acknowledged: Yes
Decision to publish in: 8 months
Accepted manuscript published in: 10 months
Rejected manuscript returned: Yes, with return postage paid by publication.
Rejected manuscript criticized: Sometimes
Submit to:
Dr. Edwin A. Quain
Fordham University
Bronx, New York 10458

Dr. Elizabeth A. R. Brown
CUNY Brooklyn College
Brooklyn, New York 11210
Editorial Board Members

SPECIAL STIPULATIONS
Manuscripts are considered on an annual basis only, with March as the deadline for submissions.

TRIVIUM [121]
St. David's University College
Lampeter, Cards., Wales Great Britain
351

First published in 1966

SUBSCRIPTION DATA
Issues and rates: Published annually.
Average paid circulation: 250
Annual rate(s): Individuals £2, Institutions £3
Managing Editor: Rhys S. Jones

EDITORIAL DESCRIPTION
Concerned with research in the humanities, particularly languages and literature, including Celtic studies.
Articles per average issue: 11
Audience: Professors of arts and theology
Manuscripts accepted in English, Welsh, French, German

MANUSCRIPT INFORMATION
Subject field(s): European literature, theology, history
Manuscript requirements: Will edit to suit own style.
Preferred length: 12 pages maximum
Number of copies to be submitted: One
Abstract: Yes.
Author information and reprints: Payment: None.
Is simultaneous submission of article to other journals permitted: No
Exclusive manuscript rights between acceptance and publication: No
Copyright: Held by publication.
Reprints: Available, first 30 free
Additional information: Manuscript should be typed, double-spaced with ample margins; footnotes on a separate sheet.
Disposition of manuscript:
Query letter: Not necessary.
Receipt of manuscript acknowledged: Yes
Decision to publish in: 3-4 weeks
Accepted manuscript published in: 6-18 months
Rejected manuscript returned: Yes
Rejected manuscript criticized: Sometimes
Submit to:
Rhys S. Jones
General Editor
(See address above)

UNIVERSITY OF TORONTO QUARTERLY [122]
A Canadian Journal of the Humanities
University of Toronto Press
Front Campus
Toronto, Ontario MSS 1A6, Canada
(416) 928-2240

First published in 1931

SUBSCRIPTION DATA
Issues and rates: Published quarterly.
Average paid circulation: 71; 1500 controlled
Annual rate(s): Foreign $8.00

Managing Editor: W. F. Blissett

EDITORIAL DESCRIPTION
Contains scholarly articles and reviews of books in the humanities.
Articles per average issue: 5
Audience: Academics
Manuscripts accepted in English, French

MANUSCRIPT INFORMATION
Subject field(s): English literature, philosophy, French literature, other literatures
Manuscript requirements: See latest issue.
Preferred length: 20-30 pages
Number of copies to be submitted: One
Author information and reprints: Payment: By publication to author. $50.00 per article.
Is simultaneous submission of article to other journals permitted: No
Exclusive manuscript rights between acceptance and publication: No
Copyright: Held by publication.
Reprints: Available, cost varies with length
Additional information: Manuscript should be accompanied by self-addressed envelope and international reply coupons.
Disposition of manuscript:
Query letter: Not necessary.
Receipt of manuscript acknowledged: Yes
Decision to publish in: 4-6 weeks
Accepted manuscript published in: 1-1 ½ years
Rejected manuscript returned: Yes, if return postage is supplied by author.
Rejected manuscript criticized: Yes
Submit to:
W. F. Blissett
Editor
(See address above)

VICTORIAN PERIODICALS NEWSLETTER [123]
English Department
University of Toronto
Toronto 5, Ontario, Canada
(416) 928-3190

First published in 1968

SUBSCRIPTION DATA
Issues and rates: Published quarterly.
Average paid circulation: 900
Annual rate(s): Individuals $5.00; Institutions $7.00
Publisher or Sponsor: Research Society for Victorian Periodicals

EDITORIAL DESCRIPTION
Provides an informal means of exchanging information among scholars in the field of Victorian periodicals.
Articles per average issue: 3
Audience: Academic
Manuscripts accepted in English

MANUSCRIPT INFORMATION
Subject field(s): Victorian England
Manuscript requirements: See latest issue for style requirements.
Preferred length: 5-20 pages

Number of copies to be submitted: Two
Abstract: Yes
Author information and reprints: Payment:
None.
Is simultaneous submission of article to
other journals permitted: No
Exclusive manuscript rights between
acceptance and publication: Yes
Copyright: Held by publication.
Reprints: Available
Disposition of manuscript:
Query letter: No
Receipt of manuscript acknowledged: Yes
Decision to publish in: 1 month
Accepted manuscript published in: 12
months
Rejected manuscript returned: Yes, if
return postage is supplied by author.
Rejected manuscript criticized: Yes
Submit to:
N. Merrill Distad
(See address above)

VICTORIAN STUDIES [124]
Ballantine Hall 338
Indiana University
Bloomington, Indiana 47401
(812) 337-9533

SUBSCRIPTION DATA
Issues and rates: Published quarterly.
Average paid circulation: 2800
Annual rate(s): Individuals $7.00;
Institutions $12.00

EDITORIAL DESCRIPTION
An interdisciplinary journal about
nineteenth century Great Britain. Articles
are considered in the fields of English
literature, history, history of science,
history of art, sociology, economics, etc.
Articles should be interdisciplinary in
approach and be of general interest to
scholars.

MANUSCRIPT INFORMATION
Subject field(s): Literature, history
Manuscript requirements: MLA
Preferred length: 30 pages maximum
Number of copies to be submitted: Two
Author information and reprints: Payment:
None.
Is simultaneous submission of article to
other journals permitted: No
Exclusive manuscript rights between
acceptance and publication: Yes
Copyright: Held by publication.
Reprints: Available
Additional information: Return postage or
international reply coupons must be
included if author wishes manuscript
returned.
Disposition of manuscript:
Receipt of manuscript acknowledged: Yes
Decision to publish in: 2-3 months
Accepted manuscript published in: 6-12
months
Rejected manuscript returned: Yes, if
self-addressed, stamped envelope is sent
with manuscript.
Rejected manuscript criticized: Yes
Submit to:
Martha Vicinus

Editor
(See address above)

WESTERN HUMANITIES
REVIEW [125]
University of Utah
Salt Lake City, Utah 84112
(801) 581-7438

First published in 1947

SUBSCRIPTION DATA
Issues and rates: Published quarterly.
Average paid circulation: 900
Annual rate(s): $6.00
Publisher or Sponsor: University of Utah
Managing Editor: Jack Garlington

EDITORIAL DESCRIPTION
Contains articles, short stories, poems,
film criticism, book reviews.
Articles per average issue: 15
Audience: Educated, general
Manuscripts accepted in English

MANUSCRIPT INFORMATION
Subject field(s): Articles on subjects in the
humanities, short stories, poetry, book
reviews (usually assigned), film criticism
Manuscript requirements: MLA
Preferred length: 3000 words; 15 pages
Number of copies to be submitted: One
Abstract: Not necessary.
Author information and reprints: Payment:
By publication to author. $75- $100 per
article. $35 per poem.
Is simultaneous submission of article to
other journals permitted: Yes
Exclusive manuscript rights between
acceptance and publication: Yes
Copyright: Held by publication.
Reprints: Available, 25 furnished free
Disposition of manuscript:
Query letter: Not necessary.
Receipt of manuscript acknowledged: No
Decision to publish in: One month
Accepted manuscript published in: 4-5
months
Rejected manuscript returned: Yes, if
return postage is supplied by author.
Rejected manuscript criticized: No
Submit to:
Editor
(See address above)

THE YALE REVIEW [126]
1902A Yale Station
New Haven, Connecticut 06520
(203) 436-8307

First published in 1911

SUBSCRIPTION DATA
Issues and rates: Published quarterly.
Average paid circulation: 6328; 192
controlled
Annual rate(s): $8.00, Pan-Am $9.00,
Foreign $9.00

Publisher or Sponsor: Yale University
Managing Editor: Mary Price

EDITORIAL DESCRIPTION
Foreign and domestic affairs, literary
criticism, science for the layman, fiction
and poetry.
Articles per average issue: 5
Audience: Scholarly world
Manuscripts accepted in English

MANUSCRIPT INFORMATION
Manuscript requirements: See latest issue for
style requirements.
Preferred length: 5000 words; 20 pages
(typewritten, double-spaced) or less
Number of copies to be submitted: One
Abstract:
Author information and reprints: Payment:
By publication to author.
Is simultaneous submission of article to
other journals permitted: No
Exclusive manuscript rights between
acceptance and publication: Yes
Copyright: Held by publication.
Reprints: Available at cost, should be
ordered before publication.
Additional information: Footnotes should be
incorporated in text before submission of
manuscript.
Disposition of manuscript:
Query letter: Not necessary.
Receipt of manuscript acknowledged: No
Decision to publish in: 1-3 months
Accepted manuscript published in: 2
years
Rejected manuscript returned: Yes, if
return postage is supplied by author.
Rejected manuscript criticized: No
Submit to:
John J. E. Palmer
Editor
(See address above)

Creative and performing arts

AFRICAN ARTS [127]
African Studies Center, Bunche Hall 10377
University of California
Los Angeles, California 90024
(213) 825-1218

Previously entitled *African Arts/Arts
D'Afrique*

First published in 1967

SUBSCRIPTION DATA
Issues and rates: Published quarterly.
Average paid circulation: 5,000
Annual rate(s): $14.00
Publisher or Sponsor: University of
California, Los Angeles, African Studies
Center

EDITORIAL DESCRIPTION
Journal of traditional and contemporary
African art.

Articles per average issue: 10
Manuscripts accepted in English

MANUSCRIPT INFORMATION

Subject field(s): Literary, graphic, plastic and performing arts of Africa
Manuscript requirements: Chicago
Preferred length: 5000-7000 words
Number of copies to be submitted: One
Abstract: No
Author information and reprints: Payment: By publication to author. $50.00 per article for Africans; $25.00 for non-Africans
Is simultaneous submission of article to other journals permitted: No
Exclusive manuscript rights between acceptance and publication: Yes
Copyright: Held by publication.
Reprints: Not available.
Additional information: Good quality photographs desirable. Typewritten, double-spaced; footnotes on separate sheet at end.
Disposition of manuscript:
Receipt of manuscript acknowledged: Yes
Decision to publish in: 2 months
Accepted manuscript published in: Varies
Rejected manuscript returned: Yes
Rejected manuscript criticized: No
Submit to:
John F. Povey
Editor
(See address above)

AFRICAN MUSIC [128]

Journal of the African Music Society
P.O. Box 138
Roodepoort, Transvaal 1725, South Africa
763-4164

Previously entitled *African Music Society Newsletter*

First published in 1954

SUBSCRIPTION DATA

Issues and rates: Published annually.
Average paid circulation: 750; 25 controlled
Annual rate(s): $15.00
Publisher or Sponsor: The African Music Society
Managing Editor: Andrew T. N. Tracey

EDITORIAL DESCRIPTION

Contains articles on all aspects of the music of Africa south of the Sahara; analysis of the music as part of society, organology, music in dance and other art forms in national life, education, religion, history, etc.

MANUSCRIPT INFORMATION

Subject field(s): Contributions arising from first-hand research or experience, especially by Africans.
Manuscript requirements: See latest issue for style requirements.
Preferred length: 2,000 to 4,000 words
Number of copies to be submitted: Two

Author information and reprints: Payment: None.
Is simultaneous submission of article to other journals permitted: Preferably not
Exclusive manuscript rights between acceptance and publication: Yes
Copyright: Held by author.
Reprints: Available, 20 copies free.
Additional information: Articles to be submitted in English, or French with summary in English.
Disposition of manuscript:
Receipt of manuscript acknowledged: Yes
Decision to publish in: 1 month
Accepted manuscript published in: In following edition
Rejected manuscript returned: Yes
Rejected manuscript criticized: If requested.
Submit to:
Andrew Tracey
Editor
(See address above)

SPECIAL STIPULATIONS

Reports on original, first hand research in African music, on any aspect of the music, songs, and associated activities such as dancing, costume, ritual and religious associations are particularly important.

AIA JOURNAL [129]

1735 New York Avenue, N.W.
Washington, D.C. 20006
(202) 785-7277

First published in 1944

SUBSCRIPTION DATA

Issues and rates: Published monthly.
Average paid circulation: 26,756
Annual rate(s): $10.00, Students $4.00, Members $5.00, Foreign $20.00
Publisher or Sponsor: American Institute of Architects

EDITORIAL DESCRIPTION

Seeks to report, interpret and disseminate the happenings in the world of architecture in the United States to active architects.
Articles per average issue: 8-12
Audience: Architects
Manuscripts accepted in English

MANUSCRIPT INFORMATION

Subject field(s): Practice of architecture from programming through construction
Manuscript requirements: See latest issue for style requirements.
Preferred length: Varies
Number of copies to be submitted: Two
Abstract: Not necessary.
Author information and reprints: Payment: None. Except to professional writers.
Exclusive manuscript rights between acceptance and publication: Yes
Copyright: Held by publication.
Reprints: Available, rates on request

Additional information: Manuscript should be typewritten, double-spaced.
Disposition of manuscript:
Query letter: Necessary.
Receipt of manuscript acknowledged: Yes
Decision to publish in: 2-3 months
Accepted manuscript published in: Varies
Rejected manuscript returned: Yes
Rejected manuscript criticized: Occasionally
Submit to:
Donald Canty
Editor
(See address above)

ALPHA PSI OMEGA PLAYBILL [130]

Delta Psi Omega Playbill
Department of Speech Communication
Eastern Illinois University
Charleston, Illinois 61920
(217) 581-2016

First published in 1926

SUBSCRIPTION DATA

Issues and rates: Published semi-annually.
Average paid circulation: 8,500 controlled
Publisher or Sponsor: Alpha Psi Omega National Honorary in Theatre
Managing Editor: Donald P. Garner

EDITORIAL DESCRIPTION

Half of the magazine is devoted to articles on theatre; other half is devoted to honoring outstanding theatre programs.
Articles per average issue: 5
Audience: Academic, students of theatre
Manuscripts accepted in English

MANUSCRIPT INFORMATION

Subject field(s): Theatre (all phases)
Manuscript requirements: MLA
Preferred length: 1000-2200 words
Number of copies to be submitted: One
Abstract: Not necessary.
Author information and reprints: Payment: None.
Is simultaneous submission of article to other journals permitted: Yes
Exclusive manuscript rights between acceptance and publication: No
Copyright: Held by author.
Reprints: Available
Additional information: Pictures, drawings, illustrations are appreciated.
Disposition of manuscript:
Query letter: Not necessary.
Receipt of manuscript acknowledged: Yes
Decision to publish in: 3-6 months
Accepted manuscript published in: 6-12 months
Rejected manuscript returned: Yes, if self-addressed, stamped envelope is sent with manuscript.
Rejected manuscript criticized: No
Submit to:
Donald P. Garner
Editor
(See address above)

THE AMERICAN ART JOURNAL [131]

40 West 57th Street, 5th Floor
New York, New York 10019
(212) 752-6384

First published in 1969

SUBSCRIPTION DATA
Issues and rates: Published semi-annually.
 Average paid circulation: 1,700
 Annual rate(s): $10.00; Foreign $11.00; Institutions $10.00; Students $10.00; Foreign institutions $11.00
Publisher or Sponsor: Kennedy Galleries, Inc.

EDITORIAL DESCRIPTION
Dedicated to the presentation of significant scholarship and the encouragement of serious research on the visual arts in the United States
Articles per average issue: 5-6
Audience: Scholars, informed laymen
 Manuscripts accepted in English only

MANUSCRIPT INFORMATION
Subject field(s): American art from the 17th to mid-20th centuries, focusing mainly on 18th, 19th and early 20th century; painting, sculpture, architecture, printmaking, and the decorative arts
Manuscript requirements: See latest issue for style requirements.
 Preferred length: 2,000-3,000 words
 Number of copies to be submitted: 2
 Abstract: Not necessary.
Author information and reprints: Payment: By publication to author. $300.00 per article. and 6 copies of the issue
 Is simultaneous submission of article to other journals permitted: Not permitted.
 Exclusive manuscript rights between acceptance and publication: Yes
 Copyright: Held by publication.
 Reprints: Available at cost.
Additional information: The author must usually obtain photographs at his own expense.
Disposition of manuscript:
 Query letter: Not necessary, but advisable.
 Receipt of manuscript acknowledged: Yes
 Decision to publish in: 1-3 months
 Accepted manuscript published in: 3-12 months
 Rejected manuscript returned: Yes, with return postage paid by publication.
 Rejected manuscript criticized: Reasons for rejections only
Submit to:
 John D. Morse;
 Jane V. Turano
 Editor and Assistant Editor
 (See address above)

AMERICAN MUSICOLOGICAL SOCIETY. JOURNAL [132]

201 South 34th Street
Philadelphia, Pennsylvania 19104
(215) 594-7544

First published in 1948

SUBSCRIPTION DATA
Issues and rates: Published three times per year.
 Average paid circulation: 3,925
 Annual rate(s): $15.00
Publisher or Sponsor: American Musicological Society, Inc.
Managing Editor: Don M. Randel

EDITORIAL DESCRIPTION
Contains research in the history of music of all periods and cultures; reviews of books and records of musicological interest.
Articles per average issue: 8
 Manuscripts accepted in English

MANUSCRIPT INFORMATION
Subject field(s): Music history, music theory
Manuscript requirements: See latest issue for style requirements.
 Preferred length: 7,500 words; 25 pages or less
 Number of copies to be submitted: One
 Abstract: Not necessary.
Author information and reprints: Payment: None.
 Is simultaneous submission of article to other journals permitted: No
 Exclusive manuscript rights between acceptance and publication: Yes
 Copyright: Held by publication.
 Reprints: Available, 100 free
Additional information: Musical examples must be supplied on separate sheets with captions and texts typed separately.
Disposition of manuscript:
 Query letter: Not necessary.
 Receipt of manuscript acknowledged: Yes
 Decision to publish in: 3 months
 Accepted manuscript published in: 9-12 months
 Rejected manuscript returned: Yes, if self-addressed, stamped envelope is sent with manuscript.
 Rejected manuscript criticized: No
Submit to:
 Lawrence F. Bernstein
 Editor-in-Chief
 Department of Music
 University of Pennsylvania
 201 South 34th Street
 Philadelphia Pennsylvania 19174
 (215) 594-7544

ARTIBUS ASIAE [133]

Quarterly of Asian Art and Archaeology
CH-6612 Ascona, Switzerland
(093) 35 22 66

SUBSCRIPTION DATA
Issues and rates: Published quarterly.
 Annual rate(s): Individuals $25.00
Publisher or Sponsor: Institute of Fine Arts, New York University

EDITORIAL DESCRIPTION
Presents new discoveries, previously unpublished objects of art
Articles per average issue: 5-6
Audience: Professional, academic, dealers
 Manuscripts accepted in English, French, German

MANUSCRIPT INFORMATION
Subject field(s): Asian art and archaeology; India and Southeast Asia; Far East; the Migrations; Near East; also detailed book reviews
Manuscript requirements: No specific style guide.
 Preferred length: None
 Number of copies to be submitted: 2
 Abstract: Not necessary
Author information and reprints: Payment: Reprints only. 20-25 copies
 Is simultaneous submission of article to other journals permitted: Not permitted.
 Exclusive manuscript rights between acceptance and publication: Yes
 Copyright: Held by publication.
Additional information: Desire good academic style; footnotes at bottom of page
Disposition of manuscript:
 Query letter: Not necessary, but advisable.
 Receipt of manuscript acknowledged: Yes
 Decision to publish in: 1-3 months
 Accepted manuscript published in: 3-9 months
 Rejected manuscript returned: Yes, with return postage paid by publication.
 Rejected manuscript criticized: Sometimes
Submit to:
 Prof. Alexander C. Soper
 Editor-in-Chief
 Institue of Fine Arts, New York University
 1 East 78th Street
 New York, New York 10021
 (212) 988-5550

ARTS IN SOCIETY [134]

728 Lowell Hall
University of Wisconsin
Madison, Wisconsin 53706
(608) 262-0646

First published in 1958

SUBSCRIPTION DATA
Issues and rates: Published three times per year.
 Annual rate(s): $7.50; Students $6.50
Publisher or Sponsor: University of Wisconsin
Managing Editor: D. Jean Collins

EDITORIAL DESCRIPTION
Dedicated to the augmentation of the arts and to the advancement of education in the arts and to present the insights of experience, research and theory on support of educational efforts to enhance the position of the arts in America.
Articles per average issue: 10
Audience: Anyone with an interest in the arts
 Manuscripts accepted in all languages

Creative and performing arts

MANUSCRIPT INFORMATION

Subject field(s): In general, four areas are dealt with: teaching and learning of the arts; aesthetics and philosophy; social analysis; significant examples of creative expression in a medium served by the printing process.

Manuscript requirements: See latest issue for style requirements. MLA

Preferred length: Varies

Number of copies to be submitted: 2

Abstract: Not necessary.

Author information and reprints: Payment: By publication to author.

Copyright: Held by publication.

Reprints: Available at cost.

Disposition of manuscript:

Query letter: Not necessary, but advisable.

Receipt of manuscript acknowledged: Yes

Decision to publish in: 2-7 weeks

Accepted manuscript published in: Varies

Rejected manuscript returned: Yes, if return postage is supplied by author.

Rejected manuscript criticized: No

Submit to:

Edward Kamarck

Editor

(See address above)

ARTS MAGAZINE [135]

Ideas in Contemporary Art
23 East 26th Street
New York, New York 10010
(212) MU 5-8500

Previously entitled *Art Digest,* until 1955

First published in 1926

SUBSCRIPTION DATA

Issues and rates: Published monthly.
Average paid circulation: 42,000
Annual rate(s): $20.00

Managing Editor: Florence Steinberg

EDITORIAL DESCRIPTION

A publication of the visual arts, with focus on ideas in contemporary art.

Articles per average issue: 10

Audience: Art and intellectual communities
Manuscripts accepted in English

MANUSCRIPT INFORMATION

Subject field(s): Visual arts: current events in the art world, new directions in art, historical and current scholarship

Manuscript requirements: See latest issue for style requirements.

Preferred length: 1000-2000 words

Number of copies to be submitted: One

Abstract: Not necessary.

Author information and reprints: Payment: By publication to author. Negotiable

Is simultaneous submission of article to other journals permitted: No

Exclusive manuscript rights between acceptance and publication: Yes

Copyright: Held by publication.

Reprints: Available at cost

Disposition of manuscript:

Query letter: Not necessary.

Receipt of manuscript acknowledged: Yes

Decision to publish in: 1 month

Accepted manuscript published in: 2 months

Rejected manuscript returned: Yes

Rejected manuscript criticized: Occasionally

Submit to:

Richard Martin

Editor

(See address above)

THE CANADIAN COMPOSER [136]

501-1407 Yonge Street
Toronto, Ontario M4T 1Y7, Canada
(416) 925-5138

First published in 1964

SUBSCRIPTION DATA

Issues and rates: 10 issues per year
Average paid circulation: 7,000 controlled
Annual rate(s): $2.00

Publisher or Sponsor: Composers, Authors and Publishers Association of Canada, Limited

EDITORIAL DESCRIPTION

Contains articles of interest to members of Canadian performing right society.

Articles per average issue: 6

Audience: Composers
Manuscripts accepted in English, French

MANUSCRIPT INFORMATION

Subject field(s): Activities of members, activities of affiliated societies, international copyright of music

Manuscript requirements: No specific style guide.

Preferred length: 2,500 words

Number of copies to be submitted: 1

Abstract: No

Author information and reprints: Payment: By publication to author.

Is simultaneous submission of article to other journals permitted: Yes

Exclusive manuscript rights between acceptance and publication: No

Copyright: Held by author.

Reprints: Available

Disposition of manuscript:

Query letter: Yes

Receipt of manuscript acknowledged: Yes

Decision to publish in: 2 months

Accepted manuscript published in: 2 months

Rejected manuscript returned: Yes

Rejected manuscript criticized: No

Submit to:

Richard Flohil

Editor

(See address above)

CHILDREN'S THEATRE REVIEW [137]

American Theatre Association
1317 F Street, N. W.
Washington, D. C. 20004
(202) 737-5606

First published in 1945

SUBSCRIPTION DATA

Issues and rates: Published quarterly.
Average paid circulation: 1,000
Annual rate(s): $8.00; Students $10.00; Members 17.50

Publisher or Sponsor: National Children's Theatre Association

Managing Editor: Sharon Davis

EDITORIAL DESCRIPTION

An overview of child drama as it is developing in the U. S. and abroad. Highlighted is the work being done in children's theatres and creative drama activities

Articles per average issue: 5

Audience: The membership of the National Children's Theatre Association
Manuscripts accepted in English only

MANUSCRIPT INFORMATION

Subject field(s): Historical, current, international and philosophical articles in the field of children's theatre; creative drama programs, ideas, research; special interests in new approaches, theatre-in-education and book reviews

Manuscript requirements: See latest issue for style requirements. MLA

Preferred length: 6-10 pages

Number of copies to be submitted: 1

Abstract: Not necessary.

Author information and reprints: Payment: None.

Is simultaneous submission of article to other journals permitted: Permitted

Exclusive manuscript rights between acceptance and publication: No

Copyright: Held by author.

Reprints: Not available.

Disposition of manuscript:

Query letter: Not necessary, but advisable.

Receipt of manuscript acknowledged: Yes

Decision to publish in: 2 months

Accepted manuscript published in: 6 months

Rejected manuscript returned: Yes, with return postage paid by publication.

Rejected manuscript criticized: Sometimes

Submit to:

Tom F. Behm

Editor

Department of Speech and Drama, Taylor Building

University of North Carolina at Greensboro

Greensboro, North Carolina 27412

(919) 275-1817

THE CHORAL JOURNAL [138]
P.O. Box 17736
Tampa, Florida 33612
(813) 935-9381

First published in 1959

SUBSCRIPTION DATA

Issues and rates: Published monthly.
    Average paid circulation: 5,000
    Annual rate(s): Institutions $4, Foreign $5
Publisher or Sponsor: The American Choral Directors Association
Managing Editor: R. Wayne Hugoboom

EDITORIAL DESCRIPTION

    Contains articles concerned with the choral area
Articles per average issue: 4-6
Audience: Choral directors, students
    Manuscripts accepted in English only

MANUSCRIPT INFORMATION

Subject field(s): Historical research, performance practices, technique, composers, special choral work, book reviews, record reviews, association news; all fields of choral endeavor.
Manuscript requirements: Chicago
    Preferred length: 4,000-8,000 words; 16-32 pages
    Number of copies to be submitted: Two
    Abstract: Yes.
Author information and reprints: Payment: None.
    Is simultaneous submission of article to other journals permitted: No
    Exclusive manuscript rights between acceptance and publication: Yes
    Copyright: Held by publication.
    Reprints: Not available.
Disposition of manuscript:
    Query letter: Necessary.
    Receipt of manuscript acknowledged: Yes
    Decision to publish in: 1-2 months
    Accepted manuscript published in: 2-4 months
    Rejected manuscript returned: Yes
    Rejected manuscript criticized: Occasionally
Submit to:
    Louis Diercks
    Chairman, Editorial Board
    Route 2
    Box 29
    West Finley, Pennsylvania 15377

CHURCH MUSIC [139]
Concordia Publishing House
3558 South Jefferson
St. Louis, Missouri 63118
(314) 664-7000

First published in 1966

SUBSCRIPTION DATA

Issues and rates: Published semi-annually.
    Average paid circulation: 3,000; 3,500 controlled
    Annual rate(s): $4.50

EDITORIAL DESCRIPTION

    Contains articles for professional church musicians.
Articles per average issue: 8
Audience: Church musicians, pastors, laymen interested in subject
    Manuscripts accepted in English

MANUSCRIPT INFORMATION

Subject field(s): Contemporary, scholarly, historical
Manuscript requirements: Style sheet sent on request.
    Preferred length: Supplied on request
    Number of copies to be submitted: Two
    Abstract: No
Author information and reprints: Payment: None.
    Is simultaneous submission of article to other journals permitted: Yes
    Exclusive manuscript rights between acceptance and publication: Yes
    Copyright: Held by publication.
    Reprints: Not available.
Additional information: Double-spaced typescript
Disposition of manuscript:
    Query letter: No
    Receipt of manuscript acknowledged: Yes
    Decision to publish in: 3 months
    Accepted manuscript published in: 6 months
    Rejected manuscript returned: Yes
    Rejected manuscript criticized: No
Submit to:
    Carl Schalk
    Editor
    Concordia Teachers College
    7400 Augusta
    River Forest, Illinois 60305
    (312) 771-8300

CLAVIER [140]
A Magazine for Pianists & Organists
1418 Lake Street
The Instrumentalist Company
Evanston, Illinois 60204
(312) 328-6000

First published in 1962

SUBSCRIPTION DATA

Issues and rates: Published monthly.
    Average paid circulation: 18,919
    Annual rate(s): $7.00
Managing Editor: Dorothy Packard

EDITORIAL DESCRIPTION

    Contains articles and features of interest to keyboard teachers, performers, and students; reviews of new music publications (piano and organ music, books on music); interviews with well-known professionals regarding musical interpretation and keyboard technique; complete pieces of music in the centerfold pages.
Articles per average issue: 9
    Manuscripts accepted in English

MANUSCRIPT INFORMATION

Subject field(s): Private or group keyboard teaching, keyboard technique, interpretation of keyboard music, studio management practices, music theory, music history and biography, performance practices, new developments in keyboard instruments as well as study of older or rare instruments, instrument maintenance.
Manuscript requirements: Chicago
    Preferred length: Open
    Number of copies to be submitted: One
    Abstract: Not necessary.
Author information and reprints: Payment: By publication to author. $18.00 per page.
    Is simultaneous submission of article to other journals permitted: No
    Exclusive manuscript rights between acceptance and publication: Yes
    Copyright: Held by publication.
    Reprints: Not available.
Additional information: Manuscripts should be neatly typed with double spacing and with ample left and right margins. Music examples, photographs or other supporting material should accompany the manuscript. Author should include short biographical sketch.
Disposition of manuscript:
    Receipt of manuscript acknowledged: Yes
    Decision to publish in: Varies
    Accepted manuscript published in: Varies
    Rejected manuscript returned: Yes
    Rejected manuscript criticized: No
Submit to:
    Dorothy R. Packard
    Editor and Advertising Manager
    (See address above)

SPECIAL STIPULATIONS

    Prior to submitting manuscripts, authors must obtain permission from proper source for use of copyrighted material and include a statement of such clearance with the manuscript.

CMA/AMC GAZETTE [141]
56 Sparks Street, Suite 505
Ottawa, Ontario K1P 5A9, Canada
(613) 233-5653

SUBSCRIPTION DATA

Issues and rates: Published quarterly.
    Average paid circulation: 1,100
    Annual rate(s): Under revision
Publisher or Sponsor: Canadian Museums Association
Managing Editor: André Déry

EDITORIAL DESCRIPTION

    Contains information on the development of national and provincial museums and art galleries, as well as technical and museological articles. Seeks to aid in the improvement of museums as collecting, educational, exhibiting and research institutions and act as a clearing house for information of interest to museums.
Articles per average issue: 4
Audience: Museum and art gallery personnel
    Manuscripts accepted in English, French

Creative and performing arts

MANUSCRIPT INFORMATION
Subject field(s): Museography, collections care, training museum staff, extension services, technical skills related to museum work, exhibition design, museum management, Canadiana, environmental control
Manuscript requirements: See latest issue for style requirements.
   Preferred length: 1500-3500 words; 20 pages maximum
   Number of copies to be submitted: Two
Author information and reprints: Payment: By publication to author. $.05 per word.
   Is simultaneous submission of article to other journals permitted: No
   Exclusive manuscript rights between acceptance and publication: Yes
   Copyright: Held by publication.
   Reprints: Not available.
Additional information: Manuscripts must be typewritten and double-spaced, with footnotes at bottom of page. Include relevant photographs (glossy) if possible.
Disposition of manuscript:
   Receipt of manuscript acknowledged: Yes
   Decision to publish in: 1 month
   Accepted manuscript published in: 3 months
   Rejected manuscript returned: Yes, if self-addressed, stamped envelope is sent with manuscript.
   Rejected manuscript criticized: No
Submit to:
   André Déry
   Publications Editor
   (See address above)

SPECIAL STIPULATIONS
Accepted manuscripts are subject to editing for consistency of style.

CODA [142]
Canada's Jazz Magazine
P.O. Box 87, Station J
Toronto, Ontario M4J 4X8, Canada
(416) 929-5065

First published in 1958

SUBSCRIPTION DATA
Issues and rates: 10 times per year
   Annual rate(s): $3.50
Managing Editor: John W. Norris

EDITORIAL DESCRIPTION
   Contains articles on jazz; record reviews; jazz literature reviews.
Articles per average issue: 4
Audience: Specialists in jazz and blues music
   Manuscripts accepted in English, French

MANUSCRIPT INFORMATION
Subject field(s): Jazz, blues
Manuscript requirements: See latest issue for style requirements.
   Preferred length: Varies
   Number of copies to be submitted: One
Author information and reprints: Payment: None.
   Is simultaneous submission of article to other journals permitted: Yes
   Exclusive manuscript rights between acceptance and publication: No
   Copyright: Not copyrighted
   Reprints: Not available.
Additional information: If photographs are included, good quality prints (glossies) are needed with credits on reverse side.
Disposition of manuscript:
   Receipt of manuscript acknowledged: No
   Decision to publish in: 2-24 months
   Accepted manuscript published in: 2-24 months
   Rejected manuscript returned: No
   Rejected manuscript criticized: No
Submit to:
   John W. Norris
   Editor
   (See address above)

SPECIAL STIPULATIONS
Prefer articles on jazz subjects which have received little coverage.

COMPARATIVE DRAMA [143]
Department of English
Western Michigan University
Kalamazoo, Michigan 49001
(616) 383-1685

First published in 1967

SUBSCRIPTION DATA
Issues and rates: Published quarterly.
   Average paid circulation: 700
   Annual rate(s): Individuals $4.00; Institutions $6.00; Foreign individuals $5.00; Foreign institutions $7.00
Managing Editor: Clifford Davidson; C.J. Gianakaris; John H. Stroupe

EDITORIAL DESCRIPTION
   Contains critical studies of drama of all nations and all periods. Especially encourages studies that are international in spirit and interdisciplinary in scope.
Articles per average issue: 5
Audience: Scholars and students of drama
   Manuscripts accepted in English only

MANUSCRIPT INFORMATION
Manuscript requirements: MLA
   Preferred length: 2000-5000 words
   Number of copies to be submitted: 1
   Abstract: Optional
Author information and reprints: Payment: Reprints only. 2 copies of issue and 10-20 offprints
   Is simultaneous submission of article to other journals permitted: No
   Exclusive manuscript rights between acceptance and publication: Yes
   Copyright: Held by publication.
   Reprints: Available, no cost
Disposition of manuscript:
   Receipt of manuscript acknowledged: Yes
   Decision to publish in: 2-4 weeks
   Accepted manuscript published in: Within six months
   Rejected manuscript returned: Yes, if return postage is supplied by author.
   Rejected manuscript criticized: Yes

Submit to:
   Editors
   (See address above)

THE CONSORT [144]
Annual Journal of the Dolmetsch Foundation
14 Chestnut Way, Home Farm Road
Godalming, Surrey GU7 1TS, England
7725

First published in 1929

SUBSCRIPTION DATA
Issues and rates: Published annually.
   Average paid circulation: 900
   Annual rate(s): £ 2.10
Publisher or Sponsor: Dolmetsch Foundation
Managing Editor: Shelagh M. Godwin

EDITORIAL DESCRIPTION
   Contains articles principally (but not exclusively) about early music, its performance, the instruments used; reviews of books on early music, and new editions of early music.
Articles per average issue: 5
Audience: Scholars and lovers of early music
   Manuscripts accepted in English, French, German, Russian

MANUSCRIPT INFORMATION
Subject field(s): Composers, instruments, manuscripts
Manuscript requirements: Style sheet sent on request.
   Preferred length: 2,500-8,000 words
   Number of copies to be submitted: Two
Author information and reprints: Payment: By publication to author. Honorarium to author
   Is simultaneous submission of article to other journals permitted: No
   Exclusive manuscript rights between acceptance and publication: Yes
   Copyright: Held by publication.
   Reprints: Not available.
Additional information: Manuscripts should be in the proper style, with relevant musical examples set apart from the text, and a comprehensive list of sources should be included as a footnote.
Disposition of manuscript:
   Receipt of manuscript acknowledged: Yes
   Decision to publish in: 4 weeks
   Accepted manuscript published in: 10 weeks
   Rejected manuscript returned: Yes
   Rejected manuscript criticized: No
Submit to:
   Editor
   (See address above)

CURATOR [145]
American Museum of Natural History
79th Street and Central Park West
New York, New York 10024
(212) 873-1300

First published in 1958

SUBSCRIPTION DATA
Issues and rates: Published quarterly.
  Average paid circulation: 1,000
  Annual rate(s): $11.00; Foreign $12.00
Publisher or Sponsor: American Museum of Natural History

EDITORIAL DESCRIPTION
Covers all aspects of the museum field, from detailed preparation techniques to the role of museums in general
Articles per average issue: 8
Audience: Museum professionals
  Manuscripts accepted in English

MANUSCRIPT INFORMATION
Subject field(s): Any museum-related subject
Manuscript requirements: See latest issue for style requirements.
  Preferred length: No preference
  Number of copies to be submitted: 3
  Abstract: Not necessary.
Author information and reprints: Payment: None.
  Is simultaneous submission of article to other journals permitted: Permitted, but not encouraged.
  Exclusive manuscript rights between acceptance and publication: No
  Copyright: Held by publication.
  Reprints: Available at cost.
Additional information: Illustrations are encouraged.
Disposition of manuscript:
  Query letter: Not necessary.
  Receipt of manuscript acknowledged: Yes
  Decision to publish in: 2 months
  Accepted manuscript published in: 3 months
  Rejected manuscript returned: Yes, with return postage paid by publication.
  Rejected manuscript criticized: Sometimes
Submit to: Thomas D. Nicholson
  Editor-in-Chief
  (See address above)

CURRENT MUSICOLOGY [146]
Department of Music
Columbia University
New York, New York 10027
(212) 280-3826

First published in 1965

SUBSCRIPTION DATA
Issues and rates: Published semi-annually.
  Average paid circulation: 1,000; 100 controlled
  Annual rate(s): Institutions $8.50, Individuals $6.00
Publisher or Sponsor: Columbia University, Graduate School of Music
Managing Editor: Richard Koprowski

EDITORIAL DESCRIPTION
Contains reports of musical events at North American and foreign college and university campuses; articles on historical musicology, theory, ethnomusicology, etc.; reviews on recent dissertations; bibliographies; projects on special themes.
Articles per average issue: 7 articles; 10 reports
Audience: Graduate students and professors of music
  Manuscripts accepted in English

MANUSCRIPT INFORMATION
Subject field(s): Scholarly investigations of music of all periods
Manuscript requirements: Chicago and MLA
  Preferred length: 12-15 pages
  Number of copies to be submitted: Two
  Abstract: Not necessary.
Author information and reprints: Payment: Two free copies
  Is simultaneous submission of article to other journals permitted: No
  Exclusive manuscript rights between acceptance and publication: Yes
  Copyright: Held by publication.
  Reprints: Available at cost
Additional information: Notes must be double-spaced at the end of the article. Musical examples must be placed on separate sheets and be camera-ready.
Disposition of manuscript:
  Query letter: Not necessary.
  Receipt of manuscript acknowledged: Yes
  Decision to publish in: 6 months
  Accepted manuscript published in: 1 year
  Rejected manuscript returned: Yes, if self-addressed, stamped envelope is sent with manuscript.
  Rejected manuscript criticized: No
Submit to:
  Editor
  (See address above)

DANCE MAGAZINE [147]
10 Columbus Circle
New York, New York 10019
(212) 977-9770

First published in 1922

SUBSCRIPTION DATA
Issues and rates: Published monthly.
  Average paid circulation: 30,000
  Annual rate(s): $12.00, Foreign $14.00
Managing Editor: Richard Philp

EDITORIAL DESCRIPTION
Contains dance reviews, photos, feature material.
Articles per average issue: 10
Audience: Dancers, teachers, students, general public
  Manuscripts accepted in English

MANUSCRIPT INFORMATION
Subject field(s): Dancers, dance companies
Manuscript requirements: See latest issue for style requirements.
  Preferred length: 2,500 words
  Number of copies to be submitted: One
  Abstract: Not necessary.
Author information and reprints: Payment: By publication to author. $50.00 per article.
  Is simultaneous submission of article to other journals permitted: No
  Exclusive manuscript rights between acceptance and publication: No
  Copyright: Held by publication.
  Reprints: Available
Disposition of manuscript:
  Query letter: Necessary.
  Receipt of manuscript acknowledged: No
  Decision to publish in: 1 month
  Accepted manuscript published in: 6 weeks
  Rejected manuscript returned: Yes, if self-addressed, stamped envelope is sent with manuscript.
  Rejected manuscript criticized: Sometimes
Submit to:
  William Como
  Editor-in-Chief
  (See address above)

DANCE PERSPECTIVES [148]
29 East 9th Street
New York, New York 10003
(212) 777-1594

First published in 1959

SUBSCRIPTION DATA
Issues and rates: Published quarterly.
  Average paid circulation: 2000
  Annual rate(s): $10.00

EDITORIAL DESCRIPTION
An illustrated scholarly journal of dance.
Articles per average issue: 1
Audience: Dance audience
  Manuscripts accepted in English

MANUSCRIPT INFORMATION
Subject field(s): Critical and historical aspects of dance and allied arts in relation to dance; film, decor, etc.
Manuscript requirements: MLA. Full documentation but not academic style.
  Preferred length: 15,000-20,000 words
  Number of copies to be submitted: Two
  Abstract: Not necessary.
Author information and reprints: Payment: By publication to author. $250 per article.
  Is simultaneous submission of article to other journals permitted: Permitted.
  Exclusive manuscript rights between acceptance and publication: Yes
  Copyright: Held by publication.
  Reprints: Available at no cost.
Additional information: Illustrations are essential. Prefer to have manuscripts submitted first in summary or outline form. Revisions are frequently requested.
Disposition of manuscript:
  Receipt of manuscript acknowledged: Yes
  Decision to publish in: 1-2 months
  Accepted manuscript published in: 1-2 years
  Rejected manuscript returned: Yes
  Rejected manuscript criticized: Sometimes
Submit to:
  Selma Jeanne Cohen
  Editor
  (See address above)

Creative and performing arts 47

DANCE SCOPE [149]
245 West 52d Street
New York, New York 10019
(212) 245-4833

First published in 1965

SUBSCRIPTION DATA
Issues and rates: Published semi-annually.
  Average paid circulation: 2,000
  Annual rate(s): $3.50; Foreign $4.00
Publisher or Sponsor: The American Dance Guild
Managing Editor: Richard Lorber

EDITORIAL DESCRIPTION
  Explores all aspects of past, present and future dance; to reveal the unity within the multiplicity of performing art forms.
Articles per average issue: 6
Audience: Dancers, educators, general audience
  Manuscripts accepted in English

MANUSCRIPT INFORMATION
Subject field(s): All areas relating to dance: ethnic ritual forms, personal essay, memoir, critical in-depth studies, historical scholarship, ballet, anthropological research, intermedia art, performance documentation, interviews, therapy, theory
Manuscript requirements: No specific style guide. See latest issue for style requirements.
  Preferred length: 1,500-3,500 words; 6-15 pages
  Number of copies to be submitted: 1
  Abstract: Not necessary.
Author information and reprints: Payment: By publication to author. $20.00 per article.
  Is simultaneous submission of article to other journals permitted: Not permitted.
  Exclusive manuscript rights between acceptance and publication: Yes
  Copyright: Held by publication unless author specifically requests it
  Reprints: Available at no cost. 5 copies of magazine
Disposition of manuscript:
  Query letter: Not necessary, but advisable.
  Receipt of manuscript acknowledged: Yes
  Decision to publish in: 4-6 weeks
  Accepted manuscript published in: 2 months
  Rejected manuscript returned: Yes, if return postage is supplied by author.
  Rejected manuscript criticized: Sometimes
Submit to:
  Richard Lorber
  Editor
  (See address above)

DESIGN [150]
The Magazine of Creative Art
1100 Waterway Boulevard
Indianapolis, Indiana 46202
(317) 634-1100

First published in 1879

SUBSCRIPTION DATA
Issues and rates: Published bi-monthly.
  Average paid circulation: 9,000; 500 controlled
  Annual rate(s): $7.00; Foreign $8.00; Institutions $7.00
Managing Editor: Barbara L. Albert

EDITORIAL DESCRIPTION
  Creative ideas for arts and crafts for the individual and the classroom in addition to conveying theoretical, historical design and artistic concepts.
Articles per average issue: 10
Audience: Teachers of art, students, those interested in crafts.
  Manuscripts accepted in English only

MANUSCRIPT INFORMATION
Subject field(s): Any area in fine and graphic arts
Manuscript requirements: Style sheet sent on request.
  Preferred length: 1,000 to 1,500 words
  Number of copies to be submitted: 1
  Abstract: Not necessary.
Author information and reprints: Payment: By publication to author. $20.00 to $75.00 per article.
  Is simultaneous submission of article to other journals permitted: Not permitted.
  Exclusive manuscript rights between acceptance and publication: Yes
  Copyright: Held by publication unless pre-arranged with author
  Reprints: Available at cost. Varies
Disposition of manuscript:
  Query letter: Not necessary, but advisable.
  Receipt of manuscript acknowledged: Yes
  Decision to publish in: 6-8 weeks
  Accepted manuscript published in: 8-16 weeks
  Rejected manuscript returned: Yes, if return postage is supplied by author.
  Rejected manuscript criticized: Yes
Submit to:
  Barbara L. Albert
  Editor
  (See address above)

DETROIT INSTITUTE OF ARTS. BULLETIN [151]
5200 Woodward
Detroit, Michigan 48202
(313) 831-0360 ext. 42

SUBSCRIPTION DATA
Issues and rates: Published quarterly.
  Average paid circulation: 9,000 controlled
  Annual rate(s): $4.00
Publisher or Sponsor: Detroit Institute of Arts, Founders Society
Managing Editor: Susan F. Rossen

EDITORIAL DESCRIPTION
  Publishes scholarly, educational articles on newly acquisitioned objects or groups of objects in the permanent collections of the D.I.A., or reassessment, important recontributions and discoveries or works of art in the collections.

MANUSCRIPT INFORMATION
Subject field(s): Art history, museum problems
Manuscript requirements: Style sheet sent on request.
  Preferred length: 2,000 words
  Number of copies to be submitted: One
Author information and reprints: Payment: By publication to author. $200.00 per article.
  Is simultaneous submission of article to other journals permitted: No
  Exclusive manuscript rights between acceptance and publication: Yes
  Copyright: No copyright
  Reprints: Available at no cost.
Additional information: Publication is directed mainly at the membership and a limited public, not to scholars even though the articles published must be complete and thorough.
Disposition of manuscript:
  Receipt of manuscript acknowledged: Yes
  Decision to publish in: 3 weeks
  Accepted manuscript published in: 3-9 months
Submit to:
  Editor
  (See address above)

DRAMA & THEATRE [152]
Department of English
SUNY at Fredonia
Fredonia, New York 14063
(716) 673-3587

Previously entitled *First Stage*

First published in 1961

SUBSCRIPTION DATA
Issues and rates: Published semi-annually.
  Average paid circulation: 1500
  Annual rate(s): $4.50, Foreign $5.00
Publisher or Sponsor: State University of New York, Fredonia
Managing Editor: James Shokoff

EDITORIAL DESCRIPTION
  Contents include articles on contemporary theatre and drama; interviews with dramatists and directors; new plays and translations of new plays; play reviews; book reviews.
Articles per average issue: 8
Audience: Theatre, drama students, scholars and professionals
  Manuscripts accepted in English

MANUSCRIPT INFORMATION
Subject field(s): New plays, translations, articles, interviews, book reviews, play reviews
Manuscript requirements: MLA; also see latest issue of publication
  Preferred length: 2,000-3,000 words; 8-10 pages
  Number of copies to be submitted: One
  Abstract: Not necessary.
Author information and reprints: Payment: By publication to author.
  Is simultaneous submission of article to other journals permitted: No

Exclusive manuscript rights between acceptance and publication: No
Copyright: Held by author.
Reprints: Not available.
Additional information: For plays, follow standard dramatic form.
Disposition of manuscript:
Query letter: Not necessary.
Receipt of manuscript acknowledged: Yes
Decision to publish in: 2-3 months
Accepted manuscript published in: 6-12 months
Rejected manuscript returned: Yes, if self-addressed, stamped envelope is sent with manuscript.
Rejected manuscript criticized: Sometimes
Submit to:
For Articles:
Henry F. Salerno
Editor

For Reviews:
James Shokoff
Managing Editor
(See address above)

THE DRAMA REVIEW [153]
51 West 4th Street, Room 300
New York, New York 10012
(212) 598-2597

Previously entitled *Tulane Drama Review*

First published in 1955

SUBSCRIPTION DATA
Issues and rates: Published quarterly.
Average paid circulation: 15,000
Annual rate(s): $9.50, Foreign $11.50
Publisher or Sponsor: New York University, School of the Arts

EDITORIAL DESCRIPTION
Covers contemporary and historical trends in the full range of the performing arts.
Articles per average issue: 9-15
Audience: Practitioners, professors, students, theatregoers
Manuscripts accepted in all languages

MANUSCRIPT INFORMATION
Subject field(s): Theatre, dance, film, TV, music, fine arts
Manuscript requirements: Chicago
Preferred length: None
Number of copies to be submitted: One
Author information and reprints: Payment: By publication to author. $.02-$.03 per word.
Is simultaneous submission of article to other journals permitted: No
Exclusive manuscript rights between acceptance and publication: Yes
Copyright: Held by publication.
Reprints: Available, cost on request
Disposition of manuscript:
Receipt of manuscript acknowledged: Yes
Decision to publish in: One month
Accepted manuscript published in: 3-6 months
Rejected manuscript returned: Yes, if return postage is supplied by author.
Submit to:
Paul R. Ryan
Executive Editor
(See address above)

DRAMATICS [154]
An Educational Magazine for Students, Teachers, and Directors of Theatre Arts
Box E, College Hill Station
Cincinnati, Ohio 45224
(513) 541-7379

First published in 1929

SUBSCRIPTION DATA
Issues and rates: Monthly, October through May
Average paid circulation: 50,000
Annual rate(s): $5.00, Pan-Am $5.25, Foreign $5.50, Students $3.00
Publisher or Sponsor: International Thespian Society
Managing Editor: Thomas A. Barker

EDITORIAL DESCRIPTION
Feature articles on theatre projects and play productions; world-wide theatre innovations; technical, acting and directing hints; dance; mime; touring groups; children's theatre; focus on educational theatre. Contains practical and helpful hints to offer creative ideas for high school theatre students and teachers.
Articles per average issue: 5-8
Audience: Teachers and students of secondary school theatre
Manuscripts accepted in English only

MANUSCRIPT INFORMATION
Subject field(s): One-act plays, practical technical information, acting/directing hints, unusual play productions, mime, dance and movement, children's theatre; all areas that relate to the performing arts.
Manuscript requirements: Style sheet sent on request.
Preferred length: 2000 words
Number of copies to be submitted: One
Author information and reprints: Payment: By publication to author. $15 to $40.00 per article. Free copies for feature, technicalities article or one-act play.
Is simultaneous submission of article to other journals permitted: No
Exclusive manuscript rights between acceptance and publication: Yes
Copyright: First North American Serial Rights only
Reprints: Available, 10 copies free; $1.00 per each additional 10.
Additional information: Photos accompanying article are most helpful. Clear, crisp black and white glossies 5 by 7 or larger preferred. Not interested in critiques of specific productions
Disposition of manuscript:
Query letter: Not necessary, but advisable.
Receipt of manuscript acknowledged: Yes
Decision to publish in: Three months
Accepted manuscript published in: Two months
Rejected manuscript returned: Yes, if return postage is supplied by author.
Rejected manuscript criticized: Sometimes
Submit to:
Thomas A. Barker
Editor and Director of Publications
(See address above)

DRAMATIKA [155]
370 Riverside Drive
New York, New York 10025
(212) RI 9-5092

First published in 1967

SUBSCRIPTION DATA
Issues and rates: Published semi-annually.
Annual rate(s): $4.00; Institutions $5.00
Publisher or Sponsor: COSMEP; CCLM
Managing Editor: John Pyros

EDITORIAL DESCRIPTION
Publishes pieces ready for performance: plays, songs, film scripts, etc.
Articles per average issue: 6
Audience: Those interested in the performing arts
Manuscripts accepted in English

MANUSCRIPT INFORMATION
Manuscript requirements: No specific style guide.
Preferred length: 20 pages maximum
Number of copies to be submitted: 1
Abstract: Not necessary.
Author information and reprints: Payment: Reprints only. 1
Is simultaneous submission of article to other journals permitted: Not permitted.
Exclusive manuscript rights between acceptance and publication: Yes
Copyright: Held by publication.
Reprints: Not available.
Disposition of manuscript:
Query letter: Not necessary.
Receipt of manuscript acknowledged: No
Decision to publish in: 1 month
Accepted manuscript published in: 6 months
Rejected manuscript returned: Yes, if return postage is supplied by author.
Rejected manuscript criticized: Sometimes
Submit to:
John Pyros
Editor-Publisher
(See address above)

EDUCATIONAL THEATRE JOURNAL [156]
ATA National Office
1317 F Street, N. W.
Washington, D. C. 20004
(202) 737-5606

SUBSCRIPTION DATA
Issues and rates: Published quarterly.
Annual rate(s): Members $15.00

Creative and performing arts

Publisher or Sponsor: American Theatre Association; University and College Theatre Association
Managing Editor: Anthony Reid

EDITORIAL DESCRIPTION
Publishes articles on theatre and education.
Audience: Academic
Manuscripts accepted in English

MANUSCRIPT INFORMATION
Subject field(s): Theatre history, dramatic literature, audience research, theatre education, contemporary theatre, theatre around the world, interviews, reviews
Manuscript requirements: MLA
Preferred length: 8-38 pages
Number of copies to be submitted: 2
Abstract: Not necessary.
Author information and reprints: Payment: Reprints only. 5 issues
Is simultaneous submission of article to other journals permitted: Not permitted.
Exclusive manuscript rights between acceptance and publication: Yes
Copyright: Held by the Association; right to reprint is always granted to author.
Reprints: Available at no cost. Minimum of 100 Available at cost.
Disposition of manuscript:
Receipt of manuscript acknowledged: Yes
Decision to publish in: About 8 weeks
Accepted manuscript published in: 6-12 months
Rejected manuscript returned: Yes, if return postage is supplied by author.
Rejected manuscript criticized: Sometimes
Submit to:
Virginia Scott
Co-Editor
82 Perham Street
Farmington, Maine 04938

ETHNOMUSICOLOGY [157]
Room 513, 201 South Main Street
Ann Arbor, Michigan 48108
(504) 451-4659

First published in 1953

SUBSCRIPTION DATA
Issues and rates: Published three times per year.
Average paid circulation: 1600
Annual rate(s): Individuals $12.50, Institutions $15.00, Students $7.50
Publisher or Sponsor: Society for Ethnomusicology, Inc.
Managing Editor: Gerard Behague

EDITORIAL DESCRIPTION
Contains works of interest to ethnomusicologists, musicologists, and folklorists, on a professional basis, usually based upon actual research on the subjects covered.
Articles per average issue: 4-5
Audience: Scholars, students, professional musicians
Manuscripts accepted in English only

MANUSCRIPT INFORMATION
Subject field(s): Ethnomusicology, ethnic dance, bibliography, discography, musical instruments, historical documents, linguistic texts of music
Manuscript requirements: See latest issue for style requirements. MLA
Preferred length: 10-40 pages
Number of copies to be submitted: Two
Abstract: Yes. An abstract of 50-100 words.
Author information and reprints: Payment: None.
Is simultaneous submission of article to other journals permitted: Yes
Exclusive manuscript rights between acceptance and publication: No
Copyright: Held jointly by author and publication
Reprints: Available at cost.
Additional information: Presently not accepting papers on single folksongs from Appalachia or other American or English repertoires, or the summaries of the work of others.
Disposition of manuscript:
Query letter: Not necessary.
Receipt of manuscript acknowledged: Yes
Decision to publish in: 6-18 months
Accepted manuscript published in: 12-18 months
Rejected manuscript returned: Yes
Rejected manuscript criticized: Yes
Submit to:
Gerard Behague
Editor
Department of Music
University of Texas at Austin
Austin, Texas 78712
(512) 471-1985

THE HARPSICHORD [158]
P. O. Box 4323
Denver, Colorado 80204
(303) 244-4971

First published in 1968

SUBSCRIPTION DATA
Issues and rates: Published quarterly.
Average paid circulation: 2,000
Annual rate(s): $10.00; Foreign $11.00; Institutions $10.00; Students $10.00; Foreign institutions $11.00
Publisher or Sponsor: International Harpsichord Society
Managing Editor: Harold L. Haney

EDITORIAL DESCRIPTION
Devoted to the keyboard instruments of the Baroque period with emphasis on the harpsichord and clavichord
Articles per average issue: 5
Audience: Musicians, academic
Manuscripts accepted in English only

MANUSCRIPT INFORMATION
Subject field(s): Interpretation of early music, record reviews, tuning methods, repair, restoration, and construction; some music published

Manuscript requirements: See latest issue for style requirements.
Preferred length: 100-8,000 words
Number of copies to be submitted: 1
Abstract: Not necessary.
Author information and reprints: Payment: Reprints only. 6
Is simultaneous submission of article to other journals permitted: Permitted, but not encouraged.
Exclusive manuscript rights between acceptance and publication: No
Copyright: Held by publication. Author is freely given the rights to re-publish or sell if desired.
Reprints: Available at no cost. 6
Additional information: High quality material desired. Articles must be timeless, not related to one performance or event. Include also a short biography of the author and a photograph, if possible.
Disposition of manuscript:
Query letter: Not necessary.
Receipt of manuscript acknowledged: Yes
Decision to publish in: Several months
Accepted manuscript published in: 12 months or more
Rejected manuscript returned: Yes, if return postage is supplied by author.
Rejected manuscript criticized: Sometimes
Submit to:
Harold L. Haney
Editor
(See address above)

THE INSTRUMENTALIST [159]
The School Band and Orchestra Director's Magazine
1418 Lake Street
Evanston, Illinois 60204
(312) 328-6000

First published in 1946

SUBSCRIPTION DATA
Issues and rates: Monthly except July
Average paid circulation: 19,000
Annual rate(s): $8.00, Foreign $8.90
Managing Editor: Kenneth L. Neidig

EDITORIAL DESCRIPTION
"In-service education" for school band and orchestra directors and instrumental music teachers; professional help for instrumentalists in the form of instrumental clinics, how-to articles, new trends, practical philosophy, interested in practical information of immediate use to instrumentalists, by musicians who are sharing knowledge, techniques, experiences.
Articles per average issue: 15
Audience: School band and orchestra directors
Manuscripts accepted in English

MANUSCRIPT INFORMATION
Manuscript requirements: Chicago
Preferred length: 6-8 pages
Number of copies to be submitted: One

Author information and reprints: Payment: By publication to author. $10-$100 per article.
Is simultaneous submission of article to other journals permitted: No
Exclusive manuscript rights between acceptance and publication: Yes
Copyright: Held by publication.
Reprints: Available, 2-3 copies of issue free; reprints at cost
Disposition of manuscript:
Query letter: Not necessary, but advisable.
Receipt of manuscript acknowledged: Yes
Decision to publish in: 2-4 weeks
Accepted manuscript published in: 3-12 months
Rejected manuscript returned: Yes
Rejected manuscript criticized: No
Submit to:
Kenneth L. Neidig
Editor
(See address above)

INTERNATIONAL MUSICIAN [160]
220 Mt. Pleasant Avenue
Newark, New Jersey 07104
(201) 484-6600

Previously entitled *American Musician*

First published in 1898

SUBSCRIPTION DATA
Issues and rates: Published monthly.
Average paid circulation: 295,000
Annual rate(s): $5.00
Publisher or Sponsor: American Federation of Musicians
Managing Editor: Stanley Ballard

EDITORIAL DESCRIPTION
Material pertains to professional musicians: news items, biographies, symphonic notes, obituaries, Nashville news, pop and jazz.
Articles per average issue: 3
Audience: Professional musicians
Manuscripts accepted in English

MANUSCRIPT INFORMATION
Subject field(s): Music
Manuscript requirements: See latest issue for style requirements.
Preferred length: 2,000 to 2,500 words; 6 pages
Number of copies to be submitted: One
Author information and reprints: Payment: By publication to author.
Is simultaneous submission of article to other journals permitted: No
Exclusive manuscript rights between acceptance and publication: Yes
Copyright: No
Reprints: Available at no cost
Disposition of manuscript:
Query letter: Not necessary.
Receipt of manuscript acknowledged: No
Decision to publish in: 1 month
Accepted manuscript published in: Varies
Rejected manuscript returned: Yes, if return postage is supplied by author.
Rejected manuscript criticized: No
Submit to:
Stanley Ballard
Editor
(See address above)

JAZZ MAGAZINE [161]
63 Champs Elysees
Paris, France 75008
359-01-79

SUBSCRIPTION DATA
Issues and rates: Published monthly.
Average paid circulation: 12,000
Annual rate(s): Fr. 50; Foreign Fr. 57
Managing Editor: Philippe Carles

EDITORIAL DESCRIPTION
Contains articles in the jazz field. Mainly concerned with the new tendencies in Afro-American music.
Articles per average issue: 6
Audience: General
Manuscripts accepted in English, French

MANUSCRIPT INFORMATION
Subject field(s): Interviews of musicians, studies on musical problems
Manuscript requirements: See latest issue for style requirements.
Preferred length: 4-10 pages
Number of copies to be submitted: One
Abstract: No
Author information and reprints: Payment: By publication to author. $20-$50 per article.
Is simultaneous submission of article to other journals permitted: Not to another French publication.
Exclusive manuscript rights between acceptance and publication: No
Copyright: Held by publication.
Reprints: Available at minimal cost
Additional information: Payment may be lower if translation into French has to be made by the publication.
Disposition of manuscript:
Query letter: No
Receipt of manuscript acknowledged: Yes
Decision to publish in: 2 weeks
Accepted manuscript published in: At least one month
Rejected manuscript returned: Yes, if return postage is supplied by author.
Rejected manuscript criticized: Yes
Submit to:
Philippe Carles
Chief Editor
(See address above)
225-99-62

JEMF QUARTERLY [162]
John Edwards Memorial Foundation,
Folklore & Mythology Center
University of California
Los Angeles, California 90024
(213) 825-3777

Previously entitled *JEMF Newsletter*

First published in 1965

SUBSCRIPTION DATA
Issues and rates: Published quarterly.
Average paid circulation: 600; 75 controlled
Annual rate(s): 7.50; Institutions $9.00; Members $7.50
Publisher or Sponsor: John Edwards Memorial Foundation
Managing Editor: Norm Cohen

EDITORIAL DESCRIPTION
To provide coverage of all areas of commercially recorded and published American folk music and genres of folk-derived music, such as hillbilly, blues, cajun, cowboy, western, gospel.
Articles per average issue: 6
Audience: Scholars, fans and collectors
Manuscripts accepted in English

MANUSCRIPT INFORMATION
Subject field(s): Individual performers, songs, styles, or combinations of these. Can be written from various perspectives: historical, folkloristic, sociological, musicological. Also published are bibliographies, discographies, and related reference materials.
Manuscript requirements: See latest issue for style requirements.
Preferred length: 500-2500 words
Number of copies to be submitted: One
Abstract: Not necessary.
Author information and reprints: Payment: Reprints only. 5-10
Is simultaneous submission of article to other journals permitted: Permitted, but not encouraged.
Exclusive manuscript rights between acceptance and publication: Yes
Copyright: Not standardized
Reprints: Not available.
Disposition of manuscript:
Query letter: Not necessary.
Receipt of manuscript acknowledged: Yes
Decision to publish in: 1-2 months
Accepted manuscript published in: 2-3 months
Rejected manuscript returned: Yes, if return postage is supplied by author.
Rejected manuscript criticized: Sometimes
Submit to:
Norm Cohen
Editor
(See address above)

SPECIAL STIPULATIONS
Authors are encouraged to provide photographs or any other illustrative material.

THE JOURNAL OF AESTHETICS AND ART CRITICISM [163]
Department of Philosophy
Temple University
Philadelphia, Pennsylvania 19122
(215) 787-8290

Creative and performing arts

SUBSCRIPTION DATA
Issues and rates: Published quarterly.
  Average paid circulation: 2800
  Annual rate(s): $15.00, Foreign $16.00
Publisher or Sponsor: American Society for Aesthetics

EDITORIAL DESCRIPTION
Contains studies of the arts and related types of experience from a philosophic, scientific or other theoretical standpoint, including those of psychology, sociology, anthropology, and education, as well as examinations of the nature and function of criticism, aesthetic judgments and aesthetic value.
Articles per average issue: 10
Manuscripts accepted in English

MANUSCRIPT INFORMATION
Subject field(s): Aesthetics, theory of criticism
Manuscript requirements: Chicago
  Preferred length: 3000-7000 words
  Number of copies to be submitted: 2 ribbon copies
  Abstract: Not necessary.
Author information and reprints: Payment: None. 50 free reprints
  Is simultaneous submission of article to other journals permitted: No
  Exclusive manuscript rights between acceptance and publication: Yes
  Reprints: Available, over 50 at cost
Disposition of manuscript:
  Query letter: Not necessary.
  Receipt of manuscript acknowledged: Yes
  Decision to publish in: 2 months
  Accepted manuscript published in: 2 years
  Rejected manuscript returned: Yes, if return postage is supplied by author.
  Rejected manuscript criticized: Sometimes
Submit to:
  John Fisher
  Editor
  (See address above)

JOURNAL OF BAND RESEARCH [164]
Iowa State University Press
South State Avenue
Ames, Iowa 50010
(515) 294-5280

Previously entitled *The ABA Journal of Band Research*

First published in 1964

SUBSCRIPTION DATA
Issues and rates: Published semi-annually.
  Average paid circulation: 900
  Annual rate(s): $5.00
Publisher or Sponsor: American Bandmasters Association

EDITORIAL DESCRIPTION
Historical, descriptive, analytical, and experimental research relating to the development of bands
Articles per average issue: 5
Audience: Band directors and researchers
Manuscripts accepted in English

MANUSCRIPT INFORMATION
Subject field(s): Band music, band instrumentation, composers for band
Manuscript requirements: Style sheet sent on request.
  Preferred length: 2,000-5,000 words
  Number of copies to be submitted: 2
  Abstract: Not necessary.
Author information and reprints: Payment: None. Two copies of issue in which article appears.
  Is simultaneous submission of article to other journals permitted: No
  Exclusive manuscript rights between acceptance and publication: Yes
  Copyright: Held by publication.
  Reprints: Not available.
Additional information: Illustrations or musical examples should be in a form ready for printing. Include also a biographical sketch of author.
Disposition of manuscript:
  Query letter: Not necessary.
  Receipt of manuscript acknowledged: Yes
  Decision to publish in: Several months
  Accepted manuscript published in: Varies
  Rejected manuscript returned: Yes
  Rejected manuscript criticized: Yes
Submit to:
  Warren E. George
  Editor
  Department of Music Education
  Pennsylvania State University
  University Park, Pennsylvania 16802
  (814) 863-0418

JOURNAL OF CHURCH MUSIC [165]
2900 Queen Lane
Philadelphia, Pennsylvania 19129
(215) 848-6800 ext. 251

First published in 1959

SUBSCRIPTION DATA
Issues and rates: Published monthly.
  Average paid circulation: 4,800
  Annual rate(s): $7.00, Foreign $8.00
Publisher or Sponsor: Lutheran Church in America
Managing Editor: Robert A. Camburn

EDITORIAL DESCRIPTION
Contains articles directed principally toward organists and choir directors in small to medium-sized churches who have limited opportunities for music study; also directed toward ministers of music and members of music committees.
Articles per average issue: 4
Audience: Church organists, choir directors, ministers of music
Manuscripts accepted in English

MANUSCRIPT INFORMATION
Subject field(s): Choir training (all ages), choral techniques, organ techniques, church music administration, handbell choir techniques, biographies of contemporary church music composers.
Manuscript requirements: Chicago
  Preferred length: 1500-2500 words
  Number of copies to be submitted: One
  Abstract: Not necessary.
Author information and reprints: Payment: By publication to author. $.02 per word. 3-5 complimentary author's copies also.
  Is simultaneous submission of article to other journals permitted: No
  Exclusive manuscript rights between acceptance and publication: Yes
  Copyright: Held by publication.
  Reprints: Available, cost depends on length
Additional information: Any references to previously published material should be fully cited including title, author, place, date and name of publisher; number of pages and price. Special mention should be made if any works cited are out of print.
Disposition of manuscript:
  Query letter: Not necessary, but advisable.
  Receipt of manuscript acknowledged: Yes
  Decision to publish in: 1 month
  Accepted manuscript published in: 6 months
  Rejected manuscript returned: Yes
  Rejected manuscript criticized: Sometimes
Submit to:
  Robert A. Camburn
  (See address above)

SPECIAL STIPULATIONS
Welcome articles by writers from any denomination.

JOURNAL OF JAZZ STUDIES [166]
Rutgers Institute of Jazz Studies
Dana Library
Newark, New Jersey 07102
(201) 648-5595

SUBSCRIPTION DATA
Issues and rates: Published semi-annually.
  Average paid circulation: 1,000
  Annual rate(s): $7.00
Publisher or Sponsor: Rutgers Institute of Jazz Studies
Managing Editor: Charles Nanry; David Cayer

EDITORIAL DESCRIPTION
Contains scholarly articles on jazz and related musical topics.

MANUSCRIPT INFORMATION
Subject field(s): Sociology, discography, history, psychology, literature, anthropology, political science, economics, musicology, ethnomusicology, Black studies
Manuscript requirements: Chicago
  Preferred length: 15-25 pages
  Number of copies to be submitted: Three
Author information and reprints: Payment: None.
  Is simultaneous submission of article to other journals permitted: No

Exclusive manuscript rights between acceptance and publication: Yes
Copyright: Held by publication.
Reprints: Not available.
Disposition of manuscript:
  Receipt of manuscript acknowledged: Yes
  Decision to publish in: 2 months
  Accepted manuscript published in: 6 months
  Rejected manuscript returned: Yes, if self-addressed, stamped envelope is sent with manuscript.
  Rejected manuscript criticized: Yes
Submit to:
  Charles Nanry
  Editor
  (See address above)
  (201) 249-4479

JOURNAL OF MUSIC THEORY [167]
Yale School of Music
New Haven, Connecticut 06520
(203) 436-1348

First published in 1957

SUBSCRIPTION DATA
Issues and rates: Published semi-annually.
  Average paid circulation: 1500
  Annual rate(s): $6.00
Publisher or Sponsor: Yale University
Managing Editor: James M. Baker

EDITORIAL DESCRIPTION
Contains scholarly articles in the field of music theory in the broadest sense; analyses, newly developed theoretical constructs, historical studies, theory translations, acoustical studies, aesthetic studies, reviews of the most important current books on music. Strives to select articles of the highest scholarly and technical competence, representing the broadest range of topics.
Articles per average issue: 4-5
Audience: Scholars, theorists, historians, composers, educators
  Manuscripts accepted in English, French, German

MANUSCRIPT INFORMATION
Subject field(s): Book reviews, translations, aesthetics, set-theory analysis, studies of early theory, Schenker analysis, acoustics
Manuscript requirements: Chicago
  Preferred length: 20-40 typewritten, double-spaced pages
  Number of copies to be submitted: Two
  Abstract: Not necessary.
Author information and reprints: Payment: Reprints only. 30 offprints
  Is simultaneous submission of article to other journals permitted: No
  Exclusive manuscript rights between acceptance and publication: Yes
  Copyright: Held by publication.
  Reprints: Available
Disposition of manuscript:
  Query letter: Not necessary.
  Receipt of manuscript acknowledged: Yes
  Decision to publish in: 1-3 months
  Accepted manuscript published in: 6 months
  Rejected manuscript returned: Yes
  Rejected manuscript criticized: No
Submit to:
  James M. Baker
  Managing Editor
  (See address above)
  (203) 777-0906

LEONARDO [168]
International Journal of the Contemporary Artist
Pergamon Press, Inc.
Maxwell House, Fairview Park
Elmsford, New York 10523
(914) 592-7700

First published in 1966

SUBSCRIPTION DATA
Issues and rates: Published quarterly.
  Annual rate(s): $50.00
Managing Editor: Frank J. Malina

EDITORIAL DESCRIPTION
Tries to reflect the developing world impact of contemporary art on mankind in a world made small by modern means of communication and transportation and where the diversity of community life is being given a unifying basis by the universality of scientific and technological achievements.
Articles per average issue: 8-10
Audience: Artists, art teachers, all those interested in international arts
  Manuscripts accepted in English, French

MANUSCRIPT INFORMATION
Subject field(s): Any branch of visual fine art, whether static, kinetic or mixed media; new developments; new materials and scientific techniques of possible use to artists or on subjects in the fields of physics, psychology, cinema, theatre, anesthetics, architecture, etc.
Manuscript requirements: See latest issue for style requirements.
  Preferred length: 2,000 to 6,000 words
  Number of copies to be submitted: 2
  Abstract: Yes. Not to exceed 300 words that gives the essential points of the text, it should be supplied in English and French.
Author information and reprints: Payment: Reprints only. 50
  Is simultaneous submission of article to other journals permitted: Not permitted.
  Exclusive manuscript rights between acceptance and publication: Yes
  Copyright: Held by publication.
  Reprints: Available at cost.
Disposition of manuscript:
  Query letter: Not necessary.
  Receipt of manuscript acknowledged: Yes
  Decision to publish in: 4 weeks
  Accepted manuscript published in: 5 months
  Rejected manuscript returned: Yes, if return postage is supplied by author.
  Rejected manuscript criticized: Sometimes
Submit to:
  Frank J. Malina
  Founder-Editor
  17 rue Emile Dunois
  92100-Boulogne sur Seine, France

MASTER DRAWINGS [169]
33 East 36th Street
New York New York 10016
(212) 685-0008

First published in 1963

SUBSCRIPTION DATA
Issues and rates: Published quarterly.
  Annual rate(s): $20.00; Foreign $21.00
Managing Editor: Felice Stampfle

EDITORIAL DESCRIPTION
Devoted to the study and illustration of Western draughtsmanship from the fourteenth century through the nineteenth century. Primarily, it is concerned with the publication of unknown material and significant new attributions and findings. From time to time articles on collections of the past and present are included.
Articles per average issue: 5-8
Audience: Scholars and students of art history, collectors and individuals with an interest in drawings.
  Manuscripts accepted in all European languages

MANUSCRIPT INFORMATION
Subject field(s): Drawings by artists or schools of the fourteenth through nineteenth centuries.
Manuscript requirements: See latest issue for style requirements.
  Preferred length: None
  Number of copies to be submitted: One
  Abstract: Not necessary.
Author information and reprints: Payment: Honorarium and 2 complimentary copies of the magazine.
  Exclusive manuscript rights between acceptance and publication: Yes
  Copyright: Held by publication.
  Reprints: Available at cost. Based on length
Disposition of manuscript:
  Query letter: Not necessary, but advisable.
  Receipt of manuscript acknowledged: Yes
  Decision to publish in: 1-3 months
  Accepted manuscript published in: 3-12 months
  Rejected manuscript returned: Yes, with return postage paid by publication.
  Rejected manuscript criticized: No
Submit to:
  Felice Stampfle
  Editor
  (See address above)

Creative and performing arts

MISSISSIPPI MUSIC EDUCATOR [170]
P.O. Box 5284
University of Southern Mississippi
Hattiesburg, Mississippi 39401
(601) 266-4185

SUBSCRIPTION DATA
Issues and rates: October, December, February, May
  Average paid circulation: 850; 200 controlled
  Annual rate(s): $3.00
Publisher or Sponsor: Mississippi Music Educators Association
Managing Editor: Robert J. Tuley

EDITORIAL DESCRIPTION
  Publishes articles in music education; reports and notices of activities of music education in schools and colleges of Mississippi; editorials; information provided by Music Educators National Conference; some reviews of music, books, etc.; photos. Strives for promotion of music education in schools of Mississippi; services and information for members of Mississippi Music Educators Association.
Articles per average issue: Varies
Audience: Professional educators
  Manuscripts accepted in English

MANUSCRIPT INFORMATION
Subject field(s): Music education, fine arts
Manuscript requirements: See latest issue for style requirements.
  Preferred length: 3 to 5 pages
  Number of copies to be submitted: One
Author information and reprints: Payment: None.
  Is simultaneous submission of article to other journals permitted: Yes
  Exclusive manuscript rights between acceptance and publication: No
  Copyright: Held by author.
  Reprints: Available; complimentary copies of publication
Disposition of manuscript:
  Query letter: Necessary.
  Receipt of manuscript acknowledged: Yes
  Decision to publish in: One month maximum
  Accepted manuscript published in: 1-3 months
  Rejected manuscript returned: Yes, if return postage is supplied by author.
  Rejected manuscript criticized: No
Submit to:
  Robert J. Tuley
  Editor
  (See address above)

MODERN DRAMA [171]
Hakkert
554 Spadina Crescent
Toronto M5S 2J9, Canada
966-5196

First published in 1958

SUBSCRIPTION DATA
Issues and rates: Published quarterly.
  Average paid circulation: 2,800
  Annual rate(s): $10.00; Individuals $10.00; Institutions $15.00
Publisher or Sponsor: University of Toronto, Graduate Center for the Study of Drama
Managing Editor: Frederick Marker

EDITORIAL DESCRIPTION
  Academic articles on modern drama, international studies of plays, dramatists, and aspects of the genre
Articles per average issue: 12
Audience: High-school to university
  Manuscripts accepted in English; French

MANUSCRIPT INFORMATION
Subject field(s): All aspects of modern drama.
Manuscript requirements: MLA
  Preferred length: 4000 pages maximum
  Number of copies to be submitted: 1
  Abstract: Not necessary.
Author information and reprints: Payment: Reprints only. 15 reprints
  Is simultaneous submission of article to other journals permitted: Not permitted.
  Exclusive manuscript rights between acceptance and publication: Yes
  Copyright: Held by publication.
  Reprints: Available at cost.
Additional information: Will not publish anything previously published
Disposition of manuscript:
  Query letter: Not necessary.
  Receipt of manuscript acknowledged: Yes
  Decision to publish in: 1-2 months
  Accepted manuscript published in: 12-18 months
  Rejected manuscript returned: Yes, if return postage is supplied by author.
  Rejected manuscript criticized: Sometimes
Submit to:
  Prof. Frederick Marker
  Editor
  Graduate Centre for Study of Drama
  University of Toronto
  Toronto, Canada

MUSEUMS JOURNAL [172]
Museums Association
87 Charlotte Street
London W1P 2BX, England
(01) 636-4600

First published in 1901

SUBSCRIPTION DATA
Issues and rates: Published quarterly.
  Average paid circulation: 2,700
  Annual rate(s): £5.00; Foreign £6.00
Publisher or Sponsor: The Museums Association
Managing Editor: Mary E. Pettman

EDITORIAL DESCRIPTION
  Contains articles, technical notes and book reviews relating to the work of museums and art galleries
Articles per average issue: 10
Audience: Professional
  Manuscripts accepted in English

MANUSCRIPT INFORMATION
Manuscript requirements: Style sheet sent on request.
  Number of copies to be submitted: 2
  Abstract: Not necessary.
Author information and reprints: Payment: Reprints only. 25
  Is simultaneous submission of article to other journals permitted: Not permitted.
  Exclusive manuscript rights between acceptance and publication: Yes
  Copyright: Held by publication.
Disposition of manuscript:
  Query letter: Not necessary, but advisable.
  Receipt of manuscript acknowledged: Yes
  Decision to publish in: 1-3 months
  Accepted manuscript published in: 2-12 months
  Rejected manuscript returned: Yes, with return postage paid by publication.
  Rejected manuscript criticized: Reasons for rejections only
Submit to:
  Mary E. Pettman
  Editor
  (See address above)

MUSIC JOURNAL [173]
370 Lexington Avenue
New York, New York 10017
(212) 889-9350

First published in 1942

SUBSCRIPTION DATA
Issues and rates: Ten times per year
  Average paid circulation: 33,000
  Annual rate(s): $9.00, Pan-Am $10.00, Foreign $10.50

EDITORIAL DESCRIPTION
  Contains articles dealing with any aspect of music, light or serious, with equal emphasis on educational and entertainment values.
Articles per average issue: 10
Audience: Music educators, artists, students
  Manuscripts accepted in English

MANUSCRIPT INFORMATION
Subject field(s): Band, orchestral, folk, rock, jazz, vocal, piano, recreational, opera, dance, concert, musicals
Manuscript requirements: No specific style guide.
  Preferred length: 1000 words
  Number of copies to be submitted: Two
  Abstract: Not necessary.
  Is simultaneous submission of article to other journals permitted: Yes
  Exclusive manuscript rights between acceptance and publication: Yes
  Copyright: Held by publication, but will transfer to author
  Reprints: Not available.
Disposition of manuscript:
  Query letter: Not necessary.
  Receipt of manuscript acknowledged: No
  Decision to publish in: 2 weeks

Accepted manuscript published in: 2-4 months
Rejected manuscript returned: Yes
Rejected manuscript criticized: No
Submit to:
Robert Cumming
Editor-in-Chief
(See address above)

SPECIAL STIPULATIONS
Enclose stamped, self-addressed envelope for immediate acknowledgment.

MUSIC MINISTRY [174]
201 Eighth Avenue South
Nashville, Tennessee 37202
(615) 749-6308

First published in 1959

SUBSCRIPTION DATA
Issues and rates: Published monthly.
  Average paid circulation: 12,000
  Annual rate(s): $7.25
Publisher or Sponsor: The United Methodist Church
Managing Editor: H. Myron Braun

EDITORIAL DESCRIPTION
Contains articles and practical helps for all persons with music and worship responsibility in church and church schools.
Articles per average issue: 3
Audience: Church musicians
  Manuscripts accepted in English

MANUSCRIPT INFORMATION
Subject field(s): Music (concerning specific or theory for church music), worship, theology, choral, organ, hymnology, music education, current trends; reviews of new resources.
Manuscript requirements: No specific style guide.
  Number of copies to be submitted: One
Author information and reprints: Payment: By publication to author. $.03 per word. Poetry about $.50 per line
  Is simultaneous submission of article to other journals permitted: No
  Exclusive manuscript rights between acceptance and publication: Yes
  Copyright: Held by publication.
  Reprints: Not available.
Disposition of manuscript:
  Query letter: No
  Receipt of manuscript acknowledged: No
  Decision to publish in: Three months
  Accepted manuscript published in: Six months
  Rejected manuscript returned: Yes, if self-addressed, stamped envelope is sent with manuscript.
  Rejected manuscript criticized: No
Submit to:
H. Myron Braun
Editor
(See address above)

MUSICAL ANALYSIS [175]
Box 7652, NT Station
Denton, Texas 76203

First published in 1972

SUBSCRIPTION DATA
Issues and rates: Published semi-annually.
  Average paid circulation: 100
  Annual rate(s): $5.00
Managing Editor: James Siddons

EDITORIAL DESCRIPTION
Contributions on any subject of musical scholarship as long as it pursues a systematic or logical mode of inquiry
Articles per average issue: 3-5
Audience: Music scholars, informed professionals, and amateurs
  Manuscripts accepted in English

MANUSCRIPT INFORMATION
Subject field(s): All fields of musicology, ethnomusicology, publishing and bibliography, music criticism and aesthetics
Manuscript requirements: See latest issue for style requirements.
  Preferred length: 2,000-3,000 words
  Number of copies to be submitted: 1
  Abstract: Yes. Of 50-150 words
Author information and reprints: Payment: Reprints only. 3 copies of issue
  Is simultaneous submission of article to other journals permitted: Not permitted.
  Exclusive manuscript rights between acceptance and publication: No
  Copyright: Held by editor
  Reprints: Not available.
Disposition of manuscript:
  Query letter: Not necessary.
  Receipt of manuscript acknowledged: Yes
  Decision to publish in: 2-4 months
  Accepted manuscript published in: 2-6 months
  Rejected manuscript returned: Yes, if return postage is supplied by author.
  Rejected manuscript criticized: Sometimes
Submit to:
James Siddons
Editor
(See address above)

THE MUSICAL TIMES [176]
38a Beak Street
London W1R 4BP, England
01-437-1222

First published in 1844

SUBSCRIPTION DATA
Issues and rates: Published monthly.
  Average paid circulation: 12,000
  Annual rate(s): $10.45
Managing Editor: Stanley Sadie

EDITORIAL DESCRIPTION
Contains reviews of books, records, music, concerts, festivals; articles on all aspects of music; reports on London and the provinces and overseas events.
Articles per average issue: 5
Audience: Specialist, academic
  Manuscripts accepted in English

MANUSCRIPT INFORMATION
Manuscript requirements: See latest issue for style requirements.
  Preferred length: 1000-2500 words
  Number of copies to be submitted: One
  Abstract: No
Author information and reprints: Payment: By publication to author. £10 per 1000 words.
  Is simultaneous submission of article to other journals permitted: No
  Exclusive manuscript rights between acceptance and publication: Yes
  Copyright: Held by author.
  Reprints: Not available.
Disposition of manuscript:
  Query letter: No
  Receipt of manuscript acknowledged: Yes
  Decision to publish in: 6 months
  Accepted manuscript published in: Varies
  Rejected manuscript returned: Yes
  Rejected manuscript criticized: No
Submit to:
Stanley Sadie
Editor
(See address above)

NACWPI JOURNAL [177]
Official Publication of the National Association of College Wind and Percussion Instructors
Division of Fine Arts
Northeast Missouri State University
Kirksville, Missouri 63501
(816) 665-5121 ext. 3426

SUBSCRIPTION DATA
Issues and rates: Published quarterly.
  Average paid circulation: 1,100; 1,000 controlled
  Annual rate(s): $6.00
Publisher or Sponsor: National Association of College Wind and Percussion Instructors
Managing Editor: Richard Weerts

EDITORIAL DESCRIPTION
Contains monographs, papers and articles dealing with the playing and teaching of all wind and percussion instruments on the university level.

MANUSCRIPT INFORMATION
Subject field(s): Playing and teaching of the wind and percussion instruments.
Manuscript requirements: See latest issue for style requirements.
  Preferred length: 2 to 10 pages
  Number of copies to be submitted: One
Author information and reprints: Payment: None.
  Is simultaneous submission of article to other journals permitted: No
  Exclusive manuscript rights between acceptance and publication: Yes
  Copyright: Held by publication.
  Reprints: Available, $1.00 per page

Creative and performing arts

Additional information: All materials must be typewritten and double-spaced, of college and university quality.
Disposition of manuscript:
  Receipt of manuscript acknowledged: Yes
  Decision to publish in: 4-6 weeks
  Accepted manuscript published in: 3-24 months
  Rejected manuscript returned: Yes
  Rejected manuscript criticized: No
Submit to:
  Richard Kenneth Weerts
  Editor
  (See address above)

THE NATS BULLETIN [178]
The Official Magazine of the National Association of Teachers of Singing
Chicago Musical College
Roosevelt University
Chicago, Illinois 60605
(312) 341-3780

Previously entitled *The Bulletin*

First published in 1944

SUBSCRIPTION DATA
Issues and rates: 4 times per year: October, December, February/March and May/June
  Average paid circulation: 3,650
  Annual rate(s): $6.00; Pan-Am $6.50; Foreign $7.00
Publisher or Sponsor: National Association of Teachers of Singing, Inc.
Managing Editor: Harvey Ringel

EDITORIAL DESCRIPTION
Deals exclusively with matters pertinent to singers and teachers of singing. Research and development in voice science, even when controversial is given extensive coverage. Presents the authoritative views of outstanding laryngologists, acousticians and musicologists as well as timely contributions by the foremost members of the voice teaching profession.
Articles per average issue: 5 plus discussions, reviews
Audience: Teachers of singing, singers, graduate students of vocal pedagogy
  Manuscripts accepted in English, French, German

MANUSCRIPT INFORMATION
Subject field(s): Pedagogy, repertoire, voice science, teachers preparation, inter-related disciplines
Manuscript requirements: Chicago
  Preferred length: 14 pages
  Number of copies to be submitted: One
Author information and reprints: Payment: None.
  Is simultaneous submission of article to other journals permitted: No
  Exclusive manuscript rights between acceptance and publication: Yes
  Copyright: Held by publication.

Additional information: Reprint arrangements are made directly between author and printer.
Disposition of manuscript:
  Query letter: Not necessary.
  Receipt of manuscript acknowledged: Yes
  Decision to publish in: 3 months
  Accepted manuscript published in: 9 months
  Rejected manuscript returned: Yes
  Rejected manuscript criticized: Yes
Submit to:
  Harvey Ringel
  Editor
  (See address above)

NEW JERSEY MUSIC & ARTS MAGAZINE [179]
P.O. Box 567
572 Main Street
Chatham, New Jersey 07928
(201) 635-6116

First published in 1945

SUBSCRIPTION DATA
Issues and rates: Published monthly.
  Average paid circulation: 5,000
  Annual rate(s): $4.00

EDITORIAL DESCRIPTION
Contains monthly calendar of events in all the arts; feature articles; personality profiles, news; all relating to the arts and artists. Main concentration is on New Jersey and its citizens.
Articles per average issue: 5
Audience: Those interested in the arts
  Manuscripts accepted in English

MANUSCRIPT INFORMATION
Subject field(s): Art, music, dance, drama, literature, film, poetry, photography, anything relating to the arts
Manuscript requirements: No specific style guide.
  Preferred length: Open
  Number of copies to be submitted: Two
  Abstract: Not necessary.
Author information and reprints: Payment: By publication to author. $15 to $50 per article.
  Is simultaneous submission of article to other journals permitted: No
  Exclusive manuscript rights between acceptance and publication: Yes
  Copyright: Held by publication.
  Reprints: Available, first one hundred free
Disposition of manuscript:
  Query letter: Not necessary.
  Receipt of manuscript acknowledged: Yes
  Decision to publish in: 60 days
  Accepted manuscript published in: 1-3 months
  Rejected manuscript returned: Yes, if self-addressed, stamped envelope is sent with manuscript.
  Rejected manuscript criticized: No
Submit to:
  Ruthann Williams
  Editor
  (See address above)

THE OPERA JOURNAL [180]
University of Mississippi
University, Mississippi 38677
(601) 232-7268 ext. 4

Previously entitled *NOA Newsletter*

First published in 1968

SUBSCRIPTION DATA
Issues and rates: Published quarterly.
  Average paid circulation: 1000
Publisher or Sponsor: The National Opera Association
Managing Editor: Leland Fox

EDITORIAL DESCRIPTION
Contains articles related to the subject of opera, reviews of books on opera, reviews of new scores, information relating to the activities of the parent organization.
Articles per average issue: 3
Audience: Persons interested in musical scholarship and opera
  Manuscripts accepted in English, French, German

MANUSCRIPT INFORMATION
Subject field(s): Aesthetics, musicology, commentary, review, general information
Manuscript requirements: No specific style guide.
  Preferred length: 1500-3000 words
  Number of copies to be submitted: One
  Abstract: Not necessary.
Author information and reprints: Payment: None.
  Is simultaneous submission of article to other journals permitted: Yes
  Exclusive manuscript rights between acceptance and publication: No
  Copyright: Held by publication.
  Reprints: Available at no cost
Additional information: Footnotes are discouraged; the information should be incorporated into the article. Photographs are welcomed.
Disposition of manuscript:
  Query letter: Not necessary.
  Receipt of manuscript acknowledged: Yes
  Decision to publish in: 3 months
  Accepted manuscript published in: 6 months
  Rejected manuscript returned: Yes
  Rejected manuscript criticized: Yes
Submit to:
  Leland S. Fox
  Editor
  (See address above)

ORIENTAL ART [181]
12 Ennerdale Road
Richmond, Surrey, England

SUBSCRIPTION DATA
Issues and rates: Published quarterly.
  Annual rate(s): £4.50, Foreign $12.00

EDITORIAL DESCRIPTION
Contains articles on all forms of Oriental art.

MANUSCRIPT INFORMATION
Author information and reprints: Payment:
By publication to author.
Disposition of manuscript:
Receipt of manuscript acknowledged: Yes
Rejected manuscript returned: Yes
Submit to:
Edmund Capon
Editor
8, The Gateway
Park Lane
Richmond, Surrey, England

PERCUSSIONIST [182]
Percussive Arts Society
130 Carol Drive
Terre Haute, Indiana 47805
(812) 466-2982

First published in 1963

SUBSCRIPTION DATA
Issues and rates: Published quarterly.
Average paid circulation: 3,500
Annual rate(s): Individuals $7.00;
Institutions $5.00; Students $7.00;
Members $10.00
Publisher or Sponsor: The Percussive Arts Society
Managing Editor: Neal L. Fluegel

EDITORIAL DESCRIPTION
Percussion education and performance
Articles per average issue: 6-8
Audience: Musicians and educators
Manuscripts accepted in English

MANUSCRIPT INFORMATION
Manuscript requirements: No specific style guide.
Preferred length: As required
Number of copies to be submitted: 1
Abstract: Not necessary.
Author information and reprints: Payment:
None.
Is simultaneous submission of article to other journals permitted: Permitted, but not encouraged.
Exclusive manuscript rights between acceptance and publication: No
Reprints: Available at cost. $1.50 per issue
Disposition of manuscript:
Query letter: Not necessary.
Receipt of manuscript acknowledged: Yes
Decision to publish in: 3 months
Accepted manuscript published in: 1 year
Rejected manuscript returned: Yes, if return postage is supplied by author.
Rejected manuscript criticized: No
Submit to:
Neal L. Fluegel
Editor
(See address above)

PERFORMING ARTS IN CANADA MAGAZINE [183]
52 Avenue Road, 2nd Floor
Toronto, Ontario M5R 2G3, Canada
(416) 921-2601

SUBSCRIPTION DATA
Issues and rates: Published quarterly.
Average paid circulation: 30,000
Annual rate(s): $3.00

EDITORIAL DESCRIPTION
Contains articles on theatre, dance and music; play reviews, interviews, one-act plays, forum section, technical articles on theatre.
Articles per average issue: 7
Audience: People involved or interested in the performing arts
Manuscripts accepted in English

MANUSCRIPT INFORMATION
Subject field(s): Theatre, dance, music, one-act plays
Manuscript requirements: Style sheet sent on request.
Preferred length: Varies
Number of copies to be submitted: One
Abstract: Yes.
Author information and reprints: Payment:
By publication to author. $15.00 to $75.00 per article.
Is simultaneous submission of article to other journals permitted: No
Exclusive manuscript rights between acceptance and publication: No
Copyright: Held by author.
Reprints: Available, free to author
Disposition of manuscript:
Query letter: Necessary.
Receipt of manuscript acknowledged: Yes
Decision to publish in: 4 weeks
Rejected manuscript returned: Yes
Rejected manuscript criticized: Upon request
Submit to:
Arnold Edinborough
Editor
(See address above)

PERSPECTIVES OF NEW MUSIC [184]
Box 271
Yardley, Pennsylvania 19067
(914) 758-6740

First published in 1962

SUBSCRIPTION DATA
Issues and rates: Published semi-annually.
Average paid circulation: 3,000
Annual rate(s): $9.50
Managing Editor: Eve Hanle

EDITORIAL DESCRIPTION
Devoted to the dissemination of thought and information in the areas of contemporary music, composition and theory, and in all other music-intellectual concerns. New compositions are published in score in conjunction with critical articles; innovative approaches are encouraged
Articles per average issue: 15
Audience: Professional musicians, academic, scholarly
Manuscripts accepted in English

MANUSCRIPT INFORMATION
Subject field(s): Not limited except by prior obligations.
Manuscript requirements: No specific style guide.
Preferred length: Author's discretion
Number of copies to be submitted: Original and 1 copy
Abstract: Not necessary.
Author information and reprints: Payment:
Reprints only. 25 reprints
Is simultaneous submission of article to other journals permitted: Not permitted.
Exclusive manuscript rights between acceptance and publication: Yes
Copyright: Held by publication.
Reprints: Available at no cost. 25
Disposition of manuscript:
Query letter: Not necessary, but advisable.
Receipt of manuscript acknowledged: Yes
Decision to publish in: 6 months
Accepted manuscript published in: 1-2 years
Rejected manuscript returned: Yes, with return postage paid by publication.
Rejected manuscript criticized: Sometimes
Submit to:
Benjamin Boretz
Editor
Department of Music
Bard College
Annandale-on-Hudson, New York 12504
(914) 758-6740

THE PIANO QUARTERLY [185]
P.O. Box 815
Wilmington, Vermont 05363
(802) 464-5149

First published in 1951

SUBSCRIPTION DATA
Issues and rates: Published quarterly.
Average paid circulation: 3,100 4,000 controlled
Annual rate(s): $7.00; Foreign $8.00;
Individuals $8.00; Institutions $7.00;
Foreign individuals $8.00; Foreign institutions $8.00
Managing Editor: Robert J. Silverman

EDITORIAL DESCRIPTION
Directed toward the world of the piano. Contains feature articles and interviews with leading pianists, reviews of new music, records and books; particularly directed toward the piano teacher and performer.
Articles per average issue: 9
Audience: Pianists on all levels
Manuscripts accepted in English, German, French

MANUSCRIPT INFORMATION
Subject field(s): Piano pedagogy, master lessons, performance problems, research; the entire spectrum of the piano world.
Manuscript requirements: See latest issue for style requirements.
Preferred length: 3,000 to 5,000 words
Number of copies to be submitted: 1

Creative and performing arts

Abstract: Not necessary.
Author information and reprints: Payment: None.
Is simultaneous submission of article to other journals permitted: Not permitted.
Exclusive manuscript rights between acceptance and publication: Yes
Copyright: Held by publication but exceptions are made
Reprints: Not available.
Disposition of manuscript:
Query letter: Not necessary.
Receipt of manuscript acknowledged: Yes
Decision to publish in: 2 weeks
Accepted manuscript published in: 6 months
Rejected manuscript returned: Yes, with return postage paid by publication.
Rejected manuscript criticized: Yes
Submit to:
Robert J. Silverman
Editor
(See address above)

RESTORATION AND EIGHTEENTH CENTURY THEATRE RESEARCH [186]
820 N. Michigan Avenue
Chicago, Illinois 60611
(312) 670-3071

First published in 1962

SUBSCRIPTION DATA
Issues and rates: Published semi-annually.
Average paid circulation: 950; 50 controlled
Annual rate(s): $3.00
Publisher or Sponsor: Loyola University, Chicago; Department of English

EDITORIAL DESCRIPTION
Devoted to research in theatre and on all aspects of theatre activity. It includes an annual annotated bibliography of books, periodicals, and dissertations concerned with Restoration and Eighteenth century theatre research. Works in progress in the field are published regularly.
Articles per average issue: 4-9
Audience: Academic
Manuscripts accepted in English

MANUSCRIPT INFORMATION
Subject field(s): Theatre, play publication, acting, relationship of theatre to social conditions
Manuscript requirements: MLA
Preferred length: Less than 5,000 words
Number of copies to be submitted: One
Abstract: Yes. 100 words or less
Author information and reprints: Payment: None.
Is simultaneous submission of article to other journals permitted: No
Exclusive manuscript rights between acceptance and publication: No
Copyright: Held by Loyola University
Reprints: Not available.
Disposition of manuscript:
Query letter: Not necessary.
Receipt of manuscript acknowledged: Yes
Decision to publish in: 4-6 weeks
Accepted manuscript published in: One year or less
Rejected manuscript returned: Yes
Rejected manuscript criticized: Yes
Submit to:
John S. Shea
Editor
(See address above)

SACRED MUSIC [187]
Route 2, Box 1
Irving, Texas 75062
(214) 254-8176

Previously entitled *Caecilia; Catholic Choirmaster*

First published in 1874

SUBSCRIPTION DATA
Issues and rates: Published quarterly.
Average paid circulation: 1100
Annual rate(s): $7.50
Publisher or Sponsor: Church Music Association of America

EDITORIAL DESCRIPTION
Contains articles on subjects dealing with church music; sample music; choral reviews; magazine reviews; book and record reviews; news of national and international interest; editorials and letters from readers.
Articles per average issue: 4
Audience: Catholic church musicians
Manuscripts accepted in English, French, German, Latin, Italian

MANUSCRIPT INFORMATION
Subject field(s): Church music, choral music, organ music, liturgical matters, practical articles
Manuscript requirements: See latest issue for style requirements.
Preferred length: 10-12 pages
Number of copies to be submitted: One
Abstract: Not necessary.
Author information and reprints: Payment: By publication to author. Nominal honorarium is offered.
Is simultaneous submission of article to other journals permitted: Yes
Reprints: Not available.
Additional information: Manuscript should be typewritten, double-spaced.
Disposition of manuscript:
Receipt of manuscript acknowledged: Yes
Decision to publish in: 4-5 weeks
Accepted manuscript published in: 4-5 weeks
Rejected manuscript returned: Yes
Rejected manuscript criticized: No
Submit to:
Rev. Ralph S. March, S.O. Cist.
Editor
(See address above)

SOURCE: MUSIC OF THE AVANT GARDE [188]
2101 22nd Street
Sacramento, California 95818
(916) 457-3173

First published in 1967

SUBSCRIPTION DATA
Issues and rates: Irregularly, approximately 2 per year
Average paid circulation: 2,000
Annual rate(s): $13.00, Foreign $15.00
Managing Editor: Stanley G. Lunetta

EDITORIAL DESCRIPTION
Contains articles, scores, records, reportage, interviews, computer flow charts, etc. by composer/performers on the leading edge of music.
Articles per average issue: 10-15
Audience: New Music composers, teachers, performers, students
Manuscripts accepted in English

MANUSCRIPT INFORMATION
Subject field(s): New music
Manuscript requirements: No specific style guide.
Preferred length: Depends on subject matter
Number of copies to be submitted: One
Author information and reprints: Payment: By publication to author. 10 per cent of total sales of the issue, divided by the number of contributors to it.
Is simultaneous submission of article to other journals permitted: Yes
Exclusive manuscript rights between acceptance and publication: No
Copyright: Held by publication.
Reprints: Available, cost varies per article.
Disposition of manuscript:
Query letter: Not necessary.
Receipt of manuscript acknowledged: Yes
Decision to publish in: Varies
Accepted manuscript published in: 6-12 months
Rejected manuscript returned: Yes
Rejected manuscript criticized: No
Submit to:
Editor
(See address above)

SOUTHWESTERN MUSICIAN AND TEXAS MUSIC EDUCATOR [189]
P.O. Box 9908
Houston, Texas 77015
(713) 453-7833

First published in 1919

SUBSCRIPTION DATA
Issues and rates: Ten times per year
Average paid circulation: 6300
Annual rate(s): $2.50
Publisher or Sponsor: Texas Music Educators Association
Managing Editor: J. F. Lenzo

EDITORIAL DESCRIPTION
To serve the music educators in Texas as a means of communication among the membership, as a publicity medium for various educational or professional music activities, as a stimulant to professional thought and action through the

publication of editorials and articles and to promote the field of music education within the state.
Articles per average issue: 2
Audience: Music educators
Manuscripts accepted in English only

MANUSCRIPT INFORMATION
Subject field(s): Reviews of band, choral and orchestral publications, new books on music, and reports on significant research in music education and music in general
Manuscript requirements: Literary works: free style; scholarly works: Chicago
Preferred length: 1200 to 1500 words
Number of copies to be submitted: One
Author information and reprints: Payment: By publication to author. $20.00 to $75.00 based on evaluation of article
Is simultaneous submission of article to other journals permitted: No
Exclusive manuscript rights between acceptance and publication: Yes
Copyright: Held by publication.
Reprints: Not available.
Additional information: Manuscripts should be typewritten, double-spaced.
Disposition of manuscript:
Query letter: Not necessary.
Receipt of manuscript acknowledged: Yes
Decision to publish in: 2-4 weeks
Accepted manuscript published in: 18-24 months
Rejected manuscript returned: Yes
Rejected manuscript criticized: No
Submit to:
J. F. Lenzo
Editor
(See address above)

STUDIO INTERNATIONAL [190]
Journal of Modern Art
Subscription Department
Watling Street
Bletchley, Bucks., England
(09) 087-1981

Previously entitled *The Studio*

First published in 1893

SUBSCRIPTION DATA
Issues and rates: Published bi-monthly.
Annual rate(s): £10.00; Foreign $29.00; Students £7.50; $24.00
Managing Editor: Peter Townsend

EDITORIAL DESCRIPTION
Covers the international development, criticism, and exhibition of art from impressionism to the contemporary avant-grade; reviews and articles by world-known critics, historians and especially by artists themselves on the problems and developments in the international visual arts
Articles per average issue: 8; 20 reviews
Audience: Those with interests in the international art world: collectors, artists, laymen
Manuscripts accepted in English

MANUSCRIPT INFORMATION
Manuscript requirements: No specific style guide.
Preferred length: 3,000 words
Number of copies to be submitted: 2
Abstract: Not necessary.
Author information and reprints: Payment: By publication to author.
Is simultaneous submission of article to other journals permitted: Not permitted.
Exclusive manuscript rights between acceptance and publication: Yes
Copyright: Held by publication.
Reprints: Available at no cost.
Disposition of manuscript:
Query letter: Not necessary, but advisable.
Receipt of manuscript acknowledged: Yes
Decision to publish in: 1-2 weeks
Accepted manuscript published in: 2-3 months
Rejected manuscript returned: Yes, with return postage paid by publication.
Rejected manuscript criticized: Sometimes
Submit to:
Peter Townsend;
John McEwen
Editor and Assistant Editor
Studio International Publications, Ltd.
14 West Central Street
London WC1A 1JH, England

THEATRE CRAFTS [191]
250 West 57th Street
New York, New York 10019
(212) 582-4110

First published in 1967

SUBSCRIPTION DATA
Issues and rates: Published bi-monthly.
Average paid circulation: 30,000
Annual rate(s): $6.00

EDITORIAL DESCRIPTION
Contains articles on the technical/craft aspect of theatre and film including makeup, costume, scenic design, theatre architecture, and lighting. Two special issues a year focus on themes such as Church theatre, street theatre, Shakespeare festivals, circus, etc.

MANUSCRIPT INFORMATION
Subject field(s): Sets, costumes, lighting, administration, architecture
Manuscript requirements: See latest issue for style requirements.
Preferred length: 12 pages
Number of copies to be submitted: One
Author information and reprints: Payment: None.
Is simultaneous submission of article to other journals permitted: Yes
Exclusive manuscript rights between acceptance and publication: Yes
Copyright: Held by publication.
Reprints: Available at no cost
Disposition of manuscript:
Receipt of manuscript acknowledged: Yes
Decision to publish in: 3 months
Accepted manuscript published in: 2-6 months
Rejected manuscript returned: Yes
Rejected manuscript criticized: No
Submit to:
Patricia J. MacKay
Editor
(See address above)

THEATRE DESIGN AND TECHNOLOGY [192]
Journal of the U.S. Institute for Theatre Technology
245 West 52nd Street
New York, New York 10019
(212) 757-7138

First published in 1965

SUBSCRIPTION DATA
Issues and rates: Published quarterly.
Average paid circulation: 2,100
Annual rate(s): Institutions $12.00
Publisher or Sponsor: U.S. Institute for Theatre Technology
Managing Editor: Donald Swinney

EDITORIAL DESCRIPTION
Concerned with the physical aspects of the theatre: architecture, engineering, administration, and the basic conditions of presentation. A reasonable balance is maintained between theoretical and practical articles.
Articles per average issue: 5
Audience: Theatrical designers, technicians, architects, engineers
Manuscripts accepted in English, French, German, Russian, Polish

MANUSCRIPT INFORMATION
Subject field(s): Theatre technology, architecture, engineering, production, management, and history
Manuscript requirements: Chicago; Editorial Guide sent on request
Preferred length: 1500-2000 words; 10-15 pages
Number of copies to be submitted: Two
Abstract: Not necessary.
Author information and reprints: Payment: Reprints only. 2 copies of issue and 2 tear sheets
Is simultaneous submission of article to other journals permitted: No
Exclusive manuscript rights between acceptance and publication: Yes
Copyright: Held by publication.
Reprints: Available, $75.00 per 100
Additional information: Include all graphics and proof of right to publish them.
Disposition of manuscript:
Query letter: Not necessary, but advisable.
Receipt of manuscript acknowledged: Yes
Decision to publish in: 3-6 months
Accepted manuscript published in: 12 months
Rejected manuscript returned: Yes, if self-addressed, stamped envelope is sent with manuscript.
Rejected manuscript criticized: Yes

Submit to:
Thomas S. Watson
Editor
1 Hillside Road
Newark, Delaware 19711
(302) 731-5468

THEATRE NOTEBOOK [193]
A Journal of the History and Technique of the British Theatre
103 Ralph Court
Queensway
London W2 5HU, England
01 229 5150

First published in 1945

SUBSCRIPTION DATA

Issues and rates: Published three times per year.
Average paid circulation: 1,000
Annual rate(s): £4.00; Foreign $12.00
Publisher or Sponsor: The Society for Theatre Research

EDITORIAL DESCRIPTION

Contains articles on research into British theatre history including technical aspects; reviews; notes and queries.
Articles per average issue: 6
Audience: Students and historians of theatre history
Manuscripts accepted in English

MANUSCRIPT INFORMATION

Subject field(s): History of theatres; actors and acting; plays in performance; scene and costume design; ballet, opera, music hall, toy theatre; lighting and other techniques
Manuscript requirements: See latest issue for style requirements.
Preferred length: 3000 words
Number of copies to be submitted: One
Abstract: Not necessary.
Author information and reprints: Payment: Reprints only. 6 copies of journal
Is simultaneous submission of article to other journals permitted: No
Exclusive manuscript rights between acceptance and publication: Yes
Copyright: Held by publication.
Reprints: Available, cost according to length
Additional information: Illustrations accepted, whole plate, glossy. Manuscript should be typewritten.
Disposition of manuscript:
Query letter: Not necessary, but advisable.
Receipt of manuscript acknowledged: Yes
Decision to publish in: 1 month
Accepted manuscript published in: Up to one year
Rejected manuscript returned: Yes
Rejected manuscript criticized: No
Submit to:
Sybil Rosenfeld
Joint Editor
(See address above)

THEATRE QUARTERLY [194]
30 Prince of Wales Crescent
London NW1, England
(01) 485-2320

First published in 1971

SUBSCRIPTION DATA

Issues and rates: Published quarterly.
Average paid circulation: 4,000
Annual rate(s): $17.50; Institutions $30.00
Publisher or Sponsor: British Theatre Institute

EDITORIAL DESCRIPTION

This is a serious, performance oriented journal devoted to all aspects of theatre, historical or contemporary, with a strong emphasis on documentation, source material, rehearsal logs, interviews, etc., of a practical rather than theoretical nature.
Articles per average issue: 7
Audience: Theatre workers, students, and academics
Manuscripts accepted in English only

MANUSCRIPT INFORMATION

Subject field(s): Theatre, preferably treated with an emphasis on performing aspects.
Manuscript requirements: See latest issue for style requirements. Style sheet sent on request.
Preferred length: 3,000-7,000 words
Number of copies to be submitted: 1
Abstract: Not necessary.
Author information and reprints: Payment: By publication to author.
Is simultaneous submission of article to other journals permitted: Permitted, but not encouraged.
Exclusive manuscript rights between acceptance and publication: Yes
Copyright: First serial rights only. In the event of reprint, a fee is payable.
Reprints: Not available.
Additional information: A study of the journal is strongly recommended.
Disposition of manuscript:
Query letter: Not necessary, but advisable.
Receipt of manuscript acknowledged: Yes
Decision to publish in: 8 weeks
Accepted manuscript published in: 6-9 months
Rejected manuscript returned: Yes, if return postage is supplied by author.
Rejected manuscript criticized: Reasons for rejections only
Submit to:
Catherine Itzin,
Simon Trussler
Editors
(See address above)

THE TRACKER [195]
Journal of the Organ Historical Society
421 S. South Street
Wilmington, Ohio 45177
(513) 382-3124

First published in 1956

SUBSCRIPTION DATA

Issues and rates: Published quarterly.
Average paid circulation: 600; 100 controlled
Annual rate(s): $7.50
Publisher or Sponsor: Organ Historical Society, Inc.
Managing Editor: Albert Robinson

EDITORIAL DESCRIPTION

Contains articles pertaining to the history of organ building in America; biographies of builders of pipe organs; accounts of historic instruments, their removal, restoration, disposition.
Articles per average issue: 7
Audience: Organists, organ builders, musicologists, historians
Manuscripts accepted in English

MANUSCRIPT INFORMATION

Subject field(s): Organ building, specific organs, builder's biography, changes in organ construction or location, organ tonal design, construction technicalities, organ book reviews, organ record reviews, organ recital reviews
Manuscript requirements: No specific style guide.
Preferred length: 10,000 words maximum
Number of copies to be submitted: One
Abstract: Not necessary.
Author information and reprints: Payment: None.
Is simultaneous submission of article to other journals permitted: No
Exclusive manuscript rights between acceptance and publication: Yes
Copyright: Held by publication.
Reprints: Not available.
Additional information: Deadlines: Summer-May 1; Fall-July 1; Winter-September 1; Spring-January 1.
Disposition of manuscript:
Query letter: Not necessary.
Receipt of manuscript acknowledged: Yes
Decision to publish in: One month
Accepted manuscript published in: One month
Rejected manuscript returned: Yes
Rejected manuscript criticized: No
Submit to:
Albert F. Robinson
Editor
c/o First Presbyterian Church
20 Kings Highway East
Haddonfield, New Jersey 08033
(609) 429-1960

Language and linguistics

AMERICAN SPEECH [196]
A Quarterly of Linguistic Usage
Columbia University Press
562 West 113th Street
New York, New York 10025
(212) 865-2000

First published in 1925

SUBSCRIPTION DATA
Issues and rates: Published quarterly.
   Annual rate(s): $10.00
Publisher or Sponsor: American Dialect Society

EDITORIAL DESCRIPTION
Publishes scholarly articles and notes on the English language in the western hemisphere. Contributions dealing with English in other parts of the world and with other languages influencing English or influenced by it are also considered.
Articles per average issue: 15
Audience: Scholarly
   Manuscripts accepted in English

MANUSCRIPT INFORMATION
Subject field(s): Current usage, dialectology, phonology, lexicon, syntax, history of English, sociolinguistics, general linguistics, lexicography
Manuscript requirements: MLA; Chicago; style sheet for glossaries sent upon request
   Preferred length: Under 10,000 words
   Number of copies to be submitted: Two
   Abstract: Not necessary.
Author information and reprints: Payment: Reprints only. 10 copies of the issue for full-length articles.
   Is simultaneous submission of article to other journals permitted: No
   Exclusive manuscript rights between acceptance and publication: Yes
   Copyright: Held by publication.
   Reprints: Available at cost
Additional information: Manuscripts must be double-spaced throughout, with footnotes and tables on separate sheets at the end.
Disposition of manuscript:
   Receipt of manuscript acknowledged: Yes
   Decision to publish in: 3-4 months
   Accepted manuscript published in: 9-12 months
   Rejected manuscript returned: Yes
   Rejected manuscript criticized: Sometimes
Submit to:
   John Algeo
   Editor
   Department of English, Park Hall
   University of Georgia
   Athens, Georgia 30602
   (404) 542-1261 ext. 303

ANTHROPOLOGICAL LINGUISTICS [197]

Department of Anthropology, Rawles Hall 108
Indiana University
Bloomington, Indiana 47401
(812) 337-1472

SUBSCRIPTION DATA
Issues and rates: 9 times per year
   Average paid circulation: 1100
   Annual rate(s): $4.00
Publisher or Sponsor: Archives of Languages of the World, Indiana University, Anthropology Department
Managing Editor: Florence M. Voegelin

EDITORIAL DESCRIPTION
Contains papers in descriptive linguistics, sociolinguistics and psycholinguistics.
Articles per average issue: 3-4
Audience: Professional, academic
   Manuscripts accepted in English

MANUSCRIPT INFORMATION
Manuscript requirements: See latest issue for style requirements.
   Preferred length: 10-30 pages
   Number of copies to be submitted: One
Author information and reprints: Payment: None.
   Is simultaneous submission of article to other journals permitted: No
   Exclusive manuscript rights between acceptance and publication: Yes
   Copyright: Held by author.
   Reprints: Available, 50 free
Disposition of manuscript:
   Query letter: Not necessary.
   Receipt of manuscript acknowledged: Yes
   Decision to publish in: 3 months
   Accepted manuscript published in: 6-9 months
   Rejected manuscript returned: Yes
   Rejected manuscript criticized: Sometimes
Submit to:
   Florence M. Voegelin
   Editor
   (See address above)

AUMLA [198]

Department of Modern Languages
James Cook University
Townsville 4811, Queensland, Australia
793711 ext. 306

First published in 1953

SUBSCRIPTION DATA
Issues and rates: Published semi-annually.
   Average paid circulation: 1,200; 300 controlled
   Annual rate(s): $A4.00
Publisher or Sponsor: Australian Universities Language and Literature Association

EDITORIAL DESCRIPTION
Contains articles on languages and linguistics, philology, and literary criticism.
Articles per average issue: 6-7, plus reviews
Audience: Academic
   Manuscripts accepted in English, French, German

MANUSCRIPT INFORMATION
Manuscript requirements: Style sheet sent on request.
   Preferred length: 8000 words; 20 pages
   Number of copies to be submitted: One
   Abstract: Yes
Author information and reprints: Payment: None.
   Is simultaneous submission of article to other journals permitted: No
   Exclusive manuscript rights between acceptance and publication: Yes
   Copyright: Held by publication.
   Reprints: Available
Disposition of manuscript:
   Query letter: No
   Receipt of manuscript acknowledged: Yes
   Decision to publish in: 3 months
   Accepted manuscript published in: 6-12 months
   Rejected manuscript returned: Yes, if self-addressed, stamped envelope is sent with manuscript.
   Rejected manuscript criticized: Yes
Submit to:
   R.T. Sussex
   Editor
   (See address above)

THE BILINGUAL REVIEW/LA REVISTA BILINGÜE [199]

Department of Foreign Languages
York College, CUNY
Jamaica, New York 11451
(212) 969-4036

First published in 1974

SUBSCRIPTION DATA
Issues and rates: Published three times per year.
   Average paid circulation: 4,000
   Annual rate(s): $6.00
Publisher or Sponsor: York College, City University of New York
Managing Editor: Mary M. Keller

EDITORIAL DESCRIPTION
Dedicated to the study of the linguistics and literature of English-Spanish bi-lingualism in the United States and Hispanic life in the U. S.
Articles per average issue: 10-12
Audience: Professional, academic
   Manuscripts accepted in All major languages

MANUSCRIPT INFORMATION
Subject field(s): Research and scholarly articles dealing with bi-lingualism, primarily but not exclusively Spanish-English; U.S.-Hispanic literature; English-Spanish contrastive linguistics or problems in translation; fiction, poetry, etc., concerning Hispanic life in the U.S.
Manuscript requirements: MLA
   Preferred length: 4-40 pages
   Number of copies to be submitted: 2
   Abstract: Not necessary. Recommended in the case of research papers.
Author information and reprints: Payment: Reprints only. 2 issues
   Is simultaneous submission of article to other journals permitted: Not permitted.
   Exclusive manuscript rights between acceptance and publication: Yes
   Copyright: Held by publication. with generous reprint allowances to author.

Language and linguistics

Reprints: Not available.
Additional information: Short reviews treating only one title are not accepted. Usually reviews treat more than one title.
Disposition of manuscript:
  Query letter: Not necessary.
  Receipt of manuscript acknowledged: Yes
  Decision to publish in: 6-8 weeks
  Accepted manuscript published in: 6 months or more
  Rejected manuscript returned: Yes, if return postage is supplied by author.
  Rejected manuscript criticized: Yes
Submit to:
  Prof. Gary D. Keller
  Editor-in-Chief
  (See address above)

THE BRITISH JOURNAL OF DISORDERS OF COMMUNICATION [200]

Longman Group Ltd., Journals Division
Burnt Mill
Harlow, Essex, England
26721

SUBSCRIPTION DATA
Issues and rates: Published semi-annually.
  Annual rate(s): £2.50, Foreign $7.50
Publisher or Sponsor: College of Speech Therapists, London
Managing Editor: Betty Byers Brown

EDITORIAL DESCRIPTION
  Scope includes the receptive and expressive aspects of language, audiology, articulation and personal, social and environmental conditions relating to communication through spoken and written language.
Submit to:
  Betty Byers Brown
  Editor
  (See address above)

SPECIAL STIPULATIONS
  Request additional information from editor.

BULLETIN OF HISPANIC STUDIES [201]

Liverpool University Press
123 Grove Street
Liverpool L77AF, England
(051) 709-3630

Previously entitled *Bulletin of Spanish Studies*

First published in 1923

SUBSCRIPTION DATA
Issues and rates: Published quarterly.
  Average paid circulation: 1000
  Annual rate(s): £6.00; Foreign $15.00; 900 Pesetas
Publisher or Sponsor: Liverpool University Press
Managing Editor: Geoffrey Ribbans

EDITORIAL DESCRIPTION
  Contains scholarly articles and book-reviews on the language, literature, and occasionally history of Spain, Portugal and Latin America.
Articles per average issue: 4-5
Audience: Hispanists
  Manuscripts accepted in English, Spanish, Portuguese, Catalan

MANUSCRIPT INFORMATION
Subject field(s): Spanish language, Spanish literature, Spanish-American literature, Portuguese literature, Portuguese language, Catalan language
Manuscript requirements: See latest issue for style requirements.
  Preferred length: 4,000-9,000 words
  Number of copies to be submitted: Two
  Abstract: No
Author information and reprints: Payment: None.
  Is simultaneous submission of article to other journals permitted: No
  Exclusive manuscript rights between acceptance and publication: Yes
  Copyright: Held by publication.
  Reprints: Available, 25 free; extra cost on application.
Disposition of manuscript:
  Query letter: No
  Receipt of manuscript acknowledged: Yes
  Decision to publish in: 2-3 months
  Accepted manuscript published in: 2 years
  Rejected manuscript returned: Yes
  Rejected manuscript criticized: Sometimes
Submit to:
  Editor
  School of Hispanic Studies
  The University
  P.O. Box 147
  Liverpool L69 3BX, England
  (051) 709-6022 ext. 713

CANADIAN MODERN LANGUAGE REVIEW [202]

34 Butternut Street
Toronto, Ontario M4K 1T7, Canada
(416) 465-8929

First published in 1943

SUBSCRIPTION DATA
Issues and rates: Published quarterly.
  Average paid circulation: 3,200
  Annual rate(s): $10.00
Publisher or Sponsor: Ontario Modern Language Teachers' Association

EDITORIAL DESCRIPTION
  Contains practical articles on linguistics, literature, methodology, critical studies, sample tests, lesson plans, teaching hints, dissent, book reviews (foreign languages only).
Articles per average issue: 10
Audience: Teachers of modern language at all levels
  Manuscripts accepted in English, French, German, Italian, Spanish

MANUSCRIPT INFORMATION
Manuscript requirements: See latest issue for style requirements. MLA
  Preferred length: 10-12 pages
  Number of copies to be submitted: 3
  Abstract: Abstract should be in English
Author information and reprints: Payment: Reprints only. 4 copies of issue
  Is simultaneous submission of article to other journals permitted: No
  Exclusive manuscript rights between acceptance and publication: Yes
  Copyright: Held jointly by author and publication.
  Reprints: Available from printer
Disposition of manuscript:
  Query letter: Not necessary.
  Receipt of manuscript acknowledged: Yes
  Decision to publish in: 6-8 weeks
  Accepted manuscript published in: 6 months
  Rejected manuscript returned: Yes, if self-addressed, stamped envelope is sent with manuscript.
  Rejected manuscript criticized: No
Submit to:
  Anthony S. Mollica
  Editor
  4 Oakmount Road
  Welland, Ontario L3C 4X8, Canada
  (416) 732-2149

CLA JOURNAL* [203]

Official Publication of the College Language Association
Morgan State College
Baltimore, Maryland 21239
(301) 323-2270 ext. 266

SUBSCRIPTION DATA
Issues and rates: Published quarterly.
  Average paid circulation: 1000; 1100 controlled
  Annual rate(s): $6.00, Pan-Am $6.50, Foreign $7.00
Publisher or Sponsor: The College Language Association
Managing Editor: Therman B. O'Daniel

EDITORIAL DESCRIPTION
  Includes articles of any type which relate to the various aspects of language and literature in English and foreign languages.

MANUSCRIPT INFORMATION
Subject field(s): American literature, English literature, American and English language, linguistics, black studies, bibliography, criticism, foreign languages, foreign literature, Caribbean studies, any type of article dealing with languages and literature.
Manuscript requirements: MLA, footnotes at bottom of page preferred.
  Preferred length: 10 to 12 pages
  Number of copies to be submitted: Two

Author information and reprints: Payment: None.
Is simultaneous submission of article to other journals permitted: No
Exclusive manuscript rights between acceptance and publication: Yes
Copyright: Held by publication.
Reprints: Available
Additional information: Excessively long articles must be unusually meritorious and timely.
Disposition of manuscript:
Receipt of manuscript acknowledged: Yes
Decision to publish in: Two to three months
Accepted manuscript published in: One year
Rejected manuscript returned: Yes, if self-addressed, stamped envelope is sent with manuscript.
Rejected manuscript criticized: Occasionally
Submit to:
Editor
(See address above)

DIMENSION [204]
Contemporary German Arts and Letters
Department of Germanic Languages
University of Texas at Austin
P.O. Box 7939
Austin, Texas 78712
(512) 471-4314

First published in 1968

SUBSCRIPTION DATA

Issues and rates: Published three times per year.
Average paid circulation: 550
Annual rate(s): $7.50
Publisher or Sponsor: University of Texas, Department of Germanic Languages

EDITORIAL DESCRIPTION

Each issue offers contributions in German with the English translation and the German original side by side. Contents vary from poetry, prose and drama to critical comments on current writers, political events and social developments.
Articles per average issue: 12-20
Audience: Those interested in contemporary German writing
Manuscripts accepted in English, German

MANUSCRIPT INFORMATION

Subject field(s): Original literary works by contemporary German-speaking authors; translations into English of contemporary German-speaking authors; a few essays on contemporary literature in German-speaking lands.
Manuscript requirements: See latest issue for style requirements.
Preferred length: 5000 words maximum; 20 pages
Number of copies to be submitted: One
Abstract: Not necessary.

Author information and reprints: Payment: By publication to author. $2 to $5 per page.
Is simultaneous submission of article to other journals permitted: No
Exclusive manuscript rights between acceptance and publication: Yes
Copyright: Held by publication.
Reprints: Available at cost
Disposition of manuscript:
Query letter: Necessary.
Receipt of manuscript acknowledged: Yes
Decision to publish in: One month
Accepted manuscript published in: One year
Rejected manuscript returned: Yes, if self-addressed, stamped envelope is sent with manuscript.
Rejected manuscript criticized: No
Submit to:
A. Leslie Willson
Editor
(See address above)

SPECIAL STIPULATIONS

Few unsolicited translations accepted, and none if German authors are not contemporary.

ENGLISH LANGUAGE TEACHING JOURNAL [205]
English as a Foreign or Second Language
16 Alexandra Gardens
Hounslow, Middlesex, England

First published in 1946

SUBSCRIPTION DATA

Issues and rates: Published quarterly.
Average paid circulation: 8,200
Annual rate(s): $7.50

EDITORIAL DESCRIPTION

Publishes articles on various aspects of the teaching of English as a foreign language. Preference is given to articles of direct value to the classroom instructor.
Articles per average issue: 14
Audience: Academic
Manuscripts accepted in English

MANUSCRIPT INFORMATION

Manuscript requirements: See latest issue for style requirements.
Preferred length: 2,000-2,500 words
Number of copies to be submitted: One
Abstract: No
Author information and reprints: Payment: By publication to author. £5.25 per thousand words.
Is simultaneous submission of article to other journals permitted: No
Exclusive manuscript rights between acceptance and publication: Yes
Copyright: Held by publication.
Reprints: Available at cost.
Disposition of manuscript:
Receipt of manuscript acknowledged: Yes
Decision to publish in: 4 weeks
Accepted manuscript published in: 20 months

Rejected manuscript returned: Yes, if return postage is supplied by author.
Rejected manuscript criticized: No
Submit to:
W. R. Lee
Editor
(See address above)

FORUM ITALICUM [206]
Department of Spanish, Italian, and Portuguese
State University of New York
Buffalo, New York 14214
(716) 636-2189

SUBSCRIPTION DATA

Issues and rates: Published quarterly.
Average paid circulation: 1000
Annual rate(s): $4.00, Foreign $4.75

EDITORIAL DESCRIPTION

Contains articles on Italian literature, linguistics, fiction and poetry; translations and book reviews.
Articles per average issue: 25
Audience: Students, professors, critics, writers
Manuscripts accepted in English, Italian, French, Spanish

MANUSCRIPT INFORMATION

Subject field(s): Literature, arts, criticism dealing with Italian
Manuscript requirements: MLA
Preferred length: 15 pages
Number of copies to be submitted: One
Abstract: Not necessary.
Author information and reprints: Payment: None.
Is simultaneous submission of article to other journals permitted: No
Exclusive manuscript rights between acceptance and publication: Yes
Copyright: Held by publication.
Reprints: Available at cost
Disposition of manuscript:
Query letter: Not necessary.
Receipt of manuscript acknowledged: Yes
Decision to publish in: One month
Accepted manuscript published in: One year
Rejected manuscript returned: Yes
Rejected manuscript criticized: Yes
Submit to:
Michael Ricciardelli
Editor
(See address above)

THE FRENCH REVIEW [207]
P.O. Box 149
Chapel Hill, North Carolina 27514
(919) 933-2062

First published in 1927

SUBSCRIPTION DATA

Issues and rates: 6 issues per year
Average paid circulation: 13,933
Annual rate(s): $10.00; Foreign $11.00

Language and linguistics

Publisher or Sponsor: American Association of Teachers of French

EDITORIAL DESCRIPTION

Publishes articles on French literature, civilization, and the teaching of French; Association news; book reviews (literary history and criticism, creative works, civilization, textbooks, linguistics).
Articles per average issue: 9-10
Audience: Teachers of French language and literature
Manuscripts accepted in English, French

MANUSCRIPT INFORMATION

Subject field(s): Literature, civilization, pedagogy, book reviews
Manuscript requirements: MLA
Preferred length: Articles: 3,600 words; book reviews: 650 words
Number of copies to be submitted: One
Abstract: Not necessary.
Author information and reprints: Payment: None.
Is simultaneous submission of article to other journals permitted: No
Exclusive manuscript rights between acceptance and publication: Yes
Copyright: Held by publication.
Reprints: Available, cost on request
Disposition of manuscript:
Query letter: Not necessary.
Receipt of manuscript acknowledged: Yes
Decision to publish in: 2 months
Accepted manuscript published in: 18-24 months
Rejected manuscript returned: Yes, if return postage is supplied by author.
Rejected manuscript criticized: Yes
Submit to:
Stirling Haig
Editor
(See address above)

SPECIAL STIPULATIONS

Membership in American Association of Teachers of French is required for submission of articles.

GENERAL LINGUISTICS [208]
Pennsylvania State University Press
University Park, Pennsylvania 16802

First published in 1955

SUBSCRIPTION DATA

Issues and rates: Published quarterly.
Average paid circulation: 700
Annual rate(s): $13.50
Managing Editor: Janet Dietz

EDITORIAL DESCRIPTION

Contains articles in linguistics: comparative and historical linguistics, psycholinguistics, sociolinguistics; generative linguistics, interpretive semantics, comparative and historical linguistics, language specific articles
Articles per average issue: 3-4
Audience: Linguists
Manuscripts accepted in English, French, German

MANUSCRIPT INFORMATION

Manuscript requirements: LSA; see also back cover of publication
Preferred length: 1-50 pages
Number of copies to be submitted: Three
Abstract: Not necessary.
Author information and reprints: Payment: None.
Is simultaneous submission of article to other journals permitted: No
Exclusive manuscript rights between acceptance and publication: Yes
Copyright: Held by publication.
Reprints: Available
Disposition of manuscript:
Query letter: Not necessary.
Receipt of manuscript acknowledged: Yes
Decision to publish in: 6-12 months
Accepted manuscript published in: One year
Rejected manuscript returned: Yes, if return postage is supplied by author.
Rejected manuscript criticized: Yes
Submit to:
William Riegel Schmalstieg
Editor
N-438 Burrowes Building
University Park, Pennsylvania 16802
(814) 865-1352

THE GERMANIC REVIEW [209]
Columbia University Press
136 South Broadway
Irving-on-Hudson, New York 10533
(212) 280-3201

First published in 1926

SUBSCRIPTION DATA

Issues and rates: Published quarterly.
Average paid circulation: 1,400
Annual rate(s): $7.50, Foreign $7.80
Publisher or Sponsor: Columbia University, Department of Germanic Languages
Managing Editor: Joseph Padur Bauke

EDITORIAL DESCRIPTION

Publishes scholarly contributions that give greater understanding of the form and meaning of German literature and the language itself. Also includes book reviews.
Articles per average issue: 4 articles; 6 reviews
Audience: Specialists in the field
Manuscripts accepted in English only

MANUSCRIPT INFORMATION

Manuscript requirements: MLA
Preferred length: 6,000-7,000 words
Number of copies to be submitted: One
Abstract: Not necessary.
Author information and reprints: Payment: Reprints only. 10 free copies of magazine to manuscript authors; 2 free to authors of book reviews.
Is simultaneous submission of article to other journals permitted: Permitted, but not encouraged.
Exclusive manuscript rights between acceptance and publication: Yes
Copyright: Held by Columbia University Press
Reprints: Available at cost.
Additional information: Limited to contributions in English except in the most unusual cases. Illustrations are paid for by the author.
Disposition of manuscript:
Query letter: Not necessary.
Receipt of manuscript acknowledged: Yes
Decision to publish in: 6 weeks
Accepted manuscript published in: 1 year
Rejected manuscript returned: Yes, if return postage is supplied by author.
Rejected manuscript criticized: No
Submit to:
Editor
320 Hamilton Hall
Columbia University
New York, New York 10027

GLOSSA [210]
An International Journal of Linguistics
Department of Modern Languages
Simon Fraser University
Burnaby 2, British Columbia V5A 1S6, Canada
(604) 291-3544 ext. 3626

First published in 1967

SUBSCRIPTION DATA

Issues and rates: Published semi-annually.
Average paid circulation: 600; 750 controlled
Annual rate(s): $7.00
Publisher or Sponsor: Glossa Society

EDITORIAL DESCRIPTION

Contains scholarly contributions to all aspects of general linguistics as they apply to theory and human communication systems. No particular linguistic school of thought is favored, nor any particular branch of linguistics.
Articles per average issue: 7-9
Manuscripts accepted in English, French, languages using Roman or Cyrillic fonts

MANUSCRIPT INFORMATION

Subject field(s): General linguistics, linguistic theory, psycholinguistics, sociolinguistics, language acquisition, data presentation, anthropological linguistics, mathematical linguistics, history of linguistics
Manuscript requirements: LSA
Preferred length: 6 to 70 pages
Number of copies to be submitted: One
Abstract: Yes. Only after acceptance for publication.
Author information and reprints: Payment: Reprints only. 25 offprints
Is simultaneous submission of article to other journals permitted: No
Exclusive manuscript rights between acceptance and publication: Yes
Copyright: Held by publication.
Reprints: Not available.
Disposition of manuscript:
Query letter: Not necessary.
Receipt of manuscript acknowledged: Yes
Decision to publish in: 2 months
Accepted manuscript published in: 6-9 months

Rejected manuscript returned: Yes, if return postage is supplied by author.
Rejected manuscript criticized: No
Submit to:
Editorial Board
(See address above)

HISPANIA [211]
A Journal Devoted to the Interests of Teaching Spanish and Portugese
Department of Romance Languages
University of Cincinnati
Cincinnati, Ohio 45221
(513) 475-3888

First published in 1917

SUBSCRIPTION DATA
Issues and rates: Published quarterly.
Average paid circulation: 16,500
Annual rate(s): Students $4.00, Members $8.00
Publisher or Sponsor: American Association of Teachers of Spanish and Portugese

EDITORIAL DESCRIPTION
Contains articles of interest to teachers of Spanish and Portugese at all levels. Contributors are encouraged to present their own opinion regarding the literature, language, pedagogy, book reviews, research, professional news, foreign language directions, films, and news from the Hispanic world.
Articles per average issue: 15
Audience: Academic
Manuscripts accepted in English, Spanish, Portuguese

MANUSCRIPT INFORMATION
Subject field(s): Hispanic literature, Hispanic linguistics, teaching Spanish/Portuguese, professional concerns, Hispanic culture
Manuscript requirements: MLA; see latest issue
Preferred length: 15-20 pages
Number of copies to be submitted: One original
Abstract: No
Author information and reprints: Payment: None.
Is simultaneous submission of article to other journals permitted: No
Exclusive manuscript rights between acceptance and publication: No
Copyright: Held by publication.
Reprints: Available at cost
Additional information: Articles on Hispanic literature must be at least 12 manuscript pages in length.
Disposition of manuscript:
Query letter: No
Receipt of manuscript acknowledged: Yes
Decision to publish in: 3 months
Accepted manuscript published in: 18-24 months
Rejected manuscript returned: Yes, if return postage is supplied by author.
Submit to:
Donald W. Bleznick
Editor
(See address above)

SPECIAL STIPULATIONS
Only members of the Association may submit articles for consideration.

HISPANIC REVIEW [212]
Williams Hall
University of Pennsylvania
Philadelphia, Pennsylvania 19174
(215) 594-7420

SUBSCRIPTION DATA
Issues and rates: Published quarterly.
Average paid circulation: 1200
Annual rate(s): $9.50
Publisher or Sponsor: University of Pennsylvania, Department of Romance Languages
Managing Editor: José M. Regueiro

EDITORIAL DESCRIPTION
Devoted to research in the Hispanic languages and literatures. Publishes articles on all aspects of Spanish language and Spanish-American literatures, with no particular preference as to critical or historical method, provided the work is of the highest scholarly caliber.
Articles per average issue: 3
Audience: College students and professors
Manuscripts accepted in English, French, German, Spanish, Portuguese

MANUSCRIPT INFORMATION
Manuscript requirements: MLA
Preferred length: Reviews: 1500 words; Articles 7,500 words, 6 pages maximum
Number of copies to be submitted: One
Abstract: Yes. MLA
Author information and reprints: Payment: Reprints only. 15 unbound offprints of articles, 10 unbound offprints of Varia and Reviews.
Is simultaneous submission of article to other journals permitted: No
Exclusive manuscript rights between acceptance and publication: Yes
Reprints: Available
Disposition of manuscript:
Query letter: Not necessary.
Receipt of manuscript acknowledged: Yes
Decision to publish in: 4-6 weeks
Accepted manuscript published in: 18 months
Rejected manuscript returned: Yes
Rejected manuscript criticized: Yes
Submit to:
Editorial Office
(See address above)

HISPANÓFILA [213]
Department of Romance Languages
University of North Carolina
Chapel Hill, North Carolina 27514
(919) 933-2062 ext. 218

First published in 1957

SUBSCRIPTION DATA
Issues and rates: Published three times per year.
Annual rate(s): $8.00

EDITORIAL DESCRIPTION
Contains critical essays in Spanish and Spanish-American literature.
Articles per average issue: 8
Manuscripts accepted in English, Spanish, Portuguese

MANUSCRIPT INFORMATION
Manuscript requirements: MLA
Preferred length: 12 pages
Number of copies to be submitted: One
Abstract: Not necessary.
Author information and reprints: Payment: None.
Is simultaneous submission of article to other journals permitted: Expect author to notify of simultaneous submission.
Exclusive manuscript rights between acceptance and publication: Yes
Copyright: Registered under Spanish copyright laws
Reprints: Available, $.04 per page
Disposition of manuscript:
Query letter: Not necessary.
Receipt of manuscript acknowledged: Yes
Decision to publish in: 1 month
Accepted manuscript published in: Two years
Rejected manuscript returned: Yes
Rejected manuscript criticized: Yes
Submit to:
A. V. Ebersole
Editor
(See address above)

HISTORIOGRAPHIA LINGUISTICA [214]
International Journal for the History of Linguistics
John Benjamins B. V.
Amsteldijk 44
Amsterdam-Z., The Netherlands
(020) 73 81 56

First published in 1974

SUBSCRIPTION DATA
Issues and rates: Published three times per year.
Annual rate(s): Dfl. 55; Institutions Dfl. 90

EDITORIAL DESCRIPTION
The central objectives are the discussion of the epistemiological and methodological foundations of historiography of the language sciences and the critical presentation of particular areas or aspects of actual or potential research; intended to serve linguists, psycholinguists, and philosophers of language of divergent persuasions in the history of linguistic thought.
Articles per average issue: 12; 1 review
Audience: Professional linguists, philosophers of language, historians, scientists
Manuscripts accepted in English, French, German, Italian, Spanish

MANUSCRIPT INFORMATION
Subject field(s): History of linguistics, philosophy of language, psycholinguistics,

history of ideas, history of science, epistemiology
Manuscript requirements: See latest issue for style requirements. LSA
   Preferred length: 20-40 pages
   Number of copies to be submitted: 2
   Abstract: Yes. An abstract of about 300 words containing the main theme of the argument. It must be in English for all articles.
Author information and reprints: Payment: Reprints only. 50 reprints
   Is simultaneous submission of article to other journals permitted: Not permitted.
   Exclusive manuscript rights between acceptance and publication: Yes
   Copyright: Held by publication.
Disposition of manuscript:
   Query letter: Not necessary, but advisable.
   Receipt of manuscript acknowledged: Yes
   Decision to publish in: 4-8 weeks
   Accepted manuscript published in: 6-10 months
   Rejected manuscript returned: Yes, if return postage is supplied by author.
   Rejected manuscript criticized: Sometimes
Submit to:
   Dr. E.F.K. Koerner
   Editor
   Fachbereich Sprachwissenschaft
   Universität Regensburg
   D-8400 Regensburg, Federal Republic of Germany
   (0941) 943-3427

THE INCORPORATED LINGUIST [215]
Institute of Linguists
Lloyds Bank Chambers
91 Newington Causeway
London SE1 6BN, England
01-407-4755

Previously entitled *The Linguists' Review*

First published in 1962

SUBSCRIPTION DATA
Issues and rates: Published quarterly.
   Average paid circulation: 5,500
   Annual rate(s): £2.50
Managing Editor: D. Cook-Radmore

EDITORIAL DESCRIPTION
Contains articles of general linguistic interest to professional linguists and all people interested in languages.
Articles per average issue: 3
Audience: Professional and amateur linguists
   Manuscripts accepted in English, French, German, Spanish, Italian, Russian

MANUSCRIPT INFORMATION
Subject field(s): Language teaching, translating, interpreting; applied linguistics
Manuscript requirements: No specific style guide.
   Preferred length: 2,500-3,000 words
   Number of copies to be submitted: Three

Abstract: Yes.
Author information and reprints: Payment: None.
   Is simultaneous submission of article to other journals permitted: No
   Exclusive manuscript rights between acceptance and publication: Yes
   Copyright: Held by author.
   Reprints: Depends on quantity; must be requested at time of submission of article.
Disposition of manuscript:
   Query letter: Necessary.
   Receipt of manuscript acknowledged: Yes
   Decision to publish in: One month
   Accepted manuscript published in: 3-6 months
   Rejected manuscript returned: Yes
   Rejected manuscript criticized: No
Submit to:
   S. D. Beaumont
   The Assistant Editor
   (See address above)

INTERNATIONAL JOURNAL OF AMERICAN LINGUISTICS [216]
University of Chicago Press
5801 Ellis Avenue
Chicago Illinois 60637
(312) 753-3347

First published in 1917

SUBSCRIPTION DATA
Issues and rates: Published quarterly.
   Average paid circulation: 2,200
   Annual rate(s): $12.00; Institutions $16.00
Publisher or Sponsor: Linguistic Society of America, American Anthropological Association
Managing Editor: Alma Dean Rumsey

EDITORIAL DESCRIPTION
Contains articles on American Indian languages; abstracts, notes and reviews.
Articles per average issue: 10-15
Audience: Professional linguists and anthropologists
   Manuscripts accepted in English

MANUSCRIPT INFORMATION
Subject field(s): American Indian languages, theoretical linguistic topics if applicable
Manuscript requirements: Chicago; see back issues
   Preferred length: 20 pages
   Number of copies to be submitted: Ribbon copy (one)
   Abstract: Not necessary.
Author information and reprints: Payment: None.
   Is simultaneous submission of article to other journals permitted: No
   Exclusive manuscript rights between acceptance and publication: Yes
   Copyright: Held by publication.
   Reprints: Available, 50 reprints free

Additional information: Publisher has a royalty sharing arrangement under which authors receive 50 percent royalties after expense deductions.
Disposition of manuscript:
   Query letter: Not necessary.
   Receipt of manuscript acknowledged: Sometimes
   Decision to publish in: Varies
   Rejected manuscript returned: Yes
   Rejected manuscript criticized: Sometimes
Submit to:
   C. F. Voegelin
   (See address above)

ITALICA [217]
601 Casa Italiana
Columbia University
New York, New York 10027

First published in 1924

SUBSCRIPTION DATA
Issues and rates: Published quarterly.
   Average paid circulation: 1,800
   Annual rate(s): $8.00
Publisher or Sponsor: American Association of Teachers of Italian

EDITORIAL DESCRIPTION
Contains articles and reviews dealing with Italian literature, language and pedagogy.
Audience: Members of Association
   Manuscripts accepted in English, Italian, French, Spanish, German

MANUSCRIPT INFORMATION
Manuscript requirements: MLA
   Preferred length: 25 pages
   Number of copies to be submitted: Two
Author information and reprints: Payment: None.
   Is simultaneous submission of article to other journals permitted: No
   Exclusive manuscript rights between acceptance and publication: Yes
   Reprints: Available
Disposition of manuscript:
   Query letter: Not necessary.
   Receipt of manuscript acknowledged: No
   Decision to publish in: One month
   Accepted manuscript published in: One year or more
   Rejected manuscript returned: Yes
   Rejected manuscript criticized: No
Submit to:
   Olga Ragusa
   Editor
   (See address above)

THE JOURNAL OF ENGLISH AND GERMANIC PHILOLOGY [218]
100 English Building
University of Illinois
Urbana, Illinois 61801
(217) 333-3989

First published in 1897

SUBSCRIPTION DATA
Issues and rates: Published quarterly.
  Average paid circulation: Not available.
  Annual rate(s): $10.00; Foreign $10.50
Publisher or Sponsor: University of Illinois, Graduate College
Managing Editor: P. M. Mitchell

EDITORIAL DESCRIPTION
  Publishes scholarly and critical articles on English, American, German, and Scandinavian literature and language; also reviews on the same subjects.
Articles per average issue: 5
Audience: Teachers, scholars, students
  Manuscripts accepted in English, German, Scandinavian languages

MANUSCRIPT INFORMATION
Subject field(s): English literature, German literature, Scandinavian literature, American literature, philology
Manuscript requirements: MLA
  Preferred length: 12-30 pages, 9 pages minimum (typewritten, double-spaced)
  Number of copies to be submitted: One (no Xerox)
  Abstract: Yes.
Author information and reprints: Payment: Reprints only. 6 copies of the magazine
  Is simultaneous submission of article to other journals permitted: No
  Exclusive manuscript rights between acceptance and publication: Yes
  Copyright: Held by Board of Trustees of the University of Illinois
  Reprints: Available; price list sent with proofs
Disposition of manuscript:
  Query letter: Not necessary.
  Receipt of manuscript acknowledged: Yes
  Decision to publish in: 1-6 months
  Accepted manuscript published in: Two years
  Rejected manuscript returned: Yes
  Rejected manuscript criticized: Sometimes
Submit to:
  Dale Kramer
  Chairman, Board of Editors

  For articles in German and Scandinavian:
  P. M. Mitchell
  Editorial Board
  (See address above)

JOURNAL OF LINGUISTICS [219]
Cambridge University Press
32 East 57th Street
New York, New York 10022

SUBSCRIPTION DATA
  Annual rate(s): £4.50; Pan-Am $15.00
Publisher or Sponsor: Linguistics Association of Great Britain

EDITORIAL DESCRIPTION
  Articles of a general theoretical nature in all three branches of linguistics (including phonetics).
Audience: Linguists
  Manuscripts accepted in English, French, German

MANUSCRIPT INFORMATION
Manuscript requirements: See latest issue for style requirements.
  Preferred length: No preference
  Number of copies to be submitted: 2
  Abstract: Not necessary.
Author information and reprints: Payment: None.
  Copyright: Held by Cambridge University Press
Disposition of manuscript:
  Query letter: Not necessary, but advisable.
Submit to:
  Professor F. R. Palmer
  Editor
  Department of Linguistic Science
  The University of Reading, Whiteknights
  Reading RG6 2AA, England

JOURNAL OF VERBAL LEARNING AND VERBAL BEHAVIOR [220]
Academic Press, Inc.
111 Fifth Avenue
New York, New York 10003

First published in 1962

SUBSCRIPTION DATA
Issues and rates: Published bi-monthly.
  Average paid circulation: Not available.
  Annual rate(s): $32.00; Foreign $35.00
Managing Editor: Roselle Coviello

EDITORIAL DESCRIPTION
  Publishes original experimental, theoretical and review papers concerned with problems of verbal learning, human memory and psycholinguistics and other closely related verbal processes. Published papers are expected to make a significant contribution to the shaping of scientific issues and theories.
Articles per average issue: 10
Audience: Researchers, academicians
  Manuscripts accepted in English

MANUSCRIPT INFORMATION
Manuscript requirements: See latest issue for style requirements. APA
  Number of copies to be submitted: Four
Author information and reprints: Payment: Reprints only. 50 reprints
  Is simultaneous submission of article to other journals permitted: No
  Exclusive manuscript rights between acceptance and publication: Yes
  Copyright: Held by publication.
  Reprints: Available
Disposition of manuscript:
  Query letter: No
  Receipt of manuscript acknowledged: Yes
  Decision to publish in: 30 days
  Accepted manuscript published in: 7 months
  Rejected manuscript returned: Yes, with return postage paid by publication.
  Rejected manuscript criticized: Yes
Submit to:
  Edwin Martin
  Editor
  Department of Psychology
  University of Kansas
  Lawrence, Kansas 66045

LA CORONICA [221]
Department of Romance Languages
Emory University
Atlanta, Georgia 30322
(404) 377-2411

First published in 1972-73

SUBSCRIPTION DATA
Issues and rates: Published semi-annually.
  Average paid circulation: 200
  Annual rate(s): $2.00; Foreign $2.00; Individuals $2.00; Institutions $3.00; Foreign individuals $2.00; Foreign institutions $3.00
Publisher or Sponsor: Modern Language Association Sp. I
Managing Editor: Harvey L. Sharrer

EDITORIAL DESCRIPTION
  A newsletter dedicated to the dissemination of news of interest to scholars of the Hispanic Medieval period
Articles per average issue: 4
Audience: Medieval Hispanists
  Manuscripts accepted in English or Spanish

MANUSCRIPT INFORMATION
Subject field(s): Medieval Spanish language and literature; welcomed are feature articles, reports on major conferences, colloquia, research projects, opportunities for research in the United States and abroad, abstracts of papers and Ph. D. dissertations, articles of pedagogical interest, special bibliographies and items not normally included in existing journals.
Manuscript requirements: MLA
  Preferred length: 3-4 pages
Author information and reprints: Payment: None.
  Reprints: Not available.
Disposition of manuscript:
  Query letter: Not necessary, but advisable.
  Receipt of manuscript acknowledged: Yes
  Decision to publish in: 2 weeks
  Accepted manuscript published in: 6 months
  Rejected manuscript returned: Yes, if return postage is supplied by author.
  Rejected manuscript criticized: Yes
Submit to:
  Harvey L. Sharrer
  Editor
  Department of Spanish and Portuguese
  University of California
  Santa Barbara, California 93106

LANGUAGE [222]
1611 North Kent Street
Arlington, Virginia 22209
(703) 933-3756

First published in 1924

Language and linguistics

SUBSCRIPTION DATA
Issues and rates: Published quarterly.
  Average paid circulation: 6400
  Annual rate(s): $25.00
Publisher or Sponsor: Linguistic Society of America

EDITORIAL DESCRIPTION
  Contains technical articles dealing with problems of linguistic science and reviews of recently published linguistic works.
Audience: Linguistic community

MANUSCRIPT INFORMATION
Subject field(s): Linguistics
Manuscript requirements: LSA
  Preferred length: None
  Number of copies to be submitted: One
Author information and reprints: Payment: None.
  Copyright: Held by publication.
  Reprints: Available, 100 free
Disposition of manuscript:
  Receipt of manuscript acknowledged: Yes
  Decision to publish in: One month
  Accepted manuscript published in: One year
  Rejected manuscript returned: Yes
  Rejected manuscript criticized: Sometimes
Submit to:
  William Bright
  Editor
  Department of Anthropology
  University of California
  Los Angeles, California 90024
  (213) 825-2739

LANGUAGE LEARNING [223]
A Journal of Applied Linguistics
2001 North University Building
University of Michigan
Ann Arbor, Michigan 48104
(313) 764-2413

SUBSCRIPTION DATA
Issues and rates: Published semi-annually.
  Average paid circulation: 2,800
  Annual rate(s): Individuals $5.00, Institutions $9.00

EDITORIAL DESCRIPTION
  Contains experimental and theoretical research in first and second language acquisition, psycholinguistics, language pedagogy, and related areas of applied linguistics.
Articles per average issue: 10
Audience: University and secondary school language teachers; researchers
  Manuscripts accepted in English

MANUSCRIPT INFORMATION
Subject field(s): Second language acquisition, foreign language teaching, psycholinguistics, first language acquisition
Manuscript requirements: APA
  Preferred length: 15-20 pages
  Number of copies to be submitted: Two
  Abstract: Yes. See APA

Author information and reprints: Payment: None.
  Is simultaneous submission of article to other journals permitted: Yes, if so notified upon submission of manuscript.
  Exclusive manuscript rights between acceptance and publication: Yes
  Copyright: Held by publication.
  Reprints: Available, minimum of 100 at $24.00
Disposition of manuscript:
  Receipt of manuscript acknowledged: Yes
  Decision to publish in: 2 months
  Accepted manuscript published in: 3-5 months
  Rejected manuscript returned: Yes
  Rejected manuscript criticized: No
Submit to:
  H. Douglas Brown
  Editor
  (See address above)

LANGUAGE SCIENCES [224]
Research Center for the Language Sciences
516 East Sixth Street
Bloomington, Indiana 47401
(812) 337-6193

First published in 1968

SUBSCRIPTION DATA
Issues and rates: Five times per year
  Average paid circulation: 1,000
  Annual rate(s): $5.00

EDITORIAL DESCRIPTION
  Publishes articles, reviews, announcements of interest to linguists, and others interested in language sciences; theoretical and research materials, commentary on current trends. Focus is on scholarly but informal consideration of developments in the subject fields; encouragement of younger scholars.
Articles per average issue: 4-5 articles; 4-6 reviews
Audience: Professionals and graduate students in linguistics
  Manuscripts accepted in English, French, Spanish

MANUSCRIPT INFORMATION
Subject field(s): Linguistics, language teaching, English as second language, semiotics
Manuscript requirements: See latest issue for style requirements.
  Preferred length: 5,000 words maximum; 20 pages
  Number of copies to be submitted: One
  Abstract: Yes. MLA
Author information and reprints: Payment: Reprints only. 20 copies of issue
  Is simultaneous submission of article to other journals permitted: No
  Exclusive manuscript rights between acceptance and publication: Yes
  Copyright: Held by author.
  Reprints: Available, 20 free to U.S., 10 to foreign, $.25 each additional copy

Additional information: Prefer footnotes, references, figures on separate pages.
Disposition of manuscript:
  Query letter: Not necessary.
  Receipt of manuscript acknowledged: Yes
  Decision to publish in: 4 weeks maximum
  Accepted manuscript published in: 10-12 months
  Rejected manuscript returned: Yes, if self-addressed, stamped envelope is sent with manuscript.
  Rejected manuscript criticized: Yes
Submit to:
  Kathleen M. Fenton
  Editor
  (See address above)

THE LINGUISTIC REPORTER [225]
Newsletter In Applied Linguistics
1611 North Kent Street
Arlington, Virginia 22209
(703) 528-4312

SUBSCRIPTION DATA
Issues and rates: Monthly, except July and August
  Average paid circulation: 3500; 500 controlled
  Annual rate(s): $4.50
Publisher or Sponsor: Center for Applied Linguistics
Managing Editor: Allene Guss Grognet

EDITORIAL DESCRIPTION
  Contains news about languages and linguistics, national and international.
Audience: Language teachers, linguists

MANUSCRIPT INFORMATION
Manuscript requirements: No specific style guide.
  Preferred length: 2000 words or less
  Number of copies to be submitted: One
  Abstract: Not necessary.
Author information and reprints: Payment: None.
  Is simultaneous submission of article to other journals permitted: Yes
  Exclusive manuscript rights between acceptance and publication: No
  Copyright: Held by author.
  Reprints: Available
Additional information: Publication is basically a newsletter, not a journal.
Disposition of manuscript:
  Query letter: Necessary.
  Receipt of manuscript acknowledged: Yes
  Decision to publish in: One week
  Accepted manuscript published in: 1-2 months
  Rejected manuscript returned: Yes
  Rejected manuscript criticized: No
Submit to:
  Allene Guss Grognet
  Director of Publications
  (See address above)

LINGUISTICS [226]
An International Review
Mouton Publishers,
Herderstraat 5, P.O. Box 1132
The Hague, Netherlands
070 924 451

First published in 1963

SUBSCRIPTION DATA
Issues and rates: Published semi-monthly.
  Average paid circulation: 1000; 1300 controlled
  Annual rate(s): Dfl. 18 per issue
Publisher or Sponsor: EDICOM, The Hague
Managing Editor: Paul M. Waszink

EDITORIAL DESCRIPTION
Attempts to give as broad a survey as possible of all activities carried out in the field of linguistics. Primary attention is paid to investigations dealing with current themes in linguistic theory, but reports on particular language systems and descriptive analyses of theses are equally acceptable.
Articles per average issue: 2-6
Audience: Professional, academic
  Manuscripts accepted in English, French, Spanish

MANUSCRIPT INFORMATION
Subject field(s): Theory of linguistics, description and analysis of particular languages, neurolinguistics, psycholinguistics, historical languages.
Manuscript requirements: Style sheet sent on request.
  Preferred length: 20,000 words, maximum
  Number of copies to be submitted: One
  Abstract: No
Author information and reprints: Payment: None.
  Is simultaneous submission of article to other journals permitted: Permitted after written permission of the publishers has been obtained.
  Exclusive manuscript rights between acceptance and publication: Yes
  Copyright: Held by publication.
  Reprints: Available, at a rate of Dfl. 0.10 per printed page
Disposition of manuscript:
  Query letter: No
  Receipt of manuscript acknowledged: Yes
  Decision to publish in: 1 month
  Accepted manuscript published in: 9 months
  Rejected manuscript returned: Yes, if return postage is supplied by author.
  Rejected manuscript criticized: No
Submit to:
  Paul M. Waszink
  Editor
  (See address above)

LYRICA GERMANICA [227]
Journal for German Lyric Poetry
3307 Cornwall Drive
Lexington, Kentucky 40503

First published in 1966

SUBSCRIPTION DATA
Issues and rates: Published semi-annually.
  Annual rate(s): $1.50; Foreign $2.00
Managing Editor: A. Wayne Wonderley

EDITORIAL DESCRIPTION
Publishes previously unpublished, original German lyric poetry; translations into English of German lyric poetry created before 1880; reviews.
Articles per average issue: 6-8
Audience: Friends of German lyric poetry
  Manuscripts accepted in German, English

MANUSCRIPT INFORMATION
Subject field(s): Brief German lyric poems (original and unpublished), short translations
Manuscript requirements: See latest issue for style requirements.
  Preferred length: 4-8 lines
  Number of copies to be submitted: Two
  Abstract: Not necessary.
Author information and reprints: Payment: None.
  Is simultaneous submission of article to other journals permitted: No
  Reprints: Available, rates available on application; reprints well in advance of publication.
Disposition of manuscript:
  Receipt of manuscript acknowledged: Yes
  Decision to publish in: 6-12 months
  Accepted manuscript published in: One year
  Rejected manuscript returned: Yes, if return postage is supplied by author.
  Rejected manuscript criticized: No
Submit to:
  A. Wayne Wonderley
  Editor
  (See address above)

SPECIAL STIPULATIONS
Publication is a non-profit journal whose editors and staff serve without compensation. The journal is primarily handset and printed letterpress.

MIDWEST MODERN LANGUAGE ASSOCIATION BULLETIN [228]
English/Philosophy Building 311
University of Iowa
Iowa City, Iowa 52242
(319) 353-3291

First published in 1968

SUBSCRIPTION DATA
Issues and rates: Published semi-annually.
  Average paid circulation: 2000
  Annual rate(s): $4.00
Publisher or Sponsor: Midwest Modern Language Association
Managing Editor: Delaine Heynen

EDITORIAL DESCRIPTION
Contains critical and scholarly articles on the study and teaching of language and literature, particularly in relation to political, cultural, and historical issues, as well as essays on critical methodology, literary history, and the theory of language.
Articles per average issue: 4-6
Audience: Teachers of English and modern foreign languages of all levels
  Manuscripts accepted in English

MANUSCRIPT INFORMATION
Subject field(s): English literature; French, German, Spanish, Slavic, and American literature; Black literature; Italian literature; comparative literature; literary criticism; literature and film; American studies; medieval studies; Shakespeare
Manuscript requirements: MLA
  Preferred length: 6000-8000 words
  Number of copies to be submitted: One
  Abstract: Not necessary.
Author information and reprints: Payment: None.
  Is simultaneous submission of article to other journals permitted: No
  Exclusive manuscript rights between acceptance and publication: Yes
  Copyright: Held by publication.
  Reprints: Available, $15.00 per 25 copies
Disposition of manuscript:
  Query letter: Not necessary.
  Receipt of manuscript acknowledged: Yes
  Decision to publish in: 60 days
  Accepted manuscript published in: One year
  Rejected manuscript returned: Yes, if return postage is supplied by author.
  Rejected manuscript criticized: No
Submit to:
  Gerald L. Bruns
  Executive Secretary
  (See address above)

THE MODERN LANGUAGE JOURNAL [229]
13149 Cannes Drive
St. Louis, Missouri 63141
(314) 434-2158

First published in 1916

SUBSCRIPTION DATA
Issues and rates: 6 times a year
  Average paid circulation: 9000; 500 controlled
  Annual rate(s): Individuals $6.00; Institutions $8.00; Foreign $8.00
Publisher or Sponsor: National Federation of Modern Language Teachers Associations

EDITORIAL DESCRIPTION
Contains articles concerning methods, pedagogical research and topics of professional interest to all foreign language teachers (with emphasis on secondary educators).
Articles per average issue: 6
Audience: Foreign language teachers
  Manuscripts accepted in English

MANUSCRIPT INFORMATION
Subject field(s): Teaching strategies, applied linguistics, innovative foreign language programs, book reviews, psycholinguistics, teacher education,

foreign language curricula, achievement testing, bilingualism, aptitude and aptitude testing
Manuscript requirements: MLA
　Preferred length: 3,700 words
　Number of copies to be submitted: Two
　Abstract: Not necessary.
Author information and reprints: Payment: Reprints only. 2 copies of journal
　Is simultaneous submission of article to other journals permitted: No
　Exclusive manuscript rights between acceptance and publication: Yes
　Copyright: Held by publication.
　Reprints: Available, 100 minimum
Additional information: Paper must be original, previously unpublished and styled according to MLA Style Sheet, double-spaced throughout, including footnotes which should be typed at the end of the paper.
Disposition of manuscript:
　Query letter: Not necessary.
　Receipt of manuscript acknowledged: Yes
　Decision to publish in: At least 3 months
　Accepted manuscript published in: 2-12 months
　Rejected manuscript returned: Yes, if return postage is supplied by author.
　Rejected manuscript criticized: Yes
Submit to:
　Charles L. King
　Editor
　University of Colorado
　McKenna 30A
　Boulder, Colorado 80302
　(303) 492-7036 ext. 7036

MODERN LANGUAGE REVIEW [230]
King's College, Strand
London, WC2R 2LS, England

First published in 1905

SUBSCRIPTION DATA

Issues and rates: Published quarterly.
　Average paid circulation: 2,500
　Annual rate(s): Members $7.50
Publisher or Sponsor: Modern Humanities Research Association

EDITORIAL DESCRIPTION

　Publishes original articles on language and literature containing the results of research and criticism for the advanced researcher in the English, Romance, Germanic, and Slavonic languages.
Articles per average issue: 11
Audience: Academic
　Manuscripts accepted in English

MANUSCRIPT INFORMATION

Manuscript requirements: Modern Humanitites Research Association Style Book
　Number of copies to be submitted: One original
Author information and reprints: Payment: By author to publication. For excessive corrections in proof.
　Is simultaneous submission of article to other journals permitted: No
　Exclusive manuscript rights between acceptance and publication: Yes
　Reprints: Available, 20 offprints free
Disposition of manuscript:
　Receipt of manuscript acknowledged: Yes
　Rejected manuscript returned: Yes
Submit to:
　C. P. Brand
　General Editor
　David Hume Tower
　George Square
　Edinburgh, Scotland

MODERN LANGUAGE STUDIES [231]
NEMLA, English Department
University of Massachusetts
Amherst, Massachusetts 01002

First published in 1970
　Average paid circulation: 1,000; 200 controlled
　Annual rate(s): $6.00; Foreign $6.00; Institutions $6.00; Students $3.00; Members $6.00
Publisher or Sponsor: Northeast Modern Language Association of America

EDITORIAL DESCRIPTION

　The official organ of the Association, it publishes articles of interest to teachers and scholars in the areas of English, American, and comparative literature, and of the modern foreign languages; to foster a broad interest in the humanities and to forward effective teaching and research in this area.
Articles per average issue: 8-12
Audience: Scholars and teachers of English and language
　Manuscripts accepted in All languages

MANUSCRIPT INFORMATION

Manuscript requirements: MLA
　Preferred length: No limitations, 10-25 pages are preferred
Additional information: Good academic, scholarly style is preferred. Place footnotes at the end.
Disposition of manuscript:
　Decision to publish in: 1 month
　Accepted manuscript published in: 3-6 months
Submit to:
　Edna L. Steeves,
　Armand B. Chartier
　Editors
　Department of English
　University of Rhode Island
　Kingston, Rhode Island 02881
　792-5931

MODERN LANGUAGES [232]
Journal of the Modern Language Association
35 Lewisham Way
New Cross
London SE14 6PP, England
(01) 691-2086

First published in 1919

SUBSCRIPTION DATA

Issues and rates: Published quarterly.
　Average paid circulation: 3,800; 3,000 controlled
　Annual rate(s): £3.00; Foreign $9.00
Publisher or Sponsor: Modern Language Association

EDITORIAL DESCRIPTION

　Language, literature, civilization, applied linguistics, teaching methodology, reports of national conferences all as related to French, German, Spanish, Russian, and Italian
Articles per average issue: 7
Audience: Academic
　Manuscripts accepted in English (French, German)

MANUSCRIPT INFORMATION

Manuscript requirements: No specific style guide.
　Preferred length: 4,000 words; 15 pages
　Number of copies to be submitted: 1
　Abstract: Not necessary.
Author information and reprints: Payment: Reprints only. 6 offprints and 1 copy of issue
　Is simultaneous submission of article to other journals permitted: Not permitted.
　Exclusive manuscript rights between acceptance and publication: Yes
　Copyright: Held by the Association
　Reprints: Available at cost.
Additional information: Typewritten; quotations of more than 2 lines should be indented without quotation marks; footnotes, numbered consecutively, at the end.
Disposition of manuscript:
　Query letter: Not necessary.
　Receipt of manuscript acknowledged: Yes
　Decision to publish in: Maximum 3 months
　Accepted manuscript published in: 6-9 months
　Rejected manuscript returned: Yes, with return postage paid by publication.
　Rejected manuscript criticized: Sometimes
Submit to:
　Edward M. Batley
　Editor
　(See address above)

MONATSHEFTE FÜR DEUTSCHEN UNTERRICHT, DEUTSCHE SPRACHE UND LITERATUR [233]
Department of German, Van Hise Hall
University of Wisconsin
Madison, Wisconsin 53706
(608) 262-9747

Previously entitled *Pädagogische Monatshefte*

First published in 1899

SUBSCRIPTION DATA

Issues and rates: Published quarterly.

Average paid circulation: 1350; 20 controlled
Annual rate(s): Institutions $20.00, Individuals $9.00, Foreign $9.50
Managing Editor: Valters Nollendorfs

EDITORIAL DESCRIPTION

Contains scholarly articles dealing with German language and literature; book reviews; annual listing of college and university German departments and their faculties.
Articles per average issue: 5
Audience: College German teachers
Manuscripts accepted in English, German

MANUSCRIPT INFORMATION

Subject field(s): German literature, German language, German culture and civilization, pedagogy
Manuscript requirements: MLA
Preferred length: 15-20 pages
Number of copies to be submitted: One
Abstract: Yes. 150 words
Author information and reprints: Payment: Reprints only. Authors of articles receive 10 free copies; authors of reviews receive 1 free copy.
Is simultaneous submission of article to other journals permitted: No
Exclusive manuscript rights between acceptance and publication: Yes
Copyright: Held by the Regents of the University of Wisconsin System
Reprints: Available, cost per schedule
Additional information: No previously published material (including parts of dissertations) is accepted.
Disposition of manuscript:
Receipt of manuscript acknowledged: Yes
Decision to publish in: 2-3 months
Accepted manuscript published in: 2 years
Rejected manuscript returned: Yes
Rejected manuscript criticized: Usually
Submit to:
Valters Nollendorfs
Editor
(See address above)

MOREHEAD STATE UNIVERSITY BULLETIN OF APPLIED LINGUISTICS [234]
Box 681
Morehead State University
Morehead, Kentucky 40351
(606) 783-3166

First published in 1964

SUBSCRIPTION DATA

Issues and rates: Published semi-monthly.
Average paid circulation: 1000
Annual rate(s): $2.50, Foreign $4.00
Managing Editor: L. W. Barnes

EDITORIAL DESCRIPTION

Publishes articles on applied linguistics.
Articles per average issue: 1
Audience: Academic
Manuscripts accepted in English

MANUSCRIPT INFORMATION

Subject field(s): Psycholinguistics, literary style, sociolinguistics, phonology, grammar, dialectology, morphemics, semantics, programming language, structure of literature, reading and linguistics
Manuscript requirements: MLA
Preferred length: 1500 words; 3-4 pages
Number of copies to be submitted: Two
Abstract: Not necessary.
Author information and reprints: Payment: Reprints only. Contributor's copies
Is simultaneous submission of article to other journals permitted: No
Exclusive manuscript rights between acceptance and publication: Yes
Copyright: Held by publication.
Reprints: Available
Disposition of manuscript:
Query letter: Necessary.
Receipt of manuscript acknowledged: Yes
Decision to publish in: 2 weeks
Accepted manuscript published in: 3 months
Rejected manuscript returned: Yes, if self-addressed, stamped envelope is sent with manuscript.
Rejected manuscript criticized: No
Submit to:
Lewis W. Barnes
Editor
(See address above)

NALLD JOURNAL [235]
Newsletter of the National Association of Language Laboratory Directors
Ohio University
Athens, Ohio 45701
(614) 594-5795

First published in 1966

SUBSCRIPTION DATA

Issues and rates: Published quarterly.
Average paid circulation: 700; 300 controlled
Annual rate(s): $6.00, Pan-Am $7.00, Foreign $9.00
Publisher or Sponsor: National Association of Language Laboratory Directors
Managing Editor: C. P. Richardson

EDITORIAL DESCRIPTION

Contains articles concerning use of media in classroom, language lab usage, and current research in use of instructional media; tape market; materials review; NALLD business.
Articles per average issue: 4
Audience: Teachers, media directors
Manuscripts accepted in English, German, French, Spanish

MANUSCRIPT INFORMATION

Subject field(s): Language lab usage, instructional media in classroom, methodology
Manuscript requirements: MLA
Preferred length: 1,000 to 5,000 words
Number of copies to be submitted: One
Abstract: Yes.
Author information and reprints: Payment: None.
Is simultaneous submission of article to other journals permitted: No
Exclusive manuscript rights between acceptance and publication: Yes
Copyright: Held by publication.
Reprints: Available, cost quoted upon request
Additional information: Use of drawings and photographs to illustrate articles is encouraged. Prefer articles dealing with practical applications of instructional media.
Disposition of manuscript:
Query letter: Not necessary.
Receipt of manuscript acknowledged: Yes
Decision to publish in: 1-2 months
Accepted manuscript published in: 3-6 months
Rejected manuscript returned: Yes, if self-addressed, stamped envelope is sent with manuscript.
Rejected manuscript criticized: No
Submit to:
Charles P. Richardson
Editor
(See address above)

NUSA [236]
Studies in Indonesian and Languages in Indonesia
P. O. Box 2811/Jkt
Jakarta-Pusat, Indonesia

First published in Spring 1975

SUBSCRIPTION DATA

Issues and rates: Irregular
Average paid circulation: 300

EDITORIAL DESCRIPTION

Deals with the linguistics of the languages of Indonesia, including diachronic; areal (Indonesia) only.
Audience: Linguists, professional, academic
Manuscripts accepted in English

MANUSCRIPT INFORMATION

Manuscript requirements: Any widely used linguistic styleguide.
Preferred length: None
Number of copies to be submitted: 2
Abstract: Not necessary.
Author information and reprints: Payment: None.
Is simultaneous submission of article to other journals permitted: Not permitted.
Exclusive manuscript rights between acceptance and publication: Yes
Copyright: Held by author.
Reprints: Available at no cost. Only for authors residing in Indonesia
Additional information: This periodical is a series. All material must be camera-ready when submitted. Shipments exceeding single rate should be sent registered mail.
Disposition of manuscript:
Query letter: Not necessary.
Receipt of manuscript acknowledged: Yes
Decision to publish in: 1-3 months
Rejected manuscript returned: Yes, if return postage is supplied by author.

Rejected manuscript criticized: Yes
Submit to:
John W. M. Verhaar
Editor
(See address above)

OCEANIC LINGUISTICS [237]
The University Press of Hawaii
535 Ward Avenue
Honolulu, Hawaii 96814
(808) 536-6051

First published in 1962

SUBSCRIPTION DATA
Issues and rates: Published semi-annually.
  Average paid circulation: 342; 61 controlled
  Annual rate(s): Institutions $7.00, Individuals $5.00
Publisher or Sponsor: The University of Hawaii
Managing Editor: Byron W. Bender

EDITORIAL DESCRIPTION
Articles discuss issues in linguistic theory that pertain to languages of the area, report current research on historical relations, or furnish new information about inadequately described languages.
Articles per average issue: 5
Audience: Linguists
  Manuscripts accepted in English

MANUSCRIPT INFORMATION
Subject field(s): Austronesian linguistics, Papuan linguistics, descriptive linguistics, comparative linguistics, lexicostatistics, lexicography of the Pacific Basin and islands of South East Asia.
Manuscript requirements: Chicago; LSA
  Preferred length: 5000-10,000 words; 20-40 pages
  Number of copies to be submitted: Two
  Abstract: Optional
Author information and reprints: Payment: None.
  Is simultaneous submission of article to other journals permitted: Subject to approval of editor.
  Exclusive manuscript rights between acceptance and publication: Yes
  Copyright: Held by publication.
  Reprints: Available, 50 free; additional at cost
Disposition of manuscript:
  Query letter: Not necessary.
  Receipt of manuscript acknowledged: Yes
  Decision to publish in: Varies
  Accepted manuscript published in: 1 year
  Rejected manuscript returned: Yes
  Rejected manuscript criticized: Yes
Submit to:
George W. Grace
Editor
Department of Linguistics
University of Hawaii
Honolulu, Hawaii 96822
(808) 948-8307

OLD ENGLISH NEWSLETTER [238]
Center for Medieval and Renaissance Studies
320 Main Library, 1858 Neil Avenue
Columbus, Ohio 43210
(614) 422-7495

First published in 1967

SUBSCRIPTION DATA
Issues and rates: Published semi-annually.
  Average paid circulation: 100; 1,000 controlled
  Annual rate(s): Institutions $3.00
Publisher or Sponsor: Modern Language Association of America, Group I, Old English
Articles per average issue: 1
Audience: Anglo-Saxon scholars
  Manuscripts accepted in English

EDITORIAL DESCRIPTION
Contains annual bibliography for Old English; work in Old English studies; news of general interest; pedagogical articles.

MANUSCRIPT INFORMATION
Subject field(s): Pedagogy, research in Old English
Manuscript requirements: MLA
  Preferred length: 12 pages maximum
  Number of copies to be submitted: One
  Abstract: No
Author information and reprints: Payment: None.
  Is simultaneous submission of article to other journals permitted: No
  Exclusive manuscript rights between acceptance and publication: Yes
  Copyright: Held by author.
  Reprints: Not available.
Additional information: Manuscript must be clean, original copy, double-spaced.
Disposition of manuscript:
  Query letter: Yes
  Receipt of manuscript acknowledged: Yes
  Decision to publish in: 1 month
  Accepted manuscript published in: 6-12 months
  Rejected manuscript returned: Yes, if self-addressed, stamped envelope is sent with manuscript.
  Rejected manuscript criticized: Yes
Submit to:
Stanley J. Kahrl
Editor
(See address above)

PHI SIGMA IOTA NEWSLETTER [239]
Department of Modern Languages
Boston University
Boston, Massachusetts 02215
(617) 353-2641

SUBSCRIPTION DATA
Issues and rates: Published semi-annually.
  Average paid circulation: 4,000
  Annual rate(s): $10 for 3 years
Publisher or Sponsor: Phi Sigma Iota Romance Language Honor Society

EDITORIAL DESCRIPTION
Contains articles, reports, book reviews, etc. on five Romance languages and Latin cultures and civilizations: French, Spanish, Italian, Portuguese, Rumanian.
Articles per average issue: Varies
Audience: Membership, academic
  Manuscripts accepted in English

MANUSCRIPT INFORMATION
Subject field(s): Romance literatures, Romance languages, Romance cultures, Romance linguistics
Manuscript requirements: See latest issue for style requirements.
  Preferred length: 500-700 words
  Number of copies to be submitted: One
  Abstract: No
Author information and reprints: Payment: By publication to author. Scholarship competition each year: $1,000 for best graduate study, $500 for runner-up.
  Is simultaneous submission of article to other journals permitted: No
  Exclusive manuscript rights between acceptance and publication: Yes
  Copyright: Held by author.
  Reprints: Available, $2.50 per reprint
Additional information: Scholarship conditions available upon request.
Disposition of manuscript:
  Query letter: Yes
  Receipt of manuscript acknowledged: No
  Decision to publish in: 2 months
  Accepted manuscript published in: 1 year
  Rejected manuscript returned: Yes
  Rejected manuscript criticized: Yes
Submit to:
Warren Wilder;
Herbert Golden
Editors
(See address above)

PHILOLOGICAL QUARTERLY [240]
The University of Iowa
210 Graphic Services Building
Iowa City, Iowa 52242
(319) 353-3413

First published in 1922

SUBSCRIPTION DATA
Issues and rates: Published quarterly.
  Average paid circulation: 1,800; 450 controlled
  Annual rate(s): $10.00; Institutions $15.00
Publisher or Sponsor: The University of Iowa
Managing Editor: William Kupfersmith

EDITORIAL DESCRIPTION
Devoted to scholarly investigation of the classical and modern languages and literatures.
Articles per average issue: 12
Audience: Literary scholars
  Manuscripts accepted in English, Spanish, French

Subject field(s): Modern and classical philology
Manuscript requirements: See latest issue for style requirements. MLA
   Preferred length: 4,500-6,500 words; 8,000 maximum
   Number of copies to be submitted: One
   Abstract: Not necessary.
Author information and reprints: Payment: None.
   Is simultaneous submission of article to other journals permitted: No
   Exclusive manuscript rights between acceptance and publication: Yes
   Copyright: Held by publication.
   Reprints: Available at nominal cost
Disposition of manuscript:
   Query letter: Not necessary.
   Receipt of manuscript acknowledged: Yes
   Decision to publish in: 1-3 months
   Accepted manuscript published in: 12-24 months
   Rejected manuscript returned: Yes, if return postage is supplied by author.
   Rejected manuscript criticized: Yes
Submit to:
   Editors
   323 EPB
   University of Iowa
   Iowa City, Iowa 52242
   (319) 353-3547

PHONETICA [241]
Journal of the International Society of Phonetic Sciences
S. Karger AG
Arnold-Boecklin Strasse 25
CH-4011 Basel, Switzerland
061-390880

SUBSCRIPTION DATA
Issues and rates: 8 times per year (2 volumes)
   Average paid circulation: 710; 57 controlled
   Annual rate(s): SFr. 132.00; Foreign $54.00 per volume
Publisher or Sponsor: International Society of Phonetic Sciences

EDITORIAL DESCRIPTION
International journal devoted to the science of phonetics, including all sub-disciplines. It is concerned both with the phonetic description and historical development of the languages of the world and with the theory and methodology of phonetic research as such.
Articles per average issue: 4
Audience: Professional, academic
   Manuscripts accepted in English, French, German

MANUSCRIPT INFORMATION
Subject field(s): Phonology, acoustic phonetics, application of phonetics in medicine, telecommunication, etc.
Manuscript requirements: See latest issue for style requirements.
   Preferred length: 10 printed pages
   Number of copies to be submitted: 2
   Abstract: A short summary
Author information and reprints: Payment: Reprints only. 25 reprints
Disposition of manuscript:
   Query letter: No
   Receipt of manuscript acknowledged: Yes
   Decision to publish in: 1 month
   Accepted manuscript published in: 5 months
   Rejected manuscript returned: Yes
   Rejected manuscript criticized: Yes
Submit to:
   W. Bethge
   Deutsches Spracharchiv
   Adenauerallee 96
   D-53 Bonn, Federal Republic of Germany

ROMANCE NOTES [242]
Department of Romance Languages
University of North Carolina
Chapel Hill, North Carolina 27514
(919) 933-2032 ext. 218

First published in 1959

SUBSCRIPTION DATA
Issues and rates: Published three times per year.
   Average paid circulation: 700
   Annual rate(s): $8.00; Students $4.00
Publisher or Sponsor: University of North Carolina, Department of Romance Languages
Managing Editor: George B. Daniel

EDITORIAL DESCRIPTION
Contains articles on language and literature in the Romance Languages. Encourages publication of articles by beginning scholars as well as by those already established.
Articles per average issue: 34
Audience: Professionals
   Manuscripts accepted in French, Spanish, Italian, Portuguese, English

MANUSCRIPT INFORMATION
Manuscript requirements: MLA
   Preferred length: 8 to 10 pages
   Number of copies to be submitted: One
   Abstract: Not necessary.
Author information and reprints: Payment: None.
   Exclusive manuscript rights between acceptance and publication: Yes
   Copyright: Held by publication.
   Reprints: Available, $7.00 per 50 copies
Disposition of manuscript:
   Receipt of manuscript acknowledged: Yes
   Decision to publish in: 1-7 months
   Accepted manuscript published in: 2 years
   Rejected manuscript returned: Yes
   Rejected manuscript criticized: Sometimes
Submit to:
   Editor
   (See address above)

ROMANCE PHILOLOGY [243]
University of California Press
2223 Fulton Street
Berkeley, California 94720
(415) 642-4247

First published in 1947

SUBSCRIPTION DATA
Issues and rates: Published quarterly.
   Average paid circulation: 1,200
   Annual rate(s): Individuals $12, Institutions $18, Foreign $19.00
Publisher or Sponsor: University of California
Managing Editor: Yakov Malkiel

EDITORIAL DESCRIPTION
Contains studies of Romance culture through historical linguistics and Medieval literature, with some attention paid to general theory of linguistics and literary analysis. Emphasis is placed on those Old World and New World areas where Romance culture has developed most vigorously.
Articles per average issue: 8
Audience: Scholars
   Manuscripts accepted in English, French, Spanish, Portuguese, Italian

MANUSCRIPT INFORMATION
Manuscript requirements: See latest issue for style requirements.
   Preferred length: 10-25 pages
   Number of copies to be submitted: Two
   Abstract: Not necessary.
Author information and reprints: Payment: None.
   Is simultaneous submission of article to other journals permitted: No
   Exclusive manuscript rights between acceptance and publication: Yes
   Copyright: Held by publication.
   Reprints: Available
Disposition of manuscript:
   Query letter: Necessary.
   Receipt of manuscript acknowledged: Yes
   Decision to publish in: 1-2 months
   Accepted manuscript published in: 12-20 months
   Rejected manuscript returned: Yes, if return postage is supplied by author.
   Rejected manuscript criticized: Sometimes
Submit to:
   Yakov Malkiel
   Editor
   Department of Linguistics
   University of California
   Berkeley, California 94720
   (415) 642-2757

SPECIAL STIPULATIONS
The journal is strictly a scholarly medium.

SEMINAR [244]
A Journal of Germanic Studies
University of Toronto Press
Toronto 5, Ontario, Canada
(604) 228-2550

First published in 1965

SUBSCRIPTION DATA
Issues and rates: Published quarterly.
   Average paid circulation: 750
   Annual rate(s): $6.00
Publisher or Sponsor: Canadian Association of University Teachers of German,
   Australasian Universities Language and Literature Association
Managing Editor: M. S. Batts

EDITORIAL DESCRIPTION
   Contains essays on Germanic languages and literatures, reviews.
Articles per average issue: 4-5
Audience: Academic
   Manuscripts accepted in English, French, German

MANUSCRIPT INFORMATION
Subject field(s): Germanic literature, Germanic language
Manuscript requirements: MLA
   Preferred length: 5,000 words; 15 pages
   Number of copies to be submitted: One
Author information and reprints: Payment: None.
   Is simultaneous submission of article to other journals permitted: No
   Exclusive manuscript rights between acceptance and publication: Yes
   Copyright: Held by sponsoring association
   Reprints: Available, first 15 free
Disposition of manuscript:
   Query letter: Not necessary.
   Receipt of manuscript acknowledged: Yes
   Decision to publish in: 10 weeks
   Accepted manuscript published in: 12 months
   Rejected manuscript returned: Yes
   Rejected manuscript criticized: Yes
Submit to:
   M. S. Batts
   Editor
   Department of German
   University of British Columbia
   Vancouver 8, British Columbia, Canada

SLAVIC AND EAST EUROPEAN JOURNAL [245]
Department of Slavic Languages and Literatures
University of Illinois at Urbana-Champaign
Urbana, Illinois 61801
(217) 333-1204

First published in 1957

SUBSCRIPTION DATA
Issues and rates: Published quarterly.
   Average paid circulation: 2,000
   Annual rate(s): Individuals $15.00, Institutions $17.50

Publisher or Sponsor: American Association of Teachers of Slavic and East European Languages
Managing Editor: Frank Y. Gladney

EDITORIAL DESCRIPTION
   Contains articles on Slavic and East European languages, literatures, and pedagogy.
Articles per average issue: 7
Audience: Scholars, teachers, students
   Manuscripts accepted in English

MANUSCRIPT INFORMATION
Manuscript requirements: Style sheet sent on request.
   Preferred length: 20 pages
   Number of copies to be submitted: One
   Abstract: Not necessary.
Author information and reprints: Payment: None.
   Is simultaneous submission of article to other journals permitted: No
   Exclusive manuscript rights between acceptance and publication: Yes
   Copyright: Held by publication.
   Reprints: Available, 25 free
Disposition of manuscript:
   Query letter: Not necessary.
   Receipt of manuscript acknowledged: Yes
   Decision to publish in: 2-3 months
   Accepted manuscript published in: 6-12 months
   Rejected manuscript returned: Yes
   Rejected manuscript criticized: Yes
Submit to:
   Editor
   (See address above)

STUDIES IN AFRICAN LINGUISTICS [246]
Department of Linguistics
University of California
Los Angeles, California 90024
(213) 825-0634

First published in 1970

SUBSCRIPTION DATA
Issues and rates: Published three times per year.
   Average paid circulation: 225
   Annual rate(s): $8.00; Institutions $12.00
Publisher or Sponsor: African Studies Center, UCLA
Managing Editor: Thomas J. Hinnebusch

EDITORIAL DESCRIPTION
   For those interested in syntactic and phonological theory, linguistic analysis, African languages and linguistics universally
Articles per average issue: 4 to 5
Audience: Linguists specializing in African languages
   Manuscripts accepted in French, English, German

MANUSCRIPT INFORMATION
Subject field(s): African languages and linguistics: phonology, syntax, historical-comparative, sociolinguistics, linguistic theory in the light of African language data.
Manuscript requirements: See latest issue for style requirements. Style sheet sent on request.
   Preferred length: 25 to 30 pages
   Number of copies to be submitted: 2
   Abstract: Not necessary
Author information and reprints: Payment: Reprints only. 50
   Is simultaneous submission of article to other journals permitted: Permitted.
   Copyright: Held by the Regents of the University of California
   Reprints: Not available.
Disposition of manuscript:
   Query letter: Not necessary, but advisable.
   Receipt of manuscript acknowledged: Yes
   Decision to publish in: 3 to 6 weeks
   Accepted manuscript published in: 3 months
   Rejected manuscript returned: Yes, if return postage is supplied by author.
   Rejected manuscript criticized: Yes
Submit to:
   Thomas J. Hinnebusch
   Editor
   (See address above)

STUDIES IN LINGUISTICS [247]
Box 85
Taos, New Mexico 87571
(505) 758-8414

First published in 1942

SUBSCRIPTION DATA
Issues and rates: Published annually.
   Average paid circulation: 700
   Annual rate(s): $10.00
Managing Editor: George L. Trager

EDITORIAL DESCRIPTION
   Contains articles in all areas of general and anthropological linguistics.
Articles per average issue: 6-10
Audience: Linguists
   Manuscripts accepted in English

MANUSCRIPT INFORMATION
Subject field(s): Any area of descriptive or historical or other linguistics with emphasis on anthropological and ethnological connections.
Manuscript requirements: Authors may request use of their own style if explained clearly. Spelling variations also permitted.
   Preferred length: 2-25 pages
   Number of copies to be submitted: One
   Abstract: Yes.
Author information and reprints: Payment: None.
   Is simultaneous submission of article to other journals permitted: No
   Exclusive manuscript rights between acceptance and publication: Yes
   Copyright: Not copyrighted
   Reprints: Available, 50 free; additional at cost
Disposition of manuscript:
   Query letter: Not necessary.
   Receipt of manuscript acknowledged: Yes

Decision to publish in: Varies
Accepted manuscript published in: Varies
Rejected manuscript returned: Yes
Rejected manuscript criticized: If requested
Submit to:
George L. Trager
Editor
(See address above)

VISIBLE LANGUAGE [248]
The Journal for Research on the Visual Media of Language Expression
The Cleveland Museum of Art
Cleveland, Ohio 44106
(216) 421-7340 ext. 300

First published in 1967

SUBSCRIPTION DATA
Issues and rates: Published quarterly.
Average paid circulation: 1,100
Annual rate(s): $11.00
Managing Editor: Merald E. Wrolstad

EDITORIAL DESCRIPTION
Devoted to research on the visual media of language expression —a new interdisciplinary concept involving the generation and organization of man's graphic forms —writing, typography, signing, as well as physical and mental response to these forms.
Articles per average issue: 5
Audience: Scholarly, reading researchers, linguists, graphic designers
Manuscripts accepted in English

MANUSCRIPT INFORMATION
Subject field(s): Linguistics, reading/literacy, graphic design, typography, paleography, semiotics, concrete poetry, electronic alphabets, descriptive bibliography, environmental signing
Manuscript requirements: Style sheet sent on request.
Preferred length: None
Number of copies to be submitted: Three
Abstract: Yes. 75-100 words
Author information and reprints: Payment: Reprints only. Subscription plus 20 offprints
Is simultaneous submission of article to other journals permitted: No
Exclusive manuscript rights between acceptance and publication: Yes
Copyright: Held by either author or publication
Reprints: Not available.
Additional information: Manuscripts should be in the proper style, with footnotes, references, tables and charts on separate pages. Illustrations are encouraged.
Disposition of manuscript:
Query letter: Not necessary, but advisable.
Receipt of manuscript acknowledged: Yes
Decision to publish in: 1-2 months
Accepted manuscript published in: 6-8 months
Rejected manuscript returned: Yes
Rejected manuscript criticized: Sometimes

Submit to:
Merald E. Wrolstad
Editor
(See address above)

WEST VIRGINIA UNIVERSITY PHILOLOGICAL PAPERS [249]
201C Chitwood Hall
West Virginia University
Morgantown, West Virginia 26506
(304) 293-5121

First published in 1936

SUBSCRIPTION DATA
Issues and rates: Published annually.
Average paid circulation: 300 controlled
Publisher or Sponsor: West Virginia University
Managing Editor: Armand E. Singer

EDITORIAL DESCRIPTION
Contains articles on any phase of language or literature, ancient or modern. Articles must be original contributions to literary or linguistic scholarship.
Articles per average issue: 10
Audience: Scholars
Manuscripts accepted in English

MANUSCRIPT INFORMATION
Manuscript requirements: MLA; typewritten, double-spaced with footnotes at end
Preferred length: 20-25 pages maximum
Number of copies to be submitted: Two
Author information and reprints: Payment: None.
Is simultaneous submission of article to other journals permitted: No
Exclusive manuscript rights between acceptance and publication: Yes
Copyright: Held by publication.
Reprints: Available at cost
Disposition of manuscript:
Query letter: Not necessary.
Receipt of manuscript acknowledged: Yes
Decision to publish in: 1-5 months
Accepted manuscript published in: 12-18 months
Rejected manuscript returned: Yes
Rejected manuscript criticized: Yes
Submit to:
Armand E. Singer
Editor-in-Chief
(See address above)

SPECIAL STIPULATIONS
Contributions limited to institutions of higher learning in West Virginia. No book reviews unless original contributions to learning; no regular book review section.

Library

THE AMERICAN ARCHIVIST [250]
Society of American Archivists, Box 8198
University of Illinois, Chicago Circle
Chicago, Illinois 60680
(312) 996-3370

First published in 1938

SUBSCRIPTION DATA
Issues and rates: Published quarterly.
Average paid circulation: 3,000
Annual rate(s): Foreign $20.00; Institutions $20.00; Students $10.00
Publisher or Sponsor: Society of American Archivists
Managing Editor: Fred W. Coker

EDITORIAL DESCRIPTION
Publication of articles and news of professional interest to archivists, records managers, and manuscripts curators
Articles per average issue: 6
Audience: Professional archivists, members of the Society
Manuscripts accepted in English

MANUSCRIPT INFORMATION
Manuscript requirements: See latest issue for style requirements. Chicago
Abstract: Yes. Of about 75 words
Author information and reprints: Payment: None.
Is simultaneous submission of article to other journals permitted: Not permitted.
Exclusive manuscript rights between acceptance and publication: Yes
Copyright: Held by publication.
Reprints: Available at cost.
Disposition of manuscript:
Query letter: Not necessary, but advisable.
Receipt of manuscript acknowledged: Yes
Decision to publish in: 6-8 weeks
Accepted manuscript published in: 6-9 months
Rejected manuscript returned: Yes, with return postage paid by publication.
Rejected manuscript criticized: Sometimes
Submit to:
The Editor
National Archives Building
7th Street and Pennsylvania Avenue
Washington, D. C. 20408
(202) 962-3264

AMERICAN LIBRARIES [251]
50 East Huron Street
Chicago, Illinois 60611
(312)944-6780

Previously entitled *ALA Bulletin*

First published in 1882 as part of Library Journal. It became a separate magazine in 1907.

SUBSCRIPTION DATA
Issues and rates: Published monthly.
  Average paid circulation: 36,077; 1,190 controlled
  Annual rate(s): Institutions $20.00
Publisher or Sponsor: American Library Association
Managing Editor: Arthur Plotnik

EDITORIAL DESCRIPTION
The official bulletin of the American Library Association, it is the only magazine published by the Association which goes to all of the membership. Its primary objectives are communicating with the membership about the goals, activities, and business of the Association; providing news of developments in librarianship and advances in library service; and serving as a forum for the discussion of issues and problems of interest to the library profession at large.
Articles per average issue: 20; short, solicited
Audience: ALA Membership
  Manuscripts accepted in English

MANUSCRIPT INFORMATION
Subject field(s): Libraries, librarians, education, publishing, legislation affecting any of the preceding
Manuscript requirements: No specific style guide.
  Preferred length: None
  Number of copies to be submitted: 1
Author information and reprints: Payment: By publication to author.
  Is simultaneous submission of article to other journals permitted: Not permitted.
  Exclusive manuscript rights between acceptance and publication: Yes
  Copyright: First serial rights only
  Reprints: Available at cost.

SPECIAL STIPULATIONS
Unsolicited manuscripts not encouraged.

AMERICAN SOCIETY FOR INFORMATION SCIENCE. JOURNAL [252]
JASIS
1155 16th Street, N. W., Suite 210
Washington, D. C. 20015
(202) 656-1893

Previously entitled *American Documentation*

First published in 1950

SUBSCRIPTION DATA
Issues and rates: Published bi-monthly.
  Average paid circulation: 6,500
  Annual rate(s): $45.00; Foreign $50.00
Publisher or Sponsor: American Society for Information Science
Managing Editor: Jack Lass

EDITORIAL DESCRIPTION
Publishes technical and scientific research in a wide variety of information-related fields

Articles per average issue: 7-10
Audience: Professional, academic
  Manuscripts accepted in English

MANUSCRIPT INFORMATION
Subject field(s): Library science, linguistics, computers, abstracting, indexing, cybernetics, operations research, management research, etc.
Manuscript requirements: Style sheet sent on request.
  Preferred length: As required
  Number of copies to be submitted: 3
  Abstract: Yes. 200 words maximum describing the main points and conclusions of the paper.
Author information and reprints: Payment: None.
  Is simultaneous submission of article to other journals permitted: Not permitted.
  Exclusive manuscript rights between acceptance and publication: Yes
  Copyright: Held by the Society
  Reprints: Available at cost.
Additional information: Any artwork required is to be in a finished form suitable for reduction; black and white line art, glossy prints
Disposition of manuscript:
  Query letter: Not necessary.
  Receipt of manuscript acknowledged: Yes
  Decision to publish in: 3-9 weeks
  Accepted manuscript published in: 6-9 months
  Rejected manuscript returned: Yes, if return postage is supplied by author.
  Rejected manuscript criticized: Yes
Submit to:
  Arthur W. Elias
  Editor
  (See address above)

ARCHIVES [253]
Journal of the British Records Association
79 Whitwell Way
Coton,
Cambridge CB3 7PW, England

First published in 1949

SUBSCRIPTION DATA
Issues and rates: Published semi-annually.
  Average paid circulation: 1,100
  Annual rate(s): £2.25, Members £1.50
Publisher or Sponsor: British Records Association

EDITORIAL DESCRIPTION
Contains articles on archives and other documentary source materials; descriptions of archive repositories; reviews of publications based on archival sources; reports of conferences and activities of Association and other bodies concerned with custody or use of archives.
Articles per average issue: 2-4
Audience: Custodians, users, owners of archives
  Manuscripts accepted in English

MANUSCRIPT INFORMATION
Subject field(s): All aspects of the ownership, custody, preservation, study and publication of archives.
Manuscript requirements: See latest issue for style requirements.
  Preferred length: 5000 words maximum
  Number of copies to be submitted: One
  Abstract: No
Author information and reprints: Payment: None.
  Is simultaneous submission of article to other journals permitted: By prior arrangement only
  Exclusive manuscript rights between acceptance and publication: Yes
  Copyright: Held by publication.
  Reprints: Available, 6 free; additional at cost
Additional information: One or two illustrations may be accepted with manuscript.
Disposition of manuscript:
  Query letter: Preferred
  Receipt of manuscript acknowledged: Yes
  Decision to publish in: 3 to 4 weeks
  Accepted manuscript published in: 6 to 12 months
  Rejected manuscript returned: Yes, if return postage is supplied by author.
  Rejected manuscript criticized: Sometimes
Submit to:
  A.E.B. Owen
  Honorary Editor
  (See address above)

ARKANSAS LIBRARIES [254]
701 North McAdoo Street
Little Rock, Arkansas 72205
(501) 663-6633

SUBSCRIPTION DATA
Issues and rates: Published quarterly.
  Average paid circulation: 950; 100 controlled
  Annual rate(s): $10.00; Foreign $10.00
Publisher or Sponsor: Arkansas Library Association; Arkansas Library Commission
Managing Editor: Katherine Stanick

EDITORIAL DESCRIPTION
Primary focus is on items of interest to the library professionals of Arkansas, with national coverage as well of the field of librarianship
Audience: Library profession
  Manuscripts accepted in English

MANUSCRIPT INFORMATION
Manuscript requirements: See latest issue for style requirements. Style sheet sent on request.
  Preferred length: 500-2,000 words; 1-4 pages
  Number of copies to be submitted: 2
  Abstract: Not necessary.
Author information and reprints: Payment: None.
  Is simultaneous submission of article to other journals permitted: Permitted.

Exclusive manuscript rights between acceptance and publication: No
Copyright: No provisions
Reprints: Not available.
Disposition of manuscript:
Query letter: Not necessary.
Receipt of manuscript acknowledged: No
Decision to publish in: 6 weeks
Accepted manuscript published in: 3 months
Rejected manuscript returned: Yes, if return postage is supplied by author.
Rejected manuscript criticized: No
Submit to:
Katherine C. Stanick
Executive Secretary
(See address above)

ASLIB PROCEEDINGS [255]
3 Belgrave Square
London SW1X 8PL, England
(01) 235-5050

First published in 1948

SUBSCRIPTION DATA
Issues and rates: Published monthly.
Average paid circulation: 3,300
Annual rate(s): £12.50 Members £4.00
Publisher or Sponsor: ASLIB
Managing Editor: Margaret J. Bidnead

EDITORIAL DESCRIPTION
Presents papers of a practical nature with some relevence to the problems incountered in the every day operation of library and information units and services
Articles per average issue: 3-4
Audience: Special librarians and information scientists
Manuscripts accepted in English

MANUSCRIPT INFORMATION
Subject field(s): Special librarianship, information science, practical problems solved, technical notes
Manuscript requirements: No specific style guide.
Number of copies to be submitted: 2
Abstract: Yes. Of about 200 words
Author information and reprints: Payment: Reprints only. 25
Is simultaneous submission of article to other journals permitted: Permitted, but not encouraged.
Exclusive manuscript rights between acceptance and publication: Yes
Copyright: Held jointly by publication and author
Disposition of manuscript:
Query letter: Not necessary.
Receipt of manuscript acknowledged: Yes
Decision to publish in: 2-3 months
Accepted manuscript published in: 2-3 months
Rejected manuscript returned: Yes, with return postage paid by publication.
Rejected manuscript criticized: No
Submit to:
Margaret J. Bidnead
Editor
(See address above)

THE ASSISTANT LIBRARIAN [256]
Official Journal of the Association of Assistant Librarians
Central Library
Southgate
Stevenage, Herts. SG1 1HD, England
2941/42

Previously entitled *The Library Assistant*

First published in 1898

SUBSCRIPTION DATA
Issues and rates: 11 issues per annum
Annual rate(s): £5.00; Foreign $14.00 (U.S.)
Publisher or Sponsor: Association of Assistant Librarians

EDITORIAL DESCRIPTION
Contains articles on librarianship, bibliography, literature, and censorship from a radical point of view.
Articles per average issue: 2
Audience: Librarians, especially the younger assistant
Manuscripts accepted in English

MANUSCRIPT INFORMATION
Subject field(s): Librarianship, bibliography, communications, mass media, social responsibility, literature, intellectual freedom
Manuscript requirements: No specific style guide.
Preferred length: 1,500-3,000 words; 2-4 pages
Number of copies to be submitted: One
Abstract: No
Author information and reprints: Payment: None.
Is simultaneous submission of article to other journals permitted: No
Exclusive manuscript rights between acceptance and publication: Yes
Copyright: Held by publication.
Reprints: Not available.
Additional information: Everything typewritten, double-spaced, wide margins; black and white photos only
Disposition of manuscript:
Query letter: No
Receipt of manuscript acknowledged: Yes
Decision to publish in: One month
Accepted manuscript published in: 6 months
Rejected manuscript returned: Yes, if return postage is supplied by author.
Rejected manuscript criticized: Yes
Submit to:
Brian C. Arnold
Editor
(See address above)

THE BAY STATE LIBRARIAN [257]
Massachusetts Library Association
P.O. Box 7
Nahant, Massachusetts 01908
(617) 581-1562

SUBSCRIPTION DATA
Issues and rates: Published quarterly.
Average paid circulation: 1700
Annual rate(s): $4.00
Publisher or Sponsor: Massachusetts Library Association
Managing Editor: Jane Lopes

EDITORIAL DESCRIPTION
Contains articles of interest to librarians both locally and nation-wide.

MANUSCRIPT INFORMATION
Subject field(s): Library interests
Manuscript requirements: Style sheet sent on request.
Preferred length: Varies
Number of copies to be submitted: One
Author information and reprints: Payment: None.
Exclusive manuscript rights between acceptance and publication: No
Disposition of manuscript:
Receipt of manuscript acknowledged: Yes
Decision to publish in: Varies
Rejected manuscript returned: Yes, if return postage is supplied by author.
Submit to:
Jane Lopes
Editor
Morse-Slanger Library
Boston City Hospital
Boston, Massachusetts 02118

BIBLIOGRAPHICAL SOCIETY OF AMERICA. PAPERS [258]
Box 397, Grand Central Station
New York, New York 10017

First published in 1907

SUBSCRIPTION DATA
Issues and rates: Published quarterly.
Average paid circulation: 1700
Annual rate(s): $15.00
Publisher or Sponsor: The Bibliographical Society of America

EDITORIAL DESCRIPTION
Contains articles pertaining to descriptive, analytical or historical bibliography, textual criticism, history of the press, questions of censorship, and related subjects.
Articles per average issue: 15
Audience: Those interested in books and book production.
Manuscripts accepted in English

MANUSCRIPT INFORMATION
Manuscript requirements: MLA
Preferred length: 3,000-10,000 for articles; shorter for notes
Number of copies to be submitted:
Abstract: Yes
Author information and reprints: Payment: Reprints only. 40 copies for articles; 20 for notes and reviews
Is simultaneous submission of article to other journals permitted: No

Exclusive manuscript rights between acceptance and publication: No
Copyright: Held by publication. but assigned to author upon request.
Reprints: Not available.
Additional information: See the statement of editorial policy in the first issue of each year.
Disposition of manuscript:
Query letter: No
Receipt of manuscript acknowledged: Yes
Decision to publish in: 3 months
Accepted manuscript published in: 8-16 months
Rejected manuscript returned: Yes, if return postage is supplied by author.
Rejected manuscript criticized: Yes
Submit to:
William B. Todd
Editor
Parlin Hall 110
University of Texas
Austin, Texas 78712

BODLEIAN LIBRARY RECORD [259]
Bodleian Library
Oxford OX1 3BG, England
(0865) 44675

Previously entitled *Bodleian Quarterly Record*

First published in 1938

SUBSCRIPTION DATA
Issues and rates: Irregular
  Average paid circulation: 2,000
  Annual rate(s): £.50
Publisher or Sponsor: Bodleian Library
Managing Editor: Miss G. M. Briggs

EDITORIAL DESCRIPTION
  Contains current Bodleian library news; articles on books and manuscripts, bibliography, printing history, library history, wholly or partly related to the library and its collections.
Articles per average issue: Varies
Audience: Scholarly
  Manuscripts accepted in English (French)

MANUSCRIPT INFORMATION
Manuscript requirements: See latest issue for style requirements.
  Preferred length: 5000 words maximum
  Number of copies to be submitted: One
Author information and reprints: Payment: Reprints only. 25 offprints
  Is simultaneous submission of article to other journals permitted: No
  Exclusive manuscript rights between acceptance and publication: Yes
  Copyright: Held jointly by the Library and author.
  Reprints: Available
Disposition of manuscript:
  Query letter: No
  Receipt of manuscript acknowledged: Yes
  Decision to publish in: Varies
  Accepted manuscript published in: Varies
  Rejected manuscript returned: Yes

Rejected manuscript criticized: Yes
Submit to:
The Editor
(See address above)

BRIO [260]
Journal of the United Kingdom Branch of the International Association of Music Libraries
BBC Music Library
Yalding House
156 Great Portland Street London W1N 6AJ, England
(01) 580-4468, ex. 2414

First published in 1964

SUBSCRIPTION DATA
Issues and rates: Published semi-annually.
  Average paid circulation: 500
  Annual rate(s): £1.00, Foreign $2.70
Publisher or Sponsor: International Association of Music Libraries

EDITORIAL DESCRIPTION
  Contains articles relating to music libraries and all aspects of music librarianship, musical bibliography.
Articles per average issue: 3
Audience: Professional music librarians
  Manuscripts accepted in English

MANUSCRIPT INFORMATION
Manuscript requirements: See latest issue for style requirements.
  Preferred length: 1,000-2,000 words
  Number of copies to be submitted: One
  Abstract: No
Author information and reprints: Payment: None.
  Is simultaneous submission of article to other journals permitted: No
  Exclusive manuscript rights between acceptance and publication: Yes
  Copyright: Held jointly by author and publication
  Reprints: Not available.
Disposition of manuscript:
  Query letter: Desirable
  Receipt of manuscript acknowledged: Yes
  Decision to publish in: One week
  Accepted manuscript published in: 6-12 months
  Rejected manuscript returned: Yes, if self-addressed, stamped envelope is sent with manuscript.
  Rejected manuscript criticized: Occasionally
Submit to:
Clifford Bartlett
Editor
(See address above)

BRITISH COLUMBIA LIBRARY QUARTERLY [261]
2425 MacDonald Street
Vancouver, British Columbia V6K 3Y9
Canada

First published in 1937

SUBSCRIPTION DATA
Issues and rates: Published quarterly.
  Annual rate(s): Institutions $25.00; Students $5.00; Members $20.00; Foreign individuals $15.00
Publisher or Sponsor: British Columbia Library Association
Managing Editor: Ross Carter

EDITORIAL DESCRIPTION
  To publish articles of interest to British Columbia librarians, and to review media, books, records, usually by British Columbians about British Columbia and the library profession.
Articles per average issue: 1 to 2; 20 reviews
Audience: Librarians
  Manuscripts accepted in English

MANUSCRIPT INFORMATION
Subject field(s): British Columbia, librarianship
Manuscript requirements: Chicago
  Preferred length: 15-20 pages
  Number of copies to be submitted: 2
  Abstract: Not necessary.
Author information and reprints: Payment: None.
  Is simultaneous submission of article to other journals permitted: Permitted, but not encouraged.
  Copyright: Held by author.
  Reprints: Available at cost.
Disposition of manuscript:
  Query letter: Not necessary.
  Receipt of manuscript acknowledged: Yes
  Decision to publish in: 3 months
  Accepted manuscript published in: 3-6 months
  Rejected manuscript returned: Yes, with return postage paid by publication.
  Rejected manuscript criticized: No
Submit to:
Ross Carter;
Lee Windriech
Editors
(See address above)

BULLETIN OF BIBLIOGRAPHY AND MAGAZINE NOTES [262]
15 Southwest Park
Westwood, Massachusetts 02090
(617) 329-3350 ext. 68

First published in 1897

SUBSCRIPTION DATA
Issues and rates: Published quarterly.
  Average paid circulation: 2000; 30 controlled
  Annual rate(s): $15.00

EDITORIAL DESCRIPTION
  Publishes bibliographies, checklists and research studies on subjects in the humanities and social sciences useful to students, professors, librarians and other library users. A record of new, changed and discontinued periodical titles is a regular feature.
Articles per average issue: 6-7
Audience: Academic, general librarians

Manuscripts accepted in English

MANUSCRIPT INFORMATION
Manuscript requirements: MLA
Preferred length: 34 pages maximum
Number of copies to be submitted: One
Abstract: No
Author information and reprints: Payment: Reprints only. Ten copies of issue in which article appears.
Is simultaneous submission of article to other journals permitted: No
Exclusive manuscript rights between acceptance and publication: Yes
Copyright: Held by author.
Reprints: Available at cost
Additional information: Manuscripts should contain an introductory statement, as well as the author's name and affiliation.
Disposition of manuscript:
Query letter: Not necessary, but advisable.
Receipt of manuscript acknowledged: Yes
Decision to publish in: 2 months
Accepted manuscript published in: 12 months
Rejected manuscript returned: Yes, if return postage is supplied by author.
Rejected manuscript criticized: Yes
Submit to:
Eleanor Cavanaugh Jones
Editor
(See address above)

CALIFORNIA SCHOOL LIBRARIES [263]
Box 1277
Burlingame, California 94010
(415) 692-2350

Previously entitled *Bulletin of the School Library Association of California*

First published in 1925

SUBSCRIPTION DATA
Issues and rates: Published quarterly.
Average paid circulation: 2,000
Annual rate(s): $5.00; Foreign $5.00; Institutions $5.00; Foreign institutions $5.00
Publisher or Sponsor: California Association of School Librarians
Managing Editor: Chase Dane

EDITORIAL DESCRIPTION
Especially interested in articles describing actual and model school library programs throughout the state. Articles commenting on the philosophy of school librarianship, describing new developments, and listing multimedia materials in specific subject areas will be welcomed.
Articles per average issue: 6 to 8
Audience: School librarians
Manuscripts accepted in English

MANUSCRIPT INFORMATION
Subject field(s): School librarianship

Manuscript requirements: No specific style guide.
Preferred length: 1,000-1,500 words; 4-6 pages
Number of copies to be submitted: One
Abstract: Not necessary.
Author information and reprints: Payment: None.
Is simultaneous submission of article to other journals permitted: Permitted.
Exclusive manuscript rights between acceptance and publication: No
Copyright: Held by author.
Reprints: Available at cost.
Disposition of manuscript:
Query letter: Not necessary.
Receipt of manuscript acknowledged: Yes
Decision to publish in: 1-2 weeks
Accepted manuscript published in: 1-2 months
Rejected manuscript returned: Yes, with return postage paid by publication.
Rejected manuscript criticized: Reasons for rejections only
Submit to:
Chase Dane
Editor
Santa Monica Unified School District
1723 Fourth Street
Santa Monica, California 90401
(213) 393-2785 Ex. 228

CANADIAN LIBRARY JOURNAL [264]
Canadian Library Association
151 Sparks Street
Ottawa, Ontario K1P 5E3, Canada
(613) 232-9625

First published in 1944

SUBSCRIPTION DATA
Issues and rates: Published bi-monthly.
Average paid circulation: 5,000
Annual rate(s): $10.00
Publisher or Sponsor: Canadian Library Association
Managing Editor: Pamela Lee MacRae

EDITORIAL DESCRIPTION
Publishes articles of interest to the professional librarian
Articles per average issue: 12
Audience: Librarians and those in related professions
Manuscripts accepted in English

MANUSCRIPT INFORMATION
Subject field(s): Unions, women's rights, public lending right, intellectual freedom, as well as library science and practical advice on library management, budgets, collections, etc.
Manuscript requirements: See latest issue for style requirements. Style sheet sent on request.
Preferred length: Up to 2,500 words
Number of copies to be submitted: 2
Abstract: Not necessary.

Author information and reprints: Payment: By publication to author. $25.00 honorarium
Is simultaneous submission of article to other journals permitted: Not permitted.
Exclusive manuscript rights between acceptance and publication: No
Copyright: Held by author.
Reprints: Not available.
Additional information: Especially encourage articles that are erudite, but fast-paced with strong opening paragraph, bringing in human interest whenever possible.
Disposition of manuscript:
Query letter: Not necessary.
Receipt of manuscript acknowledged: No
Decision to publish in: 4 weeks
Accepted manuscript published in: 4-8 weeks
Rejected manuscript returned: Yes, if return postage is supplied by author.
Rejected manuscript criticized: Sometimes
Submit to:
Pamela Lee MacRae
Editor
(See address above)

CATALOGUE & INDEX [265]
Periodical of the Library Association Cataloguing and Indexing Group
Department of Librarianship
Leeds Polytechnic
Leeds BS1 2SY, England
0532-26696

First published in 1966

SUBSCRIPTION DATA
Issues and rates: Published quarterly.
Average paid circulation: 2,500 controlled
Annual rate(s): £ 2.50

EDITORIAL DESCRIPTION
Contains articles on cataloguing, classification, indexing, information storage and retrieval.
Articles per average issue: 4-5
Audience: Librarians
Manuscripts accepted in English

MANUSCRIPT INFORMATION
Manuscript requirements: See latest issue for style requirements.
Preferred length: Maximum 2,500 words
Number of copies to be submitted: Two
Abstract: No
Author information and reprints: Payment: None.
Is simultaneous submission of article to other journals permitted: No
Exclusive manuscript rights between acceptance and publication: No
Copyright: Held by publication.
Reprints: Not available.
Disposition of manuscript:
Query letter: Yes
Receipt of manuscript acknowledged: Yes
Decision to publish in: 2 months
Accepted manuscript published in: 3 months

Rejected manuscript returned: Yes
Rejected manuscript criticized: No
Submit to:
Russell Sweeney
Editor
(See address above)

CATHOLIC LIBRARY WORLD [266]
461 West Lancaster Avenue
Haverford, Pennsylvania 19041
(215) MI 9-5251

First published in 1929

SUBSCRIPTION DATA
Issues and rates: Published monthly.
Average paid circulation: 4,000; 3,500 controlled
Annual rate(s): $10.00; Foreign $11.00; Institutions $10.00
Publisher or Sponsor: Catholic Library Association
Managing Editor: John T. Corrigan

EDITORIAL DESCRIPTION
Monthly themes which express specific interests of members and the library profession. Current book reviews.
Articles per average issue: 5
Audience: Professional librarians
Manuscripts accepted in English only

MANUSCRIPT INFORMATION
Subject field(s): Library and educational media concerns, children, young adult
Manuscript requirements: Style sheet sent on request.
Preferred length: As required
Number of copies to be submitted: 2
Abstract: Yes. 100 words or less
Author information and reprints: Payment: Reprints only. 50 free reprints
Is simultaneous submission of article to other journals permitted: Not permitted.
Exclusive manuscript rights between acceptance and publication: Yes
Copyright: Held by publication.
Reprints: Available at cost.
Disposition of manuscript:
Query letter: Not necessary.
Receipt of manuscript acknowledged: Yes
Decision to publish in: 1-3 months
Accepted manuscript published in: 9-12 months
Rejected manuscript returned: Yes, with return postage paid by publication.
Rejected manuscript criticized: Sometimes
Submit to:
Howard W. Winger
Managing Editor
University of Chicago, Graduate Library School
1100 East 57th Street
Chicago Illinois 60637
(312) 753-3486

SPECIAL STIPULATIONS
Publisher has a royalty sharing arrangement under which authors receive 50 per cent of reprint royalties after deduction of expenses.

COLLEGE & RESEARCH LIBRARIES [267]
50 East Huron Street
Chicago, Illinois 60611

First published in 1939

SUBSCRIPTION DATA
Issues and rates: Bi-monthly, with 11 monthly News issues
Average paid circulation: 16,000
Annual rate(s): Members $7.50, $15.00
Publisher or Sponsor: Association of College and Research Libraries

EDITORIAL DESCRIPTION
Contains articles on the whole range of professional librarianship.
Articles per average issue: 7
Audience: Academic librarians
Manuscripts accepted in English

MANUSCRIPT INFORMATION
Subject field(s): Bibliography, cataloging, acquisitions and other topics of interest to librarians
Manuscript requirements: See latest issue for style requirements.
Preferred length: 3,000-5,000 words
Number of copies to be submitted: 2
Abstract: Yes, of 75-100 words double-spaced
Author information and reprints: Payment: None.
Is simultaneous submission of article to other journals permitted: No
Exclusive manuscript rights between acceptance and publication: Yes
Copyright: Held by the American Library Association
Reprints: Author receives complimentary offprints
Additional information: Manuscript should be typewritten, double-spaced, with notes numbered consecutively at the end.
Disposition of manuscript:
Query letter: No
Receipt of manuscript acknowledged: Yes
Decision to publish in: 8 weeks
Accepted manuscript published in: 6-8 months
Rejected manuscript returned: Yes
Rejected manuscript criticized: Yes
Submit to:
Richard D. Johnson
Editor
James M. Milne Library
State University College
Oneonta, New York 13820

Material for News issue:
Mary Frances Collins
News Editor
University Library
State University of New York at Albany
Albany, New York 12222

DREXEL LIBRARY QUARTERLY [268]
Graduate School of Library Science
Drexel University
Philadelphia, Pennsylvania 19104
(215) 895-2483

First published in 1965

SUBSCRIPTION DATA
Issues and rates: Published quarterly.
Average paid circulation: 900
Annual rate(s): $12.00
Publisher or Sponsor: Drexel University, Graduate School of Library Science

EDITORIAL DESCRIPTION
Each issue is devoted to some topic or sub-area within the field of library science and is edited by a special issue editor who usually invites contributors to write a specific article.
Audience: Directed toward working librarians.
Manuscripts accepted in English

MANUSCRIPT INFORMATION
Subject field(s): General library science, information science, school librarianship, academic libraries, special libraries, cataloging, indexing and abstracting
Manuscript requirements: GPO; Chicago
Preferred length: 10 pages
Number of copies to be submitted: Two
Author information and reprints: Payment: Reprints only. 5 copies of issue in which material appears
Is simultaneous submission of article to other journals permitted: No
Exclusive manuscript rights between acceptance and publication: Yes
Copyright: Held by publication.
Reprints: Not available.
Disposition of manuscript:
Query letter: Yes
Receipt of manuscript acknowledged: Yes
Decision to publish in: 2 months
Rejected manuscript returned: Yes, if self-addressed, stamped envelope is sent with manuscript.
Rejected manuscript criticized: No
Submit to:
Barbara P. Casini
Managing Editor
(See address above)

SPECIAL STIPULATIONS
Contact managing editor if interested in editing an issue.

FID NEWS BULLETIN [269]
International Federation for Documentation
7 Hofweg
The Hague, Netherlands
070 180081

Previously entitled *FID Informations*

First published in 1951

SUBSCRIPTION DATA
Issues and rates: Published monthly.

Average paid circulation: 2000
Annual rate(s): 40 Dfl
Publisher or Sponsor: International Federation for Documentation
Managing Editor: W. van der Brugghen

EDITORIAL DESCRIPTION

Contains news on organization of information, calendars and reports of conferences, mechanization, reprography, training, standardization, classification, documentation literature, bibliographies, abstracting and indexing services.
Articles per average issue: 50 items
Audience: Scientists, information officers, documentalists, librarians
Manuscripts accepted in English

MANUSCRIPT INFORMATION

Subject field(s): News items only
Manuscript requirements: No specific style guide.
Preferred length: 200 words
Number of copies to be submitted: One
Abstract: No
Author information and reprints: Payment: None.
Is simultaneous submission of article to other journals permitted: Yes
Exclusive manuscript rights between acceptance and publication: No
Copyright: Not copyrighted
Reprints: Not available.
Disposition of manuscript:
Query letter: No
Receipt of manuscript acknowledged: Yes
Decision to publish in: 2 weeks
Accepted manuscript published in: 2-4 weeks
Rejected manuscript returned: No
Rejected manuscript criticized: Yes
Submit to:
W. van der Brugghen
Editor
(See address above)

SPECIAL STIPULATIONS

Manuscripts should be received before the 25th of the month preceeding publication.

FILM LIBRARY QUARTERLY [270]
Box 348, Radio City Station
New York, New York 10019
(212) 790-6418

SUBSCRIPTION DATA

Issues and rates: Published quarterly.
Average paid circulation: 1,200; 1,400 controlled
Annual rate(s): $8.00
Publisher or Sponsor: Film Library Information Council
Emma Cohn

EDITORIAL DESCRIPTION

Contains articles on non-theatrical, non-narrative film; includes the documentary, informational-cultural, and experimental film. Contains information and articles on new nonprint technology as they apply to public library service.
Articles per average issue: 8
Audience: Film librarians, film specialists, educators
Manuscripts accepted in English

MANUSCRIPT INFORMATION

Subject field(s): Film, video, nonprint services in libraries.
Manuscript requirements: Style sheet sent on request.
Preferred length: 2,000 to 3,000 words; 5 to 6 pages
Number of copies to be submitted: One
Abstract: No
Author information and reprints: Payment: Reprints only. All the free copies the author wants.
Is simultaneous submission of article to other journals permitted: No
Exclusive manuscript rights between acceptance and publication: Yes
Copyright: Held by publication.
Reprints: Not available.
Disposition of manuscript:
Query letter: No
Receipt of manuscript acknowledged: Yes
Decision to publish in: 2 weeks
Accepted manuscript published in: 1-6 months
Rejected manuscript returned: Yes
Rejected manuscript criticized: Yes
Submit to:
William Sloan
Editor
Donnell Film Library
20 West 53rd Street
New York, New York 10019
(212) 790-6549

FOCUS ON INDIANA LIBRARIES [271]
Monroe County Public Library
303 East Kirkwood Avenue
Bloomington, Indiana 47401
(812) 339-2271

SUBSCRIPTION DATA

Issues and rates: Published quarterly.
Average paid circulation: 1,600
Annual rate(s): $6.00
Publisher or Sponsor: Indiana Library Association

EDITORIAL DESCRIPTION

Contains articles on librarianship, media and library users; progress and final program reports; news items; ILA activity reports.
Articles per average issue: 3-4
Audience: Professional
Manuscripts accepted in English

MANUSCRIPT INFORMATION

Subject field(s): Librarians, readers, media, technical applications in libraries, library buildings, studies/surveys
Manuscript requirements: Style sheet sent on request.
Preferred length: 1,200 words minimum
Number of copies to be submitted: One
Abstract: No
Author information and reprints: Payment: None. Four copies of issue carrying article
Is simultaneous submission of article to other journals permitted: Yes, to state or local level only.
Exclusive manuscript rights between acceptance and publication: No
Copyright: Held by publication.
Reprints: Available, order from printer
Additional information: Typewritten, double-spaced, on 40 characters per line.
Disposition of manuscript:
Query letter: No
Receipt of manuscript acknowledged: Yes
Decision to publish in: One month
Accepted manuscript published in: 6-9 months
Rejected manuscript returned: Yes, if self-addressed, stamped envelope is sent with manuscript.
Rejected manuscript criticized: Yes
Submit to:
Sally Hunt
Editor
(See address above)

HARVARD LIBRARY BULLETIN [272]
Journals Dept. Harvard University Press
79 Garden Street
Cambridge, Massachusetts 02138
(617) 495-2438

First published in 1947

SUBSCRIPTION DATA

Issues and rates: Published quarterly.
Average paid circulation: 1,500
Annual rate(s): $15.00; Pan-Am $15.00; Foreign $15.00

EDITORIAL DESCRIPTION

To make known to the scholarly world the collections and experience of the Harvard University Library.
Articles per average issue: 5-7
Audience: All persons interested in the Harvard Library and in subjects covered by its collections
Manuscripts accepted in English, French, German

MANUSCRIPT INFORMATION

Subject field(s): Nearly all fields are covered by the Library's collections.
Manuscript requirements: MLA
Preferred length: 1,000 to 15,000 words; 3-50 pages
Number of copies to be submitted: One
Abstract: Not necessary.
Author information and reprints: Payment: Reprints only. 50 reprints, 2 copies of issue
Is simultaneous submission of article to other journals permitted: Permitted, but not encouraged.
Exclusive manuscript rights between acceptance and publication: Yes
Copyright: Held by publication.
Reprints: Available at no cost. first 50 free

Disposition of manuscript:
  Query letter: Not necessary.
  Receipt of manuscript acknowledged: Yes
  Decision to publish in: 2 weeks
  Accepted manuscript published in: 9-12 months
  Rejected manuscript returned: Yes, if return postage is supplied by author.
  Rejected manuscript criticized: Sometimes
Submit to:
  Edwin E. Williams
  Editor
  Lamont Library 505
  Harvard University
  Cambridge, Massachusetts 02138
  (617) 495-2457

ILLINOIS LIBRARIES [273]
Centennial Building
Illinois State Library
Springfield, Illinois 62756
(217) 782-5870

First published in 1919

SUBSCRIPTION DATA
Issues and rates: Monthly except July and August
  Average paid circulation: 10,000 controlled
  Annual rate(s): Free
Publisher or Sponsor: Illinois State Library

EDITORIAL DESCRIPTION
  Contains articles dealing with all types of libraries and the library profession as a whole.
Articles per average issue: 20
Audience: All types of libraries
  Manuscripts accepted in English

MANUSCRIPT INFORMATION
Subject field(s): Library science and service
Manuscript requirements: See latest issue for style requirements.
  Preferred length: 5-10 pages
  Number of copies to be submitted: One
  Abstract: No
Author information and reprints: Payment: None.
  Is simultaneous submission of article to other journals permitted: Yes
  Exclusive manuscript rights between acceptance and publication: No
  Reprints: Not available.
Additional information: Manuscripts should be typewritten, double-spaced.
Disposition of manuscript:
  Query letter: No
  Receipt of manuscript acknowledged: Yes
  Decision to publish in: 3 to 5 weeks
  Accepted manuscript published in: Six months
  Rejected manuscript returned: Yes
  Rejected manuscript criticized: No
Submit to:
  Irma R. Bostian
  Editor
  (See address above)

INFORMATION NEWS AND SOURCES [274]
23 East 26th Street
New York, New York 10010
(212) 532-1955

Previously entitled *Information News/Sources/Profiles*

First published in 1969

SUBSCRIPTION DATA
Issues and rates: Published monthly.
  Annual rate(s): $35.00
Publisher or Sponsor: Science Associates/International, Inc.

EDITORIAL DESCRIPTION
  Publishes news and articles on all aspects of information science, library science and related interests. Seeks to keep information users abreast of new data files, legislation, proposals, and opportunities.
Articles per average issue: 2
Audience: Information specialists
  Manuscripts accepted in English only

MANUSCRIPT INFORMATION
Subject field(s): Opinion; profiles; information centers, information organizations, information personalities
Manuscript requirements: See latest issue for style requirements.
  Preferred length: 3,500 words; 10 pages
  Number of copies to be submitted: One
  Abstract: No
Author information and reprints: Payment: None.
  Is simultaneous submission of article to other journals permitted: Yes, in case of opinion papers only
  Exclusive manuscript rights between acceptance and publication: Yes
  Copyright: Held by publication.
  Reprints: Available at cost
Disposition of manuscript:
  Query letter: No
  Receipt of manuscript acknowledged: Yes
  Decision to publish in: Two weeks
  Accepted manuscript published in: Two months
  Rejected manuscript returned: Yes, if self-addressed, stamped envelope is sent with manuscript.
  Rejected manuscript criticized: No
Submit to:
  Marilyn G. McCormick
  Managing Editor
  (See address above)

THE INFORMATION SCIENTIST [275]
657 High Road Tottenham N17 8AA, England
(01) 808-6399

Previously entitled *Bulletin*

First published in 1961

SUBSCRIPTION DATA
Issues and rates: Published quarterly.
  Average paid circulation: 1400
  Annual rate(s): £3.50
Publisher or Sponsor: The Institute of Information Scientists
Managing Editor: A.D.B. Gilchrist

EDITORIAL DESCRIPTION
  Purpose is to promote and maintain high standards in scientific and technical information work.
Articles per average issue: 3
Audience: Scientists, librarians
  Manuscripts accepted in English

MANUSCRIPT INFORMATION
Subject field(s): Contains papers on information retrieval, information dissemination, systems design, indexing, classification, microforms, information science in general.
Manuscript requirements: Style sheet sent on request.
  Preferred length: 6,000 words maximum
  Number of copies to be submitted: Two
  Abstract: Yes, an author-abstract of up to 200 words
Author information and reprints: Payment: None.
  Is simultaneous submission of article to other journals permitted: No
  Exclusive manuscript rights between acceptance and publication: Yes
  Copyright: Held by publication.
  Reprints: Available
Additional information: Typewritten, double-spaced, standard sized paper; author's name, affiliation, and address.
Disposition of manuscript:
  Query letter: No
  Receipt of manuscript acknowledged: Yes
  Decision to publish in: 6-8 weeks
  Accepted manuscript published in: 3-6 months
  Rejected manuscript returned: Yes
  Rejected manuscript criticized: Yes
Submit to:
  Editor
  (See address above)

INFORMATION STORAGE AND RETRIEVAL [276]
Libraries and Information Centers-Systems and Networks-An International Journal
Pergamon Press, Inc.
Fairview Park
Elmsford, New York 10523
(914) 592-7700

First published in 1963

SUBSCRIPTION DATA
Issues and rates: Published monthly.
  Annual rate(s): Institutions $15.00

EDITORIAL DESCRIPTION
  Provides a forum for the publication of advances in theory, techniques and practice of information storage and retrieval which deals as a branch of information science.
Articles per average issue: 3-5
Audience: Professional, academic

Manuscripts accepted in English, French, German, Italian

MANUSCRIPT INFORMATION

Subject field(s): Library and information center processes, research, indexing policy, mechanized applications, searching strategy, interaction between the system and its users, etc.
Manuscript requirements: See latest issue for style requirements.
  Preferred length: None
  Number of copies to be submitted: 2, double-spaced
  Abstract: Yes. The essential contents briefly recapitulated in a summary.
Author information and reprints: Payment: By author to publication. $35.00 per page. Voluntary
  Is simultaneous submission of article to other journals permitted: Not permitted.
  Exclusive manuscript rights between acceptance and publication: Yes
  Copyright: Held by publication.
  Reprints: Available at cost.
Disposition of manuscript:
  Query letter: Not necessary.
  Receipt of manuscript acknowledged: Yes
  Decision to publish in: 4 weeks
  Accepted manuscript published in: 6 months
  Rejected manuscript returned: Yes, if return postage is supplied by author.
  Rejected manuscript criticized: Reasons for rejections only
Submit to:
  Prof. Bernard Fry
  Editor-in-Chief
  Graduate Library School
  Indiana University
  Bloomington, Indiana 47401

THE JOURNAL OF ACADEMIC LIBRARIANSHIP [277]
P. O. Box 3496
Boulder, Colorado 80303
(303) 494-6360

First published in March, 1975

SUBSCRIPTION DATA

Issues and rates: Published bi-monthly.
  Annual rate(s): $14.00; Foreign $16.00; Institutions $25.00
Managing Editor: Dr. Richard M. Dougherty

EDITORIAL DESCRIPTION

To provide academic librarians with the results of research findings in the field; to address the current issues confronting the profession; keys to literature in the field of librarianship, information science, and administration in higher education; photo essays to highlight and demonstrate innovations in an academic library
Articles per average issue: 4
Audience: Academic librarians
  Manuscripts accepted in English only

MANUSCRIPT INFORMATION

Subject field(s): Library management, technological developments, public and technical services, collection development, international librarianship, educational administration
Manuscript requirements: Style sheet sent on request. Chicago
  Number of copies to be submitted: 2
  Abstract: Yes. A short abstract of 100 words or less presenting the scope, methodology and conclusions of the paper.
Author information and reprints: Payment: By publication to author. An honorarium of $50.00
  Is simultaneous submission of article to other journals permitted: Not permitted.
  Exclusive manuscript rights between acceptance and publication: Yes
  Copyright: Held by publication.
  Reprints: Available at cost.
Additional information: Manuscripts to be typewritten, double-spaced on standard white paper.
Disposition of manuscript:
  Query letter: Not necessary.
  Receipt of manuscript acknowledged: Yes
  Decision to publish in: 4-6 weeks
  Accepted manuscript published in: 4-6 months
  Rejected manuscript returned: Yes, if return postage is supplied by author.
  Rejected manuscript criticized: Reasons for rejections only
Submit to:
  Dr. Richard M. Dougherty
  Editor
  P. O. Box 6146
  Albany, California 94706

JOURNAL OF EDUCATION FOR LIBRARIANSHIP [278]
471 Park Lane
State College, Pennsylvania 16801
(814) 238-0254

First published in 1960

SUBSCRIPTION DATA

Issues and rates: Published quarterly.
  Average paid circulation: 2,000
  Annual rate(s): $8.00
Publisher or Sponsor: Association of American Library Schools
Managing Editor: Janet Phillips

EDITORIAL DESCRIPTION

Contains articles on all aspects of education for librarianship.
Articles per average issue: 4-5
Audience: Librarians and library educators
  Manuscripts accepted in English

MANUSCRIPT INFORMATION

Subject field(s): Library education, teaching methods, research in library science
Manuscript requirements: See latest issue for style requirements.
  Preferred length: Up to 25 pages
  Number of copies to be submitted: Three
  Abstract: Preferable

Author information and reprints: Payment: None.
  Is simultaneous submission of article to other journals permitted: No
  Exclusive manuscript rights between acceptance and publication: Yes
  Copyright: Held by author.
  Reprints: Available
Additional information: Manuscripts should be neatly typewritten, double-spaced with bibliography included at the end when applicable.
Disposition of manuscript:
  Receipt of manuscript acknowledged: Yes
  Decision to publish in: 4 weeks
  Accepted manuscript published in: 6 months
  Rejected manuscript returned: Yes
  Rejected manuscript criticized: Yes
Submit to:
  Norman Horrocks
  Editor
  School of Library Service
  Dalhousie University
  Halifax, Nova Canada
  (902) 424-3656

JOURNAL OF LIBRARIANSHIP [279]
Quarterly of the Library Association
7 Ridgmount Street
London WC1E 7AE, England
(01) 636-7543

First published in 1969

SUBSCRIPTION DATA

Issues and rates: Published quarterly.
  Average paid circulation: 1,300
  Annual rate(s): £7.00; Foreign £7.00; Students £2.00; Members £6.00
Publisher or Sponsor: The Library Association

EDITORIAL DESCRIPTION

Concerned with the publication of the results of research in the field of librarianship, information science and bibliography
Articles per average issue: 4-5
Audience: Librarians and information officers
  Manuscripts accepted in English

MANUSCRIPT INFORMATION

Manuscript requirements: Style sheet sent on request.
  Preferred length: 4,000-7,000 words
  Number of copies to be submitted: 2
  Abstract: Yes.
Author information and reprints: Payment: By publication to author.
  Is simultaneous submission of article to other journals permitted: Not permitted.
  Exclusive manuscript rights between acceptance and publication: Yes
  Copyright: Held jointly by the Association and the contributor
  Reprints: Available at no cost. 25 Available at cost.
Disposition of manuscript:
  Query letter: Necessary.

Receipt of manuscript acknowledged: Yes
Decision to publish in: 3 months
Accepted manuscript published in: 3 months
Rejected manuscript returned: Yes, with return postage paid by publication.
Rejected manuscript criticized: Reasons for rejections only
Submit to:
F. J. Cornell
Editor of Publications
(See address above)

JOURNAL OF LIBRARY AUTOMATION [280]

American Library Association
50 East Huron Street
Chicago, Illinois 60611
(312) 944-6780

First published in 1968

SUBSCRIPTION DATA

Issues and rates: Published quarterly.
  Average paid circulation: 5,637
  Annual rate(s): $15.00
Publisher or Sponsor: American Library Association, Information Science and Automation Division
Managing Editor: Susan K. Martin

EDITORIAL DESCRIPTION

Contains scholarly papers and technical reports on findings in the following fields: research and development in library automation, including inter-library communications; research in information science related to library activities; and the history and teaching of these subjects; educational technology of all aspects of audio-visual communication, including both software and hardware.
Articles per average issue: 5
Audience: Librarians, information scientists, and systems analysists
  Manuscripts accepted in English, and any modern European language

MANUSCRIPT INFORMATION

Subject field(s): Library automation, information science, library networks, educational technology, cable television, telecommunications, library systems analysis
Manuscript requirements: Chicago
  Preferred length: 4,000-5,000 words
  Number of copies to be submitted: Two
  Abstract: Yes
Author information and reprints: Payment: None.
  Is simultaneous submission of article to other journals permitted: Yes
  Exclusive manuscript rights between acceptance and publication: Yes
  Copyright: Held by publication.
  Reprints: Available, rates vary
Additional information: Instructions to authors available upon request. Manuscript should be typewritten, double-spaced with title page and references, if any.
Disposition of manuscript:
  Query letter: No
  Receipt of manuscript acknowledged: Yes

Decision to publish in: Two months
Accepted manuscript published in: 6-12 months
Rejected manuscript returned: Yes
Rejected manuscript criticized: Yes
Submit to:
Susan K. Martin
Head, Library Systems Office
General Library
University of California
Berkeley, California 94720
(415) 642-3773

JOURNAL OF LIBRARY HISTORY, PHILOSOPHY, AND COMPARATIVE LIBRARIANSHIP [281]

School of Library Science
Florida State University
Tallahassee, Florida 32306
(904) 644-2294

First published in 1966

SUBSCRIPTION DATA

Issues and rates: Published quarterly.
  Average paid circulation: 1,200
  Annual rate(s): Individuals $15.00
Publisher or Sponsor: Florida State University, School of Library Science
Managing Editor: Dr. Lee Warner

EDITORIAL DESCRIPTION

Contains articles on library history, library philosophy, and comparative librarianship.
Articles per average issue: 3-5
Audience: Librarians, historians
  Manuscripts accepted in English

MANUSCRIPT INFORMATION

Manuscript requirements: Chicago
  Preferred length: Research studies: 2,000-5,000; essays: 1,000-3,000 words
  Number of copies to be submitted: Two
  Abstract: No
Author information and reprints: Payment: None.
  Is simultaneous submission of article to other journals permitted: No
  Exclusive manuscript rights between acceptance and publication: Yes
  Copyright: Held by publication.
  Reprints: Not available.
Disposition of manuscript:
  Query letter: No
  Receipt of manuscript acknowledged: Yes
  Decision to publish in: 2-4 months
  Accepted manuscript published in: 6-12 months
  Rejected manuscript returned: Yes, if return postage is supplied by author.
  Rejected manuscript criticized: Yes
Submit to:
Harold Goldstein
Editor
(See address above)

LEARNING TODAY [282]

An Educational Magazine of Library-College Thought
Box 956
Norman, Oklahoma 73069
(405) 325-3923

Previously entitled *Library-College Journal*

First published in 1968

SUBSCRIPTION DATA

Issues and rates: 8 times per year
  Average paid circulation: 2,500
  Annual rate(s): $10
Publisher or Sponsor: Library-College Associates, Inc.

EDITORIAL DESCRIPTION

Contains observation, opinion, research concerning the educational function of libraries in the American school.
Articles per average issue: 3
Audience: Educators in all fields
  Manuscripts accepted in English

MANUSCRIPT INFORMATION

Subject field(s): Education, school libraries
Manuscript requirements: No specific style guide.
  Preferred length: 1,500-3,000 words
  Number of copies to be submitted: One
  Abstract: No
Author information and reprints: Payment: None.
  Is simultaneous submission of article to other journals permitted: No
  Exclusive manuscript rights between acceptance and publication: Yes
  Copyright: Held by publication.
  Reprints: Available
Disposition of manuscript:
  Query letter: No
  Receipt of manuscript acknowledged: Yes
  Decision to publish in: 3 or 4 weeks
  Accepted manuscript published in: One year
  Rejected manuscript returned: Yes
  Rejected manuscript criticized: No
Submit to:
Howard Clayton
Editor
(See address above)

LIBRARY ASSOCIATION OF ALBERTA. BULLETIN [283]

Box 1000
Lacombe, Alberta Canada
(403) 328-9857

SUBSCRIPTION DATA

Issues and rates: Published quarterly.
  Average paid circulation: 500 controlled
  Annual rate(s): $10.00
Publisher or Sponsor: Library Association of Alberta
Managing Editor: P. H. Connolly

EDITORIAL DESCRIPTION

Publishes material of interest to librarians serving in public, college, university, and special libraries. Issues are frequently

concerned with specific themes, e.g. the problem of handling and making use of audio-visual equipment.
Articles per average issue: 2-4
Audience: Librarians, interested parties
Manuscripts accepted in English, French

MANUSCRIPT INFORMATION

Subject field(s): Library and information science, book reviews, Canadian subjects
Manuscript requirements: See latest issue for style requirements.
　Preferred length: 4,000 words; 3 to 10 pages
　Number of copies to be submitted: One
　Abstract: Not necessary
Author information and reprints: Payment: None.
　Is simultaneous submission of article to other journals permitted: Yes
　Exclusive manuscript rights between acceptance and publication: No
　Copyright: Held by author.
　Reprints: Available at cost
Additional information: Any of the generally recognized methods for footnoting and for listing sources used is acceptable. Black and white photos and line drawings are accepted; color photos are not.
Disposition of manuscript:
　Query letter: No
　Receipt of manuscript acknowledged: Yes
　Decision to publish in: 2 weeks
　Accepted manuscript published in: 4 to 8 weeks
　Rejected manuscript returned: Yes
　Rejected manuscript criticized: Sometimes
Submit to:
　Editor
　(See address above)

SPECIAL STIPULATIONS

Librarians in adjacent provinces and states are invited to submit theoretical articles of general interest; also articles in other disciplines providing their articles relate in some way to librarianship.

LIBRARY HISTORY [284]

Journal of the Library History Group of the Library Association
Library Association
7 Ridgemount Street
London WC1E 7AE, England

First published in 1967

SUBSCRIPTION DATA

Issues and rates: Published semi-annually.
　Average paid circulation: 400; 1,500 controlled
　Annual rate(s): Pan-Am $5.00
Publisher or Sponsor: Library Association, Library History Group
Managing Editor: Peter A. Hoare

EDITORIAL DESCRIPTION

Contains scholarly articles on the history of libraries, librarianship, and book-collecting; surveys of recent publications and research are regular features
Articles per average issue: 1-2
Audience: Librarians, book-collectors, historians
Manuscripts accepted in English

MANUSCRIPT INFORMATION

Subject field(s): Primarily European and British Isles in scope, but wider fields are not excluded. No period limitations.
Manuscript requirements: See latest issue for style requirements.
　Preferred length: Under 10,000 words
　Number of copies to be submitted: 2
　Abstract: Not necessary.
Author information and reprints: Payment: Reprints only.
　Is simultaneous submission of article to other journals permitted: Permitted, with notification of the editor
　Exclusive manuscript rights between acceptance and publication: Yes
　Copyright: Held jointly by the author and the Library History Group
Disposition of manuscript:
　Query letter: Not necessary, but advisable.
　Receipt of manuscript acknowledged: Yes
　Decision to publish in: Varies
　Accepted manuscript published in: Varies
　Rejected manuscript returned: Yes, with return postage paid by publication.
　Rejected manuscript criticized: Sometimes
Submit to:
　Peter A. Hoare
　Editor
　Glasgow University
　Hillhead Street
　Glasgow G12 0E, Scotland
　(041) 334-2122

LIBRARY JOURNAL [285]

1180 Avenue of the Americas
New York, New York 10036
(212) 581-8800

First published in 1876

SUBSCRIPTION DATA

Issues and rates: Published semi-monthly.
　Average paid circulation: 40,000
　Annual rate(s): $16.20
Publisher or Sponsor: American Library Association

EDITORIAL DESCRIPTION

A multi-purpose journal which contains articles on all aspects of librarianship and extensive reviews.
Articles per average issue: Varies
Audience: Professional librarians
Manuscripts accepted in English

MANUSCRIPT INFORMATION

Subject field(s): Librarianship, information storage and retrieval, bibliographic essays on current literature and other subjects, censorship
Manuscript requirements: Chicago, Turabian for bibliographic style; prefer minimum footnotes.
　Preferred length: 2,000 words
　Number of copies to be submitted: Two
　Abstract: No
Author information and reprints: Payment: By publication to author. $25- $300 per article. Depending on nature of contribution.
　Is simultaneous submission of article to other journals permitted: No
　Exclusive manuscript rights between acceptance and publication: Yes
　Copyright: Held by publication.
　Reprints: Not available.
Additional information: Double-space typescript with wide margins
Disposition of manuscript:
　Query letter: No
　Receipt of manuscript acknowledged: Yes
　Decision to publish in: 1-4 months
　Accepted manuscript published in: Varies
　Rejected manuscript returned: Yes
Submit to:
　John N. Berry III
　Editor
　(See address above)
　(212) 764-5175

LIBRARY OCCURRENT [286]

Indiana State Library
140 North Senate
Indianapolis, Indiana 46204
(317) 633-5620

First published in 1906

SUBSCRIPTION DATA

Issues and rates: Published quarterly.
　Average paid circulation: 3475 controlled
Publisher or Sponsor: Indiana State Library
Managing Editor: Mary Jeanette Smith

EDITORIAL DESCRIPTION

Contains articles primarily of interest to Indiana librarians and trustees; lists of library science books, books on and about Indiana, reference works and documents.
Articles per average issue: 3
Audience: Librarians, students in library science
Manuscripts accepted in English

MANUSCRIPT INFORMATION

Subject field(s): Librarianship, library-related, book-related
Manuscript requirements: See latest issue for style requirements.
　Preferred length: 2500-3000 words
　Number of copies to be submitted: Two
　Abstract: No
Author information and reprints: Payment: None.
　Is simultaneous submission of article to other journals permitted: No
　Exclusive manuscript rights between acceptance and publication: No
　Copyright: Held by publication.
　Reprints: Available, cost varies

Additional information: Prefer footnotes at end of article.
Disposition of manuscript:
  Query letter: Not necessary, but advisable.
  Receipt of manuscript acknowledged: Yes
  Decision to publish in: 2-4 weeks
  Accepted manuscript published in: Varies considerably
  Rejected manuscript returned: Yes
  Rejected manuscript criticized: If requested.
Submit to:
  Mary Jeanette Smith
  Publications Editor
  (See address above)

LIBRARY QUARTERLY [287]
Uiversity of Chicago Press
5801 Ellis Avenue
Chicago, Illinois 60637
(312) 753-2591

First published in 1931

SUBSCRIPTION DATA
Issues and rates: Published quarterly.
  Average paid circulation: 4,000
  Annual rate(s): $10.00; Foreign $11.00; Institutions $14.00; Foreign institutions $15.00
Managing Editor: Howard W. Winger

EDITORIAL DESCRIPTION
  A channel for the publication of library research
Articles per average issue: 4
Audience: Professional librarians, professors of librarianship
  Manuscripts accepted in English only

MANUSCRIPT INFORMATION
Subject field(s): Objective and thorough treatment of any problem of general importance to librarianship
Manuscript requirements: See latest issue for style requirements.
  Preferred length: 1,200-1,500 words; 8 pages
  Number of copies to be submitted: 2
  Abstract: Yes. One or two paragraphs to identify the scope of the article as well as a brief biography.
Author information and reprints: Payment: Reprints only. 3 copies upon publication and 100-250 reprints
  Is simultaneous submission of article to other journals permitted: Permitted, but not encouraged.
  Exclusive manuscript rights between acceptance and publication: Yes
  Copyright: Held by author.
  Reprints: Available at cost. $10.00 per page.
Additional information: Bibliographies are appreciated. Headings for the individual sections in articles are requested as well as black and white photographs.
Disposition of manuscript:
  Query letter: Not necessary.
  Receipt of manuscript acknowledged: Yes
  Decision to publish in: 1 week
  Accepted manuscript published in: 1 month
  Rejected manuscript returned: Yes, if return postage is supplied by author.
  Rejected manuscript criticized: Sometimes
Submit to:
  John T. Corrigan
  Editor
  (See address above)

LIBRARY RESOURCES & TECHNICAL SERVICES [288]
American Library Association
50 East Huron Street
Chicago, Illinois 60611
(312) 944-6780 ext. 228

First published in 1957

SUBSCRIPTION DATA
Issues and rates: Published quarterly.
  Average paid circulation: 10,000
  Annual rate(s): $15.00
Publisher or Sponsor: American Library Association, Resources and Technical Services Division

EDITORIAL DESCRIPTION
  Contains articles of interest to personnel in library technical services departments and to administrators.
Articles per average issue: 6-8
Audience: Librarians in technical services
  Manuscripts accepted in English

MANUSCRIPT INFORMATION
Subject field(s): Library technical services, library cataloging and classification, library reproduction, preservation of materials, library resources and acquisitions, serial publications in libraries
Manuscript requirements: Chicago
  Number of copies to be submitted: Two
  Abstract: Yes; An abstract of 75-100 words with the name and affiliation of the author.
Author information and reprints: Payment: None.
  Is simultaneous submission of article to other journals permitted: No
  Copyright: Not copyrighted
  Reprints: Available, cost varies with length
Disposition of manuscript:
  Query letter: No
  Receipt of manuscript acknowledged: Yes
  Decision to publish in: Several months
  Accepted manuscript published in: Several months
  Rejected manuscript returned: Yes
  Rejected manuscript criticized: Sometimes
Submit to:
  Wesley Simonton
  Editor
  Library School
  University of Minnesota
  Minneapolis, Minnesota 55455
  (612) 373-5254

MEDIA: LIBRARY SERVICES JOURNAL [289]
127 Ninth Avenue North
Nashville, Tennessee 37234
(615) 254-5461 ext. 471

Previously entitled *Church Library Magazine*

First published in 1960

SUBSCRIPTION DATA
Issues and rates: Published quarterly.
  Average paid circulation: 16,200
  Annual rate(s): $2.75
Publisher or Sponsor: Southern Baptist Convention, Sunday School Board
Managing Editor: Wayne E. Todd

EDITORIAL DESCRIPTION
  Provides administrative assistance to church library workers.
Articles per average issue: 25
Audience: Church library workers
  Manuscripts accepted in English

MANUSCRIPT INFORMATION
Subject field(s): Administration, promotion
Manuscript requirements: See latest issue for style requirements.
  Preferred length: 650 words
  Number of copies to be submitted: One
  Abstract: No
Author information and reprints: Payment: By publication to author. $.025 per word.
  Is simultaneous submission of article to other journals permitted: No
  Exclusive manuscript rights between acceptance and publication: Yes
  Copyright: Held by the Sunday School Board of the Southern Baptist Convention
  Reprints: Not available.
Additional information: Type 55 characters per line, double-spaced.
Disposition of manuscript:
  Query letter: No
  Receipt of manuscript acknowledged: Yes
  Decision to publish in: 1 month
  Accepted manuscript published in: 9-12 months
  Rejected manuscript returned: Yes
  Rejected manuscript criticized: No
Submit to:
  Wanda C. Lineberry
  Assistant Editor
  (See address above)

MEDICAL LIBRARY ASSOCIATION BULLETIN [290]
Medical Library Association, Suite 3208
919 North Michigan Avenue
Chicago, Illinois 60611
(312) 266-2456

First published in 1911

SUBSCRIPTION DATA
Issues and rates: Published quarterly.
  Average paid circulation: 4,184

Annual rate(s): $20.00; Members $30.00; Foreign individuals $20.00; Foreign institutions $50.00
Publisher or Sponsor: Medical Library Association
Managing Editor: John S. LoSasso

EDITORIAL DESCRIPTION

Contains contributions of value to medical bibliography, medical librarianship, and the history of medical books, libraries, and librarians
Articles per average issue: 15
Audience: Professionals
Manuscripts accepted in English

MANUSCRIPT INFORMATION

Subject field(s): Health sciences librarianship, health sciences bibliography
Manuscript requirements: Chicago
  Preferred length: 25 pages maximum
  Number of copies to be submitted: 3
  Abstract: An abstract, not exceeding 150 words, stating the paper's major points rather than merely indicating topics discussed.
Author information and reprints: Payment: None.
  Is simultaneous submission of article to other journals permitted: Not permitted.
  Exclusive manuscript rights between acceptance and publication: Yes
  Copyright: Held by the Association
  Reprints: Available at cost.
Disposition of manuscript:
  Query letter: Not necessary.
  Receipt of manuscript acknowledged: Yes
  Decision to publish in: 6 weeks
  Accepted manuscript published in: 6-7 months
  Rejected manuscript returned: Yes, with return postage paid by publication.
  Rejected manuscript criticized: Yes
Submit to:
  Robert Lewis
  Biomedical Library
  University of California, San Diego
  La Jolla, California 92037
  (714) 452-3245

THE MICHIGAN LIBRARIAN [291]
226 West Washtenaw
Lansing, Michigan 48933
(517) 484-7274

First published in 1934

SUBSCRIPTION DATA

Issues and rates: Published quarterly.
  Average paid circulation: 2,100
  Annual rate(s): $6.00; Members $4.00
Publisher or Sponsor: Michigan Library Association
Managing Editor: Frances H. Pletz

EDITORIAL DESCRIPTION

To provide a continuing education to the membership of the Michigan Library Association in the form of articles and membership news of current interest to them.
Articles per average issue: 5

Audience: Librarians, trustees and friends
Manuscripts accepted in English

MANUSCRIPT INFORMATION

Subject field(s): Any current library-associated problems or programs
Manuscript requirements: No specific style guide.
  Preferred length: 4 pages
  Number of copies to be submitted: 1
  Abstract: Not necessary.
Author information and reprints: Payment: None.
  Is simultaneous submission of article to other journals permitted: Permitted.
  Exclusive manuscript rights between acceptance and publication: No
  Reprints: Available at cost.
Additional information: Manuscripts must be typewritten double-spaced, 72 letters to the line
Disposition of manuscript:
  Query letter: Not necessary, but advisable.
  Receipt of manuscript acknowledged: No
  Decision to publish in: 6 months
  Accepted manuscript published in: 9 months
  Rejected manuscript returned: Yes, if return postage is supplied by author.
  Rejected manuscript criticized: Sometimes
Submit to:
  Frances H. Pletz
  Editor
  (See address above)

MICROFORM REVIEW [292]
Box 1297
Weston, Connecticut 06880
(203) 227-2229

First published in 1972

SUBSCRIPTION DATA

Issues and rates: Published quarterly.
Managing Editor: Allen B. Veaner

EDITORIAL DESCRIPTION

Provides a review medium for microforms published for the academic and scholarly community, especially libraries. Seeks reviews of all published microforms regardless of subject. Orientation is that of the consumer of the finished product.
Audience: Librarians, book selection officers, micropublishers
Manuscripts accepted in English

MANUSCRIPT INFORMATION

Subject field(s): Microform Review seeks reviews of the Form of the material, quite independently of the subject. Reviewed are materials on roll film, fiche, ultrafiche, and all other formats. Micropublished material can include books, journals, manuscripts, facsimiles, photographs—anything representable on microforms.
Manuscript requirements: Style sheet sent on request.
  Preferred length: No preference
  Number of copies to be submitted: Two

  Abstract: Yes. For articles only.
Author information and reprints: Payment: None.
Additional information: Preference is shown for articles written clearly, grammatically, and with good syntax. Only in the case of exceptionally cogent content will the editor substantially rewrite a poorly written article.
Disposition of manuscript:
  Query letter: Not necessary.
  Decision to publish in: 1-2 months
  Rejected manuscript criticized: Sometimes
Submit to:
  Alan M. Meckler;
  Allen B. Veaner
  Publisher, Editor-in-Chief, respectively
  (See address above)

SPECIAL STIPULATIONS

Articles of a promotional character prepared by commercial organizations mainly to assist in the marketing of specific products or publishing ventures are generally not accepted. However, factual articles or controversial articles from commercial organizations are welcomed. It is the practice of Microform Review to invite additional views on controversial subjects.

MISSOURI LIBRARY ASSOCIATION NEWSLETTER [293]
Missouri Library Association Executive Office
403 South Sixth Street
Columbia, Missouri 65201
(314) 449-4627

Previously entitled *MLA Quarterly*

First published in 1971

SUBSCRIPTION DATA

Issues and rates: Published bi-monthly.
  Average paid circulation: 1,000
  Annual rate(s): $3.00; Foreign $3.00; Institutions $3.00; Students Free; Foreign individuals $3.00; Foreign institutions $3.00
Publisher or Sponsor: Missouri Library Association
Managing Editor: Marilyn H. Lake

EDITORIAL DESCRIPTION

All and any material relevant to libraries and the profession of library science are considered.
Audience: Librarians, staff, trustees of libraries, and general citizens
Manuscripts accepted in English

MANUSCRIPT INFORMATION

Subject field(s): All library related matters
Manuscript requirements: No specific style guide.
  Preferred length: 2 pages
  Number of copies to be submitted: 1
  Abstract: Not necessary.

Author information and reprints: Payment: None.
  Is simultaneous submission of article to other journals permitted: Permitted if other publication is not copyrighted
  Exclusive manuscript rights between acceptance and publication: No
  Reprints: Available at cost.
Disposition of manuscript:
  Query letter: Not necessary.
  Receipt of manuscript acknowledged: Yes
  Decision to publish in: 4 weeks
  Accepted manuscript published in: 8 weeks
  Rejected manuscript returned: Yes, with return postage paid by publication.
  Rejected manuscript criticized: Reasons for rejections only
Submit to:
  Marilyn H. Lake
  Editor-in-Chief
  (See address above)

MOUNTAIN-PLAINS LIBRARY QUARTERLY [294]
106 South 55th Street
Omaha, Nebraska 68132
(402) 556-5793

First published in 1956

SUBSCRIPTION DATA

Issues and rates: Published quarterly.
  Average paid circulation: 900
  Annual rate(s): $8.00
Publisher or Sponsor: Mountain Plains Library Association

EDITORIAL DESCRIPTION

  Contains articles, short stories, poetry, book reviews, cartoons, items of interests, editorial.
Articles per average issue: 3
Audience: Professional librarians and interested laymen
  Manuscripts accepted in English

MANUSCRIPT INFORMATION

Subject field(s): Librarianship, library science, literary-bibliographic
Manuscript requirements: See latest issue for style requirements.
  Preferred length: None
  Number of copies to be submitted: One
Author information and reprints: Payment: None.
  Is simultaneous submission of article to other journals permitted: No
  Exclusive manuscript rights between acceptance and publication: Yes
  Copyright: Held by author.
  Reprints: Available, minimal cost
Additional information: Mainly concerned with the states of North and South Dakota, Nebraska, Kansas, Wyoming, Colorado, Nevada, and Utah.
Disposition of manuscript:
  Receipt of manuscript acknowledged: Yes
  Decision to publish in: Three weeks
  Accepted manuscript published in: Four weeks
  Rejected manuscript returned: Yes, if return postage is supplied by author.

  Rejected manuscript criticized: Yes
Submit to:
  John M. Christ
  Editor-in-Chief
  (See address above)
  (402) 553-4700 ext. 640

NEBRASKA LIBRARY ASSOCIATION QUARTERLY [295]
3420 South 37th Street
Lincoln, Nebraska 68506
(802) 488-2712

First published in 1970

SUBSCRIPTION DATA

Issues and rates: Published quarterly.
  Average paid circulation: 50; 700 controlled
  Annual rate(s): $5.00
Publisher or Sponsor: Nebraska Library Association

EDITORIAL DESCRIPTION

  Contains reports of committees, sections and officers, articles by librarians; news items, etc.
Articles per average issue: 5
Audience: Librarians
  Manuscripts accepted in English

MANUSCRIPT INFORMATION

Manuscript requirements: See latest issue for style requirements.
  Preferred length: 2-3 pages
  Number of copies to be submitted: One
  Abstract: No
Author information and reprints: Payment: None.
  Is simultaneous submission of article to other journals permitted: Yes
  Exclusive manuscript rights between acceptance and publication: No
  Reprints: Not available.
Disposition of manuscript:
  Query letter: No
  Receipt of manuscript acknowledged: No
  Rejected manuscript returned: Yes, if return postage is supplied by author.
  Rejected manuscript criticized: No
Submit to:
  Louise B. Shelledy
  Executive Secretary and Editor
  (See address above)

NETWORK INTERNATIONAL COMMUNICATIONS IN LIBRARY AUTOMATION [296]
P. O. Box 27235
1024 Vista Del Cerro
Tempe, Arizona 85282
(602) 968-2023

First published in 1974

SUBSCRIPTION DATA

Issues and rates: Published monthly.

  Annual rate(s): $24.00; Foreign $26.00; Individuals $24.00; Students $24.00; Members Free; Foreign individuals $26.00
Publisher or Sponsor: The Association for Library Automation Research Communications (LARC)
Managing Editor: Allen Pratt

EDITORIAL DESCRIPTION

  A link in the LARC effort to establish a World Information System for Library Automation Developments (WISLAD). The editorial policies of Network are controlled by a panel of prominent librarians and systems scientists from both eastern and western countries. An international corps of editors and correspondents forms the nucleus of the editorial staff, covering the entire scope of library automation activities.
Articles per average issue: 4
Audience: Library and Information Scientists
  Manuscripts accepted in English

MANUSCRIPT INFORMATION

Subject field(s): Worldwide information in the field of Library Automation and related developments.
Manuscript requirements: No specific style guide.
  Preferred length: Maximum 600 words; 3 pages
  Abstract: Not necessary.
Author information and reprints: Payment: None.
  Is simultaneous submission of article to other journals permitted: Permitted, but not encouraged.
  Exclusive manuscript rights between acceptance and publication: Yes
  Copyright: Held by publication.
  Reprints: Not available.
Disposition of manuscript:
  Query letter: Not necessary, but advisable.
  Receipt of manuscript acknowledged: Yes
  Decision to publish in: 6 weeks
  Accepted manuscript published in: 90 days
  Rejected manuscript returned: Yes, with return postage paid by publication.
Submit to:
  Allan Pratt
  Managing Editor
  Graduate Library School
  Indiana University
  Bloomington, Indiana 47401

NEW YORK PUBLIC LIBRARY. BULLETIN [297]
Readex Books
101 Fifth Avenue
New York, New York 10003

First published in 1897

SUBSCRIPTION DATA

Issues and rates: Published quarterly.
  Average paid circulation: 2,150
  Annual rate(s): $7.50

Publisher or Sponsor: New York Public Library
Managing Editor: William L. Coakley

EDITORIAL DESCRIPTION

Open to original critical study of anything in, about, or in back of books and manuscripts; any useful bibliographical tools for such study. Especially welcome are studies of new or neglected material in the New York Public Library.
Articles per average issue: 4
Audience: Scholarly, general
Manuscripts accepted in English

MANUSCRIPT INFORMATION

Subject field(s): American publishing history, American history and literature, certain fields of English literature, theatre, dance, music, the Near and Far East
Manuscript requirements: Style sheet sent on request.
Preferred length: None
Number of copies to be submitted: One
Author information and reprints: Payment: Reprints only. 4 copies of issue
Is simultaneous submission of article to other journals permitted: No
Exclusive manuscript rights between acceptance and publication: Yes
Copyright: Held by publication.
Reprints: Available, cost based on length.
Disposition of manuscript:
Query letter: Not necessary, but advisable.
Receipt of manuscript acknowledged: Yes
Decision to publish in: 3 months
Accepted manuscript published in: 6-24 months
Rejected manuscript returned: Yes
Rejected manuscript criticized: Yes
Submit to:
David V. Erdman
Editor
New York Public Library
Fifth Avenue and 42nd Street
New York, New York 10018

NEWSLETTER ON INTELLECTUAL FREEDOM [298]
American Library Association
50 East Huron Street
Chicago Illinois 60611
(312) 944-6780

First published in 1952

SUBSCRIPTION DATA

Issues and rates: Published bi-monthly.
Average paid circulation: 3,000
Annual rate(s): $6.00
Publisher or Sponsor: American Library Association
Managing Editor: Judith F. Krug

EDITORIAL DESCRIPTION

Devoted to freedom of speech and the press.
Articles per average issue: 2
Audience: Librarians, teachers, publishers
Manuscripts accepted in English

MANUSCRIPT INFORMATION

Subject field(s): First Amendment history, First Amendment rights (of reporters, teachers, students, prisoners, et al.), censorship
Manuscript requirements: Chicago
Preferred length: 15 pages
Number of copies to be submitted: 2
Abstract: Not necessary.
Author information and reprints: Payment: Reprints only. 10
Is simultaneous submission of article to other journals permitted: Permitted, but not encouraged.
Exclusive manuscript rights between acceptance and publication: Yes
Copyright: Held by author.
Reprints: Available at no cost. 10
Disposition of manuscript:
Query letter: Not necessary.
Receipt of manuscript acknowledged: Yes
Decision to publish in: 2-4 weeks
Accepted manuscript published in: 2-4 months
Rejected manuscript returned: Yes, if return postage is supplied by author.
Rejected manuscript criticized: Sometimes
Submit to:
Judith F. Krug
Editor
(See address above)

THE NORTH COUNTRY LIBRARIAN [299]
The Journal of the Minnesota Library Association
319 15th Avenue Southeast
Minneapolis, Minnesota 55455
(612) 333-9123

Previously entitled *Lakeland Librarian; Bulletin of the Minnesota Library Association*

First published in 1952

SUBSCRIPTION DATA

Issues and rates: Published quarterly.
Average paid circulation: 1,500
Annual rate(s): $2.00
Publisher or Sponsor: Minnesota Library Association

EDITORIAL DESCRIPTION

Coverage of Minesota Library Association activities primarily; also library activities around the state of Minnesota. Includes general and research-type articles of interest to librarians and trustees.

MANUSCRIPT INFORMATION

Subject field(s): Library science
Manuscript requirements: See latest issue for style requirements.
Preferred length: 300 to 600 words; 1 to 2 pages
Number of copies to be submitted: Two

Author information and reprints: Payment: None.
Is simultaneous submission of article to other journals permitted: Not to national publications or those in this area.
Exclusive manuscript rights between acceptance and publication: No
Copyright: Not copyrighted
Reprints: Available at cost of duplication and mailing
Disposition of manuscript:
Receipt of manuscript acknowledged: Yes
Decision to publish in: One month
Accepted manuscript published in: 3 months
Rejected manuscript returned: Yes, if self-addressed, stamped envelope is sent with manuscript.
Rejected manuscript criticized: No
Submit to:
Judith Overmier
Editor
(See address above)

NOTES [301]
Quarterly Journal of the Music Library Association
Room 205
343 South Main Street
Ann Arbor, Michigan 48108
(313) 761-6350

First published in 1934

SUBSCRIPTION DATA

Issues and rates: Published quarterly.
Average paid circulation: 3,000; 3,950 controlled
Annual rate(s): $10.00; Foreign $11.00; Institutions $15.00; Students $4.50; Members $12.00; Foreign institutions $16.00
Publisher or Sponsor: Music Library Association, Inc.

EDITORIAL DESCRIPTION

Renders as comprehensive a report on new music materials as possible; contains articles, book reviews, indexes
Articles per average issue: 4 articles
Audience: Librarians, musicologists, bibliographers, discographers
Manuscripts accepted in English

MANUSCRIPT INFORMATION

Subject field(s): Music bibliography, music library problems, technical programs, histories of music librarianship, library-related articles in music history
Manuscript requirements: See latest issue for style requirements. Chicago
Preferred length: None
Number of copies to be submitted: 1
Abstract: Not necessary.
Author information and reprints: Payment: None.
Is simultaneous submission of article to other journals permitted: Not permitted.
Exclusive manuscript rights between acceptance and publication: Yes
Copyright: Held by publication.
Reprints: Available at cost.

PNLA QUARTERLY [305]
Southern Oregon College Library
Ashland, Oregon 97520
(502) 482-6445

First published in 1936

SUBSCRIPTION DATA
Issues and rates: Published quarterly.
  Average paid circulation: 1,425
  Annual rate(s): $5.00; Foreign $5.50;
  Individuals $5.00; Institutions $5.00;
  Students $5.00; Members Free; Foreign
  individuals $5.50; Foreign institutions
  $5.50

Publisher or Sponsor: Pacific Northwest
  Library Association
Managing Editor: Richard E. Moore

EDITORIAL DESCRIPTION
  Library topics relating to northwest
  libraries
Articles per average issue: 3
Audience: Northwest librarians
  Manuscripts accepted in English

MANUSCRIPT INFORMATION
Subject field(s): Contemporary and historical
  problems affecting libraries in Oregon,
  Washington, Idaho, Montana, Alaska
  and British Columbia
Manuscript requirements: No specific style
  guide.
  Preferred length: 3,000 words or less
  Number of copies to be submitted: 1
  Abstract: Not necessary.
Author information and reprints: Payment:
  None.
  Is simultaneous submission of article to
  other journals permitted: Permitted, but
  not encouraged.
  Exclusive manuscript rights between
  acceptance and publication: Yes
  Copyright: Held by author.
  Reprints: Not available.
Disposition of manuscript:
  Query letter: Not necessary.
  Receipt of manuscript acknowledged: Yes
  Decision to publish in: 1 month
  Accepted manuscript published in: 6
  months
  Rejected manuscript returned: Yes, with
  return postage paid by publication.
  Rejected manuscript criticized:
  Sometimes
Submit to:
  Richard E. Moore
  Editor and Business Manager
  (See address above)

THE PRIVATE LIBRARY [306]
37, Lombardy Drive
Berkhamsted, Hertfordshire, England
5819

First published in 1957

SUBSCRIPTION DATA
Issues and rates: Published quarterly.
  Average paid circulation: 1,400; 50
  controlled
  Annual rate(s): $13.00
Publisher or Sponsor: The Private Libraries
  Association

EDITORIAL DESCRIPTION
  Contains articles on all aspects of book
  collecting, private presses, bookplates.
Articles per average issue: 5
Audience: Book collectors, libraries
  Manuscripts accepted in English

MANUSCRIPT INFORMATION
Subject field(s): Book illustrations,
  collections, private presses, bookplates,
  libraries
Manuscript requirements: See latest issue for
  style requirements.
  Preferred length: 2000-4000 words
  Number of copies to be submitted: One
  Abstract: No
Author information and reprints: Payment:
  Reprints only.
  Is simultaneous submission of article to
  other journals permitted: No
  Exclusive manuscript rights between
  acceptance and publication: Yes
  Copyright: Held by author.
  Reprints: Not available.
Additional information: Manuscript should
  be typewritten, double-spaced.
Disposition of manuscript:
  Query letter: Not necessary, but
  advisable.
  Receipt of manuscript acknowledged: Yes
  Decision to publish in: One month
  Accepted manuscript published in: Six
  months
  Rejected manuscript returned: Yes, if
  return postage is supplied by author.
  Rejected manuscript criticized: No
Submit to:
  John Cotton
  Editor
  (See address above)

PROOF [307]
The Yearbook of American Bibliographical
and Textual Studies
Editorial Offices
University of South Carolina
Columbia, South Carolina 29208
(803) 777-4843

First published in 1971

SUBSCRIPTION DATA
Issues and rates: Published annually.
  Annual rate(s): $20

EDITORIAL DESCRIPTION
  Publishes articles on books and
  manuscripts and their contributions to
  American culture. Concerned with works
  by Americans published here and abroad,
  and with foreign works published in
  America. Emphasizes essays on the
  theory and practice of bibliography and
  textual criticism, and on printing,
  publishing, and bookselling history.
Articles per average issue: 12-16
  Manuscripts accepted in English

MANUSCRIPT INFORMATION
Subject field(s): Textual studies,
  bibliography, American literature, films,
  history, librarianship, publishing,
  journalism, music
Manuscript requirements: See latest issue for
  style requirements. MLA
  Preferred length: None
  Number of copies to be submitted: One
  Abstract: Yes
Author information and reprints: Payment:
  Reprints only. 2 copies of issue
  Is simultaneous submission of article to
  other journals permitted: No
  Exclusive manuscript rights between
  acceptance and publication: Yes
  Copyright: Held by publication.
  Reprints: Available, cost depends on
  length.
Additional information: Manuscripts should
  be in proper style, with footnotes on
  separate pages. All text matter and
  footnotes must be double-spaced.
Disposition of manuscript:
  Query letter: No
  Receipt of manuscript acknowledged: Yes
  Decision to publish in: 3 months
  Rejected manuscript returned: Yes, if
  return postage is supplied by author.
  Rejected manuscript criticized: No
Submit to:
  Joseph Katz
  Editor
  (See address above)

SPECIAL STIPULATIONS
  Deadline for current issue is May 30 of
  each year.

RQ [308]
American Library Association
Reference and Adult Services Division
50 East Huron Street
Chicago, Illinois 60611
(312) 944-6780 ext. 293

First published in 1960

SUBSCRIPTION DATA
Issues and rates: Published quarterly.
  Average paid circulation: 9500 controlled
Publisher or Sponsor: American Library
  Association, Reference and Adult
  Services

EDITORIAL DESCRIPTION
  Purpose is to disseminate materials of
  interest to reference librarians,
  bibliographers, adult services librarians,
  and others interested in user-oriented
  library services.
Articles per average issue: 5-10
Audience: Membership
  Manuscripts accepted in English

MANUSCRIPT INFORMATION
Subject field(s): Reference services in
  libraries, services to adults in libraries
Manuscript requirements: Style sheet sent
  on request.

Additional information: See "Directions to Contributors" in each issue.
Disposition of manuscript:
Query letter: Not necessary.
Receipt of manuscript acknowledged: Yes
Decision to publish in: 6-8 weeks
Accepted manuscript published in: 6-8 months
Rejected manuscript returned: Yes, with return postage paid by publication.
Rejected manuscript criticized: Sometimes
Submit to:
James W. Pruett
Editor
Music Library, Hill Hall
University of North Carolina
Chapel Hill, North Carolina 27514
(919) 933-1030

OCCASIONAL PAPERS [302]
249 Armory Building
University of Illinois
Graduate School of Library Science
Champaign, Illinois 61820
(217) 333-1359

SUBSCRIPTION DATA
Issues and rates: Irregular
Average paid circulation: 800
Annual rate(s): Individuals $5.00
Publisher or Sponsor: University of Illinois, Graduate School of Library Science

EDITORIAL DESCRIPTION
These papers deal with any aspect of librarianship and consist of manuscripts which are too long or too detailed for publication in a library periodical or which are of temporary or specialized interest.
Articles per average issue: 6
Audience: Librarians
Manuscripts accepted in English only

MANUSCRIPT INFORMATION
Subject field(s): Any field of librarianship
Manuscript requirements: Style sheet sent on request.
Preferred length: 20-100 pages
Number of copies to be submitted: One
Author information and reprints: Payment: 12 free copies
Is simultaneous submission of article to other journals permitted: No
Exclusive manuscript rights between acceptance and publication: Yes
Copyright: Not copyrighted
Reprints: Available

Disposition of manuscript:
Query letter: No
Receipt of manuscript acknowledged: Yes
Decision to publish in: 6 weeks
Accepted manuscript published in: 6 months

Rejected manuscript returned: Yes
Rejected manuscript criticized: Yes
Submit to:
Herbert Goldhor
Managing Editor
(See address above)

OHIO LIBRARY ASSOCIATION BULLETIN [303]
Publications Office
40 South Third Street
Columbus, Ohio 43215
(614) 221-9057/8

First published in 1931

SUBSCRIPTION DATA
Issues and rates: Published quarterly.
Average paid circulation: 2,650
Annual rate(s): Individuals $5.00
Publisher or Sponsor: Ohio Library Association
Managing Editor: Robert F. Cayton

EDITORIAL DESCRIPTION
Library oriented, the bulletin publishes articles covering the spectrum of the library world: interviews, solutions to library problems, types of libraries, reports of conferences, book publishing and reviews, special libraries, special services, biographies, bibliographies, automation.
Articles per average issue: 5
Audience: Librarians - college, public, school and special, and those interested in library matters or careers.
Manuscripts accepted in English only

MANUSCRIPT INFORMATION
Subject field(s): All areas of learning are the province of libraries and library journals. The bulletin does not limit itself geographically to Ohio libraries or personnel, but welcomes informative and concisely written articles from other sources.
Manuscript requirements: MLA
Preferred length: 1500-3000 words
Number of copies to be submitted: 1
Abstract: Not necessary.
Author information and reprints: Payment: None.
Is simultaneous submission of article to other journals permitted: Not permitted.
Exclusive manuscript rights between acceptance and publication: Yes
Reprints: Available at cost.
Disposition of manuscript:
Query letter: Not necessary, but advisable.
Receipt of manuscript acknowledged: Yes
Decision to publish in: 1-2 weeks
Accepted manuscript published in: 3-6 months
Rejected manuscript returned: Yes, with return postage paid by publication.

Rejected manuscript criticized: Reasons for rejections only
Submit to:
Robert F. Cayton
Editor
Dawes Memorial Library
Marietta College
Marietta, Ohio 45750
(614) 373-4643

PLA BULLETIN [304]
Pennsylvania Library Association
200 South Craig Street
Pittsburgh, Pennsylvania 15213
(412) 687-6664

First published in 1945

SUBSCRIPTION DATA
Issues and rates: Published bi-monthly.
Average paid circulation: 3,000
Annual rate(s): $5.00
Publisher or Sponsor: Pennsylvania Library Association
Managing Editor: Dr. Mary E. Stillman

EDITORIAL DESCRIPTION
Library service, especially as it relates to Pennsylvania
Articles per average issue: 3
Audience: Pennsylvania librarians
Manuscripts accepted in English

MANUSCRIPT INFORMATION
Subject field(s): Library Science
Manuscript requirements: No specific style guide.
Preferred length: 3-6 pages
Number of copies to be submitted: 1
Abstract: Not necessary.

Author information and reprints: Payment: None.
Is simultaneous submission of article to other journals permitted: Permitted, but not encouraged.
Exclusive manuscript rights between acceptance and publication: No
Copyright: Not copyrighted
Reprints: Available at cost.

Disposition of manuscript:
Query letter: Not necessary.
Receipt of manuscript acknowledged: Yes
Decision to publish in: 30 days
Accepted manuscript published in: 6 months
Rejected manuscript returned: Yes, with return postage paid by publication.
Rejected manuscript criticized: Sometimes

Submit to:
Dr. Mary E. Stillman
Editor
Albright College Library
Reading, Pennsylvania 19604
215-921-2381 x223

Preferred length: 2,000 words
Number of copies to be submitted: One
Abstract: No
Author information and reprints: Payment: None.
Is simultaneous submission of article to other journals permitted: Decided on an individual basis
Exclusive manuscript rights between acceptance and publication: Same as above
Copyright: Not copyrighted
Reprints: Available at cost
Disposition of manuscript:
Query letter: No
Receipt of manuscript acknowledged: Yes
Decision to publish in: Three months
Accepted manuscript published in: Six months
Rejected manuscript returned: Yes
Rejected manuscript criticized: No
Submit to:
Dennis N. Ribbens
Editor
P.O. Box 1847
Lawrence University Library
Appleton, Wisconsin 54911
(414) 739-3681 ext. 264

THE SCHOOL LIBRARIAN [309]
Victoria House
29-31 George Street
Oxford OX1 2AY, England
(0865) 722 746

First published in 1937

SUBSCRIPTION DATA
Issues and rates: Published quarterly.
Average paid circulation: 7,000
Annual rate(s): £6.40; Foreign $20.00 (U.S., Can.)
Publisher or Sponsor: School Library Association

EDITORIAL DESCRIPTION
Contains articles on school libraries: use, administration, book selection, children's authors; book reviews.
Articles per average issue: 4
Audience: Librarians, academic
Manuscripts accepted in English

MANUSCRIPT INFORMATION
Manuscript requirements: See latest issue for style requirements.
Preferred length: 2,500 words
Number of copies to be submitted: 2
Author information and reprints: Payment: By publication to author. By arrangement.
Is simultaneous submission of article to other journals permitted: No
Exclusive manuscript rights between acceptance and publication: Yes
Copyright: Held by author.
Reprints: Available by arrangement
Disposition of manuscript:
Receipt of manuscript acknowledged: Yes
Decision to publish in: 6 weeks
Accepted manuscript published in: 6-9 months
Rejected manuscript returned: Yes
Rejected manuscript criticized: Yes
Submit to:
Norman Furlong
Editor

Submit reviews to:
Margaret Meek
Review Editor

SCHOOL LIBRARY JOURNAL [310]
For Children's, Young Adult, and School Librarians
1180 Avenue of the Americas
New York, New York 10036
(212) 764-5200
Previously entitled *Junior Libraries*

First published in 1954

SUBSCRIPTION DATA
Issues and rates: Monthly, September through May
Average paid circulation: 31,000
Annual rate(s): $10.80, Pan-Am $11.80, Foreign $12.80

EDITORIAL DESCRIPTION
Contains articles of interest to librarians serving children and young people in schools and public libraries.
Articles per average issue: 3
Audience: Librarians in children's and young adult's services
Manuscripts accepted in English

MANUSCRIPT INFORMATION
Manuscript requirements: No specific style guide.
Preferred length: 3,500 words
Author information and reprints: Payment: By publication to author. $100.00 per article.
Is simultaneous submission of article to other journals permitted: No
Exclusive manuscript rights between acceptance and publication: Yes
Copyright: Held by publication.
Reprints: Not available.
Additional information: Manuscripts should be typewritten, double-spaced.
Disposition of manuscript:
Query letter: No
Receipt of manuscript acknowledged: Yes
Decision to publish in: 2 months
Accepted manuscript published in: 2 to 3 months
Rejected manuscript returned: Yes, if return postage is supplied by author.
Rejected manuscript criticized: No
Submit to:
Lillian N. Gerhardt
Editor-in-Chief
(See address above)

SCHOOL MEDIA QUARTERLY* [311]
Journal of the American Association of School Librarians
50 East Huron Street
Chicago, Illinois 60611
(312) 944-6780

SUBSCRIPTION DATA
Issues and rates: Published quarterly.
Average paid circulation: 10,000
Publisher or Sponsor: American Association of School Librarians

EDITORIAL DESCRIPTION
Contains articles which provide practical suggestions to school librarians; articles which report trends in school library service and which help librarians discover new horizons; and scholarly articles which summarize research results or important sources of library information for improved services. Various special columns focus on interests and news.

MANUSCRIPT INFORMATION
Subject field(s): Media program, research, library improvement, evaluation, facilities, intellectual freedom, utilization, technology, curriculum, media personnel, reviews

Manuscript requirements: Chicago
Number of copies to be submitted: Two
Author information and reprints: Payment: None.
Is simultaneous submission of article to other journals permitted: No
Reprints: Available, cost varies with length and order volume
Disposition of manuscript:
Receipt of manuscript acknowledged: Yes
Accepted manuscript published in: Set up by agreement between editor and author
Rejected manuscript returned: Yes
Rejected manuscript criticized: Sometimes
Submit to:
Editor
(See address above)

SOUTH CAROLINA LIBRARIAN [312]
P.O. Box 11322
Columbia, South Carolina 29210

SUBSCRIPTION DATA
Issues and rates: Published semi annually.
Average paid circulation: 1,000
Annual rate(s): $2.00
Publisher or Sponsor: South Carolina Library Association

EDITORIAL DESCRIPTION
Contains articles on books, libraries and librarians in South Carolina.
Articles per average issue: 4
Manuscripts accepted in English only

MANUSCRIPT INFORMATION
Subject field(s): Librarianship, book reviews
Manuscript requirements: No specific style guide.
Preferred length: None
Number of copies to be submitted: Two
Abstract: No
Author information and reprints: Payment: None.

Is simultaneous submission of article to other journals permitted: Yes
Exclusive manuscript rights between acceptance and publication: No
Copyright: Held by author.
Reprints: Not available.
Disposition of manuscript:
Query letter: No
Receipt of manuscript acknowledged: Yes
Decision to publish in: 1 month
Accepted manuscript published in: 3 months
Rejected manuscript returned: Yes, if self-addressed, stamped envelope is sent with manuscript.
Rejected manuscript criticized: No
Submit to:
Lester E. Duncan
Editor
(See address above)

THE SOUTHEASTERN LIBRARIAN [313]
Southeastern Library Association
P.O. Box 987
Tucker, Georgia 30084
(404) 939-5080

First published in 1951

SUBSCRIPTION DATA
Issues and rates: Published quarterly.
Average paid circulation: 3,300
Annual rate(s): $6.00
Publisher or Sponsor: The Southeastern Library Association
Managing Editor: Carl W. Franklin

EDITORIAL DESCRIPTION
Contains articles on librarianship in the southeastern United States; news, notes about people, institutions, events in the region.
Articles per average issue: 4
Audience: Librarians
Manuscripts accepted in English

MANUSCRIPT INFORMATION
Subject field(s): Libraries, librarianship, library education
Manuscript requirements: Chicago
Preferred length: None
Number of copies to be submitted: Two
Abstract: No
Author information and reprints: Payment: None.
Is simultaneous submission of article to other journals permitted: Yes
Exclusive manuscript rights between acceptance and publication: No
Copyright: Not copyrighted
Reprints: Not available.
Additional information: Photographs to accompany articles should be glossy prints, as large or larger than the final reproduction. Art work (graphs, line drawings, etc.) must be black on white and camera-ready.
Disposition of manuscript:
Query letter: No
Receipt of manuscript acknowledged: Yes
Decision to publish in: 2-3 months
Accepted manuscript published in: 2-3 months
Rejected manuscript returned: Yes
Rejected manuscript criticized: Sometimes
Submit to:
H. Joanne Harrar
Editor
University of Georgia Libraries
Athens, Georgia 30601
(404) 542-2716

SPECIAL LIBRARIES [314]
Special Libraries Association
235 Park Avenue South
New York, New York 10003
(212) 777-8136

SUBSCRIPTION DATA
Issues and rates: Monthly, except bi-monthly for May through June
Average paid circulation: 10,000
Annual rate(s): $22.50, Foreign $24.50
Publisher or Sponsor: Special Libraries Association

EDITORIAL DESCRIPTION
Publishes material on all important subject areas, methods and techniques for "putting knowledge to work"; new and developing areas of librarianship, information science and information technology; administration, organization and operation of special libraries and information centers; scholarly reports of research in the field; professional standards, etc.
Articles per average issue: 6-7
Audience: Special librarians and information scientists
Manuscripts accepted in English

MANUSCRIPT INFORMATION
Manuscript requirements: Chicago
Preferred length: 1,000 to 5,000 words; 20 pages
Number of copies to be submitted: One original and three copies
Abstract: Yes; 50-100 words

Author information and reprints: Payment: None.
Is simultaneous submission of article to other journals permitted: No
Exclusive manuscript rights between acceptance and publication: Yes
Copyright: Held by publication.
Reprints: Not available

Disposition of manuscript:
Query letter: No
Receipt of manuscript acknowledged: Yes
Decision to publish in: At least 6 weeks
Accepted manuscript published in: 3-5 months
Rejected manuscript returned: Yes
Rejected manuscript criticized: Sometimes
Submit to:
Janet Dee Bailey
Editor
(See address above)

TENNESSEE LIBRARIAN [315]
P. O. Box 12085
Nashville, Tennessee 37212
(615) 256-1630

First published in 1948

SUBSCRIPTION DATA
Issues and rates: Published quarterly.
Average paid circulation: 1,500
Annual rate(s): $4.00
Publisher or Sponsor: Tennessee Library Association
Managing Editor: Danny R. Hatcher

EDITORIAL DESCRIPTION
To provide a communication and information link between the members of the Tennessee Library Association and a similar link with the national library community.
Articles per average issue: 3 to 4
Audience: Members of the Tennessee Library Association and the Library community in general.
Manuscripts accepted in English

MANUSCRIPT INFORMATION
Subject field(s): Library and Information Science and other areas as they apply to Libraries (i.e. data processing, collecting rare books & manuscripts, etc.)
Manuscript requirements: See latest issue for style requirements.
Preferred length: 1500 to 2000 words
Number of copies to be submitted: 1
Abstract: Not necessary.
Author information and reprints: Payment: None.
Is simultaneous submission of article to other journals permitted: Not permitted.
Exclusive manuscript rights between acceptance and publication: Yes
Copyright: Held by author.
Reprints: Not available.
Disposition of manuscript:
Query letter: Not necessary.
Receipt of manuscript acknowledged: Yes
Decision to publish in: 2-4 weeks
Accepted manuscript published in: 3-6 months
Rejected manuscript returned: Yes, with return postage paid by publication.
Rejected manuscript criticized: Reasons for rejections only
Submit to:
Danny R. Hatcher
Editor
700 16th Avenue South
Nashville, Tennessee 37203
(615) 256-1630

TEXAS LIBRARY JOURNAL [316]
Box 7763, University Station
Austin, Texas 78712
471-1040

Previously entitled *New Notes*

First published in 1924

SUBSCRIPTION DATA

Issues and rates: Published quarterly.
  Average paid circulation: 3200
  Annual rate(s): $8.00
Publisher or Sponsor: Texas Library Association
Managing Editor: Ronald Seeliger

EDITORIAL DESCRIPTION

Publication contains library science articles with a specific interest to Texas librarians.
Articles per average issue: 4
Audience: Librarians and interested laymen
  Manuscripts accepted in English only

MANUSCRIPT INFORMATION

Subject field(s): Library science, bibliography, publishing
Manuscript requirements: See latest issue for style requirements.
  Preferred length: 500-1000 words
  Number of copies to be submitted: One
  Abstract: No

Author information and reprints: Payment: None.
  Is simultaneous submission of article to other journals permitted: No
  Exclusive manuscript rights between acceptance and publication: Yes
  Reprints: Available

Disposition of manuscript:
  Query letter: Preferred
  Receipt of manuscript acknowledged: Yes
  Decision to publish in: 3 weeks
  Accepted manuscript published in: 3 months
  Rejected manuscript returned: Yes
  Rejected manuscript criticized: No
Submit to:
  Mary Pound
  Editor
  (See address above)

TOP OF THE NEWS [317]

American Library Association
50 East Huron Street
Chicago, Illinois 60611
(312) 948-0740

First published in 1941

SUBSCRIPTION DATA

Issues and rates: Published quarterly.
  Annual rate(s): $15.00; Foreign $15.00; Institutions $15.00
Publisher or Sponsor: The American Library Association, Children's and Young Adult's Services Division
Managing Editor: Mary J. Anderson

EDITORIAL DESCRIPTION

Directed toward, and contains articles of interest to those librarians responsible for evaluating, selecting reading and listening materials and planning programs and services for children and young adults in all types of libraries
Articles per average issue: 6
Audience: Librarians
  Manuscripts accepted in English

MANUSCRIPT INFORMATION

Manuscript requirements: Style sheet sent on request.
  Preferred length: None
  Number of copies to be submitted: 1
  Abstract: Not necessary.

Author information and reprints: Payment: None.
  Is simultaneous submission of article to other journals permitted: Permitted, but not encouraged.
  Exclusive manuscript rights between acceptance and publication: Yes
  Copyright: Normally not copyrighted.
  Reprints: Available at cost.

Disposition of manuscript:
  Query letter: Not necessary, but advisable.
  Receipt of manuscript acknowledged: Yes
  Decision to publish in: 2-4 months
  Accepted manuscript published in: 3-8 months

  Rejected manuscript returned: Yes, if return postage is supplied by author.
  Rejected manuscript criticized: Sometimes
Submit to:
  Mary J. Anderson
  CDS/YASD Executive Secretary
  (See address above)

UTAH LIBRARIES [318]

2150 South Second West, Suite 16
Salt Lake City, Utah 84115

First published in 1957

SUBSCRIPTION DATA

Issues and rates: Published semi-annually.
  Annual rate(s): $2.00
Publisher or Sponsor: Utah Library Association

EDITORIAL DESCRIPTION

Deals with ideas, problems, programs, and other matters of philosophical or practical interest to Utah librarians.
Articles per average issue: 5
Audience: Professional
  Manuscripts accepted in English

MANUSCRIPT INFORMATION

Subject field(s): Librarianship and related matters: publishing, writing, information, retrieval, computers, technology, educational media, etc.
Manuscript requirements: MLA
  Preferred length: 1,000-2,500 words
  Number of copies to be submitted: 1
  Abstract: Not necessary.
Author information and reprints: Payment: Reprints only. 2 copies
  Is simultaneous submission of article to other journals permitted: Permitted, but not encouraged.
  Exclusive manuscript rights between acceptance and publication: Yes
  Copyright: Held by publication.
  Reprints: Available at no cost.
Additional information: The use of graphic and other illustrative material is especially encouraged.

Disposition of manuscript:
  Query letter: Not necessary, but advisable.
  Receipt of manuscript acknowledged: Yes
  Decision to publish in: 2 months
  Accepted manuscript published in: 1-6 months
  Rejected manuscript returned: Yes, with return postage paid by publication.
  Rejected manuscript criticized: Yes
Submit to:
  Blaine H. Hall
  Editor
  Brigham Young University
  505B HBLL
  Provo, Utah 84601

VERMONT LIBRARIES [319]

Vermont Department of Libraries
111 State Street
Montpelier, Vermont 05602
(802) 828-3261
Previously entitled *Vermont Library Association Bulletin*

First published in 1970

SUBSCRIPTION DATA

Issues and rates: Published bi-monthly.
  Average paid circulation: 1,750 controlled
  Annual rate(s): No charge
Publisher or Sponsor: Vermont Department of Libraries Vermont Library Association, Vermont Library Trustees Association

EDITORIAL DESCRIPTION

Contains library and library-related news of particular interest to Vermont librarians and library trustees.
Articles per average issue: 2
  Manuscripts accepted in English only

MANUSCRIPT INFORMATION

Subject field(s): Vermont library news, issue/topic applicable to Vermont libraries, librarianship generally
Manuscript requirements: No specific style guide.
  Preferred length: 3-8 pages
  Number of copies to be submitted: One
  Abstract: No

Author information and reprints: Payment: None.
  Is simultaneous submission of article to other journals permitted: Yes, as long as editor is so informed.
  Exclusive manuscript rights between acceptance and publication: No
  Copyright: Not copyrighted
  Reprints: Available at no cost
Additional information: manuscripts should be typewritten, double-spaced.
Disposition of manuscript:
  Query letter: No
  Receipt of manuscript acknowledged: Yes
  Decision to publish in: 1-8 weeks

Accepted manuscript published in: 2-4 months
Rejected manuscript returned: Yes
Rejected manuscript criticized: Yes
Submit to:
Henry O. Marcy
Editor
(See address above)

WILSON LIBRARY BULLETIN [320]
950 University Avenue
Bronx, New York 10452
(212) 588-8400

First published in 1914

SUBSCRIPTION DATA
Issues and rates: Published monthly.
Average paid circulation: 33,000
Annual rate(s): $11.00; Foreign $13.00; Individuals $11.00

EDITORIAL DESCRIPTION
To provide "indispensable matter for the library-minded." Since the modern library provides information and aids to recreation in a wide variety of format—films, filmstrips, recordings, tapes, art prints, realia, pamphlets, newspapers, periodicals, and books; review columns are inclusive. Articles are theoretical, practical, or both.
Articles per average issue: 6
Audience: Librarians, publishers, book sellers
Manuscripts accepted in English, except by special arrangement

MANUSCRIPT INFORMATION
Subject field(s): Librarianship, information science, publishing, reading censorship, freedom of information
Manuscript requirements: Chicago
Preferred length: 12 to 18 pages
Number of copies to be submitted: Two
Abstract: Not necessary.
Author information and reprints: Payment: By publication to author. $25.00-$150.00 per article.
Is simultaneous submission of article to other journals permitted: Not permitted.
Exclusive manuscript rights between acceptance and publication: Yes
Copyright: First serial rights only.
Reprint requests are first referred to the author for permission.
Reprints: Not available.
Additional information: As a popular magazine, rather than a scholarly journal, articles must be written in lively style. All factual data and bibliographic data must be accurate.
Disposition of manuscript:
Query letter: Not necessary.
Receipt of manuscript acknowledged: Yes
Decision to publish in: 2 months
Accepted manuscript published in: 2-4 months
Rejected manuscript returned: Yes, if return postage is supplied by author.
Rejected manuscript criticized: Sometimes

Submit to:
William R. Eshelman
Editor
(See address above)

WISCONSIN LIBRARY BULLETIN [321]
126 Langdon Street
Madison, Wisconsin 53702
(608) 266-2582

First published in 1905

SUBSCRIPTION DATA
Issues and rates: Published bi-monthly.
Average paid circulation: 4000
Annual rate(s): $3.50
Publisher or Sponsor: Wisconsin Department of Public Instruction, Division for Library Services

EDITORIAL DESCRIPTION
Contains professional articles in the field of libraries, media centers; news of Wisconsin libraries, media centers and their personnel; materials lists.
Articles per average issue: 12
Audience: Librarians, media specialists
Manuscripts accepted in English

MANUSCRIPT INFORMATION
Subject field(s): Library information science, including audiovisuals
Manuscript requirements: Style sheet sent on request.
Preferred length: 200 to 1500 words; 1 to 7 pages
Number of copies to be submitted: One
Abstract: No

Author information and reprints: Payment: None. Complimentary copy of issue including article
Is simultaneous submission of article to other journals permitted: No
Exclusive manuscript rights between acceptance and publication: Yes
Copyright: Not copyrighted
Reprints: Not available.

Additional information: Use ordinary typeface on bond paper, double-space, with wide margins; give author's professional title and position as well as address and telephone number.

Disposition of manuscript:
Query letter: No
Receipt of manuscript acknowledged: Yes
Decision to publish in: 1 to 4 weeks
Accepted manuscript published in: 3 months
Rejected manuscript returned: Yes
Rejected manuscript criticized: No

Submit to:
Beryl E. Hoyt
Editor
(See address above)

Literature

AMERICAN LITERARY REALISM, 1870-1910 [322]
Department of English
University of Texas at Arlington
Arlington, Texas 76010
(817) 273-2785

First published in 1967

SUBSCRIPTION DATA
Issues and rates: Published quarterly.
Average paid circulation: 600
Annual rate(s): $5.00, Foreign $6.00
Publisher or Sponsor: University of Texas at Arlington, Department of English
Managing Editor: Kenneth M. Roemer

EDITORIAL DESCRIPTION
Contains articles on American literature, 1870-1910; bibliographic focus. Bibliographies of secondary comment and bibliographic or textual notes preferred.
Articles per average issue: 4
Audience: Specialists in American Literature and culture
Manuscripts accepted in English

MANUSCRIPT INFORMATION
Subject field(s): American Literature, 1870-1910: bibliographies of secondary comment; bibliographies of primary works; brief textual studies; notes with bibliographical or textual slants; publication of brief unpublished material by period authors; critical articles
Manuscript requirements: See latest issue for style requirements.
Preferred length: 1000-5000 words
Number of copies to be submitted: Bibliographies: one; articles: two
Abstract: Not necessary.
Author information and reprints: Payment: Reprints only. 2 copies of issue; 5-10 tear sheets.
Is simultaneous submission of article to other journals permitted: No
Exclusive manuscript rights between acceptance and publication: Yes
Copyright: Held by publication.
Reprints: Available at production cost
Additional information: Footnotes should be kept to a minimum. Return postage required. Most contributions are invited, but unsolicited material is welcome, especially if it has a bibliographic or textual slant.
Disposition of manuscript:
Query letter: Necessary.
Receipt of manuscript acknowledged: Yes
Decision to publish in: 4 weeks
Accepted manuscript published in: One year maximum
Rejected manuscript returned: Yes, if self-addressed, stamped envelope is sent with manuscript.
Rejected manuscript criticized: Sometimes
Submit to:
Clayton L. Eichelberger
Editor
(See address above)

Literature

SPECIAL STIPULATIONS
Annotators with access to major libraries are needed.

AMERICAN LITERATURE [323]
A Journal of Literary History, Criticism, and Bibliography
6667 College Station
Durham, North Carolina 27708
(919) 684-3948

First published in 1929

SUBSCRIPTION DATA
Issues and rates: Published quarterly.
Average paid circulation: 5,964
Annual rate(s): $8.00; Students $4.00; Institutions $10.00
Publisher or Sponsor: Modern Language Association of America, American Literature Section

EDITORIAL DESCRIPTION
Contains articles on American literary history, criticism, and bibliography; book reviews and notices; research in progress; bibliographical listing of articles on American literature appearing in current periodicals.
Articles per average issue: 5-6 articles; 5-6 notes
Audience: Professional scholars
Manuscripts accepted in English

MANUSCRIPT INFORMATION
Manuscript requirements: MLA; Chicago
Preferred length: Not over 25 pages
Number of copies to be submitted: Two
Abstract: Yes
Author information and reprints: Payment: Reprints only. 50 reprints
Is simultaneous submission of article to other journals permitted: No
Exclusive manuscript rights between acceptance and publication: Yes
Copyright: Held by publication.
Reprints: Available at cost.
Disposition of manuscript:
Query letter: No
Receipt of manuscript acknowledged: Yes
Decision to publish in: 90 days
Accepted manuscript published in: 6 months
Rejected manuscript returned: Yes, if return postage is supplied by author.
Rejected manuscript criticized: Yes
Submit to:
Arlin Turner
Editor
(See address above)

ARIZONA QUARTERLY [324]
University of Arizona
Tucson, Arizona 85721
(602) 884-1029

First published in 1945

SUBSCRIPTION DATA
Issues and rates: Published quarterly.
Annual rate(s): $2.00
Publisher or Sponsor: University of Arizona

EDITORIAL DESCRIPTION
Publishes articles on literary topics; short stories, poems, book reviews.
Articles per average issue: 4-8
Audience: Literary and general readers
Manuscripts accepted in English

MANUSCRIPT INFORMATION
Subject field(s): Literary criticism, general essays, fiction, poetry, book reviews
Manuscript requirements: MLA
Preferred length: 2,000-3,500 words
Number of copies to be submitted: One
Abstract: Yes.
Author information and reprints: Payment: Reprints only. Copies of publication, subscription, annual awards
Is simultaneous submission of article to other journals permitted: No
Exclusive manuscript rights between acceptance and publication: Yes
Copyright: Held by publication.
Reprints: Available at printer's charge

Disposition of manuscript:
Query letter: Not necessary.
Receipt of manuscript acknowledged: On request
Decision to publish in: 4-6 weeks
Accepted manuscript published in: Varies
Rejected manuscript returned: Yes, if self-addressed, stamped envelope is sent with manuscript.
Rejected manuscript criticized: No
Submit to:
Editor
(See address above)

BIBLIOGRAPHICAL SOCIETY OF AMERICA. PAPERS [325]
University of Texas
English Building 110
Austin, Texas 78712
(512) 471-3561

First published in 1907

SUBSCRIPTION DATA
Issues and rates: Published quarterly.
Average paid circulation: 1700
Annual rate(s): $15.00

EDITORIAL DESCRIPTION
Contains articles, notes, news and notes of professional interest, reviews, brief mention of other publications.
Articles per average issue: 15-20
Audience: Scholars
Manuscripts accepted in English

MANUSCRIPT INFORMATION
Subject field(s): Bibliography (analytical, descriptive, historical, and occasionally enumerative); editorial problems, history of printing, addenda or corrigenda to bibliographies
Manuscript requirements: See "Statement of Editorial Policy," first issue of the year
Preferred length: Articles 3000-6000, notes 100-3000 words

Number of copies to be submitted: One
Abstract: Yes, 50-200 words
Author information and reprints: Payment: None.
Is simultaneous submission of article to other journals permitted: No
Exclusive manuscript rights between acceptance and publication: Yes
Copyright: Held by publication.
Reprints: Available, 40 free for articles, 20 free for notes and reviews
Disposition of manuscript:
Query letter: No
Receipt of manuscript acknowledged: Yes
Decision to publish in: Four months
Accepted manuscript published in: One year
Rejected manuscript returned: Yes, if return postage is supplied by author.
Rejected manuscript criticized: Yes
Submit to:
William B. Todd
Editor
(See address above)

SPECIAL STIPULATIONS
Authors receive 75 per cent of a fee required of publishers who reprint their articles. Authors may also submit book-length material for consideration as a separate issue by the Society.

BLAKE NEWSLETTER [326]
An Illustrated Quarterly
Department of Language and Literature
University of New Mexico
Albuquerque, New Mexico 87131
(505) 277-3103

First published in 1967

SUBSCRIPTION DATA
Issues and rates: Published quarterly.
Annual rate(s): $5.00; Foreign $5.00; Institutions $5.00; Students Free (on campus); Members $5.00; Foreign institutions $5.00

EDITORIAL DESCRIPTION
Contains material on the life and work of William Blake, both his literary and artistic endeavors.
Articles per average issue: 10-12; including reviews
Audience: Blake scholars
Manuscripts accepted in English

MANUSCRIPT INFORMATION
Subject field(s): Art criticism, literary criticism, biography and bibliography
Manuscript requirements: MLA
Preferred length: Less than 25 pages
Number of copies to be submitted: Two
Author information and reprints: Payment: None.
Is simultaneous submission of article to other journals permitted: No
Exclusive manuscript rights between acceptance and publication: Yes
Copyright: Held by publication.
Reprints: Available, cost varies
Disposition of manuscript:
Receipt of manuscript acknowledged: Yes
Decision to publish in: 4-6 weeks

Accepted manuscript published in: 3 months
Rejected manuscript returned: Yes
Rejected manuscript criticized: Yes
Submit to:
Morris Eaves
Associate Editor
(See address above)

Morton D. Palex
Associate Editor
Department of English
University of California
Berkeley, California 94720

BLAKE STUDIES [327]
An International Journal Devoted to the Study of the Poetry and Painting of William Blake, 1757-1827
Department of English
Illinois State University
Normal, Illinois 61761
(309) 438-2475

First published in 1968

SUBSCRIPTION DATA
Issues and rates: Published semi-annually.
　Average paid circulation: 660
　Annual rate(s): $7.50, Foreign $8.50
Publisher or Sponsor: The American Blake Foundation
Managing Editor: Kay Parkhurst Easson

EDITORIAL DESCRIPTION
　Contains original critical essays on Blake's biography, painting, poetry, and engravings; bibliographical studies of Blake's publications; essays on the relationship of Blake's work to the works of Samuel Palmer, Henry Fuseli, John Flaxman and others of his circle; review essays of major publications in the field.
Articles per average issue: 4
Audience: Blake literary and art scholars
　Manuscripts accepted in English

MANUSCRIPT INFORMATION
Subject field(s): Literary history, art history, bibliography, literary criticism
Manuscript requirements: MLA
　Preferred length: 2,000 to 8,000 words; 8-30 pages
　Number of copies to be submitted: One original and one Xerox.
　Abstract: Not necessary.
Author information and reprints: Payment: Reprints only. 2 copies of the journal
　Is simultaneous submission of article to other journals permitted: No
　Exclusive manuscript rights between acceptance and publication: Yes
　Copyright: Held by publication.
　Reprints: Available at cost
Additional information: Manuscripts should be in the proper style with footnotes on separate pages. Author's name should appear only on the cover letter so that articles may be sent to readers anonymously.
Disposition of manuscript:
　Query letter: Not necessary.

Receipt of manuscript acknowledged: Yes
Decision to publish in: 6-12 weeks
Accepted manuscript published in: 3-9 months
Rejected manuscript returned: Yes, if return postage is supplied by author.
Rejected manuscript criticized: Yes
Submit to:
Kay Parkhurst Easson
Co-Editor
(See address above)

SPECIAL STIPULATIONS
　Illustrations to accompany the paper must be secured by the author. Color transparencies and permission for their use will be secured by the journal. All photographs become the property of The American Blake Foundation and remain on file in the Foundation's research library.

BOOKS ABROAD [328]
An International Literary Quarterly
University of Oklahoma Press
1005 Asp Avenue
Norman, Oklahoma 73069
(405) 325-5111 ext. 32

SUBSCRIPTION DATA
Issues and rates: Published quarterly.
　Average paid circulation: 3,000
　Annual rate(s): Individuals $8.00, Institutions $15.00
Managing Editor: Ivar Ivask

EDITORIAL DESCRIPTION
　Covers fiction, drama, literary criticism, biography, essay, poetry, and any other genre that might be considered *belles-lettres*.

MANUSCRIPT INFORMATION
Subject field(s): Contemporary non-English literatures, non-English writers, non-English critics, comparative literature, literary problems, literary events, publishing, literary prizes, unpublished correspondence, literary journalism, interviews with literary people, photos of literary people
Manuscript requirements: Chicago
　Preferred length: 1,200-3,000 words; 5-12 pages
　Number of copies to be submitted: One
Author information and reprints: Payment: None.
　Is simultaneous submission of article to other journals permitted: No
　Exclusive manuscript rights between acceptance and publication: Yes
　Copyright: Held by publication.
　Reprints: Available, 25 free reprints for an article; 10 free reprints for a commentary
Disposition of manuscript:
　Receipt of manuscript acknowledged: Yes
　Decision to publish in: 5-10 days
　Accepted manuscript published in: 2-10 months
　Rejected manuscript returned: Yes
　Rejected manuscript criticized: Sometimes

Submit to:
Ivar Ivask
Editor
(See address above)
(405) 325-4531

BULLETIN BAUDELAIRIEN [329]
Box 1514, Station B
Vanderbilt University
Nashville, Tennessee 37235
(615) 322-2657

First published in 1965

SUBSCRIPTION DATA
Issues and rates: Published semi-annually.
　Average paid circulation: 200; 400 controlled
　Annual rate(s): $2.00, Foreign $3.00

Publisher or Sponsor: W. T. Bandy Center for Baudelaire Studies

EDITORIAL DESCRIPTION
　Contains short articles and notes on Baudelaire's life and works; bibliographies. Emphasis is on literary history and bibliography.

Articles per average issue: 6-7
Audience: Scholars and students of 19th century French literature, Baudelaire in particular

　Manuscripts accepted in French only

MANUSCRIPT INFORMATION
Subject field(s): Baudelaire or his circle
Manuscript requirements: MLA
　Preferred length: 1,000 words; 3-5 pages; typewritten, double-spaced
　Number of copies to be submitted: One

Author information and reprints: Payment: Reprints only. Limited number of author's copies
　Is simultaneous submission of article to other journals permitted: No
　Exclusive manuscript rights between acceptance and publication: Yes
　Copyright: Held by author.
　Reprints: Not available.

Disposition of manuscript:
　Receipt of manuscript acknowledged: Yes
　Decision to publish in: 2-4 weeks
　Accepted manuscript published in: 6-12 months
　Rejected manuscript returned: Yes, if return postage is supplied by author.
　Rejected manuscript criticized: Sometimes

Submit to:
W. T. Bandy;
Claude Pichois
Editors
(See address above)

SPECIAL STIPULATIONS
　All articles submitted must be in French.

BULLETIN OF THE COMEDIANTES [330]
Department of Spanish and Portuguese
University of Southern California
Los Angeles, California 90007
(213) 746-2516

First published in 1949

SUBSCRIPTION DATA
Issues and rates: Published semi-annually.
  Average paid circulation: 500
  Annual rate(s): Individuals $3.50,
  Institutions $4.00

EDITORIAL DESCRIPTION
  Contains researched essays about the *Comedia,* Spanish drama from the *Celestina* through Calderón, roughly 1500-1700; annual bibliography of publications on the drama of this period; *Mentidero de Comediantes*
Articles per average issue: 6-8
Audience: Specialists in the Spanish *Comedia*
  Manuscripts accepted in English and all Romance languages

MANUSCRIPT INFORMATION
Subject field(s): Spanish drama, 1500-1700
Manuscript requirements: MLA
  Preferred length: 4-12 pages
  Number of copies to be submitted: One
  Abstract: Yes.
Author information and reprints: Payment: None.
  Is simultaneous submission of article to other journals permitted: No
  Exclusive manuscript rights between acceptance and publication: Yes
  Copyright: Held by author.
  Reprints: Available
Disposition of manuscript:
  Query letter: Not necessary.
  Receipt of manuscript acknowledged: Yes
  Decision to publish in: 4-6 weeks
  Accepted manuscript published in: 12-18 months
  Rejected manuscript returned: Yes, if self-addressed, stamped envelope is sent with manuscript.
  Rejected manuscript criticized: No
Submit to:
  Karl C. Gregg
  Department of Romance Languages
  University of Arizona
  Tucson, Arizona 85721

THE BURROUGHS BULLETIN [331]
House of Greystoke
6657 Locust
Kansas City, Missouri 64131
(816) 523-5176

SUBSCRIPTION DATA
Issues and rates: Published monthly.
  Average paid circulation: 2,500; 200 controlled
  Annual rate(s): $15.00
Publisher or Sponsor: The Burroughs Bibliophiles
Managing Editor: Vern Coriell

EDITORIAL DESCRIPTION
  Contains articles, reviews, reprints, and original material concerning the works of Edgar Rice Burroughs.
Articles per average issue: 1-5
Audience: Those interested in the works of Burroughs
  Manuscripts accepted in English only

MANUSCRIPT INFORMATION
Manuscript requirements: No specific style guide.
  Preferred length: Open
  Number of copies to be submitted: One
  Abstract: Not necessary.
Author information and reprints: Payment: Reprints only. Copies of issue.
  Is simultaneous submission of article to other journals permitted: No
  Exclusive manuscript rights between acceptance and publication: Yes
  Copyright: Held by Edgar Rice Burroughs, Inc.
  Reprints: Available in limited number
Disposition of manuscript:
  Query letter: Not necessary.
  Receipt of manuscript acknowledged: Yes
  Decision to publish in: 6-8 weeks
  Accepted manuscript published in: 6-12 months
  Rejected manuscript returned: Yes, if return postage is supplied by author.
  Rejected manuscript criticized: No
Submit to:
  Vern W. Coriell
  Editor
  (See address above)

THE BYRON JOURNAL [332]
6 Gertrude Street
London SW10 0JN, England
(01) 352-5112

First published in 1973

SUBSCRIPTION DATA
Issues and rates: Published annually.
  Average paid circulation: 2,000
  Annual rate(s): £0.50
Publisher or Sponsor: The Byron Society

EDITORIAL DESCRIPTION
  Contains scholarly articles on Lord Byron's life and work.
Articles per average issue: 8
Audience: Byron scholars
  Manuscripts accepted in English

MANUSCRIPT INFORMATION
Manuscript requirements: No specific style guide.
  Preferred length: 1,000-2,000 words
  Number of copies to be submitted: 2
  Abstract: Not necessary.
Author information and reprints: Payment: None.
  Is simultaneous submission of article to other journals permitted: Permitted.
  Exclusive manuscript rights between acceptance and publication: Yes
  Copyright: Held by author.
  Reprints: Available at cost.
Disposition of manuscript:
  Query letter: Not necessary.
  Receipt of manuscript acknowledged: Yes
  Decision to publish in: 4 months
  Accepted manuscript published in: 6 months
  Rejected manuscript returned: Yes, if return postage is supplied by author.
  Rejected manuscript criticized: No
Submit to:
  Dennis Walwin-Jones
  Executive Editor
  (See address above)

CANADIAN LITERATURE [333]
A Journal of Criticism and Review
University of British Columbia
Vancouver 8, British Columbia, Canada
(604) 228-2780

First published in 1959

SUBSCRIPTION DATA
Issues and rates: Published quarterly.
  Average paid circulation: 2,300
  Annual rate(s): $5.50
Managing Editor: George Woodcock

EDITORIAL DESCRIPTION
  Contains critical articles and reviews on writers and books in Canada.

MANUSCRIPT INFORMATION
Subject field(s): Canadian writing and writers
Manuscript requirements: See latest issue for style requirements.
  Preferred length: 5,000 words maximum
  Number of copies to be submitted: One
Author information and reprints: Payment: By publication to author. $6.00 per page.
  Is simultaneous submission of article to other journals permitted: No
  Exclusive manuscript rights between acceptance and publication: Yes
  Copyright: Held by author.
  Reprints: Not available.
Additional information: Neither photocopies nor carbon copies will be considered.
Disposition of manuscript:
  Receipt of manuscript acknowledged: No
  Decision to publish in: 1 month
  Accepted manuscript published in: 1 year
  Rejected manuscript returned: Yes, if self-addressed, stamped envelope is sent with manuscript.
  Rejected manuscript criticized: No
Submit to:
  George Woodcock
  Editor
  (See address above)

CLAUDEL STUDIES [334]
University of Dallas
Irving, Texas 75061
(229) 253-1123

Previously entitled *Claudel Newsletter*

First published in 1972

SUBSCRIPTION DATA
Issues and rates: Published semi-annually.
Average paid circulation: 500
Annual rate(s): $3.00
Managing Editor: Robert S. Dupree;
Moses M. Nagy

EDITORIAL DESCRIPTION
Contains articles, monographs, notes, and reviews relating directly or indirectly to Paul Claudel.
Articles per average issue: 4-5
Audience: Professors, students, theatre people
Manuscripts accepted in English, French

MANUSCRIPT INFORMATION
Subject field(s): Research on Claudel, monographs, influence of Claudel, the theatre of Claudel, translations into English
Manuscript requirements: MLA
Preferred length: 15-20 pages
Number of copies to be submitted: One
Abstract: Not necessary.
Author information and reprints: Payment: None.
Is simultaneous submission of article to other journals permitted: Yes
Exclusive manuscript rights between acceptance and publication: Yes
Copyright: Held by publication.
Reprints: Not available.

Disposition of manuscript:
Query letter: Not necessary.
Receipt of manuscript acknowledged: Yes
Decision to publish in: 1-2 months
Accepted manuscript published in: 6 months
Rejected manuscript returned: Yes
Rejected manuscript criticized: Yes
Submit to:
Moses M. Nagy
Editor-in-Chief
University of Dallas Station
Department of French
Irving, Texas 75061
(214) 253-1123 Ext. 229

COLBY LIBRARY QUARTERLY [335]
Colby College
Waterville, Maine 04901
(207) 873-1131 ext. 207

First published in 1943

SUBSCRIPTION DATA
Issues and rates: Published quarterly.
Average paid circulation: 700
Annual rate(s): $3.00
Publisher or Sponsor: Colby College Library
Managing Editor: Richard Cary

EDITORIAL DESCRIPTION
Interested in Maine authors (i.e., Edwin Arlington Robinson, Sarah Orne Jewett, Edna St. Vincent Millay, Kenneth Roberts, Jacob Abbott, Henry Wadsworth Longfellow, Mary Ellen Chase, Robert P. Tristram Coffin) and in Maine history.
Articles per average issue: 5-6
Audience: Scholars of literature and history
Manuscripts accepted in English

MANUSCRIPT INFORMATION
Subject field(s): Literary criticism, history, interpretation, bibliography, and biography
Manuscript requirements: See latest issue for style requirements.
Preferred length: 20 pages maximum
Number of copies to be submitted: One
Abstract: Yes.
Author information and reprints: Payment: Reprints only. Ten copies of issue in which essay is printed.
Exclusive manuscript rights between acceptance and publication: No
Copyright: Not copyrighted
Reprints: Available at current prices
Disposition of manuscript:
Query letter: Not necessary.
Receipt of manuscript acknowledged: No
Decision to publish in: 3 weeks
Accepted manuscript published in: 12 months
Rejected manuscript returned: Yes, if return postage is supplied by author.
Rejected manuscript criticized: No
Submit to:
Richard Cary
Editor
(See address above)

COLLEGE LITERATURE [336]
Department of English
West Chester State College
West Chester, Pennsylvania 19380
(215) 436-2901

First published in 1974

SUBSCRIPTION DATA
Issues and rates: Published three times per year.
Average paid circulation: 800
Annual rate(s): $3.00; Foreign $4.50; Institutions $3.00; Students $3.00

EDITORIAL DESCRIPTION
Contains scholarly, pedagogical articles intended to serve as a *vade mecum* to the works most often taught in literature courses in American colleges and universities, from Homer to the present.
Articles per average issue: 6
Audience: Academic: professors and students
Manuscripts accepted in English

MANUSCRIPT INFORMATION
Subject field(s): Western literature
Manuscript requirements: MLA
Preferred length: 20-25 pages
Number of copies to be submitted: 2
Abstract: Not necessary. It will be requested upon acceptance for publication.
Author information and reprints: Payment: Reprints only. 5 copies of journal, 25 tear sheets
Is simultaneous submission of article to other journals permitted: Permitted, but not encouraged.
Exclusive manuscript rights between acceptance and publication: Yes
Copyright: Author's agreement provides for his full use of the article later, and a sharing upon resale.
Reprints: Available at cost.
Disposition of manuscript:
Query letter: Necessary.
Receipt of manuscript acknowledged: Yes
Decision to publish in: 1-2 months
Accepted manuscript published in: 5-6 months
Rejected manuscript returned: Yes, if return postage is supplied by author.
Rejected manuscript criticized: Sometimes
Submit to:
Dr. Bernard Oldsey
Editor
(See address above)

COMPARATIVE LITERATURE STUDIES [337]
University of Illinois,
2054 Foreign Language Building
Urbana, Illinois 61801
(217) 333-0830

First published in 1963

SUBSCRIPTION DATA
Issues and rates: Published quarterly.
Average paid circulation: 1,000
Annual rate(s): $7.50, Foreign $8.50
Publisher or Sponsor: University of Illinois
Managing Editor: A. Owen Aldridge

EDITORIAL DESCRIPTION
Contains articles on literary history and the history of ideas, with particular emphasis on European literary relations with both North and South America.
Articles per average issue: 6
Audience: Academic
Manuscripts accepted in English, French, Spanish, German

MANUSCRIPT INFORMATION
Subject field(s): Comparative literature
Manuscript requirements: MLA
Preferred length: 12 pages
Number of copies to be submitted: One
Abstract: Not necessary.
Author information and reprints: Payment: None.
Is simultaneous submission of article to other journals permitted: No
Exclusive manuscript rights between acceptance and publication: Yes
Copyright: Held by publication.
Reprints: Available, 25 free
Disposition of manuscript:
Query letter: Not necessary.
Receipt of manuscript acknowledged: Yes
Decision to publish in: 3 months
Accepted manuscript published in: 12 months

Rejected manuscript returned: Yes
Rejected manuscript criticized: Yes
Submit to:
A. Owen Aldridge
(See address above)

CONRADIANA [338]

P.O. Box 4229
Texas Technological University
Lubbock, Texas 79409
(806) 742-4211

SUBSCRIPTION DATA
Issues and rates: Published three times per year.
Average paid circulation: 700
Annual rate(s): $7.50, Foreign $8.50
Publisher or Sponsor: Texas Technological University, Textual Studies Institute, Department of English

EDITORIAL DESCRIPTION
Publishes original criticism of Conrad: biographical materials, bibliography, news, notes, queries, anything else concerning the life and work of the English novelist Joseph Conrad (1857-1924). Publication strives to be as objective as possible.
Articles per average issue: 7
Audience: Conrad scholars
Manuscripts accepted in English only

MANUSCRIPT INFORMATION
Subject field(s): Criticism, interpretation, explication de texte, textual studies, biography, bibliography, poetry, translations, reviews, thesis abstracts, article notes, book notes
Manuscript requirements: MLA with citations of Conrad's works appearing within the text whenever possible. Margins of 1 ½ inches at sides and at top required.
Preferred length: 3,000 to 6,000 words; 10-20 pages
Number of copies to be submitted: 3
Abstract: 300 word abstract of paper required plus short biographical sketch of author.
Author information and reprints: Payment: None.
Is simultaneous submission of article to other journals permitted: Yes, by prior arrangement with the editor.
Exclusive manuscript rights between acceptance and publication: Yes
Copyright: Held by publication.
Reprints: Available at cost of printing
Additional information: Each manuscript is read by at least three experts in the field before decision is reached.
Disposition of manuscript:
Query letter: Not necessary.
Receipt of manuscript acknowledged: Yes
Decision to publish in: 3 months
Accepted manuscript published in: 1 year
Rejected manuscript returned: Yes, if self-addressed, stamped envelope is sent with manuscript.
Rejected manuscript criticized: No
Submit to:
David L. Higdon
Editor

Box 4530, Texas Technological University
Lubbock, Texas 79409
(817) 273-2692

CONTEMPORARY LITERATURE [339]

Helen C. White Hall
600 North Park Street
Madison, Wisconsin 53706
(608) 263-3775

Previously entitled *Wisconsin Studies in Contemporary Literature*

First published in 1960

SUBSCRIPTION DATA
Issues and rates: Published quarterly.
Average paid circulation: 2,000
Annual rate(s): Individuals $10.00, Institutions $20.00
Managing Editor: Julie Wosk

EDITORIAL DESCRIPTION
Contains critical and/or scholarly articles about all aspects of literature since 1940.
Articles per average issue: 5-6
Audience: Academic
Manuscripts accepted in English

MANUSCRIPT INFORMATION
Subject field(s): Anglo-American and continental poetry, fiction, drama and criticism
Manuscript requirements: MLA, Chicago
Preferred length: 15-30 pages
Number of copies to be submitted: One
Abstract: Only upon acceptance
Author information and reprints: Payment: None.
Is simultaneous submission of article to other journals permitted: No
Exclusive manuscript rights between acceptance and publication: Yes
Copyright: Held by publication.
Reprints: Available, free
Disposition of manuscript:
Query letter: Not necessary.
Receipt of manuscript acknowledged: Yes
Decision to publish in: 6-12 weeks
Accepted manuscript published in: 6-18 months
Rejected manuscript returned: Yes, if self-addressed, stamped envelope is sent with manuscript.
Rejected manuscript criticized: No
Submit to:
L. S. Dembo
Editor
(See address above)

CRITICAL QUARTERLY [340]

Department of English
University of Manchester
Manchester M13 9PL, England
(061) 273-3333

SUBSCRIPTION DATA
Issues and rates: Published quarterly.
Average paid circulation: 5,000
Annual rate(s): £3.50
Managing Editor: C. B. Cox;
A. E. Dyson

EDITORIAL DESCRIPTION
Contains literary criticism and poetry.
Articles per average issue: 6
Audience: General
Manuscripts accepted in English

MANUSCRIPT INFORMATION
Subject field(s): 20th century literature, literature pre-1900
Manuscript requirements: MLA
Preferred length: 3,000-8,000 words
Number of copies to be submitted: One
Abstract: Not necessary.
Author information and reprints: Payment: Reprints only. 10 offprints
Is simultaneous submission of article to other journals permitted: No
Exclusive manuscript rights between acceptance and publication: Yes
Copyright: Held by author.
Reprints: Available
Disposition of manuscript:
Query letter: Not necessary.
Receipt of manuscript acknowledged: Yes
Decision to publish in: 8 weeks
Accepted manuscript published in: 6 months
Rejected manuscript returned: Yes, if return postage is supplied by author.
Rejected manuscript criticized: No
Submit to:
C. B. Cox
(See address above)

THE CRITICAL REVIEW [341]

Melbourne
English Department
University of Melbourne
Parkville, Victoria 3052, Australia
34-0484

Previously entitled *Melbourne Critical Review*

First published in 1958

SUBSCRIPTION DATA
Issues and rates: Published annually.
Average paid circulation: 1500; 100 controlled
Annual rate(s): $A1.20, Foreign $A1.40
Managing Editor: T. B. Tomlinson

EDITORIAL DESCRIPTION
Contains articles on English, American and some European literatures and culture.
Articles per average issue: 10
Audience: Academic
Manuscripts accepted in English

MANUSCRIPT INFORMATION
Subject field(s): Literary criticism and related matters

Manuscript requirements: Rules for Compositors and Printers, Oxford University Press
  Preferred length: 7000 to 8000 words
  Number of copies to be submitted: One
Author information and reprints: Payment: None.
  Is simultaneous submission of article to other journals permitted: Yes
  Exclusive manuscript rights between acceptance and publication: No
  Copyright: Held by author.
  Reprints: Available at no cost
Additional information: No footnotes printed
Disposition of manuscript:
  Query letter: No
  Receipt of manuscript acknowledged: Yes
  Decision to publish in: Two months
  Accepted manuscript published in: Maximum twelve months
  Rejected manuscript returned: Yes, if self-addressed, stamped envelope is sent with manuscript.
  Rejected manuscript criticized: Sometimes
Submit to:
  S. L. Goldberg
  Editor
  (See address above)

CRITIQUE [342]
Studies in Modern Fiction
Department of English
Georgia Institute of Technology
Atlanta, Georgia 30332
(404) 894-2739

Previously entitled *Faulkner Studies*

First published in 1956

SUBSCRIPTION DATA
Issues and rates: Published three times per year.
  Average paid circulation: 1,400
  Annual rate(s): $7.50, Foreign $8.00
Managing Editor: James Dean Young

EDITORIAL DESCRIPTION
  Publishing critical essays on the fiction of contemporary writers of all countries, the journal is principally interested in essays on writers who are alive and without great reputations. Bibliographies of individual writers are occasionally published.
Articles per average issue: 9
Audience: Students and teachers of literature
  Manuscripts accepted in English

MANUSCRIPT INFORMATION
Subject field(s): Literary criticism, formal analysis, thematic analysis, survey of individual development, comparative studies
Manuscript requirements: MLA
  Preferred length: 4,000 to 6,000 words; 15 to 25 pages
  Number of copies to be submitted: One
  Abstract: Only upon acceptance

Author information and reprints: Payment: Reprints only. Five copies of issue, and 25 reprints
  Is simultaneous submission of article to other journals permitted: No
  Exclusive manuscript rights between acceptance and publication: Yes
  Copyright: Held by publication.
  Reprints: Available
Additional information: MSS. should have necessary footnotes on separate pages. All quotations in other languages should be translated into English.
Disposition of manuscript:
  Receipt of manuscript acknowledged: No
  Decision to publish in: 4-6 months
  Accepted manuscript published in: 12 months
  Rejected manuscript returned: Yes, if self-addressed, stamped envelope is sent with manuscript.
  Rejected manuscript criticized: Yes
Submit to:
  James Dean Young
  Editor
  (See address above)

THE D. H. LAWRENCE REVIEW [343]
Box 2474, University of Arkansas
Fayetteville, Arkansas 72701
(501) 575-4301

First published in 1968

SUBSCRIPTION DATA
Issues and rates: Published three times per year.
  Average paid circulation: 500
  Annual rate(s): $5.00

Managing Editor: James C. Cowan

EDITORIAL DESCRIPTION
  Contains criticism, historical scholarship, reviews, and bibliography of D. H. Lawrence and his circle; Lawrence's tradition and influences; column of news and announcements of publications, seminars, symposia of interest to Lawrence scholars. Occasional special issues deal with specific areas of Lawrence's work or with other figures related to him.
Articles per average issue: 7
Audience: Scholars and general readers
  Manuscripts accepted in English (others will be translated)

MANUSCRIPT INFORMATION
Subject field(s): D. H. Lawrence, his influence, images or traditions used (e.g., the phoenix)
Manuscript requirements: MLA; Chicago
  Preferred length: 8 to 15 pages
  Number of copies to be submitted: Two
  Abstract: MLA
Author information and reprints: Payment: Reprints only. 2 copies of issue and 25 reprints of article

  Is simultaneous submission of article to other journals permitted: No
  Exclusive manuscript rights between acceptance and publication: Yes
  Copyright: Held by publication, but permission to reprint elsewhere is usually granted on request and without fee.
  Reprints: Available at no cost
Additional information: Manuscripts should be literate, and make an original contribution to knowledge of the topic.
Disposition of manuscript:
  Query letter: Not necessary, but advisable.
  Receipt of manuscript acknowledged: Yes
  Decision to publish in: 3 months
  Accepted manuscript published in: One year
  Rejected manuscript returned: Yes, if return postage is supplied by author.
  Rejected manuscript criticized: Yes
Submit to:
  James C. Cowan
  Editor
  (See address above)

DANTE STUDIES [344]
State University of New York Press
99 Washington Avenue
Albany, New York 12210
(518) 474-6050

Previously entitled *Annual Report of the Dante Society*

First published in 1882

SUBSCRIPTION DATA
Issues and rates: Published annually.
  Average paid circulation: 600
  Annual rate(s): $5.00

Publisher or Sponsor: Dante Society of America, Inc.
Managing Editor: Anthony L. Pellegrini

EDITORIAL DESCRIPTION
  Contains articles on the life and works of Dante Alighieri; annual bibliography of American Dante scholarship.
Articles per average issue: 12
Audience: Literary and academic
  Manuscripts accepted in English, Italian, French, Spanish

MANUSCRIPT INFORMATION
Manuscript requirements: See latest issue for style requirements.
  Preferred length: 35 pages maximum
  Number of copies to be submitted: One
Author information and reprints: Payment: None.
  Is simultaneous submission of article to other journals permitted: No
  Exclusive manuscript rights between acceptance and publication: Yes
  Copyright: Held by publication.
  Reprints: Available, $.25 per copy
Disposition of manuscript:
  Query letter: Not necessary.

Receipt of manuscript acknowledged: Yes
Decision to publish in: 3 months
Accepted manuscript published in: 1 year
Rejected manuscript returned: Yes
Rejected manuscript criticized: Yes
Submit to:
Anthony L. Pellegrini
Editor
Department of Romance Languages
SUNY at Binghamton
Binghamton, New York 13901
(607) 798-2543

DICKENS STUDIES NEWSLETTER [345]
Department of English
Southern Illinois University
Carbondale, Illinois 62901
(618) 453-5321

First published in 1970

SUBSCRIPTION DATA
Issues and rates: Published quarterly.
  Average paid circulation: 500
  Annual rate(s): $7.00
Publisher or Sponsor: The Dickens Society
Managing Editor: Robert B. Partlow, Jr.

EDITORIAL DESCRIPTION
Publishes short critical essays about Dickens' work; reviews of books about Dickens and the Victorian era; bibliographical check list of Dickens' works and secondary sources.
Articles per average issue: 7
Audience: Scholars and students
  Manuscripts accepted in English, French, German

MANUSCRIPT INFORMATION
Manuscript requirements: MLA
  Preferred length: Under 4000 words
  Number of copies to be submitted: Two
  Abstract: No
Author information and reprints: Payment: None.
  Is simultaneous submission of article to other journals permitted: No
  Exclusive manuscript rights between acceptance and publication: Yes
  Copyright: Held by author.
  Reprints: Not available.
Disposition of manuscript:
  Query letter: Not necessary.
  Receipt of manuscript acknowledged: Yes
  Decision to publish in: 2-4 weeks
  Accepted manuscript published in: 4-6 months
  Rejected manuscript returned: Yes, if return postage is supplied by author.
  Rejected manuscript criticized: Yes
Submit to:
Robert B. Partlow, Jr.
Production Editor
(See address above)

THE DICKENSIAN [346]
48 Doughty Street
London, WC1N 2LF England
01 405-2127

First published in 1905

SUBSCRIPTION DATA
Issues and rates: Published three times per year.
  Average paid circulation: 2,000
  Annual rate(s): £2.50; Foreign £3.00; Institutions £3.50; Foreign institutions £4.00
Publisher or Sponsor: The Dickens Fellowship

EDITORIAL DESCRIPTION
Contains articles (preferably illustrated) on all aspects of Dicken's life, character and writings; reviews of recent books on Dickens.
Articles per average issue: 6-10
Audience: Academic, general
  Manuscripts accepted in English

MANUSCRIPT INFORMATION
Manuscript requirements: Style sheet sent on request.
  Preferred length: 2,000-3,000 words; 4-6 pages
  Number of copies to be submitted: 1
  Abstract: Yes
Author information and reprints: Payment: None.
  Is simultaneous submission of article to other journals permitted: Yes
  Exclusive manuscript rights between acceptance and publication: Yes
  Copyright: Held by author.
  Reprints: Available, 25 free
Additional information: Spelling should be anglicised throughout. Double-spaced typescript throughout.
Disposition of manuscript:
  Query letter: Yes
  Receipt of manuscript acknowledged: Yes
  Decision to publish in: 6 weeks
  Accepted manuscript published in: 12-18 months
  Rejected manuscript returned: Yes, if return postage is supplied by author.
  Rejected manuscript criticized: No
Submit to:
Michael Slater
Honorary Editor
Birkbeck College
Malet Street
London WC1E 7HX, England
01-580-6622 ext. 315

EARLY AMERICAN LITERATURE [347]
Department of English, Bartlett Hall
University of Massachusetts
Amherst, Massachusetts 01002
(413) 545-1382

SUBSCRIPTION DATA
Issues and rates: Published three times per year.
  Average paid circulation: 650; 700 controlled
  Annual rate(s): $5.00
Publisher or Sponsor: Modern Language Association of America, Early American Literature Group
Managing Editor: Everett Emerson

EDITORIAL DESCRIPTION
Contains studies of literature, culture, intellectual history, American literature through early national period.
Articles per average issue: 7
Audience: Teachers of American Literature
  Manuscripts accepted in English

MANUSCRIPT INFORMATION
Subject field(s): Literary studies, cultural studies, intellectual studies, editions
Manuscript requirements: MLA
  Preferred length: 1-40 pages
  Number of copies to be submitted: One
  Abstract: Yes; MLA
Author information and reprints: Payment: None.
  Is simultaneous submission of article to other journals permitted: No
  Exclusive manuscript rights between acceptance and publication: Yes
  Copyright: Held by publication.
  Reprints: Available, $2 per page per 50 copies
Disposition of manuscript:
  Query letter: No
  Receipt of manuscript acknowledged: Yes
  Decision to publish in: 3 months
  Accepted manuscript published in: 15 months
  Rejected manuscript returned: Yes
  Rejected manuscript criticized: Yes
Submit to:
Everett Emerson
Editor
(See address above)

ELH [348]
The Johns Hopkins University
Baltimore, Maryland 21218

Previously entitled *A Journal of English Literary History*

First published in 1934

SUBSCRIPTION DATA
Issues and rates: Published quarterly.
  Average paid circulation: 1900; 500 controlled
  Annual rate(s): Institutions $12.00; Individuals $15.00
Managing Editor: Arnold Stein

EDITORIAL DESCRIPTION
Contains essays on major texts in English and American literature making important critical contributions.
Articles per average issue: 9
Audience: Professional scholars, critics and advanced students
  Manuscripts accepted in English

MANUSCRIPT INFORMATION
Subject field(s): Critical articles on literature
Manuscript requirements: MLA
   Preferred length: None
   Number of copies to be submitted: One
   Abstract: Not necessary.
Author information and reprints: Payment: None.
   Is simultaneous submission of article to other journals permitted: No
   Exclusive manuscript rights between acceptance and publication: Yes
   Copyright: Held by publication.
   Reprints: Available; 10 free; additional at cost
Disposition of manuscript:
   Query letter: Not necessary.
   Receipt of manuscript acknowledged: Yes
   Decision to publish in: 30 days
   Accepted manuscript published in: One year
   Rejected manuscript returned: Yes, if return postage is supplied by author.
   Rejected manuscript criticized: No
Submit to:
   The Editors
   (See address above)

EMILY DICKENSON BULLETIN [349]
A Semi-Annual Review
4508 38th Street
Brentwood, Maryland 20722
864-8527

First published in 1968

SUBSCRIPTION DATA
Issues and rates: Published semi-annually.
   Annual rate(s): $10.00

Publisher or Sponsor: Modern Language Association, Conference of Learned Editors

EDITORIAL DESCRIPTION
   A scholarly journal devoted to Emily Dickinson. Includes bibliography lists, reviews of new and classic books, notes and queries, articles, translations
Articles per average issue: 6
Audience: Academic
   Manuscripts accepted in English, translations

MANUSCRIPT INFORMATION
Subject field(s): Emily Dickinson, her life, times and works, influences, etc.
Manuscript requirements: MLA
   Preferred length: 4,000 words; 10 pages
   Number of copies to be submitted: 1
   Abstract: Yes. Of about 200 words summarizing the thrust of the article.
Author information and reprints: Payment: Reprints only. 1 copy of issue
   Is simultaneous submission of article to other journals permitted: Permitted.
   Exclusive manuscript rights between acceptance and publication: Yes
   Copyright: No copyright
   Reprints: Available at cost.
Additional information: There is a current two year backlog of material. Single poem explications are discouraged. Two or more poems, preferably an entire series, should be explored together. Grouping by theme or subject is ideal.
Disposition of manuscript:
   Query letter: Not necessary.
   Receipt of manuscript acknowledged: No
   Decision to publish in: 2-3 weeks
   Accepted manuscript published in: 2 years
   Rejected manuscript returned: Yes, if return postage is supplied by author.
   Rejected manuscript criticized: Yes
Submit to:
   Dr. Frederick L. Morey
   Editor and Publisher
   (See address above)

ENGLISH LANGUAGE NOTES [350]
The University of Colorado
101D Hellems
Boulder, Colorado 80302
(303) 492-7624

First published in 1963

SUBSCRIPTION DATA
Issues and rates: Published quarterly.
   Average paid circulation: 1,000; 100 controlled
   Annual rate(s): $11.00; Institutions $20.00
Publisher or Sponsor: The University of Colorado

EDITORIAL DESCRIPTION
   Provides an outlet for short articles and scholarly notes pertaining to English and American language and literature. Ordinarily explication unsupported by biographical, historical or bibliographical evidence will not be accepted.
Articles per average issue: 10-15
Audience: Scholarly
   Manuscripts accepted in English

MANUSCRIPT INFORMATION
Manuscript requirements: MLA
   Preferred length: 10 pages
   Number of copies to be submitted: 1
   Abstract: Not necessary.
Author information and reprints: Payment: Reprints only. 2 copies of issue
   Is simultaneous submission of article to other journals permitted: Not permitted.
   Exclusive manuscript rights between acceptance and publication: Yes
   Copyright: Held by publication.
   Permission to reprint given upon request.
   Reprints: Available at cost.
Additional information: Typewritten, original manuscripts, please
Disposition of manuscript:
   Query letter: Not necessary.
   Receipt of manuscript acknowledged: Yes
   Decision to publish in: 3-6 months
   Accepted manuscript published in: 6-12 months
   Rejected manuscript returned: Yes, if return postage is supplied by author.
   Rejected manuscript criticized: Sometimes
Submit to:
   Charles L. Proudfit
   Editor
   (See address above)

ENGLISH LITERARY RENAISSANCE [351]
Department of English
Amherst, Massachusetts 01002
(413) 545-2520

First published in 1970

SUBSCRIPTION DATA
Issues and rates: Published three times per year.
   Average paid circulation: 650; 800 controlled
   Annual rate(s): $10.00; Institutions $15.00
Managing Editor: Roberts French

EDITORIAL DESCRIPTION
   Publishes rare texts and manuscripts, critical and scholarly essays on the English literary achievement, 1485-1668
Articles per average issue: 6
Audience: Students and scholars in the Renaissance
   Manuscripts accepted in Any modern language

MANUSCRIPT INFORMATION
Subject field(s): Literature of the English Renaissance, related literatures and fields of intellectual background
Manuscript requirements: See latest issue for style requirements. MLA
   Preferred length: 15-40 typewritten pages
   Number of copies to be submitted: 2
   Abstract: Not necessary.
Author information and reprints: Payment: Reprints only. 2 copies of the issue
   Is simultaneous submission of article to other journals permitted: Not permitted.
   Exclusive manuscript rights between acceptance and publication: Yes
   Copyright: Held by publication, first rights only
   Reprints: Available at cost.
Additional information: Texts or transcriptions of manuscripts should be in diplomatic old-spelling with introduction, textual and explanatory notes typed separately. Illustrations may accompany submissions.
Disposition of manuscript:
   Query letter: Not necessary.
   Receipt of manuscript acknowledged: Yes
   Decision to publish in: 8-10 weeks
   Accepted manuscript published in: 1 year or less
   Rejected manuscript returned: Yes, if return postage is supplied by author.
   Rejected manuscript criticized: Yes
Submit to:
   Arthur F. Kinney
   Editor
   (See address above)

ENGLISH LITERATURE IN TRANSITION [352]
1880-1920
Department of English
Arizona State University
Tempe, Arizona 85281
(602) 965-4116

Previously entitled *English Fiction in Transition*

First published in 1957

SUBSCRIPTION DATA
Issues and rates: 4 times a year irregularly
  Average paid circulation: 850
  Annual rate(s): $4.00, Foreign $5.00
Managing Editor: Helmut E. Gerber

EDITORIAL DESCRIPTION
  Contains scholarly critical articles on authors whose work was published between 1880 and 1920; secondary annotated bibliographies; primary checklists; previously unpublished primary short works, with notes and commentary; book reviews.
Articles per average issue: 4
Audience: College and university teachers and students
  Manuscripts accepted in English

MANUSCRIPT INFORMATION
Manuscript requirements: See latest issue for style requirements.
  Preferred length: Under 8,000 to 10,000 words
  Number of copies to be submitted: Original and one copy
  Abstract: Yes; MLA Abstract Systems Form
Author information and reprints: Payment: Reprints only. 2 free copies
  Is simultaneous submission of article to other journals permitted: No
  Exclusive manuscript rights between acceptance and publication: Yes
  Copyright: Held by publication.
  Reprints: Available, cut sheets and copies at special rates
Additional information: Double-spaced, notes gathered at end, full bibliographical data in notes.
Disposition of manuscript:
  Query letter: No
  Receipt of manuscript acknowledged: Yes
  Decision to publish in: 6-8 weeks
  Accepted manuscript published in: Within a year
  Rejected manuscript returned: Yes, if self-addressed, stamped envelope is sent with manuscript.
  Rejected manuscript criticized: Yes
Submit to:
  Helmut E. Gerber
  Editor
  (See address above)

SPECIAL STIPULATIONS
  Inquire first about submission of bibliographies, primary checklists and book reviews.

ENGLISH STUDIES [353]
A Journal of English Language and Literature
Swets & Zeitlinger
347B, Heereweg
Lisse, The Netherlands
(02521) 19113

First published in 1919

SUBSCRIPTION DATA
Issues and rates: Published bi-monthly.
  Annual rate(s): Dfl. 69; Institutions Dfl. 69
Managing Editor: Prof. R. Derolez

EDITORIAL DESCRIPTION
  To publish articles dealing with the study of English language and literature
Articles per average issue: 6-8
Audience: Academic
  Manuscripts accepted in English

MANUSCRIPT INFORMATION
Manuscript requirements: Style sheet sent on request.
  Preferred length: 4-6 pages
  Abstract: Not necessary.
Author information and reprints: Payment: None.
  Is simultaneous submission of article to other journals permitted: Not permitted.
  Exclusive manuscript rights between acceptance and publication: Yes
  Copyright: Held by publication.
  Reprints: Available at no cost. 20
Disposition of manuscript:
  Query letter: Not necessary.
  Receipt of manuscript acknowledged: Yes
Submit to:
  Prof. R. Derolez
  Editor-in-Chief
  Rozier 44
  B-9000 Ghent, Belgium

ESQ: A JOURNAL OF THE AMERICAN RENAISSANCE [354]
Department of English
Washington State University
Pullman, Washington 99163
(509) 335-4795

Previously entitled *Emerson Society Quarterly*

First published in 1955

SUBSCRIPTION DATA
Issues and rates: Published quarterly.
  Average paid circulation: 1000
  Annual rate(s): $10.00
Publisher or Sponsor: Washington State University

EDITORIAL DESCRIPTION
  Publishes scholarly, critical papers on 19th century American literature and thought, general Romanticism and American Transcendentalism, including critical and historical essays and reviews, and stresses the need to view American writing in an international context.
Articles per average issue: 8
Audience: Students of American Literature
  Manuscripts accepted in English

MANUSCRIPT INFORMATION
Subject field(s): 19th century American literature, Romanticism, Transcendentalism, 19th century American philosophy and theology in relation to the arts, 19th century American arts in relation to literature, 19th century American history in relation to the arts.
Manuscript requirements: MLA
  Preferred length: 3000-10,000 words; 10-35 pages
  Number of copies to be submitted: Two
  Abstract: Not necessary.
Author information and reprints: Payment: Reprints only. A free copy of the journal
  Is simultaneous submission of article to other journals permitted: Not permitted.
  Exclusive manuscript rights between acceptance and publication: Yes
  Reprints: Available at no cost.
Disposition of manuscript:
  Query letter: Not necessary.
  Receipt of manuscript acknowledged: Yes
  Decision to publish in: 2 to 4 months
  Accepted manuscript published in: 1 year
  Rejected manuscript returned: Yes, if return postage is supplied by author.
  Rejected manuscript criticized: Yes
Submit to:
  G. R. Thompson
  Editor
  (See address above)

ESSAYS IN CRITICISM [355]
Keble College
Oxford, England
55062

First published in 1951

SUBSCRIPTION DATA
Issues and rates: Published quarterly.
  Average paid circulation: 2,500
  Annual rate(s): £3
Managing Editor: Stephen Wall

EDITORIAL DESCRIPTION
  Contains papers on literary criticism.

MANUSCRIPT INFORMATION
Subject field(s): English literature before 1940
Manuscript requirements: No specific style guide.
  Preferred length: 5,000 words
  Number of copies to be submitted: One
Author information and reprints: Payment: None.
  Is simultaneous submission of article to other journals permitted: Yes
  Exclusive manuscript rights between acceptance and publication: Yes

Copyright: Held by author.
Reprints: Available, 12 free

Disposition of manuscript:
Receipt of manuscript acknowledged: Yes
Decision to publish in: 1 month
Accepted manuscript published in: 12 months
Rejected manuscript returned: Yes, if return postage is supplied by author.
Rejected manuscript criticized: Yes
Submit to:
Stephen Wall
(See address above)

SPECIAL STIPULATIONS
Articles by English academics preferred.

EVELYN WAUGH NEWSLETTER [356]
c/o English Department
Nassau Community College
State University of New York
Garden City, New York 11530
(516) 741-6817 ext. 348

First published in 1967

SUBSCRIPTION DATA
Issues and rates: Published three times per year.
Average paid circulation: 200; 25 controlled
Annual rate(s): $2.50; Foreign £1.10
Managing Editor: Paul A. Doyle

EDITORIAL DESCRIPTION
Contains critical analysis, biographical information, bibliography, notes, news items and publication data relating to the life and writings of Evelyn Waugh; also book reviews and articles about other books and authors related to Evelyn Waugh. Emphasis is on the importance of Evelyn Waugh as a 20th century novelist, a comic and fascinating character in his own right.
Articles per average issue: 4-5
Audience: Teachers, librarians, researchers, students
Audience: English, French

MANUSCRIPT INFORMATION
Subject field(s): Critical analysis, biographical information, bibliography, book reviews, news items, notes, publication data
Manuscript requirements: MLA
Preferred length: 200 to 800 words; 3 pages
Number of copies to be submitted: One
Abstract: Yes; MLA
Author information and reprints: Payment: Reprints only. 3 copies of article
Is simultaneous submission of article to other journals permitted: No
Exclusive manuscript rights between acceptance and publication: Yes
Copyright: Held by author.
Reprints: Available, $.75 each
Disposition of manuscript:
Query letter: No
Receipt of manuscript acknowledged: No

Decision to publish in: 2 to 3 weeks
Accepted manuscript published in: One year
Rejected manuscript returned: Yes, if self-addressed, stamped envelope is sent with manuscript.
Rejected manuscript criticized: Yes
Submit to:
Paul A. Doyle
Editor-in-Chief
(See address above)

SPECIAL STIPULATIONS
Editors answer questions for scholars working on Evelyn Waugh; publication serves as a clearing house for information.

THE EXPLICATOR [357]
Virginia Commonwealth University
901 West Franklin Street
Richmond, Virginia 23284
(804) 770-6522

SUBSCRIPTION DATA
Issues and rates: Published monthly.
Average paid circulation: 2600
Annual rate(s): 4.00, Foreign $4.50; Institutions $6.00
Publisher or Sponsor: The Explicator Literary Foundation, Inc.
Managing Editor: J. Edwin Whitesell

EDITORIAL DESCRIPTION
Contains *explications de texte* in English of standard works of literature in any language.
Articles per average issue: 7-8
Audience: Teachers and students of literature
Manuscripts accepted in English only

MANUSCRIPT INFORMATION
Subject field(s): Any anthologized literature
Manuscript requirements: MLA
Preferred length: 2 typed pages
Number of copies to be submitted: Two
Author information and reprints: Payment: None.
Is simultaneous submission of article to other journals permitted: No
Exclusive manuscript rights between acceptance and publication: Yes
Copyright: Held by publication.
Reprints: Available, first ten free, $.25 per additional reprint
Additional information: Articles must be typewritten and double-spaced.
Disposition of manuscript:
Query letter: No
Receipt of manuscript acknowledged: Yes
Decision to publish in: 6 months
Accepted manuscript published in: One year
Rejected manuscript returned: Yes, if return postage is supplied by author.
Rejected manuscript criticized: Sometimes
Submit to:
Managing Editor
(See address above)

SPECIAL STIPULATIONS
Nothing but explication will be considered. No original poetry or fiction will even be read.

EXTRAPOLATION [358]
A Journal of Science Fiction and Fantasy
Box 3186
The College of Wooster
Wooster, Ohio 44691
(216) 264-1234 ext. 397

First published in 1959

SUBSCRIPTION DATA
Issues and rates: Published semi-annually.
Average paid circulation: 1,200
Annual rate(s): $3.00
Publisher or Sponsor: Modern Language Association of America, Seminar on Science Fiction,
Science Fiction Research Association, Inc.

EDITORIAL DESCRIPTION
Contains studies of science fiction and fantasy, world literature; bibliography, history, criticism.
Articles per average issue: 9-11
Audience: Scholars, teachers, students
Manuscripts accepted in English

MANUSCRIPT INFORMATION
Subject field(s): History of fantasy and science fiction; criticism and bibliography of fantasy and science fiction; other media treatment of fantasy and science fiction.
Manuscript requirements: MLA
Preferred length: 2000-5000 words; 8-20 pages
Number of copies to be submitted: Two
Abstract: Yes; MLA
Author information and reprints: Payment: None.
Is simultaneous submission of article to other journals permitted: No
Exclusive manuscript rights between acceptance and publication: Yes
Copyright: Held by publication.
Reprints: Available at no cost.
Disposition of manuscript:
Receipt of manuscript acknowledged: Yes
Decision to publish in: 6 weeks to 2 months
Accepted manuscript published in: Within year
Rejected manuscript returned: Yes
Rejected manuscript criticized: Yes
Submit to:
Thomas D. Clareson
Editor
(See address above)

THE GEORGIA REVIEW [359]
Lustrat House
University of Georgia
Athens, Georgia 30602
(404) 542-3481

First published in 1947

Literature

SUBSCRIPTION DATA
Issues and rates: Published quarterly.
   Average paid circulation: 1,800
   Annual rate(s): $3.00, Foreign $3.50
Publisher or Sponsor: University of Georgia

EDITORIAL DESCRIPTION
   Contains articles dealing with 19th and 20th century literature, literary criticism, art, and the history of ideas; short stories; poetry; book reviews.
Articles per average issue: 23
Audience: Intelligent reader
   Manuscripts accepted in English

MANUSCRIPT INFORMATION
Manuscript requirements: MLA
   Preferred length: Prose: 1,500 to 8,000 words; poetry up to 200 lines
   Number of copies to be submitted: One
   Abstract: No
Author information and reprints: Payment: By publication to author. $.01 per word. Poems: $.50 per line
   Is simultaneous submission of article to other journals permitted: No
   Exclusive manuscript rights between acceptance and publication: Yes
   Copyright: Held by publication.
   Reprints: Available, $3.25 per page for 100 copies.
Disposition of manuscript:
   Query letter: No
   Receipt of manuscript acknowledged: No
   Decision to publish in: 6-8 weeks
   Accepted manuscript published in: 3-12 months
   Rejected manuscript returned: Yes, if self-addressed, stamped envelope is sent with manuscript.
   Rejected manuscript criticized: Sometimes
Submit to:
   Editor
   (See address above)

GERMAN-AMERICAN STUDIES [360]
A Journal of History, Literature, Biography and Genealogy
7204 Langerford Drive
Cleveland, Ohio 44129
(216) 888-7293

First published in 1969

SUBSCRIPTION DATA
Issues and rates: Published semi-annually.
   Average paid circulation: 300
   Annual rate(s): $10.00; Pan-Am $12.00; Institutions $10.00; Foreign individuals $12.00
Publisher or Sponsor: The Society for German-American Studies
Managing Editor: Dr. Robert E. Ward

EDITORIAL DESCRIPTION
   Treats the history, language and literature of the German-Speaking people in the U. S. and assists genealogists, biographers, and bibliographers

Articles per average issue: 6-8
Audience: Scholars, students
   Manuscripts accepted in English, German

MANUSCRIPT INFORMATION
Subject field(s): History, literary history, original German poetry, biography, bibliography, linguistics, sociology, education, book reviews, genealogy, German immigration to U. S.
Manuscript requirements: See latest issue for style requirements. MLA
   Preferred length: 1,000 to 6,250 words; 4-25 pages
   Number of copies to be submitted: 2
   Abstract: Yes.
Author information and reprints: Payment: Reprints only. 10
   Is simultaneous submission of article to other journals permitted: Permitted, but not encouraged.
   Exclusive manuscript rights between acceptance and publication: Yes
   Copyright: Held by publication.
   Reprints: Not available.
Disposition of manuscript:
   Query letter: Not necessary, but advisable.
   Receipt of manuscript acknowledged: Yes
   Decision to publish in: 6 weeks
   Accepted manuscript published in: 4 months
   Rejected manuscript returned: Yes, if return postage is supplied by author.
   Rejected manuscript criticized: Sometimes
Submit to:
   Dr. Robert E. Ward
   Editor-in-Chief
   (See address above)

THE GYPSY SCHOLAR [361]
A Graduate Forum of Literary Criticism
Department of English
Michigan State University
East Lansing, Michigan 48824
(517) 355-7578

First published in 1973

SUBSCRIPTION DATA
Issues and rates: Published three times per year.
   Average paid circulation: 100; 50 controlled
   Annual rate(s): Individuals $5.00; Institutions $7.00; Foreign individuals $16.50; Foreign institutions $8.50
Managing Editor: George W. Perabo

EDITORIAL DESCRIPTION
   Articles written by graduate students which deal with literary works and pedagogical techniques; especially interested in approaches which are speculative, venturesome, inquiring, or controversial.
Articles per average issue: 4-6

Audience: Graduate students and faculty in departments of literature and language
   Manuscripts accepted in English only

MANUSCRIPT INFORMATION
Subject field(s): Critical articles, employing any approach, on any work of literature from any country or period; brief notes and short articles on pedagogy or other professional concerns of graduate students.
Manuscript requirements: MLA
   Preferred length: 6,000 words
   Number of copies to be submitted: 1
   Abstract: Not necessary.
Author information and reprints: Payment: None.
   Is simultaneous submission of article to other journals permitted: Not permitted.
   Exclusive manuscript rights between acceptance and publication: Yes
   Copyright: Held by publication.
   Reprints: Available at cost.
Additional information: Primary interest in articles dealing with a major work, author, genre, or theme so as to be of interest to a wide, not a specialized audience.
Disposition of manuscript:
   Query letter: Not necessary.
   Receipt of manuscript acknowledged: Yes
   Decision to publish in: 6 weeks
   Accepted manuscript published in: 6 months
   Rejected manuscript returned: Yes, if return postage is supplied by author.
   Rejected manuscript criticized: Reasons for rejections only
Submit to:
   George W. Perabo
   Managing Editor
   (See address above)

SPECIAL STIPULATIONS
   Only articles submitted by graduate students are considered for publication.

HARTFORD STUDIES IN LITERATURE [362]
A Journal of Interdisciplinary Criticism
200 Bloomfield Avenue
West Hartford, Connecticut 06117
(203) 243-4259

First published in 1968

SUBSCRIPTION DATA
Issues and rates: Published three times per year.
   Average paid circulation: 350
   Annual rate(s): Individuals $4.50, Institutions $6.00
Publisher or Sponsor: University of Hartford

EDITORIAL DESCRIPTION
   A journal of literary criticism as informed by any other art, science, or related scholarly discipline. It carries articles, book reviews, listing of books, journals, and offprints, with brief comments.

Articles per average issue: 3-7
Audience: General, scholarly
Manuscripts accepted in English

MANUSCRIPT INFORMATION
Subject field(s): Literature in any language, art, music, psychology, history, political science, economics, philosophy

Manuscript requirements: MLA
Preferred length: 10-20 pages
Number of copies to be submitted: One or two
Abstract: Yes

Author information and reprints: Payment: None.
Is simultaneous submission of article to other journals permitted: Preferably not without notice.
Exclusive manuscript rights between acceptance and publication: No
Copyright: Held by publication.
Reprints: Available, cost according to length

Disposition of manuscript:
Query letter: Yes
Receipt of manuscript acknowledged: Yes
Decision to publish in: 90 days
Accepted manuscript published in: Indefinite
Rejected manuscript returned: Yes, if return postage is supplied by author.
Rejected manuscript criticized: Yes

Submit to:
Leonard F. Manheim
General Editor
(See address above)

HORN BOOK MAGAZINE [363]
About Children's Books and Reading
585 Boylston
Boston, Massachusetts 02116
(617) 536-3145

First published in 1924

SUBSCRIPTION DATA
Issues and rates: Published bi-monthly.
Average paid circulation: 27,000
Annual rate(s): $8.50, Foreign $9.50

Managing Editor: Ethel Heins

EDITORIAL DESCRIPTION
Contains articles about children's literature and reviews of recently published children's books.

Articles per average issue: 3

Audience: Children's librarians, parents, teachers

MANUSCRIPT INFORMATION
Subject field(s): Children's literature, library programs for children

Manuscript requirements: No specific style guide.

Preferred length: 2,000 words; 7-9 pages
Number of copies to be submitted: One
Abstract: No

Author information and reprints: Payment: By publication to author. $5.00 per page.
Is simultaneous submission of article to other journals permitted: No
Exclusive manuscript rights between acceptance and publication: Yes
Copyright: Held by publication.
Reprints: Not available.

Disposition of manuscript:
Query letter: Yes
Receipt of manuscript acknowledged: Yes
Decision to publish in: 2 months
Accepted manuscript published in: 3 months
Rejected manuscript returned: Yes
Rejected manuscript criticized: No

Submit to:
Ethel Heins
Editor
(See address above)

INTERNATIONAL ARTHURIAN SOCIETY. BIOGRAPHICAL BULLETIN [364]
Department of French
University of Nottingham
Nottingham, England
(0602) 56101

First published in 1949

SUBSCRIPTION DATA
Issues and rates: Published annually.
Average paid circulation: 1200
Annual rate(s): Foreign $5.00

Publisher or Sponsor: International Arthurian Society
Managing Editor: Lewis Thorpe

EDITORIAL DESCRIPTION
Contains a world wide bibliography of literature published in all languages on the "Matter of Britain," romances of the Round Table; critical and research articles; news of congresses, list of members.

Articles per average issue: 4

Audience: Scholars and those interested in this topic

Manuscripts accepted in English, French

MANUSCRIPT INFORMATION
Subject field(s): World literature relating to Arthurian topics

Manuscript requirements: No specific style guide.

Preferred length: 1 to 10 pages; typewritten, double-spaced with footnotes numbered consecutively.

Number of copies to be submitted: Two
Abstract: Not necessary.

Author information and reprints: Payment: None.
Is simultaneous submission of article to other journals permitted: No
Exclusive manuscript rights between acceptance and publication: Yes
Copyright: Held by publication.
Reprints: Available, cost varies

Disposition of manuscript:
Query letter: Not necessary.
Receipt of manuscript acknowledged: Yes
Decision to publish in: 2 months
Accepted manuscript published in: Within a year
Rejected manuscript returned: Yes
Rejected manuscript criticized: Yes

Submit to:
Lewis Thorpe
International Secretary
(See address above)

SPECIAL STIPULATIONS
Authors are almost invariably members of the International Arthurian Society.

INTERRACIAL BOOKS FOR CHILDREN [365]
1841 Broadway
New York, New York 10023
(212) 757-5339

First published in 1965

SUBSCRIPTION DATA
Issues and rates: 8 times a year
Average paid circulation: 5000
Annual rate(s): Individuals $8.00, Institutions $15.00

Publisher or Sponsor: Council on Interracial Books for Children, Inc.

Managing Editor: Bradford Chambers

EDITORIAL DESCRIPTION
Re-evaluation of classic literature for racist and sexist stereotypes; reviews new books on multiracial themes; publishes the findings of Council studies and research projects.

Articles per average issue: 5

Audience: Parents, teachers, editors, librarians, authors
Manuscripts accepted in English

MANUSCRIPT INFORMATION
Subject field(s): Book reviews, articles on current publishing and educational matters with emphasis on identification of racist-sexist bias found in children's books.

Manuscript requirements: See latest issue for style requirements.
Preferred length: 1,000-2,000 words

Author information and reprints: Payment: By publication to author. $50.00-150.00 per article. short book reviews $10.00-$15.00

Literature

Is simultaneous submission of article to other journals permitted: Yes
Exclusive manuscript rights between acceptance and publication: No
Copyright: Held by author.
Reprints: Available

Disposition of manuscript:
Query letter: Yes
Receipt of manuscript acknowledged: Yes
Decision to publish in: 4 weeks

Submit to:
Jean Carey Bond
(See address above)

JACK LONDON NEWSLETTER [366]
c/o H.C. Woodbridge
Department of Foreign Languages
Southern Illinois University
Carbondale, Illinois, 62901

SUBSCRIPTION DATA
Issues and rates: Published three times per year.
Average paid circulation: 300
Annual rate(s): $5.00
Managing Editor: Hensley C. Woodbridge

EDITORIAL DESCRIPTION
Devoted to the study, i.e. life, works, bibliography, of Jack London and Jesse Stuart.
Articles per average issue: 6
Audience: Students of London and Stuart
Manuscripts accepted in English only

MANUSCRIPT INFORMATION
Subject field(s): Articles, notes and bibliographies
Manuscript requirements: MLA
Preferred length: Up to 10,000 words
Number of copies to be submitted: One
Abstract: No

Author information and reprints: Payment: None.
Is simultaneous submission of article to other journals permitted: No
Copyright: Not copyrighted
Reprints: 2 copies of issue given to contributors; other copies may be purchased at $1.00 per copy.
Disposition of manuscript:
Query letter: No
Receipt of manuscript acknowledged: Yes
Decision to publish in: 1 week
Accepted manuscript published in: 6-9 months
Rejected manuscript returned: Yes
Rejected manuscript criticized: Sometimes
Submit to:
Hensley Charles Woodbridge
Editor and Publisher
(See address above)

JAMES JOYCE QUARTERLY [367]
University of Tulsa
600 South College
Tulsa, Oklahoma 74104
(918) 939-6351 ext. 501

First published in 1963

SUBSCRIPTION DATA
Issues and rates: Published quarterly.
Average paid circulation: 1,150
Annual rate(s): $5.00, Foreign $6.00
Publisher or Sponsor: University of Tulsa
Managing Editor: Charlotte C. Stewart

EDITORIAL DESCRIPTION
Contains academic criticism, notes and essays, of Joyce's works and the work of his critics; reviews of books dealing with Joyce's works; essays on Joyce and the Irish Renaissance and his relationship with the writers of his time. Occasional special issues on other major Anglo-Irish writers contemporary with Joyce.
Articles per average issue: 15
Audience: People interested in Joyce
Manuscripts accepted in English

MANUSCRIPT INFORMATION
Subject field(s): Joyce studies
Manuscript requirements: MLA, plus "Special Note to Contributors" which is carried on back of contents page in each issue.
Preferred length: Notes: 900-1500 words; articles: 4500-6000 words
Number of copies to be submitted: One
Abstract: No
Author information and reprints: Payment: Reprints only. 5 contributor's copies; special rate on additional copies
Is simultaneous submission of article to other journals permitted: No
Exclusive manuscript rights between acceptance and publication: Yes
Copyright: Held by publication.
Reprints: 25 offprints at time of publication
Disposition of manuscript:
Query letter: No
Receipt of manuscript acknowledged: Yes
Decision to publish in: 6-12 weeks
Accepted manuscript published in: 6-8 months
Rejected manuscript returned: Yes, if self-addressed, stamped envelope is sent with manuscript.
Rejected manuscript criticized: Yes
Submit to:
Thomas F. Staley
Editor
(See address above)
(918) 939-6351 ext. 335

JOHNSONIAN NEWSLETTER [368]
610 Philosophy Hall
Columbia University
New York, New York 10027
(212) 280-3215

First published in 1940

SUBSCRIPTION DATA
Issues and rates: Published quarterly.
Average paid circulation: 1,200
Annual rate(s): $3.00, Foreign $3.50
Managing Editor: James L. Clifford;
John H. Middendorf

EDITORIAL DESCRIPTION
Contains news of scholarly work on the 18th century; new books about life and literature from 1660 to 1800, and Samuel Johnson and contemporaries.
Audience: Scholars and collectors interested in the 18th century

MANUSCRIPT INFORMATION
Subject field(s): 18th-century literature, work of Samuel Johnson, history of period
Manuscript requirements: No specific style guide.
Preferred length: Not over 400 words
Number of copies to be submitted: One
Abstract: No
Author information and reprints: Payment: None.
Is simultaneous submission of article to other journals permitted: No
Exclusive manuscript rights between acceptance and publication: No
Copyright: Held by author.
Reprints: Not available.
Disposition of manuscript:
Query letter: No
Receipt of manuscript acknowledged: Yes
Decision to publish in: 2-3 months
Accepted manuscript published in: 6 months
Rejected manuscript returned: Yes
Rejected manuscript criticized: Yes
Submit to:
Editor
(See address above)

SPECIAL STIPULATIONS
Poetry is sometimes accepted but must be on 18th century, or imitate 18th century style.

THE JOURNAL OF COMMONWEALTH LITERATURE [369]
Oxford University Press
Press Road
Neasden, London NW10 ODD, England

First published in 1965

SUBSCRIPTION DATA
Issues and rates: Published three times per year.
Average paid circulation: 1,000
Annual rate(s): £3.50; Foreign $9.50
Publisher or Sponsor: University of Leeds

EDITORIAL DESCRIPTION
Contains bibliographies, articles, interviews and reviews concerned with literature from anywhere in the world except Britain, Ireland and U.S. Chiefly scholarly, critical, but not merely academic in function.
Articles per average issue: 6-7 plus reviews

Audience: Readers with literary, bibliographic, general, historical, and third world interests
Manuscripts accepted in English

MANUSCRIPT INFORMATION
Subject field(s): Literature of present and past commonwealth countries except Britain and Ireland
Manuscript requirements: See latest issue for style requirements. APA
　Preferred length: 4,500 words maximum
　Number of copies to be submitted: 2
　Abstract: Yes
Author information and reprints: Payment: By publication to author. £4.00 per 1,000 words
　Is simultaneous submission of article to other journals permitted: Not permitted.
　Exclusive manuscript rights between acceptance and publication: Yes
　Copyright: Held by publication.
　Reprints: Not available.
Additional information: Double-spaced typescript; quotations of more than one line single-spaced, beginning against left margin; footnotes on separate page; use British spelling.
Disposition of manuscript:
　Query letter: Not necessary, but advisable.
　Receipt of manuscript acknowledged:
　Decision to publish in: 2-3 months
　Accepted manuscript published in: 30 months
　Rejected manuscript returned: Yes, if return postage is supplied by author.
　Rejected manuscript criticized: No
Submit to:
　Arthur Ravenscroft
　Editor
　School of English
　University of Leeds
　Leeds, LS2 9JT, England

JOURNAL OF MODERN LITERATURE [370]
Temple University
Philadelphia, Pennsylvania 19122
(215) 787-8505

First published in 1970

SUBSCRIPTION DATA
Issues and rates: 5 times a year
　Average paid circulation: 2,000
　Annual rate(s): $8.00
Managing Editor: Kathleen Morgan

EDITORIAL DESCRIPTION
　Contains scholarly studies of the literature of the past century with emphasis on the Modernist period from 1880 to 1950.
Articles per average issue: 10-12
Audience: Literary scholars
　Manuscripts accepted in English

MANUSCRIPT INFORMATION
Subject field(s): Modernist literature
Manuscript requirements: MLA
　Preferred length: None

　Number of copies to be submitted: One
　Abstract: No
Author information and reprints: Payment: By publication to author. Varies
　Is simultaneous submission of article to other journals permitted: Yes
　Exclusive manuscript rights between acceptance and publication: Yes
　Copyright: Held by publication.
　Reprints: Available at no cost.
Disposition of manuscript:
　Query letter: No
　Receipt of manuscript acknowledged: Yes
　Decision to publish in: 4-6 weeks
　Accepted manuscript published in: 6 months
　Rejected manuscript returned: Yes, if return postage is supplied by author.
　Rejected manuscript criticized: No
Submit to:
　Maurice Beebe
　Editor-in-Chief
　(See address above)

THE JOURNAL OF NARRATIVE TECHNIQUE [371]
Department of English
Eastern Michigan University
Ypsilanti, Michigan 48197
(313) 487-0165

First published in 1971

SUBSCRIPTION DATA
Issues and rates: Published three times per year.
　Average paid circulation: 500
　Annual rate(s): $3.00; Foreign $1.25
Managing Editor: George Perkins

EDITORIAL DESCRIPTION
　Scholarly essays on narrative literature in English.
Articles per average issue: 6
Audience: Scholars in English and American literature
　Manuscripts accepted in English

MANUSCRIPT INFORMATION
Subject field(s): All periods and all literary genres in English, provided that in each instance the focus of the critic is on the author's management of his narrative elements.
Manuscript requirements: MLA
　Preferred length: 3,000-6,500 words; 10-25 pages
　Number of copies to be submitted: One
　Abstract: Not necessary. Authors must prepare MLA abstracts for articles accepted for publication.
Author information and reprints: Payment: Reprints only. 10 copies of relevant issue
　Is simultaneous submission of article to other journals permitted: Not permitted.
　Copyright: By Eastern Michigan University Press
　Reprints: Not available.
Disposition of manuscript:
　Query letter: Not necessary.
　Receipt of manuscript acknowledged: Yes
　Decision to publish in: 2-3 months

　Accepted manuscript published in: 3-6 months
　Rejected manuscript returned: Yes, if return postage is supplied by author.
　Rejected manuscript criticized: Sometimes
Submit to:
　George Perkins
　General Editor
　(See address above)

JOURNAL OF SOUTH ASIAN LITERATURE [372]
Asian Studies Center
Center for International Programs 101, Michigan State University
East Lansing, Michigan 48824
(517) 353-1680

Previously entitled *Mahfil*

First published in 1965

SUBSCRIPTION DATA
Issues and rates: Published quarterly.
　Annual rate(s): Foreign $8.00; Individuals $6.00; Institutions $7.00; Students $6.00; Foreign individuals $8.00; Foreign institutions $8.00
Managing Editor: Marilyn M. Wilcox

EDITORIAL DESCRIPTION
　Devoted to the dissemination of the best of South Asian literature in English translation; publishes a large number of reviews, critical studies, bibliographies, poetry, short stories, plays, novellas, etc.
Articles per average issue: Varies
Audience: Those interested in South Asian literature
　Manuscripts accepted in English

MANUSCRIPT INFORMATION
Manuscript requirements: See latest issue for style requirements.
　Preferred length: As required
　Number of copies to be submitted: 2
　Abstract: Not necessary.
Author information and reprints: Payment: Consult Editor
　Copyright: Held by Asian Studies Center
　Reprints: Available at no cost.
Disposition of manuscript:
　Query letter: Necessary.
　Receipt of manuscript acknowledged: Yes
　Decision to publish in: Varies
　Rejected manuscript returned: Yes, with return postage paid by publication.
　Rejected manuscript criticized: Sometimes
Submit to:
　Carlo Coppola;
　C. M. Naim
　Editors
　Modern Language Department
　Oakland University
　Rochester, Minnesota 48663

JOURNAL OF SPANISH STUDIES: TWENTIETH CENTURY [373]
Department of Modern Languages
Kansas State University, Eisenhower Hall
Manhattan, Kansas 66506
(913) 532-6760

First published in 1973

SUBSCRIPTION DATA
Issues and rates: Published three times per year.
  Average paid circulation: 1,000
  Annual rate(s): $6.00 for all
Managing Editor: Luis González-del-Valle

EDITORIAL DESCRIPTION
  Contains important scholarly articles dealing with the literatures of Spain and Spanish America in this century, with emphasis on the esthetic characteristics; book reviews, both creative and critical.
Articles per average issue: 6
Audience: Academic, specialist, general
  Manuscripts accepted in English, Spanish

MANUSCRIPT INFORMATION
Subject field(s): Literary theory, individual authors, comparative literature, themes, esthetics, humanities
Manuscript requirements: MLA, with all notes at the end
  Preferred length: 12-25 pages
  Number of copies to be submitted: Original and 1 copy
  Abstract: Yes. Brief
Author information and reprints: Payment: Reprints only. 25, 50, 75, 100
  Is simultaneous submission of article to other journals permitted: Not permitted.
  Exclusive manuscript rights between acceptance and publication: Yes
  Copyright: Held by publication.
  Reprints: Available at cost.
Disposition of manuscript:
  Query letter: Not necessary.
  Receipt of manuscript acknowledged: Yes
  Decision to publish in: 2 months
  Accepted manuscript published in: 1 year
  Rejected manuscript returned: Yes, if return postage is supplied by author.
  Rejected manuscript criticized: Yes
Submit to:
  Vincente Cabrera;
  Luis T. González-del-Valle
  Editors
  Department of Foreign Languages
  Colorado State University
  Fort Collins, Colorado 80521
  (313) 491-6370

KALKI [374]
Studies in James Branch Cabell
Department of English
University of Cincinnati
Cincinnati, Ohio 45221
(513) 475-4075

Previously entitled *The Cabellian Quarterly*

First published in 1967

SUBSCRIPTION DATA
Issues and rates: Published quarterly.
  Average paid circulation: 250
  Annual rate(s): $5.00
Publisher or Sponsor: The James Branch Cabell Society
Managing Editor: Paul Spencer

EDITORIAL DESCRIPTION
  Publishes articles relating to the life, works, and milieu of James Branch Cabell; also functions as a newsletter with letters, enquiries, and reviews.
Articles per average issue: 3-4
Audience: Scholarly, general
  Manuscripts accepted in English

MANUSCRIPT INFORMATION
Subject field(s): J. B. Cabell, sources, criticism, influence, historical research
Manuscript requirements: MLA
  Preferred length: None
  Number of copies to be submitted: Two
  Abstract: No
Author information and reprints: Payment: By publication to author. Copies upon request
  Is simultaneous submission of article to other journals permitted: Yes, with permissions and agreement
  Exclusive manuscript rights between acceptance and publication: No
  Copyright: Held by publication.
  Reprints: Not available.
Disposition of manuscript:
  Query letter: No
  Receipt of manuscript acknowledged: Yes
  Decision to publish in: 30 days
  Accepted manuscript published in: 12 to 18 months
  Rejected manuscript returned: Yes
  Rejected manuscript criticized: No
Submit to:
  William Leigh Godshalk
  Editor
  (See address above)
  (513) 751-6549

THE KIPLING JOURNAL [375]
18 Northumberland Avenue
London WC2N 5BJ, England
01-930-6733

First published in 1927

SUBSCRIPTION DATA
Issues and rates: Published quarterly.
  Average paid circulation: 1000
  Annual rate(s): Individuals $5.00, Institutions $6.00
Publisher or Sponsor: The Kipling Society
Managing Editor: Roger Lancelyn Green

EDITORIAL DESCRIPTION
  Contains articles on the life and works of Rudyard Kipling; book reviews and letters
Articles per average issue: 4
Audience: Academic, general
  Manuscripts accepted in English

MANUSCRIPT INFORMATION
Manuscript requirements: See latest issue for style requirements.
  Preferred length: 2,000 words
  Number of copies to be submitted: One
  Abstract: No
Author information and reprints: Payment: None.
  Is simultaneous submission of article to other journals permitted: Yes
  Exclusive manuscript rights between acceptance and publication: No
  Copyright: Held by author.
  Reprints: Not available.
Disposition of manuscript:
  Query letter: No
  Receipt of manuscript acknowledged: Yes
  Decision to publish in: Six weeks
  Accepted manuscript published in: Varies
  Rejected manuscript returned: Yes, if return postage is supplied by author.
  Rejected manuscript criticized: Yes
Submit to:
  Roger Lancelyn Green
  Poulton Hall
  Poulton-Lancelyn
  Wirral, Cheshire L63 9LN, England

L'ESPRIT CRÉATEUR [376]
Box 222
Lawrence, Kansas 66044
(913) 864-3164

First published in 1961

SUBSCRIPTION DATA
Issues and rates: Published quarterly.
  Average paid circulation: 1200
  Annual rate(s): $5.00

EDITORIAL DESCRIPTION
  Contains critical interpretation of French literature. Each issue presents analyses of the literary production of a single author or of works falling within a literary movement or mode. Reviews and review articles are accepted, as well as interviews with contemporary French or Francophone critics.
Articles per average issue: 8
Audience: Persons interested in French literature
  Manuscripts accepted in English, French

MANUSCRIPT INFORMATION
Subject field(s): Literature: French, Francophone
Manuscript requirements: MLA
  Preferred length: 4,000 words; 15 pages
  Number of copies to be submitted: Two
  Abstract: No
Author information and reprints: Payment: Reprints only. Five copies
  Is simultaneous submission of article to other journals permitted: No
  Exclusive manuscript rights between acceptance and publication: Yes
  Copyright: Held by publication.
  Reprints: Available, cost by page and length

Additional information: Avoid footnotes
Disposition of manuscript:
Query letter: Only for reviews
Receipt of manuscript acknowledged: Yes
Decision to publish in: 3-6 months
Accepted manuscript published in: 3-6 months
Rejected manuscript returned: Yes
Rejected manuscript criticized: Yes
Submit to:
John D. Erickson
Editor
(See address above)

THE LITERARY REVIEW [377]
Fairleigh Dickinson University
Rutherford, New Jersey 07070
(201) 933-5000 ext. 353

First published in 1957

SUBSCRIPTION DATA
Issues and rates: Published quarterly.
Average paid circulation: 2,000
Annual rate(s): $7.00, Foreign $8.00
Managing Editor: Charles Angoff

EDITORIAL DESCRIPTION
Concerns itself chiefly with contemporary writing in the field of *belles lettres* both in the U.S. and abroad. Although essays of analytical or explicatory nature are frequently published, the review stresses creative rather than critical writing.
Articles per average issue: Varies
Manuscripts accepted in English

MANUSCRIPT INFORMATION
Subject field(s): Poetry, stories, articles, plays, sketches, epigrams
Manuscript requirements: No specific style guide.
Number of copies to be submitted: One
Abstract: No
Author information and reprints: Payment: Reprints only. Two copies of the issue in which material appears.
Is simultaneous submission of article to other journals permitted: No
Exclusive manuscript rights between acceptance and publication: Yes
Copyright: Held by publication.
Reprints: Available, cost depends upon length
Disposition of manuscript:
Query letter: No
Receipt of manuscript acknowledged: No
Decision to publish in: 6 to 8 weeks
Accepted manuscript published in: 12-18 months
Rejected manuscript returned: Yes, if return postage is supplied by author.
Rejected manuscript criticized: No
Submit to:
Charles Angoff
Editor
(See address above)

LITERARY SKETCHES [378]
P.O. Box 711
Williamsburg, Virginia 23185
(804) 229-2901

Previously entitled *Books*

First published in 1961

SUBSCRIPTION DATA
Issues and rates: Published monthly.
Average paid circulation: 1,000
Annual rate(s): $1.50, Foreign $2.00
Managing Editor: Mary Lewis Chapman

EDITORIAL DESCRIPTION
Contains sketches of literary personalities.
Articles per average issue: 1
Manuscripts accepted in English

MANUSCRIPT INFORMATION
Subject field(s): Literary
Manuscript requirements: See latest issue for style requirements.
Preferred length: Not over 1,000 words
Number of copies to be submitted: One
Abstract: No
Author information and reprints: Payment: By publication to author. $.005 per word.
Is simultaneous submission of article to other journals permitted: Yes
Exclusive manuscript rights between acceptance and publication: Yes
Copyright: Held by publication.
Reprints: Not available.
Disposition of manuscript:
Query letter: No
Receipt of manuscript acknowledged: No
Decision to publish in: One month
Accepted manuscript published in: 1-6 months
Rejected manuscript returned: Yes, if return postage is supplied by author.
Rejected manuscript criticized: No
Submit to:
Mary Lewis Chapman
Publisher-Editor
(See address above)

LITERATURE/FILM QUARTERLY [379]
Salisbury State College
Salisbury, Maryland 21801
(301) 749-8810

First published in 1973

SUBSCRIPTION DATA
Issues and rates: Published quarterly.
Average paid circulation: 600
Annual rate(s): $6.00; Foreign $6.00; Individuals $5.00; Students $4.00
Managing Editor: Thomas L. Erskine

EDITORIAL DESCRIPTION
Articles on the complex interrelationships between literature and film. Also publish interviews and reviews of film books and contemporary films with literary ties.
Articles per average issue: 10
Audience: Students of literature and film

Manuscripts accepted in English only

MANUSCRIPT INFORMATION
Subject field(s): Literature and film
Manuscript requirements: MLA
Preferred length: 2,500 words; 10 pages
Number of copies to be submitted: 2
Abstract: Not necessary.
Author information and reprints: Payment: Reprints only. 1 issue, 6 offprints
Is simultaneous submission of article to other journals permitted: Permitted, but not encouraged.
Exclusive manuscript rights between acceptance and publication: Yes
Copyright: Held by publication.
Reprints: Available at no cost. 6
Disposition of manuscript:
Query letter: Not necessary.
Receipt of manuscript acknowledged: Yes
Decision to publish in: 3 months
Accepted manuscript published in: 3 months
Rejected manuscript returned: Yes, if return postage is supplied by author.
Rejected manuscript criticized: Sometimes
Submit to:
Thomas L. Erskine
Editor
(See address above)

THE LONDON COLLECTOR [380]
1420 Pontiac Road S. E.
Grand Rapids, Michigan 49506
(616) 452-2531

First published in 1971

SUBSCRIPTION DATA
Issues and rates: Irregular
Average paid circulation: 200
Annual rate(s): $1.00
Managing Editor: Richard L. Weiderman

EDITORIAL DESCRIPTION
All articles of interest pertaining to the life and work of Jack London
Articles per average issue: 4
Audience: Anyone interested in the life and works of Jack London
Manuscripts accepted in English

MANUSCRIPT INFORMATION
Subject field(s): Jack London and his times; San Francisco writers at the turn of the century; London collecting and bibliography
Manuscript requirements: No specific style guide.
Preferred length: None
Number of copies to be submitted: 1
Abstract: Not necessary.
Author information and reprints: Payment: Reprints only. 12
Is simultaneous submission of article to other journals permitted: Permitted.
Exclusive manuscript rights between acceptance and publication: Yes
Copyright: Held by publication.
Reprints: Available at cost.

Disposition of manuscript:
Query letter: Not necessary.
Receipt of manuscript acknowledged: Yes
Decision to publish in: 1 week
Accepted manuscript published in: A long time
Rejected manuscript returned: Yes, with return postage paid by publication.
Rejected manuscript criticized: Yes
Submit to:
Richard L. Weiderman
Editor
(See address above)

MARK TWAIN JOURNAL [381]
Kirkwood, Missouri 63122
(314) 822-0852

Previously entitled *Mark Twain Quarterly*

First published in 1936

SUBSCRIPTION DATA
Issues and rates: Published semi-annually.
Average paid circulation: Not available.
Annual rate(s): $3.00 for four issues
Managing Editor: Cyril Clemens

EDITORIAL DESCRIPTION
Publishes articles on Mark Twain and other noted authors, both foreign and domestic; some verse in each issue.
Articles per average issue: 10-12
Audience: scholars, and students of Mark Twain
Manuscripts accepted in English

MANUSCRIPT INFORMATION
Subject field(s): Mark Twain, English authors, foreign authors, recollections of noted people and accounts of visits with noted people
Manuscript requirements: See latest issue for style requirements.
Preferred length: 2 to 10 pages
Number of copies to be submitted: One
Abstract: No
Author information and reprints: Payment: None.
Is simultaneous submission of article to other journals permitted: No
Exclusive manuscript rights between acceptance and publication: Yes
Copyright: Held by author.
Reprints: Not available.
Disposition of manuscript:
Query letter: No
Receipt of manuscript acknowledged: Yes
Decision to publish in: Two weeks
Accepted manuscript published in: 6-12 months
Rejected manuscript returned: Yes
Rejected manuscript criticized: No
Submit to:
Cyril Clemens
Editor
(See address above)

SPECIAL STIPULATIONS
New authors are given special consideration.

MASSACHUSETTS STUDIES IN ENGLISH [382]
Journal of the University of Massachusetts Graduate English Program
Department of English, Bartlett Hall
University of Massachusetts
Amherst, Massachusetts 01002
(413) 545-0978

First published in 1967

SUBSCRIPTION DATA
Issues and rates: Published semi-annually.
Average paid circulation: 150; 250 controlled
Annual rate(s): $2.00
Publisher or Sponsor: University of Massachusetts, Graduate English Program
Managing Editor: Susan Currier

EDITORIAL DESCRIPTION
Publishes articles of original criticism in all areas of English and American literature, stylistics, aesthetic theory and linguistics.
Articles per average issue: 3-4
Audience: Academic
Manuscripts accepted in English

MANUSCRIPT INFORMATION
Subject field(s): English and American literature, English and American linguistics, American dialectology
Manuscript requirements: MLA; Chicago
Preferred length: 5000 words; 20 pages maximum
Number of copies to be submitted: One
Abstract: No
Author information and reprints: Payment: None.
Is simultaneous submission of article to other journals permitted: No
Exclusive manuscript rights between acceptance and publication: Yes
Copyright: Held by publication.
Reprints: Not available.
Additional information: Manuscripts should conform to the MLA Style Sheet, with double-spaced footnotes at the end.
Disposition of manuscript:
Query letter: No
Receipt of manuscript acknowledged: No
Decision to publish in: 3 months
Accepted manuscript published in: 1-3 months
Rejected manuscript returned: Yes
Rejected manuscript criticized: No
Submit to:
Marcia S. Curtis
Editor
(See address above)

SPECIAL STIPULATIONS
Accepts manuscripts only from students enrolled in a recognized graduate English program.

MILTON QUARTERLY [383]
Department of English
Ohio University
Athens, Ohio 45701
(614) 594-6422

Previously entitled *Milton Newsletter*

First published in 1967

SUBSCRIPTION DATA
Issues and rates: Published quarterly.
Average paid circulation: 800-1000
Annual rate(s): Individuals $4.00; Institutions $5.00; Foreign $4.50
Managing Editor: Markland G. Lloyd

EDITORIAL DESCRIPTION
Contains articles on the life and works of John Milton; reviews of current books (or tapes or recordings) concerned with Milton or the seventeenth-century milieu; abstracts of articles appearing in other journals. Point of view is objective, non-biased.
Articles per average issue: 4-6
Audience: Scholars, interested readers
Manuscripts accepted in English

MANUSCRIPT INFORMATION
Subject field(s): Milton's life, poetry, cultural milieu
Manuscript requirements: MLA
Preferred length: 15 pages or less
Number of copies to be submitted: One
Abstract: Yes; MLA
Author information and reprints: Payment: Reprints only. Five complimentary issues
Is simultaneous submission of article to other journals permitted: No
Exclusive manuscript rights between acceptance and publication: Yes, but exceptions are occasionally made
Copyright: Held by Editor
Reprints: Available through printer
Disposition of manuscript:
Query letter: No
Receipt of manuscript acknowledged: Yes
Decision to publish in: 4-6 weeks
Accepted manuscript published in: Generally less than one year
Rejected manuscript returned: Yes
Rejected manuscript criticized: Yes
Submit to:
Markland G. Lloyd
Assistant Editor
(See address above)

MODERN FICTION STUDIES [384]
Department of English
Purdue University
West Lafayette, Indiana 47907
(317) 493-1684

First published in 1955

SUBSCRIPTION DATA
Issues and rates: Published quarterly.
Average paid circulation: 4200
Annual rate(s): Individuals $6.00, Institutions $7.00, Foreign $8.00

EDITORIAL DESCRIPTION
Publishes criticism, scholarship, and bibliographies of American, English, and European fiction since 1880; articles, notes and comments, correspondence, and book reviews. Spring and Autumn

issues are often special numbers dealing with individual writers; Summer and Winter issues are generally concerned with various writers and subjects.
Articles per average issue: 10
Audience: Teachers and scholars of modern fiction
Manuscripts accepted in All modern languages

MANUSCRIPT INFORMATION
Subject field(s): Critical articles, critical notes, literary criticism of fiction in all languages since 1880
Manuscript requirements: MLA
Preferred length: 3000-6000 words (for articles); 500-2000 words (for notes)
Number of copies to be submitted: One
Abstract: Only after acceptance
Author information and reprints: Payment: Reprints only. 2 copies of the journal and 15-40 off-prints, depending on length.
Is simultaneous submission of article to other journals permitted: No
Exclusive manuscript rights between acceptance and publication: Yes
Copyright: Author has specified right to reprint his own material and receives 50 per cent of reprint sales of specific articles.
Reprints: Not available.
Disposition of manuscript:
Query letter: No
Receipt of manuscript acknowledged: Yes
Decision to publish in: 2-4 months
Accepted manuscript published in: 18-24 months for general issues, 3-4 months for special issues.
Rejected manuscript returned: Yes, if return postage is supplied by author.
Rejected manuscript criticized: Rarely
Submit to:
William T. Stafford;
Margaret Church
Editors
(See address above)

MODERN PHILOLOGY [385]
University of Chicago Press
5801 Ellis Avenue
Chicago, Illinois 60637
(312) 753-2592

First published in 1903

SUBSCRIPTION DATA
Issues and rates: Published quarterly.
Average paid circulation: 1800
Annual rate(s): $8.00, Foreign $9.00
Publisher or Sponsor: University of Chicago, Division of Humanities

EDITORIAL DESCRIPTION
Devoted to research in medieval and modern literature. Interested in all significant developments in the fields of literary study. Short notes are used only when of exceptional importance.
Articles per average issue: 7
Audience: Scholars, critics, and students of medieval and modern literature and language

Manuscripts accepted in all modern languages

MANUSCRIPT INFORMATION
Manuscript requirements: See latest issue for style requirements.
Preferred length: 50 pages maximum
Number of copies to be submitted: One; typewritten
Abstract: No
Author information and reprints: Payment: None.
Is simultaneous submission of article to other journals permitted: No
Exclusive manuscript rights between acceptance and publication: Yes
Copyright: Held by publication.
Reprints: Available, cost varies according to length.
Disposition of manuscript:
Query letter: No
Receipt of manuscript acknowledged: Yes
Decision to publish in: 1-3 months
Accepted manuscript published in: 18-30 months
Rejected manuscript returned: Yes, if self-addressed, stamped envelope is sent with manuscript.
Rejected manuscript criticized: Occasionally
Submit to:
Gwin J. Kolb;
Edward W. Rosenheim, Jr.
Editors
University of Chicago
1050 East 59th Street
Chicago, Illinois 60637
(312) 753-2503

MOSAIC [386]
A Journal for the Comparative Study of Literature and Ideas
208 Tier Building
University of Manitoba
Winnipeg, Manitoba, Canada
(204) 474-9763

First published in 1967

SUBSCRIPTION DATA
Issues and rates: Published quarterly.
Average paid circulation: 1,900
Annual rate(s): $8.00
Managing Editor: R. G. Collins; John Wortley

EDITORIAL DESCRIPTION
A journal for the comparative study of literature and ideas.
Articles per average issue: 12
Audience: Literary, academic
Manuscripts accepted in English, French

MANUSCRIPT INFORMATION
Subject field(s): Literature, art, psychology, sociology
Manuscript requirements: MLA
Preferred length: 5,000 words
Number of copies to be submitted: One
Abstract: Yes; MLA

Author information and reprints: Payment: None. Payment in special instances only.
Is simultaneous submission of article to other journals permitted: No
Exclusive manuscript rights between acceptance and publication: Yes
Copyright: Held by publication.
Reprints: Available, 25 free
Disposition of manuscript:
Query letter: No
Receipt of manuscript acknowledged: Yes
Decision to publish in: 8 to 10 weeks
Accepted manuscript published in: Six months
Rejected manuscript returned: Yes
Rejected manuscript criticized: Yes
Submit to:
R.G. Collins;
John Wortley
Co-Editors
(See address above)

MÉLANGES MALRAUX MISCELLANY [387]
Box 3231
University of Wyoming
Laramie, Wyoming 82071
(307) 766-4177

First published in 1969

SUBSCRIPTION DATA
Issues and rates: Published semi-annually.
Average paid circulation: 275; 25 controlled
Annual rate(s): $4.00
Publisher or Sponsor: The Malraux Society

EDITORIAL DESCRIPTION
Contains biographical, bibliographical, critical studies related to the life or work of André Malraux.
Articles per average issue: 4-6
Audience: Scholars, general
Manuscripts accepted in English, French, German

MANUSCRIPT INFORMATION
Subject field(s): Anything related to Malraux.
Manuscript requirements: MLA
Preferred length: 10 to 25 pages
Number of copies to be submitted: One
Abstract: Yes, 1 page with footnotes at end of article
Author information and reprints: Payment: Reprints only. 10 issues
Is simultaneous submission of article to other journals permitted: No
Exclusive manuscript rights between acceptance and publication: Yes
Copyright: Held by publication.
Reprints: Not available.
Disposition of manuscript:
Query letter: No
Receipt of manuscript acknowledged: Yes
Decision to publish in: One month to six weeks
Accepted manuscript published in: Less than one year
Rejected manuscript returned: Yes

Literature

Rejected manuscript criticized: Sometimes
Submit to:
Walter G. Langlois
Editor
(See address above)

NEGRO AMERICAN LITERATURE FORUM [388]
For School and University Teachers
School of Education
Indiana State University
Terre Haute, Indiana 47809
(812) 232-6311 ext. 2851

First published in 1967

SUBSCRIPTION DATA
Issues and rates: Published quarterly.
  Average paid circulation: 750
  Annual rate(s): $4, Foreign $5
Managing Editor: Hannah Hedrick

EDITORIAL DESCRIPTION
  Contains literary, critical, pedagogical, curricular articles on literature by or about Black Americans.
Articles per average issue: 6
Audience: Teachers in secondary and undergraduate programs

MANUSCRIPT INFORMATION
Subject field(s): Literary criticism, curricula, creative writing
Manuscript requirements: MLA
  Preferred length: 15 pages maximum
  Number of copies to be submitted: One
  Abstract: No
Author information and reprints: Payment: Reprints only. 3 copies to each contributor
  Is simultaneous submission of article to other journals permitted: Yes
  Exclusive manuscript rights between acceptance and publication: No
  Copyright: Held by publication.
  Reprints: Not available.
Additional information: Guest editors for special issues are paid $60 for expenses.
Disposition of manuscript:
  Query letter: No
  Receipt of manuscript acknowledged: Yes
  Decision to publish in: 2 weeks
  Accepted manuscript published in: One year
  Rejected manuscript returned: Yes
  Rejected manuscript criticized: Yes
Submit to:
  Hannah Hedrick
  (See address above)

NEUVA NARRATIVA HISPANOAMERICA [389]
Latin American Studies Program
Adelphi University
Garden City, New York 11530

First published in 1971

SUBSCRIPTION DATA
Issues and rates: Published semi-annually.
  Annual rate(s): Institutions $15.00; Students $12.00; Foreign individuals $20.00; Foreign institutions $20.00
Managing Editor: Helmy F. Giacoman

EDITORIAL DESCRIPTION
  Theoretical and critical studies of contemporary Latin American fiction.
Articles per average issue: 20
Audience: University professors and graduate students.
  Manuscripts accepted in Spanish

MANUSCRIPT INFORMATION
Subject field(s): Contemporary Latin American fiction
Manuscript requirements: MLA
  Preferred length: 20 pages
  Number of copies to be submitted: 2
  Abstract: Not necessary.
Author information and reprints: Payment: None.
  Is simultaneous submission of article to other journals permitted: Not permitted.
  Copyright: Held by publication first and author second.
  Reprints: Available at cost. Varies
Disposition of manuscript:
  Query letter: Not necessary.
  Receipt of manuscript acknowledged: Yes
  Decision to publish in: 60 days
  Accepted manuscript published in: 60 days
  Rejected manuscript returned: Yes, if return postage is supplied by author.
  Rejected manuscript criticized: No
Submit to:
  Helmy F. Giacoman
  Editor
  P.O. Box 70
  Malverne, New York 11565

SPECIAL STIPULATIONS
  Articles must be highly scientific and original.

THE NEW ENGLAND QUARTERLY* [390]
A Historical Review of New England Life and Letters
Hubbard Hall, Bowdoin College
Brunswick, Maine 04001
(207) 725-8731 ext. 289

SUBSCRIPTION DATA
Issues and rates: Published quarterly.
  Average paid circulation: 2000
  Annual rate(s): $8.00
Publisher or Sponsor: The Colonial Society of Massachusetts

EDITORIAL DESCRIPTION
  Contains essays and reviews on New England life and literature.

MANUSCRIPT INFORMATION
Subject field(s): Literature and history
Manuscript requirements: See latest issue for style requirements.
  Preferred length: Twenty-five pages
  Number of copies to be submitted: One or two
Author information and reprints: Payment: None.
  Is simultaneous submission of article to other journals permitted: No
  Exclusive manuscript rights between acceptance and publication: No
  Copyright: Held by publication.
  Reprints: Available, authors receive 25 copies and a year subscription
Disposition of manuscript:
  Receipt of manuscript acknowledged: Yes
  Decision to publish in: One month
  Accepted manuscript published in: One year
  Rejected manuscript returned: Yes
  Rejected manuscript criticized: No
Submit to:
  Herbert Ross Brown
  Managing Editor
  (See address above)

NEW LITERARY HISTORY [391]
A Journal of Theory and Interpretation
Wilson Hall
University of Virginia
Charlottesville, Virginia 22903
(804) 924-3887

First published in Autumn 1969

SUBSCRIPTION DATA
Issues and rates: Published three times per year.
  Average paid circulation: 1,571; 100 controlled
  Annual rate(s): $9.00, Foreign $9.75, Institutions $12.00

EDITORIAL DESCRIPTION
  Focus is on the theory and interpretation of literature, not confined to English or American literature.
Articles per average issue: 12
Audience: Academic
  Manuscripts accepted in English, French, German, Russian

MANUSCRIPT INFORMATION
Subject field(s): Reasons for literary change; the definitions of periods and their uses in interpretation; the evolution of styles, conventions, genres and their relationship to each other and to the periods in which they flourished; the interconnection between national literary histories; the place of evaluation in literary history, etc. and articles from other disciplines that help interpret or define the problems of literary history.
Manuscript requirements: MLA
  Preferred length: 5,000 to 6,000 words; 20 pages
  Number of copies to be submitted: One
  Abstract: No
Author information and reprints: Payment: Reprints only. 25 offprints of article and copy of journal
  Is simultaneous submission of article to other journals permitted: No
  Exclusive manuscript rights between acceptance and publication: Yes
  Copyright: Held by publication.

Reprints: Available, $.50 each
Disposition of manuscript:
  Query letter: No
  Receipt of manuscript acknowledged: Yes
  Decision to publish in: 3-6 months
  Accepted manuscript published in: Varies
  Rejected manuscript returned: Yes
  Rejected manuscript criticized: No
Submit to:
  Ralph Cohen
  Editor
  (See address above)

SPECIAL STIPULATIONS
  Articles must be primarily theoretical.

THE NEWSBOY [392]
440 Palace Street
Aurora, Illinois 60506

First published in 1961

SUBSCRIPTION DATA
Issues and rates: Published monthly.
  Average paid circulation: 300
  Annual rate(s): $5.00, Foreign $6.00
Publisher or Sponsor: Horatio Alger Society

EDITORIAL DESCRIPTION
  Contains articles on or about Horatio Alger, Jr.: his life, writing, times and places.
Articles per average issue: 1
Audience: Libraries and members of the Society
  Manuscripts accepted in English

MANUSCRIPT INFORMATION
Subject field(s): Horatio Alger, Jr.
Manuscript requirements: No specific style guide.
  Preferred length: None
  Number of copies to be submitted: One
  Abstract: No
Author information and reprints: Payment: None.
  Is simultaneous submission of article to other journals permitted: Yes
  Exclusive manuscript rights between acceptance and publication: No
  Copyright: Held by author.
  Reprints: Available, 5 free
Additional information: Articles must be authenticated with proper credit for sources. Sources must be open for approval.
Disposition of manuscript:
  Query letter: No
  Receipt of manuscript acknowledged: Yes
  Decision to publish in: 1-2 months
  Accepted manuscript published in: 1-2 months
  Rejected manuscript returned: Yes
  Rejected manuscript criticized: Sometimes
Submit to:
  Jack Bales
  Editor
  (See address above)

NINETEENTH-CENTURY FICTION [393]
Department of English
Rolfe Hall 3336
University of California
Los Angeles, California 90024
(213) 825-4920

Previously entitled *The Trollopian*

First published in 1945

SUBSCRIPTION DATA
Issues and rates: Published quarterly.
  Average paid circulation: 2,300
  Annual rate(s): Individuals $8.00, Institutions $12.00

EDITORIAL DESCRIPTION
  Contains scholarly and critical articles on English language fiction of the period 1800-1900; notes on historical and critical aspects of that fiction; reviews of scholarly and critical books about the fiction and the authors of the period.
Articles per average issue: 7-8
Audience: Scholarly
  Manuscripts accepted in English

MANUSCRIPT INFORMATION
Subject field(s): 19th-century fiction, individual authors of such fiction.
Manuscript requirements: MLA
  Preferred length: 5000 words; 20 pages
  Number of copies to be submitted: One
  Abstract: No
Author information and reprints: Payment: None.
  Is simultaneous submission of article to other journals permitted: No
  Exclusive manuscript rights between acceptance and publication: Yes
  Copyright: Held by publication.
  Reprints: Available; 25 free, additional $.56 per copy
Additional information: Desire manuscripts that make a significant contribution to the scholarly and critical understanding of the works and authors treated. Authors are expected to be in full command of the existing scholarship and criticism on their subjects. Everything typewritten, double-spaced including footnotes at end.
Disposition of manuscript:
  Query letter: No
  Receipt of manuscript acknowledged: Yes
  Decision to publish in: 1-3 months
  Accepted manuscript published in: 12-18 months
  Rejected manuscript returned: Yes, if return postage is supplied by author.
  Rejected manuscript criticized: Sometimes
Submit to:
  Alexander Welsh
  Editor
  (See address above)

NINETEENTH-CENTURY FRENCH STUDIES [394]
Department of Foreign Languages
State University College
Fredonia, New York 14063
(716) 672-3385

First published in 1972

SUBSCRIPTION DATA
Issues and rates: Published quarterly.
  Average paid circulation: 550
  Annual rate(s): $5.50; Foreign $5.50

EDITORIAL DESCRIPTION
  Publishes studies of French literature of the 19th century from a philosophical, psychological, sociological, anthropological, cultural, historical, or other critical standpoint.
Articles per average issue: 8
Audience: Students and scholars of French literature
  Manuscripts accepted in English, French

MANUSCRIPT INFORMATION
Subject field(s): Literature, criticism, short story, poetry, theater, novel
Manuscript requirements: MLA
  Preferred length: 2,000 to 5,000 words; 10 to 20 pages
  Number of copies to be submitted: One
  Abstract: Yes; MLA abstract of 200 words or less in English
Author information and reprints: Payment: Reprints only. copies of issue
  Is simultaneous submission of article to other journals permitted: No
  Exclusive manuscript rights between acceptance and publication: Yes
  Copyright: Held by publication.
  Reprints: Available; cost depends on length
Disposition of manuscript:
  Query letter: No
  Receipt of manuscript acknowledged: Yes
  Decision to publish in: 1-3 months
  Accepted manuscript published in: 6-12 months
  Rejected manuscript returned: Yes, if self-addressed, stamped envelope is sent with manuscript.
  Rejected manuscript criticized: Yes
Submit to:
  Thomas H. Goetz
  Editor
  (See address above)

NOTES ON MISSISSIPPI WRITERS [395]
Box 433, Southern Station
Hattiesburg, Mississippi 39401
(601) 266-7189

First published in 1968

SUBSCRIPTION DATA
Issues and rates: Published three times per year.
  Average paid circulation: 300
  Annual rate(s): $2.00, Foreign $2.50

Managing Editor: Hilton Anderson

EDITORIAL DESCRIPTION
Contains material about Mississippi authors.
Articles per average issue: 4-6
Audience: Academic
Manuscripts accepted in English

MANUSCRIPT INFORMATION
Subject field(s): Literature, biography, bibliography, criticism
Manuscript requirements: MLA
Preferred length: 500-600 words; 1-20 pages
Number of copies to be submitted: One
Abstract: No
Author information and reprints: Payment: Reprints only. 5 copies of issue
Is simultaneous submission of article to other journals permitted: No
Exclusive manuscript rights between acceptance and publication: Yes
Copyright: Held by publication.
Reprints: Not available.
Disposition of manuscript:
Query letter: No
Receipt of manuscript acknowledged: Yes
Decision to publish in: 2-3 months
Accepted manuscript published in: 2-6 months
Rejected manuscript returned: Yes, if return postage is supplied by author.
Rejected manuscript criticized: Yes
Submit to:
Hilton Anderson
Editor
(See address above)

NOTTINGHAM FRENCH STUDIES [396]
The University
Nottingham, NG7 2RD, England
(0602) 56101-2476

First published in 1962

SUBSCRIPTION DATA
Issues and rates: Published semi-annually.
Average paid circulation: 500
Annual rate(s): $4.00; Individuals $4.00
Publisher or Sponsor: The University of Nottingham

EDITORIAL DESCRIPTION
Contains articles on the literature of France, from 1500 to the present
Articles per average issue: 4
Audience: Academic
Manuscripts accepted in English, French

MANUSCRIPT INFORMATION
Manuscript requirements: See latest issue for style requirements.
Preferred length: 5,000-6,000 words; 10 pages
Number of copies to be submitted: One
Abstract: No

Author information and reprints: Payment: None.
Is simultaneous submission of article to other journals permitted: Permitted, but not encouraged.
Exclusive manuscript rights between acceptance and publication: Yes
Copyright: Held by publication.
Reprints: Available, 50 without charge
Disposition of manuscript:
Query letter: Not necessary, but advisable.
Receipt of manuscript acknowledged: Yes
Decision to publish in: 2-3 months
Accepted manuscript published in: 2-3 months
Rejected manuscript returned: Yes
Rejected manuscript criticized: No
Submit to:
Lewis Thorpe
(See address above)

NOVEL: A FORUM ON FICTION [397]
P.O. Box 1984
Brown University
Providence, Rhode Island 02912
(401) 863-2133

First published in 1967

SUBSCRIPTION DATA
Issues and rates: Published three times per year.
Average paid circulation: 1500; 250 controlled
Annual rate(s): $5.00, Foreign £1.80

EDITORIAL DESCRIPTION
Contains critical and theoretical essays and reviews on the fiction of all countries in all ages; promotes debate on novel theory, the novel's history in all literatures, and invites critical readings which accommodate the novel's breadth and depth.
Articles per average issue: 6 plus reviews
Audience: Academic
Manuscripts accepted in English

MANUSCRIPT INFORMATION
Subject field(s): Theory of the novel, comprehensive critical readings, comparative and historical essays, close readings of single works
Manuscript requirements: See latest issue for style requirements. MLA
Preferred length: 4000-6000 words; 15-25 pages
Number of copies to be submitted: One
Abstract: No
Author information and reprints: Payment: By publication to author. $50.00 per article. $35.00 for review essays; $10.00 for book reviews
Is simultaneous submission of article to other journals permitted: No
Exclusive manuscript rights between acceptance and publication: Yes
Copyright: Held by publication.
Reprints: Not available.
Disposition of manuscript:
Query letter: No
Receipt of manuscript acknowledged: Yes
Decision to publish in: Three months
Accepted manuscript published in: 6-12 months
Rejected manuscript returned: Yes, if self-addressed, stamped envelope is sent with manuscript.
Rejected manuscript criticized: Occasionally
Submit to:
Mark Spilka
Managing Editor
(See address above)
(401) 863-2391

PAPERS ON LANGUAGE AND LITERATURE [398]
A Journal for Scholars and Critics of Language and Literature
Southern Illinois University at Edwardsville
Edwardsville, Illinois 62025
692-2119

Previously entitled *Papers on English Language and Literature*

First published in 1965

SUBSCRIPTION DATA
Issues and rates: Published quarterly.
Annual rate(s): $7.00
Publisher or Sponsor: Southern Illinois University, Edwardsville

EDITORIAL DESCRIPTION
Devoted to literary history, analysis, stylistics, and evaluation.
Articles per average issue: 10
Audience: Academic
Manuscripts accepted in English, German, modern Romance languages

MANUSCRIPT INFORMATION
Subject field(s): Original materials relating to *belles lettres,* journals, notebooks, and similar documents pertaining to all periods, and all national literatures
Manuscript requirements: Chicago
Preferred length: 15-18 pages; 3-8 notes.
Number of copies to be submitted: 2
Abstract: No
Author information and reprints: Payment: None.
Is simultaneous submission of article to other journals permitted: No
Exclusive manuscript rights between acceptance and publication: No
Copyright: Held by Southern Illinois University Board of Trustees
Reprints: Available
Disposition of manuscript:
Query letter: No
Receipt of manuscript acknowledged: Yes
Decision to publish in: 2-3 months
Accepted manuscript published in: 3-12 months
Rejected manuscript returned: Yes, if self-addressed, stamped envelope is sent with manuscript.
Rejected manuscript criticized: Usually
Submit to:
Alvin Sullivan
Editor

(See address above)
(618) 692-2119

PAUNCH [399]
123 Woodward Avenue
Buffalo, New York 14214
(716) 836-7332
    Average paid circulation: 150; 450 controlled
    Annual rate(s): $3.00; Institutions $4.00; Students $3.00; Foreign individuals $3.00; Foreign institutions $4.00
Managing Editor: Arthur Efron

EDITORIAL DESCRIPTION
    Problems in aesthetics are considered from a radical point of view: that modern society has become the insane project that D. H. Lawrence thought it to be.
Articles per average issue: 8
Audience: College teachers of English and comparative literature, and students
    Manuscripts accepted in English

MANUSCRIPT INFORMATION
Subject field(s): Literature and the human body; literature and anarchism; literature and the aesthetics of Dewey and S. C. Pepper
Manuscript requirements: No specific style guide.
    Preferred length: No preference
    Number of copies to be submitted: 1
    Abstract: Not necessary.
Author information and reprints: Payment: Reprints only. 25
    Is simultaneous submission of article to other journals permitted: Not permitted.
    Exclusive manuscript rights between acceptance and publication: Yes
    Copyright: Held by publication.
    Reprints: Not available.
Disposition of manuscript:
    Query letter: Not necessary, but advisable.
    Receipt of manuscript acknowledged: No
    Decision to publish in: 60 days
    Accepted manuscript published in: up to 8 months
    Rejected manuscript returned: Yes, if return postage is supplied by author.
    Rejected manuscript criticized: Sometimes
Submit to:
    Arthur Efron
    Editor
    (See address above)

PMLA [400]
Publications of the Modern Language Association of America
62 Fifth Avenue
New York, New York 10011
(212) 691-3200 ext. 730

SUBSCRIPTION DATA
Issues and rates: Six times a year
    Average paid circulation: 33,500
    Annual rate(s): Members $25, Students $7, Foreign $18, Institutions $20
Publisher or Sponsor: Modern Language Association of America
Managing Editor: William Pell

EDITORIAL DESCRIPTION
    Publishes scholarship and criticism on the modern languages and literatures. Articles normally employ a widely applicable approach or methodology, use an interdisciplinary approach of importance to the interpretation of literature, treat a broad subject or theme, treat a major author or work, or discuss a minor author or work in such a way as to bring insight to a major author, work, genre, period, or critical method.
Articles per average issue: 10
Audience: Membership of MLA
    Manuscripts accepted in All modern languages

MANUSCRIPT INFORMATION
Subject field(s): all modern languages and literatures
Manuscript requirements: MLA
    Preferred length: 2,500-12,500 words
    Number of copies to be submitted: One
    Abstract: Yes
Author information and reprints: Payment: Reprints only. 25 offprints
    Is simultaneous submission of article to other journals permitted: No
    Exclusive manuscript rights between acceptance and publication: Yes
    Copyright: Held by publication.
    Reprints: Available
Additional information: Only members of MLA may submit papers; all papers must be accompanied by an abstract on the standard form obtainable from the Editor.
Disposition of manuscript:
    Query letter: No
    Receipt of manuscript acknowledged: Yes
    Decision to publish in: 60 days
    Accepted manuscript published in: 2 years
    Rejected manuscript returned: Yes
    Rejected manuscript criticized: Yes
Submit to:
    William D. Schaefer
    Editor
    (See address above)

SPECIAL STIPULATIONS
    Each paper submitted will be sent to at least one consultant reader and one member of the Advisory Committee. If recommended by these readers, it will be forwarded to the Editor and the Editorial Board for final decision.

POE STUDIES [401]
Department of English
Washington State University
Pullman, Washington 99163
(509) 335-4795

Previously entitled *Poe Newsletter*

First published in 1968

SUBSCRIPTION DATA
Issues and rates: Published semi-annually.
    Average paid circulation: 1100
    Annual rate(s): $3.00
Publisher or Sponsor: Washington State University
Managing Editor: G. R. Thompson

EDITORIAL DESCRIPTION
    Contains articles on the life and works of Edgar Allen Poe and his contemporaries; Gothic tradition in literature; critical and historical essays; bibliographies; reviews.
Articles per average issue: 15
Audience: Students of Poe and American Literature
    Manuscripts accepted in English

MANUSCRIPT INFORMATION
Manuscript requirements: MLA
    Preferred length: Under 5,000 words
    Number of copies to be submitted: Two
    Abstract: No
Author information and reprints: Payment: Reprints only. Ten copies of journal
    Is simultaneous submission of article to other journals permitted: No
    Exclusive manuscript rights between acceptance and publication: Yes
    Copyright: Not copyrighted
    Reprints: Not available.
Disposition of manuscript:
    Query letter: No
    Receipt of manuscript acknowledged: Yes
    Decision to publish in: 2-4 months
    Accepted manuscript published in: One year
    Rejected manuscript returned: Yes, if return postage is supplied by author.
    Rejected manuscript criticized: Yes
Submit to:
    G. R. Thompson
    Editor
    (See address above)

QUARTERLY REVIEW OF LITERATURE [402]
26 Haslet Avenue
Princeton, New Jersey 08540
(609) 452-4703

First published in 1943

SUBSCRIPTION DATA
Issues and rates: Published semi-annually.
    Average paid circulation: 2,500
    Annual rate(s): $10.00
Managing Editor: René Weiss

EDITORIAL DESCRIPTION
    Contains prose, fiction and poetry.
Articles per average issue: Varies
Audience: Academic, general
    Manuscripts accepted in English

MANUSCRIPT INFORMATION
Manuscript requirements: See latest issue for style requirements.
    Preferred length: None
Author information and reprints: Payment: By publication to author.
    Exclusive manuscript rights between acceptance and publication: Yes
    Copyright: Held by publication.

Reprints: Not available.
Disposition of manuscript:
  Query letter: No
  Receipt of manuscript acknowledged: No
  Rejected manuscript returned: Yes, if self-addressed, stamped envelope is sent with manuscript.
  Rejected manuscript criticized: Sometimes
Submit to:
  T. Weiss
  Editor
  (See address above)

SPECIAL STIPULATIONS
  Due to the present 30th Anniversary Special Retrospective Issue, no manuscripts will be read until late in 1975.

RESEARCH IN AFRICAN LITERATURES [403]
African and Afro-American Research Institute
2609 University Avenue, University of Texas at Austin
Austin, Texas 78712
(512) 471-3857

First published in 1970

SUBSCRIPTION DATA
Issues and rates: Published semi-annually.
  Average paid circulation: 1,000; 300 controlled
  Annual rate(s): $6.00 to all
Publisher or Sponsor: Modern Language Association, African Studies Association
Managing Editor: Bernth O. Lindfors

EDITORIAL DESCRIPTION
  Interested in scholarship on African oral and written literatures—articles, bibliographies, conference reports, research in progress, book reviews. Prefer theoretical, biographical and historical articles.
Articles per average issue: 10 Articles, 16 book reviews
Audience: Scholars and students of African literatures
  Manuscripts accepted in English and French

MANUSCRIPT INFORMATION
Subject field(s): Oral and written African literatures
Manuscript requirements: See latest issue for style requirements. MLA
  Preferred length: No restrictions
  Number of copies to be submitted: Two
  Abstract: Yes. Yes
Author information and reprints: Payment: Reprints only. 5 Issues
  Is simultaneous submission of article to other journals permitted: Not permitted.
  Exclusive manuscript rights between acceptance and publication: Yes
  Copyright: Held by publication.
  Reprints: Available at no cost. 25
Disposition of manuscript:
  Query letter: Not necessary.

Receipt of manuscript acknowledged: Yes
Decision to publish in: 2 months
Accepted manuscript published in: 6 months
Rejected manuscript returned: Yes, if return postage is supplied by author.
Rejected manuscript criticized: Sometimes
Submit to:
  Bernth O. Lindfors
  Editor
  (See address above)

THE REVIEW OF ENGLISH STUDIES [404]
A Quarterly Journal of English Literature and the English Language
Oxford University Press
37 Dover Street
London W1, England

First published in 1925

SUBSCRIPTION DATA
Issues and rates: Published quarterly.

EDITORIAL DESCRIPTION
  Contains scholarly articles in the field of English language and literature; reviews of works of scholarship
Articles per average issue:
Audience: Scholarly
  Manuscripts accepted in English

MANUSCRIPT INFORMATION
Subject field(s): English language and literature
Manuscript requirements: Style sheet sent on request.
  Preferred length: 6,000-7,000 words; 12-14 pages
  Number of copies to be submitted: One
  Abstract: No
Author information and reprints: Payment: None.
  Is simultaneous submission of article to other journals permitted: No
  Exclusive manuscript rights between acceptance and publication: Yes
  Copyright: Held by publication.
  Reprints: Available, 25 free
Disposition of manuscript:
  Query letter: No
  Receipt of manuscript acknowledged: Yes
  Decision to publish in: One month
  Accepted manuscript published in: Six months
  Rejected manuscript returned: Yes, if return postage is supplied by author.
  Rejected manuscript criticized: No
Submit to:
  John B. Bamborough
  Editor
  (See address above)

REVISTA DE ESTUDIOS HISPÁNICOS [405]
P.O. Box 3544
University, Alabama 35486
(205) 348-5059

First published in 1967

SUBSCRIPTION DATA
Issues and rates: Published three times per year.
  Average paid circulation: 600
  Annual rate(s): $6.00
Managing Editor: Paul Kennedy

EDITORIAL DESCRIPTION
  Focuses on Spain, Hispanic-America, other Hispanic-speaking areas and groups, and Portugal and Brazil. It allows those who dedicate themselves to research in and study of the Hispanic world to know and consider different points of view concerning literary and linguistic themes from any period.
Articles per average issue: 10
Audience: Academic
  Manuscripts accepted in English, Spanish, Portuguese, and all other modern Romance languages

MANUSCRIPT INFORMATION
Subject field(s): Spanish literature, Spanish-American literature
Manuscript requirements: MLA
  Preferred length: 25 pages maximum
  Number of copies to be submitted: One
  Abstract: No
Author information and reprints: Payment: None.
  Is simultaneous submission of article to other journals permitted: No
  Exclusive manuscript rights between acceptance and publication: Yes
  Copyright: None
  Reprints: Not available.
Disposition of manuscript:
  Query letter: No
  Receipt of manuscript acknowledged: Yes
  Decision to publish in: Up to two weeks
  Accepted manuscript published in: 2-3 years
  Rejected manuscript returned: Yes
  Rejected manuscript criticized: Yes
Submit to:
  Enrique Ruiz-Fornells
  Editor
  (See address above)

REVISTA IBEROAMERICANA [406]
612 AIR Building, University of Pittsburgh
135 North Bellefield Avenue
Pittsburgh, Pennsylvania 15213
(412) 624-5227

First published in 1938

SUBSCRIPTION DATA
Issues and rates: Published quarterly.
  Average paid circulation: 2,500
  Annual rate(s): Pan-Am $13.00; Foreign $12.00; Institutions $15.00; Students $10.00; Members $12.00

Publisher or Sponsor: Instituto Internacional de Literatura Iberoamericana
Managing Editor: Alfredo A. Roggiano

EDITORIAL DESCRIPTION

Latin American literature, criticism, scholarly documents, bibliography and reviews
Audience: Scholars, universities, colleges, higher educational institutions
Manuscripts accepted in Spanish and Portuguese

MANUSCRIPT INFORMATION

Manuscript requirements: Style sheet sent on request. MLA
  Preferred length: Articles 15 to 40 pages; Notes 5 to 14 pages
  Number of copies to be submitted: Original and one copy
  Abstract: Not necessary.
Author information and reprints: Payment: By publication to author. $50.00 per article.
  Is simultaneous submission of article to other journals permitted: Not permitted.
  Exclusive manuscript rights between acceptance and publication: Yes
  Copyright: Held by the International Institute
  Reprints: Available at no cost. 25
Disposition of manuscript:
  Query letter: Not necessary, but advisable.
  Receipt of manuscript acknowledged: Yes
  Decision to publish in: 10 to 40 days
  Accepted manuscript published in: 40 to 60 days
  Rejected manuscript returned: Yes, if return postage is supplied by author.
  Rejected manuscript criticized: Sometimes
Submit to:
  Alfredo Roggiano
  Director
  (See address above)

ROCKY MOUNTAIN REVIEW OF LANGUAGE AND LITERATURE [407]
Rocky Mountain Modern Language Association Bulletin
2056 Annex
University of Utah
Salt Lake City Utah 84112
(801)581-6070

First published in 1966

SUBSCRIPTION DATA

Issues and rates: Published quarterly.
  Average paid circulation: 700
  Annual rate(s): $6.00
Publisher or Sponsor: Rocky Mountain Modern Language Association
Managing Editor: Phillip Johnson

EDITORIAL DESCRIPTION

Contains articles on literary scholarship and pedagogical matters relating to the teaching of literature.
Articles per average issue: 5
Audience: Teachers of English, foreign languages and literatures
Manuscripts accepted in English

MANUSCRIPT INFORMATION

Subject field(s): Literary scholarship, related pedagogical matters
Manuscript requirements: MLA
  Preferred length: 2000-5000 words
  Number of copies to be submitted: Two
  Abstract: After acceptance only
Author information and reprints: Payment: None.
  Is simultaneous submission of article to other journals permitted: No
  Exclusive manuscript rights between acceptance and publication: Yes
  Copyright: Held by publication.
  Reprints: Available at cost
Additional information: All contributors must be members of the Association.
Disposition of manuscript:
  Query letter: Not necessary.
  Receipt of manuscript acknowledged: Yes
  Decision to publish in: 8 weeks
  Accepted manuscript published in: Within six months
  Rejected manuscript returned: Yes, if return postage is supplied by author.
  Rejected manuscript criticized: Sometimes
Submit to:
  Franklin Fisher;
  Rosemary Beless
  The Editors
  (See address above)

ROMANIC REVIEW [408]
Columbia University Press
562 West 113th Street
New York, New York 10025
(212) 865-2000

First published in 1910

SUBSCRIPTION DATA

Issues and rates: Published quarterly.
  Average paid circulation: 1300
  Annual rate(s): $10.00, Foreign $10.30
Managing Editor: Susan Tiefenbrun

EDITORIAL DESCRIPTION

Publication is devoted to study of the Romance literatures.
Articles per average issue: 4-5 articles; 5-10 reviews
Audience: Scholarly
Manuscripts accepted in English, French, Spanish

MANUSCRIPT INFORMATION

Subject field(s): French literature, Spanish and Italian literature, poetics
Manuscript requirements: MLA
  Preferred length: 6-20 pages
  Number of copies to be submitted: One
  Abstract: Not necessary.
Author information and reprints: Payment: None.
  Is simultaneous submission of article to other journals permitted: No
  Copyright: Held by publication.
  Reprints: Available, cost depends on length
Additional information: Manuscript should be typewritten, double-spaced with footnotes at the end.
Disposition of manuscript:
  Query letter: Not necessary.
  Receipt of manuscript acknowledged: Yes
  Decision to publish in: 2 months
  Accepted manuscript published in: 12-18 months
  Rejected manuscript returned: Yes, if self-addressed, stamped envelope is sent with manuscript.
  Rejected manuscript criticized: Sometimes
Submit to:
  Michael Riffaterre
  General Editor
  518 Philosophy Hall
  Columbia University
  New York, New York 10027
  (212) 280-3906

RUSSIAN LITERATURE TRIQUARTERLY [409]
2901 Heatherway
Ann Arbor, Michigan 48104
(313) 971-2367

First published in 1971

SUBSCRIPTION DATA

Issues and rates: Published three times per year.
  Average paid circulation: 1,000
  Annual rate(s): Individuals $15.95; Institutions $25.00; Students $12.95; Foreign individuals $16.95; Foreign institutions $26 all paper
Managing Editor: Carl R. & Ellendea Proffer

EDITORIAL DESCRIPTION

Translations, criticism and original documents pertaining to Russian literature, reviews of books currently published in field of Slavic studies
Articles per average issue: 25
Audience: Adult layman, but particularly those specializing in Russian or other literatures.
Manuscripts accepted in English & Russian

MANUSCRIPT INFORMATION

Subject field(s): Russian literature
Manuscript requirements: Style sheet sent on request.
  Preferred length: Under 40 pages preferred
  Number of copies to be submitted: 1
  Abstract: Not necessary.
Author information and reprints: Payment: Reprints only. 1 free issue, 5 free offprints
  Is simultaneous submission of article to other journals permitted: Permitted.
  Exclusive manuscript rights between acceptance and publication: Yes
  Copyright: Held by publication.
  Reprints: Available at cost. Varies

Disposition of manuscript:
  Query letter: Not necessary.
  Receipt of manuscript acknowledged: No
  Decision to publish in: 2 months
  Accepted manuscript published in: 3-12 months
  Rejected manuscript returned: Yes, with return postage paid by publication.
  Rejected manuscript criticized: Sometimes
Submit to:
  Carl R. Proffer;
  Ellendea Proffer
  Editors
  (See address above)

THE SCRIBLERIAN AND THE KIT-CATS [410]
English Department
Temple University
Philadelphia, Pennsylvania 19122
(215) 787-7539

Previously entitled *The Scriblerian*

First published in 1968

SUBSCRIPTION DATA
Issues and rates: Published semi-annually.
  Average paid circulation: 1,300; 1,700 controlled
  Annual rate(s): Individuals $3, Foreign $4

EDITORIAL DESCRIPTION
Concerned with material about the original Kit-Cats, Scriblerians and their associates in the late seventeenth and early eighteenth centuries.
Articles per average issue: 2
Audience: Scholarly
  Manuscripts accepted in English

MANUSCRIPT INFORMATION
Subject field(s): Scriblerians, Kit-Cats, 18th century contemporaries
Manuscript requirements: MLA
  Preferred length: 500 words
  Number of copies to be submitted: One
  Abstract: No
Author information and reprints: Payment: None.
  Is simultaneous submission of article to other journals permitted: No
  Exclusive manuscript rights between acceptance and publication: Yes
  Copyright: Held by publication.
  Reprints: Not available.
Additional information: Extra copies of news journal sent to authors.
Disposition of manuscript:
  Query letter: No
  Receipt of manuscript acknowledged: Yes
  Decision to publish in: Six weeks
  Accepted manuscript published in: Six months
  Rejected manuscript returned: Yes
  Rejected manuscript criticized: Sometimes
Submit to:
  The Editors
  (See address above)

THE SEWANEE REVIEW [411]
University of the South
Sewanee, Tennessee 37375
(615) 598-5142

SUBSCRIPTION DATA
Issues and rates: Published quarterly.
  Average paid circulation: 3750; 125 controlled
  Annual rate(s): $7.00
Publisher or Sponsor: The University of the South

EDITORIAL DESCRIPTION
Contains previously unpublished short fiction and verse, essays on literature and related subjects, book reviews.

MANUSCRIPT INFORMATION
Subject field(s): Creative writing (fiction and poetry), world literature, literary trends, evaluation of individual authors and books, philosophy, religion, music, English and American literature
Manuscript requirements: MLA, with slight variations
  Preferred length: 2500-10,000 words
  Number of copies to be submitted: One
Author information and reprints: Payment: By publication to author. $10.00-$12.00 per page.
  Is simultaneous submission of article to other journals permitted: No
  Exclusive manuscript rights between acceptance and publication: Yes
  Copyright: Held by publication.
  Reprints: Not available.
Disposition of manuscript:
  Receipt of manuscript acknowledged: No
  Decision to publish in: 2 weeks to 2 months
  Accepted manuscript published in: 3-24 months
  Rejected manuscript returned: Yes, if self-addressed, stamped envelope is sent with manuscript.
  Rejected manuscript criticized: No
Submit to:
  Editor
  (See address above)

THE SHAKESPEARE NEWSLETTER [412]
University of Illinois at Chicago Circle
Department of English
Chicago, Illinois 60680
(312) 996-3289

First published in 1951

SUBSCRIPTION DATA
Issues and rates: Six times during the academic year
  Average paid circulation: 2100
  Annual rate(s): $2.00, Foreign $2.25

EDITORIAL DESCRIPTION
Contains news of Shakespeare scholarship and drama, Shakespeare festivals, digests of scholarly and popular articles, digests of dissertations, digests of papers delivered at scholarly meetings, book reviews, biographies of Shakespeareans, brief original articles, occasional poems, news of Shakespeare associations.
Articles per average issue: 2
Audience: Teachers of Shakespeare and students
  Manuscripts accepted in English

MANUSCRIPT INFORMATION
Manuscript requirements: See latest issue for style requirements.
  Preferred length: 1500 words or less
  Number of copies to be submitted: One
  Abstract: Yes
Author information and reprints: Payment: Reprints only. Several copies
  Is simultaneous submission of article to other journals permitted: No
  Exclusive manuscript rights between acceptance and publication: Yes
  Copyright: Not copyrighted
  Reprints: Available at cost.
Additional information: Article must give ample evidence that other scholarship on the subject has been read and evaluated.
Disposition of manuscript:
  Query letter: Necessary.
  Receipt of manuscript acknowledged: Yes
  Decision to publish in: A week or more
  Accepted manuscript published in: Within a few weeks
  Rejected manuscript returned: Yes, if self-addressed, stamped envelope is sent with manuscript.
  Rejected manuscript criticized: Yes
Submit to:
  Louis Marder
  Editor and Publisher
  (See address above)
  (312) 475-7550

SPECIAL STIPULATIONS
Brief biographical statement would be interesting if author is not of established reputation.

SHAKESPEARE QUARTERLY [413]
201 East Capitol Street
Washington, D.C. 20003
(202) 546-4800

First published in 1950

SUBSCRIPTION DATA
Issues and rates: Published quarterly.
  Average paid circulation: 3000
  Annual rate(s): $12.50, Foreign $15.00
Publisher or Sponsor: Folger Shakespeare Library

EDITORIAL DESCRIPTION
Contains articles, notes and comments, reviews, an annual International Shakespeare bibliography and an annual review of Shakespeare festivals.
Articles per average issue: 10
Audience: Students and teachers of English literature, the Renaissance and Shakespeare
  Manuscripts accepted in English

MANUSCRIPT INFORMATION
Subject field(s): Shakespeare, all aspects

Manuscript requirements: See latest issue for style requirements.
　Preferred length: Not over 25 pages
　Number of copies to be submitted: Two
　Abstract: Yes
Author information and reprints: Payment: Reprints only. 5 copies of Journal
　Is simultaneous submission of article to other journals permitted: No
　Copyright: Held by publication.
　Reprints: Not available.
Disposition of manuscript:
　Query letter: No
　Receipt of manuscript acknowledged: Yes
　Decision to publish in: 4 months
　Accepted manuscript published in: Varies
　Rejected manuscript returned: Yes, if self-addressed, stamped envelope is sent with manuscript.
　Rejected manuscript criticized: Yes
Submit to:
　John F. Andrews
　Editor
　(See address above)
　(202) 546-8866

SPECIAL STIPULATIONS
　Highest standards of scholarship are expected.

THE SHAVIAN [414]
Journal of the Shaw Society
High Orchard
125 Markyate Road
Dagenham, Essex RM8 2LB, England
(01) 593-7209

SUBSCRIPTION DATA
Issues and rates: Published semi-annually.
　Annual rate(s): $4.00; Institutions $5.00
Publisher or Sponsor: The Shaw Society
Managing Editor: Eric F. J. Ford

EDITORIAL DESCRIPTION
　Publishes articles on the life and work of George Bernard Shaw; his influences and influence; his contemporaries and milieu; his relevance to society then and now, etc.
Articles per average issue: 14
Audience: Researchers, students,
　Manuscripts accepted in English

MANUSCRIPT INFORMATION
Manuscript requirements: MLA
　Preferred length: 5,000 words; 8-10 typewritten pages
　Number of copies to be submitted: 3
　Abstract: Yes. Up to 250 words outlining argument
Author information and reprints: Payment: Reprints only. 6 copies of article
　Is simultaneous submission of article to other journals permitted: Not permitted.
　Exclusive manuscript rights between acceptance and publication: Yes
　Copyright: Held by author.
　Reprints: Available at cost.
Additional information: Bibliographies and notes listed at end.
Disposition of manuscript:
　Query letter: Not necessary.
　Receipt of manuscript acknowledged: No
　Decision to publish in: 3 months
　Accepted manuscript published in: 12 months
　Rejected manuscript returned: No
　Rejected manuscript criticized: Sometimes
Submit to:
　Eric F. J. Ford
　Executive Editor
　(See address above)

THE SHAW REVIEW [415]
S-234 Burrowes Building
The Pennsylvania State University
University Park, Pennsylvania 16802
(814) 865-4242

Previously entitled *The Shaw Bulletin*, until 1959

First published in 1951

SUBSCRIPTION DATA
Issues and rates: Published three times per year.
　Average paid circulation: 700
　Annual rate(s): $6.75

EDITORIAL DESCRIPTION
　Perspective is Bernard Shaw and his milieu; personalities, works relevant to his age and to ours.
Articles per average issue: 10 including reviews
Audience: Literary and theatrical scholars
　Manuscripts accepted in English only

MANUSCRIPT INFORMATION
Subject field(s): Shaw
Manuscript requirements: MLA, but first footnote should be number 2
　Preferred length: Under 5,000 words
　Number of copies to be submitted: One
　Abstract: No
Author information and reprints: Payment: Reprints only. Ten copies of issue in which the article appears.
　Is simultaneous submission of article to other journals permitted: No
　Exclusive manuscript rights between acceptance and publication: Yes
　Copyright: Held by publication.
　Reprints: Available.
Disposition of manuscript:
　Receipt of manuscript acknowledged: Yes
　Decision to publish in: 2 months
　Accepted manuscript published in: 1 year
　Rejected manuscript returned: Yes, if self-addressed, stamped envelope is sent with manuscript.
　Rejected manuscript criticized: Yes
Submit to:
　Stanley Weintraub
　Editor
　(See address above)

THE SOUTH CAROLINA REVIEW [416]
Department of English
Clemson University
Clemson, South Carolina 29631
(803) 656-3229

First published in 1968

SUBSCRIPTION DATA
Issues and rates: Published semi-annually.
　Annual rate(s): $2.00; Foreign $2.50
Publisher or Sponsor: Clemson University, College of Liberal Arts
Managing Editor: William Koon

EDITORIAL DESCRIPTION
　Publishes essays, scholarly articles, criticism, poetry and stories. Not limited to regional topics.
Articles per average issue: 15
Audience: Professional literary, general
　Manuscripts accepted in English

MANUSCRIPT INFORMATION
Subject field(s): Essays on any literary topic, no geographical considerations
Manuscript requirements: No specific style guide.
　Preferred length: 8,000 words; 25 pages
　Number of copies to be submitted: 1
　Abstract: Not necessary.
Author information and reprints: Payment: Reprints only. 6
　Is simultaneous submission of article to other journals permitted: Permitted, but not encouraged.
　Exclusive manuscript rights between acceptance and publication: No
　Copyright: Held by Clemson University, reassigned to author upon request.
　Reprints: Not available.
Submit to:
　William Koon
　Editor
　(See address above)

SOUTHWESTERN AMERICAN LITERATURE [417]
Box 13646, N. T. Station
Denton, Texas 76203
(817) 788-2025

First published in 1971

SUBSCRIPTION DATA
Issues and rates: Published three times per year.
　Average paid circulation: 225
　Annual rate(s): $3.00
Publisher or Sponsor: Southwestern American Literature Association
Managing Editor: Helen Lang Leath

EDITORIAL DESCRIPTION
　Contains articles and book reviews on Southwestern literature and folklore.
Articles per average issue: 5 articles; 3-10 book reviews
Audience: Regional
　Manuscripts accepted in English

MANUSCRIPT INFORMATION
Subject field(s): Survey of genre, biography, critical, folklore, minority works
Manuscript requirements: MLA
 Preferred length: 15-20 pages
 Number of copies to be submitted: One
 Abstract: No
Author information and reprints: Payment: None.
 Is simultaneous submission of article to other journals permitted: No
 Exclusive manuscript rights between acceptance and publication: Yes
 Copyright: Held by publication.
 Reprints: Not available.
Disposition of manuscript:
 Query letter: No
 Receipt of manuscript acknowledged: Yes
 Decision to publish in: 60 days
 Accepted manuscript published in: One year
 Rejected manuscript returned: Yes
 Rejected manuscript criticized: No
Submit to:
 Helen Lang Leath
 Editor
 (See address above)

STEINBECK QUARTERLY [418]
English Department
Ball State University
Muncie, Indiana 47306
(317) 285-4044

Previously entitled *Steinbeck Newsletter*

First published in 1968

SUBSCRIPTION DATA
Issues and rates: Published quarterly.
 Average paid circulation: 350
 Annual rate(s): $6.00
Publisher or Sponsor: John Steinbeck Society of America

EDITORIAL DESCRIPTION
 Contains articles on Steinbeck, bibliographical checklists, miscellaneous reports on works in progress, recent publications, etc.
Articles per average issue: 3-5
Audience: Academic
 Manuscripts accepted in English

MANUSCRIPT INFORMATION
Subject field(s): John Steinbeck
Manuscript requirements: MLA
 Preferred length: 8-10 typewritten pages
 Number of copies to be submitted: Two
Author information and reprints: Payment: Reprints only. 5 copies of the issue
 Is simultaneous submission of article to other journals permitted: No
 Exclusive manuscript rights between acceptance and publication: Yes
 Copyright: Held by the editor for the Steinbeck Society
 Reprints: Not available.
Disposition of manuscript:
 Receipt of manuscript acknowledged: Yes
 Decision to publish in: 2 months
 Accepted manuscript published in: 12-24 months
 Rejected manuscript returned: Yes, if return postage is supplied by author.
 Rejected manuscript criticized: Sometimes
Submit to:
 Dr. Tetsumaro Hayashi
 Editor-in-Chief
 (See address above)

STUDIES IN BLACK LITERATURE [419]
Box 3425
Fredericksburg, Virginia 22401
(703) 373-7250 ext. 287

First published in 1970

SUBSCRIPTION DATA
Issues and rates: Published three times per year.
 Average paid circulation: 400
 Annual rate(s): Institutions $7.00, Individuals $4.00
Managing Editor: Raman Singh

EDITORIAL DESCRIPTION
 Contains scholarly articles on Black literature, largely literature from America and Africa. Creative work is also accepted.
Articles per average issue: 5-7
Audience: Academic
 Manuscripts accepted in English

MANUSCRIPT INFORMATION
Subject field(s): Black literature, creative work
Manuscript requirements: MLA
 Preferred length: 10 to 15 pages
 Number of copies to be submitted: 1
 Abstract: No
Author information and reprints: Payment: Reprints only. Contributor's copies
 Is simultaneous submission of article to other journals permitted: Yes, must inform publication.
 Exclusive manuscript rights between acceptance and publication: No
 Copyright: Held by publication.
 Reprints: Available
Additional information: Manuscripts must be typewritten, double-spaced with footnotes at the end.
Disposition of manuscript:
 Query letter: No
 Receipt of manuscript acknowledged: No
 Decision to publish in: 4-8 weeks
 Accepted manuscript published in: Six months or more
 Rejected manuscript returned: Yes
 Rejected manuscript criticized: No
Submit to:
 Raman K. Singh
 Editor
 (See address above)

SPECIAL STIPULATIONS
 Desire bold concepts in literary analysis.

STUDIES IN BROWNING AND HIS CIRCLE [420]
Armstrong Browning Library
P. O. Box 6336
Waco, Texas 76706
(817) 755-3566

Previously entitled *The Browning Newsletter*

First published in 1968

SUBSCRIPTION DATA
Issues and rates: Published semi-annually.
 Average paid circulation: 350
 Annual rate(s): $5.00
Publisher or Sponsor: Armstrong Browning Library, Baylor University
Managing Editor: Jack W. Herring

EDITORIAL DESCRIPTION
 A journal of history, criticism, and bibliography pertaining to Robert Browning and the Victorian period.
Articles per average issue: 11-12
Audience: All students of Robert Browning
 Manuscripts accepted in English

MANUSCRIPT INFORMATION
Subject field(s): Robert Browning, Elizabeth Barrett Browning, Browning family, friends and correspondents, Victorian poets in relation to the Brownings
Manuscript requirements: MLA
 Preferred length: None
 Number of copies to be submitted: Two
 Abstract: No
Author information and reprints: Payment: Reprints only. 10 copies of the journal
 Is simultaneous submission of article to other journals permitted: Yes
 Exclusive manuscript rights between acceptance and publication: No
 Copyright: Held by publication.
 Reprints: Not available.
Additional information: Manuscripts will be submitted to one member of a five-member editorial board, who accepts or rejects the paper.
Disposition of manuscript:
 Query letter: No
 Receipt of manuscript acknowledged: Yes
 Decision to publish in: 4 months
 Accepted manuscript published in: 5-6 months
 Rejected manuscript returned: Yes, if return postage is supplied by author.
 Rejected manuscript criticized: Sometimes
Submit to:
 Jack W. Herring
 Editor
 (See address above)

STUDIES IN ENGLISH LITERATURE 1500-1900 [421]
Rice University
Houston, Texas 77001
(713) 528-4141 ext. 303

First published in 1961

SUBSCRIPTION DATA
Issues and rates: Published quarterly.
Managing Editor: Edward Doughtie

EDITORIAL DESCRIPTION
A quarterly journal of historical and critical studies. Each issue will be devoted to one of four fields: winter, English Renaissance; spring, Elizabethan and Jacobean Drama; summer, Restoration and Eighteenth Century; autumn, Nineteenth Century.
Articles per average issue: 11
Audience: Scholars and graduate students
Manuscripts accepted in English

MANUSCRIPT INFORMATION
Manuscript requirements: MLA
Preferred length: 12-24 pages
Number of copies to be submitted: One original copy
Abstract: Upon acceptance only
Author information and reprints: Payment: None.
Is simultaneous submission of article to other journals permitted: No
Exclusive manuscript rights between acceptance and publication: Yes
Copyright: Held by Rice University. Fees for further publication are passed on to the author.
Reprints: Available, 25 provided free
Additional information: Typewritten, double-spaced with endnotes
Disposition of manuscript:
Receipt of manuscript acknowledged: Yes
Decision to publish in: 1-3 months
Accepted manuscript published in: 2-3 years
Rejected manuscript returned: Yes, if return postage is supplied by author.
Rejected manuscript criticized: Occasionally
Submit to:
Editor
(See address above)

STUDIES IN THE NOVEL [422]
P.O. Box 13706
North Texas State University
Denton, Texas 76201
(817) 788-2025

First published in 1969

SUBSCRIPTION DATA
Issues and rates: Published quarterly.
Average paid circulation: 1650
Annual rate(s): $4.00
Publisher or Sponsor: North Texas State University

EDITORIAL DESCRIPTION
Contains scholarly articles on various aspects of the novel.
Articles per average issue: 12
Audience: Scholarly
Manuscripts accepted in English

MANUSCRIPT INFORMATION
Manuscript requirements: MLA
Preferred length: 10-20 pages
Number of copies to be submitted: Two

Abstract: Yes
Author information and reprints: Payment: Reprints only. Two copies of the issue in which the article appears.
Is simultaneous submission of article to other journals permitted: No
Exclusive manuscript rights between acceptance and publication: Yes
Copyright: Held by publication.
Reprints: Available
Disposition of manuscript:
Query letter: No
Receipt of manuscript acknowledged: Yes
Decision to publish in: Two months
Accepted manuscript published in: Twelve months
Rejected manuscript returned: Yes
Rejected manuscript criticized: Yes
Submit to:
James W. Lee
Editor
(See address above)

STUDIES IN PHILOLOGY* [423]
University of North Carolina Press
P. O. Box 2288
Chapel Hill, North Carolina 27514
(919) 933-2105

SUBSCRIPTION DATA
Issues and rates: Five times a year

EDITORIAL DESCRIPTION
Contains studies of classical, medieval, and modern literature.

MANUSCRIPT INFORMATION
Subject field(s): English Renaissance literature; medieval English, neo-classical and Victorian, continental literature, classical literature
Manuscript requirements: MLA; Chicago
Preferred length: 15-25 pages
Number of copies to be submitted: One
Author information and reprints: Payment: None.
Is simultaneous submission of article to other journals permitted: No
Exclusive manuscript rights between acceptance and publication: Yes
Copyright: Held by publication.
Reprints: Available, 20 free
Disposition of manuscript:
Receipt of manuscript acknowledged: Yes
Decision to publish in: 2-3 months
Accepted manuscript published in: 18 months
Rejected manuscript returned: Yes
Rejected manuscript criticized: No
Submit to:
Editor
(See address above)

STUDIES IN SCOTTISH LITERATURE [424]
English Department
University of South Carolina
Columbia, South Carolina 29208
(803) 777-2239

First published in 1963

SUBSCRIPTION DATA
Issues and rates: Published quarterly.
Average paid circulation: 500
Annual rate(s): $5.00
Managing Editor: G. Ross Roy

EDITORIAL DESCRIPTION
Contains critical articles, notes and book reviews pertaining to Scottish literature.
Articles per average issue: 8
Audience: Academic, general
Manuscripts accepted in English

MANUSCRIPT INFORMATION
Manuscript requirements: See latest issue for style requirements.
Preferred length: None
Number of copies to be submitted: One
Author information and reprints: Payment: None.
Is simultaneous submission of article to other journals permitted: No
Exclusive manuscript rights between acceptance and publication: Yes
Copyright: Held by Editor.
Reprints: Available, first 20 free.
Disposition of manuscript:
Query letter: No
Receipt of manuscript acknowledged: Yes
Decision to publish in: 3-5 months
Accepted manuscript published in: 6-12 months
Rejected manuscript returned: Yes
Rejected manuscript criticized: Yes
Submit to:
G. Ross Roy
Editor
(See address above)

STUDIES IN SHORT FICTION [425]
2100 College Street
Newberry, South Carolina 29108
(803) 276-5010 ext. 284

First published in 1963

SUBSCRIPTION DATA
Issues and rates: Published quarterly.
Average paid circulation: 1,300
Annual rate(s): $8.00
Publisher or Sponsor: Newberry College

EDITORIAL DESCRIPTION
Contains articles and notes on short fiction; reviews of books on short fiction; special numbers, cross-indexed listing of short-story anthologies by tables of contents and by individual writers.
Articles per average issue: 8-12
Audience: Academic
Manuscripts accepted in English, French, Spanish, German

MANUSCRIPT INFORMATION
Subject field(s): Short fiction exclusively: short story, novella, short novel, short-short, long short story
Manuscript requirements: MLA
Preferred length: 15 pages maximum including notes
Number of copies to be submitted: One

Abstract: No
Author information and reprints: Payment: None.
Is simultaneous submission of article to other journals permitted: No
Exclusive manuscript rights between acceptance and publication: Yes
Copyright: Held by Newberry College
Reprints: $5.00 a page for first five pages; $1.00 a page additional
Disposition of manuscript:
Query letter: No
Receipt of manuscript acknowledged: Yes
Decision to publish in: 3-4 weeks
Accepted manuscript published in: 18-24 months
Rejected manuscript returned: Yes, if return postage is supplied by author.
Rejected manuscript criticized: Sometimes
Submit to:
Frank L. Hoskins, Jr.
Editor
(See address above)
(803) 276-5010 ext. 206

STYLE [426]
Department of English
University of Arkansas
Fayetteville, Arkansas 72701
(501) 575-4301

First published in 1967

SUBSCRIPTION DATA
Issues and rates: Published three times per year.
Average paid circulation: 400
Annual rate(s): $7.00
Publisher or Sponsor: University of Arkansas, Department of English
Managing Editor: James R. Bennett

EDITORIAL DESCRIPTION
Contains articles dealing with varying aspects of literary style, reviews of books concerned with style, pertinent announcements, bibliographies of books and articles dealing with style.
Articles per average issue: 8
Audience: Literary scholars, linguists
Manuscripts accepted in English

MANUSCRIPT INFORMATION
Subject field(s): Literature in the English language, evaluation of style
Manuscript requirements: MLA
Preferred length: 15-35 pages
Number of copies to be submitted: One
Abstract: Yes, of about 200 words
Author information and reprints: Payment: None.
Is simultaneous submission of article to other journals permitted: No
Exclusive manuscript rights between acceptance and publication: Yes
Copyright: Held by publication.
Reprints: Available, 15 free
Disposition of manuscript:
Query letter: No
Receipt of manuscript acknowledged: No
Decision to publish in: 2 weeks to 1 month

Accepted manuscript published in: Varies
Rejected manuscript returned: Yes, if self-addressed, stamped envelope is sent with manuscript.
Rejected manuscript criticized: Occasionally
Submit to:
The Editors
(See address above)

SYMPOSIUM [427]
A Quarterly Journal in Modern Foreign Literatures
210 H. B. Crouse Hall
Syracuse University
Syracuse, New York 13210
(315) 476-5541 ext. 2309

SUBSCRIPTION DATA
Issues and rates: Published quarterly.
Average paid circulation: 1,000
Annual rate(s): $8.00
Managing Editor: J. H. Matthews

EDITORIAL DESCRIPTION
Devoted primarily to modern foreign literature. Dramatists, novelists and poets are covered.
Articles per average issue: 7
Audience: Academic
Manuscripts accepted in Any modern language

MANUSCRIPT INFORMATION
Manuscript requirements: MLA
Preferred length: 20-35 pages
Number of copies to be submitted: One
Abstract: No
Author information and reprints: Payment: Reprints only. 5 copies of issue
Is simultaneous submission of article to other journals permitted: No
Exclusive manuscript rights between acceptance and publication: Yes
Copyright: Held by publication.
Reprints: Not available. complimentary
Disposition of manuscript:
Query letter: No
Receipt of manuscript acknowledged: Yes
Decision to publish in: One week
Accepted manuscript published in: One year
Rejected manuscript returned: Yes, if return postage is supplied by author.
Rejected manuscript criticized: Frequently
Submit to:
J. H. Matthews
(See address above)

TEXAS STUDIES IN LITERATURE AND LANGUAGE [428]
A Journal of the Humanities
University Station, Box 7577
Austin, Texas 78712
(512) 471-1149

Previously entitled *Texas Studies in English*

First published in 1911

SUBSCRIPTION DATA
Issues and rates: Published quarterly.
Average paid circulation: 900
Annual rate(s): Individuals $8, Institutions $10

EDITORIAL DESCRIPTION
Contains scholarly and critical articles on English and American literature; also some articles in other areas of the humanities.
Articles per average issue: 12
Audience: Professional, academic
Manuscripts accepted in English

MANUSCRIPT INFORMATION
Manuscript requirements: MLA
Preferred length: None
Number of copies to be submitted: One
Author information and reprints: Payment: None.
Is simultaneous submission of article to other journals permitted: No
Exclusive manuscript rights between acceptance and publication: Yes
Copyright: Held by publication.
Reprints: Available
Disposition of manuscript:
Query letter: No
Receipt of manuscript acknowledged: Yes
Decision to publish in: Two months or less
Accepted manuscript published in: 18-20 months
Rejected manuscript returned: Yes, if self-addressed, stamped envelope is sent with manuscript.
Rejected manuscript criticized: Yes
Submit to:
Ernest J. Lovell, Jr.
Executive Editor
(See address above)

THOREAU JOURNAL [429]
Box 551
Old Town, Maine 04468
(207) 827-7683

First published in 1969

SUBSCRIPTION DATA
Issues and rates: Published quarterly.
Average paid circulation: 400
Annual rate(s): $6.00, Members $4.00
Publisher or Sponsor: The Thoreau Fellowship, Inc.
Managing Editor: Mary P. Sherwood

EDITORIAL DESCRIPTION
Contains articles, poems, letters to the editor. All material about Thoreau or his interests. Emphasis on Thoreau's integrity, and his natural history interests.
Articles per average issue: 4-8
Audience: Thoreau devoteés, literary Thoreauvians
Manuscripts accepted in English

MANUSCRIPT INFORMATION
Subject field(s): Ecology, philosophy, literature, American Indians literature.

Manuscript requirements: No specific style guide.
Preferred length: Maximum 10 pages
Number of copies to be submitted: One
Abstract: Not necessary.
Author information and reprints: Payment: Reprints only. Complimentary copy (2 copies for longer papers).
Is simultaneous submission of article to other journals permitted: No
Exclusive manuscript rights between acceptance and publication: Yes
Copyright: No copyright
Reprints: Available if author orders them and pays costs.
Additional information: Double space manuscript.
Disposition of manuscript:
Query letter: Not necessary.
Receipt of manuscript acknowledged: Yes
Decision to publish in: 2-3 months
Accepted manuscript published in: 6-12 months
Rejected manuscript returned: Yes, if return postage is supplied by author.
Rejected manuscript criticized: Sometimes
Submit to:
Dr. Richard Fleck
Editor
English Department
University of Wyoming
Laramie, Wyoming 82071

THE THOREAU SOCIETY BULLETIN [430]
State University College
Geneseo, New York 14454
(716) 245-5513

First published in 1941

SUBSCRIPTION DATA
Issues and rates: Published quarterly.
Average paid circulation: 1,000
Annual rate(s): $2.00
Publisher or Sponsor: The Thoreau Society Inc.
Managing Editor: Walter Harding

EDITORIAL DESCRIPTION
Contains short articles about Henry David Thoreau, his writings, his influence, etc.
Articles per average issue: 5
Audience: Students of Thoreau
Manuscripts accepted in English

MANUSCRIPT INFORMATION
Subject field(s): Thoreau
Manuscript requirements: MLA
Preferred length: 4,000 words maximum
Number of copies to be submitted: One
Abstract: Yes
Author information and reprints: Payment: None.
Is simultaneous submission of article to other journals permitted: No
Exclusive manuscript rights between acceptance and publication: Yes
Copyright: Will copyright for author if he arranges in advance
Reprints: Available at no cost
Additional information: Articles must be typewritten, double-spaced.
Disposition of manuscript:
Query letter: No
Decision to publish in: Several weeks
Accepted manuscript published in: 3 to 6 months
Rejected manuscript returned: Yes, if return postage is supplied by author.
Rejected manuscript criticized: Yes
Submit to:
Walter Harding
(See address above)

TRIQUARTERLY [431]
University Hall 101
Northwestern University
Evanston, Illinois 60201
(312) 492-3490

SUBSCRIPTION DATA
Issues and rates: Published three times per year.
Average paid circulation: 5,000
Annual rate(s): $7.00, Foreign $7.75
Publisher or Sponsor: Northwestern University
Managing Editor: Theresa Maylone

EDITORIAL DESCRIPTION
An international journal of arts, letters and opinion, primarily concentrating on contemporary American fiction. Does not publish poetry.

MANUSCRIPT INFORMATION
Subject field(s): Fiction (excerpts from novels), short stories, criticism of modern fiction, others depend on subject of special issues planned
Manuscript requirements: MLA preferred but not required
Preferred length: None
Number of copies to be submitted: One
Author information and reprints: Payment: By publication to author. $10.00 per page.
Is simultaneous submission of article to other journals permitted: With permission from Editor
Exclusive manuscript rights between acceptance and publication: Yes
Copyright: Held by publication.
Reprints: Not available.
Disposition of manuscript:
Receipt of manuscript acknowledged: No
Decision to publish in: Six weeks
Accepted manuscript published in: Varies enormously but is explained to author upon acceptance
Rejected manuscript returned: Yes, if self-addressed, stamped envelope is sent with manuscript.
Rejected manuscript criticized: Sometimes
Submit to:
Editor
(See address above)

TWENTIETH CENTURY LITERATURE [432]
A Scholarly and Critical Journal
Hofstra University Press
Hofstra University
Hempstead, New York 11550
(516) 560-3882

SUBSCRIPTION DATA
Issues and rates: Published quarterly.
Average paid circulation: 2150
Annual rate(s): Individuals $7.00, Institutions $10.00, Foreign individuals $8.00, Foreign institutions $11.00

EDITORIAL DESCRIPTION
Contains articles on all aspects of modern and contemporary literature, including articles on authors in other languages.

MANUSCRIPT INFORMATION
Manuscript requirements: MLA
Preferred length: 20 to 30 pages
Number of copies to be submitted: One
Abstract: Yes
Author information and reprints: Payment: Reprints only. 25 reprints
Is simultaneous submission of article to other journals permitted: No
Exclusive manuscript rights between acceptance and publication: Yes
Copyright: Held by publication.
Reprints: Available at cost, if notified before publishing
Additional information: Footnotes should be numbered consecutively at end of article.
Disposition of manuscript:
Query letter: No
Receipt of manuscript acknowledged: Yes
Decision to publish in: Ten to twelve weeks
Accepted manuscript published in: Less than 1 year
Rejected manuscript returned: Yes
Rejected manuscript criticized: Sometimes
Submit to:
William McBrien
Editor
(See address above)

VERGILIUS [433]
Department of Foreign Languages
Georgia State University
Atlanta, Georgia 30303
(404) 658-2448

SUBSCRIPTION DATA
Issues and rates: Published annually.
Average paid circulation: 1700
Annual rate(s): $3.50
Publisher or Sponsor: Vergilian Society Inc.

EDITORIAL DESCRIPTION
Contains articles on Vergilian studies, Roman archaeology.
Articles per average issue: 5-8
Audience: Classicists, academic
Manuscripts accepted in English

MANUSCRIPT INFORMATION
Subject field(s): Vergilian studies, Latin literature, Roman archaeology
Manuscript requirements: See latest issue for style requirements.
   Preferred length: 1500-2000 words
   Number of copies to be submitted: One
Author information and reprints: Payment: None.
   Is simultaneous submission of article to other journals permitted: No
   Exclusive manuscript rights between acceptance and publication: Yes
   Copyright: Held by author.
   Reprints: Not available.
Disposition of manuscript:
   Receipt of manuscript acknowledged: Yes
   Decision to publish in: 1 month
   Accepted manuscript published in: 1 year
   Rejected manuscript returned: Yes
   Rejected manuscript criticized: No
Submit to:
   Dr. Janice M. Benario
   Editor
   (See address above)

VICTORIAN POETRY [434]
A Critical Journal of Victorian Literature
129 Armstrong Hall
West Virginia University
Morgantown, West Virginia 26206
(304) 293-4070

First published in 1953

SUBSCRIPTION DATA
Issues and rates: Published quarterly.
   Average paid circulation: 1300
   Annual rate(s): Institutions $8.00, Individuals $6.00
Managing Editor: John F. Stasny

EDITORIAL DESCRIPTION
   Contains long and short articles, reviews, brief articles and notes.
Articles per average issue: 8
Audience: Professional
   Manuscripts accepted in English

MANUSCRIPT INFORMATION
Subject field(s): Victorian poetry (any point of view)
Manuscript requirements: MLA
   Preferred length: Long articles: less than 30 pages; short articles: less than 10 pages
   Number of copies to be submitted: Two
   Abstract: Only for manuscripts over 10 pages
Author information and reprints: Payment: None.
   Is simultaneous submission of article to other journals permitted: No
   Exclusive manuscript rights between acceptance and publication: Yes
   Copyright: Held by publication.
   Reprints: Available at cost
Additional information: See inside front cover of the journal.
Disposition of manuscript:
   Query letter: No
   Receipt of manuscript acknowledged: Yes
   Decision to publish in: 3 months
   Accepted manuscript published in: Long articles: 2 years
   Rejected manuscript returned: Yes, if self-addressed, stamped envelope is sent with manuscript.
   Rejected manuscript criticized: Sometimes
Submit to:
   Editor
   (See address above)

VORTICE [435]
Literatura y Crítica
Spanish Department
Stanford University
Stanford, California 94305
(415) 497-4414

First published in 1974

SUBSCRIPTION DATA
Issues and rates: Published three times per year.
   Annual rate(s): $4.50; Institutions $10.00; Foreign individuals $6.00; Foreign institutions $10.00
Publisher or Sponsor: Stanford University
Managing Editor: Elena Laborde Schwab

EDITORIAL DESCRIPTION
   Publishes narrative, poetry, and criticism on Latin American or Spanish literature
Articles per average issue: 15
Audience: Academic
   Manuscripts accepted in English, Spanish, Portuguese, French

MANUSCRIPT INFORMATION
Manuscript requirements: See latest issue for style requirements. MLA
   Preferred length: No preference
   Number of copies to be submitted: 2
   Abstract: Not necessary.
Author information and reprints: Payment: None.
   Is simultaneous submission of article to other journals permitted: Not permitted.
   Exclusive manuscript rights between acceptance and publication: Yes
   Copyright: Held by the University
   Reprints: Not available.
Disposition of manuscript:
   Query letter: Not necessary.
   Receipt of manuscript acknowledged: Yes
   Decision to publish in: 1 month
   Accepted manuscript published in: 1 month
   Rejected manuscript returned: Yes, if return postage is supplied by author.
   Rejected manuscript criticized: No
Submit to:
   Editor
   (See address above)

WALT WHITMAN REVIEW [436]
Journalism Program
Oakland University
Rochester, Michigan 48063

Previously entitled *Walt Whitman Newsletter*

First published in 1955

SUBSCRIPTION DATA
Issues and rates: Published quarterly.
   Average paid circulation: 700
   Annual rate(s): $7.00 per 2 years
Managing Editor: William White; Charles E. Feinberg

EDITORIAL DESCRIPTION
   Contains articles, notes, bibliographies, and book reviews dealing with Walt Whitman and his writings: new material (poems, prose, letters) or reinterpretation of old material (criticism of his poems and prose), relationships with contemporaries, influence, reputation.
Articles per average issue: 10
Audience: Specialists in Whitman and 19th and 20th century literature
   Manuscripts accepted in English

MANUSCRIPT INFORMATION
Subject field(s): Walt Whitman: life, writings, friends, associates, influence, reputation, bibliography.
Manuscript requirements: MLA, modified slightly
   Preferred length: 500-6,000 words; 2 to 20 pages
   Number of copies to be submitted: One
   Abstract: Yes
Author information and reprints: Payment: Reprints only. Three copies of the issue
   Is simultaneous submission of article to other journals permitted: No
   Exclusive manuscript rights between acceptance and publication: Yes
   Copyright: Author may reprint his own material without fee; others pay $10 a page, shared equally between author and the publisher.
   Reprints: Not available.
Additional information: Typewritten, double-spaced
Disposition of manuscript:
   Query letter: No
   Receipt of manuscript acknowledged: Yes
   Decision to publish in: Few days
   Accepted manuscript published in: About 2 years
   Rejected manuscript returned: Yes, if self-addressed, stamped envelope is sent with manuscript.
   Rejected manuscript criticized: Yes
Submit to:
   William White
   Editor
   (See address above)

WELLSIANA [437]
The World of H. G. Wells
High Orchard
125 Markyate Road
Dagenham, Essex RM8 2LB, England
(01) 593-7209

SUBSCRIPTION DATA
Issues and rates: Published semi-annually.
   Average paid circulation: 800; 1,000 controlled
   Annual rate(s): $4.00; Institutions $5.00
Publisher or Sponsor: H. G. Wells Society International

EDITORIAL DESCRIPTION
   Studies on the life and work of H. G. Wells, his influences, contemporaries, milieu; his relevance to his age and ours
Articles per average issue: 1-4
Audience: Researchers, students, literature enthusiasts
   Manuscripts accepted in English

MANUSCRIPT INFORMATION
Manuscript requirements: MLA
   Preferred length: 3,000 words; 6-8 pages
   Number of copies to be submitted: 3
   Abstract: Yes. Up to 250 words outlining arguement
Author information and reprints: Payment: Reprints only. 6 copies of article
   Is simultaneous submission of article to other journals permitted: Not permitted.
   Exclusive manuscript rights between acceptance and publication: Yes
   Copyright: Held by publication.
   Reprints: Available at cost.
Additional information: All fields of study are encouraged. Bibliographies and notes at end please.
Disposition of manuscript:
   Query letter: Not necessary.
   Receipt of manuscript acknowledged: No
   Decision to publish in: 3 months
   Accepted manuscript published in: 12 months
   Rejected manuscript returned: Yes, if return postage is supplied by author.
   Rejected manuscript criticized: Sometimes
Submit to:
   Eric F. J. Ford
   Executive Editor
   (See address above)

WESTERN AMERICAN LITERATURE [438]
UMC 32
Utah State University
Logan, Utah 84322
(801) 752-4100 ext. 7514

First published in 1966

SUBSCRIPTION DATA
Issues and rates: Published quarterly.
   Average paid circulation: 639; 639 controlled
   Annual rate(s): $7.00 for all
Publisher or Sponsor: Western Literature Association
Managing Editor: Thomas J. Lyon

EDITORIAL DESCRIPTION
   To stimulate interest and critical study of Western regional literature
Articles per average issue: Five
Audience: Students and teachers of Western literature
   Manuscripts accepted in English

MANUSCRIPT INFORMATION
Subject field(s): Western writers and writing
Manuscript requirements: MLA
   Preferred length: 2,500-3,000 words; 10-18 pages
   Number of copies to be submitted: One
   Abstract: Not necessary.
Author information and reprints: Payment: Reprints only. 5 Copies, 30 Off-prints
   Copyright: Western Literature Association
   Reprints: Available at no cost.
Disposition of manuscript:
   Query letter: Not necessary.
   Receipt of manuscript acknowledged: Yes
   Decision to publish in: 2-3 Months
   Accepted manuscript published in: 3-6 Months
   Rejected manuscript returned: Yes, if return postage is supplied by author.
   Rejected manuscript criticized: Reasons for rejections only
Submit to:
   Thomas J. Lyon
   Editor
   (See address above)

THE WORDSWORTH CIRCLE [439]
Department of English
Temple University
Philadelphia Pennsylvania 19122
(215) 787-7344

First published in 1970

SUBSCRIPTION DATA
Issues and rates: Published quarterly.
   Average paid circulation: 800
   Annual rate(s): Institutions $5.00, Students $4.00, Individuals $5.00
Managing Editor: Marilyn S. Gaull

EDITORIAL DESCRIPTION
   Contains notes, queries, abstracts of papers, research in progress, exhibitions, library collection checklists and essays dealing with the writings and times of the First Generation English Romantics: Wordsworth, Coleridge, Hazlitt, DeQuincey, Lamb, Southey, the minor poets and popular writers. A news journal founded to improve communication among colleagues interested in the writings and times of the first generation English Romantics.
Articles per average issue: 10
Audience: Academic
   Manuscripts accepted in English

MANUSCRIPT INFORMATION
Subject field(s): Wordsworth, Coleridge, Lamb, Southey, DeQuincey, Hazlitt
Manuscript requirements: MLA
   Preferred length: 2000 5000 words
   Number of copies to be submitted: Two
   Abstract: Yes
Author information and reprints: Payment: Reprints only. 3 copies of issue
   Is simultaneous submission of article to other journals permitted: No
   Exclusive manuscript rights between acceptance and publication: Yes
   Copyright: Held by publication.
   Reprints: Available at $1.50 each.
Additional information: Contributors must subscribe to the journal.
Disposition of manuscript:
   Query letter: No
   Receipt of manuscript acknowledged: Yes
   Decision to publish in: 1 month
   Accepted manuscript published in: 3 months
   Rejected manuscript returned: Yes
   Rejected manuscript criticized: Yes
Submit to:
   Marilyn S. Gaull
   Editor
   (See address above)

YALE FRENCH STUDIES [440]
Yale University
323 William L. Harkness Hall
New Haven, Connecticut 06520
(203) 432-4655

First published in 1948

SUBSCRIPTION DATA
Issues and rates: Published semi-annually.
   Average paid circulation: 1300
   Annual rate(s): $4.00
Managing Editor: Joseph H. Halpern

EDITORIAL DESCRIPTION
   Contains scholarly articles devoted to French literature and culture and relevant areas. Each issue is organized around a specific theme, subject, author, etc.
Articles per average issue: 15
   Manuscripts accepted in English

MANUSCRIPT INFORMATION
Subject field(s): French literature, French culture
Manuscript requirements: MLA
   Preferred length: 15 pages
   Number of copies to be submitted: One
   Abstract: Not necessary.
Author information and reprints: Payment: None.
   Is simultaneous submission of article to other journals permitted: No
   Exclusive manuscript rights between acceptance and publication: Yes
   Copyright: Held by publication.
   Reprints: Available, 25 free
Disposition of manuscript:
   Query letter: Yes
   Receipt of manuscript acknowledged: Yes
   Decision to publish in: One month

Accepted manuscript published in: One year
Rejected manuscript returned: Yes
Rejected manuscript criticized: No
Submit to:
Joseph Halpern
Managing Editor
(See address above)

SPECIAL STIPULATIONS
Unsolicited manuscripts usually not accepted.

ZEITSCHRIFT FÜR DEUTSCHAMERIKANISCHE LITERATUR [441]
The Magazine of German-American Literature
2545 Harrison Avenue
Cincinnati, Ohio 45211
662-3621

Previously entitled *Das Mitteilungsblatt*

First published in 1974

SUBSCRIPTION DATA
Issues and rates: Published three times per year.
  Annual rate(s): $3.00
Publisher or Sponsor: Verband deutschsprachiger Autoren in Amerika, The Association of German-speaking Authors in America

EDITORIAL DESCRIPTION
Publishes prose and poetry written in German by German-American authors.
Articles per average issue: 10-12
Audience: German-American authors, students, teachers
  Manuscripts accepted in German, Dutch, English

MANUSCRIPT INFORMATION
Subject field(s): German-American prose and poetry from the 17th century to the present covering the entire western hemisphere
Manuscript requirements: No specific style guide.
  Preferred length: 10 pages
  Number of copies to be submitted: 2
  Abstract: Not necessary.
Author information and reprints: Payment: Reprints only. 5 copies of the issue
  Is simultaneous submission of article to other journals permitted: Permitted, but not encouraged.
  Exclusive manuscript rights between acceptance and publication: Yes
  Copyright: First serial rights only
  Reprints: Available at cost.
Additional information: Not interested in German literature on America, but German literature written in America.
Disposition of manuscript:
  Query letter: Not necessary, but advisable.
  Receipt of manuscript acknowledged: Yes
  Decision to publish in: 2-3 months
  Accepted manuscript published in: 3-6 months
  Rejected manuscript returned: Yes, if return postage is supplied by author.
  Rejected manuscript criticized: Sometimes
Submit to:
Don H. Tolzmann
Editor/Redacteur
(See address above)

Philosophy

AUSTRALASIAN JOURNAL OF PHILOSOPHY [442]
Philosophy Department
Research School of Social Science
Australian National University
Canberra, Australia
Canberra 49-2341

Previously entitled *Australasian Journal of Psychology and Philosophy*

First published in 1923

SUBSCRIPTION DATA
Issues and rates: Published three times per year.
  Average paid circulation: 1,300
  Annual rate(s): Members A $5.00; Institutions A $8.00
Publisher or Sponsor: Australasian Association of Philosophy
Managing Editor: Robert Brown

EDITORIAL DESCRIPTION
Professional journal of current philosophy articles for a technically trained audience.
Articles per average issue: 7
Audience: Professional, academic
  Manuscripts accepted in English only

MANUSCRIPT INFORMATION
Subject field(s): Epistemology, metaphysics, philosophical logic, ethics, political philosophy
Manuscript requirements: See latest issue for style requirements.
  Preferred length: 20,000 words maximum
  Number of copies to be submitted: One
  Abstract: No
Author information and reprints: Payment: None.
  Is simultaneous submission of article to other journals permitted: No
  Exclusive manuscript rights between acceptance and publication: Yes
  Copyright: Held by author.
  Reprints: Available
Additional information: International reply coupon required for air mail return of manuscript.
Disposition of manuscript:
  Query letter: No
  Receipt of manuscript acknowledged: Yes
  Decision to publish in: 2-10 weeks
  Accepted manuscript published in: 4-8 months
  Rejected manuscript returned: Yes
  Rejected manuscript criticized: Frequently
Robert Brown
Editor
(See address above)

DIALOGUE [443]
Canadian Philosophical Review
Canadian Philosophical Association
1390 Sherbrooke W.
Montreal, Quebec H36 1K2, Canada

First published in 1962

SUBSCRIPTION DATA
Issues and rates: Published quarterly.
  Average paid circulation: 1500
  Annual rate(s): $16.00
Publisher or Sponsor: Canadian Philosophical Association
Managing Editor: John Woods; Francois Duchesneau

EDITORIAL DESCRIPTION
Contains articles, reviews, critical notices in all general areas of philosophical interest.
Audience: Professional
  Manuscripts accepted in English, French

MANUSCRIPT INFORMATION
Subject field(s): Philosophy
Manuscript requirements: Chicago
  Preferred length: 25 pages
  Number of copies to be submitted: One
Author information and reprints: Payment: None.
  Is simultaneous submission of article to other journals permitted: No
  Exclusive manuscript rights between acceptance and publication: Yes
  Copyright: Held by author.
  Reprints: Available
Disposition of manuscript:
  Query letter: Not necessary.
  Receipt of manuscript acknowledged: Yes
  Decision to publish in: 3 months
  Accepted manuscript published in: 1 year or more
  Rejected manuscript returned: Yes, if return postage is supplied by author.
  Rejected manuscript criticized: Yes
Submit to:
Manuscripts in English:
Dr. John Woods
Department of Philosophy
University of Victoria
Victoria, British Columbia Canada

Manuscripts in French:
Dr. Francois Duchesneau
Departemente de Philosophie
Université Ottawa
Ottawa, Ontario Canada

INQUIRY [444]
An Interdisciplinary Journal of Philosophy and the Social Sciences
Department of Philosophy
College of Arts & Science, Blindern
University of Trondheim
7000 Trondheim, Norway
(075)16900

First published in 1958

SUBSCRIPTION DATA
Issues and rates: Published quarterly.
 Average paid circulation: 1500
 Annual rate(s): Individuals $12, Institutions $15
Managing Editor: Arne Naess; Alastair Hannay

EDITORIAL DESCRIPTION
 Contains scholarly articles, discussions, and review discussions in all areas of philosophy and from all points of view; focuses principally on the articulation of philosophical perspectives and a broadening of the notion of philosophical inquiry itself.
Articles per average issue: 8
Audience: Professional philosophers and general readers with philosophical interests
 Manuscripts accepted in English and German

MANUSCRIPT INFORMATION
Subject field(s): Philosophy
Manuscript requirements: See latest issue for style requirements.
 Preferred length: 10,000 words; 20-25 pages
 Number of copies to be submitted: Two
 Abstract: Yes.
Author information and reprints: Payment: None.
 Is simultaneous submission of article to other journals permitted: No
 Exclusive manuscript rights between acceptance and publication: Yes
 Copyright: Held by publication.
 Reprints: Available at no cost.
Additional information: Manuscripts must be typewritten, double-spaced. Notes should be separated from the main body of the article.
Disposition of manuscript:
 Query letter: Not necessary.
 Receipt of manuscript acknowledged: Yes
 Decision to publish in: 1-3 months
 Accepted manuscript published in: 1 year
 Rejected manuscript returned: Yes, if return postage is supplied by author.
 Rejected manuscript criticized: Yes
Submit to:
 Alastair Hannay
 Editor
 (See address above)

INTERNATIONAL PHILOSOPHICAL QUARTERLY [445]
Fordham University
New York, New York 10458
(212) 933-2233

First published in 1961

SUBSCRIPTION DATA
Issues and rates: Published quarterly.
 Average paid circulation: 1850; 50 controlled
 Annual rate(s): $10.00
Publisher or Sponsor: Foundation for International Philosophical Exchange
Managing Editor: Norris Clarke

EDITORIAL DESCRIPTION
 To provide an international forum in English for the interchange of basic philosophical ideas between the Americas and Europe and between East and West; to encourage vital contemporary expression (creative, critical, and historical) in the intercultural tradition of theistic, spiritualist, and personalist humanism, but without further restriction of school within these broad perspectives.
Articles per average issue: 6 to 7
Audience: General, philosophical audience
 Manuscripts accepted in English, French, German, Italian, Spanish

MANUSCRIPT INFORMATION
Subject field(s): Philosophy: problems, history, East-West, interdisciplinary
Manuscript requirements: See latest issue for style requirements.
 Preferred length: 5,000-10,000 words (typewritten, double-spaced)
 Number of copies to be submitted: One
 Abstract: Not necessary.
Author information and reprints: Payment: None.
 Is simultaneous submission of article to other journals permitted: No
 Exclusive manuscript rights between acceptance and publication: Yes
 Copyright: Held by publication.
 Reprints: Available at no cost.
Additional information: Footnotes should be at the end of article.
Disposition of manuscript:
 Query letter: Not necessary.
 Receipt of manuscript acknowledged: Yes
 Decision to publish in: 1-2 months
 Accepted manuscript published in: One year
 Rejected manuscript returned: Yes, if return postage is supplied by author.
 Rejected manuscript criticized: Yes
Submit to:
 Editor
 (See address above)

THE JOURNAL OF CRITICAL ANALYSIS [446]
Jersey City State College
2039 Kennedy Boulevard
Jersey City, New Jersey 07305
(201) 547-3238

First published in 1969

SUBSCRIPTION DATA
Issues and rates: Published quarterly.
 Average paid circulation: 400
 Annual rate(s): $12.00
Publisher or Sponsor: The National Council for Critical Analysis

EDITORIAL DESCRIPTION
 Contains articles on philosophical issues.
Articles per average issue: 5 to 9
Audience: Philosophers and educators
 Manuscripts accepted in English

MANUSCRIPT INFORMATION
Subject field(s): Philosophy
Manuscript requirements: MLA
 Preferred length: 15 pages
 Number of copies to be submitted: Three
 Abstract: Yes.
Author information and reprints: Payment: None.
 Is simultaneous submission of article to other journals permitted: No
 Exclusive manuscript rights between acceptance and publication: Yes
 Copyright: Held by publication.
 Reprints: Available at cost.
Additional information: Manuscripts should be typewritten, double-spaced (23 lines per page).
Disposition of manuscript:
 Query letter: Not necessary.
 Receipt of manuscript acknowledged: Yes
 Decision to publish in: 1 to 4 months
 Accepted manuscript published in: 4 to 6 months
 Rejected manuscript returned: Yes, if return postage is supplied by author.
 Rejected manuscript criticized: No
Submit to:
 P. S. Schievella
 Editor
 (See address above)

THE JOURNAL OF PHILOSOPHY [447]
720 Philosophy Hall
Columbia University
New York, New York 10027
(212) 280-3188

Previously entitled *Journal of Philosophy, Psychology and Scientific Methods*

First published in 1904

SUBSCRIPTION DATA
Issues and rates: Published bi-weekly.
 Average paid circulation: 4500
 Annual rate(s): Students $7.00, Individuals $10.00, Institutions $12.00

EDITORIAL DESCRIPTION
 Encourages philosophical exchange and progress through prompt publication of articles of current interest. Particularly interested in papers that explore the borderline between philosophy and the special disciplines. Not interested in articles that are primarily expository in character.
Articles per average issue: 3
Audience: Academic philosophers and readers who are keenly interested in philosophy
 Manuscripts accepted in English

MANUSCRIPT INFORMATION
Subject field(s): Philosophy
Manuscript requirements: See latest issue for style requirements.
  Preferred length: 4000 words; 10 printed pages
  Number of copies to be submitted: One
  Abstract: Not necessary.
Author information and reprints: Payment: None.
  Is simultaneous submission of article to other journals permitted: No
  Exclusive manuscript rights between acceptance and publication: Yes
  Copyright: Held by publication.
  Reprints: Available to author, at publication time.
Additional information: See latest issue for footnote style. No bibliographies.
Disposition of manuscript:
  Query letter: Not necessary.
  Receipt of manuscript acknowledged: Yes
  Decision to publish in: 3 months
  Accepted manuscript published in: 3-8 months
  Rejected manuscript returned: Yes, if self-addressed, stamped envelope is sent with manuscript.
  Rejected manuscript criticized: No
Submit to:
  Leigh S. Cauman
  Managing Editor
  (See address above)

THE JOURNAL OF SYMBOLIC LOGIC [449]
P. O. Box 6248
201 Charles Street
Providence, Rhode Island 02940
(401) 272-9500

First published in 1936

SUBSCRIPTION DATA
Issues and rates: Published quarterly.
  Annual rate(s): $40.00 per volume; Foreign $40.00; Institutions $40.00; Members Free with dues
Publisher or Sponsor: Association for Symbolic Logic
Managing Editor: Alfons Borgers

EDITORIAL DESCRIPTION
  The official organ of the Association, it invites original technical papers in the field of symbolic logic, expository papers, and philosophical papers which bear upon the field and make use of its methods; studies in the history of logic in which modern developments are taken into account.
Articles per average issue: 15
Audience: Symbolic logicians, philosophers, mathematicians
  Manuscripts accepted in English, French

MANUSCRIPT INFORMATION
Manuscript requirements: See latest issue for style requirements.
  Preferred length: Less than 32 pages
  Number of copies to be submitted: 1
  Abstract: Not necessary.

Author information and reprints: Payment: By author to publication. $30.00 per page.
  Is simultaneous submission of article to other journals permitted: Not permitted.
  Exclusive manuscript rights between acceptance and publication: Yes
  Copyright: Held by publication.
  Reprints: Available at no cost. 50
Disposition of manuscript:
  Query letter: Not necessary.
  Receipt of manuscript acknowledged: Yes
  Accepted manuscript published in: 9-12 months
Submit to:
  Editor
  (See address above)

MAIN CURRENTS IN MODERN THOUGHT [450]
12 Church Street
New Rochelle, New York 10805
(914) 636-3150

SUBSCRIPTION DATA
Issues and rates: Published quarterly.
  Annual rate(s): $6.50; Institutions $14.50
Publisher or Sponsor: The Center for Integrative Education
Managing Editor: Emily Sellon

EDITORIAL DESCRIPTION
  Presents significant contributions to contemporary thought which point to a unified vision of the world by bringing the universal principles and modes of knowing in terms of which all cultures, ancient and modern, find their unique expressions.
  Manuscripts accepted in English

MANUSCRIPT INFORMATION
Subject field(s): Interdisciplinary relating to the educational process
Manuscript requirements: Style sheet sent on request.
  Preferred length: 5,000-6,000 words
  Number of copies to be submitted: 2
  Abstract: Not necessary.
Author information and reprints: Payment: Reprints only. 25
  Is simultaneous submission of article to other journals permitted: Permitted, but not encouraged.
  Exclusive manuscript rights between acceptance and publication: Yes
  Copyright: Held by publication.
  Reprints: Available at cost.
Disposition of manuscript:
  Query letter: Not necessary.
  Receipt of manuscript acknowledged: Yes
  Decision to publish in: Varies
  Accepted manuscript published in: Varies
  Rejected manuscript returned: Yes, if return postage is supplied by author.
  Rejected manuscript criticized: Yes
Submit to:
  Emily Sellon;
  Patrick Milburn
  Editor and Associate Editor
  (See address above)

MAN AND WORLD [451]
An International Philosophical Review
Martinus Nyhoff, P. O. Box 269
Lange Voorhout 9-11
The Hague, The Netherlands
(070) 469-460

First published in 1968

SUBSCRIPTION DATA
Issues and rates: Published quarterly.
  Annual rate(s): Individuals Dfl.34.20; Institutions Dfl.54.00

EDITORIAL DESCRIPTION
  Dedicated to a discussion of fundamental philosophical problems and original solutions to them; concerned with reflecting the philosophical dimensions of all areas of human experience.
  Manuscripts accepted in English, French, German

MANUSCRIPT INFORMATION
Subject field(s): Politics, the arts, morality, science, religion as reflected philosophically
Manuscript requirements: No specific style guide. See latest issue for style requirements.
  Preferred length: As required
  Number of copies to be submitted: 2
  Abstract: Not necessary.
Additional information: Manuscripts should be typewritten, double-spaced throughout with wide margins.
Submit to:
  Editor
  P. O. Box 173
  State College, Pennsylvania 16801

MIND [452]
A Quarterly Review of Philosophy
Department of Philosophy
Birkbeck College, Malet Street
London WC1E 7HX, England
01.580.6622

First published in 1876

SUBSCRIPTION DATA
Issues and rates: Published quarterly.
  Average paid circulation: 5,000
  Annual rate(s): $7.50
Publisher or Sponsor: The Mind Association

EDITORIAL DESCRIPTION
  Publishes articles, discussion notes, critical notices and reviews in the general field of philosophy.
Articles per average issue: 6 to 10
Audience: Philosophers
  Manuscripts accepted in English

MANUSCRIPT INFORMATION
Subject field(s): Philosophy
Manuscript requirements: No specific style guide.
  Preferred length: Articles: 6000 words; Notes: 500-2000 words
  Number of copies to be submitted: One
  Abstract: Not necessary.

Author information and reprints: Payment: By publication to author. Reviews only at £1.50 per page.
Is simultaneous submission of article to other journals permitted: Permitted, but not encouraged.
Exclusive manuscript rights between acceptance and publication: Yes
Copyright: Held by publication.
Reprints: Available, 25 free

Additional information: Proofs are read by author and editor. Contributors are asked to retain copy of typescript so that typescript need not be sent with galley proofs.

Disposition of manuscript:
Query letter: Not necessary.
Receipt of manuscript acknowledged: Yes, if requested
Decision to publish in: 1-2 months
Accepted manuscript published in: 15 months
Rejected manuscript returned: Yes, if return postage is supplied by author.
Rejected manuscript criticized: Often

Submit to:
David W. Hamlyn
Editor
(See address above)

THE MONIST [453]
International Journal of General Philosophical Inquiry
P. O. Box 599
LaSalle, Illinois 61401
(815) 223-2520

First published in 1888

SUBSCRIPTION DATA
Issues and rates: Published quarterly.
Average paid circulation: 1,400; 100 controlled
Annual rate(s): $10.00; Foreign $11.00; Institutions $10.00; Students $7.50
Managing Editor: Ann Freeman

EDITORIAL DESCRIPTION
Deals with philosophical problems arising in any area of philosophy and its related disciplines. Each issue is sharply limited within the scope of a general preassigned topic. Topics are announced two years in advance.
Articles per average issue: 8
Audience: Professional, academic
Manuscripts accepted in English

MANUSCRIPT INFORMATION
Manuscript requirements: Chicago
Preferred length: 6,000-8,000 words; 15-20 pages
Number of copies to be submitted: 2
Abstract: Yes. After acceptance, a form is issued to the author for guidance in preparing the abstract.

Author information and reprints: Payment: Reprints only. 25 reprints and 2 copies of issue
Is simultaneous submission of article to other journals permitted: Not permitted.
Exclusive manuscript rights between acceptance and publication: Yes
Copyright: Held by publication. Equal reprint rights held jointly with author.
Reprints: Available at no cost. 50, if author is subscriber. Available at cost.

Additional information: Write for details on the forthcoming topics. No paper is published that has been or is being considered elsewhere for publication.

Disposition of manuscript:
Query letter: Necessary.
Receipt of manuscript acknowledged: Yes
Decision to publish in: 2 months
Accepted manuscript published in: 9 months
Rejected manuscript returned: Yes, if return postage is supplied by author.
Rejected manuscript criticized: Sometimes

Submit to:
Prof. Eugene Freeman
Editor
P. O. Box 1908
Los Gatos, California 95030
(408) 354-7727

THE NEW SCHOLASTICISM [454]
A Quarterly of Philosophy
University of Notre Dame
Notre Dame, Indiana 46556
(219) 283-7534

First published in 1927

SUBSCRIPTION DATA
Issues and rates: Published quarterly.
Average paid circulation: 2650
Annual rate(s): $9.00
Publisher or Sponsor: American Catholic Philosophical Association

EDITORIAL DESCRIPTION
Contains discussion articles, review articles, book reviews, chronicles in all areas of philosophy.
Articles per average issue: 8-10
Audience: Academic and philosophy community
Manuscripts accepted in English

MANUSCRIPT INFORMATION
Subject field(s): All areas of philosophy
Manuscript requirements: Style sheet sent on request. Chicago
Preferred length: 1,000 to 3,000 words; 10-20 pages
Number of copies to be submitted: One
Abstract: Yes, of 100-150 words (in duplicate)

Author information and reprints: Payment: None.
Is simultaneous submission of article to other journals permitted: No

Exclusive manuscript rights between acceptance and publication: Yes
Copyright: Held by publication.
Reprints: Available, 25 reprints free

Additional information: Manuscripts should be typewritten and double-spaced, with footnotes and author's affiliation at the end on separate sheets.

Disposition of manuscript:
Receipt of manuscript acknowledged: Yes
Decision to publish in: One to two months
Accepted manuscript published in: One year
Rejected manuscript returned: Yes
Rejected manuscript criticized: Yes

Submit to:
John A. Oesterle
Editor
(See address above)

NOÛS [455]
Nihil philosophici a nobis alienum putamus
126 Sycamore
Indiana University
Bloomington, Indiana 47401
(812) 337-5676

First published in 1966

SUBSCRIPTION DATA
Issues and rates: Published quarterly.
Average paid circulation: 1,200
Annual rate(s): Individuals $9.00; Institutions $16.00; Foreign $16.50
Publisher or Sponsor: Indiana University
Managing Editor: Hector-Neri Castañeda

EDITORIAL DESCRIPTION
Publishes quality essays and brief discussions on philosophical problems regardless of the author's philosophical school or point of view. From time to time, will publish symposia, surveys of work recently done on specially selected philosophical topics, critical studies of recent books (rather than reviews), and catalogues of recent publications in philosophy.
Articles per average issue: 7
Audience: Professional philosophers, teachers of philosophy, serious students
Manuscripts accepted in English

MANUSCRIPT INFORMATION
Subject field(s): Philosophy
Manuscript requirements: See latest issue for style requirements.
Preferred length: 2,000-5,000 words
Number of copies to be submitted: Two
Abstract: Not necessary.

Author information and reprints: Payment: None. There is a processing fee of $2.00 for non-subscribers
Is simultaneous submission of article to other journals permitted: No

Exclusive manuscript rights between acceptance and publication: Yes
Copyright: Held by publication.
Reprints: Available

Disposition of manuscript:
Receipt of manuscript acknowledged: Yes
Decision to publish in: 1-2 months
Accepted manuscript published in: 12-18 months
Rejected manuscript returned: Yes
Rejected manuscript criticized: Sometimes

Submit to:
Secretary
(See address above)

THE PERSONALIST [456]
An International Review of Philosophy
School of Philosophy
University of Southern California
Los Angeles, California 90007
(213) 746-2378

First published in 1909

SUBSCRIPTION DATA
Issues and rates: Published quarterly.
Average paid circulation: Not available.
Annual rate(s): $6.00
Publisher or Sponsor: University of Southern California
Managing Editor: Lucy Helbock

EDITORIAL DESCRIPTION
Contains articles pertaining to all areas of philosophy; annual table of contents; book reviews appear occasionally in Autumn issue only.
Articles per average issue: 10
Audience: Professors and students of philosophy
Manuscripts accepted in English

MANUSCRIPT INFORMATION
Subject field(s): Philosophy
Manuscript requirements: MLA, footnotes at end of article
Preferred length: 25 printed pages maximum
Number of copies to be submitted: One
Abstract: Not necessary.
Author information and reprints: Payment: None.
Is simultaneous submission of article to other journals permitted: No
Exclusive manuscript rights between acceptance and publication: Yes
Copyright: Held by publication.
Reprints: Available, price list sent with proofs
Disposition of manuscript:
Receipt of manuscript acknowledged: Yes
Decision to publish in: 4 months
Accepted manuscript published in: 12-24 months

Rejected manuscript returned: Yes, if self-addressed, stamped envelope is sent with manuscript.
Rejected manuscript criticized: Yes

Submit to:
John Hospers
Editor
(See address above)

PHILOSOPHIA [457]
Philosophical Quarterly of Israel
Bar-Ilan University
Ramat-Gan, Israel
(03) 718 558

First published in 1971

SUBSCRIPTION DATA
Issues and rates: Published quarterly.
Annual rate(s): $10.00; Institutions $14.00

EDITORIAL DESCRIPTION
Publishes contributions in analytical philosophy from all over the world; is especially interested in application of formal logic and linguistics to philosophy.
Articles per average issue: 12
Audience: Professional
Manuscripts accepted in English

MANUSCRIPT INFORMATION
Subject field(s): Analytical and formal logic
Manuscript requirements: No specific style guide.
Preferred length: 15 pages or less
Number of copies to be submitted: 2
Abstract: Yes. of up to 100 words

Author information and reprints: Payment: Reprints only. 20 free reprints and 1 issue
Is simultaneous submission of article to other journals permitted: Not permitted.
Exclusive manuscript rights between acceptance and publication: Yes
Copyright: Held by publication.
Permission for republication granted after notice with reference to this publication.
Reprints: Available at cost.

Disposition of manuscript:
Query letter: Not necessary.
Receipt of manuscript acknowledged: Yes
Decision to publish in: 3-6months
Accepted manuscript published in: 1-2years
Rejected manuscript returned: Yes, if return postage is supplied by author.
Rejected manuscript criticized: Reasons for rejections only

Submit to:
Dr. Asa Kasher
Editor
(See address above)

THE PHILOSOPHICAL QUARTERLY [458]
Journals Manager, Scottish Academic Press
25 Perth Street
Edinburgh EH3 5DW, Scotland

First published in 1950

SUBSCRIPTION DATA
Issues and rates: Published quarterly.
Average paid circulation: 1,800
Annual rate(s): £3.00; Foreign $8.50; Institutions £5.00; $14.00
Publisher or Sponsor: The University of St. Andrews; Scots Philosophical Club

Managing Editor: Bernard Mayo

EDITORIAL DESCRIPTION
Contains articles of general interest in all fields of philosophy and discussions of recent contributions.
Articles per average issue: 6-8
Audience: Professional, academic
Manuscripts accepted in English

MANUSCRIPT INFORMATION
Subject field(s): All philosophical fields, but not purely historical work.

Manuscript requirements: MLA
Preferred length: 8,000 words maximum
Number of copies to be submitted: 1
Abstract: Not necessary.

Author information and reprints: Payment: Reprints only. 20
Is simultaneous submission of article to other journals permitted: Not permitted.
Exclusive manuscript rights between acceptance and publication: Yes
Copyright: Held jointly by author and the journal.
Reprints: Available at cost.

Additional information: Confine footnotes as far as possible to references. Type them separately with long quotations indented, double-spaced. Photo copies are acceptable.

Disposition of manuscript:
Query letter: Not necessary.
Receipt of manuscript acknowledged: No
Decision to publish in: 4 weeks
Accepted manuscript published in: 5 months
Rejected manuscript returned: Yes, if return postage is supplied by author.
Rejected manuscript criticized: Sometimes

Submit to:
Christopher Bryant
Assistant Editor
Department of Moral Philosophy
University of St. Andrews
Fife KY16 9AL, Scotland

THE PHILOSOPHICAL REVIEW [459]
218 Goldwin Smith Hall
Cornell University
Ithaca, New York 14850
(607) 256-5000

First published in 1892

SUBSCRIPTION DATA
Issues and rates: Published quarterly.
  Average paid circulation: 3950
  Annual rate(s): Institutions $8.00,
  Individuals $5.00
Publisher or Sponsor: Cornell University, Sage School of Philosophy
Managing Editor: Norman Kretzmann

EDITORIAL DESCRIPTION
Contains articles and discussions on topics in philosophy and the history of philosophy; reviews of recently published books in philosophy and the history of philosophy; list of books received.
Articles per average issue: 4 plus reviews
Audience: Professional philosophers and students of philosophy
  Manuscripts accepted in English

MANUSCRIPT INFORMATION
Subject field(s): Philosophy, history of philosophy
Manuscript requirements: Chicago
  Preferred length: 20-30 pages for articles; 5-10 pages for discussions
  Number of copies to be submitted: One
  Abstract: No

Author information and reprints: Payment: Reprints only. 50 free reprints; authors of book reviews receive $25.00.
  Is simultaneous submission of article to other journals permitted: Yes
  Exclusive manuscript rights between acceptance and publication: No
  Copyright: Not copyrighted
  Reprints: Available, first 50 free; additional at cost.

Disposition of manuscript:
  Receipt of manuscript acknowledged: Yes
  Decision to publish in: Within a month
  Accepted manuscript published in: Within a year
  Rejected manuscript returned: Yes
  Rejected manuscript criticized: Sometimes

Submit to:
  Editor
  (See address above)

PHILOSOPHY & PUBLIC AFFAIRS [460]
P.O. Box 231
Princeton University Press
Princeton, New Jersey 08540
(609) 452-4880

First published in 1971

SUBSCRIPTION DATA
Issues and rates: Published quarterly.
  Average paid circulation: 2,700
  Annual rate(s): Individuals $8.50; Institutions $3.50; Students $5.00
Publisher or Sponsor: Princeton University Press
Managing Editor: Scotia W. MacRae

EDITORIAL DESCRIPTION
Designed to fill the need for a periodical in which philosophers with different viewpoints and philosophically inclined writers from various disciplines, including law, political science, economics, and sociology, can bring their distinctive methods to bear on problems that concern everyone.
Articles per average issue: Four
  Manuscripts accepted in English

MANUSCRIPT INFORMATION
Subject field(s): Law, philosophy, political science, economics, sociology public affairs, government.
Manuscript requirements: See latest issue for style requirements.
  Preferred length: 15-35 pages
  Number of copies to be submitted: One
  Abstract: Not necessary.
Author information and reprints: Payment: Reprints only. 100
  Is simultaneous submission of article to other journals permitted: Not permitted.
  Exclusive manuscript rights between acceptance and publication: Yes
  Copyright: Held by publication.
  Reprints: Not available.
Additional information: Contributions should be typewritten and double-spaced with wide margins throughout. Footnotes should be double-spaced and gathered at the end. Camera-ready copy must be submitted for figures.
Disposition of manuscript:
  Query letter: Not necessary.
  Receipt of manuscript acknowledged: Yes
  Decision to publish in: 1-3 months
  Accepted manuscript published in: 3-9 months
  Rejected manuscript returned: Yes, if return postage is supplied by author.
  Rejected manuscript criticized: No
Submit to:
  Scotia W. MacRae
  Managing Editor
  (See address above)

SPECIAL STIPULATIONS
Publisher has a royalty sharing arrangement under which authors receive 50 per cent of reprint royalties.

PHILOSOPHY EAST AND WEST [461]
A Quarterly of Asian and Comparative Thought
University Press of Hawaii
535 Ward Avenue
Honolulu, Hawaii 96814
(808) 537-1581

First published in 1951

SUBSCRIPTION DATA
Issues and rates: Published quarterly.
  Average paid circulation: 1300
  Annual rate(s): Individuals $8.00, Institutions $10.00
Publisher or Sponsor: University of Hawaii
Managing Editor: John S. Howe, Jr.

EDITORIAL DESCRIPTION
Contains articles dealing with the relevance of philosophy to art, literature, science, and social practice of Asian civilizations, and original contributions to philosophy which work from an intercultural basis. Presents, in a comparative manner, the distinctive characteristics of the various philosophical traditions in the East and West.
Articles per average issue: 6
Audience: Scholars and students of Asian comparative thought
  Manuscripts accepted in English

MANUSCRIPT INFORMATION
Subject field(s): Philosophy, art, literature, science, social practice of Asian civilizations
Manuscript requirements: See latest issue for style requirements.
  Preferred length: 5,000 words or less
  Number of copies to be submitted: 2
  Abstract: Optional

Author information and reprints: Payment: None.
  Is simultaneous submission of article to other journals permitted: No
  Exclusive manuscript rights between acceptance and publication: Yes
  Copyright: Held by publication.
  Reprints: Available, 50 free to authors

Disposition of manuscript:
  Query letter: Necessary.
  Receipt of manuscript acknowledged: Yes
  Decision to publish in: 4 weeks
  Accepted manuscript published in: 6 months
  Rejected manuscript returned: Yes
  Rejected manuscript criticized: Yes

Submit to:
  Eliot Deutsch
  Editor
  2424 Maile Way
  Honolulu, Hawaii 96822
  (808) 948-8323

PHILOSOPHY IN CONTEXT [462]
Cashier's Office
Cleveland State University
Cleveland, Ohio 44115
(216) 687-3900

SUBSCRIPTION DATA

Issues and rates: Published semi-annually.
   Annual rate(s): $3.00; Institutions $3.00; Students $3.00

EDITORIAL DESCRIPTION

Examines philosophical issues with a primarily student audience in mind.
Articles per average issue: 8
Audience: Academic
   Manuscripts accepted in English

MANUSCRIPT INFORMATION

Manuscript requirements: No specific style guide.
   Preferred length: 10-12 pages
   Number of copies to be submitted: 2
   Abstract: Not necessary.

Author information and reprints: Payment: None.
   Is simultaneous submission of article to other journals permitted: Not permitted.
   Exclusive manuscript rights between acceptance and publication: Yes
   Copyright: Held by publication.
   Reprints: 12 Available at no cost.

Disposition of manuscript:
   Query letter: Not necessary.
   Receipt of manuscript acknowledged: Yes
   Decision to publish in: 2-3 months
   Accepted manuscript published in: 1 year
   Rejected manuscript returned: Yes, if return postage is supplied by author.
   Rejected manuscript criticized: Yes

Submit to:
   Joseph P. De Marco
   Associate Editor
   Department of Philosophy
   Cleveland State University
   Cleveland, Ohio 44115

PHILOSOPHY OF SCIENCE [463]
Official Journal of the Philosophy of Science Association
18 Morrill Hall
Department of Philosophy
Michigan State University
East Lansing, Michigan 48823
(517) 353-9392

First published in 1933

SUBSCRIPTION DATA

Issues and rates: Published quarterly.
   Average paid circulation: 2600
   Annual rate(s): Institutions $17.50, Individuals $15.00

Publisher or Sponsor: Philosophy of Science Association
Managing Editor: Peter D. Asquith

EDITORIAL DESCRIPTION

Contributions deal with knowledge, scientific method, causality, and other subjects of general philosophical interest.
Articles per average issue: 4, plus 2-4 discussions
Audience: Philosophers and scientists
   Manuscripts accepted in English

MANUSCRIPT INFORMATION

Subject field(s): Philosophy of Science
Manuscript requirements: See latest issue for style requirements.
   Preferred length: Less than 30 pages
   Number of copies to be submitted: Two
   Abstract: Yes

Author information and reprints: Payment: None.
   Is simultaneous submission of article to other journals permitted: No
   Exclusive manuscript rights between acceptance and publication: Yes
   Copyright: Held by publication.
   Reprints: Available

Disposition of manuscript:
   Query letter: Not necessary.
   Receipt of manuscript acknowledged: Yes
   Decision to publish in: 6 months
   Accepted manuscript published in: 1 year
   Rejected manuscript returned: Yes, if return postage is supplied by author.
   Rejected manuscript criticized: Yes

Submit to:
   Editorial Board
   (See address above)

PHILOSOPHY AND RHETORIC [464]
215 Wagner Building
University Park, Pennsylvania 16802
(814) 865-1327

First published in 1968

SUBSCRIPTION DATA

Issues and rates: Published quarterly.
   Average paid circulation: 800
   Annual rate(s): $10.00, Foreign $13.00
Managing Editor: Henry W. Johnstone, Jr.

EDITORIAL DESCRIPTION

Contains papers on the philosophical aspects of rhetoric.
Articles per average issue: 4
Audience: Philosophers and rhetoricians
   Manuscripts accepted in English

MANUSCRIPT INFORMATION

Manuscript requirements: No specific style guide.
   Preferred length: 5000 words; 15 pages
   Number of copies to be submitted: Two
Author information and reprints: Payment: None.
   Is simultaneous submission of article to other journals permitted: No
   Exclusive manuscript rights between acceptance and publication: Yes
   Copyright: Held by publication.
   Reprints: Available, 25 free

Disposition of manuscript:
   Query letter: Not necessary.
   Receipt of manuscript acknowledged: Yes
   Decision to publish in: 3 months
   Accepted manuscript published in: 1 year
   Rejected manuscript returned: Yes, if return postage is supplied by author.
   Rejected manuscript criticized: No
Submit to:
   Henry W. Johnstone, Jr.
   Editor
   246 Sparks Building
   University Park, Pennsylvania 16802
   (814) 865-3200

PHILOSOPHY TODAY [465]
Carthagena Station
Celina, Ohio 45822
(419) 925-4121

First published in 1957

SUBSCRIPTION DATA

Issues and rates: Published quarterly.
   Average paid circulation: 1345 controlled
   Annual rate(s): $7.00, Foreign $7.50
Managing Editor: Robert F. Lechner

EDITORIAL DESCRIPTION

Contains articles on problems and issues in contemporary philosophy.
Articles per average issue: 7-10
Audience: Professional philosophers, educators
   Manuscripts accepted in English

MANUSCRIPT INFORMATION

Subject field(s): Philosophy, philosophy-theology
Manuscript requirements: No specific style guide.
   Preferred length: 5000-7000 words
   Number of copies to be submitted: One
   Abstract: Yes; 1 typed page

Author information and reprints: Payment: Reprints only. Two copies of issue in which article appears, plus 30 off-prints.
   Is simultaneous submission of article to other journals permitted: No
   Exclusive manuscript rights between acceptance and publication: Yes
   Copyright: Held by author or publication
   Reprints: Available

Disposition of manuscript:
   Query letter: Not necessary.
   Receipt of manuscript acknowledged: Yes
   Decision to publish in: One month
   Accepted manuscript published in: Within a year
   Rejected manuscript returned: Yes, if return postage is supplied by author.
   Rejected manuscript criticized: No
Submit to:
   Robert F. Lechner
   Editor
   (See address above)

PROCESS STUDIES [466]
1325 North College Avenue
Claremont, California 91711
(714) 621-3144

First published in 1971

SUBSCRIPTION DATA
Issues and rates: Published quarterly.
Average paid circulation: 800
Annual rate(s): Individuals $6.00,
Institutions $10.00
Managing Editor: Robert W. Hutton

EDITORIAL DESCRIPTION
Publishes major articles dealing with process philosophy, most notably that of Alfred North Whitehead, and application of process conceptualizations to other fields.
Articles per average issue: 4-6
Audience: Philosophers, theologians
Manuscripts accepted in English, will translate others

MANUSCRIPT INFORMATION
Subject field(s): Process philosophy; process philosophy as related to: theology, aesthetics, mathematics, physics, biology, cosmology, history of religion, social science, literary criticism
Manuscript requirements: See latest issue for style requirements.
Preferred length: 10-30 pages
Number of copies to be submitted: One
Abstract: Yes, on the form supplied by editor.
Author information and reprints: Payment: Reprints only. 25 reprints
Is simultaneous submission of article to other journals permitted: Consult editor.
Exclusive manuscript rights between acceptance and publication: Yes
Copyright: Held by publication.
Reprints: Available
Disposition of manuscript:
Receipt of manuscript acknowledged: Yes
Decision to publish in: 3-5 weeks
Accepted manuscript published in: 3-9 months
Rejected manuscript returned: Yes, if self-addressed, stamped envelope is sent with manuscript.
Rejected manuscript criticized: Sometimes
Submit to:
Lewis S. Ford
Co-Editor
3157 Trumpet Road
Chesapeake, Virginia 23321
(804) 488-6791

RESEARCH IN PHENOMENOLOGY [467]
Humanities Press, Inc.
Atlantic Highlands, New Jersey 07716

SUBSCRIPTION DATA
Issues and rates: Published annually.
Average paid circulation: Not available.
Managing Editor: John Sallis

EDITORIAL DESCRIPTION
Contains papers presenting original research, interpretive and critical studies of the work of major phenomenological thinkers; historical studies relevant to phenomenology.

MANUSCRIPT INFORMATION
Subject field(s): Philosophy
Manuscript requirements: See latest issue for style requirements.
Preferred length: 20-30 pages
Number of copies to be submitted: One
Author information and reprints: Payment: None.
Is simultaneous submission of article to other journals permitted: No
Exclusive manuscript rights between acceptance and publication: Yes
Copyright: Held by publication.
Reprints: Available
Disposition of manuscript:
Receipt of manuscript acknowledged: Yes
Decision to publish in: 6 weeks
Accepted manuscript published in: Maximum 1 year
Rejected manuscript returned: Yes
Rejected manuscript criticized: No
Submit to:
John Sallis
Editor
Department of Philosophy
Duquesne University
Pittsburgh, Pennsylvania 15219
(412) 434-6504

REVIEW OF METAPHYSICS [468]
The Catholic University of America
Washington, D.C. 20017
(202) 635-8778

SUBSCRIPTION DATA
Issues and rates: Published quarterly.
Average paid circulation: 3400
Annual rate(s): Institutions $12.00, Individuals $7.00, Students $4.00
Publisher or Sponsor: Philosophy Education Society, Inc.
Managing Editor: William A. Frank

EDITORIAL DESCRIPTION
Devoted to the promotion of technically competent, definitive contributions to philosophical knowledge. Not associated with any school or group, nor the organ of any association or institution, it is interested in persistent, resolute inquiries into root questions.
Articles per average issue: 6
Audience: Philosophers of all persuasions
Manuscripts accepted in English

MANUSCRIPT INFORMATION
Subject field(s): Philosophy
Manuscript requirements: Chicago
Preferred length: 20 pages
Number of copies to be submitted: One
Author information and reprints: Payment: None.
Is simultaneous submission of article to other journals permitted: No
Exclusive manuscript rights between acceptance and publication: Yes
Copyright: Held by publication.
Reprints: Available, at cost
Additional information: A stamped self-addressed envelope should accompany each manuscript.
Disposition of manuscript:
Receipt of manuscript acknowledged: Yes
Decision to publish in: 3-4 weeks
Accepted manuscript published in: 2-3 months
Rejected manuscript returned: Yes, if return postage is supplied by author.
Rejected manuscript criticized: Sometimes
Submit to:
Jude P. Dougherty
Editor
(See address above)
(202) 635-5259

RUSSELL: THE JOURNAL OF THE BERTRAND RUSSELL ARCHIVES [469]
McMaster University Library Press
Russell Archives, Mills Memorial Library
Hamilton, Ontario L8S 4L6, Canada
(416) 525-9140

First published in 1971

SUBSCRIPTION DATA
Issues and rates: Published quarterly.
Average paid circulation: 350; 100 controlled
Annual rate(s): $3.50; Foreign $4.50; Individuals $3.00; Institutions $3.50; Students $3.00; Foreign individuals $4.00; Foreign institutions $4.50
Publisher or Sponsor: McMaster University; The Bertrand Russell Society
Managing Editor: Kenneth Blackwell

EDITORIAL DESCRIPTION
A clearing-house for the scholarly resources of the Russell Archives. Articles include bibliographies of writings by and about Russell, book reviews, details of current research topics, news of publication projects and articles related to his life and work.
Articles per average issue: 4
Audience: Persons with special interest in Bertrand Russell
Manuscripts accepted in English

MANUSCRIPT INFORMATION
Subject field(s): Any topic related to the life, work or study of Bertrand Russell.
Manuscript requirements: No specific style guide.
Preferred length: 1,000 words
Number of copies to be submitted: 1
Abstract: Not necessary.
Author information and reprints: Payment: None.

Is simultaneous submission of article to other journals permitted: Permitted.
Exclusive manuscript rights between acceptance and publication: No
Copyright: Held by author.
Reprints: Available at no cost. 10

Disposition of manuscript:
Query letter: Not necessary, but advisable.
Receipt of manuscript acknowledged: Yes
Decision to publish in: 1 month
Accepted manuscript published in: 4 months
Rejected manuscript returned: Yes, with return postage paid by publication.
Rejected manuscript criticized: Reasons for rejections only
Submit to:
Kenneth Blackwell
Editor
(See address above)

Poetry and contemporary literature

AGENDA [470]
5 Cranbourne Court
Albert Bridge Road
London SW11 4PE, England
01-228-0700

First published in 1959

SUBSCRIPTION DATA
Issues and rates: Published quarterly.
Average paid circulation: 2,000
Annual rate(s): £3 ($9.00)
Managing Editor: Peter Dale

EDITORIAL DESCRIPTION
Contains poetry and criticism. Special issues on particular poets and writers.

MANUSCRIPT INFORMATION
Subject field(s): Poetry, critical articles
Manuscript requirements: See latest issue for style requirements.
Preferred length: 3,000 to 5,000 words
Number of copies to be submitted: One
Author information and reprints: Payment: Reprints only. 6 complimentary copies
Is simultaneous submission of article to other journals permitted: No
Exclusive manuscript rights between acceptance and publication: Yes
Copyright: Held by author.
Reprints: Not available.
Disposition of manuscript:
Query letter: Not necessary.
Receipt of manuscript acknowledged: No
Decision to publish in: 4 weeks
Accepted manuscript published in: 3 months
Rejected manuscript returned: Yes, if return postage is supplied by author.
Rejected manuscript criticized: Sometimes
Submit to:
William Cookson
Editor
(See address above)

ANTAEUS [471]
One West 30th Street, Room 203
New York, New York 10001
(212) 736-2599

First published in 1970

SUBSCRIPTION DATA
Issues and rates: Published quarterly.
Average paid circulation: 5,000
Annual rate(s): $10.00
Managing Editor: Gail S. Rosenblum

EDITORIAL DESCRIPTION
Publishes articles on literature, some poetry as well as prose.
Articles per average issue: 3-4 stories; 2 documents; 40 poems
Audience: Readers of serious literature
Manuscripts accepted in English

MANUSCRIPT INFORMATION
Subject field(s): Poetry, prose, fiction, some documents of special literary interest, interviews
Manuscript requirements: No specific style guide.
Preferred length: None
Number of copies to be submitted: 1
Abstract: Not necessary.
Author information and reprints: Payment: None.
Is simultaneous submission of article to other journals permitted: Permitted, but not encouraged.
Exclusive manuscript rights between acceptance and publication: Yes
Copyright: Held by publication.
Reprints: Not available.
Disposition of manuscript:
Query letter: Not necessary.
Receipt of manuscript acknowledged: No
Decision to publish in: 1 month
Accepted manuscript published in: 6 months
Rejected manuscript returned: Yes, if return postage is supplied by author.
Rejected manuscript criticized: No
Submit to:
Daniel Halpern
Editor
(See address above)

THE ANTIGONISH REVIEW [472]
St. Francis Xavier University
Antigonish, Nova Scotia, Canada
(902) 867-2221

SUBSCRIPTION DATA
Issues and rates: Published quarterly.
Average paid circulation: 500
Annual rate(s): $5.00
Publisher or Sponsor: St. Francis Xavier University

EDITORIAL DESCRIPTION
Contains short stories, poems, essays, interviews and book reviews.
Articles per average issue: 25
Audience: Literary
Manuscripts accepted in English, French

MANUSCRIPT INFORMATION
Subject field(s): Literary and philosophical
Manuscript requirements: No specific style guide.
Preferred length: 1000 words; 5 pages
Number of copies to be submitted: One
Abstract: Not necessary.
Author information and reprints: Payment: None.
Is simultaneous submission of article to other journals permitted: Yes
Exclusive manuscript rights between acceptance and publication: No
Copyright: Held by author.
Reprints: Available
Disposition of manuscript:
Query letter: Not necessary.
Receipt of manuscript acknowledged: Yes
Decision to publish in: 6 weeks
Accepted manuscript published in: 4 months
Rejected manuscript returned: Yes, if self-addressed, stamped envelope is sent with manuscript.
Rejected manuscript criticized: No
Submit to:
R. J. MacSween
Editor
(See address above)

THE ARK RIVER REVIEW [473]
519 Montgomery
Haverford, Pennsylvania 19041
(215) 896-8812

First published in 1971

SUBSCRIPTION DATA
Issues and rates: Published quarterly.
Average paid circulation: 800; 2,400 controlled
Annual rate(s): $2.00; Pan-Am $2.50; Foreign $2.50; Individuals $2.00; Institutions $2.50; Students $2.00; Foreign individuals $2.50; Foreign institutions $2.50
Publisher or Sponsor: Kansas Arts Commission

EDITORIAL DESCRIPTION
Open to a wide range of styles. New and unusual work is preferred.

Articles per average issue: 20
Audience: Those interested in language and literature, fiction and poetry.
Manuscripts accepted in English

MANUSCRIPT INFORMATION

Manuscript requirements: No specific style guide.
Preferred length: 1 to 20; average of 6 pages
Number of copies to be submitted: 2
Abstract: Not necessary.
Author information and reprints: Payment: By publication to author. Reprints only. 2 Other Fiction $3.00 per page; poetry 20 cents per line, $5.00 minimum
Is simultaneous submission of article to other journals permitted: Not permitted.
Exclusive manuscript rights between acceptance and publication: Yes
Copyright: Held by publication.
Reprints: Available at cost. 50 cents each
Additional information: Name and address should be given in upper right-hand corner of each page of the manuscript. Title and page number of each subsequent page also in upper right hand corner.
Disposition of manuscript:
Query letter: Not necessary.
Receipt of manuscript acknowledged: No
Decision to publish in: 1 month
Accepted manuscript published in: 6 months
Rejected manuscript returned: Yes, if return postage is supplied by author.
Rejected manuscript criticized: Sometimes
Submit to:
Arthur Vogelsang
Editor
(See address above)

BARDIC ECHOES [474]
1036 Emerald Avenue, N.E.
Grand Rapids, Michigan 49503
(616) 454-9120

First published in 1960

SUBSCRIPTION DATA

Issues and rates: Published quarterly.
Average paid circulation: 350; 150 controlled
Annual rate(s): $2.00
Publisher or Sponsor: The Bards of Grand Rapids
Managing Editor: Clarence L. Weaver

EDITORIAL DESCRIPTION

Contains poetry; listing with brief comment or review books of verse from authors or publishers; news of poetry contests; listing of exchange periodicals.
Articles per average issue: Varies
Audience: Those who enjoy poetry
Manuscripts accepted in English

MANUSCRIPT INFORMATION

Subject field(s): Poetry: modern themes, seasonal themes; any theme acceptable, depending on its handling.

Manuscript requirements: No specific style guide.
Preferred length: One page; 40 lines
Number of copies to be submitted: One
Author information and reprints: Payment: Reprints only. 1 copy of issue
Is simultaneous submission of article to other journals permitted: No
Exclusive manuscript rights between acceptance and publication: Yes
Copyright: Held by author.
Reprints: Not available.
Additional information: Each poem should be on a separate 8 ½x11 sheet with author's name and address.
Disposition of manuscript:
Query letter: Not necessary.
Receipt of manuscript acknowledged: No
Decision to publish in: 1-10 weeks
Accepted manuscript published in: 4-12 months
Rejected manuscript returned: Yes, if self-addressed, stamped envelope is sent with manuscript.
Rejected manuscript criticized: No
Submit to:
Clarence L. Weaver
Editor
(See address above)

BELOIT POETRY JOURNAL [475]
Box 2
Beloit, Wisconsin 53511
(608) 362-2907

First published in 1950

SUBSCRIPTION DATA

Issues and rates: Published quarterly.
Average paid circulation: 800; 200 controlled
Annual rate(s): $3.00

EDITORIAL DESCRIPTION

Contains contemporary poetry, including some translations; aims to represent the growing tip of poetry; occasional chapbook issues, such as recent volumes of concrete poetry, Asian poetry, and works of single poets.
Articles per average issue: 15
Audience: Highly literate
Manuscripts accepted in English

MANUSCRIPT INFORMATION

Subject field(s): Poetry
Manuscript requirements: See latest issue for style requirements.
Preferred length: Any length
Number of copies to be submitted: One
Author information and reprints: Payment: Reprints only. 3 copies of issue
Is simultaneous submission of article to other journals permitted: No
Exclusive manuscript rights between acceptance and publication: Yes
Copyright: Held by publication.
Reprints: Not available.
Additional information: Submit with self-addressed stamped envelope.
Disposition of manuscript:
Query letter: Not necessary.

Receipt of manuscript acknowledged: No
Decision to publish in: 1-12 weeks
Accepted manuscript published in: One month
Rejected manuscript returned: Yes, if self-addressed, stamped envelope is sent with manuscript.
Rejected manuscript criticized: No
Submit to:
Editorial Board
(See address above)

SPECIAL STIPULATIONS

Familiarity with the magazine would prevent many unsuitable submissions.

BOUNDARY 2 [476]
A Journal of Postmodern Literature
State University of New York at Binghamton
Binghamton, New York 13901
(607) 798-2743

First published in 1972

SUBSCRIPTION DATA

Issues and rates: Published three times per year.
Average paid circulation: 850; 150 controlled
Annual rate(s): Individuals $7.00; Institutions $9.00; Foreign individuals $8.00; Foreign institutions $10.00

EDITORIAL DESCRIPTION

Postmodern criticism, poetry, fiction, drama
Articles per average issue: 10
Audience: Academic
Manuscripts accepted in English

MANUSCRIPT INFORMATION

Manuscript requirements: No specific style guide.
Number of copies to be submitted: 1
Abstract: Not necessary.
Author information and reprints: Payment: None.
Is simultaneous submission of article to other journals permitted: Not permitted.
Exclusive manuscript rights between acceptance and publication: Yes
Copyright: Held by publication.
Reprints: Available at cost.
Disposition of manuscript:
Query letter: Not necessary.
Receipt of manuscript acknowledged: Yes
Decision to publish in: 2 months
Accepted manuscript published in: 9-12 months
Rejected manuscript returned: Yes, if return postage is supplied by author.
Rejected manuscript criticized: Sometimes
Submit to:
William V. Spanos;
Robert Kroetsch
Co-Editors
(See address above)

Poetry and contemporary literature 137

CALIFORNIA QUARTERLY [477]
100 Sproul Hall
University of California at Davis
Davis, California 95616

First published in 1971

SUBSCRIPTION DATA
Issues and rates: Published quarterly.
Average paid circulation: 300
Annual rate(s): $5.00; Foreign $5.00;
Institutions $5.00
Managing Editor: Elliot L. Gilbert

EDITORIAL DESCRIPTION
Contains fiction and poetry, with occasional criticism
Articles per average issue: Fiction 2-4; poetry 20-25
Manuscripts accepted in English

MANUSCRIPT INFORMATION
Subject field(s): No subject limitation
Manuscript requirements: No specific style guide.
Preferred length: 8,000 words
Number of copies to be submitted: 1
Abstract: Not necessary.
Author information and reprints: Payment:
By publication to author. Prose: $2.00 per page; poetry: $3.00 per page
Is simultaneous submission of article to other journals permitted: Not permitted.
Exclusive manuscript rights between acceptance and publication: Yes
Copyright: Held by publisher, but transferred to author upon request
Reprints: Available at no cost. 2
Disposition of manuscript:
Query letter: Not necessary.
Receipt of manuscript acknowledged: No
Decision to publish in: 6-8 weeks
Accepted manuscript published in: 3-6 months
Rejected manuscript returned: Yes, if return postage is supplied by author.
Rejected manuscript criticized: Sometimes
Submit to:
Poetry:
Karl Shapiro

Fiction:
Elliot Gilbert
Editors
(See address above)

CANADIAN SHORT STORY MAGAZINE [478]
518 26th Street South
Lethbridge, Alberta T1J 3R4, Canada
(403) 329-0493

SUBSCRIPTION DATA
Issues and rates: Published quarterly.
Annual rate(s): $2.00; Pan-Am $3.00; Foreign $5.00

EDITORIAL DESCRIPTION
Publishes short stories for Canadians, by Canadians, about Canada.
Articles per average issue: Varies

Audience: General Canadian
Manuscripts accepted in English, French

MANUSCRIPT INFORMATION
Subject field(s): All morally sound fields with a Canadian location.
Manuscript requirements: See latest issue for style requirements. Style sheet sent on request.
Preferred length: 1,500 words; 6 pages
Number of copies to be submitted: 1
Abstract: Not necessary.
Author information and reprints: Payment:
By publication to author. Varies
Is simultaneous submission of article to other journals permitted: Not permitted.
Exclusive manuscript rights between acceptance and publication: Yes
Copyright: Held by publication. first serial rights only
Reprints: Not available.
Additional information: Double-spaced typescript, wide margins, accepted forms of mechanics in spelling, punctuations, etc.
Disposition of manuscript:
Query letter: Necessary.
Receipt of manuscript acknowledged: No
Decision to publish in: 1 month
Accepted manuscript published in: About 1 year
Rejected manuscript returned: Yes, if return postage is supplied by author.
Rejected manuscript criticized: Reasons for rejections only
Submit to:
Louis Burke
Editor
(See address above)

SPECIAL STIPULATIONS
Author must be a Canadian citizen.

CARAVEL MAGAZINE [479]
315 Kneale Avenue South
Thief River Falls, Minnesota 56701
(218) 681-5965

First published in 1957

SUBSCRIPTION DATA
Issues and rates: Irregular
Average paid circulation: 550
Annual rate(s): $2.00; Foreign $2.25

EDITORIAL DESCRIPTION
Contains prose accounts of the poet's relation to the world; verse dealing with people and places, with what peoples of world have in common.
Articles per average issue: 20
Audience: Academic
Manuscripts accepted in English (occasional translation)

MANUSCRIPT INFORMATION
Manuscript requirements: Chicago; Webster 3
Preferred length: 1000 words
Number of copies to be submitted: One original
Abstract: Not necessary.

Author information and reprints: Payment:
By publication to author. $.05 per line
Is simultaneous submission of article to other journals permitted: No
Exclusive manuscript rights between acceptance and publication: Yes
Reprints: Not available.
Disposition of manuscript:
Query letter: Not necessary.
Receipt of manuscript acknowledged: No
Decision to publish in: 1 month
Accepted manuscript published in: 6 months
Rejected manuscript returned: Yes, if self-addressed, stamped envelope is sent with manuscript.
Rejected manuscript criticized: No
Submit to:
Ben Hagglund
Editor and Publisher
(See address above)

THE CARLETON MISCELLANY [480]
Carleton College
Northfield, Minnesota 55057
(507) 645-4431 ext. 208

First published in 1960

SUBSCRIPTION DATA
Issues and rates: Published semi-annually.
Average paid circulation: 800; 1,000 controlled
Annual rate(s): $3.00; Foreign $3.00; Individuals $3.00
Managing Editor: Wayne M. Carver

EDITORIAL DESCRIPTION
An informal but serious tone directed toward evaluation, criticism, and depiction of contemporary culture, poetry, fiction, essays and reviews
Articles per average issue: 25
Audience: Academics who have not given up or in to pedantry and despair; all friends of the casual, informal, satiric, and rationally eccentric.
Manuscripts accepted in English

MANUSCRIPT INFORMATION
Subject field(s): Lively, informal but not unstrung poetry, fiction and essays on any subject
Manuscript requirements: See latest issue for style requirements.
Preferred length: 10,000 words maximum
Number of copies to be submitted: 1
Abstract: Not necessary.
Author information and reprints: Payment:
By publication to author. $8.00 per page.
Is simultaneous submission of article to other journals permitted: Not permitted.
Exclusive manuscript rights between acceptance and publication: Yes
Copyright: Held by publication but assigned to author upon request
Reprints: Not available.
Disposition of manuscript:
Query letter: Not necessary.
Receipt of manuscript acknowledged: No
Decision to publish in: 6 to 8 weeks

Accepted manuscript published in: 6 months to 1 year
Rejected manuscript returned: Yes, if return postage is supplied by author.
Rejected manuscript criticized: Sometimes
Submit to:
Wayne M. Carver
Editor
(See address above)

SPECIAL STIPULATIONS
No queries please. First copies only, in readable condition. No graphics.

CAROLINA QUARTERLY [481]
Box 1117
Chapel Hill, North Carolina 27514
(919) 933-0136

Previously entitled *Carolina Magazine*

First published in 1948

SUBSCRIPTION DATA
Issues and rates: Published three times per year.
   Average paid circulation: 2000
   Annual rate(s): $4.00, Foreign $5.00
Managing Editor: Jeff Richards

EDITORIAL DESCRIPTION
Contains original poetry, fiction, graphics, and reviews.
Articles per average issue: 5-7 fiction; 8-12 poems
Audience: University, literary
   Manuscripts accepted in English

MANUSCRIPT INFORMATION
Subject field(s): Fiction, poetry
Manuscript requirements: See latest issue for style requirements.
   Preferred length: Under 8000 words
   Number of copies to be submitted: One
   Abstract: Not necessary.
Author information and reprints: Payment: By publication to author. $5.00 per page.
   Is simultaneous submission of article to other journals permitted: No
   Reprints: Available, 3 issues free
Additional information: Manuscripts should be typewritten, double-spaced and clearly marked on the envelope for fiction or poetry. There is no Fall issue.
Disposition of manuscript:
   Query letter: Not necessary.
   Receipt of manuscript acknowledged: No
   Decision to publish in: 6-8 weeks
   Accepted manuscript published in: Next issue
   Rejected manuscript returned: Yes, if self-addressed, stamped envelope is sent with manuscript.
   Rejected manuscript criticized: Sometimes
Submit to:
Fiction or Poetry Editor
(See address above)
(919) 933-0136

CHICAGO REVIEW [482]
The University of Chicago
Chicago, Illinois 60637
(312) 753-3571

SUBSCRIPTION DATA
Issues and rates: Published quarterly.
   Average paid circulation: 3,000 controlled
   Annual rate(s): $6.95, Foreign $8.00
Managing Editor: Thomas Joyce

EDITORIAL DESCRIPTION
Seeks out new writers of fiction and poetry as well as more established authors. Publishes book reviews and essays, along with photography and graphic art in general.
Articles per average issue: 25
Audience: Literary
   Manuscripts accepted in English

MANUSCRIPT INFORMATION
Subject field(s): Fiction, poetry, reviews, essays, art
Manuscript requirements: See latest issue for style requirements.
   Preferred length: Open
   Number of copies to be submitted: One
   Abstract: Not necessary.
Author information and reprints: Payment: By publication to author. Currently offering a $100 prize each in fiction, poetry, and other categories; also occasional individual arrangement.
   Is simultaneous submission of article to other journals permitted: Discouraged
   Exclusive manuscript rights between acceptance and publication: Yes
   Copyright: Depends on situation
   Reprints: Not available.
Additional information: Will not return manuscripts without full return postage and appropriate envelope.
Disposition of manuscript:
   Receipt of manuscript acknowledged: No
   Decision to publish in: 3-8 weeks
   Accepted manuscript published in: 2-7 months
   Rejected manuscript returned: Yes, if self-addressed, stamped envelope is sent with manuscript.
   Rejected manuscript criticized: Sometimes
Submit to:
Fiction, Poetry, Art, or Nonfiction Departments
(See address above)

CONCERNING POETRY [483]
English Department
Western Washington State College
Bellingham, Washington 98225

SUBSCRIPTION DATA
Issues and rates: Published semi-annually.
   Average paid circulation: 350; 100 controlled
   Annual rate(s): $3.00, Foreign $3.50

EDITORIAL DESCRIPTION
Contains explications of poems, general articles on poetry, original poems, reviews. Articles are aimed at helping people to better read poetry.

MANUSCRIPT INFORMATION
Manuscript requirements: MLA
   Preferred length: 10 pages maximum
   Number of copies to be submitted: One
Author information and reprints: Payment: Reprints only. Copies of the journal.
   Is simultaneous submission of article to other journals permitted: Yes
   Exclusive manuscript rights between acceptance and publication: Yes
   Copyright: Held by publication.
   Reprints: Not available.
Disposition of manuscript:
   Receipt of manuscript acknowledged: No
   Decision to publish in: 1 to 2 months
   Accepted manuscript published in: 6-12 months
   Rejected manuscript returned: Yes, if self-addressed, stamped envelope is sent with manuscript.
   Rejected manuscript criticized: No
Submit to:
L. L. Lee
Editor

Poetry to:
Robert Huff
Poetry Editor
(See address above)

DECEMBER [484]
A Magazine of the Arts and Opinion
Box 274
Western Springs, Illinois 60558
(312) 246-1918

SUBSCRIPTION DATA
Issues and rates: Irregular
   Average paid circulation: 2,000
   Annual rate(s): $8.00 per 4 issues

EDITORIAL DESCRIPTION
Contains prose, poetry, fiction, movie criticism.
Articles per average issue: 75
Audience: Literary and artistic community
   Manuscripts accepted in English

MANUSCRIPT INFORMATION
Manuscript requirements: No specific style guide.
   Preferred length: 5,000 words maximum
   Number of copies to be submitted: 1, typewritten, double-spaced
   Abstract: No
Author information and reprints: Payment: Reprints only. 2 copies of issue.
   Is simultaneous submission of article to other journals permitted: No
   Exclusive manuscript rights between acceptance and publication: Yes
   Copyright: Held by author.
   Reprints: Not available.
Disposition of manuscript:
   Query letter: Not necessary.
   Receipt of manuscript acknowledged: No
   Decision to publish in: 8 weeks
   Accepted manuscript published in: 1 year

Rejected manuscript returned: Yes, if
return postage is supplied by author.
Rejected manuscript criticized: No
Submit to:
Curt Johnson
Editor and Publisher
(See address above)

DEKALB LITERARY ARTS
JOURNAL [485]
DeKalb College
555 North Indian Creek Drive
Clarkston, Georgia 30021
(404) 292-1520

SUBSCRIPTION DATA
Issues and rates: Published quarterly.
  Average paid circulation: 1500
  Annual rate(s): $5.00
Publisher or Sponsor: DeKalb College

EDITORIAL DESCRIPTION
  Contains stories, critical articles, poems,
  songs, reviews, Illustrations.
Articles per average issue: Varies
Audience: Academic
  Manuscripts accepted in any language.

MANUSCRIPT INFORMATION
Subject field(s): Literary
Manuscript requirements: No specific style
  guide.
  Preferred length: Open
  Number of copies to be submitted: One
  Abstract: Not necessary.
Author information and reprints: Payment:
  Reprints only. Copy of issue
  Is simultaneous submission of article to
  other journals permitted: No
  Exclusive manuscript rights between
  acceptance and publication: Yes
  Copyright: Held by author.
  Reprints: Not available.
Additional information: Manuscripts must
  be typewritten, double-spaced; no
  xeroxes, carbons
Disposition of manuscript:
  Query letter: Not necessary.
  Receipt of manuscript acknowledged: No
  Decision to publish in: 6 weeks
  Accepted manuscript published in: 1 year
  Rejected manuscript returned: Yes, if
  self-addressed, stamped envelope is sent
  with manuscript.
  Rejected manuscript criticized: No
Submit to:
Gayle Goodin
Editor
(See address above)

DESCANT [486]
The Literary Journal of Texas Christian
University
Department of English
Texas Christian University
Fort Worth, Texas 76129
(817) 962-2461

SUBSCRIPTION DATA
Issues and rates: Published quarterly.
  Average paid circulation: 600
  Annual rate(s): $2.00
Publisher or Sponsor: Texas Christian
  University
Managing Editor: Betsy Colquitt

EDITORIAL DESCRIPTION
  Contains short stories and poetry and
  essays on modern literature.
Articles per average issue: 12
  Manuscripts accepted in English

MANUSCRIPT INFORMATION
Subject field(s): Short stories, poetry, essays
Manuscript requirements: MLA
  Preferred length: Up to 6000 words for
  short fiction; poetry: 50 lines
  Number of copies to be submitted: One
  Abstract: Not necessary.
Author information and reprints: Payment:
  Reprints only. copies of the magazine
  Is simultaneous submission of article to
  other journals permitted: No
  Exclusive manuscript rights between
  acceptance and publication: Yes
  Copyright: Held by publication.
  Reprints: Not available.
Disposition of manuscript:
  Query letter: Not necessary.
  Receipt of manuscript acknowledged: No
  Decision to publish in: Six weeks
  Accepted manuscript published in: Six
  months
  Rejected manuscript returned: Yes, if
  self-addressed, stamped envelope is sent
  with manuscript.
  Rejected manuscript criticized: No
Submit to:
Betsy Feagan Colquitt
(See address above)

DRIFTWOOD EAST
QUARTERLY [487]
95 Carter Avenue
Pawtucket, Rhode Island 02861
(401)724-5690

First published in 1973

SUBSCRIPTION DATA
Issues and rates: Published quarterly.
  Average paid circulation: Not available.
  Annual rate(s): $5.00
Managing Editor: Marjorie Look Drake

EDITORIAL DESCRIPTION
  Contains poetry.
Articles per average issue: 125-150
Audience: Poets, teachers, therapists
  Manuscripts accepted in English only

MANUSCRIPT INFORMATION
Subject field(s): Any style of poem except
  avant garde.
Manuscript requirements: See latest issue for
  style requirements.
  Preferred length: 16-20 lines
Author information and reprints: Payment:
  None.
  Is simultaneous submission of article to
  other journals permitted: No
  Exclusive manuscript rights between
  acceptance and publication: Yes
  Copyright: Held by author.
  Reprints: Available at cost.
Disposition of manuscript:
  Query letter: Not necessary.
  Decision to publish in: 2 weeks
  Accepted manuscript published in: 3
  months
  Rejected manuscript returned: Yes, if
  return postage is supplied by author.
  Rejected manuscript criticized: Yes
Submit to:
Editor
(See address above)

ENCORE [488]
A Quarterly of Verse and Poetic Arts
1121 Major Avenue NW
Albuquerque, New Mexico 87107
(505) 344-5615

SUBSCRIPTION DATA
Issues and rates: Published quarterly.
  Average paid circulation: 500; 100
  controlled
  Annual rate(s): $3.00

EDITORIAL DESCRIPTION
  Contains verse of every type presented as
  a "program" in a performance; all types
  from traditional to avant garde; poems by
  well-known, established poets as well as
  beginners and students; some music with
  lyrics; articles or prose pieces of interest
  to poets; pen and ink sketches and
  photographs. Strives to illustrate that
  poetry is still one of the performing arts.
Articles per average issue: 80
Audience: General
  Manuscripts accepted in English

MANUSCRIPT INFORMATION
Subject field(s): Poetry, pen and ink
  sketches, photographs
Manuscript requirements: No specific style
  guide.
  Preferred length: None
  Number of copies to be submitted: 2
  Abstract: No
Author information and reprints: Payment:
  None. Complimentary copy of issue in
  which work appears.
  Is simultaneous submission of article to
  other journals permitted: No
  Exclusive manuscript rights between
  acceptance and publication: Yes
  Copyright: Held by publication.
  Reprints: Not available.
Additional information: Since publication
  uses quite a bit of re-printed materials, it
  requests full information about previous
  place of publication so that proper credit
  may be given.
Disposition of manuscript:
  Query letter: No
  Receipt of manuscript acknowledged: Yes
  Decision to publish in: 2-3 weeks
  Accepted manuscript published in: 12
  months
  Rejected manuscript returned: Yes, if
  return postage is supplied by author.
  Rejected manuscript criticized:
  Sometimes

Submit to:
   Alice S. Briley
   Editor
   (See address above)

EPOCH [489]
245 Goldwin Smith Hall
Cornell University
Ithaca, New York 14850
(607) 256-3385

First published in 1947

SUBSCRIPTION DATA
Issues and rates: Published three times per year.
   Average paid circulation: 1,000; 1,300 controlled
   Annual rate(s): $4.00
Publisher or Sponsor: Cornell University
Managing Editor: Clara Graves

EDITORIAL DESCRIPTION
   Presents contemporary writing, both fiction and poetry, of the highest quality
Articles per average issue: 25
   Manuscripts accepted in English

MANUSCRIPT INFORMATION
Subject field(s): Fiction, poetry, critical opinion concerning contemporary writing
Manuscript requirements: No specific style guide.
   Preferred length: Fiction 10,000 words maximum
   Number of copies to be submitted: 2
   Abstract: Not necessary.
Author information and reprints: Payment: Reprints only. A limited number of subscriptions
   Is simultaneous submission of article to other journals permitted: Not permitted.
   Exclusive manuscript rights between acceptance and publication: Yes
   Copyright: Held by publisher, but assigned to author upon request
   Reprints: Not available.
Disposition of manuscript:
   Query letter: Not necessary.
   Receipt of manuscript acknowledged: No
   Decision to publish in: 3 months
   Accepted manuscript published in: 6 months
   Rejected manuscript returned: Yes, if return postage is supplied by author.
   Rejected manuscript criticized: Sometimes
Submit to:
   Baxter Hathaway
   Editor-in-Chief
   (See address above)

ESSENCE [490]
26 Fowler Street
New Haven, Connecticut 06515

First published in 1950

SUBSCRIPTION DATA
Issues and rates: Irregular

Managing Editor: Joseph Payne Brennan

EDITORIAL DESCRIPTION
   Contains only poetry, both traditional and free forms, on almost any subject.
Articles per average issue: 12-15
Audience: Those with interest in poetry
   Manuscripts accepted in English only

MANUSCRIPT INFORMATION
Subject field(s): Poetry
Manuscript requirements: See latest issue for style requirements.
   Preferred length: One page or less
   Number of copies to be submitted: One
   Abstract: No
Author information and reprints: Payment: None.
   Is simultaneous submission of article to other journals permitted: No
   Exclusive manuscript rights between acceptance and publication: Yes
   Copyright: Held by publication.
   Reprints: Not available.
Disposition of manuscript:
   Query letter: No
   Receipt of manuscript acknowledged: No
   Decision to publish in: Two weeks
   Accepted manuscript published in: Six months
   Rejected manuscript returned: Yes, if return postage is supplied by author.
   Rejected manuscript criticized: No
Submit to:
   Joseph Payne Brennan
   Editor and Publisher
   (See address above)

THE FREE LANCE [491]
A Magazine of Poetry and Prose
6005 Grand Avenue
Cleveland, Ohio 44104
(216) 431-7116

First published in 1950

SUBSCRIPTION DATA
Issues and rates: Published semi-annually.
   Average paid circulation: 500; 1000 controlled
   Annual rate(s): $2.00

EDITORIAL DESCRIPTION
   Emphasis is mainly avant-garde, modern literary techniques and ideas. Work should be experimental. Aesthetics and philosophical-scientific articles invited.
Articles per average issue: 2 Articles; 20 poems
Audience: Writers, students, teachers
   Manuscripts accepted in English and occasional translations

MANUSCRIPT INFORMATION
Subject field(s): Poetry; music; aesthetic theories of philosophy, poetry, science
Manuscript requirements: Style sheet sent on request.
   Preferred length: 5000 words
   Number of copies to be submitted: One
   Abstract: No

Author information and reprints: Payment: Reprints only. Copies only
   Is simultaneous submission of article to other journals permitted: No
   Copyright: Held by publication.
   Reprints: Not available.
Additional information: Formerly published by the Free Lance Poets and Prose Workshop.
Disposition of manuscript:
   Query letter: Not necessary, but advisable.
   Receipt of manuscript acknowledged: No
   Decision to publish in: 6 months
   Accepted manuscript published in: 1-3 months
   Rejected manuscript returned: Yes, if self-addressed, stamped envelope is sent with manuscript.
   Rejected manuscript criticized: No
Submit to:
   Russell Atkins;
   Casper Jordan
   Editors
   (See address above)

SPECIAL STIPULATIONS
   Author's name and address should appear on front of incoming mailing envelope and on each page of manuscript and covering letter. Do not place publication's address on return envelope.

GHOST DANCE [492]
The International Quarterly of Experimental Poetry
ATL, EBH
Michigan State University
East Lansing, Michigan 48823
(517) 351-5977

First published in 1968

SUBSCRIPTION DATA
Issues and rates: Published quarterly.
   Average paid circulation: 1,000
   Annual rate(s): $2.50

EDITORIAL DESCRIPTION
   Dedicated to rather difficult, avant-garde poetry, nothing traditional in form or content.
Articles per average issue: 20-30
Audience: "Snobs and elitists"
   Manuscripts accepted in all languages.

MANUSCRIPT INFORMATION
Subject field(s): Poetry
Manuscript requirements: Avant garde
   Preferred length: Short
Author information and reprints: Payment: None.
   Is simultaneous submission of article to other journals permitted: No
   Exclusive manuscript rights between acceptance and publication: Yes
   Copyright: Held by author.
   Reprints: Not available.
Disposition of manuscript:
   Query letter: No
   Receipt of manuscript acknowledged: Yes
   Decision to publish in: 1 day

Accepted manuscript published in: 3-4 months
Rejected manuscript returned: Yes, if self-addressed, stamped envelope is sent with manuscript.
Rejected manuscript criticized: Sometimes
Submit to:
Hugh Bernard Fox
Editor
(See address above)

SPECIAL STIPULATIONS

Suggest poet becomes acquainted with Hart Crane, W.C. Williams, A.L. Gillespie, the French Symbolists and D.A. Levy to familiarize himself with the meaning given the word "experimental."

THE HIRAM POETRY REVIEW [493]

P.O. Box 162
Hiram, Ohio 44234
(216) 569-3211

First published in 1966

SUBSCRIPTION DATA
Issues and rates: Published semi-annually.
Average paid circulation: 500
Annual rate(s): $2.00, Foreign $2.25
Publisher or Sponsor: Hiram College, Department of English

EDITORIAL DESCRIPTION
Contains poetry, reviews, articles. (Reviews and articles by invitation only).
Articles per average issue: 25-30
Audience: Readers of serious poetry
Manuscripts accepted in English

MANUSCRIPT INFORMATION
Subject field(s): Original poems
Manuscript requirements: No specific style guide.
Preferred length: None
Number of copies to be submitted: One
Abstract: No
Author information and reprints: Payment: Reprints only. Two copies plus one year's subscription
Is simultaneous submission of article to other journals permitted: No
Exclusive manuscript rights between acceptance and publication: Yes
Copyright: Held by publication. but assigned to author upon written request
Reprints: Not available.
Disposition of manuscript:
Query letter: No
Receipt of manuscript acknowledged: No
Decision to publish in: One month
Accepted manuscript published in: Up to six months
Rejected manuscript returned: Yes, if return postage is supplied by author.
Rejected manuscript criticized: No
Submit to:
David Fratus
Editor
(See address above)

THE IOWA REVIEW [494]

EPB 321, University of Iowa
Iowa City, Iowa 52242
(319) 353-6048

First published in 1970

SUBSCRIPTION DATA
Issues and rates: Published quarterly.
Average paid circulation: 1,000; 300 controlled
Annual rate(s): $7.50, Foreign $8.50
Publisher or Sponsor: University of Iowa, Graduate College, School of Letters
Managing Editor: Kim Merker

EDITORIAL DESCRIPTION
Contains poetry, fiction, literary interviews, and literary criticism. Interested in current poetry and criticism, plus contemporary fiction of all schools, especially experimental.
Audience: Academic
Manuscripts accepted in English

MANUSCRIPT INFORMATION
Subject field(s): Literature
Manuscript requirements: No specific style guide.
Preferred length: 1-2 pages, poetry; 10-30 pages, fiction
Number of copies to be submitted: One
Abstract: No
Author information and reprints: Payment: By publication to author. $10.00 per page for fiction and criticism; $1.00 per line for poetry
Is simultaneous submission of article to other journals permitted: No
Exclusive manuscript rights between acceptance and publication: No
Copyright: Held by publication.
Reprints: Not available.
Disposition of manuscript:
Query letter: No
Receipt of manuscript acknowledged: No
Decision to publish in: 2-4 weeks
Accepted manuscript published in: 3-6 months
Rejected manuscript returned: Yes
Rejected manuscript criticized: Yes
Submit to:
Thomas Whitaker
Editor
(See address above)

KANSAS QUARTERLY [495]

Denison Hall
Kansas State University
Manhattan, Kansas 66506
(913) 532-6716

SUBSCRIPTION DATA
Issues and rates: Published quarterly.
Average paid circulation: 600; 400 controlled
Annual rate(s): $7.50, Foreign $8.00
Managing Editor: Harold Schneider, Ben Nyberg

EDITORIAL DESCRIPTION
Contains articles on art, history and literary criticism with special interest in fiction and poetry.
Articles per average issue: 20-100
Audience: Humanists, general
Manuscripts accepted in English

MANUSCRIPT INFORMATION
Subject field(s): Short stories, poetry, U.S. history, one-act plays, special topics in art and literary criticism
Manuscript requirements: MLA
Preferred length: 10-25 pages
Number of copies to be submitted: One
Author information and reprints: Payment: Reprints only. Two copies of issue
Is simultaneous submission of article to other journals permitted: No
Exclusive manuscript rights between acceptance and publication: Yes
Copyright: Held by publication.
Reprints: Not available.
Disposition of manuscript:
Receipt of manuscript acknowledged: No
Decision to publish in: 2-3 months
Accepted manuscript published in: 18 months
Rejected manuscript returned: Yes, if self-addressed, stamped envelope is sent with manuscript.
Rejected manuscript criticized: Yes
Submit to:
The Editors
(See address above)

SPECIAL STIPULATIONS
Prospective contributors are asked to examine past copies of the magazine.

KARAMU [496]

English Department
Eastern Illinois University
Charleston, Illinois 61920
(217) 581-5013

First published in 1966

SUBSCRIPTION DATA
Issues and rates: Published annually.
Average paid circulation: 300
Annual rate(s): $3.00 per 4 issues

EDITORIAL DESCRIPTION
Contains art, poetry, short stories, criticism on contemporary writing.
Articles per average issue: 15-20
Audience: Those with interests in literature and poetry
Manuscripts accepted in English

MANUSCRIPT INFORMATION
Subject field(s): Literature
Manuscript requirements: MLA
Preferred length: Article: 10,000 words; short story: 3,000-8,000 words
Number of copies to be submitted: One
Abstract: No

Author information and reprints: Payment:
Reprints only. 2 copies of issue
Is simultaneous submission of article to
other journals permitted: No
Exclusive manuscript rights between
acceptance and publication: Yes
Copyright: Held by publication.
Reprints: Not available.
Disposition of manuscript:
Query letter: No
Receipt of manuscript acknowledged: No
Decision to publish in: 4-5 months
Accepted manuscript published in: 9-12
months
Rejected manuscript returned: Yes, if
return postage is supplied by author.
Rejected manuscript criticized: No
Submit to:
Allen Neff
Editor
(See address above)

THE LITTLE MAGAZINE [497]
Box 207, Cathedral Station
New York, New York 10025

Previously entitled *The Quest*

First published in 1966

SUBSCRIPTION DATA
Issues and rates: Published quarterly.
Average paid circulation: 900
Annual rate(s): $5.00; Foreign $7.50;
Institutions $5.00; Foreign individuals
$7.50
Managing Editor: Ormond A. Seavey

EDITORIAL DESCRIPTION
Publishes poetry and fiction of superior
quality.
Articles per average issue: 20-30
Audience: Those interested in contemporary
poetry and fiction
Manuscripts accepted in English

MANUSCRIPT INFORMATION
Manuscript requirements: See latest issue for
style requirements.
Preferred length: None
Number of copies to be submitted: 1
Abstract: Not necessary.
Author information and reprints: Payment:
Reprints only.
Is simultaneous submission of article to
other journals permitted: Not permitted.
Exclusive manuscript rights between
acceptance and publication: Yes
Copyright: Held by publication.
Reprints: Not available.
Additional information: Do not send more
than 10 poems or 2 stories at once.
Disposition of manuscript:
Query letter: Not necessary.
Receipt of manuscript acknowledged: No
Decision to publish in: 6-10 weeks
Accepted manuscript published in: 4-12
months
Rejected manuscript returned: Yes, if
return postage is supplied by author.
Rejected manuscript criticized: No

Submit to:
Editorial Board
(See address above)

THE MALAHAT REVIEW [498]
University of Victoria
Victoria, British Columbia, Canada
(604) 477-6911 ext. 468

SUBSCRIPTION DATA
Issues and rates: Published quarterly.
Annual rate(s): $5.00
Publisher or Sponsor: University of Victoria
Managing Editor: Robin Skelton

EDITORIAL DESCRIPTION
Contains poetry, short stories,
translations, criticism, book reviews and
an art section.

MANUSCRIPT INFORMATION
Subject field(s): Poetry, poetry in
translation, modern fiction, critical
articles, only work that has never
appeared before in English
Manuscript requirements: See latest issue for
style requirements.
Preferred length: Under 5,000 words
prose
Number of copies to be submitted: One
Author information and reprints: Payment:
By publication to author. $25.00 per
1000 words of prose; $10.00 per poem
per page
Is simultaneous submission of article to
other journals permitted: No
Exclusive manuscript rights between
acceptance and publication: Yes
Copyright: Held by publication.
Reprints: Available, at cost
Disposition of manuscript:
Receipt of manuscript acknowledged: No
Decision to publish in: 6 weeks
Accepted manuscript published in: 1 year
Rejected manuscript returned: Yes
Rejected manuscript criticized: No
Submit to:
Editor
(See address above)

SPECIAL STIPULATIONS
Only work not previously published in
English should be submitted.

MISSISSIPPI REVIEW [499]
Box 37, South Station
Hattiesburg, Mississippi 39401
(601) 266-7180

First published in 1972

SUBSCRIPTION DATA
Issues and rates: Published three times per
year.
Average paid circulation: 300
Annual rate(s): $3.00 for all

Publisher or Sponsor: University of
Southern Mississippi
Managing Editor: Gordon Weaver

EDITORIAL DESCRIPTION
Original literature, quality short fiction
and poetry
Audience: Academic, literary

MANUSCRIPT INFORMATION
Manuscript requirements: See latest issue for
style requirements.
Preferred length: 5,000 words
Number of copies to be submitted: 1
Abstract: Not necessary.
Author information and reprints: Payment:
By publication to author. $5.00 per
poem; $3.00 per page.
Exclusive manuscript rights between
acceptance and publication: Yes
Copyright: Held by publication.
Reprints: Not available.
Disposition of manuscript:
Query letter: Not necessary.
Receipt of manuscript acknowledged: No
Decision to publish in: 2 months
Accepted manuscript published in: 6
months
Rejected manuscript returned: Yes, if
return postage is supplied by author.
Rejected manuscript criticized:
Sometimes
Submit to:
Gordon Weaver
Editor
(See address above)

MONUMENT IN CANTOS
AND ESSAYS [500]
4508 Mexico Gravel Road
Columbia, Missouri 65201
(314) 474-4736

First published in 1968

SUBSCRIPTION DATA
Issues and rates: Published annually.
Annual rate(s): $10.00; Foreign $1.00;
Institutions $2.00; Students $1.00

EDITORIAL DESCRIPTION
Publishes the best of poetry and short
fiction available; terse, vivid imagery,
strong on particularity
Articles per average issue: 40
Audience: Persons interested in poetry and
fiction
Manuscripts accepted in English

MANUSCRIPT INFORMATION
Manuscript requirements: No specific style
guide.
Preferred length: 10 pages maximum
Number of copies to be submitted: 1
Abstract: Not necessary.
Author information and reprints: Payment:
Reprints only. An annual prize of $25.00
for the best work or series
Is simultaneous submission of article to
other journals permitted: Not permitted.
Exclusive manuscript rights between
acceptance and publication: Yes
Copyright: First serial rights only

Poetry and contemporary literature

Disposition of manuscript:
Query letter: Not necessary.
Receipt of manuscript acknowledged: No
Decision to publish in: 3 months
Accepted manuscript published in: 1 year
Rejected manuscript returned: Yes, if return postage is supplied by author.
Rejected manuscript criticized: Yes
Submit to:
Victor C. Myers
Editor
(See address above)

MUSTANG REVIEW [501]
212 South Broadway
Denver, Colorado 80209

First published in 1967

SUBSCRIPTION DATA
Issues and rates: Published semi-annually.
Average paid circulation: 400
Annual rate(s): $2.00
Managing Editor: Karl Edd

EDITORIAL DESCRIPTION
Contains poetry, art sketches, miscellania, odd historical bits.

MANUSCRIPT INFORMATION
Subject field(s): Poetry, occasionally good pen and ink sketches are accepted
Manuscript requirements: See latest issue for style requirements.
Preferred length: 14-20 line poems
Number of copies to be submitted: One
Author information and reprints: Payment: Reprints only. One copy to author and half price on additional.
Is simultaneous submission of article to other journals permitted: No
Exclusive manuscript rights between acceptance and publication: Yes
Copyright: Held by publication. Automatically reverts to author on first publication.
Reprints: Not available.
Disposition of manuscript:
Receipt of manuscript acknowledged: No
Decision to publish in: 2 weeks maximum
Accepted manuscript published in: One year
Rejected manuscript returned: Yes
Rejected manuscript criticized: Occasionally
Submit to:
Editor
(See address above)

SPECIAL STIPULATIONS
Items in the style of Sandburg, Hart Crane, Jarrell, Rimbaud, are welcome.

NASSAU REVIEW [502]
The Faculty Journal of Nassau Community College Devoted to Arts, Letters and Sciences
Nassau Community College
State University of New York
Garden City, New York 11530
(516) 742-0600, ext. 348

First published in 1964

SUBSCRIPTION DATA
Issues and rates: Published annually.
Average paid circulation: 1200 controlled
Publisher or Sponsor: Nassau Community College

EDITORIAL DESCRIPTION
Contains poems; short stories; one act plays; critical analyses on literary, historical, philosophical subjects.
Articles per average issue: 25, including poems
Audience: Teachers, scholars, librarians, general readers
Manuscripts accepted in English, French, Spanish

MANUSCRIPT INFORMATION
Subject field(s): Poems, critical analyses, short stories, one act plays
Manuscript requirements: MLA
Preferred length: 1000-4000 words; 8 pages
Number of copies to be submitted: One
Abstract: Yes; MLA
Author information and reprints: Payment: Reprints only. 10 copies given to author.
Is simultaneous submission of article to other journals permitted: No
Exclusive manuscript rights between acceptance and publication: Yes
Copyright: Held by publication.
Reprints: Not available.
Additional information: Additional copies of complete issue supplied free.
Disposition of manuscript:
Query letter: No
Receipt of manuscript acknowledged: Yes
Decision to publish in: 2-4 months
Accepted manuscript published in: 6 months
Rejected manuscript returned: Yes, if return postage is supplied by author.
Rejected manuscript criticized: No
Submit to:
Paul A. Doyle
Editor-in-Chief
(See address above)

NEW LETTERS [503]
University of Missouri, Kansas City
5346 Charlotte Street
Kansas City, Missouri 64110
(816) 276-1168

Previously entitled *The University Review*, 1934

First published in 1971

SUBSCRIPTION DATA
Issues and rates: Published quarterly.
Annual rate(s): $8.00; Pan-Am $8.00; Institutions $10.00
Publisher or Sponsor: University of Missouri, Kansas City

EDITORIAL DESCRIPTION
Publishes high quality fiction, photography and artwork of permanent value
Articles per average issue: 2-3 stories; 2-3 articles; 10-15 poems
Audience: General
Manuscripts accepted in English

MANUSCRIPT INFORMATION
Subject field(s): Literature, history, sociology, autobiography, biography, letters, memoirs
Manuscript requirements: Chicago
Preferred length: Cogent
Number of copies to be submitted: 1
Abstract: Not necessary.
Author information and reprints: Payment: By publication to author.
Is simultaneous submission of article to other journals permitted: Not permitted.
Exclusive manuscript rights between acceptance and publication: Yes
Copyright: Held by Curators of the University of Missouri, but assigned to the author on request.
Reprints: Not available.
Additional information: Footnotes should be incorporated into the text. Only work of high quality is desired. Original typescripts only, no xeroxes or carbons.
Disposition of manuscript:
Query letter: Necessary for articles only
Receipt of manuscript acknowledged: No
Decision to publish in: 1 month
Accepted manuscript published in: 4-6 months
Rejected manuscript returned: Yes, if return postage is supplied by author.
Rejected manuscript criticized: No
Submit to:
David Ray
Editor
(See address above)

NEW WRITERS [504]
Literary Workshop Publications, Inc.
507 Fifth Avenue
New York, New York 10017
(212) OX 7-5895

First published in 1973

SUBSCRIPTION DATA
Issues and rates: Published quarterly.
Average paid circulation: 250; 250 controlled
Annual rate(s): $8.00; Foreign $12.00; Institutions $10.00; Students $8.00
Managing Editor: Miriam Easton

EDITORIAL DESCRIPTION
Devoted to the short story written by new, unpublished writers, individuals, or members of groups, classes; also contains critiques of previously published works.

Articles per average issue: 9-10
Audience: Those interested in contemporary literature
Manuscripts accepted in English

MANUSCRIPT INFORMATION

Subject field(s): No subject limitations
Manuscript requirements: See latest issue for style requirements. MLA
Preferred length: None
Number of copies to be submitted: 2
Abstract: Not necessary.
Author information and reprints: Payment: By publication to author. $10.00-$50.00 per 10 pages and 1 copy of issue
Is simultaneous submission of article to other journals permitted: Permitted.
Exclusive manuscript rights between acceptance and publication: No
Copyright: Held by publication. first serial rights only
Reprints: Available at no cost. to authors of critiques
Additional information: Give complete biographical details of author. If student, give name of teacher, school and time of attendance.
Disposition of manuscript:
Query letter: Not necessary.
Receipt of manuscript acknowledged: Yes
Decision to publish in: 3 months
Accepted manuscript published in: Varies
Rejected manuscript returned: Yes, if return postage is supplied by author.
Rejected manuscript criticized: Yes
Submit to:
Constance Glickman
Literary Editor
Drawer S
Gravesend Station
Brooklyn, New York 11223
(212) OX 7-5895

THE NORTH AMERICAN REVIEW [505]
The University of Northern Iowa
Cedar Falls, Iowa 50613
(319) 273-2681

First published in 1815

SUBSCRIPTION DATA

Issues and rates: Published quarterly.
Average paid circulation: 3,000
Annual rate(s): $6.00; Pan-Am $6.15; Foreign $7.00
Managing Editor: Robley Wilson, Jr.

EDITORIAL DESCRIPTION

A literary magazine publishing both fiction and poetry with a strong bias toward non-fiction dealing with environmental concerns.
Articles per average issue: 20-30
Audience: Literate, young adult
Manuscripts accepted in English

MANUSCRIPT INFORMATION

Subject field(s): Literature, ecology, and/or general interest, including politics
Manuscript requirements: See latest issue for style requirements.
Preferred length: No limitations
Number of copies to be submitted: 1
Abstract: Not necessary.
Author information and reprints: Payment: By publication to author.
Is simultaneous submission of article to other journals permitted: Not permitted.
Exclusive manuscript rights between acceptance and publication: Yes
Copyright: First serial rights only
Reprints: Not available.
Disposition of manuscript:
Query letter: Necessary for non-fiction
Receipt of manuscript acknowledged: No
Decision to publish in: 6-10 weeks
Accepted manuscript published in: 3-9 months
Rejected manuscript returned: Yes, if return postage is supplied by author.
Rejected manuscript criticized: Sometimes
Submit to:
Robley Wilson, Jr.
Editor
(See address above)

NORTHERN LIGHT [506]
605 Fletcher Argue Building
University of Manitoba
Winnipeg, Manitoba, Canada
(204) 474-8145

Previously entitled *The Far Point*

First published in 1968

SUBSCRIPTION DATA

Issues and rates: Published semi-annually.
Average paid circulation: 1,000; 350 controlled
Annual rate(s): $2.50
Publisher or Sponsor: University of Manitoba
Managing Editor: George Amabile

EDITORIAL DESCRIPTION

Contains contemporary poetry.
Articles per average issue: 40
Audience: General
Manuscripts accepted in English

MANUSCRIPT INFORMATION

Subject field(s): Poetry, reviews of recent books of Canadian poetry
Manuscript requirements: See latest issue for style requirements.
Preferred length: Poetry: no limit; reviews: 2-3 pages
Number of copies to be submitted: One
Abstract: No
Author information and reprints: Payment: Reprints only. 5 contributors' copies
Is simultaneous submission of article to other journals permitted: No
Exclusive manuscript rights between acceptance and publication: Yes
Copyright: Held by publication.
Reprints: Not available.
Additional information: Manuscripts must be accompanied by self-addressed, stamped envelope.
Disposition of manuscript:
Query letter: No
Receipt of manuscript acknowledged: No
Decision to publish in: 4-6 weeks
Accepted manuscript published in: 6-12 months
Rejected manuscript returned: Yes, if self-addressed, stamped envelope is sent with manuscript.
Rejected manuscript criticized: If requested
Submit to:
George Amabile
Editor
(See address above)

NORTHWEST REVIEW [507]
369 P. L. C.
University of Oregon
Eugene, Oregon 97403
(503) 686-3957

First published in 1956

SUBSCRIPTION DATA

Issues and rates: Published three times per year.
Average paid circulation: 600
Annual rate(s): $4.00; Students $3.00
Publisher or Sponsor: CCLM, COSMEP, University of Oregon
Managing Editor: Michael H. Strelow

EDITORIAL DESCRIPTION

A literary magazine with a Northwest emphasis in reviews and occasional special regional issues; also poetry and fiction of high literary quality without regional regard.
Articles per average issue: 5 stories; 25 poems
Audience: Literary and others interested in special issues
Manuscripts accepted in English

MANUSCRIPT INFORMATION

Subject field(s): Fiction and poetry, book reviews from small presses and Northwest authors and subject matter
Manuscript requirements: No specific style guide.
Preferred length: None
Number of copies to be submitted: 1
Abstract: Not necessary.
Author information and reprints: Payment: By publication to author.
Is simultaneous submission of article to other journals permitted: Not permitted.
Exclusive manuscript rights between acceptance and publication: Yes
Copyright: First serial rights only
Reprints: Available at cost.
Disposition of manuscript:
Query letter: Not necessary.
Receipt of manuscript acknowledged: No
Decision to publish in: 1 month-6 weeks
Accepted manuscript published in: 3-5 months
Rejected manuscript returned: Yes, if return postage is supplied by author.
Rejected manuscript criticized: Sometimes
Submit to:
Fiction:
Donald Bodey

Poetry and Reviews
Jim Heynen
Editors
(See address above)

OUTPOSTS [508]
72 Burwood Road
Walton-on-Thames, Surrey, KT12 4AL
England
Walton 40712

First published in 1944

SUBSCRIPTION DATA
Issues and rates: Published quarterly.
  Average paid circulation: 2,000
  Annual rate(s): £1.20; Foreign $6.00
Managing Editor: Howard Sergeant

EDITORIAL DESCRIPTION
  Publishes contemporary poetry, articles on poetry, book reviews, etc.

MANUSCRIPT INFORMATION
Manuscript requirements: Style sheet sent on request.
  Preferred length: 40 lines
  Number of copies to be submitted: One
  Abstract: No
Author information and reprints: Payment: By publication to author.
  Is simultaneous submission of article to other journals permitted: No
  Exclusive manuscript rights between acceptance and publication: Yes
  Copyright: Held by author.
  Reprints: Not available.
Additional information: Authors outside the U.K. must include international postage coupons for return of manuscript.
Disposition of manuscript:
  Query letter: No
  Receipt of manuscript acknowledged: No
  Decision to publish in: 1-2 weeks
  Accepted manuscript published in: Varies
  Rejected manuscript returned: Yes, if return postage is supplied by author.
  Rejected manuscript criticized: No
Submit to:
  Howard Sergeant
  Editor
  (See address above)

PERSPECTIVE [509]
A Magazine of Modern Literature
Washington University
P.O. Box 1122
St. Louis, Missouri 63130
(314) 863-0100 ext. 4217

First published in 1947

SUBSCRIPTION DATA
Issues and rates: Irregular
  Average paid circulation: 1000
  Annual rate(s): $4.00, Foreign $4.50
Managing Editor: Jarvis Thurston; Mona Van Duyn

EDITORIAL DESCRIPTION
  Contains fiction, poetry, criticism of literature and special issues on well-known writers, e.g., Wallace Stevens, William Carlos Williams.
Articles per average issue: 15
Audience: Academic
  Manuscripts accepted in English

MANUSCRIPT INFORMATION
Subject field(s): Poems, short stories, criticism
Manuscript requirements: No specific style guide.
  Preferred length: 3000-4000 words; 14-25 pages
  Number of copies to be submitted: 1
  Abstract: No
Author information and reprints: Payment: None.
  Is simultaneous submission of article to other journals permitted: No
  Exclusive manuscript rights between acceptance and publication: Yes
  Copyright: Held by publication.
  Reprints: Not available.
Additional information: Annual award of $150 for best poem and for best short story.
Disposition of manuscript:
  Query letter: No
  Receipt of manuscript acknowledged: No
  Decision to publish in: 2 months
  Decision to publish in: 6 months
  Accepted manuscript published in: 6-12 months
  Rejected manuscript returned: Yes, if self-addressed, stamped envelope is sent with manuscript.
  Rejected manuscript criticized: No
Submit to:
  Editors
  (See address above)

POET AND CRITIC [510]
Department of English
Iowa State University
Ames, Iowa 50010
(515) 294-6963

First published in 1964

SUBSCRIPTION DATA
Issues and rates: Published three times per year.
  Average paid circulation: 600
  Annual rate(s): $3.00
Publisher or Sponsor: Iowa State University

EDITORIAL DESCRIPTION
  Contains poetry, articles, reviews.

MANUSCRIPT INFORMATION
Manuscript requirements: MLA
  Preferred length: 2000-3000 words
  Number of copies to be submitted: 1
  Abstract: No
Author information and reprints: Payment: By publication to author. $30 prize poem award
  Is simultaneous submission of article to other journals permitted: No
  Exclusive manuscript rights between acceptance and publication: Yes
  Copyright: Held by author.
  Reprints: Not available.
Disposition of manuscript:
  Query letter: No
  Receipt of manuscript acknowledged: No
  Decision to publish in: 1 month
  Accepted manuscript published in: 2-3 months
  Rejected manuscript returned: Yes, if self-addressed, stamped envelope is sent with manuscript.
  Rejected manuscript criticized: No
Submit to:
  Richard Gustafson
  (See address above)

POETRY VENTURE [511]
8245 26th Avenue North
St. Petersburg, Florida 33710
(813) 345-8864

First published in 1968

SUBSCRIPTION DATA
Issues and rates: Published semi-annually.
  Average paid circulation: 1000; 500 controlled
  Annual rate(s): $3.00; Foreign $3.18; Institutions $3.00

EDITORIAL DESCRIPTION
  Poetry of all types: Traditional and modern, original and unpublished. Poems with modern lyricism, intelligible content, displaying an awareness of the craft and presenting some knowledge of technique. Features established and aspiring poets from America and abroad.
Articles per average issue: 40
  Manuscripts accepted in All languages

MANUSCRIPT INFORMATION
Subject field(s): Poetry; small magazine publishing; editorship; poetry reviews; criticism, analysis, commentaries, articles, etc.
Manuscript requirements: No specific style guide.
  Preferred length: Poetry: 112 lines maximum; articles: 2,000 words
  Number of copies to be submitted: 1
  Abstract: Not necessary.
Author information and reprints: Payment: Reprints only, as well as a one year subscription
  Is simultaneous submission of article to other journals permitted: Not permitted.
  Copyright: Held by Editor
Additional information: Foreign language manuscripts should be accompanied by an English translation, as they will be published simultaneously.
Disposition of manuscript:
  Query letter: Not necessary.
  Receipt of manuscript acknowledged: No
  Decision to publish in: 4-24 weeks

Accepted manuscript published in: 6-12 months
Rejected manuscript returned: Yes, if return postage is supplied by author.
Rejected manuscript criticized: Sometimes
Submit to:
Marjorie Schuck
Editor & Publisher
(See address above)

PRISM INTERNATIONAL [512]
A Journal of Contemporary Writing
Creative Writing Department
University of British Columbia
Vancouver, British Columbia V6T 1W5, Canada
(604) 228-2712

SUBSCRIPTION DATA
Issues and rates: Published three times per year.
  Average paid circulation: 1,500
  Annual rate(s): $5.00
Publisher or Sponsor: University of British Columbia; The Canada Council

EDITORIAL DESCRIPTION
Poetry, fiction, drama and occasional non-fiction with a bias toward the avant garde and experimental
Articles per average issue: 25
Audience: Academic, general
  Manuscripts accepted in English

MANUSCRIPT INFORMATION
Manuscript requirements: No specific style guide.
  Preferred length: Maximum of 8,000 words
  Number of copies to be submitted: 1
  Abstract: Not necessary.
Author information and reprints: Payment: By publication to author. $5.00 per page.
  Is simultaneous submission of article to other journals permitted: Not permitted.
  Exclusive manuscript rights between acceptance and publication: Yes
  Copyright: First serial rights only
  Reprints: Not available.
Disposition of manuscript:
  Query letter: Not necessary.
  Receipt of manuscript acknowledged: No
  Decision to publish in: 1-3 months
  Accepted manuscript published in: Next issue
  Rejected manuscript returned: Yes, if return postage is supplied by author.
  Rejected manuscript criticized: No
Submit to:
Michael Bullock
Editor-in-Chief
(See address above)

SALT LICK [513]
P.O. Box 1064
Quincy, Illinois 62301
(217) 222-1331

First published in 1969

SUBSCRIPTION DATA
Issues and rates: Irregular
  Average paid circulation: 500; 1200 controlled
  Annual rate(s): Institutions $5.00, Individuals $3.00
Managing Editor: James Haining

EDITORIAL DESCRIPTION
Contains new literature in its various forms; each issue is accompanied by a portfolio of art works, usually in edition.
Articles per average issue: 20-28
Audience: Academic
  Manuscripts accepted in English, computer

MANUSCRIPT INFORMATION
Subject field(s): Poetry, fiction, graphics, non-fiction, statements, essays, reviews
Manuscript requirements: No specific style guide.
  Preferred length: 10 pages; typewritten, single poem to page
  Number of copies to be submitted: One
  Abstract: Yes.
Author information and reprints: Payment: Reprints only. Contributor's copies.
  Is simultaneous submission of article to other journals permitted: No
  Exclusive manuscript rights between acceptance and publication: Yes
  Copyright: Held by publication.
  Reprints: Available
Disposition of manuscript:
  Receipt of manuscript acknowledged: No
  Decision to publish in: Two weeks
  Accepted manuscript published in: 6-12 months
  Rejected manuscript returned: Yes, if return postage is supplied by author.
  Rejected manuscript criticized: Sometimes
Submit to:
James Haining
Editor
(See address above)

THE SMALL POND MAGAZINE OF LITERATURE [514]
10 Overland Drive
Stratford, Connecticut 06497
(203) 378-9259

First published in 1964

SUBSCRIPTION DATA
Issues and rates: Published three times per year.
  Average paid circulation: 275
  Annual rate(s): $2.50
Managing Editor: Napoleon St. Cyr

EDITORIAL DESCRIPTION
Contains short reviews, poetry, prose, usually fiction, contributors' page and editorial.
Articles per average issue: 35
Audience: General poetry readers
  Manuscripts accepted in English

MANUSCRIPT INFORMATION
Subject field(s): Poetry, fiction, articles, essays, art work, miscellaneous
Manuscript requirements: See latest issue for style requirements.
  Preferred length: Fiction: 2500 words; verse: 100 lines maximum
  Number of copies to be submitted: One; typewritten, including a short curriculum vitae
  Abstract: No
Author information and reprints: Payment: Reprints only. 2 copies of issue
  Is simultaneous submission of article to other journals permitted: No
  Exclusive manuscript rights between acceptance and publication: Yes
  Copyright: Held by editor
  Reprints: Available, inquire on cost
Additional information: Articles and essays must be backed with proof of authority of the author.
Disposition of manuscript:
  Query letter: No
  Receipt of manuscript acknowledged: No
  Decision to publish in: 7-15 days
  Accepted manuscript published in: 2-12 months
  Rejected manuscript returned: Yes, if return postage is supplied by author.
  Rejected manuscript criticized: Sometimes
Submit to:
Napoleon St. Cyr
Editor
(See address above)

SOUTH DAKOTA REVIEW [515]
University of South Dakota
Vermillion, South Dakota 57069
(605) 677-5220

SUBSCRIPTION DATA
Issues and rates: Published quarterly.
  Average paid circulation: 600; 200 controlled
  Annual rate(s): $6.00
Publisher or Sponsor: University of South Dakota

EDITORIAL DESCRIPTION
Contains fiction, poetry, articles, occasional photos, art work, book reviews. Emphasis is on the American West, or on regionalism (Upper Midwest), but not confined to it.
Articles per average issue: 15
Audience: General, academic
  Manuscripts accepted in English

MANUSCRIPT INFORMATION
Subject field(s): Western American literature, Midwestern and contemporary American literature, American literature, contemporary European, world British history, culture.
Manuscript requirements: Style should be reasonably informal. Footnotes to be internal, if possible.
  Preferred length: 3,000 to 5,000 words; 10 to 17 pages
  Number of copies to be submitted: One
  Abstract: No

Accepted manuscript published in: 6-12 months
Rejected manuscript returned: Yes, if return postage is supplied by author.
Rejected manuscript criticized: Sometimes
Submit to:
Marjorie Schuck
Editor & Publisher
(See address above)

PRISM INTERNATIONAL [512]
A Journal of Contemporary Writing
Creative Writing Department
University of British Columbia
Vancouver, British Columbia V6T 1W5, Canada
(604) 228-2712

SUBSCRIPTION DATA
Issues and rates: Published three times per year.
Average paid circulation: 1,500
Annual rate(s): $5.00
Publisher or Sponsor: University of British Columbia; The Canada Council

EDITORIAL DESCRIPTION
Poetry, fiction, drama and occasional non-fiction with a bias toward the avant garde and experimental
Articles per average issue: 25
Audience: Academic, general
Manuscripts accepted in English

MANUSCRIPT INFORMATION
Manuscript requirements: No specific style guide.
Preferred length: Maximum of 8,000 words
Number of copies to be submitted: 1
Abstract: Not necessary.
Author information and reprints: Payment: By publication to author. $5.00 per page.
Is simultaneous submission of article to other journals permitted: Not permitted.
Exclusive manuscript rights between acceptance and publication: Yes
Copyright: First serial rights only
Reprints: Not available.
Disposition of manuscript:
Query letter: Not necessary.
Receipt of manuscript acknowledged: No
Decision to publish in: 1-3 months
Accepted manuscript published in: Next issue
Rejected manuscript returned: Yes, if return postage is supplied by author.
Rejected manuscript criticized: No
Submit to:
Michael Bullock
Editor-in-Chief
(See address above)

SALT LICK [513]
P.O. Box 1064
Quincy, Illinois 62301
(217) 222-1331

First published in 1969

SUBSCRIPTION DATA
Issues and rates: Irregular
Average paid circulation: 500; 1200 controlled
Annual rate(s): Institutions $5.00, Individuals $3.00
Managing Editor: James Haining

EDITORIAL DESCRIPTION
Contains new literature in its various forms; each issue is accompanied by a portfolio of art works, usually in edition.
Articles per average issue: 20-28
Audience: Academic
Manuscripts accepted in English, computer

MANUSCRIPT INFORMATION
Subject field(s): Poetry, fiction, graphics, non-fiction, statements, essays, reviews
Manuscript requirements: No specific style guide.
Preferred length: 10 pages; typewritten, single poem to page
Number of copies to be submitted: One
Abstract: Yes.
Author information and reprints: Payment: Reprints only. Contributor's copies.
Is simultaneous submission of article to other journals permitted: No
Exclusive manuscript rights between acceptance and publication: Yes
Copyright: Held by publication.
Reprints: Available
Disposition of manuscript:
Receipt of manuscript acknowledged: No
Decision to publish in: Two weeks
Accepted manuscript published in: 6-12 months
Rejected manuscript returned: Yes, if return postage is supplied by author.
Rejected manuscript criticized: Sometimes
Submit to:
James Haining
Editor
(See address above)

THE SMALL POND MAGAZINE OF LITERATURE [514]
10 Overland Drive
Stratford, Connecticut 06497
(203) 378-9259

First published in 1964

SUBSCRIPTION DATA
Issues and rates: Published three times per year.
Average paid circulation: 275
Annual rate(s): $2.50
Managing Editor: Napoleon St. Cyr

EDITORIAL DESCRIPTION
Contains short reviews, poetry, prose, usually fiction, contributors' page and editorial.
Articles per average issue: 35
Audience: General poetry readers
Manuscripts accepted in English

MANUSCRIPT INFORMATION
Subject field(s): Poetry, fiction, articles, essays, art work, miscellaneous
Manuscript requirements: See latest issue for style requirements.
Preferred length: Fiction: 2500 words; verse: 100 lines maximum
Number of copies to be submitted: One; typewritten, including a short curriculum vitae
Abstract: No
Author information and reprints: Payment: Reprints only. 2 copies of issue
Is simultaneous submission of article to other journals permitted: No
Exclusive manuscript rights between acceptance and publication: Yes
Copyright: Held by editor
Reprints: Available, inquire on cost
Additional information: Articles and essays must be backed with proof of authority of the author.
Disposition of manuscript:
Query letter: No
Receipt of manuscript acknowledged: No
Decision to publish in: 7-15 days
Accepted manuscript published in: 2-12 months
Rejected manuscript returned: Yes, if return postage is supplied by author.
Rejected manuscript criticized: Sometimes
Submit to:
Napoleon St. Cyr
Editor
(See address above)

SOUTH DAKOTA REVIEW [515]
University of South Dakota
Vermillion, South Dakota 57069
(605) 677-5220

SUBSCRIPTION DATA
Issues and rates: Published quarterly.
Average paid circulation: 600; 200 controlled
Annual rate(s): $6.00
Publisher or Sponsor: University of South Dakota

EDITORIAL DESCRIPTION
Contains fiction, poetry, articles, occasional photos, art work, book reviews. Emphasis is on the American West, or on regionalism (Upper Midwest), but not confined to it.
Articles per average issue: 15
Audience: General, academic
Manuscripts accepted in English

MANUSCRIPT INFORMATION
Subject field(s): Western American literature, Midwestern and contemporary American literature, American literature, contemporary European, world British history, culture.
Manuscript requirements: Style should be reasonably informal. Footnotes to be internal, if possible.
Preferred length: 3,000 to 5,000 words; 10 to 17 pages
Number of copies to be submitted: One
Abstract: No

Poetry and Reviews
Jim Heynen
Editors
(See address above)

OUTPOSTS [508]
72 Burwood Road
Walton-on-Thames, Surrey, KT12 4AL
England
Walton 40712

First published in 1944

SUBSCRIPTION DATA
Issues and rates: Published quarterly.
  Average paid circulation: 2,000
  Annual rate(s): £1.20; Foreign $6.00
Managing Editor: Howard Sergeant

EDITORIAL DESCRIPTION
  Publishes contemporary poetry, articles on poetry, book reviews, etc.

MANUSCRIPT INFORMATION
Manuscript requirements: Style sheet sent on request.
  Preferred length: 40 lines
  Number of copies to be submitted: One
  Abstract: No
Author information and reprints: Payment: By publication to author.
  Is simultaneous submission of article to other journals permitted: No
  Exclusive manuscript rights between acceptance and publication: Yes
  Copyright: Held by author.
  Reprints: Not available.
Additional information: Authors outside the U.K. must include international postage coupons for return of manuscript.
Disposition of manuscript:
  Query letter: No
  Receipt of manuscript acknowledged: No
  Decision to publish in: 1-2 weeks
  Accepted manuscript published in: Varies
  Rejected manuscript returned: Yes, if return postage is supplied by author.
  Rejected manuscript criticized: No
Submit to:
  Howard Sergeant
  Editor
  (See address above)

PERSPECTIVE [509]
A Magazine of Modern Literature
Washington University
P.O. Box 1122
St. Louis, Missouri 63130
(314) 863-0100 ext. 4217

First published in 1947

SUBSCRIPTION DATA
Issues and rates: Irregular
  Average paid circulation: 1000
  Annual rate(s): $4.00, Foreign $4.50

Managing Editor: Jarvis Thurston;
Mona Van Duyn

EDITORIAL DESCRIPTION
  Contains fiction, poetry, criticism of literature and special issues on well-known writers, e.g., Wallace Stevens, William Carlos Williams.
Articles per average issue: 15
Audience: Academic
  Manuscripts accepted in English

MANUSCRIPT INFORMATION
Subject field(s): Poems, short stories, criticism
Manuscript requirements: No specific style guide.
  Preferred length: 3000-4000 words; 14-25 pages
  Number of copies to be submitted: 1
  Abstract: No
Author information and reprints: Payment: None.
  Is simultaneous submission of article to other journals permitted: No
  Exclusive manuscript rights between acceptance and publication: Yes
  Copyright: Held by publication.
  Reprints: Not available.
Additional information: Annual award of $150 for best poem and for best short story.
Disposition of manuscript:
  Query letter: No
  Receipt of manuscript acknowledged: No
  Decision to publish in: 2 months
  Decision to publish in: 6 months
  Accepted manuscript published in: 6-12 months
  Rejected manuscript returned: Yes, if self-addressed, stamped envelope is sent with manuscript.
  Rejected manuscript criticized: No
Submit to:
  Editors
  (See address above)

POET AND CRITIC [510]
Department of English
Iowa State University
Ames, Iowa 50010
(515) 294-6963

First published in 1964

SUBSCRIPTION DATA
Issues and rates: Published three times per year.
  Average paid circulation: 600
  Annual rate(s): $3.00
Publisher or Sponsor: Iowa State University

EDITORIAL DESCRIPTION
  Contains poetry, articles, reviews.

MANUSCRIPT INFORMATION
Manuscript requirements: MLA
  Preferred length: 2000-3000 words
  Number of copies to be submitted: 1
  Abstract: No

Author information and reprints: Payment: By publication to author. $30 prize poem award
  Is simultaneous submission of article to other journals permitted: No
  Exclusive manuscript rights between acceptance and publication: Yes
  Copyright: Held by author.
  Reprints: Not available.
Disposition of manuscript:
  Query letter: No
  Receipt of manuscript acknowledged: No
  Decision to publish in: 1 month
  Accepted manuscript published in: 2-3 months
  Rejected manuscript returned: Yes, if self-addressed, stamped envelope is sent with manuscript.
  Rejected manuscript criticized: No
Submit to:
  Richard Gustafson
  (See address above)

POETRY VENTURE [511]
8245 26th Avenue North
St. Petersburg, Florida 33710
(813) 345-8864

First published in 1968

SUBSCRIPTION DATA
Issues and rates: Published semi-annually.
  Average paid circulation: 1000; 500 controlled
  Annual rate(s): $3.00; Foreign $3.18; Institutions $3.00

EDITORIAL DESCRIPTION
  Poetry of all types: Traditional and modern, original and unpublished. Poems with modern lyricism, intelligible content, displaying an awareness of the craft and presenting some knowledge of technique. Features established and aspiring poets from America and abroad.
Articles per average issue: 40
  Manuscripts accepted in All langugaes

MANUSCRIPT INFORMATION
Subject field(s): Poetry; small magazine publishing; editorship; poetry reviews; criticism, analysis, commentaries, articles, etc.
Manuscript requirements: No specific style guide.
  Preferred length: Poetry: 112 lines maximum; articles: 2,000 words
  Number of copies to be submitted: 1
  Abstract: Not necessary.
Author information and reprints: Payment: Reprints only. as well as a one year subscription
  Is simultaneous submission of article to other journals permitted: Not permitted.
  Copyright: Held by Editor
Additional information: Foreign language manuscripts should be accompanied by an English translation, as they will be published simultaneously.
Disposition of manuscript:
  Query letter: Not necessary.
  Receipt of manuscript acknowledged: No
  Decision to publish in: 4-24 weeks

Poetry and contemporary literature

Author information and reprints: Payment: None. Payment in copies of the magazine
Is simultaneous submission of article to other journals permitted: No
Exclusive manuscript rights between acceptance and publication: Yes
Copyright: Held by publication.
Reprints: Not available.
Disposition of manuscript:
Query letter: No
Receipt of manuscript acknowledged: No
Decision to publish in: 10-30 days
Accepted manuscript published in: 3-12 months
Rejected manuscript returned: Yes, if self-addressed, stamped envelope is sent with manuscript.
Rejected manuscript criticized: Occasionally
Submit to:
John R. Milton
Editor
(See address above)

SOUTHERN LITERARY JOURNAL [516]
Greenlaw Hall
University of North Carolina at Chapel Hill
Chapel Hill, North Carolina 27514
(919) 933-5481

First published in 1968

SUBSCRIPTION DATA
Issues and rates: Published semi-annually.
  Average paid circulation: 550
  Annual rate(s): $5.00; Foreign $5.00; Institutions $5.50

EDITORIAL DESCRIPTION
Essays and reviews on the literature of the South
Articles per average issue: 9
Audience: Primarily academic
  Manuscripts accepted in English

MANUSCRIPT INFORMATION
Subject field(s): Southern literature
Manuscript requirements: MLA
  Preferred length: 4,000 to 5,000 words
  Abstract: Not necessary.
Author information and reprints: Payment: By publication to author. $5.00 per page.
  Is simultaneous submission of article to other journals permitted: Not permitted.
  Exclusive manuscript rights between acceptance and publication: Yes
  Copyright: Held by publication.
  Reprints: Available at cost.
Disposition of manuscript:
  Query letter: Not necessary.
  Receipt of manuscript acknowledged: No
  Decision to publish in: 2 months
  Accepted manuscript published in: 6 months
  Rejected manuscript returned: Yes, if return postage is supplied by author.
  Rejected manuscript criticized: Sometimes
Submit to:
  Louis D. Rubin, Jr.;
  C. Hugh Holman
Co-Editors
(See address above)

SOUTHERN POETRY REVIEW [517]
Department of English
North Carolina State University
Raleigh, North Carolina 27607
(919) 737-3336

Previously entitled *Impetus*

First published in 1958

SUBSCRIPTION DATA
Issues and rates: Published semi-annually.
  Average paid circulation: 500; 100 controlled
  Annual rate(s): $3.00
Managing Editor: Mary C. Williams

EDITORIAL DESCRIPTION
Contains poems, usually short, in the modern idiom from any region, although it tries to provide a showcase for young Southern poets.
Articles per average issue: 60
  Manuscripts accepted in English only

MANUSCRIPT INFORMATION
Subject field(s): Poetry
Manuscript requirements: No specific style guide.
  Preferred length: Short poems
  Number of copies to be submitted: One
  Abstract: No
Author information and reprints: Payment: By publication to author. $3 per poem and one copy of issue
  Is simultaneous submission of article to other journals permitted: No
  Exclusive manuscript rights between acceptance and publication: Yes
  Copyright: Held by publication. Reverts to author after publication.
  Reprints: Not available.
Additional information: Manuscripts not considered during the summer.
Disposition of manuscript:
  Query letter: No
  Receipt of manuscript acknowledged: No
  Decision to publish in: 2-4 weeks
  Accepted manuscript published in: 3-12 months
  Rejected manuscript returned: Yes, if self-addressed, stamped envelope is sent with manuscript.
  Rejected manuscript criticized: No
Submit to:
  Guy Owen
  Editor
  (See address above)

SPECIAL STIPULATIONS
Include name and address on each poem.

THE SOUTHERN REVIEW [518]
Drawer D, University Station
Baton Rouge, Louisiana 70803
(504) 388-5108

First published in 1965

SUBSCRIPTION DATA
Issues and rates: Published quarterly.
  Average paid circulation: 3000
  Annual rate(s): $5.00
Publisher or Sponsor: Louisiana State University

EDITORIAL DESCRIPTION
Contains critical essays, poetry, fiction. Primarily a literary magazine.
Manuscripts accepted in English

MANUSCRIPT INFORMATION
Subject field(s): Critical essays, poetry, fiction, book reviews, history of ideas, history and culture of the South
Manuscript requirements: See latest issue for style requirements.
  Preferred length: Poetry: 1-3 pages; Prose: 3000-6000 words
  Number of copies to be submitted: One
  Abstract: No
Author information and reprints: Payment: By publication to author. Maximum of $.05 per word for prose; $50 for poetry
  Is simultaneous submission of article to other journals permitted: No
  Exclusive manuscript rights between acceptance and publication: Yes
  Copyright: Held by publication.
  Reprints: Available, $3.50 per page
Disposition of manuscript:
  Query letter: No
  Receipt of manuscript acknowledged: No
  Decision to publish in: One month
  Accepted manuscript published in: 3-9 months
  Rejected manuscript returned: Yes, if return postage is supplied by author.
  Rejected manuscript criticized: No
Submit to:
  Donald E. Stanford;
  Lewis P. Simpson
  Editors
  (See address above)

THE SPARROW MAGAZINE [519]
Vagrom Chap Books
103 Waldron Street
West Lafayette, Indiana 47906
(317) 743-1991

First published in 1954

SUBSCRIPTION DATA
Issues and rates: Published semi-annually.
  Average paid circulation: 400; 600 controlled
  Annual rate(s): Individuals $2.50, Institutions $3.00
Managing Editor: Felix Stefanile

EDITORIAL DESCRIPTION
Devoted to poetry: about 75% creative work, and 25% seriously critical work, in-depth essays on poetics or poets.
Articles per average issue: 32
Audience: Poets, teachers, libraries
  Manuscripts accepted in English

MANUSCRIPT INFORMATION
Subject field(s): Original poems, translations, critical essays, book reviews, poetry "news"
Manuscript requirements: Prose should conform to MLA requirements
  Preferred length: None
  Number of copies to be submitted: One original
  Abstract: No
Author information and reprints: Payment: By publication to author. $25.00 prize per issue.
  Is simultaneous submission of article to other journals permitted: No
  Exclusive manuscript rights between acceptance and publication: Yes
  Copyright: Held by publication.
  Reprints: Not available.
Additional information: Poems one to a page, no Xeroxes
Disposition of manuscript:
  Query letter: No
  Receipt of manuscript acknowledged: No
  Decision to publish in: 4-8 weeks
  Accepted manuscript published in: 6 months
  Rejected manuscript returned: Yes, if return postage is supplied by author.
  Rejected manuscript criticized: Sometimes
Submit to:
  Felix and Selma Stefanile
  Editors and Publishers
  (See address above)

SPRING RAIN [520]
P.O. Box 15319
Seattle, Washington 98115

First published in 1971

SUBSCRIPTION DATA
Issues and rates: Published semi-annually.
  Average paid circulation: Not available.
  Annual rate(s): $4.00, Foreign $7.00
Managing Editor: John and Karen Sollid

EDITORIAL DESCRIPTION
  Publishes modern, lyric poetry.
Articles per average issue: 8 Poets
Audience: Academic
  Manuscripts accepted in English

MANUSCRIPT INFORMATION
Subject field(s): Poetry (modern lyric)
Manuscript requirements: See latest issue for style requirements.
  Preferred length: None
  Number of copies to be submitted: One
  Abstract: No
Author information and reprints: Payment: Reprints only. Two copies of issue
  Is simultaneous submission of article to other journals permitted: No
  Exclusive manuscript rights between acceptance and publication: Yes
  Copyright: Held by publication.
  Reprints: Not available.

Additional information: Unpublished poetry only, is acceptable. Send five different poems and enclose return postage.
Disposition of manuscript:
  Query letter: No
  Receipt of manuscript acknowledged: Yes
  Decision to publish in: 1-6 weeks
  Accepted manuscript published in: 1-3 months
  Rejected manuscript returned: Yes, if self-addressed, stamped envelope is sent with manuscript.
  Rejected manuscript criticized: Yes
Submit to:
  John and Karen Sollid
  Editors
  (See address above)

STAR WEST OF AMERICA [521]
P.O. Box 731
Sausalito, California 94965
692-0421

Previously entitled *S-B Gazette*

First published in 1963

SUBSCRIPTION DATA
Issues and rates: Published semi-annually.
  Average paid circulation: 1,000 controlled
  Annual rate(s): $6.60
Managing Editor: Leon Spiro

EDITORIAL DESCRIPTION
  Publishes poetry in nine languages, prose, artwork (black and white), satire, etc. Point of view is free, liberal and humanistic.
Articles per average issue: 9-12
Audience: Academic; editors, poets

MANUSCRIPT INFORMATION
Subject field(s): Poetry, multi-lingual; satire, sex, humor
Manuscript requirements: No specific style guide.
  Preferred length: 3/6 stanza or free verse
  Number of copies to be submitted: One
  Rejected manuscript returned: No
Author information and reprints: Payment: Reprints only. Five copies of issue
  Is simultaneous submission of article to other journals permitted: No
  Exclusive manuscript rights between acceptance and publication: Yes
  Copyright: Held by publication.
  Reprints: Available free for less than 20 reprints
Additional information: Publication prefers camera ready material; IBM-typed, single-spaced, signed.
Disposition of manuscript:
  Receipt of manuscript acknowledged: No
  Decision to publish in: 30 days
  Accepted manuscript published in: 4 months
  Rejected manuscript returned: Yes, if self-addressed, stamped envelope is sent with manuscript.
  Rejected manuscript criticized: Yes
Submit to:
  Leon Spiro

Director
(See address above)

SPECIAL STIPULATIONS
  Publication consents to immediate reprints in foreign cultural papers, encouraged by overseas staff.

VOICES INTERNATIONAL [522]
An International Literary Quarterly
6804 Cloverdale Drive
Little Rock, Arkansas 72209
(501) 565-6305

First published in 1966

SUBSCRIPTION DATA
Issues and rates: Published quarterly.
  Average paid circulation: 300
  Annual rate(s): $6.00
Publisher or Sponsor: South and West, Inc.

EDITORIAL DESCRIPTION
  Contains literary quality poetry and occasional essays on poetry.
Articles per average issue: 50-60
Audience: Poetry enthusiasts
  Manuscripts accepted in All languages, if English translation is supplied

MANUSCRIPT INFORMATION
Subject field(s): Poetry, all subjects
Manuscript requirements: No specific style guide.
  Preferred length: 30 lines or less
  Number of copies to be submitted: One
Author information and reprints: Payment: Reprints only. One contributor's copy
  Is simultaneous submission of article to other journals permitted: No
  Exclusive manuscript rights between acceptance and publication: Yes
  Copyright: Held by publication.
  Reprints: Available
Additional information: One poem per page, with name and address in upper left-hand corner
Disposition of manuscript:
  Query letter: No
  Receipt of manuscript acknowledged: Yes
  Decision to publish in: 3-4 weeks
  Accepted manuscript published in: 6-12 months
  Rejected manuscript returned: Yes, if self-addressed, stamped envelope is sent with manuscript.
  Rejected manuscript criticized: Yes
Submit to:
  Clovita Rice
  Editor
  (See address above)

SPECIAL STIPULATIONS
  Publication encourages the beginning poet as well as the established author.

WEBSTER REVIEW [523]
Webster College
Webster Groves, Missouri 63119
(314) 432-2657

First published in 1974

SUBSCRIPTION DATA
Issues and rates: Published quarterly.
  Average paid circulation: 500
  Annual rate(s): $5.00; Foreign $5.00
Publisher or Sponsor: Webster College

EDITORIAL DESCRIPTION
  A literary quarterly with an emphasis on international literature in English; contemporary fiction, poetry, interviews, essays.
Articles per average issue: 20
Audience: Academic, general
  Manuscripts accepted in English

MANUSCRIPT INFORMATION
Subject field(s): Serious, imaginative contemporary writing on any topic.
Manuscript requirements: No specific style guide.
  Preferred length: None
  Number of copies to be submitted: 1
  Abstract: Not necessary.
Author information and reprints: Payment: Reprints only. 2 copies
  Is simultaneous submission of article to other journals permitted: Permitted, but not encouraged.
  Exclusive manuscript rights between acceptance and publication: Yes
  Copyright: Held by author.
Disposition of manuscript:
  Query letter: Not necessary.
  Receipt of manuscript acknowledged: No
  Decision to publish in: 1 month
  Accepted manuscript published in: 3 months
  Rejected manuscript returned: Yes, if return postage is supplied by author.
  Rejected manuscript criticized: Sometimes
Submit to:
  Nancy Shapiro
  Editor
  (See address above)

WEID [524]
The Sensibility Revue
P.O. Drawer 1409
Homestead, Florida 33030

SUBSCRIPTION DATA
Issues and rates: Published three times per year.
  Average paid circulation: 500
  Annual rate(s): $5.00
Managing Editor: D. V. Smith

EDITORIAL DESCRIPTION
  Contains articles on language and literature; essays, poetry, short stories.

MANUSCRIPT INFORMATION
Subject field(s): Poetry, any subject relevant to language and literature
Manuscript requirements: See latest issue for style requirements.
  Preferred length: None
  Number of copies to be submitted: One

Author information and reprints: Payment: None. Copy of issue
  Is simultaneous submission of article to other journals permitted: No
  Exclusive manuscript rights between acceptance and publication: Yes
  Copyright: Held by publication.
  Reprints: Not available.
Additional information: Manuscript must be clean and legible.
Disposition of manuscript:
  Receipt of manuscript acknowledged: No
  Decision to publish in: 3 months
  Accepted manuscript published in: One year
  Rejected manuscript returned: Yes, if self-addressed, stamped envelope is sent with manuscript.
  Rejected manuscript criticized: No
Submit to:
  Charles Guenther
  2935 Russell Boulevard
  St. Louis, Missouri 63104

  Submit book reviews to:
  E. N. Fortner
  Route 1, Box 259
  Estacada, Oregon 97023

YALE LIT [525]
243A Yale Station
New Haven, Connecticut 06511
(203) 624-1600

Previously entitled *The Yale Literary Magazine*

First published in 1836

SUBSCRIPTION DATA
Issues and rates: 5 times per year
  Average paid circulation: 1,000
  Annual rate(s): $7.50, Foreign $9.50
Managing Editor: Jeff Rider

EDITORIAL DESCRIPTION
  Contains short stories, poetry, reviews of the arts.
Articles per average issue: 2-3 articles; 10-20 poems; 3-6 reviews
Audience: Academic
  Manuscripts accepted in English

MANUSCRIPT INFORMATION
Subject field(s): Short stories, poetry
Manuscript requirements: No specific style guide.
  Preferred length: None
  Number of copies to be submitted: One
  Abstract: No
Author information and reprints: Payment: None.
  Is simultaneous submission of article to other journals permitted: No
  Exclusive manuscript rights between acceptance and publication: Yes
  Copyright: Held by publication.
  Reprints: Not available.
Disposition of manuscript:
  Query letter: No
  Receipt of manuscript acknowledged: Yes
  Decision to publish in: 1-3 months

  Accepted manuscript published in: 2-3 months
  Rejected manuscript returned: Yes, if self-addressed, stamped envelope is sent with manuscript.
  Rejected manuscript criticized: No
Submit to:
  Jeff Rider
  Managing Editor
  (See address above)

Religion and theology

ADRIS NEWSLETTER [526]
Department of Sociology and Anthropology
Marquette University
Milwaukee, Wisconsin 53233
(414) 224-6838

First published in 1971-72

SUBSCRIPTION DATA
Issues and rates: Published quarterly.
  Average paid circulation: 117; 6 controlled
  Annual rate(s): $5.00
Publisher or Sponsor: Association for the Development of Religious Information Systems (ADRIS)
Managing Editor: David O. Moberg

EDITORIAL DESCRIPTION
  Contains news reports, information about new and existing information systems pertinent to religion; reports of appropriate meetings; book reviews; letters to the editor, etc. All content is relevant in some manner to information systems dealing with religion.
Articles per average issue: Varies
Audience: Academic, clerical
  Manuscripts accepted in English

MANUSCRIPT INFORMATION
Subject field(s): Religion, computer software, social science archives with religion contents, information management
Manuscript requirements: See latest issue for style requirements.
  Preferred length: 200 words
  Number of copies to be submitted: Two
  Abstract: No
Author information and reprints: Payment: None.
  Is simultaneous submission of article to other journals permitted: Yes
  Exclusive manuscript rights between acceptance and publication: No
  Copyright: Held by author.
  Reprints: Not available.
Additional information: Source of additional information on the topic is essential.
  Everything typewritten, double-spaced
Disposition of manuscript:
  Receipt of manuscript acknowledged: Yes
  Decision to publish in: 2 months
  Accepted manuscript published in: 3 months
  Rejected manuscript returned: No

Rejected manuscript criticized: No
Submit to:
David O. Moberg
Coordinator, ADRIS
(See address above)

AMERICA [527]
National Catholic Weekly Review
106 West 56th Street
New York, New York 10019
(212) 581-4640

First published in 1909

SUBSCRIPTION DATA
Issues and rates: Published weekly.
  Average paid circulation: 46,000
  Annual rate(s): $14.00
Managing Editor: Thomas H. Stahel

EDITORIAL DESCRIPTION
  A weekly journal of opinion devoted to analysis of, and comment on, current developments and trends in the fields of politics, economics, culture, religion. Contents: editorials, letters, articles, regular columns, criticism of books, film and theatre. Edited and published by a group of Jesuits viewing the world scene from a Christian point of view.
Articles per average issue: 4-5
Audience: Educated readership
  Manuscripts accepted in English

MANUSCRIPT INFORMATION
Subject field(s): Current events, trends in thought, theology, criticism
Manuscript requirements: See latest issue for style requirements.
  Preferred length: 1,500 words
  Number of copies to be submitted: One
  Abstract: Not necessary.
Author information and reprints: Payment: By publication to author. $60 to $75 per article.
  Is simultaneous submission of article to other journals permitted: No
  Exclusive manuscript rights between acceptance and publication: Yes
  Copyright: Held by publication.
  Reprints: Available in limited number
Disposition of manuscript:
  Query letter: Not necessary.
  Receipt of manuscript acknowledged: Yes
  Decision to publish in: Three weeks
  Accepted manuscript published in: Three to six weeks
  Rejected manuscript returned: Yes, if return postage is supplied by author.
  Rejected manuscript criticized: No
Submit to:
Donald R. Campion
Editor-in-Chief
(See address above)

SPECIAL STIPULATIONS
  Publication is not interested in fiction or purely informational (travel or other) pieces.

AMERICAN ACADEMY OF RELIGION. JOURNAL [528]
Council on the Study of Religion
Wilfrid Laurier University
Waterloo, Ontario N2L 3C5, Canada
(519) 884-7300

Previously entitled *Journal of Bible and Religion*

First published in 1934

SUBSCRIPTION DATA
Issues and rates: Published quarterly.
  Average paid circulation: 4,950; 5,500 controlled
  Annual rate(s): $20.00; Foreign $20.00; Institutions $20.00; Students $7.50
Publisher or Sponsor: American Academy of Religion
Managing Editor: Ray L. Hart

EDITORIAL DESCRIPTION
  Publishes articles in all areas of the academic study of religion
Articles per average issue: 12
Audience: Researchers and instructors in the field of religion
  Manuscripts accepted in English

MANUSCRIPT INFORMATION
Subject field(s): All areas: literature and religion; Asian religions; Biblical literature; ethics; history; religion and the social sciences; philosophy, etc.
Manuscript requirements: Style sheet sent on request.
  Preferred length: 5,000 words
  Number of copies to be submitted: 2
  Abstract: Not necessary.
Author information and reprints: Payment: Reprints only. 50
  Is simultaneous submission of article to other journals permitted: Not permitted.
  Exclusive manuscript rights between acceptance and publication: Yes
  Copyright: Held by publication.
  Reprints: Available at cost.
Disposition of manuscript:
  Query letter: Not necessary.
  Receipt of manuscript acknowledged: Yes
  Decision to publish in: 3 months
  Accepted manuscript published in: 3-6 months
  Rejected manuscript returned: Yes, if return postage is supplied by author.
  Rejected manuscript criticized: Sometimes
Submit to:
Ray L. Hart
Editor
Department of Religious Studies
University of Montana
Missoula, Montana 59801
(406) 243-5563

THE AMERICAN BENEDICTINE REVIEW [529]
2nd and Division Streets
Atchison, Kansas 66002
(913) 367-5340 ext. 298

First published in 1950

SUBSCRIPTION DATA
Issues and rates: Published quarterly.
  Average paid circulation: 1,250
  Annual rate(s): $10.00, Foreign $10.50
Publisher or Sponsor: American Benedictine Review
Managing Editor: Timothy P. Fry

EDITORIAL DESCRIPTION
  Publishes articles on the whole range of knowledge, with particular emphasis on the history, theory and practice of Benedictinism, theology and philosophy.
Articles per average issue: 6-8
Audience: College educated
  Manuscripts accepted in English

MANUSCRIPT INFORMATION
Manuscript requirements: MLA
  Preferred length: 20-30 pages
  Number of copies to be submitted: Two
Author information and reprints: Payment: None. Two copies of publication with accepted article.
  Is simultaneous submission of article to other journals permitted: No
  Exclusive manuscript rights between acceptance and publication: Yes
  Copyright: Held by publication.
  Reprints: Available; Six tearsheets provided author; additional from printer at cost.
Disposition of manuscript:
  Query letter: No
  Receipt of manuscript acknowledged: Yes
  Decision to publish in: 5-6 months
  Accepted manuscript published in: One year or more
  Rejected manuscript returned: Yes
  Rejected manuscript criticized: Yes
Submit to:
Timothy P. Fry
Editor
(See address above)

AMERICAN JEWISH HISTORICAL QUARTERLY [530]
Publication of the American Jewish Historical Society
2 Thornton Road
Waltham, Massachusetts 02154
(617) 891-8110

Previously entitled *Publication of The American Jewish Historical Society*

First published in 1893

SUBSCRIPTION DATA
Issues and rates: Published quarterly.
  Average paid circulation: 3300
  Annual rate(s): $15.00
Publisher or Sponsor: American Jewish Historical Society
Managing Editor: Bernard Wax

EDITORIAL DESCRIPTION
  Publishes articles based on original research that provide insight on the

Religion and theology

American Jewish experience in the broadest context.
Articles per average issue: 4
Audience: Academic, general
Manuscripts accepted in English

MANUSCRIPT INFORMATION
Subject field(s): American Jewish history
Manuscript requirements: MLA
Preferred length: Up to 30 pages typed, double-spaced
Number of copies to be submitted: Two
Abstract: No
Author information and reprints: Payment: None.
Is simultaneous submission of article to other journals permitted: No
Exclusive manuscript rights between acceptance and publication: Yes
Copyright: Held by publication.
Reprints: Available free
Disposition of manuscript:
Query letter: No
Receipt of manuscript acknowledged: Yes
Decision to publish in: 2-3 months
Accepted manuscript published in: 12 months
Rejected manuscript returned: Yes
Rejected manuscript criticized: Yes
Submit to:
Nathan M. Kaganoff
Librarian-Editor
(See address above)

SPECIAL STIPULATIONS
Publisher has royalty sharing arrangement under which author receives 50% of reprint royalties

AMERICAN SCIENTIFIC AFFILIATION JOURNAL [531]
5 Douglas Avenue
Elgin, Illinois 60120
(312) 697-5466

First published in 1949

SUBSCRIPTION DATA
Issues and rates: Published quarterly.
Average paid circulation: 2,700
Annual rate(s): $8.00
Publisher or Sponsor: American Scientific Affiliation
Managing Editor: William D. Sisterson

EDITORIAL DESCRIPTION
The purpose of the organization is to explore any and every area relating Christian faith and science. The journal publishes results of such study, with an evangelical Christian perspective. Science is broadly defined.
Articles per average issue: 8
Audience: General
Manuscripts accepted in English

MANUSCRIPT INFORMATION
Subject field(s): Any article on the relationship of science to Christian faith
Manuscript requirements: Style sheet sent on request.
Preferred length: 3,000-6,000 words
Number of copies to be submitted: Two
Abstract: Yes
Author information and reprints: Payment: None.
Is simultaneous submission of article to other journals permitted: Yes
Copyright: Held by publication.
Reprints: Not available.
Disposition of manuscript:
Query letter: No, but advisable
Receipt of manuscript acknowledged: Yes
Rejected manuscript returned: Yes, if self-addressed, stamped envelope is sent with manuscript.
Rejected manuscript criticized: Usually
Submit to:
Richard H. Bube
Editor
753 Mayfield Avenue
Stanford, California 94305
(415) 321-5796

THE AMERICAN SEPHARDI [532]
Sephardic Studies Program
Yeshiva University
500 West 185th Street
New York, New York 10033
(212) 208-8400

First published in 1966
Average paid circulation: 5,000

SUBSCRIPTION DATA
Issues and rates: Published semi-annually.
Annual rate(s): $5.00
Publisher or Sponsor: Yeshiva University, Sephardic Studies Program
Managing Editor: Dr. Herman P. Salomon

EDITORIAL DESCRIPTION
Contains articles on Sephardic heritage and Sephardic activities.
Audience: General
Manuscripts accepted in English (Ladino)

MANUSCRIPT INFORMATION
Subject field(s): Sephardic religious, social and cultural activities
Manuscript requirements: See latest issue for style requirements.
Number of copies to be submitted: Three
Abstract: No
Author information and reprints: Payment: None.
Is simultaneous submission of article to other journals permitted: Must be discussed with publication.
Exclusive manuscript rights between acceptance and publication: Yes
Copyright: Held by publication.
Reprints: Not available.
Disposition of manuscript:
Query letter: Yes
Receipt of manuscript acknowledged: Yes
Decision to publish in: 4 weeks
Accepted manuscript published in: One year or less
Rejected manuscript returned: Yes, if return postage is supplied by author.
Rejected manuscript criticized: No
Submit to:
Herbert Dobrinsky
(See address above)

ANGLICAN THEOLOGICAL REVIEW [533]
600 Haven Street
Evanston, Illinois 60201
(312) 328-9300

First published in 1918

SUBSCRIPTION DATA
Issues and rates: Published quarterly.
Average paid circulation: 1,825; 50 controlled
Annual rate(s): $8.00

EDITORIAL DESCRIPTION
Contains articles in contemporary theology, ethics, biblical studies, and various interdisciplinary studies.
Articles per average issue: 6 articles plus reviews
Audience: Academic, clergy, informed laity
Manuscripts accepted in English only

MANUSCRIPT INFORMATION
Subject field(s): Theology, ethics, theology of culture, biblical studies, philosophy of religion, history of religions, historical theology
Manuscript requirements: Chicago
Preferred length: 4000-6000 words; 15-25 pages
Number of copies to be submitted: Two
Abstract: Yes; of 100-200 words
Author information and reprints: Payment: None.
Is simultaneous submission of article to other journals permitted: No
Exclusive manuscript rights between acceptance and publication: Yes
Copyright: Held by publication.
Reprints: Available, first 25 free.
Additional information: Heavily footnoted essays not encouraged. Limited publication of material for specialists.
Disposition of manuscript:
Query letter: No
Receipt of manuscript acknowledged: Yes
Decision to publish in: 6-8 weeks
Accepted manuscript published in: 6-9 months
Rejected manuscript returned: Yes
Rejected manuscript criticized: Yes
Submit to:
W. Taylor Stevenson
Editor-in-Chief
Theology Department
Marquette University
Milwaukee, Wisconsin 53233
(414) 964-5298

APPLIED CHRISTIANITY [534]
Relating Christian Principles to Crucial National Issues
7960 Crescent Avenue
Buena Park, California 90620
(714) 821-5770

First published in 1974

SUBSCRIPTION DATA

Issues and rates: Published monthly.
  Average paid circulation: 30,000
  Annual rate(s): $7.00
Publisher or Sponsor: Christian Freedom Foundation, Inc.

EDITORIAL DESCRIPTION

Seeks to relate the Christian ethic to economics, government, social problems and controversial issues.
Articles per average issue: 5-7
Audience: Evangelical Christians
  Manuscripts accepted in English only

MANUSCRIPT INFORMATION

Subject field(s): Economics, government, poverty, abortion, euthanasia, capital punishment, media morals, crime, race relations, social issues, public leadership roles for Christian citizens
Manuscript requirements: Style sheet sent on request.
  Preferred length: 1,500-2000 words; 6-8 pages
  Number of copies to be submitted: Two
  Abstract: No
Author information and reprints: Payment: By publication to author. $75.00-$125.00 per article.
  Is simultaneous submission of article to other journals permitted: No
  Exclusive manuscript rights between acceptance and publication: Yes
  Copyright: Held by publication.
  Reprints: Not available.
Disposition of manuscript:
  Query letter: Preferred
  Receipt of manuscript acknowledged: Yes
  Decision to publish in: 3 weeks
  Accepted manuscript published in: 3-10 months
  Rejected manuscript returned: Yes, if self-addressed, stamped envelope is sent with manuscript.
  Rejected manuscript criticized: If requested
Submit to:
  David J. June
  Assistant Editor
  (See address above)

BIBLICAL THEOLOGY BULLETIN [535]

Piazza del Gesù 45
00186 Rome, Italy
(06) 6795131

First published in 1971

SUBSCRIPTION DATA

Issues and rates: Published three times per year.
  Average paid circulation: Not available.
  Annual rate(s): $5.00

Publisher or Sponsor: International Team of Scripture Scholars
Managing Editor: Leopold Sabourin

EDITORIAL DESCRIPTION

The articles, notes and views, and book reviews intend to bring out the main trends of present-day debates and expound the theological meaning of the inspired texts in a language accessible also to non-specialists.
Articles per average issue: 5
Audience: Academic, clerical, students
  Manuscripts accepted in English only

MANUSCRIPT INFORMATION

Subject field(s): Biblical theology, Biblical exegesis, related fields
Manuscript requirements: No specific style guide.
  Preferred length: 15 to 25 pages
  Number of copies to be submitted: One
  Abstract: No
Author information and reprints: Payment: None.
  Is simultaneous submission of article to other journals permitted: No
  Exclusive manuscript rights between acceptance and publication: Yes
  Copyright: Held by publication.
  Reprints: Available, 25 free
Additional information: Notify writing project in advance, to avoid duplication. Manuscripts must be typewritten, double-spaced, with footnotes on separate pages.
Disposition of manuscript:
  Query letter: Yes
  Receipt of manuscript acknowledged: Yes
  Decision to publish in: One week
  Accepted manuscript published in: 3-5 months
  Rejected manuscript returned: Yes
  Rejected manuscript criticized: Yes
Submit to:
  Leopold Sabourin
  (See address above)

BIJDRAGEN [536]

Tydschrift vor Filosofie en Theologie
Redaktie Bijdragen
Keizersgracht 105
Amsterdam, The Netherlands
020-242752

First published in 1938

SUBSCRIPTION DATA

Issues and rates: Published quarterly.
  Average paid circulation: 370; 630 controlled
  Annual rate(s): 60 Dutch guilders
Managing Editor: H. van Luijk; P. Fransen

EDITORIAL DESCRIPTION

Contains articles on theology, philosophy and social sciences.
Articles per average issue: 5
Audience: Philosophers and theologians
  Manuscripts accepted in Dutch, English, German, French

MANUSCRIPT INFORMATION

Subject field(s): Philosophy, theology, history of dogma, church history, canon law, biblical studies.
Manuscript requirements: Style sheet sent on request.
  Preferred length: 20 pages
  Number of copies to be submitted: One
  Abstract: Yes. Should be in English, French or German
Author information and reprints: Payment: None.
  Is simultaneous submission of article to other journals permitted: Should get permission of the Editors
  Exclusive manuscript rights between acceptance and publication: No
  Copyright: Held by publication.
  Reprints: Available
Disposition of manuscript:
  Query letter: Not necessary.
  Receipt of manuscript acknowledged: Yes
  Decision to publish in: 3 months
  Accepted manuscript published in: 3 months
  Rejected manuscript returned: Yes
  Rejected manuscript criticized: Yes
Submit to:
  Dr. H. van Luijk
  Editor
  (See address above)

BRIGHAM YOUNG UNIVERSITY STUDIES [537]

A Voice for the Community of LDS Scholars
Brigham Young University A-283 JKBA
Provo, Utah 84602
(801) 374-1211 ext. 3448

First published in 1959

SUBSCRIPTION DATA

Issues and rates: Published quarterly.
  Average paid circulation: 4,000; 400 controlled
  Annual rate(s): $7.00
Publisher or Sponsor: Brigham Young University

EDITORIAL DESCRIPTION

Interest in all fields with special interest and priority to articles dealing with Mormon thought, history, theology, literature, and related fields
Articles per average issue: 8
Audience: Scholars
  Manuscripts accepted in English

MANUSCRIPT INFORMATION

Subject field(s): Mormon history, thought, theology, literature; general history, thought, theology, literature, poetry, short story, and drama
Manuscript requirements: Chicago
  Preferred length: 2,500 to 4,000 words; 10-15 pages
  Number of copies to be submitted: One
  Abstract: No

Author information and reprints: Payment: Reprints only. Twenty reprints and three copies of issue containing article
Is simultaneous submission of article to other journals permitted: Yes but prefer not
Exclusive manuscript rights between acceptance and publication: Yes
Copyright: Held by publication.
Reprints: Available at printing costs
Additional information: Double-spaced typescript with footnotes on a separate page at the end.
Disposition of manuscript:
Query letter: No
Receipt of manuscript acknowledged: Yes
Decision to publish in: 3-4 months
Accepted manuscript published in: 6-12 months
Rejected manuscript returned: Yes
Rejected manuscript criticized: Sometimes
Submit to:
Charles D. Tate, Jr.
Editor
(See address above)

THE CATHOLIC BIBLICAL QUARTERLY [538]

The Catholic University of America
Washington, D.C. 20064
(202) 635-5519

First published in 1939

SUBSCRIPTION DATA
Issues and rates: Published quarterly.
Average paid circulation: 3,300; 200 controlled
Annual rate(s): $10.00
Publisher or Sponsor: The Catholic Biblical Association of America

EDITORIAL DESCRIPTION
Contains scholarly articles on Scripture and related fields (e.g., Biblical archaeology, ancient Near Eastern history, literary criticism, textual criticism, interpretation, Qumran, Ugaritic and other cognate language studies, Biblical theology).
Audience: Scripture specialists, students
Manuscripts accepted in English

MANUSCRIPT INFORMATION
Subject field(s): Scripture and related fields
Manuscript requirements: See CBQ 33 (1971), pp. 85-88
Preferred length: Up to 10 pages for short articles; up to 30 pages for major articles
Number of copies to be submitted: Two
Abstract: No
Author information and reprints: Payment: Fifty offprint copies of the article
Is simultaneous submission of article to other journals permitted: No
Exclusive manuscript rights between acceptance and publication: Yes
Copyright: Held by Catholic Biblical Association of America
Reprints: Available

Disposition of manuscript:
Query letter: Not necessary, but advisable.
Receipt of manuscript acknowledged: Yes
Decision to publish in: Three months
Accepted manuscript published in: Nine months
Rejected manuscript returned: Yes
Rejected manuscript criticized: Yes
Submit to:
George T. Montague
General Editor
St. Basil's College
95 St. Joseph Street
Toronto, Ontario M5S 2R9, Canada

SPECIAL STIPULATIONS
Due to an abundant supply of manuscripts, only those of very high quality can be considered.

CATHOLIC HISTORICAL REVIEW [539]

The Catholic University of America
Washington, D.C. 20064
(202) 635-5079

First published in 1915

SUBSCRIPTION DATA
Issues and rates: Published quarterly.
Average paid circulation: 2100; 2250 controlled
Annual rate(s): $12.00
Publisher or Sponsor: The Catholic University of America

EDITORIAL DESCRIPTION
Contains scholarly articles on the history of the Catholic Church broadly considered; critical reviews of books; bibliography of recent periodical literature.
Articles per average issue: 3
Audience: Scholars, historians
Manuscripts accepted in English

MANUSCRIPT INFORMATION
Subject field(s): History of the Catholic Church broadly considered
Manuscript requirements: See latest issue for style requirements.
Preferred length: 10,000 words maximum; 30 typed pages double spaced with footnotes on last page(s).
Number of copies to be submitted: One
Abstract: No
Author information and reprints: Payment: None.
Is simultaneous submission of article to other journals permitted: No
Exclusive manuscript rights between acceptance and publication: Yes
Copyright: Held by publication.
Reprints: Available, 25 free
Disposition of manuscript:
Query letter: No
Receipt of manuscript acknowledged: Yes
Decision to publish in: 4-8 weeks
Accepted manuscript published in: 2-3 years
Rejected manuscript returned: Yes, if return postage is supplied by author.
Rejected manuscript criticized: Yes
Submit to:
Robert Trisco
Editor
(See address above)

CHICAGO STUDIES [540]

An Archdiocesan Review
Box 665
Mundelein, Illinois 60060
(312) 566-6401 ext. 37

First published in 1962

SUBSCRIPTION DATA
Issues and rates: 3 times per year, May, September and December
Average paid circulation: 5,000
Annual rate(s): $5.00, Foreign $5.50

EDITORIAL DESCRIPTION
An articulate presentation of the best in modern scholarship that can contribute to the professional knowledge of the priest.
Articles per average issue: 9
Audience: Religious educators
Manuscripts accepted in English

MANUSCRIPT INFORMATION
Subject field(s): Theology, scripture, liturgy, catechetics, philosophy, canon law, sociology and related sciences
Manuscript requirements: See latest issue for style requirements.
Preferred length: 3,000 words
Number of copies to be submitted: One
Abstract: No
Author information and reprints: Payment: By publication to author. $.02 per word.
Is simultaneous submission of article to other journals permitted: No
Exclusive manuscript rights between acceptance and publication: Yes
Copyright: Held by publication.
Reprints: Available at cost
Additional information: Two free copies of journal given to each author.
Disposition of manuscript:
Query letter: No
Receipt of manuscript acknowledged: Yes
Decision to publish in: 6 to 8 weeks
Accepted manuscript published in: 1 to 6 months
Rejected manuscript returned: Yes, if return postage is supplied by author.
Rejected manuscript criticized: No
Submit to:
George J. Dyer
Editor
(See address above)

CHINA NOTES [541]
Room 616
475 Riverside Drive
New York, New York 10027

Previously entitled *China Bulletin* (before 1962)

First published in 1947

SUBSCRIPTION DATA
Issues and rates: Published quarterly.
   Average paid circulation: 1,500
   Annual rate(s): $2.00; Foreign $3.00
Publisher or Sponsor: The National Council of Churches, USA
Managing Editor: Donald MacInnis

EDITORIAL DESCRIPTION
   Primary concerns are religion in contemporary China, and developments in the life of man and society.
Articles per average issue: 5
Audience: People with Chinese and Asian concerns

MANUSCRIPT INFORMATION
Manuscript requirements: No specific style guide.
   Preferred length: 1,500 to 2,000 words
   Number of copies to be submitted: 1
   Abstract: Not necessary.
Author information and reprints: Payment: None.
   Is simultaneous submission of article to other journals permitted: Subsequent publication permitted
   Exclusive manuscript rights between acceptance and publication: Yes
   Reprints: Available at cost.
Disposition of manuscript:
   Query letter: Necessary.
   Receipt of manuscript acknowledged: Yes
   Decision to publish in: 3 months
   Accepted manuscript published in: 6 months
   Rejected manuscript returned: Yes, with return postage paid by publication.
   Rejected manuscript criticized: Sometimes
Submit to:
   Donald MacInnis
   Editor
   (See address above)

CHRISTIAN CENTURY [542]
407 South Dearborn Street
Chicago, Illinois 60605
(312) 427-5380

SUBSCRIPTION DATA
Issues and rates: Published weekly.
   Average paid circulation: 30,000
   Annual rate(s): $12.00; Foreign $13.50
Publisher or Sponsor: Christian Century Foundation

EDITORIAL DESCRIPTION
   Publication is a religious journal for the liberal community, both secular and religious.
Articles per average issue: 6

Audience: General, educated readership
   Manuscripts accepted in English

MANUSCRIPT INFORMATION
Subject field(s): Social issues, theology, art and culture
Manuscript requirements: See latest issue for style requirements.
   Preferred length: 2000 words
   Number of copies to be submitted: One
   Abstract: No
Author information and reprints: Payment: By publication to author. Open
   Is simultaneous submission of article to other journals permitted: No
   Exclusive manuscript rights between acceptance and publication: Yes
   Copyright: Held by publication.
   Reprints: Available
Disposition of manuscript:
   Query letter: Preferred
   Receipt of manuscript acknowledged: Yes
   Decision to publish in: Four weeks
   Accepted manuscript published in: Two months
   Rejected manuscript returned: Yes, if self-addressed, stamped envelope is sent with manuscript.
   Rejected manuscript criticized: No
Submit to:
   James M. Wall
   Editor
   (See address above)

CHRISTIANITY TODAY [543]
1014 Washington Building
Washington, D.C. 20005
(202) 347-1753

First published in 1956

SUBSCRIPTION DATA
Issues and rates: Published bi-weekly.
   Average paid circulation: 167,234; 1,695 controlled
   Annual rate(s): $8.50, Foreign $9.50
Managing Editor: David E. Kucharsky

EDITORIAL DESCRIPTION
   Contains articles, reviews, poetry, columns, etc. Point of view is evangelical, theologically conservative.
Articles per average issue: 3-4
Audience: Ministers and laity
   Manuscripts accepted in English

MANUSCRIPT INFORMATION
Subject field(s): Theology, ethics, philosophy, religion
Manuscript requirements: Chicago
   Preferred length: 2000 words
   Number of copies to be submitted: One
   Abstract: No
Author information and reprints: Payment: By publication to author. $75.00 up per article.
   Is simultaneous submission of article to other journals permitted: No
   Exclusive manuscript rights between acceptance and publication: Yes
   Copyright: Held by publication.
   Reprints: Available ocassionally

Additional information: Readers expect contents to be presented in a Biblically oriented way.
Disposition of manuscript:
   Query letter: No
   Receipt of manuscript acknowledged: Yes
   Decision to publish in: 2 month
   Accepted manuscript published in: 2 months or more
   Rejected manuscript returned: Yes, if self-addressed, stamped envelope is sent with manuscript.
   Rejected manuscript criticized: No
Submit to:
   Harold Lindsell
   Editor-Publisher
   (See address above)

THE CHURCH HERALD [544]
630 Myrtle Street N.W.
Grand Rapids, Michigan 49504
(616) 458-5156

Previously entitled *The Christian Intelligencer*

First published in 1826

SUBSCRIPTION DATA
Issues and rates: Published bi-weekly.
   Average paid circulation: 74,500; 500 controlled
   Annual rate(s): Individuals $3.75
Publisher or Sponsor: The Reformed Church in America

EDITORIAL DESCRIPTION
   Features articles on Biblical themes and contemporary issues.
Articles per average issue: 8
Audience: General
   Manuscripts accepted in English

MANUSCRIPT INFORMATION
Subject field(s): Christian life, Christian doctrine, Christianity and culture, forms of worship, communication between peoples, Christian education, ethics and business relations, death and dying, creative use of leisure
Manuscript requirements: Chicago
   Preferred length: 700 to 1300 words
   Number of copies to be submitted: One
Author information and reprints: Payment: By publication to author. $.02 and up per word.
   Is simultaneous submission of article to other journals permitted: Yes
   Exclusive manuscript rights between acceptance and publication: Yes
   Reprints: Not available.
Disposition of manuscript:
   Query letter: No
   Receipt of manuscript acknowledged: No
   Decision to publish in: 1-2 weeks
   Accepted manuscript published in: 1-12 weeks
   Rejected manuscript returned: Yes, if return postage is supplied by author.
   Rejected manuscript criticized: Occasionally
Submit to:
   John A. Stapert

Religion and theology

Editor
(See address above)

CHURCH HISTORY [545]
Swift Hall
University of Chicago
Chicago, Illinois 60637
(312) 753-4026

SUBSCRIPTION DATA
Issues and rates: Published quarterly.
 Average paid circulation: 3000
 Annual rate(s): $10, Students $6
Publisher or Sponsor: American Society of Church History

EDITORIAL DESCRIPTION
 Contains articles on Church historical materials of every type in the various distinguishable areas of the discipline.
Articles per average issue: 7-8
Audience: Academic
 Manuscripts accepted in English only

MANUSCRIPT INFORMATION
Subject field(s): Church history
Manuscript requirements: Chicago
 Preferred length: 25-30 pages including footnotes
 Number of copies to be submitted: One
 Abstract: No
Author information and reprints: Payment: None.
 Is simultaneous submission of article to other journals permitted: No
 Exclusive manuscript rights between acceptance and publication: Yes
 Copyright: Held by publication.
 Reprints: Available, cost depends on number of pages
Disposition of manuscript:
 Query letter: No
 Receipt of manuscript acknowledged: Yes
 Decision to publish in: 3 months
 Accepted manuscript published in: 12-18 months
 Rejected manuscript returned: Yes
 Rejected manuscript criticized: Yes
Submit to:
 Editors
 (See address above)

CHURCH AND STATE [546]
8120 Fenton Street
Silver Springs, Maryland 20910
(301) 589-3707

First published in 1948

SUBSCRIPTION DATA
Issues and rates: Published monthly.
 Average paid circulation: 130,000
 Annual rate(s): $5.00; Foreign $6.00;
 Individuals $5.00; Institutions $3.00;
 Students $1.50

Publisher or Sponsor: Americans United for the Separation of Church and State
Managing Editor: Edd Doerr

EDITORIAL DESCRIPTION
 Vigorous advocacy of church-state separation and opposition to clericalism
Articles per average issue: Varies
 Manuscripts accepted in English only

MANUSCRIPT INFORMATION
Subject field(s): Past issues have included: Vatican diplomacy; religious factors in adoption procedures; the origins of church-state separation in 18th century America; early American Baptists and religious liberty; religious education in British schools.
Manuscript requirements: See latest issue for style requirements.
 Preferred length: 800 to 2,000 words
 Number of copies to be submitted: 1
 Abstract: Not necessary.
Author information and reprints: Payment: By publication to author. $50.00 per article.
 Is simultaneous submission of article to other journals permitted: Permitted.
 Exclusive manuscript rights between acceptance and publication: Yes
 Copyright: Held by publication-first serial rights only
 Reprints: Available at no cost.
Disposition of manuscript:
 Query letter: Not necessary, but advisable.
 Receipt of manuscript acknowledged: Yes
 Decision to publish in: 2 to 3 months
 Accepted manuscript published in: 2 to 3 months
 Rejected manuscript returned: Yes, with return postage paid by publication.
 Rejected manuscript criticized: Reasons for rejections only
Submit to:
 Albert J. Menendez
 Assistant Editor
 (See address above)

THE CHURCHMAN [547]
1074 23rd Avenue North
St. Petersburg, Florida 33704
(813) 894-0097

First published in 1804

SUBSCRIPTION DATA
Issues and rates: Published monthly.
 Average paid circulation: 6,000
 Annual rate(s): $6.50,
Managing Editor: Edna Ruth Johnson

EDITORIAL DESCRIPTION
 Focuses on current social issues, freedom of ideas and contains editorials, book reviews, open forum, special articles.
Articles per average issue: 7 to 10
Audience: People of all faiths and denominations.
 Manuscripts accepted in English

MANUSCRIPT INFORMATION
Subject field(s): Social issues, international affairs, world peace and brotherhood, philosophy, religion, politics, history, humanism, economics
Manuscript requirements: See latest issue for style requirements.
 Preferred length: 800-1000 words (typewritten double-spaced)
 Number of copies to be submitted: One
 Abstract: Not necessary.
Author information and reprints: Payment: Reprints only. Copies of the issue containing article.
 Is simultaneous submission of article to other journals permitted: No
 Exclusive manuscript rights between acceptance and publication: Yes
 Copyright: Not copyrighted
 Reprints: Available at cost.
Additional information: Manuscript should have one and a quarter inch margins and name and address of author(s)
Disposition of manuscript:
 Query letter: No
 Receipt of manuscript acknowledged: Yes
 Decision to publish in: One week
 Accepted manuscript published in: Varies
 Rejected manuscript returned: Yes, if return postage is supplied by author.
 Rejected manuscript criticized: Yes
Submit to:
 Edna Ruth Johnson
 Editor
 (See address above)

COMMONWEAL [548]
A Review of Public Affairs, Literature and the Arts
232 Madison Avenue
New York, New York 10016
(212) 683-2042

SUBSCRIPTION DATA
Issues and rates: Published bi-weekly.
 Average paid circulation: 25,000
 Annual rate(s): $15.00; Foreign $17.00
Managing Editor: John Deedy

EDITORIAL DESCRIPTION
 Principal focus is on politics and social problems, religion, books and the arts with a liberal point of view; edited by Catholic laymen.
Articles per average issue: 5-10
Audience: General
 Manuscripts accepted in English

MANUSCRIPT INFORMATION
Manuscript requirements: See latest issue for style requirements.
 Preferred length: 1,200-3,000 words
 Number of copies to be submitted: One
Author information and reprints: Payment: By publication to author. $.02 per word.
 Is simultaneous submission of article to other journals permitted: No
 Copyright: Held by publication.
 Reprints: Not available.
Disposition of manuscript:
 Query letter: No, but helpful
 Receipt of manuscript acknowledged: Yes
 Decision to publish in: 2 to 3 weeks

Rejected manuscript returned: Yes, if return postage is supplied by author.
Rejected manuscript criticized: No
Submit to:
James O'Gara
Editor
(See address above)

CONCORDIA HISTORICAL INSTITUTE QUARTERLY [549]
A Journal for the History of Lutheranism in America
801 DeMun Avenue
St. Louis, Missouri 63105
(314) 721-5934, ext. 297

First published in 1928

SUBSCRIPTION DATA
Issues and rates: Published quarterly.
 Average paid circulation: 1300; 1600 controlled
 Annual rate(s): $5.00
Publisher or Sponsor: Concordia Historical Institute, The Lutheran Church Missouri Synod

EDITORIAL DESCRIPTION
 Contains articles on the history, biography, autobiography, chronology, geography, congregational and other historical subjects dealing with Lutheranism in America.
Articles per average issue: 4
Audience: Academic, clergy
 Manuscripts accepted in English

MANUSCRIPT INFORMATION
Subject field(s): Synodical organizations, geographical areas, institutional histories, persons, teachings, and other activities
Manuscript requirements: MLA, Chicago
 Preferred length: 4,500 words
 Number of copies to be submitted: One
Author information and reprints: Payment: 6-8 free issues
 Is simultaneous submission of article to other journals permitted: No
 Exclusive manuscript rights between acceptance and publication: Yes
 Copyright: Held by publication.
 Reprints: Available only by special arrangement
Disposition of manuscript:
 Query letter: No
 Receipt of manuscript acknowledged: Yes
 Decision to publish in: 3-6 months
 Accepted manuscript published in: 6-9 months
 Rejected manuscript returned: Yes, if return postage is supplied by author.
 Rejected manuscript criticized: No
Submit to:
 Ronald J. Schlegel
 Acting Editor
 (See address above)

CONSERVATIVE JUDAISM [550]
3080 Broadway
New York, New York 10027
(212) 749-8000 ext. 330

First published in 1945

SUBSCRIPTION DATA
Issues and rates: Published quarterly.
 Average paid circulation: 2,700; 3,000 controlled
 Annual rate(s): $5.00
Publisher or Sponsor: The Rabbinical Assembly, Jewish Theological Seminary

EDITORIAL DESCRIPTION
 Contains articles on contemporary Jewish life and letters, Jewish theology, education, philosophy and Israel-Diaspora relationships.
Articles per average issue: 15-20
Audience: Rabbis, Academic
 Manuscripts accepted in English

MANUSCRIPT INFORMATION
Subject field(s): Contemporary Jewish life and letters, Jewish theology, Jewish education, Israel
Manuscript requirements: See latest issue for style requirements.
 Preferred length: 2,000 to 6,000 words
 Number of copies to be submitted: Two
 Abstract: No
Author information and reprints: Payment: None.
 Is simultaneous submission of article to other journals permitted: No
 Exclusive manuscript rights between acceptance and publication: Yes
 Copyright: Held by publication.
 Reprints: Available at printer's fee
Disposition of manuscript:
 Query letter: No
 Receipt of manuscript acknowledged: Yes
 Decision to publish in: 1-3 months
 Accepted manuscript published in: 3-12 months
 Rejected manuscript returned: Yes
 Rejected manuscript criticized: No
Submit to:
 Deborah Brodie
 Managing Editor
 (See address above)

THE CORD [551]
A Franciscan Spiritual Review
The Franciscan Institute
St. Bonaventure, New York 14778
(716) 375-2105

First published in 1950

SUBSCRIPTION DATA
Issues and rates: Published monthly.
 Average paid circulation: 1,225; 40 controlled
 Annual rate(s): $3.00
Publisher or Sponsor: The Franciscan Institute

EDITORIAL DESCRIPTION
 Publishes material of theoretical and practical nature either directly or at least closely related to the spiritual needs of Franciscan religious in particular, but also lay Catholics interested in the Franciscan viewpoint of theology and spirituality.
Articles per average issue: 4
 Manuscripts accepted in English only

MANUSCRIPT INFORMATION
Subject field(s): Franciscan spirituality, doctrine, history; Catholic spirituality, doctrine; Christian spirituality, doctrine, history, and philosophy
Manuscript requirements: See latest issue for style requirements.
 Preferred length: 8-12 pages
 Number of copies to be submitted: One
 Abstract: No
Author information and reprints: Payment: None.
 Is simultaneous submission of article to other journals permitted: Yes
 Exclusive manuscript rights between acceptance and publication: No
 Copyright: Only if obtained by author for himself.
 Reprints: Not available.
Disposition of manuscript:
 Query letter: No
 Receipt of manuscript acknowledged: Yes
 Decision to publish in: One week
 Accepted manuscript published in: 3-6 months
 Rejected manuscript returned: Yes
 Rejected manuscript criticized: Yes
Submit to:
 Michael D. Meilach
 Editor
 Siena College Friary
 Loudonville, New York 12211
 (518) 783-2300

CROSS AND CROWN [552]
P.O. Box 627
Oak Park, Illinois 60303
(312) 771-6050

First published in 1949

SUBSCRIPTION DATA
Issues and rates: Published quarterly.
 Average paid circulation: 6,500
 Annual rate(s): $4.00, Pan-Am $4.50, Foreign $5.00
Publisher or Sponsor: Province St. Albert the Great
Managing Editor: Stanley J. Gaines

EDITORIAL DESCRIPTION
 Presentation of spiritual material.
Articles per average issue: 7
Audience: Clergy, educated laity
 Manuscripts accepted in English

Religion and theology

MANUSCRIPT INFORMATION
Subject field(s): Religious subjects, liturgy, church renewal, ecumenism, studies of the Bible
Manuscript requirements: See latest issue for style requirements.
  Preferred length: 3000 words
  Number of copies to be submitted: One
  Abstract: No
Author information and reprints: Payment: By publication to author. $4.00 per page.
  Is simultaneous submission of article to other journals permitted: No
  Exclusive manuscript rights between acceptance and publication: Yes
  Copyright: Held by publication but permission to reprint is granted without charge.
  Reprints: Sometimes available
Disposition of manuscript:
  Query letter: No
  Receipt of manuscript acknowledged: Yes
  Decision to publish in: 3 weeks or less
  Accepted manuscript published in: 3-9 months
  Rejected manuscript returned: Yes, if return postage is supplied by author.
  Rejected manuscript criticized: Yes
Submit to:
  John J. McDonald
  Editor
  1909 South Ashland Avenue
  Chicago, Illinois 60608
  (312) 226-0074

CRUX [553]
A Quarterly Journal of Christian Thought and Opinion
745 Mount Pleasant Road
Toronto, Ontario, Canada
(416) 487-3431

First published in 1963

SUBSCRIPTION DATA
Issues and rates: Published quarterly.
  Annual rate(s): $3.00
Publisher or Sponsor: Graduate Christian Fellowship

EDITORIAL DESCRIPTION
  Each issue explores a central theme of Christian understanding and practice; Biblical and Christian insights are related to other areas of study and life.
Articles per average issue: 4-5
Audience: General, academic
  Manuscripts accepted in English

MANUSCRIPT INFORMATION
Manuscript requirements: See latest issue for style requirements.
  Preferred length: 5,000 to 6,000 words
  Number of copies to be submitted: Two
  Abstract: No
Author information and reprints: Payment: None.
  Is simultaneous submission of article to other journals permitted: No
  Exclusive manuscript rights between acceptance and publication: Yes
  Copyright: Held by publication.
  Reprints: Not available.

Disposition of manuscript:
  Query letter: No, but useful
  Receipt of manuscript acknowledged: Yes
  Decision to publish in: 4 weeks
  Accepted manuscript published in: 6 to 9 months
  Rejected manuscript returned: Yes, if return postage is supplied by author.
  Rejected manuscript criticized: Sometimes
Submit to:
  P. W. Gooch
  Editor
  Scarborough College
  University of Toronto
  West Hill, Ontario M1C 1A4, Canada
  (416) 284-3144

DIALOGUE: A JOURNAL OF MORMON THOUGHT [554]
1081 Westwood Boulevard, #215
Los Angeles, California 90024
(213) 477-5713

First published in 1966

SUBSCRIPTION DATA
Issues and rates: Published quarterly.
  Average paid circulation: 3,000
  Annual rate(s): $20.00; Foreign $26.00
Publisher or Sponsor: Dialogue Foundation

EDITORIAL DESCRIPTION
  Contains articles and essays (historical, literary, social, scientific, theological, etc.), book reviews, sermons, bibliography, notes and comments, fiction, poetry, music, graphics.

MANUSCRIPT INFORMATION
Subject field(s): Mormonism: culture, history, theology, literature, arts; religion (general); ecumenism; contemporary events; moral issues
Manuscript requirements: See latest issue for style requirements.
  Preferred length: 10 pages
  Number of copies to be submitted: Two
Author information and reprints: Payment: None. 2 copies of journal
  Is simultaneous submission of article to other journals permitted: No
  Exclusive manuscript rights between acceptance and publication: Yes
  Copyright: Held by publication.
  Reprints: Available
Disposition of manuscript:
  Receipt of manuscript acknowledged: Yes
  Decision to publish in: 1-2 months
  Rejected manuscript returned: Yes, if return postage is supplied by author.
  Rejected manuscript criticized: Yes
Submit to:
  Robert A. Rees
  Editor
  (See address above)

THE DREW GATEWAY [555]
A Journal of Comment and Criticism
Drew University
Madison, New Jersey 07940
(201) 377-3000 ext. 246

SUBSCRIPTION DATA
Issues and rates: Published three times per year.
  Average paid circulation: 3800 controlled
Publisher or Sponsor: The Drew University Theological School

EDITORIAL DESCRIPTION
  Publishes articles and reviews that cover a broad range of religious subjects for the benefit of pastors and teachers.

MANUSCRIPT INFORMATION
Subject field(s): Biblical studies, Church history, theology, ethics, philosophy of religion, the Church, ministry, humanities, the arts, world religions
Manuscript requirements: Chicago
  Preferred length: 3,000 to 6,000 words; 12-25 pages
  Number of copies to be submitted: One
Author information and reprints: Payment: None. Three copies of issue in which article appears.
  Is simultaneous submission of article to other journals permitted: No
  Exclusive manuscript rights between acceptance and publication: Yes
  Copyright: Held by author.
  Reprints: Available at cost
Disposition of manuscript:
  Query letter: No
  Receipt of manuscript acknowledged: Yes
  Decision to publish in: 6 to 8 weeks
  Accepted manuscript published in: 3 to 6 months
  Rejected manuscript returned: Yes
  Rejected manuscript criticized: No
Submit to:
  Charles Courtney
  Editor
  (See address above)

EASTERN CHURCHES REVIEW [556]
A Journal of Eastern Christendom
1 Canterbury Road
Oxford OX2 6LU, England
0865-54023

First published in 1966

SUBSCRIPTION DATA
Issues and rates: Published semi-annually.
  Average paid circulation: 1,000
  Annual rate(s): £3.50, Foreign $10.00
Publisher or Sponsor: Eastern Churches Review Trust

EDITORIAL DESCRIPTION
  Contains articles on the history and present situation of the Eastern Churches (Orthodox, non-Chalcedonian, Eastern Catholic). The journal aims at furthering Christian unity through fair and objective comment.
Articles per average issue: 4-5

Audience: Academic specialists
Manuscripts accepted in English

MANUSCRIPT INFORMATION
Subject field(s): Theology, history, art, liturgy, current affairs, spirituality
Manuscript requirements: See latest issue for style requirements.
Preferred length: 4,000-6,000 words; 15-25 pages
Number of copies to be submitted: One
Abstract: No
Author information and reprints: Payment: None.
Is simultaneous submission of article to other journals permitted: No
Exclusive manuscript rights between acceptance and publication: Yes
Copyright: Held by publication.
Reprints: Available, 20 free
Additional information: Manuscripts are to be typed with double spacing; footnotes typed on additional sheets at end (also in double spacing).
Disposition of manuscript:
Query letter: No
Receipt of manuscript acknowledged: Yes
Decision to publish in: 6-12 weeks
Accepted manuscript published in: 6-12 months
Rejected manuscript returned: Yes
Rejected manuscript criticized: No
Submit to:
Kallistos Timothy Ware
(See address above)

ENCOUNTER [557]
A Journal of Creative Theological Scholarship
Christian Theological Seminary
Box 88267
Indianapolis, Indiana 46208
(317) 924-1331 ext. 33

Previously entitled *Shane Quarterly*

First published in 1940

SUBSCRIPTION DATA
Issues and rates: Published quarterly.
Average paid circulation: 659; 50 controlled
Annual rate(s): $6.00
Publisher or Sponsor: Christian Theological Seminary
Managing Editor: Leslie R. Galbraith

EDITORIAL DESCRIPTION
Contains scholarly articles of theological interest.
Articles per average issue: 8
Audience: Scholars, clergy, laymen
Manuscripts accepted in English

MANUSCRIPT INFORMATION
Subject field(s): Theology, Biblical scholarship, ethics, Church history
Manuscript requirements: See latest issue for style requirements.
Preferred length: 10-20 pages
Number of copies to be submitted: One
Abstract: No

Author information and reprints: Payment: None.
Exclusive manuscript rights between acceptance and publication: Yes
Copyright: Held by publication.
Reprints: Available at minimal cost if ordered before publication
Disposition of manuscript:
Query letter: No
Receipt of manuscript acknowledged: Yes
Decision to publish in: 2 months
Accepted manuscript published in: 6 months
Rejected manuscript returned: Yes
Rejected manuscript criticized: Yes
Submit to:
Clark M. Williamson
Editor
(See address above)

EVANGELICAL MISSIONS QUARTERLY [558]
Box 267
Springfield, Pennsylvania 19064

First published in 1964

SUBSCRIPTION DATA
Issues and rates: Published quarterly.
Average paid circulation: 4300
Annual rate(s): $4.25
Publisher or Sponsor: Evangelical Missions Information Service
Managing Editor: James W. Reapsome

EDITORIAL DESCRIPTION
Contains articles about evangelical Protestant missionary work overseas; book reviews.
Articles per average issue: 6
Audience: Professional, missionaries, scholars, students, pastors
Manuscripts accepted in English

MANUSCRIPT INFORMATION
Subject field(s): Evangelical Protestant missionary work overseas
Manuscript requirements: See latest issue for style requirements.
Preferred length: 2,000 words
Number of copies to be submitted: One
Abstract: No
Author information and reprints: Payment: By publication to author. $.01 per word.
Is simultaneous submission of article to other journals permitted: No
Exclusive manuscript rights between acceptance and publication: Yes
Copyright: Held by author.
Reprints: Not available.
Additional information: Manuscripts to be typewritten, double-spaced.
Disposition of manuscript:
Query letter: No
Receipt of manuscript acknowledged: Yes
Decision to publish in: One week
Accepted manuscript published in: 3-12 months
Rejected manuscript returned: Yes
Rejected manuscript criticized: For revision purposes

Submit to:
James W. Reapsome
Editor
(See address above)

THE EVANGELICAL QUARTERLY [559]
A Theological Review
Paternoster House
3 Mount Radford Crescent
Exeter, Devon EX2 4JW, England
(0392) 50631

First published in 1929

SUBSCRIPTION DATA
Issues and rates: Published quarterly.
Average paid circulation: 1,900
Annual rate(s): Foreign $8.00

EDITORIAL DESCRIPTION
Contains Biblical, theological, historical articles; extensive and in-depth book reviews.
Articles per average issue: 4
Audience: Interdenominational
Manuscripts accepted in English, French, German

MANUSCRIPT INFORMATION
Manuscript requirements: See latest issue for style requirements.
Preferred length: Up to 10,000 words
Number of copies to be submitted: One
Abstract: No
Author information and reprints: Payment: None.
Is simultaneous submission of article to other journals permitted: No
Exclusive manuscript rights between acceptance and publication: Yes
Copyright: Held by author.
Reprints: Available by arrangement
Disposition of manuscript:
Query letter: No
Receipt of manuscript acknowledged: Yes
Decision to publish in: 2 months
Accepted manuscript published in: Up to 24 months
Rejected manuscript returned: Yes, if return postage is supplied by author.
Rejected manuscript criticized: Yes
Submit to:
F. F. Bruce
The Crossways, Temple Road
Buxton, Derbyshire, England
Buxton: 3250

FOUNDATIONS [560]
A Baptist Journal of History and Theology
1106 South Goodman
Rochester, New York 14620
(716) 473-1740

Previously entitled *The Chronicle*

First published in 1938

SUBSCRIPTION DATA
Issues and rates: Published quarterly.

Religion and theology

Average paid circulation: 1100
Annual rate(s): $5.00, Foreign $5.50
Publisher or Sponsor: American Baptist Historical Society

EDITORIAL DESCRIPTION

Contains articles related to Baptist history and theology.
Articles per average issue: 6
Audience: Ministers, theological students, interested laymen
Manuscripts accepted in English

MANUSCRIPT INFORMATION

Manuscript requirements: Chicago
Preferred length: 10-12 pages
Number of copies to be submitted: One
Abstract: No
Author information and reprints: Payment: None.
Is simultaneous submission of article to other journals permitted: No
Exclusive manuscript rights between acceptance and publication: Yes
Copyright: Held by publication.
Reprints: Available at cost.
Additional information: Double-spaced with wide margins.
Disposition of manuscript:
Query letter: Desirable
Receipt of manuscript acknowledged: Yes
Decision to publish in: 3 months
Accepted manuscript published in: 6-12 months
Rejected manuscript returned: Yes, if return postage is supplied by author.
Rejected manuscript criticized: No
Submit to:
Dr. Eldon Ernst
Editor
2465 Le Conte Avenue
Berkeley, California 94709

HARVARD THEOLOGICAL REVIEW* [561]
45 Francis Avenue
Cambridge, Massachusetts 02138
(617) 495-5259

SUBSCRIPTION DATA

Issues and rates: Published quarterly.
Average paid circulation: 1000; 800 controlled
Annual rate(s): $8.00, Foreign $9.00
Publisher or Sponsor: Harvard Divinity School

EDITORIAL DESCRIPTION

Contains articles and brief notes on theological, religious and Biblical subjects.

MANUSCRIPT INFORMATION

Subject field(s): Theology, Biblical studies, Church history, ethics, history of religion, sociology of religion and related subjects
Manuscript requirements: See latest issue for style requirements.
Preferred length: Articles: 10-30 pages; Notes: 2-10 pages
Number of copies to be submitted: One

Author information and reprints: Payment: None. 50 offprints.
Is simultaneous submission of article to other journals permitted: Yes
Copyright: Held by publication.
Reprints: Not available.
Additional information: Footnotes on separate pages, numbered consecutively.
Disposition of manuscript:
Receipt of manuscript acknowledged: Yes
Decision to publish in: 8-10 weeks
Accepted manuscript published in: 2-6 months
Rejected manuscript returned: Yes
Rejected manuscript criticized: Sometimes
Submit to:
Editor
(See address above)

THE HEYTHROP JOURNAL [562]
A Quarterly Review of Philosophy and Theology
Heythrop College,
Cavendish Square
London W1M OAN, England
01-580-6941 ext. 42

First published in 1960

SUBSCRIPTION DATA

Issues and rates: Published quarterly.
Annual rate(s): £4.00; Foreign $12.50

EDITORIAL DESCRIPTION

Contains articles on philosophy and theology and related subjects.
Articles per average issue: 4-5
Manuscripts accepted in English

MANUSCRIPT INFORMATION

Subject field(s): Philosophy, theology, Biblical, Christian origins, Church history, historical theology, patristics, Newman/Tyrrell, ecumenical, canon law, religious sociology, missions
Manuscript requirements: Style sheet sent on request.
Preferred length: 6,000-8,000 words
Number of copies to be submitted: One
Abstract: No
Author information and reprints: Payment: None.
Is simultaneous submission of article to other journals permitted: No
Exclusive manuscript rights between acceptance and publication: Yes
Copyright: Held by publication.
Reprints: Available, 24 only
Additional information: Everything, including footnotes, typewritten double-spaced.
Disposition of manuscript:
Query letter: No
Receipt of manuscript acknowledged: Yes
Decision to publish in: 3-4 weeks
Accepted manuscript published in: 4-6 months
Rejected manuscript returned: Yes, if return postage is supplied by author.
Rejected manuscript criticized: Yes

Submit to:
Dr. Robert Murray
Editor
(See address above)

HISTORICAL MAGAZINE OF THE PROTESTANT EPISCOPAL CHURCH [563]
607 Rathervue Place, Box 2247
Austin, Texas 78767
(512) 472-6816

First published in 1932

SUBSCRIPTION DATA

Issues and rates: Published quarterly.
Average paid circulation: 1,250
Annual rate(s): $10.00
Publisher or Sponsor: Church Historical Society
Managing Editor: Lawrence L. Brown

EDITORIAL DESCRIPTION

Contains articles on Church history with particular emphasis on the American Episcopal Church, the Anglican Church and American Christianity in general. A publication of the Episcopal Church, it allows authors to speak for their own viewpoint and thus strives for a breadth of interpretation.

MANUSCRIPT INFORMATION

Subject field(s): American Episcopal Church, Church of England, Anglican Churches, American and English Christianity
Manuscript requirements: Chicago, Typewritten, double-spaced
Preferred length: 8,000-10,000 words
Number of copies to be submitted: Two
Author information and reprints: Payment: None.
Is simultaneous submission of article to other journals permitted: No
Exclusive manuscript rights between acceptance and publication: Yes
Copyright: Held by publication.
Reprints: Available, orders must be placed from author direct to printer.
Disposition of manuscript:
Query letter: Desirable
Receipt of manuscript acknowledged: Yes
Decision to publish in: 6-8 weeks
Accepted manuscript published in: 6-9 months
Rejected manuscript returned: Yes, if self-addressed, stamped envelope is sent with manuscript.
Rejected manuscript criticized: Sometimes
Submit to:
Lawrence L. Brown
Editor
(See address above)

HISTORY OF RELIGION* [564]

An International Journal for Comparative Historical Studies
University of Chicago Press
5801 Ellis Avenue
Chicago, Illinois 60637
(312) 753-3347

SUBSCRIPTION DATA

Issues and rates: Published quarterly.
 Average paid circulation: 1250
 Annual rate(s): $10.00, Foreign $11.00

EDITORIAL DESCRIPTION

Devoted to the study of historical religious phenomena. Its primary aim is the integration of results of the several disciplines of the science of religion. Articles of a synthetical character are intended to acquaint readers with progress being made in the general area of history of religions.

MANUSCRIPT INFORMATION

Subject field(s): Synthetic presentations, hermeneutic analysis of religious phenomena, review articles, problems of methodology, comparative studies, articles on less-known or neglected religions (Slavic, Altaic, etc.)
Manuscript requirements: Chicago
 Preferred length: 20-50 pages
 Number of copies to be submitted: One
Author information and reprints: Payment: None.
 Is simultaneous submission of article to other journals permitted: No
 Reprints: Available
Disposition of manuscript:
 Receipt of manuscript acknowledged: Yes
 Decision to publish in: 5 weeks
 Accepted manuscript published in: 9 months
 Rejected manuscript returned: Yes
 Rejected manuscript criticized: No
Submit to:
 Editor
 Divinity School, University of Chicago
 Chicago, Illinois 60637

THE ILIFF REVIEW [565]

2201 South University Boulevard
Denver, Colorado 80210
(303) 744-1287

First published in 1944

SUBSCRIPTION DATA

Issues and rates: Published three times per year.
 Average paid circulation: 500; 100 controlled
 Annual rate(s): $1.50
Managing Editor: Charles S. Milligan

EDITORIAL DESCRIPTION

Contains scholarly articles and book reviews in the various fields of religious studies.
Articles per average issue: 4
Audience: Scholars
 Manuscripts accepted in English

MANUSCRIPT INFORMATION

Subject field(s): Theology, philosophy, history, Biblical, sociology, psychology, ethics
Manuscript requirements: Turabian
 Preferred length: 10 to 15 pages
 Number of copies to be submitted: One
 Abstract: No
Author information and reprints: Payment: None.
 Is simultaneous submission of article to other journals permitted: Yes, wish to be informed if submitted elsewhere.
 Exclusive manuscript rights between acceptance and publication: Yes
 Copyright: No
 Reprints: Available, 85 free
Disposition of manuscript:
 Query letter: No
 Receipt of manuscript acknowledged: Yes
 Decision to publish in: 4 to 6 weeks
 Accepted manuscript published in: 3 months
 Rejected manuscript returned: Yes, if return postage is supplied by author.
 Rejected manuscript criticized: No
Submit to:
 Charles S. Milligan
 Editor
 (See address above)

INTERNATIONAL REVIEW OF MISSION [566]

150 Route de Ferney
1211 Geneva 20, Switzerland
33 34 00

First published in 1912

SUBSCRIPTION DATA

Issues and rates: Published quarterly.
 Average paid circulation: 5,000
 Annual rate(s): $9.00
Publisher or Sponsor: World Council of Churches, Commission on World Mission and Evangelism

EDITORIAL DESCRIPTION

Contains scholarly articles reflecting on problems and changing patterns in the mission of the Church. Some articles are descriptive of what is happening in world mission on all six continents; book reviews, and a bibliography on world mission and evangelism.
Articles per average issue: 10
Audience: Religious, missionaries, general
 Manuscripts accepted in English, French, German, Spanish

MANUSCRIPT INFORMATION

Manuscript requirements: See latest issue for style requirements.
 Preferred length: 2,000 to 5,000 words
 Number of copies to be submitted: One
 Abstract: No
Author information and reprints: Payment: By publication to author. 40 Swiss francs per article.
 Is simultaneous submission of article to other journals permitted: Yes, with notification of publication
 Exclusive manuscript rights between acceptance and publication: Yes
 Copyright: Held by publication.
 Reprints: Available
Additional information: Typewritten, double-spaced
Disposition of manuscript:
 Query letter: No
 Receipt of manuscript acknowledged: Yes
 Decision to publish in: 2-3 weeks
 Accepted manuscript published in: 3-6 months
 Rejected manuscript returned: Yes
 Rejected manuscript criticized: No
Submit to:
 Ruth Sovik
 Editorial Assistant
 (See address above)

JOURNAL FOR THE SCIENTIFIC STUDY OF RELIGION [567]

Box U68A
University of Connecticut
Storrs, Connecticut 06268
(203) 486-4424

First published in 1961

SUBSCRIPTION DATA

Issues and rates: Published quarterly.
 Average paid circulation: 3000
 Annual rate(s): $15.00
Publisher or Sponsor: Society for the Scientific Study of Religion

EDITORIAL DESCRIPTION

Publishes scholarly articles on religion written from a scientific perspective. The journal is interdisciplinary, though most of its contributors are sociologists or psychologists, or have some training in those fields. Emphasis is placed on empirical studies of religious phenomena, on theoretical interpretation of research findings, on clarification of methodological and conceptual problems in studying religion, and in presentation of testable theories.
Articles per average issue: 6-8
Audience: Academic
 Manuscripts accepted in English

MANUSCRIPT INFORMATION

Manuscript requirements: Style sheet published in December, 1972 issue
 Preferred length: 5-35 pages
 Number of copies to be submitted: Two
 Abstract: Yes; 100 words or less
Author information and reprints: Payment: None.
 Is simultaneous submission of article to other journals permitted: Permitted only with express permission of the Editor.
 Exclusive manuscript rights between acceptance and publication: No
 Copyright: Held by publication.
 Reprints: Available, cost depends on length.
Additional information: Name and affiliation on a separate sheet.
Disposition of manuscript:
 Query letter: No

Receipt of manuscript acknowledged: Yes
Decision to publish in: 3-5 months
Accepted manuscript published in: 2-3 months
Rejected manuscript returned: Yes
Rejected manuscript criticized: Yes
Submit to:
Richard Gorsuch
Editor
Institute of Behavioral Research
Texas Christian University
Ft. Worth, Texas 76129

JOURNAL OF CHURCH AND STATE [568]
A Scholarly Journal for Matters Relating to Church-State Affairs
Baylor University, Box 380
Waco, Texas 76703
(817) 755-1519

First published in 1959

SUBSCRIPTION DATA
Issues and rates: Published three times per year.
Average paid circulation: 1,200
Annual rate(s): $6.00

EDITORIAL DESCRIPTION
Contains articles on Church-State relationships.
Articles per average issue: 6
Audience: Academic, legal, clergy, government
Manuscripts accepted in English

MANUSCRIPT INFORMATION
Subject field(s): Historical, legal, constitutional, theological, philosophical, and sociological aspects of Church-State affairs and religious freedom.
Manuscript requirements: Chicago Style sheet sent on request.
Preferred length: 30 pages maximum
Number of copies to be submitted: 2
Abstract: No
Author information and reprints: Payment: None. 50 tear-sheets free to author
Is simultaneous submission of article to other journals permitted: Yes, but not dual
Exclusive manuscript rights between acceptance and publication: Yes
Copyright: Held by publication.
Reprints: Available, cost quoted on publication
Disposition of manuscript:
Receipt of manuscript acknowledged: Yes
Decision to publish in: 3-9 months
Accepted manuscript published in: 6-8 months
Rejected manuscript returned: Yes
Rejected manuscript criticized: Sometimes
Submit to:
Dr. James L. Garrett, Jr.
Editor
(See address above)

JOURNAL OF ECUMENICAL STUDIES [569]
Temple University
Philadelphia, Pennsylvania 19122
(215) 787-7714

First published in 1964

SUBSCRIPTION DATA
Issues and rates: Published quarterly.
Average paid circulation: 3000; 850 controlled
Annual rate(s): $10.00, Students $5.00, Foreign $11.00
Managing Editor: Paul Mojzes

EDITORIAL DESCRIPTION
Contains articles, book reviews, article abstracts (from over 500 periodicals published around the world), worldwide reports on interreligious dialogue and study and discussion questions for each article.
Articles per average issue: 5
Audience: Academic, clergy, laity
Manuscripts accepted in English

MANUSCRIPT INFORMATION
Manuscript requirements: MLA, Chicago
Preferred length: 15-30 pages
Number of copies to be submitted: One
Abstract: No
Author information and reprints: Payment: None.
Is simultaneous submission of article to other journals permitted: No
Exclusive manuscript rights between acceptance and publication: Yes
Copyright: Held by publication.
Reprints: 40 reprints free; additional copies are at cost to author.
Disposition of manuscript:
Query letter: No
Receipt of manuscript acknowledged: Yes
Decision to publish in: Several months
Accepted manuscript published in: Up to 1 year
Rejected manuscript returned: Yes
Rejected manuscript criticized: Occasionally
Submit to:
Leonard Swidler
Editor
(See address above)

JOURNAL OF PASTORAL CARE* [570]
475 Riverside Drive, Suite 450
New York, New York 10027
(212) 870-2558

SUBSCRIPTION DATA
Issues and rates: Published quarterly.
Average paid circulation: 5487; 1646 controlled
Annual rate(s): $8.00, Foreign $8.80
Publisher or Sponsor: Association for Clinical Pastoral Education, Inc., American Association of Pastoral Counselors

EDITORIAL DESCRIPTION
Contains articles on ministry of pastoral care and counseling, clinical pastoral education, research studies, and relationship to other professions.

MANUSCRIPT INFORMATION
Subject field(s): Pastoral work, ministry and mission of the Church, clinical pastoral education, pastoral counseling, characteristics of the ministry in relation to other helping professions of institutions
Manuscript requirements: See latest issue for style requirements.
Preferred length: Length of article depends on contents; communications and abstracts should not exceed six double-spaced typed pages.
Number of copies to be submitted: Original and two copies
Author information and reprints: Payment: Payment per article when the article is requested.
Is simultaneous submission of article to other journals permitted: No
Exclusive manuscript rights between acceptance and publication: Yes
Copyright: Held by publication.
Reprints: Available from publisher
Disposition of manuscript:
Receipt of manuscript acknowledged: Yes
Decision to publish in: 1-2 months
Accepted manuscript published in: 6 months to 2 years
Rejected manuscript returned: Yes
Rejected manuscript criticized: No
Submit to:
Managing Editor
(See address above)

JOURNAL OF RELIGION [571]
Swift Hall 005
1025 East 58th Street
University of Chicago
Chicago, Illinois 60637
(312) 753-4021

First published in 1921

SUBSCRIPTION DATA
Issues and rates: Published quarterly.
Average paid circulation: Not available.
Annual rate(s): $10.00; Students $8.00; Foreign $11.00
Publisher or Sponsor: University of Chicago, Divinity School

EDITORIAL DESCRIPTION
Contributions in the various modes of theological scholarship that touch in some vital way on questions concerning the role of religion in the general life of culture. Seeks to promote systematic inquiry into the manifold dimensions of the meaning and import of religion.
Articles per average issue: 4-5
Audience: Students, teachers, theologians
Manuscripts accepted in English

MANUSCRIPT INFORMATION
Subject field(s): Theology (Biblical, historical, constructive); Biblical studies; theology of culture; religion in interdiscipline: with literature, with psychology; ethics; religion and society; comparative religions
Manuscript requirements: Chicago; also, consult the preliminary pages of each issue
  Preferred length: 20-30 pages
  Number of copies to be submitted: Two
  Abstract: No
Author information and reprints: Payment: Reprints only. 50 free reprints
  Is simultaneous submission of article to other journals permitted: No
  Exclusive manuscript rights between acceptance and publication: Yes
  Copyright: Held by the University of Chicago Press
  Reprints: Available, at cost, depending on length
Additional information: All submitted papers should be double-spaced, including footnotes which should appear at the end of the paper.
Disposition of manuscript:
  Query letter: No
  Receipt of manuscript acknowledged: Yes
  Decision to publish in: Within three months
  Accepted manuscript published in: Within one year
  Rejected manuscript returned: Yes, if return postage is supplied by author.
  Rejected manuscript criticized: Yes
Submit to:
  Nathan A. Scott, Jr.
  Editor
  (See address above)

JOURNAL OF RELIGION AND HEALTH [572]
Institutes of Religion and Health
3 West 29th Street
New York, New York 10001
(212) 725-7924

First published in 1961

SUBSCRIPTION DATA
Issues and rates: Published quarterly.
  Average paid circulation: 3,000; 4,000 controlled
  Annual rate(s): $8.00
Publisher or Sponsor: Institutes of Religion and Health
Managing Editor: Harry C. Meserve

EDITORIAL DESCRIPTION
  Seeks to present a balanced view of important issues in the relationship between religion and the health and psychological sciences.
Articles per average issue: 7
Audience: Clergy, physicians, psychologists, psychiatrists, counsellors
  Manuscripts accepted in English

MANUSCRIPT INFORMATION
Subject field(s): Religion, counseling, psychiatry, psychology, medicine, social sciences
Manuscript requirements: Chicago except for references
  Preferred length: 3,000 to 5,000 words; 12 to 20 pages
  Number of copies to be submitted: Two
  Abstract: No
Author information and reprints: Payment: None.
  Is simultaneous submission of article to other journals permitted: No
  Exclusive manuscript rights between acceptance and publication: Yes
  Copyright: Held by publication.
  Reprints: Available
Additional information: Manuscripts must be typewritten, double-spaced, on one side of regular typewriter paper. Titles should be brief with references at the end of the paper. Author's biographical information should be furnished.
Disposition of manuscript:
  Receipt of manuscript acknowledged: Yes
  Decision to publish in: 90 days
  Accepted manuscript published in: 6-12 months
  Rejected manuscript returned: Yes, if self-addressed, stamped envelope is sent with manuscript.
  Rejected manuscript criticized: Sometimes
Submit to:
  Harry C. Meserve
  Editor
  P.O. Box 428
  Southwest Harbor, Maine 04679

JOURNAL OF RELIGIOUS THOUGHT [573]
Howard University
Washington, D. C. 20059
636-7673

First published in 1934

SUBSCRIPTION DATA
Issues and rates: Published semi-annually.

EDITORIAL DESCRIPTION
  An interdisciplinary approach to all religions
Articles per average issue: 5

MANUSCRIPT INFORMATION
Manuscript requirements: Chicago
  Preferred length: 15 to 20 pages
  Number of copies to be submitted: 3
  Abstract: Yes
Author information and reprints: Payment: None.
  Is simultaneous submission of article to other journals permitted: Permitted, but not encouraged.
  Exclusive manuscript rights between acceptance and publication: Yes
  Copyright: Held by publication.
Additional information: Please include a brief biographical sketch.
Disposition of manuscript:
  Query letter: Necessary.
  Receipt of manuscript acknowledged: Yes
  Decision to publish in: 60 days
  Accepted manuscript published in: 60 days
  Rejected manuscript returned: Yes, if return postage is supplied by author.
  Rejected manuscript criticized: No
Submit to:
  J. Deotis Roberts
  Editor
  (See address above)

JUDAISM [574]
A Quarterly Journal
15 East 84th Street
New York, New York 10028
(212) 879-4500 ext. 850

First published in 1952

SUBSCRIPTION DATA
Issues and rates: Published quarterly.
  Average paid circulation: 3,500
  Annual rate(s): $8.00, Foreign $9.00
Publisher or Sponsor: American Jewish Congress
Managing Editor: Ruth B. Waxman

EDITORIAL DESCRIPTION
  Dedicated to the creative discussion and exposition of the religious, moral and philosophical concepts of Judaism and their relevance to the problems of modern society.

MANUSCRIPT INFORMATION
Subject field(s): Anything relevant to Judaism
Manuscript requirements: No specific style guide.
  Preferred length: 5,500 words
  Number of copies to be submitted: One
Author information and reprints: Payment: None. 2 copies of the issue in which article appears and 25 reprints
  Is simultaneous submission of article to other journals permitted: No
  Exclusive manuscript rights between acceptance and publication: No
  Copyright: Held by publication.
  Reprints: Available, first 25 free
Disposition of manuscript:
  Query letter: No
  Receipt of manuscript acknowledged: Yes
  Decision to publish in: One month
  Accepted manuscript published in: 6 months
  Rejected manuscript returned: Yes
  Rejected manuscript criticized: Yes
Submit to:
  Editor
  (See address above)

LEXINGTON THEOLOGICAL QUARTERLY [575]
631 South Limestone Street
Lexington, Kentucky 40508
(606) 252-0361 ext. 29

Religion and theology

SUBSCRIPTION DATA
Issues and rates: Published quarterly.
  Average paid circulation: 2400 controlled
Publisher or Sponsor: Lexington Theological Seminary
Managing Editor: William R. Barr

EDITORIAL DESCRIPTION
Contains essays having religious themes, or relating religious concepts or perspective to contemporary issues; scholarly, although generally not technical, in nature.
Articles per average issue: 3
Audience: Alumni of Lexington Seminary
  Manuscripts accepted in English

MANUSCRIPT INFORMATION
Subject field(s): Creative religious thought, reports of important developments within religion, reports of local experiments in developing a new religious life style, critiques of religious thought and institutions
Manuscript requirements: Chicago
  Preferred length: 16 pages
  Number of copies to be submitted: One
  Abstract: No
Author information and reprints: Payment: None.
  Is simultaneous submission of article to other journals permitted: No
  Exclusive manuscript rights between acceptance and publication: Yes
  Copyright: Held by author.
  Reprints: Available, 20 free to author
Additional information: All quoted or paraphrased material should be footnoted. A few lines of biographical information identifying the author are helpful.
Disposition of manuscript:
  Query letter: No
  Receipt of manuscript acknowledged: Yes
  Decision to publish in: Three weeks
  Accepted manuscript published in: Within six months
  Rejected manuscript returned: Yes
  Rejected manuscript criticized: Yes
Submit to:
  William R. Barr
  Editor
  (See address above)

SPECIAL STIPULATIONS
Most manuscripts are solicited, although unsolicited manuscripts are considered and evaluated by the Editorial Committee.

THE LIVING LIGHT [576]
An Interdisciplinary Review of Christian Education
1312 Massachusetts Avenue, N.W.
Washington, D.C. 20005
(202) 635-5705

First published in 1964

SUBSCRIPTION DATA
Issues and rates: Published quarterly.
  Annual rate(s): $8.00, Foreign $8.50
Publisher or Sponsor: United States Catholic Conference

EDITORIAL DESCRIPTION
Presents development and trends, reports on research, and encourages critical thinking in the field of religious education and pastoral action. Under Roman Catholic auspices, it seeks to promote dialogue with educators of other religious traditions as well as those in secular pursuits.
Articles per average issue: 10
Audience: Professional religious educators

MANUSCRIPT INFORMATION
Subject field(s): Religious education, theology, educational theory and practice
Manuscript requirements: See latest issue for style requirements.
  Preferred length: 3,000 to 4,000 words
  Number of copies to be submitted: One
  Abstract: No
Author information and reprints: Payment: By publication to author. $10.00 per page.
  Is simultaneous submission of article to other journals permitted: No
  Exclusive manuscript rights between acceptance and publication: Yes
  Copyright: Held by publication.
  Reprints: Not available.
Disposition of manuscript:
  Query letter: No
  Receipt of manuscript acknowledged: Yes
  Decision to publish in: 60 to 90 days
  Accepted manuscript published in: 60 to 90 days
  Rejected manuscript returned: Yes, if return postage is supplied by author.
  Rejected manuscript criticized: No
Submit to:
  Berard L. Marthaler
  Executive Editor
  Catholic University of America
  420 Michigan Avenue
  Washington, D.C. 20064

LOUVAIN STUDIES [577]
100 Naamsestraat
B-3000 Leuven, Belgium
016/21955

SUBSCRIPTION DATA
Issues and rates: Published semi-annually.
  Average paid circulation: 1500
  Annual rate(s): 150 Belgian francs, Foreign $3.00
Publisher or Sponsor: Catholic University of Louvain, Faculty of Theology
Managing Editor: Raymond F. Collins

EDITORIAL DESCRIPTION
Articles and reviews published reflect the spirit of theology at the University of Louvain, but it is not necessary that the authors be affiliated with the University.
  Abstract: 5-6
Audience: Students of theology, clergy
  Manuscripts accepted in English

MANUSCRIPT INFORMATION
Subject field(s): Theology, including systematic theology; biblical science; Christian ethics; ecclesiastical history; religious sociology; philosophy of religion
Manuscript requirements: Style sheet sent on request.
  Preferred length: 8000-11000 words; 15-20 pages
  Number of copies to be submitted: One
  Abstract: No
Author information and reprints: Payment: By publication to author. 1000 Belgian francs per article.
  Is simultaneous submission of article to other journals permitted: No
  Exclusive manuscript rights between acceptance and publication: Yes
  Copyright: Held by publication.
  Reprints: Available
Disposition of manuscript:
  Receipt of manuscript acknowledged: Yes
  Decision to publish in: 4-6 weeks
  Accepted manuscript published in: 8 months
  Rejected manuscript returned: Yes
  Rejected manuscript criticized: No
Submit to:
  Raymond F. Collins
  Managing Editor
  (See address above)

MAITREYA [578]
A Series on the Potential of Man's Inner Evolution
2045 Francisco Street
Berkeley, California 94709
(415) 549-3900

First published in 1969

SUBSCRIPTION DATA
Issues and rates: Published annually.
  Average paid circulation: 7,500
  Annual rate(s): $2.95
Managing Editor: Samuel Bercholz

EDITORIAL DESCRIPTION
Each volume of the series focuses on an aspect of the potential development of man's inner evolution.
Articles per average issue: 12-15
Audience: Teachers and students of comparative religion, psychology and consciousness
  Manuscripts accepted in English only

MANUSCRIPT INFORMATION
Subject field(s): Dependent on the theme of each particular volume.
Manuscript requirements: See latest issue for style requirements.
  Preferred length: 5-40 pages
  Number of copies to be submitted: 2
Author information and reprints: Payment: Dependent on agreement between publisher and author.
  Is simultaneous submission of article to other journals permitted: No
  Exclusive manuscript rights between acceptance and publication: Yes
  Copyright: Held by publication.
  Reprints: Available at cost

Additional information: Authors should inquire concerning the theme of future issues.
Disposition of manuscript:
Query letter: Recommended
Receipt of manuscript acknowledged: Yes
Decision to publish in: 1-3 months
Accepted manuscript published in: 3-8 months
Rejected manuscript returned: Yes, if self-addressed, stamped envelope is sent with manuscript.
Rejected manuscript criticized: Sometimes
Submit to:
Hazel Silber
Associate Editor
(See address above)

THE MENNONITE [579]
600 Shaftesbury Boulevard
Winnipeg, Manitoba, R3P OM4, Canada
(204) 888-6781

First published in 1885

SUBSCRIPTION DATA
Issues and rates: Published weekly.
Average paid circulation: 15,000
Annual rate(s): $5.50, Foreign $6.50
Publisher or Sponsor: Mennonite Church, General Conference

EDITORIAL DESCRIPTION
Publishes articles about happenings in the Mennonite Church as well as the church at large and the relationship of various political, social, and economic events to the Christian faith.
Articles per average issue: 2
Audience: Membership
Manuscripts accepted in English

MANUSCRIPT INFORMATION
Subject field(s): Current theological issues, social issues, family life, international understanding, meditations, poems, fiction
Manuscript requirements: Chicago; also *Manual of Style* published by Faith and Life Press, Newton, Kansas
Preferred length: 1000-1500 words
Number of copies to be submitted: One
Abstract: No
Author information and reprints: Payment: By publication to author. $.01-$.02 per word.
Is simultaneous submission of article to other journals permitted: Yes
Exclusive manuscript rights between acceptance and publication: No
Copyright: Not copyrighted
Reprints: Not available.
Disposition of manuscript:
Receipt of manuscript acknowledged: No
Decision to publish in: Two months
Accepted manuscript published in: 6-12 months
Rejected manuscript returned: Yes, if self-addressed, stamped envelope is sent with manuscript.
Rejected manuscript criticized: No

Submit to:
Larry Kehler
Editor
(See address above)

METANOIA [580]
An Independent Journal of Radical Lutheranism
2126 University Avenue
Dubuque, Iowa 52001

First published in 1969

SUBSCRIPTION DATA
Issues and rates: Published quarterly.
Annual rate(s): $3.00, Foreign $3.50
Managing Editor: Douglas C. Stange

EDITORIAL DESCRIPTION
Inculcates a point of view which follows most closely the Christian Socialist heritage. Seeks to restore a forum wherein privatism and apathy may be vigorously answered.
Articles per average issue: 4-7
Audience: Academic, religious, social activists
Manuscripts accepted in French, German, Spanish, English

MANUSCRIPT INFORMATION
Subject field(s): Religion, politics, society (social welfare)
Manuscript requirements: MLA
Preferred length: 1250-1500 words; 5-6 pages
Number of copies to be submitted: One
Abstract: No
Author information and reprints: Payment: None. 3 copies of the journal
Is simultaneous submission of article to other journals permitted: Yes
Exclusive manuscript rights between acceptance and publication: Yes
Copyright: Not copyrighted
Reprints: Available
Disposition of manuscript:
Query letter: No
Receipt of manuscript acknowledged: Yes
Decision to publish in: 2-3 weeks
Accepted manuscript published in: 6-9 months
Rejected manuscript returned: Yes
Rejected manuscript criticized: Sometimes
Submit to:
Douglas C. Stange
Editor
(See address above)

METHODIST HISTORY [581]
Box 488
Lake Junaluska, North Carolina 28745
(704) 456-9433

First published in 1962

SUBSCRIPTION DATA
Issues and rates: Published quarterly.
Average paid circulation: 700
Annual rate(s): $5.00
Publisher or Sponsor: United Methodist Church, Commission on Archives and History

EDITORIAL DESCRIPTION
Contains scholarly articles on Methodist history, not solely United Methodist.
Articles per average issue: 4-5
Audience: Scholarly community
Manuscripts accepted in English

MANUSCRIPT INFORMATION
Subject field(s): Methodist history, history of education, social action within Methodism, Methodist biography
Manuscript requirements: No specific style guide.
Preferred length: 5000 words; 10-15 pages
Number of copies to be submitted: One
Author information and reprints: Payment: None. Subscription to journal and 25 free reprints
Is simultaneous submission of article to other journals permitted: Yes
Exclusive manuscript rights between acceptance and publication: No
Copyright: Not copyrighted
Reprints: Not available.
Additional information: Typewritten, double-spaced manuscripts
Disposition of manuscript:
Query letter: Helpful, but not necessary
Receipt of manuscript acknowledged: Yes
Decision to publish in: 6 months
Accepted manuscript published in: 6-9 months
Rejected manuscript returned: Yes
Rejected manuscript criticized: Yes
Submit to:
John H. Ness
Editor
(See address above)

MONASTIC STUDIES [582]
Mount Saviour Monastery
Pine City, New York 14871

First published in 1963

SUBSCRIPTION DATA
Issues and rates: Irregular
Average paid circulation: 1000
Annual rate(s): $5.00 Brother Peter

EDITORIAL DESCRIPTION
Contains essays on monastic spirituality and life, chiefly of the Benedictine tradition of Western Christendom, but with contributions concerning Hindu and Buddhist traditions of the East.
Articles per average issue: 12
Audience: General
Manuscripts accepted in English, others considered for translation

MANUSCRIPT INFORMATION
Subject field(s): Spirituality, history, ecumenism, liturgy
Manuscript requirements: MLA
Preferred length: None
Number of copies to be submitted: 2
Abstract: No

Author information and reprints: Payment: None.
Is simultaneous submission of article to other journals permitted: No
Exclusive manuscript rights between acceptance and publication: Yes
Copyright: No
Reprints: Available 10 free
Additional information: Typewritten, double-spaced with footnotes and quotations at the end.
Disposition of manuscript:
Query letter: Yes
Receipt of manuscript acknowledged: Yes
Decision to publish in: One month
Accepted manuscript published in: Up to one year
Rejected manuscript returned: Yes, if self-addressed, stamped envelope is sent with manuscript.
Rejected manuscript criticized: Yes
Submit to: Brother Peter
Editor
(See address above)

THE MONTH [583]
A Review of Christian Thought and World Affairs
114 Mount Street
London W1Y 6AH, England
(01) 493-7811

First published in 1864

SUBSCRIPTION DATA
Issues and rates: Published monthly.
Average paid circulation: 5,600; 1,800 controlled
Annual rate(s): $15.00

EDITORIAL DESCRIPTION
Concerned with trends and events particularly affecting the Roman Catholic Church throughout the world. Contains articles on the relationships between theology and politics, sociology, psychology.
Articles per average issue: 5
Audience: General
Manuscripts accepted in English, French, German, Spanish

MANUSCRIPT INFORMATION
Subject field(s): Church events, theology, sociology, psychology, literature
Manuscript requirements: See latest issue for style requirements.
Preferred length: 3,000-4,000 words
Number of copies to be submitted: One
Abstract: No
Author information and reprints: Payment: By publication to author.
Is simultaneous submission of article to other journals permitted: No
Exclusive manuscript rights between acceptance and publication: Yes
Copyright: Held by publication.
Reprints: Available at cost.
Disposition of manuscript:
Receipt of manuscript acknowledged: No
Decision to publish in: 4-6 weeks
Accepted manuscript published in: 2-3 months

Rejected manuscript returned: Yes
Rejected manuscript criticized: Sometimes
Submit to:
Michael J. Walsh
Editor
(See address above)

NEW BLACKFRIARS [584]
Blackfriars
Oxford OX1 3LY, England
Oxford 57607

Previously entitled *Blackfriars*

First published in 1920

SUBSCRIPTION DATA
Issues and rates: Published monthly.
Average paid circulation: 2,000
Annual rate(s): $12.50, Foreign £3.90
Publisher or Sponsor: English Dominicans
Managing Editor: Rosemary Eagleton

EDITORIAL DESCRIPTION
Primarily a theological journal, but with special interests in the relationships between theology, culture and politics. A politically and theologically radical approach to issues and events with concern toward Christian faith and the Church as revolutionary challenge; criticism and commitment.
Articles per average issue: 5 articles; 5-8 reviews
Audience: Educated, general
Manuscripts accepted in English

MANUSCRIPT INFORMATION
Subject field(s): Theology, philosophy, politics, literature, other arts, sociology, anthropology
Manuscript requirements: No specific style guide.
Preferred length: 2,000-4,000 words
Number of copies to be submitted: One
Abstract: No
Author information and reprints: Payment: By publication to author. $15 per article.
Is simultaneous submission of article to other journals permitted: Yes, with editorial permission
Exclusive manuscript rights between acceptance and publication: Yes
Copyright: Held by publication.
Reprints: Not available.
Disposition of manuscript:
Query letter: No
Receipt of manuscript acknowledged: Yes
Decision to publish in: 1 month
Accepted manuscript published in: 4-6 months
Rejected manuscript returned: Yes, if return postage is supplied by author.
Rejected manuscript criticized: No
Submit to:
Herbert McCabe
(See address above)

OHIO JOURNAL OF RELIGIOUS STUDIES [585]
Department of Religious Studies
Cleveland State University
Cleveland, Ohio 44115
(216) 687-2170

First published in 1972

SUBSCRIPTION DATA
Issues and rates: Published semi-annually.
Average paid circulation: 1,200
Annual rate(s): $3.00; Institutions $3.00
Publisher or Sponsor: Ohio Academy of Religion
Managing Editor: Dr. Frederick Holck

EDITORIAL DESCRIPTION
Articles reflecting original scholarly research in any given area of religion
Articles per average issue: 5-7
Audience: Academic
Manuscripts accepted in English

MANUSCRIPT INFORMATION
Subject field(s): Biblical studies; history of Christianity and Judaism, Hinduism, Buddhism; myths, methodology, and philosophy of religion, etc.
Manuscript requirements: See latest issue for style requirements.
Preferred length: 15-20 pages
Number of copies to be submitted: 3
Abstract: Yes. Of one page
Author information and reprints: Payment: Reprints only. 10 free copies
Is simultaneous submission of article to other journals permitted: Permitted, but not encouraged.
Exclusive manuscript rights between acceptance and publication: Yes
Copyright: Held by publication. Exceptions are made
Reprints: Available at cost.
Disposition of manuscript:
Query letter: Not necessary, but advisable.
Receipt of manuscript acknowledged: Yes
Decision to publish in: 4-6 weeks
Accepted manuscript published in: 3-5 months
Rejected manuscript returned: Yes, if return postage is supplied by author.
Rejected manuscript criticized: Sometimes
Submit to:
Dr. Frederick Holck
Editor
(See address above)

PASTORAL COUNSELING [586]
2832 East Desert Cove Avenue
Phoenix, Arizona 85028
(602) 992-6185

First published in 1973

SUBSCRIPTION DATA
Issues and rates: Published quarterly.
Average paid circulation: 753
Annual rate(s): $5.00

Publisher or Sponsor: Christ Catholic Church, Diocese of Boston
Managing Editor: Karl Pruter

EDITORIAL DESCRIPTION

Every phase of practical theology, pastoral counseling, confession, hospital and sick calls, etc.
Articles per average issue: 5
Audience: Clergy of every denomination, and active laymen
Manuscripts accepted in English

MANUSCRIPT INFORMATION

Subject field(s): Pastoral care, counseling, confessions, specialized ministries to the aged, shut-in, young people, divorced, etc.
Manuscript requirements: No specific style guide.
  Preferred length: 1,500 words; 7 pages
  Number of copies to be submitted: 1
  Abstract: Not necessary.
Author information and reprints: Payment: None.
  Is simultaneous submission of article to other journals permitted: Permitted, but not encouraged.
  Exclusive manuscript rights between acceptance and publication: No
  Copyright: None
  Reprints: Not available.
Disposition of manuscript:
  Query letter: Not necessary.
  Receipt of manuscript acknowledged: Yes
  Decision to publish in: 2 weeks
  Accepted manuscript published in: 60 days
  Rejected manuscript returned: Yes, if return postage is supplied by author.
  Rejected manuscript criticized: Yes
Submit to:
  Fr. Karl Pruter
  Editor
  (See address above)

PASTORAL LIFE MAGAZINE [587]

The Magazine for Today's Ministry
St. Paul Monastery
Canfield, Ohio 44406
(216) 533-5503 ext. 37

First published in 1953

SUBSCRIPTION DATA

Issues and rates: Monthly except July
  Average paid circulation: 8,000
  Annual rate(s): $6.00; Foreign $7.00
Publisher or Sponsor: Society of St. Paul
Managing Editor: Victor L. Viberti

EDITORIAL DESCRIPTION

Focuses attention on the current problems, needs, issues and important activities related to all phases of pastoral work and life. Avoids academic treatments on abstract and controversial subjects.
Articles per average issue: 12
Audience: Clergy
  Manuscripts accepted in English

MANUSCRIPT INFORMATION

Subject field(s): Pastoral, theological, religious education, spiritual
Manuscript requirements: See latest issue for style requirements.
  Preferred length: 1000-3000 words; not to exceed 12 pages
  Number of copies to be submitted: One
  Abstract: Only upon request
Author information and reprints: Payment: By publication to author. $.03 per word.
  Is simultaneous submission of article to other journals permitted: No
  Exclusive manuscript rights between acceptance and publication: Yes
  Copyright: Held by publication.
  Reprints: Available, cost varies
Disposition of manuscript:
  Query letter: Preferred
  Receipt of manuscript acknowledged: Yes
  Decision to publish in: Two weeks
  Accepted manuscript published in: 2-4 months
  Rejected manuscript returned: Yes, if self-addressed, stamped envelope is sent with manuscript.
  Rejected manuscript criticized: Yes
Submit to:
  Victor L. Viberti
  Editor
  (See address above)

PERKINS JOURNAL [588]

Perkins School of Theology
Southern Methodist University
Dallas, Texas 75275
(214) 692-2209

Previously entitled *Perkins School of Theology Journal*

First published in 1947

SUBSCRIPTION DATA

Issues and rates: Published quarterly.
  Average paid circulation: 7,800 controlled

EDITORIAL DESCRIPTION

A vehicle for communicating with alumni and friends of Perkins, and ministers and teachers on matters of current theological concern which are important to the Church's ministry.
Articles per average issue: 4
Audience: United Methodist clergy of the South Central Jurisdiction
  Manuscripts accepted in English

MANUSCRIPT INFORMATION

Subject field(s): The ministry, theology, Bible, ethics, historical theology, religion
Manuscript requirements: No specific style guide.
  Preferred length: 3000-5000 words
  Number of copies to be submitted: Two
  Abstract: No
Author information and reprints: Payment: None.
  Is simultaneous submission of article to other journals permitted: Yes
  Exclusive manuscript rights between acceptance and publication: yes
  Copyright: Held by publication.
  Reprints: Available
Additional information: Typewritten, double-spaced manuscripts
Disposition of manuscript:
  Query letter: No
  Receipt of manuscript acknowledged: Yes
  Decision to publish in: One month
  Accepted manuscript published in: Six months
  Rejected manuscript returned: Yes
  Rejected manuscript criticized: Yes
Submit to:
  Leroy T. Howe
  Editor
  (See address above)

PRACTICAL PAPERS FOR THE BIBLE TRANSLATOR [589]

Bible Society in Australia
P.O. Box 507
Canberra City ACT 2601, Australia

First published in 1950

SUBSCRIPTION DATA

Issues and rates: April and October
  Average paid circulation: 2,500
  Annual rate(s): £.50; Foreign $1.25
Publisher or Sponsor: United Bible Societies

EDITORIAL DESCRIPTION

Contains articles and book reviews on biblical and linguistic subjects relevant to the work of Bible translation.
Articles per average issue: 8
Audience: Translators
  Manuscripts accepted in English

MANUSCRIPT INFORMATION

Subject field(s): Theory and practice of translation, Biblical studies, history of Bible translation, general linguistics
Manuscript requirements: Style sheet sent on request.
  Preferred length: 4000-5000 words; 8-10 pages
  Number of copies to be submitted: Two
  Abstract: No
Author information and reprints: Payment: Reprints only. 12 offprints of the article
  Is simultaneous submission of article to other journals permitted: Permission to be obtained in advance from editor
  Exclusive manuscript rights between acceptance and publication: Yes
  Copyright: Held by publication.
  Reprints: Not available.
Additional information: The contributor is asked to indicate whether American or British spelling is preferred. Greek and Hebrew quotations are transliterated.
Disposition of manuscript:
  Receipt of manuscript acknowledged: Yes
  Decision to publish in: 1-2 months
  Accepted manuscript published in: 6-12 months
  Rejected manuscript returned: Yes
  Rejected manuscript criticized: Yes
Submit to:
  Rev. E. McG. Fry
  Editor
  (See address above)

Religion and theology

THE PRIEST [590]
Noll Plaza
Huntington, Indiana 46750
(219) 356-8400 ext. 332

Previously entitled *The Acolyte*

First published in 1925

SUBSCRIPTION DATA
Issues and rates: Published monthly.
   Average paid circulation: 10,244
   Annual rate(s): $7.00, Foreign $8.00
Managing Editor: Paul A. Manoski

EDITORIAL DESCRIPTION
   Publishes articles which are primarily of interest and help to the Roman Catholic clergy and seminarians: articles in dogmatic and moral theology, pastoral theology, spiritual life, human interest and humorous situations.

MANUSCRIPT INFORMATION
Subject field(s): Priestly ministry, pastoral problems, moral theology, spirituality, liturgy, homiletics, applied psychology, sociology, humor
Manuscript requirements: Chicago
   Preferred length: 2,000 words; 8 pages
   Number of copies to be submitted: One
Author information and reprints: Payment: By publication to author. $.02 per word. $5.00 per page.
   Is simultaneous submission of article to other journals permitted: No
   Exclusive manuscript rights between acceptance and publication: Yes
   Copyright: Held by publication.
   Reprints: Not available.
Disposition of manuscript:
   Receipt of manuscript acknowledged: Yes
   Decision to publish in: 2 weeks
   Accepted manuscript published in: 4 to 6 months
   Rejected manuscript returned: Yes
   Rejected manuscript criticized: No
Submit to:
   Jordan Aumann
   Editor
   1111 North Richmond Street
   Chicago, Illinois 60622
   (312) 276-1111

RCDA: RELIGION IN COMMUNIST DOMINATED AREAS [591]
475 Riverside Drive, Suite 452
New York, New York 10027
(212) 870-2481

First published in 1962

SUBSCRIPTION DATA
Issues and rates: Published bi-monthly
   Average paid circulation: 1,000
   Annual rate(s): $15.00

Publisher or Sponsor: Research Center for Religion and Human Rights in Closed Societies, Ltd.

EDITORIAL DESCRIPTION
   Publishes and analyses information on the attitudes and practices of Communist Parties with respect to the life, work and vital concerns of believers in Communist countries. Particular attention is given to the violation of religious freedom and other human rights in all closed societies.
Articles per average issue: 10-15
Audience: Academic, organizational, general
   Manuscripts accepted in English, French, German, all languages of the communist countries

MANUSCRIPT INFORMATION
Subject field(s): Violation of religious freedom and other human rights in Communist and other totalitarian countries; Church-State relations, Christian-Marxist dialogue
Manuscript requirements: See latest issue for style requirements.
   Preferred length: 2,000 to 8,000 words
   Number of copies to be submitted: Three
   Abstract: Yes
Author information and reprints: Payment: None. Complimentary copies to author
   Is simultaneous submission of article to other journals permitted: Yes
   Exclusive manuscript rights between acceptance and publication: No
   Copyright: Held by author.
   Reprints: Not available.
Additional information: Articles written in English or previously translated have priority.
Disposition of manuscript:
   Receipt of manuscript acknowledged: Yes
   Decision to publish in: Six months
   Accepted manuscript published in: Six to eight months
   Rejected manuscript returned: Yes, if self-addressed, stamped envelope is sent with manuscript.
   Rejected manuscript criticized: No
Submit to:
   Blahoslav Hrubéy
   Editor
   (See address above)
   (212) 663-6771

REFORMED REVIEW [592]
A Journal of the Seminaries of the Reformed Church in America
Western Theological Seminary
86 East 12th Street
Holland, Michigan 49423
(616) 392-8555 ext. 26

Previously entitled *Western Seminary Review*

First published in 1947

SUBSCRIPTION DATA
Issues and rates: Published three times per year.
   Average paid circulation: 300; 1,800 controlled
   Annual rate(s): $3.00

Publisher or Sponsor: The Reformed Church in America, Theological Seminaries

EDITORIAL DESCRIPTION
   Contains articles of a theological and ecclesiastical nature; book reviews of theological and religious books. Seeks to set forth the historic Christian faith as understood within the Reformed tradition.
Articles per average issue: 4
Audience: Ministers, laymen
   Manuscripts accepted in English

MANUSCRIPT INFORMATION
Subject field(s): Theology, plight of man, religion, social needs
Manuscript requirements: Chicago
   Preferred length: 3,000-7,000 words
   Number of copies to be submitted: One
   Abstract: No
Author information and reprints: Payment: None.
   Is simultaneous submission of article to other journals permitted: Yes
   Exclusive manuscript rights between acceptance and publication: No
   Copyright: Not copyrighted
   Reprints: Entire issue available
Additional information: Typewritten, double-spaced manuscripts
Disposition of manuscript:
   Query letter: No
   Receipt of manuscript acknowledged: Yes
   Decision to publish in: 1 month
   Accepted manuscript published in: 6 months
   Rejected manuscript returned: Yes, if return postage is supplied by author.
   Rejected manuscript criticized: Yes
Submit to:
   M. Eugene Osterhaven
   Editor
   (See address above)

RELIGION AND SOCIETY [593]
St. Croix Review
Box 244
Stillwater, Minnesota 55082
(612) 439-7190

Previously entitled *Religion and Society*

First published in 1968

SUBSCRIPTION DATA
Issues and rates: Published semi-monthly.
   Average paid circulation: 500; 2000 controlled
   Annual rate(s): $10.00
Publisher or Sponsor: Religion and Society, Inc.
Managing Editor: Angus McDonald

EDITORIAL DESCRIPTION
   Contains articles which have a bearing on contemporary moral problems. Advocates "sound" economics and moral freedom.
Articles per average issue: 6
Audience: Upper income
   Manuscripts accepted in English

MANUSCRIPT INFORMATION
Manuscript requirements: Chicago
  Preferred length: 10-12 pages
  Number of copies to be submitted: One
  Rejected manuscript returned: No
Author information and reprints: Payment: None.
  Is simultaneous submission of article to other journals permitted: Yes
  Exclusive manuscript rights between acceptance and publication: Yes
  Copyright: Held by publication.
  Reprints: Sometimes available
Disposition of manuscript:
  Query letter: No
  Receipt of manuscript acknowledged: No
  Decision to publish in: Less than 2 weeks
  Accepted manuscript published in: Up to 12 months
  Rejected manuscript returned: Yes, if self-addressed, stamped envelope is sent with manuscript.
  Rejected manuscript criticized: Sometimes
Submit to:
  Editor
  (See address above)

RELIGIOUS HUMANISM [594]
105 West North College Street
P.O. Box 278
Yellow Springs, Ohio 45387
(513) 767-1324

First published in 1966

SUBSCRIPTION DATA
Issues and rates: Published quarterly.
  Average paid circulation: 1500
  Annual rate(s): $5.00
Publisher or Sponsor: Fellowship of Religious Humanists
Managing Editor: Robert S. Hoagland

EDITORIAL DESCRIPTION
  To provide a forum for liberal religious, naturalistic and humanistic points of view.
Articles per average issue: 10
Audience: Naturalistic humanists
  Manuscripts accepted in English

MANUSCRIPT INFORMATION
Subject field(s): Religion, philosophy, history, sociology, science, etc.
Manuscript requirements: See latest issue for style requirements.
  Preferred length: 6 to 10 pages
  Number of copies to be submitted: One
  Abstract: No
Author information and reprints: Payment: None.
  Is simultaneous submission of article to other journals permitted: No
  Exclusive manuscript rights between acceptance and publication: Yes
  Copyright: Held by publication.
  Reprints: Available at printer's cost
Additional information: No footnotes or bibliography.
Disposition of manuscript:
  Query letter: No
  Receipt of manuscript acknowledged: Yes
  Decision to publish in: 2 weeks
  Accepted manuscript published in: 3 months
  Rejected manuscript returned: Yes, if self-addressed, stamped envelope is sent with manuscript.
  Rejected manuscript criticized: Sometimes
Submit to:
  Robert S. Hoagland
  Editor
  218 North Blackhawk Avenue
  Madison, Wisconsin 53705
  (608) 238-3954

THE REVIEW OF BOOKS AND RELIGION [595]
Box 86
White River Junction, Vermont 05001
(802) 295-5323

SUBSCRIPTION DATA
Issues and rates: Published monthly.
  Average paid circulation: 2,500
  Annual rate(s): $5.00; Foreign $5.00; Institutions $5.00

EDITORIAL DESCRIPTION
  A comprehensive review medium covering books in religion and related fields; focus is on objectivity about religion, yet positive; ecumenical, yet appreciative of distinctive traditions; the style is lively, yet searching; trenchant, yet urbane
Articles per average issue: 40-50 reviews
Audience: Academic, religious, lay
  Manuscripts accepted in English

MANUSCRIPT INFORMATION
Subject field(s): Religion, philosophy, sociology, general interdisciplinary studies, books, humanities
Manuscript requirements: No specific style guide. See latest issue for style requirements.
  Preferred length: 450-950 words
  Number of copies to be submitted: Original and 1 carbon copy
  Abstract: Not necessary.
Author information and reprints: Payment: Reprints only. 2 copies
  Is simultaneous submission of article to other journals permitted: Not permitted.
  Exclusive manuscript rights between acceptance and publication: Yes
  Copyright: Held by publication.
  Reprints: Available at cost.
Additional information: Most of the reviews are solicited by the editors.
Disposition of manuscript:
  Query letter: Not necessary.
  Receipt of manuscript acknowledged: No
  Decision to publish in: 1 month
  Accepted manuscript published in: 3 months
  Rejected manuscript returned: Yes, with return postage paid by publication.
  Rejected manuscript criticized: Sometimes
Submit to:
  Iris V. Cully;
  Kendig Brubaker Cully
  Editors
  (See address above)

REVIEW OF RELIGIOUS RESEARCH [596]
P. O. Box 228, Cathedral Station
New York, New York 10025
(414) 224-6846

SUBSCRIPTION DATA
Issues and rates: Published three times per year.
  Average paid circulation: 1,050; 50 controlled
  Annual rate(s): $11.00
Publisher or Sponsor: The Religious Research Association, Inc.
Managing Editor: Michael McCloskey

EDITORIAL DESCRIPTION
  Contains articles pertaining to religion and the social sciences; church planning; reviews of religious research; book reviews pertaining to the areas of religion and general social science; church planning abstracts.

MANUSCRIPT INFORMATION
Subject field(s): Sociology of religion, church planning and church planning studies, psychology of religion, religion and the social sciences
Manuscript requirements: ASA
  Preferred length: 4,000 words or up to 16 pages
  Number of copies to be submitted: Three
Author information and reprints: Payment: None.
  Is simultaneous submission of article to other journals permitted: No
  Exclusive manuscript rights between acceptance and publication: Yes
  Copyright: Held by publication.
  Reprints: Available
Disposition of manuscript:
  Receipt of manuscript acknowledged: Yes
  Decision to publish in: 45-90 days
  Accepted manuscript published in: 3-6 months
  Rejected manuscript returned: Yes
  Rejected manuscript criticized: Yes
Submit to:
  Richard D. Knudten
  Editor
  Department of Sociology and Anthropology
  Marquette University
  Milwaukee, Wisconsin 53233

SEPHARDIC SCHOLAR [597]
American Society of Sephardic Studies,
Yeshiva University
500 West 185th Street
New York, New York 10033
(212) 568-8400

Previously entitled *Journal of the American Society of Sephardic Studies*

First published in 1968

Religion and theology

SUBSCRIPTION DATA
Issues and rates: Bi-annually
  Average paid circulation: 1,200
  Annual rate(s): Individuals $5.00
Publisher or Sponsor: Yeshiva University, Sephardic Studies Program
Managing Editor: Dr. Rachel Dalven

EDITORIAL DESCRIPTION
Contains articles of Sephardic heritage and languages for academicians.
Articles per average issue: 6-8
Audience: Academicians
  Manuscripts accepted in English, French, Spanish

MANUSCRIPT INFORMATION
Subject field(s): Sephardic social, linguistic, and cultural backgrounds, as well as its contributions to other cultures
Manuscript requirements: See latest issue for style requirements.
  Preferred length: No preference
  Number of copies to be submitted: 3
  Abstract: Not necessary.
Author information and reprints: Payment: None.
  Is simultaneous submission of article to other journals permitted: Please contact the publication concerning submission to other periodicals
  Exclusive manuscript rights between acceptance and publication: Yes
  Copyright: Held by publication.
  Reprints: Not available.
Disposition of manuscript:
  Query letter: Necessary.
  Receipt of manuscript acknowledged: Yes
  Decision to publish in: 4 weeks
  Accepted manuscript published in: 1 year
  Rejected manuscript returned: Yes, if return postage is supplied by author.
  Rejected manuscript criticized: No
Submit to:
  Dr. Rachel Dalven
  Managing Editor
  (See address above)

SISTERS TODAY [598]
St. John's Abbey
Collegeville, Minnesota 56321
(612) 363-2643

SUBSCRIPTION DATA
Issues and rates: Monthly except July and August
  Average paid circulation: 20,851
  Annual rate(s): $5.00, Foreign $5.50
Publisher or Sponsor: St. John's Abbey, Collegeville, Minnesota
Managing Editor: Daniel Durken

EDITORIAL DESCRIPTION
Contains articles on various aspects of religious life for Roman Catholic religious women (sisters and nuns). Topics such as community life; the religious vows of poverty, chastity and obedience. A balance between liberal and conservative positions is hopefully maintained while an effort is made to further the continual renewal of religious life according to the teachings of the Catholic Church.
Articles per average issue: 5
Audience: Sisters, nuns
  Manuscripts accepted in English only

MANUSCRIPT INFORMATION
Subject field(s): Prayer and worship, community life, the vows, Scriptural comments, new apostolates, old apostolates renewed
Manuscript requirements: See latest issue for style requirements.
  Preferred length: 8-12 pages; typewritten, double-spaced
  Number of copies to be submitted: One
  Abstract: No
Author information and reprints: Payment: By publication to author. $5.00 per page.
  Is simultaneous submission of article to other journals permitted: No
  Exclusive manuscript rights between acceptance and publication: Yes
  Copyright: None
  Reprints: Not available.
Additional information: Articles by free-lance writers who are unfamiliar with religious women's life as it is being lived today are rarely acceptable. Poetry is not needed at this time due to backlog of unpublished poems.
Disposition of manuscript:
  Query letter: Not necessary, but helpful
  Receipt of manuscript acknowledged: Yes
  Decision to publish in: 1-12 months
  Accepted manuscript published in: 1-12 months or longer
  Rejected manuscript returned: Yes, if self-addressed, stamped envelope is sent with manuscript.
  Rejected manuscript criticized: No
Submit to:
  Daniel Durken
  Editor
  (See address above)

SOCIOLOGICAL ANALYSIS [599]
A Journal in the Sociology of Religion
Roger D. Irle, Executive Secretary
Association for the Sociology of Religion
Northern Illinois University
De Kalb, Illinois 60115
(815) 753-0694

SUBSCRIPTION DATA
Issues and rates: Published quarterly.
  Average paid circulation: 1175; 1300 controlled
  Annual rate(s): $15.00, Foreign $17.00
Publisher or Sponsor: Association for the Sociology of Religion

EDITORIAL DESCRIPTION
Publishes sociological and anthropological research, theory, comparative analyses in the field of religion. The journal seeks studies that attend to both historical and contemporary materials within a sociological framework broadly defined. Thus religion is explored, analysed and explained in a variety of contexts and cultures.

MANUSCRIPT INFORMATION
Subject field(s): Religious research, social theory of religion, religion and politics, religion and values, religious careers, institutions, myths, symbols, religious consciousness
Manuscript requirements: Style sheet sent on request.
  Preferred length: 10,000 words; 40 pages maximum
  Number of copies to be submitted: Two
  Abstract: No
Author information and reprints: Payment: None.
  Is simultaneous submission of article to other journals permitted: No
  Exclusive manuscript rights between acceptance and publication: Yes
  Copyright: Held by publication.
  Reprints: Available, consult editor
Additional information: Manuscripts should be according to style, with footnotes, references, tables and charts on separate pages. Figures should be prepared for submission to printer. Author's name and affiliation should appear only on a separate cover page so articles can be sent out anonymously for editorial evaluation.
Disposition of manuscript:
  Receipt of manuscript acknowledged: Yes
  Decision to publish in: Four weeks
  Accepted manuscript published in: Six months
  Rejected manuscript returned: Yes
  Rejected manuscript criticized: Yes
Submit to:
  Carroll J. Bourg
  Editor
  Department of Sociology
  Box 813, Fisk University
  Nashville, Tennessee 37203

SPIRITUAL LIFE [600]
A Quarterly of Contemporary Spirituality
2131 Lincoln Road, N.E.
Washington, D.C. 20002
(202) 832-6622

SUBSCRIPTION DATA
Issues and rates: Published quarterly.
  Average paid circulation: 12,200; 14,100 controlled
  Annual rate(s): $4.00, Foreign $4.50
Publisher or Sponsor: Washington Province of Discalced Carmelite Fathers, Inc.
Managing Editor: Christopher Latimer

EDITORIAL DESCRIPTION
Publishes high quality articles about man's encounter with God in the present-day world. Articles reflecting a wide range of religious and philosophical beliefs are published.
Articles per average issue: 8
Audience: Those interested in spiritual theology
  Manuscripts accepted in English, French, German, Spanish, Italian

MANUSCRIPT INFORMATION
Subject field(s): Spiritual theology, religious life, lay spirituality

Manuscript requirements: Chicago
Preferred length: 3,000-5,000 words, typewritten, double-spaced
Number of copies to be submitted: One
Abstract: Not necessarily
Author information and reprints: Payment: By publication to author. $50.00 to $100.00 per article.
Is simultaneous submission of article to other journals permitted: No
Exclusive manuscript rights between acceptance and publication: Yes
Copyright: Held by author.
Reprints: Not available.
Additional information: Author may have reprints made at his own expense.
Disposition of manuscript:
Query letter: No
Receipt of manuscript acknowledged: No
Decision to publish in: Two weeks
Accepted manuscript published in: Six months
Rejected manuscript returned: Yes, if self-addressed, stamped envelope is sent with manuscript.
Rejected manuscript criticized: No
Submit to:
Christopher Latimer
Editor
(See address above)

SPECIAL STIPULATIONS
Sample copy of magazine plus guidelines sent upon request to prospective authors.

THE SPRINGFIELDER [601]
Concordia Theological Seminary
Springfield, Illinois 62702
(217) 544-7401

First published in 1937

SUBSCRIPTION DATA
Issues and rates: Published quarterly.
Average paid circulation: 8,400
Publisher or Sponsor: Concordia Theological Seminary
Managing Editor: David P. Scaer

EDITORIAL DESCRIPTION
Contains theological articles written for use by the parish pastors of the Missouri Synod and the Lutheran Church in general; articles deal with union negotiations in world Lutheranism and with current exegetical problems.
Articles per average issue: 5
Audience: Pastors of the Missouri Synod
Manuscripts accepted in English

MANUSCRIPT INFORMATION
Subject field(s): Contemporary theology, Biblical studies, Lutheranism today, European Church developments, problems in the Missouri Synod, Martin Luther, Lutheran confessions, ecumenical theology
Manuscript requirements: Chicago
Preferred length: 1250-2500 words; 5-10 pages
Number of copies to be submitted: Three
Abstract: No

Author information and reprints: Payment: None.
Is simultaneous submission of article to other journals permitted: No
Exclusive manuscript rights between acceptance and publication: No
Copyright: None
Reprints: Not available.
Disposition of manuscript:
Query letter: No
Receipt of manuscript acknowledged: Yes
Decision to publish in: 6-12 months
Accepted manuscript published in: 12 months
Rejected manuscript returned: Yes
Rejected manuscript criticized: No
Submit to:
David P. Scaer
Editor
(See address above)

TECHNICAL PAPERS FOR THE BIBLE TRANSLATOR [602]
United Bible Societies
146 Queen Victoria Street
London EC4B 4BX, England
(01) 248-4751

Previously entitled *The Bible Translator*

First published in 1950

SUBSCRIPTION DATA
Issues and rates: January and July
Average paid circulation: 2,500
Annual rate(s): £1.00, Foreign $2.50
Publisher or Sponsor: United Bible Societies

EDITORIAL DESCRIPTION
Contains articles and book reviews on Biblical and linguistic subjects relevant to the work of Bible translation.
Articles per average issue: 6-7; and reviews
Audience: Translators, scholars
Manuscripts accepted in English (French, German)

MANUSCRIPT INFORMATION
Subject field(s): Theory and practice of translation, applied linguistics, Biblical studies, history of Bible translation, general linguistics
Manuscript requirements: Style sheet sent on request.
Preferred length: 4000-5000 words; 8-10 pages
Number of copies to be submitted: Two
Abstract: No
Author information and reprints: Payment: Reprints only. 12 offprints
Is simultaneous submission of article to other journals permitted: If permission is obtained in advance from editor.
Exclusive manuscript rights between acceptance and publication: Yes
Copyright: Held by publication.
Reprints: Not available.
Additional information: Contributor is asked to indicate whether American or British spelling is preferred.
Disposition of manuscript:
Query letter: No
Receipt of manuscript acknowledged: Yes
Decision to publish in: 1-2 months
Accepted manuscript published in: 6-12 months
Rejected manuscript returned: Yes
Rejected manuscript criticized: Yes
Submit to:
P. Ellingworth
Editor
(See address above)

THEOLOGICAL STUDIES [603]
3520 Prospect Street, N.W., Room 401
Washington, D.C. 20007
(202) 338-0754

First published in 1940

SUBSCRIPTION DATA
Issues and rates: Published quarterly.
Average paid circulation: 6,800; 7,100 controlled
Annual rate(s): $8.00, Foreign $8.50
Managing Editor: Joseph N. Tylenda

EDITORIAL DESCRIPTION
Contains scholarly research in various theological and related disciplines.
Articles per average issue: 7
Audience: Theologians, clergy, laity with some theological background
Manuscripts accepted in English

MANUSCRIPT INFORMATION
Subject field(s): Systematic theology, historical theology, biblical theology, pastoral theology
Manuscript requirements: Style sheet sent on request.
Preferred length: Articles: 5,000-20,000 words; notes: 1,500-5,000 words
Number of copies to be submitted: One
Abstract: Optional
Author information and reprints: Payment: None.
Is simultaneous submission of article to other journals permitted: No
Exclusive manuscript rights between acceptance and publication: Yes
Copyright: Held by publication.
Reprints: Available; 100 copies free to author.
Additional information: Entire manuscript (including footnotes and long quotations within text) must be typewritten, double-spaced.
Disposition of manuscript:
Query letter: No
Receipt of manuscript acknowledged: Yes
Decision to publish in: 2 to 6 weeks
Accepted manuscript published in: 3 to 9 months
Rejected manuscript returned: Yes
Rejected manuscript criticized: Sometimes
Submit to:
Walter J. Burghardt
Editor-in-Chief
(See address above)

Religion and theology

UNION SEMINARY QUARTERLY REVIEW [604]
3041 Broadway
New York, New York 10027
(212) 662-7100 ext. 343

SUBSCRIPTION DATA
Issues and rates: Published quarterly.
  Average paid circulation: 1200; 7600 controlled
  Annual rate(s): $7.00
Publisher or Sponsor: Union Theological Seminary

EDITORIAL DESCRIPTION
  A scholarly, ecumenical journal of theology, containing articles and book reviews which focus on the biblical, historical, and theological foundations of Christian faith, and on the church in contemporary society.
Articles per average issue: 3
Audience: Clergy, seminarians, informed laypeople, libraries
  Manuscripts accepted in English

MANUSCRIPT INFORMATION
Subject field(s): Theology, ethics, biblical studies, church history, Jewish-Christian dialogue, psychiatry and religion, religion and the arts
Manuscript requirements: No specific style guide.
  Preferred length: 10-20 pages
  Number of copies to be submitted: One
  Abstract: No
Author information and reprints: Payment: None.
  Is simultaneous submission of article to other journals permitted: No
  Exclusive manuscript rights between acceptance and publication: Yes
  Copyright: Held by author.
  Reprints: Available, on request
Additional information: Unsolicited manuscripts must be accompanied by stamped, self-addressed envelope.
Disposition of manuscript:
  Receipt of manuscript acknowledged: Yes
  Decision to publish in: 12-15 weeks
  Accepted manuscript published in: 6-10 months
  Rejected manuscript returned: Yes, if self-addressed, stamped envelope is sent with manuscript.
  Rejected manuscript criticized: Yes
Submit to:
  Mark A. Zier
  Editor
  (See address above)

ZYGON [605]
Journal of Religion and Science
University of Chicago Press
5801 Ellis Avenue
Chicago, Illinois 60637
(312) 753-2592

First published in 1966

SUBSCRIPTION DATA
Issues and rates: Published quarterly.
  Average paid circulation: 1350
  Annual rate(s): $10.00; Institutions $14.00; Foreign $11.00; Foreign institutions $15.00
Publisher or Sponsor: Institute on Religion in an Age of Science, Center for Advanced Study in Religion and Science

EDITORIAL DESCRIPTION
  Articles revolve around attempts to reach a better understanding on scientific grounds of the various theological and philosophical questions
Articles per average issue: 5
Audience: Academic, clergy, educators, laymen
  Manuscripts accepted in English only

MANUSCRIPT INFORMATION
Subject field(s): Man's origins, history, nature, and destiny in the cosmos, life and death, freedom and responsibility, right and wrong, good and evil, salvation and sin, reward and punishment, valid bases for improving man's awareness, feelings, motivations, and beliefs about matters most sacred to him.
Manuscript requirements: Chicago
  Preferred length: 1-100 pages
  Number of copies to be submitted: Three
  Abstract: Yes
Author information and reprints: Payment: None.
  Is simultaneous submission of article to other journals permitted: Yes
  Exclusive manuscript rights between acceptance and publication: Yes
  Copyright: Held by publication.
  Reprints: Available at cost
Additional information: Typewritten, double-spaced, with ample margins
Disposition of manuscript:
  Query letter: No
  Receipt of manuscript acknowledged: Yes
  Decision to publish in: Varies
  Accepted manuscript published in: Varies
  Rejected manuscript returned: Yes
  Rejected manuscript criticized: No
Submit to:
  Ralph Wendell Burhoe
  Editor
  1524 East 59th Street
  Chicago, Illinois 60637
  (312) 753-3163

Interdisciplinary and area studies

Interdisciplinary

ANTARCTIC JOURNAL OF THE UNITED STATES [606]
National Science Foundation
Polar Information Service
Washington, D.C. 20550
(202) 632-4076

First published in 1966

SUBSCRIPTION DATA
Issues and rates: Published bi-monthly.
  Average paid circulation: 4,000; 1,500 controlled
  Annual rate(s): $6.50, Foreign $8.25
Publisher or Sponsor: National Science Foundation

EDITORIAL DESCRIPTION
  Contains articles on U.S. activities in Antarctica, related activities elsewhere, and trends in the U.S. antarctic research program.
Articles per average issue: 20
Audience: Scientists, administrators, public
  Manuscripts accepted in English

MANUSCRIPT INFORMATION
Subject field(s): Physical sciences, social and medical sciences, technology, logistics, political science, international cooperation, history
Manuscript requirements: GPO
  Preferred length: 2 to 20 pages
  Number of copies to be submitted: Three
  Abstract: No
Author information and reprints: Payment: None.
  Is simultaneous submission of article to other journals permitted: No
  Exclusive manuscript rights between acceptance and publication: Yes
  Copyright: No copyright
  Reprints: Available
Additional information: Photographs and drawings accepted.
Disposition of manuscript:
  Query letter: No
  Receipt of manuscript acknowledged: Yes
  Decision to publish in: 1 month
  Accepted manuscript published in: 3 months
  Rejected manuscript returned: Yes
  Rejected manuscript criticized: Yes
Submit to:
  Guy G. Guthridge
  Director
  (See address above)

ARCTIC AND ALPINE RESEARCH [607]
Institute of Arctic and Alpine Research
University of Colorado
Boulder, Colorado 80302
(303) 492-6387

First published in 1969

SUBSCRIPTION DATA
Issues and rates: Published quarterly.
  Annual rate(s): Institutions $20.00, Individuals $12.00, Students $8.00
Publisher or Sponsor: University of Colorado, Institute of Arctic and Alpine Research
Managing Editor: Kathleen A. Salzberg

EDITORIAL DESCRIPTION
  Contains original research papers, resulting correspondence, and short notes dealing with any scientific or cultural aspect of arctic and alpine environments and related topics on the subarctic and subalpine and the Pleistocene era.
Articles per average issue: 8-9
Audience: Postgraduate, research
  Manuscripts accepted in English

MANUSCRIPT INFORMATION
Subject field(s): Geology, geography, glaciology, biology, ecology, meteorology, climatology, archaeology, sociology, history
Manuscript requirements: Style sheet sent on request.
  Preferred length: 4,000-5,000 words; 15-20 pages
  Number of copies to be submitted: Two
  Abstract: Yes
Author information and reprints: Payment: By author to publication. $40.00 per page. Voluntary
  Is simultaneous submission of article to other journals permitted: No
  Exclusive manuscript rights between acceptance and publication: Yes
  Copyright: Held by publication.
  Reprints: Available, 50 free
Additional information: Manuscript should be in proper style with footnotes, references, tables and figures on separate pages. Two copies of all figures are required for review.
Disposition of manuscript:
  Query letter: No
  Receipt of manuscript acknowledged: Yes
  Decision to publish in: 4-8 weeks
  Accepted manuscript published in: 3-6 months
  Rejected manuscript returned: Yes
  Rejected manuscript criticized: Yes
Submit to:
  Kathleen A. Salzberg
  Editor
  (See address above)

ARCTIC BULLETIN [608]
Officer of Polar Programs
National Science Foundation
1800 G Street, N.W.
Washington, D.C. 20550
(202) 632-4076

First published in 1973

SUBSCRIPTION DATA
Issues and rates: Published quarterly.
  Average paid circulation: 1,500 controlled
Publisher or Sponsor: National Science Foundation, Interagency Arctic Research Coordinating Committee
Managing Editor: Jerry R. Stringer

EDITORIAL DESCRIPTION
  Contains information on federally funded or sponsored research in Alaska and the Arctic.
Articles per average issue: 6
Audience: Researchers
  Manuscripts accepted in English

MANUSCRIPT INFORMATION
Subject field(s): Federal Arctic research
Manuscript requirements: Style sheet sent on request.
  Preferred length: None
  Number of copies to be submitted: Three
  Abstract: No
Author information and reprints: Payment: None.
  Is simultaneous submission of article to other journals permitted: No, except in symposia compilations
  Exclusive manuscript rights between acceptance and publication: Yes
  Copyright: Not copyrighted
  Reprints: Not available.
Additional information: Summary and survey articles of federally sponsored or funded research rather than technical reports of research are desired. All should be typewritten, double-spaced.
Disposition of manuscript:
  Query letter: No
  Receipt of manuscript acknowledged: Yes
  Decision to publish in: 2-4 weeks
  Accepted manuscript published in: 3 months
  Rejected manuscript returned: Yes
  Rejected manuscript criticized: Sometimes
Submit to:
  Editor
  (See address above)

THE BLACK SCHOLAR [609]
Journal of Black Studies and Research
P.O. Box 908
Sausalito, California 94965
(415) 332-3130

SUBSCRIPTION DATA
Issues and rates: Monthly, except July and August
  Average paid circulation: 15,000
  Annual rate(s): $10.00
Publisher or Sponsor: Black World Foundation
Managing Editor: Robert L. Allen

EDITORIAL DESCRIPTION
  Publishes articles on political, economic, social and cultural topics of interest to black scholars and black activists. The journal serves as a forum for serious

discussion of various issues and theories within the black struggle.
Articles per average issue: 6
Audience: Academic
Manuscripts accepted in English

MANUSCRIPT INFORMATION
Subject field(s): Black studies, black psychology, black literature, black soldier, black politics, black prisoners, the black colony, black church, black writers, black culture, black labor, black women
Manuscript requirements: Style sheet sent on request.
  Preferred length: 8 to 25 pages
  Number of copies to be submitted: One
Author information and reprints: Payment: None. 10 copies of issue and a subscription to the journal.
  Is simultaneous submission of article to other journals permitted: No
  Exclusive manuscript rights between acceptance and publication: Yes
  Copyright: Held by publication.
  Reprints: Not available.
Disposition of manuscript:
  Query letter: Preferred
  Receipt of manuscript acknowledged: Yes
  Decision to publish in: 2 months
  Accepted manuscript published in: 2-5 months
  Rejected manuscript returned: Yes, if self-addressed, stamped envelope is sent with manuscript.
  Rejected manuscript criticized: Sometimes
Submit to:
  Robert Chrisman
  Editor
  (See address above)

SPECIAL STIPULATIONS
  Articles by non-black authors upon request only.

THE GERONTOLOGIST [610]
Gerontological Society
One Dupont Circle, Suite 520
Washington, D.C. 20036
(202) 659-4698

First published in 1961

SUBSCRIPTION DATA
Issues and rates: Published bi-monthly.
  Average paid circulation: 5,600
  Annual rate(s): $20.00
Publisher or Sponsor: Gerontological Society
Managing Editor: Marjorie Adler

EDITORIAL DESCRIPTION
  Contains articles of general interest; interprets and applies research to the field of practice; and keeps the reader abreast of developments in gerontology; special monographs.
Articles per average issue: 17
Audience: Professional
  Manuscripts accepted in English

MANUSCRIPT INFORMATION
Subject field(s): Biology, medicine, psychology and social sciences, social welfare
Manuscript requirements: APA
  Preferred length: Not to exceed 15 typewritten, double-spaced pages
  Number of copies to be submitted: 3
  Abstract: Yes, not to exceed 4 sentences. It should indicate the essence of the findings, methodology, and implications or relationship to professional practice.
Author information and reprints: Payment: None.
  Is simultaneous submission of article to other journals permitted: No
  Exclusive manuscript rights between acceptance and publication: Yes
  Copyright: Held by publication.
  Reprints: Available, price list sent with galley proof
Additional information: A maximum of two small tables or graphs is suggested for complete manuscript. Tables should be typed on separate sheets.
Disposition of manuscript:
  Query letter: No
  Receipt of manuscript acknowledged: Yes
  Rejected manuscript returned: Yes, if self-addressed, stamped envelope is sent with manuscript.
  Rejected manuscript criticized: No
Submit to:
  Jerome Kaplan
  Editor-in-Chief
  770 Dickson Parkway
  Mansfield, Ohio 44907
  (419) 524-4178

INTERNATIONAL AFFAIRS [611]
Oxford University Press
Press Road
Neasden, London NW10 0DD, England

First published in 1922

SUBSCRIPTION DATA
Issues and rates: Published quarterly.
  Annual rate(s): £5.00; Foreign $15.00 (U.S.A.)
Publisher or Sponsor: Royal Institute of International Affairs

EDITORIAL DESCRIPTION
  Contains original articles on matters of broad international interest from an economic, monetary and political viewpoint, as well as an extensive book review section covering both British and foreign publications
Articles per average issue: 6
Audience: Professional, governmental, legal, business, academic
  Manuscripts accepted in English

MANUSCRIPT INFORMATION
Manuscript requirements: See latest issue for style requirements. Style sheet sent on request.
  Preferred length: 4,000-6,000 words
  Number of copies to be submitted: 1
  Abstract: Not necessary.
Author information and reprints: Payment: By publication to author. £25.00-£40.00 per article.
  Is simultaneous submission of article to other journals permitted: Not permitted.
  Exclusive manuscript rights between acceptance and publication: Yes
  Copyright: Held jointly by the author and the publication
  Reprints: Available at cost.
Disposition of manuscript:
  Query letter: Not necessary, but advisable.
  Receipt of manuscript acknowledged: No
  Decision to publish in: 3 weeks
  Accepted manuscript published in: 3-6 months
  Rejected manuscript returned: Yes, with return postage paid by publication.
  Rejected manuscript criticized: Reasons for rejections only
Submit to:
  Wendy Hinde
  Editor
  Chatham House
  10 St. James' Square
  London SW1Y 4LE, England
  (01) 930-2233

INTERNATIONAL JOURNAL [612]
31 Wellesley Street East
Toronto, Ontario M4Y 1G9, Canada
(416) 923-7369

First published in 1946

SUBSCRIPTION DATA
Issues and rates: Published quarterly.
  Average paid circulation: 3,000
  Annual rate(s): $12.00; Foreign $12.00; Institutions $12.00; Students $5.00; Foreign institutions $12.00
Publisher or Sponsor: Canadian Institute of International Affairs

EDITORIAL DESCRIPTION
  To provide articles of interest to both the specialist and general reader. Each issue is centered on a broad theme, e.g. economy, diplomatic method, Pacific affairs, NATO.
Articles per average issue: 8-10
Audience: Academics and interested public
  Manuscripts accepted in English and French

MANUSCRIPT INFORMATION
Subject field(s): International affairs since 1914
Manuscript requirements: See latest issue for style requirements.
  Preferred length: 3,500-5,000 words
  Number of copies to be submitted: 2
  Abstract: Not necessary.
Author information and reprints: Payment: By publication to author. $100.00 per article.
  Is simultaneous submission of article to other journals permitted: Permitted, but not encouraged.

Interdisciplinary

Exclusive manuscript rights between acceptance and publication: Yes
Copyright: Held jointly with publication
Reprints: Available at no cost. 25
Available at cost. Varies

Additional information: Complete manuscript, including footnotes, is to be submitted typewritten and double-spaced.

Disposition of manuscript:
Query letter: Not necessary, but advisable.
Receipt of manuscript acknowledged: Yes
Decision to publish in: 2 weeks to 3 months
Accepted manuscript published in: 3-6 months
Rejected manuscript returned: Yes, with return postage paid by publication.
Rejected manuscript criticized: Reasons for rejections only

Submit to:
James Eayrs;
Robert Spencer
Editors
(See address above)

INTERNATIONAL PROBLEMS [613]

The Journal of the Israeli Institute for the Study of International Affairs
POB 17027
Tel Aviv 61170, Israel
41-42-56

First published in 1963

SUBSCRIPTION DATA

Issues and rates: Published quarterly.
Average paid circulation: 3190; 4000 controlled
Annual rate(s): $10.00

Publisher or Sponsor: The Israeli Institute for the Study of International Affairs

Managing Editor: A. Segal

EDITORIAL DESCRIPTION

Contains articles on international law, international relations, peace and future research, Middle East conflict, problems of developing countries and all other legal, social and economic research that aids in the understanding of war and peace.

Articles per average issue: 15-17
Audience: Politicians, journalists, researchers, students
Manuscripts accepted in English, French, Hebrew

MANUSCRIPT INFORMATION

Subject field(s): International politics, international law, Middle East conflict, peace research, future oriented studies

Manuscript requirements: No specific style guide.
Preferred length: 6000-9000 words; 12-15 pages
Number of copies to be submitted: Two
Abstract: Yes. For articles in Hebrew, abstract should be submitted in English or French.

Author information and reprints: Payment: None. Two copies of issue in which articles appears.
Is simultaneous submission of article to other journals permitted: No
Exclusive manuscript rights between acceptance and publication: Yes
Copyright: Held by author.
Reprints: Available, cost depends on length

Additional information: Manuscript should be in the proper style with footnotes, references and tables on separate pages at the end.

Disposition of manuscript:
Query letter: Not necessary
Receipt of manuscript acknowledged: Yes
Decision to publish in: 6-8 weeks
Accepted manuscript published in: 6-9 months
Rejected manuscript returned: Yes
Rejected manuscript criticized: No

Submit to:
Mushkat Marion
Editor-in-Chief
(See address above)
623-585

INTERNATIONAL STUDIES QUARTERLY [614]

Sage Publications
275 South Beverly Drive
Beverly Hills, California 90202
(213) 274-8003

Previously entitled *Background: The Journal of the International Studies Association*

First published in 1963

SUBSCRIPTION DATA

Issues and rates: Published quarterly.
Average paid circulation: 3,200
Annual rate(s): $12.00; Institutions $20.00; Students $5.00; Members $12.00; Foreign institutions $16.50

Publisher or Sponsor: International Studies Association

Managing Editor: Jonathan Wilkenfield

EDITORIAL DESCRIPTION

To promote scholarly research in international studies, including cross-cultural, legal, historical, and behavioral analyses; to promote the publication of manuscripts by non-North American authors

Articles per average issue: 5
Audience: The scholarly community in the field of international studies
Manuscripts accepted in English

MANUSCRIPT INFORMATION

Subject field(s): International politics; international law and organization; cross-cultural studies; strategy; foreign policy analysis; conflict and peace research; quantitative international relations

Manuscript requirements: See latest issue for style requirements.
Preferred length: 2,500 to 12,500 words; 10-50 pages

Number of copies to be submitted: 3
Abstract: Not necessary.

Author information and reprints: Payment: None.
Is simultaneous submission of article to other journals permitted: Permitted, provided author informs editor
Exclusive manuscript rights between acceptance and publication:
Copyright: Held by publisher and the International Studies Association
Reprints: Available at no cost. 25

Disposition of manuscript:
Query letter: Not necessary.
Receipt of manuscript acknowledged: Yes
Decision to publish in: 8 weeks
Accepted manuscript published in: 6 months
Rejected manuscript returned: Yes, with return postage paid by publication.
Rejected manuscript criticized: Yes

Submit to:
Jonathan Wilkenfield
Editor
Department of Government
University of Maryland
College Park, Maryland 20742

JOURNAL OF BLACK STUDIES [615]

Sage Publications, Inc.
275 South Beverly Drive
Beverly Hills, California 90212
(213) 274-2423

SUBSCRIPTION DATA

Issues and rates: Published quarterly.
Average paid circulation: Not available.
Annual rate(s): Institutions $15.00; Individuals $10.00; Students $8.00; Foreign individuals $11.50; Foreign institutions $16.50

EDITORIAL DESCRIPTION

Concerns the broad range of questions involving persons of African descent: economic, political, sociological, historical, literary, and philosophical.

MANUSCRIPT INFORMATION

Subject field(s): Black studies, sociology, history, literature, politics, economics, philosophy

Manuscript requirements: Style sheet sent on request.
Preferred length: 6,250-7,500 words; 25 to 30 pages
Number of copies to be submitted: Two

Author information and reprints: Payment: Reprints only. 25 tear sheets
Is simultaneous submission of article to other journals permitted: Permitted, but not encouraged. Author must notify publisher that manuscript is under consideration elsewhere.
Exclusive manuscript rights between acceptance and publication: Yes
Copyright: Held by publication.
Reprints: Available if purchased by special order in amounts no fewer than 100

Disposition of manuscript:
Receipt of manuscript acknowledged: Yes

Decision to publish in: 6-8 weeks
Accepted manuscript published in: 6-9 months
Rejected manuscript returned: Yes
Rejected manuscript criticized: Yes
Submit to:
Arthur L. Smith
Editor
Communication Department
SUNY, Buffalo
Buffalo, New York

THE JOURNAL OF DEVELOPING AREAS [616]
Western Illinois University
Macomb, Illinois 61455
(309) 295-2014

First published in 1966

SUBSCRIPTION DATA
Issues and rates: Published quarterly.
  Average paid circulation: 1,515; 135 controlled
  Annual rate(s): Individuals $12.00; Institutions $16.00

EDITORIAL DESCRIPTION
  Contains articles, bibliography section, news and notes, book review section, editorial comment. International scope, interdisciplinary with the intention of stimulating the descriptive, theoretical, and comparative study of regional development, past and present, with the object of promoting fuller understanding of man's relationship to the developmental process.
Articles per average issue: 5
Audience: Professional, students
  Manuscripts accepted in English, French

MANUSCRIPT INFORMATION
Subject field(s): Economics, political science, sociology, geography, international business, agriculture, anthropology, history, literature, education, law
Manuscript requirements: Chicago
  Preferred length: 5,000 to 9,000 words; 20-30 pages
  Number of copies to be submitted: Three
  Abstract: Optional
Author information and reprints: Payment: None. 2 copies of the issue and 50 offprints.
  Is simultaneous submission of article to other journals permitted: Yes, must be so notified
  Exclusive manuscript rights between acceptance and publication: Yes
  Copyright: Held by publication.
  Reprints: Not available.
Additional information: Keep tabular material to a minimum. All figures must be professionally prepared and be in a camera-ready form. Author's name and affiliation should appear only on the title page. Everything typewritten, double-spaced.
Disposition of manuscript:
  Receipt of manuscript acknowledged: Yes
  Decision to publish in: 2-4 months
  Accepted manuscript published in: One year

Rejected manuscript returned: Yes, if return postage is supplied by author.
Rejected manuscript criticized: Yes
Submit to:
Spencer H. Brown
General Editor
(See address above)

JOURNAL OF GERONTOLOGY [617]
Gerontological Society
One Dupont Circle, Suite 520
Washington, D.C. 20036
(202) 659-4698

First published in 1946

SUBSCRIPTION DATA
Issues and rates: Published bi-monthly.
  Average paid circulation: 5,600
  Annual rate(s): $30.00
Publisher or Sponsor: Gerontological Society
Managing Editor: Marjorie Adler

EDITORIAL DESCRIPTION
  Contains original research in the biological sciences, clinical medicine, psychological and social sciences, social welfare; book reviews, and an extensive current bibliography in gerontology.
Articles per average issue: 15
Audience: Professional
  Manuscripts accepted in English

MANUSCRIPT INFORMATION
Subject field(s): Biology, medicine, psychology and social sciences, social welfare
Manuscript requirements: APA
  Preferred length: Not to exceed 15 pages
  Number of copies to be submitted: One
  Abstract: Yes, brief and at the end
Author information and reprints: Payment: None.
  Is simultaneous submission of article to other journals permitted: No
  Exclusive manuscript rights between acceptance and publication: Yes
  Copyright: Held by publication.
  Reprints: Available, costs sent with galley proofs
Additional information: Everything should be typewritten, double-spaced, with tables on separate sheets; each plate must be arranged by the author.
Disposition of manuscript:
  Receipt of manuscript acknowledged: Yes
  Rejected manuscript returned: Yes, if self-addressed, stamped envelope is sent with manuscript.
  Rejected manuscript criticized: No
Submit to:
Dr. Harold Brody
Editor-in-Chief
State University of New York at Buffalo
School of Medicine
Buffalo, New York 14214
(716) 831-2912

JOURNAL OF SAFETY RESEARCH [618]
National Safety Council
425 North Michigan Avenue
Chicago, Illinois 60611
(312) 527-4800

Previously entitled *Traffic Safety Research Review*

First published in 1969

SUBSCRIPTION DATA
Issues and rates: Published quarterly.
  Average paid circulation: 2,000
  Annual rate(s): $15.00, Foreign $15.23
Publisher or Sponsor: National Safety Council
Managing Editor: Jean Stephenson

EDITORIAL DESCRIPTION
  Publishes articles based on research experience in all areas of safety.
Articles per average issue: 5
Audience: Researchers, professionals
  Manuscripts accepted in English

MANUSCRIPT INFORMATION
Subject field(s): Traffic, industry, farm, home, school, and public; human error and accidents, methods of accident investigation and analysis, evaluation of accident countermeasures, or the relationship between man-machine-environment factors and hazards.
Manuscript requirements: Style sheet sent on request.
  Preferred length: 10-20 pages
  Number of copies to be submitted: Three
  Abstract: Yes
Author information and reprints: Payment: None. Five complimentary copies of publication.
  Is simultaneous submission of article to other journals permitted: No
  Exclusive manuscript rights between acceptance and publication: Yes
  Copyright: Held by publication.
  Reprints: Available, cost according to number of pages
Additional information: Typewritten double-spaced, with each table and figure on separate sheet, black and white only.
Disposition of manuscript:
  Query letter: No
  Receipt of manuscript acknowledged: Yes
  Decision to publish in: 6-8 weeks
  Accepted manuscript published in: 6-9 months
  Rejected manuscript returned: Yes
  Rejected manuscript criticized: Yes
Submit to:
Thomas W. Planek
Editor
(See address above)

NORTH-NORD [619]
Information Canada, Serials and Periodicals, Vanguard Building
171 Slater Street
Ottawa, Ontario K1A 0S9, Canada
(613) 996-5064

Interdisciplinary

First published in 1956

SUBSCRIPTION DATA
Issues and rates: Published bi-monthly.
   Average paid circulation: 4,000
   Annual rate(s): $6.00; Foreign $7.50
Managing Editor: Robert F. J. Shannon

EDITORIAL DESCRIPTION
Journal of information and opinion. Scientific, historical, sociological, adventure and exploration articles make up most of the content.
Articles per average issue: 10-12
Audience: General public, educational and scientific institutions
   Manuscripts accepted in English or French

MANUSCRIPT INFORMATION
Subject field(s): Must be on events north of the 60th parallel, mainly on the Canadian north, but stories are accepted from and on Alaska, Northern Scandinavia, Iceland, Greenland and the USSR above the 60th parallel.
Manuscript requirements: See latest issue for style requirements. Style sheet sent on request. Canadian Press Style Manual
   Preferred length: 1,500-2,000 words
   Number of copies to be submitted: One original
   Abstract: Yes. Typewritten, double or triple spaced, on plain white bond, one and one-half inch margins.
Author information and reprints: Payment: By publication to author. Request rate sheet
   Is simultaneous submission of article to other journals permitted: Not permitted.
   Exclusive manuscript rights between acceptance and publication: Yes
   Copyright: Canadian copyright - full rights
   Reprints: Available at cost.
Additional information: No hunting or fishing sports stories that are suitable for outdoors magazines are accepted. However, native life and hunting methods are acceptable.
Disposition of manuscript:
   Query letter: Not necessary, but advisable.
   Receipt of manuscript acknowledged: Yes
   Decision to publish in: 2 months
   Accepted manuscript published in: 3 months
   Rejected manuscript returned: Yes, with return postage paid by publication.
   Rejected manuscript criticized: Sometimes
Submit to:
   Robert F. J. Shannon
   Managing Editor
   Indian and Northern Affairs, Room 354
   400 Laurier Ave. West
   Ottawa, Ontario K1A 0H4, Canada
   (613) 995-6206

ORBIS [620]
A Journal of World Affairs
Foreign Policy Research Institute
3508 Market Street, Suite 350
Philadelphia, Pennsylvania 19104
(215) 382-0685

First published in 1957

SUBSCRIPTION DATA
Issues and rates: Published quarterly.
   Average paid circulation: 4,000; 4800 controlled
   Annual rate(s): $10.00
Publisher or Sponsor: Foreign Policy Research Institute
Managing Editor: Robert C. Herber

EDITORIAL DESCRIPTION
Each issue contains articles on various subjects in world affairs, modern history, country and area studies, foreign policy, international economic and strategic affairs, etc.
Articles per average issue: 11 articles, 5 reviews
Audience: Scholars, statesmen, students concerned laymen
   Manuscripts accepted in English

MANUSCRIPT INFORMATION
Subject field(s): World affairs, foreign policy, diplomacy, strategy, area and country studies, military affairs, science and technology, modern history
Manuscript requirements: Chicago with a few variations. Divide manuscript into several sections.
   Preferred length: 5,000 to 7,500 words; 20-30 pages
   Number of copies to be submitted: Three
   Abstract: No
Author information and reprints: Payment: None. 3 copies of the issue and 10 reprints free.
   Is simultaneous submission of article to other journals permitted: No
   Exclusive manuscript rights between acceptance and publication: Yes
   Copyright: Held by publication.
   Reprints: Available, at printer's cost
Additional information: Footnotes typed double-space and placed at end of manuscript; manuscript also typed double-space.
Disposition of manuscript:
   Query letter: No
   Receipt of manuscript acknowledged: Yes
   Decision to publish in: 6 weeks
   Accepted manuscript published in: 3-6 months
   Rejected manuscript returned: Yes, if return postage is supplied by author.
   Rejected manuscript criticized: Yes, if specific criticism is supplied by Editorial Board
Submit to:
   Managing Editor
   (See address above)
   (215) 382-0685

PERCEPTION [621]
Pion Limited
207 Brondesbury Park
London NW2 5JN, England

SUBSCRIPTION DATA
Issues and rates: Published quarterly.
   Annual rate(s): £10.00; Foreign £11.25
Managing Editor: Richard L. Gregory, Bristol

EDITORIAL DESCRIPTION
This rigorously scientific and scholarly journal brings together papers devoted to physiological, psychological, cognitive, and philosophical aspects of perception. It reports experimental results and theoretical ideas ranging over the fields of animal, human and machine perception. Emphasis is on theoretical cross-disciplinary approaches
Audience: Professional, academic
   Manuscripts accepted in English (French, German)

MANUSCRIPT INFORMATION
Subject field(s): Physiological mechanisms; role of experience in developing perception; skills, such as driving or flying; effects of culture on perception and aesthetics; errors, illusions and perceptual phenomena occurring in controlled conditions; cognitive experiments; verbal and non-verbal skills; reading; philosophical implications of experiments and theories of perception for epistemology, aesthetics, and art.
Manuscript requirements: See latest issue for style requirements. Style sheet sent on request.
   Preferred length: None
   Number of copies to be submitted: 2
   Abstract: Yes
Author information and reprints: Payment: None.
Additional information: Papers may be full experimental reports or preliminary results, critical reviews, descriptions of novel apparatus and techniques. Notes for authors are available upon request.
Submit to:
   P. Bach-y-Rita
   Smith-Kettlewell Institute of Visual Sciences
   University of the Pacific
   2232 Webster Street
   San Francisco, California 94115

H. Barlow
Department of Physiology-Anatomy
University of California
Berkeley, California 94720
Editorial Board Members

THE THIRD WORLD REVIEW [622]
Department of Sociology and Anthropology
State University of New York
Cortland, New York 13045
(607) 753-2724

First published in 1974

SUBSCRIPTION DATA
Issues and rates: Published semi-annually.
 Annual rate(s): Institutions $8.00;
 Students $6.00; Members $6.00

EDITORIAL DESCRIPTION
Focuses on the social, political, cultural and economic aspects of the developing societies and the dynamics of their relationships with the developed societies.
Articles per average issue: 7-8
Audience: Social scientists
 Manuscripts accepted in English

MANUSCRIPT INFORMATION
Subject field(s): Political sociology, political anthropology, political science, international relations, economics, history
Manuscript requirements: See latest issue for style requirements. ASR,AAA
 Preferred length: 25-30 pages
 Number of copies to be submitted: 3
 Abstract: Yes. Not to exceed 200 words, on a separate sheet of paper
Author information and reprints: Payment: Reprints only. 3 copies of the issue
 Is simultaneous submission of article to other journals permitted: Not permitted.
 Exclusive manuscript rights between acceptance and publication: Yes
 Copyright: Held jointly by author and publication
 Reprints: Available at cost.
Disposition of manuscript:
 Query letter: Not necessary, but advisable.
 Receipt of manuscript acknowledged: Yes
 Decision to publish in: 1 month
 Accepted manuscript published in: 12-18 months
 Rejected manuscript returned: Yes, with return postage paid by publication.
 Rejected manuscript criticized: Reasons for rejections only
Submit to:
 Ilyas Ba-Yunus
 Chief Editor
 (See address above)

WAR/PEACE REPORT [623]
Fact and Opinion on Progress Toward a World of Peace with Justice
218 East 18th Street
New York, New York 10003
(212) 228-2470

First published in 1961

SUBSCRIPTION DATA
Issues and rates: Published bi-monthly.
 Average paid circulation: 6,000
 Annual rate(s): Individuals $9.50, Institutions $19.50
Publisher or Sponsor: Center for War/Peace Studies
Managing Editor: Richard Hudson

EDITORIAL DESCRIPTION
A journal of fact and opinion on progress toward a world of peace with justice. Covers current developments in world affairs, critical issues affecting war and peace, and general information useful to teachers.
Articles per average issue: 6-8
Audience: Well-informed general readers especially interested in world problems
 Manuscripts accepted in English

MANUSCRIPT INFORMATION
Subject field(s): United Nations, arms control, development, population control, environment, human rights, peace action, energy crisis, world economy
Manuscript requirements: See latest issue for style requirements. New York Times
 Preferred length: 500-3,000 words
 Number of copies to be submitted: One
 Abstract: No
Author information and reprints: Payment: None.
 Is simultaneous submission of article to other journals permitted: Yes
 Exclusive manuscript rights between acceptance and publication: Yes
 Copyright: Held by publication.
 Reprints: Available
Disposition of manuscript:
 Query letter: Not necessary
 Receipt of manuscript acknowledged: Yes
 Decision to publish in: 2 months
 Accepted manuscript published in: 3 months
 Rejected manuscript returned: Yes, if return postage is supplied by author.
 Rejected manuscript criticized: No
Submit to:
 Richard Hudson
 Editor
 (See address above)

WORLD AFFAIRS REPORT [624]
Box 4434
Stanford, California 94305
(415) 322-2026

Previously entitled *Report of the California Institute of International Studies*

First published in 1970

SUBSCRIPTION DATA
Issues and rates: Published quarterly.
 Annual rate(s): $4.00; Institutions $4.00; Students $4.00; Members $4.00
Publisher or Sponsor: California Institute of International Studies
Managing Editor: Ronald Hilton

EDITORIAL DESCRIPTION
Provides a running survey of international affairs, with special interest in the Soviet role in the world
Audience: Academic, professional
 Manuscripts accepted in English

MANUSCRIPT INFORMATION
Manuscript requirements: Chicago
 Preferred length: Open
 Number of copies to be submitted: 1
 Abstract: Yes. Suitable for *Historical Abstract*
Author information and reprints: Payment: By author to publication.
 Is simultaneous submission of article to other journals permitted: Not permitted.
 Exclusive manuscript rights between acceptance and publication: Yes
 Copyright: Held by author.
 Reprints: Available at cost.
Disposition of manuscript:
 Query letter: Necessary.
 Receipt of manuscript acknowledged: Yes
 Decision to publish in: 1 month
 Accepted manuscript published in: 2 months
 Rejected manuscript returned: Yes, if return postage is supplied by author.
 Rejected manuscript criticized: Reasons for rejections only
Submit to:
 Ronald Hilton
 Editor
 (See address above)

WORLD POLITICS [625]
A Quarterly Journal of International Relations
Corwin Hall, Princeton University
Princeton, New Jersey 08540
(609) 452-4865

First published in 1948

SUBSCRIPTION DATA
Issues and rates: Published quarterly.
 Average paid circulation: 4,366
 Annual rate(s): $10.00, Foreign $13.50
Publisher or Sponsor: Princeton University, Center of International Studies

EDITORIAL DESCRIPTION
Contains scholarly research having broad theoretical significance in international relations or comparative politics.
Articles per average issue: 7
Audience: Scholars of international relations and comparative politics
 Manuscripts accepted in English

MANUSCRIPT INFORMATION
Subject field(s): International relations, comparative politics, government, history, economics, geography, ecology, sociology/anthropology, international law, strategic studies, area studies
Manuscript requirements: MLA, Chicago. Manuscripts should be double-spaced throughout and submitted in duplicate. Footnotes should be numbered consecutively, typed double-spaced, and added at the end of the manuscript.
 Preferred length: 3,000-5,000 words; 20-30 pages
 Number of copies to be submitted: Two
 Abstract: Yes
Author information and reprints: Payment: By publication to author. $50.00 per article.
 Is simultaneous submission of article to other journals permitted: No
 Exclusive manuscript rights between acceptance and publication: Yes
 Copyright: Held by Princeton University Press

Reprints: Available, 100 free; additional in multiples of 100 if ordered in advance; cost depends on length of article.
Additional information: For anonomous editorial evaluation author's name and affiliation should appear only on a separate cover page.
Disposition of manuscript:
Query letter: No
Receipt of manuscript acknowledged: Yes
Decision to publish in: 1-3 months
Accepted manuscript published in: 6-12 months
Rejected manuscript returned: Yes
Rejected manuscript criticized: No
Submit to:
Elsbeth G. Lewin
Executive Editor
(See address above)

THE WORLD TODAY [626]
Chatham House
10 St. James's Square
London SW1, England
(01) 920-2233

First published in 1945

SUBSCRIPTION DATA
Issues and rates: Published monthly.
Average paid circulation: 5,000
Annual rate(s): £4.75, Foreign $15.00,
Publisher or Sponsor: Royal Institute of International Affairs

EDITORIAL DESCRIPTION
Deals mainly with international events but contains articles on internal political and economic conditions in individual countries, written by authors with first-hand knowledge. Short comment in "Notes of the Month" puts current developments in perspective and provides a background to events of international significance.
Articles per average issue: 5-6
Audience: Academics, journalists, politicians, businessmen, interested in international affairs
Manuscripts accepted in English, French, German

MANUSCRIPT INFORMATION
Subject field(s): Political or economic aspects of international affairs
Manuscript requirements: See latest issue for style requirements.
Preferred length: 3,500 words (articles); 1200 to 1500 words (Notes)
Number of copies to be submitted: One
Abstract: Not necessary
Author information and reprints: Payment: By publication to author. £12.60 to £15.75 per page.
Is simultaneous submission of article to other journals permitted: Permitted only for restricted number of non-English language journals by previous arrangement
Exclusive manuscript rights between acceptance and publication: Yes
Copyright: Held jointly by author and publication
Reprints: Not available.

Disposition of manuscript:
Query letter: Advisable
Receipt of manuscript acknowledged: Yes
Decision to publish in: One month
Accepted manuscript published in: 1-4 months
Rejected manuscript returned: Yes
Rejected manuscript criticized: No
Submit to:
The Editor
(See address above)

African studies

AFRICA REPORT [627]
833 United Nations Plaza
New York, New York 10017

SUBSCRIPTION DATA
Issues and rates: Published bi-monthly.
Average paid circulation: 12,000
Annual rate(s): $9.00
Publisher or Sponsor: African-American Institute
Managing Editor: Robert L. Denerstein

EDITORIAL DESCRIPTION
A general journal covering contemporary Africa.
Articles per average issue: 10
Audience: Americans interested in Africa
Manuscripts accepted in English

MANUSCRIPT INFORMATION
Subject field(s): Africa and any Africa-related material in any subject area
Manuscript requirements: See latest issue for style requirements.
Preferred length: 2,500-3,500 words
Number of copies to be submitted: One
Author information and reprints: Payment: By publication to author. $100.00-$150.00 per article.
Is simultaneous submission of article to other journals permitted: No
Exclusive manuscript rights between acceptance and publication: Yes
Copyright: Held by publication.
Reprints: Not available.
Disposition of manuscript:
Query letter: No
Receipt of manuscript acknowledged: No
Decision to publish in: One month
Accepted manuscript published in: 1-3 months
Rejected manuscript returned: Yes
Rejected manuscript criticized: Yes
Submit to:
Anthony J. Hughes
Editor
(See address above)

AFRICA TODAY [628]
The Center for International Race Relations
University of Denver
Denver, Colorado 80210
(303) 753-3678

First published in 1953

SUBSCRIPTION DATA
Issues and rates: Published quarterly.
Average paid circulation: 3000
Annual rate(s): $8.00; Foreign $12.00
Managing Editor: Edward A. Hawley

EDITORIAL DESCRIPTION
Contains articles analyzing current political, social, economic, and literary developments in Africa, book reviews, listing of periodical and pamphlet publications, letters to the editor.
Articles per average issue: 5-6
Audience: Academic
Manuscripts accepted in English only

MANUSCRIPT INFORMATION
Subject field(s): Politics, economics, sociology, anthropology, literature, art, biography
Manuscript requirements: See latest issue for style requirements.
Preferred length: 1,500-6,000 words
Number of copies to be submitted: Two
Abstract: No
Author information and reprints: Payment: None. 2-5 copies of issue in which article appears.
Is simultaneous submission of article to other journals permitted: No
Exclusive manuscript rights between acceptance and publication: Yes
Copyright: Held by publication.
Reprints: Available at cost
Additional information: Typewritten, double-spaced
Disposition of manuscript:
Query letter: No
Receipt of manuscript acknowledged: Yes
Decision to publish in: 6-10 weeks
Accepted manuscript published in: 3-9 months
Rejected manuscript returned: Yes
Rejected manuscript criticized: Sometimes
Submit to:
Edward A. Hawley
Executive Editor
(See address above)
(303) 753-2755

AFRICAN AFFAIRS [629]
The Journal of the Royal African Society
18 Northumberland Avenue
London WC2N 5BJ, England
(01) 930-6733 ext. 89

First published in 1906

SUBSCRIPTION DATA
Issues and rates: Published quarterly.
Average paid circulation: 2,365; 2,550 controlled
Annual rate(s): £7.50

Managing Editor: Michael Twaddle;
A.E. Atmore
Publisher or Sponsor: Royal African Society

EDITORIAL DESCRIPTION

Contains articles on all phases of African life and conditions.
Articles per average issue: 5
Audience: General
Manuscripts accepted in English

MANUSCRIPT INFORMATION

Subject field(s): African history, economic and social affairs, international relations
Manuscript requirements: See latest issue for style requirements.
Preferred length: 6000 words
Number of copies to be submitted: Two
Abstract: No
Author information and reprints: Payment: None.
Is simultaneous submission of article to other journals permitted: No
Exclusive manuscript rights between acceptance and publication: Yes
Copyright: Held by publication.
Reprints: Available at cost
Disposition of manuscript:
Query letter: No
Receipt of manuscript acknowledged: Yes
Decision to publish in: Varies
Accepted manuscript published in: Varies
Rejected manuscript returned: Yes
Rejected manuscript criticized: No
Submit to:
The Editors
(See address above)

AFRICAN PROGRESS [630]

11 East 44th Street
New York, New York 10017
(212) 682-3972

First published in 1971

SUBSCRIPTION DATA

Issues and rates: Published monthly.
Average paid circulation: 125,000
Annual rate(s): $10.00; Foreign $10.00 plus postage; Institutions $10.00; Students $10.00
Managing Editor: Linus A. Bassey

EDITORIAL DESCRIPTION

Provides American and African businessmen and government officials information on events in both continents
Articles per average issue: 8
Audience: Business and government officials
Manuscripts accepted in English

MANUSCRIPT INFORMATION

Subject field(s): Export-import, technology, finance, transportation, agriculture, new product developments
Manuscript requirements: Style sheet sent on request.
Preferred length: 1,500 words; 6 pages
Number of copies to be submitted: 2
Abstract: Not necessary.

Author information and reprints: Payment: By publication to author. Varies per page.
Is simultaneous submission of article to other journals permitted: Not permitted.
Exclusive manuscript rights between acceptance and publication: Yes
Copyright: Held by publication.
Reprints: Not available.
Disposition of manuscript:
Query letter: Not necessary, but advisable.
Receipt of manuscript acknowledged: Yes
Decision to publish in: 2 months
Accepted manuscript published in: 3 months
Rejected manuscript returned: Yes, if return postage is supplied by author.
Rejected manuscript criticized: No
Submit to:
L. A. Bassey
Publisher
(See address above)

AFRICAN STUDIES [631]

Witwatersrand University Press
Jan Smuts Avenue
Johannesburg, South Africa
724-1311 Ext. 794

Previously entitled *Bantu Studies*

First published in 1921

SUBSCRIPTION DATA

Issues and rates: Published quarterly.
Average paid circulation: 800
Annual rate(s): R7.50
Managing Editor: D. T. Cole;
W. D. Hammond-Tooke

EDITORIAL DESCRIPTION

Contains articles on African anthropology, government and languages.

MANUSCRIPT INFORMATION

Manuscript requirements: Oxford English Dictionary and Oxford University Press (London) Style Guide
Preferred length: 5,000 words
Number of copies to be submitted: One
Abstract: Yes
Author information and reprints: Payment: Reprints only. 45 offprints
Is simultaneous submission of article to other journals permitted: Yes, but publication would prefer about 2 months for an option on the article.
Exclusive manuscript rights between acceptance and publication: Yes
Copyright: Held by publication.
Reprints: Available at cost.
Additional information: Typewritten, double-spaced, full references in footnotes.
Disposition of manuscript:
Query letter: No
Receipt of manuscript acknowledged: Yes
Decision to publish in: 6 weeks
Accepted manuscript published in: 3 months
Rejected manuscript returned: Yes
Rejected manuscript criticized: No

Submit to:
Mrs. N. H. Wilson
Publications Officer
(See address above)

AFRICAN STUDIES REVIEW [632]

Program of Eastern African Studies
Syracuse University
Syracuse, New York 13210

SUBSCRIPTION DATA

Issues and rates: Published three times per year.
Average paid circulation: 2125 controlled
Annual rate(s): Individuals $25.00, Institutions $40.00
Publisher or Sponsor: African Studies Association

EDITORIAL DESCRIPTION

Contains academic and scholarly articles and book reviews in African studies (all disciplines).
Manuscripts accepted in English

MANUSCRIPT INFORMATION

Subject field(s): African Studies
Manuscript requirements: See latest issue for style requirements.
Preferred length: Articles: More than 12 pages
Number of copies to be submitted: 2
Author information and reprints: Payment: None.
Is simultaneous submission of article to other journals permitted: No
Exclusive manuscript rights between acceptance and publication: No
Copyright: Held by publication.
Reprints: Available at no cost. 25 to author
Disposition of manuscript:
Query letter: No
Receipt of manuscript acknowledged: Yes
Decision to publish in: 6 weeks
Accepted manuscript published in: 3-6 months
Rejected manuscript returned: Yes
Rejected manuscript criticized: Sometimes
Submit to:
Alan K. Smith
Editor
(See address above)

THE CONCH [633]

A Sociological Journal of African Cultures and Literatures
Department of African Studies
State University of New York at New Paltz
New Paltz, New York 12561
(914) 257-2073

Previously entitled *A Biafran Journal of Literary and Cultural Analysis*

First published in 1969
Average paid circulation: 1,000

Annual rate(s): Individuals $7.00;
Institutions $9.00; Foreign individuals
$9.00; Foreign institutions $11.00
Managing Editor: Lynda S. Anozie

EDITORIAL DESCRIPTION

Dedicated to the pursuit of truth and
excellence in African history and cultural
criticism. Multidisciplinary and
comparative in scope, it explores
problems related to African sociology,
literature, sociolinguistics and cognitive
psychology.
Articles per average issue: 8
Audience: Academic, well-informed
Manuscripts accepted in English, French

MANUSCRIPT INFORMATION

Subject field(s): African literature
(traditional and modern); linguistics
(structural and generative); principles of
communication in Africa; cultural
anthropology and sociology with an
emphasis on methodology
Manuscript requirements: See latest issue for
style requirements. MLA
Preferred length: 2-25 pages
Number of copies to be submitted: 2
Abstract: Yes. An abstract in English is
necessary for articles written in French.
Author information and reprints: Payment:
Reprints only. 10 offprints and 1 copy of
issue
Is simultaneous submission of article to
other journals permitted: Permitted, with
notification of publication.
Exclusive manuscript rights between
acceptance and publication: Yes
Copyright: Held by publication. But
permission is always granted to authors
to reprint.
Reprints: Available at cost.
Additional information: All manuscripts
should be typewritten, double-spaced.
Disposition of manuscript:
Query letter: Not necessary, but
advisable.
Receipt of manuscript acknowledged: No
Decision to publish in: 3-6 months
Accepted manuscript published in: 2
months
Rejected manuscript returned: Yes, if
return postage is supplied by author.
Rejected manuscript criticized: Reasons
for rejections only
Submit to:
Dr. Sunday O. Anozie
Editor
(See address above)

SPECIAL STIPULATIONS

Articles are frequently contracted or
assigned to known experts.

THE CONCH REVIEW OF BOOKS [634]

A Literary Supplement on Africa
Department of African Studies
State University of New York, College at
New Paltz
New Paltz, New York 12561
(914) 257-2073

First published in 1973

SUBSCRIPTION DATA

Issues and rates: Published quarterly.
Average paid circulation: 1,000
Annual rate(s): Individuals $10.00;
Institutions $15.00; Foreign individuals
$12.00; Foreign institutions $17.00
Managing Editor: Lynda S. Anozie

EDITORIAL DESCRIPTION

An international quarterly devoted to
in-depth and timely reviews of books,
films, and recordings, relating to Africa
in particular, and the Third World in
general
Articles per average issue: 10-15 reviews
Audience: Academic, business, tourism,
library
Manuscripts accepted in English, French

MANUSCRIPT INFORMATION

Subject field(s): Recent publications on
Africa-related subjects, both recent and
previously published, based on aspects of
African and Black experience, including
traditional and modern music from
Africa and the West Indies
Manuscript requirements: MLA
Preferred length: 1,500 words
Number of copies to be submitted: 1
Abstract: Not necessary.
Author information and reprints: Payment:
Reprints only. 2 copies of issue
Is simultaneous submission of article to
other journals permitted: Not permitted.
Exclusive manuscript rights between
acceptance and publication: Yes
Copyright: Held by publication.
Permission to reprint is always granted to
the author who applies.
Reprints: Not available.
Additional information: Contributing editors
and reviewers are required to fill out an
official reviewer's form.
Disposition of manuscript:
Query letter: Necessary.
Receipt of manuscript acknowledged: No
Decision to publish in: 2 weeks
Accepted manuscript published in: 3
weeks
Rejected manuscript returned: Yes, if
return postage is supplied by author.
Rejected manuscript criticized: No
Submit to:
Dr. Sunday O. Anozie
Editor and Publisher
(See address above)

JOURNAL OF MODERN AFRICAN STUDIES [635]

Cambridge University Press
32 East 57th Street
New York, New York 10022
Annual rate(s): $23.50 per volume

EDITORIAL DESCRIPTION

All areas of African studies, with notes
on centers, research projects, and reports
of recent conferences are also welcome.
Manuscripts accepted in English

MANUSCRIPT INFORMATION

Manuscript requirements: See latest issue for
style requirements. Style sheet sent on
request.
Preferred length: 3,000 to 6,000 words
Number of copies to be submitted: 2
Abstract: Not necessary.
Author information and reprints: Payment:
Reprints only. 25 offprints
Is simultaneous submission of article to
other journals permitted: Not permitted.
Exclusive manuscript rights between
acceptance and publication: Yes
Copyright: Held by publication.
Reprints: Available at cost.
Disposition of manuscript:
Query letter: Not necessary, but
advisable.
Receipt of manuscript acknowledged: Yes
Rejected manuscript returned: Yes, if
return postage is supplied by author.
Rejected manuscript criticized:
Sometimes
Submit to:
Prof. David Kimble
Editor
University of Botswana, Lesotho, and
Swaziland
P. O. Roma
Maseru, Lesotho, South Africa

Asian and Pacific studies

ASIAN SURVEY [636]

University of California Press
Berkeley, California 94720
(415) 642-0978

First published in 1961

SUBSCRIPTION DATA

Issues and rates: Published monthly.
Average paid circulation: 3300
Annual rate(s): $15.00; Institutions
$21.00
Publisher or Sponsor: University of
California, Berkeley

EDITORIAL DESCRIPTION

Contains articles on contemporary Asian
affairs: political, social, economic.
Articles per average issue: 6
Audience: Academic
Manuscripts accepted in English

MANUSCRIPT INFORMATION

Subject field(s): Political science, economics,
sociology
Manuscript requirements: Chicago
Preferred length: 7500 words; 25-30
pages
Number of copies to be submitted: Two
Abstract: No
Author information and reprints: Payment:
None.
Is simultaneous submission of article to
other journals permitted: Yes

Exclusive manuscript rights between acceptance and publication: Yes
Copyright: Held by Regents of University of California
Reprints: Available, $.90 per reprint
Additional information: Can publish only limited numbers of tables or maps. Author must provide camera-ready black and white line drawings. Footnotes should be appended at end and typed double-spaced.
Disposition of manuscript:
Query letter: No
Receipt of manuscript acknowledged: Yes
Decision to publish in: Two to three months
Accepted manuscript published in: 6 months to one year
Rejected manuscript returned: Yes
Rejected manuscript criticized: Yes
Submit to:
Robert A. Scalapino;
Leo E. Rose
Associate Editors
(See address above)

BULLETIN OF CONCERNED ASIAN SCHOLARS [637]
Bay Area Institute
604 Mission Street, Room 1001
San Francisco, California 94105
(415) 986-5690

Previously entitled *C.C.A.S. Newsletter*

First published in 1969

SUBSCRIPTION DATA
Issues and rates: Published quarterly.
   Average paid circulation: 2,000
   Annual rate(s): Individuals $6.00, Foreign $7.00, Students $4.00, Institutions $10.00
Publisher or Sponsor: Committee of Concerned Asian Scholars
Managing Editor: Jon Livingston

EDITORIAL DESCRIPTION
Publishes interdisciplinary articles on politics, history, societies, and international relations of contemporary Asia; also American-Asian relations. Attempts to deal with effects of imperialism on modern Asia.
Articles per average issue: 5-7
Audience: Asia Specialist, general
   Manuscripts accepted in English only

MANUSCRIPT INFORMATION
Subject field(s): Politics, history, sociology, international relations, imperialism, economics, America in Asia
Manuscript requirements: Generally *Far Eastern Quarterly* and Association for Asian Studies Stylesheet
   Preferred length: 10-60 pages
   Number of copies to be submitted: Three
Author information and reprints: Payment: Reprints only. 5 copies of issue
   Is simultaneous submission of article to other journals permitted: Yes

Exclusive manuscript rights between acceptance and publication: No
Copyright: Held by publication.
Reprints: Available at no cost. Upon request
Disposition of manuscript:
Query letter: No
Receipt of manuscript acknowledged: Yes
Decision to publish in: 1-3 months
Accepted manuscript published in: 6-9 months; special topic issues are 1 year usually.
Rejected manuscript returned: Yes
Rejected manuscript criticized: Usually
Submit to:
Jon Livingston
(See address above)

CONTRIBUTIONS TO ASIAN STUDIES [638]
Department of Sociology and Anthropology
York University
Toronto, Ontario, Canada
(416) 667-3720

First published in 1972

SUBSCRIPTION DATA
Issues and rates: Published semi-annually.
   Annual rate(s): $16.00
Publisher or Sponsor: Canadian Association for South Asian Studies
Managing Editor: K. Ishwaran

EDITORIAL DESCRIPTION
Intended as a forum for scholarly analyses of Asian societies and cultures, past and contemporary, from the diverse standpoints of the international community of scholars in all the social sciences and humanities.
Articles per average issue: 20
   Manuscripts accepted in English

MANUSCRIPT INFORMATION
Manuscript requirements: See latest issue for style requirements.
   Preferred length: 8,500 words; 25 pages
   Number of copies to be submitted: Two
   Abstract: No
Author information and reprints: Payment: None.
   Is simultaneous submission of article to other journals permitted: No
   Exclusive manuscript rights between acceptance and publication: Yes
   Copyright: Held by publication.
   Reprints: Available
Disposition of manuscript:
Query letter: No
Receipt of manuscript acknowledged: 1-2 months
Decision to publish in: 1-2 months
Accepted manuscript published in: One year
Rejected manuscript returned: Yes, if return postage is supplied by author.
Rejected manuscript criticized: If requested
Submit to:
K. Ishwaran
General Editor
(See address above)

HARVARD JOURNAL OF ASIATIC STUDIES [639]
2 Divinity Avenue
Cambridge, Massachusetts 02138
(617) 495-2758

First published in 1936

SUBSCRIPTION DATA
Issues and rates: Published annually.
   Average paid circulation: 1200
   Annual rate(s): $10.00
Publisher or Sponsor: Harvard-Yenching Institute
Managing Editor: Glenn W. Baxter

EDITORIAL DESCRIPTION
Contains articles based primarily on materials in Asian languages and dealing with the languages, literature, pre-contemporary history or culture of East Asia; critical book reviews and descriptive notices of scholarly works in this area.
Articles per average issue: 8-10
Audience: Scholars
   Manuscripts accepted in English only

MANUSCRIPT INFORMATION
Subject field(s): Languages, literature, history (premodern), sociology, art
Manuscript requirements: HJAS Stylesheet (price $.35), MLA, Turabian
   Preferred length: 20-60 pages
   Number of copies to be submitted: One
   Abstract: No
Author information and reprints: Payment: None.
   Is simultaneous submission of article to other journals permitted: No
   Exclusive manuscript rights between acceptance and publication: Yes
   Copyright: Held by author.
   Reprints: Available, 50 free reprints to author.
Additional information: Chinese characters and Japanese *kana* can be accommodated, but must be used sparingly and only where necessary.
Disposition of manuscript:
Query letter: No
Receipt of manuscript acknowledged: Yes
Decision to publish in: 2-6 months
Accepted manuscript published in: 1-3 years
Rejected manuscript returned: Yes
Rejected manuscript criticized: No
Submit to:
Timothy Connor
Assistant Editor
(See address above)

SPECIAL STIPULATIONS
Articles must be based on primary source materials in one of the Asian languages specified (Chinese, Japanese, Mongolian, Korean), not wholly on secondary source materials in Western languages.

Asian and Pacific studies

JOURNAL OF ASIAN AND AFRICAN STUDIES [640]
Department of Sociology and Anthropology
York University
Toronto, Ontario M3J 1P3, Canada
(416) 667-3720

First published in 1965

SUBSCRIPTION DATA
Issues and rates: Published quarterly.
  Annual rate(s): $16.00

EDITORIAL DESCRIPTION
  Edited by a board of scholars from all over the world who are specialists in Asian and African studies, it presents a scholarly account of studies of man and society in the developing nations of Asia and Africa. It endeavours to fill a need in the field in that it unites contributions from anthropology, sociology, history, and related social sciences into a concerted emphasis upon building up systematic knowledge and using the knowledge derived from pure research for the reconstruction of societies entering a phase of advanced technology.
Articles per average issue: 4-6
Audience: Teachers, students
  Manuscripts accepted in English

MANUSCRIPT INFORMATION
Manuscript requirements: See latest issue for style requirements.
  Preferred length: 8,500 words; 25 pages
  Number of copies to be submitted: Two
  Abstract: No
Author information and reprints: Payment: None.
  Is simultaneous submission of article to other journals permitted: No
  Exclusive manuscript rights between acceptance and publication: Yes
  Copyright: Held by publication.
  Reprints: 25 free reprints
Additional information: Use graphs, tables, and diagrams sparingly. Indicate current professional affiliation and mailing address.
Disposition of manuscript:
  Query letter: No
  Receipt of manuscript acknowledged: Yes
  Decision to publish in: 1-2 months
  Accepted manuscript published in: One year
  Rejected manuscript returned: Yes, if return postage is supplied by author.
  Rejected manuscript criticized: If requested
Submit to:
  K. Ishwaran
  General Editor
  (See address above)

JOURNAL OF ASIAN STUDIES [641]
University of Chicago
Chicago, Illinois 60637

Previously entitled *Far Eastern Quarterly*

SUBSCRIPTION DATA
Issues and rates: Published quarterly.
  Average paid circulation: 7,679
  Annual rate(s): Institutions $30; Members $20; Students $10
Publisher or Sponsor: Association for Asian Studies, Inc.

EDITORIAL DESCRIPTION
  Contains materials dealing with East, South, and South East Asia in general.
Audience: Members, academic
  Manuscripts accepted in English

MANUSCRIPT INFORMATION
Subject field(s): Humanities, social sciences
Manuscript requirements: MLA and *Journal of Asian Studies* Style Sheet (sent upon request).
  Preferred length: 35 pages
  Number of copies to be submitted: Three
  Abstract: No
Author information and reprints: Payment: None.
  Is simultaneous submission of article to other journals permitted: No
  Exclusive manuscript rights between acceptance and publication: No
  Copyright: Held by publication.
  Reprints: Available
Disposition of manuscript:
  Receipt of manuscript acknowledged: Yes
  Decision to publish in: 4 months
  Accepted manuscript published in: 3-12 months
  Rejected manuscript returned: Yes
  Rejected manuscript criticized: Yes
Submit to:
  H. D. Harootunian
  Editor
  (See address above)

THE JOURNAL OF PACIFIC HISTORY [642]
Research School of Pacific Studies
National University, P. O. Box 4
Canberra, A.C.T 2600, Australia

First published in 1966

SUBSCRIPTION DATA
Issues and rates: Published semi-annually.
  Average paid circulation: 1,000; 5
  Annual rate(s): $6.50; Foreign US$10.00
Managing Editor: Jennifer A. K. Terrell

EDITORIAL DESCRIPTION
  Contains articles on original research in the field of Pacific history, defined in its broadest sense
Articles per average issue: 4-6
Audience: Professional, academic
  Manuscripts accepted in English

MANUSCRIPT INFORMATION
Subject field(s): Archaeology, prehistory and ethnohistory, as well as contemporary government and political development; Pacific islands, including Hawaii and New Guinea

Manuscript requirements: See latest issue for style requirements. Style sheet sent on request.
  Preferred length: 8,000 words
  Number of copies to be submitted: 2
  Abstract: Not necessary.
Author information and reprints: Payment: Reprints only. 25 reprints
  Is simultaneous submission of article to other journals permitted: Not permitted.
  Exclusive manuscript rights between acceptance and publication: Yes
  Copyright: Held by publication.
  Reprints: Available at cost. Ordered in advance of publication
Additional information: Doublespacing, quarto, wide margins on all sides, footnotes consecutively at the end.
Disposition of manuscript:
  Query letter: Not necessary.
  Receipt of manuscript acknowledged: Yes
  Decision to publish in: 2-3 months
  Accepted manuscript published in: 3-9 months
  Rejected manuscript returned: Yes, with return postage paid by publication.
  Rejected manuscript criticized: Sometimes
Submit to:
  The Editors
  (See address above)

JOURNAL OF SOUTHEAST ASIAN STUDIES [643]
Department of History
University of Singapore
Singapore 10, Republic of Singapore
50451 ext. 229

Previously entitled *Journal of Southeast Asian History*

First published in 1960

SUBSCRIPTION DATA
Issues and rates: Published semi-annually.
  Average paid circulation: 2000
  Annual rate(s): $25.00 (Singapore)
Publisher or Sponsor: University of Singapore, History Department

EDITORIAL DESCRIPTION
  Contains interdisciplinary articles on Southeast Asian countries.
Articles per average issue: 7-9
Audience: Academic
  Manuscripts accepted in English

MANUSCRIPT INFORMATION
Manuscript requirements: Style sheet sent on request.
  Preferred length: 4000 to 8000 words
  Number of copies to be submitted: Two
  Abstract: No
Author information and reprints: Payment: Reprints only. 13 Reprints, 1 copy of issue
  Is simultaneous submission of article to other journals permitted: No
  Exclusive manuscript rights between acceptance and publication: Yes
  Copyright: Held by publication.

Reprints: Not available.
Additional information: Articles based on original research are given priority.
Disposition of manuscript:
  Receipt of manuscript acknowledged: Yes
  Decision to publish in: 1-6 months
  Accepted manuscript published in: 6-9 months
  Rejected manuscript returned: Yes
  Rejected manuscript criticized: No
Submit to:
  Editor
  (See address above)

MODERN ASIAN STUDIES [644]
Cambridge University Press
32 East 57th Street
New York, New York 10022

Managing Editor: Dr. Gordon Johnson

EDITORIAL DESCRIPTION
  Concerned with the history, geography, politics, sociology, literature, economics and social anthropology of South Asia, Southeast Asia, China and Japan.
  Manuscripts accepted in English

MANUSCRIPT INFORMATION
Manuscript requirements: See latest issue for style requirements. Style sheet sent on request.
  Preferred length: 2,000 to 8,000 words
  Number of copies to be submitted: 2 typewritten
  Abstract: Not necessary.
Author information and reprints: Payment: Reprints only. 25
  Is simultaneous submission of article to other journals permitted: Not permitted.
  Exclusive manuscript rights between acceptance and publication: Yes
  Copyright: Held by publication
Submit to:
  Dr. Gordon Johnson
  Editor
  Selwyn College
  Cambridge CB3 9DQ, England

SOUTH ASIAN STUDIES [645]
South Asia Studies Centre
University of Rajasthan
Jaipur 302004, India
63211-267

SUBSCRIPTION DATA
Issues and rates: Published semi-annually.
  Average paid circulation: Not available.
  Annual rate(s): Rs. 15.00, Foreign $2.50
Publisher or Sponsor: University of Rajasthan, South Asia Studies Centre

EDITORIAL DESCRIPTION
  Contains articles based on or focused on the domestic or external politics in South Asia. Also contains book reviews and review articles.
Articles per average issue: 6
Audience: Academic
  Manuscripts accepted in English

MANUSCRIPT INFORMATION
Subject field(s): South Asian studies
Manuscript requirements: See latest issue for style requirements.
  Preferred length: 5000 words
  Number of copies to be submitted: Two
  Abstract: No
Author information and reprints: Payment: None.
  Is simultaneous submission of article to other journals permitted: No
  Exclusive manuscript rights between acceptance and publication: Yes
  Copyright: Held by publication.
  Reprints: Available, 25 free
Disposition of manuscript:
  Query letter: No
  Receipt of manuscript acknowledged: Yes
  Decision to publish in: 3 months
  Accepted manuscript published in: 3-6 months
  Rejected manuscript returned: Yes
  Rejected manuscript criticized: No
Submit to:
  Shanti Prasad Varma
  Chief Editor
  (See address above)

European studies

AUSTRIAN HISTORY YEARBOOK [646]
Rice University
Houston, Texas 77001
(713) 528-4141

Previously entitled *Austrian History Newsletter*

First published in 1965

SUBSCRIPTION DATA
Issues and rates: Published annually.
  Average paid circulation: 800; 100 controlled
  Annual rate(s): $11.00; Foreign $11.00; Institutions $11.00; Students $11.00
Publisher or Sponsor: Conference Group for Central European History; Rice University

EDITORIAL DESCRIPTION
  Publishes research articles, bibliographies, and book reviews dealing with the history of the Habsburg monarchy and all of the constituent lands as well as the history of Austria and Hungary since World War I
Articles per average issue: 6-8
Audience: Academic, professional
  Manuscripts accepted in English, German, Italian, French

MANUSCRIPT INFORMATION
Manuscript requirements: No specific style guide.
  Preferred length: 7,000-15,000 words
  Number of copies to be submitted: 1
  Abstract: Not necessary, but helpful.
Author information and reprints: Payment: None
  Is simultaneous submission of article to other journals permitted: Permitted, but not encouraged.
  Exclusive manuscript rights between acceptance and publication: Yes
  Copyright: Held by Rice University
  Reprints: Available at cost.
Additional information: Manuscripts presented in English should be in good literary English.
Disposition of manuscript:
  Query letter: Not necessary.
  Receipt of manuscript acknowledged: Yes
  Decision to publish in: Varies
  Accepted manuscript published in: 2-3 years
  Rejected manuscript returned: Yes, with return postage paid by publication.
  Rejected manuscript criticized: Yes
Submit to:
  Prof. R. John Rath
  Editor
  (See address above)

CANADIAN SLAVONIC PAPERS [647]
Revue Canadienne des Slavistes
256 Paterson Hall
Carleton University
Ottawa, Ontario K1S 5B6, Canada
(613) 231-2685

First published in 1956

SUBSCRIPTION DATA
Issues and rates: Published quarterly.
  Average paid circulation: 800; 200 controlled
  Annual rate(s): $12.00; Pan-Am $12.25; Institutions $25.00; Students $9.00; Members $15.00
Publisher or Sponsor: Canadian Association of Slavists
Managing Editor: John W. Strong

EDITORIAL DESCRIPTION
  Contains articles, assigned book reviews, and review articles of high scholarly quality in all disciplines related to the field of Slavic studies, Eastern Europe, Russia, and the USSR.
Articles per average issue: 6
Audience: Scholars in Slavic studies
  Manuscripts accepted in English, French

MANUSCRIPT INFORMATION
Subject field(s): History, political science, sociology, geography, literature, linguistics; no chronological requirements.
Manuscript requirements: No specific style guide. See latest issue for style requirements.
  Preferred length: 2,000-3,000 words; 20-25 typewritten, double-spaced pages
  Number of copies to be submitted: 2
  Abstract: Yes. Short abstracts of 150-200 words in French for English articles and in English for French articles.

Author information and reprints: Payment: Reprints only. 25 reprints
Is simultaneous submission of article to other journals permitted: Not permitted.
Exclusive manuscript rights between acceptance and publication: Yes
Copyright: Held by publication.
Reprints: Available at cost.
Additional information: Use the Cyrillic transliteration system of the Library of Congress. Cyrillic is printed only in exeptional cases. Footnotes should be on separate pages.
Disposition of manuscript:
Query letter: Not necessary, but advisable.
Receipt of manuscript acknowledged: Yes
Decision to publish in: 3-4 months
Accepted manuscript published in: 6 months
Rejected manuscript returned: Yes, with return postage paid by publication.
Rejected manuscript criticized: Sometimes
Submit to:
R. Carter Elwood
Managing Editor
(See address above)

CANADIAN-AMERICAN REVIEW OF HUNGARIAN STUDIES [648]

Hungarian Reader's Service, Inc.
908-1356 Meadowlands Drive East
Ottawa, Ontario K2E 6K6, Canada

First published in 1974

SUBSCRIPTION DATA
Issues and rates: Published semi-annually.
Annual rate(s): $12.00; Foreign $12.00; Students $8.00
Publisher or Sponsor: Magyar Lektoratus, Inc.

EDITORIAL DESCRIPTION
Publishes articles and book reviews in all fields of Hungarian studies.
Articles per average issue: 4
Audience: Professional, academic
Manuscripts accepted in English (Hungarian, French)

MANUSCRIPT INFORMATION
Subject field(s): Hungarian history, sociology, geography, politics, linguistics; Hungarians outside Hungary, especially North America; book reviews on East European affairs
Manuscript requirements: See latest issue for style requirements. Style sheet sent on request.
Preferred length: 6,000-9, words
Number of copies to be submitted: 2
Abstract: Not necessary.
Author information and reprints: Payment: Reprints only. 12 issues, 50 offprints
Is simultaneous submission of article to other journals permitted: Not permitted.
Exclusive manuscript rights between acceptance and publication: No
Copyright: Held by the Hungarian Reader's Service, Inc.
Reprints: Available at cost.
Disposition of manuscript:
Query letter: Not necessary, but advisable.
Receipt of manuscript acknowledged: Yes
Decision to publish in: A few months
Accepted manuscript published in: Up to a year
Rejected manuscript returned: Yes, with return postage paid by publication.
Rejected manuscript criticized: Sometimes
Submit to:
Nandor F. Dreisziger
Editor
Department of History
The Royal Military College of Canada
Kingston, Ontario Canada
(613) 545-7243

EAST EUROPEAN QUARTERLY [649]

Box 29, Regent Hall
University of Colorado
Boulder, Colorado 80302
(303) 492-6183

First published in 1967

SUBSCRIPTION DATA
Issues and rates: Published quarterly.
Annual rate(s): $12.00; Foreign $12.00; Institutions $12.00

EDITORIAL DESCRIPTION
A scholarly journal devoted to the publication of articles, documents, and reviews related to the history, politics, society, economics, and civilization of Eastern Europe
Articles per average issue: 7
Audience: Specialists, academic
Manuscripts accepted in English, French, German, Italian

MANUSCRIPT INFORMATION
Subject field(s): The social sciences and humanities as related to Eastern Europe
Manuscript requirements: Any professional stylistic manual.
Preferred length: 5,000-10,000 words; 12-24 pages
Number of copies to be submitted: 1
Abstract: Not necessary.
Author information and reprints: Payment: Reprints only.
Is simultaneous submission of article to other journals permitted: Permitted.
Exclusive manuscript rights between acceptance and publication: Yes
Copyright: In the public domain
Reprints: Almost any quantity desired available at cost.
Disposition of manuscript:
Query letter: Not necessary.
Receipt of manuscript acknowledged: Yes
Decision to publish in: 6 weeks
Accepted manuscript published in: 18 months
Rejected manuscript returned: Yes, with return postage paid by publication.
Rejected manuscript criticized: Reasons for rejections only
Submit to:
Stephen Fischer-Galati
Editor
(See address above)

EIRE-IRELAND [650]

A Journal of Irish Studies
683 Osceola Avenue
St. Paul, Minnesota 55105
(612) 647-5678

First published in 1966

SUBSCRIPTION DATA
Issues and rates: Published quarterly.
Average paid circulation: 4,800
Annual rate(s): $10.00
Publisher or Sponsor: Irish American Cultural Institute
Managing Editor: Eoin McKiernan

EDITORIAL DESCRIPTION
Contains articles dealing with Irish culture (history, literature, science, art, etc.) treated objectively and in a scholarly manner.
Articles per average issue: 12
Audience: General, Academic
Manuscripts accepted in English

MANUSCRIPT INFORMATION
Manuscript requirements: MLA
Preferred length: 2,000-5,000 words
Number of copies to be submitted: One
Abstract: Helpful, but not necessary
Author information and reprints: Payment: None.
Is simultaneous submission of article to other journals permitted: If advised
Copyright: Held by publication.
Reprints: Not available.
Disposition of manuscript:
Query letter: Helpful
Receipt of manuscript acknowledged: Yes
Decision to publish in: Up to 4 months
Accepted manuscript published in: Up to 8 months
Rejected manuscript returned: Yes, if return postage is supplied by author.
Rejected manuscript criticized: Yes
Submit to:
Eoin McKiernan
Editor
(See address above)

ITALIAN QUARTERLY [651]

University of Massachusetts, Boston
Harbor Campus
Boston, Massachusetts 02125

First published in 1957

SUBSCRIPTION DATA
Issues and rates: Published quarterly.
Annual rate(s): $8.00

EDITORIAL DESCRIPTION
Publishes scholarly articles and reviews in the area of Italian studies

Articles per average issue: 4-5
Audience: Academic
  Manuscripts accepted in English, some Italian, French

MANUSCRIPT INFORMATION

Manuscript requirements: See latest issue for style requirements.
  Preferred length: 20-25 pages
  Number of copies to be submitted: 2
  Abstract: Not necessary.
Author information and reprints: Payment: None.
  Is simultaneous submission of article to other journals permitted: Not permitted.
  Exclusive manuscript rights between acceptance and publication: Yes
  Copyright: Held by publication.
  Reprints: Available at cost.
Disposition of manuscript:
  Query letter: Not necessary.
  Receipt of manuscript acknowledged: Yes
  Decision to publish in: 3 months
  Accepted manuscript published in: 12-24 months
  Rejected manuscript returned: Yes, if return postage is supplied by author.
  Rejected manuscript criticized: Sometimes
Submit to:
  Spencer Di Scala
  Executive Editor
  (See address above)

JOURNAL OF BALTIC STUDIES [652]

AABS Executive Office
366 86th Street
Brooklyn, New York 11209
(212) 745-3893

Previously entitled *Bulletin of Baltic Studies*

First published in 1970

SUBSCRIPTION DATA

Issues and rates: Published quarterly.
  Average paid circulation: 1,300
  Annual rate(s): Individuals $15.00; Institutions $20.00; Students $7.50; Members $15.00
Publisher or Sponsor: Association for the Advancement of Baltic Studies, Inc. (AABS)

EDITORIAL DESCRIPTION

  An interdisciplinary scholarly publication featuring articles, reviews, bibliographical notes, news, research in progress on the Baltic area and related studies and events
Articles per average issue: 6-8
Audience: Academic
  Manuscripts accepted in English, German

MANUSCRIPT INFORMATION

Manuscript requirements: MLA
  Preferred length: 12-30 pages double-spaced
  Number of copies to be submitted: 2
  Abstract: Yes. Up to 200 words for literature, linguistics and folklore articles

Author information and reprints: Payment: Reprints only. 1 gratis copy plus offprints
  Is simultaneous submission of article to other journals permitted: Not permitted.
  Exclusive manuscript rights between acceptance and publication: Yes
  Copyright: Held by publication.
  Reprints: Not available.
Additional information: Desire a good academic or scholarly style, footnotes following the body of the article. Cyrillic transliterations should follow the MLA style.
Disposition of manuscript:
  Query letter: Not necessary.
  Receipt of manuscript acknowledged: Yes
  Decision to publish in: 3 months
  Accepted manuscript published in: 3-9 months
  Rejected manuscript returned: Yes, with return postage paid by publication.
  Rejected manuscript criticized: Yes
Submit to:
  Arvids Ziedonis, Jr.
  Editor
  Muhlenburg College
  Allentown, Pennsylvania 18104
  (215) 433-3191

JOURNAL OF INDO-EUROPEAN STUDIES [653]

Montana College of Mineral Science and Technology
Butte, Montana 59701
(406) 792-8321

First published in 1973

SUBSCRIPTION DATA

Issues and rates: Published quarterly.
  Annual rate(s): Institutions $18.00; Students $9.00
Managing Editor: Dr. Roger Pearson

EDITORIAL DESCRIPTION

  An academic publication synthesizing archaeological, linguistic, mythological and historical material relating to the prehistory and early history of the culture and migration of the Indo-European speaking peoples of Europe and Asia.
Articles per average issue: 8
Audience: Academic
  Manuscripts accepted in English

MANUSCRIPT INFORMATION

Manuscript requirements: Style sheet sent on request.
  Preferred length: 8,000 words maximum
  Number of copies to be submitted: 2
  Abstract: Yes. Of about 50-100 words
Author information and reprints: Payment: Reprints only. 75
  Is simultaneous submission of article to other journals permitted: Permitted.
  Exclusive manuscript rights between acceptance and publication: Yes
  Copyright: Held by publication.
  Reprints: Available at no cost. 75 free

Additional information: Suggest contacting the editorial office with outline of the proposed article for advice and guidance.
Submit to:
  The Editor
  (See address above)

LITUANUS [654]

Lithuanian Quarterly Journal of Arts and Sciences
6621 South Troy Avenue
Chicago, Illinois 60629

First published in 1954

SUBSCRIPTION DATA

Issues and rates: Published quarterly.
  Average paid circulation: 4,100
  Annual rate(s): $8.00
Managing Editor: John A. Rackauskas

EDITORIAL DESCRIPTION

  Includes interdisciplinary articles and essays, art reproductions, book reviews, comments, documentary material, and a presentation of *belles lettres*. Limited to the examination of all questions pertaining to the countries and people of the Baltic States, particularly Lithuania (in general, Latvia and Estonia).
Articles per average issue: 5-6
Audience: Academic
  Manuscripts accepted in English

MANUSCRIPT INFORMATION

Subject field(s): Political science, bibliographic material, archeology, history, literature, poetry, religion, education, philosophy, geography
Manuscript requirements: Chicago or MLA
  Preferred length: 10-12 pages
  Number of copies to be submitted: Two
  Abstract: No
Author information and reprints: Payment: None.
  Is simultaneous submission of article to other journals permitted: No
  Exclusive manuscript rights between acceptance and publication: Yes
  Copyright: Held by publication.
  Reprints: Not available.
Additional information: Typewritten, double-spaced, footnotes numbered at end on separate sheet.
Disposition of manuscript:
  Query letter: No
  Receipt of manuscript acknowledged: Yes
  Decision to publish in: 2-4 weeks
  Accepted manuscript published in: 6-12 months
  Rejected manuscript returned: Yes
  Rejected manuscript criticized: No
Submit to:
  John A. Rackauskes
  General and Managing Editor
  Chicago State University (E-328)
  Chicago, Illinois 60628
  (312) 995-2349

NEW WORLD REVIEW [655]
Suite 308
156 Fifth Avenue
New York, New York 10010
(212) CH 3-0666

SUBSCRIPTION DATA

Issues and rates: Published bi-monthly.
Annual rate(s): $4.00; Foreign $5.00; Institutions $4.00; Foreign institutions $5.00

Managing Editor: Jessica Smith

EDITORIAL DESCRIPTION

Devoted to a sympathetic review of life and thought in the Soviet Union and other socialist countries; of national liberation movements and the issues of peace, war and social change; international relations as applied to the socialist countries

Articles per average issue: 8-10
Audience: Specialists, professional, academic, general
Manuscripts accepted in English

MANUSCRIPT INFORMATION

Subject field(s): World peace, detente, U.S.-Soviet relations, cultural change, trade, poetry if pertinent
Manuscript requirements: No specific style guide.
Preferred length: 1,000-3,000 words
Number of copies to be submitted: 1
Abstract: Not necessary.
Author information and reprints: Payment: Reprints only. By arrangement
Is simultaneous submission of article to other journals permitted: Permitted, with knowledge of the publication
Exclusive manuscript rights between acceptance and publication: Yes
Copyright: None
Reprints: Available at cost.
Additional information: All articles should be accompanied by a biographical description of the author.
Disposition of manuscript:
Query letter: Not necessary, but advisable.
Receipt of manuscript acknowledged: Yes
Decision to publish in: 1-4 weeks
Accepted manuscript published in: Varies
Rejected manuscript returned: Yes, if return postage is supplied by author.
Rejected manuscript criticized: Sometimes
Submit to:
Jessica Smith
Editor
(See address above)

RUNDSCHAU [656]
An American German Review
339 Walnut Street
Philadelphia, Pennsylvania 19106
WA 3-7230

First published in 1970

SUBSCRIPTION DATA

Issues and rates: 9 times a year
Average paid circulation: 100,000 controlled
Annual rate(s): $4.50; Students Free
Publisher or Sponsor: National Carl Schurz Association
Managing Editor: Hans W. Henzel

EDITORIAL DESCRIPTION

Publishes reports on social, political, and cultural events in Germany and other German-speaking areas of the world.

Articles per average issue: 8
Audience: Students
Manuscripts accepted in English, German

MANUSCRIPT INFORMATION

Subject field(s): Almost anything having to do with Germany except of a very technical or scholarly nature.
Manuscript requirements: No specific style guide.
Preferred length: 2,000 words maximum
Number of copies to be submitted: 1
Abstract: Not necessary.
Author information and reprints: Payment: By publication to author. $.05 per word.
Is simultaneous submission of article to other journals permitted: Permitted.
Exclusive manuscript rights between acceptance and publication: Yes
Copyright: Held by publication.
Reprints: Not available.
Additional information: Welcomes photographs. These are paid for separately.
Disposition of manuscript:
Query letter: Not necessary, but advisable.
Receipt of manuscript acknowledged: No
Decision to publish in: 2-4 weeks
Accepted manuscript published in: Varies
Rejected manuscript returned: Yes, if return postage is supplied by author.
Rejected manuscript criticized: Reasons for rejections only
Submit to:
Editor
(See address above)

THE RUSSIAN REVIEW [657]
An American Quarterly devoted to Russia Past and Present
LHH 216
Hoover Institution
Stanford, California 94305
(415) 497-2067

First published in 1942

SUBSCRIPTION DATA

Issues and rates: Published quarterly.
Average paid circulation: 1,700
Annual rate(s): $12.00; Foreign $13.00; Institutions $12.00; Students $8.00
Publisher or Sponsor: The Hoover Institution
Managing Editor: Terence Emmons

EDITORIAL DESCRIPTION

Provides a forum for work on Russian-American and Soviet-American relations past and present

Articles per average issue: 5
Audience: Academic, scholarly
Manuscripts accepted in English, French, German, Russian

MANUSCRIPT INFORMATION

Subject field(s): Russian history, political science, literature, linguistics, sociology, psychology, the arts
Manuscript requirements: Chicago
Preferred length: 7,000
Number of copies to be submitted: 2
Abstract: Not necessary.
Author information and reprints: Payment: Reprints only. Occasional cash payments to free-lance writers
Is simultaneous submission of article to other journals permitted: Not permitted.
Exclusive manuscript rights between acceptance and publication: Yes
Copyright: First serial rights
Reprints: Not available.
Disposition of manuscript:
Query letter: Not necessary.
Receipt of manuscript acknowledged: No
Decision to publish in: 4-6 weeks
Accepted manuscript published in: 3-6 months
Rejected manuscript returned: Yes, if return postage is supplied by author.
Rejected manuscript criticized: Reasons for rejections only
Submit to:
Terence Emmons;
W. Thomas Wilfong
Editors
(See address above)

SCANDINAVIAN REVIEW [658]
127 East 73rd Street
New York, New York 10021
(212) 879-9779

Previously entitled *The American-Scandinavian Review*

First published in 1913

SUBSCRIPTION DATA

Issues and rates: Published quarterly.
Average paid circulation: 7,500
Annual rate(s): $9.00; Foreign $10.00; Members $20.00
Publisher or Sponsor: The American-Scandinavian Foundation

EDITORIAL DESCRIPTION

Contains articles about modern Scandinavian history, life, culture, arts, and science, Nordic area studies.

Articles per average issue: 7
Audience: General
Manuscripts accepted in English

MANUSCRIPT INFORMATION

Manuscript requirements: MLA
Preferred length: 2500-3000 words; 8-10 pages
Number of copies to be submitted: One
Abstract: No

Author information and reprints: Payment: By publication to author. $75.00 or more per article.
Is simultaneous submission of article to other journals permitted: No
Exclusive manuscript rights between acceptance and publication: Yes
Copyright: Held by publication.
Reprints: Available, price on application
Additional information: Copy deadlings are the first of December, March, June, and September.
Disposition of manuscript:
Query letter: Preferred
Receipt of manuscript acknowledged: No
Decision to publish in: 2 weeks
Accepted manuscript published in: 4-6 weeks
Rejected manuscript returned: Yes
Rejected manuscript criticized: No
Submit to:
Erik J. Friis
Editor
(See address above)

SLAVIC REVIEW [659]
American Quarterly of Soviet and East European Studies
409 East Chalmers, Room 352
University of Illinois
Champaign, Illinois 61820
(217) 333-9253

Previously entitled *American Slavic and East European Review*

First published in 1941

SUBSCRIPTION DATA
Issues and rates: Published quarterly.
Average paid circulation: 3,800; 100 controlled
Annual rate(s): $20.00
Publisher or Sponsor: American Association for the Advancement of Slavic Studies

EDITORIAL DESCRIPTION
Contains contributions on Russia and Eastern Europe, past and present (discussion, articles, notes and comment, reviews, news of the profession, books received, etc.)
Articles per average issue: 7
Audience: Slavic area specialists
Manuscripts accepted in English

MANUSCRIPT INFORMATION
Subject field(s): History, literature, political science, international affairs, economics, sociology, geography, arts, language and linguistics, anthropology, philosophy, law
Manuscript requirements: Chicago, Library of Congress transliteration system (with modifications).
Preferred length: 25 pages
Number of copies to be submitted: 3
Abstract: Yes
Author information and reprints: Payment: Reprints only. A copy of the issue and 15 tearsheets of article
Is simultaneous submission of article to other journals permitted: No

Exclusive manuscript rights between acceptance and publication: Yes
Copyright: Held by publication.
Reprints: Available
Additional information: Manuscript should be typed clearly on white paper of good quality (erasable bond is not recommended). Everything should be double-spaced, including the footnotes, which should be numbered consecutively and placed at the end of the manuscript.
Disposition of manuscript:
Query letter: No
Receipt of manuscript acknowledged: Yes
Decision to publish in: 2 months
Accepted manuscript published in: 8-9 months
Rejected manuscript returned: Yes
Rejected manuscript criticized: Yes
Submit to:
James R. Millar
Editor
(See address above)

SOVIET STUDIES [660]
Publications Office
University of Glasgow
Glasgow G12 8QG, Scotland
(041) 339-8855

SUBSCRIPTION DATA
Issues and rates: Published quarterly.
Annual rate(s): £6.00; $18.00
Publisher or Sponsor: University of Glasgow
Managing Editor: J. Miller, M.A.

EDITORIAL DESCRIPTION
An academic journal publishing articles pertaining to the social and economic structure and institutions of the USSR and Eastern Europe
Articles per average issue: 7
Audience: University staff and students
Manuscripts accepted in English

MANUSCRIPT INFORMATION
Manuscript requirements: Style sheet sent on request.
Preferred length: 10,000 words maximum
Number of copies to be submitted: 2
Abstract: Not necessary.
Author information and reprints: Payment: None. Authors receive 75 per cent of any royalties from reprinting elsewhere.
Is simultaneous submission of article to other journals permitted: Not permitted.
Exclusive manuscript rights between acceptance and publication: Yes
Copyright: Held by the University of Glasgow
Reprints: Available at no cost. 25 Available at cost.
Disposition of manuscript:
Query letter: Not necessary.
Receipt of manuscript acknowledged: Yes
Decision to publish in: 1 month
Accepted manuscript published in: 6 months
Rejected manuscript returned: Yes, if return postage is supplied by author.
Rejected manuscript criticized: Sometimes

Submit to:
The Editor
9 Southhark Terrace
Glasgow, Scotland

SURVEY [661]
A Journal of East and West Studies
Oxford University Press
Press Road
Neasden, London NW10, England
(01) 450-8080

First published in 1956

SUBSCRIPTION DATA
Issues and rates: Published quarterly.
Average paid circulation: 3,000
Annual rate(s): £4.00; $10.00; Institutions £4.00; $10.00
Publisher or Sponsor: International Association for Cultural Freedom, Stanford University
Managing Editor: Leopold Ladebz

EDITORIAL DESCRIPTION
Discusses contemporary problems within the framework of East-West relations. Contributions cover a broad range of academic disciplines.
Articles per average issue: 10-12
Audience: Academic, general public interested in current affairs
Manuscripts accepted in English preferred, Russian, French, German accepted

MANUSCRIPT INFORMATION
Subject field(s): Political and current affairs in relation to Eastern Europe and other communist countries, East-West relations, contemporary and social issues in the same areas; comparative analyses of political, cultural and socio-economic issues with special emphasis on specialized studies, and of current ideological trends.
Manuscript requirements: See latest issue for style requirements.
Preferred length: None
Number of copies to be submitted: 2
Abstract: Not necessary.
Author information and reprints: Payment: By publication to author. £6.00 per 1,000 words, with a £30.00 limit
Is simultaneous submission of article to other journals permitted: Not permitted.
Exclusive manuscript rights between acceptance and publication: Yes
Copyright: Held by publication.
Reprints: Available at no cost. 25 Available at cost.
Disposition of manuscript:
Query letter: Not necessary, but advisable.
Receipt of manuscript acknowledged: Yes
Decision to publish in: Varies
Accepted manuscript published in: Varies
Rejected manuscript returned: Yes, with return postage paid by publication.
Rejected manuscript criticized: Reasons for rejections only
Submit to:
Leopold Labedz

Editor
Ilford House
133 Oxford Street
London W1R 1TD, England
(01) 734-0592/3

TODAY IN FRANCE [662]
Box 551, Cathedral Station
New York, New York 10025
(212) 749-3843

First published in 1961

SUBSCRIPTION DATA
Issues and rates: Published bi-monthly.
  Average paid circulation: 750; 1200 controlled
  Annual rate(s): $4.00 1 year; $7, 2 years
Publisher or Sponsor: Society for French-American Affairs
Managing Editor: Benjamin Protter

EDITORIAL DESCRIPTION
Contains information pertinent to French politics and international affairs, articles by prominent French political writers; also analysis of news. Covers general information concerning educational field in France.
Articles per average issue: 3-4
Audience: Academic, political
  Manuscripts accepted in English, French

MANUSCRIPT INFORMATION
Subject field(s): French domestic and foreign affairs, international matters affecting American-French relations, conditions in French schools, etc.
Manuscript requirements: See latest issue for style requirements. brevity; must also have verifiable material
  Preferred length: 1000 words
  Number of copies to be submitted: One
  Abstract: No
Author information and reprints: Payment: None.
  Is simultaneous submission of article to other journals permitted: No
  Exclusive manuscript rights between acceptance and publication: Yes
  Copyright: Held by publication.
  Reprints: 5 copies free to author, additional at cost depending on quantity
Disposition of manuscript:
  Query letter: Preferable
  Receipt of manuscript acknowledged: Yes
  Decision to publish in: 2 weeks
  Accepted manuscript published in: 2 months
  Rejected manuscript returned: Yes, if return postage is supplied by author.
  Rejected manuscript criticized: No
Submit to:
  Editor
  (See address above)

SPECIAL STIPULATIONS
Request that articles give facts and analysis and avoid personal opinions as such.

THE UKRAINIAN HISTORIAN [663]
P.O. Box 312
Kent, Ohio 44240

First published in 1965

SUBSCRIPTION DATA
Issues and rates: Published quarterly.
  Annual rate(s): $12.00
Publisher or Sponsor: Ukrainian Historical Association, Inc.

EDITORIAL DESCRIPTION
Contains articles on the political, cultural and social history of the Ukraine and Eastern Europe.
Articles per average issue: 10-12
Audience: Academic
  Manuscripts accepted in English, Ukrainian

MANUSCRIPT INFORMATION
Subject field(s): History, historiography, ecclesiastical history, social history, history of ideas, history of immigration to the U.S., archaeology, bibliography, biography and related studies
Manuscript requirements: Turabian
  Preferred length: 10-25 pages
  Number of copies to be submitted: Two
  Abstract: Yes
Author information and reprints: Payment: None.
  Is simultaneous submission of article to other journals permitted: No
  Exclusive manuscript rights between acceptance and publication: Yes
  Copyright: Held by publication.
  Reprints: Available
Additional information: Typewritten, double-spaced manuscript
Disposition of manuscript:
  Query letter: Yes
  Receipt of manuscript acknowledged: Yes
  Decision to publish in: 1-3 months
  Accepted manuscript published in: 3-5 months
  Rejected manuscript returned: Yes, if return postage is supplied by author.
  Rejected manuscript criticized: Yes
Submit to:
  Dr. L. R. Wynar
  Editor
  (See address above)

Latin American studies

HISPANIC AMERICAN HISTORICAL REVIEW* [665]
Duke University Press
6697 College Station
Durham, North Carolina 27708
(919) 684-2173

SUBSCRIPTION DATA
Issues and rates: Published quarterly.
  Average paid circulation: 2657; 96 controlled
  Annual rate(s): Individuals $10.00, Institutions $12.00, Foreign $4.00
Publisher or Sponsor: American Historical Association, Conference on Latin American History

EDITORIAL DESCRIPTION
Contains articles, book reviews, book notices, other books received, professional notes, correspondence, notes and comments items.

MANUSCRIPT INFORMATION
Subject field(s): Latin American history; Spanish and Portuguese history, if related to Latin America; other European history or U.S. history as it relates to Latin American history; focus on the impingement on Latin America is required, as well as (normally) the use of Latin American sources.
Manuscript requirements: Style sheet sent on request.
  Preferred length: 35 pages
  Number of copies to be submitted: One
Author information and reprints: Payment: None.
  Is simultaneous submission of article to other journals permitted: No
  Exclusive manuscript rights between acceptance and publication: Yes
  Copyright: Held by publication.
  Reprints: Available, 25 free, schedule of rates for additional copies.
Additional information: Any graphs used in articles accepted for publication must be submitted by the author as camera-ready copy; tables in articles should be kept as mechanically simple as possible.
Disposition of manuscript:
  Receipt of manuscript acknowledged: Yes
  Decision to publish in: Two to six months
  Accepted manuscript published in: Varies
  Rejected manuscript returned: Yes
  Rejected manuscript criticized: Frequently
Submit to:
  Stanley R. Ross
  Managing Editor
  Sid W. Richardson Hall, Unit I
  The University of Texas
  Austin, Texas 78712
  (512) 471-5551

JOURNAL OF INTERAMERICAN STUDIES AND WORLD AFFAIRS* [666]
Sage Publications, Inc.
275 South Beverly Drive
Beverly Hills, California 90212
(213) 274-2423

SUBSCRIPTION DATA
Issues and rates: Published quarterly.
  Average paid circulation: Not available.
  Annual rate(s): Institutions $15.00; Individuals $10.00; Students $8.00; Foreign individuals $11.50; Foreign institutions $16.50

Publisher or Sponsor: University of Miami, Center for Advanced International Studies

EDITORIAL DESCRIPTION

Concerned with social, economic, political, and cultural aspects of life in Latin America, including the Caribbean, particularly when the subject is of concern to more than one of the traditional disciplines.

MANUSCRIPT INFORMATION

Subject field(s): Sociology, politics, culture, economics
Manuscript requirements: Style sheet sent on request.
  Preferred length: 6,250-7,500 words; 25 to 30 pages
  Number of copies to be submitted: Two
Author information and reprints: Payment: None. 25 tear-sheets free to author.
  Is simultaneous submission of article to other journals permitted: Permitted, but not encouraged. Author must notify publisher that manuscript is under consideration elsewhere.
  Exclusive manuscript rights between acceptance and publication: Yes
  Copyright: Held by publication.
  Reprints: Available if purchased by special order in amounts no fewer than 100
Disposition of manuscript:
  Receipt of manuscript acknowledged: Yes
  Decision to publish in: Six to eight weeks
  Accepted manuscript published in: Six to nine months
  Rejected manuscript returned: Yes
  Rejected manuscript criticized: Yes
Submit to:
  John P. Harrison
  Editor
  Institute of Inter-American Studies
  Center for Advanced International Studies
  University of Miami, Box 8134
  Coral Gables, Florida 33124

JOURNAL OF LATIN AMERICAN STUDIES [667]
Cambridge University Press
32 East 57th Street
New York, New York 10022

SUBSCRIPTION DATA

Issues and rates: Published semi-annually.
Publisher or Sponsor: Institutes of Latin American Studies at the Universities of Cambridge, Glasgow, Liverpool, London and Oxford

EDITORIAL DESCRIPTION

Free discussion of all topics pertaining to Latin American studies
Manuscripts accepted in English

MANUSCRIPT INFORMATION

Subject field(s): The study of Latin America from the standpoint of the social sciences, including anthropology, archaeology, economics, geography, history, international relations, politics, sociology, etc.
Manuscript requirements: See latest issue for style requirements.
  Preferred length: 8,000 words maximum
  Number of copies to be submitted: 2, typewritten, double-spaced
  Abstract: Yes.
Author information and reprints: Payment: Reprints only. 25 offprints
  Is simultaneous submission of article to other journals permitted: Not permitted.
  Exclusive manuscript rights between acceptance and publication: Yes
  Copyright: Held by publication.
  Reprints: Available at cost.
Additional information: Not concerned with linguistic or literary studies
Disposition of manuscript:
  Query letter: Not necessary, but advisable.
  Receipt of manuscript acknowledged: Yes
  Rejected manuscript returned: Yes, if return postage is supplied by author.
  Rejected manuscript criticized: Sometimes
Submit to:
  The Editors
  Institute of Latin American Studies
  31 Tavistock Square
  London WC1H 9HA, England

LATIN AMERICAN RESEARCH REVIEW [668]
Hamilton Hall
University of North Carolina
Chapel Hill, North Carolina 27514
(919)933-3041

First published in 1965

SUBSCRIPTION DATA

Issues and rates: Published three times per year.
  Average paid circulation: 3000
  Annual rate(s): Institutions $8.00; Individuals $5.00; Students $8.00
Publisher or Sponsor: Latin American Studies Association
Managing Editor: Leah Florence

EDITORIAL DESCRIPTION

Contains interdisciplinary articles on Latin America.
Articles per average issue: 8
Audience: Scholars
  Manuscripts accepted in English, Spanish, Portuguese

MANUSCRIPT INFORMATION

Subject field(s): All fields with Latin American content.
Manuscript requirements: Style sheet sent on request.
  Preferred length: None
  Number of copies to be submitted: Two
  Abstract: No
Author information and reprints: Payment: None.
  Is simultaneous submission of article to other journals permitted: No
  Exclusive manuscript rights between acceptance and publication: Yes
  Copyright: Held by publication.
  Reprints: Available to author only
Additional information: Everything typewritten, double-spaced.
Disposition of manuscript:
  Query letter: Yes
  Receipt of manuscript acknowledged: Yes
  Decision to publish in: 60-90 days
  Accepted manuscript published in: 9 months
  Rejected manuscript returned: Yes
  Rejected manuscript criticized: Yes
Submit to:
  John D. Martz
  Editor-in-Chief
  (See address above)

LUSO-BRAZILIAN REVIEW [669]
University of Wisconsin Press
Box 1379
Madison, Wisconsin 53701
(608) 262-1116

SUBSCRIPTION DATA

Issues and rates: Published semi-annually.
  Average paid circulation: 600; 10 controlled
  Annual rate(s): $8.00, Individuals $5.00

EDITORIAL DESCRIPTION

Contains articles on history, language, economics, geography, literature, sociology, and civilization of Portuguese-speaking areas of the world.
Articles per average issue: 10
Audience: Scholars
  Manuscripts accepted in English, Spanish, Portuguese, French

MANUSCRIPT INFORMATION

Manuscript requirements: MLA; Chicago
  Preferred length: 20 pages
  Number of copies to be submitted: One
  Abstract: No
Author information and reprints: Payment: None.
  Is simultaneous submission of article to other journals permitted: Yes
  Exclusive manuscript rights between acceptance and publication: Yes
  Copyright: Held by Regents of the University of Wisconsin
  Reprints: Available
Disposition of manuscript:
  Query letter: No
  Receipt of manuscript acknowledged: Yes
  Decision to publish in: 60 days
  Accepted manuscript published in: Depends on field
  Rejected manuscript returned: Yes
  Rejected manuscript criticized: Yes
Submit to:
  Managing Editor
  1107 Van Hise Hall
  1220 Linden Drive
  Madison, Wisconsin 53706
  (608) 262-2529

SOCIAL AND ECONOMIC STUDIES [670]

Institute of Social and Economic Research
University of the West Indies
Mona
Kingston 7, Jamaica
927-6661 ext. 409

First published in 1953

SUBSCRIPTION DATA

Issues and rates: Published quarterly.
Annual rate(s): $6.00; Foreign $7.50 (U. S.)

EDITORIAL DESCRIPTION

A journal devoted to the publication of research and discussion on agricultural, anthropological, demographic, economic, educational, monetary, political and sociological questions with emphasis on the problems of the developing territories, particular those in the Caribbean.

Articles per average issue: 5
Audience: Academic
Manuscripts accepted in English

MANUSCRIPT INFORMATION

Manuscript requirements: See latest issue for style requirements.
Number of copies to be submitted: 3
Abstract: Yes
Author information and reprints: Payment: Reprints only. 25 reprints
Is simultaneous submission of article to other journals permitted: No
Exclusive manuscript rights between acceptance and publication: No
Copyright: Held by publication.
Reprints: Available at cost
Disposition of manuscript:
Query letter: No
Receipt of manuscript acknowledged: Yes
Decision to publish in: 3 months
Accepted manuscript published in: 6-12 months
Rejected manuscript returned: Yes
Rejected manuscript criticized: No
Submit to:
Alister McIntyre
Publications Editor
(See address above)

Middle Eastern studies

INTERNATIONAL JOURNAL OF MIDDLE EAST STUDIES [671]

Middle East Studies Association, New York University
50 Washington Square
New York, New York 10003
(212) 598-2400

First published in 1970

SUBSCRIPTION DATA

Issues and rates: Published quarterly.
Average paid circulation: 1,500
Annual rate(s): Institutions $40.00; Students $12.50; Members $30.00
Publisher or Sponsor: Middle East Studies Association

EDITORIAL DESCRIPTION

Devoted to the publication of original monographs concerning the middle eastern world from the 7th century to modern times

Articles per average issue: 6
Audience: Professional, academic
Manuscripts accepted in English (quotes in middle eastern languages)

MANUSCRIPT INFORMATION

Subject field(s): History, political science, economics, anthropology, sociology, philology, law, philosophy and literature of the area encompassing Iran, Turkey, Afghanistan, Israel, Pakistan, and the Arab countries, mostly in the social sciences and humanities.
Manuscript requirements: See latest issue for style requirements.
Preferred length: 20 typewritten pages
Number of copies to be submitted: 1
Abstract: Not necessary.
Author information and reprints: Payment: Reprints only. 50
Is simultaneous submission of article to other journals permitted: Not permitted.
Exclusive manuscript rights between acceptance and publication: Yes
Copyright: Held by publication.
Disposition of manuscript:
Query letter: Not necessary, but advisable.
Receipt of manuscript acknowledged: Yes
Decision to publish in: 2-3 months
Accepted manuscript published in: 1 year
Rejected manuscript returned: Yes, if return postage is supplied by author.
Rejected manuscript criticized: Reasons for rejections only
Submit to:
Stanford J. Shaw
Editor
Department of History
University of California, Los Angeles
Los Angeles, California 90024
(213) 825-1571

JOURNAL OF NEAR EASTERN STUDIES [672]

University of Chicago Press
5801 Ellis Avenue
Chicago, Illinois 60637
(312) 753-2493

Previously entitled *Hebraica*, 1884-95; *American Journal of Semitic Languages and Literatures*, 1895-1941

First published in 1884

SUBSCRIPTION DATA

Issues and rates: Published quarterly.
Average paid circulation: 2,500; 100 controlled
Annual rate(s): $10.00; Foreign $13.00; Institutions $12.00; Students $7.00
Publisher or Sponsor: University of Chicago, Department of Near Eastern Languages and Civilizations

EDITORIAL DESCRIPTION

Contains scholarly articles and book reviews dealing with the ancient and medieval Near East, especially ancient Egypt, Babylonia, Palestine, and Iran, including archaeology, languages, literature, history, Old Testament and Islam

Articles per average issue: 4-8
Audience: Professional, academic
Manuscripts accepted in English, French, German

MANUSCRIPT INFORMATION

Manuscript requirements: Chicago
Preferred length: As required
Number of copies to be submitted: 2
Abstract: Not necessary.
Author information and reprints: Payment: Reprints only. 50
Is simultaneous submission of article to other journals permitted: Not permitted.
Exclusive manuscript rights between acceptance and publication: Yes
Copyright: Held by publication.
Reprints: Available at cost.
Additional information: Everything typewritten, double-spaced, with footnotes listed separately and numbered consecutively throughout.
Disposition of manuscript:
Query letter: Not necessary.
Receipt of manuscript acknowledged: Yes
Decision to publish in: 1-2 months
Accepted manuscript published in: 18-24 months
Rejected manuscript returned: Yes, if return postage is supplied by author.
Rejected manuscript criticized: Sometimes
Submit to:
Robert D. Biggs
Editor
1155 East 58th Street
Chicago, Illinois 60637

SPECIAL STIPULATIONS

No articles on modern political problems of the Near East are accepted.

JOURNAL OF PALESTINE STUDIES [673]

Institute for Palestine Studies
P.O. Box 11-7164
Ashqar Building, Clemenceau Street
Beirut, Lebanon
236547

First published in 1971

SUBSCRIPTION DATA

Issues and rates: Published quarterly.
Average paid circulation: 4,127; 4,800 controlled
Annual rate(s): £4.90; Foreign $12.00

Publisher or Sponsor: Institute for Palestine Studies, Kuwait University

EDITORIAL DESCRIPTION

Provides analytical articles in all disciplines on the Palestine problem and the Arab-Israeli conflict; includes pertinent Arab political documents and surveys of the Arab and Hebrew press as well as a bibliographical survey of relevent international periodical literature.
Articles per average issue: 7
Audience: Academic
Manuscripts accepted in Arabic, English, German, French

MANUSCRIPT INFORMATION

Subject field(s): Zionism, Arab-Israeli conflict, Israel, the Palestinians, energy crisis, treated from the standpoint of the various social science disciplines and focusing on current or recent developments.
Manuscript requirements: See latest issue for style requirements.
Preferred length: 6,000-7,000 words; 25 double-spaced pages
Number of copies to be submitted: 1
Abstract: Not necessary.
Author information and reprints: Payment: By publication to author. $100.00 per article.
Is simultaneous submission of article to other journals permitted: Permitted, but not encouraged.
Exclusive manuscript rights between acceptance and publication: Yes
Copyright: Held by publication.
Reprints: Available at no cost. 75
Disposition of manuscript:
Query letter: Not necessary.
Receipt of manuscript acknowledged: Yes
Decision to publish in: 2 months
Accepted manuscript published in: 6-12 months
Rejected manuscript returned: Yes, with return postage paid by publication.
Rejected manuscript criticized: Reasons for rejections only
Submit to:
Hisham B. Sharabi
Editor
(See address above)

MERIP REPORTS [674]
P.O. Box 48, Harvard Square Station
Cambridge, Massachusetts 02138
(617) 491-3261

SUBSCRIPTION DATA

Issues and rates: Published monthly.
Average paid circulation: 2,000 controlled
Annual rate(s): Individuals $6.00, Institutions $10.00
Publisher or Sponsor: Middle East Research and Information Project

EDITORIAL DESCRIPTION

Each issue presents information and analysis on the political economy of the Middle East, on the role of the United States in the area, and on the class and national struggles of the people. Also featured are sections on current events in the Middle East and book reviews. Point of view is anti-imperialist and socialist (independent). The Middle East in its broadest sense includes the Levant, North Africa, Arabian peninsula, Persian-Arab Gulf & surrounding areas: Indian Ocean, Red Sea, and Northeast Africa.
Articles per average issue: 1
Audience: General
Manuscripts accepted in English

MANUSCRIPT INFORMATION

Subject field(s): US involvement in the Middle East, political economy of Middle East, liberation struggles in region, book reviews
Manuscript requirements: Style sheet sent on request.
Preferred length: 10,000 words or less; 40 pages
Number of copies to be submitted: Two
Abstract: No
Author information and reprints: Payment: None.
Is simultaneous submission of article to other journals permitted: Permitted as long as publication is notified in advance
Exclusive manuscript rights between acceptance and publication: No
Copyright: Held by publication.
Reprints: Available
Disposition of manuscript:
Query letter: Helpful
Receipt of manuscript acknowledged: Yes
Decision to publish in: 3 weeks
Accepted manuscript published in: 3 to 6 months
Rejected manuscript returned: Yes
Rejected manuscript criticized: Yes
Submit to:
Editor
(See address above)

THE MIDDLE EAST JOURNAL [675]
1761 N Street, N. W.
Washington, D. C. 20036
(202) 785-1141

First published in 1947

SUBSCRIPTION DATA

Issues and rates: Published quarterly.
Average paid circulation: 3,200
Annual rate(s): $10.00; Pan-Am $10.50; Foreign $10.50; Institutions $10.00; Members $16.00
Publisher or Sponsor: The Middle East Institute

EDITORIAL DESCRIPTION

Takes no stand on the problems of the Middle East; its sole criterion is that material published be sound, informative, and presented without emotional bias.
Articles per average issue: 5
Audience: Specialists, academic, governmental
Manuscripts accepted in English

MANUSCRIPT INFORMATION

Subject field(s): Social sciences, contemporary, covering the Middle East from North Africa to Afghanistan and Pakistan
Manuscript requirements: Style sheet sent on request.
Preferred length: 5,000 words
Number of copies to be submitted: 1
Abstract: Not necessary.
Author information and reprints: Payment: Reprints only. 100
Is simultaneous submission of article to other journals permitted: Not permitted.
Exclusive manuscript rights between acceptance and publication: Yes
Copyright: Held by publication.
Reprints: Available at cost.
Disposition of manuscript:
Query letter: Not necessary, but advisable.
Receipt of manuscript acknowledged: Yes
Decision to publish in: 12 weeks
Accepted manuscript published in: 6 months
Rejected manuscript returned: Yes, with return postage paid by publication.
Rejected manuscript criticized: Sometimes
Submit to:
William Sands
Editor
(See address above)

MIDDLE EAST STUDIES ASSOCIATION BULLETIN [676]
New York University
Hagop Kevorkian Center for Near Eastern Studies
New York, New York 10003
(212) 598-2400

First published in 1967

SUBSCRIPTION DATA

Issues and rates: Published quarterly.
Average paid circulation: 1,500
Annual rate(s): Members $20.00, Students $9.00, Institutions $30.00
Publisher or Sponsor: Middle East Studies Association

EDITORIAL DESCRIPTION

Contains sources of information on research activities in Middle East studies; also articles on teaching materials, research climate and facilities, and model syllabi.
Articles per average issue: 3
Audience: Academic
Manuscripts accepted in English only

MANUSCRIPT INFORMATION

Subject field(s): Teaching materials, research facilities, syllabi of courses on the Middle East, literature in translation
Manuscript requirements: See latest issue for style requirements.
Preferred length: 30 pages
Number of copies to be submitted: One
Abstract: No

Author information and reprints: Payment: None.
  Is simultaneous submission of article to other journals permitted: No
  Copyright: Held by publication.
  Reprints: Not available.
Disposition of manuscript:
  Query letter: Not necessary, but advisable.
  Receipt of manuscript acknowledged: No
  Decision to publish in: 2 weeks
  Accepted manuscript published in: 2-3 months
  Rejected manuscript returned: Yes
  Rejected manuscript criticized: Yes
Submit to:
  I. William Zartman
  Executive Secretary
  (See address above)

MIDDLE EASTERN STUDIES [677]
67 Great Russell Street
London WC1 3BT, England
01-405-9405 ext. 16

First published in 1964

SUBSCRIPTION DATA
Issues and rates: Published three times per year.
  Annual rate(s): £7.50; Foreign $22.50; Institutions £10.00; Foreign institutions $30.00

EDITORIAL DESCRIPTION
Contains articles on contemporary Middle East and its recent past.
Articles per average issue: 5
Audience: Academic political scientists and historians
  Manuscripts accepted in English

MANUSCRIPT INFORMATION
Subject field(s): Middle Eastern studies
Manuscript requirements: See latest issue for style requirements.
  Preferred length: 8,000 words
  Number of copies to be submitted: Two
  Abstract: No
Author information and reprints: Payment: None.
  Is simultaneous submission of article to other journals permitted: No
  Exclusive manuscript rights between acceptance and publication: Yes
  Copyright: Held by publication.
  Reprints: Available, 25 free
Disposition of manuscript:
  Query letter: No
  Receipt of manuscript acknowledged: Yes
  Decision to publish in: 1 month
  Accepted manuscript published in: Varies
  Rejected manuscript returned: Yes
  Rejected manuscript criticized: No
Submit to:
  Elie Kedourie
  Editor
  London School of Economics
  Moughton Street, Aldwych
  London WC2A 2AE, England

North American studies

AFRO-AMERICAN STUDIES* [678]
An Interdisciplinary Journal
Gordon and Breach Science Publishers
One Park Avenue
New York, New York 10016
(212) 689-0360

SUBSCRIPTION DATA
Issues and rates: Published quarterly.
  Average paid circulation: Not available.
  Annual rate(s): Institutions $41.00, Individuals $11.00, Students $5.00

EDITORIAL DESCRIPTION
Published for educators and professionals in colleges and other educational institutions initiating and developing curricula, programs and faculties in Black Studies.

MANUSCRIPT INFORMATION
Subject field(s): History, sociology, economics, psychology, education in their interdisciplinary aspects; information about developing Black Studies programs
Manuscript requirements: Style sheet sent on request.
Additional information: Letter of inquiry should be sent to editor before submission of manuscript.
Submit to:
  Richard D. Trent
  Editor
  Medgar Evers College
  City University of New York
  Brooklyn, New York 11225

AKWESASNE NOTES [679]
Mohawk Nation at Akwesasne
Rooseveltown, New York 13683
(518) 358-4697

First published in 1969

SUBSCRIPTION DATA
Issues and rates: Eight times a year
  Average paid circulation: 69,000
Publisher or Sponsor: Program in American Indian Studies, SUNY at Buffalo

EDITORIAL DESCRIPTION
Contains Indian material: news, graphics, book and film review, poetry; today, yesterday and tomorrow's Indian people. Provides a unifying element in communications between Indian peoples of North and South America. Seeks to make them aware of one another, their problems.
Articles per average issue: 10
Audience: General
  Manuscripts accepted in English

MANUSCRIPT INFORMATION
Subject field(s): Anything related to native peoples around the world.
Manuscript requirements: No specific style guide.
  Preferred length: None
  Number of copies to be submitted: One
  Abstract: No
Author information and reprints: Payment: None.
  Is simultaneous submission of article to other journals permitted: Yes
  Exclusive manuscript rights between acceptance and publication: No
  Copyright: Held by author.
  Reprints: Available at cost.
Additional information: Publication is news oriented. If a manuscript is relevant to an existing situation it is used right away.
Disposition of manuscript:
  Receipt of manuscript acknowledged: No
  Decision to publish in: Varies
  Accepted manuscript published in: Varies
  Rejected manuscript returned: Yes, if self-addressed, stamped envelope is sent with manuscript.
  Rejected manuscript criticized: Sometimes
Submit to: Rarihokwats
  Editor
  (See address above)

AMERICAN INDIAN CULTURE AND RESEARCH JOURNAL [680]
American Indian Culture and Research Center
University of California at Los Angeles
Los Angeles, California 90024
(213) 825-7315

Previously entitled *American Indian Culture Center Journal*

SUBSCRIPTION DATA
Issues and rates: Published quarterly.
  Annual rate(s): $4.00
Publisher or Sponsor: University of California at Los Angeles

EDITORIAL DESCRIPTION
Provides a research forum for scholars and innovators in the areas of historical and contemporary American Indian life and culture; emphasis is on the 'here and now' and how the past has brought us here.
Articles per average issue: 5
Audience: Academic
  Manuscripts accepted in English

MANUSCRIPT INFORMATION
Subject field(s): All academic fields that pertain to American Indians: economics, political science, sociology, literature, history, philosophy, etc.
Manuscript requirements: MLA
  Preferred length: None
  Number of copies to be submitted: 2
  Abstract: Not necessary.

Author information and reprints: Payment: None.
  Is simultaneous submission of article to other journals permitted: Not permitted.
  Exclusive manuscript rights between acceptance and publication: Yes
  Copyright: Held by author.
  Reprints: Available at cost.
Disposition of manuscript:
  Query letter: Not necessary.
  Receipt of manuscript acknowledged: Yes
  Decision to publish in: 6 months
  Accepted manuscript published in: 4-6 months
  Rejected manuscript returned: Yes, with return postage paid by publication.
  Rejected manuscript criticized: Yes
Submit to:
  Kogee Thomas
  Editor
  (See address above)

AMERICAN INDIAN QUARTERLY [681]
A Journal of Anthropology, History and Literature
P. O. Box 443
Hurst, Texas 76053
(817) 281-3784

First published in 1974

SUBSCRIPTION DATA

Issues and rates: Published quarterly.
  Annual rate(s): $7.00; Foreign $7.65; Institutions $7.00; Students $5.00; Members $7.00
Publisher or Sponsor: Southwestern American Indian Society, Fort Worth Museum of Science and History

EDITORIAL DESCRIPTION

A scholarly professional journal dealing with the Indian in North America, Canada, U. S., Mexico, Central America, and the Caribbean; book reviews, bibliography, current research, and professional news
Articles per average issue: 2-3
Audience: Research, academic, students, general
  Manuscripts accepted in English

MANUSCRIPT INFORMATION

Subject field(s): Anthropology, history and literature from prehistoric to modern on the subject of Native Americans
Manuscript requirements: See latest issue for style requirements. Style sheet sent on request. MLA
  Preferred length: 5,000-6,000 words; 20-26 pages
  Number of copies to be submitted: 2 typscripts, double-spaced
  Abstract: Not necessary.
Author information and reprints: Payment: Reprints only. 10 reprints
  Is simultaneous submission of article to other journals permitted: Permitted, but not encouraged.
  Exclusive manuscript rights between acceptance and publication: Yes
  Copyright: Held by publication.
  Reprints: Available at cost.
Disposition of manuscript:
  Query letter: Not necessary, but advisable.
  Receipt of manuscript acknowledged: Yes
  Decision to publish in: 4 weeks
  Accepted manuscript published in: 4-6 months
  Rejected manuscript returned: Yes, if return postage is supplied by author.
  Rejected manuscript criticized: Yes, if requested
Submit to:
  William L. Turnbull
  Editor
  (See address above)

AMERICAN QUARTERLY [682]
Box 1, Logan Hall
University of Pennsylvania
Philadelphia, Pennsylvania 19174
(215) 594-6252

First published in 1949

SUBSCRIPTION DATA

Issues and rates: Published quarterly.
  Average paid circulation: 4,600
  Annual rate(s): $10.00, Foreign $12.00
Publisher or Sponsor: American Studies Association; University of Pennsylvania

EDITORIAL DESCRIPTION

Publishes scholarly articles on American civilization, past and present.
Articles per average issue: 6
Audience: Professional
  Manuscripts accepted in English only

MANUSCRIPT INFORMATION

Subject field(s): History, literature, anthropology, religion, art, music, sociology, philosophy, interdisciplinary approach
Manuscript requirements: MLA
  Preferred length: 5000-7000 words; 20-25 pages
  Number of copies to be submitted: Two
  Abstract: No
Author information and reprints: Payment: None.
  Is simultaneous submission of article to other journals permitted: No
  Exclusive manuscript rights between acceptance and publication: Yes
  Copyright: Held by publication.
  Reprints: Available, 25 copies free, additional at cost
Disposition of manuscript:
  Query letter: No
  Receipt of manuscript acknowledged: Yes
  Decision to publish in: 5 months
  Accepted manuscript published in: Less than one year
  Rejected manuscript returned: Yes, if self-addressed, stamped envelope is sent with manuscript. As well as a postcard for acknowledging receipt of manuscript.
  Rejected manuscript criticized: Yes
Submit to:
  Bruce Kuklick
  Editor
  (See address above)

AMERICAN STUDIES* [683]
1135 Maine Street
Lawrence, Kansas 66044
(913) 864-4263

SUBSCRIPTION DATA

Issues and rates: Published semi-annually.
  Average paid circulation: 600; 400 controlled
  Annual rate(s): $6.25
Publisher or Sponsor: Midcontinent American Studies Association
Managing Editor: Stuart Levine

EDITORIAL DESCRIPTION

Contains articles on aspects of U.S. society and/or culture; essay reviews of American studies books; brief reviews of books in the component disciplines.

MANUSCRIPT INFORMATION

Manuscript requirements: MLA, but footnotes double-spaced at end.
  Preferred length: 17 pages
  Number of copies to be submitted: Two
Author information and reprints: Payment: None.
  Is simultaneous submission of article to other journals permitted: No
  Exclusive manuscript rights between acceptance and publication: Yes
  Copyright: Held by publication.
  Reprints: Available, $25.00 per 100 copies
Additional information: Journal allows republication only with consent of author. Journal removes author's name before submitting manuscript to editorial commentators. Journal helps author place good articles deemed too specialized for an American Studies audience.
Disposition of manuscript:
  Receipt of manuscript acknowledged: Yes
  Decision to publish in: 45 days
  Accepted manuscript published in: Within the year
  Rejected manuscript returned: Yes
  Rejected manuscript criticized: Yes
Submit to:
  Stuart Levine
  Editor
  (See address above)

THE AMERICAN WEST [684]
American West Publishing Company
599 College Avenue
Palo Alto, California 94306
(415) 327-4660

First published in 1964

SUBSCRIPTION DATA

Issues and rates: Published bi-monthly.
  Average paid circulation: 29,521; 412 controlled
  Annual rate(s): $12.00; Foreign $13.00

Managing Editor: Ed Holm

EDITORIAL DESCRIPTION

Contains articles on the past, present, and future of the American West: historical, geographical, natural history, ecological, environmental, conservation articles.

Articles per average issue: 7
Manuscripts accepted in English

MANUSCRIPT INFORMATION

Subject field(s): Man-history, natural history, conservation, ecology
Manuscript requirements: Style sheet sent on request.
Preferred length: 2,500-4,000 words
Number of copies to be submitted: One
Author information and reprints: Payment: By publication to author. $100.00-$300.00 per article.
Is simultaneous submission of article to other journals permitted: No
Exclusive manuscript rights between acceptance and publication: Yes
Copyright: Held by publication.
Reprints: Not available.
Disposition of manuscript:
Query letter: Preferred
Receipt of manuscript acknowledged: Yes
Decision to publish in: 4 weeks
Accepted manuscript published in: 3-6 months
Rejected manuscript returned: Yes, if return postage is supplied by author.
Rejected manuscript criticized: No
Submit to:
Ed Holm
Managing Editor
(See address above)

CANADIAN NOTES AND QUERIES [685]

Questions & Réponses Canadiennes
Douglas Library
Queen's University
Kingston, Ontario K7L 5C4, Canada
(613) 547-3030

First published in 1968

SUBSCRIPTION DATA

Issues and rates: Published three times per year.
Average paid circulation: 500 controlled
Annual rate(s): Free
Publisher or Sponsor: Antiquarian Booksellers Association of Canada
Managing Editor: William F. E. Morley

EDITORIAL DESCRIPTION

A medium for the exchange of information in the field of Canadian studies.
Articles per average issue: 20
Audience: Scholars anywhere interested in Canadian studies and institutions with special collections of Canadiana
Manuscripts accepted in English, French

MANUSCRIPT INFORMATION

Subject field(s): Canadian studies in the humanities and social sciences of any period
Manuscript requirements: No specific style guide.
Preferred length: 200 pages maximum
Number of copies to be submitted: 1
Abstract: Not necessary.
Author information and reprints: Payment: None.
Is simultaneous submission of article to other journals permitted: Permitted, but not encouraged.
Exclusive manuscript rights between acceptance and publication: Yes
Copyright: Held by publication.
Reprints: Not available.
Additional information: Queries should be concise, yet include specific references necessary to identify the problem fully. Replies should be authenticated by sources.
Disposition of manuscript:
Query letter: Not necessary.
Receipt of manuscript acknowledged: Yes
Decision to publish in: 1 month
Accepted manuscript published in: 4-6 months
Rejected manuscript returned: Yes, with return postage paid by publication.
Rejected manuscript criticized: Sometimes
Submit to:
William F. E. Morley
English Editor
(See address above)
Michel Thériault
Redactor française
Directeur des Acquisitions, La Bibliothéque
Université de Montreal
Montreal C.P. 6128, Québec, Canada

THE CANADIAN REVIEW OF AMERICAN STUDIES [686]

Stong College, York University
4700 Keele Street
Downsview, Ontario, Canada
(416) 667-3465

SUBSCRIPTION DATA

Issues and rates: Published semi-annually.
Average paid circulation: 600
Annual rate(s): Members $10.00; Institutions $8.00
Publisher or Sponsor: Canadian Association of American Studies

EDITORIAL DESCRIPTION

Contains articles dealing with American society, culture, art, literature, intellectual history; interdisciplinary articles on the Americas; cultural relations between Canada and the United States; geography, history and geology of North America.
Articles per average issue: 8-10
Audience: Academic
Manuscripts accepted in English, French

MANUSCRIPT INFORMATION

Manuscript requirements: MLA
Preferred length: 2000-5000 words
Number of copies to be submitted: Two
Abstract: No
Author information and reprints: Payment: Reprints only. 50 offprints
Is simultaneous submission of article to other journals permitted: No
Exclusive manuscript rights between acceptance and publication: Yes
Copyright: Held by publication.
Reprints: Available
Disposition of manuscript:
Query letter: No
Receipt of manuscript acknowledged: Yes
Decision to publish in: 3-8 weeks
Accepted manuscript published in: 3-9 months
Rejected manuscript returned: Yes
Rejected manuscript criticized: Yes
Submit to:
Robert L. White
Editor
(See address above)

GREAT PLAINS JOURNAL [687]

Museum of the Great Plains
P.O. Box 68
Lawton, Oklahoma 73501
(405) 353-5675

First published in 1961

SUBSCRIPTION DATA

Issues and rates: Published semi-annually.
Average paid circulation: 800
Annual rate(s): $7.50
Publisher or Sponsor: Museum of the Great Plains

EDITORIAL DESCRIPTION

An interdisciplinary journal devoted to the enhancement of knowledge of the Great Plains of North America. Its special interests are history, anthropology, archaeology, natural history, and ecology of the 10-state Great Plains region, southern Canada and northern Mexico.
Articles per average issue: 3
Audience: Professional and nonprofessional historians
Manuscripts accepted in English

MANUSCRIPT INFORMATION

Subject field(s): History, anthropology, archaeology, natural history, ecology, geography, ethnology
Manuscript requirements: Chicago
Preferred length: 5,000 words; 20 pages
Number of copies to be submitted: One
Abstract: No
Author information and reprints: Payment: None.
Is simultaneous submission of article to other journals permitted: No
Exclusive manuscript rights between acceptance and publication: Yes
Copyright: Held by publication.
Reprints: Available at printing cost only

Additional information: Style should follow that of latest issues. All footnotes should appear at end of manuscript.
Disposition of manuscript:
Query letter: No
Receipt of manuscript acknowledged: Yes
Decision to publish in: 1-2 months
Accepted manuscript published in: 6-12 months
Rejected manuscript returned: Yes, if self-addressed, stamped envelope is sent with manuscript.
Rejected manuscript criticized: Yes
Submit to:
Steve Wilson
Editor
(See address above)

THE INDIAN HISTORIAN [688]
1451 Masonic Avenue
San Francisco, California 94117
(415) 626-5236

First published in 1964

SUBSCRIPTION DATA
Issues and rates: Published quarterly.
Average paid circulation: 10,109
Annual rate(s): $6.00
Publisher or Sponsor: American Indian Historical Society

EDITORIAL DESCRIPTION
Edited and published by American Indian scholars.
Articles per average issue: 7
Audience: Academic, general
Manuscripts accepted in English

MANUSCRIPT INFORMATION
Subject field(s): Native American anthropology, archaeology, economic situation, history, culture, short fiction, poetry, current affairs
Manuscript requirements: See latest issue for style requirements.
Preferred length: 40 pages maximum
Number of copies to be submitted: One
Author information and reprints: Payment: None.
Is simultaneous submission of article to other journals permitted: No
Exclusive manuscript rights between acceptance and publication: Yes
Copyright: Held by either author or publication.
Reprints: Available, 20 free to author
Disposition of manuscript:
Query letter: Yes
Receipt of manuscript acknowledged: Yes
Decision to publish in: 1-3 months
Accepted manuscript published in: 3-6 months
Rejected manuscript returned: Yes, if self-addressed, stamped envelope is sent with manuscript.
Rejected manuscript criticized: No
Submit to:
Jeannette Henry
Editor
(See address above)

INDIAN TRUTH [689]
Room 519
1505 Race Street
Philadelphia, Pennsylvania 19102
(215) 563-8349

First published in 1920

SUBSCRIPTION DATA
Issues and rates: Published three times per year.
Average paid circulation: 3,500
Annual rate(s): $10.00; Students $5.00
Publisher or Sponsor: The Indian Rights Association
Managing Editor: Theodore B. Hetzel

EDITORIAL DESCRIPTION
Articles and news relating to Native Americans and to the Indian Rights Association
Audience: Members of the Association and officials of Indian tribes and the Bureau of Indian Affairs
Manuscripts accepted in English

MANUSCRIPT INFORMATION
Subject field(s): Editorials, policy, news about the affairs of American Indians
Manuscript requirements: See latest issue for style requirements.
Preferred length: 1,000 words
Abstract: Not necessary.
Author information and reprints: Payment: None.
Is simultaneous submission of article to other journals permitted: Permitted.
Exclusive manuscript rights between acceptance and publication: No
Copyright: No copyright
Reprints: Available at no cost. Several
Disposition of manuscript:
Query letter: Necessary.
Decision to publish in: Varies
Accepted manuscript published in: Varies
Rejected manuscript returned: Yes, if return postage is supplied by author.
Rejected manuscript criticized: Reasons for rejections only
Submit to:
Editor
(See address above)

JOURNAL OF AMERICAN STUDIES [690]
Cambridge University Press
32 East 57th Street
New York, New York 10022

First published in 1955
Publisher or Sponsor: British Association for American Studies

EDITORIAL DESCRIPTION
Contributions in the history, society, government, politics, economics, geography, literature and thought of the United States
Manuscripts accepted in English

MANUSCRIPT INFORMATION
Subject field(s): American studies
Manuscript requirements: See latest issue for style requirements. Style sheet sent on request.
Preferred length: 5,000 words
Number of copies to be submitted: 2
Abstract: Not necessary.
Author information and reprints: Payment: Reprints only. 25
Is simultaneous submission of article to other journals permitted: Not permitted.
Exclusive manuscript rights between acceptance and publication: Yes
Copyright: Held by publication.
Reprints: Available at no cost.
Submit to:
Editor
Department of American Studies
The University
Manchester M13 9PL, England

JOURNAL OF CANADIAN STUDIES/REVUE D'ÉTUDES CANADIENNES [691]
Trent University
Peterborough, Ontario K9J 7B8, Canada
(705) 748-1369

First published in 1966

SUBSCRIPTION DATA
Issues and rates: Published quarterly.
Average paid circulation: 1,200
Annual rate(s): Individuals $6.00; Institutions $10.00; Students $4.50
Publisher or Sponsor: Trent University

EDITORIAL DESCRIPTION
An academic review of Canadian studies. Its selection of articles is intended, in both subject and approach, to be of general as well as scholarly interest
Articles per average issue: 4-8
Audience: Academic, general
Manuscripts accepted in English, French

MANUSCRIPT INFORMATION
Subject field(s): Canadian history, politics, literature, society and the arts
Manuscript requirements: No specific style guide.
Preferred length: 2,000-10,,000 words
Number of copies to be submitted: 1
Abstract: Not necessary.
Author information and reprints: Payment: By publication to author. $10.00 per page.
Is simultaneous submission of article to other journals permitted: Permitted, but not encouraged.
Exclusive manuscript rights between acceptance and publication: Yes
Copyright: Held jointly by author and publication
Reprints: Not available.
Disposition of manuscript:
Query letter: Not necessary.
Receipt of manuscript acknowledged: Yes
Submit to:
Denis Smith
Editor
(See address above)

North American studies

THE JOURNAL OF NEGRO HISTORY* [692]
1407 14th Street, N.W.
Washington, D.C. 20005
(202) 667-2822

SUBSCRIPTION DATA

Issues and rates: Published quarterly.
 Average paid circulation: 6,500; 500 controlled
 Annual rate(s): $10.00, Foreign $10.50
Publisher or Sponsor: The Association for the Study of Negro Life and History, Inc.
Managing Editor: W. Augustus Low

EDITORIAL DESCRIPTION

Designed to meet the needs of students of history and Black studies at the college level and above. It is a scientific, historical periodical which treats definitively the history of the Black man both in this country and throughout the world.

MANUSCRIPT INFORMATION

Subject field(s): African-American history, race relations, documents, slavery, anti-slavery, changing historical traditions, new light in history, politics, religion, education, mis-education
Manuscript requirements: See latest issue for style requirements.
 Preferred length: No longer than twenty pages
 Number of copies to be submitted: Two
Author information and reprints: Payment: None. Five complimentary copies are sent to author
 Is simultaneous submission of article to other journals permitted: No
 Exclusive manuscript rights between acceptance and publication: Yes
 Copyright: Held by publication.
 Reprints: Available only upon prior request
Disposition of manuscript:
 Receipt of manuscript acknowledged: Yes
 Decision to publish in: A month or more
 Accepted manuscript published in: Varies
 Rejected manuscript returned: Yes, if self-addressed, stamped envelope is sent with manuscript.
 Rejected manuscript criticized: No
Submit to:
 Editor
 (See address above)

THE MASTERKEY [693]
For Indian Lore and History
Southwest Museum, Highland Park
Los Angeles, California 90042
(213) 221-2163

SUBSCRIPTION DATA

Issues and rates: Published quarterly.
 Average paid circulation: 1000
 Annual rate(s): $3.50
Publisher or Sponsor: Southwest Museum

EDITORIAL DESCRIPTION

Contains articles on the archaeology, ethnology, history, arts and handicrafts of the American Indian in North, Central and South America.
Articles per average issue: 4-6
Audience: Academic, general
 Manuscripts accepted in English only

MANUSCRIPT INFORMATION

Manuscript requirements: No specific style guide.
 Preferred length: 2500-3500 words
 Number of copies to be submitted: One
 Abstract: No
Author information and reprints: Payment: None.
 Is simultaneous submission of article to other journals permitted: No
 Exclusive manuscript rights between acceptance and publication: Yes
 Copyright: Held by publication.
 Reprints: Not available.
Additional information: As few illustrations and references as possible.
Disposition of manuscript:
 Query letter: No
 Receipt of manuscript acknowledged: Yes
 Decision to publish in: Two weeks
 Accepted manuscript published in: Up to one year
 Rejected manuscript returned: Yes, if self-addressed, stamped envelope is sent with manuscript.
 Rejected manuscript criticized: Occasionally
Submit to:
 Bruce Bryan
 Curator and Editor
 (See address above)

MISSISSIPPI QUARTERLY [694]
The Journal of Southern Culture
Box 5272
Mississippi State University, Mississippi 39762
(601) 325-4730

SUBSCRIPTION DATA

Issues and rates: Published quarterly.
 Average paid circulation: 600
 Annual rate(s): $6.00, Foreign $7.00
Managing Editor: Peyton W. Williams, Jr.

EDITORIAL DESCRIPTION

Accepts articles, notes, queries, documents, and collections of letters dealing with the culture of the American South. Most of the material deals with literature, history, sociology, and speech.
Articles per average issue: 5-6
Audience: Academic
 Manuscripts accepted in English

MANUSCRIPT INFORMATION

Subject field(s): Literature, history, sociology, economics, folklore, speechways, politics, art, music
Manuscript requirements: MLA
 Preferred length: 12-15 pages
 Number of copies to be submitted: Two
 Abstract: Yes, of 150 words
Author information and reprints: Payment: None.
 Is simultaneous submission of article to other journals permitted: No
 Exclusive manuscript rights between acceptance and publication: Yes
 Copyright: Held by publication.
 Reprints: Available, 20 free, others at variable cost.
Disposition of manuscript:
 Query letter: No
 Receipt of manuscript acknowledged: Yes
 Decision to publish in: 2-4 months
 Accepted manuscript published in: 6-24 months
 Rejected manuscript returned: Yes, if return postage is supplied by author.
 Rejected manuscript criticized: No
Submit to:
 Peyton W. Williams, Jr.
 Editor
 (See address above)

MONARCHY CANADA [695]
2 Wedgewood Crescent
Ottawa, Ontario K1B 4B4, Canada
(613) 824-5225

Previously entitled *Canadian Monarchist*

First published in 1970

SUBSCRIPTION DATA

Issues and rates: 5 times yearly
 Average paid circulation: 2,300
 Annual rate(s): $5.00 (and U.S.); Foreign $9.50; Institutions $5.00
Publisher or Sponsor: Monarchist League of Canada
Managing Editor: Ronald Frye

EDITORIAL DESCRIPTION

Deals with all aspects of the Canadian constitution with focus on the value of the Monarchy to Canada
Articles per average issue: 2-3
Audience: Academic, professional, governmental, students
 Manuscripts accepted in English, French

MANUSCRIPT INFORMATION

Subject field(s): Historical articles on the Monarchy, its value to Canada
Manuscript requirements: No specific style guide.
 Preferred length: 1,000-2,000 words; 4-8 pages
 Number of copies to be submitted: 1
 Abstract: Not necessary.
Author information and reprints: Payment: Reprints only. 5 reprints
Disposition of manuscript:
 Query letter: Necessary.
 Decision to publish in: 2-4 months
 Rejected manuscript returned: Yes, if return postage is supplied by author.
 Rejected manuscript criticized: Sometimes
Submit to:
 Ronald Frye;
 John Gould
 Editors
 (See address above)

PLATEAU [696]
The Quarterly of the Museum of Northern Arizona
Museum of Northern Arizona
P.O. Box 1389
Flagstaff, Arizona 86001
(602) 774-5211

Previously entitled *Museum Notes*

First published in 1928

SUBSCRIPTION DATA
Issues and rates: Published quarterly.
  Average paid circulation: 1200
  Annual rate(s): $7.50
Publisher or Sponsor: Northern Arizona Society of Science and Art, Inc.
Managing Editor: Evelyn C. Roat

EDITORIAL DESCRIPTION
  Contains original research on subjects relating to the plateau of northern Arizona
Articles per average issue: 4
Audience: Members, scientists
  Manuscripts accepted in English

MANUSCRIPT INFORMATION
Subject field(s): Archaeology, ethnology, geology, biology, history and art.
Manuscript requirements: See latest issue for style requirements.
  Preferred length: 3,000 words
  Number of copies to be submitted: Two
Author information and reprints: Payment: None.
  Is simultaneous submission of article to other journals permitted: No
  Exclusive manuscript rights between acceptance and publication: Yes
  Copyright: Held by publication.
  Reprints: Available, cost quoted to author when pages known.
Disposition of manuscript:
  Query letter: No
  Receipt of manuscript acknowledged: Yes
  Decision to publish in: One month
  Accepted manuscript published in: One year
  Rejected manuscript returned: Yes
  Rejected manuscript criticized: No
Submit to:
  Editor
  (See address above)

Social sciences

Social sciences (general)

ADOLESCENCE [697]
P.O. Box 165, 391 Willets Road
Roslyn Heights, New York 11577
(516) 484-4950

First published in 1966

SUBSCRIPTION DATA
Issues and rates: Published quarterly.
  Average paid circulation: 3000
  Annual rate(s): $10.00

EDITORIAL DESCRIPTION
  An international quarterly devoted to the physiological, psychological, psychiatric, sociological, and educational aspects of the second decade of human life.
Articles per average issue: 14
Audience: Professional
  Manuscripts accepted in English

MANUSCRIPT INFORMATION
Manuscript requirements: See latest issue for style requirements.
  Preferred length: 1200-6000 words; 4-20 pages
  Number of copies to be submitted: Two
  Abstract: Yes
Author information and reprints: Payment: None.
  Is simultaneous submission of article to other journals permitted: Yes
  Exclusive manuscript rights between acceptance and publication: Yes
  Copyright: Held by publication.
  Reprints· Available; cost depends on length
Additional information: Typewritten, double-spaced
Disposition of manuscript:
  Query letter: Preferable
  Receipt of manuscript acknowledged: Yes
  Decision to publish in: 10 days to 2 weeks
  Accepted manuscript published in: 8 months
  Rejected manuscript returned: Yes
  Rejected manuscript criticized: Yes
Submit to:
  William Kroll
  Editor and Publisher
  (See address above)

BEHAVIOR SCIENCE RESEARCH [698]
HRAF Journal of Comparative Studies
Human Relations Area Files, Inc.
Box 2015, Yale Station
New Haven, Connecticut 06520
(203) 777-2334

Previously entitled *Behavior Science Notes*

First published in 1966

SUBSCRIPTION DATA
Issues and rates: Published quarterly.
  Average paid circulation: 350; 450 controlled
  Annual rate(s): Individuals $3.00, Institutions $5.00
Publisher or Sponsor: Human Relations Area Files, Inc.
Managing Editor: Elizabeth P. Swift

EDITORIAL DESCRIPTION
  Welcome contributions from scholars, in particular those reporting methodological or theoretical results of cross-cultural research, preliminary results of field research, and descriptive or theoretical research based on substantive ethnographic data. Annotated bibliographies on specific areas or topics of ethnographic interest are especially welcome.
Articles per average issue: 3
Audience: Social sciences, anthropologists, cross-culturalists

MANUSCRIPT INFORMATION
Subject field(s): Cross-cultural studies, ethnography, ethnographic bibliographies
Manuscript requirements: Chicago, AAA
  Preferred length: 25-30 pages
  Number of copies to be submitted: Two
  Abstract: Yes; 50-75 words
Author information and reprints: Payment: None.
  Is simultaneous submission of article to other journals permitted: No
  Exclusive manuscript rights between acceptance and publication: No
  Copyright: Held by publication.
  Reprints: Available, first 100 free
Disposition of manuscript:
  Query letter: No
  Receipt of manuscript acknowledged: Yes
  Decision to publish in: 3 months
  Accepted manuscript published in: 6-9 months
  Rejected manuscript returned: Yes
  Rejected manuscript criticized: No
Submit to:
  Elizabeth P. Swift
  Managing Editor
  (See address above)

BEHAVIORAL SCIENCES AND COMMUNITY DEVELOPMENT [699]
National Institute of Community Development
Rajendranagar
Hyderabad, Andhrapradesh, India 48001

SUBSCRIPTION DATA
Issues and rates: Published three times per year.
  Average paid circulation: 400
  Annual rate(s): £20.00; Foreign $8.00, £3.00
Publisher or Sponsor: Institute of Community Development
Managing Editor: V.R.K. Paramahamsa

EDITORIAL DESCRIPTION
  Covers research findings in all aspects of community development and change in rural India.
Articles per average issue: 5-7
Audience: Research, academic, administrators
  Manuscripts accepted in English

MANUSCRIPT INFORMATION
Subject field(s): All aspects of economic, sociological, political and administrative changes in rural India
Manuscript requirements: See latest issue for style requirements.
  Preferred length: 20 pages maximum
  Number of copies to be submitted: Three
  Abstract: Yes
Author information and reprints: Payment: Reprints only. 25 reprints
  Is simultaneous submission of article to other journals permitted: No
  Exclusive manuscript rights between acceptance and publication: Yes
  Copyright: Held by publication.
  Reprints: Available
Disposition of manuscript:
  Receipt of manuscript acknowledged: Yes
  Decision to publish in: Three months
  Accepted manuscript published in: Nine months
  Rejected manuscript returned: Yes
Submit to:
  Editor
  (See address above)

CATALYST [700]
A Journal of Social Science
Otonabee College
Trent University
Peterborough, Ontario K9J 7B8, Canada
(705) 748-1580

First published in 1965

SUBSCRIPTION DATA
Issues and rates: Published semi-annually.
  Average paid circulation: 2,000
  Annual rate(s): $3.00; Institutions $6.00

EDITORIAL DESCRIPTION
  Publishes articles which critically assess theoretical developments in the social sciences (espec. sociology) which elaborate the theoretical issues for science and demonstrate how substantive problems can be dealt with scientifically.
Articles per average issue: 7
Audience: Social scientists in general
  Manuscripts accepted in English

MANUSCRIPT INFORMATION
Subject field(s): Theoretical, methodological and substantive problems in sociology and social science; critical assessment of theoretical positions.
Manuscript requirements: Style sheet sent on request.
  Preferred length: 3,000-15,000 words

Number of copies to be submitted: 2
Abstract: Not necessary.
Author information and reprints: Payment.
Reprints only. 25
Is simultaneous submission of article to other journals permitted: Not permitted.
Exclusive manuscript rights between acceptance and publication: Yes
Copyright: Held by publication.
Reprints: Available at cost.
Disposition of manuscript:
Query letter: Not necessary.
Receipt of manuscript acknowledged: Yes
Decision to publish in: 2 months
Accepted manuscript published in: 3-5 months
Rejected manuscript returned: Yes, with return postage paid by publication.
Rejected manuscript criticized: Yes
Submit to:
John Hillman
Editor
(See address above)

CORNELL JOURNAL OF SOCIAL RELATIONS [701]
Department of Sociology, Uris Hall
Cornell University
Ithaca, New York 14850
(607) 256-3834

First published in 1966

SUBSCRIPTION DATA
Issues and rates: Published semi-annually.
Average paid circulation: 300
Annual rate(s): Institutions $4.00, Students $2.00, Individuals $3.00

EDITORIAL DESCRIPTION
Contains empirical, theoretical, and methodological papers in the various fields of the behavioral sciences and social relations.
Articles per average issue: 5
Audience: Academic
Manuscripts accepted in English

MANUSCRIPT INFORMATION
Subject field(s): Social relations and behavioral sciences, including psychology, sociology, anthropology, organizational behavior, human development and family studies.
Manuscript requirements: AJS Style sheet sent on request.
Preferred length: 15-30 pages
Number of copies to be submitted: Two
Abstract: Yes; 200 words or less
Author information and reprints: Payment: None.
Is simultaneous submission of article to other journals permitted: No
Exclusive manuscript rights between acceptance and publication: Yes
Copyright: Held by publication.
Reprints: Available, 20 free
Additional information: Everything typewritten, double-spaced with author's full name and affiliation
Disposition of manuscript:
Query letter: No, but helpful
Receipt of manuscript acknowledged: Yes
Decision to publish in: 3 months
Accepted manuscript published in: 2-6 months
Rejected manuscript returned: Yes, if return postage is supplied by author.
Rejected manuscript criticized: Yes
Submit to:
Gregory B. Appling
Coordinating Editor
(See address above)

EKISTICS [702]
The Problems and Science of Human Settlements
Page Farm Road
Lincoln, Massachusetts 01773
(413) 259-9144

First published in 1955

SUBSCRIPTION DATA
Issues and rates: Published monthly.
Annual rate(s): $24.00
Managing Editor: Gwen K. Bell

EDITORIAL DESCRIPTION
Ekistics, as developed by C.A. Doxiadis, studies the elements of nature, anthropos, society, shells, and networks, and their synthesis in human settlements; offers both original and reprinted articles, with each issue devoted to a particular theme.
Articles per average issue: 12
Audience: Professionals in disciplines concerned with human settlements: architects, economists, environmentalists, urban planners, etc.
Manuscripts accepted in English

MANUSCRIPT INFORMATION
Subject field(s): Nature (geology, geography); anthropics (psychiatry, religion, etc.); society (demography, administration, economics, etc.) shells (architecture, engineering etc.); networks (transportation, communications, etc.)
Manuscript requirements: No specific style guide.
Preferred length: None
Number of copies to be submitted: 2
Author information and reprints: Payment: Reprints only. 10 reprints, 1 copy of issue
Is simultaneous submission of article to other journals permitted: Permitted.
Exclusive manuscript rights between acceptance and publication: No
Copyright: Held by author.
Reprints: Available at cost.
Disposition of manuscript:
Query letter: Not necessary, but advisable.
Receipt of manuscript acknowledged: Yes
Decision to publish in: 1 week to 1 year
Rejected manuscript returned: Yes, with return postage paid by publication.
Rejected manuscript criticized: Yes
Submit to:
Gwen K. Bell
Editor
(See address above)

HISTORICAL METHODS NEWSLETTER [703]
UCIS Publications
University of Pittsburgh
Pittsburgh, Pennsylvania 15260
(412) 624-6023

First published in 1967

SUBSCRIPTION DATA
Issues and rates: Published quarterly.
Average paid circulation: 1,250
Annual rate(s): $5.00; Institutions $9.00; Students $3.50

EDITORIAL DESCRIPTION
An international scholarly publication dealing with concepts and methods relevant to historical social science
Articles per average issue: 4
Audience: Academic, professional
Manuscripts accepted in English, French

MANUSCRIPT INFORMATION
Subject field(s): History as related to the social sciences
Manuscript requirements: See latest issue for style requirements. Style sheet sent on request.
Preferred length: 30 pages, typewritten, double-spaced
Number of copies to be submitted: 2
Abstract: Not necessary.
Author information and reprints: Payment: None.
Is simultaneous submission of article to other journals permitted: Permitted, but not encouraged.
Exclusive manuscript rights between acceptance and publication: Yes
Copyright: Held by publication.
Reprints: Available at cost.
Disposition of manuscript:
Query letter: Not necessary, but advisable.
Receipt of manuscript acknowledged: Yes
Decision to publish in: 8 weeks
Accepted manuscript published in: 3-6 months
Rejected manuscript returned: Yes, with return postage paid by publication.
Rejected manuscript criticized: Sometimes
Submit to:
Jonathan Levine
Editor
Department of History
University of Pittsburgh
Pittsburgh, Pennsylvania 15260
(412) 624-5544

HUMAN RELATIONS* [704]
A Journal of Studies towards the Integration of the Social Sciences
Plenum Publishing Corporation
227 West 17th Street
New York, New York 10011
(212) 255-0713

SUBSCRIPTION DATA
Issues and rates: Published bi-monthly.
Average paid circulation: Not available.

Social sciences (general)

Annual rate(s): $30.00
Publisher or Sponsor: Tavistock Institute of Human Relations
Managing Editor: Robert Rapoport

EDITORIAL DESCRIPTION
Publishes interdisciplinary and widely applicable research in social sciences; papers on systems analysis and integrated problems of sociology, psychology, group dynamics and operations research.

MANUSCRIPT INFORMATION
Subject field(s): Sociology; industrial research; systems analysis; psychology; social work
Manuscript requirements: See latest issue for style requirements.
  Number of copies to be submitted: Two
Author information and reprints: Payment: None.
  Copyright: Held by Tavistock Institute of Human Relations
  Reprints: Available, 50 free
Disposition of manuscript:
  Receipt of manuscript acknowledged: Yes
  Decision to publish in: 6-8 weeks
  Accepted manuscript published in: 6-8 months
  Rejected manuscript returned: Yes
Submit to:
  Eric Trist
  Co-ordinating Editor
  University of Pennsylvania
  Wharton School of Finance and Commerce
  Management Science Center
  Philadelphia, Pennsylvania 19104

INTERNATIONAL DEVELOPMENT REVIEW [705]
1346 Connecticut Avenue, N.W.
Washington, D.C. 20036
(202) 296-3810

First published in 1959

SUBSCRIPTION DATA
Issues and rates: Published quarterly.
  Average paid circulation: 8,000; 300 controlled
  Annual rate(s): Institutions $10.00
Publisher or Sponsor: Society for International Development
Managing Editor: Andrew E. Rice

EDITORIAL DESCRIPTION
Contains articles on economic and social development, dealing with practical experience or applied theory, as well as inter-disciplinary articles and those dealing with new concepts or approaches.
Articles per average issue: 5
Audience: People engaged in work connected with the economic and social development of less developed countries.
  Manuscripts accepted in English, French, Spanish

MANUSCRIPT INFORMATION
Subject field(s): International development: economics, agriculture, sociology, international administration
Manuscript requirements: See latest issue for style requirements.
  Preferred length: 3000-5000 words
  Number of copies to be submitted: Two
  Abstract: No
Author information and reprints: Payment: None. 25 copies of issue in which article appears.
  Is simultaneous submission of article to other journals permitted: No
  Exclusive manuscript rights between acceptance and publication: Yes
  Copyright: Held by Society for International Development
  Reprints: Not available.
Disposition of manuscript:
  Receipt of manuscript acknowledged: Yes
  Decision to publish in: 1-2 months
  Accepted manuscript published in: 3-6 months
  Rejected manuscript returned: Yes
  Rejected manuscript criticized: Sometimes
Submit to:
  Andrew E. Rice
  Editor
  (See address above)

INTERNATIONAL REVIEW OF COMMUNITY DEVELOPMENT [706]
Piazza Cavalieri di Malta 2
Rome, Italy 00153
5740411

SUBSCRIPTION DATA
Issues and rates: Published annually.
  Annual rate(s): $8.50
Publisher or Sponsor: Università di Roma, Centro Educazione Professionale Assistenti Società

EDITORIAL DESCRIPTION
Deals with problems of socio-economic development and publishes articles by experts and practitioners in this field, discussing socio-anthropological implications of principles and methods of development interventions.
Articles per average issue: 14
Audience: Professional
  Manuscripts accepted in English, French, Spanish, Italian

MANUSCRIPT INFORMATION
Subject field(s): Sociology, anthropology, regional planning, urban problems, group conflict, intervention methods
Manuscript requirements: See latest issue for style requirements.
  Preferred length: 10-25 pages
  Number of copies to be submitted: Two
  Abstract: Yes
Author information and reprints: Payment: Reprints only. One copy of the volume and 40 reprints
  Is simultaneous submission of article to other journals permitted: Yes, if the article appears in a different language.
  Exclusive manuscript rights between acceptance and publication: No
  Copyright: Held by publication.
  Reprints: Available
Additional information: The articles are usually published in the original language; if the contents appear of considerable interest, translation in other languages can be arranged.
Disposition of manuscript:
  Receipt of manuscript acknowledged: Yes
  Decision to publish in: 6-8 weeks
  Accepted manuscript published in: Within one year
  Rejected manuscript returned: Yes
  Rejected manuscript criticized: Sometimes
Submit to:
  Anna Maria Levi
  Editor
  (See address above)

INTERNATIONAL SOCIAL SCIENCE JOURNAL [707]
Revue International des Sciences Sociales
UNESCO Publications Center
P. O. Box 433
New York, New York 10016

Previously entitled *International Social Science Bulletin* (until 1958)

First published in 1948

SUBSCRIPTION DATA
Issues and rates: Published quarterly.
  Average paid circulation: 5,000
  Annual rate(s): 52 French Francs or equivalent
Publisher or Sponsor: United Nations Educational, Scientific and Cultural Organization (UNESCO)
Managing Editor: Peter Lengyel

EDITORIAL DESCRIPTION
Each issue deals with a theme within the social sciences (disciplinary or inter-disciplinary), to which a panel of eminent specialists representing different national, regional, substantive or ideological approaches are invited to contribute. The periodical seeks to mediate between different communities of social scientists, schools of thought, traditions or emerging interests.
Articles per average issue: 10
Audience: Academic, professional or administrative social scientists
  Manuscripts accepted in principally English, French and Arabic

MANUSCRIPT INFORMATION
Subject field(s): According to themes of successive issues; see announcement of forthcoming topics on inside front cover, and past topics on back cover.
Manuscript requirements: Style sheet sent on request.
  Preferred length: 5,000 words; 20-25 pages
  Number of copies to be submitted: 3
  Abstract: Not necessary.
Author information and reprints: Payment: By publication to author. Reprints only. $250.00 per article.
  Is simultaneous submission of article to other journals permitted: Permitted, but not encouraged.

Exclusive manuscript rights between acceptance and publication: Yes
Copyright: Held by publisher, but liberal conditions for cession.
Reprints: Available at no cost. 25 in English or French

Additional information: Most manuscripts are commissioned directly but occasional papers relating to current topics may be accepted. Short communications on professional developments or trends of international significance are encouraged. From 1975 there will be a special section on data and information problems in social science, to which contributions may be made.

Disposition of manuscript:
Query letter: Not necessary, but advisable.
Receipt of manuscript acknowledged: Yes
Decision to publish in: 1 month
Accepted manuscript published in: 7-10 months
Rejected manuscript returned: Yes, with return postage paid by publication.
Rejected manuscript criticized: Reasons for rejections only

Submit to:
Peter Lengyl
Editor
UNESCO
Place de Fontenoy
75700 Paris, France
566 57-57 ext. 4631

JOURNAL OF THE HISTORY OF THE BEHAVIORAL SCIENCES [708]

4 Conant Square
Brandon, Vermont 05733
(802) 247-6871

First published in 1965

SUBSCRIPTION DATA

Issues and rates: Published quarterly.
Average paid circulation: 1,000
Annual rate(s): $25.00; Foreign $26.00
Managing Editor: Charles S. Jakiela

EDITORIAL DESCRIPTION

Contains papers discussing the history of the social sciences.
Articles per average issue: 10
Audience: Historians of the behavioral sciences
Manuscripts accepted in English

MANUSCRIPT INFORMATION

Subject field(s): Psychology, medicine, anthropology, linguistics, neurology, history, neurophysiology
Manuscript requirements: Style sheet sent on request.
Preferred length: 6-10 pages
Number of copies to be submitted: 3
Abstract: Yes
Author information and reprints: Payment: None.
Is simultaneous submission of article to other journals permitted: Yes

Exclusive manuscript rights between acceptance and publication: Yes
Copyright: Held by publication.
Reprints: Available

Disposition of manuscript:
Query letter: No
Receipt of manuscript acknowledged: Yes
Decision to publish in: 8 weeks
Accepted manuscript published in: 12-15 months
Rejected manuscript returned: Yes, if return postage is supplied by author.
Rejected manuscript criticized: Yes

Submit to:
Robert I. Watson
Editor
Psychology Department
University of New Hampshire
Durham, New Hampshire 03824
(603) 862-1234

JOURNAL OF PEASANT STUDIES [709]

67 Great Russell Street
London WC1B 3BT, England
01-405-9405 ext. 16

First published in 1973

SUBSCRIPTION DATA

Issues and rates: Published quarterly.
Annual rate(s): £10.50; Foreign $31.50
Managing Editor: C. A. Curwen, T. J. Byres, Teodor Shanin

EDITORIAL DESCRIPTION

An interdisciplinary journal of peasant studies.
Articles per average issue: 5
Audience: Academic
Manuscripts accepted in English

MANUSCRIPT INFORMATION

Subject field(s): Peasant sociology, peasant economics, peasant values, history, etc.
Manuscript requirements: Style sheet sent on request.
Preferred length: 8,000 words
Number of copies to be submitted: Two
Abstract: Yes, of 100 words
Author information and reprints: Payment: None.
Is simultaneous submission of article to other journals permitted: Yes
Exclusive manuscript rights between acceptance and publication: Yes
Copyright: Held by publication.
Reprints: Available, first 25 free and 1 copy of issue

Disposition of manuscript:
Query letter: No
Receipt of manuscript acknowledged: Yes
Decision to publish in: 1 month
Accepted manuscript published in: Varies
Rejected manuscript returned: Yes. By surface mail

Submit to:
The Secretary
(See address above)

JOURNAL OF RESEARCH IN CRIME AND DELINQUENCY [710]

NCCD Research Center
609 Second Street, Suite D
Davis, California 95616
(916) 756-0808

First published in 1964

SUBSCRIPTION DATA

Issues and rates: Published semi-annually.
Average paid circulation: 2,200
Annual rate(s): $10.00
Publisher or Sponsor: National Council on Crime and Delinquency

EDITORIAL DESCRIPTION

Contains reports of original research in crime and delinquency, new theory, and the critical analysis of theories and concepts especially pertinent to research development in this field.
Articles per average issue: 8
Audience: Researchers

MANUSCRIPT INFORMATION

Subject field(s): Survey research, personality classification, statistical methodology, biochemical methods, psychotherapy, general psychology, sociology of institutions, general sociology, mathematical models, social theory, social psychology, law, public administration, police science
Manuscript requirements: Style sheet sent on request.
Preferred length: 7,200 words; 30 pages
Number of copies to be submitted: Four
Abstract: Yes; 300 words
Author information and reprints: Payment: None.
Is simultaneous submission of article to other journals permitted: No
Exclusive manuscript rights between acceptance and publication: Yes
Copyright: Held by publication.
Reprints: Available, cost depends on length

Additional information: Manuscript should be typewritten, double-spaced, with footnotes and tables on separate pages following text. Page one of the text is to include the following: title of manuscript, name of author, present position, highest academic degrees, college awarding degrees, date, specific requirements for tables and line drawings.

Disposition of manuscript:
Query letter: No
Receipt of manuscript acknowledged: Yes
Decision to publish in: 3-12 months
Accepted manuscript published in: 6 months
Rejected manuscript returned: Yes
Rejected manuscript criticized: No

Submit to:
Editor
(See address above)

Social sciences (general)

JOURNAL OF SEX RESEARCH [711]
138 East 94th Street
New York, New York 10028
(212) 534-7721

First published in 1965

SUBSCRIPTION DATA
Issues and rates: Published quarterly.
  Annual rate(s): $17.00; Foreign $18.00
Publisher or Sponsor: Society for the Scientific Study of Sex
Managing Editor: Hugo G. Beigel

EDITORIAL DESCRIPTION
  Contains scientific studies of sexuality in all its aspects.
Articles per average issue: 8-10
Audience: Professional
  Manuscripts accepted in English

MANUSCRIPT INFORMATION
Subject field(s): Sexuality, problems and cure, new insights into its development, history, legal aspects, social and individual, deviations, disturbances, therapeutics, medical, psychological, aesthetic, social, sociological, legal, criminal, demographic, etc.
Manuscript requirements: APA, Style sheet sent on request.
  Preferred length: 3,000 to 5,000 words
  Number of copies to be submitted: Two
  Abstract: Yes
Author information and reprints: Payment: None.
  Is simultaneous submission of article to other journals permitted: No
  Exclusive manuscript rights between acceptance and publication: Yes
  Copyright: Held by publication.
  Reprints: Available at printer's cost
Additional information: Manuscript should be legible, double-spaced, with tables, references and charts on separate pages, no footnotes except grants received. Author's title and present function or occupation should be on separate page.
Disposition of manuscript:
  Receipt of manuscript acknowledged: Yes
  Decision to publish in: 2-6 weeks
  Accepted manuscript published in: One year
  Rejected manuscript returned: Yes, if self-addressed, stamped envelope is sent with manuscript.
  Rejected manuscript criticized: Yes
Submit to:
  Hugo G. Beigel
  Editor-in-Chief
  (See address above)

KYKLOS [712]
International Review for the Social Sciences
Kyklos Verlag
Postfach 524
CH-4000 Basel 2, Switzerland

First published in 1947

SUBSCRIPTION DATA
Issues and rates: Published quarterly.
  Average paid circulation: 4,100
  Annual rate(s): Sfr. 50.00; Foreign Sfr. 50.00; Institutions Sfr. 50.00
Publisher or Sponsor: Genossenschaftliche Zentralbank, Basel; List Gesellschaft, Dülsseldorf
Managing Editor: Bruno S. Frey

EDITORIAL DESCRIPTION
  Publishes articles and notes of general interest, not too technical, treating problems of relevance and containing new results of research in the social sciences
Articles per average issue: 7
Audience: Professional, academic
  Manuscripts accepted in German, English, French

MANUSCRIPT INFORMATION
Manuscript requirements: No specific style guide.
  Preferred length: 25 pages
  Number of copies to be submitted: 2
  Abstract: Yes. Half a page, in English, and if possible, in German and French as well as one of about 100 words for the *Journal of Economic Literature.*
Author information and reprints: Payment: By publication to author. SFr. 10.00 per page.
  Is simultaneous submission of article to other journals permitted: Not permitted.
  Exclusive manuscript rights between acceptance and publication: Yes
  Copyright: Held by publication.
  Reprints: Available at no cost. 10
Additional information: Typewritten, double-spaced fair drawings of all graphs
Disposition of manuscript:
  Query letter: Not necessary.
  Receipt of manuscript acknowledged: Yes
  Accepted manuscript published in: Next issue
  Rejected manuscript returned: Yes, if return postage is supplied by author.
  Rejected manuscript criticized: No
Submit to:
  René Frey
  Redaktion
  Institut für Sozialwissenschaft
  Petersgraben 29
  CH-4051 Basel, Switzerland
  (06) 25 26 05

THE NEW SCHOLAR [713]
Studies, Essays & Reviews in the Social Sciences
College of Arts and Letters
San Diego State University
San Diego, California 92115
(714) 286-6280

First published in 1969

SUBSCRIPTION DATA
Issues and rates: Published semi-annually.
  Average paid circulation: 800; 25 controlled
  Annual rate(s): Individuals $4.00; Institutions $9.00; Foreign individuals $7.00; Foreign institutions $10.00

Managing Editor: Michael Arguello

EDITORIAL DESCRIPTION
  Contains original research or new interpretations in the social sciences.
Articles per average issue: 12
Audience: Professional and Laypeople
  Manuscripts accepted in English, Spanish

MANUSCRIPT INFORMATION
Subject field(s): Anthropology, sociology, geography, political science, economics, history, minority studies, psychology
Manuscript requirements: Chicago; See latest issue for style requirements.
  Preferred length: 35 pages or less
  Number of copies to be submitted: Original and two copies
Author information and reprints: Payment: None. Two copies of issue and 10 offprints.
  Is simultaneous submission of article to other journals permitted: No
  Exclusive manuscript rights between acceptance and publication: Yes
  Copyright: Held by publication.
  Reprints: Available
Additional information: Leave generous margins; illustrations and drawings to be done in India ink
Disposition of manuscript:
  Query letter: Preferred
  Receipt of manuscript acknowledged: Yes
  Decision to publish in: 60 days
  Accepted manuscript published in: 3-4 months
  Rejected manuscript returned: Yes
  Rejected manuscript criticized: Yes
Submit to:
  Vernon H. Kjonegaard
  Editor
  (See address above)

SPECIAL STIPULATIONS
  Publication has a continuing need for competent book reviewers. Address inquiries to Book Review Editor.

POPULATION STUDIES [714]
A Journal of Demography
Population Investigation Committee
The London School of Economics, Houghton Street
Aldwych, London WC2A 2AE, England
(01) 405-7686

First published in 1947

SUBSCRIPTION DATA
Issues and rates: Published three times per year.
  Average paid circulation: 2,900
  Annual rate(s): £6.00; Foreign $18.00

EDITORIAL DESCRIPTION
  Contains articles within or bordering on the field of demography
Articles per average issue: 12
Audience: Professional, academic
  Manuscripts accepted in English

MANUSCRIPT INFORMATION
Subject field(s): Results of new research, surveys, historical surveys, book reviews, new techniques, etc.
Manuscript requirements: Style sheet sent on request.
  Preferred length: As required
  Number of copies to be submitted: 2
  Abstract: Yes. A short summary of about 200 words
Author information and reprints: Payment: Reprints only. 25
  Is simultaneous submission of article to other journals permitted: Not permitted.
  Exclusive manuscript rights between acceptance and publication: Yes
  Copyright: Held jointly by publication and author
  Reprints: Available at cost.
Disposition of manuscript:
  Query letter: Not necessary.
  Receipt of manuscript acknowledged: Yes
  Decision to publish in: 2 months
  Accepted manuscript published in: 2-6 months
  Rejected manuscript returned: Yes, with return postage paid by publication.
  Rejected manuscript criticized: Sometimes
Submit to:
  Prof. David V. Glass
  Editor
  (See address above)

THE POTOMAC REVIEW [715]
Graduate Studies in the Social Sciences
429 Marvin Center
George Washington University
Washington, D.C. 20037
(301) 337-5600 ext. 106

Previously entitled *Journal of International and Comparative Studies*

First published in 1968

SUBSCRIPTION DATA
Issues and rates: Published three times per year.
  Average paid circulation: 1,000
  Annual rate(s): $3.00, Foreign $5.00; Students $2.50
Managing Editor: Jonathan Sanford

EDITORIAL DESCRIPTION
  Contains graduate scholarship in the social sciences.
Articles per average issue: 5
Audience: Academic
  Manuscripts accepted in English

MANUSCRIPT INFORMATION
Subject field(s): Social sciences and history
Manuscript requirements: See latest issue for style requirements.
  Preferred length: 15-20 pages
  Number of copies to be submitted: One or two
  Abstract: No

Author information and reprints: Payment: None.
  Is simultaneous submission of article to other journals permitted: Not without written permission from editor.
  Exclusive manuscript rights between acceptance and publication: No
  Copyright: Held by publication.
  Reprints: Available
Disposition of manuscript:
  Query letter: No
  Receipt of manuscript acknowledged: Yes
  Decision to publish in: 3 months
  Accepted manuscript published in: 1-2 months
  Rejected manuscript returned: Yes, if return postage is supplied by author.
  Rejected manuscript criticized: Yes
Submit to:
  Jonathan E. Sanford
  Manuscript Editor
  (See address above)

THE PUBLIC INTEREST [716]
10 East 53rd Street
New York, New York 10022
(212) 593-7123

SUBSCRIPTION DATA
Issues and rates: Published quarterly.
  Average paid circulation: 10,000
  Annual rate(s): $9.50; Foreign $10.50
Publisher or Sponsor: National Affairs Inc.

EDITORIAL DESCRIPTION
  Contains readable articles for the informed public on all areas of social policy.

MANUSCRIPT INFORMATION
Subject field(s): Social policy, political science, sociology, economics
Manuscript requirements: See latest issue for style requirements.
  Preferred length: 3,000-10,000 words
  Number of copies to be submitted: Three
Author information and reprints: Payment: By publication to author. $100 per article.
  Is simultaneous submission of article to other journals permitted: No
  Exclusive manuscript rights between acceptance and publication: Yes
  Copyright: Held by publication.
  Reprints: Available only to author who deals directly with reprint firm
Disposition of manuscript:
  Receipt of manuscript acknowledged: Yes
  Decision to publish in: 4-6 weeks
  Accepted manuscript published in: 2-6 months
  Rejected manuscript returned: Yes, if self-addressed, stamped envelope is sent with manuscript.
  Rejected manuscript criticized: Occasionally
Submit to:
  Marc F. Plattner
  Managing Editor
  (See address above)

SOCIAL BIOLOGY [717]
1180 Observatory Drive, Room 5440
Madison, Wisconsin 53706
(608) 262-5818

Previously entitled *Eugenics Quarterly*

First published in 1954

SUBSCRIPTION DATA
Issues and rates: Published quarterly.
  Average paid circulation: 1,635
  Annual rate(s): $25.00; Foreign $25.00; Institutions $25.00; Members $61.00
Publisher or Sponsor: Society for the Study of Social Biology

EDITORIAL DESCRIPTION
  Contains articles which further knowledge of the biological and socio-cultural forces affecting human populations and their evolution.
Articles per average issue: 9
  Manuscripts accepted in English

MANUSCRIPT INFORMATION
Subject field(s): Anthropology, demography, medical genetics, public health, sociology and other fields
Manuscript requirements: See latest issue for style requirements.
  Preferred length: None
  Number of copies to be submitted: 2
  Abstract: Not necessary.
Author information and reprints: Payment: None. There are excess page and table charges.
  Is simultaneous submission of article to other journals permitted: Not permitted.
  Exclusive manuscript rights between acceptance and publication: Yes
  Copyright: Held by publication.
  Reprints: Available at cost.
Disposition of manuscript:
  Query letter: Not necessary.
  Receipt of manuscript acknowledged: Yes
  Decision to publish in: 3-6 months
  Accepted manuscript published in: 9 months
  Rejected manuscript returned: Yes, if return postage is supplied by author.
  Rejected manuscript criticized: Sometimes
Submit to:
  Richard H. Osborne
  Editor
  (See address above)

SOCIAL CHANGE: IDEAS AND APPLICATIONS [718]
Box 9155
Arlington, Virginia 22209
(703) 527-1500

Previously entitled *Human Relations Training News*

First published in 1954

SUBSCRIPTION DATA
Issues and rates: Published quarterly.

Average paid circulation: 3,000; 100 controlled
Annual rate(s): $7.00 for two years
Publisher or Sponsor: The NTL Institute for Applied Behavioral Science

EDITORIAL DESCRIPTION

Contains articles on the theory and application of the laboratory method of training and consultation as applied to the dynamics of social change. It explores the relationship of group dynamics to the development and implementation of meaningful social change.
Articles per average issue: 3-4
Manuscripts accepted in English

MANUSCRIPT INFORMATION

Subject field(s): Social change, training techniques, consultation theory, training theory, anecdotal experience, individual change
Manuscript requirements: See latest issue for style requirements.
Preferred length: 1800-2000 words; 6 pages
Number of copies to be submitted: Two
Abstract: No
Author information and reprints: Payment: None.
Is simultaneous submission of article to other journals permitted: No
Exclusive manuscript rights between acceptance and publication: Yes
Copyright: Held by publication.
Reprints: Not available.
Disposition of manuscript:
Query letter: No
Receipt of manuscript acknowledged: Yes
Decision to publish in: Three months
Accepted manuscript published in: Six months
Rejected manuscript returned: Yes
Rejected manuscript criticized: No
Submit to:
Lawrence Porter
Editor
(See address above)

SOCIAL SCIENCE [719]

1719 Ames
Winfield, Kansas 67156

First published in 1924

SUBSCRIPTION DATA

Issues and rates: Published quarterly.
Average paid circulation: 8,000; 50 controlled
Annual rate(s): $3.00 for all
Publisher or Sponsor: Pi Gamma Mu
Managing Editor: Effie B. Urquhart

EDITORIAL DESCRIPTION

A unique international and interdisciplinary journal which covers both theory and application, historical and contemporary, qualitative and quantitative data from the fields of economics, history, political science, and sociology.
Articles per average issue: 6-10

Audience: Students, educators and other professionals

MANUSCRIPT INFORMATION

Subject field(s): Any social science subject and geographical area
Manuscript requirements: See latest issue for style requirements. Style sheet sent on request.
Preferred length: 4,000-5,000; 10-15 pages
Number of copies to be submitted: 2
Abstract: Yes. An abstract of about 80 words on the problem, methodology and most important findings.
Author information and reprints: Payment: Reprints only. 6
Is simultaneous submission of article to other journals permitted: Not permitted.
Exclusive manuscript rights between acceptance and publication: Yes
Copyright: Held by publication but author may reprint articles with the permission of the Editor.
Reprints: Not available.
Additional information: Original, interesting and well-written articles, free from pretentiousness are desired. Manuscripts must be submitted typewritten, double-spaced, with the footnotes at the end of the article.
Disposition of manuscript:
Query letter: Not necessary, but advisable.
Receipt of manuscript acknowledged: No
Decision to publish in: 10 days
Accepted manuscript published in: 2-9 months
Rejected manuscript returned: Yes, with return postage paid by publication.
Rejected manuscript criticized: Sometimes
Submit to:
Dr. Panos D. Bardis
Editor and Book Review Editor
Sociology-Anthropology Number 21
The University of Toledo
Toledo, Ohio 43606
(419) 537-2791

SOCIAL SCIENCE AND MEDICINE [720]

Pergamon Press, Inc.
Fairview Park
Elmsford, New York 10523
(914) 592-7700

First published in 1967

SUBSCRIPTION DATA

Issues and rates: Published monthly.
Annual rate(s): $25.00; Institutions $65.00

EDITORIAL DESCRIPTION

Contains important research and theoretical papers in all areas of common interest to the socio-behavioral sciences and medicine, including psychiatry and epidemiology.
Articles per average issue: Varies
Audience: Professional, academic
Manuscripts accepted in English, French, German, Spanish

MANUSCRIPT INFORMATION

Subject field(s): All aspects of anthropology, economics, education, psychology, and sociology which relate directly to mental and physical health, public health, and nursing studies.
Manuscript requirements: See latest issue for style requirements.
Preferred length: None
Number of copies to be submitted: Original and 1 copy, double-spaced
Abstract: Yes. Not to exceed 400 words
Author information and reprints: Payment: Reprints only. 50 reprints
Is simultaneous submission of article to other journals permitted: Not permitted.
Exclusive manuscript rights between acceptance and publication: Yes
Copyright: Held by publication.
Reprints: Available at cost.
Disposition of manuscript:
Query letter: Not necessary.
Receipt of manuscript acknowledged: Yes
Decision to publish in: 4 weeks
Accepted manuscript published in: 5 months
Rejected manuscript returned: Yes, if return postage is supplied by author.
Rejected manuscript criticized: Reasons for rejections only
Submit to:
Research, notes and announcements to:
René C. Fox
University of Pennsylvania
Philadelphia, Pennsylvania 19104

For book reviews to:
John Stoeckle
Massachusetts General Hospital
Boston, Massachusetts 02114

SOCIAL SCIENCE QUARTERLY [721]

University of Texas at Austin
Austin, Texas 78712
(512) 471-4384

Previously entitled *Southwestern Social Science*

First published in 1920

SUBSCRIPTION DATA

Issues and rates: Published quarterly.
Average paid circulation: 3,200
Annual rate(s): $8.00, Foreign $16.00; Institutions $15.00
Publisher or Sponsor: Southwestern Social Science Association
Managing Editor: Cynthia Gardner

EDITORIAL DESCRIPTION

Contains articles of interdisciplinary appeal in the fields of sociology, political science, economics, history, geography, and business.
Articles per average issue: 16
Audience: Social scientists
Manuscripts accepted in English

MANUSCRIPT INFORMATION
Subject field(s): Business, history, economics, political science, geography, sociology
Manuscript requirements: Style sheet sent on request.
 Preferred length: 30 pages maximum
 Number of copies to be submitted: Three
 Abstract: Yes; of 50-75 words
Author information and reprints: Payment: None.
 Is simultaneous submission of article to other journals permitted: No
 Exclusive manuscript rights between acceptance and publication: Yes
 Copyright: Held by publication.
 Reprints: Available at no cost. 25 free reprints
Disposition of manuscript:
 Query letter: No
 Receipt of manuscript acknowledged: Yes
 Decision to publish in: 2-3 months
 Accepted manuscript published in: 3-6 months
 Rejected manuscript returned: No
 Rejected manuscript criticized: Yes
Submit to:
 Charles M. Bonjean
 Editor
 (See address above)

SOCIAL THEORY AND PRACTICE [722]
International and Interdisciplinary Journal of Social Philosophy
Department of Philosophy
Florida State University
Tallahasee, Florida 32306
(904) 644-1483

First published in 1970

SUBSCRIPTION DATA
Issues and rates: Published semi-annually.
 Annual rate(s): $10.00; Foreign $10.60; Institutions $21.00; Foreign institutions $21.60
Publisher or Sponsor: Florida State University, Department of Philosophy
Managing Editor: Robert Biles

EDITORIAL DESCRIPTION
 Provides a forum for the expression of important and controversial social and political issues; constructive and critical work at all levels and on all social issues is welcomed.
Articles per average issue: 5-9
Audience: Interdisciplinary academic
 Manuscripts accepted in English

MANUSCRIPT INFORMATION
Manuscript requirements: Chicago
 Number of copies to be submitted: 2
 Abstract: Not necessary.
Author information and reprints: Payment: None.
 Is simultaneous submission of article to other journals permitted: Not permitted.
 Exclusive manuscript rights between acceptance and publication: Yes
 Copyright: Held by publication.
 Reprints: Available at no cost. 150 Available at cost.
Disposition of manuscript:
 Query letter: Not necessary.
 Receipt of manuscript acknowledged: Yes
 Decision to publish in: 3-4 months
 Accepted manuscript published in: 6 months
 Rejected manuscript returned: Yes, with return postage paid by publication.
 Rejected manuscript criticized: Yes
Submit to:
 Managing Editor
 (See address above)

SOCIETY [723]
Transaction/Social Science and Modern Society
Box A
Rutgers-The State University
New Brunswick, New Jersey 08903
(201) 932-2280

Previously entitled *Transaction* (first 9 volumes)

First published in 1963

SUBSCRIPTION DATA
Issues and rates: Published bi-monthly.
 Average paid circulation: 50,000
 Annual rate(s): $9.75; Pan-Am $9.75; Foreign $12.00; Individuals $9.75; Institutions $9.75; Students $7.25; Members $7.25; Foreign individuals $12.00; Foreign institutions $12.00
Managing Editor: Irving Louis Horowitz

EDITORIAL DESCRIPTION
 The dissemination of social science information of wide policy consequences to the general and interested public.
Articles per average issue: 8-10
 Manuscripts accepted in English

MANUSCRIPT INFORMATION
Subject field(s): Sociology, social work, anthropology, political science, economics, psychology, urban affairs, and social history.
Manuscript requirements: Style sheet sent on request. Chicago
 Preferred length: 10,000 words; 15 pages
 Number of copies to be submitted: Minimum of 2
 Abstract: Not necessary.
Author information and reprints: Payment: Reprints only. Varies by article and reprint purpose
 Is simultaneous submission of article to other journals permitted: Permitted, but not encouraged.
 Copyright: Held by publication.
 Reprints: Available at cost. Varies
Additional information: Be certain to read previous issues for "style" guidance.
Disposition of manuscript:
 Query letter: Not necessary.
 Receipt of manuscript acknowledged: Yes
 Decision to publish in: 3-4 months
 Accepted manuscript published in: 6-10 months
 Rejected manuscript returned: Yes, with return postage paid by publication.
 Rejected manuscript criticized: Sometimes
Submit to:
 Doreen Ferrazzarra
 Assistant to the Editor
 (See address above)

SOCIETY FOR RESEARCH IN CHILD DEVELOPMENT. MONOGRAPHS [724]
University of Chicago Press
5801 Ellis Avenue
Chicago, Illinois 60637
(312) 753-3370

First published in 1935

SUBSCRIPTION DATA
Issues and rates: Published quarterly.
 Annual rate(s): $15.00
Publisher or Sponsor: Society for Research in Child Development

EDITORIAL DESCRIPTION
 Contains research studies on child development, especially longitudinal studies.
Articles per average issue: 1
Audience: Professional, academic
 Manuscripts accepted in English

MANUSCRIPT INFORMATION
Subject field(s): Psychology, sociology, physical growth, psychiatry, pediatrics, anthropology
Manuscript requirements: APA
 Preferred length: 60-300 pages
 Number of copies to be submitted: 3
 Abstract: Yes. 300 words maximum
Author information and reprints: Payment: Reprints only. 10 reprints
 Is simultaneous submission of article to other journals permitted: Not permitted.
 Exclusive manuscript rights between acceptance and publication: Yes
 Copyright: Held by publication.
 Reprints: Available at cost.
Additional information: Procure instruction memo from editor.
Disposition of manuscript:
 Query letter: Not necessary.
 Receipt of manuscript acknowledged: Yes
 Decision to publish in: 3 months
 Accepted manuscript published in: 5 months
 Rejected manuscript returned: Yes, if return postage is supplied by author.
 Rejected manuscript criticized: Sometimes
Submit to:
 Through 1975:
 Robert R. Sears
 Editor
 (See address above)

 Effective 1976:
 Frances D. Horowitz
 Editor
 Department of Human Development

Social sciences (general)

University of Kansas
Lawrence, Kansas 66045

STUDIES IN COMPARATIVE INTERNATIONAL DEVELOPMENT [725]

Transaction, Inc.
Rutgers, The State University
New Brunswick, New Jersey 08903
(201) 932-2280

SUBSCRIPTION DATA

Issues and rates: Published three times per year.
   Average paid circulation: 1500; 100 controlled
   Annual rate(s): $15.00, Students $10.00, Foreign $16.50
Publisher or Sponsor: Transaction, Inc.
Managing Editor: Danielle Salti

EDITORIAL DESCRIPTION

Contains papers in the field of comparative international development from the perspective of each social science. The main section on Development Research usually includes four or five papers; another section on Development Policy presents a basic social scientific policy recommendation in any given area of development. Special emphasis is on the application of political sociology to Third World problems and events.

Articles per average issue: Varies
Audience: Professional, academic
   Manuscripts accepted in English

MANUSCRIPT INFORMATION

Subject field(s): Sociology, political science, economics, anthropology, psychology, history, geography
Manuscript requirements: Chicago; see Notice to Contributors in publication.
   Preferred length: 20-25 pages
   Number of copies to be submitted: Original and 1 copy
Author information and reprints: Payment: None.
   Is simultaneous submission of article to other journals permitted: No
   Exclusive manuscript rights between acceptance and publication: Yes
   Copyright: Held by publication.
   Reprints: Available, $5.00 per page for 100 copies
Additional information: Questions on technical aspects of a manuscript after acceptance for publication but prior to actual publication, should be addressed to the Associate Editor. Queries may be addressed in French, Spanish, Italian, Portuguese or German; but all manuscripts must be submitted in English for final approval.
Disposition of manuscript:
   Receipt of manuscript acknowledged: Yes
   Decision to publish in: 2-6 months
   Accepted manuscript published in: 6-12 months
   Rejected manuscript returned: Yes, if self-addressed, stamped envelope is sent with manuscript.
   Rejected manuscript criticized: Sometimes
Submit to:
   Irving Louis Horowitz
   Chief Editor
   (See address above)

URBAN STUDIES [726]

Longman Group Ltd., Journals Division
Burnt Mill
Harlow, Essex, England
26721

First published in 1964

SUBSCRIPTION DATA

Issues and rates: Published three times per year.
   Annual rate(s): £7.00, Foreign $21.00

EDITORIAL DESCRIPTION

Provides social and economic contributions dealing with urban matters and with urban planning.
Submit to:
   J.T. Hughes
   Editor
   (See address above)

SPECIAL STIPULATIONS

Request additional information from editor.

WORKING PAPERS FOR A NEW SOCIETY [727]

123 Mt. Auburn Street
Cambridge, Massachusetts 02138
(617) 547-4474

First published in 1973

SUBSCRIPTION DATA

Issues and rates: Published quarterly.
   Average paid circulation: 3,500
   Annual rate(s): $10.00, Foreign $15.00
Publisher or Sponsor: The Cambridge Policy Studies Institute, Inc.
Managing Editor: John Case;
Nancy Lyons

EDITORIAL DESCRIPTION

Contains articles on social and political "alternatives": new policy proposals (e.g., a credit income tax), descriptions of alternative institutions (e.g., communes, food co-ops), proposals for political programs (community ownership, land reform), "utopian" speculation.
Articles per average issue: 10, including reviews
Audience: Left of center
   Manuscripts accepted in English

MANUSCRIPT INFORMATION

Manuscript requirements: Chicago
   Preferred length: 3000-5000 words; 15-25 typewritten, double-spaced pages
   Number of copies to be submitted: Two
   Abstract: No
Author information and reprints: Payment: By publication to author. $100 per article.
   Is simultaneous submission of article to other journals permitted: No
   Exclusive manuscript rights between acceptance and publication: Yes
   Copyright: Held by publication.
   Reprints: Reprints planned
Additional information: Manuscripts are subject to extensive editing, in consultation with author, as necessary.
Disposition of manuscript:
   Receipt of manuscript acknowledged: Yes
   Decision to publish in: Four weeks
   Accepted manuscript published in: Three months
   Rejected manuscript returned: Yes, if self-addressed, stamped envelope is sent with manuscript.
   Rejected manuscript criticized: No
Submit to:
   John Case;
   Nancy Lyons
   Managing Editors
   (See address above)

YOUTH AND SOCIETY* [728]

Sage Publications, Inc.
275 South Beverly Drive
Beverly Hills, California 90212
(213) 274-2423

SUBSCRIPTION DATA

Issues and rates: Published quarterly.
   Average paid circulation: Not available.
   Annual rate(s): Institutions $15.00; Individuals $10.00; Students $8.00; Foreign individuals $11.50; Foreign institutions $16.50

EDITORIAL DESCRIPTION

Publishes articles concerned with the social and political implications of youth culture and development; focus on middle adolescence through young adulthood; empirical and theoretical studies relevant to socialization, processes of development, impact of youth culture on society, patterns of adult role acquisition.

MANUSCRIPT INFORMATION

Subject field(s): Sociology, psychology, political science, anthropology, history, economics
Manuscript requirements: Style sheet sent on request.
   Preferred length: 6,250-7,500 words; 25 to 30 pages
   Number of copies to be submitted: Two
Author information and reprints: Payment: None. 25 tear-sheets free to author.
   Is simultaneous submission of article to other journals permitted: Permitted, but not encouraged. Author must notify publisher that manuscript is under consideration elsewhere.
   Exclusive manuscript rights between acceptance and publication: Yes
   Copyright: Held by publication.
   Reprints: Available if purchased by special order in amounts no fewer than 100

Disposition of manuscript:
  Receipt of manuscript acknowledged: Yes
  Decision to publish in: Six to eight weeks
  Accepted manuscript published in: Six to nine months
  Rejected manuscript returned: Yes
  Rejected manuscript criticized: Yes
Submit to:
  Alex W. McEachern
  Editor
  Youth Studies Center
  University of Southern California
  Los Angeles, California 90007

Accounting

ACCOUNTANCY [729]
City House
56/66 Goswell Road
London EC1, England
(O1) 628-7060

Previously entitled *The Incorporated Accountants Journal*

First published in 1889

SUBSCRIPTION DATA
Issues and rates: Published monthly.
  Average paid circulation: 40,648
  Annual rate(s): £7.50; Foreign £7.50; Institutions £7.50; Students £3.00; Members $6.00
Publisher or Sponsor: The Institute of Chartered Accountants in England and Wales
Managing Editor: Geoffrey A. Holmes

EDITORIAL DESCRIPTION
Covers all the interests of accountants, whether in practice, in industry, commerce or the public service; and of general management interest in financial problems and their solutions
Articles per average issue: 40
Audience: Professional
  Manuscripts accepted in English

MANUSCRIPT INFORMATION
Subject field(s): Accounting, finance, banking, taxation, auditing, business machines and computers, investment, statistics, marketing, budget, coporate strategy, mathematical analysis, law, take-overs and amalgamations, etc.
Manuscript requirements: Style sheet sent on request.
  Preferred length: 1,100-5,700 words; 1-5 pages
  Number of copies to be submitted: 2
  Abstract: Not necessary.
Author information and reprints: Payment: By publication to author.
  Is simultaneous submission of article to other journals permitted: Permitted, but not encouraged.
  Exclusive manuscript rights between acceptance and publication: No
  Copyright: First serial rights only
  Reprints: Available at cost.

Disposition of manuscript:
  Query letter: Not necessary, but advisable.
  Receipt of manuscript acknowledged: Yes
  Decision to publish in: 7-28 days
  Accepted manuscript published in: 2 months
  Rejected manuscript returned: Yes, with return postage paid by publication.
  Rejected manuscript criticized: Reasons for rejections only
Submit to:
  Geoffrey A. Holmes
  Editor
  (See address above)

THE CALIFORNIA CPA QUARTERLY [730]
1000 Welch Road
Palo Alto, California 94304
(415) 321-9545

First published in 1959

SUBSCRIPTION DATA
Issues and rates: Published quarterly.
  Average paid circulation: 12,500
  Annual rate(s): $3.00
Publisher or Sponsor: The California Society of Certified Public Accountants

EDITORIAL DESCRIPTION
Contains articles and columns of interest and concern to professional accountants.
Articles per average issue: 3
Audience: Certified public accountants
  Manuscripts accepted in English

MANUSCRIPT INFORMATION
Subject field(s): Accounting, auditing, taxation, management advisory services, computer science, communications arts, economics, business law, functional fields of business
Manuscript requirements: Wireservice Stylebooks, See latest issue for style requirements.
  Preferred length: 2500-3500 words
  Number of copies to be submitted: One
  Abstract: No
Author information and reprints: Payment: None. Complimentary copies of issue.
  Is simultaneous submission of article to other journals permitted: No
  Exclusive manuscript rights between acceptance and publication: Yes
  Copyright: Held by author.
  Reprints: Not available.
Additional information: Typewritten, double-spaced, with subheads and other graphics clearly indicated.
Disposition of manuscript:
  Query letter: No
  Receipt of manuscript acknowledged: Yes
  Decision to publish in: 1-4 months
  Accepted manuscript published in: 4-8 months
  Rejected manuscript returned: Yes
  Rejected manuscript criticized: No
Submit to:
  Gerald J. Sirocky
  Managing Editor
  (See address above)

COST AND MANAGEMENT [731]
P. O. Box 176
Hamilton, Ontario L8N 3C3, Canada
(416) 525-4100

First published in 1926

SUBSCRIPTION DATA
Issues and rates: Published bi-monthly.
  Average paid circulation: 19,593
  Annual rate(s): $7.50; Foreign $10.00
Publisher or Sponsor: Society of Industrial Accountants of Canada
Managing Editor: Dan R. Hicks

EDITORIAL DESCRIPTION
Seeks practical and conceptual articles designed to foster the development of the accountant in management.
Articles per average issue: 6-7
Audience: Accountants and managers
  Manuscripts accepted in English, French

MANUSCRIPT INFORMATION
Subject field(s): Accounting (especially management accounting), finance, economics, management, and related areas.
Manuscript requirements: No specific style guide.
  Preferred length: 5,000 words
  Number of copies to be submitted: 2
  Abstract: Not necessary.
Author information and reprints: Payment: None.
  Is simultaneous submission of article to other journals permitted: Not permitted.
  Exclusive manuscript rights between acceptance and publication: Yes
  Copyright: Held by publication.
  Reprints: Available at no cost. 12
Disposition of manuscript:
  Query letter: Not necessary, but advisable.
  Receipt of manuscript acknowledged: Yes
  Decision to publish in: 1 month
  Accepted manuscript published in: 6 months
  Rejected manuscript returned: Yes, with return postage paid by publication.
  Rejected manuscript criticized: Yes
Submit to:
  Dan R. Hicks
  Managing Editor
  (See address above)

THE CPA JOURNAL [732]
600 Third Avenue
New York, New York 10016
(212) 953-1388

SUBSCRIPTION DATA
Issues and rates: Published monthly.
  Average paid circulation: 32,000
  Annual rate(s): $18.00; Foreign $21.00; Students $9.00

Publisher or Sponsor: New York State Society of Certified Public Accountants

EDITORIAL DESCRIPTION

Publishes articles of interest to practicing CPA's

Articles per average issue: 5

Audience: Professional
Manuscripts accepted in English

MANUSCRIPT INFORMATION

Subject field(s): Accounting, auditing, estate planning, management advisory services, administration; practical applications are preferred, but some theoretical discussions are accepted, along with articles on trends within the profession.

Manuscript requirements: No specific style guide.
Preferred length: 2,500 words
Number of copies to be submitted: 1
Abstract: Not necessary.

Author information and reprints: Payment: None.
Is simultaneous submission of article to other journals permitted: Not permitted.
Exclusive manuscript rights between acceptance and publication: Yes
Copyright: Held by publication.
Reprints: Available at cost.

Disposition of manuscript:
Query letter: Not necessary.
Receipt of manuscript acknowledged: Yes
Decision to publish in: 1 month
Accepted manuscript published in: 4 months
Rejected manuscript returned: Yes, if return postage is supplied by author.
Rejected manuscript criticized: Reasons for rejections only

Submit to:
Allen Weiss
Managing Editor
(See address above)

THE INTERNAL AUDITOR [733]

The Institute of Internal Auditors, Inc.
5500 Diplomat Circle
Orlando, Florida 32810
(305) 647-4700

First published in 1944

SUBSCRIPTION DATA

Issues and rates: Published bi-monthly.
Average paid circulation: 13,500; 500 controlled
Annual rate(s): $10.00

Publisher or Sponsor: The Institute of Internal Auditors, Inc.

EDITORIAL DESCRIPTION

Publishes articles on the theory and practice of modern internal auditing in government and industry.

Articles per average issue: 10-12

Audience: Internal auditors, business managers
Manuscripts accepted in English

MANUSCRIPT INFORMATION

Subject field(s): Internal auditing, behavioral sciences, statistical sampling

Manuscript requirements: Style sheet sent on request.
Preferred length: 2,000-3,000 words; 8-15 pages
Number of copies to be submitted: 2

Author information and reprints: Payment: Reprints only. 5 free copies of Journal
Is simultaneous submission of article to other journals permitted: Yes
Exclusive manuscript rights between acceptance and publication: Yes
Copyright: Held by publication.
Reprints: Available, $.50 each

Additional information: Everything is to be typewritten, double-spaced, clean copy with clear originals of artwork or charts.

Disposition of manuscript:
Query letter: No
Receipt of manuscript acknowledged: Yes
Decision to publish in: 60 days
Accepted manuscript published in: 3-9 months
Rejected manuscript returned: Yes
Rejected manuscript criticized: No

Submit to:
Don Anders
Director of Communications
(See address above)

THE INTERNATIONAL JOURNAL OF ACCOUNTING EDUCATION AND RESEARCH [734]

320 Commerce West
University of Illinois
Urbana, Illinois 61801
(217) 333-4545

First published in 1965

SUBSCRIPTION DATA

Issues and rates: Published semi-annually.
Average paid circulation: 1,000
Annual rate(s): $3.00

Publisher or Sponsor: Center for International Education and Research in Accounting

Managing Editor: V. K. Zimmerman

EDITORIAL DESCRIPTION

Welcomes articles dealing particularly with the international developments of accounting but also accepts articles of broad interest to accounting theory which may not have any designated international focus. Features articles that describe particular national accounting practices.

Articles per average issue: 8-10

Audience: Academic and professional accountants
Manuscripts accepted in English

MANUSCRIPT INFORMATION

Subject field(s): International theory development, contrasting international practice, comparative accounting education, special international accounting problems, international economic influences, international financial influences, international history, general accounting theory, general accounting practice

Manuscript requirements: See latest issue for style requirements.
Preferred length: 4500 to 6000 words; 18-24 pages
Number of copies to be submitted: Two
Abstract: No

Author information and reprints: Payment: None.
Is simultaneous submission of article to other journals permitted: Yes, but wish to be informed of the other review process.
Exclusive manuscript rights between acceptance and publication: Yes
Copyright: Held by publication.
Reprints: Available

Disposition of manuscript:
Query letter: No
Receipt of manuscript acknowledged: Yes
Decision to publish in: 6-12 months
Accepted manuscript published in: 6 months
Rejected manuscript returned: Yes
Rejected manuscript criticized: Yes

Submit to:
V. K. Zimmerman
Director
(See address above)

THE JOURNAL OF ACCOUNTANCY [735]

1211 Avenue of the Americas
New York, New York 10036
(212) 581-8440 ext. 256

First published in 1905

SUBSCRIPTION DATA

Issues and rates: Published monthly.
Average paid circulation: 176,000 controlled
Annual rate(s): $10.00

Publisher or Sponsor: American Institute of Certified Public Accountants

EDITORIAL DESCRIPTION

Concerns accounting policy and research, opinions and practical experience on current accounting, auditing, financial reporting and professional developments.

Articles per average issue: 4

Audience: Professional accountants
Manuscripts accepted in English

MANUSCRIPT INFORMATION

Subject field(s): Accounting standards and theory, auditing standards and practice, management of an accounting practice, management accounting, systems and procedures, taxes, professional affairs, government accounting, education, recruitment

Manuscript requirements: Chicago
Preferred length: 2,500-4,000 words
Number of copies to be submitted: Three
Abstract: Yes

Author information and reprints: Payment: None.
Is simultaneous submission of article to other journals permitted: No

Exclusive manuscript rights between acceptance and publication: Yes
Copyright: Held by American Institute of Certified Public Accountants, Inc.
Reprints: Available
Additional information: Typewritten, double-spaced
Disposition of manuscript:
 Query letter: No
 Receipt of manuscript acknowledged: Yes
 Decision to publish in: Four weeks
 Accepted manuscript published in: Two months
 Rejected manuscript returned: Yes
 Rejected manuscript criticized: Yes
Submit to:
 William O. Doherty
 Editor
 (See address above)

JOURNAL OF ACCOUNTING RESEARCH [736]
Graduate School of Business
University of Chicago
5836 Greenwood Avenue
Chicago, Illinois 60637
(312) 753-3693

First published in 1963

SUBSCRIPTION DATA
Issues and rates: Published three times per year.
 Average paid circulation: 2,500
 Annual rate(s): $10.00, Students $7.50
Managing Editor: Nicholas Dopuch

EDITORIAL DESCRIPTION
Contains research in accounting and auditing.
Manuscripts accepted in English

MANUSCRIPT INFORMATION
Subject field(s): Accounting, auditing
Manuscript requirements: No specific style guide.
 Preferred length: None
 Number of copies to be submitted: Two
Author information and reprints: Payment: None.
 Is simultaneous submission of article to other journals permitted: No
 Exclusive manuscript rights between acceptance and publication: No
 Copyright: Held by publication.
 Reprints: Available, 100 minimum
Additional information: Typewritten, double-spaced, with tables and footnotes at the end.
Disposition of manuscript:
 Receipt of manuscript acknowledged: Yes
 Decision to publish in: 3 months
 Accepted manuscript published in: 6 months
 Rejected manuscript returned: Yes
 Rejected manuscript criticized: Sometimes
Submit to:
 Nicholas Dopuch
 Editor
 (See address above)

THE JOURNAL OF TAXATION [737]
125 East 56th Street
New York, New York 10022
(212) 421-6740

First published in 1954

SUBSCRIPTION DATA
Issues and rates: Published monthly.
 Average paid circulation: 16,500
 Annual rate(s): $36.00
Managing Editor: Leo J. Northart

EDITORIAL DESCRIPTION
Contains sophisticated analysis of new developments in taxation, with emphasis on practical problems of corporate and personal federal income, estate and gift taxation.
Articles per average issue: 6
Audience: Professional tax practitioners
Manuscripts accepted in English

MANUSCRIPT INFORMATION
Subject field(s): Taxation
Manuscript requirements: See latest issue for style requirements.
 Preferred length: 4,000 to 5,000 words typewritten, double-spaced
 Number of copies to be submitted: Two
 Abstract: No
Author information and reprints: Payment: None.
 Is simultaneous submission of article to other journals permitted: No
 Exclusive manuscript rights between acceptance and publication: Yes
 Copyright: Held by publication.
 Reprints: Available, 100 free
Disposition of manuscript:
 Query letter: Yes
 Receipt of manuscript acknowledged: Yes
 Decision to publish in: 3-4 weeks
 Accepted manuscript published in: 1-3 months
 Rejected manuscript returned: Yes
 Rejected manuscript criticized: Yes
Submit to:
 Editor
 (See address above)

THE NATIONAL PUBLIC ACCOUNTANT [738]
1717 Pennsylvania Avenue NW, Suite 1200
Washington, D.C. 20006
(202) 298-9040

First published in 1947

SUBSCRIPTION DATA
Issues and rates: Published monthly.
 Average paid circulation: 1,815; 16,185 controlled
 Annual rate(s): $9.00, Foreign $10.00
Publisher or Sponsor: National Society of Public Accountants

EDITORIAL DESCRIPTION
Editorially directed toward accountants in public practice, to expose them to the current thinking in the areas of tax practice, accounting, auditing, and professional ethics.
Articles per average issue: 4
Audience: Accountants, bankers, lawyers, students, government officials
Manuscripts accepted in English

MANUSCRIPT INFORMATION
Subject field(s): Accounting, auditing, tax practice, tax law, more efficient practices, new books and products, ethics, IRS regulations
Manuscript requirements: Style sheet sent on request.
 Preferred length: 2500-5000 words; 7-10 pages
 Number of copies to be submitted: Two
 Rejected manuscript returned: Not necessary
Author information and reprints: Payment: None.
 Is simultaneous submission of article to other journals permitted: Yes, if author makes this known
 Exclusive manuscript rights between acceptance and publication: Yes
 Copyright: Held by publication.
 Reprints: Available; cost depends on length
Additional information: Manuscripts to be typewritten, double-spaced, including good copies of illustrations.
Disposition of manuscript:
 Query letter: No
 Receipt of manuscript acknowledged: Yes
 Decision to publish in: Two weeks
 Accepted manuscript published in: Usually 2-3 months
 Rejected manuscript returned: Yes, if self-addressed, stamped envelope is sent with manuscript.
 Rejected manuscript criticized: No
Submit to:
 Linda A. Taxis
 Managing Editor
 (See address above)

THE TAX ADVISER [739]
1211 Avenue of the Americas
New York, New York 10036
(212) 581-8440

First published in 1970

SUBSCRIPTION DATA
Issues and rates: Published monthly.
 Average paid circulation: 12,000
 Annual rate(s): $36.00
Publisher or Sponsor: American Institute of Certified Public Accountants

EDITORIAL DESCRIPTION
Contains articles and departments devoted to federal tax planning, trends and techniques.
Articles per average issue: 3
Audience: Tax professionals
Manuscripts accepted in English only

MANUSCRIPT INFORMATION
Subject field(s): Federal tax

Manuscript requirements: See latest issue for style requirements.
  Preferred length: At least 16 pages
  Number of copies to be submitted: Two
  Rejected manuscript returned: No
Author information and reprints: Payment: None.
  Is simultaneous submission of article to other journals permitted: Yes, if submitted to noncommercial publications
  Exclusive manuscript rights between acceptance and publication: No
  Copyright: Held by publication.
  Reprints: Available, no cost to author
Additional information: Author should indicate whether manuscript has been submitted to other publications. Manuscripts to be typewritten, double-spaced, with footnotes listed separately.
Disposition of manuscript:
  Query letter: No
  Receipt of manuscript acknowledged: Yes
  Decision to publish in: 1-2 months
  Accepted manuscript published in: 2-3 months
  Rejected manuscript returned: Yes
  Rejected manuscript criticized: No
Submit to:
  E. S. Linett
  Editor
  (See address above)

TAXATION FOR ACCOUNTANTS [740]

A National Monthly Professional Tax Magazine for the Accountant in General Practice
125 East 56th Street
New York, New York 20022
(212) 421-6740

First published in 1970

SUBSCRIPTION DATA

Issues and rates: Published monthly.
  Average paid circulation: 15,500
  Annual rate(s): $24.00

EDITORIAL DESCRIPTION

Contains discussion of practical problems in determining a particular taxpayer's correct tax liability, and planning related to control of tax liability. Contents are aimed at the accountant in general practice who is not a tax specialist.
Articles per average issue: 6
Audience: Accounts in general practice
  Manuscripts accepted in English

MANUSCRIPT INFORMATION

Subject field(s): Taxation
Manuscript requirements: See latest issue for style requirements.
  Preferred length: 4,000 to 5,000 words
  Number of copies to be submitted: Two
  Abstract: No
Author information and reprints: Payment: None.
  Is simultaneous submission of article to other journals permitted: No
  Exclusive manuscript rights between acceptance and publication: Yes
  Copyright: Held by publication.
  Reprints: Available, 100 free
Additional information: Edited by the staff of *The Journal of Taxation*.
Disposition of manuscript:
  Query letter: Yes
  Receipt of manuscript acknowledged: Yes
  Decision to publish in: 2-4 weeks
  Accepted manuscript published in: 1-2 months
  Rejected manuscript returned: Yes
  Rejected manuscript criticized: Yes
Submit to:
  Editor
  (See address above)

THE VIRGINIA ACCOUNTANT [741]

Suite 1010
700 East Main Street Building
Richmond, Virginia 23219
(703) 643-1489

First published in 1948

SUBSCRIPTION DATA

Issues and rates: Published quarterly.
  Average paid circulation: 200; 2,000 controlled
  Annual rate(s): $4.00, Foreign $5.00
Publisher or Sponsor: Virginia Society of Certified Public Accountants
Managing Editor: John B. Sperry

EDITORIAL DESCRIPTION

The official publication of the Virginia Society of Public Accountants, it contains technical material on accounting, auditing, taxation and management services.
Articles per average issue: 4-5
Audience: Membership, students, financial subscribers
  Manuscripts accepted in English

MANUSCRIPT INFORMATION

Preferred length: 10-12 pages, typewritten, double-spaced. Style sheet sent on request.
Number of copies to be submitted: Two
Abstract: No
Author information and reprints: Payment: None.
  Is simultaneous submission of article to other journals permitted: No
  Exclusive manuscript rights between acceptance and publication: No
  Copyright: Held by publication.
  Reprints: Not available.
Disposition of manuscript:
  Query letter: No
  Receipt of manuscript acknowledged: Yes
  Decision to publish in: 60 days
  Accepted manuscript published in: 60 days
  Rejected manuscript returned: Yes
  Rejected manuscript criticized: No
Submit to:
  Patricia P. Koontz
  Business Manager
  (See address above)

Business and economics

THE ACES BULLETIN [742]

Indiana University
1005 East Tenth Street
Bloomington, Indiana 47401
(812) 337-2824

Previously entitled *ASTE Bulletin*

First published in 1959

SUBSCRIPTION DATA

Issues and rates: Published three times per year.
  Average paid circulation: 700
  Annual rate(s): $7.50; Institutions $10.00
Publisher or Sponsor: Association for Comparative Economic Studies
Managing Editor: John P. Hardt; Robert W. Campbell

EDITORIAL DESCRIPTION

Publishes articles on comparative studies of economic systems, planning and economic development as well as acts as an information exchange to further the growth of systematic knowledge in the above areas and items related to these fields concerning research, instruction and publication.
Articles per average issue: 4-5
Audience: Academic, research specialists
  Manuscripts accepted in English

MANUSCRIPT INFORMATION

Subject field(s): Foreign economies and related disciplines.
Manuscript requirements: See latest issue for style requirements.
  Preferred length: Up to 30 pages
  Number of copies to be submitted: Two
  Abstract: No
Author information and reprints: Payment: None.
  Is simultaneous submission of article to other journals permitted: No
  Exclusive manuscript rights between acceptance and publication: Yes
  Copyright: Held by publication.
  Reprints: Not available.
Disposition of manuscript:
  Query letter: No
  Receipt of manuscript acknowledged: Yes
  Decision to publish in: 1-2 months
  Accepted manuscript published in: 1-4 months
  Rejected manuscript returned: No
  Rejected manuscript criticized: Yes
Submit to:
  John P. Hardt
  Editor
  Congressional Research Service
  The Library of Congress
  Washington, D.C. 20540
  (202) 426-5000

  Robert W. Campbell
  Specialist in Soviet Economics

Department of Economics
Ballantine Hall, Indiana University
Bloomington, Indiana 47401
(812) 337-7808

ADMINISTRATIVE SCIENCE QUARTERLY [743]

Malott Hall, Cornell University
Ithaca, New York 14853
(607) 256-5117

First published in 1956

SUBSCRIPTION DATA

Issues and rates: Published quarterly.
  Average paid circulation: 4,500; 4,600 controlled
  Annual rate(s): Individuals $12.00, Institutions $20.00
Publisher or Sponsor: Cornell University, Graduate School of Business and Public Administration
Managing Editor: K. Schwartz

EDITORIAL DESCRIPTION

  Contains articles, book reviews, news and notes, and publications received on the subject of organizational behavior.
Articles per average issue: 8-10
Audience: Academic, professional
  Manuscripts accepted in English, French, German, Spanish, Russian, Dutch, Norwegian

MANUSCRIPT INFORMATION

Subject field(s): Organizational behavior, social psychology, political science, sociology, business administration
Manuscript requirements: Chicago
  Preferred length: 7,500-10,500 words; 25-35 pages
  Number of copies to be submitted: 2 copies if less than 7500 words; otherwise 3 copies
  Abstract: Yes; of 100 words or less
Author information and reprints: Payment: None.
  Is simultaneous submission of article to other journals permitted: Only in special cases based upon specific requests.
  Exclusive manuscript rights between acceptance and publication: Yes
  Copyright: Held by publication.
  Reprints: Available to authors
Additional information: Manuscripts are to be typewritten, double-spaced, with a cover letter and detachable identification sheet.
Disposition of manuscript:
  Query letter: Not necessary, but advisable.
  Receipt of manuscript acknowledged: Yes
  Decision to publish in: 3 months
  Accepted manuscript published in: 3-4 months
  Rejected manuscript returned: Yes
  Rejected manuscript criticized: Yes
Submit to:
  Katherine B. Schwartz
  Managing Editor
  (See address above)

ALABAMA BUSINESS [744]

Center for Business and Economic Research
The University of Alabama
Box AK
University, Alabama 35486
(205) 348-6191

First published in 1930

SUBSCRIPTION DATA

Issues and rates: Published monthly.
  Average paid circulation: 6,303 controlled
Publisher or Sponsor: The University of Alabama

EDITORIAL DESCRIPTION

  Contains statistics on business conditions in Alabama as well as articles of interest to businessmen and others interested in the economy of the state and nation.
Articles per average issue: 2-3
Audience: Businessmen, economists

MANUSCRIPT INFORMATION

Subject field(s): Business, economics, sociology, demography, transportation, travel, finance, environment, etc.
Manuscript requirements: Style sheet sent on request.
  Preferred length: 10-15 pages
  Number of copies to be submitted: One
  Abstract: No
Author information and reprints: Payment: None.
  Is simultaneous submission of article to other journals permitted: No
  Exclusive manuscript rights between acceptance and publication: Yes
  Copyright: Not copyrighted
  Reprints: Available
Disposition of manuscript:
  Query letter: No
  Receipt of manuscript acknowledged: Yes
  Decision to publish in: 2-3 months
  Accepted manuscript published in: 2-3 months
  Rejected manuscript returned: Yes
  Rejected manuscript criticized: No
Submit to:
  Editor
  (See address above)

AMERICAN ECONOMIC REVIEW [745]

Box Q
Brown University
Providence, Rhode Island 02912
(401) 863-2787

First published in 1911

SUBSCRIPTION DATA

Issues and rates: Published quarterly.
  Average paid circulation: 26,000
  Annual rate(s): $30.00, Members $20.00
Publisher or Sponsor: American Economic Association
Managing Editor: George H. Borts

EDITORIAL DESCRIPTION

  Contains articles on economic research, economic policy, economic measurement and analysis.
Articles per average issue: 30
Audience: Professional economists
  Manuscripts accepted in English

MANUSCRIPT INFORMATION

Manuscript requirements: Style sheet sent on request.
  Preferred length: 50 pages maximum
  Number of copies to be submitted: Two
Author information and reprints: Payment: By author to publication. $10.00 per article.
  Is simultaneous submission of article to other journals permitted: No
  Exclusive manuscript rights between acceptance and publication: Yes
  Copyright: Held by publication.
  Reprints: Available, 100 free; additional copies at cost
Disposition of manuscript:
  Receipt of manuscript acknowledged: Yes
  Decision to publish in: 2-6 months
  Accepted manuscript published in: One year
  Rejected manuscript returned: Yes
  Rejected manuscript criticized: Yes
Submit to:
  George H. Borts
  Editor
  (See address above)

THE AMERICAN ECONOMIST [746]

Journal of Omicron Delta Epsilon
Department of Economics
Box 3985, University Station
Laramie, Wyoming 82071
(307) 766-3384

First published in 1957

SUBSCRIPTION DATA

Issues and rates: Published semi-annually.
  Average paid circulation: 6,000
  Annual rate(s): $5.00, non-members; Members $3.00; Institutions $6.00
Publisher or Sponsor: Omicron Delta Epsilon, International Honor Society in Economics
Managing Editor: John Guilfoil; Curtis Cramer

EDITORIAL DESCRIPTION

  Contains scholarly articles in all fields of economics.
Articles per average issue: 18-22
Audience: Professional economists and students of economics

MANUSCRIPT INFORMATION

Manuscript requirements: See latest issue for style requirements.
  Preferred length: Shorter articles preferred

Number of copies to be submitted: One
Abstract: No
Author information and reprints: Payment: None.
Is simultaneous submission of article to other journals permitted: No
Exclusive manuscript rights between acceptance and publication: Yes
Copyright: Held by publication.
Reprints: Available, cost depending of length
Disposition of manuscript:
Query letter: No
Receipt of manuscript acknowledged: Yes
Decision to publish in: 2-4 months
Accepted manuscript published in: 6 months
Rejected manuscript returned: Yes
Rejected manuscript criticized: Yes
Submit to:
John D. Guilfoil
Editor
Department of Economics
New York University
New York, New York 10003
(212) 598-2225

AMERICAN INDUSTRIAL DEVELOPMENT COUNCIL. JOURNAL [747]

AIDC Journal
Suite 707
215 West Pershing Road
Kansas City, Missouri 64108
(816)474-4558

First published in 1966

SUBSCRIPTION DATA

Issues and rates: Published quarterly.
  Average paid circulation: 1,250
  Annual rate(s): $15.00; Pan-Am $15.00; Foreign $20.00
Publisher or Sponsor: American Industrial Development Council, Inc.
Managing Editor: Dr. Howard G. Roepke

EDITORIAL DESCRIPTION

Publishes articles on applied economic development
Articles per average issue: 6
Audience: Those responsible for local and regional economic development
Manuscripts accepted in English only

MANUSCRIPT INFORMATION

Subject field(s): Economic growth, industrial location, community development, industrial land use, government actions affecting economic development, rural and urban land use problems, economic location theory
Manuscript requirements: See latest issue for style requirements.
  Preferred length: 3,000 to 5,000 words; 15-25 pages
  Number of copies to be submitted: 2
  Abstract: Not necessary.
Author information and reprints: Payment: Reprints only. 50 reprints
  Is simultaneous submission of article to other journals permitted: Not permitted.
  Exclusive manuscript rights between acceptance and publication: Yes
  Copyright: Held by publisher, but reprint permission to the author is automatic
  Reprints: 50
Disposition of manuscript:
  Query letter: Not necessary.
  Receipt of manuscript acknowledged: Yes
  Decision to publish in: 1 month
  Accepted manuscript published in: 3-6 monhs
  Rejected manuscript returned: Yes, with return postage paid by publication.
  Rejected manuscript criticized: Yes
Submit to:
  Professor Howard G. Roepke
  Department of Geography
  University of Illinois
  Urbana, Illinois 61801
  (217) 333-1322

THE ANTITRUST BULLETIN [748]

95 Morton Street
New York, New York 10014
(212) 243-5775

First published in 1956

SUBSCRIPTION DATA

Issues and rates: Published quarterly.
  Average paid circulation: 2100
  Annual rate(s): $37.50
Publisher or Sponsor: Federal Legal Publications, Inc.
Managing Editor: Martin Greenberg

EDITORIAL DESCRIPTION

Contains scholarly articles on antitrust law, industrial economics, foreign antitrust and trade regulation, domestic trade regulation; book reviews and occasional symposia.
Articles per average issue: 6-8
Audience: Attorneys and industrial economists
Manuscripts accepted in English

MANUSCRIPT INFORMATION

Subject field(s): Antitrust law, foreign trade regulation, industrial economics, trade regulation
Manuscript requirements: HLRA for legal articles; GPO, Chicago
  Preferred length: As required to explore subject
  Number of copies to be submitted: 2
  Abstract: No
Author information and reprints: Payment: None. 50 reprints of article
  Is simultaneous submission of article to other journals permitted: No
  Exclusive manuscript rights between acceptance and publication: Yes
  Copyright: Held by publication.
  Reprints: Available, contact publisher
Additional information: Submit original copy with reproducible charts and graphs on separate sheets. Double space all material. Use opaque white paper.
Disposition of manuscript:
  Query letter: Preferred
  Receipt of manuscript acknowledged: Yes
  Decision to publish in: 6 weeks
  Accepted manuscript published in: 6-9 months
  Rejected manuscript returned: Yes
  Rejected manuscript criticized: Sometimes
Submit to:
  James M. Clabault
  Vice-President, Legal
  Burroughs Corporation
  Burroughs Place
  Detroit, Michigan 48232

SPECIAL STIPULATIONS

Authors have free access to their own materials for reprinting. 50% of reprint royalty goes to authors.

ATLANTA ECONOMIC REVIEW [749]

Georgia State University
University Plaza
Atlanta, Georgia 30303
(404) 658-2622

First published in 1951

SUBSCRIPTION DATA

Issues and rates: Published bi-monthly.
  Average paid circulation: 8,000
  Annual rate(s): $8.00, Foreign $11.00
Publisher or Sponsor: Georgia State University, School of Business Administration
Managing Editor: Carolyn R. Pollard

EDITORIAL DESCRIPTION

Publishes articles on business, economics and the business sciences as well as articles on environment and urban development.
Articles per average issue: 16
Audience: Business executives, government officials, professors
Manuscripts accepted in English

MANUSCRIPT INFORMATION

Subject field(s): General business, banking, management, marketing, health care, environment, organizational structure, labor relations, minority business
Manuscript requirements: Style sheet sent on request.
  Preferred length: 25 pages
  Number of copies to be submitted: Two
  Abstract: Yes
Author information and reprints: Payment: None.
  Is simultaneous submission of article to other journals permitted: Yes
  Exclusive manuscript rights between acceptance and publication: Yes
  Copyright: Held by publication.
  Reprints: Available
Disposition of manuscript:
  Query letter: No
  Receipt of manuscript acknowledged: Yes
  Decision to publish in: 6-8 weeks
  Accepted manuscript published in: 3-4 months
  Rejected manuscript returned: Yes
  Rejected manuscript criticized: No

Submit to:
Carolyn R. Pollard
Associate Editor
(See address above)

BAYLOR BUSINESS STUDIES [750]
Hankamer School of Business
P.O. Box 6278
Waco, Texas 76706
(817) 755-3495

First published in 1949

SUBSCRIPTION DATA

Issues and rates: Published quarterly.
Average paid circulation: 200; 1,300 controlled
Annual rate(s): $1.50
Publisher or Sponsor: Hankamer School of Business, Baylor University
Managing Editor: Burke A. Parsons

EDITORIAL DESCRIPTION

Contains articles dealing with business or economics.
Articles per average issue: 3
Audience: Business, academic

MANUSCRIPT INFORMATION

Subject field(s): Business (all functional areas), economics
Manuscript requirements: No specific style guide.
Preferred length: 2000-5000 words; 12-30 pages
Number of copies to be submitted: Two
Abstract: No
Author information and reprints: Payment: None. 6-10 copies of article free to author
Is simultaneous submission of article to other journals permitted: No
Exclusive manuscript rights between acceptance and publication: No
Copyright: Not copyrighted
Reprints: Not available.
Additional information: manuscripts are to be typewritten, double-spaced, with sources fully documented; author identified by job title.
Disposition of manuscript:
Query letter: No
Receipt of manuscript acknowledged: Yes
Decision to publish in: Three weeks
Accepted manuscript published in: Two months
Rejected manuscript returned: Yes
Rejected manuscript criticized: Yes
Submit to:
Burke A. Parsons
Director of Research
(See address above)

BUSINESS AND ECONOMIC DIMENSIONS [751]
Bureau of Economic and Business Research
University of Florida
Gainesville, Florida 32611
(904) 392-0171

First published in 1965

SUBSCRIPTION DATA

Issues and rates: Published bi-monthly.
Average paid circulation: 1150
Annual rate(s): $8.00
Publisher or Sponsor: University of Florida, Bureau of Economic and Business Research
Managing Editor: Alan K. Whiteleather

EDITORIAL DESCRIPTION

Contains articles on business and economic matters of interest to academicians, laymen, especially those in business, labor and government.
Articles per average issue: 6-7
Manuscripts accepted in English

MANUSCRIPT INFORMATION

Subject field(s): Any topic touching on the formation, distribution or conservation of wealth, including non-monetary wealth, and business education.
Manuscript requirements: GPO; Chicago
Preferred length: None
Number of copies to be submitted: 2
Author information and reprints: Payment: Reprints only. 5 copies supplied free
Is simultaneous submission of article to other journals permitted: Permitted, but not encouraged.
Exclusive manuscript rights between acceptance and publication: No
Copyright: Not copyrighted
Reprints: Available at no cost.
Additional information: Manuscripts should be typewritten, triple-spaced, with footnotes at the end.
Disposition of manuscript:
Query letter: No
Receipt of manuscript acknowledged: Yes
Decision to publish in: 1 month
Accepted manuscript published in: 2 months
Rejected manuscript returned: Yes
Rejected manuscript criticized: No
Submit to:
Ralph B. Thompson
Editor
(See address above)

BUSINESS HISTORY [752]
67 Great Russell Street
London WC1 3BT, England
01-4051/9405 ext. 16

SUBSCRIPTION DATA

Issues and rates: Published semi-annually.
Annual rate(s): £4.50, $13.50; Institutions £6.50, $19.50
Managing Editor: F. E. Hyde

EDITORIAL DESCRIPTION

Contains articles on business history, industrial management, commercial enterprise and cognate areas of economic development.
Articles per average issue: 4
Audience: Academics, historians of business and economics

MANUSCRIPT INFORMATION

Manuscript requirements: See latest issue for style requirements.
Preferred length: 8,000
Number of copies to be submitted: Two
Abstract: No
Author information and reprints: Payment: None.
Is simultaneous submission of article to other journals permitted: No
Exclusive manuscript rights between acceptance and publication: Yes
Copyright: Held by publication.
Reprints: Available, first 25 free
Disposition of manuscript:
Query letter: No
Receipt of manuscript acknowledged: Yes
Decision to publish in: 1 month
Accepted manuscript published in: Varies
Rejected manuscript returned: Yes
Rejected manuscript criticized: No
Submit to:
F. E. Hyde
Department of Economic History
University of Liverpool
Liverpool L69 3BX, England

BUSINESS HISTORY REVIEW* [753]
An International Journal of Business and Economic History
214-16 Baker Library
Harvard Business School
Boston, Massachusetts 02163
(617) 495-6367

SUBSCRIPTION DATA

Issues and rates: Published quarterly.
Average paid circulation: 2200
Annual rate(s): $15.00
Publisher or Sponsor: Harvard Graduate School of Business Administration

EDITORIAL DESCRIPTION

Publishes articles, notes, book reviews, and special issues on the history of business and the interaction of business and its social and political environment throughout the world.

MANUSCRIPT INFORMATION

Subject field(s): Business and economic history, archival and bibliographic contributions relating to business and economic history
Manuscript requirements: Chicago
Preferred length: 9,000 words
Number of copies to be submitted: Two
Author information and reprints: Payment: None. One copy of the issue in which the material appears, plus 20 reprints
Is simultaneous submission of article to other journals permitted: No
Exclusive manuscript rights between acceptance and publication: Yes
Copyright: Held by publication.
Reprints: Available
Additional information: Manuscript and footnotes at the end of the text should be double-spaced.
Disposition of manuscript:
Receipt of manuscript acknowledged: Yes

Business and economics

Decision to publish in: 8 weeks
Accepted manuscript published in: 6 months to 12 months
Rejected manuscript returned: Yes
Rejected manuscript criticized: Yes
Submit to:
Editor
(See address above)

BUSINESS HORIZONS [754]
School of Business, Room 436
Indiana University
Bloomington, Indiana 47401
(812) 337-5507

First published in 1957

SUBSCRIPTION DATA
Issues and rates: Published bi-monthly.
Average paid circulation: 5,200; 200 controlled
Annual rate(s): $10.00; Pan-Am $12.00; Foreign $12.00; Institutions $10.00; Students $5.00; Members $12.00; Foreign individuals $12.00; Foreign institutions $12.00
Publisher or Sponsor: Indiana University, Graduate School of Business
Managing Editor: William G. Ryan

EDITORIAL DESCRIPTION
Bridges the gap between academic and real life, between theory and practice, brings the world the clearest exposition of theory and practice of business, always looking to the future.
Articles per average issue: 11
Audience: Middle and upper management, as well as scholars and students of the practice of business
Manuscripts accepted in English only

MANUSCRIPT INFORMATION
Subject field(s): Any area of business
Manuscript requirements: Chicago
Preferred length: 18 pages
Number of copies to be submitted: 2
Abstract: Yes.
Author information and reprints: Payment: Reprints only. 50 offprints, one year subscription, 3 copies of issue
Is simultaneous submission of article to other journals permitted: Not permitted.
Exclusive manuscript rights between acceptance and publication: Yes
Copyright: Held by publication
Reprints: Available at cost.
Disposition of manuscript:
Query letter: Not necessary.
Receipt of manuscript acknowledged: Yes
Decision to publish in: 12 weeks
Accepted manuscript published in: 4 months
Rejected manuscript returned: Yes, if return postage is supplied by author.
Rejected manuscript criticized: No
Submit to:
William G. Ryan
Executive Editor
(See address above)

BUSINESS AND SOCIETY REVIEW [755]
Tower Suite
870 7th Avenue
New York, New York 10019
(212) 977-7436

First published in 1972

SUBSCRIPTION DATA
Issues and rates: Published quarterly.
Annual rate(s): $28.00
Managing Editor: Paul London

EDITORIAL DESCRIPTION
Deals with the social context of business, environment, corporate size, discrimination, consumer issues, etc.
Articles per average issue: 14
Audience: Business professionals, academics, public interest groups
Manuscripts accepted in English

MANUSCRIPT INFORMATION
Subject field(s): Social responsibility, consumerism, ecology and business, discrimination, corporate power, business and politics, corporate size, work ethic, corporate democracy
Manuscript requirements: Style sheet sent on request.
Preferred length: 2000-4000 words
Number of copies to be submitted: One
Author information and reprints: Payment: By publication to author. $50-$200 per article.
Is simultaneous submission of article to other journals permitted: Yes
Exclusive manuscript rights between acceptance and publication: Yes
Copyright: Held by publication.
Reprints: Available at cost
Additional information: Should be typewritten, double-spaced. No footnotes or charts unless essential.
Disposition of manuscript:
Query letter: No
Receipt of manuscript acknowledged: Yes
Decision to publish in: One month
Accepted manuscript published in: 3 months
Rejected manuscript returned: Yes, if self-addressed, stamped envelope is sent with manuscript.
Rejected manuscript criticized: No
Submit to:
Paul London
Managing Editor
(See address above)

BUSINESS TODAY [756]
Green Hall Annex
Princeton, New Jersey 08540
(609) 921-1111

SUBSCRIPTION DATA
Issues and rates: Published three times per year.
Average paid circulation: 1,000; 200,000 controlled
Annual rate(s): $6.00; Institutions $6.00; Students $6.00

Publisher or Sponsor: Foundation for Student Communication
Managing Editor: Ellen D. Harvey

EDITORIAL DESCRIPTION
Provides a means of communication between business and students
Audience: Students
Manuscripts accepted in English

MANUSCRIPT INFORMATION
Subject field(s): Student business relations; interesting, but unknown aspects of business
Manuscript requirements: No specific style guide.
Preferred length: 1,200 words
Number of copies to be submitted: 1
Abstract: Not necessary.
Author information and reprints: Payment: By publication to author. Varies
Is simultaneous submission of article to other journals permitted: Permitted.
Exclusive manuscript rights between acceptance and publication: No
Copyright: Held by publication
Reprints: Not available.
Disposition of manuscript:
Query letter: Not necessary.
Receipt of manuscript acknowledged: No
Decision to publish in: 2 weeks
Accepted manuscript published in: Varies
Rejected manuscript returned: Yes, if return postage is supplied by author.
Rejected manuscript criticized: No
Submit to:
Ellen D. Harvey
Editor
(See address above)

CALIFORNIA MANAGEMENT REVIEW [757]
350 Barrows Hall
University of California
Berkeley, California 94720
(415) 642-7159

First published in 1958

SUBSCRIPTION DATA
Issues and rates: Published quarterly.
Average paid circulation: 5,000
Annual rate(s): $12.00; Foreign $15.00
Publisher or Sponsor: University of California at Berkeley, Los Angeles, and Irvine; Schools of Business Administration
Managing Editor: Robert N. Katz

EDITORIAL DESCRIPTION
Publishes articles by active managers, executives, professors of Business Administration. Seeks to provide a bridge between academicians and active business managers.
Articles per average issue: 12
Audience: Managers, academicians
Manuscripts accepted in English

MANUSCRIPT INFORMATION
Subject field(s): Management and all related fields

Manuscript requirements: See latest issue for style requirements.
Preferred length: Flexible
Number of copies to be submitted: Three
Author information and reprints: Payment: None.
Is simultaneous submission of article to other journals permitted: No
Exclusive manuscript rights between acceptance and publication: Yes
Copyright: Held by publication.
Reprints: Available; 50 free to authors
Additional information: Manuscripts should be typewritten, double-spaced, with references double-spaced on separate page, each table on a separate page.
Disposition of manuscript:
Query letter: No
Receipt of manuscript acknowledged: Yes
Decision to publish in: 2 months
Accepted manuscript published in: 6-9 months
Rejected manuscript returned: Yes
Rejected manuscript criticized: No
Submit to:
Robert N. Katz
Managing Editor
(See address above)

CANADIAN JOURNAL OF ECONOMICS [758]
Revue Canadienne D'Economique
University of Vancouver
Vancouver, British Columbia V6T 1W5, Canada
(604) 228-2839

Previously entitled *Canadian Journal of Economics and Political Science*

First published in 1968

SUBSCRIPTION DATA
Issues and rates: Published quarterly.
Average paid circulation: 4,700
Annual rate(s): $15.00
Publisher or Sponsor: Canadian Economics Association
Managing Editor: G. Rosenbluth

EDITORIAL DESCRIPTION
Contains significant contributions to knowledge in all areas of economics, excluding highly technical papers addressed to small specialist audiences.
Articles per average issue: 10
Audience: Economists
Manuscripts accepted in French, English

MANUSCRIPT INFORMATION
Subject field(s): Economics
Manuscript requirements: See latest issue for style requirements.
Preferred length: 4000 words; 16 pages
Number of copies to be submitted: Three
Abstract: Yes, 100 words
Author information and reprints: Payment: Submission fee of $13 for manuscripts from non-members.
Is simultaneous submission of article to other journals permitted: No
Exclusive manuscript rights between acceptance and publication: Yes
Copyright: Held by Canadian Economics Association
Reprints: Available, 50 free
Disposition of manuscript:
Query letter: No
Receipt of manuscript acknowledged: Yes
Decision to publish in: Four months
Accepted manuscript published in: Six months
Rejected manuscript returned: Yes
Rejected manuscript criticized: Yes
Submit to:
Gideon Rosenbluth
Managing Editor
Department of Economics
University of British Columbia
Vancouver 8, British Columbia V6T 1W5, Canada

CHALLENGE [759]
The Magazine of Economic Affairs
901 North Broadway
White Plains, New York 10603
(914) 428-8700

First published in Reinaugural issue 1973

SUBSCRIPTION DATA
Issues and rates: Published bi-monthly.
Average paid circulation: 15,000 controlled
Annual rate(s): $10.00, Foreign $15.00
Managing Editor: Fred Ablin

EDITORIAL DESCRIPTION
A magazine of economic affairs written by economists for economists and laymen. Deals in depth with the whole gamut of economic issues: inflation; taxation; the budget; welfare; money; trade; employment; the world economy.
Articles per average issue: 10
Audience: Enlightened laymen
Manuscripts accepted in English

MANUSCRIPT INFORMATION
Subject field(s): Open, but with emphasis on policy-oriented subjects
Manuscript requirements: See latest issue for style requirements.
Preferred length: 2,000-4,000 words
Number of copies to be submitted: 2
Abstract: No
Author information and reprints: Payment: By publication to author. Honorarium
Is simultaneous submission of article to other journals permitted: No
Exclusive manuscript rights between acceptance and publication: Yes
Copyright: Held by publication.
Reprints: Available at cost
Disposition of manuscript:
Query letter: No
Receipt of manuscript acknowledged: Yes
Decision to publish in: 1 month
Accepted manuscript published in: Varies
Rejected manuscript returned: Yes
Rejected manuscript criticized: No
Submit to:
Myron E. Sharpe
Editor
(See address above)

COLORADO BUSINESS REVIEW [760]
Business Research Division
307 College of Business
University of Colorado
Boulder, Colorado 80302
(303) 492-8221

Previously entitled *Better Business*

First published in 1928

SUBSCRIPTION DATA
Issues and rates: Published monthly.
Average paid circulation: 50; 2,300 controlled
Annual rate(s): $5.00
Publisher or Sponsor: University of Colorado, Business Research Division
Managing Editor: C. R. Goeldner

EDITORIAL DESCRIPTION
Contains articles of interest to Colorado businessmen, on local business conditions, and Colorado economic indicators.
Articles per average issue: 1
Audience: Business, government, professional leaders in the Rocky Mountain states
Manuscripts accepted in English

MANUSCRIPT INFORMATION
Subject field(s): Manpower, marketing, finance, forecasting, tourism and recreation, small business, growth, economic development, business statistics, management, organization
Manuscript requirements: Chicago
Preferred length: 8 to 10 pages
Number of copies to be submitted: Three
Abstract: No
Author information and reprints: Payment: None.
Is simultaneous submission of article to other journals permitted: No
Exclusive manuscript rights between acceptance and publication: Yes
Copyright: Not copyrighted
Reprints: Not available.
Additional information: Typewritten, double-spaced, with footnotes on separate page at the end
Disposition of manuscript:
Query letter: No
Receipt of manuscript acknowledged: Yes
Decision to publish in: Six weeks
Accepted manuscript published in: 3 months
Rejected manuscript returned: Yes
Rejected manuscript criticized: Yes
Submit to:
C. R. Goeldner
Editor
(See address above)

Business and economics

COMMODITIES [761]
The Magazine of Futures Trading
1000 Century Plaza
Columbia, Maryland 21044
(301) 730-5359

First published in 1972

SUBSCRIPTION DATA
Issues and rates: Published monthly.
  Average paid circulation: 5,500; 9,500 controlled
  Annual rate(s): $34.00
Managing Editor: Edgar K. Lofton, Jr.

EDITORIAL DESCRIPTION
Publishes articles for the private individual futures traders, to help them better understand and succeed in the trading of commodities.
Articles per average issue: 4
Audience: Professional, academic
  Manuscripts accepted in English only

MANUSCRIPT INFORMATION
Subject field(s): Fundamental analysis of specific commodities and markets; technical studies of markets; "how-to" articles on trading strategy; interviews with successful (and unsuccessful) traders; book reviews
Manuscript requirements: No specific style guide.
  Preferred length: 2,000-2,500 words
  Number of copies to be submitted: 2
  Abstract: Not necessary.
Author information and reprints: Payment: By publication to author. $.08 per word.
  Is simultaneous submission of article to other journals permitted: Not permitted.
  Exclusive manuscript rights between acceptance and publication: Yes
  Copyright: First serial and individual reprints rights held by publication
  Reprints: Available at cost.
Disposition of manuscript:
  Query letter: Not necessary, but advisable.
  Decision to publish in: 3 weeks
  Accepted manuscript published in: 6 weeks
  Rejected manuscript returned: Yes, if return postage is supplied by author.
  Rejected manuscript criticized: Sometimes
Submit to:
  Edgar K. Lofton, Jr.;
  Daniel C. Ruck
  Senior Editors
  (See address above)

THE DIRECTOR [762]
10 Belgrave Square
London SW1X 8PW, England
01-235-3601

First published in 1949

SUBSCRIPTION DATA
Issues and rates: Published monthly.
  Average paid circulation: 45,000
  Annual rate(s): £14.00
Publisher or Sponsor: Institute of Directors

EDITORIAL DESCRIPTION
Contains articles on management of general and specific interest to directors.
Articles per average issue: 30
Audience: Company directors
  Manuscripts accepted in English

MANUSCRIPT INFORMATION
Manuscript requirements: See latest issue for style requirements.
  Preferred length: 1600-1800 words
  Number of copies to be submitted: One
  Abstract: Yes
Author information and reprints: Payment: By publication to author.
  Is simultaneous submission of article to other journals permitted: No
  Exclusive manuscript rights between acceptance and publication: Yes
  Copyright: Held by publication.
  Reprints: Available, cost depends on length
Disposition of manuscript:
  Query letter: Not necessary, but advisable.
  Receipt of manuscript acknowledged: Yes
  Decision to publish in: 2 weeks
  Accepted manuscript published in: 6 weeks
  Rejected manuscript returned: Yes
  Rejected manuscript criticized: No
Submit to:
  George Bull
  Editor
  (See address above)

ECONOMIC INQUIRY [763]
Journal of the Western Economic Association
Department of Economics
University of California
Los Angeles, California 90024
(213) 825-4422

Previously entitled *Western Economic Journal*

First published in 1962

SUBSCRIPTION DATA
Issues and rates: Published quarterly.
  Average paid circulation: 3,500; 100 controlled
  Annual rate(s): $20.00, Foreign $22.00
Publisher or Sponsor: Western Economic Association

EDITORIAL DESCRIPTION
Contains scholarly articles on all facets of economics.
Articles per average issue: 12-14
Audience: Professional economists
  Manuscripts accepted in English

MANUSCRIPT INFORMATION
Subject field(s): Economics
Manuscript requirements: Style sheet sent on request.
  Preferred length: Less than 30 pages
  Number of copies to be submitted: Three
  Abstract: Only upon acceptance
Author information and reprints: Payment: By author to publication. $12.50 per article. $7.50 for Association members
  Is simultaneous submission of article to other journals permitted: No
  Exclusive manuscript rights between acceptance and publication: Yes
  Copyright: Held by publication.
  Reprints: Available, price list sent upon request
Disposition of manuscript:
  Query letter: No
  Receipt of manuscript acknowledged: Yes
  Decision to publish in: 2 months
  Accepted manuscript published in: 3-6 months
  Rejected manuscript returned: Yes
  Rejected manuscript criticized: Yes
Submit to:
  Robert W. Clower
  Editor
  (See address above)

ECONOMIC NOTES [764]
80 East 11th Street
New York, New York 10003
(212) 473-1042

First published in 1927

SUBSCRIPTION DATA
Issues and rates: Published monthly.
  Average paid circulation: 1500
  Annual rate(s): $3.00, Foreign $4.50
Publisher or Sponsor: Labor Research Association
Managing Editor: Robert W. Dunn

EDITORIAL DESCRIPTION
Contains articles on labor, economics, social conditions from a leftist point of view.
Audience: General
  Manuscripts accepted in English only

MANUSCRIPT INFORMATION
Manuscript requirements: No specific style guide.
  Preferred length: 600-1200 words
  Number of copies to be submitted: One
Author information and reprints: Payment: None.
  Is simultaneous submission of article to other journals permitted: Yes
  Reprints: Available
Disposition of manuscript:
  Query letter: Yes
  Receipt of manuscript acknowledged: Yes
  Decision to publish in: 1 month
  Rejected manuscript returned: Yes
  Rejected manuscript criticized: No
Submit to:
  Editor
  (See address above)

EXPLORATIONS IN ECONOMIC HISTORY [765]
Kent State University Press
Kent, Ohio 44242
(216) 672-7913

SUBSCRIPTION DATA
Issues and rates: Published quarterly.
  Average paid circulation: 900
  Annual rate(s): $20.00

EDITORIAL DESCRIPTION
A journal of research in economic history defined in its broadest terms to encompass all work in applied economics which has a significant historical dimension.

MANUSCRIPT INFORMATION
Subject field(s): Economic history, economic development, income distribution, poverty and human resources development
Manuscript requirements: Chicago
  Preferred length: 20 pages
  Number of copies to be submitted: Two
Author information and reprints: Payment: None.
  Is simultaneous submission of article to other journals permitted: No
  Exclusive manuscript rights between acceptance and publication: Yes
  Copyright: Held by publication.
  Reprints: Available at time of publication
Disposition of manuscript:
  Receipt of manuscript acknowledged: Yes
  Decision to publish in: Few months
  Rejected manuscript returned: Yes
  Rejected manuscript criticized: No
Submit to:
  Gary Walton
  Editor
  Department of Economics
  University of Indiana
  Bloomington, Indiana 47401

THE FREEMAN [766]
Ideas on Liberty
Foundation for Economic Education, Inc.
Irvington-on-Hudson, New York 10533
(914) 591-7230

SUBSCRIPTION DATA
Issues and rates: Published monthly.
  Average paid circulation: 45,000 controlled
  Annual rate(s): $5.00
Publisher or Sponsor: Foundation for Economic Education, Inc.
Managing Editor: Paul L. Poirot

EDITORIAL DESCRIPTION
Articles on the economic, political, and moral principles of private property, voluntary exchange, and limited government, plus one or more book reviews. Point of view is conservative or libertarian.
Articles per average issue: 8
Audience: Friends of liberty
  Manuscripts accepted in English

MANUSCRIPT INFORMATION
Subject field(s): Economics, political science, moral issues
Manuscript requirements: Copy on request
  Preferred length: 3000 words maximum
  Number of copies to be submitted: One
  Abstract: No

Author information and reprints: Payment: By publication to author. $.05 per word
  Is simultaneous submission of article to other journals permitted: Yes
  Exclusive manuscript rights between acceptance and publication: Yes
  Copyright: Rights reserved to author on request
  Reprints: Available depending on quantity
Additional information: Manuscripts should be typewritten, double-spaced.
Disposition of manuscript:
  Query letter: No
  Receipt of manuscript acknowledged: Yes
  Decision to publish in: 1 week
  Accepted manuscript published in: 3 months
  Rejected manuscript returned: Yes, if return postage is supplied by author.
  Rejected manuscript criticized: Yes
Submit to:
  Paul L. Poirot
  Managing Editor
  (See address above)

HARVARD BUSINESS REVIEW [767]
Soldiers Field
Boston, Massachusetts 02163
(617) 495-6800

First published in 1922

SUBSCRIPTION DATA
Issues and rates: Published bi-monthly.
  Average paid circulation: 160,000
  Annual rate(s): $15.00, Foreign $18.00
Publisher or Sponsor: Harvard Graduate School of Business Administration
Managing Editor: Virginia B. Fales

EDITORIAL DESCRIPTION
Publishes articles on a broad range of management topics.

MANUSCRIPT INFORMATION
Subject field(s): Business, government and society; business planning, strategy, structure and policy formulation; finance; international business; labor relations, human relations; organizational development and personnel administration; managerial economics, control, reporting and accounting; marketing, advertising, retailing and sales management
Manuscript requirements: Style sheet sent on request.
  Preferred length: 6-25 pages
  Number of copies to be submitted: One
Author information and reprints: Payment: By publication to author. $100.00 per article.
  Is simultaneous submission of article to other journals permitted: No
  Exclusive manuscript rights between acceptance and publication: Yes
  Copyright: Held by publication.
  Reprints: Available, 100 complimentary copies
Disposition of manuscript:
  Query letter: No

  Receipt of manuscript acknowledged: Yes
  Decision to publish in: Several weeks
  Accepted manuscript published in: 2-5 months
  Rejected manuscript returned: Yes
  Rejected manuscript criticized: Sometimes
Submit to:
  The Editors
  (See address above)

INSPECTION NEWS [768]
P.O. Box 4081
Atlanta, Georgia 30302
(404) 875-8321

SUBSCRIPTION DATA
Issues and rates: Published quarterly.
  Average paid circulation: 137,000 controlled
Publisher or Sponsor: Retail Credit Company

EDITORIAL DESCRIPTION
Contains articles on insurance, law, medicine, the humanities.

MANUSCRIPT INFORMATION
Subject field(s): Insurance, general
Manuscript requirements: See latest issue for style requirements.
  Preferred length: 2,000 words; 10-12 pages
  Number of copies to be submitted: One
Author information and reprints: Payment: By publication to author. $.02 per word. $25.00 minimum per article.
  Is simultaneous submission of article to other journals permitted: No
  Exclusive manuscript rights between acceptance and publication: Yes
  Copyright: Held by author.
  Reprints: Available at no cost
Additional information: Two to three articles per issue are from outside sources, rest of magazine is staff prepared. Query on articles before submission of manuscript is suggested.
Disposition of manuscript:
  Query letter: Necessary
  Receipt of manuscript acknowledged: No
  Decision to publish in: 2-3 weeks
  Accepted manuscript published in: 3-6 months
  Rejected manuscript returned: Yes, if self-addressed, stamped envelope is sent with manuscript.
  Rejected manuscript criticized: No
Submit to:
  H. A. McQuade
  Editor
  (See address above)

SPECIAL STIPULATIONS
Publication desires unpublished manuscripts by educators and well-placed professionals in fields of insurance, law, medicine, the humanities, etc.

Business and economics 223

INTERNATIONAL INSURANCE MONITOR [769]
150 West 28th Street
New York, New York 10001
(212) 255-6112

First published in 1947

SUBSCRIPTION DATA
Issues and rates: Published monthly.
 Average paid circulation: 2,150; 1,175 controlled
 Annual rate(s): $18.50

EDITORIAL DESCRIPTION
 Contains articles on international insurance and reinsurance worldwide; analytical articles, news items, research.
Articles per average issue: 5
Audience: International insurers
 Manuscripts accepted in English

MANUSCRIPT INFORMATION
Subject field(s): Market reports, conventions, seminars, educational reports, news items
Manuscript requirements: Webster 3, Skillin
 Preferred length: 1500 to 2000 words
 Number of copies to be submitted: One
 Abstract: No
Author information and reprints: Payment: By publication to author. $5-$10 per column
 Is simultaneous submission of article to other journals permitted: No
 Exclusive manuscript rights between acceptance and publication: Yes
 Copyright: Held by publication.
 Reprints: Available upon agreement
Disposition of manuscript:
 Query letter: Yes
 Receipt of manuscript acknowledged: Yes
 Decision to publish in: 10-14 days
 Accepted manuscript published in: Variable
 Rejected manuscript returned: Yes
 Rejected manuscript criticized: No
Submit to:
 Thomas J. Lewis
 Publisher
 (See address above)

JOURNAL OF BUSINESS [770]
University of Chicago Press
5801 Ellis Avenue
Chicago, Illinois 60637
(312) 753-2592

First published in 1928

SUBSCRIPTION DATA
Issues and rates: Published quarterly.
 Average paid circulation: 4,200
 Annual rate(s): $11.00; Foreign $12.00; Institutions $16.00
Managing Editor: Irving Schweiger

EDITORIAL DESCRIPTION
 Publishes articles of high academic quality, presenting new theory, new data or new methodology on any topic of interest to business researchers, practitioners and students.
Articles per average issue: 1
 Manuscripts accepted in English

MANUSCRIPT INFORMATION
Manuscript requirements: See latest issue for style requirements.
 Preferred length: None
 Number of copies to be submitted: Two
Author information and reprints: Payment: None. 50 free reprints
 Is simultaneous submission of article to other journals permitted: No
 Exclusive manuscript rights between acceptance and publication: Yes
 Copyright: Held by publication.
 Reprints: Available, cost based on length
Additional information: Double-spaced, with footnotes at end, no separate reference list.
Disposition of manuscript:
 Query letter: No
 Receipt of manuscript acknowledged: Yes
 Decision to publish in: 1-4 months
 Accepted manuscript published in: 3-9 months
 Rejected manuscript returned: Yes
 Rejected manuscript criticized: Yes
Submit to:
 Editor
 Graduate School of Business
 University of Chicago
 Chicago, Illinois 60637
 (312) 753-3660

SPECIAL STIPULATIONS
 Publisher has a royalty sharing arrangement under which authors receive 50 per cent of reprint royalties after deduction of expenses.

JOURNAL OF BUSINESS ADMINISTRATION [771]
Faculty of Commerce
University of British Columbia
Vancouver, British Columbia V6T 1W5, Canada
(604) 228-2222

First published in 1969

SUBSCRIPTION DATA
Issues and rates: Published semi-annually.
 Annual rate(s): $3.50; Institutions $3.50
Publisher or Sponsor: University of British Columbia, Faculty of Commerce
Managing Editor: Ilan Vertinsky

EDITORIAL DESCRIPTION
 The aim is toward the scholarly point of view in looking at problems in marketing, accounting, and exchange of research ideas.
Articles per average issue: 6-7
Audience: Scholars of commerce and business administration
 Manuscripts accepted in English

MANUSCRIPT INFORMATION
Subject field(s): Commerce and business administration
Manuscript requirements: No specific style guide.
 Number of copies to be submitted: Two
 Abstract: Not necessary.
Author information and reprints: Payment: None.
 Is simultaneous submission of article to other journals permitted: Not permitted.
 Exclusive manuscript rights between acceptance and publication: Yes
 Copyright: Held by Faculty of Commerce and Business Administration, University of British Columbia
 Reprints: Not available.
Disposition of manuscript:
 Query letter: Not necessary.
 Receipt of manuscript acknowledged: Yes
 Decision to publish in: 8 weeks
 Accepted manuscript published in: 6 months
 Rejected manuscript returned: Yes, with return postage paid by publication.
 Rejected manuscript criticized: Sometimes
Submit to:
 Ilan Vertinsky
 Editor
 (See address above)

JOURNAL OF CONSUMER AFFAIRS [772]
American Council on Consumer Interests-Stanley Hall
University of Missouri
Columbia, Missouri 65201
(314) 882-7724

First published in 1967

SUBSCRIPTION DATA
Issues and rates: Published semi-annually.
 Average paid circulation: 3,000
 Annual rate(s): $10.00; Foreign $10.00; Individuals $10.00; Institutions $10.00; Students $10.00
Publisher or Sponsor: American Council on Consumer Interests
Managing Editor: Joseph N. Uhl

EDITORIAL DESCRIPTION
 To stimulate writing furthering the definition, understanding and advancement of the consumer interests. Directed to a multi-discipline, professional readership of educators, researchers, policy makers, and other professionals.
Articles per average issue: 10-12
Audience: Educators, researchers and government personnel
 Manuscripts accepted in English only

MANUSCRIPT INFORMATION
Subject field(s): Consumer economics, consumer behavior, consumer policy, consumer education
Manuscript requirements: See latest issue for style requirements. Style sheet sent on request.
 Preferred length: No preference
 Number of copies to be submitted: 3
 Abstract: Yes. Headnote required, not to exceed 175 words.

Author information and reprints: Payment: Reprints only.
 Is simultaneous submission of article to other journals permitted: Permitted, but not encouraged.
 Exclusive manuscript rights between acceptance and publication: No
 Copyright: Held by University of Wisconsin Press
 Reprints: Available at cost. Varies by length
Disposition of manuscript:
 Query letter: Not necessary.
 Receipt of manuscript acknowledged: Yes
 Decision to publish in: 2-4 months
 Accepted manuscript published in: 5-10 months
 Rejected manuscript returned: Yes, if return postage is supplied by author.
 Rejected manuscript criticized: Sometimes
Submit to:
 Joseph N. Uhl
 Editor
 Krannert Building, Room 647
 Purdue University, Department of Agricultural Economics
 West Lafayette, Indiana 47907
 (317) 494-4004

JOURNAL OF DEVELOPMENT STUDIES [773]
67 Great Russell Street
London WC1B 3BT, England
01-405-9405 ext. 16

First published in 1964

SUBSCRIPTION DATA
Issues and rates: Published quarterly.
 Annual rate(s): £8.50 ($36.00),
 Institutions £12.00 ($25.00)
Managing Editor: Michael Lipton

EDITORIAL DESCRIPTION
 Devoted to economic, political and social development.
Articles per average issue: 6
Audience: Academic social scientists
 Manuscripts accepted in English

MANUSCRIPT INFORMATION
Subject field(s): Economics, sociology
Manuscript requirements: Style sheet sent on request.
 Preferred length: 8,000 words
 Number of copies to be submitted: Two
 Abstract: Yes; 100 words
Author information and reprints: Payment: None.
 Is simultaneous submission of article to other journals permitted: No
 Exclusive manuscript rights between acceptance and publication: Yes
 Copyright: Held by publication.
 Reprints: Available, 25 free
Disposition of manuscript:
 Query letter: No
 Receipt of manuscript acknowledged: Yes
 Decision to publish in: 2 months
 Accepted manuscript published in: Varies
 Rejected manuscript returned: Yes
 Rejected manuscript criticized: No
Submit to:
 The Secretary
 (See address above)

JOURNAL OF ECONOMIC HISTORY [774]
22 South 18th Street
Allentown, Pennsylvania 18104
(215) 434-4742

SUBSCRIPTION DATA
Issues and rates: Published quarterly.
 Average paid circulation: 3,600
 Annual rate(s): $15.00; Individuals $10.00; Institutions $15.00; Students $3.00; Foreign individuals $10.50
Publisher or Sponsor: Economic History Association

EDITORIAL DESCRIPTION
 Contains articles on the history of economics, and related areas.
Articles per average issue: 4
Audience: Educators, professionals
 Manuscripts accepted in English

MANUSCRIPT INFORMATION
Manuscript requirements: Style sheet sent on request.
 Preferred length: 20 pages
 Number of copies to be submitted: 2
 Abstract: Not necessary.
Author information and reprints: Payment: None.
 Is simultaneous submission of article to other journals permitted: Permitted, but not encouraged.
 Exclusive manuscript rights between acceptance and publication: No
 Copyright: Held by the Association
Disposition of manuscript:
 Decision to publish in: Varies
 Accepted manuscript published in: 6 months
 Rejected manuscript returned: Yes, if return postage is supplied by author.
 Rejected manuscript criticized: Sometimes
Submit to:
 Louis Galambos,
 Rondo Cameron
 Editors
 Milton S. Eisenhower Library
 The Johns Hopkins University
 Baltimore, Maryland 21218

JOURNAL OF ECONOMIC ISSUES [775]
AFEE/JEI Fiscal Office, 509-J Business Administration Bldg.
The Pennsylvania State University
University Park, Pennsylvania 16802
(814) 865-2872

First published in 1967

SUBSCRIPTION DATA
Issues and rates: Published quarterly.
 Average paid circulation: 1,400
 Annual rate(s): Individuals $9.50; Institutions $12.00; Members $9.50
Publisher or Sponsor: Association for Evolutionary Economics, Michigan State University
Managing Editor: Warren J. Samuels

EDITORIAL DESCRIPTION
 General economics, with special emphasis on an institutional and evolutionary point of view.
Articles per average issue: 8
Audience: Professors of economics
 Manuscripts accepted in English

MANUSCRIPT INFORMATION
Subject field(s): Economics, including history of economic thought and related law, philosophy, history, and social science.
Manuscript requirements: Style sheet sent on request. Chicago
 Preferred length: 20 pages
 Number of copies to be submitted: Three
 Abstract: Not necessary.
Author information and reprints: Payment: Reprints only. 1 Copy, 25 reprints
 Is simultaneous submission of article to other journals permitted: Not permitted.
 Exclusive manuscript rights between acceptance and publication: Yes
 Copyright: By publication; author able to republish freely
 Reprints: 25 Gratis to author available at cost set by printing firm
Additional information: Paper must make substantive contribution to its field.
Disposition of manuscript:
 Query letter: Not necessary.
 Receipt of manuscript acknowledged: Yes
 Decision to publish in: 1 week to 3 months
 Accepted manuscript published in: 1 Year
 Rejected manuscript returned: Yes, with return postage paid by publication.
 Rejected manuscript criticized: Yes
Submit to:
 Warren J. Samuels
 Editor
 Department of Economics
 Michigan State University
 East Lansing, Michigan 48824
 (517) 355-1860

JOURNAL OF ECONOMICS AND BUSINESS [776]
Temple University
School of Business Administration, Room 6
Philadelphia, Pennsylvania 19462
(215) 787-8101

Previously entitled *Economic and Business Bulletin*

First published in 1948

SUBSCRIPTION DATA
Issues and rates: Published three times per year.

Business and economics 225

Average paid circulation: 600; 2900 controlled
Annual rate(s): $7.00, Foreign $9.00
Managing Editor: Robert H. Deans

EDITORIAL DESCRIPTION
Devoted to professional and academic thinking and research in economics, business, and related matters, it contains articles in business and economics with a section on notes and communications. From time to time it also includes a special feature on a timely topic.
Audience: Academic, business and government researchers
Manuscripts accepted in any language

MANUSCRIPT INFORMATION
Subject field(s): Finance, economics, management, marketing, health administration
Manuscript requirements: See latest issue for style requirements.
  Preferred length: 15-60 pages
  Number of copies to be submitted: Two
  Abstract: No
Author information and reprints: Payment: None.
  Is simultaneous submission of article to other journals permitted: No
  Exclusive manuscript rights between acceptance and publication: Yes
  Copyright: Held by publication.
  Reprints: Available, free to author
Additional information: Reprints are available for nominal charge of $1.00. Additional copies of reprints are discounted by number purchased.
Disposition of manuscript:
  Query letter: No
  Receipt of manuscript acknowledged: Yes
  Decision to publish in: 6 to 8 weeks
  Accepted manuscript published in: No more than one year
  Rejected manuscript returned: Yes
  Rejected manuscript criticized: Yes
Submit to:
  Robert H. Deans
  Editor
  (See address above)

SPECIAL STIPULATIONS
Journal does not limit size of issue nor attempt to accumulate manuscripts beyond three issues. Size of journal predicated on accepted manuscripts.

THE JOURNAL OF HUMAN RESOURCES [777]
Education, Manpower, and Welfare Policies
University of Wisconsin
4315 Social Science Building
Madison, Wisconsin 53706
(608) 262-4867

First published in 1966

SUBSCRIPTION DATA
Issues and rates: Published quarterly.
  Average paid circulation: 2150; 15 controlled
  Annual rate(s): Individuals $10.50, Foreign $10.50, Institutions $20.00
Publisher or Sponsor: University of Wisconsin
Managing Editor: Barbara D. Dennis

EDITORIAL DESCRIPTION
Provides a forum for analysis of the role of education and training in enhancing production skills, employment opportunities, and income, as well as for analysis of manpower, health, and welfare policies as they relate to the labor market and to economic and social development. Gives priority to studies having empirical content.
Articles per average issue: 5-9
Audience: Academic economists, demographers, policy-makers
Manuscripts accepted in English

MANUSCRIPT INFORMATION
Subject field(s): Discrimination in employment; vocational education/occupational training; economics of education; health economics; welfare economics; labor market/labor supply; earnings/wages/income; professions, other than medical; income transfers; theoretical/methodological; migration/mobility; socioeconomic status
Manuscript requirements: Chicago
  Preferred length: 20 pages
  Number of copies to be submitted: Three
  Abstract: Upon acceptance only
Author information and reprints: Payment: None. 2 copies of journal and 25 tear sheets
  Is simultaneous submission of article to other journals permitted: No
  Exclusive manuscript rights between acceptance and publication: Yes
  Copyright: Held by Regents of the University of Wisconsin
  Reprints: Available at cost
Disposition of manuscript:
  Query letter: No
  Receipt of manuscript acknowledged: Yes
  Decision to publish in: 6-12 weeks
  Accepted manuscript published in: 6-8 months
  Rejected manuscript returned: Yes, if it is an original; not carbons or Xerox copies
  Rejected manuscript criticized: Yes, if it reaches the referee stage
Submit to:
  Glen G. Cain
  Editor
  (See address above)

THE JOURNAL OF INSURANCE [778]
Insurance Information Institute
110 William Street
New York, New York 10038
(212) 233-7650

First published in 1960

SUBSCRIPTION DATA
Issues and rates: Published bi-monthly.
  Average paid circulation: 80,000 controlled
  Annual rate(s): $4.00
Publisher or Sponsor: Insurance Information Institute
Managing Editor: Bernard Kaapcke

EDITORIAL DESCRIPTION
Contains articles on property-liability insurance, and related subjects such as highway safety, natural disasters, crime prevention, etc.
Articles per average issue: 5-6
Audience: Insurance brokers, agents, management
Manuscripts accepted in English

MANUSCRIPT INFORMATION
Subject field(s): Insurance, highways, autos, fire, hurricanes, crime, etc.
Manuscript requirements: Style sheet sent on request.
  Preferred length: 1500 words; 5-6 pages
  Number of copies to be submitted: One
  Abstract: No
Author information and reprints: Payment: By publication to author.
  Is simultaneous submission of article to other journals permitted: Require exclusive submission if payment is given.
  Exclusive manuscript rights between acceptance and publication: Yes
  Copyright: Held by publication.
  Reprints: Available at printing cost
Additional information: Typewritten, double-spaced
Disposition of manuscript:
  Query letter: No
  Receipt of manuscript acknowledged: Yes
  Decision to publish in: Two weeks
  Accepted manuscript published in: Three months
  Rejected manuscript returned: Yes, if return postage is supplied by author.
  Rejected manuscript criticized: Yes
Submit to:
  Bernard Kaapcke
  Editor
  (See address above)

JOURNAL OF MARKETING [779]
American Marketing Association
222 South Riverside Plaza
Chicago, Illinois 60606
(312) 648-0536

First published in 1936

SUBSCRIPTION DATA
Issues and rates: Published quarterly.
  Average paid circulation: 24,000
  Annual rate(s): Individuals $9.00, members, $18.00 non-members; Foreign $20.00
Publisher or Sponsor: American Marketing Association
Managing Editor: Edward W. Cundiff

EDITORIAL DESCRIPTION
Contains reports on recent developments in marketing management and in research on marketing theory and practice.
Articles per average issue: 10

Audience: Business, academic interested in marketing
Manuscripts accepted in English

MANUSCRIPT INFORMATION

Subject field(s): Marketing (all aspects)
Manuscript requirements: Style sheet sent on request.
Preferred length: 4,000 to 6,000 words; 15 pages
Number of copies to be submitted: Four
Abstract: Yes, of 150 words or less
Author information and reprints: Payment: None. 15 free reprints of article.
Is simultaneous submission of article to other journals permitted: No
Exclusive manuscript rights between acceptance and publication: Yes
Copyright: Held by publication.
Reprints: Available, 25 free; others according to cost schedule
Disposition of manuscript:
Query letter: No
Receipt of manuscript acknowledged: Yes
Decision to publish in: 8-12 weeks
Accepted manuscript published in: 9 months
Rejected manuscript returned: Yes, if self-addressed, stamped envelope is sent with manuscript.
Rejected manuscript criticized: Yes
Submit to:
Edward W. Cundiff
Editor
Universiy of Texas
Business-Economics Building 707
Austin, Texas 78712
(312) 471-4198

JOURNAL OF MARKETING RESEARCH [780]

222 South Riverside Plaza
Chicago, Illinois 60606
(312) 648-0536

First published in 1964

SUBSCRIPTION DATA

Issues and rates: Published quarterly.
Average paid circulation: 12,000
Annual rate(s): $18.00, members $ 9.00
Publisher or Sponsor: American Marketing Association
Managing Editor: Frank M. Bass

EDITORIAL DESCRIPTION

The focus of the journal is on methodology and the philosophical, conceptual, and technical problems of research in marketing. Its purpose is to serve as a medium for exchanging ideas and keeping up with the latest developments in marketing research.
Articles per average issue: 8-10
Audience: Marketing researchers, analysts, directors, planners, consultants, educators
Manuscripts accepted in English

MANUSCRIPT INFORMATION

Subject field(s): Presentation of new techniques for solving marketing problems, demonstration of different ways in which known techniques may be used with marketing problems, clarification of marketing theories or of methodology, contributions to marketing knowledge, reviews of developments and concepts in related fields
Manuscript requirements: Style sheet sent on request.
Preferred length: None
Number of copies to be submitted: Three
Abstract: Yes
Author information and reprints: Payment: None. 25 free reprints
Is simultaneous submission of article to other journals permitted: No
Exclusive manuscript rights between acceptance and publication: Yes
Copyright: Held by publication.
Reprints: Available
Additional information: Manuscripts should be submitted in proper style. Camera-ready artwork is required for all figures in accepted manuscripts.
Disposition of manuscript:
Query letter: No
Receipt of manuscript acknowledged: Yes
Decision to publish in: 6-8 weeks
Accepted manuscript published in: 6 months
Rejected manuscript returned: Yes
Rejected manuscript criticized: Yes
Submit to:
Frank M. Bass
Purdue University
Krannert Graduate School of Industrial Administration
West Lafayette, Indiana 47907
(317) 494-8456

JOURNAL OF POLITICAL ECONOMY* [781]

University of Chicago Press
5801 Ellis Avenue
Chicago, Illinois 60637
(312) 753-2592

SUBSCRIPTION DATA

Issues and rates: Published bi-monthly.
Average paid circulation: 5500
Annual rate(s): $15.00, Foreign $16.00

EDITORIAL DESCRIPTION

Contains articles on all fields of economics.

MANUSCRIPT INFORMATION

Subject field(s): Macroeconomics, microeconomics, monetary theory, price theory, econometrics, international trade, economic history, industrial organization, agricultural economics, business economics
Manuscript requirements: Chicago
Author information and reprints: Payment: By author to publication. $10 per article.
Is simultaneous submission of article to other journals permitted: No
Exclusive manuscript rights between acceptance and publication: Yes
Copyright: Held by publication.
Reprints: Available, $8 per 4 pages
Disposition of manuscript:
Receipt of manuscript acknowledged: Yes
Decision to publish in: 6-8 weeks
Accepted manuscript published in: 8-10 months
Submit to:
Editor
(See address above)

JOURNAL OF PURCHASING AND MATERIALS MANAGEMENT [782]

College of Business Administration
Arizona State University
Tempe, Arizona 85281
(602) 965-3432

Previously entitled *Journal of Purchasing*

First published in 1965

SUBSCRIPTION DATA

Issues and rates: Published quarterly.
Average paid circulation: 4100
Annual rate(s): $8.00; Foreign $9.00
Publisher or Sponsor: National Association of Purchasing Management, Inc.

EDITORIAL DESCRIPTION

Presents concepts from business, statistics, economics, engineering, behavioral science, or any discipline which contribute to the advancement of knowledge in business or governmental purchasing, materials management, or related areas. Articles may discuss theories, principles, or philosophies; analyze business, economic, political, or social issues and trends; describe and evaluate techniques and practices; examine legal considerations, or report relevant research.
Articles per average issue: 6
Audience: Professors and purchasing managers
Manuscripts accepted in English

MANUSCRIPT INFORMATION

Subject field(s): Purchasing, materials management, inventory control, production scheduling, traffic, quality control, economics
Manuscript requirements: Chicago
Preferred length: 4000-6000 words
Number of copies to be submitted: Four
Abstract: No
Author information and reprints: Payment: None.
Is simultaneous submission of article to other journals permitted: Yes
Exclusive manuscript rights between acceptance and publication: No
Copyright: Held by publication.
Reprints: Available; 50 free to author, others at cost
Disposition of manuscript:
Query letter: No
Receipt of manuscript acknowledged: Yes
Decision to publish in: 6 weeks
Accepted manuscript published in: 6 months
Rejected manuscript returned: Yes
Rejected manuscript criticized: Yes

Business and economics

Submit to:
Harold Fearon
Editor
(See address above)

JOURNAL OF RETAILING [783]
New York University, Tisch Hall
Washington Square
New York, New York 10003

SUBSCRIPTION DATA
Issues and rates: Published quarterly.
  Average paid circulation: 3,000
  Annual rate(s): $10.00
Publisher or Sponsor: New York University, Institute of Retail Management
Managing Editor: Sallie W. Sewell

EDITORIAL DESCRIPTION
  Presents articles, concepts, ideas or research methodology that will be of significant value to retailers and teachers of retailing.
Audience: Primarily retailers and teachers of retailing, as well as related fields
  Manuscripts accepted in English

MANUSCRIPT INFORMATION
Subject field(s): Retailing, teaching of retailing, research in retailing
Manuscript requirements: See latest issue for style requirements. Style sheet sent on request.
  Preferred length: No excessive length, typewritten, double-spaced
  Number of copies to be submitted: 2
  Abstract: Yes. Of 150 words summarizing the article
Author information and reprints: Payment: None.
  Is simultaneous submission of article to other journals permitted: Not permitted.
  Exclusive manuscript rights between acceptance and publication: Yes
  Copyright: Held by publication; permission to reuse usually granted upon written request.
  Reprints: Available at no cost.
Disposition of manuscript:
  Query letter: Not necessary.
  Receipt of manuscript acknowledged: Yes
  Decision to publish in: Varies
  Accepted manuscript published in: Varies
  Rejected manuscript returned: Yes, if return postage is supplied by author.
  Rejected manuscript criticized: Sometimes
Submit to:
Sallie W. Sewell
Editor
(See address above)

JOURNAL OF RISK AND INSURANCE [784]
One State Farm Plaza
Bloomington, Illinois 61701
(309) 662-2614

Previously entitled *Journal of Insurance*

First published in 1932

SUBSCRIPTION DATA
Issues and rates: Published quarterly.
  Average paid circulation: 2200; 40 controlled
  Annual rate(s): $20.00
Publisher or Sponsor: American Risk and Insurance Association

EDITORIAL DESCRIPTION
  Publishes scholarly articles on the theory and practice of risk and insurance; book reviews, review articles and communications.
Articles per average issue: 15-20
Audience: Anyone interested in risk or insurance
  Manuscripts accepted in English

MANUSCRIPT INFORMATION
Subject field(s): Risk theory, insurance theory, risk management, insurance practice
Manuscript requirements: Style sheet sent on request.
  Preferred length: 12-30 pages
  Number of copies to be submitted: One original and 3 copies
  Abstract: Yes
Author information and reprints: Payment: None.
  Is simultaneous submission of article to other journals permitted: No
  Exclusive manuscript rights between acceptance and publication: Yes
  Copyright: Held by publication.
  Reprints: Available; 25 free, additional at cost
Disposition of manuscript:
  Query letter: No
  Receipt of manuscript acknowledged: Yes
  Decision to publish in: 6-8 weeks
  Accepted manuscript published in: 6-9 months
  Rejected manuscript returned: Yes
  Rejected manuscript criticized: Yes
Submit to:
William T. Beadles
Administrative Editor
(See address above)

JOURNAL OF TRAVEL RESEARCH [785]
Business Research Division
Graduate School of Business Administration, University of Colorado
Boulder, Colorado 80302
(303) 492-8227

Previously entitled *Travel Research Bulletin*

First published in 1962

SUBSCRIPTION DATA
Issues and rates: Published quarterly.
  Average paid circulation: 50; 1500 controlled
  Annual rate(s): $25.00; Pan-Am $25.00; Foreign $25 plus $10 for air mail; Individuals $25.00; Institutions $25.00; Students $25.00; Members Free
Publisher or Sponsor: The Travel Research Association
Managing Editor: Charles R. Goeldner

EDITORIAL DESCRIPTION
  Strives to advance the level and standards used in travel research by providing readers with new and helpful information about travel research, new techniques, creative views, generalizations about travel research thought and practice, and synthesis of travel research material.
Articles per average issue: 3-4
Audience: Users and producers of travel research
  Manuscripts accepted in English

MANUSCRIPT INFORMATION
Subject field(s): Travel, tourism, recreation, leisure. International and domestic.
Manuscript requirements: Style sheet sent on request.
  Preferred length: 4,000 words; 12 double-spaced pages
  Number of copies to be submitted: 4
  Abstract: Yes. Abstract required is more like a headnote and should run between 75-100 words.
Author information and reprints: Payment: None.
  Is simultaneous submission of article to other journals permitted: Not permitted.
  Exclusive manuscript rights between acceptance and publication: Yes
  Copyright: Not copyrighted
  Reprints: Available at cost. $1.00 per copy
Disposition of manuscript:
  Query letter: Not necessary.
  Receipt of manuscript acknowledged: Yes
  Decision to publish in: 6 months
  Accepted manuscript published in: 6-9 months
  Rejected manuscript returned: Yes, with return postage paid by publication.
  Rejected manuscript criticized: No
Submit to:
Charles R. Goeldner;
Karen P. Dicke
Editors
(See address above)

LOUISIANA BUSINESS REVIEW [786]
College of Business Administration, LSU
P.O. Box 17350-A
Baton Rouge, Louisiana 70803
(504) 388-5830

First published in 1937

SUBSCRIPTION DATA
Issues and rates: Published monthly.
  Average paid circulation: 4,500 controlled
Publisher or Sponsor: Louisiana State University, Division of Research, College of Business Administration

EDITORIAL DESCRIPTION
  Contains articles on business and economic indicators for Louisiana and its

metropolitan areas; articles related to business and economic interests.
Articles per average issue: 1
Audience: Business and academic community
Manuscripts accepted in English

MANUSCRIPT INFORMATION

Subject field(s): Economics, regional science, management, marketing, finance, other business areas
Manuscript requirements: No specific style guide.
Preferred length: 10 pages
Number of copies to be submitted: Two
Author information and reprints: Payment: None.
Is simultaneous submission of article to other journals permitted: Yes
Exclusive manuscript rights between acceptance and publication: Yes
Copyright: Not copyrighted
Reprints: Available, 5 free
Additional information: Manuscripts are to be typewritten, double-spaced on paper supplied by periodical. Graphs or charts should be in camera-ready form.
Disposition of manuscript:
Receipt of manuscript acknowledged: Yes
Decision to publish in: One month
Accepted manuscript published in: 3 to 6 months
Rejected manuscript returned: Yes
Rejected manuscript criticized: Yes
Submit to:
Loren C. Scott
Associate Director
(See address above)

MARKETING [787]
Haymarket Publishing, Ltd.
Craven House, 34 Fouberts Place
London W1, England
636-3600

SUBSCRIPTION DATA

Issues and rates: Published monthly.
Average paid circulation: 20,000
Annual rate(s): £5.00; Members £13.50
Publisher or Sponsor: Institute of Marketing

EDITORIAL DESCRIPTION

Focuses on matters of topical interest to those dealing with all areas of the marketing field.
Articles per average issue: 6
Audience: Management
Manuscripts accepted in English

MANUSCRIPT INFORMATION

Subject field(s): Topical and or controversial material written in a simple, direct, non-academic style.
Manuscript requirements: No specific style guide.
Preferred length: 2,000 words
Number of copies to be submitted: 2
Abstract: Yes. Of about 100 words as well as paragraph headings.

Author information and reprints: Payment: By publication to author, £20.00 per 1,000 words
Is simultaneous submission of article to other journals permitted: Not permitted.
Exclusive manuscript rights between acceptance and publication: Yes
Copyright:
Reprints: Available at cost.
Disposition of manuscript:
Query letter: Not necessary, but advisable.
Receipt of manuscript acknowledged: Yes
Decision to publish in: 2 weeks
Accepted manuscript published in: 10 weeks
Rejected manuscript returned: No
Rejected manuscript criticized: Sometimes
Submit to:
Michael Rines
Editor
(See address above)

MARQUETTE BUSINESS REVIEW [788]
College of Business Administration
Marquette University
Milwaukee, Wisconsin 53233
(414) 224-7331

First published in 1957

SUBSCRIPTION DATA

Issues and rates: Published quarterly.
Average paid circulation: 2,800 controlled
Publisher or Sponsor: Marquette University, College of Business Administration
Managing Editor: Thomas F. Divine

EDITORIAL DESCRIPTION

Contains well-documented articles that appear to make a new contribution to the literature of business and economics. Editorial interest in academic freedom and encouragement of research.
Articles per average issue: 6
Manuscripts accepted in English only

MANUSCRIPT INFORMATION

Subject field(s): Management, control, marketing, finance, economics, statistical studies, business education
Manuscript requirements: Style sheet sent on request.
Preferred length: 2,000 to 4,000 words
Number of copies to be submitted: Two
Abstract: No
Author information and reprints: Payment: None. Ten copies of issue in which article appears.
Is simultaneous submission of article to other journals permitted: Yes
Exclusive manuscript rights between acceptance and publication: Yes, if author agrees to publication date assigned
Copyright: Not copyrighted
Reprints: Available, cost paid by author
Disposition of manuscript:
Query letter: No
Receipt of manuscript acknowledged: Yes
Decision to publish in: Four weeks

Accepted manuscript published in: One year
Rejected manuscript returned: Yes
Rejected manuscript criticized: Yes, if requested by author
Submit to:
The Editor
(See address above)

MAY TRENDS [789]
111 South Washington Street
Park Ridge, Illinois 60025
(312) 825-8806

First published in 1967

SUBSCRIPTION DATA

Issues and rates: Published three times per year.
Average paid circulation: 10,000 controlled
Publisher or Sponsor: George S. May International Company

EDITORIAL DESCRIPTION

Each issue carries original articles dealing with the problems or trends of specific businesses - manufacturers, wholesalers, retailers. Seeks to assist in the development of business and marketing trends through the presentation of ideas and viewpoints of leading authorities.
Articles per average issue: 5
Audience: Professional, business
Manuscripts accepted in English

MANUSCRIPT INFORMATION

Subject field(s): Problems of manufacturers, wholesalers, and retailers
Manuscript requirements: No specific style guide.
Preferred length: 2,500-3,000 words
Number of copies to be submitted: One
Abstract: No
Author information and reprints: Payment: By publication to author. $100- $250 per article.
Is simultaneous submission of article to other journals permitted: No
Exclusive manuscript rights between acceptance and publication: Yes
Copyright: Held by publication.
Reprints: Available in limited number.
Additional information: Articles are to be submitted on speculation. Decisions on acceptability are made promptly and author informed. Payment is made upon acceptance.
Disposition of manuscript:
Query letter: Advisable
Receipt of manuscript acknowledged: Yes
Decision to publish in: 1 week
Accepted manuscript published in: 45 days
Rejected manuscript returned: Yes
Rejected manuscript criticized: Yes
Submit to:
John J. Coffey, Jr.
Editor
(See address above)

Business and economics

MONTANA BUSINESS QUARTERLY [790]
Bureau of Business and Economic Research
University of Montana, School of Business Administration
Missoula, Montana 59801
(406) 243-5113

First published in 1962

SUBSCRIPTION DATA
Issues and rates: Published quarterly.
 Average paid circulation: 550; 800
 Annual rate(s): $4.00; Foreign $4.00; Institutions $4.00
Publisher or Sponsor: University of Montana, Bureau of Business and Economic Research

EDITORIAL DESCRIPTION
A regional journal of business and public affairs, including economic, educational, public, social and environmental issues of Montana and the Rocky Mountain west.
Articles per average issue: 5
Audience: Professional, academic, business, general
 Manuscripts accepted in English

MANUSCRIPT INFORMATION
Manuscript requirements: See latest issue for style requirements. Chicago
 Preferred length: 10-20 pages typescript
 Number of copies to be submitted: 2
 Abstract: Not necessary.
Author information and reprints: Payment: Reprints only. 10 per article
 Is simultaneous submission of article to other journals permitted: Permitted, but not encouraged.
 Copyright: Not copyrighted
 Reprints: Available at cost.
Disposition of manuscript:
 Query letter: Not necessary, but advisable.
 Receipt of manuscript acknowledged: Yes
 Decision to publish in: 1 month
 Accepted manuscript published in: 3-6 months
 Rejected manuscript returned: Yes, if return postage is supplied by author.
 Rejected manuscript criticized: Sometimes
Submit to:
 Joyce D. Zacek
 Editor
 (See address above)

MSU BUSINESS TOPICS [791]
5A Berkey Hall, Division of Research
Michigan State University
East Lansing, Michigan 48824
(517) 355-9585

First published in 1952

SUBSCRIPTION DATA
Issues and rates: Published quarterly.
 Average paid circulation: 24,500 controlled
Publisher or Sponsor: Michigan State University, Division of Research, Graduate School of Business Administration
Managing Editor: Dole A. Anderson

EDITORIAL DESCRIPTION
A service of the University for all those interested in business and economic matters.
Articles per average issue: 8-9
Audience: Business generalist
 Manuscripts accepted in English only

MANUSCRIPT INFORMATION
Subject field(s): International, economics, finance, accounting, marketing, urban affairs, management, small business, personnel, transportation, government, environment and society, consumerism, education, taxation, labor-management relations, and other related subjects.
Manuscript requirements: See latest issue for style requirements. Style sheet sent on request. Chicago
 Preferred length: 15-30 typewritten pages
 Number of copies to be submitted: Two
 Abstract: Not necessary.
Author information and reprints: Payment: Reprints only. Two copies of journal and 25 reprints of article to author.
 Is simultaneous submission of article to other journals permitted: Not permitted.
 Exclusive manuscript rights between acceptance and publication: Yes
 Copyright: Held by publication.
 Reprints: Available at cost.
Disposition of manuscript:
 Query letter: Not necessary.
 Receipt of manuscript acknowledged: Yes
 Decision to publish in: Sixty days
 Rejected manuscript returned: Yes, with return postage paid by publication.
 Rejected manuscript criticized: Sometimes
Submit to:
 Mary Lu Hough
 Executive Editor
 (See address above)

THE NEW ENGLANDER [792]
New England's Business Magazine
Yankee, Inc.
Dublin, New Hampshire 03444
(603) 563-8111

First published in 1953

SUBSCRIPTION DATA
Issues and rates: Published monthly.
 Average paid circulation: 12,400; 9,600 controlled
 Annual rate(s): $10.00

EDITORIAL DESCRIPTION
Contains feature articles on business subjects, major economic issues and careers of interest to business executives in New England.
Articles per average issue: 25
 Manuscripts accepted in English only

MANUSCRIPT INFORMATION
Subject field(s): New England economic affairs, company profiles, New England industry analysis, personality profiles
Manuscript requirements: See latest issue for style requirements.
 Preferred length: 1500 words; 4-10 pages
 Number of copies to be submitted: One
 Abstract: No
Author information and reprints: Payment: By publication to author. $150 per article.
 Is simultaneous submission of article to other journals permitted: No
 Exclusive manuscript rights between acceptance and publication: Yes
 Copyright: Held by publication.
 Reprints: Available
Additional information: Typewritten, double-spaced; photographs and line art invited
Disposition of manuscript:
 Query letter: No
 Receipt of manuscript acknowledged: Yes
 Decision to publish in: 2-3 weeks
 Accepted manuscript published in: 2-3 months
 Rejected manuscript returned: Yes
 Rejected manuscript criticized: No
Submit to:
 Bradford W. Ketchum, Jr.
 Editor
 (See address above)

NORTH CAROLINA REVIEW OF BUSINESS AND ECONOMICS [793]
Center for Applied Research, School of Business and Economics
University of North Carolina at Greensboro
Greensboro, North Carolina 27412
(919) 379-5430

First published in 1974

SUBSCRIPTION DATA
Issues and rates: Published quarterly.
 Average paid circulation: 2,200 controlled
 Annual rate(s): Free upon request
Publisher or Sponsor: University of North Carolina at Greensboro

EDITORIAL DESCRIPTION
General topics in business and economics focusing primarily on those problems which are relevent to North Carolina
Articles per average issue: 4
Audience: Professional, academic, business
 Manuscripts accepted in English

MANUSCRIPT INFORMATION
Manuscript requirements: Style sheet sent on request.
 Preferred length: 10 pages
 Number of copies to be submitted: 2
 Abstract: Not necessary.
Author information and reprints: Payment: None.
 Is simultaneous submission of article to other journals permitted: Permitted, but not encouraged.

Exclusive manuscript rights between acceptance and publication: Yes
Copyright: Not copyrighted
Reprints: Available at cost.
Additional information: Typewritten (elite), double-spaced
Disposition of manuscript:
Query letter: Not necessary, but advisable.
Receipt of manuscript acknowledged: Yes
Decision to publish in: 2 weeks
Accepted manuscript published in: 3 months
Rejected manuscript returned: Yes, with return postage paid by publication.
Rejected manuscript criticized: Reasons for rejections only
Submit to:
G. Donald Jud
Director, Center for Applied Research
(See address above)

PITTSBURGH BUSINESS REVIEW [794]
402 Bruce Hall
University of Pittsburgh
Pittsburgh, Pennsylvania 15213
(412) 624-6437

SUBSCRIPTION DATA
Issues and rates: Published bi-monthly.
Average paid circulation: 9500 controlled
Publisher or Sponsor: University of Pittsburgh, Bureau of Business Research, Graduate School of Business

EDITORIAL DESCRIPTION
Contains facts and commentary exploring trends in the Pittsburgh district and the nation.
Articles per average issue: 1
Audience: Business executives
Manuscripts accepted in English

MANUSCRIPT INFORMATION
Subject field(s): General business
Manuscript requirements: No specific style guide.
Preferred length: 2000-4000 words; 12-20 pages
Number of copies to be submitted: Two
Abstract: Yes
Author information and reprints: Payment: None.
Is simultaneous submission of article to other journals permitted: No
Exclusive manuscript rights between acceptance and publication: Yes
Copyright: Held by publication.
Reprints: Available
Disposition of manuscript:
Query letter: No
Receipt of manuscript acknowledged: Yes
Decision to publish in: 4-6 weeks
Accepted manuscript published in: 2 months
Rejected manuscript returned: Yes
Rejected manuscript criticized: Sometimes
Submit to:
Margaret M. Walsh
Editor
(See address above)

PLANNING REVIEW [795]
Crane, Russak & Company, Inc.
347 Madison Avenue
New York, New York 10017
(212) 899-1403

First published in October, 1972

SUBSCRIPTION DATA
Issues and rates: Published bi-monthly.
Average paid circulation: 2,000; 1,500 controlled
Annual rate(s): Individuals $30.00
Publisher or Sponsor: North American Society for Corporate Planning, Inc.
Managing Editor: Robert J. Allio

EDITORIAL DESCRIPTION
Seeks to publish significant and useful articles dealing with the broad field of strategy and long range planning for the corporate community.
Articles per average issue: 6
Audience: Planners and business executives

MANUSCRIPT INFORMATION
Subject field(s): Economics, book reviews, behavioral sciences, international issues of the 1980's, management sciences, mergers & acquisitions, news, research and relevant editorials and articles relating to planning and decision making
Manuscript requirements: See latest issue for style requirements. Style sheet sent on request.
Preferred length: 1,200-3,600 words
Number of copies to be submitted: One
Abstract: Yes. Intended purpose of article
Author information and reprints: Payment: Reprints only.
Is simultaneous submission of article to other journals permitted: Permitted, but not encouraged.
Exclusive manuscript rights between acceptance and publication: Yes
Copyright: Held by North American Society for Corporate Planning, Inc.
Reprints: Available at cost.
Disposition of manuscript:
Query letter: Not necessary, but advisable.
Receipt of manuscript acknowledged: Yes
Decision to publish in: 2-3 Weeks
Accepted manuscript published in: 8-12 Weeks
Rejected manuscript returned: Yes, with return postage paid by publication.
Rejected manuscript criticized: Reasons for rejections only
Submit to:
Robert J. Allio
Editor
c/o Babcock & Wilcox
161 East 42nd Street
New York, New York 10017
(212) 687-6700

QUARTERLY JOURNAL OF ECONOMICS [796]
Journals Dept., Harvard University Press
79 Garden Street
Cambridge, Massachusetts 02138
(617) 495-2438

First published in 1886

SUBSCRIPTION DATA
Issues and rates: Published quarterly.
Average paid circulation: Average of 5200
Annual rate(s): $15.00
Managing Editor: Professor Richard A. Musgrave

EDITORIAL DESCRIPTION
Analytical contributions to economic research. Articles should deal with basic issues in economic analysis, utilization of technical skills, but substance rather than technique important.
Articles per average issue: 15
Audience: Graduate students, teachers, and researchers in economics
Manuscripts accepted in English

MANUSCRIPT INFORMATION
Subject field(s): Economic analysis of basic interest involving theory, concept development, policy, methodology, economy and society, social indicators.
Manuscript requirements: No specific style guide. See latest issue for style requirements. Style sheet sent on request. Chicago
Preferred length: Under 30 pages
Number of copies to be submitted: 2
Abstract: Abstract requested after article accepted—style should conform to *Journal of Economic Abstracts* requirements
Author information and reprints: Payment: Reprints only. 25 reprints
Is simultaneous submission of article to other journals permitted: Not permitted.
Exclusive manuscript rights between acceptance and publication: Yes
Copyright: The Journal holds exclusive world rights; permission to reprint or translate must be obtained from both the QJE and the author.
Reprints: Available at cost. Depends on length of published article and quantity ordered
Disposition of manuscript:
Query letter: Not necessary.
Receipt of manuscript acknowledged: Yes
Decision to publish in: 4-5 months
Accepted manuscript published in: 12 months
Rejected manuscript returned: Yes, with return postage paid by publication.
Rejected manuscript criticized: Sometimes
Submit to:
Professor Richard A. Musgrave
Editor
Littauer 227
Harvard University
Cambridge, Massachusetts 02138
(617) 495-2142

Business and economics

QUARTERLY REVIEW OF ECONOMICS AND BUSINESS [797]
408 David Kinley Hall
University of Illinois
Urbana, Illinois 61801
(217) 333-2330

First published in 1961

SUBSCRIPTION DATA
Issues and rates: Published quarterly.
  Average paid circulation: 1,780
  Annual rate(s): Individuals $6.00, Institutions $8.00, Foreign individuals $7.00, Foreign institutions $9.00
Publisher or Sponsor: University of Illinois, Bureau of Economic and Business Research
Managing Editor: Joseph D. Phillips

EDITORIAL DESCRIPTION
  Contains factual information and interpretative comment on economic and business questions.
Articles per average issue: 7
Audience: Business specialists, academic economists
  Manuscripts accepted in English

MANUSCRIPT INFORMATION
Subject field(s): Economics, business
Manuscript requirements: See latest issue for style requirements.
  Preferred length: 3,200-4,000 words; 12-15 pages
  Number of copies to be submitted: Two
  Abstract: No
Author information and reprints: Payment: None.
  Is simultaneous submission of article to other journals permitted: No
  Exclusive manuscript rights between acceptance and publication: Yes
  Copyright: Held by publication.
  Reprints: Available, 25 free
Disposition of manuscript:
  Query letter: No
  Receipt of manuscript acknowledged: Yes
  Decision to publish in: 3 months
  Accepted manuscript published in: 9 months
  Rejected manuscript returned: Yes
  Rejected manuscript criticized: Sometimes
Submit to:
  Joseph D. Phillips
  Editor
  (See address above)

THE REVIEW OF BLACK POLITICAL ECONOMY [798]
Transaction Periodical Consortium
Rutgers University
New Brunswick, New Jersey 08903
(201) 932-2280

First published in 1970

SUBSCRIPTION DATA
Issues and rates: Published quarterly.
  Average paid circulation: 1,000; 1,300 controlled
  Annual rate(s): $12.50; Pan-Am $12.50; Foreign $14.50; Institutions $17.00; Students $8.00; Foreign institutions $19.00
Publisher or Sponsor: Black Economic Research Center, Rutgers University

EDITORIAL DESCRIPTION
  Publishes technical analyses or studied opinions of Black economic development
Articles per average issue: 5
Audience: Academic, professional
  Manuscripts accepted in English

MANUSCRIPT INFORMATION
Subject field(s): The economics of Black America, Caribbean, Africa, and the Third World countries
Manuscript requirements: Chicago
  Preferred length: 20 pages or less
  Number of copies to be submitted: Original and 1 copy
  Abstract: Yes. Of one or two short paragraphs as well as a short author's vitae.
Author information and reprints: Payment: Reprints only. 5 copies of issue
  Is simultaneous submission of article to other journals permitted: Permitted.
  Exclusive manuscript rights between acceptance and publication: No
  Reprints: Available at cost.
Additional information: Footnotes should be grouped together on separate pages.
Disposition of manuscript:
  Query letter: Not necessary.
  Receipt of manuscript acknowledged: Yes
  Decision to publish in: 3 months
  Accepted manuscript published in: 6 months
  Rejected manuscript returned: No
  Rejected manuscript criticized: Sometimes
Submit to:
  Lloyd Hogan
  Editor
  112 West 120th Street
  New York, New York 10027
  (212) 666-0310

THE REVIEW OF ECONOMIC STUDIES [799]
Journal of the Society for Economic Analysis
Longman Group Ltd.
43-45 Annandale Street
Edinburgh EH7 4AT, Scotland

First published in 1933

SUBSCRIPTION DATA
Issues and rates: Published quarterly.
  Average paid circulation: 3,000
  Annual rate(s): $15.00, Students $4.00
Publisher or Sponsor: Society for Economic Analysis, Ltd.
Managing Editor: G. M. Heal; D. F. Hendry

EDITORIAL DESCRIPTION
  Encourages research in theoretical and applied economics, especially by young economists.
Articles per average issue: 15
Audience: Research, academic, governmental, business
  Manuscripts accepted in English

MANUSCRIPT INFORMATION
Subject field(s): Theoretical and applied economics
Manuscript requirements: See latest issue for style requirements.
  Preferred length: 20-25 pages
  Number of copies to be submitted: Three
  Abstract: Yes, less than 100 words
Author information and reprints: Payment: By author to publication. For alterations to proofs.
  Is simultaneous submission of article to other journals permitted: No
  Exclusive manuscript rights between acceptance and publication: Yes
  Copyright: Held by publication.
  Reprints: 25 free, extra at cost
Additional information: Place footnotes at end. Diagrams should be in black India ink on white paper.
Disposition of manuscript:
  Query letter: No
  Receipt of manuscript acknowledged: Yes
  Decision to publish in: 4 months
  Accepted manuscript published in: 6 months
  Rejected manuscript returned: No
  Rejected manuscript criticized: Yes
Submit to:
  M. K. Majum Dar
  Editor
  Department of Economics, Uris Hall
  Cornell University
  Ithaca, New York 14853

  Manuscripts from the United Kingdom should be submitted to:
  Editorial Committee
  School of Social Studies,
  Falmer,
  Brighton, BN1 9QN, England

THE REVIEW OF ECONOMICS AND STATISTICS [800]
Harvard University Press
79 Garden Street
Cambridge, Massachusetts 02138
(617) 495-2614

Previously entitled *The Review of Economic Statistics*

First published in 1922

SUBSCRIPTION DATA
Issues and rates: Published quarterly.

Average paid circulation: 6,000
Annual rate(s): $15.00; Foreign $16.00;
Institutions $15.00; Students $7.50;
Foreign institutions $16.00
Publisher or Sponsor: Harvard College
Managing Editor: Virginia W. Leahy

EDITORIAL DESCRIPTION
Publishes the results of scientific studies in economics from all fields, of any school of thought, so long as they make a significant contribution to the understanding of the processes which govern the American and other economies.
Articles per average issue: 15 plus
Audience: Economists
Manuscripts accepted in English

MANUSCRIPT INFORMATION
Manuscript requirements: See latest issue for style requirements. Style sheet sent on request.
Preferred length: 6,000 words for articles; 3,000 words for notes
Number of copies to be submitted: 2
Abstract: Not necessary.
Author information and reprints: Payment: None.
Is simultaneous submission of article to other journals permitted: Not permitted.
Exclusive manuscript rights between acceptance and publication: Yes
Copyright: Held by publication. A fee of $10.00 per page for reprint privileges is divided equally with the author.
Reprints: Available at cost.
Disposition of manuscript:
Query letter: Not necessary.
Receipt of manuscript acknowledged: Yes
Decision to publish in: 3 months
Accepted manuscript published in: 1 year
Rejected manuscript returned: Yes, with return postage paid by publication.
Rejected manuscript criticized: Yes
Submit to:
Hendrik S. Houthakker
Editor
211 Littauer Center
Harvard University Cambridge, Massachusetts 02138
(617) 495-2113

REVIEW OF SOCIAL ECONOMY [801]
DePaul University
2323 North Seminary
Chicago, Illinois 60614
(312) 321-8172

First published in 1944

SUBSCRIPTION DATA
Issues and rates: Published semi-annually.
Average paid circulation: 980; 1100 controlled
Annual rate(s): $10.00, Foreign $11.00

Publisher or Sponsor: Association for Social Economics
Managing Editor: William R. Waters

EDITORIAL DESCRIPTION
Contains articles with emphasis upon ethical or normative aspects of the nature of economics and economic policy and in the general area of social economics.
Articles per average issue: 10
Audience: Academic
Manuscripts accepted in English

MANUSCRIPT INFORMATION
Subject field(s): Ethical aspects of economic science, health economics, development, evaluation of economic policy, economic education
Manuscript requirements: Style sheet sent on request.
Preferred length: 5,000-10,000 words
Number of copies to be submitted: Three
Abstract: Preferred
Author information and reprints: Payment: None.
Is simultaneous submission of article to other journals permitted: Yes
Exclusive manuscript rights between acceptance and publication: Yes
Copyright: Held by publication.
Reprints: Available, 10 free
Additional information: Membership in Association for Social Economics allows one free submission per year; otherwise, $10.00 submission fee.
Disposition of manuscript:
Query letter: No
Receipt of manuscript acknowledged: Yes
Decision to publish in: 2-3 months
Accepted manuscript published in: 6 months
Rejected manuscript returned: Yes
Rejected manuscript criticized: Yes
Submit to:
Editor
(See address above)
(312) 248-2580

SAN FRANCISCO BUSINESS MAGAZINE [802]
465 California Street
San Francisco, California 94104
(415) 392-4511

First published in 1965

SUBSCRIPTION DATA
Issues and rates: Published monthly.
Average paid circulation: 5000; 7000 controlled
Annual rate(s): $8.00
Publisher or Sponsor: Greater San Francisco Chamber of Commerce
Managing Editor: Jim Haynes

EDITORIAL DESCRIPTION
Contains articles on business, government and trade in the Bay Area.
Articles per average issue: 8
Audience: Business men and women
Manuscripts accepted in English

MANUSCRIPT INFORMATION
Manuscript requirements: No specific style guide.
Preferred length: 1500 words
Number of copies to be submitted: One
Abstract: Yes
Author information and reprints: Payment: None.
Is simultaneous submission of article to other journals permitted: No
Exclusive manuscript rights between acceptance and publication: Yes
Copyright: Held by publication.
Reprints: Not available.
Disposition of manuscript:
Query letter: Not necessary, but advisable.
Receipt of manuscript acknowledged: Yes
Decision to publish in: 60 days
Accepted manuscript published in: 4 months
Rejected manuscript returned: Yes
Rejected manuscript criticized: No
Submit to:
Jim Haynes
Editor
(See address above)

SCOTTISH JOURNAL OF POLITICAL ECONOMY [803]
Longman Group Ltd., Journals Division
Burnt Mill
Harlow, Essex, England
26721

SUBSCRIPTION DATA
Issues and rates: Published three times per year.
Annual rate(s): £7.00, Foreign $22.00
Managing Editor: L. C. Hunter

EDITORIAL DESCRIPTION
Coverage of current problems in policy and theory, notably in relation to industry, labor and management, and regional economics.
Submit to:
L. C. Hunter
Editor
(See address above)

SPECIAL STIPULATIONS
Request additional information from editor.

THE SOUTH MAGAZINE [804]
P. O. Box 2350
1306 West Kennedy Boulevard
Tampa, Florida 33609
(813) 251-1081

First published in 1974

SUBSCRIPTION DATA
Issues and rates: Published bi-monthly.
Average paid circulation: 10,000
Annual rate(s): $5.95

Business and economics

Managing Editor: Roy B. Bain

EDITORIAL DESCRIPTION
  Primarily interested in the economic and urban affairs that originate in the ten-state area of the South
Articles per average issue: 8
Audience: Businessmen, government officials, community leaders
  Manuscripts accepted in English only

MANUSCRIPT INFORMATION
Subject field(s): Commerce, cities, companies, politics, people, culture
Manuscript requirements: Style sheet sent on request.
  Preferred length: 700-1600 words; 12 pages
  Number of copies to be submitted: 1
  Abstract: Not necessary.
Author information and reprints: Payment: By publication to author.
  Is simultaneous submission of article to other journals permitted: Not permitted.
  Exclusive manuscript rights between acceptance and publication: Yes
  Copyright: First serial rights only
  Reprints: Available at cost.
Disposition of manuscript:
  Query letter: Not necessary, but advisable.
  Receipt of manuscript acknowledged: Yes
  Decision to publish in: 2-3 weeks
  Accepted manuscript published in: 2-3 months
  Rejected manuscript returned: Yes, if return postage is supplied by author.
  Rejected manuscript criticized: Sometimes
Submit to:
  Roy B. Bain
  Editor
  (See address above)

SOUTHERN ECONOMIC JOURNAL [805]
Carroll Hall
University of North Carolina
Chapel Hill, North Carolina 27514
(919) 933-8301

First published in 1932

SUBSCRIPTION DATA
Issues and rates: Published quarterly.
  Average paid circulation: 4,000
  Annual rate(s): $20.00; Foreign $20.00; Individuals $20.00; Institutions $20.00; Students $20.00; Members $12.00; Foreign institutions $20.00
Publisher or Sponsor: Southern Economic Association
Managing Editor: Vincent J. Tarascio

EDITORIAL DESCRIPTION
  A technical journal dealing with current economic trends.
Articles per average issue: 20
Audience: Teachers, researchers, and other professionals in business, economics, and related fields
  Manuscripts accepted in English

MANUSCRIPT INFORMATION
Subject field(s): Any subject within the general field of economics
Manuscript requirements: Chicago
  Preferred length: 25-30 pages
  Number of copies to be submitted: 2
  Abstract: Yes. Specifications are included in the style sheet which is sent to authors whose manuscripts have been accepted for publication.
Author information and reprints: Payment: By author to publication. $10.00 per article.
  Is simultaneous submission of article to other journals permitted: Permitted, but not encouraged.
  Exclusive manuscript rights between acceptance and publication: Yes
  Copyright: Held by publication.
  Reprints: Not available.
Disposition of manuscript:
  Query letter: Not necessary.
  Receipt of manuscript acknowledged: Yes
  Decision to publish in: 6 months
  Accepted manuscript published in: 3 months
  Rejected manuscript returned: Yes, with return postage paid by publication.
  Rejected manuscript criticized: Yes
Submit to:
  Vincent J. Tarascio
  Managing Editor
  (See address above)

UNIVERSITY OF MICHIGAN BUSINESS REVIEW [806]
The University of Michigan
Graduate School of Business Administration
Ann Arbor, Michigan 48104
(313) 763-4510

First published in 1949

SUBSCRIPTION DATA
Issues and rates: Published bi-monthly.
  Average paid circulation: 32,000 controlled
  Annual rate(s): $6.00
Publisher or Sponsor: University of Michigan, Graduate School of Business Administration

EDITORIAL DESCRIPTION
  Contains articles on business and economics.
Articles per average issue: 6
Audience: Business and academic
  Manuscripts accepted in English

MANUSCRIPT INFORMATION
Subject field(s): Business, economics
Manuscript requirements: No specific style guide.
  Preferred length: Maximum 3,900 words; 13 pages
  Number of copies to be submitted: Two
  Abstract: No
Author information and reprints: Payment: None. 50 copies of the magazine containing article
  Is simultaneous submission of article to other journals permitted: No

  Exclusive manuscript rights between acceptance and publication: Yes
  Copyright: Held by publication.
  Reprints: Not available.
Disposition of manuscript:
  Query letter: No
  Receipt of manuscript acknowledged: Yes
  Decision to publish in: One month
  Accepted manuscript published in: Three months
  Rejected manuscript returned: Yes
  Rejected manuscript criticized: No
Submit to:
  Patricia J. Shontz
  Editor
  (See address above)

THE WHARTON QUARTERLY [807]
517 Franklin Building
University of Pennsylvania
Philadelphia, Pennsylvania 19174
(215) 594-5742

First published in Winter 1966

SUBSCRIPTION DATA
Issues and rates: Published quarterly.
  Average paid circulation: 3,500; 30,000 controlled
  Annual rate(s): $6.00, Foreign $9.00
Publisher or Sponsor: The Wharton School, University of Pennsylvania

EDITORIAL DESCRIPTION
  Contains reports on academic research and management; studies of management, business, and finance.
Articles per average issue: 4 and Economic Newsletter
Audience: Management
  Manuscripts accepted in English

MANUSCRIPT INFORMATION
Subject field(s): Economics, marketing, finance, management, forecasting, insurance, behavioral sciences
Manuscript requirements: See latest issue for style requirements.
  Preferred length: 1,500-3,000 words; 10-14 pages
  Number of copies to be submitted: One
  Abstract: No
Author information and reprints: Payment: Negotiable
  Is simultaneous submission of article to other journals permitted: Yes
  Exclusive manuscript rights between acceptance and publication: No
  Copyright: Held by Trustees of the University of Pennsylvania
  Reprints: Available
Disposition of manuscript:
  Query letter: No
  Receipt of manuscript acknowledged: Yes
  Decision to publish in: One month
  Accepted manuscript published in: Four months
  Rejected manuscript returned: Yes
  Rejected manuscript criticized: Sometimes

Submit to:
William M. Alrich
Editor
(See address above)

Finance and banking

THE BANKERS MAGAZINE [808]
89 Beach Street
Boston, Massachusetts 02111
(617) 423-2020

First published in 1846

SUBSCRIPTION DATA
Issues and rates: Published quarterly.
  Average paid circulation: Not available.
  Annual rate(s): $38.00
Managing Editor: Richard B. Miller

EDITORIAL DESCRIPTION
Contains articles on banking and finance for the professional.
Articles per average issue: 15-20
Audience: Professional bankers
  Manuscripts accepted in English

MANUSCRIPT INFORMATION
Manuscript requirements: See latest issue for style requirements.
  Preferred length: 3,000-5,000 words; 15-20 pages
  Number of copies to be submitted: Two
  Abstract: No
Author information and reprints: Payment: By publication to author. Modest honorarium
  Is simultaneous submission of article to other journals permitted: No
  Exclusive manuscript rights between acceptance and publication: Yes
  Copyright: Held by publication.
  Reprints: Available at cost
Disposition of manuscript:
  Query letter: Not necessary, but advisable.
  Receipt of manuscript acknowledged: Yes
  Decision to publish in: 2-4 weeks
  Accepted manuscript published in: 3 months
  Rejected manuscript returned: Yes
  Rejected manuscript criticized: Yes
Submit to:
  Richard B. Miller
  Managing Editor
  (See address above)

BURROUGHS CLEARING HOUSE [809]
P.O. Box 418
Detroit, Michigan 48232
(313) 972-7932

SUBSCRIPTION DATA
Issues and rates: Published monthly.
  Average paid circulation: 74,000 controlled
Publisher or Sponsor: Burroughs Corporation, Detroit
Managing Editor: Norman E. Douglas

EDITORIAL DESCRIPTION
Contains feature length articles on financial subjects; columns devoted to banking news, international banking, legislative reporting, personnel advancements and new products.

MANUSCRIPT INFORMATION
Subject field(s): Management, operations, personnel, business development, credit-loans, international banking, features
Manuscript requirements: See latest issue for style requirements.
  Preferred length: 1800-2000 words
  Number of copies to be submitted: One
Author information and reprints: Payment: By author to publication. $.10 per word. Plus payment for photos.
  Is simultaneous submission of article to other journals permitted: Not within financial field.
  Exclusive manuscript rights between acceptance and publication: Yes
  Copyright: Held by publication.
  Reprints: Not available.
Disposition of manuscript:
  Receipt of manuscript acknowledged: Yes
  Decision to publish in: 10 days
  Accepted manuscript published in: Three months
  Rejected manuscript returned: Yes
  Rejected manuscript criticized: Yes
Submit to:
  Norman Douglas
  Managing Editor
  (See address above)

CREDIT AND FINANCIAL MANAGEMENT [810]
475 Park Avenue South
New York, New York 10016
(212) 725-1700 ext. 35

First published in 1896

SUBSCRIPTION DATA
Issues and rates: 11 times per year
  Average paid circulation: 42,000
  Annual rate(s): Institutions $4.50, Members $5.00, Foreign $6.00
Publisher or Sponsor: National Association of Credit Management

EDITORIAL DESCRIPTION
A monthly publication for credit and financial executives, representing manufacturers, banks, insurance, factoring, financial organizations and institutions.
Articles per average issue: 5-6
Audience: Executives, treasurers, controllers, and management personnel in the U.S. and overseas.
  Manuscripts accepted in English

MANUSCRIPT INFORMATION
Subject field(s): Credit, finance, management, insurance, international monetary trends, banking, manufacturing, office management, advertising, apparel industry and commerce, financial institutions
Manuscript requirements: Style sheet sent on request.
  Preferred length: 8-10 pages
  Number of copies to be submitted: Three
  Abstract: No
Author information and reprints: Payment: By publication to author. Open
  Is simultaneous submission of article to other journals permitted: No
  Exclusive manuscript rights between acceptance and publication: Yes
  Copyright: Held by publication.
  Reprints: Available
Disposition of manuscript:
  Query letter: No
  Receipt of manuscript acknowledged: Yes
  Decision to publish in: 6-8 weeks
  Accepted manuscript published in: 6 months
  Rejected manuscript returned: Yes, if self-addressed, stamped envelope is sent with manuscript.
  Rejected manuscript criticized: No
Submit to:
  James J. Andover
  Editorial Director
  (See address above)

THE CREDIT WORLD [811]
375 Jackson Avenue
St. Louis, Missouri 63130
(314) 727-4045

First published in 1912

SUBSCRIPTION DATA
Issues and rates: Published monthly.
  Average paid circulation: 55,000 controlled
  Annual rate(s): Members $5.00
Publisher or Sponsor: International Consumer Credit Association
Managing Editor: William Henry Blake

EDITORIAL DESCRIPTION
Publication contains Association editorials, pertinent feature articles on subjects of consumer credit management as well as articles of interest to middle and top management in consumer credit granting field. Viewpoint is that of trade association striving to gain best interests of its membership.
Articles per average issue: 3-4
  Manuscripts accepted in English

MANUSCRIPT INFORMATION
Subject field(s): Credit granting management techniques, future trends within industry, credit scoring techniques, skip tracing, credit counseling, development of new electronic machinery to improve service to customers and improve credit functions at credit granters' establishments.

Manuscript requirements: See latest issue for style requirements.
Preferred length: 8-10 pages.
Number of copies to be submitted: Three
Abstract: No
Author information and reprints: Payment: None.
Is simultaneous submission of article to other journals permitted: No
Exclusive manuscript rights between acceptance and publication: Yes
Copyright: Held by publication.
Reprints: Not available.
Disposition of manuscript:
Receipt of manuscript acknowledged: Yes
Decision to publish in: 6-8 weeks
Accepted manuscript published in: 3-4 months
Rejected manuscript returned: Yes, if return postage is supplied by author.
Rejected manuscript criticized: No
Submit to:
Richard K. Klein
Editor
(See address above)

SPECIAL STIPULATIONS

If photographs accompany manuscript, they should be 8x10 black and white glossy prints, must carry proper identifications. Footnotes, references, etc., and should be on separate pages. Tables and charts must be camera-ready copy.

ESTATE PLANNING [812]
512 North Florida Avenue
Tampa, Florida 33602

First published in 1973

SUBSCRIPTION DATA

Issues and rates: Published quarterly.
Average paid circulation: 16,000
Annual rate(s): $18.00; Foreign $18.00; Institutions $18.00; Students $9.00; Foreign institutions $18.00

EDITORIAL DESCRIPTION

Serious technical discussion of estate planning, trust and estate administration, and family asset management: law, accounting, investment, insurance, trusts.
Articles per average issue: 10
Manuscripts accepted in English

MANUSCRIPT INFORMATION

Manuscript requirements: See latest issue for style requirements.
Preferred length: 5,000 words
Number of copies to be submitted: 2
Abstract: Not necessary.
Author information and reprints: Payment: None.
Is simultaneous submission of article to other journals permitted: Not permitted.
Exclusive manuscript rights between acceptance and publication: Yes
Copyright: Held by publication.
Reprints: Available at no cost. 100
Disposition of manuscript:
Query letter: Not necessary, but advisable.
Receipt of manuscript acknowledged: Yes
Decision to publish in: 3 weeks
Accepted manuscript published in: 2 months
Rejected manuscript returned: Yes, with return postage paid by publication.
Rejected manuscript criticized: Sometimes
Submit to:
Editor
125 East 56th Street
New York, New York 10022

EUROMONEY [813]
A Journal of the International Money and Capital Markets
14 Finsbury Circus
London EC2M 7AB, England
(01) 606-1234

SUBSCRIPTION DATA

Issues and rates: Published monthly.
Average paid circulation: 5,500
Annual rate(s): £15.00; Foreign $60.00
Managing Editor: Pedraic Fallon

EDITORIAL DESCRIPTION

Provides a forum for views on the international money and capital markets as well as a source of information on trends and developments in the domestic markets, from all centers of international importance
Articles per average issue: 30
Audience: International banking community, corporate treasurers
Manuscripts accepted in English

MANUSCRIPT INFORMATION

Subject field(s): Finance, economics
Manuscript requirements: See latest issue for style requirements. Style sheet sent on request.
Preferred length: 800-2,500 words
Number of copies to be submitted: 1
Abstract: Not necessary.
Author information and reprints: Payment: By publication to author. By arrangement
Is simultaneous submission of article to other journals permitted: Not permitted.
Exclusive manuscript rights between acceptance and publication: Yes
Copyright: Held by author.
Reprints: Available at cost.
Disposition of manuscript:
Query letter: Necessary.
Receipt of manuscript acknowledged: Yes
Decision to publish in: 1 week
Accepted manuscript published in: 3 weeks
Rejected manuscript returned: No
Rejected manuscript criticized: Sometimes
Submit to:
The Editor
(See address above)

FINANCIAL ANALYSTS JOURNAL [814]
The Magazine for Investment Management
219 East 42nd Street
New York, New York 10017
(212) 557-0067

First published in 1945

SUBSCRIPTION DATA

Issues and rates: Published bi-monthly.
Average paid circulation: 21,000
Annual rate(s): $16.00; Foreign $18.00
Publisher or Sponsor: Financial Analysts Federation
Managing Editor: Jack L. Treynor

EDITORIAL DESCRIPTION

Contains discussions of the technical and policy problems of the investment professional.
Articles per average issue: 7
Audience: Investment professionals, educators, trust officers, CPA's, fund managers
Manuscripts accepted in English

MANUSCRIPT INFORMATION

Subject field(s): Economics, money and banking, security valuation, portfolio themes, industry technology, financial planning, international finance
Manuscript requirements: Chicago
Preferred length: 2,500-10,000 words
Number of copies to be submitted: Three
Abstract: Not necessary
Author information and reprints: Payment: None.
Is simultaneous submission of article to other journals permitted: No
Exclusive manuscript rights between acceptance and publication: Yes
Copyright: Held by publication.
Reprints: 300 available at no cost
Additional information: Manuscript should be typewritten, double-spaced, with footnotes at the end. Graphs and charts should be on separate sheets.
Disposition of manuscript:
Query letter: No
Receipt of manuscript acknowledged: Yes
Decision to publish in: 3 months
Accepted manuscript published in: 9 months
Rejected manuscript returned: Yes, if self-addressed, stamped envelope is sent with manuscript.
Rejected manuscript criticized: Yes
Submit to:
Jack L. Treynor
Editor
(See address above)

THE JOURNAL OF COMMERCIAL BANK LENDING [815]
Room 1432, PNB Building
Philadelphia, Pennsylvania 19107
(215) 563-0267

SUBSCRIPTION DATA

Issues and rates: Published monthly.

Average paid circulation: 16,000; 6,000 controlled
Annual rate(s): $10.00
Publisher or Sponsor: The National Association of Bank Loan and Credit

EDITORIAL DESCRIPTION

Contains articles relating to commercial bank lending, accounting principles, international lending, bank assets, liability and capital management. Strives for educational and professional enlightenment of bank commercial loan and credit officers.
Articles per average issue: 7
Audience: Commercial loan and credit officers, bank managers, examiners, educators
Manuscripts accepted in English only

MANUSCRIPT INFORMATION

Manuscript requirements: Style sheet sent on request.
Preferred length: 20-30 pages
Number of copies to be submitted: Two
Author information and reprints: Payment: None. 6 copies of issue in which article appears.
Is simultaneous submission of article to other journals permitted: No
Exclusive manuscript rights between acceptance and publication: Yes
Copyright: Held by publication.
Reprints: Available, 20 free; others at cost
Disposition of manuscript:
Query letter: No
Receipt of manuscript acknowledged: Yes
Decision to publish in: 6-8 weeks
Accepted manuscript published in: 3-6 months
Rejected manuscript returned: Yes, with return postage paid by publication.
Rejected manuscript criticized: No
Submit to:
Theodore C. McDaniels
Managing Editor
(See address above)
(215) 563-2067

JOURNAL OF FINANCE [816]

Graduate School of Business
100 Trinity Place
New York, New York 10006
(212) 285-6140

First published in 1946

SUBSCRIPTION DATA

Issues and rates: 5 times per year
Average paid circulation: 6,500
Annual rate(s): $17.00, Institutions $25.00
Publisher or Sponsor: American Finance Association

EDITORIAL DESCRIPTION

Publishes articles that touch on every aspect of finance from international banking to consumer credit. The journal is written for teachers and the professional financier. The book reviews give a relatively current check on works in the field. Dissertation abstracts and proceedings of the annual meeting are also published.
Articles per average issue: 15
Audience: Professionals in finance
Manuscripts accepted in English

MANUSCRIPT INFORMATION

Manuscript requirements: See latest issue for style requirements.
Preferred length: 30 pages or less
Number of copies to be submitted: Two
Abstract: Yes
Author information and reprints: Payment: None.
Copyright: Held jointly by author and publication
Disposition of manuscript:
Query letter: No
Receipt of manuscript acknowledged: Yes
Decision to publish in: 6 to 7 weeks
Submit to:
For articles:
Professor J. Guttentag
Editor
Wharton School
University of Pennsylvania
Philadelphia Pennsylvania 19174

For Book Reviews:
Professor A. Cohan
Book Review Editor
University of Georgia
Athens, Georgia 30602

JOURNAL OF MONEY, CREDIT, AND BANKING [817]

Ohio State University Press
2070 Neil Avenue
Columbus, Ohio 43210
(614) 422-6930

Previously entitled *National Banking Review*

First published in 1969

SUBSCRIPTION DATA

Issues and rates: Published quarterly.
Average paid circulation: 2,250
Annual rate(s): $14.00, Foreign $15.00; Students $8.00
Managing Editor: Richard A. McKee

EDITORIAL DESCRIPTION

A scholarly journal devoted to analysis of recent policy in government and commercial banking sectors.
Articles per average issue: 8
Audience: Economists, monetarists, academic, government, banking
Manuscripts accepted in English only

MANUSCRIPT INFORMATION

Subject field(s): Monetary theory, government policy, commercial banking
Manuscript requirements: Style sheet sent on request.
Preferred length: 10-40 pages
Number of copies to be submitted: Two
Abstract: Yes
Author information and reprints: Payment: None.
Is simultaneous submission of article to other journals permitted: No
Exclusive manuscript rights between acceptance and publication: Yes
Copyright: Held by publication.
Reprints: Available, cost upon request
Disposition of manuscript:
Query letter: No
Receipt of manuscript acknowledged: Yes
Decision to publish in: 6-8 weeks
Accepted manuscript published in: 6-10 months
Rejected manuscript returned: Yes, if return postage is supplied by author.
Rejected manuscript criticized: Sometimes
Submit to:
Journals Department
(See address above)

THE MAGAZINE OF BANK ADMINISTRATION [818]

P. O. Box 500
303 South Northwest Highway
Park Ridge, Illinois 60068
(312) 775-5344

Previously entitled *Auditgram*

First published in 1924

SUBSCRIPTION DATA

Issues and rates: Published monthly.
Average paid circulation: 35,000
Annual rate(s): $10.00; Foreign $10.00; Institutions $10.00; Students $10.00
Publisher or Sponsor: Bank Administration Institute
Managing Editor: Frank G. McCabe

EDITORIAL DESCRIPTION

Edited for bankers engaged in management, operations, automation, accounting, safeguarding, controllership, and auditing
Articles per average issue: 6
Audience: Professional bankers
Manuscripts accepted in English

MANUSCRIPT INFORMATION

Subject field(s): Modernizing banking, improving operations, bank efficiency, cost centers, management, personnel administration, internal safeguards, profitability
Manuscript requirements: Chicago
Preferred length: 6-10 pages
Number of copies to be submitted: 2
Abstract: Not necessary.
Author information and reprints: Payment: By publication to author. $100.00 per article.
Is simultaneous submission of article to other journals permitted: Not permitted.
Exclusive manuscript rights between acceptance and publication: Yes
Copyright: Held by publication.
Reprints: Available at cost.
Disposition of manuscript:
Query letter: Not necessary, but advisable.

Receipt of manuscript acknowledged: Yes
Decision to publish in: 10 days
Accepted manuscript published in: 3-4 months
Rejected manuscript returned: Yes, with return postage paid by publication.
Rejected manuscript criticized: Reasons for rejections only
Submit to:
Frank McCabe
Editor
(See address above)

PUBLIC FINANCE QUARTERLY* [819]
Sage Publications, Inc.
275 South Beverly Drive
Beverly Hills, California 90212
(213) 274-2423

SUBSCRIPTION DATA
Issues and rates: Published quarterly.
 Average paid circulation: Not available.
 Annual rate(s): Institutions $18.00; Individuals $12.00; Students $9.00; Foreign individuals $13.00; Foreign institutions $19.00

EDITORIAL DESCRIPTION
Publishes broadly-based articles covering theoretical, quantitative and institutional problems relating to the allocation, distribution, and stabilization functions within the public sector of the economy.

MANUSCRIPT INFORMATION
Subject field(s): Public choice, human resources, foreign trade, tax burdens, inflation, environmental economics, raising of public revenues and their use by government
Manuscript requirements: Style sheet sent on request.
 Preferred length: 6,250-7,500 words; 25 to 30 pages
 Number of copies to be submitted: Two
Author information and reprints: Payment: None. 25 tear-sheets free to author.
 Is simultaneous submission of article to other journals permitted: Permitted, but not encouraged. Author must notify publisher that manuscript is under consideration elsewhere.
 Exclusive manuscript rights between acceptance and publication: Yes
 Copyright: Held by publication.
 Reprints: Available if purchased by special order in amounts no fewer than 100
Disposition of manuscript:
 Receipt of manuscript acknowledged: Yes
 Decision to publish in: Six to eight weeks
 Accepted manuscript published in: Six to nine months
 Rejected manuscript returned: Yes
 Rejected manuscript criticized: Yes
Submit to:
Editor
(See address above)

REAL ESTATE REVIEW [820]
P.O. Box 522
Manhasset, New York 11030
(516) 627-4810

First published in 1971

SUBSCRIPTION DATA
Issues and rates: Published quarterly.
 Average paid circulation: 25,000
 Annual rate(s): $28.00, Foreign $32.00

EDITORIAL DESCRIPTION
Publishes articles directed to sophisticated real estate professionals, investors or lenders. Subject matter should be "how-to" studies: views on future trends in real estate, or the relationship between real estate and social problems.
Articles per average issue: 16
 Manuscripts accepted in English

MANUSCRIPT INFORMATION
Subject field(s): Investment, financing, management, tax aspects, legal aspects, housing, brokerage
Manuscript requirements: Style sheet sent on request.
 Preferred length: 3000-6000 words; 12-24 pages
 Number of copies to be submitted: One
 Abstract: No
Author information and reprints: Payment: By publication to author. $50.00 per article. 2 complimentary copies of issue.
 Is simultaneous submission of article to other journals permitted: No
 Exclusive manuscript rights between acceptance and publication: Yes
 Copyright: Held by publication.
 Reprints: Available at cost
Disposition of manuscript:
 Query letter: No
 Receipt of manuscript acknowledged: Yes
 Decision to publish in: 6 to 8 weeks
 Accepted manuscript published in: 3 to 6 months
 Rejected manuscript returned: Yes
 Rejected manuscript criticized: If requested
Submit to:
Alvin L. Arnold
Editor
(See address above)

Labor

INDUSTRIAL AND LABOR RELATIONS REVIEW [821]
Research Building, Room 201
Cornell University
Ithaca, New York 14853
(607) 256-3295

First published in 1947

SUBSCRIPTION DATA
Issues and rates: Published quarterly.
 Average paid circulation: 5,000
 Annual rate(s): $10.00 Foreign $11.00 Students $5.00
Publisher or Sponsor: Cornell University
Managing Editor: Donald E. Cullen

EDITORIAL DESCRIPTION
Foremost scholars discuss their research findings in manpower development, labor economics, collective bargaining, labor law, and organizational behavior. Each issue features a comprehensive listing of current publications, book reviews, and reports of on-going research.
Articles per average issue: 7-8
Audience: Scholars and practitioners in industrial and labor relations and related fields
 Manuscripts accepted in English

MANUSCRIPT INFORMATION
Subject field(s): Social insurance, private welfare plans, politics, government and industrial relations, labor problems in the U. S. and internationally.
Manuscript requirements: Style sheet sent on request. Chicago
 Preferred length: 25-30 typewritten pages
 Number of copies to be submitted: 1-2
 Abstract: Not necessary.
Author information and reprints: Payment: Reprints only. 100 reprints and one year's subscription
 Is simultaneous submission of article to other journals permitted: Not permitted.
 Exclusive manuscript rights between acceptance and publication: Yes
 Copyright: Held by Cornell University
 Reprints: Available at cost. $5.00 per page
Disposition of manuscript:
 Query letter: Not necessary.
 Receipt of manuscript acknowledged: Yes
 Decision to publish in: 1 year
 Accepted manuscript published in: 6 months
 Rejected manuscript returned: No
 Rejected manuscript criticized: Reasons for rejections only
Submit to:
Prof. Donald E. Cullen
Editor
(See address above)

INDUSTRIAL RELATIONS [822]
A Journal of Economy and Society
Institute of Industrial Relations
University of California
Berkeley, California 94720
(415) 642-5452

First published in October, 1961

SUBSCRIPTION DATA
Issues and rates: Published three times per year.
 Average paid circulation: 2250; 80 controlled
 Annual rate(s): $8.00

Publisher or Sponsor: Institute of Industrial Relations, University of California, Berkeley

EDITORIAL DESCRIPTION

Source of information and ideas on all aspects of the employment relationship; emphasis on developments in labor economics, sociology, psychology, political science, and law.
Articles per average issue: 4-8
Audience: Academic, management, labor
Manuscripts accepted in English

MANUSCRIPT INFORMATION

Subject field(s): Collective bargaining, employment, labor economics, industrial psychology, organizational psychology, training and development, comparative industrial relations systems
Manuscript requirements: Style sheet sent on request.
Preferred length: 5,000-7,000 words; 20-25 pages
Number of copies to be submitted: Two
Abstract: No
Author information and reprints: Payment: None.
Is simultaneous submission of article to other journals permitted: No
Exclusive manuscript rights between acceptance and publication: Yes
Copyright: Held by publication.
Reprints: Available on order
Additional information: Manuscript should be typed, double-spaced with tables, charts and figures on separate pages. Charts should be camera ready.
Disposition of manuscript:
Query letter: No
Receipt of manuscript acknowledged: Yes
Decision to publish in: 2 months
Accepted manuscript published in: 6 months or more
Rejected manuscript returned: Yes
Rejected manuscript criticized: Sometimes
Submit to:
Barbara Porter
Managing Editor
(See address above)

INTERNATIONAL LABOUR REVIEW [823]
International Labour Office
CH-1211 Geneva 22, Switzerland
022 985 211 ext. 3651

First published in 1921

SUBSCRIPTION DATA

Issues and rates: Published monthly.
Average paid circulation: 4,400; 4,350 controlled
Annual rate(s): 50 Swiss francs
Publisher or Sponsor: International Labour Office

EDITORIAL DESCRIPTION

Publishes the results of original research, international comparative studies and articles analysing experience of international interest with the aim of contributing to wider understanding of questions of labor and social policy and administration.
Articles per average issue: 5
Audience: Academic, business, labor, governmental
Manuscripts accepted in English, French, Spanish

MANUSCRIPT INFORMATION

Subject field(s): Labor economics, education and training, social security, collective bargaining, income promotion, labor-management relations, national and international legislation
Manuscript requirements: Style sheet sent on request.
Preferred length: 5,000 to 8,000 words; 20 to 32 pages
Number of copies to be submitted: Two
Abstract: Yes, of 100 words or less
Author information and reprints: Payment: None.
Is simultaneous submission of article to other journals permitted: Yes, but only unpublished manuscripts accepted.
Exclusive manuscript rights between acceptance and publication: Yes
Copyright: Held by publication.
Reprints: Available, 25 free
Additional information: Most articles are specifically commissioned.
Disposition of manuscript:
Query letter: No
Receipt of manuscript acknowledged: Yes
Decision to publish in: 2-3 months
Accepted manuscript published in: 3-5 months
Rejected manuscript returned: On request
Rejected manuscript criticized: No
Submit to:
Chief Editor
(See address above)

SPECIAL STIPULATIONS

Published in English, French and Spanish editions.

JOURNAL OF COLLECTIVE NEGOTIATIONS IN THE PUBLIC SECTOR [824]
Baywood Publishing Company, Inc.
43 Central Drive
Farmingdale, New York 11735
(516) 293-7130

First published in 1972

SUBSCRIPTION DATA

Issues and rates: Published quarterly.
Annual rate(s): $30.00; Foreign $32.00

EDITORIAL DESCRIPTION

Emphasizes practical ideas guiding readers toward usable techniques for the negotiation process and contract administration for dealing with the complexities and ramifications of public sector labor relations.
Articles per average issue: 7
Audience: Those involved in the negotiations process

Manuscripts accepted in English

MANUSCRIPT INFORMATION

Subject field(s): Preparations for bargaining, composition of negotiation teams, technique at the table, impasse procedures, mediation, fact finding
Manuscript requirements: See latest issue for style requirements. Style sheet sent on request.
Preferred length: Up to 5,000 words
Abstract: Yes, 150 words
Author information and reprints: Payment: Reprints only. 20 copies
Is simultaneous submission of article to other journals permitted: Not permitted.
Exclusive manuscript rights between acceptance and publication: Yes
Copyright: Held by publication.
Reprints: Available at cost.
Disposition of manuscript:
Query letter: Not necessary, but advisable.
Receipt of manuscript acknowledged: Yes
Decision to publish in: 4-6 weeks
Accepted manuscript published in: 6 months
Rejected manuscript returned: Yes, with return postage paid by publication.
Rejected manuscript criticized: Sometimes
Submit to:
Dr. Harry Kershen
Executive Editor
(See address above)

JOURNAL OF INDUSTRIAL RELATIONS [825]
The Journal of the Industrial Relations Society of Australia
c/o School of Industrial Relations
University of Sydney
Sydney, N.S.W. 2006, Australia
660-0522 ext. 3077

First published in 1959

SUBSCRIPTION DATA

Issues and rates: Published quarterly.
Average paid circulation: 3,200
Annual rate(s): $7.00
Publisher or Sponsor: Industrial Relations Society of New South Wales
Managing Editor: Kingsley Laffer

EDITORIAL DESCRIPTION

Contains articles and notes dealing with industrial relations broadly defined to include the contributions of all relevant disciplines. Emphasis is on Australian material but some overseas material is desired.
Articles per average issue: 9
Audience: Industrial, academic
Manuscripts accepted in English

MANUSCRIPT INFORMATION

Subject field(s): Industrial relations, labor economics, industrial sociology, industrial law, industrial psychology

Manuscript requirements: See latest issue for style requirements.
  Preferred length: 5000-6000 words; 12-15 pages
  Number of copies to be submitted: Two
  Abstract: No
Author information and reprints: Payment: None.
  Is simultaneous submission of article to other journals permitted: No
  Exclusive manuscript rights between acceptance and publication: Yes
  Copyright: Held by author.
  Reprints: Available, 50 free
Disposition of manuscript:
  Query letter: No
  Receipt of manuscript acknowledged: Yes
  Decision to publish in: 2-3 weeks
  Accepted manuscript published in: 6-12 months
  Rejected manuscript returned: Yes
  Rejected manuscript criticized: Yes
Submit to:
  Kingsley Laffer
  Editor
  (See address above)

LABOR TODAY [826]
The Rank and File in Action
343 South Dearborn Street
Chicago, Illinois 60604
(312) 922-5560

SUBSCRIPTION DATA
Issues and rates: Published monthly.
  Average paid circulation: Not available.
  Annual rate(s): $3.00, Foreign $6.00
Publisher or Sponsor: Labor Today Association
Managing Editor: John Kailin

EDITORIAL DESCRIPTION
  A monthly tabloid of fact and controversy, written by and for trade unionists.

MANUSCRIPT INFORMATION
Subject field(s): Organizing in plants, strikes, the labor movement, international trade union movement, women workers, black and white workers unity
Manuscript requirements: No specific style guide.
  Preferred length: Four pages maximum
  Number of copies to be submitted: Two
Author information and reprints: Payment: None.
  Is simultaneous submission of article to other journals permitted: Yes
  Exclusive manuscript rights between acceptance and publication: No
  Copyright: Held by publication.
  Reprints: Available, $.15 per copy
Disposition of manuscript:
  Receipt of manuscript acknowledged: Yes
  Decision to publish in: One month
  Accepted manuscript published in: One month
  Rejected manuscript returned: Yes, if self-addressed, stamped envelope is sent with manuscript.
  Rejected manuscript criticized: Sometimes

Submit to:
  Jim Williams
  Co-Editor
  (See address above)

MONTHLY LABOR REVIEW [827]
U.S. Department of Labor
Bureau of Labor Statistics
Washington, D.C. 20212
(202) 961-2327

Previously entitled *Monthly Review*

First published in 1915

SUBSCRIPTION DATA
Issues and rates: Published monthly.
  Average paid circulation: 19,769
  Annual rate(s): $16.25 Foreign $20.35
Managing Editor: Robert W. Fisher

EDITORIAL DESCRIPTION
  Publishes research, analysis, and current statistics on prices, wages, productivity, industrial relations, employment and the labor force
Articles per average issue: 12
Audience: Management, union officials, arbitrators, educators, attorneys,
  Manuscripts accepted in English

MANUSCRIPT INFORMATION
Subject field(s): Economics, social sciences
Manuscript requirements: GPO; Style sheet sent on request.
  Preferred length: 3,000 to 3,500 words
  Number of copies to be submitted: Original and two copies
  Abstract: Yes; should be about 100 words giving a clear idea of the main conclusions, methods, and line of reasoning.
Author information and reprints: Payment: None.
  Is simultaneous submission of article to other journals permitted: No
  Exclusive manuscript rights between acceptance and publication: Yes
  Copyright: Not copyrighted
  Reprints: Available
Additional information: Manuscripts should be factual and analytical, not polemical in tone.
Disposition of manuscript:
  Query letter: No
  Receipt of manuscript acknowledged: Yes
  Decision to publish in: 3-4 weeks
  Accepted manuscript published in: 3-4 months
  Rejected manuscript returned: Yes
  Rejected manuscript criticized: No
Submit to:
  Herbert C. Morton
  Editor-in-Chief
  (See address above)

RELATIONS INDUSTRIELLES [828]
Presses de l'Université Laval
Université Laval
Québec, Québec G1K 7R4, Canada
(418) 656-4092

First published in 1945

SUBSCRIPTION DATA
Issues and rates: Published quarterly.
  Annual rate(s): $12.00; Foreign $13.00
Publisher or Sponsor: Canadian Industrial Relations Research Institute
Managing Editor: Gérard Dion

EDITORIAL DESCRIPTION
  Publishes articles of quality on all aspects of industrial and labor relations with a particular, but not exclusive, emphasis on the Canadian.
Articles per average issue: 10
Audience: Academic, union leaders, personnel and industrial relations managers
  Manuscripts accepted in French, English

MANUSCRIPT INFORMATION
Subject field(s): Labor economics, sociology of work, industrial psychology, trade unionism, personnel management, labor law, labor history, etc.
Manuscript requirements: See latest issue for style requirements. Style sheet sent on request.
  Preferred length: 6,000 words
  Number of copies to be submitted: 3
  Abstract: Yes. A short abstract of about 60 words presenting the object of the article. In addition, a summary of about 900 words to be translated into English or French.
Author information and reprints: Payment: Reprints only. 25 reprints and 4 issues
  Is simultaneous submission of article to other journals permitted: Not permitted.
  Exclusive manuscript rights between acceptance and publication: Yes
  Copyright: Held by publication.
  Reprints: Available at cost.
Disposition of manuscript:
  Query letter: Not necessary, but advisable.
  Receipt of manuscript acknowledged: Yes
  Decision to publish in: 1-3 months
  Accepted manuscript published in: 6-12 months
  Rejected manuscript returned: No
  Rejected manuscript criticized: No
Submit to:
  Gérard Dion
  Editor
  Départment des relations industrielles
  Université Laval
  Québec, Québec G1K 7P4, Canada
  (418) 656-3358

SPECIAL STIPULATIONS
  Due to the bilingual character of the journal, once the manuscript has been accepted, a summary must be presented for translation in the other language.

Management and personnel

AACSB BULLETIN [829]
Suite 50
760 Office Parkway
St. Louis, Missouri 63141
(314) 872-8481

First published in 1964

SUBSCRIPTION DATA
Issues and rates: Published quarterly.
  Average paid circulation: 2,000
Publisher or Sponsor: American Assembly
  of Collegiate Schools of Business
Managing Editor: Jesse M. Smith, Jr.

EDITORIAL DESCRIPTION
  Contains papers of current interest in
  business administration and management.
Articles per average issue: 5-6
Audience: Administrators, faculty,
  businessmen, libraries
  Manuscripts accepted in English only

MANUSCRIPT INFORMATION
Subject field(s): All topics relating to
  business administration and management
Manuscript requirements: Style sheet sent
  on request.
  Preferred length: 10 to 15 pages
  Number of copies to be submitted: 4
Author information and reprints: Payment:
  Reprints only. 5 copies of issue.
  Is simultaneous submission of article to
  other journals permitted: No
  Exclusive manuscript rights between
  acceptance and publication: Yes
  Copyright: Held by publication.
  Reprints: Available, cost on request
Disposition of manuscript:
  Query letter: No
  Receipt of manuscript acknowledged: Yes
  Decision to publish in: 1 to 2 months
  Accepted manuscript published in: 6-9
  months
  Rejected manuscript returned: Yes
  Rejected manuscript criticized:
  Sometimes
Submit to:
  Eunice K. Lange
  Publications Coordinator
  (See address above)

ACADEMY OF MANAGEMENT JOURNAL [830]
Department of Management
Georgia State University
University Plaza
Atlanta, Georgia 30303
(301) 454-4721

Previously entitled *Journal of the Academy
of Management*

First published in 1958

SUBSCRIPTION DATA
Issues and rates: Published quarterly.
  Average paid circulation: 4,000
  Annual rate(s): $20.00
Publisher or Sponsor: Academy of
  Management
Managing Editor: John B. Miner

EDITORIAL DESCRIPTION
  Contains articles in the field of
  management and administration, broadly
  defined.
Articles per average issue: 20
Audience: Scholars and practitioners
  Manuscripts accepted in English

MANUSCRIPT INFORMATION
Subject field(s): Business policy and
  planning, international management,
  management consulting, management
  development, management history and
  theory, organizational behavior
Manuscript requirements: Style sheet sent
  on request.
  Preferred length: Papers: 10-15 printed
  pages; notes: 2-4 printed pages
  Number of copies to be submitted: Three
  Abstract: Yes, 50 words; none for notes
Author information and reprints: Payment:
  None.
  Is simultaneous submission of article to
  other journals permitted: No
  Exclusive manuscript rights between
  acceptance and publication: Yes
  Copyright: Held by publication.
  Reprints: Available, cost depends on
  length.
Disposition of manuscript:
  Query letter: No
  Receipt of manuscript acknowledged: Yes
  Decision to publish in: Within two
  months
  Accepted manuscript published in:
  Within one year
  Rejected manuscript returned: Yes
  Rejected manuscript criticized: If
  requested
Submit to:
  John B. Miner
  Editor
  (See address above)

ASSOCIATION & SOCIETY MANAGER [831]
825 South Barrington Avenue
Los Angeles, California 90049
(213) 826-8388

First published in 1969

SUBSCRIPTION DATA
Issues and rates: Published bi-monthly.
  Average paid circulation: 1,403; 13,203
  controlled
  Annual rate(s): $20.00; Foreign $40.00
Managing Editor: Hal Spector;
  Martin H. Waldman

EDITORIAL DESCRIPTION
  Articles deal with methods of
  professional management, plus problems
  and solutions on accommodations, travel,
  exhibit space, group insurance, etc.
Audience: Managers of professional
  membership societies who are responsible
  for all facets of executive management of
  professional association and societies.
  Manuscripts accepted in English

MANUSCRIPT INFORMATION
Manuscript requirements: Style sheet sent
  on request.
  Preferred length: 3000-5000 words
  Number of copies to be submitted: Two
Author information and reprints: Payment:
  None.
  Is simultaneous submission of article to
  other journals permitted: No
  Exclusive manuscript rights between
  acceptance and publication: Yes
  Copyright: Held by author.
  Reprints: Available at cost
Additional information: Desire camera-ready
  artwork.
Disposition of manuscript:
  Receipt of manuscript acknowledged: Yes
  Decision to publish in: Varies
  Accepted manuscript published in: Varies
  Rejected manuscript returned: Yes
  Rejected manuscript criticized: No
Submit to:
  Roberta Atchison
  Editorial Coordinator
  (See address above)

JOURNAL OF SMALL BUSINESS MANAGEMENT [832]
General Secretary, NCSBMD
University of Wisconsin Extension
Milwaukee, Wisconsin 53203
(414) 224-1818

First published in 1963

SUBSCRIPTION DATA
Issues and rates: Published quarterly.
  Average paid circulation: 300; 700
  controlled
  Annual rate(s): $7.50; Pan-Am $8.16;
  Institutions $50.00; Students $4.00;
  Members $15.00
Publisher or Sponsor: National Council for
  Small Business Management;
  West Virginia University, Bureau of
  Business Research
Managing Editor: Stanley J. Kloc

EDITORIAL DESCRIPTION
  Devoted to fostering progress in all
  phases of management development for
  small business. Each issue is structured
  around a theme of special interest.
  Features probe current trends and report
  on innovations.
Articles per average issue: 8
Audience: Business, professional, academic,
  governmental
  Manuscripts accepted in English

MANUSCRIPT INFORMATION
Subject field(s): Management assistance,
  financing, location, crime, franchising,
  failure, minorities, marketing, advertising,
  consumerism, legal problems, ecological
  and environmental problems.

Manuscript requirements: Style sheet sent on request. Chicago
   Preferred length: 2,000 words; 8 pages
   Number of copies to be submitted: 3
   Abstract: Not necessary.
Author information and reprints: Payment: Reprints only. 5 copies of issue
   Is simultaneous submission of article to other journals permitted: Permitted, but not encouraged.
   Exclusive manuscript rights between acceptance and publication: Yes
   Copyright: Held by publication.
   Reprints: Not available.
Additional information: Effective use of tables, graphs, illustrations is encouraged. Footnotes should be in complete form. A brief biographical sketch of the author should accompany the manuscript.
Disposition of manuscript:
   Query letter: Not necessary.
   Receipt of manuscript acknowledged: Yes
   Decision to publish in: 6-8 weeks
   Accepted manuscript published in: 3 months
   Rejected manuscript returned: Yes, with return postage paid by publication.
   Rejected manuscript criticized: Yes
Submit to:
   James H. Thompson;
   Stanley J. Kloc
   Editor and Managing Editor
   Bureau of Business Research
   West Virginia University
   Morgantown, West Virginia 26506
   (304) 293-6371

MANAGEMENT SCIENCE [833]
Journal of the Institute of Management Sciences
146 Westminister Street
Providence, Rhode Island 02903
(401) 274-2525

First published in 1954

SUBSCRIPTION DATA
Issues and rates: Published monthly.
   Average paid circulation: 11,000
   Annual rate(s): $32.00, Members $25.00, Students $12.00
Publisher or Sponsor: Institute of Management Sciences

EDITORIAL DESCRIPTION
Specialized journal concerned with methods and theory of managerial decision making. Two sections are published: theory series is devoted to reporting of new methodological developments, whether analytical or philosophical; the application series is concerned with the application of theory to real problems.
Articles per average issue: 12-15
Audience: Managers, educators, business
   Manuscripts accepted in English

MANUSCRIPT INFORMATION
Manuscript requirements: See latest issue for style requirements.
   Preferred length: 10 printed pages maximum
   Number of copies to be submitted: 3
   Abstract: Yes, 100-200 words
Author information and reprints: Payment: None.
   Is simultaneous submission of article to other journals permitted: No
   Exclusive manuscript rights between acceptance and publication: Yes
   Copyright: Held by publication.
   Reprints: Available at cost
Disposition of manuscript:
   Query letter: No
   Receipt of manuscript acknowledged: Yes
   Decision to publish in: 6 months
   Accepted manuscript published in: 12 months
   Rejected manuscript returned: If requested
   Rejected manuscript criticized: Yes
Submit to:
   M. K. Starr
   Editor
   Graduate School of Business
   Columbia University
   New York, New York 10027

MANAGEMENT TODAY [834]
Regent House
54-62 Regent Street
London W1A 4YJ, England
(01)439-4242

Previously entitled *The Manager*

First published in 1966

SUBSCRIPTION DATA
Issues and rates: Published monthly.
   Average paid circulation: 65,000
   Annual rate(s): £9.00

EDITORIAL DESCRIPTION
Contains articles on management theory, technique, economic forecasts, studies in key areas of business management, national policy, case histories of companies in Britain, the U.S., Europe.
Articles per average issue: 8
Audience: Managers at all levels
   Manuscripts accepted in English only

MANUSCRIPT INFORMATION
Subject field(s): Management theory and practice
Manuscript requirements: See latest issue for style requirements.
   Preferred length: 4000-5000 words or 2500 words
   Number of copies to be submitted: One
   Abstract: No
Author information and reprints: Payment: By publication to author. Varies
   Is simultaneous submission of article to other journals permitted: No
   Exclusive manuscript rights between acceptance and publication: Yes
   Copyright: Held by publication.
   Reprints: Available at cost.
Additional information: Author should send details of current appointment, etc.
Disposition of manuscript:
   Query letter: No
   Decision to publish in: 2 weeks
   Accepted manuscript published in: 1-6 months
   Rejected manuscript returned: Yes
   Rejected manuscript criticized: Sometimes
Submit to:
   Robert Heller
   Editor
   (See address above)

MANAGEMENT WORLD [835]
Administrative Management Society
Maryland Road
Willow Grove, Pennsylvania 19090
(215) 659-4300

Previously entitled *Professional Management Bulletin*

First published in 1972

SUBSCRIPTION DATA
Issues and rates: Published monthly.
   Average paid circulation: 13,500
   Annual rate(s): $12.00
Publisher or Sponsor: Administrative Management Society
Managing Editor: James N. Bruno

EDITORIAL DESCRIPTION
Offers in-depth material on the diverse disciplines of administrative management.
Articles per average issue: 5
Audience: Administrative managers, leaders in all the services, industry, education and government
   Manuscripts accepted in English

MANUSCRIPT INFORMATION
Subject field(s): Administrative services, financial management, general management, education, office management, office design and layout, micrographics, word processing
Manuscript requirements: See latest issue for style requirements.
   Preferred length: 2000 words; 8-10 pages
   Number of copies to be submitted: 2
   Abstract: Not necessary.
Author information and reprints: Payment: None.
   Is simultaneous submission of article to other journals permitted: Not permitted.
   Exclusive manuscript rights between acceptance and publication: Yes
   Copyright: Held by publication.
   Reprints: Available at cost.
Disposition of manuscript:
   Query letter: Not necessary, but advisable.
   Receipt of manuscript acknowledged: Yes
   Decision to publish in: 1 week
   Rejected manuscript returned: Yes, if return postage is supplied by author.
   Rejected manuscript criticized: Sometimes
Submit to:
   James N. Bruno
   Director of Publications
   (See address above)

MEDICAL GROUP MANAGEMENT [836]
Journal of the M.G.M.A.
4101 East Louisiana Avenue
Denver, Colorado 80222
(303) 753-1111

First published in 1954

SUBSCRIPTION DATA
Issues and rates: Published bi-monthly.
   Average paid circulation: 100; 2,900 controlled
   Annual rate(s): $12.00
Publisher or Sponsor: Medical Group Management Association
Managing Editor: Diane Spera

EDITORIAL DESCRIPTION
   Publishes material on clinic administration and group practice that includes historical, current, theoretical and practice-oriented information. Articles do not necessarily represent the position of the Association.
Articles per average issue: 6
Audience: Administrators, medical directors
   Manuscripts accepted in English

MANUSCRIPT INFORMATION
Manuscript requirements: See latest issue for style requirements.
   Preferred length: 8 to 12 typewritten, double-spaced pages
   Number of copies to be submitted: Two
Author information and reprints: Payment: None.
   Is simultaneous submission of article to other journals permitted: No
   Exclusive manuscript rights between acceptance and publication: Yes
   Copyright: Held by publication.
   Reprints: Available, cost based on length and quantity
Additional information: Illustrative material, including drawings, charts and tables are acceptable. A biographical sketch and a photograph of the author will be requested when a manuscript is accepted for publication.
Disposition of manuscript:
   Query letter: No
   Receipt of manuscript acknowledged: Yes
   Decision to publish in: 2-4 weeks
   Accepted manuscript published in: 3-5 months
   Rejected manuscript returned: Yes
   Rejected manuscript criticized: Yes
Submit to:
   Fred E. Graham, II
   Executive Editor
   (See address above)

OMEGA [837]
The International Journal of Management Science
Pergamon Press, Inc.
Fairview Park
Elmsford, New York 10523
(914) 592-7700

First published in 1973

SUBSCRIPTION DATA
Issues and rates: Published bi-monthly.
   Annual rate(s): $25.00; Institutions $75.00

EDITORIAL DESCRIPTION
   Contains articles, short papers reporting developments in management science, operational research and managerial economics, including research results describing state of the art in specific areas.
Articles per average issue: 10-15
Audience: Professional, academic
   Manuscripts accepted in English

MANUSCRIPT INFORMATION
Manuscript requirements: See latest issue for style requirements.
   Preferred length: About 5,000 words for articles
   Number of copies to be submitted: 3
   Abstract: Yes. Of about 250-500 words
Author information and reprints: Payment: Reprints only. 50 reprints
   Is simultaneous submission of article to other journals permitted: Not permitted.
   Exclusive manuscript rights between acceptance and publication: Yes
   Copyright: Held by publication.
   Reprints: Available at cost.
Disposition of manuscript:
   Query letter: Not necessary.
   Receipt of manuscript acknowledged: Yes
   Decision to publish in: 4 weeks
   Accepted manuscript published in: 5 months
   Rejected manuscript returned: Yes, if return postage is supplied by author.
   Rejected manuscript criticized: Reasons for rejections only
Submit to:
   Prof. Samuel Eilon
   Editor
   Department of Management Science
   Imperial College of Science and Technology
   London SW7 2BX, England

OPERATIONAL RESEARCH QUARTERLY [838]
Pergamon Press, Inc.
Fairview Park
Elmsford, New York 10523
(914) 592-7700

First published in 1950

SUBSCRIPTION DATA
Issues and rates: Published bi-monthly.
   Annual rate(s): $25.00; Institutions $40.00
Publisher or Sponsor: Operational Research Society, Ltd.

EDITORIAL DESCRIPTION
   Contains contributions on any matter relevant to the theory, practice, history or methodology of operational research or the affairs of the Society, practical case studies, reviews of the art.
Articles per average issue: 12-15
Audience: Practitioners in operational research, academicians
   Manuscripts accepted in English

MANUSCRIPT INFORMATION
Manuscript requirements: See latest issue for style requirements.
   Preferred length: None
   Number of copies to be submitted: 3
   Abstract: Yes. Not to exceed 150 words to precede the article.
Author information and reprints: Payment: Reprints only. 50 reprints
   Is simultaneous submission of article to other journals permitted: Not permitted.
   Exclusive manuscript rights between acceptance and publication: Yes
   Copyright: Held by publication.
   Reprints: Available at cost.
Disposition of manuscript:
   Query letter: Not necessary.
   Receipt of manuscript acknowledged: Yes
   Decision to publish in: 4 weeks
   Accepted manuscript published in: 5 months
   Rejected manuscript returned: Yes, if return postage is supplied by author.
   Rejected manuscript criticized: Reasons for rejections only
Submit to:
   Prof. K. B. Haley,
   Mrs. Carol Williams
   Editor and Editorial Assistant
   Department of Engineering Production
   University of Birmingham
   Birmingham B15 2TT, England
   (021) 472-1301, ext. 3029 or 2467

PERSONNEL [839]
The Management of People at Work
135 West 50th Street
New York, New York 10020
(212) 586-8100 ext. 260

First published in 1923

SUBSCRIPTION DATA
Issues and rates: Published bi-monthly.
   Average paid circulation: 58,000
   Annual rate(s): $15.00, Members $12.00
Publisher or Sponsor: American Management Associations, Inc.

EDITORIAL DESCRIPTION
   Contains articles on new developments in theory and application in the personnel field, behavioral sciences, industrial relations, compensation.
Audience: Managers
   Manuscripts accepted in English

MANUSCRIPT INFORMATION
Manuscript requirements: See latest issue for style requirements.
   Preferred length: 2,000-5,000 words
   Number of copies to be submitted: Two
   Abstract: Yes
Author information and reprints: Payment: None.
   Is simultaneous submission of article to other journals permitted: No

Exclusive manuscript rights between acceptance and publication: Yes
Copyright: Held by publication.
Reprints: Available
Disposition of manuscript:
  Query letter: No
  Receipt of manuscript acknowledged: Yes
  Decision to publish in: 1-2 weeks
  Accepted manuscript published in: 2-4 months
  Rejected manuscript returned: Yes
  Rejected manuscript criticized: Sometimes
Submit to:
  Ernest C. Miller
  Editor-in-chief
  (See address above)

THE PERSONNEL ADMINISTRATOR [840]
The Magazine of People
American Society for Personnel Administration
19 Church Street
Berea, Ohio 44017
(216) 234-2500

First published in 1950

SUBSCRIPTION DATA
Issues and rates: 8 times a year
  Average paid circulation: 12,250; 650 controlled
  Annual rate(s): $10.00, Foreign $12.00
Publisher or Sponsor: The American Society for Personnel Administration

EDITORIAL DESCRIPTION
Editorial content informs the Society's members and subscribers of developments, trends, innovations and opinions in the field of recruitment, training and development, motivation, employer-employee relations, labor relations, communications, safety, employee services, feeding, automation, computerization of records.
Articles per average issue: 10
Audience: Human resource managers in business, education, industry, institutions and government

MANUSCRIPT INFORMATION
Subject field(s): All areas of human resource management: personnel, labor, industrial relations
Manuscript requirements: Style sheet sent on request.
  Preferred length: 500-2,500 words
  Number of copies to be submitted: One
  Abstract: No
Author information and reprints: Payment: None.
  Is simultaneous submission of article to other journals permitted: No
  Exclusive manuscript rights between acceptance and publication: No
  Copyright: Held by publication.
  Reprints: Available, write for costs
Disposition of manuscript:
  Query letter: Helpful, not necessary
  Receipt of manuscript acknowledged: Yes
  Decision to publish in: 2 weeks
  Accepted manuscript published in: 2-4 months
  Rejected manuscript returned: Yes
  Rejected manuscript criticized: No
Submit to:
  Catherine Bower
  Editor
  (See address above)

PERSONNEL JOURNAL [841]
The Magazine of Industrial Relations and Personnel Management
150 Pico Boulevard
Santa Monica, California 90405
(213) 396-0551

SUBSCRIPTION DATA
Issues and rates: Published monthly.
  Average paid circulation: 13,500
  Annual rate(s): $16.00; Foreign $35.00
Managing Editor: Trevor Hodges

EDITORIAL DESCRIPTION
Devoted editorially to employment and recruiting, employee and labor relations, training, testing and evaluation, communications, safety, insurance, employee benefit and retirement programs, recreation, in-plant feeding, personnel records, electronic data processing, automation, etc.
Articles per average issue: 10
Audience: Personnel and industrial relations specialists
Manuscripts accepted in English

MANUSCRIPT INFORMATION
Subject field(s): All subjects pertaining to employment and recruiting, employee and labor relations, training, testing and evaluation, etc.
Manuscript requirements: Style sheet sent on request.
  Preferred length: 3500 words; five pages
  Number of copies to be submitted: Original and copy
  Abstract: No
Author information and reprints: Payment: None.
  Is simultaneous submission of article to other journals permitted: No
  Exclusive manuscript rights between acceptance and publication: Yes
  Copyright: Held by publication.
  Reprints: Available, $.50 each
Additional information: Everything, including references, should be typewritten, double-spaced, with wide margins, on standard bond paper.
Disposition of manuscript:
  Query letter: No
  Receipt of manuscript acknowledged: Yes
  Decision to publish in: 2-6 months
  Accepted manuscript published in: 6-12 months
  Rejected manuscript returned: Yes
  Rejected manuscript criticized: No
Submit to:
  Arthur C. Croft
  Editor
  (See address above)

SALES MANAGEMENT [842]
The Marketing Magazine
633 Third Avenue
New York, New York 10017
(212) 986-4800

First published in 1918

SUBSCRIPTION DATA
Issues and rates: Published semi-monthly.
  Average paid circulation: 43,168
  Annual rate(s): $18.00
Managing Editor: Robert H. Albert

EDITORIAL DESCRIPTION
Short or long articles on the sales and marketing operations of companies, concerning the evaluation of markets for products and services; the planning, packaging, advertising, promotion, distribution and servicing of them, and the management and training of the sales force.
Audience: Sales and marketing and other business executives responsible for the sale and marketing of their products and services.
Manuscripts accepted in English

MANUSCRIPT INFORMATION
Subject field(s): Marketing, Sales Management, Advertising, Packaging
Manuscript requirements: See latest issue for style requirements.
  Preferred length: 500-1,800
  Number of copies to be submitted: One
  Abstract: Not necessary.
Author information and reprints: Payment: By publication to author.
  Reprints: Available at cost.
Disposition of manuscript:
  Query letter: Not necessary, but advisable.
  Receipt of manuscript acknowledged: No
  Decision to publish in: 1 month
  Accepted manuscript published in: 2 months
  Rejected manuscript returned: Yes, with return postage paid by publication.
  Rejected manuscript criticized: No
Submit to:
  Robert H. Albert
  Editor
  (See address above)

SLOAN MANAGEMENT REVIEW [843]
Alfred P. Sloan School of Management
Massachusetts Institute of Technology
Cambridge, Massachusetts 02139
(617) 253-7170

Previously entitled *Industrial Management Review*

SUBSCRIPTION DATA
Issues and rates: Published three times per year.
  Average paid circulation: Not available.
  Annual rate(s): $12.00, Foreign $14.00

Publisher or Sponsor: Industrial Management Review Association
Managing Editor: Gay Van Ausdall

EDITORIAL DESCRIPTION

To promote the exchange of information between the academic and business worlds by informing the practicing manager of ongoing research in management. Articles are selected to provide the reader with an analytical, application-oriented approach to managerial problems.

Articles per average issue: 6
Manuscripts accepted in English

MANUSCRIPT INFORMATION

Subject field(s): Planning and control, data processing, R & D, operations research, production, organization studies and applications, industrial relations, marketing, finance, accounting and economics, general papers on the interface between society and management
Manuscript requirements: Style sheet sent on request.
  Preferred length: 3000-6000 words
  Number of copies to be submitted: Two
  Abstract: Yes
Author information and reprints: Payment: None.
  Is simultaneous submission of article to other journals permitted: No
  Exclusive manuscript rights between acceptance and publication: Yes
  Copyright: Held by publication.
  Reprints: Available, 5 free; additional available at cost
Disposition of manuscript:
  Receipt of manuscript acknowledged: Yes
  Decision to publish in: 6-8 weeks
  Accepted manuscript published in: 3-7 months
  Rejected manuscript returned: Yes, if self-addressed, stamped envelope is sent with manuscript.
  Rejected manuscript criticized: Sometimes
Submit to:
  Gay Van Ausdall
  Managing Editor
  (See address above)

TRAINING [844]

The Magazine of Manpower and Management Development
One Park Avenue
New York, New York 10016
(212) 725-3936

Previously entitled *Training in Business and Industry*

First published in 1964

SUBSCRIPTION DATA

Issues and rates: Published monthly.
  Average paid circulation: 4,000; 39,500 controlled
  Annual rate(s): $10.00, Foreign $15.00

Managing Editor: Harold Littledale

EDITORIAL DESCRIPTION

Contains articles dealing with the field of training and management development in organizations, including business, industry, finance, government and military, as well as hospitals, trade associations and universities.
Articles per average issue: 10
Audience: People who train other people
  Manuscripts accepted in English

MANUSCRIPT INFORMATION

Subject field(s): Training (frequently in-house) of employees and managers.
Manuscript requirements: See latest issue for style requirements.
  Preferred length: 1,000-3,000 words typewritten double-spaced
  Number of copies to be submitted: One
  Abstract: No
Author information and reprints: Payment: By publication to author. $.05 per word.
  Is simultaneous submission of article to other journals permitted: No
  Exclusive manuscript rights between acceptance and publication: Yes
  Copyright: Held by publication.
  Reprints: Not available.
Disposition of manuscript:
  Query letter: Helpful
  Receipt of manuscript acknowledged: No
  Decision to publish in: 1-6 weeks
  Accepted manuscript published in: 1-6 months
  Rejected manuscript returned: Yes, if return postage is supplied by author.
  Rejected manuscript criticized: No
Submit to:
  Editor
  (See address above)

TRAINING AND DEVELOPMENT JOURNAL [845]

P.O. Box 5307
Madison, Wisconsin 53705
(608) 274-3440

First published in 1947

SUBSCRIPTION DATA

Issues and rates: Published monthly.
  Average paid circulation: 12,000
  Annual rate(s): $20.00, Foreign $24.00
Publisher or Sponsor: American Society for Training and Development, Inc.
Managing Editor: Joel H. Bradtke

EDITORIAL DESCRIPTION

Contains articles on human resources, management, training and development.
Articles per average issue: 8
Audience: Professionals in field
  Manuscripts accepted in English only

MANUSCRIPT INFORMATION

Subject field(s): Personnel, transactional analysis, audio-visual training, educational programs, management, career education, hospital training, experienced based, organizational development, organizational psychology, professionalism, corporate role in training
Manuscript requirements: AP
  Preferred length: 3,000 words
  Number of copies to be submitted: Two
Author information and reprints: Payment: None. 10 copies of issue in which article is published.
  Is simultaneous submission of article to other journals permitted: Only if author notifies of publication
  Exclusive manuscript rights between acceptance and publication: Yes
  Copyright: Held by publication.
  Reprints: Available, cost varies
Additional information: All manuscripts to be typewritten, double-spaced, on one side of paper. Include biography.
Disposition of manuscript:
  Query letter: Yes
  Receipt of manuscript acknowledged: Yes
  Decision to publish in: 3-6 months
  Accepted manuscript published in: 3-6 months
  Rejected manuscript returned: Yes
  Rejected manuscript criticized: No
Submit to:
  Joel H. Bradtke
  Editor
  (See address above)

Public relations and advertising

JOURNAL OF ADVERTISING [846]

Donald R. Glover
School of Journalism, University of Kansas
Lawrence, Kansas 66045

First published in 1972

SUBSCRIPTION DATA

Issues and rates: Published quarterly.
  Average paid circulation: 700
  Annual rate(s): $10.00; Foreign $15.00; Institutions $10.00; Students $8.00
Publisher or Sponsor: The American Academy of Advertising
Managing Editor: Daniel K. Stewart

EDITORIAL DESCRIPTION

Encourages the discovery and development of valid theory and relevant facts regarding the psychological and philosophical aspects of communications and the relationship between these and other components of the advertising process.
Articles per average issue: 8
Audience: Advertisers, agencies of advertising, academicians
  Manuscripts accepted in English

MANUSCRIPT INFORMATION

Subject field(s): Philosophy of advertising, psychology, research, management, social issues, government affairs, in advertising

Manuscript requirements: See latest issue for style requirements. Style sheet sent on request.
  Preferred length: 12-14 pages
  Number of copies to be submitted: 3
  Abstract: Yes. Abstract should be of 100 to 120 words on a separate sheet of paper.
Author information and reprints: Payment: None.
  Is simultaneous submission of article to other journals permitted: Permitted, but not encouraged.
  Exclusive manuscript rights between acceptance and publication: Yes
  Copyright: Held by publication.
  Reprints: Available at cost.
Disposition of manuscript:
  Query letter: Not necessary.
  Receipt of manuscript acknowledged: Yes
  Decision to publish in: 1-3 months
  Accepted manuscript published in: 9-12 months
  Rejected manuscript returned: Yes, if return postage is supplied by author.
  Rejected manuscript criticized: Sometimes
Submit to:
  Dr. Daniel K. Stewart
  Editor-in-Chief
  Department of Marketing
  Northern Illinois University
  DeKalb, Illinois 60115
  (815) 753-1287

JOURNAL OF ADVERTISING RESEARCH [847]
3 East 54th Street
New York, New York 10022
(212) 751-5656

SUBSCRIPTION DATA
Issues and rates: Published bi-monthly.
  Average paid circulation: 2,000; 1800 controlled
  Annual rate(s): $20.00; Institutions $20.00
Publisher or Sponsor: Advertising Research Foundation, Inc.

EDITORIAL DESCRIPTION
  Publishes papers treating various facets of advertising and market research primarily for users and managers of research.
Articles per average issue: 8
Audience: Marketing and advertising researchers
  Manuscripts accepted in English only

MANUSCRIPT INFORMATION
Subject field(s): Advertising research, marketing research
Manuscript requirements: Style sheet sent on request.
  Preferred length: 10-20 pages
  Number of copies to be submitted: Three
  Abstract: No
Author information and reprints: Payment: None.
  Is simultaneous submission of article to other journals permitted: No
  Exclusive manuscript rights between acceptance and publication: Yes
  Copyright: Held by publication.
  Reprints: Available; $3.00 each
Disposition of manuscript:
  Query letter: No
  Receipt of manuscript acknowledged: Yes
  Decision to publish in: 6 months
  Accepted manuscript published in: 1-6 months
  Rejected manuscript returned: No
  Rejected manuscript criticized: Yes
Submit to:
  William S. Hale
  Managing Editor
  (See address above)

PUBLIC RELATIONS JOURNAL [848]
845 Third Avenue
New York, New York 10022
(212) 751-1940

SUBSCRIPTION DATA
Issues and rates: Published monthly.
  Average paid circulation: 10,500
  Annual rate(s): $9.50, Members $7.50, Foreign $10.50
Publisher or Sponsor: Public Relations Society of America, Inc.

EDITORIAL DESCRIPTION
  Contains articles pertaining to public relations.
Articles per average issue: 7
Audience: Public relations practitioners
  Manuscripts accepted in English

MANUSCRIPT INFORMATION
Subject field(s): Public relations
Manuscript requirements: See latest issue for style requirements.
  Preferred length: 1000-1500 words; 11 pages
  Number of copies to be submitted: One
  Abstract: No
Author information and reprints: Payment: None.
  Is simultaneous submission of article to other journals permitted: No
  Exclusive manuscript rights between acceptance and publication: Yes
  Copyright: Held by publication.
  Reprints: Available, cost depends on quantity
Disposition of manuscript:
  Query letter: No
  Receipt of manuscript acknowledged: Yes
  Decision to publish in: 3 weeks
  Accepted manuscript published in: Varies
  Rejected manuscript returned: Yes
  Rejected manuscript criticized: No
Submit to:
  Joyce M. Campbell
  Executive Editor
  (See address above)

Communications

Communications (general)

AB BOOKMAN'S WEEKLY [849]
For the Specialist Book World
P.O. Box 1100
Newark, New Jersey 07101
(201) 624-4454

First published in 1948

SUBSCRIPTION DATA
Issues and rates: Published weekly.
  Average paid circulation: 7,100
  Annual rate(s): $20.00

EDITORIAL DESCRIPTION
  Contains features and news on the book trade, out-of-print, rare books, book reviews, bibliography, history of the book trade and publishing, printing, library notes, news about bookmen and trade.
Articles per average issue: 1-2
Audience: Booksellers, librarians
  Manuscripts accepted in English

MANUSCRIPT INFORMATION
Subject field(s): Bibliography, rare books, trade features, out-of-print market, biographical about bookmen
Manuscript requirements: See latest issue for style requirements.
  Preferred length: 2,000-3,000 words
  Number of copies to be submitted: 1
  Abstract: No
Author information and reprints: Payment: None.
  Is simultaneous submission of article to other journals permitted: No
  Exclusive manuscript rights between acceptance and publication: Yes
  Copyright: Held by publication.
  Reprints: Not available.
Disposition of manuscript:
  Receipt of manuscript acknowledged: No
  Decision to publish in: 1 month
  Accepted manuscript published in: Varies
  Rejected manuscript returned: Yes, if self-addressed, stamped envelope is sent with manuscript.
  Rejected manuscript criticized: No
Submit to:
  Jacob L. Chernofsky
  Editor
  (See address above)

ABCA BULLETIN [850]
317B David Kinley Hall
University of Illinois
Urbana, Illinois 61801
(217) 333-2960

First published in 1936

SUBSCRIPTION DATA
Issues and rates: Irregular
  Average paid circulation: 1,100
  Annual rate(s): Free to subscribers of *The Journal of Business Communication*
Publisher or Sponsor: American Business Communication Association
Managing Editor: George H. Douglas

EDITORIAL DESCRIPTION
  Contains practical materials primarily for teachers of business communication, but also some how-to information for businessmen interested in communication.
Audience: Teachers, businessmen
  Manuscripts accepted in English

MANUSCRIPT INFORMATION
Subject field(s): Business communication, technical and professional writing, teaching in the above areas
Manuscript requirements: Style sheet sent on request.
  Preferred length: 1,500 to 6,000 words
  Number of copies to be submitted: Two
  Abstract: No
Author information and reprints: Payment: None.
  Is simultaneous submission of article to other journals permitted: No
  Exclusive manuscript rights between acceptance and publication: None
  Reprints: Not available.
Disposition of manuscript:
  Query letter: No
  Receipt of manuscript acknowledged: Yes
  Decision to publish in: 4 weeks
  Accepted manuscript published in: 1 year
  Rejected manuscript returned: Yes, if self-addressed, stamped envelope is sent with manuscript.
  Rejected manuscript criticized: Yes
Submit to:
  George H. Douglas
  Editor
  (See address above)

COMMUNICATION [851]
Gordon and Breach
One Park Avenue
New York, New York 10016

First published in 1974

SUBSCRIPTION DATA
Issues and rates: Published semi-annually.

EDITORIAL DESCRIPTION
  Devoted to the exploration of the role of communication in human affairs.
Articles per average issue: 6-8
Audience: Those interested in people, human affairs, politics, institutions, society, etc.
  Manuscripts accepted in English only

MANUSCRIPT INFORMATION
Manuscript requirements: See latest issue for style requirements.
  Preferred length: 10-20 pages
  Number of copies to be submitted: 2
  Abstract: Not necessary.
Author information and reprints: Payment: Reprints only. 50
  Is simultaneous submission of article to other journals permitted: Not permitted.
  Exclusive manuscript rights between acceptance and publication: Yes
  Copyright: Held by publication.
  Reprints: Available at cost.
Additional information: Each issue is devoted to a special topic. Consult current issue for list of Issues-in-Progress
Disposition of manuscript:
  Query letter: Not necessary, but advisable.
  Receipt of manuscript acknowledged: Yes
  Decision to publish in: 2-4 weeks
  Accepted manuscript published in: 6 months to 1 year
  Rejected manuscript returned: Yes, with return postage paid by publication.
  Rejected manuscript criticized: Sometimes
Submit to:
  Editor
  Department of Communication Studies
  Simon Fraser University
  Burnaby 2, British Columbia, Canada
  (604) 922-4818

THE JOURNAL OF BUSINESS COMMUNICATION [852]
317B David Kinley Hall
University of Illinois
Urbana, Illinois 61801
(217) 333-2960

First published in 1963

SUBSCRIPTION DATA
Issues and rates: Published quarterly.
  Average paid circulation: 1,000
  Annual rate(s): $15.00
Publisher or Sponsor: American Business Communication Association

EDITORIAL DESCRIPTION
  Articles pertaining to research in the fields of business and technical writing and communication.
Articles per average issue: 5
  Manuscripts accepted in English

MANUSCRIPT INFORMATION
Subject field(s): Business communication, teaching of business communications, business writing, technical writing and communications
Manuscript requirements: MLA or Chicago
  Preferred length: 3,000 words
  Number of copies to be submitted: Two
  Abstract: Yes
Author information and reprints: Payment: None.
  Is simultaneous submission of article to other journals permitted: No
  Exclusive manuscript rights between acceptance and publication: Yes
  Copyright: Held by publication.
  Reprints: Available

Disposition of manuscript:
  Query letter: No
  Receipt of manuscript acknowledged: Yes
  Decision to publish in: 6 weeks
  Accepted manuscript published in: 8 months
  Rejected manuscript returned: Yes, if return postage is supplied by author.
  Rejected manuscript criticized: Yes
Submit to:
  George H. Douglas
  Editor
  (See address above)

JOURNAL OF COMMUNICATION [853]

Post Office Box 13358
Philadelphia, Pennsylvania 19101
(212) 594-6685

SUBSCRIPTION DATA
Issues and rates: Published quarterly.
  Average paid circulation: 5,000
  Annual rate(s): $15.00
Publisher or Sponsor: International Communication Association and Annenberg School of Communications

EDITORIAL DESCRIPTION
  Contains scholarly articles on information systems, interpersonal communication, mass communication, organizational communication, and intercultural communication.
Articles per average issue: 10
Audience: Academic, professional
  Manuscripts accepted in English, French, Spanish

MANUSCRIPT INFORMATION
Manuscript requirements: Style sheet sent on request.
  Preferred length: Ten pages
  Number of copies to be submitted: Three
  Abstract: No
Author information and reprints: Payment: None.
  Is simultaneous submission of article to other journals permitted: Yes
  Exclusive manuscript rights between acceptance and publication: Yes
  Copyright: Held by publication.
  Reprints: Available from printer directly at time of publication.
Disposition of manuscript:
  Query letter: No
  Receipt of manuscript acknowledged: Yes
  Decision to publish in: Varies
  Accepted manuscript published in: Varies
  Rejected manuscript returned: Yes
  Rejected manuscript criticized: Yes
Submit to:
  George Gerbner
  Editor
  (See address above)

JOURNAL OF PSYCHOLINGUISTIC RESEARCH [854]

Plenum Publishing Corporation
227 West 17th Street
New York, New York 10011
(212) 255-0713

First published in 1971

SUBSCRIPTION DATA
Issues and rates: Published quarterly.
  Average paid circulation: Not available.
  Annual rate(s): Institutions $28.00, Foreign institutions $29.80, Individuals $18.00, Foreign individuals $19.80

EDITORIAL DESCRIPTION
  Contains theoretical and experimental papers, critical surveys, book reviews covering a broad range of approaches to the study of the communicative process. Seeks to publish papers from the several disciplines engaged in psycholinguistic research; to provide a single medium for communication among linguists, psychologists, biologists, sociologists.
Articles per average issue: 7
Audience: Professional, academic
  Manuscripts accepted in English

MANUSCRIPT INFORMATION
Subject field(s): Social and anthropological bases of communications, development of speech and languages, semantics, biological foundations, psychopathological aspects, educational psycholinguistics
Manuscript requirements: APA
  Preferred length: None
  Number of copies to be submitted: Original and 3 copies
  Abstract: Yes
Author information and reprints: Payment: None.
  Copyright: Held by publication.
  Reprints: Available, cost varies
Disposition of manuscript:
  Query letter: No
  Receipt of manuscript acknowledged: Yes
  Decision to publish in: 6-8 weeks
  Accepted manuscript published in: 6-8 months
  Rejected manuscript returned: Yes
  Rejected manuscript criticized: If requested
Submit to:
  R. W. Rieber
  Editor
  The John Jay College
  City University of New York
  315 Park Avenue South
  New York, New York 10010

JOURNAL OF TECHNICAL WRITING AND COMMUNICATION [855]

Baywood Publishing Co.
43 Central Drive
Farmingdale, New York 11735
(516) 293-7130

First published in 1971

SUBSCRIPTION DATA
Issues and rates: Published quarterly.
  Annual rate(s): $33.00
Managing Editor: Jay R. Gould

EDITORIAL DESCRIPTION
  Devoted to technical and scientific communication and to the views and developments of communicators.
Articles per average issue: 8
Audience: Technical writers and communicators, scientists, teachers, industrial managers, students
  Manuscripts accepted in English

MANUSCRIPT INFORMATION
Subject field(s): Development of technical and scientific communication, news, teaching methods, graphics, oral presentations, style guides, research, book reviews, announcements
Manuscript requirements: See latest issue for style requirements.
  Preferred length: 5,000 words maximum
  Number of copies to be submitted: 2
  Abstract: Yes. An abstract of not more than 100 words, with headings
Author information and reprints: Payment: Reprints only.
  Is simultaneous submission of article to other journals permitted: Not permitted.
  Exclusive manuscript rights between acceptance and publication: Yes
  Copyright: Held by publication.
Disposition of manuscript:
  Query letter: Not necessary.
  Receipt of manuscript acknowledged: Yes
  Decision to publish in: 2 weeks
  Accepted manuscript published in: 2 issues
  Rejected manuscript returned: Yes, if return postage is supplied by author.
  Rejected manuscript criticized: Reasons for rejections only
Submit to:
  Jay R. Gould
  Editor
  Department of Language and Literature
  Rensselaer Polytechnic Institute
  Troy, New York 12181
  (517) 270-6469

MARGINS [856]

A Review of Little Magazines & Small Press Books
2912 North Hackett
Milwaukee, Wisconsin 53211

SUBSCRIPTION DATA
Issues and rates: Published bi-monthly.
  Average paid circulation: 500
  Annual rate(s): $6.00 for all
Managing Editor: Tom Montag

EDITORIAL DESCRIPTION
  A survey of alternative/small press publishing in America and elsewhere; features significant books and magazines; looks at presses and various publishing ventures and concerns relevant to small publishing; intent is to report on, evaluate, criticize, create alternatives in

Communications (general)

contemporary writing, publishing and reading.
Articles per average issue: Varies
Audience: Institutions, libraries and individuals interested in the condition of alternative publishing today
Manuscripts accepted in English

MANUSCRIPT INFORMATION
Subject field(s): Reviews of small press books and little magazines; interviews with poets and publishers; overviews of publishing ventures of small presses and little magazines; reports on publishing activities of particular literary communities
Manuscript requirements: See latest issue for style requirements.
 Preferred length: No preference
 Number of copies to be submitted: 1
 Abstract: Not necessary.
Author information and reprints: Payment: Reprints only. 3-5
 Is simultaneous submission of article to other journals permitted: Permitted.
 Exclusive manuscript rights between acceptance and publication: No
 Copyright: Held by publication, but released at author's request
 Reprints: Not available.
Additional information: Manuscripts should be typewritten, double-spaced, clean copy with no carbons
Disposition of manuscript:
 Query letter:
 Receipt of manuscript acknowledged: No
 Decision to publish in: 2 weeks to 2 months
 Accepted manuscript published in: 2-4 months
 Rejected manuscript returned: Yes, if return postage is supplied by author.
 Rejected manuscript criticized: No
Submit to:
 Tom Montag
 Editor
 (See address above)

NEWSLETTER ON INTELLECTUAL FREEDOM [857]
50 East Huron Street
Chicago, Illinois 60611
(312) 944-6780

First published in 1952

SUBSCRIPTION DATA
Issues and rates: Published bi-monthly.
 Average paid circulation: 3,000
 Annual rate(s): $6.00
Publisher or Sponsor: American Library Association, Intellectual Freedom Committee

EDITORIAL DESCRIPTION
 Publishes articles on censorship, the First Amendment, and related topics. Expresses editorial opposition to abridgements of freedom of expression.
Articles per average issue: 1-2
Audience: Library Personnel
 Manuscripts accepted in English

MANUSCRIPT INFORMATION
Subject field(s): Censorship, First Amendment, obscenity law, rights of minors, prisoners' right to read
Manuscript requirements: Chicago
 Preferred length: 15 pages maximum
 Number of copies to be submitted: Two
 Abstract: No
Author information and reprints: Payment: None.
 Is simultaneous submission of article to other journals permitted: No
 Exclusive manuscript rights between acceptance and publication: Yes
 Copyright: Not copyrighted
 Reprints: Available, 10 free
Disposition of manuscript:
 Query letter: No
 Receipt of manuscript acknowledged: Yes
 Decision to publish in: 1 month
 Accepted manuscript published in: 3-6 months
 Rejected manuscript returned: Yes, if self-addressed, stamped envelope is sent with manuscript.
 Rejected manuscript criticized: Sometimes
Submit to:
 Judith F. Krug
 Editor
 (See address above)

PUBLISHERS WEEKLY [858]
1180 Avenue of the Americas
New York, New York 10036
(212) 764-5100

First published in 1872

SUBSCRIPTION DATA
Issues and rates: Published weekly.
 Average paid circulation: 30,000; 32,000 controlled
 Annual rate(s): $20.00; Pan-Am $23.00; Foreign $25.00; Individuals $20.00
Managing Editor: John F. Baker

EDITORIAL DESCRIPTION
 The trade journal of the American industry, providing ideas and information for all who handle books professionally. Articles and news items cover new publishing firms and book outlets, legislation and legal action dealing with censorship, copyright, plagiarism, etc., reports of conventions and conferences, literary awards, trends and statistics, major advertising and promotion, best seller lists, interviews with authors and industry figures, personnel changes, obituaries, advance reviews of fiction, nonfiction, children's books and paperbacks, seasonal announcement issues, monthly section on book design and production.
Articles per average issue: 1-2
Audience: Publishers, booksellers, librarians, agents, book manufacturers, authors, educators, lawyers dealing with literary property.
 Manuscripts accepted in English

MANUSCRIPT INFORMATION
Subject field(s): Writing, editing, publishing, marketing, manufacturing, promotion, distribution of books in the United States and Canada, and to some extent in other parts of the world, e.g., Western Europe. Emphasis on advance news, forthcoming books, future projections of sales trends, etc.
Manuscript requirements: See latest issue for style requirements.
 Number of copies to be submitted: Two
 Abstract: Not necessary.
Author information and reprints: Payment: By publication to author. 10 cents per word. $50.00 per page.
 Is simultaneous submission of article to other journals permitted: Not permitted.
 Exclusive manuscript rights between acceptance and publication: Yes
 Copyright: First serial rights only
 Reprints: Not available.
Additional information: Most material is staff written.
Disposition of manuscript:
 Query letter: Not necessary, but advisable.
 Receipt of manuscript acknowledged: No
 Rejected manuscript returned: Yes, if return postage is supplied by author.
 Rejected manuscript criticized: Sometimes
Submit to:
 Arnold W. Ehrlich;
 John F. Baker
 Editor-in-Chief and Managing Editor respectively
 (See address above)

QUILL & QUIRE [859]
59 Front Street East
Toronto, Ontario M5E 1B3, Canada
(416) 364-3333

First published in 1935

SUBSCRIPTION DATA
Issues and rates: Published monthly.
 Average paid circulation: 12,000
 Annual rate(s): $12.00

EDITORIAL DESCRIPTION
 Contains book reviews, author interviews, articles and news on book publishing, book selling, libraries, education.
 Manuscripts accepted in English

MANUSCRIPT INFORMATION
Subject field(s): Publishing, bookselling or librarianship in Canada.
Manuscript requirements: See latest issue for style requirements.
 Preferred length: 1,000-2,000 words
 Number of copies to be submitted: 1
 Abstract: Not necessary.
Author information and reprints: Payment: By publication to author. $65-$100.00 per article.
 Is simultaneous submission of article to other journals permitted: Permitted, but not encouraged.
 Exclusive manuscript rights between acceptance and publication: Yes

Copyright: Held by publication.
Reprints: Available at no cost.
Disposition of manuscript:
  Query letter: Necessary.
  Receipt of manuscript acknowledged: Yes
  Decision to publish in: 2 weeks
  Accepted manuscript published in: 4 weeks
  Rejected manuscript returned: Yes, with return postage paid by publication.
  Rejected manuscript criticized: Reasons for rejections only
Submit to:
  Fiona Mee
  Editor
  (See address above)

SCHOLARLY PUBLISHING [860]
A Journal for Authors and Publishers
University of Toronto Press
Front Campus
Toronto, Ontario M5S 1A6, Canada
(416) 928-2238

SUBSCRIPTION DATA
Issues and rates: Published quarterly.
  Average paid circulation: 1200
  Annual rate(s): $10.00
Managing Editor: Eleanor Harman

EDITORIAL DESCRIPTION
Contains articles devoted to various aspects of the publishing of serious non-fiction, from the viewpoint of the writer and reader, the librarian, and publishing personnel in all areas. International in interest and scope. Also carries book reviews in this field, letters, and news reports.
Articles per average issue: 12
Audience: Authors, publishers, librarians
  Manuscripts accepted in English

MANUSCRIPT INFORMATION
Manuscript requirements: Chicago
  Preferred length: 1500 to 5000 words
  Number of copies to be submitted: One
  Abstract: No
Author information and reprints: Payment: By publication to author. Varies depending on length, subject and treatment
  Is simultaneous submission of article to other journals permitted: Under exceptional circumstances, and if reported by author.
  Exclusive manuscript rights between acceptance and publication: Yes
  Copyright: Held by publication.
  Reprints: Available, 100 free
Disposition of manuscript:
  Query letter: Desirable
  Receipt of manuscript acknowledged: Yes
  Decision to publish in: 3 weeks
  Accepted manuscript published in: 3-6 months
  Rejected manuscript returned: Yes
  Rejected manuscript criticized: Yes
Submit to:
  Eleanor Harman
  Editor
  (See address above)

SIPAPU [861]
Route 1, Box 216
Winters, California 95694
(916) 662-3364

First published in 1970

SUBSCRIPTION DATA
  Annual rate(s): $2.00 for all

EDITORIAL DESCRIPTION
A newsletter for librarians and others interested in Third World Studies, the counter-culture, and the alternative press.
Articles per average issue: 1
Audience: Librarians
  Manuscripts accepted in English

MANUSCRIPT INFORMATION
Subject field(s): Reports on alternative presses and their editors; interviews; American and contemporary emphasis
  Preferred length: 2,000 words
  Number of copies to be submitted: 1
Author information and reprints: Payment: By publication to author. $0.02 per word.
Disposition of manuscript:
  Decision to publish in: 3 weeks
  Accepted manuscript published in: 6 months
Submit to:
  General articles:
  Noel R. Peattie

  Material on Feminism:
  Dora Biblarz
  Co-Editors and Publishers
  (See address above)

SMALL PRESS REVIEW [862]
Box 1056
Paradise, California 95969
(916) 877-6110

First published in 1967

SUBSCRIPTION DATA
Issues and rates: Published monthly.
  Average paid circulation: 2,000
  Annual rate(s): $10.00, Foreign $15.00
Managing Editor: Len Fulton

EDITORIAL DESCRIPTION
Contains news, reviews, essays on little magazine-small press scene worldwide.

MANUSCRIPT INFORMATION
Manuscript requirements: See latest issue for style requirements.
  Preferred length: 100-300 words
  Number of copies to be submitted: One
  Abstract: No
Author information and reprints: Payment: By publication to author. By arrangement.
  Is simultaneous submission of article to other journals permitted: Yes
  Exclusive manuscript rights between acceptance and publication: Yes
  Copyright: Held jointly by author and publication
  Reprints: Not available.

Disposition of manuscript:
  Receipt of manuscript acknowledged: Yes
  Decision to publish in: 1 week
  Accepted manuscript published in: 1 month
  Rejected manuscript returned: Yes, if self-addressed, stamped envelope is sent with manuscript.
  Rejected manuscript criticized: No
Submit to:
  Len Fulton
  Publisher
  (See address above)

TECHNICAL COMMUNICATION [863]
Society for Technical Communication
1010 Vermont Avenue, N.W.
Washington, D.C. 20005
(202) 737-0035

Previously entitled *STWP Review*

First published in 1953

SUBSCRIPTION DATA
Issues and rates: Published quarterly.
  Average paid circulation: 4000
  Annual rate(s): $15.00
Publisher or Sponsor: Society for Technical Communication

EDITORIAL DESCRIPTION
Contains articles on the theory and practice of technical communications in all media.
Articles per average issue: 5
Audience: Technical writers, editors, managers, educators
  Manuscripts accepted in English

MANUSCRIPT INFORMATION
Subject field(s): Technical writing, technical editing, technical publishing, technical illustrating, management communications
Manuscript requirements: No specific style guide.
  Preferred length: 4000-5000 words
  Number of copies to be submitted: Three
  Abstract: Yes
Author information and reprints: Payment: None.
  Is simultaneous submission of article to other journals permitted: Yes
  Exclusive manuscript rights between acceptance and publication: Yes
  Copyright: Held by publication.
  Reprints: Available at cost.
Additional information: Double-spaced, generous margins; original art work desired.
Disposition of manuscript:
  Query letter: No
  Receipt of manuscript acknowledged: Yes
  Decision to publish in: 3-6 months
  Accepted manuscript published in: 3 months
  Rejected manuscript returned: Yes, if self-addressed, stamped envelope is sent with manuscript.
  Rejected manuscript criticized: Yes
Submit to:
  A. Stanley Higgins

Editor
Westinghouse Research Laboratories
Pittsburgh, Pennsylvania 15235
(412) 256-7580

TODAY'S SPEECH [864]
Journal of the Eastern Communication Association
Department of Communication Studies
University of Massachusetts
Amherst, Massachusetts 01002
(413) 545-0140

First published in 1952

SUBSCRIPTION DATA
Issues and rates: Published quarterly.
   Average paid circulation: 3,000
Publisher or Sponsor: Eastern Communication Association
Managing Editor: Hermann G. Stelzner

EDITORIAL DESCRIPTION
   Carries articles dealing with theoretical and applied studies of communication: public discourse, media, theatre, etc.
Articles per average issue: 6-8
Audience: Teachers of communication
   Manuscripts accepted in English only

MANUSCRIPT INFORMATION
Subject field(s): Rhetoric, experimental studies of communication, speech communication, radio and television, oral interpretation, theatre
Manuscript requirements: MLA
   Preferred length: 3,000 to 4,000 words
   Number of copies to be submitted: Two
   Abstract: Yes, of about 100 words
Author information and reprints: Payment: None.
   Is simultaneous submission of article to other journals permitted: Yes
   Exclusive manuscript rights between acceptance and publication: No
   Copyright: Held by publication.
   Reprints: Available, $17.50 for 50 reprints
Disposition of manuscript:
   Query letter: No
   Receipt of manuscript acknowledged: Yes
   Decision to publish in: 4-6 weeks
   Accepted manuscript published in: 6 months
   Rejected manuscript returned: Yes
   Rejected manuscript criticized: Yes
Submit to:
   Hermann G. Stelzner
   Editor
   (See address above)

THE WRITER [865]
The Pioneer Magazine for Literary Workers
8 Arlington Street
Boston, Massachusetts 02116
(617) 536-7420

First published in 1887

SUBSCRIPTION DATA
Issues and rates: Published monthly.
   Average paid circulation: 45,000
   Annual rate(s): $9.00; Pan-Am $10.00; Foreign $10.00
Managing Editor: A. S. Burack

EDITORIAL DESCRIPTION
   Articles of instruction by leading authors, editors and teachers, plus up-to-date and accurate markets for manuscript sales.
Articles per average issue: 6
Audience: Free-lance writers, all fields, including short stories, novels, nonfiction, poetry, drama.
   Manuscripts accepted in English

MANUSCRIPT INFORMATION
Subject field(s): Manuscripts accepted from writers, editors, and teachers, on free-lance writing only.
Manuscript requirements: See latest issue for style requirements.
   Preferred length: 2,000 words
   Number of copies to be submitted: One
   Abstract: Not necessary.
Author information and reprints: Payment: By publication to author.
   Is simultaneous submission of article to other journals permitted: Not permitted.
   Exclusive manuscript rights between acceptance and publication: Yes
   Copyright: Held by publication. Will transfer after publication by special request.
   Reprints: Not available.
Disposition of manuscript:
   Query letter: Not necessary, but advisable.
   Receipt of manuscript acknowledged: Yes
   Decision to publish in: 30 Days
   Accepted manuscript published in: Varies
   Rejected manuscript returned: Yes, if return postage is supplied by author.
   Rejected manuscript criticized: No
Submit to:
   A. S. Burack
   Editor
   (See address above)

SPECIAL STIPULATIONS
   With few exceptions, articles are written by published writers, editors or literary agents.

Audio-visual

AUDIOVISUAL INSTRUCTION [866]
1201 Sixteenth Street N.W.
Washington, D.C. 20036
(202) 833-4180

First published in 1956

SUBSCRIPTION DATA
Issues and rates: Published monthly.
   Average paid circulation: 20,000
   Annual rate(s): $18.00, Foreign $20.00
Publisher or Sponsor: Association for Educational Communications and Technology
Managing Editor: Carol Bruce

EDITORIAL DESCRIPTION
   Contains articles pertaining to educational technology and the use of media for education and training. Emphasizes use of media and technology for the improvement of instruction.
Articles per average issue: 6-8
Audience: Professionals in educational technology, educators, librarians

MANUSCRIPT INFORMATION
Subject field(s): Educational technology, educational media, educational innovation (new theme each issue)
Manuscript requirements: Style sheet sent on request.
   Preferred length: 1,000-1,200 words
   Number of copies to be submitted: Two
   Abstract: Yes
Author information and reprints: Payment: None.
   Is simultaneous submission of article to other journals permitted: Permitted, but not encouraged.
   Exclusive manuscript rights between acceptance and publication: Yes
   Copyright: Held by publication.
   Reprints: Not available.
Additional information: List of themes for each issue and style requirements are published in the June/July issue each year. Deadlines are four months before publication of issue.
Disposition of manuscript:
   Receipt of manuscript acknowledged: Yes
   Decision to publish in: 4-6 weeks
   Accepted manuscript published in: 2-3 months minimum
   Rejected manuscript returned: Yes
   Rejected manuscript criticized: No
Submit to:
   H. B. Hitchens
   Editor
   (See address above)

SPECIAL STIPULATIONS
   Galleys not sent to authors. Manuscripts are sometimes held for future issues if author permits and are sometimes referred to other AECT publications, author permitting. Previously copyrighted or published material not generally used.

AV COMMUNICATION REVIEW [867]
1201 16th Street NW
Washington, D.C. 20036
(202) 833-4180

Previously entitled *Audio-Visual Communication Review*

First published in 1953

SUBSCRIPTION DATA
Issues and rates: Published quarterly.
   Average paid circulation: 8000
   Annual rate(s): $19.50, Foreign $20.50

Publisher or Sponsor: Association for Educational Communications and Technology, Inc.
Managing Editor: Vita Pariente

EDITORIAL DESCRIPTION

Contains articles on theory, development, research, comment related to technological processes in education and learning. Book reviews discuss a wider range of topics: education, technology, communications, film art, educational systems, educational evaluation.
Articles per average issue: 5
Audience: Researchers and Educators
Manuscripts accepted in English

MANUSCRIPT INFORMATION

Subject field(s): Instructional technology, learning, communication, information theory, systems, perception, audiovisual research
Manuscript requirements: APA (for reference style); other information sent on request
Preferred length: 8-30 pages
Number of copies to be submitted: Three
Abstract: Yes, of 2-5 sentences
Author information and reprints: Payment: None.
Is simultaneous submission of article to other journals permitted: No
Exclusive manuscript rights between acceptance and publication: Yes
Copyright: Held by publication.
Reprints: Not available.
Additional information: Author receives three copies of issue containing article.
Disposition of manuscript:
Receipt of manuscript acknowledged: Yes
Decision to publish in: 2-6 months
Accepted manuscript published in: 6-12 months
Rejected manuscript returned: Yes
Rejected manuscript criticized: No
Submit to:
Robert Heinich
Editor
Audio-Visual Center
Indiana University
Bloomington, Indiana 47401
(812) 337-3875

SPECIAL STIPULATIONS

Author must provide an English translation of articles written in other languages; recommend submission of abstract of article (in English) first.

COMMUNICATION ARTS INTERNATIONAL [868]
P. O. Box 2801
Washington, D. C. 20013
(202) 638-5568

Previously entitled *Film & Sound Journal*

First published in 1932

SUBSCRIPTION DATA

Issues and rates: Published quarterly.
Average paid circulation: 2,000; 10,000 controlled
Annual rate(s): $6.00; Foreign $8.00; Members $25.00
Publisher or Sponsor: International Association of Independent Producers
Managing Editor: Dr. Edward J. Rothkirch

EDITORIAL DESCRIPTION

Gives complete coverage of all aspects of the Audio-Visual field
Articles per average issue: 8
Audience: Producers and distributors, and users of A-V material
Manuscripts accepted in English

MANUSCRIPT INFORMATION

Manuscript requirements: No specific style guide.
Preferred length: 400-800 words
Number of copies to be submitted: 1
Abstract: Not necessary.
Author information and reprints: Payment: By publication to author. $25-$50.00 per article.
Is simultaneous submission of article to other journals permitted: Permitted, but not encouraged.
Exclusive manuscript rights between acceptance and publication: No
Copyright: First serial rights only
Reprints: Available at cost.
Disposition of manuscript:
Query letter: Not necessary, but advisable.
Receipt of manuscript acknowledged: No
Decision to publish in: 30 days
Accepted manuscript published in: 90 days
Rejected manuscript returned: Yes, if return postage is supplied by author.
Rejected manuscript criticized: Sometimes
Submit to:
Duarte J. Martinau
Associate Editor
(See address above)

DB: THE SOUND ENGINEERING MAGAZINE [869]
1120 Old Country Road
Plainview, New York 11803
(516) 433-6530

First published in 1967

SUBSCRIPTION DATA

Issues and rates: Published monthly.
Average paid circulation: 6300; 14,000 controlled
Annual rate(s): $6.00, Foreign $12.00
Managing Editor: Alex Porianda

EDITORIAL DESCRIPTION

Provides technical information for the professional audio engineer and technician in recording, broadcasting, film-sound, audio visual and sound reinforcement fields. Contains articles on applications, product design, new techniques, typical installations, educational and background information.
Articles per average issue: 4
Audience: Sound engineers and technicians
Manuscripts accepted in English

MANUSCRIPT INFORMATION

Subject field(s): Recording, broadcast audio, film sound, sound reinforcement, articles of audio interest.
Manuscript requirements: No specific style guide.
Preferred length: 10 pages
Number of copies to be submitted: One
Abstract: No
Author information and reprints: Payment: By publication to author. $25.00 per page.
Is simultaneous submission of article to other journals permitted: Yes
Exclusive manuscript rights between acceptance and publication: No
Copyright: Held by publication.
Reprints: Available
Disposition of manuscript:
Query letter: No
Receipt of manuscript acknowledged: Yes
Decision to publish in: 2 weeks
Accepted manuscript published in: 3 months
Rejected manuscript returned: No
Rejected manuscript criticized: No
Submit to:
Robert Bach
Publisher
(See address above)
(516) 433-6530

Film

AUDIENCE [870]
The Wilson Associates
Box 5804, Grand Central Station
New York, New York 10017
(201) 869-7395

First published in 1968

SUBSCRIPTION DATA

Issues and rates: Published monthly.
Average paid circulation: 2,800; 75 controlled
Annual rate(s): $4.80 for all
Managing Editor: Robert A. Wilson, Jr.

EDITORIAL DESCRIPTION

Cinema as a reflection and extension of personal experience; the popular arts as mirrors of the viewer's psyche; film criticism as conversation between friends rather than announcements from an ivory tower.
Articles per average issue: 8
Audience: Cinema enthusiasts who do not necessarily see everything that is released.
Manuscripts accepted in English

MANUSCRIPT INFORMATION

Subject field(s): Cinema current or past; poetry and short stories; theatre, television, books related to the popular arts.
Manuscript requirements: See latest issue for style requirements.
Preferred length: 800 to 1,000 words; 2-3 pages

Number of copies to be submitted: 1
Abstract: Not necessary.
Author information and reprints: Payment: Reprints only. Subject to availability
Is simultaneous submission of article to other journals permitted: Not permitted.
Exclusive manuscript rights between acceptance and publication: Yes
Copyright: Reverts to author upon publication
Additional information: A relaxed conversational style; emotional commitment to the arts, but without pomposity.
Disposition of manuscript:
Query letter: Not necessary.
Receipt of manuscript acknowledged: Yes
Decision to publish in: 1 week
Accepted manuscript published in: 2 months
Rejected manuscript returned: Yes, with return postage paid by publication.
Rejected manuscript criticized: Yes
Submit to:
Robert A. Wilson, Jr.
Editor
(See address above)

CINEMA JOURNAL [871]

17 West College Street
Iowa City, Iowa 52242

Previously entitled *Journal of the Society of Cinematologists*

First published in 1966

SUBSCRIPTION DATA

Issues and rates: Published semi-annually.
Annual rate(s): $4.00; Foreign $4.00
Publisher or Sponsor: Society for Cinema Studies

EDITORIAL DESCRIPTION

Publishes articles for scholars and others with a highly specialized interest in film, primarily in film history, theory, criticism
Articles per average issue: 5
Audience: Academic, professional
Manuscripts accepted in English

MANUSCRIPT INFORMATION

Subject field(s): Film history, theory, criticism, American and foreign, ficitional experimental, documentary, silent and sound
Manuscript requirements: No specific style guide.
Preferred length: 5,000 words
Number of copies to be submitted: 2
Abstract: Not necessary.
Author information and reprints: Payment: Reprints only. 6 copies of magazine
Is simultaneous submission of article to other journals permitted: Permitted, if kept informed
Exclusive manuscript rights between acceptance and publication: Yes
Copyright: Held by publication.
Permissions policy is liberal for authors using material in his own book.
Reprints: Not available.

Additional information: No reviews of recent film releases or special studies of individual films of the past.
Disposition of manuscript:
Query letter: Not necessary, but advisable.
Receipt of manuscript acknowledged: Yes
Decision to publish in: 2 months
Accepted manuscript published in: 6 months
Rejected manuscript returned: Yes, if return postage is supplied by author.
Rejected manuscript criticized: Sometimes
Submit to:
Richard Dyer MacCann
Editor
Department of Broadcasting and Film
University of Iowa
Iowa City, Iowa 52242
(319) 353-4404

FILM CULTURE [872]

G.P.O. Box 1499
New York, New York 10001
(212) 226-0010

First published in 1955

SUBSCRIPTION DATA

Issues and rates: Published quarterly.
Average paid circulation: 1500; 2000 controlled
Annual rate(s): $4, Foreign $5, Institutions $20.00
Managing Editor: Jonas Mekas

EDITORIAL DESCRIPTION

Contains articles on film history, aesthetics and criticism with emphasis on the new American cinema.
Audience: Film students, filmmakers, scholars, historians
Manuscripts accepted in English only

MANUSCRIPT INFORMATION

Subject field(s): Film (all aspects)
Manuscript requirements: No specific style guide.
Number of copies to be submitted: One
Abstract: Not necessary.
Author information and reprints: Payment: None.
Is simultaneous submission of article to other journals permitted: No
Exclusive manuscript rights between acceptance and publication: Yes
Copyright: Held by publication.
Reprints: Available
Additional information: Manuscripts should be typewritten, double-spaced, including name, address of author
Disposition of manuscript:
Query letter: Not necessary.
Receipt of manuscript acknowledged: Yes
Decision to publish in: Varies
Accepted manuscript published in: Varies
Rejected manuscript returned: Yes, if self-addressed, stamped envelope is sent with manuscript.
Rejected manuscript criticized: No
Submit to:
Jonas Mekas

Editor-in-Chief
(See address above)

FILM HERITAGE [873]

College of Liberal Arts
Wright State University
Dayton, Ohio 45431
(513) 426-6650 ext. 553

First published in 1965

SUBSCRIPTION DATA

Issues and rates: Published quarterly.
Average paid circulation: 2000
Annual rate(s): $3.00, Foreign $3.50
Publisher or Sponsor: Wright State University
Managing Editor: F. Anthony Macklin

EDITORIAL DESCRIPTION

Devoted to analyses of films and rediscoveries of underrated films; reviews and interviews.
Articles per average issue: 4-5
Audience: Anyone interested in film.
Manuscripts accepted in English

MANUSCRIPT INFORMATION

Subject field(s): Film
Manuscript requirements: Chicago
Preferred length: 10 pages
Number of copies to be submitted: One
Abstract: Not necessary.
Author information and reprints: Payment: Reprints only. 3 copies of issue
Is simultaneous submission of article to other journals permitted: No
Exclusive manuscript rights between acceptance and publication: Yes
Copyright: Held by Editor
Reprints: Not available
Disposition of manuscript:
Query letter: Not necessary.
Receipt of manuscript acknowledged: No
Decision to publish in: 6-8 weeks
Accepted manuscript published in: 6-9 months
Rejected manuscript returned: Yes
Rejected manuscript criticized: Sometimes
Submit to:
F. Anthony Macklin
Editor
(See address above)

THE FILM JOURNAL [874]

Box 9602
Hollins College, Virginia 24020
(703) 362-4757

First published in Spring 1971

SUBSCRIPTION DATA

Issues and rates: Published semi-annually.
Average paid circulation: 7,000
Annual rate(s): $5.00; Foreign $7.00;
Individuals $5.00; Institutions $7.00;
Students $5.00; Foreign institutions $9.00

Managing Editor: Thomas R. Atkins

EDITORIAL DESCRIPTION

This is an educational journal publishing original essays, interviews, documents, photographs, graphics, and poetry related to the history and aesthetics of motion pictures with special emphasis on the relationship between film and the humanities, particularly writing and graphic arts.
Articles per average issue: Four to six
Audience: Film scholars, teachers, students, professionals, as well as general film readers.
Manuscripts accepted in English

MANUSCRIPT INFORMATION

Subject field(s): Significant films of all types, American and foreign, classics and contemporary; interviews with directors, and other film artists; film and the liberal arts; film and the graphic arts.
Manuscript requirements: See latest issue for style requirements.
Preferred length: Approximately 2,500 words; eight to twelve pages
Number of copies to be submitted: One
Abstract: Not necessary.
Author information and reprints: Payment: Reprints only. Issues only
Is simultaneous submission of article to other journals permitted: Permitted.
Exclusive manuscript rights between acceptance and publication: No
Copyright: All rights reserved by Editor-Publisher
Reprints: Not available.
Disposition of manuscript:
Query letter: Necessary.
Receipt of manuscript acknowledged: No
Decision to publish in: Six weeks
Accepted manuscript published in: One year
Rejected manuscript returned: Yes, if return postage is supplied by author.
Rejected manuscript criticized: Sometimes
Submit to:
Thomas R. Atkins
Editor-Publisher
(See address above)

SPECIAL STIPULATIONS

If possible, author should submit photographs or film stills illustrating his essay.

FILM QUARTERLY [875]

University of California Press
Berkeley, California 94720
(412) 642-6333

Previously entitled *Quarterly of Film, Radio and Television; Hollywood Quarterly*

First published in 1945

SUBSCRIPTION DATA

Issues and rates: Published quarterly.
Average paid circulation: 8,000
Annual rate(s): $6.00; Pan-Am $6.00; Foreign $7.00; Institutions $10.00;
Foreign individuals $7.00; Foreign institutions $11.00

EDITORIAL DESCRIPTION

A journal of criticism, history and theory of motion pictures and materials written from diverse points of view.
Articles per average issue: 10
Audience: Students, teachers, film-makers, critics, historians
Manuscripts accepted in English

MANUSCRIPT INFORMATION

Subject field(s): Film criticism, history, theory, experimental film, documentary, feature-narrative, etc.
Manuscript requirements: See latest issue for style requirements.
Preferred length: Under 3,500 words
Number of copies to be submitted: 1
Abstract: Not necessary.
Author information and reprints: Payment: By publication to author. 15 cents per word.
Is simultaneous submission of article to other journals permitted: Not permitted.
Exclusive manuscript rights between acceptance and publication: Yes
Copyright: Held by the Regents of the University of California
Reprints: Available at no cost. 2 copies
Disposition of manuscript:
Query letter: Not necessary, but advisable.
Receipt of manuscript acknowledged: Yes
Decision to publish in: 3 months
Accepted manuscript published in: 3 months
Rejected manuscript returned: Yes, if return postage is supplied by author.
Rejected manuscript criticized: Sometimes
Submit to:
Ernest Callenbach
Editor
(See address above)

FILMMAKERS NEWSLETTER [876]

41 Union Square West
New York, New York 10003
(212) 989-5170

First published in 1967

SUBSCRIPTION DATA

Issues and rates: Published monthly.
Average paid circulation: 18,000
Annual rate(s): $7.00, Foreign $12.00
Managing Editor: H. Whitney Bailey

EDITORIAL DESCRIPTION

Contains feature articles on film techniques and the production of feature films; technical articles on new equipment and production methods; information and events for professional and independent filmmakers.
Articles per average issue: 5
Audience: Professional filmmakers
Manuscripts accepted in English

MANUSCRIPT INFORMATION

Subject field(s): Filmmaking
Manuscript requirements: See latest issue for style requirements.
Preferred length: 16 pages
Number of copies to be submitted: One
Abstract: Not necessary.
Author information and reprints: Payment: None.
Is simultaneous submission of article to other journals permitted: No
Exclusive manuscript rights between acceptance and publication: Yes
Copyright: Held by publication.
Reprints: Available
Disposition of manuscript:
Query letter: Not necessary.
Receipt of manuscript acknowledged: No
Decision to publish in: 4 weeks
Accepted manuscript published in: 2-3 months
Rejected manuscript returned: Yes
Rejected manuscript criticized: No
Submit to:
Harold W. Bailey
(See address above)

FILMOGRAPH [877]

Illustrated Quarterly of American Film History and Research
Orlean, Virginia 22128
(703) 364-1275

First published in 1970

SUBSCRIPTION DATA

Issues and rates: Published quarterly.
Average paid circulation: Not available.
Annual rate(s): $7.00
Managing Editor: Murray Summers

EDITORIAL DESCRIPTION

Devoted to the history of American film, giving attention to its personalities, directors, and technicians; to individual films; to certain aspects or phases of its history; and to its contributions to art and culture.
Articles per average issue: 5
Audience: Filmgoers
Manuscripts accepted in English

MANUSCRIPT INFORMATION

Subject field(s): Directors, personalities, interviews, filmographies, essays on film subjects, producers, discussions of individual films, reviews of past and current films, technicians, reviews of books and articles on film, surveys of the literature on film, contributions of film to art and life
Manuscript requirements: No specific style guide.
Preferred length: As required
Number of copies to be submitted: One
Author information and reprints: Payment: Reprints only. 2 copies of issue
Is simultaneous submission of article to other journals permitted: No
Exclusive manuscript rights between acceptance and publication: Yes
Copyright: Held by publication.
Reprints: Not available.

Additional information: Wherever possible, relevant photographs should be submitted along with articles. Photographs should be captioned. Manuscripts should be typed and double-spaced.
Disposition of manuscript:
  Query letter: Necessary.
  Receipt of manuscript acknowledged: Yes
  Decision to publish in: One week
  Accepted manuscript published in: 3-6 months
  Rejected manuscript returned: Yes, if self-addressed, stamped envelope is sent with manuscript.
  Rejected manuscript criticized: Yes
Submit to:
  Murray Summers
  Editor
  (See address above)

SPECIAL STIPULATIONS
  Although contributors should provide complete source acknowledgements and, where helpful, notes and bibliographies, they should follow their own dictates as to style.

JOURNAL OF POPULAR FILM [878]
100 University Hall
Bowling Green State University
Bowling Green, Ohio 43403
(419) 372-2664

First published in Winter 1972

SUBSCRIPTION DATA
Issues and rates: Published quarterly.
  Average paid circulation: 2,500
  Annual rate(s): $5.00; Students $3.50

EDITORIAL DESCRIPTION
  Publishes articles and related materials pertaining to popular films and their reflection of cultural values and attitudes
Articles per average issue: 5
Audience: Academic, film buffs
  Manuscripts accepted in English

MANUSCRIPT INFORMATION
Subject field(s): Film history, genre study, cultural analysis, criticism; no film reviews
Manuscript requirements: MLA
  Preferred length: 3,000 words
  Number of copies to be submitted: 2
  Abstract: Not necessary.
Author information and reprints: Payment: Reprints only. 25
  Is simultaneous submission of article to other journals permitted: Permitted, but not encouraged.
  Exclusive manuscript rights between acceptance and publication: Yes
  Copyright: Held by publication. all reprint fees shared 50-50 with author
  Reprints: Available at no cost. 25
Disposition of manuscript:
  Query letter: Not necessary.
  Receipt of manuscript acknowledged: Yes
  Decision to publish in: 2 months
  Accepted manuscript published in: 6-10 months
  Rejected manuscript returned: Yes, if return postage is supplied by author.
  Rejected manuscript criticized: Yes
Submit to:
  Sam L. Grogg, Jr.;
  Michael T. Marsden;
  John G. Nachbar
  Editors
  (See address above)

Journalism

AUTHORSHIP [879]
1365 Logan Street, Suite 100
Denver, Colorado 80203
(303) 266-9811

First published in 1944

SUBSCRIPTION DATA
Issues and rates: Published quarterly.
  Average paid circulation: 2,000 controlled
  Annual rate(s): $3.50, Foreign $5.00
Publisher or Sponsor: The National Writers Club
Managing Editor: David Raffelock

EDITORIAL DESCRIPTION
  Contains helpful information for freelance writers; reports on malpractices in area of creative writing on editors who hold manuscripts overly long, fail to report on them or fail to pay for them.
Articles per average issue: 5
Audience: Freelance writers
  Manuscripts accepted in English

MANUSCRIPT INFORMATION
Subject field(s): Personal experiences, editorial contacts, "how-to" articles, humorous incidents
Manuscript requirements: No specific style guide.
  Preferred length: 300-500 words; 2 to 4 pages
  Number of copies to be submitted: One
  Abstract: No
Author information and reprints: Payment: By publication to author. $.01 per word.
  Is simultaneous submission of article to other journals permitted: No
  Exclusive manuscript rights between acceptance and publication: Yes
  Copyright: Held by author.
  Reprints: Not available.
Additional information: All serious articles must be authentic and helpful to freelance writers.
Disposition of manuscript:
  Query letter: No
  Receipt of manuscript acknowledged: Yes
  Decision to publish in: 2-3 weeks
  Accepted manuscript published in: 6 months
  Rejected manuscript returned: Yes, if return postage is supplied by author.
  Rejected manuscript criticized: Yes
Submit to:
  Donald E. Bower
  Editor
  (See address above)

CHICAGO JOURNALISM REVIEW [880]
Room 509
192 North Clark Street
Chicago, Illinois 60601
(312) 332-3102

First published in 1968

SUBSCRIPTION DATA
Issues and rates: Published monthly.
  Average paid circulation: 3,500
  Annual rate(s): $7.00; Foreign $8.50; Individuals $7.00; Institutions $7.00
Publisher or Sponsor: Association of Working Press, Inc.

EDITORIAL DESCRIPTION
  A forum for the issues and problems involved in the news media
Articles per average issue: 7
Audience: Journalists, media-related people, educators, anyone interested in the news media
  Manuscripts accepted in English

MANUSCRIPT INFORMATION
Subject field(s): All aspects of journalism and the media, newspapers, radio, television, magazines, book publishing; locally or nationally oriented.
Manuscript requirements: No specific style guide.
  Preferred length: Varies
  Number of copies to be submitted: 1
  Abstract: Not necessary.
Author information and reprints: Payment: None.
  Is simultaneous submission of article to other journals permitted: Permitted, but not encouraged.
  Exclusive manuscript rights between acceptance and publication: No
  Reprints: Available at cost.
Disposition of manuscript:
  Query letter: Not necessary, but advisable.
  Receipt of manuscript acknowledged: Yes
  Decision to publish in: Varies
  Rejected manuscript returned: Yes, with return postage paid by publication.
  Rejected manuscript criticized: No
Submit to:
  Leonard Aronson;
  Michael Miner
  Editors
  (See address above)

COLLEGE PRESS REVIEW [881]
Department of Technical Journalism
Colorado State University
Fort Collins, Colorado 80523

First published in 1955

SUBSCRIPTION DATA
Issues and rates: Published quarterly.

Average paid circulation: 1,000; 50 controlled
Annual rate(s): $15.00; Foreign $16.00
Publisher or Sponsor: National Council of College Publications Advisers

EDITORIAL DESCRIPTION

Contains articles by, about and of interest to college publications staffs, editors and faculty advisors.
Articles per average issue: 10-12
Audience: Academic, professional
Manuscripts accepted in English

MANUSCRIPT INFORMATION

Subject field(s): College press, student press, media
Manuscript requirements: See latest issue for style requirements.
Preferred length: 1,200-3,000 words
Number of copies to be submitted: 3
Abstract: No
Author information and reprints: Payment: Reprints only. 5 free
Is simultaneous submission of article to other journals permitted: Permitted with approval of editor only.
Exclusive manuscript rights between acceptance and publication: Yes
Copyright: Held by publication.
Reprints: Available
Additional information: Illustrations especially desired
Disposition of manuscript:
Query letter: Yes
Receipt of manuscript acknowledged: No
Decision to publish in: 1-3 months
Accepted manuscript published in: 6-12 months
Rejected manuscript returned: Yes, if self-addressed, stamped envelope is sent with manuscript.
Rejected manuscript criticized: Reasons for rejections only
Submit to:
John Windhauser
Editor
(See address above)

COLLEGIATE JOURNALIST [882]
School of Journalism
Ohio University
Athens, Ohio 45701
(614) 594-7312

First published in 1963

SUBSCRIPTION DATA

Issues and rates: Published three times per year.
Average paid circulation: 1100 controlled
Annual rate(s): $5.00 for 3 years
Publisher or Sponsor: Alpha Phi Gamma, National Honorary Journalism Fraternity

EDITORIAL DESCRIPTION

Devoted to articles that attempt to make the editing and production of college newspapers, magazines and yearbooks easier and more professionally satisfying.
Articles per average issue: 5

Audience: Editors of college newspapers, yearbooks, magazines
Manuscripts accepted in English

MANUSCRIPT INFORMATION

Subject field(s): College newspapers, campus yearbooks, campus magazines, related concerns

MANUSCRIPT INFORMATION

Manuscript requirements: Chicago, GPO
Preferred length: 600-800 words, typewritten double-spaced
Number of copies to be submitted: 2
Abstract: No
Author information and reprints: Payment: Reprints only.
Is simultaneous submission of article to other journals permitted: Not permitted.
Exclusive manuscript rights between acceptance and publication: Yes
Copyright: No copyright
Reprints: Not available
Disposition of manuscript:
Query letter: No, but helpful
Receipt of manuscript acknowledged: If postpaid card is included
Decision to publish in: 1-6 months
Accepted manuscript published in: 3-15 months
Rejected manuscript returned: Yes, if return postage is supplied by author.
Rejected manuscript criticized: No
Submit to:
Professor J. W. Click
Editor
(See address above)

JOURNALISM QUARTERLY [883]
School of Journalism
Ohio University
Athens, Ohio 45701
(614) 594-7311

First published in 1924

SUBSCRIPTION DATA

Issues and rates: Published quarterly.
Average paid circulation: 4,417
Annual rate(s): $12.00
Publisher or Sponsor: Association for Education in Journalism
Managing Editor: Randall Murray

EDITORIAL DESCRIPTION

Contains research in journalism and mass communication.
Articles per average issue: 25
Audience: Academic and research
Manuscripts accepted in English

MANUSCRIPT INFORMATION

Manuscript requirements: See latest issue.
Preferred length: 10-12 pages
Number of copies to be submitted: Three
Abstract: No
Author information and reprints: Payment: None.
Is simultaneous submission of article to other journals permitted: No

Exclusive manuscript rights between acceptance and publication: Yes
Copyright: Held by publication.
Reprints: Available, cost varies depending on length
Disposition of manuscript:
Query letter: No
Receipt of manuscript acknowledged: Yes
Decision to publish in: 3-4 months
Accepted manuscript published in: 9-12 months
Rejected manuscript returned: Yes
Rejected manuscript criticized: Yes
Submit to:
Guido H. Stempel, III
Acting Editor
(See address above)
(614) 594-6710

SCHOLASTIC EDITOR-GRAPHICS/COMMUNICATIONS [884]
720 Washington SE
University of Minnesota
Minneapolis, Minnesota 55414
(612) 373-3180

SUBSCRIPTION DATA

Issues and rates: Monthly, September to May
Average paid circulation: 3,000
Annual rate(s): $6.50
Publisher or Sponsor: National Scholastic Press Association and the Associated Collegiate Press
Managing Editor: Wally Wikoff

EDITORIAL DESCRIPTION

Contains how-to articles of interest to the editors, staffs and advisers of college and high school publications (yearbooks, newspapers and magazines); also recent developments in the field of journalism and mass communication.

MANUSCRIPT INFORMATION

Subject field(s): Yearbooks, newspapers, photography, magazines, CCTV, campus radio, articles on all phases of production and content
Manuscript requirements: See latest issue for style requirements.
Preferred length: 10-20 pages
Number of copies to be submitted: One
Author information and reprints: Payment: None. Contributor's copies only.
Is simultaneous submission of article to other journals permitted: No
Exclusive manuscript rights between acceptance and publication: Yes
Copyright: Held by publication.
Reprints: Available, cost depends upon length
Disposition of manuscript:
Receipt of manuscript acknowledged: Yes
Decision to publish in: 1-4 weeks
Accepted manuscript published in: A year at most
Rejected manuscript returned: Yes, if self-addressed, stamped envelope is sent with manuscript.
Rejected manuscript criticized: No

Submit to:
Kristi Hedstrom
Editor
(See address above)

ST. LOUIS JOURNALISM REVIEW [885]
P.O. Box 3086
St. Louis, Missouri 63130
(314) 991-1698

First published in 1970

SUBSCRIPTION DATA
Issues and rates: Published bi-monthly.
  Average paid circulation: 5,000
  Annual rate(s): $5.00, Foreign $7.00
Managing Editor: Charles L. Klotzer

EDITORIAL DESCRIPTION
A critique of St. Louis metropolitan media and broadcasting by St. Louis working journalists. Also open to lay critics of the press and those denied access to the regular media or whose stories have been distorted.
Manuscripts accepted in English only

MANUSCRIPT INFORMATION
Subject field(s): Printed media, broadcasting, journalism reviews of any publication and broadcasting industry.
Manuscript requirements: See latest issue for style requirements.
  Preferred length: None
  Number of copies to be submitted: One
Author information and reprints: Payment: None.
  Is simultaneous submission of article to other journals permitted: Yes
  Exclusive manuscript rights between acceptance and publication: Yes
  Copyright: Held by publication.
  Reprints: Available
Disposition of manuscript:
  Receipt of manuscript acknowledged: No
  Decision to publish in: 4-6 weeks
  Accepted manuscript published in: 3-4 months
  Rejected manuscript returned: Yes
  Rejected manuscript criticized: No
Submit to:
Editorial Board
(See address above)

WRITER'S DIGEST [886]
America's Leading Writer's Magazine
9933 Alliance Road
Cincinnati, Ohio 45242
(513) 984-0710

Previously entitled *Successful Writing*

First published in 1920

SUBSCRIPTION DATA
Issues and rates: Published monthly.
  Average paid circulation: 100,0000
  Annual rate(s): $5.95, Foreign $6.95

EDITORIAL DESCRIPTION
Contains practical instruction articles on specific types of writing for the freelance market; in-depth market features on major magazine categories and book publishing firms; interviews with well known U.S. writers.
Articles per average issue: 10-12
Audience: Free-lance writers
  Manuscripts accepted in English

MANUSCRIPT INFORMATION
Manuscript requirements: See latest issue for style requirements.
  Preferred length: 2,500 words maximum
  Number of copies to be submitted: One
  Abstract: No
Author information and reprints: Payment: By publication to author. $.03 per word.
  Is simultaneous submission of article to other journals permitted: No
  Exclusive manuscript rights between acceptance and publication: Yes
  Copyright: Held by publication.
  Reprints: Not available.
Disposition of manuscript:
  Receipt of manuscript acknowledged: No
  Decision to publish in: 3 weeks
  Accepted manuscript published in: 6-12 months
  Rejected manuscript returned: Yes
  Rejected manuscript criticized: No
Submit to:
Skip Weiner
Editor
(See address above)

Radio and television

EBU REVIEW [887]
Programmes, Administration, Law
Geneva Edition
Case postale 193
CH-1211 Geneva 20, Switzerland
332400

Previously entitled *EBU Review, Part B*

First published in 1958

SUBSCRIPTION DATA
Issues and rates: Published bi-monthly.
  Average paid circulation: 3000; 4000 controlled
  Annual rate(s): 45 Swiss francs
Publisher or Sponsor: European Broadcasting Union

EDITORIAL DESCRIPTION
Contains feature articles and news items covering all programme, administrative and legal aspects of radio and television throughout the world. Editorial material must be highly professional, written by broadcasting executives for broadcasting executives.
Manuscripts accepted in English, French, German, Italian

MANUSCRIPT INFORMATION
Manuscript requirements: No specific style guide.
  Preferred length: To be agreed
  Number of copies to be submitted: Two
  Abstract: No
Author information and reprints: Payment: By publication to author. To be agreed
  Is simultaneous submission of article to other journals permitted: No
  Exclusive manuscript rights between acceptance and publication: Yes
  Copyright: Held by publication.
  Reprints: Available, at cost depending on number and format
Disposition of manuscript:
  Query letter: No, but advisable
  Receipt of manuscript acknowledged: Yes
  Decision to publish in: 1-2 months
  Accepted manuscript published in: 3-6 months
  Rejected manuscript returned: Yes
  Rejected manuscript criticized: No
Submit to:
J. Straschnov
Editor-in-Chief
(See address above)

EDUCATIONAL & INDUSTRIAL TELEVISION [888]
607 Main Street
Ridgefield, Connecticut 06877
(203) 438-3774

Previously entitled *Educational Television*

First published in 1968

SUBSCRIPTION DATA
Issues and rates: Published monthly.
  Average paid circulation: 3,500; 13,500 controlled
  Annual rate(s): $12.00, Foreign $16.00
Managing Editor: Mary Woolf

EDITORIAL DESCRIPTION
Provides specific and practical information on how to use television for teaching, training, communicating, surveillance, as well as methods, equipment, materials, programs, costs, etc.
Articles per average issue: 5-6
Audience: Audio-visual professionals in schools, industry, hospitals, armed forces, public television
  Manuscripts accepted in English

MANUSCRIPT INFORMATION
Manuscript requirements: Chicago
  Preferred length: 15 pages maximum
  Number of copies to be submitted: One
  Abstract: No
Author information and reprints: Payment: None. 10 copies of issue plus one year complimentary subscription
  Is simultaneous submission of article to other journals permitted: No
  Exclusive manuscript rights between acceptance and publication: Yes
  Copyright: Held by publication.
  Reprints: Available

Additional information: Include biographical data of author. If photographs are not applicable to the manuscript, drawings, cartoons, diagrams or charts may be used. No footnotes or bibliographies.
Disposition of manuscript:
Query letter: No, but helpful
Receipt of manuscript acknowledged: Yes
Decision to publish in: 8-12 weeks
Accepted manuscript published in: 2-12 months
Rejected manuscript returned: Yes
Rejected manuscript criticized: Yes
Submit to:
Mary M. Woolf
Managing Editor

SPECIAL STIPULATIONS
There is a backlog of general pieces. Especially needed are articles with practical, specific information as well as cassette/cartridge formats.

EDUCATIONAL BROADCASTING [889]
The International Journal of Audio and Visual Learning
825 South Barrington Avenue
Los Angeles, California 90049
(213) 826-8388

First published in 1968

SUBSCRIPTION DATA
Issues and rates: Published bi-monthly.
Average paid circulation: 903; 13,306 controlled
Annual rate(s): $20; Foreign $40
Managing Editor: Hal Spector; Martin Waldman

EDITORIAL DESCRIPTION
Emphasis is on technological advances in the educational broadcasting field, with feature articles stressing new and more effective applications of hardware and software for filming, transmitting and viewing, thereby making the broadcaster and audio-visual director better informed, more efficient and effective. An application-oriented publication.
Audience: Educational directors, ETV station managers, ITV operators, military instructional coordinators, government broadcasters and industrial training directors.
Manuscripts accepted in English

MANUSCRIPT INFORMATION
Subject field(s): Educational broadcasting practices and techniques, industrial training practices and techniques, facility and system reports, equipment techniques, financing, programming, medical and military applications, public policy
Manuscript requirements: Style sheet sent on request.
Preferred length: 3000-5000 words
Number of copies to be submitted: Two
Author information and reprints: Payment: None.
Is simultaneous submission of article to other journals permitted: No

Exclusive manuscript rights between acceptance and publication: Yes
Copyright: Held by author.
Reprints: Available, cost varies with length
Additional information: Desire camera-ready artwork.
Disposition of manuscript:
Receipt of manuscript acknowledged: Yes
Decision to publish in: Varies
Accepted manuscript published in: Varies
Rejected manuscript returned: Yes
Rejected manuscript criticized: No
Submit to:
Roberta Atchison
Editorial Coordinator
(See address above)
(213) 826-8388 ext. 247

FEEDBACK [890]
School of Public Communication
Boston University
640 Commonwealth Avenue
Boston, Massachusetts 02215
(617) 353-3483

First published in 1965

SUBSCRIPTION DATA
Issues and rates: Published quarterly.
Average paid circulation: 600 controlled
Publisher or Sponsor: Broadcast Education Association

EDITORIAL DESCRIPTION
Contains news of interest to broadcast educators, articles concerning current issues in broadcast education, notes on activities of the organization.
Articles per average issue: 5
Audience: Educators, broadcasters
Manuscripts accepted in English only

MANUSCRIPT INFORMATION
Subject field(s): Focuses on university level broadcast education. Broadcasting, television, management, sales, instruction, cable television
Manuscript requirements: MLA, Chicago
Preferred length: 750 words; 3 pages
Number of copies to be submitted: Two
Abstract: No
Author information and reprints: Payment: None.
Is simultaneous submission of article to other journals permitted: Yes
Exclusive manuscript rights between acceptance and publication: No
Copyright: Held by publication.
Reprints: Available
Disposition of manuscript:
Receipt of manuscript acknowledged: Yes
Decision to publish in: 2 weeks
Accepted manuscript published in: 2 months
Rejected manuscript returned: Yes
Rejected manuscript criticized: Yes
Submit to:
Robert R. Smith
Editor
(See address above)

GP NEWSLETTER [891]
Great Plains National Instructional Television Library
Box 80669
Lincoln, Nebraska 68501
(402) 467-2502

First published in 1962

SUBSCRIPTION DATA
Issues and rates: Published monthly.
Average paid circulation: 10,000 controlled
Publisher or Sponsor: Great Plains National Instructional Television Library

EDITORIAL DESCRIPTION
Contains informational, promotional reviews of recorded (video tape, video cassette, 16mm film) instruction acquired for distribution by GPN; articles pertinent to the use of television in the classroom; general ITV items of news relative to GPN and its customer-users.
Articles per average issue: Varies
Audience: Those with a practical interest in instructional television and related media
Manuscripts accepted in English

MANUSCRIPT INFORMATION
Subject field(s): Use of instructional television in the classroom
Manuscript requirements: See latest issue for style requirements.
Preferred length: 1,200-1,500 words typewritten, double-spaced, with one inch margins
Number of copies to be submitted: One
Abstract: No
Author information and reprints: Payment: By publication to author. Payment varies
Is simultaneous submission of article to other journals permitted: No, but after GPN article is in general circulation, then author may use at will.
Exclusive manuscript rights between acceptance and publication: Yes
Copyright: No copyright restrictions
Reprints: Available, singles free; large quantities, at cost
Additional information: Inquiries are requested.
Disposition of manuscript:
Query letter: Yes
Receipt of manuscript acknowledged: Yes
Decision to publish in: 10 days
Accepted manuscript published in: 6-8 weeks
Rejected manuscript returned: Yes, if self-addressed, stamped envelope is sent with manuscript.
Rejected manuscript criticized: No
Submit to:
Richard L. Spence
Information Coordinator
(See address above)
(402) 467-2502 ext. 28

HAM RADIO MAGAZINE [892]
Focus on Communications Technology
Greenville, New Hampshire 03048
(603) 878-1441

First published in 1968

SUBSCRIPTION DATA
Issues and rates: Published monthly.
  Average paid circulation: 45,000
  Annual rate(s): $8.00, Foreign $10.00

EDITORIAL DESCRIPTION
  Covers the technical and home construction aspects of amateur radio. Brings the hobbiest up to date on the latest products and techniques.
Articles per average issue: 10
Audience: Serious amateur radio enthusiasts
  Manuscripts accepted in English

MANUSCRIPT INFORMATION
Subject field(s): Construction, theory
Manuscript requirements: Style sheet sent on request.
  Preferred length: Up to 20 pages
  Number of copies to be submitted: One
  Abstract: No
Author information and reprints: Payment: By publication to author. $1.00 per column inch in the magazine.
  Is simultaneous submission of article to other journals permitted: No
  Exclusive manuscript rights between acceptance and publication: Yes
  Copyright: Held by publication.
  Reprints: Available at publisher's cost
Disposition of manuscript:
  Query letter: Helpful
  Receipt of manuscript acknowledged: Yes
  Decision to publish in: One month
  Accepted manuscript published in: Four months
  Rejected manuscript returned: Yes
  Rejected manuscript criticized: No
Submit to:
  James R. Fisk
  (See address above)

JOURNAL OF BROADCASTING [893]

Temple University
Philadelphia, Pennsylvania 19122
(215) 787-8432

SUBSCRIPTION DATA
Issues and rates: Published quarterly.
  Average paid circulation: 1,800; 60 controlled
  Annual rate(s): $17.50, Students $5.00
Publisher or Sponsor: Association for Professional Broadcasting Education
Managing Editor: Christopher H. Sterling

EDITORIAL DESCRIPTION
  A scholarly and research journal devoted to study and comment on all aspects of broadcasting and allied fields (such as cable, video recording, etc.), covering history, technology, regulation, content, audience research, public policy, bibliographies, etc. Includes critical, research, policy, theoretical and other kinds of articles.
Articles per average issue: 8-10
Audience: Academic
  Manuscripts accepted in English only

MANUSCRIPT INFORMATION
Subject field(s): Broadcasting, mass communications, cable television, other electronic media, education about media, bibliographies, book reviews
Manuscript requirements: Chicago
  Preferred length: 10-20 pages
  Number of copies to be submitted: Two
  Abstract: Yes
Author information and reprints: Payment: None. $25 if reprinted elsewhere (paid to author)
  Is simultaneous submission of article to other journals permitted: No
  Exclusive manuscript rights between acceptance and publication: Yes
  Copyright: Held by publication.
  Reprints: Available, $1.00 per page per 100 copies
Additional information: Manuscript should include minimum graphic material; footnotes at end of paper on separate sheet(s); name of author on top page only.
Disposition of manuscript:
  Query letter: No
  Receipt of manuscript acknowledged: Yes
  Decision to publish in: 2-4 weeks
  Accepted manuscript published in: 3-6 months
  Rejected manuscript returned: Yes, if self-addressed, stamped envelope is sent with manuscript.
  Rejected manuscript criticized: Yes
Submit to:
  Christopher H. Sterling
  Editor
  (See address above)

JOURNAL OF COLLEGE RADIO [894]

Department of Oral Communication
Central State University
Edmond, Oklahoma 73034
(405) 341-6166

SUBSCRIPTION DATA
Issues and rates: Monthly (7 times during the academic year)
  Average paid circulation: 5,000
  Annual rate(s): $5.00, Foreign $6.00
Publisher or Sponsor: Intercollegiate Broadcasting System

EDITORIAL DESCRIPTION
  Content of articles should help improve skills and add to the practical knowledge of college radio station operation and/or broadcasting in general; also research in the broadcast communication area.

MANUSCRIPT INFORMATION
Subject field(s): Campus radio, campus TV, regulation, engineering, advertising, promotion, research, broadcast education, music industry
Manuscript requirements: Style sheet sent on request.
  Preferred length: Open
  Number of copies to be submitted: One
Author information and reprints: Payment: None.
  Is simultaneous submission of article to other journals permitted: No
  Exclusive manuscript rights between acceptance and publication: Yes
  Copyright: Held by both author and publication
  Reprints: Available, cost upon request
Disposition of manuscript:
  Receipt of manuscript acknowledged: Yes
  Decision to publish in: 3 weeks
  Accepted manuscript published in: 1-3 months
  Rejected manuscript returned: Yes
  Rejected manuscript criticized: Yes
Submit to:
  Craig Marrs
  Editor/Publisher
  (See address above)

SOCIETY OF MOTION PICTURE AND TELEVISION ENGINEERS JOURNAL [895]

862 Scarsdale Avenue
Scarsdale, New York 10583
(914) 472-6606

Previously entitled *SMPTE Transactions*

First published in 1916

SUBSCRIPTION DATA
Issues and rates: Published monthly.
  Average paid circulation: 10,000
  Annual rate(s): $35.00
Publisher or Sponsor: Society of Motion Picture and Television Engineers
Managing Editor: Victor H. Allen

EDITORIAL DESCRIPTION
  Contains articles on engineering, science, technology for motion pictures, television, instrumentation, high-speed photography.
Articles per average issue: 8
Audience: Engineers, researchers, producers
  Manuscripts accepted in English, French, Spanish, German, Russian

MANUSCRIPT INFORMATION
Manuscript requirements: Style sheet sent on request.
  Preferred length: None
  Number of copies to be submitted: Three
  Abstract: Yes
Author information and reprints: Payment: None.
  Is simultaneous submission of article to other journals permitted: No
  Exclusive manuscript rights between acceptance and publication: Yes
  Copyright: Held by publication.
  Reprints: Available at cost.
Additional information: Arrangements for reprints of a published paper can be made by the author or his company.
Disposition of manuscript:
  Query letter: No
  Receipt of manuscript acknowledged: Yes
  Decision to publish in: 5-8 weeks
  Accepted manuscript published in: 8-12 weeks
  Rejected manuscript returned: Yes
  Rejected manuscript criticized: Yes

Submit to:
  Victor H. Allen
  Editor
  (See address above)

Speech

AMERICAN FORENSIC ASSOCIATION JOURNAL [896]
Eastern Montana College
Billings, Montana 59101
(406) 657-2178

First published in 1964

SUBSCRIPTION DATA
Issues and rates: Published quarterly.
  Average paid circulation: 1,300
  Annual rate(s): Individuals $10.00; Institutions $12.00; Members $10.00; Foreign individuals $10.00; Foreign institutions $12.00
Publisher or Sponsor: American Forensic Association
Managing Editor: George W. Ziegelmueller

EDITORIAL DESCRIPTION
  Is designed to increase knowledge in those areas of communication theory, practice, and instruction relevant to forensics in schools and college.
Articles per average issue: 4
Audience: Forensics personnel
  Manuscripts accepted in English

MANUSCRIPT INFORMATION
Subject field(s): Argumentation, persuasion, discussion, debate, parliamentary speaking, forensic activities, and appropriate aspects of speech education
Manuscript requirements: MLA
  Preferred length: 4,000 words maximum
  Number of copies to be submitted: 2
  Abstract: Not necessary.
Author information and reprints: Payment: None.
  Is simultaneous submission of article to other journals permitted: Permitted.
  Exclusive manuscript rights between acceptance and publication: Yes
  Copyright: Held by publication.
  Reprints: Available at cost. $3.00 each
Additional information: Submit a title page that includes title of the essay, author's identification (title, institution). This should be separate from the body of the article. Footnotes and tables on separate pages at the end.
Disposition of manuscript:
  Query letter: Not necessary, but advisable.
  Receipt of manuscript acknowledged: Yes
  Decision to publish in: 1-3 months
  Accepted manuscript published in: 3-12 months
  Rejected manuscript returned: Yes, with return postage paid by publication.
  Rejected manuscript criticized: Sometimes
Submit to:
  George W. Ziegelmueller

Editor
Department of Speech Communication and Theatre
Wayne State University
Detroit, Michigan 48202
(313) 577-2950

SPECIAL STIPULATIONS
  Publisher has a royalty sharing arrangement under which authors receive 50 per cent of royalties after the deduction of expenses.

FOLIA PHONIATRICA [897]
International Journal of Phoniatrics, Speech Therapy and Communication Pathology
S. Karger AG
Arnold-Boecklin Strasse 25
CH-4011 Basel, Switzerland
061-390880

First published in 1947

SUBSCRIPTION DATA
Issues and rates: Published bi-monthly.
  Average paid circulation: 1,003; 25 controlled
  Annual rate(s): SFr.132.00; Foreign $54.00

EDITORIAL DESCRIPTION
  Furthers the study, general instruction, and acquaintance with up-to-date scientific results in physiology and pathology of speech and voice in all countries of the world. Not purely experimental, but also quantitative methods are dealt with, and initial consideration is given to the physiology and action of voice organs.
Articles per average issue: 6-7
Audience: Professional
  Manuscripts accepted in English, German, French

MANUSCRIPT INFORMATION
Manuscript requirements: Style sheet sent on request.
  Preferred length: No limit
  Number of copies to be submitted: 2
  Abstract: Yes, a summary in the original language and one in English.
Author information and reprints: Payment: None.
  Is simultaneous submission of article to other journals permitted: No
  Exclusive manuscript rights between acceptance and publication: Yes
  Copyright: Held by publication.
  Reprints: Available at cost
Disposition of manuscript:
  Query letter: No
  Receipt of manuscript acknowledged: Yes
  Decision to publish in: 1-2 months
  Accepted manuscript published in: 6-7 months
  Rejected manuscript returned: Yes
Submit to:
  Prof. Dr. E. Loebell
  Editor
  Universitätsklinik für Hals-, Nasen- und Ohrenleiden
  Inselspital
  CH-3008 Bern, Switzerland

QUARTERLY JOURNAL OF SPEECH [898]
Department of Communication Arts
University of Wisconsin
Madison, Wisconsin 53706
(608) 262-2543

SUBSCRIPTION DATA
Issues and rates: Published quarterly.
  Average paid circulation: 7225
  Annual rate(s): $15
Publisher or Sponsor: Speech Communication Association

EDITORIAL DESCRIPTION
  Contains articles on communication theory and research, drama, history of public address, oral interpretation of literature.
Articles per average issue: 10
Audience: Academic, researchers
  Manuscripts accepted in English

MANUSCRIPT INFORMATION
Subject field(s): Communication theory, communication research, history of theatre, theatre criticism, rhetorical criticism, mass media theory, history of broadcasting, argumentation
Manuscript requirements: MLA
  Preferred length: 3,000-6,000 words
  Number of copies to be submitted: Two
Author information and reprints: Payment: None.
  Is simultaneous submission of article to other journals permitted: No
  Exclusive manuscript rights between acceptance and publication: Yes
  Copyright: Held by Association
  Reprints: Available, 25-50 free
Additional information: See current copies of the journal. Double space throughout. Author's name only on a separate cover page.
Disposition of manuscript:
  Query letter: No
  Receipt of manuscript acknowledged: Yes
  Decision to publish in: 6 weeks
  Accepted manuscript published in: 6-12 months
  Rejected manuscript returned: Yes
  Rejected manuscript criticized: Yes
Submit to:
  Robert L. Scott
  Editor
  (See address above)

SOUTHERN SPEECH COMMUNICATION JOURNAL [899]
Auburn University
Department of Speech Communication
Auburn, Alabama 36830
(205) 826-4682

Previously entitled *Southern Speech Journal*

First published in 1935

SUBSCRIPTION DATA
Issues and rates: Published quarterly.
  Average paid circulation: 2500; 2800 controlled
  Annual rate(s): $10.00
Publisher or Sponsor: Southern Speech Communication Association

EDITORIAL DESCRIPTION
Publishes historical and scientific research on speech communication, dramatic art, and radio and television.
Articles per average issue: 7-8
Audience: Scholars
  Manuscripts accepted in English

MANUSCRIPT INFORMATION
Subject field(s): Southern public address, rhetorical theory, dramatic art, radio and television, communication theory, American public address, voice science, oral interpretation
Manuscript requirements: MLA; See latest issue for style requirements.
  Preferred length: 4000 words maximum, everything typewritten, double-spaced. No use of *Ibid.*
  Number of copies to be submitted: Two
  Abstract: Yes
Author information and reprints: Payment: None.
  Is simultaneous submission of article to other journals permitted: No
  Exclusive manuscript rights between acceptance and publication: Yes
  Copyright: Held by publication.
  Reprints: Available, cost is variable
Disposition of manuscript:
  Query letter: No
  Receipt of manuscript acknowledged: Yes
  Decision to publish in: 6-8 weeks
  Accepted manuscript published in: 6-12 months
  Rejected manuscript returned: Yes
  Rejected manuscript criticized: Sometimes
Submit to:
  Bert E. Bradley
  Editor
  (See address above)

SPEECH MONOGRAPHS [900]
Speech Communication Association
Statler Hilton Hotel
33rd Street and Seventh Avenue
New York, New York 10001
(212) 736-6625

First published in 1934

SUBSCRIPTION DATA
Issues and rates: Published quarterly.
  Average paid circulation: 3,700
  Annual rate(s): $20.00 (includes membership)
Publisher or Sponsor: Speech Communication Association

EDITORIAL DESCRIPTION
Contains research studies concerned with speech and related communicative behaviors.
Articles per average issue: 10

Audience: Research, academic
  Manuscripts accepted in English

MANUSCRIPT INFORMATION
Subject field(s): Communication, rhetoric, small groups, persuasion, interpersonal relations
Manuscript requirements: MLA
  Preferred length: 5000-8000 words
  Number of copies to be submitted: Three
Author information and reprints: Payment: None.
  Is simultaneous submission of article to other journals permitted: No
  Exclusive manuscript rights between acceptance and publication: Yes
  Copyright: Held by publication.
  Reprints: Available from printer
Disposition of manuscript:
  Query letter: No
  Receipt of manuscript acknowledged: Yes
  Decision to publish in: 10-12 weeks
  Accepted manuscript published in: 6-9 months
  Rejected manuscript returned: Yes
  Rejected manuscript criticized: Yes
Submit to:
  Roger E. Nebergall
  Editor
  Department of Speech Communication
  University of Illinois
  Urbana, Illinois, 61801

Education

Education

ACADEMIC THERAPY [901]
1539 Fourth Street
San Rafael, California 94904
(415) 456-1394

Previously entitled *Academic Therapy Quarterly*

SUBSCRIPTION DATA
Issues and rates: Quarterly, plus 2 newsletters
  Average paid circulation: 8000
  Annual rate(s): $6.00

EDITORIAL DESCRIPTION
  Contains practical and theoretical viewpoints on methods for helping intellectually capable but academically underachieving children and youth.
Articles per average issue: 15
Audience: Educational therapists and diagnosticians
  Manuscripts accepted in English

MANUSCRIPT INFORMATION
Subject field(s): Learning disabilities
Manuscript requirements: Chicago
  Preferred length: 1500-1800 words; 6-8 pages
  Number of copies to be submitted: Original and one copy
  Abstract: No
Author information and reprints: Payment: None.
  Is simultaneous submission of article to other journals permitted: No
  Exclusive manuscript rights between acceptance and publication: Yes
  Copyright: Held by publication.
  Reprints: Available, 50 free
Disposition of manuscript:
  Query letter: Helpful
  Receipt of manuscript acknowledged: Yes
  Decision to publish in: Four weeks
  Accepted manuscript published in: Three to four issues
  Rejected manuscript returned: Yes
  Rejected manuscript criticized: No
Submit to:
  John I. Arena
  Editor
  (See address above)

ADE BULLETIN [902]
62 Fifth Avenue
New York, New York 10011
(212) 691-3200 ext. 722

SUBSCRIPTION DATA
Issues and rates: Published quarterly.
  Average paid circulation: 1,500
  Annual rate(s): $5.00
Publisher or Sponsor: Association of Departments of English

EDITORIAL DESCRIPTION
  Contains essays, surveys, reviews on matters of interest to two and four-year college and university departments teaching English. Attempts to provide department chairpersons with accurate information about new directions in the teaching and learning of language and literature in college.

MANUSCRIPT INFORMATION
Subject field(s): College English, departmental management, career opportunities for students with work in English
Manuscript requirements: MLA
  Preferred length: 2,500 words; 10 pages
  Number of copies to be submitted: One
  Abstract: No
Author information and reprints: Payment: None.
  Is simultaneous submission of article to other journals permitted: No
  Exclusive manuscript rights between acceptance and publication: Yes
  Copyright: Held by publication.
  Reprints: Available, ten free; reprint cost varies
Disposition of manuscript:
  Receipt of manuscript acknowledged: No
  Decision to publish in: 2-4 weeks
  Accepted manuscript published in: 6 months
  Rejected manuscript returned: Yes, if return postage is supplied by author.
  Rejected manuscript criticized: No
Submit to:
  Elizabeth Wooten
  Editor
  (See address above)

AEDS JOURNAL [903]
1201 16th Street, N.W.
Washington, D.C. 20036
(202) 833-4100

First published in 1965

SUBSCRIPTION DATA
Issues and rates: Published quarterly.
  Average paid circulation: 1500
  Annual rate(s): $10.00
Publisher or Sponsor: Association for Educational Data Systems

EDITORIAL DESCRIPTION
  Contains articles, research papers, book reviews, historical reviews, expository or tutorial articles on computors, data processing and education.
Articles per average issue: 4
Audience: Educators
  Manuscripts accepted in English

MANUSCRIPT INFORMATION
Subject field(s): Research in educational data processing, description of projects in educational data processing, educational data processing theory, educational planning
Manuscript requirements: Style sheet sent on request.
  Preferred length: 20 pages maximum
  Number of copies to be submitted: Three
  Abstract: No
Author information and reprints: Payment: None.
  Is simultaneous submission of article to other journals permitted: No
  Exclusive manuscript rights between acceptance and publication: Yes
  Copyright: Held by publication.
  Reprints: Available
Additional information: Send biographical sketch of author.
Disposition of manuscript:
  Query letter: Preferred
  Receipt of manuscript acknowledged: Yes
  Decision to publish in: 3 months
  Accepted manuscript published in: 3-6 months
  Rejected manuscript returned: Yes, if self-addressed, stamped envelope is sent with manuscript.
  Rejected manuscript criticized: Yes
Submit to:
  Robin C. Smith
  Editor
  American Technological University
  Box 1416
  Killeen, Texas 76541
  (817) 634-8728

ALBERTA JOURNAL OF EDUCATIONAL RESEARCH [904]
Faculty of Education, Room 949
University of Alberta
Edmonton, Alberta T6G 2E1, Canada
(403) 432-5869

First published in 1955

SUBSCRIPTION DATA
Issues and rates: Published quarterly.
  Average paid circulation: 720
  Annual rate(s): $6.00
Publisher or Sponsor: University of Alberta, Faculty of Education
Managing Editor: Thomas E. Kieren

EDITORIAL DESCRIPTION
  Devoted to the dissemination, criticism, interpretation and encouragement of all forms of systematic inquiry into education and fields related to education.
Articles per average issue: 8
Audience: Educational researchers
  Manuscripts accepted in English

MANUSCRIPT INFORMATION
Subject field(s): Education, child development, learning, intellectual development
Manuscript requirements: APA
  Preferred length: 2,500-7,000 words; 10-30 pages typewritten, double-spaced
  Number of copies to be submitted: Two
  Abstract: Yes

Author information and reprints: Payment: None.
Is simultaneous submission of article to other journals permitted: No
Exclusive manuscript rights between acceptance and publication: Yes
Copyright: Held by author.
Reprints: Available, first 20 free
Additional information: Tables and diagrams should be strictly limited.
Disposition of manuscript:
Query letter: No
Receipt of manuscript acknowledged: Yes
Decision to publish in: 3 months
Accepted manuscript published in: 6 months
Rejected manuscript returned: Yes
Rejected manuscript criticized: Yes
Submit to:
Thomas E. Kieren
Editor
(See address above)

THE ALBERTA SCHOOL TRUSTEE [905]
311, 10106-111 Avenue
Edmonton, Alberta, Canada
(403) 479-1921

SUBSCRIPTION DATA
Issues and rates: Published quarterly.
Average paid circulation: 2,500
Annual rate(s): $3.00
Publisher or Sponsor: Alberta School Trustees Association

EDITORIAL DESCRIPTION
Contains articles on all aspects of public education.
Articles per average issue: 5
Audience: Educators
Manuscripts accepted in English

MANUSCRIPT INFORMATION
Subject field(s): Finance, teachers, curriculum, school buildings, pupil transportation, school administration, school law, salary negotiations, local autonomy, school organization, colleges and universities, other educational institutions
Manuscript requirements: Style sheet sent on request.
Preferred length: 1,500-2,000 words; 8-10 pages
Number of copies to be submitted: One
Author information and reprints: Payment: None.
Is simultaneous submission of article to other journals permitted: Yes
Exclusive manuscript rights between acceptance and publication: No
Copyright: Held by author.
Reprints: Not available.
Disposition of manuscript:
Query letter: Yes
Receipt of manuscript acknowledged: Yes
Decision to publish in: 1 week
Accepted manuscript published in: One to two months
Rejected manuscript returned: Yes
Rejected manuscript criticized: No

Submit to:
Hal Martin
Editor
(See address above)

AMERICAN ANNALS OF THE DEAF [906]
5034 Wisconsin Avenue NW
Washington, D.C. 20016
(203) 363-1327

First published in 1847

SUBSCRIPTION DATA
Issues and rates: Published bi-monthly.
Average paid circulation: 5500
Annual rate(s): $12.50
Publisher or Sponsor: Conference of Executives of American Schools for the Deaf and Convention of American Instructors of the Deaf
Managing Editor: McCay Vernon

EDITORIAL DESCRIPTION
Contains articles on educational matters concerning the deaf.
Articles per average issue: 6
Audience: Teachers, specialists, administrators working with the deaf
Manuscripts accepted in English

MANUSCRIPT INFORMATION
Manuscript requirements: Style sheet sent on request.
Number of copies to be submitted: Three
Abstract: Yes
Author information and reprints: Payment: None.
Is simultaneous submission of article to other journals permitted: No
Exclusive manuscript rights between acceptance and publication: No
Reprints: Available at nominal cost
Disposition of manuscript:
Query letter: No
Receipt of manuscript acknowledged: Yes
Decision to publish in: Not over 30 days
Accepted manuscript published in: Three months
Rejected manuscript returned: Yes
Rejected manuscript criticized: Yes
Submit to:
McCay Vernon
Editor
Western Maryland College
Westminster, Maryland 21157
(301) 848-7000 ext. 233

AMERICAN ASSOCIATION OF TEACHER EDUCATORS IN AGRICULTURE. JOURNAL [907]
Virginia Polytechnic Institute and State University
2113 Derring Hall
Blacksburg, Virginia 24061
(703) 951-6836

First published in 1961

SUBSCRIPTION DATA
Issues and rates: Published three times per year.
Average paid circulation: 300
Annual rate(s): $4.50
Publisher or Sponsor: American Association of Teacher Educators in Agriculture
Managing Editor: Larry E. Miller

EDITORIAL DESCRIPTION
Contains articles on developments, innovations, and trends in teacher education in agriculture.
Articles per average issue: 4-5
Audience: Academic
Manuscripts accepted in English only

MANUSCRIPT INFORMATION
Subject field(s): Vocational education, agricultural education, vocational guidance, research, teacher education
Manuscript requirements: See latest issue for style requirements.
Preferred length: 900-3000 words; 3-10 pages
Number of copies to be submitted: One
Abstract: No
Author information and reprints: Payment: None. Two copies of issue in which article appears.
Is simultaneous submission of article to other journals permitted: No
Exclusive manuscript rights between acceptance and publication: Yes
Copyright: Held by publication.
Reprints: Not available.
Additional information: Manuscript should be accompanied by footnotes and references. Author's name, title and position should appear.
Disposition of manuscript:
Query letter: No
Receipt of manuscript acknowledged: Yes
Decision to publish in: 6-8 weeks
Accepted manuscript published in: 6-9 months
Rejected manuscript returned: Yes, if return postage is supplied by author.
Rejected manuscript criticized: Yes
Submit to:
Larry E. Miller
Managing Editor
(See address above)

THE AMERICAN BIOLOGY TEACHER [908]
1420 N Street, N.W.
Washington, D.C. 20005
(202) 667-8268

SUBSCRIPTION DATA
Issues and rates: Published monthly.
Average paid circulation: 14,500
Annual rate(s): $15, Foreign $17
Publisher or Sponsor: National Association of Biology Teachers, Inc.
Managing Editor: Jerry P. Lightner

EDITORIAL DESCRIPTION
Contains articles on biology curricula, laboratory facilities, laboratory techniques, biology education research,

new teaching methods, book reviews, audio-visual reviews.

MANUSCRIPT INFORMATION
Subject field(s): Biologic curriculum, biologic teaching methods, laboratory facilities, laboratory techniques, biology education philosophy
Manuscript requirements: AIBS
  Preferred length: 4-12 pages
  Number of copies to be submitted: One
Author information and reprints: Payment: None.
  Is simultaneous submission of article to other journals permitted: No
  Exclusive manuscript rights between acceptance and publication: Yes
  Copyright: Held by publication.
  Reprints: Available at cost set by printer
Disposition of manuscript:
  Receipt of manuscript acknowledged: Yes
  Decision to publish in: Six weeks
  Accepted manuscript published in: Four to six months
  Rejected manuscript returned: Yes
  Rejected manuscript criticized: No
Submit to:
  Jack L. Carter
  Editor
  Department of Biology
  The Colorado College
  Colorado Springs, Colorado 80903
  (303) 473-2233 ext. 317

AMERICAN EDUCATION [909]
U.S. Office of Education
400 Maryland Avenue S.W.
Washington, D.C. 20202
(202) 963-7785

SUBSCRIPTION DATA
Issues and rates: 10 issues per year
  Average paid circulation: 20,000; 25,000 controlled
  Annual rate(s): $9.95, Foreign $12.45
Publisher or Sponsor: U.S. Office of Education
Managing Editor: William A. Horn

EDITORIAL DESCRIPTION
Articles discuss innovative and exemplary programs or activities covering the full range of education and having some federal involvement (a requirement) though not necessarily funding. Interested in factual presentation of successful programs that educators may want to adapt to their own situations.
Articles per average issue: 6
Audience: Educational Administrators
Manuscripts accepted in English

MANUSCRIPT INFORMATION
Subject field(s): Education in all its aspects with federal involvement
Manuscript requirements: Style sheet sent on request.
  Preferred length: 2500 words
  Number of copies to be submitted: One
  Abstract: No
Author information and reprints: Payment: By publication to author. $150 per article. Usually $300 for an assigned article, $225.00 for unsolicited work depending upon length
  Is simultaneous submission of article to other journals permitted: No
  Exclusive manuscript rights between acceptance and publication: Yes
  Copyright: Not copyrighted
  Reprints: Not available.
Disposition of manuscript:
  Query letter: Yes, recommended
  Receipt of manuscript acknowledged: Yes
  Decision to publish in: 2 to 4 weeks
  Accepted manuscript published in: 3 to 4 months
  Rejected manuscript returned: Yes
  Rejected manuscript criticized: No
Submit to:
  Leroy V. Goodman
  Editor
  (See address above)

AMERICAN EDUCATIONAL RESEARCH JOURNAL [910]
1126 Sixteenth Street, NW
Washington, D.C. 20036
(202) 223-9485

SUBSCRIPTION DATA
Issues and rates: Published quarterly.
  Average paid circulation: 14,000
  Annual rate(s): $10.00
Publisher or Sponsor: American Educational Research Association
Managing Editor: Patricia E. Stivers

EDITORIAL DESCRIPTION
Contains original research, both empirical and theoretical; extensive selective bibliographies; review of appropriate publications and published and experimental test instruments.
Articles per average issue: 6
Manuscripts accepted in English

MANUSCRIPT INFORMATION
Subject field(s): Reports of original studies in any aspect of education
Manuscript requirements: APA and current issue
  Preferred length: 20 pages
  Number of copies to be submitted: Three
  Abstract: Yes
Author information and reprints: Payment: Reprints only. 50 free to author
  Is simultaneous submission of article to other journals permitted: No
  Exclusive manuscript rights between acceptance and publication: Yes
  Copyright: Held by publication.
  Reprints: Available, cost quoted individually
Disposition of manuscript:
  Query letter: No
  Receipt of manuscript acknowledged: Yes
  Decision to publish in: 4-8 weeks
  Accepted manuscript published in: 4-6 months
  Rejected manuscript returned: Yes
Submit to:
  Kaoru Yamamoto
  College of Education
  Arizona State University
  Tempe, Arizona 85281
  (602) 965-7456

AMERICAN JOURNAL OF PHYSICS [911]
American Institute of Physics
335 East 45th Street
New York, New York 10017
(212) 685-1940

First published in 1933

SUBSCRIPTION DATA
Issues and rates: Published monthly.
  Average paid circulation: 12,300
  Annual rate(s): $25.00; Foreign $27.00
Publisher or Sponsor: American Association of Physics Teachers

EDITORIAL DESCRIPTION
Devoted to the instructional and cultural aspects of physical science rather than to research.
Articles per average issue: 10-12
Audience: Teachers and students of physics, primarily at the college and university level
Manuscripts accepted in English

MANUSCRIPT INFORMATION
Manuscript requirements: See latest issue for style requirements. AIP
  Preferred length: Varies
  Number of copies to be submitted: 3
  Abstract: Yes. Each regular article must be prefaced by an abstract between 50 and 100 words long. Notes and Discussions do not carry abstracts.
Author information and reprints: Payment: By author to publication. $70.00 per page.
  Is simultaneous submission of article to other journals permitted: An article or note is accepted for publication with the understanding that it has not been published elsewhere.
  Exclusive manuscript rights between acceptance and publication: Yes
  Copyright: Held by the Association.
  Reprints: Available at no cost. 100 Available at cost.
Additional information: See "Information for Contributors" on the inside front cover of the January issue.
Disposition of manuscript:
  Query letter: Not necessary.
  Receipt of manuscript acknowledged: Yes
  Decision to publish in: 8 weeks
  Accepted manuscript published in: 6 months
  Rejected manuscript returned: Yes, if return postage is supplied by author.
  Rejected manuscript criticized: Yes
Submit to:
  Edwin F. Taylor
  Editor
  Room 20B-136
  Massachusetts Institute of Technology
  Cambridge, Massachusetts 02139
  (617) 253-1491

THE AMERICAN SCHOOL BOARD JOURNAL [912]

State National Bank Plaza
Evanston, Illinois 60201
(312) 869-7730

First published in 1891

SUBSCRIPTION DATA

Issues and rates: Published monthly.
  Average paid circulation: 46,000
  Annual rate(s): $16.00, Foreign $24.00
Publisher or Sponsor: National School Boards Association
Managing Editor: David Martin

EDITORIAL DESCRIPTION

  Contains information and interpretation of nearly all aspects (legal, political, financial, administrative, operational) of the public school system. Stresses the importance for all concerned (citizens, children and society in general) that local control of public education be maintained.
Articles per average issue: 10
Audience: School Boards, Superintentents, Administrators
  Manuscripts accepted in English

MANUSCRIPT INFORMATION

Subject field(s): Operation of school boards; financial operation of schools; rights of children, teachers, administrators; political aspects of local control
Manuscript requirements: See latest issue for style requirements.
  Preferred length: 5 to 15 pages
  Number of copies to be submitted: One original
  Abstract: No
Author information and reprints: Payment: By publication to author. Usually pay only for assigned work, but occasionally pay small honorarium for unsolicited material.
  Is simultaneous submission of article to other journals permitted: No
  Exclusive manuscript rights between acceptance and publication: Yes
  Copyright: Held by publication.
  Reprints: Not available.
Disposition of manuscript:
  Receipt of manuscript acknowledged: Yes
  Decision to publish in: 3 months
  Accepted manuscript published in: 3 to 6 months
  Rejected manuscript returned: Yes
  Rejected manuscript criticized: No
Submit to:
  James Betchkal
  Editor and Assistant Publisher
  (See address above)

AMERICAN SCHOOL AND UNIVERSITY [913]

134 North Thirteenth Street
Philadelphia, Pennsylvania 19107
(215) 564-5170

SUBSCRIPTION DATA

Issues and rates: Published monthly.
  Average paid circulation: 5,089; 37,007 controlled
  Annual rate(s): $15.00, Foreign $13.00

EDITORIAL DESCRIPTION

  Written for administrators, architects and others involved in construction, operation and maintenance of the nation's public schools, private schools, colleges and universities. The articles are entirely centered on educational facilities: their construction and maintainence.

MANUSCRIPT INFORMATION

Subject field(s): Construction techniques, ways of remodeling and modernizing, case histories, practical ways to accomplish jobs, interviews, innovative facilities, new equipment
Manuscript requirements: Style sheet sent on request.
  Preferred length: 2000 words maximum
Author information and reprints: Payment: By publication to author. Amount per page varies.
  Is simultaneous submission of article to other journals permitted: No
  Exclusive manuscript rights between acceptance and publication: Yes
  Copyright: Held by publication.
  Reprints: Available; 3 free
Additional information: No curriculum-oriented topics.
Disposition of manuscript:
  Receipt of manuscript acknowledged: Yes
  Decision to publish in: 2 to 6 weeks
  Accepted manuscript published in: 2 to 4 months
  Rejected manuscript returned: Yes, if self-addressed, stamped envelope is sent with manuscript.
  Rejected manuscript criticized: Sometimes
Submit to:
  James R. Russo
  Editor
  (See address above)
  (215) 564-5170 ext. 311

AMERICAN SECONDARY EDUCATION [914]

College of Education
The University of Akron
Akron, Ohio 44325
(216) 375-7772

First published in 1970

SUBSCRIPTION DATA

Issues and rates: Published quarterly.
  Average paid circulation: 2,000; 2,600 controlled
  Annual rate(s): $12.00; Foreign $12.00; Institutions $12.00
Publisher or Sponsor: Ohio Association of Secondary School Principals

EDITORIAL DESCRIPTION

  To promote change in education at the secondary level
Articles per average issue: 10
Audience: Secondary school principals and teachers
  Manuscripts accepted in English

MANUSCRIPT INFORMATION

Manuscript requirements: APA
  Preferred length: 2,000-4,000 words
  Number of copies to be submitted: 4
  Abstract: Not necessary.
Author information and reprints: Payment: None.
  Is simultaneous submission of article to other journals permitted: Permitted, but not encouraged.
  Exclusive manuscript rights between acceptance and publication: Yes
  Copyright: Held by publication.
  Reprints: Available at cost.
Additional information: Research should be defined in layman's terms. How-to and practical articles are desired.
Disposition of manuscript:
  Query letter: Not necessary.
  Receipt of manuscript acknowledged: Yes
  Decision to publish in: 4 months
  Accepted manuscript published in: 6 months
  Rejected manuscript returned: Yes, with return postage paid by publication.
  Rejected manuscript criticized: Sometimes
Submit to:
  Charles L. Wood
  Editor
  (See address above)

AMERICAN TEACHER [915]

1012 14th Street NW
Washington, D.C. 20005
(202) 737-6141 ext. 32

First published in 1916

SUBSCRIPTION DATA

Issues and rates: Monthly except July and August
  Average paid circulation: 425,000
  Annual rate(s): $7.00, includes *Changing Education*
Publisher or Sponsor: American Federation of Teachers, AFL-CIO
Managing Editor: David Elsila

EDITORIAL DESCRIPTION

  Contains news of the teacher union movement and concerns of classroom teachers.
Articles per average issue: 6
Audience: Classroom Teachers
  Manuscripts accepted in English

MANUSCRIPT INFORMATION

Subject field(s): Economics affecting teachers, academic freedom and teacher rights, educational problems of minorities
Manuscript requirements: See latest issue for style requirements.
  Preferred length: 1,000 words typewritten, double-spaced
  Number of copies to be submitted: One
  Abstract: No

Author information and reprints: Payment: By publication to author. $25-$100 per article.
Is simultaneous submission of article to other journals permitted: Yes
Exclusive manuscript rights between acceptance and publication: No
Copyright: Held by author.
Reprints: Available at cost
Disposition of manuscript:
Query letter: No
Receipt of manuscript acknowledged: No
Decision to publish in: 3-6 months
Accepted manuscript published in: 3-6 months
Rejected manuscript returned: Yes, if return postage is supplied by author.
Rejected manuscript criticized: No
Submit to:
David A. Elsila
Editor
(See address above)

THE ARITHMETIC TEACHER [916]

1906 Association Drive
Reston, Virginia 22091
(703) 620-9840

First published in 1954

SUBSCRIPTION DATA

Issues and rates: 8 times per year
Average paid circulation: 45,000
Annual rate(s): $13.00, Members $11.00
Publisher or Sponsor: National Council of Teachers of Mathematics

EDITORIAL DESCRIPTION

Concerned with the teaching of mathematics in kindergarten and elementary school.
Articles per average issue: 8
Audience: Elementary school teachers and teacher educators

MANUSCRIPT INFORMATION

Subject field(s): Elementary school mathematics: methods and content
Manuscript requirements: Chicago
Preferred length: 2000-2500 words typewritten double-spaced, on one side with generous margins
Number of copies to be submitted: Two
Abstract: No
Author information and reprints: Payment: None.
Is simultaneous submission of article to other journals permitted: No
Exclusive manuscript rights between acceptance and publication: Yes
Disposition of manuscript:
Receipt of manuscript acknowledged: Yes
Decision to publish in: 6-8 weeks
Accepted manuscript published in: 6 months
Rejected manuscript returned: Yes
Rejected manuscript criticized: Yes
Submit to:
Jane M. Hill
Managing Editor
(See address above)

ARIZONA ENGLISH BULLETIN [917]

English Department
Arizona State University
Tempe, Arizona 85281
(602) 965-6130

SUBSCRIPTION DATA

Issues and rates: Published three times per year.
Average paid circulation: Not available.
Annual rate(s): $4.00
Publisher or Sponsor: Arizona English Teachers Association

EDITORIAL DESCRIPTION

Publishes articles on teaching English in the secondary school, occasionally elementary or junior college.
Articles per average issue: 20
Audience: Secondary English teachers
Manuscripts accepted in English

MANUSCRIPT INFORMATION

Subject field(s): English for the secondary teacher
Manuscript requirements: See latest issue for style requirements.
Preferred length: 4 to 12 pages
Number of copies to be submitted: One
Author information and reprints: Payment: None. Three copies of the issue containing the article.
Is simultaneous submission of article to other journals permitted: No
Exclusive manuscript rights between acceptance and publication: Yes
Copyright: Not copyrighted
Reprints: Not available.
Additional information: Articles are grouped around one theme each issue. Inquire of the Editor for future themes. Articles should be practical and based on sound theory and pedagogy. Theoretical articles are occasionally used, usually solicited.
Disposition of manuscript:
Query letter: Helpful
Receipt of manuscript acknowledged: No
Decision to publish in: One week or more
Accepted manuscript published in: Varies
Rejected manuscript returned: Yes, if self-addressed, stamped envelope is sent with manuscript.
Rejected manuscript criticized: No
Submit to:
Kenneth L. Donelson
Editor
(See address above)

ART EDUCATION [918]

National Art Education Association
1916 Association Drive
Reston, Virginia 22091
(703) 620-3855

First published in 1948

SUBSCRIPTION DATA

Issues and rates: 8 times a year
Average paid circulation: 9,500
Annual rate(s): $15.00 for all; Members $25.00
Publisher or Sponsor: National Art Education Association
Managing Editor: Beverly Jeanne Davis

EDITORIAL DESCRIPTION

Current trends, problems, and philosophies in art education, including all levels, preprimary through university and adult education, in the visual arts.
Articles per average issue: 5
Audience: Elementary and secondary art teachers and art consultants; university art education faculty; art education students.
Manuscripts accepted in English

MANUSCRIPT INFORMATION

Subject field(s): Articles on art education: current issues, problems, trends, philosophies concerning education in the visual arts; aesthetic education; the art curriculum; art teacher education; interdisciplinary approaches in the fine arts.
Manuscript requirements: Style sheet sent on request.
Preferred length: 8-14 pages
Number of copies to be submitted: Original and 2 copies
Abstract: Not necessary.
Author information and reprints: Payment: None.
Is simultaneous submission of article to other journals permitted: Not permitted.
Copyright: Author and publisher.
Reprints: Available at no cost. 2 copies at no cost Available at cost.
Additional information: Primary emphasis should be on education through and in the visual arts, with concern for underlying philosophy. No how-to-do-it type articles are accepted.
Disposition of manuscript:
Query letter: Not necessary.
Receipt of manuscript acknowledged: Yes
Decision to publish in: 6 weeks
Accepted manuscript published in: Within a year
Rejected manuscript returned: Yes, with return postage paid by publication.
Rejected manuscript criticized: Sometimes
Submit to:
Editor
(See address above)

ASSOCIATION OF COLLEGIATE SCHOOLS OF PLANNING BULLETIN [919]

School of Urban Planning
Michigan State University
East Lansing, Michigan 48823
(517) 353-5321

First published in 1963

SUBSCRIPTION DATA

Issues and rates: Published quarterly.
Average paid circulation: 100; 700 controlled
Annual rate(s): $5.00

Publisher or Sponsor: Association of Collegiate Schools of Planning
Managing Editor: Carl Goldschmidt

EDITORIAL DESCRIPTION

Contains articles on urban planning education, often spanning a wide variety of contemporary and controversial subjects.
Articles per average issue: 3-5
Audience: Planning educators
Manuscripts accepted in English

MANUSCRIPT INFORMATION

Subject field(s): Urban and regional planning
Manuscript requirements: No specific style guide.
   Preferred length: 6 pages or less
   Number of copies to be submitted: Two
   Abstract: Yes
Author information and reprints: Payment: None.
   Is simultaneous submission of article to other journals permitted: Yes
   Exclusive manuscript rights between acceptance and publication: No
   Copyright: Not copyrighted
   Reprints: Not available.
Disposition of manuscript:
   Query letter: Preferred
   Receipt of manuscript acknowledged: Yes
   Decision to publish in: 1 month
   Accepted manuscript published in: 3 months maximum
   Rejected manuscript returned: No
   Rejected manuscript criticized: No
Submit to:
   Carl Goldschmidt
   Editor
   (See address above)

ATE NEWSLETTER [920]

1701 K Street, N.W.
Washington, D.C. 20006
(202) 223-1068

SUBSCRIPTION DATA

Issues and rates: Published bi-monthly.
   Average paid circulation: 3500
   Annual rate(s): Members $25.00
Publisher or Sponsor: Association of Teacher Educators

EDITORIAL DESCRIPTION

Contains in-house and other materials relative to improving teacher education.
Audience: Those who teach teachers and to the supervisors and directors of student teaching and field experiences in teacher education.
Manuscripts accepted in English

MANUSCRIPT INFORMATION

Subject field(s): Teacher education; student teaching; human relations; education of teachers; methodology: performance-based, simulation, open classroom, etc.
Manuscript requirements: Style sheet sent on request.
   Preferred length: 3-4 pages
   Number of copies to be submitted: Two

Author information and reprints: Payment: None. Two copies of issue in which article appears.
   Is simultaneous submission of article to other journals permitted: No
   Exclusive manuscript rights between acceptance and publication: No
   Copyright: Not copyrighted
   Reprints: Available at no cost, limited
Additional information: Manuscripts should be in proper style, double-spaced, typewritten, with appropriate references if needed.
Disposition of manuscript:
   Receipt of manuscript acknowledged: Yes
   Decision to publish in: 4-6 weeks
   Accepted manuscript published in: Up to six months
   Rejected manuscript returned: Yes, if return postage is supplied by author.
   Rejected manuscript criticized: No
Submit to:
   Melvin C. Buller
   Executive Secretary
   (See address above)

ATHLETIC JOURNAL [921]

Athletic Journal Publishing Company
1729 Howard Street
Evanston, Illinois 60202
(312) 328-8545

First published in 1921

SUBSCRIPTION DATA

Issues and rates: Monthly except July and August
   Average paid circulation: 31,000
   Annual rate(s): $4.00, Foreign $5.00

EDITORIAL DESCRIPTION

Contains technical articles on athletic coaching, athletic technique and athletic training.
Articles per average issue: 15-18
Audience: Athletic directors, all levels
Manuscripts accepted in English

MANUSCRIPT INFORMATION

Subject field(s): Sports, sports administration, athletic training
Manuscript requirements: No specific style guide.
   Preferred length: 1500 words; 5 pages
   Number of copies to be submitted: One
   Abstract: No
Author information and reprints: Payment: By publication to author. $25.00 per article. Plus 3 copies of issue in which article appears.
   Is simultaneous submission of article to other journals permitted: No
   Exclusive manuscript rights between acceptance and publication: Yes
   Copyright: Held by publication.
   Reprints: Available
Additional information: Articles accepted only from men/women actively engaged in coaching or administration of high school or college athletics.
Disposition of manuscript:
   Query letter: No
   Receipt of manuscript acknowledged: Yes

   Decision to publish in: 2 weeks
   Accepted manuscript published in: 6-12 months
   Rejected manuscript returned: Yes, if return postage is supplied by author.
   Rejected manuscript criticized: No
Submit to:
   John L. Griffith
   Publisher
   (See address above)

BEHAVIORAL & SOCIAL SCIENCE TEACHER [922]

Behavioral Publications
72 Fifth Avenue
New York, New York 10011
(212) 243-6000

First published in 1974

SUBSCRIPTION DATA

Issues and rates: Published semi-annually.
   Average paid circulation: 2,000
   Annual rate(s): $6.00; Foreign $14.00; Institutions $12.00
Publisher or Sponsor: City College, CUNY, School of Education
Managing Editor: Jean Blackburn

EDITORIAL DESCRIPTION

Devoted to the growing needs of high school and two-year college teachers of the social sciences, it presents materials designed to enrich the teacher and help develope new and exciting teaching strategies, to increase awareness of new research and developments, and illuminate theoretical and practical issues.
Articles per average issue: 8
Audience: Academic
Manuscripts accepted in English

MANUSCRIPT INFORMATION

Manuscript requirements: APA
   Preferred length: 16 pages
   Number of copies to be submitted: 3
   Abstract: Yes.
Author information and reprints: Payment: None.
   Is simultaneous submission of article to other journals permitted: Not permitted.
   Exclusive manuscript rights between acceptance and publication: Yes
   Copyright: Held by publication.
   Reprints: Available at cost.
Disposition of manuscript:
   Query letter: Not necessary.
   Receipt of manuscript acknowledged: Yes
   Decision to publish in: 3 months
   Accepted manuscript published in: 6 months
   Rejected manuscript returned: Yes, if return postage is supplied by author.
   Rejected manuscript criticized: Sometimes
Submit to:
   Prof. Harwood Fisher
   Editor-in Chief
   School of Education, Klapper Hall, CUNY
   135th Street and Convent Avenue
   New York, New York 10031
   (212) 621-2164

BRITISH JOURNAL OF EDUCATIONAL PSYCHOLOGY [923]

B. J. E. P. Department
25 Perth Street
Edinburgh EH3 5DW, Scotland

First published in 1931

SUBSCRIPTION DATA

Issues and rates: Published three times per year.
Average paid circulation: 4,000
Annual rate(s): £4.00; Foreign £13.50; post free; Members £1.50
Publisher or Sponsor: British Psychological Society
Managing Editor: Prof. Noel J. Entwistle

EDITORIAL DESCRIPTION

Publishes empirical studies of education or educational psychology, with some theoretical papers, review articles or position papers
Articles per average issue: 12
Audience: Educational researchers, undergraduate and graduate teachers, educational psychologists
Manuscripts accepted in English only

MANUSCRIPT INFORMATION

Subject field(s): Studies of students of any age range which make use of psychological or social psychological methodologies; learning, personality, measurement, observation, linguistic development: all as they apply to education
Manuscript requirements: See November issue
Preferred length: 2,500-4,00 words
Number of copies to be submitted: 2
Abstract: Yes. should give an indication of the size and nature of the sample and mention the aim, scope and results of the inquiry in not more than 200 words.
Author information and reprints: Payment: Reprints only. 50 reprints
Is simultaneous submission of article to other journals permitted: Not permitted.
Exclusive manuscript rights between acceptance and publication: Yes
Copyright: Held jointly by author and publication
Reprints: Available at cost. £7.00 per 100
Additional information: Keep tabular material to a minimum. Relate length to the international significance of the study, note style of references used, and check these references carefully.
Disposition of manuscript:
Query letter: Not necessary.
Receipt of manuscript acknowledged: Yes
Decision to publish in: 8 weeks
Accepted manuscript published in: 9 months
Rejected manuscript returned: Yes, with return postage paid by publication.
Rejected manuscript criticized: Sometimes
Submit to:
Prof. Noel J. Entwistle
The Editor
Department of Educational Research
Cartmel College
Bailrigg, Lancaster LA1 4YL, England
0524-65201

BUSINESS EDUCATION WORLD [924]

1221 Avenue of the Americas
New York, New York 10020
(212) 997-3216

First published in 1919

SUBSCRIPTION DATA

Issues and rates: Published bi-monthly.
Average paid circulation: 90,000 controlled

EDITORIAL DESCRIPTION

Contains articles dealing with innovative application of teaching methods, educational theories, trends in business and office education, collegiate business education.
Articles per average issue: 7
Audience: Teachers of business education
Manuscripts accepted in English

MANUSCRIPT INFORMATION

Subject field(s): Accounting, data processing, computing, office education, shorthand, typing, career education, collegiate business and consumer education programs
Manuscript requirements: Style sheet sent on request.
Preferred length: 1,600-2,500 words, typewritten, double-spaced
Number of copies to be submitted: 2
Abstract: No
Author information and reprints: Payment: By publication to author. $50.00 per article. Advance copies of issue in which article appears.
Is simultaneous submission of article to other journals permitted: No
Exclusive manuscript rights between acceptance and publication: Yes
Copyright: Held by publication.
Reprints: Not available.
Additional information: Manuscript should be typewritten (60 spaces to a line), double spaced, with author's name, title and professional affiliation all on first page only.
Disposition of manuscript:
Query letter: No
Receipt of manuscript acknowledged: Yes
Decision to publish in: 6-8 weeks
Accepted manuscript published in: Up to one year
Rejected manuscript returned: Yes
Rejected manuscript criticized: Sometimes
Submit to:
Susan S. Schrumpf
Editor
(See address above)

THE CABE JOURNAL [925]

410 Asylum Street 532
Hartford, Connecticut 06103
(203) 522-8201

Previously entitled *Concerns of CABE*

First published in 1969

SUBSCRIPTION DATA

Issues and rates: Published bi-weekly.
Average paid circulation: 2500 controlled
Publisher or Sponsor: Connecticut Association of Boards of Education, Inc.

EDITORIAL DESCRIPTION

Contains articles of general educational interest for school board members.
Articles per average issue: 5
Audience: Connecticut school board members
Manuscripts accepted in English only

MANUSCRIPT INFORMATION

Subject field(s): Educational innovation, management, philosophy, or opinion
Manuscript requirements: No specific style guide.
Preferred length: 4-8 pages
Number of copies to be submitted: Two
Abstract: Yes
Author information and reprints: Payment: None.
Is simultaneous submission of article to other journals permitted: Yes
Exclusive manuscript rights between acceptance and publication: No
Copyright: Held by author.
Reprints: Up to 6 reprints provided, additional at cost.
Disposition of manuscript:
Query letter: Preferred
Receipt of manuscript acknowledged: Yes
Decision to publish in: 1 month
Accepted manuscript published in: 6 months maximum
Rejected manuscript returned: Yes, if return postage is supplied by author.
Rejected manuscript criticized: No
Submit to:
Steven Mansfield
Director of Communications
(See address above)

THE CANADIAN ADMINISTRATOR [926]

Department of Educational Administration
The University of Alberta
Edmonton, Alberta, Canada
(403) 432-5241

SUBSCRIPTION DATA

Issues and rates: Published monthly.
Annual rate(s): Individuals $3.00

EDITORIAL DESCRIPTION

Contains articles on research in educational administration.
Articles per average issue: 1
Audience: Scholars, administrators
Manuscripts accepted in English

MANUSCRIPT INFORMATION

Subject field(s): Organizational theory, administration, program development, evaluation, human relations, group dynamics, change and innovation

Manuscript requirements: See latest issue for style requirements.
  Preferred length: 2500-3000 words; 11 pages
  Number of copies to be submitted: One
  Abstract: No
Author information and reprints: Payment: None.
  Is simultaneous submission of article to other journals permitted: No
  Exclusive manuscript rights between acceptance and publication: Yes
  Copyright: Held by publication.
  Reprints: Available
Disposition of manuscript:
  Query letter: No
  Receipt of manuscript acknowledged: Yes
  Decision to publish in: 3 months
  Accepted manuscript published in: 6 months
  Rejected manuscript returned: Yes
  Rejected manuscript criticized: Yes
Submit to:
  C.S. Bumbarger
  (See address above)

CANADIAN AND INTERNATIONAL EDUCATION [927]
Education Canadienne et Internationale
Faculty of Education, Althouse College
University of Western Ontario
London, Ontario N6G 1G7, Canada
(519) 679-3480

First published in 1972

SUBSCRIPTION DATA
Issues and rates: Published semi-annually.
  Average paid circulation: 500
  Annual rate(s): $6.00; Pan-Am $6.00; Foreign $6.00; Individuals $6.00; Institutions $6.00; Students $3.00; Foreign institutions $6.00
Publisher or Sponsor: The Comparative and International Education Society of Canada
Managing Editor: Dr. David J. Radcliffe

EDITORIAL DESCRIPTION
  The study of education and society in Canada and other nations, educational theories and practices as they develop and change in various societies, clarification of the role of education in promoting understanding within and between nations.
Articles per average issue: 8
Audience: Scholars interested in comparative education
  Manuscripts accepted in English and French

MANUSCRIPT INFORMATION
Subject field(s): Education; stress on the contemporary, but historical articles acceptable. Canada, all other nations and societies, international and intercultural.
Manuscript requirements: See latest issue for style requirements.
  Preferred length: 3,000 to 5,000 words; 15-20 pages
  Number of copies to be submitted: Two

Abstract: Yes. Would also welcome English abstract for French submission, French abstract for English submission, but this is not required.
Author information and reprints: Payment: Reprints only. 3 copies of Journal
  Is simultaneous submission of article to other journals permitted: Permitted, but not encouraged.
  Exclusive manuscript rights between acceptance and publication: Yes
  Copyright: Held by publication.
  Reprints: Not available.
Disposition of manuscript:
  Query letter: Not necessary.
  Receipt of manuscript acknowledged: Yes
  Decision to publish in: 1-2 months
  Accepted manuscript published in: 3-9 months
  Rejected manuscript returned: Yes, if return postage is supplied by author.
  Rejected manuscript criticized: Reasons for rejections only
Submit to:
  Dr. David Radcliffe
  Editor
  (See address above)

CATECHIST [928]
2285 Arbor Boulevard
Dayton, Ohio 45439
(513) 294-3636

SUBSCRIPTION DATA
Issues and rates: Eight issues during school year
  Average paid circulation: 30,000
  Annual rate(s): $6.00, Foreign $7.00 (Canada)

EDITORIAL DESCRIPTION
  Contains major articles dealing with religious education (essentially Catholic) and related areas: theology, Scripture, pedagogy, child and adolescent psychology, media materials and techniques, ecclesiology, ecumenism, social problems.
Articles per average issue: 6
Audience: Teachers of religion
  Manuscripts accepted in English

MANUSCRIPT INFORMATION
Subject field(s): Catechetics, learning psychology, classroom techniques, Scripture, Christian living, theology, education, materials
Manuscript requirements: See latest issue for style requirements.
  Preferred length: 1500-1800 words
  Number of copies to be submitted: One
  Abstract: No
Author information and reprints: Payment: By publication to author. $50-$100 per article.
  Is simultaneous submission of article to other journals permitted: No
  Exclusive manuscript rights between acceptance and publication: Yes
  Copyright: Held by publication.
  Reprints: Not available.
Additional information: Manuscripts must be double-spaced, typewritten with wide margins left, right, top and bottom. Only

the original copy, not carbon or duplicated copies, will be accepted. Author's name, address, phone number and credentials should accompany manuscript.
Disposition of manuscript:
  Query letter: No
  Receipt of manuscript acknowledged: Yes
  Decision to publish in: One month
  Accepted manuscript published in: Varies
  Rejected manuscript returned: Yes
  Rejected manuscript criticized: Yes
Submit to:
  Robert J. Hawking
  Editor
  (See address above)

THE CEA CRITIC [929]
Centenary College
P. O. Box 4188
Shreveport, Louisiana 71104
(318) 869-5254

Previously entitled *College English Association Newsletter*

First published in 1939

SUBSCRIPTION DATA
Issues and rates: Bi-monthly, November through May
  Average paid circulation: 2800; 200 controlled
  Annual rate(s): Individuals $8.00, Institutions $10.00
Publisher or Sponsor: The College English Association, Inc.

EDITORIAL DESCRIPTION
  Contains brief critical essays treating literary materials used in the teaching of college English; creative work, particularly poetry, related to the teaching of literature; reviews of books concerned with literary criticism and scholarship.
Articles per average issue: 20
Audience: Teachers of college English
  Manuscripts accepted in English

MANUSCRIPT INFORMATION
Subject field(s): Literary criticism, poetry
Manuscript requirements: See latest issue for style requirements.
  Preferred length: 500-2000 words; 2-8 pages
  Number of copies to be submitted: One
  Abstract: No
Author information and reprints: Payment: Reprints only. 2 Complimentary copies of issue
  Is simultaneous submission of article to other journals permitted: No
  Exclusive manuscript rights between acceptance and publication: Yes
  Copyright: Held by publication.
  Reprints: Available at cost
Disposition of manuscript:
  Query letter: No
  Receipt of manuscript acknowledged: Yes
  Decision to publish in: 2 months
  Accepted manuscript published in: 6-12 months

Education

Rejected manuscript returned: Yes, if return postage is supplied by author.
Rejected manuscript criticized: Yes
Submit to:
Earle Labor
Editor of Publications, College English Association
(See address above)

SPECIAL STIPULATIONS
Publication reserved for CEA members.

THE CEA FORUM [930]
Centenary College
P. O. Box 4188
Shreveport, Louisiana 71104
(318) 869-5254

First published in 1970

SUBSCRIPTION DATA
Issues and rates: Published bi-monthly.
  Average paid circulation: 2,800; 200 controlled
  Annual rate(s): Individuals $8.00; Institutions $10.00; Students $5.00; Foreign individuals $8.00; Foreign institutions $10.00
Publisher or Sponsor: The College English Association, Inc.

EDITORIAL DESCRIPTION
News and views relating to the teaching of college English, along with reports of national and regional CEA activities; encourages dialogue on timely academic issues and innovations in college teaching.
Articles per average issue: 20
Audience: College English teachers
  Manuscripts accepted in English

MANUSCRIPT INFORMATION
Subject field(s): All fields related to the teaching of college English; literature, grammar, linguistics, rhetoric. Creative work related to college English is also welcome.
Manuscript requirements: See latest issue for style requirements.
  Preferred length: 100-500 words; 1-2 pages
  Number of copies to be submitted: 1
  Abstract: Not necessary.
Author information and reprints: Payment: Reprints only. 2
  Is simultaneous submission of article to other journals permitted: Not permitted.
  Exclusive manuscript rights between acceptance and publication: Yes
  Copyright: Held by publication.
  Reprints: Available at cost.
Disposition of manuscript:
  Query letter: Not necessary.
  Receipt of manuscript acknowledged: Yes
  Decision to publish in: 2 months
  Accepted manuscript published in: 1-6 months
  Rejected manuscript returned: Yes, if return postage is supplied by author.
  Rejected manuscript criticized: Sometimes

Submit to:
Earle Labor
Editor
(See address above)

SPECIAL STIPULATIONS
Publication reserved for members of the College English Association

CHANGE [931]
The Magazine of Higher Learning
NBW Tower
New Rochelle, New York 10801
(914) 235-8700

SUBSCRIPTION DATA
Issues and rates: Published monthly.
  Average paid circulation: 32,000
  Annual rate(s): $14.00; Foreign $18.00

EDITORIAL DESCRIPTION
A leading monthly in higher education, providing commentary and criticism on higher education and general cultural and intellectual aspects of society. In addition to major articles, it features monthly columns which are assigned on outside viewpoints, Washington, research, science and book review-essays. Editors accept all ideological views, with editorial views confined to positions on the editorial page.
Articles per average issue: 4
Audience: Academic
  Manuscripts accepted in English

MANUSCRIPT INFORMATION
Subject field(s): Pedagogic issues, socio-political issues, philosophic pieces
Manuscript requirements: See latest issue for style requirements.
  Preferred length: 2,000-6,000 words; 5-15 pages typewritten, double-spaced
  Number of copies to be submitted: One
  Abstract: No
Author information and reprints: Payment: By publication to author. $350 per article. $100 for columns.
  Is simultaneous submission of article to other journals permitted: No
  Exclusive manuscript rights between acceptance and publication: Yes
  Copyright: Held by publication.
Additional information: Less than 5 per cent of all unsolicited manuscripts submitted are accepted.
Disposition of manuscript:
  Query letter: Advisable
  Receipt of manuscript acknowledged: Yes
  Decision to publish in: 1 month
  Accepted manuscript published in: 3-5 months
  Rejected manuscript returned: Yes, if self-addressed, stamped envelope is sent with manuscript.
  Rejected manuscript criticized: Yes
Submit to:
Celia Morris
Senior Editor
(See address above)

CHANGING EDUCATION [932]
1012 14th Street NW
Washington, D.C. 20005
(202) 737-6141 ext. 32

First published in 1966

SUBSCRIPTION DATA
Issues and rates: Published quarterly.
  Average paid circulation: 425,000
  Annual rate(s): $7.00, includes *American Teacher*
Publisher or Sponsor: American Federation of Teachers, AFL-CIO

EDITORIAL DESCRIPTION
Contains articles in all areas of education: motivation, educational policies, HEW programs, academic freedom, racism and sexism, educational concerns of minorities.
Articles per average issue: 15
Audience: Classroom teachers
  Manuscripts accepted in English

MANUSCRIPT INFORMATION
Manuscript requirements: See latest issue for style requirements.
  Preferred length: 2,000 words or less
  Number of copies to be submitted: One
  Abstract: No
Author information and reprints: Payment: By publication to author. $25-$100 per article.
  Is simultaneous submission of article to other journals permitted: Yes
  Exclusive manuscript rights between acceptance and publication: No
  Copyright: Not copyrighted
  Reprints: Available at cost
Disposition of manuscript:
  Query letter: No
  Receipt of manuscript acknowledged: Yes
  Decision to publish in: 6 months
  Accepted manuscript published in: 6 months
  Rejected manuscript returned: Yes, if return postage is supplied by author.
  Rejected manuscript criticized: If requested
Submit to:
David Elsila
Editor
(See address above)

CHILDHOOD EDUCATION [933]
3615 Wisconsin Avenue, N.W.
Washington, D.C. 20016
(202) 363-6963

First published in 1924

SUBSCRIPTION DATA
Issues and rates: Published bi-monthly.
  Average paid circulation: 27,000
  Annual rate(s): Members $15.00; Students $7.50; Institutions $18.00; Individuals $18.00

Publisher or Sponsor: Association for Childhood Education International
Managing Editor: Lucy Prete Martin

EDITORIAL DESCRIPTION
Brings to teachers, administrators, parents, day care and family/social/community workers helpful, stimulating and professional articles on children's experiences, human relationships, programs and problems.
Articles per average issue: 6
Audience: Professional, academic, students, general
Manuscripts accepted in English

MANUSCRIPT INFORMATION
Subject field(s): Child growth and development, innovative teaching practices, school-community relations, teacher education, research, international/intercultural education, literature and other creative arts, special education, day care, parenting, environmental education, releasing human potentials
Manuscript requirements: Chicago
 Preferred length: 950-1950 words; 2-4 printed pages
 Number of copies to be submitted: Three
 Abstract: No
Author information and reprints: Payment: Reprints only. 5 copies
 Is simultaneous submission of article to other journals permitted: No
 Exclusive manuscript rights between acceptance and publication: Yes
 Copyright: Held by publication.
 Reprints: Available at cost.
Additional information: Most of the articles used are solicited and developed monthly themes planned by the ACEI Publications Committee. Flexibility is built into the schedule to allow for use of quality unsolicited manuscripts.
Disposition of manuscript:
 Query letter: No
 Receipt of manuscript acknowledged: Yes
 Decision to publish in: 1-3 months
 Accepted manuscript published in: Varies
 Rejected manuscript returned: Yes, if self-addressed, stamped envelope is sent with manuscript.
 Rejected manuscript criticized: Occasionally
Submit to:
 Dr. Monroe D. Cohen
 Editor/Director of Publications
 (See address above)

THE CHRONICLE OF HIGHER EDUCATION [934]
Room 201
1717 Massachusetts Avenue, N. W.
Washington, D. C. 20036
(202) 667-3344

First published in 1966

SUBSCRIPTION DATA
Issues and rates: Published weekly.
 Average paid circulation: 35,000
 Annual rate(s): Foreign $21.00

Managing Editor: John Crowl

EDITORIAL DESCRIPTION
An independent newspaper, it covers news of higher education and related fields throughout the country.
Articles per average issue: 2
Audience: Academic
Manuscripts accepted in English

MANUSCRIPT INFORMATION
Subject field(s): Most of the issue is written by staff reporters, but the "Weekly Point of View" section will consider essays in virtually any topic relating to higher education or academic disciplines.
Manuscript requirements: See latest issue for style requirements.
 Preferred length: 800-1,600 words
 Number of copies to be submitted: 2
 Abstract: Not necessary.
Author information and reprints: Payment: By publication to author. $50.00-$215.00 per article.
 Is simultaneous submission of article to other journals permitted: Not permitted.
 Exclusive manuscript rights between acceptance and publication: Yes
 Copyright: Held by publication.
Additional information: Essays must be written in clear language. Avoid jargon. Controversial viewpoints are welcomed, if well-presented.
Disposition of manuscript:
 Query letter: Not necessary, but advisable.
 Receipt of manuscript acknowledged: Yes
 Decision to publish in: 1 month
 Accepted manuscript published in: 2 months
 Rejected manuscript returned: Yes, if return postage is supplied by author.
 Rejected manuscript criticized: No
Submit to:
 Edward R. Weidlein
 Senior Editor
 (See address above)

THE COACHING CLINIC [935]
Prentice-Hall, Inc.
Englewood Cliffs, New Jersey 07632
(201) 947-1000 ext. 2841

First published in 1963

SUBSCRIPTION DATA
Issues and rates: Published monthly.
 Average paid circulation: 5500
 Annual rate(s): $24

EDITORIAL DESCRIPTION
Contains practical coaching articles on high school and college sports.
Articles per average issue: 1012
Audience: Academic
Manuscripts accepted in English

MANUSCRIPT INFORMATION
Subject field(s): All interscholastic and intercollegiate sports; emphasis on football, basketball, track, and minor sports.

Manuscript requirements: See latest issue for style requirements.
 Preferred length: 1500 to 2000 words
 Number of copies to be submitted: One
 Abstract: No
Author information and reprints: Payment: Reprints only. 5 complimentary copies of issue
 Is simultaneous submission of article to other journals permitted: No
 Exclusive manuscript rights between acceptance and publication: Yes
 Copyright: Held by publication.
Disposition of manuscript:
 Query letter: No
 Receipt of manuscript acknowledged: Yes
 Decision to publish in: 1 to 2 weeks
 Accepted manuscript published in: At least 6 months
 Rejected manuscript returned: Yes
 Rejected manuscript criticized: Yes
Submit to:
 Dwight Wardell
 Editor
 (See address above)

COLLEGE COMPOSITION AND COMMUNICATION [936]
National Council of Teachers of English
1111 Kenyon Road
Urbana, Illinois 61801
(217) 328-3870

First published in 1950

SUBSCRIPTION DATA
Issues and rates: Published quarterly.
 Average paid circulation: 6,000
 Annual rate(s): $5.00; Foreign $6.50
Publisher or Sponsor: National Council of Teachers of English

EDITORIAL DESCRIPTION
Contains articles on the teaching of written composition and speech, language and literature, professional reviews (by assignment). Provides a professional forum for teachers of college freshman English.
Articles per average issue: 15
Audience: Teachers of undergraduate English
Manuscripts accepted in English only

MANUSCRIPT INFORMATION
Subject field(s): Rhetoric, literature, teaching, and language
Manuscript requirements: MLA; See latest issue for style requirements.
 Preferred length: 10-12 pages
 Number of copies to be submitted: One
 Abstract: Upon acceptance
Author information and reprints: Payment: None. Share permissions fees with publisher.
 Is simultaneous submission of article to other journals permitted: Yes
 Exclusive manuscript rights between acceptance and publication: Yes
 Copyright: Held by publication.
 Reprints: Available at printer's rates

Disposition of manuscript:
  Query letter: No
  Receipt of manuscript acknowledged: No
  Decision to publish in: 30-60 days
  Accepted manuscript published in: 6-9 months
  Rejected manuscript returned: Yes
  Rejected manuscript criticized: Yes
Submit to:
  Edward P. J. Corbett
  Editor
  Department of English
  Ohio State University
  164 West 17th Avenue
  Columbus, Ohio 43210
  (614) 422-6866

SPECIAL STIPULATIONS

NCTE acts as publisher but exercises no substantial editorial control; the latter is in the hands of the editor.

COLLEGE ENGLISH [937]

National Council of Teachers of English
1111 Kenyon Road
Urbana, Illinois 61801
(217) 328-3870

First published in 1939

SUBSCRIPTION DATA

Issues and rates: 8 issues per year
  Average paid circulation: 15,000
  Annual rate(s): $15.00; Pan-Am $16.50; Foreign $16.50
Publisher or Sponsor: National Council of Teachers of English

EDITORIAL DESCRIPTION

Contains essays, criticism, on educational theory, language, rhetoric and literature directed to teachers of English at the college level.
Articles per average issue: 18-20
Audience: College English teachers
  Manuscripts accepted in English only

MANUSCRIPT INFORMATION

Subject field(s): Literature, language, educational theory, pedagogy, rhetoric
Manuscript requirements: See latest issue for style requirements.
  Preferred length: 20-30 pages typewritten, double-spaced
  Number of copies to be submitted: Two
Author information and reprints: Payment: None. Share permissions fees with publisher.
  Is simultaneous submission of article to other journals permitted: Yes, with notification thereof.
  Exclusive manuscript rights between acceptance and publication: Yes
  Copyright: Held by NCTE
  Reprints: Available at printer's rates
Disposition of manuscript:
  Query letter: No, but helpful
  Receipt of manuscript acknowledged: Yes
  Decision to publish in: 4 months
  Accepted manuscript published in: Varies
  Rejected manuscript returned: Yes, if return postage is supplied by author.
  Rejected manuscript criticized: No
Submit to:
  Richard Ohmann
  Editor
  Wesleyan University
  Middletown, Connecticut 06457
  (203) 347-9411

SPECIAL STIPULATIONS

NCTE acts as publisher but exercises no substantial editorial control; the latter is in the hands of the editor.

COLLEGE STUDENT JOURNAL [938]

A Journal Pertaining to College Students
1362 Santa Cruz Court
Chula Vista, California 92010
(414) 421-9377

Previously entitled *College Student Survey*

First published in 1966

SUBSCRIPTION DATA

Issues and rates: Published quarterly.
  Average paid circulation: 1,000
  Annual rate(s): Institutions $10.00, Individuals $7.50, Foreign institutions $11.50, Foreign individuals $9.00
Publisher or Sponsor: Project Innovation
Managing Editor: Lan M. Cassel

EDITORIAL DESCRIPTION

Contains original investigations and theoretical papers dealing with college student values, attitudes, opinions, and learnings. This includes the areas of graduate school and professional education, and select areas pertinent to college preparation. Preference is given to studies dealing with attitude and ideas of students, and pertinent research.
Articles per average issue: 22-24
Audience: Academic
  Manuscripts accepted in English

MANUSCRIPT INFORMATION

Subject field(s): Student attitudes, student life, professional preparation, management, organizational climate, student learning, evaluation, leadership, college management, faculty evaluation, learning, drug abuse education
Manuscript requirements: APA
  Preferred length: 1,500 words; 5 pages
  Number of copies to be submitted: Two
  Abstract: Yes, of 120 words or less.
Author information and reprints: Payment: By author to publication.
  Is simultaneous submission of article to other journals permitted: No
  Exclusive manuscript rights between acceptance and publication: Yes
  Copyright: Held by publication.
  Reprints: Available, $2 per page for 50
Disposition of manuscript:
  Query letter: No
  Receipt of manuscript acknowledged: Yes
  Decision to publish in: 30 days
  Accepted manuscript published in: 6-12 months
  Rejected manuscript returned: Yes
  Rejected manuscript criticized: No
Submit to:
  Russell N. Cassel
  Editor
  (See address above)

COLLEGE AND UNIVERSITY [939]

Journal of the American Association of Collegiate Registrars and Admissions Officers
One Du Pont Circle, N. W., Suite 330
Washington, D. C. 20036
(202) 293-6230

First published in 1910

SUBSCRIPTION DATA

Issues and rates: Published quarterly.
  Average paid circulation: 6,493 controlled
  Annual rate(s): $14.00; Foreign $14.00; Institutions $14.00
Publisher or Sponsor: American Association of Collegiate Registrars and Admissions Officers (AACRAO)
Managing Editor: Robert E. Mahn

EDITORIAL DESCRIPTION

To advance professionally the work positions in offices of admissions, financial aid, institutional research, records, registration, and closely related functions among institutions of higher learning
Articles per average issue: 10
  Manuscripts accepted in English

MANUSCRIPT INFORMATION

Subject field(s): Emerging issues pertaining to the responsibilities and functions of AACRAO members and new patterns for dealing with them are desired.
Manuscript requirements: See latest issue for style requirements.
  Preferred length: Brief
  Number of copies to be submitted: 1 original
  Abstract: Not necessary.
Author information and reprints: Payment: None.
  Is simultaneous submission of article to other journals permitted: Permitted, but not encouraged.
  Exclusive manuscript rights between acceptance and publication: No
  Copyright: No arrangements made.
  Reprints: Available at no cost. 2 issues Available at cost.
Disposition of manuscript:
  Query letter: Not necessary.
  Receipt of manuscript acknowledged: Yes
  Decision to publish in: 5 weeks
  Accepted manuscript published in: 4 months
  Rejected manuscript returned: Yes, with return postage paid by publication.
  Rejected manuscript criticized: Sometimes
Submit to:
  Robert E. Mahn
  Editor
  Cutler Hall

Ohio University
Athens, Ohio 45701
(614) 594-5461

COMMUNITY EDUCATION JOURNAL [940]
P.O. Box 1666
Midland, Michigan 48640
(517) 631-0500

First published in 1971

SUBSCRIPTION DATA
Issues and rates: Published bi-monthly.
Average paid circulation: 5,000
Annual rate(s): $7.50, Foreign $12.00

EDITORIAL DESCRIPTION
Contains articles related to the field of community education.

MANUSCRIPT INFORMATION
Subject field(s): Community education
Manuscript requirements: No specific style guide.
Preferred length: 1500-3000 words typewritten, double-spaced
Number of copies to be submitted: One
Abstract: No
Author information and reprints: Payment: None. Two copies of journal.
Is simultaneous submission of article to other journals permitted: No
Exclusive manuscript rights between acceptance and publication: Yes
Copyright: Held by publication.
Reprints: Available, rates supplied
Additional information: Photos that would enhance the article should be submitted with the article; in addition, a picture of the author and a brief biographical sketch.
Disposition of manuscript:
Receipt of manuscript acknowledged: Yes
Decision to publish in: Six weeks
Accepted manuscript published in: 2 to 6 months
Rejected manuscript returned: Yes
Rejected manuscript criticized: Sometimes
Submit to:
Richard C. Pendell
Editor and Publisher
(See address above)

SPECIAL STIPULATIONS
Articles are accepted or rejected on the basis of relevance to community education, professionalism and impact.

COMPARATIVE EDUCATION REVIEW [941]
Comparative and International Education Society
Graduate School of Education
University of California
Los Angeles, California 90024
(213) 825-2621

First published in 1956

SUBSCRIPTION DATA
Issues and rates: Published three times per year.
Average paid circulation: 3000
Annual rate(s): Members $15.00
Publisher or Sponsor: Comparative and International Education Society
Managing Editor: Andreas M. Kazamias

EDITORIAL DESCRIPTION
Publishes analytic and/or interpretative articles dealing with all aspects of education across nations and cultures.
Articles per average issue: 7
Audience: Academic
Manuscripts accepted in English

MANUSCRIPT INFORMATION
Subject field(s): Any aspect of education
Manuscript requirements: Chicago
Preferred length: 5000-7000 words; 20-25 pages
Number of copies to be submitted: Three
Abstract: No
Author information and reprints: Payment: None.
Is simultaneous submission of article to other journals permitted: No
Exclusive manuscript rights between acceptance and publication: Yes
Copyright: Held by publication.
Reprints: Not available.
Disposition of manuscript:
Receipt of manuscript acknowledged: Yes
Decision to publish in: Three months
Accepted manuscript published in: Six months
Rejected manuscript returned: Yes, if self-addressed, stamped envelope is sent with manuscript.
Rejected manuscript criticized: Yes
Submit to:
Andreas M. Kazamias
Editor
Box 71, Education Building
University of Wisconsin
Madison, Wisconsin 53706

THE COMPUTER EDUCATOR [942]
Box 460
Chicago Heights, Illinois
(312) 754-6669

First published in 1974

SUBSCRIPTION DATA
Issues and rates: Published monthly.
Average paid circulation: 10,000
Annual rate(s): $6.00; Foreign individuals $9.00 plus postage
Managing Editor: Newell E. Usher

EDITORIAL DESCRIPTION
News, perspective, business data processing, education hardware and delivery systems, learning resources, software and courseware, letters, groups, standards, testing, certification, CAI/CMI, calendar, people, international, future, government, research/development of topics related to computer education in all areas.
Audience: Management and persons responsible for and contributing to all areas of computers and education.
Manuscripts accepted in English

MANUSCRIPT INFORMATION
Subject field(s): Computers and education with emphasis on using computers to assist in and manage the education function with future perspective and further emphasis on opening communication lines between research/development, resources and funds and end-users.
Manuscript requirements: No specific style guide.
Author information and reprints: Payment: None, but will negotiate
Is simultaneous submission of article to other journals permitted: Permitted.
Copyright: By publication unless otherwise negotiated.
Reprints: Available at cost. $1.00 per issue or special arrangements negotiated.
Disposition of manuscript:
Query letter: Not necessary, but advisable.
Receipt of manuscript acknowledged: No
Decision to publish in: Varies
Accepted manuscript published in: Varies
Rejected manuscript returned: Yes, if return postage is supplied by author.
Rejected manuscript criticized: Sometimes
Submit to:
Newell E. Usher
Editorial Director
(See address above)

CONTEMPORARY EDUCATION [943]
Reeve Hall, Room 201
Indiana State University
Terre Haute, Indiana 47809
(812) 232-6311 ext. 2508

Previously entitled *Teacher's College Journal*

First published in 1929

SUBSCRIPTION DATA
Issues and rates: Published quarterly.
Average paid circulation: 3,600 controlled
Annual rate(s): $7.00, Foreign $10.00
Publisher or Sponsor: Indiana State University, School of Education
Managing Editor: M. Dale Baughman

EDITORIAL DESCRIPTION
Editorial point of view is that all children must be educated and that educational practices must be sufficiently varied to accommodate all children.
Articles per average issue: 12-15
Audience: Prospective and in-service teachers and administrators in public schools
Manuscripts accepted in English only

Education

MANUSCRIPT INFORMATION
Subject field(s): Teacher education, supervision, research in education, instruction, guidance and counseling, higher education, secondary education, elementary education
Manuscript requirements: APA
  Preferred length: 6-10 pages
  Number of copies to be submitted: One or two
  Abstract: Yes, 1-2 brief paragraphs
Author information and reprints: Payment: None.
  Is simultaneous submission of article to other journals permitted: Prefer to be notified in advance
  Exclusive manuscript rights between acceptance and publication: No
  Copyright: Held by publication.
  Reprints: Available, cost varies with length
Disposition of manuscript:
  Query letter: Encouraged
  Receipt of manuscript acknowledged: Yes
  Decision to publish in: 4-8 weeks
  Accepted manuscript published in: 6-12 months
  Rejected manuscript returned: Yes, if return postage is supplied by author.
  Rejected manuscript criticized: Sometimes
Submit to:
  M. Dale Baughman
  Editor
  (See address above)

CONTINUING HIGHER EDUCATION [944]
1700 Asp Avenue
Norman, Oklahoma 73069
(405) 325-1021

First published in 1952

SUBSCRIPTION DATA
Issues and rates: Published quarterly.
  Average paid circulation: 437; 38 controlled
  Annual rate(s): $7.50
Publisher or Sponsor: Association for Continuing Higher Education

EDITORIAL DESCRIPTION
  Contains articles and information regarding collegiate continuing education.
Articles per average issue: 3
Audience: Educators
  Manuscripts accepted in English

MANUSCRIPT INFORMATION
Subject field(s): Higher adult education, adult education, higher education, legislation, regional activities of member institutions, institutional practices
Manuscript requirements: No specific style guide.
  Preferred length: 1000-1500 words; 4-6 pages
  Number of copies to be submitted: One
  Abstract: No

Author information and reprints: Payment: None.
  Is simultaneous submission of article to other journals permitted: Yes
  Exclusive manuscript rights between acceptance and publication: Yes
  Copyright: Held by author.
  Reprints: Not available.
Disposition of manuscript:
  Receipt of manuscript acknowledged: Yes
  Decision to publish in: 2 to 3 weeks
  Accepted manuscript published in: 1 to 2 months
  Rejected manuscript returned: Yes, if self-addressed, stamped envelope is sent with manuscript.
  Rejected manuscript criticized: No
Submit to:
  Clarence H. Thompson
  Editor
  P.O. Box 207
  North Dartmouth, Massachusetts 02747
  (617) 993-2206

THE CORE TEACHER [945]
404F Education Building
Kent State University
Kent, Ohio 44242
(216) 672-2472

First published in 1951

SUBSCRIPTION DATA
Issues and rates: Published quarterly.
  Average paid circulation: 300
  Annual rate(s): $4.00
Publisher or Sponsor: National Association for Core Curriculum, Inc.

EDITORIAL DESCRIPTION
  Publishes news of NACC and affiliates; substantive articles on core curriculum and other interdisciplinary programs; summaries of research and other publications; reviews of instructional materials useful in such programs. Generally supportive of common learning programs that emphasize problem solving, inquiry, and a major input of student needs and concerns in instruction.
Articles per average issue: 1-2
Audience: teachers, administrators, curriculum specialists, professors of education
  Manuscripts accepted in English only

MANUSCRIPT INFORMATION
Subject field(s): Core, block-time, humanities, social studies, language arts, team teaching
Manuscript requirements: No specific style guide.
  Preferred length: No restrictions
  Number of copies to be submitted: One
  Abstract: Not necessary
Author information and reprints: Payment: None.
  Is simultaneous submission of article to other journals permitted: No
  Exclusive manuscript rights between acceptance and publication: No
  Copyright: Not copyrighted
  Reprints: Not available.
Disposition of manuscript:
  Query letter: No
  Receipt of manuscript acknowledged: Yes
  Decision to publish in: 2 weeks
  Accepted manuscript published in: 3 months
  Rejected manuscript returned: Yes, if self-addressed, stamped envelope is sent with manuscript.
  Rejected manuscript criticized: Yes
Submit to:
  Gordon F. Vars
  Executive Secretary-Treasurer, NACC
  (See address above)

THE DECA DISTRIBUTOR [946]
200 Park Avenue
Falls Church, Virginia 22046
(703) 532-7672

SUBSCRIPTION DATA
Issues and rates: Published quarterly.
  Average paid circulation: 160,000; 1,000 controlled
  Annual rate(s): $3.00
Publisher or Sponsor: Distributive Education Clubs of America

EDITORIAL DESCRIPTION
  Contains news related to the members of the Distributive Education Clubs of America.

MANUSCRIPT INFORMATION
Subject field(s): Students, business, government
Manuscript requirements: See latest issue for style requirements.
  Preferred length: 800 words; 3 pages
  Number of copies to be submitted: One
Author information and reprints: Payment: None.
  Is simultaneous submission of article to other journals permitted: Yes
  Exclusive manuscript rights between acceptance and publication: No
  Copyright: Held by publication.
  Reprints: Not available.
Disposition of manuscript:
  Receipt of manuscript acknowledged: Yes
  Decision to publish in: 2 months
  Accepted manuscript published in: 3 months
  Rejected manuscript returned: Yes, if self-addressed, stamped envelope is sent with manuscript.
  Rejected manuscript criticized: Yes
Submit to:
  Phil Hayes
  Editor
  (See address above)

EdCENTRIC MAGAZINE [947]
A Journal of Educational Change
PO Box 1802
Eugene, Oregon 97401
(503) 343-0810

First published in 1969

SUBSCRIPTION DATA
Issues and rates: Published bi-monthly.
  Average paid circulation: 5,000
  Annual rate(s): Individuals $6.00,
    Institutions $10.00
Publisher or Sponsor: U.S. National Student
  Association

EDITORIAL DESCRIPTION
  A study of education in the U.S.,
  critiques of the U.S. educational system,
  radical alternatives of education in the
  U.S. and abroad.
Articles per average issue: 6
Audience: People interested in educational
  liberation, organizers and activists in
  educational change
  Manuscripts accepted in English only

MANUSCRIPT INFORMATION
Subject field(s): Educational alternatives and
  critiques, case studies of good programs,
  radical analysis of education
Manuscript requirements: See latest issue for
  style requirements.
  Preferred length: 2000 to 4500 words; 10
    pages
  Number of copies to be submitted: Two
  Abstract: Not necessary, but desirable
Author information and reprints: Payment:
  By publication to author. Occasionally;
    less than $100 per article.
  Is simultaneous submission of article to
    other journals permitted: Yes
  Exclusive manuscript rights between
    acceptance and publication: No
  Copyright: Held by publication for
    author
  Reprints: Available
Disposition of manuscript:
  Query letter: No
  Receipt of manuscript acknowledged: Yes
  Decision to publish in: One month
  Accepted manuscript published in: Two
    months or more
  Rejected manuscript returned: No
  Rejected manuscript criticized:
    Sometimes
Submit to:
  Editorial Collective
  (See address above)

EDUCATION [948]
1362 Santa Cruz Court
Chula Vista, California 92010
(714) 421-9377

First published in 1880

SUBSCRIPTION DATA
Issues and rates: Published quarterly.
  Average paid circulation: 3,500
  Annual rate(s): Institutions $10.00,
    Individuals $7.50, Foreign institutions
    $11.50, Foreign individuals $9.00
Publisher or Sponsor: Project Innovation
Managing Editor: Lan M. Cassel

EDITORIAL DESCRIPTION
  Contains original investigations and
  theoretical papers dealing with
  worthwhile notions on learning, teaching,
  and education. Preference is given to
  innovations in the public or private
  schools, proposed or actual, theoretical or
  evaluative.
Articles per average issue: 22
Audience: Educators, psychologists
  Manuscripts accepted in English

MANUSCRIPT INFORMATION
Subject field(s): Material concerns all levels
  and every area of education. Intended for
  use primarily in teacher education:
  secondary, special, administration, adult,
  elementary, guidance, industry, college;
  psychology; learning;
Manuscript requirements: APA
  Preferred length: 1500 words; 5 pages
  Number of copies to be submitted: Two
  Abstract: Yes, of 120 words or less
Author information and reprints: Payment:
  By author to publication. Varies
    depending on article.
  Is simultaneous submission of article to
    other journals permitted: No
  Exclusive manuscript rights between
    acceptance and publication: Yes
  Copyright: Held by publication.
  Reprints: Available, $2 per page for 50
Disposition of manuscript:
  Query letter: No
  Receipt of manuscript acknowledged: Yes
  Decision to publish in: 30 days
  Accepted manuscript published in: 6-12
    months
  Rejected manuscript returned: Yes
  Rejected manuscript criticized: No
Submit to:
  Russell N. Cassel
  Editor
  (See address above)

EDUCATION CANADA [949]
252 Bloor Street West
Toronto, Ontario M5S 1V5, Canada
(416) 924-7721

Previously entitled *Canadian Education and
Research Digest*

First published in 1945

SUBSCRIPTION DATA
Issues and rates: Published quarterly.
  Average paid circulation: 2,600
  Annual rate(s): $5.00
Publisher or Sponsor: Canadian Education
  Association

EDITORIAL DESCRIPTION
  Filling a role between the scholarly
  research journal and the commercial
  magazine, the objective is to serve as a
  forum for the thoughtful expression of
  views on issues and problems of practical
  concern to an audience that must day to
  day come to grips with the major
  educational problems of the times.
Articles per average issue: 8
Audience: School officials and state
  department of education officers
  Manuscripts accepted in English, French

MANUSCRIPT INFORMATION
Subject field(s): Trends, objectives, practices
  and programs in Canadian elementary
  and secondary schools.
Manuscript requirements: See latest issue for
  style requirements.
  Preferred length: 2000-3000 words
  Number of copies to be submitted: Two
  Abstract: No
Author information and reprints: Payment:
  None.
  Is simultaneous submission of article to
    other journals permitted: No
  Exclusive manuscript rights between
    acceptance and publication: Yes
  Copyright: Held by publication.
  Reprints: Available at time of publication
    if ordered in advance
Additional information: Photographs
  welcomed.
Disposition of manuscript:
  Query letter: Not necessary
  Receipt of manuscript acknowledged: Yes
  Decision to publish in: 2-3 months
  Accepted manuscript published in: 3
    months
  Rejected manuscript returned: Yes, with
    return postage paid by publication.
  Rejected manuscript criticized: No
Submit to:
  Harriett Goldsborough
  Editor
  (See address above)

EDUCATION AND TRAINING [950]
Dryden Chambers
119 Oxford Street
London W1R 1PA, England
(01) 437-3063

SUBSCRIPTION DATA
Issues and rates: Published monthly.
  Average paid circulation: 3,000
  Annual rate(s): £8.20

EDITORIAL DESCRIPTION
  Contains articles on all aspects of further
  education, review section on books, films,
  audio-visual, etc.
Articles per average issue: 8
Audience: Academic, professional
  Manuscripts accepted in English

MANUSCRIPT INFORMATION
Subject field(s): All topics relevant to
  continuing education
Manuscript requirements: See latest issue for
  style requirements.
  Preferred length: 2000 words
  Number of copies to be submitted: One
Author information and reprints: Payment:
  By publication to author.
  Is simultaneous submission of article to
    other journals permitted: Yes
  Exclusive manuscript rights between
    acceptance and publication: Yes
  Copyright: Held by publication.
Disposition of manuscript:
  Receipt of manuscript acknowledged: Yes
  Accepted manuscript published in: One
    month minimum
  Rejected manuscript returned: Yes

Rejected manuscript criticized: No
Submit to:
  Derek Bradley
  Editor
  (See address above)

EDUCATIONAL COURIER [951]
Suite 315, 207 Queen's Quay
West Toronto, Onatrio M5J 1A7, Canada
(416) 368-3807

First published in 1930

SUBSCRIPTION DATA
Issues and rates: 8 issues per year
  Average paid circulation: 55,000
  Annual rate(s): $4.00
Publisher or Sponsor: Federation of Women Teachers of Ontario, Ontario Public School Men Teachers Federation

EDITORIAL DESCRIPTION
  Contains articles on elementary education.
Articles per average issue: 8
Audience: Ontario teachers
  Manuscripts accepted in English

MANUSCRIPT INFORMATION
Subject field(s): Educational theory and practice, current educational issues.
Manuscript requirements: Style sheet sent on request.
  Preferred length: 5-10 pages
  Number of copies to be submitted: One
Author information and reprints: Payment: By publication to author. Honorarium
  Is simultaneous submission of article to other journals permitted: No
  Reprints: Not available.
Disposition of manuscript:
  Query letter: No
  Receipt of manuscript acknowledged: Yes
  Decision to publish in: 1-2 months
  Accepted manuscript published in: Varies
  Rejected manuscript returned: Yes
  Rejected manuscript criticized: Upon request
Submit to:
  Edward Hynas
  Editor
  (See address above)

EDUCATIONAL HORIZONS [952]
2000 East 8th Street
Bloomington, Indiana 47401
(812) 339-3411

Previously entitled *Pi Lambda Theta Journal*

First published in 1921

SUBSCRIPTION DATA
Issues and rates: Published quarterly.
  Average paid circulation: 600; 18,000 controlled
  Annual rate(s): $5.00, Foreign $5.50
Publisher or Sponsor: Pi Lambda Theta
Managing Editor: Mary Margaret Carney

EDITORIAL DESCRIPTION
  Contains articles on topics having to do with education, all aspects, all levels.
Articles per average issue: 8
Audience: Educators
  Manuscripts accepted in English

MANUSCRIPT INFORMATION
Subject field(s): Education: administration, supervision, counseling, teaching, teacher-training, etc.
Manuscript requirements: Chicago; Webster 3; APA
  Preferred length: 4000-6000 words; 15-20 pages; 50 characters per line, 25 lines per page
  Number of copies to be submitted: Three
  Abstract: No
Author information and reprints: Payment: None. 5 copies of journal
  Is simultaneous submission of article to other journals permitted: Yes
  Exclusive manuscript rights between acceptance and publication: No
  Copyright: Not copyrighted
  Reprints: Available at cost
Additional information: Three issues each year are done with the help of a guest editor. For these issues all articles are solicited. Unsolicited articles are limited to a single issue.
Disposition of manuscript:
  Query letter: Helpful
  Receipt of manuscript acknowledged: Yes
  Decision to publish in: 2 months
  Accepted manuscript published in: 6 months
  Rejected manuscript returned: Yes
  Rejected manuscript criticized: Yes
Submit to:
  Miriam M. Bryan
  Editor
  17 Executive Drive NE, Suite 100
  Atlanta, Georgia 30329
  (404) 325-3131

EDUCATIONAL RECORD [953]
American Council on Education
One Dupont Circle
Washington, D.C. 20036
(202) 833-4784

SUBSCRIPTION DATA
Issues and rates: Published quarterly.
  Average paid circulation: 2,000; 10,000 controlled
  Annual rate(s): $10.00, Foreign $16.00
Publisher or Sponsor: American Council on Education
Managing Editor: Clifford B. Fair

EDITORIAL DESCRIPTION
  Contains articles and other materials of interest to college and university administrators.
Articles per average issue: 10

MANUSCRIPT INFORMATION
Subject field(s): Academic administration, accreditation, collective bargaining, curricula, financing, federal relations, grades, tenure and promotion, admissions, equal opportunity
Manuscript requirements: Chicago
  Preferred length: 15-20 pages; typewritten, double-spaced
  Number of copies to be submitted: Two
  Abstract: No
Author information and reprints: Payment: None.
  Is simultaneous submission of article to other journals permitted: No
  Exclusive manuscript rights between acceptance and publication: Yes
  Copyright: Held by publication.
  Reprints: Available, 100 free
Disposition of manuscript:
  Query letter: No
  Receipt of manuscript acknowledged: Yes
  Decision to publish in: 2 months
  Accepted manuscript published in: 2-3 months
  Rejected manuscript returned: Yes
  Rejected manuscript criticized: No
Submit to:
  Editor
  (See address above)

EDUCATIONAL RESEARCHER [954]
1126 Sixteenth Street, NW
Washington, D.C. 20036
(202) 223-9485

First published in 1972

SUBSCRIPTION DATA
Issues and rates: Published monthly.
  Average paid circulation: 12,200
  Annual rate(s): $10.00
Publisher or Sponsor: American Educational Research Association
Managing Editor: Patricia E. Stivers

EDITORIAL DESCRIPTION
  Contains news and commentary on events in the field of educational research; articles which synthesize or analyze in a scholarly fashion matters of general significance to research in education. Special features include interviews with prominent individuals in the field and review essays on significant publications.
Articles per average issue: 4
Audience: Professors and researchers in education
  Manuscripts accepted in English

MANUSCRIPT INFORMATION
Manuscript requirements: Chicago
  Preferred length: 10-15 pages
  Number of copies to be submitted: Two
Author information and reprints: Payment: Reprints only. 10 copies of issue.
  Is simultaneous submission of article to other journals permitted: No
  Exclusive manuscript rights between acceptance and publication: Yes
  Copyright: Held by publication.
  Reprints: Available, cost quoted individually

Disposition of manuscript:
  Query letter: No
  Receipt of manuscript acknowledged: Yes
  Decision to publish in: 2-4 weeks
  Accepted manuscript published in: 1-3 months
  Rejected manuscript returned: Yes
  Rejected manuscript criticized: No
Submit to:
  Richard E. Schutz
  Southwest Regional Laboratory for R & D
  4665 Lampson Avenue
  Los Alamitos, California 90720
  (213) 598-7661

EDUCATIONAL REVIEW [955]
School of Education
University of Birmingham
P.O. Box 363
Birmingham B15 2TT, England
(021) 472-1301 ext. 3384

First published in 1948

SUBSCRIPTION DATA
Issues and rates: Published three times per year.
  Average paid circulation: 1650
  Annual rate(s): £1.50
Publisher or Sponsor: University of Birmingham School of Education

EDITORIAL DESCRIPTION
  Contains general articles and accounts of research of interest to teachers, lecturers, research workers in education and educational psychology and to students of education; articles dealing with research, with descriptions of experimental work in schools, with critical reviews of teaching methods or curriculum content in schools; articles on administrative problems, on tests and measurement, on child growth and development and on the relation of schools to the community.
Articles per average issue: 6
Audience: Research, academic
  Manuscripts accepted in English

MANUSCRIPT INFORMATION
Manuscript requirements: Style sheet sent on request.
  Preferred length: 3,000 words
  Number of copies to be submitted: One
  Abstract: Yes
Author information and reprints: Payment: None.
  Is simultaneous submission of article to other journals permitted: No
  Exclusive manuscript rights between acceptance and publication: Yes
  Copyright: Held by publication.
  Reprints: Not available.
Additional information: Typewritten, double-spaced. Material should not have been published elsewhere
Disposition of manuscript:
  Query letter: No
  Receipt of manuscript acknowledged: Yes
  Decision to publish in: 3 months
  Accepted manuscript published in: 3 months
  Rejected manuscript returned: Yes
  Rejected manuscript criticized: No
Submit to:
  C.B. Wade
  Executive Editor
  (See address above)

EDUCATIONAL SIGNPOST [956]
663 Fifth Avenue
New York, New York 10022
(212) 687-6865

First published in 1938

SUBSCRIPTION DATA
Issues and rates: Yearly report, special editions during year
  Annual rate(s): $10.00, Members $5.00
Publisher or Sponsor: American Education Association
Managing Editor: Timothy A. Mitchell

EDITORIAL DESCRIPTION
  Contains articles on education: philosophy of, curriculum; text books, parent groups, community relations, elementary, secondary, college, reading reform. Upholds religion in education, opposes sex education.
  Manuscripts accepted in English

MANUSCRIPT INFORMATION
Subject field(s): Manuscript must be of interest to teachers, parents, school administrators and contain specific examples.
Manuscript requirements: APA
  Preferred length: 500 words
  Number of copies to be submitted: One
  Abstract: No
Author information and reprints: Payment: Normally none, $25 per article if highly important
  Is simultaneous submission of article to other journals permitted: Yes
  Exclusive manuscript rights between acceptance and publication: No
  Copyright: Held by author.
  Reprints: Available, cost varies
Additional information: Not accepted unless it upholds policy of organization-American constitution as opposed to world government.
Disposition of manuscript:
  Query letter: Not necessary, but advisable.
  Receipt of manuscript acknowledged: Yes
  Decision to publish in: 3 weeks
  Accepted manuscript published in: Varies
  Rejected manuscript returned: Yes, if self-addressed, stamped envelope is sent with manuscript.
  Rejected manuscript criticized: Yes
Submit to:
  Cathryn Laurentia Dorney
  Executive Director
  (See address above)

EDUCATIONAL STUDIES [957]
A Journal of Book Reviews in the Foundations of Education
Box 8088
University of Texas
Austin, Texas 78712
(512) 471-4295

First published in 1970

SUBSCRIPTION DATA
Issues and rates: Published quarterly.
  Average paid circulation: 1,700; 1,870 controlled
  Annual rate(s): $6.00; Institutions $10.00; Students $2.50
Publisher or Sponsor: The American Educational Studies Association

EDITORIAL DESCRIPTION
  Short book reviews of all current publications in the foundations of education; longer articles on books or subjects of particular interest to professors and students in education.
Articles per average issue: 6-8 long articles; 50-60 short reviews
Audience: Professors and students in education, reference librarians and researchers
  Manuscripts accepted in English

MANUSCRIPT INFORMATION
Subject field(s): Statements on the intellectual dimensions of educational studies as a field of study and teaching; foundations approaches to topics of general interest; lengthy review of new major books
Manuscript requirements: See latest issue for style requirements.
  Number of copies to be submitted: 2
  Abstract: Not necessary.
Author information and reprints: Payment: None.
  Exclusive manuscript rights between acceptance and publication: Yes
  Copyright: Held by publication.
  Reprints: Available at no cost. 100
Disposition of manuscript:
  Query letter: Not necessary.
  Receipt of manuscript acknowledged: Yes
  Decision to publish in: 1 month
  Accepted manuscript published in: 3-9 months
  Rejected manuscript returned: Yes, if return postage is supplied by author.
  Rejected manuscript criticized: Sometimes
Submit to:
  John A. Laska
  Editor
  (See address above)

EDUCATIONAL THEORY [958]
Education Building
University of Illinois
Urbana, Illinois 61801
(217) 333-3003

First published in 1950

Education

SUBSCRIPTION DATA
Issues and rates: Published quarterly.
  Average paid circulation: 2,500
  Annual rate(s): $10.00, Foreign $11.00
Publisher or Sponsor: Philosophy of Education Society, John Dewey Society, University of Illinois
Managing Editor: Joe R. Burnett

EDITORIAL DESCRIPTION
To foster the continuing development of educational theory and to encourage wide and effective discussion of theoretical problems within the educational profession. Devoted to publishing scholarly articles and studies in the foundation of education, and in related disciplines outside the field of education, which contribute to the advancement of educational theory.
Articles per average issue: 8-10
Audience: Academic
  Manuscripts accepted in English

MANUSCRIPT INFORMATION
Subject field(s): Philosophy of education, social foundations of education, history of education, philosophy related disciplines
Manuscript requirements: MLA
  Preferred length: 6,000-8,000 words
  Number of copies to be submitted: Original plus 3 copies
  Abstract: No
Author information and reprints: Payment: None.
  Is simultaneous submission of article to other journals permitted: Yes
  Exclusive manuscript rights between acceptance and publication: Yes
  Copyright: Held by publication.
  Reprints: Available, author must order from printer
Additional information: Footnotes at end; negatives must be provided for any charts.
Disposition of manuscript:
  Query letter: No
  Receipt of manuscript acknowledged: Yes
  Decision to publish in: 8-10 weeks
  Accepted manuscript published in: 9-12 months
  Rejected manuscript returned: Yes
  Rejected manuscript criticized: Sometimes
Submit to:
  Editor
  (See address above)

EDUCATORS GUIDE TO MEDIA AND METHODS [959]
134 North Thirteenth Street
Philadelphia, Pennsylvania 19107
(215) 564-5170

First published in 1964

SUBSCRIPTION DATA
Issues and rates: Monthly, September through May
  Average paid circulation: 42,416; 5,242 controlled
  Annual rate(s): $9.00

EDITORIAL DESCRIPTION
Editorials and reviews involving films, paperbacks, records, tapes, television, video-tape recording, slides and film books--new equipment to encourage the more effective use of contemporary teaching materials in grades 8 through college and university years.
Articles per average issue: 7
Audience: Secondary and college level educators; audio-visual directors
  Manuscripts accepted in English

MANUSCRIPT INFORMATION
Subject field(s): Contemporary teaching materials, films, paperbacks, records, tapes, television, videotape recording, slides, film books
Manuscript requirements: See latest issue of publication and submit outline prior to submission of manuscript.
  Preferred length: Not to exceed 2000 words
  Number of copies to be submitted: Two
Author information and reprints: Payment: By publication to author. Amount varies.
  Is simultaneous submission of article to other journals permitted: No
  Exclusive manuscript rights between acceptance and publication: Yes
  Copyright: Held by publication.
  Reprints: Available, sometimes
Additional information: Must be typewritten, double-spaced, including all references to publishers and film distributors with price and address information.
Disposition of manuscript:
  Query letter: No
  Receipt of manuscript acknowledged: Yes
  Decision to publish in: 2-6 months
  Accepted manuscript published in: 2-4 months
  Rejected manuscript returned: Yes, if self-addressed, stamped envelope is sent with manuscript.
  Rejected manuscript criticized: Sometimes
Submit to:
  Frank McLaughlin
  Editor
  (See address above)

EDUCOM [960]
Bulletin of the Interuniversity Communications Council Inc.
P.O. Box 364
Princeton, New Jersey 08540
(609) 921-7575

First published in 1966

SUBSCRIPTION DATA
Issues and rates: Published quarterly.
  Average paid circulation: 500; 10,000 controlled
  Annual rate(s): $5 to educators, $10 to others
Publisher or Sponsor: Interuniversity Communications Council

EDITORIAL DESCRIPTION
Contains articles on the application of computing and other technology in higher education; reports on EDUCOM activities.
Articles per average issue: 3
Audience: Academic
  Manuscripts accepted in English

MANUSCRIPT INFORMATION
Subject field(s): Computer science in higher education, television in higher education
Manuscript requirements: Chicago
  Preferred length: 2000-3000 words
  Number of copies to be submitted: Two
  Abstract: Optional
Author information and reprints: Payment: None.
  Is simultaneous submission of article to other journals permitted: No
  Exclusive manuscript rights between acceptance and publication: Yes
  Copyright: Held by publication.
  Reprints: Available at cost
Disposition of manuscript:
  Query letter: Suggested
  Receipt of manuscript acknowledged: Yes
  Decision to publish in: Two months
  Accepted manuscript published in: 2 to 6 months
  Rejected manuscript returned: Yes
  Rejected manuscript criticized: No
Submit to:
  Carolyn Landis
  (See address above)

ELEMENTARY ENGLISH [961]
National Council of Teachers of English
1111 Kenyon Road
Urbana, Illinois 61801
(217) 328-3870

First published in 1924

SUBSCRIPTION DATA
Issues and rates: 8 issues per year
  Average paid circulation: 30,000
  Annual rate(s): $15.00; Pan-Am $12.50, Foreign $13.00, Students $4.00
Publisher or Sponsor: National Council of Teachers of English

EDITORIAL DESCRIPTION
Contains articles, research reports, reviews of professional books, all related to the concerns of the elementary school teacher as teacher of the language arts.
Articles per average issue: 20
  Manuscripts accepted in English

MANUSCRIPT INFORMATION
Subject field(s): Elementary teaching, children's literature, reading and the language arts
Manuscript requirements: See latest issue for style requirements.
  Preferred length: 10-12 pages typewritten, double-spaced
  Number of copies to be submitted: Two
  Abstract: No

Author information and reprints: Payment: None. Share reprint fees with publisher.
Is simultaneous submission of article to other journals permitted: Yes
Exclusive manuscript rights between acceptance and publication: Yes
Copyright: Held by publisher
Reprints: Available at printer's rates
Additional information: Articles not accepted that have been published previously. The right to edit is reserved for clarity, sexism, excessive length.
Disposition of manuscript:
Receipt of manuscript acknowledged: No
Decision to publish in: 30-60 days
Accepted manuscript published in: Four months
Rejected manuscript returned: Yes
Rejected manuscript criticized: No
Submit to:
Dr. Iris M. Tiedt
Editor
University of Santa Clara
Santa Clara, California 95053

ELEMENTARY SCHOOL GUIDANCE AND COUNSELING [962]
American Personnel and Guidance Association
1607 New Hampshire Avenue N.W.
Washington, D.C. 20009
(202) 483-4633

SUBSCRIPTION DATA

Issues and rates: Published quarterly.
Average paid circulation: 18,000
Annual rate(s): $8.00, Members $6.00
Publisher or Sponsor: American School Counselor Association
Managing Editor: Robert D. Myrick

EDITORIAL DESCRIPTION

Directed to the interests of counselors, educators and pupil personnel specialists involved in the counseling and guidance of elementary school children. Features articles that range from theory, research and professional statements to practical procedures and techniques.
Articles per average issue: 5
Audience: Counselors, teachers, pupil personnel specialists
Manuscripts accepted in English

MANUSCRIPT INFORMATION

Subject field(s): Counseling; guidance programs; child development theory, concepts and research; problems confronting counselors and teachers
Manuscript requirements: APA
Preferred length: 3,000-5,000 words; 10-12 pages
Number of copies to be submitted: Three
Abstract: No
Author information and reprints: Payment: None.
Is simultaneous submission of article to other journals permitted: No
Exclusive manuscript rights between acceptance and publication: Yes
Copyright: Held by publication.
Reprints: Available at cost.

Additional information: Authors should see guidelines published in recent issue.
Disposition of manuscript:
Query letter: No
Receipt of manuscript acknowledged: Yes
Decision to publish in: 2-3 months
Accepted manuscript published in: 6 months to a year
Rejected manuscript returned: Yes
Rejected manuscript criticized: Yes
Submit to:
Robert D. Myrick
Editor
College of Education
University of Florida
Gainesville, Florida 32611
(904) 392-0731

ELEMENTARY SCHOOL JOURNAL [963]
University of Chicago Press
5801 Ellis Avenue
Chicago, Illinois 60637
(312) 753-3347

Previously entitled *Elementary School Teacher*

First published in 1900

SUBSCRIPTION DATA

Issues and rates: Monthly, from October through May
Average paid circulation: 19,000
Annual rate(s): $8.00, Foreign $9.00
Managing Editor: Josephine Costantino
Publisher or Sponsor: University of Chicago, Department of Education, and Graduate School of Education

EDITORIAL DESCRIPTION

Contains articles of concern to the professional in elementary education.
Articles per average issue: 10
Audience: Professional, academic
Manuscripts accepted in English

MANUSCRIPT INFORMATION

Subject field(s): Research, school subjects, innovative classroom practice, teacher education, child development, supervision, school and social change, administration
Manuscript requirements: Style sheet sent on request.
Preferred length: 2,000 words
Number of copies to be submitted: One or two
Author information and reprints: Payment: Reprints only. Choice of 50 reprints or year's subscription to Journal.
Is simultaneous submission of article to other journals permitted: No
Exclusive manuscript rights between acceptance and publication: Yes
Copyright: Held by University of Chicago
Reprints: Available, 50 free

Additional information: Interested in black-and-white photos. Prefer simple, uncluttered pictures of children of elementary-school age.
Disposition of manuscript:
Query letter: No
Receipt of manuscript acknowledged: Yes
Decision to publish in: 2-6 weeks
Accepted manuscript published in: Minimum of 3 months
Rejected manuscript returned: Yes
Rejected manuscript criticized: Sometimes
Submit to:
Richard E. Hodges
Editor
5835 Kimbark Avenue, Judd Hall
University of Chicago
Chicago, Illinois 60637
(312) 743-3872

ENGLISH EDUCATION [964]
National Council of Teachers of English
1111 Kenyon Road
Urbana, Illinois 61801
(217) 328-3870

First published in 1964

SUBSCRIPTION DATA

Issues and rates: Published three times per year.
Average paid circulation: 2,400
Annual rate(s): $5.00, Pan-Am $5.50, Foreign $6.00
Publisher or Sponsor: National Council of Teachers of English

EDITORIAL DESCRIPTION

Contains professional essays concerning the content and methodology of professional courses for the preparation of English teachers.

MANUSCRIPT INFORMATION

Subject field(s): Education, English, educational psychology
Manuscript requirements: See latest issue for style requirements.
Preferred length: 12-18 pages
Number of copies to be submitted: Two
Author information and reprints: Payment: None.
Is simultaneous submission of article to other journals permitted: Yes
Exclusive manuscript rights between acceptance and publication: Yes
Copyright: Held by publication.
Reprints: Available at printer's rates
Disposition of manuscript:
Receipt of manuscript acknowledged: No
Decision to publish in: 30-60 days
Accepted manuscript published in: Four months
Rejected manuscript returned: Yes
Rejected manuscript criticized: No
Submit to:
Ben F. Nelms
Editor
University of Missouri
227 Mark Twain

Columbia, Missouri 65201
(314) 882-2121

ENGLISH JOURNAL [965]
National Council of Teachers of English
1111 Kenyon Road
Urbana, Illinois 61801

First published in 1912

SUBSCRIPTION DATA

Issues and rates: Monthly, September through May
Average paid circulation: 55,000
Annual rate(s): $15.00
Publisher or Sponsor: National Council of Teachers of English

EDITORIAL DESCRIPTION

Contains articles, research reports, reviews of professional books (by assignment) related to the teaching of English grades 6-12.
Articles per average issue: 18-20
Audience: English teachers
Manuscripts accepted in English

MANUSCRIPT INFORMATION

Subject field(s): Language, literature, rhetoric
Manuscript requirements: See latest issue for style requirements. Chicago
Preferred length: 6-14 pages
Number of copies to be submitted: One
Abstract: No
Author information and reprints: Payment: None. Share permissions with publisher.
Is simultaneous submission of article to other journals permitted: Yes, with notification thereof
Exclusive manuscript rights between acceptance and publication: Yes
Copyright: Held by publication.
Reprints: Available at printer's rates
Disposition of manuscript:
Query letter: No
Receipt of manuscript acknowledged: Yes
Decision to publish in: 30-60 days
Accepted manuscript published in: Four months
Rejected manuscript returned: Yes
Rejected manuscript criticized: No
Submit to:
Stephen N. Judy
Editor
P.O. Box 112
East Lansing, Michigan 48823
(517) 353-6657

ENGLISH RECORD [966]
State University of New York
Oneonta, New York 13820
(607) 431-3514

First published in 1950

SUBSCRIPTION DATA

Issues and rates: Published quarterly.
Average paid circulation: 1,500; 500 controlled
Annual rate(s): $10.00
Publisher or Sponsor: New York State English Council

EDITORIAL DESCRIPTION

Contains articles on the teaching of English.
Articles per average issue: 15
Audience: English teachers of all levels
Manuscripts accepted in English

MANUSCRIPT INFORMATION

Subject field(s): Literary criticism, language, composition, rhetoric, English as a foreign language, English education research
Manuscript requirements: MLA
Preferred length: 3000 words; 12 pages
Number of copies to be submitted: One
Abstract: No
Author information and reprints: Payment: None.
Is simultaneous submission of article to other journals permitted: No
Exclusive manuscript rights between acceptance and publication: Yes
Copyright: Held by publication.
Reprints: Available at cost
Disposition of manuscript:
Query letter: No
Receipt of manuscript acknowledged: Yes
Decision to publish in: 6 weeks
Accepted manuscript published in: Current volume
Rejected manuscript returned: Yes, if return postage is supplied by author.
Rejected manuscript criticized: No
Submit to:
Richard L. Knudson
(See address above)

FOREIGN LANGUAGE ANNALS [967]
A Review of Current Progress in Teaching Foreign Languages
62 Fifth Avenue
New York, New York 10011
(212) 741-7868

First published in 1967

SUBSCRIPTION DATA

Issues and rates: Four times yearly-October, December, March, May
Average paid circulation: 11,500
Annual rate(s): $10.00, Foreign $12.00
Publisher or Sponsor: American Council on the Teaching of Foreign Languages

EDITORIAL DESCRIPTION

Publishes information of current significance to the teacher, administrator, or researcher, whatever the educational level or the language with which he is concerned. Dedicated to advancing all phases of the profession of foreign language teaching.
Articles per average issue: 7
Audience: Foreign language teachers
Manuscripts accepted in English, with exceptions

MANUSCRIPT INFORMATION

Subject field(s): Teaching techniques, language teacher education, methodology, research
Manuscript requirements: MLA
Preferred length: 25 pages maximum
Number of copies to be submitted: Two
Abstract: Yes
Author information and reprints: Payment: None. Five copies of the issue in which article appears
Is simultaneous submission of article to other journals permitted: No
Exclusive manuscript rights between acceptance and publication: Yes
Copyright: Held by publication.
Reprints: Available, cost based on number of pages
Disposition of manuscript:
Query letter: No
Receipt of manuscript acknowledged: Yes
Decision to publish in: Three months
Accepted manuscript published in: Six months
Rejected manuscript returned: Yes
Rejected manuscript criticized: Yes
Submit to:
C. Edward Scebold
Editor
(See address above)

FORUM [968]
For the Discussion of New Trends in Education
APS Publications, Inc.
150 Fifth Avenue
New York New York 10011

First published in 1956

SUBSCRIPTION DATA

Issues and rates: Published three times per year.
Average paid circulation: 2000
Annual rate(s): £1.50

EDITORIAL DESCRIPTION

Contains articles on new trends in education: primary, secondary and further. Originally founded to promote growth of comprehensive schools and non-streaming.
Articles per average issue: 8
Audience: Professional, academic
Manuscripts accepted in English

MANUSCRIPT INFORMATION

Subject field(s): Education
Manuscript requirements: No specific style guide.
Number of copies to be submitted: One
Abstract: No
Author information and reprints: Payment: None.
Is simultaneous submission of article to other journals permitted: Yes
Exclusive manuscript rights between acceptance and publication: No
Copyright: Held by author.
Reprints: Not available.
Disposition of manuscript:
Receipt of manuscript acknowledged: Yes
Rejected manuscript returned: Yes

Rejected manuscript criticized: No
Submit to:
Brian Simon
Editor
11 Pendene Road
Leicester LE2 3DQ England

THE GIFTED CHILD QUARTERLY [969]
8080 Springvalley Drive
Cincinnati, Ohio 45236
(513) 631-1777

First published in 1957

SUBSCRIPTION DATA
Issues and rates: Published quarterly.
Annual rate(s): $20.00, Pan-Am $24.00, Foreign $24.00
Publisher or Sponsor: The National Association for Gifted Children
Managing Editor: Ann F. Isaacs

EDITORIAL DESCRIPTION
Contains articles on research, programs and practices in the education and psychology of gifted children.
Articles per average issue: 8-10
Audience: Academic
Manuscripts accepted in English

MANUSCRIPT INFORMATION
Subject field(s): Giftedness: philosophy, creativity and talent, how to develop and improve it
Manuscript requirements: See latest issue for style requirements.
Preferred length: 3000 words
Number of copies to be submitted: Two
Abstract: No
Author information and reprints: Payment: By author to publication. $15 per page.
Is simultaneous submission of article to other journals permitted: No
Exclusive manuscript rights between acceptance and publication: Yes
Copyright: Held by publication.
Reprints: Available, cost depends on quantity
Disposition of manuscript:
Query letter: No
Receipt of manuscript acknowledged: Yes
Decision to publish in: 1 week to several months
Accepted manuscript published in: 3-6 months
Rejected manuscript returned: Yes, if return postage is supplied by author.
Rejected manuscript criticized: Yes
Submit to:
Ann Fabe Isaacs
Editor-Publisher
(See address above)

THE GUIDANCE CLINIC [970]
Parker Publishing Company, Inc.
West Nyack, New York 10994
(201) 947-1000 ext. 572

First published in 1969

SUBSCRIPTION DATA
Issues and rates: Monthly except July and August
Average paid circulation: 5000
Annual rate(s): $36

EDITORIAL DESCRIPTION
Contains articles on successful programs and techniques that can be adapted by counselors at all educational levels. Emphasis is on practical applicability rather than on theory or scholarly research.
Articles per average issue: 7-8
Audience: Secondary and undergraduate counselors
Manuscripts accepted in English

MANUSCRIPT INFORMATION
Subject field(s): Counseling practices, policies and programs, career education, exceptional students, faculty relations, counselor and community
Manuscript requirements: See latest issue for style requirements.
Preferred length: 5-6 pages; 2000-2500 words
Number of copies to be submitted: One
Abstract: No
Author information and reprints: Payment: None. Five complimentary copies to author.
Is simultaneous submission of article to other journals permitted: No
Exclusive manuscript rights between acceptance and publication: No
Copyright: Held by publication.
Reprints: Not available.
Disposition of manuscript:
Query letter: No
Receipt of manuscript acknowledged: Yes
Decision to publish in: One month
Accepted manuscript published in: 6-9 months
Rejected manuscript returned: Yes
Rejected manuscript criticized: Yes
Submit to:
Ellen Massarsky
Editor
(See address above)

HARVARD EDUCATIONAL REVIEW [971]
Longfellow Hall, 13 Appian Way
Cambridge, Massachusetts 02138
(617) 495-3432

Previously entitled *The Harvard Teachers Record,* 1931-1936

First published in 1931

SUBSCRIPTION DATA
Issues and rates: Published quarterly.
Average paid circulation: 14,000
Annual rate(s): $14.00, Foreign $16.00
Publisher or Sponsor: Harvard Graduate School of Education

EDITORIAL DESCRIPTION
A forum for research, analysis, and discussion of vital issues in educational theory, policy, and practice.
Articles per average issue: 3-4
Audience: Academic
Manuscripts accepted in English

MANUSCRIPT INFORMATION
Subject field(s): Education; psychology, history, anthropology, sociology, and politics of education
Manuscript requirements: See latest issue for style requirements.
Preferred length: 20-40 pages
Number of copies to be submitted: Two
Abstract: Yes
Author information and reprints: Payment: Reprints only. 25 free to author
Is simultaneous submission of article to other journals permitted: No
Exclusive manuscript rights between acceptance and publication: Yes
Copyright: Held by publication.
Reprints: Available, cost varies by length
Disposition of manuscript:
Query letter: No
Receipt of manuscript acknowledged: Yes
Decision to publish in: 1-2 months
Accepted manuscript published in: 3-6 months
Rejected manuscript returned: Yes
Rejected manuscript criticized: No
Submit to:
Rochelle Beck;
Marshall J. Hirano
Co-Chairpersons, Editorial Board
(See address above)

HIGHER EDUCATION [972]
An International Journal of Higher Education and Educational Planning
Elsevier Scientific Publishing Company
P. O. Box 211, Jan van Galenstraat 335
Amsterdam, The Netherlands
(20) 515-9222

First published in 1972

SUBSCRIPTION DATA
Issues and rates: Published quarterly.
Average paid circulation: 1,000
Annual rate(s): Individuals $20.00; Institutions $37.50
Managing Editor: Alec M. Ross

EDITORIAL DESCRIPTION
Creates a forum for discussion based on contributions from different countries in all areas of higher (or tertiary) education.
Articles per average issue: 7
Audience: Educators
Manuscripts accepted in English

MANUSCRIPT INFORMATION
Subject field(s): The journal is divided into four sections: Original articles; reports of significant innovation, experiments or developments; information with special reference to current developments; book reviews
Manuscript requirements: See latest issue for style requirements. Style sheet sent on request. Chicago
Preferred length: 8,000 words maximum
Number of copies to be submitted: 3
Abstract: Yes. 200 words maximum

Education

Author information and reprints: Payment: Reprints only. 50
Is simultaneous submission of article to other journals permitted: Not permitted.
Exclusive manuscript rights between acceptance and publication: Yes
Copyright: Held by publication, but author himself is free to republish elsewhere
Reprints: Available at no cost. 50 Available at cost.
Disposition of manuscript:
Query letter: Not necessary, but advisable.
Receipt of manuscript acknowledged: Yes
Decision to publish in: 3 months
Accepted manuscript published in: 6-8 months
Rejected manuscript returned: Yes, if return postage is supplied by author.
Rejected manuscript criticized: Reasons for rejections only
Submit to:
Philip G. Altbach
North American Editor
Department of Higher Education
State University of New York at Buffalo
Buffalo, New York 14214

HIGHER EDUCATION BULLETIN [973]
Center for Educational Research and Development
The University
Lancaster LA1 4YL, England
0524-65201, ext. 4409

First published in 1967

SUBSCRIPTION DATA
Issues and rates: Published three times per year.
Annual rate(s): Individuals £2.00; Institutions £2.00

EDITORIAL DESCRIPTION
Publishes contributions on all aspects of higher education, with strong emphasis on survey articles, reviews of the literature, and "state of the art" papers which attempt to bring together for evaluation and comparison the wide range of material in a given area.
Articles per average issue: 3
Audience: Academic, professional
Manuscripts accepted in English

MANUSCRIPT INFORMATION
Subject field(s): Policy and planning, faculty and students, teaching, learning and the curriculum, with emphasis on Britain.
Manuscript requirements: No specific style guide.
Preferred length: 4,000-5,000 words
Number of copies to be submitted: 2
Abstract: Yes.
Author information and reprints: Payment: Reprints only. 25 reprints
Is simultaneous submission of article to other journals permitted: Permitted.
Exclusive manuscript rights between acceptance and publication: No
Copyright: Held by author.

Disposition of manuscript:
Query letter: Not necessary, but advisable.
Receipt of manuscript acknowledged: Yes
Decision to publish in: 1-2 months
Accepted manuscript published in: 3-9 months
Rejected manuscript returned: Yes, with return postage paid by publication.
Rejected manuscript criticized: Yes
Submit to:
D. J. Hounsell
Editor
(See address above)

THE HISTORY TEACHER [974]
California State University
Long Beach, California 90840
(213) 498-4431

First published in 1967

SUBSCRIPTION DATA
Issues and rates: Published quarterly.
Average paid circulation: 4000
Annual rate(s): Individuals $8.00; Institutions $10.00
Publisher or Sponsor: Society for History Education

EDITORIAL DESCRIPTION
A professional journal devoted to the teaching of history at the university, community college and secondary levels.
Articles per average issue: 8
Manuscripts accepted in English

MANUSCRIPT INFORMATION
Subject field(s): Historiography, teaching techniques, curricula, media materials in the teaching of history
Manuscript requirements: No specific style guide.
Preferred length: 2,500-7,500 words; everything typewritten, double-spaced with footnotes at end
Number of copies to be submitted: One
Abstract: No
Author information and reprints: Payment: None. 25 off-prints to author.
Is simultaneous submission of article to other journals permitted: No
Exclusive manuscript rights between acceptance and publication: Yes
Copyright: Held by the Society for History Education
Reprints: Available, cost by special quotation
Additional information: Illustrations accepted.
Disposition of manuscript:
Query letter: No
Receipt of manuscript acknowledged: Yes
Decision to publish in: 1-2 months
Accepted manuscript published in: 3-9 months
Rejected manuscript returned: Yes
Rejected manuscript criticized: Yes
Submit to:
Keith Ian Polakoff
Editor
(See address above)

IAPPW JOURNAL [975]
International Association of Pupil Personnel Workers
850 Hungerford Drive
Rockville, Maryland 20850
(301) 279-3189

Previously entitled *National League to Promote School Attendance*

First published in 1911-1948

SUBSCRIPTION DATA
Issues and rates: Published quarterly.
Annual rate(s): $15.00, Foreign $20.00
Publisher or Sponsor: International Association of Pupil Personnel Workers

EDITORIAL DESCRIPTION
The journal is committed to the promotion of pupil personnel services and programs which help children succeed in education. Every child should be encouraged to feel a sense of worth and value to himself, his family, and his community.
Articles per average issue: 7
Audience: Professional, academic
Manuscripts accepted in English only

MANUSCRIPT INFORMATION
Subject field(s): Child abuse, child labor laws, counseling single parents, school attendance, special education, juvenile court, family court, training schools, mental health hospitals, mental health clinics, drug abuse, family relations
Manuscript requirements: Style sheet sent on request.
Number of copies to be submitted: Four
Abstract: Yes
Author information and reprints: Payment: Reprints only. Two complimentary copies of issue in which article appears
Is simultaneous submission of article to other journals permitted: No
Exclusive manuscript rights between acceptance and publication: Yes
Copyright: Held by publication.
Reprints: Available; 100 for $25.00 plus postage
Disposition of manuscript:
Query letter: No
Receipt of manuscript acknowledged: Yes
Decision to publish in: 2 months
Accepted manuscript published in: 4-6 months
Rejected manuscript returned: Yes, if return postage is supplied by author.
Rejected manuscript criticized: Sometimes
Submit to:
William Edwin Myer
Supervisor of Pupil Personnel

Martin Bach
Managing Editor
1713 62nd Street
Kenosha, Wisconsin 53140

IAVA JOURNAL [976]
Learning Resources Service
Southern Illinois University
Carbondale, Illinois 62901
(618) 453-2258

SUBSCRIPTION DATA
Issues and rates: Published quarterly.
  Average paid circulation: 1,000 controlled
  Annual rate(s): Members $8.00, Students $4.00
Publisher or Sponsor: Illinois Audiovisual Association

EDITORIAL DESCRIPTION
  Contains state-wide announcements and national updates; feature articles: instructional media design, development, utilization and evaluation; conference summary; affiliate reports; advice from the pros (professional guidelines).
Articles per average issue: 7
Audience: Instructional media personnel
  Manuscripts accepted in English

MANUSCRIPT INFORMATION
Subject field(s): instructional media, educational communications and technology, media utilization, innovative media programs, learning theory as related to educational media
Manuscript requirements: See latest issue for style requirements.
  Preferred length: 500-1500 words
  Number of copies to be submitted: Two
Author information and reprints: Payment: None.
  Is simultaneous submission of article to other journals permitted: No
  Exclusive manuscript rights between acceptance and publication: No
  Copyright: Not copyrighted.
  Reprints: Not available.
Disposition of manuscript:
  Receipt of manuscript acknowledged: No
  Decision to publish in: 4 months
  Accepted manuscript published in: 6 months
  Rejected manuscript returned: No
  Rejected manuscript criticized: No
Submit to:
  Joe Gary
  Associate Editor
  Lakeland College
  U.S. 4 South
  Mattoon, Illinois 61938

IMPROVING COLLEGE AND UNIVERSITY TEACHING [977]
Oregon State University Press
P.O. Box 689
Oregon State University
Corvallis, Oregon 97331
(503) 754-3166

First published in 1953

SUBSCRIPTION DATA
Issues and rates: Published quarterly.
  Average paid circulation: 3,000
  Annual rate(s): $9.00
Publisher or Sponsor: Oregon State University, Graduate School

EDITORIAL DESCRIPTION
  This international quarterly features articles on college and university teaching written by college and university teachers and administrators.
Articles per average issue: 20-30
Audience: Academic
  Manuscripts accepted in English only

MANUSCRIPT INFORMATION
Subject field(s): Higher education
Manuscript requirements: See latest issue for style requirements.
  Preferred length: 1700 words, 2 pages
  Number of copies to be submitted: One
  Abstract: No
Author information and reprints: Payment: None.
  Is simultaneous submission of article to other journals permitted: Yes
  Exclusive manuscript rights between acceptance and publication: No
  Copyright: Held by publication.
  Reprints: Available, $5.00 per article page per 100 copies
Disposition of manuscript:
  Query letter: preferred
  Receipt of manuscript acknowledged: Yes
  Decision to publish in: 6 months
  Accepted manuscript published in: 2 years
  Rejected manuscript returned: Yes, if self-addressed, stamped envelope is sent with manuscript.
  Rejected manuscript criticized: No
Submit to:
  Delmer M. Goode
  Editor
  (See address above)

IMPROVING HUMAN PERFORMANCE [978]
A Research Quarterly
Catholic University
P. O. Box 137, Cardinal Station
Washington, D.C. 20017
(202) 635-5825

First published in 1972

SUBSCRIPTION DATA
Issues and rates: Published quarterly.
  Average paid circulation: 1,500
  Annual rate(s): $30.00, Foreign $32.00
Publisher or Sponsor: National Society for Performance and Instruction

EDITORIAL DESCRIPTION
  Deals with programmed instruction and the improvement of human performance in training and education areas.
Articles per average issue: 6
  Manuscripts accepted in English

MANUSCRIPT INFORMATION
Subject field(s): Programmed instruction, training, education, performance improvement
Manuscript requirements: APA
  Preferred length: None
  Number of copies to be submitted: 3
  Abstract: Helpful
Author information and reprints: Payment: None.
  Is simultaneous submission of article to other journals permitted: No
  Exclusive manuscript rights between acceptance and publication: Yes
  Copyright: Held by publication.
  Reprints: Available, cost varies
Additional information: Figures and charts should be camera-ready.
Disposition of manuscript:
  Query letter: No
  Receipt of manuscript acknowledged: No
  Decision to publish in: 2-6 months
  Accepted manuscript published in: 2-6 months
  Rejected manuscript returned: Yes, if return postage is supplied by author.
  Rejected manuscript criticized: Yes
Submit to:
  Jeanine Lee
  Managing Editor
  (See address above)

THE INDEPENDENT SCHOOL BULLETIN [979]
4 Liberty Square
Boston, Massachusetts 02109
(617) 542-1988

First published in 1941

SUBSCRIPTION DATA
Issues and rates: Published quarterly.
  Average paid circulation: 9,400
  Annual rate(s): $7.00, Members $5.00
Publisher or Sponsor: National Association of Independent Schools
Managing Editor: Blair McElroy

EDITORIAL DESCRIPTION
  Contains articles of general educational interest or on specific subject fields in elementary and secondary education.
Articles per average issue: 17
  Manuscripts accepted in English

MANUSCRIPT INFORMATION
Manuscript requirements: No specific style guide.
  Preferred length: 2,000-2,500 words; 8-10 pages
  Number of copies to be submitted: One
  Abstract: No
Author information and reprints: Payment: None.
  Is simultaneous submission of article to other journals permitted: Yes
  Exclusive manuscript rights between acceptance and publication: Yes
  Copyright: Held by publication.
  Reprints: Not available.
Disposition of manuscript:
  Query letter: No
  Receipt of manuscript acknowledged: Yes
  Decision to publish in: Two months
  Accepted manuscript published in: 2-9 months

Rejected manuscript returned: Yes
Rejected manuscript criticized: No
Submit to:
Blair McElroy
Editor
(See address above)

INSTRUCTOR [980]
Instructor Park
Dansville, New York 14437
(716) 987-2221

First published in 1890

SUBSCRIPTION DATA
Issues and rates: Monthly except July and August
  Average paid circulation: 255,000
  Annual rate(s): $10.00

EDITORIAL DESCRIPTION
A periodical planned to assist elementary classroom teachers in their work.
Articles per average issue: 18
Audience: Academic, classroom teachers, supervisors
  Manuscripts accepted in English

MANUSCRIPT INFORMATION
Subject field(s): Elementary education practices, teaching procedures, subject matter ideas, new trends and opportunities in elementary education
Manuscript requirements: Style sheet sent on request.
  Preferred length: 500-1200 words
  Number of copies to be submitted: 1
  Abstract: No
Author information and reprints: Payment: By publication to author. $5.00-$15.00 for short articles; $20.00-$200.00 for full length articles
  Is simultaneous submission of article to other journals permitted: No
  Exclusive manuscript rights between acceptance and publication: Yes
  Copyright: Held by publication.
  Reprints: Not available.
Disposition of manuscript:
  Query letter: No
  Receipt of manuscript acknowledged: Yes
  Decision to publish in: Within 4 months
  Accepted manuscript published in: 3-24 months
  Rejected manuscript returned: Yes
  Rejected manuscript criticized: No
Submit to:
Rosemary Alexander
Executive Editor
(See address above)
(716) 987-2221 ext. 22

INTEGRATED EDUCATION [981]
Report on Race and Schools
School of Education
Northwestern University
2003 Sheridan Road
Evanston, Illinois 60201
(312) 492-5102

First published in 1963

SUBSCRIPTION DATA
Issues and rates: Published bi-monthly.
  Average paid circulation: 5,000
  Annual rate(s): $10.00, Foreign $11.50
Publisher or Sponsor: Integrated Education Associates

EDITORIAL DESCRIPTION
Reports current developments, new court decisions, literature of the field; all bearing on equal educational opportunities for Black, Chicano, Indian-American, and Puerto Rican children.
Articles per average issue: 6-10
Audience: Teachers, parents
  Manuscripts accepted in English

MANUSCRIPT INFORMATION
Subject field(s): Classroom practice, law, sociology, psychology, history
Manuscript requirements: See latest issue for style requirements.
  Preferred length: 10-20 typewritten, double-spaced pages
  Number of copies to be submitted: Two
Author information and reprints: Payment: None.
  Is simultaneous submission of article to other journals permitted: No
  Exclusive manuscript rights between acceptance and publication: Yes
  Copyright: Held by publication.
  Reprints: Available, at cost
Disposition of manuscript:
  Receipt of manuscript acknowledged: Yes
  Decision to publish in: 4-6 weeks
  Accepted manuscript published in: 2-6 months
  Rejected manuscript returned: Yes, if return postage is supplied by author.
  Rejected manuscript criticized: Yes
Submit to:
Meyer Weinberg
Editor
(See address above)

INTERCHANGE [982]
A Journal of Educational Studies
Ontario Institute for Studies in Education
252 Bloor Street West
Toronto, Ontario M5S 1V6, Canada
(416) 923-6641 ext. 288

First published in 1970

SUBSCRIPTION DATA
Issues and rates: Published quarterly.
  Average paid circulation: 2,000
  Annual rate(s): Students $5.00, Individuals $7.00, Institutions $10.00
Publisher or Sponsor: The Ontario Institute for Studies in Education

EDITORIAL DESCRIPTION
Contains theoretical, empirical, and policy-oriented work relating to education.
Articles per average issue: 8
Audience: Researchers, educators
  Manuscripts accepted in English

MANUSCRIPT INFORMATION
Subject field(s): Education
Manuscript requirements: APA
  Preferred length: 25 pages
  Number of copies to be submitted: Three
Author information and reprints: Payment: None.
  Is simultaneous submission of article to other journals permitted: No
  Exclusive manuscript rights between acceptance and publication: Yes
  Copyright: Held by publication.
  Reprints: Available
Additional information: Typewritten, double-spaced manuscripts
Disposition of manuscript:
  Query letter: No
  Receipt of manuscript acknowledged: Yes
  Decision to publish in: 8 weeks
  Accepted manuscript published in: 3 months
  Rejected manuscript returned: Yes
  Rejected manuscript criticized: Yes
Submit to:
Andrew Effrat
Editor
(See address above)

INTERNATIONAL EDUCATIONAL AND CULTURAL EXCHANGE [983]
U. S. Government Printing Office
Superintendent of Documents
Washington, D.C. 20402
(202) 541-2051

First published in 1965

SUBSCRIPTION DATA
Issues and rates: Published quarterly.
  Average paid circulation: 500; 8,500 controlled
  Annual rate(s): $5.75; Foreign $7.20
Publisher or Sponsor: U.S. Advisory Committee on International Educational and Cultural Affairs

EDITORIAL DESCRIPTION
Provides information on a wide range of international exchange activities; serves as a forum for the discussion of issues in international educational and cultural affairs, both feature-length and shorter articles. Also reports on books, films, conferences, and opportunities for funding.
Articles per average issue: 8
Audience: Those actively engaged in international exchange activities: foreign student advisors, teachers, community volunteers, exchanges, administrators, cultural attaches
  Manuscripts accepted in English

MANUSCRIPT INFORMATION
Manuscript requirements: See latest issue for style requirements. GPO but not strictly
  Preferred length: 1,000-4,000 words
  Number of copies to be submitted: 1
  Abstract: Not necessary.

Author information and reprints: Payment: Reprints only. 10 copies of issue and 100 reprints
Is simultaneous submission of article to other journals permitted: Not permitted.
Exclusive manuscript rights between acceptance and publication: Yes
Copyright: Not copyrighted
Additional information: Typewritten, double-spaced manuscripts
Disposition of manuscript:
Query letter: Not necessary.
Receipt of manuscript acknowledged: Yes
Decision to publish in: 2-3 weeks
Accepted manuscript published in: 3 months
Rejected manuscript returned: Yes, with return postage paid by publication.
Rejected manuscript criticized: Reasons for rejections only
Submit to:
Nancy J. Fritz
Editor
CU/ACS, Room 420 SA-2
Department of State
Washington, D.C. 20520
(202) 632-2835

INTERNATIONAL JOURNAL OF INSTRUCTIONAL MEDIA [984]

Baywood Publishing Company, Inc.
43 Central Drive
Farmingdale, New York 11735
(516) 293-7130

First published in 1973

SUBSCRIPTION DATA

Issues and rates: Published quarterly.
Annual rate(s): $27.50; Foreign $29.50

EDITORIAL DESCRIPTION

Publishes papers applying instructional media to the learning process producing communication between teacher and student; supplements this relationship with an educational interface between curriculum and learning material.
Articles per average issue: 11
Audience: Academic, professional, media directors, consultants
Manuscripts accepted in English

MANUSCRIPT INFORMATION

Subject field(s): Utilization of media in work of individuals; experimental testing and effective programs in instructional media; articles which provide new ideas and encourage broader use of media in education.
Manuscript requirements: See latest issue for style requirements. Style sheet sent on request.
Preferred length: 5,000 words maximum
Number of copies to be submitted: 2
Abstract: Yes. Of about 150 words
Author information and reprints: Payment: Reprints only. 20 copies
Is simultaneous submission of article to other journals permitted: Not permitted.
Exclusive manuscript rights between acceptance and publication: Yes

Copyright: Held by publication.
Reprints: Available at cost.
Disposition of manuscript:
Query letter: Not necessary.
Receipt of manuscript acknowledged: Yes
Decision to publish in: 4-6 months
Accepted manuscript published in: 6 months
Rejected manuscript returned: Yes
Rejected manuscript criticized: Sometimes
Submit to:
Dr. Phillip J. Sleeman
Executive Editor
Instructional Media Center
University of Connecticut
Storrs, Connecticut 06268

INTERNATIONAL REVIEW OF EDUCATION [985]

Martinus Nyhoff
P. O. Box 269, Lange Voorhout 9-11
The Hague, The Netherlands
(070) 469660

First published in 1955

SUBSCRIPTION DATA

Issues and rates: Published quarterly.
Annual rate(s): Individuals Dfl 40.00; Institutions Dfl 40.00

EDITORIAL DESCRIPTION

Devoted to the publication of scholarly articles, reviews, communications, and reports on all questions of education and related fields as far as they are of international interest.
Manuscripts accepted in English

MANUSCRIPT INFORMATION

Manuscript requirements: See latest issue for style requirements.
Preferred length: As required
Number of copies to be submitted: 3
Abstract: Not necessary.
Disposition of manuscript:
Query letter: Not necessary, but advisable.
Rejected manuscript returned: Yes, if return postage is supplied by author.
Rejected manuscript criticized: Sometimes
Submit to:
Editorial Office
UNESCO Institute for Children
Feldbrunnerstrasse 70
2 Hamburg 13, Federal Republic of Germany

JGE: THE JOURNAL OF GENERAL EDUCATION [986]

215 Wagner Building
The Pennsylvania State University Press
University Park, Pennsylvania 16802
(814) 865-1327

Previously entitled *The Journal of General Education*

First published in 1946

SUBSCRIPTION DATA

Issues and rates: Published quarterly.
Average paid circulation: 1,700; 2100 controlled
Annual rate(s): $9.00; Pan-Am $9.50
Foreign $10.50; Individuals $9.00
Managing Editor: Carol Sams

EDITORIAL DESCRIPTION

A unique journal devoted to general and liberal education giving specialists a forum for the exchange of ideas.
Articles per average issue: 7
Audience: Teachers and students in colleges, junior colleges, and universities.
Manuscripts accepted in English

MANUSCRIPT INFORMATION

Subject field(s): All fields, particularly interdisciplinary, interdepartmental
Manuscript requirements: Chicago
Preferred length: No limitations
Number of copies to be submitted: 1
Abstract: Yes. An MLA form is sent to each author upon acceptance of manuscript.
Author information and reprints: Payment: None.
Is simultaneous submission of article to other journals permitted: Permitted.
Request that the information be given upon submission.
Exclusive manuscript rights between acceptance and publication: Yes
Copyright: Held by the Pennsylvania State University Press
Reprints: Available at no cost. 25
Disposition of manuscript:
Query letter: Not necessary, but advisable.
Receipt of manuscript acknowledged: Yes
Decision to publish in: 3 weeks
Accepted manuscript published in: 9 months
Rejected manuscript returned: Yes, if return postage is supplied by author.
Rejected manuscript criticized: Sometimes
Submit to:
Caroline D. Eckhardt;
Robert B. Eckhardt
Co-editors
(See address above)

THE JOURNAL OF AESTHETIC EDUCATION [987]

288B Education
University of Illinois at Urbana-Champaign
Urbana, Illinois 61801
(217) 333-6584

First published in 1966

SUBSCRIPTION DATA

Issues and rates: Published quarterly.
Average paid circulation: 1500
Annual rate(s): $7.50

Education

Publisher or Sponsor: University of Illinois

EDITORIAL DESCRIPTION
Publication contains articles devoted to an understanding of problem areas critical to education in the arts and the humanities; articles which comment upon the aesthetic character of other disciplines, such as mathematics and the sciences; articles which focus on the aesthetic import of the new communications media and environmental arts; articles dealing with the aesthetic aspects of the art and craft of teaching.
Articles per average issue: 7
Audience: Academic
Manuscripts accepted in English

MANUSCRIPT INFORMATION
Manuscript requirements: Style sheet sent on request.
Preferred length: 5,000-6,000 words
Number of copies to be submitted: Two
Abstract: No
Author information and reprints: Payment: None.
Is simultaneous submission of article to other journals permitted: No
Exclusive manuscript rights between acceptance and publication: Yes
Copyright: Held by publication.
Reprints: Available, cost on request
Disposition of manuscript:
Query letter: No
Receipt of manuscript acknowledged: Yes
Decision to publish in: One to two months
Accepted manuscript published in: Varies
Rejected manuscript returned: Yes
Rejected manuscript criticized: No
Submit to:
Ralph A. Smith
Editor
(See address above)

JOURNAL OF AMERICAN INDIAN EDUCATION [988]
Bureau of Educational Research and Services
Arizona State University
Tempe, Arizona 85281
(602) 965-3538

SUBSCRIPTION DATA
Issues and rates: Published three times per year.
Average paid circulation: 1,000
Annual rate(s): $3.50
Publisher or Sponsor: Arizona State University, Bureau of Educational Research and Services

EDITORIAL DESCRIPTION
Publishes manuscripts and research concerning the broad area of American Indian education and Indian affairs of North American Indians.
Articles per average issue: 4
Audience: Those with interests in Indian affairs
Manuscripts accepted in English

MANUSCRIPT INFORMATION
Subject field(s): Efforts are made to include a geographic representation of items relevant to the American Indian.
Manuscript requirements: See latest issue for style requirements.
Preferred length: 1,000-1,500 words; 8-10 pages
Number of copies to be submitted: 2
Abstract: No
Author information and reprints: Payment: None.
Is simultaneous submission of article to other journals permitted: Yes, prefer notification of other submissions
Exclusive manuscript rights between acceptance and publication: Yes
Copyright: Clearance for re-printing of articles to be received from Bureau of Educational Research and Services
Reprints: Available, cost negotiated
Additional information: Manuscript should be typewritten, double-spaced; original and 1 copy to be forwarded to editor; information on author to be included.
Disposition of manuscript:
Query letter: No
Receipt of manuscript acknowledged: Yes
Decision to publish in: 4-6 weeks
Accepted manuscript published in: 2-3 months
Rejected manuscript returned: Yes
Rejected manuscript criticized: Yes
Submit to:
George A. Gill
Editor
Center for Indian Education
College of Education
Arizona State University
Tempe, Arizona 85281
(602) 965-6292

JOURNAL OF BIOLOGICAL EDUCATION [989]
Institute of Biology
41 Queen's Gate
London SW7 5HU, England
(01) 589-9076

First published in 1967

SUBSCRIPTION DATA
Issues and rates: Published bi-monthly.
Average paid circulation: 2,000
Annual rate(s): £100.00; $25.00
Publisher or Sponsor: Institute of Biology London
Managing Editor: Rob Dixon

EDITORIAL DESCRIPTION
A Forum for news and new ideas in teaching biology.
Articles per average issue: 6
Audience: Educators
Manuscripts accepted in English

MANUSCRIPT INFORMATION
Subject field(s): Curriculum development and details of projects or work undertaken.
Manuscript requirements: Style sheet sent on request.
Preferred length: As required
Number of copies to be submitted: 2
Abstract: Yes
Author information and reprints: Payment: Reprints only. 25 free reprints
Is simultaneous submission of article to other journals permitted: Permitted, but not encouraged.
Exclusive manuscript rights between acceptance and publication: Yes
Copyright: Held by publication.
Reprints: Available at cost.
Disposition of manuscript:
Query letter: Not necessary.
Receipt of manuscript acknowledged: Yes
Decision to publish in: 1 month
Accepted manuscript published in: 2-4 months
Rejected manuscript returned: Yes, with return postage paid by publication.
Rejected manuscript criticized: Sometimes
Submit to:
Editor
(See address above)

THE JOURNAL OF BUSINESS EDUCATION [990]
The Magazine for Teachers of Business Subjects
15 South Franklin Street
Wilkes Barre, Pennsylvania 18701
(717) 823-6258

First published in 1928

SUBSCRIPTION DATA
Issues and rates: Published monthly.
Average paid circulation: 14,000 controlled
Annual rate(s): $7.00; Foreign $8.00
Managing Editor: Robert C. Trethaway

EDITORIAL DESCRIPTION
Subjects concern the teaching of business subjects in all levels.
Articles per average issue: 8-10
Audience: Teachers of business subjects
Manuscripts accepted in English

MANUSCRIPT INFORMATION
Subject field(s): Automation, bookkeeping/accounting, distributive education, general business, law, management, office practice, stenography, teacher education, curriculum, etc.
Manuscript requirements: See latest issue for style requirements.
Preferred length: 1,500
Number of copies to be submitted: 2
Abstract: Not necessary.
Author information and reprints: Payment: None.
Is simultaneous submission of article to other journals permitted: Not permitted.
Exclusive manuscript rights between acceptance and publication: Yes
Copyright: Held by publication.
Reprints: Available at cost.

Additional information: An original typed copy of the manuscript is preferred, double-spaced, with subheads every two or three hundred words. Illustrations are welcome.
Disposition of manuscript:
　Query letter: Not necessary, but advisable.
　Receipt of manuscript acknowledged: Yes
　Decision to publish in: 1-3 months
　Accepted manuscript published in: 3 months
　Rejected manuscript returned: Yes, with return postage paid by publication.
　Rejected manuscript criticized: Yes
Submit to:
　Dr. Elizabeth V. Tonne
　Editor
　(See address above)

JOURNAL OF COLLEGE SCIENCE TEACHING [991]
National Science Teachers Association
1742 Connecticut Avenue
Washington, D.C. 20009
(202) 265-4150

First published in 1971

SUBSCRIPTION DATA
Issues and rates: 5 times a year
　Average paid circulation: 3,400
　Annual rate(s): $12.00
Publisher or Sponsor: National Science Teachers Association
Managing Editor: Rosemary Amidei

EDITORIAL DESCRIPTION
　Addressed to college science teachers at introductory level; educational philosophy and techniques; science.
Articles per average issue: 10
Audience: College science teachers
　Manuscripts accepted in English

MANUSCRIPT INFORMATION
Subject field(s): Course descriptions, educational philosophy, educational techniques, science topics
Manuscript requirements: Style sheet sent on request.
　Preferred length: 2,500 words
　Number of copies to be submitted: Three
　Abstract: Yes
Author information and reprints: Payment: None.
　Is simultaneous submission of article to other journals permitted: No
　Exclusive manuscript rights between acceptance and publication: Yes
　Copyright: Held by publication.
　Reprints: Available
Disposition of manuscript:
　Query letter: No
　Receipt of manuscript acknowledged: Yes
　Decision to publish in: 2 months
　Accepted manuscript published in: 6 months
　Rejected manuscript returned: Yes
　Rejected manuscript criticized: Yes
Submit to:
　Leo Schubert
　Editor
　The American University
　Department of Chemistry
　Washington, D.C. 20016

JOURNAL OF CREATIVE BEHAVIOR [992]
1300 Elmwood Avenue, Chase Hall
State University College
Buffalo, New York 14222
(716) 862-6221

First published in 1967

SUBSCRIPTION DATA
Issues and rates: Published quarterly.
　Annual rate(s): $9.00, Foreign $10.00
Publisher or Sponsor: Creative Education Foundation, Inc.
Managing Editor: Angelo M. Biondi

EDITORIAL DESCRIPTION
　Contributions relating to creativity and problem-solving are invited. Articles should be of interest to individuals who have either a vocational or avocational interest in these areas.
Articles per average issue: 6-8
　Manuscripts accepted in English

MANUSCRIPT INFORMATION
Manuscript requirements: See latest issue for style requirements.
　Preferred length: 8,000 words maximum
　Number of copies to be submitted: Two
Author information and reprints: Payment: None. Two copies of issue in which article appears.
　Is simultaneous submission of article to other journals permitted: No
　Reprints: Available at nominal cost
Additional information: Diagrams should be drawn in India ink on white cover stock in the exact size that would appear in the journal. Tables should be typed on separate sheets of paper with appropriate title.
Disposition of manuscript:
　Query letter: No
　Receipt of manuscript acknowledged: Yes
　Decision to publish in: Up to six months
　Accepted manuscript published in: 6 months
　Rejected manuscript returned: Yes
　Rejected manuscript criticized: No
Submit to:
　The Editor
　(See address above)

THE JOURNAL OF ECONOMIC EDUCATION [993]
1212 Avenue of the Americas
New York, New York 10036
(212) 582-5150

First published in 1969

SUBSCRIPTION DATA
Issues and rates: Published semi-annually.
　Average paid circulation: 2,000; 5,000 controlled
　Annual rate(s): $4.00
Publisher or Sponsor: The Joint Council on Economic Education
Managing Editor: George G. Dawson

EDITORIAL DESCRIPTION
　Contains articles dealing with economic education stressing research and evaluation of the teaching of economics at all educational levels; short notes and communications; book reviews; notices of new audio-visual materials in economics.
Articles per average issue: 12
Audience: Teachers of economics
　Manuscripts accepted in English

MANUSCRIPT INFORMATION
Subject field(s): Economic education
Manuscript requirements: Style sheet sent on request.
　Preferred length: 3500 words; 12 pages
　Number of copies to be submitted: Three
　Abstract: Yes
Author information and reprints: Payment: None.
　Is simultaneous submission of article to other journals permitted: Yes
　Exclusive manuscript rights between acceptance and publication: Yes
　Copyright: Held by publication.
　Reprints: Available, cost varies
Disposition of manuscript:
　Query letter: No
　Receipt of manuscript acknowledged: Yes
　Decision to publish in: Five months
　Accepted manuscript published in: Eight months
　Rejected manuscript returned: No
　Rejected manuscript criticized: Yes
Submit to:
　George G. Dawson
　Managing Editor
　(See address above)

JOURNAL OF EDUCATION [994]
Department of Education
P.O. Box 578
Halifax, Nova Scotia, Canada
(902) 424-5570

First published in 1851

SUBSCRIPTION DATA
Issues and rates: Published quarterly.
　Average paid circulation: 13,500 controlled
Publisher or Sponsor: Nova Scotia Department of Education
Managing Editor: R. A. Simpson

EDITORIAL DESCRIPTION
　Contains articles concerning education generally; education in Nova Scotia; articles on history and natural history of Nova Scotia; articles of general cultural interest.
Articles per average issue: 8
Audience: Educators
　Manuscripts accepted in English

MANUSCRIPT INFORMATION
Subject field(s): Educational practices and projects in Nova Scotia, trends in educational thought, educational opinion in Nova Scotia, Nova Scotia history and natural history.
Manuscript requirements: See latest issue for style requirements.
  Preferred length: 1,500-4,000 words
  Number of copies to be submitted: One
  Abstract: Not necessary
Author information and reprints: Payment: None.
  Is simultaneous submission of article to other journals permitted: Yes
  Exclusive manuscript rights between acceptance and publication: Yes
  Copyright: Held by author.
  Reprints: Not available.
Additional information: Typescript, double-spaced, with ample margins.
Disposition of manuscript:
  Query letter: No
  Receipt of manuscript acknowledged: Yes
  Decision to publish in: Up to 3 months.
  Accepted manuscript published in: Up to 6 months
  Rejected manuscript returned: Yes
  Rejected manuscript criticized: No
Submit to:
  Raymond A. Simpson
  Director, Publication and Reference Service
  (See address above)

SPECIAL STIPULATIONS
  Highly technical or research papers should not be submitted; most articles published are such as would interest the majority of classroom teachers in a large school system.

JOURNAL OF EDUCATION [995]
765 Commonwealth Avenue
Boston, Massachusetts 02215
(617) 353-3730

First published in 1875

SUBSCRIPTION DATA
Issues and rates: Published quarterly.
  Average paid circulation: 1,550
  Annual rate(s): $5.00
Publisher or Sponsor: Boston University, School of Education
Managing Editor: Joel Rakow

EDITORIAL DESCRIPTION
  Addresses students and educators with regard to pertinent issues in contemporary education.
Articles per average issue: 4-6
Audience: Educators
  Manuscripts accepted in English

MANUSCRIPT INFORMATION
Subject field(s): Education: any subject field
Manuscript requirements: APA
  Preferred length: None
  Number of copies to be submitted: Original plus two copies
  Abstract: Yes, 100-200 words

Author information and reprints: Payment: Reprints only. 2 complimentary copies
  Is simultaneous submission of article to other journals permitted: No
  Exclusive manuscript rights between acceptance and publication: Yes
  Copyright: Held by the Trustees of Boston University
  Reprints: Not available.
Disposition of manuscript:
  Query letter: No
  Receipt of manuscript acknowledged: Yes
  Decision to publish in: 4-6 weeks
  Accepted manuscript published in: 3-6 months
  Rejected manuscript returned: Yes
  Rejected manuscript criticized: Sometimes
Submit to:
  The Editor
  (See address above)

SPECIAL STIPULATIONS
  Require very brief vita of author.

JOURNAL OF EDUCATIONAL MEASUREMENT [996]
Evaluation Services
Michigan State university
East Lansing, Michigan 48824
(517) 355-1912

First published in 1964

SUBSCRIPTION DATA
Issues and rates: Published quarterly.
  Average paid circulation: 3,000
  Annual rate(s): $15.00, Foreign $16.00
Publisher or Sponsor: National Council on Measurement in Education
Managing Editor: Irvin J. Lehmann

EDITORIAL DESCRIPTION
  Contains reports and research articles of applications of measurement in an educational context; solicited reviews of current standardized educational and psychological tests and of other important measurement works
Articles per average issue: 6-10
Audience: Those with interest in application of measurement
  Manuscripts accepted in English

MANUSCRIPT INFORMATION
Subject field(s): Educational measurement, other measurement
Manuscript requirements: APA
  Preferred length: 1500-2100 words; 5-7 pages
  Number of copies to be submitted: Three
  Abstract: Yes
Author information and reprints: Payment: None.
  Is simultaneous submission of article to other journals permitted: Yes
  Exclusive manuscript rights between acceptance and publication: Yes
  Copyright: Held by publication.
  Reprints: Available, $3.00 per page for 100 reprints

Disposition of manuscript:
  Receipt of manuscript acknowledged: Yes
  Decision to publish in: 2-3 months
  Accepted manuscript published in: 10-12 months
  Rejected manuscript returned: Yes
  Rejected manuscript criticized: Yes
Submit to:
  Richard Jaeger
  Editor
  College of Education
  University of South Florida
  Tampa, Florida 33620

JOURNAL OF EDUCATIONAL TECHNOLOGY SYSTEMS [997]
Baywood Publishing Company, Inc.
43 Central Drive
Farmingdale, New York 11735
(516) 293-7130

First published in 1972

SUBSCRIPTION DATA
Issues and rates: Published quarterly.
  Annual rate(s): $33.00; Foreign $35.00
Publisher or Sponsor: Society for Applied Learning Technology

EDITORIAL DESCRIPTION
  Deals with systems in which technology and education interface, along with the nature of technological advances useful for teaching and learning. It focuses on the techniques and approaches for using technology in the educational process.
Articles per average issue: 7
Audience: Educators
  Manuscripts accepted in English

MANUSCRIPT INFORMATION
Subject field(s): Actual classroom practice and experimentation with educational use, innovative papers dealing with systems for individualizing instruction.
Manuscript requirements: See latest issue for style requirements. Style sheet sent on request.
  Preferred length: Up to 5,000 words
  Number of copies to be submitted: 2
  Abstract: Yes. Of about 150 words
Author information and reprints: Payment: Reprints only. 20 copies
  Is simultaneous submission of article to other journals permitted: Not permitted.
  Exclusive manuscript rights between acceptance and publication: Yes
  Copyright: Held by publication.
  Reprints: Available at cost.
Disposition of manuscript:
  Query letter: Not necessary, but advisable.
  Receipt of manuscript acknowledged: Yes
  Decision to publish in: 4-6 weeks
  Accepted manuscript published in: 6 months
  Rejected manuscript returned: Yes, with return postage paid by publication.
  Rejected manuscript criticized: Sometimes
Submit to:
  Dr. Thomas T. Liao;

Dr. David C. Miller
Editors
(See address above)

THE JOURNAL OF
EDUCATIONAL THOUGHT [998]
Room 1304, Education Tower
The University of Calgary
Calgary, Alberta T2N 1N4, Canada
284-5629

First published in 1967

SUBSCRIPTION DATA
Issues and rates: Published three times per year.
  Annual rate(s): $5.00
Publisher or Sponsor: The University of Calgary, Faculty of Education

EDITORIAL DESCRIPTION
Attempts to complement empirical research by publishing speculative, critical articles on education. Draws specifically upon philosophical, social and historical insights, but is receptive to other approaches, theoretical and practical, including those of teachers and administrators. Does not represent any particular viewpoint on educational issues, but does try to maintain a balance between criticism of existing educational programs and practices and suggestions for alternatives. Consideration of alternatives can include both speculation about proposed alternatives and reporting upon innovations actually being attempted.
Articles per average issue: 3-5
Manuscripts accepted in English

MANUSCRIPT INFORMATION
Subject field(s): Relating to the educational field
Manuscript requirements: Chicago
  Preferred length: 4,000 words; 15 pages
  Number of copies to be submitted: One or more.
  Abstract: Yes, including a biographical sketch of author
Author information and reprints: Payment: None.
  Is simultaneous submission of article to other journals permitted: Publication expects to be advised if manuscript is being submitted elsewhere.
  Exclusive manuscript rights between acceptance and publication: Yes
  Copyright: Held by author.
  Reprints: Available
Disposition of manuscript:
  Query letter: No
  Receipt of manuscript acknowledged: Yes
  Decision to publish in: Two months
  Accepted manuscript published in: Three to six months
  Rejected manuscript returned: Yes
  Rejected manuscript criticized: Sometimes
Submit to:
  The Editor
  (See address above)

JOURNAL OF ENGLISH
TEACHING TECHNIQUES [999]
Division of Humanities
Southwest Minnesota State College
Marshall, Minnesota 56258
(507) 537-7155

First published in 1968

SUBSCRIPTION DATA
Issues and rates: Published quarterly.
  Average paid circulation: 325
  Annual rate(s): $4.00, Foreign $5.00
Publisher or Sponsor: Southeast Minnesota State College, Literature and American Language Program
Managing Editor: Delbert Wylder

EDITORIAL DESCRIPTION
Contains articles and book reviews of scholarly merit dealing with any and all teaching techniques used in the English classroom at all educational levels.
Articles per average issue: 6
Audience: Teachers of English
Manuscripts accepted in English

MANUSCRIPT INFORMATION
Subject field(s): Literature, poetry and drama, composition, linguistics, creative writing, English teaching techniques, reading skills
Manuscript requirements: MLA
  Preferred length: Not to exceed 20 pages
  Number of copies to be submitted: Two
  Abstract: No
Author information and reprints: Payment: None.
  Is simultaneous submission of article to other journals permitted: Yes
  Exclusive manuscript rights between acceptance and publication: Yes
  Copyright: Held by publication.
  Reprints: Available upon specific request
Additional information: Typewritten, double-spaced. Photographs should be glossy prints. Drawings should be done in black ink.
Disposition of manuscript:
  Query letter: No
  Receipt of manuscript acknowledged: Yes
  Decision to publish in: 6-8 weeks
  Accepted manuscript published in: 6 months
  Rejected manuscript returned: Yes, if return postage is supplied by author.
  Rejected manuscript criticized: No
Submit to:
  P.J. Hickerson, Jr.
  Editor
  (See address above)

JOURNAL OF EXTENSION [1000]
807 Extension Building
Madison, Wisconsin 53706
(608) 262-1974

Previously entitled *Journal of Cooperative Education*

First published in 1963

SUBSCRIPTION DATA
Issues and rates: Published bi-monthly.
  Average paid circulation: 6,000
  Annual rate(s): $9.00
Managing Editor: Patrick J. Borich

EDITORIAL DESCRIPTION
Articles are published that bridge the gap between theory and practice for the extension practitioner.
Articles per average issue: 2
Audience: Adult and extension educators
Manuscripts accepted in English

MANUSCRIPT INFORMATION
Subject field(s): Extension work, programming, adult/continuing education, change process, human behavior, group processes, administration/supervision, teaching/learning
Manuscript requirements: See latest issue for style requirements.
  Preferred length: 12-20 typewritten, double-spaced
  Number of copies to be submitted: Four
  Abstract: No
Author information and reprints: Payment: None.
  Is simultaneous submission of article to other journals permitted: No
  Exclusive manuscript rights between acceptance and publication: No
  Copyright: Held by publication.
  Reprints: Available
Disposition of manuscript:
  Query letter: No
  Receipt of manuscript acknowledged: Yes
  Decision to publish in: Six weeks
  Accepted manuscript published in: 3-6 months
  Rejected manuscript returned: Yes
  Rejected manuscript criticized: Yes
Submit to:
  Patrick J. Borich
  Editor
  260 Coffey
  St. Paul, Minnesota 55101
  (612) 373-1223

JOURNAL OF FINANCIAL
EDUCATION [1001]
School of Business
San Jose State University
San Jose, California 95192
(408) 277-3495

Previously entitled *Financial Education*

First published in 1972

SUBSCRIPTION DATA
Issues and rates: Published annually.
  Average paid circulation: 350
  Annual rate(s): Foreign $3.00; Individuals $3.00; Institutions $6.00; Students $3.00; Members $30.00
Managing Editor: George R. Sanderson

EDITORIAL DESCRIPTION
Publishes innovative articles on how to better teach courses in corporate finance,

investments, financial institutions, and related subjects
Articles per average issue: 16
Audience: Professors of finance, libraries, and financial managers
Manuscripts accepted in English

MANUSCRIPT INFORMATION
Subject field(s): Corporate finance; investments; financial institutions; case studies; international finance
Manuscript requirements: See latest issue for style requirements.
  Preferred length: 4-8 pages
  Number of copies to be submitted: 3
  Abstract: Not necessary.
Author information and reprints: Payment: None.
  Is simultaneous submission of article to other journals permitted: Not permitted.
  Exclusive manuscript rights between acceptance and publication: Yes
  Copyright: Held by publication.
  Reprints: Not available.
Disposition of manuscript:
  Query letter: Not necessary.
  Receipt of manuscript acknowledged: Yes
  Decision to publish in: 2 months
  Accepted manuscript published in: varies
  Rejected manuscript returned: No
  Rejected manuscript criticized: Yes
Submit to:
  Dr. George R. Sanderson
  Editor
  (See address above)

THE JOURNAL OF GEOGRAPHY [1002]
National Council for Geographic Education
115 North Marion Street
Oak Park, Illinois 60301
(312) 383-5633

First published in 1898

SUBSCRIPTION DATA
Issues and rates: Monthly, September-May
  Average paid circulation: 6,500; 500 controlled
  Annual rate(s): Individuals $12, Institutions $16
Publisher or Sponsor: National Council for Geographic Education
Managing Editor: Ronald E. Nelson

EDITORIAL DESCRIPTION
  The official publication of the National Council for Geographic Education, it contains substantive, philosophical, and methodological articles.
Articles per average issue: 4-5
Audience: Geographic educators at all levels
  Manuscripts accepted in English

MANUSCRIPT INFORMATION
Subject field(s): Geographic education, environmental education, conservation, earth sciences, social studies and related fields
Manuscript requirements: See latest issue for style requirements.
  Preferred length: None
  Number of copies to be submitted: One
  Abstract: No
Author information and reprints: Payment: None.
  Is simultaneous submission of article to other journals permitted: Yes
  Exclusive manuscript rights between acceptance and publication: Yes
  Copyright: Held by publication.
  Reprints: Available, cost on request.
Additional information: Place footnotes in the text immediately following the line of reference. Maps and drawings should be done in black ink and be of professional quality. Photographs, if any, should be clear and sharply focused, with good contrast and printed on glossy, firm paper.
Disposition of manuscript:
  Query letter: No
  Receipt of manuscript acknowledged: Yes
  Decision to publish in: Six weeks
  Accepted manuscript published in: 6-9 months
  Rejected manuscript returned: Yes
  Rejected manuscript criticized: Yes
Submit to:
  Ronald E. Nelson
  Editor
  Department of Geography
  Western Illinois University
  Macomb, Illinois 61455
  (309) 298-1648

JOURNAL OF GEOLOGICAL EDUCATION [1003]
c/o Larry Martin
1118 South Carnegie Drive
Tuscon, Arizona 85710
(602) 296-1768

SUBSCRIPTION DATA
Issues and rates: 5 per year
  Average paid circulation: 3,300
  Annual rate(s): $12.50; Members $10.00; Students $4.50
Publisher or Sponsor: National Association of Geology Teachers

EDITORIAL DESCRIPTION
  Contains geological reviews and articles, college and secondary school level teaching aids, philosophies of teaching, status reports (for secondary level mainly).
Articles per average issue: 8-10
Audience: Academic
  Manuscripts accepted in English only

MANUSCRIPT INFORMATION
Manuscript requirements: See latest issue for style requirements.
  Preferred length: Less than 15 pages
  Number of copies to be submitted: Two
  Abstract: Yes
Author information and reprints: Payment: By author to publication. $50 per page. Where author has institutional or grant funds available.
  Is simultaneous submission of article to other journals permitted: No
  Copyright: Held by publication.
  Reprints: Available at cost
Disposition of manuscript:
  Query letter: No
  Receipt of manuscript acknowledged: Yes
  Decision to publish in: 2-4 months
  Accepted manuscript published in: 2 months
  Rejected manuscript returned: Yes
  Rejected manuscript criticized: Yes
Submit to:
  James H. Shea
  Editor
  Division of Science
  University of Wisconsin, Parkside
  Kenosha, Wisconsin 53140
  (414) 553-2449

THE JOURNAL OF HIGHER EDUCATION [1004]
Ohio State University Press
2070 Neil Avenue
Columbus, Ohio 43210
(614) 422-6930

First published in 1930

SUBSCRIPTION DATA
Issues and rates: Published bi-monthly.
  Average paid circulation: 5,850; 6,000 controlled
  Annual rate(s): Institutions $12.00, Individuals $10.00, Foreign $11.00
Publisher or Sponsor: American Association for Higher Education
Managing Editor: Richard A. McKee

EDITORIAL DESCRIPTION
  A scholarly journal devoted to the professional and academic concerns of college and university administrators, faculty, trustees, and students. Presents professional views on the most significant and recent developments in higher education. Aimed at broad coverage of problems of recent interest.
Articles per average issue: 6
Audience: Student personnel administrators, academic
  Manuscripts accepted in English

MANUSCRIPT INFORMATION
Subject field(s): Policy issues in administration, organizational development trends, research studies, faculty and student viewpoints, organization in higher education, administration behavior, college teaching, evaluation, current issues, university finances
Manuscript requirements: Chicago
  Preferred length: 15-20 pages
  Number of copies to be submitted: Three
  Abstract: Yes
Author information and reprints: Payment: None.
  Is simultaneous submission of article to other journals permitted: No
  Exclusive manuscript rights between acceptance and publication: Yes
  Copyright: Held by publication.
  Reprints: Available on request
Disposition of manuscript:
  Query letter: No
  Receipt of manuscript acknowledged: Yes

Decision to publish in: 2-6 weeks
Accepted manuscript published in: 3-6 months
Rejected manuscript returned: Yes, if return postage is supplied by author.
Rejected manuscript criticized: Sometimes
Submit to:
Robert J. Silverman
Editor
(See address above)

JOURNAL OF INSTRUCTIONAL PSYCHOLOGY [1005]
P. O. Box 5630
Milwaukee, Wisconsin 53211
(414) 278-0701

First published in 1974

SUBSCRIPTION DATA
Issues and rates: Published quarterly.
  Annual rate(s): Individuals $7.50; Institutions $10.00; Foreign individuals $9.00; Foreign institutions $11.50
Managing Editor: Dr. George E. Uhlig

EDITORIAL DESCRIPTION
Publishes manuscripts related to the instructional process at all levels of education.
Articles per average issue: 8
Audience: Public and private school teachers, college and University instructors.
  Manuscripts accepted in English

MANUSCRIPT INFORMATION
Subject field(s): General instructional methodology, instructional case studies, evaluation
Manuscript requirements: Style sheet sent on request. APA
  Preferred length: 1,500 to 2,500 words
  Number of copies to be submitted: 2
  Abstract: Yes. It should be written on a separate sheet of paper, about 120 words in length. Should contain (a) the problem, (b) the method, (c) the results, and (d) the conclusions.
Author information and reprints: Payment: By author to publication. $8.00 per page.
  Is simultaneous submission of article to other journals permitted: Permitted, but not encouraged.
  Exclusive manuscript rights between acceptance and publication: Yes
  Copyright: Held by author and publication
  Reprints: Available at cost.
Disposition of manuscript:
  Receipt of manuscript acknowledged: Yes
  Decision to publish in: 2 months
  Accepted manuscript published in: 3-6 months
  Rejected manuscript returned: Yes, if return postage is supplied by author.
  Rejected manuscript criticized: Reasons for rejections only
Submit to:
  Dr. George E. Uhlig;
  Alma G. Vasquez

Editors
(See address above)
(414) 278-0701

JOURNAL OF LEARNING DISABILITIES [1006]
101 East Ontario Street
Chicago, Illinois 60611
(312) 337-7800

SUBSCRIPTION DATA
Issues and rates: Monthly except July and August
  Average paid circulation: 15,000
  Annual rate(s): $12.00; Foreign $25.00
Managing Editor: Patricia E. Lane

EDITORIAL DESCRIPTION
Publishes clinical applications, research and theoretical articles on specific learning disabilities. The journal is a multidisciplinary, international exchange of information, covering over 20 disciplines which contribute to the study of the nature and remediation of specific learning disabilities.
Articles per average issue: 8-10
Audience: Clinicians, teachers, researchers
  Manuscripts accepted in English

MANUSCRIPT INFORMATION
Subject field(s): Specific learning disabilities
Manuscript requirements: Style sheet sent on request.
  Preferred length: Maximum 20 pages
  Number of copies to be submitted: Three
  Abstract: Yes
Author information and reprints: Payment: None. Five copies of issue in which article appears.
  Is simultaneous submission of article to other journals permitted: No
  Exclusive manuscript rights between acceptance and publication: Yes
  Copyright: Held by publication.
  Reprints: Available at cost, depending on length of article
Additional information: Authors not familiar with the publication or the exact nature of the field that it serves should first query the editor with an explanatory letter and brief outline.
Disposition of manuscript:
  Query letter: No
  Receipt of manuscript acknowledged: Yes
  Decision to publish in: 8-10 weeks
  Accepted manuscript published in: 9-12 months
  Rejected manuscript returned: Yes, if self-addressed, stamped envelope is sent with manuscript.
  Rejected manuscript criticized: Sometimes
Submit to:
  P. E. Lane
  Editor-in-Chief
  (See address above)

THE JOURNAL OF NEGRO EDUCATION [1007]
P. O. Box 311
Howard University
Washington, D. C. 20059
(202) 636-6751

First published in 1932

SUBSCRIPTION DATA
Issues and rates: Published quarterly.
  Average paid circulation: 3,000
  Annual rate(s): $7.50; Foreign $8.50
Publisher or Sponsor: Howard University
Managing Editor: Theresa A. Rector

EDITORIAL DESCRIPTION
Purposes: to stimulate the collection and facilitate the dissemination of facts about the education of black people; to present discussions of proposals and practices relating to the education of black people; to stimulate and sponsor investigations of issues incident to the education of black people
Articles per average issue: 12
Audience: Educators, researchers
  Manuscripts accepted in English

MANUSCRIPT INFORMATION
Subject field(s): Education, sociology, language development, educational psychology, economics; material must be of current interest or historical value; especially interested in articles dealing with blacks in the Americas, Caribbean and Africa
Manuscript requirements: See latest issue for style requirements. Chicago
  Preferred length: 15-18 pages
  Number of copies to be submitted: 2
  Abstract: Not necessary.
Author information and reprints: Payment: None.
  Is simultaneous submission of article to other journals permitted: Permitted, but not encouraged.
  Exclusive manuscript rights between acceptance and publication: Yes
  Copyright: Held by publication.
  Reprints: Available at no cost.
Disposition of manuscript:
  Query letter: Not necessary.
  Receipt of manuscript acknowledged: Yes
  Decision to publish in: 8-10 weeks
  Accepted manuscript published in: 24 months
  Rejected manuscript returned: Yes, with return postage paid by publication.
  Rejected manuscript criticized: Sometimes
Submit to:
  Charles A. Martin
  Editor-in-Chief
  (See address above)

JOURNAL OF NUTRITION EDUCATION [1008]
2140 Shattuck Avenue, Suite #1110
Berkeley, California 94704
(415) 548-1363

First published in 1969

Education

SUBSCRIPTION DATA

Issues and rates: Published quarterly.
  Average paid circulation: 9,000
  Annual rate(s): $10.00, Institutions $14.00
Publisher or Sponsor: Society for Nutrition Education

EDITORIAL DESCRIPTION

Contains research articles, critiques, reviews, and features relevant to nutrition education to help the nutrition educator to be more effective in communicating with and motivating his students, patients, colleagues, or the lay public.
Articles per average issue: 4-6
Audience: Academic
  Manuscripts accepted in English only

MANUSCRIPT INFORMATION

Subject field(s): Background data affecting nutrition education, nutrition education methods from preschool to old age, evaluation of nutrition education
Manuscript requirements: GPO
  Preferred length: Up to 16 pages typewritten, double-spaced
  Number of copies to be submitted: Original and 4 copies
  Abstract: Yes; up to 150 words discussing content and findings.
Author information and reprints: Payment: By author to publication. $55.00 per page. for first 3 pages; $110.00 per page. for over 3 pages
  Is simultaneous submission of article to other journals permitted: No
  Exclusive manuscript rights between acceptance and publication: Yes
  Copyright: Held by publication.
  Reprints: Available at cost
Additional information: All submitted manuscripts are reviewed for significance and soundness by a panel of expert reviewers. Occasional supplements published if funding is obtained by author.
Disposition of manuscript:
  Query letter: No
  Receipt of manuscript acknowledged: Yes
  Decision to publish in: 2 months
  Accepted manuscript published in: 6-12 months
  Rejected manuscript returned: Yes
  Rejected manuscript criticized: Yes
Submit to:
  Helen D. Ullrich
  Editor
  (See address above)

JOURNAL OF PHYSICAL EDUCATION* [1009]

Lee Circle YMCA
New Orleans, Louisiana 70130
(504) 524-1574

SUBSCRIPTION DATA

Issues and rates: Published bi-monthly.
  Average paid circulation: 2500
  Annual rate(s): $6.00, Foreign $6.50, Students $3.00
Publisher or Sponsor: The National Physical Education Society
Managing Editor: Philip W. Wortman

EDITORIAL DESCRIPTION

Contains articles on health, physical education, recreation, sports, dance, research theory and practice; philosophical, art forms, programmatic, inspirational.

MANUSCRIPT INFORMATION

Subject field(s): Physical education, health, recreation, sports, spirit-mind-body relationships, human development
Manuscript requirements: No specific style guide.
  Preferred length: 700-1500 words; 1-2 pages
  Number of copies to be submitted: Two
Author information and reprints: Payment: None. Two copies of issue in which article appears.
  Is simultaneous submission of article to other journals permitted: Yes
  Exclusive manuscript rights between acceptance and publication: Yes
  Copyright: Held by author.
  Reprints: Available to author
Additional information: Manuscripts may be sent out for evaluation, so author's name should appear only on separate covering page.
Disposition of manuscript:
  Receipt of manuscript acknowledged: Yes
  Decision to publish in: 4 to 6 weeks
  Accepted manuscript published in: 1 to 6 months
  Rejected manuscript returned: Yes
  Rejected manuscript criticized: No
Submit to:
  Leonard Rosewarren
  Editor
  90 North Newberry Street
  York, Pennsylvania 17401
  (717) 843-7884

JOURNAL OF READING [1010]

International Reading Association
800 Barksdale Road
Newark, Delaware 19711
(302) 731-1600

Previously entitled *Journal of Developmental Reading*

First published in 1957

SUBSCRIPTION DATA

Issues and rates: Monthly, October through May
  Average paid circulation: 17,500
  Annual rate(s): $15.00
Publisher or Sponsor: International Reading Association

EDITORIAL DESCRIPTION

Contains articles on reading at secondary school level and up.
Articles per average issue: 10
  Manuscripts accepted in English

MANUSCRIPT INFORMATION

Subject field(s): Reading, related fields
Manuscript requirements: MLA, other requirements sent on request
  Preferred length: Variable
  Number of copies to be submitted: Three
  Abstract: No
Author information and reprints: Payment: None. Five complimentary copies.
  Is simultaneous submission of article to other journals permitted: No
  Exclusive manuscript rights between acceptance and publication: Yes
  Copyright: Held by publication.
  Reprints: Not available.
Disposition of manuscript:
  Query letter: No
  Receipt of manuscript acknowledged: Yes
  Decision to publish in: Six weeks
  Accepted manuscript published in: Two to twelve months
  Rejected manuscript returned: Yes, if return postage is supplied by author.
  Rejected manuscript criticized: Yes
Submit to:
  Lloyd W. Kline
  Editor
  (See address above)
  (302) 731-1600 ext. 65

JOURNAL OF READING BEHAVIOR [1011]

Clemson University
Clemson, South Carolina 29631
(803) 656-3482

SUBSCRIPTION DATA

Issues and rates: Published quarterly.
  Average paid circulation: 2000
  Annual rate(s): Individuals $10.00, Institutions $10.00
Publisher or Sponsor: National Reading Conference, Inc.

EDITORIAL DESCRIPTION

Publishes original experimental and theoretical articles concerned with reading behavior. Special emphasis is placed on articles dealing with issues related to the understanding of prose and learning through reading. Reports in this area may deal either with related basis cognitive processes or with instructional issues, provided the latter are specifically related to a theoretical base.
Articles per average issue: 10
Audience: Teachers of reading
  Manuscripts accepted in English

MANUSCRIPT INFORMATION

Subject field(s): Reading research, prose learning
Manuscript requirements: See latest issue for style requirements.
  Preferred length: 3,000-10,000 words
  Number of copies to be submitted: Five
  Abstract: Yes
Author information and reprints: Payment: None.
  Is simultaneous submission of article to other journals permitted: No
  Exclusive manuscript rights between acceptance and publication: Yes

Copyright: Held by publication.
Reprints: Available
Disposition of manuscript:
Query letter: Yes
Receipt of manuscript acknowledged: Yes
Decision to publish in: 3 months
Accepted manuscript published in: 6 months
Rejected manuscript returned: Yes
Rejected manuscript criticized: Yes
Submit to:
J. Jaap Tuinman
Editor
Institute for Child Study
Indiana University
Bloomington, Indiana 47401
(812) 337-1732

JOURNAL OF RESEARCH IN MUSIC EDUCATION [1012]
MENC
1201 Sixteenth Street, N.W.
Washington, D.C. 20036
(202) 833-4243

First published in 1953

SUBSCRIPTION DATA
Issues and rates: Published quarterly.
Average paid circulation: 9,000
Annual rate(s): $8.00, Foreign $9.00
Publisher or Sponsor: Society for Research in Music Education of the Music Educators National Conference
Managing Editor: Michele J. Brace

EDITORIAL DESCRIPTION
Contains articles of a philosophical, historical, or scientific nature that report the results of research pertinent in any way to instruction in music.
Articles per average issue: 10
Audience: Academic
Manuscripts accepted in English

MANUSCRIPT INFORMATION
Subject field(s): Music education, music
Manuscript requirements: MLA for text; Chicago for tables, charts, and figures.
Preferred length: 5-35 pages
Number of copies to be submitted: One
Abstract: Yes, of 50-150 words
Author information and reprints: Payment: None.
Is simultaneous submission of article to other journals permitted: No
Exclusive manuscript rights between acceptance and publication: Yes
Copyright: Held by publication.
Reprints: Available at cost.
Disposition of manuscript:
Query letter: No
Receipt of manuscript acknowledged: Yes
Decision to publish in: 6-8 weeks
Accepted manuscript published in: Up to one year
Rejected manuscript returned: Yes, if self-addressed, stamped envelope is sent with manuscript.
Rejected manuscript criticized: Yes
Submit to:
Robert G. Petzold

Editor
5545 Humanities Building
The University of Wisconsin
Madison, Wisconsin 53706
(608) 263-2530

THE JOURNAL OF SPECIAL EDUCATION [1013]
3515 Woodhaven Road
Philadelphia, Pennsylvania 19154
(215) 632-5900

First published in 1966

SUBSCRIPTION DATA
Issues and rates: Published quarterly.
Average paid circulation: 3,150; 350 controlled
Annual rate(s): $18.50, Students $13.50

EDITORIAL DESCRIPTION
Contains articles of research, theory, opinion, and review respecting special education and areas of special concern to general education.
Articles per average issue: 8-9
Audience: Academic
Manuscripts accepted in English

MANUSCRIPT INFORMATION
Subject field(s): Education, medicine, psychiatry, psychology
Manuscript requirements: APA
Number of copies to be submitted: 3 copies
Abstract: Yes, not exceeding 300 words
Author information and reprints: Payment: None.
Is simultaneous submission of article to other journals permitted: No
Exclusive manuscript rights between acceptance and publication: Yes
Copyright: Held by publication.
Reprints: Available, 20 free reprints given to author.
Additional information: Original art work should not be sent until manuscript is accepted.
Disposition of manuscript:
Query letter: No
Receipt of manuscript acknowledged: No
Decision to publish in: 3 months
Accepted manuscript published in: Varies
Rejected manuscript returned: Yes
Rejected manuscript criticized: Not always
Submit to:
Lester Mann
Executive Editor
3515 Woodhaven Road
Philadelphia, Pennsylvania 19154
632-5900

JOURNAL OF TEACHER EDUCATION [1014]
One Dupont Circle, Suite 610
Washington, D.C. 20036
(202) 293-2450

First published in 1950

SUBSCRIPTION DATA
Issues and rates: Published quarterly.
Average paid circulation: 12,000
Annual rate(s): $10.00
Publisher or Sponsor: American Association of Colleges for Teacher Education

EDITORIAL DESCRIPTION
Each issue features current themes central to teacher education. The Journal relies more on solicited manuscripts because of its thematic content.
Articles per average issue: 19
Audience: Professional, academic
Manuscripts accepted in English

MANUSCRIPT INFORMATION
Subject field(s): Broad field of education, academic specialties which contribute to education.
Manuscript requirements: Chicago
Preferred length: 6 to 12 double-spaced pages
Number of copies to be submitted: Two
Author information and reprints: Payment: None.
Is simultaneous submission of article to other journals permitted: Yes
Exclusive manuscript rights between acceptance and publication: Yes
Copyright: Held by publication.
Reprints: Available
Additional information: Authors are urged to present their ideas and information in analytical and provocative as well as descriptive form. Absolute accuracy is required for all references and quoted material.
Disposition of manuscript:
Query letter:
Receipt of manuscript acknowledged: Yes
Decision to publish in: 6-12 months
Accepted manuscript published in: 12 months
Rejected manuscript returned: Yes
Rejected manuscript criticized: No
Submit to:
Joel L. Burdin
Editor
(See address above)

SPECIAL STIPULATIONS
Rejected manuscripts have the option of being processed into the ERIC (Educational Resources Information Center) system for publication through the ERIC Clearinghouse on Teacher Education.

JOURNAL OF TRAFFIC SAFETY EDUCATION [1015]
2784 West Wilberta Lane
Anaheim, California 92804
(714) 527-8933

Previously entitled *CALDEA Calendar*

First published in 1953

SUBSCRIPTION DATA
Issues and rates: Published quarterly.
Average paid circulation: 5,000-8,000
Annual rate(s): $4.00, Foreign $5.00

Publisher or Sponsor: California Driver Education Association
Managing Editor: Richard Kaywood

EDITORIAL DESCRIPTION

Devoted to traffic safety education for teachers, supervisors, administrators, state department of education consultants, research organizations, and related fields of enforcement, education, insurance, traffic engineering, motor vehicle administration.

Articles per average issue: 20
Audience: Academic
Manuscripts accepted in English

MANUSCRIPT INFORMATION

Subject field(s): Pedestrian, passenger, bicycle, motorcycle, beginning and advanced driver education; driver improvement, teacher preparation; alcohol education; preventive maintenance for automobiles; auto insurance; driving simulators; multiple car driving range; multi-media instruction.
Manuscript requirements: No specific style guide.
  Preferred length: 4-10 pages
  Number of copies to be submitted: Two
  Abstract: No
Author information and reprints: Payment: None. Two copies of the issue in which article appears
Is simultaneous submission of article to other journals permitted: No
Exclusive manuscript rights between acceptance and publication: Yes
Copyright: Held by publication.
Reprints: Available from printer with advance arrangements.
Disposition of manuscript:
  Query letter: No
  Receipt of manuscript acknowledged: Yes
  Decision to publish in: 3-6 weeks
  Accepted manuscript published in: 2-6 months
  Rejected manuscript returned: Yes
  Rejected manuscript criticized: Yes
Submit to:
  Richard Kaywood
  Publications Editor
  (See address above)
  (213) 498-4014

JOURNAL OF VERBAL LEARNING AND VERBAL BEHAVIOR [1016]

Academic Press, Inc.
111 Fifth Avenue
New York, New York 10003

First published in 1962

SUBSCRIPTION DATA

Issues and rates: Published bi-monthly.
  Annual rate(s): $37.50; Foreign $42.50

EDITORIAL DESCRIPTION

Publishes conceptually and theoretically important papers on the cognitive processes underlying human learning and memory

Articles per average issue: 11
Audience: Psychologists, educators
Manuscripts accepted in English

MANUSCRIPT INFORMATION

Subject field(s): Human verbal cognition, learning and memory, psycholinguistics, reading
Manuscript requirements: See latest issue for style requirements.
  Preferred length: No preference
  Number of copies to be submitted: 4
  Abstract: Yes. A concise summary of 120 words maximum.
Author information and reprints: Payment: None.
Is simultaneous submission of article to other journals permitted: Not permitted.
Exclusive manuscript rights between acceptance and publication: Yes
Copyright: Held by publication.
Disposition of manuscript:
  Query letter: Not necessary.
  Receipt of manuscript acknowledged: Yes
  Decision to publish in: 30 days
  Accepted manuscript published in: 7 months
  Rejected manuscript returned: Yes, with return postage paid by publication.
  Rejected manuscript criticized: Yes
Submit to:
  Edwin Martin
  Editor
  Department of Psychology
  University of Kansas
  Lawrence, Kansas 66045
  (913) 864-4131

JOURNALISM EDUCATOR [1017]

AEJ Publications Office
University of Minnesota, School of Journalism
Minneapolis, Minnesota 55455
(612) 373-3565

First published in 1945

SUBSCRIPTION DATA

Issues and rates: Published quarterly.
  Average paid circulation: 2,000
  Annual rate(s): $6.00; Foreign $6.40
Publisher or Sponsor: Association for Education in Journalism
Managing Editor: LaRue W. Gilleland

EDITORIAL DESCRIPTION

A journal promoting excellence in teaching to prepare men and women for careers in print and broadcast journalism, advertising, and public relations.
Articles per average issue: About 15
Audience: Administrators and professors in journalism and mass communications departments and schools in major universities.
Manuscripts accepted in Only English

MANUSCRIPT INFORMATION

Subject field(s): Teaching ideas that have worked in the classroom; improving relations between journalism education and news media; journalism education programs abroad and how they compare with those in American universities
Manuscript requirements: See latest issue for style requirements.
  Preferred length: 2,500 words maximum
  Number of copies to be submitted: 2
  Abstract: Not necessary.
Author information and reprints: Payment: None.
Is simultaneous submission of article to other journals permitted: Permitted, but not encouraged.
Exclusive manuscript rights between acceptance and publication: No
Copyright: First serial rights only
Reprints: Available at no cost. Three copies of magazine
Disposition of manuscript:
  Query letter: Not necessary, but advisable.
  Receipt of manuscript acknowledged: Yes
  Decision to publish in: 2 months
  Accepted manuscript published in: 6-12 months
  Rejected manuscript returned: Yes, if return postage is supplied by author.
  Rejected manuscript criticized: Sometimes
Submit to:
  LaRue W. Gilleland
  Editor
  Department of Journalism, University of Nevada, Reno
  Mack Social Science Building
  Reno, Nevada 89507
  784-6531

JUCO REVIEW [1018]

P.O. Box 1586
Hutchinson, Kansas 67501
(316) 663-5445

SUBSCRIPTION DATA

Issues and rates: Nine issues, September through May
  Average paid circulation: 3000
  Annual rate(s): $4.00
Publisher or Sponsor: National Junior College Athletic Association

EDITORIAL DESCRIPTION

Publishes articles on all phases of athletics, athletic administration, specific sports, etc., with emphasis in the field of junior and community colleges.

MANUSCRIPT INFORMATION

Manuscript requirements: No specific style guide.
  Preferred length: 3 pages maximum
  Number of copies to be submitted: Three
Author information and reprints: Payment: None.
Is simultaneous submission of article to other journals permitted: No
Exclusive manuscript rights between acceptance and publication: Yes
Reprints: Available, 5 per author
Disposition of manuscript:
  Receipt of manuscript acknowledged: Yes
  Decision to publish in: 2-3 months
  Accepted manuscript published in: 3-4 months

Rejected manuscript returned: Yes, if self-addressed, stamped envelope is sent with manuscript.
Rejected manuscript criticized: No
Submit to:
George E. Killian
Executive Director
(See address above)

KANSAS SCHOOL BOARD JOURNAL [1019]
825 Western Avenue
Topeka, Kansas 66606
(913) 357-1144

SUBSCRIPTION DATA
Issues and rates: Published quarterly.
Average paid circulation: 4,500
Annual rate(s): $2.50
Publisher or Sponsor: Kansas Association of School Boards
Managing Editor: M. A. McGhehey

EDITORIAL DESCRIPTION
Publishes articles of fact or opinion of interest to school board members or school administrators. Articles apply to conduct of school affairs in Kansas.
Articles per average issue: 5
Audience: Academic administrators
Manuscripts accepted in English

MANUSCRIPT INFORMATION
Subject field(s): Education
Manuscript requirements: No specific style guide.
Preferred length: 1,500 to 5,000 words
Number of copies to be submitted: One
Abstract: No
Author information and reprints: Payment: None.
Is simultaneous submission of article to other journals permitted: Yes
Exclusive manuscript rights between acceptance and publication: No
Copyright: Held by author.
Reprints: Not available.
Additional information: Articles should have application to conduct of school affairs in Kansas.
Disposition of manuscript:
Query letter: No
Receipt of manuscript acknowledged: Yes
Decision to publish in: One month
Accepted manuscript published in: One to six months
Rejected manuscript returned: Yes
Rejected manuscript criticized: No
Submit to:
John William Koepke
Director of Publications
(See address above)

K-EIGHT [1020]
Grade School Management, Materials and Methods
134 North 13th Street
Philadelphia, Pennsylvania 19107
(215) 564-5170

SUBSCRIPTION DATA
Issues and rates: Published three times per year.
Average paid circulation: 30,000 controlled
Annual rate(s): $10.00

EDITORIAL DESCRIPTION
Contains articles on teaching materials, films, paperbacks, records, tapes, TV, videotape, slides, film loops, drug education, learning games and kits.
Articles per average issue: 5
Audience: Principals in grades K-Eight
Manuscripts accepted in English only

MANUSCRIPT INFORMATION
Manuscript requirements: Style sheet sent on request.
Preferred length: Up to 2,000 words
Number of copies to be submitted: Two
Abstract: Yes
Author information and reprints: Payment: By publication to author. Negotiable.
Is simultaneous submission of article to other journals permitted: No
Exclusive manuscript rights between acceptance and publication: Yes
Copyright: Held by publication.
Reprints: Available, 3 free
Disposition of manuscript:
Query letter: No
Receipt of manuscript acknowledged: Yes
Decision to publish in: 2-6 weeks
Accepted manuscript published in: 2-4 months
Rejected manuscript returned: Yes, if self-addressed, stamped envelope is sent with manuscript.
Rejected manuscript criticized: Sometimes
Submit to:
Stuart Miller
Editorial Director
(See address above)

THE KENTUCKY ENGLISH BULLETIN [1021]
Department of English
University of Kentucky
1239 Office Tower
Lexington, Kentucky 40506
(602) 257-1313

First published in 1936

SUBSCRIPTION DATA
Issues and rates: Published three times per year.
Average paid circulation: 1200
Annual rate(s): $4.00
Publisher or Sponsor: Kentucky Council of Teachers of English

EDITORIAL DESCRIPTION
Contains articles on literature, composition, linguistics.
Articles per average issue: 5-6
Audience: Addressed mainly to Kentucky elementary and high school teachers.
Manuscripts accepted in English

MANUSCRIPT INFORMATION
Manuscript requirements: See latest issue for style requirements.
Preferred length: 5-10 pages
Number of copies to be submitted: One
Abstract: No
Author information and reprints: Payment: None.
Is simultaneous submission of article to other journals permitted: Yes
Exclusive manuscript rights between acceptance and publication: No
Copyright: Held by publication.
Reprints: Available
Disposition of manuscript:
Query letter: No
Receipt of manuscript acknowledged: Yes
Decision to publish in: One week
Accepted manuscript published in: Up to 3 months
Rejected manuscript returned: Yes, if self-addressed, stamped envelope is sent with manuscript.
Rejected manuscript criticized: Yes
Submit to:
Editor
(See address above)

LE MAGISTER [1022]
Saint-Nicolas
Co. Lévis, Québec GOS 2Z0, Canada
(418) 832-4102

First published in 1965

SUBSCRIPTION DATA
Issues and rates: 10 issues per year
Average paid circulation: 29,980; 44,900 controlled
Annual rate(s): $3.00
Managing Editor: Albert Gervais

EDITORIAL DESCRIPTION
Contains articles concerning education, on any academic level.
Articles per average issue: 10-13
Audience: French speaking teachers of Quebec
Manuscripts accepted in French, English

MANUSCRIPT INFORMATION
Subject field(s): Education, literature, sociology, any topic linked with education
Manuscript requirements: No specific style guide.
Preferred length: 3 pages
Number of copies to be submitted: One
Abstract: No
Author information and reprints: Payment: None.
Is simultaneous submission of article to other journals permitted: Yes
Exclusive manuscript rights between acceptance and publication: No
Reprints: Available
Disposition of manuscript:
Query letter: No
Receipt of manuscript acknowledged: No
Decision to publish in: 1 month
Accepted manuscript published in: 2-3 months

Rejected manuscript returned: No
Rejected manuscript criticized: No
Submit to:
Albert Gervais
Editor
(See address above)

LEARNING [1023]
The Magazine for Creative Teaching
Subscription Department
1255 Portland Place
Boulder, Colorado 80320

First published in 1972

SUBSCRIPTION DATA
Issues and rates: Published monthly.
  Average paid circulation: 220,000
  Annual rate(s): $12.00; Pan-Am $14.00; Foreign $14.00
Managing Editor: Morton Malkofsky

EDITORIAL DESCRIPTION
Articles focus on hard-headed evaluations of creative teaching practices and practical steps for implementing good ones, but also span "why-to" explanations of psychology and sociology underlying good teaching, and public affairs pieces on trends with direct impact on classroom teachers.
Articles per average issue: 6
Audience: Alert, well-educated classroom teachers
  Manuscripts accepted in English only

MANUSCRIPT INFORMATION
Subject field(s): Successful teachers in action dealing with tough contemporary education problems; roundups and assessments of educational policies, movements and trends; how-to pieces on tested teaching strategies; educational psychology for the classroom teacher.
Manuscript requirements: See latest issue for style requirements. Style sheet sent on request.
  Preferred length: 1,500-3,500 words
  Number of copies to be submitted: 1
  Abstract: Not necessary.
Author information and reprints: Payment: By publication to author.
  $150.00-$250.00 per article.
  Is simultaneous submission of article to other journals permitted: Not permitted.
  Exclusive manuscript rights between acceptance and publication: Yes
  Copyright: Held by publication.
  Reprints: Available at cost. Varies
Additional information: Aim for a clear, jargon-free style. Writers should propose stories in one or two-page query letters outlining thrust, major judgments and some sample anecdotes, examples or teaching activities.
Disposition of manuscript:
  Query letter: Not necessary, but advisable.
  Receipt of manuscript acknowledged: No
  Decision to publish in: 1-2 months
  Accepted manuscript published in: 2-8 months
  Rejected manuscript returned: Yes, if return postage is supplied by author.

Rejected manuscript criticized: Sometimes
Submit to:
Manuscript Submissions
530 University Avenue
Palo Alto, California 94301
(415) 321-1770

LOUISIANA SCHOOLS [1024]
Journal of the Louisiana Teachers' Association
P.O. Box 1906
Baton Rouge, Louisiana 70821
(504) 343-9243 ext. 7

First published in 1923

SUBSCRIPTION DATA
Issues and rates: 9 times a year
  Average paid circulation: 28,000
  Annual rate(s): $3.00
Publisher or Sponsor: Louisiana Teachers' Association
Managing Editor: William C. Baker

EDITORIAL DESCRIPTION
Contains educational articles of general interest from K-12 and higher education; official proceedings of the Louisiana Teachers' Association.
Articles per average issue: 7
Audience: Educators of all levels
  Manuscripts accepted in English

MANUSCRIPT INFORMATION
Subject field(s): Education
Manuscript requirements: Style sheet sent on request.
  Preferred length: 2500 words; 7 pages typewritten, double-spaced, third person
  Number of copies to be submitted: One
  Abstract: No
Author information and reprints: Payment: None.
  Is simultaneous submission of article to other journals permitted: Yes
  Exclusive manuscript rights between acceptance and publication: No
  Copyright: Held by author.
  Reprints: Not available.
Disposition of manuscript:
  Query letter: No
  Receipt of manuscript acknowledged: Yes
  Decision to publish in: 1 week
  Accepted manuscript published in: 1-6 months
  Rejected manuscript returned: Yes
  Rejected manuscript criticized: No
Submit to:
William C. Baker
Managing Editor
(See address above)

LUTHERAN EDUCATION [1025]
3558 South Jefferson Avenue
St. Louis, Missouri 63118
(314) 664-7000

Previously entitled *Schulblatt*

First published in 1865

SUBSCRIPTION DATA
Issues and rates: 5 times per year
  Average paid circulation: 4800
  Annual rate(s): $5.00
Managing Editor: M. L. Radke

EDITORIAL DESCRIPTION
Publishes articles on educational practice and research, church-related education. Devoted to the in-service training of teachers, primarily those in schools of the Lutheran Church-Missouri Synod.
Articles per average issue: 12
Audience: Teachers and administrators
  Manuscripts accepted in English

MANUSCRIPT INFORMATION
Subject field(s): Educational practice, educational research, applied psychology, educational methods, religious education, theology applied to education
Manuscript requirements: MLA
  Preferred length: 10-12 pages
  Number of copies to be submitted: One
  Abstract: No
Author information and reprints: Payment: None.
  Is simultaneous submission of article to other journals permitted: No
  Exclusive manuscript rights between acceptance and publication: Yes
  Copyright: Held by publication.
  Reprints: Available
Additional information: Typewritten, double-spaced, standard paper
Disposition of manuscript:
  Query letter: No
  Receipt of manuscript acknowledged: Yes
  Decision to publish in: 4 weeks
  Accepted manuscript published in: 6 months
  Rejected manuscript returned: Yes, if return postage is supplied by author.
  Rejected manuscript criticized: Yes
Submit to:
Merle Louis Radke
Editor
7400 Augusta Street
River Forest, Illinois 60305
(312) 771-8300 ext. 247.

THE MANITOBA TEACHER [1026]
191 Harcourt Street
Winnipeg, Manitoba R3J 3H2, Canada
(204) 888-7961

First published in 1919

SUBSCRIPTION DATA
Issues and rates: Monthly, except July and August
  Average paid circulation: 100; 15,900 controlled
  Annual rate(s): $3.00
Publisher or Sponsor: The Manitoba Teachers' Society

EDITORIAL DESCRIPTION
Contains news stories, features, announcements primarily dealing with public education in Manitoba, geared to

majority of readership: teachers in public schools in Manitoba.
Manuscripts accepted in English

MANUSCRIPT INFORMATION

Subject field(s): Public school education in Manitoba, education outside Manitoba, general educational trends
Manuscript requirements: See latest issue for style requirements.
  Preferred length: 1,000-1,500 words
  Number of copies to be submitted: Two
  Abstract: No
Author information and reprints: Payment: None.
  Is simultaneous submission of article to other journals permitted: Yes, but information should be submitted with submission of article
  Copyright: Held by both author and publication
  Reprints: Available, free as long as supply lasts
Additional information: Manuscripts to be typed double-spaced with All margins of about 1 ½ inch width. Brief biographical sketch of author(s) to accompany manuscripts.
Disposition of manuscript:
  Query letter: Preferred
  Receipt of manuscript acknowledged: Yes
  Decision to publish in: One to three months
  Accepted manuscript published in: 1-12 months
  Rejected manuscript returned: Yes, if self-addressed, stamped envelope is sent with manuscript.
  Rejected manuscript criticized: Upon request
Submit to:
  Mrs. Miep van Raalte
  Assistant Editor
  (See address above)

MAN/SOCIETY/TECHNOLOGY [1027]

A Journal of Industrial Arts Education
American Industrial Arts Association
1201 16th Street, N.W.
Washington, D.C. 20036
(202) 833-4211

SUBSCRIPTION DATA

Issues and rates: 8 times per year
  Average paid circulation: 9,000
  Annual rate(s): $9.00
Publisher or Sponsor: American Industrial Arts Association

EDITORIAL DESCRIPTION

Publishes material related to industrial arts education. Acceptable articles could be based on philosophy, curriculum, research, support systems, teacher education, classroom techniques, etc.
Articles per average issue: 6-8
Audience: Teachers of industrial arts
  Manuscripts accepted in English

MANUSCRIPT INFORMATION

Subject field(s): Request specific issue themes from editor.
Manuscript requirements: See latest issue for style requirements.
  Preferred length: 10 to 15 pages
  Number of copies to be submitted: 2
  Abstract: No
Author information and reprints: Payment: None.
  Is simultaneous submission of article to other journals permitted: No
  Exclusive manuscript rights between acceptance and publication: Yes
  Copyright: Held by publication.
  Reprints: Not available.
Additional information: Typewritten, double-spaced, one side only; clear black and white photos appreciated; author's name on cover letter only to allow anonymous review.
Disposition of manuscript:
  Query letter: No
  Receipt of manuscript acknowledged: Yes
  Decision to publish in: 1 to 3 months
  Accepted manuscript published in: Depends on schedule of issue themes
  Rejected manuscript returned: Yes, if return postage is supplied by author.
  Rejected manuscript criticized: Sometimes
Submit to:
  Colleen P. Stamm
  Editor
  (See address above)

MASSACHUSETTS MUSIC NEWS [1028]

Post Office Box 532
West Springfield, Massachusetts 01089
(413) 739-9065

Previously entitled *MMEA Music News*

First published in 1941

SUBSCRIPTION DATA

Issues and rates: Published quarterly.
  Average paid circulation: 2000 controlled
  Annual rate(s): $5.00
Publisher or Sponsor: Massachusetts Music Educators Association
Managing Editor: J. Anthony Di Giore

EDITORIAL DESCRIPTION

Contains articles on any aspect of music education.
Articles per average issue: 5-6
Audience: Professional educators
  Manuscripts accepted in English

MANUSCRIPT INFORMATION

Subject field(s): Instrumental methods, choral materials, performance, electronic
Manuscript requirements: No specific style guide.
  Preferred length: Three to four pages
  Number of copies to be submitted: One
  Abstract: No
Author information and reprints: Payment: None.
  Is simultaneous submission of article to other journals permitted: Yes
  Exclusive manuscript rights between acceptance and publication: No
  Copyright: Held by author.
  Reprints: Available
Additional information: Accompanying photographs should be black and white glossies.
Disposition of manuscript:
  Query letter: No
  Receipt of manuscript acknowledged: Yes
  Decision to publish in: 2 weeks
  Accepted manuscript published in: 6-8 weeks
  Rejected manuscript returned: Yes
  Rejected manuscript criticized: Yes
Submit to:
  J. Anthony Di Giore
  Editor
  (See address above)

THE MATHEMATICS TEACHER [1029]

1906 Association Drive
Reston, Virginia 22091
(703) 620-9840 ext. 202

First published in 1908

SUBSCRIPTION DATA

Issues and rates: Published monthly.
  Average paid circulation: 50,000
  Annual rate(s): Members $11.00; Institutions $13.00
Publisher or Sponsor: National Council of Teachers of Mathematics
Managing Editor: Carol V. McCamman

EDITORIAL DESCRIPTION

Contains articles on mathematics and the teaching of mathematics, junior high school, senior high school, two-year college, and teacher education college.
Articles per average issue: 15
Audience: Academic
  Manuscripts accepted in English only

MANUSCRIPT INFORMATION

Subject field(s): Mathematics education, grades 7-14; mathematics, grades 7-14
Manuscript requirements: Style sheet sent on request.
  Preferred length: Less than 2000 words
  Number of copies to be submitted: Two
  Abstract: No
Author information and reprints: Payment: None.
  Is simultaneous submission of article to other journals permitted: No
  Exclusive manuscript rights between acceptance and publication: Yes
  Copyright: Held by publication.
  Reprints: Available
Disposition of manuscript:
  Query letter: No
  Receipt of manuscript acknowledged: Yes
  Decision to publish in: 2-3 months
  Accepted manuscript published in: Over a year
  Rejected manuscript returned: Yes
  Rejected manuscript criticized: Sometimes
Submit to:
  Editorial Panel
  (See address above)

MEASUREMENT AND EVALUATION IN GUIDANCE [1030]

American Personnel and Guidance Association
1607 New Hampshire Avenue, N. W.
Washington, D. C. 20009
(202) 483-4633

First published in 1968

SUBSCRIPTION DATA

Issues and rates: Published quarterly.
   Average paid circulation: 3,000
   Annual rate(s): $12.00
Publisher or Sponsor: Association for Measurement and Evaluation in Guidance

EDITORIAL DESCRIPTION

Contains manuscripts that deal with theoretical and other problems of the measurement specialist to those directed to the administrator, counselor, or personnel worker, having clearly described implications for the practitioner in measurement and evaluation.
Articles per average issue: 8
Audience: Professionals in schools, public and private agencies, business, industry and government
Manuscripts accepted in English

MANUSCRIPT INFORMATION

Subject field(s): Measurement and testing
Manuscript requirements: APA
   Preferred length: 1,500-3,000 words
   Number of copies to be submitted: Original and 2 copies
   Abstract: Yes. Of about 175 words
Author information and reprints: Payment: Reprints only. 5
   Is simultaneous submission of article to other journals permitted: Not permitted.
   Exclusive manuscript rights between acceptance and publication: Yes
   Copyright: Held by the Association
Additional information: Tabular presentation must be well-organized, tight and clear, camera-ready on standard-sized, white bond paper.
Disposition of manuscript:
   Query letter: Not necessary.
   Receipt of manuscript acknowledged: Yes
   Decision to publish in: 2 months
   Accepted manuscript published in: 4 months
   Rejected manuscript returned: Yes, with return postage paid by publication.
   Rejected manuscript criticized: Reasons for rejections only
Submit to:
   Dr. William A. Mehrens
   Editor
   Michigan State University, College of Education
   460 Erickson Hall
   East Lansing, Michigan 48824

MIDDLE SCHOOL JOURNAL [1031]

P. O. Box 968
Fairborn, Ohio 45324
(517) 774-3517

Previously entitled *Midwest Middle School Journal*

First published in 1970

SUBSCRIPTION DATA

Issues and rates: Published quarterly.
   Average paid circulation: 700; 1,000 controlled
   Annual rate(s): $6.00
Publisher or Sponsor: National Middle School Association
Managing Editor: Glenn Maynard

EDITORIAL DESCRIPTION

Furthers the dissemination of new ideas, practices, and analyzes controversial issues in the subject of middle school education.
Articles per average issue: 6-8
Audience: Principals, teachers, supervisors, counselors, college faculty dealing with middle schools
Manuscripts accepted in English

MANUSCRIPT INFORMATION

Subject field(s): Any topic related to middle school programs, practices, and philosophy
Manuscript requirements: See latest issue for style requirements.
   Preferred length: 1,200-1,500 words; 6-8 pages
   Number of copies to be submitted: 3
   Abstract: Not necessary.
Author information and reprints: Payment: None.
   Is simultaneous submission of article to other journals permitted: Permitted, but not encouraged.
   Exclusive manuscript rights between acceptance and publication: Yes
   Copyright: Held by publication.
   Reprints: Not available.
Additional information: All manuscripts to be typewritten, double-spaced.
Disposition of manuscript:
   Query letter: Not necessary, but advisable.
   Receipt of manuscript acknowledged: Yes
   Decision to publish in: 8 weeks
   Accepted manuscript published in: 3-6 months
   Rejected manuscript returned: Yes, with return postage paid by publication.
   Rejected manuscript criticized: Sometimes
Submit to:
   Thomas E. Gatewood
   Editor
   Department of Secondary Education
   Central Michigan University
   Mt. Pleasant, Michigan 48859

MINNESOTA READING QUARTERLY [1032]

Post Office Box 22467
Minneapolis, Minnesota 55429
(612) 561-9297

Previously entitled *MRA Newsletter*

First published in 1956

SUBSCRIPTION DATA

Issues and rates: Published quarterly.
   Average paid circulation: 900
   Annual rate(s): $6.00
Publisher or Sponsor: Minnesota Reading Association, Inc.
Managing Editor: Tracy F. Tyler, Jr.

EDITORIAL DESCRIPTION

Contains reading-oriented material dealing with local research relating to reading; descriptions of current school programs and practices; abstracts of papers, theses, etc.; and viewpoints on various aspects of reading, reading instructional practice, and related topics.
Articles per average issue: 3-5
Audience: Reading teachers, and MRA members
Manuscripts accepted in English

MANUSCRIPT INFORMATION

Subject field(s): Teaching of reading; psychology of reading; history, philosophy, and sociology of reading; reading-related articles of any nature
Manuscript requirements: Chicago
   Preferred length: 1200 to 3000 words; 6 to 12 pages
   Number of copies to be submitted: Two
   Abstract: No
Author information and reprints: Payment: None. 6 copies of issue in which article appears.
   Is simultaneous submission of article to other journals permitted: No
   Exclusive manuscript rights between acceptance and publication: Yes
   Copyright: Held by publication.
   Reprints: Not available.
Additional information: Prepared to assist authors in developing ideas to the point of publication. A short biographical sketch about the author should accompany the article. Include full name, present position, location, and something about background. Appropriate pictures to accompany an article are always welcome.
Disposition of manuscript:
   Query letter: No
   Receipt of manuscript acknowledged: Yes
   Decision to publish in: One week
   Accepted manuscript published in: 3 to 6 months
   Rejected manuscript returned: Yes
   Rejected manuscript criticized: Yes
Submit to:
   Tracy F. Tyler, Jr.
   Editor
   (See address above)

MOMENTUM [1033]
Journal of the National Catholic Educational Association
Suite 350, One Dupont Circle
Washington, D.C. 20036
(202) 293-5954 ext. 68

Previously entitled *NCEA Bulletin*

First published in 1970

SUBSCRIPTION DATA
Issues and rates: Published quarterly.
   Average paid circulation: 14,500
   Annual rate(s): $8.00
Publisher or Sponsor: National Catholic Educational Association
Managing Editor: Carl Balcerak

EDITORIAL DESCRIPTION
Contains articles on current topics of interest to professional Catholic educators; innovative programs in Catholic schools.
Articles per average issue: 7 with shorts and book reviews
Audience: Teachers, administrators, parents
   Manuscripts accepted in English

MANUSCRIPT INFORMATION
Subject field(s): Catholic education, education
Manuscript requirements: No specific style guide.
   Preferred length: 2,500-3,000 words
   Number of copies to be submitted: One
   Abstract: No
Author information and reprints: Payment: By publication to author. $.02 per word.
   Is simultaneous submission of article to other journals permitted: Yes
   Copyright: Held by publication.
   Reprints: Available
Additional information: For innovative programs in Catholic schools, author should zero in on such a program in a specific school. The article should have lots of quotes, reactions of people to program, and several 8 1/2 X 10 glossy photos.
Disposition of manuscript:
   Query letter: Yes
   Receipt of manuscript acknowledged: Yes
   Decision to publish in: 2 weeks
   Accepted manuscript published in: 2-3 months
   Rejected manuscript returned: Yes
   Rejected manuscript criticized: Sometimes
Submit to:
   Editor
   (See address above)

MUSIC EDUCATORS JOURNAL [1034]
Official Magazine of the Music Educators National Conference
8150 Leesburg Pike,
Vienna, Virginia 22180
(703) 790-8500

Previously entitled *Music Supervisors Journal*

First published in 1914

SUBSCRIPTION DATA
Issues and rates: Monthly except June, July, August
   Average paid circulation: 70,000 controlled
Publisher or Sponsor: Music Educators National Conference
Managing Editor: Malcolm E. Bessom

EDITORIAL DESCRIPTION
Contains articles about all aspects of music, education, and music education.
Articles per average issue: 115
Audience: Music educators, preschool through university
   Manuscripts accepted in English only

MANUSCRIPT INFORMATION
Subject field(s): Philosophy of music education, the arts, aesthetics, instrumental music instruction, vocal music instruction, music in elementary education, music in secondary education, music in higher education, ethnic musics, learning theory, community music programs, the international music scene
Manuscript requirements: See latest issue for style requirements.
   Preferred length: 8-12 pages
   Number of copies to be submitted: One
   Abstract: No
Author information and reprints: Payment: None.
   Is simultaneous submission of article to other journals permitted: No
   Exclusive manuscript rights between acceptance and publication: Yes
   Copyright: Held by publication.
   Reprints: Not available.
Disposition of manuscript:
   Query letter: No
   Receipt of manuscript acknowledged: Yes
   Decision to publish in: 3-6 months
   Accepted manuscript published in: 3-6 months
   Rejected manuscript returned: Yes
   Rejected manuscript criticized: No
Submit to:
   Malcolm E. Bessom
   Editor
   (See address above)

NATIONAL ASSOCIATION OF COLLEGES AND TEACHERS OF AGRICULTURE. JOURNAL [1035]
NACTA Journal
Secretary-Treasurer
Sam Houston State University, P. O. Box 2088
Huntsville, Texas 77340
(713) 295-6211

First published in 1957

SUBSCRIPTION DATA
Issues and rates: Published quarterly.
   Average paid circulation: 1,200 controlled
   Annual rate(s): Institutions $30.00
Publisher or Sponsor: National Association of Colleges and Teachers of Agriculture

EDITORIAL DESCRIPTION
Directed toward the professional advancement of the college teacher of agriculture, its total offering includes something for every college teacher regardless of the size of his institution and subject matter.
Audience: Academic
   Manuscripts accepted in English

MANUSCRIPT INFORMATION
Subject field(s): All aspects of the teaching of college agriculture: methods, problems, philosophy, and rewards.
Manuscript requirements: See latest issue for style requirements.
   Preferred length: 3,000 words typescript
   Number of copies to be submitted: 4
   Abstract: Not necessary. Only if there are doubts about the suitability of the article.
Author information and reprints: Payment: Reprints only. 5 copies of the issue
   Is simultaneous submission of article to other journals permitted: Permitted.
   Exclusive manuscript rights between acceptance and publication: No
   Copyright: Not copyrighted
   Reprints: Available at cost.
Disposition of manuscript:
   Query letter: Not necessary, but advisable.
   Receipt of manuscript acknowledged: Yes
   Accepted manuscript published in: 12 months
   Rejected manuscript returned: Yes, with return postage paid by publication.
   Rejected manuscript criticized: Sometimes
Submit to:
   Dr. Jack C. Everly
   Editor
   Office of Instructional Resources
   University of Illinois, 608 West Vermont
   Urbana, Illinois 61801
   (217) 333-3690

NATIONAL ELEMENTARY PRINCIPAL [1036]
National Association of Elementary School Principals
1801 North Moore Street
Arlington, Virginia 22209
(703) 528-5639

First published in 1906

SUBSCRIPTION DATA
Issues and rates: 6 issues per year
   Average paid circulation: 30,000
   Annual rate(s): Members $35.00, Foreign $40.00
Publisher or Sponsor: National Association of Elementary School Principals
Managing Editor: Paul L. Houts

EDITORIAL DESCRIPTION
Publishes articles on all phases of early childhood, elementary, and middle school education; school administration; and

social issues affecting education and educational reform.
Articles per average issue: 10
Audience: Teachers, administrators
Manuscripts accepted in English

MANUSCRIPT INFORMATION

Subject field(s): Educational reform, elementary education, school administration, social issues, school facilities, early education, special education, school/community relations, administrator preparation, interviews
Manuscript requirements: Style sheet sent on request.
  Preferred length: 2,000-3,500 words; 10-15 pages
  Number of copies to be submitted: Original and 2 carbons
  Abstract: No
Author information and reprints: Payment: None. Six complimentary copies of issue in which article appears.
  Is simultaneous submission of article to other journals permitted: No
  Exclusive manuscript rights between acceptance and publication: Yes
  Copyright: Held by publication.
  Reprints: Available at cost
Disposition of manuscript:
  Query letter: No
  Receipt of manuscript acknowledged: Yes
  Decision to publish in: 6-8 weeks
  Accepted manuscript published in: 2-12 months
  Rejected manuscript returned: Yes
  Rejected manuscript criticized: No
Submit to:
  Paul L. Houts
  Director of Publications and Editor
  (See address above)

NATURE STUDY [1037]
Journal of Environmental Education and Interpretation
R.D. 1
Homer, New York 13077
(607) 749-3655

Previously entitled *A.N.S.S. Newsletter*

First published in 1946

SUBSCRIPTION DATA

Issues and rates: Published quarterly.
  Average paid circulation: 900
  Annual rate(s): $5.00
Publisher or Sponsor: American Nature Study Society

EDITORIAL DESCRIPTION

Contains articles, news and notes, book reviews on environmental education, nature study, outdoor education.
Articles per average issue: 6
Audience: Academic, general
Manuscripts accepted in English

MANUSCRIPT INFORMATION

Subject field(s): Environmental education, nature study

Manuscript requirements: No specific style guide.
  Preferred length: 1500-1800 words; 6-10 pages
  Number of copies to be submitted: One
  Abstract: No
Author information and reprints: Payment: None.
  Is simultaneous submission of article to other journals permitted: Yes
  Exclusive manuscript rights between acceptance and publication: No
  Copyright: Held by author.
  Reprints: Available
Additional information: Illustrations may be pen and ink or black and white glossy photographs.
Disposition of manuscript:
  Query letter: No, but helpful
  Receipt of manuscript acknowledged: Yes
  Decision to publish in: 4 months
  Accepted manuscript published in: 9 months
  Rejected manuscript returned: Yes, if return postage is supplied by author.
  Rejected manuscript criticized: On request
Submit to:
  John A. Gustafson
  Editor
  (See address above)

NCAA NEWS [1038]
U.S. Highway 50 and Nall Avenue
P.O. Box 1906
Shawnee Mission, Kansas 66222
(913) 384-3220

First published in 1964

SUBSCRIPTION DATA

Issues and rates: Irregular, 18 issues per year
  Average paid circulation: 10,000 controlled
  Annual rate(s): $6.00
Publisher or Sponsor: National Collegiate Athletic Association

EDITORIAL DESCRIPTION

Publishes articles and features on college athletics: teams, personalities, rules, games, all sports. Favors all collegiate interests in sports.
Articles per average issue: 20-25
Audience: Administrators, coaches
Manuscripts accepted in English

MANUSCRIPT INFORMATION

Subject field(s): Personalities, teams, any phase of sports
Manuscript requirements: AP
  Preferred length: 600 words; 3 pages
  Number of copies to be submitted: One
  Abstract: No
Author information and reprints: Payment: None.
  Is simultaneous submission of article to other journals permitted: Yes
  Exclusive manuscript rights between acceptance and publication: No
  Copyright: Held by author.
  Reprints: Available at no cost

Additional information: Stories should be relatively short, newspaper style. Publication has a tabloid layout.
Disposition of manuscript:
  Query letter: No
  Receipt of manuscript acknowledged: No
  Decision to publish in: 1 week
  Accepted manuscript published in: 1-2 months
  Rejected manuscript returned: No
  Rejected manuscript criticized: No
Submit to:
  Dave R. Daniel
  Editor
  (See address above)

SPECIAL STIPULATIONS

Circulated among every major college and university campus in the U.S. with an athletic program.

THE NEGRO EDUCATIONAL REVIEW [1039]
A Forum for Discussion of Afro-American Issues
P.O. Box 2895, West Bay Annex
Jacksonville, Florida 32203
(904) 646-2870

First published in 1950

SUBSCRIPTION DATA

Issues and rates: Published quarterly.
  Average paid circulation: 3,000
  Annual rate(s): $10.00; Foreign $12.00
Managing Editor: R. Grann Lloyd

EDITORIAL DESCRIPTION

Provides scholarly treatments of Negro education and the black experience and implications, plus the consequences of racial discrimination in American society.
Articles per average issue: 6-8
Manuscripts accepted in English

MANUSCRIPT INFORMATION

Subject field(s): Education, sociology, history, political science, economics, language and literature, geography, business, art, music, psychology, other fields, depending on nature and contents of manuscripts
Manuscript requirements: Chicago
  Preferred length: 3000-4000 words; 10-15 pages
  Number of copies to be submitted: Two
Author information and reprints: Payment: None.
  Is simultaneous submission of article to other journals permitted: No
  Exclusive manuscript rights between acceptance and publication: Yes
  Copyright: Held by publication.
  Reprints: Available
Disposition of manuscript:
  Query letter: No
  Receipt of manuscript acknowledged: Yes
  Decision to publish in: 3-4 weeks
  Accepted manuscript published in: Depends on publication schedule.
  Rejected manuscript returned: Yes, if self-addressed, stamped envelope is sent with manuscript.

Rejected manuscript criticized: Yes
Submit to:
R. Grann Lloyd
(See address above)
(904) 765-3189

NEW JERSEY SCHOOL LEADER [1040]
New Jersey School Boards Association
P.O. Box 909
Trenton, New Jersey 08605
(609) 695-7600

Previously entitled *School Board Notes*

First published in 1954

SUBSCRIPTION DATA
Issues and rates: Published bi-monthly.
  Average paid circulation: 7,000
  Annual rate(s): $4.50
Publisher or Sponsor: New Jersey School Boards Association

EDITORIAL DESCRIPTION
  Contains articles and information on public education; association news, information on school law and regulations, etc. Content mainly concerns New Jersey schools. Emphasizes support of public education.
Articles per average issue: 2-3
Audience: School Administrators, board members, government officials
  Manuscripts accepted in English

MANUSCRIPT INFORMATION
Subject field(s): Education, federal and state aid
Manuscript requirements: See latest issue for style requirements.
  Preferred length: 1500 to 2000 words; 2-4 pages
  Number of copies to be submitted: 1
  Abstract: No
Author information and reprints: Payment: Payment only for commissioned articles.
  Is simultaneous submission of article to other journals permitted: Yes, upon special request
  Exclusive manuscript rights between acceptance and publication: Yes
  Copyright: Held by publication.
  Reprints: Available, cost depends upon scarcity.
Additional information: Association also publishes a monthly newsletter, *School Board Notes,* which contains news on happenings in education.
Disposition of manuscript:
  Query letter: No
  Receipt of manuscript acknowledged: Yes
  Decision to publish in: 1 month
  Accepted manuscript published in: 2-4 months
  Rejected manuscript returned: Yes, if self-addressed, stamped envelope is sent with manuscript.
Submit to:
  Clyde E. Leib
  Editor
  (See address above)

NEW YORK STATE SCHOOL BOARDS ASSOCIATION. JOURNAL [1041]
111 Washington Avenue
Albany, New York 12210
(518) 465-3474

SUBSCRIPTION DATA
Issues and rates: Published monthly.
  Average paid circulation: 8,000
  Annual rate(s): $10.00
Publisher or Sponsor: New York State School Boards Association, Inc.
Managing Editor: Donald G. Brossman

EDITORIAL DESCRIPTION
  Contains articles in all areas of education.
Articles per average issue: 2
Audience: School board members, administrators
  Manuscripts accepted in English

MANUSCRIPT INFORMATION
Subject field(s): Educational subjects
Manuscript requirements: See latest issue for style requirements.
  Preferred length: 1200 to 1500 words
  Number of copies to be submitted: One
  Abstract: No
Author information and reprints: Payment: None.
  Is simultaneous submission of article to other journals permitted: Yes
  Exclusive manuscript rights between acceptance and publication: No
  Copyright: None
  Reprints: Available occasionally
Disposition of manuscript:
  Query letter: No
  Receipt of manuscript acknowledged: Yes
  Decision to publish in: 3 months
  Accepted manuscript published in: 6 months
  Rejected manuscript returned: Yes
  Rejected manuscript criticized: No
Submit to:
  George E. Lowe
  Director of Public Relations
  (See address above)

NJEA REVIEW [1042]
180 West State Street
Trenton, New Jersey 08608
(509) 599-4561 ext. 46

SUBSCRIPTION DATA
Issues and rates: Nine issues, September through May
  Average paid circulation: 106,000 controlled
Publisher or Sponsor: New Jersey Education Association

EDITORIAL DESCRIPTION
  Prefer articles describing educational practices. Articles should be timely, broad enough to appeal to entire profession, well-researched but not too technical and not footnoted. Articles are especially valuable if they concern New Jersey experiences.
Articles per average issue: 8-10
Audience: Teachers
  Manuscripts accepted in English

MANUSCRIPT INFORMATION
Subject field(s): New trends in education, teaching requirements, curriculum experiments, subject areas
Manuscript requirements: Style sheet sent on request.
  Preferred length: 500 to 1000 words double-spaced
  Number of copies to be submitted: One
  Abstract: No
Author information and reprints: Payment: None.
  Is simultaneous submission of article to other journals permitted: No
  Exclusive manuscript rights between acceptance and publication: Yes
  Copyright: Held by publication.
  Reprints: Available at nominal cost
Disposition of manuscript:
  Query letter: No
  Receipt of manuscript acknowledged: Yes
  Decision to publish in: Varies
  Accepted manuscript published in: Varies
  Rejected manuscript returned: Yes
  Rejected manuscript criticized: No
Submit to:
  George M. Adams
  Associate Editor
  (See address above)

NSPI NEWSLETTER [1043]
P.O. Box 137, Cardinal Station
Catholic University
Washington, D.C. 20064
(202) 635-5825

Previously entitled *NSPI Journal*

First published in 1961

SUBSCRIPTION DATA
Issues and rates: 10 times yearly
  Average paid circulation: 2000
  Annual rate(s): $30.00, Foreign $32.00.
  Both include a subscription to *Improving Human Performance*
Publisher or Sponsor: National Society for Performance and Instruction

EDITORIAL DESCRIPTION
  Contains articles on education and training.
Articles per average issue: 1
  Manuscripts accepted in English

MANUSCRIPT INFORMATION
Manuscript requirements: Style sheet sent on request.
  Preferred length: Open
  Number of copies to be submitted: Two or three
  Abstract: Helpful
Author information and reprints: Payment: None.
  Is simultaneous submission of article to other journals permitted: Yes
  Exclusive manuscript rights between acceptance and publication: Yes

Education

Copyright: Held by publication.
Reprints: Available
Additional information: Photographs and charts should be camera ready.
Disposition of manuscript:
  Query letter: No
  Receipt of manuscript acknowledged: Yes
  Decision to publish in: 3 to 9 months
  Accepted manuscript published in: Two to four months
  Rejected manuscript returned: No
  Rejected manuscript criticized: Sometimes
Submit to:
  Jeanine Lee
  Managing Editor
  (See address above)

N.Y.S. JOURNAL OF H.P.E.R. [1044]
138 Washington Avenue
Albany, New York 12210
(518) 434-8179

SUBSCRIPTION DATA
Issues and rates: Published semi-annually.
  Average paid circulation: 3500; 3750 controlled
  Annual rate(s): $9.00
Publisher or Sponsor: New York State Association for Health, Physical Education and Recreation

EDITORIAL DESCRIPTION
Contains research articles and articles on current trends in health, physical education, and recreation.
Articles per average issue: 10
Audience: Professional, academic
  Manuscripts accepted in English

MANUSCRIPT INFORMATION
Subject field(s): Physical education, health, research, related fields
Manuscript requirements: See latest issue for style requirements.
  Preferred length: 3 pages
  Number of copies to be submitted: Two
Author information and reprints: Payment: None.
  Is simultaneous submission of article to other journals permitted: No
  Exclusive manuscript rights between acceptance and publication: Yes
  Copyright: Not copyrighted
  Reprints: Not available.
Disposition of manuscript:
  Receipt of manuscript acknowledged: Yes
  Decision to publish in: 6-8 weeks
  Accepted manuscript published in: 6-8 weeks
  Rejected manuscript returned: Yes
  Rejected manuscript criticized: No
Submit to:
  Millard G. Roberts
  Editor
  (See address above)

OREGON ASCD CURRICULUM BULLETIN [1045]
P.O. Box 421
Salem, Oregon 97308
(503) 838-1220

Previously entitled *Curriculum Bulletin*

First published in 1939

SUBSCRIPTION DATA
Issues and rates: Published bi-monthly.
  Average paid circulation: 800; 50 controlled
  Annual rate(s): $5.00, Foreign $7.50, Canada $6.50
Publisher or Sponsor: Oregon Association for Supervision and Curriculum Development

EDITORIAL DESCRIPTION
Contains monographs on topics concerned with the development of school curriculum.
Articles per average issue: 1
Audience: Teachers, administrators
  Manuscripts accepted in English only

MANUSCRIPT INFORMATION
Subject field(s): School curriculum and related topics
Manuscript requirements: See latest issue for style requirements.
  Preferred length: 10,000 to 25,000 words; 25 to 60 pages
  Number of copies to be submitted: One
  Abstract: No
Author information and reprints: Payment: None. 5 free copies to author
  Is simultaneous submission of article to other journals permitted: No
  Exclusive manuscript rights between acceptance and publication: Held by publication for one year only afterwhich publication is encouraged.
  Copyright: Held by author.
  Reprints: Available, cost varies depending on length
Disposition of manuscript:
  Receipt of manuscript acknowledged: Yes
  Decision to publish in: 6-12 weeks
  Accepted manuscript published in: 2-6 months
  Rejected manuscript returned: Yes
  Rejected manuscript criticized: No
Submit to:
  Charles Gengler
  Oregon College of Education
  Monmouth, Oregon 97361

PEABODY JOURNAL OF EDUCATION [1046]
George Peabody College for Teachers
Nashville, Tennessee 37203
615-327-8080

First published in 1923

SUBSCRIPTION DATA
Issues and rates: Published quarterly.
  Average paid circulation: 2100
  Annual rate(s): Institutions $10.00, Foreign individuals $9.00, Individuals $8.00, Foreign institutions $11.00
Publisher or Sponsor: George Peabody College for Teachers

EDITORIAL DESCRIPTION
A professional publication designed to foster the professional development of classroom teachers, college and university professors and leaders in education. Each issue contains editorial comment, a section focused on a current issue in education, articles of general educational interest, and book reviews. Emphasizes higher education and its role in promoting and improving education at all levels.
Articles per average issue: 10
Audience: Teachers, Administrators
  Manuscripts accepted in English

MANUSCRIPT INFORMATION
Subject field(s): Education, all levels and all areas such as: educational research, junior and community colleges, international education, innovations in education, special education, etc.
Manuscript requirements: MLA
  Preferred length: 5-12 pages
  Number of copies to be submitted: Three
Author information and reprints: Payment: None. 4 copies of the issue in which article appears.
  Is simultaneous submission of article to other journals permitted: Yes
  Exclusive manuscript rights between acceptance and publication: Yes
  Copyright: Held by George Peabody College for Teachers
  Reprints: Articles are reprinted only upon request.
Disposition of manuscript:
  Query letter: No
  Receipt of manuscript acknowledged: Yes
  Decision to publish in: 35 days
  Accepted manuscript published in: Accepted manuscripts are usually published in the first or second issue following date of acceptance.
  Rejected manuscript returned: Yes, if return postage is supplied by author.
  Rejected manuscript criticized: No
Submit to:
  Ralph E. Kirkman
  Editor
  (See address above)

PENMEN'S NEWSLETTER [1047]
34 Broadway Avenue
Ottawa, Ontario K1S 2U6, Canada
(613) 232-3014

First published in 1949

SUBSCRIPTION DATA
Issues and rates: Published bi-monthly.
  Average paid circulation: 200
  Annual rate(s): $5.00

Publisher or Sponsor: International Association of Master Penmen and Teachers of Handwriting

EDITORIAL DESCRIPTION

Contains news and articles on and by penmen and teachers of handwriting.
Articles per average issue: 1-2
Audience: Penmen, teachers, engrossers
Manuscripts accepted in English

MANUSCRIPT INFORMATION

Subject field(s): Modern 20th century style of writing, teaching of handwriting, engraving and illumination, ornamental writing
Manuscript requirements: See latest issue for style requirements.
  Preferred length: One page
  Number of copies to be submitted: One
Author information and reprints: Payment: None.
  Is simultaneous submission of article to other journals permitted: Yes
  Copyright: Held by publication.
  Reprints: Available
Disposition of manuscript:
  Query letter: No
  Receipt of manuscript acknowledged: Yes
  Decision to publish in: One week
  Accepted manuscript published in: 2-3 months
  Rejected manuscript returned: Yes
  Rejected manuscript criticized: Yes
Submit to:
  Eileen Richardson
  Editor
  (See address above)

PERCUSSIVE NOTES [1048]

Percussive Arts Society
130 Carol Drive
Terre Haute, Indiana 47805
(812) 466-2982

First published in 1963

SUBSCRIPTION DATA

Issues and rates: Published three times per year.
  Average paid circulation: 3,500
  Annual rate(s): Foreign $7.00; Individuals $7.00; Institutions $5.00; Students $7.00; Members $10.00
Publisher or Sponsor: Percussive Arts Society
Managing Editor: James L. Moore

EDITORIAL DESCRIPTION

Deals with the education and performance of percussion instruments.
Articles per average issue: 6-8
Audience: Musicians and educators
Manuscripts accepted in English

MANUSCRIPT INFORMATION

Manuscript requirements: No specific style guide.
  Preferred length: No preference
  Number of copies to be submitted: One
  Abstract: Not necessary.
Author information and reprints: Payment: None.
  Is simultaneous submission of article to other journals permitted: Permitted, but not encouraged.
  Exclusive manuscript rights between acceptance and publication: No
  Reprints: Available at cost. $1.50 per issue
Disposition of manuscript:
  Query letter: Not necessary.
  Receipt of manuscript acknowledged: Yes
  Decision to publish in: 3 months
  Accepted manuscript published in: 1 year
  Rejected manuscript returned: Yes, if return postage is supplied by author.
  Rejected manuscript criticized: No
Submit to:
  James L. Moore
  Editor
  (See address above)

THE PERSONNEL AND GUIDANCE JOURNAL [1049]

1607 New Hampshire Avenue, N. W.
Washington, D. C. 20009
(202) 483-4633

Previously entitled *Occupations*

First published in 1921

SUBSCRIPTION DATA

Issues and rates: Published monthly.
  Annual rate(s): $20.00; Foreign $20.00; Members $23.00
Publisher or Sponsor: The American Personnel and Guidance Association
Managing Editor: Jaclyn J. Alexander

EDITORIAL DESCRIPTION

Publishes manuscripts directed to the common interests of counselors and personnel workers in schools, colleges, community agencies and government.
Articles per average issue: 7
Manuscripts accepted in English

MANUSCRIPT INFORMATION

Subject field(s): Stimulating writing dealing with current professional and scientific issues, new techniques or innovative programs, the APGA as an association and its role in society, critical integrations of published research, research reports of unusual significance to practitioners
Manuscript requirements: See latest issue for style requirements. Style sheet sent on request. APA
  Preferred length: 3,500 words maximum
  Number of copies to be submitted: 3
  Abstract: Yes For full-length articles only, of about 100 words stating the central idea in nontechnical language
Author information and reprints: Payment: Reprints only. 10 copies of journal
  Is simultaneous submission of article to other journals permitted: Not permitted.
  Exclusive manuscript rights between acceptance and publication: Yes
  Copyright: Held by publication.
  Reprints: Available at cost.
Disposition of manuscript:
  Query letter: Not necessary.
  Receipt of manuscript acknowledged: Yes
  Decision to publish in: 2 months
  Accepted manuscript published in: 5-6 months
  Rejected manuscript returned: No
  Rejected manuscript criticized: Yes
Submit to:
  Leo Goldman
  Editor
  (See address above)

PERSONNEL NEWS FOR SCHOOL SYSTEMS [1050]

Educational Service Bureau
1835 K Street, N.W.
Washington, D.C. 20006
(202) 683-5080

First published in 1965

SUBSCRIPTION DATA

Issues and rates: Published monthly.
  Average paid circulation: 500
  Annual rate(s): $70
Publisher or Sponsor: Educational Service Bureau, Inc.
Managing Editor: Don Keefer

EDITORIAL DESCRIPTION

Contains news and counsel for public school personnel administrators in such areas as negotiations, board policies and regulations implementation; EEOC Guidelines; management by objectives; tenure; evaluation.
Articles per average issue: 3
Audience: Public school personnel administrators
Manuscripts accepted in English

MANUSCRIPT INFORMATION

Manuscript requirements: See latest issue for style requirements.
  Preferred length: 1000-2000 words
  Number of copies to be submitted: Two
  Abstract: No
Author information and reprints: Payment: By publication to author. Small honorarium possible, not guaranteed.
  Is simultaneous submission of article to other journals permitted: No
  Exclusive manuscript rights between acceptance and publication: Yes
  Copyright: Held by publication.
  Reprints: Available for $3.00
Additional information: Typewritten, double-spaced
Disposition of manuscript:
  Query letter: No
  Receipt of manuscript acknowledged: Yes
  Decision to publish in: 6 weeks
  Accepted manuscript published in: 6 weeks
  Rejected manuscript returned: Yes, if self-addressed, stamped envelope is sent with manuscript.
  Rejected manuscript criticized: No
Submit to:
  Dr. Eric F. Rhodes

Education

Editor
(See address above)

PHYSICS EDUCATION [1051]
The Institute of Physics
1 Lowther Gardens, Prince Consort Road
London SW7 2AB, United Kingdom
01-589 0048

SUBSCRIPTION DATA

Issues and rates: 7 issues a year
Average paid circulation: 3,100
Annual rate(s): £10.00, Foreign $35.00
Publisher or Sponsor: The Institute of Physics

EDITORIAL DESCRIPTION

Contains practical information on teaching methods and aids, educational developments, physics applications, news sections and reviews. Aimed at teachers of physics in schools, universities and colleges at a level bridging school and first year university teaching.
Articles per average issue: 14
Audience: Teachers and lecturers in physics
Manuscripts accepted in English

MANUSCRIPT INFORMATION

Subject field(s): Teaching methods and apparatus, specialized physics for the general reader, applications of physics, difficult points in physics teaching, news items
Manuscript requirements: Style sheet sent on request.
Preferred length: 2000-4000 words; 2-4 typeset pages
Number of copies to be submitted: Two
Abstract: No
Author information and reprints: Payment: None.
Is simultaneous submission of article to other journals permitted: Only by prior arrangement
Exclusive manuscript rights between acceptance and publication: Yes
Copyright: Held by author.
Reprints: Available, 50 free
Disposition of manuscript:
Query letter: No
Receipt of manuscript acknowledged: Yes
Decision to publish in: 4-6 weeks
Accepted manuscript published in: 2-6 months
Rejected manuscript returned: Yes
Rejected manuscript criticized: Yes
Submit to:
Neil Warnock-Smith
Staff Editor
(See address above)

THE PHYSICS TEACHER [1052]
Department of Physics
State University of New York
Stony Brook, New York 11790
(516) 246-6058

First published in 1961

SUBSCRIPTION DATA

Issues and rates: 9 issues per year
Average paid circulation: 10,500
Annual rate(s): $5.00, Foreign $17.00
Publisher or Sponsor: American Association of Physics Teachers
Managing Editor: Arthlyn Ferguson

EDITORIAL DESCRIPTION

Contains articles, notes, apparatus evaluations, book reviews of interest to teachers of physics on the introductory level, high school and college.
Audience: High school and college teachers of introductory physics
Manuscripts accepted in English

MANUSCRIPT INFORMATION

Subject field(s): Physics
Manuscript requirements: See latest issue for style requirements.
Preferred length: Articles: 5,000 words; notes: 1,000 words
Number of copies to be submitted: Two
Abstract: No
Author information and reprints: Payment: None.
Is simultaneous submission of article to other journals permitted: No
Exclusive manuscript rights between acceptance and publication: Yes
Copyright: Held by publication.
Reprints: Available, cost on request
Additional information: Photographs, drawings solicited to be used with articles and notes. Manuscripts must be double-spaced.
Disposition of manuscript:
Query letter: No
Receipt of manuscript acknowledged: Yes
Decision to publish in: 6-8 weeks
Accepted manuscript published in: 6-8 months
Rejected manuscript returned: Yes
Rejected manuscript criticized: Yes
Submit to:
Clifford Swartz
Editor
(See address above)

PLANNING FOR HIGHER EDUCATION [1053]
Suite 1-A
3 Washington Square Village
New York, New York 10025
(212) 673-4320

Previously entitled *SCUP Journal*

First published in 1970

SUBSCRIPTION DATA

Issues and rates: Published bi-monthly.
Average paid circulation: 14,500
Annual rate(s): $15.00
Publisher or Sponsor: Society for College and University Planning; Educational Facilities Laboratories
Managing Editor: Lawrence F. Kramer

EDITORIAL DESCRIPTION

Concerned with all aspects of educational planning and the relationship of all the elements: academic, financial, physical and community aspects; focuses on long-range planning achievements and developments underway; a looseleaf format, to facilitate reproduction and distribution within institutions
Articles per average issue: 5
Audience: College and university planners, educational consultants, administrators, trustees, governmental
Manuscripts accepted in English

MANUSCRIPT INFORMATION

Subject field(s): Comprehensive, physical, financial, academic, statewide, facilities, community, inter-institutional planning; institutional research; management; futurology. A case-study orientation is encouraged, as are reports from other nations.
Manuscript requirements: See latest issue for style requirements. Style sheet sent on request.
Preferred length: 3,400 words
Number of copies to be submitted: 3
Abstract: Not necessary.
Author information and reprints: Payment: None.
Is simultaneous submission of article to other journals permitted: Permitted, but not encouraged.
Exclusive manuscript rights between acceptance and publication: Yes
Copyright: Held by publication.
Reprints: Available at no cost. 30 Available at cost.
Additional information: In depth, critical discussions are preferred, describing past, present and future problems, alternatives, solutions, modifications, expectations.
Disposition of manuscript:
Query letter: Not necessary, but advisable.
Receipt of manuscript acknowledged: Yes
Decision to publish in: 2 months
Accepted manuscript published in: Maximum 4 months
Rejected manuscript returned: Yes
Rejected manuscript criticized: Yes
Submit to:
Lawrence F. Kramer
Publications Editor
(See address above)

SPECIAL STIPULATIONS

Submission of a preliminary outline is recommended.

PSBA BULLETIN [1054]
Pennsylvania School Boards Association
412 North Second Street
Harrisburg, Pennsylvania 17101
(717) 233-1642

First published in 1959

SUBSCRIPTION DATA

Issues and rates: Published bi-monthly.
Average paid circulation: 8,700 controlled
Annual rate(s): $5.00

Publisher or Sponsor: Pennsylvania School Boards Association

EDITORIAL DESCRIPTION

Contains a variety of informative and "how to" articles concerning all aspects of basic education and school management. Includes studies, feature articles and school management techniques.
Articles per average issue: 4
Audience: School Board members, administrators, lawyers, business managers, general public
Manuscripts accepted in English only

MANUSCRIPT INFORMATION

Subject field(s): Public education, school law, school finance, public labor relations, lay governance, communications, curriculum
Manuscript requirements: See latest issue for style requirements.
Preferred length: 1,000 to 1,400 words; 7-8 pages
Number of copies to be submitted: One
Abstract: Yes
Author information and reprints: Payment: None. Copies of the publication.
Is simultaneous submission of article to other journals permitted: Yes
Exclusive manuscript rights between acceptance and publication: No
Copyright: Not copyrighted
Reprints: Available
Additional information: Manuscripts should be written in a clear journalistic style, double-spaced and typed. Charts, photographs, and artwork welcomed.
Disposition of manuscript:
Query letter: No
Receipt of manuscript acknowledged: Yes
Decision to publish in: 2 weeks
Accepted manuscript published in: One month
Rejected manuscript returned: Yes, if self-addressed, stamped envelope is sent with manuscript.
Rejected manuscript criticized: No
Submit to:
Nicholas L. Goble
Director of Public Relations
(See address above)

QUEST [1055]

Dr. Francis Bleick, Business Manager
1419 Ninth Avenue South
St. Cloud, Minnesota 56301
(612) 252-5682

First published in 1963

SUBSCRIPTION DATA

Issues and rates: Published semi-annually.
Average paid circulation: 4,500 controlled
Annual rate(s): $8.00 (and Canada); Foreign $10.00; Institutions $8.00

Publisher or Sponsor: National Association for Physical Education of College Women; National College Physical Education for Men

EDITORIAL DESCRIPTION

Designed to present articles on current issues in physical education, sport, the science of exercise and human movement. Most monographs are thematic. Each issue is devoted to a previously announced single topic.
Articles per average issue: 15-25
Audience: Professional, academic
Manuscripts accepted in English

MANUSCRIPT INFORMATION

Manuscript requirements: APA
Preferred length: 10-20 typewritten, double-spaced pages
Number of copies to be submitted: 2
Abstract: Not necessary.
Author information and reprints: Payment: None.
Is simultaneous submission of article to other journals permitted: Permitted, but not encouraged.
Exclusive manuscript rights between acceptance and publication: No
Copyright:
Reprints: Not available.
Additional information: Future topics of issues may be obtained from the editor. Research findings are not ordinarily reported.
Disposition of manuscript:
Query letter: Not necessary, but advisable.
Receipt of manuscript acknowledged: Yes
Decision to publish in: 1 month after deadline
Accepted manuscript published in: 6-12 months
Rejected manuscript returned: Yes, with return postage paid by publication.
Rejected manuscript criticized: No
Submit to:
Dr. Betty Spears
Editor
Curry Hicks Building
University of Massachusetts
Amherst, Massachusetts 01002
(413) 545-2514

READING HORIZONS [1056]

Reading Center and Clinic
Western Michigan University
Kalamazoo, Michigan 49008
(616) 383-1992

First published in 1960

SUBSCRIPTION DATA

Issues and rates: Published quarterly.
Average paid circulation: 400; 250 controlled
Annual rate(s): $4.00

EDITORIAL DESCRIPTION

Contains material of interest to teachers of reading at the elementary, secondary, college, and adult levels.

Articles per average issue: 3-4
Audience: Professionals interested in reading
Manuscripts accepted in English

MANUSCRIPT INFORMATION

Subject field(s): Teaching of reading, diagnosis and treatment of the disabled reader, reading in the content areas, preparation of reading teachers, and parents
Manuscript requirements: Style sheet sent on request. Double-space, use references rather than footnotes
Preferred length: 2,000 to 4,000 words; 10-20 pages
Number of copies to be submitted: Two
Abstract: No
Author information and reprints: Payment: Reprints only. 6 copies; microfilm issues are available
Is simultaneous submission of article to other journals permitted: No
Exclusive manuscript rights between acceptance and publication: Yes
Copyright: Held by Reading Center and Clinic, Western Michigan University
Reprints: Not available.
Disposition of manuscript:
Query letter: No
Receipt of manuscript acknowledged: Yes
Decision to publish in: 8 weeks
Accepted manuscript published in: 6-9 months
Rejected manuscript returned: Yes
Rejected manuscript criticized: No
Submit to:
Dorothy J. McGinnis
Director, Reading Center and Clinic
(See address above)

READING IMPROVEMENT [1057]

A Journal Devoted to the Teaching of Reading
Project Innovation
1362 Santa Cruz Court
Chula Vista, California 92010

SUBSCRIPTION DATA

Issues and rates: Published quarterly.
Average paid circulation: 2,500
Annual rate(s): Institutions $8.00, Individuals $6.00, Foreign institutions $9.50, Foreign individuals $7.50
Publisher or Sponsor: Project Innovation
Managing Editor: Lan M. Cassel

EDITORIAL DESCRIPTION

Includes reports of investigation and theoretical papers dealing with reading improvement at all levels of education, and in every area of concern. Preference is given to manuscripts that present meaningful and practical ways for dealing with the problem of reading instruction. Research and theory are equally acceptable.
Articles per average issue: 16
Audience: Teachers, educators and reading personnel
Manuscripts accepted in English

Education

MANUSCRIPT INFORMATION
Subject field(s): Reading instruction, language arts, reading lab, comprehension, group testing-reading, learning problems-reading, communication, spelling, diagnostic reading
Manuscript requirements: APA
  Preferred length: 1,500 words; 5 pages
  Number of copies to be submitted: Two
  Abstract: Yes. Include abstract of less than 120 words.
Author information and reprints: Payment: By author to publication. Depends on article.
  Is simultaneous submission of article to other journals permitted: No
  Exclusive manuscript rights between acceptance and publication: Yes
  Copyright: Held by publication.
  Reprints: Available, $2 for 50
Disposition of manuscript:
  Query letter: No
  Receipt of manuscript acknowledged: Yes
  Decision to publish in: 30 days
  Accepted manuscript published in: 6-12 months
  Rejected manuscript returned: Yes
  Rejected manuscript criticized: No
Submit to:
  Russell N. Cassel
  Editor
  (See address above)

READING RESEARCH QUARTERLY [1058]
International Reading Association
800 Barksdale Road
Newark, New Jersey 17911
(302) 731-1600

First published in 1965

SUBSCRIPTION DATA
Issues and rates: Published quarterly.
  Average paid circulation: 10,500
  Annual rate(s): $15.00; Foreign $17.00; Institutions $15.00
Publisher or Sponsor: International Reading Association

EDITORIAL DESCRIPTION
  Reading at all levels as it relates to linguistics, psychology, and other disciplines
Articles per average issue: 6-8
Audience: Reading researcher

MANUSCRIPT INFORMATION
Subject field(s): Education, psychology, linguistics, language, arts, medical areas that relate to reading
Manuscript requirements: See latest issue for style requirements. Style sheet sent on request.
  Preferred length: 25-35 pages
  Number of copies to be submitted: 4
  Abstract: Yes. Of 100-150 words as well as a biographical sketch of 25-50 words
Author information and reprints: Payment: None.
  Is simultaneous submission of article to other journals permitted: Not permitted.
  Exclusive manuscript rights between acceptance and publication: Yes
  Copyright: Held by publication.
  Reprints: Available at cost.
Additional information: Manuscript should be typewritten, triple-spaced throughout.
Disposition of manuscript:
  Query letter: Not necessary.
  Receipt of manuscript acknowledged: Yes
  Decision to publish in: 3-6 weeks
  Accepted manuscript published in: 3-6 months
  Rejected manuscript returned: Yes, if return postage is supplied by author.
  Rejected manuscript criticized: Reasons for rejections only
Submit to:
  Dr. Roger Farr;
  Samuel Weintraub
  Co-Editors
  207 Education Building
  Indiana University
  Bloomington, 47401
  (812) 337-7167

THE READING TEACHER [1059]
International Reading Association
800 Barksdale Road
Newark, Delaware 19711
(302) 731-1600 ext. 65

First published in 1948

SUBSCRIPTION DATA
Issues and rates: Monthly, October through May
  Average paid circulation: 47,500
  Annual rate(s): $15.00 with membership
Publisher or Sponsor: International Reading Association

EDITORIAL DESCRIPTION
  Contains articles on reading at elementary level.
Articles per average issue: 10
Audience: Reading teachers, elementary classroom teachers, supervisors, principals
  Manuscripts accepted in English

MANUSCRIPT INFORMATION
Subject field(s): Reading, related fields
Manuscript requirements: MLA; other requirements sent on request
  Preferred length: Varies
  Number of copies to be submitted: 3
  Abstract: No
Author information and reprints: Payment: None. 5 free copies of issue.
  Is simultaneous submission of article to other journals permitted: No
  Exclusive manuscript rights between acceptance and publication: Yes
  Copyright: Held by publication.
  Reprints: Not available.
Disposition of manuscript:
  Query letter: No
  Receipt of manuscript acknowledged: Yes
  Decision to publish in: 6 weeks
  Accepted manuscript published in: 2-12 months
  Rejected manuscript returned: Yes, if return postage is supplied by author.
  Rejected manuscript criticized: Yes
Submit to:
  Lloyd W. Kline
  Editor
  (See address above)

RELIGIOUS EDUCATION [1060]
409 Prospect Street
New Haven, Connecticut
(203) 864-6141

First published in 1906

SUBSCRIPTION DATA
Issues and rates: Published bi-monthly.
  Average paid circulation: 5,000; 482 controlled
  Annual rate(s): $15.00
Publisher or Sponsor: The Religious Education Association
Managing Editor: Boardman W. Kathan

EDITORIAL DESCRIPTION
  A platform for the free discussion of religious issues and their bearing on education. Includes articles, symposia, scholarly papers and research findings in all aspects of religion and education, from a multi-faith and inter-disciplinary perspective.
Articles per average issue: 9
Audience: Professional, academic
  Manuscripts accepted in English, French

MANUSCRIPT INFORMATION
Manuscript requirements: Chicago
  Preferred length: 3,000-5,000 words; 12-20 pages
  Number of copies to be submitted: One
  Abstract: No
Author information and reprints: Payment: Reprints only. 3 copies of issue
  Is simultaneous submission of article to other journals permitted: No
  Exclusive manuscript rights between acceptance and publication: Yes
  Copyright: Held by publication.
  Reprints: Available, cost depends on length
Additional information: Prefer footnotes at bottom of page and numbered serially.
Disposition of manuscript:
  Receipt of manuscript acknowledged: Yes
  Decision to publish in: 2-3 months
  Accepted manuscript published in: 6-12 months
  Rejected manuscript returned: Yes
  Rejected manuscript criticized: No
Submit to:
  Randolph Crump Miller
  Editor
  (See address above)

RESEARCH IN THE TEACHING OF ENGLISH [1061]
National Council of Teachers of English
1111 Kenyon Road
Urbana, Illinois 61801
(217) 328-3870

First published in 1967

SUBSCRIPTION DATA
Issues and rates: Published semi-annually.
  Average paid circulation: 3,500
  Annual rate(s): $5.00
Publisher or Sponsor: National Council of Teachers of English

EDITORIAL DESCRIPTION
  Contains research reports on the teaching of English or on the effect of English teaching on students. Presents a forum for circulating the latest research studies in the teaching of English.
Audience: Professors of English

MANUSCRIPT INFORMATION
Manuscript requirements: See latest issue for style requirements.
  Preferred length: 14-20 pages
  Number of copies to be submitted: Two
Author information and reprints: Payment: None. Share permissions fees with publisher.
  Is simultaneous submission of article to other journals permitted: Yes
  Exclusive manuscript rights between acceptance and publication: Yes
  Copyright: Held by publication.
  Reprints: Available at printer's rates
Disposition of manuscript:
  Receipt of manuscript acknowledged: No
  Decision to publish in: 30-60 days
  Accepted manuscript published in: 4 months
  Rejected manuscript returned: Yes
  Rejected manuscript criticized: No
Submit to:
  Alan C. Purves
  Editor
  310 West Delaware
  Urbana, Illinois 61801

SPECIAL STIPULATIONS
  NCTE acts as publisher but exercises no substantial editorial control; the latter is in the hands of the editor.

RESEARCH QUARTERLY* [1062]
1201 16th Street, N.W.
Room 222
Washington, D.C. 20036
(202) 833-5553

SUBSCRIPTION DATA
Issues and rates: Published quarterly.
  Average paid circulation: 10,000
  Annual rate(s): $15.00, Foreign $16.00
Publisher or Sponsor: American Association for Health, Physical Education, and Recreation

EDITORIAL DESCRIPTION
  Contains research articles contributing to knowledge and the development of theory, either as new information, substantiation or contradiction of previous findings, or application of new or improved techniques.

MANUSCRIPT INFORMATION
Subject field(s): Physiology, motivation, physiological psychology, motor skills acquisition, teaching techniques, health education, kinesiology, statistical techniques
Manuscript requirements: Style sheet sent on request.
  Preferred length: None
  Number of copies to be submitted: Three
Author information and reprints: Payment: None.
  Is simultaneous submission of article to other journals permitted: No
  Exclusive manuscript rights between acceptance and publication: Yes
  Copyright: Held by publication.
  Reprints: Available
Disposition of manuscript:
  Receipt of manuscript acknowledged: Yes
  Decision to publish in: 3 months
  Accepted manuscript published in: 9 months
  Rejected manuscript returned: Yes
  Rejected manuscript criticized: Yes
Submit to:
  Editor
  (See address above)

REVIEW OF EDUCATIONAL RESEARCH [1063]
1126 Sixteenth Street, NW
Washington, D.C. 20036
(202) 223-9485

First published in 1931

SUBSCRIPTION DATA
Issues and rates: Published quarterly.
  Average paid circulation: 15,200
  Annual rate(s): $10.00
Publisher or Sponsor: American Educational Research Association
Managing Editor: Patricia E. Stivers

EDITORIAL DESCRIPTION
  Contains critical, integrative reviews of research literature. Important studies are identified, summarized and critically analyzed.
Articles per average issue: 6
Audience: Professors and researchers in education
  Manuscripts accepted in English

MANUSCRIPT INFORMATION
Subject field(s): Reviews of any aspect of research in education.
Manuscript requirements: APA, 1974
  Preferred length: 20-30 pages
  Number of copies to be submitted: 3
  Abstract: Yes
Author information and reprints: Payment: None.
  Is simultaneous submission of article to other journals permitted: No
  Exclusive manuscript rights between acceptance and publication: Yes
  Copyright: Held by publication.
  Reprints: Available, cost quoted individually, 50 provided free to author

Disposition of manuscript:
  Receipt of manuscript acknowledged: Yes
  Decision to publish in: 4 months
  Accepted manuscript published in: 3-4 months
  Rejected manuscript returned: Yes
  Rejected manuscript criticized: Yes
Submit to:
  Samuel J. Messick
  Educational Testing Service
  Princeton, New Jersey 08540
  (609) 921-9000 ext. 2040

SALARY AND MERIT [1064]
Information and Research for More Effective Compensation In Public Education
1835 K Street NW
Suite 908
Washington, D.C. 20006
(202) 683-5080

First published in 1969

SUBSCRIPTION DATA
Issues and rates: Published monthly.
  Average paid circulation: 500
  Annual rate(s): $48.00
Publisher or Sponsor: Educational Service Bureau, Inc.

EDITORIAL DESCRIPTION
  Contains sample teacher compensation plans, salary schedules; articles on merit pay, differential staffing, management by objectives, performance contracting.
Articles per average issue: 3
Audience: Salary administrators
  Manuscripts accepted in English

MANUSCRIPT INFORMATION
Manuscript requirements: Style sheet sent on request.
  Preferred length: 1500-2000 words; 3 typed pages double-spaced
  Number of copies to be submitted: One
  Abstract: No
Author information and reprints: Payment: None.
  Is simultaneous submission of article to other journals permitted: Yes
  Exclusive manuscript rights between acceptance and publication: No
  Copyright: Held by publication.
  Reprints: Available at cost. $2.50 per copy
Additional information: Letter granting permission to publish article must accompany manuscript.
Disposition of manuscript:
  Query letter: No
  Receipt of manuscript acknowledged: Yes
  Decision to publish in: One month
  Accepted manuscript published in: One month
  Rejected manuscript returned: Yes, if self-addressed, stamped envelope is sent with manuscript.
  Rejected manuscript criticized: No
Submit to:
  Norman Burnett
  Director of Publications
  (See address above)

Education

SPECIAL STIPULATIONS
Annual prizes awarded for Best Merit Pay Plans (prizes awarded to school districts, not individuals).

SCHOOL BUSINESS AFFAIRS [1065]
ASBO's Newsmagazine/Journal
2424 West Lawrence
Chicago, Illinois 60625
(312) 728-3204

First published in 1934

SUBSCRIPTION DATA
Issues and rates: Published monthly.
Average paid circulation: 5,500; 1,000 controlled
Annual rate(s): Members $40.00 part of ASBO membership
Publisher or Sponsor: Association of School Business Officials

EDITORIAL DESCRIPTION
Contains professional articles on school business management, public and non-public schools.
Articles per average issue: 3
Audience: Practitioners and professors of school business management
Manuscripts accepted in English

MANUSCRIPT INFORMATION
Subject field(s): Finance, accounting, budgeting, food service, personnel, bus transportation, insurance, federal aid, college management, maintenance, purchasing, office management
Manuscript requirements: See latest issue for style requirements.
Preferred length: 500-2000 words; 3-8 typed pages double-spaced
Number of copies to be submitted: Two
Author information and reprints: Payment: None.
Is simultaneous submission of article to other journals permitted: Yes
Exclusive manuscript rights between acceptance and publication: No
Copyright: Not copyrighted
Reprints: Available, cost on request
Additional information: Manuscript should be accompanied by picture and biography of author. Articles are solicited primarily from ASBO members.
Disposition of manuscript:
Query letter: Not necessary but helpful
Receipt of manuscript acknowledged: Yes
Decision to publish in: 1 week
Accepted manuscript published in: 2-4 weeks
Rejected manuscript returned: Yes
Rejected manuscript criticized: Yes
Submit to:
Dwight B. Esau
Managing Editor
(See address above)

SCHOOL AND COMMUNITY [1066]
P.O. Box 458
Columbia, Missouri 65201
(314) 422-3127 ext. 58

SUBSCRIPTION DATA
Issues and rates: Monthly, September through May
Average paid circulation: 44,000
Annual rate(s): $4.50, Foreign $5.25
Publisher or Sponsor: Missouri State Teachers Association

EDITORIAL DESCRIPTION
Contains articles of interest to elementary, secondary and higher education teachers; important events, research, legislation, innovative educational practices. Strives to advance educational program at the elementary, secondary and higher education levels; to promote the profession of teaching. Content is limited to the state of Missouri.
Articles per average issue: 10
Audience: Educators
Manuscripts accepted in English

MANUSCRIPT INFORMATION
Subject field(s): School finance, classroom practice, experimentation, research, workshops, inservice
Manuscript requirements: Type, double-space, wide margins
Preferred length: 900 words; 3 pages
Number of copies to be submitted: One
Abstract: No
Author information and reprints: Payment: None. Copy of issue is sent to author.
Is simultaneous submission of article to other journals permitted: No
Exclusive manuscript rights between acceptance and publication: Yes
Copyright: Held by publication.
Reprints: Available, cost depends on length.
Disposition of manuscript:
Query letter: No, but advisable
Receipt of manuscript acknowledged: Yes
Decision to publish in: One week
Accepted manuscript published in: 1-4 months
Rejected manuscript returned: Yes, if return postage is supplied by author.
Rejected manuscript criticized: No
Submit to:
Inks Franklin
Editor
(See address above)

THE SCHOOL COUNSELOR [1067]
1607 New Hampshire Avenue N.W.
Washington, D.C. 20009
(202) 483-4633

First published in 1953

SUBSCRIPTION DATA
Issues and rates: 5 times per year
Average paid circulation: 19,000
Annual rate(s): $10.00
Publisher or Sponsor: American School Counselor Association

EDITORIAL DESCRIPTION
Contains articles on guidance and counseling.
Articles per average issue: 8
Audience: School counselors
Manuscripts accepted in English only

MANUSCRIPT INFORMATION
Manuscript requirements: See latest issue for style requirements.
Preferred length: 12 to 14 pages
Number of copies to be submitted: Three
Abstract: No
Author information and reprints: Payment: None.
Is simultaneous submission of article to other journals permitted: No
Exclusive manuscript rights between acceptance and publication: Yes
Copyright: Held by publication.
Reprints: Available
Disposition of manuscript:
Receipt of manuscript acknowledged: Yes
Decision to publish in: 3 months
Accepted manuscript published in: 6 months
Rejected manuscript returned: Yes
Rejected manuscript criticized: Yes
Submit to:
Marguerite R. Carroll
Editor
Fairfield University
Fairfield, Connecticut 06430
(203) 255-5411

THE SCHOOL GUIDANCE WORKER [1068]
1000 Yonge Street, Suite 304
Toronto, Ontario M4W 2K8 Canada
(416) 928-3210

SUBSCRIPTION DATA
Issues and rates: Published bi-monthly.
Annual rate(s): $7.00

EDITORIAL DESCRIPTION
Contents of interest to school guidance personnel particularly and to educators generally.

MANUSCRIPT INFORMATION
Subject field(s): School guidance, school counselling
Manuscript requirements: Style sheet sent on request.
Preferred length: 2,500-3,500 words; 8-10 pages
Number of copies to be submitted: Two
Author information and reprints: Payment: By publication to author. $50.00 per article.
Is simultaneous submission of article to other journals permitted: Yes
Exclusive manuscript rights between acceptance and publication: Yes
Reprints: Available, $.50 each

Additional information: Present policy involves theme issues, hence unsolicited manuscripts get second priority to solicited ones.
Disposition of manuscript:
Query letter: Yes
Receipt of manuscript acknowledged: Yes
Decision to publish in: 2 months
Accepted manuscript published in: 4-6 months
Rejected manuscript returned: Yes
Rejected manuscript criticized: No
Submit to:
Carl L. Bedal
Editor
(See address above)

SCHOOL SCIENCE AND MATHEMATICS [1069]
P.O. Box 1614
Indiana University of Pennsylvania
Indiana, Pennsylvania 15701
(412) 357-3000

First published in 1901

SUBSCRIPTION DATA
Issues and rates: 8 issues per year
Average paid circulation: 10,000
Annual rate(s): $10.00, Foreign $12.00
Publisher or Sponsor: School Science and Mathematics Association, Inc.
Managing Editor: Dale M. Shafer

EDITORIAL DESCRIPTION
Articles deal with current topics of interest in science and mathematics education.
Articles per average issue: 15
Audience: Junior, senior high school and college teachers and students of science and mathematics
Manuscripts accepted in English

MANUSCRIPT INFORMATION
Subject field(s): All areas of science and mathematics education
Manuscript requirements: Style sheet sent on request.
Preferred length: 4 journal pages
Number of copies to be submitted: Two
Abstract: No
Author information and reprints: Payment: None.
Is simultaneous submission of article to other journals permitted: No
Exclusive manuscript rights between acceptance and publication: Yes
Copyright: Held by publication.
Reprints: Available
Disposition of manuscript:
Query letter: No
Receipt of manuscript acknowledged: Yes
Decision to publish in: 3 months
Accepted manuscript published in: 1 year
Rejected manuscript returned: Yes
Rejected manuscript criticized: Yes
Submit to:
George G. Mallinson
Editor
535 Kendall Avenue
Kalamazoo, Michigan 49007
(616) 342-2255

SCHOOL SHOP [1070]
Industrial-Technical Education
416 Longshore Drive
P. O. Box 623
Ann Arbor, Michigan 48107
(313) 769-1211

First published in 1940

SUBSCRIPTION DATA
Issues and rates: Monthly except July and August
Average paid circulation: 4,000; 45,000 controlled
Annual rate(s): $8.00, Foreign $9.00

EDITORIAL DESCRIPTION
Serves the field of industrial, vocational and technical education. This includes automotive, drafting, general shop, graphic arts, electricity, electronics, metal working, machine shop, welding, woodworking and other industrial-technical skills, trades and specialities.
Articles per average issue: 16
Audience: Professionals in industrial-technical trades and specialties
Manuscripts accepted in English

MANUSCRIPT INFORMATION
Subject field(s): Industrial arts, trade and industrial education, vocational education, technical education
Manuscript requirements: Style sheet sent on request.
Preferred length: 6-8 pages
Number of copies to be submitted: 2
Author information and reprints: Payment: By publication to author. Varies
Is simultaneous submission of article to other journals permitted: No
Exclusive manuscript rights between acceptance and publication: Yes
Copyright: Held by publication.
Reprints: Available
Additional information: Authors only from editorial interest field
Disposition of manuscript:
Query letter: No
Receipt of manuscript acknowledged: Yes
Decision to publish in: 3-6 weeks
Accepted manuscript published in: 3-9 months
Rejected manuscript returned: Yes
Rejected manuscript criticized: Occasionally
Submit to:
Howard Kahn
Managing Editor
(See address above)

THE SCHOOL TRUSTEE [1071]
Saskatchewan School Trustees Association
570 Avord Tower
Regina, Saskatchewan S4P 0R7, Canada
(306) 522-7685

First published in 1930

SUBSCRIPTION DATA
Issues and rates: 5 per year
Average paid circulation: 5,000
Annual rate(s): $3.00
Publisher or Sponsor: Saskatchewan School Trustees Association

EDITORIAL DESCRIPTION
Contains articles on education: innovation, finance, theory, opinion, trends.
Articles per average issue: 3
Audience: Trustees, educators
Manuscripts accepted in English

MANUSCRIPT INFORMATION
Subject field(s): Education
Manuscript requirements: Canadian Press style
Preferred length: 1500 words; 6-8 typed pages double-spaced
Number of copies to be submitted: Two
Abstract: No
Author information and reprints: Payment: None.
Is simultaneous submission of article to other journals permitted: Yes
Exclusive manuscript rights between acceptance and publication: No
Copyright: Held by author.
Reprints: Available in limited number at no cost
Disposition of manuscript:
Query letter: No
Receipt of manuscript acknowledged: Yes
Decision to publish in: 30 days
Accepted manuscript published in: 45-60 days
Rejected manuscript returned: Yes
Rejected manuscript criticized: No
Submit to:
Norman John Elliott
Editorial Assistant
(See address above)

SCIENCE AND CHILDREN [1072]
1742 Connecticut Avenue, N.W.
Washington, D.C. 20003
(202) 265-4150

First published in 1963

SUBSCRIPTION DATA
Issues and rates: 8 times a year
Average paid circulation: 27,000
Annual rate(s): $8.00
Publisher or Sponsor: National Science Teachers Association

EDITORIAL DESCRIPTION
Journal of science designed with emphasis on K-8 and teacher trainers in elementary science.
Articles per average issue: 9
Audience: Elementary science educators, classroom teachers and administrators
Manuscripts accepted in English

MANUSCRIPT INFORMATION
Subject field(s): Classroom activities, feature stories, editorials, poetry, program designs, science content, interdiscipline

Education

teaching, reviews and research, anything related to the teaching of science in elementary school
Manuscript requirements: Style sheet sent on request. manuscripts typed, double-spaced.
  Preferred length: 1200-1500 words
  Number of copies to be submitted: Two
  Abstract: No
Author information and reprints: Payment: None.
  Is simultaneous submission of article to other journals permitted: No
  Exclusive manuscript rights between acceptance and publication: Yes
  Copyright: Held by publication.
  Reprints: Available
Additional information: Black & white photographs are encouraged
Disposition of manuscript:
  Query letter: No
  Receipt of manuscript acknowledged: Yes
  Decision to publish in: 3-6 months
  Accepted manuscript published in: 3-12 months
  Rejected manuscript returned: Yes
  Rejected manuscript criticized: Yes
Submit to:
  Phyllis R. Marcuccio
  Editor
  (See address above)

SPECIAL STIPULATIONS
  Published manuscripts represent the opinions of the authors and do not necessarily represent the policies of the National Science Teachers Association.

SCIENCE EDUCATION [1073]
John Wiley and Sons, Inc.
605 Third Avenue
New York, New York 10016
(212) 867-9800

First published in 1919

SUBSCRIPTION DATA
Issues and rates: Published quarterly.
  Annual rate(s): $20.00; Foreign $20.00 plus postage
Publisher or Sponsor: AEIS
Managing Editor: N. E. Bingham

EDITORIAL DESCRIPTION
  Innovations in curricula, materials, and evaluative procedures in both the classroom and laboratory situations
  Audience: Science educators
  Manuscripts accepted in English

MANUSCRIPT INFORMATION
Subject field(s): Educational matters pertinent to science educators; applied and basic research, pilot studies, innovations in approach, organization, content or evaluation.
Manuscript requirements: Style sheet sent on request.
  Number of copies to be submitted: 2
  Abstract: Yes. A synopsis of the main points of the paper.
Author information and reprints: Payment: Reprints only. 25 copies
  Copyright: Held by publication.
  Reprints: Available at cost.
Submit to:
  Prof. N. E. Bingham
  Editor
  1718 N. W. 10th Avenue
  Gainesville, Florida 32601

THE SCIENCE TEACHER [1074]
Journal of the National Science Teachers Association
1742 Connecticut Avenue, NW
Washington, D.C. 20009
(202) 265-4150

First published in 1933

SUBSCRIPTION DATA
Issues and rates: 9 times per year: September through May
  Average paid circulation: 22,476
  Annual rate(s): $15
Publisher or Sponsor: National Science Teachers Association

EDITORIAL DESCRIPTION
  Contains background articles on educational and scientific topics; ideas for classroom and laboratory work; reviews of books, filmstrips, etc.; news of legislation and other matters of interest to persons in science education; news of the NSTA.
  Articles per average issue: 12
  Audience: Teachers and others engaged in science education principally at the secondary school level
  Manuscripts accepted in English

MANUSCRIPT INFORMATION
Subject field(s): Science education, science, classroom ideas
Manuscript requirements: Style sheet sent on request.
  Preferred length: 1000-2000 words
  Number of copies to be submitted: Two
  Abstract: No
Author information and reprints: Payment: None.
  Is simultaneous submission of article to other journals permitted: No
  Exclusive manuscript rights between acceptance and publication: Yes
  Copyright: Held by publication.
  Reprints: Available, cost depends on quantity
Disposition of manuscript:
  Query letter: No
  Receipt of manuscript acknowledged: Yes
  Decision to publish in: 1 month
  Accepted manuscript published in: 3-8 months
  Rejected manuscript returned: Yes
  Rejected manuscript criticized: No
Submit to:
  Mary E. Hawkins
  Editor
  (See address above)
  (202) 265-4150

SLOW LEARNER WORKSHOP [1075]
Parker Publishing Company, Inc.
West Nyack, New York 10994
(201) 947-1000 ext. 572

SUBSCRIPTION DATA
Issues and rates: Monthly except July and August
  Average paid circulation: 5000
  Annual rate(s): $36

EDITORIAL DESCRIPTION
  Contains practical, classroom-tested techniques for helping students who have difficulty learning whatever the cause.

MANUSCRIPT INFORMATION
Subject field(s): Teaching and counseling students with learning problems, using instructional resources, developing methods and techniques, maximizing personnel efficiency, expanding the role of special education, special remedial programs
Manuscript requirements: See latest issue for style requirements.
  Preferred length: 5-6 pages; 2000-2500 words
  Number of copies to be submitted: One
Author information and reprints: Payment: None. 5 complimentary copies to author.
  Is simultaneous submission of article to other journals permitted: No
  Exclusive manuscript rights between acceptance and publication: No
  Copyright: Held by publication.
  Reprints: Not available.
Disposition of manuscript:
  Receipt of manuscript acknowledged: Yes
  Decision to publish in: One month
  Accepted manuscript published in: 6-9 months
  Rejected manuscript returned: Yes
  Rejected manuscript criticized: Yes
Submit to:
  Budd Theobald
  Editor
  (See address above)

THE SLOW LEARNING CHILD [1076]
Schonell Educational Research Centre
University of Queensland
St. Lucia, Queensland 4067, Australia
71-3611

First published in 1954

SUBSCRIPTION DATA
Issues and rates: Published three times per year.
  Average paid circulation: 1,200; 400 controlled
  Annual rate(s): $A9.00
Publisher or Sponsor: Fred and Eleanor Schonell Educational Research Centre

EDITORIAL DESCRIPTION
  Contains articles on all aspects of special education practice, curriculum, organization, methods, materials, research.

Articles per average issue: 6
Audience: Professional, academic
  Manuscripts accepted in English

MANUSCRIPT INFORMATION

Subject field(s): Learning disability, reading, exceptional children, mental retardation psycholinguistics
Manuscript requirements: APS Publication Manual
  Preferred length: 3000 words; 8 pages
  Number of copies to be submitted: Two
  Abstract: Yes
Author information and reprints: Payment: Reprints only. 12 free copies
  Is simultaneous submission of article to other journals permitted: No
  Exclusive manuscript rights between acceptance and publication: Yes
  Copyright: Held by publication.
  Reprints: Available at cost.
Additional information: Double-spaced typescript, wide margins, good academic style.
Disposition of manuscript:
  Query letter: No
  Receipt of manuscript acknowledged: Yes
  Decision to publish in: Up to 3 months
  Accepted manuscript published in: 6 months
  Rejected manuscript returned: Yes, if self-addressed, stamped envelope is sent with manuscript.
  Rejected manuscript criticized: No
Submit to:
  Dr. Robert J. Andrews
  Editor
  (See address above)

THE SOCIAL STUDIES [1077]
A Periodical for Teachers and Administrators
4000 South Albemarle Street, N.W.
Washington, D. C. 20016
(202) 362-6445

First published in 1909

SUBSCRIPTION DATA

Issues and rates: Published bi-monthly.
  Average paid circulation: 6000
  Annual rate(s): $8.50; Foreign $9.50

EDITORIAL DESCRIPTION

  Contains articles of interest to teachers and educators in the field of the social studies.
Articles per average issue: 10
Audience: Educators
  Manuscripts accepted in English

MANUSCRIPT INFORMATION

Subject field(s): Social studies in general, history, geography, economics, methods, techniques
Manuscript requirements: See latest issue for style requirements.
  Preferred length: 15 pages
  Number of copies to be submitted: 2
  Abstract: No

Author information and reprints: Payment: Reprints only. 2 copies of the magazine
  Is simultaneous submission of article to other journals permitted: Not encouraged
  Exclusive manuscript rights between acceptance and publication: Yes
  Copyright: Held by publication.
  Reprints: Not available.
Disposition of manuscript:
  Query letter: No
  Receipt of manuscript acknowledged: No
  Decision to publish in: 4-6 weeks
  Accepted manuscript published in: 12 months
  Rejected manuscript returned: Yes
  Rejected manuscript criticized: Sometimes
Submit to:
  Editor
  105 Hutchinson Avenue
  Haddonfield, New Jersey 08033

SOUTHERN ASSOCIATION OF COLLEGES AND SCHOOLS. PROCEEDINGS [1078]
795 Peachtree Street NE
Atlanta, Georgia 30308
(404) 875-8011

SUBSCRIPTION DATA

Issues and rates: 8 times per year
  Average paid circulation: 14,000; 400 controlled
  Annual rate(s): $4.00
Publisher or Sponsor: Southern Association of Colleges and Schools, Inc.
Managing Editor: Marian G. Lord

EDITORIAL DESCRIPTION

  Contains association news and news of accreditation in general, education news of interest to Southern educators.
Audience: Educators at all levels
  Manuscripts accepted in English

MANUSCRIPT INFORMATION

Subject field(s): Accreditation, educational improvement, accountability, educational financing
Manuscript requirements: Chicago
  Preferred length: 500 words; 1-2 pages
  Number of copies to be submitted: One
  Abstract: No
Author information and reprints: Payment: None.
  Is simultaneous submission of article to other journals permitted: Yes
  Exclusive manuscript rights between acceptance and publication: No
  Copyright: Not copyrighted
  Reprints: Available in limited supply
Disposition of manuscript:
  Query letter: No
  Receipt of manuscript acknowledged: No
  Decision to publish in: 1 month
  Accepted manuscript published in: 1-2 months
  Rejected manuscript returned: Yes, if self-addressed, stamped envelope is sent with manuscript.
  Rejected manuscript criticized: No

Submit to:
  Marian G. Lord
  Editor
  (See address above)
  (404) 875-8011

SPECIAL EDUCATION: FORWARD TRENDS [1079]
12 Hollycroft Avenue
London NW3 7QL, England

Previously entitled *Special Education*

First published in 1974

SUBSCRIPTION DATA

Issues and rates: Published quarterly.
  Average paid circulation: 6,800
  Annual rate(s): £3.00; Institutions £6.00; Foreign £5.50 Foreign institutions £11.00
Publisher or Sponsor: National Council for Special Education
Managing Editor: Margaret Peter

EDITORIAL DESCRIPTION

  Professional journal for those concerned with special education. Reports new developments, including teaching techniques and educational research; articles on the medical, therapeutic, psychological and sociological aspects of special education.
Articles per average issue: 6-8
Audience: Academic, professional
  Manuscripts accepted in English

MANUSCRIPT INFORMATION

Subject field(s): Education, educational psychology, psychiatry with reference to disturbed children, medical aspects of handicap, sociology of education, other subjects related to education of the handicapped.
Manuscript requirements: Style sheet sent on request.
  Preferred length: 1,100-3,300 words
  Number of copies to be submitted: 3
  Abstract: No
Author information and reprints: Payment: None, except commissioned articles.
  Is simultaneous submission of article to other journals permitted: No
  Reprints: Not available.
Disposition of manuscript:
  Query letter: Advisable
  Receipt of manuscript acknowledged: Yes
  Decision to publish in: 1 month
  Accepted manuscript published in: 3-9 months
  Rejected manuscript returned: Yes
  Rejected manuscript criticized: No
Submit to:
  Margaret Peter
  Editor
  (See address above)

SPELLING PROGRESS BULLETIN [1080]

Dedicated to Finding the Causes of Difficulties in Learning, Reading and Spelling
5848 Alcove Avenue
North Hollywood, California 91607
(213) 763-9397

SUBSCRIPTION DATA

Issues and rates: Published quarterly.
Average paid circulation: Not available.
Annual rate(s): $3.00; Foreign $5.00
Publisher or Sponsor: Phonemic Spelling Council
Managing Editor: Newell W. Tune

EDITORIAL DESCRIPTION

Publishes various phases of research in reading, spelling, spelling reform, phonetics, language reform, artificial alphabets, etc. Editorial point of view emphasizes usefulness of simplification of English spelling.
Articles per average issue: 4-5
Audience: Educators
Manuscripts accepted in English

MANUSCRIPT INFORMATION

Subject field(s): Reading research, spelling research, spelling reform, reading difficulties, spelling difficulties, alphabet reform, phonetics, allied subjects
Manuscript requirements: See latest issue for style requirements.
Preferred length: 1000 to 10,000 words
Number of copies to be submitted: One
Abstract: Not necessary. Reprints only. Six copies of issue
Is simultaneous submission of article to other journals permitted: Yes
Exclusive manuscript rights between acceptance and publication: Yes
Copyright: Held by author.
Reprints: Available at $.75 per issue
Additional information: Title page of any issue will be supplied on request.
Disposition of manuscript:
Query letter: Not necessary.
Receipt of manuscript acknowledged: Yes
Decision to publish in: 2-4 weeks
Accepted manuscript published in: 1-4 months
Rejected manuscript returned: Yes
Rejected manuscript criticized: Yes, if requested
Submit to:
Newell W. Tune
Editor
(See address above)

STUDENT PERSONNEL ASSOCIATION FOR TEACHER EDUCATION. JOURNAL [1081]

1607 New Hampshire Avenue, N.W.
Washington, D.C. 20009
(202) 483-4633

Previously entitled *SPATE*

First published in 1961

SUBSCRIPTION DATA

Issues and rates: Published quarterly.
Average paid circulation: 850
Annual rate(s): $6.50
Publisher or Sponsor: Student Personnel Association for Teacher Education
Managing Editor: Judith Mattson

EDITORIAL DESCRIPTION

Contains articles on teacher and school administrator characteristics, recruitment and selective retention strategies, teacher placement, systems analysis of teacher education, personnel practices for teacher education students. Prefer empirical reports on variables associated with teacher performance.
Articles per average issue: 6
Manuscripts accepted in English only

MANUSCRIPT INFORMATION

Subject field(s): Teacher characteristics, student teaching, selection of students, selection of administrators, perceptions of school environments, teacher employment, career aspirations of teachers, minorities in teaching
Manuscript requirements: APA
Preferred length: Not more than 20 pages
Number of copies to be submitted: Three
Abstract: No
Author information and reprints: Payment: None.
Is simultaneous submission of article to other journals permitted: No
Exclusive manuscript rights between acceptance and publication: Yes
Copyright: Held by publication.
Reprints: Available
Disposition of manuscript:
Query letter: No
Receipt of manuscript acknowledged: Yes
Decision to publish in: 1-3 months
Accepted manuscript published in: 2-4 months
Rejected manuscript returned: Yes
Rejected manuscript criticized: Yes
Submit to:
James C. Dickinson
Editor
3415 Latama Drive
Carrollwood
Tampa, Florida 33618
(813) 933-4111

STUDIES IN ART EDUCATION [1082]

National Art Education Association
1916 Association Drive
Reston, Virginia 22091
(703) 620-3855

First published in 1958

SUBSCRIPTION DATA

Issues and rates: Published three times per year.
Average paid circulation: 3,000
Annual rate(s): $15.00; Foreign $15.00; Individuals $15.00; Institutions $15.00; Students $15.00; Members $10.00 with active membership

Publisher or Sponsor: National Art Education Association
Managing Editor: Beverly Jeanne Davis

EDITORIAL DESCRIPTION

Research in art education; philosophical and historical materials; empirical research studies; a scholarly examination of issues and research in the field of art education.
Articles per average issue: 8-10
Audience: College and university art education faculty, especially those involved in or interested in research, philosophy, and theory; elementary and secondary art teachers and consultants; art education college students.
Manuscripts accepted in English

MANUSCRIPT INFORMATION

Subject field(s): Scholarly reports and discussions of current research in the field of art education; scholarly papers on the philosophy of art education or on the historical development of art education; reports of empirical research in the field of art education.
Manuscript requirements: See latest issue for style requirements. Style sheet sent on request. APA
Preferred length: 10-25 pages
Number of copies to be submitted: Original and two copies
Abstract: Not necessary.
Author information and reprints: Payment: None.
Is simultaneous submission of article to other journals permitted: Not permitted.
Exclusive manuscript rights between acceptance and publication: Yes
Copyright: Author and publisher
Reprints: Available at cost. 1 free copy of issue sent to author
Disposition of manuscript:
Query letter: Not necessary.
Receipt of manuscript acknowledged: Yes
Decision to publish in: 8 months
Accepted manuscript published in: 6 months
Rejected manuscript returned: Yes, with return postage paid by publication.
Rejected manuscript criticized: Yes
Submit to:
Dr. Marylou Kuhn
Editor
Department of Art Education
The Florida State University
Tallahassee, Florida 32306

STUDIES IN PHILOSOPHY AND EDUCATION [1083]

Southern Illinois University
Edwardsville, Illinois 62025
(618) 692-2808

First published in 1960

SUBSCRIPTION DATA

Issues and rates: Published three times per year.
Annual rate(s): $8.00; Foreign $9.50; Institutions $9.00; Students $8.00; Foreign institutions $9.50

Publisher or Sponsor: Philosophy of
   Education Society
Managing Editor: Francis Villemain

EDITORIAL DESCRIPTION

Technical discussions in the field of the
philosophy of education
Articles per average issue: Varies
Audience: Educators, philosophers
   Manuscripts accepted in English

MANUSCRIPT INFORMATION

Subject field(s): Fairly technical statements
   in the philosophy of education dealing
   with the growing edge of thought therein.
Manuscript requirements: MLA
   Preferred length: 3,000-5,000 words;
      12-15 typewritten pages
   Number of copies to be submitted: 3
   Abstract: Yes. A brief, objective
      description of the contents of the paper.
Author information and reprints: Payment:
      None.
   Is simultaneous submission of article to
      other journals permitted: Not permitted.
   Exclusive manuscript rights between
      acceptance and publication: Yes
Additional information: Articles should be
   scholarly, documented, well written. Case
   studies are welcome, as long as they are
   analyzed for clinical application by
   readers.
Disposition of manuscript:
   Query letter: Not necessary.
   Receipt of manuscript acknowledged: Yes
   Decision to publish in: 1-2 months
   Accepted manuscript published in: 1 year
   Rejected manuscript returned: Yes, if
      return postage is supplied by author.
   Rejected manuscript criticized: Reasons
      for rejections only
Submit to:
   Editor-in-Chief
   (See address above)

TEACHER [1084]

The Professional Magazine of the
Elementary Grades
P. O. Box 800
Cos Cob, Connecticut 06807
(203) 869-8585

Previously entitled *Grade Teacher*

First published in 1882

SUBSCRIPTION DATA

Issues and rates: 9 issues per school year
   Average paid circulation: 255,712
   Annual rate(s): $10.00; Foreign $13.50
Managing Editor: Dianne M. Shannon

EDITORIAL DESCRIPTION

Presents articles and ideas that can be
adapted by the individual teacher for
classroom use.
Articles per average issue: 36
Audience: Elementary school teachers
   Manuscripts accepted in English only

MANUSCRIPT INFORMATION

Subject field(s): Any field with direct
   classroom interest and application
Manuscript requirements: Style sheet sent
   on request.
   Preferred length: As required
   Number of copies to be submitted: 2
   Abstract: Not necessary.
Author information and reprints: Payment:
   By publication to author.
   Is simultaneous submission of article to
      other journals permitted: Not permitted.
   Exclusive manuscript rights between
      acceptance and publication: Yes
   Copyright: Held by publication.
   Reprints: Available at cost.
Additional information: Typewritten,
   double-spaced, with wide margins.
Disposition of manuscript:
   Query letter: Not necessary, but
      advisable.
   Receipt of manuscript acknowledged: No
   Decision to publish in: 1 month
   Rejected manuscript returned: Yes, if
      return postage is supplied by author.
   Rejected manuscript criticized: No
Submit to:
   Manuscript Editor
   One Fawcett Place
   Greenwich, Connecticut 06830

THE TEACHER OF THE DEAF [1085]

The Journal of the National College of
Teachers of the Deaf
32, Merston Drive
East Didsbury
Manchester M20 0WT, England
061-434-2704

First published in 1902

SUBSCRIPTION DATA

Issues and rates: Published bi-monthly.
   Average paid circulation: 500; 1500
      controlled
   Annual rate(s): £2.90
Publisher or Sponsor: National College of
   Teachers of the Deaf

EDITORIAL DESCRIPTION

Contains articles on the practice,
administration, curriculum and history of
the education of the deaf.
Articles per average issue: 4
Audience: Teachers of the deaf,
   administrators, medical workers,
   researchers, speech therapists,
   audiologists
   Manuscripts accepted in English

MANUSCRIPT INFORMATION

Subject field(s): Education of deaf: teaching,
   methods, curriculum, administration,
   research, history, audiology
Manuscript requirements: Style sheet sent
   on request.
   Preferred length: 8000 words maximum
   Number of copies to be submitted: Two
   Abstract: Yes. Details for preparation
      sent on request
Author information and reprints: Payment:
      None.
   Is simultaneous submission of article to
      other journals permitted: No
   Exclusive manuscript rights between
      acceptance and publication: Yes
   Copyright: Held by publication.
   Reprints: Available at cost if ordered
      when manuscript is submitted
Additional information: Use brackets in text
   rather than footnotes.
Disposition of manuscript:
   Query letter: No, but helpful
   Receipt of manuscript acknowledged: Yes
   Decision to publish in: 2 weeks
   Accepted manuscript published in: 2-12
      months
   Rejected manuscript returned: Yes
   Rejected manuscript criticized: Yes
Submit to:
   John Kenneth Reeves
   Editor
   (See address above)

THE TEACHER PAPER [1086]

2221 N. E. 23rd Street
Portland, Oregon 97212
(203) 282-2443

First published in 1968

SUBSCRIPTION DATA

Issues and rates: 5 times per year
   Average paid circulation: 2,500
   Annual rate(s): $8.00; Foreign $15.00;
      Institutions $8.00; Students $8.00;
      Foreign individuals $5.00; Foreign
      institutions $15.00
Managing Editor: Robin B. Staab

EDITORIAL DESCRIPTION

A journal of fact and opinion published
for classroom teachers by classroom
teachers in hopes of humanizing the
public schools.
Articles per average issue: 8
Audience: Classroom teachers (pre-school to
   12 grade), parents, citizens
   Manuscripts accepted in English

MANUSCRIPT INFORMATION

Subject field(s): Any subject concerning
   human beings in schools or learning
   situations
Manuscript requirements: See latest issue for
   style requirements.
   Preferred length: 500 to 2,500 words
   Number of copies to be submitted: 1
   Abstract: Not necessary.
Author information and reprints: Payment:
   By publication to author. 1 cent per
   word.
   Is simultaneous submission of article to
      other journals permitted: Permitted.
   Exclusive manuscript rights between
      acceptance and publication: No
   Copyright: Held by publication.
   Reprints: Available at no cost. Available
      at cost.
Additional information: No jargon please.
Disposition of manuscript:
   Query letter: Not necessary.
   Receipt of manuscript acknowledged: No
   Decision to publish in: 2-3 months
   Accepted manuscript published in: Varies
   Rejected manuscript returned: Yes, if
      return postage is supplied by author.

Rejected manuscript criticized:
Sometimes
Submit to:
Robin B. Staab;
Fred L. Staab
Editors/Publishers
(See address above)

TEACHER'S VOICE [1087]
1216 Kendale Boulevard, Box 673
East Lansing, Michigan 48823
(517) 332-6551 ext. 277

Previously entitled *Michigan Education Journal*

First published in 1923

SUBSCRIPTION DATA
Issues and rates: Published bi-weekly.
 Average paid circulation: 84,893
 Annual rate(s): $4.00, Foreign $4.50
Publisher or Sponsor: Michigan Education Association

EDITORIAL DESCRIPTION
 Contains articles on current state and federal issues of concern to teachers, administrators, and school-related personnel.
Articles per average issue: Unsolicited manuscripts are not published in every issue
Audience: K-12, higher education teachers
 Manuscripts accepted in English

MANUSCRIPT INFORMATION
Subject field(s): Education or topics relevant to educators, such as political action, etc.
Manuscript requirements: Style sheet sent on request.
 Preferred length: 1,500 words maximum
 Number of copies to be submitted: One
 Abstract: No
Author information and reprints: Payment: None.
 Is simultaneous submission of article to other journals permitted: No
 Exclusive manuscript rights between acceptance and publication: Yes
 Copyright: No copyright
 Reprints: Available at minimal cost.
Disposition of manuscript:
 Query letter: No, but recommended
 Receipt of manuscript acknowledged: Yes
 Decision to publish in: Within a month
 Accepted manuscript published in: As soon as possible.
 Rejected manuscript returned: Yes
 Rejected manuscript criticized: No
Submit to:
 Elwood W. Landis
 Managing Editor
 (See address above)

TEACHING POLITICAL SCIENCE [1088]
Sage Publications, Inc.
275 South Beverly Drive
Beverly Hills, California 90212
(213) 274-2423

First published in 1974

SUBSCRIPTION DATA
Issues and rates: Published quarterly.
 Average paid circulation: Not available.
 Annual rate(s): Institutions $20.00; Individuals $12.00

EDITORIAL DESCRIPTION
 Emphasizes teaching with direct application to the subject matter of political science.
Articles per average issue: 8-10
Audience: Academic
 Manuscripts accepted in English

MANUSCRIPT INFORMATION
Subject field(s): Teaching, political science
Manuscript requirements: Style sheet sent on request.
 Preferred length: 6,250-7,500 words; 25 to 30 pages
 Number of copies to be submitted: Two
 Abstract: No
Author information and reprints: Payment: Reprints only. 25 tear-sheets
 Is simultaneous submission of article to other journals permitted: Permitted, but not encouraged. Author must notify publisher that manuscript is under consideration elsewhere.
 Exclusive manuscript rights between acceptance and publication: Yes
 Copyright: Held by publication.
 Reprints: Available if purchased by special order in amounts no fewer than 100
Disposition of manuscript:
 Query letter: No
 Receipt of manuscript acknowledged: Yes
 Decision to publish in: 6-8 weeks
 Accepted manuscript published in: 12-18 months
 Rejected manuscript returned: Yes
 Rejected manuscript criticized: Yes
Submit to:
 Samuel Krislov
 Editor
 Department of Political Science
 University of Minnesota
 Minneapolis, Minnesota 55455

THE TEXAS ELEMENTARY PRINCIPALS AND SUPERVISORS ASSOCIATION. JOURNAL [1089]
316 West Twelfth Street
Austin, Texas 78701
(817) 382-3702

First published in 1970

SUBSCRIPTION DATA
Issues and rates: December and April
 Average paid circulation: 2000
 Annual rate(s): $2.00, Foreign $3.00
Publisher or Sponsor: Texas Elementary Principals and Supervisors Association

EDITORIAL DESCRIPTION
 Contents are primarily directed toward the improvement of administrative and supervisory leadership roles at the various elementary school levels.
Articles per average issue: 8-10
Audience: Elementary principals, supervisors, and teachers
 Manuscripts accepted in English

MANUSCRIPT INFORMATION
Subject field(s): All elementary subject matter and role levels.
Manuscript requirements: Style sheet sent on request.
 Preferred length: 8 pages
 Number of copies to be submitted: Two
 Abstract: No
Author information and reprints: Payment: Reprints only. 3 copies
 Is simultaneous submission of article to other journals permitted: No
 Exclusive manuscript rights between acceptance and publication: Yes
 Copyright: Held by publication.
 Reprints: Not available.
Additional information: The editor and editorial review committee favor articles which are well researched, written from a writer's particular point of view. Contents should be of a practical nature, able to withstand critical review and analysis.
Disposition of manuscript:
 Query letter: No
 Receipt of manuscript acknowledged: Yes
 Decision to publish in: 3 weeks
 Accepted manuscript published in: 3-6 months
 Rejected manuscript returned: Yes, if self-addressed, stamped envelope is sent with manuscript.
 Rejected manuscript criticized: If requested
Submit to:
 R. C. Bradley
 Editor-in-Chief
 2032 Houston Place
 Denton, Texas 76201

THEOLOGICAL EDUCATION [1090]
Box 396
Vandalia, Ohio 45377
(513) 898-4654

First published in 1964

SUBSCRIPTION DATA
Issues and rates: Published quarterly.
 Average paid circulation: 3,900
 Annual rate(s): $4.50
Publisher or Sponsor: Association of Theological Schools in the U.S. and Canada
Managing Editor: Jesse H. Ziegler

EDITORIAL DESCRIPTION
 Primary interest is to address faculty, administrative staff, boards of trustees, and students of theological schools engaged primarily in education for ministry, priesthood, or rabbinate, regarding the nature of such education.
Articles per average issue: 7 or 8
 Manuscripts accepted in English

MANUSCRIPT INFORMATION
Subject field(s): Theological education: teaching method, curriculum design, field work, evaluation, models of organization, place of special groups, relationship to churches, etc.
Manuscript requirements: See latest issue for style requirements. Chicago
  Preferred length: 3,500 words
  Number of copies to be submitted: 1
  Abstract: Not necessary.
Author information and reprints: Payment: Reprints only. 5
  Is simultaneous submission of article to other journals permitted: Permitted, but not encouraged.
  Exclusive manuscript rights between acceptance and publication: No
  Copyright: Material is not copyrighted
  Reprints: Available at cost.
Additional information: Manuscript should be typed, double-spaced
Disposition of manuscript:
  Query letter: Not necessary, but advisable.
  Receipt of manuscript acknowledged: Yes
  Decision to publish in: 30 to 60 days
  Accepted manuscript published in: 6 to 15 months
  Rejected manuscript returned: Yes, if return postage is supplied by author.
  Rejected manuscript criticized: No
Submit to:
  Jesse H. Ziegler
  Editor-in-chief
  (See address above)

TODAY'S CATHOLIC TEACHER [1091]
2451 East River Road
Dayton, Ohio 45439
(513) 294-5785

First published in 1967

SUBSCRIPTION DATA
Issues and rates: 8 issues per year
  Average paid circulation: 4,000; 63,000 controlled
  Annual rate(s): $6.00, Foreign $7.00

EDITORIAL DESCRIPTION
  Publishes articles, features, and columns pertaining to educational philosophy and practice, particularly as they relate to the nonpublic school in general and Catholic school in particular.
Articles per average issue: 5
Audience: Catholic educators
  Manuscripts accepted in English

MANUSCRIPT INFORMATION
Subject field(s): Curriculum, school philosophy, educational innovation, professional concerns, parent-teacher relationships
Manuscript requirements: Style sheet sent on request.
  Preferred length: 800-1200, 1500-3000 words
  Number of copies to be submitted: One
  Abstract: No
Author information and reprints: Payment: By publication to author. $20.00 to $75.00 per article.
  Is simultaneous submission of article to other journals permitted: No
  Exclusive manuscript rights between acceptance and publication: Yes
  Copyright: Held by publication.
  Reprints: Available, $.25 each
Disposition of manuscript:
  Query letter: Preferred
  Receipt of manuscript acknowledged: No
  Decision to publish in: 1-2 months
  Accepted manuscript published in: 2-3 months
  Rejected manuscript returned: Yes, if return postage is supplied by author.
  Rejected manuscript criticized: Sometimes
Submit to:
  Ruth A. Matheny
  Editor
  (See address above)
  (513) 294-5785

SPECIAL STIPULATIONS
  Articles dealing with Catholic school situations are given preference.

TODAY'S EDUCATION [1092]
NEA Journal
1201 16th Street NW
Washington, D.C. 20036
(202) 833-5442

Previously entitled *NEA Journal*

First published in 1913

SUBSCRIPTION DATA
Issues and rates: Published quarterly.
  Average paid circulation: 1,600,000
  Annual rate(s): $7.00
Publisher or Sponsor: National Education Association of the U.S.
Executive Editor: Walter Graves

EDITORIAL DESCRIPTION
  Includes both articles of general educational interest and on special subjects.
Articles per average issue: 25
Audience: Public school teachers and administrators
  Manuscripts accepted in English

MANUSCRIPT INFORMATION
Subject field(s): Critical issues in American education
Manuscript requirements: Typed, double-spaced; further details available on request
  Preferred length: 1,200-2,500 words
  Number of copies to be submitted: One original
Author information and reprints: Payment: None.
  Is simultaneous submission of article to other journals permitted: No
  Exclusive manuscript rights between acceptance and publication: Yes
  Copyright: Held by publication.
  Reprints: Available at minimal cost
Disposition of manuscript:
  Query letter: No
  Receipt of manuscript acknowledged: Yes
  Decision to publish in: 2 months
  Accepted manuscript published in: Varies
  Rejected manuscript returned: Yes
  Rejected manuscript criticized: No
Submit to:
  Mildred S. Fenner
  Editor
  (See address above)

SPECIAL STIPULATIONS
  Include a self-addressed stamped envelope with submission.

UNITED STATES TRACK AND FIELD QUARTERLY REVIEW [1093]
745 State Circle
Ann Arbor, Michigan 48104
(616) 349-1008

Previously entitled *Track & Field Clinic Notes,* 1932

First published in 1964

SUBSCRIPTION DATA
Issues and rates: Published quarterly.
  Average paid circulation: 1500; 500 controlled
  Annual rate(s): $15.00; Foreign $10.00; Students $8.00
Publisher or Sponsor: U.S. Track Coaches Association

EDITORIAL DESCRIPTION
  Contains articles on professional technical coaching of track and field.
Articles per average issue: 10-12
Audience: Academic
  Manuscripts accepted in English

MANUSCRIPT INFORMATION
Subject field(s): Track and field, research, scientific, book reviews
Manuscript requirements: Style sheet sent on request.
  Preferred length: No limit
  Number of copies to be submitted: One
  Abstract: Yes
Author information and reprints: Payment: None.
  Is simultaneous submission of article to other journals permitted: Yes, with approval
  Exclusive manuscript rights between acceptance and publication: No
  Copyright: Held by both author and publication.
  Reprints: Available at cost.
Disposition of manuscript:
  Query letter: No
  Receipt of manuscript acknowledged: Yes
  Decision to publish in: One month
  Accepted manuscript published in: 1 to 6 months
  Rejected manuscript returned: Yes
  Rejected manuscript criticized: Yes

Submit to:
G. G. Dales
Editor
Department of Physical Education and Athletics
Western Michigan University
Kalamazoo, Michigan 49001
(616) 349-1008

UNIVERSITY OF CHICAGO SCHOOL REVIEW* [1094]

University of Chicago Press
5801 Ellis Avenue
Chicago, Illinois 60637
(312) 753-2592

SUBSCRIPTION DATA

Issues and rates: Published quarterly.
  Average paid circulation: 4,000
  Annual rate(s): Individuals $10, Institutions $14
Publisher or Sponsor: University of Chicago, Department of Education

EDITORIAL DESCRIPTION

Seeks to develop and maintain a lively forum for the communication and discussion of vital issues in education.

MANUSCRIPT INFORMATION

Subject field(s): Higher education, all levels of education, psychology, sociology
Manuscript requirements: Chicago
  Preferred length: None
  Number of copies to be submitted: Three
Author information and reprints: Payment: None.
  Exclusive manuscript rights between acceptance and publication: Yes
  Copyright: Held by the University of Chicago
  Reprints: Available, cost varies by length
Disposition of manuscript:
  Receipt of manuscript acknowledged: Yes
  Decision to publish in: 1-2 months
  Accepted manuscript published in: 3-12 months
  Rejected manuscript returned: Yes, if self-addressed, stamped envelope is sent with manuscript.
  Rejected manuscript criticized: No
Submit to:
  Benjamin D. Wright
  Editor
  5835 Kimbark Avenue
  Chicago, Illinois 60637
  (312) 753-3814

URBAN EDUCATION [1095]

Sage Publications, Inc.
275 South Beverly Drive
Beverly Hills, California 90212
(213) 274-2423

First published in 1965

SUBSCRIPTION DATA

Issues and rates: Published quarterly.
  Average paid circulation: 1,000; 30 controlled
  Annual rate(s): Institutions $15.00; Individuals $10.00; Students $8.00; Foreign individuals $11.50; Foreign institutions $16.50

EDITORIAL DESCRIPTION

Publishes articles concerned with the measurement and evaluation of pupil learning
Articles per average issue: 6-8
Audience: Scholars, researchers, school administrators
Manuscripts accepted in English

MANUSCRIPT INFORMATION

Subject field(s): assessment of administrative organization, expenditures, relationships with community and clientele, and of anticipated results. Relevant fields include jurisprudence, psychology, sociology, political science, anthropology, economics, philosophy, medicine, administration, and history.
Manuscript requirements: Style sheet sent on request. ASA modified
  Preferred length: 2,500-5,000 words; 10-20 pages
  Number of copies to be submitted: Two
  Abstract: No
Author information and reprints: Payment: Reprints only. 25 tear-sheets
  Is simultaneous submission of article to other journals permitted: Permitted, but discouraged. Author must notify publisher that manuscript is under consideration elsewhere.
  Exclusive manuscript rights between acceptance and publication: Yes
  Copyright: Held by publication.
  Reprints: Available if purchased by special order in amounts no fewer than 100
Disposition of manuscript:
  Query letter: No
  Receipt of manuscript acknowledged: Yes
  Decision to publish in: 8-12 weeks
  Accepted manuscript published in: 6-9 months
  Rejected manuscript returned: Yes
  Rejected manuscript criticized: Yes
Submit to:
  Warren Button
  Editor
  Department of Social Foundations of Education
  305 Foster Hall
  State University of New York at Buffalo
  Buffalo, New York 14214

THE VOCATIONAL GUIDANCE QUARTERLY [1096]

1607 New Hampshire Avenue NW
Washington, D.C. 20009
(202) 483-4633

First published in 1952

SUBSCRIPTION DATA

Issues and rates: Published quarterly.
  Average paid circulation: 20,000
  Annual rate(s): $10.00, Foreign $10.50
Publisher or Sponsor: National Vocational Guidance Association
Managing Editor: Robert A. Malone

EDITORIAL DESCRIPTION

Concerned with the role of work in the life of man. Work is interpreted as meaningful activity which plays a role during all stages of life, from childhood to retirement years.
Articles per average issue: 15
Audience: Counselors and guidance workers
Manuscripts accepted in English only

MANUSCRIPT INFORMATION

Subject field(s): Vocational development, vocational planning, occupational choice, preparation for occupations, labor market dynamics, job finding, job satisfaction
Manuscript requirements: Style sheet sent on request.
  Preferred length: 2500 words; 10 pages
  Number of copies to be submitted: Three
  Abstract: Yes, of 30 words
Author information and reprints: Payment: None. 5 copies of the journal.
  Is simultaneous submission of article to other journals permitted: No
  Exclusive manuscript rights between acceptance and publication: Yes
  Copyright: Held by publication.
  Reprints: Available at no cost.
Additional information: Reports of research and discussions of theory are welcome, but authors are expected to extend conclusions to practical applications.
Disposition of manuscript:
  Query letter: No
  Receipt of manuscript acknowledged: Yes
  Decision to publish in: 2-3 months
  Accepted manuscript published in: 6-9 months
  Rejected manuscript returned: Yes
  Rejected manuscript criticized: Yes
Submit to:
  Daniel Sinick
  Editor
  George Washington University
  Washington, D.C. 20006
  (202) 676-6376

THE VOLTA REVIEW [1097]

3417 Volta Place, N.W.
Washington, D.C. 20007
(202) 337-5220

Previously entitled *The Association Review*

First published in 1899

SUBSCRIPTION DATA

Issues and rates: Monthly except June, July, or August
  Average paid circulation: 7000
  Annual rate(s): $15.00; Students $10.00, Pan-Am $16.00, Foreign $16.50
Publisher or Sponsor: The Alexander Graham Bell Association for the Deaf
Managing Editor: Dr. George W. Fellendorf

EDITORIAL DESCRIPTION

Publishes articles related to speech and hearing, education of the deaf, social and

vocational development of deaf and hard of hearing children and adults.
Articles per average issue: 6
Audience: Professionals in speech and hearing, parents of communication-handicapped children, deaf individuals
Manuscripts accepted in English

MANUSCRIPT INFORMATION
Subject field(s): Speech, hearing-auditory training, education of the hearing impaired, language development of children with auditory impairment, social adjustment of the hearing handicapped, audiology-otology, linguistics, parent education, teacher training, research in communication sciences, legislation for handicapped, personal accomplishments of deaf children/adults
Manuscript requirements: APA. Also request "Information for Authors." Footnotes, references, tables and charts, photos on separate pages.
  Preferred length: 2400 words; 9 pages
  Number of copies to be submitted: Three
  Abstract: Yes. 100-200 word abstract
Author information and reprints: Payment: None.
  Is simultaneous submission of article to other journals permitted: No
  Exclusive manuscript rights between acceptance and publication: Yes
  Copyright: Held by publication.
  Reprints: Available on request in quantities of 50 or more for new reprints.
Additional information: For anonymous editorial evaluation, the author's name and affiliation should appear only on a separate covering page.
Disposition of manuscript:
  Query letter: No
  Receipt of manuscript acknowledged: Yes
  Decision to publish in: 60-90 days
  Accepted manuscript published in: 1-5 months
  Rejected manuscript returned: Yes
  Rejected manuscript criticized: No
Submit to:
  Robin Wittusen
  Associate Editor
  (See address above)

YOUNG CHILDREN [1098]
1834 Connecticut Avenue NW
Washington, D.C. 20009
(202) 232-8777

Previously entitled *Journal of Nursery Education*

First published in 1956

SUBSCRIPTION DATA
Issues and rates: Published bi-monthly.
  Average paid circulation: 24,000
  Annual rate(s): $10.00, Members $15.00
Publisher or Sponsor: National Association for the Education of Young Children

EDITORIAL DESCRIPTION
  Contains articles related to the needs, development and education of children from birth to eight years.

Articles per average issue: 6
Audience: Persons engaged in working with young children
Manuscripts accepted in English

MANUSCRIPT INFORMATION
Subject field(s): Child development, early education, teacher training, curriculum ideas, research
Manuscript requirements: No specific style guide.
  Preferred length: 5,000-10,000 words
  Number of copies to be submitted: Two
  Abstract: No
Author information and reprints: Payment: None.
  Is simultaneous submission of article to other journals permitted: No
  Exclusive manuscript rights between acceptance and publication: Yes
  Copyright: Held by publication.
  Reprints: Available, cost depends on length.
Disposition of manuscript:
  Query letter: No
  Receipt of manuscript acknowledged: Yes
  Decision to publish in: 10-12 weeks
  Accepted manuscript published in: Varies
  Rejected manuscript returned: Yes
  Rejected manuscript criticized: Yes
Submit to:
  Georgiana Engstrom
  Editor
  (See address above)

Geography

Geography

THE ASSOCIATION OF AMERICAN GEOGRAPHERS ANNALS [1099]
1710 Sixteenth Street, N.W.
Washington, D.C. 20009
(612) 373-0273

First published in 1911

SUBSCRIPTION DATA
Issues and rates: Published quarterly.
  Average paid circulation: 8,000
  Annual rate(s): $20.00, Foreign $24.00
Publisher or Sponsor: The Association of American Geographers
Managing Editor: John Fraser Hart

EDITORIAL DESCRIPTION
  Contains results of scholarly geographic research.
Articles per average issue: 6-12
Audience: Geographers
  Manuscripts accepted in English

MANUSCRIPT INFORMATION
Subject field(s): Geography
Manuscript requirements: See latest issue for style requirements.
  Preferred length: Maximum 20,000 words
  Number of copies to be submitted: One
  Abstract: Yes
Author information and reprints: Payment: None.
  Is simultaneous submission of article to other journals permitted: No
  Exclusive manuscript rights between acceptance and publication: Yes
  Copyright: Held by Association of American Geographers
  Reprints: Available, cost varies with length
Disposition of manuscript:
  Query letter: No
  Receipt of manuscript acknowledged: Yes
  Decision to publish in: Four months
  Accepted manuscript published in: Four months
  Rejected manuscript returned: Yes
  Rejected manuscript criticized: Yes
Submit to:
  John Fraser Hart
  Editor
  Department of Geography
  University of Minnesota
  Minneapolis, Minnesota 55455
  (612) 373-0273

DIRECTIONS [1100]
The New Jersey Journal of Geography
Department of Geography
Trenton State College
Trenton, New Jersey 08625
(609) 771-2197

First published in 1973

SUBSCRIPTION DATA
Issues and rates: Published quarterly.
  Average paid circulation: 220; 460 controlled
  Annual rate(s): $2.00 for all; Students $1.00 Members $2.00
Publisher or Sponsor: New Jersey Council for Geographic Education
Managing Editor: Percy H. Dougherty

EDITORIAL DESCRIPTION
  Intended to act as a forum for New Jersey geographers and advance the statis of the discipline.
Articles per average issue: 2
Audience: Geographers
  Manuscripts accepted in English

MANUSCRIPT INFORMATION
Subject field(s): Geography with a stress on New Jersey and teacher education topics, earth science, cartography, environmental studies, regional science, spatial analysis, theoretical geography, and computer graphics.
Manuscript requirements: See latest issue for style requirements. AAG
  Preferred length: Varied words; less than 10 pages
  Abstract: Yes. 100 words or less
Author information and reprints: Payment: None.
  Is simultaneous submission of article to other journals permitted: Permitted, but not encouraged.
  Exclusive manuscript rights between acceptance and publication: No
  Reprints: Available at cost.
Disposition of manuscript:
  Query letter: Not necessary, but advisable.
  Receipt of manuscript acknowledged: Yes
  Decision to publish in: 3 months
  Accepted manuscript published in: 3 months
  Rejected manuscript returned: Yes, with return postage paid by publication.
  Rejected manuscript criticized: Yes
Submit to:
  Percy H. Dougherty
  Editor
  (See address above)

GEOFORUM [1101]
The International Multi-disciplinary Journal of Physical, Human and Regional Geosciences
Pergamon Press Ltd.
Headington Hill Hall
Oxford OX3 OBW, England
(0865) Oxford 64881

First published in 1970

SUBSCRIPTION DATA
Issues and rates: Published quarterly.
  Annual rate(s): $42.60(U.S.)

EDITORIAL DESCRIPTION
  A platform on which to build an efficient system for the close evaluation and dissemination of knowledge of our geographical environment by closely monitoring the state of current and future research. Individual issues are devoted to a specific topic.
Articles per average issue: 10-12
Audience: Professional geoscientists in all disciplines
  Manuscripts accepted in English, French, German

MANUSCRIPT INFORMATION
Subject field(s): All fields of geoscience: cities and urbanism, land reclamation, aerial and spatial observation techniques, economic geography, etc.
Manuscript requirements: See latest issue for style requirements. Style sheet sent on request.
  Preferred length: 9,000 words; 30 pages
  Number of copies to be submitted: 2
  Abstract: Yes. A summary is required in English, French as well as German. Figure and table captions also in these languages.
Author information and reprints: Payment: Reprints only. main articles, 50 reprints; reports, 25 reprints
  Is simultaneous submission of article to other journals permitted: Permitted, but not encouraged.
  Exclusive manuscript rights between acceptance and publication: Yes
  Copyright: Held by publication.
  Reprints: Available at cost.

Disposition of manuscript:
  Query letter: Not necessary, but advisable.
  Receipt of manuscript acknowledged: Yes
  Decision to publish in: 1-3 months
  Accepted manuscript published in: 9 months
  Rejected manuscript returned: Sometimes

Submit to:
  Dr. Wolf Tietze
  Executive Editor
  Einsteinstrasse 5
  D-3180 Wolfsburg, Federal Republic of Germany
  (05361) 49589

GEOGRAPHICAL ANALYSIS [1102]
An International Journal of Theoretical Geography
Ohio State University Press
2070 Neil Avenue
Columbus, Ohio 43210
(614) 422-6930

First published in 1969

SUBSCRIPTION DATA
Issues and rates: Published quarterly.
  Average paid circulation: 1,150
  Annual rate(s): Individuals $12.00, Institutions $14.00, Students $8.00
Managing Editor: Richard A. McKee

EDITORIAL DESCRIPTION
  Contains formulation and verification of geographic theory through mathematical analysis and model-building.
Articles per average issue: 8

Audience: Geographers, regional planners
Manuscripts accepted in English

MANUSCRIPT INFORMATION

Subject field(s): Regional analysis, location theory, migration patterns, demographics, network analysis, spatial trends, growth patterns
Manuscript requirements: Style sheet sent on request.
Preferred length: 10-25 pages
Number of copies to be submitted: Two
Abstract: Yes
Author information and reprints: Payment: None.
Is simultaneous submission of article to other journals permitted: No
Exclusive manuscript rights between acceptance and publication: Yes
Copyright: Held by publication.
Reprints: Available, cost upon request
Disposition of manuscript:
Receipt of manuscript acknowledged: Yes
Decision to publish in: 6-8 weeks
Accepted manuscript published in: 2-6 months
Rejected manuscript returned: Yes, if self-addressed, stamped envelope is sent with manuscript.
Rejected manuscript criticized: Sometimes
Submit to:
R.G. Golledge
Department of Geography
Ohio State University
Columbus, Ohio 43210
(614) 422-8744

THE GEOGRAPHICAL JOURNAL [1103]

The Royal Geographical Society
1, Kensington Gore
London SW1 2AR, England

First published in 1893

SUBSCRIPTION DATA

Issues and rates: Published three times per year.
Average paid circulation: 10,000
Annual rate(s): £10.00; Foreign $27.00
Publisher or Sponsor: The Royal Geographical Society
Managing Editor: Sir Laurence Kirwan, K.C.M.G.

EDITORIAL DESCRIPTION

Concerned with all aspects of geographical research and exploration; includes book reviews.
Articles per average issue: 12
Audience: Academic and those geographically informed
Manuscripts accepted in English, French

MANUSCRIPT INFORMATION

Subject field(s): No limitations
Manuscript requirements: See latest issue for style requirements. Style sheet sent on request.
Preferred length: Up to 6,000 words
Number of copies to be submitted: 2
Abstract: Yes, 150-200 words
Author information and reprints: Payment: Reprints only. 25 free offprints
Is simultaneous submission of article to other journals permitted: Not permitted.
Exclusive manuscript rights between acceptance and publication: Yes
Copyright: Held by the Royal Geographic Society
Reprints: Available at cost.
Additional information: Maps or diagrams may be prepared by the author or in the Society's drawing office.
Disposition of manuscript:
Query letter: Not necessary.
Receipt of manuscript acknowledged: Yes
Decision to publish in: 1-4 months
Accepted manuscript published in: 3-9 months
Rejected manuscript returned: Yes, with return postage paid by publication.
Rejected manuscript criticized: No
Submit to:
The Editor
(See address above)

THE GEOGRAPHICAL MAGAZINE [1104]

128 Long Acre
London WC2E 9QH, England
836-2468

First published in 1935

SUBSCRIPTION DATA

Issues and rates: Published monthly.
Annual rate(s): £5.70; Foreign £6.90
Publisher or Sponsor: Royal Geographical Society

EDITORIAL DESCRIPTION

Publishes items appealing to people interested in the world from the geographer's viewpoint.
Articles per average issue: Varies
Audience: Professional, academic, general
Manuscripts accepted in English only

MANUSCRIPT INFORMATION

Subject field(s): Any interest in the entire geographic discipline
Manuscript requirements: No specific style guide. See latest issue for style requirements.
Preferred length: 1,500-2,500 words
Number of copies to be submitted: 1
Abstract: Not necessary.
Author information and reprints: Payment: By publication to author. Payment by arrangement
Copyright: By arrangement
Reprints: Available at no cost. 100 minimum Available at cost.
Disposition of manuscript:
Query letter: Not necessary, but advisable.
Receipt of manuscript acknowledged: Yes
Rejected manuscript returned: Yes, if return postage is supplied by author.
Rejected manuscript criticized: Sometimes
Submit to:
Derek Weber
Editor
(See address above)

THE GEOGRAPHICAL REVIEW [1105]

Broadway at 156th Street
New York, New York 10032
(212) 234-8100

First published in 1916

SUBSCRIPTION DATA

Issues and rates: Published quarterly.
Average paid circulation: 6,500
Annual rate(s): $30.00; Foreign $25.00; Institutions $30.00; Students $10.00; Members $25.00
Publisher or Sponsor: The American Geographical Society

EDITORIAL DESCRIPTION

This is an interdisciplinary, international quarterly that publishes original, scholarly, and authoritative articles on topics of geographical significance; also some notes and reviews
Articles per average issue: 6
Audience: Professional, academic
Manuscripts accepted in English

MANUSCRIPT INFORMATION

Subject field(s): Cultural, economic, historical, environmental, biographical, and lesser-known fields of geography as well as specialized fields such as meteorology, climatology and cartography
Manuscript requirements: Chicago
Preferred length: 20-25 pages
Number of copies to be submitted: Original and 1 copy
Abstract: Yes. Of about 125 words
Author information and reprints: Payment: Reprints only. 50 reprints
Is simultaneous submission of article to other journals permitted: Not permitted.
Exclusive manuscript rights between acceptance and publication: Yes
Copyright: Held by publication.
Reprints: Available at cost. $2.00 each
Additional information: Typewritten, double-spaced, footnotes numbered consecutively throughout; authors accepted for publication will be asked to provide finished maps, graphs, and diagrams that are camera-ready copy of previously-sent rough sketches.
Disposition of manuscript:
Query letter: Not necessary.
Receipt of manuscript acknowledged: Yes
Decision to publish in: 4-6 weeks
Accepted manuscript published in: 9-12 months
Rejected manuscript returned: Yes, if return postage is supplied by author.
Rejected manuscript criticized: Sometimes
Submit to:
Dr. Sarah K. Myers
Editor
(See address above)

ILLINOIS GEOGRAPHICAL SOCIETY BULLETIN [1106]

University of Illinois, Chicago Circle
Department of Geography
Chicago, Illinois 60680
(312) 996-3112

SUBSCRIPTION DATA

Issues and rates: Published semi-annually.
  Average paid circulation: 400; 475 controlled
  Annual rate(s): Individuals $4.00, Institutions $5.00, Students $2.50
Publisher or Sponsor: Illinois Geographical Society

EDITORIAL DESCRIPTION

Contains articles on various aspects of geography, including geographic education; news from Illinois geographic centers; coverage of affairs of the Illinois Geographical Society; and various other items of interest to geographers and geographic educators.
Articles per average issue: 4
Audience: Professional geographers and social scientists
  Manuscripts accepted in English

MANUSCRIPT INFORMATION

Subject field(s): Geography, geographic education
Manuscript requirements: See latest issue for style requirements.
  Preferred length: Up to 25 pages
  Number of copies to be submitted: Two
  Abstract: Not necessary
Author information and reprints: Payment: None.
  Is simultaneous submission of article to other journals permitted: No
  Exclusive manuscript rights between acceptance and publication: Yes
  Copyright: Not copyrighted
  Reprints: Not available.
Additional information: All illustrations (maps, photos, etc.) must be suitable for reproduction on 5½ x 8½ inch page.
Disposition of manuscript:
  Receipt of manuscript acknowledged: Yes
  Decision to publish in: One to two months
  Accepted manuscript published in: Six months
  Rejected manuscript returned: Yes
  Rejected manuscript criticized: Yes
Submit to:
  Dr. Albert J. Larson Nelson
  Editor
  (See address above)

JOURNAL OF BIOGEOGRAPHY [1107]

Blackwell Scientific Publications, Ltd.
Osney Mead
Oxford OX2 OEL, England

First published in 1974

SUBSCRIPTION DATA

Issues and rates: Published quarterly.
  Annual rate(s): $34.00

Managing Editor: Dr. David Watts

EDITORIAL DESCRIPTION

Contains multidisciplinary papers in geography and the several areas of biology, including medicine and paleontology.
Articles per average issue: 6
Audience: Professional biologists and geographers
  Manuscripts accepted in English, German, French

MANUSCRIPT INFORMATION

Subject field(s): Biogeography, ecology, distributional ecology, evolutionary ecology
Manuscript requirements: See latest issue for style requirements.
  Preferred length: 10-30 pages
  Number of copies to be submitted: 3
  Abstract: Yes. Of about 50-300 words
Author information and reprints: Payment: Reprints only. 50 reprints
  Is simultaneous submission of article to other journals permitted: Permitted.
  Exclusive manuscript rights between acceptance and publication: Yes
  Copyright: Held by publication.
Disposition of manuscript:
  Query letter: Not necessary.
  Receipt of manuscript acknowledged: Yes
  Decision to publish in: 2-3 months
  Accepted manuscript published in: 6-12 months
  Rejected manuscript returned: Yes, with return postage paid by publication.
  Rejected manuscript criticized: Sometimes
Submit to:
  Daniel Simberloff
  Associate Editor
  Department of Biological Science
  Florida State University
  Tallahassee, Florida 32306
  (904) 644-6739

NATIONAL GEOGRAPHIC [1108]

17th and M Streets, N.W.
Washington, D.C. 20036
(202) 296-7500

First published in 1888

SUBSCRIPTION DATA

Issues and rates: Published monthly.
  Average paid circulation: 8,000,000
  Annual rate(s): $10.00, Members $8.50
Publisher or Sponsor: National Geographic Society
Managing Editor: Gilbert M. Grosvenor

EDITORIAL DESCRIPTION

Publishes first-person articles on human geography, including travel and exploration, mountaineering and seafaring, archeological discoveries, natural history, important or unusual industries, occupations, or commodities, advances in science, and notable festivals and folkways all profusely illustrated in color. The world of today and its people are viewed with interest and sympathetic understanding, without politics and controversy, or criticism and invidious comparisons of morals, religion, and customs.
Articles per average issue: 6-7
Audience: General
  Manuscripts accepted in any language; editor will translate. before publication.

MANUSCRIPT INFORMATION

Subject field(s): Travel, exploration, natural history, science, archaeology, festivals and folkways, industries and occupations
Manuscript requirements: Style sheet sent on request.
  Preferred length: 2000-4000 words
  Number of copies to be submitted: One
Author information and reprints: Payment: By publication to author. $1,500 to $3,000 for text; page rate for unsolicited color photographs, $300.
  Is simultaneous submission of article to other journals permitted: No
  Exclusive manuscript rights between acceptance and publication: Yes
  Copyright: Held by publication.
  Reprints: Not available.
Additional information: Manuscript accompanied by original color transparencies of high quality and interest has a better chance of acceptance.
Disposition of manuscript:
  Query letter: Necessary.
  Receipt of manuscript acknowledged: Yes
  Decision to publish in: 3-4 weeks
  Accepted manuscript published in: 3-4 months
  Rejected manuscript returned: Yes
  Rejected manuscript criticized: No
Submit to:
  Andrew H. Brown
  Assistant Editor
  (See address above)

SPECIAL STIPULATIONS

Articles are not essays, but first-person narratives relating authors' own experiences and observations.

THE PROFESSIONAL GEOGRAPHER [1109]

1710 Sixteenth Street, N.W.
Washington, D.C. 20009
(202) 234-1450

First published in 1949

SUBSCRIPTION DATA

Issues and rates: Published quarterly.
  Average paid circulation: 8,000
  Annual rate(s): $10.00, Foreign $12.00
Publisher or Sponsor: Association of American Geographers

EDITORIAL DESCRIPTION

Contains articles on subjects relating to professional geography.
Articles per average issue: 10-12
Audience: Geographers
  Manuscripts accepted in English

MANUSCRIPT INFORMATION
Manuscript requirements: See latest issue for style requirements.
  Preferred length: 4,000 words; 6 pages, maximum
  Number of copies to be submitted: One
Author information and reprints: Payment: None.
  Is simultaneous submission of article to other journals permitted: No
  Exclusive manuscript rights between acceptance and publication: Yes
  Copyright: Held by publication.
  Reprints: Available on order
Additional information: See Editorial Policy Statement.
Disposition of manuscript:
  Query letter: No
  Receipt of manuscript acknowledged: Yes
  Decision to publish in: 3 months
  Accepted manuscript published in: 6 months
  Rejected manuscript returned: Yes
  Rejected manuscript criticized: Yes
Submit to:
  Donald J. Patton
  Editor
  Department of Geography
  The Florida State University
  Tallahassee, Florida 32306
  (904) 599-2351

REVUE DE GEOGRAPHIE DE MONTREAL [1110]
Les Presses de L'Université de Montreal
Box 6128
Montreal 11, Quebec Canada
(514) 343-7143

Previously entitled *Revue Canadienne de Geographie*

First published in 1947

SUBSCRIPTION DATA
Issues and rates: Published quarterly.
  Annual rate(s): $5.00; Foreign $15.00
Publisher or Sponsor: Ministere de L'Education du Quebec, Conseil National de Recherches du Canada
Managing Editor: Camille Laverdiere

EDITORIAL DESCRIPTION
  Articles, notes, bibliographies and essays based on the works of geographers, environmentalists, urbanists, etc., for the advancement of fundamental research and applied geography
Articles per average issue: 8
Audience: Geographers
  Manuscripts accepted in French and English

MANUSCRIPT INFORMATION
Subject field(s): Physical geography of cold climates, urban geography, economic geography, transportation, ecology
Manuscript requirements: See latest issue for style requirements.
  Preferred length: No preference
  Number of copies to be submitted: 3
  Abstract: Yes. Three abstracts of 18 lines each, one in French, second in English, and the third in the language of the author's choice
Author information and reprints: Payment: Reprints only. 50 reprints, 1 issue
  Is simultaneous submission of article to other journals permitted: Not permitted.
  Exclusive manuscript rights between acceptance and publication: Yes
  Copyright: Held by Les Presses de L'Université de Montreal
  Reprints: Available at no cost. 50 (articles); 25 (notes)
Disposition of manuscript:
  Receipt of manuscript acknowledged: Yes
  Decision to publish in: 3 months
  Accepted manuscript published in: 3-6 months
  Rejected manuscript returned: Yes, with return postage paid by publication.
  Rejected manuscript criticized: Yes
Submit to:
  Camille Laverdiere;
  Nicole Carette
  (See address above)

SOUTHEASTERN GEOGRAPHER [1111]
Journal of the Southeastern Division, Association of American Geographers
Department of Geography
University of North Carolina
Chapel Hill, North Carolina 27514
(919) 933-8901

First published in 1961

SUBSCRIPTION DATA
Issues and rates: Published semi-annually.
  Average paid circulation: 800
  Annual rate(s): $5.00; Foreign $5.00; Institutions $5.00; Students $2.50; Members $5.00; Foreign institutions $5.00
Publisher or Sponsor: Association of American Geographers, Southeastern Division
Managing Editor: Stephen S. Birdsall

EDITORIAL DESCRIPTION
  Publishes research papers of general topical or methodological interest as well as those concerned with the South.
Articles per average issue: Varies; generally 6-10
Audience: Professors and students of geography, others with an interest in the physical and human geography of the South
  Manuscripts accepted in English

MANUSCRIPT INFORMATION
Subject field(s): Primary emphasis on geographic aspects of the South; others should be of special topical or methodological interest to geographers.
Manuscript requirements: See latest issue for style requirements.
  Preferred length: 2,000 to 4,000 words
  Number of copies to be submitted: One
  Abstract: Yes. An abstract is required only for accepted manuscripts; 150-200 words
Author information and reprints: Payment: None.
  Is simultaneous submission of article to other journals permitted: Not permitted.
  Exclusive manuscript rights between acceptance and publication: Yes
  Reprints: Available at cost.
Disposition of manuscript:
  Query letter: Not necessary.
  Receipt of manuscript acknowledged: Yes
  Decision to publish in: 6-8 weeks
  Accepted manuscript published in: Less than 1 year
  Rejected manuscript returned: Yes, with return postage paid by publication.
  Rejected manuscript criticized: Yes
Submit to:
  Stephen S. Birdsall
  Editor
  (See address above)

History

History

ACADIENSIS [1112]
Journal of the History of the Atlantic Region
Dept. of History
University of New Brunswick
Fredericktown, New Brunswick Canada
453-4621/453-4622

First published in Fall 1971

SUBSCRIPTION DATA
Issues and rates: Published semi-annually.
   Annual rate(s): Individuals $5.00;
   Institutions $8.00
Managing Editor: T. William Acheson

EDITORIAL DESCRIPTION
   History and society of the Atlantic provinces of Canada and northern New England
Articles per average issue: 4-5
Audience: University
   Manuscripts accepted in French and English

MANUSCRIPT INFORMATION
Subject field(s): History, literary history, historical demography, economic history, historical geography of the northern seaboard of North America
Manuscript requirements: See latest issue for style requirements.
   Preferred length: 8,000 to 10,000 words
   Number of copies to be submitted: One
   Abstract: Not necessary.
Author information and reprints: Payment: None.
   Is simultaneous submission of article to other journals permitted: Permitted, but not encouraged.
   Exclusive manuscript rights between acceptance and publication: Yes
   Copyright: Held by publication.
   Reprints: Available at no cost. 15 Available at cost.
Disposition of manuscript:
   Query letter: Not necessary.
   Receipt of manuscript acknowledged: Yes
   Decision to publish in: 3 months
   Accepted manuscript published in: 6 months
   Rejected manuscript returned: Yes, with return postage paid by publication.
   Rejected manuscript criticized: Yes
Disposition of manuscript:
   T. William Acheson
   Editor
   (See address above)

AEROSPACE HISTORIAN [1113]
History Department
Kansas State University
Manhattan, Kansas 66506
(913) 532-6733

Previously entitled *The Air Power Historian*

First published in 1954

SUBSCRIPTION DATA
Issues and rates: Published quarterly.
   Average paid circulation: 5,200; 120 controlled
   Annual rate(s): Individuals $10.00, Institutions $20.00
Publisher or Sponsor: Air Force Historical Foundation
Managing Editor: Carol Brandt

EDITORIAL DESCRIPTION
   Contains a wide variety of articles on aviation history with emphasis on personal experience, lessons of history.
Articles per average issue: 6-7
Audience: Aerospace buffs and historians
   Manuscripts accepted in English

MANUSCRIPT INFORMATION
Subject field(s): Aviation history, aviation politics, military/aviation theory, naval aviation
Manuscript requirements: Type, double-space, ample margins, for more details see latest issue
   Preferred length: Not to exceed 5000 words
   Number of copies to be submitted: 3
Author information and reprints: Payment: None. 10 copies of issue.
   Is simultaneous submission of article to other journals permitted: No
   Exclusive manuscript rights between acceptance and publication: Yes
   Copyright: Held by publication.
   Reprints: Instructions on acceptance of manuscript
Disposition of manuscript:
   Query letter: No
   Receipt of manuscript acknowledged: Yes
   Decision to publish in: 2 months
   Accepted manuscript published in: 3-9 months
   Rejected manuscript returned: Yes
   Rejected manuscript criticized: Yes
Submit to:
   Robin Higham
   Editor
   (See address above)

ALBERTA HISTORICAL REVIEW [1114]
95 Holmwood Avenue NW
Calgary, Alberta, T2K 2G7, Canada
289-8149

First published in 1953

SUBSCRIPTION DATA
Issues and rates: Published quarterly.
   Average paid circulation: 2000; 2400 controlled
   Annual rate(s): $4.00
Publisher or Sponsor: Historical Society of Alberta
Managing Editor: Hugh A. Dempsey

EDITORIAL DESCRIPTION
   Contains articles and papers on the history of Alberta.
Articles per average issue: 3-4
Audience: General
   Manuscripts accepted in English

MANUSCRIPT INFORMATION
Subject field(s): History of Alberta
Manuscript requirements: Type, double-space, one-side of sheet. Use of footnotes acceptable, but within reason. Authors check galleys only. For further details see latest issue of periodical
   Preferred length: 6,000 words
   Number of copies to be submitted: One
Author information and reprints: Payment: None.
   Is simultaneous submission of article to other journals permitted: Yes
   Exclusive manuscript rights between acceptance and publication: No
   Copyright: Held by author.
   Reprints: Available at printer's cost
Disposition of manuscript:
   Query letter: No
   Receipt of manuscript acknowledged: Yes
   Decision to publish in: One month
   Accepted manuscript published in: 6 months
   Rejected manuscript returned: Yes
   Rejected manuscript criticized: If requested
Submit to:
   Editor
   (See address above)

AMERICAN AVIATION HISTORICAL SOCIETY. JOURNAL [1115]
P.O. Box 99
Garden Grove, California 92642
(805) 649-1139

First published in 1956

SUBSCRIPTION DATA
Issues and rates: Published quarterly.
   Average paid circulation: 4500
   Annual rate(s): $12.50
Publisher or Sponsor: American Aviation Historical Society
Managing Editor: James J. Sloan

EDITORIAL DESCRIPTION
   Contains articles on all aspects of aviation.
Articles per average issue: 15
Audience: General
   Manuscripts accepted in English

MANUSCRIPT INFORMATION
Manuscript requirements: See latest issue for style requirements.
   Preferred length: As required
   Number of copies to be submitted: One
   Abstract: No
Author information and reprints: Payment: None.
   Is simultaneous submission of article to other journals permitted: Yes
   Exclusive manuscript rights between acceptance and publication: Yes
   Copyright: Held by publication.
   Reprints: Available

Disposition of manuscript:
  Query letter: No
  Receipt of manuscript acknowledged: Yes
  Decision to publish in: One year
  Accepted manuscript published in: One year
  Rejected manuscript returned: Yes
  Rejected manuscript criticized: Yes
Submit to:
  Martin Cole
  Editor
  (See address above)

THE AMERICAN GENEALOGIST [1116]
1232 39th Street
Des Moines, Iowa 50311
(515) 255-4513

Previously entitled *The New Haven Genealogical Magazine*, 1922-1932

First published in 1922

SUBSCRIPTION DATA
Issues and rates: Published quarterly.
  Annual rate(s): $7.00 Foreign $7.00

EDITORIAL DESCRIPTION
  Devoted genealogy, and to a very limited extent, heraldry; articles deal with the dissemination of genealogical knowledge, the improvement of the genealogical method, the correction of widely printed errors, and reviews of books.
Articles per average issue: 25
Audience: General
  Manuscripts accepted in English (French, German, Italian)

MANUSCRIPT INFORMATION
Subject field(s): Subsidiary and ancillary disciplines of genealogy. In general the period after 1800 is less desired, but all will be judged on their own merits.
Manuscript requirements: No specific style guide. See latest issue for style requirements.
  Preferred length: 10 printed pages
  Number of copies to be submitted: 1
  Abstract: Not necessary.
Author information and reprints: Payment: Reprints only. 1 complimentary copy
  Exclusive manuscript rights between acceptance and publication: Yes
  Copyright: Not copyrighted
  Reprints: Not available.
Additional information: Double-spaced typescript, not a carbon. Previously unpublished material only.
Disposition of manuscript:
  Query letter: Not necessary.
  Receipt of manuscript acknowledged: Yes
  Decision to publish in: Promptly
  Accepted manuscript published in: Varies
  Rejected manuscript returned: Yes, if return postage is supplied by author.
  Rejected manuscript criticized: Yes
Submit to:
  George E. McCracken
  Editor
  (See address above)

AMERICAN HERITAGE [1117]
The Magazine of History
1221 Avenue of the Americas
New York, New York 10020
(212) 997-1221

First published in 1954

SUBSCRIPTION DATA
Issues and rates: Published bi-monthly.
  Average paid circulation: 210,000
  Annual rate(s): $24.00
Managing Editor: Oliver Jensen

EDITORIAL DESCRIPTION
  Devoted to American history and culture.
Articles per average issue: 12
Audience: Anyone interested in American history
  Manuscripts accepted in English

MANUSCRIPT INFORMATION
Subject field(s): American history, American culture
Manuscript requirements: Precise and nonacademic
  Preferred length: 5000 words or less
  Number of copies to be submitted: One
  Abstract: No
Author information and reprints: Payment: By publication to author. On acceptance.
  Copyright: Held by publication.
  Reprints: Occasional tearsheets available
Additional information: No fiction, poetry or fictionalized history accepted.
Disposition of manuscript:
  Query letter: Preferred
  Receipt of manuscript acknowledged: No
  Decision to publish in: 1-2 months
  Accepted manuscript published in: Varies
  Rejected manuscript returned: Yes
  Rejected manuscript criticized: No
Submit to:
  E. M. Halliday
  Articles Editor
  (See address above)

SPECIAL STIPULATIONS
  Also publishes appropriate book excerpts which are to be submitted to Barbara Klaw at least 6 months prior to publication.

THE AMERICAN HISTORICAL REVIEW [1118]
400 A Street, S.E.
Washington, D.C. 20003
(202) 544-2422

First published in 1895

SUBSCRIPTION DATA
Issues and rates: Five per year
  Average paid circulation: 25,000
  Annual rate(s): $20.00, Students $10.00
Publisher or Sponsor: American Historical Association
Managing Editor: Nancy Lane

EDITORIAL DESCRIPTION
  The official publication of the American Historical Association. Reviews are arranged according to period and area of historical interest.
Articles per average issue: 3 articles-175 book reviews
Audience: Historians
  Manuscripts accepted in English

MANUSCRIPT INFORMATION
Subject field(s): Any historical field
Manuscript requirements: Chicago
  Preferred length: 40 printed pages maximum
  Number of copies to be submitted: One original
  Abstract: No
Author information and reprints: Payment: None.
  Is simultaneous submission of article to other journals permitted: No
  Exclusive manuscript rights between acceptance and publication: Yes
  Copyright: Held by publication.
  Reprints: Available at printer's cost
Disposition of manuscript:
  Query letter: No
  Receipt of manuscript acknowledged: Yes
  Decision to publish in: 3-4 months
  Accepted manuscript published in: 6 months
  Rejected manuscript returned: Yes
  Rejected manuscript criticized: Yes
Submit to:
  Robert K. Webb
  Editor
  (See address above)

THE AMERICAN NEPTUNE [1119]
A Quarterly Journal of Maritime History
Peabody Museum
161 Essex Street
Salem, Massachusetts 01970
(617) 745-1876

First published in 1941

SUBSCRIPTION DATA
Issues and rates: Published quarterly.
  Average paid circulation: 1,200
  Annual rate(s): $15.00
Publisher or Sponsor: Peabody Museum of Salem

EDITORIAL DESCRIPTION
  Contains scholarly articles on the various aspects of American maritime history. Documents of maritime interests, notes and book review are included.
Articles per average issue: 4-5
Audience: Maritime and naval historians

MANUSCRIPT INFORMATION
Subject field(s): Maritime history

Manuscript requirements: Double-spaced typed pages with footnotes on separate pages
Preferred length: 10-30 pages
Number of copies to be submitted: One
Author information and reprints: Payment: None.
Is simultaneous submission of article to other journals permitted: No
Exclusive manuscript rights between acceptance and publication: Yes
Copyright: Held by publication.
Reprints: 4 copies of the particular issue available gratis to authors.
Additional information: The original top copy of the manuscript should be sent. No Xerox or photocopies. Illustrations limited to black and white or line cut material. Articles are printed by letterpress.
Disposition of manuscript:
Query letter: Not necessary but desirable
Receipt of manuscript acknowledged: Yes
Decision to publish in: 2-3 months
Accepted manuscript published in: One and half years
Rejected manuscript returned: Yes
Rejected manuscript criticized: No
Submit to:
Philip C.F. Smith
Managing Editor
(See address above)

SPECIAL STIPULATIONS
The Editors assume no responsibility for unsolicited manuscripts.

ANNALS OF IOWA [1120]
Historical Building
East 12th and Grand Avenue
Des Moines, Iowa 50319
(515) 281-5229

First published in 1865

SUBSCRIPTION DATA
Issues and rates: Published quarterly.
Average paid circulation: 1,500; 250 controlled
Annual rate(s): $2.00; Foreign $2.50
Publisher or Sponsor: Iowa Historical Department
Managing Editor: Judith A. Gildner

EDITORIAL DESCRIPTION
To present material that is pertinent to the history of Iowa and the Midwest
Articles per average issue: 4-6
Audience: Academic, general
Manuscripts accepted in English

MANUSCRIPT INFORMATION
Subject field(s): Iowa history, sociology, archaeology, biographies of Iowans past and present, diaries, memoirs, letters
Manuscript requirements: See latest issue for style requirements. Style sheet sent on request.
Preferred length: 6,000-7,500 words; 20-25 pages
Number of copies to be submitted: 1
Abstract: Not necessary.

Author information and reprints: Payment: Reprints only. 4 issues
Is simultaneous submission of article to other journals permitted: Permitted, but not encouraged.
Exclusive manuscript rights between acceptance and publication: Yes
Copyright: Held by author.
Reprints: Available at cost.
Additional information: Manuscripts typewritten, double-spaced with footnotes on separate pages at the end.
Disposition of manuscript:
Query letter: Not necessary.
Receipt of manuscript acknowledged: Yes
Decision to publish in: 2 weeks
Accepted manuscript published in: 6-12 months
Rejected manuscript returned: Yes, with return postage paid by publication.
Rejected manuscript criticized: Sometimes
Submit to:
Judith A. Gildner
Editor
(See address above)

ANNALS OF WYOMING [1121]
Wyoming State Archives and Historical Department
State Office Building
Cheyenne, Wyoming 82002
(307) 777-7518

Previously entitled *Quarterly Bulletin*

First published in 1923

SUBSCRIPTION DATA
Issues and rates: Published semi-annually.
Average paid circulation: 1100
Annual rate(s): Members $5.00; Institutions $10.00
Publisher or Sponsor: Wyoming State Archives and Historical Department

EDITORIAL DESCRIPTION
Contains articles of a scholarly nature on the history of Wyoming, related events or areas adjacent to Wyoming; book reviews in same areas of interest as articles in journal.
Articles per average issue: 5
Audience: Historians, members
Manuscripts accepted in English

MANUSCRIPT INFORMATION
Subject field(s): All phases of Wyoming history, general area Western history
Manuscript requirements: See latest issue for style requirements.
Preferred length: 1000 words or more
Number of copies to be submitted: One
Abstract: No
Author information and reprints: Payment: Reprints only. 2 copies of issue in which material is published
Is simultaneous submission of article to other journals permitted: No
Exclusive manuscript rights between acceptance and publication: Yes
Copyright: Held by publication.

Reprints: Available at printer's cost if arrangements made prior to publication
Additional information: Double-spaced typescript on standard bond paper; footnotes at end, numbered consecutively.
Disposition of manuscript:
Query letter: No
Receipt of manuscript acknowledged: Yes
Decision to publish in: 4-6 weeks
Accepted manuscript published in: 1-2 years
Rejected manuscript returned: Yes
Rejected manuscript criticized: No
Submit to:
Katherine Halverson
Editor
(See address above)

ARIZONA AND THE WEST [1122]
A Quarterly Journal of History
Library 310, University of Arizona
Tucson, Arizona 85721
(602) 884-2484

First published in 1959

SUBSCRIPTION DATA
Issues and rates: Published quarterly.
Average paid circulation: 1,400
Annual rate(s): $7.50, Foreign $8.00
Publisher or Sponsor: University of Arizona

EDITORIAL DESCRIPTION
Publication is devoted to the history of the Trans-Mississippi West. Each issue contains articles; a dedication to an outstanding figure in Western *belles-lettres;* book reviews; short book notes; and an edited document.
Articles per average issue: 4
Audience: Scholars and history buffs
Manuscripts accepted in English

MANUSCRIPT INFORMATION
Subject field(s): History
Manuscript requirements: See latest issue for style requirements.
Preferred length: 15-30 pages double-spaced, footnotes on separate pages
Number of copies to be submitted: One
Abstract: No
Author information and reprints: Payment: None.
Is simultaneous submission of article to other journals permitted: No
Exclusive manuscript rights between acceptance and publication: Yes
Copyright: Held by Board of Regents, University of Arizona
Reprints: Available, 25 in covers free
Additional information: The author should advise of location of illustrations pertinent to his article.
Disposition of manuscript:
Query letter: No
Receipt of manuscript acknowledged: Yes
Decision to publish in: 4-6 weeks
Accepted manuscript published in: 6-9 months
Rejected manuscript returned: Yes
Rejected manuscript criticized: Sometimes

Submit to:
Harwood P. Hinton
Editor
(See address above)

THE ARKANSAS HISTORICAL QUARTERLY [1123]

Department of History
University of Arkansas
Fayetteville, Arkansas 72701
(501) 575-3001

First published in 1942

SUBSCRIPTION DATA
Issues and rates: Published quarterly.
  Average paid circulation: 1400
  Annual rate(s): $6.00, Foreign $6.40
Publisher or Sponsor: Arkansas Historical Association

EDITORIAL DESCRIPTION
Contains articles on Arkansas history; book reviews of books either dealing with Arkansas, or by Arkansas writers, or dealing with a subject thought to be of interest to Arkansans.
Articles per average issue: 4
Audience: Adult
  Manuscripts accepted in English

MANUSCRIPT INFORMATION
Subject field(s): Arkansas history
Manuscript requirements: Manuscript typed, double spaced, footnotes on separate sheet(s) at end of article
  Preferred length: 6,000 words; 20-25 pages
  Number of copies to be submitted: One
Author information and reprints: Payment: None. Two copies of the issue in which article appears.
  Is simultaneous submission of article to other journals permitted: No
  Exclusive manuscript rights between acceptance and publication: Yes
  Copyright: Held by publication.
  Reprints: Available, $2 per page.
Disposition of manuscript:
  Query letter: No
  Receipt of manuscript acknowledged: Yes
  Decision to publish in: 6 months
  Accepted manuscript published in: 6-12 months
  Rejected manuscript returned: Yes
  Rejected manuscript criticized: Sometimes
Submit to:
Walter L. Brown
Managing Editor
(See address above)

THE ARLINGTON HISTORICAL MAGAZINE [1124]

P. O. Box 402
Arlington, Virginia 22210
(703) 528-1305

First published in 1957

SUBSCRIPTION DATA
Issues and rates: Published annually.
  Average paid circulation: 300
  Annual rate(s): $4.00 Plus Postage; Foreign $4.00 Plus Postage
Publisher or Sponsor: The Arlington Historical Society
Managing Editor: Catherine L. Bahn

EDITORIAL DESCRIPTION
To promote the discovery and preservation of the history of Arlington County, Virginia through research, reminiscences, pictures, letters, proclamations, newspapers, publications that might otherwise be lost and to promote the Museum
Articles per average issue: 6
Audience: Those interested in the history of Arlington and Virginia
  Manuscripts accepted in English

MANUSCRIPT INFORMATION
Subject field(s): Life in the 18th and 19th centuries, changes in real estate sections, records of governmental changes, schools, recreation, historical buildings
Manuscript requirements: See latest issue for style requirements.
  Preferred length: 3,000 to 5,000 words
  Number of copies to be submitted: 1
  Abstract: Not necessary.
Author information and reprints: Payment: None.
  Is simultaneous submission of article to other journals permitted: Permitted, but not encouraged.
  Exclusive manuscript rights between acceptance and publication: Yes
  Copyright: Held by the Arlington Historical Society
  Reprints: Available at cost.
Disposition of manuscript:
  Query letter: Not necessary, but advisable.
  Receipt of manuscript acknowledged: Yes
  Decision to publish in: 1 month
  Rejected manuscript returned: Yes, if return postage is supplied by author.
  Rejected manuscript criticized: Reasons for rejections only
Submit to:
Catherine I. Bahn;
Sandra Doyle
Editors
(See address above)

CALIFORNIA HISTORICAL QUARTERLY [1125]

2090 Jackson Street
San Francisco, California 94109
(415) 567-1848

Previously entitled *California Historical Society Quarterly*

First published in 1922

SUBSCRIPTION DATA
Issues and rates: Published quarterly.
  Average paid circulation: 6,900
  Annual rate(s): $17.50, Students $10.00
Publisher or Sponsor: California Historical Society

EDITORIAL DESCRIPTION
Contains scholarly articles on the history of California and of the West as related to California. Primary focus on historical events or trends that have a bearing on life in present-day California. Prefer readable scholarship, i.e., writing that can be appreciated outside the academic community as well as within campus boundaries.
Articles per average issue: 5
Audience: Scholars, history buffs, general
  Manuscripts accepted in English

MANUSCRIPT INFORMATION
Subject field(s): Social economic, political, ethnic group, popular culture and literary histories; biographies, interpretations, etc.
Manuscript requirements: See latest issue for style requirements.
  Preferred length: Up to 25 pages
  Number of copies to be submitted: Two
  Abstract: No
Author information and reprints: Payment: None. Two copies of issue in which article appears, plus 25 reprints.
  Is simultaneous submission of article to other journals permitted: No
  Exclusive manuscript rights between acceptance and publication: Yes
  Copyright: Held by publication.
  Reprints: Available; 25 free, more at cost.
Additional information: Include footnotes for all quotations; sources for graphics submitted with article. Articles with interesting graphics given preference over non-illustrated material; graphic resources list may suffice.
Disposition of manuscript:
  Query letter: No
  Receipt of manuscript acknowledged: Yes
  Decision to publish in: 8 weeks
  Accepted manuscript published in: Up to one year
  Rejected manuscript returned: Yes
  Rejected manuscript criticized: Usually
Submit to:
Marilyn Ziebarth
Managing Editor
(See address above)

CANADIAN FRONTIER [1126]

The Canadian Natural History Magazine
P. O. Box 157
New Westminster, British Columbia V3L 4Y4, Canada
(604) 588-4991

First published in 1971

SUBSCRIPTION DATA
Issues and rates: Published quarterly.
  Average paid circulation: 5,000; 250 controlled
  Annual rate(s): $3.50; Foreign $3.50; Institutions $3.50; Foreign institutions $3.50

EDITORIAL DESCRIPTION
Contains articles on the life and times of pre-1900 Canada, the pioneer

personalities and early events which shaped the nation; the Indians, explorers and settlers as well as the land, forts, townsites and homesteads.
Articles per average issue: 6-7
Audience: General, academic
Manuscripts accepted in English

MANUSCRIPT INFORMATION

Subject field(s): Items from all 10 provinces
Manuscript requirements: No specific style guide.
Preferred length: 2,000-3,000 words
Number of copies to be submitted: 1
Abstract: Not necessary.
Author information and reprints: Payment: By publication to author. $30.00-$75.00 per article.
Is simultaneous submission of article to other journals permitted: Permitted, but not encouraged.
Exclusive manuscript rights between acceptance and publication: Yes
Copyright: First serial rights only; further use must acknowledge this publication
Reprints: Available at cost.
Additional information: Outlines are first considered before authors are given a firm commitment of acceptance. Illustrated articles given primary consideration.
Disposition of manuscript:
Query letter: Not necessary.
Receipt of manuscript acknowledged: Yes
Decision to publish in: 5 weeks
Accepted manuscript published in: 3 months
Rejected manuscript returned: Yes, if return postage is supplied by author.
Rejected manuscript criticized: Sometimes
Submit to:
Rick Antonson
Publisher
(See address above)

CANADIAN HISTORICAL REVIEW [1127]
University of Toronto Press
Toronto, Ontario M5S 1A6, Canada
(416) 928-2240

First published in 1920

SUBSCRIPTION DATA

Issues and rates: Published quarterly.
Average paid circulation: 5000
Annual rate(s): $8.00
Managing Editor: Michael Cross

EDITORIAL DESCRIPTION

Publishes articles on all aspects of Canadian history and foreign policy.
Articles per average issue: 3-4
Audience: Canadian historians
Manuscripts accepted in English or French

MANUSCRIPT INFORMATION

Subject field(s): Canadian history, Canadian foreign relations.

Manuscript requirements: Style sheet sent on request.
Preferred length: 6000-9000 words; 25-35 pages
Number of copies to be submitted: 2
Abstract: No
Author information and reprints: Payment: None. 25 offprints and 2 copies of issue.
Is simultaneous submission of article to other journals permitted: No
Exclusive manuscript rights between acceptance and publication: Yes
Copyright: Held by publication.
Reprints: Available
Disposition of manuscript:
Query letter: No
Receipt of manuscript acknowledged: Yes
Decision to publish in: 6 weeks
Accepted manuscript published in: 1 year
Rejected manuscript returned: Yes
Rejected manuscript criticized: Yes
Submit to:
The Editor
(See address above)

SPECIAL STIPULATIONS

Scholarly articles only

CANADIAN JOURNAL OF HISTORY [1128]
Annales Canadiennes D'Histoire
Box 384 Sub Post Office No. 6
Saskatoon, Saskatchewan S7N 0W0, Canada
(306) 343-5270

First published in 1966

SUBSCRIPTION DATA

Issues and rates: Published three times per year.
Average paid circulation: 700
Annual rate(s): $5.50 for all
Managing Editor: J. Michael Hayden

EDITORIAL DESCRIPTION

Publishes contributions in all fields of history other than Canadian.
Articles per average issue: 4
Audience: Professional historians
Manuscripts accepted in English, French

MANUSCRIPT INFORMATION

Manuscript requirements: See latest issue for style requirements.
Number of copies to be submitted: 1
Abstract: Not necessary.
Author information and reprints: Payment: None.
Is simultaneous submission of article to other journals permitted: Permitted, but not encouraged.
Exclusive manuscript rights between acceptance and publication: Yes
Copyright: Held by publication.
Reprints: Available at no cost. 25; Available at cost. $.25 each
Disposition of manuscript:
Query letter: Not necessary.
Receipt of manuscript acknowledged: Yes
Decision to publish in: 1-2 months
Accepted manuscript published in: 6-12 months
Rejected manuscript returned: Yes, with return postage paid by publication.
Rejected manuscript criticized: Yes
Submit to:
J. Michael Hayden
Managing Editor
Department of History
University of Saskatchewan
Saskatoon, Saskatchewan S7W 0W0, Canada
(306) 343-5278

CENTAURUS [1129]
International Magazine of the History of Mathematics, Science and Technology
Munksgaard
Norre Sogade 35
1370 Copenhagen, Denmark
06 12 71 88

First published in 1950

SUBSCRIPTION DATA

Issues and rates: Published quarterly.
Average paid circulation: 600
Annual rate(s): 210.00 Danish Crowns
Managing Editor: Mogens Pihl

EDITORIAL DESCRIPTION

Contains research papers in the history of the exact sciences, technology and medicine; reviews of books.
Articles per average issue: 4-7
Audience: Historians
Manuscripts accepted in English, French, German

MANUSCRIPT INFORMATION

Manuscript requirements: See latest issue for style requirements.
Preferred length: 10-30 pages; brief communications 1-2 pages
Number of copies to be submitted: 1
Author information and reprints: Payment: None.
Is simultaneous submission of article to other journals permitted: No
Exclusive manuscript rights between acceptance and publication: Yes
Copyright: Held by publication.
Reprints: Available, 50 copies free
Additional information: References should be placed at end of paper and contain no reading matter.
Disposition of manuscript:
Query letter: No
Receipt of manuscript acknowledged: Yes
Decision to publish in: 1-2 months
Accepted manuscript published in: 6-8 months
Rejected manuscript returned: Yes
Rejected manuscript criticized: Yes
Submit to:
Olaf Pedersen
Institute for the History of Science
Ny Munkegade
DK-8000 Aarhus C, Denmark

CENTRAL EUROPEAN HISTORY [1130]

Emory University
Atlanta, Georgia 30322
(404) 377-2411, ext. 7501

First published in 1968

SUBSCRIPTION DATA

Issues and rates: Published quarterly.
 Average paid circulation: 1200
 Annual rate(s): Individuals $12.00, Institutions $18.00, Students $6.00
Publisher or Sponsor: American Historical Association, Conference Group for Central European History

EDITORIAL DESCRIPTION

Publishes bibliographical articles, and review articles on Central European history, some dealing with the history of German-speaking Central Europe. All approaches to history and all historical periods are acceptable.
Articles per average issue: 3 articles, 2-5 reviews
Audience: International scholars
 Manuscripts: Prefer English but German accepted

MANUSCRIPT INFORMATION

Subject field(s): History of German-speaking Central Europe, including interdisciplinary and comparative approaches.
Manuscript requirements: Chicago
 Preferred length: 10-30 pages
 Number of copies to be submitted: Two
 Abstract: Desirable. 2 copies, footnotes double-spaced and separate
Author information and reprints: Payment: None.
 Is simultaneous submission of article to other journals permitted: No
 Exclusive manuscript rights between acceptance and publication: Yes
 Copyright: Held by Emory University; authors consulted about reprints and paid
 Reprints: Available, 25 free; additional at cost
Additional information: Unsolicited book reviews not accepted. Consult editor before preparing bibliographical articles. Manuscripts should be double-spaced throughout, including footnotes. Footnotes should be numbered consecutively, and placed at the end of the manuscript.
Disposition of manuscript:
 Query letter: Welcome
 Receipt of manuscript acknowledged: Yes
 Decision to publish in: 3 months
 Accepted manuscript published in: 1-2 years
 Rejected manuscript returned: Yes, if self-addressed, stamped envelope is sent with manuscript.
Submit to:
 Douglas A. Unfug
 Editor
 (See address above)

THE CHRONICLE OF ABA [1131]

Official Publication of the Aaron Burr Association
Tremont, Inca Road
Linden, Virginia 22642
(703) 635-6095

First published in 1948

SUBSCRIPTION DATA

Issues and rates: Published quarterly.
 Average paid circulation: 100; 1,000 controlled
 Annual rate(s): $1.00
Publisher or Sponsor: The Aaron Burr Association

EDITORIAL DESCRIPTION

Contains comments concerning any newspaper or magazine articles which deal with the life and career of Colonel Aaron Burr and the members of his immediate family. Favorable to the cause of Colonel Aaron Burr. Also includes news of the Aaron Burr Association and its activities.
Articles per average issue: 1
Audience: To anyone interested in the life and career of Aaron Burr
 Manuscripts accepted in English

MANUSCRIPT INFORMATION

Manuscript requirements: See latest issue for style requirements.
 Preferred length: 250 words maximum type double-space on one side of page
 Number of copies to be submitted: One
 Abstract: No
Author information and reprints: Payment: None.
 Is simultaneous submission of article to other journals permitted: Yes
 Exclusive manuscript rights between acceptance and publication: No
 Copyright: Not copyrighted.
 Reprints: Reprints are available at printing and postage costs.
Additional information: Author should retain a copy for himself.
Disposition of manuscript:
 Receipt of manuscript acknowledged: Yes. Desirable but not required
 Decision to publish in: One week
 Accepted manuscript published in: Next issue
 Rejected manuscript returned: Yes, if self-addressed, stamped envelope is sent with manuscript.
 Rejected manuscript criticized: No
Submit to:
 Samuel Engle Burr, Jr.
 Editor
 (See address above)

SPECIAL STIPULATIONS

Prepare material about one month before publication date. Almost everything is staff written.

CIVIL WAR HISTORY [1132]

A Journal of the Middle Period
Kent State University Press
Kent, Ohio 44242
(216) 672-7913

First published in 1955

SUBSCRIPTION DATA

Issues and rates: Published quarterly.
 Average paid circulation: 1652
 Annual rate(s): $7.50, Students $6.50
Managing Editor: John T. Hubbell

EDITORIAL DESCRIPTION

Contains scholarly articles and reviews dealing with subjects pertaining to the Civil War era.
Articles per average issue: 4
Audience: Educated, usually college and professional
 Manuscripts accepted in English

MANUSCRIPT INFORMATION

Subject field(s): U.S. History 1820-1880, Civil War.
Manuscript requirements: Chicago
 Preferred length: 15-25 pages
 Number of copies to be submitted: Two
 Abstract: No
Author information and reprints: Payment: Reprints only. 6 copies
 Is simultaneous submission of article to other journals permitted: No
 Exclusive manuscript rights between acceptance and publication: Yes
 Copyright: Held by publication.
 Reprints: Available, cost for offprints of article varies with number of pages.
Disposition of manuscript:
 Query letter: No
 Receipt of manuscript acknowledged: Yes
 Decision to publish in: 6-8 weeks
 Accepted manuscript published in: One year
 Rejected manuscript returned: Yes, if self-addressed, stamped envelope is sent with manuscript.
 Rejected manuscript criticized: Yes
Submit to:
 Editor
 Department of History
 Kent State University
 Kent, Ohio 44242
 (216) 672-2492

THE COLORADO MAGAZINE [1133]

Colorado State Museum
200 Fourteenth Avenue
Denver, Colorado 80203
(303) 892-2138

First published in 1923

SUBSCRIPTION DATA

Issues and rates: Published quarterly.
 Average paid circulation: 3,400
 Annual rate(s): Members $5

History

Publisher or Sponsor: State Historical Society of Colorado

EDITORIAL DESCRIPTION

The journal contains scholarly, well-documented, and illustrated manuscripts; edited documents and reminiscences; society's news notes and book notes; and a section of books reviews by notable historians. The material discusses all aspects of the history (social, cultural, economic, and political) of Colorado and the Rocky Mountain Region.

Articles per average issue: 3-4
Audience: Society membership; professors of western history; students of all educational institutions
Manuscripts accepted in English

MANUSCRIPT INFORMATION

Subject field(s): Colorado History, Rocky Mountain region history
Manuscript requirements: Chicago, style sheet sent on request
  Preferred length: 20-25 pages typed double-spaced
  Number of copies to be submitted: One
  Abstract: No
Author information and reprints: Payment: Reprints only. 10 copies of journal
  Is simultaneous submission of article to other journals permitted: No
  Exclusive manuscript rights between acceptance and publication: Yes
  Copyright: Held by publication.
  Reprints: Available
Additional information: Desire scholarly, well-documented manuscripts
Disposition of manuscript:
  Receipt of manuscript acknowledged: Yes
  Decision to publish in: 8-10 weeks
  Accepted manuscript published in: 4-12 months
  Rejected manuscript returned: Yes
  Rejected manuscript criticized: Yes
Submit to:
  Cathryne Christine Johnson
  Editor
  (See address above)

DELAWARE HISTORY [1134]
Historical Society of Delaware
505 Market Street
Wilmington, Delaware 19801
(302) 655-7161

First published in 1946

SUBSCRIPTION DATA
Issues and rates: Published semi-annually.
  Average paid circulation: 1,400
  Annual rate(s): $10.00
Publisher or Sponsor: Historical Society of Delaware

EDITORIAL DESCRIPTION
Contains articles and edited documents on the history of Delaware.
Articles per average issue: 3
Audience: History enthusiasts
Manuscripts accepted in English

MANUSCRIPT INFORMATION
Subject field(s): Any aspect of Delaware history
Manuscript requirements: Style sheet sent on request.
  Preferred length: 20-30 pages
  Number of copies to be submitted: One
  Abstract: No
Author information and reprints: Payment: None.
  Is simultaneous submission of article to other journals permitted: No
  Exclusive manuscript rights between acceptance and publication: Yes
  Copyright: Held by publication.
  Reprints: Available, 20 free
Disposition of manuscript:
  Query letter: No
  Receipt of manuscript acknowledged: Yes
  Decision to publish in: 3 months
  Accepted manuscript published in: 12-18 months
  Rejected manuscript returned: Yes
  Rejected manuscript criticized: Yes
Submit to:
  George H. Gibson
  Managing Editor
  (See address above)

DETROIT SOCIETY FOR GENEALOGICAL RESEARCH MAGAZINE [1135]
Containing Records of Michigan and Michigan Source States
c/o The Burton Historical Collection
Detroit Public Library
5201 Woodward Avenue at Kirby
Detroit, Michigan 48202

SUBSCRIPTION DATA
Issues and rates: Published quarterly.
  Average paid circulation: 1000
  Annual rate(s): $8.00
Publisher or Sponsor: The Detroit Society for Genealogical Research, Inc.
Managing Editor: Harriette M Wheeler

EDITORIAL DESCRIPTION
Contains genealogical materials: family histories, transcriptions of vital records, Bible records, tombstone inscriptions, guides and aids, historical background articles, queries, etc.

MANUSCRIPT INFORMATION
Subject field(s): Genealogy, historical background
Manuscript requirements: Chicago
  Preferred length: Various
  Number of copies to be submitted: One
Author information and reprints: Payment: None. 2 complimentary copies of issue.
  Is simultaneous submission of article to other journals permitted: No
  Exclusive manuscript rights between acceptance and publication: Yes
  Copyright: Held by publication.
  Reprints: Not available.
Additional information: This magazine publishes material submitted by members only. Writers must join the society. At present there is an abundance of manuscripts awaiting publication; therefore only outstanding pieces will be considered.
Disposition of manuscript:
  Receipt of manuscript acknowledged: Yes
  Decision to publish in: 6-8 weeks
  Accepted manuscript published in: 12-14 months
  Rejected manuscript returned: Yes
  Rejected manuscript criticized: No
Submit to:
  Eva Murell Harmison
  Editor
  830 North Wilson
  Royal Oak, Michigan 48067
  (313) 542-6411

THE FILSON CLUB HISTORY QUARTERLY [1136]
118 West Breckinridge Street
Louisville, Kentucky 40203
(502) 582-3727

First published in 1926

SUBSCRIPTION DATA
Issues and rates: Published quarterly.
  Average paid circulation: 2500
  Annual rate(s): $8.00
Publisher or Sponsor: The Filson Club, Inc.

EDITORIAL DESCRIPTION
Publishes research papers and articles dealing with regional historical topics; also biography, genealogy, and archaeology so long as they relate to Kentucky or the surrounding states. The connection with Kentucky can be tenuous. Publication is interested in sound original research on almost any aspect of history.
Articles per average issue: 5
Audience: Membership
Manuscripts accepted in English only

MANUSCRIPT INFORMATION
Subject field(s): History, biography, genealogy, archaeology
Manuscript requirements: Style sheet sent on request.
  Preferred length: 2000-6000 words; 25 pages
  Number of copies to be submitted: One
Author information and reprints: Payment: None.
  Is simultaneous submission of article to other journals permitted: No
  Exclusive manuscript rights between acceptance and publication: Yes
  Copyright: Held by publication.
  Reprints: Available at cost
Disposition of manuscript:
  Query letter: Useful, but not required
  Receipt of manuscript acknowledged: Yes
  Decision to publish in: 2-4 weeks
  Accepted manuscript published in: 6-12 months
  Rejected manuscript returned: Yes
  Rejected manuscript criticized: No
Submit to:
  Robert E. McDowell
  Editor
  (See address above)

FRENCH HISTORICAL STUDIES [1137]

Society for French Historical Studies
Department of History, Louisiana State University
Baton Rouge, Louisiana 70803

First published in 1958

SUBSCRIPTION DATA

Issues and rates: Published semi-annually.
  Average paid circulation: 1,300
  Annual rate(s): $12.00; Institutions $12.00; Students $5.00
Publisher or Sponsor: Society for French Historical Studies
Managing Editor: David H. Pinkney

EDITORIAL DESCRIPTION

  The journal publishes articles on all aspects of French history.
Articles per average issue: 8
Audience: Historians of France
  Manuscripts accepted in English and French

MANUSCRIPT INFORMATION

Manuscript requirements: Chicago
  Preferred length: 20-30 pages
  Number of copies to be submitted: 1
  Abstract: Not necessary.
Author information and reprints: Payment: None.
  Is simultaneous submission of article to other journals permitted: Not permitted.
  Exclusive manuscript rights between acceptance and publication: Yes
  Copyright: Held by publication.
  Reprints: Available at cost. Varies according to length
Disposition of manuscript:
  Query letter: Not necessary.
  Receipt of manuscript acknowledged: Yes
  Decision to publish in: 2-3 months
  Accepted manuscript published in: 18 months
  Rejected manuscript returned: Yes, with return postage paid by publication.
  Rejected manuscript criticized: Yes
Submit to:
  David H. Pinkney
  Editor
  Parrington Hall, DE-05
  University of Washington
  Seattle, Washington 98105
  (206) 543-2992

THE GEORGIA HISTORICAL QUARTERLY [1138]

Le Conte 122-C, Uga
Athens, Georgia 30602
(404) 542-8813

First published in 1917

SUBSCRIPTION DATA

Issues and rates: Published quarterly.
  Average paid circulation: 2,100
  Annual rate(s): $10.00
Publisher or Sponsor: Georgia Historical Society

EDITORIAL DESCRIPTION

  Contains historical articles primarily on Georgia, but also on the South, Civil War, Reconstruction. Articles should pertain to Georgia or the South in some respect.
Articles per average issue: 4-5
Audience: Georgia and Southern
  Manuscripts accepted in English

MANUSCRIPT INFORMATION

Subject field(s): Georgia, Southern states, Civil War, Reconstruction, recent South, all articles must be historical and scholarly
Manuscript requirements: Style sheet sent on request. Manuscripts should be typed double-spaced, footnotes grouped at end of article under "Notes."
  Preferred length: 3,000 to 6,000, not over 9,000 words
  Number of copies to be submitted: One
  Abstract: No
Author information and reprints: Payment: None. Two copies of issue in which article appears.
  Is simultaneous submission of article to other journals permitted: No
  Exclusive manuscript rights between acceptance and publication: Yes
  Copyright: Held by author.
  Reprints: Available at author's expense.
Disposition of manuscript:
  Query letter: No, but is desirable
  Receipt of manuscript acknowledged: Yes
  Decision to publish in: Not more than a month
  Accepted manuscript published in: 1-2 years
  Rejected manuscript returned: Yes
  Rejected manuscript criticized: Yes
Submit to:
  Phinizy Spaulding
  Editor
  (See address above)

THE HISTORIAN [1139]

A Journal of History
Phi Alpha Theta
2812 Livingston Street
Allentown, Pennsylvania 18104
(215) 432-2452

First published in 1938

SUBSCRIPTION DATA

Issues and rates: Published quarterly.
  Average paid circulation: 10,000
  Annual rate(s): $7.50; Foreign $9.00; Institutions $7.50; Members $6.00; Foreign institutions $9.00
Publisher or Sponsor: Phi Alpha Theta
Managing Editor: Dr. Gerald Nash

EDITORIAL DESCRIPTION

  Publishes articles in all areas of history.
Articles per average issue: 5
Audience: Historians, general
  Manuscripts accepted in English

MANUSCRIPT INFORMATION

Subject field(s): All topics in the field of history
Manuscript requirements: See latest issue for style requirements. Chicago
  Preferred length: As required
  Number of copies to be submitted: 1
  Abstract: Not necessary.
Author information and reprints: Payment: Reprints only. 25 reprints
  Is simultaneous submission of article to other journals permitted: Not permitted.
  Exclusive manuscript rights between acceptance and publication: Yes
  Copyright: Held by publication.
  Reprints: Available at cost.
Disposition of manuscript:
  Query letter: Not necessary, but advisable.
  Receipt of manuscript acknowledged: Yes
  Decision to publish in: 2-3 months
  Accepted manuscript published in: 6-12 months
  Rejected manuscript returned: Yes, if return postage is supplied by author.
  Rejected manuscript criticized: Sometimes
Submit to:
  Dr. Gerald Nash
  Editor
  University of New Mexico
  Albuquerque, New Mexico 87106

THE HISTORICAL JOURNAL [1140]

Cambridge University Press
32 East 57th Street
New York, New York 10022

Previously entitled *The Cambridge Historical Journal*

SUBSCRIPTION DATA

Issues and rates: Published quarterly.
  Annual rate(s): Individuals $27.00 per volume
Publisher or Sponsor: Cambridge Historical Society
Managing Editor: D. E. D. Beales

EDITORIAL DESCRIPTION

  Concerned mainly with the period from the fifteenth century to the present
Audience: Historians
  Manuscripts accepted in English

MANUSCRIPT INFORMATION

Subject field(s): Research articles, reviews of recent books or groups of books, short communications from all over the world
Manuscript requirements: See latest issue for style requirements.
  Preferred length: 5,000-10,000 words
  Number of copies to be submitted: 2
Author information and reprints: Payment: None.
  Is simultaneous submission of article to other journals permitted: Not permitted.
  Exclusive manuscript rights between acceptance and publication: Yes
  Copyright: Held by publication.
Additional information: Manuscripts should be typewritten, double-spaced with

generous margins on conventional size paper.
Disposition of manuscript:
  Query letter: Not necessary, but advisable.
Submit to:
  D. E. D. Beales
  Editor
  Sidney Sussex College
  Cambridge CB2 3HU, England

HISTORICAL REFLECTIONS [1141]
Réflexions Historiques
Department of History
University of Waterloo
Waterloo, Ontario N2L 3G1, Canada

First published in 1974

SUBSCRIPTION DATA
Issues and rates: Published semi-annually.
  Average paid circulation: 2,000 controlled
  Annual rate(s): $5.00; Foreign $5.00; Institutions $10.00; Students $5.00

EDITORIAL DESCRIPTION
Readable, interpretive essays in history of sufficient significant interest to professional historians
Articles per average issue: 6
Audience: Professional historians
  Manuscripts accepted in English, French

MANUSCRIPT INFORMATION
Subject field(s): All fields of history
Manuscript requirements: No specific style guide.
  Preferred length: 5,000-20,000 words
  Number of copies to be submitted: 1
  Abstract: Not necessary.
Author information and reprints: Payment: None.
  Is simultaneous submission of article to other journals permitted: Permitted, but not encouraged.
  Copyright: Held by author.
  Reprints: Available at no cost. 10
Disposition of manuscript:
  Query letter: Not necessary, but advisable.
  Receipt of manuscript acknowledged: No
  Decision to publish in: 3-4 weeks
  Accepted manuscript published in: 6-12 months
  Rejected manuscript returned: Yes, with return postage paid by publication.
  Rejected manuscript criticized: Reasons for rejections only
Submit to:
  John F. H. New;
  Gilman M. Ostrander
  Co-Editors
  (See address above)

HISTORY OF EDUCATION QUARTERLY [1142]
School of Education
New York University
New York, New York 10003
(212) 598-2593

First published in 1961

SUBSCRIPTION DATA
Issues and rates: Published quarterly.
  Average paid circulation: 2000
  Annual rate(s): Institutions $15.00, Members $12.50
Publisher or Sponsor: History of Education Society

EDITORIAL DESCRIPTION
Contains articles and book reviews on the history of education defined broadly to include formal and informal, ancient and modern, and American, Western, and non-Western education.
Articles per average issue: 4
Audience: Historians and educators
  Manuscripts accepted in Prefer English

MANUSCRIPT INFORMATION
Subject field(s): Educational history-all countries and eras
Manuscript requirements: Chicago
  Number of copies to be submitted: Two
  Abstract: No
Author information and reprints: Payment: None.
  Is simultaneous submission of article to other journals permitted: No
  Copyright: Held by publication.
  Reprints: Available, 25 free
Disposition of manuscript:
  Query letter: No
  Receipt of manuscript acknowledged: Yes
  Decision to publish in: 2 months
  Accepted manuscript published in: Within a year
  Rejected manuscript returned: Yes
  Rejected manuscript criticized: Yes
Submit to:
  Paul H. Mattingly
  Editor
  (See address above)

HISTORY AND THEORY [1143]
Studies in the Philosophy of History
Wesleyan Station
Middletown, Connecticut 06457
(203) 347-6965

First published in 1960

SUBSCRIPTION DATA
Issues and rates: Published quarterly.
  Average paid circulation: 2600
  Annual rate(s): Individuals $10.00, Institutions $16.00
Managing Editor: Jane K. Parker

EDITORIAL DESCRIPTION
International journal publishing monographs, essays, reviews, and bibliographies in four areas: theory of history; method of history; historiography; and relationship between problems in historical theory and method and those in economics, psychology, and other social sciences.
Articles per average issue: 8, including review essays
Audience: Historians, philosophers, social scientists
  Manuscripts accepted in English and French

MANUSCRIPT INFORMATION
Subject field(s): History, historiography, historicism, philosophy of history, theories of history
Manuscript requirements: Chicago, with certain style changes. Footnotes should follow text of article.
  Preferred length: None
  Number of copies to be submitted: One
  Abstract: No
Author information and reprints: Payment: None. 25 free offprints of article.
  Is simultaneous submission of article to other journals permitted: No
  Exclusive manuscript rights between acceptance and publication: Yes
  Copyright: Held by Wesleyan University
  Reprints: Available at cost
Disposition of manuscript:
  Query letter: No
  Receipt of manuscript acknowledged: Yes
  Decision to publish in: 6 weeks
  Accepted manuscript published in: Within a few months
  Rejected manuscript returned: Yes
  Rejected manuscript criticized: Yes
Submit to:
  Richard T. Vann
  Executive Editor
  (See address above)

ILLINOIS STATE HISTORICAL SOCIETY JOURNAL [1144]
Old State Capitol
Springfield, Illinois 62706
(217) 782-4836

First published in 1908

SUBSCRIPTION DATA
Issues and rates: 5 times a year
  Average paid circulation: 4000
  Annual rate(s): $7.50
Publisher or Sponsor: Illinois State Historical Society
Managing Editor: Ellen M. Whitney

EDITORIAL DESCRIPTION
Publishes articles concerned with the history of Illinois in its broadest sense.
Articles per average issue: 4-6
Audience: History professors and general public
  Manuscripts accepted in English

MANUSCRIPT INFORMATION
Subject field(s): All subject fields related to Illinois history
Manuscript requirements: MLA, Chicago
  Preferred length: 5000-7000 words
  Number of copies to be submitted: One

Abstract: Yes, but not required. Style guide available on request
Author information and reprints: Payment: None.
Is simultaneous submission of article to other journals permitted: No
Exclusive manuscript rights between acceptance and publication: Yes
Copyright: Held by publication.
Reprints: Available at no cost
Additional information: Each article is expected to make an original contribution to Illinois history. All articles must be fully documented.
Disposition of manuscript:
Query letter: No
Receipt of manuscript acknowledged: Yes
Decision to publish in: 8-10 weeks
Accepted manuscript published in: 2-3 years
Rejected manuscript returned: Yes
Rejected manuscript criticized: Yes, if a revision might be accepted
Submit to:
Ellen M. Whitney
Editor
(See address above)

INDIANA MAGAZINE OF HISTORY [1145]

Ballantine Hall 742
Indiana University
Bloomington, Indiana 47401
(812) 337-4139

First published in 1905

SUBSCRIPTION DATA

Issues and rates: Published quarterly.
Average paid circulation: 5,000
Annual rate(s): Individuals $5
Publisher or Sponsor: Indiana Historical Society

EDITORIAL DESCRIPTION

Publishes articles and documents on the political, economic, social, and cultural history of Indiana and the Middle West. Consideration is also given to items in the general fields of American and Canadian history if they have obvious relevance to Indiana or the Middle West.
Articles per average issue: 3
Audience: Scholarly and general
Manuscripts accepted in English

MANUSCRIPT INFORMATION

Subject field(s): Indiana, Midwest, American, and Canadian histories
Manuscript requirements: Chicago with modifications; see recent issues
Preferred length: Maximum 7,500 words; 30 pages
Number of copies to be submitted: Two
Abstract: No
Author information and reprints: Payment: None. 25 copies of the issue in which article appears.
Is simultaneous submission of article to other journals permitted: No
Exclusive manuscript rights between acceptance and publication: Yes
Copyright: Held by publication.

Reprints: Available at cost, depending on length
Additional information: Tables, maps, and charts on separate pages and footnotes, double-spaced, grouped at the end.
Disposition of manuscript:
Query letter: No
Receipt of manuscript acknowledged: Yes
Decision to publish in: 90-120 days
Accepted manuscript published in: 1-2 year
Rejected manuscript returned: Yes
Submit to:
Donald F. Carmony
Editor
(See address above)

INTERNATIONAL REVIEW OF SOCIAL HISTORY [1146]

Van Gorcum
Industrieweg 38
Assen, The Netherlands
05920-15647

First published in 1956

SUBSCRIPTION DATA

Issues and rates: Published three times per year.
Average paid circulation: 1,000; 400 controlled
Annual rate(s): Dfl. 40
Publisher or Sponsor: Internationaal Instituut voor Sociale Geschiedenis, International Institute for Social History

EDITORIAL DESCRIPTION

Contains articles on social history; previously unpublished documents and descriptive bibliography of current socio-historical literature.
Articles per average issue: 5
Audience: Historians
Manuscripts accepted in English, German, French

MANUSCRIPT INFORMATION

Subject field(s): History of the labor movements, history of social classes
Manuscript requirements: Style sheet sent on request.
Preferred length: 5,000-12,000 words; 20-50 pages
Number of copies to be submitted: One
Abstract: No
Author information and reprints: Payment: By publication to author. $1.50 per page.
Is simultaneous submission of article to other journals permitted: No
Exclusive manuscript rights between acceptance and publication: Yes
Copyright: Held by publication.
Reprints: Available, 20 free, additional at cost
Disposition of manuscript:
Query letter: No
Receipt of manuscript acknowledged: Yes
Decision to publish in: 3-6 months
Accepted manuscript published in: 12-18 months
Rejected manuscript returned: Yes
Rejected manuscript criticized: Occasionally

Submit to:
A.V.N. van Woerden
Editorial Secretary
Herengracht 262-266
Amsterdam, The Netherlands

ISIS [1147]

An International Review Devoted to the History of Science and Its Cultural Influences
Smithsonian Institution
Washington, D.C. 20560
(202) 381-5691

First published in 1913

SUBSCRIPTION DATA

Issues and rates: Published quarterly.
Average paid circulation: 2,800
Annual rate(s): Institutions $21.00, Individuals $18.00, Students $9.00
Publisher or Sponsor: History of Science Society, Inc.
Managing Editor: Bernard S. Finn

EDITORIAL DESCRIPTION

Contains essays of original research in the history of science and technology, book reviews.
Articles per average issue: 7
Manuscripts accepted in English, French, German

MANUSCRIPT INFORMATION

Subject field(s): History of science, history of technology, social influence of science
Manuscript requirements: See latest issue for style requirements.
Preferred length: None
Number of copies to be submitted: Two
Abstract: No
Author information and reprints: Payment: None.
Is simultaneous submission of article to other journals permitted: No
Exclusive manuscript rights between acceptance and publication: Yes
Copyright: Held by publication.
Reprints: Available, 25 free reprints; extra copies $.03 per page
Disposition of manuscript:
Query letter: No
Receipt of manuscript acknowledged: Yes
Decision to publish in: 2-3 months
Accepted manuscript published in: 6-12 months
Rejected manuscript returned: Yes
Rejected manuscript criticized: Yes
Submit to:
Robert P. Multhauf
Editor
(See address above)

JOURNAL OF AFRICAN HISTORY [1148]

Cambridge University Press
32 East 57th Street
New York, New York 10022

EDITORIAL DESCRIPTION

Presents articles and papers on all aspects of African history
Manuscripts accepted in English

MANUSCRIPT INFORMATION

Manuscript requirements: See latest issue for style requirements.
  Preferred length: 6,000 words maximum
  Number of copies to be submitted: 2
  Abstract: Yes. A summary of the article, not exceeding 300 words
Author information and reprints: Payment: Reprints only. 25 separates
  Is simultaneous submission of article to other journals permitted: Not permitted.
  Exclusive manuscript rights between acceptance and publication: Yes
  Copyright: Held by publication.
  Reprints: Available at cost.
Additional information: Observe closely the conventions listed in the Notes to Contributors, inside the back cover.
Disposition of manuscript:
  Query letter: Not necessary, but advisable.
  Receipt of manuscript acknowledged: Yes
  Rejected manuscript returned: Yes, if return postage is supplied by author.
  Rejected manuscript criticized: Sometimes
Submit to:
  The Editors
  School of Oriental and African Studies
  University of London
  London W. C. 1, England

JOURNAL OF AMERICAN HISTORY [1149]

Indiana University
Ballantine Hall
Bloomington, Indiana 47401
(812) 337-3034

Previously entitled *Mississippi Valley Historical Review*

First published in 1914

SUBSCRIPTION DATA

Issues and rates: Published quarterly.
  Average paid circulation: 12,500
  Annual rate(s): Institutions $15.00, Individuals $12.00, Students $6.00
Publisher or Sponsor: Organization of American Historians

EDITORIAL DESCRIPTION

Contains articles written by professional historians on the history of the United States.
Articles per average issue: 5
Audience: Members
  Manuscripts accepted in English

MANUSCRIPT INFORMATION

Subject field(s): Historical
Manuscript requirements: MLA; Chicago
  Preferred length: 7,000-7,500 words
  Number of copies to be submitted: Two
  Abstract: No
Author information and reprints: Payment: By publication to author. $5.00 per page.
  Is simultaneous submission of article to other journals permitted: No
  Exclusive manuscript rights between acceptance and publication: Yes
  Copyright: Held by publication.
  Reprints: Available
Disposition of manuscript:
  Query letter: No
  Receipt of manuscript acknowledged: Yes
  Decision to publish in: 12 weeks
  Accepted manuscript published in: 15 months
  Rejected manuscript returned: Yes
Submit to:
  Martin Ridge
  Managing Editor
  (See address above)

JOURNAL OF ASIAN HISTORY [1150]

Otto Harrassowitz Verlag
Taunusstrasse 6
D-62 Wiesbaden, Federal Republic of Germany
(06121) 521 046

First published in 1967

SUBSCRIPTION DATA

Issues and rates: Published semi-annually.
  Average paid circulation: 1,000
  Annual rate(s): DM 48 worldwide

EDITORIAL DESCRIPTION

Covers historical research on any period and all the regions of Asia with the exception of the ancient Near East
Articles per average issue: 3-4
Audience: Professional, academic
  Manuscripts accepted in English, French, German

MANUSCRIPT INFORMATION

Manuscript requirements: See latest issue for style requirements. Style sheet sent on request.
  Preferred length: 10-15 pages
  Number of copies to be submitted: 1
  Abstract: Not necessary.
Author information and reprints: Payment: Reprints only. 25 reprints
  Is simultaneous submission of article to other journals permitted: Not permitted.
  Exclusive manuscript rights between acceptance and publication: Yes
  Copyright: Held by publication.
Disposition of manuscript:
  Query letter: Not necessary.
  Receipt of manuscript acknowledged: Yes
  Decision to publish in: 30 days
  Accepted manuscript published in: 6 months
  Rejected manuscript returned: Yes, with return postage paid by publication.
  Rejected manuscript criticized: Yes
Submit to:
  Prof. Denis Sinor
  Editor
  Asian Studies Research Institute
  Indiana University, Goodbody Hall
  Bloomington, Indiana 47401

JOURNAL OF CONTEMPORARY HISTORY [1151]

4 Devonshire Street
London W1N 2BH, England
(01) 636-7247

First published in 1966

SUBSCRIPTION DATA

Issues and rates: Published quarterly.
  Average paid circulation: Not available.
  Annual rate(s): Institutions $22.00 (£8.50); Individuals $14.00 (£4.50)
Managing Editor: Walter Laqueur; George L. Mosse

EDITORIAL DESCRIPTION

Concentrates on the study and discussion of twentieth-century European history, particularly those trends and events which have influenced political, social, economic and administrative developments.
Articles per average issue: 8
Audience: Specialist and general student
  Manuscripts accepted in English only

MANUSCRIPT INFORMATION

Subject field(s): Post 1914 history
Manuscript requirements: Style sheet sent on request.
  Preferred length: 6,250-7,500 words; 25-30 pages
  Number of copies to be submitted: Two
  Abstract: No
Author information and reprints: Payment: None. 25 tear-sheets free to author.
  Is simultaneous submission of article to other journals permitted: Permitted, but not encouraged. Author must notify publisher that manuscript is under consideration elsewhere.
  Exclusive manuscript rights between acceptance and publication: Yes
  Copyright: Held by publication.
  Reprints: Available if purchased by special order at time of publication
Disposition of manuscript:
  Query letter: No
  Receipt of manuscript acknowledged: Yes
  Decision to publish in: 6-8 weeks
  Accepted manuscript published in: 15 months
  Rejected manuscript returned: No
  Rejected manuscript criticized: No
Submit to:
  Walter Laqueur
  Editor
  (See address above)

JOURNAL OF IMPERIAL AND COMMONWEALTH HISTORY [1152]

67 Great Russell Street
London WC1B 3BT, England
01-405-9405

First published in 1972

SUBSCRIPTION DATA
Issues and rates: Published three times per year.
  Annual rate(s): £10.00 ($30)
Managing Editor: Trevor Reese

EDITORIAL DESCRIPTION
  Contains articles on empire and its evolution into the modern commonwealth; broad issues of commonwealth: British imperial policy, colonial rule, local response; rise of nationalism, decolonization, transfer of power.
Articles per average issue: 5
Audience: Academic historians
  Manuscripts accepted in English

MANUSCRIPT INFORMATION
Subject field(s): Empire evolution, commonwealth and related topics
Manuscript requirements: Style sheet sent on request.
  Preferred length: 8000 words
  Number of copies to be submitted: Two
  Abstract: No
Author information and reprints: Payment: None.
  Is simultaneous submission of article to other journals permitted: No
  Exclusive manuscript rights between acceptance and publication: Yes
  Copyright: Held by publication.
  Reprints: Available, first 25 free
Disposition of manuscript:
  Query letter: No
  Receipt of manuscript acknowledged: Yes
  Decision to publish in: 1 month
  Accepted manuscript published in: Varies
  Rejected manuscript returned: Yes
  Rejected manuscript criticized: No
Submit to:
  The Secretary
  (See address above)

JOURNAL OF MEDIEVAL HISTORY [1153]

North Holland Publishing Company
P. O. Box 211
Amsterdam, The Netherlands

First published in 1975

SUBSCRIPTION DATA
Issues and rates: Published quarterly.
  Annual rate(s): Individuals $13.50; Institutions $32.95

EDITORIAL DESCRIPTION
  Papers cover all aspects of medieval European history.
Articles per average issue: 5
Audience: Academic
  Manuscripts accepted in English, French, German

MANUSCRIPT INFORMATION
Subject field(s): Medieval Europe, North Africa, Middle East, including the British Isles, c. 400-1500 A.D.
Manuscript requirements: See latest issue for style requirements. Style sheet sent on request.
  Preferred length: 7,000-10,000 words; 30 pages
  Number of copies to be submitted: 3
  Abstract: Yes
Author information and reprints: Payment: Reprints only. 25 free reprints
  Is simultaneous submission of article to other journals permitted: Permitted, but not encouraged.
  Exclusive manuscript rights between acceptance and publication: Yes
  Copyright: No specific arrangements
  Reprints: Available at cost.
Disposition of manuscript:
  Query letter: Not necessary, but advisable.
  Receipt of manuscript acknowledged: Yes
  Decision to publish in: 1-2 weeks
  Accepted manuscript published in: 6 months
  Rejected manuscript returned: Yes, if return postage is supplied by author.
  Rejected manuscript criticized: Sometimes
Submit to:
  Prof. Richard Vaughan
  Editor
  Department of History
  University of Hull
  Hull HU6 7RX, England

JOURNAL OF MEXICAN-AMERICAN HISTORY [1154]

P.O. Box 13861, UCSB
Santa Barbara, California 93107
(805) 968-5915

First published in 1970

SUBSCRIPTION DATA
Issues and rates: Published annually.
  Average paid circulation: 1,000
  Annual rate(s): $12.50

EDITORIAL DESCRIPTION
  Contains articles, reviews, bibliography concerning Mexicans in the United States, 1848-present. Strong preference for rigorous, thoroughly documented research. Polemical articles strictly held accountable for documentation.

MANUSCRIPT INFORMATION
Subject field(s): History, social science, other disciplines
Manuscript requirements: See latest issue for style requirements.
  Preferred length: 20,000 words maximum; 40 pages
  Number of copies to be submitted: Two
  Abstract: No
Author information and reprints: Payment: None.
  Is simultaneous submission of article to other journals permitted: No
  Exclusive manuscript rights between acceptance and publication: Yes
  Copyright: Held by either author or publication
  Reprints: Not available.
Additional information: Require thorough documentation, consistent style, notes at back of manuscript.
Disposition of manuscript:
  Query letter: Preferred
  Receipt of manuscript acknowledged: Yes
  Decision to publish in: Varies
  Accepted manuscript published in: 1-9 months
  Rejected manuscript returned: Yes, if self-addressed, stamped envelope is sent with manuscript.
  Rejected manuscript criticized: Yes
Submit to:
  Joseph P. Navarro
  Editor
  (See address above)

THE JOURNAL OF MISSISSIPPI HISTORY [1155]

Box 571
Jackson, Mississippi 39205
(601) 354-6218

First published in 1939

SUBSCRIPTION DATA
Issues and rates: Published quarterly.
  Average paid circulation: 2,100
  Annual rate(s): $6.50
Publisher or Sponsor: Mississippi Historical Society; Mississippi Department of Archives and History
Managing Editor: John E. Gonzales

EDITORIAL DESCRIPTION
  Contains articles relating to Mississippi history; genealogical articles on Mississippians.
Articles per average issue: 6-7
Audience: Historians and other scholars.
  Manuscripts accepted in English only

MANUSCRIPT INFORMATION
Subject field(s): All areas of Mississippi history
Manuscript requirements: Chicago
  Preferred length: 20-25 pages
  Number of copies to be submitted: One
  Abstract: No
Author information and reprints: Payment: None.
  Is simultaneous submission of article to other journals permitted: No
  Exclusive manuscript rights between acceptance and publication: Yes
  Copyright: Held by publication.
  Reprints: Available
Disposition of manuscript:
  Query letter: No
  Receipt of manuscript acknowledged: Yes
  Decision to publish in: 6 months

Accepted manuscript published in: 2-3 years
Rejected manuscript returned: Yes
Rejected manuscript criticized: Yes
Submit to:
John E. Gonzales
Editor
Box 181, Southern Station
University of Southern Mississippi
Hattiesburg, Mississippi 39401
(601) 266-7197

THE JOURNAL OF MODERN HISTORY [1156]

5801 South Ellis Avenue
Chicago, Illinois 60637
(312) 753-3347

First published in 1929

SUBSCRIPTION DATA

Issues and rates: Published quarterly.
Average paid circulation: 5,000
Annual rate(s): Individuals $10.00; Institutions $14.00; Students $8.50; Members $8.50; Foreign individuals $11.00; Foreign institutions $15.00
Publisher or Sponsor: American Historical Association, Modern European History Section
Managing Editor: William H. McNeill

EDITORIAL DESCRIPTION

European history since 1500
Articles per average issue: Four
Audience: University and professional
Manuscripts accepted in English

MANUSCRIPT INFORMATION

Manuscript requirements: Style sheet sent on request.
Preferred length: 40 Typewritten pages maximum
Number of copies to be submitted: Two
Abstract: Not necessary.
Author information and reprints: Payment: Reprints only. 50 reprints
Is simultaneous submission of article to other journals permitted: Not permitted.
Exclusive manuscript rights between acceptance and publication: Yes
Copyright: Held by The University of Chicago Press
Reprints: Available at cost. $2.50 per page
Disposition of manuscript:
Query letter: Not necessary.
Receipt of manuscript acknowledged: Yes
Decision to publish in: 2 Months
Accepted manuscript published in: 2 Years
Rejected manuscript returned: Yes, with return postage paid by publication.
Rejected manuscript criticized: Sometimes
Submit to:
William H. McNeill
Editor
1126 East 59th Street
Chicago, Illinois 60637
(312) 753-2627

JOURNAL OF SOCIAL HISTORY [1157]

Carnegie-Mellon University
Pittsburgh, Pennsylvania 15213
(412) 621-2600

First published in 1967

SUBSCRIPTION DATA

Issues and rates: Published quarterly.
Average paid circulation: 1500
Annual rate(s): $15.00; Institutions $18.00
Managing Editor: Peter N. Stearns

EDITORIAL DESCRIPTION

Contains articles and extensive reviews on topics of substantive and methodological concern to social historians. Focus on problems of modernization, particularly but not exclusively in Europe and the U.S. Interested in encouraging new kinds of research and analysis in the field of social history.
Articles per average issue: 5
Audience: Social scientists and historians
Manuscripts accepted in English

MANUSCRIPT INFORMATION

Subject field(s): Social protest, stratification, mobility, family history, cultural values
Manuscript requirements: Chicago
Preferred length: 25-35 pages
Number of copies to be submitted: One
Abstract: No
Author information and reprints: Payment: None.
Is simultaneous submission of article to other journals permitted: No
Exclusive manuscript rights between acceptance and publication: Yes
Copyright: Held by publication.
Reprints: Available, $.75 each after first 25
Disposition of manuscript:
Query letter: No
Receipt of manuscript acknowledged: No
Decision to publish in: 2 months or less
Accepted manuscript published in: One year
Rejected manuscript returned: Yes, if return postage is supplied by author.
Rejected manuscript criticized: Yes
Submit to:
Editor
(See address above)

JOURNAL OF SOUTHERN HISTORY [1158]

Rice University
Houston, Texas 77001
(713) 528-4141 ext. 293

First published in 1935

SUBSCRIPTION DATA

Issues and rates: Published quarterly.
Average paid circulation: 5,000
Annual rate(s): $10.00
Publisher or Sponsor: Southern Historical Association
Managing Editor: S. W. Higginbotham

EDITORIAL DESCRIPTION

Contains documented research articles in the field of Southern history; reviews of books on Southern and general American history and historiography; book notes; historical news and notices.
Articles per average issue: 4
Audience: Professional historians and students
Manuscripts accepted in English

MANUSCRIPT INFORMATION

Subject field(s): Southern history; slavery, abolition, and the Negro; Civil War and Confederacy; reconstruction
Manuscript requirements: See latest issue for style requirements.
Preferred length: 6,500-11,000 words
Number of copies to be submitted: Two
Abstract: No
Author information and reprints: Payment: None.
Is simultaneous submission of article to other journals permitted: No
Exclusive manuscript rights between acceptance and publication: Yes
Copyright: Held by publication.
Reprints: Available at no cost, unless special covers are requested
Disposition of manuscript:
Query letter: No
Receipt of manuscript acknowledged: Yes
Decision to publish in: 6 weeks
Accepted manuscript published in: 9-15 months
Rejected manuscript returned: Yes
Rejected manuscript criticized: Sometimes
Submit to:
S. W. Higginbotham
Managing Editor
(See address above)

JOURNAL OF THE WEST [1159]

1915 South Western Avenue
Los Angeles, California 90018
(213) 734-1911

First published in 1962

SUBSCRIPTION DATA

Issues and rates: Published quarterly.
Average paid circulation: 4,200
Annual rate(s): $12.00; Foreign $16.00; Institutions $10.00

EDITORIAL DESCRIPTION

Publishes articles on western history and geography from the Mississippi River west including Canada, Alaska, Mexico, and Central America
Articles per average issue: 6-12
Audience: Academic, general
Manuscripts accepted in English, Spanish

MANUSCRIPT INFORMATION

Subject field(s): All phases of western history and geography, including archaeology, anthropology, geology, etc.

Manuscript requirements: No specific style guide. Chicago
   Preferred length: 5,000-7,000 words
   Number of copies to be submitted: 2
   Abstract: Not necessary.
Author information and reprints: Payment: Reprints only. 10
   Is simultaneous submission of article to other journals permitted: Not permitted.
   Exclusive manuscript rights between acceptance and publication: Yes
   Copyright: Held by publication.
   Reprints: Not available.
Disposition of manuscript:
   Query letter: Not necessary.
   Receipt of manuscript acknowledged: Yes
   Decision to publish in: 6-12 months
   Rejected manuscript returned: Yes, if return postage is supplied by author.
   Rejected manuscript criticized: Sometimes
Submit to:
   Lorrin L. Morrison
   Editor and Publisher
   (See address above)

KENTUCKY HISTORICAL SOCIETY REGISTER [1160]
P.O. Box H
Frankfort, Kentucky 40601
(502) 564-3016

First published in 1903

SUBSCRIPTION DATA
Issues and rates: Published quarterly.
   Average paid circulation: 9,500
   Annual rate(s): $5.00
Publisher or Sponsor: The Kentucky Historical Society
Managing Editor: Hambleton Tapp

EDITORIAL DESCRIPTION
   Publishes scholarly articles on Kentucky history, or with a bearing upon Kentucky history. Scholars in the United States review books written in the field of history, largely, but not altogether, American history.
Articles per average issue: 5
Audience: Persons interested in Kentucky history; local, state, national historians, scholars, writers
   Manuscripts accepted in English

MANUSCRIPT INFORMATION
Subject field(s): Social, political, military, economic, educational, religious, legal, cultural, biographical; interstate relations as concerns Kentucky
Manuscript requirements: Chicago
   Preferred length: 25-30 pages
   Number of copies to be submitted: One
   Abstract: No
Author information and reprints: Payment: None.
   Is simultaneous submission of article to other journals permitted: Yes
   Exclusive manuscript rights between acceptance and publication: No
   Copyright: Held by publication.
   Reprints: Available

Disposition of manuscript:
   Query letter: Yes
   Receipt of manuscript acknowledged: Yes
   Decision to publish in: 2 weeks
   Accepted manuscript published in: 6-12 months
   Rejected manuscript returned: Yes
   Rejected manuscript criticized: No
Submit to:
   Hambleton Tapp
   Editor
   (See address above)

LANCASTER COUNTY HISTORICAL SOCIETY JOURNAL [1161]
230 North President Avenue
Lancaster, Pennsylvania 17603
(717) 392-4633

Previously entitled *Papers Read Before the LCHS 1896-1955*

First published in 1896

SUBSCRIPTION DATA
Issues and rates: Published quarterly.
   Average paid circulation: 2350
   Annual rate(s): $10.00
Publisher or Sponsor: Lancaster County Historical Society
Managing Editor: John Ward Willson Loose

EDITORIAL DESCRIPTION
   Contains a mixture of scholarly research papers, theses, dissertations, and less formal essays and memoirs, pertaining primarily to Lancaster County history and biography. Protection of both scholars' freedom and responsible scholarship is the editorial point of view.
Articles per average issue: 3
Audience: Academic and general history interest
   Manuscripts accepted in English

MANUSCRIPT INFORMATION
Subject field(s): Economic history, intellectual history, political history, social history, technological history, biography, historiography (methods), primarily pertaining to Southeastern Pennsylvania.
Manuscript requirements: Chicago, MLA
   Preferred length: 32-80 pages
   Number of copies to be submitted: One
   Abstract: No
Author information and reprints: Payment: None.
   Is simultaneous submission of article to other journals permitted: Yes
   Exclusive manuscript rights between acceptance and publication: Yes
   Copyright: Held by publication.
   Reprints: Available, 20 free; additional at cost
Additional information: Illustrative material accepted.
Disposition of manuscript:
   Query letter: No
   Receipt of manuscript acknowledged: Yes
   Decision to publish in: 2 months
   Accepted manuscript published in: 2-8 months
   Rejected manuscript returned: Yes
   Rejected manuscript criticized: Yes
Submit to:
   John Ward Willson Loose
   Editor-in-Chief
   3311 Columbia Pike
   Lancaster, Pennsylvania 17603
   (717) 392-4513

MANITOBA PAGEANT [1162]
M211-190 Rupert Avenue
Winnipeg, Manitoba R3B0N2, Canada
(204) 943-7037

SUBSCRIPTION DATA
Issues and rates: Published three times per year.
   Average paid circulation: 1000
   Annual rate(s): $2.50
Publisher or Sponsor: Manitoba Historical Society
Managing Editor: W.J. Fraser

EDITORIAL DESCRIPTION
   Contains historical articles pertaining to the history of the province of Manitoba, Canada.
Articles per average issue: Depends on length of manuscript
Audience: Mainly in Canada but also in U.S.
   Manuscripts accepted in English

MANUSCRIPT INFORMATION
Subject field(s): History of Manitoba
Manuscript requirements: See latest issue for style requirements.
   Preferred length: Varies
   Number of copies to be submitted: One
   Abstract: No
Author information and reprints: Payment: None.
   Is simultaneous submission of article to other journals permitted: No
   Exclusive manuscript rights between acceptance and publication: Yes, unless otherwise authorized
   Copyright: Held by publication.
   Reprints: Not available.
Disposition of manuscript:
   Query letter: Not necessary
   Receipt of manuscript acknowledged: Yes
   Decision to publish in: 6 months
   Accepted manuscript published in: Up to one year
   Rejected manuscript returned: Yes, if return postage is supplied by author.
   Rejected manuscript criticized: No
Submit to:
   Editor
   (See address above)

MANKIND [1163]
The Magazine of Popular History
8060 Melrose Avenue
Los Angeles, California 90046
(213) 653-8060

First published in 1967

History

SUBSCRIPTION DATA

Issues and rates: Published bi-monthly.
  Average paid circulation: 150,000
  Annual rate(s): $6.50, Foreign $8.50

EDITORIAL DESCRIPTION

Contains articles of significant historical, cultural or artistic value which are accurate and involve the reader immediately in the excitement of human events. Open to any aspect of man's history that is professionally handled and involves a fresh point of view.

Articles per average issue: 8
Audience: History buffs and students
  Manuscripts accepted in English only

MANUSCRIPT INFORMATION

Subject field(s): Query
Manuscript requirements: See latest issue for style requirements.
  Preferred length: 3,000 to 4,000 words; 12 to 15 pages
  Number of copies to be submitted: One
  Abstract: Not necessary
Author information and reprints: Payment: By publication to author. From $150-$250 per article.
  Is simultaneous submission of article to other journals permitted: No
  Exclusive manuscript rights between acceptance and publication: Yes
  Copyright: Held by publication.
  Reprints: Not available.
Additional information: Magazine is pictorially oriented, so articles should be geared toward this and author should, if possible, indicate good sources of pictorial material and even provide these himself.
Disposition of manuscript:
  Query letter: Preferable
  Receipt of manuscript acknowledged: No, unless return card is enclosed
  Decision to publish in: 6-8 weeks
  Accepted manuscript published in: 6 months to a year
  Rejected manuscript returned: Yes, if return postage is supplied by author.
  Rejected manuscript criticized: No
Submit to:
  Alvaro Cardona-Hine
  Editor
  (See address above)

THE MARYLAND HISTORIAN [1164]

History Department
University of Maryland
College Park, Maryland 20742
(301) 454-2843

First published in 1970

SUBSCRIPTION DATA

Issues and rates: Published semi-annually.
  Average paid circulation: 350; 100 controlled
  Annual rate(s): Individuals $3.00; Institutions $8.00

EDITORIAL DESCRIPTION

Offers scholarly articles, review essays, and special features of interest to historians and general readers.

Articles per average issue: 5
Audience: Historians and general readers
  Manuscripts accepted in English

MANUSCRIPT INFORMATION

Subject field(s): All fields of history
Manuscript requirements: See latest issue for style requirements.
  Preferred length: 25 pages
  Number of copies to be submitted: 1
  Abstract: Not necessary.
Author information and reprints: Payment: Reprints only. 25 reprints
  Is simultaneous submission of article to other journals permitted: Not permitted.
  Copyright: Held by publication.
  Reprints: Available at cost.
Additional information: Both student and faculty articles accepted; not a "house organ" for the University of Maryland nor strictly a journal of Maryland history. Will consider appropriate illustrations.
Disposition of manuscript:
  Query letter: Not necessary.
  Receipt of manuscript acknowledged: Yes
  Decision to publish in: 2 months
  Rejected manuscript returned: Yes, with return postage paid by publication.
  Rejected manuscript criticized: Yes
Submit to:
  Editor
  (See address above)

MICHIGAN HISTORY [1165]

Michigan History Division
Department of State
208 North Capital
Lansing, Michigan 48918
(517) 373-0510

First published in 1917

SUBSCRIPTION DATA

Issues and rates: Published quarterly.
  Average paid circulation: 5,000
  Annual rate(s): $5.00

EDITORIAL DESCRIPTION

Publication has as its primary purpose the publication of scholarly articles, documents, and reviews contributing to the knowledge and the study of the history of the state of Michigan.

Articles per average issue: 3-4
Audience: Scholars, general
  Manuscripts accepted in English

MANUSCRIPT INFORMATION

Subject field(s): Old Northwest, state of Michigan, Great Lakes, Middle West, Canadian History
Manuscript requirements: Chicago
  Preferred length: 5,000-6,000 words; 20 pages
  Number of copies to be submitted: Two, original and carbon or machine copy
  Abstract: No

Author information and reprints: Payment: None.
  Is simultaneous submission of article to other journals permitted: No
  Exclusive manuscript rights between acceptance and publication: Yes
  Copyright: Held by publication.
  Reprints: Available; publication holds the final rights for reprinting any material but consults the author for his wishes and generally follows them.
Additional information: Typescript to be double-spaced. Place footnotes separately after the text.
Disposition of manuscript:
  Receipt of manuscript acknowledged:
  Decision to publish in: 6-9 weeks
  Accepted manuscript published in: 6-12 months
  Rejected manuscript returned: Yes
  Rejected manuscript criticized: Yes
Submit to:
  John Hoffmann
  Editor
  (See address above)

SPECIAL STIPULATIONS

Often publishes thematic issues and will hold articles for a longer period of time, in this instance. However, the author is notified of such a possibility, and may request the return of his manuscript if the time span involved is unacceptable to him.

MID-AMERICA [1166]

An Historical Review
Loyola University
6525 Sheridan Road
Chicago, Illinois 60626
(312) 274-3000

Previously entitled *Illinois Catholic Historical Review*

First published in 1918

SUBSCRIPTION DATA

Issues and rates: Published quarterly.
  Average paid circulation: 700
  Annual rate(s): $5.00, Foreign $6.00
Publisher or Sponsor: Loyola University, Chicago
Managing Editor: John V. Mentag

EDITORIAL DESCRIPTION

Contains articles dealing with U.S. history; book reviews, notes and comments. In recent years preference has been given to topics treating events of the late 19th century and 20th century to 1933.

Articles per average issue: 3-4
Audience: College and university professors and students
  Manuscripts accepted in English

MANUSCRIPT INFORMATION

Subject field(s): U.S. political, diplomatic history; religion in politics, topics at editor's discretion.

Manuscript requirements: See latest issue for style requirements.
Preferred length: 5000-7000 words; 20-30 pages
Number of copies to be submitted: One
Abstract: No
Author information and reprints: Payment: None.
Is simultaneous submission of article to other journals permitted: No
Exclusive manuscript rights between acceptance and publication: Yes
Copyright: Held by publication.
Reprints: Available at author's expense
Disposition of manuscript:
Query letter: No, but would be helpful
Receipt of manuscript acknowledged: Yes
Decision to publish in: 2 months
Accepted manuscript published in: 6 months to 2 years
Rejected manuscript returned: Yes, if return postage is supplied by author.
Rejected manuscript criticized: Sometimes
Submit to:
Editor
(See address above)

MINNESOTA HISTORY [1167]

The Quarterly of the Minnesota Historical Society
690 Cedar Street
St. Paul, Minnesota 55101
(612) 296-2264

Previously entitled *Minnesota History Bulletin*

First published in 1915

SUBSCRIPTION DATA

Issues and rates: Published quarterly.
Average paid circulation: 7,000
Annual rate(s): Members $10.00, Institutions $10.00
Publisher or Sponsor: Minnesota Historical Society

EDITORIAL DESCRIPTION

Publishes scholarly articles, book reviews, and news notes relating to the history of Minnesota and the upper Midwest. It is directed to both professional and general readers with an interest in the history of the state and the region.
Articles per average issue: 2-3
Audience: Professional, general
Manuscripts accepted in English only

MANUSCRIPT INFORMATION

Subject field(s): Midwest: exploration, Indians, pioneers, folklore, fur trade; Minnesota political history, economic history, archaeology, agriculture, ethnic groups, social history; historic sites
Manuscript requirements: Style sheet sent on request.
Preferred length: 5,000 to 8,000 words; 15 to 35 pages
Number of copies to be submitted: One
Abstract: No

Author information and reprints: Payment: None.
Is simultaneous submission of article to other journals permitted: No
Exclusive manuscript rights between acceptance and publication: Yes
Copyright: Held by publication.
Reprints: Available
Additional information: Manuscripts should be footnoted and in proper style. Author requested to furnish pictures pertinent to subject, map suggestions, graphs if appropriate.
Disposition of manuscript:
Query letter: No
Receipt of manuscript acknowledged: Yes
Decision to publish in: Up to three months
Accepted manuscript published in: Varies
Rejected manuscript returned: Yes
Rejected manuscript criticized: Sometimes
Submit to:
Kenneth A. Carley
Editor
(See address above)

MONTANA: THE MAGAZINE OF WESTERN HISTORY [1168]

225 North Roberts Street
Helena, Montana 59601
(406) 449-2694

Previously entitled *Montana Magazine of History*

First published in 1951

SUBSCRIPTION DATA

Issues and rates: Published quarterly.
Average paid circulation: 4,000
Annual rate(s): $7.50, Foreign $9.00
Publisher or Sponsor: The Montana Historical Society
Managing Editor: Vivian A. Paladin

EDITORIAL DESCRIPTION

Contains history of the Trans-Mississippi West, authentically written and backed by valid research, but not overly-scholarly approach. Heavily illustrated with authentic pictures and/or documentary art.
Articles per average issue: 5
Audience: general
Manuscripts accepted in English only

MANUSCRIPT INFORMATION

Subject field(s): History of American West, all facets: exploration, fur trade, mining, homesteading, open range cattle period, politics, industrial history, etc.
Manuscript requirements: Style sheet sent on request.
Preferred length: 3,500 to 7,000 words; 12 to 22 pages
Number of copies to be submitted: One
Abstract: No
Author information and reprints: Payment: By publication to author.
Is simultaneous submission of article to other journals permitted: No

Exclusive manuscript rights between acceptance and publication: Yes
Copyright: Held by publication.
Reprints: Not available.
Additional information: Release of articles for inclusion in book-length treatments given without charge if arrangements are made at time of manuscript acquisition.
Disposition of manuscript:
Query letter: Preferred, but not necessary
Receipt of manuscript acknowledged: Yes
Decision to publish in: 2 months
Accepted manuscript published in: Within the coming two volume years.
Rejected manuscript returned: Yes, if return postage is supplied by author.
Rejected manuscript criticized: Yes
Submit to:
Vivian A. Paladin
Editor
(See address above)

NEBRASKA HISTORY [1169]

Nebraska State Historical Society
1500 R Street
Lincoln, Nebraska 68508
(402) 432-2793 ext. 002

First published in 1918

SUBSCRIPTION DATA

Issues and rates: Published quarterly.
Average paid circulation: Not available.
Annual rate(s): $3.00
Publisher or Sponsor: Nebraska State Historical Society

EDITORIAL DESCRIPTION

Publishes articles relating to history, politics, and anthropology in Nebraska and the plains.
Articles per average issue: 4-6
Manuscripts accepted in English

MANUSCRIPT INFORMATION

Subject field(s): History (Nebraska), politics (Nebraska), anthropology (Plains), biography (Nebraskans), reminiscences
Manuscript requirements: See latest issue for style requirements.
Preferred length: 6,000 words; 25 pages
Number of copies to be submitted: One
Abstract: No
Author information and reprints: Payment: None. Six copies of the issue in which the manuscript is published
Is simultaneous submission of article to other journals permitted: No, author may withdraw manuscript upon request
Exclusive manuscript rights between acceptance and publication: Yes
Reprints: Available, by special arrangement
Additional information: Manuscripts should be in proper style with footnotes on separate pages. Authors should include a resume for contributors section.
Disposition of manuscript:
Query letter: No
Receipt of manuscript acknowledged: Yes
Decision to publish in: 6-8 weeks
Accepted manuscript published in: 12-24 months

Rejected manuscript returned: Yes
Rejected manuscript criticized: Sometimes
Submit to:
Marvin F. Kivett
Editor
(See address above)

NEW JERSEY HISTORY [1170]

The New Jersey Historical Society
230 Broadway
Newark, New Jersey 07104
(201) 483-3939

Previously entitled *Proceedings of the New Jersey Historical Society*

First published in 1845

SUBSCRIPTION DATA

Issues and rates: Published quarterly.
Average paid circulation: 2,800
Annual rate(s): Institutions $10.00; Members $15.00
Publisher or Sponsor: The New Jersey Historical Society
Managing Editor: Joseph F. Mahoney

EDITORIAL DESCRIPTION

All aspects of the history of the colony and state of New Jersey.
Articles per average issue: 3
Audience: Professional and avocational historians of New Jersey
Manuscripts accepted in English

MANUSCRIPT INFORMATION

Subject field(s): Any aspect of New Jersey history
Manuscript requirements: See latest issue for style requirements. MLA, slightly modified
Preferred length: 20-25 pages
Number of copies to be submitted: One, two preferred
Abstract: Not necessary.
Author information and reprints: Payment: Reprints only. 25 Reprints
Is simultaneous submission of article to other journals permitted: Not permitted.
Exclusive manuscript rights between acceptance and publication: Yes
Copyright: Held by publication.
Reprints: Not available.
Disposition of manuscript:
Query letter: Not necessary.
Receipt of manuscript acknowledged: Yes
Decision to publish in: 90-120 days
Accepted manuscript published in: 6-12 Months
Rejected manuscript returned: Yes, if return postage is supplied by author.
Rejected manuscript criticized: Sometimes
Submit to:
Joseph F. Mahoney
Editor
(See address above)

NEW MEXICO HISTORICAL REVIEW [1171]

Bandelier 122, University of New Mexico
Albuquerque, New Mexico 87131
(505) 277-2027

First published in 1926

SUBSCRIPTION DATA

Issues and rates: Published quarterly.
Annual rate(s): $6.00
Publisher or Sponsor: University of New Mexico

EDITORIAL DESCRIPTION

For the publication of legitimate historical material of New Mexican and regional interest, including scholarly articles, documents, bibliographies and book reviews. Geographically, the region comprises the area of the Spanish Colonial Viceroyalty of New Spain north from Mexico City. This does not exclude the publication of material deemed relevant to the general background and understanding of this region even though not dealing specifically with it.
Articles per average issue: 3
Audience: Professional, general
Manuscripts accepted in English

MANUSCRIPT INFORMATION

Manuscript requirements: Style sheet sent on request.
Preferred length: 10-35 pages
Number of copies to be submitted: Two
Author information and reprints: Payment: A small honorarium and 2 copies of whole issue, 25 offprints
Is simultaneous submission of article to other journals permitted: No
Exclusive manuscript rights between acceptance and publication: Yes
Copyright: Held by publication.
Reprints: Available at cost.
Additional information: Use of information sheet requested, or consult current issues. Double-space all copy and leave ample margins.
Disposition of manuscript:
Query letter: No
Receipt of manuscript acknowledged: Yes
Decision to publish in: Up to two months
Accepted manuscript published in: 6 to 18 months
Rejected manuscript returned: Yes
Rejected manuscript criticized: On occasion
Submit to:
Eleanor B. Adams
Editor
(See address above)

THE NEW YORK HISTORICAL SOCIETY QUARTERLY [1172]

170 Central Park West
New York, New York 10024
(212) 873-3400

First published in 1917

SUBSCRIPTION DATA

Issues and rates: Published quarterly.
Average paid circulation: 400; 1,700 controlled
Annual rate(s): Individuals $10.00; Members Free
Managing Editor: Kathleen Luhrs

EDITORIAL DESCRIPTION

Contains well-researched, scholarly articles pertaining to New York City and State history, and reviews of current books on United States history.
Articles per average issue: 3-4
Audience: Scholars in American history and art, librarians, and curators
Manuscripts accepted in English

MANUSCRIPT INFORMATION

Subject field(s): United States history and art, New York City and State, chronologically ranging from 1660 through World War II.
Manuscript requirements: Style sheet sent on request. Chicago
Preferred length: 8,000-9,000 words; 30-35 typed pages
Number of copies to be submitted: Two
Abstract: Not necessary.
Author information and reprints: Payment: Reprints only. 3 Issues, 25 offprints
Is simultaneous submission of article to other journals permitted: Not permitted.
Exclusive manuscript rights between acceptance and publication: No
Copyright: Held by publication
Reprints: Available at cost. $.75
Additional information: Require thoroughly documented footnotes, double-spaced in a separate grouping at the end of the article.
Disposition of manuscript:
Query letter: Not necessary, but advisable.
Receipt of manuscript acknowledged: Yes
Decision to publish in: 1-3 Months
Accepted manuscript published in: 4-12 Months
Rejected manuscript returned: Yes, with return postage paid by publication.
Rejected manuscript criticized: Sometimes
Submit to:
Kathleen Luhrs
Editor
(See address above)

NEW YORK HISTORY [1173]

Quarterly Journal of the N.Y.S.H.A.
Fenimore House
Cooperstown, New York 13326
(607) 547-2533 ext. 74

Previously entitled *Quarterly Journal of the N.Y.S.H.A.*

First published in 1919

SUBSCRIPTION DATA

Issues and rates: Published quarterly.
Average paid circulation: 2600; 200 controlled
Annual rate(s): $12.00

Publisher or Sponsor: New York State Historical Association
Managing Editor: Wendell Tripp

EDITORIAL DESCRIPTION

Contains articles relating to various aspects of the history of New York state and of aspects of national history that have influenced the history of New York state. Articles are directed to the professional historian and to the knowledgeable amateur historian.
Articles per average issue: 4
Audience: Academic and amateur historians
Manuscripts accepted in English

MANUSCRIPT INFORMATION

Subject field(s): New York history, New York literature, Northeast history, national history
Manuscript requirements: Chicago, with slight modifications available upon request.
  Preferred length: 4500 words; 25 pages
  Number of copies to be submitted: One
  Abstract: No
Author information and reprints: Payment: None. Ten copies of issue free to author.
  Is simultaneous submission of article to other journals permitted: No
  Exclusive manuscript rights between acceptance and publication: Yes
  Copyright: Held by publication.
  Reprints: Available, cost varies with length
Additional information: Footnotes should be on separate pages.
Disposition of manuscript:
  Query letter: No
  Receipt of manuscript acknowledged: Yes
  Decision to publish in: 6-8 weeks
  Accepted manuscript published in: 6-9 months
  Rejected manuscript returned: Yes, if return postage is supplied by author.
  Rejected manuscript criticized: Yes
Submit to:
  Wendell Tripp
  Editorial Associate
  (See address above)

THE NORTH CAROLINA HISTORICAL REVIEW [1174]
Division of Archives and History
109 East Jones Street
Raleigh, North Carolina 27611
(919) 829-7442

SUBSCRIPTION DATA

Issues and rates: Published quarterly.
  Average paid circulation: 2,500
  Annual rate(s): $6.00
Publisher or Sponsor: North Carolina Division of Archives and History
Managing Editor: Memory F. Mitchell

EDITORIAL DESCRIPTION

Contains articles on many phases of North Carolina and Southern history, documentary materials, book reviews; illustrated; each volume indexed. The editorial board is interested in articles and documents pertaining to the history of North Carolina and adjacent states. Articles on the history of other sections will be considered when there are ties with North Carolinians or events significant in the history of the state. Materials primarily genealogical are not accepted.

MANUSCRIPT INFORMATION

Subject field(s): History
Manuscript requirements: Chicago
  Preferred length: 15-25 pages
  Number of copies to be submitted: Two
Author information and reprints: Payment: By publication to author. $10.00 per article.
  Is simultaneous submission of article to other journals permitted: No
  Exclusive manuscript rights between acceptance and publication: Yes
  Copyright: Held by publication.
  Reprints: Available at cost set by printer.
Additional information: Ten copies of issue containing article are sent to author.
Disposition of manuscript:
  Receipt of manuscript acknowledged: Yes
  Decision to publish in: 2 months
  Accepted manuscript published in: 1-2 years
  Rejected manuscript returned: Yes
  Rejected manuscript criticized: Usually
Submit to:
  Memory F. Mitchell
  Editor
  (See address above)

OHIO HISTORY [1175]
Ohio Historical Center
1982 Velma Avenue
Columbus, Ohio 43211
(614) 466-5282

Previously entitled *Ohio Archaeological and Historical Society Quarterly; Ohio Historical Quarterly*

First published in 1887

SUBSCRIPTION DATA

Issues and rates: Published quarterly.
  Average paid circulation: 9000; 350 controlled
  Annual rate(s): $10.00
Publisher or Sponsor: Ohio Historical Society
Managing Editor: Helen M. Thurston

EDITORIAL DESCRIPTION

Contains articles, documents, and reviews which contribute to the knowledge of the history of Ohio and its people.
Articles per average issue: 4-5
Audience: General public as well as academic
Manuscripts accepted in English only

MANUSCRIPT INFORMATION

Subject field(s): Political history, social history, cultural history, economic history, institutional history, folk history, architectural history, natural history, biography, prehistory
Manuscript requirements: See latest issue for style requirements.
  Preferred length: 6500 words; 25 pages
  Number of copies to be submitted: One
  Abstract: No
Author information and reprints: Payment: None.
  Is simultaneous submission of article to other journals permitted: No
  Exclusive manuscript rights between acceptance and publication: No
  Copyright: Held by publication.
  Reprints: Not available. but 25 copies of an issue given to author
Additional information: Original research required.
Disposition of manuscript:
  Query letter: No
  Receipt of manuscript acknowledged: Yes
  Decision to publish in: One month
  Accepted manuscript published in: Varies
  Rejected manuscript returned: Yes, if return postage is supplied by author.
  Rejected manuscript criticized: Yes
Submit to:
  Helen M. Thurston
  Managing Editor
  (See address above)

OREGON HISTORICAL QUARTERLY [1176]
1230 SW Park Avenue
Portland, Oregon 97205
(503) 222-1741

First published in 1900

SUBSCRIPTION DATA

Issues and rates: Published quarterly.
  Average paid circulation: 5100
  Annual rate(s): $10.00
Publisher or Sponsor: Oregon Historical Society
Managing Editor: P. Knuth

EDITORIAL DESCRIPTION

Contains articles dealing with history and life in the Oregon country and history of the Pacific Northwest after 1859, related events in the nation and the world.
Articles per average issue: 3-5
Manuscripts accepted in English

MANUSCRIPT INFORMATION

Manuscript requirements: See latest issue for style requirements.
  Preferred length: 4,000-10,000 words
  Number of copies to be submitted: One
  Abstract: No
Author information and reprints: Payment: None. 10 copies of publication
  Is simultaneous submission of article to other journals permitted: No
  Exclusive manuscript rights between acceptance and publication: Yes
  Copyright: Held by publication.
  Reprints: Available, cost depends on length
Disposition of manuscript:
  Query letter: No
  Receipt of manuscript acknowledged: Yes
  Decision to publish in: 4-6 weeks

Accepted manuscript published in: 2-3 years
Rejected manuscript returned: Yes, if return postage is supplied by author.
Submit to:
P. Knuth
Executive Editor
(See address above)

THE PACIFIC HISTORIAN [1177]
University of the Pacific
3601 Pacific Avenue
Stockton, California 95204
(209) 946-2405

First published in 1957

SUBSCRIPTION DATA
Issues and rates: Published quarterly.
  Average paid circulation: 1800; 2500 controlled
  Annual rate(s): $6.00
Publisher or Sponsor: University of the Pacific
Managing Editor: Martha Seffer O'Bryon

EDITORIAL DESCRIPTION
  A quarterly of Western history and ideas.

MANUSCRIPT INFORMATION
Subject field(s): History, literature, Western art
Manuscript requirements: See latest issue for style requirements.
  Preferred length: 500 to 4,000 words
  Number of copies to be submitted: Two
Author information and reprints: Payment: None.
  Is simultaneous submission of article to other journals permitted: No
  Exclusive manuscript rights between acceptance and publication: Yes
  Copyright: Held by publication.
  Reprints: Available, $10 for 1000.
Additional information: Include photo of writer and biography. All material must be original research and footnotes and bibliography are appreciated.
Disposition of manuscript:
  Receipt of manuscript acknowledged: Yes
  Decision to publish in: 1 month
  Accepted manuscript published in: 1 year maximum
  Rejected manuscript returned: Yes
  Rejected manuscript criticized: No
Submit to:
Martha Seffer O'Bryon
Editor
(See address above)
(209) 466-8807

PACIFIC HISTORICAL REVIEW [1178]
Ralph Bunche Hall
University of California
Los Angeles, California 90024
(213) 825-3579

First published in 1932

SUBSCRIPTION DATA
Issues and rates: Published quarterly.
  Average paid circulation: 2000
  Annual rate(s): Individuals $8.00, Institutions $12.00, Students $4.00
Publisher or Sponsor: American Historical Association, Pacific Coast Branch
Managing Editor: Norris Hundley

EDITORIAL DESCRIPTION
  Devoted to the history of American expansionism to the Pacific and beyond, and to the post frontier developments of the 20th century American West. Also publishes articles on the methodologies and philosophies of historians.
Articles per average issue: Varies; usually 5
Manuscripts accepted in English

MANUSCRIPT INFORMATION
Manuscript requirements: See latest issue for style requirements. Manuscripts must be double spaced and notes must be submitted on separate sheets and double spaced.
  Preferred length: 5000 t0 7000 words
  Number of copies to be submitted: Three
  Abstract: No
Author information and reprints: Payment: None. 25 reprints and copy of the issue in which the article appears and a year's gratis subscription to the journal.
  Is simultaneous submission of article to other journals permitted: No
  Exclusive manuscript rights between acceptance and publication: Yes
  Copyright: Held by Association.
  Reprints: Available, 25 free
Disposition of manuscript:
  Query letter: No
  Receipt of manuscript acknowledged: Yes
  Decision to publish in: 4-12 weeks
  Accepted manuscript published in: Varies, but nearly always less than a year
  Rejected manuscript returned: Yes
  Rejected manuscript criticized: Yes
Submit to:
Norris C. Hundley
Managing Editor
(See address above)

PALIMPSEST [1179]
402 Iowa Avenue
Iowa City, Iowa 52240
(319) 338-5471

First published in 1920

SUBSCRIPTION DATA
Issues and rates: Published semi-monthly.
  Average paid circulation: 8,850 controlled
  Annual rate(s): Free with $5 membership
Publisher or Sponsor: State Historical Society of Iowa

EDITORIAL DESCRIPTION
  Articles published on the history of Iowa and the surrounding region which may be of interest to the general reading public.
Articles per average issue: 3
Audience: General
Manuscripts accepted in English

MANUSCRIPT INFORMATION
Subject field(s): Iowa: history, literature, biography, education, art, sociology, political science
Manuscript requirements: MLA
  Preferred length: 25-30 pages
  Number of copies to be submitted: Two
  Abstract: No
Author information and reprints: Payment: None.
  Is simultaneous submission of article to other journals permitted: No
  Exclusive manuscript rights between acceptance and publication: Yes
  Copyright: Held by publication.
  Reprints: Available, 24 free
Additional information: Photographic illustrations desired to accompany published article.
Disposition of manuscript:
  Query letter: No
  Receipt of manuscript acknowledged: Yes
  Decision to publish in: Varies
  Accepted manuscript published in: 2-6 months
  Rejected manuscript returned: Yes
  Rejected manuscript criticized: Sometimes
Submit to:
L. Edward Purcell
Editor
(See address above)

PROLOGUE: THE JOURNAL OF THE NATIONAL ARCHIVES [1180]
National Archives Building
Washington, D.C. 20408
(202) 963-4275

First published in 1969

SUBSCRIPTION DATA
Issues and rates: Published quarterly.
  Average paid circulation: 6,000; 8,000 controlled
  Annual rate(s): $5.00
Publisher or Sponsor: National Archives and Records Service
Managing Editor: John J. Rumbarger

EDITORIAL DESCRIPTION
  Contains scholarly articles in history, based on federal records in the custody of the National Archives, presidential libraries and federal records centers.
Articles per average issue: 4-5
Audience: Historians and general public
Manuscripts accepted in English

MANUSCRIPT INFORMATION
Subject field(s): History
Manuscript requirements: Chicago
  Preferred length: 20-30 pages
  Number of copies to be submitted: One
  Abstract: No
Author information and reprints: Payment: None.
  Is simultaneous submission of article to other journals permitted: No

Exclusive manuscript rights between acceptance and publication: Yes
Copyright: Author may elect to apply for copyright
Reprints: Available, 50 complimentary
Disposition of manuscript:
Query letter: Helpful
Receipt of manuscript acknowledged: Yes
Decision to publish in: 6-8 weeks
Accepted manuscript published in: 6-9 months
Rejected manuscript returned: Yes
Rejected manuscript criticized: Sometimes
Submit to:
John J. Rumbarger
Editor
(See address above)

REPORT AND HISTORICAL COLLECTIONS [1181]
South Dakota Department of History
Soldiers' and Sailors' Memorial
Pierre, South Dakota 57501
(605) 224-3615

First published in 1902

SUBSCRIPTION DATA
Issues and rates: Biennial
Average paid circulation: 1500
Annual rate(s): $9.00
Publisher or Sponsor: South Dakota State Historical Society
Managing Editor: Dayton W. Canaday

EDITORIAL DESCRIPTION
Publishes articles and documents on all aspects of the history of South Dakota and the surrounding region.
Articles per average issue: 5
Audience: General public and professionals
Manuscripts accepted in English only

MANUSCRIPT INFORMATION
Subject field(s): Pioneer history, Indian history, and all aspects of South Dakota history
Manuscript requirements: Chicago
Preferred length: 12,000-18,000 words; 50-80 pages
Number of copies to be submitted: One
Abstract: No
Author information and reprints: Payment: None. Two copies of issue in which article appears
Is simultaneous submission of article to other journals permitted: No
Exclusive manuscript rights between acceptance and publication: Yes
Copyright: Held by publication.
Reprints: Available at cost
Additional information: Manuscripts must be double-spaced and in the proper style, with footnotes, references, tables, and charts on separate pages.
Disposition of manuscript:
Query letter: No
Receipt of manuscript acknowledged: Yes
Decision to publish in: 1-2 months
Accepted manuscript published in: 9-12 months

Rejected manuscript returned: Yes
Rejected manuscript criticized: Yes
Submit to:
Dayton W. Canaday
Editor
(See address above)

THE SIXTEENTH CENTURY JOURNAL [1182]
Center for Reformation Research
6477 San Bonita Avenue
Saint Louis, Missouri 63105
(314) 727-6655

Previously entitled *Sixteenth Century Essays and Studies*

First published in 1970

SUBSCRIPTION DATA
Issues and rates: Published semi-annually.
Average paid circulation: 650; 150 controlled
Annual rate(s): $8.00; Institutions $12.50; Students $8.00; Members $7.00; Foreign individuals $12.00; Foreign institutions $15.00
Publisher or Sponsor: The Sixteenth Century Studies Conference and the Center for Reformation Research
Managing Editor: Robert V. Schnucker

EDITORIAL DESCRIPTION
Principal focus is upon European civilization of the 16th century, in particular upon the intellectual and ecclesiastical and political changes which accompanied the Reformation.
Articles per average issue: Seven
Audience: Scholars and students of the Renaissance and Reformation
Manuscripts accepted in English

MANUSCRIPT INFORMATION
Subject field(s): Sacred and secular history, intellectual, political, social, economic, theological, etc.; topics that relate to Europe and Europeans from the late 15th to the early 17th centuries.
Manuscript requirements: Chicago
Preferred length: None
Number of copies to be submitted: Two
Abstract: Not necessary.
Author information and reprints: Payment: None.
Is simultaneous submission of article to other journals permitted: Permitted, but not encouraged.
Exclusive manuscript rights between acceptance and publication: No
Copyright: Held by publication.
Reprints: Available at no cost. 25
Additional information: Footnotes at the bottom of the page and provide translation of any foreign language used in the manuscript.
Disposition of manuscript:
Query letter: Not necessary.
Receipt of manuscript acknowledged: Yes
Decision to publish in: 2-3 months
Accepted manuscript published in: 6-12 months

Rejected manuscript returned: Yes, with return postage paid by publication.
Rejected manuscript criticized: Yes
Submit to:
Robert M. Kingdon
Editor
(See address above)

SOUTH DAKOTA HISTORY [1183]
South Dakota State Historical Society
Quarterly
Soldiers' and Sailors' Memorial
Pierre, South Dakota 57501
(605) 224-3615

First published in 1970

SUBSCRIPTION DATA
Issues and rates: Published quarterly.
Average paid circulation: 2100
Annual rate(s): $5.00
Managing Editor: Janice M. Dykshorn

EDITORIAL DESCRIPTION
Publishes articles and documents on all aspects of the history of South Dakota and the surrounding region. Genealogical studies are not accepted.
Articles per average issue: 3
Audience: General public and professionals
Manuscripts accepted in English only

MANUSCRIPT INFORMATION
Subject field(s): Pioneer history, Indian history and all aspects of South Dakota history
Manuscript requirements: Chicago
Preferred length: 6,000 to 9,000 words; 25 to 35 pages typed double-spaced
Number of copies to be submitted: One
Abstract: No
Author information and reprints: Payment: None. three copies of issue in which article appears and 25 additional at cost
Is simultaneous submission of article to other journals permitted: No
Exclusive manuscript rights between acceptance and publication: Yes
Copyright: Held by publication.
Reprints: Not available.
Additional information: Manuscripts should be in the proper style, with footnotes, references, tables, and charts on separate pages. A short biographical statement should be enclosed, as well as any photographs that are intended to illustrate the article.
Disposition of manuscript:
Query letter: No
Receipt of manuscript acknowledged: Yes
Decision to publish in: 4-6 weeks
Accepted manuscript published in: 9-12 months
Rejected manuscript returned: Yes
Rejected manuscript criticized: Yes
Submit to:
Janice M. Dykshorn
Managing Editor
(See address above)

History

TECHNOLOGY AND CULTURE [1184]
The International Quarterly of the Society for the History of Technology
University of Chicago Press
5801 Ellis Avenue
Chicago, Illinois 60637
(312) 753-3347

First published in 1960

SUBSCRIPTION DATA
Issues and rates: Published quarterly.
   Average paid circulation: 2,000
   Annual rate(s): $15.00; Foreign $20.00
Publisher or Sponsor: Society for the History of Technology

EDITORIAL DESCRIPTION
Contains historical studies of the development of technology, and its relationship to economics, society, art, literature, politics, philosophy, etc. Also contains exhibit reviews, book reviews, bibliographies, and reports of conferences and meetings.
Articles per average issue: 6
Audience: Scholarly
   Manuscripts accepted in English

MANUSCRIPT INFORMATION
Manuscript requirements: Chicago
   Preferred length: 3000 words
   Number of copies to be submitted: Two
   Abstract: No
Author information and reprints: Payment: None.
   Is simultaneous submission of article to other journals permitted: No
   Exclusive manuscript rights between acceptance and publication: Yes
   Copyright: Held by publication.
   Reprints: Available, 25 free
Disposition of manuscript:
   Receipt of manuscript acknowledged: Yes
   Decision to publish in: 3 months
   Accepted manuscript published in: 8 months
   Rejected manuscript returned: Yes
   Rejected manuscript criticized: Yes
Submit to:
   Melvin Kranzberg
   Editor-in-Chief
   Department of Social Sciences
   Georgia Institute of Technology
   Atlanta, Georgia 30332
   (404) 894-3198

VERMONT HISTORY [1185]
Vermont Historical Society
Montpelier, Vermont 05602
(802) 828-2291

First published in 1895

SUBSCRIPTION DATA
Issues and rates: Published quarterly.
   Average paid circulation: 3,000
   Annual rate(s): $7.50; Foreign $7.50; Institutions $7.50
Publisher or Sponsor: Vermont Historical Society

EDITORIAL DESCRIPTION
Presents articles pertaining to Vermont from the earliest explorations to the present time.
Articles per average issue: 8
Audience: Academic, general
   Manuscripts accepted in English

MANUSCRIPT INFORMATION
Subject field(s): The history of Vermont and its citizens in national affairs
Manuscript requirements: No specific style guide.
   Preferred length: 10-30 pages
   Number of copies to be submitted: 2
   Abstract: Not necessary.
Author information and reprints: Payment: None.
   Is simultaneous submission of article to other journals permitted: Permitted, but not encouraged.
   Exclusive manuscript rights between acceptance and publication: No
   Copyright: Held by publication.
   Reprints: Available at cost.
Disposition of manuscript:
   Query letter: Not necessary.
   Receipt of manuscript acknowledged: Yes
   Decision to publish in: 2-8 weeks
   Accepted manuscript published in: 4-12 months
   Rejected manuscript returned: Yes, with return postage paid by publication.
   Rejected manuscript criticized: Yes
Submit to:
   Charles T. Morrissey
   Editor and Director
   (See address above)

VIRGINIA CAVALCADE [1186]
Virginia State Library
Richmond, Virginia 23219
(804) 770-2311

First published in 1951

SUBSCRIPTION DATA
Issues and rates: Published quarterly.
   Average paid circulation: 16,700
   Annual rate(s): $3.00
Publisher or Sponsor: Virginia State Library

EDITORIAL DESCRIPTION
Contains articles on Virginia history.
Articles per average issue: 4-5
   Manuscripts accepted in English

MANUSCRIPT INFORMATION
Subject field(s): Virginia history
Manuscript requirements: Chicago
   Preferred length: 2500 words; 10 pages
   Number of copies to be submitted: One
   Abstract: No
Author information and reprints: Payment: By publication to author. $100.00 per article.
   Is simultaneous submission of article to other journals permitted: No
   Exclusive manuscript rights between acceptance and publication: Yes
   Copyright: Held by publication.
   Reprints: Not available.
Additional information: "Invitation to Authors" available on request
Disposition of manuscript:
   Query letter: No
   Receipt of manuscript acknowledged: Yes
   Decision to publish in: 1-3 months
   Accepted manuscript published in: 3-12 months
   Rejected manuscript returned: Yes
   Rejected manuscript criticized: Yes
Submit to:
   Jon Kukla
   Managing Editor
   (See address above)

THE VIRGINIA MAGAZINE OF HISTORY AND BIOGRAPHY [1187]
P.O. Box 7311
Richmond, Virginia 23221
(804) 358-4901

First published in 1893

SUBSCRIPTION DATA
Issues and rates: Published quarterly.
   Average paid circulation: 3,100; 50 controlled
   Annual rate(s): $8.00
Publisher or Sponsor: The Virginia Historical Society

EDITORIAL DESCRIPTION
Contains articles on all phases of Virginia history and well-edited source materials on Virginia history. Some articles on Virginians whose importance is outside the bounds of Virginia are accepted.
Articles per average issue: 5
Audience: Scholars and Virginia history fans
   Manuscripts accepted in English

MANUSCRIPT INFORMATION
Subject field(s): Virginia history
Manuscript requirements: MLA, Chicago
   Preferred length: 5,000 words; 15-25 pages
   Number of copies to be submitted: One
   Abstract: No
Author information and reprints: Payment: By publication to author. $2.00 per printed page
   Is simultaneous submission of article to other journals permitted: No
   Exclusive manuscript rights between acceptance and publication: Yes
   Copyright: Held by publication.
   Reprints: Available, about $36.00 per 100. Price varies with length.
Additional information: Footnotes are required, should be typed double-spaced. All articles should be based on original research and should advance the frontiers of history.
Disposition of manuscript:
   Query letter: No
   Receipt of manuscript acknowledged: Yes
   Decision to publish in: 6 weeks

Accepted manuscript published in: 2 years
Rejected manuscript returned: Yes, if self-addressed, stamped envelope is sent with manuscript.
Rejected manuscript criticized: No
Submit to:
William M. E. Rachal
Editor
(See address above)

THE WESTERN HISTORICAL QUARTERLY [1188]
Utah State University, UMC 07
Logan, Utah 84322
(801) 752-4100 ext. 7517

First published in 1970

SUBSCRIPTION DATA
Issues and rates: Published quarterly.
 Average paid circulation: 3,000
 Annual rate(s): $9.00 Foreign $12.00; membership in WHA, $16.00 (includes subscriptions to all publications sponsored by WHA.)
Publisher or Sponsor: Western History Association

EDITORIAL DESCRIPTION
 The American West in all its varied aspects; westward movement from coast to coast, settlement development of society in the west to the present.
Articles per average issue: 4
Audience: All persons interested in American history, particularly the westward movement and the West
 Manuscripts accepted in English

MANUSCRIPT INFORMATION
Subject field(s): History, related disciplines; studies of all aspects of the westward movement in American history; frontier themes relating to the regional West in recent times.
Manuscript requirements: Chicago; Editorial Policy Statement will be sent upon request
 Preferred length: 5,000-6,500 words; 20 to 25 pages
 Number of copies to be submitted: Two
 Abstract: No
Author information and reprints: Payment: None. 3 copies of issue in which article appears.
 Is simultaneous submission of article to other journals permitted: No
 Exclusive manuscript rights between acceptance and publication: No
 Copyright: Held by Western History Association
 Reprints: Available at cost
Disposition of manuscript:
 Query letter: No
 Receipt of manuscript acknowledged: Yes
 Decision to publish in: 8-10 weeks
 Accepted manuscript published in: 6-12 months
 Rejected manuscript returned: Yes
 Rejected manuscript criticized: No
Submit to:
 S. George Ellsworth
Editor
(See address above)

WESTERN STATES JEWISH HISTORICAL QUARTERLY [1189]
2429 23rd Street
Santa Monica, California 90405
(213) 399-3585

First published in 1968

SUBSCRIPTION DATA
Issues and rates: Published quarterly.
 Average paid circulation: 1,000
 Annual rate(s): $9.00, Foreign $11.00
Publisher or Sponsor: Southern California Jewish Historical Society

EDITORIAL DESCRIPTION
 Contains articles on Jewish history in the Western States, including Hawaii, Alaska, and Western Canada, and Western Mexico.
Articles per average issue: 6
Audience: Universities, historical societies, historical libraries, and individuals interested in western Jewish history.
 Manuscripts accepted in English

MANUSCRIPT INFORMATION
Subject field(s): Western Jewish history
Manuscript requirements: See latest issue for style requirements.
 Preferred length: None
 Number of copies to be submitted: One
 Abstract: No
Author information and reprints: Payment: None.
 Is simultaneous submission of article to other journals permitted: No
 Exclusive manuscript rights between acceptance and publication: Yes
 Copyright: Held by publication.
 Reprints: Not available; $2.00 for whole copies, for authors. Two copies provided gratis for authors
Additional information: Manuscripts should be documented, typed, double-spaced, and footnotes should appear at bottom of each page.
Disposition of manuscript:
 Query letter: No
 Receipt of manuscript acknowledged: Yes
 Decision to publish in: One month
 Accepted manuscript published in: 2 years
 Rejected manuscript returned: Yes
 Rejected manuscript criticized: Yes
Submit to:
 Norton B. Stern
Editor
(See address above)
(213) 396-0946

THE WILLIAM AND MARY QUARTERLY [1190]
A Magazine of Early American History
P.O. Box 220
Williamsburg, Virginia 23185
(703) 229-2771

First published in 1892

SUBSCRIPTION DATA
Issues and rates: Published quarterly.
 Average paid circulation: 4100
 Annual rate(s): $8.00, Students $5.00
Publisher or Sponsor: Institute of Early American History and Culture
Managing Editor: Michael McGiffert

EDITORIAL DESCRIPTION
 Contains articles, documents, and book reviews in the field of early American history and culture and related topics in English or European history.
Articles per average issue: 7
Audience: Scholarly
 Manuscripts accepted in English

MANUSCRIPT INFORMATION
Subject field(s): American studies to 1815, related subjects in European history
Manuscript requirements: Style sheet sent on request.
 Preferred length: 45 pages maximum
 Number of copies to be submitted: Two
 Abstract: No
Author information and reprints: Payment: None. 2 copies of issue in which article appears; 90 offprints; year's subscription to journal
 Is simultaneous submission of article to other journals permitted: Strongly discouraged
 Exclusive manuscript rights between acceptance and publication: Yes
 Copyright: Held by publication.
 Reprints: Available
Additional information: Manuscripts should be in the proper style, with footnotes, references, tables, and charts on separate pages.
Disposition of manuscript:
 Query letter: No
 Receipt of manuscript acknowledged: Yes
 Decision to publish in: 60-90 days
 Accepted manuscript published in: 12 months
 Rejected manuscript returned: Yes
 Rejected manuscript criticized: Yes
Submit to:
 Michael McGiffert
Editor
(See address above)

Law and public administration

Law and public administration

ALBERTA LAW REVIEW [1191]
The University of Alberta
Edmonton, Alberta, Canada
(403) 432-5558

SUBSCRIPTION DATA
Issues and rates: Published three times per year.
  Average paid circulation: 2,750
  Annual rate(s): $12.00

EDITORIAL DESCRIPTION
  Publishes law oriented materials. Emphasis is on both academic and practical writing. All fields of law are covered.

MANUSCRIPT INFORMATION
Subject field(s): All areas of law, in-depth analysis of a particular area of law
Manuscript requirements: Style sheet sent on request.
  Preferred length: None
  Number of copies to be submitted: One
Author information and reprints: Payment: None.
  Is simultaneous submission of article to other journals permitted: No
  Exclusive manuscript rights between acceptance and publication: Yes
  Copyright: Held by author.
  Reprints: Available, 50 free
Disposition of manuscript:
  Receipt of manuscript acknowledged: Yes
  Decision to publish in: 6-8 weeks
  Accepted manuscript published in: 6-9 months
  Rejected manuscript returned: Yes
  Rejected manuscript criticized: No
Submit to:
  Christopher R Head
  Editor-in-Chief
  (See address above)

AMERICAN BAR ASSOCIATION JOURNAL [1192]
Official Publication of the American Bar Association
1155 East 60th Street
Chicago, Illinois 60637
(312) 493-0533

First published in 1915

SUBSCRIPTION DATA
Issues and rates: Published monthly.
  Average paid circulation: 193,568
  Annual rate(s): $5.00, Members $2.50
Publisher or Sponsor: American Bar Association

EDITORIAL DESCRIPTION
  Contains articles dealing with the law, its development, new legislation, court decisions, and with professional responsibility and activities of lawyers. In addition, there are a number of regular monthly departments covering the U.S. Supreme Court, other courts, Washington, current legal literature, the U.N., law office management, tax developments. The editorial point of view reflects positions taken on various issues by the Board of Governors and the House of Delegates of the American Bar Association.
Articles per average issue: 9
Audience: Members of legal profession
  Manuscripts accepted in English

MANUSCRIPT INFORMATION
Subject field(s): Law, public affairs, legal profession, legal history
Manuscript requirements: Chicago
  Preferred length: 3,000-3,500 words; 12-15 pages
  Number of copies to be submitted: One (must be ribbon or good machine copy)
  Abstract: No
Author information and reprints: Payment: None.
  Is simultaneous submission of article to other journals permitted: Under specific arrangement
  Exclusive manuscript rights between acceptance and publication: Yes
  Copyright: Held by publication.
  Reprints: Not available.
Additional information: Authors are expected and requested to disclose any financial, economic or professional interests or affiliations that may have influenced positions taken or advocated in their articles. That they have done so is an implied representation by authors submitting manuscripts.
Disposition of manuscript:
  Query letter: No
  Receipt of manuscript acknowledged: Yes
  Decision to publish in: 4 weeks
  Accepted manuscript published in: 1-4 months
  Rejected manuscript returned: Yes
  Rejected manuscript criticized: No
Submit to:
  Richard B. Allen
  Editor
  (See address above)

AMERICAN BUSINESS LAW JOURNAL [1193]
Graduate School of Business
Bloomington, Indiana 47401
(812) 337-9308

First published in 1963

SUBSCRIPTION DATA
Issues and rates: Published three times per year.
  Average paid circulation: 1,300
  Annual rate(s): Institutions $8.00; Students $7.00; Members $10.00
Publisher or Sponsor: American Business Law Association
Managing Editor: John D. Donnell

EDITORIAL DESCRIPTION
  Contains material related to the law that is likely to be of interest to teachers of business law or legal studies at the college level, excluding professional law schools
Articles per average issue: 7-8
Audience: College teachers of law
  Manuscripts accepted in English

MANUSCRIPT INFORMATION
Subject field(s): Jurisprudence, current legislation of concern to business; international, urban, environmental, trade, corporation, real estate, insurance law
Manuscript requirements: Style sheet sent on request. HLRA
  Preferred length: 4,000-8,000 words
  Number of copies to be submitted: 3
  Abstract: Yes. Of 100-150 words, for articles only
Author information and reprints: Payment: Reprints only. 25 reprints
  Is simultaneous submission of article to other journals permitted: Permitted, but not encouraged.
  Exclusive manuscript rights between acceptance and publication: Yes
  Copyright: Held by publication. with free use to author
  Reprints: Available at cost.
Disposition of manuscript:
  Query letter: Not necessary.
  Receipt of manuscript acknowledged: Yes
  Decision to publish in: 4-5 weeks
  Accepted manuscript published in: 3-6 months
  Rejected manuscript returned: Yes, with return postage paid by publication.
  Rejected manuscript criticized: Yes
Submit to:
  John D. Donnell
  (See address above)

AMERICAN CITY MAGAZINE [1194]
Magazine of Municipal Management and Engineering
Berkshire Common
Pittsfield, Massachusetts 01201
(413) 499-2550

SUBSCRIPTION DATA
Issues and rates: Published monthly.
  Average paid circulation: 36,000 controlled
  Annual rate(s): $15.00, Foreign $30.00

EDITORIAL DESCRIPTION
  Articles pinpoint urban problems and tell how local governments have solved them. Covers all areas of municipal concern: parks, streets, lighting, fire, police, refuse disposal, public works, etc. Attempts to provide material that is reliable, proved, practical and sufficiently inspiring to give confidence to the men and women facing the responsibility of providing urban administration and carrying it out.

Articles per average issue: 30
Audience: Municipal, urban and county officials

MANUSCRIPT INFORMATION

Subject field(s): Water and wastewater treatment, street maintenance, street lighting, parks and playgrounds, traffic control, parking, mass transit, fire and police, municipal administration and government, business machines and city purchasing, municipal airports, street cleaning and snow removal, refuse disposal, pest and weed control
Manuscript requirements: See latest issue for style requirements.
  Preferred length: 500 to 1,000 words; 3-5 pages typewritten
  Number of copies to be submitted: Two
Author information and reprints: Payment: By publication to author. Amount depends on material.
  Is simultaneous submission of article to other journals permitted: No
  Exclusive manuscript rights between acceptance and publication: Yes
  Copyright: Held by publication.
  Reprints: Available, cost quotation on request
Disposition of manuscript:
  Receipt of manuscript acknowledged: Yes
  Decision to publish in: 2-3 weeks
  Accepted manuscript published in: 2-6 months
  Rejected manuscript returned: Yes
  Rejected manuscript criticized: No
Submit to:
  Curtis R. Buttenheim
  Publisher
  (See address above)

AMERICAN JOURNAL OF COMPARATIVE LAW [1195]
School of Law
University of California
Berkeley, California 94720
(415) 642-2913

SUBSCRIPTION DATA

Issues and rates: Published quarterly.
  Average paid circulation: 2000
  Annual rate(s): $15.00
Publisher or Sponsor: American Association for the Comparative Study of Law

EDITORIAL DESCRIPTION

Contains articles, comments, book reviews concerning comparative law.
Articles per average issue: 6

MANUSCRIPT INFORMATION

Subject field(s): Law, if of comparative interest
Manuscript requirements: See latest issue for style requirements.
  Preferred length: 30 pages maximum
  Number of copies to be submitted: One
Author information and reprints: Payment: None.
  Is simultaneous submission of article to other journals permitted: Yes
  Exclusive manuscript rights between acceptance and publication: Yes
  Copyright: Held by publication.
  Reprints: Available, first 50 free
Disposition of manuscript:
  Receipt of manuscript acknowledged: Yes
  Decision to publish in: 1-4 weeks
  Accepted manuscript published in: Up to 6 months
  Rejected manuscript returned: Yes
  Rejected manuscript criticized: Sometimes
Submit to:
  John G. Fleming
  Editor-in-Chief
  (See address above)
  (415) 642-1870

AMERICAN JOURNAL OF CRIMINAL LAW [1196]
2500 Red River
Austin, Texas 78705

First published in 1972

SUBSCRIPTION DATA

Issues and rates: Published three times per year.
  Average paid circulation: 850
Managing Editor: Max Addison

EDITORIAL DESCRIPTION

Presents the general developments in case law as well as empirical studies, well-written opinion and "diatribe" on current issues
Articles per average issue: 1-2
Audience: Students and practicing criminal lawyers
  Manuscripts accepted in English

MANUSCRIPT INFORMATION

Subject field(s): A broad range of articles is featured; submmissions should have some legal relevance; there is a slight geographical bias toward the Southwest.
Manuscript requirements: No specific style guide.
  Preferred length: 40 pages maximum
  Number of copies to be submitted: 1
  Abstract: Not necessary.
Author information and reprints: Payment: None.
  Is simultaneous submission of article to other journals permitted: Permitted.
  Exclusive manuscript rights between acceptance and publication: Yes
  Copyright: Held by publication.
  Reprints: Available at cost.
Disposition of manuscript:
  Query letter: Not necessary.
  Receipt of manuscript acknowledged: No
  Decision to publish in: 1-2 months
  Accepted manuscript published in: 6-9 months
  Rejected manuscript returned: No
  Rejected manuscript criticized: Reasons for rejections only
Submit to:
  Editor-in-Chief
  (See address above)

AMERICAN JOURNAL OF INTERNATIONAL LAW [1197]
2223 Massachusetts Avenue, N.W.
Washington, D.C. 20008
(202) 265-4313 ext. 26

First published in 1907

SUBSCRIPTION DATA

Issues and rates: Published quarterly.
  Average paid circulation: 8,000
  Annual rate(s): $30.00
Publisher or Sponsor: American Society of International Law

EDITORIAL DESCRIPTION

Provides for the laymen and professionals interested in international law and relations a source of authoritatve current thought, trends, and material affecting international legal matters.
Audience: Lawyers, government personnel, professors, university graduate students in field
  Manuscripts accepted in English

MANUSCRIPT INFORMATION

Subject field(s): International law, international relations, international organization, international trade and investment
Manuscript requirements: GPO for form; HLRA for footnotes.
  Preferred length: 10,000-20,000 words
  Number of copies to be submitted: 3
Author information and reprints: Payment: None. 50 free offprints
  Is simultaneous submission of article to other journals permitted: No
  Exclusive manuscript rights between acceptance and publication: Yes
  Copyright: Held by publication.
  Reprints: Not available.
Disposition of manuscript:
  Query letter: No
  Receipt of manuscript acknowledged: Yes
  Decision to publish in: 3 months
  Accepted manuscript published in: 3-6 months
  Rejected manuscript returned: Yes
  Rejected manuscript criticized: Yes
Submit to:
  Richard R. Baxter
  Editor-in-Chief
  Harvard Law School
  Cambridge, Massachusetts 02138

AMERICAN JOURNAL OF JURISPRUDENCE [1198]
University of Notre Dame Law School
Notre Dame, Indiana 46556
(219) 283-3354

Previously entitled *Natural Law Forum*

First published in 1956

SUBSCRIPTION DATA

Issues and rates: Published annually.
  Average paid circulation: 850
  Annual rate(s): $7.50

Law and public administration

Publisher or Sponsor: Natural Law Forum, Inc.
Managing Editor: Aniela Murphy

EDITORIAL DESCRIPTION

Dedicated to a critical examination of the significance of natural law for our times. It seeks to provide a meeting ground for discussion and a clearinghouse for information. Scholarly contributions from the point of view of any intellectual discipline, whether scientific, historical, political, legal, philosophical or theological, and whether favorable or unfavorable to the natural law approach, will be welcome.
Articles per average issue: 10
Audience: Professional, academic, historical, legal
Manuscripts accepted in English

MANUSCRIPT INFORMATION

Subject field(s): Any topic pertaining to natural law, whether legal, philosophical theological, political, scientific, etc.
Manuscript requirements: No specific style guide.
Preferred length: 40 pages
Number of copies to be submitted: One
Abstract: Yes, of 1 paragraph
Author information and reprints: Payment: Reprints only. 50 reprints
Is simultaneous submission of article to other journals permitted: No
Exclusive manuscript rights between acceptance and publication: Yes
Copyright: Held by publication.
Reprints: Available at cost.
Disposition of manuscript:
Query letter: No
Receipt of manuscript acknowledged: Yes
Decision to publish in: 8 weeks
Rejected manuscript returned: Yes
Rejected manuscript criticized: Occasionally
Submit to:
Aniela Murphy
Managing Editor
(See address above)

THE ARBITRATION JOURNAL [1199]

140 West 51st Street
New York, New York 10020
(212) 582-6620

First published in 1937

SUBSCRIPTION DATA

Issues and rates: Published quarterly.
Average paid circulation: 5000
Annual rate(s): $10.00, Foreign $12.00
Publisher or Sponsor: American Arbitration Association

EDITORIAL DESCRIPTION

Contains articles on the law and practice of all types of arbitration in the United States and abroad.
Articles per average issue: 5
Audience: Lawyers, businessmen, academics
Manuscripts accepted in English

MANUSCRIPT INFORMATION
Subject field(s): Labor relations, arbitration laws, business problems, community disputes, international trade
Manuscript requirements: See latest issue for style requirements.
Preferred length: 4000 words; 12 pages
Number of copies to be submitted: One
Abstract: No
Author information and reprints: Payment: None.
Is simultaneous submission of article to other journals permitted: Occasionally, if special arrangements are made
Exclusive manuscript rights between acceptance and publication: Yes
Copyright: Held by publication.
Reprints: Available, if paid for by author
Disposition of manuscript:
Query letter: No
Receipt of manuscript acknowledged: Yes
Decision to publish in: One month
Accepted manuscript published in: 6 months
Rejected manuscript returned: Yes
Rejected manuscript criticized: No
Submit to:
Morris Stone
Editor
(See address above)

THE BANKING LAW JOURNAL [1200]

Warren, Gorham and Lamont, Inc.
870 Seventh Avenue
New York, New York 10019

First published in 1889

SUBSCRIPTION DATA
Issues and rates: Published monthly.
Average paid circulation: 5,000
Annual rate(s): $44; Foreign $47

EDITORIAL DESCRIPTION

Contains articles and essays on commercial banking law and bank regulation. Provides practical knowledge of developments in all areas of the law affecting banks.
Audience: Bankers, bank attorneys
Manuscripts accepted in English

MANUSCRIPT INFORMATION
Subject field(s): Commercial banking law, bank regulation, consumer credit regulation
Manuscript requirements: See latest issue for style requirements.
Preferred length: 15-30 pages
Number of copies to be submitted: Two
Abstract: No
Author information and reprints: Payment: None. 6 free copies of issue.
Is simultaneous submission of article to other journals permitted: Yes
Exclusive manuscript rights between acceptance and publication: Yes
Copyright: Held by publication.
Reprints: Available, cost depends on length
Additional information: Manuscript should be typed, double-spaced, on 8 ½ by 11-inch white bond. Footnotes should be typed on separate pages.
Disposition of manuscript:
Receipt of manuscript acknowledged: Yes
Decision to publish in: 2-3 weeks
Accepted manuscript published in: 2-4 months
Rejected manuscript returned: Yes
Rejected manuscript criticized: No
Submit to:
Gerald T. Dunne
Editor-in-Chief
7301 Princeton
University City, Missouri 63130
(314) 535-3300 ext. 340

BAYLOR LAW REVIEW [1201]

Box 6262
Waco, Texas 76706
(817) 755-3487

First published in 1948

SUBSCRIPTION DATA
Issues and rates: Published quarterly.
Average paid circulation: 1200; 75 controlled
Annual rate(s): $10.00
Managing Editor: David Bragg

EDITORIAL DESCRIPTION

Publishes articles concerning legal subjects of national and state interest. Although the journal's primary emphasis is on Texas law, topics of national concern also receive intensive treatment.
Articles per average issue: 15
Audience: Legal profession, scholars, judges, and students
Manuscripts accepted in English

MANUSCRIPT INFORMATION
Subject field(s): Legal subjects of state and national interest
Manuscript requirements: See latest issue for style requirements. triple-space manuscript
Preferred length: 6,000 to 9,000 words; 15-25 pages
Number of copies to be submitted: Two
Abstract: No
Author information and reprints: Payment: None. 20 reprints and 2 copies of issue.
Is simultaneous submission of article to other journals permitted: No
Exclusive manuscript rights between acceptance and publication: Yes
Copyright: Held by publication.
Reprints: Available, 20 free
Disposition of manuscript:
Query letter: No
Receipt of manuscript acknowledged: Yes
Decision to publish in: 3-4 weeks
Accepted manuscript published in: 4-6 months
Rejected manuscript returned: Yes, if self-addressed, stamped envelope is sent with manuscript.
Rejected manuscript criticized: No
Submit to:
Articles Editor
(See address above)

BEYOND TIME [1202]

Connecticut Quarterly Journal of Criminal Justice
P. O. Box 38
Haddam, Connecticut 06438
(203) 345-4547

First published in 1973

SUBSCRIPTION DATA

Issues and rates: Published three times per year.
Average paid circulation: 20; 300 controlled
Annual rate(s): $10.00; Individuals $10.00; Institutions $10.00; Students $10.00
Managing Editor: Robert J. Brooks

EDITORIAL DESCRIPTION

Concerned with research, commentary, new approaches and fiction dealing with the offender and offender rehabilitation; directed toward the layman as well as the professional interested in improving the criminal justice system.

Articles per average issue: 7
Audience: Professionals and laymen interested in criminal justice reform
Manuscripts accepted in English

MANUSCRIPT INFORMATION

Subject field(s): All subjects dealing with the justice system with an emphasis on treatment or new approaches to the administration of justice. There are no strict chronological or geographical considerations if the manuscript can be related to contemporary issues in American justice.

Manuscript requirements: Professional terminology should be limited or explained so that article can be understood easily by non-professionals.
Preferred length: 20 pages
Number of copies to be submitted: 2
Abstract: Not necessary.

Author information and reprints: Payment: None.
Is simultaneous submission of article to other journals permitted: Permitted, but not encouraged.
Exclusive manuscript rights between acceptance and publication: Yes
Copyright: No copyright
Reprints: Available at no cost. 5

Disposition of manuscript:
Query letter: Not necessary.
Receipt of manuscript acknowledged: Yes
Decision to publish in: 2 months
Accepted manuscript published in: 4 months
Rejected manuscript returned: No
Rejected manuscript criticized: Reasons for rejections only

Submit to:
Peggy J. Signorelli;
Robert J. Brooks
Associate Editors
(See address above)

BOSTON COLLEGE INDUSTRIAL AND COMMERCIAL LAW REVIEW [1203]

Boston College Law School
St. Thomas More Drive
Brighton, Massachusetts 02135
(617) 969-0100 ext. 2417

First published in 1958

SUBSCRIPTION DATA

Issues and rates: 6 times per year
Average paid circulation: 1400; 1600 controlled
Annual rate(s): $10.50
Publisher or Sponsor: Boston College Law School
Managing Editor: James McGuire

EDITORIAL DESCRIPTION

Contains articles dealing with industrial and commercial law. Also interested in articles dealing with the academic and practical sides of legal issues. No predisposition as to point of view. Good scholarship is the most important criterion.

Articles per average issue: 4
Audience: Lawyers involved in industrial, commercial, and labor matters
Manuscripts accepted in English

MANUSCRIPT INFORMATION

Subject field(s): Taxation, environmental law, commercial law, labor law, antitrust, patents, banking, securities, administrative law, mutual funds, corporate law, trusts and estates
Manuscript requirements: HLRA, Whitebook
Preferred length: None
Number of copies to be submitted: Three
Abstract: If possible

Author information and reprints: Payment: None.
Is simultaneous submission of article to other journals permitted: Yes, but not preferred
Exclusive manuscript rights between acceptance and publication: Yes
Copyright: Held by publication.
Reprints: Available; 25 free, additional at cost, depending on length
Additional information: Manuscripts should be triple-spaced with a two-inch left margin.

Disposition of manuscript:
Query letter: No
Receipt of manuscript acknowledged: Yes
Decision to publish in: 2-3 weeks
Accepted manuscript published in: 2-6 months
Rejected manuscript returned: Yes
Rejected manuscript criticized: Sometimes

Submit to:
William P. Robinson
Solicitations and Articles Editor
(See address above)

BUFFALO LAW REVIEW [1204]

John Lord O'Brien Hall
SUNY/Buffalo Amherst Campus
Buffalo, New York 14260
(716) 852-4326

SUBSCRIPTION DATA

Issues and rates: Published three times per year.
Average paid circulation: 700
Annual rate(s): $9.00
Managing Editor: Shelly Scott Friedman

EDITORIAL DESCRIPTION

Publishes articles and comments on subjects in the legal field.
Articles per average issue: 8
Audience: International legal community
Manuscripts accepted in English only

MANUSCRIPT INFORMATION

Subject field(s): Law, law-related
Manuscript requirements: HLRA
Preferred length: 100 pages maximum
Number of copies to be submitted: One
Abstract: Yes

Author information and reprints: Payment: None.
Is simultaneous submission of article to other journals permitted: Yes
Exclusive manuscript rights between acceptance and publication: Yes
Copyright: Held by publication.
Reprints: Available, first reprints free

Disposition of manuscript:
Query letter: No
Receipt of manuscript acknowledged: Yes
Decision to publish in: 10 days
Accepted manuscript published in: 4 months
Rejected manuscript returned: Yes
Rejected manuscript criticized: Sometimes

Submit to:
Alan Ahart;
Judith Levitt
Articles Editors
(See address above)

CALIFORNIA LAW REVIEW [1205]

School of Law
University of California
Berkeley, California 94720
(415) 642-7562

First published in 1912

SUBSCRIPTION DATA

Issues and rates: Published bi-monthly.
Average paid circulation: 2715
Annual rate(s): $12.50
Managing Editor: H. Lee Watson

EDITORIAL DESCRIPTION

Publishes articles of a general legal nature of interest to the bench, the bar, and academics.
Articles per average issue: 6
Audience: Scholars, judges, attorneys, students
Manuscripts accepted in English

Law and public administration

MANUSCRIPT INFORMATION

Subject field(s): Legal analysis, comment, history and other topics of a general legal nature

Manuscript requirements: GPO and HLRA
Preferred length: Up to 200 pages
Number of copies to be submitted: One
Abstract: No

Author information and reprints: Payment: Reprints only. Two copies of issue and 25 reprints
Is simultaneous submission of article to other journals permitted: Yes, however, will not consider material appearing in other law reviews
Exclusive manuscript rights between acceptance and publication: Yes
Copyright: Held by publication.
Reprints: Available, 25 free; additional at cost

Additional information: Double or triple spaced manuscripts preferred. Footnotes should be on separate pages.

Disposition of manuscript:
Query letter: No
Receipt of manuscript acknowledged: Yes
Decision to publish in: 2-6 weeks
Accepted manuscript published in: 2-6 months
Rejected manuscript returned: Yes
Rejected manuscript criticized: Sometimes

Submit to:
Articles Department
(See address above)

CALIFORNIA SCHOOL LAW DIGEST [1206]

P. O. Box 6220
San Mateo, California 94403
(415) 574-1839

First published in 1973

SUBSCRIPTION DATA

Issues and rates: Published monthly.
Annual rate(s): $30.00; Institutions $30.00

Managing Editor: Jay E. Grenig

EDITORIAL DESCRIPTION

Publishes articles on California school law, judicial decisions of California courts affecting the public schools of California

Articles per average issue: 1
Audience: California educators and attorneys
Manuscripts accepted in English

MANUSCRIPT INFORMATION

Subject field(s): Legal problems of California public schools

Manuscript requirements: No specific style guide.
Preferred length: 2-6 typewritten, double-spaced pages
Number of copies to be submitted: 1
Abstract: Not necessary.

Author information and reprints: Payment: Reprints only. 10 reprints
Is simultaneous submission of article to other journals permitted: Not permitted.

Exclusive manuscript rights between acceptance and publication: Yes
Copyright: Held by publication.

Disposition of manuscript:
Query letter: Not necessary, but advisable.
Receipt of manuscript acknowledged: Yes
Decision to publish in: 60 days
Accepted manuscript published in: 90 days
Rejected manuscript returned: Yes, with return postage paid by publication.
Rejected manuscript criticized: Yes

Submit to:
Jay E. Grenig
Editor
(See address above)

CALIFORNIA STATE BAR JOURNAL [1207]

1230 West Third Street
Los Angeles, California 90017
(213) 482-8220

First published in 1925

SUBSCRIPTION DATA

Issues and rates: Published bi-monthly.
Average paid circulation: 48,000
Annual rate(s): $5.00; Foreign $5.00; Institutions $5.00

Publisher or Sponsor: State Bar Association of California

Managing Editor: Darlene L. Lima

EDITORIAL DESCRIPTION

Articles dealing with all areas of the legal profession

Articles per average issue: 3-6
Audience: Legal profession
Manuscripts accepted in English

MANUSCRIPT INFORMATION

Manuscript requirements: See latest issue for style requirements.
Preferred length: 4,000 words maximum
Number of copies to be submitted: 3
Abstract: Not necessary.

Author information and reprints: Payment: None.
Is simultaneous submission of article to other journals permitted: Not permitted.
Exclusive manuscript rights between acceptance and publication: Yes
Copyright: Held by publication.
Reprints: Not available.

Disposition of manuscript:
Query letter: Not necessary.
Receipt of manuscript acknowledged: Yes
Decision to publish in: 1-3 months
Accepted manuscript published in: 3-6 months
Rejected manuscript returned: Yes, with return postage paid by publication.
Rejected manuscript criticized: No

Submit to:
Darlene L. Lima
Managing Editor
(See address above)

CALIFORNIA WESTERN LAW REVIEW [1208]

California Western School of Law
3902 Lomaland Drive
San Diego, California 92106
(714) 224-3211

First published in 1965

SUBSCRIPTION DATA

Issues and rates: Published three times per year.
Average paid circulation: 1000
Annual rate(s): $6.00

Publisher or Sponsor: United States International University

Managing Editor: Wayne D. Wilson

EDITORIAL DESCRIPTION

Presents a detailed discussion of practical legal topics.

Articles per average issue: 3
Audience: Legal community
Manuscripts accepted in English

MANUSCRIPT INFORMATION

Subject field(s): Legal, jurisprudence, political science

Manuscript requirements: See latest issue for style requirements.
Preferred length: 50-70 Typed pages exclusive of footnotes
Number of copies to be submitted: One
Abstract: No

Author information and reprints: Payment: None.
Is simultaneous submission of article to other journals permitted: No
Exclusive manuscript rights between acceptance and publication: Yes
Copyright: Held by publication.
Reprints: Available, 50 free, additional at cost

Disposition of manuscript:
Query letter: Advisable
Receipt of manuscript acknowledged: Yes
Decision to publish in: 3 weeks
Accepted manuscript published in: 3 months
Rejected manuscript returned: Yes
Rejected manuscript criticized: No

Submit to:
Lead Articles Editor
(See address above)

CANADIAN CONSTITUTIONAL JOURNAL [1209]

2 Wedgewood Crescent
Ottawa KIB 4B4, Canada
(613) 824-5225

First published in 1970

SUBSCRIPTION DATA

Issues and rates: 5 times per year
Average paid circulation: 2,300
Annual rate(s): $5.00; Individuals $5.00; Foreign individuals $10.00; Foreign institutions $10.00

Publisher or Sponsor: The Monarchist League of Canada
Managing Editor: Ronald P. Frye

EDITORIAL DESCRIPTION

A discussion of the political and historical aspects of the Canadian constitution with special emphasis on the Canadian Monarchy.
Articles per average issue: 2
Audience: Those interested in a discussion of Canadian constitutional problems
Manuscripts accepted in English and French

MANUSCRIPT INFORMATION

Subject field(s): History of the Canadian monarchy including biographies of different Canadian Governor Generals; aspects of the Canadian constitution
Manuscript requirements: MLA
Preferred length: 2,000 to 5,000 words
Number of copies to be submitted: 1
Abstract: Yes.
Author information and reprints: Payment: None.
Is simultaneous submission of article to other journals permitted: Permitted, but not encouraged.
Exclusive manuscript rights between acceptance and publication: Yes
Copyright: Held by publication.
Reprints: Not available.
Additional information: Consideration will be given to articles which argue for forms of government other than constitutional monarchy.
Disposition of manuscript:
Query letter: Not necessary, but advisable.
Receipt of manuscript acknowledged: Yes
Decision to publish in: 3-4 months
Accepted manuscript published in: 6-12 months
Rejected manuscript returned: Yes, if return postage is supplied by author.
Rejected manuscript criticized: Sometimes
Submit to:
Ronald P. Frye
Editor
Suite 11
8 Paisley Avenue North
Hamilton, Ontario L8S 4G4, Canada

SPECIAL STIPULATIONS

All articles must be of a scholarly nature.

CANADIAN PUBLIC ADMINISTRATION [1210]

Administration Publique du Canada
897 Bay Street
Toronto, Ontario M5S 127, Canada
(416) 923-7319

First published in 1958

SUBSCRIPTION DATA

Issues and rates: Published quarterly.
Average paid circulation: 2,800
Annual rate(s): $25.00

Publisher or Sponsor: The Institute of Public Administration of Canada
Managing Editor: Douglas V. Smiley

EDITORIAL DESCRIPTION

Contains articles on theory and practice of public administration with relevance for Canada; Broad interpretation of public administration.
Articles per average issue: 8
Audience: Teachers of public administration, senior civil servants, general academae, general government
Manuscripts accepted in English and French

MANUSCRIPT INFORMATION

Subject field(s): Canadian government, politics, public policy-process and areas of public administration: Theory organization and theory management, Canadian and comparative British and U.S. etc.
Manuscript requirements: Style sheet sent on request.
Preferred length: 20 pages
Number of copies to be submitted: Three
Abstract: Yes. 250 words, typed double-spaced on letter sized paper
Author information and reprints: Payment: None.
Is simultaneous submission of article to other journals permitted: No
Exclusive manuscript rights between acceptance and publication: Yes
Copyright: Held by publication.
Reprints: Available, 50 free to author
Additional information: Manuscripts should be in the proper style, with footnotes, references, tables and charts on separate pages. Author's name and affiliation should appear only on a separate cover page so articles can be sent out anonymously for editorial evaluation.
Disposition of manuscript:
Query letter: No
Receipt of manuscript acknowledged: Yes
Decision to publish in: Varies
Accepted manuscript published in: 3 months
Rejected manuscript returned: Yes
Rejected manuscript criticized: Sometimes
Submit to:
Douglas V. Smiley
Editor
(See address above)

CASE WESTERN RESERVE JOURNAL OF INTERNATIONAL LAW [1211]

Case Western Reserve University
11075 East Boulevard
Cleveland, Ohio 44106
(216) 368-3291

First published in 1969

SUBSCRIPTION DATA

Issues and rates: Published semi-annually.
Average paid circulation: 300
Annual rate(s): $7.00 for all

Publisher or Sponsor: Case Western Reserve University, Franklin Thomas Backus School of Law
Managing Editor: Gregory J. Lavelle

EDITORIAL DESCRIPTION

A scholarly periodical edited and published by the students of the Franklin Thomas Backus School of Law, it draws upon manuscripts submitted by scholars and practitioners as well as law students for making up each issue; devoted exclusively to legal analyses in the international and comparative law field.
Articles per average issue: 4
Audience: The legal community both academic and practicing, as well as the international business community, and those interested in international relations and politics.
Manuscripts accepted in English

MANUSCRIPT INFORMATION

Subject field(s): Manuscripts dealing with any aspect of international/comparative law are published. There are no chronological or geographical limitations.
Manuscript requirements: See latest issue for style requirements. GPO
Preferred length: 30 pages
Number of copies to be submitted: 3
Abstract: Not necessary. Will request if article is accepted for publication.
Author information and reprints: Payment: Reprints only. Five copies of issue in which article appears
Is simultaneous submission of article to other journals permitted: Permitted, but publication must be so informed and given a deadline for action.
Exclusive manuscript rights between acceptance and publication: Yes
Copyright: Held by publication, but will negotiate reprint rights.
Reprints: Available at cost.
Disposition of manuscript:
Query letter: Not necessary.
Receipt of manuscript acknowledged: Yes
Decision to publish in: 1 month
Accepted manuscript published in: 6 months
Rejected manuscript returned: Yes, with return postage paid by publication.
Rejected manuscript criticized: Sometimes
Submit to:
John E. Codrea
Editor-in-Chief
(See address above)

CATHOLIC UNIVERSITY LAW REVIEW [1212]

Catholic University of America
Washington, D.C. 20017
(202) 635-5157

SUBSCRIPTION DATA

Issues and rates: Published quarterly.
Average paid circulation: 1500
Annual rate(s): $10.00

EDITORIAL DESCRIPTION

Scholarly legal publication of articles that contribute to the development of the law

Law and public administration

and make the profession aware of subjects of law that are matters of current interest.

MANUSCRIPT INFORMATION

Subject field(s): Current legal topics, federal legislation, recent legal developments, book reviews, commentaries
Manuscript requirements: See latest issue for style requirements.
  Preferred length: Maximum 100 tripled spaced pages
  Number of copies to be submitted: Original plus 2 copies
Author information and reprints: Payment: None.
  Is simultaneous submission of article to other journals permitted: No
  Exclusive manuscript rights between acceptance and publication: Yes
  Copyright: Held by publication.
  Reprints: Available, 25 free; additional reprint prices quoted
Additional information: Contributing authors are requested to disclose any financial, economic, or professional interests or affiliations that may have influenced positions taken or advocated in their articles.
Disposition of manuscript:
  Receipt of manuscript acknowledged: Yes
  Decision to publish in: Two to six weeks
  Accepted manuscript published in: One to six months
  Rejected manuscript returned: Yes
  Rejected manuscript criticized: Sometimes
Submit to:
  Thomas P. Gilliss
  Editor-in-Chief
  (See address above)

COLUMBIA JOURNAL OF TRANSNATIONAL LAW [1213]

Columbia Law School
435 West 116th Street, Box 8
New York, New York 10027
(212) 280-3742

First published in 1961

SUBSCRIPTION DATA

Issues and rates: Published three times per year.
  Average paid circulation: 1,000
  Annual rate(s): $10.00, Foreign $11.00

EDITORIAL DESCRIPTION

Contains articles on public and private international law; foreign and comparative law.
Articles per average issue: 4 plus casenotes
Audience: Academic, legal, general
  Manuscripts accepted in English

MANUSCRIPT INFORMATION

Subject field(s): International law, international finance, international trade, conflict of laws, international development, East-West affairs, human rights

Manuscript requirements: HLRA, GPO
  Preferred length: 10,000 words; 40 pages double-spaced
  Number of copies to be submitted: Two
  Abstract: No
Author information and reprints: Payment: None.
  Is simultaneous submission of article to other journals permitted: No
  Exclusive manuscript rights between acceptance and publication: Yes
  Copyright: Held by publication.
  Reprints: Available, at no cost
Disposition of manuscript:
  Receipt of manuscript acknowledged: Yes
  Decision to publish in: 1 month
  Accepted manuscript published in: 3 months
  Rejected manuscript returned: Yes
  Rejected manuscript criticized: No
Submit to:
  Stefan R. Boshkov
  Articles Editor
  (See address above)

THE COLUMBIA LAW REVIEW [1214]

435 West 116th Street
New York, New York 10027
(212) 280-4398

First published in 1901

SUBSCRIPTION DATA

Issues and rates: 8 times per year
  Average paid circulation: 4100
  Annual rate(s): $15, Foreign $16
Managing Editor: Robert P. Feldman; Jonathan A. Lindsey

EDITORIAL DESCRIPTION

Contains student and professional articles dealing with current legal issues.
Articles per average issue: 3
Audience: Legal profession
  Manuscripts accepted in English

MANUSCRIPT INFORMATION

Subject field(s): Legal
Manuscript requirements: HLRA
  Preferred length: Varies
  Number of copies to be submitted: Two
  Abstract: No
Author information and reprints: Payment: None.
  Is simultaneous submission of article to other journals permitted: Yes
  Exclusive manuscript rights between acceptance and publication: Yes
  Copyright: Held by publication.
  Reprints: Available, 50 free
Additional information: Manuscript must be typewritten and triple-spaced.
Disposition of manuscript:
  Query letter: No
  Receipt of manuscript acknowledged: Yes
  Decision to publish in: 1 month
  Accepted manuscript published in: Varies
  Rejected manuscript returned: Yes
  Rejected manuscript criticized: No
Submit to:
  Articles Editor
  (See address above)

COMMON MARKET LAW REVIEW [1215]

A. W. Sijthoff International Publishing Company
Doezastraat 1, P. O. Box 26
Leiden, The Netherlands
(071) 21845; Telex 32447

First published in 1963

SUBSCRIPTION DATA

Issues and rates: Published quarterly.
  Average paid circulation: 1,450; 200 controlled
  Annual rate(s): Dfl. 98.00; Foreign $40.00

Publisher or Sponsor: British Institute of International and Comparative Law, London; The Europa Institute; University of Leiden

EDITORIAL DESCRIPTION

Publishes comments on the law of the European communities
Articles per average issue: 7
Audience: Professional, academic, business.
  Manuscripts accepted in English

MANUSCRIPT INFORMATION

Manuscript requirements: See latest issue for style requirements. Style sheet sent on request.
  Preferred length: None
  Number of copies to be submitted: 3
  Abstract: Yes. Of about 150 words

Author information and reprints: Payment: Reprints only. 1 issue and 50 offprints
  Is simultaneous submission of article to other journals permitted: Not permitted.
  Exclusive manuscript rights between acceptance and publication: Yes
  Copyright: Held by publication.
  Reprints: Available at cost.

Disposition of manuscript:
  Query letter: Not necessary, but advisable.
  Receipt of manuscript acknowledged: Yes
  Decision to publish in: 1 month
  Accepted manuscript published in: 3 months
  Rejected manuscript returned: Yes, if return postage is supplied by author.
  Rejected manuscript criticized: Reasons for rejections only

Submit to:
  Prof. Paul J. G. Kapteyn
  Executive Editor
  Europa Institute
  Hugo de Grootlaan 27
  Leiden, The Netherlands
  (071) 49 641

COMPUTER LAW SERVICE [1216]

28 State Street, Suite 2200
Boston, Massachusetts 02109
(617) 742-8300

SUBSCRIPTION DATA
Issues and rates: 4 times per year
　Average paid circulation: Not available.
　Annual rate(s): $465.00
Managing Editor: Robert P. Bigelow

EDITORIAL DESCRIPTION
　Contains articles, reference material and decisions of all types of tribunals on the legal problems engendered by the computer. Designed to be an aid to the practicing lawyer as well as a source book of information for general researchers.
Articles per average issue: 3
Audience: Lawyers
　Manuscripts accepted in English

MANUSCRIPT INFORMATION
Subject field(s): Contract problems, software protection, taxation, privacy, communications law, liability for computer mistakes, licensing, industry problems
Manuscript requirements: See latest issue for style requirements.
　Preferred length: 3000 words; 10 typed pages
　Number of copies to be submitted: Two
　Abstract: No
Author information and reprints: Payment: None. Free reprints for original articles.
　Is simultaneous submission of article to other journals permitted: Depends on distribution of the publication.
　Exclusive manuscript rights between acceptance and publication: Yes
　Copyright: Negotiable
　Reprints: Available, cost depends on length
Additional information: Photographs, charts, etc. are usable.
Disposition of manuscript:
　Query letter: No
　Receipt of manuscript acknowledged: Yes
　Decision to publish in: 1-2 months
　Accepted manuscript published in: 3-12 months
　Rejected manuscript returned: Yes
　Rejected manuscript criticized: No
Submit to:
　Editor
　(See address above)

CONNECTICUT LAW REVIEW [1217]
1800 Asylum Avenue
West Hartford, Connecticut 06117
(203) 232-7593

Previously entitled *Connecticut Bar Journal* 1948-1968

First published in 1948

SUBSCRIPTION DATA
Issues and rates: Published quarterly.
　Average paid circulation: 1200; 300 controlled
　Annual rate(s): $8.00

Managing Editor: Gary S. Starr

EDITORIAL DESCRIPTION
　Publishes articles, both practical and theoretical, on law and related topics.
Articles per average issue: 6-8
Audience: Lawyers, judges, legislators, academics, and students
　Manuscripts accepted in English

MANUSCRIPT INFORMATION
Subject field(s): Law related fields, legal education
Manuscript requirements: See latest issue for style requirements. Text and footnotes typed separately; triple-space with 2 inch margin left; citations should conform to White Book style.
　Preferred length: 20-60 pages plus footnotes
　Number of copies to be submitted: One
　Abstract: Yes
Author information and reprints: Payment: None.
　Is simultaneous submission of article to other journals permitted: Discouraged
　Exclusive manuscript rights between acceptance and publication: Yes
　Copyright: Held by University of Connecticut Press unless author wishes to hold copyright.
　Reprints: Available, first 50 free
Additional information: If simultaneous submission to other journals, indicate in cover letter.
Disposition of manuscript:
　Query letter: No
　Receipt of manuscript acknowledged: Yes
　Decision to publish in: 3-6 weeks
　Accepted manuscript published in: 2-5 months
　Rejected manuscript returned: Yes
　Rejected manuscript criticized: Sometimes
Submit to:
　George E. O'Brien, Jr.
　Editor-in-Chief
　(See address above)

CORNELL LAW REVIEW [1218]
Cornell Law School
Ithaca, New York 14853
(607) 256-3387

Previously entitled *Cornell Law Quarterly*

First published in 1915

SUBSCRIPTION DATA
Issues and rates: Published semi-monthly.
　Average paid circulation: 3300; 100 controlled
　Annual rate(s): $12.50 Foreign $13.70
Managing Editor: Leslie Locke;
Carol Bartlett

EDITORIAL DESCRIPTION
　Contains articles on current topics in the law.
Articles per average issue: 3
Audience: Lawyers and scholars of Law
　Manuscripts accepted in English

MANUSCRIPT INFORMATION
Subject field(s): Law, other related fields
Manuscript requirements: See latest issue for style requirements.
　Number of copies to be submitted: One
Author information and reprints: Payment: None.
　Is simultaneous submission of article to other journals permitted: Arrangements made on an individual basis.
　Exclusive manuscript rights between acceptance and publication: Yes
　Copyright: Held by publication.
　Reprints: Available, 50 free
Disposition of manuscript:
　Receipt of manuscript acknowledged: Yes
　Decision to publish in: 2 weeks
　Rejected manuscript returned: Yes
　Rejected manuscript criticized: Yes
Submit to:
　Michael Brady
　Article and Book Review Editor
　(See address above)

COURT REVIEW [1219]
Box 1399
Holyoke, Massachusetts 01040
(413) 534-1506

Previously entitled *Municipal Court Briefs and Review*

SUBSCRIPTION DATA
Issues and rates: Published bi-monthly.
　Average paid circulation: 2,100
　Annual rate(s): $20.00
Publisher or Sponsor: American Judges Association
Managing Editor: Judge Michael J. Donohue

EDITORIAL DESCRIPTION
　Contains articles on all aspects of the law and related areas of interest to judges.
Articles per average issue: 4
Audience: Judges in the U. S. and Canada
　Manuscripts accepted in English

MANUSCRIPT INFORMATION
Manuscript requirements: No specific style guide.
　Preferred length: As required
　Number of copies to be submitted: 2
　Abstract: Not necessary.
Author information and reprints: Payment: By author to publication.
　Is simultaneous submission of article to other journals permitted: Permitted.
　Exclusive manuscript rights between acceptance and publication: No
　Reprints: Available at no cost.
Disposition of manuscript:
　Query letter: Not necessary, but advisable.
　Decision to publish in: 2 months
　Accepted manuscript published in: 4 months
　Rejected manuscript returned: Yes, with return postage paid by publication.
　Rejected manuscript criticized: Sometimes
Submit to:
　Judge Michael J. Donohue

Law and public administration

Editor
(See address above)

CREIGHTON LAW REVIEW [1220]
2200 California
Omaha, Nebraska 68178
(402) 536-2980

First published in 1968

SUBSCRIPTION DATA
Issues and rates: Published quarterly.
  Average paid circulation: 3,600
  Annual rate(s): $7.00
Publisher or Sponsor: Creighton University School of Law

EDITORIAL DESCRIPTION
Publishes lead articles by practitioners and professors, comments and case notes by students, on a broad range of legal topics.
Articles per average issue: 10-15
Audience: Professional, academic
  Manuscripts accepted in English

MANUSCRIPT INFORMATION
Subject field(s): Taxation, corporations, constitutional law, torts, securities, international law
Manuscript requirements: HLRA
  Preferred length: 15-25 pages
  Number of copies to be submitted: Two
  Abstract: No
Author information and reprints: Payment: Reprints only. Free copies of issue in which article appears.
  Is simultaneous submission of article to other journals permitted: Yes
  Exclusive manuscript rights between acceptance and publication: No
  Copyright: Held by publication.
  Reprints: Available at cost.
Disposition of manuscript:
  Query letter: No
  Receipt of manuscript acknowledged: Yes
  Decision to publish in: 3-6 weeks
  Accepted manuscript published in: 2-4 months
  Rejected manuscript returned: Yes
  Rejected manuscript criticized: Yes
Submit to:
  Joyce A. Dixon
  Editor
  (See address above)

CRIMINAL LAW BULLETIN [1221]
Warren, Gorham and Lamont, Inc.
89 Beach Street
Boston, Massachusetts 02111
(518) 457-3224

First published in 1965

SUBSCRIPTION DATA
Issues and rates: 6 times per year
  Average paid circulation: 5,000
  Annual rate(s): $34.00

Managing Editor: Lily Pilgrim

EDITORIAL DESCRIPTION
Contains articles on the criminal justice system with both a legal and sociological perspective; digests of recent court decisions; digests of law review articles; book reviews, and practical guides for lawyers.
Articles per average issue: 4
Audience: Professional, academic
  Manuscripts accepted in English

MANUSCRIPT INFORMATION
Subject field(s): Legal, sociological, psychological, police science and corrections
  Preferred length: 20 to 40 pages
  Number of copies to be submitted: Two
  Abstract: No
Author information and reprints: Payment: None.
  Is simultaneous submission of article to other journals permitted: No
  Exclusive manuscript rights between acceptance and publication: Yes
  Copyright: Held by publication.
  Reprints: Available
Disposition of manuscript:
  Query letter: No
  Receipt of manuscript acknowledged: Yes
  Decision to publish in: 2 weeks to 1 month
  Accepted manuscript published in: Two months
  Rejected manuscript returned: No
  Rejected manuscript criticized: Occasionally
Submit to:
  Fred Cohen
  Editor-in-chief
  SUNY at Albany
  School of Criminal Justice
  Albany, New York 12203

THE CRIMINAL LAW REVIEW [1222]
11 New Fetter Lane
London EC4, England
(01) 583-9855

First published in 1954

SUBSCRIPTION DATA
Issues and rates: Published monthly.
  Average paid circulation: 6,000
  Annual rate(s): £6.75

EDITORIAL DESCRIPTION
Covers all aspects of criminal law in England as well as internationally, with articles on practical applications, and new developments in the law
Articles per average issue: 3
Audience: Legal practitioners, criminologists, law students
  Manuscripts accepted in English

MANUSCRIPT INFORMATION
Manuscript requirements: See latest issue for style requirements. Style sheet sent on request.
  Preferred length: 4,000 words
  Number of copies to be submitted: 1
Author information and reprints: Payment: By publication to author. £2.00 per page.
  Is simultaneous submission of article to other journals permitted: Permitted, but not encouraged.
  Exclusive manuscript rights between acceptance and publication: Yes
  Copyright: Held by publication.
  Reprints: Available at cost.
Additional information: Welcomes contributions from the United States. All manuscripts are to be typewritten, double-spaced.
Disposition of manuscript:
  Query letter: Not necessary.
  Receipt of manuscript acknowledged: Yes
  Decision to publish in: 2-3 weeks
  Accepted manuscript published in: 3-4 months
  Rejected manuscript returned: Yes, with return postage paid by publication.
  Rejected manuscript criticized: Reasons for rejections only
Submit to:
  Jane Slater
  Assistant Editor
  (See address above)

DEFENSE LAW JOURNAL [1223]
1435 North Meridian Street
Indianapolis, Indiana 46202
(317) 634-4098 ext. 32

SUBSCRIPTION DATA
Issues and rates: 6 times per year
  Annual rate(s): $45

EDITORIAL DESCRIPTION
Contains reviews of decisions from various jurisdictions which are of interest to attorneys engaged in defense of civil cases in the tort, products liability, or insurance fields; lead articles are written by experienced attorneys, willing to share their expertise with other attorneys.

MANUSCRIPT INFORMATION
Subject field(s): Tort law
Manuscript requirements: Style sheet sent on request.
  Is simultaneous submission of article to other journals permitted: No
  Exclusive manuscript rights between acceptance and publication: Yes
  Copyright: Held by publication.
  Reprints: Available, 25 free to author.
Disposition of manuscript:
  Receipt of manuscript acknowledged: Yes
  Decision to publish in: Three weeks
  Accepted manuscript published in: Varies greatly
  Rejected manuscript returned: No
  Rejected manuscript criticized: Yes
Submit to:
  Robert Alan Scalf
  Editor
  (See address above)

DENVER LAW JOURNAL [1224]
200 West 14th Avenue
Denver, Colorado 80204
(303) 753-2651

Previously entitled *Dicta*

First published in 1923

SUBSCRIPTION DATA
Issues and rates: Published quarterly.
  Average paid circulation: 1500; 1500 controlled
  Annual rate(s): $9.00
Managing Editor: Charles P Leder

EDITORIAL DESCRIPTION
  Contains articles of interest to the national legal community.
Articles per average issue: 7
  Manuscripts accepted in English

MANUSCRIPT INFORMATION
Subject field(s): Any topic in the legal or legal empirical fields.
Manuscript requirements: No specific style guide.
  Preferred length: None
  Number of copies to be submitted: Two
  Abstract: No
Author information and reprints: Payment: Reprints only. 25 reprints
  Is simultaneous submission of article to other journals permitted: No
  Exclusive manuscript rights between acceptance and publication: Yes
  Copyright: Held by publication.
  Reprints: Available, variable cost
Disposition of manuscript:
  Query letter: No
  Receipt of manuscript acknowledged: Yes
  Decision to publish in: 2 weeks
  Accepted manuscript published in: 3 months
  Rejected manuscript returned: Yes
  Rejected manuscript criticized: Yes
Submit to:
  Editor-in-Chief
  (See address above)

DePAUL LAW REVIEW [1225]
25 East Jackson, Room 1735
Chicago, Illinois 60604
(312) 321-7758

First published in 1951

SUBSCRIPTION DATA
Issues and rates: Published quarterly.
  Average paid circulation: 2,500
  Annual rate(s): $10.00
Managing Editor: Roslyn Corenzwit Lieb

EDITORIAL DESCRIPTION
  Contains scholarly legal articles.
Articles per average issue: 5-7 (varies)
Audience: Legal practitioners, professors and students
  Manuscripts accepted in English

MANUSCRIPT INFORMATION
Subject field(s): Law and related fields

Manuscript requirements: Style sheet sent on request.
  Preferred length: None
  Number of copies to be submitted: 1
  Abstract: Preferably triple-spaced with footnotes appended to body; must conform to HLRA
Author information and reprints: Payment: None.
  Is simultaneous submission of article to other journals permitted: Yes
  Exclusive manuscript rights between acceptance and publication: Yes
  Copyright: Held by publication.
  Reprints: Available cost based on length
Disposition of manuscript:
  Query letter: No
  Receipt of manuscript acknowledged: Yes
  Decision to publish in: 1-2 months
  Accepted manuscript published in: 3 months
  Rejected manuscript returned: only if requested
  Rejected manuscript criticized: Yes
Submit to:
  Bradford E. Block
  Editor-in-Chief
  (See address above)

EARTH LAW JOURNAL [1226]
Journal of International and Comparative Environmental Law
A. W. Sijthoff International Publishing Company
Doezastraat 1, P. O. Box 26
Leiden, The Netherlands
(071) 21 845; Telex 32447

First published in 1975

SUBSCRIPTION DATA
Issues and rates: Published quarterly.
  Average paid circulation: 1,200; 500 controlled
  Annual rate(s): Dfl. 82.00; Foreign $33.00
Publisher or Sponsor: I.U.C.N., Morges, Switzerland; Friends of the Earth, London; Environmental Law Institute, Washington

EDITORIAL DESCRIPTION
  Focuses on environmental law as developed by national governments, their political subdivisions and by regional and international organizations; the legal systems of civil law, common law and socialist law being explored equally.
Articles per average issue: 6
Audience: Professional, governmental, conservation, academic
  Manuscripts accepted in English

MANUSCRIPT INFORMATION
Manuscript requirements: See latest issue for style requirements. Style sheet sent on request.
  Preferred length: None
  Number of copies to be submitted: 3
  Abstract: Yes. Of about 150 words

Author information and reprints: Payment: Reprints only. 1 issue and 50 reprints
  Is simultaneous submission of article to other journals permitted: Consultation with publisher conditional
  Exclusive manuscript rights between acceptance and publication: Yes
  Copyright: Held by publication.
  Reprints: Available at cost.
Disposition of manuscript:
  Query letter: Not necessary, but advisable.
  Receipt of manuscript acknowledged: Yes
  Decision to publish in: 1 month
  Accepted manuscript published in: 3 months
  Rejected manuscript returned: Yes, if return postage is supplied by author.
  Rejected manuscript criticized: Sometimes
Submit to:
  Nicholas A. Robinson
  Editor-in-Chief
  P. O. Box 2849
  Grand Central Station
  New York, New York 10017
  (212) 421-7200

EMORY LAW JOURNAL [1227]
Emory University School of Law
1722 North Decatur Road
Atlanta, Georgia 30322
(404) 377-2411 Ex. 7908

Previously entitled *Journal of Public Law*

First published in 1952

SUBSCRIPTION DATA
Issues and rates: Published quarterly.
  Average paid circulation: 925 850 controlled
  Annual rate(s): $10.00 Foreign $10.00 Individuals $10.00
Publisher or Sponsor: Emory University, School of Law
Managing Editor: Ronald J. Davis

EDITORIAL DESCRIPTION
  A scholarly legal review focusing on public law broadly defined as encompassing any legal topic discussing the relationship of the individual to society and government as it is affected by the laws of that society. The editorial policy is somewhat broader than that of a traditional law review.
Articles per average issue: 4 professional, 6 student
Audience: Legal scholars, practicing attorneys, judges and social scientists
  Manuscripts accepted in English

MANUSCRIPT INFORMATION
Subject field(s): Constitutional law, administrative law, criminal law, antitrust law, securities law, public law, comparative law, employment & labor law and other related areas of law
Manuscript requirements: Harvard Whitebook
  Preferred length: 40-80 pages
  Number of copies to be submitted: 1

Abstract: Not necessary.
Author information and reprints: Payment: Reprints only. 2 copies of issue & 50 reprints of article
Is simultaneous submission of article to other journals permitted: Permitted.
Exclusive manuscript rights between acceptance and publication: Yes
Copyright: Held by publication.
Reprints: Available at cost.
Additional information: Double-space manuscript; triple-space footnotes
Disposition of manuscript:
Query letter: Not necessary.
Receipt of manuscript acknowledged: Yes
Decision to publish in: 4-6 weeks
Accepted manuscript published in: 3-5 months
Rejected manuscript returned: Yes, with return postage paid by publication.
Rejected manuscript criticized: Reasons for rejections only
Submit to:
Executive Articles Editor
(See address above)

FEDERAL BAR NEWS [1228]
Mr. Russell McKinnon, Suite 420
1815 H Street, N. W.
Washington, D. C. 20006
(202) 638-0253

First published in 1953

SUBSCRIPTION DATA
Issues and rates: Published monthly.
Average paid circulation: 14,000
Annual rate(s): $6.00; Foreign $7.00
Publisher or Sponsor: The Federal Bar Association

EDITORIAL DESCRIPTION
Contains substantive articles on any aspect of federal law or pending legislation of federal concern; the only requirement is that all viewpoints be well documented in the text.
Articles per average issue: 2
Audience: Attorneys and libraries
Manuscripts accepted in English only

MANUSCRIPT INFORMATION
Subject field(s): Any area of concern to federal lawyers dealing with federal law
Manuscript requirements: No specific style guide.
Preferred length: 2,000 words; 8-10 pages
Number of copies to be submitted: 2
Abstract: Not necessary.
Author information and reprints: Payment: Reprints only. 2-3 copies
Is simultaneous submission of article to other journals permitted: Not permitted.
Exclusive manuscript rights between acceptance and publication: Yes
Copyright: Held by author.
Additional information: Everything must be typewritten, double-spaced.
Disposition of manuscript:
Query letter: Necessary.
Receipt of manuscript acknowledged: No
Decision to publish in: 15 days
Accepted manuscript published in: 30 days
Rejected manuscript returned: Yes, if return postage is supplied by author.
Rejected manuscript criticized: Sometimes
Submit to:
Russell F. McKinnon
Associate Editor
(See address above)

THE GEORGE WASHINGTON LAW REVIEW [1229]
2000 H Street, N.W.
Washington, D.C. 20006
(202) 676-6835

First published in 1932

SUBSCRIPTION DATA
Issues and rates: 5 times annually
Average paid circulation: 2373; 40 controlled
Annual rate(s): $10.00, Foreign $11.50
Managing Editor: Mark E. Alberts

EDITORIAL DESCRIPTION
Contains lead articles, student notes, and book reviews on topics within the broad area of public law.
Articles per average issue: 8-10
Manuscripts accepted in English only

MANUSCRIPT INFORMATION
Subject field(s): All areas of public law
Manuscript requirements: Strunk, HLRA
Preferred length: None
Number of copies to be submitted: Two
Author information and reprints: Payment: None.
Is simultaneous submission of article to other journals permitted: Simultaneous submission of an article to other publications is permitted, but will not publish any article accepted and published elsewhere.
Exclusive manuscript rights between acceptance and publication: Yes
Copyright: Held by publication.
Reprints: Available, first 50 free; each additional 50 at $.80 per page
Additional information: Excessive use of quotations in the text is discouraged.
Disposition of manuscript:
Query letter: No
Receipt of manuscript acknowledged: Yes
Decision to publish in: 2-3 weeks
Accepted manuscript published in: Three months
Rejected manuscript returned: Yes
Rejected manuscript criticized: Occasionally
Submit to:
Editor-in-Chief
(See address above)

SPECIAL STIPULATIONS
Each volume has a new editorial board.

GEORGIA STATE BAR JOURNAL [1230]
State Bar of Georgia
1510 Fulton National Bank Building
55 Marietta Street NW
Atlanta, Georgia 30303
(404) 522-6255

First published in 1964

SUBSCRIPTION DATA
Issues and rates: Published quarterly.
Average paid circulation: 9,000
Annual rate(s): $4.00
Publisher or Sponsor: State Bar of Georgia

EDITORIAL DESCRIPTION
Publishes articles on due process, judiciary problems, estate planning, habeas corpus, antitrust practice, sales and use tax, legal aid, corporation law, etc.; also casenotes and decisions are included from Georgia law school students.
Articles per average issue: 4-6
Audience: Members of Georgia State Bar
Manuscripts accepted in English only

MANUSCRIPT INFORMATION
Subject field(s): General practice, specific fields of practice, miscellaneous biographies, speeches
Manuscript requirements: Style sheet sent on request.
Preferred length: 15 pages double or triple-spaced including any footnotes
Number of copies to be submitted: 2
Abstract: No
Author information and reprints: Payment: None.
Is simultaneous submission of article to other journals permitted: No
Exclusive manuscript rights between acceptance and publication: Yes
Copyright: Held by publication.
Reprints: Available, through printer
Disposition of manuscript:
Query letter: No
Receipt of manuscript acknowledged: Yes
Decision to publish in: 6-9 weeks
Accepted manuscript published in: 4-6 months
Rejected manuscript returned: Yes
Rejected manuscript criticized: No
Submit to:
Mary Henry
Managing Editor
(See address above)

HARVARD CIVIL RIGHTS-CIVIL LIBERTIES LAW REVIEW [1231]
Langdell Hall, Harvard Law School
Cambridge, Massachusetts 02138
(617) 495-4500

First published in 1966

SUBSCRIPTION DATA
Issues and rates: Published three times per year.
Average paid circulation: 2200

Annual rate(s): $8.50 per year

EDITORIAL DESCRIPTION

Publishes material on civil rights, civil liberties, poverty and welfare law, housing and consumer law, environmental law, criminal law, and employment and education. Material may be either legal analysis or political, economic, sociological, or scientific analysis as it bears on legal problems.

Articles per average issue: 5-7

Audience: Legal service offices, public interest organizations, university libraries, private law firms
Manuscripts accepted in English

MANUSCRIPT INFORMATION

Manuscript requirements: Triple-space text, footnotes and quotes with 3 inch margin on left. Footnotes appended to text, conform to "The Bluebook" (A Uniform System of Citation)
Preferred length: None
Number of copies to be submitted: One

Author information and reprints: Payment: None.
Is simultaneous submission of article to other journals permitted: Yes, if notified it is being done
Exclusive manuscript rights between acceptance and publication: Yes
Copyright: Held by publication.
Reprints: Available at no cost

Disposition of manuscript:
Query letter: No
Receipt of manuscript acknowledged: Yes
Decision to publish in: 3-6 weeks
Accepted manuscript published in: 1-6 months
Rejected manuscript returned: Yes, if self-addressed, stamped envelope is sent with manuscript.
Rejected manuscript criticized: Yes

Submit to:
John W. Handley, Jr.
Managing Editor
(See address above)

HARVARD INTERNATIONAL LAW JOURNAL [1232]
Austin Hall
Harvard Law School
Cambridge, Massachusetts 02178
(617) 495-3146

First published in 1959

SUBSCRIPTION DATA

Issues and rates: Published three times per year.
Average paid circulation: 1000; 100 controlled
Annual rate(s): $8.50, Foreign $9.50

EDITORIAL DESCRIPTION

Journal is composed of articles, comments, and notes on public international law and foreign and comparative law. Interest is in all aspects of international law; attempting to provide a balanced perspective on current developments.

Articles per average issue: 2-4

Audience: International lawyers and scholars
Manuscripts accepted in English

MANUSCRIPT INFORMATION

Subject field(s): International law

Manuscript requirements: Style sheet sent on request.
Preferred length: 50-100 pages
Number of copies to be submitted: Three
Abstract: No

Author information and reprints: Payment: None.
Is simultaneous submission of article to other journals permitted: Yes
Exclusive manuscript rights between acceptance and publication: Yes
Copyright: Held by publication.
Reprints: Available, cost depends on length.

Disposition of manuscript:
Receipt of manuscript acknowledged: Yes
Decision to publish in: One month
Accepted manuscript published in: 3-6 months
Rejected manuscript returned: Yes, if return postage is supplied by author.
Rejected manuscript criticized: No

Submit to:
Editor-in-Chief
(See address above)

HARVARD JOURNAL ON LEGISLATION [1233]
Langdell Hall, Harvard Law School
Cambridge, Massachusetts 02138
(617) 495-4400

First published in 1964

SUBSCRIPTION DATA

Issues and rates: Published quarterly.
Average paid circulation: 1000; 100 controlled
Annual rate(s): $7.50, Foreign $9.00

Publisher or Sponsor: Harvard Legislative Research Bureau

Managing Editor: Cary H. Hall

EDITORIAL DESCRIPTION

Publishes legal articles, statutory comments, model statutes and book reviews. Primary emphasis is on legislative response to current legal and social problems.

Articles per average issue: 6

Audience: Legislators, Law students and professors
Manuscripts accepted in English

MANUSCRIPT INFORMATION

Subject field(s): Federal, state and local legislation; legislative solutions to current problems; statutory analysis and comment; model statutes; legislative process; foreign legislation; legal process; legislative history

Manuscript requirements: Style sheet sent on request.
Preferred length: 7,500 to 15,000 words; 50 to 100 pages
Number of copies to be submitted: Two

Abstract: No

Author information and reprints: Payment: None.
Is simultaneous submission of article to other journals permitted: Yes, with notice
Exclusive manuscript rights between acceptance and publication: Yes
Copyright: Held by publication.
Reprints: Available if ordered before publication

Additional information: All citations must conform to HLRA. Manuscript must be triple-spaced.

Disposition of manuscript:
Query letter: No
Receipt of manuscript acknowledged: Yes
Decision to publish in: 1 month
Accepted manuscript published in: 3 months
Rejected manuscript returned: Yes, if return postage is supplied by author.
Rejected manuscript criticized: If requested

Submit to:
Kenneth Burns;
Cary Hall
(See address above)

HARVARD LAW REVIEW [1234]
Gannett House
Cambridge, Massachusetts 02138
(617) 495-4425

SUBSCRIPTION DATA

Issues and rates: Published monthly.
Average paid circulation: 10,000
Annual rate(s): $15.00, Foreign $16.50

Publisher or Sponsor: Harvard Law Review Association

Managing Editor: Daniel J Meltzer

EDITORIAL DESCRIPTION

Contains articles by lawyers and professors on legal and related topics; student notes and casenotes on the law; book reviews.

MANUSCRIPT INFORMATION

Subject field(s): All areas of legal scholarship

Manuscript requirements: Style sheet sent on request.
Preferred length: None
Number of copies to be submitted: One

Author information and reprints: Payment: None.
Is simultaneous submission of article to other journals permitted: Yes
Exclusive manuscript rights between acceptance and publication: Yes
Copyright: Held by publication.
Reprints: Available, $3.30 per number

Disposition of manuscript:
Receipt of manuscript acknowledged: Yes
Decision to publish in: 1-2 months
Accepted manuscript published in: Varies
Rejected manuscript returned: Yes
Rejected manuscript criticized: No

Submit to:
Articles Editor
(See address above)
(617) 661-1373

HUMAN RIGHTS [1235]

American Bar Association, Circulation Department
1155 East 60th Street
Chicago, Illinois 60637
(312) 493-0533

First published in 1971

SUBSCRIPTION DATA

Issues and rates: Published three times per year.
Average paid circulation: 400; 4,300 controlled
Annual rate(s): $10.00; Free to members

Publisher or Sponsor: American Bar Association, Section on Individual Rights and Responsibilities,
Southern Methodist University

EDITORIAL DESCRIPTION

Contains articles, comments, notes, speeches, reports, symposia on rights and responsibilities of individuals.
Articles per average issue: 5-6
Audience: Lawyers, law students and teachers
Manuscripts accepted in English

MANUSCRIPT INFORMATION

Subject field(s): Open to all fields as long as submission is within the editorial description.
Manuscript requirements: See latest issue for style requirements.
Preferred length: None
Number of copies to be submitted: 1
Abstract: Not necessary.
Author information and reprints: Payment: Reprints only. 20 reprints
Is simultaneous submission of article to other journals permitted: Permitted.
Exclusive manuscript rights between acceptance and publication: Yes
Copyright: Held by the American Bar Association
Additional information: Place footnotes on a separate sheet.
Disposition of manuscript:
Query letter: Not necessary, but advisable.
Receipt of manuscript acknowledged: Yes
Decision to publish in: 2-3 weeks
Accepted manuscript published in: 1-4 months
Rejected manuscript returned: Yes, if return postage is supplied by author.
Rejected manuscript criticized: Sometimes
Submit to:
Neil H. Cogan
Faculty Editor
School of Law
Southern Methodist University
Dallas, Texas 75275
(214) 692-2579

INDIANA LAW JOURNAL [1236]

Law Building Annex
Indiana University School of Law
Bloomington, Indiana 47401
(812) 337-5175

First published in 1926

SUBSCRIPTION DATA

Issues and rates: Published quarterly.
Average paid circulation: 1500
Annual rate(s): $10.00; Foreign $12.00
Managing Editor: Jan Bianchi; Grant Shipley

EDITORIAL DESCRIPTION

Contains articles related directly or indirectly to areas of primary concern to the legal community.
Articles per average issue: 5
Audience: Lawyers and legal scholars
Manuscripts accepted in English

MANUSCRIPT INFORMATION

Subject field(s): Law, business, social science
Manuscript requirements: Type, triple-space; footnotes governed by *Harvard Citator*
Number of copies to be submitted: One
Abstract: No
Author information and reprints: Payment: None.
Is simultaneous submission of article to other journals permitted: No
Exclusive manuscript rights between acceptance and publication: Yes
Reprints: Available, 50 free
Disposition of manuscript:
Query letter: No
Receipt of manuscript acknowledged: Yes
Decision to publish in: 2 weeks
Accepted manuscript published in: 2 months
Rejected manuscript returned: Yes
Rejected manuscript criticized: No
Submit to:
Editor-In-Chief
(See address above)

INTERNATIONAL LEGAL MATERIALS [1237]

Current Documents
2223 Massachusetts Ave., N. W.
Washington, D. C. 20008
(202) 265-4313

First published in 1962

SUBSCRIPTION DATA

Issues and rates: Published bi-monthly.
Average paid circulation: 2,000
Annual rate(s): $45.00; Foreign $45.00; Institutions $45.00; Students $15.00; Members $15.00; Foreign institutions $45.00
Publisher or Sponsor: American Society of International Law
Managing Editor: Marilou M. Righini

EDITORIAL DESCRIPTION

Introductory notes to documents, and current documents providing up-to-date information on international relations. These current materials are not available in permanent collections until later but are likely to be of interest to a broad group of readers working in the field.
Articles per average issue: 27
Audience: International lawyers, legal scholars, and officials dealing with international matters
Manuscripts accepted in English

MANUSCRIPT INFORMATION

Subject field(s): International Law, both public and private on all subjects including environment, investment, energy, natural resources, law of the sea, consular relations, recognition, etc.
Manuscript requirements: No specific style guide.
Number of copies to be submitted: One
Abstract: Yes. Sample sent on request
Author information and reprints: Payment: None.
Is simultaneous submission of article to other journals permitted: Permitted, but not encouraged.
Exclusive manuscript rights between acceptance and publication:
Copyright: None
Reprints: Not available.
Disposition of manuscript:
Query letter: Not necessary.
Receipt of manuscript acknowledged: Yes
Decision to publish in: 1-2 months
Accepted manuscript published in: 1-2 months
Rejected manuscript returned: No
Submit to:
Marilou M. Righini
Editor
(See address above)

INTERNATIONAL ORGANIZATION [1238]

Center for Research in International Studies
Stanford University
Stanford California 94305
(415) 321-2300

SUBSCRIPTION DATA

Issues and rates: Published quarterly.
Average paid circulation: 2,700
Annual rate(s): Individuals $12.50; Institutions $25.00
Publisher or Sponsor: World Peace Foundation, Boston, Massachusetts; University of Wisconsin Press

EDITORIAL DESCRIPTION

Publishes analytical articles, review essays and brief notes dealing primarily with development, functioning, or political factors associated with international agencies and regional arrangements, or their dynamic relationships with the international political and economic environments in which they operate.
Articles per average issue: 10
Audience: Professional students of international politics and organizations
Manuscripts accepted in English (French)

MANUSCRIPT INFORMATION

Subject field(s): International agencies, regional arrangements
Manuscript requirements: Style sheet sent on request.
Preferred length: Notes: 2,000 words; articles: 35 pages

Number of copies to be submitted: Three
Abstract: Yes, substantial
Author information and reprints: Payment: None.
Is simultaneous submission of article to other journals permitted: No
Exclusive manuscript rights between acceptance and publication: Yes
Copyright: Held by publication.
Reprints: Available, first 10 free
Disposition of manuscript:
Receipt of manuscript acknowledged: Yes
Decision to publish in: Six weeks
Accepted manuscript published in: 6 months
Rejected manuscript returned: Yes, if self-addressed, stamped envelope is sent with manuscript.
Rejected manuscript criticized: Yes
Submit to:
Robert O. Keohane
Editor
(See address above)

IUSTITIA [1239]
Indiana University
School of Law
Bloomington, Indiana 47401
(812) 337-2902

First published in 1973

SUBSCRIPTION DATA
Issues and rates: Published semi-annually.
Average paid circulation: 150; 75 controlled
Annual rate(s): $10.00; Institutions $10.00
Publisher or Sponsor: Indiana University School of Law, Bloomington

EDITORIAL DESCRIPTION
A forum for increasing communication between the law and other disciplines. Its philosophy constitutes a strong commitment to the evaluation of key social, economic and political issues on the basis of their ultimate legal implication. This continuing dialogue is intended to be the basis for new perspectives and solutions.
Articles per average issue: 8-12
Audience: Academic, legal
Manuscripts accepted in English only

MANUSCRIPT INFORMATION
Subject field(s): Interdisciplinary topics with some relation to law or legal considerations
Manuscript requirements: MLA, HLRA
Preferred length: 25 typewritten pages
Number of copies to be submitted: Original and 1 copy
Abstract: Not necessary. Helpful for editorial decision.
Author information and reprints: Payment: Reprints only. Several, upon request
Is simultaneous submission of article to other journals permitted: Permitted, but not encouraged.
Exclusive manuscript rights between acceptance and publication: Yes

Copyright: Held by publication.
Exceptions considered
Reprints: Not available.
Additional information: Student manuscripts are encouraged.
Disposition of manuscript:
Query letter: Not necessary, but advisable.
Receipt of manuscript acknowledged: No
Decision to publish in: 2-4 weeks
Accepted manuscript published in: 2 months
Rejected manuscript returned: Yes, if return postage is supplied by author.
Rejected manuscript criticized: Sometimes
Submit to:
Editors
(See address above)

JOHN MARSHALL JOURNAL OF PRACTICE AND PROCEDURE [1240]
315 South Plymouth Court
Chicago, Illinois 60604
(312) 427-2737 ext. 259

First published in 1967

SUBSCRIPTION DATA
Issues and rates: Published three times per year.
Average paid circulation: 1200; 500 controlled
Annual rate(s): $7.50
Managing Editor: Michael J. Meyer

EDITORIAL DESCRIPTION
Publishes articles and student comments on current developments in the law.
Articles per average issue: 8
Audience: Attorneys, judges, legislators
Manuscripts accepted in English

MANUSCRIPT INFORMATION
Subject field(s): Legal-concentration on practice and procedure
Manuscript requirements: HLRA
Preferred length: 30-40 pages
Number of copies to be submitted: One
Abstract: No
Author information and reprints: Payment: None.
Is simultaneous submission of article to other journals permitted: No
Exclusive manuscript rights between acceptance and publication: Yes
Copyright: Held by publication.
Reprints: Available
Disposition of manuscript:
Query letter: No
Receipt of manuscript acknowledged: Yes
Decision to publish in: 3 months
Accepted manuscript published in: 6-9 months
Rejected manuscript returned: Yes
Rejected manuscript criticized: Yes
Submit to:
Editor-in-Chief
(See address above)

JOURNAL OF AIR LAW AND COMMERCE [1241]
Southern Methodist University
School of Law
Dallas, Texas 75275
(214) 692-3465

First published in 1930

SUBSCRIPTION DATA
Issues and rates: Published quarterly.
Average paid circulation: 1,400; 100 controlled
Annual rate(s): $21.00; Foreign $13.00
Publisher or Sponsor: Southern Methodist University, School of Law
Managing Editor: Peter B. Heister

EDITORIAL DESCRIPTION
The only scholarly publication in English devoted to legal and economical problems of aviation and space.
Articles per average issue: 3-5; plus student work
Audience: Professional, academic, aviation
Manuscripts accepted in English

MANUSCRIPT INFORMATION
Manuscript requirements: GPO; *Texas Law Review Manual on Style*
Preferred length: 40 pages
Number of copies to be submitted: 1
Abstract: Not necessary.
Author information and reprints: Payment: Reprints only. 25
Is simultaneous submission of article to other journals permitted: Permitted, but not encouraged.
Exclusive manuscript rights between acceptance and publication: No
Copyright: Held by publication.
Additional information: Manuscripts should be triple-spaced on standard heavy bond, ample margins, footnotes on separate pages following the text.
Disposition of manuscript:
Query letter: Not necessary, but advisable.
Receipt of manuscript acknowledged: No
Decision to publish in: 1-2 months
Accepted manuscript published in: Varies
Rejected manuscript returned: Yes, if return postage is supplied by author.
Rejected manuscript criticized: No
Submit to:
Stephen B. Early
Articles Editor
(See address above)
(214) 350-4860

JOURNAL OF COMPARATIVE ADMINISTRATION* [1242]
Sage Publications, Inc.
275 South Beverly Drive
Beverly Hills, California 90212
(213) 274-2423

SUBSCRIPTION DATA
Issues and rates: Published quarterly.
Average paid circulation: Not available.

Law and public administration

Annual rate(s): Institutions $18.00;
Individuals $12.00; Students $9.00;
Foreign individuals $13.00; Foreign
institutions $19.00
Publisher or Sponsor: American Society for
Public Administration, Comparative
Administration Group

EDITORIAL DESCRIPTION
Publishes theoretical and empirical
research articles focusing on the
interdisciplinary or international concerns
of public organizations. Also includes
research notes reporting on ongoing
research projects, research designs, and
preliminary findings; review articles also
sought.

MANUSCRIPT INFORMATION
Subject field(s): Public administration
Manuscript requirements: Style sheet sent
on request.
  Preferred length: 6,250-7,500 words; 25
  to 30 pages
  Number of copies to be submitted: Two
Author information and reprints: Payment:
Reprints only. 25 tear-sheets
  Is simultaneous submission of article to
  other journals permitted: Permitted, but
  not encouraged. Author must notify
  publisher that manuscript is under
  consideration elsewhere.
  Exclusive manuscript rights between
  acceptance and publication: Yes
  Copyright: Held by publication.
  Reprints: Available if purchased by
  special order in amounts no fewer than
  100
Disposition of manuscript:
  Receipt of manuscript acknowledged: Yes
  Decision to publish in: Six to eight weeks
  Accepted manuscript published in: Six to
  nine months
  Rejected manuscript returned: Yes
  Rejected manuscript criticized: Yes
Submit to:
  Peter Savage
  Editor
  Department of Political Science
  University of Houston, Cullen Boulevard
  Houston, Texas 77004

JOURNAL OF CRIMINAL LAW AND CRIMINOLOGY [1243]
428 East Preston Street
Baltimore, Maryland 21202
(301) 528-4116

First published in 1910

SUBSCRIPTION DATA
Issues and rates: Published quarterly.
  Average paid circulation: 3800
  Annual rate(s): $15.00, Foreign $16.25
Publisher or Sponsor: Northwestern
University School of Law

EDITORIAL DESCRIPTION
Contains papers on criminal law and
criminology.
Articles per average issue: 10
Audience: Criminal lawyers, criminologists
  Manuscripts accepted in English

MANUSCRIPT INFORMATION
Manuscript requirements: Style sheet sent
on request.
  Preferred length: None
  Number of copies to be submitted: Two
Author information and reprints: Payment:
None.
  Is simultaneous submission of article to
  other journals permitted: No
  Exclusive manuscript rights between
  acceptance and publication: Yes
  Copyright: Held by publication.
  Reprints: Available, 100 free
Disposition of manuscript:
  Query letter: No
  Receipt of manuscript acknowledged: Yes
  Decision to publish in: 2 months
  Accepted manuscript published in: 6-9
  months
  Rejected manuscript returned: Yes
  Rejected manuscript criticized: Yes
Submit to:
  Marie D. Christiansen
  Business Manager
  Northwestern University School of Law
  357 East Chicago Avenue
  Chicago, Illinois 60611
  (312) 649-8467

JOURNAL OF FAMILY LAW [1244]
University of Louisville School of Law
Louisville, Kentucky 40208
(502) 636-4288

First published in 1961

SUBSCRIPTION DATA
Issues and rates: Published quarterly.
  Average paid circulation: 1,000
  Annual rate(s): $15.00

EDITORIAL DESCRIPTION
Contains articles and student notes
dealing with all aspects of family law;
short abstracts of recent cases in the area
of family law; book reviews on recent
books touching on legal problems
affecting or concerning the family.
Articles per average issue: 4
Audience: Academic, professional
  Manuscripts accepted in English only

MANUSCRIPT INFORMATION
Subject field(s): Manuscripts dealing with
any phase of family law are accepted,
including but not limited to the following
areas of topics: juveniles, divorce,
adoption, illegitimacy, support payments,
etc.
Manuscript requirements: HLRA
  Preferred length: None
  Number of copies to be submitted: Two
  Abstract: No
Author information and reprints: Payment:
Reprints only. Two copies of the issue in
which article appears and reprints
furnished on request.
  Is simultaneous submission of article to
  other journals permitted: No
  Exclusive manuscript rights between
  acceptance and publication: Yes
  Copyright: Held by publication.
  Reprints: Available, cost varies depending
  on length
Additional information: Biographical
information on author should be sent
with manuscript. Footnotes should be on
separate pages.
Disposition of manuscript:
  Query letter: No
  Receipt of manuscript acknowledged: Yes
  Decision to publish in: 2-3 weeks
  Accepted manuscript published in: 6-8
  weeks
  Rejected manuscript returned: Yes
  Rejected manuscript criticized: No
Submit to:
  Editor-in-Chief
  (See address above)

JOURNAL OF INTERNATIONAL LAW AND ECONOMICS [1245]
National Law Center
George Washington University
Washington, D.C. 20006
(202) 676-7164

Previously entitled *Studies in Law and
Economic Development; Journal of Law
and Economic Development*

First published in 1966

SUBSCRIPTION DATA
Issues and rates: Published three times per
year.
  Average paid circulation: 700
  Annual rate(s): $10.00, Foreign $11.00
Publisher or Sponsor: George Washington
University, National Law Center

EDITORIAL DESCRIPTION
Contains articles on international legal
problems as they apply to economics
problems, international business and
economic development.
Articles per average issue: 6-7
Audience: Legal practitioners,
administrators, scholars, businessmen
throughout world.
  Manuscripts accepted in English

MANUSCRIPT INFORMATION
Subject field(s): International law, foreign
investment, economic development,
foreign trade
Manuscript requirements: See latest issue for
style requirements. Double-space with
footnotes appended to manuscript;
citation form *Harvard Citator*.
  Preferred length: 40-60 pages
  double-spaced
  Number of copies to be submitted: Two
  Abstract: No
Author information and reprints: Payment:
None.
  Is simultaneous submission of article to
  other journals permitted: No
  Exclusive manuscript rights between
  acceptance and publication: Yes
  Copyright: Held by publication.
  Reprints: Available, first 15 free
Disposition of manuscript:
  Query letter: No

Receipt of manuscript acknowledged: Yes
Decision to publish in: 3 weeks
Accepted manuscript published in: 4 months
Rejected manuscript returned: Yes
Rejected manuscript criticized: No
Submit to:
Kenneth S. Levinson
Editor-in-Chief
(See address above)

SPECIAL STIPULATIONS

Journal reserves the right to return for revision or reject articles previously conditionally accepted for publication.

JOURNAL OF INTERNATIONAL LAW AND POLITICS [1246]

249 Sullivan Street
New York, New York 10012
(212) 598-3789

First published in 1968

SUBSCRIPTION DATA

Issues and rates: Published three times per year.
Average paid circulation: Not available.
Annual rate(s): $7.50, Pan-Am $7.75, Foreign $8.00
Publisher or Sponsor: New York University School of Law
Managing Editor: Jo-Una Spadafora

EDITORIAL DESCRIPTION

Publishes articles dealing with all aspects of public and private international law.
Articles per average issue: 2-4
Manuscripts accepted in English only

MANUSCRIPT INFORMATION

Manuscript requirements: HLRA
Preferred length: No preferred length
Number of copies to be submitted: 2
Author information and reprints: Payment: None.
Is simultaneous submission of article to other journals permitted: Yes, but the Journal wishes to be notified of such.
Exclusive manuscript rights between acceptance and publication: Yes
Copyright: Held by publication.
Reprints: Available, 25 free to author
Disposition of manuscript:
Query letter: No
Receipt of manuscript acknowledged: Yes
Decision to publish in: 3 weeks
Accepted manuscript published in: 3-4 months
Accepted manuscript published in: Yes on request
Rejected manuscript criticized: No
Submit to:
Editor
(See address above)

JOURNAL OF POLICE SCIENCE AND ADMINISTRATION [1247]

11 Firstfield Road
Gaithersburg, Maryland 20760
(301) 948-0922 ext. 201

First published in 1972

SUBSCRIPTION DATA

Issues and rates: Published quarterly.
Average paid circulation: 4,000
Annual rate(s): $15.00
Publisher or Sponsor: International Association of Chiefs of Police, Northwestern University
Managing Editor: Fred E. Inbau

EDITORIAL DESCRIPTION

Contains feature articles, case studies, research projects and technical data in the fields of police science and police administration.
Articles per average issue: 14
Audience: Police administrators, law enforcement educators
Manuscripts accepted in English only

MANUSCRIPT INFORMATION

Subject field(s): Police science and administration
Manuscript requirements: See latest issue for style requirements. footnotes, not references. Include original and copy
Preferred length: Varies
Number of copies to be submitted: 2
Abstract: No
Author information and reprints: Payment: None.
Is simultaneous submission of article to other journals permitted: No
Exclusive manuscript rights between acceptance and publication: Yes
Copyright: Held by publication.
Reprints: Not available.
Disposition of manuscript:
Query letter: No
Receipt of manuscript acknowledged: Yes
Decision to publish in: 6-8 weeks
Accepted manuscript published in: Contact editor
Rejected manuscript returned: Yes
Rejected manuscript criticized: No
Submit to:
Glen D. King
Associate Editor
(See address above)

SPECIAL STIPULATIONS
Exclusive rights only

JOURNAL OF PSYCHIATRY AND LAW [1248]

95 Morton Street
New York, New York 10014
(212) 243-5775

First published in 1973

SUBSCRIPTION DATA

Issues and rates: Published quarterly.
Average paid circulation: 1,500
Annual rate(s): $20.00; Foreign $26.00; Institutions $24.00; Students $20.00; Foreign institutions $26.00
Managing Editor: Dianne Nashel

EDITORIAL DESCRIPTION

Examines the interfaces of psychiatry and studies of human behavior with law; investigates law through the lens of man's knowledge of his mind
Articles per average issue: 4-6
Audience: Professional, academic, legal
Manuscripts accepted in English

MANUSCRIPT INFORMATION

Subject field(s): Psychiatry and the law, rights of mental patients, suicide in prison, forensic psychiatry, crime and punishment and super ego
Manuscript requirements: Style sheet sent on request.
Preferred length: As is necessary
Number of copies to be submitted: 2
Abstract: Yes.
Author information and reprints: Payment: Reprints only. 50 copies of article and 2 issues
Is simultaneous submission of article to other journals permitted: Not permitted.
Exclusive manuscript rights between acceptance and publication: Yes
Copyright: Held by publication. Author receives 50 per cent of reprint royalties.
Reprints: Available at cost.
Disposition of manuscript:
Query letter: Not necessary, but advisable.
Receipt of manuscript acknowledged: Yes
Decision to publish in: 30 days
Accepted manuscript published in: 3-6 months
Rejected manuscript returned: Yes, with return postage paid by publication.
Rejected manuscript criticized: Sometimes
Submit to:
Dianne Nashel
Managing Editor
28 Morris Road
Tenafly, New Jersey 07670
(201) 568-1159

JOURNAL OF URBAN LAW [1249]

University of Detroit
651 East Jefferson Avenue
Detroit, Michigan 48226
(313) 927-1568

Previously entitled *University of Detroit Law Journal*

First published in 1966

SUBSCRIPTION DATA

Issues and rates: 5 times per year
Average paid circulation: 1,200; 50 controlled
Annual rate(s): $10.00; Foreign $12.00

Law and public administration

Publisher or Sponsor: University of Detroit, School of Law
Managing Editor: Marc E. Thomas

EDITORIAL DESCRIPTION
Any legal topic as it relates to urban or public law
Articles per average issue: 4-5
Audience: Lawyers, professors, academicians
Manuscripts accepted in English

MANUSCRIPT INFORMATION
Manuscript requirements: HLRA
Preferred length: As required
Number of copies to be submitted: 1
Abstract: Not necessary.
Author information and reprints: Payment: Reprints only. 10 issues
Is simultaneous submission of article to other journals permitted: Permitted.
Exclusive manuscript rights between acceptance and publication: Yes
Copyright: Held by publication.
Reprints: Available at cost.
Additional information: Footnotes and text are to be kept separate. Everything, including quotations, is to be triple-spaced.
Disposition of manuscript:
Query letter: Not necessary.
Receipt of manuscript acknowledged: Yes
Decision to publish in: 2 weeks
Accepted manuscript published in: 3-9 months
Rejected manuscript returned: Yes, if return postage is supplied by author.
Rejected manuscript criticized: No
Submit to:
Article and Book Review Editor
(See address above)

JUDICATURE [1250]

The Journal of the American Judicature Society
1155 East 60th Street
Chicago, Illinois 60637
(312) 667-2727

SUBSCRIPTION DATA
Issues and rates: Ten times yearly (bi-monthly issues are June through September)
Average paid circulation: 47,000; 4,000 controlled
Annual rate(s): $6.00
Publisher or Sponsor: The American Judicature Society

EDITORIAL DESCRIPTION
Publishes original articles on means of improving the administration of justice, reviews of selected books, review of current events and developments in the field of court improvement.
Articles per average issue: 5
Audience: General
Manuscripts accepted in English

MANUSCRIPT INFORMATION
Subject field(s): Courtroom procedure, judicial and legal ethics; court administration, courtroom design, judicial compensation, selection, retirement and removal; correctional systems, juvenile justice, fair trial and free press
Manuscript requirements: Typewritten, double-spaced; footnotes, if any, appended. See latest issue for further style details.
Preferred length: 3000 words
Number of copies to be submitted: Two
Author information and reprints: Payment: None. 50 free copies of issue in which article appears.
Is simultaneous submission of article to other journals permitted: No
Exclusive manuscript rights between acceptance and publication: Yes
Copyright: Held by publication.
Reprints: Available
Disposition of manuscript:
Query letter: No
Receipt of manuscript acknowledged: Yes
Decision to publish in: One month
Accepted manuscript published in: 2-6 months
Rejected manuscript returned: Yes
Rejected manuscript criticized: Sometimes
Submit to:
Barbara R. Schulert
Managing Editor
(See address above)

JUVENILE JUSTICE [1251]

The Journal of the National Council of Juvenile Court Judges
Box 8000
Reno, Nevada 89507
(702) 784-6012

Previously entitled *Juvenile Court Judges Journal*

SUBSCRIPTION DATA
Issues and rates: Published quarterly.
Average paid circulation: 3,100
Annual rate(s): $9, Foreign $11
Publisher or Sponsor: National Council of Juvenile Court Judges
Managing Editor: Penny Landell

EDITORIAL DESCRIPTION
Contains articles on juvenile justice, juvenile and family courts, juvenile delinquency, juvenile probation, juvenile detention, alternatives to juvenile detention, police juvenile enforcement, and juvenile court administration, children with problems, learning disabilities.
Articles per average issue: 5-7
Audience: Juvenile justice agencies, corrections, behavioral sciences, police, courts, professors of law and sociology
Manuscripts accepted in English

MANUSCRIPT INFORMATION
Subject field(s): Juvenile justice, delinquency, courts; family courts; court administration; juvenile probation; adolescent behavior; juvenile court law; juvenile enforcement
Manuscript requirements: Style sheet sent on request. AP
Preferred length: 4,000-8,000 words; 15-30 pages
Number of copies to be submitted: Two
Author information and reprints: Payment: None. 12 copies of issue.
Is simultaneous submission of article to other journals permitted: No
Exclusive manuscript rights between acceptance and publication: Yes
Copyright: Held by publication.
Reprints: Not available. but an author may make copies at his own expense providing proper credit is given to the periodical.
Disposition of manuscript:
Query letter: No
Receipt of manuscript acknowledged: Yes
Decision to publish in: 6-10 weeks
Accepted manuscript published in: 3-6 months
Rejected manuscript returned: Yes
Rejected manuscript criticized: If requested
Submit to:
Gerald P. Wittman
Acting Editor
(See address above)

LAW & SOCIETY REVIEW [1252]

University of Denver
200 West 14th Avenue
Denver, Colorado 80204
(303) 753-2653

First published in 1964

SUBSCRIPTION DATA
Issues and rates: Published quarterly.
Average paid circulation: 2200
Annual rate(s): Individuals $15.00, Institutions $20.00, Foreign $21.00
Publisher or Sponsor: Law and Society Association

EDITORIAL DESCRIPTION
Publishes scholarly articles in the fields of law and society, dealing with research, methodology, and theory.
Articles per average issue: 6-7
Audience: Scholars and practitioners in law and social sciences
Manuscripts accepted in English

MANUSCRIPT INFORMATION
Subject field(s): Sociology of law, legal anthropology, political studies of legal order, psychology and law, law enforcement processes, comparative legal studies, development of legal institutions
Manuscript requirements: Style sheet sent on request.
Preferred length: None
Number of copies to be submitted: Two
Abstract: No
Author information and reprints: Payment: Reprints only. 25 copies
Is simultaneous submission of article to other journals permitted: Exclusive submission receives preference.
Exclusive manuscript rights between acceptance and publication: No
Copyright: Held by publication.
Reprints: Available from author

Additional information: Articles should be academic and scholarly. Footnotes appended

Disposition of manuscript:
Query letter: No
Receipt of manuscript acknowledged: Yes
Decision to publish in: 2-3 months
Accepted manuscript published in: 6 months
Rejected manuscript returned: Yes
Rejected manuscript criticized: Sometimes

Submit to:
Marc Galanter
Editor-in-Chief
Faculty of Law and Jurisprudence
State University of New York
Buffalo, New York 14202
(716) 852-4372

SPECIAL STIPULATIONS
Publisher shares royalties with authors or reprints of articles

LAW AND CONTEMPORARY PROBLEMS [1253]

Duke University School of Law
Duke Station
Durham, North Carolina 27706
(919) 684-2636

First published in 1933

SUBSCRIPTION DATA
Issues and rates: Published quarterly.
Average paid circulation: 2,400
Annual rate(s): $12.00; Individuals $12.00; Institutions $12.00; Students $12.00; Foreign institutions $13.00
Publisher or Sponsor: Duke University, School of Law

EDITORIAL DESCRIPTION
Each issue is devoted to a symposium on a particular topic of contempory interest. These topics are approached from an interdisciplinary perspective with contributions by legal scholars, economists, social scientists, and public officials.
Articles per average issue: 8-12
Audience: Primarily the legal profession, although subscribers include general university libraries, government agencies, and foreign educational institutions
Manuscripts accepted in English

MANUSCRIPT INFORMATION
Subject field(s): Recent symposia have dealt with such diverse subjects as judicial ethics, health care, police practices, expansion of the common market and athletics.
Manuscript requirements: Style sheet sent on request.
Preferred length: 8,000-15,000 words; 15-20 pages
Number of copies to be submitted: 2
Abstract: Not necessary.

Author information and reprints: Payment: None.
Is simultaneous submission of article to other journals permitted: Permitted, but not encouraged.
Exclusive manuscript rights between acceptance and publication: Yes
Copyright: Held by publication.
Reprints: Available at no cost. 100
Additional information: Nearly 95 per cent of our authors are solicited by the publication.

Disposition of manuscript:
Query letter: Necessary.
Receipt of manuscript acknowledged: Yes
Decision to publish in: 1-2 weeks
Accepted manuscript published in: 2-3 months
Rejected manuscript returned: Yes, with return postage paid by publication.
Rejected manuscript criticized: No

Submit to:
Chairman, Editorial Committee
(See address above)

SPECIAL STIPULATIONS
Future topics are decided upon 2 volume years ahead of publication.

LAW OFFICE ECONOMICS AND MANAGEMENT [1254]

Room 2200, 28 State Street
Boston, Massachusetts 02109
(617) 742-8300

First published in 1960

SUBSCRIPTION DATA
Issues and rates: Published quarterly.
Average paid circulation: 2000
Annual rate(s): $52.50

EDITORIAL DESCRIPTION
Contains articles and items of interest to law office managers.
Articles per average issue: 2
Audience: Law office managers
Manuscripts accepted in English

MANUSCRIPT INFORMATION
Subject field(s): Forms of practice, personnel, methods of practice, office environment, the legal profession
Manuscript requirements: See latest issue for style requirements.
Preferred length: 2000-2500 words; 6-8 pages
Number of copies to be submitted: Two
Abstract: No

Author information and reprints: Payment: None.
Is simultaneous submission of article to other journals permitted: No
Exclusive manuscript rights between acceptance and publication: Yes
Copyright: Negotiable
Reprints: Available, 100 free per original

Disposition of manuscript:
Query letter: No
Receipt of manuscript acknowledged: Yes
Decision to publish in: 2-3 months
Accepted manuscript published in: Varies

Rejected manuscript returned: Yes
Rejected manuscript criticized: Sometimes

Submit to:
Robert P. Bigelow
Editor
(See address above)

LAWYER OF THE AMERICAS [1255]

University of Miami, School of Law
P.O. Box 8087
Coral Gables, Florida 33124
(305) 284-5562

First published in 1969

SUBSCRIPTION DATA
Issues and rates: Published three times per year.
Average paid circulation: 600
Annual rate(s): $8.50
Publisher or Sponsor: Miami School of Law, Institute for Inter-American Legal Studies

EDITORIAL DESCRIPTION
Contains articles and reports on inter-American legal developments; regional and international activities; Latin American economic integration; taxation; economic developments; Inter-American Bar Association.
Articles per average issue: 4
Audience: Jurists and others interested in inter-American law
Manuscripts accepted in English

MANUSCRIPT INFORMATION
Subject field(s): All legal areas, particularly those relating to the Western Hemisphere and its legal systems.
Manuscript requirements: Style sheet sent on request.
Preferred length: 6,000 words; 25 pages
Number of copies to be submitted: Original and one carbon
Abstract: No
Author information and reprints: Payment: None.
Is simultaneous submission of article to other journals permitted: No objection if advised at proper time.
Exclusive manuscript rights between acceptance and publication: Yes
Copyright: Held by publication.
Reprints: Available; 25 free, additional at cost.
Additional information: Curriculum vitae of author should accompany article.

Disposition of manuscript:
Query letter: No
Receipt of manuscript acknowledged: Yes
Decision to publish in: 2 weeks
Accepted manuscript published in: 4 months or less
Rejected manuscript returned: Yes, if self-addressed, stamped envelope is sent with manuscript.
Rejected manuscript criticized: No

Submit to:
Susana B. Lacy
Managing Editor
(See address above)
(305) 284-4551

Law and public administration

LOUISIANA LAW REVIEW [1256]
Louisiana State University
Baton Rouge, Louisiana 70803
(504) 388-8701

SUBSCRIPTION DATA
Issues and rates: Published quarterly.
  Average paid circulation: 1250
  Annual rate(s): $10.00, Foreign $12.00
Managing Editor: Randy McClanahan

EDITORIAL DESCRIPTION
  Legal periodical consisting of lead articles, student comment and notes. Second issue of each volume is devoted to a symposium of the work of the Louisiana Appellate Courts.
Articles per average issue: 15
Audience: Lawyers, judges, law students
  Manuscripts accepted in English triple space manuscript

MANUSCRIPT INFORMATION
Subject field(s): Legal

Manuscript requirements: See latest issue for style requirements.
  Preferred length: 20 pages
  Number of copies to be submitted: 2
  Abstract: No

Author information and reprints: Payment: None.
  Reprints: Available, 50 free

Disposition of manuscript:
  Query letter: No
  Receipt of manuscript acknowledged: Yes
  Decision to publish in: 2 weeks
  Accepted manuscript published in: varies
  Rejected manuscript returned: Yes, if return postage is supplied by author.
  Rejected manuscript criticized: No

Submit to:
  Editorial Board
  (See address above)

SPECIAL STIPULATIONS
  Manuscripts are usually invited.

MARYLAND LAW REVIEW [1257]
University of Maryland School of Law
500 West Baltimore Street
Baltimore, Maryland 21201
(301) 528-7414

First published in 1936

SUBSCRIPTION DATA
Issues and rates: Published quarterly.
  Average paid circulation: 5600; 500 controlled
  Annual rate(s): $5.00
Publisher or Sponsor: University of Maryland School of Law
Managing Editor: Jeffrey A. Hammond

EDITORIAL DESCRIPTION
  Contains student and non-student articles on cases and legal topics.
Articles per average issue: 5-6
Audience: Lawyers and law students
  Manuscripts accepted in English

MANUSCRIPT INFORMATION
Subject field(s): Law, political science, sociology
Manuscript requirements: HLRA
  Preferred length: Minimum 15,000 words
  Number of copies to be submitted: Two
Author information and reprints: Payment: None.
  Is simultaneous submission of article to other journals permitted: Yes
  Exclusive manuscript rights between acceptance and publication: Yes
  Copyright: Held by publication.
  Reprints: 50 available free, additional ones at cost
Disposition of manuscript:
  Receipt of manuscript acknowledged: Yes
  Decision to publish in: One month
  Accepted manuscript published in: 3-4 months
  Rejected manuscript returned: Yes, if return postage is supplied by author.
  Rejected manuscript criticized: No
Submit to:
  Stewart Webb
  Articles Editor
  (See address above)

McGILL LAW JOURNAL [1258]
3644 Peel Street
Montreal, Quebec H3A 1W9, Canada
(514) 845-8824

First published in 1952

SUBSCRIPTION DATA
Issues and rates: Published quarterly.
  Average paid circulation: 1,800
  Annual rate(s): $10.00

EDITORIAL DESCRIPTION
  Contains articles, notes and book reviews with special emphasis upon international law, and civil and common law of Canada.
Articles per average issue: 8-12
Audience: Professional, scholars, students
  Manuscripts accepted in English, French

MANUSCRIPT INFORMATION
Manuscript requirements: Style sheet sent on request.
  Preferred length: 15-35 pages
  Number of copies to be submitted: One
  Abstract: No
Author information and reprints: Payment: None.
  Exclusive manuscript rights between acceptance and publication: Yes
  Copyright: Held by publication.
  Reprints: Available, 50 free
Additional information: Prefer footnotes double-spaced, bound separately from text.
Disposition of manuscript:
  Query letter: No
  Receipt of manuscript acknowledged: Yes
  Decision to publish in: 3-4 weeks
  Accepted manuscript published in: 3-6 months
  Rejected manuscript returned: No
  Rejected manuscript criticized: No
Submit to:
  The Editor
  (See address above)

MICHIGAN LAW REVIEW [1259]
Hutchins Hall
Ann Arbor, Michigan 48104
(313) 764-0542

First published in 1902

SUBSCRIPTION DATA
Issues and rates: 8 times per year
  Average paid circulation: 3100
  Annual rate(s): $15.00; Foreign $17.00
Publisher or Sponsor: Michigan Law Review Association

EDITORIAL DESCRIPTION
  Contains legal articles, comments and notes, and book reviews and periodical index.
Articles per average issue: 2
Audience: Professional, academic
  Manuscripts accepted in English

MANUSCRIPT INFORMATION
Subject field(s): Legal
Manuscript requirements: HLRA
  Preferred length: None
  Number of copies to be submitted: One
  Abstract: No
Author information and reprints: Payment: None.
  Is simultaneous submission of article to other journals permitted: Yes
  Exclusive manuscript rights between acceptance and publication: Yes
  Copyright: Held by publication.
  Reprints: Not available.
Additional information: Triple-spaced typescript; footnotes should detail as much as possible; note unpublished support.
Disposition of manuscript:
  Query letter: No
  Receipt of manuscript acknowledged: Yes
  Decision to publish in: Varies
  Accepted manuscript published in: Varies
  Rejected manuscript returned: Yes
  Rejected manuscript criticized: No
Submit to:
  Articles Editors
  (See address above)

MISSISSIPPI LAW JOURNAL [1260]
P.O. Box 146
University, Mississippi 38677
(601) 232-7455

First published in 1928

SUBSCRIPTION DATA
Issues and rates: 6 times per year
  Average paid circulation: 4,000
  Annual rate(s): $12.00

Publisher or Sponsor: Mississippi State Bar, University of Mississippi Law School
Managing Editor: Stephen W. Rosenblatt

EDITORIAL DESCRIPTION

Contains University of Mississippi law student comments on current topics of legal interest and notes on significant recent court decisions; reviews of books of legal interest.
Articles per average issue: 3
Audience: Lawyers, law professors and law students
Manuscripts accepted in English

MANUSCRIPT INFORMATION

Subject field(s): Any topic of current legal importance
Manuscript requirements: Style sheet sent on request.
Preferred length: 10,000-15,000 words; 40-60 pages
Number of copies to be submitted: Two
Author information and reprints: Payment: None. 25 reprints of article
Is simultaneous submission of article to other journals permitted: No
Exclusive manuscript rights between acceptance and publication: Yes
Copyright: Held by publication.
Reprints: Available, cost determined at time of publication
Additional information: Manuscript should be typed on right-hand two-thirds of page. Footnotes should be typed separately, also on right-hand two-thirds of page.
Disposition of manuscript:
Receipt of manuscript acknowledged: Yes
Decision to publish in: 2 weeks
Accepted manuscript published in: 2-4 months
Rejected manuscript returned: Yes
Rejected manuscript criticized: No
Submit to:
David Howarth
Articles Editor
(See address above)

MONTANA LAW REVIEW [1261]
University of Montana School of Law
Missoula, Montana 59801
(406) 243-2023

First published in 1941

SUBSCRIPTION DATA

Issues and rates: Published semi-annually.
Average paid circulation: 1700
Annual rate(s): $7.00
Managing Editor: Joel E. Guthals

EDITORIAL DESCRIPTION

Contains professional and student articles on law and related topics; emphasis on Montana law.
Articles per average issue: 20
Audience: Lawyers and judges
Manuscripts accepted in English

MANUSCRIPT INFORMATION
Subject field(s): Law

Manuscript requirements: HLRA
Preferred length: 4,000-5,000 words; 20-25 pages
Number of copies to be submitted: One
Abstract: No
Author information and reprints: Payment: None.
Is simultaneous submission of article to other journals permitted: No
Exclusive manuscript rights between acceptance and publication: No
Copyright: Held by publication.
Reprints: Available, $.75 each
Disposition of manuscript:
Query letter: Yes
Receipt of manuscript acknowledged: Yes
Decision to publish in: 2 weeks
Accepted manuscript published in: 3-4 months
Rejected manuscript returned: Yes, if self-addressed, stamped envelope is sent with manuscript.
Rejected manuscript criticized: Yes
Submit to:
Editor-in-Chief
(See address above)

NETHERLANDS INTERNATIONAL LAW REVIEW [1262]
A. W. Sijthoff International Publishing Company
Doezastraat 1., P. O. Box 26
Leiden, The Netherlands
(070) 21845; Telex 32447

First published in 1954

SUBSCRIPTION DATA
Issues and rates: Published quarterly.
Average paid circulation: 1,000; 200 controlled
Annual rate(s): Dfl. 78.00; Foreign $32.00
Publisher or Sponsor: T. M. C. Asser Institute, Interuniversity Research Center of International Law

EDITORIAL DESCRIPTION

Presents an international platform for the legal scholarly community in the field of international law
Articles per average issue: 6
Audience: Legal specialists
Manuscripts accepted in English

MANUSCRIPT INFORMATION
Manuscript requirements: No specific style guide. See latest issue for style requirements.
Number of copies to be submitted: 3
Abstract: Yes. Of about 150 words.
Author information and reprints: Payment: Reprints only. 1 issue and 50 offprints
Is simultaneous submission of article to other journals permitted: Not permitted.
Exclusive manuscript rights between acceptance and publication: Yes
Copyright: Held by publication.
Reprints: Available at cost.

Disposition of manuscript:
Query letter: Not necessary, but advisable.
Receipt of manuscript acknowledged: Yes
Decision to publish in: 2 months
Accepted manuscript published in: 4 months
Rejected manuscript returned: Yes, if return postage is supplied by author.
Rejected manuscript criticized: Sometimes
Submit to:
L. Erades
Editor-in-Chief
Bergselaan 232
Rotterdam, The Netherlands
(010) 243-618

NEW ENGLAND JOURNAL ON PRISON LAW [1263]
126 Newbury Street
Boston, Massachusetts 02116
(617) 267-9655

First published in 1974

SUBSCRIPTION DATA
Issues and rates: Published semi-annually.
Annual rate(s): Institutions $10.00; Students and Prisoners $6.00
Managing Editor: Kenneth R. Hamm

EDITORIAL DESCRIPTION

Focuses on problems inherent to prison systems and related areas; a forum for scholarly thinking for airing diverse views, testing reform; designed to examine the application, within the prison systems, of substantive and procedural law in the light of constitutional guarantees
Articles per average issue: 3-4
Audience: Professional, governmental, legal, academic, students, prisoners
Manuscripts accepted in English

MANUSCRIPT INFORMATION
Subject field(s): Any prison-related topic is acceptable; historical perspectives as well as contemporary treatments of prison issues; emphasizes law, but will not exclude any topic having substantial impact on the study of the prison community
Manuscript requirements: HLRA
Preferred length: 30-80
Number of copies to be submitted: 1
Abstract: Not necessary.
Author information and reprints: Payment: None.
Is simultaneous submission of article to other journals permitted: Not permitted.
Exclusive manuscript rights between acceptance and publication: Yes
Copyright: Held by publication.
Reprints: Not available.
Additional information: Must be typewritten, triple-spaced, with footnotes at the end, conforming to HLRA.
Disposition of manuscript:
Query letter: Not necessary.
Receipt of manuscript acknowledged: Yes

Law and public administration

Decision to publish in: 4-6 weeks
Accepted manuscript published in: Up to 6 months
Rejected manuscript returned: Yes, if return postage is supplied by author.
Rejected manuscript criticized: Sometimes
Submit to:
Jon H. Kurland
Articles Editor
(See address above)

NEW JERSEY STATE BAR JOURNAL [1264]
172 West State Street
Trenton, New Jersey 08608
(609) 394-1101

First published in 1957

SUBSCRIPTION DATA
Issues and rates: Published quarterly.
  Average paid circulation: 10,000
  Annual rate(s): $3.00
Publisher or Sponsor: New Jersey State Bar Association

EDITORIAL DESCRIPTION
Contains articles of interest to the practicing attorney.
Articles per average issue: 12
Audience: Attorney members of New Jersey State Bar Association
Manuscripts accepted in English

MANUSCRIPT INFORMATION
Subject field(s): Practice of law, legal philosophy, law reform, general material involving lawyers.
Manuscript requirements: See latest issue for style requirements.
  Preferred length: 2,500 words
  Number of copies to be submitted: 6
  Abstract: No
Author information and reprints: Payment: None.
  Is simultaneous submission of article to other journals permitted: No
  Exclusive manuscript rights between acceptance and publication: Yes
  Copyright: Held by publication.
  Reprints: available at author's expense
Disposition of manuscript:
  Query letter: Preferred
  Receipt of manuscript acknowledged: Yes
  Decision to publish in: 3 months
  Accepted manuscript published in: 6 months
  Rejected manuscript returned: Yes
  Rejected manuscript criticized: Yes
Submit to:
R. Bruce Gebhardt
Managing Editor
(See address above)

NEW YORK LAW FORUM [1265]
New York Law School
57 Worth Street
New York, New York 10013
(212) 925-9830

First published in 1955

SUBSCRIPTION DATA
Issues and rates: Published quarterly.
  Average paid circulation: 550; 1100 controlled
  Annual rate(s): $12.00
Publisher or Sponsor: New York Law School
Managing Editor: John Greene

EDITORIAL DESCRIPTION
Contains articles of a legal nature; analysis of current legal problems; cover symposium topics.
Articles per average issue: 6
Audience: Lawyers; legal researchers, judges, legislators
Manuscripts accepted in English

MANUSCRIPT INFORMATION
Subject field(s): Legal
Manuscript requirements: HLRA
  Preferred length: Variable
  Number of copies to be submitted: 3
  Abstract: No
Author information and reprints: Payment: None.
  Is simultaneous submission of article to other journals permitted: No
  Exclusive manuscript rights between acceptance and publication: Yes
  Copyright: Held by publication.
  Reprints: Available
Additional information: Manuscript should be triple spaced, footnotes typed separately from text.
Disposition of manuscript:
  Query letter: No
  Receipt of manuscript acknowledged: Yes
  Decision to publish in: 2 weeks
  Accepted manuscript published in: 4 months
  Rejected manuscript returned: Yes
  Rejected manuscript criticized: Sometimes
Submit to:
Clifford Wasserman
Articles Editor
(See address above)

NEW YORK STATE BAR JOURNAL [1266]
One Marine Midland Plaza
Binghamton, New York 13901
(607) 723-9511

Previously entitled *New York State Bar Bulletin*

SUBSCRIPTION DATA
Issues and rates: 8 times a year
  Average paid circulation: 24,000
Publisher or Sponsor: New York State Bar Association

EDITORIAL DESCRIPTION
Contains articles on legal or related subjects of interest to members; legal lore; obiter dicta; lawyer placement service; calendar of association events. Reflects official action taken by the New York State Bar Association.
Articles per average issue: Varies
Manuscripts accepted in English only

MANUSCRIPT INFORMATION
Subject field(s): Law; related to law; general, but of interest to legal profession
Manuscript requirements: See latest issue for style requirements.
  Preferred length: 3,000 words
  Number of copies to be submitted: One
Author information and reprints: Payment: None.
  Is simultaneous submission of article to other journals permitted: No
  Exclusive manuscript rights between acceptance and publication: Yes
  Copyright: Held by publication.
  Reprints: Available, some free
Additional information: Footnotes should be added at end of article. Photograph of author and short biographical sketch should accompany manuscript.
Disposition of manuscript:
  Receipt of manuscript acknowledged: Yes
  Decision to publish in: Varies
  Accepted manuscript published in: Varies
  Rejected manuscript returned: Yes
  Rejected manuscript criticized: On occasion.
Submit to:
Eugene C. Gerhart
Editor-in-Chief
(See address above)

NEW YORK UNIVERSITY LAW REVIEW [1267]
249 Sullivan Street
New York, New York 10012
(212) 777-7560

First published in 1924

SUBSCRIPTION DATA
Issues and rates: 6 times per year
  Average paid circulation: 3500; 2500 controlled
  Annual rate(s): $12.50, Foreign $13.00
Managing Editor: Laureen Bedell

EDITORIAL DESCRIPTION
Publication is a law review.
Articles per average issue: 5 plus book reviews
Audience: Lawyers, law students, bar association and general legal community
Manuscripts accepted in English

MANUSCRIPT INFORMATION
Subject field(s): Any law-related field
Manuscript requirements: GPO, HLRA
  Preferred length: Minimum 40-50 pages (including footnotes)
  Number of copies to be submitted: 2
  Abstract: Yes, on bonded paper, triple-spaced, 1/3 page left hand margin-same criteria as manuscript
Author information and reprints: Payment: None.
  Is simultaneous submission of article to other journals permitted: No
  Exclusive manuscript rights between acceptance and publication: Yes
  Copyright: Held by N.Y.U. Law School

Reprints: Available, 50 free covers at authors expense; additional reprints at cost.
Disposition of manuscript:
Query letter: No
Receipt of manuscript acknowledged: Yes
Decision to publish in: 1-4 weeks, depending on season
Accepted manuscript published in: 2-3 months
Rejected manuscript returned: Yes, if self-addressed, stamped envelope is sent with manuscript.
Rejected manuscript criticized: Sometimes
Submit to:
Articles and Book Review Editor
(See address above)
(212) 598-3507

NOLPE SCHOOL LAW JOURNAL [1268]
825 Western Avenue
Topeka, Kansas 66606
(913) 357-7242

First published in 1971

SUBSCRIPTION DATA
Issues and rates: Published semi-annually.
Average paid circulation: 100; 3327 controlled
Annual rate(s): $2.50
Publisher or Sponsor: National Organization on Legal Problems of Education
Managing Editor: M. A. McGhehey

EDITORIAL DESCRIPTION
Attempts to provide broad information about current issues in school law.
Articles per average issue: 5-6
Audience: School administrators, Board members, attorneys, law-ed students, teachers
Manuscripts accepted in English

MANUSCRIPT INFORMATION
Subject field(s): Current issues in school law
Manuscript requirements: HLRA footnotes according to Harvard's Uniform System of Citation
Preferred length: 8,000 words; 20-24 pages
Number of copies to be submitted: One
Author information and reprints: Payment: None. 2 copies of issue
Is simultaneous submission of article to other journals permitted: Yes
Exclusive manuscript rights between acceptance and publication: Yes
Copyright: Held by National Organization on Legal Problems of Education
Reprints: Available, price quoted at time of publication
Disposition of manuscript:
Query letter: No
Receipt of manuscript acknowledged: Yes
Decision to publish in: Within one month
Accepted manuscript published in: 6 months
Rejected manuscript returned: Yes, if return postage is supplied by author.

Rejected manuscript criticized: No
Submit to:
Susan C. Tillett
Editor
(See address above)

NORTH CAROLINA LAW REVIEW [1269]
University of North Carolina School of Law
Chapel Hill, North Carolina 27514
(919) 933-3926

SUBSCRIPTION DATA
Issues and rates: 6 times a year: November, December, February, March, June, October
Average paid circulation: 2400; 2600 controlled
Annual rate(s): $12.50
Publisher or Sponsor: North Carolina Law Review Association
Managing Editor: I.W. Hankins

EDITORIAL DESCRIPTION
Publishes articles on current developments in all fields of law. Authors are usually advanced law students, professors and prominent practitioners.
Articles per average issue: 2
Audience: Attorneys
Manuscripts accepted in English

MANUSCRIPT INFORMATION
Subject field(s): All areas of law
Manuscript requirements: HLRA
Preferred length: 40 pages of text; 40 pages of footnotes
Number of copies to be submitted: Two
Author information and reprints: Payment: None. Copy of the issue in which article appears
Is simultaneous submission of article to other journals permitted: Simultaneous submission is permitted but simultaneous publication is not.
Exclusive manuscript rights between acceptance and publication: Yes
Copyright: Held by publication.
Reprints: Available, 50 free
Disposition of manuscript:
Receipt of manuscript acknowledged: Yes
Decision to publish in: Almost immediately
Accepted manuscript published in: 3-5 months
Rejected manuscript returned: Yes, if self-addressed, stamped envelope is sent with manuscript.
Rejected manuscript criticized: Sometimes
Submit to:
J Goodman
Articles Editor
(See address above)

NORTH DAKOTA LAW REVIEW [1270]
Journal of the North Dakota State Bar Association
UND School of Law
Grand Forks, North Dakota 58201
(701) 777-2941

Previously entitled *North Dakota Bar Briefs*

First published in 1927

SUBSCRIPTION DATA
Issues and rates: Published quarterly.
Average paid circulation: 1600
Annual rate(s): $10.00
Publisher or Sponsor: University of North Dakota School of Law, North Dakota State Bar Association
Managing Editor: Robert L. Manley

EDITORIAL DESCRIPTION
Contains articles on law and related topics.
Articles per average issue: 10
Audience: Attorneys, judges and legislators
Manuscripts accepted in English

MANUSCRIPT INFORMATION
Subject field(s): Law
Manuscript requirements: HLRA; also see publication
Number of copies to be submitted: One
Abstract: No
Author information and reprints: Payment: None. 25 reprints
Is simultaneous submission of article to other journals permitted: Yes
Exclusive manuscript rights between acceptance and publication: Yes
Copyright: Held by publication.
Reprints: Available
Disposition of manuscript:
Query letter: No
Receipt of manuscript acknowledged: Yes
Decision to publish in: 2 weeks
Accepted manuscript published in: 3-8 weeks
Rejected manuscript returned: Yes, if self-addressed, stamped envelope is sent with manuscript.
Rejected manuscript criticized: No
Submit to:
Soliciting Editors
(See address above)

NORTHWESTERN UNIVERSITY LAW REVIEW [1271]
357 East Chicago Avenue
Chicago, Illinois 60611
(312) 649-8467

Previously entitled *Illinois Law Review*

First published in 1906

SUBSCRIPTION DATA
Issues and rates: Published bi-monthly.
Average paid circulation: 2,200 controlled
Annual rate(s): $10.00, Foreign $10.75
Managing Editor: M. D. Christiansen

EDITORIAL DESCRIPTION
A scholarly, yet practical, publication covering developments in all areas of law, as well as related fields. It contains reports and interpretations of current legislative enactments and judicial

decisions and also, helps readers to ascertain significant trends in the law through the publication of papers by scholars and leading lawyers.
Articles per average issue: 8
Audience: Legal profession,
Manuscripts accepted in English

MANUSCRIPT INFORMATION

Subject field(s): Legal; corporate law; criminal law; national, international law; general; international, property law
Manuscript requirements: See latest issue for style requirements.
  Preferred length: 28 pages
  Number of copies to be submitted: Two
  Abstract: No
Author information and reprints: Payment: None.
  Is simultaneous submission of article to other journals permitted: No
  Exclusive manuscript rights between acceptance and publication: Yes
  Copyright: Held by Northwestern University School of Law
  Reprints: Available, 25 copies free to author; others on cost basis
Additional information: Manuscripts should be submitted on 8 ½ x 11 paper, triple-spaced.
Disposition of manuscript:
  Query letter: No, but advisable
  Receipt of manuscript acknowledged: Yes
  Decision to publish in: 6-8 weeks
  Accepted manuscript published in: Possibly six months.
  Rejected manuscript returned: Yes, if return postage is supplied by author.
  Rejected manuscript criticized: Yes
Submit to:
  Editor-in-Chief
  (See address above)
  (312) 649-8429

OKLAHOMA LAW REVIEW [1272]
University of Oklahoma College of Law
630 Parrington Oval
Norman, Oklahoma 73069
(405) 325-5191

First published in 1948

SUBSCRIPTION DATA

Issues and rates: Published quarterly.
  Average paid circulation: 1300; 600 controlled
  Annual rate(s): $8.00
Publisher or Sponsor: Oklahoma University College of Law
Managing Editor: John N Hermes

EDITORIAL DESCRIPTION

Contains scholarly articles on law and related topics.
Articles per average issue: 3-4 plus student written material
Audience: Practicing attorneys, legal scholars, students
Manuscripts accepted in English

MANUSCRIPT INFORMATION

Subject field(s): Law
Manuscript requirements: Style sheet sent on request.
  Preferred length: No limit
  Number of copies to be submitted: Two
  Abstract: No
Author information and reprints: Payment: None.
  Is simultaneous submission of article to other journals permitted: No
  Exclusive manuscript rights between acceptance and publication: Yes
  Copyright: Held by publication.
  Reprints: 25 free; additional reprints at cost
Additional information: Manuscripts should follow the style prescribed by HLRA and should be triple spaced. Biographical matters should accompany manuscript.
Disposition of manuscript:
  Query letter: No
  Receipt of manuscript acknowledged: Yes
  Decision to publish in: 2-4 weeks
  Accepted manuscript published in: 3 months
  Rejected manuscript returned: Yes
  Rejected manuscript criticized: No
Submit to:
  Editor-in-Chief
  (See address above)

OTTAWA LAW REVIEW [1273]
University of Ottawa
Faculty of Law
Ottawa K1N 6N5, Canada
(613) 231-5717

First published in 1966

SUBSCRIPTION DATA

Issues and rates: Published three times per year.
  Annual rate(s): $8.00
Managing Editor: Gerard A. Ferguson

EDITORIAL DESCRIPTION

Contains original research on law and law-related disciplines.
Articles per average issue: 10-15
Audience: Professionals and Academics in law and law-related fields
Manuscripts accepted in English and French

MANUSCRIPT INFORMATION

Subject field(s): Law, law-related disciplines
Manuscript requirements: Style sheet sent on request.
  Preferred length: 6,000-9,000 words; 25-35 pages
  Number of copies to be submitted: Two
  Abstract: No
Author information and reprints: Payment: None.
  Is simultaneous submission of article to other journals permitted: No
  Exclusive manuscript rights between acceptance and publication: Yes
  Copyright: Held by publication.
  Reprints: Available, 40 free
Additional information: Manuscripts should be typewritten, double-spaced, with footnotes, references, tables and charts on separate pages. For anonymous editorial evaluation author's name and affiliation should appear only on a separate cover page.
Disposition of manuscript:
  Query letter: No
  Receipt of manuscript acknowledged: Yes
  Decision to publish in: Two weeks
  Accepted manuscript published in: 3-6 months
  Rejected manuscript returned: Yes
  Rejected manuscript criticized: Sometimes
Submit to:
  Faculty Editor
  (See address above)

PLANNING [1274]
The ASPO Magazine
1313 East 60th Street
Chicago, Illinois 60637
(312) 947-2100

Previously entitled *Planning Newsletter*

First published in 1972

SUBSCRIPTION DATA

Issues and rates: 11 times per year
  Average paid circulation: 13,000
  Annual rate(s): $25.00; Foreign $25.00; Institutions $25.00; Students $10.00; Foreign institutions $25.00
Publisher or Sponsor: American Society of Planning Officials
Managing Editor: Robert Cassidy

EDITORIAL DESCRIPTION

To provide sociological, economical and political information concerning city and regional planning and environmental issues
Articles per average issue: 4
Audience: Officials and staff of federal, state, county, regional, and city planning offices and planning commissions
Manuscripts accepted in English

MANUSCRIPT INFORMATION

Subject field(s): City planning, environment
Manuscript requirements: No specific style guide.
  Preferred length: 2,000 words; 9 pages
  Number of copies to be submitted: 2
  Abstract: Not necessary.
Author information and reprints: Payment: Only when the editors request the story. Then payment is $125.00
  Is simultaneous submission of article to other journals permitted: Permitted with approval of editor
  Exclusive manuscript rights between acceptance and publication: Yes
  Copyright: Held by publication.
  Reprints: Available at no cost. 10
Disposition of manuscript:
  Query letter: Not necessary.
  Receipt of manuscript acknowledged: Yes
  Decision to publish in: 2 months
  Accepted manuscript published in: 2 months
  Rejected manuscript returned: Yes, with return postage paid by publication.
  Rejected manuscript criticized: No

Submit to:
Ed McCahill
Editor
(See address above)

THE POLICE CHIEF [1275]
The Professional Voice of Law Enforcement
Eleven Firstfield Road
Gaithersburg, Maryland 20760
(301) 948-0922 ext. 291

Previously entitled *Police Chief's Newsletter*

First published in 1932

SUBSCRIPTION DATA
Issues and rates: Published monthly.
Average paid circulation: 20,000; 1,900 controlled
Annual rate(s): $9.00
Publisher or Sponsor: International Association of Chiefs of Police
Managing Editor: Alice C. Pitcher

EDITORIAL DESCRIPTION
Contains articles on practitioners' experiences in developing new techniques, developments in entire field of criminal justice with emphasis on law enforcement technology.
Articles per average issue: 6
Audience: Law enforcement field
Manuscripts accepted in English

MANUSCRIPT INFORMATION
Subject field(s): Police standards, police administration, police personnel, crime prevention, highway safety, technology, citizen cooperation, police training, police procedures, juveniles and police, theory and principles, practitioners' experiences
Manuscript requirements: Chicago
Preferred length: Maximum 20 pages; minimum 8 pages
Number of copies to be submitted: One
Abstract: No
Author information and reprints: Payment: None. 5 author's copies
Is simultaneous submission of article to other journals permitted: No
Exclusive manuscript rights between acceptance and publication: Yes
Copyright: Held by publication.
Reprints: Available at actual cost plus 20%
Additional information: Prefer original writing based on knowledge and experience rather than extensive quotes and citations of published works. The latter are usually rejected.
Disposition of manuscript:
Query letter: No
Receipt of manuscript acknowledged: Yes
Decision to publish in: 3-5 months
Accepted manuscript published in: 2-12 months
Rejected manuscript returned: Yes
Rejected manuscript criticized: No
Submit to:
Editor
(See address above)

THE PRACTICAL LAWYER [1276]
4025 Chestnut Street
Philadelphia, Pennsylvania 19104
(215) 387-3000

First published in 1955

SUBSCRIPTION DATA
Issues and rates: Monthly, October through May
Average paid circulation: 17,000
Annual rate(s): $12.00
Publisher or Sponsor: The American Law Institute and the American Bar Association, Committee on Continuing Education

EDITORIAL DESCRIPTION
Contains informative articles for the legal profession, aimed at solving the kinds of problems lawyers encounter day to day.
Articles per average issue: 6
Audience: Lawyers
Manuscripts accepted in English

MANUSCRIPT INFORMATION
Subject field(s): Law office management, general legal skills, trial and appellate practice, taxation, corporate and business law, personal injury law, real estate law, commercial law, estate planning, criminal law, legal ethics, other areas of law practice
Manuscript requirements: Style sheet sent on request.
Preferred length: 3,000- 7,000 words
Number of copies to be submitted: One
Abstract: No
Author information and reprints: Payment: None. 12 copies of issue, 1-year free subscription, and commemorative certificate.
Is simultaneous submission of article to other journals permitted: No
Exclusive manuscript rights between acceptance and publication: Yes
Copyright: Copyright by The American Law Institute
Reprints: Available, price list established by printer
Additional information: An attorney must author or co-author articles giving advice on substantive law and other aspects of legal practice.
Disposition of manuscript:
Query letter: No
Receipt of manuscript acknowledged: Yes
Decision to publish in: 1-3 weeks
Accepted manuscript published in: 3-4 months
Rejected manuscript returned: Yes
Rejected manuscript criticized: No
Submit to:
Paul A. Wolkin
Editor
(See address above)

PUBLIC ADMINISTRATION REVIEW [1277]
American Society for Public Administration
1225 Connecticut Ave., N.W.
Washington, D.C. 20036
(202) 785-3255

First published in 1940

SUBSCRIPTION DATA
Issues and rates: Published bi-monthly.
Average paid circulation: 15,000
Annual rate(s): $25, Foreign $30
Publisher or Sponsor: American Society for Public Administration

EDITORIAL DESCRIPTION
Source of opinion, comment and information on public administration.
Articles per average issue: 10-12
Audience: Practitioners, teachers and students of public administration

MANUSCRIPT INFORMATION
Subject field(s): The science, processes and art of public administration and related policy matters.
Manuscript requirements: See latest issue for style requirements.
Preferred length: 2,000 to 3,000 words; 15 to 20 pages
Number of copies to be submitted: 4
Abstract: Yes, see latest issue for style
Author information and reprints: Payment: None. 3 copies of issue.
Is simultaneous submission of article to other journals permitted: No
Exclusive manuscript rights between acceptance and publication: Yes
Copyright: Held by publication.
Reprints: Available at cost.
Additional information: As there are different editors for different features, consult "Communication and Routing" on back cover of most recent issue. "Regular" submissions submitted to Managing Editor.
Disposition of manuscript:
Query letter: No
Receipt of manuscript acknowledged: Yes
Decision to publish in: Two months
Accepted manuscript published in: 6-12 months
Rejected manuscript returned: Yes
Rejected manuscript criticized: In most cases
Submit to:
Frank Marini
Managing Editor
School of Public Administration and Urban Studies
San Diego State University
San Diego, California 92115

PUBLIC MANAGEMENT [1278]
PM
1140 Connecticut Avenue, Suite 201
Washington, D.C. 20036
(202) 293-2200 ext. 36

First published in 1918

Law and public administration

SUBSCRIPTION DATA
Issues and rates: Published monthly.
  Average paid circulation: 15,412
  Annual rate(s): $8.00
Publisher or Sponsor: International City Management Association

EDITORIAL DESCRIPTION
Contains articles by local, state, and federal officials and authorities on subjects of professional interest to municipal administrators.

MANUSCRIPT INFORMATION
Subject field(s): Local government and all areas pertaining thereto.
Manuscript requirements: Style sheet sent on request.
  Preferred length: 1,500-2,500 words; 6-10 pages
  Number of copies to be submitted: One
Author information and reprints: Payment: None.
  Is simultaneous submission of article to other journals permitted: No
  Exclusive manuscript rights between acceptance and publication: Yes
  Copyright: Held by publication.
  Reprints: Available; single copies free; quantity reprints available at cost.
Disposition of manuscript:
  Receipt of manuscript acknowledged: Yes
  Decision to publish in: 6-8 weeks
  Accepted manuscript published in: 6-8 months
  Rejected manuscript returned: Yes
  Rejected manuscript criticized: No
Submit to:
  Mary Margaret Grant
  Director, Communication Services
  (See address above)

PUBLIC POWER [1279]
Suite 212, 2600 Virginia Avenue NW
Washington, D.C. 20037
(202) 333-9200

First published in 1942

SUBSCRIPTION DATA
Issues and rates: Published bi-monthly.
  Average paid circulation: 10,000 controlled
  Annual rate(s): $8.50
Publisher or Sponsor: American Public Power Association

EDITORIAL DESCRIPTION
Information on trends and developments relating to management, operation, engineering, research, accounting, legislation, legal, marketing, etc.
Articles per average issue: 6
Audience: Managers and policy-making officials of municipal and other local publicly owned electric systems
  Manuscripts accepted in English only.

MANUSCRIPT INFORMATION
Subject field(s): All fields of interest to local publicly owned electric utilities
Manuscript requirements: No specific style guide.
  Preferred length: 500-2,500 words
  Number of copies to be submitted: One
  Abstract: No
Author information and reprints: Payment: By publication to author. $15 per page. Negotiable.
  Is simultaneous submission of article to other journals permitted: Yes
  Exclusive manuscript rights between acceptance and publication: Yes
  Copyright: Held by author.
  Reprints: Available at cost
Disposition of manuscript:
  Query letter: Suggested
  Receipt of manuscript acknowledged: Yes
  Decision to publish in: Varies
  Accepted manuscript published in: Varies
  Rejected manuscript returned: Yes, if return postage is supplied by author.
  Rejected manuscript criticized: No
Submit to:
  Ron Ross
  Editor
  (See address above)

THE REVIEW OF SOCIALIST LAW [1280]
A. W. Sijthoff Publishing Company
Doezastraat 1, P. O. Box 26
Leiden, The Netherlands
(071) 21845; Telex 32447

First published in 1975

SUBSCRIPTION DATA
Issues and rates: Published quarterly.
  Annual rate(s): Dfl. 70.00; Foreign $28.00
Publisher or Sponsor: Documentation Office for East European Law, Leiden
Managing Editor: Prof. F. J. M. Feldbrugge

EDITORIAL DESCRIPTION
Covers all areas of the legal systems in Eastern Europe, China and other socialist states
Articles per average issue: 4
Audience: Specialist legal, business
  Manuscripts accepted in English

MANUSCRIPT INFORMATION
Manuscript requirements: See latest issue for style requirements. Style sheet sent on request.
  Preferred length: None
  Number of copies to be submitted: 3
  Abstract: Yes. Of about 150 words
Author information and reprints: Payment: Reprints only. 1 issue and 50 offprints
  Is simultaneous submission of article to other journals permitted: Not permitted.
  Exclusive manuscript rights between acceptance and publication: Yes
  Copyright: Held by publication.
  Reprints: Available at cost.
Disposition of manuscript:
  Query letter: Necessary.
  Receipt of manuscript acknowledged: Yes
  Decision to publish in: 1 month
  Accepted manuscript published in: 4 months
  Rejected manuscript returned: Yes, if return postage is supplied by author.
  Rejected manuscript criticized: Sometimes

Submit to:
  Ger P. van den Berg
  Secretary to the Editor
  Documentation Office for East European Law
  Rappenburg 82
  Leiden, The Netherlands
  (071) 26822

RUTGERS JOURNAL OF COMPUTERS AND THE LAW [1281]
180 University Avenue
Newark, New Jersey 07102
(201) 648-5549

First published in 1970

SUBSCRIPTION DATA
Issues and rates: Published semi-annually.
  Average paid circulation: 750; 800 controlled
  Annual rate(s): $20.00
Managing Editor: Raymond Storch

EDITORIAL DESCRIPTION
Concerned with the interaction of technology and the law with a special interest in computers.
Audience: Attorneys, computer firms
  Manuscripts accepted in English

MANUSCRIPT INFORMATION
Subject field(s): Legal aspects of the computer industry; antitrust, government regulation; legal ramifications of the use of computers in insurance, securities, liability for computer error; application of computers to the legal profession and research
Manuscript requirements: See latest issue for style requirements. Style sheet sent on request.
  Preferred length: 25 pages
  Number of copies to be submitted: 2
  Abstract: Not necessary.
Author information and reprints: Payment: None.
  Is simultaneous submission of article to other journals permitted: Permitted, but not encouraged.
  Exclusive manuscript rights between acceptance and publication: No
  Copyright: Unless previously secured by the author, it is held by the publication.
  Reprints: Available at cost.
Disposition of manuscript:
  Query letter: Not necessary.
  Receipt of manuscript acknowledged:
  Decision to publish in: 3 weeks
  Accepted manuscript published in: 6 months
  Rejected manuscript returned: No
  Rejected manuscript criticized: Sometimes

Submit to:
Richard McGill;
Ruth Ann Weidel
Managing Editors
(See address above)

RUTGERS LAW REVIEW [1282]
180 University Avenue
Newark, New Jersey 07102
(201) 648-5391

SUBSCRIPTION DATA
Issues and rates: 5 times per year
Average paid circulation: 3000
Annual rate(s): $12.00

EDITORIAL DESCRIPTION
Contains articles of legal scholarship.
Articles per average issue: 3-4

MANUSCRIPT INFORMATION
Subject field(s): Any area of the law
Manuscript requirements: See latest issue for style requirements.
Preferred length: None
Number of copies to be submitted: Two
Author information and reprints: Payment: None.
Is simultaneous submission of article to other journals permitted: Yes
Exclusive manuscript rights between acceptance and publication: No
Copyright: Held by either author or publication
Reprints: Available
Disposition of manuscript:
Query letter: No
Decision to publish in: One week
Accepted manuscript published in: 6 months
Rejected manuscript returned: Yes, if self-addressed, stamped envelope is sent with manuscript.
Rejected manuscript criticized: Yes
Submit to:
Lee Hilles Wertheim
Editor
(See address above)

RUTGERS-CAMDEN LAW JOURNAL [1283]
Rutgers-Camden Law School
Fifth and Penn Streets
Camden, Pennsylvania 08102
(609) 964-9101

First published in 1969

SUBSCRIPTION DATA
Issues and rates: Published quarterly.
Average paid circulation: 600; 700 controlled
Annual rate(s): $10.00
Publisher or Sponsor: Rutgers-Camden School of Law
Managing Editor: Minna J. Kotkin

EDITORIAL DESCRIPTION
Articles of interest to the legal community
Articles per average issue: 3-4

Audience: Attorneys, law students, professors of law
Manuscripts accepted in English only

MANUSCRIPT INFORMATION
Manuscript requirements: HLRA; Texas Law Review Manual on Style, 2nd Edition
Number of copies to be submitted: 2
Abstract: Not necessary.
Author information and reprints: Payment: None.
Is simultaneous submission of article to other journals permitted: Permitted.
Reprints: Available at no cost. 50
Disposition of manuscript:
Query letter: Not necessary.
Receipt of manuscript acknowledged: Yes
Decision to publish in: 1 week
Accepted manuscript published in: 3 months
Rejected manuscript returned: Yes, if return postage is supplied by author.
Rejected manuscript criticized: Sometimes
Submit to:
Karl Baker;
Harriet Dalton
Articles Editors
(See address above)

SAGE PROFESSIONAL PAPERS IN ADMINISTRATIVE AND POLICY STUDIES* [1284]
Sage Publications, Inc.
275 South Beverly Drive
Beverly Hills, California 90212
(213) 274-2423

SUBSCRIPTION DATA
Issues and rates: 3 times per year. Each volume contains 12 papers which are released in groups of 4.
Annual rate(s): Institutions $18; Individuals $12; Students $9; Foreign individuals $13; Foreign institutions $19

EDITORIAL DESCRIPTION
Publishes theoretical and empirical works in many disciplines as they bear on policy-making and policy implementation. Some relevant areas include national security; criminal, legal, and judicial systems; health services, environment, regulation of the economy, poverty and social services, corporate affairs and urban affairs.

MANUSCRIPT INFORMATION
Subject field(s): Business and public administration, sociology, economics, political science, psychology
Manuscript requirements: Style sheet sent on request.
Preferred length: 12,000 to 36,000 words; 40-120 pages
Number of copies to be submitted: Three
Author information and reprints: Payment: By publication to author. $100 per article.
Is simultaneous submission of article to other journals permitted: No

Exclusive manuscript rights between acceptance and publication: Yes
Copyright: Held by publication.
Reprints: Authors receive 25 copies of their own paper free.
Disposition of manuscript:
Receipt of manuscript acknowledged: Yes
Decision to publish in: Six to eight weeks
Accepted manuscript published in: Six to nine months
Rejected manuscript returned: Yes
Rejected manuscript criticized: Yes
Submit to:
H. George Frederickson
Editor
School of Public and Environmental Affairs
Indiana University
400 East Seventh Street
Bloomington, Indiana 47401

SAINT LOUIS UNIVERSITY LAW JOURNAL [1285]
3642 Lindell Boulevard
St. Louis, Missouri 63108
(314) 535-3300 ext. 357

Previously entitled *Intramural Law Review of St. Louis University*

SUBSCRIPTION DATA
Issues and rates: Published quarterly.
Average paid circulation: 600; 500 controlled
Annual rate(s): $8.00, Foreign $9.50
Managing Editor: Leslie R. Melman

EDITORIAL DESCRIPTION
Contains lead law articles; comments on contemporary issues; recent developments in case law.
Articles per average issue: 3 lead articles
Audience: Law students and legal profession
Manuscripts accepted in English

MANUSCRIPT INFORMATION
Subject field(s): Law
Manuscript requirements: See latest issue for style requirements.
Preferred length: No limit
Number of copies to be submitted: Two
Author information and reprints: Payment: None.
Is simultaneous submission of article to other journals permitted: Yes
Exclusive manuscript rights between acceptance and publication: Yes
Copyright: Held by publication.
Reprints: Available, cost supplied on request
Disposition of manuscript:
Receipt of manuscript acknowledged: Yes
Decision to publish in: 3 weeks
Accepted manuscript published in: 3 months
Rejected manuscript returned: Yes
Rejected manuscript criticized: Yes
Submit to:
William Sitzer
Editor-in-Chief
(See address above)

SECURITIES REGULATION LAW JOURNAL [1286]

Warren, Gorham and Lamont, Inc.
89 Beach Street
Boston, Massachusetts 02111
(617) 423-2020

First published in 1973

SUBSCRIPTION DATA

Issues and rates: Published quarterly.
  Average paid circulation: 2500
  Annual rate(s): $34.00
Managing Editor: Gerald Kaplan

EDITORIAL DESCRIPTION

Features articles by leading practitioners and regulators in area of securities regulation. Aim is to provide the securities specialist with workable and practical knowledge.
Audience: Law professionals

MANUSCRIPT INFORMATION

Subject field(s): Federal regulation of securities
Manuscript requirements: See latest issue for style requirements.
  Preferred length: 10-30 pages
  Number of copies to be submitted: Two
  Abstract: Yes
Author information and reprints: Payment: None. 6 copies of issue.
  Is simultaneous submission of article to other journals permitted: Yes
  Exclusive manuscript rights between acceptance and publication: Yes
  Copyright: Held by publication.
  Reprints: Available, cost depends on length.
Additional information: Manuscript should be typed, double-spaced, on 8½ x 11 bond. Footnotes should be typed on separate pages.
Disposition of manuscript:
  Receipt of manuscript acknowledged: No
  Decision to publish in: 2-4 weeks
  Accepted manuscript published in: 2-6 months
  Rejected manuscript returned: Yes
  Rejected manuscript criticized: No
Submit to:
  Donald E. Schwartz
  Editor-in-Chief
  Georgetown University Law Center
  600 New Jersey Avenue N.W.
  Washington, D.C. 20001
  (202) 624-8000

SOCIETY OF PROFESSIONAL INVESTIGATORS. BULLETIN [1287]

P. O. Box 1197
Church Street Station
New York, New York 10008

SUBSCRIPTION DATA

Issues and rates: Published annually.
  Annual rate(s): Members Free

Publisher or Sponsor: The Society of Professional Investigators

EDITORIAL DESCRIPTION

Dedicated to the principles of law enforcement and police science
Articles per average issue: Varies
Audience: Law enforcement officials
  Manuscripts accepted in English

MANUSCRIPT INFORMATION

Subject field(s): Any topic dealing with law enforcement
Manuscript requirements: No specific style guide.
  Preferred length: 40 pages
  Number of copies to be submitted: 2
  Abstract: Not necessary.
Author information and reprints: Payment: None.
  Is simultaneous submission of article to other journals permitted: Not permitted.
  Exclusive manuscript rights between acceptance and publication: Yes
  Copyright: Held by publication.
Submit to:
  Ralph Vollono
  Secretary and Assistant Editor
  (See address above)

SOUTH DAKOTA LAW REVIEW [1288]

School of Law
University of South Dakota
Vermillion, South Dakota 57069
(605) 677-5646

First published in 1956

SUBSCRIPTION DATA

Issues and rates: Published three times per year.
  Average paid circulation: 1200
  Annual rate(s): $7.00
Managing Editor: Vance R Goldammer

EDITORIAL DESCRIPTION

Contains developments and trends in all areas of the law.
Articles per average issue: 10-15
Audience: Legal
  Manuscripts accepted in English

MANUSCRIPT INFORMATION

Subject field(s): All areas of legal interest
Manuscript requirements: Texas Manual on Style, HLRA
  Preferred length: None
  Number of copies to be submitted: Two
  Abstract: No
Author information and reprints: Payment: None. 5 reprints and two copies of issue.
  Is simultaneous submission of article to other journals permitted: No
  Exclusive manuscript rights between acceptance and publication: Yes
  Copyright: Held by publication.
  Reprints: Available at cost
Disposition of manuscript:
  Query letter: No
  Receipt of manuscript acknowledged: Yes
  Decision to publish in: 1 month
  Accepted manuscript published in: 1-3 months
  Rejected manuscript returned: Yes
  Rejected manuscript criticized: Yes
Submit to:
  Editor
  (See address above)

SOUTHERN CALIFORNIA LAW REVIEW [1289]

Law Center
University of Southern California
Los Angeles, California 90007
(213) 746-6366

First published in 1927

SUBSCRIPTION DATA

Issues and rates: Published quarterly.
  Average paid circulation: 1,600
  Annual rate(s): $14.50; Institutions $14.50; Students $14.50

EDITORIAL DESCRIPTION

General law and law-related articles in the forefront of developing law
Articles per average issue: 3
Audience: Legal practitioners, judges, professors, legislators, students
  Manuscripts accepted in English

MANUSCRIPT INFORMATION

Manuscript requirements: See latest issue for style requirements.
  Preferred length: None
  Number of copies to be submitted: 1
  Abstract: Not necessary.
Author information and reprints: Payment: Reprints only. 50
  Is simultaneous submission of article to other journals permitted: Permitted, but not encouraged.
  Exclusive manuscript rights between acceptance and publication: Yes
  Copyright: Held by publication.
  Reprints: Available at cost.
Additional information: Articles should be typewritten, triple-spaced.
Disposition of manuscript:
  Query letter: Not necessary, but advisable.
  Receipt of manuscript acknowledged: Yes
  Decision to publish in: 10 days
  Accepted manuscript published in: 60 days
  Rejected manuscript returned: Yes, with return postage paid by publication.
  Rejected manuscript criticized: Reasons for rejections only
Submit to:
  James L. Feder
  Editor-in-Chief
  (See address above)

STATE GOVERNMENT [1290]

The Journal of State Affairs
The Council of State Governments
Iron Works Pike
Lexington, Kentucky 40511
(606) 252-2291 ext. 252

First published in 1930

SUBSCRIPTION DATA
Issues and rates: Published quarterly.
  Average paid circulation: 9,291; 867 controlled
  Annual rate(s): $7.00 annually
Publisher or Sponsor: The Council of State Governments

EDITORIAL DESCRIPTION
  Uses articles on any phase of state government.
Articles per average issue: 12
Audience: Elected and professional state government officials and staffers and scholars of state government.
  Manuscripts accepted in English

MANUSCRIPT INFORMATION
Subject field(s): Any phase of state government
Manuscript requirements: Chicago, with additions.
  Preferred length: 2,000 to 3,000 words; 8-12 pages
  Number of copies to be submitted: One
  Abstract: No
Author information and reprints: Payment: None.
  Is simultaneous submission of article to other journals permitted: No
  Exclusive manuscript rights between acceptance and publication: Yes
  Copyright: Held by publication.
  Reprints: Available, 50 free to author
Disposition of manuscript:
  Query letter: No
  Receipt of manuscript acknowledged: Yes
  Decision to publish in: 2 to 4 weeks
  Accepted manuscript published in: 3 months
  Rejected manuscript returned: Yes
  Rejected manuscript criticized: No
Submit to:
  Paul Albright
  Editor
  (See address above)

STUDENT LAWYER [1291]
1155 East 60th Street
Chicago, Illinois 60637
(312) 493-0533

SUBSCRIPTION DATA
Issues and rates: September through May (9 issues)
  Average paid circulation: 24,000
  Annual rate(s): $3.00
Publisher or Sponsor: American Bar Association, Law Student Division
Managing Editor: David Martin

EDITORIAL DESCRIPTION
  Contains articles on legal and social problems of interest to law students. Special emphasis given to articles telling law students how to bring about specific changes.
Articles per average issue: 12
Audience: Law students
  Manuscripts accepted in English

MANUSCRIPT INFORMATION
Manuscript requirements: See latest issue for style requirements.
  Preferred length: 3,000 words maximum
  Number of copies to be submitted: One
Author information and reprints: Payment: Three issues and sometimes small honorarium
  Is simultaneous submission of article to other journals permitted: Yes, if notified of this.
  Exclusive manuscript rights between acceptance and publication: Yes
  Copyright: Held by publication.
  Reprints: Available, cost passed on to author
Additional information: Photos and illustrations accepted with article.
Disposition of manuscript:
  Query letter: Preferred
  Receipt of manuscript acknowledged: Yes
  Decision to publish in: 3 weeks
  Accepted manuscript published in: 2-3 months
  Rejected manuscript returned: Yes, if self-addressed, stamped envelope is enclosed.
  Rejected manuscript criticized: No
Submit to:
  Editor
  (See address above)

TAXATION FOR LAWYERS [1292]
A National Professional Tax Journal for the Lawyer in General Practice who is not a Tax Specialist
125 East 56th Street
New York, New York 10022
(212) 421-6740

First published in 1972

SUBSCRIPTION DATA
Issues and rates: Published bi-monthly.
  Average paid circulation: 10,000
  Annual rate(s): $18.00
Publisher or Sponsor: Tax Research Group Ltd.
Managing Editor: Leo J. Northart

EDITORIAL DESCRIPTION
  Contains discussion of practical problems in taxation as they affect law practice and the lawyer's client.
Articles per average issue: 4
Audience: Lawyers in general practice
  Manuscripts accepted in English

MANUSCRIPT INFORMATION
Subject field(s): Taxation
Manuscript requirements: See latest issue for style requirements.
  Preferred length: 4,000 to 5,000 words
  Number of copies to be submitted: Two
  Abstract: No
Author information and reprints: Payment: None.
  Is simultaneous submission of article to other journals permitted: No
  Exclusive manuscript rights between acceptance and publication: Yes
  Copyright: Held by publication.
  Reprints: Available, 100 free
Disposition of manuscript:
  Query letter: Yes
  Receipt of manuscript acknowledged: Yes
  Decision to publish in: 2-4 weeks
  Accepted manuscript published in: 1-2 months
  Rejected manuscript returned: Yes
  Rejected manuscript criticized: Yes
Submit to:
  Editor
  (See address above)

TEXAS BAR JOURNAL [1293]
Box 12487, Capitol Station
Austin, Texas 78711
(512) 476-6823

First published in 1938

SUBSCRIPTION DATA
Issues and rates: Monthly except July
  Average paid circulation: 27,000
  Annual rate(s): $11.00, Foreign $12.00
Publisher or Sponsor: State Bar of Texas
Managing Editor: Virginia Parton

EDITORIAL DESCRIPTION
  Contains legal articles and news items of interest to the legal profession.
Articles per average issue: 4-5
Audience: Lawyers and judges
  Manuscripts accepted in English

MANUSCRIPT INFORMATION
Subject field(s): Legal articles dealing with Texas law and practice
Manuscript requirements: Style sheet sent on request.
  Preferred length: 3,000 words
  Number of copies to be submitted: One
Author information and reprints: Payment: None.
  Is simultaneous submission of article to other journals permitted: No
  Exclusive manuscript rights between acceptance and publication: Yes
  Copyright: Held by publication.
  Reprints: Available, $2 plus $.10 a page
Disposition of manuscript:
  Query letter: No
  Receipt of manuscript acknowledged: Yes
  Decision to publish in: 2-3 weeks
  Accepted manuscript published in: No set time, when space available
  Rejected manuscript returned: Yes
  Rejected manuscript criticized: No
Submit to:
  Editor
  (See address above)

TEXAS INTERNATIONAL LAW JOURNAL [1294]
2500 Red River
Austin, Texas 78705
(512) 474-5151

SUBSCRIPTION DATA
Issues and rates: Published three times per year.
  Average paid circulation: 500

Annual rate(s): $6.50, Foreign $7.50
Publisher or Sponsor: University of Texas School of Law
Managing Editor: Gary Rosin

EDITORIAL DESCRIPTION

Contains articles on public and private international law and world trade.
Articles per average issue: 2-4
Audience: Attorneys
  Manuscripts accepted in English, French, Spanish, German

MANUSCRIPT INFORMATION

Subject field(s): International commerce, public international law, comparative law
Manuscript requirements: No specific style guide.
  Preferred length: Approximately 30 pages
  Number of copies to be submitted: Two
  Abstract: No
Author information and reprints: Payment: None.
  Is simultaneous submission of article to other journals permitted: Yes
  Exclusive manuscript rights between acceptance and publication: Yes
  Copyright: Held by publication.
  Reprints: Available
Disposition of manuscript:
  Query letter: Yes
  Receipt of manuscript acknowledged: Yes
  Decision to publish in: 1 month
  Accepted manuscript published in: 1-6 months
  Rejected manuscript returned: Yes
  Rejected manuscript criticized: No
Submit to:
  Charles Maynard
  Articles Editor
  (See address above)

TRAFFIC QUARTERLY [1295]

An Independent Journal for Better Traffic Operations
Box 55, Saugatuck Station
Westport, Connecticut 06880
(203) 227-4852

First published in 1947

SUBSCRIPTION DATA

Issues and rates: Published quarterly.
  Average paid circulation: 5500 controlled
Publisher or Sponsor: Eno Foundation for Transportation, Inc.
Managing Editor: Robert S. Holmes

EDITORIAL DESCRIPTION

Publishes theoretical and empirical research articles on transportation planning, design, operation, and regulation.
Articles per average issue: 10
Audience: Transportation professionals,
  Manuscripts accepted in English

MANUSCRIPT INFORMATION

Subject field(s): Transportation
Manuscript requirements: Chicago
  Preferred length: 4,000-5,000 words; 20 pages
  Number of copies to be submitted: Two
  Abstract: No
Author information and reprints: Payment: None.
  Is simultaneous submission of article to other journals permitted: No, will not publish articles that have been published elsewhere
  Exclusive manuscript rights between acceptance and publication: Yes
  Copyright: Held by Eno Foundation for Transportation, Inc.
  Reprints: Available, up to 100 copies, at no cost
Additional information: Submit 100-word biographical sketch and original art work, if any, for illustrations black and white glossy photos only. Tables and figures camera-ready
Disposition of manuscript:
  Query letter: No
  Receipt of manuscript acknowledged: Yes
  Decision to publish in: 2-3 months
  Accepted manuscript published in: 6-9 months
  Rejected manuscript returned: Yes
  Rejected manuscript criticized: No
Submit to:
  Editor-in-Chief
  (See address above)

SPECIAL STIPULATIONS

Author is responsible for permission to quote. Author's Guide available on request.

TRANSPORTATION JOURNAL [1296]

547 West Jackson Boulevard
Chicago, Illinois 60606
(312) 939-2491

First published in 1961

SUBSCRIPTION DATA

Issues and rates: Published quarterly.
  Average paid circulation: 800; 3,700 controlled
  Annual rate(s): $10.00
Publisher or Sponsor: American Society of Traffic and Transportation Inc

EDITORIAL DESCRIPTION

Devoted to the publication of articles which will contribute to a clear understanding of the management of transportation and stimulate interest in critical appraisals of practices and techniques of transportation and related fields; dissemination of information designed to advance the traffic, transportation and physical distribution management profession.
Articles per average issue: 12
Audience: Professional
  Manuscripts accepted in English

MANUSCRIPT INFORMATION

Subject field(s): Transportation, physical distribution, logistics, education, traffic management
Manuscript requirements: See latest issue for style requirements.
  Preferred length: 1500-4000 words double-spaced
  Number of copies to be submitted: Two
  Abstract: No
Author information and reprints: Payment: None.
  Is simultaneous submission of article to other journals permitted: No
  Exclusive manuscript rights between acceptance and publication: Yes
  Copyright: Held by publication.
  Reprints: Available, rates on request
Disposition of manuscript:
  Query letter: No
  Receipt of manuscript acknowledged: Yes
  Decision to publish in: 6 months
  Accepted manuscript published in: 6 months
  Rejected manuscript returned: Yes
  Rejected manuscript criticized: Yes
Submit to:
  Charles A. Taff
  Editor
  College of Business and Management
  University of Maryland
  College Park, Maryland 20742
  (301) 277-3460

TRIAL MAGAZINE [1297]

20 Garden Street
Cambridge, Massachusetts 02138
(617) 868-6900

First published in 1965

SUBSCRIPTION DATA

Issues and rates: Published bi-monthly.
  Average paid circulation: 33,400; 35,826 controlled
  Annual rate(s): $5.00
Publisher or Sponsor: The Association of Trial Lawyers of America
Managing Editor: Barbara E. Sullivan

EDITORIAL DESCRIPTION

Contains articles of contemporary social/legal/political issues as well as practical information relevant to a legally oriented readership and "news" of developments in the law and law-related disciplines.
Articles per average issue: 8
Audience: Legal and related fields
  Manuscripts accepted in English

MANUSCRIPT INFORMATION

Subject field(s): Legal, legislative, social, political/legal, consumer, crime, safety, workmen's compensation, legal education, insurance, environment
Manuscript requirements: No specific style guide.
  Preferred length: 3,000-4500 words; 2 pages
  Number of copies to be submitted: Two
  Abstract: No
Author information and reprints: Payment: None.
  Is simultaneous submission of article to other journals permitted: Yes

Exclusive manuscript rights between acceptance and publication: Yes
Copyright: Held by publication.
Reprints: Available, $50.00 per thousand
Disposition of manuscript:
 Query letter: No
 Receipt of manuscript acknowledged: Yes
 Decision to publish in: 2 weeks
 Accepted manuscript published in: Up to two months
 Rejected manuscript returned: Yes
 Rejected manuscript criticized: No
Submit to:
 Managing Editor
 (See address above)
 (627) 868-6900 ext. 37

UNAUTHORIZED PRACTICE NEWS [1298]
1155 East 60th Street
Chicago, Illinois 60637
(312) 493-0533 ext. 489

SUBSCRIPTION DATA
Issues and rates: Published quarterly.
 Average paid circulation: 150; 3,350 controlled
 Annual rate(s): $5.00
Publisher or Sponsor: American Bar Association

EDITORIAL DESCRIPTION
 A current review of activities to curb the unlawful practice of the law. Also interested in considering articles written from the prospective of any academic discipline.

MANUSCRIPT INFORMATION
Subject field(s): Unlawful practice of the law
Manuscript requirements: No specific style guide.
 Preferred length: None
 Number of copies to be submitted: One
Author information and reprints: Payment: None.
 Is simultaneous submission of article to other journals permitted: No
 Exclusive manuscript rights between acceptance and publication: Yes
 Copyright: Held by publication.
 Reprints: Not available.
Disposition of manuscript:
 Receipt of manuscript acknowledged: Yes
 Decision to publish in: 6 weeks
 Accepted manuscript published in: 12 weeks
 Rejected manuscript returned: Yes
 Rejected manuscript criticized: No
Submit to:
 Standing Committee on Unauthorized Practice of the Law
 (See address above)

UNIFORM COMMERCIAL CODE LAW JOURNAL [1299]
Warren, Gorham and Lamont, Inc.
870 Seventh Avenue
New York, New York 10019
(212) 977-7400

First published in 1968

SUBSCRIPTION DATA
Issues and rates: Published quarterly.
 Average paid circulation: 1863
 Annual rate(s): $32.50
Managing Editor: Elijah E Jhirad

EDITORIAL DESCRIPTION
 Contains articles and essays of interest to attorneys and others concerned with developments in commercial law. Provides practitioners in area of commercial law with an overview of developments in the law as well as practical advice.
Audience: Law professionals
 Manuscripts accepted in English

MANUSCRIPT INFORMATION
Subject field(s): Commercial law
Manuscript requirements: See latest issue for style requirements.
 Preferred length: 10-25 pages
 Number of copies to be submitted: One
Author information and reprints: Payment: None. 6 copies of issue.
 Is simultaneous submission of article to other journals permitted: Yes
 Exclusive manuscript rights between acceptance and publication: Yes
 Copyright: Held by publication.
 Reprints: Available, cost depends on length
Additional information: Manuscript should be typed, double-spaced, on 8 ½ by 11 white bond. Footnotes should be typed on separate pages.
Disposition of manuscript:
 Receipt of manuscript acknowledged: No
 Decision to publish in: 2-4 weeks
 Accepted manuscript published in: 2-4 months
 Rejected manuscript returned: Yes
 Rejected manuscript criticized: No
Submit to:
 Editor-in-Chief
 (See address above)

UNIVERSITY OF CHICAGO LAW REVIEW [1300]
1111 East 60th Street
Chicago, Illinois, 60637
(312) 753-2427

First published in 1933

SUBSCRIPTION DATA
Issues and rates: Published quarterly.
 Average paid circulation: 2200; 300 controlled
 Annual rate(s): $10.00, Pan-Am $10.50, Foreign $11.00
Publisher or Sponsor: University of Chicago Law School

EDITORIAL DESCRIPTION
 Contains general legal literature of interest to both scholar and practitioner.
Articles per average issue: 6-8
Audience: Legal profession
 Manuscripts accepted in English

MANUSCRIPT INFORMATION
Subject field(s): Law
Manuscript requirements: Chicago; HLRA
 Preferred length: 100 triple-spaced pages
 Number of copies to be submitted: One
 Abstract: No
Author information and reprints: Payment: None.
 Is simultaneous submission of article to other journals permitted: Yes
 Exclusive manuscript rights between acceptance and publication: Yes
 Copyright: Held by publication.
 Reprints: Available, first 25 free
Disposition of manuscript:
 Query letter: No
 Receipt of manuscript acknowledged: Yes
 Decision to publish in: Less than one month
 Accepted manuscript published in: Three months
 Rejected manuscript returned: Yes, if return postage is supplied by author.
 Rejected manuscript criticized: Sometimes
Submit to:
 Ronald M. Levin
 Article and Book Review Editor
 (See address above)

UNIVERSITY OF CINCINNATI LAW REVIEW [1301]
University of Cincinnati
Cincinnati, Ohio 45221
(513) 475-2801

First published in 1927

SUBSCRIPTION DATA
Issues and rates: Published quarterly.
 Average paid circulation: 1350
 Annual rate(s): $8.00
Publisher or Sponsor: University of Cincinnati

EDITORIAL DESCRIPTION
 Contains articles on law and related fields.
Articles per average issue: 2-8
Audience: the legal profession
 Manuscripts accepted in English only

MANUSCRIPT INFORMATION
Manuscript requirements: No specific style guide.
 Preferred length: None
 Number of copies to be submitted: One
 Abstract: Required on only selected articles: Triple-space manuscript, append footnotes.
Author information and reprints: Payment: None.
 Is simultaneous submission of article to other journals permitted: No
 Exclusive manuscript rights between acceptance and publication: Yes
 Copyright: Held by publication.
 Reprints: Available, 50 free
Disposition of manuscript:
 Query letter: No
 Receipt of manuscript acknowledged: Yes

Decision to publish in: 2-4 weeks
Accepted manuscript published in: Varies
Rejected manuscript returned: Yes
Rejected manuscript criticized: Yes
Submit to:
James B. Helmer, Jr.
Editor-in-Chief
(See address above)

UNIVERSITY OF COLORADO LAW REVIEW [1302]

Fleming Law Building
University of Colorado
Boulder, Colorado 80302
(303) 492-6145

Previously entitled *Rocky Mountain Law Review*

First published in 1928

SUBSCRIPTION DATA
Issues and rates: Published quarterly.
Average paid circulation: approximately 950
Annual rate(s): $8.00, Foreign $9.00; Single issues $3.50
Publisher or Sponsor: University of Colorado

EDITORIAL DESCRIPTION
Contains articles by authors from the legal profession or related fields on topics of interest to the legal profession. Welcomes submission of articles on topics across the entire spectrum of the legal field.
Articles per average issue: 2
Audience: Lawyers, law students, judges, law professors
Manuscripts accepted in English

MANUSCRIPT INFORMATION
Subject field(s): Entire spectrum of legal field
Manuscript requirements: HLRA
Preferred length: No specific limit
Number of copies to be submitted: Two
Abstract: No
Author information and reprints: Payment: None.
Is simultaneous submission of article to other journals permitted: Policy is to seek a right of first refusal before thorough article evaluation is done if the article is submitted to other law reviews.
Exclusive manuscript rights between acceptance and publication: Yes
Copyright: Held by publication.
Reprints: Available, 50 free, additional copies billed at cost
Additional information: Manuscripts must be typed, triple-spaced. Footnotes should be on separate page at end of text.
Disposition of manuscript:
Query letter: Desirable
Receipt of manuscript acknowledged: Yes
Decision to publish in: 3 weeks
Accepted manuscript published in: 2-6 months depending on time of submission
Rejected manuscript returned: Yes
Rejected manuscript criticized: Reasons for rejection given.

Submit to:
Matthew D. Skeen
Editor-in-Chief
(See address above)

UNIVERSITY OF ILLINOIS LAW FORUM [1303]

College of Law
University of Illinois
Champaign, Illinois 61820
(217) 333-6756

SUBSCRIPTION DATA
Issues and rates: Published quarterly.
Average paid circulation: 2,200; 200 controlled
Annual rate(s): $10.00
Publisher or Sponsor: University of Illinois College of Law

EDITORIAL DESCRIPTION
Publication is divided into a lead section and a student section. Lead section is generally written by law professors, practicing attorneys, and judges and consists of articles on all areas of the law and of reviews of books of interest to the legal profession. Publication seeks to provide a scholarly treatment of legal issues which may be of interest to the practicing attorney as well as the academician. Articles relating to Illinois are of special interest.

MANUSCRIPT INFORMATION
Subject field(s): Law (all areas)
Manuscript requirements: HLRA
Preferred length: 30-80 pages, double spaced
Number of copies to be submitted: One
Author information and reprints: Payment: None. 5 copies of issue in which article appears
Is simultaneous submission of article to other journals permitted: Yes
Exclusive manuscript rights between acceptance and publication: Yes
Copyright: Held by publication.
Reprints: Available, 50 free
Disposition of manuscript:
Receipt of manuscript acknowledged: Yes
Decision to publish in: One to two weeks
Accepted manuscript published in: Varies, from 2-12 months
Rejected manuscript returned: Yes
Rejected manuscript criticized: No
Submit to:
Articles Editor
(See address above)

UNIVERSITY OF MICHIGAN JOURNAL OF LAW REFORM [1304]

731 Legal Research Building
Ann Arbor, Michigan 48104
(313) 763-2195

Previously entitled *Prospectus*

First published in 1968

SUBSCRIPTION DATA
Issues and rates: Published three times per year.
Average paid circulation: 1300
Annual rate(s): $7.50, Foreign $8.00
Publisher or Sponsor: University of Michigan Law School

EDITORIAL DESCRIPTION
General legal journal with emphasis on law reform proposals and significant legal experimentation.
Articles per average issue: 11
Audience: Entire profession; courts, legislators, lawyers, students.
Manuscripts accepted in English

MANUSCRIPT INFORMATION
Subject field(s): Open
Manuscript requirements: Style sheet sent on request.
Preferred length: None
Number of copies to be submitted: One
Abstract: Optional, details for preparation sent on request
Author information and reprints: Payment: None. 5 copies of issue in which article appears and 20 reprints.
Is simultaneous submission of article to other journals permitted: Yes
Exclusive manuscript rights between acceptance and publication: Yes
Copyright: Held by University of Michigan Law School
Reprints: Available, 20 copies free
Disposition of manuscript:
Query letter: No
Receipt of manuscript acknowledged: Yes
Decision to publish in: 2-4 weeks
Accepted manuscript published in: Approx. 15 weeks
Rejected manuscript returned: Upon request
Rejected manuscript criticized: Sometimes
Submit to:
I. Scott Bass
Articles Editor
(See address above)

UNIVERSITY OF PENNSYLVANIA LAW REVIEW [1305]

3440 Chestnut Street
Philadelphia, Pennsylvania 19174
(215) 243-7060

SUBSCRIPTION DATA
Issues and rates: Published bi-monthly.
Average paid circulation: 1800
Annual rate(s): $15.00, Foreign $17.50
Managing Editor: Michael C. Keley

EDITORIAL DESCRIPTION
Contains law related articles, short student commentary, book reviews.
Articles per average issue: 6
Audience: Students, scholars, practitioners
Manuscripts accepted in English

MANUSCRIPT INFORMATION
Subject field(s): Law, any related topics

Manuscript requirements: See latest issue for style requirements.
Number of copies to be submitted: One
Author information and reprints: Payment: None. 30 reprints.
Is simultaneous submission of article to other journals permitted: Yes
Exclusive manuscript rights between acceptance and publication: Yes
Copyright: Held by University of Pennsylvania
Reprints: Available, for some articles, $2.00 each.
Additional information: Triple space copy, footnotes on separate pages.
Disposition of manuscript:
Query letter: No
Receipt of manuscript acknowledged: Yes
Decision to publish in: Several weeks
Accepted manuscript published in: 2-3 months
Rejected manuscript returned: Yes
Rejected manuscript criticized: No
Submit to:
Articles and Book Review Editor
(See address above)

UNIVERSITY OF SAN FRANCISCO LAW REVIEW [1306]

University of San Francisco
School of Law
San Francisco, California 94117
(415) 666-6154

First published in 1966

SUBSCRIPTION DATA
Issues and rates: Published quarterly.
Average paid circulation: 1850
Annual rate(s): $8.00 per year, $3.50 per issue
Publisher or Sponsor: University of San Francisco, School of Law

EDITORIAL DESCRIPTION
Publishes a range of articles by members of the Bench and Bar, comments by students, and book reviews of publications of interest to students, practicing attorneys and members of both state and federal judiciaries. Articles and comments focus upon particularized areas of the law in which conflict, ambiguity or discrepancies presently exist.
Articles per average issue: 8
Audience: Legal profession
Manuscripts accepted in English

MANUSCRIPT INFORMATION
Subject field(s): Criminal and civil law and procedure, administrative agency review, constitutional law (1st Amendment rights), consumer protection.
Manuscript requirements: See latest issue for style requirements.
Preferred length: 7,500 words; 30 pages
Number of copies to be submitted: One
Abstract: Optional, triple-space if possible
Author information and reprints: Payment: None.
Is simultaneous submission of article to other journals permitted: No

Exclusive manuscript rights between acceptance and publication: Yes
Copyright: Held by publication.
Reprints: Available
Disposition of manuscript:
Query letter: No
Receipt of manuscript acknowledged: Yes
Decision to publish in: Two weeks
Accepted manuscript published in: 2-3 months
Rejected manuscript returned: Yes
Rejected manuscript criticized: Optional
Submit to:
Gary Halling
Articles Editor
(See address above)

UNIVERSITY OF TORONTO LAW JOURNAL [1307]

University of Toronto Press
Front Campus
Toronto, Ontario H5S 1A6, Canada

SUBSCRIPTION DATA
Issues and rates: Published quarterly.
Annual rate(s): $10.00

EDITORIAL DESCRIPTION
Contains articles on law and related social sciences.
Articles per average issue: 4
Audience: Professional
Manuscripts accepted in English, French

MANUSCRIPT INFORMATION
Manuscript requirements: Chicago
Number of copies to be submitted: Two
Author information and reprints: Payment: Reprints only. 25 reprints
Is simultaneous submission of article to other journals permitted: No
Exclusive manuscript rights between acceptance and publication: Yes
Copyright: Held by publication.
Reprints: Available
Additional information: Manuscript should be double-spaced typescript.

Disposition of manuscript:
Query letter: Yes
Receipt of manuscript acknowledged: Yes
Decision to publish in: Varies
Accepted manuscript published in: 1 year
Rejected manuscript returned: Yes
Rejected manuscript criticized: Yes

Submit to:
R.C.B. Risk
Editor
Faculty of Law
University of Toronto
Toronto, Ontario Canada
(416) 928-8579

URBAN AFFAIRS QUARTERLY* [1308]

Sage Publications, Inc.
275 South Beverly Drive
Beverly Hills, California 90212
(213) 274-2423

SUBSCRIPTION DATA
Issues and rates: Published quarterly.
Annual rate(s): Institutions $15.00; Individuals $10.00; Students $8.00; Foreign individuals $11.50; Foreign institutions $16.50

EDITORIAL DESCRIPTION
Publishes articles concerned with basic or applied research in urban problems as well as implementation of policy and programs.

MANUSCRIPT INFORMATION
Subject field(s): Urban affairs, policy, sociology
Manuscript requirements: Style sheet sent on request.
Preferred length: 6,250-7,500 words; 25 to 30 pages
Number of copies to be submitted: Two
Author information and reprints: Payment: None. 25 tear-sheets free to author.
Is simultaneous submission of article to other journals permitted: Permitted, but not encouraged. Author must notify publisher that manuscript is under consideration elsewhere.
Exclusive manuscript rights between acceptance and publication: Yes
Copyright: Held by publication.
Reprints: Available if purchased by special order in amounts no fewer than 100
Disposition of manuscript:
Receipt of manuscript acknowledged: Yes
Decision to publish in: Six to eight weeks
Accepted manuscript published in: Six to nine months
Rejected manuscript returned: Yes
Rejected manuscript criticized: Yes
Submit to:
Peter Bouxsein
Editor
Institute of Public Policy Studies
1516 Rackham Building
University of Michigan
Ann Arbor, Michigan 48104

UTAH LAW REVIEW [1309]

College of Law
University of Utah
Salt Lake City, Utah 84112
(801) 581-7337

First published in 1949

SUBSCRIPTION DATA
Issues and rates: Published quarterly.
Average paid circulation: 1100
Annual rate(s): $12.00
Publisher or Sponsor: Utah Law Review Society
Managing Editor: Michael O. Terry

EDITORIAL DESCRIPTION
Publishes articles; student notes and comments on legal problems; book reviews and case notes on decisions by Utah Supreme Court.
Articles per average issue: 15
Audience: Legal profession, legislators
Manuscripts accepted in English

Law and public administration

MANUSCRIPT INFORMATION
Subject field(s): Any law related field
Manuscript requirements: HLRA
   Number of copies to be submitted: Two
   Abstract: No
Author information and reprints: Payment: None.
   Is simultaneous submission of article to other journals permitted: Yes
   Exclusive manuscript rights between acceptance and publication: No
   Copyright: Held by publication unless author specifically requests
   Reprints: Available at $2.00 per reprint
Disposition of manuscript:
   Query letter: No
   Receipt of manuscript acknowledged: Yes
   Decision to publish in: 3 months
   Accepted manuscript published in: 6 months
   Rejected manuscript returned: Yes
   Rejected manuscript criticized: Yes
Submit to:
   Editor-in-Chief
   (See address above)

VIRGINIA MUNICIPAL REVIEW [1310]
The Municipal Officials' Magazine
8th Floor, 1108 East Main Street
Richmond, Virginia 23219
(703) 643-1113

First published in 1921

SUBSCRIPTION DATA
Issues and rates: Published monthly.
   Average paid circulation: 10,000
   Annual rate(s): $5.00
Managing Editor: Ralph L. Dombrower

EDITORIAL DESCRIPTION
   Contains articles on governmental subjects.

MANUSCRIPT INFORMATION
Subject field(s): Governmental
Manuscript requirements: MLA; Chicago
   Preferred length: 500 words
   Number of copies to be submitted: Two
Author information and reprints: Payment: By publication to author.
   Is simultaneous submission of article to other journals permitted: Yes
   Exclusive manuscript rights between acceptance and publication: Yes
   Copyright: Held by publication.
   Reprints: Available at cost
Disposition of manuscript:
   Receipt of manuscript acknowledged: Yes
   Decision to publish in: 60 days
   Accepted manuscript published in: 60 days
   Rejected manuscript returned: Yes, if return postage is supplied by author.
Submit to:
   Editor
   P.O. Box 100
   Richmond, Virginia 23201

WAKE FOREST LAW REVIEW [1311]
P.O. Box 7206, Reynolda Station
Winston-Salem, North Carolina 27109
(919) 725-9711, ext. 429

First published in 1965

SUBSCRIPTION DATA
Issues and rates: Published quarterly.
   Average paid circulation: Not available.
   Annual rate(s): $8.00
Managing Editor: Albert R. H. Bell, Jr.

EDITORIAL DESCRIPTION
   A legal periodical providing the legal profession with useful material on timely legal topics. Non-student writing consists of leading articles by one of recognized stature in a particular field of law and book reviews by promient legal scholars on works of interest to the legal profession.
Articles per average issue: 4
Audience: Legal profession
   Manuscripts accepted in English

MANUSCRIPT INFORMATION
Subject field(s): Legal topics
Manuscript requirements: Style sheet sent on request.
   Preferred length: 50 pages maximum
   Number of copies to be submitted: One
   Abstract: No
Author information and reprints: Payment: None.
   Is simultaneous submission of article to other journals permitted: No
   Exclusive manuscript rights between acceptance and publication: Yes
   Copyright: Held by publication.
   Reprints: Available, 50 free reprints
Additional information: Manuscript should be in proper style, double spaced with footnotes in legal form. Footnotes, references, table and charts should be on separate pages.
Disposition of manuscript:
   Query letter: No
   Receipt of manuscript acknowledged: Yes
   Decision to publish in: 3 months
   Accepted manuscript published in: 3 months
   Rejected manuscript returned: Yes
   Rejected manuscript criticized: Sometimes
Submit to:
   Donald J. McFadyen
   Editor-in-Chief
   (See address above)

WASHINGTON LAW REVIEW [1312]
JB-20 Condon
University of Washington
Seattle, Washington 98195
(206) 543-4097

Previously entitled *Washington Law Review & State Bar Journal*

First published in 1926

SUBSCRIPTION DATA
Issues and rates: Published quarterly.
   Average paid circulation: 1,600
   Annual rate(s): $12.00, Foreign $12.60

EDITORIAL DESCRIPTION
   Contains articles, comments, casenotes, statutory notes, book reviews.
Articles per average issue: 8
Audience: Legal professional
   Manuscripts accepted in English

MANUSCRIPT INFORMATION
Subject field(s): Law
Manuscript requirements: HLRA
Author information and reprints: Payment: Reprints only. Free bound reprints furnished to authors.
   Is simultaneous submission of article to other journals permitted: Yes
   Exclusive manuscript rights between acceptance and publication: Yes
   Copyright: Held by publication.
   Reprints: Available
Disposition of manuscript:
   Query letter: No
   Receipt of manuscript acknowledged: Yes
   Decision to publish in: 2-4 weeks
   Accepted manuscript published in: 4 months
   Rejected manuscript returned: No
   Rejected manuscript criticized: No
Submit to:
   The Editor
   (See address above)

WASHINGTON AND LEE LAW REVIEW [1313]
Washington and Lee University
Lexington, Virginia 24450
(703) 463-5507

First published in 1938

SUBSCRIPTION DATA
Issues and rates: Published quarterly.
   Average paid circulation: 2100
   Annual rate(s): $12.00

EDITORIAL DESCRIPTION
   Contains notes and comments on current problems in law as portrayed in recent cases. Articles are written by lawyers, professors and students.
Articles per average issue: Up to six
Audience: Legal profession
   Manuscripts accepted in English

MANUSCRIPT INFORMATION
Subject field(s): All fields of law including international and comparative law
Manuscript requirements: See latest issue for style requirements.
   Preferred length: 15-100 pages
   Number of copies to be submitted: One
   Abstract: If possible
Author information and reprints: Payment: None.
   Is simultaneous submission of article to other journals permitted: Yes
   Exclusive manuscript rights between acceptance and publication: Yes

Copyright: Held by publication.
Reprints: Available, first 50 free
Disposition of manuscript:
  Query letter: No
  Receipt of manuscript acknowledged: Yes
  Decision to publish in: One week
  Accepted manuscript published in: 1-3 months
  Rejected manuscript returned: Yes
  Rejected manuscript criticized: Yes
Submit to:
  Lead Articles Editor
  (See address above)

WISCONSIN LAW REVIEW [1314]
University of Wisconsin Law School
975 Bascom Mall
Madison, Wisconsin 53706
(608) 262-2109

SUBSCRIPTION DATA
Issues and rates: Published quarterly.
  Average paid circulation: 2300
  Annual rate(s): $10.00
Managing Editor: Gregory S. Pokrass

EDITORIAL DESCRIPTION
  Contains lead articles on law and society.
Articles per average issue: 3-4 lead articles
Audience: Legal profession
  Manuscripts accepted in English only

MANUSCRIPT INFORMATION
Subject field(s): Legal analysis, law and society, legal history, book reviews of legal books
Manuscript requirements: Style sheet sent on request.
  Preferred length: No less than 30 pages
  Number of copies to be submitted: One
  Abstract: No
Author information and reprints: Payment: None.
  Is simultaneous submission of article to other journals permitted: Yes
  Exclusive manuscript rights between acceptance and publication: Yes
  Copyright: Held by publication.
  Reprints: Available, first 50 free
Additional information: Triple space everything, including footnotes. Use 2½ inch margin on left-hand side.
Disposition of manuscript:
  Query letter: No
  Receipt of manuscript acknowledged: Yes
  Decision to publish in: 2-3 weeks
  Accepted manuscript published in: 3-4 months
  Rejected manuscript returned: Yes
  Rejected manuscript criticized: No
Submit to:
  Articles Editor
  (See address above)

YALE LAW JOURNAL [1315]
401-A Yale Station
New Haven, Connecticut 06520
(203) 436-8243

First published in 1891

SUBSCRIPTION DATA
Issues and rates: Monthly, November through July
  Average paid circulation: 4,500
  Annual rate(s): $18.00; Foreign $20.00
Managing Editor: W. Duane Benton

EDITORIAL DESCRIPTION
  Contains legal articles written by professors, lawyers and students.
Articles per average issue: 8
Audience: Legal profession; lawyers, students, etc.
  Manuscripts accepted in English

MANUSCRIPT INFORMATION
Subject field(s): Legal subjects, all aspects
Manuscript requirements: HLRA
  Preferred length: 15,000 words or 100 pages maximum
  Number of copies to be submitted: One
  Abstract: No
Author information and reprints: Payment: None.
  Is simultaneous submission of article to other journals permitted: Yes
  Exclusive manuscript rights between acceptance and publication: Yes
  Copyright: Held by publication.
  Reprints: Available, 50 free
Additional information: Place footnotes on separate page at end. Triple space and leave wide left hand margin.
Disposition of manuscript:
  Query letter: No
  Receipt of manuscript acknowledged: Yes
  Decision to publish in: 6 weeks
  Accepted manuscript published in: 3-5 months
  Rejected manuscript returned: Yes, if return postage is supplied by author.
  Rejected manuscript criticized: No
Submit to:
  Editor
  (See address above)

Military

Military

AIR FORCE LAW REVIEW [1316]
AVIPO/JA
Maxwell AFB, Alabama 36112
(305) 293-2802

Previously entitled *USAF JAG Law Review*

First published in 1959

SUBSCRIPTION DATA
Issues and rates: Published quarterly.
  Average paid circulation: 4,000
  Annual rate(s): $2.50, Foreign $3.25
Publisher or Sponsor: Judge Advocate General's Department, United States Air Force

EDITORIAL DESCRIPTION
  Provides a forum for articles on military law or related subjects of interest to judge advocate officers on active duty in the Air Force. This publication does not contain editorial articles and articles included are selected on merit rather than on the basis of a particular point of view.
Articles per average issue: 10
Audience: Lawyers, particularly military lawyers
  Manuscripts accepted in English only

MANUSCRIPT INFORMATION
Subject field(s): Military justice, procurement, claims, labor law, tax, international law, any topic which has a direct or indirect relationship with the practice of law in the Air Force.
Manuscript requirements: See latest issue for style requirements.
  Preferred length: Any reasonable length
  Number of copies to be submitted: Two
  Abstract: No
Author information and reprints: Payment: None.
  Is simultaneous submission of article to other journals permitted: Yes
  Exclusive manuscript rights between acceptance and publication: Yes
  Copyright: Held by publication.
  Reprints: Not available. Copies of entire issue will be furnished to the author.
Additional information: Only articles which have not been printed will be accepted.
Disposition of manuscript:
  Query letter: No
  Receipt of manuscript acknowledged: Yes
  Decision to publish in: 2-4 weeks
  Accepted manuscript published in: 1-6 months
  Rejected manuscript returned: Yes if requested
  Rejected manuscript criticized: Yes
Submit to:
  Richard J Erickson
  Editor
  (See address above)

AIR UNIVERSITY REVIEW [1317]
The Professional Journal of the United States Air Force
REV, Bldg. 1211
Maxwell Air Force Base, Alabama 36112
(205) 293-7641

Previously entitled *Air University Quarterly Review*

First published in 1947

SUBSCRIPTION DATA
Issues and rates: Published bi-monthly.
  Average paid circulation: 650; 18,500 controlled
  Annual rate(s): $8.00, Foreign $10.00
Publisher or Sponsor: United States Air Force
Managing Editor: Jack H. Mooney

EDITORIAL DESCRIPTION
  Contains articles dealing with Air Force programs, plans, technical development, strategy, tactics, management, and history selected for publication solely on their relevance to U.S. Air Force professional interests.
Articles per average issue: 11
Audience: Air Force and Department of Defense Officials
  Manuscripts accepted in English

MANUSCRIPT INFORMATION
Subject field(s): Procurement of aircraft, strategy, tactics, personnel management, historical articles, Air Force doctrine, racial relations in the Air Force, technical development, professional military education, Air Force programs in space, foreign air forces, uses of airpower
Manuscript requirements: Style sheet sent on request.
  Preferred length: 3000 to 3500 words; 10 to 15 pages
  Number of copies to be submitted: Original only
  Abstract: No
Author information and reprints: Payment: By publication to author.
  Is simultaneous submission of article to other journals permitted: No
  Exclusive manuscript rights between acceptance and publication: Yes
  Copyright: No copyright is involved as this is a government publication.
  Reprints: Not available.
Additional information: Also published quarterly in Spanish and Brazilian Portuguese
Disposition of manuscript:
  Query letter: No
  Receipt of manuscript acknowledged: Yes
  Decision to publish in: 3 weeks
  Accepted manuscript published in: 2-6 months
  Rejected manuscript returned: Yes
  Rejected manuscript criticized: No
Submit to:
  Colonel Eldon W. Downs, USAF
  (See address above)

SPECIAL STIPULATIONS
  Articles accepted for publication (if written by other than federal personnel on duty time) qualify for cash awards ranging from $40 to $100. The best article in each issue also receives a $50 prize and a plaque. Articles submitted for publication and written by U.S. military personnel on active duty require military clearance prior to publication.

ARMY [1318]
1529 18th Street, N.W.
Washington, D.C. 20036
(202) 483-1800

First published in 1950

SUBSCRIPTION DATA
Issues and rates: Published monthly.
  Average paid circulation: 92,000
  Annual rate(s): $10.00
Publisher or Sponsor: The Association of the U.S. Army
Managing Editor: M.T. Walker

EDITORIAL DESCRIPTION
  Publishes articles and editorial comment about military affairs.
Articles per average issue: 10
Audience: Professional military personnel
  Manuscripts accepted in English

MANUSCRIPT INFORMATION
Subject field(s): Military
Manuscript requirements: NYT
  Preferred length: Up to 3,000 words; typewritten
  Number of copies to be submitted: One
  Abstract: No
Author information and reprints: Payment: By publication to author. $.07- $.10 per word.
  Is simultaneous submission of article to other journals permitted: No
  Exclusive manuscript rights between acceptance and publication: Yes
  Copyright: Held by publication.
  Reprints: Not available.
Disposition of manuscript:
  Query letter: No
  Receipt of manuscript acknowledged: Yes
  Decision to publish in: Six weeks
  Accepted manuscript published in: Usually not more than three months
  Rejected manuscript returned: Yes
  Rejected manuscript criticized: Varies, depending on whether there are possibilities in rewrite.
Submit to:
  L. James Binder
  Editor-in-Chief
  (See address above)

DEFENSE MANAGEMENT JOURNAL [1319]
OASD(I&L) Cameron Station
Alexandria, Virginia 22314
(202) 274-7558

Previously entitled *Cost Reduction Journal*

First published in 1965

SUBSCRIPTION DATA
Issues and rates: Published quarterly.
  Average paid circulation: 3,628; 39,191 controlled
  Annual rate(s): $3.10; Foreign $3.90
Publisher or Sponsor: Office of the Secretary of Defense
Managing Editor: Robert F. Goerlich

EDITORIAL DESCRIPTION
  Seeks to stimulate management improvement and encourage administrative excellence through an interchange of ideas and techniques.
Articles per average issue: 12
Audience: Executive and supervisor levels
  Manuscripts accepted in English

MANUSCRIPT INFORMATION
Subject field(s): Management, defense weapon systems acquisition
Manuscript requirements: See latest issue for style requirements.
  Preferred length: 1500 to 2000 words
  Number of copies to be submitted: Four
  Abstract: No
Author information and reprints: Payment: None. Copies supplied to author.
  Is simultaneous submission of article to other journals permitted: Yes
  Exclusive manuscript rights between acceptance and publication: No
  Copyright: None
  Reprints: Not available.
Disposition of manuscript:
  Query letter: No
  Receipt of manuscript acknowledged: No
  Decision to publish in: 10 days
  Accepted manuscript published in: 3-6 months
  Rejected manuscript returned: Yes
  Rejected manuscript criticized: Yes
Submit to:
  Editor
  (See address above)

INFANTRY MAGAZINE [1320]
The Professional Magazine for Infantrymen
Post Office Box 2005
Fort Benning, Georgia 31905
(404) 545-5400

Previously entitled *The Mailing List*

First published in 1922

SUBSCRIPTION DATA
Issues and rates: Published bi-monthly.
  Average paid circulation: 15,000
  Annual rate(s): $5.95, Foreign $7.95
Publisher or Sponsor: U.S. Army Infantry School
Managing Editor: Ltc. Thomas J. Barham

EDITORIAL DESCRIPTION
  Contains current information on organization, weapons, equipment, tactics, and techniques and provides forum for progressive military thinking; to present the latest military developments and trends of particular interest to infantrymen.
Articles per average issue: 15
Audience: Infantry, U.S. Army
  Manuscripts accepted in English

MANUSCRIPT INFORMATION
Subject field(s): Weapons, equipment, training, tactics, foreign armies organization, employment, tactics, equipment
Manuscript requirements: MLA; AP
  Preferred length: 2,000 to 3,500 words
  Number of copies to be submitted: Original and copy
  Abstract: Not necessary.
Author information and reprints: Payment: By publication to author. At rate determined by Editor
  Is simultaneous submission of article to other journals permitted: No
  Exclusive manuscript rights between acceptance and publication: Yes
  Copyright: Not copyrighted
  Reprints: Available
Additional information: Include one-half page biographical sketch of author.
Disposition of manuscript:
  Receipt of manuscript acknowledged: Yes
  Decision to publish in: 30 days
  Accepted manuscript published in: 2 to 6 months
  Rejected manuscript returned: Yes, if self-addressed, stamped envelope is sent with manuscript.
  Rejected manuscript criticized: If requested
Submit to:
  Editor
  (See address above)

INTERCEPTOR [1321]
HQ ADC/SED, Box 46
Ent Air Force Base, Colorado 80912
(303) 635-8911 ext. 3186

SUBSCRIPTION DATA
Issues and rates: Published monthly.
  Average paid circulation: 7,000 controlled
Managing Editor: Kay Kiekhoefer

EDITORIAL DESCRIPTION
  Publishes flying safety articles related to military aircraft with applications to the entire flying community.
Articles per average issue: 8
Audience: Pilots
  Manuscripts accepted in English only

MANUSCRIPT INFORMATION
Subject field(s): Flying safety, limitations of man, supervision, management
Manuscript requirements: No specific style guide.
  Preferred length: 3-4 pages
  Number of copies to be submitted: One
  Abstract: No
Author information and reprints: Payment: None.
  Is simultaneous submission of article to other journals permitted: Simultaneous submission permitted but with separate publishing dates
  Exclusive manuscript rights between acceptance and publication: No
  Copyright: Held by author.
  Reprints: Available
Additional information: Any article printed in this publication can be printed in any other military magazine.
Disposition of manuscript:
  Query letter: No
  Receipt of manuscript acknowledged: Yes
  Decision to publish in: 1 week
  Accepted manuscript published in: 6 weeks
  Rejected manuscript returned: Yes
  Rejected manuscript criticized: Yes
Submit to:
  Editor
  (See address above)

MILITARY AFFAIRS [1322]
History Department
Kansas State University
Manhattan, Kansas 66506
(913) 532-6733

Previously entitled *Journal of the American Military History Society*

First published in 1937

SUBSCRIPTION DATA
Issues and rates: Published quarterly.
  Average paid circulation: 1,020; 100 controlled
  Annual rate(s): Individuals $10.00, Institutions $14.00
Publisher or Sponsor: American Military Institute
Managing Editor: Carol Brandt

EDITORIAL DESCRIPTION
  Contains scholarly articles on all aspects of military history plus academic intelligence, museums perspectives, bibliography of recent articles, and book reviews.
Articles per average issue: 5-6
Audience: Scholars, professionals and buffs
  Manuscripts accepted in English

MANUSCRIPT INFORMATION
Subject field(s): Military history broadly interpreted.
Manuscript requirements: See latest issue for style requirements.
  Preferred length: Not to exceed 5000 words
  Number of copies to be submitted: Three
  Abstract: No
Author information and reprints: Payment: None. 10 copies of issue.
  Is simultaneous submission of article to other journals permitted: No
  Exclusive manuscript rights between acceptance and publication: Yes
  Copyright: Held by publication.
  Reprints: Instructions on acceptance
Additional information: No illustrations, but maps or charts may be submitted
Disposition of manuscript:
  Query letter: No

Receipt of manuscript acknowledged: Yes
Decision to publish in: 2-3 months
Accepted manuscript published in: 9 months
Rejected manuscript returned: Yes
Rejected manuscript criticized: Yes
Submit to:
Robin Higham
Editor
(See address above)

MILITARY LAW REVIEW [1323]
The Judge Advocate General's School
Department of the Army
Charlottesville, Virginia 22901
(804) 293-7376

First published in 1958

SUBSCRIPTION DATA
Issues and rates: Published quarterly.
Average paid circulation: 2000; 6,000 controlled
Annual rate(s): $5.90, Foreign $7.45
Publisher or Sponsor: U.S. Department of the Army

EDITORIAL DESCRIPTION
Contains articles of direct interest to the military lawyer. Edited for those interested in military law to share the product of their experiences and research.
Articles per average issue: 5
Audience: Attorneys
Manuscripts accepted in English

MANUSCRIPT INFORMATION
Subject field(s): Any legal subject having some relevance to military law.
Manuscript requirements: See latest issue for style requirements.
Preferred length: 50 to 100 pages
Number of copies to be submitted: Two
Abstract: Yes, triple-spaced; footnotes conform to HLRA
Author information and reprints: Payment: None.
Is simultaneous submission of article to other journals permitted: No
Exclusive manuscript rights between acceptance and publication: Yes
Copyright: Held by publication.
Reprints: Not available.
Additional information: Triple space all copy.
Disposition of manuscript:
Query letter: No
Receipt of manuscript acknowledged: Yes
Decision to publish in: 3-4 weeks
Accepted manuscript published in: 2 months
Rejected manuscript returned: Yes
Rejected manuscript criticized: No
Submit to:
Editor
(See address above)

SPECIAL STIPULATIONS
The opinions and conclusions presented in the articles published do not necessarily represent the views of The Judge Advocate General's School or any other governmental agency.

MILITARY POLICE JOURNAL [1324]
Box 7500
Fort Gordon, Georgia 30905
(404) 791-6921

SUBSCRIPTION DATA
Issues and rates: Published monthly.
Average paid circulation: 12,000
Annual rate(s): $5.00, Foreign $7.00
Publisher or Sponsor: Military Police Association

EDITORIAL DESCRIPTION
Publication includes feature articles about law enforcement and current happenings in the Military Police Corps.

MANUSCRIPT INFORMATION
Subject field(s): Law enforcement in the armed forces
Manuscript requirements: Style sheet sent on request.
Preferred length: None
Number of copies to be submitted: By publication to author. $.01 per word.
Is simultaneous submission of article to other journals permitted: Yes
Exclusive manuscript rights between acceptance and publication: Yes
Copyright: Held by publication.
Reprints: Available, $3.00 per page
Disposition of manuscript:
Receipt of manuscript acknowledged: Yes
Decision to publish in: 1 month
Accepted manuscript published in: 2-3 months
Rejected manuscript returned: Yes, if self-addressed, stamped envelope is sent with manuscript.
Rejected manuscript criticized: No
Submit to:
Daniel R. Perry
Editor
(See address above)

MILITARY REVIEW [1325]
USACGSC
Fort Leavenworth, Kansas 66027
(913) 684-5642

First published in 1922

SUBSCRIPTION DATA
Issues and rates: Published monthly.
Average paid circulation: 7,500; 13,700 controlled
Annual rate(s): $6.00; Foreign $7.50
Publisher or Sponsor: United States Army Command and General Staff College
Managing Editor: Robert C. McDonald

EDITORIAL DESCRIPTION
Contains articles on national and military strategy, national defense affairs, international relations, military doctrine at the higher levels of command, organization, leadership and management.
Articles per average issue: 7
Audience: Students of military affairs
Manuscripts accepted in English

MANUSCRIPT INFORMATION
Subject field(s): Defense policy, leadership, management, strategy, logistics, weapons, foreign forces, tactics, defense economics, international affairs, great leaders, military history
Manuscript requirements: See latest issue for style requirements.
Preferred length: 3,000-5,000 words
Number of copies to be submitted: 2
Abstract: No
Author information and reprints: Payment: By publication to author. $50- $100 per article.
Is simultaneous submission of article to other journals permitted: No
Exclusive manuscript rights between acceptance and publication: Yes
Copyright: Held by author.
Reprints: Available, cost varies with number
Additional information: Typewritten, double-spaced, on one side of standard-sized paper.
Disposition of manuscript:
Receipt of manuscript acknowledged: Yes
Decision to publish in: 2-4 weeks
Accepted manuscript published in: 3-4 months
Rejected manuscript returned: Yes
Rejected manuscript criticized: No
Submit to:
Editor
(See address above)

NATIONAL DEFENSE [1326]
The Journal of the American Defence Preparedness Association
819 Union Trust Building
Washington, D.C. 20005
(202) 347-7250

Previously entitled *Ordnance*

First published in 1920

SUBSCRIPTION DATA
Issues and rates: Published bi-monthly.
Average paid circulation: 34,000; 1,800 controlled
Annual rate(s): $8.00, Foreign $10.00
Publisher or Sponsor: The American Defence Preparedness Association

EDITORIAL DESCRIPTION
Designed to reflect the position and policy of the Association, which is a nonpartisan but conservative scientific, technical, educational, and non-profit-making association of individuals who support the concept of industrial preparedness for the national defense.
Articles per average issue: 8-10
Audience: Business, military
Manuscripts accepted in English

MANUSCRIPT INFORMATION
Subject field(s): Defense problems and policies (from authoritative spokesmen), domestic and foreign weapons and materiel, national security, strategy and tactics, new technology (materials, R&D,

etc.) related to national defense, foreign technology
Manuscript requirements: See latest issue for style requirements.
  Preferred length: 2,000 words typewritten, double-spaced
  Number of copies to be submitted: Two
  Abstract: Optional
Author information and reprints: Payment: By publication to author. $25 per page.
  Is simultaneous submission of article to other journals permitted: No
  Exclusive manuscript rights between acceptance and publication: Yes
  Copyright: Held by publication.
  Reprints: Available, cost depends on process used for reprint.
Additional information: Prefer a selection of 8 X 10 glossy photos, original line drawings or charts, unscreened, to select suitable illustrations for the layout. Figures for technical articles follow the same format: original art or clean, offset-reproducible copy, clearly referenced in the text or annotated by author for reference.
Disposition of manuscript:
  Query letter: Not necessary, but helpful.
  Receipt of manuscript acknowledged: Yes
  Decision to publish in: 4-8 weeks
  Accepted manuscript published in: 9 months average
  Rejected manuscript returned: Yes
  Rejected manuscript criticized: No
Submit to:
  R. E. Lewis
  Editor
  (See address above)

THE NATIONAL GUARDSMAN [1327]
1 Massachusetts Avenue N.W.
Washington, D.C. 20001
(202) 7-0341

First published in 1947

SUBSCRIPTION DATA
Issues and rates: Published monthly.
  Average paid circulation: 68,000
  Annual rate(s): $2.00, Foreign $2.50
Publisher or Sponsor: National Guard Association of the United States

EDITORIAL DESCRIPTION
Contains feature articles on military matters: defense policy, strategy, tactics, training, logistics, administration, unusual activities and accomplishments of individuals, with the focus on the Army National Guard and Air National Guard.
Articles per average issue: 2-4
Audience: Military officers
  Manuscripts accepted in English

MANUSCRIPT INFORMATION
Subject field(s): National defense, civil disturbance duty, disaster duty
Manuscript requirements: No specific style guide.
  Preferred length: Maximum 3,000 words
  Number of copies to be submitted: One
  Abstract: Optional

Author information and reprints: Payment: By publication to author. Up to $.05 per word.
  Is simultaneous submission of article to other journals permitted: No
  Exclusive manuscript rights between acceptance and publication: Yes
  Copyright: Held by publication.
  Reprints: Available at cost.
Additional information: Typewritten, double-spaced. Advise use certified or registered mail as insurance against loss.
Disposition of manuscript:
  Receipt of manuscript acknowledged: Yes
  Decision to publish in: 1 week
  Accepted manuscript published in: 2-6 months
  Rejected manuscript returned: Yes, if return postage is supplied by author.
  Rejected manuscript criticized: No
Submit to:
  Editor
  (See address above)

PARAMETERS [1328]
The Journal of the U.S. Army War College
U.S. Army War College
Carlisle Barracks, Pennsylvania 17013
(717) 245-4943

First published in 1971

SUBSCRIPTION DATA
Issues and rates: Published semi-annually.
  Average paid circulation: 5,800 controlled
Publisher or Sponsor: U.S. Army War College
Managing Editor: Col. Alfred J. Mock

EDITORIAL DESCRIPTION
Provides a vehicle for continuing education and professional development of War College graduates and other military officers and civilians concerned with military affairs.
Articles per average issue: 6
Audience: Military, government officials, civilian academicians

MANUSCRIPT INFORMATION
Manuscript requirements: Style sheet sent on request.
  Preferred length: 5,000-7,000 words
  Number of copies to be submitted: One
  Abstract: Yes.
Author information and reprints: Payment: By publication to author. Up to $50.00 per page.
  Is simultaneous submission of article to other journals permitted: No
  Exclusive manuscript rights between acceptance and publication: Yes
  Copyright: Held by author.
  Reprints: Available, 25 free and 5 issues
Disposition of manuscript:
  Query letter: Not necessary.
  Receipt of manuscript acknowledged: Yes
  Decision to publish in: 2-8 weeks
  Accepted manuscript published in: 3-6 months
  Rejected manuscript returned: Yes
  Rejected manuscript criticized: No

Submit to:
  Editor
  (See address above)

ROYAL UNITED SERVICES INSTITUTE FOR DEFENCE STUDIES JOURNAL [1329]
Whitehall
London SW1A 2ET, England
01-930-5854

First published in 1857

SUBSCRIPTION DATA
Issues and rates: Published quarterly.
  Average paid circulation: 6,250
  Annual rate(s): £4.80.
Publisher or Sponsor: Royal United Services Institute for Defence Studies
Managing Editor: R.G.S. Bidwell

EDITORIAL DESCRIPTION
Contains articles on defence and military matters, military history, reviews of military books. For the study of British defence and overseas policy and for the promotion and advancement of the science and literature of the services.
Articles per average issue: 12
Audience: Those interested in and working in the field of defence, military

MANUSCRIPT INFORMATION
Subject field(s): Defence, military history
Manuscript requirements: See latest issue for style requirements. "Times" style
  Preferred length: 3000-5000 words maximum
  Number of copies to be submitted: Two
  Abstract: No
Author information and reprints: Payment: By publication to author. £5.00 per 1,000 words
  Is simultaneous submission of article to other journals permitted: No. Only original material considered for publication
  Exclusive manuscript rights between acceptance and publication: Yes
  Copyright: Available, cost on request
  Reprints: Available, only at time of printing
Additional information: Illustrative material to be supplied separately with indication on manuscript for positioning.
Disposition of manuscript:
  Query letter: No
  Receipt of manuscript acknowledged: Yes
  Decision to publish in: 2-4 weeks
  Accepted manuscript published in: Minimum of 3 months
  Rejected manuscript returned: Yes, if return postage is supplied by author.
  Rejected manuscript criticized: Sometimes
Submit to:
  R.G.S. Bidwell
  (See address above)

Political science

Political science

THE ACTIVIST [1330]
A Student Journal of Politics and Opinion
Box 29
Oberlin, Ohio 44074

SUBSCRIPTION DATA
Issues and rates: Published semi-annually.
  Average paid circulation: 500; 2000 controlled
  Annual rate(s): Individuals $2.00, Institutions $1.50, Foreign $3.00
Managing Editor: Lucille J. Schwartz

EDITORIAL DESCRIPTION
  Contains articles on political issues facing the Left; book reviews; some literary pieces with political significance. Student-run independent of student opinion in the U.S.
Articles per average issue: 6

MANUSCRIPT INFORMATION
Subject field(s): Left strategy, political economy, social history, socialist feminism, radical perspectives in the arts
Manuscript requirements: No specific style guide.
  Preferred length: 2500-5000 words; 5 to 20 pages
  Number of copies to be submitted: One
Author information and reprints: Payment: None.
  Is simultaneous submission of article to other journals permitted: Yes
  Exclusive manuscript rights between acceptance and publication: No
  Copyright: Held by author.
  Reprints: Not available.
Additional information: Publication reserves the right to edit.
Disposition of manuscript:
  Query letter: No
  Receipt of manuscript acknowledged: No
  Decision to publish in: 2 months
  Accepted manuscript published in: 3 months
  Rejected manuscript returned: Yes, if return postage is supplied by author.
  Rejected manuscript criticized: No
Submit to:
  Editor
  (See address above)

AMERICAN JOURNAL OF POLITICAL SCIENCE [1331]
Quarterly Journal of the Midwest Political Science Association
Department of Political Science
Ohio State University
Columbus, Ohio 43210
(614) 422-5358

Previously entitled *Midwest Journal of Political Science*

First published in 1957

SUBSCRIPTION DATA
Issues and rates: Published quarterly.
  Average paid circulation: 2,500
  Annual rate(s): $15.00, Students $6.00, Members $12.00, Foreign $15.75
Publisher or Sponsor: Midwest Political Science Association

EDITORIAL DESCRIPTION
  A general journal of political science. Open to all members of the political science profession, and to all areas of the discipline of political science.
Articles per average issue: 10
Audience: Professional political scientists
  Manuscripts accepted in English

MANUSCRIPT INFORMATION
Subject field(s): Comparative politics, American politics, political theory, international politics, public administration, research methods
Manuscript requirements: Style sheet sent on request.
  Preferred length: 20-25 pages
  Number of copies to be submitted: Three
  Abstract: Yes, all references to author should be excised from 2 copies.
Author information and reprints: Payment: None.
  Is simultaneous submission of article to other journals permitted: No
  Exclusive manuscript rights between acceptance and publication: Yes
  Copyright: Held by publication.
  Reprints: Available, 25 free
Disposition of manuscript:
  Query letter: No
  Receipt of manuscript acknowledged: Yes
  Decision to publish in: Average time 2 months
  Accepted manuscript published in: 12-15 months
  Rejected manuscript returned: No
  Rejected manuscript criticized: Yes
Submit to:
  John H. C. Kessel
  Editor
  (See address above)

AMERICAN OPINION [1332]
395 Concord Avenue
Belmont, Massachusetts 02178
(617) 489-0600

First published in 1958

SUBSCRIPTION DATA
Issues and rates: Published monthly.
  Average paid circulation: 40,000
  Annual rate(s): $10, Foreign $12
Managing Editor: Scott Stanley, Jr.

EDITORIAL DESCRIPTION
  Features articles dealing with contemporary political affairs, book reviews, and poetry.
Articles per average issue: 6
Audience: Conservative
  Manuscripts accepted in English

MANUSCRIPT INFORMATION
Subject field(s): Conservative politics
Manuscript requirements: See latest issue for style requirements.
  Preferred length: 3,000 words
  Number of copies to be submitted: one
  Abstract: No
Author information and reprints: Payment: By publication to author. $25 per page.
  Is simultaneous submission of article to other journals permitted: No
  Exclusive manuscript rights between acceptance and publication: Yes
  Copyright: Held by publication.
  Reprints: Available
Additional information: Manuscripts should be double-spaced.
Disposition of manuscript:
  Query letter: Desirable
  Receipt of manuscript acknowledged: No
  Decision to publish in: 2 months
  Accepted manuscript published in: 2-3 months
  Rejected manuscript returned: Yes, if return postage is supplied by author.
  Rejected manuscript criticized: No
Submit to:
  Managing Editor
  (See address above)

THE AMERICAN POLITICAL SCIENCE REVIEW [1333]
1527 New Hampshire Avenue, N.W.
Washington, D.C. 20036
(202) 483-2512

First published in 1906

SUBSCRIPTION DATA
Issues and rates: Published quarterly.
  Average paid circulation: 18,000
  Annual rate(s): $50.00
Publisher or Sponsor: The American Political Science Association
Managing Editor: Nelson W. Polsby

EDITORIAL DESCRIPTION
  Contains scholarly articles and book reviews within the discipline of political science.
Articles per average issue: 10
Audience: political scientists, specifically

MANUSCRIPT INFORMATION
Subject field(s): All areas of political science
Manuscript requirements: See latest issue for style requirements.
  Number of copies to be submitted: Two
Author information and reprints: Payment: None.
  Is simultaneous submission of article to other journals permitted: Yes, if noted that it is being done
  Exclusive manuscript rights between acceptance and publication: Yes
  Copyright: Held by American Political Science Association
  Reprints: Available
Disposition of manuscript:
  Query letter: No
  Receipt of manuscript acknowledged: Yes
  Decision to publish in: 3 months

Accepted manuscript published in: One Year
Rejected manuscript returned: Yes
Rejected manuscript criticized: Yes
Submit to:
Nelson W. Polsby
Department of Political Science
University of California
Berkeley, California 94720
(415) 642-1017

AMERICAN POLITICS QUARTERLY [1334]
Sage Publications, Inc.
275 South Beverly Drive
Beverly Hills, California 90212
(213) 274-2423

First published in 1973

SUBSCRIPTION DATA
Issues and rates: Published quarterly.
Average paid circulation: Not available.
Annual rate(s): Institutions $18.00; Individuals $12.00; Students $9.00; Foreign individuals $13.00; Foreign institutions 19.00

EDITORIAL DESCRIPTION
Publishes basic research in all areas of American government
Articles per average issue: 5
Audience: Professional, academic, general
Manuscripts accepted in English

MANUSCRIPT INFORMATION
Subject field(s): Urban, state, and national politics, political parties, public opinion, political theory, legislative behavior, the legal process, administrative organizations, intergovernmental relations.
Manuscript requirements: Style sheet sent on request.
Preferred length: 6,250-7,500 words; 25 to 30 pages
Number of copies to be submitted: 3
Abstract: No
Author information and reprints: Payment: Reprints only. 25 tear-sheets
Is simultaneous submission of article to other journals permitted: Permitted, but not encouraged; author must notify publisher that manuscript is under consideration elsewhere.
Exclusive manuscript rights between acceptance and publication: Yes
Copyright: Held by publication.
Reprints: Available if purchased by special order in amounts no fewer than 100
Disposition of manuscript:
Query letter: No
Receipt of manuscript acknowledged: Yes
Decision to publish in: 6-8 weeks
Accepted manuscript published in: 6-9 months
Rejected manuscript returned: Yes
Rejected manuscript criticized: Yes
Submit to:
Harlan Hanh
Editor
Department of Political Science
University of Southern California
Los Angeles, California 90007
(213) 746-2653

CALIFORNIA JOURNAL [1335]
The Monthly Report on State Government and Politics
1617 10th Street
Sacramento, California 95814
(916) 444-2840

First published in 1970

SUBSCRIPTION DATA
Issues and rates: Published monthly.
Average paid circulation: 6,500
Annual rate(s): Individuals $15.00; Institutions $30.00
Publisher or Sponsor: California Center for Research and Education in Government
Managing Editor: Ed Salzman

EDITORIAL DESCRIPTION
Objective reporting and analysis of issues, events and politics in California
Articles per average issue: Varies; 2-4
Audience: Those with an interest in California government and politics
Manuscripts accepted in English

MANUSCRIPT INFORMATION
Manuscript requirements: See latest issue for style requirements.
Preferred length: 1,000-4,000 words; 1-5 pages
Number of copies to be submitted: 1
Abstract: Not necessary.
Author information and reprints: Payment: By publication to author. $50.00 per page.
Is simultaneous submission of article to other journals permitted: Permitted.
Exclusive manuscript rights between acceptance and publication: No
Copyright: Held by publication.
Reprints: Not available.
Disposition of manuscript:
Query letter: Not necessary, but advisable.
Receipt of manuscript acknowledged: Yes
Decision to publish in: 2 weeks
Accepted manuscript published in: 2 months
Rejected manuscript returned: Yes, with return postage paid by publication.
Rejected manuscript criticized: Sometimes
Submit to:
Ed Salzman
Editor
(See address above)

COMPARATIVE POLITICS [1336]
City University of New York Graduate Center
33 West 42nd Street, Room 908
New York, New York 10036
(212) 790-4248

First published in 1968

SUBSCRIPTION DATA
Issues and rates: Published quarterly.
Average paid circulation: 2,200, complimentary and exchange 41
Annual rate(s): Students $7, Individuals $10, Foreign individuals $11, Foreign institutions $17, Institutions $15
Publisher or Sponsor: City University of New York
Managing Editor: Margaret C. Bayldon

EDITORIAL DESCRIPTION
Contains articles, research notes, and review articles devoted to comparative analysis of political institutions and behavior. The journal is open to all schools of thought and trends within the discipline.
Articles per average issue: About 5, plus research notes and review of articles
Audience: Political sciences, international relations, related field

MANUSCRIPT INFORMATION
Manuscript requirements: Style sheet sent on request.
Preferred length: 6,000-9,000 words; 25-35 pages
Number of copies to be submitted: Three
Abstract: Not necessary, manuscripts published are abstracted in *International Political Science Abstracts*
Author information and reprints: Payment: None. $50.00 honorarium for requested review articles.
Is simultaneous submission of article to other journals permitted: No
Exclusive manuscript rights between acceptance and publication: Yes
Copyright: Held by publication.
Reprints: 50 free to authors, more available at cost, depending on length of article.
Additional information: Style sheet sould be requested before submission of manuscripts; footnotes, references, tables and charts on separate pages. For anonymous editorial evaluation author's name and affiliation should appear only on a separate cover page.
Disposition of manuscript:
Query letter: No
Receipt of manuscript acknowledged: Yes
Decision to publish in: 2-3 months
Accepted manuscript published in: 9-12 months
Rejected manuscript returned: Yes
Rejected manuscript criticized: Yes
Submit to:
Managing Editor
(See address above)
(212) 790-4249

EUROPEAN JOURNAL OF POLITICAL RESEARCH [1337]
Elsevier Scientific Publishing Company
P. O. Box 211, Jan van Galenstraat 335
Amsterdam, The Netherlands
(20) 515-9222

First published in 1973

SUBSCRIPTION DATA
Issues and rates: Published quarterly.

Average paid circulation: 600
Annual rate(s): Individuals $18.00;
Institutions $32.50
Publisher or Sponsor: The European
Consortium for Political Research
Managing Editor: Arend Lyphart

EDITORIAL DESCRIPTION

Fosters communication and collaboration
among political scientists and the
dissemination of research findings and
information across national and linquistic
boundaries
Articles per average issue: 4
Audience: Academics, political scientists
Manuscripts accepted in English

MANUSCRIPT INFORMATION

Manuscript requirements: Style sheet sent
on request. Chicago
Preferred length: 8,000 words maximum
Number of copies to be submitted: 3
Abstract: Yes. Maximum of 200 words
Author information and reprints: Payment:
Reprints only. 50 reprints
Is simultaneous submission of article to
other journals permitted: Not permitted.
Exclusive manuscript rights between
acceptance and publication: Yes
Copyright: Held by publication, but later
publication elsewhere is permitted
Reprints: Available at cost

Disposition of manuscript:
Query letter: Not necessary.
Receipt of manuscript acknowledged: Yes
Decision to publish in: 2 months
Accepted manuscript published in: 6-8
months
Rejected manuscript returned: Yes, if
return postage is supplied by author.
Rejected manuscript criticized: Reasons
for rejections only

Submit to:
Arend Lyphart
Editor-in-Chief
Department of Political Science,
University of Leyden
27 Hugo de Grootstraat
Leyden, The Netherlands
(71) 49641

FOREIGN AFFAIRS* [1338]
58 East 68th Street
New York, New York 10021

SUBSCRIPTION DATA

Issues and rates: Published quarterly.
Average paid circulation: 70,000
Annual rate(s): $10.00

EDITORIAL DESCRIPTION

Publishes articles on the political,
economic and social aspects of U.S.
foreign policy.

MANUSCRIPT INFORMATION

Subject field(s): Politics, economics, U.S.
foreign policy
Manuscript requirements: See latest issue for
style requirements.
Preferred length: 4000-5000 words
Number of copies to be submitted: One

Author information and reprints: Payment:
By publication to author. $250 per
article.
Copyright: Held by publication.
Reprints: Available at cost
Disposition of manuscript:
Receipt of manuscript acknowledged: Yes
Decision to publish in: 2-3 weeks
Accepted manuscript published in: Varies
Submit to:
Editor
(See address above)

FOREIGN SERVICE
JOURNAL [1339]
2101 E Street NW
Washington, D.C. 20037
(202) 338-4045

Previously entitled *American Consular
Bulletin*

First published in 1919

SUBSCRIPTION DATA

Issues and rates: Published monthly.
Average paid circulation: 8,500; 500
controlled
Annual rate(s): $6.00; Foreign $7.00
Publisher or Sponsor: American Foreign
Service Association
Managing Editor: Shirley R. Newhall

EDITORIAL DESCRIPTION

Contents include diplomacy, foreign
affairs, foreign policy; the internal and
external operations of the foreign affairs
agencies. Publication is directed toward
fostering an *esprit de corps* among
foreign affairs personnel.
Articles per average issue: 5
Audience: Employees of the foreign affairs
agencies of the U.S. and others with
interest in diplomacy and foreign affairs
Manuscripts accepted in English

MANUSCRIPT INFORMATION

Subject field(s): Making of foreign policy,
diplomatic studies, administration,
personnel, history, literature
Manuscript requirements: See latest issue for
style requirements.
Preferred length: 2500-3500 words
Number of copies to be submitted: One
Abstract: No
Author information and reprints: Payment:
By publication to author. $.02 per word.
Is simultaneous submission of article to
other journals permitted: No
Exclusive manuscript rights between
acceptance and publication: No
Copyright: Held by publication, but
assigned or transferred to author on
request
Reprints: Available, at cost
Disposition of manuscript:
Query letter: No
Receipt of manuscript acknowledged: Yes
Decision to publish in: 2-4 weeks
Accepted manuscript published in: 1-6
months

Rejected manuscript returned: Yes, if
self-addressed, stamped envelope is sent
with manuscript.
Rejected manuscript criticized: Yes
Submit to:
Editor
(See address above)

SPECIAL STIPULATIONS

Much of publication's material is received
from people actively working in the
foreign affairs field, but it welcomes
informative material from others.

GLOBAL DIALOGUE [1340]
11 Fifth Avenue
P.O. Box 385
Pelham, New York 10803
(914) 738-0321

First published in 1968

SUBSCRIPTION DATA

Issues and rates: Published monthly.
Average paid circulation: Not available.
Annual rate(s): Individuals $8.00
Managing Editor: E. Weinfeld

EDITORIAL DESCRIPTION

Publishes articles on international
relations, economic topics, social
questions; ecology.
Articles per average issue: varies
Audience: Colleges, high schools, public
libraries, institutions, individuals
Manuscripts accepted in English

MANUSCRIPT INFORMATION

Subject field(s): Economics, Common
Market, free trade, power blocks, balance
of power, birth control and church,
former colonies, Japan and its policy,
Japan and its economics, China, ecology
Manuscript requirements: Lively as opposed
to textbook-presentation
Preferred length: 6,000 to 10,000 words
Number of copies to be submitted: 2
Abstract: Not necessary
Author information and reprints: Payment:
None.
Is simultaneous submission of article to
other journals permitted: No
Exclusive manuscript rights between
acceptance and publication: Yes
Copyright: Held by publication.
Reprints: Up to 20 available at no cost,
additional copies at cost
Additional information: Author's name and
affiliation will appear if article published.
Disposition of manuscript:
Query letter: No
Receipt of manuscript acknowledged: No
Decision to publish in: 1-2 months
Accepted manuscript published in: 2-6
months
Rejected manuscript returned: Yes, if
self-addressed, stamped envelope is sent
with manuscript.
Rejected manuscript criticized:
Occasionally
Submit to:
Editor
(See address above)

SPECIAL STIPULATIONS
Publication is not party oriented, and is therefore not interested in manuscripts which attempt to influence votes.

INSTANT RESEARCH ON PEACE AND VIOLENCE [1341]

Tammelanpuistokatu 58 B
33100 Tampere 10, Finland
931 23571

First published in 1971

SUBSCRIPTION DATA
Issues and rates: Published quarterly.
Average paid circulation: 350; 700 controlled
Annual rate(s): Individuals $5.00, Institutions $7.00
Publisher or Sponsor: Tampere Peace Research Institute
Managing Editor: Unto Vesa

EDITORIAL DESCRIPTION
Concentrates on actual problems from the point of view of peace research. Theme issues thus far: Indochina; Southern Africa; European security and cooperation; disarmament; ocean policies; international humanitarian law; conventional weaponry ban, etc.
Articles per average issue: 4-5
Audience: Academic, journalists, peace movement
Manuscripts accepted in English

MANUSCRIPT INFORMATION
Subject field(s): Peace research, international politics, political science, economics, sociology, philosophy, etc.
Manuscript requirements: See latest issue for style requirements.
Preferred length: 15-25 pages
Number of copies to be submitted: Two
Abstract: No
Author information and reprints: Payment: None.
Is simultaneous submission of article to other journals permitted: Yes
Exclusive manuscript rights between acceptance and publication: No
Copyright: Held by author.
Reprints: Available
Disposition of manuscript:
Query letter: No
Receipt of manuscript acknowledged: No
Decision to publish in: 2-8 weeks
Accepted manuscript published in: 2-4 months
Rejected manuscript returned: Yes
Rejected manuscript criticized: Yes
Submit to:
Raimo Vëayrynen
Editor-in-Chief
(See address above)

INTERNATIONAL SOCIALIST REVIEW [1342]

14 Charles Lane
New York, New York 10014
(212) 929-3486

Previously entitled *New International; Fourth International*

First published in 1934

SUBSCRIPTION DATA
Issues and rates: Published monthly.
Average paid circulation: 8,000
Annual rate(s): $5.00, Foreign $6.00
Managing Editor: Les Evans

EDITORIAL DESCRIPTION
A monthly Marxist journal with articles on contemporary politics, national and international. Accepts articles on Marxist economics, good muckraking journalism, feminism, and literary criticism of social significance. While views expressed in signed articles are the responsibility of the authors, editorial policy encourages the building of an independent socialist movement in the United States, in opposition to the Democratic and Republican parties. In regard to international politics, the magazine is critical of the bureaucratic regimes of The Soviet Union and China.
Articles per average issue: 5-6
Audience: Radical political milieu, trade unionists, college students
Manuscripts accepted in English, French or Spanish preferred. Publish in English. Will translate if article is accepted for publication.

MANUSCRIPT INFORMATION
Subject field(s): Political analysis, economics, The Black movement, etc.
Manuscript requirements: Style sheet sent on request.
Preferred length: Up to 50 pages, triple-spaced
Number of copies to be submitted: One
Abstract: No
Author information and reprints: Payment: None.
Is simultaneous submission of article to other journals permitted: No
Exclusive manuscript rights between acceptance and publication: Yes
Copyright: Held by publication. unless otherwise specified by author
Reprints: Up to 30 copies
Disposition of manuscript:
Query letter: No, but it is suggested
Receipt of manuscript acknowledged: Yes
Decision to publish in: 2 weeks
Accepted manuscript published in: 3 months, sometimes less.
Rejected manuscript returned: Yes, if return postage is supplied by author.
Rejected manuscript criticized: on request
Submit to:
Les Evans
Editor
(See address above)

JOURNAL OF CONFLICT RESOLUTION [1343]

Research on War and Peace between and within Nations
Sage Publications, Inc.
275 South Beverly Drive
Beverly Hills, California 90212
(213) 274-2423

First published in 1957

SUBSCRIPTION DATA
Issues and rates: Published quarterly.
Average paid circulation: Not available.
Annual rate(s): Individuals $14.40; Institutions $24.00; Foreign individuals $15.50; Foreign institutions $25.00

EDITORIAL DESCRIPTION
Publishes social-scientific research and theory on human conflict. The journal's primary focus is on international conflict within as well as between nations, that may help in understanding problems of war and peace.
Articles per average issue: 8
Audience: Interdisciplinary social scientists
Manuscripts accepted in English

MANUSCRIPT INFORMATION
Subject field(s): International conflict, intra-nation conflict, inter-group conflict, peace research, gaming and simulation
Manuscript requirements: Style sheet sent on request.
Preferred length: 6,000 to 9,000 words; 25 to 30 pages
Number of copies to be submitted: Three
Abstract: Yes, of 150 words maximum
Author information and reprints: Payment: Reprints only. 24 reprints and two copies of the issue in which article appears.
Is simultaneous submission of article to other journals permitted: No
Exclusive manuscript rights between acceptance and publication: Yes
Copyright: Held by publication.
Reprints: available at cost
Additional information: Manuscripts should be in proper style, with footnotes, references, tables and charts on separate pages. Author's name and affiliation should appear only on a separate page.
Disposition of manuscript:
Receipt of manuscript acknowledged: Yes
Decision to publish in: 6-8 weeks
Accepted manuscript published in: 6-9 months
Rejected manuscript returned: Yes
Rejected manuscript criticized: Sometimes
Submit to:
Bruce M. Russett
Editor
Department of Political Science
Yale University
124 Prospect Street
New Haven, Connecticut 06520
(203) 436-0187

MATCHBOX [1344]

An International Journal on Human Rights
3618 Sacramento Street
San Francisco, California 94114
(415) 563-3733

First published in 1974

SUBSCRIPTION DATA

Issues and rates: Published quarterly.
  Average paid circulation: 20,000 controlled
  Annual rate(s): Institutions $15.00; Students $10.00; Members $15.00
Publisher or Sponsor: Amnesty International of the U.S.A.

EDITORIAL DESCRIPTION

An international journal on human rights, it deals specifically with those who have been imprisoned, tortured or killed for nonviolently expressing their beliefs or exercising their rights guaranteed under the Universal Declaration of Human Rights of the United Nations.

Articles per average issue: 4-10
Audience: Membership, general
  Manuscripts accepted in English only

MANUSCRIPT INFORMATION

Subject field(s): Prison conditions, political prisoners (non-violent) outside the U.S.; The majority of the information is cleared through Amnesty-London
Manuscript requirements: MLA
  Preferred length: 2,000-3,00 words
  Number of copies to be submitted: 1
  Abstract: Not necessary.
Author information and reprints: Payment: Reprints only. 2 copies, more on request
  Is simultaneous submission of article to other journals permitted: Permitted, only when advised of it
  Exclusive manuscript rights between acceptance and publication: Yes
  Copyright: Held by author.
  Reprints: Available at no cost.
Additional information: Articles regarding U.S. prisoners or lobbying for legislation are not accepted.
Disposition of manuscript:
  Query letter: Necessary.
  Receipt of manuscript acknowledged: Yes
  Decision to publish in: 2 months
  Accepted manuscript published in: 1-3 months
  Rejected manuscript returned: Yes, if return postage is supplied by author.
  Rejected manuscript criticized: Sometimes
Submit to:
  Grace L. Harwood
  Editor
  (See address above)

MONTHLY REVIEW [1345]

An Independent Socialist Magazine
62 West 14th Street
New York, New York 10011
(212) 691-2555

First published in 1949

SUBSCRIPTION DATA

Issues and rates: 11 issues per year
  Average paid circulation: 10,000
  Annual rate(s): Institutions $12.00, Individuals $9.00, Foreign $10.00

EDITORIAL DESCRIPTION

Contains articles on world affairs from a socialist and Marxist point of view; book reviews.

Articles per average issue: 6-8
  Manuscripts accepted in English, Spanish, French, German, Portuguese, Italian

MANUSCRIPT INFORMATION

Subject field(s): Economics, political science, sociology, analyses of capitalism, analyses of Third World struggles, problems of socialism
Manuscript requirements: Chicago
  Preferred length: 5,000 words maximum
  Number of copies to be submitted: Two
  Abstract: Not necessary
Author information and reprints: Payment: By publication to author. $50 per article. Book reviews: $25
  Is simultaneous submission of article to other journals permitted: No
  Exclusive manuscript rights between acceptance and publication: Yes
  Copyright: Held by publication.
  Reprints: Not available.
Disposition of manuscript:
  Query letter: Yes
  Receipt of manuscript acknowledged: Yes
  Decision to publish in: 2 months
  Accepted manuscript published in: 3 months
  Rejected manuscript returned: Yes
  Rejected manuscript criticized: No
Submit to:
  Harry Magdoff;
  Paul Sweezy
  Co-editors
  (See address above)

POLICY STUDIES JOURNAL [1346]

The Journal of the Policy Studies Organization
361 Lincoln Hall
University of Illinois
Urbana, Illinois 61801
(217) 359-2831 and
(703) 532-6021

First published in 1972

SUBSCRIPTION DATA

Issues and rates: Published quarterly.
  Average paid circulation: 1,200
  Annual rate(s): Individuals $6; Institutions $12
Publisher or Sponsor: Policy Studies Organization
Managing Editor: Stuart S. Nagel

EDITORIAL DESCRIPTION

Each issue has contained a section on "Organization and Journal Developments," a symposium on a policy studies topic, and "Comments from the Field."

Articles per average issue: 12
Audience: Political and social scientists also policy makers and appliers
  Manuscripts accepted in English

MANUSCRIPT INFORMATION

Subject field(s): Environment, civil liberties, economic regulation, elections, foreign policy, crime policy, education, poverty, policy administration, comparative policy, policy theory, research methods health, science policy, urban policy, research utilization, and policy studies teaching
Manuscript requirements: No specific style guide.
  Preferred length: 1500 words; 6 pages
  Number of copies to be submitted: Two
  Abstract: Not necessary
Author information and reprints: Payment: None.
  Is simultaneous submission of article to other journals permitted: Yes, if editor is informed
  Exclusive manuscript rights between acceptance and publication: Yes
  Copyright: Held by publication.
  Reprints: Not available.
Disposition of manuscript:
  Query letter: No
  Receipt of manuscript acknowledged: Yes
  Decision to publish in: One month
  Accepted manuscript published in: Three months
  Rejected manuscript returned: Yes
  Rejected manuscript criticized: Yes
Submit to:
  Stuart S. Nagel
  Coordinator
  (See address above)

THE POLITICAL QUARTERLY [1347]

48 Lanchester Road
London N6, England
01-883-1331

First published in 1930

SUBSCRIPTION DATA

Issues and rates: Published quarterly.
  Average paid circulation: 3,000
  Annual rate(s): £4

EDITORIAL DESCRIPTION

Contains articles on topical issues of politics and public administration, international as well as British. Basically radical but concerned with comment from every political viewpoint.

Articles per average issue: 8
  Manuscripts accepted in English

MANUSCRIPT INFORMATION

Subject field(s): Politics, government
Manuscript requirements: No specific style guide.
  Preferred length: 4,000 words
  Number of copies to be submitted: Two

Author information and reprints: Payment:
By publication to author. $7.50 per page.
Is simultaneous submission of article to
other journals permitted: No
Exclusive manuscript rights between
acceptance and publication: Yes
Copyright: Held by publication.
Reprints: Not available.
Disposition of manuscript:
Query letter: No
Receipt of manuscript acknowledged: Yes
Decision to publish in: 2 months
Accepted manuscript published in: 3
months
Rejected manuscript returned: Yes
Rejected manuscript criticized: No
Submit to:
Editor
(See address above)

POLITICAL SCIENCE QUARTERLY [1348]

The Academy of Political Science
2852 Broadway
New York, New York 10025
(212) 866-6754

First published in 1886

SUBSCRIPTION DATA

Issues and rates: Published quarterly.
Average paid circulation: 11,000
Annual rate(s): $14.00; Institutions
$17.00; Students $10.00. All include a
subscription to *Proceedings of the
Academy of Political Science*
Publisher or Sponsor: The Academy of
Political Science
Managing Editor: Demetrios Caraley

EDITORIAL DESCRIPTION

It provides a background of facts and
documented opinions that enables the
reader to make a contribution to any
discussion of today's most critical issues;
articles on contemporary and historical
aspects of government, politics, and
public affairs; book reviews
Articles per average issue: 6
Audience: Scholar, general
Manuscripts accepted in English

MANUSCRIPT INFORMATION

Manuscript requirements: Style sheet sent
on request.
Preferred length: 6,000 words
Number of copies to be submitted: 2
Abstract: Yes. Of 100-200 words
specifying the major themes and
conclusions of the article.
Author information and reprints: Payment:
Reprints only. 50 reprints and 3 issues
Is simultaneous submission of article to
other journals permitted: Not permitted.
Exclusive manuscript rights between
acceptance and publication: Yes
Copyright: Held by publication. reprint
permission is subject to author's approval
Reprints: Available at cost.

Additional information: Everything is to be
typewritten, double-spaced, with ample
margins, tables on separate pages,
author's name on separate page also.
Disposition of manuscript:
Query letter: Not necessary.
Receipt of manuscript acknowledged: Yes
Decision to publish in: 4-6 weeks
Accepted manuscript published in: 3
months
Rejected manuscript returned: Yes, if
return postage is supplied by author.
Rejected manuscript criticized:
Sometimes
Submit to:
Demetrios Caraley
Managing Editor
(See address above)

PS [1349]

American Political Science Association
1527 New Hampshire Avenue, N. W.
Washington, D. C. 20036
(202) 483-2512

SUBSCRIPTION DATA

Issues and rates: Published quarterly.
Annual rate(s): $50.00
Publisher or Sponsor: The American
Political Science Association
Managing Editor: Walter E. Beach

EDITORIAL DESCRIPTION

News of the association and articles on
subjects related to political science
Articles per average issue: 3-4
Audience: Political scientists and members
of the American Association of Political
Scientists
Manuscripts accepted in English

MANUSCRIPT INFORMATION

Subject field(s): All areas of political science
and related interests
Manuscript requirements: See latest issue for
style requirements.
Preferred length: No preference
Number of copies to be submitted: 2
Abstract: Not necessary.
Author information and reprints: Payment:
None.
Is simultaneous submission of article to
other journals permitted: Permitted, if
publication is informed
Exclusive manuscript rights between
acceptance and publication: Yes
Copyright: Held by the American
Political Science Association
Reprints: Available at no cost.
Additional information: Subscribers receive
both *PS* and *The American Political
Science Review*
Disposition of manuscript:
Query letter: Not necessary.
Receipt of manuscript acknowledged: Yes
Decision to publish in: 3 months
Accepted manuscript published in: 1 year
Rejected manuscript returned: Yes, if
return postage is supplied by author.
Rejected manuscript criticized: Yes
Submit to:
Walter E. Beach
Editor
(See address above)

PUBLIC POLICY [1350]

Littauer 119, Harvard University
Cambridge, Massachusetts 02138
(617) 495-2103

First published in 1940

SUBSCRIPTION DATA

Issues and rates: Published quarterly.
Average paid circulation: 1200
Annual rate(s): $10.00, Foreign $11.00

Publisher or Sponsor: Kennedy School of
Government

Managing Editor: David A. Wise;
Lawrence D. Brown

EDITORIAL DESCRIPTION

Contains articles about public policy
based on studies primarily in political
science and economics.
Articles per average issue: 6
Manuscripts accepted in English

MANUSCRIPT INFORMATION

Subject field(s): Any field in public policy

Manuscript requirements: See latest issue for
style requirements.
Preferred length: None
Number of copies to be submitted: 2
Abstract: No

Author information and reprints: Payment:
None.
Is simultaneous submission of article to
other journals permitted: No
Exclusive manuscript rights between
acceptance and publication: Yes
Copyright: Held by publication.
Reprints: Available

Disposition of manuscript:
Query letter: No
Receipt of manuscript acknowledged: Yes
Decision to publish in: 1-2 months
Accepted manuscript published in: 3-4
months
Rejected manuscript returned: Yes
Rejected manuscript criticized: Yes

Submit to:
Editor
(See address above)

THE REVIEW OF POLITICS [1351]

Box B
Notre Dame, Indiana 46556
(219) 283-6623

First published in 1939

SUBSCRIPTION DATA

Issues and rates: Published quarterly.
Average paid circulation: 2200; 400
controlled
Annual rate(s): $7.00, Foreign $7.50
Publisher or Sponsor: University of Notre
Dame

EDITORIAL DESCRIPTION

Devoted to the study of political realities
and to political community in an

Aristotelian sense. Articles and reviews present critical analyses of institutions and techniques. Distinctive emphasis is a concern with the philosophical and historical aspects of current problems.
Articles per average issue: 5
Audience: Scholars
Manuscripts accepted in English only

MANUSCRIPT INFORMATION

Manuscript requirements: Chicago
Preferred length: 5000-9000 words; 12 to 26 pages
Number of copies to be submitted: Two
Abstract: No
Author information and reprints: Payment: None. 2 copies of issue and 50 offprints of article
Is simultaneous submission of article to other journals permitted: No
Exclusive manuscript rights between acceptance and publication: Yes
Copyright: Held by publication.
Reprints: Available at cost
Disposition of manuscript:
Query letter: No
Receipt of manuscript acknowledged: Yes
Decision to publish in: 3 month
Accepted manuscript published in: 6-9 months
Rejected manuscript returned: Yes
Rejected manuscript criticized: Sometimes
Submit to:
Thomas Stritch
Editor
(See address above)

RISING UP ANGRY [1352]
Box 3746
Merchandise Mart
Chicago, Illinois 60654
(312) 472-1791

SUBSCRIPTION DATA

Issues and rates: Every 3 weeks
Average paid circulation: 17,500; 2,000 controlled
Annual rate(s): $5.00

EDITORIAL DESCRIPTION

Concerned especially with the lack of justice in the courts, lack of health care, with police brutality and the struggle for change.
Articles per average issue: 17
Audience: Working and poor people
Manuscripts accepted in English, Spanish

MANUSCRIPT INFORMATION

Subject field(s): Any topics that move the people closer to revolution and freedom.
Manuscript requirements: No specific style guide.
Preferred length: 1,000 words
Number of copies to be submitted: One
Abstract: No
Author information and reprints: Payment: None.
Is simultaneous submission of article to other journals permitted: Yes
Exclusive manuscript rights between acceptance and publication: No

Copyright: Held by publication.
Reprints: Not available.
Disposition of manuscript:
Query letter: No
Receipt of manuscript acknowledged: No
Decision to publish in: Varies
Accepted manuscript published in: Varies
Rejected manuscript returned: No
Rejected manuscript criticized: No
Submit to:
Editor
(See address above)

SAGE PROFESSIONAL PAPERS IN AMERICAN POLITICS [1353]
Sage Publications, Inc.
275 South Beverly Drive
Beverly Hills, California 90212
(213) 274-2423

First published in 1973

SUBSCRIPTION DATA

Issues and rates: 3 times per year. Each volume contains 12 papers which are released in groups of 4.
Average paid circulation: Not available.
Annual rate(s): Institutions $18; Individuals $12; Students $9; Foreign individuals $13; Foreign institutions $19

EDITORIAL DESCRIPTION

Publishes papers focusing on empirical research, or on methodological or theoretical concerns in such areas as public policy, political parties, public opinion, political socialization, legislative behavior, urban politics, judicial behavior, and the legal process.
Manuscripts accepted in English

MANUSCRIPT INFORMATION

Subject field(s): Political science, history, psychology, sociology
Manuscript requirements: Style sheet sent on request.
Preferred length: 12,000 to 36,000 words; 40-120 pages
Number of copies to be submitted: 2
Abstract: Optional
Author information and reprints: Payment: By publication to author. $100 per article.
Is simultaneous submission of article to other journals permitted: No
Exclusive manuscript rights between acceptance and publication: Yes
Copyright: Held by publication.
Reprints: Authors receive 25 copies of their own paper free
Disposition of manuscript:
Query letter: No
Receipt of manuscript acknowledged: Yes
Decision to publish in: 6-8 weeks
Accepted manuscript published in: 6-9 months months
Rejected manuscript returned: Yes
Rejected manuscript criticized: Yes
Submit to:
Randall B. Ripley
Editor
Department of Political Science

Ohio State University
Columbus, Ohio 43210

SAGE PROFESSIONAL PAPERS IN COMPARATIVE POLITICS* [1354]
Sage Publications, Inc.
275 South Beverly Drive
Beverly Hills, California 90212
(213) 274-2423

SUBSCRIPTION DATA

Issues and rates: 3 times per year; each volume contains 12 papers which are published in groups of 4.
Annual rate(s): Institutions $18; Individuals $12; Students $9; Foreign individuals $13; Foreign institutions $19

EDITORIAL DESCRIPTION

Contains cross-national or cross-cultural studies including case studies and abstract papers that formulate valid theoretical generalizations about the structures, behavior, and performance of politics.

MANUSCRIPT INFORMATION

Subject field(s): Political science
Manuscript requirements: Style sheet sent on request.
Preferred length: 12,000 to 36,000 words; 40-120 pages
Number of copies to be submitted: Three
Author information and reprints: Payment: By publication to author. $100 per article.
Is simultaneous submission of article to other journals permitted: No
Exclusive manuscript rights between acceptance and publication: Yes
Copyright: Held by publication.
Reprints: Authors receive 25 copies of their own papers free
Disposition of manuscript:
Receipt of manuscript acknowledged: Yes
Decision to publish in: Six to eight weeks
Accepted manuscript published in: Six to nine months
Rejected manuscript returned: Yes
Rejected manuscript criticized: Yes
Submit to:
Harry Eckstein
Editor
Center for International Affairs, Corwin Hall
Princeton University
Princeton, New Jersey 08540

SAGE PROFESSIONAL PAPERS IN INTERNATIONAL STUDIES [1355]
Sage Publications, Inc.
275 South Beverly Drive
Beverly Hills, California 90212
(213) 274-2423

SUBSCRIPTION DATA
Issues and rates: 3 times per year. Each volume contains 12 papers which are released in groups of 4.
Average paid circulation: Not available.
Annual rate(s): Institutions $18; Individuals $12; Students $9; Foreign individuals $13; Foreign institutions $19
Managing Editor: Vincent Davis, Maurice East

EDITORIAL DESCRIPTION
Concentrates on studies of theoretical or empirical significance in the field of international studies.

MANUSCRIPT INFORMATION
Subject field(s): International studies, politics, administration
Manuscript requirements: Style sheet sent on request.
Preferred length: 12,000 to 36,000 words; 50-120 double-spaced pages
Number of copies to be submitted: Three
Author information and reprints: Payment: By publication to author. $100 per article.
Is simultaneous submission of article to other journals permitted: No
Exclusive manuscript rights between acceptance and publication: Yes
Copyright: Held by publication.
Reprints: Authors receive 25 copies of their own paper free.
Disposition of manuscript:
Query letter: No
Receipt of manuscript acknowledged: Yes
Decision to publish in: 8-12 weeks
Accepted manuscript published in: 6-9 months
Rejected manuscript returned: Yes
Rejected manuscript criticized: Yes
Submit to:
Vincent Davis
Editor
Patterson School of Diplomacy
University of Kentucky
Lexington, Kentucky 40506
(606) 257-4667

SOCIALIST REVOLUTION [1356]
396 Sanchez Street
San Francisco, California 94114
(415) 621-7046

First published in 1969

SUBSCRIPTION DATA
Issues and rates: Published bi-monthly.
Average paid circulation: 5,000
Annual rate(s): $10.00; Foreign $11.00

EDITORIAL DESCRIPTION
Contains political and historical articles, Marxist in outlook.
Articles per average issue: 6
Audience: Academic
Manuscripts accepted in English

MANUSCRIPT INFORMATION
Subject field(s): History, culture, politics
Manuscript requirements: No specific style guide.
Preferred length: Varies
Author information and reprints: Payment: None.
Is simultaneous submission of article to other journals permitted: Yes
Exclusive manuscript rights between acceptance and publication: Yes
Copyright: Held by author.
Reprints: Not available.
Disposition of manuscript:
Query letter: No
Receipt of manuscript acknowledged: Yes
Decision to publish in: 2 months
Accepted manuscript published in: 6 months
Rejected manuscript returned: Yes, if self-addressed, stamped envelope is sent with manuscript.
Rejected manuscript criticized: Sometimes
Submit to:
Eli Zaretsky
Editor
(See address above)

STUDIES IN BURKE AND HIS TIME [1357]
Alfred University
Alfred, New York 14802
(607) 871-2256

Previously entitled *The Burke Newsletter*

First published in 1959

SUBSCRIPTION DATA
Issues and rates: Published three times per year.
Average paid circulation: 800
Annual rate(s): $7.00
Publisher or Sponsor: Alfred University
Managing Editor: Steven R. Phillips

EDITORIAL DESCRIPTION
Contains essays on Burke's life, thought, continuing influence, or milieu, on ideas which support or oppose Burke, or on other major figures or issues of the period 1750-1800.
Articles per average issue: 3
Audience: Academic
Manuscripts accepted in English

MANUSCRIPT INFORMATION
Subject field(s): Interdisciplinary
Manuscript requirements: See latest issue for style requirements.
Preferred length: 20 pages
Number of copies to be submitted: Two
Abstract: No
Author information and reprints: Payment: None.
Is simultaneous submission of article to other journals permitted: No
Exclusive manuscript rights between acceptance and publication: No
Copyright: None
Reprints: Available
Disposition of manuscript:
Query letter: No
Receipt of manuscript acknowledged: Yes
Decision to publish in: Two months
Accepted manuscript published in: One year
Rejected manuscript returned: Yes
Rejected manuscript criticized: Yes
Submit to:
Steven R. Phillips
Editor
(See address above)

STUDIES IN COMPARATIVE COMMUNISM [1358]
An International Interdisciplinary Journal
School of International Relations
University of Southern California
Los Angeles, California 90007
(213) 746-2651

First published in 1968

SUBSCRIPTION DATA
Issues and rates: Published quarterly.
Average paid circulation: Not available.
Annual rate(s): Institutions $16.00; Individuals $10.00
Publisher or Sponsor: University of Southern California, School of International Relations
Managing Editor: Peter Berton

EDITORIAL DESCRIPTION
Contains scholarly articles, review articles, research notes, documents, bibliographical section on political, economic, social and cultural developments in the Communist world; Communist movements in non-Communist countries. Preference is given to manuscripts which are comparative and interdisciplinary in nature.
Articles per average issue: 5-8
Audience: Professional
Manuscripts accepted in English

MANUSCRIPT INFORMATION
Subject field(s): Communist movement and ideology, countries and parties; not limited to intra-communist comparisons.
Manuscript requirements: See latest issue for style requirements. Style sheet sent on request.
Preferred length: Articles: 6,000-10,000 words
Number of copies to be submitted: 3 copies
Abstract: Yes
Author information and reprints: Payment: None. Free issue, also free reprints
Is simultaneous submission of article to other journals permitted: No
Exclusive manuscript rights between acceptance and publication: Yes
Copyright: Held by publication.
Reprints: Available, 25 free; additional at cost
Disposition of manuscript:
Query letter: No
Receipt of manuscript acknowledged: Yes
Decision to publish in: 1-3 months

Accepted manuscript published in: 3-18 months
Rejected manuscript returned: Yes, if self-addressed, stamped envelope is sent with manuscript.
Rejected manuscript criticized: Sometimes
Submit to:
For articles:
Peter A. Berton
Editor
(See address above)
(213) 746-6065

For review articles, research notes, and graduate student essays:
Rudolf L. Tokes
Associate Editor
Department of Political Science
University of Connecticut
Storrs, Connecticut 06268

TACTICS [1359]
P.O. Box 3541
Arlington, Virginia 22203
(703) 524-7857

First published in 1964

SUBSCRIPTION DATA
Issues and rates: Published monthly.
Average paid circulation: 1,750
Annual rate(s): $10

EDITORIAL DESCRIPTION
Contains articles on news analysis, focusing on attitudes, ideologies, tactics. The only professional publication in the cold-hot (psychological) war.
Articles per average issue: 4-6 articles, always in-depth by knowledgeable persons of influence
Manuscripts accepted in English only

MANUSCRIPT INFORMATION
Manuscript requirements: See latest issue for style requirements.
Preferred length: 1000-6000 words with preference for 2000-4000
Number of copies to be submitted: one
Abstract: No
Author information and reprints: Payment: By publication to author. $25 to $100 per article.
Is simultaneous submission of article to other journals permitted: No
Exclusive manuscript rights between acceptance and publication: Yes
Copyright: Held by publication.
Reprints: Available at specified rates
Disposition of manuscript:
Query letter: Preferred
Receipt of manuscript acknowledged: Yes
Decision to publish in: 2 weeks
Accepted manuscript published in: One or two issues ahead
Rejected manuscript returned: Yes, if return postage is supplied by author.
Rejected manuscript criticized: Yes
Submit to:
Edward Hunter
Editor
(See address above)

SPECIAL STIPULATIONS
Always use most common & simplest forms: Theater, not Theatre etc.

WESTERN POLITICAL QUARTERLY [1360]
214 Orson Spencer Hall
University of Utah
Salt Lake City, Utah 84112
(801) 581-7137

First published in 1948

SUBSCRIPTION DATA
Issues and rates: Published quarterly.
Average paid circulation: 2,300
Annual rate(s): $9.00; Institutions $15.00; Students $9.00; Foreign individuals $10.00; Foreign institutions $16.00
Publisher or Sponsor: Western Political Science Association
Managing Editor: Donald W. Hanson

EDITORIAL DESCRIPTION
Publishes articles in all areas, international and domestic, which are of interest to political scientists.
Articles per average issue: 9
Audience: Scholars, professionals
Manuscripts accepted in English only

MANUSCRIPT INFORMATION
Manuscript requirements: No specific style guide.
Preferred length: Not specified
Number of copies to be submitted: 2
Abstract: Yes. Of about 150 words briefly describing the article's content.
Author information and reprints: Payment: None.
Is simultaneous submission of article to other journals permitted: Permitted, but not encouraged.
Exclusive manuscript rights between acceptance and publication: No
Copyright: Held by the University of Utah
Reprints: Available at no cost. In multiples of 25
Additional information: Author's name and affiliation should appear on a separate cover page. All footnotes on a separate page.
Disposition of manuscript:
Query letter: Not necessary.
Receipt of manuscript acknowledged: Yes
Decision to publish in: 3 months
Accepted manuscript published in: 3-4 months
Rejected manuscript returned: Yes, with return postage paid by publication.
Rejected manuscript criticized: Yes
Submit to:
Donald W. Hanson
Editor
(See address above)

Psychology and mental health

Psychology and mental health

ADOLESCENT PSYCHIATRY [1361]
Annals of the American Society for Adolescent Psychiatry
24 Green Valley Road
Wallingford, Pennsylvania 19086
(215) LO 6-1054

First published in 1971

SUBSCRIPTION DATA
Issues and rates: Published annually.
  Average paid circulation: 4,000
  Annual rate(s): $17.50; Institutions $17.50; Students $12.00; Foreign individuals $19.00
Publisher or Sponsor: American Society for Adolescent Psychiatry

EDITORIAL DESCRIPTION
  An encyclopedic collection of papers on the clinical and research aspects of the adolescent and his development and growth.
Articles per average issue: 25-30
Audience: Professional, academic, etc.
  Manuscripts accepted in English

MANUSCRIPT INFORMATION
Manuscript requirements: Style sheet sent on request.
  Preferred length: 25-30 pages
  Number of copies to be submitted: Original and 3 copies
  Abstract: Not necessary.
Author information and reprints: Payment: None.
  Is simultaneous submission of article to other journals permitted: Not permitted.
  Exclusive manuscript rights between acceptance and publication: Yes
  Copyright: Held by publication.
  Reprints: Available at cost.
Disposition of manuscript:
  Query letter: Not necessary, but advisable.
  Receipt of manuscript acknowledged: Yes
  Decision to publish in: 2 months
  Accepted manuscript published in: 1 year
  Rejected manuscript returned: Yes, with return postage paid by publication.
  Rejected manuscript criticized: Sometimes
Submit to:
  Sherman C. Feinstein, M. D.
  Managing Editor
  741 St. Johns
  Highland Park, Illinois 60035
  (312) 433-0690

AMERICAN ACADEMY OF PSYCHOANALYSIS. JOURNAL [1362]
Periodicals Department, John Wiley & Sons, Inc.
605 Third Avenue
New York, New York 10016
(212) 867-9800

First published in 1973

SUBSCRIPTION DATA
Issues and rates: Published quarterly.
  Annual rate(s): Individuals $25.00; Members $13.00
Publisher or Sponsor: American Academy of Psychoanalysis
Managing Editor: Silvano Arieti, M.D.

EDITORIAL DESCRIPTION
  Is devoted to the psychoanalytic exploration of man in its broadest possible sense, without adherence to the tenets of any one school and is open to anyone with a contribution to make in this ever expanding field.
Articles per average issue: 7
Audience: Behavioral scientists
  Manuscripts accepted in English

MANUSCRIPT INFORMATION
Subject field(s): Changes occuring in society and culture which stimulate a re-evaluation of psychoanalytic theories; new biological and cultural innovations that are related to the human psyche
Manuscript requirements: Style sheet sent on request.
  Preferred length: 30 pages maximum
  Number of copies to be submitted: 3
  Abstract: Not necessary.
Author information and reprints: Payment: Reprints only. 20
  Is simultaneous submission of article to other journals permitted: Not permitted.
  Exclusive manuscript rights between acceptance and publication: Yes
  Copyright: Held by publication.
Disposition of manuscript:
  Query letter: Not necessary.
  Receipt of manuscript acknowledged: Yes
  Decision to publish in: 6 weeks
  Accepted manuscript published in: 3-5 months
  Rejected manuscript returned: Yes, with return postage paid by publication.
  Rejected manuscript criticized: Yes
Submit to:
  Silvano Arieti, M.D.
  Editor
  American Academy of Psychoanalysis
  40 Gramercy Park North
  New York, New York 10010
  (212) 477-4250

AMERICAN IMAGO [1363]
A Psychoanalytic Journal for Culture, Science and the Arts
Wayne State University Press
46 East 73rd Street
New York, New York 10021
(212) 879-8466

First published in 1939

SUBSCRIPTION DATA
Issues and rates: Published quarterly.
  Average paid circulation: 1,000
  Annual rate(s): $10.00
Managing Editor: Harry Slochower

EDITORIAL DESCRIPTION
  Contains articles on the application of psychoanalysis to the humanities.
Articles per average issue: 4-5
  Manuscripts accepted in English only

MANUSCRIPT INFORMATION
Subject field(s): Literature, art, sociology, philosophy, politics
Manuscript requirements: See latest issue for style requirements.
  Preferred length: 6,000-10,000 words; 20-30 pages
  Number of copies to be submitted: 2
  Abstract: Yes, see latest issue
Author information and reprints: Payment: None.
  Is simultaneous submission of article to other journals permitted: No
  Exclusive manuscript rights between acceptance and publication: Yes
  Copyright: Held by publication.
  Reprints: 25 reprints gratis, additional available, cost on request
Disposition of manuscript:
  Query letter: No
  Receipt of manuscript acknowledged: Yes
  Decision to publish in: 1-3 months
  Accepted manuscript published in: 6-9 months
  Rejected manuscript returned: Yes, if return postage is supplied by author.
  Rejected manuscript criticized: Yes
Submit to:
  Harry Slochower
  Editor-in-Chief
  (See address above)

AMERICAN JOURNAL OF ART THERAPY [1364]
Art in Education, Rehabilitation, and Psychotherapy
P.O. Box 4918
Washington, D.C. 20008
(202) 363-2638

Previously entitled *Bulletin of Art Therapy*

First published in 1961

SUBSCRIPTION DATA
Issues and rates: Published quarterly.
  Average paid circulation: 2300; 100 controlled
  Annual rate(s): $10.00, Foreign $12.00
Managing Editor: Elinor Ulman

EDITORIAL DESCRIPTION
  Deals with the visual arts as they contribute to human understanding and mental health. Contents regularly include new theoretical formulations, reports of research, case studies, descriptions of actual programs.

Articles per average issue: 3
Audience: Art therapists, art educators, psychologists, psychiatrists
Manuscripts accepted in English

MANUSCRIPT INFORMATION
Subject field(s): Art therapy: diagnostic and therapeutic applications; art in special education; rehabilitation through art; psychology and psychopathology of art; expressive therapies.
Manuscript requirements: See latest issue for style requirements.
  Preferred length: 10 to 20 pages
  Number of copies to be submitted: Two
Author information and reprints: Payment: None.
  Is simultaneous submission of article to other journals permitted: No
  Exclusive manuscript rights between acceptance and publication: Yes
  Copyright: Held by publisher.
  Reprints: Available at cost
Additional information: Illustrations may be considered in the form of slides or color prints but for publication they must be submitted as black and white glossy prints approximately 4 x 5 inches or larger.
Disposition of manuscript:
  Query letter: No
  Receipt of manuscript acknowledged: Yes
  Decision to publish in: 3 months
  Accepted manuscript published in: 9-12 months
  Rejected manuscript returned: Yes
  Rejected manuscript criticized: Yes
Submit to:
  Elinor Ulman
  Editor
  (See address above)

AMERICAN JOURNAL OF CLINICAL HYPNOSIS [1365]
Suite 218
2400 East Devon Avenue
Des Plaines, Illinois 60018
(312) 297-3317

First published in 1958

SUBSCRIPTION DATA
Issues and rates: Published quarterly.
  Average paid circulation: 3,400
  Annual rate(s): $12.00; Foreign $12.00; Institutions $12.00; Members $6.00
Publisher or Sponsor: American Society of Clinical Hypnosis
Managing Editor: Dr. William E. Edmonston, Jr.

EDITORIAL DESCRIPTION
Publishes original articles in clinical and experimental hypnosis in addition to brief clinical reports on the uses of hypnosis in cases, book reviews, and abstracts of current literature in the field.
Articles per average issue: 10
Audience: Professional
  Manuscripts accepted in English

MANUSCRIPT INFORMATION
Manuscript requirements: APA
  Preferred length: None
  Number of copies to be submitted: Original and 2 copies
  Abstract: Yes.
Author information and reprints: Payment: None.
  Is simultaneous submission of article to other journals permitted: Not permitted.
  Exclusive manuscript rights between acceptance and publication: Yes
  Copyright: Held by the Society
  Reprints: Available at cost.
Disposition of manuscript:
  Query letter: Not necessary.
  Receipt of manuscript acknowledged: Yes
  Decision to publish in: 1-3 months
  Accepted manuscript published in: 6-9 months
  Rejected manuscript returned: Yes, if return postage is supplied by author.
  Rejected manuscript criticized: Reasons for rejections only
Submit to:
  Dr. William E. Edmonston, Jr.
  Editor
  Department of Psychology
  Colgate University
  Hamilton, New York 13346
  (315) 824-4354

AMERICAN JOURNAL OF ORTHOPSYCHIATRY [1366]
1775 Broadway
New York, New York 10019
(212) 586-5690

SUBSCRIPTION DATA
Issues and rates: Published quarterly.
  Average paid circulation: 8300
  Annual rate(s): $16.00, Foreign $17.00
Publisher or Sponsor: American Orthopsychiatric Association, Inc.
Managing Editor: Ernest Herman

EDITORIAL DESCRIPTION
Contains articles especially concerned with preventive aspects of mental health
Articles per average issue: 18
Audience: Social and behavioral scientists; mental health workers
  Manuscripts accepted in English only

MANUSCRIPT INFORMATION
Subject field(s): Psychiatry, psychology, community mental health, social problems, learning and cognition, schools and mental health, urban problems
Manuscript requirements: See latest issue for style requirements.
  Preferred length: 5000-7000 words; 10 pages
  Number of copies to be submitted: Three
  Abstract: Yes
Author information and reprints: Payment: None.
  Is simultaneous submission of article to other journals permitted: No
  Exclusive manuscript rights between acceptance and publication: Yes
  Copyright: Held by publication.
  Reprints: Available

Disposition of manuscript:
  Query letter: No
  Receipt of manuscript acknowledged: Yes
  Decision to publish in: 3-4 months
  Accepted manuscript published in: Six months
  Rejected manuscript returned: Often, but not always
Submit to:
  Ernest Herman
  Managing Editor
  (See address above)

THE AMERICAN JOURNAL OF PSYCHIATRY [1367]
1700 18th Street, N.W.
Washington, D.C. 20009
(202) 232-7878

First published in 1844

SUBSCRIPTION DATA
Issues and rates: Published monthly.
  Average paid circulation: 27,878
  Annual rate(s): $18.00; Foreign $22.00; Canada and South America $19
Publisher or Sponsor: American Psychiatric Association
Managing Editor: Evelyn S. Myers

EDITORIAL DESCRIPTION
Contains scientific and other scholarly material of interest to psychiatrists: clinical, research, psychiatric education, health care, etc.
Articles per average issue: 3
Audience: Psychiatrists, other mental health professionals
  Manuscripts accepted in English

MANUSCRIPT INFORMATION
Subject field(s): Psychiatry, other mental health disciplines, health care
Manuscript requirements: See latest issue for style requirements.
  Preferred length: 10-12 pages
  Number of copies to be submitted: Two
  Abstract: Optional
Author information and reprints: Payment: None.
  Is simultaneous submission of article to other journals permitted: No
  Exclusive manuscript rights between acceptance and publication: Yes
  Copyright: Held by publication.
  Reprints: Available
Additional information: Rejection rate is 3 of 4 manuscripts submitted; only findings of high interest considered.
Disposition of manuscript:
  Query letter: No
  Receipt of manuscript acknowledged: Yes
  Decision to publish in: 3-4 months
  Accepted manuscript published in: 6 months
  Rejected manuscript returned: Yes
  Rejected manuscript criticized: Yes
Submit to:
  Francis J. Braceland
  Editor
  (See address above)

Psychology and mental health

THE AMERICAN JOURNAL OF PSYCHOLOGY [1368]
University of Illinois Press
Urbana, Illinois 61801
(217) 333-0955

First published in 1888

SUBSCRIPTION DATA
Issues and rates: Published quarterly.
  Average paid circulation: 3,200
  Annual rate(s): $15.00, Foreign $15.50
Publisher or Sponsor: University of Illinois
Managing Editor: Sharon Ferguson

EDITORIAL DESCRIPTION
  General experimental psychology; publishes reports of original research, shorter notes and discussions, and pertinent book reviews.
Articles per average issue: 17
Audience: Experimental psychologists
  Manuscripts accepted in English

MANUSCRIPT INFORMATION
Subject field(s): General experimental psychology
Manuscript requirements: APA
  Preferred length: None
  Number of copies to be submitted: Two
  Abstract: Yes
Author information and reprints: Payment: None.
  Is simultaneous submission of article to other journals permitted: No
  Exclusive manuscript rights between acceptance and publication: Yes
  Copyright: Held by publication.
  Reprints: Available to author at publication only
Disposition of manuscript:
  Query letter: No
  Receipt of manuscript acknowledged: Yes
  Decision to publish in: 1-3 months
  Accepted manuscript published in: One year
  Rejected manuscript returned: Yes, if return postage is supplied by author.
  Rejected manuscript criticized: Yes
Submit to:
  Lloyd G. Humphreys
  Editor
  Psychology Building
  University of Illinois at Urbana
  Champaign, Illinois 61820

AMERICAN PSYCHOANALYTIC ASSOCIATION JOURNAL [1369]
239 Park Avenue South
New York, New York 10003
(212) 621-2021

First published in 1953

SUBSCRIPTION DATA
Issues and rates: Published quarterly.
  Average paid circulation: 5,000
  Annual rate(s): $20.00; Institutions $30.00
Publisher or Sponsor: American Psychoanalytic Association

EDITORIAL DESCRIPTION
  Covers a broad scope of psychoanalysis including its applications to psychiatry, general medicine, sociology, education, etc.
Articles per average issue: Varies
Audience: Professional, scientific
  Manuscripts accepted in English

MANUSCRIPT INFORMATION
Subject field(s): Psychoanalysis, psychiatric education and research, application of psychoanalysis
Manuscript requirements: See latest issue for style requirements.
  Preferred length: None
  Number of copies to be submitted: Four
  Abstract: No
Author information and reprints: Payment: None.
  Is simultaneous submission of article to other journals permitted: No
  Exclusive manuscript rights between acceptance and publication: Yes
  Copyright: Held by publication.
  Reprints: Available
Additional information: Very long manuscripts may be considered for a monograph.
Disposition of manuscript:
  Query letter: Yes
  Receipt of manuscript acknowledged: Yes
  Decision to publish in: 6 weeks
  Accepted manuscript published in: Within one year
  Rejected manuscript returned: Yes
  Rejected manuscript criticized: Yes
Submit to:
  Harold P. Blum
  Editor
  23 The Hemlocks
  Roslyn Estates, New York 11576
  (516) 621-3215

AMERICAN PSYCHOLOGIST [1370]
American Psychological Association
1200 17th Street, N.W.
Washington, D.C. 20036
(202) 833-7670

SUBSCRIPTION DATA
Issues and rates: Published monthly.
  Annual rate(s): $12.00, Members $5.00, Foreign $13.00
Publisher or Sponsor: American Psychological Association

EDITORIAL DESCRIPTION
  The official publication of the association contains archival documents, comments, a Psychology in Action section, announcements, convention calendars, and regular articles. Articles should be timely and of broad general interest to psychologists of all scientific and professional persuasions.

MANUSCRIPT INFORMATION
Manuscript requirements: APA; Chicago; Webster's Seventh New Collegiate Dictionary
  Number of copies to be submitted: Three
  Abstract: Yes, 100-120 words
Author information and reprints: Payment: None.
  Is simultaneous submission of article to other journals permitted: No
  Exclusive manuscript rights between acceptance and publication: Yes
  Copyright: Held by APA; author's permission required to reprint.
  Reprints: Available in minimum orders of 100
Disposition of manuscript:
  Receipt of manuscript acknowledged: Yes
  Decision to publish in: 2 months
  Accepted manuscript published in: 12 month maximum
  Rejected manuscript returned: Yes
  Rejected manuscript criticized: Yes
Submit to:
  Kenneth B. Little
  Editor
  (See address above)

APA MONITOR [1371]
1200 17th Street NW
Washington, D.C. 20036
(202) 833-7555

SUBSCRIPTION DATA
Issues and rates: Published monthly.
  Average paid circulation: 40,000
  Annual rate(s): $5.00, Members $1.00
Publisher or Sponsor: American Psychological Association
Managing Editor: Sharland Trotter

EDITORIAL DESCRIPTION
  Contains news and features of interest to psychologists, including coverage of APA activities, legislation and agency action affecting science and health, new appointments of psychologists, grants, awards, meetings, workshops, new publications, studies and opinion on major issues facing psychology. As the official newspaper of the American Psychological Association, the *Monitor* represents the scientists and professionals who make up the field.
Audience: Psychologists and other behavioral scientists
  Manuscripts accepted in English

MANUSCRIPT INFORMATION
Subject field(s): Psychology and related disciplines
Manuscript requirements: See latest issue for style requirements.
  Preferred length: 1000 words; 4 pages
  Number of copies to be submitted: 2
  Abstract: No
Author information and reprints: Payment: By publication to author.
  Is simultaneous submission of article to other journals permitted: No
  Exclusive manuscript rights between acceptance and publication: Yes
  Copyright: Held by publication.

Reprints: Not available.
Disposition of manuscript:
  Query letter: Yes
  Receipt of manuscript acknowledged: Yes
  Decision to publish in: 1 month
  Accepted manuscript published in: 2 months
  Rejected manuscript returned: Yes, if self-addressed, stamped envelope is sent with manuscript.
  Rejected manuscript criticized: No
Submit to:
  Sharland Trotter
  Editor
  (See address above)
  (202) 833-7634

SPECIAL STIPULATIONS
  Unsolicited manuscripts not encouraged.

ARCHIVES OF SEXUAL BEHAVIOR [1372]
An Interdisciplinary Research Journal
Plenum Publishing Corporation
227 West 17th Street
New York, New York 10011
(212) 255-0713

SUBSCRIPTION DATA
Issues and rates: Published bi-monthly.
  Average paid circulation: Not available.
  Annual rate(s): Individuals $19.00, Institutions $40.00
Managing Editor: Richard Green

EDITORIAL DESCRIPTION
  Contains original research, review articles, book reviews and current studies in the field of human sexual behavior.
Articles per average issue: 8-9
Audience: Professional
  Manuscripts accepted in English

MANUSCRIPT INFORMATION
Subject field(s): Psychology, psychiatry, biology, ethology, neurophysiology, sociology
Manuscript requirements: AIBS
  Preferred length: 1-25 pages
  Number of copies to be submitted: Original and 3 copies
  Abstract: Yes, 1 page, double-spaced
Author information and reprints: Payment: None.
  Is simultaneous submission of article to other journals permitted: No
  Exclusive manuscript rights between acceptance and publication: Yes
  Copyright: Held by publication.
  Reprints: Available at cost
Disposition of manuscript:
  Query letter: No
  Receipt of manuscript acknowledged: Yes
  Decision to publish in: 6-8 weeks
  Accepted manuscript published in: 8-12 months
  Rejected manuscript returned: Yes
  Rejected manuscript criticized: Yes
Submit to:
  Richard Green
  Editor

Department of Psychiatry and Behavioral Science
State University of New York at Stony Brook
Stony Brook, New York 11794

AUSTRALIAN PSYCHOLOGIST [1373]
Department of Psychology
University of Queensland
St. Lucia, 94067 Australia
(073) 706222

SUBSCRIPTION DATA
Issues and rates: Published three times per year.
  Average paid circulation: 2,600
  Annual rate(s): $9.00
Publisher or Sponsor: Australian Psychological Society

EDITORIAL DESCRIPTION
  Contains articles related to professional issues and practice in psychology. Policy is to cover wide range of psychological activities and interest. Both research and comment are acceptable.
Articles per average issue: 8
Audience: Professional
  Manuscripts accepted in English

MANUSCRIPT INFORMATION
Subject field(s): All areas of psychological practice, teaching of psychology
Manuscript requirements: APA
  Preferred length: 1,500-6000 words; 15 to 30 pages
  Number of copies to be submitted: Two
  Abstract: No
Author information and reprints: Payment: None.
  Is simultaneous submission of article to other journals permitted: No
  Exclusive manuscript rights between acceptance and publication: Yes
  Copyright: Held by publication.
  Reprints: Available; 25 free, additional at cost.
Additional information: Manuscripts should be prepared in proper style with footnotes, references, tables and figures on separate pages.
Disposition of manuscript:
  Receipt of manuscript acknowledged: Yes
  Decision to publish in: 1-3 months
  Accepted manuscript published in: 6-8 months
  Rejected manuscript returned: Yes
  Rejected manuscript criticized: Yes
Submit to:
  George E. Kearney
  Editor
  (See address above)

BEHAVIOR RESEARCH METHODS & INSTRUMENTATION [1374]
Psychonomic Society, Inc.
1108 West 34th Street
Austin, Texas 78705
(512) 454-7848

First published in 1968-1969

SUBSCRIPTION DATA
Issues and rates: Published bi-monthly.
  Average paid circulation: 1000
  Annual rate(s): Individuals $10.00, Institutions $20.00
Publisher or Sponsor: Psychonomic Society, Inc.
Managing Editor: Clifford T. Morgan

EDITORIAL DESCRIPTION
  Contains articles on experimental psychology.
Articles per average issue: 15-20
Audience: Experimental psychologists
  Manuscripts accepted in English

MANUSCRIPT INFORMATION
Subject field(s): Method, techniques, and instrumentation of research in experimental psychology
Manuscript requirements: Style sheet sent on request.
  Preferred length: None
  Number of copies to be submitted: 3
  Abstract: Yes; 100-150 words, using American Psychological Association form
Author information and reprints: Payment: None.
  Is simultaneous submission of article to other journals permitted: Yes
  Copyright: Held by publication.
  Reprints: Available
Disposition of manuscript:
  Query letter: No
  Receipt of manuscript acknowledged: Yes
  Decision to publish in: 1 month
  Accepted manuscript published in: 3-5 months
  Rejected manuscript returned: Yes
  Rejected manuscript criticized: Yes
Submit to:
  Joseph B. Sidowski
  Editor
  Department of Psychology
  University of South Florida
  Tampa, Florida 33620

BEHAVIOR RESEARCH AND THERAPY [1375]
An International Multi-Disciplinary Journal
Pergamon Press
Fairview Park
Elmsford, New York 10523
(914) 592-7700

First published in 1963

SUBSCRIPTION DATA
Issues and rates: Published quarterly.
  Annual rate(s): $25.00; Institutions $50.00

EDITORIAL DESCRIPTION
  An interdisciplinary journal in the behavioral sciences.
Articles per average issue: 15
Audience: Professional, academic
  Manuscripts accepted in English

MANUSCRIPT INFORMATION
Manuscript requirements: See latest issue for style requirements.
  Preferred length: None
  Number of copies to be submitted: Original and 1 copy
  Abstract: Yes. A summary of not more than 200 words at the beginning of the article.
Author information and reprints: Payment: None.
  Is simultaneous submission of article to other journals permitted: Not permitted.
  Exclusive manuscript rights between acceptance and publication: Yes
  Copyright: Held by publication.
  Reprints: Available at cost.
Disposition of manuscript:
  Query letter: Not necessary.
  Receipt of manuscript acknowledged: Yes
  Decision to publish in: 4 weeks
  Accepted manuscript published in: 5 months
  Rejected manuscript returned: Yes, if return postage is supplied by author.
  Rejected manuscript criticized: Reasons for rejections only
Submit to:
  Prof. H. J. Eysenck,
  Dr. S. Rachman
  Editor-in-Chief and Assistant Editor
  Institute of Psychiatry
  De Crespigny Park Road
  Denmark Hill
  London SE5 8AZ, England

BEHAVIOR THERAPY [1376]
Rutgers University
New Brunswick, New Jersey 08903
(201) 932-2000

First published in 1970

SUBSCRIPTION DATA
Issues and rates: 5 times per year
  Average paid circulation: 2800; 50 controlled
  Annual rate(s): $18, Foreign $20. Members of the Association for Advancement of Behavior Therapy may purchase at reduced cost.
Managing Editor: R. Van Frank

EDITORIAL DESCRIPTION
  Contains clinical and research articles for the professional in the fields of clinical psychology and psychiatry and social work which deal with behavior therapy and behavior change.
Articles per average issue: 20
Audience: Psychologists, psychiatrists, social workers, educators, speech and reading therapists
  Manuscripts accepted in English

MANUSCRIPT INFORMATION
Subject field(s): Experimental clinical psychology, experimental clinical psychiatry
Manuscript requirements: APA
  Preferred length: 15 pages maximum
  Number of copies to be submitted: Two
  Abstract: Yes
Author information and reprints: Payment: None.
  Is simultaneous submission of article to other journals permitted: No
  Exclusive manuscript rights between acceptance and publication: Yes
  Copyright: Held by publication.
  Reprints: 50 gratis, additional at cost
Disposition of manuscript:
  Query letter: No
  Receipt of manuscript acknowledged: Yes
  Decision to publish in: 6-10 weeks
  Accepted manuscript published in: 8-12 months
  Rejected manuscript returned: Yes
  Rejected manuscript criticized: Yes
Submit to:
  Cyril M. Franks
  Editor
  (See address above)

BIOLOGICAL PSYCHIATRY* [1377]
The Journal of the Society of Biological Psychiatry
Plenum Publishing Corporation
227 West 17th Street
New York, New York 10011
(212) 255-0713

SUBSCRIPTION DATA
Issues and rates: Published bi-monthly.
  Annual rate(s): $36.00, Foreign $38.70
Publisher or Sponsor: Society of Biological Psychiatry

EDITORIAL DESCRIPTION
  Covers a whole range of psychiatric research; occasional theoretical and review papers, brief reports, correspondence, news and notes and editorials; psychiatric research from all sources, disciplines and research areas.

MANUSCRIPT INFORMATION
Subject field(s): Psychiatry, pathology, physiology, pharmacology, biochemical, genetic, clinical, psychological
Manuscript requirements: AIBS
  Number of copies to be submitted: Original and 2 copies
  Copyright: Held by publication.
  Reprints: Available, cost varies
Disposition of manuscript:
  Receipt of manuscript acknowledged: Yes
  Decision to publish in: 6-8 weeks
  Accepted manuscript published in: 6-8 months
  Rejected manuscript returned: Yes
Submit to:
  Joseph Wortis
  Editor
  Department of Psychiatry
  Maimonides Medical Center
  4802 Tenth Avenue
  Brooklyn, New York 11219

THE BRITISH JOURNAL OF PSYCHIATRY [1378]
17 Belgrave Square
London SW1X 8PG, England
(01) 235-8857

Previously entitled *Journal of Mental Science; The Asylum Journal*

First published in 1853

SUBSCRIPTION DATA
Issues and rates: Published monthly.
  Average paid circulation: 4,900; 5,000 controlled
  Annual rate(s): £25.00; Foreign $75.00
Publisher or Sponsor: The Royal College of Psychiatrists
Managing Editor: Edward H. Hare

EDITORIAL DESCRIPTION
  Endeavours to include work done in every psychiatric field, and to reflect every school of thought within the specialty. Contributions on psychology, sociology, anthropology and other related subjects are welcome insofar as they have relevance to clinical psychiatry.
Articles per average issue: 15
Audience: Professional
  Manuscripts accepted in English

MANUSCRIPT INFORMATION
Manuscript requirements: See latest issue for style requirements.
  Preferred length: 1000 to 4000 words
  Number of copies to be submitted: 3
  Abstract: Yes, a synopsis of about 120 words at the beginning of the article.
Author information and reprints: Payment: None.
  Is simultaneous submission of article to other journals permitted: No
  Exclusive manuscript rights between acceptance and publication: Yes
  Copyright: Held by publication.
  Reprints: Available
Additional information: Manuscripts must be typed on quarto paper with double spacing and generous margins. The title, with the names only of the authors, should be brief and to the point so as to give a clear idea of the nature of the work.
Disposition of manuscript:
  Query letter: No
  Receipt of manuscript acknowledged: Yes
  Decision to publish in: 4 weeks
  Accepted manuscript published in: 6-12 months
  Rejected manuscript returned: Yes
  Rejected manuscript criticized: Yes
Submit to:
  E. H. Hare
  Editor
  (See address above)

CANADIAN COUNSELLOR/CONSEILLER CANADIEN [1379]
Suite 302
1000 Yonge Street
Toronto 289, Ontario, Canada

First published in 1967

SUBSCRIPTION DATA

Issues and rates: Published quarterly.
Average paid circulation: 1,200
Annual rate(s): $9.00
Publisher or Sponsor: Canadian Guidance and Counselling Association
Managing Editor: Myrne B. Nevison

EDITORIAL DESCRIPTION

Publishes papers of particular interest to counsellors in Canada
Articles per average issue: 10
Audience: Counsellors
Manuscripts accepted in English, French

MANUSCRIPT INFORMATION

Subject field(s): Counselling psychology
Manuscript requirements: APA
Preferred length: 3,000 words; 10-12 pages
Number of copies to be submitted: 2
Abstract: Yes. In both French and English
Author information and reprints: Payment: None.
Exclusive manuscript rights between acceptance and publication: Yes
Copyright: Held by publication.
Reprints: Available at cost.
Disposition of manuscript:
Query letter: Not necessary.
Receipt of manuscript acknowledged: Yes
Decision to publish in: 3 months
Accepted manuscript published in: 6 months
Rejected manuscript returned: Yes, with return postage paid by publication.
Rejected manuscript criticized: Reasons for rejections only
Submit to:
Dr. Myrne B. Nevison
Editor
(See address above)

CANADIAN JOURNAL OF BEHAVIOURAL SCIENCE [1380]
Revue Canadienne Des Sciences Du Comportement
1390 Sherbrooke Street West
Montreal, Quebec H3G 1K2, Canada
(514) 845-5616

First published in 1969

SUBSCRIPTION DATA

Issues and rates: Published quarterly.
Annual rate(s): Individuals $20.00
Publisher or Sponsor: Canadian Psychological Association
Managing Editor: Park O. Davidson

EDITORIAL DESCRIPTION

The Journal publishes articles in the applied areas of psychology and research articles in the areas of social, personality, abnormal, education, developmental and child psychology. Brief case reports with theoretical or practical implications will be considered, in particular programme evaluation studies.
Articles per average issue: 9 to 10
Audience: Psychology, Sociology and other behavioural sciences
Manuscripts accepted in English and French

MANUSCRIPT INFORMATION

Subject field(s): Social, personality, abnormal, educational, developmental, child, environmental, organisational, community and cross-cultural psychology
Manuscript requirements: APA See latest issue for style requirements.
Preferred length: 12-15 Typed pages
Number of copies to be submitted: Three
Abstract: Yes. Up to 100 words
Author information and reprints: Payment: None.
Is simultaneous submission of article to other journals permitted: Not permitted.
Exclusive manuscript rights between acceptance and publication: Yes
Reprints: Available at no cost.
Disposition of manuscript:
Query letter: Not necessary.
Receipt of manuscript acknowledged: Yes
Decision to publish in: Two months
Accepted manuscript published in: Six months
Rejected manuscript returned: Yes, with return postage paid by publication.
Rejected manuscript criticized: Yes
Submit to:
Park O. Davidson
Editor
Department of Psychology
University of British Columbia
Vancouver, British Columbia V6T 1W5, Canada
(604) 228-6327

CHARACTER POTENTIAL [1381]
A Record of Research
207 State Street
Schenectady, New York 12305
(518) 370-2466

First published in 1962

SUBSCRIPTION DATA

Issues and rates: Irregularly
Average paid circulation: 500; 500 controlled
Annual rate(s): $4.00, Foreign $5.00 for 4 issues
Publisher or Sponsor: Union College Character Research Project
Managing Editor: Herman Williams

EDITORIAL DESCRIPTION

Publishes theoretical and applied research reports that are concerned with attitudes, values, moral development or character. The primary concern is dissemination of information of research in human moral or character development.
Articles per average issue: 8-10
Audience: Educational researchers, religious, education professionals, psychological researchers in attitudes and values.
Manuscripts accepted in English

MANUSCRIPT INFORMATION

Subject field(s): Psychology, education, religion, religious education
Manuscript requirements: Style sheet sent on request.
Preferred length: Varies
Number of copies to be submitted: One
Abstract: Not necessary
Author information and reprints: Payment: None. 15 copies to author.
Is simultaneous submission of article to other journals permitted: If prior permission obtained
Exclusive manuscript rights between acceptance and publication: Yes
Copyright: Held by publication.
Reprints: Available, cost on request
Disposition of manuscript:
Query letter: No
Receipt of manuscript acknowledged: Yes
Decision to publish in: 2-4 months
Accepted manuscript published in: Varies greatly
Rejected manuscript returned: Yes
Rejected manuscript criticized: No
Submit to:
Herman J. Williams
Editor
(See address above)

CHILD DEVELOPMENT [1382]
University of Chicago Press
5801 Ellis Avenue
Chicago, Illinois 60637
(312) 753-3370

SUBSCRIPTION DATA

Issues and rates: Published quarterly.
Average paid circulation: 5,000
Annual rate(s): $25.00, Foreign $26.00

EDITORIAL DESCRIPTION

A publication outlet for reports of empirical research and for theoretical articles, or reviews that have theoretical implications for developmental research. Contributions from all disciplines concerned with developmental processes are welcome.
Articles per average issue: 35
Manuscripts accepted in English

MANUSCRIPT INFORMATION

Manuscript requirements: Chicago, APA
Preferred length: 20 pages maximum
Number of copies to be submitted: Two

Abstract: Yes, of 100 words
Is simultaneous submission of article to other journals permitted: No
Copyright: Held by publication.
Reprints: Available
Additional information: Authors may suggest names of persons particularly qualified to review their manuscripts.
Disposition of manuscript:
Query letter: No
Receipt of manuscript acknowledged: Yes
Decision to publish in: 3 months maximum
Accepted manuscript published in: One year maximum
Rejected manuscript returned: Yes
Submit to:
W. E. Jeffrey
Editor
Department of Psychology
University of California
Los Angeles, California 90024

CHILD PSYCHIATRY AND HUMAN DEVELOPMENT [1383]

Behavioral Publications, Inc.
72 Fifth Avenue
New York, New York 10011
(212) 243-6000

First published in 1970

SUBSCRIPTION DATA

Issues and rates: Published quarterly.
Average paid circulation: 2,000
Annual rate(s): Institutions $35.00, Individuals $17.50
Managing Editor: Jean Blackburn

EDITORIAL DESCRIPTION

To serve the allied professional groups represented by the specialties of child psychiatry, pediatrics, psychology, social science and human development in their task; to define the developing child and adolescent in health and in conflict.
Articles per average issue: 5
Audience: Psychiatrists, psychologists, pediatricians.
Manuscripts accepted in English

MANUSCRIPT INFORMATION

Subject field(s): Psychiatry, child psychiatry, psychology, medicine, pediatrics
Manuscript requirements: IM
Preferred length: 16 pages maximum
Number of copies to be submitted: Two
Abstract: Yes
Author information and reprints: Payment: None.
Is simultaneous submission of article to other journals permitted: No
Exclusive manuscript rights between acceptance and publication: Yes
Copyright: Held by publication.
Reprints: Available, cost depends on length of article
Disposition of manuscript:
Query letter: No
Receipt of manuscript acknowledged: Yes
Decision to publish in: 6-8 weeks
Accepted manuscript published in: 5 months
Rejected manuscript returned: Yes, if return postage is supplied by author.
Rejected manuscript criticized: No
Submit to:
John C. Duffy, MD
US Public Health Service
Governor's Island
New York, New York 10004
(212) 264-8620

CHILD STUDY JOURNAL [1384]

Child Study Center
State University College at Buffalo
Buffalo, New York 14222
(716) 862-6315

Previously entitled *Child Study Center Bulletin*

First published in 1970

SUBSCRIPTION DATA

Issues and rates: Published quarterly.
Annual rate(s): $8.00
Publisher or Sponsor: SUNY College at Buffalo, Child Study Center

EDITORIAL DESCRIPTION

The journal serves as a publication medium for the theory and research on child and adolescent development. Particular attention will be given to articles devoted to the educational and psychological aspects of human development.
Articles per average issue: 5
Audience: Professional, academic
Manuscripts accepted in English

MANUSCRIPT INFORMATION

Subject field(s): Educational psychology, psychology, child development, counseling
Manuscript requirements: APA
Preferred length: 15 pages
Number of copies to be submitted: Two
Abstract: Yes
Author information and reprints: Payment: None.
Is simultaneous submission of article to other journals permitted: No
Exclusive manuscript rights between acceptance and publication: Yes
Copyright: Held jointly by author and publication.
Reprints: Available, cost depends on article length
Disposition of manuscript:
Query letter: No
Receipt of manuscript acknowledged: Yes
Decision to publish in: 6-12 weeks
Accepted manuscript published in: 9-12 months
Rejected manuscript returned: Yes
Rejected manuscript criticized: Yes
Submit to:
Donald E. Carter
Editor
(See address above)

COGNITIVE PSYCHOLOGY [1385]

Academic Press, Inc.
111 Fifth Avenue
New York, New York 10003

SUBSCRIPTION DATA

Issues and rates: Published bi-monthly.
Average paid circulation: Not available.
Annual rate(s): $39.50; Foreign $42.50

EDITORIAL DESCRIPTION

Publishes original empirical, theoretical and tutorial papers, methodological articles and critical reviews dealing with memory, language processing, perception, problem solving and thinking. Emphasizes work on the organization of human information processing. Papers dealing with relevant problems in linguistics, artificial intelligence and neurophysiology are welcome if they are of direct interest to cognitive psychologists.

MANUSCRIPT INFORMATION

Manuscript requirements: APA; see Information for Authors in latest issue.
Preferred length: None
Number of copies to be submitted: Three
Author information and reprints: Payment: None.
Copyright: Held by publication.
Reprints: Available
Submit to:
Tom Trabasso
Editor
Princeton University
Department of Psychology
Princeton, New Jersey 08540

COMMUNITY MENTAL HEALTH JOURNAL [1386]

Behavioral Publications, Inc.
72 Fifth Avenue
New York, New York 10011
(212) 243-6000

First published in 1965

SUBSCRIPTION DATA

Issues and rates: Published quarterly.
Average paid circulation: 4,000
Annual rate(s): Institutions $30.00, Individuals $12.00
Managing Editor: Jean Blackburn

EDITORIAL DESCRIPTION

Devoted to emergent approaches in mental health research, theory, and practice as they relate to community, broadly defined. Mental health is seen as more or less congruent with the general concept of social well-being.
Articles per average issue: 10
Audience: Psychologists, mental health workers, social workers
Manuscripts accepted in English

MANUSCRIPT INFORMATION

Subject field(s): Psychology, mental health, psychiatry

Manuscript requirements: APA
  Preferred length: 16 pages maximum
  Number of copies to be submitted: Two
  Abstract: Yes, of about 100 words
Author information and reprints: Payment: None.
  Is simultaneous submission of article to other journals permitted: No
  Exclusive manuscript rights between acceptance and publication: Yes
  Copyright: Held by publication.
  Reprints: Available, cost depends on length of article
Disposition of manuscript:
  Query letter: No
  Receipt of manuscript acknowledged: Yes
  Decision to publish in: 6-8 weeks
  Accepted manuscript published in: 5 months
  Rejected manuscript returned: Yes, if return postage is supplied by author.
  Rejected manuscript criticized: No
Submit to:
  Lenin A. Baler
  University of Michigan
  School of Public Health
  Community Mental Health Program
  Ann Arbor, Michigan 48104

CONFINIA PSYCHIATRICA [1387]
Borderland of Psychiatry
S. Karger AG
Arnold-Boecklin Strasse 25
CH-4011 Basel, Switzerland
061-390880

First published in 1958

SUBSCRIPTION DATA
Issues and rates: Published quarterly.
  Average paid circulation: 797; 53 controlled
  Annual rate(s): SFr. 88.00; Foreign $36.00
Publisher or Sponsor: The International Society of Art and Psychopathology
Managing Editor: H. Heimann, Tübingen

EDITORIAL DESCRIPTION
Emphasizes the relationship of the sciences and humanities to psychopathology but is also available for disciplines which so far do not have journals of their own.
Articles per average issue: 5
  Manuscripts accepted in English, German, French

MANUSCRIPT INFORMATION
Subject field(s): Psychology, research on behavior, sociology, theology, history of art and literature, history of medicine, statistics, pharmacology and endocrinology
Manuscript requirements: See latest issue for style requirements.
  Preferred length: 12 printed pages
  Number of copies to be submitted: 2
  Abstract: Yes, a summary in the original language, English title.
Author information and reprints: Payment: Reprints only.
  Is simultaneous submission of article to other journals permitted: No
  Exclusive manuscript rights between acceptance and publication: Yes
  Copyright: Held by publication.
  Reprints: Available
Disposition of manuscript:
  Receipt of manuscript acknowledged: Yes
  Rejected manuscript returned: Yes
Submit to:
  H. Heimann
  Editor
  (See address above)

SPECIAL STIPULATIONS
Request additional manuscript information from publisher.

CONTEMPORARY PSYCHOLOGY* [1388]
American Psychological Association
1200 17th Street, N.W.
Washington, D.C. 20036
(202) 833-7670

SUBSCRIPTION DATA
Issues and rates: Published monthly.
  Average paid circulation: 14,600
  Annual rate(s): $15.00; Members $5.00, Foreign $16.00
Publisher or Sponsor: American Psychological Association

EDITORIAL DESCRIPTION
A journal of critical reviews of books, films, and other material in the field of psychology. Material reviewed is selected by the editorial staff to represent a world-wide cross-section of psychological works. The reviews are prepared by those who have competence in specialized fields in psychology, but are written for a broad and varied audience. It provides a means by which the reader may keep abreast of current psychological thought and opinion.

MANUSCRIPT INFORMATION
Manuscript requirements: APA; Chicago; *Webster's Seventh New Collegiate Dictionary*
  Number of copies to be submitted: Two
Author information and reprints: Payment: None.
  Is simultaneous submission of article to other journals permitted: No
  Exclusive manuscript rights between acceptance and publication: Yes
  Copyright: Held by APA; author's permission required to reprint.
  Reprints: Available in minimum orders of 100
Disposition of manuscript:
  Receipt of manuscript acknowledged: Yes
  Decision to publish in: 2 months
  Accepted manuscript published in: 12 month maximum
  Rejected manuscript returned: Yes
  Rejected manuscript criticized: Yes
Submit to:
  Janet Spence
  Editor
  Department of Psychology
  University of Texas
  Austin, Texas 78712

CORRECTIVE AND SOCIAL PSYCHIATRY [1389]
122 North Cooper Street
Olathe, Kansas 66061
(913) 782-4282

Previously entitled *Corrective Psychiatry*

First published in 1950

SUBSCRIPTION DATA
Issues and rates: Published quarterly.
  Average paid circulation: 1,000; 100 controlled
  Annual rate(s): $15.00; Institutions $20.00; Students $15.00; Foreign individuals $18.00; Foreign institutions $23.00
Publisher or Sponsor: Martin Psychiatric Research Foundation, Inc.
Managing Editor: Jack D. Rash

EDITORIAL DESCRIPTION
An eclectic forum for the publication of original papers contributing to the advancement of the therapeutic community in all its settings: correctional institutions, hospitals, churches, schools, family, and industry
Articles per average issue: 5
Audience: Practitioners and researchers in the mental health community
  Manuscripts accepted in English only

MANUSCRIPT INFORMATION
Subject field(s): Psychology, psychiatry, sociology, behavior modification, analysis, humanism, Gestalt, etc.
Manuscript requirements: APA
  Preferred length: 5-15 pages
  Number of copies to be submitted: 3
  Abstract: Not necessary.
Author information and reprints: Payment: Reprints only. 2 issues
  Is simultaneous submission of article to other journals permitted: Not permitted.
  Exclusive manuscript rights between acceptance and publication: Yes
  Copyright: Held by publication.
Disposition of manuscript:
  Query letter: Not necessary, but advisable.
  Receipt of manuscript acknowledged: Yes
  Decision to publish in: 1 month
  Accepted manuscript published in: 3-6 months
  Rejected manuscript returned: Yes, if return postage is supplied by author.
  Rejected manuscript criticized: Yes
Submit to:
  Jack D. Rash
  Managing Editor
  (See address above)

THE COUNSELING PSYCHOLOGIST [1390]

Box 1180, Washington University
St. Louis, Missouri 63130
(314) 863-0100 ext. 4277

SUBSCRIPTION DATA

Issues and rates: Published quarterly.
  Average paid circulation: 4100; 2400 controlled
  Annual rate(s): $10.00, Foreign $12.00, Students $8.00
Publisher or Sponsor: American Psychological Association, Division 17
Managing Editor: Arthur Resnikoff

EDITORIAL DESCRIPTION

  Contents include counseling psychology and related areas. Lead article focuses on one topic, followed by responses from solicited authors. Also includes a Professional Forum for which contributions are not solicited. Attempts to present diverse points of view on main topic.
Articles per average issue: 8-10
Audience: Counseling psychologists, clinical psychologists, social workers.
  Manuscripts accepted in English only

MANUSCRIPT INFORMATION

Subject field(s): Counseling psychology, guidance, counselor training
Manuscript requirements: APA
  Preferred length: Cannot be specified on major items. 5-10 pages for forum
  Number of copies to be submitted: Three
  Abstract: Yes, two copies
Author information and reprints: Payment: None.
  Is simultaneous submission of article to other journals permitted: No
  Exclusive manuscript rights between acceptance and publication: No
  Copyright: Held by publication.
  Reprints: Not available.
Disposition of manuscript:
  Query letter: Yes
  Receipt of manuscript acknowledged: Yes
  Decision to publish in: One month
  Accepted manuscript published in: 3-6 months
  Rejected manuscript returned: Yes, if self-addressed, stamped envelope is sent with manuscript.
  Rejected manuscript criticized: Yes
Submit to:
  Arthur Resnikoff
  Managing Editor
  (See address above)
  (314) 863-0100 ext. 4784

DEVELOPMENTAL PSYCHOLOGY [1391]

American Psychological Association
1200 17th Street, N.W.
Washington, D.C. 20036
(202) 833-7670

SUBSCRIPTION DATA

Issues and rates: Published bi-monthly.
  Average paid circulation: 5,920
  Annual rate(s): $30.00, Members $10.00, Foreign $31.00
Publisher or Sponsor: American Psychological Association
Managing Editor: Anita DeVivo

EDITORIAL DESCRIPTION

  Primarily intended for reports of empirical research in which the development implications are clear and convincing, the journal publishes articles that significantly advance knowledge about growth and development. Any variable or set of variables that helps to promote understanding of psychological processes and their development within the life-span is appropriate.
Articles per average issue: 23
Audience: Professional, academic
  Manuscripts accepted in English

MANUSCRIPT INFORMATION

Manuscript requirements: APA; Chicago
  Preferred length: 15-20 pages
  Number of copies to be submitted: Two
  Abstract: Yes, of 100-175 words on a separate sheet.
Author information and reprints: Payment: None.
  Is simultaneous submission of article to other journals permitted: No
  Exclusive manuscript rights between acceptance and publication: Yes
  Copyright: Held by APA; author's permission required to reprint.
  Reprints: Available in minimum orders of 100
Disposition of manuscript:
  Query letter: No
  Receipt of manuscript acknowledged: Yes
  Decision to publish in: 2 months
  Accepted manuscript published in: 12 month maximum
  Rejected manuscript returned: Yes
  Rejected manuscript criticized: Yes
Submit to:
  Richard D. Odom
  Editor
  Department of Psychology
  Vanderbilt University
  134 Wesley Hall
  Nashville, Tennessee 37240

GENETIC PSYCHOLOGY MONOGRAPHS [1392]

The Journal Press
2 Commercial Street
Provincetown, Massachusetts 02657
(617) 487-0133

SUBSCRIPTION DATA

Issues and rates: Published quarterly.
  Average paid circulation: 1156; 32 controlled
  Annual rate(s): $26.00
Managing Editor: Powell Murchison

EDITORIAL DESCRIPTION

  Devoted to developmental and clinical psychology.
Articles per average issue: 3-5
Audience: Developmental and clinical psychologists
  Manuscripts accepted in English only

MANUSCRIPT INFORMATION

Subject field(s): Developmental psychology, clinical psychology
Manuscript requirements: Style sheet sent on request.
  Preferred length: 9,000-15,000 words
  Number of copies to be submitted: Two
  Abstract: As summary only
Author information and reprints: Payment: By author to publication. Author pays only for unusual expenses, such as tables, figures, equation, and special fonts, and for excess pages beyond 50 in final printing.
  Is simultaneous submission of article to other journals permitted: No
  Exclusive manuscript rights between acceptance and publication: Yes
  Copyright: Held by publication.
  Reprints: Available, 200 free to author.
Additional information: All copy must be double-spaced and the original typewritten manuscript must be submitted with a legible carbon copy or photocopy.
Disposition of manuscript:
  Query letter: No
  Receipt of manuscript acknowledged: Yes
  Decision to publish in: 2-4 weeks
  Accepted manuscript published in: 1 year
  Rejected manuscript returned: Yes
  Rejected manuscript criticized: Occasionally
Submit to:
  Powell Murchison
  Managing Editor
  (See address above)

GROUP PROCESS [1393]

Gordon and Breach
One Park Avenue South
New York, New York 10016
(212) 689-0360

Previously entitled *Journal of Group Psychoanalysis and Process*

First published in 1968

SUBSCRIPTION DATA

Issues and rates: Published semi-annually.
  Annual rate(s): Individuals $9.00, Institutions $18.00

EDITORIAL DESCRIPTION

  Published for social and behavioral scientists, practieners and students. Presents articles on significant features of current group processes.
Articles per average issue: 8-10
Audience: Professional, academic
  Manuscripts accepted in English, French, Spanish, Portuguese

MANUSCRIPT INFORMATION

Manuscript requirements: Style sheet sent on request.
  Preferred length: None specified
  Number of copies to be submitted: Three, double-spaced
  Abstract: Yes

Author information and reprints: Payment: Reprints only. 50 reprints
Is simultaneous submission of article to other journals permitted: No
Exclusive manuscript rights between acceptance and publication: Yes
Copyright: Held by publication.
Reprints: Available
Additional information: Figures submitted must be of a quality high enough for standard reproduction. Should be prepared in India ink on white paper or tracing cloth.
Disposition of manuscript:
Query letter: No
Receipt of manuscript acknowledged: Yes
Decision to publish in: 3-6 months
Accepted manuscript published in: 1 year
Rejected manuscript returned: Yes, if return postage is supplied by author.
Rejected manuscript criticized: Yes
Submit to:
Dr. Max Rosenbaum
Editor
P.O. Box 1078
Grand Central Station
New York, New York 10017

GROUP PSYCHOTHERAPY AND PSYCHODRAMA [1394]
P. O. Box 311
259 Wolcott Avenue
Beacon, New York 12508
(914) 831-2318

Previously entitled *Group Psychotherapy*

First published in 1947

SUBSCRIPTION DATA
Issues and rates: Published semi-annually.
Average paid circulation: 1,000
Annual rate(s): $14.00; Pan-Am $14.00 plus postage; Institutions $14.00
Managing Editor: Zerka T. Moreno

EDITORIAL DESCRIPTION
Contributions by professionals in the field of psychodrama, role-playing, group dynamics, group methods, psychotherapy, sociometry, and allied fields.
Articles per average issue: 20
Audience: Professional workers, students, teachers
Manuscripts accepted in English

MANUSCRIPT INFORMATION
Manuscript requirements: See latest issue for style requirements.
Number of copies to be submitted: 2
Abstract: Not necessary.
Author information and reprints: Payment: None.
Is simultaneous submission of article to other journals permitted: Not permitted.
Exclusive manuscript rights between acceptance and publication:
Copyright: Held by author.
Reprints: Available at cost.
Disposition of manuscript:
Query letter: Not necessary.

Receipt of manuscript acknowledged: Yes
Decision to publish in: 2 weeks
Accepted manuscript published in: 2 years
Rejected manuscript returned: Yes, with return postage paid by publication.
Rejected manuscript criticized: Sometimes
Submit to:
Editor
(See address above)

HISTORY OF CHILDHOOD QUARTERLY [1395]
The Journal of Psychohistory
2315 Broadway
New York, New York 10024
(212) 873-3331

First published in 1973

SUBSCRIPTION DATA
Issues and rates: Published quarterly.
Average paid circulation: 6,000
Annual rate(s): $14.00; Individuals $14.00; Institutions $20.00; Students 14.00; Foreign individuals $14.00; Foreign institutions $20.00
Managing Editor: Lloyd de Mause

EDITORIAL DESCRIPTION
Scholarly articles on childhood past and present and psychological studies of history
Articles per average issue: 6
Audience: College and general readership
Manuscripts accepted in English

MANUSCRIPT INFORMATION
Subject field(s): History of childhood, past and present, psychological studies of historical movements or individuals
Manuscript requirements: See latest issue for style requirements.
Preferred length: 5,000 words
Number of copies to be submitted: 1
Abstract: Not necessary.
Author information and reprints: Payment: None.
Is simultaneous submission of article to other journals permitted: Permitted.
Exclusive manuscript rights between acceptance and publication: No
Copyright: Held by publication.
Reprints: Available at no cost. 50
Disposition of manuscript:
Query letter: Not necessary.
Receipt of manuscript acknowledged: Yes
Decision to publish in: 1 week
Accepted manuscript published in: 4 months
Rejected manuscript returned: Yes, with return postage paid by publication.
Rejected manuscript criticized: Yes
Submit to:
Lloyd de Mause
Editor
(See address above)

HUMAN DEVELOPMENT [1396]
S. Karger AG
Arnold Boecklin Strasse 25
CH-4011 Basel, Switzerland
061-390880

Previously entitled *Vita Humana*

SUBSCRIPTION DATA
Issues and rates: Published bi-monthly.
Average paid circulation: 1,121; 45 controlled
Annual rate(s): Sfr. 132.00; Foreign $54.00

EDITORIAL DESCRIPTION
Publishes original articles on psychological differences and changes during the whole lifespan. Preference is given to theoretical contributions and scholarly reviews of the literature concerning research of diverse psychological variables, multidisciplinary investigations, and cross-cultural comparisons.
Articles per average issue: 6
Manuscripts accepted in English, French, German

MANUSCRIPT INFORMATION
Subject field(s): Psychology, education, sociology, anthropology, biology, psychiatry, special education, medicine
Manuscript requirements: See latest issue for style requirements.
Preferred length: 10-12 pages, maximum
Number of copies to be submitted: Two
Abstract: Yes, with 6 key words.
Author information and reprints: Payment: Reprints only. 100 reprints
Is simultaneous submission of article to other journals permitted: No
Exclusive manuscript rights between acceptance and publication: Yes
Copyright: Held by publication.
Reprints: Available at cost
Disposition of manuscript:
Query letter: No
Receipt of manuscript acknowledged: Yes
Decision to publish in: 3 weeks
Accepted manuscript published in: 6 months
Rejected manuscript returned: Yes
Rejected manuscript criticized: Yes
Submit to:
Klaus F. Riegel
Executive Editor
Department of Psychology
University of Michigan
Ann Arbor, Michigan 48104
(313) 764-0430

INDIVIDUAL PSYCHOLOGIST [1397]
Room 306-Hill Hall
West Virginia College of Graduate Studies
Institute, West Virginia 25112
(304 768-9711 ext. 284

First published in 1963

SUBSCRIPTION DATA
Issues and rates: Published semi-annually.

Annual rate(s): $2.00; Foreign $4.00;
Individuals $2.00; Institutions $2.00;
Students $2.00; Foreign individuals $4.00;
Foreign institutions $4.00
Publisher or Sponsor: American Society of Adlerian Psychology
Managing Editor: William H. Culp

EDITORIAL DESCRIPTION

Scholarly but non-technical descriptions of research in the field of Adlerian psychology. Non-technical research articles that conform to the theory of Adlerian Psychology as well as book reviews.
Articles per average issue: 5-6
Audience: Counselors and teachers
Manuscripts accepted in English

MANUSCRIPT INFORMATION

Subject field(s): Psychology, counseling, and application of Adlerian psychology to the classroom
Manuscript requirements: APA See latest issue for style requirements.
Preferred length: 12 to 15 Double-spaced typewritten pages
Number of copies to be submitted: 3
Abstract: Not necessary.
Author information and reprints: Payment: None.
Is simultaneous submission of article to other journals permitted: Not permitted.
Exclusive manuscript rights between acceptance and publication: Yes
Reprints: Available at cost.
Disposition of manuscript:
Query letter: Not necessary.
Receipt of manuscript acknowledged: Yes
Decision to publish in: 4 months
Accepted manuscript published in: 6-8 months
Rejected manuscript returned: Yes, if return postage is supplied by author.
Rejected manuscript criticized: Yes
Submit to:
William H. Culp;
Manford A. Sonstegard
Editor
(See address above)

INDIVIDUAL PSYCHOLOGY NEWSLETTER [1398]

Organ of the International Association of Individual Psychology
6 Vale Rise
London NW11 8SD, England
(01) 455-5064

SUBSCRIPTION DATA

Issues and rates: Published bi-monthly.
Average paid circulation: 450; 500 controlled
Annual rate(s): £1.50, Foreign $5.00
Publisher or Sponsor: International Association of Individual Psychology
Managing Editor: Paul Rom

EDITORIAL DESCRIPTION

Contains news about events in individual psychology the world over; Adlerian bibliography; book reviews; papers on literary, educational, psychotherapeutical points; discussion with other schools of psychology.
Audience: Adlerians and sympathizers

MANUSCRIPT INFORMATION

Subject field(s): Individual Psychology
Manuscript requirements: No specific style guide.
Preferred length: 200 to 1000 words
Number of copies to be submitted: Two
Abstract: No
Author information and reprints: Payment: None.
Is simultaneous submission of article to other journals permitted: Yes
Exclusive manuscript rights between acceptance and publication: No
Copyright: Held by publication.
Reprints: Available
Disposition of manuscript:
Query letter: No
Receipt of manuscript acknowledged: Yes
Decision to publish in: One week
Accepted manuscript published in: 2 months
Rejected manuscript returned: Yes, if return postage is supplied by author.
Rejected manuscript criticized: Yes
Submit to:
Paul Rom
Editor
(See address above)

INTERAMERICAN JOURNAL OF PSYCHOLOGY [1399]

Revista Interamericana de Psicologia
P.O. Box 88 UTEP
El Paso, Texas 79968
(915) 747-5834

First published in 1967

SUBSCRIPTION DATA

Issues and rates: Published quarterly
Average paid circulation: 900
Annual rate(s): $8.00
Managing Editor: Jacqueline W. Calkins

EDITORIAL DESCRIPTION

Publishes representative papers in the various areas of psychological research and practice. Serves as a primary medium of communication among psychologists in North, Central and South America. Also includes book reviews and announcements of Interamerican interest.
Articles per average issue: 10
Audience: Psychologists in the Americas
Manuscripts accepted in English, Spanish and Portuguese

MANUSCRIPT INFORMATION

Subject field(s): Psychological research
Manuscript requirements: Style sheet sent on request. and published in first issue each year
Preferred length: 10-20 pages
Number of copies to be submitted: Two
Abstract: Yes. no more than 200 words.
Author information and reprints: Payment: None.
Is simultaneous submission of article to other journals permitted: No
Exclusive manuscript rights between acceptance and publication: Yes
Copyright: Held by publication.
Reprints: Available, 50 reprints free, additional at cost
Additional information: Manuscript should be typed, double-spaced, preferably on white bond paper of good quality and standard size; mechanically reproduced papers acceptable if easily legible. Abstract, footnotes, references, tables, figures and legends should be submitted on separate pages. Camera-ready originals of tables and figures should be included.
Disposition of manuscript:
Query letter: No
Receipt of manuscript acknowledged: Yes
Decision to publish in: 2-4 months
Accepted manuscript published in: 9 months
Rejected manuscript returned: Yes
Rejected manuscript criticized: Yes
Submit to:
Luiz F.S. Natalicio
(See address above)
(915) 747-5834

SPECIAL STIPULATIONS

Only original articles not previously published elsewhere are accepted.

INTERNATIONAL JOURNAL OF AGING AND HUMAN DEVELOPMENT [1400]

An International Journal of Psycho-social Gerontology
Baywood Publishing Company, Inc.
43 Central Drive
Farmingdale, New York 11735
(516) 293-7130

Previously entitled *Aging and Human Development*

First published in 1970

SUBSCRIPTION DATA

Issues and rates: Published quarterly.
Average paid circulation: 1,000
Annual rate(s): $30.00; Foreign $32.00

EDITORIAL DESCRIPTION

Investigates the psychological and social aspects of aging and the aged.
Articles per average issue: 12
Audience: Professional, academic, medical, geriatrical
Manuscripts accepted in English

MANUSCRIPT INFORMATION

Manuscript requirements: See latest issue for style requirements. Style sheet sent on request.
Preferred length: 5,000 words maximum
Number of copies to be submitted: 3
Abstract: Yes. 100 words or less

Author information and reprints: Payment: Reprints only. 20 copies
Is simultaneous submission of article to other journals permitted: Not permitted.
Exclusive manuscript rights between acceptance and publication: Yes
Copyright: Held by publication.
Reprints: Available at cost.
Disposition of manuscript:
Query letter: Not necessary, but advisable.
Receipt of manuscript acknowledged: Yes
Decision to publish in: 4-6 weeks
Accepted manuscript published in: 6 months
Rejected manuscript returned: Yes, with return postage paid by publication.
Rejected manuscript criticized: Sometimes
Submit to:
Dr. Robert J. Kastenbaum
Editor
Psychology I
University of Massachusetts
Columbia Point Campus
Dorchester, Massachusetts 02125

INTERNATIONAL JOURNAL OF CLINICAL AND EXPERIMENTAL HYPNOSIS [1401]

Institute of the Pennsylvania Hospital
111 North 49th Street
Philadelphia, Pennsylvania 19139
(215) 829-2776

Previously entitled *Journal of Clinical and Experimental Hypnosis*

First published in 1953

SUBSCRIPTION DATA

Issues and rates: Published quarterly.
Average paid circulation: 1,600
Annual rate(s): Institutions $25.00; Individuals $16.00
Publisher or Sponsor: Society for Clinical and Experimental Hypnosis, Inc.
Managing Editor: Martin T. Orne

EDITORIAL DESCRIPTION

Publishes only original research papers dealing with hypnosis in psychology, psychiatry, the medical and dental specialties, and allied areas of science. Articles include clinical and experimental studies, discussions of theory, significant historical and cultural material, and related data.
Articles per average issue: 9
Audience: Professional
Manuscripts accepted in English

MANUSCRIPT INFORMATION

Subject field(s): Psychotherapeutic applications of hypnosis, general medical applications of hypnosis, dentistry and hypnosis, research in hypnosis, general theory and history of hypnosis
Manuscript requirements: APA
Preferred length: 5-20 typewritten, double-spaced pages
Number of copies to be submitted: Four
Abstract: Yes
Author information and reprints: Payment: None. Except if immediate publication is requested; charge is $15 per page.
Is simultaneous submission of article to other journals permitted: No
Exclusive manuscript rights between acceptance and publication: Yes
Copyright: Held by the Society
Reprints: Available
Additional information: All illustrations must be of a professional quality and in glossy form.
Disposition of manuscript:
Query letter: No, cover letter is sufficient
Receipt of manuscript acknowledged: Yes
Decision to publish in: 3-4 months
Accepted manuscript published in: 10-14 months
Rejected manuscript returned: Yes
Rejected manuscript criticized: Yes
Submit to:
Martin T. Orne, M.D.
Editor
(See address above)

INTERNATIONAL JOURNAL OF GROUP PSYCHOTHERAPY [1402]

239 Park Avenue South
New York, New York 10003
(212) 674-2021

First published in 1951

SUBSCRIPTION DATA

Issues and rates: Published quarterly.
Average paid circulation: 5000
Annual rate(s): Individuals $18.50, Institutions $28.50
Publisher or Sponsor: American Group Psychotherapy Association
Managing Editor: Saul Scheidlinger

EDITORIAL DESCRIPTION

Devoted to reporting and interpreting research and practice of group psychotherapy in various settings in the United States and other countries.
Articles per average issue: Varies
Audience: Scientific
Manuscripts accepted in English

MANUSCRIPT INFORMATION

Subject field(s): Group psychotherapy and related fields
Manuscript requirements: See latest issue for style requirements.
Number of copies to be submitted: Two
Abstract: No
Author information and reprints: Payment: None.
Is simultaneous submission of article to other journals permitted: No
Exclusive manuscript rights between acceptance and publication: Yes
Copyright: Held by the Association
Reprints: Available, cost varies
Disposition of manuscript:
Query letter: Yes
Receipt of manuscript acknowledged: Yes
Decision to publish in: 2-3 months
Accepted manuscript published in: 3 months
Rejected manuscript returned: Yes
Rejected manuscript criticized: No
Submit to:
Saul Scheidlinger
Editor
Box 230, 150 Christopher Street
New York, New York 10014

INTERNATIONAL PHARMACOPSYCHIATRY [1403]

Topical Problems
S. Karger AG
Arnold-Boecklin Strasse 25
CH-4011 Basel, Switzerland
061-390880

First published in 1968

SUBSCRIPTION DATA

Issues and rates: Published quarterly.
Average paid circulation: 482; 58 controlled
Annual rate(s): SFr. 88.00; Foreign $36.00

EDITORIAL DESCRIPTION

Recognition of clinical psychopharmacology as an integral part of psychiatry is inherent in concept and publication. It is very evident today that psychiatric pharmacotherapy has not only influenced symptomatology and pattern of psychiatric disorders, but has also shed new light on problems of etiology, diagnosis and principles of therapeutic evaluation. It is the main purpose of this journal to bridge the still existing gaps between clinical psychopharmacology and the general body of psychiatric science.
Articles per average issue: 6
Manuscripts accepted in English, French, German

MANUSCRIPT INFORMATION

Manuscript requirements: See latest issue for style requirements.
Preferred length: 8 printed pages
Number of copies to be submitted: 3
Abstract: Yes, in the original language, including an English title and 6-9 key words
Author information and reprints: Payment: Reprints only.
Is simultaneous submission of article to other journals permitted: No
Exclusive manuscript rights between acceptance and publication: Yes
Copyright: Held by publication.
Disposition of manuscript:
Query letter: No
Receipt of manuscript acknowledged: Yes
Decision to publish in: 2 months
Accepted manuscript published in: 5 months
Rejected manuscript returned: Yes
Rejected manuscript criticized: No
Submit to:
Editor
(See address above)

SPECIAL STIPULATIONS
Request any additional manuscript information from publisher.

THE INTERNATIONAL PSYCHOLOGIST [1404]
Newsletter of the International Council of Psychologists
2472 South Kearney
Denver, Colorado 80722
(303) 758-3180

First published in 1960

SUBSCRIPTION DATA
Issues and rates: Published quarterly.
   Average paid circulation: 600; 200 controlled
   Annual rate(s): $15
Publisher or Sponsor: International Council of Psychologists, Inc.

EDITORIAL DESCRIPTION
Contains psychological news of international interest
Articles per average issue: 10
Audience: Psychologists with interests beyond their own country
Manuscripts accepted in English

MANUSCRIPT INFORMATION
Subject field(s): Psychology
Manuscript requirements: Factual news notes
   Preferred length: 1000 words maximum
   Number of copies to be submitted: 1
   Abstract: No
Author information and reprints: Payment: None.
   Is simultaneous submission of article to other journals permitted: Yes
   Exclusive manuscript rights between acceptance and publication: No
   Copyright: Held by author.
   Reprints: Not available.
Disposition of manuscript:
   Query letter: Preferred
   Receipt of manuscript acknowledged: No
   Decision to publish in: 3 months
   Accepted manuscript published in: 6 months
   Rejected manuscript returned: Yes, if return postage is supplied by author.
   Rejected manuscript criticized: No
Submit to:
   Dr. Constance Nelson
   Editor
   (See address above)

INTERNATIONAL UNDERSTANDING [1405]
International Council of Psychologists, Inc.
4014 Cody Road
Sherman Oaks, California 91403

SUBSCRIPTION DATA
Issues and rates: Published annually.
   Average paid circulation: 800
Publisher or Sponsor: International Council of Psychologists, Inc.
   Annual rate(s): $14.00

EDITORIAL DESCRIPTION
Contains essays and research articles on psychological topics of international interest.
Articles per average issue: Varies
Audience: Professional
Manuscripts accepted in English

MANUSCRIPT INFORMATION
Subject field(s): Psychology, peace
Manuscript requirements: No specific style guide.
   Preferred length: 2,000 words
   Number of copies to be submitted: One
   Abstract: Yes
Author information and reprints: Payment: None.
   Is simultaneous submission of article to other journals permitted: Yes
   Exclusive manuscript rights between acceptance and publication: No
   Copyright: Held by author.
   Reprints: Not available.
Disposition of manuscript:
   Query letter: Yes
   Receipt of manuscript acknowledged: Yes
   Decision to publish in: 1 month
   Accepted manuscript published in: 1 year or less
   Rejected manuscript returned: Yes, if return postage is supplied by author.
   Rejected manuscript criticized: No
Submit to:
   Frances A. Mullen
   Editor
   (See address above)

INTERPERSONAL DEVELOPMENT [1406]
International Journal for Humanistic Approaches to Group Psychotherapy, Sensitivity Training and Organizational Development
S. Karger AG
Arnold-Boecklin Strasse 25
CH-4011 Basel, Switzerland
061-390880

First published in 1970

SUBSCRIPTION DATA
Issues and rates: Published quarterly.
   Average paid circulation: 345; 55 controlled
   Annual rate(s): SFr.88.00; Foreign $36.00

EDITORIAL DESCRIPTION
Sensitivity training, encounter groups, T-groups, etc., seek to increase personal insight and understanding of others as well as effectiveness in social group situations. These methods reflect an affirmative rather than a remedial philosophy and stress available and potential capabilities of the human being. The journal hopes to deepen understanding of the methods of interpersonal development by rigorous enquiry, insightful observation, careful reporting, responsible criticism, and occasionally belles-lettres and poetry.
Articles per average issue: 4-5
Manuscripts accepted in English, German, French

MANUSCRIPT INFORMATION
Manuscript requirements: See latest issue for style requirements.
   Preferred length: None
   Number of copies to be submitted: 2
   Abstract: Yes, with key words
Author information and reprints: Payment: None.
   Is simultaneous submission of article to other journals permitted: No
   Exclusive manuscript rights between acceptance and publication: Yes
   Copyright: Held by publication.
   Reprints: Available at cost
Disposition of manuscript:
   Query letter: No
   Receipt of manuscript acknowledged: Yes
   Decision to publish in: 1-3 months
   Accepted manuscript published in: 6-9 months
   Rejected manuscript returned: Yes
   Rejected manuscript criticized: Yes
Submit to:
   Dr. F. Massarik
   6245 Scenic Avenue
   Hollywood, California 90068

   In Europe:
   Dr. Cary L. Cooper
   University of Manchester
   Institute of Science and Technology
   Department of Management Sciences
   Manchester M60 1QD, England

ISSUES IN RADICAL THERAPY [1407]
P. O. Box 23544
Oakland, California 94705
(415) 841-8023

First published in 1973

SUBSCRIPTION DATA
Issues and rates: Published quarterly.
   Average paid circulation: 2,500
   Annual rate(s): Individuals $4.00; Institutions $10.00; Students $4.00; Foreign individuals $5.00; Foreign institutions $12.00
Publisher or Sponsor: IRT Collective

EDITORIAL DESCRIPTION
A journal of practical politics which serves as a forum for dialogue and exchange of information among people involved in the radical therapy movement; expose and stop oppressive misuse of psychiatry by the establishment; a vehicle of exchange of practical experience and theory on how to be psychiatrists for each other.
Articles per average issue: 12
Audience: People in or interested in the radical therapy movement and people involved in giving therapy

MANUSCRIPT INFORMATION

Subject field(s): Anything relating to psychology, personal experiences of psychiatric oppression, political or social analysis of various modes of therapy, psychological warfare, and misuse of psychology in prisons, etc.

Manuscript requirements: No specific style guide.
   Preferred length: Up to 3,500 words; 5 to 15 pages
   Number of copies to be submitted: Three typewritten
   Abstract: Not necessary.

Author information and reprints: Payment: None.
   Is simultaneous submission of article to other journals permitted: Permitted, but not encouraged.
   Exclusive manuscript rights between acceptance and publication: No
   Copyright: Held by publication but freely transferred to author
   Reprints: Available at no cost. 10

Disposition of manuscript:
   Query letter: Not necessary.
   Receipt of manuscript acknowledged: Yes
   Decision to publish in: 2-6 Months
   Accepted manuscript published in: 3-6 Months
   Rejected manuscript returned: Yes, if return postage is supplied by author.
   Rejected manuscript criticized: Yes

Submit to:
Editor
(See address above)

JOURNAL OF ABNORMAL CHILD PSYCHOLOGY [1408]
Plenum Publishing Corporation
227 West 17th Street
New York, New York 10011
(212) 255-0713

First published in 1972

SUBSCRIPTION DATA

Issues and rates: Published quarterly.
   Annual rate(s): $16.00; Foreign $16.00; Institutions $32.00; Members $12.50; Foreign institutions $33.80

EDITORIAL DESCRIPTION

Devoted to research and theory concerned with psychopathology in childhood and adolescence emphasizing original experimental and correlational research

Articles per average issue: 10-12
Audience: Professional, academic
Manuscripts accepted in English

MANUSCRIPT INFORMATION

Manuscript requirements: APA
   Preferred length: None
   Number of copies to be submitted: 3
   Abstract: Yes. Of about 150 words

Author information and reprints: Payment: None.
   Is simultaneous submission of article to other journals permitted: Not permitted.
   Exclusive manuscript rights between acceptance and publication: Yes
   Copyright: Held by publication.
   Reprints: Available at cost.

Disposition of manuscript:
   Query letter: Not necessary.
   Receipt of manuscript acknowledged: Yes
   Decision to publish in: 2 months
   Accepted manuscript published in: 9 months
   Rejected manuscript returned: Yes, with return postage paid by publication.
   Rejected manuscript criticized: Yes

Submit to:
Dr. Herbert C. Quay
Editor
P. O. Box 24-8245
University of Miami
Coral Gables, Florida 33124
(305) 284-5208

JOURNAL OF ABNORMAL PSYCHOLOGY [1409]
American Psychological Association
1200 17th Street, N.W.
Washington, D.C. 20036
(202) 833-7670

Previously entitled *Journal of Abnormal and Social Psychology*

First published in 1906

SUBSCRIPTION DATA

Issues and rates: Published bi-monthly.
   Average paid circulation: 8,000
   Annual rate(s): $24.00, Members $10.00, Foreign $25.00

Publisher or Sponsor: American Psychological Association

Managing Editor: Anita DeVivo

EDITORIAL DESCRIPTION

Devoted to basic research and theory in the broad field of abnormal behavior, its determinants, and its correlates.

Articles per average issue: 15-20
Audience: Psychologists, health professionals, academic
Manuscripts accepted in English

MANUSCRIPT INFORMATION

Manuscript requirements: APA; Chicago
   Preferred length: 10-20 manuscript pages
   Number of copies to be submitted: Three
   Abstract: Yes

Author information and reprints: Payment: None.
   Is simultaneous submission of article to other journals permitted: No
   Exclusive manuscript rights between acceptance and publication: Yes
   Copyright: Held by APA; author's permission required to reprint.
   Reprints: Available in minimum orders of 100

Disposition of manuscript:
   Query letter: No
   Receipt of manuscript acknowledged: Yes
   Decision to publish in: 2 months
   Accepted manuscript published in: 12 month maximum
   Rejected manuscript returned: Yes
   Rejected manuscript criticized: Yes

Submit to:
Leonard Eron
Editor
Department of Psychology, Box 4348
University of Illinois, Chicago Circle
Chicago, Illinois 60680

THE JOURNAL OF ANALYTICAL PSYCHOLOGY [1410]
30 Devonshire Place
London W.1, England
01-486 2321

First published in 1955

SUBSCRIPTION DATA

Issues and rates: Published semi-annually.
   Average paid circulation: 1,200
   Annual rate(s): $10.00

Publisher or Sponsor: The Society of Analytical Psychology, Ltd.

EDITORIAL DESCRIPTION

Contains articles on all aspects of analytical psychology, as exemplified in the writings of C. G. Jung.

Articles per average issue: 6
Audience: Anyone interested in the work of C.G. Jung
Manuscripts accepted in English

MANUSCRIPT INFORMATION

Subject field(s): Psycho-therapy, clinical papers, academic psychology, psychiatry (all aspects of this field), theology, comparative religion, philosophy, anthropology, education, art, literature

Manuscript requirements: Style sheet sent on request.
   Preferred length: 3,000 to 6,000 words
   Number of copies to be submitted: Two
   Abstract: No

Author information and reprints: Payment: None.
   Is simultaneous submission of article to other journals permitted: No
   Exclusive manuscript rights between acceptance and publication: No
   Copyright: Held by publication.
   Reprints: Available, 50 free

Additional information: Papers to be typewritten, double-spaced on A4 paper. Full list of references required to be laid out in accordance with Notes for Authors (sent on request).

Disposition of manuscript:
   Query letter: No
   Receipt of manuscript acknowledged: Yes
   Decision to publish in: 4 weeks
   Accepted manuscript published in: 6-18 months
   Rejected manuscript returned: Yes
   Rejected manuscript criticized: No

Submit to:
A. Plaut
Editor
(See address above)

JOURNAL OF APPLIED BEHAVIOR ANALYSIS [1411]

Department of Human Development
University of Kansas
Lawrence, Kansas 66044
(913) 843-0008

First published in 1968

SUBSCRIPTION DATA

Issues and rates: Published quarterly.
　Average paid circulation: 7,000
　Annual rate(s): $18.00
Publisher or Sponsor: Society for the Experimental Analysis of Behavior, Inc.
Managing Editor: H. Garth Hopkins

EDITORIAL DESCRIPTION

　Original publication of reports of experimental research involving applications of the analysis of behavior to problems of social importance as well as technical articles relevant to such research and discussions of issues arising from behavioral applications.
Articles per average issue: 18
Audience: Psychologists, psychiatrists, educators, social workers
　Manuscripts accepted in English

MANUSCRIPT INFORMATION

Manuscript requirements: See latest issue for style requirements.
　Number of copies to be submitted: Five
　Abstract: Yes
Author information and reprints: Payment: None.
　Is simultaneous submission of article to other journals permitted: No
　Exclusive manuscript rights between acceptance and publication: Yes
　Copyright: Held by publication.
　Reprints: Available, cost based on number of pages and prints.
Disposition of manuscript:
　Receipt of manuscript acknowledged: Yes
　Decision to publish in: 3-6 months
　Accepted manuscript published in: 3 months
　Rejected manuscript returned: Yes
　Rejected manuscript criticized: Yes
Submit to:
　Dr. Stewart Agras
　Editor
　Department of Psychiatry
　Stanford University
　Stanford, California

JOURNAL OF APPLIED PSYCHOLOGY* [1412]

American Psychological Association
1200 17th Street, N.W.
Washington, D.C. 20036
(202) 833-7670

SUBSCRIPTION DATA

Issues and rates: Published bi-monthly.
　Average paid circulation: 8,100
　Annual rate(s): $24.00, Members $10.00, Foreign $25.00
Publisher or Sponsor: American Psychological Association

EDITORIAL DESCRIPTION

　Devoted primarily to original investigations, contributing new knowledge and understanding to any field of applied psychology, except clinical psychology. Consideration will be given to quantitative investigations of interest to psychologists,

MANUSCRIPT INFORMATION

Subject field(s): Business, industry, government, urban affairs, police and correctional systems, health systems and institutions, transportation and defense systems, space and other new environments, educational systems and consumer affairs. A theoretical or review article may be accepted if it represents a special contribution to an applied field.
Manuscript requirements: APA; Chicago
　Number of copies to be submitted: Three
Author information and reprints: Payment: None.
　Is simultaneous submission of article to other journals permitted: No
　Exclusive manuscript rights between acceptance and publication: Yes
　Copyright: Held by APA; author's permission required to reprint.
　Reprints: Available in minimum orders of 100
Disposition of manuscript:
　Receipt of manuscript acknowledged: Yes
　Decision to publish in: 2 months
　Accepted manuscript published in: 12 month maximum
　Rejected manuscript returned: Yes
　Rejected manuscript criticized: Yes
Submit to:
　Editor
　(See address above)

JOURNAL OF BEHAVIOR THERAPY AND EXPERIMENTAL PSYCHIATRY [1413]

An Interdisciplinary Journal
Pergamon Press, Inc.
Fairview Park
Elmsford, New York 10523
(914) 592-7700

First published in 1970

SUBSCRIPTION DATA

Issues and rates: Published quarterly.
　Annual rate(s): $25.00; Institutions $45.00

EDITORIAL DESCRIPTION

　Publishes original research papers in behavior therapy and psychiatry, intending to overcome the training gap in behavior therapy for the medically trained therapist.
Articles per average issue: 2-10
Audience: Professional, academic
　Manuscripts accepted in English

MANUSCRIPT INFORMATION

Subject field(s): Expositions of technical details not found in textbooks; case reports and transcriptions of interviews, new procedures, disquitions on theory of behavior, disorders in particular and theory of behavior change in general.
Manuscript requirements: See latest issue for style requirements.
　Preferred length: None
　Number of copies to be submitted: Original and 2 copies
　Abstract: Yes. A summary not exceeding 200 words on a separate sheet in duplicate.
Author information and reprints: Payment: Reprints only. 50 reprints
　Is simultaneous submission of article to other journals permitted: Not permitted.
　Exclusive manuscript rights between acceptance and publication: Yes
　Copyright: Held by publication.
　Reprints: Available at cost.
Disposition of manuscript:
　Query letter: Not necessary.
　Receipt of manuscript acknowledged: Yes
　Decision to publish in: 4 weeks
　Accepted manuscript published in: 5 months
　Rejected manuscript returned: Yes, if return postage is supplied by author.
　Rejected manuscript criticized: Reasons for rejections only
Submit to:
　Prof. Joseph Wolpe
　Editor
　Eastern Pennsylvania Psychiatric Institute
　3300 Henry Avenue
　Philadelphia, Pennsylvania 19129

JOURNAL OF CHILD PSYCHOLOGY AND PSYCHIATRY [1414]

Pergamon Press, Inc.
Fairview Park
Elmsford, New York 10523
(914) 592-7700

First published in 1960

SUBSCRIPTION DATA

Issues and rates: Published bi-monthly.
　Annual rate(s): $25.00; Institutions $40.00
Publisher or Sponsor: Association for Child Psychology and Psychiatry

EDITORIAL DESCRIPTION

　Contains original articles, reviews and correspondence primarily in child psychology and psychiatry, including developmental and experimental studies, but recognizes that many other disciplines have an important contribution to make in the mental life and behaviour of children.
Articles per average issue: 5-8
Audience: Professional, academic
　Manuscripts accepted in English

MANUSCRIPT INFORMATION
Subject field(s): Such related fields as animal behavior, anthropology, education, family studies, pediatrics, physiology and sociology
Manuscript requirements: See latest issue for style requirements.
   Preferred length: None
   Number of copies to be submitted: 2 double-spaced on quarto paper
   Abstract: Yes
Author information and reprints: Payment: Reprints only. 50 reprints
   Is simultaneous submission of article to other journals permitted: Not permitted.
   Exclusive manuscript rights between acceptance and publication: Yes
   Copyright: Held by publication.
   Reprints: Available at cost.
Disposition of manuscript:
   Query letter: Not necessary.
   Receipt of manuscript acknowledged: Yes
   Decision to publish in: 4 weeks
   Accepted manuscript published in: 5 months
   Rejected manuscript returned: Yes, if return postage is supplied by author.
   Rejected manuscript criticized: Reasons for rejections only
Submit to:
   Prof. Leon Eisenberg
   Harvard Medical School
   Boston, Massachusetts 02114

   Prof. S. H. White
   Department of Psychology and Social Relations
   Harvard University
   Cambridge, Massachusetts 02138
   Corresponding Editors

JOURNAL OF CLINICAL PSYCHOLOGY [1415]
4 Conant Square
Brandon, Vermont 05733
(802) 247-6871

First published in 1946

SUBSCRIPTION DATA
Issues and rates: Published quarterly.
   Average paid circulation: 2500
   Annual rate(s): $25.00; Foreign $26.00
Managing Editor: Patricia A. Germeles

EDITORIAL DESCRIPTION
   Contains basic research studies in clinical psychology areas of psychodiagnosis, psychodynamics, psychopathology, clinical judgment, objective tests, personality tests, projective tests, and psychological case handling.
Articles per average issue: 30
Audience: Clinical psychologists
   Manuscripts accepted in English

MANUSCRIPT INFORMATION
Manuscript requirements: Style sheet sent on request.
   Preferred length: 4-6 pages
   Number of copies to be submitted: Original and 2 carbons
   Abstract: Yes
Author information and reprints: Payment: By author to publication. per page.
   Is simultaneous submission of article to other journals permitted: Yes
   Exclusive manuscript rights between acceptance and publication: Yes
   Copyright: Held by publication.
   Reprints: Available at regular prices
Additional information: Only objective research studies are considered.
Disposition of manuscript:
   Query letter: No
   Receipt of manuscript acknowledged: Yes
   Decision to publish in: 14 days
   Accepted manuscript published in: 3-6 months
   Rejected manuscript returned: Yes
   Rejected manuscript criticized: Yes
Submit to:
   Vladimir Pishkin
   Editor
   VA Hospital
   921 Northeast 13th Street
   Oklahoma City, Oklahoma 73104

JOURNAL OF COMMUNITY PSYCHOLOGY [1416]
4 Conant Square
Brandon, Vermont 05733
(802) 247-6871

First published in 1973

SUBSCRIPTION DATA
Issues and rates: Published quarterly.
   Average paid circulation: 750
   Annual rate(s): $25.00, Foreign $26.00
Managing Editor: C. S. Jakiela

EDITORIAL DESCRIPTION
   Contains research reports of interest to community mental health.
Articles per average issue: 15
Audience: Psychologists of the community
   Manuscripts accepted in English

MANUSCRIPT INFORMATION
Subject field(s): Community Psychology
Manuscript requirements: Style sheet sent on request.
   Preferred length: 4-6 pages
   Number of copies to be submitted: Three
   Abstract: Yes
Author information and reprints: Payment: By author to publication. Determined by editor
   Is simultaneous submission of article to other journals permitted: Yes
   Exclusive manuscript rights between acceptance and publication: Yes
   Copyright: Held by publication.
   Reprints: Available
Disposition of manuscript:
   Query letter: No
   Receipt of manuscript acknowledged: Yes
   Decision to publish in: 2 weeks
   Accepted manuscript published in: 6 months
   Rejected manuscript returned: Yes, if return postage is supplied by author.
   Rejected manuscript criticized: Yes
Submit to:
   J.R. Newbrough
   Box 319
   George Peabody College
   Nashville, Tennessee 37203

JOURNAL OF COMPARATIVE AND PHYSIOLOGICAL PSYCHOLOGY [1417]
American Psychological Association
1200 17th Street, N.W.
Washington, D.C. 20036
(202) 833-7670

Previously entitled *Journal of Animal Behavior, Psychobiology*

First published in Present title since 1947

SUBSCRIPTION DATA
Issues and rates: Published monthly.
   Average paid circulation: 3,720
   Annual rate(s): $60.00, Members $25.00, Foreign $61.00
Publisher or Sponsor: American Psychological Association
Managing Editor: Anita DeVivo

EDITORIAL DESCRIPTION
   Publishes original research reports in the field of comparative and physiological psychology, including animal learning, conditioning, and sensory processes. Editorial policies favor articles reporting studies of substantial scope, usually involving a series of related experiments.
Articles per average issue: 10
Audience: Research, academic
   Manuscripts accepted in English

MANUSCRIPT INFORMATION
Manuscript requirements: APA; Chicago
   Preferred length: 20-50 typewritten pages
   Number of copies to be submitted: 3
   Abstract: Yes, under 175 words
Author information and reprints: Payment: None.
   Is simultaneous submission of article to other journals permitted:
   Exclusive manuscript rights between acceptance and publication: Yes
   Copyright: Held by APA; author's permission required to reprint.
   Reprints: Available in minimum orders of 100
Disposition of manuscript:
   Query letter: No
   Receipt of manuscript acknowledged: Yes
   Decision to publish in: 2 months
   Accepted manuscript published in: 12 months maximum
   Rejected manuscript returned: Yes
   Rejected manuscript criticized: Yes
Submit to:
   Garth J. Thomas
   Editor
   Center for Brain Research
   University of Rochester Medical Center
   Rochester, New York 14642

JOURNAL OF CONSULTING AND CLINICAL PSYCHOLOGY* [1418]

American Psychological Association
1200 17th Street, N.W.
Washington, D.C. 20036
(202) 833-7670

SUBSCRIPTION DATA

Issues and rates: Published bi-monthly.
  Average paid circulation: 12,255
  Annual rate(s): $24.00, Members $10.00, Foreign $25.00
Publisher or Sponsor: American Psychological Association

EDITORIAL DESCRIPTION

Publishes original contributions on the development, validity, and use of techniques of diagnosis and treatment in disordered behavior; studies of populations of clinical interest.

MANUSCRIPT INFORMATION

Subject field(s): Hospital, prison, rehabilitation, geriatric, and similar samples; cross-cultural and demographic studies of interest for the behaviour disorders; studies of personality and of its assessment and development where these have a clear bearing on problems of consulting and clinical psychology; the etiology and characteristics of psychopathological states; or case studies pertinent to the preceding topics.
Manuscript requirements: APA; Chicago
  Number of copies to be submitted: Three
Author information and reprints: Payment: None.
  Is simultaneous submission of article to other journals permitted: No
  Exclusive manuscript rights between acceptance and publication: Yes
  Copyright: Held by APA; author's permission required to reprint.
  Reprints: Available in minimum orders of 100
Disposition of manuscript:
  Receipt of manuscript acknowledged: Yes
  Decision to publish in: 2 months
  Accepted manuscript published in: 12 month maximum
  Rejected manuscript returned: Yes
  Rejected manuscript criticized: Yes
Submit to:
  Editor
  (See address above)

JOURNAL OF COUNSELING PSYCHOLOGY* [1419]

American Psychological Association
1200 17th Street, N.W.
Washington, D.C. 20036
(202) 833-7670

SUBSCRIPTION DATA

Issues and rates: Published bi-monthly.
  Average paid circulation: 11,350
  Annual rate(s): $15.00, Members $5.00, Foreign $16.00
Publisher or Sponsor: American Psychological Association

EDITORIAL DESCRIPTION

Serves as a primary publication medium for theory and research on counseling and related activities carried on by counselors and personnel workers. Developmental aspects of counseling as well as diagnostic, remedial, and therapeutic approaches.
Audience: Psychologists and counselors

MANUSCRIPT INFORMATION

Manuscript requirements: APA; Chicago
  Number of copies to be submitted: Two
Author information and reprints: Payment: None.
  Is simultaneous submission of article to other journals permitted: No
  Exclusive manuscript rights between acceptance and publication: Yes
  Copyright: Held by APA; author's permission required to reprint.
  Reprints: Available in minimum orders of 100
Disposition of manuscript:
  Receipt of manuscript acknowledged: Yes
  Decision to publish in: 2 months
  Accepted manuscript published in: 12 month maximum
  Rejected manuscript returned: Yes
  Rejected manuscript criticized: Yes
Submit to:
  Editor
  (See address above)

  Beginning 1976:
  Dr. Samuel H. Osipow
  Editor
  Department of Psychology
  Ohio State University
  Columbus, Ohio 43210

JOURNAL OF CROSS-CULTURAL PSYCHOLOGY [1420]

Sage Publications, Inc.
275 South Beverly Drive
Beverly Hills, California 90212
(213) 274-2423

First published in 1970

SUBSCRIPTION DATA

Issues and rates: Published quarterly.
  Average paid circulation: Not available.
  Annual rate(s): Institutions $20.00; Individuals $12.00; Students $10.00; Foreign individuals $11.50; Foreign institutions $16.50
Publisher or Sponsor: International Association of Cross-Cultural Psychology, Western Washington State College

EDITORIAL DESCRIPTION

Publishes work in cross-cultural behavioral and social research; studies of psychological phenomena (including motivation, learning, attitudes, and perception) as conditioned by cultures and subcultures; comparative correlational and experimental inferential research as well as theoretical and critical papers.
Articles per average issue: 9-10
Audience: Psychologists, anthropologists
  Manuscripts accepted in English

MANUSCRIPT INFORMATION

Subject field(s): Psychology, culture, sociology, political science, anthropology
Manuscript requirements: Style sheet sent on request. and APA
  Preferred length: 6,250-7,500 words; 10 to 30 pages
  Number of copies to be submitted: 3
  Abstract: Yes
Author information and reprints: Payment: Reprints only. 25 tear-sheets
  Is simultaneous submission of article to other journals permitted: Permitted, but not encouraged. Author must notify publisher that manuscript is under consideration elsewhere.
  Exclusive manuscript rights between acceptance and publication: Yes
  Copyright: Held by Department of Psychology, Western Washington State College
  Reprints: Available if purchased by special order in amounts no fewer than 100
Disposition of manuscript:
  Query letter: No
  Receipt of manuscript acknowledged: Yes
  Decision to publish in: 6-8 weeks
  Accepted manuscript published in: 6-9 months
  Rejected manuscript returned: Yes
  Rejected manuscript criticized: Yes
Submit to:
  Walter J. Lonner
  Editor
  Department of Psychology
  Western Washington State College
  Bellingham, Washington 98225

JOURNAL OF EDUCATIONAL PSYCHOLOGY* [1421]

American Psychological Association
1200 17th Street, N.W.
Washington, D.C. 20036
(202) 833-7670

SUBSCRIPTION DATA

Issues and rates: Published bi-monthly.
  Average paid circulation: 9,800
  Annual rate(s): $24.00, Members $10.00, Foreign $25.00
Publisher or Sponsor: American Psychological Association

EDITORIAL DESCRIPTION

Publishes original investigations and theoretical papers dealing with problems of learning, teaching, and the psychological development, relationships, and adjustment of the individual.

MANUSCRIPT INFORMATION

Subject field(s): Preference is given to studies of the more complex types of behaviour, especially in or relating to

educational settings. Papers concern all levels of education and all age groups.
Manuscript requirements: APA; Chicago
  Number of copies to be submitted: Two
Author information and reprints: Payment: None.
  Is simultaneous submission of article to other journals permitted: No
  Exclusive manuscript rights between acceptance and publication: Yes
  Copyright: Held by APA; author's permission required to reprint.
  Reprints: Available in minimum orders of 100
Disposition of manuscript:
  Receipt of manuscript acknowledged: Yes
  Decision to publish in: 2 months
  Accepted manuscript published in: 12 month maximum
  Rejected manuscript returned: Yes
  Rejected manuscript criticized: Yes
Submit to:
  Joanna Williams
  Editor
  Department of Psychology
  Teachers College, Columbia University
  New York, New York 10027

JOURNAL OF THE EXPERIMENTAL ANALYSIS OF BEHAVIOR [1422]

Department of Psychology
Indiana University
Bloomington, Indiana 47401
(812) 336-5416

First published in 1958

SUBSCRIPTION DATA

Issues and rates: Published bi-monthly.
  Average paid circulation: 4,100
  Annual rate(s): Individuals $10.00; Institutions $22.00; Students $5.00; Foreign individuals $10.00
Publisher or Sponsor: Society for the Experimental Analysis of Behavior, Inc.
Managing Editor: H. Garth Hopkins

EDITORIAL DESCRIPTION

Primarily for the original publication of experiments relevant to the behavior of individual organisms. Review articles and theoretical papers will also be considered for publication.
Articles per average issue: 21
Audience: Experimental psychologists, research, academic
  Manuscripts accepted in English only

MANUSCRIPT INFORMATION

Subject field(s): Psychology, biology
Manuscript requirements: APA; See January issue.
  Preferred length: No limits
  Number of copies to be submitted: Two
  Abstract: Yes, a maximum of 200 words.
Author information and reprints: Payment: None.
  Is simultaneous submission of article to other journals permitted: No
  Exclusive manuscript rights between acceptance and publication: Yes
  Copyright: Held by publication.
  Reprints: Available, cost depends on length
Disposition of manuscript:
  Query letter: No
  Receipt of manuscript acknowledged: Yes
  Decision to publish in: 1-3 months
  Accepted manuscript published in: 4-6 months
  Rejected manuscript returned: Yes
  Rejected manuscript criticized: Yes
Submit to:
  Victor G. Laties
  Editor
  Department of Radiation Biology and Biophysics
  University of Rochester School of Medicine and Biophysics
  Rochester, New York 14642
  (716) 275-3791

THE JOURNAL OF EXPERIMENTAL CHILD PSYCHOLOGY [1423]

Academic Press, Inc.
111 Fifth Avenue
New York, New York 10003

SUBSCRIPTION DATA

Issues and rates: Published bi-monthly.
  Annual rate(s): $67.00, Foreign $75.00
Managing Editor: Harry Beilin

EDITORIAL DESCRIPTION

Contains papers in which the behavior and development of children is clearly related to its determining variables. Typically this would mean that a variable has been manipulated in an experimental manner.

MANUSCRIPT INFORMATION

Manuscript requirements: APA
  Number of copies to be submitted: Two
  Abstract: Include a concise abstract not to exceed 300 words.
Author information and reprints: Payment: None.
  Is simultaneous submission of article to other journals permitted: No
  Exclusive manuscript rights between acceptance and publication: Yes
  Copyright: Held by publication.
  Reprints: First 50 free
Disposition of manuscript:
  Rejected manuscript returned: Yes
Submit to:
  Harry Beilin
  Editor
  City University of New York
  Graduate Center
  33 West 42nd Street
  New York, New York 10036

JOURNAL OF EXPERIMENTAL PSYCHOLOGY* [1424]

American Psychological Association
1200 17th Street, N.W.
Washington, D.C. 20036
(202) 833-7670

SUBSCRIPTION DATA

Issues and rates: Published monthly.
  Average paid circulation: 4,150
  Annual rate(s): $60.00, Members $25.00, Foreign $61.00
Publisher or Sponsor: American Psychological Association

EDITORIAL DESCRIPTION

Publishes original experimental investigations which contribute substantially toward the development of psychology as an experimental science.

MANUSCRIPT INFORMATION

Subject field(s): Studies with normal human subjects are favored over studies involving abnormal or animal subjects, except when the latter are specifically oriented toward the extension of general psychological theory. Experimental psychometric studies and studies in applied experimental psychology or engineering psychology may be accepted if they have broad implications for experimental and theoretical psychology.
Manuscript requirements: APA; Chicago
  Preferred length: 20 pages maximum
  Number of copies to be submitted: Two
Author information and reprints: Payment: None.
  Is simultaneous submission of article to other journals permitted: No
  Exclusive manuscript rights between acceptance and publication: Yes
  Copyright: Held by APA; author's permission required to reprint.
  Reprints: Available in minimum orders of 100
Disposition of manuscript:
  Receipt of manuscript acknowledged: Yes
  Decision to publish in: 2 months
  Accepted manuscript published in: 12 month maximum
  Rejected manuscript returned: Yes
  Rejected manuscript criticized: Yes
Submit to:
  David Grant
  Editor
  Department of Psychology
  University of Wisconsin
  Madison, Wisconsin 53706

JOURNAL OF FAMILY COUNSELING [1425]

Transaction, Inc.
Rutgers University
New Brunswick, New Jersey 08903
(201) 932-2280

First published in 1973

SUBSCRIPTION DATA

Issues and rates: Published semi-annually.
  Average paid circulation: 2,000; 1,000 controlled
  Annual rate(s): Individuals $6.00; Institutions $12.00; Students $6.00; Members $5.00; Foreign individuals $7.00; Foreign institutions $13.00

Publisher or Sponsor: National Alliance for Family Life, Inc.
Managing Editor: Dr. Daniel L. Araoz

EDITORIAL DESCRIPTION

Published for the busy clinician in the general field of family counseling; from premarital to divorce counseling and psychotherapy, sex education, child rearing, marriage enrichment and counseling. Articles having a practical, clinical orientation.
Articles per average issue: 15
Audience: Practicing psychotherapists
Manuscripts accepted in any language

MANUSCRIPT INFORMATION

Subject field(s): Any article which deals with clinical techniques and methodology in treating couples and families.
Manuscript requirements: See latest issue for style requirements.
Preferred length: As required
Number of copies to be submitted: 2
Abstract: Yes.
Author information and reprints: Payment: None.
Is simultaneous submission of article to other journals permitted: Not permitted.
Exclusive manuscript rights between acceptance and publication: Yes
Copyright: Held by publication.
Reprints: Available at cost.
Disposition of manuscript:
Query letter: Necessary.
Receipt of manuscript acknowledged: Yes
Decision to publish in: Up to 6 months
Accepted manuscript published in: 6 months
Rejected manuscript returned: Yes, if return postage is supplied by author.
Rejected manuscript criticized: Sometimes
Submit to:
Zerka T. Moreno
Editor
(See address above)

THE JOURNAL OF GENERAL PSYCHOLOGY [1426]

Experimental, Physiological and Comparative Psychology
The Journal Press
2 Commercial Street
Provincetown, Massachusetts 02657
(617) 487-0133

First published in 1928

SUBSCRIPTION DATA

Issues and rates: Published quarterly.
Average paid circulation: 1653; 37 controlled
Annual rate(s): $26.00
Managing Editor: Powell Murchison

EDITORIAL DESCRIPTION

Devoted to experimental, physiological, and comparative psychology, with briefly reported replications, refinements, and comments.
Articles per average issue: 15

Audience: Experimental and comparative psychologists
Manuscripts accepted in English only

MANUSCRIPT INFORMATION

Subject field(s): Experimental psychology, comparative psychology, physiological psychology
Manuscript requirements: Style sheet sent on request.
Preferred length: 3000-6000 words
Number of copies to be submitted: Two
Abstract: As summary only
Author information and reprints: Payment: By author to publication. Author pays only for unusual expenses, such as tables, figures, equations, and special fonts.
Is simultaneous submission of article to other journals permitted: No
Exclusive manuscript rights between acceptance and publication: Yes
Copyright: Held by publication.
Reprints: Available, 100 free to author.
Additional information: All copy must be double-spaced and the original typewritten manuscript must be submitted with a legible carbon copy or photocopy.
Disposition of manuscript:
Query letter: No
Receipt of manuscript acknowledged: Yes
Decision to publish in: 2-4 weeks
Accepted manuscript published in: 1 year
Rejected manuscript returned: Yes
Rejected manuscript criticized: Occasionally
Submit to:
Powell Murchison
Managing Editor
(See address above)

THE JOURNAL OF GENETIC PSYCHOLOGY [1427]

Developmental and Clinical Psychology
The Journal Press
2 Commercial Street
Provincetown, Massachusetts 02657
(617) 487-0133

Previously entitled *The Pedagogical Seminary*

First published in 1891

SUBSCRIPTION DATA

Issues and rates: Published quarterly.
Average paid circulation: 1602; 31 controlled
Annual rate(s): $26.00
Managing Editor: Powell Murchison

EDITORIAL DESCRIPTION

Devoted to developmental and clinical psychology, with briefly reported replications and refinements and occasional book reviews.
Articles per average issue: 17
Audience: Developmental and clinical psychologists
Manuscripts accepted in English only

MANUSCRIPT INFORMATION

Subject field(s): Developmental psychology, clinical psychology
Manuscript requirements: Style sheet sent on request.
Preferred length: 3000-6000 words
Number of copies to be submitted: Two
Abstract: As summary only; everything typewritten, double-spaced, original plus one carbon or photocopy.
Author information and reprints: Payment: By author to publication. Author pays only for unusual expenses, such as tables, figures, equations, and special fonts.
Is simultaneous submission of article to other journals permitted: No
Exclusive manuscript rights between acceptance and publication: Yes
Copyright: Held by publication.
Reprints: Available, 100 free to author.
Additional information: All copy must be double-spaced and the original typewritten manuscript must be submitted with a legible carbon copy or photocopy.
Disposition of manuscript:
Query letter: No
Receipt of manuscript acknowledged: Yes
Decision to publish in: 2-4 weeks
Accepted manuscript published in: 18 months
Rejected manuscript returned: Yes
Rejected manuscript criticized: Occasionally
Submit to:
Powell Murchison
Managing Editor
(See address above)

JOURNAL OF GERIATRIC PSYCHIATRY [1428]

International Universities Press, Inc.
239 Park Avenue South
New York, New York 10003
(212) 674-2021

First published in 1967

SUBSCRIPTION DATA

Issues and rates: Published semi annually.
Annual rate(s): $12.00; Foreign £6.00; Institutions $20.00
Publisher or Sponsor: The Boston Society for Gerontologic Psychiatry, Inc.

EDITORIAL DESCRIPTION

Designed to set before psychiatrists, psychologists, social workers, social scientists, and medical personnel the new thinking and recent findings in the field of geriatric psychiatry
Articles per average issue: 7-8
Manuscripts accepted in English

MANUSCRIPT INFORMATION

Manuscript requirements: See latest issue for style requirements. Style sheet sent on request.
Preferred length: Unspecified
Number of copies to be submitted: Original and 3 copies
Abstract: Not necessary.

Author information and reprints: Payment: None.
Is simultaneous submission of article to other journals permitted: Not permitted.
Exclusive manuscript rights between acceptance and publication: Yes
Copyright: Held by International Universities Press, Inc.
Reprints: Available at cost.
Disposition of manuscript:
Query letter: Not necessary.
Receipt of manuscript acknowledged: Yes
Decision to publish in: 3-4 weeks
Accepted manuscript published in: 6-12 months
Rejected manuscript returned: Yes, with return postage paid by publication.
Rejected manuscript criticized: Reasons for rejections only
Submit to:
Martin A. Berezin, M.D.;
Sidney Levin, M.D.
90 Forest Avenue
West Newton, Massachusetts 02165

JOURNAL OF GRAPHOANALYSIS [1429]
Scientific Handwriting Analysis
325 West Jackson Boulevard
Chicago, Illinois 60606
(312) 922-0856

First published in 1929

SUBSCRIPTION DATA
Issues and rates: Published monthly.
Average paid circulation: 50,000
Annual rate(s): $10.00
Publisher or Sponsor: International Graphoanalysis Society
Managing Editor: V. Peter Ferrara

EDITORIAL DESCRIPTION
Contains articles on topics closely related to behavioral sciences, applied psychology.
Articles per average issue: 5
Audience: Psychologists, students
Manuscripts accepted in English, French

MANUSCRIPT INFORMATION
Subject field(s): Psychology, marriage, child rearing, health, vocational, effective living
Manuscript requirements: Chicago
Preferred length: 1500 words
Number of copies to be submitted: One
Abstract: Yes
Author information and reprints: Payment: By publication to author. $25-$75 depending on value of article.
Is simultaneous submission of article to other journals permitted: Yes
Exclusive manuscript rights between acceptance and publication: No
Copyright: Held by publication.
Reprints: Available at cost
Disposition of manuscript:
Query letter: No
Receipt of manuscript acknowledged: Yes
Decision to publish in: Two weeks
Accepted manuscript published in: 3 months
Rejected manuscript returned: Yes, if self-addressed, stamped envelope is sent with manuscript.
Rejected manuscript criticized: No
Submit to:
V. Peter Ferrara
Managing Editor
(See address above)

JOURNAL OF HOMOSEXUALITY [1430]
Haworth Press
130 West 72nd Street
New York, New York 10023

First published in 1974

SUBSCRIPTION DATA
Issues and rates: Published quarterly.
Average paid circulation: 5,000
Annual rate(s): $12.00; Pan-Am $17.00; Foreign $17.00
Managing Editor: Margaret Morewhite

EDITORIAL DESCRIPTION
Publishes original research, and clinical articles on homosexuality and gender identity, from the fields of psychology, sociology, anthropology, medicine, social work and law.
Articles per average issue: 7
Audience: Psychologists, mental health professionals, sociologists and other behavioral and social scientists
Manuscripts accepted in English

MANUSCRIPT INFORMATION
Subject field(s): Psychology, sociology, anthropology, law
Manuscript requirements: Style sheet sent on request. APA
Preferred length: 15-20 pages
Number of copies to be submitted: 2
Abstract: Yes. APA Manual
Author information and reprints: Payment: None.
Is simultaneous submission of article to other journals permitted: Not permitted.
Exclusive manuscript rights between acceptance and publication: Yes
Copyright: Held by publication.
Reprints: Available at no cost. 50
Disposition of manuscript:
Query letter: Necessary.
Receipt of manuscript acknowledged: Yes
Decision to publish in: 3 months
Accepted manuscript published in: Varies
Rejected manuscript returned: Yes, if return postage is supplied by author.
Rejected manuscript criticized: Sometimes
Submit to:
Charles Silverstein
Editor
Institute for Human Identity, Inc.
490 West End Avenue, Suite 3-B
New York, New York 10023
(212) 799-9432

JOURNAL OF HUMANISTIC PSYCHOLOGY [1431]
Suite 206, 1314 Westwood Boulevard
Los Angeles, California 90024
(213) 474-6545

First published in 1961

SUBSCRIPTION DATA
Issues and rates: Published quarterly.
Average paid circulation: 6000; 100 controlled
Annual rate(s): $10.00
Publisher or Sponsor: Association for Humanistic Psychology
Managing Editor: Thomas C. Greening

EDITORIAL DESCRIPTION
Concerned with the publication of experiential reports, theoretical papers, research studies, applications of humanistic psychology, and humanistic analyses of contemporary culture. Topics of special interest are authenticity, encounter, self-actualization, search for meaning, creativity, intentionality, psychological health, being motivation, values, love, identity, and commitment.
Articles per average issue: 8
Audience: Humanistic psychologists, psychotherapists, teachers, general public
Manuscripts accepted in English

MANUSCRIPT INFORMATION
Subject field(s): Psychology, humanistic psychology, education, psychotherapy, philosophy, personal growth
Manuscript requirements: APA
Preferred length: 2 to 30 pages
Number of copies to be submitted: Two
Abstract: Not necessary
Author information and reprints: Payment: None.
Is simultaneous submission of article to other journals permitted: No
Exclusive manuscript rights between acceptance and publication: Yes
Copyright: Held by Association
Reprints: Available, 100 free
Disposition of manuscript:
Query letter: No
Receipt of manuscript acknowledged: Yes
Decision to publish in: 3 months
Accepted manuscript published in: 3 months
Rejected manuscript returned: Yes
Rejected manuscript criticized: Occasionally
Submit to:
Thomas C. Greening
Editor
(See address above)

JOURNAL OF INDIVIDUAL PSYCHOLOGY [1432]
140 Niviki Circle
Honolulu, Hawaii 96821
(802) 373-1839

Previously entitled *The American Journal of Individual Psychology*

Psychology and mental health

First published in 1945

SUBSCRIPTION DATA

Issues and rates: Published semi-annually.
Annual rate(s): $7.00
Publisher or Sponsor: American Society of Adlerian Psychology
Managing Editor: H. L. Ansbacher

EDITORIAL DESCRIPTION

Contains theoretical papers, research reports, case material and methods of psychotherapy. Point of view is holistic, goal-oriented, Adlerian psychology.
Articles per average issue: 15
Audience: General public
Manuscripts accepted in English

MANUSCRIPT INFORMATION

Subject field(s): Practice of psychotherapy, personality theory
Manuscript requirements: APA
Preferred length: Up to 5000 words
Number of copies to be submitted: Two
Abstract: No
Author information and reprints: Payment: None.
Is simultaneous submission of article to other journals permitted: No
Exclusive manuscript rights between acceptance and publication: Yes
Copyright: Held by publication.
Reprints: Available
Disposition of manuscript:
Query letter: No
Receipt of manuscript acknowledged: No
Decision to publish in: 2-3 months
Accepted manuscript published in: 6 months
Rejected manuscript returned: Yes
Rejected manuscript criticized: Yes
Submit to:
Raymond J. Corsini
Editor
(See address above)

JOURNAL OF MENTAL HEALTH [1433]

1341 G Street N.W., Room 426
Washington, D.C. 20005
(202) 628-4379

SUBSCRIPTION DATA

Issues and rates: Published monthly.
Average paid circulation: 1,200
Annual rate(s): $3.50, Foreign $4.50
Publisher or Sponsor: Neurotics Anonymous International Liaison, Inc.
Managing Editor: Grover Boydston

EDITORIAL DESCRIPTION

Contains editorials and articles about mental and emotional illness and recovery, recovery stories from members.
Articles per average issue: 3
Audience: Professional
Manuscripts accepted in English

MANUSCRIPT INFORMATION

Subject field(s): Mental health and illness

Manuscript requirements: See latest issue for style requirements.
Preferred length: 1,200 to 1,500 words; 3 to 5 printed pages
Number of copies to be submitted: One
Abstract: Yes
Author information and reprints: Payment: None.
Is simultaneous submission of article to other journals permitted: No
Exclusive manuscript rights between acceptance and publication: Yes
Copyright: Held by publication.
Reprints: Available, $.30 per copy
Disposition of manuscript:
Receipt of manuscript acknowledged: Yes
Decision to publish in: One month
Accepted manuscript published in: Two months
Rejected manuscript returned: No
Rejected manuscript criticized: No
Submit to:
Editor
(See address above)

JOURNAL OF MOTOR BEHAVIOR [1434]

727 De La Guerra Plaza
Santa Barbara, California 93101
(805) 963-4321

SUBSCRIPTION DATA

Issues and rates: Published quarterly.
Average paid circulation: 1015; 55 controlled
Annual rate(s): Individuals $10; Institutions $25
Managing Editor: Richard A. Schmidt

EDITORIAL DESCRIPTION

Publishes papers which contribute to a basic understanding of human motor behavior. The areas of motor learning and skilled performance predominate, but studies on other factors such as kinesthetic perception, fatigue, growth and maturation, and anthropometric variables related to skilled performance are acceptable.
Articles per average issue: 8

MANUSCRIPT INFORMATION

Subject field(s): Motor learning, human performance, motor memory, human factors, information processing
Manuscript requirements: APA
Preferred length: 1000-5000 words
Number of copies to be submitted: Three
Abstract: Yes
Author information and reprints: Payment: None.
Is simultaneous submission of article to other journals permitted: No
Exclusive manuscript rights between acceptance and publication: Yes
Copyright: Held by publication.
Reprints: Available, cost depending on article length
Disposition of manuscript:
Query letter: Yes
Receipt of manuscript acknowledged: Yes
Decision to publish in: Two months

Accepted manuscript published in: Six months
Rejected manuscript returned: Yes
Rejected manuscript criticized: Yes
Submit to:
Richard A. Schmidt
Managing Editor
Department of Physical Education
University of Southern California
Los Angeles, California 90007

JOURNAL OF MUSIC THERAPY [1435]

P.O. Box 610
Lawrence, Kansas 66044
(913) 842-1909

First published in 1964

SUBSCRIPTION DATA

Issues and rates: Published quarterly.
Average paid circulation: 2500
Annual rate(s): $7.00, Foreign $8.50
Publisher or Sponsor: National Association for Music Therapy, Inc.
Managing Editor: Margaret Sears

EDITORIAL DESCRIPTION

Contains professional articles concerning music therapy, book reviews, editorials, letters to editor, music therapy materials reviews.
Articles per average issue: 6
Audience: College level (generally) interested in music therapy
Manuscripts accepted in English

MANUSCRIPT INFORMATION

Subject field(s): Music therapy, allied health fields
Manuscript requirements: See latest issue for style requirements.
Preferred length: None
Number of copies to be submitted: Two
Abstract: Yes, see latest issue
Author information and reprints: Payment: None.
Is simultaneous submission of article to other journals permitted: Each case handled individually by editor.
Exclusive manuscript rights between acceptance and publication: No
Copyright: Held by publication.
Reprints: Available, author assumes cost
Additional information: Must be double spaced, on 8 ½ x 11 inch paper of medium weight.
Disposition of manuscript:
Query letter: No
Receipt of manuscript acknowledged: Yes
Decision to publish in: 2-3 months
Accepted manuscript published in: One year
Rejected manuscript returned: Yes
Rejected manuscript criticized: Only if possibility of acceptance upon revision
Submit to:
David E. Wolfe
Editor
Golden Valley Health Center
4101 Golden Valley Road
Minneapolis, Minnesota 55422
(612) 588-2771

JOURNAL OF PARAPSYCHOLOGY [1436]

Box 6847, College Station
Durham, North Carolina 27708
(919) 688-8241

First published in 1937

SUBSCRIPTION DATA

Issues and rates: Published quarterly.
Average paid circulation: 1250; 135 controlled
Annual rate(s): $8.00

Publisher or Sponsor: Foundation for Research on the Nature of Man

Managing Editor: Anne Carroll

EDITORIAL DESCRIPTION

Contains experimental reports, book reviews, parapsychological abstracts, correspondence, news and comments. Publishes reports of experimental research in parapsychology. Theoretical articles not usually acceptable unless accompanied by supporting data.
Articles per average issue: 4

Audience: Those interested in parapsychology
Manuscripts accepted in English

MANUSCRIPT INFORMATION

Subject field(s): Parapsychology

Manuscript requirements: See latest issue for style requirements.
Preferred length: 2400 to 3600 words; 10-15 printed pages
Number of copies to be submitted: Two
Abstract: Yes, 1-2 paragraph summary including all essential information: hypothesis, procedure, results, conclusion

Author information and reprints: Payment: None.
Is simultaneous submission of article to other journals permitted: No
Exclusive manuscript rights between acceptance and publication: Yes
Copyright: No copyright
Reprints: Available, half cost up to 200 reprints

Disposition of manuscript:
Query letter: No
Receipt of manuscript acknowledged: Yes
Decision to publish in: 1-2 months
Accepted manuscript published in: 6 months
Rejected manuscript returned: Yes, if return postage is supplied by author.
Rejected manuscript criticized: Yes
Submit to:
Dorothy H. Pope
Editor
(See address above)

JOURNAL OF PERSONALITY ASSESSMENT [1437]

Society for Personality Assessment, Inc.
1070 East Angeleno Avenue
Burbank, California 91501
(213) 848-6060

Previously entitled *Journal of Projective Techniques and Personality Assessment*

First published in 1936 (as *Rorschach Research Exchange*)
Average paid circulation: 2,700
Annual rate(s): $18.00; Foreign $19.00
Publisher or Sponsor: Society for Personality Assessment, Inc.
Managing Editor: Dr. Walter G. Klopfer

EDITORIAL DESCRIPTION

For the study and advancement of projective and other assessment techniques; research articles, reviews of literature, case studies, new tests, theoretical studies, comments, rebuttals and book reviews related to personality assessment
Articles per average issue: 10
Audience: Professionals concerned with the assessment of personality, clinical psychologists, psychiatrists, mental health scientists, students
Manuscripts accepted in English

MANUSCRIPT INFORMATION

Manuscript requirements: See latest issue for style requirements. APA
Preferred length: As required
Number of copies to be submitted: 3
Abstract: Yes.
Author information and reprints: Payment: None.
Is simultaneous submission of article to other journals permitted: Permitted, but not encouraged.
Exclusive manuscript rights between acceptance and publication: Yes
Copyright: Held by the Society
Reprints: Available at no cost. 50
Additional information: See the inside cover for stylistic requirements.
Disposition of manuscript:
Query letter: Not necessary.
Receipt of manuscript acknowledged: Yes
Decision to publish in: 2 months
Accepted manuscript published in: 1 year
Rejected manuscript returned: Yes, with return postage paid by publication.
Rejected manuscript criticized: Yes
Submit to:
Dr. Walter D. Klopfer
Editor
7840 S. W. 51st Street
Portland, Oregon 97219
(503) 246-6371

JOURNAL OF PERSONALITY AND SOCIAL PSYCHOLOGY [1438]

American Psychological Association
1200 17th Street, N.W.
Washington, D.C. 20036
(202) 833-7670

Previously entitled *Journal of Abnormal and Social Psychology*

SUBSCRIPTION DATA
Issues and rates: Published monthly.
Average paid circulation: 6,450
Annual rate(s): $48.00 Members $20.00, Foreign $49.00
Publisher or Sponsor: American Psychological Association
Managing Editor: Harold P. Van Cott

EDITORIAL DESCRIPTION

Publishes original research reports in the areas of social psychology and personality dynamics.
Articles per average issue: 18
Audience: Professional social scientists
Manuscripts accepted in English

MANUSCRIPT INFORMATION

Subject field(s): Methodological articles, studies primarily concerned with the development of measuring instruments, replications, and reports of negative results or failures to replicate published work are acceptable if they are judged to make a substantial contribution to knowledge.
Manuscript requirements: APA; Chicago
Preferred length: 9 pages maximum
Number of copies to be submitted: Two
Abstract: Yes, see APA
Author information and reprints: Payment: None.
Is simultaneous submission of article to other journals permitted: No
Exclusive manuscript rights between acceptance and publication: Yes
Copyright: Held by APA; author's permission required to reprint.
Reprints: Available in minimum orders of 100
Disposition of manuscript:
Query letter: No
Receipt of manuscript acknowledged: Yes
Decision to publish in: 2 months
Accepted manuscript published in: 12 month maximum
Rejected manuscript returned: Yes
Rejected manuscript criticized: Yes
Submit to:
John Lanzetta
Editor
Department of Psychology
Dartmouth College
Hanover, New Hampshire 03755

JOURNAL OF PHENOMENOLOGICAL PSYCHOLOGY [1439]

Studies in the Science of Human Experience and Behavior
Humanities Press, Inc.
Atlantic Highlands, New Jersey 07716
(201) 872-1441

First published in 1970

SUBSCRIPTION DATA
Issues and rates: Published semi-annually.
Annual rate(s): $9.00, Foreign $10.00
Managing Editor: Amedeo Giorgi

EDITORIAL DESCRIPTION

Contains theoretical and empirical articles demonstrating the value of phenomenological approach to psychology.

Psychology and mental health

Articles per average issue: 6
Audience: Psychologists, professionals
   Manuscripts accepted in English, French and German

MANUSCRIPT INFORMATION
Subject field(s): Psychology, philosophy, sociology, anthropology
Manuscript requirements: See latest issue for style requirements.
   Preferred length: 15-20 pages
   Number of copies to be submitted: 3
   Abstract: Yes
Author information and reprints: Payment: None.
   Is simultaneous submission of article to other journals permitted: No
   Exclusive manuscript rights between acceptance and publication: Yes
   Copyright: Held by publication.
   Reprints: Available
Disposition of manuscript:
   Query letter: Yes
   Receipt of manuscript acknowledged: Yes
   Decision to publish in: 6 months
   Accepted manuscript published in: 6-9 months
   Rejected manuscript returned: No
   Rejected manuscript criticized: Yes
Submit to:
   Amedeo P. Giorgi
   Editor
   Psychology Department
   Duquesne University
   Pittsburgh, Pennsylvania 15219
   (412) 434-6518

JOURNAL OF PSYCHIATRY AND LAW [1440]
95 Morton Street
New York, New York 10014
(212) 243-5775

First published in 1973

SUBSCRIPTION DATA
Issues and rates: Published quarterly.
   Average paid circulation: 1,500
   Annual rate(s): $20.00; Foreign $26.00; Institutions $24.00; Students $20.00; Foreign institutions $26.00
Managing Editor: Dianne Nashel

EDITORIAL DESCRIPTION
   Examines the interfaces of psychiatry and studies of human behavior with law; investigates law through the lens of man's knowledge of his mind
Articles per average issue: 4-6
Audience: Professional, academic, legal
   Manuscripts accepted in English

MANUSCRIPT INFORMATION
Subject field(s): Psychiatry and the law, rights of mental patients, suicide in prison, forensic psychiatry, crime and punishment and super ego
Manuscript requirements: Style sheet sent on request.
   Preferred length: As is necessary
   Number of copies to be submitted: 2
   Abstract: Yes
Author information and reprints: Payment: Reprints only. 50 copies of article and 2 issues
   Is simultaneous submission of article to other journals permitted: Not permitted.
   Exclusive manuscript rights between acceptance and publication: Yes
   Copyright: Held by publication. Author receives 50 per cent of reprint royalties.
   Reprints: Available at cost.
Disposition of manuscript:
   Query letter: Not necessary, but advisable.
   Receipt of manuscript acknowledged: Yes
   Decision to publish in: 30 days
   Accepted manuscript published in: 3-6 months
   Rejected manuscript returned: Yes, with return postage paid by publication.
   Rejected manuscript criticized: Sometimes
Submit to:
   Dianne Nashel
   Managing Editor
   28 Morris Road
   Tenafly, New Jersey 07670
   (201) 568-1159

THE JOURNAL OF PSYCHOLOGY [1441]
The General Field of Psychology
2 Commercial Street
Provincetown, Massachusetts 02657
(617) 487-0133

First published in 1936

SUBSCRIPTION DATA
Issues and rates: Published bi-monthly.
   Average paid circulation: 1726; 30 controlled
   Annual rate(s): $39.00
Managing Editor: Powell Murchison

EDITORIAL DESCRIPTION
   Devoted to all branches of psychology.
Articles per average issue: 20
Audience: All psychologists
   Manuscripts accepted in English only

MANUSCRIPT INFORMATION
Manuscript requirements: Style sheet sent on request.
   Preferred length: 1,000-10,000 words
   Number of copies to be submitted: Two
   Abstract: As summary only
Author information and reprints: Payment: By author to publication.
   Is simultaneous submission of article to other journals permitted: No
   Exclusive manuscript rights between acceptance and publication: Yes
   Copyright: Held by publication.
   Reprints: Available, 200 free to author.
Additional information: All copy must be double-spaced and the original typewritten manuscript must be submitted with a legible carbon copy or photocopy.
Disposition of manuscript:
   Query letter: No
   Receipt of manuscript acknowledged: Yes
   Decision to publish in: 1-2 weeks
   Accepted manuscript published in: 2 months or less
   Rejected manuscript returned: Yes
   Rejected manuscript criticized: Occasionally
Submit to:
   Powell Murchison
   Managing Editor
   (See address above)

SPECIAL STIPULATIONS
   This journal features very prompt publication.

JOURNAL OF SCHOOL PSYCHOLOGY [1442]
Behavioral Publications
72 Fifth Avenue
New York, New York 10011
(212) 243-6000

First published in 1963

SUBSCRIPTION DATA
Issues and rates: Published quarterly.
   Average paid circulation: 2,500
   Annual rate(s): Individuals $12.00, Institutions $30.00, Foreign individuals $14.00, Foreign institutions $32.00
Managing Editor: Jean Blackburn

EDITORIAL DESCRIPTION
   Publishes articles on research, opinions and practice in school psychology aimed toward fostering the continued development of school psychology as a scientific and professional specialty.
Articles per average issue: 8
   Manuscripts accepted in English

MANUSCRIPT INFORMATION
Subject field(s): Education, psychology
Manuscript requirements: APA
   Preferred length: 1500-4500 words; 5-15 pages
   Number of copies to be submitted: Two
   Abstract: Yes
Author information and reprints: Payment: None.
   Is simultaneous submission of article to other journals permitted: No
   Exclusive manuscript rights between acceptance and publication: Yes
   Copyright: Held by publication.
   Reprints: Available; cost varies
Disposition of manuscript:
   Query letter: No
   Receipt of manuscript acknowledged: Yes
   Decision to publish in: 6 weeks
   Accepted manuscript published in: 5 months
   Rejected manuscript returned: Yes, if return postage is supplied by author.
   Rejected manuscript criticized: Yes
Submit to:
   Beeman N. Phillips
   College of Education
   Department of Educational Psychology
   The University of Texas
   Austin, Texas 78712
   (512) 471-3653

JOURNAL OF SEX AND MARITAL THERAPY [1443]
Behavioral Publications
72 Fifth Avenue
New York, New York 10011
(212) 243-6000

First published in 1974

SUBSCRIPTION DATA
Issues and rates: Published quarterly.
  Average paid circulation: 2,000
  Annual rate(s): $15.00; Institutions $30.00
Managing Editor: Jean Blackburn

EDITORIAL DESCRIPTION
  Provides an active and contemporary forum for new clinical techniques and revolutionary ideas rapidly emerging from the practice of sex and marital therapy.
Articles per average issue: 6-8
  Manuscripts accepted in English

MANUSCRIPT INFORMATION
Subject field(s): New therapeutics techniques, outcome studies, special clinical problems, and innovative conceptualizations of sexual functioning and marital relationships.
Manuscript requirements: IM
  Preferred length: 10-15 typewritten pages
  Number of copies to be submitted: 2
  Abstract: Yes.
Author information and reprints: Payment: None.
  Is simultaneous submission of article to other journals permitted: Not permitted.
  Exclusive manuscript rights between acceptance and publication: Yes
  Copyright: Held by publication.
  Reprints: Available at cost.
Disposition of manuscript:
  Query letter: Not necessary.
  Receipt of manuscript acknowledged: Yes
  Decision to publish in: 3-6 months
  Accepted manuscript published in: 6 months
  Rejected manuscript returned: Yes, if return postage is supplied by author.
  Rejected manuscript criticized: No
Submit to:
  Helen S. Kaplan, M. D.;
  Clifford J. Sager, M. D.;
  Harold A. Lear, M. D.
  Editors
  Suite 1A
  65 East 76th Street
  New York, New York 10021

THE JOURNAL OF SOCIAL PSYCHOLOGY [1444]
2 Commercial Street
Provincetown, Massachusetts 02657
(617) 487-0133

First published in 1930

SUBSCRIPTION DATA
Issues and rates: Published bi-monthly.
  Average paid circulation: 2381; 31 controlled
  Annual rate(s): $39.00
Managing Editor: Powell Murchison

EDITORIAL DESCRIPTION
  Devoted to studies of persons in group settings and of culture and personality; special attention to cross-cultural articles and notes, and to briefly reported replications and refinements.
Articles per average issue: 25
Audience: Social psychologists
  Manuscripts accepted in English only

MANUSCRIPT INFORMATION
Subject field(s): Cross-cultural studies, group studies field research
Manuscript requirements: Style sheet sent on request.
  Preferred length: 500-5000 words
  Number of copies to be submitted: Two
  Abstract: As summary only
Author information and reprints: Payment: None. Author pays only for unusual expenses, such as tables, figures, equations, and special fonts.
  Is simultaneous submission of article to other journals permitted: No
  Exclusive manuscript rights between acceptance and publication: Yes
  Copyright: Held by publication.
  Reprints: Available, 100 free to author.
Additional information: All copy must be double-spaced and the original typewritten manuscript must be submitted with a legible carbon copy or photocopy.
Disposition of manuscript:
  Query letter: No
  Receipt of manuscript acknowledged: Yes
  Decision to publish in: 2-3 weeks
  Accepted manuscript published in: 1 year
  Rejected manuscript returned: Yes
  Rejected manuscript criticized: Occasionally
Submit to:
  Powell Murchison
  Managing Editor
  (See address above)

JOURNAL OF VOCATIONAL BEHAVIOR [1445]
Academic Press, Inc.
111 Fifth Avenue
New York, New York 10003
(212) 677-6713

SUBSCRIPTION DATA
Issues and rates: Published quarterly.
  Annual rate(s): Institutions $51.00, Individuals $51.00

EDITORIAL DESCRIPTION
  Publishes empirical, methodological, and theoretical articles related to vocational behavior.

MANUSCRIPT INFORMATION
Subject field(s): Validation of theoretical constructs, developments in instrumentation, program comparisons, and research methodology as related to vocational development, preference, choice, and selection, implementation, satisfaction, and effectiveness throughout the life span and across cultural, national, sex, and other demographic boundaries.
Manuscript requirements: APA; see latest issue.
  Number of copies to be submitted: Two
Author information and reprints: Payment: By author to publication. Alterations in excess of 10% of the cost of composition.
  Copyright: Held by publication.
  Reprints: Available; 50 free
Additional information: Author should not place name on the manuscript itself.
Submit to:
  Samuel H. Osipow
  Editor
  Department of Psychology
  The Ohio State University
  Columbus, Ohio 43210

LEARNING & MOTIVATION [1446]
Academic Press, Inc.
111 Fifth Avenue
New York, New York 10003

First published in 1970

SUBSCRIPTION DATA
Issues and rates: Published quarterly.
  Average paid circulation: 1,000
  Annual rate(s): $17.50; Foreign $19.50; Institutions $34.50; Foreign institutions $37.50

EDITORIAL DESCRIPTION
  Publishes original experimental and theoretical papers addressed to the analysis of basic phenomena and mechanisms of learning and motivation, including papers on biological and evolutionary influences upon the learning and motivation processes
Articles per average issue: 11
Audience: Professional
  Manuscripts accepted in English

MANUSCRIPT INFORMATION
Subject field(s): Behavioral psychology in the field of learning and motivation
Manuscript requirements: APA. See latest issue for style requirements.
  Number of copies to be submitted: 4
  Abstract: Yes. Of about 100-150 words
Author information and reprints: Payment: Reprints only. 50
  Is simultaneous submission of article to other journals permitted: Not permitted.
  Exclusive manuscript rights between acceptance and publication: Yes
  Copyright: Held by publication.
  Reprints: Available at cost.
Disposition of manuscript:
  Query letter: Not necessary.
  Receipt of manuscript acknowledged: Yes
  Decision to publish in: 2 months
  Accepted manuscript published in: 6 months
  Rejected manuscript returned: Yes, with return postage paid by publication.

Rejected manuscript criticized: Yes
Submit to:
 J. Bruce Overmier
 Editor
 Department of Psychology, Elliott Hall
 University of Minnesota
 Minneapolis, Minnesota 55455
 (612) 373-3430

MASSACHUSETTS JOURNAL OF MENTAL HEALTH [1447]
Department of Mental Health
190 Portland Street
Boston, Massachusetts 02114
(617) 727-8608

First published in 1970

SUBSCRIPTION DATA

Issues and rates: Published quarterly.
 Average paid circulation: 4000 controlled
 Annual rate(s): Free
Publisher or Sponsor: Massachusetts Department of Mental Health
Managing Editor: Evelyn M. Stone

EDITORIAL DESCRIPTION

Contains descriptions of programs, research and ideas pertaining to the area of mental health; editorial; research abstracts; book reviews; special features.
Articles per average issue: 2
Audience: Mental health professionals
 Manuscripts accepted in English

MANUSCRIPT INFORMATION

Subject field(s): Psychiatry, psychology, psychopharmacology, legal medicine, community medicine, mental retardation, psychiatric administration, psychiatric social work, psychiatric nursing, history
Manuscript requirements: Style sheet sent on request.
 Preferred length: 2500 to 5000 words; 10 to 20 pages
 Number of copies to be submitted: Three
 Abstract: No
Author information and reprints: Payment: None.
 Is simultaneous submission of article to other journals permitted: No
 Exclusive manuscript rights between acceptance and publication: Yes
 Copyright: Held by publication.
 Reprints: Available, limited
Additional information: Contributors should be residents of Massachusetts. Manuscript should be typed, double-spaced with full name, title, degrees, and affiliations on title page.
Disposition of manuscript:
 Query letter: No
 Receipt of manuscript acknowledged: Yes
 Decision to publish in: One month
 Accepted manuscript published in: 3-6 months
 Rejected manuscript returned: Yes
 Rejected manuscript criticized: Yes on some occasions
Submit to:
 Evelyn M. Stone
 Managing Editor
 (See address above)

MEMORY AND COGNITION [1448]
1108 West 34th Street
Austin, Texas 78705
(512) 454-7848

First published in 1973

SUBSCRIPTION DATA

Issues and rates: Published bi-monthly.
 Average paid circulation: 1,300
 Annual rate(s): $30.00; Institutions $30.00; Students $12.00; Foreign individuals $15.00; Foreign institutions $30.00
Publisher or Sponsor: Psychonomic Society, Inc.
Managing Editor: Ann L. Sanford

EDITORIAL DESCRIPTION

Covers human learning and memory, conceptual processes, psycholinguistics, problem solving, thinking, decision making and skilled performance as well as work directly related to these topics in the areas of computer simulation, information processing, mathematical psychology, etc.
Articles per average issue: Varies
Audience: Professional psychologists, academic
 Manuscripts accepted in English

MANUSCRIPT INFORMATION

Manuscript requirements: See latest issue for style requirements. Style sheet sent on request. APA
 Preferred length: None
 Number of copies to be submitted: 2
 Abstract: Yes. A concise paragraph of not more than 100-150 words
Author information and reprints: Payment: None.
 Reprints: Available at cost.
Disposition of manuscript:
 Query letter: Not necessary.
 Receipt of manuscript acknowledged: Yes
 Decision to publish in: 2-4 weeks
 Accepted manuscript published in: 4 months
 Rejected manuscript returned: Yes, with return postage paid by publication.
 Rejected manuscript criticized: Sometimes
Submit to:
 Dr. Rudolph Schultz
 Department of Psychology
 University of Iowa
 Iowa City, Iowa 52240

MENNINGER CLINIC BULLETIN [1449]
The Menninger Foundation
Box 829
Topeka, Kansas 66601
(913) 234-9566, ext. 3604

SUBSCRIPTION DATA

Issues and rates: Published bi-monthly.
 Average paid circulation: 3,400
 Annual rate(s): $15.00
Publisher or Sponsor: The Menninger Foundation
Managing Editor: Virginia T. Eicholtz

EDITORIAL DESCRIPTION

A scientific journal containing articles on psychiatry, psychology, neurology, psychoanalysis, child psychiatry, and related subjects.
Articles per average issue: 6
 Manuscripts accepted in English

MANUSCRIPT INFORMATION

Subject field(s): Psychiatry, psychology, neurology, psychoanalysis, child psychiatry, and related subjects
Manuscript requirements: See latest issue for style requirements.
 Preferred length: 6,000 to 9,000 words; 25 to 35 pages
 Number of copies to be submitted: Original, plus three copies
 Abstract: No
Author information and reprints: Payment: None. Ten copies of issue in which article appears.
 Is simultaneous submission of article to other journals permitted: No
 Exclusive manuscript rights between acceptance and publication: Yes
 Copyright: Held by The Menninger Foundation
 Reprints: Available, cost depends on length
Disposition of manuscript:
 Receipt of manuscript acknowledged: Yes
 Decision to publish in: 6-8 weeks
 Accepted manuscript published in: 6-9 months
 Rejected manuscript returned: Yes
 Rejected manuscript criticized: Yes
Submit to:
 Sydney R. Smith
 Editor-in-Chief
 (See address above)

MENTAL HEALTH AND SOCIETY [1450]
International Journal of Community Mental Health
S. Karger, A.G.
Arnold Boecklin Strasse 25
CH-4011 Basel, Switzerland

First published in 1974

SUBSCRIPTION DATA

Issues and rates: Published bi-monthly.
 Annual rate(s): $26.00; Foreign £10.80; DM 68.00; SFr. 72.00

EDITORIAL DESCRIPTION

Reflects the developing interdisciplinary approach and practice in the fields of social and community psychiatry, psychology and the social sciences as well as education; provides a forum for the reporting on and the examination of theory, research and experience of socio-cultural facts on the development and function of the human being and his malaise.
Articles per average issue: Varies

Audience: Professional, academic
Manuscripts accepted in English only

MANUSCRIPT INFORMATION

Subject field(s): The influences on the person of childrearing, education, family and community life, social policy, economic pressures, occupation, bureaucratic and political institutions and belief systems. Inter-group and cross-cultural comparisons will receive special attention.
Manuscript requirements: Style sheet sent on request.
Preferred length: 8 printed pages
Number of copies to be submitted: 2
Abstract: Yes. Not more than 10 lines
Author information and reprints: Payment: Reprints only. 100 reprints; there is an excess page charge.
Is simultaneous submission of article to other journals permitted: Not permitted.
Exclusive manuscript rights between acceptance and publication: Yes
Copyright: Held by publication.
Reprints: Available at cost.
Disposition of manuscript:
Query letter: Not necessary, but advisable.
Receipt of manuscript acknowledged: Yes
Decision to publish in: Varies
Accepted manuscript published in: 4-6 months
Rejected manuscript returned: Yes, if return postage is supplied by author.
Rejected manuscript criticized: Yes
Submit to:
Louis Miller
Editor-in-Chief
Jerusalem Academic Press
P. O. Box 2390
Jerusalem, Israel

MENTAL RETARDATION [1451]
5201 Connecticut Avenue N.W.
Washington, D.C. 20015
(202) 244-8143

First published in 1963

SUBSCRIPTION DATA
Issues and rates: Published bi-monthly.
Average paid circulation: 11,500
Annual rate(s): $15.00, Foreign $16.00
Publisher or Sponsor: American Association on Mental Deficiency
Managing Editor: Susan J. Annis

EDITORIAL DESCRIPTION
Contains new approaches to methodology; critical summaries; interpretation of essays on current topics; program descriptions; case studies illustrating philosophy or theory; research reports.
Articles per average issue: 13
Manuscripts accepted in English only

MANUSCRIPT INFORMATION
Subject field(s): Psychology, sociology, education

Manuscript requirements: APA
Preferred length: 9 pages
Number of copies to be submitted: Three
Abstract: Yes
Author information and reprints: Payment: By author to publication. Only very expensive tables and graphs
Is simultaneous submission of article to other journals permitted: No
Copyright: Held by publication.
Reprints: Available, 50 copies of 4 pages or less for $18.00.
Disposition of manuscript:
Query letter: No
Receipt of manuscript acknowledged: Yes
Decision to publish in: 2-5 months
Accepted manuscript published in: 2-5 months
Rejected manuscript returned: Yes
Rejected manuscript criticized: No
Submit to:
Sue Allen Warren
Editor
Boston University
765 Commonwealth Avenue
Boston, Massachusetts 02215
(617) 353-3208

MERRILL-PALMER QUARTERLY OF BEHAVIOR AND DEVELOPMENT [1452]
71 East Ferry Avenue
Detroit, Michigan 48202
(313) 875-7450, Ext. 309

First published in 1954

SUBSCRIPTION DATA
Issues and rates: Published quarterly.
Average paid circulation: 2,000
Annual rate(s): $11.00, Foreign $12.00
Publisher or Sponsor: The Merrill-Palmer Institute
Managing Editor: Dr. Douglas R. Powell

EDITORIAL DESCRIPTION
Contains conceptual analyses of problems under investigation; results of exploratory studies in new areas, and case material illustrative of general principles, as well as completed research reports. Papers which develop new approaches to theory and research are particularly welcomed, as are those which critically examine existing approaches or place them within a broader perspective.
Articles per average issue: 7
Audience: Researchers, psychologists
Manuscripts accepted in English only

MANUSCRIPT INFORMATION
Subject field(s): Developmental psychology, child psychology
Manuscript requirements: APA
Preferred length: None
Number of copies to be submitted: Two
Abstract: Yes
Author information and reprints: Payment: None.
Is simultaneous submission of article to other journals permitted: Not preferable

Copyright: Held by the Merrill-Palmer Institute
Reprints: Available
Disposition of manuscript:
Query letter: No
Receipt of manuscript acknowledged: Yes
Accepted manuscript published in: 1 year
Submit to:
Martin L. Hoffman
Editor
Department of Psychology
University of Michigan
Ann Arbor, Michigan 48104
(313) 764-7472

NEUROPSYCHOBIOLOGY [1453]
International Journal for Basic and Clinical Studies in Psychiatric Research
S. Karger, A.G.
Arnold Boecklin Strasse 25
CH-4011 Basel, Switzerland

First published in 1975

SUBSCRIPTION DATA
Issues and rates: Published bi-monthly.
Annual rate(s): $48.00; Foreign SFr. 132.00; DM 125.00

EDITORIAL DESCRIPTION
Devoted to the publication of original papers applying the principles and approaches of biology to the study of psychopathology, with a strong emphasis on methodology; also short reports, new observations and correspondence.
Articles per average issue: Varies
Audience: Research psychiatrists
Manuscripts accepted in English, French, German

MANUSCRIPT INFORMATION
Subject field(s): High quality research in biochemistry, physiology, endocrinology, pathology, pharmacology, biometry, genetics, epidemiology and related fields as they apply to psychiatry
Manuscript requirements: Style sheet sent on request.
Preferred length: 10 printed pages
Number of copies to be submitted: 2
Abstract: Yes. Not more than 10 lines, also in English; a list of 3-9 words for indexing purposes, and a title in English as well as original language.
Author information and reprints: Payment: None.
Is simultaneous submission of article to other journals permitted: Not permitted.
Exclusive manuscript rights between acceptance and publication: Yes
Copyright: Held by publication.
Reprints: Available at cost.
Disposition of manuscript:
Query letter: Not necessary, but advisable.
Receipt of manuscript acknowledged: Yes
Decision to publish in: Varies
Accepted manuscript published in: Varies
Rejected manuscript returned: Yes, if return postage is supplied by author.
Rejected manuscript criticized: Yes

Submit to:
J. Mendlewicz, Brussels
Main Editor
(See address above)

OMEGA-THE JOURNAL OF DEATH AND DYING [1454]

Baywood Publishing Company, Inc.
43 Central Drive
Farmingdale, New York 11735
(516) 293-7130

First published in 1970

SUBSCRIPTION DATA
Issues and rates: Published quarterly.
Annual rate(s): $30.00; Foreign $32.00
Publisher or Sponsor: Ars Moriendi

EDITORIAL DESCRIPTION
Concerned with the impact of death on the human being and on the human community.
Articles per average issue: 11
Audience: Professional
Manuscripts accepted in English

MANUSCRIPT INFORMATION
Subject field(s): Original research reports, critical reviews of the literature, descriptions of therapeutic and educational programs, philosophical analyses, and historical surveys.
Manuscript requirements: See latest issue for style requirements. Style sheet sent on request.
Preferred length: 5,000 words maximum
Number of copies to be submitted: 3
Abstract: Yes. Up to 100 words
Author information and reprints: Payment: Reprints only. 20 copies
Is simultaneous submission of article to other journals permitted: Not permitted.
Exclusive manuscript rights between acceptance and publication: Yes
Copyright: Held by publication.
Reprints: Available at cost.
Disposition of manuscript:
Query letter: Not necessary, but advisable.
Receipt of manuscript acknowledged: Yes
Decision to publish in: 4-6 weeks
Accepted manuscript published in: 6 months
Rejected manuscript returned: Yes, with return postage paid by publication.
Rejected manuscript criticized: Sometimes
Submit to:
Dr. Robert Kastenbaum
Editor
Psychology I
University of Massachusetts
Columbia Point Campus
Dorchester, Massachusetts 02125

THE ONTARIO PSYCHOLOGIST [1455]

245 Old Forest Hill Road
Toronto, Ontario M6C 2H5, Canada
(416) 781-3791

First published in 1969

SUBSCRIPTION DATA
Issues and rates: Published bi-monthly.
Average paid circulation: 1,000
Annual rate(s): $12.00
Publisher or Sponsor: Ontario Psychological Association
Managing Editor: Susan Cravitz

EDITORIAL DESCRIPTION
Contains papers on issues in professional and academic psychology.
Articles per average issue: Varies
Audience: Psychological community
Manuscripts accepted in English

MANUSCRIPT INFORMATION
Subject field(s): Professional affairs, current issues in psychology, ethics, privacy, image of psychologist, papers of general interest
Manuscript requirements: See latest issue for style requirements.
Preferred length: 10 pages
Number of copies to be submitted: Two
Abstract: Not necessary
Author information and reprints: Payment: None.
Is simultaneous submission of article to other journals permitted: No
Exclusive manuscript rights between acceptance and publication: Yes
Copyright: Held by publication.
Reprints: Available, cost on request
Disposition of manuscript:
Query letter: Good idea
Receipt of manuscript acknowledged: Yes
Decision to publish in: 1 month
Accepted manuscript published in: 2-4 months
Rejected manuscript returned: Yes
Rejected manuscript criticized: Yes
Submit to:
James M. Ricks
44 Whitby Psychiatric Hospital
Box 613
Whitby, Ontario L1N 5S9, Canada
(416) 668-5881

OTTO RANK ASSOCIATION JOURNAL [1456]

58 East Court Street
Doylestown, Pennsylvania 18901
(215) 378-8300

First published in 1966

SUBSCRIPTION DATA
Issues and rates: Published semi-annually.
Average paid circulation: 500
Annual rate(s): $5.00
Publisher or Sponsor: The Otto Rank Association
Managing Editor: Virginia P. Robinson; Anita J. Faatz

EDITORIAL DESCRIPTION
The purpose of the association is to foster and develop interest in the writings of Dr. Otto Rank (1884-1939); to promote further explorations of his concepts and their meaning for art, literature, psychology, psychotherapy and the history of culture
Articles per average issue: 10

MANUSCRIPT INFORMATION
Subject field(s): Psychology, literature, folklore
Manuscript requirements: No specific style guide.
Preferred length: 3,000 to 6,000 words; 3 pages
Number of copies to be submitted: Two
Author information and reprints: Payment: None.
Is simultaneous submission of article to other journals permitted: Yes
Exclusive manuscript rights between acceptance and publication: No
Copyright: Held by publication.
Reprints: Available
Disposition of manuscript:
Query letter: No
Receipt of manuscript acknowledged: Yes
Accepted manuscript published in: Six months
Rejected manuscript returned: Yes
Rejected manuscript criticized: No
Submit to:
Executive Director
(See address above)

PARAPSYCHOLOGY REVIEW [1457]

29 West 57th Street
New York, New York 10019
(212) 751-5940

First published in 1970

SUBSCRIPTION DATA
Issues and rates: Published bi-monthly.
Average paid circulation: 3000
Annual rate(s): $4.00
Publisher or Sponsor: Parapsychology Foundation

EDITORIAL DESCRIPTION
Contains articles, book reviews pertaining to the scientific study of the paranormal; news of psychical research and related developments.
Articles per average issue: 3-4 articles
Audience: Academic and general
Manuscripts accepted in English

MANUSCRIPT INFORMATION
Subject field(s): Psychical research
Manuscript requirements: Chicago
Preferred length: 200 to 2000 words
Number of copies to be submitted: One
Abstract: No
Author information and reprints: Payment: By publication to author. $50 up per article.
Is simultaneous submission of article to other journals permitted: No
Exclusive manuscript rights between acceptance and publication: Yes
Copyright: Held by publication.
Reprints: Not available

Disposition of manuscript:
  Query letter: Advisable
  Receipt of manuscript acknowledged: No
  Decision to publish in: 5-10 days
  Accepted manuscript published in: 1-6 months
  Rejected manuscript returned: Yes, if return postage is supplied by author.
  Rejected manuscript criticized: No
Submit to:
  Betty Shapin
  Editor
  (See address above)

PERCEPTION & PSYCHOPHYSICS [1458]
Psychonomic Society, Inc.
1108 West 34th Street
Austin, Texas 78705
(512) 454-7848

SUBSCRIPTION DATA
Issues and rates: Published bi-monthly.
  Average paid circulation: 1500
  Annual rate(s): Institutions $50.00, Individuals $25.00
Publisher or Sponsor: Psychonomic Society, Inc.
Managing Editor: Clifford T. Morgan

EDITORIAL DESCRIPTION
  Contains papers on perception, sensory psychology and psychophysics.
Audience: Experimental psychologists
  Manuscripts accepted in English

MANUSCRIPT INFORMATION
Manuscript requirements: Style sheet sent on request.
  Preferred length: Any reasonable length
  Number of copies to be submitted: Two
  Abstract: Yes. 100-150 words in *Psychological Abstracts* form
Author information and reprints: Payment: None.
  Is simultaneous submission of article to other journals permitted: Not preferred.
  Copyright: Held by publication.
  Reprints: Available, cost depends on length
Disposition of manuscript:
  Query letter: No
  Receipt of manuscript acknowledged: Yes
  Decision to publish in: 1 month
  Accepted manuscript published in: 3 to 5 months
  Rejected manuscript returned: Yes
  Rejected manuscript criticized: Yes
Submit to:
  Charles W. Ericksen
  Editor
  Department of Psychology
  University of Illinois
  Champaign, Illinois 61820

PERSONNEL PSYCHOLOGY [1459]
Box 6965, College Station
Durham, North Carolina 27708
(919) 688-3227

First published in 1948

SUBSCRIPTION DATA
Issues and rates: Published quarterly.
  Average paid circulation: 3,000
  Annual rate(s): $15.00, Foreign $16.00
Managing Editor: Geraldine R. Thomas

EDITORIAL DESCRIPTION
  Publishes manuscripts reporting research methods, research results, or the application of research results to the solution of personnel problems in business, industry, and government. Equally acceptable are critical surveys of the literature giving current status of knowledge and research on various phases of personnel psychology such as aspects of training and worker analysis, employee relations, morale, etc.
Articles per average issue: 10
Audience: Personnel Managers, libraries, etc.
  Manuscripts accepted in English

MANUSCRIPT INFORMATION
Subject field(s): Psychology in industry
Manuscript requirements: APA
  Preferred length: None
  Number of copies to be submitted: Three
  Abstract: Yes
Author information and reprints: Payment: By author to publication. $30.00 per page. $40.00 per printed page of tabular material.
  Is simultaneous submission of article to other journals permitted: No
  Exclusive manuscript rights between acceptance and publication: Yes
  Copyright: Held by publication.
  Reprints: Available
Disposition of manuscript:
  Query letter: No
  Receipt of manuscript acknowledged: Yes
  Decision to publish in: 6 weeks
  Accepted manuscript published in: One year
  Rejected manuscript returned: Yes
  Rejected manuscript criticized: No
Submit to:
  Dr. Milton D. Hakel
  Editor
  Department of Psychology
  Ohio State University
  1945 North High Street
  Columbus, Ohio 43210
  (614) 422-3038

PROFESSIONAL PSYCHOLOGY* [1460]
American Psychological Association
1200 17th Street, N.W.
Washington, D.C. 20036
(202) 833-7670

SUBSCRIPTION DATA
Issues and rates: Published quarterly.
  Average paid circulation: 8,500
  Annual rate(s): $12.00; Members $5.00, Foreign $13.00
Publisher or Sponsor: American Psychological Association

EDITORIAL DESCRIPTION
  Covers the range of psychology as a profession, particularly in the areas of training, practice, and teaching, and their relationship to issues of human welfare.

MANUSCRIPT INFORMATION
Subject field(s): Applications of research, standards of practice, teaching practices, interprofessional relations, delivery of services, and innovative approaches to training.
Manuscript requirements: APA; Chicago
  Number of copies to be submitted: Three
Author information and reprints: Payment: None.
  Is simultaneous submission of article to other journals permitted: No
  Exclusive manuscript rights between acceptance and publication: Yes
  Copyright: Held by APA; author's permission required to reprint.
  Reprints: Available in minimum orders of 100
Disposition of manuscript:
  Receipt of manuscript acknowledged: Yes
  Decision to publish in: 2 months
  Accepted manuscript published in: 12 month maximum
  Rejected manuscript returned: Yes
  Rejected manuscript criticized: Yes
Submit to:
  Donald Freedheim
  Editor
  Department of Psychology
  Case Western Reserve University
  Cleveland, Ohio 44106

PSYCHIATRIA CLINICA [1461]
S. Karger AG
Arnold-Boecklin Strasse 25
CH-4011 Basel, Switzerland
061-390880

SUBSCRIPTION DATA
Issues and rates: Published bi-monthly.
  Average paid circulation: 675; 55 controlled
  Annual rate(s): SFr. 132.00; Foreign $54.00

EDITORIAL DESCRIPTION
  The journal publishes reports in the fields of psychopharmacology, psychotherapy and social psychiatry, with an emphasis on clinical practice. It is primarily concerned with the various developments on the European scene.
Articles per average issue: 6
  Manuscripts accepted in English, German, French

MANUSCRIPT INFORMATION
Manuscript requirements: See latest issue for style requirements.
  Preferred length: 8 printed pages
  Number of copies to be submitted: 2
  Abstract: Yes, a summary in the original including a title in English.

Psychology and mental health

Author information and reprints: Payment: Reprints only.
Is simultaneous submission of article to other journals permitted: No
Exclusive manuscript rights between acceptance and publication: Yes
Copyright: Held by publication.
Disposition of manuscript:
Query letter: Yes
Receipt of manuscript acknowledged: Yes
Decision to publish in: 1 month
Accepted manuscript published in: 6 months
Rejected manuscript returned: Yes
Rejected manuscript criticized: No
Submit to:
Prof. Dr. P. Berner
Director
Psychiatrische Universitätsklinik
Lazarettgasse 14
A-1097 Wien, Austria

THE PSYCHIATRIC FORUM [1462]
P.O. Box 119
Columbia, South Carolina 29202
(803) 758-7511

SUBSCRIPTION DATA
Issues and rates: Published semi-annually.
Average paid circulation: 3,000 controlled
Publisher or Sponsor: Hall Psychiatric Institute of the South Carolina Department of Mental Health
Managing Editor: Lucius C. Pressley

EDITORIAL DESCRIPTION
Contains articles related to the field of mental health.

MANUSCRIPT INFORMATION
Subject field(s): Psychiatry, psychology, psychiatric social work, psychiatric history and book reviews
Manuscript requirements: See latest issue for style requirements.
Preferred length: 6-12 pages
Number of copies to be submitted: Two
Author information and reprints: Payment: None.
Is simultaneous submission of article to other journals permitted: No
Exclusive manuscript rights between acceptance and publication: Yes
Copyright: Held by publication.
Reprints: Available from printer
Additional information: Only original articles that have not been published elsewhere are eligible.
Disposition of manuscript:
Receipt of manuscript acknowledged: Yes
Decision to publish in: 1 month
Accepted manuscript published in: Up to 6 months
Rejected manuscript returned: Yes
Rejected manuscript criticized: No
Submit to:
Lucius C. Pressley
Editor
(See address above)

PSYCHIATRIC QUARTERLY [1463]
44 Holland Avenue
Albany, New York 12208
(518) 474-1769

First published in 1927

SUBSCRIPTION DATA
Issues and rates: Published quarterly.
Average paid circulation: 1800
Annual rate(s): $8.00, Foreign $8.50
Publisher or Sponsor: New York State Department of Mental Hygiene

EDITORIAL DESCRIPTION
Publishes articles, editorials, book reviews and "news notes" within the field of clinical psychiatry. Special emphasis is placed on the education and training of mental health professionals.
Articles per average issue: 12
Audience: Psychiatrists, psychologists
Manuscripts accepted in English only

MANUSCRIPT INFORMATION
Subject field(s): Hospital and private practice, community clinics, social psychiatry, neurology, mental retardation
Manuscript requirements: See latest issue for style requirements.
Preferred length: 4,500 words; 15 pages
Number of copies to be submitted: Two
Abstract: Yes
Author information and reprints: Payment: None.
Is simultaneous submission of article to other journals permitted: No
Exclusive manuscript rights between acceptance and publication: Yes
Copyright: Held by publication.
Reprints: Available; 25 free
Additional information: Authors must begin article with a brief "Identifier Paragraph" so that readers will be able to decide which articles they wish to read.
Disposition of manuscript:
Query letter: No
Receipt of manuscript acknowledged: Yes
Decision to publish in: 6 weeks
Accepted manuscript published in: 2-6 months
Rejected manuscript returned: Yes
Rejected manuscript criticized: No
Submit to:
Austin C. Smith
Assistant Editor
(See address above)

PSYCHIATRY [1464]
Journal for the Study of Interpersonal Processes
1610 New Hampshire Avenue NW
Washington, D.C. 20009
(202) 667-3008

First published in 1938

SUBSCRIPTION DATA
Issues and rates: Published quarterly.
Average paid circulation: 3,400
Annual rate(s): $12.50; U.S., Canada, Mexico; $13.50 all other countries; Institutions $20.00 U.S., Canada, Mexico; $21.00 all other countries
Publisher or Sponsor: William Alanson White Psychiatric Foundation, Inc.
Managing Editor: Gloria H. Parloff

EDITORIAL DESCRIPTION
Contents include interdisciplinary clinical and research studies. The journal seeks to integrate psychiatry with psychology, sociology, anthropology, philosophy, etc. It attempts to be broadly communicative without sacrificing technical quality.
Articles per average issue: 8
Audience: professional
Manuscripts accepted in English

MANUSCRIPT INFORMATION
Subject field(s): Psychiatry, psychology, sociology, anthropology, philosophy, and related areas
Manuscript requirements: See latest issue for style requirements.
Preferred length: 20 to 40 pages
Number of copies to be submitted: Two
Abstract: No
Author information and reprints: Payment: None.
Is simultaneous submission of article to other journals permitted: No
Exclusive manuscript rights between acceptance and publication: Yes
Copyright: Held by publication.
Reprints: Available at cost
Additional information: Authors must defray cost of unusually expensive illustrative material. Stamped return envelope should be enclosed with submitted manuscript.
Disposition of manuscript:
Receipt of manuscript acknowledged: Yes
Decision to publish in: 3-4 months
Accepted manuscript published in: 9-12 months
Rejected manuscript returned: Yes, if self-addressed, stamped envelope is sent with manuscript.
Rejected manuscript criticized: Sometimes criticized if the remarks of the Editorial Board might be helpful.
Submit to:
Donald L. Burnham, M.D.
Editor
(See address above)

PSYCHIC [1465]
Exploring the Extended Nature of Man and the Universe
680 Beach Street 408
San Francisco, California 94109
(415) 776-2600

First published in 1969

SUBSCRIPTION DATA
Issues and rates: Published bi-monthly.
Average paid circulation: 45,000
Annual rate(s): $5.50

Managing Editor: James Grayson Bolen

EDITORIAL DESCRIPTION

Straightforward approach to psychic phenomena, parapsychology, consciousness research and other areas that explore the nature of man and human potential.
Articles per average issue: 6
Audience: professionals
　Manuscripts accepted in English

MANUSCRIPT INFORMATION

Subject field(s): Psychic phenomena, parapsychology, consciousness research, ESP and human potential
Manuscript requirements: See latest issue for style requirements.
　Preferred length: 2,000-3,500 words
　Number of copies to be submitted: One
　Abstract: Yes, outline requested
Author information and reprints: Payment: By publication to author. $75-$350 per article.
　Is simultaneous submission of article to other journals permitted: No
　Exclusive manuscript rights between acceptance and publication: Yes
　Copyright: Held by publication.
　Reprints: Not available.
Additional information: Queries desired.
Disposition of manuscript:
　Query letter: Yes
　Receipt of manuscript acknowledged: No
　Decision to publish in: 4 to 6 weeks
　Accepted manuscript published in: 4 months
　Rejected manuscript returned: Yes, if self-addressed, stamped envelope is sent with manuscript.
　Rejected manuscript criticized: No
Submit to:
　Alan Vaughan
　Articles Editor
　(See address above)

THE PSYCHOANALYTIC QUARTERLY [1466]

57 West 57th Street
New York, New York 10019
(212) 753-5223

First published in 1932

SUBSCRIPTION DATA

Issues and rates: Published quarterly.
　Average paid circulation: 4,500
　Annual rate(s): $20.00, Foreign $21.00

EDITORIAL DESCRIPTION

Publishes clinical studies, papers on the development of psychoanalytic theory and on the application of psychoanalysis to art, education, sociology, literature and anthropology as well as book reviews, abstracts of current psychiatric journals and notes.
Articles per average issue: 6
Audience: Psychoanalysts, and related professionals
　Manuscripts accepted in Englisn only

MANUSCRIPT INFORMATION

Subject field(s): Psychoanalysis, psychiatry, psychology, related disciplines
Manuscript requirements: See latest issue for style requirements.
　Preferred length: 6000 words; 25 pages maximum
　Number of copies to be submitted: 2
　Abstract: Yes, no more than 100 words to preface article
Author information and reprints: Payment: None. Complimentary copy of issue in which article appears.
　Is simultaneous submission of article to other journals permitted: No
　Exclusive manuscript rights between acceptance and publication: Yes
　Copyright: Held by publication. in trust for author
　Reprints: Available, cost depends on length of article
Disposition of manuscript:
　Query letter: No
　Receipt of manuscript acknowledged: Yes
　Decision to publish in: Three months
　Accepted manuscript published in: Six months or more
　Rejected manuscript returned: Yes
　Rejected manuscript criticized: Sometimes
Submit to:
　Jacob A. Arlow, M.D.
　Editor
　(See address above)

THE PSYCHOANALYTIC REVIEW [1467]

150 West 13th Street
New York, New York 10011
(212) 924-7440

Previously entitled *Psychoanalysis*

First published in 1913

SUBSCRIPTION DATA

Issues and rates: Published quarterly.
　Average paid circulation: 2000
　Annual rate(s): $16.00, Foreign $18.00
Publisher or Sponsor: National Psychological Association for Psychoanalysis
Managing Editor: Murray H. Sherman

EDITORIAL DESCRIPTION

An American journal of psychoanalytic psychology devoted to the understanding of behavior and culture. Rather eclectic in psychoanalytic theory but tending to include a primarily Freudian viewpoint. Publications include theoretical and clinical contributions with a strong emphasis upon psychoanalysis as applied to literature and the arts.
Articles per average issue: 9-12
Audience: Libraries, hospitals, clinics, professionals
　Manuscripts accepted in English only

MANUSCRIPT INFORMATION

Subject field(s): Psychoanalysis, psychiatry, sociology, psychology

Manuscript requirements: See latest issue for style requirements.
　Preferred length: 15-28 pages
　Number of copies to be submitted: Three
Author information and reprints: Payment: None.
　Is simultaneous submission of article to other journals permitted: No
　Exclusive manuscript rights between acceptance and publication: Yes
　Copyright: Held by publication.
　Reprints: Available at cost
Disposition of manuscript:
　Query letter: No
　Receipt of manuscript acknowledged: Yes
　Decision to publish in: Six weeks
　Accepted manuscript published in: Two years
　Rejected manuscript returned: Yes
　Rejected manuscript criticized: Sometimes
Submit to:
　Murray H. Sherman
　Managing Editor
　(See address above)

PSYCHOENERGETIC SYSTEMS [1468]

An International Journal
Gordon and Breach
One Park Avenue
New York, New York 10016

First published in 1974

SUBSCRIPTION DATA

Issues and rates: Published quarterly.
　Average paid circulation: 200
　Annual rate(s): $19.50; Pan-Am $19.50; Foreign $19.50; Institutions $58.00; Students $19.50; Members $15.00; Foreign institutions $58.00
Publisher or Sponsor: International Association for Psychotronic Research
Managing Editor: Brian H. Washburn

EDITORIAL DESCRIPTION

Pinpoints the critical anomalies in science, and their impact on our understanding of living systems; investigates phenomena which are being observed on the frontiers of science, and finds how anomalies of any given area relate to one another-if they do.
Articles per average issue: 7
Audience: Scientists
　Manuscripts accepted in English

MANUSCRIPT INFORMATION

Subject field(s): Consciousness, matter and energy interaction, acupuncture, brain research, bioelectric fields, Kirlian photography, auric fields, unorthodox healing, biocommunication, quasi-sensory communication, psi processes, subliminal perception, paraphysics, and psychokenetic effects
Manuscript requirements: APA
　Preferred length: Varies
　Number of copies to be submitted: 5
　Abstract: Yes

Psychology and mental health 439

Author information and reprints: Payment: Reprints only. 50
Is simultaneous submission of article to other journals permitted: Permitted, but not encouraged.
Exclusive manuscript rights between acceptance and publication: Yes
Copyright: Held by publication.
Reprints: Not available.
Disposition of manuscript:
Query letter: Not necessary.
Receipt of manuscript acknowledged: Yes
Decision to publish in: 3 months
Accepted manuscript published in: 6 months
Rejected manuscript returned: Yes, if return postage is supplied by author.
Rejected manuscript criticized: Yes
Submit to:
Michael Maliszewski
Executive Editor
Suite 347, International House
1414 East 59th Street
Chicago, Illinois 60637
(312) 753-0096

PSYCHOLOGICAL BULLETIN* [1469]
American Psychological Association
1200 17th Street, N.W.
Washington, D.C. 20036
(202) 833-7670

SUBSCRIPTION DATA
Issues and rates: Published monthly.
Average paid circulation: 11,550
Annual rate(s): $24.00, Members $10.00
Foreign $25.00
Publisher or Sponsor: American Psychological Association

EDITORIAL DESCRIPTION
Publishes evaluative reviews of the research literature in psychology; reviews and interpretations of substantive and methodological issues; reports of original research only when these are used to illustrate some methodological problem or issue. Methodological issues discussed in the journal should be aimed at the solution of some particular research problem in psychology, but these issues should be of sufficient breadth to interest a wide readership among psychologists.

MANUSCRIPT INFORMATION
Manuscript requirements: APA; Chicago
Number of copies to be submitted: Two
Author information and reprints: Payment: None.
Is simultaneous submission of article to other journals permitted: No
Exclusive manuscript rights between acceptance and publication: Yes
Copyright: Held by APA; author's permission required to reprint.
Reprints: Available in minimum orders of 100
Disposition of manuscript:
Receipt of manuscript acknowledged: Yes
Decision to publish in: 2 months
Accepted manuscript published in: 12 month maximum
Rejected manuscript returned: Yes
Rejected manuscript criticized: Yes
Submit to:
James Deese
Editor
Department of Psychology
Gilmer Hall, University of Virginia
Charlottesville, Virginia 22901

PSYCHOLOGICAL ISSUES [1470]
239 Park Avenue South
New York, New York 10003
(212) 674-2021

First published in 1959

SUBSCRIPTION DATA
Issues and rates: Four numbers per volume published irregularly
Average paid circulation: 1500
Annual rate(s): Individuals $15.00
Institutions $32.50
Managing Editor: Herbert J. Schlesinger

EDITORIAL DESCRIPTION
Publishes a diversity of source materials for a general psychoanalytic theory of behavior.
Articles per average issue: Varies
Audience: Scientific
Manuscripts accepted in English

MANUSCRIPT INFORMATION
Manuscript requirements: See latest issue for style requirements.
Preferred length: Varies
Number of copies to be submitted: Two
Abstract: No
Author information and reprints: Payment: None.
Is simultaneous submission of article to other journals permitted: No
Exclusive manuscript rights between acceptance and publication: Yes
Copyright: Held by publisher
Reprints: Not available.
Disposition of manuscript:
Query letter: Yes
Receipt of manuscript acknowledged: Yes
Decision to publish in: Varies
Accepted manuscript published in: Varies
Rejected manuscript returned: Yes
Rejected manuscript criticized: No
Submit to:
Herbert J. Schlesinger
Editor
4200 East Ninth Avenue
Denver, Colorado 80220

PSYCHOLOGICAL MEDICINE [1471]
Journal for Research in Psychiatry and the Allied Sciences
B.M.A. House
Tavistock Square
London WC1H 9JR, England
01-387 4499

First published in 1970

SUBSCRIPTION DATA
Issues and rates: Published quarterly.
Average paid circulation: Not available.
Annual rate(s): $22.00
Publisher or Sponsor: British Medical Journal Group

EDITORIAL DESCRIPTION
Contains articles on medical research.
Manuscripts accepted in English

MANUSCRIPT INFORMATION
Manuscript requirements: See latest issue for style requirements.
Preferred length: None
Number of copies to be submitted: Two
Abstract: Yes
Author information and reprints: Payment: None.
Is simultaneous submission of article to other journals permitted: No
Exclusive manuscript rights between acceptance and publication: Yes
Copyright: Held by publication.
Reprints: Available
Disposition of manuscript:
Query letter: No
Receipt of manuscript acknowledged: Yes
Decision to publish in: One month
Accepted manuscript published in: Six months
Rejected manuscript returned: Yes
Rejected manuscript criticized: No
Submit to:
The Editor
(See address above)

THE PSYCHOLOGICAL RECORD [1472]
Denison University
Granville, Ohio 43023
(614) 587-0810

First published in 1937

SUBSCRIPTION DATA
Issues and rates: Published quarterly.
Average paid circulation: 1,800
Annual rate(s): Institutions $10.00;
Students $4.00; Members $6.00
Managing Editor: Paul T. Mountjoy

EDITORIAL DESCRIPTION
Publishes theoretical & experimental articles and commentary on current developments in psychology. Interested in papers that develop new approaches and methods.
Articles per average issue: 15
Audience: Academic and professional psychologists, psychiatrists, sociologists.
Manuscripts accepted in English

MANUSCRIPT INFORMATION
Subject field(s): General psychology
Manuscript requirements: See latest issue for style requirements. APA
Preferred length: 8-12 typed pages
Abstract: Yes.

Author information and reprints: Payment:
By author to publication. $12.00-$16.00
per page.
Is simultaneous submission of article to
other journals permitted: Not permitted.
Exclusive manuscript rights between
acceptance and publication: Yes
Copyright: Held by publication.
Reprints: Available at cost.
Disposition of manuscript:
Query letter: Not necessary.
Receipt of manuscript acknowledged: Yes
Decision to publish in: 1-3 months
Accepted manuscript published in: 1-2
months after acceptance
Rejected manuscript returned: Yes, with
return postage paid by publication.
Rejected manuscript criticized: Yes
Submit to:
Dr. Irvin S. Wolf
Editor
(See address above)

PSYCHOLOGICAL REPORTS [1473]
Box 1441
Missoula, montana 59801
(406) 243-5091

SUBSCRIPTION DATA

Issues and rates: Published bi-monthly.
Average paid circulation: Not available.
Annual rate(s): $56.00
Managing Editor: Carol H. Ammons

EDITORIAL DESCRIPTION

Seeks to encourage scientific originality
and creativity in the field of general
psychology, for the person who is first a
psychologist, then a specialist.

MANUSCRIPT INFORMATION

Manuscript requirements: APA
Preferred length: 2 to 20 pages
Number of copies to be submitted: Two
Author information and reprints: Payment:
By author to publication.
Is simultaneous submission of article to
other journals permitted: No
Exclusive manuscript rights between
acceptance and publication: Yes
Copyright: Held by publication.
Reprints: Available, $20 per page for 200
Disposition of manuscript:
Receipt of manuscript acknowledged: Yes
Decision to publish in: 6 weeks
Accepted manuscript published in: Two
months
Submit to:
Editor
(See address above)

PSYCHOLOGICAL RESEARCH [1474]
An International Journal of Perception,
Learning and Communication
Springer-Verlag
175 Fifth Aveue
New York, New York 10010

First published in 1921

Annual rate(s): DM 140 per volume
Managing Editor: Professor H. W.
Leibowitz

EDITORIAL DESCRIPTION
See sub-title
Manuscripts accepted in English, German

MANUSCRIPT INFORMATION

Manuscript requirements: See latest issue for
style requirements. Style sheet sent on
request.
Preferred length: 32 pages maximum
Number of copies to be submitted: 2
Abstract: Yes. Papers in French and
German should also include a summary
in English as well as translation into
English of the title.
Author information and reprints: Payment:
Reprints only. 75 offprints
Is simultaneous submission of article to
other journals permitted: Not permitted.
Exclusive manuscript rights between
acceptance and publication: Yes
Copyright: Held by publication.
Reprints: Available at cost.
Submit to:
Professor H. W. Leibowitz
Co-Editor
Department of Psychology, The
Pennsylvania State University
417 Psychology Building
University Park, Pennsylvania 16802

PSYCHOLOGICAL REVIEW [1475]
American Psychological Association
1200 17th Street NW
Washington, D.C. 20036
(202) 833-7670

SUBSCRIPTION DATA

Issues and rates: Published bi-monthly.
Average paid circulation: 12,075
Annual rate(s): $15.00, Members $5.00,
Foreign $16.00
Publisher or Sponsor: American
Psychological Association
Managing Editor: Anita DeVivo

EDITORIAL DESCRIPTION

Devoted to articles of theoretical
significance to any area of scientific
endeavor in psychology. Ordinarily,
manuscripts which consist primarily of
original reports of research or of reviews
of the literature should be submitted to
other journals. Methodological and
statistical articles are not appropriate.

MANUSCRIPT INFORMATION

Manuscript requirements: APA; Chicago;
Webster's New Collegiate Dictionary
Preferred length: 7,500 words maximum
Number of copies to be submitted: Three
Author information and reprints: Payment:
None.
Is simultaneous submission of article to
other journals permitted: No
Exclusive manuscript rights between
acceptance and publication: Yes
Copyright: Held by APA; author's
permission required to reprint.

Reprints: Available in minimum orders
of 100
Disposition of manuscript:
Receipt of manuscript acknowledged: Yes
Decision to publish in: 2 months
Accepted manuscript published in: 12
month maximum
Rejected manuscript returned: Yes
Rejected manuscript criticized: Yes
Submit to:
George Mandler
Editor
Department of Psychology
University of California
La Jolla, California 92037

PSYCHOLOGY [1476]
A Journal of Human Behavior
P.O. Box 6495
Savannah, Georgia 31405
(912) 355-7927

First published in 1964

SUBSCRIPTION DATA

Issues and rates: Published quarterly.
Average paid circulation: 4,000
Annual rate(s): $7.00; Foreign $8.00
Managing Editor: John A. Blazer

EDITORIAL DESCRIPTION

Publishes articles concerning all areas of
human behavior.
Articles per average issue: 8
Audience: Mental health professionals
Manuscripts accepted in English

MANUSCRIPT INFORMATION

Subject field(s): Psychology, psychiatry,
marriage, testing, diagnostics, sociology,
child guidance
Manuscript requirements: APA
Number of copies to be submitted: Two
Abstract: Yes APA style
Author information and reprints: Payment:
By author to publication.
Is simultaneous submission of article to
other journals permitted: No
Exclusive manuscript rights between
acceptance and publication: Yes
Copyright: Held by publication.
Reprints: Available at cost
Disposition of manuscript:
Query letter: No
Receipt of manuscript acknowledged: No
Decision to publish in: 10 days
Accepted manuscript published in: 3-6
months
Rejected manuscript returned: Yes, if
return postage is supplied by author.
Rejected manuscript criticized: Yes
Submit to:
John A. Blazer
Editor
(See address above)

PSYCHOLOGY IN THE SCHOOLS [1477]
4 Conant Square
Brandon, vermont 05733
(802) 247-6871

Psychology and mental health

First published in 1965

SUBSCRIPTION DATA

Issues and rates: Published quarterly.
    Average paid circulation: 2500
    Annual rate(s): $26.00, Foreign $25.00
Managing Editor: Eleanor C. Thorne

EDITORIAL DESCRIPTION

Contains papers on the applications of psychology to education.
Articles per average issue: 25
Audience: Educational psychologists
    Manuscripts accepted in English

MANUSCRIPT INFORMATION

Subject field(s): Educational psychology, learning problems, guidance
Manuscript requirements: See latest issue for style requirements.
    Preferred length: 4-6 pages
    Number of copies to be submitted: Three
    Abstract: Yes
Author information and reprints: Payment: By author to publication. Determined by editor
    Is simultaneous submission of article to other journals permitted: Yes
    Exclusive manuscript rights between acceptance and publication: Yes
    Copyright: Held by publication.
    Reprints: Available, cost determined by length
Disposition of manuscript:
    Receipt of manuscript acknowledged: Yes
    Decision to publish in: 3-4 weeks
    Accepted manuscript published in: 6 months
    Rejected manuscript returned: Yes
    Rejected manuscript criticized: Yes
Submit to:
    Gerald B. Fuller
    Editor
    Department of Psychology
    Central Michigan University
    Mt. Pleasant, Michigan 48858

PSYCHOLOGY TODAY [1478]

317 Fourteenth Street
Del Mar, California 92014
(714) 453-5000

First published in 1967

SUBSCRIPTION DATA

Issues and rates: Published monthly.
    Average paid circulation: 1,000,000
    Annual rate(s): $12.00, Foreign $14.00
Managing Editor: Elizabeth Hall

EDITORIAL DESCRIPTION

Contains articles written by professionals in the social sciences and based on laboratory work or clinical experience; interviews with prominent social scientists.
Audience: Educated laymen
    Manuscripts accepted in English

MANUSCRIPT INFORMATION

Subject field(s): Psychology, sociology, anthropology, other social sciences

Manuscript requirements: No specific style guide.
    Preferred length: 3,000 words
    Number of copies to be submitted: One
    Abstract: No
Author information and reprints: Payment: By publication to author. $500.00 per article.
    Is simultaneous submission of article to other journals permitted: Yes
    Exclusive manuscript rights between acceptance and publication: Yes
    Copyright: Held by publication.
    Reprints: Available, cost depends on quantity
Disposition of manuscript:
    Query letter: Helpful
    Receipt of manuscript acknowledged: No
    Decision to publish in: 1 month
    Accepted manuscript published in: 3-6 months
    Rejected manuscript returned: Yes
    Rejected manuscript criticized: Sometimes
Submit to:
    Paul B. Chance
    Manuscript Editor
    (See address above)
    (714) 453-5000 ext. 457

PSYCHOPHARMACOLOGIA [1479]

Springer-Verlag
175 Fifth Avenue
New York, New York 10010
    Annual rate(s): DM 96 per volume
Managing Editor: H. Barry, III

EDITORIAL DESCRIPTION

Provides a medium for the prompt publication of scientific contributions concerned with the analysis and synthesis of the effects of drugs on behavior, in the broadest sense of the term.
    Manuscripts accepted in English, French, German

MANUSCRIPT INFORMATION

Subject field(s): May be of a clinical nature, or may deal with specialized investigations in the fields of experimental psychology, neuropsychology, neurochemistry, general pharmacology and cognate disciplines.
Manuscript requirements: See latest issue for style requirements.
    Preferred length: As required
    Number of copies to be submitted: 3
    Abstract: Yes. A brief abstract in English concerned with the methods used and with the experimental results presented in a way for easy accessability and should not exceed 200 words. Include also an English translation of the title.
Author information and reprints: Payment: Reprints only. 75 offprints
    Is simultaneous submission of article to other journals permitted: Not permitted.
    Exclusive manuscript rights between acceptance and publication: Yes
    Copyright: Held by publication.
    Reprints: Available at cost.
Submit to:
    Professor Jonathan O. Cole, M. D.

Editorial Board
Department of Mental Health, Boston State Hospital
591 Morton Street
Boston, Massachusetts 02124

PSYCHOSOMATICS [1480]

Official Publication of the Academy of Psychosomatic Medicine
1921 Newkirk Avenue
Brooklyn, New York 11226
(212) 284-2888

First published in 1960

SUBSCRIPTION DATA

Issues and rates: Published bi-monthly.
    Average paid circulation: 1000; 2500-3500 controlled
    Annual rate(s): $15, Foreign $17
Publisher or Sponsor: Academy of Psychosomatic Medicine

EDITORIAL DESCRIPTION

Devoted to the concept of total or comprehensive medicine. Attempts to close the gap between medicine and psychiatry through psychotherapeutic and psychopharmacologic means. Articles emphasize relation of body to mind.
Articles per average issue: 9-10
Audience: Professional
    Manuscripts accepted in English

MANUSCRIPT INFORMATION

Subject field(s): Reviews of psychosomatic relationships, use of psychopharmaceuticals, case studies, methods of psychotherapy
Manuscript requirements: See latest issue for style requirements.
    Preferred length: 10-12 pages
    Number of copies to be submitted: 2
    Abstract: Yes
Author information and reprints: Payment: None.
    Is simultaneous submission of article to other journals permitted: No
    Exclusive manuscript rights between acceptance and publication: Yes, except for release to medical press
    Copyright: Held by publication.
    Reprints: Available
Disposition of manuscript:
    Query letter: Preferable
    Receipt of manuscript acknowledged: Yes
    Decision to publish in: 6 weeks
    Accepted manuscript published in: 6-12 months
    Rejected manuscript returned: Yes
    Rejected manuscript criticized: No
Submit to:
    Wilfred Dorfman, M.D.
    Editor-in-Chief
    (See address above)

PSYCHOTHERAPY AND PSYCHOSOMATICS [1481]

S. Karger AG
Arnold-Boecklin Strasse 25
CH-4011 Basel, Switzerland
061-390880

Previously entitled *Acta Psychotherapeutica et Psychomatica*

First published in 1953

SUBSCRIPTION DATA

Issues and rates: Published bi-monthly.
  Average paid circulation: 532; 54 controlled
  Annual rate(s): SFr. 132.00; Foreign $54.00 per volume
Publisher or Sponsor: International Federation for Medical Psychotherapy

EDITORIAL DESCRIPTION

Within a strictly scientific framework, the journal presents a variety of views reflecting contemporary ideas in the fields of psychotherapy, psychosomatic medicine and special education.
Articles per average issue: 15
Manuscripts accepted in English

MANUSCRIPT INFORMATION

Manuscript requirements: See latest issue for style requirements.
  Preferred length: 12 printed pages
  Number of copies to be submitted: 2
  Abstract: Yes
Author information and reprints: Payment: Reprints only.
  Is simultaneous submission of article to other journals permitted: No
  Exclusive manuscript rights between acceptance and publication: Yes
  Copyright: Held by publication.
Disposition of manuscript:
  Query letter: Yes
  Receipt of manuscript acknowledged: Yes
  Decision to publish in: 1 month
  Accepted manuscript published in: 6 months
  Rejected manuscript returned: Yes
  Rejected manuscript criticized: No
Submit to:
  Peter E. Sifneos, M.D.
  Editor
  Harvard Medical School Department of Psychology
  Beth Israel Hospital
  Boston, Massachusetts 02215

PSYCHOTHERAPY AND SOCIAL SCIENCE REVIEW [1482]
A Journal of Book Reviews
59 Fourth Avenue
New York, New York 10003
(212) 677-1280

First published in 1969

SUBSCRIPTION DATA

Issues and rates: Published monthly.
  Average paid circulation: 50,000
Publisher or Sponsor: Psychiatry and Social Science Book Club

EDITORIAL DESCRIPTION

Contains essays and extended book reviews of current books in fields of interest. Publication is psychoanalytically oriented.
Audience: Professional

Manuscripts accepted in English only

MANUSCRIPT INFORMATION

Subject field(s): Psychiatry, social sciences
Manuscript requirements: Style sheet sent on request.
  Preferred length: 1,000-5000
  Number of copies to be submitted: 2
  Abstract: Yes words
Author information and reprints: Payment: By publication to author. By arrangement.
  Is simultaneous submission of article to other journals permitted: No
  Exclusive manuscript rights between acceptance and publication: Yes
  Copyright: By arrangement
  Reprints: Not available.
Disposition of manuscript:
  Query letter: Preferred
  Receipt of manuscript acknowledged: Yes
  Decision to publish in: One month
  Accepted manuscript published in: Three months
  Rejected manuscript returned: Yes, if return postage is supplied by author.
  Rejected manuscript criticized: No
Submit to:
  Valerie Andrews
  Managing Editor
  (See address above)

SPECIAL STIPULATIONS

Mental health professionals are the only authors seriously considered.

PSYCHOTHERAPY: THEORY, RESEARCH AND PRACTICE* [1483]
University of Chicago
5848 South University Avenue
Chicago, Illinois 60637
(312) 753-4742

SUBSCRIPTION DATA

Issues and rates: Published quarterly.
  Average paid circulation: 5,000
  Annual rate(s): $10.00, Foreign $11.00
Publisher or Sponsor: American Psychological Association, Psychotherapy Division
Managing Editor: Charlotte Z. Rosen

EDITORIAL DESCRIPTION

Publishes articles relevant to psychotherapy. Is not limited to research but also specializes in theory and in direct descriptions of cases with emphasis on the therapist describing problems and choices. Open to all the different viewpoints in the field.

MANUSCRIPT INFORMATION

Subject field(s): Psychotherapy
Manuscript requirements: APA
  Preferred length: 10-12 pages
  Number of copies to be submitted: Two
Author information and reprints: Payment: None.
  Is simultaneous submission of article to other journals permitted: No
  Reprints: Available, cost depends on length

Disposition of manuscript:
  Receipt of manuscript acknowledged: Yes
  Decision to publish in: Six months
  Accepted manuscript published in: Six months
  Rejected manuscript returned: Yes
  Rejected manuscript criticized: Yes
Submit to:
  Eugene T. Gendlin
  Editor
  (See address above)

REPRESENTATIVE RESEARCH IN SOCIAL PSYCHOLOGY [1484]
Department of Psychology
University of North Carolina
Chapel Hill, North Carolina 27514
(919) 933-7636

First published in 1970

SUBSCRIPTION DATA

Issues and rates: Published semi-annually.
  Average paid circulation: 300
  Annual rate(s): $4.00; Institutions $12.00; Foreign individuals $7.00; Foreign institutions $15.00
Managing Editor: Robert G. Folger

EDITORIAL DESCRIPTION

To promote methodological improvement within the field of social psychology. The decision to publish is based solely on the adequacy of the design and research methods and the relevance to theoretical issues. Especially encouraged are positive and negative replications, methodological notes and theoretical comments on the direction of social psychology.
Articles per average issue: 8
Audience: Social psychologists
Manuscripts accepted in English

MANUSCRIPT INFORMATION

Subject field(s): Personality, social motivation, communication, social interaction and socialization
Manuscript requirements: APA
  Preferred length: 10-15 pages
  Number of copies to be submitted: 3
  Abstract: Yes Up to 125 words
Author information and reprints: Payment: None.
  Is simultaneous submission of article to other journals permitted: Not permitted.
  Exclusive manuscript rights between acceptance and publication: Yes
  Copyright: Held by publication.
  Reprints: Available at cost.
Disposition of manuscript:
  Query letter: Not necessary.
  Receipt of manuscript acknowledged: Yes
  Decision to publish in: 2 months
  Accepted manuscript published in: 6 months
  Rejected manuscript returned: Yes, with return postage paid by publication.
  Rejected manuscript criticized: Yes
Submit to:
  Robert G. Folger
  Review Coordinator
  (See address above)

THE SCANDINAVIAN JOURNAL OF PSYCHOLOGY [1485]

Almqvist & Wiksell Periodical Company
Box 62
S-101 20 Stockholm 1, Sweden
08/23 79 90

SUBSCRIPTION DATA

Issues and rates: Published quarterly.
  Average paid circulation: Not available.
  Average paid circulation: 2,000
  Annual rate(s): Sw.Kr. 98.00; Foreign $25.75
Publisher or Sponsor: The Psychological Association of Scandinavia

EDITORIAL DESCRIPTION

Devoted to original scientific contributions in all fields of psychology.

MANUSCRIPT INFORMATION

Subject field(s): Psychology
Manuscript requirements: Style sheet sent on request.
  Number of copies to be submitted: Original and one copy
Author information and reprints: Payment: None. 100 free reprints
  Is simultaneous submission of article to other journals permitted: No
  Exclusive manuscript rights between acceptance and publication: Yes
  Copyright: Held by the Psychological Association of Scandinavia
  Reprints: Available
Additional information: Manuscripts should be typewritten with double spacing and in the form in which the author wishes the paper to appear.
Submit to:
  Lars Kebbon
  Editor
  Ulleaker Sjukhus
  S-75017 Uppsala, Sweden

SOCIAL BEHAVIOR AND PERSONALITY [1486]

An International Journal
Editorial Services Ltd.
P.O. Box 6443
Wellington, New Zealand

First published in 1973

SUBSCRIPTION DATA

Issues and rates: Published semi-annually.
  Average paid circulation: Not available.
  Annual rate(s): Individuals $NZ8.00; Institutions $12.00
Publisher or Sponsor: Society for Personality Research Incorporated

EDITORIAL DESCRIPTION

Publishes research and theoretical articles on all aspects of personality and social psychology.
Articles per average issue: 15
Audience: Professional
  Manuscripts accepted in English

MANUSCRIPT INFORMATION

Subject field(s): Educational, developmental, and social psychology, psychology of personality, clinical psychology, psychiatry, sociology, industrial and community psychology, cultural anthropology and management science.
Manuscript requirements: APA
  Preferred length: 5000 words or less
  Number of copies to be submitted: Two
  Is simultaneous submission of article to other journals permitted: No
  Exclusive manuscript rights between acceptance and publication: Yes
  Copyright: Held by publication.
  Reprints: Available at cost price
Disposition of manuscript:
  Query letter: No
  Receipt of manuscript acknowledged: Yes
  Decision to publish in: 3-4 weeks
  Accepted manuscript published in: 6-8 weeks
  Rejected manuscript returned: Yes
  Rejected manuscript criticized: Yes
Submit to:
  Dr. Robert A. C. Stewart
  Editor
  For Jan.-Nov., 1975:
  Memorial University
  St. John's Newfoundland, Canada

  After Nov., 1975:
  Massey University
  Palmerston North, New Zealand

SOCIAL PSYCHIATRY [1487]

Springer-Verlag
175 Fifth Avenue
New York, New York 10010

SUBSCRIPTION DATA

Issues and rates: Published quarterly.
  Annual rate(s): DM 98 per volume
Managing Editor: N. Kreitman

EDITORIAL DESCRIPTION

To provide a medium for the prompt publication of scientific contributions concerned with the effects of social conditions upon behavior and the relationship between psychiatric disorder and the social environment.
Manuscripts accepted in English, French, German

MANUSCRIPT INFORMATION

Subject field(s): May be original investigations, clinical reports, conference proceedings, or specialized investigations into the fields of social psychology, sociology, anthropology, epidemiology or social administration.
Manuscript requirements: See latest issue for style requirements.
  Preferred length: 20 maximum pages
  Number of copies to be submitted: 3
  Abstract: Yes. A short summary in English giving the most important results. French and German manuscripts should include an abstract in English as well as a translation of the title.

Author information and reprints: Payment: Reprints only. 75 offprints
  Is simultaneous submission of article to other journals permitted: Not permitted.
  Exclusive manuscript rights between acceptance and publication: Yes
  Copyright: Held by publication.
  Reprints: Available at cost.
Submit to:
  Dr. Stephen Fleck
  Editor
  Department of Psychiatry
  333 Cedar Street
  New Haven, Connecticut 06510

SUICIDE [1488]

Behavioral Publications
72 Fifth Avenue
New York, New York 10011
(212) 243-6000

Previously entitled *Life-Threatening Behavior*

First published in 1971

SUBSCRIPTION DATA

Issues and rates: Published quarterly.
  Average paid circulation: 2,000
  Annual rate(s): Individuals $15.00; Institutions $35.00
Managing Editor: Jean Blackburn

EDITORIAL DESCRIPTION

Devoted to emergent approaches to self and other destructive behaviors. It is multi-disciplinary and concerned with suicide prevention, death, accidents, sub-intentioned destruction, and threats to life's length and breadth from within and without.
Articles per average issue: 5
Audience: Psychiatrists and other human service professionals.
  Manuscripts accepted in English

MANUSCRIPT INFORMATION

Subject field(s): Psychology, psychiatry
Manuscript requirements: APA
  Preferred length: 10-15 typed pages
  Number of copies to be submitted: Two
  Abstract: Yes
Author information and reprints: Payment: None.
  Is simultaneous submission of article to other journals permitted: No
  Exclusive manuscript rights between acceptance and publication: Yes
  Copyright: Held by publication.
  Reprints: Available
Disposition of manuscript:
  Query letter: No
  Receipt of manuscript acknowledged: Yes
  Decision to publish in: 3 months
  Accepted manuscript published in: 6 months
  Rejected manuscript returned: Yes
  Rejected manuscript criticized: Upon request
Submit to:
  Edwin S. Shneidman
  Editor

Neuropsychiatric Institute
760 Westwood Plaza
Los Angeles, California 90024

THE TRAINING SCHOOL BULLETIN [1489]

1667 East Landis Avenue
Vineland, New Jersey 08360
(609) 691-0021 Ext. 285

First published in 1904

SUBSCRIPTION DATA
Issues and rates: Published quarterly.
 Average paid circulation: 2,000; 8,000 controlled
 Annual rate(s): $4.00, Foreign $6.50
Publisher or Sponsor: American Institute for Mental Studies, Training School Unit

EDITORIAL DESCRIPTION
 Open to original articles for the professional worker dealing with mental retardation and those areas having a direct relationship to mental retardation.
Articles per average issue: 7-9
Audience: Professionals
 Manuscripts accepted in English

MANUSCRIPT INFORMATION
Manuscript requirements: See latest issue for style requirements.
 Preferred length: 10 pages
 Number of copies to be submitted: Two
 Abstract: Yes
Author information and reprints: Payment: None.
 Is simultaneous submission of article to other journals permitted: Yes
 Exclusive manuscript rights between acceptance and publication: No
 Copyright: Not copyrighted
 Reprints: Available, 25 free
Disposition of manuscript:
 Query letter: No
 Receipt of manuscript acknowledged: Yes
 Decision to publish in: 1 month
 Accepted manuscript published in: 4 months
 Rejected manuscript returned: Yes, if self-addressed, stamped envelope is sent with manuscript.
 Rejected manuscript criticized: Yes
Submit to:
 Thomas J. Fanning
 Managing Editor
 (See address above)

TRANSACTIONAL ANALYSIS JOURNAL [1490]

3155 College Avenue
Berkeley, California 94705
(415) 653-9672

Previously entitled *Transactional Analysis Bulletin*

First published in 1971

SUBSCRIPTION DATA
Issues and rates: Published quarterly.
 Average paid circulation: 6,700
 Annual rate(s): $15.00, Foreign $7.50
Publisher or Sponsor: International Transactional Analysis Association
Managing Editor: Stephen B. Karpman, M.D.

EDITORIAL DESCRIPTION
 Publishes articles of clinical and scientific interest to members and practitioners of transactional analysis.
Articles per average issue: 10
 Manuscripts accepted in English

MANUSCRIPT INFORMATION
Subject field(s): Any applications of transactional analysis
Manuscript requirements: See latest issue for style requirements.
 Number of copies to be submitted: Ten
 Abstract: Not necessary
Author information and reprints: Payment: None.
 Is simultaneous submission of article to other journals permitted: No
 Exclusive manuscript rights between acceptance and publication: Yes
 Copyright: Held by publication.
 Reprints: Available, cost depends on length
Disposition of manuscript:
 Query letter: No
 Receipt of manuscript acknowledged: Yes
 Decision to publish in: 90 days
 Accepted manuscript published in: 90 days
 Rejected manuscript returned: No
 Rejected manuscript criticized: Yes
Submit to:
 Editorial Board
 (See address above)

TRANSCULTURAL PSYCHIATRIC RESEARCH REVIEW [1491]

Beatty Hall
1266 Pine Avenue, West
Montreal, Quebec H3G 1A8,
(514) 392-5165

Previously entitled *Review and Newsletter*

SUBSCRIPTION DATA
Issues and rates: Published semi-annually.
 Annual rate(s): $7.00; Foreign $7.00; Institutions $7.00; Foreign institutions $7.00
Publisher or Sponsor: Canada Council
Managing Editor: Eric D. Wittkower

EDITORIAL DESCRIPTION
 Abstracts and original articles dealing with the borderline area between psychiatry and anthropology
Articles per average issue: 34
Audience: Psychiatrists and cultural anthropologists
 Manuscripts accepted in any language (will be translated)

MANUSCRIPT INFORMATION
Subject field(s): Clinical observations, research, theoretical issues, presented from all over the world.
Manuscript requirements: APA
 Preferred length: 1,000 words; 4-5 pages
 Number of copies to be submitted: 2
 Abstract: Yes. A brief, objective description of the contents of the paper.
Author information and reprints: Payment: None.
 Is simultaneous submission of article to other journals permitted: Permitted.
 Exclusive manuscript rights between acceptance and publication: No
 Copyright: Held by publication.
Disposition of manuscript:
 Query letter: Not necessary, but advisable.
 Receipt of manuscript acknowledged: Yes
 Decision to publish in: 2-3 months
 Accepted manuscript published in: Varies
 Rejected manuscript returned: No
 Rejected manuscript criticized: Sometimes
Submit to:
 Eric D. Wittkower
 Editor-in-Chief
 (See address above)

Social welfare

Social welfare

AFB RESEARCH BULLETIN [1492]
15 West 16th Street
New York, New York 10011
(212) 924-0420 ext. 745

First published in 1962

SUBSCRIPTION DATA
Issues and rates: Published semi-annually.
  Average paid circulation: 200; 450 controlled
  Annual rate(s): $6.00
Publisher or Sponsor: American Foundation for the Blind
Managing Editor: Leslie L. Clark

EDITORIAL DESCRIPTION
Contains research articles and reports relevant to problems caused by visual handicaps; information on prototypes and new devices.
Articles per average issue: 12-15
Audience: Researchers
  Manuscripts accepted in English

MANUSCRIPT INFORMATION
Subject field(s): Blindness, low vision, psychology, education, technology, neurology
Manuscript requirements: Style sheet sent on request.
  Number of copies to be submitted: Two
Author information and reprints: Payment: Reprints only. 10 free reprints to author
  Is simultaneous submission of article to other journals permitted: No
  Exclusive manuscript rights between acceptance and publication: Yes
  Copyright: Held by author.
  Reprints: Available at $.10 per page
Disposition of manuscript:
  Query letter: No
  Receipt of manuscript acknowledged: Yes
  Decision to publish in: 3 months
  Accepted manuscript published in: One year
  Rejected manuscript returned: Yes
  Rejected manuscript criticized: Sometimes
Submit to:
  Leslie L. Clark
  (See address above)

THE ALCOHOLISM DIGEST [1493]
P. O. Box 6318
5632 Connecticut Avenue, N. W.
Washington, D. C. 20015
(319) 948-0740

First published in 1973

SUBSCRIPTION DATA
Issues and rates: Published monthly.
  Average paid circulation: 2,500
Publisher or Sponsor: Information Planning Associates, Inc.
Managing Editor: Clarence M. Johnson

EDITORIAL DESCRIPTION
Presents articles on any aspect of alcoholism and alcohol abuse; treatment and rehabilitation; traffic safety; abuse in government and industry; alcohol education, etc.
Articles per average issue: 12
Audience: Professional, general, academic
  Manuscripts accepted in English

MANUSCRIPT INFORMATION
Manuscript requirements: No specific style guide.
  Preferred length: None
  Number of copies to be submitted: 2
  Abstract: Not necessary.
Author information and reprints: Payment: None.
  Is simultaneous submission of article to other journals permitted: Permitted.
  Exclusive manuscript rights between acceptance and publication: No
  Copyright: Held by the Library of Congress
  Reprints: Available at no cost.
Additional information: All articles accepted for publication will also appear in the annual compilation.
Disposition of manuscript:
  Query letter: Not necessary, but advisable.
  Receipt of manuscript acknowledged: Yes
  Decision to publish in: 2 weeks
  Accepted manuscript published in: 3 months
  Rejected manuscript returned: Yes, if return postage is supplied by author.
  Rejected manuscript criticized: Reasons for rejections only
Submit to:
  Clarence M. Johnson
  Director of Publications
  (See address above)

AMERICAN ARCHIVES OF REHABILITATION THERAPY [1494]
Official Publication of the American Association for Rehabilitation Therapy
W. 32 Ferndale Road
Paramus, New Jersey 07652

First published in 1950

SUBSCRIPTION DATA
Issues and rates: Published quarterly.
  Average paid circulation: 250; 250 controlled
  Annual rate(s): $6.00, Foreign $7.00
Publisher or Sponsor: American Association for Rehabilitation Therapy, Inc.
Managing Editor: Elwood A. Cavalier

EDITORIAL DESCRIPTION
Contains articles on all aspects of the rehabilitation field.
Articles per average issue: 4
Audience: Professionals
  Manuscripts accepted in English only

MANUSCRIPT INFORMATION
Subject field(s): Rehabilitation, any related field to rehabilitation
Manuscript requirements: See latest issue for style requirements.
  Preferred length: 5000 words
  Number of copies to be submitted: One original and one carbon
  Abstract: No
Author information and reprints: Payment: None.
  Is simultaneous submission of article to other journals permitted: No
  Exclusive manuscript rights between acceptance and publication: Yes
  Copyright: Held by publication.
  Reprints: Available
Disposition of manuscript:
  Query letter: No
  Receipt of manuscript acknowledged: Yes
  Decision to publish in: 1 month
  Accepted manuscript published in: 6 months
  Rejected manuscript returned: Yes
  Rejected manuscript criticized: Yes
Submit to:
  George J. Goldin
  Editor
  c/o Department of Rehabilitation and Special Education
  Northeastern University
  Boston, Massachusetts 02115
  (617) 437-2485

ASHA [1495]
A Journal of the American Speech and Hearing Association
9030 Old Georgetown Road
Washington, D.C. 20014
(301) 530-3400

First published in 1959

SUBSCRIPTION DATA
Issues and rates: Published monthly.
  Average paid circulation: 25,000
  Annual rate(s): $28.00, Foreign $31.00
Publisher or Sponsor: American Speech and Hearing Association
Managing Editor: Frederick T. Spahr

EDITORIAL DESCRIPTION
Contains articles, book reviews, etc.
Audience: Speech pathologists, audiologists
  Manuscripts accepted in English

MANUSCRIPT INFORMATION
Subject field(s): Speech, hearing, language
Manuscript requirements: Chicago
  Preferred length: 5-10 pages
  Number of copies to be submitted: Five
  Abstract: No
Author information and reprints: Payment: None.
  Is simultaneous submission of article to other journals permitted: No
  Exclusive manuscript rights between acceptance and publication: Yes
  Copyright: Held by author.
  Reprints: Available
Disposition of manuscript:
  Query letter: No

Receipt of manuscript acknowledged: Yes
Decision to publish in: Varies
Accepted manuscript published in: Varies
Rejected manuscript criticized: Yes
Submit to:
Frank R. Kleffner
Assistant Editor
Central Institute for the Deaf
818 South Euclid Avenue
St. Louis, Missouri 63110

BRITISH JOURNAL OF ADDICTION [1496]

Longman Group Ltd., Journals Division
Burnt Mill
Harlow, Essex, England
26721

SUBSCRIPTION DATA

Issues and rates: Published quarterly.
Annual rate(s): £8.00, Foreign $24.00
Publisher or Sponsor: Society for the Study of Addiction

EDITORIAL DESCRIPTION

Contains original research papers in the field of science and medicine which contribute to an understanding and evaluation of the problems of dependence on alcohol and other drugs.
Submit to:
M. M. Glatt
Editor
(See address above)

SPECIAL STIPULATIONS

Request additional information from editor.

CANADIAN JOURNAL OF OCCUPATIONAL THERAPY [1497]

Canadian Association of Occupational Therapists
4 New Street
Toronto, Ontario M5R 1P6, Canada
(416) 922-3701

SUBSCRIPTION DATA

Issues and rates: Published quarterly.
Annual rate(s): $10.00; Foreign $11.25
Publisher or Sponsor: The Canadian Association of Occupational Therapists
Managing Editor: Rosalie Kupfer-Halstuck

EDITORIAL DESCRIPTION

Publishes all articles relating to the practice and teaching of occupational therapy
Articles per average issue: 5
Audience: Professional, academic
Manuscripts accepted in English, French

MANUSCRIPT INFORMATION

Subject field(s): Psychiatry, physical medicine, education, reviews, personal experiences
Manuscript requirements: See latest issue for style requirements. Style sheet sent on request.
Preferred length: 4,500 words; 12-15 pages
Number of copies to be submitted: 3
Abstract: Yes.
Author information and reprints: Payment: None.
Is simultaneous submission of article to other journals permitted: Not permitted.
Exclusive manuscript rights between acceptance and publication: Yes
Copyright: Held by publication.
Reprints: Available at cost.
Disposition of manuscript:
Query letter: Not necessary.
Receipt of manuscript acknowledged: Yes
Decision to publish in: 1 month
Accepted manuscript published in: 2-4 months
Rejected manuscript returned: Yes, with return postage paid by publication.
Rejected manuscript criticized: Yes
Submit to:
Mrs. Rosalie Kupfer-Halstuck
Editor
4660 Queen Mary Road, No. 36
Montreal, Quebec, Canada
(514) 735-3345

CANADIAN WELFARE [1498]

Box 3505, Station C
Ottawa, Ontario K1Y 4G1, Canada
(613) 728-1865

SUBSCRIPTION DATA

Issues and rates: Published bi-monthly.
Average paid circulation: 4,300; 4,600 controlled
Annual rate(s): $5.00
Publisher or Sponsor: The Canadian Council on Social Development
Managing Editor: Norman Dahl

EDITORIAL DESCRIPTION

Contains articles on social welfare generally, including social policy development (income security, housing, corrections, personal social services, particularly for the most vulnerable members of society). Point of view is that an extension of social services and a continual updating of social policy measures is necessary for the well-being of all, particularly the oppressed, alienated, aged, disabled and deprived members of society.
Articles per average issue: 5
Audience: General
Manuscripts accepted in English

MANUSCRIPT INFORMATION

Subject field(s): Social services, income security, housing (social aspects), health services (social aspects), social justice, corrections and criminology, work and leisure, environment
Manuscript requirements: See latest issue for style requirements.
Preferred length: 2,000 to 3,000 words; 8 to 12 pages
Number of copies to be submitted: Two
Abstract: No
Author information and reprints: Payment: None.
Is simultaneous submission of article to other journals permitted: No
Exclusive manuscript rights between acceptance and publication: Yes
Copyright: Held by publication.
Reprints: Available, $15.00 per 1000
Additional information: Typescript required. Avoid jargon. References to be kept to a minimum.
Disposition of manuscript:
Query letter: Desirable
Receipt of manuscript acknowledged: Yes
Decision to publish in: One month
Accepted manuscript published in: 2-12 months
Rejected manuscript returned: Yes
Rejected manuscript criticized: Yes
Submit to:
Norman Dahl
Editor
(See address above)

CHILD CARE QUARTERLY [1499]

Behavioral Publications
72 Fifth Avenue
New York, New York 10011
(212) 662-3100

First published in 1973

SUBSCRIPTION DATA

Issues and rates: Published quarterly.
Average paid circulation: 2,000
Annual rate(s): $12.00; Institutions $30.00

EDITORIAL DESCRIPTION

Dedicated to the improvement of child care practice in a variety of settings; designed to serve child workers, their supervisors, agency administrators, and instructors in this rapidly accelerating field.
Articles per average issue: 8-10
Audience: Administrators, workers in residential treatment and day care centers
Manuscripts accepted in English

MANUSCRIPT INFORMATION

Subject field(s): Psychology, psychiatry, social services, welfare, children
Manuscript requirements: APA
Preferred length: 10-15 typewritten pages
Number of copies to be submitted: Two
Abstract: No
Author information and reprints: Payment: None.
Is simultaneous submission of article to other journals permitted: No
Exclusive manuscript rights between acceptance and publication: Yes
Copyright: Held by publication.
Reprints: Available
Disposition of manuscript:
Query letter: No
Receipt of manuscript acknowledged: Yes
Decision to publish in: 3-6 months
Accepted manuscript published in: 6-8 months

Social welfare

Rejected manuscript returned: Yes, if return postage is supplied by author.
Rejected manuscript criticized: No
Submit to:
Jerome Beker
Editor
11 Ross Avenue
Spring Valley, New York 10977

CHILD WELFARE [1500]
Journal of the Child Welfare League of America
67 Irving Place
New York, New York 10003
(212) 254-7410

First published in 1920

SUBSCRIPTION DATA
Issues and rates: Monthly except August and September
Average paid circulation: 7,500; 1,500 controlled
Annual rate(s): $8.00, Foreign $9.00, Students $6.00
Publisher or Sponsor: Child Welfare League of America, Inc.

EDITORIAL DESCRIPTION
Contains articles in all areas of child welfare or related service: administration, supervision, casework, groupwork, community organization, teaching; interdisciplinary approaches to the field of child welfare; issues of social policy which bear on child welfare.
Articles per average issue: 6-7
Audience: Child welfare personnel
Manuscripts accepted in English

MANUSCRIPT INFORMATION
Subject field(s): Standards of practice, group care, group homes, residential treatment, foster family care, child neglect, child development, institutional care, adoption, unmarried parent, child care worker training
Manuscript requirements: Style sheet sent on request.
Preferred length: 3,000-4,000 words
Number of copies to be submitted: Two
Author information and reprints: Payment: None.
Is simultaneous submission of article to other journals permitted: No
Exclusive manuscript rights between acceptance and publication: Yes
Copyright: Held by publication.
Reprints: Available at no cost.
Additional information: Typewritten, double-spaced
Disposition of manuscript:
Query letter: No
Receipt of manuscript acknowledged: Yes
Decision to publish in: 2-4 weeks
Accepted manuscript published in: 6-9 months
Rejected manuscript returned: Yes, if return postage is supplied by author.
Rejected manuscript criticized: No
Submit to:
Carl Schoenberg
Editor
(See address above)

CLINICAL SOCIAL WORK JOURNAL [1501]
Behavioral Publications
72 Fifth Avenue
New York, New York 10011
(212) 243-6000

First published in 1973

SUBSCRIPTION DATA
Issues and rates: Published quarterly.
Average paid circulation: 5,000
Annual rate(s): $12.00, Institutions $30.00
Publisher or Sponsor: National Federation of Societies for Clinical Social Work
Managing Editor: Jean Blackburn

EDITORIAL DESCRIPTION
Objectives are to broaden the understanding and skill of the clinical social work practitioner or teacher concerned with individuals, couples, families and groups.
Articles per average issue: 8
Manuscripts accepted in English

MANUSCRIPT INFORMATION
Subject field(s): Social work, sociology, psychology, psychiatry
Manuscript requirements: APA
Preferred length: 10-15 typewritten pages
Number of copies to be submitted: Two
Abstract: No
Author information and reprints: Payment: None.
Is simultaneous submission of article to other journals permitted: No
Exclusive manuscript rights between acceptance and publication: Yes
Copyright: Held by publication.
Reprints: Available
Disposition of manuscript:
Query letter:
Receipt of manuscript acknowledged: Yes
Decision to publish in: 6-8 weeks
Accepted manuscript published in: 6 months
Rejected manuscript returned: Yes
Rejected manuscript criticized: No
Submit to:
Mary L. Gottesfeld
Editor
285 West End Avenue
New York, New York 10023

CONTEMPORARY DRUG PROBLEMS [1502]
95 Morton Street
New York, New York 10014
(212) 243-5775

First published in 1972

SUBSCRIPTION DATA
Issues and rates: Published quarterly.
Annual rate(s): Individuals $20, Institutions $24, Foreign $26

EDITORIAL DESCRIPTION
Contains interdisciplinary articles on drug use and abuse.
Rejected manuscript returned: 4-6
Audience: Professional
Manuscripts accepted in English

MANUSCRIPT INFORMATION
Subject field(s): Public health, law, treatment, education, psychology, sociology, medicine, pharmacology, politics/political science
Manuscript requirements: Style sheet sent on request.
Preferred length: As required
Number of copies to be submitted: 2
Abstract: No
Author information and reprints: Payment: None. 50 reprints
Is simultaneous submission of article to other journals permitted: No
Exclusive manuscript rights between acceptance and publication: Yes
Copyright: Held by publication.
Reprints: Available from publisher
Additional information: Submit on white opaque stock. Include original art for charts, graphs, tables. All art should be on separate pages. Send original and one copy of manuscript, double-spaced throughout. There is a royalty-sharing agreement whereby the author and publication share royalties after deduction of expenses. Author has free access to his material.
Disposition of manuscript:
Query letter: No
Receipt of manuscript acknowledged: Yes
Decision to publish in: 4 weeks
Accepted manuscript published in: 3-6 months
Rejected manuscript returned: Yes
Rejected manuscript criticized: Sometimes
Submit to:
Roberta London
Managing Editor
515 Oxford Street
Westbury, New York 11590
(516) 333-4418

DRUG FORUM [1503]
The Journal of Human Issues
Baywood Publishing Company, Inc.
43 Central Drive
Farmingdale, New York 11735
(516) 293-7130

First published in 1971
Average paid circulation: 1,500
Annual rate(s): $30.00; Foreign $32.00
Publisher or Sponsor: Institute for the Study of Drug Addiction

EDITORIAL DESCRIPTION
Provides insights into the increasing problems of the misuse of drugs and presents successes and failures that individuals, programs, institutions and communities have experienced. Concerns itself with changing drug-oriented ways of living.
Articles per average issue: 14

Audience: Professionals involved in the treatment, rehabilitation and supervision of drug abuse programs.
Manuscripts accepted in English

MANUSCRIPT INFORMATION
Subject field(s): Drug treatment, cultural aspects of drug use, legal issues
Manuscript requirements: See latest issue for style requirements. Style sheet sent on request.
  Preferred length: 5,000 words maximum
  Number of copies to be submitted: 2
  Abstract: Yes. Of about 150 words at the beginning of paper.
Author information and reprints: Payment: Reprints only. 20 copies
  Is simultaneous submission of article to other journals permitted: Not permitted.
  Exclusive manuscript rights between acceptance and publication: Yes
  Copyright: Held by publication.
  Reprints: Available at cost.
Disposition of manuscript:
  Query letter: Not necessary, but advisable.
  Receipt of manuscript acknowledged: Yes
  Decision to publish in: 4-6 weeks
  Accepted manuscript published in: 6 months
  Rejected manuscript returned: Yes, with return postage paid by publication.
  Rejected manuscript criticized: Sometimes
Submit to:
  Dr. Stanley Einstein
  Executive Editor
  (See address above)

THE FAMILY COORDINATOR [1504]
Journal of Education, Counseling and Services
National Council on Family Relations
1219 University Avenue Southeast
Minneapolis, Minnesota 55414
(612) 331-2774

Previously entitled *Family Life Coordinator*

First published in 1952

SUBSCRIPTION DATA
Issues and rates: Published quarterly.
  Average paid circulation: 6,800
  Annual rate(s): $15.00, Foreign $17.00
Publisher or Sponsor: National Council on Family Relations
Managing Editor: William C. Nichols, Jr.

EDITORIAL DESCRIPTION
Directed to practitioners serving marriage and the family through education, counseling, and community services. A medium for disseminating reports of experiences in teaching, counseling, or other community services that provide leads for others to explore; evaluation of work utilizing innovative methods; or the application of research and theory to practice.
Articles per average issue: 15
Audience: Professionals, students

Manuscripts accepted in English

MANUSCRIPT INFORMATION
Subject field(s): Anything dealing with the family field
Manuscript requirements: Style sheet sent on request.
  Preferred length: 5-8 pages
  Number of copies to be submitted: Two
  Abstract: Yes
Author information and reprints: Payment: None.
  Is simultaneous submission of article to other journals permitted: Yes
  Exclusive manuscript rights between acceptance and publication: Yes
  Copyright: Held by publication.
  Reprints: Available, $24.00 per hundred copies for 5-8 pages.
Disposition of manuscript:
  Receipt of manuscript acknowledged: Yes
  Decision to publish in: 3 months
  Accepted manuscript published in: 9 months
  Rejected manuscript returned: Yes
  Rejected manuscript criticized: Yes
Submit to:
  The Editor
  228-A Sandels Building
  Florida State University
  Tallahassee, Florida 32306

FAMILY PLANNING PERSPECTIVES [1505]
The Alan Guttmacher Institute
515 Madison Avenue
New York, New York 10022
(212) 752-2100 ext. 254

First published in 1969

SUBSCRIPTION DATA
Issues and rates: Published bi-monthly.
  Average paid circulation: 24,000 controlled
Publisher or Sponsor: Planned Parenthood Federation of America, Inc.
Managing Editor: Richard Lincoln

EDITORIAL DESCRIPTION
Contains original research and book reviews in fields related to family planning: social and biomedical research, demography, program planning and evaluation, clinical technique, current attitudes and practice.
Articles per average issue: 8-10
Audience: Professionals
Manuscripts accepted in English

MANUSCRIPT INFORMATION
Subject field(s): Family planning programs planning and evaluation; contraception knowledge, attitudes, practice; abortion; social and biomedical research in reproduction; federal and local government policy; population; legislation and legal aspects of family planning; clinical guidelines in providing family planning
Manuscript requirements: Chicago; Style sheet sent on request.
  Preferred length: 5,000-10,000 words

  Number of copies to be submitted: Two
  Abstract: No
Author information and reprints: Payment: None.
  Is simultaneous submission of article to other journals permitted: Yes
  Exclusive manuscript rights between acceptance and publication: Yes
  Copyright: Held by publication.
  Reprints: Available, cost depends on length
Disposition of manuscript:
  Query letter: No
  Receipt of manuscript acknowledged: Yes
  Decision to publish in: 4-6 weeks
  Accepted manuscript published in: 2-6 months
  Rejected manuscript returned: Yes
  Rejected manuscript criticized: Occasionally
Submit to:
  Richard Lincoln
  Editor
  (See address above)

FAMILY PROCESS [1506]
149 East 78th Street
New York, New York 10021
(212) 879-4900

First published in 1962

SUBSCRIPTION DATA
Issues and rates: Published quarterly.
  Average paid circulation: 4,200
  Annual rate(s): $12.00, Foreign $13.00, Institutions $20.00
Publisher or Sponsor: Family Institute, New York; Mental Research Institute, Palo Alto
Managing Editor: Judith Lieb

EDITORIAL DESCRIPTION
Contains interdisciplinary articles in the areas of family study and treatment.
Articles per average issue: 7-8
Audience: Social and behavioral scientists
Manuscripts accepted in English

MANUSCRIPT INFORMATION
Subject field(s): Family psychotherapy; family research; problems relating to family: anthropology, sociology, psychology
Manuscript requirements: Style sheet sent on request.
  Preferred length: None
  Number of copies to be submitted: Two
  Abstract: Yes, a lead-in summary of 150 words
Author information and reprints: Payment: None.
  Is simultaneous submission of article to other journals permitted: No
  Exclusive manuscript rights between acceptance and publication: Yes
  Copyright: Held by publication.
  Reprints: Available, cost varies with length
Disposition of manuscript:
  Query letter: No
  Receipt of manuscript acknowledged: Yes
  Decision to publish in: 6-10 weeks

Social welfare

Accepted manuscript published in: 2-3 months
Rejected manuscript returned: Yes
Rejected manuscript criticized: Yes
Submit to:
Donald A. Bloch
Editor
Stockbridge, Massachusetts 01262
(413) 637-1810

FRIDAY LETTER [1507]
National Council on Alcoholism
2 Park Avenue
New York, New York 10016
(212) 889-3160

Previously entitled *NCA Newsletter*

First published in 1970

SUBSCRIPTION DATA
Issues and rates: Published monthly.
  Average paid circulation: 3700
Publisher or Sponsor: National Council on Alcoholism, Inc.

EDITORIAL DESCRIPTION
Contains news items related to the National Council on Alcoholism and alcoholism generally.
Manuscripts accepted in English

MANUSCRIPT INFORMATION
Manuscript requirements: No specific style guide.
  Preferred length: Brief
  Number of copies to be submitted: One
  Abstract: Yes
Author information and reprints: Payment: None.
  Is simultaneous submission of article to other journals permitted: Yes
  Exclusive manuscript rights between acceptance and publication: No
  Copyright: Held by publication.
  Reprints: Available
Disposition of manuscript:
  Query letter: No
  Receipt of manuscript acknowledged: No
  Decision to publish in: 2 months
  Accepted manuscript published in: 1-2 months
  Rejected manuscript returned: No
  Rejected manuscript criticized: No
Submit to:
  Sally Rothkopf
  Editor
  (See address above)

INDUSTRIAL GERONTOLOGY [1508]
Problems and Potentials of Work and Age
The National Council on the Aging
1828 L Street, N. W., Room 504
Washington, D. C. 20036
(202) 223-6250

First published in 1969

SUBSCRIPTION DATA
Issues and rates: Published quarterly.
  Average paid circulation: 3,500
  Annual rate(s): $20.00; Foreign $20.00
Publisher or Sponsor: National Council on the Aging; U. S. Department of Labor
Managing Editor: Nancy C. Peavy

EDITORIAL DESCRIPTION
Contains articles on the relationship between work and age, research and factual information about programs and policies affecting middle-aged and older persons
Articles per average issue: 6-10
Audience: Academic, business, government
Manuscripts accepted in English

MANUSCRIPT INFORMATION
Subject field(s): Age discrimination, job counseling, physical capacity and job performance, retraining, employment and unemployment, second careers, retirement preparation, pensions, legislation.
Manuscript requirements: Style sheet sent on request.
  Preferred length: 3,000-4,000 words; 15-20 pages
  Number of copies to be submitted: 2
  Abstract: Not necessary.
Author information and reprints: Payment: None.
  Is simultaneous submission of article to other journals permitted: Not permitted.
  Exclusive manuscript rights between acceptance and publication: Yes
  Copyright: Held by publication unless permission granted otherwise
  Reprints: Available at cost.
Additional information: See summary in the Summer 1974 issue.
Disposition of manuscript:
  Query letter: Not necessary, but advisable.
  Receipt of manuscript acknowledged: Yes
  Decision to publish in: 2-3 months
  Accepted manuscript published in: 6 months
  Rejected manuscript returned: Yes, with return postage paid by publication.
  Rejected manuscript criticized: Reasons for rejections only
Submit to:
  Elizabeth L. Meier;
  Nancy C. Peavy
  Executive Editor and Editor
  (See address above)

INTERNATIONAL SOCIAL WORK [1509]
Post Box 1496
Bombay 400001, India
266034

First published in 1958

SUBSCRIPTION DATA
Issues and rates: Published quarterly.
  Average paid circulation: 800
  Annual rate(s): $5.00
Publisher or Sponsor: International Council on Social Welfare; International Association of Schools of Social Work; International Federation of Social Workers
Managing Editor: S. D. Gokhale

EDITORIAL DESCRIPTION
Covers all topics in social welfare.
Articles per average issue: Varies
Audience: Professional
Manuscripts accepted in English, French

MANUSCRIPT INFORMATION
Subject field(s): Social welfare topics in developing countries, professional and voluntary work.
Manuscript requirements: No specific style guide.
  Preferred length: 5-6 pages
  Number of copies to be submitted: Two
  Abstract: No
Author information and reprints: Payment: Reprints only. 2 copies of journal
  Is simultaneous submission of article to other journals permitted: Yes
  Exclusive manuscript rights between acceptance and publication: No
  Copyright: None
  Reprints: Available. Order at time of submission.
Disposition of manuscript:
  Query letter: No
  Receipt of manuscript acknowledged: Yes
  Decision to publish in: 2 weeks
  Accepted manuscript published in: 2-3 months
  Rejected manuscript returned: Yes, if self-addressed, stamped envelope is sent with manuscript.
  Rejected manuscript criticized: Yes
Submit to:
  E. E. Irvine
  Editor-in-Chief
  28 Church Street
  Wing, nr. Leighton Buzzard Beds., England

JOURNAL OF DRUG EDUCATION [1510]
Baywood Publishing Company, Inc.
43 Central Drive
Farmingdale, New York 11735
(516) 293-7130

First published in 1971

SUBSCRIPTION DATA
Issues and rates: Published quarterly.
  Annual rate(s): $30.00; Foreign $32.00

EDITORIAL DESCRIPTION
Addresses itself to those charged with the responsibility of disseminating accurate information on the subject of drug abuse to various segments of our society.
Articles per average issue: 13
Audience: Academic, law enforcement professionals, clergy, military
Manuscripts accepted in English

MANUSCRIPT INFORMATION
Subject field(s): Innovations and the role of the educator in drug education, school and community drug education programs, drug research.
Manuscript requirements: See latest issue for style requirements. Style sheet sent on request.
   Preferred length: 5,000 words maximum
   Number of copies to be submitted: 2
   Abstract: Yes. 100 words maximum.
Author information and reprints: Payment: Reprints only. 20 copies
   Is simultaneous submission of article to other journals permitted: Not permitted.
   Exclusive manuscript rights between acceptance and publication: Yes
   Copyright: Held by publication.
   Reprints: Available at cost.
Disposition of manuscript:
   Query letter: Not necessary, but advisable.
   Receipt of manuscript acknowledged: Yes
   Decision to publish in: 4-6 weeks
   Accepted manuscript published in: 6 months
   Rejected manuscript returned: Yes, with return postage paid by publication.
   Rejected manuscript criticized: Sometimes
Submit to:
   Albert E. Bedworth;
   Joseph A. D'Elia
   Executive Editors
   (See address above)

JOURNAL OF DRUG ISSUES [1511]
P.O. Box 4021
Tallahassee, Florida 32303
(904) 385-6524

First published in 1971

SUBSCRIPTION DATA
Issues and rates: Published quarterly.
   Average paid circulation: 3600
   Annual rate(s): $20.00, Foreign $23.00

EDITORIAL DESCRIPTION
   Contains articles on drug issues with appeal to a broad cross section of both professional and lay readers. Advocates a reasoned, unemotional examination of drug matters.
Articles per average issue: 12
   Manuscripts accepted in English

MANUSCRIPT INFORMATION
Manuscript requirements: See latest issue for style requirements.
   Preferred length: 5,000-10,000 words
   Number of copies to be submitted: Two
   Abstract: Yes, of 100-150 words
Author information and reprints: Payment: None.
   Is simultaneous submission of article to other journals permitted: No
   Exclusive manuscript rights between acceptance and publication: Yes
   Copyright: Held by publication.
   Reprints: Available, cost dependent on pages

Additional information: Manuscripts should be typewritten, double-spaced with notes and references collated on the final page. Sub-headings should be placed appropriately.
Disposition of manuscript:
   Query letter: No
   Receipt of manuscript acknowledged: Yes
   Decision to publish in: 4-6 weeks
   Accepted manuscript published in: Varies
   Rejected manuscript returned: Yes, if return postage is supplied by author.
   Rejected manuscript criticized: Sometimes
Submit to:
   Richard L. Rachin
   Editor
   (See address above)

JOURNAL OF LEISURABILITY [1512]
Box 281, Station A
Ottawa, Ontario K1N 8V2, Canada
(613) 231-5943

First published in 1974

SUBSCRIPTION DATA
Issues and rates: Published quarterly.
   Average paid circulation: 800; 100 controlled
   Annual rate(s): $9.00; Students $7.50
Publisher or Sponsor: Leisure and Disability Publications Steering Committee

EDITORIAL DESCRIPTION
   Devoted to supplying professionals in the fields of leisure and or disability with a source of stimulation for improved practice and conceptualization in the general area of recreation sciences for the disabled.
Articles per average issue: 5-6
Audience: Professionals, educators, students
   Manuscripts accepted in English

MANUSCRIPT INFORMATION
Subject field(s): Recreation for the disabled
Manuscript requirements: Style sheet sent on request.
   Preferred length: 2,500 words maximum
   Number of copies to be submitted: 2
   Abstract: Not necessary.
Author information and reprints: Payment: None.
   Is simultaneous submission of article to other journals permitted: Permitted, but not encouraged.
   Exclusive manuscript rights between acceptance and publication: Yes
   Copyright: Held by publication.
   Reprints: Not available.
Disposition of manuscript:
   Query letter: Not necessary.
   Receipt of manuscript acknowledged: Yes
   Decision to publish in: 1 month
   Accepted manuscript published in: 6 months
   Rejected manuscript returned: Yes, with return postage paid by publication.
   Rejected manuscript criticized: Yes
Submit to:
   Dr. Peter A. Witt

Editor
(See address above)

JOURNAL OF MARRIAGE AND THE FAMILY [1513]
National Council on Family Relations
1219 University Avenue S.E.
Minneapolis, Minnesota 55414
(612) 331-2774

Previously entitled *Marriage and Family Living*

First published in 1939

SUBSCRIPTION DATA
Issues and rates: Published quarterly.
   Average paid circulation: 9,500
   Annual rate(s): $20.00; Foreign $22.00
Publisher or Sponsor: National Council on Family Relations

EDITORIAL DESCRIPTION
   A medium for the presentation of original theory, research interpretation, and critical discussion of materials related to marriage and the family.
Articles per average issue: 20
Audience: Professionals, students
   Manuscripts accepted in English

MANUSCRIPT INFORMATION
Subject field(s): Any aspect of the family area
Manuscript requirements: Style sheet sent on request.
   Preferred length: 5-8 pages
   Number of copies to be submitted: Two
   Abstract: Yes
Author information and reprints: Payment: None.
   Is simultaneous submission of article to other journals permitted: Yes
   Exclusive manuscript rights between acceptance and publication: Yes
   Copyright: Held by publication.
   Reprints: Available; $24.00 per hundred copies for 5-8 pages. The cost varies by page number and number of copies wanted.
Disposition of manuscript:
   Query letter: No
   Receipt of manuscript acknowledged: Yes
   Decision to publish in: 3 months
   Accepted manuscript published in: 9 months
   Rejected manuscript returned: Yes, if self-addressed, stamped envelope is sent with manuscript.
   Rejected manuscript criticized: Yes
Submit to:
   Carlfred B. Broderick
   Department of Sociology and Anthropology
   University of Southern California
   Los Angeles, California 90007
   (213) 746-2658

Social welfare 453

JOURNAL OF PSYCHEDELIC DRUGS [1514]
118 South Bedford Street
Madison, Wisconsin 53703
(608) 362-8848

First published in 1967

SUBSCRIPTION DATA
Issues and rates: Published quarterly.
  Average paid circulation: 4,200
  Annual rate(s): $27.00, Foreign $40.00, Institutions $30.00
Publisher or Sponsor: Student Association for the Study of Hallucinogens, Inc.

EDITORIAL DESCRIPTION
Contains critical and historical reviews, theoretical analyses, speculative papers with a systematic focus and a limited number of reports of original empirical research (basic or applied), all with regard to drug use, drug misuse, drug education, drug abuse prevention and related areas.
Articles per average issue: 7-14
Audience: Academic, professional
  Manuscripts accepted in English

MANUSCRIPT INFORMATION
Subject field(s): Drug abuse, drug education, hallucinogens, narcotics, psychology and psychiatry, social work, pharmacology
Manuscript requirements: Style sheet sent on request.
  Preferred length: 5-20 pages
  Number of copies to be submitted: Three
  Abstract: Yes, of 150-300 words
Author information and reprints: Payment: None.
  Is simultaneous submission of article to other journals permitted: No
  Exclusive manuscript rights between acceptance and publication: Yes
  Copyright: Held by publication.
  Reprints: Available, 75 free offprints, 2 issues
Additional information: Tables and figures should be kept to an absolute minimum. Figures should be submitted in a camera-ready form.
Disposition of manuscript:
  Query letter: No
  Receipt of manuscript acknowledged: Yes
  Decision to publish in: 1-3 months
  Accepted manuscript published in: 2-5 months
  Rejected manuscript returned: Yes
  Rejected manuscript criticized: Yes
Submit to:
  Nancy Gottlieb
  Co-Editor
  (See address above)

JOURNAL OF REHABILITATION [1515]
1522 K Street, N.W.
Washington, D.C. 20005
(202) 659-2430

SUBSCRIPTION DATA
Issues and rates: Published bi-monthly.
  Average paid circulation: 36,000
  Annual rate(s): $5.00, Pan-Am $5.50, Foreign $6.00
Publisher or Sponsor: National Rehabilitation Association

EDITORIAL DESCRIPTION
Publishes social-medical-scientific research and theory which results in a practical application that leads to the employment and well being of physically and/or mentally handicapped people.

MANUSCRIPT INFORMATION
Subject field(s): Job placement, job stability (follow-up studies), agency problems, legislation, rehabilitation counseling, sheltered workshops, occupational therapy, physical therapy, physical medicine, nursing
Manuscript requirements: Style sheet sent on request.
  Preferred length: 3000 words; 12 pages
  Number of copies to be submitted: Three
  Abstract: Yes
Author information and reprints: Payment: Reprints only. 15 copies of the issue in which the article appears.
  Is simultaneous submission of article to other journals permitted: No
  Exclusive manuscript rights between acceptance and publication: Yes
  Copyright: Held by publication.
  Reprints: Tearsheets are provided free.
Disposition of manuscript:
  Receipt of manuscript acknowledged: Yes
  Decision to publish in: 3-6 months
  Accepted manuscript published in: 3-6 months
  Rejected manuscript returned: Yes, if self-addressed, stamped envelope is sent with manuscript.
  Rejected manuscript criticized: Sometimes
Submit to:
  Betty Winkler Roberts
  Editor
  (See address above)

JOURNAL OF REHABILITATION OF THE DEAF [1516]
814 Thayer Avenue
Silver Spring, Maryland 20910
(301) 589-0880

First published in 1967

SUBSCRIPTION DATA
Issues and rates: Published quarterly.
  Average paid circulation: 1,300
  Annual rate(s): $10.00, Foreign $12.00
Publisher or Sponsor: Professional Rehabilitation Workers with the Adult Deaf, Inc.
Managing Editor: Charles R. Hill

EDITORIAL DESCRIPTION
Contains articles having to do with rehabilitation of deaf people.
Articles per average issue: 5
Audience: Professionals
  Manuscripts accepted in English

MANUSCRIPT INFORMATION
Subject field(s): Counseling, psychology, psychiatry, vocational rehabilitation, professional training, audiology, speech, communication
Manuscript requirements: APA
  Preferred length: 2000-3000 words, typewritten, double-spaced
  Number of copies to be submitted: Two
  Abstract: No
Author information and reprints: Payment: None.
  Is simultaneous submission of article to other journals permitted: No
  Exclusive manuscript rights between acceptance and publication: Yes
  Copyright: Not copyrighted
  Reprints: Available, 5 copies free
Disposition of manuscript:
  Query letter: No
  Receipt of manuscript acknowledged: Yes
  Decision to publish in: 1 month
  Accepted manuscript published in: 3 months
  Rejected manuscript returned: Yes
  Rejected manuscript criticized: Yes
Submit to:
  Glenn T. Lloyd
  Editor
  (See address above)

SPECIAL STIPULATIONS
A professional journal; articles must be soundly based; opinion papers are not wanted.

JOURNAL OF STUDIES ON ALCOHOL [1517]
Rutgers Center of Alcohol Studies
Rutgers University
New Brunswick, New Jersey 08903
(201) 932-3510

Previously entitled *Quarterly Journal of Studies on Alcohol*

First published in 1940

SUBSCRIPTION DATA
Issues and rates: Published monthly
  Average paid circulation: 2900
  Annual rate(s): $20.00, Foreign $21.00
Publisher or Sponsor: Center of Alcohol Studies, Rutgers University

EDITORIAL DESCRIPTION
Contains original reports of new research on all aspects of alcohol and alcohol problems; abstracts and bibliography of current literature, book reviews and author and subject indexes.
Articles per average issue: 15-20
Audience: Scholars, researchers
  Manuscripts accepted in English

MANUSCRIPT INFORMATION
Subject field(s): Biochemistry, physiology, experimental psychology, clinical psychology, psychiatry, medicine, sociology, epidemiology, anthropology, economics, law, history

Manuscript requirements: Style sheet sent on request.
   Preferred length: 1,000 to 9,000 words; 4 to 35 pages
   Number of copies to be submitted: Two
   Abstract: Yes
Author information and reprints: Payment: None.
   Is simultaneous submission of article to other journals permitted: No
   Exclusive manuscript rights between acceptance and publication: Yes
   Copyright: Held by publication.
   Reprints: Available, 25 free; additional at cost.
Additional information: Everything typewritten, double-spaced; tables on separate sheets; figures and illustrations in the form of camera-ready glossy prints; references numbered consecutively at end.
Disposition of manuscript:
   Query letter: No
   Receipt of manuscript acknowledged: Yes
   Decision to publish in: 2 months
   Accepted manuscript published in: 12-18 months
   Rejected manuscript returned: Yes
   Rejected manuscript criticized: Yes
Submit to:
   Timothy G. Coffey
   Managing Editor
   (See address above)

KEYNOTE [1518]
The Quarterly Magazine of Boys' Clubs of America
771 First Avenue
New York, New York 10017
(212) 684-4400 ext. 51

First published in 1966

SUBSCRIPTION DATA
Issues and rates: Published quarterly.
   Average paid circulation: 1,000; 6,000 controlled
   Annual rate(s): $6.00
Publisher or Sponsor: Boys' Clubs of America

EDITORIAL DESCRIPTION
Contains information related to current trends and social conditions of interest to those actively engaged in work with today's youth, especially disadvantaged boys. Written for the adult professionals who operate the nation's more than 1,100 Boys' Clubs.
Articles per average issue: 10
Audience: professional youth workers
   Manuscripts accepted in English

MANUSCRIPT INFORMATION
Subject field(s): Program ideas, child development, funding, promotion techniques, physical activities, health and nutrition
Manuscript requirements: See latest issue for style requirements.
   Preferred length: 2,000 words; 8 pages
   Number of copies to be submitted: One
   Abstract: No

Author information and reprints: Payment: Reprints only. Complimentary copies of issue in which material appears.
   Is simultaneous submission of article to other journals permitted: No
   Exclusive manuscript rights between acceptance and publication: Yes
   Copyright: Held by publication.
   Reprints: Available, cost on request
Additional information: Generally information submitted is specifically geared to Boys' Club work. Those outside the field should check with editor first on relevance of material.
Disposition of manuscript:
   Query letter: Yes
   Receipt of manuscript acknowledged: Yes
   Decision to publish in: 3-6 months
   Accepted manuscript published in: 3-6 months
   Rejected manuscript returned: No
   Rejected manuscript criticized: Yes
Submit to:
   John W. Owen
   Editor
   (See address above)

LABOR-MANAGEMENT ALCOHOLISM JOURNAL [1519]
National Council on Alcoholism, Inc.
2 Park Avenue
New York, New York 10016
(212) 889-3160

Previously entitled *Labor-Management Alcoholism Newsletter*

First published in 1971

SUBSCRIPTION DATA
Issues and rates: Published bi-monthly.
   Annual rate(s): $18.00
Publisher or Sponsor: National Council on Alcoholism, Inc., Labor-Management Division
Managing Editor: William S. Dunkin

EDITORIAL DESCRIPTION
The only publication which focuses exclusively and authoritatively on the broad problem of dealing effectively with alcoholism of the employee including news stories and features
Articles per average issue: 12-15
Audience: Labor and management interested in the problem of alcoholism and allied fields
   Manuscripts accepted in English

MANUSCRIPT INFORMATION
Subject field(s): Current employee alcoholism programs; reports on alcoholism arbitration cases; statistical results; cost-benefit analyses; recovery and prevalence rates; new techniques in the field including identification and motivational techniques; effective treatment methods, innovative insurance coverages; legislation, legal hazards, disability, early retirement, etc.
Manuscript requirements: See latest issue for style requirements.
   Preferred length: No preference
   Abstract: Not necessary.

Author information and reprints: Payment: None.
   Is simultaneous submission of article to other journals permitted: Not permitted.
   Exclusive manuscript rights between acceptance and publication: Yes
   Copyright: Held by publication. Held by the National Council on Alcoholism, Inc.
Disposition of manuscript:
   Query letter: Necessary.
Submit to:
   William S. Dunkin
   Editor
   (See address above)

SPECIAL STIPULATIONS
   Highly specialized reporting required

MENTAL RETARDATION/DÉFICIENCE MENTALE [1520]
Kinsemn NIMR Building
York University Campus
Toronto, Ontario M3J 1P3, Canada
(416) 661-9611 ext. 39

Previously entitled *The Bulletin*

First published in 1958

SUBSCRIPTION DATA
Issues and rates: Published quarterly.
   Average paid circulation: 14,000
   Annual rate(s): $2.00, Foreign $2.00
Publisher or Sponsor: Canadian Association for the Mentally Retarded

EDITORIAL DESCRIPTION
Contains informative articles on subject featured for the particular issue. Encourages associations and workers in field of mental retardation to report and therefore see the comprehensive nature of services for the mentally retarded.
Articles per average issue: 5
Audience: Professionals
   Manuscripts accepted in English, French

MANUSCRIPT INFORMATION
Subject field(s): Mental retardation, developmental handicap, multi-handicap, human rights, how to operate successful programs in these fields.
Manuscript requirements: See latest issue for style requirements.
   Preferred length: 2000 words; 4 pages maximum
   Number of copies to be submitted: Two
   Abstract: No
Author information and reprints: Payment: None.
   Is simultaneous submission of article to other journals permitted: Yes
   Exclusive manuscript rights between acceptance and publication: Yes
   Copyright: Held by author.
   Reprints: Available, about 300 for $20.
Additional information: Correspond with editor for topics featured in particular issues. Manuscripts are to be typewritten, double-spaced.
Disposition of manuscript:
   Query letter: No

Social welfare

Receipt of manuscript acknowledged: Yes
Decision to publish in: 1 week to 3 months
Accepted manuscript published in: 3-12 months
Rejected manuscript returned: Yes, if return postage is supplied by author.
Rejected manuscript criticized: Only on request
Submit to:
  Betty Anglin
  Editor
  (See address above)

MSHA [1521]
Journal of the Michigan Speech and Hearing Association
724 Abbott Road
East Lansing, Michigan 48823
(517) 337-1646

First published in 1965

SUBSCRIPTION DATA
Issues and rates: Published semi-annually.
  Average paid circulation: 1,400
  Annual rate(s): $3.00
Publisher or Sponsor: Michigan Speech and Hearing Association
Managing Editor: Ralph Rupp

EDITORIAL DESCRIPTION
Publishes research, case studies, innovative rehabilitational approaches related to human communication and disordered human communication, in the areas of speech pathology, audiology and education of the hearing impaired
Articles per average issue: 6-10
Audience: Professionals in communications pathology
  Manuscripts accepted in English only

MANUSCRIPT INFORMATION
Subject field(s): Speech pathology, audiology, education of the hearing impaired.
Manuscript requirements: Style sheet sent on request.
  Preferred length: 10-12 pages
  Number of copies to be submitted: Two
  Abstract: Yes
Author information and reprints: Payment: None.
  Is simultaneous submission of article to other journals permitted: No
  Exclusive manuscript rights between acceptance and publication: No
  Copyright: Not copyrighted
  Reprints: Not available.
Additional information: In case of excessive manuscript flow, some preference is given to Association members.
Disposition of manuscript:
  Query letter: No
  Receipt of manuscript acknowledged: Yes
  Decision to publish in: 8 weeks
  Accepted manuscript published in: 6-8 months
  Rejected manuscript returned: Yes
  Rejected manuscript criticized: Yes
Submit to:
  Ralph R. Rupp

Editor
Speech Clinic of the Medical School
University of Michigan
1111 East Catherine
Ann Arbor, Michigan 48104
(313) 764-8446

THE NEW OUTLOOK FOR THE BLIND [1522]
15 West 16th Street
New York, New York 10011
(212) 924-0420 Ext. 826

Previously entitled *Outlook for the Blind*

First published in 1907

SUBSCRIPTION DATA
Issues and rates: Published monthly.
  Average paid circulation: 3,200
  Annual rate(s): $6.00, Foreign $7.50
Publisher or Sponsor: American Foundation for the Blind, Inc.

EDITORIAL DESCRIPTION
Contains articles and features on all aspects of services to blind and visually handicapped persons of all ages; manuscripts accepted from any relevant subject field. A journal for professionals in service to blind and visually handicapped persons and an impartial forum for all views.
Articles per average issue: 5
Audience: Professionals
  Manuscripts accepted in English

MANUSCRIPT INFORMATION
Subject field(s): Education, rehabilitation, psychology, social work, gerontology, counseling, recreation
Manuscript requirements: Style sheet sent on request.
  Preferred length: 2,500-4,000 words; 10-14 pages
  Number of copies to be submitted: Two
  Abstract: Yes
Author information and reprints: Payment: None.
  Is simultaneous submission of article to other journals permitted: No
  Exclusive manuscript rights between acceptance and publication: Yes
  Copyright: Held by publication.
  Reprints: Available, 50 free to author
Additional information: Shorter manuscripts (350-1,000 words) may be considered for the "Comment" section.
Disposition of manuscript:
  Query letter: No
  Receipt of manuscript acknowledged: Yes
  Decision to publish in: 4 to 6 weeks
  Accepted manuscript published in: 4 to 6 months
  Rejected manuscript returned: Yes
  Rejected manuscript criticized: No
Submit to:
  Patricia Scherf Smith
  Managing Editor
  (See address above)

SPECIAL STIPULATIONS
Also available in a braille edition and a recorded edition.

PUBLIC WELFARE [1523]
The Journal of the American Public Welfare Association
1155 16th Street, N.W.
Washington, D.C. 20036
(202) 833-9250

First published in 1943

SUBSCRIPTION DATA
Issues and rates: Published quarterly.
  Average paid circulation: 9,828; 1,200 controlled
  Annual rate(s): $8.00, Foreign $9.00
Publisher or Sponsor: The American Public Welfare Association

EDITORIAL DESCRIPTION
Contains comment, opinion and book reviews dealing with social work practice, public welfare administration, SSI, social welfare programming, poverty, mental health, legal services to poor people, family planning, child welfare, health care, prison reform, civil rights, housing for the poor; includes examinations of priorities at the national level and political implications. Generally supportive of expansion of social welfare programs to meet the needs of people in a rapidly changing technological society.
Articles per average issue: 8-10
Audience: Academic, government, professionals in field
  Manuscripts accepted in English

MANUSCRIPT INFORMATION
Manuscript requirements: Chicago
  Preferred length: 25 pages maximum
  Number of copies to be submitted: Two
  Abstract: Not necessary
Author information and reprints: Payment: None.
  Is simultaneous submission of article to other journals permitted: No
  Exclusive manuscript rights between acceptance and publication: Yes
  Copyright: Held by publication.
  Reprints: Available at cost of printing
Additional information: Typewritten, double-spaced
Disposition of manuscript:
  Query letter: No
  Receipt of manuscript acknowledged: Yes
  Decision to publish in: 1-3 months
  Accepted manuscript published in: 1-3 months
  Rejected manuscript returned: Yes
  Rejected manuscript criticized: Yes
Submit to:
  Perry
  Frank
  Editor
  (See address above)

THE REHABILITATION TEACHER [1524]

National Braille Press
88 St. Stephen Street
Boston, Massachusetts 02115
(617) 266-6160

Previously entitled *Home Teacher*

First published in 1937

SUBSCRIPTION DATA

Issues and rates: Published monthly.
   Average paid circulation: 250 Inkprint; 450 Braille
   Annual rate(s): Inkprint $5.00; Braille $2.00; Foreign Free Braille

EDITORIAL DESCRIPTION

A professional journal for rehabilitation teachers and workers with the adult blind
Articles per average issue: 4
Audience: Rehabilitation teachers
   Manuscripts accepted in English, French

MANUSCRIPT INFORMATION

Subject field(s): Techniques of daily living for visually handicapped; social work; counseling; technical skills, crafts; sensory aids
Manuscript requirements: No specific style guide.
   Preferred length: 2,500-4,000 words
   Number of copies to be submitted: 2
   Abstract: Not necessary.
Author information and reprints: Payment: None.
   Is simultaneous submission of article to other journals permitted: Permitted.
   Exclusive manuscript rights between acceptance and publication: No
   Copyright: No arrangement
   Reprints: Available at no cost. 2 Braill; 2 Inkprint
Disposition of manuscript:
   Query letter: Not necessary.
   Receipt of manuscript acknowledged: Yes
   Decision to publish in: 2 weeks
   Accepted manuscript published in: 1 month
   Rejected manuscript returned: Yes, if return postage is supplied by author.
   Rejected manuscript criticized: Sometimes
Submit to:
   Margaret K. Bisbee
   Editor
   (See address above)

SMITH COLLEGE STUDIES IN SOCIAL WORK [1525]

Smith College School for Social Work
Northampton, Massachusetts 01060
(413) 584-2700 ext. 298

First published in 1930

SUBSCRIPTION DATA

Issues and rates: Published three times per year.
   Average paid circulation: 2000
   Annual rate(s): $4.50

Publisher or Sponsor: Smith College School for Social Work
Managing Editor: Kenneth H. McCartney

EDITORIAL DESCRIPTION

Publishes empirical and theoretical work designed to clarify the connections between ego psychological perspectives on behavior and aspects of clinical practice.
Articles per average issue: 4
Audience: Clinical social workers
   Manuscripts accepted in English

MANUSCRIPT INFORMATION

Subject field(s): Clinical social work, ego psychology, social work education, clinical research
Manuscript requirements: See latest issue for style requirements.
   Preferred length: 10-30 pages
   Number of copies to be submitted: Two
   Abstract: Yes
Author information and reprints: Payment: None.
   Is simultaneous submission of article to other journals permitted: No
   Exclusive manuscript rights between acceptance and publication: Yes
   Copyright: Held by publication.
   Reprints: Available at printing cost
Additional information: Typewritten, double-spaced; in-text citations; reference list at end.
Disposition of manuscript:
   Query letter: No
   Receipt of manuscript acknowledged: Yes
   Decision to publish in: Six weeks
   Accepted manuscript published in: Three months
   Rejected manuscript returned: Yes
   Rejected manuscript criticized: No
Submit to:
   Roger R. Miller
   Editor
   (See address above)

THE SOCIAL AND REHABILITATION RECORD [1526]

Room 5334, 330 C Street, S.W.
Washington, D.C. 20201
(202) 962-0310

Previously entitled *Rehabilitation Record*

First published in 1960

SUBSCRIPTION DATA

Issues and rates: 10 times per year
   Average paid circulation: 6,000; 4,000 controlled
   Annual rate(s): $5.50, Foreign $7.00
Publisher or Sponsor: Social and Rehabilitation Service, Department of HEW

EDITORIAL DESCRIPTION

Contains articles on all aspects of vocational rehabilitation; program, theory, practice, philosophy of rehabilitation and all physical or mental handicapping conditions.
Articles per average issue: 5
Audience: Professionals in the field
   Manuscripts accepted in English only

MANUSCRIPT INFORMATION

Subject field(s): Homebound, mental retardation, mental illness, blindess, deafness, cerebral palsy, epilepsy, correctional rehabilitation, public assistance, Medicaid, HMO, PSRO, management, all handicapping conditions
Manuscript requirements: GPO
   Preferred length: 8 pages
   Number of copies to be submitted: One original
   Abstract: No
Author information and reprints: Payment: None.
   Is simultaneous submission of article to other journals permitted: No
   Exclusive manuscript rights between acceptance and publication: Yes
   Copyright: Not copyrighted
   Reprints: Available for limited articles.
Additional information: Typewritten, double-spaced; figures and tables welcomed.
Disposition of manuscript:
   Query letter: No
   Receipt of manuscript acknowledged: Yes
   Decision to publish in: 4-6 weeks
   Accepted manuscript published in: 6 months
   Rejected manuscript returned: Yes
   Rejected manuscript criticized: No
Submit to:
   Ron Bourgea
   Editor
   (See address above)

SOCIAL SERVICE REVIEW [1527]

969 East 60th Street
Chicago, Illinois 60637
(312) 753-4628

First published in 1927

SUBSCRIPTION DATA

Issues and rates: Published quarterly.
   Average paid circulation: 6,310; 9,867 controlled
   Annual rate(s): Institutions $12.00; Individuals $10.00
Publisher or Sponsor: University of Chicago, School of Social Service Administration

EDITORIAL DESCRIPTION

Publishes research and analytical articles on social work and social welfare and related social sciences.
Articles per average issue: 8
Audience: Professionals
   Manuscripts accepted in English

MANUSCRIPT INFORMATION

Subject field(s): Social welfare and related social sciences
Manuscript requirements: Style sheet sent on request.
   Preferred length: As required
   Number of copies to be submitted: Two
   Abstract: Yes

Social welfare

Author information and reprints: Payment: None.
Is simultaneous submission of article to other journals permitted: No
Exclusive manuscript rights between acceptance and publication: Yes
Copyright: Held by publication.
Reprints: Available; cost dependent on length
Disposition of manuscript:
Query letter: No
Receipt of manuscript acknowledged: Yes
Decision to publish in: 4-8 weeks
Accepted manuscript published in: 4-6 months
Rejected manuscript returned: Yes
Rejected manuscript criticized: No
Submit to:
Frank R. Breul
Editor
(See address above)

TENNESSEE PUBLIC WELFARE RECORD [1528]

Department of Public Welfare
410 State Office Building
Nashville, Tennessee 37219
(615) 741-3692

First published in 1938

SUBSCRIPTION DATA

Issues and rates: Published quarterly.
Average paid circulation: 8,000 controlled
Publisher or Sponsor: Tennessee Department of Public Welfare
Managing Editor: Malinda Jones

EDITORIAL DESCRIPTION

Contains articles on social services, public assistance, rehabilitation, day care, child development, program for children and the aging, case stories.
Articles per average issue: 8-10
Audience: Legislators, social agencies, citizens, librarians
Manuscripts accepted in English

MANUSCRIPT INFORMATION

Subject field(s): Social services, public assistance, rehabilitation, day care, child development, program for children and the aging, case stories
Manuscript requirements: See latest issue for style requirements.
Preferred length: 5 to 10 pages
Number of copies to be submitted: Two
Abstract: No
Author information and reprints: Payment: None.
Is simultaneous submission of article to other journals permitted: Yes
Exclusive manuscript rights between acceptance and publication: No
Copyright: Not copyrighted
Reprints: Not available.
Additional information: Everything typewritten, double-spaced.
Disposition of manuscript:
Query letter: No
Receipt of manuscript acknowledged: Yes
Decision to publish in: 2 weeks
Accepted manuscript published in: 2 to 4 months
Rejected manuscript returned: Yes
Rejected manuscript criticized: No
Submit to:
Malinda Jones
Director of Information and Publications
(See address above)

TOXICOMANIES [1529]

969, route de l'Eglise
Québec G1V 3V4, Canada
(418) 653-8771 ext. 63

First published in 1968

SUBSCRIPTION DATA

Issues and rates: Published quarterly.
Average paid circulation: 2,000 controlled
Annual rate(s): Foreign $10.00
Publisher or Sponsor: Office de la Prévention l'Alcoolisme et des Autres Toxicomanies

EDITORIAL DESCRIPTION

Publishes articles from all fields of knowledge that contribute to the understanding of the problems of alcohol and other drugs.
Articles per average issue: 5
Audience: Researchers, professionals on the field
Manuscripts accepted in English, French, Spanish

MANUSCRIPT INFORMATION

Subject field(s): Toxicomanias (alcoholism, drugs)
Manuscript requirements: No specific style guide.
Preferred length: 6,250 words; 25 pages
Number of copies to be submitted: 1
Abstract: Yes, in English and in French
Author information and reprints: Payment: None.
Is simultaneous submission of article to other journals permitted: Yes
Exclusive manuscript rights between acceptance and publication: No
Copyright: Held by author.
Reprints: Available, 25 free
Additional information: Manuscripts should be typewritten and double spaced, with references collated on the final page in alphabetical order of the author's name. Tables should be numbered in Roman figures and should be accompanied by a short and concise legend.
Disposition of manuscript:
Query letter: No
Receipt of manuscript acknowledged: Yes
Decision to publish in: 1 to 2 months
Accepted manuscript published in: 5 months
Rejected manuscript returned: No
Rejected manuscript criticized: Yes
Submit to:
Rénald Chabot
Responsable des publications de l'Optat
(See address above)

Sociology and anthropology

Sociology and anthropology

AMERICAN ANTHROPOLOGIST [1530]
1703 New Hampshire Avenue, N.W.
Washington, D.C. 20009
(202) 232-8800

SUBSCRIPTION DATA
Issues and rates: Published quarterly.
  Average paid circulation: 6,000
  Annual rate(s): $25.00
Publisher or Sponsor: American Anthropological Association

EDITORIAL DESCRIPTION
  Publishes scholarly articles of general interest to professional anthropologists from all disciplines of anthropology. Contains comprehensive review coverage of new publications of significance in the field.

MANUSCRIPT INFORMATION
Subject field(s): Any subject field in anthropology
Manuscript requirements: Style sheet sent on request.
  Preferred length: 15-25 pages, flexible
  Number of copies to be submitted: Three
Author information and reprints: Payment: None.
  Is simultaneous submission of article to other journals permitted: No
  Exclusive manuscript rights between acceptance and publication: Yes
  Copyright: Held by publication.
  Reprints: Available at cost
Disposition of manuscript:
  Receipt of manuscript acknowledged: Yes
  Decision to publish in: Few months
  Accepted manuscript published in: Up to 18 months
  Rejected manuscript returned: Yes
  Rejected manuscript criticized: Yes
Submit to:
  Editor

AMERICAN ETHNOLOGIST [1531]
American Anthropological Association
1703 New Hampshire Avenue, N.W.
Washington, D.C. 20009

First published in 1974

SUBSCRIPTION DATA
Issues and rates: Published quarterly.
  Average paid circulation: 3,000
  Annual rate(s): $20.00
Publisher or Sponsor: American Anthropological Association
Managing Editor: Elsa L. Vorwerk

EDITORIAL DESCRIPTION
  Contains research papers and articles on ethnology.
Articles per average issue: 11
Audience: Cultural anthropologists
  Manuscripts accepted in English

MANUSCRIPT INFORMATION
Subject field(s): Ethnology
Manuscript requirements: Style sheet sent on request.
  Preferred length: 30 pages
  Number of copies to be submitted: Three
  Abstract: Yes, with a list of key words.
Author information and reprints: Payment: None.
  Is simultaneous submission of article to other journals permitted: No
  Exclusive manuscript rights between acceptance and publication: Yes
  Copyright: Held by publication.
  Reprints: Available at cost
Disposition of manuscript:
  Query letter: No
  Receipt of manuscript acknowledged: Yes
  Decision to publish in: 6-8 weeks
  Accepted manuscript published in: 5 months
  Rejected manuscript returned: Yes
  Rejected manuscript criticized: Yes
Submit to:
  Victoria Bricker
  Editor
  Department of Anthropology
  Tulane University
  New Orleans, Louisiana 70118
  (504) 865-4306

AMERICAN JOURNAL OF SOCIOLOGY [1532]
1130 East 59th Street
Chicago, Illinois 60637
(301) 753-4377

First published in 1895

SUBSCRIPTION DATA
Issues and rates: Published bi-monthly.
  Average paid circulation: 9200
  Annual rate(s): $12.00, Foreign $13.00, Students $8.00, Institutions $16.00

EDITORIAL DESCRIPTION
  Contains research and theory in the field of sociology primarily, with some work in political science and anthropology.
Articles per average issue: 7-8
Audience: General sociological audience
  Manuscripts accepted in English only

MANUSCRIPT INFORMATION
Manuscript requirements: See latest issue for style requirements.
  Preferred length: 40 pages
  Number of copies to be submitted: 3
  Abstract: Yes
Author information and reprints: Payment: None.
  Is simultaneous submission of article to other journals permitted: No
  Exclusive manuscript rights between acceptance and publication: No
  Copyright: Held by publication.
  Reprints: Available
Disposition of manuscript:
  Query letter: No
  Receipt of manuscript acknowledged: Yes
  Decision to publish in: 6 months
  Accepted manuscript published in: 1 year
  Rejected manuscript returned: Yes
  Rejected manuscript criticized: Yes
Submit to:
  Charles E. Bidwell
  Editor
  (See address above)

AMERICAN SOCIOLOGICAL REVIEW [1533]
1722 N Street, N.W.
Washington, D.C. 20036
(202) 833-3410

First published in 1935

SUBSCRIPTION DATA
Issues and rates: Published bi-monthly.
  Average paid circulation: 18,000
  Annual rate(s): $15.00, Institutions $30.00
Publisher or Sponsor: American Sociological Association
Managing Editor: Otto N. Larsen

EDITORIAL DESCRIPTION
  Reflects the basic research interests of professional sociologists. Reports innovations and developments across the field drawing on historical perspectives, theoretical analyses, and rigorous empirical research in seeking explanations for social phenomena.
  Manuscripts accepted in English

MANUSCRIPT INFORMATION
Manuscript requirements: Style sheet sent on request.
  Number of copies to be submitted: 3
  Abstract: Yes
Author information and reprints: Payment: None.
  Is simultaneous submission of article to other journals permitted: No
  Exclusive manuscript rights between acceptance and publication: Yes
  Copyright: Held by publication.
  Reprints: Not available.
Disposition of manuscript:
  Query letter: No
  Receipt of manuscript acknowledged: Yes
  Decision to publish in: Varies
  Accepted manuscript published in: 6-12 months
  Rejected manuscript returned: Yes, if self-addressed, stamped envelope is sent with manuscript.
Submit to:
  Morris Zelditch, Jr.
  Editor
  Department of Sociology

Stanford University
Stanford, California 94305
(415) 497-0141

THE AMERICAN SOCIOLOGIST [1534]
1722 N Street, N.W.
Washington, D.C. 20036
(202) 833-3410

SUBSCRIPTION DATA

Issues and rates: Published quarterly.
  Average paid circulation: 18,000
  Annual rate(s): $10.00; Institutions $15.00
Publisher or Sponsor: American Sociological Association
Managing Editor: Otto N. Larsen

EDITORIAL DESCRIPTION

Contains research reports and scholarly commentary on developments and new directions in the discipline and probes problems confronting sociology as a profession. Provides current assessments of teaching innovations, research challenges, and the relationship of sociology to social policy.
Manuscripts accepted in English

MANUSCRIPT INFORMATION

Manuscript requirements: Style sheet sent on request.
  Number of copies to be submitted: Three
  Abstract: No
Author information and reprints: Payment: None.
  Is simultaneous submission of article to other journals permitted: No
  Exclusive manuscript rights between acceptance and publication: Yes
  Copyright: Held by publication.
  Reprints: Not available.
Disposition of manuscript:
  Query letter: No
  Receipt of manuscript acknowledged: Yes
  Decision to publish in: Varies
  Accepted manuscript published in: 3-6 months
  Rejected manuscript returned: Yes, if self-addressed, stamped envelope is sent with manuscript.
  Rejected manuscript criticized: No
Submit to:
  Leon Mayhew
  Editor
  Department of Sociology
  University of California
  Davis, California 95616
  (916) 752-0782

ANTHROPOLOGICAL JOURNAL OF CANADA [1535]
1575 Forlan Drive
Ottawa, Ontario K2C 0R8, Canada
(613) 225-3405

First published in 1963

SUBSCRIPTION DATA

Issues and rates: Published quarterly.
  Average paid circulation: Not available.
  Annual rate(s): $6.00 (and U.S.), Foreign $7.00
Publisher or Sponsor: Anthropological Association of Canada

EDITORIAL DESCRIPTION

Contains anthropological articles with emphasis on archaeology; any aspect of anthropology, any part of the world, with related problems of history, geology, geography, or other.
Articles per average issue: 4-8
Audience: Academic, professional
Manuscripts accepted in English, French

MANUSCRIPT INFORMATION

Subject field(s): Anthropology, archaeology, history, geology, geography
Manuscript requirements: No specific style guide.
  Preferred length: 600-3000 words; 2 to 20 pages
  Number of copies to be submitted: One
Author information and reprints: Payment: None.
  Is simultaneous submission of article to other journals permitted: No
  Exclusive manuscript rights between acceptance and publication: Yes
  Copyright: Held by author.
  Reprints: Available at cost
Additional information: Avoid technical jargon. Double spacing, original manuscript, illustrations or line drawings.
Disposition of manuscript:
  Query letter: No
  Receipt of manuscript acknowledged: Yes
  Decision to publish in: 2 weeks
  Accepted manuscript published in: 3-6 months
  Rejected manuscript returned: Yes
  Rejected manuscript criticized: Sometimes
Submit to:
  Thomas E. Lee
  Editor
  (See address above)

ANTHROPOLOGICAL QUARTERLY [1536]
Catholic University Press
Catholic University
Washington, D. C. 20017
(202) 635-5052

Previously entitled *Primitive Man*

First published in 1929

SUBSCRIPTION DATA

Issues and rates: Published quarterly.
  Average paid circulation: 1,000; 100 controlled
  Annual rate(s): $8.00; Foreign $8.00; Individuals $8.00; Institutions $10.00; Students $5.50;
Managing Editor: Dr. Michael Kenny

EDITORIAL DESCRIPTION

Seeks to reflect the mainstreams of anthropological thought. A world-wide scope with emphasis on Circum-Mediterranean and Latin America areas is focused on socio-cultural anthropology. It's goal is the rapid dissemination of durable, scholarly materials which blend scientific precision with humanism and scrupulous analysis with meticulous description.
Articles per average issue: 5
Audience: Social and cultural anthropologists, sociologists, area specialists
Manuscripts accepted in English

MANUSCRIPT INFORMATION

Subject field(s): Social and cultural anthropology
Manuscript requirements: See latest issue for style requirements. AAA
  Preferred length: 4,000-8,000 words
  Number of copies to be submitted: 2
  Abstract: Yes. Abstract of 150 words or less
Author information and reprints: Payment: None.
  Is simultaneous submission of article to other journals permitted: Not permitted.
  Exclusive manuscript rights between acceptance and publication: Yes
  Copyright: Held by Catholic University of America Press
  Reprints: Available at cost.
Additional information: Articles based on recent fieldwork are preferred.
Disposition of manuscript:
  Query letter: Not necessary.
  Receipt of manuscript acknowledged: Yes
  Decision to publish in: 2-5 months
  Accepted manuscript published in: 6 months
  Rejected manuscript returned: Yes, if return postage is supplied by author.
  Rejected manuscript criticized: Sometimes
Submit to:
  Dr. Michael Kenny
  Editor
  MacMahon Building
  Catholic University
  Washington, D. C. 20017
  (202) 635-5080

ARCTIC ANTHROPOLOGY [1537]
University of Wisconsin Press
Box 1379
Madison, Wisconsin 53701
(608) 262-1116

First published in 1962

SUBSCRIPTION DATA

Issues and rates: Published semi-annually.
  Average paid circulation: 625; 10 controlled
  Annual rate(s): Individuals $15.00, Institutions $25.00

EDITORIAL DESCRIPTION

Publishes papers and longer studies in all fields of anthropology and prehistory of the arctic, sub-arctic and contiguous regions of the world.
Articles per average issue: 1-6
Audience: Professional

Sociology and anthropology

Manuscripts accepted in English

MANUSCRIPT INFORMATION

Subject field(s): Prehistory, archaeology, ethnography, acculturation, applied anthropology, physical anthropology, human biology
Manuscript requirements: AA, Style sheet sent on request.
  Preferred length: None
  Number of copies to be submitted: 2
  Abstract: Yes
Author information and reprints: Payment: None. Partial subsidy may be required for monograph-length works.
  Is simultaneous submission of article to other journals permitted: No
  Exclusive manuscript rights between acceptance and publication: Yes
  Copyright: Held by publication.
  Reprints: Available
Disposition of manuscript:
  Receipt of manuscript acknowledged: Yes
  Decision to publish in: 1-2 months
  Accepted manuscript published in: One year
  Rejected manuscript returned: Yes
  Rejected manuscript criticized: Yes
Submit to:
  Catherine McClellan
  Editor
  5454 Social Science Building
  University of Wisconsin
  Madison, Wisconsin 53706
  (608) 262-7395

THE CANADIAN REVIEW OF SOCIOLOGY AND ANTHROPOLOGY [1538]

Revue Canadienne de Sociologie et d'Anthropologie
P.O. Box 878
Quebec, Canada
(514) 343-7314

First published in 1964

SUBSCRIPTION DATA

Issues and rates: Published quarterly.
  Average paid circulation: 1600; 100 controlled
  Annual rate(s): $32.00, Institutions $37.00
Publisher or Sponsor: Canadian Sociology and Anthropology Association
Managing Editor: John Jackson

EDITORIAL DESCRIPTION

Contains articles concerning theory and research in all areas of sociology and cultural and social anthropology. Review articles and book reviews are also published. Particularly concerned with the presentation of materials about Canadian society although the policy does not exclude articles on other cultures and societies.
Articles per average issue: 6
  Manuscripts accepted in English, French

MANUSCRIPT INFORMATION

Subject field(s): Sociology, cultural anthropology, social anthropology

Manuscript requirements: See latest issue for style requirements.
  Preferred length: 20-25 pages
  Number of copies to be submitted: Two
  Abstract: Yes
Author information and reprints: Payment: None.
  Is simultaneous submission of article to other journals permitted: No
  Exclusive manuscript rights between acceptance and publication: Yes
  Copyright: Held by publication.
  Reprints: Available, 25 free
Additional information: Everything typewritten, double-spaced. Reprint royalties are shared 50-50 with author.
Disposition of manuscript:
  Query letter: No
  Receipt of manuscript acknowledged: Yes
  Decision to publish in: 3-4 months
  Accepted manuscript published in: Varies
  Rejected manuscript returned: Yes
  Rejected manuscript criticized: Yes
Submit to:
  Raymond Breton
  Editor
  Department of Sociology
  University of Toronto
  Toronto, Ontario M5S A1, Canada
  (416) 522-4971 ext. 481

CRIME AND DELINQUENCY [1539]

Continental Plaza
411 Hackensack Avenue
Hackensack, New Jersey 07601
(201) 488-0400

Previously entitled *NPPA Journal*

First published in 1955

SUBSCRIPTION DATA

Issues and rates: Published quarterly.
  Average paid circulation: 10,600
  Annual rate(s): $15.00
Publisher or Sponsor: National Council on Crime and Delinquency
Managing Editor: Matthew Matlin

EDITORIAL DESCRIPTION

Contains articles on all aspects of the criminal justice system.
Articles per average issue: 8
Audience: Professionals
  Manuscripts accepted in English

MANUSCRIPT INFORMATION

Subject field(s): Criminal justice, law enforcement, juvenile and criminal courts, correctional institutions, correctional programs, sentencing, decisions, statutes, probation and parole
Manuscript requirements: Style sheet sent on request.
  Preferred length: 12-30 pages
  Number of copies to be submitted: Two
  Abstract: Yes

Author information and reprints: Payment: None.
  Is simultaneous submission of article to other journals permitted: No
  Exclusive manuscript rights between acceptance and publication: Yes
  Copyright: Held by publication.
  Reprints: Available at cost
Disposition of manuscript:
  Query letter: No
  Receipt of manuscript acknowledged: Yes
  Decision to publish in: 2 weeks to 3 months
  Accepted manuscript published in: 3-24 months
  Rejected manuscript returned: Yes
  Rejected manuscript criticized: Sometimes
Submit to:
  Matthew Matlin
  Editor
  (See address above)

CURRENT ANTHROPOLOGY [1540]

A World Journal of the Sciences of Man
University of Chicago
1126 East 59th Street
Chicago, Illinois 60637
(312) 753-3718

First published in 1960

SUBSCRIPTION DATA

Issues and rates: Published quarterly.
  Average paid circulation: 5246; 8109 controlled
  Annual rate(s): $21.00, Members $7.00
Publisher or Sponsor: Wenner-Gren Foundation for Anthropological Research

EDITORIAL DESCRIPTION

An international journal of general anthropology which is a published record of a unique experiment in communication within a world-wide community of individual scholars known as "Associates". At present there are more than 3,000 Associates, representing all the various disciplines of the sciences of man. They correspond directly with the editor and each other.
Articles per average issue: 4-5
  Manuscripts accepted in English

MANUSCRIPT INFORMATION

Manuscript requirements: Chicago
  Number of copies to be submitted: One
  Abstract: Yes
Author information and reprints: Payment: None.
  Is simultaneous submission of article to other journals permitted: No
  Exclusive manuscript rights between acceptance and publication: Yes
  Copyright: Held by the Foundation
  Reprints: Available, quotes on request
Additional information: The suitability of an article for publication is determined by a process of multiple refereeing.
Disposition of manuscript:
  Query letter: No
  Receipt of manuscript acknowledged: Yes

Decision to publish in: 6 weeks
Accepted manuscript published in: 9 months
Rejected manuscript returned: Yes
Rejected manuscript criticized: Yes

Submit to:
Cyril S. Belshaw
Editor
Department of Anthropology and Sociology
University of British Columbia
Vancouver, British Columbia V6T 1W5, Canada

CURRENT SOCIOLOGY/LA SOCIOLOGIE CONTEMPORAINE [1541]

Journal of the International Sociological Association
Mouton & Company
P. O. Box 482
The Hague, The Netherlands

First published in 1952

SUBSCRIPTION DATA

Issues and rates: Published three times per year.
Annual rate(s): Foreign £6.20 Individuals £6.20; Institutions £8.30; Students £6.20

Publisher or Sponsor: The International Sociological Association

EDITORIAL DESCRIPTION

Provides an overview of a specialized area in sociology, a concept, method, issue or theory; the aim is to provide a general outline of the topic together with the author's assessment of its most important aspects.

Articles per average issue: 1

Audience: Professional sociologists throughout the world
Manuscripts accepted in English, French

MANUSCRIPT INFORMATION

Subject field(s): Any specialist field of sociology, e.g. sociology of religion; theoretical perspective, e.g. structuralism; theoretical concept, e.g. nationalism; sociological method, e.g. mathematical sociology, etc.

Manuscript requirements: See latest issue for style requirements.
Preferred length: 40,000 words and annotated bibliography
Number of copies to be submitted: 2
Abstract: Not necessary.

Author information and reprints: Payment: By publication to author. $500.00 per trend report
Is simultaneous submission of article to other journals permitted: Not permitted.
Exclusive manuscript rights between acceptance and publication: Yes
Copyright: Held by publication.
Reprints: Available at cost.

Additional information: Publishes only extended trend reports which provide an overview of the topic and an annotated bibliography on the literature, not articles as such.

Disposition of manuscript:
Query letter: Not necessary, but advisable.
Receipt of manuscript acknowledged: Yes
Decision to publish in: 1 month
Accepted manuscript published in: 6 months
Rejected manuscript returned: Yes, with return postage paid by publication.
Rejected manuscript criticized: Reasons for rejections only

Submit to:
Dr. Margaret S. Archer
Editor
Department of Sociology
University of Warwick
Coventry, Warwickshire CV4 7AL, England
0203-24011 2499

ETHNOLOGY [1542]

An International Journal of Social and Cultural Anthropology
Department of Anthropology
University of Pittsburgh
Pittsburgh, Pennsylvania 15213
(412) 624-4092

First published in 1962

SUBSCRIPTION DATA

Issues and rates: Published quarterly.
Average paid circulation: 3,500
Annual rate(s): $10.00

Publisher or Sponsor: University of Pittsburgh

Managing Editor: E. Dolores Donohue

EDITORIAL DESCRIPTION

Contains articles on cultural and social anthropology.

MANUSCRIPT INFORMATION

Manuscript requirements: See latest issue for style requirements.
Preferred length: 2-35 pages
Number of copies to be submitted: One
Abstract: No

Author information and reprints: Payment: None.
Is simultaneous submission of article to other journals permitted: No
Exclusive manuscript rights between acceptance and publication: Yes
Copyright: None
Reprints: Available at cost.

Disposition of manuscript:
Receipt of manuscript acknowledged: Yes
Decision to publish in: 2 months
Accepted manuscript published in: 1 month
Rejected manuscript returned: Yes
Rejected manuscript criticized: Sometimes

Submit to:
Editor
(See address above)

INTERNATIONAL JOURNAL OF COMPARATIVE SOCIOLOGY [1543]

Department of Sociology and Anthropology
York University
Toronto, Ontario, Canada
(416) 667-3720

First published in 1966

SUBSCRIPTION DATA

Issues and rates: Published quarterly.
Annual rate(s): $16.00

Managing Editor: K. Ishwaran

EDITORIAL DESCRIPTION

This journal presents a detailed and scholarly account of studies made in different cultures on a comparative basis, with a view to reaching a common level of abstraction, and thereby showing areas where cultural bias might be involved. The primary aim of the publication is the furtherance of pure research in the interests of truth. Secondly, the policy is one of encouragement of those areas of research, inquiry into which is in the interest of man and society.

Articles per average issue: 24-30

Audience: Social scientists
Manuscripts accepted in English

MANUSCRIPT INFORMATION

Subject field(s): Comparative sociology, social sciences

Manuscript requirements: See latest issue for style requirements.
Preferred length: 8,500 words; 25 pages
Number of copies to be submitted: Two

Author information and reprints: Payment: None.
Is simultaneous submission of article to other journals permitted: No
Exclusive manuscript rights between acceptance and publication: Yes
Copyright: Held by publication.
Reprints: Available

Disposition of manuscript:
Query letter: No
Receipt of manuscript acknowledged: Yes
Decision to publish in: 1-2 months
Accepted manuscript published in: One year
Rejected manuscript returned: Yes, if return postage is supplied by author.
Rejected manuscript criticized: If requested

Submit to:
K. Ishwaran
General Editor
(See address above)

INTERNATIONAL JOURNAL OF CONTEMPORARY SOCIOLOGY [1544]

An International Quarterly of Contemporary Research in Sociology
Department of Sociology
Auburn University
Auburn, Alabama 36830

Previously entitled *Indian Sociological Bulletin*

First published in 1963

SUBSCRIPTION DATA
Issues and rates: Published quarterly.
  Average paid circulation: 1,698
  Annual rate(s): $12.00

EDITORIAL DESCRIPTION
  Publishes papers and research reports and findings of both quantitative and qualitative research; inter-disciplinary, encyclopedic and synthetic studies. Emphasis on theory as well as the application of the principles of sociology; publication of studies with inter-cultural and cross-cultural approach.
Articles per average issue: 6
Audience: Professionals
  Manuscripts accepted in English

MANUSCRIPT INFORMATION
Subject field(s): Sociological theory, social stratification, cross-cultural studies, social change, sociology in different countries, innovations in methodology, medical sociology, sociology of religion
Manuscript requirements: Sociological Abstracts, Style sheet sent on request.
  Preferred length: 3000 to 5000 words
  Number of copies to be submitted: Two
  Abstract: Yes
Author information and reprints: Payment: None. Two copies of the journal and 20 reprints.
  Is simultaneous submission of article to other journals permitted: No
  Exclusive manuscript rights between acceptance and publication: Yes
  Copyright: Held by publication.
  Reprints: Available, 20 free
Additional information: Manuscripts should be in the proper style, with footnotes, references, tables and charts on separate pages. Author's name and affiliation should appear only on a separate cover page so articles can be sent out anonymously for editorial evaluation.
Disposition of manuscript:
  Query letter: Yes
  Receipt of manuscript acknowledged: Yes
  Decision to publish in: 6-8 weeks
  Accepted manuscript published in: 6-9 months
  Rejected manuscript returned: Yes, if self-addressed, stamped envelope is sent with manuscript.
  Rejected manuscript criticized: Sometimes
Submit to:
  Raj P. Mohan
  Editor and Book Review Editor
  (See address above)

INTERNATIONAL JOURNAL OF SOCIOLOGY OF THE FAMILY [1545]

Department of Sociology
Northern Illinois University
DeKalb, Illinois 60115
(815) 753-0234

First published in 1971

SUBSCRIPTION DATA
Issues and rates: Published semi-annually.
  Annual rate(s): $7.00; Foreign Asia Rs 25.00; India Rs 20.00; Institutions $8.50; Students $5.50

EDITORIAL DESCRIPTION
  Devoted to the encouragement of cross-cultural, cross-national, and interdisciplinary research and exchange concerning significant developments in general sociology and sociology of the family
Articles per average issue: 15
Audience: Professional, clergy
  Manuscripts accepted in English

MANUSCRIPT INFORMATION
Manuscript requirements: Style sheet sent on request.
  Preferred length: 10-15 pages
  Number of copies to be submitted: 3
  Abstract: Yes. Of 200-250 words
Author information and reprints: Payment: None.
  Is simultaneous submission of article to other journals permitted: Not permitted.
  Exclusive manuscript rights between acceptance and publication: Yes
  Copyright: Held by publication.
  Reprints: Available at cost.
Disposition of manuscript:
  Query letter: Not necessary.
  Receipt of manuscript acknowledged: Yes
  Decision to publish in: 2 months
  Accepted manuscript published in: 1 year
  Rejected manuscript returned: Yes, with return postage paid by publication.
  Rejected manuscript criticized: Yes
Submit to:
  Man Singh Das
  Editor
  (See address above)

INTERNATIONAL MIGRATION REVIEW [1546]

209 Flagg Place
Staten Island, New York 10304
(212) 351-8800

Previously entitled *International Migration Digest*

First published in 1964

SUBSCRIPTION DATA
Issues and rates: Published quarterly.
  Average paid circulation: 2,157
  Annual rate(s): $14.50, Foreign $15.50, Institutions $19.50, Foreign institutions $20.50
Publisher or Sponsor: Center for Migration Studies of New York, Inc.

EDITORIAL DESCRIPTION
  A quarterly studying sociological, demographic, historical, and legislative aspects of human migration movements and ethnic group relations.
Articles per average issue: 6
Audience: Sociologists, economists, historians, political scientists, lawyers, psychologists
  Manuscripts accepted in English

MANUSCRIPT INFORMATION
Subject field(s): Demography, sociology, history, immigration law
Manuscript requirements: See latest issue for style requirements. Style sheet sent on request.
  Preferred length: 25 pages
  Number of copies to be submitted: Two
  Abstract: No
Author information and reprints: Payment: None.
  Is simultaneous submission of article to other journals permitted: No
  Exclusive manuscript rights between acceptance and publication: Yes
  Copyright: Held by publication.
  Reprints: Available
Disposition of manuscript:
  Query letter: No
  Receipt of manuscript acknowledged: Yes
  Decision to publish in: 8-10 weeks
  Accepted manuscript published in: 4-8 months
  Rejected manuscript returned: Yes
  Rejected manuscript criticized: Yes
Submit to:
  S. M. Tomasi
  Editor
  (See address above)

JOURNAL OF AMERICAN FOLKLORE [1547]

Box 7819
University of Texas Press
Austin, Texas 78712

First published in 1888

SUBSCRIPTION DATA
Issues and rates: Published quarterly.
  Average paid circulation: 2,500
  Annual rate(s): Individuals $10.00, Institutions $12.00
Publisher or Sponsor: American Folklore Society
Managing Editor: Lois Rankin

EDITORIAL DESCRIPTION
  Offers articles on all aspects of world folklore, reviews of books, records and films of current interest to folklorists.
Articles per average issue: 5 articles; 6 notes and queries
Audience: Folklorists
  Manuscripts accepted in English

MANUSCRIPT INFORMATION
Subject field(s): Folklore, ethnology, Americana, folk music, literature and folklore
Manuscript requirements: MLA and Chicago
  Preferred length: 6,000-7,000 words
  Number of copies to be submitted: Two
  Abstract: Optional
Author information and reprints: Payment: None.
  Is simultaneous submission of article to other journals permitted: No
  Exclusive manuscript rights between acceptance and publication: Yes
  Copyright: Held by publication.
  Reprints: Available, 25 free
Disposition of manuscript:
  Query letter: No
  Receipt of manuscript acknowledged: Yes
  Decision to publish in: Two months
  Accepted manuscript published in: Five months
  Rejected manuscript returned: Yes
Submit to:
  J. Barre Toelken
  Editor
  Department of English
  University of Oregon
  Eugene, Oregon 97403
  (512) 471-7233

JOURNAL OF ANTHROPOLOGICAL RESEARCH [1548]
Department of Anthropology
University of New Mexico
Albuquerque, New Mexico 87131
(505) 277-4544

Previously entitled *Southwestern Journal of Anthropology*

First published in 1945

SUBSCRIPTION DATA
Issues and rates: Published quarterly.
  Average paid circulation: 2,253
  Annual rate(s): Individuals $7.00, Institutions $12.00
Publisher or Sponsor: The University of New Mexico
Managing Editor: Harry Basehart

EDITORIAL DESCRIPTION
  Contains articles in the four major sub-disciplines of anthropology (ethnology, archeology, physical anthropology, linguistics). The majority of papers submitted for consideration are in ethnology. Problem-oriented articles which present substantive data in a theoretical context are preferred. Papers with a descriptive emphasis are published rarely; highly specialized articles usually are not considered appropriate for this general journal of anthropology.
Articles per average issue: 4
Audience: Professional anthropologists
  Manuscripts accepted in English

MANUSCRIPT INFORMATION
Subject field(s): Ethnology, archeology, linguistics, physical anthropology
Manuscript requirements: See latest issue for style requirements.
  Preferred length: 12,000 words; 25 pages
  Number of copies to be submitted: One
  Abstract: Yes, not to exceed 150 words.
Author information and reprints: Payment: None.
  Is simultaneous submission of article to other journals permitted: No
  Exclusive manuscript rights between acceptance and publication: Yes
  Copyright: Held by publication.
  Reprints: Available
Disposition of manuscript:
  Query letter: No
  Receipt of manuscript acknowledged: Yes
  Decision to publish in: Two months
  Accepted manuscript published in: Six months
  Rejected manuscript returned: Yes
  Rejected manuscript criticized: No
Submit to:
  Editor
  (See address above)
  (505) 277-2200

JOURNAL OF COMPARATIVE FAMILY STUDIES [1549]
Department of Sociology, University of Calgary
2920 24th Avenue, N. W.
Calgary, Alberta T2N 1N4, Canada
(403) 284-6501

First published in 1970

SUBSCRIPTION DATA
Issues and rates: Published semi-annually.
  Annual rate(s): $8.00; Foreign $8.00; Institutions $8.00; Students $6.00

EDITORIAL DESCRIPTION
  Publishes articles on rational as well as international cross-cultural family studies
Articles per average issue: 12
Audience: Professional, academic
  Manuscripts accepted in English

MANUSCRIPT INFORMATION
Subject field(s): Comparative family studies in anthropology, sociology, medical sociology, and psychology
Manuscript requirements: ASA
  Preferred length: 5,000 words
  Number of copies to be submitted: 3
  Abstract: Yes. Of about 200 words covering the general theme of the paper and the major findings.
Author information and reprints: Payment: By author to publication. $.05 per word. $10.00 per page. $50.00 per article.
  Is simultaneous submission of article to other journals permitted: Permitted, but not encouraged.
  Exclusive manuscript rights between acceptance and publication: Yes
  Copyright: Held by publication.
  Reprints: Available at cost.

Additional information: Keep tables and graphs to a minimum to reduce cost of printing.
Disposition of manuscript:
  Query letter: Not necessary.
  Receipt of manuscript acknowledged: Yes
  Accepted manuscript published in: 4 months
  Rejected manuscript returned: Yes, if return postage is supplied by author.
  Rejected manuscript criticized: Sometimes
Submit to:
  Dr. George Kurian
  Editor
  (See address above)

JOURNAL OF HEALTH AND SOCIAL BEHAVIOR [1550]
1722 N Street, N.W.
Washington, D.C. 20036
(202) 833-3410

SUBSCRIPTION DATA
Issues and rates: Published quarterly.
  Average paid circulation: 3,000
  Annual rate(s): $10.00, Institutions $15.00
Publisher or Sponsor: American Sociological Association
Managing Editor: Otto N. Larsen

EDITORIAL DESCRIPTION
  Emphasizes the sociological analysis of all aspects of social life bearing on human health, mental and physical, including studies of the institutions and occupations devoted to diagnosis, treatment, rehabilitation and the delivery of health services generally. Empirical studies, theoretical analyses and general reviews of problem areas in health and medical practice are published.
Articles per average issue: 5
Audience: Those in the sociology of medicine field
  Manuscripts accepted in English

MANUSCRIPT INFORMATION
Manuscript requirements: Style sheet sent on request.
  Number of copies to be submitted: Three
  Abstract: Yes
Author information and reprints: Payment: None.
  Is simultaneous submission of article to other journals permitted: No
  Exclusive manuscript rights between acceptance and publication: Yes
  Copyright: Held by publication.
  Reprints: Not available.
Disposition of manuscript:
  Query letter: No
  Receipt of manuscript acknowledged: Yes
  Decision to publish in: Varies
  Accepted manuscript published in: 6-12 months
  Rejected manuscript returned:
  Rejected manuscript criticized: Yes Yes, if self-addressed, stamped envelope is sent with manuscript.
Submit to:
  Jacquelyne J. Jackson

Sociology and anthropology

Editor
Box 3003
Duke University Medical Center
Durham, North Carolina 27706
(919) 684-3175

JOURNAL OF POPULAR CULTURE [1551]
101 University Hall
Bowling Green State University
Bowling Green, Ohio 43403
(419) 372-4610

First published in 1967

SUBSCRIPTION DATA
Issues and rates: Published quarterly.
   Average paid circulation: 2,000; 250 controlled
   Annual rate(s): Members $15.00
Managing Editor: Ray B. Browne

EDITORIAL DESCRIPTION
   Contains articles pertaining to the area of popular culture broadly defined as the voice and muscle of the people, the movements of its past, present and future.
Articles per average issue: 20
Audience: Academic and professional

MANUSCRIPT INFORMATION
Subject field(s): Popular culture in the broadest sense.
Manuscript requirements: MLA
   Preferred length: 10-15 pages
   Number of copies to be submitted: One original
   Abstract: Yes
Author information and reprints: Payment: None.
   Is simultaneous submission of article to other journals permitted: Yes
   Exclusive manuscript rights between acceptance and publication: Yes
   Copyright: Held by publication.
   Reprints: Available
Disposition of manuscript:
   Query letter: No
   Receipt of manuscript acknowledged: Yes
   Decision to publish in: 6 weeks
   Accepted manuscript published in: 12-24 months
   Rejected manuscript returned: Yes
   Rejected manuscript criticized: Occasionally
Submit to:
   Ray B. Browne
   Editor
   (See address above)

KENTUCKY FOLKLORE RECORD [1552]
Box U-169
Western Kentucky University
Bowling Green, Kentucky 42101
(502) 745-3855

First published in 1955

SUBSCRIPTION DATA
Issues and rates: Published quarterly.
   Average paid circulation: 450
   Annual rate(s): $3.00
Publisher or Sponsor: Kentucky Folklore Society
Managing Editor: Charles Snow Guthrie

EDITORIAL DESCRIPTION
   Contains articles dealing with any aspect of folklore current in the Commonwealth of Kentucky including the history of folklore study and the use of folklore in education, creative writing, etc.; reports of folklore activities in Kentucky and the surrounding areas; reviews of publications dealing with Kentucky folklore, the folklore of other regions, and any other related area of interest.
Articles per average issue: 10
Audience: Academic
   Manuscripts accepted in English only

MANUSCRIPT INFORMATION
Subject field(s): Folktale, folksong, folklife, folk speech, superstitions, local legends, folklore in literature, book reviews, record reviews, children's lore, folk poetry, folk arts and crafts
Manuscript requirements: MLA
   Preferred length: 600 words and up
   Number of copies to be submitted: One
   Abstract: No
Author information and reprints: Payment: Reprints only. Three copies of issue
   Is simultaneous submission of article to other journals permitted: No
   Exclusive manuscript rights between acceptance and publication: Yes
   Copyright: Held by publication.
   Reprints: Not available.
Additional information: Most reviews done are on assignment.
Disposition of manuscript:
   Query letter: Not necessary, but advisable.
   Receipt of manuscript acknowledged: Yes
   Decision to publish in: 4 weeks
   Accepted manuscript published in: 6-12 months
   Rejected manuscript returned: Yes, if self-addressed, stamped envelope is sent with manuscript.
   Rejected manuscript criticized: No
Submit to:
   Charles S. Guthrie
   Editor
   (See address above)

SPECIAL STIPULATIONS
   Contributions are not limited to professional folklorists and are both welcomed and received from any source.

MAN [1553]
The Journal of the Royal Anthropological Institute
6 Burlington Gardens
London W1X 2EX, England
(01) 920-6328

Previously entitled *Journal of the Royal Anthropological Institute*

First published in 1871

SUBSCRIPTION DATA
Issues and rates: Published quarterly.
   Average paid circulation: 3,000
   Annual rate(s): £12.00; Foreign $31.50
Publisher or Sponsor: Royal Anthropological Institute

EDITORIAL DESCRIPTION
   Contains articles on anthropology in the broadest sense (including physical anthropology, archaeology, ethnography, linguistics).
Articles per average issue: 10
Audience: Professional, academic
   Manuscripts accepted in English only

MANUSCRIPT INFORMATION
Manuscript requirements: Style sheet sent on request.
   Preferred length: 10,000 words maximum
   Number of copies to be submitted: One
   Abstract: Yes
Author information and reprints: Payment: Reprints only. 25 reprints
   Is simultaneous submission of article to other journals permitted: No
   Exclusive manuscript rights between acceptance and publication: Yes
   Copyright: Held by publication.
   Reprints: Available
Additional information: Double-spaced typescript on quarto with note, references, and artwork on separate pages.
Disposition of manuscript:
   Query letter: No
   Receipt of manuscript acknowledged: Yes
   Decision to publish in: 3 months
   Accepted manuscript published in: 6 months
   Rejected manuscript returned: Yes
   Rejected manuscript criticized: Sometimes
Submit to:
   P. G. Rivière
   Editor
   (See address above)
   (0582) 83-3331

THE MISSISSIPPI FOLKLORE REGISTER [1554]
Ovid S. Vickers
East Central Junior College
Decatur, Mississippi 39327
635-2949

First published in 1967

SUBSCRIPTION DATA
Issues and rates: Published quarterly.
   Average paid circulation: 500
   Annual rate(s): $3.00 for all
Publisher or Sponsor: The Mississippi Folklore Society
Managing Editor: Marice C. Brown

EDITORIAL DESCRIPTION
   To record folklore of any state or country.
Articles per average issue: 6

Audience: Those interested in folklore
Manuscripts accepted in English

MANUSCRIPT INFORMATION
Subject field(s): Any subject related to folklore
Manuscript requirements: MLA
Preferred length: 8 pages
Number of copies to be submitted: 1
Abstract: Not necessary.
Author information and reprints: Payment: None.
Is simultaneous submission of article to other journals permitted: Permitted, but not encouraged.
Exclusive manuscript rights between acceptance and publication: Yes
Copyright: Held by publication.
Reprints: Available at no cost. 10
Disposition of manuscript:
Query letter: Not necessary.
Receipt of manuscript acknowledged: Yes
Decision to publish in: 1 month
Accepted manuscript published in: 3 months
Rejected manuscript returned: Yes, if return postage is supplied by author.
Rejected manuscript criticized: Sometimes
Submit to:
Dr. Marice C. Brown
Editor
Box 133, Southern Station
University of Southern Mississippi
Hattiesburg, Mississippi 39401

NORTHWEST ANTHROPOLOGICAL RESEARCH NOTES [1555]
Department of Sociology/Anthropology
University of Idaho
Moscow, Idaho 83843
(208) 885-6751

First published in 1967

SUBSCRIPTION DATA
Issues and rates: Published semi-annually.
Average paid circulation: 350
Annual rate(s): $4.00
Managing Editor: Roderick Sprague

EDITORIAL DESCRIPTION
Contains articles on the anthropology of the Northwest.
Articles per average issue: 8
Manuscripts accepted in English

MANUSCRIPT INFORMATION
Subject field(s): Anthropology, social anthropology, cultural anthropology, archaeology, physical anthropology, ethnohistory, anthropological linguistics
Manuscript requirements: See latest issue for style requirements.
Preferred length: 20 to 150 pages
Number of copies to be submitted: Two
Abstract: Yes
Author information and reprints: Payment: None.
Is simultaneous submission of article to other journals permitted: No

Exclusive manuscript rights between acceptance and publication: Yes
Copyright: Held by publication.
Reprints: Available, 100 free
Disposition of manuscript:
Query letter: No
Receipt of manuscript acknowledged: Yes
Decision to publish in: 6 weeks
Accepted manuscript published in: 1 year
Rejected manuscript returned: Yes
Rejected manuscript criticized: Yes
Submit to:
Roderick Sprague
Editor
(See address above)

OCEANIA [1556]
Mackie Building
University of Sydney
Sydney, N.S.W. 2006, Australia

SUBSCRIPTION DATA
Issues and rates: Published quarterly.
Average paid circulation: Not available.
Annual rate(s): $11.25, Foreign $17.00
Publisher or Sponsor: University of Sydney
Managing Editor: A. P. Elkin

EDITORIAL DESCRIPTION
A journal devoted to the study of the native peoples of Australia, New Guinea and the islands of the Pacific Ocean.
Articles per average issue: 5
Audience: Anthropologists
Manuscripts accepted in English

MANUSCRIPT INFORMATION
Subject field(s): Social anthropology, linguistics
Manuscript requirements: See latest issue for style requirements.
Preferred length: 5,000-10,000 words
Number of copies to be submitted: One
Abstract: Yes
Author information and reprints: Payment: None.
Is simultaneous submission of article to other journals permitted: No
Exclusive manuscript rights between acceptance and publication: Yes
Copyright: Held by publication.
Reprints: Available at cost
Additional information: Manuscripts should be in the proper style, with references, tables and charts on separate pages. Footnotes in text. Author's name and affiliation should appear on a separate cover page.
Disposition of manuscript:
Query letter: No
Receipt of manuscript acknowledged: Yes
Decision to publish in: 6-8 weeks
Accepted manuscript published in: 6-9 months
Rejected manuscript returned: Yes
Rejected manuscript criticized: Yes
Submit to:
A. P. Elkin
Editor
(See address above)

RESEARCHES IN POPULATION ECOLOGY [1557]
The Society of Population Ecology
c/o Japan Academic Societies Center
Yayoi 2-4-16, Bunkyo-ku, Tokyo 113, Japan

First published in Spring 1961

SUBSCRIPTION DATA
Issues and rates: Published semi-annually.
Annual rate(s): Institutions $20.00; Members $10.00
Publisher or Sponsor: The Society of Population Ecology
Managing Editor: Shun'iti Iwao

EDITORIAL DESCRIPTION
Promotes and fosters the study of population ecology; publishes original papers dealing with the various aspects of this field.
Articles per average issue: 10
Audience: Members of the Society
Manuscripts accepted in English only

MANUSCRIPT INFORMATION
Manuscript requirements: See latest issue for style requirements. Style sheet sent on request.
Preferred length: 20 pages maximum
Number of copies to be submitted: 2
Abstract: Yes.
Author information and reprints: Payment: None. A fee of $20.00 for any pages over 20 is charged.
Is simultaneous submission of article to other journals permitted: Not permitted.
Exclusive manuscript rights between acceptance and publication: No
Copyright: Not specified
Reprints: Available at no cost. 50
Available at cost. $3.00 per 100 copies
Additional information: Typewritten, double-spaced with ample margins
Disposition of manuscript:
Query letter: Not necessary.
Receipt of manuscript acknowledged: Yes
Decision to publish in:
Accepted manuscript published in:
Rejected manuscript returned: Yes, with return postage paid by publication.
Rejected manuscript criticized: Reasons for rejections only
Submit to:
Shun'iti Iwao
Managing Editor
Laboratory of Applied Entomology
Faculty of Agriculture, Nagoya University
Chikusa-ku, Nagoya 464, Japan

RURAL SOCIOLOGY [1558]
207 Weaver Building
The Pennsylvania State University
University Park, Pennsylvania 16801
(814) 865-0455

First published in 1936

SUBSCRIPTION DATA
Issues and rates: Published quarterly.

Sociology and anthropology

Average paid circulation: 3000
Annual rate(s): $12.00
Publisher or Sponsor: Rural Sociological Society
Managing Editor: Robert C. Bealer

EDITORIAL DESCRIPTION

Contains research reports; theoretical essays; policy analysis, pertinent book reviews; index of pertinent research bulletins and monographs.
Articles per average issue: 28
Audience: Sociologists
Manuscripts accepted in English

MANUSCRIPT INFORMATION

Subject field(s): Rural sociology, social organization, social change, community development, applied theory, methodology, urbanization, comparative analysis
Manuscript requirements: Contained in Spring issue of each year.
Preferred length: 25 pages maximum
Number of copies to be submitted: Four
Abstract: Yes
Author information and reprints: Payment: None.
Is simultaneous submission of article to other journals permitted: No
Exclusive manuscript rights between acceptance and publication: Yes
Copyright: Held by Rural Sociological Society
Reprints: Available, $20 for 100 of 4 page article
Disposition of manuscript:
Receipt of manuscript acknowledged: Yes
Decision to publish in: 2-3 months
Accepted manuscript published in: 6-9 months
Rejected manuscript returned: Yes, if self-addressed, stamped envelope is sent with manuscript.
Rejected manuscript criticized: Yes
Submit to:
Robert C. Bealer
Editor
(See address above)

SIMULATION AND GAMES* [1559]

An International Journal of Theory, Design, and Research
Sage Publications, Inc.
275 South Beverly Drive
Beverly Hills, California 90212
(213) 784-2423

SUBSCRIPTION DATA

Issues and rates: Published quarterly.
Average paid circulation: Not available.
Annual rate(s): Institutions $18; Individuals $12; Students $9; Foreign individuals $13; Foreign institutions $19

EDITORIAL DESCRIPTION

Publishes theoretical papers about simulations in research and teaching, empirical studies, and technical papers about new gaming techniques; includes coverage of man, man-machine, and machine simulations of social processes.
Each issue includes book reviews, listing of newly available simulations, and "simulation reviews."

MANUSCRIPT INFORMATION

Subject field(s): Gaming, human behavior, teaching, research design
Manuscript requirements: Style sheet sent on request.
Preferred length: 6,250-7,500 words; 25 to 30 pages
Number of copies to be submitted: Two
Author information and reprints: Payment: None. 25 tear-sheets free to author.
Is simultaneous submission of article to other journals permitted: Permitted, but not encouraged. Author must notify publisher that manuscript is under consideration elsewhere.
Exclusive manuscript rights between acceptance and publication: Yes
Copyright: Held by publication.
Reprints: Available if purchased by special order in amounts no fewer than 100
Disposition of manuscript:
Receipt of manuscript acknowledged: Yes
Decision to publish in: Six to eight weeks
Accepted manuscript published in: Six to nine months
Rejected manuscript returned: Yes
Rejected manuscript criticized: Yes
Submit to:
Keith J. Edwards,
James Coleman
Editors
Center for Social Organization of Schools
Johns Hopkins university
Baltimore, Maryland 21218

SOCIAL FORCES [1560]

Room 168, Hamilton Hall
The University of North Carolina
Chapel Hill, North Carolina 27514
(919) 933-5502

First published in 1922

SUBSCRIPTION DATA

Issues and rates: Published quarterly.
Average paid circulation: 5,000
Annual rate(s): Individuals $10.00, Foreign $11.00, Institutions $12.00, Foreign institutions $13.00
Managing Editor: Norma C. Scofield

EDITORIAL DESCRIPTION

Contains sociological articles which explore new data, new methods of analysis, new theoretical orientations.
Articles per average issue: 13
Audience: Social scientists
Manuscripts accepted in English

MANUSCRIPT INFORMATION

Subject field(s): Theory; methodology; studies in social structure; studies in social psychology; studies in social problems, social and cultural change; applications of sociology.
Manuscript requirements: Style sheet sent on request.
Preferred length: 15-20 pages
Number of copies to be submitted: Two
Abstract: Yes, 125 words or less
Author information and reprints: Payment: None.
Is simultaneous submission of article to other journals permitted: No
Exclusive manuscript rights between acceptance and publication: Yes
Copyright: Held by publication.
Reprints: Available, 25 free; extra at cost
Disposition of manuscript:
Query letter: No
Receipt of manuscript acknowledged: Yes
Decision to publish in: 3 months
Accepted manuscript published in: One year
Rejected manuscript returned: Yes, if return postage is supplied by author.
Rejected manuscript criticized: Yes
Submit to:
Everett K. Wilson
Editor
(See address above)

SOCIOLOGICAL INQUIRY [1561]

Journal of the Sociology Honor Society
Ontario Institute for Studies in Education
252 Bloor Street West
Toronto 181, Ontario Canada
(416) 923-6641 ext. 288

Previously entitled *Alpha Kappa Deltan*

First published in 1930

SUBSCRIPTION DATA

Issues and rates: Published quarterly.
Average paid circulation: 6,000
Annual rate(s): Institutions $6.00, Individuals $4.00, Members $3.40
Publisher or Sponsor: Alpha Kappa Delta

EDITORIAL DESCRIPTION

Contains primarily theory and interesting new developments in sociology.
Articles per average issue: 8
Manuscripts accepted in English

MANUSCRIPT INFORMATION

Subject field(s): Sociology
Manuscript requirements: See latest issue for style requirements.
Preferred length: 20 pages
Number of copies to be submitted: Three
Abstract: Yes
Author information and reprints: Payment: None.
Is simultaneous submission of article to other journals permitted: No
Exclusive manuscript rights between acceptance and publication: Yes
Copyright: Held by publication.
Reprints: Available
Disposition of manuscript:
Query letter: No
Receipt of manuscript acknowledged: Yes
Decision to publish in: 6-8 weeks
Accepted manuscript published in: 3 months
Rejected manuscript returned: Yes
Rejected manuscript criticized: Yes

Submit to:
Andrew Effrat
Editor
(See address above)

SOCIOLOGICAL METHODS AND RESEARCH [1562]

Sage Publications, Inc.
275 South Beverly Drive
Beverly Hills, California 90212
(213) 273-2423

First published in 1972

SUBSCRIPTION DATA
Issues and rates: Published quarterly.
Average paid circulation: Not available.
Annual rate(s): Institutions $18; Individuals $12; Students $9; Foreign individuals $13; Foreign institutions $19
Managing Editor: Edgar F. Borgatta, George W. Bohrnstedt

EDITORIAL DESCRIPTION
Emphasizes articles that advance the understanding of sociology as a cumulative empirical science, through systematic presentations that clarify methodological problems and assist in ordering known facts and their implications.
Articles per average issue: 6
Audience: Professional
Manuscripts accepted in English

MANUSCRIPT INFORMATION
Subject field(s): Sociology, methodology
Manuscript requirements: Style sheet sent on request.
Preferred length: 6,250-7,500 words; 25 to 30 pages
Number of copies to be submitted: 3
Abstract: Yes
Author information and reprints: Payment: Reprints only. 25 tear-sheets free to author
Is simultaneous submission of article to other journals permitted: Permitted, but not encouraged. Author must notify publisher that manuscript is under consideration elsewhere.
Exclusive manuscript rights between acceptance and publication: Yes
Copyright: Held by publication.
Reprints: Available if purchased by special order in amounts no fewer than 100
Disposition of manuscript:
Query letter: No
Receipt of manuscript acknowledged: Yes
Decision to publish in: 6-12 weeks
Accepted manuscript published in: 6-9 months
Rejected manuscript returned: Yes
Rejected manuscript criticized: Yes
Submit to:
Edgar F. Borgatta
Editor
Department of Sociology
Queens College, CUNY
Flushing, New York 11367

THE SOCIOLOGICAL QUARTERLY [1563]

1004 Elm Street
Columbia, Missouri 65201
(314) 882-3776

Previously entitled *The Midwest Sociologist*

First published in 1953

SUBSCRIPTION DATA
Issues and rates: Published quarterly.
Average paid circulation: 2,498
Annual rate(s): Individuals $10.00, Institutions $12.00, Foreign institutions $13.00
Publisher or Sponsor: Midwest Sociological Society
Managing Editor: James L. McCartney

EDITORIAL DESCRIPTION
Publishes articles of theoretical and methodological significance to sociologists; special series on state of the field of sociology; selected topics.
Articles per average issue: 10
Manuscripts accepted in English

MANUSCRIPT INFORMATION
Subject field(s): All fields of specialization in sociology, material of interest to sociologists
Manuscript requirements: ASA; Chicago
Preferred length: 10-20 pages
Number of copies to be submitted: Three
Abstract: Yes
Author information and reprints: Payment: None.
Is simultaneous submission of article to other journals permitted: No
Exclusive manuscript rights between acceptance and publication: Yes
Copyright: Held by publication.
Reprints: Available at cost
Disposition of manuscript:
Query letter: No
Receipt of manuscript acknowledged: Yes, if postcard is provided by author.
Decision to publish in: 2-3 months
Accepted manuscript published in: 6-9 months
Rejected manuscript returned: Yes, if self-addressed, stamped envelope is sent with manuscript.
Rejected manuscript criticized: No
Submit to:
James L. McCartney
Editor
(See address above)

THE SOCIOLOGICAL REVIEW [1564]

University of Keele
Keele, Staffordshire ST5 5BG, England
Keele Park 371

SUBSCRIPTION DATA
Issues and rates: Published quarterly.
Average paid circulation: 2,000
Annual rate(s): $10.00
Managing Editor: W. M. Williams; Ronald Frankenberg

EDITORIAL DESCRIPTION
Contains articles and book reviews.
Articles per average issue: 6
Manuscripts accepted in English

MANUSCRIPT INFORMATION
Subject field(s): Sociology
Manuscript requirements: Style sheet sent on request.
Number of copies to be submitted: One
Author information and reprints: Payment: None.
Is simultaneous submission of article to other journals permitted: Yes
Exclusive manuscript rights between acceptance and publication: Yes
Copyright: Held by author.
Reprints: Available, cost varies
Disposition of manuscript:
Receipt of manuscript acknowledged: Yes
Decision to publish in: 3 months
Accepted manuscript published in: 6 months
Rejected manuscript returned: Yes
Rejected manuscript criticized: No
Submit to:
The Managing Editors' Secretary
(See address above)

SOCIOLOGICAL SYMPOSIUM [1565]

Department of Sociology, McBryde Hall
Virginia Polytechnic Institute and State University
Blacksburg, Virginia 24061
(703) 951-6878

First published in 1968

SUBSCRIPTION DATA
Issues and rates: Published semi-annually.
Average paid circulation: Not available.
Annual rate(s): Individuals $5.00, Institutions $8.00, Foreign $9.00

EDITORIAL DESCRIPTION
Publishes research and theory on topics significant to social scientists. Each issue is devoted to a single topic.
Articles per average issue: 8
Audience: Social scientists
Manuscripts accepted in English

MANUSCRIPT INFORMATION
Subject field(s): Sociology, political science, psychology, other social sciences
Manuscript requirements: ASR
Preferred length: 15-20 pages
Number of copies to be submitted: Two
Abstract: No
Author information and reprints: Payment: None.
Is simultaneous submission of article to other journals permitted: No
Exclusive manuscript rights between acceptance and publication: Yes
Copyright: Held by publication.
Reprints: Not available.

Additional information: Manuscripts should be in the proper style, with footnotes, references, tables and charts on separate pages. Author's name and affiliation should appear only on a separate cover page so articles can be sent out anonymously for editorial evaluation.

Disposition of manuscript:
Query letter: No
Receipt of manuscript acknowledged: Yes
Decision to publish in: 6-8 weeks
Accepted manuscript published in: 6-8 months
Rejected manuscript returned: Yes, if self-addressed, stamped envelope is sent with manuscript.
Rejected manuscript criticized: Yes

Submit to:
John Nelson Edwards
Editor
(See address above)
(703) 951-5360

SOCIOLOGY [1566]
The Journal of the British Sociological Association
Medical Sociology Unit
Centre for Social Studies, Westburn Road
Aberdeen, AB9 2ZE Scotland
0224 23423 ext. 2422

First published in 1967

SUBSCRIPTION DATA
Issues and rates: Published three times per year.
Average paid circulation: 1900
Annual rate(s): £6.00; Foreign $16.00
Publisher or Sponsor: British Sociological Association

EDITORIAL DESCRIPTION
Publishes main-line sociology, anthropology, and social psychology: theoretical and/or empirical.
Articles per average issue: 5-6; notes, correspondence
Audience: Professional
Manuscripts accepted in English

MANUSCRIPT INFORMATION
Subject field(s): Sociology, social anthropology, social psychology
Manuscript requirements: See latest issue for style requirements.
Preferred length: 9000 words maximum
Number of copies to be submitted: Two
Abstract: Short abstract of 100-200 words.
Author information and reprints: Payment: Reprints only. 25
Is simultaneous submission of article to other journals permitted: Yes, with knowledge of editor.
Exclusive manuscript rights between acceptance and publication: Yes
Copyright: Held by author.
Reprints: Available
Additional information: Articles must be set out in style according to details printed in first number of each volume. Author's name and biographical note should appear on separate cover sheet. Authors pay cost of alterations to text made at proof stage. American authors should use English spellings where possible.

Disposition of manuscript:
Query letter: No
Receipt of manuscript acknowledged: Yes
Decision to publish in: 6-8 weeks
Accepted manuscript published in: 9 months
Rejected manuscript returned: Yes, if self-addressed, stamped envelope is sent with manuscript.
Rejected manuscript criticized: Yes

Submit to:
Gordon Horobin
Editor
(See address above)

SOCIOLOGY OF EDUCATION [1567]
1722 N Street, N.W.
Washington, D.C. 20036
(202) 833-3410

SUBSCRIPTION DATA
Issues and rates: Published quarterly.
Average paid circulation: 3,000
Annual rate(s): $10.00, Institutions $15.00
Publisher or Sponsor: American Sociological Association
Managing Editor: Otto N. Larsen

EDITORIAL DESCRIPTION
Presents sociological research that penetrates issues over the whole spectrum of the education enterprise from nursery school to higher education. Family, peer, school, and other societal structures are analyzed in relation to educational aspirations, plans, performance, and consequences as they occur in various national and cultural contexts.
Manuscripts accepted in English

MANUSCRIPT INFORMATION
Manuscript requirements: Style sheet sent on request.
Number of copies to be submitted: Three
Abstract: Yes
Author information and reprints: Payment: None.
Is simultaneous submission of article to other journals permitted: No
Exclusive manuscript rights between acceptance and publication: Yes
Copyright: Held by publication.
Reprints: Not available.
Disposition of manuscript:
Query letter: No
Receipt of manuscript acknowledged: Yes
Decision to publish in: Varies
Accepted manuscript published in: 6-12 months
Rejected manuscript returned: Yes, if self-addressed, stamped envelope is sent with manuscript.

Submit to:
John I. Kitsuse
Editor
Department of Sociology
Northwestern University
Evanston, Illinois 60201
(312) 492-5415

SOCIOLOGY AND SOCIAL RESEARCH [1568]
An International Journal
University of Southern California
Los Angeles, California 90007
(213) 746-2658

Previously entitled *Studies of Sociology*

First published in 1915

SUBSCRIPTION DATA
Issues and rates: Published quarterly.
Average paid circulation: 2,200; 2,100 controlled
Annual rate(s): $10.00, Foreign $13.00, Institutions $15.00, Foreign institutions $18.00
Publisher or Sponsor: University of Southern California
Managing Editor: Lourdes A. Ongkeko

EDITORIAL DESCRIPTION
A scholarly quarterly in the field of social science with emphasis on sociology. Articles encompass a broad spectrum of interest with occasional issues of special focus.
Articles per average issue: 10-12
Audience: Sociologists, social psychologists
Manuscripts accepted in English

MANUSCRIPT INFORMATION
Subject field(s): Narcotics addiction, race relations, juvenile delinquency, social class, leisure and recreation, alienation, aging, predicting marital adjustment, interracial marriage, research methodology, role and status, sociological theory, and public opinion.
Manuscript requirements: Style sheet sent on request.
Preferred length: 10 pages
Number of copies to be submitted: Three
Abstract: Yes
Author information and reprints: Payment: None.
Is simultaneous submission of article to other journals permitted: No
Exclusive manuscript rights between acceptance and publication: Yes
Copyright: Held by publication.
Reprints: Not always available
Disposition of manuscript:
Query letter: No
Receipt of manuscript acknowledged: Yes
Decision to publish in: 6 weeks
Accepted manuscript published in: 4 months
Rejected manuscript returned: Yes, if self-addressed, stamped envelope is sent with manuscript.
Rejected manuscript criticized: Yes

Submit to:
The Editor
(See address above)
(213) 746-6302

SOCIOMETRY [1569]
A Journal of Research in Social Psychology
1722 N Street, N.W.
Washington, D.C. 20036
(202) 833-3410

SUBSCRIPTION DATA
Issues and rates: Published quarterly.
   Average paid circulation: 3,000
   Annual rate(s): $10.00, Institutions $15.00
Publisher or Sponsor: American Sociological Association
Managing Editor: Otto N. Larsen

EDITORIAL DESCRIPTION
Drawing on contributions from any sector or discipline of the scientific community, this journal reports investigations of the processes and products of social interaction to develop knowledge in social psychology. The editors are especially receptive to creative thought and rigorous research that can shape the theoretical structure of the field.
Manuscripts accepted in English

MANUSCRIPT INFORMATION
Subject field(s): A wide-range of concerns with interpersonal behavior including reference groups, communication networks, risk-taking, aggression, attitude change, alienation, self-conception, peer and family influences, norms and social cohesion.
Manuscript requirements: Style sheet sent on request.
   Number of copies to be submitted: Three
   Abstract: Yes
Author information and reprints: Payment: None.
   Is simultaneous submission of article to other journals permitted: No
   Exclusive manuscript rights between acceptance and publication: Yes
   Copyright: Held by publication.
   Reprints: Not available.
Disposition of manuscript:
   Query letter: No
   Receipt of manuscript acknowledged: Yes
   Decision to publish in: Varies
   Accepted manuscript published in: Varies
   Rejected manuscript returned: Yes, if self-addressed, stamped envelope is sent with manuscript.
   Rejected manuscript criticized: Yes
Submit to:
   Richard J. Hill
   Editor
   Department of Sociology
   University of Oregon
   Eugene, Oregon 94703
   (503) 686-5002

STEWARD ANTHROPOLOGICAL SOCIETY. JOURNAL [1570]
Department of Anthropology, 109
Davenport Hall
University of Illinois
Urbana, Illinois 61801

First published in 1969

SUBSCRIPTION DATA
Issues and rates: Published semi-annually.
   Average paid circulation: 200
   Annual rate(s): $4.00; Institutions $10.00
Publisher or Sponsor: Steward Anthropological Society

EDITORIAL DESCRIPTION
Provides an outlet for articles with a theoretical viewpoint in the various fields anthropology and related disciplines.
Articles per average issue: 5
Audience: Anthropologists, social scientists
Manuscripts accepted in English

MANUSCRIPT INFORMATION
Manuscript requirements: See latest issue for style requirements.
   Preferred length: Under 5,000 words; Under 20 pages
   Number of copies to be submitted: 2
   Abstract: Not necessary.
Author information and reprints: Payment: None.
   Is simultaneous submission of article to other journals permitted: Permitted, but not encouraged.
   Exclusive manuscript rights between acceptance and publication: No
   Copyright: Held by publication.
   Reprints: Available at no cost. 15
Additional information: Manuscripts must be submitted in a camera-ready form. The use of photographs is discouraged.
Disposition of manuscript:
   Query letter: Not necessary.
   Receipt of manuscript acknowledged: Yes
   Decision to publish in: 3 months
   Accepted manuscript published in: 6 months
   Rejected manuscript returned: No
   Rejected manuscript criticized: Yes
Submit to:
   Editor
   (See address above)

TENNESSEE FOLKLORE SOCIETY BULLETIN [1571]
Box 234
Middle Tennessee State University
Murfreesboro, Tennessee 37130
(615) 898-2576

First published in 1935

SUBSCRIPTION DATA
Issues and rates: Published quarterly.
   Average paid circulation: 375
   Annual rate(s): Individuals $3.00; Institutions $4.00
Publisher or Sponsor: Tennessee Folklore Society

EDITORIAL DESCRIPTION
Publishes articles in folklore, book and record reviews, announcements, summary of articles in other magazines. Roughly two-thirds of material is about the Southeast.
Articles per average issue: 3
Audience: Teachers, general
Manuscripts accepted in English only

MANUSCRIPT INFORMATION
Subject field(s): Folklore only
Manuscript requirements: MLA; full bibliographical information on books and records reviewed
   Preferred length: 1500-4000 words; 6-16 pages
   Number of copies to be submitted: One
Author information and reprints: Payment: None. 3 copies of issue
   Is simultaneous submission of article to other journals permitted: No
   Exclusive manuscript rights between acceptance and publication: Yes
   Copyright: Held by the Society
   Reprints: Available at price of individual copy
Disposition of manuscript:
   Query letter: No
   Receipt of manuscript acknowledged: Yes
   Decision to publish in: Two weeks
   Accepted manuscript published in: 3-6 months
   Rejected manuscript returned: Yes, if return postage is supplied by author.
   Rejected manuscript criticized: Yes
Submit to:
   Ralph W. Hyde
   Secretary-Editor
   (See address above)

URBAN LIFE [1572]
A Journal of Ethnographic Research
Sage Publications, Inc.
275 South Beverly Drive
Beverly Hills, California 90212
(213) 274-2423

Previously entitled *Urban Life and Culture*

First published in 1972

SUBSCRIPTION DATA
Issues and rates: Published quarterly.
   Annual rate(s): Institutions $15.00; Individuals $10.00; Students $8.00; Foreign individuals $11.50; Foreign institutions $16.50

EDITORIAL DESCRIPTION
Publishes works of urban ethnography, employing participant-observation and intensive qualitative interviewing and conveying the inner life and texture of the diverse social enclaves and personal circumstances of urban societies.
Articles per average issue: 5
Audience: Professional, academic
Manuscripts accepted in English

MANUSCRIPT INFORMATION
Subject field(s): Sociology, anthropology, political science, geography, criminology, psychology
Manuscript requirements: Style sheet sent on request.
   Preferred length: 6,250-7,500 words; 25 to 30 pages
   Number of copies to be submitted: Two
   Abstract: No
Author information and reprints: Payment: Reprints only. 25 tear-sheets
   Is simultaneous submission of article to other journals permitted: Permitted, but not encouraged. Author must notify

publisher that manuscript is under consideration elsewhere.
Exclusive manuscript rights between acceptance and publication: Yes
Copyright: Held by publication.
Reprints: Available if purchased by special order in amounts no fewer than 100

Disposition of manuscript:
Query letter: No
Receipt of manuscript acknowledged: Yes
Decision to publish in: 6-8 weeks
Accepted manuscript published in: 6-9 months
Rejected manuscript returned: Yes
Rejected manuscript criticized: Yes

Submit to:
John Irwin
Editor
Department of Sociology
San Francisco State University
San Francisco, California 94132

URBAN AND SOCIAL CHANGE REVIEW [1573]

McGuinn Hall, Room 202
Boston College
Chestnut Hill, Massachusetts 02167
(617) 969-0100 ext. 2132

SUBSCRIPTION DATA

Issues and rates: Published semi-annually.
Average paid circulation: 1,500
Annual rate(s): Individuals $4.00, Institutions $6.00

Publisher or Sponsor: Boston College, Graduate School of Social Work

EDITORIAL DESCRIPTION

Contains review articles on issues of interest to researchers and practitioners in the areas of urban and social change; provides an urban information clearinghouse of selected reference materials, including books, periodicals, bibliographies, information services, simulation games, films, etc.; interdisciplinary interest in urban affairs issues, primarily oriented toward social science research.

Articles per average issue: 3-4
Audience: Managers of human service programs
Manuscripts accepted in English

MANUSCRIPT INFORMATION

Subject field(s): Urban problems, social change, urban education, planning, urban history, human service, ethnic problems

Manuscript requirements: No specific style guide.
Preferred length: 4000 words; 12-16 pages
Number of copies to be submitted: Two

Author information and reprints: Payment: None.
Is simultaneous submission of article to other journals permitted: Yes
Exclusive manuscript rights between acceptance and publication: Yes
Copyright: Held by publication.
Reprints: Available, cost on request

Disposition of manuscript:
Query letter: No
Receipt of manuscript acknowledged: Yes
Decision to publish in: 1-2 months
Accepted manuscript published in: Up to six months
Rejected manuscript returned: Yes
Rejected manuscript criticized: Sometimes

Submit to:
Karen Wolk Feinstein
Managing Editor
(See address above)

WESTERN FOLKLORE [1574]

University of California Press
Berkeley, California 74720
(415) 642-4245

Previously entitled *California Folklore Quarterly*

First published in 1942

SUBSCRIPTION DATA

Issues and rates: Published quarterly.
Average paid circulation: 865; 41 controlled
Annual rate(s): Institutions $12.00, Foreign institutions $13.00, Individuals $10.00, Foreign individuals $11.00

Publisher or Sponsor: California Folklore Society

Managing Editor: D. K. Wilgus

EDITORIAL DESCRIPTION

Contains analysis and criticism of world folklore; short items of collectanea; notes and queries; book and record reviews.

Articles per average issue: 6
Audience: Scholars, general laymen
Manuscripts accepted in English

MANUSCRIPT INFORMATION

Subject field(s): Folklore

Manuscript requirements: Chicago
Preferred length: 3000-4000 words
Number of copies to be submitted: One
Rejected manuscript returned: No

Author information and reprints: Payment: Reprints only. 25 offprints
Is simultaneous submission of article to other journals permitted: No
Exclusive manuscript rights between acceptance and publication: Yes
Copyright: Held by publication.
Reprints: Available

Additional information: Footnotes should be consecutive at the end of the article and double-spaced.

Disposition of manuscript:
Query letter: No
Receipt of manuscript acknowledged: Yes
Decision to publish in: 1 month
Accepted manuscript published in: 9 months
Rejected manuscript returned: Yes
Rejected manuscript criticized: Yes

Submit to:
D. K. Wilgus
Editor
11377 Bunche Hall
University of California
Los Angeles, California 90024
(213) 825-3962

Women's studies

Women's studies

CANADIAN NEWSLETTER OF RESEARCH ON WOMEN [1575]
Sociology Department
University of Waterloo
Waterloo, Ontario N2L 3G1, Canada
(416) 885-1211

First published in May 1972

SUBSCRIPTION DATA

Issues and rates: Published three times per year.
Annual rate(s): $5.00; Foreign $6.00 (U.S.); Institutions $12.00; Students $5.00

EDITORIAL DESCRIPTION

Strives to improve communication among people doing research in women's studies; publishes information on the status of women in institutions and countries; provides for exchange of ideas about courses on sexroles or women. Regular sections on research, reports, periodicals, book reviews, bibliographies, abstracts, etc.
Audience: Research oriented
Manuscripts accepted in English

MANUSCRIPT INFORMATION

Subject field(s): Only book reviews are accepted from outside sources. Balance of material is solicited. Books must have been published since 1970, both internationally and Canadian (excluding U.S.), dealing with sexroles or about women.
Manuscript requirements: No specific style guide. See latest issue for style requirements.
Preferred length: Maximum of 3 double-spaced pages
Number of copies to be submitted: 1
Abstract: Not necessary.
Author information and reprints: Payment: None.
Is simultaneous submission of article to other journals permitted: Permitted.
Exclusive manuscript rights between acceptance and publication: No
Copyright: None
Reprints: Available at cost.
Disposition of manuscript:
Query letter: Necessary.
Receipt of manuscript acknowledged: Yes
Decision to publish in: 1 month
Accepted manuscript published in: 3 months
Rejected manuscript returned: No
Rejected manuscript criticized: Sometimes
Submit to:
Margrit Eichler,
Patricia Carter
Editors
(See address above)

THE FEMINIST ART JOURNAL [1576]
41 Montgomery Place
Brooklyn, New York 11215
(212) 857-9456

First published in 1972

SUBSCRIPTION DATA

Issues and rates: Published quarterly.
Average paid circulation: 4,000
Annual rate(s): $4.00; Pan-Am $6.00; Foreign $6.00; Institutions $10.00; Students $4.00; Foreign individuals $6.00; Foreign institutions $12.00
Publisher or Sponsor: College Art Association
Managing Editor: Charles S. Nemser

EDITORIAL DESCRIPTION

To present the arts of women past and present in all fields with an emphasis on visual arts; to deal with issues of interest to the contemporary art scene.
Articles per average issue: 8-10
Audience: Artists of both sexes as well as students and those interested in women's studies
Manuscripts accepted in English, French

MANUSCRIPT INFORMATION

Subject field(s): The entire field of the arts: the link being articles with a feminist slant or of particular interest to women; scholarly pieces, controversial articles, book reviews, film, theatre, poetry

Manuscript requirements: See latest issue for style requirements.
Preferred length: 3,750 words; 15 pages
Number of copies to be submitted: 1
Abstract: Not necessary.

Author information and reprints: Payment: By publication to author. Reprints only. 5 $25.00 per article.
Is simultaneous submission of article to other journals permitted: Not permitted.
Exclusive manuscript rights between acceptance and publication: Yes
Copyright: First serial rights only
Reprints: Available at no cost. 5

Additional information: Manuscripts should be typewritten, double-spaced, in a clear readable style; photographs must be very sharp and clearly titled.

Disposition of manuscript:
Query letter: Not necessary, but advisable.
Receipt of manuscript acknowledged: Yes
Decision to publish in: 1 month
Accepted manuscript published in: 3 months
Rejected manuscript returned: Reasons for rejections only
Rejected manuscript criticized: Sometimes

Submit to:
Cindy Nemser
Editor-in-Chief
(See address above)

NATIONAL ASSOCIATION FOR WOMEN DEANS, ADMINISTRATORS, AND COUNSELORS. JOURNAL [1577]
1028 Connecticut Avenue, N. W.
Washington, D. C. 20036
(202) 659-9330

First published in 1937

SUBSCRIPTION DATA

Issues and rates: Published quarterly.
Annual rate(s): $8.50; Foreign $10.00; Institutions $8.50
Publisher or Sponsor: National Association for Women Deans, Administrators, and Counselors
Managing Editor: Joan M. McCall

EDITORIAL DESCRIPTION

Articles of special interest to women in fields dealing with students; student personnel administrators, etc.
Articles per average issue: 5-8
Audience: Professional
Manuscripts accepted in English

MANUSCRIPT INFORMATION

Subject field(s): Student personnel, educational administration, counseling, women, sexism, continuing education, career development
Manuscript requirements: APA
Preferred length: 2,500-3,000 words; 10-12 pages
Number of copies to be submitted: 2
Abstract: Not necessary.
Author information and reprints: Payment: Reprints only. 3 copies of issue
Is simultaneous submission of article to other journals permitted: Permitted, but not encouraged.
Exclusive manuscript rights between acceptance and publication: No
Copyright: Held by publication.
Reprints: Available at cost.
Disposition of manuscript:
Query letter: Not necessary.
Receipt of manuscript acknowledged: Yes
Decision to publish in: 6 months
Accepted manuscript published in: 1 year
Rejected manuscript criticized: Sometimes
Submit to:
Dr. Margaret C. Berry
Editor
P. O. Box 7699, U. T. Station
University of Texas at Austin
Austin, Texas 78712

SPECIAL STIPULATIONS

Due to the large number of manuscripts, the publication is running about one year behind.

NATIONAL BUSINESS WOMAN [1578]
2012 Massachusetts Avenue NW
Washington, D.C. 20036
(202) 293-1100 ext. 43

Previously entitled *Independent Woman*

First published in 1919

SUBSCRIPTION DATA
Issues and rates: 11 times per year
   Average paid circulation: 900; 170,000 controlled
   Annual rate(s): $5.00
Publisher or Sponsor: The National Federation of Business and Professional Women's Clubs, Inc.
Managing Editor: Lola S. Tilden

EDITORIAL DESCRIPTION
To speak for the interests of all business and professional women. Contains articles on educational means by which skills for employment may be developed.
Articles per average issue: 2
Audience: Employed women
   Manuscripts accepted in English only

MANUSCRIPT INFORMATION
Subject field(s): Participation in government; financial and/or retirement planning; new business trends, such as converting to the metric system; emerging careers for women; trends in employment of women; consumer issues
Manuscript requirements: Good journalistic style, no breeziness or cuteness; no "first person" experiences.
   Preferred length: 1,200 words
   Number of copies to be submitted: One
   Abstract: No
Author information and reprints: Payment: By publication to author. $.03 per word.
   Is simultaneous submission of article to other journals permitted: No
   Exclusive manuscript rights between acceptance and publication: Yes
   Copyright: Held by publication.
   Reprints: Not available.
Additional information: Include preferred byline (e.g., freelance writer, teacher, lecturer, etc.).
Disposition of manuscript:
   Query letter: No
   Receipt of manuscript acknowledged: No
   Decision to publish in: 6 weeks
   Accepted manuscript published in: 3 months
   Rejected manuscript returned: Yes, if return postage is supplied by author.
   Rejected manuscript criticized: No
Submit to:
   Lola S. Tilden
   Editor
   (See address above)

SPECIAL STIPULATIONS
Sample copy of magazine available for $1.00 to cover postage.

PRESS WOMAN [1579]
1105 Main Street
Blue Springs, Missouri 64015
(816) 229-8191

First published in 1937

SUBSCRIPTION DATA
Issues and rates: Published monthly.
   Average paid circulation: 3600
   Annual rate(s): $3.00

Publisher or Sponsor: National Federation of Press Women, Inc.
Managing Editor: Lois Lauer Wolfe

EDITORIAL DESCRIPTION
Contains articles on journalistic subjects pertaining to women in the profession; news of membership activities of women journalists in general and NFPW members in particular.
Articles per average issue: 1-2
Audience: Women journalists
   Manuscripts accepted in English

MANUSCRIPT INFORMATION
Subject field(s): Journalism, communications
Manuscript requirements: See latest issue for style requirements.
   Preferred length: 5-10 pages
   Number of copies to be submitted: One
   Abstract: No
Author information and reprints: Payment: None.
   Is simultaneous submission of article to other journals permitted: Yes
   Copyright: Not copyrighted
   Reprints: Available
Disposition of manuscript:
   Query letter: No
   Receipt of manuscript acknowledged: Yes
   Decision to publish in: 2 weeks
   Accepted manuscript published in: 2 months
   Rejected manuscript returned: Yes, if self-addressed, stamped envelope is sent with manuscript.
   Rejected manuscript criticized: No
Submit to:
   Lois Lauer Wolfe
   Editor
   (See address above)

PROSE [1580]
National Law Women's Newsletter
400 Huntington Avenue
Boston, Massachusetts 02115

First published in 1971

SUBSCRIPTION DATA
Issues and rates: Published bi-monthly.
   Average paid circulation: 2,700
   Annual rate(s): $5.00; Institutions $25.00; Students $3.00

EDITORIAL DESCRIPTION
Maintains communication and sisterhood among women at law school and gives coverage to events, projects and conferences which concern law women and women in general.
Articles per average issue: 4
Audience: Professional, academic, legal
   Manuscripts accepted in English

MANUSCRIPT INFORMATION
Subject field(s): All areas of current interest to women as related to the legal profession, and legal practice
Manuscript requirements: No specific style guide. See latest issue for style requirements.
   Preferred length: 1,000 words

   Number of copies to be submitted: 1
   Abstract: Not necessary.
Author information and reprints: Payment: None.
   Is simultaneous submission of article to other journals permitted: Permitted.
   Exclusive manuscript rights between acceptance and publication: No
   Copyright: Held by publication.
   Reprints: Available at cost.
Disposition of manuscript:
   Query letter: Not necessary.
   Receipt of manuscript acknowledged: Yes
   Decision to publish in: 1 month
   Accepted manuscript published in: 2 months
   Rejected manuscript returned: Yes, with return postage paid by publication.
   Rejected manuscript criticized: No
Submit to:
   Lin Horowitz
   Editor
   (See address above)

WOMEN [1581]
A Journal of Liberation
3028 Greenmount Avenue
Baltimore, Maryland 21218
(301) 235-5245

First published in 1969

SUBSCRIPTION DATA
Issues and rates: Published three times per year.
   Average paid circulation: 20,000; 4,000 controlled
   Annual rate(s): Individuals $4.00, Institutions $10.00, Foreign $6.00

EDITORIAL DESCRIPTION
A women's liberation magazine with a thematic focus; past issues have been on such themes as Women in History, Women in Revolution, Women in the Arts, Women as Workers, Sexuality.
Articles per average issue: 20
Audience: General
   Manuscripts accepted in English

MANUSCRIPT INFORMATION
Subject field(s): All kinds of women: Third-World, foreign, ethnic, older women, poor women, organizing women, aging, poetry, health care
Manuscript requirements: See latest issue for style requirements.
   Preferred length: 4000 words or less; 16 pages
   Number of copies to be submitted: 1
   Abstract: No
Author information and reprints: Payment: Reprints only. Copy of issue in which article appears.
   Is simultaneous submission of article to other journals permitted: Yes, if informed and notified as soon as it is accepted by someone else.
   Exclusive manuscript rights between acceptance and publication: Yes
   Copyright: Held by publication.
   Reprints: Not available.

Disposition of manuscript:
  Query letter: No
  Receipt of manuscript acknowledged: Yes
  Decision to publish in: 3-5 months
  Accepted manuscript published in: 1-2 months
  Rejected manuscript returned: Yes, if self-addressed, stamped envelope is sent with manuscript.
  Rejected manuscript criticized: Sometimes
Submit to:
  Material Committee
  (See address above)

WOMEN IN BUSINESS [1582]
9100 Ward Parkway
Kansas City, Missouri 64114
(816) 361-6621

First published in 1949

SUBSCRIPTION DATA
Issues and rates: 9 times per year
  Average paid circulation: 80,000
  Annual rate(s): $7.00
Publisher or Sponsor: American Business Women's Association
Managing Editor: Joanne H. Mordus

EDITORIAL DESCRIPTION
Designed to educate and inform working women of subjects that effect their business and personal lives.
Articles per average issue: 2
  Manuscripts accepted in English

MANUSCRIPT INFORMATION
Subject field(s): Business relations, techniques and products, kitchen, fashion or career guides for the working woman; government regulations which affect women, etc.
Manuscript requirements: No specific style guide.
  Preferred length: 1,500 words maximum
  Number of copies to be submitted: 1
  Abstract: Not necessary.
Author information and reprints: Payment: By publication to author. $.03-$.05 per word.
  Is simultaneous submission of article to other journals permitted: Not permitted.
  Exclusive manuscript rights between acceptance and publication: Yes
  Copyright: Held by publication.
  Reprints: Available at no cost. Flexible Available at cost.
Additional information: Articles about outstanding women are accepted only if the subject is a member of the Association
Disposition of manuscript:
  Query letter: Not necessary.
  Receipt of manuscript acknowledged: No
  Decision to publish in: 2 weeks-2 months
  Accepted manuscript published in: 3-6 months
  Rejected manuscript returned: Yes, if return postage is supplied by author.
  Rejected manuscript criticized: Sometimes

Submit to:
  Joanne H. Mordus
  Editor
  (See address above)

WOMEN STUDIES ABSTRACTS [1583]
P. O. Box 1
Rush, New York 14543
(716) 533-1376

First published in 1972

SUBSCRIPTION DATA
Issues and rates: Published quarterly.
  Average paid circulation: 1,500
  Annual rate(s): Individuals $8.50; Institutions $15.00; Students $7.00

EDITORIAL DESCRIPTION
Contains essays, bibliographies, and abstracts of scholarly articles on women.
Articles per average issue: 1
Audience: Academic, professional
  Manuscripts accepted in English, French, Spanish

MANUSCRIPT INFORMATION
Subject field(s): Education and socialization; sex roles; characteristics and differences; employment; sexuality; mental and physical health; family planning; childbirth; abortion; women's liberation movement
Manuscript requirements: No specific style guide.
  Preferred length: 20-30 pages
  Number of copies to be submitted: 2
  Abstract: Not necessary.
Author information and reprints: Payment: By publication to author. Up to $200.00 per article.
  Is simultaneous submission of article to other journals permitted: Permitted, with knowledge of this publication
  Exclusive manuscript rights between acceptance and publication: Yes
  Copyright: Held by publication.
  Reprints: Available at cost.
Disposition of manuscript:
  Query letter: Not necessary, but advisable.
  Receipt of manuscript acknowledged: Yes
  Decision to publish in: 2 weeks
  Accepted manuscript published in: 4 months
  Rejected manuscript returned: Yes, if return postage is supplied by author.
  Rejected manuscript criticized: Reasons for rejections only
Submit to:
  Sara S. Whaley
  Editor-Publisher
  (See address above)

WOMEN'S STUDIES [1584]
An Interdisciplinary Journal
Gordon and Breach Science Publishers
One Park Avenue
New York, New York 10016
(212) 689-0360

First published in 1972

SUBSCRIPTION DATA
Issues and rates: Published semi-annually.
  Average paid circulation: 800
  Annual rate(s): Individuals $10.00, Institutions $29.00

EDITORIAL DESCRIPTION
Provides a forum for the presentation of scholarship and criticism by and about women in the fields of literature, history, art, sociology, psychology, political science, economics, anthropology, law and the sciences.
Articles per average issue: 10
Audience: Scholars
  Manuscripts accepted in English

MANUSCRIPT INFORMATION
Manuscript requirements: MLA, Style sheet sent on request.
  Preferred length: 5-10 pages
  Number of copies to be submitted: 3
  Abstract: Yes
Author information and reprints: Payment: None.
  Is simultaneous submission of article to other journals permitted: Yes
  Exclusive manuscript rights between acceptance and publication: Yes
  Copyright: Held by publication.
  Reprints: Available
Additional information: Must be original unpublished work not under consideration elsewhere.
Disposition of manuscript:
  Query letter: No
  Receipt of manuscript acknowledged: Yes
  Decision to publish in: 3 months
  Accepted manuscript published in: 1 year
  Rejected manuscript returned: Yes, if self-addressed, stamped envelope is sent with manuscript.
  Rejected manuscript criticized: No
Submit to:
  Wendy Martin
  Editor
  Queen's College
  City University of New York
  Flushing, New York 11367

Science and technology

Science and technology (general)

AMERICAN CERAMIC SOCIETY JOURNAL [1585]
65 Ceramic Drive
Columbus, Ohio 43214
(614) 268-8645

SUBSCRIPTION DATA
Issues and rates: Published monthly.
  Average paid circulation: 9,500
  Annual rate(s): $45.00; Foreign $48.00.
  All include subscription to *Ceramic Bulletin*
Publisher or Sponsor: American Ceramic Society, Inc.
Managing Editor: M. Geraldine Smith

EDITORIAL DESCRIPTION
  Publishes original fundamental research on ceramic materials. Ceramic Abstracts Section offers a broad reference and abstract coverage of the entire ceramic field.
Articles per average issue: 19
Audience: Professional, scientific, research
  Manuscripts accepted in English

MANUSCRIPT INFORMATION
Subject field(s): Physical chemistry, crystal chemistry, high temperature reactions, analytic chemistry, solid state physics, colloid chemistry, materials development, materials properties
Manuscript requirements: Style sheet sent on request.
  Preferred length: 10 pages maximum
  Number of copies to be submitted: Three
  Abstract: Yes
Author information and reprints: Payment: By author to publication. $60.00 per page. Voluntary page charge.
  Is simultaneous submission of article to other journals permitted: No
  Exclusive manuscript rights between acceptance and publication: Yes
  Copyright: Held by publication.
  Reprints: Available, 100 copies on payment of page charge, otherwise rates on publication.
Additional information: Manuscripts receive at least two reviews for technical evaluation.
Disposition of manuscript:
  Query letter: No
  Receipt of manuscript acknowledged: Yes
  Decision to publish in: 3-4 months
  Accepted manuscript published in: 3-4 months
  Rejected manuscript returned: Yes
  Rejected manuscript criticized: Yes
Submit to:
  Margie K. Reser
  Technical Editor
  (See address above)

AMERICAN CONCRETE INSTITUTE JOURNAL [1586]
Box 19150
Detroit, Michigan 48219
(313) 532-2600

First published in 1929

SUBSCRIPTION DATA
Issues and rates: Published monthly.
  Average paid circulation: 16,000
  Annual rate(s): $22.00
Publisher or Sponsor: American Concrete Institute
Managing Editor: Robert G. Wiedyke

EDITORIAL DESCRIPTION
  Contains technical papers on concrete technology, design, construction information.
Articles per average issue: 6
Audience: Engineers, contractors
  Manuscripts accepted in English

MANUSCRIPT INFORMATION
Subject field(s): Concrete technology
Manuscript requirements: Chicago, with modifications
  Preferred length: 6000 words; 20 pages or less
  Number of copies to be submitted: Three
  Abstract: Yes
Author information and reprints: Payment: None.
  Is simultaneous submission of article to other journals permitted: No
  Exclusive manuscript rights between acceptance and publication: Yes
  Copyright: Held by publication.
  Reprints: Available, cost on request
Additional information: Follow ACI Publications Policy.
Disposition of manuscript:
  Query letter: No
  Receipt of manuscript acknowledged: Yes
  Decision to publish in: 3-4 months
  Accepted manuscript published in: 10-12 months
  Rejected manuscript returned: Yes
  Rejected manuscript criticized: No
Submit to:
  Secretary, Technical Activities Committee
  (See address above)

SPECIAL STIPULATIONS
  All technical material is refereed by Technical Activities Committee reviewers expert in field of submitted manuscript.

AMERICAN SCIENTIST [1587]
345 Whitney Avenue
New Haven, Connecticut 06511
(203) 624-2566

SUBSCRIPTION DATA
Issues and rates: Published bi-monthly.
  Average paid circulation: 130,000
  Annual rate(s): $12.00, Foreign $14.00
Publisher or Sponsor: The Society of the Sigma Xi, The Scientific Research Company of North America, Inc.

EDITORIAL DESCRIPTION
  Contains reports, scientific research and review papers; book reviews and society news.

MANUSCRIPT INFORMATION
Subject field(s): Physical sciences, earth sciences, life sciences, behavioral sciences, mathematics, computer science, history of science, engineering
Manuscript requirements: Chicago
  Preferred length: 8000 words; 20 to 25 pages
  Number of copies to be submitted: Two
Author information and reprints: Payment: None.
  Is simultaneous submission of article to other journals permitted: No
  Exclusive manuscript rights between acceptance and publication: Yes
  Copyright: Held by publication.
  Reprints: Available; 100 free, more at cost
Disposition of manuscript:
  Receipt of manuscript acknowledged: Yes
  Decision to publish in: 4 to 6 weeks
  Accepted manuscript published in: 1 or 2 issues after acceptance
  Rejected manuscript returned: Yes, if return postage is supplied by author.
  Rejected manuscript criticized: Sometimes
Submit to:
  Jane V. Olson
  Editor
  (See address above)

ARCHIVE FOR HISTORY OF EXACT SCIENCES [1588]
Springer Verlag
175 Fifth Avenue
New York, New York 10010

SUBSCRIPTION DATA
  Annual rate(s): DM 136 per volume
Managing Editor: C. Truesdell

EDITORIAL DESCRIPTION
  Nourishes historical research meeting the standards of the mathematical sciences; gives rapid and full publication to writings of exceptional depth, scope and permanence; advances the course of mathematical thought and precise theory of nature.
Audience: Mathematicians, physical scientists
  Manuscripts accepted in English, French, German, Italian, Latin, Spanish

MANUSCRIPT INFORMATION
Subject field(s): Primarily mathematics and natural philosophy, but also some experimentation in the physical sciences
Manuscript requirements: See latest issue for style requirements. Chapter 609, *The*

Complete Plain Words by Sir Ernest Gowers
Preferred length: As required
Number of copies to be submitted: 2
Abstract: Yes. In English
Author information and reprints: Payment: Reprints only. 75 offprints
Is simultaneous submission of article to other journals permitted: Not permitted.
Exclusive manuscript rights between acceptance and publication: Yes
Copyright: Held by publication.
Additional information: Authors should reflect clear thought through chosen, specific words composed in direct, responsible, and active syntax. The vague and verbose style called "scholarly" is not acceptable.
Submit to:
A. Aaboe;
M. J. Klein
Editorial Board members
Department of History of Science and Medicine
Yale University
New Haven, Connecticut

BRITISH INTERPLANETARY SOCIETY JOURNAL [1589]

12 Bessborough Gardens
London SW1V 2JJ, England
(01) 828-9371

First published in 1934

SUBSCRIPTION DATA
Issues and rates: Published monthly.
  Average paid circulation: 1500
  Annual rate(s): $33.00
Publisher or Sponsor: British Interplanetary Society
Managing Editor: G. V. Groves

EDITORIAL DESCRIPTION
  Contains papers on space research and space technology.
Articles per average issue: 8
Audience: General scientific and technical
  Manuscripts accepted in English

MANUSCRIPT INFORMATION
Subject field(s): Advanced propulsion systems, aerospace vehicles, extraterrestrial life, ground testing facilities, guidance and control, instrumentation for space vehicles, interstellar communication, life-support systems, lunar and planetary research, navigation in space, orbital theory, rocket propulsion, space environment, space medicine
Manuscript requirements: See latest issue for style requirements.
  Preferred length: 3500-5000 words
  Number of copies to be submitted: One
  Abstract: No
Author information and reprints: Payment: None.
  Is simultaneous submission of article to other journals permitted: No
  Exclusive manuscript rights between acceptance and publication: Yes

Copyright: Held by publication.
Reprints: Available at cost.
Disposition of manuscript:
  Receipt of manuscript acknowledged: yes
  Decision to publish in: One month
  Accepted manuscript published in: Three months
  Rejected manuscript returned: Yes
  Rejected manuscript criticized: Yes
Submit to:
Editor
(See address above)

BULLETIN OF THE ATOMIC SCIENTISTS [1590]

1020-24 East 58th Street
Chicago, Illinois 60637
(312) 363-5225

Previously entitled *Science and Public Affairs*

First published in 1945

SUBSCRIPTION DATA
Issues and rates: 10 issues per year
  Average paid circulation: 20,500; 58 controlled
  Annual rate(s): $10.00; Foreign $12.00
Managing Editor: Richard S. Lewis
Publisher or Sponsor: Educational Foundation for Nuclear Science, Inc.

EDITORIAL DESCRIPTION
  Contains articles and commentaries on the impact of science and technology on public affairs, with emphasis on developments in arms control and disarmament, nuclear energy and the interaction of technology and the environment.

MANUSCRIPT INFORMATION
Subject field(s): Arms control, environment, scientific exploration, science education, technology impact, international development
Manuscript requirements: No specific style guide.
  Preferred length: 3,500 to 4,000 words
  Number of copies to be submitted: Two
Author information and reprints: Payment: None.
  Is simultaneous submission of article to other journals permitted: No
  Exclusive manuscript rights between acceptance and publication: No
  Copyright: Held by publication.
  Reprints: Available at cost
Disposition of manuscript:
  Receipt of manuscript acknowledged: Yes
  Decision to publish in: 30 to 60 days
  Accepted manuscript published in: 30 to 120 days
Submit to:
Editor
(See address above)

CALIFORNIA ACADEMY OF SCIENCES. OCCASIONAL PAPERS [1591]

Golden Gate Park
San Francisco, California 94118
(415) 221-5100 ext. 74

First published in 1890

SUBSCRIPTION DATA
Issues and rates: Irregular
  Average paid circulation: 125; 725 controlled
  Annual rate(s): $7.50
Publisher or Sponsor: California Academy of Sciences

EDITORIAL DESCRIPTION
  Individual papers are published which deal with various aspects of biology and geology; work in systematics predominates.
Articles per average issue: 1
Audience: Scientific
  Manuscripts accepted in English

MANUSCRIPT INFORMATION
Subject field(s): Biology, geology
Manuscript requirements: Style sheet sent on request.
  Preferred length: None
  Number of copies to be submitted: One
  Abstract: Yes
Author information and reprints: Payment: None.
  Is simultaneous submission of article to other journals permitted: No
  Exclusive manuscript rights between acceptance and publication: Yes
  Copyright: No copyright held
  Reprints: Available; 50 free, cost for more depends on length of paper
Disposition of manuscript:
  Query letter: Yes
  Receipt of manuscript acknowledged: Yes
  Decision to publish in: 6 weeks
  Accepted manuscript published in: 12 months
  Rejected manuscript returned: Yes
  Rejected manuscript criticized: No
Submit to:
Diana R. Young
Editor
(See address above)

SPECIAL STIPULATIONS
  Normally, authors must be members of the Academy.

CALIFORNIA ACADEMY OF SCIENCES. PROCEEDINGS [1592]

Golden Gate Park
San Francisco, California 94118
(415) 221-5100 ext. 74

First published in 1854

SUBSCRIPTION DATA
Issues and rates: Irregular
  Average paid circulation: 175; 725 controlled

Science and technology (general)

Annual rate(s): $7.50
Publisher or Sponsor: California Academy of Sciences

EDITORIAL DESCRIPTION

Contains papers dealing with biology and geology; emphasis on systematic studies.
Articles per average issue: 1
Audience: Scientific
Manuscripts accepted in English

MANUSCRIPT INFORMATION

Subject field(s): Biology, geology
Manuscript requirements: Style sheet sent on request.
Preferred length: None
Number of copies to be submitted: One
Abstract: Yes
Author information and reprints: Payment: None.
Is simultaneous submission of article to other journals permitted: No
Exclusive manuscript rights between acceptance and publication: Yes
Copyright: Not copyrighted
Reprints: Available; 50 free, cost of others depends on length
Disposition of manuscript:
Query letter: Yes
Receipt of manuscript acknowledged: Yes
Decision to publish in: 6 weeks
Accepted manuscript published in: 12 months
Rejected manuscript returned: Yes
Rejected manuscript criticized: No
Submit to:
Diana R. Young
Editor
(See address above)

SPECIAL STIPULATIONS

Authors must be Academy members or treat Academy material.

COASTAL RESEARCH [1593]

Notes
Geology Department
Florida State University
Tallahassee, Florida 32306
(904) 644-3208

First published in 1962

SUBSCRIPTION DATA

Issues and rates: Published three times per year.
Average paid circulation: 400; 500 controlled
Annual rate(s): $3.00, Foreign $4.00
Publisher or Sponsor: Florida State University, Geology Department

EDITORIAL DESCRIPTION

Publishes news and technical reports on coastal research in many areas.
Articles per average issue: 5-10
Audience: Professional
Manuscripts accepted in English

MANUSCRIPT INFORMATION

Subject field(s): Geology, biology, geography, meteorology, climatology, engineering, archeology, economics, law, ecology, planning, history
Manuscript requirements: No specific style guide.
Preferred length: 1000-1500 words
Number of copies to be submitted: One
Abstract: No
Author information and reprints: Payment: None.
Is simultaneous submission of article to other journals permitted: Yes
Exclusive manuscript rights between acceptance and publication: No
Reprints: Not available.
Additional information: No illustrations or lengthy bibliographies; AGI reference style.
Disposition of manuscript:
Receipt of manuscript acknowledged: Yes
Decision to publish in: 1-3 months
Accepted manuscript published in: 2-6 months
Rejected manuscript returned: Yes
Rejected manuscript criticized: No
Submit to:
W. F. Tanner
Editor
(See address above)

COMBUSTION AND FLAME [1594]

The Journal of the Combustion Institute
American Elsevier Publishing Co., Inc.
52 Vanderbilt Avenue
New York, New York 10017
(212)686-5277

First published in 1957

SUBSCRIPTION DATA

Issues and rates: Published bi-monthly.
Average paid circulation: 1,800
Annual rate(s): $52.00; Foreign $52.00; Institutions $52.00; Members $18.00
Publisher or Sponsor: The Combustion Institute
Managing Editor: Howard B. Palmer

EDITORIAL DESCRIPTION

For the communication of research in combustion science, it presents experimental and theoretical results in all areas concerned with flames, explosions, and detonations.
Articles per average issue: 15
Audience: Researchers in the combustion process
Manuscripts accepted in English

MANUSCRIPT INFORMATION

Subject field(s): Flame ignition, inhibition, propagation, stability, structure; deflagration and detonation; fire phenomena; pollution from combustion; kinetics and mechanisms of combustion reactions; heterogeneous combustion; heat transfer and radiation in combustion; propellants; fluid dynamics and combustion; electrical aspects of flames.
Manuscript requirements: See latest issue for style requirements.
Preferred length: 2,500 to 4,500 words; 10 to 20 pages
Number of copies to be submitted: 3
Abstract: Yes. One paragraph of 100 to 300 words
Author information and reprints: Payment: None.
Is simultaneous submission of article to other journals permitted: Not permitted.
Exclusive manuscript rights between acceptance and publication: Yes
Copyright: American Elsevier Publishing Co., Inc.
Reprints: Available at no cost. 50
Disposition of manuscript:
Query letter: Not necessary.
Receipt of manuscript acknowledged: Yes
Decision to publish in: 1 to 3 months
Accepted manuscript published in: 4 to 5 months
Rejected manuscript returned: Yes, with return postage paid by publication.
Rejected manuscript criticized: Yes
Submit to:
Professor Howard B. Palmer
Editor
Fuel Science Section, M. I. Building
Pennsylvania State University
University Park, Pennsylvania 16802
(814) 865-6512

DESALINATION [1595]

An International Journal on the Science and Technology of Desalination and Water Purification
Elsevier/Excerpta Medica/North Holland
P. O. Box 211
Amsterdam, The Netherlands

First published in 1966

SUBSCRIPTION DATA

Issues and rates: Published bi-monthly.
Annual rate(s): Institutions $102.30 per volume
Managing Editor: Miriam Balaban

EDITORIAL DESCRIPTION

Covers the broad area of water purification, pollution control, desalination techniques as applied to food, chemical, drugs and metallurgy.
Articles per average issue: 8
Audience: Desalination researchers and engineers
Manuscripts accepted in English

MANUSCRIPT INFORMATION

Manuscript requirements: See latest issue for style requirements.
Preferred length: As required
Number of copies to be submitted: 2
Abstract: Yes. Not to exceed 100 words
Author information and reprints: Payment: None.
Is simultaneous submission of article to other journals permitted:
Exclusive manuscript rights between acceptance and publication: Yes
Copyright: Held by publication.
Reprints: Available at cost.
Disposition of manuscript:
Query letter: Not necessary, but advisable.

Receipt of manuscript acknowledged: Yes
Decision to publish in: 2 weeks
Accepted manuscript published in: 4 months
Rejected manuscript returned: Yes, with return postage paid by publication.
Rejected manuscript criticized: Reasons for rejections only
Submit to:
Miriam Balaban
Editor
P. O. Box 4122
Jerusalem, Israel

H. C. Simpson
Regional Editor for Europe
Department of Thermodynamics and Fluid Mechanics
University of Strathclyde
Montrose Street
Glasgow, Scotland

EXPLOSIVES AND PYROTECHNICS [1596]
Franklin Institute Research Laboratories
Philadelphia, Pennsylvania 19103
(215) 448-1236

First published in 1968

SUBSCRIPTION DATA
Issues and rates: Published monthly.
  Average paid circulation: Not available.
  Annual rate(s): $19.00; Foreign $17.00 plus $7.00 airmail postage
Publisher or Sponsor: Franklin Institute Research Laboratories

EDITORIAL DESCRIPTION
A technical newsletter of explosives, pyrotechnics and their devices.
Articles per average issue: 1
Audience: Professional
  Manuscripts accepted in English

MANUSCRIPT INFORMATION
Subject field(s): Explosives, pyrotechnics, blasting, aerospace, safety, related military topics
Manuscript requirements: See latest issue for style requirements.
  Preferred length: 250-500 words
  Number of copies to be submitted: One
  Abstract: No
Author information and reprints: Payment: None.
  Is simultaneous submission of article to other journals permitted: Yes
  Exclusive manuscript rights between acceptance and publication: No
  Copyright: Held by The Institute
Additional information: Manuscripts typewritten, double-spaced, with illustrations in camera-ready form.
Disposition of manuscript:
  Query letter: No
  Receipt of manuscript acknowledged: No
  Decision to publish in: 1 month
  Accepted manuscript published in: 1-4 months

Rejected manuscript returned: No
Rejected manuscript criticized: No
Submit to:
Gunther Cohn
Editor
(See address above)

FLORIDA SCIENTIST [1597]
Quarterly Journal of the Florida Academy of Sciences
810 East Rollins Street
Orlando, Florida 32803
(305) 275-2141

Previously entitled *Quarterly Journal*

First published in 1936

SUBSCRIPTION DATA
Issues and rates: Published quarterly.
  Average paid circulation: 1000
  Annual rate(s): $10.00
Publisher or Sponsor: Florida Academy of Sciences

EDITORIAL DESCRIPTION
Publishes original research articles in any field of science.
Articles per average issue: 12
Audience: Scientific
  Manuscripts accepted in English

MANUSCRIPT INFORMATION
Subject field(s): Scientific research
Manuscript requirements: CBE, See latest issue for style requirements.
  Preferred length: 1-20 pages
  Number of copies to be submitted: Two
  Abstract: Yes
Author information and reprints: Payment: By author to publication. Page charge on tables and plates.
  Is simultaneous submission of article to other journals permitted: No
  Exclusive manuscript rights between acceptance and publication: Yes
  Reprints: Available at printer's cost
Additional information: Members of the Academy are given preference.
Disposition of manuscript:
  Query letter: No
  Receipt of manuscript acknowledged: Yes
  Decision to publish in: 3 months
  Accepted manuscript published in: 6-12 months
  Rejected manuscript returned: Yes
  Rejected manuscript criticized: Yes
Submit to:
Harvey A. Miller
Editor
(See address above)

GEORGIA ACADEMY OF SCIENCE BULLETIN [1598]
Department of Biology
Georgia State University
Atlanta, Georgia 30303
(404) 658-3107

SUBSCRIPTION DATA
Issues and rates: Published quarterly.

Average paid circulation: 950; 150 controlled
Annual rate(s): $5.00
Publisher or Sponsor: Georgia Academy of Science

EDITORIAL DESCRIPTION
Contains articles reporting original scientific research. Authors do not have to be members of the Georgia Academy of Science.
Articles per average issue: 7
Audience: Scientific
  Manuscripts accepted in English

MANUSCRIPT INFORMATION
Subject field(s): Biology, chemistry, earth sciences, physics, mathematics, engineering, psychology, medicine, philosophy, history of science, anthropology, archaeology, science education
Manuscript requirements: See latest issue for style requirements.
  Preferred length: 15 pages
  Number of copies to be submitted: Two
  Abstract: A summary
Author information and reprints: Payment: None.
  Is simultaneous submission of article to other journals permitted: No
  Exclusive manuscript rights between acceptance and publication: Yes
  Copyright: Held by publication.
  Reprints: Available, cost depends on length.
Disposition of manuscript:
  Query letter: No
  Receipt of manuscript acknowledged: Yes
  Decision to publish in: Six weeks
  Accepted manuscript published in: Six months
  Rejected manuscript returned: Yes
  Rejected manuscript criticized: Yes
Submit to:
Marvin D. Whitehead
Editor
(See address above)

HIGH SPEED GROUND TRANSPORTATION JOURNAL [1599]
Box 4824, Duke Station
Durham, North Carolina 27704
(919) 477-7801

First published in 1967

SUBSCRIPTION DATA
Issues and rates: Published three times per year.
  Annual rate(s): $45.00, Foreign $46.50
Publisher or Sponsor: Planning Transport Associates, Inc.

EDITORIAL DESCRIPTION
Contains articles on the sociological, psychological, planning, engineering, legal, environmental, economic aspects of ground transportation.
Articles per average issue: 10
Audience: Professional governmental
  Manuscripts accepted in English

MANUSCRIPT INFORMATION
Manuscript requirements: Style sheet sent on request.
  Preferred length: 10,000 words
  Number of copies to be submitted: Two
  Abstract: Yes
Author information and reprints: Payment: None.
  Is simultaneous submission of article to other journals permitted: No
  Exclusive manuscript rights between acceptance and publication: Yes
  Copyright: Held by publication.
  Reprints: Available, by order, 100 minimum
Additional information: All papers are reviewed.
Disposition of manuscript:
  Query letter: No
  Receipt of manuscript acknowledged: Yes
  Decision to publish in: 1-2 months
  Accepted manuscript published in: 5-8 months
  Rejected manuscript returned: Yes
  Rejected manuscript criticized: Yes
Submit to:
  James J. Murray
  Editor
  (See address above)

HIGH TEMPERATURE SCIENCE [1600]
An International Journal
Academic Press, Inc.
111 Fifth Avenue
New York, New York 10003
(212) 677-6713

SUBSCRIPTION DATA
Issues and rates: Published bi-monthly.
  Annual rate(s): $42.50; Foreign $47.50

EDITORIAL DESCRIPTION
Publishes articles that treat of original studies in all areas of high-temperature science

MANUSCRIPT INFORMATION
Subject field(s): Chemistry, ceramics, metallurgy, physics and the various types of engineering; also brief communications which present unusual new results or novel viewpoints on important high-temperature problems.
Manuscript requirements: See latest issue for style requirements.
  Preferred length: Brief communications: not to exceed 1000 words
  Number of copies to be submitted: Three
  Copyright: Held by publication.
Submit to:
  John L. Margrave
  Editor
  Department of Chemistry
  Rice University
  Houston, Texas 77001

THE INFO JOURNAL [1601]
Science and the Unknown
P.O. Box 367
Arlington, Virginia 22210
(703) 538-1263

First published in 1967

SUBSCRIPTION DATA
Issues and rates: Published quarterly.
  Average paid circulation: 2,000
  Annual rate(s): $6.00; Foreign $7.00
Publisher or Sponsor: The International Fortean Organization (INFO)

EDITORIAL DESCRIPTION
Contains articles on the sciences and philosophy of science; Forteana; "cryptoscience" and the growing fringes of knowledge; all natural phenomena of controversial nature. Not interested in sensationalism or material lacking any useful references; ideas presented may be highly speculative but thoughtful scholarship is always required; the journal is first and foremost a forum for skeptical expression.
Articles per average issue: 5
Audience: Scientific, general
  Manuscripts accepted in English

MANUSCRIPT INFORMATION
Subject field(s): Forteana; current science problems; historical subjects; skeptical essays; astronomy and space research; biology (evolutionary theory, exobiology, zoological mysteries, etc.); archaeology; earth sciences; cosmology; psychic phenomena, poltergeists, etc.; the sociology of science
Manuscript requirements: No specific style guide.
  Preferred length: 2,000-5,000 words
  Number of copies to be submitted: One
  Abstract: Not necessary
Author information and reprints: Payment: By publication to author. Payment by arrangement, usually limited to contributor's copies.
  Is simultaneous submission of article to other journals permitted: No
  Exclusive manuscript rights between acceptance and publication: Yes
  Copyright: Held by author.
  Reprints: Available, cost on application
Disposition of manuscript:
  Query letter: No
  Receipt of manuscript acknowledged: No
  Decision to publish in: 2-6 weeks
  Accepted manuscript published in: Varies
  Rejected manuscript returned: Yes
  Rejected manuscript criticized: Yes
Submit to:
  Paul J. Willis
  Secretary-Editor
  (See address above)

ISRAEL JOURNAL OF TECHNOLOGY [1602]
P.O.B. 801
Jerusalem, Israel 91000
227375

Previously entitled *Bulletin of the Research Council, Section C*

SUBSCRIPTION DATA
Issues and rates: Published semi-monthly.
  Average paid circulation: 650
  Annual rate(s): $36.00
Publisher or Sponsor: Research Council of Israel
Managing Editor: L. Lester

EDITORIAL DESCRIPTION
Contains articles on engineering, technology, applied mathematics.
Articles per average issue: 8
Audience: Scientific
  Manuscripts accepted in English

MANUSCRIPT INFORMATION
Manuscript requirements: See latest issue for style requirements.
  Preferred length: About 20 pages
  Number of copies to be submitted: Three
  Abstract: Yes
Author information and reprints: Payment: None.
  Is simultaneous submission of article to other journals permitted: No
  Exclusive manuscript rights between acceptance and publication: Yes
  Copyright: Held by publication.
  Reprints: Available, cost depends on length
Additional information: Typewritten, double-spaced
Disposition of manuscript:
  Query letter: No
  Receipt of manuscript acknowledged: Yes
  Decision to publish in: 6 months
  Accepted manuscript published in: 9 months
  Rejected manuscript returned: Yes
  Rejected manuscript criticized: Yes
Submit to:
  Editor
  (See address above)

JOURNAL OF ELASTICITY [1603]
Academic Book Services Holland
P. O. Box 66
Groningen, The Netherlands

First published in 1970

SUBSCRIPTION DATA
Issues and rates: Published quarterly.
  Annual rate(s): Institutions Dfl. 135.00

EDITORIAL DESCRIPTION
Reports original and significant discoveries in elasticity.
Articles per average issue: 5
Audience: Professional, academic
  Manuscripts accepted in English

MANUSCRIPT INFORMATION
Manuscript requirements: See latest issue for style requirements.
  Preferred length: 20 pages
  Number of copies to be submitted: 2
  Abstract: Yes

Author information and reprints: Payment: Reprints only. 50 reprints
Is simultaneous submission of article to other journals permitted: Not permitted.
Exclusive manuscript rights between acceptance and publication: Yes
Copyright: Held by publication.
Reprints: Available at cost.
Disposition of manuscript:
Query letter: Not necessary, but advisable.
Receipt of manuscript acknowledged: Yes
Decision to publish in: 2 months
Accepted manuscript published in: 3 months
Rejected manuscript returned: Yes, if return postage is supplied by author.
Rejected manuscript criticized: Sometimes
Submit to:
Marvin Stippes
Editor
Department of Theoretical and Applied Mechanics
University of Illinois
Urbana, Illinois 61801

JOURNAL OF FOOD SCIENCE [1604]
221 North LaSalle Street
Chicago, Illinois 60601
(312) 782-8424

Previously entitled *Food Research*

First published in 1936

SUBSCRIPTION DATA
Issues and rates: 6 times per year
Average paid circulation: 10,000
Annual rate(s): $30.00; Foreign $35.00
Publisher or Sponsor: Institute of Food Technologists
Managing Editor: Bernard Schukraft

EDITORIAL DESCRIPTION
Publishes papers which report the results of original research related to foods. It contains two major sections: Basic Science and Applied Science and Engineering.
Articles per average issue: 55
Audience: Professional
Manuscripts accepted in English

MANUSCRIPT INFORMATION
Subject field(s): Basic food science, applied food science, food engineering
Manuscript requirements: Style sheet sent on request.
Preferred length: None
Number of copies to be submitted: Three
Abstract: Yes, see style guide
Author information and reprints: Payment: By author to publication. $50 per page. Unless such payment would be a hardship.
Is simultaneous submission of article to other journals permitted: No
Exclusive manuscript rights between acceptance and publication: Yes
Copyright: Held by publication.
Reprints: Available at cost.

Disposition of manuscript:
Query letter: No
Receipt of manuscript acknowledged: Yes
Decision to publish in: 2 months
Accepted manuscript published in: 6 months
Rejected manuscript returned: Yes
Rejected manuscript criticized: Yes
Submit to:
Bernard J. Liska
Scientific Editor
P.O. Box 3067
Lafayette, Indiana 47906
(317) 743-1176

JOURNAL OF FORENSIC SCIENCES [1605]
The Official Publication of the American Academy of Forensic Sciences
1916 Race Street
Philadelphia, Pennsylvania 19103
(215) 569-4200

First published in 1954

SUBSCRIPTION DATA
Issues and rates: Published quarterly.
Average paid circulation: 2,000
Annual rate(s): $33.00
Publisher or Sponsor: American Society for Testing and Materials
Managing Editor: S. Etris

EDITORIAL DESCRIPTION
Publishes original investigations, observations, and research articles, as well as reviews, in the various branches of the forensic sciences, including forensic pathology, toxicology, psychiatry, immunology, jurisprudence, criminalistics, questioned documents, anthropology and odontology. Similar articles dealing with forensic-oriented aspects of the social sciences are also considered.
Articles per average issue: 15
Manuscripts accepted in English

MANUSCRIPT INFORMATION
Subject field(s): Forensic pathology, forensic biology, toxicology, criminalistics, questioned documents, jurisprudence, forensic odontology, physical anthropology, forensic psychiatry
Manuscript requirements: ASMT, Style sheet sent on request.
Preferred length: 6,000 to 9,000 words; 25 to 35 pages
Number of copies to be submitted: Four
Abstract: Yes
Author information and reprints: Payment: None. Three copies of issue in which article appears.
Is simultaneous submission of article to other journals permitted: No
Exclusive manuscript rights between acceptance and publication: Yes
Copyright: Held by publication.
Reprints: Available at cost
Additional information: Manuscripts should be in the proper style, typewritten, double-spaced, with legends for photographs, references, tables, and charts on separate pages. Glossy prints of photographs and original line drawings of any illustrations should accompany original manuscript.
Disposition of manuscript:
Receipt of manuscript acknowledged: Yes
Decision to publish in: 2-3 months
Accepted manuscript published in: 6-9 months
Rejected manuscript returned: Yes
Rejected manuscript criticized: Sometimes
Submit to:
Charles J. Stahl, III
Editor
Armed Forces Institute of Pathology
Washington, D.C. 20306
(202) 576-3287

JOURNAL OF MATERIALS SCIENCE [1606]
Book Publishers Ltd., Periodicals Department
North Way
Andover, Hampshire SP10 5BE, England
65563

SUBSCRIPTION DATA
Issues and rates: Published monthly.
Annual rate(s): £42.25; Foreign $108.00
Managing Editor: B. Noel Hughes

EDITORIAL DESCRIPTION
Provides a forum for all kinds of materials scientists to learn more effectively from each other.
Articles per average issue: 20
Audience: Research scientists
Manuscripts accepted in English

MANUSCRIPT INFORMATION
Subject field(s): All aspects of materials science and related disciplines
Manuscript requirements: Style sheet sent on request.
Preferred length: None
Number of copies to be submitted: 1
Abstract: Not necessary.
Author information and reprints: Payment: None.
Is simultaneous submission of article to other journals permitted: Not permitted.
Exclusive manuscript rights between acceptance and publication: Yes
Copyright: Held by publication.
Reprints: Available at cost.
Disposition of manuscript:
Query letter: Not necessary.
Receipt of manuscript acknowledged: Yes
Decision to publish in: Varies
Submit to:
Editorial Board
(See address above)

JOURNAL OF PAINT TECHNOLOGY [1607]
121 South Broad Street
Philadelphia, Pennsylvania 19107
(215) 545-1507

Previously entitled *Official Digest*

Science and technology (general)

First published in 1922

SUBSCRIPTION DATA

Issues and rates: Published monthly.
Average paid circulation: 8,600
Annual rate(s): $16.00; Foreign $22.00
Publisher or Sponsor: Federation of Societies for Paint Technology

EDITORIAL DESCRIPTION

Publishes technical and scientific articles relating to various areas of paint technology, research and manufacture, supplemented by general news of interest to the industry, as well as Federation and educational news.
Articles per average issue: 6
Audience: Research, professional
Manuscripts accepted in English

MANUSCRIPT INFORMATION

Subject field(s): Color and color measuring, corrosion, grinding and dispersion, fire retardance, formulation of coatings, raw materials analysis, testing methods, safety, exposure studies of pigments, viscosity measurements
Manuscript requirements: Style sheet sent on request.
Preferred length: 2500 words; 15 pages
Number of copies to be submitted: Four
Abstract: Yes, 75-100 words
Author information and reprints: Payment: None.
Is simultaneous submission of article to other journals permitted: No
Exclusive manuscript rights between acceptance and publication: Yes
Copyright: Held by publication.
Reprints: Available at cost.
Additional information: Manuscripts should be submitted in accepted style, with captions, references, tables, charts and appendices on separate sheets.
Disposition of manuscript:
Query letter: Yes
Receipt of manuscript acknowledged: Yes
Decision to publish in: 3 to 4 months
Accepted manuscript published in: 2 months
Rejected manuscript returned: Yes
Rejected manuscript criticized: Yes
Submit to:
Thomas A. Kocis
Editor
(See address above)

SPECIAL STIPULATIONS

Editorial Review Committee, composed of experts in various areas of paint technology and manufacture, evaluates scientific merit and timeliness of all manuscripts submitted for publication.

JOURNAL OF TESTING AND EVALUATION [1608]

1916 Race Street
Philadelphia, Pennsylvania 19103
(215) 569-4200

Previously entitled *Journal of Materials,* 1966

First published in 1973

SUBSCRIPTION DATA

Issues and rates: Published bi-monthly.
Average paid circulation: 3000
Annual rate(s): $18.00, Members $14.40
Publisher or Sponsor: American Society for Testing and Materials

EDITORIAL DESCRIPTION

Contains original research and some special surveys on the testing and evaluation of materials, products, systems, and services.
Articles per average issue: 10
Audience: Professional
Manuscripts accepted in English

MANUSCRIPT INFORMATION

Subject field(s): Testing, measurement, testing techniques, standard tests, test data on materials, product evaluation, systems evaluation
Manuscript requirements: ASMT
Preferred length: 4500 words; 30 pages
Number of copies to be submitted: Four, one with original photos and drawings
Abstract: Yes
Author information and reprints: Payment: None.
Is simultaneous submission of article to other journals permitted: No
Exclusive manuscript rights between acceptance and publication: Yes
Copyright: Held by publication.
Reprints: Available at cost.
Disposition of manuscript:
Query letter: No
Receipt of manuscript acknowledged: Yes
Decision to publish in: 2 months
Accepted manuscript published in: 6-8 months
Rejected manuscript returned: Yes
Rejected manuscript criticized: Yes
Submit to:
Samuel F. Etris
Editor
(See address above)

LABORATORY ANIMAL SCIENCE [1609]

2317 West Jefferson Street, Suite 208
Joliet, Illinois 60435
(815) 729-1261

Previously entitled *Laboratory Animal Care*

First published in 1951

SUBSCRIPTION DATA

Issues and rates: Published bi-monthly.
Average paid circulation: 3,300; 145 controlled
Annual rate(s): $45.00; Foreign $28.00; Institutions $25.00
Publisher or Sponsor: American Association for Laboratory Animal Science

EDITORIAL DESCRIPTION

Covers the field of laboratory animal production, care and techniques of use including topics ranging from design of animal facilities and equipment to anesthesia and restraint, transportation problems, post-operative care, and the introduction of new species.
Articles per average issue: 20
Audience: Professional, academic
Manuscripts accepted in English

MANUSCRIPT INFORMATION

Subject field(s): Laboratory animal facility management, animal models, veterinary medicine, animal diseases, animal breeding and reproduction, anesthesia, nutrition, supply purchasing and housing.
Manuscript requirements: See latest issue for style requirements. Style sheet sent on request.
Preferred length: 3-10 journal pages
Number of copies to be submitted: 2
Abstract: Yes
Author information and reprints: Payment: By author to publication. $20.00 per page.
Is simultaneous submission of article to other journals permitted: Permitted, but not encouraged.
Exclusive manuscript rights between acceptance and publication: No
Copyright: Held by the Association
Reprints: Available at cost.
Disposition of manuscript:
Query letter: Not necessary.
Receipt of manuscript acknowledged: Yes
Decision to publish in: 1-4 months
Accepted manuscript published in: 2-6 months
Rejected manuscript returned: Yes, with return postage paid by publication.
Rejected manuscript criticized: Reasons for rejections only
Submit to:
Aaron M. Leash, D.V.M.
Editor
Case Western Reserve University, School of Medicine
2119 Adington Road
Cleveland, Ohio 44106
(216) 368-3490

THE MICROSCOPE [1610]

2 McCrone Mews, Belsize Lane
London NW3 5BG, England
01 435 2282

SUBSCRIPTION DATA

Issues and rates: Published quarterly.
Average paid circulation: 900; 50 controlled
Annual rate(s): £12.00, Foreign $30.00
Managing Editor: G. D. Woodard

EDITORIAL DESCRIPTION

An international journal dedicated to the advancement of light, electron, X-ray, biological, metallographic, mineralogical or chemical microscopy.
Articles per average issue: 8
Audience: Microscopists
Manuscripts accepted in English

MANUSCRIPT INFORMATION

Subject field(s): Microscopy

Manuscript requirements: See latest issue for style requirements.
  Preferred length: 2000 words; 10 pages
  Number of copies to be submitted: Two
  Abstract: Yes.
Author information and reprints: Payment: By author to publication. $24 per page.
  Is simultaneous submission of article to other journals permitted: No
  Exclusive manuscript rights between acceptance and publication: Yes
  Copyright: Held by publication.
  Reprints: Available, 100 pieces - $2.00 per page, if paying page charges. $10.00 per page, if not.
Disposition of manuscript:
  Query letter:
  Receipt of manuscript acknowledged: Yes
  Decision to publish in: 2 months
  Accepted manuscript published in: 3 months
  Rejected manuscript returned: Yes
  Rejected manuscript criticized: Yes
Submit to:
  W. C. McCrone
  Editor
  2820 South Michigan Avenue
  Chicago, Illinois 60616
  (312) 842-7100

NATIONAL ACADEMY OF SCIENCES OF THE UNITED STATES PROCEEDINGS* [1611]
2101 Constitution Avenue
Washington, D.C. 20418
(202) 961-1871

SUBSCRIPTION DATA
Issues and rates: Published monthly.
  Average paid circulation: 8,200; 900 controlled
  Annual rate(s): $35.00
Publisher or Sponsor: National Academy of Sciences

EDITORIAL DESCRIPTION
Contains papers in all the sciences, major portion of which are the biological sciences.

MANUSCRIPT INFORMATION
Subject field(s): Any science named in the titles of the sections of the Academy, also immunology, cell biology, pathology, and statistics
Manuscript requirements: See latest issue for style requirements.
  Preferred length: 5,500 words; 5 printed pages maximum
  Number of copies to be submitted: Two
Author information and reprints: Payment: By author to publication. $75 per page. Members of the Academy have a number of free pages per year.
  Is simultaneous submission of article to other journals permitted: No
  Reprints: Available
Additional information: Any author who is not a member of the Academy must submit his paper through a member.
Disposition of manuscript:
  Receipt of manuscript acknowledged: Yes
  Decision to publish in: Few days
  Accepted manuscript published in: 8 weeks
  Rejected manuscript returned: Yes
Submit to:
  Member of the Academy or Editor
  (See address above)

NATURAL HISTORY MAGAZINE [1612]
Central Park West at 79th Street
New York, New York 10024
(212) 873-1498

First published in 1900

SUBSCRIPTION DATA
Issues and rates: Published monthly.
  Average paid circulation: 350,000
  Annual rate(s): $8, Foreign $9
Publisher or Sponsor: American Museum of Natural History
Managing Editor: Alan Ternes

EDITORIAL DESCRIPTION
Publication contains an ecologically-oriented survey of natural history and anthropology. Also covers environment, earth sciences, and astronomy. Combines well-written, clear, interesting presentations with significant content, preferably related to current research.
Articles per average issue: 8
Audience: Professional, informed laymen
  Manuscripts accepted in English

MANUSCRIPT INFORMATION
Subject field(s): Natural history, wildlife, ecology, anthropology, astronomy, earth sciences, environment, human ecology
Manuscript requirements: Chicago See latest issue for style requirements.
  Preferred length: 2,000-3,500 words
  Number of copies to be submitted: Two
  Abstract: Not necessary
Author information and reprints: Payment: By publication to author. $300-$500 per article.
  Is simultaneous submission of article to other journals permitted: No
  Exclusive manuscript rights between acceptance and publication: Yes
  Copyright: Held by publication.
  Reprints: Available, 25 free tear sheets
Additional information: Need beautiful illustrations, preferably in color; 35mm transparencies welcome, if sharp and well exposed.
Disposition of manuscript:
  Query letter: No, but helpful
  Receipt of manuscript acknowledged: Yes
  Decision to publish in: 1-4 weeks
  Accepted manuscript published in: Varies
  Rejected manuscript returned: Yes
  Rejected manuscript criticized: No
Submit to:
  Editor
  (See address above)

NATURE [1613]
Macmillan Journals Ltd.
Brunel Road
Basingstoke, Hampshire, England
(01) 836-6633

First published in 1869

SUBSCRIPTION DATA
Issues and rates: Published weekly.
  Average paid circulation: 20,000
  Annual rate(s): £22.00; Pan-Am £28.00
Managing Editor: Dr. David Davies

EDITORIAL DESCRIPTION
An international journal of general science
Articles per average issue: 40
Audience: Professional scientists
  Manuscripts accepted in English

MANUSCRIPT INFORMATION
Subject field(s): All sciences
Manuscript requirements: See latest issue for style requirements.
  Preferred length: 1,000 words
  Number of copies to be submitted: 3
  Abstract: Not necessary.
Author information and reprints: Payment: None.
  Is simultaneous submission of article to other journals permitted: Not permitted.
  Exclusive manuscript rights between acceptance and publication: Yes
  Copyright: Held by publication
  Reprints: Available at cost.
Disposition of manuscript:
  Query letter: Not necessary.
  Receipt of manuscript acknowledged: Yes
  Decision to publish in: 1 month
  Accepted manuscript published in: 3 months
  Rejected manuscript returned: No
  Rejected manuscript criticized: Sometimes
Submit to:
  Editor
  4 Little Essex Street
  London, England
  (01) 836-6633

NORTHWEST SCIENCE [1614]
Washington State University Press
Pullman, Washington 99163
(509) 335-3518

First published in 1926

SUBSCRIPTION DATA
Issues and rates: Published quarterly.
  Average paid circulation: 1000
  Annual rate(s): $5.00
Publisher or Sponsor: Northwest Scientific Association
Managing Editor: Bruce Ettling

EDITORIAL DESCRIPTION
Contains articles based upon research carried out in or of interest to scholars in the Pacific Northwest.
Articles per average issue: 6

Science and technology (general)

Audience: Scientific
  Manuscripts accepted in English

MANUSCRIPT INFORMATION
Subject field(s): Zoology, forestry, geology, agronomy, wildlife management, anthropology
Manuscript requirements: Style sheet sent on request.
  Preferred length: 3000-5000 words; 10-20 pages
  Number of copies to be submitted: Two
  Abstract: Yes
Author information and reprints: Payment: None.
  Is simultaneous submission of article to other journals permitted: No
  Exclusive manuscript rights between acceptance and publication: No
  Copyright: Not copyrighted.
  Reprints: Available, supplied at cost.
Disposition of manuscript:
  Query letter: No
  Receipt of manuscript acknowledged: Yes
  Decision to publish in: 3-6 months
  Accepted manuscript published in: 6-9 months
  Rejected manuscript returned: Yes
  Rejected manuscript criticized: Yes
Submit to:
  Bruce V. Ettling
  Editor
  (See address above)
  (509) 335-4525

THE OHIO JOURNAL OF SCIENCE [1615]
Ohio Academy of Science
445 King Avenue
Columbus, Ohio 43201
(614) 299-9097

SUBSCRIPTION DATA
Issues and rates: Published bi-monthly.
  Average paid circulation: 3000
  Annual rate(s): $15.00; Foreign $16.50
Publisher or Sponsor: Ohio Academy of Science

EDITORIAL DESCRIPTION
  Materials published are scientific professional papers and reviews of scientific books.

MANUSCRIPT INFORMATION
Subject field(s): All fields of science
Manuscript requirements: AIBS
  Preferred length: None
  Number of copies to be submitted: Two
Author information and reprints: Payment: By author to publication. requested in cases of excessive length.
  Is simultaneous submission of article to other journals permitted: No
  Exclusive manuscript rights between acceptance and publication: Yes
  Copyright: Not copyrighted
  Reprints: Available at cost
Disposition of manuscript:
  Receipt of manuscript acknowledged: Yes
  Decision to publish in: 2-3 months
  Accepted manuscript published in: 2-4 months
  Rejected manuscript returned: Yes
  Rejected manuscript criticized: Yes
Submit to:
  M.A. Lessler
  Editor
  Department of Physiology
  Ohio State University
  Columbus, Ohio 43210

PACIFIC DISCOVERY [1616]
California Academy of Sciences
Golden Gate Park
San Francisco, California 94118
(415) 221-5100

First published in 1948

SUBSCRIPTION DATA
Issues and rates: Published bi-monthly.
  Average paid circulation: 10,000
  Annual rate(s): $4.00; Foreign $4.75
Publisher or Sponsor: California Academy of Sciences
Managing Editor: George E. Lindsay

EDITORIAL DESCRIPTION
  A semi-popular journal of nature and culture around the world, its purpose is to convey scientific information in a lively, interesting manner.
Articles per average issue: 4-5
Audience: Scientific, informed laymen
  Manuscripts accepted in English

MANUSCRIPT INFORMATION
Subject field(s): Natural history, ecology, anthropology, geology, paleontology, animal behavior, biogeography, taxonomy
Manuscript requirements: Style sheet sent on request.
  Preferred length: 1,500-3,000 words
  Number of copies to be submitted: 1
  Abstract: Not necessary.
Author information and reprints: Payment: By publication to author. $.05 per word. $10.00 per photograph
  Is simultaneous submission of article to other journals permitted: Not permitted.
  Exclusive manuscript rights between acceptance and publication: Yes
  Copyright: First serial rights only
  Reprints: Not available.
Disposition of manuscript:
  Query letter: Not necessary, but advisable.
  Receipt of manuscript acknowledged: Yes
  Decision to publish in: 2-4 months
  Accepted manuscript published in: 2-4 months
  Rejected manuscript returned: Yes, if return postage is supplied by author.
  Rejected manuscript criticized: Reasons for rejections only
Submit to:
  Bruce Finson
  Editor
  (See address above)

PACIFIC SCIENCE [1617]
The University Press of Hawaii
535 Ward Avenue
Honolulu, Hawaii 96814
(808) 537-1581

First published in 1947

SUBSCRIPTION DATA
Issues and rates: Published quarterly.
  Average paid circulation: 860
  Annual rate(s): Institutions $20.00; Individuals $10.00
Publisher or Sponsor: University of Hawaii
Managing Editor: E. Alison Kay

EDITORIAL DESCRIPTION
  A multidisciplinary quarterly which publishes reports of current research in the biological and physical sciences of the Pacific basin.
Articles per average issue: 10
Audience: Academic, scientific
  Manuscripts accepted in English

MANUSCRIPT INFORMATION
Subject field(s): Zoology, botany, oceanography, geology
Manuscript requirements: AIBS
  Number of copies to be submitted: Original and one carbon or photocopy
  Abstract: Optional
Author information and reprints: Payment: None.
  Is simultaneous submission of article to other journals permitted: No
  Exclusive manuscript rights between acceptance and publication: Yes
  Copyright: Held by publication.
  Reprints: Available, 50 reprints free
Additional information: Manuscript should be typed on standard sized, nonerasable, white bond paper, double-spaced throughout. A reasonable number of line drawings and black and white photographs will be accepted. Illustrations in color will be accepted only if the author bears the costs of reproduction of such photographs.
Disposition of manuscript:
  Query letter: Permitted.
  Receipt of manuscript acknowledged: Yes
  Decision to publish in: Varies
  Accepted manuscript published in: 1 year or less
  Rejected manuscript returned: Yes
  Rejected manuscript criticized: Sometimes
Submit to:
  E. Alison Kay
  Editor
  Department of General Science
  University of Hawaii
  Honolulu, Hawaii 96822
  (808) 948-8303

POWDER TECHNOLOGY [1618]
An International Journal on the Science and Technology of Wet and Dry Particulate Systems
Elsevier Sequoia SA
P.O. Box 851 1001 Lausanne 1, Switzerland
(021) 20 73 81

First published in 1967

SUBSCRIPTION DATA
Issues and rates: Published bi-monthly.
  Annual rate(s): SFr. 280.00

EDITORIAL DESCRIPTION
  Publishes papers on all aspects of the formation of particles and their characterization and on the study of systems containing particulate solids; size of particles may range from sub-micron to that of mined or quarried materials.
Articles per average issue: 15
  Manuscripts accepted in English, French, and German (Abstracts in English only)

MANUSCRIPT INFORMATION
Subject field(s): Results of research into the fundamental properties and behavior of powders and granular materials and the exploitation of this knowledge for handling and using them. (The scope of the journal ranges from such fundamental aspects as the surface physics and chemistry of solid particles to essentially practical topics such as design of equipment for processing and storing powders.)
Manuscript requirements: Style sheet sent on request.
  Number of copies to be submitted: 3
  Abstract: Yes.
Author information and reprints: Payment: None.
  Is simultaneous submission of article to other journals permitted: No
  Exclusive manuscript rights between acceptance and publication: Yes
  Copyright: Held by publication.
  Reprints: Available at cost. 25 free to authors.
Disposition of manuscript:
  Query letter:
  Receipt of manuscript acknowledged: Yes
  Decision to publish in: 8 weeks
  Accepted manuscript published in: 6 months
  Rejected manuscript returned: Yes
  Rejected manuscript criticized: Yes
Submit to:
  J. C. Williams
  Editor-in-Chief
  School of Powder Technology
  University of Bradford
  Bradford 7, Yorkshire, England
  (274) 33466

Authors in U.S.A. and Canada should submit their manuscript to:
  A. Lieberman
  Royco Instruments, Inc.
  141 Jefferson Drive
  Menlo Park, California

Authors in Australia to:
  D. F. Kelsall, C.S.I.R.O.
  Division of Chemical Engineering
  P.O. Box 4321
  Melbourne, Victoria Australia

RESEARCH MANAGEMENT [1619]

International Journal of Research Management
Box 8, Saugatuck Station
Westport, Connecticut 06880
(203) 226-6350

First published in 1958

SUBSCRIPTION DATA
Issues and rates: Published bi-monthly.
  Average paid circulation: 300
  Annual rate(s): $18.00; Foreign $20.00; Institutions $18.00; Students $18.00; Members Free; Foreign institutions $20.00
Publisher or Sponsor: The Industrial Research Institute
Managing Editor: H. R. Clauser

EDITORIAL DESCRIPTION
  Devoted exclusively to providing information on all aspects of the management of science, research and development and technology.
Articles per average issue: 7
Audience: Managers of science, research, development and engineering
  Manuscripts accepted in English

MANUSCRIPT INFORMATION
Subject field(s): Planning, budgeting, personnel administration, project selection and management, creativity, organization, science policy. etc.
Manuscript requirements: No specific style guide. See latest issue for style requirements.
  Preferred length: 1,500-4,000 words
  Number of copies to be submitted: 2
  Abstract: Not necessary.
Author information and reprints: Payment: None.
  Is simultaneous submission of article to other journals permitted: Permitted, but not encouraged.
  Exclusive manuscript rights between acceptance and publication: Yes
  Copyright: Held by publication.
  Reprints: Available at cost.
Disposition of manuscript:
  Query letter: Not necessary, but advisable.
  Receipt of manuscript acknowledged: Yes
  Decision to publish in: 6-8 weeks
  Accepted manuscript published in: 6-9 months
  Rejected manuscript returned: Yes, if return postage is supplied by author.
  Rejected manuscript criticized: No
Submit to:
  H. R. Clauser
  Editor
  1 Valley Lane
  Armonk, New York 10504
  (914) 273-8530

RESEARCH/DEVELOPMENT [1620]

Technical Publishing Company
1301 South Grove Avenue
Barrington, Illinois 60110
(312) 381-1840

Previously entitled *Industrial Laboratories*

First published in 1950

SUBSCRIPTION DATA
Issues and rates: Published monthly.
  Average paid circulation: 70,000 controlled
Managing Editor: R.K. Springborn

EDITORIAL DESCRIPTION
  Contains articles describing tools and techniques useful to the scientists and engineers engaged in research and development.
Articles per average issue: 5
Audience: Scientific
  Manuscripts accepted in English

MANUSCRIPT INFORMATION
Manuscript requirements: See latest issue for style requirements.
  Preferred length: None
  Number of copies to be submitted: 2
  Abstract: No
Author information and reprints: Payment: None.
  Is simultaneous submission of article to other journals permitted: No
  Exclusive manuscript rights between acceptance and publication: Yes
  Copyright: Held by publication.
  Reprints: Available
Disposition of manuscript:
  Query letter: No
  Receipt of manuscript acknowledged: Yes
  Decision to publish in: Varies
  Accepted manuscript published in: Varies
  Rejected manuscript returned: Yes
  Rejected manuscript criticized: No
Submit to:
  C. J. Mosbacher
  Editor
  (See address above)

SCIENCE [1621]

1515 Massachusetts Avenue N.W.
Washington, D.C. 20005
(202) 467-4354

First published in 1848

SUBSCRIPTION DATA
Issues and rates: Published weekly.
  Average paid circulation: 152,471
  Annual rate(s): $30.00, Institutions $40.00; Members $21.00
Publisher or Sponsor: American Association for the Advancement of Science
Managing Editor: Robert V. Ormes

EDITORIAL DESCRIPTION
  Publishes short technical reports and longer review articles in the sciences.

Science and technology (general)

Articles per average issue: 3 articles; 10-12 reports
Audience: Academic, scientific, industrial
Manuscripts accepted in English

MANUSCRIPT INFORMATION
Subject field(s): Physical and life sciences
Manuscript requirements: Chicago; other information on request
Preferred length: 20 pages maximum for articles; 7 pages for reports
Number of copies to be submitted: Three
Abstract: Yes, only for reports
Author information and reprints: Payment: None.
Is simultaneous submission of article to other journals permitted: No
Exclusive manuscript rights between acceptance and publication: Yes
Copyright: Held by the American Association for the Advancement of Science
Reprints: Available, 100 free
Additional information: Most articles are solicited, but unsolicited articles are given fair reviews and if the material is excellent, it will be published.
Disposition of manuscript:
Query letter: No
Receipt of manuscript acknowledged: Yes
Decision to publish in: 4-6 weeks
Accepted manuscript published in: 2-3 months
Rejected manuscript returned: Yes
Rejected manuscript criticized: No
Submit to:
Philip H. Abelson
Editor
(See address above)
(202) 467-4350

SCIENCE FOR THE PEOPLE [1622]
9 Walden Street
Jamaica Plain, Massachusetts 02130
(617) 427-0642

First published in 1970

SUBSCRIPTION DATA
Issues and rates: Published bi-monthly.
Average paid circulation: Not available.
Annual rate(s): $12.00
Publisher or Sponsor: Scientists and Engineers for Social and Political Action

EDITORIAL DESCRIPTION
Publishes material describing the anti-human nature of American science and technology and relates efforts to confront and change the present uses of science. Publication reflects belief that science is inherently political, being used by those who have access to it to exploit and control the majority.
Articles per average issue: 6-8
Audience: Scientific
Manuscripts accepted in English

MANUSCRIPT INFORMATION
Subject field(s): Scientific work places, debunking oppressive science

Manuscript requirements: See latest issue for style requirements.
Preferred length: 1,000-3,000 words
Number of copies to be submitted: Six
Abstract: Desirable
Author information and reprints: Payment: None.
Is simultaneous submission of article to other journals permitted: Yes
Exclusive manuscript rights between acceptance and publication: No
Copyright: Held by author.
Reprints: Some are available
Disposition of manuscript:
Receipt of manuscript acknowledged: Yes
Decision to publish in: 2-3 months
Accepted manuscript published in: At least 2 months
Rejected manuscript returned: Yes, if return postage is supplied by author.
Rejected manuscript criticized: Yes
Submit to:
Editorial Collective
(See address above)

SCIENCE FORUM [1623]
A Canadian Journal of Science and Technology
University of Toronto Press, Journals Department
5201 Dufferin Street
Downsview, Ontario M3H 5T8, Canada
(416) 667-7781

First published in 1968

SUBSCRIPTION DATA
Issues and rates: Published bi-monthly.
Average paid circulation: 2,500
Annual rate(s): $10.00

EDITORIAL DESCRIPTION
Deals with the interaction between science, technology, and society, including science policy discussions; provides a forum for the scientific community from the grass roots to the policy makers
Articles per average issue: 4-8 articles; 8-10 comments; 1-2 book reviews
Audience: Professional, academic, governmental, general
Manuscripts accepted in English, French

MANUSCRIPT INFORMATION
Manuscript requirements: See latest issue for style requirements. Style must be straight forward and free of jargon.
Preferred length: 2,500 words for an article; 800 for comments
Number of copies to be submitted: 2
Abstract: Not necessary.
Author information and reprints: Payment: By publication to author. 25.00-$100.00 per article.
Is simultaneous submission of article to other journals permitted: Permitted, but not encouraged.
Exclusive manuscript rights between acceptance and publication: Yes
Reprints: Available at cost.

Disposition of manuscript:
Query letter: Not necessary, but advisable.
Receipt of manuscript acknowledged: Yes
Decision to publish in: 2 months
Accepted manuscript published in: 8-12 months
Rejected manuscript returned: Yes, with return postage paid by publication.
Rejected manuscript criticized: Reasons for rejections only
Submit to:
David C. Spurgeon
Editor
P. O. Box 8500
Ottawa, Ontario K1G 3H9, Canada
966-2321

STATEN ISLAND INSTITUTE OF ARTS & SCIENCES. PROCEEDINGS [1624]
75 Stuyvesant Place
Staten Island, New York 10301
(212) 727-1135

First published in 1883

SUBSCRIPTION DATA
Issues and rates: Published three times per year.
Average paid circulation: 300
Annual rate(s): $7.50
Publisher or Sponsor: Staten Island Institute of Arts and Sciences

EDITORIAL DESCRIPTION
Contains articles on natural and earth sciences, ecology and environment (problems and solutions), history of science, articles about local environment.
Articles per average issue: 5
Audience: Professional, general
Manuscripts accepted in English

MANUSCRIPT INFORMATION
Subject field(s): Environment, geology, archaeology, botany, entomology, astronomy, space, history of science, scientific biography, parks and city planning, general natural science, education (higher)
Manuscript requirements: Style sheet sent on request.
Preferred length: 1500-2000 words
Number of copies to be submitted: One
Author information and reprints: Payment: None. 10 copies of issue in which article appears
Is simultaneous submission of article to other journals permitted: No
Exclusive manuscript rights between acceptance and publication: Yes
Copyright: Held by publication.
Reprints: Not available.
Additional information: Footnotes, charts, references, (All typewritten, double-spaced) tables, illustrations (drawings and photos) curriculum vitae should accompany the manuscript.
Disposition of manuscript:
Query letter: No
Receipt of manuscript acknowledged: Yes

Decision to publish in: 3-5 weeks
Accepted manuscript published in: Varies
Rejected manuscript returned: Yes, if self-addressed, stamped envelope is sent with manuscript.
Rejected manuscript criticized: If required
Submit to:
C. K. Schneider
Editor
(See address above)

SYNTHESIS [1625]
The University Journal in the History and Philosophy of Science
838 Holyoke Center
Cambridge, Massachusetts 02138
(617) 495-3742

First published in 1971

SUBSCRIPTION DATA
Issues and rates: Published quarterly.
   Average paid circulation: 500; 2,000 controlled
   Annual rate(s): $6.00; Students $3.00
Managing Editor: Suzanne Koch-Weser

EDITORIAL DESCRIPTION
Publishes the best of all graduate and undergraduate research in the field of the history and philosophy of science; functions as a clearinghouse for educational information in the field
Articles per average issue: 3
Audience: Academic, interested laymen
   Manuscripts accepted in English only

MANUSCRIPT INFORMATION
Manuscript requirements: Style sheet sent on request. MLA
   Preferred length: 20-30 pages
   Number of copies to be submitted: 2
   Abstract: Not necessary.
Author information and reprints: Payment: None.
   Is simultaneous submission of article to other journals permitted: Permitted, but not encouraged.
   Exclusive manuscript rights between acceptance and publication: Yes
   Copyright: Held by publication.
   Reprints: Available at cost.
Disposition of manuscript:
   Query letter: Not necessary.
   Receipt of manuscript acknowledged: Yes
   Decision to publish in: 2-3 weeks
   Accepted manuscript published in: 1 month
   Rejected manuscript returned: Yes, if return postage is supplied by author.
   Rejected manuscript criticized: No
Submit to:
   Editor
   (See address above)

TECHNOLOGY REVIEW [1626]
Room E19-430
Massachusetts Institute of Technology
Cambridge, Massachusetts 02139
(617) 253-4872

First published in 1899

SUBSCRIPTION DATA
Issues and rates: 8 per year
   Average paid circulation: 45,000
   Annual rate(s): $9, Foreign $10
Publisher or Sponsor: Massachusetts Institute of Technology, Alumni Association
Managing Editor: Dennis Meredith

EDITORIAL DESCRIPTION
Contains new developments in science, engineering, management, and the related social sciences, with emphasis on their impact on human affairs and the environment in which they are conducted. A semi-technical journal, written for readers with some sense of science or engineering but with no special background in any one of these fields.
Articles per average issue: 5
Audience: Scientific, general
   Manuscripts accepted in English

MANUSCRIPT INFORMATION
Manuscript requirements: Style sheet sent on request.
   Preferred length: 5,000-8,000 words
   Number of copies to be submitted: One
   Rejected manuscript returned: Not necessary
Author information and reprints: Payment: By publication to author. Depending on subject and treatment
   Is simultaneous submission of article to other journals permitted: No
   Exclusive manuscript rights between acceptance and publication: Yes
   Copyright: Held by publication.
   Reprints: Available
Disposition of manuscript:
   Query letter: No
   Receipt of manuscript acknowledged: Yes
   Decision to publish in: 4-6 weeks
   Accepted manuscript published in: Varies
   Rejected manuscript returned: Yes
   Rejected manuscript criticized: Sometimes
Submit to:
   John I. Mattill
   Editor
   (See address above)

TEXAS JOURNAL OF SCIENCE [1627]
P.O. Box 10979
Angelo State University Station
San Angelo, Texas 76901
(915) 944-1717

First published in 1949

SUBSCRIPTION DATA
Issues and rates: Published quarterly.
   Average paid circulation: 1,500
   Annual rate(s): $9.00
Publisher or Sponsor: Texas Academy of Science

EDITORIAL DESCRIPTION
Contains original research papers in physics, chemistry, mathematical sciences, earth sciences, biological sciences, environmental sciences, social sciences, computer science, science education; symposia on various topics.
Articles per average issue: 15
Audience: Academic, general
   Manuscripts accepted in English

MANUSCRIPT INFORMATION
Subject field(s): Science
Manuscript requirements: See latest issue for style requirements.
   Preferred length: Varies
   Number of copies to be submitted: Three
   Abstract: Yes
Author information and reprints: Payment: By author to publication. $10.00 per page. If funds from a grant or institution are available.
   Is simultaneous submission of article to other journals permitted: No
   Exclusive manuscript rights between acceptance and publication: No
   Copyright: No copyright
   Reprints: Available
Disposition of manuscript:
   Receipt of manuscript acknowledged: Yes
   Decision to publish in: Varies
   Accepted manuscript published in: 6 to 12 months
   Rejected manuscript returned: No
   Rejected manuscript criticized: Yes
Submit to:
   Gerald G. Raun
   Editor
   (See address above)

THIN SOLID FILMS [1628]
An International Journal on the Science and Technology of Thin and Thick Films
Elsevier Sequoia SA
P.O. Box 851
1001 Lausanne 1, Switzerland
(021) 20 73 81

First published in 1965

SUBSCRIPTION DATA
Issues and rates: Published monthly.
   Average paid circulation: 1100
   Annual rate(s): SFr. 810.00

EDITORIAL DESCRIPTION
Publishes papers on all aspects of the science and technology of thin films including industrial applications.
Articles per average issue: 11
   Manuscripts accepted in English, French and German (Abstracts in English only)

MANUSCRIPT INFORMATION
Subject field(s): Substrates, deposition techniques, structural properties, physical and physicochemical properties, applications
Manuscript requirements: Style sheet sent on request.
   Number of copies to be submitted: Two
   Abstract: Yes.
Author information and reprints: Payment: None.
   Is simultaneous submission of article to other journals permitted: No

Exclusive manuscript rights between acceptance and publication: Yes
Copyright: Held by publication.
Reprints: Available, cost quoted upon publication
Disposition of manuscript:
  Query letter:
  Receipt of manuscript acknowledged: Yes
  Decision to publish in: 2 to 4 weeks
  Accepted manuscript published in: 4 months
  Rejected manuscript returned: Yes
  Rejected manuscript criticized: Sometimes
Submit to:
  George Siddall
  Editor
  10 Little Crabtree, West Green
  Crawley, Sussex RH11 7HW, England
  (3723) 74151

For authors in the U.S.A. and Canada, submit manuscripts to:
  Jay N. Zemel
  The Moore School of Electrical Engineering
  University of Pennsylvania
  Philadelphia, Pennsylvania

WASHINGTON ACADEMY OF SCIENCES. JOURNAL [1629]
9650 Rockville Pike
Bethesda, Maryland
(301) 530-1402

Previously entitled *Proceedings of the Washington Academy of Sciences*

First published in 1911

SUBSCRIPTION DATA
Issues and rates: Published quarterly.
  Average paid circulation: 1,600
  Annual rate(s): $14.00; Foreign $15.00
Publisher or Sponsor: Washington Academy of Sciences
Managing Editor: Richard H. Foote

EDITORIAL DESCRIPTION
Publishes historical articles, critical reviews, and scholarly scientific articles, notices of meetings and abstract proceedings of the meetings of the Academy and its affiliated societies as well as regional news items.

MANUSCRIPT INFORMATION
Manuscript requirements: No specific style guide.
Author information and reprints: Payment: None.
  Copyright: Washington Academy of Sciences
  Reprints: Available at cost.
Disposition of manuscript:
  Query letter: Not necessary.
  Receipt of manuscript acknowledged: Yes
  Rejected manuscript returned: Yes, if return postage is supplied by author.
  Rejected manuscript criticized: Sometimes

Submit to:
  Richard H. Foote
  Editor
  (See address above)

Archaeology

AMERICAN ANTIQUITY* [1630]
1703 New Hampshire Avenue, N.W.
Washington, D.C. 20009

SUBSCRIPTION DATA
Issues and rates: Published quarterly.
  Average paid circulation: 4,125
  Annual rate(s): Members $15.00, Institutions $20.00, Students $10.00
Publisher or Sponsor: Society for American Archaeology

EDITORIAL DESCRIPTION
Covers the archaeology of the Western Hemisphere and related fields of significance to American archaeologists.

MANUSCRIPT INFORMATION
Subject field(s): Archaeology of the New World and related subjects
Manuscript requirements: See latest issue for style requirements.
  Number of copies to be submitted: Three
  Abstract: Yes, less than 500 words.
Author information and reprints: Payment: None.
  Is simultaneous submission of article to other journals permitted: No
  Exclusive manuscript rights between acceptance and publication: Yes
  Copyright: Held by the Society for American Archaeology
Additional information: Footnotes are not permitted; text citations should be set in parentheses.
Submit to:
  Edwin N. Wilmsen
  Editor
  Museum of Anthropology
  University of Michigan
  Ann Arbor, Michigan 48104
  (313) 764-0481

AMERICAN JOURNAL OF ARCHAEOLOGY [1631]
Box 1967, Yale Station
New Haven, Connecticut 06520
(203) 436-3415

First published in 1885

SUBSCRIPTION DATA
Issues and rates: Published quarterly.
  Average paid circulation: 5,200
  Annual rate(s): $20.00
Publisher or Sponsor: Archaeological Institute of America

EDITORIAL DESCRIPTION
Contains articles on archaeology, mainly Mediterranean and Near Eastern, prehistoric through late Roman Empire.

Articles per average issue: 10
Audience: Professional archaeologists
  Manuscripts accepted in English

MANUSCRIPT INFORMATION
Subject field(s): Classical and Near Eastern archaeology
Manuscript requirements: Style sheet sent on request.
  Number of copies to be submitted: One
  Abstract: Yes
Author information and reprints: Payment: None.
  Is simultaneous submission of article to other journals permitted: No
  Exclusive manuscript rights between acceptance and publication: Yes
  Copyright: Not copyrighted
  Reprints: Not available.
Disposition of manuscript:
  Query letter: No
  Receipt of manuscript acknowledged: Yes
  Decision to publish in: 1 month
  Accepted manuscript published in: 12-18 months
  Rejected manuscript returned: Yes
  Rejected manuscript criticized: Sometimes
Submit to:
  Jerome J. Pollitt
  Editor-in-Chief
  (See address above)

ARCHAEOLOGICAL SOCIETY OF VIRGINIA. QUARTERLY BULLETIN [1632]
1946 Lansing Avenue
Richmond, Virginia 23225
(703) 232-6144

First published in 1946

SUBSCRIPTION DATA
Issues and rates: Published quarterly.
  Average paid circulation: 1300
  Annual rate(s): Institutions $4.00
Publisher or Sponsor: Archaeological Society of Virginia

EDITORIAL DESCRIPTION
Contains articles on Indians, archaeology and related matters, usually limited to Virginia area.
Articles per average issue: 4
Audience: Professional and non-professional archaeologists
  Manuscripts accepted in English

MANUSCRIPT INFORMATION
Subject field(s): Archaeology, Indians, colonial history, related matters
Manuscript requirements: See latest issue for style requirements.
  Preferred length: 300 to 20,000 words
  Number of copies to be submitted: One
Author information and reprints: Payment: None.
  Is simultaneous submission of article to other journals permitted: Yes
  Exclusive manuscript rights between acceptance and publication: No
  Copyright: None

Reprints: Available, 2 copies free to authors, others at cost.
Additional information: Typewritten, double-spaced, one side only; all pictures and line drawing to be camera-ready copy at scale to be published.
Disposition of manuscript:
  Query letter: No
  Receipt of manuscript acknowledged: Yes, on request
  Decision to publish in: 3 months
  Accepted manuscript published in: 6-12 months
  Rejected manuscript returned: Yes
  Rejected manuscript criticized: Yes
Submit to:
  Merle D. Kerby
  Editor
  (See address above)

ARCHAEOLOGY [1633]
A Magazine Dealing with the Antiquity of the World
260 West Broadway
New York, New York 10013
(212) 925-7333

First published in 1948

SUBSCRIPTION DATA
Issues and rates: Published quarterly.
  Average paid circulation: 16,500
  Annual rate(s): $8.50, Foreign $9.50
Publisher or Sponsor: Archaeological Institute of America
Managing Editor: Phyllis Pollak Katz

EDITORIAL DESCRIPTION
  Articles include field reports, museum articles, studies of archaeological material; news items on recent finds; book reviews.
Articles per average issue: 10
Audience: Laymen
  Manuscripts accepted in English, any European

MANUSCRIPT INFORMATION
Subject field(s): Archaeology, art history, history, anthropology
Manuscript requirements: Style sheet sent on request.
  Preferred length: 2500 words; 10 pages
  Number of copies to be submitted: One
  Abstract: No
Author information and reprints: Payment: By publication to author. $6 per printed page for articles only.
  Is simultaneous submission of article to other journals permitted: No
  Exclusive manuscript rights between acceptance and publication: Yes
  Copyright: Held by the Institute
  Reprints: Available, 50 free; additional at cost
Additional information: No footnotes; author should include brief *vita* and may include bibliography.
Disposition of manuscript:
  Query letter: No
  Receipt of manuscript acknowledged: Yes
  Decision to publish in: 3 months
  Accepted manuscript published in: 6 months
  Rejected manuscript returned: Yes
  Rejected manuscript criticized: Sometimes
Submit to:
  Phyllis Pollak Katz
  Editor
  (See address above)

ART AND ARCHAEOLOGY NEWSLETTER [1634]
243 East 39th Street
New York, New York 10016
(212) 686-0591

First published in 1965

SUBSCRIPTION DATA
Issues and rates: Published quarterly.
  Average paid circulation: 1,600
  Annual rate(s): $4.50 (4 issues)
Managing Editor: Otto F. Reiss

EDITORIAL DESCRIPTION
  Contains news about archaeology and ancient history, mainly concerning the Old World; a forum for intriguing new hypotheses and theories in these fields.
Articles per average issue: 5
Audience: Laymen, academicians, professional, general
  Manuscripts accepted in English, German, French

MANUSCRIPT INFORMATION
Subject field(s): Excavations, new advances in scholarship and research, unsolved problems, manners and mores in antiquity, ancient technology, myths and the factual core that they may contain
Manuscript requirements: Style sheet sent on request.
  Preferred length: 2000 words
  Number of copies to be submitted: One
Author information and reprints: Payment: By publication to author. $20-$25 per article.
  Is simultaneous submission of article to other journals permitted: Yes
  Exclusive manuscript rights between acceptance and publication: Yes
  Copyright: Held by publication.
  Reprints: Available at cost
Additional information: Like articles to be accompanied by at least one black and white photograph. Authors must be able to supply precise sources for all factual statements. Travel pieces about sites on the Amexco circuit are not desired.
Disposition of manuscript:
  Query letter: Advisable
  Receipt of manuscript acknowledged: Yes
  Decision to publish in: 2 months
  Accepted manuscript published in: 9-12 months
  Rejected manuscript returned: Yes, if return postage is supplied by author.
  Rejected manuscript criticized: No
Submit to:
  Otto F. Reiss
  Editor
  (See address above)

ASIAN PERSPECTIVES [1635]
A Journal of Archaeology and Prehistory of Asia and the Pacific
The University Press of Hawaii
535 Ward Avenue
Honolulu, Hawaii 96814
(808) 537-1581

Previously entitled *The Bulletin of the Far-Eastern Prehistory Association*

First published in 1957

SUBSCRIPTION DATA
Issues and rates: Published semi-annually.
  Average paid circulation: 456; 40 controlled
  Annual rate(s): $7.50, Institutions $12.00
Managing Editor: John Howe

EDITORIAL DESCRIPTION
  Contains regional reports summarizing current research, topical studies and reports of significant sites, book reviews. Area covered includes island areas from Madagascar to Hawaii and continental areas from Pakistan to Siberia.
Articles per average issue: 8
Audience: Archaeologists, anthropologists, prehistorians
  Manuscripts accepted in English

MANUSCRIPT INFORMATION
Subject field(s): Archaeology, prehistory
Manuscript requirements: Chicago
  Preferred length: 2500-5000 words; 10-15 pages
  Number of copies to be submitted: Two
  Abstract: Optional
Author information and reprints: Payment: None.
  Is simultaneous submission of article to other journals permitted: No
  Exclusive manuscript rights between acceptance and publication: Yes
  Copyright: Held by publisher
  Reprints: Available, 50 free; additional at cost.
Disposition of manuscript:
  Query letter: No
  Receipt of manuscript acknowledged: No
  Decision to publish in: Varies
  Accepted manuscript published in: Varies
  Rejected manuscript returned: Yes
  Rejected manuscript criticized: Sometimes
Submit to:
  Wilhelm G. Solheim, II
  Editor
  Department of Anthropology
  University of Hawaii
  Honolulu, Hawaii 96822
  (808) 948-8994

THE CHESOPIEAN* [1636]
A Journal of North American Archaeology
7507 Pennington Road
Norfolk, Virginia 23505
(703) 588-4254

SUBSCRIPTION DATA
Issues and rates: Published bi-monthly.

Average paid circulation: 800
Annual rate(s): $7.50, Foreign $8.00
Publisher or Sponsor: The Chesopiean Archaeological Association

EDITORIAL DESCRIPTION

Contains reports, articles, papers concerning archaeology, anthropology, linguistics, ethnology, geology, paleontology, palynology or any other field having to do with the study of archaeology/anthropology.

MANUSCRIPT INFORMATION

Subject field(s): North American archaeology, ethnology, anthropology, linguistics, paleontology, geology
Manuscript requirements: No specific style guide.
Preferred length: 40 pages maximum
Number of copies to be submitted: One
Author information and reprints: Payment: None.
Is simultaneous submission of article to other journals permitted: Yes
Exclusive manuscript rights between acceptance and publication: No
Copyright: Held by author.
Reprints: Available at cost
Additional information: Include line drawings, black and white glossy prints, tables, maps, etc.
Disposition of manuscript:
Receipt of manuscript acknowledged: Yes
Decision to publish in: Immediate
Accepted manuscript published in: Three to six months
Rejected manuscript returned: Yes
Rejected manuscript criticized: No
Submit to:
Floyd Painter
Editor
(See address above)

ISRAEL EXPLORATION JOURNAL [1637]
3 Shmuel Hanagid Street
P. O. Box 7041
Jerusalem, Israel
02/227991

First published in 1951

SUBSCRIPTION DATA

Issues and rates: Published quarterly.
Average paid circulation: 2100
Annual rate(s): $9.00
Publisher or Sponsor: Israel Exploration Society
Managing Editor: Joseph Aviram

EDITORIAL DESCRIPTION

Includes papers from contributors from all over the world on ancient, especially Biblical, history and archaeology; history and archaeology of later periods; preliminary reports on excavations; book reviews, etc.
Articles per average issue: 10
Manuscripts accepted in English

MANUSCRIPT INFORMATION

Subject field(s): Archaeology

Manuscript requirements: See latest issue for style requirements.
Preferred length: 8 pages
Number of copies to be submitted: One
Author information and reprints: Payment: None.
Is simultaneous submission of article to other journals permitted: No
Exclusive manuscript rights between acceptance and publication: Yes
Copyright: Held by publication.
Reprints: Available, 50 free
Disposition of manuscript:
Receipt of manuscript acknowledged: Yes
Decision to publish in: 6 months
Accepted manuscript published in: Two years or less
Rejected manuscript returned: Yes
Rejected manuscript criticized: No
Submit to:
Editor
(See address above)

THE KIVA [1638]
Arizona State Museum
The University of Arizona
Tucson, Arizona 85721
(602) 884-2445

First published in 1935

SUBSCRIPTION DATA

Issues and rates: Published quarterly.
Average paid circulation: Not available.
Annual rate(s): $10.00
Publisher or Sponsor: Arizona Archaeological and Historical Society, Inc.

EDITORIAL DESCRIPTION

Contains original papers related to the archaeology of the southwestern United States and northern Mexico.
Articles per average issue: 6
Audience: Professional archaeologists
Manuscripts accepted in English

MANUSCRIPT INFORMATION

Subject field(s): Archaeology, ethnology, history.
Manuscript requirements: Chicago; Style sheet sent on request.
Preferred length: 20-50 pages
Number of copies to be submitted: Two
Abstract: Yes
Author information and reprints: Payment: None.
Is simultaneous submission of article to other journals permitted: No
Exclusive manuscript rights between acceptance and publication: Yes
Copyright: Held by publication.
Reprints: Available
Disposition of manuscript:
Query letter: No
Receipt of manuscript acknowledged: Yes
Decision to publish in: One month
Accepted manuscript published in: 6-9 months
Rejected manuscript returned: Yes
Rejected manuscript criticized: No

Submit to:
William J. Robinson
Editor
(See address above)

SOUTHWESTERN LORE [1639]
Department of Anthropology
University of Colorado
Boulder, Colorado 80302
(303) 443-2211 ext. 7419

First published in 1935

SUBSCRIPTION DATA

Issues and rates: Published quarterly.
Average paid circulation: 650
Annual rate(s): Individuals $4.00, Family $6.00, Institutions $6.00
Publisher or Sponsor: Colorado Archaeological Society

EDITORIAL DESCRIPTION

Contains articles on Colorado and the American Southwest; field reports and synthetic works. Articles are for a professional audience as well as for the informed amateur archaeologist.
Articles per average issue: 2-3
Manuscripts accepted in English

MANUSCRIPT INFORMATION

Subject field(s): Archaeology
Manuscript requirements: See latest issue for style requirements.
Preferred length: 1000 to 5000 words; 5-20 pages
Number of copies to be submitted: One
Abstract: Yes
Author information and reprints: Payment: Reprints only. 5 copies of issue
Is simultaneous submission of article to other journals permitted: No
Exclusive manuscript rights between acceptance and publication: Yes
Copyright: Held by publication.
Reprints: Available at cost.
Additional information: All artwork should be of a camera-ready, publishable quality.
Disposition of manuscript:
Query letter: No
Receipt of manuscript acknowledged: Yes
Decision to publish in: 1-3 months
Accepted manuscript published in: 4-6 months
Rejected manuscript returned: Yes
Rejected manuscript criticized: No
Submit to:
James J. Hester
Editor
(See address above)

Architecture

ARCHITECTURAL DESIGN [1640]
AD
26 Bloomsbury Way
London WC1A 2SS, England
(01) 405-6325

First published in 1930

SUBSCRIPTION DATA

Issues and rates: Published monthly.
Average paid circulation: 10,534
Annual rate(s): £8.70, Foreign $21.50

EDITORIAL DESCRIPTION

Concerned with breaking down the notion that architecture is a formal, fine art based on relationships of volume, form and silhouette. Shows that architecture is an organizational framework which can grow and transform itself, in step with change; allows and encourages people to develop their own life styles to maximum effect.

Articles per average issue: Varies
Audience: Professional, general, academic
Manuscripts accepted in English

MANUSCRIPT INFORMATION

Subject field(s): Architecture, building, construction
Manuscript requirements: All style requirements sent on request.
Preferred length: 1,500-2,000 words maximum
Number of copies to be submitted: 2
Abstract: Helpful
Author information and reprints: Payment: By publication to author. By arrangement
Is simultaneous submission of article to other journals permitted: Permitted, abroad only
Exclusive manuscript rights between acceptance and publication: Yes
Copyright: First British rights
Reprints: Not available.
Additional information: Typewritten copy; black and white photos
Disposition of manuscript:
Query letter: No
Receipt of manuscript acknowledged: Yes
Decision to publish in: 6-8 weeks
Accepted manuscript published in: Varies
Rejected manuscript returned: Yes, if self-addressed, stamped envelope is sent with manuscript.
Rejected manuscript criticized: No
Submit to:
Monica Pidgeon
Editor
(See address above)

CATHEDRAL AGE [1641]

Washington Cathedral
Mount Saint Alban
Washington, D.C. 20015
(202) 966-3500

First published in 1925

SUBSCRIPTION DATA

Issues and rates: Published quarterly.
Average paid circulation: 1,500; 16,500 controlled
Annual rate(s): $5.00

Publisher or Sponsor: Protestant Episcopal Cathedral Foundation

EDITORIAL DESCRIPTION

Cathedrals around the world: their architecture, stained glass, other fine arts, music, etc.
Articles per average issue: 5-6
Manuscripts accepted in English

MANUSCRIPT INFORMATION

Manuscript requirements: See latest issue for style requirements. NYT
Preferred length: 1,800 words
Number of copies to be submitted: 2
Abstract: Not necessary.
Author information and reprints: Payment: By publication to author. $35.00 per article.
Is simultaneous submission of article to other journals permitted: Permitted, but not encouraged.
Exclusive manuscript rights between acceptance and publication: Yes
Copyright: Held by publication.
Reprints: Available at cost.
Disposition of manuscript:
Query letter: Necessary.
Receipt of manuscript acknowledged: Yes
Decision to publish in: 2-3 weeks
Accepted manuscript published in: 6 months
Rejected manuscript returned: Yes, with return postage paid by publication.
Rejected manuscript criticized: Sometimes
Submit to:
Nancy S. Montgomery
Editor
(See address above)

PROGRESSIVE ARCHITECTURE [1642]

600 Summer Street
Stamford, Connecticut 06904
(203) 348-7531

Previously entitled *Pencil Points*

First published in 1920

SUBSCRIPTION DATA

Issues and rates: Published monthly.
Average paid circulation: 65,000
Annual rate(s): $7.00; Foreign $18.00
Managing Editor: James A. Murphy

EDITORIAL DESCRIPTION

Contains articles on innovations, basic principles and developments in architecture and urban planning: planning, design, engineering, technology, use of materials, methods of practice, research.
Articles per average issue: Varies
Audience: Professional
Manuscripts accepted in English

MANUSCRIPT INFORMATION

Subject field(s): Architectural engineering, building materials, architectural business, office practice

Manuscript requirements: See latest issue for style requirements.
Preferred length: 1500-2400 words
Number of copies to be submitted: Two
Abstract: Yes
Author information and reprints: Payment: By publication to author. Negotiated.
Is simultaneous submission of article to other journals permitted: No
Exclusive manuscript rights between acceptance and publication: Yes
Copyright: Held by publication.
Additional information: Almost all articles are staff written; other submissions should be by letter of inquiry plus outline.
Disposition of manuscript:
Receipt of manuscript acknowledged: Yes
Decision to publish in: 4-6 weeks
Accepted manuscript published in: 4-6 months
Rejected manuscript returned: Yes
Rejected manuscript criticized: No
Submit to:
John Morris Dixon
Editor
(See address above)

SOCIETY OF ARCHITECTURAL HISTORIANS. JOURNAL [1643]

Room 716
Walnut Street
Philadelphia, Pennsylvania 19103
(215) PE 5-0224

Previously entitled *American Society of Architectural Historians Journal*

First published in 1941

SUBSCRIPTION DATA

Issues and rates: Published quarterly.
Average paid circulation: 3,900
Annual rate(s): $20.00 with membership; Pan-Am $22.00; Individuals $22.00; Institutions $20.00; Students $12.50; Foreign individuals $22.00; Foreign institutions $22.00
Publisher or Sponsor: Society of Architectural Historians

EDITORIAL DESCRIPTION

Contains articles on architectural history and criticism; book reviews; publication of symposia; letters; notes
Articles per average issue: 4-5
Audience: Professors of art history and architecture, architects, museum personnel, preservationists, etc.
Manuscripts accepted in English, French

MANUSCRIPT INFORMATION

Subject field(s): All aspects of architectural history, including links with archaeology, and the history of engineering
Manuscript requirements: See latest issue for style requirements.
Preferred length: As required
Number of copies to be submitted: 1
Abstract: Not necessary.

Author information and reprints: Payment: None.
　Is simultaneous submission of article to other journals permitted: Not permitted.
　Exclusive manuscript rights between acceptance and publication: Yes
　Copyright: Held by publication.
　Reprints: Available at no cost. 25 Available at cost.

Disposition of manuscript.
　Query letter: Not necessary, but advisable.
　Receipt of manuscript acknowledged: Yes
　Decision to publish in: Varies
　Accepted manuscript published in: 1 year
　Rejected manuscript returned: Yes, with return postage paid by publication.

Submit to:
　Christian F. Otto
　Editor
　College of Architecture, Art, and Planning
　Cornell University
　Ithaca, New York 14850

Earth sciences

Earth sciences (general)

AMERICAN METEOROLOGICAL SOCIETY BULLETIN [1644]
45 Beacon Street
Boston, Massachusetts 02108
(617) 227-2425

First published in 1920

SUBSCRIPTION DATA
Issues and rates: Published monthly.
　Average paid circulation: 10,000
　Annual rate(s): $20.00, Foreign $25.00
Publisher or Sponsor: American Meteorological Society
Managing Editor: Kenneth C. Spengler

EDITORIAL DESCRIPTION
　Official organ of the Society featuring broad review articles, government agency survey papers, editorials, meeting programs and summaries, professional and membership news, announcements, book reviews, advertisements and Society activities.
Articles per average issue: 5
Audience: Professional, membership
　Manuscripts accepted in English

MANUSCRIPT INFORMATION
Subject field(s): Atmospheric sciences, oceanography
Manuscript requirements: See latest issue for style requirements.
　Preferred length: 3-8 pages: notes; 8-30 pages: papers
　Number of copies to be submitted: Three
　Abstract: Yes
Author information and reprints: Payment: By author to publication. $70.00 per printed page is requested from author's organization.
　Is simultaneous submission of article to other journals permitted: No
　Exclusive manuscript rights between acceptance and publication: Yes
　Copyright: No copyright
　Reprints: First 100 free if page charge honored
Disposition of manuscript:
　Query letter: No
　Receipt of manuscript acknowledged: Yes
　Decision to publish in: 2-3 months
　Accepted manuscript published in: 3-4 months
　Rejected manuscript returned: Yes
　Rejected manuscript criticized: Yes
Submit to:
　Kenneth C. Spengler
　Editor
　(See address above)

CANADIAN GEOTECHNICAL JOURNAL [1645]
National Research Council of Canada
100 Sussex Drive
Ottawa, Ontario K1A OR6, Canada
(613) 992-5411

SUBSCRIPTION DATA
Issues and rates: Published quarterly.
　Average paid circulation: 1,700
　Annual rate(s): Individuals $5, Institutions $10
Publisher or Sponsor: National Research Council of Canada
Managing Editor: H. W. Williamson

EDITORIAL DESCRIPTION
　Publishes the results of original scientific research in the fields of soil engineering, as well as those in geology, soil science, and snow and ice mechanics as they relate to civil engineering.
Articles per average issue: 18
Audience: Professional
　Manuscripts accepted in English, French

MANUSCRIPT INFORMATION
Manuscript requirements: Style sheet sent on request.
　Preferred length: Under 25 pages
　Number of copies to be submitted: Two
　Abstract: Yes
Author information and reprints: Payment: None.
　Is simultaneous submission of article to other journals permitted: No
　Exclusive manuscript rights between acceptance and publication: Yes
　Copyright: Held by publication.
　Reprints: Available, only at time of publication. Cost based on length.
Disposition of manuscript:
　Query letter: No
　Receipt of manuscript acknowledged: Yes
　Decision to publish in: 3 months
　Accepted manuscript published in: 4 months
　Rejected manuscript returned: Yes
　Rejected manuscript criticized: Yes
Submit to:
　D. J. Bazett
　Editor
　C.B.A. Engineering, Ltd.
　1425 West Pender Street
　Vancouver, British Columbia V6G 2S3, Canada
　(604) 683-4131

CANADIAN JOURNAL OF EARTH SCIENCES [1646]
National Research Council of Canada
100 Sussex Drive
Ottawa, Ontario K1A OR6, Canada
(613) 992-5411

First published in 1964

SUBSCRIPTION DATA
Issues and rates: Published monthly.
　Average paid circulation: 3500
　Annual rate(s): Individuals $12.00, Institutions $24.00
Publisher or Sponsor: National Research Council of Canada
Managing Editor: S. E. Jenness

EDITORIAL DESCRIPTION
　Publishes the results of original scientific research in any field of earth sciences.
Articles per average issue: 14
Audience: Professional
　Manuscripts accepted in English, French

MANUSCRIPT INFORMATION
Manuscript requirements: Style sheet sent on request.
　Preferred length: Under 25 pages
　Number of copies to be submitted: Two
　Abstract: Yes
Author information and reprints: Payment: None.
　Is simultaneous submission of article to other journals permitted: No
　Exclusive manuscript rights between acceptance and publication: Yes
　Copyright: Held by publication.
　Reprints: Available only at time of publication. Cost based on length.
Disposition of manuscript:
　Query letter: No
　Receipt of manuscript acknowledged: Yes
　Decision to publish in: 3 months
　Accepted manuscript published in: 3 months
　Rejected manuscript returned: Yes
　Rejected manuscript criticized: Yes
Submit to:
　E. R. W. Neale
　Editor
　Department of Geology
　Memorial University
　St. John's, Newfoundland
　(709) 579-5081

COLORADO SCHOOL OF MINES QUARTERLY [1647]
Department of Publications
Colorado School of Mines
Golden, Colorado 80401
(303) 279-3381

First published in 1905

SUBSCRIPTION DATA
Issues and rates: Published quarterly.
　Average paid circulation: 2,400; 100 controlled
　Annual rate(s): $25.00, Foreign $30.00
Publisher or Sponsor: Colorado School of Mines

EDITORIAL DESCRIPTION
　Subjects concern mineral resources, geology, geophysics, paleontology, petroleum and gas, hydrocarbons, mining, metallurgy, energy resources.
Articles per average issue: 1-2
Audience: Professional
　Manuscripts accepted in English

MANUSCRIPT INFORMATION

Subject field(s): Future energy sources, mineral resources, mine problems and new methods for improvement, oil shale, stratigraphic, extraction of metals, pollution problems

Manuscript requirements: See latest issue for style requirements.
　Preferred length: 15 to 200 pages
　Number of copies to be submitted: Two
　Abstract: Yes

Author information and reprints: Payment: Reprints only.
　Is simultaneous submission of article to other journals permitted: No
　Exclusive manuscript rights between acceptance and publication: Yes
　Copyright: Held by Colorado School of Mines
　Reprints: Not available.

Disposition of manuscript:
　Query letter: No
　Receipt of manuscript acknowledged: Yes
　Decision to publish in: 4-6 weeks
　Accepted manuscript published in: 6-9 months
　Rejected manuscript returned: Yes
　Rejected manuscript criticized: No

Submit to:
　Jon W. Raese
　Director of Publications
　(See address above)

EARTH SCIENCE BULLETIN [1648]

Wyoming Geological Association
P.O. Box 545
Casper, Wyoming 82601
(307) 234-9133

SUBSCRIPTION DATA

Issues and rates: Published quarterly.
　Average paid circulation: 1400
　Annual rate(s): $5.00

Publisher or Sponsor: Wyoming Geological Association

EDITORIAL DESCRIPTION

Contains articles on various aspects of the earth sciences.

Articles per average issue: 3

Audience: Professional
　Manuscripts accepted in English only

MANUSCRIPT INFORMATION

Subject field(s): Geology, geophysics, petroleum, mining, energy, archaeology

Manuscript requirements: American Association of Petroleum Geologists style sheet.
　Preferred length: 15-20 pages
　Number of copies to be submitted: One
　Abstract: No

Author information and reprints: Payment: None.
　Exclusive manuscript rights between acceptance and publication: No
　Copyright: Held by author.
　Reprints: Not available.

Additional information: Illustrations should be approximately the same scale as final published scale, and should require no further drafting. Everything typewritten, double-spaced.

Disposition of manuscript:
　Query letter: No
　Receipt of manuscript acknowledged: Yes
　Decision to publish in: 3 months
　Accepted manuscript published in: 3 to 6 months
　Rejected manuscript returned: Yes
　Rejected manuscript criticized: No

Submit to:
　Earl L. Batten
　Editor
　P.O. Box 3140
　Casper, Wyoming 82601
　(307) 234-9133

EARTH-SCIENCE REVIEWS [1649]

An International Journal to bridge the gap between research articles and textbooks
Elsevier Scientific Publishing Company
P. O. Box 211, Jan van Galenstraat 335
Amsterdam, The Netherlands

First published in 1966

SUBSCRIPTION DATA

Issues and rates: Published quarterly.
　Annual rate(s): Individuals Dfl 50.00; Institutions Dfl 104.00

EDITORIAL DESCRIPTION

Provides geologists with an overall view of recent advances in the earth sciences; to allow the reader to see his particular interests related to the geological sciences as a whole; includes a large book-review section

Articles per average issue: Varies

Audience: Geologists, libraries
　Manuscripts accepted in English

MANUSCRIPT INFORMATION

Manuscript requirements: Style sheet sent on request.
　Preferred length: As required
　Number of copies to be submitted: 3
　Abstract: Yes.

Author information and reprints: Payment: None.
　Is simultaneous submission of article to other journals permitted: Not permitted.
　Exclusive manuscript rights between acceptance and publication: Yes
　Copyright: Held by publication.
　Reprints: Available at no cost. 50

Disposition of manuscript:
　Query letter: Not necessary.
　Receipt of manuscript acknowledged: Yes
　Decision to publish in: 6 weeks
　Accepted manuscript published in: 6 months
　Rejected manuscript returned: Yes, with return postage paid by publication.
　Rejected manuscript criticized: Reasons for rejections only

Submit to:
　Editorial Department
　(See address above)

GEOPHYSICAL PROSPECTING [1650]

Official Journal of the European Association of Exploration Geophysicists
30 Carel van Bylandtlaan, Postbus 162
The Hague, The Netherlands 2076

First published in 1953

SUBSCRIPTION DATA

Issues and rates: Published quarterly.
　Average paid circulation: 4,000
　Annual rate(s): Dfl. 80

Publisher or Sponsor: European Association of Exploration Geophysicists

Managing Editor: K. Helbig

EDITORIAL DESCRIPTION

Contains original articles, comments to articles previously published, abstracts of papers, book reviews.
Manuscripts accepted in English (French, German)

MANUSCRIPT INFORMATION

Subject field(s): Seismic prospecting, electric prospecting, magnetic prospecting, gravity prospecting, geophysical case histories

Manuscript requirements: See latest issue for style requirements.
　Preferred length: 20 pages
　Number of copies to be submitted: Three

Author information and reprints: Payment: Reprints only. 50
　Is simultaneous submission of article to other journals permitted: No
　Exclusive manuscript rights between acceptance and publication: Yes
　Copyright: Held by publication.
　Reprints: Available at cost.

Disposition of manuscript:
　Receipt of manuscript acknowledged: Yes
　Decision to publish in: 3 months
　Accepted manuscript published in: 9 months
　Rejected manuscript returned: Yes
　Rejected manuscript criticized: Yes

Submit to:
　Editor
　(See address above)

GEOPHYSICS [1651]

Journal of the Society of Exploration Geophysicists
P.O. Box 3098
Tulsa, Oklahoma 74101
(918) 743-1365

SUBSCRIPTION DATA

Issues and rates: Published bi-monthly.
　Average paid circulation: 9,500
　Annual rate(s): $18.00

Publisher or Sponsor: Society of Exploration Geophysicists

Managing Editor: Jerry W. Henry

EDITORIAL DESCRIPTION

Contains technical articles dedicated to the advancement of the science of geophysics and the art of geophysical prospecting.

Articles per average issue: 10
Audience: Professional
  Manuscripts accepted in English

MANUSCRIPT INFORMATION
Subject field(s): Geophysics, mining, oceanography, geothermal activity, geology, other earth sciences
Manuscript requirements: Style sheet sent on request.
  Preferred length: None
  Number of copies to be submitted: Three
  Abstract: Yes
Author information and reprints: Payment: None.
  Is simultaneous submission of article to other journals permitted: No
  Exclusive manuscript rights between acceptance and publication: Yes
  Copyright: Held by publication.
  Reprints: Available at cost.
Disposition of manuscript:
  Query letter: No
  Receipt of manuscript acknowledged: Yes
  Decision to publish in: 3 months
  Accepted manuscript published in: 8 months
  Rejected manuscript returned: Yes
  Rejected manuscript criticized: Yes
Submit to:
  Jerry W. Henry
  Publication Manager
  (See address above)

HYDROCARBON PROCESSING [1652]
Gulf Publishing Company
P.O. Box 2608
Houston, Texas 77001
(713) 529-4301

Previously entitled *Petroleum Refiner*

First published in 1924

SUBSCRIPTION DATA
Issues and rates: Published monthly.
  Average paid circulation: 36,000
  Annual rate(s): $5.00, Foreign $12.00

EDITORIAL DESCRIPTION
  Contains technical editorial articles, news, management articles, new equipment and literature for the petroleum refining, petrochemical and gas processing industries. Strives to provide informative and interesting articles for the industries covered which are not otherwise available.
Articles per average issue: 15
  Manuscripts accepted in English

MANUSCRIPT INFORMATION
Subject field(s): Process design, mechanical design, maintenance, management, equipment selection, physical property data, thermodynamic property, operations, instrumentation design, structural design, electrical design, cost data
Manuscript requirements: Style sheet sent on request.
  Preferred length: 10 pages

  Number of copies to be submitted: One
  Abstract: No
Author information and reprints: Payment: By publication to author. $25 per page.
  Is simultaneous submission of article to other journals permitted: Yes
  Exclusive manuscript rights between acceptance and publication: Yes
  Copyright: Held by publication.
  Reprints: Available, cost by quotation
Additional information: Manuscripts must be specific to oil refining, petrochemical or gas processing industries.
Disposition of manuscript:
  Receipt of manuscript acknowledged: Yes
  Decision to publish in: 1 month
  Accepted manuscript published in: 3 months
  Rejected manuscript returned: Yes
  Rejected manuscript criticized: No
Submit to:
  Frank L. Evans
  Editor
  (See address above)

INTERNATIONAL JOURNAL OF POWDER METALLURGY AND POWDER TECHNOLOGY [1653]
P.O. Box 2054
Princeton, New Jersey 08540
(609) 799-3300

SUBSCRIPTION DATA
Issues and rates: Published quarterly.
  Average paid circulation: 3,000
  Annual rate(s): $25.00
Publisher or Sponsor: American Powder Metallurgy Institute
Managing Editor: Peter K. Johnson

EDITORIAL DESCRIPTION
  Covers trends and developments in metal powders, powder consolidation techniques and P/M products from fundamental and applied points of view. Research reports, book reviews and market/business reports are also given.
Articles per average issue: 8
Audience: Professional, academic
  Manuscripts accepted in English

MANUSCRIPT INFORMATION
Subject field(s): Powder metallurgy, metal powders, carbides, composites, sintering, cermets, particulate materials, research
Manuscript requirements: See latest issue for style requirements.
  Preferred length: 2500 words
  Number of copies to be submitted: One
  Abstract: No
Author information and reprints: Payment: Reprints only. 6 reprints and 2 copies of issue
  Is simultaneous submission of article to other journals permitted: No
  Exclusive manuscript rights between acceptance and publication: Yes
  Copyright: Held by publication.
  Reprints: Available, cost on request
Disposition of manuscript:
  Query letter: No
  Receipt of manuscript acknowledged: Yes

  Decision to publish in: 6 weeks
  Accepted manuscript published in: 3-6 months
  Rejected manuscript returned: Yes
  Rejected manuscript criticized: No
Submit to:
  Henry H. Hausner
  Editor
  (See address above)

ISRAEL JOURNAL OF EARTH SCIENCES [1654]
P.O.B. 801
Jerusalem, Israel 91000
227 375

Previously entitled *Bulletin of the Research Council of Israel, Section 6*

First published in 1951

SUBSCRIPTION DATA
Issues and rates: Published quarterly.
  Average paid circulation: 700
  Annual rate(s): $18.00
Managing Editor: L. Lester

EDITORIAL DESCRIPTION
  Contains articles on all fields of earth sciences.
Articles per average issue: 20
Audience: Scientific
  Manuscripts accepted in English, French

MANUSCRIPT INFORMATION
Manuscript requirements: AIBS
  Number of copies to be submitted: Three
  Abstract: Yes
Author information and reprints: Payment: None.
  Is simultaneous submission of article to other journals permitted: No
  Exclusive manuscript rights between acceptance and publication: Yes
  Copyright: Held by publication.
  Reprints: Available, cost depends on length
Additional information: Typewritten, double-spaced, quarto with one inch margins.
Disposition of manuscript:
  Query letter: No
  Receipt of manuscript acknowledged: Yes
  Decision to publish in: 4 months
  Accepted manuscript published in: 6 months
  Rejected manuscript returned: Yes
  Rejected manuscript criticized: Yes
Submit to:
  Editor
  (See address above)

JOURNAL OF APPLIED METEOROLOGY [1655]
45 Beacon Street
Boston, Massachusetts 02108
(617) 227-2425

First published in 1962

SUBSCRIPTION DATA
Issues and rates: 8 times per year
   Average paid circulation: 6,700
   Annual rate(s). $40.00, Foreign $45.00
Publisher or Sponsor: American Meteorological Society
Managing Editor: Kenneth C. Spengler

EDITORIAL DESCRIPTION
Contains original papers and critical surveys concerned with the applications of the atmospheric sciences to operational and practical goals and to human activities.
Articles per average issue: 18
Audience: Professional
   Manuscripts accepted in English

MANUSCRIPT INFORMATION
Subject field(s): Applications of atmospheric sciences to health, economy, environment quality, air pollution, radar meteorology, climatic change, climatology and remote sensing instrumentation, air-sea interaction, urban meteorology
Manuscript requirements: See latest issue for style requirements.
   Preferred length: 3-8 pages: notes; 8-40 pages: papers
   Number of copies to be submitted: Three
   Abstract: Yes
Author information and reprints: Payment: By author to publication. $70.00 per printed page is requested from author's organization.
   Is simultaneous submission of article to other journals permitted: No
   Exclusive manuscript rights between acceptance and publication: Yes
   Copyright: No copyright
   Reprints: First 100 free if page charge is honored.
Disposition of manuscript:
   Query letter: No
   Receipt of manuscript acknowledged: Yes
   Decision to publish in: 1-2 months
   Accepted manuscript published in: 3-4 months
   Rejected manuscript returned: Yes
   Rejected manuscript criticized: Yes
Submit to:
   R. Robert Rapp
   Editor
   The Rand Corporation
   1700 Main Street
   Santa Monica, California 90406
   (213) 393-0411, Ext. 7532

THE JOURNAL OF CANADIAN PETROLEUM TECHNOLOGY [1656]
906-1117 Ste. Catherine Street West
Montreal, Quebec H3B 1J3, Canada
(514) 842-3461

SUBSCRIPTION DATA
   Average paid circulation: 1,848
   Annual rate(s): $10.00; Foreign $12.00, $15.00

Publisher or Sponsor: The Canadian Institute of Mining and Metallurgy

EDITORIAL DESCRIPTION
Contains technical papers dealing with the oil and gas industry; scientific rather than trade orientation.
Articles per average issue: 4-6
   Manuscripts accepted in English

MANUSCRIPT INFORMATION
Subject field(s): Oil production, gas production
   Preferred length: 4,000 to 6,000 words
   Number of copies to be submitted: Three
   Abstract: Yes
Author information and reprints: Payment: None.
   Is simultaneous submission of article to other journals permitted: No
   Exclusive manuscript rights between acceptance and publication: Yes
   Copyright: Held by publication.
   Reprints: Available at no cost. 50
Disposition of manuscript:
   Query letter: No
   Receipt of manuscript acknowledged: Yes
   Decision to publish in: 3 months
   Accepted manuscript published in: 6 months
   Rejected manuscript returned: Yes
   Rejected manuscript criticized: Yes
Submit to:
   E. Gordon Tapp
   Editor
   (See address above)

THE LOG ANALYST [1657]
Society of Professional Well Log Analysts
13507 Tosca Lane
Houston, Texas 77024
(713) 468-5930

SUBSCRIPTION DATA
Issues and rates: Published bi-monthly.
   Average paid circulation: 1,000; 1,000 controlled
   Annual rate(s): $10.00
Publisher or Sponsor: Society of Professional Well Log Analysts, Inc.

EDITORIAL DESCRIPTION
Publishes technical articles (research, applications, developments) of formation evaluation, primarily using well logging techniques; news of the industry and profession. Strives to promote the science and profession of formation evaluation using well logging techniques. Publication is educational and non-political.
Articles per average issue: 2-3
Audience: Geologists, engineers, earth scientists
   Manuscripts accepted in English

MANUSCRIPT INFORMATION
Subject field(s): Formation evaluation, well logging, oil and gas exploration, oil and gas evaluation and production
Manuscript requirements: See latest issue for style requirements.
   Preferred length: No requirement
   Number of copies to be submitted: Three
   Abstract: No
Author information and reprints: Payment: None.
   Is simultaneous submission of article to other journals permitted: Yes
   Exclusive manuscript rights between acceptance and publication: No
   Reprints: Available; must be ordered in advance of printing. Cost estimated on request
Additional information: Brief biographies and photos of authors should be submitted.
Disposition of manuscript:
   Receipt of manuscript acknowledged: Yes
   Decision to publish in: 6 months
   Accepted manuscript published in: 8-10 months
   Rejected manuscript returned: Yes
   Rejected manuscript criticized: No
Submit to:
   Charles Richard Glanville
   Executive Secretary
   (See address above)

MARINERS WEATHER LOG [1658]
3300 Whitehaven Street, N.W.
Washington, D.C. 20235
(202) 343-7614

First published in 1957

SUBSCRIPTION DATA
Issues and rates: Published bi-monthly.
   Average paid circulation: 4500 controlled
Publisher or Sponsor: Environmental Data Service, Department of Commerce
Managing Editor: Elwyn E. Wilson

EDITORIAL DESCRIPTION
Contains marine weather and climatology for the North Atlantic and North Pacific; articles and comments on marine meteorology, climatology, oceanography and communication.
Articles per average issue: 3
Audience: Professional
   Manuscripts accepted in English

MANUSCRIPT INFORMATION
Subject field(s): Meteorology, oceanography, climatology
Manuscript requirements: GPO
   Preferred length: 2000-4000 words; 3-6 pages
   Number of copies to be submitted: Two
Author information and reprints: Payment: None.
   Is simultaneous submission of article to other journals permitted: Yes
   Exclusive manuscript rights between acceptance and publication: No
   Copyright: Not copyrighted
   Reprints: Available at cost.
Disposition of manuscript:
   Query letter: No
   Receipt of manuscript acknowledged: No
   Decision to publish in: 2 months
   Accepted manuscript published in: 2 months
   Rejected manuscript returned: Yes

Earth sciences (general)

Rejected manuscript criticized: No
Submit to:
 Editor
 (See address above)

METEORITICS [1659]
Journal of the Meteoritic Society
Center for Meteoritic Studies
Arizona State University
Tempe, Arizona 85281
(602) 965-6511

SUBSCRIPTION DATA
Issues and rates: Published quarterly.
 Annual rate(s): Institutions $30.00; Students $4.00; Members $10.00; Foreign individuals $10.00; Foreign institutions $30.00
Publisher or Sponsor: The Meteoritic Society; Arizona State University
Managing Editor: George A. Boyd

EDITORIAL DESCRIPTION
 Presents professional and original scientific papers on meteorites, moon rocks, cosmochemistry, and geochemistry of the highest scientific order.
Articles per average issue: 6
Audience: Academic, professional, research
 Manuscripts accepted in English, French, German

MANUSCRIPT INFORMATION
Subject field(s): Geographic (solar system); chronological (past 4.5 billion years); meteoritics, asteroids, cosmochemistry and geochemistry
Manuscript requirements: See latest issue for style requirements.
 Preferred length: No limits
 Number of copies to be submitted: 2
 Abstract: Yes.
Author information and reprints: Payment: Reprints only. 100
 Is simultaneous submission of article to other journals permitted: Not permitted.
 Exclusive manuscript rights between acceptance and publication: Yes
 Copyright: None
Additional information: All papers are criticized by at least two specialists in the particular field written about before final editorial decision is made to publish.
Disposition of manuscript:
 Query letter: Not necessary.
 Receipt of manuscript acknowledged: Yes
 Decision to publish in: 2 months
 Accepted manuscript published in: 3 months
 Rejected manuscript returned: Yes, with return postage paid by publication.
 Rejected manuscript criticized: Yes
Submit to:
 Carleton B. Moore
 Editor
 (See address above)

OFFSHORE [1660]
The Journal of Ocean Business
1200 South Post Oak Road
Houston, Texas 77027
(713) 621-9720

First published in 1954

SUBSCRIPTION DATA
Issues and rates: Published monthly.
 Average paid circulation: 18,000
 Annual rate(s): $5.00, Foreign $8.00
Managing Editor: Nixon Quintrelle

EDITORIAL DESCRIPTION
 Publishes news and features of interest to operation personnel for the offshore industries, primarily oil and gas.
Articles per average issue: 6-8
Audience: Operational personnel
 Manuscripts accepted in English

MANUSCRIPT INFORMATION
Subject field(s): Oil and gas, ocean mining, boats, diving, marine construction
Manuscript requirements: See latest issue for style requirements.
 Preferred length: 2000-2500 words
 Number of copies to be submitted: One
 Abstract: Not necessary
Author information and reprints: Payment: By publication to author. Amount varies.
 Is simultaneous submission of article to other journals permitted: No
 Exclusive manuscript rights between acceptance and publication: Yes
 Copyright: Held by publication.
 Reprints: Available at cost
Disposition of manuscript:
 Query letter: Preferred
 Receipt of manuscript acknowledged: Yes
 Decision to publish in: 2 to 4 weeks
 Accepted manuscript published in: Up to a month
 Rejected manuscript returned: Yes, if self-addressed, stamped envelope is sent with manuscript.
 Rejected manuscript criticized: No
Submit to:
 Robert G. Burke
 Editor
 (See address above)

PALEOBIOS [1661]
Contributions from the University of California Museum of Paleontology
Museum of Paleontology
University of California
Berkeley, California 94720
(415) 642-1821

First published in 1967

SUBSCRIPTION DATA
Issues and rates: Irregularly
 Average paid circulation: 50; 50 controlled
 Annual rate(s): $2.00
Publisher or Sponsor: University of California, Museum of Paleontology
Managing Editor: Daryl P. Domning

EDITORIAL DESCRIPTION
 To provide quick, convenient publication for short technical articles by students or staff of the Museum of Paleontology, dealing with material in the Museum's collections or the paleontology of Western North America
Articles per average issue: 1
Audience: Professional paleontologists
 Manuscripts accepted in English

MANUSCRIPT INFORMATION
Subject field(s): Paleontology (vertebrate, invertebrate, paleobotany, or micropaleontology; articles on the history of paleontology or other topics); coverage emphasizes but is not limited to Western North America.
Manuscript requirements: See latest issue for style requirements.
 Preferred length: 30 or less pages
 Number of copies to be submitted: 2
 Abstract: Yes. Follow customary style used in comparable technical articles.
Author information and reprints: Payment: None.
 Is simultaneous submission of article to other journals permitted: Permitted, but not encouraged.
 Exclusive manuscript rights between acceptance and publication: No
 Copyright: None
 Reprints: Available at cost.
Additional information: Photographs may be included, but line drawings are preferred. Authors may be charged for cost of reproducing photograph.
Disposition of manuscript:
 Query letter: Not necessary, but advisable.
 Receipt of manuscript acknowledged: Yes
 Decision to publish in: 1 month
 Accepted manuscript published in: 1 month
 Rejected manuscript returned: Yes, with return postage paid by publication.
 Rejected manuscript criticized: Sometimes
Submit to:
 Daryl P. Domning
 Managing Editor
 (See address above)

PETROLEUM ENGINEER INTERNATIONAL [1662]
P.O. Box 1589
Dallas, Texas 75221
(214) 748-4403

First published in 1929

SUBSCRIPTION DATA
Issues and rates: Published monthly.
 Average paid circulation: 15,000; 5800 controlled
 Annual rate(s): $6.00; Foreign $10.00

Managing Editor: John Scott

EDITORIAL DESCRIPTION
Specializes in engineering/operating material covering the exploration, drilling and production of oil and gas worldwide. Objective is to engineer profits into energy operations, to obtain information to cut costs, increase efficiency, improve profitability, solve industry problems.
Articles per average issue: 5-8
Audience: Professional
Manuscripts accepted in English

MANUSCRIPT INFORMATION
Subject field(s): Operational, technical, special area, special reports
Manuscript requirements: Style sheet sent on request.
Preferred length: 2500 to 3000 words; 8 to 10 pages
Number of copies to be submitted: One
Author information and reprints: Payment: By publication to author. $25-$30 per page.
Is simultaneous submission of article to other journals permitted: No
Exclusive manuscript rights between acceptance and publication: Yes
Copyright: Held by publication.
Reprints: Available, cost quotations given
Additional information: Illustrations may be photographs, blueprints, diagrams, charts or graphs. Final art work done by magazine artists. Editorial department will edit and re-write to form and style.
Disposition of manuscript:
Receipt of manuscript acknowledged: Yes
Decision to publish in: 1 week or less
Accepted manuscript published in: Two months
Rejected manuscript returned: Yes
Rejected manuscript criticized: No
Submit to:
John Scott
Editor
(See address above)

SPECIAL STIPULATIONS
Authors should make original contact suggesting topic and work with editors to arrive at suitable approach length and intended issue ahead.

QUATERNARY RESEARCH [1663]
An Interdisciplinary Journal
Academic Press
111 Fifth Avenue
New York, New York 10003

SUBSCRIPTION DATA
Issues and rates: Published quarterly.
Average paid circulation: Not available.
Annual rate(s): $37.50; Foreign $40.50
Managing Editor: A. L. Washburn; Joe S. Creager
Publisher or Sponsor: The University of Washington

EDITORIAL DESCRIPTION
Publication is devoted to interdisciplinary articles dealing with the Quaternary Period. Articles are of basic significance to more than one discipline.

MANUSCRIPT INFORMATION
Manuscript requirements: See latest issue for style requirements.
Preferred length: 5000 words
Number of copies to be submitted: Three
Abstract: Yes, of 50-200 words on a separate page.
Is simultaneous submission of article to other journals permitted: No
Exclusive manuscript rights between acceptance and publication: Yes
Copyright: Held by University of Washington
Reprints: Available, 50 free to author
Additional information: Everything typewritten, double-spaced. Tables and figure legends should be placed at the end of the manuscript.
Disposition of manuscript:
Receipt of manuscript acknowledged: Yes
Rejected manuscript returned: Yes, if self-addressed, stamped envelope is sent with manuscript.
Rejected manuscript criticized: No
Submit to:
Editorial Office
University of Washington
Seattle, Washington 98105

SEISMOLOGICAL SOCIETY OF AMERICA BULLETIN [1664]
P. O. Box 826
Berkeley, California 94701
(415) 548-0575

First published in 1911

SUBSCRIPTION DATA
Issues and rates: Published bi-monthly.
Average paid circulation: 2,400
Annual rate(s): $36
Publisher or Sponsor: Seismological Society of America
Managing Editor: Otto W. Nuttli

EDITORIAL DESCRIPTION
Contains original research papers in all branches of earthquake studies, including earthquake engineering, geological seismology and seismological studies related to the physics of the earth's interior.
Articles per average issue: 15
Audience: Professional
Manuscripts accepted in English

MANUSCRIPT INFORMATION
Manuscript requirements: See latest issue for style requirements.
Preferred length: None
Number of copies to be submitted: Two
Abstract: Yes, not more than 250 words.
Author information and reprints: Payment: By author to publication. $40 per page.
Is simultaneous submission of article to other journals permitted: No
Exclusive manuscript rights between acceptance and publication: Yes
Copyright: Held by publication.
Reprints: Available, upon payment of page charge.
Disposition of manuscript:
Receipt of manuscript acknowledged: Yes
Decision to publish in: 1-2 months
Accepted manuscript published in: 4-6 months
Rejected manuscript returned: Yes
Rejected manuscript criticized: Yes
Submit to:
Otto W. Nuttli
Editor
Saint Louis University
P.O. Box 8099, Laclede Station
St. Louis, Missouri 63156
(314) 535-3300, Ext. 547B

TECTONOPHYSICS [1665]
Elsevier Scientific Publishing Company
P. O. Box 211, Jan van Galenstraat 335
Amsterdam, The Netherlands

SUBSCRIPTION DATA
Issues and rates: 20 issues yearly
Annual rate(s): Dfl. 150.00

EDITORIAL DESCRIPTION
Provides a medium in which all specialists in petrology, physics, and geology can present their methods and results; to encourage new reviews of their problems in a manner capable of physical interpretation
Articles per average issue: Varies
Audience: Professional geologists, physicists, and petrologists
Manuscripts accepted in English

MANUSCRIPT INFORMATION
Manuscript requirements: Style sheet sent on request.
Preferred length: None
Number of copies to be submitted: 3
Abstract: Yes.
Author information and reprints: Payment: Reprints only. 50 reprints
Is simultaneous submission of article to other journals permitted: Not permitted.
Exclusive manuscript rights between acceptance and publication: Yes
Copyright: Held by publication.
Reprints: Available at cost.
Disposition of manuscript:
Receipt of manuscript acknowledged: Yes
Decision to publish in: 6 weeks
Accepted manuscript published in: 6 months
Rejected manuscript returned: Yes, with return postage paid by publication.
Rejected manuscript criticized: Reasons for rejections only
Submit to:
Editorial Department
(See address above)

TELLUS [1666]
A Bi-monthly Journal of Geophysics
Swedish Natural Science Research Council
Wenner-Gren Center Box 23136
S-10435 Stockholm, Sweden
08-151580

First published in 1949

SUBSCRIPTION DATA
Issues and rates: Published bi-monthly.
  Average paid circulation: 1,300
  Annual rate(s): 135 Swedish Kronen; Foreign 135 Swedish Kronen; Members 80 Swedish Kronen
Publisher or Sponsor: Swedish Geophysical Society
Managing Editor: Bert Bolin

EDITORIAL DESCRIPTION
A medium for the publication of original contributions, survey articles and discussions in the field of the geophysical sciences.
Articles per average issue: 10-15
Audience: Scientists
  Manuscripts accepted in English, German, French

MANUSCRIPT INFORMATION
Subject field(s): Meteorology, atmospheric physics, oceanography, geophysical fluid dynamics, seismology, geodesy
Manuscript requirements: See latest issue for style requirements.
  Preferred length: 10 pages maximum
  Number of copies to be submitted: 3
  Abstract: Yes. One abstract in English and one in Russian. If Russian translation is impossible, the publication will arrange for a translation.
Author information and reprints: Payment: By author to publication. 100 Swedish Kronen per page.
  Is simultaneous submission of article to other journals permitted: Not permitted.
  Exclusive manuscript rights between acceptance and publication: Yes
  Copyright: Held by publication.
  Reprints: Available at no cost. 50
Disposition of manuscript:
  Query letter: Not necessary.
  Receipt of manuscript acknowledged: Yes
  Decision to publish in: 1-3 months
  Accepted manuscript published in: 1 year
  Rejected manuscript returned: Yes, with return postage paid by publication.
  Rejected manuscript criticized: Yes
Submit to:
  Bert Bolin
  Editor
  Insitiue of Meteorology, University of Stockholm
  Arrheniuslaboratoriet, Fack
  S-10405 Stockholm, Sweden
  08-150160-2410

Geology

AMERICAN ASSOCIATION OF PETROLEUM GEOLOGISTS BULLETIN [1667]
P.O. Box 979
Tulsa, Oklahoma 74101
(918) 584-2555

First published in 1917

SUBSCRIPTION DATA
Issues and rates: Published monthly.
  Average paid circulation: 18,400
  Annual rate(s): $50.00; Foreign $55.00
Publisher or Sponsor: The American Association of Petroleum Geologists

EDITORIAL DESCRIPTION
Contains articles on geology, geophysics, geochemistry, environmental science, and oceanography. Any qualified geologist, geophysicist, geochemist, physicist, chemist, biologist, and oceanographer, whether or not a member of AAPG, may submit scientific articles for review. Articles accepted for publication must undergo review and are rejected on the basis of the contents of a review or accepted for same reasons.
Articles per average issue: 10
Audience: Professional
  Manuscripts accepted in English

MANUSCRIPT INFORMATION
Subject field(s): Stratigraphy, environmental geology, organic geochemistry, sedimentology, tectonics, urban geology-geophysics, geophysics, structure, oceanography, biostratigraphy
Manuscript requirements: USGS; other information sent on request
  Preferred length: Less than 40 pages
  Number of copies to be submitted: Two
  Abstract: Yes
Author information and reprints: Payment: By author to publication. Voluntary
  Is simultaneous submission of article to other journals permitted: No
  Exclusive manuscript rights between acceptance and publication: Yes
  Copyright: Held by publication.
  Reprints: Available, cost depends on length
Additional information: Illustrations must be prepared according to AAPG style guide.
Disposition of manuscript:
  Query letter: No
  Receipt of manuscript acknowledged: Yes
  Decision to publish in: 6-8 weeks
  Accepted manuscript published in: 6-9 months
  Rejected manuscript returned: Yes
  Rejected manuscript criticized: Yes
Submit to:
  G. D. Howell
  Managing Editor
  (See address above)
  (918) 584-0278

ASSOCIATION OF ENGINEERING GEOLOGISTS. BULLETIN [1668]
8310 San Fernando Way
Dallas, Texas 75218
(214) 321-1061

SUBSCRIPTION DATA
Issues and rates: Published quarterly.
  Average paid circulation: 2,500
  Annual rate(s): $12.00, Foreign $12.50
Publisher or Sponsor: Association of Engineering Geologists

EDITORIAL DESCRIPTION
Contains case histories, new principles, techniques, or tools, discussions, and short instructive reviews in engineering geology, hydrology, and environmental geology.
Articles per average issue: 12-20
Audience: Professional
  Manuscripts accepted in English

MANUSCRIPT INFORMATION
Subject field(s): Engineering geology, hydrology, exploration geophysics, geomorphology, soils engineering, dynamic processes
Manuscript requirements: See latest issue for style requirements.
  Preferred length: 4,000-12,000 words; 10-30 pages
  Number of copies to be submitted: Two
  Abstract: Yes
Author information and reprints: Payment: None.
  Is simultaneous submission of article to other journals permitted: No
  Exclusive manuscript rights between acceptance and publication: Yes
  Copyright: Held by publication.
  Reprints: Available, cost varies
Disposition of manuscript:
  Receipt of manuscript acknowledged: Yes
  Decision to publish in: 1-3 months
  Accepted manuscript published in: 3-6 months
  Rejected manuscript returned: Yes
  Rejected manuscript criticized: Sometimes
Submit to:
  Dr. Fitzhugh T. Lee
  Editor
  U.S. Geological Survey
  Federal Center
  Denver, Colorado 80225

CALIFORNIA GEOLOGY [1669]
P.O. Box 2980
Sacramento, California 95812
(916) 445-0514

Previously entitled *Mineral Information Science*

First published in 1948

SUBSCRIPTION DATA
Issues and rates: Published monthly.
  Average paid circulation: 20,000
  Annual rate(s): $2.00
Publisher or Sponsor: California Division of Mines and Geology

EDITORIAL DESCRIPTION
Contains articles on geology in and of California; mineral resources; earthquakes, and geologic hazards; other earth science matters of interest to Californians.
Articles per average issue: 2
Audience: Professional, general
  Manuscripts accepted in English

MANUSCRIPT INFORMATION
Subject field(s): Geology, earthquake science, mines and mineral resources, earth science news
Manuscript requirements: See latest issue for style requirements.
  Preferred length: 5000 words maximum
  Number of copies to be submitted: 1 or 2
  Abstract: Yes
Author information and reprints: Payment: Reprints only.
  Is simultaneous submission of article to other journals permitted: Yes
  Exclusive manuscript rights between acceptance and publication: Yes
  Copyright: Held by publication.
  Reprints: Available at no cost
Additional information: Typewritten, double-spaced
Disposition of manuscript:
  Query letter: No
  Receipt of manuscript acknowledged: Yes
  Decision to publish in: 1-2 months
  Accepted manuscript published in: 4-6 months
  Rejected manuscript returned: Yes
  Rejected manuscript criticized: No
Submit to:
  Carl J. Hauge
  Editor-in-Chief
  1416 9th Street, Room 1341
  Sacramento, California 95814

SPECIAL STIPULATIONS
Art work should be legible. Photos should be 8 X 10 glossy or negatives. Art work is not returned.

ENGINEERING GEOLOGY [1670]
An International Journal
Elsevier Scientific Publishing Company
P. O. Box 211, Jan van Galenstraat
Amsterdam, The Netherlands

SUBSCRIPTION DATA
Issues and rates: Published quarterly.
  Annual rate(s): Institutions DFL 104.00

EDITORIAL DESCRIPTION
Publishes research articles of significant content in geology and engineering
Articles per average issue: Varies
Audience: Engineering geologists, civil engineers, geophysicists, libraries, government officials, consultants
  Manuscripts accepted in English

MANUSCRIPT INFORMATION
Subject field(s): Rock mechanics; earthquake engineering; soil mechanics; petroleum engineering; mining; civil, road and waterway engineering
Manuscript requirements: Style sheet sent on request.
  Preferred length: As required
  Number of copies to be submitted: 3
  Abstract: Yes.
Author information and reprints: Payment: None.
  Is simultaneous submission of article to other journals permitted: Not permitted.
  Exclusive manuscript rights between acceptance and publication: Yes

Copyright: Held by publication.
Reprints: Available at no cost. 50 Available at cost.
Disposition of manuscript:
  Query letter: Not necessary.
  Receipt of manuscript acknowledged: Yes
  Decision to publish in: 6 weeks
  Accepted manuscript published in: 6 months
  Rejected manuscript returned: Yes, with return postage paid by publication.
  Rejected manuscript criticized: Reasons for rejections only
Submit to:
  Editorial Department
  (See address above)

GEOTHERMICS [1671]
International Journal of Geothermal Research
SEBD Publications, Inc.
380 Saw Mill River Road
Elmsford, New York 10523
(914) 592-9141

First published in 1972

SUBSCRIPTION DATA
Issues and rates: Published quarterly.
  Annual rate(s): $25.00; Pan-Am $25.00; Foreign $25.00
Publisher or Sponsor: Italian National Research Council; International Institute for Geothermal Research, Pisa
Managing Editor: Ezio Tongiorgi

EDITORIAL DESCRIPTION
Theoretical and applied geothermics—all aspects of geothermal energy, exploration, development, utilization.
Articles per average issue: 5
Audience: Geothermal experts
  Manuscripts accepted in English, French

MANUSCRIPT INFORMATION
Subject field(s): Theoretical and applied geothermics; world-wide all aspects of geothermal energy, exploration, development and utilization.
Manuscript requirements: No specific style guide. See latest issue for style requirements.
  Preferred length: 5-40 pages
  Number of copies to be submitted: 2
  Abstract: Yes. In sufficient detail so that it provides the essential data given in the paper itself
Author information and reprints: Payment: Reprints only. 25
  Is simultaneous submission of article to other journals permitted: Not permitted.
  Exclusive manuscript rights between acceptance and publication: Yes
  Copyright: Held by publication.
  Reprints: Available at cost.
Additional information: Provide table and figure captions, and clear and complete bibliography.
Disposition of manuscript:
  Query letter: Not necessary.
  Receipt of manuscript acknowledged: Yes
  Decision to publish in: 30 days

Accepted manuscript published in: 3 months
Rejected manuscript returned: Yes, with return postage paid by publication.
Rejected manuscript criticized: Reasons for rejections only
Submit to:
  Editorial Office
  c/o Istituto Internazionale per le Ricerche Geotermiche
  Lungarno Pacinotti, 55
  Pisa, Italy 56100
  Pisa 41503

JOURNAL OF GEOLOGY [1672]
University of Chicago Press
5801 Ellis Avenue
Chicago, Illinois 60637
(312) 753-2592

First published in 1893

SUBSCRIPTION DATA
Issues and rates: Published bi-monthly.
  Average paid circulation: 2650
  Annual rate(s): $18.00, Foreign $19.00

EDITORIAL DESCRIPTION
Contains original contributions dealing with any aspect of geology, particularly those with wide appeal; geological notes; discussions and replies; book reviews.
Articles per average issue: 10
Audience: Professional
  Manuscripts accepted in English

MANUSCRIPT INFORMATION
Subject field(s): Any geological subject
Manuscript requirements: Style sheet sent on request.
  Preferred length: 25 printed pages or less
  Number of copies to be submitted: 1 original, 1 copy
  Abstract: Yes
Author information and reprints: Payment: By author to publication. $35.00 per page. Payment of page charges is not a requirement for publication.
  Is simultaneous submission of article to other journals permitted: No
  Exclusive manuscript rights between acceptance and publication: Yes
  Copyright: Held by publication.
  Reprints: Available from author
Disposition of manuscript:
  Query letter: No
  Receipt of manuscript acknowledged: Yes
  Decision to publish in: 1-3 months
  Accepted manuscript published in: 6-8 months
  Rejected manuscript returned: Yes
  Rejected manuscript criticized: Yes
Submit to:
  Peter J. Wyllie
  Editor
  Henry Hinds Laboratory
  5734 South Ellis Avenue
  Chicago, Illinois 60637
  (312) 753-3379

JOURNAL OF MATHEMATICAL GEOLOGY [1673]

Plenum Publishing Corporation
227 West 17th Street
New York, New York 10011
(212) 255-0713

Previously entitled *Journal of the International Association for Mathematical Geology*

First published in 1969

SUBSCRIPTION DATA

Issues and rates: Published bi-monthly.
 Average paid circulation: Not available.
 Annual rate(s): $60.00, Foreign $62.70, Members Special price
Publisher or Sponsor: International Association for Mathematical Geology

EDITORIAL DESCRIPTION

Covers the relation of mathematical concepts to geological models; application and use of mathematics, statistics and computers in the earth sciences.
Articles per average issue: 6
Audience: Professional
 Manuscripts accepted in English (French, German)

MANUSCRIPT INFORMATION

Manuscript requirements: See latest issue for style requirements.
 Preferred length: No more than 5000 words
 Number of copies to be submitted: Original and one copy
 Abstract: Yes, but not necessary for short notes.
Author information and reprints: Payment: None.
 Reprints: Available, cost varies
Disposition of manuscript:
 Query letter: No
 Receipt of manuscript acknowledged: Yes
 Decision to publish in: 6-8 weeks
 Accepted manuscript published in: 8-12 months
 Rejected manuscript returned: Yes
 Rejected manuscript criticized: Yes
Submit to:
 D. F. Merriam
 Editor-in-Chief
 Department of Geology
 Syracuse University
 Syracuse, New York 13210

MODERN GEOLOGY [1674]

Gordon and Breach Science Publishers
440 Park Avenue South
New York, New York 10016
(212) 689-0360

First published in 1969

SUBSCRIPTION DATA

Issues and rates: Published quarterly.
 Annual rate(s): Individuals $16.50, Institutions $63.00

EDITORIAL DESCRIPTION

Publishes experimental and theoretical papers and provides quick, easy access to the broad fields of physical, chemical, mathematical, statistical, and extra-terrestrial geology.
Articles per average issue: 7
Audience: Professional
 Manuscripts accepted in English, French, German, Italian, Spanish

MANUSCRIPT INFORMATION

Subject field(s): Mathematical geology, statistical geology, nuclear geology, isotype geology, radiation damage, thermoluminescence, new aspects of geochemistry, new aspects of geophysics, remote sensing, lunar geology, planetary geology
Manuscript requirements: See latest issue for style requirements.
 Preferred length: None
 Number of copies to be submitted: 2
 Abstract: Yes
Author information and reprints: Payment: None.
 Is simultaneous submission of article to other journals permitted: No
 Exclusive manuscript rights between acceptance and publication: Yes
 Copyright: Held by publication.
 Reprints: Available at cost
Disposition of manuscript:
 Query letter: No
 Receipt of manuscript acknowledged: Yes
 Decision to publish in: 4-6 weeks
 Accepted manuscript published in: 4-12 months
 Rejected manuscript returned: Yes
 Rejected manuscript criticized: Yes
Submit to:
 Luciano B. Ronca
 Editor
 Wayne State University
 4612 Woodward Avenue
 Detroit, Michigan 48201

OKLAHOMA GEOLOGICAL SURVEY BULLETIN [1675]

University of Oklahoma
830 Van Vleet Oval, Room 263
Norman, Oklahoma 73069
(405) 325-3031

SUBSCRIPTION DATA

Issues and rates: Irregular
Publisher or Sponsor: Oklahoma Geological Survey
Managing Editor: William D. Rose

EDITORIAL DESCRIPTION

Bulletins each consist of one paper covering one topic. A few contain two or more parts by the same author or by different authors. All are scientific works on geology.
 Manuscripts accepted in English

MANUSCRIPT INFORMATION

Subject field(s): Any phase of geology and geophysics
Manuscript requirements: USGS
 Preferred length: None
 Number of copies to be submitted: One
 Abstract: Yes
Author information and reprints: Payment: None.
 Is simultaneous submission of article to other journals permitted: No
 Exclusive manuscript rights between acceptance and publication: Yes
 Copyright: Public domain
 Reprints: Available
Disposition of manuscript:
 Query letter: No
 Receipt of manuscript acknowledged: Yes
 Decision to publish in: Three months
 Accepted manuscript published in: Two years
 Rejected manuscript returned: Yes
 Rejected manuscript criticized: Yes
Submit to:
 William D. Rose
 Editor
 (See address above)

OKLAHOMA GEOLOGY NOTES [1676]

Oklahoma Geological Survey
830 Van Vleet Oval, Room 163
Norman, Oklahoma 73069
(405) 325-3031

SUBSCRIPTION DATA

Issues and rates: Published bi-monthly.
 Average paid circulation: 500; 700 controlled
 Annual rate(s): $3.00
Publisher or Sponsor: Oklahoma Geological Survey
Managing Editor: William D. Rose

EDITORIAL DESCRIPTION

Contains short technical articles, mineral industry and petroleum news and statistics, bibliographies, reviews, and announcements of pertinence to Oklahoma geology.
Audience: Professional
 Manuscripts accepted in English

MANUSCRIPT INFORMATION

Subject field(s): Main fields of geology, geophysics, geochemistry, paleontology, geography
Manuscript requirements: Style sheet sent on request.
 Preferred length: 5 to 20 pages
 Number of copies to be submitted: One
 Abstract: Yes
Author information and reprints: Payment: None.
 Is simultaneous submission of article to other journals permitted: No
 Exclusive manuscript rights between acceptance and publication: Yes
 Copyright: Held by publication.
 Reprints: Not available.
Additional information: Artwork should be suitable for offset reproduction without additional drafting or redrafting.
Disposition of manuscript:
 Query letter: No
 Receipt of manuscript acknowledged: Yes

Decision to publish in: 1 week
Accepted manuscript published in: 2-6 months
Rejected manuscript returned: Yes
Rejected manuscript criticized: Yes
Submit to:
William D. Rose
Editor
(See address above)

SOUTHEASTERN GEOLOGY [1677]
P.O. Box 6665, College Station
Durham, North Carolina 27708
(919) 684-2206

SUBSCRIPTION DATA
Issues and rates: Published quarterly.
Average paid circulation: 550; 40 controlled
Annual rate(s): $5.00
Managing Editor: James W. Clark

EDITORIAL DESCRIPTION
Contains scientific articles on all phases of the geology, geophysics, geochemistry, etc. of the Southeast.

MANUSCRIPT INFORMATION
Subject field(s): Geology, geophysics, geochemistry, paleontology
Manuscript requirements: Style sheet sent on request.
Number of copies to be submitted: Two
Abstract: Yes
Author information and reprints: Payment: None.
Is simultaneous submission of article to other journals permitted: No
Exclusive manuscript rights between acceptance and publication: Yes
Copyright: Not copyrighted
Reprints: Available, $.15 each up to 10 pages
Disposition of manuscript:
Receipt of manuscript acknowledged: Yes
Decision to publish in: 4 months
Accepted manuscript published in: 6 months
Rejected manuscript returned: Yes
Rejected manuscript criticized: Yes
Submit to: S. Duncan Heron, Jr.
Editor-in-Chief
(See address above)

Mining and mineralogy

THE AMERICAN MINERALOGIST [1678]
Journal of the Mineralogical Society of America
1707 L Street, N.W.
Washington, D.C. 20036

First published in 1916

SUBSCRIPTION DATA
Issues and rates: Published bi-monthly.
Average paid circulation: 4,000
Annual rate(s): Students $6.00, Members $20.00, Institutions $40.00
Publisher or Sponsor: The Mineralogical Society of America
Managing Editor: Mary C. Holliman

EDITORIAL DESCRIPTION
Contains articles of original research in descriptive, theoretical, and experimental mineralogy.
Articles per average issue: 25
Audience: Professional, students
Manuscripts accepted in English

MANUSCRIPT INFORMATION
Subject field(s): Mineralogy and mineral structures, crystallography, petrology, crystal chemistry, geochemistry, isotope mineralogy, apparatus and techniques, mineral occurrences and paragenesis, topographical mineralogy
Manuscript requirements: As required
Preferred length: None
Number of copies to be submitted: Two
Abstract: Yes, of 250 words or less stating the subject, methods, and conclusions.
Author information and reprints: Payment: None.
Is simultaneous submission of article to other journals permitted: No
Exclusive manuscript rights between acceptance and publication: Yes
Copyright: Held by the Society
Reprints: Available, 100 free upon payment of page charges
Disposition of manuscript:
Query letter: No
Receipt of manuscript acknowledged: Yes
Decision to publish in: 1-3 months
Accepted manuscript published in: 2-4 months
Rejected manuscript returned: Yes
Rejected manuscript criticized: Yes
Submit to:
Dr. F. Donald Bloss
Editor
Department of Geological Sciences
Virginia Polytechnic Institute and State University
Blacksburg, Virginia 24061
(703) 951-5151

CANADIAN MINING JOURNAL [1679]
Suite 403
310 Victoria Avenue
Montreal, Quebec H3Z 2M9, Canada
487-2302

First published in 1879

SUBSCRIPTION DATA
Issues and rates: Published monthly.
Average paid circulation: 1,593; 5,473 controlled
Annual rate(s): $12.00; Foreign $30.00

EDITORIAL DESCRIPTION
Covers the technical and operating and administrative interests of Canada's mining industry.
Articles per average issue: 4
Audience: Professional
Manuscripts accepted in English

MANUSCRIPT INFORMATION
Subject field(s): Geology, geophysics, diamond drilling, mining, engineering, mine safety, mineral transportation, new operations, pollution control, new equipment developments, milling, smelting
Manuscript requirements: See latest issue for style requirements.
Preferred length: 12-15 pages
Number of copies to be submitted: 2
Abstract: Not necessary.
Author information and reprints: Payment: By publication to author. $20.00 per page.
Is simultaneous submission of article to other journals permitted: Not permitted.
Exclusive manuscript rights between acceptance and publication: Yes
Copyright: Held by publication.
Reprints: Available at cost.
Additional information: CMJ is offset, hence on acceptance originals of graphs and charts will be required. Suitable black and white photos are very helpful.
Disposition of manuscript:
Query letter: Not necessary, but advisable.
Receipt of manuscript acknowledged: Yes
Decision to publish in: 2 weeks
Accepted manuscript published in: 2 months
Rejected manuscript returned: Yes, with return postage paid by publication.
Rejected manuscript criticized: Sometimes
Submit to:
Richard H. Fish
Editor
(See address above)

THE CANADIAN MINING AND METALLURGICAL BULLETIN [1680]
CIM Bulletin
906-1117 Ste. Catherine Street West
Montreal, Quebec H3B 1J3, Canada
(514) 842-3461

SUBSCRIPTION DATA
Issues and rates: Published monthly.
Average paid circulation: 10,005
Annual rate(s): $15.00; Foreign $20.00, $25.00
Publisher or Sponsor: The Canadian Institute of Mining and Metallurgy

EDITORIAL DESCRIPTION
Publishes technical papers pertaining to all phases of the mineral industry.
Articles per average issue: 8-15
Audience: Professional
Manuscripts accepted in English

MANUSCRIPT INFORMATION

Subject field(s): Mining, metallurgy, geology, geophysics, geochemistry
Manuscript requirements: No specific style guide.
  Preferred length: 6,000 words
  Number of copies to be submitted: Three
  Abstract: No
  Is simultaneous submission of article to other journals permitted: No
  Exclusive manuscript rights between acceptance and publication: Yes
  Reprints: Available at no cost. 50
Disposition of manuscript:
  Receipt of manuscript acknowledged: Yes
  Decision to publish in: 2-3 months
  Accepted manuscript published in: 3-6 months
  Rejected manuscript returned: Yes
  Rejected manuscript criticized: Yes
Submit to:
  E. Gordon Tapp
  (See address above)

CLAYS AND CLAY MINERALS [1681]

Journal of the Clay Minerals Society
Pergamon Press, Inc.
Fairview Park
Elmsford, New York 10523
(914) 592-7700

First published in 1968

SUBSCRIPTION DATA

Issues and rates: Published bi-monthly.
  Annual rate(s): $25.00; Institutions $60.00
Publisher or Sponsor: Clay Minerals Society

EDITORIAL DESCRIPTION

  Contains contributions in all fields of clay and clay mineral technology.
Articles per average issue: Varies
Audience: Professional, academic
  Manuscripts accepted in English

MANUSCRIPT INFORMATION

Manuscript requirements: See latest issue for style requirements.
  Preferred length: None
  Number of copies to be submitted: 2
  Abstract: Yes
Author information and reprints: Payment: None.
  Is simultaneous submission of article to other journals permitted: Not permitted.
  Exclusive manuscript rights between acceptance and publication: Yes
  Copyright: Held by publication.
  Reprints: Available at cost.
Disposition of manuscript:
  Query letter: Not necessary.
  Receipt of manuscript acknowledged: Yes
  Decision to publish in: 4 weeks
  Accepted manuscript published in: 5 months
  Rejected manuscript returned: Yes, if return postage is supplied by author.
  Rejected manuscript criticized: Reasons for rejections only

Submit to:
  W. T. Granquist
  Editor-in-Chief
  P. O. Box 42286
  Houston, Texas 77042

INTERNATIONAL JOURNAL OF ROCK MECHANICS AND MINING SCIENCES [1682]

With *Geomechanics Abstracts*
Pergamon Press, Inc.
Fairview Park
Elmsford, New York 10523
(914) 592-7700

First published in 1964

SUBSCRIPTION DATA

Issues and rates: Published monthly.
  Annual rate(s): $10.00

EDITORIAL DESCRIPTION

  Contains original research papers on all aspects of mining, mineralogy and geomechanics.
Articles per average issue: Varies
Audience: Professional, academic
  Manuscripts accepted in English

MANUSCRIPT INFORMATION

Manuscript requirements: See latest issue for style requirements.
  Preferred length: None
  Number of copies to be submitted: 2 typescripts
  Abstract: Yes. Of 100-350 words immediately preceding the introduction.
Author information and reprints: Payment: Reprints only. 50 reprints
  Is simultaneous submission of article to other journals permitted: Not permitted.
  Exclusive manuscript rights between acceptance and publication: Yes
  Copyright: Held by publication.
  Reprints: Available at cost.
Disposition of manuscript:
  Query letter: Not necessary.
  Receipt of manuscript acknowledged: Yes
  Decision to publish in: 4 weeks
  Accepted manuscript published in: 5 months
  Rejected manuscript returned: Yes, if return postage is supplied by author.
  Rejected manuscript criticized: Reasons for rejections only
Submit to:
  Dr. A. Roberts
  Editor-in-Chief
  Department of Mining Engineering
  Mackay School of Mines
  University of Nevada
  Reno, Nevada 89507

MINERAL INDUSTRIES BULLETIN [1683]

Colorado School of Mines
Golden, Colorado 80401
(303) 279-3381, Ext. 219

First published in 1958

SUBSCRIPTION DATA

Issues and rates: Published bi-monthly.
  Average paid circulation: 2,200
  Annual rate(s): $4.00
Managing Editor: Jon W. Raese
Publisher or Sponsor: Colorado School of Mines Research Institute

EDITORIAL DESCRIPTION

  Contains articles on minerals, metals, earth sciences, energy, environment, extraction, production, pollution, mineral economics
Articles per average issue: 1
Audience: Professional
  Manuscripts accepted in English

MANUSCRIPT INFORMATION

Subject field(s): Availability of minerals, methods of extraction, marketing and business operations.
Manuscript requirements: See latest issue for style requirements.
  Preferred length: 50 to 60 pages
  Number of copies to be submitted: 2
  Abstract: Yes
Author information and reprints: Payment: By publication to author. $1,200.00 per article.
  Is simultaneous submission of article to other journals permitted: No
  Exclusive manuscript rights between acceptance and publication: Yes
  Copyright: Held by Colorado School of Mines
  Reprints: Available, cost varies
Additional information: Manuscript should be typewritten, double-spaced; if illustrations used from other copyrighted sources, proof of permission should be sent with manuscript; figures suitable for printing, bibliographical sources approximating that of GPO or U.S. Geological Survey style.
Disposition of manuscript:
  Query letter: Yes
  Receipt of manuscript acknowledged: Yes
  Decision to publish in: 4 weeks
  Accepted manuscript published in: 8 weeks
  Rejected manuscript returned: Yes
  Rejected manuscript criticized: No
Submit to:
  Donald Paist
  (See address above)
  (303) 279-2581

MINERALIUM DEPOSITA [1684]

International Journal for Geology, Mineralogy, and Geochemistry of Mineral Deposits
Springer-Verlag
175 Fifth Avenue
New York, New York 10010

SUBSCRIPTION DATA

Issues and rates: Published quarterly.
  Annual rate(s): DM 144 per volume; Members DM 67

Publisher or Sponsor: The Society for Geology Applied to Mineral Deposits

EDITORIAL DESCRIPTION

See sub-title
Manuscripts accepted in English, German

MANUSCRIPT INFORMATION

Preferred length: As required
Number of copies to be submitted: 2
Abstract: Yes. A summary, in English, not exceeding 15 lines in length.
Author information and reprints: Payment: Reprints only. 75 offprints
Is simultaneous submission of article to other journals permitted: Not permitted.
Exclusive manuscript rights between acceptance and publication: Yes
Copyright: Held by publication.
Submit to:
Professor Dr.-Ing. A. Maucher
Managing Editor
Institut für allgemeine und angewandte Geologie der Universität
Luisenstrasse 37
D-8000 München 2 Federal Republic of Germany

THE MINERALOGICAL RECORD [1685]

P.O. Box 783
Bowie, Maryland 20715
(301) 262-8583

First published in 1970

SUBSCRIPTION DATA

Issues and rates: Published semi-monthly.
Average paid circulation: 3,600
Annual rate(s): $6.00, Foreign $7.00

EDITORIAL DESCRIPTION

Contains original mineralogical research, mineral locality descriptions, mineral hobby information, survey articles, various topical, popular and semi-technical materials.
Articles per average issue: 4
Audience: Professional
Manuscripts accepted in English only

MANUSCRIPT INFORMATION

Manuscript requirements: See latest issue for style requirements.
Preferred length: 5 pages maximum, typewritten, double-spaced.
Number of copies to be submitted: Two
Abstract: No
Author information and reprints: Payment: None.
Is simultaneous submission of article to other journals permitted: No
Exclusive manuscript rights between acceptance and publication: No
Copyright: Held by publication.
Reprints: Available; 25 free, larger orders on request
Disposition of manuscript:
Query letter: No
Receipt of manuscript acknowledged: Yes
Decision to publish in: 6 weeks
Accepted manuscript published in: 6-12 months
Rejected manuscript returned: Yes
Rejected manuscript criticized: Yes
Submit to:
John S. White, Jr.
Editor
(See address above)

MINERALOGY AND PETROLOGY [1686]

Springer-Verlag
175 Fifth Avenue
New York, New York 10010

First published in 1947

SUBSCRIPTION DATA

Annual rate(s): DM 118 per volume
Managing Editor: J. Hoefs

EDITORIAL DESCRIPTION

Publishes contributions to the fields of geochemistry, isotope geology; the petrology and genesis of igneous, metamorphic and sedimentary rocks; experimental petrology and mineralogy; the distribution and significance of elements and their isotopes in the rocks
Manuscripts accepted in English, French, German

MANUSCRIPT INFORMATION

Manuscript requirements: See latest issue for style requirements. Style sheet sent on request.
Preferred length: As required
Number of copies to be submitted: 3
Abstract: Yes. A short abstract in English; titles of papers in French or German must also be translated into English.
Author information and reprints: Payment: Reprints only. 75 offprints
Is simultaneous submission of article to other journals permitted: Not permitted.
Exclusive manuscript rights between acceptance and publication: Yes
Copyright: Held by publication.
Reprints: Available at cost.
Submit to:
H. P. Eugster
Editorial Board Member
Department of Geology
Johns Hopkins University
Baltimore, Maryland 21218

MINERALS SCIENCE AND ENGINEERING [1687]

A Review Journal
Private Bag 7, Auckland Park
Cottesloe, Transvaal, South Africa 2006

First published in 1969

SUBSCRIPTION DATA

Issues and rates: Published quarterly.
Average paid circulation: 4500 controlled

Publisher or Sponsor: National Institute for Metallurgy

EDITORIAL DESCRIPTION

A review journal on the origin, occurrences, winning, properties, uses, and economics of minerals.
Articles per average issue: 4
Audience: Professional
Manuscripts accepted in English

MANUSCRIPT INFORMATION

Subject field(s): Chemical engineering, geology, mineralogy, pyrometallurgy, hydrometallurgy, analytical chemistry
Manuscript requirements: See latest issue for style requirements.
Preferred length: 60 pages
Number of copies to be submitted: Two
Author information and reprints: Payment: Reprints only. 25 free
Is simultaneous submission of article to other journals permitted: No
Exclusive manuscript rights between acceptance and publication: Yes
Copyright: Held by publication.
Reprints: Available at cost.
Disposition of manuscript:
Query letter: No
Receipt of manuscript acknowledged: Yes
Decision to publish in: 3 months
Accepted manuscript published in: 6 months
Rejected manuscript returned: Yes
Rejected manuscript criticized: Yes
Submit to:
E. H. Wainwright
Editor
(See address above)

MISSOURI MINERAL NEWS [1688]

Missouri Department of Natural Resources
Office of the State Geologist
Rolla, Missouri 65401
(314) 364-1752 ext. 35

Previously entitled *Missouri Mineral Industry News*

First published in 1961

SUBSCRIPTION DATA

Issues and rates: Published monthly.
Average paid circulation: 2,000 controlled
Publisher or Sponsor: Missouri Department of Natural Resources
Managing Editor: Jerry D. Vineyard

EDITORIAL DESCRIPTION

Contains brief items on Missouri geology, the water resources and mineral resources of the state and their development; includes articles on mining companies, reclamation, and pollution.
Articles per average issue: 3
Audience: Professional
Manuscripts accepted in English

MANUSCRIPT INFORMATION
Subject field(s): Geological and mineral and water resource information that would interest Missourians.
Manuscript requirements: See latest issue for style requirements.
  Preferred length: 200 to 350 words
  Number of copies to be submitted: One
  Abstract: Optional
Author information and reprints: Payment: None.
  Is simultaneous submission of article to other journals permitted: Yes
  Exclusive manuscript rights between acceptance and publication: No
  Copyright: Held by author.
  Reprints: Available at cost.
Additional information: Typewritten, double-spaced; illustrations should be camera-ready line drawings or glossy prints.
Disposition of manuscript:
  Query letter: No
  Receipt of manuscript acknowledged: Yes
  Decision to publish in: 1 week
  Accepted manuscript published in: 1 month
  Rejected manuscript returned: Yes
  Rejected manuscript criticized: No
Submit to:
  Jerry D. Vineyard
  Editor
  (See address above)

SOUTH AFRICAN INSTITUTE OF MINING AND METALLURGY JOURNAL [1689]
P.O. Box 61019
Marshalltown, Transvaal, South Africa
834-1271

First published in 1894

SUBSCRIPTION DATA
Issues and rates: Published monthly.
  Average paid circulation: 2,500
  Annual rate(s): R.20.40
Publisher or Sponsor: South African Institute of Mining and Metallurgy

EDITORIAL DESCRIPTION
  Publishes topics of interest to miners, metallurgists, engineers, mineralogists, and scientists.
Articles per average issue: 2-3
Audience: Professional
  Manuscripts accepted in English, Afrikaans

MANUSCRIPT INFORMATION
Manuscript requirements: Style sheet sent on request.
  Number of copies to be submitted: Three
  Abstract: Yes
Author information and reprints: Payment: None.
  Is simultaneous submission of article to other journals permitted: No
  Exclusive manuscript rights between acceptance and publication: Yes
  Copyright: Held by the Institute
  Reprints: Available at cost

Disposition of manuscript:
  Query letter: No
  Receipt of manuscript acknowledged: Yes
  Decision to publish in: 2 months
  Accepted manuscript published in: 3 months
  Rejected manuscript returned: Yes, if return postage is supplied by author.
  Rejected manuscript criticized: No
Submit to:
  Editor
  (See address above)

Marine sciences

AQUACULTURE [1690]
Elsevier Scientific Publishing Company
P. O. Box 211, Jan van Galenstraat 335
Amsterdam, The Netherlands
(020) 515-3365

First published in 1972

SUBSCRIPTION DATA
Issues and rates: Published semi-annually.
  Annual rate(s): Dfl. 196.00

EDITORIAL DESCRIPTION
  An international journal devoted to research on the exploration and improvement of all aquatic food resources, both floristic and faunistic, from freshwater, brackish and marine environments, related directly or indirectly to human consumption.
Articles per average issue: 9
Audience: Professional, research, academic
  Manuscripts accepted in English (French, German)

MANUSCRIPT INFORMATION
Subject field(s): Analysis of environmental requirements of animal and plant species; exploration of new food resources; breed improvement; fertilization; cultivation; havesting; diseases affecting aquatic animal and plant species and their control; conditioning of habitats; effects of water pollution, etc.
Manuscript requirements: See latest issue for style requirements. Style sheet sent on request.
  Preferred length: No preference
  Number of copies to be submitted: 3
  Abstract: Yes
Author information and reprints: Payment: Reprints only. 50 reprints
  Is simultaneous submission of article to other journals permitted: Not permitted.
  Exclusive manuscript rights between acceptance and publication: Yes
  Copyright: Held by publication.
  Reprints: Available at cost.
Disposition of manuscript:
  Query letter: Not necessary, but advisable.
  Receipt of manuscript acknowledged: Yes
  Decision to publish in: 2 months
  Accepted manuscript published in: 4-6 months

  Rejected manuscript returned: Yes, with return postage paid by publication.
  Rejected manuscript criticized: Sometimes
Submit to:
  For the Americas and Japan:
  Dr. D. F. Alderdice
  Department of the Environment
  Fisheries Research Board of Canada
  Pacific Biological Station
  Nanaimo, British Columbia, Canada

  For all other countries:
  Dr. S. J. de Groot
  Rijksinstituut voor Visserijonderzoek
  Haringkade 1, P. O. Box 68
  Ijmuiden, The Netherlands

BULLETIN OF MARINE SCIENCE [1691]
P. O. Box 368
Lawrence, Kansas 66044

Previously entitled *Bulletin of Marine Science of the Gulf and Caribbean*

First published in 1951

SUBSCRIPTION DATA
Issues and rates: Published quarterly.
  Average paid circulation: 800
  Annual rate(s): Individuals $20.00; Institutions $50.00; Students $10.00
Publisher or Sponsor: University of Miami; Rosenstiel School of Marine and Atmospheric Science
Managing Editor: William J. Richards

EDITORIAL DESCRIPTION
  Dedicated to the dissemination of high quality research in the marine sciences, primarily of biological interest dealing with the tropical and subtropical waters of the world's oceans.
Articles per average issue: 20
Audience: Academic and governmental marine scientists
  Manuscripts accepted in English

MANUSCRIPT INFORMATION
Subject field(s): Marine biology; physical, chemical and geological sciences if pertinent to marine biology; zoology, botany, microbiology, biochemistry, fisheries, ecology, systematics, evolution, biogeography and behavior.
Manuscript requirements: See latest issue for style requirements.
  Preferred length: 30 pages
  Number of copies to be submitted: Original and 2 copies
  Abstract: Yes. It should be brief and not exceed one double-spaced page. It should state the reason for the study, summarize the significant findings, and note the implications of these findings.
Author information and reprints: Payment: None.
  Is simultaneous submission of article to other journals permitted: Not permitted.

Exclusive manuscript rights between acceptance and publication: Yes
Copyright: Held by the Rosenstiel School of Marine and Atmospheric Science, The University of Miami
Reprints: Available at cost. Quoted by printer
Disposition of manuscript:
Query letter: Not necessary.
Receipt of manuscript acknowledged: Yes
Decision to publish in: 6 weeks
Accepted manuscript published in: 6 months
Rejected manuscript returned: Yes, with return postage paid by publication.
Rejected manuscript criticized: Yes
Submit to:
William J. Richards
Editor
Rosenstiel School of Marine and Atmospheric Science
4600 Rickenbacker Causeway
Miami, Florida 33149
(305) 350-7245

SPECIAL STIPULATIONS
Photographic reproductions are preferred over original illustrations. Illustrations will be requested if needed.

DEEP-SEA RESEARCH [1692]
And *Oceanographic Abstracts*
Pergamon Press
Fairview Park
Elmsford, New York 10523
(914) 592-7700

First published in 1953

SUBSCRIPTION DATA
Issues and rates: Published monthly.
Annual rate(s): $25.00; Institutions $100.00

EDITORIAL DESCRIPTION
Contains results of original scientific research, the solution of instrumental problems or research-method descriptions in the broad field of oceanography.
Articles per average issue: 5-6
Audience: Professional, academic
Manuscripts accepted in English

MANUSCRIPT INFORMATION
Manuscript requirements: See latest issue for style requirements.
Preferred length: None
Number of copies to be submitted: 3, double-spaced
Abstract: Yes. A brief abstract at the head of the paper.
Author information and reprints: Payment: Reprints only. 50 reprints
Is simultaneous submission of article to other journals permitted: Not permitted.
Exclusive manuscript rights between acceptance and publication: Yes
Copyright: Held by publication.
Reprints: Available at cost.
Disposition of manuscript:
Query letter: Not necessary.
Receipt of manuscript acknowledged: Yes
Decision to publish in: 4 weeks
Accepted manuscript published in: 5 months
Rejected manuscript returned: Yes, if return postage is supplied by author.
Rejected manuscript criticized: Reasons for rejections only
Submit to:
Mrs. J. C. Swallow
Institute of Oceanographic Sciences
Wormley
Godalming, Surrey, England

Prof. Francis A. Richards
Department of Oceanography WB-10
University of Washington
Seattle, Washington 98195
Editors

JOURNAL OF HYDRONAUTICS [1693]
1290 Avenue of Americas
New York, New York 10019
(212) 581-4300 ext. 755

First published in 1967

SUBSCRIPTION DATA
Issues and rates: Published quarterly.
Average paid circulation: 1200
Annual rate(s): $12, Foreign $14
Publisher or Sponsor: American Institute of Aeronautics and Astronautics

EDITORIAL DESCRIPTION
Dedicated to the publication of original papers which contribute to the advancement of the science and engineering of all types of marine craft, installations, and instrumentation devised to explore and make use of the oceans of the world.
Articles per average issue: 8
Audience: Professional
Manuscripts accepted in English

MANUSCRIPT INFORMATION
Subject field(s): Presents papers dealing with the hydromechanics of propulsion, the stability and control of surface vessels and submersibles, and methods for providing mobility and habitation in water. Ocean environmental characteristics, such as currents, acoustical properties, wave spectra, density, and chemical and biological aspects, are also topics insofar as they bear upon the design of bodies, structures, and instruments to be employed in the seas.
Manuscript requirements: Style sheet sent on request.
Preferred length: Synoptics: 8 pages maximum; papers: 36 pages maximum
Number of copies to be submitted: Three
Abstract: Yes
Author information and reprints: Payment: By author to publication. $85.00 per page. Voluntary.
Is simultaneous submission of article to other journals permitted: No
Exclusive manuscript rights between acceptance and publication: Yes
Copyright: Held by publication.
Reprints: 100 free if page charges are paid.
Disposition of manuscript:
Query letter: No
Receipt of manuscript acknowledged: Yes
Decision to publish in: 3 months
Accepted manuscript published in: 3 months
Rejected manuscript returned: Yes
Rejected manuscript criticized: Yes
Submit to:
Anne Huth
Managing Editor
(See address above)

JOURNAL OF MARINE RESEARCH [1694]
Sears Foundation for Marine Research
Box 2161, Yale Station
New Haven, Connecticut 06520
(203) 436-1078 ext. 61078

First published in 1937

SUBSCRIPTION DATA
Issues and rates: Published three times per year.
Average paid circulation: 1,300
Annual rate(s): $30.00
Publisher or Sponsor: Sears Foundation for Marine Research
Managing Editor: George Veronis

EDITORIAL DESCRIPTION
Contains research in all areas of oceanography: biological, chemical, geological and physical.

MANUSCRIPT INFORMATION
Manuscript requirements: See latest issue for style requirements.
Preferred length: None
Number of copies to be submitted: Original and 2 copies
Abstract: Yes
Author information and reprints: Payment: None.
Is simultaneous submission of article to other journals permitted: No
Exclusive manuscript rights between acceptance and publication: Yes
Copyright: Held by publication.
Reprints: Available at cost.
Disposition of manuscript:
Query letter: No
Receipt of manuscript acknowledged: Yes
Decision to publish in: 3 months
Accepted manuscript published in: 3 months
Rejected manuscript returned: Yes
Rejected manuscript criticized: Sometimes
Submit to:
George Veronis
Editor
(See address above)

Marine sciences

JOURNAL OF PHYSICAL OCEANOGRAPHY [1695]
45 Beacon Street
Boston, Massachusetts 02108
(617) 227-2425

First published in 1971

SUBSCRIPTION DATA
Issues and rates: Published quarterly.
  Average paid circulation: 1,500
  Annual rate(s): $20.00, Foreign $25.00
Publisher or Sponsor: American Meteorological Society
Managing Editor: Kenneth C. Spengler

EDITORIAL DESCRIPTION
Contains original theoretical and observational papers and critical surveys related to the physics, dynamics and chemistry of the oceans and of the processes coupling the sea to the atmosphere.
Articles per average issue: 20
Audience: Professional
  Manuscripts accepted in English

MANUSCRIPT INFORMATION
Subject field(s): Ocean circulation, coastal currents, surface and internal waves, air-sea interaction, turbulent mixing, vertical convection, oceanic tides, thermo-chemical properties, tracer techniques
Manuscript requirements: See latest issue for style requirements.
  Preferred length: 3-8 pages: notes; 8-40 pages: papers
  Number of copies to be submitted: Three
  Abstract: Yes
Author information and reprints: Payment: By author to publication. $70.00 per printed page is requested from author's organization.
  Is simultaneous submission of article to other journals permitted: No
  Exclusive manuscript rights between acceptance and publication: Yes
  Copyright: No copyright
  Reprints: First 100 free if page charge honored.
Disposition of manuscript:
  Query letter: No
  Receipt of manuscript acknowledged: Yes
  Decision to publish in: 2-3 months
  Accepted manuscript published in: 4-5 months
  Rejected manuscript returned: Yes
  Rejected manuscript criticized: Yes
Submit to:
  Robert O. Reid
  Editor
  Department of Meteorology
  Texas A & M University
  College Station, Texas 77843
  (713) 845-1443

MARINE BIOLOGY [1696]
International Journal of Life in Oceans and Coastal Waters
Springer-Verlag
175 Fifth Avenue
New York, New York 10010

SUBSCRIPTION DATA
Annual rate(s): DM 180 per volume
Managing Editor: R. Friedrich

EDITORIAL DESCRIPTION
Original contributions in the field of marine biology will be considered. Manuscripts accepted in English, German, French

MANUSCRIPT INFORMATION
Subject field(s): Biological oceanography, cultivation of marine organisms for scientific and commercial purposes, experimental ecology and physiology, ecological dynamics, evolution, theoretical biology related to marine environment, methods.
Manuscript requirements: See latest issue for style requirements. Style sheet sent on request.
  Preferred length: As required
  Number of copies to be submitted: 2
  Abstract: Yes. Always in English. Contributions in German and French should include a detailed summary in English.
Author information and reprints: Payment: Reprints only. 75 offprints
  Is simultaneous submission of article to other journals permitted: Not permitted.
  Exclusive manuscript rights between acceptance and publication: Yes
  Copyright: Held by publication.
Submit to:
  J. S. Pearse
  Editorial Board
  Division of Natural Sciences
  University of California
  Santa Cruz, California 95064

MARINE CHEMISTRY [1697]
An International Journal
Elsevier Scientific Publishing Company
P. O. Box 211, Jan van Galenstraat 335
Amsterdam, The Netherlands

First published in 1972

SUBSCRIPTION DATA
Issues and rates: Published annually.
  Annual rate(s): Individuals Dfl. 50.00; Institutions Dfl. 104.00

EDITORIAL DESCRIPTION
Publishes articles on all aspects of chemistry in the marine environment.
Articles per average issue: Varies
  Manuscripts accepted in English French, German

MANUSCRIPT INFORMATION
Subject field(s): Marine chemistry, oceanography, marine biology, water and environmental pollution, geochemistry
Manuscript requirements: Style sheet sent on request.
  Number of copies to be submitted: 3
  Abstract: Yes.
Author information and reprints: Payment: Reprints only. 50 reprints
  Is simultaneous submission of article to other journals permitted: Not permitted.
  Exclusive manuscript rights between acceptance and publication: Yes
  Copyright: Held by publication.
  Reprints: Available at cost.
Disposition of manuscript:
  Query letter: Not necessary.
  Receipt of manuscript acknowledged: Yes
  Decision to publish in: 6 weeks
  Accepted manuscript published in: 6 months
  Rejected manuscript returned: Yes, with return postage paid by publication.
  Rejected manuscript criticized: Reasons for rejections only
Submit to:
  Editorial Department
  (See address above)

MARINE GEOLOGY [1698]
An International Journal
Elsevier Scientific Publishing Company
P. O. Box 211, Jan van Galenstraat 335
Amsterdam, The Netherlands
515-9222

First published in 1964

SUBSCRIPTION DATA
Issues and rates: 10 issues per year
  Annual rate(s): Dfl. 60

EDITORIAL DESCRIPTION
An international medium for the publication of studies and comprehensive reviews in the fields of marine geology, geochemistry and geophysics. Preference is given to contributions of more than purely local or regional interest. Also contains a special letter section for short papers which require very rapid publication.
Articles per average issue: Varies
Audience: Professional
  Manuscripts accepted in English

MANUSCRIPT INFORMATION
Manuscript requirements: Style sheet sent on request.
  Preferred length: None
  Number of copies to be submitted: 3
  Abstract: Yes.
Author information and reprints: Payment: Reprints only. 50 reprints
  Is simultaneous submission of article to other journals permitted: Not permitted.
  Exclusive manuscript rights between acceptance and publication: Yes
  Copyright: Held by publication.
  Reprints: Available at cost.
Disposition of manuscript:
  Query letter: Not necessary.
  Receipt of manuscript acknowledged: Yes
  Decision to publish in: 6 weeks
  Accepted manuscript published in: 6 months
  Rejected manuscript returned: Yes, with return postage paid by publication.

Rejected manuscript criticized: Reasons for rejections only
Submit to:
Editorial Department
(See address above)

MARINE GEOTECHNOLOGY [1699]

An International Journal of Seafloor Science and Engineering
Crane, Russak & Company, Inc.
347 Madison Avenue
New York, New York 10017
(212) 889-1403

First published in 1975

SUBSCRIPTION DATA
Issues and rates: Published quarterly.
Annual rate(s): $34.00

EDITORIAL DESCRIPTION
Publishes the results of the theory and practice of geotechnical ocean engineering and the geotechnical aspects of marine geosciences; deals with the application of scientific methods and engineering principles to the aquisition, interpretation, and use of knowledge of seafloor soils and rocks
Articles per average issue: Varies
Audience: Professional
Manuscripts accepted in English

MANUSCRIPT INFORMATION
Subject field(s): Embraces acoustical, biological, chemical, mechanical, and physical properties affecting the electrolyte-gas-solid sedimentary system of the seafloor; also technical papers, review papers, short notes, case studies
Manuscript requirements: See latest issue for style requirements. Style sheet sent on request.
Preferred length: None
Number of copies to be submitted: 3
Abstract: Yes.
Author information and reprints: Payment: Reprints only. 50 reprints
Is simultaneous submission of article to other journals permitted: Not permitted.
Exclusive manuscript rights between acceptance and publication: Yes
Copyright: Held by publication.
Reprints: Available at cost.
Disposition of manuscript:
Query letter: Not necessary.
Receipt of manuscript acknowledged: Yes
Decision to publish in: 1 month
Accepted manuscript published in: 3-6 months
Rejected manuscript returned: Yes, with return postage paid by publication.
Rejected manuscript criticized: Sometimes
Submit to:
Dr. Adrian F. Richards
Editor-in-Chief
Marine Geotechnical Laboratory
Lehigh University
Bethlehem, Pennsylvania 18015
(215) 691-7000

SEA FRONTIERS [1700]

10 Rickenbacker Causeway, Virginia Key
Miami, Florida 33149
(305) 361-5786

First published in 1954

SUBSCRIPTION DATA
Issues and rates: Published bi-monthly.
Average paid circulation: 70,000
Annual rate(s): $10.00
Publisher or Sponsor: International Oceanographic Foundation
Managing Editor: F. May Smith

EDITORIAL DESCRIPTION
Articles pertain to recent scientific advances, to interesting life or phenomena of the sea, economical and industrial applications of marine science, historical expeditions, or scientists distinguished in the history of marine science.
Articles per average issue: 6-8
Audience: Professional
Manuscripts accepted in English

MANUSCRIPT INFORMATION
Subject field(s): All fields of marine science
Manuscript requirements: Chicago
Preferred length: 1500-2500 words
Number of copies to be submitted: One
Abstract: No
Author information and reprints: Payment: By publication to author. $.05 to $.08 per word.
Is simultaneous submission of article to other journals permitted: No
Exclusive manuscript rights between acceptance and publication: Yes
Copyright: Held by publication.
Reprints: Available at cost
Additional information: All articles must be authoritative, but written in non-technical language for the non-scientist. All manuscripts must be illustrated, preferably with photographs (color and black and white).
Disposition of manuscript:
Query letter: Preferred
Receipt of manuscript acknowledged: Yes
Decision to publish in: 6 weeks
Accepted manuscript published in: Varies
Rejected manuscript returned: Yes, if self-addressed, stamped envelope is sent with manuscript.
Rejected manuscript criticized: No
Submit to:
Jean Bradfisch
Associate Editor
(See address above)

Engineering and allied sciences

Engineering and allied sciences

ACTA METALLURGICA [1701]

Pergamon Press, Inc.
Fairview Park
Elmsford, New York 10523
(914) 592-7700

First published in 1953

SUBSCRIPTION DATA
Issues and rates: Published monthly.
  Annual rate(s): $25.00; Institutions $120.00
Publisher or Sponsor: American Society for Metals, American Institute of Mining, Metallurgical and Petroleum Engineers

EDITORIAL DESCRIPTION
  Contains original research papers in the field of metallic and non-metallic solids and related studies.
Articles per average issue: 15
Audience: Professional, academic
  Manuscripts accepted in English, French, German

MANUSCRIPT INFORMATION
Manuscript requirements: See latest issue for style requirements.
  Preferred length: None
  Number of copies to be submitted: 2
  Abstract: Yes. Not more than 200 words for all papers. Papers in German and French should carry one in English.
Author information and reprints: Payment: Reprints only. 50 reprints for single-authored papers; 100 for multiple-authored papers
  Is simultaneous submission of article to other journals permitted: Not permitted.
  Exclusive manuscript rights between acceptance and publication: Yes
  Copyright: Held by publication.
  Reprints: Available at cost.
Disposition of manuscript:
  Query letter: Not necessary.
  Receipt of manuscript acknowledged: Yes
  Decision to publish in: 4 weeks
  Accepted manuscript published in: 5 months
  Rejected manuscript returned: Yes, if return postage is supplied by author.
  Rejected manuscript criticized: Reasons for rejections only
Submit to:
  Prof. Bruce Chalmers
  Editor
  Division of Engineering and Applied Physics
  Harvard University
  Cambridge, Massachusetts 02138

AFS CAST METALS RESEARCH JOURNAL [1702]

Golf and Wolf Roads
Des Plaines, Illinois 60016
(312) 824-0181 Ext. 57

First published in 1965

SUBSCRIPTION DATA
Issues and rates: Published quarterly.
  Average paid circulation: 1000
  Annual rate(s): $25, Members $10
Publisher or Sponsor: American Foundrymen's Society
Managing Editor: Jack H. Schaum

EDITORIAL DESCRIPTION
  Contains research-level articles on metalcasting from all over the world, principally original manuscripts but numerous translations; also reports of research projects in progress at the world's principal metalcasting research labs; abstracts of metalcasting technical literature, technical notes, news.
Articles per average issue: 8
Audience: Professional
  Manuscripts accepted in English

MANUSCRIPT INFORMATION
Subject field(s): Gray iron, sand binders, inclusions, defects, sand casting, melting and pouring, arc and induction furnaces, non-ferrous metals, molding processes, solidification, mechanical testing
Manuscript requirements: Style sheet sent on request.
  Preferred length: 54,000 characters; 6 printed pages
  Number of copies to be submitted: One original: and 2 for review
  Abstract: Yes
Author information and reprints: Payment: Reprints only. 20
  Is simultaneous submission of article to other journals permitted: Yes, except for other immediately competitive journals.
  Exclusive manuscript rights between acceptance and publication: No
  Copyright: Not copyrighted
  Reprints: Available at cost.
Additional information: Please submit equation copy in camera-ready form. Linework on drawings should be good and bold for reproduction in reverse or screened.
Disposition of manuscript:
  Query letter: No
  Receipt of manuscript acknowledged: Yes
  Decision to publish in: 3 months
  Accepted manuscript published in: 6 months
  Rejected manuscript returned: No
  Rejected manuscript criticized: Yes
Submit to:
  Gerald X. Diamond
  Technical Editor
  (See address above)

SPECIAL STIPULATIONS
  Preference is for manuscripts documenting original research revealing new findings in metalcasting.

AIChE JOURNAL [1703]

Chemical Engineering Research & Development
345 East 47 Street
New York, New York 10017
(212) 752-6800 ext. 316

Previously entitled *Chemical Engineering Research & Development*

First published in 1955

SUBSCRIPTION DATA
Issues and rates: Published bi-monthly.
  Average paid circulation: 6,000
  Annual rate(s): $50.00
Publisher or Sponsor: American Institute of Chemical Engineers
Managing Editor: Sylvia Fourdrinier

EDITORIAL DESCRIPTION
  Contains articles on chemical engineering fundamentals.
Articles per average issue: 25
Audience: Research professional
  Manuscripts accepted in English

MANUSCRIPT INFORMATION
Subject field(s): Chemical engineering
Manuscript requirements: See latest issue for style requirements.
  Preferred length: 20 pages
  Number of copies to be submitted: Five
  Abstract: Yes
Author information and reprints: Payment: Reprints only. 100 reprints
  Is simultaneous submission of article to other journals permitted: No
  Exclusive manuscript rights between acceptance and publication: Yes
  Copyright: Held by publication.
  Reprints: Available, cost per page
Disposition of manuscript:
  Query letter: No
  Receipt of manuscript acknowledged: Yes
  Decision to publish in: 3 months
  Accepted manuscript published in: 4 months
  Rejected manuscript returned: Yes
  Rejected manuscript criticized: Yes
Submit to:
  Robert C. Reid
  Editor
  Massachusetts Institute of Technology
  Chemical Engineering Department
  Cambridge, Massachusetts 02139

THE AMERICAN CERAMIC SOCIETY JOURNAL [1704]

65 Ceramic Drive
Columbus, Ohio 43214
(614) 268-8645

First published in 1918

SUBSCRIPTION DATA
Issues and rates: Published bi-monthly.
  Average paid circulation: 9,500
  Annual rate(s): $45.00; Foreign $48.00; Institutions $45.00; Members $37.50;

Foreign institutions $48.00. All include subscription to *Ceramic Bulletin*
Managing Editor: M. Geraldine Smith

EDITORIAL DESCRIPTION

Contains articles on original fundamental research in ceramics
Articles per average issue: 30
Audience: Scientists, researchers, engineers
Manuscripts accepted in English

MANUSCRIPT INFORMATION

Subject field(s): Physical chemistry, crystal chemistry, high temperature reactions, analytical chemistry, solid state physics, colloid chemistry, materials development, physical and chemical properties
Manuscript requirements: See latest issue for style requirements. Style sheet sent on request.
Preferred length: 5,000 words
Abstract: Yes. A brief and factual summary, not exceeding 100 words, that contains pertinent terms suitable for indexing and information retrieval.
Author information and reprints: Payment: By author to publication. A voluntary page charge of $60.00
Is simultaneous submission of article to other journals permitted: Not permitted.
Exclusive manuscript rights between acceptance and publication: Yes
Copyright: Held by publication.
Reprints: Available at no cost. 100 Available at cost.
Additional information: Each manuscript receives at least two reviews for technical evaluation.
Disposition of manuscript:
Query letter: Not necessary, but advisable.
Receipt of manuscript acknowledged: Yes
Decision to publish in: 3-4 months
Accepted manuscript published in: 3-4 months
Rejected manuscript returned: Yes, with return postage paid by publication.
Rejected manuscript criticized: Yes
Submit to:
Margie K. Reser
Technical Editor
(See address above)

ASHRAE JOURNAL [1705]
345 East 47th Street
New York, New York 10017
(212) 752-6800

First published in 1959

SUBSCRIPTION DATA

Issues and rates: Published monthly.
Average paid circulation: 30,000
Annual rate(s): $16.00; Foreign $17.00; Institutions $16.00; Students $10.00; Members $10.00

Publisher or Sponsor: American Society of Heating, Refrigerating and Air-Conditioning Engineers
Managing Editor: James H. Cansdale

EDITORIAL DESCRIPTION

Covers research, development, design, engineering and news in the field.
Articles per average issue: 6-8
Audience: Engineers, contractors, students, educators, architects, manufacturers
Manuscripts accepted in English

MANUSCRIPT INFORMATION

Subject field(s): Heating, refrigerating, air-conditioning, ventilation, insulation, environmental control
Manuscript requirements: Style sheet sent on request.
Preferred length: 6,000 words average; 10 pages
Number of copies to be submitted: 2
Abstract: Yes.
Author information and reprints: Payment: None.
Is simultaneous submission of article to other journals permitted: Not permitted.
Exclusive manuscript rights between acceptance and publication: Yes
Copyright: Held by publication.
Reprints: Available at no cost. 100 or more Available at cost.
Disposition of manuscript:
Query letter: Necessary.
Receipt of manuscript acknowledged: Yes
Decision to publish in: 3-12 weeks
Accepted manuscript published in: 3-4 months
Rejected manuscript returned: Yes, with return postage paid by publication.
Rejected manuscript criticized: Reasons for rejections only
Submit to:
James H. Cansdale
Editor
(See address above)

ASLE TRANSACTIONS [1706]
838 Busse Highway
Park Ridge, Illinois 60068
(312) 825-5536

SUBSCRIPTION DATA

Issues and rates: Published quarterly.
Average paid circulation: 1200
Annual rate(s): $46.00; Foreign $50.00
Publisher or Sponsor: American Society of Lubrication Engineers

EDITORIAL DESCRIPTION

Reporting world-wide progress in every aspect of fundamental lubrication knowledge, with broad coverage in lubrication research, design, and development.

MANUSCRIPT INFORMATION

Subject field(s): Seals, properties of lubrication, gears and gear lubrication, petroleum and chemicals, solid lubrication, equipment and practices, metalworking fluids, bearings and bearing lubrication

Manuscript requirements: Chicago; more information sent on request
Number of copies to be submitted: Five
Abstract: Yes
Author information and reprints: Payment: None.
Is simultaneous submission of article to other journals permitted: No
Exclusive manuscript rights between acceptance and publication: Yes
Copyright: Held by publication.
Reprints: Available, cost on request
Disposition of manuscript:
Receipt of manuscript acknowledged: Yes
Decision to publish in: 4-5 months
Accepted manuscript published in: 4-12 months
Rejected manuscript returned: Yes
Rejected manuscript criticized: Yes
Submit to:
A.A. Raimondi
Editor
(See address above)

SPECIAL STIPULATIONS

Papers are usually solicited and presented at the ASLE Annual Meeting or at the ASLE/ASME Joint Lube Conference, following which they are in the journals. Contributed papers are accepted, however.

ASTM STANDARDIZATION NEWS [1707]
1916 Race Street
Philadelphia, Pennsylvania 19103
(215) 569-4200

SUBSCRIPTION DATA

Issues and rates: Published monthly.
Average paid circulation: 25,000
Annual rate(s): $9.50, Foreign $10.50
Publisher or Sponsor: American Society for Testing and Materials

EDITORIAL DESCRIPTION

Contains papers dealing with standardization, materials properties, evaluation of testing of materials.

MANUSCRIPT INFORMATION

Manuscript requirements: Style sheet sent on request.
Preferred length: 10 pages
Number of copies to be submitted: Three
Author information and reprints: Payment: None.
Is simultaneous submission of article to other journals permitted: No
Exclusive manuscript rights between acceptance and publication: Yes
Copyright: Held by publication.
Reprints: Available, cost depends on length
Disposition of manuscript:
Receipt of manuscript acknowledged: Yes
Decision to publish in: 3-6 months
Accepted manuscript published in: 2 months
Rejected manuscript returned: Yes
Rejected manuscript criticized: Yes

Submit to:
Sam F. Etris
Editor
(See address above)

AUSTRALASIAN CORROSION ENGINEERING [1708]
P.O. Box 250
North Sydney, N.S.W. 2060, Australia
69-4985

First published in 1957

SUBSCRIPTION DATA
Issues and rates: Published monthly.
   Average paid circulation: 2,400; 2,500 controlled
   Annual rate(s): Foreign $A12.50
Publisher or Sponsor: Australasian Corrosion Association

EDITORIAL DESCRIPTION
   Seeks to provide a vehicle of basic ideas in corrosion and corrosion prevention.
Articles per average issue: 2-3
Audience: Technical, managerial
   Manuscripts accepted in English

MANUSCRIPT INFORMATION
Subject field(s): Technical papers, review papers, R & D notes
Manuscript requirements: See latest issue for style requirements.
   Preferred length: None
   Number of copies to be submitted: Two
   Abstract: Optional
Author information and reprints: Payment: None.
   Is simultaneous submission of article to other journals permitted: No
   Exclusive manuscript rights between acceptance and publication: Yes
   Copyright: Held by publication.
   Reprints: Available, 30 reprints free
Disposition of manuscript:
   Query letter: Yes
   Receipt of manuscript acknowledged: No
   Decision to publish in: Four months
   Accepted manuscript published in: 6 months
   Rejected manuscript returned: Yes, if self-addressed, stamped envelope is sent with manuscript.
   Rejected manuscript criticized: Yes
Submit to:
   Francis Edward Kennedy
   General Manager
   16 Ivy Street
   Chippendale, N.S.W., 2008 Australia

AUSTRALIAN CHEMICAL ENGINEERING [1709]
P. O. Box 250
North Sydney, New South Wales 2060, Australia
(02) 699-4985

Previously entitled *Australian Journal for Chemical Engineers*

First published in 1960

SUBSCRIPTION DATA
Issues and rates: Published monthly.
   Annual rate(s): $A15.00; Foreign $A18.00
Publisher or Sponsor: University of New South Wales Chemical Engineering Association

EDITORIAL DESCRIPTION
   Publishes articles concerning new developments, techniques and technical data for managerial and technical engineering personnel in the chemical processing and allied industries.
Articles per average issue: 3-4
Audience: Professional
   Manuscripts accepted in English

MANUSCRIPT INFORMATION
Subject field(s): Chemical process engineering data, equipment details and manufacturing and installation techniques
Manuscript requirements: No specific style guide. See latest issue for style requirements.
   Preferred length: Optional
   Number of copies to be submitted: 2, typewritten, double-spaced
   Abstract: Not necessary.
Author information and reprints: Payment: Reprints only. 30 reprints
   Is simultaneous submission of article to other journals permitted: Not permitted.
   Exclusive manuscript rights between acceptance and publication: Yes
   Copyright: Held by publication. first rights only. Acknowledgement required for subsequent publication.
   Reprints: Available at cost.
Additional information: Illustrations should be twice reproduction size; original photos, graphs, etc. should be done in India ink.
Disposition of manuscript:
   Query letter: Not necessary, but advisable.
   Receipt of manuscript acknowledged: No
   Decision to publish in: 1-3 months
   Accepted manuscript published in: 6 months
   Rejected manuscript returned: No
   Rejected manuscript criticized: Sometimes
Submit to:
   F.E. Kennedy
   General Manager
   (See address above)

AUTOMATICA [1710]
The Journal of IFAC
Pergamon Press, Inc.
Fairview Park
Elmsford, New York 10523
(914) 592-7700

First published in 1963

SUBSCRIPTION DATA
Issues and rates: Published bi-monthly.
   Annual rate(s): $25.00; Institutions $70.00
Publisher or Sponsor: International Federation of Automatic Control

EDITORIAL DESCRIPTION
   Publishes detailed papers, brief papers, and correspondence on both the theoretical and experimental research work and development in the control of systems including all aspects of automatic control theory.
Articles per average issue: 10
Audience: Professional, academic
   Manuscripts accepted in English

MANUSCRIPT INFORMATION
Subject field(s): Design and characterization of components and systems; effects of instrumentation; reliability of components and systems
Manuscript requirements: See latest issue for style requirements.
   Preferred length: None
   Number of copies to be submitted: 4
   Abstract: Yes. On the first page of about 200 words or less.
Author information and reprints: Payment: None.
   Is simultaneous submission of article to other journals permitted: Not permitted.
   Exclusive manuscript rights between acceptance and publication: Yes
   Copyright: Held by publication.
   Reprints: Available at cost.
Disposition of manuscript:
   Query letter: Not necessary.
   Receipt of manuscript acknowledged: Yes
   Decision to publish in: 4 weeks
   Accepted manuscript published in: 5 months
   Rejected manuscript returned: Yes, if return postage is supplied by author.
   Rejected manuscript criticized: Reasons for rejections only
Submit to:
   George S. Axelby
   Editor
   Westinghouse Electric Corporation
   Box 746, MS-452
   Baltimore, Maryland 21203
   (301) 765-2084

AUTOMATION [1711]
The Production Engineering Magazine
Penton Plaza
1111 Chester Avenue
Cleveland, Ohio 44114
(216) 696-7000

First published in 1954

SUBSCRIPTION DATA
Issues and rates: Published monthly.
   Average paid circulation: 476; 90,000 controlled
   Annual rate(s): $12, Foreign $20
Managing Editor: Larry L. Boolden

EDITORIAL DESCRIPTION
   Technical and non-technical coverage of topics affecting the men who engineer production and are interested in manufacturing processes, handling,

controls, and manufacturing data handling.
Articles per average issue: 7-8
Audience: Professional
   Manuscripts accepted in English

MANUSCRIPT INFORMATION

Subject field(s): Manufacturing engineering, production engineering, manufacturing, production processes, industrial controls, handling, data handling
Manuscript requirements: See latest issue for style requirements.
   Preferred length: 10-30 pages
   Number of copies to be submitted: One or two
   Abstract: Not necessary
Author information and reprints: Payment: By publication to author. $25 per page.
   Is simultaneous submission of article to other journals permitted: No
   Exclusive manuscript rights between acceptance and publication: Yes
   Copyright: Held by publication.
   Reprints: Available at cost
Additional information: Typewritten, double-spaced; include photos and roughs of other illustration ideas.
Disposition of manuscript:
   Receipt of manuscript acknowledged: Yes
   Decision to publish in: 1 month
   Accepted manuscript published in: 3 months
   Rejected manuscript returned: Yes
   Rejected manuscript criticized: No
Submit to:
   John H. McRainey
   Executive Editor
   (See address above)

BALL BEARING JOURNAL [1712]
A Quarterly Review of Rolling Bearing Engineering
Aktiebolaget Svenska Kullagerfabriken
Hornsgatan 1
Göteborg, Sweden
031-840000

First published in 1926

SUBSCRIPTION DATA

Issues and rates: Published quarterly.
   Average paid circulation: 60,000 controlled
   Annual rate(s): Free
Publisher or Sponsor: Aktiebolagel Svenska Kullagerfabriken
Managing Editor: Einar Wallin

EDITORIAL DESCRIPTION

   Publishes research and development articles on rolling bearings, as well as SKF rolling, and bearing applications.
Articles per average issue: 10
Audience: Ball bearing users
   Manuscripts accepted in English, French, German and Swedish

MANUSCRIPT INFORMATION

Subject field(s): Bearing technology, bearing applications

Manuscript requirements: Style sheet sent on request.
   Preferred length: 6,000 words; 4-5 pages
   Number of copies to be submitted: One
   Abstract: Yes
Author information and reprints: Payment: By publication to author. 1 page 150 Skr.; 2-3 pages 300 Skr; over 3 pages 450 Skr. per page.
   Is simultaneous submission of article to other journals permitted: Should be discussed.
   Exclusive manuscript rights between acceptance and publication: Yes
   Copyright: Held by publication.
   Reprints: Available at cost
Disposition of manuscript:
   Query letter: Not necessary, but advisable.
   Receipt of manuscript acknowledged: Yes
   Decision to publish in: 4 weeks
   Accepted manuscript published in: 3-6 months
   Rejected manuscript returned: Yes
   Rejected manuscript criticized: Sometimes
Submit to:
   Jan-Erik Mattsson
   Editor
   (See address above)

BIOMEDICAL ENGINEERING [1713]
42/43 Gerrard Street
London W1V 7LP, England
(01) 439-2541

SUBSCRIPTION DATA

Issues and rates: Published monthly.
   Average paid circulation: 2800
   Annual rate(s): £9.50; Foreign £25.00

EDITORIAL DESCRIPTION

   An international monthly journal promoting communication between research, engineering and clinical medicine.
Articles per average issue: 4-5
Audience: Hospital clinicians, medical scientists, engineers
   Manuscripts accepted in English

MANUSCRIPT INFORMATION

Subject field(s): Biomedical engineering
Manuscript requirements: Style sheet sent on request.
   Preferred length: 3,000 to 4,000 words; 10 to 12 pages
   Number of copies to be submitted: Original and two copies
   Abstract: Yes, 100 words maximum indicating scope and significance to medical engineering and any results or conclusions obtained.
Author information and reprints: Payment: By publication to author. Between £7.35 and £5.25 per 1000 words.
   Is simultaneous submission of article to other journals permitted: No
   Exclusive manuscript rights between acceptance and publication: Yes
   Copyright: Held by publication.

   Reprints: Available, 25 free, additional at cost
Additional information: Guide to the preparation of manuscripts available from publishers.
Disposition of manuscript:
   Receipt of manuscript acknowledged: Yes
   Decision to publish in: 3 months
   Accepted manuscript published in: 6-9 months
   Rejected manuscript returned: Yes
   Rejected manuscript criticized: Yes
Submit to:
   Ian Scott
   Editor
   (See address above)

BUILDING SCIENCE [1714]
Pergamon Press, Inc.
Fairview Park
Elmsford, New York 10523
(914) 592-7700

First published in 1965

SUBSCRIPTION DATA

Issues and rates: Published quarterly.
   Annual rate(s): $25.00; Institutions $45.00

EDITORIAL DESCRIPTION

   Provides an outlet for the results of scientific research of high standard on any aspect of building science; also technical notes, letters, and some book reviews.
Articles per average issue: 7-10
Audience: Research workers and professional builders, architects
   Manuscripts accepted in English, French, German

MANUSCRIPT INFORMATION

Manuscript requirements: See latest issue for style requirements.
   Preferred length: None
   Number of copies to be submitted: 2
   Abstract: Yes. Of not more than 100 words
Author information and reprints: Payment: Reprints only. 50 reprints
   Is simultaneous submission of article to other journals permitted: Not permitted.
   Exclusive manuscript rights between acceptance and publication: Yes
   Copyright: Held by publication.
   Reprints: Available at cost.
Disposition of manuscript:
   Query letter: Not necessary.
   Receipt of manuscript acknowledged: Yes
   Decision to publish in: 4 weeks
   Accepted manuscript published in: 5 months
   Rejected manuscript returned: Yes, if return postage is supplied by author.
   Rejected manuscript criticized: Reasons for rejections only
Submit to:
   Prof. A. W. Hendry,
   Prof. C. B. Wilson
   Editor-in-Chief and Assistant Editor
   Department of Civil Engineering and Building Science

Edinburgh University
Edinburgh, Scotland

CALIFORNIA ENGINEER [1715]
Serving the Berkeley, Davis, Santa Barbara, and Los Angeles Campuses of the University of California
9 Northgate Hall
University of California
Berkeley, California 94720
(415) 642-2420

SUBSCRIPTION DATA
Issues and rates: 5 issues per academic year
  Average paid circulation: 5000
  Annual rate(s): $5.00
Publisher or Sponsor: University of California, Engineers Joint Council

EDITORIAL DESCRIPTION
  Contents include editorials, essays on engineering practice, semi-technical articles, and news. Publication tries to expand the views of engineering students to other technical disciplines and increase their social and humanistic awareness.
Audience: Students

MANUSCRIPT INFORMATION
Subject field(s): Society and engineering; environmental impact of engineering projects or ideas; semi-technical articles in engineering field
Manuscript requirements: See latest issue for style requirements.
  Preferred length: 2000 to 5000 words
  Number of copies to be submitted: One or two
Author information and reprints: Payment: None.
  Is simultaneous submission of article to other journals permitted: Yes, if publication is notified
  Exclusive manuscript rights between acceptance and publication: No
  Copyright: Author may obtain one if desired
  Reprints: Available at $.50 per reprint
Additional information: Include photo and brief resume of author.
Disposition of manuscript:
  Receipt of manuscript acknowledged: Yes
  Decision to publish in: One to four weeks
  Rejected manuscript returned: Yes, if return postage is supplied by author.
  Rejected manuscript criticized: Yes
Submit to:
  Editor
  (See address above)

SPECIAL STIPULATIONS
  Unless copyrighted, articles are available for reprinting by other publications on request.

CANADIAN JOURNAL OF CIVIL ENGINEERING [1716]
National Research Council of Canada
100 Sussex Drive
Ottawa, Ontario K1A OR6, Canada
(613) 992-5411

First published in 1974

SUBSCRIPTION DATA
Issues and rates: Published quarterly.
  Average paid circulation: 3,200
  Annual rate(s): $5.00; Institutions $10.00
Publisher or Sponsor: National Research Council of Canada
Managing Editor: H. Williamson

EDITORIAL DESCRIPTION
  Results of original scientific research in any branch of civil engineering
Articles per average issue: 8-10
Audience: Research and consulting civil engineers
  Manuscripts accepted in English, French

MANUSCRIPT INFORMATION
Manuscript requirements: Style sheet sent on request.
  Preferred length: Under 25 pages
  Number of copies to be submitted: 3
  Abstract: Yes.
Author information and reprints: Payment: None.
  Is simultaneous submission of article to other journals permitted: Not permitted.
  Exclusive manuscript rights between acceptance and publication: Yes
  Copyright: Held by publication.
  Reprints: Available at cost.
Disposition of manuscript:
  Query letter: Not necessary.
  Receipt of manuscript acknowledged: Yes
  Decision to publish in: 3 months
  Accepted manuscript published in: 4 months
  Rejected manuscript returned: Yes, if return postage is supplied by author.
  Rejected manuscript criticized: Yes
Submit to:
  Alan G. Davenport
  Editor
  Faculty of Engineering Science
  The University of Western Ontario
  London, Ontario N6A 3K7, Canada

CANADIAN METALLURGICAL QUARTERLY [1717]
Canadian Journal of Metallurgy and Material Science
906-1117 Ste. Catherine Street, West
Montreal, Quebec H3B 1J3, Canada
(514) 842-3461

SUBSCRIPTION DATA
Issues and rates: Published quarterly.
  Average paid circulation: 2,290
  Annual rate(s): $10.00; Foreign $12.00, $15.00 (air mail)
Publisher or Sponsor: The Metallurgical Society of C.I.M.

EDITORIAL DESCRIPTION
  Contains papers on all metallurgical sciences.
Articles per average issue: 15-30
  Manuscripts accepted in English

MANUSCRIPT INFORMATION
Subject field(s): Physical metallurgy, extractive metallurgy, mineral dressing, hydrometallurgy, iron and steel, general metallurgical operation
Manuscript requirements: See latest issue for style requirements.
  Preferred length: 4,000 to 6,000 words
  Number of copies to be submitted: Three
  Abstract: Yes
Author information and reprints: Payment: None.
  Is simultaneous submission of article to other journals permitted: No
  Exclusive manuscript rights between acceptance and publication: Yes
  Copyright: Held by publication.
  Reprints: Available
Disposition of manuscript:
  Query letter: Not necessary, but helpful
  Receipt of manuscript acknowledged: Yes
  Decision to publish in: 3 months
  Accepted manuscript published in: 6 months
  Rejected manuscript returned: Yes
  Rejected manuscript criticized: Yes
Submit to:
  J. M. Toguri
  Editor-in-Chief
  Department of Metallurgy and Materials Science
  University of Toronto
  Toronto, Ontario, Canada
  (416) 928-2011

CEMENT AND CONCRETE RESEARCH [1718]
An International Journal
Pergamon Press, Inc.
Fairview Park
Elmsford, New York 10523
(914) 592-7700

First published in 1971

SUBSCRIPTION DATA
Issues and rates: Published bi-monthly.
  Annual rate(s): $25.00; Institutions $45.00; Students $10.00
Publisher or Sponsor: American Concrete Institute

EDITORIAL DESCRIPTION
  Publishes papers of interest to scientists, engineers and technologists in the cement and concrete field; also some opinion and criticism, letters and notes.
Articles per average issue: 10-12
  Manuscripts accepted in English, French, German, Russian

MANUSCRIPT INFORMATION
Manuscript requirements: See latest issue for style requirements.
  Preferred length: 12 pages maximum
  Number of copies to be submitted: 2
  Abstract: Yes. A first abstract should be in English; a second in another language is encouraged.

Author information and reprints: Payment: Reprints only.
Is simultaneous submission of article to other journals permitted: Not permitted.
Exclusive manuscript rights between acceptance and publication: Yes
Copyright: Held by publication.
Reprints: Available at cost.
Additional information: Papers are photographically reduced from the original typescript, so it is important that the original be very clear. Papers cannot be retyped by the editors.
Disposition of manuscript:
Query letter: Not necessary.
Receipt of manuscript acknowledged: Yes
Decision to publish in: 4 weeks
Accepted manuscript published in: 5 months
Rejected manuscript returned: Yes, if return postage is supplied by author.
Rejected manuscript criticized: Reasons for rejections only
Submit to:
Prof. Della M. Roy
Editor-in-Chief
Materials Research Laboratory
Pennsylvania State University
University Park, Pennsylvania 16802
(814) 865-1137

CHEMICAL ENGINEERING [1719]
1221 Avenue of the Americas
New York, New York 10020
(212) 997-3198

Previously entitled *Chemical & Metallurgical Engineering*

First published in 1902

SUBSCRIPTION DATA
Issues and rates: Published bi-weekly.
Average paid circulation: 70,000
Annual rate(s): $12.00 Foreign $35.00

EDITORIAL DESCRIPTION
A trade journal for the chemical process industry, it covers the latest technical achievements from industry, government, the academic world; and makes feature reports on special aspects of chemical engineering.

MANUSCRIPT INFORMATION
Manuscript requirements: No specific style guide.
Author information and reprints: Payment: By publication to author. $25 per page.
Is simultaneous submission of article to other journals permitted: No
Exclusive manuscript rights between acceptance and publication: Yes
Copyright: Held by publication.
Disposition of manuscript:
Receipt of manuscript acknowledged: Yes
Decision to publish in: 4 weeks
Accepted manuscript published in: 3 months
Rejected manuscript returned: Yes
Rejected manuscript criticized: No
Submit to:
Robert B. Norden

Executive Editor
(See address above)

CHEMICAL ENGINEERING COMMUNICATIONS [1720]
An International Journal of Chemical Engineering and Applied Chemistry
Gordon and Breach Science Publishers
440 Park Avenue South
New York, New York 10016

First published in 1975
Annual rate(s): Individuals $16.00; Institutions $48.00; Foreign individuals £6.65; Foreign institutions £18.50

EDITORIAL DESCRIPTION
Devoted to the publication of full length research articles, letters, announcements and review papers in all the conventional areas of chemical engineering, applied chemistry and allied fields
Audience: Professional, research, academic
Manuscripts accepted in English

MANUSCRIPT INFORMATION
Subject field(s): Applied and physical chemistry, bio-engineering, molecular theory of equilibrium, transport properties, applied mathematics, etc.
Manuscript requirements: AIP, ACS
Preferred length: 35 pages maximum for articles; letters, 10 pages maximum
Number of copies to be submitted: 2
Abstract: Yes, full-length articles only giving the significant coverage and results in 100-150 words.
Author information and reprints: Payment: Reprints only. 50 reprints
Is simultaneous submission of article to other journals permitted: Not permitted.
Exclusive manuscript rights between acceptance and publication: Yes
Copyright: Held by publication.
Reprints: Available at cost.
Disposition of manuscript:
Query letter: Not necessary.
Decision to publish in: Articles 12-18 weeks
Rejected manuscript returned: Yes, if return postage is supplied by author.
Rejected manuscript criticized: Yes
Submit to:
Cornelius J. Pings,
John H. Seinfeld
Editor and Associate Editor
Division of Chemistry and Chemical Engineering
California Institute of Technology
Pasadena, California 91109

THE CHEMICAL ENGINEERING JOURNAL [1721]
An International Journal of Research and Development
Elsevier Sequoia SA
P.O. Box 851
1001 Lausanne 1, Switzerland
(021) 20 73 81

First published in 1970

SUBSCRIPTION DATA
Issues and rates: Published bi-monthly.
Annual rate(s): SFr. 280.00

EDITORIAL DESCRIPTION
Contains papers of relevance to chemical engineering (original research work not previously published, reviews on recent developments). Criteria for acceptance of papers are originality of thought, quality of work and clarity of style.
Articles per average issue: 9
Manuscripts accepted in English, French, German

MANUSCRIPT INFORMATION
Subject field(s): Chemical engineering
Manuscript requirements: See latest issue for style requirements.
Number of copies to be submitted: Two
Abstract: Yes. Papers in French and German include a summary in English.
Author information and reprints: Payment: Reprints only. 50 reprints free of charge
Is simultaneous submission of article to other journals permitted: No
Exclusive manuscript rights between acceptance and publication: Yes
Copyright: Held by publication.
Reprints: Available, cost quoted upon publication
Disposition of manuscript:
Receipt of manuscript acknowledged: Yes
Decision to publish in: 4 to 6 weeks
Accepted manuscript published in: 4 to 5 months
Rejected manuscript returned: Yes
Rejected manuscript criticized: Sometimes
Submit to:
B. A. Buffham;
D. C. Freshwater
Loughborough University of Technology
Loughborough, Leics., England
(5093) 63171

SPECIAL STIPULATIONS
Papers should be submitted to an appropriate associate editor chosen on the basis of subject matter, language and geography. The names and addresses of associate editors are given on the inside cover of the journal.

CHEMICAL ENGINEERING SCIENCE [1722]
Le Journal International de Génie Chimique
Pergamon Press, Inc.
Fairview Park
Elmsford, New York 10523
(914) 592-7700

First published in 1951

SUBSCRIPTION DATA
Issues and rates: Published monthly.
Annual rate(s): $25.00; Institutions $35.00

EDITORIAL DESCRIPTION
Publishes papers dealing with chemistry, physics and mathematics as applied to

Engineering and allied sciences

chemical engineering; topics range from general principles to new processes.
Articles per average issue: 20-30
Audience: Professional, academic
Manuscripts accepted in English, French, German

MANUSCRIPT INFORMATION

Subject field(s): Fluid mechanics, heat and mass transfer, applied reaction kinetics, chemical thermodynamics, molecular physics, phase relationships in mixtures, process control
Manuscript requirements: See latest issue for style requirements.
Preferred length: None
Number of copies to be submitted: 2
Abstract: Yes
Author information and reprints: Payment: Reprints only.
Is simultaneous submission of article to other journals permitted: Not permitted.
Exclusive manuscript rights between acceptance and publication: Yes
Copyright: Held by publication.
Reprints: Available at cost.
Additional information: Not concerned with pure science.
Disposition of manuscript:
Query letter: Not necessary.
Receipt of manuscript acknowledged: Yes
Decision to publish in: 4 weeks
Accepted manuscript published in: 5 months
Rejected manuscript returned: Yes, if return postage is supplied by author.
Rejected manuscript criticized: Reasons for rejections only
Submit to:
Prof. R. Aris
Editorial Board
Department of Chemical Engineering
University of Minnesota
Minneapolis, Minnesota 55455

CHROMATOGRAPHIA [1723]
International Journal for Rapid Communication in Chromatography and Related Techniques
Pergamon Press, Inc.
Fairview Park
Elmsford, New York 10523
(914) 592-7700

First published in 1968

SUBSCRIPTION DATA
Issues and rates: Published monthly.
Annual rate(s): Institutions $100.00

EDITORIAL DESCRIPTION
Publishes papers from the entire field of theoretical and practical chromatography.
Articles per average issue: 5-8
Audience: Professional, academic
Manuscripts accepted in English, French, German

MANUSCRIPT INFORMATION
Manuscript requirements: See latest issue for style requirements.
Preferred length: Concise
Number of copies to be submitted: 2, double- or triple-spaced
Abstract: Yes. In English
Author information and reprints: Payment: Reprints only. 75 reprints
Is simultaneous submission of article to other journals permitted: Not permitted.
Exclusive manuscript rights between acceptance and publication: Yes
Copyright: Held by publication.
Reprints: Available at cost.
Disposition of manuscript:
Query letter: Not necessary.
Receipt of manuscript acknowledged: Yes
Decision to publish in: 4 weeks
Accepted manuscript published in: 5 months
Rejected manuscript returned: Yes, if return postage is supplied by author.
Rejected manuscript criticized: Reasons for rejections only
Submit to:
L. S. Ettre
Regional Editor
157 Grumman Avenue
Norwalk, Connecticut 06851
(203) 846-9028

CIVIL ENGINEERING [1724]
Environmental Design/Engineered Construction
ASCE
345 East 47th Street
New York, New York 10017
(212) 752-6800

First published in 1930

SUBSCRIPTION DATA
Issues and rates: Published monthly.
Average paid circulation: 71,000; 2,000 controlled
Annual rate(s): $7.00; Foreign $8.50
Publisher or Sponsor: American Society of Civil Engineers

EDITORIAL DESCRIPTION
Serves the environmental design and engineered construction market penetrating its various segments
Articles per average issue: 8-13
Audience: Professional civil construction engineers
Manuscripts accepted in English

MANUSCRIPT INFORMATION
Subject field(s): Civil engineering in its various forms: highway, bridges, water supply and waste treatment facilities, buildings, missile bases, urban developments, etc.
Manuscript requirements: Style sheet sent on request.
Preferred length: 2,400 words; 8 pages
Number of copies to be submitted: 2
Abstract: Yes. Of about 120 words plus a list of key words for indexing purposes.
Author information and reprints: Payment: By publication to author. $300.00 per article.
Is simultaneous submission of article to other journals permitted: Not permitted.
Exclusive manuscript rights between acceptance and publication: Yes
Copyright: Held by publication.
Reprints: Available at cost.
Additional information: Most manuscripts are by members of the Society, but some are from outside sources.
Disposition of manuscript:
Query letter: Not necessary, but advisable.
Receipt of manuscript acknowledged: Yes
Decision to publish in: 2 weeks
Accepted manuscript published in: 6-12 months
Rejected manuscript returned: Yes, with return postage paid by publication.
Rejected manuscript criticized: No
Submit to:
Kneeland A. Godfrey, Jr.
Editor
(See address above)

CONTROL ENGINEERING [1725]
222 South Riverside Plaza
Chicago, Illinois 60606
(312) 648-5800

First published in 1954

SUBSCRIPTION DATA
Issues and rates: Published monthly.
Average paid circulation: 70,000 controlled
Annual rate(s): $10, Foreign $15
Managing Editor: Arthur Klein

EDITORIAL DESCRIPTION
Contains technical feature articles aimed at engineers and management responsible for design of instrumentation and control systems in all industries; furtherance of control system engineering, in practical and professional terms, and application of control equipments in all industry.
Articles per average issue: 10-12
Audience: Professional
Manuscripts accepted in English

MANUSCRIPT INFORMATION
Subject field(s): Control systems engineering, instrumentation and measurement, computer applications to control and test systems
Manuscript requirements: See latest issue for style requirements.
Preferred length: 2,500 words
Number of copies to be submitted: One
Abstract: Not necessary
Author information and reprints: Payment: By publication to author. $25.00 per page.
Is simultaneous submission of article to other journals permitted: No
Exclusive manuscript rights between acceptance and publication: Yes
Copyright: Held by publication.
Reprints: Available, cost dependent on quantity
Additional information: Typewritten, double-spaced; pencil drawings sufficient.
Disposition of manuscript:
Query letter: No
Receipt of manuscript acknowledged: Yes

Decision to publish in: 6-8 weeks
Accepted manuscript published in: 3-6 months
Rejected manuscript returned: Yes
Rejected manuscript criticized: No
Submit to:
Edward J. Kompass
Editor
(See address above)
(312) 648-5840

THE CORNELL ENGINEER [1726]
1 Carpenter Hall
Cornell University
Ithaca, New York 14850
(607) 256-3312

Previously entitled *The Sibley Journal of Engineering, The Cornell Civil Engineer*

First published in 1885

SUBSCRIPTION DATA
Issues and rates: 15 times per year
Average paid circulation: 4,000; 10,000 controlled
Annual rate(s): $5.00; Foreign $5.00; Institutions $5.00; Students Free (on campus)
Publisher or Sponsor: Cornell Society of Engineers
Managing Editor: James DiGiorgio

EDITORIAL DESCRIPTION
Technical engineering, general science, social implications of engineering and technology. Also news of campus events, Cornell engineers and alumni engineers, book reviews.
Articles per average issue: 4
Audience: All types of students (engineering and nonengineering), professors, engineering alumni
Manuscripts accepted in English

MANUSCRIPT INFORMATION
Subject field(s): General science, technical engineering, current research, controversial topics in technological implementation and application.
Manuscript requirements: No specific style guide.
Preferred length: 2,500 words; 10 pages
Number of copies to be submitted: 2
Abstract: Not necessary.
Author information and reprints: Payment: None.
Is simultaneous submission of article to other journals permitted: Permitted.
Exclusive manuscript rights between acceptance and publication: Yes
Copyright: Held by publication-all rights unless relinquished by publication.
Reprints: Available at no cost. 10
Disposition of manuscript:
Query letter: Not necessary, but advisable.
Receipt of manuscript acknowledged: Yes
Decision to publish in: 1 week
Accepted manuscript published in: 1 month
Rejected manuscript returned: Yes, with return postage paid by publication.
Rejected manuscript criticized: Sometimes
Submit to:
Bernarr A. Newman
Editor-in-chief
(See address above)

CORROSION [1727]
2400 West Loop South
Houston, Texas 77027
(713) 622-8980

First published in 1945

SUBSCRIPTION DATA
Issues and rates: Published monthly.
Average paid circulation: 8425; 75 controlled
Annual rate(s): $15.00, Foreign $20.00
Publisher or Sponsor: The National Association of Corrosion Engineers
Managing Editor: Thomas T. Hoke

EDITORIAL DESCRIPTION
A journal of science and engineering concerning all aspects of corrosion and corrosion control.
Articles per average issue: 6
Audience: Professional
Manuscripts accepted in English only

MANUSCRIPT INFORMATION
Subject field(s): Corrosion research, corrosion engineering, corrosion control, metallurgy
Manuscript requirements: See latest issue for style requirements.
Preferred length: 10 to 20 pages
Number of copies to be submitted: Two
Abstract: Yes
Author information and reprints: Payment: None.
Is simultaneous submission of article to other journals permitted: No
Exclusive manuscript rights between acceptance and publication: Yes
Copyright: Held by publication.
Reprints: Available
Disposition of manuscript:
Query letter: No
Receipt of manuscript acknowledged: Yes
Decision to publish in: One month
Accepted manuscript published in: 1 to 4 months
Rejected manuscript returned: Yes
Rejected manuscript criticized: Yes
Submit to:
Roger W. Staehle
The Ohio State University
Department of Metallurgy
116 West 19th Avenue
Columbus, Ohio 43210
(614) 422-6255

CORROSION SCIENCE [1728]
An International Journal of the Science and Practice of Corrosion and Protection
Pergamon Press, Inc.
Fairview Park
Elmsford, New York 10523
(914) 592-7700

First published in 1961

SUBSCRIPTION DATA
Issues and rates: Published monthly.
Annual rate(s): $25.00; Institutions $80.00
Publisher or Sponsor: Corrosion and Protection Association, Corrosion Science Society, Centre Belge d'Etude de la Corrosion

EDITORIAL DESCRIPTION
Publishes original papers and critical reviews in the field of pure and applied corrosion science, relating theoretical to practical knowledge and forming an important link between corrosion scientists and chemical and metallurgical workers.
Articles per average issue: 5
Audience: Professional, academic
Manuscripts accepted in English, French, German

MANUSCRIPT INFORMATION
Manuscript requirements: See latest issue for style requirements.
Preferred length: None
Number of copies to be submitted: 3
Abstract: Yes. Not exceeding 100 words in the language of the paper, and, if possible, in the two other languages.
Author information and reprints: Payment: Reprints only. 50 reprints
Is simultaneous submission of article to other journals permitted: Not permitted.
Exclusive manuscript rights between acceptance and publication: Yes
Copyright: Held by publication.
Reprints: Available at cost.
Disposition of manuscript:
Query letter: Not necessary.
Receipt of manuscript acknowledged: Yes
Decision to publish in: 4 weeks
Accepted manuscript published in: 5 months
Rejected manuscript returned: Yes, if return postage is supplied by author.
Rejected manuscript criticized: Reasons for rejections only
Submit to:
Papers from the U. S. and Canada to:
Dr. J. A. Ford
Editorial Board
The Olin Corporation, Metals Research Labs.
91 Shelton Avenue
New Haven, Connecticut 06504

CRYOGENICS [1729]
International Journal of Low Temperature Research and Engineering
IPC Business Press, Oakfield House
Perrymont Road
Haywards Heath, Sussex GU1 3EW, England
(0483) 71661

First published in 1960

SUBSCRIPTION DATA
Issues and rates: Published monthly.

Average paid circulation: 1,550
Annual rate(s): £36.00; Foreign $94.00
Managing Editor: Zdenek Novak

EDITORIAL DESCRIPTION

Covers all aspects of low temperature research and engineering.
Articles per average issue: 12
Audience: Scientists and engineers using temperature below -150 degrees Centigrade
Manuscripts accepted in English

MANUSCRIPT INFORMATION

Subject field(s): Properties of materials at low temperatures, superconductivity, applications of superconductivity, heat transfer, design of cryogenic equipment, industrial uses, cryobiology, cryosurgery
Manuscript requirements: Style sheet sent on request.
Preferred length: Any length
Number of copies to be submitted: 2
Abstract: Yes. It should be of 100-200 words summarizing the main points covered in the article.
Author information and reprints: Payment: Reprints only. 50 reprints plus 1 copy of issue
Is simultaneous submission of article to other journals permitted: Permitted, but not encouraged.
Exclusive manuscript rights between acceptance and publication: No
Copyright: Held by publication.
Reprints: Available at no cost. 50 Available at cost.
Additional information: Subject matter should be covered in the detail appropriate to original work.
Disposition of manuscript:
Query letter: Not necessary.
Receipt of manuscript acknowledged: Yes
Decision to publish in: 2-3 weeks
Accepted manuscript published in: 4-5 months
Rejected manuscript returned: Yes, with return postage paid by publication.
Rejected manuscript criticized: Sometimes
Submit to:
Zdenek Novak
Managing Editor
(See address above)

ELECTROMECHANICAL DESIGN [1730]

167 Corey Road
Brookline, Massachusetts 02146
(617) 232-5470

First published in 1958

SUBSCRIPTION DATA

Issues and rates: Published monthly.
Average paid circulation: 762; 35,000 controlled
Annual rate(s): $20.00; Foreign $30.00

EDITORIAL DESCRIPTION

Contains articles which deal with design of electromechanical systems and equipment and the management of the design function. Articles reflect basic design philosophies in methods of approach used to solve design problems.
Articles per average issue: 15
Audience: Professional
Manuscripts accepted in English

MANUSCRIPT INFORMATION

Subject field(s): Systems design, equipment design, research and development
Manuscript requirements: Chicago; other information sent on request
Preferred length: None
Number of copies to be submitted: One
Abstract: No
Author information and reprints: Payment: By publication to author. $25.00-$50.00 per page.
Is simultaneous submission of article to other journals permitted: No
Exclusive manuscript rights between acceptance and publication: Yes
Copyright: Held by publication.
Reprints: Available
Disposition of manuscript:
Query letter: No
Receipt of manuscript acknowledged: Yes
Decision to publish in: 1 week
Accepted manuscript published in: 2-4 months
Rejected manuscript returned: Yes, with return postage paid by publication.
Rejected manuscript criticized: Yes
Submit to:
Martin Himmelfarb
Editor
(See address above)

ELECTRONICS & POWER [1731]

Institution of Electrical Engineers
P.O. Box 8, Southgate House
Stevenage, Herts, England
(0438) 3311

Previously entitled *Journal of the Institution of Electrical Engineers*

First published in 1872

SUBSCRIPTION DATA

Issues and rates: 22 times per year
Average paid circulation: 1092; 57,443 controlled
Annual rate(s): £19.00; Foreign $49.00
Publisher or Sponsor: Institution of Electrical Engineers

EDITORIAL DESCRIPTION

Contains in-depth articles on electronics, electrical engineering, control and instrumentation, management, and general scientific articles.
Articles per average issue: 6
Audience: Membership, professional
Manuscripts accepted in English

MANUSCRIPT INFORMATION

Manuscript requirements: See latest issue for style requirements.
Preferred length: 2000 words
Number of copies to be submitted: Two
Abstract: Yes

Author information and reprints: Payment: By publication to author. £10-£12 per 1000 words.
Is simultaneous submission of article to other journals permitted: No
Exclusive manuscript rights between acceptance and publication: Yes
Copyright: Held by publication.
Reprints: Available, first 25 free.
Additional information: Typewritten, double-spaced, on one side with generous margins.
Disposition of manuscript:
Query letter: No
Receipt of manuscript acknowledged: Yes
Decision to publish in: 2-3 weeks
Accepted manuscript published in: 2-3 months
Rejected manuscript returned: Yes
Rejected manuscript criticized: Sometimes
Submit to:
John Christopher Cooper
Editor
(See address above)

ELECTRONICS LETTERS [1732]

P. O. Box 8, Southgate House
Stevenage, Herts SG1 1HQ, England
(0438) 3311

SUBSCRIPTION DATA

Issues and rates: Published bi-weekly.
Average paid circulation: 2493
Annual rate(s): £36.00
Publisher or Sponsor: Institution of Electrical Engineers

EDITORIAL DESCRIPTION

Contains original contributions in letter form on research and high-level practical applications in the fields of electronics and control engineering and science.
Articles per average issue: 20
Manuscripts accepted in English, French, German, Italian, Russian

MANUSCRIPT INFORMATION

Subject field(s): Electronics, control engineering
Manuscript requirements: Style sheet sent on request.
Preferred length: There is a strict length limit of 1½ pages (1,200 words); no mathematics and two 10cm high single column illustrations.
Number of copies to be submitted: Three
Abstract: Yes
Author information and reprints: Payment: By author to publication. £10 per letter voluntary page charge.
Is simultaneous submission of article to other journals permitted: No
Exclusive manuscript rights between acceptance and publication: Yes
Copyright: Held by publication.
Reprints: Available
Additional information: Principal aim is rapid publication. Contributions found acceptable are usually published within six weeks.
Disposition of manuscript:
Query letter: No

Receipt of manuscript acknowledged: Yes
Decision to publish in: 2-4 weeks
Accepted manuscript published in: 2-6 weeks
Rejected manuscript returned: Yes
Rejected manuscript criticized: Sometimes
Submit to:
Bernard Dunkley
Executive Editor
(See address above)

SPECIAL STIPULATIONS

All contributions must be in letter form, submitted in triplicate using double line spacing. Only SI Units may be used.

ELECTRO-OPTICAL SYSTEMS DESIGN [1733]
Everything in Electro-Optics
222 West Adams
Chicago, Illinois 60606
(312) 263-4866

First published in 1969

SUBSCRIPTION DATA

Issues and rates: Published monthly.
Average paid circulation: 27,000 controlled
Annual rate(s): $25.00, Foreign $30.00

EDITORIAL DESCRIPTION

Emphasizes information pertinent to the needs of engineers and physicists who combine optical and electronic technologies into functional systems. Emphasizes "how-to" articles, state-of-the-art articles, and other similar articles.
Articles per average issue: 3-4
Audience: Professional
Manuscripts accepted in English

MANUSCRIPT INFORMATION

Subject field(s): Lasers, optics, infra red, ultraviolet, radiometry, photometry, lowlight level television, optical memories, spectroscopy, reprography, photogramonetry
Manuscript requirements: No specific style guide.
Preferred length: 2500 words
Number of copies to be submitted: Two
Abstract: Yes
Author information and reprints: Payment: By publication to author. $30 per page.
Is simultaneous submission of article to other journals permitted: No
Exclusive manuscript rights between acceptance and publication: Yes
Copyright: Held by publication.
Reprints: Available; cost on request
Additional information: Include biography and photo of author.
Disposition of manuscript:
Query letter: No
Receipt of manuscript acknowledged: Yes
Decision to publish in: 1 week
Accepted manuscript published in: 3-6 months
Rejected manuscript returned: Yes

Submit to:
Robert D. Compton
Editor
(See address above)

ENGINEERING DIGEST [1734]
46 St. Clair Ave. East
Toronto M4T 1N2, Canada
(416) 962-4771

First published in 1954

SUBSCRIPTION DATA

Issues and rates: 10 times per year
Average paid circulation: 54,100 controlled
Annual rate(s): $15.00; Foreign $20.00; Institutions $15.00; Foreign individuals $20.00
Managing Editor: Werner H. Meyfarth

EDITORIAL DESCRIPTION

To publish in digest form, analytical and informative items of technical and professional interest for professional engineers in Canada.
Articles per average issue: Varies
Audience: Registered professional engineers in Canada
Manuscripts accepted in English

MANUSCRIPT INFORMATION

Subject field(s): News of new sciences, pollution abatement, engineering materials and techniques, technical briefs and educational matters of interest to engineers in all disciplines.
Manuscript requirements: Style sheet sent on request.
Preferred length: Varies
Number of copies to be submitted: One
Abstract: Yes. The author is advised to submit a 500 word abstract for evaluation before sending the article. The abstract accompanying the article should be 60-80 words.
Author information and reprints: Payment: None.
Is simultaneous submission of article to other journals permitted: Permitted.
Exclusive manuscript rights between acceptance and publication: No
Copyright: None
Reprints: Available at cost. Varies depending on pages
Disposition of manuscript:
Query letter: Not necessary, but advisable.
Receipt of manuscript acknowledged: No
Decision to publish in: 2 months
Accepted manuscript published in: 2 months
Rejected manuscript returned: Yes, if return postage is supplied by author.
Rejected manuscript criticized: No
Submit to:
Werner H. Meyfarth
Editor
(See address above)

ENGINEERING FRACTURE MECHANICS [1735]
An International Journal
Pergamon Press, Inc.
Fairview Park
Elmsford, New York 10523

First published in 1968

SUBSCRIPTION DATA

Issues and rates: Published quarterly.
Annual rate(s): Individuals $30.00; Institutions $70.00

EDITORIAL DESCRIPTION

Contains articles and original research papers in the field of fracture mechanics and materials science as it relates to mechanics.
Articles per average issue: 10-15
Audience: Researcher, practitioner, academic, governmental and industrial
Manuscripts accepted in English primarily

MANUSCRIPT INFORMATION

Subject field(s): Technical, theoretical papers, syntheses and utilizations of significant research results
Manuscript requirements: See latest issue for style requirements.
Preferred length: None, but concisely written
Number of copies to be submitted: 2, double-spaced
Abstract: Yes
Author information and reprints: Payment: Reprints only.
Is simultaneous submission of article to other journals permitted: Not permitted.
Exclusive manuscript rights between acceptance and publication: Yes
Copyright: Held by publication.
Reprints: Available at cost.
Disposition of manuscript:
Query letter: Not necessary.
Receipt of manuscript acknowledged: Yes
Decision to publish in: 4 weeks
Accepted manuscript published in: 5 months
Rejected manuscript returned: Yes, if return postage is supplied by author.
Rejected manuscript criticized: Reasons for rejections only
Submit to:
Prof. Harold Liebowitz
Editor-in-Chief
School of Engineering and Applied Science
The George Washington University
Washington, D.C. 20006

EXPERIMENTAL MECHANICS [1736]
Journal of the Society for Experimental Stress Analysis
21 Bridge Square
Westport, Connecticut 06880
(203) 227-0829

First published in 1961

Engineering and allied sciences

SUBSCRIPTION DATA
Issues and rates: Published monthly.
  Average paid circulation: 4200; 100 controlled
  Annual rate(s): $25.00; Foreign $28.00
Publisher or Sponsor: Society for Experimental Stress Analysis
Managing Editor: B. E. Rossi

EDITORIAL DESCRIPTION
  Contains research papers describing original investigations in mechanics which are wholly or partly experimental in nature or in which new experimental techniques are presented; applications papers describing the application of experimental-mechanics techniques to the solution of engineering problems.
Articles per average issue: 8
Audience: Professional
  Manuscripts accepted in English

MANUSCRIPT INFORMATION
Subject field(s): Photoelasticity, strain gages, moiré, material testing, fracture mechanics, holography, composites, biomechanics, fatigue, holomechanics, wave propagation, acoustic emission
Manuscript requirements: Style sheet sent on request.
  Preferred length: Technical paper: 4,000 words; technical note: 750 words or less
  Number of copies to be submitted: Three
  Abstract: Yes
Author information and reprints: Payment: By author to publication. Company sponsored voluntary page charge does not affect publication.
  Is simultaneous submission of article to other journals permitted: No
  Exclusive manuscript rights between acceptance and publication: Yes
  Copyright: Held by publication.
  Reprints: Available, cost depends on length
Additional information: In addition to publication in this journal, accepted papers are also published in the semi-annual volume of the *Proceedings of the Society for Experimental Stress Analysis.*
Disposition of manuscript:
  Receipt of manuscript acknowledged: Yes
  Decision to publish in: Several months
  Accepted manuscript published in: Six months
  Rejected manuscript returned: Yes
  Rejected manuscript criticized: Yes
Submit to:
  Editor
  (See address above)

FIRE TECHNOLOGY [1737]
National Fire Protection Association
470 Atlantic Avenue
Boston, Massachusetts 02210
(617) 482-8755

First published in 1965

SUBSCRIPTION DATA
Issues and rates: Published quarterly.
  Average paid circulation: 6300
  Annual rate(s): $10.00
Publisher or Sponsor: National Fire Protection Association

EDITORIAL DESCRIPTION
  Contains papers on fire research and fire protection engineering; reports of test results for the fire behavior of materials and effectiveness of extinguishing agents.
Articles per average issue: 7
Audience: Professional
  Manuscripts accepted in English

MANUSCRIPT INFORMATION
Subject field(s): Fire behavior, smoke and toxic hazards, extinguishing agents, equipment, fire-retardant material, fire-resistive construction, extinguishing systems, fire hazards of materials, basic research on fire.
Manuscript requirements: Chicago
  Preferred length: 4000 words; 14 pages
  Number of copies to be submitted: Three
  Abstract: Yes
Author information and reprints: Payment: None.
  Is simultaneous submission of article to other journals permitted: No
  Exclusive manuscript rights between acceptance and publication: Yes
  Copyright: Held by the Association
  Reprints: Available at cost. 300 or more copies minimum
Additional information: Illustrations for accepted articles will not be returned to author unless specifically requested. Tables, charts, and illustrations should be on separate pages. Author's name should be on title page only.
Disposition of manuscript:
  Query letter: No
  Receipt of manuscript acknowledged: Yes
  Decision to publish in: 60 days
  Accepted manuscript published in: 90 to 180 days
  Rejected manuscript returned: Yes
  Rejected manuscript criticized: No
Submit to:
  Charles A. Tuck, Jr.
  Editor
  (See address above)

SPECIAL STIPULATIONS
  Papers subject to review by the Technical Review Board.

FLUIDICS QUARTERLY [1738]
The International Forum for Research and Development in Fluidics
P.O. Box 2989
Stanford, California 94305
(415) 969-1733

First published in 1967

SUBSCRIPTION DATA
Issues and rates: Published quarterly.
  Average paid circulation: 400
  Annual rate(s): $100.00

EDITORIAL DESCRIPTION
  Contains technical papers and articles covering research and development in fluidics. Includes technical discussion and editorial comment.
Articles per average issue: 6-10
Audience: Professional
  Manuscripts accepted in English

MANUSCRIPT INFORMATION
Subject field(s): Fluidics, fluid power control, fluidic device manufacture, fluid mechanics of fluid lines
Manuscript requirements: Style sheet sent on request.
  Preferred length: None
  Number of copies to be submitted: Three
  Abstract: Yes
Author information and reprints: Payment: None.
  Is simultaneous submission of article to other journals permitted: Foreign language publication of article is permitted
  Exclusive manuscript rights between acceptance and publication: Yes
  Copyright: Held by publication.
  Reprints: Available, cost depends on article
Additional information: Complete listing of technical references, and figures suitable for reproduction are desired.
Disposition of manuscript:
  Query letter: No
  Receipt of manuscript acknowledged: Yes
  Decision to publish in: 6 weeks
  Accepted manuscript published in: 3-6 months
  Rejected manuscript returned: Yes
  Rejected manuscript criticized: Yes
Submit to:
  D. H. Tarumoto
  Editor
  (See address above)

HOSPITAL ENGINEERING [1739]
PO Box 8, Southgate House
Stevenage, Herts. SG1 1HQ, England
Stevenage 3311 ext. 49

SUBSCRIPTION DATA
Issues and rates: Published monthly.
  Average paid circulation: 200; 2000 controlled
  Annual rate(s): £10.40
Managing Editor: David Mackin

EDITORIAL DESCRIPTION
  Contains articles on the application of engineering services within hospitals and allied fields. Every third issue is international hence strong interest in international activities.
Articles per average issue: 3
Audience: Professional
  Manuscripts accepted in English, French

MANUSCRIPT INFORMATION
Subject field(s): Engineering services, hospital technology, applications, surveys, maintenance, management
Manuscript requirements: See latest issue for style requirements.
  Preferred length: 2500 words
  Number of copies to be submitted: Two
  Abstract: Yes, of about 200 words

Author information and reprints: Payment: None.
   Is simultaneous submission of article to other journals permitted: No
   Exclusive manuscript rights between acceptance and publication: Yes
   Copyright: Held by publication.
   Reprints: Available, cost varies
Disposition of manuscript:
   Query letter: Yes
   Receipt of manuscript acknowledged: Yes
   Decision to publish in: 1 month
   Accepted manuscript published in: Varies
   Rejected manuscript returned: Yes
   Rejected manuscript criticized: Yes
Submit to:
   Editor
   (See address above)

HOVERING CRAFT & HYDROFOIL [1740]
The International Review of Air Cushion Vehicles and Hydrofoils
51 Welbeck Street
London W1M 7HE, England
935-8678

SUBSCRIPTION DATA
Issues and rates: Published monthly.
   Annual rate(s): £15, Foreign $40

EDITORIAL DESCRIPTION
   Caters to engineers, research scientists, inventors, and operators in the advanced transportation and air cushion lift fields.
Articles per average issue: 4-8
Audience: Professional, academic, engineering
   Manuscripts accepted in English

MANUSCRIPT INFORMATION
Subject field(s): Hovercraft, hydrofoils, other forms of advanced transportation, relevant forms of propulsion, hoverports, philosophy of transportation systems
Manuscript requirements: See latest issue for style requirements.
   Preferred length: None
   Number of copies to be submitted: One
   Abstract: Yes
Author information and reprints: Payment: By publication to author. £7 per 1000 words.
   Is simultaneous submission of article to other journals permitted: No
   Exclusive manuscript rights between acceptance and publication: Yes
   Copyright: Held by publication.
   Reprints: Available by arrangement.
Disposition of manuscript:
   Receipt of manuscript acknowledged: Yes
   Decision to publish in: 2 weeks
   Accepted manuscript published in: 1-2 months
   Rejected manuscript returned: Yes, if return postage is supplied by author.
   Rejected manuscript criticized: No
Submit to:
   Juanita Kalerghi
   Editor
   (See address above)

IEEE PROCEEDINGS [1741]
345 East 47th Street
New York, New York 10017
(212) 752-6800

Previously entitled *IRE Proceedings*

First published in 1913

SUBSCRIPTION DATA
Issues and rates: Published monthly.
   Average paid circulation: 40,000
   Annual rate(s): Members $7.00; $48.00
Publisher or Sponsor: Institute of Electrical and Electronics Engineers
Managing Editor: W. R. Crone

EDITORIAL DESCRIPTION
   Publication is research-oriented; contains general interest papers on electrical science and technology. Emphasis on tutorial-review treatment.
Articles per average issue: 10
Audience: Professional
   Manuscripts accepted in English

MANUSCRIPT INFORMATION
Subject field(s): Electrical engineering and related areas
Manuscript requirements: Style sheet sent on request.
   Preferred length: None
   Number of copies to be submitted: Three
   Abstract: Yes
Author information and reprints: Payment: By author to publication. $60 per page. Voluntary page charge
   Is simultaneous submission of article to other journals permitted: No
   Exclusive manuscript rights between acceptance and publication: Yes
   Copyright: Held by publication.
   Reprints: Available, cost dependent on length
Additional information: Original (reproducible) figures required from author. Everything typewritten, double-spaced.
Disposition of manuscript:
   Query letter: No
   Receipt of manuscript acknowledged: Yes
   Decision to publish in: 2-3 months
   Accepted manuscript published in: 6-9 months
   Rejected manuscript returned: Yes
   Rejected manuscript criticized: Yes
Submit to:
   Editor
   (See address above)

IEEE TRANSACTIONS ON MAGNETICS [1742]
General Electric Company
Research and Development Center
P. O. Box 8
Schnectady, New York 12301
(518) 346-8771

First published in 1967

SUBSCRIPTION DATA
Issues and rates: Published quarterly.
   Average paid circulation: 4,000
   Annual rate(s): $28.00, Members $7.00
Publisher or Sponsor: Institute of Electrical and Electronics Engineers, Inc.
Managing Editor: F. E. Luborsky

EDITORIAL DESCRIPTION
   Contains papers in all fields of applied magnetics.
Articles per average issue: 50
Audience: Professional
   Manuscripts accepted in English

MANUSCRIPT INFORMATION
Subject field(s): Development, design and application of magnetic devices; magnetic materials; switching and logic devices
Manuscript requirements: See latest issue for style requirements.
   Number of copies to be submitted: Four
   Abstract: Yes
Author information and reprints: Payment: By author to publication. $60.00 per page. Voluntary.
   Is simultaneous submission of article to other journals permitted: Not permitted.
   Exclusive manuscript rights between acceptance and publication: Yes
   Copyright: Held by publication.
   Reprints: Available, 100 free if page charge honored.
Disposition of manuscript:
   Receipt of manuscript acknowledged: Yes
   Decision to publish in: 6 weeks
   Accepted manuscript published in: 6 months
   Rejected manuscript returned: Yes
   Rejected manuscript criticized: Yes
Submit to:
   Paul W. Shumate
   Reviews Editor
   Bell Laboratories, Inc.
   Murray Hill, New Jersey 07974

IEEE TRANSACTIONS ON SYSTEMS, MAN AND CYBERNETICS [1743]
345 East 47th Street
New York, New York 10017
(212) 752-6800

First published in 1970

SUBSCRIPTION DATA
Issues and rates: Published bi-monthly.
   Average paid circulation: 6,500
   Annual rate(s): $36.00; Foreign $36.00; Institutions $36.00; Members $18.00; Foreign individuals $36.00
Publisher or Sponsor: Institute of Electrical and Electronics Engineers
Managing Editor: Elwood K. Gannett

EDITORIAL DESCRIPTION
   Contains articles on the interfaces of communication, control, systems engineering in relation to man.
Articles per average issue: 12
Audience: Engineers
   Manuscripts accepted in English

MANUSCRIPT INFORMATION
Subject field(s): Integration of the theories of communication, control, cybernetics, stochastics, optimization and system structure towards the formulation of a general theory of systems; development of systems engineering technology, definition of methods, techniques, human factors, computer information, man-machine systems
Manuscript requirements: See latest issue for style requirements.
  Preferred length: 12-20 pages
  Number of copies to be submitted: 4
  Abstract: Yes.
Author information and reprints: Payment: None.
  Is simultaneous submission of article to other journals permitted: Not permitted.
  Exclusive manuscript rights between acceptance and publication: Yes
  Copyright: Held by publication.
  Reprints: Available at cost.
Disposition of manuscript:
  Query letter: Not necessary.
  Receipt of manuscript acknowledged: Yes
  Decision to publish in: 3 months
  Accepted manuscript published in: 3 months
  Rejected manuscript returned: No
  Rejected manuscript criticized: Yes
Submit to:
  Andrew P. Sage
  Editor
  School of Engineering and Applied Science
  University of Virginia
  Charlottesville, Virginia 22901
  (804) 924-3050

ILLUMINATING ENGINEERING SOCIETY. JOURNAL [1744]
345 East 47th Street
New York, New York 10017
(212) 752-6800

First published in 1971

SUBSCRIPTION DATA
Issues and rates: Published quarterly.
  Average paid circulation: 2,720
  Annual rate(s): $25.00; Foreign $25.00; Institutions $25.00; Members $10.00
Publisher or Sponsor: Illuminating Engineering Society
Managing Editor: Charles W. Beardsley

EDITORIAL DESCRIPTION
  Publishes papers in all fields of the generation and control of light, as well as the functional and environmental application of illumination.
Articles per average issue: 15
Audience: Professional, engineering
  Manuscripts accepted in English only

MANUSCRIPT INFORMATION
Subject field(s): Technical papers and reports; IES conference papers and discussion; reports of the Illuminating Engineering Research Institute;

recommended practice; ANSI-approved standards; book reviews
Manuscript requirements: Style sheet sent on request.
  Preferred length: 5,000 words
  Number of copies to be submitted: 3
  Abstract: Yes. Include the title, purpose of work, principles and procedures, results obtained, and the significance of the work.
Author information and reprints: Payment: None.
  Is simultaneous submission of article to other journals permitted: Permitted, but not encouraged.
  Exclusive manuscript rights between acceptance and publication: No
  Copyright: Held by publication.
  Reprints: Available at cost.
Disposition of manuscript:
  Query letter: Not necessary, but advisable.
  Receipt of manuscript acknowledged: Yes
  Decision to publish in: 3-6 months
  Accepted manuscript published in: 6-18 months
  Rejected manuscript returned: Yes, if return postage is supplied by author.
  Rejected manuscript criticized: Reasons for rejections only
Submit to:
  Charles W. Beardsley
  Editor
  (See address above)

INDUSTRIAL ENGINEERING [1745]
25 Technology Park
Norcross, Georgia 30071
(404) 449-0460

Previously entitled *Journal of Industrial Engineers*

First published in 1969

SUBSCRIPTION DATA
Issues and rates: Published monthly.
  Average paid circulation: 25,000
  Annual rate(s): $20.00, Foreign $22.00
Publisher or Sponsor: American Institute of Industrial Engineers

EDITORIAL DESCRIPTION
  Contains articles on new developments, new products and services, for the purposes of higher productivity, greater efficiency, and more cost effective management.
Articles per average issue: 12
Audience: Executives, general managers, and engineers in manufacturing, service industries and government.
  Manuscripts accepted in English

MANUSCRIPT INFORMATION
Subject field(s): Material handling, systems engineering, production planning, inventory control, DP systems design, costs and cost control, engineering economy, applied psychology, human factors, work measurement, methods, operations research, plant engineering

Manuscript requirements: Style sheet sent on request.
  Preferred length: 1,500-2,000 words
  Number of copies to be submitted: Two
  Abstract: Yes
Author information and reprints: Payment: None.
  Is simultaneous submission of article to other journals permitted: No
  Exclusive manuscript rights between acceptance and publication: Yes
  Copyright: Held by publication.
  Reprints: Available
Disposition of manuscript:
  Query letter: No
  Receipt of manuscript acknowledged: Yes
  Decision to publish in: 3 weeks
  Accepted manuscript published in: 2 months
  Rejected manuscript returned: Yes
  Rejected manuscript criticized: No
Submit to:
  Robert S. Rice
  Editor
  (See address above)

INSTITUTION OF ELECTRICAL ENGINEERS. PROCEEDINGS [1746]
P.O. Box 8, Southgate House
Stevenage, Herts. SG1 1HQ, England
(0438) 3311

Previously entitled *Journal of the Society of Telegraph Engineers and Electricians; Journal of the Institution of Electrical Engineers*

First published in 1872

SUBSCRIPTION DATA
Issues and rates: Published monthly.
  Average paid circulation: 6029
  Annual rate(s): £46
Publisher or Sponsor: Institution of Electrical Engineers

EDITORIAL DESCRIPTION
  Contains fully refereed papers on original research and practical applications in the fields of electronics, electrical power, control, electrical science, education and management. Published material must represent a significant addition to the literature available to the electrical engineering and control engineering professions.
Articles per average issue: 21
  Manuscripts accepted in English

MANUSCRIPT INFORMATION
Subject field(s): Electronics, electrical power engineering, control automation, electrical science, education in electrical and electronics engineering, engineering management
Manuscript requirements: Style sheet sent on request.
  Preferred length: 8 pages
  Number of copies to be submitted: Three
  Abstract: Yes

Author information and reprints: Payment: None.
Is simultaneous submission of article to other journals permitted: No
Exclusive manuscript rights between acceptance and publication: Yes
Copyright: Held by publication.
Reprints: Available, cost depends on length
Additional information: Only SI (Système Internationale) Units may be used.
Disposition of manuscript:
Query letter: No
Receipt of manuscript acknowledged: Yes
Decision to publish in: 1-3 months
Accepted manuscript published in: 3-4 months
Rejected manuscript returned: Yes
Rejected manuscript criticized: Sometimes
Submit to:
Bernard Dunkley
Group Editor
(See address above)

INTERNATIONAL JOURNAL FOR NUMERICAL METHODS IN ENGINEERING [1747]

John Wiley Sons, Ltd.
Baffins Lane
Chichester, Sussex, England
(0243) 84531

First published in 1969

SUBSCRIPTION DATA
Issues and rates: Published quarterly.
Average paid circulation: 1,500
Annual rate(s): £28.00; Foreign $72.00

EDITORIAL DESCRIPTION
Encourages the application of techniques in numerical analysis to the solution of engineering problems.
Articles per average issue: 15
Audience: Professional, academic
Manuscripts accepted in English

MANUSCRIPT INFORMATION
Manuscript requirements: See latest issue for style requirements.
Preferred length: 4,000 words
Number of copies to be submitted: 3
Abstract: Not necessary.
Author information and reprints: Payment: Reprints only. 50 reprints
Is simultaneous submission of article to other journals permitted: Not permitted.
Exclusive manuscript rights between acceptance and publication: Yes
Copyright: Held by publication.
Reprints: Available at cost.
Disposition of manuscript:
Query letter: Not necessary.
Receipt of manuscript acknowledged: Yes
Decision to publish in: 4 months
Accepted manuscript published in: 12 months
Rejected manuscript returned: No
Rejected manuscript criticized: Reasons for rejections only

Submit to:
Olgierd C. Zienkiewicz
General Editor
(See address above)

INTERNATIONAL JOURNAL OF ENGINEERING SCIENCE [1748]

Pergamon Press, Inc.
Fairview Park
Elmsford, New York 10523
(914) 592-7700

First published in 1963

SUBSCRIPTION DATA
Issues and rates: Published monthly.
Annual rate(s): $25.00; Institutions $115.00

EDITORIAL DESCRIPTION
Contains original research of the highest quality pertaining to the application of the physical, chemical and mathematical sciences to engineering.
Articles per average issue: 5-7
Audience: Researchers, professional, academic
Manuscripts accepted in English (preferred) French, German

MANUSCRIPT INFORMATION
Subject field(s): Cross-fertilization of the above fields with mechanics, electricity and magnetism, thermodynamics, physical chemistry, both from continuum and molecular points of view, either theoretical, experimental or both.
Manuscript requirements: See latest issue for style requirements.
Preferred length: None
Number of copies to be submitted: 2
Abstract: Yes
Author information and reprints: Payment: Reprints only. 50 reprints
Is simultaneous submission of article to other journals permitted: Not permitted.
Exclusive manuscript rights between acceptance and publication: Yes
Copyright: Held by publication.
Reprints: Available at cost.
Disposition of manuscript:
Query letter: Not necessary.
Receipt of manuscript acknowledged: Yes
Decision to publish in: 4 weeks
Accepted manuscript published in: 5 months
Rejected manuscript returned: Yes, if return postage is supplied by author.
Rejected manuscript criticized: Reasons for rejections only
Submit to:
Prof. A. C. Eringen
Editor-in-Chief
Solid Mechanics Program, Engineering Quadrangle
Princeton University
Princeton, New Jersey 08540

Or:
Pfof. I. N. Sneddon
Department of Mathematics
University of Glasgow
Glasgow, Scotland
Regional Editor

INTERNATIONAL JOURNAL OF HEAT AND MASS TRANSFER [1749]

Pergamon Press, Inc.
Fairview Park
Elmsford, New York 10523
(914) 592-7700

First published in 1960

SUBSCRIPTION DATA
Issues and rates: Published monthly.
Annual rate(s): $30.00; Institutions $135.00

EDITORIAL DESCRIPTION
Provides an exchange medium for analytical and experimental research in the field of heat and mass transfer and applications to engineering problems.
Articles per average issue: 13-16
Audience: Professional, academic, engineering
Manuscripts accepted in English preferred

MANUSCRIPT INFORMATION
Subject field(s): Papers on thermodynamics or fluid mechanics are not normally included.
Manuscript requirements: See latest issue for style requirements.
Preferred length: 7,000 words and 10 diagrams, all double-spaced typescript
Number of copies to be submitted: Original and 2 copies
Abstract: Yes. Of about 100 words preceding the paper. Additional abstracts in French, German or Russian will facilitate publication.
Author information and reprints: Payment: None.
Is simultaneous submission of article to other journals permitted: Not permitted.
Exclusive manuscript rights between acceptance and publication: Yes
Copyright: Held by publication.
Reprints: Available at cost.
Disposition of manuscript:
Query letter: Not necessary.
Receipt of manuscript acknowledged: Yes
Decision to publish in: 4 weeks
Accepted manuscript published in: 5 months
Rejected manuscript returned: Yes, if return postage is supplied by author.
Rejected manuscript criticized: Reasons for rejections only
Submit to:
J. P. Hartnett,
W. J. Minkowycz
Associate Editors
Department of Energy Engineering
University of Illinois
Box 4348
Chicago, Illinois 60680

Engineering and allied sciences

INTERNATIONAL JOURNAL OF MACHINE TOOL DESIGN AND RESEARCH [1750]

Pergamon Press, Inc.
Fairview Park
Elmsford, New York 10523
(914) 592-7700

First published in 1961
Annual rate(s): $25.00; Institutions $50.00

EDITORIAL DESCRIPTION

Devoted to the rapid publication of papers dealing with design, development and research relating to the field of machine tools.

Audience: Professional, academic
Manuscripts accepted in English

MANUSCRIPT INFORMATION

Subject field(s): Metal cutting, and forming processes and relevant plasticity, tool wear, machine tool vibration, mechanical engineering aspects of machine tool control, part families, manufacturing systems, automation in general, metal forming machines, explosive forming, experimental and theoretical work
Preferred length: None
Number of copies to be submitted: 2, double-spaced
Abstract: A brief recapitulation of the essential contents of the paper.
Author information and reprints: Payment: 50 reprints
Submit to:
Prof. S. A. Tobias
Joint Editor-in-Chief
Department of Mechanical Engineering
The University, Edgbaston
Birmingham, England

Prof. M. C. Shaw
Regional Editor
Department of Mechanical Engineering
Carnegie-Mellon University
Schenley Park
Pittsburgh Pennsylvania 15213

INTERNATIONAL JOURNAL OF MECHANICAL SCIENCE [1751]

Pergamon Press, Inc.
Fairview Park
Elmsford, New York 10523
(914) 592-7700

First published in 1962

SUBSCRIPTION DATA

Issues and rates: Published monthly.
Annual rate(s): $25.00; Institutions $90.00

EDITORIAL DESCRIPTION

Publishes original papers in many areas of engineering science for which there exists no well-defined heading.

Articles per average issue: 4-8
Audience: Professional, academic
Manuscripts accepted in English

MANUSCRIPT INFORMATION

Subject field(s): Mechanical and civil engineering sciences which give insight into engineering practices and processes. Papers that are purely mathematical or descriptive in nature are not normally published.
Manuscript requirements: See latest issue for style requirements.
Preferred length: None
Number of copies to be submitted: Original and 1 copy, double-spaced
Abstract: Yes. Give the essential contents of each paper at the end as well as a list of all symbols used in the paper.
Author information and reprints: Payment: Reprints only. 50 reprints
Is simultaneous submission of article to other journals permitted: Not permitted.
Exclusive manuscript rights between acceptance and publication: Yes
Copyright: Held by publication.
Reprints: Available at cost.
Disposition of manuscript:
Query letter: Not necessary.
Receipt of manuscript acknowledged: Yes
Decision to publish in: 4 weeks
Accepted manuscript published in: 5 months
Rejected manuscript returned: Yes, if return postage is supplied by author.
Rejected manuscript criticized: Reasons for rejections only
Submit to:
Prof. W. Johnson
Editor
Ridge Hall
Chapel-en-le-Firth
Stockport, Cheshire SK12 6UD, England

INTERNATIONAL JOURNAL OF MULTIPHASE FLOW [1752]

Pergamon Press, Inc.
Fairview Park
Elmsford, New York 10523
(914) 592-7700

First published in 1974

SUBSCRIPTION DATA

Issues and rates: Published bi-monthly.
Annual rate(s): $60.00

EDITORIAL DESCRIPTION

Publishes original investigations of multiphase flow, solid-fluid, fluid-fluid, etc.
Articles per average issue: 6-8
Audience: Professional, academic
Manuscripts accepted in English

MANUSCRIPT INFORMATION

Manuscript requirements: See latest issue for style requirements.
Preferred length: None
Number of copies to be submitted: 3
Abstract: Yes

Author information and reprints: Payment: Reprints only. 50 reprints
Is simultaneous submission of article to other journals permitted: Not permitted.
Exclusive manuscript rights between acceptance and publication: Yes
Copyright: Held by publication.
Reprints: Available at cost.
Disposition of manuscript:
Query letter: Not necessary.
Receipt of manuscript acknowledged: Yes
Decision to publish in: 4 weeks
Accepted manuscript published in: 5 months
Rejected manuscript returned: Yes, if return postage is supplied by author.
Rejected manuscript criticized: Reasons for rejections only
Submit to:
G. Hetsroni
Technion-Israel Institute of Technology
Haifa, Israel
Editor

Turbulent multiphase flow:
R. L. Peskin
Department of Mechanical and Aerospace Engineering
Rutgers University
New Brunswick, New Jersey 08903
Associate Editor

INTERNATIONAL JOURNAL OF NON-LINEAR MECHANICS [1753]

Pergamon Press, Inc.
Fairview Park
Elmsford, New York 10523
(914) 592-7700

First published in 1966

SUBSCRIPTION DATA

Issues and rates: Published bi-monthly.
Annual rate(s): $25.00; Institutions $75.00

EDITORIAL DESCRIPTION

Contains original research results in the various areas of theoretical and applied mechanics of solids and fluids as well as control theory wherein the phenomena are inherently non-linear.
Articles per average issue: 5-7
Audience: Professional, academic
Manuscripts accepted in English (French, German, Russian)

MANUSCRIPT INFORMATION

Subject field(s): Elasticity, plasticity, vibrations, rheology, hydrodynamics, gas dynamics, magnetohydrodynamics, astromechanics, control and stability; may be theoretical, experimental, or both.
Manuscript requirements: See latest issue for style requirements.
Preferred length: None, but concise
Number of copies to be submitted: 2
Abstract: Yes. In English for all articles.

Author information and reprints: Payment:
Reprints only. 50 reprints
Is simultaneous submission of article to
other journals permitted: Not permitted.
Exclusive manuscript rights between
acceptance and publication: Yes
Copyright: Held by publication.
Reprints: Available at cost.
Disposition of manuscript:
Query letter: Not necessary.
Receipt of manuscript acknowledged: Yes
Decision to publish in: 4 weeks
Accepted manuscript published in: 5
months
Rejected manuscript returned: Yes, if
return postage is supplied by author.
Rejected manuscript criticized: Reasons
for rejections only
Submit to:
William A. Nash
Editor-in-Chief
College of Engineering
University of Massachusetts
Amherst, Massachusetts 01002

ISA TRANSACTIONS [1754]
400 Stanwix Street
Pittsburgh, Pennsylvania 15222
(412) 281-3171

First published in 1962

SUBSCRIPTION DATA
Issues and rates: Published quarterly.
Average paid circulation: 1500
Annual rate(s): $33.00, Foreign $38.00,
Members $18.00
Publisher or Sponsor: Instrument Society of
America

EDITORIAL DESCRIPTION
Contains state-of-the-art articles in the
field of instrumentation and automatic
control. Articles describe recent advances
and applications in the areas of process
control, data handling and computation,
analysis instrumentation, chemical and
petroleum instrumentation, and
instrumentation and control systems in
other industries and sciences.
Articles per average issue: 12
Audience: Professional
Manuscripts accepted in English

MANUSCRIPT INFORMATION
Subject field(s): Instrumentation, automatic
control, testing instruments, data
handling, analysis instruments
Manuscript requirements: No specific style
guide.
Preferred length: 12-36 pages
Number of copies to be submitted: Three
Abstract: Yes
Author information and reprints: Payment:
By author to publication. $40.00
voluntary page charge
Is simultaneous submission of article to
other journals permitted: No
Exclusive manuscript rights between
acceptance and publication: Yes
Copyright: Held by publication.
Reprints: Available, price schedule
available upon request

Additional information: Illustrations should
be supplied in India ink (black) and/or
glossy photos. Illustrations and tables
should be on separate pages. Use
International System (SI) units when
designating physical quantities.
Everything typewritten, double-spaced on
white bond paper.
Disposition of manuscript:
Query letter: No
Receipt of manuscript acknowledged: Yes
Decision to publish in: 3-6 months
Accepted manuscript published in: 6-12
months
Rejected manuscript returned: Yes
Rejected manuscript criticized: No
Submit to:
Robert G. Hand
Managing Editor
(See address above)

JOURNAL OF BASIC
ENGINEERING* [1755]
Series D of the ASME Transactions
American Society of Mechanical Engineers
United Engineering Center
345 East 47th Street
New York, New York 10017
(212) 852-6800

SUBSCRIPTION DATA
Issues and rates: Published quarterly.
Annual rate(s): $30.00, Members $15.00,
Foreign $31.50
Publisher or Sponsor: American Society of
Mechanical Engineers
Managing Editor: Ronnie Heaney

EDITORIAL DESCRIPTION
Contains research papers dealing with
fluid mechanics, flow measurement,
hydrodynamics, cavitation, fracture in
metals and related topics.

MANUSCRIPT INFORMATION
Manuscript requirements: Style sheet sent
on request.
Is simultaneous submission of article to
other journals permitted: No
Exclusive manuscript rights between
acceptance and publication: Yes
Copyright: Held by the Society
Reprints: Available
Additional information: Strongly
recommended that prospective authors
discuss manuscript plans with the editor
or one of the associate editors listed in
the publication.
Submit to:
J. J. Jaklitsch, Jr.
Editor
(See address above)

JOURNAL OF COATED
FABRICS [1756]
Technomic Publishing Co., Inc.
265 West State Street
Westport, Connecticut 06880
(203) 226-6356

Previously entitled *Journal of Coated
Fibrous Materials*

First published in 1971

SUBSCRIPTION DATA
Issues and rates: Published quarterly.
Annual rate(s): $65.00; Foreign $70.00
Managing Editor: Prof. A. R. Payne

EDITORIAL DESCRIPTION
Contains articles on all aspects of the
science and technology of coated fibers.
Manuscripts accepted in English

MANUSCRIPT INFORMATION
Subject field(s): The production of coated
fibers, yarns, tapes, webs; laminating,
converting of coatings; geometry of
fibrous structures as coating substrates
Manuscript requirements: See latest issue for
style requirements.
Preferred length: As required,
typewritten, double-spaced
Number of copies to be submitted: 3
Abstract: Yes. Of approximately 100
words as well as 5-10 key words for
indexing purposes.
Author information and reprints: Payment:
None.
Is simultaneous submission of article to
other journals permitted: Permitted, but
not encouraged.
Exclusive manuscript rights between
acceptance and publication: Yes
Copyright: Held by publication.
Reprints: Available at cost.
Additional information: Title should be
brief, followed by the name, affiliation,
and address of the author as well as a
telephone number for the editor's use.
Disposition of manuscript:
Query letter: Not necessary.
Receipt of manuscript acknowledged: Yes
Decision to publish in: 3 months
Accepted manuscript published in: 3-6
months
Rejected manuscript returned: Yes, with
return postage paid by publication.
Rejected manuscript criticized:
Sometimes
Submit to:
Prof. A. R. Payne
Editor
(See address above)

JOURNAL OF
COMPOSITE MATERIALS [1757]
Technomic Publishing Co., Inc.
265 West State Street
Westport, Connecticut 06880
(203)226-6356

First published in 1966

SUBSCRIPTION DATA
Issues and rates: Published quarterly.
Annual rate(s): $65.00; Foreign $70.00
Managing Editor: Dr. Stephen W. Tsai

EDITORIAL DESCRIPTION
Provides new information on the
expanding technology of multiphase
materials.
Manuscripts accepted in English

Engineering and allied sciences

MANUSCRIPT INFORMATION
Subject field(s): Applied mechanics, chemistry, physics, metallurgy, chemical engineering, polymer science, and ceramic science, all relating to the area of composite materials
Manuscript requirements: See latest issue for style requirements.
  Preferred length: 6,000 words; 30 pages
  Number of copies to be submitted: 3
  Abstract: Yes. Of 100 words
Author information and reprints: Payment: None.
  Is simultaneous submission of article to other journals permitted: Permitted, but not encouraged.
  Exclusive manuscript rights between acceptance and publication: Yes
  Copyright: Held by publication.
  Reprints: Available at cost.
Disposition of manuscript:
  Query letter: Not necessary.
  Receipt of manuscript acknowledged: Yes
  Decision to publish in: 3 months
  Accepted manuscript published in: 3-6 months
  Rejected manuscript returned: Yes, with return postage paid by publication.
  Rejected manuscript criticized: Sometimes
Submit to:
  Dr. Stephen W. Tsai
  Editor
  Box 2334
  Dayton, Ohio 45429

JOURNAL OF ENGINEERING FOR INDUSTRY* [1758]

Series B of the ASME Transactions
American Society of Mechanical Engineers
United Engineering Center
345 East 47th Street
New York, New York 10017
(212) 852-6800

SUBSCRIPTION DATA
Issues and rates: Published quarterly.
  Annual rate(s): $30.00, Members $15.00, Foreign $31.50
Publisher or Sponsor: American Society of Mechanical Engineers
Managing Editor: Ronnie Heaney

EDITORIAL DESCRIPTION
  Devoted to articles and technical reports in the areas of management, plant engineering, machine design, materials handling, and the process industries.

MANUSCRIPT INFORMATION
Manuscript requirements: Style sheet sent on request.
  Is simultaneous submission of article to other journals permitted: No
  Exclusive manuscript rights between acceptance and publication: Yes
  Copyright: Held by the Society
  Reprints: Available
Additional information: Strongly recommended that prospective authors discuss manuscript plans with the editor or one of the associate editors listed in the publication.
Submit to:
  J. J. Jaklitsch, Jr.
  Editor
  (See address above)

JOURNAL OF ENGINEERING FOR POWER* [1759]

Series A of the ASME Transactions
American Society of Mechanical Engineers
United Engineering Center
345 East 47th Street
New York, New York 10017
(212) 852-6800

SUBSCRIPTION DATA
Issues and rates: Published quarterly.
  Average paid circulation: Not available.
  Annual rate(s): $30.00, Members $15.00, Foreign $31.50
Publisher or Sponsor: American Society of Mechanical Engineers
Managing Editor: Ronnie Heaney

EDITORIAL DESCRIPTION
  Contains technical research papers concerned with conversion of energy from fuels, gas turbines, nuclear energy, solar energy, and general power generation. Also is concerned with pollution, products from burning, etc.

MANUSCRIPT INFORMATION
Manuscript requirements: Style sheet sent on request.
  Is simultaneous submission of article to other journals permitted: No
  Exclusive manuscript rights between acceptance and publication: Yes
  Copyright: Held by the American Society of Mechanical Engineers
  Reprints: Available
Additional information: Strongly recommended that prospective authors discuss manuscript plans with the editor or one of the associate editors listed in the publication.
Submit to:
  J. J. Jaklitsch, Jr.
  Editor
  (See address above)

JOURNAL OF FIRE AND FLAMMABILITY [1760]

Technomic Publishing Co., Inc.
265 West State Street
Westport, Connecticut 06880
(203) 226-6356

First published in 1970

SUBSCRIPTION DATA
Issues and rates: Published quarterly.
  Annual rate(s): $55.00; Foreign $60.00
Managing Editor: Carlos J. Hilado

EDITORIAL DESCRIPTION
  Contains articles on all aspects of flame and fire study.

Articles per average issue: 8
  Manuscripts accepted in English

MANUSCRIPT INFORMATION
Subject field(s): Information on fire exposures and characteristics, fire and flammability in various environments, and flammability behavior of individual and composite materials, and complete systems, test methods and apparatus
Manuscript requirements: See latest issue for style requirements.
  Preferred length: None
  Number of copies to be submitted: 3
  Abstract: Yes. Of about 100 words
Author information and reprints: Payment: None.
  Is simultaneous submission of article to other journals permitted: Permitted, but not encouraged.
  Exclusive manuscript rights between acceptance and publication: Yes
  Copyright: Held by publication.
  Reprints: Available at cost.
Additional information: Include name, affiliation, biography, and address of author. Everything typewritten, double-spaced on standard paper. Illustrations should be clear, camera-ready glossies.
Disposition of manuscript:
  Query letter: Not necessary.
  Receipt of manuscript acknowledged: Yes
  Decision to publish in: 3 months
  Accepted manuscript published in: 3-6 months
  Rejected manuscript returned: Yes, with return postage paid by publication.
  Rejected manuscript criticized: Sometimes
Submit to:
  Carlos J. Hilado
  Editor-in-Chief
  312 Forest Circle
  South Charleston, West Virginia 25303

JOURNAL OF HEAT TRANSFER* [1761]

Series C of the ASME Transactions
American Society of Mechanical Engineers
United Engineering Center
345 East 47th Street
New York, New York 10017
(212) 852-6800

SUBSCRIPTION DATA
Issues and rates: Published quarterly.
  Average paid circulation: Not available.
  Annual rate(s): $30.00, Members $15.00, Foreign $31.50
Publisher or Sponsor: American Society of Mechanical Engineers
Managing Editor: Ronnie Heaney

EDITORIAL DESCRIPTION
  Contains technical reports in areas such as thermophysical properties, heat exchangers, insulation, phase changes and phase mixtures and thermometry.

MANUSCRIPT INFORMATION
Manuscript requirements: Style sheet sent on request.
Is simultaneous submission of article to other journals permitted: No
Exclusive manuscript rights between acceptance and publication: Yes
Copyright: Held by the American Society of Mechanical Engineeers
Reprints: Available
Additional information: Strongly recommended that prospective authors discuss manuscript plans with the editor or one of the associate editors listed in the publication.
Submit to:
J. J. Jaklitsch, Jr.
Editor
(See address above)

JOURNAL OF LUBRICATION TECHNOLOGY* [1762]
Series F of the ASME Transactions
American Society of Mechanical Engineers
United Engineering Center
345 East 47th Street
New York, New York 10017
(212) 852-6800

SUBSCRIPTION DATA
Issues and rates: Published quarterly.
Average paid circulation: Not available.
Annual rate(s): $30.00, Members $15.00, Foreign $31.50
Publisher or Sponsor: American Society of Mechanical Engineers
Managing Editor: Ronnie Heaney

EDITORIAL DESCRIPTION
Covers lubrication and lubricants, including bearing technology, friction and wear, seals, dry and solid lubricants and nuclear lubrication.

MANUSCRIPT INFORMATION
Manuscript requirements: Style sheet sent on request.
Is simultaneous submission of article to other journals permitted: No
Exclusive manuscript rights between acceptance and publication: Yes
Copyright: Held by the American Society of Mechanical Engineers
Reprints: Available
Additional information: Strongly recommended that prospective authors discuss manuscript plans with the editor or one of the associate editors listed in the publication.
Submit to:
J. J. Jaklitsch, Jr.
Editor
(See address above)

JOURNAL OF THE MECHANICS AND PHYSICS OF SOLIDS [1763]
Pergamon Press, Inc.
Fairview Park
Elmsford, New York 10623
(914) 592-7700

First published in 1952

SUBSCRIPTION DATA
Issues and rates: Published bi-monthly.
Annual rate(s): $25.00, Institutions $65.00

EDITORIAL DESCRIPTION
Brings together the research of mathematicians, engineers, matallurgists and physicists on the properties of constructional materials; special emphasis is on the applications and connections between continuum and micro-structural properties of materials and solutions to problems.
Articles per average issue: 6
Audience: Professional, academic
Manuscripts accepted in English

MANUSCRIPT INFORMATION
Manuscript requirements: See latest issue for style requirements.
Preferred length: None
Number of copies to be submitted: 2
Abstract: Yes
Author information and reprints: Payment: None.
Is simultaneous submission of article to other journals permitted: Not permitted.
Exclusive manuscript rights between acceptance and publication: Yes
Copyright: Held by publication.
Reprints: Available at cost.
Disposition of manuscript:
Query letter: Not necessary.
Receipt of manuscript acknowledged: Yes
Decision to publish in: 4 weeks
Accepted manuscript published in: 6 months
Rejected manuscript returned: Yes, if return postage is supplied by author.
Rejected manuscript criticized: Reasons for rejections only
Submit to:
H. G. Hopkins
Editor-in-Chief
Department of Mathematics
University of Manchester Institute of Science and Technology
Manchester M6O 1QD, England

JOURNAL OF MICROWAVE POWER [1764]
Industrial, Scientific and Medical Applications of Microwave
International Microwave Power Institute
Box 1556
Edmonton, Alberta Canada
(403) 432-5147

SUBSCRIPTION DATA
Issues and rates: Published quarterly.
Annual rate(s): $50.00
Publisher or Sponsor: International Microwave Power Institute
Managing Editor: W.A.G. Voss

EDITORIAL DESCRIPTION
Contains articles on microwave heating, microwave biology, biomedical applications of microwaves, microwave instruments, dielectric properties.
Articles per average issue: 12
Manuscripts accepted in English, French

MANUSCRIPT INFORMATION
Manuscript requirements: Style sheet sent on request.
Preferred length: 1,000-8,000 words; 3-30 pages
Number of copies to be submitted: Three
Abstract: Yes
Author information and reprints: Payment: By author to publication. $20 per page. Requested, not required.
Is simultaneous submission of article to other journals permitted: No
Exclusive manuscript rights between acceptance and publication: Yes
Copyright: Held by publication.
Reprints: Available
Additional information: SI Units to be observed.
Disposition of manuscript:
Query letter: No
Receipt of manuscript acknowledged: Yes
Decision to publish in: 2 months
Accepted manuscript published in: 4 months
Rejected manuscript returned: Yes
Rejected manuscript criticized: If requested
Submit to:
W. A. Geoffrey Voss
Editor
Department of Electrical Engineering
University of Alberta
Edmonton, Alberta Canada

JOURNAL OF STRUCTURAL MECHANICS [1765]
Marcel Dekker Journals
P. O. Box 11305, Church Street Station
New York, New York 10249

First published in 1972

SUBSCRIPTION DATA
Issues and rates: Published quarterly.
Annual rate(s): $62.50; Foreign $66.50

EDITORIAL DESCRIPTION
Addresses itself to all fields of engineering utilizing structural mechanics and presents and consolidates current developments.
Articles per average issue: 6
Audience: Professional, academic
Manuscripts accepted in English

MANUSCRIPT INFORMATION
Manuscript requirements: See latest issue for style requirements. Style sheet sent on request.
Preferred length: 5,000-10,000 words
Number of copies to be submitted: Original and 2 copies
Abstract: Yes. Of about 200 words.

Engineering and allied sciences

Author information and reprints: Payment: Reprints only. 50 reprints
Is simultaneous submission of article to other journals permitted: Not permitted.
Exclusive manuscript rights between acceptance and publication: Yes
Copyright: Held by publication.
Reprints: Available at cost.

Disposition of manuscript:
Query letter: Not necessary.
Receipt of manuscript acknowledged: Yes
Decision to publish in: 2-4 months
Accepted manuscript published in: 8-12 months
Rejected manuscript returned: Yes, with return postage paid by publication.
Rejected manuscript criticized: Yes

Submit to:
E. F. Masur
Editor
Department of Materials Engineering
University of Illinois, Chicago Circle
Chicago, Illinois 60680
(312) 996-3429

JOURNAL OF SYSTEMS ENGINEERING [1766]

Department of Systems Engineering
University of Lancaster
Bailrigg, Lancaster, England
0524 65201 ext. 4659

First published in 1969

SUBSCRIPTION DATA

Issues and rates: Published semi-annually.
Average paid circulation: 750
Annual rate(s): £5.00, Foreign $3.00
Managing Editor: G. M. Jenkins

EDITORIAL DESCRIPTION

Aims to develop and increase awareness of the effectiveness of the systems approach in bringing about improvement in real-life systems and real-life problems. Publishes papers describing how the approach has been applied to a particular area of organizational or technical activity.

Articles per average issue: 5
Audience: Professional
Manuscripts accepted in English

MANUSCRIPT INFORMATION

Subject field(s): Industrial operation and organization, public administration and environmental issues, management, planning, control and information systems

Manuscript requirements: See latest issue for style requirements.
Preferred length: 3,000-10,000 words
Number of copies to be submitted: Two
Abstract: No

Author information and reprints: Payment: Reprints only. 50 free offprints
Is simultaneous submission of article to other journals permitted: Yes, except to other journals in systems or management.
Exclusive manuscript rights between acceptance and publication: Yes
Copyright: Held by publication.
reprinting usually allowed.

Reprints: Available, first 50 free

Disposition of manuscript:
Query letter: Helpful
Receipt of manuscript acknowledged: Yes
Decision to publish in: 2-3 months
Accepted manuscript published in: 4-10 months
Rejected manuscript returned: Yes
Rejected manuscript criticized: Yes

Submit to:
Michael R. Jackson
Publishing Editor
(See address above)

JOURNAL OF TERRAMECHANICS [1767]

Pergamon Press, Inc.
Fairview Park
Elmsford, New York 10523
(914) 592-7700

First published in 1964

SUBSCRIPTION DATA

Issues and rates: Published quarterly.
Annual rate(s): $30.00; Institutions $60.00
Publisher or Sponsor: International Society for Terrain Vehicle Systems

EDITORIAL DESCRIPTION

Presents a cross-section of technical papers, reviews, comments and discussions in the field of terramechanics, the study of off-the-road locomotion and the movement of the soil; it aims to provide a common forum for discussion and exchange of ideas.

Articles per average issue: 3-5
Audience: Professional, academic
Manuscripts accepted in English, French, German

MANUSCRIPT INFORMATION

Manuscript requirements: See latest issue for style requirements.
Preferred length: None
Number of copies to be submitted: 2
Abstract: Yes

Author information and reprints: Payment: None.
Is simultaneous submission of article to other journals permitted: Not permitted.
Exclusive manuscript rights between acceptance and publication: Yes
Copyright: Held by publication.
Reprints: Available at cost.

Disposition of manuscript:
Query letter: Not necessary.
Receipt of manuscript acknowledged: Yes
Decision to publish in: 4 weeks
Accepted manuscript published in: 5 months
Rejected manuscript returned: Yes, if return postage is supplied by author.
Rejected manuscript criticized: Reasons for rejections only

Submit to:
N. W. Radforth
Editor
Muskeg Studies, University of New Brunswick
814 Montgomery Street
Fredericton, New Brunswick, Canada

LETTERS IN APPLIED AND ENGINEERING SCIENCES [1768]

An International Journal
Pergamon Press, Inc.
Fairview Park
Elmsford, New York 10523
(914) 592-7700

First published in 1973

SUBSCRIPTION DATA

Issues and rates: Published bi-monthly.
Annual rate(s): $25.00; Institutions $50.00

EDITORIAL DESCRIPTION

Established for the purpose of rapid dissemination of novel research in the fields of engineering and applied science especially research pertaining to applications of physical, chemical and mathematical sciences to engineering.

Articles per average issue: 6-8
Audience: Professional, academic
Manuscripts accepted in English, French, German, Russian

MANUSCRIPT INFORMATION

Subject field(s): Interdisciplinary research in continuum physics, continuum mechanics, electricity and magnetism, biochemistry, and biomedical engineering, and material sciences.

Manuscript requirements: See latest issue for style requirements.
Preferred length: 12 page limit, including diagrams
Number of copies to be submitted: 2
Abstract: Yes

Author information and reprints: Payment: None.
Is simultaneous submission of article to other journals permitted: Not permitted.
Exclusive manuscript rights between acceptance and publication: Yes
Copyright: Held by publication.
Reprints: Available at cost.

Additional information: All MSS. must be camera-ready copy to facilitate rapid publication.

Disposition of manuscript:
Query letter: Not necessary.
Receipt of manuscript acknowledged: Yes
Rejected manuscript returned: Yes, if return postage is supplied by author.
Rejected manuscript criticized: Reasons for rejections only

Submit to:
Prof. A. C. Eringen
Editor-in-Chief
Engineering Quadrangle, Room E-307
Princeton University
Princeton, New Jersey 08540

MACHINE DESIGN [1769]
Penton Publishing Company
1111 Chester Avenue
Cleveland, Ohio 44114
(216) 696-7000

First published in 1929

SUBSCRIPTION DATA
Issues and rates: Published bi-weekly.
　Average paid circulation: 6,000; 121,000 controlled
　Annual rate(s): $20.00; Foreign $35.00

EDITORIAL DESCRIPTION
　The purpose is to help engineers solve their everyday design problems and keep them informed of the latest developments in technology, and to provide information about leadership within the engineering profession.
Articles per average issue: 6
Audience: Design engineers
　Manuscripts accepted in English

MANUSCRIPT INFORMATION
Subject field(s): Technical articles: survey, select-and-apply; how-to-design; engineering management, survey articles, equipment
Manuscript requirements: See latest issue for style requirements. Style sheet sent on request.
　Preferred length: No preference
　Number of copies to be submitted: 1
　Abstract: Not necessary.
Author information and reprints: Payment: By publication to author. Varies with length; averages $35.00 per page
　Is simultaneous submission of article to other journals permitted: Not permitted.
　Exclusive manuscript rights between acceptance and publication: Yes
　Copyright: Held by publication. unless other arrangements specifically made.
　Reprints: Available at cost.
Disposition of manuscript:
　Query letter: Not necessary, but advisable.
　Receipt of manuscript acknowledged: Yes
　Decision to publish in: 2-3 weeks
　Accepted manuscript published in: 3 months
　Rejected manuscript returned: Yes, with return postage paid by publication.
　Rejected manuscript criticized: Reasons for rejections only
Submit to:
　Melvin E. Long
　Executive Editor
　(See address above)

MATERIALS ENGINEERING [1770]
Reinhold Publishing Company, Inc.
600 Summer Street
Stamford, Connecticut 06904
(203) 348-7531

Previously entitled *Metals & Alloys*, 1929; *Materials & Methods*, 1945; *Materials in Design Engineering*, 1957 to 1967

SUBSCRIPTION DATA
Issues and rates: Published monthly.
　Average paid circulation: 60,000 controlled
　Annual rate(s): $18; Foreign $36
Managing Editor: John A. Mock

EDITORIAL DESCRIPTION
　Contains articles on materials (metals, nonmetallics, industrial textiles, etc.), finishes and coatings, joining and fastening, testing, parts and forms.
Articles per average issue: 5
Audience: OEM specifiers of metals, non-metals, forms, finishes
　Manuscripts accepted in English

MANUSCRIPT INFORMATION
Subject field(s): Materials properties, materials applications
Manuscript requirements: See latest issue for style requirements.
　Preferred length: 2500-3000 words
　Number of copies to be submitted: Two
　Abstract: Yes
Author information and reprints: Payment: By publication to author. Varies
　Is simultaneous submission of article to other journals permitted: No
　Exclusive manuscript rights between acceptance and publication: Yes
　Copyright: Held by publication.
　Reprints: Available, cost varies
Disposition of manuscript:
　Receipt of manuscript acknowledged: Yes
　Decision to publish in: 2 weeks
　Accepted manuscript published in: 2-3 months
　Rejected manuscript returned: Yes
　Rejected manuscript criticized: No
Submit to:
　Jack E. Hauck
　Editor
　(See address above)

MATERIALS SCIENCE AND ENGINEERING [1771]
An International Journal
Elsevier Sequoia SA
P.O. Box 851
CH-1001 Lausanne, Switzerland
(021) 20 73 81

First published in 1966

SUBSCRIPTION DATA
Issues and rates: Published monthly.
　Annual rate(s): SFr. 725.00

EDITORIAL DESCRIPTION
　Contains theoretical and experimental studies and reviews of properties of materials, related both to their structure and engineering application.
Articles per average issue: 5
Audience: Professional, academic
　Manuscripts accepted in English, French, German

MANUSCRIPT INFORMATION
Subject field(s): Crystalline and non-crystalline, composte materials, glasses, liquids, organic and inorganic polymers, plasmas, vapours
Manuscript requirements: Style sheet sent on request.
　Number of copies to be submitted: Two
　Abstract: Yes. Papers in French or German should include a summary in English.
Author information and reprints: Payment: Reprints only. 50 reprints
　Is simultaneous submission of article to other journals permitted: No
　Exclusive manuscript rights between acceptance and publication: Yes
　Copyright: Held by publication.
　Reprints: Available, cost quoted upon publication
Disposition of manuscript:
　Query letter: No
　Receipt of manuscript acknowledged: Yes
　Decision to publish in: 4 weeks
　Accepted manuscript published in: 5 months
　Rejected manuscript returned: Yes
　Rejected manuscript criticized: Sometimes
Submit to:
　Robert Maddin
　Editor-in-Chief
　School of Metallurgy and Materials Science
　University of Pennsylvania
　Philadelphia, Pennsylvania 19104
　(215) 594-5000

Authors in Japan should send their manuscripts to:
　Hiroshi Kimura
　Research Institute for Iron, Steel and Other Metals
　Tohoku University
　Sendai, Japan

MATERIALS AND STRUCTURES [1772]
Research and Testing
12 rue Brancion
Paris, France
532-21-69

Previously entitled *Rilem Bulletin*

First published in 1959

SUBSCRIPTION DATA
Issues and rates: Published bi-monthly.
　Average paid circulation: 1700
　Annual rate(s): 135 Francs; Foreign 160 Francs
Publisher or Sponsor: International Union of Testing and Research
Managing Editor: R. L'Hermite; M. Fickelson

EDITORIAL DESCRIPTION
　Contains articles on construction materials, performance of structures, materials testing methods, common testing, thermal insulation and methods for the testing and observation of structures.
Articles per average issue: 5-8

Engineering and allied sciences

Audience: Researchers
 Manuscripts accepted in French, English

MANUSCRIPT INFORMATION

Manuscript requirements: See latest issue for style requirements.
 Preferred length: 10-12 pages
 Number of copies to be submitted: Two
Author information and reprints: Payment: Reprints only. 50 free
 Is simultaneous submission of article to other journals permitted: No
 Exclusive manuscript rights between acceptance and publication: Yes
 Reprints: Available
Disposition of manuscript:
 Query letter: No
 Receipt of manuscript acknowledged: Yes
 Decision to publish in: One month
 Accepted manuscript published in: 6-9 months
 Rejected manuscript returned: Yes
 Rejected manuscript criticized: No
Submit to:
 M. Fickelson
 Editor
 (See address above)

MECHANICAL ENGINEERING* [1773]

American Society of Mechanical Engineers
United Engineering Center
345 East 47th Street
New York, New York 10017
(212) 852-6800

SUBSCRIPTION DATA

Issues and rates: Published monthly.
 Average paid circulation: Not available.
 Annual rate(s): $30.00, Members $15.00, Foreign $31.50
Publisher or Sponsor: American Society of Mechanical Engineers
Managing Editor: Ronnie Heaney

EDITORIAL DESCRIPTION

A general, nonspecialist journal containing brief reports, articles and reviews in the field of mechanical engineering.

MANUSCRIPT INFORMATION

Manuscript requirements: Style sheet sent on request.
 Is simultaneous submission of article to other journals permitted: No
 Exclusive manuscript rights between acceptance and publication: Yes
 Copyright: Held by the American Society of Mechanical Engineers
 Reprints: Available
Additional information: Strongly recommended that prospective authors discuss manuscript plans with the editor or one of the associate editors listed in the publication.
Submit to:
 J. J. Jaklitsch, Jr.
 Editor
 (See address above)

MECHANICS RESEARCH COMMUNICATIONS [1774]

An International Journal
Pergamon Press, Inc.
Fairview Park
Elmsford, New York 10523
(914) 592-7700

First published in 1974

SUBSCRIPTION DATA

Issues and rates: Published monthly.
 Annual rate(s): $25.00; Institutions $35.00
Publisher or Sponsor: International Centre for Mechanical Sciences

EDITORIAL DESCRIPTION

Devoted to the rapid communication of contributions in the mechanics of fluids, solids, particles and systems.

Articles per average issue: 10
Audience: Professional, academic
 Manuscripts accepted in English

MANUSCRIPT INFORMATION

Manuscript requirements: See latest issue for style requirements.
 Preferred length: None
 Number of copies to be submitted: 2
 Abstract: Yes
Author information and reprints: Payment: None.
 Is simultaneous submission of article to other journals permitted: Not permitted.
 Exclusive manuscript rights between acceptance and publication: Yes
 Copyright: Held by publication.
 Reprints: Available at cost.
Additional information: All copy must be clean and camera-ready. It is therefore important to see the Preparation of Manuscripts section in a current issue.
Disposition of manuscript:
 Query letter: Not necessary.
 Receipt of manuscript acknowledged: Yes
 Decision to publish in: 4 weeks
 Accepted manuscript published in: 5 months
 Rejected manuscript returned: Yes, if return postage is supplied by author.
 Rejected manuscript criticized: Reasons for rejections only
Submit to:
 Prof. Bruno A. Boley, Dean
 The Technical Institute, Northwestern University
 1941 Orrington Avenue
 Evanston, Illinois 60201

 Prof. Horst Lippmann
 Institut fuer Technische Mechanik und Festigkeitslehre
 Universität Karlsruhe (TH), PB 6380
 Am Fasangarten 3
 D-75 Karlsruhe 1, Federal Republic of Germany
 (0721) 608-2661
 Editors-in-Chief

MECHANISM AND MACHINE THEORY [1775]

The Scientific Journal of IFTMM
Pergamon Press, Inc.
Fairview Park
Elmsford, New York 10523
(914) 592-7700

First published in 1966

SUBSCRIPTION DATA

Issues and rates: Published bi-monthly.
 Annual rate(s): $25.00; Institutions $70.00
Publisher or Sponsor: International Federation for the Theory of Machines and Mechanisms

EDITORIAL DESCRIPTION

Provides a medium of communication between engineers and scientists engaged in research and development within the fields of science embraced by the Federation.

Articles per average issue: 10
Audience: Professional, academic
 Manuscripts accepted in English, French, German

MANUSCRIPT INFORMATION

Subject field(s): Mechanism, dynamics of machines, applied vibration, gears and transmissions, man-machine systems and robots, applications of mathematics, graphics, and computers to machine theory and design.
Manuscript requirements: See latest issue for style requirements.
 Preferred length: 25 maximum
 Number of copies to be submitted: 2
 Abstract: Yes. A brief abstract of about 80 words in the language of the paper, and another of about 400 words in one of the other languages.
Author information and reprints: Payment: Reprints only. 50 reprints
 Is simultaneous submission of article to other journals permitted: Not permitted.
 Exclusive manuscript rights between acceptance and publication: Yes
 Copyright: Held by publication.
 Reprints: Available at cost.
Disposition of manuscript:
 Query letter: Not necessary.
 Receipt of manuscript acknowledged: Yes
 Decision to publish in: 4 weeks
 Accepted manuscript published in: 5 months
 Rejected manuscript returned: Yes, if return postage is supplied by author.
 Rejected manuscript criticized: Reasons for rejections only
Submit to:
 Prof. John J. Uiker, Jr.
 Editor-in-Chief
 Department of Mechanical Engineering
 University of Wisconsin at Madison
 1513 University Avenue
 Madison, Wisconsin 53706

METALS ENGINEERING QUARTERLY [1776]

American Society for Metals
Metals Park, Ohio 44022
(216) 338-5151

SUBSCRIPTION DATA

Issues and rates: Published quarterly.
  Average paid circulation: 3,200
  Annual rate(s): $18.00; Members $12.00; Foreign $20.00
Publisher or Sponsor: American Society for Metals

EDITORIAL DESCRIPTION

Publishes engineering articles on the processing, fabrication, and testing of metals, alloys, and related materials.

MANUSCRIPT INFORMATION

Subject field(s): Metals engineering, non-metals engineering
Manuscript requirements: Style sheet sent on request.
  Number of copies to be submitted: Two
Author information and reprints: Payment: None.
  Is simultaneous submission of article to other journals permitted: No
  Exclusive manuscript rights between acceptance and publication: No
  Copyright: Held by publication.
  Reprints: Available, cost depends on length
Disposition of manuscript:
  Receipt of manuscript acknowledged: Yes
  Decision to publish in: 1 week
  Accepted manuscript published in: 6-9 months
  Rejected manuscript returned: Yes
  Rejected manuscript criticized: No
Submit to:
  Carl R. Weymueller
  Editor
  (See address above)

MISSOURI ENGINEER [1777]

P. O. Box 365
Jefferson City, Missouri 65101
(314) 636-4861

First published in 1937

SUBSCRIPTION DATA

Issues and rates: Published monthly.
  Average paid circulation: 3,000
  Annual rate(s): $2.00; Individuals $2.00; Members $2.00
Publisher or Sponsor: Missouri Society of Professional Engineers
Managing Editor: Paul N. Doll, P.E.

EDITORIAL DESCRIPTION

Professional, non-technical, engineering material.
Articles per average issue: One
Audience: Registered professional engineers in Missouri
  Manuscripts accepted in English

MANUSCRIPT INFORMATION

Subject field(s): Registration of P.E.'s, certification of technologists, engineering education (degree & renewal); ethics; product liability; legislation; engineering manpower supply & demand
Manuscript requirements: No specific style guide.
  Preferred length: 1,200 words; 2 pages
  Number of copies to be submitted: One
  Abstract: Not necessary.
Author information and reprints: Payment: None.
  Is simultaneous submission of article to other journals permitted:
  Exclusive manuscript rights between acceptance and publication: No
Disposition of manuscript:
  Query letter: Not necessary, but advisable.
  Receipt of manuscript acknowledged: Yes
  Decision to publish in: 7 days
  Accepted manuscript published in: 20 days
  Rejected manuscript returned: No
  Rejected manuscript criticized: No
Submit to:
  Paul N. Doll
  Editor
  (See address above)

MODERN PACKAGING [1778]

The Authority on Technology and Marketing in Packaging
1221 Avenue of the Americas
New York, New York 10020
(212) 997-1221

First published in 1927

SUBSCRIPTION DATA

Issues and rates: Published monthly.
  Average paid circulation: 54,000
  Annual rate(s): $10, Foreign $25
Managing Editor: Jerome P. Frank

EDITORIAL DESCRIPTION

Contains news and articles on packaging management, research, engineering, technology, materials and containers, design, and construction, testing (including market testing), production and marketing.
Articles per average issue: 2
Audience: Professional
  Manuscripts accepted in English

MANUSCRIPT INFORMATION

Subject field(s): Technical, engineering, marketing, engineering in packaging.
Manuscript requirements: Style sheet sent on request.
  Preferred length: Maximum four pages
  Number of copies to be submitted: Original and one carbon
  Abstract: No
Author information and reprints: Payment: By publication to author. $30 per page. Or reprints of article.
  Is simultaneous submission of article to other journals permitted: No
  Exclusive manuscript rights between acceptance and publication: Yes
  Copyright: Held by publication.
  Reprints: Available, cost depends on length.
Disposition of manuscript:
  Query letter: Prefer initial inquiry with brief description of proposed article.
  Receipt of manuscript acknowledged: Yes
  Decision to publish in: 1-2 months
  Accepted manuscript published in: 3-4 months
  Rejected manuscript returned: Yes
  Rejected manuscript criticized: Yes
Submit to:
  Thomas M. James
  Editor-in-Chief
  (See address above)

NAVAL ENGINEERS JOURNAL [1779]

Suite 807
1012 14th Street, N. W.
Washington, D. C. 20005
(202) 737-0757

First published in 1889

SUBSCRIPTION DATA

Issues and rates: Published bi-monthly.
  Average paid circulation: 5,600; 150 controlled
  Annual rate(s): $20.00; Foreign $30.00; Institutions $20.00; Students $5.00; Members $5.00-$20.00
Publisher or Sponsor: The American Society of Naval Engineers
Managing Editor: Frank G. Law

EDITORIAL DESCRIPTION

To advance the profession and state of the art of engineering and to provide a large variety of technical articles.
Articles per average issue: 7
Audience: Naval and marine architects and engineers and others involved the mobile and fixed facilities of the Navy, Coast Guard, and various ship systems.
  Manuscripts accepted in English

MANUSCRIPT INFORMATION

Subject field(s): Automation, air cushion vehicles, cost effectiveness, ecological environment, electronics, education, technical data, fire safety, ship materials and procurement, systems and designs.
Manuscript requirements: Style sheet sent on request.
  Preferred length: 3,000 to 5,000 words
  Abstract: Not necessary. If abstract is included, it should not exceed 250 words.
Author information and reprints: Payment: None.
  Is simultaneous submission of article to other journals permitted: Not permitted.
  Exclusive manuscript rights between acceptance and publication: Yes
  Copyright: Held by publication.
  Reprints: Available at no cost. 20 Available at cost. Over 20

Additional information: Please request a style sheet and sample copy before submitting manuscript.
Disposition of manuscript:
Query letter: Not necessary, but advisable.
Receipt of manuscript acknowledged: Yes
Decision to publish in: 3 months
Accepted manuscript published in: 2 months
Rejected manuscript returned: Yes, with return postage paid by publication.
Rejected manuscript criticized: Sometimes
Submit to:
Frank G. Law
Editor
(See address above)

THE NORTHERN ENGINEER [1780]

Rm. 701-D, Geophysical Institute
University of Alaska
Fairbanks, Alaska 99701
(907) 479-7798

First published in 1969

SUBSCRIPTION DATA
Issues and rates: Published quarterly.
Annual rate(s): $6.00 for all
Publisher or Sponsor: University of Alaska-Fairbanks, Geophysical Institute
Managing Editor: Gina Brown

EDITORIAL DESCRIPTION
It focuses on engineering practice and technological developments in cold regions, but in the broadest sense. We will consider articles stemming from the physical, biological and behavioral sciences, also views and comments having a social or political thrust, so long as the viewpoint relates to technical problems of northern habitation, commerce, development or the environment.
Articles per average issue: Six
Audience: Engineers, contractors, geologists, homebuilders, professional engineers, architects working in Arctic and Subartic.
Manuscripts accepted in English

MANUSCRIPT INFORMATION
Subject field(s): Building in North; oil and gas engineering/developmental problems at high latitudes; energy and energy-production at high latitudes; pollution at high latitudes; water/snow hydrology at high lat.; specific problems dealing with cold, permafrost, road conditions, etc.
Manuscript requirements: Style sheet sent on request.
Preferred length: 15-20 pages; triple-spaced typewritten
Number of copies to be submitted: 1 copy. Drawings and photos must be originals.
Abstract: Not necessary.

Author information and reprints: Payment: None.
Is simultaneous submission of article to other journals permitted: Permitted, but not encouraged.
Exclusive manuscript rights between acceptance and publication: No
Copyright: No copyright
Reprints: Available at no cost. 10
Additional information: Include a brief biographical sketch of each author, of apprx. 15-20 lines. Photos and original drawings are returned in good shape. References are helpful for bibliographical information.
Disposition of manuscript:
Query letter: Not necessary.
Receipt of manuscript acknowledged: Yes
Decision to publish in: 2 weeks
Accepted manuscript published in: 3 months
Rejected manuscript returned: Yes, with return postage paid by publication.
Rejected manuscript criticized: Sometimes If requested
Submit to:
Gina Brown
Editor
(See address above)

OPTICAL ENGINEERING [1781]

The Journal of the Society of Photo-optical Instrumentation Engineers
P.O. Box 1146
Palos Verdes Estates, California 90274

First published in 1956

SUBSCRIPTION DATA
Issues and rates: Published bi-monthly.
Average paid circulation: 6,000
Annual rate(s): $25.00; Foreign $30.00
Publisher or Sponsor: Society of Photo-optical Instrumentation Engineers
Managing Editor: Joseph Yaver

EDITORIAL DESCRIPTION
Provides a medium for the publication of papers and reports on design developments of applications techniques which are of interest to those engaged in photo- and electro-optical instrumentation. Articles on general technical advances, as well as industry news, are published in the SPIE-Glass section.
Articles per average issue: 10-15
Audience: Professional
Manuscripts accepted in English

MANUSCRIPT INFORMATION
Subject field(s): Holography, space optics, range instrumentation, underwater research, image enhancement, bio-medical research, laser applications, fiber optics, computer applications, transportation studies, pattern recognition, high speed photography
Manuscript requirements: See latest issue for style requirements.
Preferred length: 20 pages
Number of copies to be submitted: Three
Abstract: Yes, of 200 words maximum.

Author information and reprints: Payment: By author to publication. $50.00 voluntary page charges.
Is simultaneous submission of article to other journals permitted: No
Exclusive manuscript rights between acceptance and publication: Yes
Copyright: Held by publication.
Reprints: Available, cost depends on length of paper
Disposition of manuscript:
Query letter: No
Receipt of manuscript acknowledged: Yes
Decision to publish in: 2-4 weeks
Accepted manuscript published in: 4-8 weeks
Rejected manuscript returned: Yes
Rejected manuscript criticized: No
Submit to:
John B. DeVelis
Merrimack College
North Andover, Massachusetts 01845

PARTICULATE MATTER [1782]

10 St. Johns Road
London NW11 OPG, England
01-458-2965

First published in 1970

SUBSCRIPTION DATA
Issues and rates: Published quarterly.
Annual rate(s): $15.00; Foreign $45.00
Publisher or Sponsor: Powder Advisory Centre
Managing Editor: Abraham S. Goldberg

EDITORIAL DESCRIPTION
An international journal for all aspects of powder and bulk granular solids technology including powder metallurgy
Articles per average issue: 6
Audience: Academicians and persons involved in industrial research and development
Manuscripts accepted in English

MANUSCRIPT INFORMATION
Subject field(s): Powder technology, powder matallurgy, powder coatings
Manuscript requirements: No specific style guide.
Preferred length: No preference
Number of copies to be submitted: 3
Abstract: Yes. 100-150 words
Author information and reprints: Payment: None.
Is simultaneous submission of article to other journals permitted: Permitted, but not encouraged.
Exclusive manuscript rights between acceptance and publication: Yes
Copyright: Held by publisher, but released for all reasonable purposes
Reprints: Available at cost.
Disposition of manuscript:
Query letter: Not necessary, but advisable.
Receipt of manuscript acknowledged: Yes
Decision to publish in: 1 month
Accepted manuscript published in: 6 months

PLASTICS ENGINEERING [1783]
Official Publication of the Society of Plastics Engineers, Inc.
656 West Putnam Avenue
Greenwich, Connecticut 06830
(203) 661-4770

Previously entitled *SPE Journal*

First published in 1934

SUBSCRIPTION DATA

Issues and rates: Published monthly.
  Average paid circulation: 18,500
  Annual rate(s): $12.00, Foreign $17.00
Publisher or Sponsor: Society of Plastics Engineers, Inc.

EDITORIAL DESCRIPTION

Contains technical and general articles on topics of interest to plastics engineers, also product news, books, people, etc.
Articles per average issue: 6
Audience: Professional
  Manuscripts accepted in English

MANUSCRIPT INFORMATION

Subject field(s): Plastics engineering, industrial management
Manuscript requirements: See latest issue for style requirements.
  Preferred length: 2500 words; 10-15 pages
  Number of copies to be submitted: Five
  Abstract: Yes
Author information and reprints: Payment: None.
  Is simultaneous submission of article to other journals permitted: No
  Exclusive manuscript rights between acceptance and publication: Yes
  Copyright: Held by publication.
  Reprints: Available, cost on request
Additional information: Typewritten, double-spaced, 37 characters per line, on one side only.
Disposition of manuscript:
  Query letter: Preferred
  Receipt of manuscript acknowledged: Yes
  Decision to publish in: 3 months
  Accepted manuscript published in: 3-6 months
  Rejected manuscript returned: Yes
  Rejected manuscript criticized: Yes
Submit to:
  A.A. Schoengood
  Editor
  (See address above)

POWER [1784]
1221 Avenue of the Americas
New York, New York 10020
(212) 997-4724

SUBSCRIPTION DATA

Issues and rates: Published monthly.
  Average paid circulation: 55,000
  Annual rate(s): Individuals $5.40, Foreign $25.00
Managing Editor: Sheldon D. Strauss

EDITORIAL DESCRIPTION

Contains articles on power generation and plant utilities engineering. Deals with the modern technology basic to the function of producing and applying energy, as well as the equipment and techniques required.
Articles per average issue: 5
Audience: Professional
  Manuscripts accepted in English only

MANUSCRIPT INFORMATION

Subject field(s): Environmental management; maintenance lubrication; air, gas and liquid handling; engines, turbines, generators; instrumentation and control; heating/cooling; plant electric systems; steam generation; energy optimization
Manuscript requirements: No specific style guide.
  Preferred length: 3,500 words; 12 pages maximum
  Number of copies to be submitted: One
Author information and reprints: Payment: By publication to author. $25.00 per page.
  Is simultaneous submission of article to other journals permitted: No
  Exclusive manuscript rights between acceptance and publication: Yes
  Copyright: Held by publication.
  Reprints: Available, write in for prices.
Additional information: Drawings to be submitted in pencil on graph paper. Illustrations and glossy photographs welcome. Typewritten, double-spaced; 75-80 characters per line; first paragraph should be a short abstract of article.
Disposition of manuscript:
  Query letter: No
  Receipt of manuscript acknowledged: Yes
  Decision to publish in: 6-8 weeks
  Accepted manuscript published in: 3 months
  Rejected manuscript returned: Yes
  Rejected manuscript criticized: No
Submit to:
  James J. O'Connor
  Editor-in-Chief
  (See address above)

PRODUCTION ENGINEER [1785]
Journal of the Institution of Production Engineers
146, Cromwell Road
London, SW7 4EF England
01-370-6981

SUBSCRIPTION DATA

Issues and rates: Published monthly.
  Average paid circulation: 700, 19,560 controlled
  Annual rate(s): £10
Publisher or Sponsor: Institution of Production Engineers
Managing Editor: Penelope Patterson

EDITORIAL DESCRIPTION

Contains technical articles, institution notes, new products on the market, abstracts of other literature in subject field.

MANUSCRIPT INFORMATION

Subject field(s): Machine tools, management, metal working.
Manuscript requirements: See latest issue for style requirements.
  Preferred length: 4,000 to 5,000 words
  Number of copies to be submitted: Three
Author information and reprints: Payment: None.
  Is simultaneous submission of article to other journals permitted: No
  Exclusive manuscript rights between acceptance and publication: Yes
  Copyright: Negotiable.
  Reprints: Available at cost
Disposition of manuscript:
  Receipt of manuscript acknowledged: Yes
  Decision to publish in: 2 months
  Accepted manuscript published in: 6 months
  Rejected manuscript returned: Yes
  Rejected manuscript criticized: No
Submit to:
  The Editor
  (See address above)

PUBLIC WORKS [1786]
200 South Broad Street
Ridgewood, New Jersey 07451
(201) 445-5800

SUBSCRIPTION DATA

Issues and rates: Published monthly.
  Average paid circulation: 1200; 30,000 controlled
  Annual rate(s): $15.00; Foreign $25.00

EDITORIAL DESCRIPTION

Contains engineering-oriented articles on design, construction, maintenance and operation of public works facilities for cities, counties and states. Subject matter includes streets and highways, traffic control, lighting, water supplies, environmental wastes control and administration.
Articles per average issue: 16
Audience: Professional
  Manuscripts accepted in English

MANUSCRIPT INFORMATION

Subject field(s): Streets and highways, water systems, wastewater systems, refuse collection and disposal, traffic control, street lighting
Manuscript requirements: Style sheet sent on request.
  Preferred length: 2500 words; 8-10 pages
  Number of copies to be submitted: One
  Abstract: No

(Rejected manuscript returned: Yes, with return postage paid by publication.
Rejected manuscript criticized: Sometimes
Submit to:
  Abraham S. Goldberg
  (See address above))

Engineering and allied sciences

Author information and reprints: Payment: By publication to author. $30.00 per page.
Is simultaneous submission of article to other journals permitted: No
Exclusive manuscript rights between acceptance and publication: Yes
Copyright: None
Reprints: Available, cost depends on length
Disposition of manuscript:
Query letter: No
Receipt of manuscript acknowledged: Yes
Decision to publish in: One week
Accepted manuscript published in: 4-5 months
Rejected manuscript returned: Yes
Rejected manuscript criticized: No
Submit to:
Edward B. Rodie
Editor
(See address above)

PURDUE ENGINEER MAGAZINE [1787]
Box 651
Stewart Center
West Fafayette, Indiana 47907
(317) 749-2957

First published in 1905

SUBSCRIPTION DATA
Issues and rates: 6 times per year
Annual rate(s): Individuals $4.00; Institutions $4.00
Managing Editor: Ronald W. Garrett

EDITORIAL DESCRIPTION
Provides undergraduates with a technical publication that will benefit them as students and as potential engineers.
Articles per average issue: 3-4
Audience: Undergraduate engineering students
Manuscripts accepted in English

MANUSCRIPT INFORMATION
Subject field(s): Technical engineering and scientific work, news concerning the engineering and scientific world, and history of famous scientists
Manuscript requirements: See latest issue for style requirements. Style sheet sent on request.
Preferred length: 10 pages
Number of copies to be submitted: 1
Abstract: Not necessary.
Author information and reprints: Payment: None.
Is simultaneous submission of article to other journals permitted: Permitted.
Exclusive manuscript rights between acceptance and publication: No
Copyright: None
Additional information: The use of photographs and diagrams is encouraged.
Disposition of manuscript:
Query letter: Not necessary.
Receipt of manuscript acknowledged: No
Decision to publish in: 4 weeks
Accepted manuscript published in: 6 weeks

Rejected manuscript returned: Yes, with return postage paid by publication.
Rejected manuscript criticized: Sometimes
Submit to:
Ronald W. Garrett;
David E. Wonn
Managing Editors
(See address above)

QUALITY ASSURANCE NEWS [1788]
Journal of the Institute of Quality Assurance
146 Cromwell Road
London SW7 4EF, England
01-370-6981

Previously entitled *Quality Engineer*

SUBSCRIPTION DATA
Issues and rates: Published monthly.
Average paid circulation: 665; 5080 controlled
Annual rate(s): £4.60
Publisher or Sponsor: The Institute of Quality Assurance
Managing Editor: Penelope Patterson

EDITORIAL DESCRIPTION
Contains technical articles in the field of quality assurance, inspection, statistical quality control, metrology.

MANUSCRIPT INFORMATION
Subject field(s): Quality control, metrology, inspection equipment
Manuscript requirements: See latest issue for style requirements.
Preferred length: 4000-5000 words
Number of copies to be submitted: Three
Author information and reprints: Payment: None.
Is simultaneous submission of article to other journals permitted: No
Exclusive manuscript rights between acceptance and publication: Yes
Copyright: Held by author.
Reprints: Available at cost
Disposition of manuscript:
Receipt of manuscript acknowledged: Yes
Decision to publish in: 2 months
Accepted manuscript published in: 4 months
Rejected manuscript returned: Yes
Rejected manuscript criticized: No
Submit to:
Editor
(See address above)

QUALITY PROGRESS [1789]
Monthly Newsmagazine of the American Society for Quality Control
American Society for Quality Control
161 West Wisconsin Avenue
Milwaukee, Wisconsin 53203
(414) 272-8575

Previously entitled *Industrial Quality Control*

First published in 1944

SUBSCRIPTION DATA
Issues and rates: Published monthly.
Average paid circulation: 20,000
Annual rate(s): $12.00, Foreign $14.00
Publisher or Sponsor: American Society for Quality Control

EDITORIAL DESCRIPTION
Contains articles on the applications of quality control and reliability techniques.
Articles per average issue: 4
Audience: Professional
Manuscripts accepted in English

MANUSCRIPT INFORMATION
Subject field(s): Quality control, reliability, standards, metrics, motivation
Manuscript requirements: Chicago
Preferred length: 1000-4000 words
Number of copies to be submitted: Three
Abstract: Yes
Author information and reprints: Payment: None.
Is simultaneous submission of article to other journals permitted: No
Exclusive manuscript rights between acceptance and publication: Yes
Copyright: Held by publication.
Reprints: Available, cost varies
Disposition of manuscript:
Query letter: No
Receipt of manuscript acknowledged: No
Decision to publish in: 2-4 months
Accepted manuscript published in: One Year
Rejected manuscript returned: Yes
Rejected manuscript criticized: Yes
Submit to:
March L. Jacques
(See address above)

THE RADIO AND ELECTRONIC ENGINEER [1790]
Journal of the Institution of Electronic and Radio Engineers
8-9 Bedford Square
London WC1B 3RG, England
01-637-2771

Previously entitled *Journal of the British Institution of Radio Engineers*

First published in 1926

SUBSCRIPTION DATA
Issues and rates: Published monthly.
Average paid circulation: 15,341
Annual rate(s): £14.00, Foreign $38.00
Publisher or Sponsor: Institution of Electronic and Radio Engineers
Managing Editor: G. D. Clifford

EDITORIAL DESCRIPTION
Contains original papers and reviews on all aspects of electronics and radio engineering.
Articles per average issue: 6-8
Audience: Professional electronic and radio engineers
Manuscripts accepted in English

MANUSCRIPT INFORMATION
Subject field(s): Electronics, radio, radar, television, computers, control, instrumentation communications, audio, nucleonics and medical electronics
Manuscript requirements: Style sheet sent on request.
  Preferred length: 10,000 words maximum
  Number of copies to be submitted: Two
  Abstract: Yes.
Author information and reprints: Payment: None.
  Is simultaneous submission of article to other journals permitted: No
  Exclusive manuscript rights between acceptance and publication: Yes
  Copyright: Held by publication.
  Reprints: Available, first 50 free
Disposition of manuscript:
  Query letter: Not necessary.
  Receipt of manuscript acknowledged: Yes
  Decision to publish in: 4-8 weeks
  Accepted manuscript published in: 4 months
  Rejected manuscript returned: Yes
  Rejected manuscript criticized: Yes
Submit to:
  Frank W. Sharp
  Editor
  (See address above)

RADIO-ELECTRONICS [1791]
The Magazine for New Ideas in Electronics
200 Park Avenue South
New York, New York 10003
(212) 777-6400

First published in 1929

SUBSCRIPTION DATA
Issues and rates: Published monthly.
  Average paid circulation: 160,000
  Annual rate(s): $7.00, Foreign $8.00

EDITORIAL DESCRIPTION
  Contains articles on electronics, TV, radio. Emphasis is on construction.
Articles per average issue: 12
Audience: Professional
  Manuscripts accepted in English

MANUSCRIPT INFORMATION
Subject field(s): Electronic servicing, construction, hi-fi, shortwave radio, solid-state, communications, test equipment
Manuscript requirements: Style sheet sent on request.
  Preferred length: 2,500 words
  Number of copies to be submitted: One
  Abstract: No
Author information and reprints: Payment: By publication to author. From $50.00 to $100.00 per page.
  Is simultaneous submission of article to other journals permitted: No
  Exclusive manuscript rights between acceptance and publication: Yes
  Copyright: Held by publication.
  Reprints: Available at cost.
Disposition of manuscript:
  Query letter: No

  Receipt of manuscript acknowledged: Yes
  Decision to publish in: 2-3 weeks
  Accepted manuscript published in: 4-8 months
  Rejected manuscript returned: Yes
  Rejected manuscript criticized: Sometimes
Submit to:
  Larry Steckler
  Editor
  (See address above)

SAMPE JOURNAL [1792]
Official Journal of the Society for the Advancement of Material and Process Engineering
P. O. Box 613
Azusa, California 91702
(213) 334-1810

SUBSCRIPTION DATA
Issues and rates: Published bi-monthly.
  Average paid circulation: 2,000; 3,000 controlled
  Annual rate(s): $25.00; Foreign $45.00
Publisher or Sponsor: Society for the Advancement of Material and Process Engineering (SAMPE)
Managing Editor: Stanley T. Peters

EDITORIAL DESCRIPTION
  Materials field, including adhesives, composites, spacecraft materials, pollution, biomedical materials, corrosion electronics, thermo-plastic fabrication, machining and fatigue testing as well as many other material-oriented fields.
Articles per average issue: Four
Audience: Material and process engineers and related fields
  Manuscripts accepted in English

MANUSCRIPT INFORMATION
Subject field(s): Recent advances in materials fields from any geographical location.
Manuscript requirements: See latest issue for style requirements.
  Number of copies to be submitted: Two
  Abstract: Yes
Author information and reprints: Payment: None.
  Is simultaneous submission of article to other journals permitted: Not permitted.
  Exclusive manuscript rights between acceptance and publication: Yes
  Copyright: Held by publication.
Additional information: All contributions must be accompanied by a stamped return envelope.
Disposition of manuscript:
  Query letter: Not necessary.
  Receipt of manuscript acknowledged: No
  Decision to publish in: 3 months
  Accepted manuscript published in: 6 months
  Rejected manuscript returned: No
  Rejected manuscript criticized: No
Submit to:
  Stanley T. Peters
  Editor
  P. O. Box 4248
  Mountain View, California 94040
  (415) 591-1414

SAMPE QUARTERLY [1793]
P.O. Box 613A
Azusa, California 91702
(213) 334-1810

First published in 1969

SUBSCRIPTION DATA
Issues and rates: Published quarterly.
  Average paid circulation: 1,000
  Annual rate(s): $20.00; Foreign $24.00;
  Individuals $20.00; Institutions $20.00;
  Students $20.00; Members $7.00; Foreign individuals $24.00; Foreign institutions $24.00
Publisher or Sponsor: Society for the Advancement of Material & Process Engineering (SAMPE)
Managing Editor: William G. Long

EDITORIAL DESCRIPTION
  The entire spectrum of materials & processes is covered, including: plastics, elastomers, adhesives, ablatives, ceramics, joining techniques, corrosion resistance, nondestructive testing, metals, advanced composites, coatings, testing & evaluation.
Articles per average issue: 5
Audience: Material and process engineers and related fields
  Manuscripts accepted in English

MANUSCRIPT INFORMATION
Subject field(s): Recent advances in plastics, elastomers, adhesives, ablatives, ceramics, joining techniques, corrosion resistance, nondestructive testing, metals, advanced composites, coatings, testing and evaluation, and related subjects from any geographical location.
Manuscript requirements: See latest issue for style requirements.
  Number of copies to be submitted: Two
  Abstract: Yes.
Author information and reprints: Payment: None.
  Is simultaneous submission of article to other journals permitted: Not permitted.
  Exclusive manuscript rights between acceptance and publication: Yes
  Copyright: Held by publication.
  Reprints: Available at cost.
Additional information: Brief descriptions of test procedure, material process, unique property determination or other aspect of materials technology too short for formal paper will be published as a technical note under author's name.
Disposition of manuscript:
  Query letter: Not necessary.
  Receipt of manuscript acknowledged: No
  Decision to publish in: 3 months
  Accepted manuscript published in: 3-6 months
  Rejected manuscript returned: No
  Rejected manuscript criticized: No
Submit to:
  William G. Long
  Editor
  1407 Brookville Lane
  Lynchburg, Virginia 24502
  (804) 384-5111 Ex. 5716

SCRIPTA METALLURGICA [1794]

Pergamon Press, Inc.
Fariview Park
Elmsford, New York 10523
(914) 592-7700

First published in 1967

SUBSCRIPTION DATA

Issues and rates: Published monthly.
  Annual rate(s): $25.00; Institutions $65.00
Publisher or Sponsor: American Society for Metals, American Institute of Mining, Metallurgical and Petroleum Engineers, American Society for Testing and Materials

EDITORIAL DESCRIPTION

The companion journal to *Acta Metallurgica*, its purpose is to provide rapid publication of letters and summaries of reports that contribute to the understanding of the properties and behavior of solids in terms of fundamental particles.
Articles per average issue: Varies
Audience: Professional, academic
  Manuscripts accepted in English

MANUSCRIPT INFORMATION

Subject field(s): Letters: Reports of new work or discussions of work already published; Summaries: Only if the full-length report is available and included with the summary.
Manuscript requirements: See latest issue for style requirements. Style sheet sent on request.
  Preferred length: 3 pages
  Number of copies to be submitted: 2, double-spaced
  Abstract: Yes, for summaries only
Author information and reprints: Payment: None.
  Is simultaneous submission of article to other journals permitted: Not permitted.
  Exclusive manuscript rights between acceptance and publication: Yes
  Copyright: Held by publication
  Reprints: Available at cost.
Additional information: Because the papers are reproduced photographically, the MSS. must conform accurately to the specifications given in each issue.
Disposition of manuscript:
  Query letter: Not necessary.
  Receipt of manuscript acknowledged: Yes
  Rejected manuscript returned: Yes, if return postage is supplied by author.
  Rejected manuscript criticized: Reasons for rejections only
Submit to:
  Prof. Bruce Chalmers
  Editor
  Division of Engineering and Applied Physics
  Harvard University
  Cambridge, Massachusetts 02138

SOLID STATE TECHNOLOGY [1795]

14 Vanderventer Avenue
Port Washington, Long Island New York 11050
(516) 883-6200

Previously entitled *Semiconductor Products*

First published in 1958

SUBSCRIPTION DATA

Issues and rates: Published monthly.
  Average paid circulation: 18,000
  Annual rate(s): $15.00, Foreign $20.00
Managing Editor: Selma Uslaner

EDITORIAL DESCRIPTION

Written by and for people engaged in designing, processing, fabrication and testing of solid state devices and circuits, e.g. transistors, diodes, integrated circuits and hybrids. Publication contains technical articles: state of the art, survey, tutorial, research and development.
Articles per average issue: 5
Audience: Professional
  Manuscripts accepted in English

MANUSCRIPT INFORMATION

Subject field(s): Semiconductor, materials, devices and circuits, processing
Manuscript requirements: Style sheet sent on request.
  Preferred length: 2,000-3,000 words; 10-15 pages
  Number of copies to be submitted: Two
  Abstract: Yes, of about 100 words
Author information and reprints: Payment: By publication to author. $30.00 per page. Payment is at editor's discretion.
  Is simultaneous submission of article to other journals permitted: No
  Exclusive manuscript rights between acceptance and publication: Yes
  Copyright: Held by publication.
  Reprints: Available, cost depends on length and quantity
Additional information: Manuscript should include: abstract, original finished artwork for line drawings, glossy photos for pictures, separate list of figure captions referenced in text.
Disposition of manuscript:
  Query letter: No
  Receipt of manuscript acknowledged: Yes
  Decision to publish in: One month
  Accepted manuscript published in: 4-9 months
  Rejected manuscript returned: Yes
  Rejected manuscript criticized: Sometimes
Submit to:
  Samuel L. Marshall
  Editor
  (See address above)

SPECIAL STIPULATIONS

Manuscript should be on a non-commercial engineering level and conform to editorial style with references listed as noted in text and should include author's name, affiliation, phone number.

SOUND AND VIBRATION [1796]

27101 East Oviatt Road
Bay Village, Ohio 44140
(216) 835-0101

First published in 1967

SUBSCRIPTION DATA

Issues and rates: Published monthly.
  Average paid circulation: 19,500 controlled
  Annual rate(s): $10.00, Foreign $20.00

EDITORIAL DESCRIPTION

Covers the fields of noise, vibration, shock control, hearing conservation, dynamic measurement instrumentation, dynamic environmental testing, and architectural acoustics.
Articles per average issue: 4
Audience: Professional
  Manuscripts accepted in English

MANUSCRIPT INFORMATION

Subject field(s): Noise control, vibration control, hearing conservation, dynamic measurements, audiometric measurements, dynamic environmental testing, architectural acoustics
Manuscript requirements: See latest issue for style requirements.
  Preferred length: 5000-8000 words
  Number of copies to be submitted: One
  Abstract: Yes
Author information and reprints: Payment: None.
  Is simultaneous submission of article to other journals permitted: Yes
  Exclusive manuscript rights between acceptance and publication: No
  Copyright: Held by publication.
  Reprints: Available
Disposition of manuscript:
  Query letter: No
  Receipt of manuscript acknowledged: Yes
  Decision to publish in: 3 months
  Accepted manuscript published in: 6 months
  Rejected manuscript returned: Yes
  Rejected manuscript criticized: Yes
Submit to:
  Jack K. Mowry
  Editor and Publisher
  (See address above)

STRAIN [1797]

Journal of the British Society for Strain Measurement
281 Heaton Road
Newcastle Upon Tyne, England
0632-655273

First published in 1965

SUBSCRIPTION DATA

Issues and rates: Published quarterly.
  Average paid circulation: 1200; 100 controlled
  Annual rate(s): £5.00, Foreign $13.75

EDITORIAL DESCRIPTION

Contains papers on strain measurement, experimental stress analysis, engineering R and D and instrumentation.
Articles per average issue: 4
Audience: Academic and industrial engineers
Manuscripts accepted in English

MANUSCRIPT INFORMATION

Subject field(s): Strain measurement, stress analysis, transducers, instrumentation, materials, high temperature strain, impacts, holography, data loggings, finite element
Manuscript requirements: Style sheet sent on request.
Preferred length: 5000 words; 6 pages
Number of copies to be submitted: Two
Abstract: Yes.
Author information and reprints: Payment: None.
Is simultaneous submission of article to other journals permitted: By agreement in advance.
Exclusive manuscript rights between acceptance and publication: Yes
Copyright: Held by publication.
Reprints: Available, cost varies
Disposition of manuscript:
Query letter: Not necessary, but advisable.
Receipt of manuscript acknowledged: Yes
Decision to publish in: 3 months
Accepted manuscript published in: 6-9 months
Rejected manuscript returned: Yes
Rejected manuscript criticized: Yes
Submit to:
I. B. Macduff
Editor
(See address above)

TELECOMMUNICATIONS [1798]
610 Washington Street
Dedham, Massachusetts 02026
(617) 326-8220

First published in 1967

SUBSCRIPTION DATA
Issues and rates: Published monthly.
Average paid circulation: 41,000 controlled
Annual rate(s): $25; Foreign $30

EDITORIAL DESCRIPTION

Contains practical systems engineering and applications articles on all facets of telecommunications, including transmission, reception, processing and display of information in both analog and digital form. Seeks to bridge the gap between telecommunications systems, equipment and service suppliers and the end users, by providing information on current and future trends in the application of systems and equipment.
Articles per average issue: 3
Audience: Professional
Manuscripts accepted in English only

MANUSCRIPT INFORMATION

Subject field(s): Transmission, reception, processing, display, analog, digital, audio, video, data
Manuscript requirements: Style sheet sent on request.
Preferred length: 15 pages
Number of copies to be submitted: Three
Abstract: Yes
Author information and reprints: Payment: By publication to author. $100.00 per article.
Is simultaneous submission of article to other journals permitted: No
Exclusive manuscript rights between acceptance and publication: Yes
Copyright: Held by publication.
Reprints: Available, at nominal cost
Disposition of manuscript:
Query letter: No
Receipt of manuscript acknowledged: Yes
Decision to publish in: One month
Accepted manuscript published in: 3-6 months
Rejected manuscript returned: Yes
Rejected manuscript criticized: Yes
Submit to:
Michael D. Sadofsky
Editor
(See address above)

TRAFFIC ENGINEERING & CONTROL [1799]
29 Newman Street
London W1P 3PE England
(01) 636-3956

First published in 1960

SUBSCRIPTION DATA
Issues and rates: Published monthly.
Average paid circulation: 5,200
Annual rate(s): £10.00; Foreign $30.00
Managing Editor: Ernest Davies

EDITORIAL DESCRIPTION

Contains articles on traffic and transportation engineering, planning, management and control, road safety, urban public transport, parking, lighting, signing, signalling and instrumentation.
Articles per average issue: 6-8
Audience: Professional
Manuscripts accepted in English only

MANUSCRIPT INFORMATION

Manuscript requirements: Style sheet sent on request.
Preferred length: 2,500-3,500 words
Number of copies to be submitted: Three
Abstract: Yes
Author information and reprints: Payment: By publication to author.
Is simultaneous submission of article to other journals permitted: Yes
Exclusive manuscript rights between acceptance and publication: Yes
Copyright: Held by publication.
Reprints: Available
Disposition of manuscript:
Query letter: No
Receipt of manuscript acknowledged: Yes
Decision to publish in: One month
Accepted manuscript published in: 3-4 months
Rejected manuscript returned: No
Rejected manuscript criticized: Yes
Submit to:
Ernest Davies
Editor
(See address above)

TRANSMISSION AND DISTRIBUTION [1800]
1 River Road
Cos Cob, Connecticut 06807
(203) 661-5000

Previously entitled *Power Equipment*

First published in 1956

SUBSCRIPTION DATA
Issues and rates: Published monthly.
Average paid circulation: 33,600 controlled

EDITORIAL DESCRIPTION

Contains articles on electric power transmission and distribution; news of industry; new products. Articles treat the subject from viewpoint of the practicing electric utility engineer.
Articles per average issue: 7-8
Audience: Professional
Manuscripts accepted in English

MANUSCRIPT INFORMATION

Subject field(s): Electric power distribution, electric power transmission, electric utility operation and maintenance, electric power line construction
Manuscript requirements: Chicago
Preferred length: 1500 words
Number of copies to be submitted: One
Abstract: No
Author information and reprints: Payment: By publication to author. Payment is based on printed page length with a decreasing rate per page. First page $30.00
Is simultaneous submission of article to other journals permitted: Yes, if submitted to a non-related field
Exclusive manuscript rights between acceptance and publication: Yes
Copyright: Held by publication.
Reprints: Available at no cost. 12 copies
Disposition of manuscript:
Query letter: No
Receipt of manuscript acknowledged: Yes
Decision to publish in: 1-3 weeks
Accepted manuscript published in: 4-9 months
Rejected manuscript returned: Yes
Rejected manuscript criticized: Sometimes
Submit to:
Stuart M. Lewis
Editor
(See address above)

WEAR [1801]

An International Journal on the Science and Technology of Friction, Lubrication and Wear
Elsevier Sequoia SA
P.O. Box 851
1001 Lausanne 1, Switzerland
(021) 20 73 81

First published in 1957

SUBSCRIPTION DATA
Issues and rates: Published monthly.
  Annual rate(s): SFr. 600.00
Managing Editor: Douglas Scott

EDITORIAL DESCRIPTION
  Contains articles on all of tribology. Aims to cover the ever-widening field of tribology and provide an international forum for discussion on an interdisciplinary basis which should help to reduce the incubation period between the availability of research results and their industrial utilisation.
Articles per average issue: 12
Audience: Professional, academic
  Manuscripts accepted in English, French, German

MANUSCRIPT INFORMATION
Subject field(s): Adhesion, friction, lubricants, lubrication, machine parts, surface properties, wear, testing
Manuscript requirements: Style sheet sent on request.
  Number of copies to be submitted: Two
  Abstract: Yes, papers in French, German should include a summary in English.
Author information and reprints: Payment: Reprints only. 50 reprints free of charge
  Is simultaneous submission of article to other journals permitted: No
  Exclusive manuscript rights between acceptance and publication: Yes
  Copyright: Held by publication.
  Reprints: Available, cost quoted upon publication
Disposition of manuscript:
  Query letter: No
  Receipt of manuscript acknowledged: Yes
  Decision to publish in: Four weeks
  Accepted manuscript published in: Four months
  Rejected manuscript returned: Yes
  Rejected manuscript criticized: Yes
Submit to:
  Douglas Scott
  Editor
  Materials Group (Z)
  National Engineering Laboratory
  East Kilbride
  Glasgow G75 OQU, Scotland

Environment and conservation

Environment and conservation

AGRO-ECOSYSTEMS [1802]
Elsevier Scientific Publishing Company
P. O. Box 211, Jan van Galenstraat
Amsterdam, The Netherlands

First published in 1974

SUBSCRIPTION DATA
Issues and rates: Published quarterly.
  Annual rate(s): Dfl. 89.00
Publisher or Sponsor: International Assocation for Ecology
Managing Editor: J. L. Harper

EDITORIAL DESCRIPTION
  Publishes reports concerned with ecological interactions within and between agricultural and managed forest systems.
Articles per average issue: 7
Audience: Professional, academic, agriculture, forestry
  Manuscripts accepted in English

MANUSCRIPT INFORMATION
Subject field(s): Historical development of agro-ecological systems; efficient management; affects of agriculture on ecosystems; pest control; long and short term effects of biocide usage; ecological consequences of intensive animal production, etc.
Manuscript requirements: See latest issue for style requirements. Style sheet sent on request.
  Preferred length: None
  Number of copies to be submitted: 3
  Abstract: Yes. Not to exceed 500 words
Author information and reprints: Payment: Reprints only. 50 reprints
  Is simultaneous submission of article to other journals permitted: Not permitted.
  Exclusive manuscript rights between acceptance and publication: Yes
  Copyright: Held by publication.
  Reprints: Available at cost.
Disposition of manuscript:
  Query letter: Not necessary.
  Receipt of manuscript acknowledged: Yes
  Decision to publish in: 2 months
  Accepted manuscript published in: 4-6 months
  Rejected manuscript returned: Yes, with return postage paid by publication.
  Rejected manuscript criticized: Yes
Submit to:
  Editor
  (See address above)

ALTERNATIVES [1803]
Perspectives on Society and Environment
Trent University
Peterborough, Ontario Canada
(705) 748-1471

SUBSCRIPTION DATA
Issues and rates: Published quarterly.
  Average paid circulation: 1800
  Annual rate(s): $3.00, Foreign $3.25
  Institutions $5.00

EDITORIAL DESCRIPTION
  Publishes articles on the full range of environmental subjects: conservation, pollution, resource depletion and wilderness primarily from social scientists.
Articles per average issue: 8
Audience: Environmentally concerned
  Manuscripts accepted in English

MANUSCRIPT INFORMATION
Subject field(s): Political science, economics, public policy, planning and resource planning, law, philosophy, sociology, journalism, psychology, anthropology, etc.
Manuscript requirements: See latest issue for style requirements.
  Preferred length: 5000 words
  Number of copies to be submitted: Two
  Abstract: No
Author information and reprints: Payment: None.
  Is simultaneous submission of article to other journals permitted: Permissible if indicated with submission.
  Exclusive manuscript rights between acceptance and publication: Yes
  Copyright: Held by publication.
  Reprints: Available, 20 free
Disposition of manuscript:
  Query letter: Preferable
  Receipt of manuscript acknowledged: No
  Decision to publish in: 2-3 months
  Accepted manuscript published in: 1 year at most
  Rejected manuscript returned: Yes
  Rejected manuscript criticized: Sometimes
Submit to:
  Robert C. Paehlke
  Editor
  (See address above)

AMERICAN FORESTS* [1804]
The Magazine of Forests, Soil, Water, Wildlife and Outdoor Recreation
1319 Eighteenth Street, N.W.
Washington, D.C. 20036
(202) 467-5810

SUBSCRIPTION DATA
Issues and rates: Published monthly.
  Average paid circulation: 75,000
  Annual rate(s): $7.50
Publisher or Sponsor: The American Forestry Association

EDITORIAL DESCRIPTION
  Contains articles on forest conservation and management, outdoor recreation, water management, soil control, wildlife management, pollution control, ecology; stories about trees in the environment.

MANUSCRIPT INFORMATION
Subject field(s): Forestry, water, wildlife, soil, recreation, pollution control, environment
Manuscript requirements: See latest issue for style requirements.
  Preferred length: 2000 words; 8 pages
  Number of copies to be submitted: One
Author information and reprints: Payment: By publication to author. $.03 per word.
  Is simultaneous submission of article to other journals permitted: No
  Exclusive manuscript rights between acceptance and publication: Yes
  Copyright: Held by publication.
  Reprints: Available to author
Disposition of manuscript:
  Receipt of manuscript acknowledged: Yes
  Decision to publish in: 2 months
  Accepted manuscript published in: 2-3 months
  Rejected manuscript returned: Yes, if self-addressed, stamped envelope is sent with manuscript.
  Rejected manuscript criticized: No
Submit to:
  James B. Craig
  Editor
  (See address above)

AMERICAN WATER WORKS ASSOCIATION JOURNAL [1805]
6666 West Quincy Avenue
Denver, Colorado 80235
(303) 988-1426

First published in 1914

SUBSCRIPTION DATA
Issues and rates: Published monthly.
  Average paid circulation: 26,000
  Annual rate(s): Members $5
Publisher or Sponsor: American Water Works Association

EDITORIAL DESCRIPTION
  Contains articles on consumptive water supply, utility management, industry control, water treatment, distribution facilities, resource development, plant operations.
Articles per average issue: 12
Audience: Professional
  Manuscripts accepted in English

MANUSCRIPT INFORMATION
Manuscript requirements: Style sheet sent on request.
  Preferred length: 3,000-4,000 words
  Number of copies to be submitted: 2-3 copies
  Abstract: No
Author information and reprints: Payment: None.
  Is simultaneous submission of article to other journals permitted: No
  Exclusive manuscript rights between acceptance and publication: Yes
  Copyright: Held by publication.
  Reprints: Available
Disposition of manuscript:
  Query letter: No

Receipt of manuscript acknowledged: Yes
Decision to publish in: 1-3 months
Accepted manuscript published in: 6-12 months
Rejected manuscript returned: Yes
Rejected manuscript criticized: No
Submit to:
Paul Hersch
Editor-in-Chief
(See address above)

AQUASPHERE [1806]
Journal of the New England Aquarium
Central Wharf
Boston, Massachusetts 02110
(617) 742-8830

First published in 1963
Average paid circulation: 12,000 controlled
Annual rate(s): $2.50
Publisher or Sponsor: New England Aquarium
Managing Editor: Jean A. Roberts

EDITORIAL DESCRIPTION

Publishes articles pertaining to water- its conditions, inhabitants, uses in food and power production, research.
Articles per average issue: 4
Audience: Academic, general
Manuscripts accepted in English

MANUSCRIPT INFORMATION

Subject field(s): Ichthyology, ecology, fishing, water-oriented historical subjects, mammals, underwater photography, water pollution research or supply. New England preferred, but not essential.
Manuscript requirements: No specific style guide.
Preferred length: 2,000 words
Number of copies to be submitted: 1
Abstract: Not necessary.
Author information and reprints: Payment: By publication to author. $50.00 per article.
Is simultaneous submission of article to other journals permitted: Permitted.
Exclusive manuscript rights between acceptance and publication: No
Copyright: Held by the New England Aquarium Corporation
Reprints: Available at no cost. 5
Additional information: High quality photographs should accompany the article.
Disposition of manuscript:
Query letter: Not necessary.
Receipt of manuscript acknowledged: Yes
Decision to publish in: 1-2 months
Accepted manuscript published in: 5 months
Rejected manuscript returned: Yes, with return postage paid by publication.
Rejected manuscript criticized: Sometimes
Submit to:
Jean A. Roberts
Editor
(See address above)

ATLANTIC NATURALIST [1807]
8940 Jones Mill Road
Washington D.C. 20015
(301) 652-9188

First published in 1946

SUBSCRIPTION DATA

Issues and rates: Published quarterly.
Average paid circulation: 1,700
Annual rate(s): $5.00; Foreign $5.00
Publisher or Sponsor: Audubon Naturalist Society of the Central Atlantic States, Inc.

EDITORIAL DESCRIPTION

Contains factual and philosophical articles on the natural history, ecology, and conservation problems of the central Atlantic states region and of areas of interest to foreign travelers.
Articles per average issue: 3-5
Audience: General
Manuscripts accepted in English

MANUSCRIPT INFORMATION

Subject field(s): Any aspect of natural history but with the larger proportion of articles devoted to ornithology, ecosystem ecology, and conservation problems of the central Atlantic states
Manuscript requirements: No specific style guide.
Preferred length: 500-3,000 words
Number of copies to be submitted: 3
Abstract: Not necessary.
Author information and reprints: Payment: None.
Is simultaneous submission of article to other journals permitted: Not permitted.
Exclusive manuscript rights between acceptance and publication: Yes
Copyright: Held by publication.
Reprints: Available at cost.
Disposition of manuscript:
Query letter: Not necessary, but advisable.
Receipt of manuscript acknowledged: Yes
Decision to publish in: 1-3 months
Accepted manuscript published in: 6-12 months
Rejected manuscript returned: Yes, with return postage paid by publication.
Rejected manuscript criticized: Reasons for rejections only
Submit to:
Ben O. Osborn
Editor
(See address above)

ATMOSPHERIC ENVIRONMENT [1808]
An International Journal
Pergamon Press, Inc.
Fairview Park
Elmsford, New York 10523
(914) 592-7700

First published in 1967

SUBSCRIPTION DATA

Issues and rates: Published monthly.
Annual rate(s): $25.00; Institutions $100.00

EDITORIAL DESCRIPTION

Covers all aspects of man's interaction with his atmospheric environment, including the administrative, economic and political aspects of these interactions.
Articles per average issue: Varies
Audience: Professional, academic
Manuscripts accepted in English, French, German

MANUSCRIPT INFORMATION

Manuscript requirements: See latest issue for style requirements.
Preferred length: None
Number of copies to be submitted: Original and 2 copies, double-spaced
Abstract: Yes
Author information and reprints: Payment: None.
Is simultaneous submission of article to other journals permitted: Not permitted.
Exclusive manuscript rights between acceptance and publication: Yes
Copyright: Held by publication.
Reprints: Available at cost.
Disposition of manuscript:
Query letter: Not necessary.
Receipt of manuscript acknowledged: Yes
Decision to publish in: 4 weeks
Accepted manuscript published in: 5 months
Rejected manuscript returned: Yes, if return postage is supplied by author.
Rejected manuscript criticized: Reasons for rejections only
Submit to:
Dr. L. P. Lodge, Jr.
Associate Executive Editor
National Center for Atmospheric Research
Boulder, Colorado

BIOLOGICAL CONSERVATION [1809]
Applied Science Publishers, Ltd.
Ripple Road
Barking, Essex, England

First published in 1968
Average paid circulation: 2,000
Annual rate(s): £12.00 for all

EDITORIAL DESCRIPTION

Contains original papers dealing with the preservation of wildlife and all Nature, and with the conservation or wise use of biological and allied natural resources.
Articles per average issue: 12
Audience: Research biologists, ecologists, and conservationists
Manuscripts accepted in English

MANUSCRIPT INFORMATION

Subject field(s): All aspects of conservation of wildlife and biological resources
Manuscript requirements: See latest issue for style requirements.
Preferred length: 3,000-5,000 words
Number of copies to be submitted: 2

Environment and conservation

Abstract: Yes. Of 80-200 words on the purpose and results of the paper. For papers in French, an abstract should be supplied in English as well.
Author information and reprints: Payment: Reprints only. 25 reprints
Is simultaneous submission of article to other journals permitted: Not permitted.
Exclusive manuscript rights between acceptance and publication: Yes
Copyright: Held by publication.
Disposition of manuscript:
Query letter: Not necessary.
Receipt of manuscript acknowledged: Yes
Decision to publish in: 4-6 weeks
Accepted manuscript published in: 3 months
Rejected manuscript returned: Yes, with return postage paid by publication.
Rejected manuscript criticized: No
Submit to:
Dr. Eric Duffey
Editor
Monks Wood Experimental Station
Institute of Terrestrial Ecology
Abbots Ripton, Huntingdon, England

CALIFORNIA FISH AND GAME [1810]
350 Golden Shore
Long Beach, California 90802
(213) 435-7741

SUBSCRIPTION DATA
Issues and rates: Published quarterly.
Average paid circulation: 600; 3,500 controlled
Annual rate(s): $2.00
Publisher or Sponsor: California Department of Fish and Game

EDITORIAL DESCRIPTION
Contains reports on research and management of fish and wildlife of California and adjacent areas.
Articles per average issue: 6-8
Audience: Wildlife managers
Manuscripts accepted in English

MANUSCRIPT INFORMATION
Subject field(s): Fish and wildlife
Manuscript requirements: AIBS
Preferred length: Maximum of 30 pages
Number of copies to be submitted: 2
Abstract: Yes
Author information and reprints: Payment: None.
Is simultaneous submission of article to other journals permitted: No
Exclusive manuscript rights between acceptance and publication: No
Copyright: Not copyrighted
Reprints: Available, first 50 free
Disposition of manuscript:
Query letter: No
Receipt of manuscript acknowledged: Yes
Decision to publish in: 6 months
Accepted manuscript published in: 12 months
Rejected manuscript returned: Yes
Rejected manuscript criticized: Yes

Submit to:
R.A. Collins
Editor
(See address above)

CALIFORNIA VECTOR VIEWS [1811]
Vector Control Section
2151 Berkeley Way
Berkeley, California 94704
(415) 843-7900

First published in 1954

SUBSCRIPTION DATA
Issues and rates: Published monthly.
Publisher or Sponsor: California Bureau of Vector Control and Solid Waste Management
Managing Editor: Thomas D. Peck

EDITORIAL DESCRIPTION
Contains information on vector control, medical entomology, waste management
Articles per average issue: 1
Audience: Professional
Manuscripts accepted in English

MANUSCRIPT INFORMATION
Subject field(s): Entomology, parasitology, zoology, chemistry, engineering
Manuscript requirements: AIBS
Preferred length: None
Number of copies to be submitted: Two
Abstract: Yes
Author information and reprints: Payment: None.
Is simultaneous submission of article to other journals permitted: Yes, if editors so informed.
Exclusive manuscript rights between acceptance and publication: No
Copyright: No copyright
Reprints: Available
Additional information: Editorial staff often requests considerable change and works with authors. Review articles are especially desired as well as research notes, scientific reports, and methods articles.
Disposition of manuscript:
Query letter: Yes
Receipt of manuscript acknowledged: Yes
Decision to publish in: 3 weeks
Accepted manuscript published in: 3-5 months
Rejected manuscript returned: Yes
Rejected manuscript criticized: Yes
Submit to:
Gail Grodhaus
Editor
(See address above)

SPECIAL STIPULATIONS
Author does not ordinarily receive proofs, he approves final manuscript revision.

CANADIAN JOURNAL OF FOREST RESEARCH [1812]
National Research Council of Canada
100 Sussex Drive
Ottawa, Ontario K1A 0R6 Canada
(613) 992-5411

First published in 1970

SUBSCRIPTION DATA
Issues and rates: Published quarterly.
Average paid circulation: 650
Annual rate(s): Individuals $5, Institutions $10
Managing Editor: H. Williamson
Publisher or Sponsor: National Research Council of Canada

EDITORIAL DESCRIPTION
Publishes the results of original scientific research in all branches of forestry.
Articles per average issue: 24
Audience: Researchers
Manuscripts accepted in English, French

MANUSCRIPT INFORMATION
Manuscript requirements: Style sheet sent on request.
Number of copies to be submitted: Three
Abstract: Yes
Author information and reprints: Payment: None.
Is simultaneous submission of article to other journals permitted: No
Exclusive manuscript rights between acceptance and publication: Yes
Copyright: Held by publication.
Reprints: Available at cost.
Disposition of manuscript:
Query letter: No
Receipt of manuscript acknowledged: Yes
Decision to publish in: 4 months
Accepted manuscript published in: 4 months
Rejected manuscript returned: Yes
Rejected manuscript criticized: Yes
Submit to:
J. L. Farrar
Editor
Faculty of Forestry
University of Toronto
Toronto, Ontario M5S 1A1 Canada
(416) 483-5487

CHEMOSPHERE [1813]
Chemistry, Physics and Biology as Focused on Environmental Problems
Pergamon Press, Inc.
Fairview Park
Elmsford, New York 10523
(914) 592-7700

First published in 1972

SUBSCRIPTION DATA
Issues and rates: Published bi-monthly.
Annual rate(s): $25.00; Institutions $40.00

EDITORIAL DESCRIPTION
Contains original and important short communications related to the fields of chemistry, physics and biology as related to changes in the atmosphere, water, and on land in relation to plants, animals and man.
Articles per average issue: 5-8
Audience: Professional, academic
Manuscripts accepted in English, French, German

MANUSCRIPT INFORMATION
Subject field(s): Aerosol formation; air quality; atmospheric chemistry; biological control of the environment; biological degradation; marine system contamination; food production and preservation; soil science; waste disposal; water quality.
Manuscript requirements: See latest issue for style requirements.
  Preferred length: None
  Number of copies to be submitted: 2, double-spaced
  Abstract: Yes. With a list of 6-9 words for indexing.
Author information and reprints: Payment: None.
  Is simultaneous submission of article to other journals permitted: Not permitted.
  Exclusive manuscript rights between acceptance and publication: Yes
  Copyright: Held by publication.
  Reprints: Available at cost. Order at time of submission
Additional information: Because of the rapid publication nature of this periodical, the MSS. must be in proper, very clear form.
Disposition of manuscript:
  Query letter: Not necessary.
  Receipt of manuscript acknowledged: Yes
  Rejected manuscript returned: Yes, if return postage is supplied by author.
  Rejected manuscript criticized: Reasons for rejections only
Submit to:
  Dr. F. Sergent
  Regional Editor
  School of Public Health
  University of Texas at Houston
  Houston, Texas 77025

CHESAPEAKE SCIENCE [1814]
Chesapeake Biological Laboratory
Box 38
Solomons, Maryland 20688
(301) 326-4281

First published in 1960

SUBSCRIPTION DATA
Issues and rates: Published quarterly.
  Average paid circulation: 400; 1200 controlled
  Annual rate(s): $6.00
Publisher or Sponsor: University of Maryland
Managing Editor: Martin L. Wiley

EDITORIAL DESCRIPTION
Presents research results and management studies dealing with the natural resources of the Chesapeake Bay region and technical papers on related subjects.
Articles per average issue: 12-15
Audience: Scientific
Manuscripts accepted in English

MANUSCRIPT INFORMATION
Subject field(s): Natural resources of estuaries, especially the Chesapeake Bay
Manuscript requirements: Style sheet sent on request.
  Preferred length: 60 pages maximum
  Number of copies to be submitted: Original and two copies
  Abstract: Yes
Author information and reprints: Payment: By author to publication. $20 per page. Voluntary.
  Is simultaneous submission of article to other journals permitted: No
  Exclusive manuscript rights between acceptance and publication: Yes
  Copyright: Not copyrighted
  Reprints: Available at no cost. 100 free
Disposition of manuscript:
  Query letter: No
  Receipt of manuscript acknowledged: Yes
  Decision to publish in: 2-3 months
  Accepted manuscript published in: 3-6 months
  Rejected manuscript returned: Yes
  Rejected manuscript criticized: Yes
Submit to:
  Martin L. Wiley
  Managing Editor
  (See address above)

THE CONSERVATIONIST [1815]
Box 2328, Grand Central Station
New York, New York 10012

First published in 1946

SUBSCRIPTION DATA
Issues and rates: Published bi-monthly.
  Average paid circulation: 185,000
  Annual rate(s): $2.00
Managing Editor: Robert F. Hall

EDITORIAL DESCRIPTION
Conservation, ecology, environment, outdoor recreation, hunting, fishing, and backpacking
Audience: English

MANUSCRIPT INFORMATION
Manuscript requirements: Style sheet sent on request. See latest issue for style requirements.
  Preferred length: 2,000 words
  Number of copies to be submitted: 1
  Abstract: Not necessary.
Author information and reprints: Payment: Reprints only.
  Is simultaneous submission of article to other journals permitted: Permitted, but not encouraged.
  Exclusive manuscript rights between acceptance and publication: No
  Copyright: Held by author.
  Reprints: Available at no cost.

Disposition of manuscript:
  Query letter: Not necessary, but advisable.
  Receipt of manuscript acknowledged: Yes
  Decision to publish in: 2 months
  Accepted manuscript published in: 2 months
  Rejected manuscript returned: Yes, with return postage paid by publication.
  Rejected manuscript criticized: Sometimes
Submit to:
  Robert F. Hall
  Editor
  Albany, New York 12201
  475-5547

CRC CRITICAL REVIEWS IN ENVIRONMENTAL CONTROL [1816]
CRC Press, Inc.
18901 Cranwood Parkway
Cleveland, Ohio 44128
(216) 475-9000

First published in 1970

SUBSCRIPTION DATA
Issues and rates: Published quarterly.
  Average paid circulation: 1,000
  Annual rate(s): $56.00, Foreign $64.00

EDITORIAL DESCRIPTION
Provides a qualitative approach to the total mass of scientific literature accomplished by utilizing outstanding experts in each field to select and critically evaluate the most significant papers published in their particular specialties. To insure accuracy and objectivity, each review is refereed prior to publication.
Articles per average issue: 3
Audience: Professional
Manuscripts accepted in English

MANUSCRIPT INFORMATION
Subject field(s): Ecology, environmental sciences, air pollution, water pollution, solid waste
Manuscript requirements: Style sheet sent on request.
  Preferred length: 75-150 pages
  Number of copies to be submitted: Three
  Abstract: Yes
Author information and reprints: Payment: Reprints only. 25
  Is simultaneous submission of article to other journals permitted: No
  Exclusive manuscript rights between acceptance and publication: Yes
  Copyright: Held by publication.
Disposition of manuscript:
  Query letter: No
  Receipt of manuscript acknowledged: Yes
  Decision to publish in: 3 weeks
  Accepted manuscript published in: 3 months
  Rejected manuscript returned: Yes
  Rejected manuscript criticized: Yes
Submit to:
  Gerald A. Becker
  Director, Editorial Operations
  (See address above)

Environment and conservation

ECOLOGICAL MODELLING [1817]
An International Journal
Elsevier Scientific Publishing Company
P. O. Box 211, Jan van Galenstraat 335
Amsterdam, The Netherlands

First published in 1975

SUBSCRIPTION DATA

Issues and rates: Published quarterly.
Annual rate(s): Individuals Dfl. 50.00; Institutions Dfl. 84.00
Managing Editor: S. E. Jorgensen

EDITORIAL DESCRIPTION

Deals with the use of mathematical models and systems analysis for the description of ecosystems and for the control of environmental pollution and resource development.
Articles per average issue: Varies
Audience: Research, professional, academic
Manuscripts accepted in English

MANUSCRIPT INFORMATION

Subject field(s): Mathematical modelling of ecosystems; systems analysis and use of computer techniques with respect to ecosystem modelling; environmental management
Manuscript requirements: See latest issue for style requirements. Style sheet sent on request.
Preferred length: As required
Number of copies to be submitted: 3
Abstract: Yes. Not to exceed 500 words
Author information and reprints: Payment: Reprints only. 50 reprints
Is simultaneous submission of article to other journals permitted: Not permitted.
Exclusive manuscript rights between acceptance and publication: Yes
Copyright: Held by publication.
Reprints: Available at cost.
Disposition of manuscript:
Query letter: Not necessary.
Receipt of manuscript acknowledged: Yes
Decision to publish in: 2 months
Accepted manuscript published in: 4-6 months
Rejected manuscript returned: Yes, with return postage paid by publication.
Rejected manuscript criticized: Yes
Submit to:
The Editor
Langkaer Vaenge 9
DK-3500 Vaerlose, Denmark

ECO-LOGOS [1818]
A Magazine of One-World Environment Concepts
Box 393
Denver, Colorado 80204
(303) 244-3578

Previously entitled *International Language Reporter*

First published in 1954

SUBSCRIPTION DATA

Issues and rates: Published quarterly.
Average paid circulation: 365; 1000 controlled
Annual rate(s): $4.00

EDITORIAL DESCRIPTION

Publishes articles on environmental/ecological subjects from an international viewpoint, including efforts toward and prospects for improved communication on a one-world basis, involving consideration of auxiliary international languages.
Articles per average issue: 5-6
Audience: Professional, general
Manuscripts accepted in English

MANUSCRIPT INFORMATION

Subject field(s): Planetary survival, ecologic interdependence, one-world communication, diminution of imperatives of national sovereignty, one-world land use and planning
Manuscript requirements: NYT
Preferred length: 3500-5000 words
Number of copies to be submitted: Two
Abstract: No
Author information and reprints: Payment: Reprints only. Six copies to author
Is simultaneous submission of article to other journals permitted: No
Exclusive manuscript rights between acceptance and publication: Yes
Copyright: Held by publication.
Reprints: Available, up to ten free
Disposition of manuscript:
Query letter: No
Receipt of manuscript acknowledged: Yes
Decision to publish in: Ten days
Accepted manuscript published in: Two months
Rejected manuscript returned: Yes, if self-addressed, stamped envelope is sent with manuscript.
Rejected manuscript criticized: No
Submit to:
John W. Ragsdale
Editor and Publisher
(See address above)

EFFLUENT AND WATER TREATMENT JOURNAL [1819]
102 College Road
Harrow, Middlesex HAI IBQ, England
01-427-9669

First published in 1960

SUBSCRIPTION DATA

Issues and rates: Published monthly.
Average paid circulation: 2209; 2102 controlled
Annual rate(s): Foreign $42.00

EDITORIAL DESCRIPTION

Publishes papers on the technical developments in the control of pollutants through the treatment and disposal of trade and municipal liquid wastes, the re-use of industrial water, and new developments in water management and the conservation of water resources.
Articles per average issue: 3
Audience: Professional
Manuscripts accepted in English

MANUSCRIPT INFORMATION

Subject field(s): Water research, effluent treatment, water management, plant design, waste treatment systems, materials
Manuscript requirements: Style sheet sent on request.
Preferred length: 3000-4000 words; 14 pages
Number of copies to be submitted: 7
Abstract: No
Author information and reprints: Payment: By publication to author. £8.00 per thousand words.
Is simultaneous submission of article to other journals permitted: No
Exclusive manuscript rights between acceptance and publication: Yes
Copyright: Held by publication.
Reprints: Available
Additional information: Does not accept articles with political, social or emotive statements concerning pollution control and the environment.
Disposition of manuscript:
Receipt of manuscript acknowledged: Yes
Decision to publish in: One month
Accepted manuscript published in: 2 to 3 months
Rejected manuscript returned: Yes
Rejected manuscript criticized: No
Submit to:
Chris D. Mole
Editor
(See address above)

THE ELEPAIO [1820]
Hawaii Audubon Society
PO Box 5032
Honolulu, Hawaii 96814

First published in 1939

SUBSCRIPTION DATA

Issues and rates: Published monthly.
Annual rate(s): $3.00
Publisher or Sponsor: Hawaii Audubon Society
Managing Editor: U. Kojima

EDITORIAL DESCRIPTION

Main concern is ecology, with the emphasis on better protection of wildlife in Hawaii.

MANUSCRIPT INFORMATION

Subject field(s): Ecology, ornithology, conservation
Manuscript requirements: No specific style guide.
Preferred length: Less than 5,000 words
Number of copies to be submitted: One
Abstract: No
Author information and reprints: Payment: None.
Is simultaneous submission of article to other journals permitted: Yes

Exclusive manuscript rights between acceptance and publication: No
Copyright: Held by publication.
Reprints: Available, $.50 each
Additional information: No facility for illustrations.
Disposition of manuscript:
  Query letter: No
  Receipt of manuscript acknowledged: Yes
  Decision to publish in: Three months
  Accepted manuscript published in: Six months
  Rejected manuscript returned: Yes, if self-addressed, stamped envelope is sent with manuscript.
  Rejected manuscript criticized: No
Submit to:
  Editor
  (See address above)

ENVIRONMENT [1821]

438 North Skinker Boulevard
St. Louis, Missouri 63130
(134) 863-6560

Previously entitled *Scientist & Citizen*

First published in 1969

SUBSCRIPTION DATA

Issues and rates: Ten per year
  Average paid circulation: 30,000
  Annual rate(s): $10.00
Publisher or Sponsor: Scientists' Institute for Public Information

EDITORIAL DESCRIPTION

Articles deal with all aspects of environmental problems and solutions to these problems; environmental education; and legal and economic information regarding the causes and cures of environmental problems. Provides technical information for laymen and professionals, but offers no opinions and takes no stand on political or economic decisions.
Articles per average issue: 5
Audience: Professional, general
  Manuscripts accepted in English

MANUSCRIPT INFORMATION

Manuscript requirements: See latest issue for style requirements.
  Preferred length: 4,000-6,000 words
  Number of copies to be submitted: Three
  Abstract: No
Author information and reprints: Payment: None.
  Is simultaneous submission of article to other journals permitted: No
  Exclusive manuscript rights between acceptance and publication: Yes
  Copyright: Held by publication.
  Reprints: Available at cost.
Disposition of manuscript:
  Query letter: No
  Receipt of manuscript acknowledged: Yes
  Decision to publish in: 4-8 weeks
  Accepted manuscript published in: 3-6 months

Rejected manuscript returned: Yes, if self-addressed, stamped envelope is sent with manuscript.
Rejected manuscript criticized: Sometimes
Submit to:
  Sheldon Novick
  Manuscript Editor
  (See address above)

ENVIRONMENT AND BEHAVIOR [1822]

An Interdisciplinary Journal
Sage Publications, Inc.
275 South Beverly Drive
Beverly Hills, California 90212
(213) 274-2423

First published in 1969

SUBSCRIPTION DATA

Issues and rates: Published quarterly.
  Average paid circulation: 1,558
  Annual rate(s): Institutions $18.00; Individuals $12.00; Students $9.00; Foreign individuals $13.00; Foreign institutions $19.00

EDITORIAL DESCRIPTION

Publishes articles concerned with the study, design, and control of the physical environment and its interaction with human behavioral systems.
Articles per average issue: 6
Audience: Architects, planners, psychologists, sociologists, geographers
  Manuscripts accepted in English

MANUSCRIPT INFORMATION

Subject field(s): Human behavior, environment, design, policy
Manuscript requirements: Style sheet sent on request.
  Preferred length: 6,250-7,500 words; 25 to 30 pages
  Number of copies to be submitted: Two
  Abstract: Yes, of 100-250 words
Author information and reprints: Payment: Reprints only. 25 tear-sheets
  Is simultaneous submission of article to other journals permitted: Permitted, but not encouraged. Author must notify publisher that manuscript is under consideration elsewhere.
  Exclusive manuscript rights between acceptance and publication: Yes
  Copyright: Held by publication.
  Reprints: Available if purchased by special order in amounts no fewer than 100
Disposition of manuscript:
  Query letter: No
  Receipt of manuscript acknowledged: Yes
  Decision to publish in: 8-15 weeks
  Accepted manuscript published in: 9-12 months
  Rejected manuscript returned: Yes
  Rejected manuscript criticized: Yes
Submit to:
  Gary H. Winkel
  Editor
  Environmental Psychology Program

City University of New York, Graduate Center
33 West 42nd Street
New York, New York 10036

ENVIRONMENT AND PLANNING-A [1823]

An International Journal of Urban and Regional Research
Pion Limited
207 Brondesbury Park
London NW2 5JN, England
01-459-0066

Previously entitled *Environment and Planning*

First published in 1969

SUBSCRIPTION DATA

Issues and rates: Published bi-monthly.
  Annual rate(s): £25; Pan-Am $70.00; Foreign £29
Managing Editor: Alan G. Wilson

EDITORIAL DESCRIPTION

An interdisciplinary journal devoted to publishing research into the analysis and study of cities and regions, and with planning processes; to ultimately foster an integrated approach to the problems of city and regional planning.
Articles per average issue: 7
Audience: Social scientists and planners with interests in urban and regional planning
  Manuscripts accepted in English, French, German

MANUSCRIPT INFORMATION

Subject field(s): All aspects of urban and regional planning as applied to geography, economics, sociology, engineering, and mathematics
Manuscript requirements: See latest issue for style requirements. Style sheet sent on request.
  Preferred length: 6,000 words; 15 pages
  Number of copies to be submitted: 3
  Abstract: Yes. Should be brief and in English
Author information and reprints: Payment: Reprints only. 50 reprints
  Is simultaneous submission of article to other journals permitted: Not permitted.
  Exclusive manuscript rights between acceptance and publication: Yes
  Copyright: Held by publication.
  Reprints: Available at cost.
Additional information: See the back cover of a recent issue.
Disposition of manuscript:
  Query letter: Not necessary.
  Receipt of manuscript acknowledged: Yes
  Decision to publish in: 1-2 months
  Accepted manuscript published in: 3-6 months
  Rejected manuscript returned: Yes, with return postage paid by publication.
  Rejected manuscript criticized: Yes
Submit to:
  Alan G. Wilson
  Editor

Department of Geography
University of Leeds
Leeds, Yorkshire LS2 9JT, England
0532-31751

ENVIRONMENT AND PLANNING-B [1824]

An International Journal of Architectural and Building Research
Pion Limited
207 Brondesbury Park
London NW2 5JN, England

SUBSCRIPTION DATA

Issues and rates: Published bi-monthly.
  Annual rate(s): £25 per volume; Pan-Am $70.00 per volume
Managing Editor: L. March

EDITORIAL DESCRIPTION

An interdisciplinary journal to advance knowledge in the fields of architectural and building research, it includes both original research and critical reviews. Quantitative and mathematical approaches are given prominence.
Articles per average issue: 7
Audience: Architects and researchers in architectural and building research
  Manuscripts accepted in English, French, German

MANUSCRIPT INFORMATION

Subject field(s): The philosophy and logic of design, the identification of problem structure, description of form and properties of combination, environmental control and energy conservation, decision making and economic evaluation in design, cultural and social aspects of architecture and building programs.
Manuscript requirements: See latest issue for style requirements. Style sheet sent on request.
  Preferred length: 6,000 words; 15 pages
  Number of copies to be submitted: 3
  Abstract: Yes.
Author information and reprints: Payment: Reprints only. 50 reprints
  Is simultaneous submission of article to other journals permitted: Not permitted.
  Exclusive manuscript rights between acceptance and publication: Yes
  Copyright: Held by publication.
  Reprints: Available at cost.
Additional information: See the back cover of any issue
Disposition of manuscript:
  Query letter: Not necessary.
  Receipt of manuscript acknowledged: Yes
  Decision to publish in: 1-2 months
  Accepted manuscript published in: 3-6 months
  Rejected manuscript returned: Yes, with return postage paid by publication.
  Rejected manuscript criticized: Yes
Submit to:
  L. March
  Editor
  Department of Systems Design
  University of Waterloo
  Waterloo, Ontario N2L 3G1; Canada

ENVIRONMENTAL CONSERVATION [1825]

An International Journal
Elsevier Sequoia, S.A.
P. O. Box 851
CH-1001 Lausanne, Switzerland
(021) 20 73 81

First published in 1974

SUBSCRIPTION DATA

Issues and rates: Published quarterly.
Publisher or Sponsor: International Union for Conservation of Nature and Natural Resources (IUCN); International Conferences on Environmental Future (ICEF); World Wildlife Fund

EDITORIAL DESCRIPTION

Advocates timely action for the protection and amelioration of the environment throughout the world.
Articles per average issue: 12
  Manuscripts accepted in English

MANUSCRIPT INFORMATION

Subject field(s): Survey articles on important aspects of ecology, resources, environmental policy, low-impact development, anti-pollution measures, environmental law and education, environmental management, case histories, short communications, summary reports, important prospects, reviews and notices, etc.
Manuscript requirements: No specific style guide. See latest issue for style requirements.
  Preferred length: Up to 6,000 words
  Number of copies to be submitted: 2
  Abstract: Not necessary. A short summary at the end of each paper to recapitulate and emphasize the main points.
Author information and reprints: Payment: None.
  Is simultaneous submission of article to other journals permitted: Not permitted.
  Exclusive manuscript rights between acceptance and publication: Yes
  Copyright: Held by publication.
  Reprints: Available at cost.
Disposition of manuscript:
  Query letter: Not necessary.
  Receipt of manuscript acknowledged: Yes
  Rejected manuscript returned: Yes, with return postage paid by publication.
Submit to:
  Prof. Dr. Nicholas Polunin
  Editor-in-Chief
  15, Chemin F.-Lehmann
  CH-1218 Grand Saconnex (Geneva), Switzerland
  (022) 98 23 83

ENVIRONMENTAL LETTERS [1826]

An International Journal for Rapid Communication
Marcel Dekker, Inc.
270 Madison Avenue
New York, New York 10016
(212) 490-7700

First published in 1971

SUBSCRIPTION DATA

Issues and rates: Published quarterly.
  Average paid circulation: 1,000
  Annual rate(s): $27.50; Foreign $31.70

EDITORIAL DESCRIPTION

Contains reports of original research, reviews, observations, legal impact in the general area of environment.
Articles per average issue: 8
Audience: Professional
  Manuscripts accepted in English

MANUSCRIPT INFORMATION

Subject field(s): Environment, water pollution, control of pollutions, effect on animal health, law
Manuscript requirements: See latest issue for style requirements.
  Preferred length: None
  Number of copies to be submitted: Two
  Abstract: Yes
Author information and reprints: Payment: None.
  Is simultaneous submission of article to other journals permitted: No
  Exclusive manuscript rights between acceptance and publication: Yes
  Copyright: Held by publication.
  Reprints: Available
Additional information: All articles are reviewed prior to acceptance. The reviewing process is a rapid one. All copy must be camera-ready.
Disposition of manuscript:
  Query letter: No
  Receipt of manuscript acknowledged: Yes
  Decision to publish in: 3 weeks
  Accepted manuscript published in: 4 weeks
  Rejected manuscript returned: Yes
  Rejected manuscript criticized: Yes
Submit to:
  James William Robinson
  Editorial Board
  Chemistry Department
  Louisiana State University
  Baton Rouge, Louisiana 70803
  (504) 388-3025

ENVIRONMENTAL POLLUTION [1827]

Applied Science Publishers, Ltd.
Ripple Road
Barking, Essex, England
(01) 595-2121

First published in 1970

SUBSCRIPTION DATA

Issues and rates: 8 times per year

Average paid circulation: 1,700
Annual rate(s): £20.00 worldwide

EDITORIAL DESCRIPTION

Contains research papers on the ecological effects of all types of environmental pollution and pollution control.

Articles per average issue: 7
Audience: Research ecologists and biologists
Manuscripts accepted in English, French, German

MANUSCRIPT INFORMATION

Subject field(s): Ecological implications of pullution problems, including the international, political, economic, social, medical, managerial, planning and engineering aspects.
Manuscript requirements: See latest issue for style requirements.
 Preferred length: 20,000 words maximum; 20 printed pages
 Number of copies to be submitted: 2
 Abstract: Yes. Of 100-150 words on the purpose and results of the paper. Papers in French and German should include an abstract in English as well.
Author information and reprints: Payment: Reprints only. 25 reprints
 Is simultaneous submission of article to other journals permitted: Not permitted.
 Exclusive manuscript rights between acceptance and publication: Yes
 Copyright: Held by publication.
Disposition of manuscript:
 Query letter: Not necessary.
 Receipt of manuscript acknowledged: Yes
 Decision to publish in: 4-6 months
 Accepted manuscript published in: 3-4 months
 Rejected manuscript returned: Yes, with return postage paid by publication.
 Rejected manuscript criticized: No
Submit to:
 Prof. Kenneth Mellanby
 Editor
 Monks Wood Experimental Station
 Abbots Ripton, Huntingdon, England

ENVIRONMENTAL RESEARCH* [1828]

An International Journal of Environmental Medicine and the Environmental Sciences
Academic Press, Inc.
111 Fifth Avenue
New York, New York 10003
(212) 677-6713

SUBSCRIPTION DATA

Issues and rates: Published quarterly.

EDITORIAL DESCRIPTION

Papers may represent original research in any of the disciplines now concerned with man-environment relationships. The relevance of the findings to broad problems of environmental biology and environmental medicine should be considered. Analytical and integrative reviews are equally eligible. Editorial emphasis is on research concerning health effects of environmental alterations, broadly considered; engineering and control efforts are well served elsewhere.

MANUSCRIPT INFORMATION

Manuscript requirements: See latest issue for style requirements.
 Number of copies to be submitted: Two
 Copyright: Held by publication.
 Reprints: Available; 50 free to senior author
Submit to:
 Editorial Offices
 Environmental Sciences Laboratory
 Mount Sinai School of Medicine
 Fifth Avenue and 100th Street
 New York, New York 10029

SPECIAL STIPULATIONS

Prior review of the paper may be undertaken with a member of the Board of Consulting Editors (see front cover of publication).

ENVIRONMENTAL SCIENCE & TECHNOLOGY [1829]

ES & T
1155 16th Street, N.W.
Washington, D. C. 20036
(202) 872-4581

First published in 1967

SUBSCRIPTION DATA

Issues and rates: Published monthly.
 Average paid circulation: 30,000
 Annual rate(s): $10.00; Foreign $15.00
Publisher or Sponsor: American Chemical Society
Managing Editor: Stanton S. Miller

EDITORIAL DESCRIPTION

Reports on all aspects of the environment and its control by scientific, engineering, and political means.
Audience: Professional
Manuscripts accepted in English

MANUSCRIPT INFORMATION

Subject field(s): Air, water, solid waste, pesticides, regulations
Manuscript requirements: See latest issue for style requirements.
Author information and reprints: Payment: None.
 Copyright: Held by publication.
 Reprints: Available at cost
Disposition of manuscript:
 Query letter: Yes
 Receipt of manuscript acknowledged: Yes
 Decision to publish in: 2-6 weeks
 Rejected manuscript returned: Yes
 Rejected manuscript criticized: Yes
Submit to:
 Research manuscripts to:
 Manuscript Reviewer

 Feature articles to:
 Managing Editor
 (See address above)

THE FLORIDA NATURALIST [1830]

P.O. Drawer 7
Maitland, Florida 32751
(305) 647-2615

SUBSCRIPTION DATA

Issues and rates: Published bi-monthly.
 Average paid circulation: 20,000
 Annual rate(s): Members $7.50
Publisher or Sponsor: The Florida Audubon Society

EDITORIAL DESCRIPTION

Contains news and feature material on conservation and natural history.
Manuscripts accepted in English

MANUSCRIPT INFORMATION

Subject field(s): Birds, animals, flora, conservation, Florida natural history, environmental education, outdoor experiences
Manuscript requirements: See latest issue for style requirements.
 Preferred length: 300-2500 words
 Number of copies to be submitted: One
Author information and reprints: Payment: None.
 Is simultaneous submission of article to other journals permitted: No
 Exclusive manuscript rights between acceptance and publication: No
 Copyright: Held by publication.
 Reprints: Available
Disposition of manuscript:
 Receipt of manuscript acknowledged: No
 Decision to publish in: 3-6 weeks
 Accepted manuscript published in: Varies
 Rejected manuscript returned: No
 Rejected manuscript criticized: No
Submit to:
 Karen G. Harrod
 Editor
 (See address above)

FOREST SCIENCE [1831]

A Quarterly Journal of Research and Technical Progress
Society of American Foresters
1010 16th Street, N. W.
Washington, D. C. 20036
(202) 296-7820

First published in 1955

SUBSCRIPTION DATA

Issues and rates: Published quarterly.
 Average paid circulation: 1,613 1,900 controlled
 Annual rate(s): $10.00; Foreign $11.00; Individuals $10.00; Institutions $20.00; Students $10.00; Members $6.00; Foreign institutions $21.00
Publisher or Sponsor: Society of American Foresters
Managing Editor: William E. Miller

EDITORIAL DESCRIPTION

Papers dealing with basic research and research techniques in forestry and fundamental related subjects

Environment and conservation

Articles per average issue: 15
Audience: Research workers and teachers of forestry
Manuscripts accepted in English only

MANUSCRIPT INFORMATION
Subject field(s): No geographical limitations
Manuscript requirements: See latest issue for style requirements.
  Preferred length: 3,000-6,000 words
  Number of copies to be submitted: 3
  Abstract: Yes.
Author information and reprints: Payment: By author to publication. $40.00 per page.
  Is simultaneous submission of article to other journals permitted:
  Exclusive manuscript rights between acceptance and publication: Yes
  Copyright: Held by publication.
  Reprints: Available at cost.
Additional information: All manuscripts are subject to critical review by the Advisory Board. Criticisms must be met before manuscript is accepted.
Disposition of manuscript:
  Query letter: Not necessary.
  Receipt of manuscript acknowledged: Yes
  Decision to publish in: 3-6 months
  Accepted manuscript published in: 12 months
  Rejected manuscript returned: Yes, with return postage paid by publication.
  Rejected manuscript criticized: Reasons for rejections only
Submit to:
  William E. Miller
  Editor
  North Central Experiment Station
  Folwell Avenue
  St. Paul, Minnesota 55101
  (612) 645-0841

FORET-CONSERVATION [1832]
915 St-Cyrille ouest, Suite 210
Québec, G1S 1T8, Canada
(418) 681-3588

First published in 1939

SUBSCRIPTION DATA
Issues and rates: Published monthly.
  Average paid circulation: 6,947
  Annual rate(s): $10.00

EDITORIAL DESCRIPTION
  Contains articles on conservation of the forest. Themes for coming issues may be obtained.
  Manuscripts accepted in French, English

MANUSCRIPT INFORMATION
Subject field(s): Conservation of forest, outdoor education, forest management, forest protection, recreation in the forest, silvicultural, logging operation, sawmilling operation, pulp and paper, major forestry problems
Manuscript requirements: No specific style guide.
  Preferred length: 4-5 pages
  Number of copies to be submitted: Two
Author information and reprints: Payment: None.
  Is simultaneous submission of article to other journals permitted: Yes, but with permission
  Exclusive manuscript rights between acceptance and publication: No
  Copyright: Held by publication.
  Reprints: Not available.
Disposition of manuscript:
  Receipt of manuscript acknowledged: No
  Decision to publish in: One week
  Accepted manuscript published in: One month
  Rejected manuscript returned: Yes
Submit to:
  Pierre Mathieu
  (See address above)

GROWTH AND CHANGE [1833]
A Journal of Regional Development
227 Commerce Building
University of Kentucky
Lexington, Kentucky 40506
(606) 257-3827

First published in 1970

SUBSCRIPTION DATA
Issues and rates: Published quarterly.
  Average paid circulation: 1,200; 20 controlled
  Annual rate(s): $7.50, Pan-Am $8.25, Foreign $8.50
Publisher or Sponsor: University of Kentucky, College of Business and Economics

EDITORIAL DESCRIPTION
  Contains articles from all disciplines concerned with regional development. The emphasis is on policy formation, analysis, and evaluation, but theoretical articles and case studies are used when they have clear policy implications. Also contains book reviews, and section of news, notes, and comments.
Articles per average issue: 8
Audience: Professional
  Manuscripts accepted in English

MANUSCRIPT INFORMATION
Subject field(s): Regional planning, race relations, ecology, industrial development, urban studies, transportation, political development, demography, poverty, social change, land use, community action
Manuscript requirements: Style sheet sent on request.
  Preferred length: 3,500 words maximum
  Number of copies to be submitted: Three
  Abstract: Yes
Author information and reprints: Payment: None.
  Is simultaneous submission of article to other journals permitted: No
  Exclusive manuscript rights between acceptance and publication: Yes
  Copyright: Held by publication.
  Reprints: Available, first 25 free
Additional information: "Guidelines for Authors" sent on request. Typewritten, double-spaced, with author's name on title page only; all references and footnotes at end.
Disposition of manuscript:
  Query letter: No
  Receipt of manuscript acknowledged: Yes
  Decision to publish in: 1-3 months
  Accepted manuscript published in: Six months
  Rejected manuscript returned: Yes, if self-addressed, stamped envelope is sent with manuscript.
  Rejected manuscript criticized: Yes
Submit to:
  David F. Ross
  Executive Editor
  (See address above)

THE INTERNATIONAL JOURNAL OF ENVIRONMENTAL STUDIES [1834]
Gordon and Breach Science Publishers
41-42 William IV Street
London WC2, England
(Editor's) 64321

First published in 1970

SUBSCRIPTION DATA
Issues and rates: Published bi-monthly.
  Average paid circulation: Not available.
  Annual rate(s): Individuals $19.50, Institutions $55.00

EDITORIAL DESCRIPTION
  Covers the relationship between man and his environment. Publishes scientific papers dealing with the many interdisciplinary aspects of environmental sciences.
Articles per average issue: 7
Audience: Academic professional and intelligent lay public.
  Manuscripts accepted in English

MANUSCRIPT INFORMATION
Subject field(s): Ecology, occupational hygiene, industrial health, social effects of technological advances, radiation, noise, pollution, city planning, transportation, population, etc.
Manuscript requirements: Style sheet sent on request.
  Preferred length: 3,000 words
  Number of copies to be submitted: 2
  Abstract: Yes.
Author information and reprints: Payment: None.
  Is simultaneous submission of article to other journals permitted:
  Exclusive manuscript rights between acceptance and publication: Yes.
  Copyright: Held by publication.
  Reprints: Available at cost. (50 free to authors)
Additional information: Letter of inquiry should be addressed to editor prior to submission of manuscript.
Disposition of manuscript:
  Query letter:
  Receipt of manuscript acknowledged: Yes.
  Decision to publish in: 4-6 weeks

Accepted manuscript published in: 1 year
Rejected manuscript returned:
Rejected manuscript criticized: Yes.
Submit to:
 J. Rose
 Editor
 College of Technology and Design
 Blackburn, England

INTERNATIONAL POLLUTION CONTROL MAGAZINE [1835]

Scranton Publishing Company
434 South Wabash
Chicago, Illinois 60605
(312) 922-4950

First published in 1972

SUBSCRIPTION DATA
Issues and rates: Published annually.
 Average paid circulation: 12,500 controlled
 Annual rate(s): $8.00

EDITORIAL DESCRIPTION
An international perspective of pollution control research and technology in the areas of water and liquid waste.
Articles per average issue: 12-20
Audience: Readers who are involved in pollution control
 Manuscripts accepted in English

MANUSCRIPT INFORMATION
Subject field(s): Water pollution control, air pollution control, solid waste management, international cooperation, cost analyses
Manuscript requirements: Style sheet sent on request.
 Preferred length: Open
 Number of copies to be submitted: 3
 Abstract:
Author information and reprints: Payment: None.
 Is simultaneous submission of article to other journals permitted: Yes
 Exclusive manuscript rights between acceptance and publication: Yes
 Copyright: Held by publication.
 Reprints: Available, cost depends on length
Additional information: The inclusion of tables and/or figures which summarize technical information is important. Editors look to the author also to supply black and white photos or color slides to go with the article.
Disposition of manuscript:
 Query letter:
 Receipt of manuscript acknowledged: Yes
 Decision to publish in: 1-3 months
 Accepted manuscript published in: 2-8 months
 Rejected manuscript returned: Yes, if return postage is supplied by author.
 Rejected manuscript criticized:
Submit to:
 Joe Ziemba
 Managing Editor
 (See address above)

JOURNAL OF ENVIRONMENTAL HEALTH [1836]

1600 Pennsylvania Street
Denver, Colorado 80203
(303) 222-4456

Previously entitled *The Sanitarian*

First published in 1937

SUBSCRIPTION DATA
Issues and rates: Published bi-monthly.
 Average paid circulation: 7,626; 343 controlled
 Annual rate(s): $10.00; Foreign $12.00
Publisher or Sponsor: National Environmental Health Association

EDITORIAL DESCRIPTION
Contains professional articles about environmental sanitation problems and solutions, professional development, organization activities, research, and various timely topics.
Articles per average issue: 10
Audience: English only

MANUSCRIPT INFORMATION
Subject field(s): Sanitation, food sanitation, potable water supply, housing, planning, solid waste disposal, air pollution control, hospital sanitation, noise, waste water disposal, radiation, radiological health, vector control, transportation, land use, recreation
Manuscript requirements: Style sheet sent on request.
 Preferred length: 5,000 words; 20 pages maximum
 Number of copies to be submitted: Three
Author information and reprints: Payment: None.
 Is simultaneous submission of article to other journals permitted: No
 Exclusive manuscript rights between acceptance and publication: Yes
 Copyright: None
 Reprints: Available, rates on request.
Additional information: Prefer articles prepared for easy reading. Pedantry is not desired. Use lead paragraph, no summary at end. If history of the subject is necessary, put somewhere other than beginning.
Disposition of manuscript:
 Query letter: No
 Receipt of manuscript acknowledged: Yes
 Decision to publish in: 2 months
 Accepted manuscript published in: 18 months
 Rejected manuscript returned: Yes
 Rejected manuscript criticized: Yes
Submit to:
 Nicholas Pohlit
 Managing Editor
 (See address above)

SPECIAL STIPULATIONS
Material prepared by or for commercial firms must not be slanted commercially, but written so the material is beneficial to professional environmental control personnel. Brand names should not be used.

JOURNAL OF ENVIRONMENTAL SCIENCES [1837]

940 East Northwest Highway
Mt. Prospect, Illinois 60056
(312) 255-1561

First published in 1959

SUBSCRIPTION DATA
Issues and rates: Published bi-monthly.
 Average paid circulation: 2,700; 1800 controlled
 Annual rate(s): Foreign $20.00; Individuals $14.00; Institutions $14.00; Members $14.00; Foreign institutions $20.00
Publisher or Sponsor: Institute of Environmental Sciences
Managing Editor: B. L. Peterson

EDITORIAL DESCRIPTION
An international authority on the many disciplines within the environmental field, it offers abstracts and technical articles on a correspondingly wide range of subjects.
Articles per average issue: 3-5
Audience: Environmental engineers, scientists and educators
 Manuscripts accepted in English

MANUSCRIPT INFORMATION
Subject field(s): Physical and earth sciences
Manuscript requirements: No specific style guide.
 Preferred length: 12 pages
 Number of copies to be submitted: 2
 Abstract: Not necessary.
Author information and reprints: Payment: None.
 Is simultaneous submission of article to other journals permitted: Not permitted.
 Exclusive manuscript rights between acceptance and publication: Yes
 Copyright: Held by publication.
 Reprints: Available at cost.
Disposition of manuscript:
 Query letter: Not necessary.
 Receipt of manuscript acknowledged: Yes
 Decision to publish in: 3-6 months
 Accepted manuscript published in: 1-3 months
 Rejected manuscript returned: Yes, if return postage is supplied by author.
 Rejected manuscript criticized: Reasons for rejections only
Submit to:
 B. L. Peterson;
 Janet Ehmann
 Editors
 (See address above)

JOURNAL OF ENVIRONMENTAL SYSTEMS [1838]

Baywood Publishing Company, Inc.
43 Central Drive
Farmingdale, New York 11735
(516) 293-7130

First published in 1971

Environment and conservation

SUBSCRIPTION DATA

Issues and rates: Published quarterly.
   Annual rate(s): $35.00; Foreign $37.00

EDITORIAL DESCRIPTION

Deals with the analysis and solution of problems which relate to the system-complexes which make up our total societal environment.

Articles per average issue: 5
Audience: Professional, governmental, academic
   Manuscripts accepted in English

MANUSCRIPT INFORMATION

Subject field(s): Concerned with the analysis, design and management of our environment
Manuscript requirements: See latest issue for style requirements. Style sheet sent on request.
   Preferred length: 5,000 words maximum
   Number of copies to be submitted: 2
   Abstract: Yes, of about 150 words
Author information and reprints: Payment: Reprints only. 20 copies
   Is simultaneous submission of article to other journals permitted: Not permitted.
   Exclusive manuscript rights between acceptance and publication: Yes
   Copyright: Held by publication.
   Reprints: Available at cost.
Disposition of manuscript:
   Query letter: Not necessary, but advisable.
   Receipt of manuscript acknowledged: Yes
   Decision to publish in: 4-6 weeks
   Accepted manuscript published in: 6 months
   Rejected manuscript returned: Yes, with return postage paid by publication.
   Rejected manuscript criticized: Sometimes
Submit to:
   Prof. Paul R. DeCicco
   Executive Editor
   Center for Urban Environmental Studies
   Polytechnic Institute of Brooklyn
   333 Jay Street
   Brooklyn, New York 11201

JOURNAL OF FOREST HISTORY [1839]

P. O. Box 1581
733 River Street
Santa Cruz, California 95061
(408) 426-3770

Previously entitled *Forest History*

First published in 1957

SUBSCRIPTION DATA

Issues and rates: Published quarterly.
   Average paid circulation: 1,200
   Annual rate(s): $10.00; Foreign $12.00; Individuals $10.00; Institutions $25.00

Publisher or Sponsor: Forest History Society
Managing Editor: Douglas F. Davis

EDITORIAL DESCRIPTION

Scholarly articles, memoirs, oral history, news, book reviews on the topic areas surrounding the history of forestry, conservation, and logging in North America, including historiographic and bibliographic material.

Articles per average issue: 3
Audience: Historians, conservationists, foresters, environmentalists—those interested in the history of man's use of forests.
   Manuscripts accepted in English

MANUSCRIPT INFORMATION

Subject field(s): Political, economic, social aspects of man's use of forests in historical context. Biographies and memoirs of historically important persons relative to these interests.
Manuscript requirements: See latest issue for style requirements. Style sheet sent on request. Chicago
   Preferred length: 6,000-8,000 words; 24-32 pages
   Number of copies to be submitted: One
   Abstract: Not necessary.
Author information and reprints: Payment: Reprints only. 10 copies of journal
   Is simultaneous submission of article to other journals permitted: Not permitted.
   Exclusive manuscript rights between acceptance and publication: Yes
   Copyright: Held by publication.
   Reprints: Available at cost. $.50 each
Additional information: Do not wish to see preliminary drafts or outlines. Chapters from doctoral theses welcome. Because of small staff, we reject many manuscripts requiring too much editorial cleanup & revision.
Disposition of manuscript:
   Query letter: Not necessary, but advisable.
   Receipt of manuscript acknowledged: Yes
   Decision to publish in: 2 to 6 months
   Accepted manuscript published in: 6 months to 1 year
   Rejected manuscript returned: Yes, if return postage is supplied by author.
   Rejected manuscript criticized: Sometimes
Submit to:
   Douglas F. Davis
   Editor
   (See address above)

SPECIAL STIPULATIONS

Type footnotes, double-spaced, at end of article. Include relevant photos, if available.

JOURNAL OF SAFETY RESEARCH [1840]

425 North Michigan Avenue
Chicago, Illinois 60610
(312) 527-4800

Previously entitled *Traffic Safety Research Review*

First published in 1969

SUBSCRIPTION DATA

Issues and rates: Published quarterly.
   Average paid circulation: 1,850
   Annual rate(s): $15.00; Pan-Am $15.15; Foreign $15.23
Publisher or Sponsor: The National Safety Council
Managing Editor: Jean T. Stephenson

EDITORIAL DESCRIPTION

Provides for the exchange of ideas and data developed through research in all areas of safety

Articles per average issue: 5
Audience: Safety professionals and researchers in related fields
   Manuscripts accepted in English

MANUSCRIPT INFORMATION

Subject field(s): Human error and accidents, accident countermeasures, man-machine environment in relationship to accidents, public health
Manuscript requirements: See latest issue for style requirements. Style sheet sent on request.
   Preferred length: As required
   Number of copies to be submitted: 3
   Abstract: Yes. 100 to 150 words in length
Author information and reprints: Payment: None.
   Is simultaneous submission of article to other journals permitted: Not permitted.
   Exclusive manuscript rights between acceptance and publication: Yes
   Copyright: Held by publication.
   Reprints: Available at no cost. 100
Disposition of manuscript:
   Query letter: Not necessary.
   Receipt of manuscript acknowledged: Yes
   Decision to publish in: 8-10 weeks
   Accepted manuscript published in: 6-12 months
   Rejected manuscript returned: Yes, with return postage paid by publication.
   Rejected manuscript criticized: Yes
Submit to:
   Jean T. Stephenson
   Managing Editor
   (See address above)

JOURNAL OF SOIL AND WATER CONSERVATION [1841]

7515 Northeast Ankeny Road
Ankeny, Iowa 50021
(515) 289-2331

First published in 1946

SUBSCRIPTION DATA

Issues and rates: Published bi-monthly.
   Average paid circulation: 14,500
   Annual rate(s): $12.50
Publisher or Sponsor: Soil Conservation Society of America
Managing Editor: Max Owen Schnepf

EDITORIAL DESCRIPTION

Dedicated to advancing the science and art of good land use. Sphere of interest includes those arts, sciences and professions that deal with land and water use; hence, the management of all renewable natural resources in an ecological sense and the relationship of these resources to human institutions and human values.

Articles per average issue: 10
Audience: Professional
   Manuscripts accepted in English

MANUSCRIPT INFORMATION
Subject field(s): Land use, water use, erosion control, resource policy, watershed management, education, land use planning, surface mining, recreation
Manuscript requirements: Style sheet sent on request.
   Preferred length: 10 to 12 pages
   Number of copies to be submitted: Three
   Abstract: Yes
Author information and reprints: Payment: Reprints only. Five copies of issue in which article appears
   Is simultaneous submission of article to other journals permitted: No
   Exclusive manuscript rights between acceptance and publication: Yes
   Copyright: Held by publication.
   Reprints: Available, cost depends on length
Disposition of manuscript:
   Query letter: No
   Receipt of manuscript acknowledged: Yes
   Decision to publish in: 6-8 weeks
   Accepted manuscript published in: 3-4 months
   Rejected manuscript returned: Yes
   Rejected manuscript criticized: Yes
Submit to:
   Max Owen Schnepf
   Editor
   (See address above)

THE JOURNAL OF WILDLIFE MANAGEMENT [1842]
3900 Wisconsin Avenue, N. W.
Washington, D. C. 20016
(202) 363-2434

First published in 1937

SUBSCRIPTION DATA
Issues and rates: Published quarterly.
   Average paid circulation: 8,000
   Annual rate(s): $30.00
Publisher or Sponsor: The Wildlife Society, Inc.
Managing Editor: Theodore A. Bookhout

EDITORIAL DESCRIPTION
   To provide information, with supporting data, on basic and applied studies of birds, mammals and to a lesser extent fishes, and their habitats with emphasis on these pursued for sport.
Articles per average issue: 30-35
Audience: Professional wildlife research and management specialists
   Manuscripts accepted in English

MANUSCRIPT INFORMATION
Subject field(s): Wildlife management techniques, ecology, biology, mammalogy, ornithology, and habitat manipulation. Studies other than current are not commonly submitted but are acceptable. The Journal is international in circulation, thus there is no restriction on study site.
Manuscript requirements: CBE
   Preferred length: Maximum of 20 pages, double-spaced
   Number of copies to be submitted: Two
   Abstract: Yes. Length should be no longer than three percent of the original article. It should be an informative digest of significant content and able to stand alone as a brief statement of the conclusions of the paper.
Author information and reprints: Payment: By author to publication. $25.00 per page.
   Exclusive manuscript rights between acceptance and publication: Yes
   Copyright: Held by publication.
   Reprints: Available at cost.
Additional information: "Instructions to Contributors" appears in each issue; these should be followed to the letter. Review papers usually are not accepted.
Disposition of manuscript:
   Query letter: A letter of intent to submit manuscript for publication is required to accompany it.
   Receipt of manuscript acknowledged: Yes
   Decision to publish in: 1-6 Months
   Accepted manuscript published in: 1-1 1/2 Years
   Rejected manuscript returned: Yes, with return postage paid by publication.
   Rejected manuscript criticized: Yes
Submit to:
   Theodore A. Bookhout
   Editor
   United States Fish and Wildlife Service,
   P.O. Box 33444
   Ohio State University
   Columbus, Ohio 43210
   (614) 422-6112

SPECIAL STIPULATIONS
   Put tables on a separate unnumbered page, with figures not exceeding 8 1/2 by 11 inches. Figure captions are to be placed on separate sheet.

LANDSCAPE PLANNING [1843]
Elsevier Scientific Publishing Company
P. O. Box 211, Jan van Galenstraat
Amsterdam, The Netherlands

First published in 1974

SUBSCRIPTION DATA
   Annual rate(s): Dfl. 89.00
Managing Editor: A. E. Weddle

EDITORIAL DESCRIPTION
   An international journal on landscape ecology, reclamation, conservation, outdoor recreation and land-use management.
Articles per average issue: 7
Audience: Professional, academic
   Manuscripts accepted in English

MANUSCRIPT INFORMATION
Subject field(s): Classification, ecology, human processes, planning, management, impact of various man-made projects, landscape architecture, economic and technical aspects of land management, environmental education, land-use legislation: all areas of landscape and planning
Manuscript requirements: See latest issue for style requirements. Style sheet sent on request. Chicago, CBE
   Preferred length: None
   Number of copies to be submitted: 3
   Abstract: Yes. Not to exceed 500 words.
Author information and reprints: Payment: Reprints only. 50 reprints
   Is simultaneous submission of article to other journals permitted: Not permitted.
   Exclusive manuscript rights between acceptance and publication: Yes
   Copyright: Held by publication.
   Reprints: Available at cost.
Disposition of manuscript:
   Query letter: Not necessary.
   Receipt of manuscript acknowledged: Yes
   Decision to publish in: 2 months
   Accepted manuscript published in: 4-6 months
   Rejected manuscript returned: Yes, with return postage paid by publication.
   Rejected manuscript criticized: Yes
Submit to:
   The Editor
   (See address above)

THE LIVING WILDERNESS [1844]
1901 Pennsylvania Avenue, N.W.
Washington, D. C. 20006
(202) 293-2732

First published in 1935

SUBSCRIPTION DATA
Issues and rates: Published quarterly.
   Average paid circulation: 75,000
Publisher or Sponsor: The Wilderness Society
Managing Editor: Richard C. Olson

EDITORIAL DESCRIPTION
   Devoted to the preservation of American Wilderness
Articles per average issue: 4

MANUSCRIPT INFORMATION
Subject field(s): Wilderness-related environmental and social concerns
Manuscript requirements: See latest issue for style requirements.
   Preferred length: 1,500 to 5,000 words
   Number of copies to be submitted: One
   Abstract: Not necessary.
Author information and reprints: Payment: By publication to author. $100.00 per page.
   Is simultaneous submission of article to other journals permitted: Permitted with permission and appropriate credit
   Copyright: Held by publication.
   Reprints: Available at cost. Cost varies

Environment and conservation 565

Disposition of manuscript:
Query letter: Not necessary, but advisable.
Accepted manuscript published in: Varies
Rejected manuscript returned: Yes, if return postage is supplied by author.
Rejected manuscript criticized: Sometimes
Submit to:
Richard C Olson
Editor
(See address above)

MAN-ENVIRONMENT SYSTEMS [1845]
A Synergistic Journal
P. O. Box 57
Orangeburg, New York 10962
(914) 634-8221

Previously entitled *Man and His Environment*

First published in 1968

SUBSCRIPTION DATA

Issues and rates: Published bi-monthly.
Average paid circulation: 600; 100 controlled
Annual rate(s): $15.00; Foreign $17.40; Institutions $18.50; Students $8.00; Members $20.00; Foreign institutions $20.90
Publisher or Sponsor: Association for the Study of Man-Environment Relations, Inc.
Managing Editor: Ada R. Esser

EDITORIAL DESCRIPTION

A forum for communications bearing on the interface between research in the behavioral and social sciences and the design and management of the sociophysical environment.
Articles per average issue: Ten
Audience: Behavioral scientists and design professionals
Manuscripts accepted in English

MANUSCRIPT INFORMATION

Subject field(s): Architecture, behavioral sciences, biological sciences, earth sciences, ecology, education, health sciences, interior design, landscape architecture, law, physical sciences, planning, social sciences
Manuscript requirements: No specific style guide.
Preferred length: 700-1600 words for shorter articles; 3,000-10,000 words for full-length articles
Number of copies to be submitted: Two
Abstract: Yes. The 700-1600 word manuscripts need no abstract and will be printed as is. The longer manuscripts need a 150 word abstract as well as short biography.
Author information and reprints: Payment: Reprints only. 25
Is simultaneous submission of article to other journals permitted: Permitted for full version of short MS., not for long MS.

Exclusive manuscript rights between acceptance and publication: No
Copyright: Held by publication.
Reprints: Available at no cost. 25 Available at cost.
Disposition of manuscript:
Query letter: Not necessary.
Receipt of manuscript acknowledged: No
Decision to publish in: 2 months
Accepted manuscript published in: 3-6 months
Rejected manuscript returned: Yes, if return postage is supplied by author.
Rejected manuscript criticized: Sometimes
Submit to:
Aristide H. Esser, M. D.
Editor
26 Park Place
Paramus, New Jersey 07652
(201) 265-8200

NATURAL RESOURCES JOURNAL [1846]
UNM School of Law
1117 Stanford NE
Albuquerque, New Mexico 87131
(505) 277-4820

First published in 1961

SUBSCRIPTION DATA

Issues and rates: Published quarterly.
Average paid circulation: 1,800; 200 controlled
Annual rate(s): $12.00; Foreign $13.00
Publisher or Sponsor: University of New Mexico, School of Law
Managing Editor: Albert E. Utton

EDITORIAL DESCRIPTION

Provides an interdisciplinary forum for the discussion of the conservation, use, regulation, and development of natural resources such as water, oil and gas, forests and public lands, air (pollution), and related subjects.
Articles per average issue: 5
Audience: Professional, governmental, legal
Manuscripts accepted in English

MANUSCRIPT INFORMATION

Subject field(s): Resource use, ecology, pollution, land use, marine problems, energy crisis, environmental policy, taxes in resource problems
Manuscript requirements: HLRA Style sheet sent on request.
Preferred length: 20 printed pages maximum
Number of copies to be submitted: Two
Author information and reprints: Payment: Reprints only. 25
Is simultaneous submission of article to other journals permitted: Yes
Exclusive manuscript rights between acceptance and publication: Yes
Copyright: Held by publication.
Reprints: Available at cost.

Additional information: Manuscript must be triple-spaced, left third of page left blank; footnotes at end.
Disposition of manuscript:
Query letter: Not necessary, but helpful
Receipt of manuscript acknowledged: Yes
Decision to publish in: 2-10 weeks
Accepted manuscript published in: 3-15 months
Rejected manuscript returned: Yes
Rejected manuscript criticized: No
Submit to:
Albert E. Utton
Editor
(See address above)
(505) 277-4910

NOT MAN APART [1847]
529 Commercial
San Francisco, California 94111
(415) 986-8100

First published in 1970

SUBSCRIPTION DATA

Issues and rates: Published bi-weekly.
Average paid circulation: 20,000; 1,000 controlled
Annual rate(s): $10.00; Pan-Am $10.00; Institutions $10.00; Students $10.00; Members $15.00
Publisher or Sponsor: Friends of the Earth
Managing Editor: Bruce E. Colman

EDITORIAL DESCRIPTION

A publication of the Friends of the Earth, it reflects the concerns and biases of the organization.
Articles per average issue: 6
Audience: Members of the Friends of the Earth
Manuscripts accepted in English

MANUSCRIPT INFORMATION

Subject field(s): Environment, conservation, energy, ecology, wildlife, natural resources, etc.
Manuscript requirements: See latest issue for style requirements.
Preferred length: Maximum 3,000 words
Number of copies to be submitted: 1
Abstract: Not necessary.
Author information and reprints: Payment: None.
Is simultaneous submission of article to other journals permitted: Permitted, with knowledge of publication
Exclusive manuscript rights between acceptance and publication: No
Copyright: Held by publication.
Reprints: Available at no cost. 25
Disposition of manuscript:
Query letter: Not necessary, but advisable.
Receipt of manuscript acknowledged: Yes
Decision to publish in: 2 weeks
Accepted manuscript published in: 1-3 months
Rejected manuscript returned: Yes, with return postage paid by publication.
Rejected manuscript criticized: Sometimes

Submit to:
Tom Turner
Editor
(See address above)

PARKS AND RECREATION MAGAZINE [1848]

1601 North Kent Street
Arlington, Virginia 22209
(703) 525-0606

SUBSCRIPTION DATA

Issues and rates: Published monthly.
   Average paid circulation: 22,000
   Annual rate(s): $10.00; Foreign $13.00
Publisher or Sponsor: National Recreation and Park Association
Managing Editor: Margaret Smith

EDITORIAL DESCRIPTION

Seeks to acquaint its readership with news, trends and features affecting the park, recreation, and conservation fields.
Articles per average issue: 6-8
Audience: Professional, general
   Manuscripts accepted in English

MANUSCRIPT INFORMATION

Subject field(s): Parks, recreation, conservation, environmental articles, urban affairs as related to parks and recreation
Manuscript requirements: Style sheet sent on request.
   Preferred length: 3000 words
   Number of copies to be submitted: Two
   Abstract: No
Author information and reprints: Payment: None.
   Is simultaneous submission of article to other journals permitted: No
   Exclusive manuscript rights between acceptance and publication: Yes
   Copyright: Held by publication.
   Reprints: Available at cost.
Disposition of manuscript:
   Query letter:
   Receipt of manuscript acknowledged: Yes
   Decision to publish in: 2-3 weeks
   Accepted manuscript published in: 2-4 months
   Rejected manuscript returned: Yes
   Rejected manuscript criticized: No
Submit to:
   Margaret F. Smith
   Managing Editor
   (See address above)
   (703) 525-0606 ext. 302

POLLUTION EQUIPMENT NEWS [1849]

8550 Babcock Road
Pittsburgh, Pennsylvania 15237
(412) 364-5366

SUBSCRIPTION DATA

Issues and rates: Published bi-monthly.
   Average paid circulation: 78,099 controlled
   Annual rate(s): $20.00; Foreign $30.00

EDITORIAL DESCRIPTION

Publishes information of all new products for pollution control.

MANUSCRIPT INFORMATION

Manuscript requirements: See latest issue for style requirements.
   Preferred length: 150 to 250 words
   Number of copies to be submitted: One
Author information and reprints: Payment: None.
   Is simultaneous submission of article to other journals permitted: Yes
   Exclusive manuscript rights between acceptance and publication: No
   Copyright: Held by publication.
Disposition of manuscript:
   Receipt of manuscript acknowledged: No
   Decision to publish in: 60-90 days
   Rejected manuscript returned: No
   Rejected manuscript criticized: No
Submit to:
   Richard Rimbach
   Editor and Publisher
   (See address above)

PROFESSIONAL SANITATION MANAGEMENT [1850]

The Magazine of Industrial Sanitation
1710 Drew Street
Clearwater, Florida 33515
(813) 446-1674

First published in 1969

SUBSCRIPTION DATA

Issues and rates: Five times a year
   Average paid circulation: 150; 2,000 controlled
Publisher or Sponsor: Environmental Management Association
Managing Editor: Russell Mark

EDITORIAL DESCRIPTION

Contains original articles on work and product environments, never published before.
Articles per average issue: 7
Audience: Professional
   Manuscripts accepted in English

MANUSCRIPT INFORMATION

Subject field(s): Work environments, product environments
Manuscript requirements: See latest issue for style requirements.
   Preferred length: 1,800 words
   Number of copies to be submitted: Two
   Abstract: Yes
Author information and reprints: Payment: None.
   Is simultaneous submission of article to other journals permitted: No
   Exclusive manuscript rights between acceptance and publication: Yes
   Copyright: Held by author.
   Reprints: Available at cost.
Additional information: Typewritten, double-spaced
Disposition of manuscript:
   Query letter: No
   Receipt of manuscript acknowledged: Yes
   Decision to publish in: Three weeks
   Accepted manuscript published in: Two months
   Rejected manuscript returned: Yes
   Rejected manuscript criticized: No
Submit to:
   Russell Mark
   Editor
   (See address above)

RECLAMATION ERA [1851]

A Water Review Quarterly
Bureau of Reclamation
U.S. Department of Interior
18th and C Streets, N.W.
Washington, D.C. 20240
(202) 343-4662

Previously entitled *Reclamation Record*

First published in 1905

SUBSCRIPTION DATA

Issues and rates: Published quarterly.
   Average paid circulation: 2,000 controlled
   Annual rate(s): $2.70; Foreign $3.40
Publisher or Sponsor: U.S. Department of the Interior, Bureau of Reclamation
Managing Editor: Kathy Wood Loveless

EDITORIAL DESCRIPTION

Publishes articles to inform the public of the activities of the Bureau of Reclamation. The contents deal primarily with the Bureau's projects: dams, reservoirs, canals, youth programs, etc. Any topic dealing with these projects in any way will be considered.
Articles per average issue: 5
Audience: Professional, governmental
   Manuscripts accepted in English

MANUSCRIPT INFORMATION

Subject field(s): Municipal, industrial, recreational uses of water; wildlife preservation, environment enhancement; natural resource conservation; flood control; power generation
Manuscript requirements: GPO See latest issue for style requirements.
   Preferred length: 500 to 3,000 words
   Number of copies to be submitted: Two
   Abstract: No
Author information and reprints: Payment: None.
   Is simultaneous submission of article to other journals permitted: Yes
   Exclusive manuscript rights between acceptance and publication: No
   Copyright: Held by author.
   Reprints: Available at no cost. 50 reprints
Additional information: All manuscripts must be typewritten, double-spaced and in 50-space lines. All graphs must be original copy and properly identified. Photographs must be black and white glossy 8 x 10 prints.
Disposition of manuscript:
   Query letter: No
   Receipt of manuscript acknowledged: Yes

Environment and conservation

Decision to publish in: 6-8 weeks
Accepted manuscript published in: 5-9 months
Rejected manuscript returned: Yes
Rejected manuscript criticized: No
Submit to:
Kathy Wood Loveless
Editor
(See address above)

REGIONAL STUDIES [1852]

Journal of the Regional Studies Association
Pergamon Press, Inc.
Maxwell House, Fairview Park
Elmsford, New York 10523
(914) 592-7700

First published in 1967

SUBSCRIPTION DATA
Issues and rates: Published quarterly.
  Annual rate(s): $25.00
Publisher or Sponsor: The Regional Studies Association
Managing Editor: Peter Hall, Reading

EDITORIAL DESCRIPTION
  Contributions reflect the application of the systematic method to the solution of problems of regional planning.
Articles per average issue: 5-6
Audience: Regional planners, researchers, government officials
  Manuscripts accepted in English

MANUSCRIPT INFORMATION
Subject field(s): The machinery of regional economic planning, its theory, its development; economic growth in developing countries; metropolitan regional planning; models of urban and regional development.
Manuscript requirements: See latest issue for style requirements.
  Preferred length: As required
  Number of copies to be submitted: 3
  Abstract: Yes. A short abstract of about 100 words should precede the introduction. Additional abstracts in French, German, and Russian will also facilitate publication.
Author information and reprints: Payment: Reprints only. 50
  Is simultaneous submission of article to other journals permitted: Not permitted.
  Exclusive manuscript rights between acceptance and publication: Yes
  Copyright: Held by publication.
  Reprints: Available at cost.
Disposition of manuscript:
  Query letter: Not necessary.
  Receipt of manuscript acknowledged: Yes
  Decision to publish in: 4 weeks
  Accepted manuscript published in: 5 months
  Rejected manuscript returned: Yes, if return postage is supplied by author.
  Rejected manuscript criticized: Reasons for rejections only
Submit to:
Prof. Peter Hall
Editor
Department of Geography
University of Reading, Whiteknights
Reading, Berkshire, England

SCIENCE OF THE TOTAL ENVIRONMENT [1853]

Elsevier Scientific Publishing Company
P. O. Box 211, Jan van Galenstraat 335
Amsterdam, The Netherlands
515-9222

First published in 1972

SUBSCRIPTION DATA
Issues and rates: Published quarterly.
  Annual rate(s): Dfl. 95 plus postage

EDITORIAL DESCRIPTION
  A medium of publication for research into those changes in the environment caused by man's activities; specifically, with the changes in natural level and distribution of chemical elements and compounds which may affect the well-being of the living world with emphasis on applied environmental chemistry.
Articles per average issue: 8
Audience: Specialists, academic, industrial, governmental
  Manuscripts accepted in English (French, German)

MANUSCRIPT INFORMATION
Subject field(s): Applications of techniques of chemistry and biolochemistry to environmental problems: air, water, soil pollution and human nutrition; medicine; environmental planning and policy
Manuscript requirements: See latest issue for style requirements. Style sheet sent on request.
  Preferred length: None
  Number of copies to be submitted: 2
  Abstract: Yes. Not to exceed 200 words. For articles written in German or French, an additional abstract in English is required.
Author information and reprints: Payment: Reprints only. 50 reprints
  Is simultaneous submission of article to other journals permitted: Not permitted.
  Exclusive manuscript rights between acceptance and publication: Yes
  Copyright: Held by publication.
  Reprints: Available at cost.
Additional information: Original figures and illustrations should accompany the manuscript.
Disposition of manuscript:
  Query letter: Not necessary.
  Receipt of manuscript acknowledged: Yes
  Decision to publish in: 2 weeks
  Accepted manuscript published in: 5 months
  Rejected manuscript returned: Yes, with return postage paid by publication.
  Rejected manuscript criticized: Reasons for rejections only
Submit to:
J. L. Monkman
Co-Editor
Air Pollution and Environmental Health Centre
Tunney's Pasture
Ottawa, Ontario K1A OH3, Canada

THE TENNESSEE CONSERVATIONIST [1854]

Tennessee Department of Conservation
2611 West End Avenue
Nashville, Tennessee 37203
(615) 741-2661

First published in 1940

SUBSCRIPTION DATA
Issues and rates: Published monthly.
  Average paid circulation: 20,000 controlled
  Annual rate(s): $2.00
Publisher or Sponsor: Tennessee Department of Conservation and Fish Commission

EDITORIAL DESCRIPTION
  Publication is oriented toward hunting, fishing, wildlife management; and toward other use, enjoyment, and preservation of Tennessee natural resources.
Articles per average issue: 10
Audience: General
  Manuscripts accepted in English

MANUSCRIPT INFORMATION
Manuscript requirements: See latest issue for style requirements.
  Preferred length: 1200-1500 words
  Number of copies to be submitted: One
Author information and reprints: Payment: By publication to author. $.05 per word.
  Is simultaneous submission of article to other journals permitted: No
  Exclusive manuscript rights between acceptance and publication: Yes
  Copyright: Not copyrighted
  Reprints: Not available.
Disposition of manuscript:
  Query letter: Preferred
  Receipt of manuscript acknowledged: Yes
  Decision to publish in: 30 days
  Accepted manuscript published in: Up to one year
  Rejected manuscript returned: Yes
Submit to:
Ardi Luther
Editor and Business Manager
(See address above)

Submit game and fish-oriented manuscripts to:
Morris Pomeroy
Editor-in-Chief
P.O. Box 40747
Nashville, Tennessee 37204
(615) 741-1421

TRANSPORTATION RESEARCH [1855]

An International Journal
Pergamon Press, Inc.
Fairview Park
Elmsford, New York 10523
(914) 592-7700

First published in 1967

SUBSCRIPTION DATA

Issues and rates: Published bi-monthly.
Annual rate(s): $25.00; Institutions $65.00

EDITORIAL DESCRIPTION

Publishes significant research which relates to the design and operation of transportation systems. Especially welcomes papers which compare or contrast modes, or analyze factors affecting modal choice, economic factors

Articles per average issue: 25-30

Audience: Professional, academic
Manuscripts accepted in English (French, German)

MANUSCRIPT INFORMATION

Subject field(s): Policy and planning, cost effectiveness, transportation and traffic engineering, urban and regional planning, control and scheduling, optimization methods, prediction of network usage and flows, noise, pollution and other environmental impacts.

Manuscript requirements: See latest issue for style requirements.
Preferred length: None
Number of copies to be submitted: 3
Abstract: Yes. In English on a separate sheet.

Author information and reprints: Payment: None.
Is simultaneous submission of article to other journals permitted: Not permitted.
Exclusive manuscript rights between acceptance and publication: Yes
Copyright: Held by publication.
Reprints: Available at cost.

Disposition of manuscript:
Query letter: Not necessary.
Receipt of manuscript acknowledged: Yes
Decision to publish in: 4 weeks
Accepted manuscript published in: 5 months
Rejected manuscript returned: Yes, if return postage is supplied by author.
Rejected manuscript criticized: Reasons for rejections only

Submit to:
Frank A. Haight
Pennsylvania Transportation Institute, Research Building B
University Park, Pennsylvania 16802

George H. Weiss
National Institutes of Health
Bethesda, Maryland 20014
Co-editors

URBAN LAND [1856]

News and Trends in Land Development
1200 18th Street NW
Washington, D.C. 20036
(202) 331-8500

First published in 1941

SUBSCRIPTION DATA

Issues and rates: Published monthly.
Average paid circulation: 5,500
Annual rate(s): Members $10.00
Publisher or Sponsor: Urban Land Institute

EDITORIAL DESCRIPTION

Contains articles on a wide range of topics of professional interest to developers, builders, realtors, architects and planners.

Articles per average issue: 3-4

Audience: Professional
Manuscripts accepted in English

MANUSCRIPT INFORMATION

Subject field(s): Land use, urban growth, housing, finance, new towns, industrial planning and development, office development, historic preservation, shopping centers, urban renewal, taxation, ecology

Manuscript requirements: Chicago
Preferred length: 15-25 pages
Number of copies to be submitted: Two
Abstract: No

Author information and reprints: Payment: Reprints only. 25 free copies to author
Is simultaneous submission of article to other journals permitted: Permitted. with knowledge of editor.
Exclusive manuscript rights between acceptance and publication: Yes
Copyright: Held by publication.
Reprints: Not available.

Additional information: An outline of the article should be sent prior to the manuscript. Everything should be typewritten, double-spaced.

Disposition of manuscript:
Query letter: Preferred
Receipt of manuscript acknowledged: Yes
Decision to publish in: 1 month
Accepted manuscript published in: 3-6 months
Rejected manuscript returned: Yes
Rejected manuscript criticized: Yes

Submit to:
Susan R. Regenbogen
Managing Editor
(See address above)
(202) 331-8500 ext. 67

WASTE AGE [1857]

6311 Gross Point Road
Niles, Illinois 60648
(312) 647-0500

SUBSCRIPTION DATA

Issues and rates: Published bi-monthly.
Average paid circulation: 1,500; 17,500 controlled
Annual rate(s): $10.00, Foreign $20.00
Managing Editor: Michael A. Oberman

EDITORIAL DESCRIPTION

Contains articles pertaining to solid or liquid waste control.

MANUSCRIPT INFORMATION

Manuscript requirements: No specific style guide.
Preferred length: None
Number of copies to be submitted: One

Author information and reprints: Payment: None.
Is simultaneous submission of article to other journals permitted: No
Exclusive manuscript rights between acceptance and publication: Yes
Copyright: Held by publication.
Reprints: Available, cost quoted

Disposition of manuscript:
Receipt of manuscript acknowledged: Yes
Decision to publish in: 1-4 weeks
Accepted manuscript published in: 1-6 months
Rejected manuscript returned: Yes
Rejected manuscript criticized: No

Submit to:
Michael A. Oberman
Editor
(See address above)

WATER & SEWAGE WORKS [1858]

Scranton Publishing Company
434 South Wabash
Chicago, Illinois 60605
(312) 922-4950

Previously entitled *Sewerage & Water Works*

First published in 1882

SUBSCRIPTION DATA

Issues and rates: Published monthly.
Average paid circulation: 32,000; 5,200 controlled
Annual rate(s): $7.50, Foreign $9.00
Managing Editor: Joseph Ziemba

EDITORIAL DESCRIPTION

Contains articles dealing with the construction, operation and maintenance of water and wastewater collection and distribution systems and treatment facilities and with the technological advances in all of these areas.

Articles per average issue: 20

Audience: Professional
Manuscripts accepted in English

MANUSCRIPT INFORMATION

Subject field(s): Wastewater treatment, water treatment, water distribution, operator training, cost analyses, government policy

Manuscript requirements: Style sheet sent on request.
Preferred length: 1000-5000 words
Number of copies to be submitted: Two
Abstract: Yes

Author information and reprints: Payment: By publication to author. $25 per page.
Is simultaneous submission of article to other journals permitted: No
Exclusive manuscript rights between acceptance and publication: Yes
Copyright: Held by publication.
Reprints: Available at cost.

Environment and conservation

Additional information: The inclusion of tables and/or figures which summarize technical information is important. Editors look to the author also to supply black and white photos or color slides to go with the article.
Disposition of manuscript:
 Query letter: No
 Receipt of manuscript acknowledged: Yes
 Decision to publish in: 1 month
 Accepted manuscript published in: 2-6 months
 Rejected manuscript returned: Yes, if return postage is supplied by author.
 Rejected manuscript criticized: No
Submit to:
 Frank Reid
 Editorial Director
 (See address above)

WATER POLLUTION CONTROL FEDERATION JOURNAL [1859]
3900 Wisconsin Avenue, N.W.
Washington, D.C. 20016
(202) 537-1320

Previously entitled *Sewage Works Journal* to 1930; *Sewage Industrial Wastes* to 1960

First published in 1928

SUBSCRIPTION DATA
Issues and rates: Published monthly.
 Average paid circulation: 20,100
 Annual rate(s): $35, Members $40
Publisher or Sponsor: Water Pollution Control Federation

EDITORIAL DESCRIPTION
 Contains technical articles, news items, product guides, new equipment.
Articles per average issue: 12-16
Audience: Professional
 Manuscripts accepted in English only

MANUSCRIPT INFORMATION
Subject field(s): Wastewater treatment, facilities design, wastewater surveys, effects of pollutants, water quality surveys, wastewater analysis, public health, pollution control legislation, public policy
Manuscript requirements: Style sheet sent on request.
 Preferred length: Less than 30 pages
 Number of copies to be submitted: Two
 Abstract: Yes, of about 150-200 words
Author information and reprints: Payment: None.
 Is simultaneous submission of article to other journals permitted: No
 Exclusive manuscript rights between acceptance and publication: Yes
 Copyright: Held by publication.
 Reprints: Available, cost varies with length
Disposition of manuscript:
 Query letter: No
 Receipt of manuscript acknowledged: Yes
 Decision to publish in: 1-3 months
 Accepted manuscript published in: 6-12 months
 Rejected manuscript returned: Yes
 Rejected manuscript criticized: No
Submit to:
 Peter J. Piecuch
 Editor
 (See address above)

WATER RESEARCH [1860]
Journal of the International Association on Water Pollution Research
Pergamon Press, Inc.
Fairview Park
Elmsford, New York 10523
(914) 592-7700

First published in 1967

SUBSCRIPTION DATA
Issues and rates: Published monthly.
 Annual rate(s): $25.00; Institutions $140.00
Publisher or Sponsor: International Association on Water Pollution Research

EDITORIAL DESCRIPTION
 Publishes original research work in the field of water quality management.
Audience: Professional, academic, governmental
 Manuscripts accepted in English, French, German

MANUSCRIPT INFORMATION
Subject field(s): Chemistry, biology, technology of water and waste-water management; analysis of the water and waste by chemical, physical, or micro-biological methods and advances in instrumentation; reviews will also be considered.
Manuscript requirements: See latest issue for style requirements.
 Preferred length: None
 Number of copies to be submitted: Original and 1 copy, double-spaced
 Abstract: Yes. All papers, regardless of language, should carry an abstract in English as well as the original language, 5 copies please.
Author information and reprints: Payment: Reprints only. 50 reprints
 Is simultaneous submission of article to other journals permitted: Not permitted.
 Exclusive manuscript rights between acceptance and publication: Yes
 Copyright: Held by publication.
 Reprints: Available at cost.
Disposition of manuscript:
 Query letter: Not necessary.
 Receipt of manuscript acknowledged: Yes
 Decision to publish in: 4 weeks
 Accepted manuscript published in: 5 months
 Rejected manuscript returned: Yes, if return postage is supplied by author.
 Rejected manuscript criticized: Reasons for rejections only
Submit to:
 Dr. S. H. Jenkins
 Executive Editor
 Upper Tame Main Drainage Authority
 156/170 Newhall Street
 Birmingham B3 1SE, England

W. W. Eckenfelder, Jr.
Editor
Box 6222, Station B
Vanderbilt University
Nashville, Tennessee 37235 453147

WATER RESOURCES RESEARCH [1861]
American Geophysical Union
1909 K Street, N.W.
Washington, D.C. 20037
(202) 331-0370

SUBSCRIPTION DATA
Issues and rates: Published bi-monthly.
 Average paid circulation: 4,500
 Annual rate(s): $20.00
Publisher or Sponsor: American Geophysical Union
Managing Editor: A.F. Spilhaus, Jr.

EDITORIAL DESCRIPTION
 Publishes papers in the areas of hydrology, fluid mechanics, geochemistry, economics, water law, thermal pollution of rivers, and biological analyses of water.
Articles per average issue: 40
 Manuscripts accepted in English only

MANUSCRIPT INFORMATION
Subject field(s): Sciences of water
Manuscript requirements: AGU
 Number of copies to be submitted: Three
 Abstract: Yes, a single paragraph of 150 words or less
Author information and reprints: Payment: By author to publication. $70.00 per page.
 Is simultaneous submission of article to other journals permitted: No
 Exclusive manuscript rights between acceptance and publication: Yes
 Copyright: Held by the American Geophysical Union
 Reprints: Available at cost.
Disposition of manuscript:
 Query letter: No
 Receipt of manuscript acknowledged: Yes
 Decision to publish in: Varies
 Accepted manuscript published in: 4-5 months
 Rejected manuscript returned: Yes
 Rejected manuscript criticized: Yes
Submit to:
 George H. Davis
 Water Resources Division
 U.S. Geological Survey, National Center
 Reston, Virginia 22092

For manuscripts on economics and water law, submit to:
 Charles W. Howe
 Department of Economics
 University of Colorado
 Boulder, Colorado 80302

Life sciences (general)

LIFE SCIENCES* [1869]
Pergamon Press
Maxwell House, Fairview Park
Elmsford, New York 10523

SUBSCRIPTION DATA
Issues and rates: Published semi-monthly.
  Average paid circulation: Not available.
  Annual rate(s): $100 combined edition

EDITORIAL DESCRIPTION
A journal devoted to short research papers discussing on-going research in the biological sciences. Part I, appearing on the first and fifteenth of the month is concerned with physiology and pharmacology. Part II, appearing on the eighth and twenty-second, is concerned with biochemistry, general and molecular biology.

MANUSCRIPT INFORMATION
Manuscript requirements: See latest issue for style requirements.
  Number of copies to be submitted: Three
  Is simultaneous submission of article to other journals permitted: No
  Exclusive manuscript rights between acceptance and publication: Yes
  Reprints: Available
Additional information: Accepted papers will be returned to the senior author with full typing instructions.
Submit to:
  Charles Matsumoto
  Executive Editor
  Lilly Research Laboratories
  Eli Lilly and Company
  Indianapolis, Indiana 46206

MECHANISMS OF AGEING AND DEVELOPMENT [1870]
Elsevier Sequoia SA
P.O. Box 851
1001 Lausanne 1, Switzerland
(021) 20 73 81

First published in 1972

SUBSCRIPTION DATA
Issues and rates: Published bi-monthly.
  Average paid circulation: 600
  Annual rate(s): SFr. 135.00
Publisher or Sponsor: Association for the Advancement of Ageing Research

EDITORIAL DESCRIPTION
Contains articles directed towards the illumination of the fundamental mechanisms underlying the processes of ageing and development in biological systems, including man. Type of articles: original research and theoretical and review articles, brief notes.
Articles per average issue: 6
  Manuscripts accepted in English, French, German

MANUSCRIPT INFORMATION
Subject field(s): Biochemistry, biophysics, molecular biology, cellular biology, neurobiology, immunology, physiology, cancer, behavioral biology
Manuscript requirements: Style sheet sent on request.
  Preferred length: 4 pages
  Number of copies to be submitted: Three
  Abstract: Yes, of about 100-200 words in English for articles written in French and German.
Author information and reprints: Payment: None. 50 reprints free of charge.
  Is simultaneous submission of article to other journals permitted: No
  Exclusive manuscript rights between acceptance and publication: Yes
  Copyright: Held by publication.
  Reprints: Available
Disposition of manuscript:
  Query letter: No
  Receipt of manuscript acknowledged: Yes
  Rejected manuscript returned: Yes
  Rejected manuscript criticized: Sometimes
Submit to:
  B. L. Strehler
  Department of Biological Sciences
  University of Southern California
  Los Angeles, California 90007

MICROPALEONTOLOGY [1871]
The American Museum of Natural History
79th Street at Central Park West
New York, New York 10024
(212) 873-1300 ext. 490

First published in 1955

SUBSCRIPTION DATA
Issues and rates: Published quarterly.
  Average paid circulation: 1,230
  Annual rate(s): Individuals $20.00; Institutions $50.00

EDITORIAL DESCRIPTION
Contains articles dealing with research results in the field of micropaleontology and related fields.
Articles per average issue: 5
Audience: Research, academic
  Manuscripts accepted in English

MANUSCRIPT INFORMATION
Subject field(s): Microfossils, biostratigraphy, ecology-microfossils, biology-microfossils, biogeography-microfossils, geochemistry of microfossils
Manuscript requirements: Style sheet sent on request.
  Preferred length: None
  Number of copies to be submitted: Two
  Abstract: Yes
Author information and reprints: Payment: By author to publication. $50 per printing plate, voluntary.
  Is simultaneous submission of article to other journals permitted: No
  Exclusive manuscript rights between acceptance and publication: Yes
  Copyright: None
  Reprints: Available at cost.
Disposition of manuscript:
  Query letter: No
  Receipt of manuscript acknowledged: Yes
  Decision to publish in: 1-2 months
  Accepted manuscript published in: One year
  Rejected manuscript returned: Yes
  Rejected manuscript criticized: Yes
Submit to:
  T. Saito
  Editor
  (See address above)

OECOLOGIA [1872]
Springer-Verlag
175 Fifth Avenue
New York, New York 10010
(212) 673-2660

SUBSCRIPTION DATA
  Annual rate(s): DM 180 per volume
Publisher or Sponsor: International Association for Ecology (Intecol)
Managing Editor: H. Remmert

EDITORIAL DESCRIPTION
Publishes original contributions and short communications dealing with the ecology of all organisms. Reports on Symposia are also published.
  Manuscripts accepted in French, German, preferably English

MANUSCRIPT INFORMATION
Subject field(s): Autecology, physiological ecology, population dynamics, production biology, demography, epidemiology, behavioral ecology, food cycles, theoretical ecology, including population genetics
Manuscript requirements: See latest issue for style requirements.
  Preferred length: 10,000 maximum words; 20 pages
  Number of copies to be submitted: 2
  Abstract: Yes. A summary of the main points should be included. Papers in French and German should in addition carry an English summary and translation of the title into English.
Author information and reprints: Payment: Reprints only. 75 offprints
  Is simultaneous submission of article to other journals permitted: Not permitted.
  Exclusive manuscript rights between acceptance and publication: Yes
  Copyright: Held by publisher
Submit to:
  D. M. Gates
  Editorial Board
  The University of Michigan Biological Station
  4051 Natural Science Building
  Ann Arbor, Michigan 48104

PHYSIOLOGY AND BEHAVIOR [1873]
An International Journal
Pergamon Press, Inc.
Fairview Park
Elmsford, New York 10523
(914) 592-7700

First published in 1966

SUBSCRIPTION DATA
Issues and rates: Published monthly.
Annual rate(s): $25.00; Institutions $175.00

EDITORIAL DESCRIPTION
Publishes original reports of systematic studies in the areas of physiology and behavior, in which at least one variable is physiological and the primary emphasis and theoretical context are behavioral; brief communications and the results of experiments.
Articles per average issue: 15-20
Audience: Professional, academic
Manuscripts accepted in English, French, German

MANUSCRIPT INFORMATION
Manuscript requirements: See latest issue for style requirements.
Preferred length: None
Number of copies to be submitted: 2
Abstract: Yes. Not to exceed 170 words, may also include copies in French and German.
Author information and reprints: Payment: Reprints only. 25 reprints
Is simultaneous submission of article to other journals permitted: Not permitted.
Exclusive manuscript rights between acceptance and publication: Yes
Copyright: Held by publication.
Reprints: Available at cost.
Disposition of manuscript:
Query letter: Not necessary.
Receipt of manuscript acknowledged: Yes
Decision to publish in: 4 weeks
Accepted manuscript published in: 6 months
Rejected manuscript returned: Yes, if return postage is supplied by author.
Rejected manuscript criticized: Reasons for rejections only
Submit to:
Matthew J. Wayner
Editor-in-Chief
Brain Research Laboratory, Syracuse University
601 University Avenue
Syracuse, New York 13210

Or to the nearest regional editor.

RESEARCH COMMUNICATIONS IN CHEMICAL PATHOLOGY AND PHARMACOLOGY [1874]
10 Oakdale Drive
Westbury, New York 11590
(516) 334-6943

First published in 1970

SUBSCRIPTION DATA
Issues and rates: Published monthly.
Annual rate(s): $54.00
Managing Editor: D. Barbara Sankar

EDITORIAL DESCRIPTION
Promotes rapid publication of important research letters, papers and reviews in chemistry, biology, pathology, pharmacology and all biomedical sciences related thereto.
Articles per average issue: 20
Audience: Professional; academic
Manuscripts accepted in English only

MANUSCRIPT INFORMATION
Subject field(s): Pathology, pharmacology, clinical chemistry, biological chemistry, physiology, toxicology, molecular mechanisms, medical biology, methodology, biochemical pathology and pharmacology, and all related sciences
Manuscript requirements: Style sheet sent on request.
Preferred length: Letters 2-4 pages; reviews 12-30 pages; articles 8-16 pages
Number of copies to be submitted: Three
Abstract: Yes
Author information and reprints: Payment: None.
Is simultaneous submission of article to other journals permitted: No
Exclusive manuscript rights between acceptance and publication: Yes
Copyright: Held by publication.
Reprints: Available, cost varies.
Disposition of manuscript:
Receipt of manuscript acknowledged: Yes
Decision to publish in: 2-6 weeks
Accepted manuscript published in: 2-6 weeks
Rejected manuscript returned: Yes
Rejected manuscript criticized: Yes
Submit to:
Editorial Board
(See address above)

SPECIAL STIPULATIONS
Due to short interval between receipt and publication of manuscript, it is preferred that authors state the number of reprints they wish at the time of submission. All research work must be original. Any legal or moral problem lies at the responsibility of the authors.

Agrology and agriculture

AGRICULTURAL HISTORY [1875]
University of California Press
2223 Fulton Street
Berkeley, California 94720
(415) 642-4269

First published in 1927

SUBSCRIPTION DATA
Issues and rates: Published quarterly.
Average paid circulation: 1,480
Annual rate(s): $8.00; Foreign $9.00; Institutions $10.00; Students $5.00; Foreign institutions $11.00

Publisher or Sponsor: Agricultural History Society
Managing Editor: James H. Shideler

EDITORIAL DESCRIPTION
A medium for the publication of research and documents pertaining to the history of agriculture in all its phases, and as a clearinghouse for information of interest and value to workers in the field.
Articles per average issue: 6
Audience: Academic, business, government
Manuscripts accepted in English

MANUSCRIPT INFORMATION
Subject field(s): History, economics, geography, land use and tenure, ecology, biology, botany, genetics, agricultural technology and political science as they relate to agriculture.
Manuscript requirements: See latest issue for style requirements. Index Mdicus
Preferred length: 10-12 pages
Number of copies to be submitted: 2
Abstract: Yes. One short paragraph summarizing manuscript content to be submitted in French and English for all manuscripts.
Author information and reprints: Payment: None.
Is simultaneous submission of article to other journals permitted: Not permitted.
Exclusive manuscript rights between acceptance and publication: Yes
Copyright: Held by publication.
Reprints: Available at cost. Depends on number of pages
Additional information: Manuscript to be typewritten, double-spaced; all charts, graphs, and photographs to be camera ready copy; references as per *Index Medicus* format.
Disposition of manuscript:
Query letter: Not necessary.
Receipt of manuscript acknowledged: Yes
Decision to publish in: 3-6 months
Accepted manuscript published in: 6-12 months
Rejected manuscript returned: No
Rejected manuscript criticized: No
Submit to:
Andrew M. Sherrington
Editor
(See address above)

AGRICULTURAL HISTORY REVIEW [1876]
Treasurer, B.A.H.S., Museum of English Rural Life
The University, Whiteknights
Reading, Berks., England

First published in 1953

SUBSCRIPTION DATA
Issues and rates: Published semi-annually.
Average paid circulation: 770; 1,000 controlled
Annual rate(s): £3.50

Publisher or Sponsor: British Agricultural History Society

EDITORIAL DESCRIPTION

Publishes new research and views on agricultural history, including land use techniques, farm structure, landownership, agricultural finance, and marketing, and rural society.

Articles per average issue: 5

Audience: Historical, academic
  Manuscripts accepted in English

MANUSCRIPT INFORMATION

Manuscript requirements: Style sheet sent on request.
  Preferred length: 8,000 words maximum
  Number of copies to be submitted: 1
  Abstract: Not necessary.

Author information and reprints: Payment: Reprints only. 25 reprints
  Is simultaneous submission of article to other journals permitted: Permitted.
  Exclusive manuscript rights between acceptance and publication: Yes
  Copyright: Held by author.
  Reprints: Available at cost.

Additional information: Articles dealing with periods other than the 19th century are preferred.

Disposition of manuscript:
  Query letter: Not necessary, but advisable.
  Receipt of manuscript acknowledged: Yes
  Decision to publish in: 1 month
  Accepted manuscript published in: 18 months
  Rejected manuscript returned: Yes, if return postage is supplied by author.
  Rejected manuscript criticized: No

Submit to:
  Prof. G. E. Mingay
  Editor
  Rutherford College
  University of Kent
  Canterbury, Kent, England
  Canterbury 66822

AGROLOGIST [1877]

151 Slater Street, Suite 907
Ottawa, Ontario, Canada K1P 5H4
(613) 232-9459

Previously entitled *AIC Review, Agricultural Institute Review*

First published in 1934

SUBSCRIPTION DATA

Issues and rates: Published bi-monthly.
  Average paid circulation: 5,300; 7,500 controlled
  Annual rate(s): $6.00, Foreign $7.00

Publisher or Sponsor: Agricultural Institute of Canada

EDITORIAL DESCRIPTION

Contains articles on trends and developments in agriculture in Canada and internationally.

Articles per average issue: 4

Audience: Professional in agricultural industry
  Manuscripts accepted in English

MANUSCRIPT INFORMATION

Subject field(s): Topics of interest to Canadian and international agriculture

Manuscript requirements: Canadian Government Style Manual for Writers and Editors.
  Preferred length: 1,000 words
  Number of copies to be submitted: 3
  Abstract:

Author information and reprints: Payment: None.
  Is simultaneous submission of article to other journals permitted: Yes
  Exclusive manuscript rights between acceptance and publication: No
  Copyright: Held by publication.
  Reprints: Available, cost on request

Disposition of manuscript:
  Query letter: Not necessary, but advisable.
  Receipt of manuscript acknowledged: Yes
  Decision to publish in: 6-8 weeks
  Accepted manuscript published in: Six months
  Rejected manuscript returned: Yes, if self-addressed, stamped envelope is sent with manuscript.
  Rejected manuscript criticized: No

Submit to:
  Wesley E. Henderson
  Managing Editor
  (See address above)

ANIMAL PRODUCTION [1878]

Journal of the British Society of Animal Production
Longman Group Ltd.
43/45 Annandale Street
Edinburgh EH7 4AT, Scotland
(031) 667-6901

First published in 1959

SUBSCRIPTION DATA

Issues and rates: Published bi-monthly.
  Average paid circulation: 2500
  Annual rate(s): £14.00, Foreign $42.00

Publisher or Sponsor: British Society of Animal Production

EDITORIAL DESCRIPTION

Contains original research articles in the field of animal science and related disciplines.

Articles per average issue: 16

Audience: Research workers, extension workers, and other workers in the field of animal science
  Manuscripts accepted in English

MANUSCRIPT INFORMATION

Subject field(s): Animal science and all related disciplines

Manuscript requirements: Style sheet sent on request.
  Preferred length: No absolute limit, but brevity is encouraged.
  Number of copies to be submitted: Two
  Abstract: Yes.

Author information and reprints: Payment: None.
  Is simultaneous submission of article to other journals permitted: No
  Exclusive manuscript rights between acceptance and publication: Yes
  Copyright: Held by publication.
  Reprints: Available, cost depends on length

Disposition of manuscript:
  Query letter:
  Receipt of manuscript acknowledged: Yes
  Decision to publish in: 1-2 months
  Accepted manuscript published in: 6-12 months
  Rejected manuscript returned: Yes
  Rejected manuscript criticized: Yes

Submit to:
  Gerald Weiner
  Senior Editor
  A.R.C. Animal Breeding Research Organization
  Kings Buildings, West Mains Road
  Edinburgh CH9 3JQ, Scotland

CANADIAN JOURNAL OF ANIMAL SCIENCE [1879]

Suite 907
151 Slater Street
Ottawa, Ontario K1P 5H4,
(613) 232-9459

Previously entitled *Canadian Journal of Agricultural Science*, 1953-1956; *Scientific Agriculture*, 1920-1952

First published in 1957

SUBSCRIPTION DATA

Issues and rates: Published quarterly.
  Average paid circulation: 1,300
  Annual rate(s): $14.00; Foreign $15.50; Members $7.00

Publisher or Sponsor: Agricultural Institute of Canada; Canadian Society of Animal Science

Managing Editor: Janet McDonald

EDITORIAL DESCRIPTION

Contains articles relating to scientific research in breeding, genetics, meats, physiology, ruminant nutrition, monogastric nutrition, and related subjects

Articles per average issue: 20-30

Audience: Professional, academic
  Manuscripts accepted in English, French

MANUSCRIPT INFORMATION

Manuscript requirements: See latest issue for style requirements. Style sheet sent on request.
  Preferred length: Up to 20 printed pages
  Number of copies to be submitted: 3
  Abstract: Yes. A resume of not more than 200 words.

Author information and reprints: Payment: By publication to author. $25.00 per page, plus illustration, table and translation charges.
Is simultaneous submission of article to other journals permitted: Permitted, but not encouraged.
Exclusive manuscript rights between acceptance and publication: Yes
Copyright: Held by publication.
Reprints: Available at cost.
Disposition of manuscript:
Query letter: Not necessary.
Receipt of manuscript acknowledged: Yes
Decision to publish in: 1-6 months
Accepted manuscript published in: 4-6 months
Rejected manuscript returned: Yes, with return postage paid by publication.
Rejected manuscript criticized: Yes
Submit to:
Dr. E. E. Lister
Editor
Animal Research Institute, Agriculture Canada
Central Experimental Farm
Ottawa, Ontario K1A 0C6, Canada
(613) 994-9723

CANADIAN JOURNAL OF SOIL SCIENCE [1880]
Suite 907
151 Slater Street
Ottawa, Ontario K1P 5H4, Canada
(613) 232-9459

Previously entitled *Canadian Journal of Agricultural Science*

First published in 1920

SUBSCRIPTION DATA
Issues and rates: Published quarterly.
Average paid circulation: 1,253
Annual rate(s): $12.00; Foreign $13.00; Institutions $18.00; Members $6.00; Foreign individuals $13.00; Foreign institutions $19.50
Publisher or Sponsor: Canadian Society of Soil Science
Managing Editor: Janet H. McDonald

EDITORIAL DESCRIPTION
Research in soil science, soil analysis, and the relationship of soil to crops.
Articles per average issue: 15
Audience: Professional agronomists
Manuscripts accepted in English, French

MANUSCRIPT INFORMATION
Manuscript requirements: See latest issue for style requirements. Chicago
Preferred length: Under 6,000 words; 20-30 pages
Abstract: Not necessary.
Author information and reprints: Payment: Reprints only. 25 offprints, 1 copy of issue
Is simultaneous submission of article to other journals permitted: Not permitted.
Exclusive manuscript rights between acceptance and publication: Yes
Copyright: Held by the Agricultural History Society
Reprints: Available at cost. 50 cents each, 50 minimum
Additional information: Typewritten, double-spaced, with all tables and footnotes on separate pages at the end. Include the publishers of works published in this century.
Disposition of manuscript:
Query letter: Not necessary.
Receipt of manuscript acknowledged: Yes
Decision to publish in: Varies
Accepted manuscript published in: 1year
Rejected manuscript returned: Yes, if return postage is supplied by author.
Rejected manuscript criticized: Yes
Submit to:
James H. Shideler
Editor
Agricultural History Center
University of California
Davis, California 95616
(916) 752-3046

GEODERMA [1881]
An International Journal of Soil Science
Elsevier Scientific Publishing Company
P. O. Box 211, Jan van Galenstraat 335
Amsterdam, The Netherlands

First published in 1967

SUBSCRIPTION DATA
Issues and rates: Published bi-monthly.
Annual rate(s): Individuals Dfl 60.00; Institutions Dfl 170.00

EDITORIAL DESCRIPTION
The entire field of soil research
Articles per average issue: Varies
Audience: Soil scientists, chemists, colleges, libraries
Manuscripts accepted in English

MANUSCRIPT INFORMATION
Subject field(s): Soil testing, agricultural chemistry, fertilizer, land development
Manuscript requirements: Style sheet sent on request.
Preferred length: As required
Number of copies to be submitted: 3
Abstract: Yes.
Author information and reprints: Payment: Reprints only. 50
Is simultaneous submission of article to other journals permitted: Not permitted.
Exclusive manuscript rights between acceptance and publication: Yes
Copyright: Held by publication.
Reprints: Available at cost.
Disposition of manuscript:
Query letter: Not necessary.
Receipt of manuscript acknowledged: Yes
Decision to publish in: 6 weeks
Accepted manuscript published in: 6 months
Rejected manuscript returned: Yes, with return postage paid by publication.
Rejected manuscript criticized: Reasons for rejections only
Submit to:
Editorial Department
(See address above)

THE INTERNATIONAL SUGAR JOURNAL [1882]
23A Easton Street
High Wycombe, Bucks, England
29408

Previously entitled *The Sugar Cane*

First published in 1869

SUBSCRIPTION DATA
Issues and rates: Published monthly.
Average paid circulation: 1100; 2200 controlled
Annual rate(s): $10.00
Managing Editor: D. Leighton

EDITORIAL DESCRIPTION
Contains articles on the technology of sugar manufacture and refining, sugar industry by-products, sugar research, beet and cane agriculture.
Articles per average issue: 3
Audience: Researchers, processors
Manuscripts accepted in English

MANUSCRIPT INFORMATION
Manuscript requirements: objective reportage
Preferred length: 3,000-6,000 words
Number of copies to be submitted: Two
Abstract: Preferably
Author information and reprints: Payment: By publication to author. $10 per page if copyright held by publishers, otherwise $5 per page.
Is simultaneous submission of article to other journals permitted: No
Exclusive manuscript rights between acceptance and publication: Yes
Copyright: Held by author.
Reprints: Available, 36 free
Additional information: No strict requirements, but thorough editing carried out with author's approval. Double-spaced, typewritten copy with drawing in Indian ink without lettering.
Disposition of manuscript:
Query letter: No
Receipt of manuscript acknowledged: Yes
Decision to publish in: Varies
Accepted manuscript published in: Varies
Rejected manuscript returned: Yes
Rejected manuscript criticized: Yes
Submit to:
Editor
(See address above)

JOURNAL OF AGRICULTURAL SCIENCE [1883]
Cambridge University Press
32 East 57th Street
New York, New York 10022

SUBSCRIPTION DATA
Issues and rates: Published quarterly.

EDITORIAL DESCRIPTION
Concise papers reporting original experimental data or methods or new analyses of already existing data, in any aspect of agricultural science.
Audience: Researchers and scientists in the agricultural sciences
Manuscripts accepted in English

MANUSCRIPT INFORMATION
Manuscript requirements: See latest issue for style requirements.
Preferred length: No preference
Number of copies to be submitted: 2
Abstract: Yes. Briefly indicate the experiments described, the main results and important conclusions
Author information and reprints: Payment: Reprints only. 25
Is simultaneous submission of article to other journals permitted: Not permitted.
Exclusive manuscript rights between acceptance and publication: Yes
Copyright: Held by publication.
Reprints: Available at no cost. 25
Additional information: A simple direct style of writing, avoiding unnecessary repetition and circumlocution is preferred.
Disposition of manuscript:
Query letter: Not necessary, but advisable.
Submit to:
Professor J. W. L. Beament
Editor
Journal of Agricultural Science
Downing Street
Cambridge CB2 3DX, England

JOURNAL OF THE SCIENCE OF FOOD & AGRICULTURE [1884]
Blackwell Scientific Publications, Ltd.
85 Marylebone High Street
London W1M 3DE England

SUBSCRIPTION DATA
Issues and rates: Published monthly.
Average paid circulation: 2,047
Annual rate(s): £20
Publisher or Sponsor: The Society of Chemical Industry
Managing Editor: T. F. West

EDITORIAL DESCRIPTION
Contains research papers in any subject related to food or agriculture.
Articles per average issue: 16
Audience: Professional, academic
Manuscripts accepted in English

MANUSCRIPT INFORMATION
Subject field(s): Any scientific field related to food or agriculture
Manuscript requirements: See latest issue for style requirements.
Number of copies to be submitted: Two
Author information and reprints: Payment: Reprints only. 25
Is simultaneous submission of article to other journals permitted: No

Copyright: Held by publication until 6 months after publication.
Reprints: Available at cost.
Disposition of manuscript:
Receipt of manuscript acknowledged: Yes
Decision to publish in: 2 months
Accepted manuscript published in: 3 months
Rejected manuscript returned: Yes
Rejected manuscript criticized: If requested
Submit to:
Editorial Secretary
14 Belgrave Square
London S.W.1., England
(01) 235-3681

LIVESTOCK PRODUCTION SCIENCE [1885]
Elsevier Scientific Publishing Company
P. O. Box 211, Jan van Galenstraat
Amsterdam, The Netherlands

First published in 1974

SUBSCRIPTION DATA
Issues and rates: Published quarterly.
Annual rate(s): Dfl. 69.00
Publisher or Sponsor: European Association for Animal Production
Managing Editor: H. de Boer

EDITORIAL DESCRIPTION
A medium for the publication of original research studies and comprehensive reviews in the field of livestock production and the exchange of current views.
Articles per average issue: 8
Audience: Researchers, livestock producers,
Manuscripts accepted in English, German, French

MANUSCRIPT INFORMATION
Subject field(s): Cattle production; breeding; housing, feeding, management, health, pollution control, advisory activities; product quality, technical and economic aspects, etc.
Manuscript requirements: See latest issue for style requirements. Style sheet sent on request.
Preferred length: As required
Number of copies to be submitted: 3
Abstract: Yes. Three abstracts, one in English, French, and German not to exceed 300 words.
Author information and reprints: Payment: Reprints only. 50 reprints
Is simultaneous submission of article to other journals permitted: Not permitted.
Exclusive manuscript rights between acceptance and publication: Yes
Copyright: Held by publication.
Reprints: Available at cost.
Disposition of manuscript:
Query letter: Not necessary.
Receipt of manuscript acknowledged: Yes
Decision to publish in: 2 months
Accepted manuscript published in: 4-6 months

Rejected manuscript returned: Yes, with return postage paid by publication.
Rejected manuscript criticized: Yes
Submit to:
The Editor
Driebergseweg 10D
Zeist, The Netherlands

SOIL SCIENCE [1886]
428 East Preston Street
Baltimore, Maryland 21202
(301) 528-4116

First published in 1916

SUBSCRIPTION DATA
Issues and rates: Published monthly.
Average paid circulation: 2700
Annual rate(s): $20.00, Foreign $23.00
Publisher or Sponsor: Rutgers University

EDITORIAL DESCRIPTION
Contains original scientific articles from all parts of the world.
Articles per average issue: 10
Audience: Professional
Manuscripts accepted in English

MANUSCRIPT INFORMATION
Subject field(s): Soil science
Manuscript requirements: See latest issue for style requirements.
Preferred length: None
Number of copies to be submitted: Two
Abstract: Yes
Author information and reprints: Payment: By author to publication. $45.00 per page. For all pages over 6.
Is simultaneous submission of article to other journals permitted: No
Exclusive manuscript rights between acceptance and publication: Yes
Copyright: Held by publication.
Reprints: Available
Disposition of manuscript:
Query letter: No
Receipt of manuscript acknowledged: Yes
Decision to publish in: 3 months
Accepted manuscript published in: 1 year
Rejected manuscript returned: Yes
Rejected manuscript criticized: Sometimes
Submit to:
J.C.F. Tedrow
Editor
College of Agriculture and Environmental Science
Rutgers University
New Brunswick, New Jersey 08903
(201) 247-1766 Ext. 1773

Biology

THE AMERICAN JOURNAL OF HUMAN GENETICS [1887]
University of Chicago Press
5801 Ellis Avenue
Chicago, Illinois 60637
(312) 753-3347

First published in 1949

SUBSCRIPTION DATA
Issues and rates: Published bi-monthly.
  Average paid circulation: 3,000
  Annual rate(s): $30.00, Foreign $31.00
Publisher or Sponsor: American Society of Human Genetics

EDITORIAL DESCRIPTION
  Contains research papers in all aspects of human and medical genetics.
Articles per average issue: 10
Audience: Human and medical geneticists, anthropologists, and physicians
  Manuscripts accepted in English

MANUSCRIPT INFORMATION
Subject field(s): Biochemical genetics; population, clinical, cytogenetics, formal genetics; immunogenetics
Manuscript requirements: Chicago
  Number of copies to be submitted: Two
  Abstract:
Author information and reprints: Payment: By author to publication. For excess tables, figures, mathematics.
  Is simultaneous submission of article to other journals permitted: No
  Exclusive manuscript rights between acceptance and publication: Yes
  Copyright: Held by American Society of Human Genetics
  Reprints: Available, cost on request
Disposition of manuscript:
  Query letter:
  Receipt of manuscript acknowledged: Yes
  Decision to publish in: 4-5 weeks
  Accepted manuscript published in: Six months
  Rejected manuscript returned: Yes
  Rejected manuscript criticized: Yes
Submit to:
  Arno G. Motulsky
  Editor
  Division of Medical Genetics, RG-20
  University of Washington
  Seattle, Washington 98195
  (206) 543-3593

ANNALS OF HUMAN BIOLOGY [1888]
Journal of the Society for the Study of Human Biology
Taylor and Francis, Ltd.
10-14 Macklin Street
London WC2B 5NF, England
(01) 405-2237

First published in 1974

SUBSCRIPTION DATA
Issues and rates: Quarterly in 1975; Bi-monthy in 1976
  Annual rate(s): £14.00; Foreign £15.75 (U.S., Can., Mex.)
Publisher or Sponsor: Society for the Study of Human Biology

EDITORIAL DESCRIPTION
  An international journal for the publication of papers concerning research into biological aspects of human populations as regards their ecology, demography, genetics, evolution and the growth, physiology, disease-patterns and behavior of the individuals comprising them.
Articles per average issue: 9
Audience: Professional, academic
  Manuscripts accepted in English

MANUSCRIPT INFORMATION
Subject field(s): Biometry, genetics, epidemiology, human ecology, evolution, physiology, anthropology, etc.
Manuscript requirements: See latest issue for style requirements. Style sheet sent on request.
  Preferred length: None
  Number of copies to be submitted: 2
  Abstract: Yes. Not to exceed 300 words in length.
Author information and reprints: Payment: Reprints only. 50 reprints
  Is simultaneous submission of article to other journals permitted: Not permitted.
  Exclusive manuscript rights between acceptance and publication: No
  Copyright: Held by publication.
  Reprints: Available at cost.
Disposition of manuscript:
  Query letter: Not necessary.
  Receipt of manuscript acknowledged: Yes
  Decision to publish in: 2 months
  Accepted manuscript published in: 6 months
  Rejected manuscript returned: Yes, with return postage paid by publication.
  Rejected manuscript criticized: Yes
Submit to:
  Prof. James M. Tanner
  Editor
  The Institute of Child Health
  Department of Growth and Development
  30 Guilford Street
  London WC1N 1EH, England

ANNALS OF HUMAN GENETICS [1889]
Cambridge University Press
32 East 57th Street
New York, New York 10022

SUBSCRIPTION DATA
Issues and rates: Published quarterly.

EDITORIAL DESCRIPTION
  Material is directly concerned with human genetics or the application of scientific principles and techniques to any aspect of human inheritance.
  Manuscripts accepted in English

MANUSCRIPT INFORMATION
Manuscript requirements: See latest issue for style requirements. Style sheet sent on request.
  Preferred length: As required
  Number of copies to be submitted: 2
  Abstract: Yes.
Author information and reprints: Payment: Reprints only. 25
  Is simultaneous submission of article to other journals permitted: Not permitted.
  Exclusive manuscript rights between acceptance and publication: Yes
  Copyright: Held by publication
  Reprints: Available at cost.
Additional information: Relevance, originality, conciseness of style and adequacy of references are major factors influencing the editors and referees.
Disposition of manuscript:
  Accepted manuscript published in: 7-8 months
Submit to:
  The Editors
  The Galton Laboratory, Department of Human Genetics and Biometry
  4 Stephenson Way
  London 1NW 2HE, England

APPLIED MICROBIOLOGY [1890]
1913 I Street, N.W.
Washington, D.C. 20006
(202) 833-9416

First published in 1953

SUBSCRIPTION DATA
Issues and rates: Published monthly.
  Average paid circulation: 12,000
  Annual rate(s): $60.00; Foreign $61.00; Institutions $60.00
Publisher or Sponsor: American Society for Microbiology
Managing Editor: Robert A. Day

EDITORIAL DESCRIPTION
  Devoted to the advancement and dissemination of applied knowledge as well as ecological knowledge, both applied and fundamental concerning microorganisms.
Articles per average issue: 39
  Manuscripts accepted in English

MANUSCRIPT INFORMATION
Manuscript requirements: See latest issue for style requirements.
  Preferred length: None
  Number of copies to be submitted: 2
  Abstract: Yes.
Author information and reprints: Payment: None.
  Is simultaneous submission of article to other journals permitted: Not permitted.
  Exclusive manuscript rights between acceptance and publication: Yes
  Copyright: Held by the Society
  Reprints: Available at cost.
Disposition of manuscript:
  Query letter: Not necessary.
  Receipt of manuscript acknowledged: Yes
  Decision to publish in: 3 months

Biology

Accepted manuscript published in: 3 months
Rejected manuscript returned: Yes, with return postage paid by publication.
Rejected manuscript criticized: Yes
Submit to:
Robert A. Day
Managing Editor
(See address above)

ARCHIVES OF BIOCHEMISTRY AND BIOPHYSICS [1891]
Academic Press, Inc.
111 Fifth Avenue
New York, New York 10003

SUBSCRIPTION DATA
Annual rate(s): $213.00 per volume;
Foreign $237.00 per volume

EDITORIAL DESCRIPTION
An international journal dedicated to the dissemination of fundamental knowledge in all areas of biochemistry and biophysics.
Manuscripts accepted in English

MANUSCRIPT INFORMATION
Manuscript requirements: See latest issue for style requirements. ACS
Preferred length: As required
Number of copies to be submitted: 3
Abstract: Yes. 50-200 words
Author information and reprints: Payment: Reprints only. 50
Is simultaneous submission of article to other journals permitted: Not permitted.
Exclusive manuscript rights between acceptance and publication: Yes
Copyright: Held by publication.
Reprints: Available at cost.
Disposition of manuscript:
Query letter: Not necessary.
Receipt of manuscript acknowledged: Yes
Rejected manuscript returned: Yes, if return postage is supplied by author.
Rejected manuscript criticized: Sometimes
Submit to:
Editorial Office
(See address above)

ARCHIVES OF MICROBIOLOGY [1892]
Journal for the Investigation of Microorganisms
Springer-Verlag
175 Fifth Avenue
New York, New York 10010

First published in 1930

SUBSCRIPTION DATA
Annual rate(s): DM 116 per volume
Managing Editor: Professor H. G. Schlegel

EDITORIAL DESCRIPTION
Publishes original papers and review articles covering the entire field of microbiology.

Audience: Microbiologists
Manuscripts accepted in English, French, German

MANUSCRIPT INFORMATION
Manuscript requirements: See latest issue for style requirements. Style sheet sent on request.
Preferred length: 32 pages maximum
Number of copies to be submitted: 2
Abstract: Yes. Should not exceed 200 words. Papers not in English should have an abstract written in English.
Author information and reprints: Payment: Reprints only. 75 offprints
Is simultaneous submission of article to other journals permitted: Not permitted.
Exclusive manuscript rights between acceptance and publication: Yes
Copyright: Held by publication.
Reprints: Available at cost.
Additional information: Full length papers as well as short communications are accepted.
Submit to:
Professor Dr. S. C. Rittenberg
Member, Editorial Board
Department of Bacteriology
University of California
Los Angeles, California 90024

AUSTRALIAN JOURNAL OF EXPERIMENTAL BIOLOGY AND MEDICAL SCIENCE [1893]
University of Adelaide
Adelaide, South Australia
2234333 ext. 2434

First published in 1924

SUBSCRIPTION DATA
Issues and rates: Published bi-monthly.
Average paid circulation: 675; 466 controlled
Annual rate(s): $A25.00
Publisher or Sponsor: University of Adelaide, South Australia
Managing Editor: Derrick Rowley

EDITORIAL DESCRIPTION
Contains full length papers describing original research in the fields of biology, biochemistry, genetics, immunology, medicine, microbiology, pathology, pharmacology and physiology.
Articles per average issue: 12
Manuscripts accepted in English

MANUSCRIPT INFORMATION
Manuscript requirements: See latest issue for style requirements.
Preferred length: As concise as possible
Number of copies to be submitted: Three
Author information and reprints: Payment: None.
Is simultaneous submission of article to other journals permitted: Yes
Exclusive manuscript rights between acceptance and publication: Yes
Copyright: Held by publication.
Reprints: Available, cost depends on content.

Disposition of manuscript:
Query letter:
Receipt of manuscript acknowledged: Yes
Decision to publish in: 4 weeks
Accepted manuscript published in: 6 months
Rejected manuscript returned: Yes
Rejected manuscript criticized: Yes
Submit to:
The Editor
(See address above)

BACTERIOLOGICAL REVIEWS [1894]
1913 I Street, N.W.
Washington, D.C. 20006
(202) 833-9416

First published in 1937

SUBSCRIPTION DATA
Issues and rates: Published quarterly.
Average paid circulation: 12,600
Annual rate(s): $16.00; Foreign $17.00; Institutions $16.00
Publisher or Sponsor: American Society for Microbiology
Managing Editor: Robert A. Day

EDITORIAL DESCRIPTION
Accepts reviews and monographs dealing with all aspects of microbiology.
Articles per average issue: 4
Audience: Microbiologists
Manuscripts accepted in English

MANUSCRIPT INFORMATION
Manuscript requirements: See latest issue for style requirements.
Preferred length: None
Number of copies to be submitted: 2
Abstract: Not necessary.
Author information and reprints: Payment: None.
Is simultaneous submission of article to other journals permitted: Not permitted.
Exclusive manuscript rights between acceptance and publication: Yes
Copyright: Held by the Society
Reprints: Available at cost.
Disposition of manuscript:
Query letter: Not necessary.
Receipt of manuscript acknowledged: Yes
Decision to publish in: 3 months
Accepted manuscript published in: 3 months
Rejected manuscript returned: Yes, with return postage paid by publication.
Rejected manuscript criticized: Yes
Submit to:
R. G. E. Murray
Editor
Department of Bacteriology
University of Western Ontario
London 72, Ontario, Canada
(519) 679-3571

BEHAVIOR GENETICS [1895]
An International Journal Devoted to Research in the Inheritance of Behavior in Animals and Man
227 West 17th Street
New York, New York 10011
(212) 255-0713

SUBSCRIPTION DATA
Issues and rates: Published quarterly.
  Average paid circulation: 1,000
  Annual rate(s): Institutions $26.00;
  Individuals $16.00; Foreign institutions
  $27.80; Foreign individuals $17.80
Managing Editor: Steven G. Vandenberg

EDITORIAL DESCRIPTION
  Contains papers which deal with the application of the various perspectives of genetics to the study of behavioral characters and the influence of behavioral differences on the genetic structure of populations.
Articles per average issue: 10
Audience: Psychologists, geneticists, psychiatrists
  Manuscripts accepted in English

MANUSCRIPT INFORMATION
Subject field(s): Animal behavior, anthropology, demography, ethnology, mental retardation, physiological psychology, psychiatric genetics
Manuscript requirements: AIBS
  Preferred length: 15 typewritten pages
  Number of copies to be submitted: Original and two copies
  Abstract: Yes, with 4-6 key words for indexing purposes.
Author information and reprints: Payment: None.
  Is simultaneous submission of article to other journals permitted: No
  Exclusive manuscript rights between acceptance and publication: Yes
  Copyright: Held by publication.
  Reprints: Available, cost varies
Additional information: All drawings in India ink.
Disposition of manuscript:
  Query letter: No
  Receipt of manuscript acknowledged: Yes
  Decision to publish in: 6-8 weeks
  Accepted manuscript published in: 6-8 months
  Rejected manuscript returned: Yes
  Rejected manuscript criticized: Yes
Submit to:
  Steven G. Vandenberg
  Executive Editor
  Department of Psychology
  University of Colorado
  Boulder, Colorado 80302

BIOCHEMICAL AND BIOPHYSICAL RESEARCH COMMUNICATIONS [1896]
Academic Press, Inc.
111 Fifth Avenue
New York, New York 10003

SUBSCRIPTION DATA
Issues and rates: Published semi-monthly.
  Annual rate(s): $177.00

EDITORIAL DESCRIPTION
  Devoted to the rapid dissemination of timely and significant observation in the fields of modern experimental biology.

MANUSCRIPT INFORMATION
Manuscript requirements: See latest issue for style requirements.
  Preferred length: 5 pages
  Number of copies to be submitted: Two
Author information and reprints: Payment: None.
  Copyright: Held by publication.
  Reprints: Available on order
Additional information: References, footnotes, figure legends should be single-spaced. Do not insert figures, figure legends, or tables into text.
Disposition of manuscript:
  Receipt of manuscript acknowledged: Yes
  Rejected manuscript returned: Yes
Submit to:
  Paul D. Boyer
  Editor
  Molecular Biology Institute
  University of California
  Los Angeles, California 90024

Also send manuscripts to:
  Esmond E. Snell
  Department of Biochemistry
  University of California
  Berkeley, California 94720

BIOCHEMICAL GENETICS [1897]
Plenum Publishing Corporation
227 West 17th Street
New York, New York 10011
(212) 255-0713

First published in 1967

SUBSCRIPTION DATA
Issues and rates: Published monthly.
  Average paid circulation: Not available.
  Annual rate(s): Institutions $72.00, Foreign institutions $77.40, Individuals $54.00, Foreign individuals $59.40
Managing Editor: Hugh S. Forrest
  Robert P. Wagner

EDITORIAL DESCRIPTION
  Contains original research in biochemical genetics, from virus to man; review articles; papers on new methods.
Articles per average issue: 8
Audience: Geneticists, biochemists
  Manuscripts accepted in English

MANUSCRIPT INFORMATION
Subject field(s): Molecular aspects of genetic variation and evolution, mutation, gene action and regulation, immunogenetics, somatic cell genetics, nucleic acid function in heredity and development, biochemical aspects of genetic defects
Manuscript requirements: See latest issue for style requirements.
  Preferred length: 8-10 pages
  Number of copies to be submitted: Three
  Abstract: Yes, of 150 words maximum
Author information and reprints: Payment: None.
  Is simultaneous submission of article to other journals permitted:
  Exclusive manuscript rights between acceptance and publication: Yes.
  Copyright: Held by publication.
  Reprints: Available, cost varies with length
Disposition of manuscript:
  Query letter:
  Receipt of manuscript acknowledged: Yes
  Decision to publish in: 6-8 weeks
  Accepted manuscript published in: 6-8 months
  Rejected manuscript returned: Yes
  Rejected manuscript criticized: Yes.
Submit to:
  R. P. Wagner;
  Hugh S. Forrest
  Editors
  Department of Zoology
  University of Texas
  Austin, Texas 78712

BIOCHEMICAL SYSTEMATICS AND ECOLOGY [1898]
Pergamon Press, Inc.
Fairview Park
Elmsford, New York 10523
(914) 592-7700

First published in 1973

SUBSCRIPTION DATA
Issues and rates: Published quarterly.
  Annual rate(s): $25.00; Institutions $40.00

EDITORIAL DESCRIPTION
  Devoted to the publication of original articles and occasional invited reviews on the application of biochemistry and chemistry to systematic problems in biology. Systematics is interpreted in the widest sense.
Articles per average issue: 8-10
Audience: Professional, academic
  Manuscripts accepted in English

MANUSCRIPT INFORMATION
Subject field(s): All classes of organisms from bacteria to higher plants, including fossils, and any type of biochemical information; feedback control, hybridization, discrete chemical compounds; classifications of living organisms, interspecific relationships, and phylogenetic affinities of major taxa.
Manuscript requirements: See latest issue for style requirements.
  Preferred length: None
  Number of copies to be submitted: 2
  Abstract: Yes
Author information and reprints: Payment: None.
  Is simultaneous submission of article to other journals permitted: Not permitted.
  Exclusive manuscript rights between acceptance and publication: Yes
  Copyright: Held by publication.
  Reprints: Available at cost.
Disposition of manuscript:
  Query letter: Not necessary.
  Receipt of manuscript acknowledged: Yes
  Decision to publish in: 4 weeks
  Accepted manuscript published in: 5 months

Rejected manuscript returned: Yes, if return postage is supplied by author.
Rejected manuscript criticized: Reasons for rejections only
Submit to:
E. Schoffeniels
Laboratoire de Biochimie
Université de Liège
Place Delcour 17
B-4000 Liège, Belgium

T. E. Swain
Biochemical Laboratory
Royal Botanic Gardens
Richmond, Surrey TW9 3DS, England

Executive Editors

Or any member of the editorial board.

BIOLOGY OF REPRODUCTION* [1899]
Official Journal of the Society for the Study of Reproduction
Academic Press, Inc.
111 Fifth Avenue
New York, New York 10003

SUBSCRIPTION DATA

Issues and rates: Monthly, except January and July
Annual rate(s): Members $20.00
Publisher or Sponsor: The Society for the Study of Reproduction

EDITORIAL DESCRIPTION

Contains papers in all areas of reproduction in the animal kingdom.

MANUSCRIPT INFORMATION

Subject field(s): Gross and microscopic anatomy, behavior, biochemistry, biophysics, pathology, pharmacology, physiology, zoology
Manuscript requirements: See latest issue for style requirements.
Number of copies to be submitted: Three
Author information and reprints: Payment: By author to publication. $20.00 per page.
Is simultaneous submission of article to other journals permitted: No
Exclusive manuscript rights between acceptance and publication: Yes
Copyright: Held by publication.
Reprints: First 50 free
Additional information: All work should have as its aim development of general principles rather than recording of specialized facts. Preliminary or inconclusive observations should not generally be described.
Disposition of manuscript:
Receipt of manuscript acknowledged: Yes
Rejected manuscript returned: Yes
Submit to:
John D. Biggers
Editor
Laboratory for Human Reproduction and Reproductive Biology
Harvard Medical School
45 Shattuck Street
Boston, Massachusetts 02115

BIOPHYSICS OF STRUCTURE AND MECHANISM [1900]
Springer-Verlag
175 Fifth Avenue
New York, New York 10010

SUBSCRIPTION DATA

Annual rate(s): DM 160 per volume
Managing Editor: F. Sauer

EDITORIAL DESCRIPTION

Papers in the field of biophysics where it is defined as the approach towards the understanding of biological functions through physical interpretation; to explain biological facts and functions by general laws of physics.
Manuscripts accepted in English, German

MANUSCRIPT INFORMATION

Subject field(s): Molecular structure, structural change and its biological function; transport phenomena and thermodynamics of irreversible processes applied to the biological phenomena; primary reactions in photosynthesis and sensory transduction.
Manuscript requirements: Style sheet sent on request.
Preferred length: As required
Number of copies to be submitted: 3
Abstract: Yes.
Author information and reprints: Payment: Reprints only. 50 offprints
Is simultaneous submission of article to other journals permitted: Not permitted.
Exclusive manuscript rights between acceptance and publication: Yes
Copyright: Held by publication.
Reprints: Available at cost.
Additional information: Theoretical treatments should only be submitted when they lead to experimentally verifiable results or when they are directly important for experimental studies in biophysics.
Submit to:
A. San Pietro
Member, Editorial Board
Department of Plant Sciences, Jordan Hall 138
Indiana University
Bloomington, Indiana 47401

BIORHEOLOGY [1901]
Journal of the International Society of Biorheology
Pergamon Press, Inc.
Fairview Park
Elmsford, New York 10523
(914) 592-7700

First published in 1962

SUBSCRIPTION DATA

Issues and rates: Published bi-monthly.
Annual rate(s): $25.00; Institutions $70.00

Publisher or Sponsor: International Society of Biorheology

EDITORIAL DESCRIPTION

Contains original research in the field of biorheology: the study of deformation and flow of biological systems or materials directly derived from living organisms. Such problems have recently assumed importance in physiology, medicine, surgery, botany and other biological disciplines.
Articles per average issue: 5-7
Audience: Professional, academic
Manuscripts accepted in English, German, French

MANUSCRIPT INFORMATION

Subject field(s): Stresses the inter-relationship between rheological properties of biological systems and their various structural aspects. However, exclusively technologically originated substances are not included.
Manuscript requirements: See latest issue for style requirements.
Preferred length: Not to exceed 15 printed pages
Number of copies to be submitted: 2
Abstract: Yes. One in the original language and one in English.
Author information and reprints: Payment: Reprints only. 50 reprints
Is simultaneous submission of article to other journals permitted: Not permitted.
Exclusive manuscript rights between acceptance and publication: Yes
Copyright: Held by publication.
Reprints: Available at cost.
Disposition of manuscript:
Query letter: Not necessary.
Receipt of manuscript acknowledged: Yes
Decision to publish in: 4 weeks
Accepted manuscript published in: 5 months
Rejected manuscript returned: Yes, if return postage is supplied by author.
Rejected manuscript criticized: Reasons for rejections only
Submit to:
A. L. Copley
Co-Editor-in-Chief
Laboratory of Biorheology
New York Medical College
New York, New York 10029

BIOS [1902]
Drew University
Madison, New Jersey 07940
(201) 273-7163

First published in 1930

SUBSCRIPTION DATA

Issues and rates: Published quarterly.
Average paid circulation: 7000; 200 controlled
Annual rate(s): $3.00, Foreign $4.00

Publisher or Sponsor: Beta Beta Beta
Biological Society
Managing Editor: Louise Bush

EDITORIAL DESCRIPTION

Contains articles on biology of interest to undergraduate students, reports of undergraduate research, history and philosophy of biology, organization news.
Articles per average issue: 6
Audience: Undergraduate biology students
Manuscripts accepted in English

MANUSCRIPT INFORMATION
Subject field(s): Biology
Manuscript requirements: AIBS
  Preferred length: 10-15 pages
  Number of copies to be submitted: Two
  Abstract:
Author information and reprints: Payment: None.
  Is simultaneous submission of article to other journals permitted: No
  Exclusive manuscript rights between acceptance and publication: Yes
  Copyright: Held by publication.
  Reprints: Available, first 50 free
Disposition of manuscript:
  Query letter: Yes.
  Receipt of manuscript acknowledged: Yes
  Decision to publish in: 3-4 months
  Accepted manuscript published in: 6 months
  Rejected manuscript returned: Yes
  Rejected manuscript criticized: No
Submit to:
  J. Teague Self
  Editor
  730 Van Vleet Oval 222
  University of Oklahoma
  Norman, Oklahoma 73069
  (405) 325-2001

BIOTROPICA [1903]
The Journal of the Association for Tropical Biology
Clifford Evans, Secretary/Treasurer
In care of The Smithsonian Institution
Washington, D. C. 20560
(202) 628-4422

First published in 1969

SUBSCRIPTION DATA
Issues and rates: Published quarterly.
  Average paid circulation: 1,200 controlled
  Annual rate(s): $10.00; Institutions $15.00; Students $10.00; Foreign institutions $15.00
Publisher or Sponsor: The Association for Tropical Biology, Inc.
Managing Editor: Michael G. Emsley

EDITORIAL DESCRIPTION
For the publication of papers on tropical biology of general interest to subscribers all over the world.
Articles per average issue: 6
Audience: Tropical biologists
  Manuscripts accepted in English, Spanish, French, Portuguese

MANUSCRIPT INFORMATION
Subject field(s): All fields of biology: the study of living organisms
Manuscript requirements: See latest issue for style requirements.
  Preferred length: 25 pages
  Number of copies to be submitted: Original and 2 copies
  Abstract: Yes.
Author information and reprints: Payment: None.
  Is simultaneous submission of article to other journals permitted: Permitted, but not encouraged.
  Exclusive manuscript rights between acceptance and publication: No
  Copyright: Not defined
  Reprints: Available at cost.
Disposition of manuscript:
  Query letter: Not necessary.
  Receipt of manuscript acknowledged: Yes
  Decision to publish in: 3-4 months
  Accepted manuscript published in: 2-3 months
  Rejected manuscript returned: Yes, with return postage paid by publication.
  Rejected manuscript criticized: Sometimes
Submit to:
  Michael G. Emsley;
  Jay C. Shaffer
  Editor and Associate Editor
  Department of Biology
  George Mason University
  Fairfax, Virginia 22030
  (703) 323-2181

CAMBRIDGE PHILOSOPHICAL SOCIETY BIOLOGICAL REVIEWS [1904]
Cambridge University Press
32 East 57th Street
New York, New York 10022

SUBSCRIPTION DATA
Issues and rates: Published bi-monthly.
  Annual rate(s): $26.50 per volume
Publisher or Sponsor: Cambridge Philosophical Society
Managing Editor: Prof. E. N. Willmer

EDITORIAL DESCRIPTION
Discusses current progress and problems in a particular area of research; an integration of different approaches to a problem in order to draw attention to gaps in knowledge; every area of biological research
Articles per average issue: 3-4
Audience: Biologists and research workers in general
  Manuscripts accepted in English

MANUSCRIPT INFORMATION
Manuscript requirements: See latest issue for style requirements.
  Preferred length: 20,000 words maximum
  Number of copies to be submitted: 2
Author information and reprints: Payment: Reprints only. 50
  Is simultaneous submission of article to other journals permitted: Not permitted.
  Exclusive manuscript rights between acceptance and publication: Yes
  Copyright: Held by publication.
  Reprints: Available at no cost.
Additional information: Manuscripts should be typewritten with numbered pages, in a style comprehensible to biologists in general and not only to specialists.
Disposition of manuscript:
  Query letter: Not necessary.
Submit to:
  Professor E. N. Willmer
  Editor
  (See address above)

CANADIAN JOURNAL OF GENETICS AND CYTOLOGY [1905]
Suite 907
151 Slater Street
Ottawa, Ontario K1P 5H4, Canada

SUBSCRIPTION DATA
Issues and rates: Published quarterly.
  Average paid circulation: 1,600
  Annual rate(s): $30.00; Foreign $30.00; Institutions $30.00; Students $6.00; Members $15.00
Publisher or Sponsor: The Genetics Society of Canada
Managing Editor: Dr. William F. Grant

EDITORIAL DESCRIPTION
The official organ of the Genetics Society of Canada
Articles per average issue: 25
Audience: Geneticists, cytologists worldwide
  Manuscripts accepted in English, French

MANUSCRIPT INFORMATION
Subject field(s): Cytology; cytogenetics; human genetics; cellular, molecular, and biochemical genetics; mutagenesis; quantitative, population and evolutionary genetics; general genetics
Manuscript requirements: See latest issue for style requirements. Style sheet sent on request.
  Preferred length: As required
  Number of copies to be submitted: 3
  Abstract: Yes. Not to exceed 200 words, giving the scope and principal findings of the work.
Author information and reprints: Payment: By author to publication. $20.00 per page.
  Is simultaneous submission of article to other journals permitted: Not permitted.
  Exclusive manuscript rights between acceptance and publication: Yes
  Copyright: Held by the Genetics Society of Canada
  Reprints: Available at cost.
Disposition of manuscript:
  Query letter: Not necessary.
  Receipt of manuscript acknowledged: Yes
  Decision to publish in: 2-3 months
  Accepted manuscript published in: 6-9 months
  Rejected manuscript returned: Yes, with return postage paid by publication.
  Rejected manuscript criticized: Yes

Biology

Submit to:
Dr. William F. Grant
Editor
Genetics Laboratory
McGill University, McDonald Campus
Sainte Anne Bellevue H9X 3M1, Canada

CANADIAN JOURNAL OF MICROBIOLOGY [1906]

National Research Council of Canada
100 Sussex Drive
Ottawa, Ontario, Canada K1A 0R6
(613) 992-5411

First published in 1954

SUBSCRIPTION DATA
Issues and rates: Published monthly.
 Average paid circulation: 2800
 Annual rate(s): Individuals $12; Institutions $24
Managing Editor: H. Williamson

EDITORIAL DESCRIPTION
 Publishes the results of original scientific research in any branch of microbiology.
Articles per average issue: 21
Audience: Research biologists
 Manuscripts accepted in English and French

MANUSCRIPT INFORMATION
Subject field(s): All fields of microbiology
Manuscript requirements: Style sheet sent on request.
 Preferred length: Under 25 pages.
 Number of copies to be submitted: Two
 Abstract: Yes.
Author information and reprints: Payment: None.
 Is simultaneous submission of article to other journals permitted: No
 Exclusive manuscript rights between acceptance and publication: Yes
 Copyright: Held by publication.
 Reprints: Available only at time of publication (cost dependent on length)
Disposition of manuscript:
 Query letter:
 Receipt of manuscript acknowledged: Yes
 Decision to publish in: 4 months
 Accepted manuscript published in: 4 months
 Rejected manuscript returned: Yes
 Rejected manuscript criticized: Yes
Submit to:
 A. Clark Blackwood
 Editor
 Department of Microbiology, Room M 213
 Macdonald College P.O.
 Montreal, Quebec, Canada
 (514) 453-6580 ext. 214

CELL AND TISSUE KINETICS [1907]

Blackwell Scientific Publications, Box 88
Osney Road
Oxford OX2 OEl, England
Oxford 40201

First published in 1968

SUBSCRIPTION DATA
Issues and rates: Published bi-monthly.
 Annual rate(s): £18.00
Managing Editor: Prof. E. H. Cooper

EDITORIAL DESCRIPTION
 Contains studies of cell proliferation and differentiation in normal and abnormal states; of control systems and mechanisms operating at intracellular as well as molecular levels.
Articles per average issue: 9
Audience: Research scientists
 Manuscripts accepted in English

MANUSCRIPT INFORMATION
Manuscript requirements: See latest issue for style requirements.
 Number of copies to be submitted: 2
 Abstract: Yes. Yes
Author information and reprints: Payment: Reprints only. 50 reprints
 Is simultaneous submission of article to other journals permitted: Not permitted.
 Exclusive manuscript rights between acceptance and publication: Yes
 Copyright: Held by publication.
 Reprints: Available at cost.
Disposition of manuscript:
 Query letter: Not necessary.
 Receipt of manuscript acknowledged: Yes
 Decision to publish in: 1-3 months
 Accepted manuscript published in: 6 months
 Rejected manuscript returned: Yes, with return postage paid by publication.
 Rejected manuscript criticized: Yes
Submit to:
 Prof. E. H. Cooper
 Editor
 Department of Pathology and Cancer Research
 School of Medicine, The University
 Leeds LS2 9NL, England

CELL AND TISSUE RESEARCH [1908]

Springer-Verlag
175 Fifth Avenue
New York, New York 10010

SUBSCRIPTION DATA
 Annual rate(s): DM 240 per volume

EDITORIAL DESCRIPTION
 Original papers in the field of descriptive and experimental cell and tissue research
 Manuscripts accepted in English

MANUSCRIPT INFORMATION
Subject field(s): Human and animal microanatomy, preference being given to papers of functional experimental content.
Manuscript requirements: Style sheet sent on request.
 Preferred length: As required
 Number of copies to be submitted: 3
 Abstract: Yes. A summary in English of not more than 200 words. Summary must be in French or German for articles written in English.
Author information and reprints: Payment: Reprints only. 75 offprints
 Is simultaneous submission of article to other journals permitted: Not permitted.
 Exclusive manuscript rights between acceptance and publication: Yes
 Copyright: Held by publication.
 Reprints: Available at cost.
Additional information: Material should be arranged under the following headings: Introduction, Materials and Methods, Results, Discussion and References.
Submit to:
 Professor Dr. D. S. Farner
 Editorial Board Member
 Department of Zoology
 University of Washington
 Seattle, Washington 98105

CHROMOSOMA [1909]

Springer-Verlag
175 Fifth Avenue
New York, New York 10010

First published in 1939

SUBSCRIPTION DATA
 Annual rate(s): DM 140 per volume

EDITORIAL DESCRIPTION
 Original contributions in the fields of nuclear and chromosome research
 Manuscripts accepted in English, French, German

MANUSCRIPT INFORMATION
Subject field(s): Articles on cytotaxonomy; mammalian and human cytogenetics are accepted only when of more general interest.
Manuscript requirements: Style sheet sent on request.
 Preferred length: As required
 Number of copies to be submitted: 3
 Abstract: Yes. An abstract in English of up to 500 syllables
Author information and reprints: Payment: Reprints only. 100 offprints
 Is simultaneous submission of article to other journals permitted: Not permitted.
 Exclusive manuscript rights between acceptance and publication: Yes
 Copyright: Held by publisher
 Reprints: Available at cost.
Submit to:
 Professor Dr. Joseph G. Hall
 Editorial Board Member
 Department of Biology
 Yale University
 New Haven, Connecticut 06520

CRITICAL REVIEWS IN BIOENGINEERING [1910]

CRC Press, Inc.
18901 Cranwood Parkway
Cleveland, Ohio 44128
(216) 475-9000

First published in 1971

SUBSCRIPTION DATA

Issues and rates: Published quarterly.
 Annual rate(s): $56.00; Foreign $64.00

EDITORIAL DESCRIPTION

Provides a qualitative approach to the total mass of scientific literature published throughout the world in this discipline.
Articles per average issue: 3
Audience: Academic, professional, library, private
 Manuscripts accepted in English

MANUSCRIPT INFORMATION

Subject field(s): Clinical applications, health care systems, basic science and instrumentation
Manuscript requirements: Style sheet sent on request.
 Preferred length: 50-75 pages
 Number of copies to be submitted: 3
 Abstract: Yes.
Author information and reprints: Payment: By author to publication. $7.50 per page. 25 reprints and 1 copy of issue
 Is simultaneous submission of article to other journals permitted: Not permitted.
 Exclusive manuscript rights between acceptance and publication: Yes
 Copyright: Held by publication.
 Reprints: Not available.
Additional information: All manuscripts are subjected to a review board.
Disposition of manuscript:
 Query letter: Not necessary.
 Receipt of manuscript acknowledged: Yes
 Decision to publish in: 3 weeks
 Accepted manuscript published in: 3 months
 Rejected manuscript returned: Yes, with return postage paid by publication.
 Rejected manuscript criticized: Yes
Submit to:
 Gerald A. Becker
 Director, Editorial Operations
 (See address above)

CRITICAL REVIEWS IN MICROBIOLOGY [1911]

CRC Press Inc.
18901 Cranwood Parkway
Cleveland, Ohio 44128
(216) 475-9000

First published in 1970

SUBSCRIPTION DATA

Issues and rates: Published quarterly.
 Annual rate(s): $56.00; Foreign $64.00

EDITORIAL DESCRIPTION

Provides a qualitative approach to the total mass of scientific literature published throughout the world in this discipline by utilizing outstanding experts in each field to select and critically evaluate the most significant papers published in their particular specialities.
Articles per average issue: 3
Audience: Academic, professional, private
 Manuscripts accepted in English

MANUSCRIPT INFORMATION

Manuscript requirements: Style sheet sent on request.
 Preferred length: 50-75 pages
 Number of copies to be submitted: 3
 Abstract: Yes.
Author information and reprints: Payment: By author to publication. $7.50 per page.
 Is simultaneous submission of article to other journals permitted: Not permitted.
 Exclusive manuscript rights between acceptance and publication: Yes
 Copyright: Held by publication.
 Reprints: Available at no cost. 25 reprints and 1 copy of issue
Additional information: Each paper is refereed prior to publication to insure accuracy and objectivity.
Disposition of manuscript:
 Query letter: Not necessary.
 Receipt of manuscript acknowledged: Yes
 Decision to publish in: 3 weeks
 Accepted manuscript published in: 3 months
 Rejected manuscript returned: Yes, with return postage paid by publication.
 Rejected manuscript criticized: Yes
Submit to:
 Gerald A. Becker
 Director, Editorial Operations
 (See address above)

CRYOBIOLOGY [1912]

International Journal of Low Temperature Biology and Medicine
Academic Press, Inc.
111 Fifth Avenue
New York, New York 10003
(212) 677-6713

SUBSCRIPTION DATA

Issues and rates: Published bi-monthly.
 Average paid circulation: 1700
 Annual rate(s): Institutions $30, Individuals $20
Publisher or Sponsor: Society for Cryobiology

EDITORIAL DESCRIPTION

Devoted to the rapid publication of research articles that relate to all aspects of low temperature biology.
Articles per average issue: 10
 Manuscripts accepted in English

MANUSCRIPT INFORMATION

Subject field(s): Studies of freezing, freeze-drying, hypothermia, hibernation, physiological effects of low environmental temperature on animals and plants, medical applications of reduced temperatures, cryosurgery, hypothermic perfusion of organs, cryoprotective agents and their pharmacological action, and pertinent methodologies.
Manuscript requirements: See latest issue for style requirements.
 Preferred length: 5 printed pages
 Number of copies to be submitted: Three
Author information and reprints: Payment: By author to publication. $10.00 per page. If contract or institution supports. No influence on editorial acceptance.
 Is simultaneous submission of article to other journals permitted: No
 Exclusive manuscript rights between acceptance and publication: No
 Copyright: Held by publication.
 Reprints: Available.
Disposition of manuscript:
 Query letter: No
 Receipt of manuscript acknowledged: Yes
 Decision to publish in: 3 weeks
 Accepted manuscript published in: 6 months
 Rejected manuscript returned: Yes
 Rejected manuscript criticized: Yes
Submit to:
 Dr. Arthur W. Rowe
 Editor-in-Chief
 The New York Blood Center
 310 East 67th Street
 New York, New York 10021
 (212) UN 1-7200

CYTOBIOLOGIE [1913]

Journal for Experimental Cell Research
Wissenschaftliche Verlagsgesellschaft mbH
Birkenwaldstrasse 44, Postfach 40
D-7 Stuttgart, Federal Republic of Germany

First published in 1969

SUBSCRIPTION DATA

Issues and rates: Published bi-monthly.
 Annual rate(s): DM 168 per volume
Publisher or Sponsor: German Society for Electronmicroscopy

EDITORIAL DESCRIPTION

Publishes papers on the structure, function and macromolecular organization of cells.
Articles per average issue: 8-12
Audience: Cell biologists
 Manuscripts accepted in English, German, French

MANUSCRIPT INFORMATION

Subject field(s): Preferred are contributions in which morphological, physiological, biochemical and biophysical data of cellular research are corellated; cellular dynamics, morphogenesis, and cytochemistry.
Manuscript requirements: Style sheet sent on request.
 Preferred length: 4-30 pages
 Number of copies to be submitted: 2
 Abstract: Yes. An abstract, in English, of 200-500 words is required for all articles. Those written in German or French should include a somewhat longer abstract in English.

Author information and reprints: Payment:
Reprints only. 75 reprints
Is simultaneous submission of article to
other journals permitted: Not permitted.
Exclusive manuscript rights between
acceptance and publication: Yes
Copyright: Held by publication.
Reprints: Available at cost.
Disposition of manuscript:
Query letter: Not necessary.
Receipt of manuscript acknowledged: Yes
Decision to publish in: 3-6 weeks
Accepted manuscript published in: 3
months
Rejected manuscript returned: Yes, with
return postage paid by publication.
Rejected manuscript criticized: Reasons
for rejections only
Submit to:
L. E. Roth
Editorial Board
Division of Biology
Kansas State University
Manhattan, Kansas 66506

CYTOBIOS [1914]
A Prestige International Journal of Cell
Biology
The Faculty Press
88 Regent Street
Cambridge, England

First published in 1969

SUBSCRIPTION DATA
Issues and rates: 3-4 times a year (3
volumes per issue)
Annual rate(s): $195.00
Managing Editor: Dr. Stuart Anderson

EDITORIAL DESCRIPTION
Publishes original investigations in all
aspects of cell biology, emphasizing work
at chemical and molecular levels.
Audience: Biomedical researchers
Manuscripts accepted in English,
occasionally French and German

MANUSCRIPT INFORMATION
Subject field(s): Cell biology, cancer
research, cytogenetics, cell pathology,
virology, molecular biology, cellular
pharmacology, immunology, radiation
biology and biophysics, biochemical
genetics, endocrinology, biodeterioration
Manuscript requirements: Style sheet sent
on request.
Preferred length: 40 pages maximum
Number of copies to be submitted: Two
Abstract: Yes.
Author information and reprints: Payment:
None.
Is simultaneous submission of article to
other journals permitted: No
Exclusive manuscript rights between
acceptance and publication: Yes
Copyright: Held by publication.
Reprints: Available, 50 free in covers.
Additional information: Manuscripts should
be in the proper style having the
following headings as appropriate:
Abstract, Introduction, Materials and
Methods, Results, Discussion,
Acknowledgements, References.
Footnotes should be avoided. Short
preliminary communications will be
accepted. Place tables and figure captions
on separate pages. Manuscripts are sent
out anonymously for editorial evaluation.
Disposition of manuscript:
Query letter:
Receipt of manuscript acknowledged: Yes
Decision to publish in: Two to four
weeks
Accepted manuscript published in: Two
to five months
Rejected manuscript returned: Yes
Rejected manuscript criticized:
Sometimes
Submit to:
The Executive Editors
(See address above)

CYTOGENETICS AND
CELL GENETICS [1915]
S. Karger AG
Arnold-Boecklin Strasse 25
CH-4011 Basel, Switzerland
061-390880

Previously entitled *Cytogenetics*

SUBSCRIPTION DATA
Issues and rates: Monthly, (2 volumes per
year)
Average paid circulation: 1250; 60
controlled
Annual rate(s): SFr. 198.00; Foreign
$80.00

EDITORIAL DESCRIPTION
Designed to provide investigators in the
field of animal cytogenetics with a
medium in which to publish their
original findings. Although emphasis has
been placed on vertebrates and
mammalian cytogenetics, with special
reference to man, papers on related
subjects are also considered by the
editors in the light of their relevance to
the general policy of the journal.
Articles per average issue: 7
Manuscripts accepted in English,
German, French

MANUSCRIPT INFORMATION
Manuscript requirements: See latest issue for
style requirements.
Preferred length: 8 printed pages
maxiimum
Number of copies to be submitted: 2
Abstract: Yes
Author information and reprints: Payment:
None.
Is simultaneous submission of article to
other journals permitted: No
Exclusive manuscript rights between
acceptance and publication: Yes
Copyright: Held by publication.
Reprints: Available
Disposition of manuscript:
Query letter: No
Receipt of manuscript acknowledged: Yes
Decision to publish in: 1 month
Accepted manuscript published in: 5
months
Rejected manuscript returned: Yes
Rejected manuscript criticized: Yes
Submit to:
H. P. Klinger
Editor
Department of Genetics
Albert Einstein College of Medicine
1300 Morris Park Avenue
Bronx, New York 10411

DEVELOPMENTAL
BIOLOGY [1916]
Academic Press, Inc.
111 Fifth Avenue
New York, New York 10003

First published in 1960

SUBSCRIPTION DATA
Issues and rates: Published monthly.
Average paid circulation: 2,300
Annual rate(s): $177.00; Foreign $195.00;
Members $39.00
Publisher or Sponsor: Society for
Developmental Biology
Managing Editor: Elizabeth D. Hay

EDITORIAL DESCRIPTION
Original papers bearing on problems of
development in the broadest sense; a
meeting ground for studies on
development that employ techniques from
a wide range of disciplines.
Articles per average issue: 20
Audience: Teachers and research workers,
students of biology
Manuscripts accepted in English

MANUSCRIPT INFORMATION
Subject field(s): Embryonic and
post-embroyonic development, growth,
regeneration and tissue repair;
reproductive biology; biology of aging;
biophysics, cytology, experimental
morphogenesis, teratology, genetics,
immunology, microbiology, pathology,
pharmacology, and physiology
Manuscript requirements: See latest issue for
style requirements.
Preferred length: 15,000 words maximum
Number of copies to be submitted: 2
Abstract: Yes. A synopsis in 200 words
or less
Author information and reprints: Payment:
None.
Is simultaneous submission of article to
other journals permitted: Not permitted.
Exclusive manuscript rights between
acceptance and publication: Yes
Copyright: Held by publisher
Reprints: Available at no cost. 50
Additional information: Conventional
format consists of Abstract, Introduction,
Methods and Materials, Results and
Discussion.
Disposition of manuscript:
Query letter: Not necessary.
Receipt of manuscript acknowledged: Yes
Decision to publish in: 1-3 months
Accepted manuscript published in: 5
months
Rejected manuscript returned: Yes, with
return postage paid by publication.
Rejected manuscript criticized: Yes

Submit to:
Elizabeth D. Hay
Editor-in-Chief
Department of Anatomy, Harvard Medical School
25 Shattuck Street
Boston, Massachusetts 02115
(617) 734-3300 ext. 619

ENZYME [1917]
Journal of Enzyme Physiology and Pathology
S. Karger AG
Arnold-Boecklin Strasse 25
CH-4011 Basel, Switzerland
061-390880

Previously entitled *Enzymologia Biologica et Clinica*

First published in 1961

SUBSCRIPTION DATA
Issues and rates: Published annually.
Average paid circulation: 507; 27 controlled
Annual rate(s): SFr.132.00; Foreign $54.00

EDITORIAL DESCRIPTION
The journal occupies itself primarily with the biological and medical problems of enzymology with direct emphasis on the pathophysiological rather than the biochemical aspects of enzymology.
Articles per average issue: 5-6
Manuscripts accepted in English

MANUSCRIPT INFORMATION
Manuscript requirements: Style sheet sent on request.
Preferred length: 12 pages
Number of copies to be submitted: 2
Abstract: Yes, with key words
Author information and reprints: Payment: None. Charges for excess pages.
Is simultaneous submission of article to other journals permitted: No
Exclusive manuscript rights between acceptance and publication: Yes
Copyright: Held by publication.
Reprints: Available
Disposition of manuscript:
Query letter: No
Receipt of manuscript acknowledged: Yes
Decision to publish in: 1-2 months
Accepted manuscript published in: 4-5 months
Rejected manuscript returned: Yes
Rejected manuscript criticized: Yes
Submit to:
Dr. J. Frei
21, rue de Bugnon
CH-1011 Lausanne, Switzerland

For articles and short reviews:
Dr. W. Eugene Knox
New England Deaconess Hospital
194 Pilgrim Road
Boston, Massachusetts 02215

For short communications:
Dr. O. Greengard
New England Deaconess Hospital
194 Pilgrim Road
Boston, Massachusetts 02215
Editors

EVOLUTION [1918]
Department of Biology
Harvard University
Cambridge, Massachusetts 02138

SUBSCRIPTION DATA
Issues and rates: Published quarterly.
Average paid circulation: 2,000
Publisher or Sponsor: The Society for the Study of Evolution
Managing Editor: Phillip W. Hedrick

EDITORIAL DESCRIPTION
Contains scientific papers on evolution.
Articles per average issue: 10-20
Audience: Evolutionists
Manuscripts accepted in English

MANUSCRIPT INFORMATION
Manuscript requirements: See latest issue for style requirements.
Preferred length: None
Number of copies to be submitted: Three
Abstract: Yes.
Author information and reprints: Payment: None.
Is simultaneous submission of article to other journals permitted: No
Exclusive manuscript rights between acceptance and publication: Yes
Copyright: Held by publication.
Reprints: Available
Disposition of manuscript:
Query letter:
Receipt of manuscript acknowledged: Yes
Decision to publish in: Three months
Accepted manuscript published in: Six months
Rejected manuscript returned: Yes
Rejected manuscript criticized: Yes.
Submit to:
Eliot B. Spiess
Editor
Department of Biological Sciences
University of Illinois at Chicago Circle
Chicago, Illinois 60680

FEDERATION PROCEEDINGS [1919]
9650 Rockville Pike
Bethesda, Maryland 20014
(301) 530-7100

First published in 1942

SUBSCRIPTION DATA
Issues and rates: Published monthly.
Average paid circulation: 18,000
Annual rate(s): $35.00, Pan-Am $38.00, Foreign $40.00

Publisher or Sponsor: Federation of American Societies for Experimental Biology

EDITORIAL DESCRIPTION
Publishes critical papers in the field of experimental biology. Also considers papers in the area of scientific public affairs.
Articles per average issue: 25
Audience: Biomedical experimenters
Manuscripts accepted in English

MANUSCRIPT INFORMATION
Subject field(s): Biology, physiology, biochemistry, pharmacology, pathology, nutrition, immunology, science news
Manuscript requirements: See latest issue for style requirements.
Preferred length: 5 printed pages
Number of copies to be submitted: Three
Abstract: Yes.
Author information and reprints: Payment: None.
Is simultaneous submission of article to other journals permitted: No
Exclusive manuscript rights between acceptance and publication: Yes
Copyright: Held by publication.
Reprints: Available at cost
Additional information: Original scientific articles concerning research are not ordinarily accepted by the journal.
Disposition of manuscript:
Query letter: Yes.
Receipt of manuscript acknowledged: Yes
Decision to publish in: 2 months
Accepted manuscript published in: 3 months
Rejected manuscript returned: Yes
Rejected manuscript criticized: Yes
Submit to:
Karl F. Heumann
Executive Editor
(See address above)

GENETICAL RESEARCH [1920]
Cambridge University Press
32 East 57th Street
New York, New York 10022

EDITORIAL DESCRIPTION
Contains original articles on research in genetics and related fields.
Articles per average issue: Varies
Audience: Scientific community
Manuscripts accepted in English

MANUSCRIPT INFORMATION
Manuscript requirements: See latest issue for style requirements. Style sheet sent on request.
Preferred length: As required
Number of copies to be submitted: 2
Abstract: Yes. A concise abstract of the significant content and conclusions of the paper, not to exceed 250 words in English, should be included. Additional summaries in French, German, Russian or Italian will be accepted.

Biology 589

Author information and reprints: Payment: Reprints only. 50 offprints
Is simultaneous submission of article to other journals permitted: Not permitted.
Exclusive manuscript rights between acceptance and publication: Yes
Copyright: Held by publication.
Reprints: Available at no cost. Available at cost.
Additional information: Submission of a paper will be taken to imply that it is unpublished and is not being considered for publication elsewhere.
Submit to:
Dr. E. C. R. Reeve
Executive Editor
Institute of Animal Genetics
West Mains Road
Edinburgh 9, Scotland

GROWTH [1921]
Southern Bio-Research Institute
Florida Southern College
Lakeland, Florida 33802
(813) 688-3755

First published in 1937

SUBSCRIPTION DATA
Issues and rates: Published quarterly.
Average paid circulation: 975
Annual rate(s): $13.50, Foreign $14.50
Managing Editor: Boris Sokoloff

EDITORIAL DESCRIPTION
Contains a broad spectrum of original investigations of normal and abnormal development and growth, both descriptive and experimental, on the levels of biochemistry, cytology, and gross anatomy. Organisms include man and other mammals, lower vertebrates, invertebrates, and occasionally plants and microorganisms.
Articles per average issue: 8-9
Audience: Physicians and researchers
Manuscripts accepted in English, French, German, Italian and Russian.

MANUSCRIPT INFORMATION
Subject field(s): Normal and abnormal growth
Manuscript requirements: AIBS
Preferred length: Ten to twenty pages
Number of copies to be submitted: Original and at least one carbon.
Abstract: Yes.
Author information and reprints: Payment: By author to publication. $16- $18 per page. Additional charge for tables, figures, photos etc.
Is simultaneous submission of article to other journals permitted: No
Exclusive manuscript rights between acceptance and publication: Yes
Copyright: Held by publication.
Reprints: Available, cost depends on length and number of copies
Additional information: Abstracts should be written in English
Disposition of manuscript:
Receipt of manuscript acknowledged: Yes
Decision to publish in: Six weeks
Accepted manuscript published in: Five months
Rejected manuscript returned: Yes
Rejected manuscript criticized: Yes
Submit to:
Gairdner B. Moment
Editor-in-Chief
Department of Biological Sciences
Goucher College
Baltimore, Maryland 21204
(301) 825-3300

HUMAN BIOLOGY [1922]
Official Publication of the Human Biology Council
Department of Anatomy
Wayne State University
540 East Canfield
Detroit, Michigan 48201
(313) 577-1081

First published in 1929

SUBSCRIPTION DATA
Issues and rates: Published quarterly.
Average paid circulation: 1,707
Annual rate(s): Institutions $15.00, Foreign $15.75; Members $10.00; Members Students $6.00

EDITORIAL DESCRIPTION
Publishes original research on human biological variation and its underlying genetic and environmental causes.
Articles per average issue: 10-15
Audience: Professional biologists
Manuscripts accepted in English

MANUSCRIPT INFORMATION
Subject field(s): Human genetics, reproduction, growth, aging, adaptation, ecology, demography and physical anthropology
Manuscript requirements: AIBS
Preferred length: 2,000-10,000 words
Number of copies to be submitted: 3
Abstract: Yes.
Author information and reprints: Payment: None.
Is simultaneous submission of article to other journals permitted: No
Exclusive manuscript rights between acceptance and publication: Yes
Copyright: Held by publication.
Reprints: Available; 25 free, charge for additional
Additional information: Illustrations (black and white) and tables must be keyed to text. Figures must bear consecutive numbers and be identified on the back. Each figure must bear a legend. The second set of figures may be xeroxes or photographs.
Disposition of manuscript:
Query letter:
Receipt of manuscript acknowledged: Yes
Decision to publish in: 3-6 weeks
Accepted manuscript published in: 6-7 months
Rejected manuscript returned: Yes
Rejected manuscript criticized: Yes
Submit to:
Gabriel W. Lasker
Editor-in-Chief
(See address above)

HUMAN GENETICS [1923]
Springer-Verlag
175 Fifth Avenue
New York, New York 10010

SUBSCRIPTION DATA
Annual rate(s): DM 148 per volume

EDITORIAL DESCRIPTION
Review articles, original investigations, short communications and clinical case reports dealing with human genetics and allied fields
Manuscripts accepted in English, German, French

MANUSCRIPT INFORMATION
Manuscript requirements: See latest issue for style requirements. Style sheet sent on request.
Preferred length: As required
Number of copies to be submitted: 3
Abstract: Yes. Papers should be preceded by a short summary. Articles in French and German should include a more detailed summary in English with translations of all titles.
Author information and reprints: Payment: Reprints only. 75 offprints
Is simultaneous submission of article to other journals permitted: Not permitted.
Exclusive manuscript rights between acceptance and publication: Yes
Copyright: Held by publication.
Reprints: Available at cost.
Submit to:
Professor Dr. A.G. Motulsky
Editorial Board
Division of Medical Genetics
University of Washington School of Medicine
Seattle, Washington 98195

HUMAN HEREDITY [1924]
S. Karger AG
Arnold-Boecklin Strasse 25
CH-4011 Basel, Switzerland
061-390880

Previously entitled *Acta Genetica et Statistica Medica*

First published in 1950

SUBSCRIPTION DATA
Issues and rates: Published bi-monthly.
Average paid circulation: 744; 56 controlled
Annual rate(s): SFr. 186.00, Foreign $54.00

EDITORIAL DESCRIPTION
Publishes a variety of papers related to human and medical genetics, especially in those fields allied with medicine and public health.
Articles per average issue: 8
Manuscripts accepted in English

MANUSCRIPT INFORMATION

Subject field(s): Research reports on the structure and composition of human populations as regards normal and pathological traits; investigations concerned with the genetics of serological and other biochemical characters as well as diseases and abnormalities; and reviews and discussions of the methods and techniques applicable in human genetic studies.

Manuscript requirements: See latest issue for style requirements.
  Preferred length: 8 pages maximum
  Number of copies to be submitted: 2
  Abstract: Yes, with 6 key words
Author information and reprints: Payment: None.
  Is simultaneous submission of article to other journals permitted: No
  Exclusive manuscript rights between acceptance and publication: Yes
  Copyright: Held by publication.
  Reprints: Available
Disposition of manuscript:
  Query letter: No
  Receipt of manuscript acknowledged: Yes
  Decision to publish in: 1 month
  Accepted manuscript published in: 4-6 months
  Rejected manuscript returned: Yes
  Rejected manuscript criticized: Yes
Submit to:
  M. Hauge
  Editor
  University Institute of Chemical Genetics
  Sygehuset
  DK-5000 Odense, Denmark

INTERNATIONAL JOURNAL OF SYSTEMATIC BACTERIOLOGY [1925]
1913 I Street, N. W.
Washington, D. C. 20006
(202) 833-9416

First published in 1951

SUBSCRIPTION DATA

Issues and rates: Published quarterly.
  Average paid circulation: 1,800
  Annual rate(s): Foreign $24.00; Individuals $8.00; Institutions $24.00; Students $8.00; Members $8.00
Publisher or Sponsor: International Association of Microbiological Societies
Managing Editor: Robert A. Day

EDITORIAL DESCRIPTION

Devoted to the advancement of the systematics of bacteria, yeasts, and yeast-like organisms and to the dissemination of information related thereto.
Articles per average issue: 20
Audience: Microbiologists
  Manuscripts accepted in English

MANUSCRIPT INFORMATION

Manuscript requirements: See latest issue for style requirements.
  Preferred length: As required
  Number of copies to be submitted: 2
  Abstract: Yes.
Author information and reprints: Payment: None.
  Is simultaneous submission of article to other journals permitted: Not permitted.
  Exclusive manuscript rights between acceptance and publication: Yes
  Copyright: Held by publication.
  Reprints: Available at cost.
Disposition of manuscript:
  Query letter: Not necessary.
  Receipt of manuscript acknowledged:
  Decision to publish in: 3 months
  Accepted manuscript published in: 3 months
  Rejected manuscript returned: Yes, with return postage paid by publication.
  Rejected manuscript criticized: Yes
Submit to:
  Robert A. Day
  Managing Editor
  (See address above)

JAPANESE JOURNAL OF MICROBIOLOGY [1926]
Igaku Shoin Ltd.
5-24-3 Hongo, Bunkyo-ku
Tokyo 113-91, Japan
(03)811-1101

First published in 1957

SUBSCRIPTION DATA

Issues and rates: Published bi-monthly.
  Annual rate(s): 13,500 Yen
Publisher or Sponsor: Japanese Society for Bacteriology; Society of Japanese Virologists

EDITORIAL DESCRIPTION

Publishes original reports of research as well as preliminary notes concerning significant findings in bacteriology, virology and related fields.
Articles per average issue: 14
  Manuscripts accepted in English, Japanese

MANUSCRIPT INFORMATION

Subject field(s): Bacteriology, virology, genetic biology, immunochemistry, carcinology, biophysical chemistry, chemical pharmacology, clinical biochemistry, mycology
Manuscript requirements: See latest issue for style requirements.
  Preferred length: 30 pages
  Number of copies to be submitted: Two
  Abstract: Yes, of about 250 words.
Author information and reprints: Payment: By author to publication. 9,000 Yen per page.
  Is simultaneous submission of article to other journals permitted: No
  Exclusive manuscript rights between acceptance and publication: Yes
  Copyright: Held by publication.
  Reprints: Available, 50 free; additional at cost.
Additional information: Articles should be divided into: Abstract, Introduction, Materials and Methods, Results, Discussion, Acknowledgements, and References.
Disposition of manuscript:
  Query letter: No
  Receipt of manuscript acknowledged: Yes
  Decision to publish in: 5-6 weeks
  Accepted manuscript published in: 4-6 months
  Rejected manuscript returned: Yes
  Rejected manuscript criticized: Sometimes
Submit to:
  Hisao Uetake
  Editor-in-Chief
  (See address above)

SPECIAL STIPULATIONS

Illustrations in full color for publication are accepted, in which case, the cost will be charged to the author.

JOURNAL OF BACTERIOLOGY [1927]
1913 I Street, N. W.
Washington, D. C. 20006
(202) 833-9416

First published in 1916

SUBSCRIPTION DATA

Issues and rates: Published monthly.
  Average paid circulation: 11,500
  Annual rate(s): $85.00; Pan-Am $87.00; Foreign $88.00; Institutions $85.00
Publisher or Sponsor: American Society for Microbiology
Managing Editor: Robert A. Day

EDITORIAL DESCRIPTION

Devoted to the dissemination of fundamental knowledge concerning bacteria and other microorganisms.
Articles per average issue: 57
Audience: Microbiologists
  Manuscripts accepted in English

MANUSCRIPT INFORMATION

Subject field(s): All areas of microbiology and related fields
Manuscript requirements: See latest issue for style requirements.
  Preferred length: As required
  Number of copies to be submitted: 2
  Abstract: Yes.
Author information and reprints: Payment: None.
  Is simultaneous submission of article to other journals permitted: Not permitted.
  Exclusive manuscript rights between acceptance and publication: Yes
  Copyright: Held by publication.
  Reprints: Available at cost.
Disposition of manuscript:
  Query letter: Not necessary.
  Receipt of manuscript acknowledged: Yes
  Decision to publish in: 3 months
  Accepted manuscript published in: 4 months

Biology

Rejected manuscript returned: Yes, with return postage paid by publication.
Rejected manuscript criticized: Yes
Submit to:
Robert A. Day
Managing Editor
(See address above)

THE JOURNAL OF CELL BIOLOGY [1928]
Rockefeller University Press
1230 York Avenue
New York, New York 10021
(212) 360-1278

SUBSCRIPTION DATA
Issues and rates: Published monthly.
  Average paid circulation: 4359; 49 controlled
  Annual rate(s): $125.00; Foreign $135.00 (Europe)
Publisher or Sponsor: The American Society for Cell Biology

EDITORIAL DESCRIPTION
  Publishes reports of original observations on the behavior, structure, and function of cells and cell products. It is especially interested in bringing to the attention of its readers discoveries arising from the application of modern techniques. Manuscripts that attempt to correlate the findings of the biophysical and biochemical disciplines with physiological and morphological information are solicited.

MANUSCRIPT INFORMATION
Manuscript requirements: CBE
  Preferred length: 15,000 words; 20 printed pages maximum
  Number of copies to be submitted: Two
Author information and reprints: Payment: By author to publication. For illustrations in excess of 4 pages
  Is simultaneous submission of article to other journals permitted: No
  Exclusive manuscript rights between acceptance and publication: Yes
  Copyright: Held by publication.
  Reprints: Available at cost. Cost on sliding scale
Disposition of manuscript:
  Receipt of manuscript acknowledged: Yes
  Rejected manuscript returned: Yes
Submit to:
Raymond B. Griffiths
Executive Editor
(See address above)
(212) 360-1539

JOURNAL OF EXPERIMENTAL BIOLOGY [1929]
Cambridge University Press
32 East 57th Street
New York, New York 10022
(212) MU 8-8885

First published in 1923

SUBSCRIPTION DATA
Issues and rates: Published bi-monthly.
  Average paid circulation: Not available.
  Annual rate(s): $30.00, Foreign £9.00
Publisher or Sponsor: Company of Biologists, Ltd.
Managing Editor: Dr. R. J. Skaer, Secretary

EDITORIAL DESCRIPTION
  Contains research reports mainly on invertebrates, but also including marine biology, neurophysiology and entomology as related to experimental zoology, physiology and biochemistry.

MANUSCRIPT INFORMATION
Manuscript requirements: See latest issue for style requirements.
  Number of copies to be submitted: 2
  Abstract: Yes. A short and concise summary of about 100 words giving the chief results of the inquiry. Submit 5 copies of abstract.
Author information and reprints: Payment: By author to publication. Excessive alteration costs, plates, etc.
  Is simultaneous submission of article to other journals permitted: No
  Exclusive manuscript rights between acceptance and publication: Yes
  Copyright: Held by the Company of Biologists, Ltd.
  Reprints: Available, first 50 free
Additional information: Line drawings should be used where possible.
Disposition of manuscript:
  Query letter: No
  Receipt of manuscript acknowledged: Yes
Submit to:
V. B. Wigglesworth;
J. A. Ramsay
Editors
Zoological Laboratory
Downing Street
Cambridge CB2 3EJ, England

JOURNAL OF GENERAL MICROBIOLOGY [1930]
Cambridge University Press
32 East 57th Street
New York, New York 10022

SUBSCRIPTION DATA
  Annual rate(s): Individuals $26.50
Publisher or Sponsor: Society for General Microbiology
Managing Editor: J. R. Postgate

EDITORIAL DESCRIPTION
  Original work on algae, bacteria, microfungi, protozoa and other microorganisms; particularly concerned with fundamental studies of these forms and their activities.
Audience: Microbiologists
  Manuscripts accepted in English

MANUSCRIPT INFORMATION
Manuscript requirements: See latest issue for style requirements.
  Preferred length: No preference
  Number of copies to be submitted: 2
  Is simultaneous submission of article to other journals permitted: Permitted.
  Exclusive manuscript rights between acceptance and publication: Yes
  Copyright: Held by publication.
Submit to:
Editorial Board
Harvest House
62 London Road
Reading, Berkshire RG1 5AS, England

JOURNAL OF HEREDITY [1931]
1028 Connecticut Avenue N.W., Suite 613
Washington, D.C. 20036
(202) 659-2096

First published in 1910

SUBSCRIPTION DATA
Issues and rates: Published bi-monthly.
  Average paid circulation: 4300
  Annual rate(s): $20.00; Foreign $21.00
Publisher or Sponsor: American Genetic Association

EDITORIAL DESCRIPTION
  Publishes theoretical, practical and review articles that focus on current research in genetics. Reports recent developments in plant, animal, and human genetics.
Articles per average issue: 20
  Manuscripts accepted in English

MANUSCRIPT INFORMATION
Subject field(s): Genetics, botany, zoology, horticulture, cytology, molecular biology, eugenics, microbiology, agronomy
Manuscript requirements: AIBS
  Preferred length: 5,000-7,000 words; 20-30 pages
  Number of copies to be submitted: Two
Author information and reprints: Payment: By author to publication. $50 per page.
  Is simultaneous submission of article to other journals permitted: No
  Exclusive manuscript rights between acceptance and publication: Yes
  Copyright: Held by publication.
  Reprints: Available at cost
Disposition of manuscript:
  Query letter: No
  Receipt of manuscript acknowledged: Yes
  Decision to publish in: 4-6 weeks
  Accepted manuscript published in: 4-6 months
  Rejected manuscript returned: Yes
  Rejected manuscript criticized: Usually
Submit to:
Barbara C. Kuhn
Managing Editor
(See address above)

JOURNAL OF MOLECULAR EVOLUTION [1932]
Springer-Verlag
175 Fifth Avenue
New York, New York 10010

SUBSCRIPTION DATA
  Annual rate(s): DM 136 per volume
Managing Editor: Dr. E. Zuckerkandl

EDITORIAL DESCRIPTION
  Publishes papers stressing experimental results with theoretical content leading to

a higher level of understanding and experimental content having implications that are clearly expressed
Manuscripts accepted in English, German, French

MANUSCRIPT INFORMATION

Subject field(s): Biogenetic evolution, evolution of informational macromolecules, evolution of genetic control mechanisms, evolution of enzyme systems and their products, evolution of macromolecular systems, and evolutionary aspects of molecular population genetics
Manuscript requirements: See latest issue for style requirements.
  Preferred length: As required
  Number of copies to be submitted: 2
  Abstract: Yes. An English summary for articles not written in English. All articles should include a summary of not more than 225 words.
Author information and reprints: Payment: Reprints only. 75 offprints
  Is simultaneous submission of article to other journals permitted: Not permitted.
  Exclusive manuscript rights between acceptance and publication: Yes
  Copyright: Held by publication.
Submit to:
  Dr. L. King
  Editorial Board
  Department of Biological Sciences
  University of California
  Santa Barbara, California 93106

JOURNAL OF THEORETICAL BIOLOGY [1933]

Academic Press Ltd.
24-28 Oval Road
London NW1, England
01-267-4466

First published in 1961

SUBSCRIPTION DATA

Issues and rates: Published monthly.
  Annual rate(s): £78.00; Foreign $201.00 plus postage

EDITORIAL DESCRIPTION

Contains papers covering all aspects of theoretical biology. A limited amount of new experimental material related to a theoretical work is acceptable.
Articles per average issue: 20
Audience: Professional, academic
  Manuscripts accepted in English

MANUSCRIPT INFORMATION

Manuscript requirements: See latest issue for style requirements.
  Number of copies to be submitted: Three
  Abstract: Yes
Author information and reprints: Payment: Negotiated between author and editor
  Is simultaneous submission of article to other journals permitted: No
  Exclusive manuscript rights between acceptance and publication: Yes
  Copyright: Held by publication.
  Reprints: Available

Disposition of manuscript:
  Receipt of manuscript acknowledged: Yes
  Decision to publish in: 3 months
  Accepted manuscript published in: 6-8 months
  Rejected manuscript returned: Yes
  Rejected manuscript criticized: Yes
Submit to:
  American papers:
  James F. Danielli
  Chief Editor
  Center for Theoretical Biology
  4248 Ridge Lea
  Amherst, New York 14226

  European papers:
  Professor L. Wolpert
  Editor
  Department of Biology as Applied to Medicine
  Middlesex Hospital Medical School
  London W1, England

LINNEAN SOCIETY BIOLOGICAL JOURNAL [1934]

Academic Press Ltd.
24-28 Oval Road
London NW1, England
01-267-4466

First published in 1969

SUBSCRIPTION DATA

Issues and rates: Published quarterly.
  Average paid circulation: 1,650
  Annual rate(s): £14.00; Foreign institutions £16.00
Publisher or Sponsor: Linnean Society of London
Managing Editor: David McClintock

EDITORIAL DESCRIPTION

Contains original scientific research in the wide general field of experimental biology, palaeontology and systematics, as well as reports of ecological and conservation studies and expeditions, also historical papers.
Articles per average issue: 6
Audience: Biologists, botanists and zoologists
  Manuscripts accepted in English

MANUSCRIPT INFORMATION

Subject field(s): General biology, botany, zoology, taxonomy and ecology
Manuscript requirements: See latest issue for style requirements.
  Number of copies to be submitted: 2
  Abstract: Yes.
Author information and reprints: Payment: None.
  Is simultaneous submission of article to other journals permitted: No
  Exclusive manuscript rights between acceptance and publication: Yes
  Copyright: Held by publication.
  Reprints: Available; 50 free, additional can be purchased
Disposition of manuscript:
  Query letter:

Receipt of manuscript acknowledged: Yes
Decision to publish in: As soon as possible
Accepted manuscript published in: 11 months
Rejected manuscript returned: Yes
Rejected manuscript criticized: Yes
Submit to:
  Editorial Secretary
  Burlington House,
  Piccadilly
  London W1V OLQ, England

MICROBIOS [1935]

International Journal of Chemical and General Microbiology
The Faculty Press
88 Regent Street
Cambridge, England

First published in 1969

SUBSCRIPTION DATA

Issues and rates: Two volumes, each of 4 numbers, per year
  Annual rate(s): Foreign $195.00
Publisher or Sponsor: The Faculty Press
Managing Editor: Dr. Stuart Anderson

EDITORIAL DESCRIPTION

An international biomedical research journal of chemical and general microbiology devoted to fundamental studies of viruses, bacteria and all micro-organisms.
Articles per average issue: Varies
Audience: Research
  Manuscripts accepted in English (French, German)

MANUSCRIPT INFORMATION

Subject field(s): Chemical microbiology, virology, bacteriology, cancer research, cellular pharmacology, micro-fungi, food manufacture and spoilage, molecular biology and biochemical genetics, immunology, biophysics and radiation biology, biodeterioration, pharmaceutical production
Manuscript requirements: Style sheet sent on request.
  Preferred length: 40 pages maximum
  Number of copies to be submitted: Two
  Abstract: Yes
Author information and reprints: Payment: None.
  Is simultaneous submission of article to other journals permitted: No
  Exclusive manuscript rights between acceptance and publication: Yes
  Copyright: Held by publication.
  Reprints: Available, 50 free in covers.

Additional information: Manuscripts should be in the proper style having the following headings as appropriate: Abstract, Introduction, Materials and Methods, Results, Discussion, Acknowledgements, References. Footnotes should be avoided. Short preliminary communications will be accepted. Place tables and figure captions on separate pages. Manuscripts are sent out anonymously for editorial evaluation.
Disposition of manuscript:
  Query letter: No
  Receipt of manuscript acknowledged: Yes
  Decision to publish in: 2-4 weeks
  Accepted manuscript published in: 2-5 months
  Rejected manuscript returned: Yes
  Rejected manuscript criticized: Sometimes
Submit to:
  The Executive Editors
  (See address above)

MOLECULAR & GENERAL GENETICS [1936]
Continuation of Zeitschrift für Vererbungslehre
Springer-Verlag
Postfach 1780 D-6900
Heidelberg, Federal Republic of Germany
49101

SUBSCRIPTION DATA
Issues and rates: Irregular
  Annual rate(s): DM 812

EDITORIAL DESCRIPTION
  Contains articles on molecular and general genetics, developmental genetics, biochemical and physical bases of genetics, animal and plant breeding, human genetics if significant for fundamental genetics.
Articles per average issue: 9
  Manuscripts accepted in English, French, and German

MANUSCRIPT INFORMATION
Subject field(s): Genetics: viral (phages), bacterial, fungus, plant, animal, cell, biochemical, biophysical, developmental
Manuscript requirements: See latest issue for style requirements.
  Preferred length: Short
Author information and reprints: Payment: None.
  Is simultaneous submission of article to other journals permitted: No
  Exclusive manuscript rights between acceptance and publication: Yes
  Copyright: Held by publication.
  Reprints: Available, 50 free
Disposition of manuscript:
  Receipt of manuscript acknowledged: Yes
  Decision to publish in: Varies
  Accepted manuscript published in: 3 months
  Rejected manuscript returned: Yes
  Rejected manuscript criticized: No
Submit to:
  Georg Melchers
  Max Planck Institut für Biologie
  Corrensstr. 41
  D-74 Tübingen, Federal Republic of Germany

MUTATION RESEARCH [1937]
Elsevier Scientific Publishing Company
Jan van Galenstraat 335, P.O. Box 211
Amsterdam, The Netherlands
(020) 515-9222

First published in 1964

SUBSCRIPTION DATA
Issues and rates: Published monthly.
  Annual rate(s): Dfl 678.00
Managing Editor: Frits H. Sobels

EDITORIAL DESCRIPTION
  International journal on mutagenesis, chromosome breakage and related subjects.
Articles per average issue: 15
Audience: Research scientists
  Manuscripts accepted in English, French, German

MANUSCRIPT INFORMATION
Manuscript requirements: See latest issue for style requirements.
  Number of copies to be submitted: 3
  Abstract: Yes. 300-400 words
Author information and reprints: Payment: Reprints only. 50 free reprints
  Is simultaneous submission of article to other journals permitted: Not permitted.
  Exclusive manuscript rights between acceptance and publication: Yes
  Copyright: ASP Biological and Medical Press B.V. Amsterdam (Elsevier Division)
  Reprints: Available at cost.
Disposition of manuscript:
  Query letter: Not necessary, but advisable.
  Receipt of manuscript acknowledged: Yes
  Decision to publish in: 2-6 weeks
  Accepted manuscript published in: 4-8 weeks
  Rejected manuscript returned: Yes, with return postage paid by publication.
  Rejected manuscript criticized: Reasons for rejections only
Submit to:
  For all sections:
  Professor F. H. Sobels
  Managing Editor
  Laboratory of Radiation Genetics and Chemical Mutagenesis
  State University
  Wassenaarseweg 62
  Leiden, The Netherlands

  For the section on Environmental Mutagenesis and Reviews on Genetic Toxicology:
  Dr. F. J. de Serres
  Associate Editor
  National Institute of Environmental Health Sciences
  P. O. Box 12233
  Research Triangle Park, North Carolina 27709

PATHOLOGIA ET MICROBIOLOGIA [1938]
S. Karger AG
Arnold-Boecklin Strasse 25
CH-4011 Basel, Switzerland
061-390880

Previously entitled *Swiss Journal of General Pathology and Bacteriology*

First published in 1938

SUBSCRIPTION DATA
Issues and rates: 8 issues per annum in 2 volumes
  Average paid circulation: 542; 28 controlled
  Annual rate(s): SFr 110.00; Foreign $44.00
Publisher or Sponsor: The International Society of Geographical Pathology

EDITORIAL DESCRIPTION
  Publishes papers dealing with the area of microbiology in all of its related disciplines.
Articles per average issue: 6
  Manuscripts accepted in English (French, German)

MANUSCRIPT INFORMATION
Manuscript requirements: See latest issue for style requirements.
  Preferred length: 8 pages
  Number of copies to be submitted: 2
  Abstract: Yes, with English title and 3-9 key words.
Author information and reprints: Payment: Reprints only.
  Is simultaneous submission of article to other journals permitted: No
  Exclusive manuscript rights between acceptance and publication: Yes
  Copyright: Held by publication.
  Reprints: Available
Disposition of manuscript:
  Query letter: No
  Receipt of manuscript acknowledged: Yes
  Decision to publish in: 1 month
  Accepted manuscript published in: 6 months
  Rejected manuscript returned: Yes
Submit to:
  H. Ramseier,
  J. R. Ruettner
  Editors
  Postfach
  CH-8028 Zürich, Switzerland

PHOTOCHEMISTRY AND PHOTOBIOLOGY [1939]
An International Journal
Pergamon Press, Inc.
Maxwell House, Fairview Park
Elmsford, New York 10523
(914) 592-7700

First published in 1962

SUBSCRIPTION DATA

Issues and rates: Published monthly.
Annual rate(s): $110.00
Publisher or Sponsor: The American Society for Photobiology
Managing Editor: Dr. John Jagger

EDITORIAL DESCRIPTION

Publishes manuscripts of the highest quality, combining scientific rigor with clarity and brevity on all aspects of photochemistry and photobiology with primary concern for analytic rather than descriptive articles having either current or foreseeable biological relevance.
Articles per average issue: 8-10
Manuscripts accepted in English

MANUSCRIPT INFORMATION

Subject field(s): The photochemistry of biological materials and related substances, and the action of infra-red, visible, and ultraviolet radiation on biological systems.
Manuscript requirements: See latest issue for style requirements. CBE
Preferred length: As required
Number of copies to be submitted: 2
Abstract: Yes. An abstract in English not exceeding 200 words; abstracts in other languages would be helpful.
Author information and reprints: Payment: By author to publication. $25.00 per page.
Is simultaneous submission of article to other journals permitted: Not permitted.
Exclusive manuscript rights between acceptance and publication: Yes
Copyright: Held by publication.
Reprints: Available at no cost.
Disposition of manuscript:
Query letter: Not necessary.
Receipt of manuscript acknowledged: Yes
Decision to publish in: 4 weeks
Accepted manuscript published in: 5 months
Rejected manuscript returned: Yes, if return postage is supplied by author.
Rejected manuscript criticized: Reasons for rejections only
Submit to:
Dr. John Jagger
Editor
P. O. Box 688
Richardson, Texas 75080

PHYSIOLOGICAL CHEMISTRY AND PHYSICS [1940]

P.O. Box 189
Portland, Oregon 97207
(503) 225-8403

First published in 1969

SUBSCRIPTION DATA

Issues and rates: Published bi-monthly.
Average paid circulation: 1000
Annual rate(s): $30.00, Foreign $31.00

EDITORIAL DESCRIPTION

Contains accounts of fundamental research of general or special interest in biological substrates.
Articles per average issue: 10
Audience: Researchers and teachers
Manuscripts accepted in English

MANUSCRIPT INFORMATION

Subject field(s): Molecular biology, biochemistry, biophysics, photo-biology
Manuscript requirements: Style sheet sent on request.
Preferred length: 6000 words maximum
Number of copies to be submitted: One original, two copies
Abstract: Yes.
Author information and reprints: Payment: None.
Is simultaneous submission of article to other journals permitted: No
Exclusive manuscript rights between acceptance and publication: Yes
Copyright: Held by publication.
Reprints: Available, cost on request
Disposition of manuscript:
Query letter:
Receipt of manuscript acknowledged: Yes
Decision to publish in: 4-6 weeks
Accepted manuscript published in: 2-4 months
Rejected manuscript returned: Yes, if self-addressed, stamped envelope is sent with manuscript.
Rejected manuscript criticized: Yes
Submit to:
Diane I. McLaughlin
Administrative Editor
(See address above)
(503) 225-8458

PREPARATIVE BIOCHEMISTRY [1941]

Marcel Dekker, Inc.
270 Madison Avenue
New York, New York 10016
(212) 490-7700

First published in 1971

SUBSCRIPTION DATA

Issues and rates: Published bi-monthly.
Annual rate(s): $30.00; Foreign $34.50; Institutions $30.00; Students $15.00; Foreign individuals $34.50
Managing Editor: Dr. Carel J. van Oss

EDITORIAL DESCRIPTION

Devoted to preparative methods and procedures in biological, immunological, pharmaceutical and clinical chemistry, molecular biology, biochemistry and biophysics
Articles per average issue: 5-8
Audience: Those involved in the disciplines enumerated above
Manuscripts accepted in English

MANUSCRIPT INFORMATION

Manuscript requirements: Style sheet sent on request.
Preferred length: No preference
Number of copies to be submitted: 1 original and 2 copies
Abstract: Yes. See style sheet or latest issue
Author information and reprints: Payment: None.
Is simultaneous submission of article to other journals permitted: Not permitted.
Exclusive manuscript rights between acceptance and publication: Yes
Copyright: Held by publication.
Reprints: Available at no cost. 20
Disposition of manuscript:
Query letter: Not necessary.
Receipt of manuscript acknowledged: Yes
Decision to publish in: 1-3 months
Accepted manuscript published in: 2-4 months
Rejected manuscript returned: Yes, with return postage paid by publication.
Rejected manuscript criticized: Yes
Submit to:
Dr. Carel J. van Oss
Executive Editor
Department of Microbiology, School of Medicine
State University of New York at Buffalo
Buffalo, New York 14214
(716) 831-2900

SPECIAL STIPULATIONS

Contributions, if accepted, are reproduced by photographing the author's typewritten manuscript; therefore, consult the style sheet in any recent issue carefully.

THE QUARTERLY REVIEW OF BIOLOGY [1942]

Division of Biological Sciences
State University of New York
Stony Brook, New York 11794
(516) 246-7704

First published in 1926

SUBSCRIPTION DATA

Issues and rates: Published quarterly.
Average paid circulation: 3000
Annual rate(s): $15
Publisher or Sponsor: The Stony Brook Foundation, Inc.
Managing Editor: Rosemary G. Smolker

EDITORIAL DESCRIPTION

Contains review articles on any of the areas of the biological sciences, plus reviews of new books in the biological sciences.
Articles per average issue: 3
Audience: Professional biologists and educated laymen
Manuscripts accepted in English

MANUSCRIPT INFORMATION

Subject field(s): Any area of the biological sciences
Manuscript requirements: AIBS
Preferred length: 25-50 pages
Number of copies to be submitted: Three
Abstract: Yes.
Author information and reprints: Payment: By author to publication. Only for pages

in excess of 20 journal pages $50.00 per page.
Is simultaneous submission of article to other journals permitted: No
Exclusive manuscript rights between acceptance and publication: Yes
Copyright: Held by publication.
Reprints: Available, cost as per schedule
Disposition of manuscript:
Query letter:
Receipt of manuscript acknowledged: Yes
Decision to publish in: 3 months
Accepted manuscript published in: Three months to one year.
Rejected manuscript returned: Yes
Rejected manuscript criticized: Yes
Submit to:
Editor
(See address above)

QUARTERLY REVIEWS OF BIOPHYSICS [1943]
Cambridge University Press
32 East 57th Street
New York, New York 10022

Publisher or Sponsor: International Union for Pure and Applied Biophysics

EDITORIAL DESCRIPTION
To provide a forum for general and specialized communication between biophysicists working in different areas.
Manuscripts accepted in English

MANUSCRIPT INFORMATION
Manuscript requirements: See latest issue for style requirements. Style sheet sent on request.
Preferred length: As required
Number of copies to be submitted: 3
Abstract: Yes.
Author information and reprints: Payment: Reprints only. 50 reprints
Is simultaneous submission of article to other journals permitted: Not permitted.
Exclusive manuscript rights between acceptance and publication: Yes
Copyright: Held by publication.
Reprints: Available at cost.
Disposition of manuscript:
Query letter: Not necessary, but advisable.
Receipt of manuscript acknowledged: Yes
Rejected manuscript returned: Yes, if return postage is supplied by author.
Rejected manuscript criticized: Sometimes
Submit to:
Editorial Board
(See address above)

THEORETICAL AND APPLIED GENETICS [1944]
International Journal for Theoretical and Applied Genetics
Springer-Verlag
175 Fifth Avenue
New York, New York 10010

Previously entitled *Der Züchter*

First published in 1929
Annual rate(s): DM 148 per volume

EDITORIAL DESCRIPTION
See sub-title
Manuscripts accepted in English, French, German

MANUSCRIPT INFORMATION
Subject field(s): Mathematical, analytic, evolutionary genetics; biochemistry of development; breeding methods; physiology of the gene; cytogenetics
Manuscript requirements: See latest issue for style requirements. Style sheet sent on request.
Preferred length: None
Number of copies to be submitted: 2
Abstract: Yes. A summary in English should precede each article. Papers not in English should also carry a summary in the language of the contribution at the end.
Author information and reprints: Payment: None.
Is simultaneous submission of article to other journals permitted: Not permitted.
Exclusive manuscript rights between acceptance and publication: Yes
Copyright: Held by publication.
Additional information: Be as concise as possible. A fundamental condition is that the manuscript has not been published nor is under consideration elsewhere for publication.
Submit to:
R. W. Allard;
H. Abplanalp
Editorial Board Members
Department of Genetics
University of California
Davis, California 95616

VIRCHOWS ARCHIV-B [1945]
Springer-Verlag
175 Fifth Avenue
New York, New York 10010

SUBSCRIPTION DATA
Annual rate(s): DM 160 per volume
Managing Editor: Dr. H. W. Altmann

EDITORIAL DESCRIPTION
Devoted primarily to cell pathology, including related questions of molecular pathology.
Manuscripts accepted in English, French, German

MANUSCRIPT INFORMATION
Manuscript requirements: See latest issue for style requirements.
Preferred length: As required
Number of copies to be submitted: 3
Abstract: Yes.
Author information and reprints: Payment: Reprints only. 75 offprints
Is simultaneous submission of article to other journals permitted: Not permitted.
Exclusive manuscript rights between acceptance and publication: Yes
Copyright: Held by publication.
Reprints: Available at cost.

Disposition of manuscript:
Accepted manuscript published in: 4 Months
Submit to:
Professor Dr. W. Kirsten
Editorial Board
Department of Pathology, University of Chicago
950 East 59th Street
Chicago, Illinois 60037

VIROLOGY [1946]
Academic Press, Inc.
111 Fifth Avenue
New York, New York 10003
(212) 677-6713

SUBSCRIPTION DATA
Issues and rates: Published monthly.
Annual rate(s): $183.00

EDITORIAL DESCRIPTION
Publishes articles on the biological, biochemical, and biophysical aspects of virus research, stressing contributions of a fundamental rather than applied nature.

MANUSCRIPT INFORMATION
Manuscript requirements: See latest issue for style requirements.
Number of copies to be submitted: One original
Copyright: Held by publication.
Reprints: Available; 50 free
Submit to:
Editorial Office
(See address above)

Botany and horticulture

AMERICAN JOURNAL OF BOTANY [1947]
Department of Botany and Microbiology
University of Oklahoma
770 Van Vleet Oval, Number 135
Norman, Oklahoma 73069
(405) 325-6234

First published in 1914

SUBSCRIPTION DATA
Issues and rates: Monthly, except May, June, November and December
Average paid circulation: 6,856
Annual rate(s): $34.00 (& Canada)
Foreign $35.00
Publisher or Sponsor: Botanical Society of America, Inc.

EDITORIAL DESCRIPTION
Contains articles in all subject fields related to botany.
Articles per average issue: 14
Audience: Botanists
Manuscripts accepted in English

MANUSCRIPT INFORMATION

Subject field(s): Related to botany: anatomy, cytology, ecology, embryology, evolution, pathology, radiation, ultrastructure, morphology, genetics, physiology, taxonomy, tissue culture, paleobotany, palynology

Manuscript requirements: Style sheet sent on request.
  Preferred length: 20 pages maximum
  Number of copies to be submitted: Two
  Abstract: Yes.

Author information and reprints: Payment: $50.00 per page.
  Is simultaneous submission of article to other journals permitted: No
  Exclusive manuscript rights between acceptance and publication: No
  Reprints: Available

Disposition of manuscript:
  Query letter:
  Receipt of manuscript acknowledged: Yes
  Decision to publish in: 8 weeks
  Accepted manuscript published in: 6 months
  Rejected manuscript returned: Yes
  Rejected manuscript criticized: Yes

Submit to:
  Dr. Ernest M. Gifford, Jr.
  Editor-in-Chief
  Department of Botany
  University of California
  Davis, California 95616
  (See address above)

SPECIAL STIPULATIONS
  Submitting author must be a member of the Botanical Society of America, Inc.

AMERICAN JOURNAL OF ENOLOGY AND VITICULTURE [1948]
P. O. Box 411
Davis, California 95616
(916) 752-0385

Previously entitled *American Journal of Enology* (1954-1958)

First published in 1950

SUBSCRIPTION DATA

Issues and rates: Published quarterly.
  Average paid circulation: 1700
  Annual rate(s): $15.00, Foreign $16.00

Publisher or Sponsor: American Society of Enologists

Managing Editor: Klayton E. Nelson

EDITORIAL DESCRIPTION
  Contains papers on original research in the field of enology, including methods of wine production, instrumentation, analytical, wine aging, technology of winemaking; grape growing problems, developments of new varieties for the production of wine.

Articles per average issue: 7

Audience: Professional enologists and viticulturists
  Manuscripts accepted in English

MANUSCRIPT INFORMATION

Subject field(s): Enology and viticulture

Manuscript requirements: Style sheet sent on request.
  Preferred length: None
  Number of copies to be submitted: Two
  Abstract: Yes.

Author information and reprints: Payment: None.
  Is simultaneous submission of article to other journals permitted: No
  Exclusive manuscript rights between acceptance and publication: Yes
  Copyright: Held by publication.
  Reprints: Available, cost per page

Disposition of manuscript:
  Query letter:
  Receipt of manuscript acknowledged: Yes
  Decision to publish in: 2 months
  Accepted manuscript published in: Within one year
  Rejected manuscript returned: Yes
  Rejected manuscript criticized: Yes

Submit to:
  Klayton E. Nelson
  Editor
  (See address above)
  (916) 752-1902

AQUATIC BOTANY [1949]
An International Scientific Journal
Elsevier Scientific Publishing Company
P. O. Box 211, Jan van Galenstraat 335
Amsterdam, The Netherlands

First published in 1975

SUBSCRIPTION DATA

Issues and rates: Published quarterly.
  Annual rate(s): Dfl. 99.00

EDITORIAL DESCRIPTION
  Concerned with fundamental studies on submerged, floating, and emergent plants in marine and fresh-water ecosystems.

Articles per average issue: 10

Audience: Professional, academic
  Manuscripts accepted in English

MANUSCRIPT INFORMATION

Subject field(s): Fundamental studies on structure, function, dynamics and classification of plant-dominated ecosystems; transplantation, herbicides, biological control, thermal pollution, uses, conservation of resources and aspects of production and decomposition. Studies on phytoplankton do not fall within the scope of the journal.

Manuscript requirements: See latest issue for style requirements. Style sheet sent on request.
  Preferred length: As required
  Number of copies to be submitted: 3
  Abstract: Yes. Not to exceed 500 words in length.

Author information and reprints: Payment: Reprints only. 50 reprints
  Is simultaneous submission of article to other journals permitted: Not permitted.
  Exclusive manuscript rights between acceptance and publication: Yes
  Copyright: Held by publication.
  Reprints: Available at cost.

Disposition of manuscript:
  Query letter: Not necessary.
  Receipt of manuscript acknowledged: Yes
  Decision to publish in: 2 months
  Accepted manuscript published in: 4-6 months
  Rejected manuscript returned: Yes, with return postage paid by publication.
  Rejected manuscript criticized: Sometimes

Submit to:
  Editorial Office
  P.O. Box 330
  Jan van Galenstraat 335
  Amsterdam, The Netherlands

AUSTRALIAN JOURNAL OF BOTANY [1950]
372 Albert Street
East Melbourne, Victoria 3002, Australia

SUBSCRIPTION DATA

Issues and rates: Published bi-monthly.
  Average paid circulation: 1342
  Annual rate(s): $A10.00

Publisher or Sponsor: Commonwealth Scientific and Industrial Research Organization

EDITORIAL DESCRIPTION
  Medium for the publication of results of original scientific research in botany.

Articles per average issue: 12

Audience: Botanists
  Manuscripts accepted in English only

MANUSCRIPT INFORMATION

Manuscript requirements: Style sheet sent on request.
  Preferred length: None
  Number of copies to be submitted: Two
  Abstract: Yes, 200 words maximum

Author information and reprints: Payment: None.
  Is simultaneous submission of article to other journals permitted: No
  Exclusive manuscript rights between acceptance and publication: Yes
  Copyright: Held by publication.
  Reprints: Available

Additional information: Manuscripts typewritten, 3 lines to inch. All manuscripts are refereed.

Disposition of manuscript:
  Query letter: No
  Receipt of manuscript acknowledged: Yes
  Decision to publish in: 8 weeks
  Accepted manuscript published in: 12 weeks
  Rejected manuscript returned: Yes
  Rejected manuscript criticized: Yes

Submit to:
  Basil Walby
  Editor-in-Chief
  (See address above)

BAILEYA [1951]
A Journal of Horticultural Taxonomy
L. H. Bailey Hortorium
Cornell University
Ithaca, New York 14853
(607) 256-2131

First published in 1953

SUBSCRIPTION DATA
Issues and rates: Irregularly, but normally 2 issues per year
  Average paid circulation: 346; 406 controlled
  Annual rate(s): $5.00
Publisher or Sponsor: Bailey Hortorium, Cornell University

EDITORIAL DESCRIPTION
Subject matter limited to cultivated plants with particular emphasis placed on their taxonomy, nomenclature, and classification. In addition, book reviews related to cultivated plants are published, and notes or articles about plantsman will be accepted.
Articles per average issue: 4-7
Audience: Persons who are interested in plant taxonomy, especially of cultivated plants.
  Manuscripts accepted in English

MANUSCRIPT INFORMATION
Subject field(s): Plant taxonomy and nomenclature
Manuscript requirements: See latest issue for style requirements.
  Preferred length: None
  Number of copies to be submitted: Two
Author information and reprints: Payment: None.
  Is simultaneous submission of article to other journals permitted: No
  Exclusive manuscript rights between acceptance and publication: No
  Copyright: Not copyrighted
  Reprints: Available at cost
Disposition of manuscript:
  Query letter:
  Receipt of manuscript acknowledged: Yes
  Decision to publish in: One month
  Accepted manuscript published in: Six months
  Rejected manuscript returned: Yes
  Rejected manuscript criticized: Yes
Submit to:
  John W. Ingram;
  Harold E. Moore, Jr.
  Editors
  (See address above)

BRITISH PHYCOLOGICAL JOURNAL [1952]
Department of Plant Sciences
University of Leeds
Leeds LS2 9JT, England
0532-31751 ext. 6573

Previously entitled *British Phycological Bulletin*

First published in 1953

SUBSCRIPTION DATA
Issues and rates: Published quarterly.
  Average paid circulation: 650; 250 controlled
  Annual rate(s): Members £3.00; Students £2.00; Institutions £8.80; Foreign £10.00 (USA and Canada $26.50)
Publisher or Sponsor: British Phycological Society

EDITORIAL DESCRIPTION
Contains articles on all aspects of study of algae: original research reports, reviews, field studies, accounts of ideas and techniques.
Articles per average issue: 12
Audience: Phycologists
  Manuscripts accepted in English

MANUSCRIPT INFORMATION
Subject field(s): Algae
Manuscript requirements: See latest issue for style requirements.
  Preferred length: None
  Number of copies to be submitted: Two
  Abstract: Yes.
Author information and reprints: Payment: None.
  Is simultaneous submission of article to other journals permitted: No
  Exclusive manuscript rights between acceptance and publication: Yes
  Copyright: Held by publication.
  Reprints: Available, 50 free.
Disposition of manuscript:
  Receipt of manuscript acknowledged: Yes
  Decision to publish in: 1-2 months, or more
  Accepted manuscript published in: 6-9 months
  Rejected manuscript returned: Yes
  Rejected manuscript criticized: Yes
Submit to:
  Gordon Frank Leedale
  (See address above)

THE BRYOLOGIST [1953]
A Quarterly Journal of Bryology and Lichenology
Department of Biology
Texas A&M University
College Station, Texas 77843
(713) 845-3116

First published in 1898

SUBSCRIPTION DATA
Issues and rates: Published quarterly.
  Average paid circulation: 980
  Annual rate(s): Individuals $15.00, Institutions $25.00
Publisher or Sponsor: American Bryological and Lichenological Society, Inc.

EDITORIAL DESCRIPTION
Contains research articles on all aspects of bryophytes and lichens but principally their biology and taxonomy; book reviews; news.
Articles per average issue: 23
Audience: Botanical scientists
  Manuscripts accepted in English, French, German, and Spanish

MANUSCRIPT INFORMATION
Subject field(s): All aspects of bryophytes and lichens
Manuscript requirements: See latest issue for style requirements.
  Preferred length: Up to 100 pages
  Number of copies to be submitted: Two
  Abstract: Yes.
Author information and reprints: Payment: None.
  Is simultaneous submission of article to other journals permitted: No
  Exclusive manuscript rights between acceptance and publication: No
  Copyright: Held by publication.
  Reprints: Available, cost determined by length
Disposition of manuscript:
  Query letter:
  Receipt of manuscript acknowledged: Yes
  Decision to publish in: One month
  Accepted manuscript published in: Within three months
  Rejected manuscript returned: Yes
  Rejected manuscript criticized: Yes
Submit to:
  Dale M.J. Mueller
  Editor
  (See address above)

CANADIAN JOURNAL OF BOTANY [1954]
National Research Council of Canada
100 Sussex Drive
Ottawa, Ontario K1A OR6, Canada
(613) 992-5411

Previously entitled *Canadian Journal of Research*

First published in 1929

SUBSCRIPTION DATA
Issues and rates: Published semi-monthly.
  Average paid circulation: 2300
  Annual rate(s): Individuals $20.00; Institutions $40.00
Managing Editor: H. Williamson

EDITORIAL DESCRIPTION
Publishes the results of original scientific research in any branch of botany.
Articles per average issue: 14
Audience: Research botanists
  Manuscripts accepted in English and French

MANUSCRIPT INFORMATION
Subject field(s): All fields of botany
Manuscript requirements: Style sheet sent on request.
  Preferred length: Under 25 pages
  Number of copies to be submitted: Two
  Abstract: Yes.
Author information and reprints: Payment: None.
  Is simultaneous submission of article to other journals permitted: No
  Exclusive manuscript rights between acceptance and publication: Yes
  Copyright: Held by publication.

Reprints: Available only at time of publication (cost dependent on length)
Disposition of manuscript:
  Query letter:
  Receipt of manuscript acknowledged: Yes
  Decision to publish in: 3 ½ months
  Accepted manuscript published in: 4 months
  Rejected manuscript returned: Yes
  Rejected manuscript criticized: Yes
Submit to:
  Michael Shaw
  Editor
  H. R. MacMillan Building
  University of British Columbia
  Vancouver, British Columbia, Canada
  (604) 228-2536

CANADIAN JOURNAL OF PLANT SCIENCE [1955]
Suite 907
151 Slater Street
Ottawa, Ontario K1P 5H4, Canada
(613) 232-9459

Previously entitled *Canadian Journal of Agricultural Science,* 1953-1956; *Scientific Agriculture* 1920-1952

First published in 1957

SUBSCRIPTION DATA
Issues and rates: Published quarterly.
  Average paid circulation: 1,500
  Annual rate(s): $14.00 Foreign $14.50 Institutions $21.50 Foreign institutions $23.50
Publisher or Sponsor: Agricultural Institute of Canada; Canadian Society of Agronomy; Canadian Society of Horticultural Science
Managing Editor: Janet McDonald

EDITORIAL DESCRIPTION
Contains articles on scientific research in cereals, forage, fruits, vegetables, weeds, ornamental plants, and other related subjects
Articles per average issue: 35-50
Audience: Professional
  Manuscripts accepted in English, French

MANUSCRIPT INFORMATION
Manuscript requirements: See latest issue for style requirements. Style sheet sent on request.
  Preferred length: Up to 20 pages
  Number of copies to be submitted: 3
  Abstract: Yes. A resume of not more than 200 words.
Author information and reprints: Payment: By publication to author. $25.00 plus illustration, table, and translation charges
  Is simultaneous submission of article to other journals permitted: Permitted, but not encouraged.
  Exclusive manuscript rights between acceptance and publication: Yes
  Copyright: Held by publication.
  Reprints: Available at cost.

Disposition of manuscript:
  Query letter: Not necessary.
  Receipt of manuscript acknowledged: Yes
  Decision to publish in: 1-6 months
  Accepted manuscript published in: 4-6 months
  Rejected manuscript returned: Yes, with return postage paid by publication.
  Rejected manuscript criticized: Yes
Submit to:
  Dr. D. H. Heinrichs
  Editor
  Agriculture Canada, Research Station
  Box 1030
  Swift Current, Saskatchewan S9H 3X2, Canada
  (306) 773-4621

THE CORNELL PLANTATIONS [1956]
100 Judd Falls Road
Ithaca, New York 14850
(607) 256-3020

First published in 1944

SUBSCRIPTION DATA
Issues and rates: Published quarterly.
  Average paid circulation: 3600 controlled
  Annual rate(s): $2.00
Publisher or Sponsor: The Cornell Plantations; Cornell University

EDITORIAL DESCRIPTION
Publishes reports on activities within the arboretum: natural area enterprise of Cornell University; articles on the Cornell physical environment and associated research; current work elsewhere in horticultural or science education, horticultural therapy, ecology, etc. Publication is devoted to plant aesthetics and the relationship between horticulture and people.
Articles per average issue: 5
Audience: Persons who are interested in plants.
  Manuscripts accepted in English

MANUSCRIPT INFORMATION
Subject field(s): Horticulture, science education, forestry, ecology
Manuscript requirements: Chicago
  Preferred length: 1200 to 1500 words
  Number of copies to be submitted: Two
  Abstract: Not necessary, but advisable.
Author information and reprints: Payment: None.
  Is simultaneous submission of article to other journals permitted: No
  Exclusive manuscript rights between acceptance and publication: Yes
  Copyright: Held by author.
  Reprints: Available; usually additional copies of issue are made available as contributor's copies, unless more than 500 are needed. Above 500, reprints are made available at printer's charge.
Disposition of manuscript:
  Query letter:
  Receipt of manuscript acknowledged: Yes

Decision to publish in: 30 days
  Accepted manuscript published in: 3-12 months
  Rejected manuscript returned: Yes, if self-addressed, stamped envelope is sent with manuscript.
  Rejected manuscript criticized: Yes
Submit to:
  Audrey H. O'Connor
  Editor
  (See address above)

FIELDIANA: BOTANY [1957]
Field Museum of Natural History
Roosevelt Road and Lake Shore Drive
Chicago, Illinois 60605
(312) 922-9410

Previously entitled *Field Museum of Natural History Botanical Series*

First published in 1895

SUBSCRIPTION DATA
Issues and rates: Irregular
Publisher or Sponsor: Field Museum of Natural History

EDITORIAL DESCRIPTION
Papers relating to the field of botany with special emphasis on Museum collections and Museum researchers.
Articles per average issue: 1
Audience: Post-doctoral
  Manuscripts accepted in English

MANUSCRIPT INFORMATION
Manuscript requirements: See latest issue for style requirements. Style sheet sent on request.
  Preferred length: As required
  Number of copies to be submitted: 1
  Abstract: Yes.
Author information and reprints: Payment: None.
  Is simultaneous submission of article to other journals permitted: Not permitted.
  Exclusive manuscript rights between acceptance and publication: Yes
  Copyright: None
  Reprints: Available at cost.
Disposition of manuscript:
  Query letter: Not necessary, but advisable.
  Receipt of manuscript acknowledged: Yes
  Decision to publish in: Varies
  Accepted manuscript published in: Varies
  Rejected manuscript returned: Yes, with return postage paid by publication.
  Rejected manuscript criticized: Sometimes
Submit to:
  James W. Van Stone
  Scientific Editor
  (See address above)

ISRAEL JOURNAL OF BOTANY [1958]
P.O.B. 801
Jerusalem, Israel 91000
227375

Previously entitled *Bulletin of the Research Council of Israel*

First published in 1951

SUBSCRIPTION DATA
Issues and rates: Published quarterly.
  Average paid circulation: 980
  Annual rate(s): $22.00
Managing Editor: L. Lester

EDITORIAL DESCRIPTION
  Contains articles on systematics and ecology of Near-Eastern flora.
Articles per average issue: 8
Audience: Botanists
  Manuscripts accepted in English

MANUSCRIPT INFORMATION
Subject field(s): Botany
Manuscript requirements: AIBS
  Preferred length: 20 pages
  Number of copies to be submitted: Three
  Abstract: Yes, double-spaced with wide margins
Author information and reprints: Payment: None.
  Is simultaneous submission of article to other journals permitted: No
  Exclusive manuscript rights between acceptance and publication: Yes
  Copyright: Held by publication.
  Reprints: Available, cost depends on length
Disposition of manuscript:
  Query letter: No
  Receipt of manuscript acknowledged: Yes
  Decision to publish in: Three months
  Accepted manuscript published in: 6 months
  Rejected manuscript returned: Yes
  Rejected manuscript criticized: Yes
Submit to:
  Editor
  (See address above)

JOURNAL OF EXPERIMENTAL BOTANY [1959]
Oxford University Press
Academic Publishing Division
Oxford OX2 GDP, England
Telex 56767

SUBSCRIPTION DATA
Issues and rates: Published bi-monthly.
  Average paid circulation: 1,600
  Annual rate(s): £28.00; Foreign $80.00
Publisher or Sponsor: Society for Experimental Biology
Managing Editor: Dr. C. P. Whittingham

EDITORIAL DESCRIPTION
  Contains research papers on any aspect of the experimental study of plants.
Articles per average issue: 20
  Manuscripts accepted in English

MANUSCRIPT INFORMATION
Subject field(s): Plant physiology, plant biochemistry, plant biophysics, developmental processes in plants from the molecular to the organismal level, fundamental aspects of experimental agronomy, experimental studies on fine structure
Manuscript requirements: Style sheet sent on request.
  Preferred length: 5,000 words; 10 pages
  Number of copies to be submitted: 2
  Abstract: Yes; not exceeding 250 words
Author information and reprints: Payment: Reprints only. 25 free offprints
  Is simultaneous submission of article to other journals permitted: No
  Exclusive manuscript rights between acceptance and publication: Yes
  Copyright: Held by publication.
  Reprints: Available
Disposition of manuscript:
  Receipt of manuscript acknowledged: Yes
  Decision to publish in: 2-3 weeks
  Accepted manuscript published in: 6 months
  Rejected manuscript returned: Yes
  Rejected manuscript criticized: Yes
Submit to:
  The Copy Assistant
  (See address above)

JOURNAL OF PHYCOLOGY [1960]
Department of Botany
Ohio State University
Columbus, Ohio 43210
(614) 422-2725

First published in 1965

SUBSCRIPTION DATA
Issues and rates: Published quarterly.
  Average paid circulation: 1,550
  Annual rate(s): Individuals $15.00, Students $7.50, Institutions $25.00
Publisher or Sponsor: Phycological Society of America

EDITORIAL DESCRIPTION
  Covers all aspects of marine and freshwater algae from taxonomy to biochemistry, physiology, molecular biology, ecology and pollution.
Articles per average issue: 20
  Manuscripts accepted in English, French, German, Spanish

MANUSCRIPT INFORMATION
Manuscript requirements: See latest issue for style requirements.
  Preferred length: 8 printed pages maximum
  Number of copies to be submitted: Three
  Abstract: Yes
Author information and reprints: Payment: By author to publication. $15.00 per page.
  Is simultaneous submission of article to other journals permitted: No
  Exclusive manuscript rights between acceptance and publication: Yes
  Copyright: Held by publication.
  Reprints: Available
Disposition of manuscript:
  Query letter: No
  Receipt of manuscript acknowledged: Yes
  Decision to publish in: 4-6 months
  Accepted manuscript published in: 6-9 months
  Rejected manuscript returned: Yes
  Rejected manuscript criticized: Yes
Submit to:
  Janet Stein
  Editor
  Department of Botany
  University of British Columbia
  Vancouver, British Columbia V6T 1W5
  Canada

LINNEAN SOCIETY BOTANICAL JOURNAL [1961]
24/28 Oval Road
London NW1 7DX, England
01-267-4466

First published in 1855

SUBSCRIPTION DATA
Issues and rates: 8 per year
  Annual rate(s): £28.00; Foreign £32.00
Publisher or Sponsor: Linnean Society of London
Managing Editor: David McClintock

EDITORIAL DESCRIPTION
  Contains original scientific research papers in the general field of experimental and descriptive botany, palaeobotany and systematics as well as reports of ecological and conservation studies, and expeditions; also papers of an historical nature.
Articles per average issue: 6
Audience: Botanists and biologists
  Manuscripts accepted in English

MANUSCRIPT INFORMATION
Subject field(s): Botany and taxonomy
Manuscript requirements: See latest issue for style requirements.
  Number of copies to be submitted: 2
  Abstract: Yes.
Author information and reprints: Payment: None.
  Is simultaneous submission of article to other journals permitted: No
  Exclusive manuscript rights between acceptance and publication: Yes
  Copyright: Held by publication.
  Reprints: Available, 50 free, additional ones can be purchased
Disposition of manuscript:
  Query letter:
  Receipt of manuscript acknowledged: Yes
  Decision to publish in: As soon as possible
  Accepted manuscript published in: 9 months
  Rejected manuscript returned: Yes
  Rejected manuscript criticized: Yes
Submit to:
  Editorial Secretary
  Burlington House, Piccadilly
  London W1V OLQ, England
  01-734-1040

MADROÑO [1962]

A West American Journal of Botany
California Botanical Society
Herbarium-Department of Botany
University of California
Berkeley, California 94720
(415) 642-2465

First published in 1917

SUBSCRIPTION DATA

Issues and rates: Published quarterly.
  Average paid circulation: 850
  Annual rate(s): Individuals $8.00; Students $4.00; Institutions $12.00
Publisher or Sponsor: California Botanical Society
Managing Editor: John L. Strother

EDITORIAL DESCRIPTION

Publishes articles dealing with western North American Botany.
Articles per average issue: 15
Audience: Botanists
  Manuscripts accepted in English, Spanish

MANUSCRIPT INFORMATION

Subject field(s): Botany
Manuscript requirements: See latest issue for style requirements.
  Preferred length: None
  Number of copies to be submitted: 2
  Abstract: No
Author information and reprints: Payment: None. There is a page charge of $30.00 per page in excess of 8 pages.
  Is simultaneous submission of article to other journals permitted: No
  Exclusive manuscript rights between acceptance and publication: No
  Copyright: None
  Reprints: Available at cost.
Disposition of manuscript:
  Query letter: No
  Receipt of manuscript acknowledged: Yes
  Decision to publish in: One month
  Accepted manuscript published in: Six months
  Rejected manuscript returned: Yes
  Rejected manuscript criticized: Yes
Submit to:
  Editor
  (See address above)

THE MICHIGAN BOTANIST [1963]

Laura T. Roberts
1509 Kearney Road
Ann Arbor, Michigan 48104
(313) 761-0021

First published in 1962

SUBSCRIPTION DATA

Issues and rates: Published quarterly.
  Average paid circulation: 1,010
  Annual rate(s): $5.00

Publisher or Sponsor: Michigan Botanical Club

EDITORIAL DESCRIPTION

A wide range of subject matter relating to both the plant kingdom and to branches of the field of botany
Articles per average issue: 5
Audience: All those with interests in the plants of the Upper Great Lakes region

MANUSCRIPT INFORMATION

Manuscript requirements: See latest issue for style requirements. Style sheet sent on request.
  Preferred length: As required
  Number of copies to be submitted: 2
  Abstract: Not necessary.
Author information and reprints: Payment: None.
  Is simultaneous submission of article to other journals permitted: Not permitted.
  Exclusive manuscript rights between acceptance and publication: Yes
  Copyright: No restriction on the author's use of his material; only occasionally are articles copyrighted.
  Reprints: Available at cost.
Additional information: Pages in excess of 20 require a subsidy of $20.00 per page. Manuscript should be typewritten, double-spaced, avoiding the use of erasable paper.
Disposition of manuscript:
  Query letter: Not necessary.
  Receipt of manuscript acknowledged: Yes
  Decision to publish in: 3-10 weeks
  Accepted manuscript published in: 1-6 months
  Rejected manuscript returned: Yes, with return postage paid by publication.
  Rejected manuscript criticized: Yes
Submit to:
  Edward G. Voss
  Editor-in-Chief
  The Herbarium, North University Building
  The University of Michigan
  Ann Arbor, Michigan 48104
  (313) 764-2431

SPECIAL STIPULATIONS

A regional orientation is strictly maintained.

MISSOURI BOTANICAL GARDEN ANNALS [1964]

2315 Tower Grove Avenue
St. Louis, Missouri 63110
(314) 865-0440 ext. 44

First published in 1914

SUBSCRIPTION DATA

Issues and rates: Published three times per year.
  Average paid circulation: 700
  Annual rate(s): $30.00; Foreign $35.00

EDITORIAL DESCRIPTION

Contains papers in systematic botany.
Audience: Botanical institutions
  Manuscripts accepted in English

MANUSCRIPT INFORMATION

Subject field(s): Systematic botany
Manuscript requirements: No specific style guide.
  Preferred length: None
  Number of copies to be submitted: Two
  Abstract: Yes.
Author information and reprints: Payment: By author to publication. $25.00 per page.
  Is simultaneous submission of article to other journals permitted: No
  Exclusive manuscript rights between acceptance and publication: Yes
  Copyright: Held by publication.
  Reprints: Available, prices sent with proof
Disposition of manuscript:
  Query letter: Yes.
  Receipt of manuscript acknowledged: Yes
  Decision to publish in: Three months
  Accepted manuscript published in: 6-12 months
  Rejected manuscript returned: Yes
  Rejected manuscript criticized: Yes
Submit to:
  Gerritt Davidse
  Editor
  (See address above)

PHYTOCHEMISTRY [1965]

Pergamon Press Ltd.
Headington Hill Hall
Oxford OX3 OBW, England

First published in 1962

SUBSCRIPTION DATA

Issues and rates: Published monthly.
  Annual rate(s): $15.00
Managing Editor: T. Swain

EDITORIAL DESCRIPTION

Covers research on all aspects of pure and applied plant biochemistry, especially that which leads to a deeper understanding of the factors underlying growth, development and differentiation of plants and the chemistry of plant products.
Audience: Plant biochemists
  Manuscripts accepted in English, French, German

MANUSCRIPT INFORMATION

Subject field(s): Biochemistry, biosynthesis, chemotaxonomy, phytochemistry, and phytochemical reports.
Manuscript requirements: See latest issue for style requirements.
  Preferred length: As required
  Number of copies to be submitted: 2
  Abstract: Yes.
Author information and reprints: Payment: None.
  Is simultaneous submission of article to other journals permitted: Not permitted.
  Exclusive manuscript rights between acceptance and publication: Yes
  Copyright: Held by publication.
  Reprints: Available at cost.

Additional information: See the "Instructions to Authors" inside the back cover of each issue.
Disposition of manuscript:
  Query letter: Not necessary.
  Receipt of manuscript acknowledged: Yes
  Decision to publish in: 4-8 weeks
  Accepted manuscript published in: 5 months
  Rejected manuscript returned: Yes, if return postage is supplied by author.
  Rejected manuscript criticized: Reasons for rejections only
Submit to:
  For papers:
  Dr. J. B. Harborne
  Department of Botany
  The University, Whiteknights
  Reading, Berkshire RG6 2AS, England

  Phytochemical reports:
  Dr. T. Swain
  Biochemical Laboratory
  Royal Botanic Gardens
  Richmond, Surrey TW9 3DS, England

PHYTOLOGIA [1966]
An International Cooperative Journal
303 Parkside Road
Plainfield, New Jersey 07060
(201) 756-8142

First published in 1933

SUBSCRIPTION DATA
Issues and rates: Published bi-monthly.
  Annual rate(s): $9.00; Foreign $9.50; Institutions $9.00
Managing Editor: Harold N. Moldenke

EDITORIAL DESCRIPTION
Devoted to original contributions in all fields of botany
Articles per average issue: 1-10
Audience: Professionnal, academic, student
  Manuscripts accepted in English

MANUSCRIPT INFORMATION
Subject field(s): No limitations
Manuscript requirements: See latest issue for style requirements. Style sheet sent on request.
  Preferred length: As required
  Number of copies to be submitted: 2
  Abstract: Not necessary.
Author information and reprints: Payment: None.
  Is simultaneous submission of article to other journals permitted: Permitted.
  Exclusive manuscript rights between acceptance and publication: No
  Copyright: Held by author.
  Reprints: Available at no cost. A few Available at cost.
Disposition of manuscript:
  Query letter: Not necessary, but advisable.
  Receipt of manuscript acknowledged: Yes
  Decision to publish in: 1 week
  Accepted manuscript published in: 2 months
  Rejected manuscript returned: Yes, if return postage is supplied by author.
  Rejected manuscript criticized: Yes
Submit to:
  Harold N. Moldenke;
  Alma L. Moldenke
  Co-Editors
  (See address above)

PLANT PHYSIOLOGY [1967]
9650 Rockville Pike
Bethesda, Maryland 20014
(301) 530-9474

First published in 1926

SUBSCRIPTION DATA
Issues and rates: Published monthly.
  Average paid circulation: 5,300
  Annual rate(s): $80.00; Institutions $80.00; Students $10.00; Members $10.00
Publisher or Sponsor: American Society of Plant Physiologists
Managing Editor: Martin Gibbs

EDITORIAL DESCRIPTION
Open to papers of merit dealing with all aspects of plant physiology.
Articles per average issue: 30
Audience: Scientists, students
  Manuscripts accepted in English

MANUSCRIPT INFORMATION
Subject field(s): Plant physiology: applied, theoretical, basic research
Manuscript requirements: See latest issue for style requirements. Style sheet sent on request. CBE
  Preferred length: 1-10 pages
  Number of copies to be submitted: 2
  Abstract: Yes.
Author information and reprints: Payment: By author to publication. per page. $70.00. No page charges to members of the Society.
  Is simultaneous submission of article to other journals permitted: Not permitted.
  Exclusive manuscript rights between acceptance and publication: Yes
  Copyright: Held by the American Society of Plant Physiologists
  Reprints: Available at cost.
Additional information: Illustrations requiring special handling carry a charge of $100.00 per page.
Disposition of manuscript:
  Query letter: Not necessary.
  Receipt of manuscript acknowledged: No
  Decision to publish in: 4-6 weeks
  Accepted manuscript published in: 5-7 months
  Rejected manuscript returned: Yes, with return postage paid by publication.
  Rejected manuscript criticized: Yes
Submit to:
  Professor Martin Gibbs
  Editor-in-Chief
  Department of Biology
  Brandeis University
  Waltham, Massachusetts 02154
  (617) 647-2741

PLANT SCIENCE BULLETIN [1968]
Plant Science Building 174
University of South Florida
Tampa, Florida 33620
(813) 935-6504

First published in 1955

SUBSCRIPTION DATA
Issues and rates: Published quarterly.
  Annual rate(s): $4.00
Publisher or Sponsor: Botanical Society of America

EDITORIAL DESCRIPTION
Publishes original contributions in all fields of general botany.
Articles per average issue: 2-3
Audience: Professional, membership
  Manuscripts accepted in English only

MANUSCRIPT INFORMATION
Manuscript requirements: No specific style guide.
  Preferred length: 2,000-3,000 words; 4-10 pages
  Number of copies to be submitted: 2
  Abstract: Not necessary.
Author information and reprints: Payment: None.
  Is simultaneous submission of article to other journals permitted: Not permitted.
  Exclusive manuscript rights between acceptance and publication: Yes
  Copyright: None
  Reprints: Available at cost.
Disposition of manuscript:
  Query letter: Not necessary.
  Receipt of manuscript acknowledged: Yes
  Decision to publish in: 2-3 months
  Accepted manuscript published in: 6-12 months
  Rejected manuscript returned: Yes, with return postage paid by publication.
  Rejected manuscript criticized: Yes
Submit to:
  Robert W. Long
  Editor
  (See address above)

PLANT SCIENCE LETTERS [1969]
An International Journal of Experimental Plant Biology
Elsevier Scientific Publishing Company
Jan van Galenstraat 335, P. O. Box 211
Amsterdam, The Netherlands
(020) 515-9222

First published in 1973

SUBSCRIPTION DATA
Issues and rates: Published monthly.
  Annual rate(s): Dfl.216 per volume
Managing Editor: Orio Ciferri, Pavia

EDITORIAL DESCRIPTION
See sub-title
Articles per average issue: 10
Audience: Researchers
  Manuscripts accepted in English (French, German)

MANUSCRIPT INFORMATION
Manuscript requirements: No specific style guide.
  Preferred length: As required
  Number of copies to be submitted: 3
  Abstract: Yes. Of about 100-200 words
Author information and reprints: Payment: Reprints only. 50 reprints
  Is simultaneous submission of article to other journals permitted: Not permitted.
  Exclusive manuscript rights between acceptance and publication: Yes
  Copyright: Held by the Biological and Medical Press B.V. (Elsevier Division)
  Reprints: Available at cost.
Disposition of manuscript:
  Query letter: Not necessary, but advisable.
  Receipt of manuscript acknowledged: Yes
  Decision to publish in: 2-4 weeks
  Accepted manuscript published in: 6-8 weeks
  Rejected manuscript returned: Yes, with return postage paid by publication.
  Rejected manuscript criticized: Reasons for rejections only
Submit to:
  Prof. C. L. F. Woodcock
  Editor
  Department of Botany
  University of Massachusetts
  Amherst, Massachusetts 01002

PLANT AND SOIL [1970]
Martinus Nyhoff
P. O. Box 269, Lange Voorhout 9-11
The Hague, The Netherlands
(070)469 460

First published in 1948

SUBSCRIPTION DATA
Issues and rates: Published bi-monthly.
  Annual rate(s): Individuals Dfl.90.00; Institutions Dfl.90.00

EDITORIAL DESCRIPTION
  Publishes articles in plant nutrition, chemistry, soil microbiology, and soil-borne diseases
Audience: Professional
  Manuscripts accepted in English, French, German

MANUSCRIPT INFORMATION
Manuscript requirements: Style sheet sent on request.
  Preferred length: As required
  Number of copies to be submitted: 2
  Abstract: Yes.
Author information and reprints: Payment: None.
  Is simultaneous submission of article to other journals permitted: Not permitted.
  Exclusive manuscript rights between acceptance and publication: Yes
  Copyright: Held by publication.
  Reprints: Available at cost.
Submit to:
  Executive Editor
  Institute for Soil Fertility
  Oosterweg 92
  Haren (Gr.), The Netherlands

PLANTA [1971]
An International Journal of Plant Biology
Springer-Verlag
175 Fifth Avenue
New York, New York 10010
  Annual rate(s): DM 108 per volume

EDITORIAL DESCRIPTION
  Publishes original articles in structural and functional biology
  Manuscripts accepted in English, French, German

MANUSCRIPT INFORMATION
Subject field(s): From biochemistry and ultrastructure to studies with tissues, organs, and whole plants, but excluding evolutionary and population botany. Papers in cytology, genetics, and phytopathology will be accepted only if they contribute to the understanding of specifically botanical problems.
Manuscript requirements: See latest issue for style requirements. Style sheet sent on request.
  Preferred length: As required
  Number of copies to be submitted: 2
  Abstract: Yes. Each contribution should be preceded by a short summary in English.
Author information and reprints: Payment: Reprints only. 75 offprints
  Is simultaneous submission of article to other journals permitted: Not permitted.
  Exclusive manuscript rights between acceptance and publication: Yes
  Copyright: Held by publication.
Submit to:
  Professor Anton Lang
  Editorial Secretary
  MSU/AEC Plant Research Laboratory
  Michigan State University
  East Lansing, Michigan 48824

PRINCIPES [1972]
Journal of the Palm Society
1320 South Venetian Way
Miami, Florida 33139
(305) 373-4279

First published in 1956

SUBSCRIPTION DATA
Issues and rates: Published quarterly.
  Annual rate(s): $8.00; Foreign $8.00; Institutions $7.00; Students $8.00; Members $15.00
Publisher or Sponsor: The Palm Society

EDITORIAL DESCRIPTION
  Presents information on palms on a world-wide scale.
Articles per average issue: 1-5
Audience: Professional, membership
  Manuscripts accepted in English

MANUSCRIPT INFORMATION
Subject field(s): Growing, cultivation, uses, unusual habitats, botanical facts, new varieties, etc.
Manuscript requirements: No specific style guide.
  Preferred length: 10 pages
  Number of copies to be submitted: 1
  Abstract: Not necessary.
Author information and reprints: Payment: Reprints only. 6 copies of issue
  Is simultaneous submission of article to other journals permitted: Not permitted.
  Exclusive manuscript rights between acceptance and publication: Yes
  Copyright: Held by publication.
  Reprints: Available at cost.
Disposition of manuscript:
  Rejected manuscript returned: Yes, if return postage is supplied by author.
  Rejected manuscript criticized: Sometimes
Submit to:
  Dr. Harold E. Moore, Jr.
  Editor
  467 Mann Library
  Cornell University
  Ithaca, New York 14850

REVIEW OF PALEOBOTANY AND PALYNOLOGY [1973]
An International Journal
Elsevier Scientific Publishing Company
P. O. Box 211, Jan van Galenstraat
Amsterdam, The Netherlands

First published in 1967

SUBSCRIPTION DATA
Issues and rates: Published bi-monthly.
  Annual rate(s): Institutions Dfl. 226 per volume

EDITORIAL DESCRIPTION
  Publishes articles to stimulate wide interdisciplinary cooperation and understanding among workers in the fields of paleobotany and palynology.
Articles per average issue: Varies
Audience: Professional, academic
  Manuscripts accepted in English

MANUSCRIPT INFORMATION
Subject field(s): Plant systematics, historical geology, coal and petroleum geology, archaeologgy, allergy research and treatment, honey research
Manuscript requirements: Style sheet sent on request.
  Preferred length: As required
  Number of copies to be submitted: 3
  Abstract: Yes.
Author information and reprints: Payment: Reprints only. 50
  Is simultaneous submission of article to other journals permitted: Not permitted.
  Exclusive manuscript rights between acceptance and publication: Yes
  Copyright: Held by publication.
  Reprints: Available at cost.
Disposition of manuscript:
  Query letter: Not necessary.

Receipt of manuscript acknowledged: Yes
Decision to publish in: 6 weeks
Accepted manuscript published in: 6 months
Rejected manuscript returned: Yes, with return postage paid by publication.
Rejected manuscript criticized: Reasons for rejections only
Submit to:
  Editor
  (See address above)

SCIENTIA HORTICULTURAE [1974]

An International Journal
Elsevier Scientific Publishing Company
P. O. Box 221, Jan van Galenstraat 335
Amsterdam, The Netherlands

First published in 1973

SUBSCRIPTION DATA
Issues and rates: Published quarterly.
  Annual rate(s): Dfl. 89.00
Publisher or Sponsor: International Society for Horticultural Science
Managing Editor: S. J. Wellensiek

EDITORIAL DESCRIPTION
A general horticultural journal, the central theme being crops and crop growing.
Articles per average issue: 11
Audience: Those involved in any aspect of horticulture
  Manuscripts accepted in English

MANUSCRIPT INFORMATION
Subject field(s): Horticulture under moderate, subtropical and tropical conditions, as well as with open and protected crop growing; soil science, plant breeding if they have direct significance to horticulture; technical aspects
Manuscript requirements: See latest issue for style requirements. Style sheet sent on request.
  Preferred length: 8 printed pages
  Number of copies to be submitted: 3
  Abstract: Yes. Not to exceed 500 words.
Author information and reprints: Payment: None.
  Is simultaneous submission of article to other journals permitted: Not permitted.
  Exclusive manuscript rights between acceptance and publication: Yes
  Copyright: Held by the Society
Disposition of manuscript:
  Query letter: Not necessary.
  Receipt of manuscript acknowledged: Yes
  Decision to publish in: 2 months
  Accepted manuscript published in: 4-6 months
  Rejected manuscript criticized: Sometimes
Submit to:
  S.J. Wellensiek
  Editorial Office
  (See address above)

SIDA [1975]

Contributions to Botany
Herbarium, Southern Methodist University
Dallas, Texas 75275
(214) 692-2257

First published in 1962

SUBSCRIPTION DATA
Issues and rates: Published semi-annually.
  Average paid circulation: 375
  Annual rate(s): $6.00

EDITORIAL DESCRIPTION
Publishes scientific papers in systematic botany.
Articles per average issue: Variable
  Manuscripts accepted in English

MANUSCRIPT INFORMATION
Subject field(s): Systematic botany
Manuscript requirements: See latest issue for style requirements.
  Preferred length: 20 to 30 pages
  Number of copies to be submitted: Two
  Abstract:
Author information and reprints: Payment: By author to publication. $15 per page.
  Is simultaneous submission of article to other journals permitted: No
  Exclusive manuscript rights between acceptance and publication: Yes
  Copyright: Held by Editor
  Reprints: Available, at cost
Disposition of manuscript:
  Query letter:
  Receipt of manuscript acknowledged: Yes
  Decision to publish in: 3 to 6 months
  Accepted manuscript published in: 1 to 3 years
  Rejected manuscript returned: Yes, if return postage is supplied by author.
  Rejected manuscript criticized: Yes
Submit to:
  William F. Mahler
  Publisher and Editor
  (See address above)

WOOD SCIENCE AND TECHNOLOGY [1976]

Springer-Verlag
175 Fifth Avenue
New York, New York 10010
(212) 673-2660

SUBSCRIPTION DATA
Issues and rates: Published quarterly.
  Annual rate(s): DM 150 per volume
Managing Editor: F. F. P. Kollmann, Munich

EDITORIAL DESCRIPTION
Research contributions and reviews covering the entire field of wood and pulp technology.
  Manuscripts accepted in English, German

MANUSCRIPT INFORMATION
Subject field(s): Wood anatomy and ultrastructure; biology of wood; cytology of cambium, xylem and phloem; tree physiology; microbiological degredation; the chemistry of wood and bark; combustion, drying, impregnation, mechanics and rheology, conversion into pulp
Manuscript requirements: No specific style guide.
  Preferred length: None
  Number of copies to be submitted: 2
  Abstract: Yes.
Author information and reprints: Payment: Reprints only.
  Is simultaneous submission of article to other journals permitted: Not permitted.
  Exclusive manuscript rights between acceptance and publication: Yes
  Copyright: Held by publication.
Submit to:
  Chemical manuscripts to:
  T. E. Timell
  State University College of Environmental Science and Forestry
  Syracuse, New York 13210

  Physical-technological manuscripts to:
  F. E. Dickenson
  University of California, Forest Products Laboratory
  1301 South 46th Street
  Richmond, California 94804
  Editorial Board Members

SPECIAL STIPULATIONS
It is a fundamental condition that manuscripts have not been, and will not be published elsewhere, either simultaneously or at a later date.

Zoology

ACTA ZOOLOGICA [1977]

International Journal for Zoology
Editorial Service/ NFR
Box 23136
S-104 Stockholm, Sweden
(08) 15 15 80

First published in 1920

SUBSCRIPTION DATA
Issues and rates: Published quarterly.
  Annual rate(s): Sw. Cr. 120; Foreign Sw. Cr. 120
Publisher or Sponsor: The Swedish Natural Science Research Council (NFR)

EDITORIAL DESCRIPTION
Publishes original reports based on all branches of animal structure research.
Articles per average issue: 7
Audience: Professional
  Manuscripts accepted in English, German, French

MANUSCRIPT INFORMATION
Subject field(s): All branches of animal structural research: cytology, histology, and gross morphology as well as the relevant techniques.
Manuscript requirements: See latest issue for style requirements. CBE
  Preferred length: 5-15 pages

Number of copies to be submitted: 2
Abstract: Yes. Not exceeding 200 words. Articles in German and French should be provided with an additional title and abstract in English.
Author information and reprints: Payment: Reprints only. 100
Is simultaneous submission of article to other journals permitted: Not permitted.
Exclusive manuscript rights between acceptance and publication: Yes
Copyright: Held by publication.
Reprints: Available at cost.
Disposition of manuscript:
Query letter: Not necessary.
Receipt of manuscript acknowledged: Yes
Decision to publish in: 3 weeks
Accepted manuscript published in: 6-8 months
Rejected manuscript returned: Yes, with return postage paid by publication.
Rejected manuscript criticized: Sometimes
Submit to:
Ragnar Olsson;
Kaj Holmberg
Editors
Box 6801
S-113 Stockholm, Sweden
(08) 34 08 60

AMERICAN BIRDS [1978]
Incorporating *Audubon Field Notes*
950 Third Avenue
New York, New York 10022
(212) 832-3200, ext. 277

Previously entitled *Audubon Field Notes*

First published in 1946

SUBSCRIPTION DATA
Issues and rates: Published bi-monthly.
Average paid circulation: 10,000
Annual rate(s): $8.00; Foreign $49.00; Institutions $48.00; Students $8.00
Publisher or Sponsor: National Audubon Society

EDITORIAL DESCRIPTION
A journal of ornithology for the serious amateur and professional. Concerned with the distribution, abundance, migration, and rare occurances of the bird life of North America.
Articles per average issue: 8-12
Audience: Professional, serious amateurs
Manuscripts accepted in English

MANUSCRIPT INFORMATION
Subject field(s): Dynamics of bird populations, distribution of species, bird identifications, unusual occurances in North America, migration, birding sites, ornithology programs in universities, etc.
Manuscript requirements: See latest issue for style requirements.
Preferred length: 3,000 words maximum unless by prior consent
Number of copies to be submitted: 2
Abstract: Not necessary.

Author information and reprints: Payment: None.
Is simultaneous submission of article to other journals permitted: Permitted, but not encouraged.
Exclusive manuscript rights between acceptance and publication: Yes
Copyright: Held by publication. with full rights to author.
Reprints: Available at cost.
Additional information: Not interested in highly technical papers with mathematical formulae or lengthy tables.
Disposition of manuscript:
Query letter: Not necessary, but advisable.
Receipt of manuscript acknowledged: Yes
Decision to publish in: 3 months
Accepted manuscript published in: 1 year
Rejected manuscript returned: Yes, with return postage paid by publication.
Rejected manuscript criticized: Yes
Submit to:
Robert Arbib
Editor
(See address above)

APPLIED ANIMAL ETHOLOGY [1979]
Elsevier Scientific Publishing Company
P. O. Box 211
Amsterdam, The Netherlands

First published in 1975

SUBSCRIPTION DATA
Issues and rates: Published quarterly.
Annual rate(s): Dfl. 91.00
Managing Editor: Andrew F. Fraser

EDITORIAL DESCRIPTION
Reports on the application of ethology to animals used by man.
Articles per average issue: 10
Audience: Professional agricultural scientists, veterinarians, zoologists, ecologists, ethologists, conservationists, curators
Manuscripts accepted in English

MANUSCRIPT INFORMATION
Subject field(s): Descriptive reports, behavior, analogues of various animals, relationships on the ecological balance, changes in the development, evolution, anomalies of behavior, etc.
Manuscript requirements: See latest issue for style requirements. Style sheet sent on request.
Preferred length: None
Number of copies to be submitted: 3
Abstract: Yes. Not to exceed 500 words.
Author information and reprints: Payment: Reprints only. 50 reprints
Is simultaneous submission of article to other journals permitted: Not permitted.
Exclusive manuscript rights between acceptance and publication: Yes
Copyright: Held by publication.
Reprints: Available at cost.
Disposition of manuscript:
Query letter: Not necessary.
Receipt of manuscript acknowledged: Yes

Decision to publish in: 2 months
Accepted manuscript published in: 4-6 months
Rejected manuscript returned: Yes, with return postage paid by publication.
Rejected manuscript criticized: Yes
Submit to:
The Editor
(See address above)

BULLETIN OF ENTOMOLOGICAL RESEARCH [1980]
Commonwealth Institute of Entomology
56 Queen's Gate
London SW7 5JR, England
(01) 584-0067

First published in 1909

SUBSCRIPTION DATA
Issues and rates: Published quarterly.
Average paid circulation: 1250; 350 controlled
Annual rate(s): £10.00, Foreign £15.00
Publisher or Sponsor: Commonwealth Institute of Entomology
Managing Editor: John R. Metcalfe

EDITORIAL DESCRIPTION
Contains research articles on applied entomology: agricultural, medical, veterinary, etc.
Articles per average issue: 15
Audience: Research workers
Manuscripts accepted in English

MANUSCRIPT INFORMATION
Manuscript requirements: See latest issue for style requirements.
Preferred length: 6000-20,000 words
Number of copies to be submitted: Two
Abstract: Yes.
Author information and reprints: Payment: None.
Is simultaneous submission of article to other journals permitted: No
Exclusive manuscript rights between acceptance and publication: Yes
Copyright: Held by Commonwealth Agricultural Bureau
Reprints: Available, 20-30 free
Disposition of manuscript:
Query letter:
Receipt of manuscript acknowledged: Yes
Decision to publish in: 2-3 months
Accepted manuscript published in: Not more than 9 months
Rejected manuscript returned: Yes
Rejected manuscript criticized: Yes
Submit to:
Director
(See address above)

CANADIAN JOURNAL OF ZOOLOGY [1981]
National Research Council of Canada
100 Sussex Drive
Ottawa, Ontario, Canada K1A 0R6
(613) 992-5411

Previously entitled *Canadian Journal of Research*

First published in 1929

SUBSCRIPTION DATA

Issues and rates: Published monthly.
   Average paid circulation: 2,000
   Annual rate(s): Individuals $12,
   Institutions $24
Managing Editor: H. Williamson

EDITORIAL DESCRIPTION

   Publishes the results of original scientific research in any field of zoology.
Articles per average issue: 16
Audience: Research zoologists
   Manuscripts accepted in English and French

MANUSCRIPT INFORMATION

Subject field(s): Behavior, biochemistry and physiology, ecology, morphology and ultrastructure, parasitology and pathology, systematics and evolution, general zoology
Manuscript requirements: Style sheet sent on request.
   Preferred length: Under 25 pages
   Number of copies to be submitted: Two
   Abstract: Yes.
Author information and reprints: Payment: None.
   Is simultaneous submission of article to other journals permitted: No
   Exclusive manuscript rights between acceptance and publication: Yes
   Copyright: Held by publication.
   Reprints: Available only at time of publication (Cost dependent on length)
Disposition of manuscript:
   Query letter:
   Receipt of manuscript acknowledged: Yes
   Decision to publish in: 3 months
   Accepted manuscript published in: 3 months
   Rejected manuscript returned: Yes
   Rejected manuscript criticized: Yes
Submit to:
   W. S. Hoar
   Editor
   Department of Zoology
   University of British Columbia
   Vancouver 8, British Columbia, Canada
   (604) 228-4881

CHELONIA [1982]

772 Spruce Street
San Francisco, California 94118
(415) 386-3254

First published in 1974

SUBSCRIPTION DATA

Issues and rates: Published bi-monthly.
   Annual rate(s): $9.00; Foreign $11.00;
   Institutions $9.00; Students $9.00

Managing Editor: Richard M. Christensen

EDITORIAL DESCRIPTION

   A conservation and research periodical devoted exclusively to the study of turtles and tortoises of the world.
Articles per average issue: 6
Audience: Veterinarians, zookeepers, zoologists
   Manuscripts accepted in English, French, Spanish, German

MANUSCRIPT INFORMATION

Subject field(s): Taxonomy, structure, pathology, breeding, care in captivity, studies in the wild, conservation efforts, laws, fossils, ecology, veterinary medicine
Manuscript requirements: Style sheet sent on request.
   Preferred length: As required
   Number of copies to be submitted: 2
   Abstract: Not necessary.
Author information and reprints: Payment: None.
   Is simultaneous submission of article to other journals permitted: Permitted.
   Exclusive manuscript rights between acceptance and publication: No
   Copyright: Held by author.
   Reprints: Available at no cost. any amount Available at cost.
Additional information: Authors need not be professional herpetologists. Manuscripts are accepted only on the basis of originality, clarity, and technical competence. Black and white photographs only.
Disposition of manuscript:
   Query letter: Not necessary, but advisable.
   Receipt of manuscript acknowledged: Yes
   Decision to publish in: 30 days
   Accepted manuscript published in: 60 days
   Rejected manuscript returned: Yes, if return postage is supplied by author.
   Rejected manuscript criticized: Yes
Submit to:
   Richard M. Christensen
   Managing Editor
   (See address above)

THE COLEOPTERISTS BULLETIN [1983]

An International Journal Devoted to the Study of Beetles
P.O. Box 1269
Gainesville, Florida 32601
(904) 372-3505 ext. 283

First published in 1947

SUBSCRIPTION DATA

Issues and rates: Published quarterly.
   Average paid circulation: 600
   Annual rate(s): Members $8.00,
   Institutions $10.00

Publisher or Sponsor: The Coleopterists Society

EDITORIAL DESCRIPTION

   Contains specialized information on beetles (coleoptera), taxonomy, ecology, morphology, biology, ethology.
Articles per average issue: 10
Audience: Entomologists, beetle collectors
   Manuscripts accepted in Any, but preferably English

MANUSCRIPT INFORMATION

Subject field(s): Entomology, biology, ecology of beetles
Manuscript requirements: AIBS
   Preferred length: 5-10 pages
   Number of copies to be submitted: Two
   Abstract: Yes.
Author information and reprints: Payment: None.
   Is simultaneous submission of article to other journals permitted: No
   Exclusive manuscript rights between acceptance and publication: Yes
   Copyright: Not copyrighted
   Reprints: Available
Disposition of manuscript:
   Query letter:
   Receipt of manuscript acknowledged: Yes
   Decision to publish in: 3 months
   Accepted manuscript published in: 3 months
   Rejected manuscript returned: Yes
   Rejected manuscript criticized: Yes
Submit to:
   Robert Eugene Woodruff
   Editor
   (See address above)

THE CONDOR [1984]

Journal of the Cooper Ornithological Society
Oakland Museum, Natural Sciences Division
1000 Oak Street
Oakland, California 94607

First published in 1898

SUBSCRIPTION DATA

Issues and rates: Published quarterly.
   Average paid circulation: 2,550
   Annual rate(s): $9.00; Students $8.00;
   Members $12.00
Publisher or Sponsor: Cooper Ornithological Society
Managing Editor: Dr. Peter R. Stettenheim

EDITORIAL DESCRIPTION

   Contains articles on scientific ornithology.
Articles per average issue: 9-10
Audience: Ornithologists
   Manuscripts accepted in English

MANUSCRIPT INFORMATION

Subject field(s): Research reports, short communications that contain new information of any subject relevant to the biology of wild species; occasional review articles; coverage of any world species.

Manuscript requirements: See latest issue for style requirements.

Preferred length: Up to 25 pages
Number of copies to be submitted: Original and 2 copies
Abstract: Not necessary.

Author information and reprints: Payment: None.

Is simultaneous submission of article to other journals permitted: Not permitted.
Exclusive manuscript rights between acceptance and publication: Yes
Copyright: Held by publication.
Reprints: Available at no cost. 100 or more Available at cost.

Additional information: Adhere to instructions that appear inside the back cover of the magazine. There is a page charge for any pages in excess of 16 printed pages.

Disposition of manuscript:
Query letter: Not necessary.
Receipt of manuscript acknowledged: Yes
Decision to publish in: 3 months
Accepted manuscript published in: 18 months
Rejected manuscript returned: Yes, with return postage paid by publication.
Rejected manuscript criticized: Reasons for rejections only

Submit to:
Dr. Peter R. Stettenheim
Editor
Meridan Road
Lebanon, New Hampshire 03766
(603) 448-4655

COPEIA [1985]

ASIH Business Office, Reptile Division
U. S. National Museum
Washington, D. C. 20560
(202) 381-6171

First published in 1913

SUBSCRIPTION DATA

Issues and rates: Published quarterly.
Average paid circulation: 3,400
Annual rate(s): $10.00; Foreign $15.00; Institutions $15.00; Students $8.00; Foreign institutions $17.00
Publisher or Sponsor: American Society of Ichthyologists and Herpetologists
Managing Editor: Dr. Clark Hubbs

EDITORIAL DESCRIPTION

Contains scientific papers on ichthyology and herpetology.
Articles per average issue: 20 papers; 20 notes
Audience: Professional scientific
Manuscripts accepted in English

MANUSCRIPT INFORMATION

Subject field(s): Systematics, ecology, anatomy, behavior worldwide
Manuscript requirements: CBE
Preferred length: 100 pages maximum
Number of copies to be submitted: Original and 2 copies
Abstract: Yes.

Author information and reprints: Payment: By author to publication. $30.00 per page.
Is simultaneous submission of article to other journals permitted: Not permitted.
Exclusive manuscript rights between acceptance and publication: Yes
Copyright: Held by the Society
Reprints: Available at cost.

Disposition of manuscript:
Query letter: Not necessary.
Receipt of manuscript acknowledged: Yes
Decision to publish in: 2 months
Accepted manuscript published in: 15 months
Rejected manuscript returned: Yes, with return postage paid by publication.
Rejected manuscript criticized: Yes

Submit to:
Dr. Clark Hubbs
Managing Editor
Department of Zoology
University of Texas
Austin, Texas 78712
(512) 471-1176

CRUSTACEANA [1986]

International Journal of Crustacean Research
E. J. Brill Publishers
Oude Rijn 33A
Leiden, The Netherlands
(071) 46-646

First published in 1960

SUBSCRIPTION DATA

Issues and rates: Published bi-monthly.
Average paid circulation: 1,100
Annual rate(s): Dfl. 76; Foreign $29.00

EDITORIAL DESCRIPTION

Publishes original scientific contributions in all branches of zoology dealing with the Crustacea.
Audience: Scientific
Manuscripts accepted in English, French, German

MANUSCRIPT INFORMATION

Subject field(s): Crustacea: Mostly taxonomy, distribution, ecology, larval life, growth, carcinology, etc.
Manuscript requirements: Style sheet sent on request.
Preferred length: 16 pages
Number of copies to be submitted: 2
Abstract: Yes. A brief summary in English, and in the original language if other than English. Editor will translate, if necessary.

Author information and reprints: Payment: None, or page charges as agreed to in advance
Is simultaneous submission of article to other journals permitted: Not permitted.
Exclusive manuscript rights between acceptance and publication: Yes
Copyright: Held by publication.
Reprints: Available at no cost. 50. Available at cost.

Additional information: Due to the large number of manuscripts, only those that

are executed in the recommended style can be considered by the referee board.
Disposition of manuscript:
Query letter: Not necessary, but advisable.
Receipt of manuscript acknowledged: Yes
Decision to publish in: 4 weeks
Accepted manuscript published in: 12-18 months
Rejected manuscript returned: Yes, with return postage paid by publication.
Rejected manuscript criticized: Reasons for rejections only

Submit to:
Dr. Jan H. Stock
Secretary, Editorial Board
Zoölogisch Museum
Plantage Middenlaan 53
Amsterdam-C, The Netherlands
(020) 974 555

SPECIAL STIPULATIONS
Biochemical articles are not accepted.

ENTOMOLOGICAL SOCIETY OF AMERICA ANNALS [1987]

4603 Calvert Road
College Park, Maryland 20740
(301) 864-1334

First published in 1908

SUBSCRIPTION DATA

Issues and rates: Published bi-monthly.
Average paid circulation: 4280
Annual rate(s): $25.00, Foreign $26.00
Publisher or Sponsor: Entomological Society of America

EDITORIAL DESCRIPTION

Contains recent research and advances in the fundamental aspects of entomology. Publishes only technical original research articles in field of basic (not applied) entomology. Chief interests are insect classification, life histories, embryology, physiology, etc.
Articles per average issue. 35
Audience: Entomologists
Manuscripts accepted in English

MANUSCRIPT INFORMATION

Subject field(s): Basic entomology
Manuscript requirements: Style sheet sent on request.
Preferred length: None
Number of copies to be submitted: Two
Abstract: Yes.

Author information and reprints: Payment: By author to publication. $40.00 per page.
Is simultaneous submission of article to other journals permitted: No
Exclusive manuscript rights between acceptance and publication: Yes
Copyright: Held by publication.
Reprints: Available

Disposition of manuscript:
Query letter:
Receipt of manuscript acknowledged: Yes
Decision to publish in: 2 to 3 months

Zoology

Accepted manuscript published in: 6 to 8 months
Rejected manuscript returned: Yes
Rejected manuscript criticized: Yes
Submit to:
James S. Packer
Managing Editor
(See address above)

EXPERIMENTAL PARASITOLOGY [1988]
Academic Press, Inc.
111 Fifth Avenue
New York, New York 10003

SUBSCRIPTION DATA
Issues and rates: Published bi-monthly.
Annual rate(s): $30.00, Foreign $33.00

EDITORIAL DESCRIPTION
Contains papers on experimental approaches to problems in the field of parasitology.
Articles per average issue: 12-15
Manuscripts accepted in English, French, German, Spanish

MANUSCRIPT INFORMATION
Subject field(s): Physiological, metabolic, biochemical, nutritional, chemotherapeutic problems of parasites and host-parasite relationships
Manuscript requirements: AIBS
Preferred length: None
Number of copies to be submitted: Original plus 2 copies
Abstract: Yes, must be factual, not indicative.
Author information and reprints: Payment: Reprints only. 50 reprints
Is simultaneous submission of article to other journals permitted: No
Copyright: Held by publication.
Reprints: Available at cost
Disposition of manuscript:
Query letter: No
Receipt of manuscript acknowledged: Yes
Decision to publish in: Several weeks
Accepted manuscript published in: Several months
Rejected manuscript returned: Yes
Rejected manuscript criticized: Yes
Submit to:
David R. Lincicome
Chairman, Editorial Board
7118 Cedar Avenue
Takoma Park, Maryland 20012

FIELDIANA: ZOOLOGY [1989]
Field Museum of Natural History
Roosevelt Road and Lake Shore Drive
Chicago, Illinois 60605
(312) 922-9410

Previously entitled *Field Museum Zoological Series*

First published in 1895

SUBSCRIPTION DATA
Issues and rates: Irregular

Publisher or Sponsor: Field Museum of Natural History
Managing Editor: Patricia M. Williams

EDITORIAL DESCRIPTION
Presents papers in all areas of zoology and natural history.
Articles per average issue: 1
Audience: Post-doctoral
Manuscripts accepted in English

MANUSCRIPT INFORMATION
Subject field(s): Special attention given work based on Museum collections or by museum researchers.
Manuscript requirements: See latest issue for style requirements. Style sheet sent on request.
Preferred length: As required
Number of copies to be submitted: 1
Abstract: Yes. Brief summary of manuscript
Author information and reprints: Payment: None.
Is simultaneous submission of article to other journals permitted: Not permitted.
Exclusive manuscript rights between acceptance and publication: Yes
Copyright: None
Reprints: Available at cost.
Disposition of manuscript:
Query letter: Not necessary, but advisable.
Receipt of manuscript acknowledged: Yes
Decision to publish in: Varies
Accepted manuscript published in: Varies
Rejected manuscript returned: Yes, with return postage paid by publication.
Rejected manuscript criticized: Sometimes
Submit to:
James W. Van Stone
Scientific Editor
(See address above)

FOLIA PRIMATOLOGICA [1990]
International Journal of Primatology
S. Karger AG
CH-4011 Basel, Switzerland
061-390880

First published in 1963

SUBSCRIPTION DATA
Issues and rates: Published monthly.
Average paid circulation: 590; 20 controlled
Annual rate(s): SFr.110.00; Foreign $44.00

EDITORIAL DESCRIPTION
An international periodical covering the entire field of contemporary primatological research ranging from phylogeny, taxonomy, anatomy, cytology, neurophysiology, immunology, biochemistry to reproduction, ecology, behaviour and psychology.
Articles per average issue: 4-6
Manuscripts accepted in English (French, German)

MANUSCRIPT INFORMATION
Manuscript requirements: See latest issue for style requirements.
Preferred length: No limit
Number of copies to be submitted: 2
Abstract: Yes, with key words (in English)
Author information and reprints: Payment: None.
Is simultaneous submission of article to other journals permitted: No
Exclusive manuscript rights between acceptance and publication: Yes
Copyright: Held by publication.
Reprints: Available at cost
Disposition of manuscript:
Query letter: No
Receipt of manuscript acknowledged: Yes
Decision to publish in: 1-2 months
Accepted manuscript published in: 6-7 months
Rejected manuscript returned: Yes
Rejected manuscript criticized: Yes
Submit to:
Prof. Dr. J. Biegert
Editor
Anthropologisches Institut der Universität
Künstlergasse 15
CH-8001 Zürich, Switzerland

GEORGIA ENTOMOLOGICAL SOCIETY. JOURNAL [1991]
Department of Entomology
University of Georgia
Athens, Georgia 30602
(404) 542-2817

First published in 1966

SUBSCRIPTION DATA
Issues and rates: Published quarterly.
Average paid circulation: 500
Annual rate(s): Individuals $5.00, Institutions $10.00
Publisher or Sponsor: Georgia Entomological Society
Managing Editor: Horace O. Lund

EDITORIAL DESCRIPTION
Contains papers on all aspects of entomology, basic and applied.
Articles per average issue: 15
Audience: Professional
Manuscripts accepted in English

MANUSCRIPT INFORMATION
Subject field(s): Entomology, physiology, ecology, evolution, systematics, morphology, toxicology, medical entomology, agricultural entomology, forest entomology, etc.
Manuscript requirements: AIBS, Style sheet sent on request.
Preferred length: 1-10 printed pages
Number of copies to be submitted: Two

Author information and reprints: Payment: By author to publication. $10.00 per page. for tables and figures $14.00 per page.
Is simultaneous submission of article to other journals permitted: No
Exclusive manuscript rights between acceptance and publication: Yes
Copyright: None
Reprints: Available, cost depends upon length.
Disposition of manuscript:
Query letter: No
Receipt of manuscript acknowledged: Yes
Decision to publish in: 2 months
Accepted manuscript published in: 6 months
Rejected manuscript returned: Yes
Rejected manuscript criticized: Yes
Submit to:
Horace O. Lund
Editor
(See address above)

THE GREAT LAKES ENTOMOLOGIST [1992]

c/o Department of Entomology
Michigan State University
East Lansing, Michigan 48823
(517) 373-3930 (office)

Previously entitled *The Michigan Entomologist*

First published in 1966

SUBSCRIPTION DATA

Issues and rates: Published quarterly.
Average paid circulation: 700
Annual rate(s): $10.00
Publisher or Sponsor: Michigan Entomological Society
Managing Editor: M. C. Nielsen (Executive Secretary)

EDITORIAL DESCRIPTION

Publishes papers of interest to amateur and professional entomologists in the Great Lakes area, including the North Central states and Canada, as well as general papers and revisions directed to a larger audience. Includes book reviews and papers dealing with historical aspects of entomology and entomologists.
Articles per average issue: 6
Audience: Professional and amateur entomologists
Manuscripts accepted in English

MANUSCRIPT INFORMATION

Subject field(s): Taxonomy, rearing methods, historical items, collecting techniques, distributional data, field observations, book reviews, insect controls, regional checklists, life histories, revisional studies, etc.
Manuscript requirements: AIBS
Preferred length: None
Number of copies to be submitted: Two
Abstract: Yes.
Author information and reprints: Payment: By author to publication. $18.00 per page. Authors without funds may apply

to the Society for financial assistance after acceptance of their manuscripts.
Is simultaneous submission of article to other journals permitted: No policy at this time
Exclusive manuscript rights between acceptance and publication: Yes
Copyright: Held by publication.
Reprints: Available
Additional information: Refer to "Information for Authors" on inside of back cover for details.
Disposition of manuscript:
Query letter:
Receipt of manuscript acknowledged: Yes
Decision to publish in: Varies
Accepted manuscript published in: 3 to 6 months
Rejected manuscript returned: Yes
Rejected manuscript criticized: Yes
Submit to:
Irving J. Cantrall
Editor
Museum of Zoology
The University of Michigan
Ann Arbor, Michigan 48104
(313) 764-0471

HERPETOLOGICA [1993]

Department of Biology
San Diego State University
San Diego, California 92182
(714) 286-5870

First published in 1936

SUBSCRIPTION DATA

Issues and rates: Published quarterly.
Average paid circulation: 2000
Annual rate(s): Individuals $10.00, Institutions $15.00
Publisher or Sponsor: Herpetologists' League

EDITORIAL DESCRIPTION

Contains original research articles on all aspects of the biology of amphibians and reptiles.
Articles per average issue: 18
Audience: Professional and non-professional herpetologists and vertebrate biologists
Manuscripts accepted in English

MANUSCRIPT INFORMATION

Subject field(s): Taxonomy, physiology, behavior, morphology, paleontology, zoogeography, evolution, ecology, parasitology, pathology, biochemistry, cytogenetics
Manuscript requirements: CBE
Preferred length: 6-30 pages
Number of copies to be submitted: Original plus 1 copy
Abstract: Yes.
Author information and reprints: Payment: None.
Is simultaneous submission of article to other journals permitted: No
Exclusive manuscript rights between acceptance and publication: No
Copyright: Not copyrighted
Reprints: Available, cost varies

Additional information: Cost of color illustrations must be borne in part by author.
Disposition of manuscript:
Query letter:
Receipt of manuscript acknowledged: Yes
Decision to publish in: 2-12 weeks
Accepted manuscript published in: 12 months (Manuscript will be published immediately if author pays full page charges.
Rejected manuscript returned: Yes
Rejected manuscript criticized: Yes
Submit to:
Crawford G. Jackson, Jr.
Editor-in-Chief
(See address above)

INTERNATIONAL JOURNAL FOR PARASITOLOGY [1994]

Pergamon Press, Inc.
Fairview Park
Elmsford, New York 10523
(914) 592-7700

First published in 1971

SUBSCRIPTION DATA

Issues and rates: Published bi-monthly.
Annual rate(s): $50.00

EDITORIAL DESCRIPTION

Provides a medium for the publication of research in any field dealing with the phenomenon of parasitism.
Articles per average issue: 12-15
Audience: Professional, academic
Manuscripts accepted in English (preferred), French, German

MANUSCRIPT INFORMATION

Subject field(s): Parasitology including life-cycles, physiology, biochemistry, ecology, immunology, cytology and ultrastructure of parasitic organisms. Taxonomic descriptions are not normally included unless part of a major review.
Manuscript requirements: See latest issue for style requirements.
Preferred length: None
Number of copies to be submitted: 2
Abstract: Yes. It should summarize the main contents and conclusions of the paper in a maximum of 150 words, on a separate page. Papers not in English should include a summary in English.
Author information and reprints: Payment: None.
Is simultaneous submission of article to other journals permitted: Not permitted.
Exclusive manuscript rights between acceptance and publication: Yes
Copyright: Held by publication.
Reprints: Available at cost.
Disposition of manuscript:
Query letter: Not necessary.
Receipt of manuscript acknowledged: Yes
Decision to publish in: 4 weeks
Accepted manuscript published in: 5 months
Rejected manuscript returned: Yes, if return postage is supplied by author.

Zoology 613

Annual rate(s): Individuals $14.00;
Institutions $20.00
Publisher or Sponsor: Institute of
Malacology

EDITORIAL DESCRIPTION
Contains articles on biology and
paleontology of mollusks.
Articles per average issue: 1-7
Audience: Professional

MANUSCRIPT INFORMATION
Subject field(s): Any aspect of study of
mollusks (malacology)
Manuscript requirements: See latest issue for
style requirements.
Preferred length: None
Number of copies to be submitted: Two
Abstract: Yes
Author information and reprints: Payment:
By arrangement with editor articles.
Is simultaneous submission of article to
other journals permitted: No
Exclusive manuscript rights between
acceptance and publication: Yes
Copyright: Held by publication.
Reprints: Available, 25 free; rest at
printing cost
Additional information: Each manuscript is
reviewed by two reviewers.
Disposition of manuscript:
Query letter: No
Receipt of manuscript acknowledged: Yes
Decision to publish in: 3 months
Accepted manuscript published in: 12-18
months
Rejected manuscript returned: Yes
Rejected manuscript criticized: Yes
Submit to:
George M. Davis
Editor
(See address above)

MALACOLOGICAL
REVIEW [2011]
P.O. Box 801
Whitmore Lake, Michigan 48189
(313) 764-0470

First published in 1968

SUBSCRIPTION DATA
Issues and rates: Published semi-annually.
Average paid circulation: 650; 50
controlled
Annual rate(s): $12.00; Foreign $13.00
Publisher or Sponsor: Society for
Experimental and Descriptive Malacology

EDITORIAL DESCRIPTION
Contains articles on biology of mollusca.

MANUSCRIPT INFORMATION
Subject field(s): Anything dealing with
mollusca
Manuscript requirements: See latest issue for
style requirements.
Preferred length: Varies
Number of copies to be submitted: Two
Is simultaneous submission of article to
other journals permitted: No

Exclusive manuscript rights between
acceptance and publication: Yes
Copyright: Held by publication.
Reprints: Available at printing costs
Disposition of manuscript:
Query letter: No
Receipt of manuscript acknowledged: Yes
Decision to publish in: 1-2 months
Accepted manuscript published in: 6-12
months
Rejected manuscript returned: Yes
Rejected manuscript criticized:
Sometimes
Submit to:
C. M. Patterson
Editor
(See address above)

MARYLAND
HERPETOLOGICAL
SOCIETY BULLETIN [2012]
Natural History Society of Maryland, Inc.
2643 North Charles Street
Baltimore, Maryland 21218
(301) 235-6116

First published in 1965

SUBSCRIPTION DATA
Issues and rates: Published quarterly.
Average paid circulation: 300-350
Annual rate(s): $3.00, Foreign $4.00

EDITORIAL DESCRIPTION
Publishes original research on the biology
distribution, zoogeography, and
systematics of amphibians and reptiles.
Articles per average issue: 8-10
Audience: Herpetologists, zoologists and
biologists.
Manuscripts accepted in English

MANUSCRIPT INFORMATION
Subject field(s): Herpetology
Manuscript requirements: AIBS
Preferred length: Maximum 50 pages
Number of copies to be submitted: Two
Author information and reprints: Payment:
None.
Is simultaneous submission of article to
other journals permitted: No
Exclusive manuscript rights between
acceptance and publication: Yes
Copyright: Held by publication.
Reprints: Available at cost
Disposition of manuscript:
Query letter: Not necessary.
Receipt of manuscript acknowledged: Yes
Decision to publish in: 1 to 3 months
Accepted manuscript published in: 1 to 3
months
Rejected manuscript returned: Yes
Rejected manuscript criticized:
Sometimes
Submit to:
Herbert S. Harris, Jr.
Executive Editor
(See address above)

THE MIGRANT [2013]
Kenneth H. Dubke
720 Bacon Trail, Apt. 1
Chattanooga, Tennessee 37412
(612) 238-4969

First published in 1930

SUBSCRIPTION DATA
Issues and rates: Published quarterly.
Average paid circulation: 800
Annual rate(s): $3.00
Publisher or Sponsor: The Tennessee
Ornithological Society
Managing Editor: Dr. Gary O. Wallace

EDITORIAL DESCRIPTION
To record observations and original
information derived from the study of
birds, primarily in Tennessee and
immediately adjacent states.
Articles per average issue: 8
Manuscripts accepted in English

MANUSCRIPT INFORMATION
Manuscript requirements: See latest issue for
style requirements.
Preferred length: As required
Number of copies to be submitted: 2
Abstract: Not necessary.
Author information and reprints: Payment:
None.
Is simultaneous submission of article to
other journals permitted: Permitted, but
not encouraged.
Exclusive manuscript rights between
acceptance and publication: No
Copyright: Held by author.
Reprints: Available at cost.
Submit to:
Query letter: Not necessary.
Receipt of manuscript acknowledged: Yes
Decision to publish in: 1-3 months
Accepted manuscript published in: 5-9
months
Rejected manuscript returned: Yes, with
return postage paid by publication.
Rejected manuscript criticized: Yes
Submit to:
Gary O. Wallace
Editor
Route 7
Sunrise Drive
Elizabethton, Tennessee 37643
(615)542-8612

THE NAUTILUS [2014]
A Quarterly Devoted to Malacology
11 Chelten Road
Havertown, Pennsylvania 19083
(215) 449-3636

First published in 1889

SUBSCRIPTION DATA
Issues and rates: Published quarterly.
Average paid circulation: 650
Annual rate(s): Institutions $12.00,
Individuals $7.00 (Subscriptions are by
calendar year only.)

EDITORIAL DESCRIPTION

Contains scientific papers on mollusks.
Articles per average issue: 9
Audience: Malacologists, zoologists,
ecologists and oceanographers
Manuscripts accepted in English

MANUSCRIPT INFORMATION

Subject field(s): Mollusks only
Manuscript requirements: AIBS
Preferred length: 4-20 ms. pages
Number of copies to be submitted: 2
Abstract: Yes.
Author information and reprints: Payment:
None.
Is simultaneous submission of article to
other journals permitted:
Exclusive manuscript rights between
acceptance and publication:
Reprints: Available, billed by printer
Disposition of manuscript:
Query letter:
Receipt of manuscript acknowledged: Yes
Decision to publish in: Varies
Accepted manuscript published in: 6-12
months
Rejected manuscript returned: Yes
Rejected manuscript criticized: Usually
Submit to:
R. Tucker Abbott
Editor
Delaware Museum of Natural History
Box 3937
Greenville, Delaware 19807
(302) 658-9111

NEW YORK ENTOMOLOGICAL SOCIETY. JOURNAL [2015]

Waksman Institute of Microbiology
Rutgers University
New Brunswick, New Jersey 08903
(201) 932-3064

First published in 1893

SUBSCRIPTION DATA

Issues and rates: Published quarterly.
Average paid circulation: 600
Annual rate(s): $8.00
Publisher or Sponsor: New York
Entomological Society

EDITORIAL DESCRIPTION

Contains articles on all subjects related to
entomology.
Articles per average issue: 10
Audience: Professional, academic
Manuscripts accepted in English

MANUSCRIPT INFORMATION

Manuscript requirements: AIBS
Preferred length: None
Number of copies to be submitted: Two
Abstract: Yes, less than 3 per cent of
article.
Author information and reprints: Payment:
By author to publication. $15.00 per
page.
Is simultaneous submission of article to
other journals permitted: No
Copyright: None

Reprints: Available at cost.
Disposition of manuscript:
Query letter: No
Receipt of manuscript acknowledged: Yes
Decision to publish in: 2-4 weeks
Accepted manuscript published in: 3-6
months
Rejected manuscript returned: Yes
Rejected manuscript criticized: Yes
Submit to:
Karl Maramorosch
Editor-in-Chief
(See address above)

OF SEA AND SHORE [2016]

P.O. Box 33
Port Gamble, Washington 98364
(206) 297-2426

First published in 1970

SUBSCRIPTION DATA

Issues and rates: Published quarterly.
Average paid circulation: 1,800; 50
controlled
Annual rate(s): $5.00 for all
Managing Editor: Thomas C. Rice

EDITORIAL DESCRIPTION

The natural history of the seas, lakes,
rivers and their shores, with special
emphasis on the molluscan life found in
these areas.
Articles per average issue: 15
Audience: Anyone interested in nature, but
especially to beginning, advanced and
professional Malacologists and
Conchologists
Manuscripts accepted in English,
German, French, Spanish

MANUSCRIPT INFORMATION

Subject field(s): Natural history-all aspects
Manuscript requirements: No specific style
guide.
Preferred length: No restrictions
Number of copies to be submitted: One
Abstract: Not necessary.
Author information and reprints: Payment:
None.
Is simultaneous submission of article to
other journals permitted: Permitted, but
not encouraged.
Exclusive manuscript rights between
acceptance and publication: Yes
Copyright: Held by publication.
Reprints: Available at no cost. Up to 50
Disposition of manuscript:
Query letter: Not necessary.
Receipt of manuscript acknowledged: Yes
Decision to publish in: 30 days
Accepted manuscript published in: 3
months
Rejected manuscript returned: Yes, with
return postage paid by publication.
Rejected manuscript criticized:
Sometimes
Submit to:
Thomas C. Rice
Editor
(See address above)

THE PAN-PACIFIC ENTOMOLOGIST [2017]

California Academy of Sciences
Golden Gate Park
San Francisco, California 94118
(415) 642-3327

First published in 1923

SUBSCRIPTION DATA

Issues and rates: Published quarterly.
Average paid circulation: 700
Annual rate(s): $6.00
Publisher or Sponsor: The Pacific Coast
Entomological Society

EDITORIAL DESCRIPTION

Contains papers on the systematic and
biological phases of entomology,
including insect taxonomy, morphology,
behavior, life history and distribution.
Articles per average issue: 15
Audience: Entomologists
Manuscripts accepted in English

MANUSCRIPT INFORMATION

Subject field(s): Systematic and biological
phases of entomology
Manuscript requirements: See latest issue for
style requirements.
Preferred length: 10 pages
Number of copies to be submitted: Two
Abstract:
Author information and reprints: Payment:
By author to publication. $18.00 per
page. Authors without institutional
support may apply for a society grant to
cover page charges.
Is simultaneous submission of article to
other journals permitted: No
Exclusive manuscript rights between
acceptance and publication: Yes
Reprints: Available, cost depends on
length
Disposition of manuscript:
Query letter:
Receipt of manuscript acknowledged: Yes
Decision to publish in: 1-2 months
Accepted manuscript published in: 6-8
months
Rejected manuscript returned: Yes
Rejected manuscript criticized: Yes
Submit to:
John I. Doyen
Editor
Division of Entomology and Parasitology
University of California
Berkeley, California 74720
(415) 642-3327

THE VELIGER [2018]

c/o Department of Zoology
University of California
Berkeley, California 94720
(415) 642-2726

First published in 1958

SUBSCRIPTION DATA

Issues and rates: Published quarterly.
Average paid circulation: Not available.

Physical sciences (general)

Submit to:
G. C. Tewinkel
Editor-in-Chief
(See address above)
(301) 593-6809

PROGRESS IN ORGANIC COATINGS [2043]

An International Review Journal
Elsevier Sequoia SA
P.O. Box 851
1001 Lausanne 1, Switzerland
(021) 20 73 81

First published in 1972

SUBSCRIPTION DATA
Issues and rates: Published quarterly.
    Average paid circulation: 750
    Annual rate(s): SFr. 155.00
Managing Editor: W. Funke

EDITORIAL DESCRIPTION
    The aim of this journal is to summarize
    and analyze the progress and current
    state of knowledge in the field of organic
    coatings and related subjects. The review
    articles are normally solicited.
    Unsolicited articles will be accepted if
    they meet the requirements.
Articles per average issue: 4
    Manuscripts accepted in English, French,
    and German (Abstracts in English only)

MANUSCRIPT INFORMATION
Subject field(s): Properties of organic
    coatings, preparation, manufacture,
    application, performance, testing, analysis
Manuscript requirements: Style sheet sent
    on request.
    Preferred length: None
    Number of copies to be submitted: Two
    Abstract: Yes.
Author information and reprints: Payment:
    By publication to author. Dfl. 10 per
    page.
    Is simultaneous submission of article to
    other journals permitted: No
    Exclusive manuscript rights between
    acceptance and publication: Yes
    Copyright: Held by publication.
    Reprints: Available, table of costs
    supplied with proofs.
Additional information: Drawings should be
    suitable for reproduction, photographs
    glossy and rich in contrast.
Disposition of manuscript:
    Query letter:
    Receipt of manuscript acknowledged: Yes
    Decision to publish in: 1 month
    Accepted manuscript published in: 6
    months
    Rejected manuscript returned: Yes
    Rejected manuscript criticized: Yes
Submit to:
    Editor
    (See address above)

SPECIAL STIPULATIONS
    See inside cover of journal for addresses
    of editors or editorial board members.

SOLAR ENERGY [2044]

The Journal of Solar Energy Science and
Technology
Pergamon Press, Inc.
Fairview Park
Elmsford, New York 10523
(914) 592-7700

First published in 1957

SUBSCRIPTION DATA
Issues and rates: Published quarterly.
    Annual rate(s): $25.00; Institutions
    $50.00
Publisher or Sponsor: International Solar
Energy Society

EDITORIAL DESCRIPTION
    Devoted exclusively to the science and
    technology of solar energy applications.

Articles per average issue: 4-6
Audience: Professional, academic
    Manuscripts accepted in English

MANUSCRIPT INFORMATION
Subject field(s): Any aspect of solar energy
    research, measurement, development, or
    application
Manuscript requirements: See latest issue for
    style requirements. AIP
    Preferred length: Papers, 4,000-6,000
    words; technical notes, 600-2,000 words
    Number of copies to be submitted:
    Original and 2 copies, double-spaced
    Abstract: Yes. Not exceeding 250 words
    to precede the paper.
Author information and reprints: Payment:
    None.
    Is simultaneous submission of article to
    other journals permitted: Not permitted.
    Exclusive manuscript rights between
    acceptance and publication: Yes
    Copyright: Held by publication.
    Reprints: Available at cost.
Disposition of manuscript:
    Query letter: Not necessary.
    Receipt of manuscript acknowledged: Yes
    Decision to publish in: 4 weeks
    Accepted manuscript published in: 5
    months
    Rejected manuscript returned: Yes, if
    return postage is supplied by author.
    Rejected manuscript criticized: Reasons
    for rejections only
Submit to:
    Dr. Peter E. Glaser
    Editor-in-Chief
    Arthur D. Little, Inc.
    Acorn Park
    Cambridge, Massachusetts 02140

SPECTROCHIMICA ACTA, PART A [2045]

Molecular Spectroscopy
Pergamon Press, Inc.
Fairview Park
Elmsford, New York 10523
(914) 592-7700

First published in 1967

SUBSCRIPTION DATA
Issues and rates: Published monthly.
    Annual rate(s): $30.00; Institutions
    $140.00

EDITORIAL DESCRIPTION
    Intended for the rapid publication of
    original work dealing with atomic and
    molecular spectroscopy (including
    photoelectron spectroscopy) with
    particular reference to problems in
    chemistry.
Articles per average issue: 10-15
Audience: Professional, academic
    Manuscripts accepted in English, French,
    German

MANUSCRIPT INFORMATION
Subject field(s): Raman spectra, nuclear
    magnetic resonance spectra, electron spin
    resonance spectra and optical rotatory
    dispersion; also high-resolution X-ray
    spectra, Mössbauer spectra, etc.
Manuscript requirements: See latest issue for
    style requirements.
    Preferred length: None
    Number of copies to be submitted:
    Original and 2 copies, double-spaced
    Abstract: Yes
Author information and reprints: Payment:
    None.
    Is simultaneous submission of article to
    other journals permitted: Not permitted.
    Exclusive manuscript rights between
    acceptance and publication: Yes
    Copyright: Held by publication.
    Reprints: Available at cost.
Disposition of manuscript:
    Query letter: Not necessary.
    Receipt of manuscript acknowledged: Yes
    Decision to publish in: 4 weeks
    Accepted manuscript published in: 5
    months
    Rejected manuscript returned: Yes, if
    return postage is supplied by author.
    Rejected manuscript criticized: Reasons
    for rejections only
Submit to:
    Prof. M. Kent Wilson
    Co-Editor
    National Science Foundation
    Chemistry Section
    Washington, D.C. 20550

SPECTROCHIMICA ACTA, PART B * [2045-1]

Fairview Park
Elmsford, New York 10523
(914) 592-7700

First published in 1967

SUBSCRIPTION DATA
Issues and rates: Published monthly.
    Annual rate(s): $25.00; Institutions
    $70.00

EDITORIAL DESCRIPTION
    Intended for rapid publication of original
    work dealing with atomic and molecular
    spectroscopy in all regions of the
    electro-magnetic spectrum and atomic

mass spectroscopy, insofar as they have direct physiochemical interest.
Articles per average issue: Varies
Audience: Professional, academic
Manuscripts accepted in English, French, German

MANUSCRIPT INFORMATION
Subject field(s): Qualitative and quantitative analysis, determination of fundamental atomic data, design and performance of equipment, new experimental procedures and general spectral theory, measurements or calculations of the properties of radiation sources or detectors, etc.
Manuscript requirements: See latest issue for style requirements.
Preferred length: None
Number of copies to be submitted: Original and 2 copies, double-spaced
Abstract: Yes
Author information and reprints: Payment: Reprints only. 50 reprints
Is simultaneous submission of article to other journals permitted: Not permitted.
Exclusive manuscript rights between acceptance and publication: Yes
Copyright: Held by publication.
Reprints: Available at cost.
Disposition of manuscript:
Query letter: Not necessary.
Receipt of manuscript acknowledged: Yes
Decision to publish in: 4 weeks
Accepted manuscript published in: 5 months
Rejected manuscript returned: Yes, if return postage is supplied by author.
Rejected manuscript criticized: Reasons for rejections only
Submit to:
Prof. V. G. Mossotti
Co-Editor
Department of Chemistry
University of Minnesota
Minneapolis, Minnesota 55455

VACUUM [2046]
An International Journal and Abstracting Service
Pergamon Press, Inc.
Fairview Park
Elmsford, New York 10523
(914) 592-7700

First published in 1951

SUBSCRIPTION DATA
Issues and rates: Published monthly.
Annual rate(s): $25.00; Institutions $55.00
Publisher or Sponsor: British Vacuum Council

EDITORIAL DESCRIPTION
Publishes original papers dealing with any of the many aspects of scientific, technical and industrial work concerned with an environment in which the total gas pressure is normally below that of the atmosphere.
Articles per average issue: 3-5
Audience: Professional, academic

Manuscripts accepted in English (French, German)

MANUSCRIPT INFORMATION
Manuscript requirements: See latest issue for style requirements.
Preferred length: None
Number of copies to be submitted: 2
Abstract: Yes
Author information and reprints: Payment: Reprints only. 50 reprints
Is simultaneous submission of article to other journals permitted: Not permitted.
Exclusive manuscript rights between acceptance and publication: Yes
Copyright: Held by publication.
Reprints: Available at cost.
Disposition of manuscript:
Query letter: Not necessary.
Receipt of manuscript acknowledged: Yes
Decision to publish in: 4 weeks
Accepted manuscript published in: 5 months
Rejected manuscript returned: Yes, if return postage is supplied by author.
Rejected manuscript criticized: Reasons for rejections only
Submit to:
J. Yarwood
Editor-in-Chief
The Polytechnic of Central London
115 New Cavendish Street
London W1M 8JS, England

Aeronautics and astronautics

ACTA ASTRONAUTICA [2047]
Journal of the International Academy of Astronautics
Pergamon Press, Inc.
Fairview Park
Elmsford, New York 10523
(914) 592-7700

Previously entitled *Astronautica Acta*

First published in 1955

SUBSCRIPTION DATA
Issues and rates: Published monthly.
Annual rate(s): $25.00; Institutions $120.00
Publisher or Sponsor: International Academy of Astronautics

EDITORIAL DESCRIPTION
Devoted to the international exchange of technical knowledge in astronautics; places before the world community of research scientists significant developments in astronautics.
Articles per average issue: 6-8
Audience: Professional, academic
Manuscripts accepted in English, French, German, Russian

MANUSCRIPT INFORMATION
Subject field(s): Current work in propulsion, astrodynamics, gas dynamics, guidance, space flight, physics of the atmosphere and space, etc.

Manuscript requirements: See latest issue for style requirements.
Preferred length: None
Number of copies to be submitted: 3, double-spaced
Abstract: Yes
Author information and reprints: Payment: Reprints only. 100 reprints
Is simultaneous submission of article to other journals permitted: Not permitted.
Exclusive manuscript rights between acceptance and publication: Yes
Copyright: Held by publication.
Reprints: Available at cost.
Disposition of manuscript:
Query letter: Not necessary.
Receipt of manuscript acknowledged: Yes
Decision to publish in: 4 weeks
Accepted manuscript published in: 5 months
Rejected manuscript returned: Yes, if return postage is supplied by author.
Rejected manuscript criticized: Reasons for rejections only
Submit to:
Prof. A. K. Oppenheim
Editor-in-Chief
Department of Engineering
University of California
Berkeley, California 94720

THE AERONAUTICAL QUARTERLY [2048]
4 Hamilton Place
London W1V OBQ, England
01-499 3515

First published in 1949

SUBSCRIPTION DATA
Issues and rates: Published quarterly.
Annual rate(s): £5.00, Members £2.60
Publisher or Sponsor: Royal Aeronautical Society
Managing Editor: E. C. Pike

EDITORIAL DESCRIPTION
Contains original papers contributing to aeronautical science and engineering, and papers developing new or improved methods of analysis and experimental techniques, but also papers on allied sciences which have a bearing on aeronautical problems.
Articles per average issue: 7-8
Audience: Research
Manuscripts accepted in English

MANUSCRIPT INFORMATION
Manuscript requirements: See latest issue for style requirements.
Preferred length: 20 pages maximum
Number of copies to be submitted: Two
Abstract: Yes
Author information and reprints: Payment: None.
Is simultaneous submission of article to other journals permitted: No
Exclusive manuscript rights between acceptance and publication: Yes
Copyright: Held by publication.
Reprints: Available
Disposition of manuscript:
Query letter: No

Aeronautics and astronautics

Receipt of manuscript acknowledged: Yes
Decision to publish in: 6 weeks
Accepted manuscript published in: 6 months
Rejected manuscript returned: Yes
Rejected manuscript criticized: Yes
Submit to:
The Editor
(See address above)

AIAA JOURNAL [2049]

1290 Avenue of the Americas
New York, New York 10019
(212) 581-4300

First published in 1963

SUBSCRIPTION DATA
Issues and rates: Published monthly.
Average paid circulation: 6,500
Annual rate(s): $79.00; Foreign $81.00; Members $7.00
Publisher or Sponsor: American Institute of Aeronautics and Astronautics

EDITORIAL DESCRIPTION
Devoted to the advancement of astronautics and aeronautics through the dissemination of original papers disclosing new technical knowledge and exploratory developments based on new knowledge, and its application to other fields.
Articles per average issue: 40
Manuscripts accepted in English

MANUSCRIPT INFORMATION
Subject field(s): Jet & rocket propulsion, space flight, hydronautics, combustion, fluid mechanics, astrodynamics, guidance, flight control, atmospheric physics, etc.
Manuscript requirements: Style sheet sent on request.
Preferred length: 36 pages
Number of copies to be submitted: Three
Abstract: Yes
Author information and reprints: Payment: By author to publication. $80.00 per page. Voluntary charge.
Is simultaneous submission of article to other journals permitted: No
Exclusive manuscript rights between acceptance and publication: Yes
Copyright: Held by publication.
Reprints: Available
Disposition of manuscript:
Query letter: No
Receipt of manuscript acknowledged: Yes
Decision to publish in: 3 months
Accepted manuscript published in: 3 months
Rejected manuscript returned: Yes
Rejected manuscript criticized: Yes
Submit to:
Anne Huth
Managing Editor
(See address above)

ASTRONAUTICS & AERONAUTICS [2050]

1290 Avenue of the Americas
New York, New York 10019
(212) 581-4300 ext. 715

SUBSCRIPTION DATA
Issues and rates: Published monthly.
Average paid circulation: 21,094; 29,224 controlled
Annual rate(s): $20.00, Foreign $22.00
Publisher or Sponsor: American Institute of Aeronautics and Astronautics

EDITORIAL DESCRIPTION
Presents the form and results of major engineering and scientific programs to show how these influence future planning; introduces the work of specialists in fields of growing importance, expected to influence R&D and design broadly; draws attention to scientific, engineering, and operational problems of unusual significance.

MANUSCRIPT INFORMATION
Subject field(s): Aircraft design, systems and operations; spacecraft design, systems and operations; space and atmospheric sciences; propulsion and power; structures and materials; guidance, control, and flight mechanics; management; communications; life support and human factors; testing and safety; marine systems and technology; urban technology
Manuscript requirements: Style sheet sent on request.
Preferred length: 3500 words
Number of copies to be submitted: Two
Author information and reprints: Payment: None.
Is simultaneous submission of article to other journals permitted: No
Exclusive manuscript rights between acceptance and publication: Yes
Copyright: Held by Institute
Reprints: Available, price list supplied on request.
Additional information: Two sets of reproducible black and white glossies to accompany editorial material; tables, if any, can be typed. Photo and biography appropriate in the context of the article necessary.
Disposition of manuscript:
Receipt of manuscript acknowledged: Yes
Decision to publish in: One month
Accepted manuscript published in: Varies
Rejected manuscript returned: Yes
Rejected manuscript criticized: Yes
Submit to:
John Newbauer
Editor-in-Chief
(See address above)

CANADIAN AERONAUTICS AND SPACE JOURNAL [2051]

77 Metcalfe Street
Ottawa K1P 5L6, Canada
(613) 234-0191

First published in 1954

SUBSCRIPTION DATA
Issues and rates: Monthly except July and August

Average paid circulation: 2100
Annual rate(s): $20.00
Publisher or Sponsor: Canadian Aeronautics and Space Institute

EDITORIAL DESCRIPTION
Contains articles on general technical and engineering subjects related to aerospace.
Articles per average issue: 4
Audience: Professional, academic
Manuscripts accepted in English, French

MANUSCRIPT INFORMATION
Subject field(s): Aerospace
Manuscript requirements: Style sheet sent on request.
Preferred length: 25 pages maximum
Number of copies to be submitted: Original and two copies
Abstract: Yes
Author information and reprints: Payment: By author to publication. $55.00 per page.
Is simultaneous submission of article to other journals permitted: No
Exclusive manuscript rights between acceptance and publication: Yes
Copyright: Held by publication.
Reprints: Available
Additional information: Double-spaced on standard-sized bond paper. Illustrations should be camera-ready glossies.
Disposition of manuscript:
Query letter: No
Receipt of manuscript acknowledged: Yes
Decision to publish in: 6 months
Accepted manuscript published in: 6 months
Rejected manuscript returned: Yes
Rejected manuscript criticized: Yes
Submit to:
Peter Albert Cobbett
Secretary
(See address above)

C.A.S.I. TRANSACTIONS [2052]

77 Metcalfe Street
Ottawa, Ontario K1P 5L6, Canada
(613) 234-0191

First published in 1968

SUBSCRIPTION DATA
Issues and rates: Published semi-monthly.
Average paid circulation: 500
Annual rate(s): $10.00, Foreign $10.50
Publisher or Sponsor: Canadian Aeronautics and Space Institute
Managing Editor: Peter Albert Cobbett

EDITORIAL DESCRIPTION
Contains articles on advanced aerospace science.
Articles per average issue: 8
Audience: Members, professional, academic
Manuscripts accepted in English, French

MANUSCRIPT INFORMATION
Manuscript requirements: Style sheet sent on request.
Preferred length: 1 to 30 pages
Number of copies to be submitted: Original and 2 copies

Abstract: Yes, of 100-300 words in non-specialist language if possible, stating the main conclusions of the paper.

Author information and reprints: Payment: By author to publication. $55.00 per page.

Is simultaneous submission of article to other journals permitted: No

Exclusive manuscript rights between acceptance and publication: Yes

Copyright: Held by publication.

Reprints: Available, details on request

Disposition of manuscript:

Query letter: No

Receipt of manuscript acknowledged: Yes

Decision to publish in: 6 months

Accepted manuscript published in: 2 months

Rejected manuscript returned: Yes

Rejected manuscript criticized: Yes

Submit to:

The Secretary

(See address above)

JOURNAL OF AIRCRAFT [2053]

1290 Avenue of the Americas
New York, New York 10019
(212) 581-4300 ext.272

First published in 1972

SUBSCRIPTION DATA

Issues and rates: Published monthly.

Average paid circulation: 4700

Annual rate(s): $59.00, Members $5,00, Foreign $61.00

Publisher or Sponsor: American Institute of Aeronautics and Astronautics

EDITORIAL DESCRIPTION

Devoted to the advancement of the science and technology of airborne flight through the dissemination of original papers describing significant advances in aircraft and the use of aircraft, and applications of aircraft technology to other fields.

Articles per average issue: 15

Audience:

Manuscripts accepted in English

MANUSCRIPT INFORMATION

Subject field(s): Aircraft systems and advanced concepts in aircraft design, flight mechanics, flight testing; flight safety, human factors, airport design, airline operation; air traffic control and flight navigation; production methods; engineering economic analyses; the development of engines, structures, control systems and other components; general aviation, military as well as civilian aircraft, ground effect machines, V/STOL airplanes, and supersonic and hypersonic airplanes.

Manuscript requirements: Style sheet sent on request.

Preferred length: 36 pages

Number of copies to be submitted: Three

Abstract: Yes.

Author information and reprints: Payment: By author to publication. $85.00 per page. Voluntary charge.

Is simultaneous submission of article to other journals permitted: No

Exclusive manuscript rights between acceptance and publication: Yes

Copyright: Held by publication.

Reprints: Available at cost.

Disposition of manuscript:

Query letter:

Receipt of manuscript acknowledged: Yes

Decision to publish in: 3 months

Accepted manuscript published in: 3 months

Rejected manuscript returned: Yes

Rejected manuscript criticized: Yes

Submit to:

Anne Huth

Managing Editor

(See address above)

JOURNAL OF SPACE CRAFT AND ROCKETS [2054]

1290 Avenue of the Americas
New York, New York 10019
(212) 581-4300 ext.272

First published in 1964

SUBSCRIPTION DATA

Issues and rates: Published monthly.

Average paid circulation: 3700

Annual rate(s): $69.00, Members $6.00, Foreign $71.00

Publisher or Sponsor: American Institute of Aeronautics and Astronautics

EDITORIAL DESCRIPTION

Devoted to the advancement of the science and technology of space flight through the dissemination of original papers describing significant advances in space technology, the use of spacecraft, and the applications of space technology to other fields.

Articles per average issue: 18

Manuscripts accepted in English

MANUSCRIPT INFORMATION

Subject field(s): Publishes qualified papers on the design, development, and missions of spacecraft, missiles, launch vehicles, and spaceplanes; system analysis; flight operations, flight testing, ground-support equipment, test facilities, field installations; manufacturing and processing techniques of unusual nature; performance testing, reliability problems, engineering economic analyses; development of propulsion systems, structures, control systems, and other components; human and environmental factors in relation to spacecraft design.

Manuscript requirements: Style sheet sent on request.

Preferred length: 36 pages

Number of copies to be submitted: Three

Abstract: Yes.

Author information and reprints: Payment: By author to publication. $85 per page. Voluntary charge.

Is simultaneous submission of article to other journals permitted: No

Exclusive manuscript rights between acceptance and publication: Yes

Copyright: Held by publication.

Reprints: Available at cost. 100 free, if page charges are paid.

Disposition of manuscript:

Query letter:

Receipt of manuscript acknowledged: Yes

Decision to publish in: 3 months

Accepted manuscript published in: 3 months

Rejected manuscript returned: Yes

Rejected manuscript criticized: Yes

Submit to:

Anne Huth

Managing Editor

(See address above)

SPACEFLIGHT [2055]

British Interplanetary Society
12 Bessborough Gardens
London SW1V 2JJ, England
(01) 828-9371

First published in 1956

SUBSCRIPTION DATA

Issues and rates: Published monthly.

Average paid circulation: 4,500

Annual rate(s): $12.50

Publisher or Sponsor: British Interplanetary Society

Managing Editor: K. W. Gatland

EDITORIAL DESCRIPTION

Contains papers in astronomy, space research and space technology.

Articles per average issue: 8

Audience: General scientific, technical readers

Manuscripts accepted in English

MANUSCRIPT INFORMATION

Subject field(s): Advanced propulsion systems, aerospace vehicles, ground testing facilities, guidance and control, materials technology, orbital theory, rocket propulsion, life-support systems, space medicine, etc.

Manuscript requirements: See latest issue for style requirements.

Preferred length: 3500-5000 words

Number of copies to be submitted: One

Abstract:

Author information and reprints: Payment: None.

Is simultaneous submission of article to other journals permitted: No

Exclusive manuscript rights between acceptance and publication: Yes

Copyright: Held by publication.

Reprints: Available at cost.

Disposition of manuscript:

Query letter:

Receipt of manuscript acknowledged: Yes

Decision to publish in: One month

Accepted manuscript published in: Three months

Rejected manuscript returned: Yes

Rejected manuscript criticized: No

Submit to:

Editor

(See address above)

Astronomy

ASSOCIATION OF LUNAR AND PLANETARY OBSERVERS. JOURNAL [2056]

The Strolling Astronomer
Box 3AZ
University Park, New Mexico 88003
(505) 522-4213

First published in 1947

SUBSCRIPTION DATA

Issues and rates: Published bi-monthly.
Average paid circulation: 1,000
Annual rate(s): $6.00; Foreign $6.00;
Institutions $6.00; Students $6.00
Publisher or Sponsor: Association of Lunar
and Planetary Observers
Managing Editor: Walter H. Haas

EDITORIAL DESCRIPTION

To present the results of research on the
moon and the planets and related topics
Articles per average issue: 8-10
Audience: Professional and amateur
astronomers, students of astronomy
Manuscripts accepted in English

MANUSCRIPT INFORMATION

Manuscript requirements: No specific style
guide.
Preferred length: 3-4 pages
Number of copies to be submitted: 1
Abstract: Not necessary.
Author information and reprints: Payment:
Reprints only. 1
Is simultaneous submission of article to
other journals permitted: Not permitted.
Exclusive manuscript rights between
acceptance and publication: Yes
Copyright: Not copyrighted
Reprints: Not available.
Disposition of manuscript:
Query letter: Not necessary, but
advisable.
Receipt of manuscript acknowledged: Yes
Decision to publish in: 2-3 weeks
Accepted manuscript published in: 4-6
months
Rejected manuscript returned: Yes, if
return postage is supplied by author.
Rejected manuscript criticized: Reasons
for rejections only
Submit to:
Walter H. Haas
Editor
(See address above)

ASTRONOMICAL SOCIETY OF THE PACIFIC. PUBLICATIONS [2057]

75 Southgate Avenue
Daly City, California 94015
(415) 755-2808

First published in 1889

SUBSCRIPTION DATA

Issues and rates: Published bi-monthly.
Average paid circulation: 2,432
Annual rate(s): $20.00; Individuals
$20.00; Institutions $25.00; Students
$16.50; Members Included in subscription
price Foreign individuals $20.00; Foreign
institutions $25.00
Publisher or Sponsor: Astronomical Society
of the Pacific
Managing Editor: D. Harold McNamara

EDITORIAL DESCRIPTION

To provide an outlet for astronomical
results of a scientific nature and serve to
keep members of the Society in touch
with current astronomical research. They
contain refereed research reports, invited
topical reviews, and abstracts of papers
given at scientific meetings.
Articles per average issue: 28
Audience: Professional and amateur
astronomers
Manuscripts accepted in English

MANUSCRIPT INFORMATION

Subject field(s): Observational,
instrumentation, radio astronomy,
theoretical (some), photometry,
spectroscopy, solar astronomy, site
testing, invited topical reviews, comets.
Manuscript requirements: See latest issue for
style requirements.
Preferred length: 9,000-18,000 words;
10-20 pages
Number of copies to be submitted: 2
(original and 1 copy)
Abstract: Yes. A brief abstract of entire
article followed by two or three key
words
Author information and reprints: Payment:
$30.00 per page.
Is simultaneous submission of article to
other journals permitted: Not permitted.
Exclusive manuscript rights between
acceptance and publication: Yes
Copyright: Held by author.
Reprints: Available at cost. Price list
available upon request
Additional information: Submit all tables in
finished form (typewritten with an
electric typewriter and carbon ribbon) in
order that all tables can be photocopied.
Be sure that references are correct.
Disposition of manuscript:
Query letter: Not necessary.
Receipt of manuscript acknowledged: Yes
Decision to publish in: 3-4 weeks
Accepted manuscript published in: 3-4
months
Rejected manuscript returned: Yes, with
return postage paid by publication.
Rejected manuscript criticized: Yes
Submit to:
Dr. D. Harold McNamara
Editor
183-A Eyring Science Center
Brigham Young University
Provo, Utah 84602
(801) 374-1211

ASTRONOMY AND ASTROPHYSICS [2058]

A European Journal
Springer-Verlag
175 Fifth Avenue
New York, New York 10010

First published in 1969
Annual rate(s): DM 166 per volume
Publisher or Sponsor: European Southern
Observatory (ESO)
Managing Editor: Dr. J. Heidmann

EDITORIAL DESCRIPTION

Publishes papers on all aspects of
astronomy and astrophysics, independent
of the techniques used to obtain the
results.
Audience: Astronomers and astrophysicists
Manuscripts accepted in English, French,
German

MANUSCRIPT INFORMATION

Subject field(s): Astronomy and
astrophysics: optical, radio, particles,
space vehicles, numerical analysis etc.,
but not observatory results.
Manuscript requirements: Style sheet sent
on request.
Preferred length: As required
Number of copies to be submitted: 2
Abstract: Yes. Papers written in French
or German should include an abstract in
English.
Author information and reprints: Payment:
None.
Is simultaneous submission of article to
other journals permitted: Not permitted.
Exclusive manuscript rights between
acceptance and publication: Yes
Copyright: Held by European Southern
Observatory
Reprints: Available at cost.
Additional information: There is a page
charge of US $25.00 for authors who do
not work in European countries.
Submit to:
Dr. S. R. Pottasch
Co-Editor-in-Chief
P. O. Box 800
Kapteyn Astronomical Institute
Groningen 8002, The Netherlands
(050) 116643

THE ASTROPHYSICAL JOURNAL [2059]

Parts 1 & 2
The University of Chicago Press
5801 Ellis Avenue
Chicago, Illinois 60637
(312) 753-3372

First published in 1895

SUBSCRIPTION DATA

Issues and rates: Published semi-monthly.
Average paid circulation: 3,400
Annual rate(s): $120.00; Foreign
$140-$180.00

Publisher or Sponsor: American
Astronomical Society

EDITORIAL DESCRIPTION

Journal is concerned with recent
astronomical developments, theories, and
discoveries. All papers in all areas of
astronomy and astrophysics are
considered for publication.
Articles per average issue: 40
Audience: Research scientists
Manuscripts accepted in English

MANUSCRIPT INFORMATION

Subject field(s): Astrophysics, relativity,
astronomy, spectroscopy, radio
astronomy, nuclear physics, solar physics,
stellar atmospheres, planetary
atmospheres, stellar and galactic
evolution, cosmology, and other related
fields
Manuscript requirements: Astrophysical
Journal Manual of Style
Preferred length: 2-60 pages (Part 1);
1-10 pages (Part 2)
Number of copies to be submitted: 2
(Part 1), 3 (Part 2)
Abstract: Yes
Author information and reprints: Payment:
By author to publication. $20.00-$55.00
per page.
Is simultaneous submission of article to
other journals permitted: No
Exclusive manuscript rights between
acceptance and publication: Yes
Copyright: Held by publication.
Reprints: Available, cost varies
Additional information: All manuscripts
must be typed double-space on regular
bond, not corrasable bond, with generous
margins for copyediting remarks.
Disposition of manuscript:
Query letter: No
Receipt of manuscript acknowledged: Yes
Decision to publish in: 1-6 months
Accepted manuscript published in: 4
months for Part 1, 2 months for Part 2
Rejected manuscript returned: Yes, with
return postage paid by publication.
Rejected manuscript criticized: Yes
Submit to:
Helmut A. Abt
Managing Editor
Kitt Peak National Observatory
Box 26732
Tucson, Arizona 85726
(602) 327-5511

THE ASTROPHYSICAL
JOURNAL, SUPPLEMENT
SERIES   [2060]

University of Chicago Press
5801 South Ellis Avenue
Chicago, Illinois 60637
(312) 753-3372

First published in 1954

SUBSCRIPTION DATA

Issues and rates: Published monthly.
Average paid circulation: 700
Annual rate(s): $16, Foreign $17 per
volume

Publisher or Sponsor: American
Astronomical Society

EDITORIAL DESCRIPTION

Contains research papers too lengthy for
the *Astrophysical Journal* on most topics
of astrophysics.
Articles per average issue: 2
Audience: Research scientists
Manuscripts accepted in English

MANUSCRIPT INFORMATION

Subject field(s): Astronomy, spectroscopy,
radio astronomy, nuclear physics, solar
physics, stellar and planetary
atmospheres, stellar and galactic
evolution, cosmology, cosmogony, and
others.
Manuscript requirements: The *Astrophysical
Journal* Manual of Style
Preferred length: 1-1,000 pages
Number of copies to be submitted: 2
Abstract: Yes
Author information and reprints: Payment:
By author to publication. $20-$50.00 per
page.
Is simultaneous submission of article to
other journals permitted: No
Exclusive manuscript rights between
acceptance and publication: Yes
Copyright: Held by publication.
Reprints: Available at varying cost
Additional information: All manuscripts
must be typed double-space on regular
bond, not corrasable bond, with generous
margins for copyediting remarks.
Disposition of manuscript:
Query letter: No
Receipt of manuscript acknowledged: Yes
Decision to publish in: 1-4 months
Accepted manuscript published in: 6
months
Rejected manuscript returned: Yes, with
return postage paid by publication.
Rejected manuscript criticized: Yes
Submit to:
Helmut A. Abt
Managing Editor
Kitt Peak National Observatory, Box
26732
Tucson, Arizona 85726
(602) 327-5511

BRITISH ASTRONOMICAL
ASSOCIATION JOURNAL   [2061]

39 Burlington House
Piccadilly,
London, England

First published in 1890

SUBSCRIPTION DATA

Issues and rates: Published bi-monthly.
Average paid circulation: 7,000
Annual rate(s): £4.50, Foreign $11.50
Managing Editor: Colin A. Ronan

EDITORIAL DESCRIPTION

Contains articles on astronomy, history
of astronomy; book reviews in astronomy
and history of astronomy.

Audience: Amateur and professional
astronomers and historians of astronomy
Manuscripts accepted in English

MANUSCRIPT INFORMATION

Subject field(s): Astronomy, history of
astronomy
Manuscript requirements: See latest issue for
style requirements.
Preferred length: 600-2,000 words
Number of copies to be submitted: Two
Abstract:
Author information and reprints: Payment:
None.
Is simultaneous submission of article to
other journals permitted: No
Exclusive manuscript rights between
acceptance and publication: Yes
Copyright: Held by author.
Reprints: Available if ordered at time of
proof correction.
Additional information: All manuscripts
must be typed with lines spaced double.
Disposition of manuscript:
Query letter:
Receipt of manuscript acknowledged: Yes
Decision to publish in: 2-3 months
Accepted manuscript published in: 6-9
months
Rejected manuscript returned: Yes, if
return postage is supplied by author.
Rejected manuscript criticized: No
Submit to:
Cmdr. H. H. Hatfield
Honorary Secretary
Lynch House
Clarendon Road
Sevenoaks, Kent, England

THE OBSERVATORY   [2062]

A Review of Astronomy
Royal Greenwich Observatory
Herstmonceux Castle
Hailsham, Sussex BN27 4RP, England
032-181-3171

First published in 1877

SUBSCRIPTION DATA

Issues and rates: Published bi-monthly.
Average paid circulation: 3300
Annual rate(s): £3.00, Foreign $9.00
Managing Editor: M. V. Penston

EDITORIAL DESCRIPTION

Contains reports of astronomical
meetings (in particular those of the Royal
Astronomical Society), original
astronomical papers, notes and letters,
book reviews, etc. All contributions are
refereed.
Articles per average issue: 25
Audience: Professional and amateur
astronomers
Manuscripts accepted in English

MANUSCRIPT INFORMATION

Subject field(s): Astronomy, related subjects
Manuscript requirements: See October 1974
issue.
Preferred length: Less than 4000 words
Number of copies to be submitted: One

Author information and reprints: Payment:
None.
  Is simultaneous submission of article to
other journals permitted: No
  Exclusive manuscript rights between
acceptance and publication: Yes
  Copyright: Held by publication.
  Reprints: Available, £1.75 per page for
50
Disposition of manuscript:
  Query letter:
  Receipt of manuscript acknowledged: Yes
  Decision to publish in: Two to six weeks
  Accepted manuscript published in: Three
to four months
  Rejected manuscript returned: Yes
  Rejected manuscript criticized: Yes
Submit to:
  Editors
  (See address above)

THE PLANETARIAN [2063]

Journal of the International Society of
Planetarium Educators
Department of Astronomy & Space Science
State University of New York at Albany
Albany, New York 12222
(518) 457-3207

First published in 1972

SUBSCRIPTION DATA

Issues and rates: Published quarterly.
  Average paid circulation: 600; 300
controlled
  Annual rate(s): $5.25; Pan-Am $5.25;
Foreign $6.25; Members $15.00
Publisher or Sponsor: International Society
of Planetarium Educators
Managing Editor: Frank C. Jettner

EDITORIAL DESCRIPTION

  Contributions should relate to
planetarium activities and/or education
or to astronomy and space sciences;
includes articles, reports, planetarium
programs, letters, humor items, pictorials
of selected planetariums, and planetarium
association news.
Articles per average issue: 3-6
Audience: Principally planetarium
specialists, but also including professional
and amateur astronomers and general
science teachers at all levels.
  Manuscripts accepted in English

MANUSCRIPT INFORMATION

Subject field(s): All aspects of planetarium
education, administration, operating
philosophy, etc. Selected papers in
astronomy education, particularly if
related to public education or
planetarium use. Also concerned with
technological reports in multi-media
which have direct application.
Manuscript requirements: Style sheet sent
on request.
  Preferred length: 300-5000 words
maximum
  Number of copies to be submitted: 1
  Abstract: Not necessary.

Author information and reprints: Payment:
Reprints only. 5 copies of issue
  Is simultaneous submission of article to
other journals permitted: Not permitted.
  Exclusive manuscript rights between
acceptance and publication: Yes
  Copyright: Held by International Society
of Planetarium Educators
  Reprints: Available at cost.
Additional information: Please see General
Instructions on flyer for contributors.
Disposition of manuscript:
  Query letter: Not necessary, but
advisable.
  Receipt of manuscript acknowledged: Yes
  Decision to publish in: 4-6 weeks
  Accepted manuscript published in: 3-12
months
  Rejected manuscript returned: Yes, if
return postage is supplied by author.
  Rejected manuscript criticized: Reasons
for rejections only
Submit to:
  Frank C. Jettner
  Executive Editor
  (See address above)

ROYAL ASTRONOMICAL SOCIETY OF CANADA JOURNAL [2064]

252 College Street
Toronto Ontario, Canada M5T 1R7
(416) 923-3784

First published in 1907

SUBSCRIPTION DATA

Issues and rates: Published bi-monthly.
  Average paid circulation: 3100
  Annual rate(s): $15.00

EDITORIAL DESCRIPTION

  Contains astronomical research.
Articles per average issue: 5
Audience: Professional and amateur
astronomers
  Manuscripts accepted in English and
French

MANUSCRIPT INFORMATION

Subject field(s): Astronomy, geophysics
Manuscript requirements: See latest issue for
style requirements.
  Number of copies to be submitted: Two
  Abstract: Yes.
Author information and reprints: Payment:
None.
  Is simultaneous submission of article to
other journals permitted: Yes
  Exclusive manuscript rights between
acceptance and publication: Yes
  Copyright: Held by publication.
  Reprints: Available
Disposition of manuscript:
  Query letter:
  Receipt of manuscript acknowledged: Yes
  Decision to publish in: 3 months
  Accepted manuscript published in: 6
months
  Rejected manuscript returned: Yes
  Rejected manuscript criticized: Yes

Submit to:
  Ian Halliday
  Editor
  Astrophysics Branch
  National Research Council
  Ottawa, Ontario K1A OR8, Canada

Chemistry

AMBIX [2065]

Journal of the Society for the History of
Alchemy and Chemistry
Dr. Smeaton, Department of the History of
Science
University College, Gower Street
London WC1, England
(O1) 387-7050

First published in 1937

SUBSCRIPTION DATA

Issues and rates: Published three times per
year.
  Annual rate(s): Institutions £7.00;
Members £3.25; Foreign institutions
£7.00
Publisher or Sponsor: Society for the
History of Alchemy and Chemistry
Managing Editor: William H. Brock

EDITORIAL DESCRIPTION

  Contains scholarly articles and reviews of
books on all aspects of the history of
chemistry and alchemy.
Articles per average issue: 4
Audience: Historians of science
  Manuscripts accepted in English

MANUSCRIPT INFORMATION

Subject field(s): Early natural philosophy
(Greeks to the scientific revolution);
history of alchemy, and of chemistry up
to recent times
Manuscript requirements: See latest issue for
style requirements.
  Preferred length: 5,000-8,000 words
  Number of copies to be submitted: 1
  Abstract: Not necessary.
Author information and reprints: Payment:
Reprints only. 25 offprints
  Is simultaneous submission of article to
other journals permitted: Not permitted.
  Exclusive manuscript rights between
acceptance and publication: Yes
  Copyright: Held by publication.
  Reprints: Available at cost.
Additional information: Desire a scholarly
style with adequate documentation.
Disposition of manuscript:
  Query letter: Not necessary, but
advisable.
  Receipt of manuscript acknowledged: Yes
  Decision to publish in: 1-3 months
  Accepted manuscript published in: 1 year
  Rejected manuscript returned: Yes, with
return postage paid by publication.
  Rejected manuscript criticized: Yes
Submit to:
  Dr. William H. Brock

Director of Victorian Studies Center
University of Leicester
University Road
Leicester LE1 7RH, England
(O5) 335-9785

AMERICAN CHEMICAL SOCIETY. JOURNAL* [2066]

1155 16th Street
Washington, D.C. 20036

SUBSCRIPTION DATA
Issues and rates: Published bi-weekly.
    Average paid circulation: 16,000
    Annual rate(s): $44.00, Members $22.00
Publisher or Sponsor: American Chemical Society

EDITORIAL DESCRIPTION
    Publishes original research in all fields of chemistry.

MANUSCRIPT INFORMATION
Subject field(s): All fields of chemistry
Manuscript requirements: ACS
    Number of copies to be submitted: Three
Author information and reprints: Payment: None.
    Is simultaneous submission of article to other journals permitted: No
    Exclusive manuscript rights between acceptance and publication: Yes
    Copyright: Held by the American Chemical Society
    Reprints: Available at cost
Additional information: Prefer papers of general interest, either because of their appeal to readers in more than one field or because they disclose findings of significance to command the interest of specialists in other fields.
Disposition of manuscript:
    Receipt of manuscript acknowledged: Yes
    Decision to publish in: Two months
    Accepted manuscript published in: Three months
    Rejected manuscript returned: Yes
    Rejected manuscript criticized: Yes
Submit to:
    Martin Styles
    Editor
    Department of Chemistry
    University of Michigan
    Ann Arbor, Michigan 48104

AMERICAN OIL CHEMISTS SOCIETY JOURNAL [2067]

508 South Sixth Street
Champaign, Illinois 61820
(217) 359-2344

Previously entitled *Oil & Soap*

First published in 1923

SUBSCRIPTION DATA
Issues and rates: Published monthly.
    Average paid circulation: 6000; 100 controlled
    Annual rate(s): $30.00, Foreign $33.00
Managing Editor: James Lyon

EDITORIAL DESCRIPTION
    Contains original papers and timely reviews of physical, chemical and processing data and methods for fats, waxes and related products such as fatty acids; information on fat deriatives, detergents, paints, proteins and oilseed products; symposia sometimes published as a unit.
Articles per average issue: 8-10
    Manuscripts accepted in English

MANUSCRIPT INFORMATION
Manuscript requirements: AIBS
    Number of copies to be submitted: Three
    Abstract: Yes.
Author information and reprints: Payment: By author to publication. $40 per page.
    Is simultaneous submission of article to other journals permitted: No
    Exclusive manuscript rights between acceptance and publication: Yes
    Copyright: Held by publication.
    Reprints: Available, cost varies with length.
Disposition of manuscript:
    Query letter:
    Receipt of manuscript acknowledged: Yes
    Decision to publish in: 1-2 months
    Accepted manuscript published in: 2-3 months
    Rejected manuscript returned: Yes
    Rejected manuscript criticized: Yes
Submit to:
    A. R. Baldwin
    Editor
    Cargill, Inc.
    Cargill Building
    Minneapolis, Minnesota 55402
    (612) 473-8811

ANALYTICAL CHEMISTRY [2068]

American Chemical Society
1155 16th Street N.W.
Washington, D.C. 20036
(202) 872-4570

SUBSCRIPTION DATA
Issues and rates: Published monthly.
    Average paid circulation: 30,000
    Annual rate(s): $7.00, Members $5.00, Foreign $15.00
Publisher or Sponsor: American Chemical Society
Managing Editor: Virginia E. Stewart

EDITORIAL DESCRIPTION
    Covers all branches of analytical chemistry including articles that are entirely theoretical with regard to analysis or reports of laboratory experiments that support, argue, refute, or extend established theory.
Articles per average issue: 45
Audience: Professional, academic
    Manuscripts accepted in English

MANUSCRIPT INFORMATION
Subject field(s): Sampling, preliminary chemical reactions, separations, instrumentation, measurements, data processing

Manuscript requirements: See latest issue for style requirements.
    Preferred length: No specific preference
    Number of copies to be submitted: Four
    Abstract: Yes, for full articles only
Author information and reprints: Payment: None.
    Is simultaneous submission of article to other journals permitted: No
    Exclusive manuscript rights between acceptance and publication: Yes
    Copyright: Held by American Chemical Society
    Reprints: Available, cost based on length
Disposition of manuscript:
    Query letter: No
    Receipt of manuscript acknowledged: Yes
    Decision to publish in: 4 months
    Accepted manuscript published in: 2 months
    Rejected manuscript returned: Yes
    Rejected manuscript criticized: Yes
Submit to:
    Herbert A. Laitinen
    Editor
    (See address above)

ANGEWANDTE CHEMIE [2069]

Applied Chemistry
Verlag Chemie
P. O. Box 129/149
D-694 Weinheim, Federal Republic of Germany
(06201) 4036

SUBSCRIPTION DATA
    Annual rate(s): DM 230; Foreign DM 230; Institutions DM 230; Students DM 65; Members DM 148
Publisher or Sponsor: Association of German Chemists; Gesellschaft Deutscher Chemiker
Managing Editor: Dr. Helmut Grünewald

EDITORIAL DESCRIPTION
    Contains articles on all aspects of the study of chemistry.
Articles per average issue: Varies
Audience: Professional
    Manuscripts accepted in German, English

MANUSCRIPT INFORMATION
Manuscript requirements: Style sheet sent on request.
    Preferred length: None
    Number of copies to be submitted: 1
    Abstract: Not necessary.
Author information and reprints: Payment: Reprints only.
    Is simultaneous submission of article to other journals permitted: Not permitted.
    Exclusive manuscript rights between acceptance and publication: Yes
    Copyright: Held by publication.
    Reprints: Available at cost.
Disposition of manuscript:
    Query letter: Necessary.
    Receipt of manuscript acknowledged: Yes
    Decision to publish in: Varies
    Accepted manuscript published in: Varies
    Rejected manuscript returned: Yes, with return postage paid by publication.

Rejected manuscript criticized:
Sometimes
Submit to:
Editor
Boschstrasse 12
D-694 Weinheim, Federal Republic of
Germany

ASSOCIATION OF OFFICIAL ANALYTICAL CHEMISTS JOURNAL [2070]

Box 540, Benjamin Franklin Station
Washington, D.C. 20044
(202) 245-1266 (Business Office); (202)
245-1526 (Editorial Office)

Previously entitled *Journal of the
Association of Official Agricultural
Chemists*

First published in 1915

SUBSCRIPTION DATA
Issues and rates: Published bi-monthly.
Average paid circulation: 4500; 15
controlled
Annual rate(s): $30.00, Foreign $32.00
Publisher or Sponsor: Association of Official
Analytical Chemists

EDITORIAL DESCRIPTION
Publishes chemical and biological assay
methods for food drugs, agricultural
products, beverages, cosmetics, coloring
materials and pesticides. Also covers the
official transactions of the Association.
Articles per average issue: 45
Audience: Scientific personnel
Manuscripts accepted in English

MANUSCRIPT INFORMATION
Subject field(s): Analytical methodology in:
fertilizers, feeds, foods, pesticides, drugs,
cosmetics, hazardous substances; forensic
sciences; colors
Manuscript requirements: Style sheet sent
on request.
Preferred length: 10-20 pages
Number of copies to be submitted: Three
Abstract: Yes.
Author information and reprints: Payment:
None.
Is simultaneous submission of article to
other journals permitted: No
Exclusive manuscript rights between
acceptance and publication: Yes
Copyright: Held by publication.
Reprints: Available; cost on sliding scale
Disposition of manuscript:
Query letter: Yes. (If subject area is in
question)
Receipt of manuscript acknowledged: Yes
Decision to publish in: 8-10 weeks
Accepted manuscript published in: 6
months
Rejected manuscript returned: Yes
Rejected manuscript criticized: Yes
Submit to:
Helen L. Reynolds
Editor
(See address above)

SPECIAL STIPULATIONS
All manuscripts subject to technical
review by 2 members of peer group.

BIOCHEMICAL JOURNAL [2071]

7 Warwick Court
London WC1R 5DP, England
01-405-4918

First published in 1906

SUBSCRIPTION DATA
Issues and rates: Published semi-monthly.
Average paid circulation: 5000
Annual rate(s): £105.00 Members £18.00
Publisher or Sponsor: The Biochemical
Society
Managing Editor: J. T. Single

EDITORIAL DESCRIPTION
Contains full-length papers and short
communications describing original
research work in all fields of
biochemistry.
Articles per average issue: 24
Audience: Research workers and students in
biochemistry and related sciences.
Manuscripts accepted in English

MANUSCRIPT INFORMATION
Subject field(s): Biochemistry
Manuscript requirements: See "Instructions
to Authors" January 1 issue
Preferred length: Papers: none; Short
Communications: 2,400 words maximum
Number of copies to be submitted:
Papers: 1, short communications: 2
Abstract: Yes.
Author information and reprints: Payment:
None. contributing members are entitled
to 25 free reprints.
Is simultaneous submission of article to
other journals permitted: No
Exclusive manuscript rights between
acceptance and publication: Yes
Copyright: Held by publication.
Reprints: Available
Disposition of manuscript:
Query letter:
Receipt of manuscript acknowledged: Yes
Decision to publish in: 5 weeks for
papers and 2 weeks for short
communications.
Accepted manuscript published in: 26
weeks for papers and 10 weeks for short
communications.
Rejected manuscript returned: Yes
Rejected manuscript criticized: Yes
Submit to:
John David Killip
Editorial Secretary
(See address above)

BIOCHEMICAL PHARMACOLOGY [2072]

Pergamon Press, Inc.
Fairview Park
Elmsford, New York 10523
(914) 592-7700

First published in 1958

SUBSCRIPTION DATA
Issues and rates: Published semi-monthly.
Annual rate(s): $40.00; Institutions
$175.00

EDITORIAL DESCRIPTION
Provides a forum for rapid publication of
original research papers, short
communications, preliminary
communications and reports in the field
of biochemical pharmacology.
Articles per average issue: Varies
Audience: Professional, academic
Manuscripts accepted in English, French,
German

MANUSCRIPT INFORMATION
Subject field(s): Research carried out with
intact animals, cells, sub-cellular
components, enzymes and model systems
if they define the mode of drug action;
antimicrobial and antiviral agents,
descriptive mathematical models,
computer techniques to elucidate
physiological and behavioral mechanisms
Manuscript requirements: See latest issue for
style requirements.
Preferred length: None for articles;
3,000-5,000 words for commentaries
Number of copies to be submitted: 2,
double-spaced
Abstract: Yes. An abstract in English.
Author information and reprints: Payment:
None.
Is simultaneous submission of article to
other journals permitted: Not permitted.
Exclusive manuscript rights between
acceptance and publication: Yes
Copyright: Held by publication.
Reprints: Available at cost.
Disposition of manuscript:
Query letter: Not necessary.
Receipt of manuscript acknowledged: Yes
Decision to publish in: 4 weeks
Accepted manuscript published in: 5
months
Rejected manuscript returned: Yes, if
return postage is supplied by author.
Rejected manuscript criticized: Reasons
for rejections only
Submit to:
Prof. Alan C. Sartorelli,
Prof. Robert L. Levine
Regional Editor and Associate Editor
Yale University School of Medicine
Sterling Hall of Medicine
333 Cedar Street
New Haven, Connecticut

BIOCHEMISTRY [2073]

1155 16th Street, N.W.
Washington, D.C. 20036

SUBSCRIPTION DATA
Issues and rates: Published bi-weekly.
Average paid circulation: 5,400
Annual rate(s): $60.00
Publisher or Sponsor: American Chemical
Society

EDITORIAL DESCRIPTION
Publishes results of original research in
all areas of biochemistry. Emphasis is

given to the relationship among chemistry, biochemistry and the other biological sciences.

MANUSCRIPT INFORMATION

Subject field(s): Subject matter includes enzymes, proteins, carbohydrates, lipids, nucleic acids and their metabolism, genetics and protein synthesis.

Manuscript requirements: ACS

Number of copies to be submitted: Four

Author information and reprints: Payment: None.

Is simultaneous submission of article to other journals permitted: No

Exclusive manuscript rights between acceptance and publication: Yes

Copyright: Held by the Society

Reprints: Available at cost

Disposition of manuscript:

Receipt of manuscript acknowledged: Yes

Decision to publish in: Two months

Accepted manuscript published in: Three months

Rejected manuscript returned: Yes

Rejected manuscript criticized: Yes

Submit to:

Hans Neurath
Editor
University of Washington
Seattle, Washington 98105

BIO-ORGANIC CHEMISTRY [2074]

An International Journal
Academic Press Inc.
111 Fifth Avenue
New York, New York 10003

First published in 1971

SUBSCRIPTION DATA

Issues and rates: Published quarterly.

Annual rate(s): $37.50; Foreign $41.50

Managing Editor: Eugene F. van Tamelen

EDITORIAL DESCRIPTION

Publishes accounts of research on the organic and physical organic chemistry of biologicaly related reactions.

Articles per average issue: 10

Audience: Organic chemists and biochemists

Manuscripts accepted in English preferred

MANUSCRIPT INFORMATION

Subject field(s): Enzyme reaction; isolation and structure mechanisms of new natural products; bio-genetic type organic synthesis; molecular structure and the behavior of enzymes; prebiotic and evolutionary organic chemistry, chemistry of biopolymers; molecular pharmacology

Manuscript requirements: See latest issue for style requirements. Style sheet sent on request.

Preferred length: As required

Number of copies to be submitted: 3

Abstract: Yes.

Author information and reprints: Payment: None.

Is simultaneous submission of article to other journals permitted: Permitted, but not encouraged.

Exclusive manuscript rights between acceptance and publication: Yes

Copyright: Held by publication.

Reprints: Available at no cost. 50

Additional information: Drawings and formulas other than routine must be of a quality suitable for direct reproduction.

Disposition of manuscript:

Query letter: Not necessary.

Receipt of manuscript acknowledged: Yes

Decision to publish in: 1 month

Accepted manuscript published in: 3 months

Rejected manuscript returned: Yes, with return postage paid by publication.

Rejected manuscript criticized: Yes

Submit to:

Eugene F. van Tamelen
Editor
Department of Chemistry
Stanford University
Stanford, California 94305
(415) 497-3507

BRITISH POLYMER JOURNAL [2075]

Society of Chemistry Industry
14 Belgrave Square
London SW1X 8PS, England
(01) 235-3681

First published in 1969

SUBSCRIPTION DATA

Issues and rates: Published bi-monthly.

Annual rate(s): £18.00; Members £10.80

Publisher or Sponsor: Society of Chemical Industry

Managing Editor: Tristram F. West

EDITORIAL DESCRIPTION

Presents original investigation from the fields of pure and applied polymer science, particularly papers dealing with the special interests of industrial macromolecular chemistry and technology including those of a theoretical nature.

Articles per average issue: 7

Audience: Professional, academic

Manuscripts accepted in English only

MANUSCRIPT INFORMATION

Manuscript requirements: Style sheet sent on request.

Preferred length: No preference

Number of copies to be submitted: 3

Abstract: Yes. A short synopsis of the main points.

Author information and reprints: Payment: Reprints only. 25

Is simultaneous submission of article to other journals permitted: Not permitted.

Exclusive manuscript rights between acceptance and publication: Yes

Reprints: Available at cost.

Disposition of manuscript:

Query letter: Not necessary.

Receipt of manuscript acknowledged: Yes

Rejected manuscript returned: Yes, with return postage paid by publication.

Rejected manuscript criticized: No

Submit to:

Editorial Secretary
(See address above)

CANADIAN JOURNAL OF BIOCHEMISTRY [2076]

National Research Council of Canada
100 Sussex Drive
Ottawa, Ontario K1A OR6, Canada
(613) 992-5411

Previously entitled *Canadian Journal of Biochemistry and Physiology* (1951-1963)

SUBSCRIPTION DATA

Issues and rates: Published monthly.

Average paid circulation: 2650

Annual rate(s): Individuals $12.00; Institutions $24.00

Publisher or Sponsor: National Research Council of Canada

Managing Editor: W. W. Hawkins

EDITORIAL DESCRIPTION

Contains papers on the results of original scientific research in any branch of biochemistry.

Articles per average issue: 18

Audience: Research biochemists

Manuscripts accepted in English and French

MANUSCRIPT INFORMATION

Subject field(s): Amino acid chemistry and metabolism, carbohydrate chemistry, cell biology (biochemical aspects), clinical biochemistry: hormone action, control of carbohydrate and lipid metabolism, enzymology, immunochemistry, lipid chemistry and biosynthesis, microbial metabolism, neurochemistry, nucleic acid chemistry, nucleic acid metabolism, nutrition and metabolism

Manuscript requirements: Style sheet sent on request.

Preferred length: Under 25 pages

Number of copies to be submitted: Two

Abstract: Yes.

Author information and reprints: Payment: None.

Is simultaneous submission of article to other journals permitted: No

Exclusive manuscript rights between acceptance and publication: Yes

Copyright: Held by publication.

Reprints: Available only at time of publication cost is dependent on length.

Disposition of manuscript:

Query letter:

Receipt of manuscript acknowledged: Yes

Decision to publish in: 3 months

Accepted manuscript published in: 3 months

Rejected manuscript returned: Yes

Rejected manuscript criticized: Yes

Submit to:

Antoine D'Iorio
Editor
Faculty of Sciences

Chemistry

Pavillion Marion, University of Ottawa
Ottawa, Ontario K1N 6N5, Canada
(613) 231-2408

CANADIAN JOURNAL OF CHEMISTRY [2077]

National Research Council of Canada
100 Sussex Drive
Ottawa, Ontario K1A OR6, Canada
(613) 992-5411

Previously entitled *Canadian Journal of Research*

First published in 1929

SUBSCRIPTION DATA
Issues and rates: Published semi-monthly.
Average paid circulation: 2900
Annual rate(s): Individuals $24;
Institutions $48.00

EDITORIAL DESCRIPTION
Publishes the results of original scientific research in any branch of chemistry.
Articles per average issue: 26
Audience: Professional, research
Manuscripts accepted in English, French

MANUSCRIPT INFORMATION
Subject field(s): Inorganic, organometallic, solution properties, electrochemistry, spectrocopy, physical organic chemistry, etc.
Manuscript requirements: Style sheet sent on request.
Preferred length: Under 25 pages
Number of copies to be submitted: Three
Abstract: Yes
Author information and reprints: Payment: None.
Is simultaneous submission of article to other journals permitted: No
Exclusive manuscript rights between acceptance and publication: Yes
Copyright: Held by publication.
Reprints: Available at cost.
Disposition of manuscript:
Query letter: No
Receipt of manuscript acknowledged: Yes
Decision to publish in: 3 months
Accepted manuscript published in: 4 months
Rejected manuscript returned: Yes
Rejected manuscript criticized: Yes
Submit to:
K. O. Kutschke
Editor
(See address above)
(613) 992-2024

CARBOHYDRATE RESEARCH [2078]

An International Journal
Elsevier Scientific Publishing Company
P. O. Box 211, Jan van Galenstraat 335
Amsterdam, The Netherlands
(020) 515-9222

First published in 1965

SUBSCRIPTION DATA
Issues and rates: Published monthly.
Annual rate(s): Dfl. 665.00 plus postage

EDITORIAL DESCRIPTION
Publishes reports of original research in carbohydrate chemistry and biochemistry; reviews of specialized topics and book reviews.
Articles per average issue: 30
Audience: Professional, academic, industrial
Manuscripts accepted in English, French, German

MANUSCRIPT INFORMATION
Subject field(s): Sugars and their derivatives; chemical synthesis; structures and stereochemistry; reactions and their mechanisms; isolation of natural products; action of enzymes; immunochemistry; biology; pharmacology; and technological aspects
Manuscript requirements: Style sheet sent on request.
Preferred length: No fixed length
Number of copies to be submitted: 3
Abstract: Yes. Full papers should include an abstract of 80-200 words. Papers in French or German should include an additional one in English.
Author information and reprints: Payment: Reprints only. 50 reprints
Is simultaneous submission of article to other journals permitted: Not permitted.
Exclusive manuscript rights between acceptance and publication: Yes
Copyright: Held by publication.
Reprints: Available at cost.
Additional information: Submit original figures with the manuscript.
Disposition of manuscript:
Query letter: Not necessary.
Receipt of manuscript acknowledged: Yes
Decision to publish in: 1 month
Accepted manuscript published in: 3 months
Rejected manuscript returned: Yes, with return postage paid by publication.
Rejected manuscript criticized: Reasons for rejections only
Submit to:
D. Horton
Department of Chemistry
The Ohio State University
Columbus, Ohio 43210

R. Stuart Tipson
10303 Parkwood Drive
Kensington, Maryland 20795

R. W. Jeanloz
Laboratory for Carbohydrate Research
Massachusetts General Hospital
Boston, Massachusetts 02114

CARBON [2079]

An International Journal
Pergamon Press, Inc.
Fairview Park
Elmsford, New York 10523
(914) 592-7700

First published in 1963

SUBSCRIPTION DATA
Issues and rates: Published bi-monthly.
Annual rate(s): $25.00; Institutions $80.00
Publisher or Sponsor: American Carbon Committee

EDITORIAL DESCRIPTION
Provides an outlet for the publication of original work in the physics and chemistry as well as the technology of the class of materials ranging from organic crystals and polymers through chars and carbons to graphite.
Articles per average issue: 7-10
Audience: Physicists, chemists, technologists
Manuscripts accepted in English, French, German

MANUSCRIPT INFORMATION
Subject field(s): Only those organic substances which are related in some way to aromatic or tetrahedrally bonded carbonaceous solids, or which can be transformed into them by heat or other means, are of interest.
Manuscript requirements: See latest issue for style requirements.
Preferred length: As required
Number of copies to be submitted: 3
Abstract: Yes. Not to exceed 200 words in English; papers in French and German should include a summary at the end in English of about 650 words.
Author information and reprints: Payment: Reprints only. 50 reprints
Is simultaneous submission of article to other journals permitted: Not permitted.
Exclusive manuscript rights between acceptance and publication: Yes
Copyright: Held by publication.
Reprints: Available at cost.
Disposition of manuscript:
Query letter: Not necessary.
Receipt of manuscript acknowledged: Yes
Decision to publish in: 4 weeks
Accepted manuscript published in: 5 months
Rejected manuscript returned: Yes, if return postage is supplied by author.
Rejected manuscript criticized: Reasons for rejections only
Submit to:
S. Mrozowski
Editor-in-Chief
Carbon Research Laboratory
State University of New York at Buffalo
Buffalo, New York 14214

CHEMICA SCRIPTA [2080]

An International Journal on Progress in Methodology and Basic Knowledge
The Almqvist & Wiksell Periodical Company
P.O. Box 62
S-101 20 Stockholm 1, Sweden
08/23 79 90

SUBSCRIPTION DATA
Issues and rates: 2 volumes of 5 issues each per year

Average paid circulation: Not available.
Annual rate(s): Sw.Kr. 310.00; Foreign $78.75
Publisher or Sponsor: The Royal Swedish Academy of Sciences
Managing Editor: Stig Claesson

EDITORIAL DESCRIPTION

Publishes articles on progress in methodology and basic knowledge, i.e., articles on new theoretical approaches and new methods of synthesis, analysis, separation and computation as well as new instruments and techniques of measurement. Review articles on recent development in these areas are occasionally included.
Articles per average issue: Varies
Manuscripts accepted in English

MANUSCRIPT INFORMATION

Manuscript requirements: See latest issue for style requirements.
Author information and reprints: Payment: None.
Is simultaneous submission of article to other journals permitted: No
Exclusive manuscript rights between acceptance and publication: Yes
Copyright: Held by publication.
Additional information: Additional information sent on request.
Submit to:
Editor
The Royal Swedish Academy of Sciences
S-104 05 Stockholm 50, Sweden

CHEMICAL TECHNOLOGY* [2081]
Bassett Building, Room 201
382 Springfield Avenue
Summit, New Jersey 07901
(201) 273-4925

SUBSCRIPTION DATA
Issues and rates: Published monthly.
Average paid circulation: 20,000
Annual rate(s): $18.00, Members $9.00
Publisher or Sponsor: American Chemical Society

EDITORIAL DESCRIPTION
Publishes articles that bear on the industrial practice of chemistry, including law; social and organizational psychology; materials and energy use and generation.

MANUSCRIPT INFORMATION
Manuscript requirements: See latest issue for style requirements.
Preferred length: 1,000 to 8,000 words
Number of copies to be submitted: Three
Author information and reprints: Payment: By publication to author. $50.00 per article.
Is simultaneous submission of article to other journals permitted: Yes
Exclusive manuscript rights between acceptance and publication: Yes
Copyright: Held by publication.
Reprints: Available, cost varies with number and length

Additional information: Publication expects high standards of style and content.
Disposition of manuscript:
Receipt of manuscript acknowledged: No
Decision to publish in: 60 days
Accepted manuscript published in: 6 months
Rejected manuscript returned: Yes, if self-addressed, stamped envelope is sent with manuscript.
Rejected manuscript criticized: Yes
Submit to:
B. J. Luberoff
Editor
(See address above)

CHEMICO-BIOLOGICAL INTERACTIONS [2082]
Elsevier Scientific Publishing Company
Jan van Galenstraat 335, P. O. Box 211
Amsterdam, The Netherlands
(020) 515-92222

First published in 1969

SUBSCRIPTION DATA
Annual rate(s): Dfl. 236
Managing Editor: G. P. Warick, London

EDITORIAL DESCRIPTION
An international journal devoted to the mechanisms by which exogenous chemicals produce changes in biological mechanisms.
Articles per average issue: 6-10
Audience: Research scientists
Manuscripts accepted in English, French, German

MANUSCRIPT INFORMATION
Subject field(s): Exogenous chemicals may be either synthetic or naturally occurring; they may include toxins, chemotherapeutic agents, carcinogens, herbicides, pesticides, teratogens, food additives, pollutants, etc.
Manuscript requirements: See latest issue for style requirements.
Preferred length: As required
Number of copies to be submitted: 3
Abstract: Yes. 200-300 words
Author information and reprints: Payment: Reprints only. 50 reprints
Is simultaneous submission of article to other journals permitted: Not permitted.
Exclusive manuscript rights between acceptance and publication: Yes
Copyright: Held by Biological and Medical Press B. V. (Elsevier Division)
Reprints: Not available.
Disposition of manuscript:
Query letter: Not necessary, but advisable.
Receipt of manuscript acknowledged: Yes
Decision to publish in: 2-6 weeks
Accepted manuscript published in: 6-8 weeks
Rejected manuscript returned: Yes, with return postage paid by publication.
Rejected manuscript criticized: Reasons for rejections only
Submit to:
Dr. J. R. Fouts
Editor

National Institutes of Environmental Health Sciences
P. O. Box 12233
Research Triangle Park, North Carolina 27709

CHEMISTRY [2083]
1155 16th Street N.W.
Washington, D.C. 20036
(202) 872-4577

Previously entitled *Chemistry Leaflet*

First published in 1927

SUBSCRIPTION DATA
Issues and rates: Eleven issues per year
Average paid circulation: 38,000
Annual rate(s): $6.00, Foreign $10.50
Publisher or Sponsor: American Chemical Society
Managing Editor: Eugenia Keller

EDITORIAL DESCRIPTION
Contains news, research developments, history, biography, survey articles in chemistry and allied sciences.
Articles per average issue: 4
Audience: Academic, professional
Manuscripts accepted in English

MANUSCRIPT INFORMATION
Manuscript requirements: See latest issue for style requirements.
Preferred length: 2,000-3,000 words; 6-10 pages
Number of copies to be submitted: Three
Abstract: No
Author information and reprints: Payment: None.
Is simultaneous submission of article to other journals permitted: No
Exclusive manuscript rights between acceptance and publication: Yes
Copyright: Held by publication.
Reprints: Available, $1.90 for 1st copy; $.35 each thereafter.
Disposition of manuscript:
Query letter: No
Receipt of manuscript acknowledged: Yes
Decision to publish in: One month
Accepted manuscript published in: Varies
Rejected manuscript returned: Yes
Rejected manuscript criticized: No
Submit to:
Eugenia Keller
Managing Editor
(See address above)

CHEMISTRY AND INDUSTRY [2084]
Society of Chemical Industry
14 Belgrave Square
London SW1X 8PS, England
(01) 235-3681

First published in 1923

SUBSCRIPTION DATA
Issues and rates: Published semi-monthly.

Chemistry

Average paid circulation: 3,328; 5,024 controlled
Annual rate(s): £28; Members Free
Publisher or Sponsor: Society of Chemical Industry
Managing Editor: Tristram F. West

EDITORIAL DESCRIPTION
To advance applied chemistry in all its branches
Articles per average issue: 7
Audience: Persons in industry and academic institutions concerned with applied and pure chemistry
Manuscripts accepted in English only

MANUSCRIPT INFORMATION
Subject field(s): Review articles on aspects of chemistry within the Society's field of interest; articles on current plant practice; short papers on new methods; apparatus and techniques and brief communications on original work having features of novelty and urgency.
Manuscript requirements: Style sheet sent on request.
Preferred length: No Preference
Number of copies to be submitted: 2
Abstract: Not necessary.
Author information and reprints: Payment: Reprints only. 25
Is simultaneous submission of article to other journals permitted: Not permitted.
Exclusive manuscript rights between acceptance and publication: Yes
Copyright: Held by publication.
Reprints: Available at cost.
Disposition of manuscript:
Query letter: Not necessary.
Receipt of manuscript acknowledged: Yes
Rejected manuscript returned: Yes, with return postage paid by publication.
Rejected manuscript criticized: No
Submit to:
Dr. T. F. West
Editor
(See address above)

CLINICA CHIMICA ACTA [2085]

International Journal of Clinical Chemistry
Elsevier Scientific Publishing Company
Jan van Galenstraat 335, P. O. Box 211
Amsterdam, The Netherlands
(020) 515-9222

First published in 1956

SUBSCRIPTION DATA
Issues and rates: Published semi-monthly.
Annual rate(s): $297.00
Managing Editor: S. C. Frazer, Aberdeen

EDITORIAL DESCRIPTION
Publishes papers reporting original research, critical reviews, and technical notes in the field of clinical chemistry, defined as the study of disease.
Articles per average issue: 20
Audience: Scientific
Manuscripts accepted in English, German, French

MANUSCRIPT INFORMATION
Subject field(s): Almost everything relevant to human or animal disease
Manuscript requirements: See latest issue for style requirements. Style sheet sent on request.
Preferred length: 4,000 words
Number of copies to be submitted: 2
Abstract: Yes. A summary in English of about 200 words.
Author information and reprints: Payment: Reprints only. 50 reprints
Is simultaneous submission of article to other journals permitted: Not permitted.
Exclusive manuscript rights between acceptance and publication: Yes
Copyright: Held by publication.
Reprints: Available at cost.
Disposition of manuscript:
Query letter: Not necessary.
Receipt of manuscript acknowledged: Yes
Decision to publish in: 1-2 months
Accepted manuscript published in: 3-4 months
Rejected manuscript returned: No
Rejected manuscript criticized: No
Submit to:
Dr. M. Rubin
Editorial Board
Department of Biochemistry
Georgetown University School of Medicine
Washington, D. C. 20007

CLINICAL CHEMISTRY [2086]

Journal of the American Association of Clinical Chemists
P.O. Box 5218
Winston-Salem, North Carolina 27103
(919) 725-0208

First published in 1955

SUBSCRIPTION DATA
Issues and rates: Published monthly.
Average paid circulation: 8300; 1000 controlled
Annual rate(s): $18.00, Pan-Am $19.00, Foreign $19.50

EDITORIAL DESCRIPTION
Welcomes contributions on the application of chemistry to the understanding of the human organism in health and disease. Articles submitted should contain original information, experimental or theoretical, that advances the science of clinical chemistry. This includes basic materials or principles, analytical techniques, instrumentation, data processing, statistical anaylses of data, clinical investigations in which chemistry has played a major role, and experimental (laboratory animal) investigations of chemically oriented problems of human disease.
Articles per average issue: 20
Manuscripts accepted in English

MANUSCRIPT INFORMATION
Subject field(s): Methods, applications to medicine, quality assurance, data processing, analytical systems, toxicology, enzymology, endocrinology, statistics

Manuscript requirements: ACS, AIBS
Preferred length: None
Number of copies to be submitted: Two
Author information and reprints: Payment: None.
Is simultaneous submission of article to other journals permitted: No
Exclusive manuscript rights between acceptance and publication: Yes
Copyright: Held by publication.
Reprints: Available
Disposition of manuscript:
Query letter:
Receipt of manuscript acknowledged: Yes
Decision to publish in: 3-4 weeks
Accepted manuscript published in: 8 weeks
Rejected manuscript returned: Yes
Rejected manuscript criticized: Yes
Submit to:
J. Stanton King, Jr.
Executive Editor
(See address above)

COMPARATIVE BIOCHEMISTRY AND PHYSIOLOGY. PARTS A, B, AND C [2087]

Pergamon Press, Inc.
Fairview Park
Elmsford, New York 10523
592-7700

First published in 1961

SUBSCRIPTION DATA
Issues and rates: Published monthly.
Annual rate(s): $55.00 (complete); $25.00 (singly); Institutions $160.00 (complete)

EDITORIAL DESCRIPTION
Presents original research in the biochemistry and physiology of animals. Particular emphasis is given to papers that approach the subject from a comparative point of view.
Audience: Professional, academic
Manuscripts accepted in English (French, German)

MANUSCRIPT INFORMATION
Manuscript requirements: See latest issue for style requirements.
Number of copies to be submitted: 2
Abstract: Yes. Of about 50 words.
Author information and reprints: Payment: None.
Is simultaneous submission of article to other journals permitted: Not permitted.
Exclusive manuscript rights between acceptance and publication: Yes
Copyright: Held by publication.
Reprints: Available at cost.
Disposition of manuscript:
Query letter: Not necessary.
Receipt of manuscript acknowledged: Yes
Decision to publish in: 4 weeks
Accepted manuscript published in: 5 months
Rejected manuscript returned: Yes, if return postage is supplied by author.

Rejected manuscript criticized: Reasons for rejections only
Submit to:
Prof. G.A. Kerkut
Editor
Department of Physiology and Biochemistry
University of Southampton
Southampton S09 3TY, England

COORDINATION CHEMISTRY REVIEWS [2088]

An International Journal
Elsevier Scientific Publishing Company
P. O. Box 211, Jan van Galenstraat 335
Amsterdam, The Netherlands
(020) 515-9222

First published in 1966

SUBSCRIPTION DATA
Issues and rates: Published monthly.
Annual rate(s): Dfl. 339 for all

EDITORIAL DESCRIPTION
Contains specialized reviews of the state of development in all aspects of coordination chemistry at the research level.
Audience: Professional, academic
Manuscripts accepted in English

MANUSCRIPT INFORMATION
Subject field(s): Coordination chemistry in its widest sense
Manuscript requirements: See latest issue for style requirements. Style sheet sent on request.
Number of copies to be submitted: 2
Abstract: Not necessary.
Author information and reprints: Payment: By publication to author.
Is simultaneous submission of article to other journals permitted: Not permitted.
Exclusive manuscript rights between acceptance and publication. Yes
Copyright: Held by publication.
Reprints: Available at cost.
Disposition of manuscript:
Query letter: Not necessary, but advisable.
Receipt of manuscript acknowledged: Yes
Decision to publish in: 4-6 weeks
Accepted manuscript published in: 5-6 months
Rejected manuscript returned: Yes, with return postage paid by publication.
Rejected manuscript criticized: Sometimes
Submit to:
Dr. A. B. P. Lever
Editor
Department of Chemistry
York University, 4700 Keel Street
Downsview, Ontario M3J 1P3, Canada

CRC CRITICAL REVIEWS IN ANALYTICAL CHEMISTRY [2089]

CRC Press, Inc.
18901 Cranwood Parkway
Cleveland, Ohio 44128
(216) 475-9000

First published in 1970

SUBSCRIPTION DATA
Issues and rates: Published quarterly.
Average paid circulation: 1,000
Annual rate(s): $56.00, Foreign $64.00

EDITORIAL DESCRIPTION
The basic concept of this program is to provide a qualitative approach to the total mass of scientific literature published throughout the world in this discipline. This is accomplished by utilizing outstanding experts in each field to select and critically evaluate the most significant papers published in their particular specialties. To insure accuracy and objectivity, each review is refereed prior to publication.
Articles per average issue: 3
Audience: Research Laboratories
Manuscripts accepted in English

MANUSCRIPT INFORMATION
Subject field(s): Analytical chemistry
Manuscript requirements: Style sheet sent on request.
Preferred length: 75-150 pages
Number of copies to be submitted: Three
Abstract: Yes.
Author information and reprints: Payment: By publication to author.
Is simultaneous submission of article to other journals permitted: No
Exclusive manuscript rights between acceptance and publication: Yes
Copyright: Held by publication.
Reprints: Available, 25 free to author
Disposition of manuscript:
Query letter:
Receipt of manuscript acknowledged: Yes
Decision to publish in: 3 weeks
Accepted manuscript published in: 3 months
Rejected manuscript returned: Yes
Rejected manuscript criticized: Yes
Submit to:
Gerald A. Becker
Director, Editorial Operations
(See address above)

EASTMAN ORGANIC CHEMICAL BULLETIN [2090]

Eastman Kodak Company
343 State Street
Rochester, New York 14650
(716) 325-2000 ext. 55105

First published in 1925

SUBSCRIPTION DATA
Issues and rates: Published quarterly.
Average paid circulation: 75,000

EDITORIAL DESCRIPTION
Publishes articles on organic chemistry in the areas of pure and applied research.
Articles per average issue: 1
Audience: Organic chemists
Manuscripts accepted in English

MANUSCRIPT INFORMATION
Subject field(s): Organic chemistry
Manuscript requirements: Style sheet sent on request.
Preferred length: 2000 words; 12-18 pages
Number of copies to be submitted: Two
Abstract:
Author information and reprints: Payment: None.
Is simultaneous submission of article to other journals permitted: No
Exclusive manuscript rights between acceptance and publication: Yes
Copyright: Held by publication.
Reprints: Available, 24 free, additional at cost.
Additional information: Manuscripts should be in proper style, with footnotes, references, tables, charts and captions on separate pages. The author is responsible for his own artwork.
Disposition of manuscript:
Query letter: Yes.
Receipt of manuscript acknowledged: Yes
Decision to publish in: 8 weeks
Accepted manuscript published in: 6 months
Rejected manuscript returned: Yes, if self-addressed, stamped envelope is sent with manuscript.
Rejected manuscript criticized: No
Submit to:
Frank C. Dixon Technical Editor
(See address above)

SPECIAL STIPULATIONS
Submitted manuscripts must be cleared and approved for publication by author's management, and such approval must be in writing.

ELECTROCHIMICA ACTA [2091]

Official Journal of the International Society of Electrochemistry
Pergamon Press, Inc.
Fairview Park
Elmsford, New York 10523
(914) 592-7700

First published in 1959

SUBSCRIPTION DATA
Issues and rates: Published monthly.
Annual rate(s): $25.00; Institutions $140.00
Publisher or Sponsor: International Society of Electrochemistry

EDITORIAL DESCRIPTION
Publishes original research and critical reviews not previously published elsewhere, in the field of pure and applied electrochemistry.
Articles per average issue: 5
Audience: Professional, academic

Chemistry

Manuscripts accepted in English preferred, French, German

MANUSCRIPT INFORMATION

Manuscript requirements: See latest issue for style requirements.

Preferred length: None

Number of copies to be submitted: 3 double-spaced, typewritten

Abstract: Yes. Not exceeding 200 words in the language of the paper. For papers written in French or German include one also in English.

Author information and reprints: Payment: Reprints only. 50 reprints

Is simultaneous submission of article to other journals permitted: Not permitted.

Exclusive manuscript rights between acceptance and publication: Yes

Copyright: Held by publication.

Reprints: Available at cost.

Disposition of manuscript:

Query letter: Not necessary.

Receipt of manuscript acknowledged: Yes

Decision to publish in: 4 weeks

Accepted manuscript published in: 5 months

Rejected manuscript returned: Yes, if return postage is supplied by author.

Rejected manuscript criticized: Reasons for rejections only

Submit to:

Prof. H. R. Thirsk
Electrochemistry Research Laboratories,
School of Chemistry
University of Newcastle upon Tyne
Newcastle upon Tyne NE1 7RU,
England

Or submit to the appropriate Sectional Editor.

EUROPEAN JOURNAL OF BIOCHEMISTRY [2092]

Springer-Verlag
175 Fifth Avenue
New York, New York 10010

First published in 1906

SUBSCRIPTION DATA

Annual rate(s): DM 105 per volume

Publisher or Sponsor: The Federation of European Biochemical Societies

EDITORIAL DESCRIPTION

Papers on fundamental aspects of biochemistry or molecular biology, provided that they describe results which make a sufficient contribution, either experimental or theoretical, to our understanding of biological problems at the chemical or physical level, or describe new methods applicable to biochemistry.

Manuscripts accepted in English, also French, German

MANUSCRIPT INFORMATION

Manuscript requirements: Style sheet sent on request.

Preferred length: As required

Number of copies to be submitted: 3

Abstract: Yes. Papers written in French or German should include an extended summary in English.

Author information and reprints: Payment: Reprints only. 40 offprints

Is simultaneous submission of article to other journals permitted: Not permitted.

Exclusive manuscript rights between acceptance and publication: Yes

Copyright: Held by the European Federation of Biochemical Societies

Reprints: Available at cost.

Submit to:

Professor Claude Liébecq
Editor-in-Chief
European Journal of Biochemistry
Boulevard de la Constitution, 69
B-4000 Liège, Belgium

GEOCHIMICA ET COSMOCHIMICA ACTA [2093]

Journal of the Geochemical Society and the Meteoritical Society
Pergamon Press, Inc.
Fairview Park
Elmsford, New York 10523
(914) 592 7700

First published in 1950

SUBSCRIPTION DATA

Issues and rates: Published monthly.

Annual rate(s): $25.00; Institutions $100.00

Publisher or Sponsor: The Geochemical Society; The Meteoritical Society

EDITORIAL DESCRIPTION

Publishes original papers in the broad areas of geochemistry and astrochemistry and their related disciplines.

Articles per average issue: 5-8

Audience: Professional, academic

Manuscripts accepted in English (French, German)

MANUSCRIPT INFORMATION

Manuscript requirements: See latest issue for style requirements.

Preferred length: None

Number of copies to be submitted: 2

Abstract: Yes

Author information and reprints: Payment: Reprints only. 50 reprints

Is simultaneous submission of article to other journals permitted: Not permitted.

Exclusive manuscript rights between acceptance and publication: Yes

Copyright: Held by publication.

Reprints: Available at cost.

Disposition of manuscript:

Query letter: Not necessary.

Receipt of manuscript acknowledged: Yes

Decision to publish in: 4 weeks

Accepted manuscript published in: 5 months

Rejected manuscript returned: Yes, if return postage is supplied by author.

Rejected manuscript criticized: Reasons for rejections only

Submit to:

Prof. D. M. Shaw
Executive Editor
Department of Geology
McMaster University
Hamilton 16, Ontario L8S 4M1, Canada

HISTOCHEMISTRY [2094]

Springer-Verlag
175 Fifth Avenue
New York, New York 10010

First published in 1958

SUBSCRIPTION DATA

Annual rate(s): DM 148 per volume

Managing Editor: Professor Dr. T. H. Schiebler

EDITORIAL DESCRIPTION

Publishes original papers dealing with problems of histo- and cytochemistry and histophysics, especially with methods thereof.

Manuscripts accepted in English, French, German

MANUSCRIPT INFORMATION

Subject field(s): Fractionation and homogenization techniques, autoradiography, polarization optics, fluorescent microscopy

Manuscript requirements: See latest issue for style requirements. Style sheet sent on request.

Preferred length: As required

Number of copies to be submitted: 2

Abstract: Yes. Each paper should include a short summary. Those written in French and German should carry in addition a more detailed summary in English.

Author information and reprints: Payment: Reprints only. 75 offprints

Is simultaneous submission of article to other journals permitted: Not permitted.

Exclusive manuscript rights between acceptance and publication: Yes

Copyright: Held by publication.

Reprints: Available at cost.

Submit to:

Professor Dr. Helen A. Padykula
Editor
Laboratory of Electron-Microscopy
Wellesley College
Wellesley, Massachusetts 02181

IMMUNOCHEMISTRY [2095]

An International Journal of Molecular Immunology
Pergamon Press, Inc.
Fairview Park
Elmsford, New York 10523
(914) 592-7700

First published in 1964

SUBSCRIPTION DATA

Issues and rates: Published monthly.

Annual rate(s): $25.00; Institutions $90.00

EDITORIAL DESCRIPTION

Publishes original research in immunology as applied to the physical, biological and medical sciences.

Articles per average issue: 4-8

Audience: Professional, academic

Manuscripts accepted in English, German, French, Spanish, Russian

MANUSCRIPT INFORMATION

Subject field(s): Chemical, physical, molecular aspects of the immunologic process.

Manuscript requirements: See latest issue for style requirements.

Preferred length: None

Number of copies to be submitted: Original and 2 copies

Abstract: Yes. In English as well as in the language used for the article.

Author information and reprints: Payment: By publication to author.

Reprints: Available at no cost. 100, if page charges paid.

Disposition of manuscript:

Query letter: Not necessary.

Receipt of manuscript acknowledged: Yes

Decision to publish in: 4 weeks

Accepted manuscript published in: 5 months

Rejected manuscript returned: Yes, if return postage is supplied by author.

Rejected manuscript criticized: Reasons for rejections only

Submit to:

Prof. Dan H. Campbell
Chairman, Editorial Board
California Institute of Technology
Department of Chemistry
Pasadena, California 91109

Prof. Fred Karush
Editorial Board
University of Pennsylvania School of Medicine
Department of Microbiology
Philadelphia, Pennsylvania 19104

INORGANIC CHEMISTRY* [2096]

American Chemical Society
1155 16th Street, N.W.
Washington, D.C. 20036

SUBSCRIPTION DATA

Issues and rates: Published monthly.

Average paid circulation: 6,000

Annual rate(s): $36.00, Members $18.00

Publisher or Sponsor: American Chemical Society

EDITORIAL DESCRIPTION

Publishes fundamental studies, both experimental and theoretical, in all phases of inorganic chemistry.

MANUSCRIPT INFORMATION

Subject field(s): Inorganic chemistry: synthesis and properties of new compounds, quantitative studies on structure, thermodynamics and kinetics of inorganic reactions.

Manuscript requirements: ACS

Number of copies to be submitted: Three

Author information and reprints: Payment: None.

Is simultaneous submission of article to other journals permitted: No

Exclusive manuscript rights between acceptance and publication: Yes

Copyright: Held by the American Chemical Society

Reprints: Available at cost

Disposition of manuscript:

Receipt of manuscript acknowledged: Yes

Decision to publish in: Three months

Accepted manuscript published in: Three months

Rejected manuscript returned: Yes

Rejected manuscript criticized: Yes

Submit to:

M. Frederick Hawthorne
Editor
Department of Chemistry
University of California
Los Angeles, California 90024

INORGANIC AND NUCLEAR CHEMISTRY LETTERS [2097]

Pergamon Press, Inc.
Fairview Park
Elmsford, New York 10523
(914) 592-7700

First published in 1965

SUBSCRIPTION DATA

Issues and rates: Published monthly.

Annual rate(s): $25.00; Institutions $95.00

EDITORIAL DESCRIPTION

Contains the results of original research in the broad fields of inorganic and nuclear chemistry.

Articles per average issue: 20-25

Audience: Professional, academic

Manuscripts accepted in English

MANUSCRIPT INFORMATION

Manuscript requirements: See latest issue for style requirements.

Preferred length: 5 pages

Number of copies to be submitted: 2

Abstract: Yes

Author information and reprints: Payment: None.

Is simultaneous submission of article to other journals permitted: Not permitted.

Exclusive manuscript rights between acceptance and publication: Yes

Copyright: Held by publication.

Reprints: Available at cost.

Disposition of manuscript:

Query letter: Not necessary.

Receipt of manuscript acknowledged: Yes

Decision to publish in: 4 weeks

Accepted manuscript published in: 5 months

Rejected manuscript returned: Yes, if return postage is supplied by author.

Rejected manuscript criticized: Reasons for rejections only

Submit to:

Joseph J. Katz
Editor-in-Chief
Argonne National Laboratory
9700 South Cass Avenue
Argonne, Illinois 60440

INTERNATIONAL JOURNAL OF PEPTIDE AND PROTEIN RESEARCH [2098]

Munksgaard International Publishers
35 Norre Sogade
DK-1370 Copenhagen K, Denmark
(01) 12 70 30

Previously entitled *International Journal of Protein Research*

First published in 1969

SUBSCRIPTION DATA

Issues and rates: Published bi-monthly.

Average paid circulation: 1000

Annual rate(s): Dkr. 336.00; Foreign $57.15

EDITORIAL DESCRIPTION

Contains original papers concerning peptides and proteins and their basic elements from every conceivable angle, such as chemical, physico-chemical, physiological, including experimental and theoretical work.

Articles per average issue: 8

Manuscripts accepted in English

MANUSCRIPT INFORMATION

Subject field(s): Peptides, proteins, amino acids

Manuscript requirements: See latest issue for style requirements.

Preferred length: 20 pages maximum

Number of copies to be submitted: Two

Abstract: Yes

Author information and reprints: Payment: None. 50 free reprints.

Is simultaneous submission of article to other journals permitted: No

Exclusive manuscript rights between acceptance and publication: Yes

Copyright: Held by author.

Reprints: Available

Disposition of manuscript:

Query letter: No

Receipt of manuscript acknowledged: Yes

Decision to publish in: 6 weeks

Accepted manuscript published in: 6-9 months

Rejected manuscript returned: Yes

Rejected manuscript criticized: Yes

Submit to:

Peter Fonss-Bech
Editor-in-Chief
Spaden B 6
DK-2630 Tastrup, Denmark
45-1 35 21 33

Chemistry

ISRAEL JOURNAL OF CHEMISTRY [2099]

P.O.B. 801
Jerusalem, Israel 91000
227375

Previously entitled *Bulletin of the Research Council of Israel, Sec. A*

First published in 1951

SUBSCRIPTION DATA
Issues and rates: Published semi-monthly.
  Average paid circulation: 1750
  Annual rate(s): $32.00
Managing Editor: L. Lester

EDITORIAL DESCRIPTION
  Contains articles on general chemistry.
Articles per average issue: 3
Audience: Chemists
  Manuscripts accepted in English and French

MANUSCRIPT INFORMATION
Subject field(s): Chemistry
Manuscript requirements: CA
  Preferred length: 20 pages
  Number of copies to be submitted: Three
  Abstract: Yes.
Author information and reprints: Payment: None.
  Is simultaneous submission of article to other journals permitted: No
  Exclusive manuscript rights between acceptance and publication: Yes
  Copyright: Held by publication.
  Reprints: Available, cost depends on length
Disposition of manuscript:
  Query letter:
  Receipt of manuscript acknowledged: Yes
  Decision to publish in: Three months
  Accepted manuscript published in: 6-9 months
  Rejected manuscript returned: Yes
  Rejected manuscript criticized: Yes
Submit to:
  Editor
  (See address above)

JOURNAL OF APPLIED CHEMISTRY AND BIOTECHNOLOGY [2100]

14 Belgrave Square
London SWIX 8PS, England
01 235-3681

Previously entitled *Journal of Applied Chemistry*

First published in 1971

SUBSCRIPTION DATA
Issues and rates: Published monthly.
  Average paid circulation: 2,100
  Annual rate(s): £28.00 Members £16.80

Publisher or Sponsor: Society of Chemical Industry
Managing Editor: Tristram F. West

EDITORIAL DESCRIPTION
  Contains papers in all areas of applied organic and inorganic chemistry.
Articles per average issue: 9
Audience: Industrial and academic chemists, and related technologists
  Manuscripts accepted in English

MANUSCRIPT INFORMATION
Subject field(s): All branches of inorganic and organic chemistry including building materials, catalysis, dyes, kinetics, ion exchange, enzyme technology
Manuscript requirements: See latest issue for style requirements.
  Preferred length: As required; normally 6 pages
  Number of copies to be submitted: 2
  Abstract: Yes. A short synopsis drawing attention to the salient points intelligible without reference to the paper itself.
Author information and reprints: Payment: Reprints only. 25 reprints
  Is simultaneous submission of article to other journals permitted: Not permitted.
  Exclusive manuscript rights between acceptance and publication: Yes
  Copyright: Held by publication.
  Reprints: Available at cost.
Additional information: See instructions to authors.
Disposition of manuscript:
  Query letter: Not necessary.
  Receipt of manuscript acknowledged: Yes
  Decision to publish in: Up to 3 months
  Accepted manuscript published in: 4 months
  Rejected manuscript returned: Yes, with return postage paid by publication.
  Rejected manuscript criticized: No
Submit to:
  Cyril A. Price
  Editorial Secretary
  (See address above)

JOURNAL OF BIOCHEMISTRY [2101]

Japan Academic Societies' Centre
Yayoi 2-4-16 Bunkyo-ku,
Tokyo 113, Japan
(03) 815-1913

First published in 1925

SUBSCRIPTION DATA
Issues and rates: Published monthly.
  Average paid circulation: 2300; 100 controlled
  Annual rate(s): Foreign $75.00
Publisher or Sponsor: Japanese Biochemical Society
Managing Editor: Ryo Sato

EDITORIAL DESCRIPTION
  Publishes original papers in the field of biochemistry in general.
Articles per average issue: 30
  Manuscripts accepted in English, French, German, Japanese

MANUSCRIPT INFORMATION
Subject field(s): Biochemistry in general
Manuscript requirements: Style sheet sent on request.
  Number of copies to be submitted: Three
Author information and reprints: Payment: By author to publication. 600 Yen per page.
  Is simultaneous submission of article to other journals permitted: No
  Exclusive manuscript rights between acceptance and publication: Yes
  Copyright: Held by publication.
  Reprints: Available
Disposition of manuscript:
  Receipt of manuscript acknowledged: Yes
  Decision to publish in: One to three months
  Accepted manuscript published in: Seven to nine months
  Rejected manuscript returned: Yes
  Rejected manuscript criticized: Yes
Submit to:
  Japanese Biochemical Society
  (See address above)

JOURNAL OF BIOLOGICAL CHEMISTRY [2102]

9650 Rockville Pike
Bethesda, Maryland 20014
(301) 530-7150

First published in 1906

SUBSCRIPTION DATA
Issues and rates: Published semi-monthly.
  Average paid circulation: 7000; 100 controlled
  Annual rate(s): $200.00
Publisher or Sponsor: American Society of Biological Chemists, Inc.

EDITORIAL DESCRIPTION
  Publishes reports of original research in biochemistry.
Articles per average issue: 45
Audience: Professional
  Manuscripts accepted in English

MANUSCRIPT INFORMATION
Subject field(s): Biochemistry
Manuscript requirements: CBE
  Preferred length: 7,000 to 10,000 words
  Number of copies to be submitted: Two
  Abstract: Yes
Author information and reprints: Payment: By publication to author. $25.00 per article.
  Is simultaneous submission of article to other journals permitted: No
  Exclusive manuscript rights between acceptance and publication: Yes
  Copyright: Held by publication.
  Reprints: Available at cost.
Disposition of manuscript:
  Query letter: No
  Receipt of manuscript acknowledged: Yes
  Decision to publish in: 2-3 months
  Accepted manuscript published in: 4-5 months
  Rejected manuscript returned: Yes
  Rejected manuscript criticized: Yes

Submit to:
Editor
(See address above)

JOURNAL OF CARBOHYDRATES-NUCLE-OSIDES-NUCLEOTIDES [2103]

An International Forum for Rapid Communication
Marcel Dekker, Inc.
270 Madison Avenue
New York, New York 10016
(212) 490-7700

First published in 1974

SUBSCRIPTION DATA
Issues and rates: Published bi-monthly.
Average paid circulation: 1,000; 25 controlled
Annual rate(s): Individuals $30.00; Institutions $60.00
Managing Editor: Dr. Robert E. Harmon

EDITORIAL DESCRIPTION
Deals with the chemistry of carbohydrates, nucleosides, and nucleotides and their biological activities.
Articles per average issue: Eight
Audience: Organic chemists, biochemists, and biologists working in the area of carbohydrates, nucleosides, and nucleotides
Manuscripts accepted in English, German, and French

MANUSCRIPT INFORMATION
Subject field(s): Chemistry, biochemistry, and biological chemistry.
Manuscript requirements: No specific style guide.
Preferred length: 8-30 pages
Number of copies to be submitted: Three-1 original and 2 copies
Abstract: Yes. Summary of research, accomplishments, result obtained and any desired conclusion.
Author information and reprints: Payment: By publication to author. $75.00 per article.
Is simultaneous submission of article to other journals permitted: Not permitted.
Exclusive manuscript rights between acceptance and publication: Yes
Copyright: Held by publication.
Reprints: Available at cost.
Disposition of manuscript:
Query letter: Not necessary.
Receipt of manuscript acknowledged: Yes
Decision to publish in: 2-3 Weeks
Accepted manuscript published in: 3 Months
Rejected manuscript returned: Yes, if return postage is supplied by author.
Rejected manuscript criticized: Reasons for rejections only
Submit to:
Dr. Robert E. Harmon
Executive Editor
Department of Chemistry
Western Michigan University
Kalamazoo, Michigan 49001
(616) 383-6134

JOURNAL OF CELLULAR PLASTICS [2104]

Technomic Publishing, Co., Inc.
265 West State Street
Westport, Connecticut 06880
(203) 226-6356

First published in 1964

SUBSCRIPTION DATA
Issues and rates: Published quarterly.
Annual rate(s): $35.00; Foreign $40.00
Managing Editor: Walter E. Becker

EDITORIAL DESCRIPTION
To provide a permanent record of achievements in the science, technology and economics of cellular plastics.
Articles per average issue: 3
Manuscripts accepted in English

MANUSCRIPT INFORMATION
Subject field(s): All areas relating to cellular plastics
Manuscript requirements: See latest issue for style requirements.
Preferred length: None
Number of copies to be submitted: 3
Abstract: Yes. Of 100 words
Author information and reprints: Payment: None.
Is simultaneous submission of article to other journals permitted: Permitted, but not encouraged.
Exclusive manuscript rights between acceptance and publication: Yes
Copyright: Held by publication.
Reprints: Available at cost.
Additional information: Include a short biography of author, affiliation, address. Appropriate captions to illustrations, as well as references are to be listed at the end.
Disposition of manuscript:
Query letter: Not necessary.
Receipt of manuscript acknowledged: Yes
Decision to publish in: 3 months
Accepted manuscript published in: 3-6 months
Rejected manuscript returned: Yes, with return postage paid by publication.
Rejected manuscript criticized: Sometimes
Submit to:
Walter E. Becker
Editor
(See address above)

JOURNAL OF CHEMICAL EDUCATION [2105]

1155 16th Street, N.W.
Washington, D.C. 20036

First published in 1924

SUBSCRIPTION DATA
Issues and rates: Published monthly.
Average paid circulation: 25,000
Annual rate(s): $7.50; Foreign $9.50

Publisher or Sponsor: American Chemical Society, Division of Chemical Education

EDITORIAL DESCRIPTION
Publishes papers on the full range of chemistry: ideas, theory, method, laboratory experimentation, philosophy, and history. Also features reports on the technical problems of teaching.
Articles per average issue: 35
Audience: High school and college chemistry teachers
Manuscripts accepted in English

MANUSCRIPT INFORMATION
Subject field(s): All aspects of chemistry that are of interest to teachers.
Manuscript requirements: Consult December, 1974 issue; use CA for abbreviations.
Preferred length: 16 pages (maximum)
Number of copies to be submitted: Three; three copies of all illustrations
Abstract:
Author information and reprints: Payment: None.
Is simultaneous submission of article to other journals permitted: No
Exclusive manuscript rights between acceptance and publication: Yes
Copyright: Held by the American Chemical Society
Reprints: Available at cost
Disposition of manuscript:
Query letter:
Receipt of manuscript acknowledged: Yes.
Decision to publish in: 3-4 months
Accepted manuscript published in: 9 months
Rejected manuscript returned: Yes.
Rejected manuscript criticized: Yes.
Submit to:
W. T. Lippincott
Editor
Department of Chemistry
University of Arizona
Tucson, Arizona 85721
(602) 884-2808

SPECIAL STIPULATIONS
Galley proofs will be submitted to author for corrections.

JOURNAL OF COORDINATION CHEMISTRY* [2106]

Gordon and Breach Science Publishers
One Park Avenue
New York, New York 10016
(212) 689-0360

SUBSCRIPTION DATA
Issues and rates: Published quarterly.
Average paid circulation: Not available.
Annual rate(s): Individuals $14.00, Institutions $32.00

EDITORIAL DESCRIPTION
Publishes original investigations on the synthesis, structure, and the physical and chemical properties of coordination compounds of metals.

Chemistry

MANUSCRIPT INFORMATION

Subject field(s): Interactions of organic and inorganic ligands with metals; equilibria, kinetics, mechanisms and catalytic effects

Manuscript requirements: Style sheet sent on request.

Additional information: Letter of inquiry should be sent to editor before submission of manuscript.

Submit to:
Arthur E. Martell
Editor
Department of Chemistry
Texas A&M University
College Station, Texas 77840

THE JOURNAL OF ELASTOMERS AND PLASTICS   [2107]

Technomic Publishing Co., Inc.
265 West State Street
Westport, Connecticut 06880
(203) 226-6356

Previously entitled *The Journal of Elastoplastics*

First published in 1969

SUBSCRIPTION DATA

Issues and rates: Published quarterly.
Annual rate(s): $55.00; Foreign $60.00

Managing Editor: Samuel Steingiser

EDITORIAL DESCRIPTION

Contains articles on all aspects of elastomers and plastics.

Articles per average issue: 6

Audience: Scientific and engineering community concerned with elastomers
Manuscripts accepted in English

MANUSCRIPT INFORMATION

Subject field(s): The research, development, and marketing of elastomers and plastics

Manuscript requirements: See latest issue for style requirements.
Preferred length: None
Number of copies to be submitted: 3
Abstract: Yes. Of 100 words

Author information and reprints: Payment: None.
Is simultaneous submission of article to other journals permitted: Permitted, but not encouraged.
Exclusive manuscript rights between acceptance and publication: Yes
Copyright: Held by publication.
Reprints: Available at cost.

Additional information: The title should be less than 10 words, followed by the name, affiliation, and address of author. A nomenclature of the principal symbols used should be provided.

Disposition of manuscript:
Query letter: Not necessary.
Receipt of manuscript acknowledged: Yes
Decision to publish in: 3 months
Accepted manuscript published in: 3-6 months
Rejected manuscript returned: Yes, if return postage is supplied by author.

Rejected manuscript criticized: Sometimes

Submit to:
Samuel Steingiser
Editor
(See address above)

JOURNAL OF ELECTROANALYTICAL CHEMISTRY AND INTERFACIAL ELECTROCHEMISTRY   [2108]

Elsevier Sequoia SA
P.O. Box 851
1001 Lausanne 1, Switzerland
(021) 20 73 81

First published in 1959

SUBSCRIPTION DATA

Issues and rates: Published semi-monthly.
Annual rate(s): SFr. 1080.00

EDITORIAL DESCRIPTION

Publishes original research work not previously published in other periodicals (regular papers), reviews on recent developments in various fields; short communications; preliminary notes; book reviews; announcements; indexes.

Articles per average issue: 12
Manuscripts accepted in English, French, and German (abstracts in English only)

MANUSCRIPT INFORMATION

Subject field(s): Electroanalytical chemistry, double-layer studies, electrokinetics, colloid stability, electrode kinetics

Manuscript requirements: Use S.I. Units throughout.
Number of copies to be submitted: Two

Author information and reprints: Payment: None.
Is simultaneous submission of article to other journals permitted: No
Exclusive manuscript rights between acceptance and publication: Yes
Copyright: Held by publication.
Reprints: Available, cost quoted upon publication

Disposition of manuscript:
Query letter:
Receipt of manuscript acknowledged: Yes
Decision to publish in: 1 month
Accepted manuscript published in: 6 months
Rejected manuscript returned: Yes
Rejected manuscript criticized: Yes

Submit to:
R. de Levie
Department of Chemistry
Georgetown University
Washington, D.C. 20007

Papers of colloid interest should be submitted to:
R. H. Ottewill
Department of Chemistry
The University
Bristol BS8 1TS, England

Others should be sent to:
R. Parsons
Department of Chemistry
The University
Bristol BS8 1TS, England

JOURNAL OF FLUORINE CHEMISTRY   [2109]

Elsevier Sequoia SA
P.O. Box 851
1001 Lausanne 1, Switzerland
(021) 20 73 81

First published in 1971

SUBSCRIPTION DATA

Issues and rates: Published quarterly.
Annual rate(s): SFr. 480.00

EDITORIAL DESCRIPTION

Contains papers concerned with research on the chemistry of fluorine and compounds where the halogen is the dominant element. Theoretical, structural or mechanistic aspects of the subject are discussed as well as the normal types of preparative and physico-chemical investigation.

Articles per average issue: 11

Audience: Professional, academic
Manuscripts accepted in English, French, German

MANUSCRIPT INFORMATION

Manuscript requirements: Style sheet sent on request.
Number of copies to be submitted: Two
Abstract: Yes. Papers in French and German should include a summary in English.

Author information and reprints: Payment: Reprints only. 50 reprints
Is simultaneous submission of article to other journals permitted: No
Exclusive manuscript rights between acceptance and publication: Yes
Copyright: Held by publication.
Reprints: Available, cost quoted upon publication

Disposition of manuscript:
Query letter: No
Receipt of manuscript acknowledged: Yes
Decision to publish in: 4 to 6 weeks
Accepted manuscript published in: 5 to 6 months
Rejected manuscript returned: Yes
Rejected manuscript criticized: Yes

Submit to:
H. J. Emeléus
University Chemical Laboratory
Lensfield Road
Cambridge CB2 1 EW, United Kingdom
(223) 56491

Manuscripts may also be submitted to:
J. C. Tatlow
Department of Chemistry
The University, P.O. Box 363
Birmingham B15 2TT, United Kingdom
(21) 4721301

JOURNAL OF HETEROCYCLIC CHEMISTRY [2110]

The International Journal of Heterocyclic Chemistry
University Station, Box 7254
Provo, Utah 84602
(801) 375-5151

First published in 1964

SUBSCRIPTION DATA

Issues and rates: Published bi-monthly.
Average paid circulation: 1500
Annual rate(s): $60.00; Foreign $64.50

EDITORIAL DESCRIPTION

Results of original research are published on any phase of heterocyclic chemistry. Informative reviews are also acceptable on any phase of heterocyclic chemistry.
Articles per average issue: 40
Manuscripts accepted in English, French, and German

MANUSCRIPT INFORMATION

Subject field(s): Any phase of heterocyclic chemistry
Manuscript requirements: See latest issue for style requirements.
Preferred length: Articles: 5 pages; notes: 3 pages; communications: 2 pages; reviews: 15 pages
Number of copies to be submitted: Three
Abstract: Yes.
Author information and reprints: Payment: By author to publication. $35.00 per page. Mandatory; waivers are not allowed.
Is simultaneous submission of article to other journals permitted: No
Exclusive manuscript rights between acceptance and publication: Yes
Copyright: Held by publication.
Reprints: Available, 100 free without covers upon payment of page charges.
Disposition of manuscript:
Query letter:
Receipt of manuscript acknowledged: Yes
Decision to publish in: 30-45 days
Accepted manuscript published in: 30-60 days
Rejected manuscript returned: Yes
Rejected manuscript criticized: Yes
Submit to:
Raymond N. Castle
Editor
(See address above)
(801) 374-1211 ext. 2227

SPECIAL STIPULATIONS

Each manuscript is reviewed by two competent reviewers who are expert in the field of research which is described in the manuscript. The technical editor will also read each manuscript.

JOURNAL OF HISTOCHEMISTRY AND CYTOCHEMISTRY [2111]

428 East Preston Street
Baltimore, Maryland 21202
(301) 528-4116

First published in 1953

SUBSCRIPTION DATA

Issues and rates: Published monthly.
Average paid circulation: 3000
Annual rate(s): $40.00, Foreign $42.00
Publisher or Sponsor: Histochemical Society, Inc.

EDITORIAL DESCRIPTION

Contains original papers in all fields of histochemistry and cytochemistry, analysis of chemical and structural organization of cells and tissues.
Articles per average issue: 8
Manuscripts accepted in English

MANUSCRIPT INFORMATION

Manuscript requirements: Style sheet sent on request.
Preferred length: None
Number of copies to be submitted: 2
Abstract: Yes.
Author information and reprints: Payment: By author to publication. $47.50 per page. In excess of 10 pages per article.
Is simultaneous submission of article to other journals permitted: No
Exclusive manuscript rights between acceptance and publication: Yes
Copyright: Held by publication.
Reprints: Available
Disposition of manuscript:
Query letter:
Receipt of manuscript acknowledged: Yes
Decision to publish in: 3 months
Accepted manuscript published in: 6 months
Rejected manuscript returned: Yes
Rejected manuscript criticized: Sometimes
Submit to:
Paul J. Anderson, M.D.
Editor
Mount Sinai School of Medicine
Fifth Avenue and 100th Street
New York, New York 10029
(212) 650-7371

JOURNAL OF INORGANIC AND NUCLEAR CHEMISTRY [2112]

Including *Bio-inorganic Chemistry*
Pergamon Press, Inc.
Fairview Park
Elmsford, New York 10523
(914) 592-7700

First published in 1955

SUBSCRIPTION DATA

Issues and rates: Published monthly.
Annual rate(s): $30.00; Institutions $220.00

EDITORIAL DESCRIPTION

Contains papers on all aspects of inorganic and nuclear chemistry.
Articles per average issue: 25
Audience: Professional, academic
Manuscripts accepted in English

MANUSCRIPT INFORMATION

Manuscript requirements: See latest issue for style requirements.
Preferred length: None
Number of copies to be submitted: 2
Abstract: Yes
Author information and reprints: Payment: None.
Is simultaneous submission of article to other journals permitted: Not permitted.
Exclusive manuscript rights between acceptance and publication: Yes
Copyright: Held by publication.
Reprints: Available at cost.
Disposition of manuscript:
Query letter: Not necessary.
Receipt of manuscript acknowledged: Yes
Decision to publish in: 4 weeks
Accepted manuscript published in: 5 months
Rejected manuscript returned: Yes, if return postage is supplied by author.
Rejected manuscript criticized: Reasons for rejections only
Submit to:
Joseph J. Katz
Editor
Argonne National Laboratory
9700 South Cass Avenue
Argonne, Illinois 60440

JOURNAL OF MACROMOLECULAR SCIENCE: PART A [2113]

Chemistry
Marcel Dekker Journals
P. O. Box 11305, Church Street Station
New York, New York 10249

SUBSCRIPTION DATA

Issues and rates: 8 issues per volume
Annual rate(s): $110.00; Foreign $118.40

EDITORIAL DESCRIPTION

Publishes original articles in molecular studies and related fields.
Audience: Scientific community
Manuscripts accepted in English

MANUSCRIPT INFORMATION

Manuscript requirements: No specific style guide. See latest issue for style requirements.
Preferred length: As required
Number of copies to be submitted: 2
Abstract: Yes. Approximately 200 words
Author information and reprints: Payment: None.
Is simultaneous submission of article to other journals permitted: Not permitted.
Exclusive manuscript rights between acceptance and publication: Yes
Copyright: Held by publication.
Reprints: Available at no cost. 50
Additional information: Typewritten, double-spaced
Submit to:
George E. Ham
Executive Editor
284 Pine Road
Briarcliff Manor, New York 10510

JOURNAL OF MEDICINAL CHEMISTRY* [2114]

American Chemical Society
1155 16th Street, N.W.
Washington, D.C. 20036

SUBSCRIPTION DATA

Issues and rates: Published monthly.
    Average paid circulation: 4,000
    Annual rate(s): $30.00, Members $15.00
Publisher or Sponsor: American Chemical
Society

EDITORIAL DESCRIPTION

    Publishes articles and notes on the
    chemistry of experimental or clinically
    useful therapeutic agents.

MANUSCRIPT INFORMATION

Subject field(s): Preparation and physical
    properties, structural elucidation,
    chemical behavior of materials of
    biological significance, structure-activity
    relationships, drug dynamics, analysis of
    medicinal agents
Manuscript requirements: ACS
    Number of copies to be submitted: Three
Author information and reprints: Payment:
    None.
    Is simultaneous submission of article to
    other journals permitted: No
    Exclusive manuscript rights between
    acceptance and publication: Yes
    Copyright: Held by the American
    Chemical Society
    Reprints: Available at cost
Disposition of manuscript:
    Receipt of manuscript acknowledged: Yes
    Decision to publish in: Two months
    Accepted manuscript published in: Three
    months
    Rejected manuscript returned: Yes
    Rejected manuscript criticized: Yes
Submit to:
    Alfred Burger
    Editor
    Department of Chemistry
    University of Virginia
    Charlottesville, Virginia 22901

THE JOURNAL OF ORGANIC CHEMISTRY* [2115]

1155 16th Street, N.W.
Washington, D.C. 20036

SUBSCRIPTION DATA

Issues and rates: Published bi-weekly.
    Average paid circulation: 10,400
    Annual rate(s): $60.00, Members $20.00,
    Foreign $66.00
Publisher or Sponsor: American Chemical
Society

EDITORIAL DESCRIPTION

    Publishes both comprehensive research
    papers and shorter notes on all aspects of
    organic chemistry.

MANUSCRIPT INFORMATION

Subject field(s): Organic reactions,
    mechanisms, natural products, synthesis
    of new compounds, theoretical organic

chemistry, spectroscopy related to
organic chemistry
Manuscript requirements: ACS
    Copyright: Held by author.
    Reprints: Available at cost
Submit to:
    Frederick D. Greene
    Editor-in-Chief
    Department of Chemistry
    Massachusetts Institute of Technology
    Cambridge, Massachusetts 02139

JOURNAL OF ORGANOMETALLIC CHEMISTRY [2116]

Incorporating *Subject Reviews and Annual
Surveys*
Elsevier Sequoia SA
P.O. Box 851
1001 Lausanne 1, Switzerland
(021) 20 73 81

First published in 1963

SUBSCRIPTION DATA

Issues and rates: Published weekly.
    Average paid circulation: 1350
    Annual rate(s): SFr. 2400.00

EDITORIAL DESCRIPTION

    Contains full papers, preliminary
    communications, subject reviews, and
    annual surveys on organometallic
    chemistry.
Articles per average issue: 18
    Manuscripts accepted in English, French
    and German (Abstracts in English only)

MANUSCRIPT INFORMATION

Subject field(s): Organometallic chemistry
Manuscript requirements: Style sheet sent
    on request.
    Number of copies to be submitted: Two
    Abstract: Yes.
Author information and reprints: Payment:
    By publication to author. For subject
    reviews and annual surveys. No payment
    for regular papers and preliminary
    communications.
    Is simultaneous submission of article to
    other journals permitted: No
    Exclusive manuscript rights between
    acceptance and publication: Yes
    Copyright: Held by publication.
    Reprints: Available, cost on request
Disposition of manuscript:
    Query letter:
    Receipt of manuscript acknowledged: Yes
    Decision to publish in: 1 month
    Accepted manuscript published in: 6
    months
    Rejected manuscript returned: Yes
    Rejected manuscript criticized: Yes
Submit to:
    C. Eaborn
    School of Molecular Sciences
    University of Sussex
    Brighton BN1 9QJ, Great Britain

Submit subject reviews to:
    D. Seyforth

Department of Chemistry
Massachusetts Institute of Technology
Cambridge, Massachusetts 02139

Submit annual surveys to:
R. B. King
Department of Chemistry
University of Georgia
Athens, Georgia 30601

JOURNAL OF PHOTOCHEMISTRY [2117]

An International Journal Devoted to the
Study of the Quantitative Aspects of
Photochemistry and Energy Transfer
Elsevier Sequoia SA
P.O. Box 851
1001 Lausanne 1, Switzerland
(021) 20 73 81

First published in 1972

SUBSCRIPTION DATA

Issues and rates: Published bi-monthly.
    Average paid circulation: 300
    Annual rate(s): SFr. 135.

EDITORIAL DESCRIPTION

    Contains papers concerned with the
    quantitative aspects of photochemistry,
    namely quantum yield determinations
    and kinetic measurements made under
    stationary and non-stationary conditions
    with reference both to elementary
    processes and to overall photochemical
    reactions.
Articles per average issue: 8
    Manuscripts accepted in English, French,
    and German (Abstracts in English only)

MANUSCRIPT INFORMATION

Manuscript requirements: Style sheet sent
    on request.
    Number of copies to be submitted: Two
    Abstract: Yes.
Author information and reprints: Payment:
    None.
    Is simultaneous submission of article to
    other journals permitted: No
    Exclusive manuscript rights between
    acceptance and publication: Yes
    Copyright: Held by publication.
    Reprints: Available, cost quoted upon
    publication
Disposition of manuscript:
    Query letter:
    Receipt of manuscript acknowledged: Yes
    Decision to publish in: 4 weeks
    Accepted manuscript published in: 4 to 5
    months
    Rejected manuscript returned: Yes
    Rejected manuscript criticized:
    Sometimes
Submit to:
    Richard P. Wayne
    Editor
    Physical Chemistry Laboratory
    South Parks Road
    Oxford OX1 3QZ, England
    (865) 53322

JOURNAL OF PHYSICAL CHEMISTRY* [2118]

American Chemical Society
1155 16th Street
Washington, D.C. 20036

SUBSCRIPTION DATA
Issues and rates: Published bi-weekly.
Average paid circulation: 6,100
Annual rate(s): $40.00, Members $20.00
Publisher or Sponsor: American Chemical Society

EDITORIAL DESCRIPTION
Contains original theoretical and experimental papers for the specialist in physical chemistry.

MANUSCRIPT INFORMATION
Subject field(s): Physical chemistry
Manuscript requirements: ACS
Number of copies to be submitted: Three
Author information and reprints: Payment: None.
Is simultaneous submission of article to other journals permitted: No
Exclusive manuscript rights between acceptance and publication: Yes
Copyright: Held by the American Chemical Society
Reprints: Available at cost
Disposition of manuscript:
Receipt of manuscript acknowledged: Yes
Decision to publish in: Two months
Accepted manuscript published in: Two months
Rejected manuscript returned: Yes
Rejected manuscript criticized: Yes
Submit to:
Bryce Crawford, Jr.
Editor
Department of Chemistry
University of Minnesota
Minneapolis, Minnesota 55455

JOURNAL OF SOLUTION CHEMISTRY [2119]

Plenum Publishing Corporation
227 West 17th Street
New York, New York 10011
(212) 255-0713

First published in 1972

SUBSCRIPTION DATA
Issues and rates: Published monthly.
Annual rate(s): $25.00; Institutions $65.00
Managing Editor: Robert L. Kay

EDITORIAL DESCRIPTION
A forum research on the physical chemistry of liquid solutions.
Articles per average issue: 7
Audience: Chemists
Manuscripts accepted in English

MANUSCRIPT INFORMATION
Subject field(s): Physical chemistry, chemical physics, molecular biology, statistical mechanics, biochemistry, biophysics; experimental investigations of the dielectric spectroscopic, thermodynamic, transport or relaxation properties of both electrolytes and nonelectrolytes in liquid solutions
Manuscript requirements: See latest issue for style requirements.
Preferred length: None
Number of copies to be submitted: Original and 2 copies
Abstract: Yes. In addition to a list of key words for indexing purposes, an abstract of about 200 words or less is required.
Author information and reprints: Payment: None.
Is simultaneous submission of article to other journals permitted: Not permitted.
Exclusive manuscript rights between acceptance and publication: Yes
Copyright: Held by publication.
Reprints: Available at cost.
Disposition of manuscript:
Query letter: Not necessary.
Receipt of manuscript acknowledged: Yes
Decision to publish in: 1 month
Accepted manuscript published in: 5 months
Rejected manuscript returned: Yes, with return postage paid by publication.
Rejected manuscript criticized: Yes
Submit to:
Robert L. Kay
Editor
Carnegie-Mellon University
4400 Fifth Avenue
Pittsburgh, Pennsylvania 15213
(412) 621-1100

THE JOURNAL OF STEROID BIOCHEMISTRY [2120]

Pergamon Press, Inc.
Fairview Park
Elmsford, New York 10523
(914) 592-7700

First published in 1970

SUBSCRIPTION DATA
Issues and rates: Published monthly.
Annual rate(s): $25.00; Institutions $80.00

EDITORIAL DESCRIPTION
Publishes original papers dealing with all aspects of steriod biochemistry including clinical papers that advance the knowledge of steroid biochemistry in Man.
Articles per average issue: 10-15
Audience: Professional, academic
Manuscripts accepted in English, French, German

MANUSCRIPT INFORMATION
Subject field(s): Structure and physico-chemical properties of steroids, methodology of their detection and measurement, their biosynthesis and catabolism, mechanisms of action of steroid hormones, comparative endocrinology of steroids, etc.
Manuscript requirements: See latest issue for style requirements.
Preferred length: 20 pages maximum for articles; 3 pages, preliminary notes; 30 pages, general reviews
Number of copies to be submitted: 3, double-spaced
Abstract: Yes. A summary in English up to 200 words followed by a maximum of 5 key words for indexing purposes.
Author information and reprints: Payment: None.
Is simultaneous submission of article to other journals permitted: Not permitted.
Exclusive manuscript rights between acceptance and publication: Yes
Copyright: Held by publication.
Reprints: Available at cost.
Disposition of manuscript:
Query letter: Not necessary.
Receipt of manuscript acknowledged: Yes
Decision to publish in: 4 weeks
Accepted manuscript published in: 5 months
Rejected manuscript returned: Yes, if return postage is supplied by author.
Rejected manuscript criticized: Reasons for rejections only
Submit to:
J. R. Pasqualini,
R. Scholler
Editors-in-Chief
Foundation for Hormone Research
26 Boulevard Brune
Paris 14e, France

LIPIDS [2121]

508 South Sixth Street
Champaign, Illinois 61820
(217) 359-2344

First published in 1965

SUBSCRIPTION DATA
Issues and rates: Published monthly.
Average paid circulation: 1800; 30 controlled
Annual rate(s): $30.00, Foreign $33.00
Publisher or Sponsor: American Oil Chemists' Society
Managing Editor: James Lyon

EDITORIAL DESCRIPTION
Contains significant original findings of physical, chemical, biochemical, pharmacological and physiological characteristics of lipids, lipoproteins and other lipid complexes. Includes methods for identification, qualitative and quantitative analysis, and other forms of characterization of these substances. Reviews on timely topics will be published occasionally.
Articles per average issue: 6-10
Manuscripts accepted in English

MANUSCRIPT INFORMATION
Manuscript requirements: AIBS
Number of copies to be submitted: Three
Abstract: Yes.

Chemistry

Author information and reprints: Payment:
By author to publication. $40 per page.
Is simultaneous submission of article to
other journals permitted: No
Exclusive manuscript rights between
acceptance and publication: Yes
Copyright: Held by publication.
Reprints: Available, cost varies with
length.
Disposition of manuscript:
Query letter:
Receipt of manuscript acknowledged: Yes
Decision to publish in: 1-2 months
Accepted manuscript published in: 2-3
months
Rejected manuscript returned: Yes
Rejected manuscript criticized: Yes
Submit to:
R. T. Holman
Editor
The Hormel Institute
801 16th Avenue, N.E.
Austin, Minnesota 55912
(507) 433-8804

MICROCHEMICAL
JOURNAL*　　　　　[2122]
Devoted to the Application of
Microtechniques in All Branches of Science
Academic Press, Inc.
111 Fifth Avenue
New York, New York 10003

SUBSCRIPTION DATA
Issues and rates: Published bi-monthly.
Publisher or Sponsor: American
Microchemical Society

EDITORIAL DESCRIPTION
Contains articles on all phases of
chemistry, including clinical and
biochemical, involving small-scale
manipulation.

MANUSCRIPT INFORMATION
Subject field(s): Organic and inorganic work
on preparation, purification, separation,
detection, determination, trace analysis,
all types of instrumentation
Manuscript requirements: See latest issue for
style requirements.
Number of copies to be submitted: Two
Author information and reprints: Payment:
By author to publication.
Is simultaneous submission of article to
other journals permitted: No
Exclusive manuscript rights between
acceptance and publication: Yes
Copyright: Held by publication.
Reprints: Available, 50 free
Additional information: Manuscripts should
be concise and consistent in style,
spelling and use of abbreviations.
Disposition of manuscript:
Receipt of manuscript acknowledged: Yes
Rejected manuscript returned: Yes
Submit to:
Al Stevermark
Editor-in-Chief
115 Beech Street
Nutley, New Jersey 07110

RUBBER CHEMISTRY
AND TECHNOLOGY　　　[2123]
Rubber Division, University of Akron
P.O. Box 123
Akron, Ohio 44325
(216) 375-7814

First published in 1928

SUBSCRIPTION DATA
Issues and rates: 5 times per year
Average paid circulation: 5000
Annual rate(s): $40.00
Publisher or Sponsor: American Chemical
Society, Rubber Division

EDITORIAL DESCRIPTION
Contains articles of interest to rubber
science; materials of rubber and its allied
substances and their chemistry, physics,
and engineering.
Articles per average issue: 22
Audience: Readers who are interested in
macromolecular science and technology.

MANUSCRIPT INFORMATION
Subject field(s): Chemistry, physics,
mathematics, engineering, production
Manuscript requirements: AIP
Preferred length: 5-50 pages
Number of copies to be submitted: Two
Author information and reprints: Payment:
None. Copy of journal containing article.
Is simultaneous submission of article to
other journals permitted: No
Exclusive manuscript rights between
acceptance and publication: Yes
Copyright: None at present
Reprints: Available
Additional information: Especially desirable
are foreign language articles of
significance. Translation furnished by
staff.
Disposition of manuscript:
Query letter:
Receipt of manuscript acknowledged: Yes
Decision to publish in: 1-3 weeks
Accepted manuscript published in: 2-4
months
Rejected manuscript returned: Yes
Rejected manuscript criticized: Yes
Submit to:
Earl C. Gregg, Jr.
Editor
B. F. Goodrich Company Research
Center
9921 Brecksville Road
Brecksville, Ohio 44141
(216) 376-3121 ext. 302

STAIN TECHNOLOGY　　　[2124]
A Journal for Microtechnic and
Histochemistry
428 East Preston Street
Baltimore, Maryland 21202
(301) 528-4116

First published in 1926

SUBSCRIPTION DATA
Issues and rates: Published bi-monthly.
Average paid circulation: 3600

Annual rate(s): $13.00, Foreign $14.50
Publisher or Sponsor: Biological Stain
Commission

EDITORIAL DESCRIPTION
Contains articles on nature and use of
dyes and other stains; histological
technics, histochemistry.

MANUSCRIPT INFORMATION
Manuscript requirements: See latest issue for
style requirements.
Number of copies to be submitted: Two
Abstract: Yes.
Author information and reprints: Payment:
None.
Is simultaneous submission of article to
other journals permitted: No
Exclusive manuscript rights between
acceptance and publication: Yes
Copyright: Held by publication.
Reprints: Available, cost depends on
length
Disposition of manuscript:
Query letter:
Receipt of manuscript acknowledged: Yes
Decision to publish in: 6 weeks
Accepted manuscript published in: 3
months
Rejected manuscript returned: Yes
Rejected manuscript criticized:
Sometimes
Submit to:
J. B. Longley, M.D.
Editor
Health Sciences Center
University of Louisville
Louisville, Kentucky 40201

STEROIDS　　　　　　　[2125]
500 Sansome Street
San Francisco, California 94111
(415) 433-0220

First published in 1963

SUBSCRIPTION DATA
Issues and rates: Published monthly.
Average paid circulation: 1,500
Annual rate(s): Individuals $36.00;
Institutions $58.00
Managing Editor: R. J. Mitchell

EDITORIAL DESCRIPTION
Designed to provide a forum for the
rapid publication of significant original
papers in organic chemistry,
biochemistry, physiology, pharmacology
and clinical or basic endocrinology in all
phases.
Articles per average issue: 12-15
Audience: Steroid researchers
Manuscripts accepted in English

MANUSCRIPT INFORMATION
Manuscript requirements: See latest issue for
style requirements.
Preferred length: None
Number of copies to be submitted:
Original and two copies
Abstract: Yes.

Author information and reprints: Payment: None.
  Is simultaneous submission of article to other journals permitted: No
  Exclusive manuscript rights between acceptance and publication: Yes
  Copyright: Held by publication.
  Reprints: Available
Disposition of manuscript:
  Receipt of manuscript acknowledged: Yes
  Decision to publish in: One to two months
  Accepted manuscript published in: Two or three months
  Rejected manuscript returned: Yes
  Rejected manuscript criticized: Yes.
Submit to:
  Albert Segaloff
  Editor
  Alton Ochsner Medical Foundation
  1520 Jefferson Highway
  New Orleans, Louisiana 70121
  (504) 837-3000

SULPHUR INSTITUTE JOURNAL [2126]
1725 K Street, N.W.
Washington, D.C. 20006
(202) 331-9660

SUBSCRIPTION DATA
Issues and rates: Published quarterly.
  Average paid circulation: 3000 controlled
Publisher or Sponsor: The Sulphur Institute

EDITORIAL DESCRIPTION
  Journal serves as a source of information on the use and importance of sulphur and its compounds. Publishes articles dealing with previously unpublished research and development work, articles based on papers which have appeared in other publications, and review articles. Does not publish detailed experimental procedures, except to the extent that they are necessary to the understanding of the subject matter.
Articles per average issue: Educated, but non-specialized readership

MANUSCRIPT INFORMATION
Subject field(s): Sulphur in general, sulphur in chemistry, sulphur in agronomy, sulphur in industry, new uses of sulphur
Manuscript requirements: Style sheet sent on request.
  Preferred length: 3000 words
  Number of copies to be submitted: One original, one copy
Author information and reprints: Payment: None.
  Is simultaneous submission of article to other journals permitted: No
  Exclusive manuscript rights between acceptance and publication: Yes
  Copyright: Held by publication.
  Reprints: Available, up to 300 free
Disposition of manuscript:
  Receipt of manuscript acknowledged: Yes
  Decision to publish in: 2 weeks
  Accepted manuscript published in: 1-4 months
  Rejected manuscript returned: Yes

Rejected manuscript criticized: No
Submit to:
  J. Platou
  Director of Information
  (See address above)

SYNTHETIC COMMUNICATIONS [2127]
An International Journal for Rapid Communication about Synthetic Organic Chemistry
Marcel Dekker, Inc.
270 Madison Avenue
New York, New York 10016
(212) 490-7700

First published in 1971

SUBSCRIPTION DATA
Issues and rates: 6 issues/volume
  Average paid circulation: 1,000
  Annual rate(s): $35.00/volume; Foreign $41.30/volume

EDITORIAL DESCRIPTION
  Contains original research papers dealing with novel synthetic organic chemistry.
Articles per average issue: 12
Audience: Synthetic organic chemists
  Manuscripts accepted in English, French, and German

MANUSCRIPT INFORMATION
Subject field(s): Synthetic organic chemistry, new methods and synthetic schemes
Manuscript requirements: See latest issue for style requirements.
  Preferred length: 2-5 pages
  Number of copies to be submitted: Two
  Abstract:
Author information and reprints: Payment: None.
  Is simultaneous submission of article to other journals permitted: No
  Exclusive manuscript rights between acceptance and publication: Yes
  Copyright: Held by publication.
  Reprints: Available, $38 for 100
Disposition of manuscript:
  Query letter:
  Receipt of manuscript acknowledged: No
  Decision to publish in: 1-4 weeks
  Accepted manuscript published in: 1-2 months
  Rejected manuscript returned: Yes
  Rejected manuscript criticized: Yes
Submit to:
  James A. Marshall
  Northwestern University
  Department of Chemistry
  Evanston, Illinois 60201
  (312) 492-5650

TALANTA [2128]
An International Journal of Analytical Chemistry
Pergamon Press, Inc.
Fairview Park
Elmsford, New York 10523
(914) 592-7700

First published in 1958

SUBSCRIPTION DATA
Issues and rates: Published monthly.
  Annual rate(s): $25.00; Institutions $110.00

EDITORIAL DESCRIPTION
  Contains original papers, communications, reviews, preliminary communications, and correspondence dealing with all aspects of analytical chemistry.
Articles per average issue: 2-3
Audience: Professional, academic
  Manuscripts accepted in English, French, German, Russian

MANUSCRIPT INFORMATION
Manuscript requirements: See latest issue for style requirements.
  Preferred length: None
  Number of copies to be submitted: 2
  Abstract: Yes. If possible, in all four languages.
Author information and reprints: Payment: None.
  Is simultaneous submission of article to other journals permitted: Not permitted.
  Exclusive manuscript rights between acceptance and publication: Yes
  Copyright: Held by publication.
  Reprints: Available at cost.
Disposition of manuscript:
  Query letter: Not necessary.
  Receipt of manuscript acknowledged: Yes
  Decision to publish in: 4 weeks
  Accepted manuscript published in: 5 months
  Rejected manuscript returned: Yes, if return postage is supplied by author.
  Rejected manuscript criticized: Reasons for rejections only
Submit to:
  H. J. Francis, Jr.
  Pennwalt Corporation
  900 First Avenue
  King of Prussia Pennsylvania 19406

  Prof. J. S. Fritz
  Department of Chemistry
  Iowa State University
  Ames, Iowa 50010
  Regional Editors

TETRAHEDRON [2129]
International Journal of Organic Chemistry
Pergamon Press, Inc.
Fairview Park
Elmsford, New York 10523
(914) 592-7700

First published in 1957
  Annual rate(s): $50.00; Institutions $280.00

EDITORIAL DESCRIPTION
  Contains original contributions of research in all areas of organic chemistry and related areas.
Articles per average issue: 25-30

Physics

Audience: Professional, academic
  Manuscripts accepted in English,
  German, French

MANUSCRIPT INFORMATION
Manuscript requirements: See latest issue for
  style requirements.
  Preferred length: None
  Number of copies to be submitted: 2
  double-spaced
  Abstract: Yes. In English for all papers
  as well as in the original language.
Author information and reprints: Payment:
  None.
  Is simultaneous submission of article to
  other journals permitted: Not permitted.
  Exclusive manuscript rights between
  acceptance and publication: Yes
  Copyright: Held by publication.
  Reprints: Available at cost.
Disposition of manuscript:
  Query letter: Not necessary.
  Receipt of manuscript acknowledged: Yes
  Decision to publish in: 4 weeks
  Accepted manuscript published in: 5
  months
  Rejected manuscript returned: Yes, if
  return postage is supplied by author.
  Rejected manuscript criticized: Reasons
  for rejections only
Submit to:
  Dr. T. Stephen
  Executive Editor
  8 Lewis Close, Risinghurst
  Headington
  Oxford OX3 8JD, England

  For papers from the Americas:
  Prof. H. H. Wasserman
  Honorary Regional Editor
  1901-A Yale Station
  New Haven, Connecticut 06520

TETRAHEDRON LETTERS [2130]
For the rapid publication of preliminary
communications in Organic Chemistry
Pergamon Press, Inc.
Fairview Park
Elmsford, New York 10523
(914) 592-7700

First published in 1959

SUBSCRIPTION DATA
Issues and rates: Published weekly.
  Annual rate(s): $45.00; Institutions
  $220.00

EDITORIAL DESCRIPTION
  This is a medium for rapid publication of
  short communications and offers
  maximum dissemination of outstanding
  developments in organic chemistry.
Articles per average issue: 20-30
Audience: Professional, academic
  Manuscripts accepted in English,
  German, French

MANUSCRIPT INFORMATION
Subject field(s): Any area of organic
  chemistry reporting new or advanced
  ideas, techniques, structures, methods or

conclusions of interest to a substantial
portion of organic chemists and the
nature of the work justifies urgent
publication.
Manuscript requirements: See latest issue for
  style requirements.
  Preferred length: 2-4 pages
  Number of copies to be submitted: 2
  Abstract: Yes. Include a list of 6-9 key
  words for indexing purposes.
Author information and reprints: Payment:
  None.
  Is simultaneous submission of article to
  other journals permitted: Not permitted.
  Exclusive manuscript rights between
  acceptance and publication: Yes
  Copyright: Held by publication.
  Reprints: Available at cost. Request at
  time of submission.
Disposition of manuscript:
  Query letter: Not necessary.
  Receipt of manuscript acknowledged: Yes
  Rejected manuscript returned: Yes, if
  return postage is supplied by author.
  Rejected manuscript criticized: Reasons
  for rejections only
Submit to:
  Dr. T. Stephen
  Executive Editor
  8 Lewis Close, Risinghurst
  Headington,
  Oxford OX3 8JD, England

  For papers from the Americas:
  Prof. H. H. Wasserman
  Honorary Regional Editor
  1901-A, Yale Station
  New Haven, Connecticut 06520

THEORETICA CHIMICA ACTA [2131]
Springer-Verlag
175 Fifth Avenue
New York, New York 10010

SUBSCRIPTION DATA
  Annual rate(s): DM 132 per volume
Publisher or Sponsor: The Academy of
  Sciences and Literature of Mainz
Managing Editor: Hermann Hartmann

EDITORIAL DESCRIPTION
  Publishes papers dealing with the
  relationship of chemical and physical
  phenomena to the deductions made from
  valence and electonics theory.
  Manuscripts accepted in French,
  German, preferably English

MANUSCRIPT INFORMATION
Subject field(s): New, experimental work,
  which brings out a new theoretical
  viewpoint.
Manuscript requirements: See latest issue for
  style requirements.
  Preferred length: As required
  Number of copies to be submitted: 3
  Abstract: Yes. See instructions to authors
  printed at the back of each issue.
Author information and reprints: Payment:
  Reprints only. 75 offprints
  Is simultaneous submission of article to
  other journals permitted: Not permitted.

Exclusive manuscript rights between
acceptance and publication: Yes
Copyright: Held by publication.
Reprints: Available at cost.
Submit to:
  Professor Dr. Ralph G. Pearson
  Editorial Board
  Department of Chemistry
  Northwestern University
  Evanston, Illinois 60201

Physics

ANNALS OF PHYSICS [2132]
Annalen der Physik
Johann Ambrosius Barth
Salomonstrasse, 18B, Postfach 109
701 Leipzig, German Democratic Republic
2 52 45

First published in 1790

SUBSCRIPTION DATA
Issues and rates: Published bi-monthly.
  Annual rate(s): 69 DM plus postage
Managing Editor: Gustav Richter

EDITORIAL DESCRIPTION
  Presents works from the general areas of
  experimental, theoretical, applied and
  mathematical physics and related
  disciplines.
Articles per average issue: 8-10
Audience: Professional
  Manuscripts accepted in English, German

MANUSCRIPT INFORMATION
Manuscript requirements: See latest issue for
  style requirements. Style sheet sent on
  request.
  Preferred length: 10-15 pages
  Number of copies to be submitted: 2
  Abstract: Yes. both English and German
Author information and reprints: Payment:
  Reprints only. 75
  Is simultaneous submission of article to
  other journals permitted: Not permitted.
  Exclusive manuscript rights between
  acceptance and publication: Yes
  Copyright: Held by publication for 6
  months
  Reprints: Available at no cost.
Disposition of manuscript:
  Query letter: Not necessary.
  Receipt of manuscript acknowledged: Yes
  Decision to publish in: 1-2 months
  Accepted manuscript published in: 6
  months
  Rejected manuscript returned: Yes, with
  return postage paid by publication.
  Rejected manuscript criticized:
  Sometimes
Submit to:
  Wilhelm Walcher
  Editor
  Renthof 5
  Marburg/Lahn, Federal Republic of
  Germany

ANNALS OF PHYSICS [2133]

Academic Press, Inc.
111 Fifth Avenue
New York, New York 10003
(212) 741-6800

SUBSCRIPTION DATA

Issues and rates: Published semi-monthly.
Annual rate(s): $248.50; Foreign $278.50

EDITORIAL DESCRIPTION

Intended to provide a medium for original work of broad significance to encourage those who have interests in several fields of physics to think of physics as a unified structure of high esthetic appeal.
Articles per average issue: 6-8
Audience: Professional physicists
Manuscripts accepted in English

MANUSCRIPT INFORMATION

Subject field(s): Plasma and fluid dynamics; statistical physics; quantum mechanics of atoms and molecules and of solid and liquid states; nuclear physics, elementary particles and field theory, classical physics, gravitation, astrophysics
Manuscript requirements: Style sheet sent on request.
Preferred length: None
Number of copies to be submitted: 2
Abstract: Yes.
Author information and reprints: Payment: None.
Is simultaneous submission of article to other journals permitted: Not permitted.
Exclusive manuscript rights between acceptance and publication: Yes
Copyright: Held by publication.
Reprints: Available at no cost.
Disposition of manuscript:
Query letter: Not necessary.
Receipt of manuscript acknowledged: Yes
Decision to publish in: 3 months
Accepted manuscript published in: 6 months
Rejected manuscript returned: Yes, with return postage paid by publication.
Rejected manuscript criticized: Sometimes
Submit to:
Philip M. Morse
Editor
Massachusetts Institute of Technology
Room 6-403
Cambridge, Massachusetts
(617) 253-7182

APPLIED PHYSICS [2134]

Springer-Verlag New York, Inc.
175 Fifth Avenue
New York, New York 10010
(212) 673-2660

Previously entitled *Zeitschrift für angewandte Physik*

First published in 1973

SUBSCRIPTION DATA

Issues and rates: Published monthly.
Average paid circulation: 1,000
Annual rate(s): $65.00 per volume
Managing Editor: Helmut K. V. Lotsch

EDITORIAL DESCRIPTION

Original reports on research frontiers in applied physics, and review and tutorial articles on research subjects of wider interest.
Articles per average issue: 15-20
Audience: Physicists, engineers, students
Manuscripts accepted in English

MANUSCRIPT INFORMATION

Subject field(s): Solid-state physics, surface physics, microwave acoustics, electrophysics, quantum electronics, laser spectroscopy, photophysical chemistry, coherent optics, integrated optics
Manuscript requirements: See latest issue for style requirements. Style sheet sent on request.
Preferred length: 6-8 pages
Number of copies to be submitted: Original and 2 copies
Abstract: Yes.
Author information and reprints: Payment: None.
Is simultaneous submission of article to other journals permitted: Not permitted.
Exclusive manuscript rights between acceptance and publication: Yes
Copyright: Held by publication.
Reprints: Available at no cost. 50
Disposition of manuscript:
Query letter: Not necessary, but advisable.
Receipt of manuscript acknowledged: Yes
Decision to publish in: 2-4 weeks
Accepted manuscript published in: 2-4 months
Rejected manuscript returned: Yes, with return postage paid by publication.
Rejected manuscript criticized: Yes
Submit to:
Helmut K. V. Lotsch
Editor
Springer Verlag
P. O. Box 105 280
D-69 Heidelberg 1, Federal Republic of Germany
(062 21) 487-253

SPECIAL STIPULATIONS

Articles must be of a high scientific level; air mail required between Europe and America.

ASTROPHYSICAL LETTERS [2135]

Gordon and Breach Science Publishers
440 Park Avenue South
New York, New York 10016
(212) 689-0360

SUBSCRIPTION DATA

Issues and rates: Published monthly.
Annual rate(s): Individuals $8.50, Institutions $28.00

EDITORIAL DESCRIPTION

The journal is devoted to the international circulation of new views and discoveries in all branches of astrophysical research. Each issue includes several short communications.

MANUSCRIPT INFORMATION

Manuscript requirements: Letter of inquiry should be sent to editor before submission of manuscript.
Submit to:
Alan Maxwell
Editor
Harvard College Observatory
Harvard University
Cambridge, Massachusetts 02138

CANADIAN JOURNAL OF PHYSICS [2136]

National Research Council of Canada
100 Sussex Drive
Ottawa, Ontario, K1A OR6 Canada
(613) 992-5411

Previously entitled *Canadian Journal of Research*

First published in 1929

SUBSCRIPTION DATA

Issues and rates: Published semi-monthly.
Average paid circulation: 2,100
Annual rate(s): Individuals $24,
Publisher or Sponsor: National Research Council of Canada

EDITORIAL DESCRIPTION

Publishes results of original scientific research in all fields of physics.
Articles per average issue: 14
Audience: Research
Manuscripts accepted in English, French

MANUSCRIPT INFORMATION

Subject field(s): Atoms, molecules and related topics; atoms, nuclei, and particles in matter; fluids, thermodynamics, and related topics; solids; nuclei; elementary particles and fields
Manuscript requirements: Style sheet sent on request.
Number of copies to be submitted: Two
Abstract: Yes
Author information and reprints: Payment: None.
Is simultaneous submission of article to other journals permitted: No
Exclusive manuscript rights between acceptance and publication: Yes
Copyright: Held by publication.
Reprints: Available at cost.
Disposition of manuscript:
Query letter: No
Receipt of manuscript acknowledged: Yes
Decision to publish in: 3 months
Accepted manuscript published in: 4 months
Rejected manuscript returned: Yes
Rejected manuscript criticized: Yes
Submit to:
P. R. Wallace

Physics

Editor
Room 313, MacDonald Physics Building
McGill University, P.O. Box 6070
Montreal 101, Quebec, Canada
(514) 392-5324

COMMUNICATIONS IN MATHEMATICAL PHYSICS [2137]

Springer-Verlag
175 Fifth Avenue
New York, New York 10010

SUBSCRIPTION DATA
Annual rate(s): DM 128 per volume
Managing Editor: K. Hepp

EDITORIAL DESCRIPTION
Publishes papers dealing with all aspects
of mathematical physics
Audience: Mathematicians and physicists
Manuscripts accepted in French,
German, preferably English

MANUSCRIPT INFORMATION
Manuscript requirements: Style sheet sent
on request
Preferred length: As required
Number of copies to be submitted: 3
Abstract: Yes.
Author information and reprints: Payment:
Reprints only. 75 offprints
Is simultaneous submission of article to
other journals permitted: Not permitted.
Exclusive manuscript rights between
acceptance and publication: Yes
Copyright: Held by publication.
Reprints: Available at cost.
Submit to:
Professor J. L. Lebowitz
Editorial Board Member
Belfer Graduate School of Science
Yeshiva University
New York, New York 10033

CRC CRITICAL REVIEWS IN SOLID STATE SCIENCES [2138]

CRC Press, Inc.
18901 Cranwood Parkway
Cleveland, Ohio 44128
(216) 475-9000

First published in 1970

SUBSCRIPTION DATA
Issues and rates: Published quarterly.
Average paid circulation: 1,000
Annual rate(s): $56.00, Foreign $64.00

EDITORIAL DESCRIPTION
The basic concept of this program is to
provide a qualitative approach to the
total mass of scientific literature
published throughout the world in this
discipline. This is accomplished by
utilizing outstanding experts in each field
to select and critically evaluate the most
significant papers published in their
particular specialties. To insure accuracy
and objectivity, each review is refereed
prior to publication.

Articles per average issue: 3
Audience: Research Laboratories
Manuscripts accepted in English

MANUSCRIPT INFORMATION
Subject field(s): Solid state physics,
macromolecular
Manuscript requirements: Style sheet sent
on request.
Preferred length: 75-150 pages
Number of copies to be submitted: Three
Abstract: Yes.
Author information and reprints: Payment:
By publication to author.
Is simultaneous submission of article to
other journals permitted: No
Exclusive manuscript rights between
acceptance and publication: Yes
Copyright: Held by publication.
Reprints: Available, 25 free to author
Disposition of manuscript:
Query letter:
Receipt of manuscript acknowledged: Yes
Decision to publish in: 3 weeks
Accepted manuscript published in: 3
months
Rejected manuscript returned: Yes
Rejected manuscript criticized: Yes
Submit to:
Gerald A. Becker
Director, Editorial Operations
(See address above)

ENERGY CONVERSION [2139]

An International Journal
Pergamon Press, Inc.
Fairview Park
Elmsford, New York 10523
(914) 592-7700

First published in 1961

SUBSCRIPTION DATA
Issues and rates: Published quarterly.
Annual rate(s): $25.00; Institutions
$50.00

EDITORIAL DESCRIPTION
Provides an interdisciplinary medium
through which advanced energy
conversion can be treated as a coherent
subject. Papers of high technical merit
concerning primary energy sources and
systems and the problems associated with
regulation and control will be accepted.
Articles per average issue: 4-5
Audience: Professional, academic
Manuscripts accepted in English, French,
German

MANUSCRIPT INFORMATION
Subject field(s): Isotope and nuclear design
principles, solar collection, advances in
the generation of heat from chemicals;
thermoelectricity, thermionic processes,
photoelectric processes, electrochemistry
associated with fuel cells and other forms
of batteries, circuitry and components,
solid state elements, etc.
Manuscript requirements: See latest issue for
style requirements.
Preferred length: None

Number of copies to be submitted: 2
double-spaced
Abstract: Yes. A brief abstract in all
three languages.
Author information and reprints: Payment:
None.
Is simultaneous submission of article to
other journals permitted: Not permitted.
Exclusive manuscript rights between
acceptance and publication: Yes
Copyright: Held by publication.
Reprints: Available at cost.
Disposition of manuscript:
Query letter: Not necessary.
Receipt of manuscript acknowledged: Yes
Decision to publish in: 4 weeks
Accepted manuscript published in: 5
months
Rejected manuscript returned: Yes, if
return postage is supplied by author.
Rejected manuscript criticized: Reasons
for rejections only
Submit to:
Dr. J. Denton
Editor-in-Chief
University of Pennsylvania
Philadelphia, Pennsylvania 19104

And appropriate regional editors.

FIELDS AND QUANTA* [2140]

Gordon and Breach Science Publishers
440 Park Avenue South
New York, New York 10016
(212) 689-0360

SUBSCRIPTION DATA
Issues and rates: Published quarterly.
Annual rate(s): Individuals $15.00,
Institutions $45.00

EDITORIAL DESCRIPTION
The journal presents critical survey
articles dealing with the nature of the
fundamental interactions of matter. The
emphasis is on subjects in the general
area of particle physics, but solid state
theory, gravitation, and other subjects
which utilize fields and quanta as a basis
and add to the understanding of the
topics are also discussed.

MANUSCRIPT INFORMATION
Subject field(s): Particle physics, solid state
theory, gravitation
Manuscript requirements: See latest issue for
style requirements.
Additional information: Letter of inquiry
should be sent to editor before
submission of manuscript.
Submit to:
E.C.G. Sudarshan
Editor
Center for Particle Theory
University of Texas at Austin
Austin, Texas 78712

GENERAL RELATIVITY AND GRAVITATION [2141]

Plenum Publishing Co., Ltd.
227 West 17th Street
New York, New York 10011

First published in 1970

SUBSCRIPTION DATA

Issues and rates: Published bi-monthly.
Annual rate(s): $55.00
Publisher or Sponsor: International
Committee on General Relativity and
Gravitation
Managing Editor: A. Held

EDITORIAL DESCRIPTION

Research and review articles connected
with the fields of general relativity and
gravitation.
Articles per average issue: 9
Audience: Specialists in the field
Manuscripts accepted in English

MANUSCRIPT INFORMATION

Manuscript requirements: No specific style
guide. See latest issue for style
requirements.
Preferred length: 15-20 pages
Number of copies to be submitted: 2
Abstract: Yes.
Author information and reprints: Payment:
None.
Is simultaneous submission of article to
other journals permitted: Not permitted.
Exclusive manuscript rights between
acceptance and publication: Yes
Copyright: Held by publication.
Reprints: Available at cost.
Additional information: No twin paradox
articles please.
Disposition of manuscript:
Query letter: Not necessary.
Receipt of manuscript acknowledged: Yes
Decision to publish in: 2-3 months
Accepted manuscript published in: 6-8
months
Rejected manuscript returned: Yes, with
return postage paid by publication.
Rejected manuscript criticized: Yes
Submit to:
A. Held
Editor
Institut für Physik, Universität Bern
Sidlerstrasse 5
CH-3012 Bern, Switzerland
(031) 65 86 33

HIGH TEMPERATURES-HIGH PRESSURES [2142]

207 Brondesbury Park
London NW2 5JN, England
(01) 459-0066

First published in 1969

SUBSCRIPTION DATA

Issues and rates: Published bi-monthly.
Annual rate(s): £30.00, $70.00 (in North
America)

EDITORIAL DESCRIPTION

Publishes research work in the fields of
high temperature and high pressure
physics, chemistry, crystallography,
metallurgy, materials science, engineering,
equipment, instrumentation, etc.
Articles per average issue: 14
Audience: Physicists, chemists, engineers,
research workers in universities and
industry.
Manuscripts accepted in English, German
and French

MANUSCRIPT INFORMATION

Manuscript requirements: See latest issue for
style requirements.
Number of copies to be submitted: Two
Abstract: Yes.
Author information and reprints: Payment:
None.
Is simultaneous submission of article to
other journals permitted: No
Exclusive manuscript rights between
acceptance and publication: Yes
Copyright: Held jointly
Reprints: Available, 50 free
Disposition of manuscript:
Query letter:
Receipt of manuscript acknowledged: Yes
Decision to publish in: 1-2 months
Accepted manuscript published in: 4-6
months
Rejected manuscript returned: Yes
Rejected manuscript criticized: Yes
Submit to:
For high temperature manuscripts:
E. Fitzer
Institut für Chemische Technik
Universität Karlsruhe
Karlsruhe, Federal Republic of Germany
(721) 608-2120

Manuscripts dealing with high pressures:
J. Lees
Standard Telecommunication
Laboratories, Ltd.
London Road
Harlow, Essex, England

INFRARED PHYSICS [2143]

Pergamon Press, Inc.
Fairview Park
Elmsford, New York 10523
(914) 592-7700

First published in 1961

SUBSCRIPTION DATA

Issues and rates: Published quarterly.
Annual rate(s): $25.00; Institutions
$40.00

EDITORIAL DESCRIPTION

Contains the results of original
investigations into infrared physics and
its allied disciplines.
Articles per average issue: 5-7
Audience: Professional, academic
Manuscripts accepted in English
preferred

MANUSCRIPT INFORMATION

Manuscript requirements: See latest issue for
style requirements.
Preferred length: None
Number of copies to be submitted: 2
Abstract: Yes. Not to exceed 200 words
at the beginning of the article; if the
original language is not English, an
abstract should be supplied in English.
Author information and reprints: Payment:
Reprints only. 50 reprints
Is simultaneous submission of article to
other journals permitted: Not permitted.
Exclusive manuscript rights between
acceptance and publication: Yes
Copyright: Held by publication.
Reprints: Available at cost. In multiples
of 50
Disposition of manuscript:
Query letter: Not necessary.
Receipt of manuscript acknowledged: Yes
Decision to publish in: 4 weeks
Accepted manuscript published in: 5
months
Rejected manuscript returned: Yes, if
return postage is supplied by author.
Rejected manuscript criticized: Reasons
for rejections only
Submit to:
T. S. Moss
Executive Editor
Royal Aircraft Establishment
Farnborough, Hampshire, England

Or:
P. Goerlich
Director for Research and Development
VEB Carl Zeiss
Jena, Federal Republic of Germany

S. Passman
National Science Foundation
Washington, D.C. 20550
Regional Editors

INTERNATIONAL JOURNAL FOR RADIATION PHYSICS AND CHEMISTRY [2144]

Pergamon Press, Inc.
Maxwell House, Fairview Park
Elmsford, New York 10523
(914) 592-7700

First published in 1969

SUBSCRIPTION DATA

Issues and rates: Published bi-monthly.
Annual rate(s): $70.00
Managing Editor: H. Hering, Sur-Yvette

EDITORIAL DESCRIPTION

A publication which groups together
articles dealing with the physical and
chemical effects of ionizing radiation, and
closely related topics.
Articles per average issue: 6-8
Audience: Researchers

Physics

Manuscripts accepted in English, French, German

MANUSCRIPT INFORMATION

Subject field(s): Radiation physics and chemistry

Manuscript requirements: See latest issue for style requirements.
Preferred length: 20-30 pages
Number of copies to be submitted: 2
Abstract: Yes. Of 100 to 300 words indicating the aim of the work, the principal results, and the major conclusions.

Author information and reprints: Payment: Reprints only. 50
Is simultaneous submission of article to other journals permitted: Not permitted.
Exclusive manuscript rights between acceptance and publication: Yes
Copyright: Held by publication.
Reprints: Available at cost.

Disposition of manuscript:
Query letter: Not necessary.
Receipt of manuscript acknowledged: Yes
Decision to publish in: 4 weeks
Accepted manuscript published in: 5 months
Rejected manuscript returned: Yes, if return postage is supplied by author.
Rejected manuscript criticized: Reasons for rejections only

Submit to:
Prof. P. J. Dyne
Associate Editor
Whiteshall Nuclear Research Laboratory
Atomic Energy of Canada, Ltd.
Pinawa, Manitoba, Canada

INTERNATIONAL JOURNAL OF MASS SPECTROMETRY AND ION PHYSICS [2145]

Elsevier Scientific Publishing Company
P. O. Box 211, Jan van Galenstraat 335
Amsterdam, The Netherlands
(020) 515-9222

First published in 1968

SUBSCRIPTION DATA

Issues and rates: Published monthly.
Annual rate(s): Dfl. 309 worldwide

EDITORIAL DESCRIPTION

Contains accounts of original research work in the field of mass spectrometry and ion physics.

Audience: Academic, professional, industrial
Manuscripts accepted in English (French, German)

MANUSCRIPT INFORMATION

Manuscript requirements: Style sheet sent on request.
Preferred length: 5-15 pages
Number of copies to be submitted: 2
Abstract: Yes. 100-200 words

Author information and reprints: Payment: Reprints only. 50 reprints
Is simultaneous submission of article to other journals permitted: Not permitted.

Exclusive manuscript rights between acceptance and publication: Yes
Copyright: Held by publication.
Reprints: Available at cost.

Disposition of manuscript:
Query letter: Not necessary.
Receipt of manuscript acknowledged: Yes
Decision to publish in: 3 weeks
Accepted manuscript published in: 4 months
Rejected manuscript returned: Yes, with return postage paid by publication.
Rejected manuscript criticized: Sometimes

Submit to:
J. Franzen
Varian MAT GmbH
Postfach 4062
28 Bremen 10, Federal Republic of Germany

A. Quayle
Thornton Research Centre
P. O. Box 1
Chester CH1 3SH, England

H. J. Svec
Department of Chemistry
Iowa State University
Ames, Iowa 50010
Editors

INTERNATIONAL JOURNAL OF THEORETICAL PHYSICS [2146]

227 West 17th Street
New York, New York 10011
(212) 255-0713

First published in 1968

SUBSCRIPTION DATA

Issues and rates: Published monthly.
Average paid circulation: Not available.
Annual rate(s): $74.00

EDITORIAL DESCRIPTION

Strives to foster and encourage development and expansion in fundamental physics. New concepts as well as standard topics are covered.

Articles per average issue: 6-10
Audience: Theoretical physics professors and researchers
Manuscripts accepted in English

MANUSCRIPT INFORMATION

Subject field(s): Physical axiomatics, general relativity theory and cosmology, high energy physics

Manuscript requirements: See latest issue for style requirements.
Number of copies to be submitted: Original and 2 copies
Abstract: Yes.
Is simultaneous submission of article to other journals permitted: No

Exclusive manuscript rights between acceptance and publication: Yes
Copyright: Held by publication.
Reprints: Available, 25 free

Disposition of manuscript:
Query letter:
Receipt of manuscript acknowledged: Yes
Decision to publish in: 6-8 weeks
Accepted manuscript published in: 6-8 months
Rejected manuscript returned: No

Submit to:
John Yates
Editor
51 Snowdon Road
Eccles, Manchester, England

JAPANESE JOURNAL OF APPLIED PHYSICS [2147]

2nd Toyo Kaiji Building
4-24-8, Shinbashi, Minato-Ku
Tokyo 105, Japan
03-432-4308

First published in 1962

SUBSCRIPTION DATA

Issues and rates: Published monthly.
Average paid circulation: 4400; 200 controlled
Annual rate(s): 20,000 Japanese Yen

Publisher or Sponsor: Physical Society of Japan, Japan Society of Applied Physics

Managing Editor: Tatsuya Niimi; Yutaka Tuzi

EDITORIAL DESCRIPTION

A monthly journal in European languages published under the cooperation of the Physical Society of Japan and the Japan Society of Applied Physics.

Articles per average issue: 20
Manuscripts accepted in English, French and German

MANUSCRIPT INFORMATION

Subject field(s): Atomic and molecular physics, structure of matter, crystal growth and phase transformations, surface and films, mechanical properties, statistical and thermal properties, electronic and electrical properties, optical properties, magnetism, magnetic materials and devices, waves and optics, semiconductors and devices, quantum electronics, nucleonics and plasma physics, technics, instrument and system

Manuscript requirements: Style sheet sent on request.
Number of copies to be submitted: one copy (original)
Abstract: Yes.

Author information and reprints: Payment: By author to publication.
Is simultaneous submission of article to other journals permitted: No
Exclusive manuscript rights between acceptance and publication: Yes
Copyright: Held by publication.
Reprints: Available

Additional information: Short Note: about 130 lines of typing, 65 strokes per line; Regular Paper: about 400 to 500 lines of typing, 65 strokes per line.
Disposition of manuscript:
Query letter: Not necessary.
Receipt of manuscript acknowledged: Yes
Decision to publish in: 3-4 4 months
Accepted manuscript published in: 1-3 months
Rejected manuscript returned: Yes
Rejected manuscript criticized: Yes
Submit to:
Editor-in-Chief
(See address above)

JOURNAL OF APPLIED PHYSICS* [2148]

American Institute of Physics
335 East 45th Street
New York, New York 10017

SUBSCRIPTION DATA
Issues and rates: Published monthly.
Average paid circulation: 10,000
Annual rate(s): $55.00, Members $17.00, Foreign $59.00
Publisher or Sponsor: American Institute of Physics

EDITORIAL DESCRIPTION
Publishes full-length articles and shorter commentaries on topics in applied physics.

MANUSCRIPT INFORMATION
Subject field(s): Applications of physics to engineering, other physical sciences and industry; solid state, optics, magnetism, spectroscopy
Manuscript requirements: AIP
Number of copies to be submitted: Two
Is simultaneous submission of article to other journals permitted: No
Exclusive manuscript rights between acceptance and publication: Yes
Copyright: Held jointly by author and publication.
Reprints: Available
Additional information: Include an abstract of less than 500 words for full-length articles.
Disposition of manuscript:
Receipt of manuscript acknowledged: Yes
Decision to publish in: Varies
Accepted manuscript published in: Varies
Submit to:
Gilbert J. Perlow
Editor
Argonne National Laboratory
P.O. Box 296
Argonne, Illinois 60439

THE JOURNAL OF CHEMICAL PHYSICS [2149]

American Institute of Physics
335 East 45th Street
New York, New York 10017
(212) 685-1940

First published in 1933

SUBSCRIPTION DATA
Issues and rates: Published semi-monthly.
Average paid circulation: 6,300
Annual rate(s): $165.00, Foreign $173.00, Members $42.00
Publisher or Sponsor: American Institute of Physics
Managing Editor: Mitchell Koch

EDITORIAL DESCRIPTION
To bridge the gap between journals of physics and journals of chemistry.
Manuscripts accepted in English

MANUSCRIPT INFORMATION
Subject field(s): Valence, quantum theory, statistical mechanics, intermolecular forces, spectroscopy, etc.
Manuscript requirements: See latest issue; Use AIP and CA for citations.
Number of copies to be submitted: One
Author information and reprints: Payment: By author to publication. $65 per page. $20 per article. To be paid by author's institution.
Is simultaneous submission of article to other journals permitted: No
Exclusive manuscript rights between acceptance and publication: Yes
Copyright: Held by the American Institute of Physics
Reprints: Available, 100 free if page charge honored
Additional information: Unavailable symbols or Greek letters should be inserted neatly in ink.
Submit to:
J. W. Stout
Editor
Department of Chemistry
University of Chicago
Chicago, Illinois 60637

SPECIAL STIPULATIONS
Non-payment of publication charge may lead to delay in publication.

JOURNAL OF COMPUTATIONAL PHYSICS [2150]

Academic Press, Inc.
111 Fifth Avenue
New York, New York 10003

First published in 1966

SUBSCRIPTION DATA
Issues and rates: Published monthly.
Average paid circulation: 1,000
Annual rate(s): $24.50; Foreign $136.50
Managing Editor: Berni J. Alder

EDITORIAL DESCRIPTION
To publish articles concerning techniques developed in the solution of data handling problems and mathematical equations, both arising in the description of physical phenomena
Articles per average issue: 10
Audience: Computational physicists
Manuscripts accepted in English

MANUSCRIPT INFORMATION
Subject field(s): Hydrodynamics, quantum mechanics, geophysics, astronomy, plasma, statistical mechanics, nuclear physics, solid state physics, aerodynamics, etc.
Manuscript requirements: Style sheet sent on request. AIP
Preferred length: 10,000 words; 20 pages
Number of copies to be submitted: 3
Abstract: Yes
Author information and reprints: Payment: None.
Is simultaneous submission of article to other journals permitted: Not permitted.
Exclusive manuscript rights between acceptance and publication: Yes
Copyright: Held by publication.
Reprints: Available at no cost. 50
Disposition of manuscript:
Query letter: Not necessary.
Receipt of manuscript acknowledged: Yes
Decision to publish in: 3 months
Accepted manuscript published in: 6 months
Rejected manuscript returned: Yes, with return postage paid by publication.
Rejected manuscript criticized: Yes
Submit to:
Sidney Fernbach;
John Killeen
Editors
P. O. Box 808
Livermore Laboratory
Livermore, California 94450
447-1100

JOURNAL OF GEOPHYSICAL RESEARCH [2151]

American Geophysical Union
1909 K Street, N.W.
Washington, D.C. 20006
(202) 331-0370

SUBSCRIPTION DATA
Issues and rates: Three per month
Average paid circulation: 9,500
Annual rate(s): $95.00
Publisher or Sponsor: American Geophysical Union
Managing Editor: A. F. Spilhaus, Jr.

EDITORIAL DESCRIPTION
On the first of the month, the issue is devoted entirely to space physics and the physics of planetary atmospheres. Papers appearing in the tenth of the month issue center around the physics and chemistry of solid earth and the geophysics of other planets. The last issue concerns the physics and chemistry of the earth's atmosphere, oceans and ocean basins and air-sea interactions.
Articles per average issue: 40, 25, 20, respectively
Audience: Scientists
Manuscripts accepted in English

MANUSCRIPT INFORMATION
Manuscript requirements: AGU
Number of copies to be submitted: Three; four for the first of the month issue

Physics

Abstract: Yes.
Is simultaneous submission of article to other journals permitted: No
Exclusive manuscript rights between acceptance and publication: Yes
Copyright: Held by the American Geophysical Union
Reprints: Available at cost
Additional information: Specific information available on request.
Disposition of manuscript:
Query letter:
Receipt of manuscript acknowledged: Yes
Decision to publish in: Varies
Accepted manuscript published in: Four months
Rejected manuscript returned: Yes
Rejected manuscript criticized: Yes
Submit to:
1st of the month:
George C. Reid
Aeronomy Laboratory
NOAA
Boulder, Colorado 80302

10th of the month:
Edward A. Flinn
Teledyne Geotech
Box 201
Alexandria, Virginia 22313

20th of the month:
Karl K. Turekian
Department of Geology and Geophysics
P.O. Box 2162, Yale Station
New Haven, Connecticut 06520

JOURNAL OF LOW TEMPERATURE PHYSICS [2152]
Plenum Publishing Corporation
227 West 17th Street
New York, New York 10011
(212) 255-0713

First published in 1969

SUBSCRIPTION DATA
Issues and rates: Published monthly.
Average paid circulation: Not available.
Annual rate(s): Institutions $195.00, Foreign institutions $205.80, Individuals $125.00, Foreign individuals $135.80

EDITORIAL DESCRIPTION
Contains original papers, letters, occasional review articles on fundamental, theoretical and experimental research developments in cryogenics and low temperature physics.
Articles per average issue: 15
Audience: Low temperature physicists
Manuscripts accepted in English

MANUSCRIPT INFORMATION
Subject field(s): Properties of Fermi and Bose systems; superfluidity and properties of quantum fluids and solids; superconductivity; phase transitions at low temperatures; thermal properties; thermodynamics
Manuscript requirements: See latest issue for style requirements.
Number of copies to be submitted: Two

Abstract: Yes.
Author information and reprints: Payment: None.
Is simultaneous submission of article to other journals permitted:
Copyright: Held by publication.
Reprints: Available, cost varies
Disposition of manuscript:
Query letter:
Receipt of manuscript acknowledged: Yes
Decision to publish in: 6-8 weeks
Accepted manuscript published in: 6 months
Rejected manuscript returned: Yes
Submit to:
John G. Daunt
Editor
Cryogenics Center
Stevens Institute of Technology
Hoboken, New Jersey 07030

JOURNAL OF MACROMOLECULAR SCIENCE, PART B [2153]
Physics
Marcel Dekker Journals
P. O. Box 11305, Church Street Station
New York, New York 10249

First published in 1967

SUBSCRIPTION DATA
Issues and rates: Published quarterly.
Average paid circulation: 1,000
Annual rate(s): $72.50

EDITORIAL DESCRIPTION
Contains original reports of basic and applied research in the physics of macromolecules-solutions and solids, synthetic and natural.
Articles per average issue: 10-12
Audience: Polymer scientists and engineers
Manuscripts accepted in English

MANUSCRIPT INFORMATION
Subject field(s): Polymer physics
Manuscript requirements: See latest issue for style requirements.
Preferred length: None
Number of copies to be submitted: 3
Abstract: Yes
Author information and reprints: Payment: Reprints only. 20 reprints
Is simultaneous submission of article to other journals permitted: Not permitted.
Exclusive manuscript rights between acceptance and publication: Yes
Copyright: Held by publication.
Disposition of manuscript:
Query letter: Not necessary.
Receipt of manuscript acknowledged: Yes
Decision to publish in: 2-3 months
Accepted manuscript published in: 8 months
Rejected manuscript returned: Yes, with return postage paid by publication.
Rejected manuscript criticized: Yes
Submit to:
Phillip H. Geir
Executive Editor

School of Engineering, Polymer Science Division
Case Western Reserve University
Cleveland, Ohio 44106
(216) 368-4186

JOURNAL OF MOLECULAR STRUCTURE [2154]
Elsevier Scientific Publishing Company
P. O. Box 330, Jan van Galenstraat 335
Amsterdam, The Netherlands
(020) 515-9222

First published in 1967

SUBSCRIPTION DATA
Issues and rates: Published monthly.
Annual rate(s): Dfl. 565 worldwide

EDITORIAL DESCRIPTION
Contains accounts of original research work in the field of molecular structure.
Audience: Professional, academic
Manuscripts accepted in English (French, German)

MANUSCRIPT INFORMATION
Manuscript requirements: See latest issue for style requirements. Style sheet sent on request.
Preferred length: 5-15 pages
Number of copies to be submitted: 2
Abstract: Yes. 100-200 words
Author information and reprints: Payment: Reprints only. 50 reprints
Is simultaneous submission of article to other journals permitted: Not permitted.
Exclusive manuscript rights between acceptance and publication: Yes
Copyright: Held by publication.
Reprints: Available at cost.
Disposition of manuscript:
Query letter: Not necessary.
Receipt of manuscript acknowledged: Yes
Decision to publish in: 3 weeks
Accepted manuscript published in: 4 months
Rejected manuscript returned: Yes, with return postage paid by publication.
Rejected manuscript criticized: Sometimes
Submit to:
W. J. Orville-Thomas
Editor
Department of Chemistry and Applied Chemistry
University of Salford
Salford, Lancashire M5 4WT, England

JOURNAL OF PHYSICS A [2155]
Mathematical and General
The Institute of Physics
Techno House
Redcliffe Way
Bristol BS1 6NX, England
0272-297481

Previously entitled *Journal of Physics A: Mathematical, Nuclear and General*

SUBSCRIPTION DATA

Issues and rates: Published monthly.

Average paid circulation: 1,934

Annual rate(s): £60.00, Foreign $180.00 (Both are joint rates for Journals of Physics A and B)

Publisher or Sponsor: The Institute of Physics

Managing Editor: D. G. Fisher

EDITORIAL DESCRIPTION

Contains research and review papers in mathematical physics, relativity and gravitation, statistical mechanics, quantum optics, plasma and discharge physics, magneto hydro-dynamics, astrophysics, space physics and cosmic rays.

Articles per average issue: 10-20

Audience: Physicists and mathematicians

Manuscripts accepted in English, French, and German

MANUSCRIPT INFORMATION

Manuscript requirements: Style sheet sent on request.

Preferred length: 8000 words; 13 pages

Number of copies to be submitted: Two

Abstract: Yes.

Author information and reprints: Payment: None.

Is simultaneous submission of article to other journals permitted: No

Exclusive manuscript rights between acceptance and publication: Yes

Copyright: Held by author.

Reprints: Available to authors

Disposition of manuscript:

Query letter:

Receipt of manuscript acknowledged: Yes

Decision to publish in: 2-4 weeks

Accepted manuscript published in: 2-3 months

Rejected manuscript returned: Yes

Rejected manuscript criticized: Sometimes

Submit to:

J. A. Revill

Staff Editor

(See address above)

JOURNAL OF PHYSICS B [2156]

Atomic and Molecular Physics
The Institute of Physics
Techno House
Redcliffe Way
Bristol BS1 6NX, England
0272-297481

First published in 1968

SUBSCRIPTION DATA

Issues and rates: 18 times a year

Average paid circulation: 2,000

Annual rate(s): UK £65.00, Foreign $195.00

Publisher or Sponsor: The Institute of Physics

Managing Editor: D. G. Fisher; Professor G. W. Series

EDITORIAL DESCRIPTION

Contains primary research papers in the the study of atoms, ions and molecules, their structure and their interactions with radiation and other particles; also those aspects of spectroscopy, surface physics, astrophysics, plasma, discharge and maser and laser physics, quantum optics, non-linear optics and other investigations where the objects of study are the elementary atomic, ionic or molecular properties of processes.

Articles per average issue: 25

Audience: Atomic and molecular physicists

Manuscripts accepted in English, French, and German

MANUSCRIPT INFORMATION

Manuscript requirements: Style sheet sent on request.

Preferred length: 8000 words maximum

Number of copies to be submitted: Two

Abstract: Yes.

Author information and reprints: Payment: None.

Is simultaneous submission of article to other journals permitted: No

Exclusive manuscript rights between acceptance and publication: Yes

Copyright: Held by both author and publication

Reprints: Available, 25 free

Disposition of manuscript:

Query letter:

Receipt of manuscript acknowledged: Yes

Decision to publish in: 2 months

Accepted manuscript published in: 6 months

Rejected manuscript returned: Yes

Rejected manuscript criticized: Yes

Submit to:

Anthony J. Cox

Staff Editor

(See address above)

JOURNAL OF PHYSICS C [2157]

Solid State Physics
The Institute of Physics
Techno House
Redcliffe Way
Bristol BS1 6NX, England
0272-297481

First published in 1968

SUBSCRIPTION DATA

Issues and rates: Published semi-monthly.

Average paid circulation: 2,030

Annual rate(s): £84.00, Foreign $270.00

Publisher or Sponsor: The Institute of Physics

Managing Editor: D. G. Fisher

EDITORIAL DESCRIPTION

Contains research papers on all aspects of solid physics other than the applied aspects and those relating exclusively to metals; liquid state theory and experiment; superfluids.

Articles per average issue: 20

Audience: Solid-state physicists in colleges and research establishments

MANUSCRIPT INFORMATION

Subject field(s): Solid state physics, liquid physics, superfluids

Manuscript requirements: Style sheet sent on request.

Preferred length: 8000 words maximum

Number of copies to be submitted: Two

Abstract: Yes.

Author information and reprints: Payment: None.

Is simultaneous submission of article to other journals permitted: No

Exclusive manuscript rights between acceptance and publication: Yes

Copyright: Held by author and publication

Reprints: 25 Free to authors

Disposition of manuscript:

Query letter:

Receipt of manuscript acknowledged: Yes

Decision to publish in: 6 weeks

Accepted manuscript published in: 12 weeks

Rejected manuscript returned: Yes

Rejected manuscript criticized: Yes

Submit to:

R. Palmer

Staff Editor

(See address above)

JOURNAL OF PHYSICS D [2158]

Applied Physics
The Institute of Physics
Techno House
Redcliffe Way
Bristol BS1 6NX, England
0272-297481

SUBSCRIPTION DATA

Issues and rates: 18 issues per year

Average paid circulation: 2,364

Annual rate(s): £39.00, Foreign $115.00

Publisher or Sponsor: The Institute of Physics

Managing Editor: D. G. Fisher

EDITORIAL DESCRIPTION

Contains research papers, very occasional review articles in crystal growth; texture and morphology of solids and their relation to properties (for metals, alloys, ceramics, polymers, composites, etc); properties of materials (magnetic, crystallographic, elastic, plastic, optical); applied metal, semiconductor and dielectric physics; radio physics, acoustics, electron optics, wave propagation; applied discharge physics, plasma physics and magnetohydrodynamics; applications of masers and lasers; neutron transport and mathematical problems in the solution of applied physical problems.

Articles per average issue: 16

Audience: Research physicists

Manuscripts accepted in English, French, and German

Physics

MANUSCRIPT INFORMATION

Manuscript requirements: Style sheet sent
on request.
Preferred length: 8000 words maximum
Number of copies to be submitted: Two
Author information and reprints: Payment:
None.
Is simultaneous submission of article to
other journals permitted: No
Exclusive manuscript rights between
acceptance and publication: Yes
Copyright: Held by both author and
publication
Reprints: Available to authors
Disposition of manuscript:
Receipt of manuscript acknowledged: Yes
Decision to publish in: 3-8 weeks
Accepted manuscript published in: 3
months
Rejected manuscript returned: Yes
Rejected manuscript criticized: Yes
Submit to:
D. F. Manley
Staff Editor
(See address above)

JOURNAL OF PHYSICS E   [2159]

Scientific Instruments
The Institute of Physics
1 Lowther Gardens
Prince Consort Road
London SW7 2AB, England
01-589 0048

Previously entitled *Journal of Scientific
Instruments*

First published in 1923

SUBSCRIPTION DATA

Issues and rates: Published monthly.
Average paid circulation: 4050
Annual rate(s): £24, Foreign $75
Publisher or Sponsor: The Institute of
Physics
Managing Editor: J. Ring;

EDITORIAL DESCRIPTION

Contains research papers on all aspects of
instrumentation and measurement; review
articles; book reviews. The journal is a
research publication with closely
controlled standards.
Articles per average issue: 27
Audience: Academic and industrial
researchers
Manuscripts accepted in English, French,
and German

MANUSCRIPT INFORMATION

Subject field(s): Theory of instrumentation
and measurement, new instruments or
research apparatus, new applications of
instruments, appraisals of instrument
design or performance
Manuscript requirements: Style sheet sent
on request.
Preferred length: 1000-5000 words; 1 to 5
typeset pages
Number of copies to be submitted: Two
Abstract: Yes.

Author information and reprints: Payment:
None.
Is simultaneous submission of article to
other journals permitted: No
Exclusive manuscript rights between
acceptance and publication: Yes
Copyright: Held by author.
Reprints: Available, 25 free
Disposition of manuscript:
Query letter:
Receipt of manuscript acknowledged: Yes
Decision to publish in: 3 months
Accepted manuscript published in: 3
months
Rejected manuscript returned: Yes
Rejected manuscript criticized: Yes
Submit to:
Neil Warnock-Smith
Staff Editor
(See address above)

JOURNAL OF PHYSICS F   [2160]

Metal Physics
The Institute of Physics
Techno House
Redcliffe Way
Bristol BS1 6NX, England
0272-297481

Previously entitled *Journal of Physics C:
Metal Physics Supplement*

First published in 1971

SUBSCRIPTION DATA

Issues and rates: Published monthly.
Average paid circulation: 1,350
Annual rate(s): £54.00, Foreign $160.00,
Japan £65.00
Publisher or Sponsor: The Institute of
Physics
Managing Editor: D. G. Fisher

EDITORIAL DESCRIPTION

Contains articles on all aspects of metal
physics including electronic band
structure and Fermi surfaces, electronic
transport in metals, optical properties
and X-ray spectra, superconductivity,
alloys, magnetic properties of metals and
alloys, dislocations, vacancies, radiation
damage and diffusion in metals and
alloys.
Articles per average issue: 20
Manuscripts accepted in English, French
and German

MANUSCRIPT INFORMATION

Manuscript requirements: Style sheet sent
on request.
Preferred length: 8000 words maximum
Number of copies to be submitted: Two
Abstract: Yes.
Author information and reprints: Payment:
None.
Is simultaneous submission of article to
other journals permitted: No
Exclusive manuscript rights between
acceptance and publication: Yes
Copyright: Held by both author and
publication
Reprints: 25 Free to authors

Disposition of manuscript:
Query letter:
Receipt of manuscript acknowledged: Yes
Decision to publish in: 2 months
Accepted manuscript published in: 4
months
Rejected manuscript returned: Yes
Rejected manuscript criticized: Yes
Submit to:
Staff Editor
(See address above)

JOURNAL OF PLASMA PHYSICS   [2161]

Cambridge University Press
32 East 57th Street
New York, New York 10022

SUBSCRIPTION DATA

Issues and rates: Published semi-monthly.
Annual rate(s): £16.00 per volume;
Foreign $21.00 per volume
Managing Editor: Dr. J. P. Dougherty

EDITORIAL DESCRIPTION

Publishes papers dealing with
experimental and theoretical plasma
physics and its applications.
Manuscripts accepted in English

MANUSCRIPT INFORMATION

Manuscript requirements: See latest issue for
style requirements. Style sheet sent on
request.
Preferred length: As required
Number of copies to be submitted: 1,
typewritten, double-spaced
Abstract: Yes.
Author information and reprints: Payment:
Reprints only. 50 offprints
Is simultaneous submission of article to
other journals permitted: Not permitted.
Exclusive manuscript rights between
acceptance and publication: Yes
Copyright: Held by publication.
Submit to:
Prof. D. Bershader
Department of Aeronautics and
Astronautics
Stanford University
Stanford, California 94305

Prof. W. B. Thompson
Department of Physics
University of California, La Jolla
La Jolla, California 92037
Associate Editors

JOURNAL OF RAMAN SPECTROSCOPY   [2162]

D. Reidel Publishing Co.
P. O. Box 17
Dordrecht, The Netherlands
078-35388

First published in 1973

SUBSCRIPTION DATA

Issues and rates: Published bi-monthly.
Average paid circulation: 1,200

Annual rate(s): $18.00; Foreign $24.00; Institutions $48.00; Students $24.00
Managing Editor: D. A. Long

EDITORIAL DESCRIPTION

An international journal for original work in all aspects of Raman spectroscopy, including high-order process and also Brillouin and Rayleigh scattering.
Articles per average issue: 10
Audience: Post-graduate students and specialists in the field.
Manuscripts accepted in English, French, German

MANUSCRIPT INFORMATION

Subject field(s): Original research papers, research notes, letters to the Editor, tabulations and contributions with a predominantly technical character, including calibration procedures
Manuscript requirements: See latest issue for style requirements.
Preferred length: No preference
Number of copies to be submitted: 2
Abstract: Yes. Each contribution should contain an abstract in English of between 150 and 250 words.
Author information and reprints: Payment: Reprints only. 25
Is simultaneous submission of article to other journals permitted: Not permitted.
Exclusive manuscript rights between acceptance and publication: Yes
Copyright: Held by publisher, unless author specifically requests to hold copyright
Reprints: Available at cost. 4 cents per page
Disposition of manuscript:
Query letter: Not necessary.
Receipt of manuscript acknowledged: Yes
Decision to publish in: 1-2 months
Accepted manuscript published in: 2-4 months
Rejected manuscript returned: Yes, if return postage is supplied by author.
Rejected manuscript criticized: Reasons for rejections only
Submit to:
Professor H. J. Bernstein
Managing Editor
National Research Council of Canada
Ottawa 7, Ontario, Canada

PHYSICA SCRIPTA [2163]

Almqvist & Wiksell Periodical Company
Box 62
S-101 20 Stockholm 1, Sweden
08/23 79 90

SUBSCRIPTION DATA
Issues and rates: Published monthly.
Average paid circulation: 1,500
Annual rate(s): Sw.Kr 400; Foreign $101.25

Publisher or Sponsor: The Royal Swedish Academy of Sciences
Managing Editor: Lamek Hulthén; Nils Robert Nilsson

EDITORIAL DESCRIPTION

Publishes articles in experimental and theoretical physics. Preferential language is English.

MANUSCRIPT INFORMATION

Subject field(s): Experimental and theoretical physics
Manuscript requirements: See latest issue for style requirements.
Author information and reprints: Payment: None.
Is simultaneous submission of article to other journals permitted: No
Exclusive manuscript rights between acceptance and publication: Yes
Copyright: Held by The Royal Swedish Academy of Sciences
Additional information: Short communications can be accepted for speedy publication. They should normally consist of not more than four double-spaced type-written pages or one journal page including tables, figures and references. Every paper should include an abstract in English.
Disposition of manuscript:
Rejected manuscript returned: Yes
Rejected manuscript criticized: No
Submit to:
Editor
The Royal Swedish Academy of Sciences
S-104 05 Stockholm 50, Sweden

PHYSICAL REVIEW LETTERS [2164]

c/o Brookhaven National Laboratory
Upton, New York 11973
(516) 345-2540

First published in 1958

SUBSCRIPTION DATA
Issues and rates: Published weekly.
Average paid circulation: 9700
Annual rate(s): $50.00, Members $20.00, Foreign $63.00
Publisher or Sponsor: American Physical Society

EDITORIAL DESCRIPTION

Contains short communications dealing with important new discoveries or topics of high current interest in rapidly changing fields of physics research.
Articles per average issue: 20
Audience: Research scientists and engineers in physics and closely related fields
Manuscripts accepted in English

MANUSCRIPT INFORMATION
Subject field(s): Physics
Manuscript requirements: AIP; see front cover of first issue of each volume
Preferred length: Under 2600 words
Number of copies to be submitted: Three
Abstract: Yes.

Author information and reprints: Payment: By author to publication. $70.00
Is simultaneous submission of article to other journals permitted: No
Exclusive manuscript rights between acceptance and publication: Yes
Copyright: Held by publication.
Reprints: Available, 100 free if publishing charge honored; otherwise, cost dependent on length of article.
Disposition of manuscript:
Query letter:
Receipt of manuscript acknowledged: Yes
Decision to publish in: 4-6 weeks
Accepted manuscript published in: 3 weeks
Rejected manuscript returned: Yes
Rejected manuscript criticized: Yes
Submit to:
J.A. Krumhansl;
George L. Trigg
Editors
(See address above)

PHYSICAL SOCIETY OF JAPAN JOURNAL [2165]

Kikai-Shinko Building, Room 211
Shiba-Koen, Minato-ku
Tokyo 105, Japan
03-434-2671

First published in 1946

SUBSCRIPTION DATA
Issues and rates: Published monthly.
Average paid circulation: 4500
Annual rate(s): 45,000 Yen

EDITORIAL DESCRIPTION

Devoted to original papers in physics and related fields which materially contribute to the progress of physics.
Articles per average issue: 40 (Full papers) 18 (short notes)
Manuscripts accepted in English, French and German

MANUSCRIPT INFORMATION

Subject field(s): Elementary particles, nuclei, cosmic rays; statistical mechanics, thermodynamics, theory of solids; magnetism; metals and alloys; semiconductors and insulators, crystal properties; X-rays, particle rays and diffraction; optics and quantum electronics; atoms and molecules, polymers and biophysics; gases, liquids and amorphous solids; plasmas, nuclear fusion and electric discharge; fluid dynamics and mathematical methods
Manuscript requirements: See latest issue for style requirements.
Preferred length: 8 pages maximum
Number of copies to be submitted: Original
Abstract: Yes.
Author information and reprints: Payment: By publication to author.
Is simultaneous submission of article to other journals permitted: No
Exclusive manuscript rights between acceptance and publication: No
Copyright: Held by author.

Physics

Reprints: Available if ordered in lots of 50.

Additional information: Short note section provided for brief reports needing prompt publication. Galley proof only will be sent to author.

Disposition of manuscript:
Query letter:
Receipt of manuscript acknowledged: Yes
Decision to publish in: 60 days
Accepted manuscript published in: 80 days
Rejected manuscript returned: Yes
Rejected manuscript criticized: Yes

Submit to:
T. Oguchi
Chief Editor
(See address above)

PHYSICS BULLETIN [2166]

The Institute of Physics
1 Lowther Gardens, Prince Consort Road
London SW7 2AB, United Kingdom
(UK) 01-589 0048

Previously entitled *Bulletin of the Institute of Physics*

First published in 1950

SUBSCRIPTION DATA

Issues and rates: Published monthly.
Average paid circulation: 500; 16,200 controlled
Annual rate(s): £15.00, Foreign $45.00

Publisher or Sponsor: The Institute of Physics

EDITORIAL DESCRIPTION

Contains articles on all aspects of physics, both technical and its wider impact; extensive news sections on meetings, books, current affairs, new technology; news of Institute of Physics.

Articles per average issue: 6
Audience: Physicists
Manuscripts accepted in English

MANUSCRIPT INFORMATION

Subject field(s): Physics, technical; physics, applications; social implications; education; science and technology news items; reports of major conferences

Manuscript requirements: See latest issue for style requirements.
Preferred length: 2000-4000 words; 2-4 typeset pages
Number of copies to be submitted: Two
Abstract:

Author information and reprints: Payment: None.
Is simultaneous submission of article to other journals permitted: Only by prior arrangement
Exclusive manuscript rights between acceptance and publication: Yes
Copyright: Held by author.
Reprints: Available, 50 free

Additional information: Diagrams and good photographs welcome. Finished artwork not required for diagrams.

Disposition of manuscript:
Query letter: Not necessary, but advisable.
Receipt of manuscript acknowledged: Yes
Decision to publish in: 2-4 weeks
Accepted manuscript published in: 2-4 months
Rejected manuscript returned: Yes
Rejected manuscript criticized: Yes

Submit to:
Kurt Paulus
Executive Editor
(See address above)

PHYSICS IN CANADA/LA PHYSIQUE AU CANADA [2167]

Canadian Association of Physicists
151 Slater Street
Ottawa, Ontario K1P 5H3, Canada
(613) 237-3392

First published in 1945

SUBSCRIPTION DATA

Issues and rates: Published bi-monthly.
Average paid circulation: 2,120
Annual rate(s): C$10.00

Publisher or Sponsor: Canadian Association of Physicists
Managing Editor: Mona L. Jento

EDITORIAL DESCRIPTION

A general interest publication containing general articles on physics, related disciplines, science policy and news of scientific activities, etc.

Articles per average issue: 2-3
Audience: Professional, academic, general
Manuscripts accepted in English, French

MANUSCRIPT INFORMATION

Manuscript requirements: See latest issue for style requirements.
Preferred length: 3,000-4,000 words
Number of copies to be submitted: 2
Abstract: Not necessary.

Author information and reprints: Payment: Reprints only. 50 reprints
Is simultaneous submission of article to other journals permitted: Permitted, but not encouraged.
Exclusive manuscript rights between acceptance and publication: No
Copyright: Held by publication.
Reprints: Available at cost.

Disposition of manuscript:
Query letter: Not necessary, but advisable.
Decision to publish in: 2 weeks
Accepted manuscript published in: 2 months
Rejected manuscript returned: Yes, with return postage paid by publication.
Rejected manuscript criticized: Reasons for rejections only

Submit to:
Robert L. Clarke
Editor
Department of Physics

Carleton University
Ottawa, Ontario K1S 5B6, Canada
(613) 231-4338

PHYSICS IN MEDICINE AND BIOLOGY [2168]

The Institute of Physics
Techno House
Redcliffe Way, Bristol BS1 6NX, England
0272-29781

First published in 1956

SUBSCRIPTION DATA

Issues and rates: Published bi-monthly.
Average paid circulation: 2,350
Annual rate(s): £27.00, Foreign $73.00

Publisher or Sponsor: The Institute of Physics; Hospital Physicists' Association; Canadian Association of Physicists, Medical & Biological Section; International Organization for Medical Physics; American Association of Physicists in Medicine

Managing Editor: D. G. Fisher

EDITORIAL DESCRIPTION

Contains review articles, research papers, notes, letters, book reviews, proceedings of associated organizations, forthcoming events diary; Abstracts Section (abstracts from 200 journals in interdisciplinary field).

Articles per average issue: 10
Audience: Physicists in hospitals and biological or medical research centers
Manuscripts accepted in English, French, and German

MANUSCRIPT INFORMATION

Subject field(s): Radiation dosimetry; radiation physics; radioisotopes; radiobiology; X-rays and other radiation in diagnosis and therapy; radiation hazards and protection; ultrasonics; thermography; bioengineering; all aspects of physics in relation to medicine, physiology and biology; instrumentation and use of computers in same fields.

Manuscript requirements: Style sheet sent on request.
Preferred length: 3000 words
Number of copies to be submitted: Two
Abstract: Yes.

Author information and reprints: Payment: None.
Is simultaneous submission of article to other journals permitted: No
Exclusive manuscript rights between acceptance and publication: Yes
Copyright: Held by both author and publication
Reprints: Available at cost. 25 free to authors

Disposition of manuscript:
Query letter:
Receipt of manuscript acknowledged: Yes
Decision to publish in: 1 month

Accepted manuscript published in: Six months from first submission to publication.
Rejected manuscript returned: Yes
Rejected manuscript criticized: Yes
Submit to:
M. Calcraft
Staff Editor
(See address above)

THE PHYSICS OF CONDENSED MATTER [2169]

Springer-Verlag
175 Fifth Avenue
New York, New York 10010

First published in 1963

SUBSCRIPTION DATA
Annual rate(s): DM 140 per volume
Managing Editor: Dr. S. Strässler

EDITORIAL DESCRIPTION
See title.
Manuscripts accepted in English, German

MANUSCRIPT INFORMATION
Manuscript requirements: See latest issue for style requirements.
Preferred length: As required
Number of copies to be submitted: 2
Abstract: Yes. An abstract of not more than 100 words in English if article is written in German and vice versa.
Author information and reprints: Payment: Reprints only. 75 offprints
Is simultaneous submission of article to other journals permitted: Not permitted.
Exclusive manuscript rights between acceptance and publication: Yes
Copyright: Held by publication.
Submit to:
Professor Dr. G. Busch
Editor
Laboratorium für Festkörperphysik
Eidgenössische Technische Hochschule
CH-8049 Zürich-Hönggerberg, Switzerland
(0 51) 57 57 70

PLASMA PHYSICS [2170]

Pergamon Press, Inc.
Fairview Park
Elmsford, New York 10523
(914) 592-7700

First published in 1959

SUBSCRIPTION DATA
Issues and rates: Published monthly.
Annual rate(s): $25.00; Institutions $85.00

EDITORIAL DESCRIPTION
Devoted to the communication of results of current research in all fields of plasma physics; review articles are also published.
Articles per average issue: 10
Audience: Professional, academic
Manuscripts accepted in English, French, German, Russian

MANUSCRIPT INFORMATION
Manuscript requirements: See latest issue for style requirements.
Preferred length: None
Number of copies to be submitted: 2
Abstract: Yes. Papers not in English should include an abstract in English.
Author information and reprints: Payment: None.
Is simultaneous submission of article to other journals permitted: Not permitted.
Exclusive manuscript rights between acceptance and publication: Yes
Copyright: Held by publication.
Reprints: Available at cost.
Disposition of manuscript:
Query letter: Not necessary.
Receipt of manuscript acknowledged: Yes
Decision to publish in: 4 weeks
Accepted manuscript published in: 5 months
Rejected manuscript returned: Yes, if return postage is supplied by author.
Rejected manuscript criticized: Reasons for rejections only
Submit to:
Prof. T. S. Chang
Regional Editor
North Carolina State University
P. O. Box 5130
Raleigh, North Carolina 27607

REVIEWS OF MODERN PHYSICS* [2171]

American Institute of Physics
335 East 45th Street
New York, New York 10017

SUBSCRIPTION DATA
Issues and rates: Published quarterly.
Average paid circulation: 11,500
Annual rate(s): $25.00, Members $10.00, Foreign $26.00
Publisher or Sponsor: American Institute of Physics
Managing Editor: Rosalind Harnett

EDITORIAL DESCRIPTION
Publishes theoretical papers of outstanding quality in physics and critical reviews of experimental literature and current research reports.

MANUSCRIPT INFORMATION
Subject field(s): Plasma physics; statistical mechanics; quantum electronics; electron, atomic and molecular physics; high-energy physics; solid state physics and astrophysics
Manuscript requirements: AIP
Number of copies to be submitted: Two
Author information and reprints: Payment: By publication to author. Modest honorarium.
Is simultaneous submission of article to other journals permitted: No
Exclusive manuscript rights between acceptance and publication: Yes
Copyright: Held jointly by author and publication.
Reprints: Available
Additional information: The editors encourage prospective authors to discuss

their plans with the appropriate associate editor.
Submit to:
David Pines
Editor
Department of Physics
University of Illinois
Urbana, Illinois 61801

SPECTROSCOPIA MOLECULAR [2172]

188 Richmond Avenue
Lexington, Kentucky 40502
(606) 266-4712

First published in 1952

SUBSCRIPTION DATA
Issues and rates: Published monthly.
Average paid circulation: 250
Annual rate(s): $2.50, Foreign $3.00

EDITORIAL DESCRIPTION
Contains information of interest and value to spectroscopists.
Articles per average issue: 1
Audience: Spectroscopists
Manuscripts accepted in English and Interlingua

MANUSCRIPT INFORMATION
Subject field(s): Spectroscopy of molecules
Manuscript requirements: AIP
Preferred length: 1000 words; 10 pages
Number of copies to be submitted: Two
Abstract: Yes.
Author information and reprints: Payment: None.
Is simultaneous submission of article to other journals permitted: No
Exclusive manuscript rights between acceptance and publication: Yes
Copyright: Not copyrighted
Reprints: Available
Additional information: Photographs not acceptable
Disposition of manuscript:
Query letter:
Receipt of manuscript acknowledged: Yes
Decision to publish in: Two weeks
Accepted manuscript published in: Two months
Rejected manuscript returned: Yes, if self-addressed, stamped envelope is sent with manuscript.
Rejected manuscript criticized: Yes
Submit to:
Forrest F. Cleveland
Editor-Publisher
(See address above)

SPECTROSCOPY LETTERS [2173]

An International Journal for Rapid Communication
Marcel Dekker, Inc.
270 Madison Avenue
New York, New York 10016
(212) 490-7700

SUBSCRIPTION DATA

Issues and rates: Published monthly.
Average paid circulation: 1,000
Annual rate(s): $60.00, Foreign $72.60

EDITORIAL DESCRIPTION

Contains reports of original research in the broad fields of spectroscopy.

Articles per average issue: 7

Audience: Spectroscopists and analytical chemists
Manuscripts accepted in English, French, German and Russian

MANUSCRIPT INFORMATION

Subject field(s): Spectroscopy, X ray, atomic absorption, UV absorption, emission spectography, fluorescence

Manuscript requirements: See latest issue for style requirements.
Preferred length: None
Number of copies to be submitted: Two
Abstract: Yes.

Author information and reprints: Payment: None.
Is simultaneous submission of article to other journals permitted: No
Exclusive manuscript rights between acceptance and publication: Yes
Copyright: Held by publication.
Reprints: Available

Disposition of manuscript:
Query letter:
Receipt of manuscript acknowledged: Yes
Decision to publish in: 3 weeks
Accepted manuscript published in: 4 weeks
Rejected manuscript returned: Yes
Rejected manuscript criticized: Yes

Submit to:
James William Robinson
Editor
Chemistry Department
Louisiana State University
Baton Rouge, Louisiana 70803
(504) 388-3025

SPECIAL STIPULATIONS

Articles must be suitable for reproduction by Photo Offset.

Nuclear sciences

ANNALS OF NUCLEAR SCIENCE AND ENGINEERING [2174]

Pergamon Press, Inc.
Fairview Park
Elmsford, New York 10523
(914) 592-7700

Previously entitled *Journal of Nuclear Energy*

First published in 1954

SUBSCRIPTION DATA

Issues and rates: Published monthly.
Annual rate(s): $30.00; Institutions $85.00

EDITORIAL DESCRIPTION

Contains papers on all aspects of nuclear energy and related disciplines.

Articles per average issue: 4-6

Audience: Professional, academic
Manuscripts accepted in English preferred (French, German)

MANUSCRIPT INFORMATION

Manuscript requirements: See latest issue for style requirements.
Preferred length: None
Number of copies to be submitted: 3
Abstract: Yes. In English for all papers.

Author information and reprints: Payment: Reprints only. 50 reprints
Is simultaneous submission of article to other journals permitted: Not permitted.
Exclusive manuscript rights between acceptance and publication: Yes
Copyright: Held by publication.
Reprints: Available at cost.

Disposition of manuscript:
Query letter: Not necessary.
Receipt of manuscript acknowledged: Yes
Decision to publish in: 4 weeks
Accepted manuscript published in: 5 months
Rejected manuscript returned: Yes, if return postage is supplied by author.
Rejected manuscript criticized: Reasons for rejections only

Submit to:
Manuscripts from the U.S. to:
J. P. Howe
Executive Editor
Gulf General Atomic Company
P. O. Box 608
San Diego, California 92112

Manuscripts from Europe to:
J. V. Dunworth, C.B.E.
Editor-in-Chief
National Physical Laboratory
Teddington, Middlesex, England

ATOMIC ABSORPTION NEWSLETTER [2175]

The Perkin-Elmer Corporation
Norwalk, Connecticut 06856
(203) 762-4089

First published in 1962

SUBSCRIPTION DATA

Issues and rates: Published bi-monthly.
Average paid circulation: 5200
Annual rate(s): $7.50

Publisher or Sponsor: The Perkin-Elmer Corporation

EDITORIAL DESCRIPTION

Contains articles on theory and applications of atomic absorption spectroscopy and its related fields of flame emission and atomic fluorescence spectroscopy.

Articles per average issue: 6-8

Audience: Professional, academic
Manuscripts accepted in English

MANUSCRIPT INFORMATION

Subject field(s): Atomic absorption applications, theory, instrumentation, flame emission, atomic fluorescence

Manuscript requirements: Style sheet sent on request.
Preferred length: Varies
Number of copies to be submitted: Original plus one or two copies
Abstract: Yes

Author information and reprints: Payment: None.
Is simultaneous submission of article to other journals permitted: No
Exclusive manuscript rights between acceptance and publication: No
Copyright: Held by publication.
Reprints: Available at no cost

Disposition of manuscript:
Query letter: No
Receipt of manuscript acknowledged: Yes
Decision to publish in: 4-8 weeks
Accepted manuscript published in: 2-4 months
Rejected manuscript returned: Yes
Rejected manuscript criticized: Yes

Submit to:
Sabina Slavin
Editor
(See address above)

ATOMIC ENERGY REVIEW [2176]

Kärntner Ring 11
P.O. Box 590
A-1011 Vienna, Austria
52 45 11 ext. 598

SUBSCRIPTION DATA

Issues and rates: Published quarterly.
Average paid circulation: 600; 1200 controlled
Annual rate(s): $20.00; Foreign £8.20

Publisher or Sponsor: International Atomic Energy Agency

Managing Editor: Dorianna Twersky

EDITORIAL DESCRIPTION

Contains critical reviews and surveys in the general field of the peaceful uses of atomic energy. Emphasis is on scientific and technological problems that are of acute interest or subject to rapid development. The editorial policy reflects the Agency's specific role to help developing countries further their science and technology.

Articles per average issue: 6

Audience: Professional, research, academic
Manuscripts accepted in English, French, German, Spanish, Russian

MANUSCRIPT INFORMATION

Subject field(s): Nuclear chemistry; reactor technology and engineering; power production; direct energy conversion; nuclear biology and medicine; dosimetry; safety, waste disposal and safeguards; nuclear geology; utilization of isotopes; nuclear data; nuclear physics

Manuscript requirements: IAEA
Information for Authors, SI Units
preferred
Preferred length: 5,000-30,000 words;
15-90 pages
Number of copies to be submitted: Three
Abstract: Yes; 200-300 words.
Author information and reprints: Payment:
By publication to author. $400- $1000
per article.
Is simultaneous submission of article to
other journals permitted: No
Exclusive manuscript rights between
acceptance and publication: Yes
Copyright: Held by publication.
Reprints: Available, 50 free; for more
than 2 authors, 100 free
Additional information: Manuscripts should
be in the proper style, with footnotes,
references, tables and charts on separate
pages. Symbols in text and on drawings
should be simple ones and internationally
recognized.
Disposition of manuscript:
Query letter: Yes
Receipt of manuscript acknowledged: Yes
Decision to publish in: 4-12 weeks
Accepted manuscript published in: 2-5
months
Rejected manuscript returned: Yes
Rejected manuscript criticized: Yes
Submit to:
The Editor
(See address above)

HEALTH PHYSICS [2177]

Official Journal of the Health Physics
Society
Pergamon Press, Inc.
Fairview Park
Elmsford, New York 10523
(914) 592-7700

First published in 1958

SUBSCRIPTION DATA
Issues and rates: Published monthly.
Annual rate(s): $25.00; Institutions
$100.00
Publisher or Sponsor: Health Physics
Society, International Radiation
Protection Association

EDITORIAL DESCRIPTION
Publishes original research, applied and
developmental work in radiation and its
relationships in the health field.
Articles per average issue: 10
Audience: Professional, academic
Manuscripts accepted in English
(preferred), French, German

MANUSCRIPT INFORMATION
Subject field(s): Radiation, radiological and
nuclear physics, dosimetry, waste
disposal, ecology, radiobiology,
monitoring techniques, air sampling,
administrative procedures, exposure data,
accident evaluation, etc.
Manuscript requirements: See latest issue for
style requirements. Typewritten,
double-spaced
Preferred length: None

Number of copies to be submitted: 2
Abstract: Yes
Author information and reprints: Payment:
By publication to author. $35.00 per
page.
Is simultaneous submission of article to
other journals permitted: Not permitted.
Exclusive manuscript rights between
acceptance and publication: Yes
Copyright: Held by publication.
Reprints: Available at no cost. 100; after
charges are paid. Available at cost.
Additional information: MSS. not in English
should be accompanied with a letter of
intent to pay page charges.
Disposition of manuscript:
Query letter: Not necessary.
Receipt of manuscript acknowledged: Yes
Decision to publish in: 4 weeks
Accepted manuscript published in: 5
months
Rejected manuscript returned: Yes, if
return postage is supplied by author.
Rejected manuscript criticized: Reasons
for rejections only
Submit to:
K. Z. Morgan
Editor-in-Chief
School of Nuclear Engineering
Georgia Institute of Technology
Atlanta, Georgia 30332

INSTITUTION OF NUCLEAR ENGINEERS. JOURNAL [2178]

The Institution of Nuclear Engineers
1 Penerly Road, Catford
London SE6, England
(O1) 695-1500

Previously entitled *Nuclear Energy*

First published in 1959

SUBSCRIPTION DATA
Issues and rates: Published bi-monthly.
Average paid circulation: 2,400
Annual rate(s): £8.00; Foreign £8.00
Managing Editor: Bruce Youngman

EDITORIAL DESCRIPTION
Seeks to encourage the advancement of
all nuclear sciences for peaceful purposes.
Articles per average issue: 4
Audience: Professional
Manuscripts accepted in English

MANUSCRIPT INFORMATION
Subject field(s): Any field of nuclear science:
research papers and reports or practical
engineering aspects of the nuclear field
Manuscript requirements: No specific style
guide.
Preferred length: Up to 5,000 words
Number of copies to be submitted: 2
Abstract: Not necessary.
Author information and reprints: Payment:
By publication to author. £4.00 per page.
£20.00 per article.
Is simultaneous submission of article to
other journals permitted: Not permitted.
Exclusive manuscript rights between
acceptance and publication: Yes

Copyright: Held by publication.
Reprints: Available at no cost.
Disposition of manuscript:
Query letter: Not necessary.
Receipt of manuscript acknowledged: Yes
Decision to publish in: 2 months
Accepted manuscript published in: 6
months
Rejected manuscript returned: Yes, with
return postage paid by publication.
Rejected manuscript criticized: Reasons
for rejections only
Submit to:
The Secretary
(See address above)

JOURNAL OF PHYSICS. PART G [2179]

Nuclear Physics
The Institute of Physics
Techno House, Redcliffe Way
Bristol BS1 6NX, England
297481

SUBSCRIPTION DATA
Issues and rates: Published monthly.
Annual rate(s): £60.00; Foreign $180.00
Publisher or Sponsor: The Institute of
Physics

EDITORIAL DESCRIPTION
Contains research papers in theoretical
and experimental nuclear and particle
physics; weak, strong and electromagnetic
interactions, and those aspects of cosmic
rays relevant to nuclear and particle
physics.
Articles per average issue: 10-20
Audience: Professional, academic
Manuscripts accepted in English, French,
German

MANUSCRIPT INFORMATION
Manuscript requirements: Style sheet sent
on request.
Preferred length: 8,000 words
Number of copies to be submitted: 2
Abstract: Yes
Author information and reprints: Payment:
None.
Is simultaneous submission of article to
other journals permitted: Not permitted.
Exclusive manuscript rights between
acceptance and publication: Yes
Copyright: Held by author.
Reprints: Available at cost.
Disposition of manuscript:
Query letter: Not necessary.
Receipt of manuscript acknowledged: Yes
Decision to publish in: 2-4 weeks
Accepted manuscript published in: 2-3
months
Rejected manuscript returned: Yes, with
return postage paid by publication.
Rejected manuscript criticized:
Sometimes
Submit to:
K. McLoughlin
Staff Editor
(See address above)

Nuclear sciences

NUCLEAR FUSION [2180]

Journal of Plasma Physics and
Thermonuclear Fusion
Kaerntner Ring 11, P.O. Box 590
A-1011 Vienna, Austria
52-45-11 ext. 598

First published in 1961

SUBSCRIPTION DATA

Issues and rates: 6 times a year
   Average paid circulation: 600; 900
   controlled
   Annual rate(s): US$49.00; £21.00;
   Austrian Schillings 920.00, DM 130.00
Publisher or Sponsor: International Atomic
   Energy Agency
Managing Editor: Dorianna Twersky

EDITORIAL DESCRIPTION

   Contains original research papers and
   reviews on plasma physics and controlled
   thermonuclear fusion, also invited reports
   on conferences in this field. Emphasis is
   placed on controlled nuclear fusion
   aspects rather than on problems of pure
   plasma physics.
Articles per average issue: 20
Audience: Plasma physics and nuclear
   fusion scientists and research workers
   Manuscripts accepted in English, French,
   Russian and Spanish

MANUSCRIPT INFORMATION

Subject field(s): Plasma experiments and
   related calculations, plasma devices and
   engineering problems, diagnostic
   techniques, plasma heating and plasma
   production, plasma reactor economy,
   plasma theory, fusion reactor technology
Manuscript requirements: IAEA
   Information for Authors, SI Units
   preferred
   Preferred length: 2,000-6,000 words
   (Reviews up to 20,000 words)
   Number of copies to be submitted: Three
   Abstract: Yes. A summary, 200-300
   words, to precede text.
Author information and reprints: Payment:
   By publication to author. For reviews
   and conference reports only
   Is simultaneous submission of article to
   other journals permitted: No
   Exclusive manuscript rights between
   acceptance and publication: Yes
   Copyright: Held by publication.
   Reprints: Available, cost depends upon
   length of article
Additional information: Manuscripts should
   be in the proper style, with footnotes,
   references, tables and charts on separate
   pages. Symbols in text and on drawings
   should be simple ones and internationally
   recognized. Manuscripts in Russian are
   translated and published in English.
   French and Spanish manuscripts can also
   be translated and published in English on
   author's request.
Disposition of manuscript:
   Query letter:
   Receipt of manuscript acknowledged: Yes
   Decision to publish in: 3-10 weeks
   Accepted manuscript published in: 1-5
   months
   Rejected manuscript returned: Yes

   Rejected manuscript criticized: Yes
Submit to:
   The Editor
   (See address above)

NUCLEAR MATERIALS MANAGEMENT [2181]

Journal of the Institute of Nuclear Materials
Management
Seaton Hall
Kansas State University
Manhattan, Kansas 66506
(913) 532-5721

Previously entitled *INMM Newsletter*

First published in 1971
   Annual rate(s): $20.00; Foreign $30.00;
   Members $15.00
Publisher or Sponsor: The Institute of
   Nuclear Materials Management, Inc.
Managing Editor: Tom Gerdis

EDITORIAL DESCRIPTION

   Contains articles on nuclear materials
   management, news, new product
   information, etc.
Articles per average issue: 4-5
Audience: Professional, membership
   Manuscripts accepted in English only

MANUSCRIPT INFORMATION

Subject field(s): Accounting, nuclear
   engineering, statistics, physics
Manuscript requirements: Style sheet sent
   on request.
   Preferred length: 10-12 pages
   Number of copies to be submitted: 5
   Abstract: Yes.
Author information and reprints: Payment:
   By author to publication. $50.00 per
   page.
   Is simultaneous submission of article to
   other journals permitted: Not permitted.
   Exclusive manuscript rights between
   acceptance and publication: Yes
   Copyright: Held by publication.
   Reprints: Available at cost.
Disposition of manuscript:
   Query letter: Necessary. Or a telephone
   call
   Decision to publish in: 4-8 weeks
   Accepted manuscript published in: Up to
   12 months
   Rejected manuscript returned: Yes, with
   return postage paid by publication.
   Rejected manuscript criticized: Reasons
   for rejections only
Submit to:
   Tom Gerdis
   Editor
   (See address above)

NUCLEAR SCIENCE AND ENGINEERING JOURNAL [2182]

A Journal of the American Nuclear Society
244 East Ogden Avenue
Hinsdale, Illinois 60521
(312) 325-1991

First published in 1956

SUBSCRIPTION DATA

Issues and rates: Published monthly.
   Average paid circulation: 2,372
   Annual rate(s): $120.00; Foreign $132.00
Publisher or Sponsor: American Nuclear
   Society
Managing Editor: Dixon Callihan

EDITORIAL DESCRIPTION

   Contains reports of research in the
   sciences and engineering related to
   nuclear energy.
Articles per average issue: 15
Audience: Scientific, academic
   Manuscripts accepted in English

MANUSCRIPT INFORMATION

Subject field(s): All disciplines in science
   and engineering related to nuclear
   energy.
Manuscript requirements: AIP
   Preferred length: None
   Number of copies to be submitted: Three
Author information and reprints: Payment:
   By author to publication. $70.00 per
   page.
   Is simultaneous submission of article to
   other journals permitted: Permitted, but
   not encouraged.
   Exclusive manuscript rights between
   acceptance and publication: Yes
   Copyright: Held by publisher
   Reprints: Available at cost
Disposition of manuscript:
   Query letter: No
   Receipt of manuscript acknowledged: Yes
   Decision to publish in: 4-6 weeks
   Accepted manuscript published in: 5
   months
   Rejected manuscript returned: Yes
   Rejected manuscript criticized: Yes
Submit to:
   Dixon Callihan
   Editor
   P.O. Box Y, Building 9213
   Oak Ridge, Tennessee 37830
   (615) 483-8611 ext. 3-5237

NUCLEAR TECHNOLOGY [2183]

American Nuclear Society
244 East Ogden Avenue
Hinsdale, Illinois 60521
(312) 325-1991

First published in 1965

SUBSCRIPTION DATA

Issues and rates: Published monthly.
   Average paid circulation: 2005
   Annual rate(s): $120.00
Publisher or Sponsor: American Nuclear
   Society

EDITORIAL DESCRIPTION

   Covers the broad spectrum of
   applications of nuclear science and
   engineering, as well as related
   technologies; publishes review papers and
   unreported work in all areas of
   fundamental research applied in the
   nuclear field: from radioisotope uses in
   industry and medicine to civil explosion
   applications, but especially in the rapidly

expanding aspects of nuclear reactor technology development.

Articles per average issue: 10

Audience: Nuclear technologists

Manuscripts accepted in English

MANUSCRIPT INFORMATION

Subject field(s): Reactor engineering, nuclear fuels, radiation, techniques, nuclear materials, fuel cycle, chemical processing, nuclear explosives, instrumentation, reactor siting, materials, nuclear education

Manuscript requirements: AIP; also "Information for Authors", back cover

Preferred length: None

Number of copies to be submitted: Three

Abstract: Yes.

Author information and reprints: Payment: By author to publication. $70.00 (per printed page)

Is simultaneous submission of article to other journals permitted: No

Exclusive manuscript rights between acceptance and publication: Yes

Copyright: Held by American Nuclear Society

Reprints: Available, 50 free

Disposition of manuscript:

Query letter:

Receipt of manuscript acknowledged: Yes

Decision to publish in: 6 to 8 weeks

Accepted manuscript published in: 4 to 6 months

Rejected manuscript returned: Yes, if self-addressed, stamped envelope is sent with manuscript.

Rejected manuscript criticized: Yes

Submit to:

Roy G. Post

Editor

Department of Nuclear Engineering

The University of Arizona

Tucson, Arizona 85721

(602) 884-1229

SPECIAL STIPULATIONS

Publishes only unpublished articles. Articles accepted only after review and recommendation of two experts selected by the editor for each paper. Authors are advised of critique.

RADIATION DATA AND REPORTS [2184]

Waterside Mall East, Room 615, AW-561

401 M Street, S.W.

Washington, D.C. 20460

(202) 755-1331

Previously entitled *Radiological Health Data and Reports*

First published in 1960

SUBSCRIPTION DATA

Issues and rates: Published monthly.

Average paid circulation: 3,800

Annual rate(s): $13.45 Foreign $16.85

Publisher or Sponsor: U.S. Environmental Protection Agency, Office of Radiation Programs

Managing Editor: Kurt L. Feldmann

EDITORIAL DESCRIPTION

Contains data on radiation from surveillance networks in the Western Hemisphere and interpretive reports of radiation data.

Articles per average issue: 2

Audience: Scientific and technical personnel with interest in radiation

Manuscripts accepted in English

MANUSCRIPT INFORMATION

Subject field(s): Ionizing radiation, nonionizing radiation

Manuscript requirements: See latest issue for style requirements.

Preferred length: 10-20 pages

Number of copies to be submitted: Two

Abstract: Yes.

Author information and reprints: Payment: None.

Is simultaneous submission of article to other journals permitted: Only to journals with different audiences.

Exclusive manuscript rights between acceptance and publication: No

Copyright: No copyrights

Reprints: Available

Disposition of manuscript:

Query letter:

Receipt of manuscript acknowledged: Yes

Decision to publish in: 2-4 months

Accepted manuscript published in: 3 months

Rejected manuscript returned: Yes

Rejected manuscript criticized: Yes

Submit to:

Samuel Wieder

Editor

(See address above)

SPECIAL STIPULATIONS

All manuscripts must be data-oriented. Papers dealing solely with instrumentation or methodology are not acceptable.

RADIATION RESEARCH [2185]

Academic Press, Inc.

111 Fifth Avenue

New York, New York 10003

(212) 677-6713

SUBSCRIPTION DATA

Issues and rates: Published monthly.

Annual rate(s): $140.00; Foreign $149.00

Publisher or Sponsor: Radiation Research Society

Managing Editor: Oddvar F. Nygaard

EDITORIAL DESCRIPTION

Publishes original articles in physics, chemistry, biology and medical research dealing with radiation effects and related subjects.

MANUSCRIPT INFORMATION

Manuscript requirements: See latest issue for style requirements.

Preferred length: 20 pages maximum

Number of copies to be submitted: Three

Author information and reprints: Payment: By author to publication. $10.00 per page. Paid by author's institution.

Copyright: Held by publication.

Additional information: Page charges are not mandatory unless reprints desired.

Submit to:

Oddvar F. Nygaard

Managing Editor

Department of Radiology

Case Western Reserve University

Cleveland, Ohio 44106

Mathematics

Mathematics (general)

ADVANCES IN APPLIED PROBABILITY [2186]

Department of Probability and Statistics
The University
Sheffield S3 7RH, England
0742 78555 ext. 269

First published in 1969

SUBSCRIPTION DATA

Issues and rates: Published quarterly.
Average paid circulation: 850; 50 controlled
Annual rate(s): £18.00; Foreign $43.20
Publisher or Sponsor: Applied Probability Trust

EDITORIAL DESCRIPTION

Contains review and expository papers, and longer research papers on applications of probability theory to the biological, physical, social and technological sciences. Publishes original contributions to the field of applied probability; these must be of general scientific interest as well as being mathematically correct.
Articles per average issue: 10-12
Audience: Research workers in universities
Manuscripts accepted in English and French

MANUSCRIPT INFORMATION

Subject field(s): Probability theory; stochastic processes (branching processes, Markov chains and processes); applications in biology; operations research (queueing, storage and traffic); applications to physical and social sciences.
Manuscript requirements: See latest issue for style requirements.
Preferred length: 20 to 35 printed pages
Number of copies to be submitted: 3
Abstract: Yes.
Author information and reprints: Payment: None.
Is simultaneous submission of article to other journals permitted: No
Exclusive manuscript rights between acceptance and publication: Yes
Copyright: Held by publication.
Reprints: Available, 50 free, additional at cost
Disposition of manuscript:
Query letter:
Receipt of manuscript acknowledged: Yes
Decision to publish in: Three months
Accepted manuscript published in: One year
Rejected manuscript returned: Yes, if return postage is supplied by author.

Rejected manuscript criticized: Yes
Submit to:
J. Gani
Editor-in-Chief
(See address above)

ADVANCES IN MATHEMATICS [2187]

Academic Press, Inc.
111 Fifth Avenue
New York, New York 10003
(212) 677-6713

SUBSCRIPTION DATA

Issues and rates: Published bi-monthly.
Annual rate(s): $122.00,

EDITORIAL DESCRIPTION

Publishes papers in any area of pure and applied mathematics. Particular regard will be given to partially or totally expository papers, but the journal will also accept reports of mathematical seminars, lecture notes, and surveys of the present state of a theory and of its history.

MANUSCRIPT INFORMATION

Manuscript requirements: AMS; see latest issue
Number of copies to be submitted: Two
Author information and reprints: Payment: By author to publication. Alterations in excess of 10 per cent of the cost of composition.
Copyright: Held by publication.
Reprints: Available; 50 free
Additional information: Inclusion of an abstract is optional (50-150 words).
Submit to:
Gian-Carlo Rota
Editor
Massachusetts Institute of Technology
Department of Mathematics
Cambridge, Massachusetts 02139

THE AMERICAN MATHEMATICAL MONTHLY [2188]

Official Journal of the Mathematical Association of America
A. B. Willcox
1225 Connecticut Avenue, N. W.
Washington, D. C. 20036
(202) 223-1977

First published in 1894

SUBSCRIPTION DATA

Issues and rates: 10 times a year
Average paid circulation: 22,000
Annual rate(s): Individuals $18.00; Institutions $50.00; Students $9.00; Members $18.00; Foreign individuals $8.00; Foreign institutions $50.00
Publisher or Sponsor: The Mathematical Association of America
Managing Editor: Alex Z. Rosenberg

EDITORIAL DESCRIPTION

To advance and promote college mathematics; exposition of topics

accessible to teachers of undergraduates; pure and applied topics. Sections include Problems, Book Reviews, and a Mathematical Education section.
Articles per average issue: 10-15
Audience: Academic, industrial and governmental mathematicians
Manuscripts accepted in English only

MANUSCRIPT INFORMATION

Subject field(s): Pure and applied mathematics at a level accessible to anyone with a first-year graduate education in mathematics. Broad exposition is especially encouraged.
Manuscript requirements: See latest issue for style requirements.
Preferred length: 5-40 printed pages
Number of copies to be submitted: 3
Abstract: Not necessary.
Author information and reprints: Payment: None.
Is simultaneous submission of article to other journals permitted: Not permitted.
Exclusive manuscript rights between acceptance and publication: Yes
Copyright: Held by the Mathematical Association of America
Reprints: Available at cost. Variable
Additional information: Authors should consult the Statement of Policy, page 1, volume 81, of January, 1974. Manuscripts to be typewritten, double-spaced, with ample margins. Indicate the various fonts desired.
Disposition of manuscript:
Query letter: Not necessary.
Receipt of manuscript acknowledged: Yes
Decision to publish in: 1-6 months
Accepted manuscript published in: 1-2 years
Rejected manuscript returned: Yes, with return postage paid by publication.
Rejected manuscript criticized: Reasons for rejections only
Submit to:
Alex Z. Rosenberg
Editor
Department of Mathematics, White Hall
Cornell University
Ithaca, New York 14853
(607) 256-3624

AMERICAN MATHEMATICAL SOCIETY BULLETIN [2189]

P.O. Box 6248
Providence, Rhode Island 02904
(401) 272-9500 ext. 218

SUBSCRIPTION DATA

Issues and rates: Published bi-monthly.
Average paid circulation: 17,245
Annual rate(s): $18.00 Members $9.00
Publisher or Sponsor: American Mathematical Society
Managing Editor: Hans F. Weinberger

EDITORIAL DESCRIPTION

Contains a record of actions of the Society, reports of meetings, short announcements of research results, and reviews of books on advanced mathematics.

Articles per average issue: 40

Audience: Mathematicians

Manuscripts accepted in English, German and Romance Languages.

MANUSCRIPT INFORMATION

Subject field(s): Research mathematics

Manuscript requirements: See latest issue for style requirements.

Preferred length: 5 pages or less

Number of copies to be submitted: One

Abstract: Not necessary.

Author information and reprints: Payment: None.

Is simultaneous submission of article to other journals permitted: No

Exclusive manuscript rights between acceptance and publication: Yes

Copyright: Held by publication.

Reprints: Available; cost at discretion of author

Disposition of manuscript:

Query letter:

Receipt of manuscript acknowledged: Yes

Decision to publish in: Six weeks

Accepted manuscript published in: 3-4 months

Rejected manuscript returned: Yes

Rejected manuscript criticized: Yes

Submit to:

John L. Kelley

Department of Mathematics

University of California, Berkeley

Berkeley, California 94720

(415) 642-6000

AMERICAN MATHEMATICAL SOCIETY PROCEEDINGS [2190]

P.O. Box 6248

Providence, Rhode Island 02940

(401) 272-9500

First published in 1950

SUBSCRIPTION DATA

Issues and rates: Published monthly.

Average paid circulation: 1729

Annual rate(s): $120.00; Members $60.00

Publisher or Sponsor: American Mathematical Society

EDITORIAL DESCRIPTION

Devoted entirely to research in pure and applied mathematics, principally to the publication of original papers of moderate length. Author and subject indexes are currently published in the last issue of each volume.

Articles per average issue: 50

Audience: Research

Manuscripts accepted in All, except Russian, Chinese

MANUSCRIPT INFORMATION

Subject field(s): Research mathematics

Manuscript requirements: AMS; See latest issue for style requirements.

Preferred length: 12 pages or less

Number of copies to be submitted: Two

Abstract: Yes

Author information and reprints: Payment: None.

Is simultaneous submission of article to other journals permitted: No

Exclusive manuscript rights between acceptance and publication: Yes

Copyright: Held by publication.

Reprints: Available at cost.

Disposition of manuscript:

Receipt of manuscript acknowledged: Yes

Decision to publish in: 3 months

Accepted manuscript published in: 13-15 months

Rejected manuscript returned: Yes

Rejected manuscript criticized: Yes

Submit to:

W. Wistar Comfort

Department of Mathematics

Wesleyan University

Middletown, Connecticut 06457

(203) 347-9411

AMERICAN MATHEMATICAL SOCIETY TRANSACTIONS [2191]

P.O. Box 6248

Providence, Rhode Island 02904

(401) 272-9500 ext. 218

First published in 1900

SUBSCRIPTION DATA

Issues and rates: Published monthly.

Average paid circulation: 1618

Annual rate(s): $210.00; Members $105.00

Publisher or Sponsor: American Mathematical Society

EDITORIAL DESCRIPTION

Devoted entirely to research in pure and applied mathematics and, in general, includes longer papers than those in the *Proceedings.*

Articles per average issue: 30

Audience: Research mathematicians

Manuscripts accepted in English, German, all Romance languages

MANUSCRIPT INFORMATION

Subject field(s): Research mathematics

Manuscript requirements: See latest issue for style requirements.

Preferred length: 12 or more pages

Number of copies to be submitted: One

Abstract: Yes

Author information and reprints: Payment: By author to publication.

Is simultaneous submission of article to other journals permitted: No

Exclusive manuscript rights between acceptance and publication: Yes

Copyright: Held by publication.

Reprints: Available

Disposition of manuscript:

Query letter: No

Receipt of manuscript acknowledged: Yes

Decision to publish in: Four months

Accepted manuscript published in: Ten months

Rejected manuscript returned: Yes

Rejected manuscript criticized: Yes

Submit to:

Harry Kesten

Department of Mathematics

Cornell University

Ithaca, New York 14850

ANNALS OF MATHEMATICS [2192]

Mathematische Annalen

Springer-Verlag

175 Fifth Avenue

New York, New York 10010

First published in 1868

SUBSCRIPTION DATA

Annual rate(s): DM 120 per volume

Managing Editor: H. Grauert

EDITORIAL DESCRIPTION

Presents papers from all fields of mathematics.

Manuscripts accepted in English, German

MANUSCRIPT INFORMATION

Manuscript requirements: See latest issue for style requirements. Style sheet sent on request.

Preferred length: As required

Number of copies to be submitted: 2

Author information and reprints: Payment: Reprints only. 75 offprints

Is simultaneous submission of article to other journals permitted: Not permitted.

Exclusive manuscript rights between acceptance and publication: Yes

Copyright: Held by publication.

Submit to:

F. John

Editorial Board

Courant Institute, New York University

251 Mercer Street

New York, New York 10012

ANNALS OF MATHEMATICS [2193]

Box 231

Princeton, New Jersey 08540

(609) 452-4964

First published in 1884

SUBSCRIPTION DATA

Issues and rates: Published bi-monthly.

Average paid circulation: 2,200

Annual rate(s): Institutions $60.00; Members $20.00

Managing Editor: Prof. Armand Borel

EDITORIAL DESCRIPTION

Contains articles on original research in mathematics.

Articles per average issue: 7

Audience: Researchers

Manuscripts accepted in English, French, German

MANUSCRIPT INFORMATION

Manuscript requirements: No specific style guide.

Preferred length: As required

Number of copies to be submitted: 2

Mathematics (general)

Abstract: Yes.
Author information and reprints: Payment:
Reprints only. 150
Is simultaneous submission of article to
other journals permitted: Not permitted.
Exclusive manuscript rights between
acceptance and publication: Yes
Copyright: Held by publication.
Disposition of manuscript:
Query letter: Not necessary.
Receipt of manuscript acknowledged: Yes
Decision to publish in: 6 months
Accepted manuscript published in: 6
months
Rejected manuscript returned: Yes, with
return postage paid by publication.
Rejected manuscript criticized:
Sometimes
Submit to:
Eleanor Weisenborn
Technical Editor
Box 231, Fine Hall
Princeton University
Princeton, New Jersey 08540
(609) 452-4191

ARCHIVE FOR RATIONAL MECHANICS AND ANALYSIS [2194]

Springer-Verlag
175 Fifth Avenue
New York, New York 10010

SUBSCRIPTION DATA
Annual rate(s): DM 144 per volume
Managing Editor: C. Truesdell

EDITORIAL DESCRIPTION
Nourishes the discipline of mechanics as
a deductive, mathematical science in the
classical tradition and promotes pure
analysis; to give rapid and full
publication to researches of exceptional
moment, depth, and permanence.
Audience: Academics
Manuscripts accepted in English,
German, French, Italian, Latin, Spanish

MANUSCRIPT INFORMATION
Manuscript requirements: See latest issue for
style requirements.
Preferred length: As required
Abstract: Yes.
Author information and reprints: Payment:
Reprints only. 75 offprints
Is simultaneous submission of article to
other journals permitted: Not permitted.
Exclusive manuscript rights between
acceptance and publication: Yes
Copyright: Held by publication.
Additional information: Authors are urged
to write clearly and well, avoiding an
excessively condensed or crabbed style.
Submit to:
R. Aris;
J. Serrin
Members Editorial Board
University of Minnesota
Minneapolis, Minnesota 55455

BIOMETRICS [2195]

Box 5962
Raleigh, North Carolina 27607
(919) 737-2534

First published in 1945

SUBSCRIPTION DATA
Issues and rates: Published quarterly.
Average paid circulation: 6,500
Annual rate(s): $18.00
Publisher or Sponsor: The Biometric Society
Managing Editor: Larry A. Nelson

EDITORIAL DESCRIPTION
The contents are devoted to the
mathematical and statistical aspects of
biology.
Articles per average issue: 14-18
Audience: Mathematicians, biologists,
biostatisticians, and statisticians
Manuscripts accepted in English

MANUSCRIPT INFORMATION
Subject field(s): Biostatistics,
biomathematics, statistics
Manuscript requirements: See latest issue for
style requirements.
Preferred length: None
Number of copies to be submitted: 4
Abstract: Yes. (150 words)
Author information and reprints: Payment:
None.
Is simultaneous submission of article to
other journals permitted: No
Exclusive manuscript rights between
acceptance and publication: Yes
Copyright: Held by publication.
Reprints: Available, prices on request
Disposition of manuscript:
Receipt of manuscript acknowledged: Yes
Decision to publish in: 3 to 6 months
Accepted manuscript published in: 18 to
21 months
Rejected manuscript returned: Yes
Rejected manuscript criticized: Yes
Submit to:
Franklin A. Graybill
Editor
Department of Statistics
Colorado State University
Fort Collins, Colorado 80521
(303) 491-6269

CANADIAN JOURNAL OF MATHEMATICS [2196]

Journal Canadien de Mathématiques
Department of Mathematics
University of Toronto
Toronto, Ontario M5S 1A1, Canada
(416) 928-3317

First published in 1949

SUBSCRIPTION DATA
Issues and rates: Published bi-monthly.
Average paid circulation: 1,400; 50
controlled
Annual rate(s): Foreign $24.00;
Individuals $24.00; Institutions $24.00;
Members $12.00

Publisher or Sponsor: The Canadian
Mathematical Congress
Managing Editor: G. de B. Robinson

EDITORIAL DESCRIPTION
Publishes original research in
mathematics. The subject scope is wide.
Articles per average issue: 24
Audience: Professional mathematicians, and
researchers
Manuscripts accepted in English, French

MANUSCRIPT INFORMATION
Subject field(s): Applied mathematics,
statistics, algebra, analysis, topology,
geometry, etc.
Manuscript requirements: See latest issue for
style requirements. Style sheet sent on
request.
Preferred length: As required
Number of copies to be submitted: 2
Abstract: Yes. A brief summary
Author information and reprints: Payment:
By author to publication. $40.00 per
page.
Is simultaneous submission of article to
other journals permitted: Not permitted.
Exclusive manuscript rights between
acceptance and publication: No
Copyright: Held by publication.
Reprints: Not available.
Disposition of manuscript:
Query letter: Not necessary.
Receipt of manuscript acknowledged: Yes
Decision to publish in: 3-6 months
Accepted manuscript published in: 12
months
Rejected manuscript returned: Yes, with
return postage paid by publication.
Rejected manuscript criticized: Yes
Submit to:
P. G. Rooney;
P. H. H. Fantham
Editors
(See address above)

GENERAL SYSTEMS [2197]

Yearbook of the Society for General
Systems Research
University of Michigan
205 Washtenaw Place
Ann Arbor, Michigan 48104
(313) 764-4200

First published in 1956

SUBSCRIPTION DATA
Issues and rates: Published annually.
Average paid circulation: 1500
Annual rate(s): $15.00
Publisher or Sponsor: Society for General
Systems Research
Managing Editor: Claire Adler

EDITORIAL DESCRIPTION
Contains original papers and reprints (the
latter mainly from European journals)
dealing with theoretical concepts and
models of systems which are applicable
to more than one of the traditional
disciplines.
Articles per average issue: 25
Audience: Research

Manuscripts accepted in English, French, Russian

MANUSCRIPT INFORMATION
Manuscript requirements: See latest issue for style requirements.
   Preferred length: 10-30 pages
   Number of copies to be submitted: Two
   Rejected manuscript returned: No
Author information and reprints: Payment: None.
   Is simultaneous submission of article to other journals permitted: May submit elsewhere providing publication is notified.
   Exclusive manuscript rights between acceptance and publication: No
   Copyright: Held by publication.
   Reprints: Available
Additional information: Complex tables (as well as all diagrams) must be submitted in form suitable for reproduction. Type composition: italics and underscores should be kept to a minimum and limited to emphasis.
Disposition of manuscript:
   Receipt of manuscript acknowledged: Yes
   Decision to publish in: 4 to 8 months
   Accepted manuscript published in: Within 1 year
   Rejected manuscript returned: Yes
   Rejected manuscript criticized: Frequently
Submit to:
   Anatol Rapoport
   Editor
   (See address above)

INDUSTRIAL MATHEMATICS [2198]
The Journal of the Industrial Mathematics Society
P.O. Box 159
Roseville, Michigan 48066
(313) 771-0403

First published in 1950

SUBSCRIPTION DATA
Issues and rates: Published semi-annually.
   Average paid circulation: 500; 700 controlled
   Annual rate(s): $8.00
Publisher or Sponsor: Industrial Mathematics Society

EDITORIAL DESCRIPTION
   Contains technical articles in the fields of applied mathematics, mechanics and engineering; book reviews.
Articles per average issue: 6
Audience: Engineers and managers
   Manuscripts accepted in English

MANUSCRIPT INFORMATION
Subject field(s): Applied mathematics, mechanics, math in engineering, design of gears.
Manuscript requirements: See latest issue for style requirements.
   Preferred length: Less than 15,000 words
   Number of copies to be submitted: Three
   Abstract: Yes.

Author information and reprints: Payment: By author to publication. $10.00 per page.
   Is simultaneous submission of article to other journals permitted: No
   Exclusive manuscript rights between acceptance and publication: Yes
   Copyright: Held by publication.
   Reprints: Available
Additional information: 50 reprints sent to author upon receipt of page charges ($10.00 per page). Additional reprints may be ordered.
Disposition of manuscript:
   Query letter:
   Receipt of manuscript acknowledged: Yes
   Decision to publish in: 2 months
   Accepted manuscript published in: 6 months
   Rejected manuscript returned: Yes, if self-addressed, stamped envelope is sent with manuscript.
   Rejected manuscript criticized: Yes
Submit to:
   Robert Schmidt
   Editor
   College of Engineering
   University of Detroit
   Detroit, Michigan 48221
   (313) 927-1042

INVENTIONES MATHEMATICAE [2199]
Springer-Verlag
175 Fifth Avenue
New York, New York 10010

SUBSCRIPTION DATA
   Annual rate(s): DM 120 per volume

EDITORIAL DESCRIPTION
   To publish new contributions to the field of mathematics
   Manuscripts accepted in English, French, German

MANUSCRIPT INFORMATION
Manuscript requirements: See latest issue for style requirements. Style sheet sent on request.
   Preferred length: As required
   Number of copies to be submitted: 3
Author information and reprints: Payment: None.
   Is simultaneous submission of article to other journals permitted: Not permitted.
   Exclusive manuscript rights between acceptance and publication: Yes
   Copyright: Held by publication.
Submit to:
   Dr. Reinhold Remmert
   Editor
   Berlinerstrasse 7
   D-4540 Lengerich, Federal Republic of Germany

ISRAEL JOURNAL OF MATHEMATICS [2200]
Weizmann Science Press of Israel
P.O. Box 801
Jerusalem, Israel 91000
227375

Previously entitled *Bulletin of the Research Council of Israel, Section F*

SUBSCRIPTION DATA
Issues and rates: Published monthly.
   Average paid circulation: 1050
   Annual rate(s): $75.00
Managing Editor: Larry Lester

EDITORIAL DESCRIPTION
   Contains articles on general mathematics.
Articles per average issue: 10
   Manuscripts accepted in English, French

MANUSCRIPT INFORMATION
Subject field(s): Mathematics
Manuscript requirements: See latest issue for style requirements.
   Preferred length: None
   Number of copies to be submitted: Two
   Abstract: Yes
Author information and reprints: Payment: None.
   Is simultaneous submission of article to other journals permitted: No
   Exclusive manuscript rights between acceptance and publication: Yes
   Copyright: Held by publication.
   Reprints: Available, cost depends on length
Disposition of manuscript:
   Query letter: No
   Receipt of manuscript acknowledged: Yes
   Decision to publish in: 3 months
   Accepted manuscript published in: 6 months
   Rejected manuscript returned: Yes
   Rejected manuscript criticized: Yes
Submit to:
   Editor
   Institute of Mathematics
   Hebrew University
   Jerusalem, Israel

JOURNAL OF APPLIED PROBABILITY [2201]
Department of Probability and Statistics
The University
Sheffield S3 7RH, England
0742 78555 ext. 269

SUBSCRIPTION DATA
Issues and rates: Published quarterly.
   Average paid circulation: 1450; 50 controlled
   Annual rate(s): £18.00; Foreign $43.20
Publisher or Sponsor: Applied Probability Trust

EDITORIAL DESCRIPTION
   Contains research papers on applications of probability theory to the biological, physical, social and technological sciences. Publishes original contributions to the field of applied probability; these must be of general scientific interest as well as being mathematically correct.
Articles per average issue: 30
Audience: Research workers
   Manuscripts accepted in English, French

Mathematics (general)

MANUSCRIPT INFORMATION

Subject field(s): Probability theory, stochastic processes (branching processes, Markov chains and processes); applications in biology; operations research (queueing, storage and traffic); applications to physical and social sciences.

Manuscript requirements: See latest issue for style requirements.
Preferred length: 10 to 20 printed pages
Number of copies to be submitted: 3
Abstract: Yes

Author information and reprints: Payment: None.
Is simultaneous submission of article to other journals permitted: No
Exclusive manuscript rights between acceptance and publication: Yes
Copyright: Held by publication.
Reprints: Available; 50 free, additional at cost

Disposition of manuscript:
Query letter: No
Receipt of manuscript acknowledged: Yes
Decision to publish in: Three months
Accepted manuscript published in: One year
Rejected manuscript returned: Yes, if return postage is supplied by author.
Rejected manuscript criticized: Yes

Submit to:
J. Gani
Editor-in-Chief
(See address above)

JOURNAL OF COMBINATORIAL THEORY [2202]

Series B
Academic Press, Inc.
111 Fifth Avenue
New York, New York 10003
(212) 677-6713

SUBSCRIPTION DATA

Issues and rates: Published bi-monthly.
Annual rate(s): $43.00; Foreign $49.00
Managing Editor: Basil Gordon;
Bruce Rothschild

EDITORIAL DESCRIPTION

Publishes original mathematical articles dealing with theoretical and physical aspects of the study of finite and discrete structures in all branches of science with particular emphasis on graph theory and matroid theory.

MANUSCRIPT INFORMATION

Manuscript requirements: AMS; see latest issue.
Number of copies to be submitted: Two

Author information and reprints: Payment: By author to publication. Alterations in excess of 10 per cent of the cost of composition.
Copyright: Held by publication.
Reprints: Available; 50 free; joint authors (up to 2): each 50 free.

Submit to:
W. I. Iutte
Editor-in-Chief

Faculty of Mathematics
University of Waterloo
Waterloo, Canada

JOURNAL OF DIFFERENTIAL GEOMETRY [2203]

Lehigh University
Bethlehem, Pennsylvania 18015
(215) 691-7000 ext. 678

First published in 1967

SUBSCRIPTION DATA

Issues and rates: Published quarterly.
Average paid circulation: 1,000; 250 controlled
Annual rate(s): $30.00
Publisher or Sponsor: Lehigh University
Managing Editor: C. C. Hsiung

EDITORIAL DESCRIPTION

Contains research papers in special topics of mathematics, differential geometry and its related topics.
Articles per average issue: Varies
Audience: Professional, academic
Manuscripts accepted in English, French, German, Italian

MANUSCRIPT INFORMATION

Manuscript requirements: See latest issue for style requirements.
Preferred length: None
Number of copies to be submitted: One

Author information and reprints: Payment: An optional page charge.
Is simultaneous submission of article to other journals permitted: No
Exclusive manuscript rights between acceptance and publication: Yes
Copyright: Held by publication.
Reprints: Not available.

Disposition of manuscript:
Query letter: No
Receipt of manuscript acknowledged: Yes
Decision to publish in: 3-6 months
Accepted manuscript published in: 15 months
Rejected manuscript returned: Yes
Rejected manuscript criticized: Yes

Submit to:
Chuan C. Hsiung
Managing Editor
(See address above)

JOURNAL OF ENGINEERING MATHEMATICS [2204]

Academic Book Services Holland
P. O. Box 66
Groningen, The Netherlands

First published in 1966

SUBSCRIPTION DATA

Issues and rates: Published quarterly.
Annual rate(s): Institutions Dfl. 130

Managing Editor: R. Timman

EDITORIAL DESCRIPTION

Promotes the application of mathematics to engineering problems.
Articles per average issue: 10
Audience: Professional, academic
Manuscripts accepted in English

MANUSCRIPT INFORMATION

Manuscript requirements: See latest issue for style requirements.
Preferred length: 20 pages
Number of copies to be submitted: 2
Abstract: Yes

Author information and reprints: Payment: Reprints only. 50 reprints
Is simultaneous submission of article to other journals permitted: Not permitted.
Exclusive manuscript rights between acceptance and publication: Yes
Copyright: Held by publication.
Reprints: Available at cost.

Disposition of manuscript:
Query letter: Not necessary, but advisable.
Receipt of manuscript acknowledged: Yes
Decision to publish in: 3 months
Accepted manuscript published in: 6 months
Rejected manuscript returned: Yes, if return postage is supplied by author.
Rejected manuscript criticized: Sometimes

Submit to:
H. W. Hoogstraten
Editorial Secretary
Department of Mathematics
University of Groningen
P. O. Box 8100
Groningen, The Netherlands

JOURNAL OF MATHEMATICAL ANALYSIS AND APPLICATIONS* [2205]

Academic Press, Inc.
111 Fifth Avenue
New York, New York 10003

SUBSCRIPTION DATA

Issues and rates: Published monthly.
Annual rate(s): $35.00, Foreign $38.00

EDITORIAL DESCRIPTION

Contains mathematical papers treating classical analysis and its manifold applications.

MANUSCRIPT INFORMATION

Subject field(s): Physics, chemistry, biology, engineering: mathematical treatment
Manuscript requirements: AMS
Number of copies to be submitted: Two
Is simultaneous submission of article to other journals permitted: No
Exclusive manuscript rights between acceptance and publication: Yes
Copyright: Held by publication.
Reprints: First 50 free

Additional information: Only papers written in lucid, expository style eligible. Do not underline tables. Figures must be submitted in form suitable for reproduction.

Disposition of manuscript:
Receipt of manuscript acknowledged: Yes
Rejected manuscript returned: Yes

Submit to:
Richard Bellman
Editor
Departments of Mathematics and Engineering
University of Southern California
Los Angeles, California 90008

JOURNAL OF MULTIVARIATE ANALYSIS [2206]

An International Journal
Academic Press, Inc.
111 Fifth Avenue
New York, New York 10003
(212) 677-6713

First published in 1971

SUBSCRIPTION DATA

Issues and rates: Published quarterly.
Annual rate(s): Individuals $20.00;
Foreign $39.50; Institutions $34.50

EDITORIAL DESCRIPTION

Provides a central medium for publication of the most significant work in the general area of multivariate analysis. The journal publishs papers on basic theoretical aspects of multivariate analysis and papers dealing with important applications.

Articles per average issue: 9
Audience: Statisticians, probabilists
Manuscripts accepted in English, French, German

MANUSCRIPT INFORMATION

Manuscript requirements: AMS; see latest issue.
Preferred length: No limits
Number of copies to be submitted: Three
Abstract: Yes
Author information and reprints: Payment: By author to publication.
Is simultaneous submission of article to other journals permitted: No
Exclusive manuscript rights between acceptance and publication: Yes
Copyright: Held by publication.
Reprints: Available, 50 free
Disposition of manuscript:
Query letter: No
Receipt of manuscript acknowledged: Yes
Decision to publish in: 6 months
Accepted manuscript published in: 12 months
Rejected manuscript returned: Yes
Rejected manuscript criticized: Yes
Submit to:
P. R. Krishnaiah
Editor
ARL (LB) Building 450
Aerospace Research Laboratories

Wright-Patterson Air Force Base, Ohio 45433

JOURNAL OF OPTIMIZATION THEORY AND APPLICATIONS [2207]

Plenum Publishing Corporation
227 West 17th Street
New York, New York 10011
(212) 255-0713

First published in 1967

SUBSCRIPTION DATA

Issues and rates: Published monthly.
Average paid circulation: Not available.
Annual rate(s): Institutions $88.00, Individuals $58.00, Foreign institutions $93.40, Foreign individuals $63.40

EDITORIAL DESCRIPTION

Publication contains survey papers; technical notes; contributed papers; technical comments; book reviews, by invitation of the editor. Emphasis is on mathematical optimization techniques and their applications to science and engineering.

Articles per average issue: 10
Audience: Engineers, scientists, mathematicians
Manuscripts accepted in English

MANUSCRIPT INFORMATION

Subject field(s): Direct methods, calculus of variations, dynamic programming, linear programming, quasilinearization, gradient methods, game theory, numerical methods, computing methods, boundary value problems
Manuscript requirements: See latest issue for style requirements.
Preferred length: 20 pages
Number of copies to be submitted: Three
Abstract: Yes
Author information and reprints: Payment: None.
Is simultaneous submission of article to other journals permitted: No
Exclusive manuscript rights between acceptance and publication: Yes
Copyright: Held by publication.
Reprints: Available, cost varies with length of paper and quantity
Subject field(s): Typewritten, triple-spaced manuscript
Disposition of manuscript:
Query letter: No
Receipt of manuscript acknowledged: Yes
Decision to publish in: 6-8 weeks
Accepted manuscript published in: 12 months
Rejected manuscript returned: No
Rejected manuscript criticized: Yes
Submit to:
Angelo Miele
Editor-in-Chief
230 Ryon Building, Rice University
Houston, Texas 77001

JOURNAL OF RECREATIONAL MATHEMATICS [2208]

Baywood Publishing Company, Inc.
43 Central Drive
Farmingdale, New York 11735
(516) 293-7130

First published in 1968

SUBSCRIPTION DATA

Issues and rates: Published quarterly.
Average paid circulation: 2,800
Annual rate(s): $18.00; Foreign $20.00

EDITORIAL DESCRIPTION

Devoted to the lighter side of mathematics, it stimulates a deeper appreciation of the values and beauty of mathematics.

Articles per average issue: 23
Audience: Academic, general
Manuscripts accepted in English

MANUSCRIPT INFORMATION

Subject field(s): Humber phenomena, alphametics, chessboard problems, number theory, puzzles, games, symbolic logic, etc.
Manuscript requirements: See latest issue for style requirements. Style sheet sent on request.
Preferred length: Up to 5,000 words
Number of copies to be submitted: 2
Abstract: Not necessary.
Author information and reprints: Payment: Reprints only. 20 copies
Is simultaneous submission of article to other journals permitted: Not permitted.
Exclusive manuscript rights between acceptance and publication: Yes
Copyright: Held by publication.
Reprints: Available at cost.
Disposition of manuscript:
Query letter: Not necessary, but advisable.
Receipt of manuscript acknowledged: Yes
Decision to publish in: 4-6 weeks
Accepted manuscript published in: 6 months
Rejected manuscript returned: Yes, with return postage paid by publication.
Rejected manuscript criticized: Sometimes
Submit to:
Joseph S. Madachy
Editor
4761 Bigger Road
Kettering, Ohio 45440

JOURNAL OF STATISTICAL PHYSICS [2209]

Plenum Publishing Corporation
227 West 17th Street
New York, New York 10011
(212) 255-0713

First published in 1969

SUBSCRIPTION DATA

Issues and rates: Published monthly.
Average paid circulation: Not available.

Mathematics (general)

Annual rate(s): Institutions $91.50, Individuals $51.00, Foreign institutions $91.05, Foreign individuals $55.05

EDITORIAL DESCRIPTION

Seeks to establish dialogues among the disciplines represented by chemists, physicists, engineers, mathematicians, biologists and econometrists.

Articles per average issue: 5-6

Audience: Physicists, engineers, mathematicians, biologists and econometrists.

Manuscripts accepted in English

MANUSCRIPT INFORMATION

Subject field(s): Statistical mechanics, kinetic theory, stochastics, information and communication theory, macroeconomics, mathematical techniques

Manuscript requirements: AIP

Preferred length: No limit

Number of copies to be submitted: Three

Abstract: Yes.

Author information and reprints: Payment: None.

Is simultaneous submission of article to other journals permitted:

Exclusive manuscript rights between acceptance and publication. Yes.

Copyright: Held by publication.

Reprints: Available, cost varies with length

Additional information: Abstracts should not exceed 150 words. A list of indexing terms (descriptive words and phrases) may be submitted with the manuscript.

Disposition of manuscript:

Query letter:

Receipt of manuscript acknowledged: Yes

Decision to publish in: 6-8 weeks

Accepted manuscript published in: 6-8 months

Rejected manuscript returned: Yes

Rejected manuscript criticized: Yes.

Submit to:

H. Reiss

Editor-in-Chief

Department of Chemistry

University of California

Los Angeles, California 90024

THE JOURNAL OF SYMBOLIC LOGIC   [2210]

P.O. Box 6248

Providence, Rhode Island 02940

(401) 272-9500 ext. 218

First published in 1936

SUBSCRIPTION DATA

Issues and rates: Published quarterly.

Average paid circulation: 3,000

Annual rate(s): $40.00; Members free

Publisher or Sponsor: Association for Symbolic Logic

Managing Editor: Alfons Borgers

EDITORIAL DESCRIPTION

Official organ of the Association for Symbolic Logic, it contains research and expository papers, philosophical papers relating to symbolic logic, and studies in

the history of logic. There is also an extensive review section.

Articles per average issue: 15-20

Audience: Professional, academic

Manuscripts accepted in English

MANUSCRIPT INFORMATION

Subject field(s): Research mathematics in symbolic logic

Manuscript requirements: See latest issue for style requirements.

Preferred length: 50 pages maximum

Number of copies to be submitted: One

Author information and reprints: Payment: Reprints only. 50 free reprints

Is simultaneous submission of article to other journals permitted: No

Exclusive manuscript rights between acceptance and publication: Yes

Copyright: Held by publication.

Reprints: Available at cost.

Disposition of manuscript:

Query letter: No

Receipt of manuscript acknowledged: Yes

Decision to publish in: Four months

Accepted manuscript published in: Twelve months

Rejected manuscript returned: Yes

Rejected manuscript criticized: Yes

Submit to:

The Editor

Room 2-274

Massachusetts Institute of Technology

Cambridge, Massachusetts 02139

(617) 864-6900

LINEAR AND MULTILINEAR ALGEBRA*   [2211]

An International Journal Publishing Articles, Reviews, and Problems

Gordon and Breach Science Publishers

440 Park Avenue South

New York, New York 10016

(212) 689-0360

SUBSCRIPTION DATA

Issues and rates: Published quarterly.

Annual rate(s): Individuals $15.00, Institutions $45.00

EDITORIAL DESCRIPTION

Publishes research papers and problems, expository and survey articles, and book reviews, in linear and multilinear algebra and certain cognate areas.

Additional information: Letter of inquiry should be sent to editors before submission of manuscript.

Submit to:

Marvin Marcus,

Robert C. Thompson

Editors

University of California

Santa Barbara, California 93107

MATHEMATICS OF COMPUTATION   [2212]

P. O. Box 6248

Providence, Rhode Island 02940

(401) 272-9500

Previously entitled *Mathematical Tables and Other Aids to Computation*

First published in 1943

SUBSCRIPTION DATA

Issues and rates: Published quarterly.

Average paid circulation: 2169

Annual rate(s): $36.00 Members $10.00

Publisher or Sponsor: American Mathematical Society

EDITORIAL DESCRIPTION

Publishes original articles on all aspects of numerical mathematics, book reviews, mathematical tables, and technical notes. Devoted to advances in numerical analysis, the application of computational methods, and high-speed calculators.

Manuscripts accepted in English, German, all Romance languages

MANUSCRIPT INFORMATION

Subject field(s): Advances in numerical analysis, the application of numerical methods, the computation of mathematical tables, the development of new disciplines related to computation, the theory of high-speed calculating devices

Manuscript requirements: AMS

Preferred length: Up to 50 pages

Number of copies to be submitted: Original and one copy

Abstract: Yes

Author information and reprints: Payment: None.

Is simultaneous submission of article to other journals permitted: No

Exclusive manuscript rights between acceptance and publication: Yes

Copyright: Held by publication.

Reprints: Available at cost.

Additional information: Typewritten, double-spaced

Disposition of manuscript:

Query letter: No

Receipt of manuscript acknowledged: Yes

Decision to publish in: Six months

Accepted manuscript published in: Six months

Rejected manuscript returned: Yes

Rejected manuscript criticized: Yes

Submit to:

James H. Bramble

Olin Hall

Cornell University

Ithaca, New York 14853

SPECIAL STIPULATIONS

The paper should be accompanied by AMS (MOS) subject classification numbers. The author may suggest the name of an editor for review of his paper. The editors are listed on the inside cover of the journal.

METROLOGIA [2213]

International Journal of Scientific Metrology
Springer-Verlag
175 Fifth Avenue
New York, New York 10010

SUBSCRIPTION DATA

Issues and rates: Published quarterly.
  Annual rate(s): DM 96 per volume
Publisher or Sponsor: International
  Committee on Weights and Measures
Managing Editor: H. Preston-Thomas

EDITORIAL DESCRIPTION

The results of original researches directed
toward the significant improvement of
fundamental measurements in any field of
physics
Manuscripts accepted in English, German

MANUSCRIPT INFORMATION

Subject field(s): Improvements in standards
  to the six units of International System of
  Units; velocity of light, gyromagnetic
  ratio of the proton, acceleration due to
  gravity; solutions to measurement
  problems in the fields of ionizing
  radiations and high frequency electrical
  phenomena
Manuscript requirements: See latest issue for
  style requirements. Style sheet sent on
  request.
  Preferred length: As required
  Number of copies to be submitted: 2
  Abstract: Yes.
Author information and reprints: Payment:
  None.
  Is simultaneous submission of article to
  other journals permitted: Not permitted.
  Exclusive manuscript rights between
  acceptance and publication: Yes
  Copyright: Held by publication.
Submit to:
  H. Preston-Thomas
  Editor
  Division of Applied Physics
  National Research Council
  Ottawa Ontario K1A OS1, Canada

MICHIGAN MATHEMATICAL JOURNAL [2214]

University of Michigan Press
615 East University
Ann Arbor, Michigan 48106
(313) 764-4392

First published in 1952

SUBSCRIPTION DATA

Issues and rates: Published quarterly.
  Average paid circulation: 780
  Annual rate(s): Institutions $12,
  Individuals $4
Publisher or Sponsor: University of
  Michigan
Managing Editor: George Piranian

EDITORIAL DESCRIPTION

Contains research papers in mathematics.
Articles per average issue: 12
  Manuscripts accepted in English

MANUSCRIPT INFORMATION

Subject field(s): All fields of mathematical
  research
Manuscript requirements: Strunk. See latest
  issue for style requirements.
  Preferred length: None
  Number of copies to be submitted: Two
  Abstract: No
Author information and reprints: Payment:
  None.
  Is simultaneous submission of article to
  other journals permitted: No
  Exclusive manuscript rights between
  acceptance and publication: Yes
  Copyright: Held by publication.
  Reprints: Available, 100 free, others at
  low cost.
Additional information: Invite contributions
  from sponsoring institutions in U.S. and
  Canada. Publication does not depend on
  payment.
Disposition of manuscript:
  Query letter: No
  Receipt of manuscript acknowledged: Yes
  Decision to publish in: 3-9 months
  Accepted manuscript published in: 9-18
  months
  Rejected manuscript returned: Yes
  Rejected manuscript criticized:
  Sometimes
Submit to:
  George Piranian
  Managing Editor
  Department of Mathematics
  University of Michigan
  Ann Arbor, Michigan 48104
  (313) 763-0151

NOTRE DAME JOURNAL OF FORMAL LOGIC [2215]

Box 5
Notre Dame, Indiana 46556
(219) 283-6157

First published in 1960

SUBSCRIPTION DATA

Issues and rates: Published quarterly.
  Average paid circulation: 850
  Annual rate(s): Individuals $10.00,
  Institutions $16.00
Publisher or Sponsor: University of Notre
  Dame

EDITORIAL DESCRIPTION

Devoted primarily to logic and the
foundations of mathematics. Papers
which are historical or philosophical in
nature will only be considered if they
employ the methods of formal logic in
their exposition.
Articles per average issue: 20
Audience: Professional, academic
  Manuscripts accepted in English, French,
  German

MANUSCRIPT INFORMATION

Subject field(s): Algebraic logic, classical
  logical systems, constructive mathematics,
  methodology of deductive systems, model
  theory, non-classical formal systems,
  proof theory, recursion theory, set theory

Manuscript requirements: Style sheet sent
  on request.
  Preferred length: None
  Number of copies to be submitted: Two
  Abstract: Yes, state methods, and results
  clearly in 200 words; no special symbols.
Author information and reprints: Payment:
  None. 1 copy of issue in which article
  appears and 50 reprints.
  Is simultaneous submission of article to
  other journals permitted: No
  Exclusive manuscript rights between
  acceptance and publication: Yes
  Copyright: Held by University of Notre
  Dame
  Reprints: Available
Additional information: Author may request
  return of accepted manuscript up to time
  it is sent for composition.
Disposition of manuscript:
  Query letter: No
  Receipt of manuscript acknowledged: Yes
  Decision to publish in: Two months
  Accepted manuscript published in: 18-24
  months.
  Rejected manuscript returned: Yes
  Rejected manuscript criticized:
  Sometimes
Submit to:
  Boleslaw Sobocinski
  Editor
  P.O. Box 28
  Notre Dame, Indiana 46556
  (219) 283-6227

ONTARIO MATHEMATICS GAZETTE [2216]

247 Bright Street
Sarnia, Ontario N7T 4E9, Canada

SUBSCRIPTION DATA

Issues and rates: Published three times per
  year.
  Average paid circulation: 1400
  Annual rate(s): Individuals $2.00,
  Institutions $3.00
Publisher or Sponsor: Ontario Association
  for Mathematics Education

EDITORIAL DESCRIPTION

Contains mathematical games, articles on
various aspects of mathematics.
Manuscripts accepted in English

MANUSCRIPT INFORMATION

Manuscript requirements: No specific style
  guide.
  Number of copies to be submitted: One
Author information and reprints: Payment:
  None.
  Is simultaneous submission of article to
  other journals permitted: Yes
  Exclusive manuscript rights between
  acceptance and publication: Yes
  Reprints: Not available.
Disposition of manuscript:
  Receipt of manuscript acknowledged: Yes
  Rejected manuscript returned: Yes
Submit to:
  William Eames
  Co-Editor
  Department of Mathematical Sciences
  Lakehead University

Mathematics (general)

Thunder Bay, Ontario, Canada
(807) 345-2121

OPERATIONS RESEARCH [2217]

Journal of the Operations Research Society
of America
428 East Preston Street
Baltimore, Maryland 21202
(301) 528-4146

First published in 1952

SUBSCRIPTION DATA

Issues and rates: Published bi-monthly.
Average paid circulation: 12,000
Annual rate(s): $20.00; Foreign $22.00;
Members $15.00
Publisher or Sponsor: Operations Research
Society of America
Managing Editor: Dr. Hugh J. Miser

EDITORIAL DESCRIPTION

Publishes papers that are of significant
interest to groups of operations research
workers.
Manuscripts accepted in English

MANUSCRIPT INFORMATION

Subject field(s): The history, policy, practice,
future, or fields of applications of
operations research.
Manuscript requirements: See latest issue for
style requirements. Style sheet sent on
request.
Preferred length: As required
Number of copies to be submitted: 4
Abstract: Yes. Of 100-200 words
summarizing the problem treated and the
principal results and conclusions.
Author information and reprints: Payment:
None.
Is simultaneous submission of article to
other journals permitted: Not permitted.
Exclusive manuscript rights between
acceptance and publication: Yes
Copyright: Held by publication.
Reprints: Available at cost.
Additional information: Everything should
be typewritten, double-spaced, no
footnotes.
Submit to:
Hugh J. Miser
Editor
P. O. Box 525
Windsor, Connecticut 06095

ROCKY MOUNTAIN JOURNAL OF MATHEMATICS [2218]

Rocky Mountain Mathematics Consortium
Arizona State University
Department of Mathematics
Tempe, Arizona 85281

SUBSCRIPTION DATA

Issues and rates: Published quarterly.
Annual rate(s): Institutions $20,
Individuals $10

Publisher or Sponsor: Rocky Mountain
Mathematics Consortium

EDITORIAL DESCRIPTION

Contains research articles and expository
articles in any branch of mathematics.
Audience: Professional, academic
Manuscripts accepted in English

MANUSCRIPT INFORMATION

Subject field(s): Mathematics (all areas)
Manuscript requirements: AMS
Preferred length: Research: at most 20
pages
Number of copies to be submitted: Two
Abstract: Yes
Author information and reprints: Payment:
By author to publication. $35 per page.
Page charge is made to author's
institution, and may be waived for survey
articles at the discretion of the editors.
Is simultaneous submission of article to
other journals permitted: No
Exclusive manuscript rights between
acceptance and publication: Yes
Copyright: Held by the Rocky Mountain
Mathematics Consortium
Reprints: Available at cost.
Additional information: Manuscripts must
be typewritten or the equivalent,
double-spaced, with ample margins. Ditto
copies are not acceptable, and
photocopies are discouraged.
Disposition of manuscript:
Query letter: No
Receipt of manuscript acknowledged: Yes
Decision to publish in: 6 months
Accepted manuscript published in: 15
months
Rejected manuscript returned: Yes
Rejected manuscript criticized: Yes
Submit to:
William R. Scott
Managing Editor
Mathematics Department
University of Utah
Salt Lake City, Utah 84112

SIAM JOURNAL ON APPLIED MATHEMATICS [2219]

33 South 17th Street
Philadelphia, Pennsylvania 19103
(215) 564-2929

Previously entitled *Journal of the Society for
Industrial and Applied Mathematics*

First published in 1953

SUBSCRIPTION DATA

Issues and rates: 8 issues per year
Average paid circulation: 1,200
Annual rate(s): $44.00, Foreign $60.00
Publisher or Sponsor: Society for Industrial
and Applied Mathematics
Managing Editor: Frederick J. Beutler

EDITORIAL DESCRIPTION

Contains research articles on all areas of
mathematics, except those more relevant
to other SIAM journals.
Articles per average issue: 20
Audience: Mathematicians

Manuscripts accepted in English

MANUSCRIPT INFORMATION

Subject field(s): Mathematical applications
in the physical, social, biological,
management and engineering sciences
Manuscript requirements: See latest issue for
style requirements.
Number of copies to be submitted: Two
Abstract: Yes
Author information and reprints: Payment:
By author to publication. $48.00 per
page. Voluntary.
Is simultaneous submission of article to
other journals permitted: No
Exclusive manuscript rights between
acceptance and publication: Yes
Copyright: Held by publication.
Reprints: Available
Disposition of manuscript:
Query letter: Yes
Receipt of manuscript acknowledged: Yes
Decision to publish in: 4 months
Accepted manuscript published in: 9
months months
Rejected manuscript returned: Yes
Rejected manuscript criticized: Yes
Submit to:
F. J. Beutler
Managing Editor
P.O. Box 7541
Philadelphia, Pennsylvania

SIAM JOURNAL ON CONTROL [2220]

33 South 17th Street
Philadelphia, Pennsylvania 19103
(215) 564-2929

First published in 1962

SUBSCRIPTION DATA

Issues and rates: Published quarterly.
Average paid circulation: 1,850
Annual rate(s): $32.00
Publisher or Sponsor: Society for Industrial
and Applied Mathematics

EDITORIAL DESCRIPTION

Contains research articles in
mathematical programming and in the
mathematical theory of control and its
applications, as well as topics in applied
probability, stochastic processes,
mathematical programming, and
differential games which are related to
control theory. It also includes English
translations of important foreign papers
on control.
Articles per average issue: 15
Audience: Mathematicians
Manuscripts accepted in English

MANUSCRIPT INFORMATION

Manuscript requirements: See latest issue for
style requirements.
Preferred length: None
Number of copies to be submitted: Two
Abstract: Yes

Author information and reprints: Payment: By author to publication. $48.00 per page.

Is simultaneous submission of article to other journals permitted: No

Exclusive manuscript rights between acceptance and publication: Yes

Copyright: Held by publication.

Reprints: Available

Disposition of manuscript:

Receipt of manuscript acknowledged: Yes

Decision to publish in: 4 months

Accepted manuscript published in: 9 months

Rejected manuscript returned: Yes

Rejected manuscript criticized: Yes

Submit to:

J. Warga

Editor

Box 7541

Philadelphia, Pennsylvania 19103

(215) 564-2929

SIAM JOURNAL ON MATHEMATICAL ANALYSIS [2221]

33 South 17th Street

Philadelphia, Pennsylvania 19103

(215) 564-2929

First published in 1970

SUBSCRIPTION DATA

Issues and rates: Published bi-monthly.

Annual rate(s): $42.00

Publisher or Sponsor: Society for Industrial and Applied Mathematics

Managing Editor: F. W. J. Olver

EDITORIAL DESCRIPTION

Contains research articles on the part of analysis which bridges abstract pure mathematics and numerical, physical and engineering applications.

Articles per average issue: 20

Audience: Mathematicians

Manuscripts accepted in English

MANUSCRIPT INFORMATION

Subject field(s): Asymptotic analysis, generalized functions, harmonic analysis, integral transforms, special functions

Manuscript requirements: Style sheet sent on request.

Preferred length: None

Number of copies to be submitted: Two

Abstract: Yes

Author information and reprints: Payment: By author to publication. $48.00 per page. Optional.

Is simultaneous submission of article to other journals permitted: No

Exclusive manuscript rights between acceptance and publication: Yes

Copyright: Held by publication.

Reprints: Available at cost

Disposition of manuscript:

Receipt of manuscript acknowledged: Yes

Decision to publish in: 4 months

Accepted manuscript published in: 9 months

Rejected manuscript returned: Yes

Rejected manuscript criticized: Yes

Submit to:

F. W. J. Olver

Managing Editor

(See address above)

SPECIAL STIPULATIONS

Abstract must accompany manuscript.

SIAM JOURNAL ON NUMERICAL ANALYSIS [2222]

33 South 17th Street

Philadelphia, Pennsylvania 19103

(215) 564-2929

First published in 1964

SUBSCRIPTION DATA

Issues and rates: Published bi-monthly.

Annual rate(s): $53.00

Publisher or Sponsor: Society for Industrial and Applied Mathematics

EDITORIAL DESCRIPTION

Contains research articles on development and analysis of numerical methods, including convergence, stability, and error analysis.

Articles per average issue: 18

Audience: Mathematicians

Manuscripts accepted in English

MANUSCRIPT INFORMATION

Subject field(s): Functional analysis, approximation theory, description of computational experiments, new types of numerical applications

Manuscript requirements: Style sheet sent on request.

Preferred length: None

Number of copies to be submitted: Two

Abstract: Yes

Author information and reprints: Payment: By author to publication. $48.00 per page. Voluntary.

Is simultaneous submission of article to other journals permitted: No

Exclusive manuscript rights between acceptance and publication: Yes

Copyright: Held by publication.

Reprints: Available

Disposition of manuscript:

Query letter: Yes

Receipt of manuscript acknowledged: Yes

Decision to publish in: 4 months

Accepted manuscript published in: 9 months

Rejected manuscript returned: Yes

Rejected manuscript criticized: Yes

Submit to:

C. B. Moler

Managing Editor

P.O. Box 7541

Philadelphia, Pennsylvania 19101

SPECIAL STIPULATIONS

Manuscripts must be accompanied by an abstract.

SIAM NEWS [2223]

33 South 17th Street

Philadelphia, Pennsylvania 19103

(215) 564-2929

First published in 1967

SUBSCRIPTION DATA

Issues and rates: Published bi-monthly.

Average paid circulation: 4,000; 4,000 controlled

Annual rate(s): $6, Members $18

Publisher or Sponsor: Society for Industrial and Applied Mathematics

EDITORIAL DESCRIPTION

Contains news articles about the society's activities; articles by prominent mathematicians and scientists on topics of interest to applied mathematicians.

Articles per average issue: 3-4

Audience: Professional, academic

Manuscripts accepted in English

MANUSCRIPT INFORMATION

Subject field(s): Significant applications of mathematics and mathematical tools, including computer facilities and techniques.

Manuscript requirements: No specific style guide.

Preferred length: 1,000 words maximum

Number of copies to be submitted: One

Abstract: No

Author information and reprints: Payment: None.

Is simultaneous submission of article to other journals permitted: Yes

Exclusive manuscript rights between acceptance and publication: No

Copyright: Held by publication.

Reprints: Not available.

Disposition of manuscript:

Query letter: No, but desirable

Receipt of manuscript acknowledged: Yes

Decision to publish in: One month

Accepted manuscript published in: 2-4 months

Rejected manuscript returned: Yes, if self-addressed, stamped envelope is sent with manuscript.

Rejected manuscript criticized: Yes

Submit to:

Robert K. Windsor

Managing Editor

(See address above)

SIAM REVIEW [2224]

33 South 17th Street

Philadelphia, Pennsylvania 19103

(215) 564-2929

First published in 1959

SUBSCRIPTION DATA

Issues and rates: Published quarterly.

Average paid circulation: 5,200

Annual rate(s): $24.00

Publisher or Sponsor: Society for Industrial and Applied Mathematics
Managing Editor: W. E. Boyce

EDITORIAL DESCRIPTION
Intended primarily for expository and survey papers. In addition, essays on topics of interest to applied mathematicians are also welcomed.
Articles per average issue: 5
Audience: Mathematicians
Manuscripts accepted in English

MANUSCRIPT INFORMATION
Manuscript requirements: See latest issue for style requirements.
Number of copies to be submitted: Two
Author information and reprints: Payment: By author to publication. $36 per page. Voluntary.
Is simultaneous submission of article to other journals permitted: No
Exclusive manuscript rights between acceptance and publication: Yes
Copyright: Held by publication.
Reprints: Available
Disposition of manuscript:
Query letter: Yes
Receipt of manuscript acknowledged: Yes
Decision to publish in: 4 months
Accepted manuscript published in: 9 months
Rejected manuscript returned: Yes
Rejected manuscript criticized: Yes
Submit to:
Editor
Box 7541
Philadelphia, Pennsylvania 19103
(215) 564-2929

TOPOLOGY [2225]
An International Journal of Mathematics
Pergamon Press, Inc.
Fairview Park
Elmsford, New York 10523
(914) 592-7700

First published in 1962

SUBSCRIPTION DATA
Issues and rates: Published quarterly.
Annual rate(s): $25.00; Institutions $40.00

EDITORIAL DESCRIPTION
Publishes papers in topology and related subjects.
Audience: Professional, academic
Manuscripts accepted in English, French, German, Italian

MANUSCRIPT INFORMATION
Manuscript requirements: See latest issue for style requirements.
Preferred length: None
Number of copies to be submitted: 2, double-spaced
Abstract: Yes
Author information and reprints: Payment: Reprints only. 150 reprints
Is simultaneous submission of article to other journals permitted: Not permitted.

Exclusive manuscript rights between acceptance and publication: Yes
Copyright: Held by publication.
Reprints: Available at cost.
Disposition of manuscript:
Query letter: Not necessary.
Receipt of manuscript acknowledged: Yes
Decision to publish in: 4 weeks
Accepted manuscript published in: 5 months
Rejected manuscript returned: Yes, if return postage is supplied by author.
Rejected manuscript criticized: Reasons for rejections only
Submit to:
Prof. R. Bott
Editorial Board Member
Department of Mathematics
Harvard University
Cambridge, Massachusetts 02138

Computer sciences

ACM COMMUNICATIONS [2226]
A Monthly Publication of the Association for Computing Machinery
1133 Avenue of the Americas
New York, New York 10036
(212) 265-6300

First published in 1958

SUBSCRIPTION DATA
Issues and rates: Published monthly.
Average paid circulation: 33,850; 35,000 controlled
Publisher or Sponsor: Association for Computing Machinery
Managing Editor: Myrtle R. Kellington

EDITORIAL DESCRIPTION
Covers timely topics of interest to the computing profession including referred technical papers, notices of professional activities, official reports of the Association, guest editorials on vital professional problems, and publication of proposed standards.
Articles per average issue: 10
Audience: Professional
Manuscripts accepted in English

MANUSCRIPT INFORMATION
Subject field(s): Computer and data processing oriented: algorithms, computer systems, education, graphics and image processing, information retrieval, management/data base systems, management science/operations research, numerical mathematics, operating systems, programming languages, programming techniques, scientific applications
Manuscript requirements: Style sheet sent on request.
Preferred length: 12 pages maximum
Number of copies to be submitted: Three
Abstract: Yes

Author information and reprints: Payment: None.
Is simultaneous submission of article to other journals permitted: No
Exclusive manuscript rights between acceptance and publication: Yes
Copyright: Held by publication.
Reprints: Available at publication time
Disposition of manuscript:
Query letter: No
Receipt of manuscript acknowledged: Yes
Decision to publish in: 3-12 months
Rejected manuscript returned: Yes
Rejected manuscript criticized: Yes
Submit to:
Robert L. Ashenhurst
Editor-in-Chief
(See address above)

AEDS MONITOR [2227]
1201 Sixteenth Street NW
Washington, D.C. 20036
(202) 833-4100

SUBSCRIPTION DATA
Issues and rates: Published monthly.
Average paid circulation: 3,000
Annual rate(s): $20.00
Publisher or Sponsor: Association for Educational Data Systems

EDITORIAL DESCRIPTION
Publishes technical articles on computers and equipment developments.
Articles per average issue: 2-3
Audience: Computer professionals
Manuscripts accepted in English

MANUSCRIPT INFORMATION
Manuscript requirements: See latest issue for style requirements.
Preferred length: 3000 words typewritten double-spaced
Number of copies to be submitted: One
Abstract: Yes
Author information and reprints: Payment: None.
Is simultaneous submission of article to other journals permitted: No
Exclusive manuscript rights between acceptance and publication: No
Copyright: Held by publication.
Reprints: Available at cost
Disposition of manuscript:
Query letter: No
Receipt of manuscript acknowledged: No
Decision to publish in: 30 days
Accepted manuscript published in: 60 days
Rejected manuscript returned: Yes, if return postage is supplied by author.
Rejected manuscript criticized: No
Submit to:
J. Foecke
Editor
5513 Brookview Avenue
Minneapolis, Minnesota 55424
(612) 926-1361

THE COMPUTER JOURNAL [2228]

The British Computer Society
29 Portland Place
London WIN 4HU, England
01-637-0471

First published in 1958

SUBSCRIPTION DATA
Issues and rates: Published quarterly.
Average paid circulation: 4,500; 12,500 controlled
Annual rate(s): £10.00; Foreign $24.00
Publisher or Sponsor: The British Computer Society

EDITORIAL DESCRIPTION
Contains reports on original research or new applications in computing; discussion, reviews, or tutorials on any aspect of new developments in computing and computer science.
Articles per average issue: 15
Audience: Professional
Manuscripts accepted in English

MANUSCRIPT INFORMATION
Subject field(s): Computer science, computer applications and theory
Manuscript requirements: Style sheet sent on request.
Preferred length: 4,000-5,000 words
Number of copies to be submitted: Two
Abstract: Yes
Author information and reprints: Payment: None.
Is simultaneous submission of article to other journals permitted: No
Exclusive manuscript rights between acceptance and publication: Yes
Copyright: Held by author.
Reprints: available; 25 free, others at cost.
Disposition of manuscript:
Query letter: No
Receipt of manuscript acknowledged: Yes
Decision to publish in: 3-6 months
Accepted manuscript published in: 12 months
Rejected manuscript returned: Yes
Rejected manuscript criticized: Yes
Submit to:
Peter Hammersley
Editor-in-Chief
University of Cambridge Computer Laboratory
Corn Exchange Street
Cambridge CB2 3QG, England
0223-45151 ext. 381

COMPUTER MAGAZINE [2229]

Suite 301
5855 Naples Plaza
Long Beach, California 90803
(213) 438-9951

Previously entitled *Computer Group News*

First published in 1966

SUBSCRIPTION DATA
Issues and rates: Published monthly.
Average paid circulation: 21,000
Annual rate(s): $30.00; Individuals $30.00; Institutions $30.00; Students $10.00; Members $46.00; Foreign individuals $41.00; Foreign institutions $30.00
Publisher or Sponsor: IEEE Computer Society
Managing Editor: H. T. Seaborn

EDITORIAL DESCRIPTION
Design, programming and use of computers, including hardware, software, and systems consideration. Emphasis is on tutorials and surveys aimed at the computer professional.
Articles per average issue: 4-5
Audience: Computer hardware and software designers
Manuscripts accepted in English

MANUSCRIPT INFORMATION
Subject field(s): Covers the entire field of computer science and engineering
Manuscript requirements: See latest issue for style requirements.
Preferred length: 2,000 to 3,000
Number of copies to be submitted: 2
Abstract: Not necessary.
Author information and reprints: Payment: None.
Is simultaneous submission of article to other journals permitted: Permitted, but not encouraged.
Exclusive manuscript rights between acceptance and publication: No
Copyright: Held by publication.
Reprints: Available at cost. Varies with length
Disposition of manuscript:
Query letter: Not necessary.
Receipt of manuscript acknowledged: Yes
Decision to publish in: 3-6 weeks
Accepted manuscript published in: 6 months
Rejected manuscript returned: Yes, if return postage is supplied by author.
Rejected manuscript criticized: Sometimes
Submit to:
Dr. Jack E. Shemer
Technical Editor
(See address above)

SPECIAL STIPULATIONS
A thorough review of the magazine before submission of manuscript is strongly recommended.

COMPUTERS AND ELECTRICAL ENGINEERING [2230]

An International Journal
Pergamon Press, Inc.
Fairview Park
Elmsford, New York 10523
(914) 592-7700

First published in 1973

SUBSCRIPTION DATA
Issues and rates: Published quarterly.
Annual rate(s): $30.00; Institutions $60.00

EDITORIAL DESCRIPTION
Recognizing the primary role of the electrical engineer in the synthesis and production of the computer, this publication is a forum for addressing the many facets of the relationship between them, publishing research and application papers, descriptive programs, tutorials, etc.
Articles per average issue: 8-10
Audience: Professional, academic
Manuscripts accepted in English

MANUSCRIPT INFORMATION
Subject field(s): The applications of analog, hybrid and digital computers, the design and development of a new generation of computers, documentations of new research, etc.
Manuscript requirements: See latest issue for style requirements.
Preferred length: None, except conciseness
Number of copies to be submitted: 2
Abstract: Yes. A short abstract on a separate sheet.
Author information and reprints: Payment: Reprints only. 50 reprints
Is simultaneous submission of article to other journals permitted: Not permitted.
Exclusive manuscript rights between acceptance and publication: Yes
Copyright: Held by publication.
Reprints: Available at cost.
Disposition of manuscript:
Query letter: Not necessary.
Receipt of manuscript acknowledged: Yes
Decision to publish in: 4 weeks
Accepted manuscript published in: 5 months
Rejected manuscript returned: Yes, if return postage is supplied by author.
Rejected manuscript criticized: Reasons for rejections only
Submit to:
John B. Slaughter
Editor
Naval Electronics Laboratory Center
San Diego, California 92152

COMPUTERS AND FLUIDS [2231]

An International Journal
Pergamon Press, Inc.
Fairview Park
Elmsford, New York 10523
(914) 592-7700

First published in 1973
Annual rate(s): $30.00; Institutions $75.00

EDITORIAL DESCRIPTION
A multidisciplinary journal that interprets the term 'fluid' in its broadest sense; the only provision is that computer technique plays a significant role in the associated studies or design methodology.

Computer sciences

Articles per average issue: 7-9
Audience: Professional, academic
Manuscripts accepted in English

MANUSCRIPT INFORMATION
Subject field(s): Computer applications to all branches of science and engineering: mechanical, civil, chemical, oceanographic, medical, geophysical, vehicular, and aeronautical
Preferred length: None
Number of copies to be submitted: 2
Author information and reprints: Payment: Reprints only. 50 reprints
Disposition of manuscript:
Decision to publish in: 4 weeks
Accepted manuscript published in: 5 months
Submit to:
Martin H. Bloom
Editor
Polytechnic Institute of Brooklyn
Graduate Center, Route 110
Farmingdale, New York 11735

COMPUTERS AND THE HUMANITIES [2232]
c/o Queens College
Flushing, New York 11367
(212) 520-7407

SUBSCRIPTION DATA
Issues and rates: Published bi-monthly.
Average paid circulation: 1900; 200 controlled
Annual rate(s): Individuals $15.00; Institutions $35.00

EDITORIAL DESCRIPTION
An international, interdisciplinary journal for scholars using the computer to study language and literature, music, history, archeology, anthropology, art history, political science, social psychology, demography, library science and related disciplines. Source of information about the computer as a tool for humanistic research and data storage and retrieval mechanism.
Articles per average issue: 5
Manuscripts accepted in English, French, German

MANUSCRIPT INFORMATION
Manuscript requirements: MLA
Preferred length: 4000-8000 words
Number of copies to be submitted: Four
Abstract: Yes
Author information and reprints: Payment: Reprints only. 50 reprints free
Is simultaneous submission of article to other journals permitted: No
Exclusive manuscript rights between acceptance and publication: Yes
Copyright: Held by publication.
Reprints: Available
Disposition of manuscript:
Query letter: No
Receipt of manuscript acknowledged: Yes
Decision to publish in: 2-3 months
Accepted manuscript published in: 2-4 months

Rejected manuscript returned: Yes, if self-addressed, stamped envelope is sent with manuscript.
Rejected manuscript criticized: Sometimes
Submit to:
Joseph Raben
Editor
(See address above)

COMPUTERS IN BIOLOGY AND MEDICINE [2233]
An International Journal
Pergamon Press, Inc.
Fairview Park
Elmsford, New York 10623
(914) 592-7700

First published in 1971

SUBSCRIPTION DATA
Issues and rates: Published quarterly.
Annual rate(s): $30.00; Institutions $45.00

EDITORIAL DESCRIPTION
A medium of international communication on the revolutionary advances being made in the application of the computer to the fields of bioscience and medicine, it publishes original articles, reviews of developments, pedagogical papers and book reviews pertinent to the field.
Articles per average issue: 8-10
Audience: Professional, academic
Manuscripts accepted in English

MANUSCRIPT INFORMATION
Subject field(s): Analysis and synthesis of biomedical systems, simulations, special processing methods, special purpose computers and data processing for clinical and experimental use, medical diagnosis and medical record processing
Manuscript requirements: See latest issue for style requirements.
Preferred length: None
Number of copies to be submitted: Original and 1 copy
Abstract: Yes. Papers should be preceded by a short abstract in English not exceeding 100 words; include a summary at the end not exceeding 500 words. Include also a list of 5-10 key words for indexing purposes.
Author information and reprints: Payment: Reprints only. 50 reprints
Is simultaneous submission of article to other journals permitted: Not permitted.
Exclusive manuscript rights between acceptance and publication: Yes
Copyright: Held by publication.
Reprints: Available at cost.
Disposition of manuscript:
Query letter: Not necessary.
Receipt of manuscript acknowledged: Yes
Decision to publish in: 4 weeks
Accepted manuscript published in: 6 months
Rejected manuscript returned: Yes, if return postage is supplied by author.
Rejected manuscript criticized: Reasons for rejections only

Submit to:
Robert S. Ledley
Editor-in-Chief
National Biomedical Research Foundation
Georgetown University Medical Center
3900 Reservoir Road, N.W.
Washington, D. C. 20007

COMPUTING SURVEYS [2234]
The Survey and Tutorial Journal of the Association for Computing Machinery
1133 Avenue of the Americas
New York, New York 10036
(212) 265-6300

First published in 1969

SUBSCRIPTION DATA
Issues and rates: Published quarterly.
Average paid circulation: 22,000
Annual rate(s): $30.00; Members $12.50
Publisher or Sponsor: Association for Computing Machinery

EDITORIAL DESCRIPTION
Contains survey and tutorial papers on all aspects of computing science and its applications.
Articles per average issue: 3
Audience: Professional
Manuscripts accepted in English

MANUSCRIPT INFORMATION
Subject field(s): Computing science and its applications, with software and programming of more interest than hardware.
Manuscript requirements: Chicago
Preferred length: 30 to 60 pages
Number of copies to be submitted: Three
Abstract: Yes
Author information and reprints: Payment: None.
Is simultaneous submission of article to other journals permitted: No
Exclusive manuscript rights between acceptance and publication: Yes
Copyright: Held by publication.
Reprints: Available at no cost.
Additional information: Typewritten, double-spaced, with special characters marked; camera-ready artwork with final draft.
Disposition of manuscript:
Query letter: Useful
Receipt of manuscript acknowledged: Yes
Decision to publish in: 2 months
Accepted manuscript published in: Six to nine months
Rejected manuscript returned: Yes
Rejected manuscript criticized: Yes
Submit to:
Lee Revens
Executive Editor
(See address above)

SPECIAL STIPULATIONS
All manuscripts are subject to a refereeing process that may require some re-working of paper recommended for publication.

DATA PROCESSING [2235]

IPC Business Press Ltd.
Oakfield House, Perrymount Road
Haywards Heath, Sussex RH16 3DH,
England
(01) 261-8404

First published in 1959

SUBSCRIPTION DATA
Issues and rates: Published bi-monthly.
  Annual rate(s): £10
Managing Editor: Nicholas Enticknap

EDITORIAL DESCRIPTION
  News and articles on developments in
  usage and on research and management
  techniques of interest to those concerned
  with management of the data processing
  function.
Articles per average issue: 10
Audience: Information data processing
  management
  Manuscripts accepted in English

MANUSCRIPT INFORMATION
Subject field(s): Data processing
Manuscript requirements: No specific style
  guide.
  Preferred length: 4,000 words maximum
  Number of copies to be submitted: 1
  Abstract: Not necessary.
Author information and reprints: Payment:
  By publication to author. Negotiable
  Is simultaneous submission of article to
  other journals permitted: Not permitted.
  Exclusive manuscript rights between
  acceptance and publication: Yes
  Copyright: Held by publication
  Reprints: Available at cost.
Disposition of manuscript:
  Query letter: Not necessary, but
  advisable.
  Receipt of manuscript acknowledged: Yes
  Decision to publish in: 1 month
  Accepted manuscript published in: 3
  months
  Rejected manuscript returned: Yes, if
  return postage is supplied by author.
  Rejected manuscript criticized:
  Sometimes
Submit to:
  Nicholas Enticknap
  Editor
  Dorset House
  Stamford Street
  London SE1 9LJ, England
  (01) 261-8404

INSTRUMENTATION TECHNOLOGY [2236]

Journal of the Instrument Society of
America
400 Stanwix Street
Pittsburgh, Pennsylvania 15222
(412) 281-3171

Previously entitled *ISA Journal*

First published in 1954

SUBSCRIPTION DATA
Issues and rates: Published monthly.
  Average paid circulation: 22,500; 4,000
  controlled
  Annual rate(s): $7.00, Foreign $14.00
Publisher or Sponsor: Instrument Society of
  America
Managing Editor: Richard K. Kaminski

EDITORIAL DESCRIPTION
  Feature articles include tutorial
  treatments of theory surveys or
  state-of-the-art reviews of current
  instrumentation equipment and
  techniques, case histories on specific
  applications, and interpretive discussions
  of new technologies, economic factors,
  etc.
Articles per average issue: 4
Audience: Professional
  Manuscripts accepted in English

MANUSCRIPT INFORMATION
Subject field(s): Process control applications,
  measurement and control hardware
  surveys, digital computer control, signal
  conditioning and handling, analog
  computing and simulation, telemetry,
  instrument maintenance and installation,
  control theory and dynamics, metrology
  and calibration, special technologies in
  instrumentation
Manuscript requirements: No specific style
  guide.
  Number of copies to be submitted: Two
  Abstract: No
Author information and reprints: Payment:
  Reprints only. Two copies of the issue in
  which article appears.
  Is simultaneous submission of article to
  other journals permitted: No
  Exclusive manuscript rights between
  acceptance and publication: Yes
  Copyright: Held by publication.
  Reprints: Available, cost depends on
  quantity
Disposition of manuscript:
  Receipt of manuscript acknowledged: Yes
  Decision to publish in: 4 weeks
  Accepted manuscript published in: 2-6
  months
  Rejected manuscript returned: Yes
  Rejected manuscript criticized:
  Occasionally
Submit to:
  Frank M. Ryan
  Editor and Associate Publisher
  (See address above)

INTERNATIONAL FORUM ON INFORMATION AND DOCUMENTATION [2237]

International Federation for Documentation
7 Hofweg
The Hague, The Netherlands
(070) 180 081

First published in 1975

SUBSCRIPTION DATA
Issues and rates: Published quarterly.
  Annual rate(s): $20.00

Publisher or Sponsor: Viniti
Managing Editor: Professor A. I. Mikhailov

EDITORIAL DESCRIPTION
  Contains articles on scientific information
  management, activities of information
  services, mechanization and automation
  of information processes, development of
  retrieval systems and indexing languages.
Articles per average issue: 5-10
Audience: Information specialists
  Manuscripts accepted in English and
  Russian

MANUSCRIPT INFORMATION
Manuscript requirements: No specific style
  guide.
  Preferred length: Maximum 5,000 words
  Number of copies to be submitted: 2
  Abstract: Yes. Up to 200 words
Author information and reprints: Payment:
  Reprints only. 25
  Is simultaneous submission of article to
  other journals permitted: Not permitted.
  Exclusive manuscript rights between
  acceptance and publication: Yes
Disposition of manuscript:
  Query letter: Necessary.
Submit to:
  Professor A. I. Mikhailov
  Editor
  (See address above)

INTERNATIONAL JOURNAL OF BIO-MEDICAL COMPUTING [2238]

22 Ripple Commercial Estate
Ripple Road
Barking, Essex, England
01-595-2121

First published in 1969

SUBSCRIPTION DATA
Issues and rates: Published quarterly.
  Annual rate(s): £16.00

EDITORIAL DESCRIPTION
  An international forum for the
  presentation of original work, interpretive
  reviews and discussion of fundamental
  research in the application of various
  types of computers in medicine and the
  biosciences.
Articles per average issue: 6
Audience: Professional, medical, bioscientific
  Manuscripts accepted in English, French,
  German

MANUSCRIPT INFORMATION
Subject field(s): Uses of computers in
  medicine and biosciences and auxiliary
  sciences
Manuscript requirements: See latest issue for
  style requirements.
  Preferred length: 3000 words; 15 pages
  Number of copies to be submitted: Two
  Abstract: Yes, 100-150 words on the
  purpose and results of paper, in English
  for papers in French and German.

Computer sciences

Author information and reprints: Payment: None.
Is simultaneous submission of article to other journals permitted: No
Exclusive manuscript rights between acceptance and publication: Yes
Copyright: Held by publication.
Reprints: Available, cost depends on length
Disposition of manuscript:
Query letter: No
Receipt of manuscript acknowledged: Yes
Decision to publish in: 2-3 weeks
Accepted manuscript published in: 3-6 months
Rejected manuscript returned: No
Rejected manuscript criticized: Yes
Submit to:
John Rose
Editor
College of Technology
Blackshire BB1 8PE, England
64321

INTERNATIONAL JOURNAL OF COMPUTER MATHEMATICS SECTION A*
[2239]

Programming Languages: Theory and Methods
Gordon and Breach Science Publishers
440 Park Avenue South
New York, New York 10016
(212) 689-0360

SUBSCRIPTION DATA

Issues and rates: Published quarterly.
Annual rate(s): Individuals $18.00, Institutions $38.50

EDITORIAL DESCRIPTION

Publishes papers concerning research and development in the theory of programming languages and their translators. The journal is intended to provide a forum for the expression of new ideas, as well as a place for exposition of knowledge.

MANUSCRIPT INFORMATION

Subject field(s): Computational linguistics, formal languages, automata, computational complexity, combinatorial algorithms, symbol manipulation
Manuscript requirements: See latest issue for style requirements.
Additional information: Letter of inquiry should be sent to editor before submission of manuscript.
Submit to:
Randall Rustin
Editor
The Courant Institute of Mathematical Sciences
New York University
100 Washington Square East
New York, New York 10003

INTERNATIONAL JOURNAL OF COMPUTER MATHEMATICS SECTION B*
[2240]

Computational Methods
Gordon and Breach Science Publishers
440 Park Avenue South
New York, New York 10016
(212) 689-0360

SUBSCRIPTION DATA

Issues and rates: Published quarterly.
Annual rate(s): Individuals $23.00, Institutions $53.50

EDITORIAL DESCRIPTION

Publishes papers concerning mathematical techniques which are of interest to computer users in the fields of numerical analysis, operations research, econometrics and applied mathematics in general.

MANUSCRIPT INFORMATION

Manuscript requirements: See latest issue for style requirements.
Additional information: Letter of inquiry should be sent to editor before submission of manuscript.
Submit to:
Randall Rustin
Editor
The Courant Institute of Mathematical Sciences
New York University
100 Washington Square East
New York, New York 10003

JOURNAL OF STATISTICAL COMPUTATION AND SIMULATION*
[2241]

Gordon and Breach Science Publishers
440 Park Avenue South
New York, New York 10016
(212) 689-0360

SUBSCRIPTION DATA

Issues and rates: Published quarterly.
Annual rate(s): Individuals $14.50, Institutions $41.50

EDITORIAL DESCRIPTION

Publishes original and significant works in areas of statistics which are related to or dependent upon the computer. The journal deals primarily with the relationship between statistics and the computer.

MANUSCRIPT INFORMATION

Manuscript requirements: Letter of inquiry should be sent to editor before submission of manuscript.
Submit to:
Richard G. Krutchkoff
Editor
Virginia Polytechnic Institute and State University
Blacksburg, Virginia 24060

JOURNAL OF SYSTEMS MANAGEMENT
[2242]

24587 Bagley Road
Cleveland, Ohio 44138
(216) 243-6900

Previously entitled *Systems & Procedures Journal*

First published in 1948

SUBSCRIPTION DATA

Issues and rates: Published monthly.
Average paid circulation: 15,000
Annual rate(s): $15, Foreign $17
Publisher or Sponsor: Association for Systems Management
Managing Editor: William Ripley

EDITORIAL DESCRIPTION

Articles are directed toward systems managers and executives involved in information processing.
Articles per average issue: 8
Audience: Systems analysts
Manuscripts accepted in English

MANUSCRIPT INFORMATION

Subject field(s): Business systems, management science, data processing, record management, training of personnel, forms design, facility planning
Manuscript requirements: Style sheet sent on request.
Preferred length: 3000 words; 6 pages
Number of copies to be submitted: Two
Abstract: No
Author information and reprints: Payment: By publication to author. $25 per article.
Is simultaneous submission of article to other journals permitted: No
Exclusive manuscript rights between acceptance and publication: Yes
Copyright: Held by publication.
Reprints: Available
Disposition of manuscript:
Query letter: No
Receipt of manuscript acknowledged: Yes
Decision to publish in: 4 weeks
Accepted manuscript published in: 2 months
Rejected manuscript returned: Yes, if return postage is supplied by author.
Rejected manuscript criticized: Yes
Submit to:
A. James Andrews
Director of Publications
(See address above)

PATTERN RECOGNITION
[2243]

Journal of the Pattern Recognition Society
Pergamon Press, Inc.
Fairview Park
Elmsford, New York 10523
(914) 592-7700

First published in 1968

SUBSCRIPTION DATA

Issues and rates: Published quarterly.
Annual rate(s): $25.00; Institutions $55.00

Publisher or Sponsor: Pattern Recognition Society

EDITORIAL DESCRIPTION

An interdisciplinary journal of research in pattern recognition in computer science, information theory, optical processing, and other fields; reviews, pedagogical papers, etc.
Articles per average issue: 4-6
Audience: Professional, academic
Manuscripts accepted in English

MANUSCRIPT INFORMATION

Subject field(s): Special issues are planned on instrumentation, theory of pattern recognition, biological taxonomy, meteorology, psychophysics, environmental sciences, high energy physics, industrial applications, physiology, space, time-dependent recognition, syntax-directed recognition, etc.
Manuscript requirements: See latest issue for style requirements.
Preferred length: None
Number of copies to be submitted: 2
Abstract: Yes. A summary of not more than 500 words should accompany MS. on separate sheet; an abstract of about 100 words should precede the introduction; and a list of 5-10 key words for indexing purposes should follow the text.
Author information and reprints: Payment: Reprints only. 50 reprints
Is simultaneous submission of article to other journals permitted: Not permitted.
Exclusive manuscript rights between acceptance and publication: Yes
Copyright: Held by publication.
Reprints: Available at cost.
Disposition of manuscript:
Query letter: Not necessary.
Receipt of manuscript acknowledged: Yes
Decision to publish in: 4 weeks
Accepted manuscript published in: 5 months
Rejected manuscript returned: Yes, if return postage is supplied by author.
Rejected manuscript criticized: Reasons for rejections only
Submit to:
Robert S. Ledley,
Louis S. Rotolo
Editor-in-Chief and Managing Editor
National Biomedical Research Foundation
Georgetown University Medical Center
Washington, D. C. 20006

SIAM JOURNAL ON COMPUTING [2244]

33 South 17th Street
Philadelphia, Pennsylvania 19103
(215) 564-2929

First published in 1972

SUBSCRIPTION DATA

Issues and rates: Published quarterly.
Average paid circulation: 1,250
Annual rate(s): $32.00

Publisher or Sponsor: Society for Industrial and Applied Mathematics
Managing Editor: John Hopcroft

EDITORIAL DESCRIPTION

Contains research articles in mathematics that apply to the problems of computer science and the non-numerical aspects of computing.
Articles per average issue: 7
Audience: Mathematicians
Manuscripts accepted in English

MANUSCRIPT INFORMATION

Subject field(s): Automation theory, analysis of algorithms, computational complexity, computational aspects of combinatorics and graph theory, the mathematical aspects of programming languages, artificial intelligence, information retrieval, data structures, and computer architecture.
Manuscript requirements: See latest issue for style requirements.
Number of copies to be submitted: Two
Abstract: Yes
Author information and reprints: Payment: By author to publication. Voluntary
Is simultaneous submission of article to other journals permitted: No
Exclusive manuscript rights between acceptance and publication: Yes
Copyright: Held by publication.
Reprints: Available
Disposition of manuscript:
Query letter: Yes
Receipt of manuscript acknowledged: Yes
Decision to publish in: 4 months
Accepted manuscript published in: 9 months
Rejected manuscript returned: Yes
Rejected manuscript criticized: Yes
Submit to:
Editor
Box 7541
Philadelphia, Pennsylvania 19103
(215) 564-2929

SIMULATION [2245]

Journal of the Society for Computer Simulation
P.O. Box 2228
La Jolla, California 92037
(714) 459-3888

First published in 1963

SUBSCRIPTION DATA

Issues and rates: Published monthly.
Average paid circulation: 3400
Annual rate(s): $32
Publisher or Sponsor: The Society for Computer Simulation

EDITORIAL DESCRIPTION

Contains technical papers on all aspects of modeling and simulation: mathematical methods; simulation languages; validation of models; simulation as an aid in teaching, designing, gaining insight; applications and programming.
Articles per average issue: 8

Audience: Professional
Manuscripts accepted in English

MANUSCRIPT INFORMATION

Subject field(s): Applications of simulation outside and inside the physical sciences and engineering, advances in methodology of simulation and modeling, validation of models and simulations.
Manuscript requirements: Style sheet sent on request.
Preferred length: 3,000-10,000 words; 10-45 pages
Number of copies to be submitted: 4
Abstract: Yes, of 50-200 words, giving the important ideas, results and conclusions
Author information and reprints: Payment: Reprints only. 50 free reprints and 2 copies of the issue
Is simultaneous submission of article to other journals permitted: No
Exclusive manuscript rights between acceptance and publication: Yes
Copyright: Held by publication. Permission is usually granted to authors to reproduce their work.
Reprints: Available at cost
Additional information: Please include a 300-500 word personalized biographical sketch.
Disposition of manuscript:
Receipt of manuscript acknowledged: Yes
Decision to publish in: 2 months
Accepted manuscript published in: 4-6 months
Rejected manuscript returned: Yes
Rejected manuscript criticized: Yes
Submit to:
Natalie Fowler
Managing Editor
(See address above)

SIMULATION COUNCILS PROCEEDINGS [2246]

P.O. Box 2228
La Jolla, California 92037
(714) 459-3888

First published in 1971

SUBSCRIPTION DATA

Issues and rates: Published semi-annually.
Average paid circulation: 250
Annual rate(s): $35
Publisher or Sponsor: The Society for Computer Simulation
Managing Editor: Natalie Fowler

EDITORIAL DESCRIPTION

Each issue is hard-bound, containing a collection of papers on a topic in the field of simulation. Topics lie mostly in the area of large-scale simulations.
Articles per average issue: 12
Audience: Professional
Manuscripts accepted in English

MANUSCRIPT INFORMATION

Subject field(s): Mathematical modeling, simulation of large-scale systems and processes, simulation language, simulation of incompletely understood

Computer sciences

systems, advanced applications of
simulation, simulation and gaming
Manuscript requirements: Style sheet sent
on request.
Preferred length: 3,000-10,000 words;
4-16 printed pages typewritten,
double-spaced
Number of copies to be submitted: Three
Abstract: Yes
Author information and reprints: Payment:
None.
Is simultaneous submission of article to
other journals permitted: No
Exclusive manuscript rights between
acceptance and publication: Yes
Copyright: Held by publication. Policy is
to grant authors the privilege of
reproducing the papers (on request to
publisher) for author's uses.
Reprints: Available at no cost.
Additional information: Each issue is
devoted to one particular topic and
edited by an expert in this field.
Disposition of manuscript:
Query letter: No
Receipt of manuscript acknowledged: Yes
Decision to publish in: 3 months
Accepted manuscript published in: 9
months
Rejected manuscript returned: Yes
Rejected manuscript criticized: Yes
Submit to:
Stanley Rogers
Editor-in-Chief
(See address above)

SPECIAL STIPULATIONS
Topics of future issues available from
Editor-in-Chief.

SOFTWARE, PRACTICE AND EXPERIENCE [2247]

John Wiley & Sons, Ltd.
Baffins Lane
Chichester, Sussex, England
84531

First published in 1971

SUBSCRIPTION DATA
Issues and rates: Published quarterly.
Average paid circulation: 1,500
Annual rate(s): £12.50; Foreign $26.25
Managing Editor: Charles A. Lang;
David W. Barron

EDITORIAL DESCRIPTION
Provides a forum for conveying the
results of practical experience in the
design, implementation, measurement and
management of software.
Articles per average issue: 10
Audience: Professional, students
Manuscripts accepted in English

MANUSCRIPT INFORMATION
Subject field(s): Computer software
Manuscript requirements: No specific style
guide.
Preferred length: 60 pages maximum
Number of copies to be submitted: 3
Abstract: A short summary of up to 150
words precedes each paper.

Author information and reprints: Payment:
Reprints only. 50 reprints
Is simultaneous submission of article to
other journals permitted: Not permitted.
Exclusive manuscript rights between
acceptance and publication: Yes
Copyright: Held by publication.
Reprints: Available at cost.
Disposition of manuscript:
Query letter: Not necessary.
Receipt of manuscript acknowledged: Yes
Decision to publish in: 3 months
Accepted manuscript published in: 3
months
Rejected manuscript returned: No
Rejected manuscript criticized: Yes
Submit to:
Prof. David W. Barron
Editor
Department of Mathematics
The University
Southampton S09 5NH, England

Medicine and medical sciences

Medicine (general)

Medicine (general)
[2248]

ACTA ANATOMICA [2249]
International Archives of Anatomy,
Histology, Embryology and Cytology
S. Karger AG
Arnold-Böcklin Strasse 25
CH-4011 Basel, Switzerland
061-390880

First published in 1945

SUBSCRIPTION DATA
Issues and rates: Published monthly.
   Average paid circulation: 970; 50
   controlled
   Annual rate(s): SFr. 242.00; Foreign
   $98.00 per volume

EDITORIAL DESCRIPTION
   Composed of important original articles
   concerning all aspects of anatomy,
   histology, embryology and cytology, as
   well as adjacent subjects, with the sole
   exception of invertebrate morphology.
   Reviews of literature in those languages
   to which access is difficult are also
   included so as to make available
   information which would not otherwise
   have received due note. Finally, reports
   on the meetings of anatomical societies in
   various countries occasionally appear, as
   well as news of personal and topical
   interest.
Articles per average issue: 10
   Manuscripts accepted in English, French,
   German

MANUSCRIPT INFORMATION
Manuscript requirements: Style sheet sent
   on request. See latest issue for style
   requirements.
   Preferred length: 12 printed pages (with
   figures); 8 printed pages (without figures)
   Number of copies to be submitted: 2
   Abstract: Yes, including an English title,
   as well as 7-9 key words.
Author information and reprints: Payment:
   Reprints only.
   Is simultaneous submission of article to
   other journals permitted: No
   Exclusive manuscript rights between
   acceptance and publication: Yes
   Copyright: Held by publication.
   Reprints: Available
Additional information: Not more than 3
   MSS. by the same author accepted per
   annum.
Disposition of manuscript:
   Receipt of manuscript acknowledged: Yes
   Rejected manuscript returned: Yes
Submit to:
   G. Wolf-Heidegger
   Anatomisches Institut der Universität
   CH-4056 Basel, Switzerland

   F. Walberg
   Anatomical Institute
   Karl Johansgate 47
   Oslo 1, Norway

A. Delmas
Institut d'Anatomie
Faculté de Médecine
F-75 Paris 6e, France
Editors

ACTA CYTOLOGICA [2250]
Journal of Clinical Cytology
428 East Preston Street
Baltimore, Maryland 21202
(301) 528-4116

First published in 1957

SUBSCRIPTION DATA
Issues and rates: Published bi-monthly.
   Average paid circulation: 5,250
   Annual rate(s): $20.00; Foreign $21.80
Publisher or Sponsor: International
   Academy of Cytology

EDITORIAL DESCRIPTION
   Contains original scientific articles
   offering significant contributions to the
   advancement of clinical cytology.
Articles per average issue: 12
   Manuscripts accepted in English

MANUSCRIPT INFORMATION
Manuscript requirements: See latest issue for
   style requirements.
   Preferred length: None
   Number of copies to be submitted: Three
   Abstract: Yes
Author information and reprints: Payment:
   None.
   Is simultaneous submission of article to
   other journals permitted: No
   Exclusive manuscript rights between
   acceptance and publication: Yes
   Copyright: Held by publication.
   Reprints: Available
Disposition of manuscript:
   Query letter: No
   Receipt of manuscript acknowledged: Yes
   Decision to publish in: 3 months
   Accepted manuscript published in: 6
   months
   Rejected manuscript returned: Yes
   Rejected manuscript criticized: Yes
Submit to:
   George L. Wied, M.D.
   Editor
   Department of Obstetrics and
   Gynecology
   5841 Maryland Avenue
   Chicago, Illinois 60637
   (312) 947-5343

ACTA HAEMATOLOGICA [2251]
Official Organ of the European Division of
the International Society of Haematology
S. Karger AG
Arnold-Böcklin Strasse 25
CH-4011 Basel, Switzerland
061-390880

SUBSCRIPTION DATA
Issues and rates: Published monthly.
   Average paid circulation: 1548; 72
   controlled

Annual rate(s): SFr. 132.00; Foreign
$98.00 per volume
Publisher or Sponsor: International Society
   of Haematology

EDITORIAL DESCRIPTION
   Publication is designed to gather and
   survey the results of hematologic research
   in Europe and America, thereby forming
   a link between the two continents. It is
   meant to facilitate a much desired
   community of work and exchange of
   thoughts, the emphasis being put on its
   international character. Clinical interest
   stands in the foreground, indicating
   thereby the general trend of this journal,
   and welcoming the discussion of
   morphologic as well as physiologic
   problems related to modern clinical
   medicine.
Articles per average issue: 6
   Manuscripts accepted in English, French
   German

MANUSCRIPT INFORMATION
Manuscript requirements: Style sheet sent
   on request.
   Preferred length: 10 printed pages
   maximum
   Number of copies to be submitted: 2
   Abstract: Yes, with 6 key words
Author information and reprints: Payment:
   None.
   Is simultaneous submission of article to
   other journals permitted: No
   Exclusive manuscript rights between
   acceptance and publication: Yes
   Copyright: Held by publication.
   Reprints: Available
Disposition of manuscript:
   Query letter: No
   Receipt of manuscript acknowledged: Yes
   Decision to publish in: 2 months
   Accepted manuscript published in: 6
   months
   Rejected manuscript returned: Yes
   Rejected manuscript criticized: Yes
Submit to:
   Dr. H. Lüdin
   Editor
   Medical Clinic
   Kantonsspital
   CH-4000 Basel, Switzerland
   (See address above)

AGENTS AND ACTIONS [2252]
Birkhäuser Publisher
P.O. Box 34
CH-4010 Basel, Switzerland
23 18 10

SUBSCRIPTION DATA
Issues and rates: 5-7 issues in free sequences
   Average paid circulation: Not available.
   Annual rate(s): Swiss francs 120.00

EDITORIAL DESCRIPTION
   Contains articles on pharmacological
   research, histamine and kinines,
   immunosuppression and inflammation,
   regulation and respiration, models in
   toxicology.
Articles per average issue: 75

Audience: Researchers in pharmacology
Manuscripts accepted in English

MANUSCRIPT INFORMATION

Subject field(s): Pharmacology, drugs, transmitters, inhibitors, histamine, kinine, immunosuppression, inflammation, regulation, respiration, toxicology

Manuscript requirements: Style sheet sent on request.
  Preferred length: 8-12 pages
  Number of copies to be submitted: Two
  Abstract: Yes.

Author information and reprints: Payment: None.
  Is simultaneous submission of article to other journals permitted: No
  Exclusive manuscript rights between acceptance and publication: Yes
  Copyright: Held by publication.
  Reprints: Available, 30 free

Additional information: Manuscripts have to be typed with double spacing. Abstracts stating the essence of the findings appear at the beginning of the articles. Illustrations should be ready for direct reproduction and accompanied by a caption. References, tables and charts should be on a separate sheet. References are to be numbered consecutively.

Disposition of manuscript:
  Query letter:
  Receipt of manuscript acknowledged: Yes
  Decision to publish in: 4-6 weeks
  Accepted manuscript published in: 3-6 months
  Rejected manuscript returned: Yes
  Rejected manuscript criticized: Yes

Submit to:
  K. Brune
  Biocentre of the University
  Klingelbergstrasse 70
  CH-4056 Basel, Switzerland
  25 38 80

AMERICAN ANNALS OF THE DEAF [2253]

5034 Wisconsin Avenue, N. W.
Washington, D. C. 20016
(202) 363-1327

First published in 1847

SUBSCRIPTION DATA

Issues and rates: Published bi-monthly.
  Average paid circulation: 6,100
  Annual rate(s): $12.50

Publisher or Sponsor: American Schools for the Deaf; American Instructors of the Deaf

EDITORIAL DESCRIPTION
  Contains professional articles on all behavioral aspects of deafness.

Articles per average issue: 8

Audience: Professional
  Manuscripts accepted in English

MANUSCRIPT INFORMATION

Subject field(s): Deafness and profound hearing loss

Manuscript requirements: See latest issue for style requirements. APA

Preferred length: As required
Number of copies to be submitted: Original and 1 copy
Abstract: Yes. A synopsis-abstract not exceeding 135 words that includes the essential features of the report, emphasizing data and avoiding generalizations.

Author information and reprints: Payment: Reprints only. 2 free issues
  Is simultaneous submission of article to other journals permitted: Not permitted.
  Exclusive manuscript rights between acceptance and publication: Yes
  Copyright: Held by publication.
  Reprints: Available at cost.

Submit to:
  Dr. McCay Vernon
  Editor
  Western Maryland College
  Westminster, Maryland 21157
  (301) 848-7000

AMERICAN COLLEGE OF EMERGENCY PHYSICIANS. JOURNAL [2254]

241 East Saginaw
East Lansing, Michigan 48823
(517) 332-6541

First published in 1972

SUBSCRIPTION DATA

Issues and rates: Published bi-monthly.
  Average paid circulation: 12,000 controlled
  Annual rate(s): $15.00; Foreign $17.00

Publisher or Sponsor: American College of Emergency Physicians

Managing Editor: Fred B. Towns

EDITORIAL DESCRIPTION
  Scientific-clinical and management material of interest to physicians and allied health personnel involved in emergency service.

Articles per average issue: 6-10

Audience: Emergency medical practitioners
  Manuscripts accepted in English

MANUSCRIPT INFORMATION

Subject field(s): Research in the fields of trauma, acute illness, EMS systems information, management articles

Manuscript requirements: Style sheet sent on request. Index Medicus
  Preferred length: 8-10 pages
  Number of copies to be submitted: 3
  Abstract: Yes.

Author information and reprints: Payment: None.
  Is simultaneous submission of article to other journals permitted: Not permitted.
  Exclusive manuscript rights between acceptance and publication: Yes
  Copyright: First serial rights
  Reprints: Available at cost.

Disposition of manuscript:
  Query letter: Not necessary, but advisable.
  Receipt of manuscript acknowledged: Yes

Decision to publish in: 4 weeks
Accepted manuscript published in: 2-3 months
Rejected manuscript returned: Yes, with return postage paid by publication.
Rejected manuscript criticized: Reasons for rejections only

Submit to:
  Fred B. Towns
  Managing Editor
  (See address above)

AMERICAN CORRECTIVE THERAPY JOURNAL [2255]

4910 Bayou Vista
Houston, Texas 77088
(713) 681-1971

Previously entitled *Journal of the Association for Physical and Mental Rehabilitation*

First published in 1947

SUBSCRIPTION DATA

Issues and rates: Published bi-monthly.
  Average paid circulation: 1,000; 100 controlled
  Annual rate(s): $12.00; Foreign $13.00; Individuals $12.00; Institutions $18.00; Students $5.00; Members $10.00; Foreign individuals $13.00; Foreign institutions $19.00

Publisher or Sponsor: American Corrective Therapy Association, Inc.

Managing Editor: Dr. Alton Hodges

EDITORIAL DESCRIPTION
  Publishes manuscripts of a professional and scientific nature in the several disciplines relating to corrective therapy: research studies, theoretical articles and systematic reviews of special areas relating to corrective or adapted physical education, psychology, physiology and special education.

Articles per average issue: 6

Audience: Physical medicine and rehabilitation personnel, adapted and developmental physical educators, exercise physiologists and therapists, athletic trainers.
  Manuscripts accepted in English

MANUSCRIPT INFORMATION

Subject field(s): Corrective, adapted, developmental, special physical education; exercise physiology; psychological considerations in stress, disease, disabilities, and rehabilitation; educational programs for preparation of personnel of these areas.

Manuscript requirements: See latest issue for style requirements.
  Preferred length: 15 pages maximum
  Number of copies to be submitted: 3
  Abstract: Not necessary.

Author information and reprints: Payment: None.
  Is simultaneous submission of article to other journals permitted: Not permitted.
  Exclusive manuscript rights between acceptance and publication: Yes
  Copyright: Held by publication.

Medicine (general)

Reprints: Available at no cost. Open
Available at cost.
Disposition of manuscript:
Query letter: Not necessary.
Receipt of manuscript acknowledged: Yes
Decision to publish in: 4 weeks
Accepted manuscript published in: 6
months
Rejected manuscript returned: Yes, with
return postage paid by publication.
Rejected manuscript criticized: Yes
Submit to:
Dr. Alton Hodges
Editor
(See address above)

AMERICAN DIETETIC
ASSOCIATION JOURNAL   [2256]
430 North Michigan Avenue
Chicago, Illinois 60611
(312) 822-0330

First published in 1925

SUBSCRIPTION DATA
Issues and rates: Published monthly.
Average paid circulation: 31,200
Annual rate(s): $18, Foreign $25
Publisher or Sponsor: The American
Dietetic Association
Managing Editor: Harriet E. Sankey

EDITORIAL DESCRIPTION
Publishes reports of original research and
other papers covering the broad aspects
of dietetics, including nutrition and diet
therapy, community nutrition, education
and training, and administration.
Articles per average issue: 7-11
Audience: Professional
Manuscripts accepted in English only

MANUSCRIPT INFORMATION
Manuscript requirements: Style sheet sent
on request.
Preferred length: 12 to 14 pages
Number of copies to be submitted: Four
Abstract: Yes, not to exceed 110 words
Author information and reprints: Payment:
None.
Is simultaneous submission of article to
other journals permitted: No
Exclusive manuscript rights between
acceptance and publication: Yes
Copyright: Held by publication.
Reprints: Available, cost varies
Disposition of manuscript:
Query letter: No
Receipt of manuscript acknowledged: Yes
Decision to publish in: 3 months
Accepted manuscript published in: 6 to 8
months
Rejected manuscript returned: Yes
Rejected manuscript criticized:
Sometimes
Submit to:
Dorothea F. Turner, R.D.
Editor
(See address above)

AMERICAN FAMILY
PHYSICIAN   [2257]
GP
1740 West 92nd Street
Kansas City, Missouri 64114
(816) 333-9700

First published in 1970

SUBSCRIPTION DATA
Issues and rates: Published monthly.
Average paid circulation: 2,000; 130,000
controlled
Annual rate(s): $10.00; Foreign $14.00
Publisher or Sponsor: American Academy
of Family Physicians

EDITORIAL DESCRIPTION
Content is essentially clinical in nature,
consisting of articles and features of
immediate practical interest to busy
family physicians. Publication strives to
promote physician education.
Articles per average issue: 8
Audience: Professional
Manuscripts accepted in English

MANUSCRIPT INFORMATION
Subject field(s): Internal medicine,
pediatrics, obstetrics, surgery, psychiatry,
gynecology, dermatology, radiology, etc.
Manuscript requirements: See latest issue for
style requirements.
Preferred length: 8-10 pages
Number of copies to be submitted: Two
Abstract: Yes
Author information and reprints: Payment:
By publication to author. $100.00 per
article.
Is simultaneous submission of article to
other journals permitted: No
Exclusive manuscript rights between
acceptance and publication: Yes
Copyright: Held by publication.
Reprints: Available, 100 free
Additional information: Typewritten,
double-spaced only on white standard
bond paper.
Disposition of manuscript:
Receipt of manuscript acknowledged: Yes
Decision to publish in: 2-3 weeks
Accepted manuscript published in: 3-6
months
Rejected manuscript returned: Yes
Rejected manuscript criticized: No
Submit to:
Walter H. Kemp
Managing Publisher
(See address above)

AMERICAN GERIATRICS
SOCIETY JOURNAL   [2258]
10 Columbus Circle, Room 1470
New York, New York 10019
(212) 582-1333

SUBSCRIPTION DATA
Issues and rates: Published monthly.
Average paid circulation: 9,000
Annual rate(s): $21.00; Foreign $24.00

Publisher or Sponsor: American Geriatrics
Society
Managing Editor: Charles E. Lyght

EDITORIAL DESCRIPTION
Publishes original articles primarily
oriented to clinical geriatric medicine,
case reports, review articles, news.
Geriatrics is interpreted in the broadest
sense and includes the etiology, diagnosis
and treatment of the aged and aging
patient.
Articles per average issue: 8
Audience: Physicians
Manuscripts accepted in English

MANUSCRIPT INFORMATION
Manuscript requirements: See latest issue for
style requirements.
Preferred length: See latest issue for style
requirements.
Number of copies to be submitted: Two
Abstract: Yes
Author information and reprints: Payment:
None.
Is simultaneous submission of article to
other journals permitted: No
Exclusive manuscript rights between
acceptance and publication: Yes
Copyright: Held by publication.
Reprints: Available, information on
acceptance
Disposition of manuscript:
Query letter: No
Receipt of manuscript acknowledged: Yes
Accepted manuscript published in: 6
months
Rejected manuscript returned: Yes
Rejected manuscript criticized: No
Submit to:
Charles E. Lyght
Editor-in-Chief
(See address above)

AMERICAN HEART
JOURNAL*   [2259]
The C.V. Mosby Company
11830 Westline Industrial Drive
St. Louis, Missouri 63141
(313) 872-8370

SUBSCRIPTION DATA
Issues and rates: Published monthly.
Average paid circulation: 8,671
Annual rate(s): $19.50, Foreign $23.25

EDITORIAL DESCRIPTION
An international publication devoted to
the study of the heart and the great
vessels. Its clinical environment is
designed to appeal to the university
affiliated clinician who lectures and
treats. Original material is presented to
the cardiologist and the internist
responsible for advanced treatment and
teaching of cardiovascular and renal
disorders.

MANUSCRIPT INFORMATION
Manuscript requirements: See latest issue for
style requirements.
Number of copies to be submitted: Two

Author information and reprints: Payment: None.

Is simultaneous submission of article to other journals permitted: No

Exclusive manuscript rights between acceptance and publication: Yes

Copyright: Held by publication.

Reprints: Available at cost

Disposition of manuscript:

Receipt of manuscript acknowledged: Yes

Rejected manuscript returned: Yes

Submit to:

George E. Burch

Editor

1430 Tulane Avenue

New Orleans, Louisiana 70112

THE AMERICAN JOURNAL OF CHINESE MEDICINE [2260]

P. O. Box 555

Garden City, New York 11530

(203) 624-7530

First published in 1973

SUBSCRIPTION DATA

Issues and rates: Published quarterly.

Annual rate(s): $25.00; Foreign $25.00; Institutions $25.00; Students $15.00

Managing Editor: John J. Kao

EDITORIAL DESCRIPTION

Devoted to scholarly and interdisciplinary study of all aspects of Chinese and related Asian medicine including history, medical theory and practice, scientific research and health-care delivery.

Articles per average issue: 8-9

Audience: Physicians, medical professionals, Sinologists, researchers, historians of science, social scientists

Manuscripts accepted in English, Chinese

MANUSCRIPT INFORMATION

Manuscript requirements: See latest issue for style requirements.

Number of copies to be submitted: 2

Abstract: Yes.

Author information and reprints: Payment: None.

Is simultaneous submission of article to other journals permitted: Not permitted.

Exclusive manuscript rights between acceptance and publication: Yes

Copyright: Held by publication.

Reprints: Available at cost.

Disposition of manuscript:

Query letter: Not necessary.

Receipt of manuscript acknowledged: Yes

Decision to publish in: Several months

Accepted manuscript published in: Varies

Rejected manuscript returned: Yes, with return postage paid by publication.

Rejected manuscript criticized: Reasons for rejections only

Submit to:

Frederick Kao, M.D.

Editor-in-Chief

(See address above)

(212) 270-1163

THE AMERICAN JOURNAL OF CLINICAL NUTRITION [2261]

9650 Rockville Pike

Bethesda, Maryland 20014

(301) 530-7111

First published in 1952

SUBSCRIPTION DATA

Issues and rates: Published monthly.

Average paid circulation: 4174; 184 controlled

Annual rate(s): $25.00, Foreign $28.00, Members $15.00

Publisher or Sponsor: The American Society for Clinical Nutrition

EDITORIAL DESCRIPTION

Contains concise reports of original research in experimental and clinical nutrition; papers dealing with nutrient, trace element, and energy metabolism and requirements; reports of scientific meetings; editorials; letters to the editor; perspectives in nutrition; papers dealing with economics and nutritional programs; and nutrition education.

Articles per average issue: 25

Audience: Professional

Manuscripts accepted in English

MANUSCRIPT INFORMATION

Subject field(s): Nutrition, as related to health and disease; biochemistry; gastroenterology; diet therapy; microbiology, as related to digestion; nutrition programs

Manuscript requirements: See latest issue for style requirements.

Preferred length: None

Number of copies to be submitted: Three

Abstract: Yes

Author information and reprints: Payment: None.

Is simultaneous submission of article to other journals permitted: No

Exclusive manuscript rights between acceptance and publication: Yes

Copyright: Held by publication.

Reprints: Available, cost dependent on length

Disposition of manuscript:

Query letter: Yes

Receipt of manuscript acknowledged: Yes

Decision to publish in: 2-4 months

Accepted manuscript published in: 4-6 months

Rejected manuscript returned: Yes

Rejected manuscript criticized: Yes

Submit to:

Robert H. Herman

Editor

Department of Medicine

Letterman Army Institute of Research

San Francisco, California 94129

(415) 561-4147

AMERICAN JOURNAL OF DISEASES OF CHILDREN [2262]

American Medical Association

535 North Dearborn Street

Chicago, Illinois 60610

First published in 1911

SUBSCRIPTION DATA

Issues and rates: Published monthly.

Average paid circulation: 25,000

Annual rate(s): $18.00; Foreign $28.00

Publisher or Sponsor: American Medical Association

Managing Editor: Robert W. Mayo

EDITORIAL DESCRIPTION

Research articles in field of bio-medical science; clinical articles in field of pediatrics.

Articles per average issue: 22

Audience: Physicians

Manuscripts accepted in English

MANUSCRIPT INFORMATION

Manuscript requirements: See latest issue for style requirements. Style sheet sent on request.

Preferred length: 700 to 7,000 words

Number of copies to be submitted: 3

Abstract: Yes.

Author information and reprints: Payment: None.

Is simultaneous submission of article to other journals permitted: Not permitted.

Copyright: Held by publication.

Reprints: Available at no cost. 200 tear sheets

Disposition of manuscript:

Query letter: Not necessary.

Receipt of manuscript acknowledged: Yes

Decision to publish in: 2 to 4 months

Accepted manuscript published in: 3 to 8 months

Rejected manuscript returned: Yes, with return postage paid by publication.

Rejected manuscript criticized: Yes

Submit to:

Gilbert B. Forbes

Chief Editor

Department of Pediatrics

University of Rochester Medical Center

Rochester, New York 14642

(716) 275-2984

AMERICAN JOURNAL OF EPIDEMIOLOGY [2263]

615 N. Wolfe Street

Baltimore, Maryland 21205

(301) 955-3441

Previously entitled *American Journal of Hygiene*

First published in 1921

SUBSCRIPTION DATA

Issues and rates: Published monthly.

Average paid circulation: 2,500

Annual rate(s): $40.00; Foreign $45.00

Medicine (general)

Managing Editor: Neal Nathanson
Publisher or Sponsor: Johns Hopkins University, School of Hygiene

EDITORIAL DESCRIPTION
Publishes original field and laboratory studies on the occurance and distribution of endemic and epidemic diseases with articles on infectious and non-infectious, acute and chronic diseases and statistical methodology.
Articles per average issue: 10
Audience: Researchers, professional
Manuscripts accepted in English only

MANUSCRIPT INFORMATION
Subject field(s): Infectious disease; chronic, non-infectious disease
Manuscript requirements: Style sheet sent on request.
Preferred length: As required
Number of copies to be submitted: Three
Abstract: Yes
Author information and reprints: Payment: By author to publication. $40 per page. For any pages over 7.
Is simultaneous submission of article to other journals permitted: No
Exclusive manuscript rights between acceptance and publication: Yes
Copyright: Held by Johns Hopkins University
Reprints: Available, schedule sent upon request
Disposition of manuscript:
Query letter: No
Receipt of manuscript acknowledged: Yes
Decision to publish in: 6 weeks
Accepted manuscript published in: 6 months
Rejected manuscript returned: Yes
Rejected manuscript criticized: Yes
Submit to:
Neal Nathanson
Editor-in-Chief
(See address above)

AMERICAN JOURNAL OF GASTROENTEROLOGY [2264]
299 Broadway
New York, New York 10007
(212) 227-7590

Previously entitled *The Review of Gastroenterology*

First published in 1934

SUBSCRIPTION DATA
Issues and rates: Published monthly.
Average paid circulation: 3,150
Annual rate(s): $15.00; Foreign $18.00
Publisher or Sponsor: American College of Gastroenterology
Managing Editor: Daniel Weiss

EDITORIAL DESCRIPTION
Contains material on digestive diseases.
Articles per average issue: 8-10
Audience: Professional, medical
Manuscripts accepted in English

MANUSCRIPT INFORMATION
Manuscript requirements: See latest issue for style requirements.
Number of copies to be submitted: Two
Abstract: Yes
Author information and reprints: Payment: Reprints only. Two copies of issue in which article appears.
Is simultaneous submission of article to other journals permitted: No
Exclusive manuscript rights between acceptance and publication: Yes
Copyright: Held by publication.
Reprints: Available, cost varies
Disposition of manuscript:
Query letter: No
Receipt of manuscript acknowledged: Yes
Decision to publish in: 2 months
Accepted manuscript published in: 9 months
Rejected manuscript returned: Yes
Rejected manuscript criticized: No
Submit to:
David A. Dreiling, M.D.
Editor-in-Chief
(See address above)

AMERICAN JOURNAL OF HOSPITAL PHARMACY [2265]
4630 Montgomery Avenue
Washington, D.C. 20014
(301) 657-3000

Previously entitled *Bulletin of the American Society of Hospital Pharmacists*

First published in 1943

SUBSCRIPTION DATA
Issues and rates: Published monthly.
Average paid circulation: 9500
Annual rate(s): $20.00
Publisher or Sponsor: American Society of Hospital Pharmacists

EDITORIAL DESCRIPTION
Contains articles pertaining to hospital pharmacy; technology; special columns; news information; new products in the industry.
Articles per average issue: 12
Audience: Professional
Manuscripts accepted in English

MANUSCRIPT INFORMATION
Subject field(s): Pharmacy practice, drug therapy, pharmaceutical technology, biopharmaceutics, radiopharmaceuticals
Manuscript requirements: See latest issue for style requirements.
Preferred length: 1500-3750 words; 6-15 pages
Number of copies to be submitted: Two
Abstract: Yes
Author information and reprints: Payment: None.
Is simultaneous submission of article to other journals permitted: No
Exclusive manuscript rights between acceptance and publication: Yes
Copyright: Held by publication.
Reprints: Available if ordered through printer

Disposition of manuscript:
Query letter: No
Receipt of manuscript acknowledged: Yes
Decision to publish in: 4-6 weeks
Accepted manuscript published in: 3-6 months
Rejected manuscript returned: Yes
Rejected manuscript criticized: Yes
Submit to:
William A. Zellmer
Editor
(See address above)

THE AMERICAN JOURNAL OF THE MEDICAL SCIENCES [2266]
Charles B. Slack, Inc.
6900 Grove Road
Thorofare, New Jersey 08086
(609) 848-1000

SUBSCRIPTION DATA
Issues and rates: Published monthly.
Annual rate(s): $22.00, Foreign $23.50
Managing Editor: Dorothy J. Love

EDITORIAL DESCRIPTION
Contains articles from all branches of medicine.
Manuscripts accepted in English

MANUSCRIPT INFORMATION
Subject field(s): All fields of medicine
Manuscript requirements: See latest issue for style requirements.
Number of copies to be submitted: Two
Author information and reprints: Payment: None.
Is simultaneous submission of article to other journals permitted: No
Exclusive manuscript rights between acceptance and publication: Yes
Copyright: Held by publication.
Reprints: Available, cost varies
Disposition of manuscript:
Receipt of manuscript acknowledged: Yes
Decision to publish in: 6-8 weeks
Accepted manuscript published in: 4-5 months
Rejected manuscript returned: Yes
Rejected manuscript criticized: Yes
Submit to:
Saul J. Farber
Editor
New York University School of Medicine
550 First Avenue
New York, New York 10016
(212) 679-3200 ext. 2840

AMERICAN JOURNAL OF OBSTETRICS AND GYNECOLOGY* [2267]
The C.V. Mosby Company
11830 Westline Industrial Drive
St. Louis, Missouri 63141
(314) 872-8370

SUBSCRIPTION DATA
Issues and rates: Published semi-monthly.
Average paid circulation: 16,504

Annual rate(s): $24.50, Foreign $30.50
Publisher or Sponsor: American Gynecological Society, American College of Obstetricians and Gynecologists

EDITORIAL DESCRIPTION
Edited for physicians specializing in OB/Gyn and those in general practice who wish to keep informed of developments in these fields. The scientific material published represents original contributions. Clinical and investigative reports are balanced in the presentation of approximately 3,000 pages of editorial material a year for prompt dissemination of current developments.

MANUSCRIPT INFORMATION
Manuscript requirements: Style sheet sent on request.
Number of copies to be submitted: 1 original, 1 copy
Author information and reprints: Payment: None.
Is simultaneous submission of article to other journals permitted: No
Exclusive manuscript rights between acceptance and publication: Yes
Copyright: Held by publication.
Reprints: Available at cost
Disposition of manuscript:
Receipt of manuscript acknowledged: Yes
Rejected manuscript returned: Yes
Submit to:
John I. Brewer
Editor-in-Chief
303 East Superior Street, Room 116
Chicago, Illinois 60611

AMERICAN JOURNAL OF OPHTHALMOLOGY [2268]
233 East Ontario Street
Suite 1401
Chicago, Illinois 60611
(312) 787-3853

First published in 1918

SUBSCRIPTION DATA
Issues and rates: Published monthly.
Average paid circulation: 15,014
Annual rate(s): $15.00; Foreign $18.00
Managing Editor: Mary L. Borysewicz

EDITORIAL DESCRIPTION
Publishes clinical and laboratory research papers and studies in the field of ophthalmology and related medical areas.
Articles per average issue: 15-20
Audience: Professional, clinicians, academic
Manuscripts accepted in English

MANUSCRIPT INFORMATION
Subject field(s): All aspects of ophthalmology, general medical information, theories and history of ophthalmic problems
Manuscript requirements: Style sheet sent on request.
Preferred length: 15-20 pages
Number of copies to be submitted: Two

Abstract: Yes; a summary of 150-250 words describing data and conclusions.
Author information and reprints: Payment: By author to publication. $500 per page charge for color figures.
Is simultaneous submission of article to other journals permitted: No
Exclusive manuscript rights between acceptance and publication: Yes
Copyright: Held by publication.
Reprints: Available, 50 provided free
Additional information: Duplicate, sized, cropped figures must be provided. Manuscripts should be in approved Journal style, references cited consecutively, separate pages for legends, references, title page.
Disposition of manuscript:
Query letter: No
Receipt of manuscript acknowledged: Yes
Decision to publish in: 4-6 weeks
Accepted manuscript published in: 6 months
Rejected manuscript returned: Yes
Rejected manuscript criticized: Sometimes
Submit to:
Frank W. Newell, M.D.
Editor
(See address above)

AMERICAN JOURNAL OF OPTOMETRY AND PHYSIOLOGICAL OPTICS [2269]
Box 441
Owatonna, Minnesota 55060
(507) 451-0009

Previously entitled *American Journal of Optometry; Archives of the American Academy of Optometry*

First published in 1924

SUBSCRIPTION DATA
Issues and rates: Published monthly.
Average paid circulation: 12,000
Annual rate(s): $15.00; Foreign $20.00; Institutions $15.00; Students $15.00
Publisher or Sponsor: American Academy of Optometry

EDITORIAL DESCRIPTION
Publishes material of interest to clinicians and researchers in visual research and its applications.
Articles per average issue: 12
Audience: Professional, academic
Manuscripts accepted in English

MANUSCRIPT INFORMATION
Subject field(s): Any subject bearing on visual sciences.
Manuscript requirements: No specific style guide.
Preferred length: 3-12 typewritten, double-spaced pages
Number of copies to be submitted: 3
Abstract: Yes.

Author information and reprints: Payment: None.
Is simultaneous submission of article to other journals permitted: Permitted, but not encouraged.
Exclusive manuscript rights between acceptance and publication: Yes
Copyright: Held by publication.
Reprints: Available at cost.
Additional information: All manuscripts are reviewed by a qualified editorial council prior to acceptance.
Disposition of manuscript:
Query letter: Not necessary, but advisable.
Receipt of manuscript acknowledged: Yes
Decision to publish in: 1-3 months
Accepted manuscript published in: 4-6 months
Rejected manuscript returned: Yes, if return postage is supplied by author.
Rejected manuscript criticized: Sometimes
Submit to:
Monroe J. Hirsch, M.D.
Editor-in-Chief
School of Optometry
University of California
Berkeley, California 94720
(415) 642-3302

AMERICAN JOURNAL OF PHARMACY AND THE SCIENCES SUPPORTING PUBLIC HEALTH [2270]
43rd Street and Kingsessing Mall
Philadelphia, Pennsylvania 19104
(215) 386-5800

First published in 1825

SUBSCRIPTION DATA
Issues and rates: Published bi-monthly.
Average paid circulation: Not available.
Annual rate(s): $4.00, Foreign $4.25
Publisher or Sponsor: Philadelphia College of Pharmacy and Science
Managing Editor: John E. Hoover

EDITORIAL DESCRIPTION
Publishes continuing education articles for pharmacists, pharmaceutical scientists, and public health scientists. Original research articles are also accepted.
Articles per average issue: 4
Manuscripts accepted in English

MANUSCRIPT INFORMATION
Manuscript requirements: Style sheet sent on request.
Preferred length: 25-50 pages
Number of copies to be submitted: Original and one copy
Abstract: Yes
Author information and reprints: Payment: None.
Is simultaneous submission of article to other journals permitted: No
Exclusive manuscript rights between acceptance and publication: Yes
Copyright: Held by publication.

Reprints: Available, cost published in each issue

Disposition of manuscript:
Query letter: No
Receipt of manuscript acknowledged: Yes
Decision to publish in: One to two months
Accepted manuscript published in: Six months
Rejected manuscript returned: Yes, if self-addressed, stamped envelope is sent with manuscript.
Rejected manuscript criticized: Sometimes

Submit to:
Linwood F. Tice
Editor
(See address above)

AMERICAN JOURNAL OF PHYSICAL MEDICINE [2271]

428 East Preston Street
Baltimore, Maryland 21202
(301) 528-4116

Previously entitled *Occupational Therapy and Rehabilitation*

First published in 1921

SUBSCRIPTION DATA

Issues and rates: Published bi-monthly.
Average paid circulation: 1,780
Annual rate(s): $12.00, Foreign $13.50
Managing Editor: H. D. Bouman

EDITORIAL DESCRIPTION

Contains original articles on all phases of physical medicine, new equipment and new products.
Manuscripts accepted in English

MANUSCRIPT INFORMATION

Manuscript requirements: See latest issue for style requirements.
Preferred length: 9000 words maximum
Number of copies to be submitted: Two
Abstract: No
Author information and reprints: Payment: None.
Is simultaneous submission of article to other journals permitted: No
Exclusive manuscript rights between acceptance and publication: Yes
Copyright: Held by publication.
Reprints: Available
Disposition of manuscript:
Query letter: No
Receipt of manuscript acknowledged: Yes
Decision to publish in: 2 months
Accepted manuscript published in: 1 year
Rejected manuscript returned: Yes
Rejected manuscript criticized: No
Submit to:
H. D. Bouman, M.D.
Editor
P.O. Box 617
Downtown Office
Phoenix, Arizona 85001
(602) 227-5229

AMERICAN MEDICAL ASSOCIATION. JOURNAL (JAMA) [2272]

535 North Dearborn Street
Chicago, Illinois 60610
(312) 751-6333

Previously entitled *Transactions of AMA*

First published in 1848

SUBSCRIPTION DATA

Issues and rates: Published weekly.
Average paid circulation: 247,000
Annual rate(s): $30.00; Students $10.00 (interns, residents)
Publisher or Sponsor: American Medical Association
Managing Editor: Robert W. Mayo

EDITORIAL DESCRIPTION

Publishes articles and reports on current research and clinical studies.
Articles per average issue: 15 plus letters, questions and answers, book reviews, comments and selected abstracts.
Audience: Professional
Manuscripts accepted in English (Spanish for Spanish language edition)

MANUSCRIPT INFORMATION

Subject field(s): General medicine, practice, socio-cultural, philosophical, historical aspects of medicine, medical advances, discussions of diagnosis, and management
Manuscript requirements: AMA
Preferred length: Reviews: 8-10 printed pages; reports: 1-2 printed pages
Number of copies to be submitted: Three
Abstract: Yes, see specifications in Advice to Authors.
Author information and reprints: Payment: None. Rare payments to medical reporters.
Is simultaneous submission of article to other journals permitted: No
Exclusive manuscript rights between acceptance and publication: Yes
Copyright: Held by the American Medical Association
Reprints: Available at cost
Additional information: Manuscripts are refereed. Some are by in-house senior editors; most by expert consultants
Disposition of manuscript:
Query letter: No
Receipt of manuscript acknowledged: Yes
Decision to publish in: 2 months or less
Accepted manuscript published in: 3-6 months
Rejected manuscript returned: Yes
Rejected manuscript criticized: Sometimes
Submit to:
Robert H. Moser, M.D.
Editor
(See address above)

AMERICAN MEDICAL TECHNOLOGISTS JOURNAL [2273]

710 Higgins Road
Park Ridge, Illinois 60068
(312) 823-5169

First published in 1939

SUBSCRIPTION DATA

Issues and rates: Published bi-monthly.
Average paid circulation: 12,500
Annual rate(s): $5.00; Foreign $6.50
Publisher or Sponsor: American Medical Technologists
Managing Editor: Chester B. Dziekonski

EDITORIAL DESCRIPTION

Presents technical and scientific articles of interest to clinical laboratory professionals with feature material on various aspects of medical laboratory work.
Articles per average issue: 3-4
Audience: Professional
Manuscripts accepted in English

MANUSCRIPT INFORMATION

Subject field(s): Any area of clinical laboratory interest
Manuscript requirements: See latest issue for style requirements. Style sheet sent on request.
Preferred length: Up to 25 pages
Number of copies to be submitted: 2
Abstract: Yes. A short summary of 4-5 sentences.
Author information and reprints: Payment: Reprints only. 50 reprints
Is simultaneous submission of article to other journals permitted: Not permitted.
Exclusive manuscript rights between acceptance and publication: Yes
Copyright: Held by publication.
Reprints: Available at cost.
Disposition of manuscript:
Query letter: Not necessary.
Receipt of manuscript acknowledged: Yes
Decision to publish in: 2 months
Accepted manuscript published in: 6 months
Rejected manuscript returned: Yes, if return postage is supplied by author.
Rejected manuscript criticized: Sometimes
Submit to:
Eleanore M. Bors
Assistant Editor
(See address above)

AMERICAN OSTEOPATHIC ASSOCIATION JOURNAL [2274]

212 East Ohio Street
Chicago, Illinois 60611
(312) 944-2713

First published in 1909

SUBSCRIPTION DATA

Issues and rates: Published monthly.
Average paid circulation: 17,899

Annual rate(s): $10.00, Foreign $14.50
Publisher or Sponsor: American Osteopathic Association

EDITORIAL DESCRIPTION
Represents the osteopathic profession in the field of scientific publication. Documents the findings and experiences of osteopathic physicians through publication of formal papers.
Articles per average issue: 10
Audience: Professional
Manuscripts accepted in English

MANUSCRIPT INFORMATION
Subject field(s): All areas of general medical practice with special emphasis on osteopathic medicine
Manuscript requirements: See latest issue for style requirements.
Preferred length: Varies
Number of copies to be submitted: Two
Abstract: Yes, substantive of about 150 words
Author information and reprints: Payment: None.
Is simultaneous submission of article to other journals permitted: No
Exclusive manuscript rights between acceptance and publication: Yes
Copyright: Held by publication.
Reprints: Available in large quantities only; 25 sets of tear sheets routinely supplied.
Additional information: Manuscripts accepted only from osteopathic physicians, faculty members or speakers at osteopathic meetings.
Disposition of manuscript:
Query letter: No
Receipt of manuscript acknowledged: Yes
Decision to publish in: 3 months
Accepted manuscript published in: 9-12 months
Rejected manuscript returned: Yes
Rejected manuscript criticized: Yes
Submit to:
George W. Northup
Editor
(See address above)

AMERICAN PODIATRY ASSOCIATION JOURNAL   [2275]
20 Chevy Chase Circle NW
Washington, D.C. 20015
(202) 362-2700

Previously entitled *Journal of the National Association of Chiropodists*

First published in 1907

SUBSCRIPTION DATA
Issues and rates: Published monthly.
Average paid circulation: 6,700
Annual rate(s): $18.00
Publisher or Sponsor: The American Podiatry Association

EDITORIAL DESCRIPTION
Publishes scientific articles on the care and treatment of diseases of the foot; case reports, research papers, reports,

editorials, book reviews, abstracts, practice management.
Articles per average issue: Varies
Audience: Professional
Manuscripts accepted in English

MANUSCRIPT INFORMATION
Subject field(s): Foot, podiatry
Manuscript requirements: Style sheet sent on request.
Number of copies to be submitted: Three
Abstract: Yes
Author information and reprints: Payment: None.
Is simultaneous submission of article to other journals permitted: No
Exclusive manuscript rights between acceptance and publication: Yes
Copyright: Held by publication.
Reprints: Available at cost determined by length of article
Additional information: Manuscripts not meeting journal requirements will be returned to author without consideration of content. Author's name and affiliation should appear on a separate cover page so manuscripts can be evaluated anonymously.
Disposition of manuscript:
Query letter: No
Receipt of manuscript acknowledged: Yes
Decision to publish in: Six to eight weeks
Accepted manuscript published in: Six months
Rejected manuscript returned: Yes
Rejected manuscript criticized: Yes
Submit to:
E. Dalton McGlamry, D.P.M.
Editor

Louis G. Buttell
Managing Editor
(See address above)

AMERICAN REVIEW OF RESPIRATORY DISEASE   [2276]
San Francisco General Hospital, Chest Service
22nd and Potrero Streets
San Francisco, California 94110
(415) 282-3909

SUBSCRIPTION DATA
Issues and rates: Published monthly.
Average paid circulation: 9,500
Annual rate(s): $25.00
Publisher or Sponsor: American Thoracic Society

EDITORIAL DESCRIPTION
Contains original manuscripts on any phase of tuberculosis or respiratory disease.
Articles per average issue: 18-20
Audience: Professional
Manuscripts accepted in English

MANUSCRIPT INFORMATION
Subject field(s): All clinical pulmonary diseases: tuberculosis, pulmonary vascular, pulmonary physiologic, diagnostic, pharmacologic

Manuscript requirements: Guide to Contributors (printed in January, March, and July); Chicago
Preferred length: 15 typewritten, double-spaced
Number of copies to be submitted: Three
Abstract: Yes
Author information and reprints: Payment: None.
Is simultaneous submission of article to other journals permitted: No
Exclusive manuscript rights between acceptance and publication: Yes
Copyright: Held by publication.
Reprints: Available
Disposition of manuscript:
Query letter: No
Receipt of manuscript acknowledged: Yes
Decision to publish in: 3 months
Accepted manuscript published in: 6 months
Rejected manuscript returned: Yes
Rejected manuscript criticized: Yes
Submit to:
John F. Murray, M.D.
Editor
(See address above)

AMERICAN SOCIETY OF PSYCHOSOMATIC DENTISTRY AND MEDICINE JOURNAL   [2277]
2802 Mermaid Avenue
Brooklyn, New York 11224
(212) 372-4569

First published in 1954

SUBSCRIPTION DATA
Issues and rates: Published quarterly.
Average paid circulation: 400
Annual rate(s): $15.00, Foreign $18.00
Publisher or Sponsor: American Society of Psychosomatic Dentistry and Medicine

EDITORIAL DESCRIPTION
Contains editorials, book reviews, scientific articles on hypnosis, psychosomatic medicine, psychology, acupuncture, etc.
Articles per average issue: 4
Audience: Medical, dental, psychological, legal
Manuscripts accepted in English, French Spanish, Japanese

MANUSCRIPT INFORMATION
Subject field(s): Hypnosis, psychosomatic medicine, dental topics, psychology, sex education, parapsychology, psychotherapy, humor
Manuscript requirements: No specific style guide.
Preferred length: 2000 words; 5 pages
Number of copies to be submitted: Two
Abstract: Yes, of one paragraph
Author information and reprints: Payment: None.
Is simultaneous submission of article to other journals permitted: No
Exclusive manuscript rights between acceptance and publication: Yes
Copyright: Held by publication.

Medicine (general)

Reprints: Available
Disposition of manuscript:
Query letter: No
Receipt of manuscript acknowledged: Yes
Decision to publish in: 6 weeks
Accepted manuscript published in: 6 months
Rejected manuscript returned: Yes, if self-addressed, stamped envelope is sent with manuscript.
Rejected manuscript criticized: No
Submit to:
Leo Wollman
Editor
(See address above)

ANNALES CHIRURGIAE ET GYNAECOLOGIAE FENNIAE [2278]

Runeberginkatu 47 A
00260 Helsinki 26, Finland

First published in 1946

SUBSCRIPTION DATA
Issues and rates: Published semi-monthly.
Average paid circulation: 1,700
Annual rate(s): $25.00
Publisher or Sponsor: Finnish Medical Society Duodecim
Managing Editor: E. Kivilaakso, M.D.

EDITORIAL DESCRIPTION
Publishes original articles, brief reports and reviews on clinical surgery and gynecology. The journal concentrates especially on fields with immediate relevance for the clinical situation.
Articles per average issue: 10-12
Audience: Medical
Manuscripts accepted in English

MANUSCRIPT INFORMATION
Subject field(s): General surgery, orthopedics, traumatology, anaesthesiology, urologic surgery, gynaecological surgery, obstetrics, vascular surgery, pathology, epidemiology
Manuscript requirements: See latest issue for style requirements.
Preferred length: 3-8 pages
Number of copies to be submitted: 2
Abstract: Yes, of less than 200 words
Author information and reprints: Payment: None.
Is simultaneous submission of article to other journals permitted: No
Exclusive manuscript rights between acceptance and publication: Yes
Copyright: Held by author.
Reprints: Available at cost.
Disposition of manuscript:
Query letter: No
Receipt of manuscript acknowledged: Yes
Decision to publish in: 1-2 months
Accepted manuscript published in: 3-8 months
Rejected manuscript returned: Yes
Rejected manuscript criticized: Yes
Submit to:
M. I. Turunen, M.D.
Editor-in-Chief
(See address above)

ANNALS OF CLINICAL RESEARCH [2279]

Runeberginkatu 47 A
00260 Helsinki 26, Finland

SUBSCRIPTION DATA
Issues and rates: Published semi-monthly.
Average paid circulation: 2,400
Annual rate(s): $25.00
Publisher or Sponsor: Finnish Medical Society Duodecim
Managing Editor: V. Valtonen

EDITORIAL DESCRIPTION
Publishes original articles, brief reports and reviews on clinical medicine including laboratory medicine. Preference on interdisciplinary subjects. One large special issue yearly on a subject selected for its new developments and actual importance in clinical medicine.
Articles per average issue: 10-12 articles
Audience: Clinical practitioners
Manuscripts accepted in English

MANUSCRIPT INFORMATION
Subject field(s): Internal medicine, dermatology, pediatrics, radiology, laboratory medicine, gynecology and obstetrics, clinical endocrinology, anesthesiology, pathology, otorhinolaryngology, epidemiology, surgery
Manuscript requirements: See latest issue for style requirements.
Preferred length: 3-8 pages
Number of copies to be submitted: Two
Abstract: Yes, of about 200 words, including a list of key words for abstracting purposes.
Author information and reprints: Payment: None.
Is simultaneous submission of article to other journals permitted: No
Exclusive manuscript rights between acceptance and publication: Yes
Copyright: Held by author.
Reprints: Available, cost varies
Disposition of manuscript:
Query letter: No
Receipt of manuscript acknowledged: Yes
Decision to publish in: 1-2 months
Accepted manuscript published in: 3-8 months
Rejected manuscript returned: Yes
Rejected manuscript criticized: Yes
Submit to:
K. K. Mustakallio
Editor-in-Chief
(See address above)

ANNALS OF INTERNAL MEDICINE [2280]

4200 Pine Street
Philadelphia, Pennsylvania 19104
(215) 243-1200

First published in 1927

SUBSCRIPTION DATA
Issues and rates: Published monthly.
Average paid circulation: 70,000
Annual rate(s): $18.00, Foreign $21.00
Publisher or Sponsor: American College of Physicians
Managing Editor: Edward J. Huth

EDITORIAL DESCRIPTION
Contains papers on clinical, laboratory, socioeconomic, cultural, and historical topics pertinent to internal medicine and related fields; announcements of courses, symposia, and other coming events. Aim is to present current developments, both clinical and investigative, and to provide a forum for a wide diversity of opinion.
Articles per average issue: 25
Audience: Physicians
Manuscripts accepted in English

MANUSCRIPT INFORMATION
Subject field(s): Internal medicine, socioeconomics of medicine, culture of medicine, pathology, dermatology, industrial medicine, pediatrics
Manuscript requirements: CBE; other instructions sent on request.
Preferred length: Request information from editor
Number of copies to be submitted: Two
Abstract: Yes, not exceeding 150 words
Author information and reprints: Payment: None.
Is simultaneous submission of article to other journals permitted: No
Exclusive manuscript rights between acceptance and publication: Yes
Copyright: Held by publication.
Reprints: Available, prices sent upon request.
Additional information: Manuscript typewritten, double-spaced; illustrations as glossy prints no larger than 8 x 10 inches and in duplicate; tables on separate sheets.
Disposition of manuscript:
Query letter: No
Receipt of manuscript acknowledged: Yes
Decision to publish in: 2-6 weeks
Accepted manuscript published in: 3-4 months
Rejected manuscript returned: Yes
Rejected manuscript criticized: Sometimes
Submit to:
Edward J. Huth, M.D.
Editor
(See address above)

ANNALS OF OTOLOGY, RHINOLOGY AND LARYNGOLOGY [2281]

4949 Forest Park Avenue
St. Louis, Missouri 63108
(314) 367-4987

First published in 1892

SUBSCRIPTION DATA
Issues and rates: Published bi-monthly.
Average paid circulation: 4,900; 200 controlled

Annual rate(s): $33.00; Foreign $35.00; Institutions $33.00; Students $17.00; Foreign institutions $35.00

Publisher or Sponsor: American Otological Society, Inc., American Laryngological Association; American Broncho-Esophagological Association

Managing Editor: Bess E. Ariek

EDITORIAL DESCRIPTION

Original clinical and research manuscripts on diseases of the ear, nose, throat and speech and hearing defects; papers read before the three otolaryngological societies; book reviews; medical notices and announcements.

Articles per average issue: 19

Audience: Otologists, laryngologists, pathologists, hospitals, libraries, clinics, medical schools, and medical clinics

Manuscripts accepted in English

MANUSCRIPT INFORMATION

Subject field(s): Clinical and scientific aspects of otolaryngology, bronchoesophagology, maxillofacial surgery, head and neck surgery, audiology, speech pathology, and related specialties

Manuscript requirements: See latest issue for style requirements. Chicago

Preferred length: 20 pages

Number of copies to be submitted: Original and 3 copies

Abstract: Yes. A comprehensive abstract-summary of 150 to 200 words

Author information and reprints: Payment: By publication to author. $50.00 per page. Payment in excess of 8 typeset pages.

Is simultaneous submission of article to other journals permitted: Not permitted.

Exclusive manuscript rights between acceptance and publication: Yes

Copyright: Held by Annals Publishing Company

Reprints: Available at no cost.

Additional information: Engravings are paid for by the author. Manuscripts too long for the conventional issue may be published as supplements.

Disposition of manuscript:

Query letter: Not necessary.

Receipt of manuscript acknowledged: Yes

Decision to publish in: 2 months

Accepted manuscript published in: 8 months

Rejected manuscript returned: Yes, with return postage paid by publication.

Rejected manuscript criticized: Reasons for rejections only

Submit to:

Ben H. Senturia, M. D.

Editor

(See address above)

ANNALS OF TROPICAL MEDICINE AND PARASITOLOGY   [2282]

Liverpool University Press
123 Grove Street
Liverpool, Lancashire L7 7AF England
051-709-7303

First published in 1906

SUBSCRIPTION DATA

Issues and rates: Published quarterly.

Average paid circulation: 900

Annual rate(s): £16.00; Foreign $40.00

Publisher or Sponsor: Liverpool School of Tropical Medicine

Managing Editor: D. R. Bell

EDITORIAL DESCRIPTION

Contains articles on tropical medicine, parasitology, entomology, tropical community health, tropical child health.

Articles per average issue: 6-9

Manuscripts accepted in English

MANUSCRIPT INFORMATION

Manuscript requirements: See latest issue for style requirements.

Preferred length: 20 pages

Number of copies to be submitted: Two

Abstract: Yes

Author information and reprints: Payment: By author to publication. £15.00 per art-page and for extra offprints (25 free).

Is simultaneous submission of article to other journals permitted: No

Exclusive manuscript rights between acceptance and publication: Yes

Copyright: Held by publication.

Reprints: Available, 25 free offprints

Additional information: SI Units should be used in typescripts, photographs, and text-figures. Illustrations for text-figures and charts should be drawn clearly and firmly in India ink (not coloured), if possible on Bristol Board. Plates and illustrations should be accompanied by short explanations.

Disposition of manuscript:

Receipt of manuscript acknowledged: Yes

Decision to publish in: One to three months

Accepted manuscript published in: One year

Rejected manuscript returned: Yes

Rejected manuscript criticized: No

Submit to:

Alison Abercromby

Editorial Secretary

Liverpool School of Tropical Medicine

Pembroke Place

Liverpool, Lancashire L7 7AF, England
051-709-7611

ANTIMICROBIAL AGENTS AND CHEMOTHERAPY   [2283]

1913 I Street, N.W.
Washington, D.C. 20006
(202) 833-9416

Previously entitled *Journal of Virology*

First published in January 1972

SUBSCRIPTION DATA

Issues and rates: Published monthly.

Average paid circulation: 4,000

Annual rate(s): $40.00; Foreign $41.00; Institutions $40.00

Publisher or Sponsor: American Society for Microbiology

Managing Editor: Robert A. Day

EDITORIAL DESCRIPTION

Devoted to the dissemination of knowledge relating to all aspects of antimicrobial agents and chemotherapy, including cancer chemotherapy.

Articles per average issue: 23

Manuscripts accepted in English

MANUSCRIPT INFORMATION

Manuscript requirements: See latest issue for style requirements.

Preferred length: None

Number of copies to be submitted: 2

Abstract: Yes.

Author information and reprints: Payment: None.

Is simultaneous submission of article to other journals permitted: Not permitted.

Exclusive manuscript rights between acceptance and publication: Yes

Copyright: Held by the Society

Reprints: Available at cost.

Disposition of manuscript:

Query letter: Not necessary.

Receipt of manuscript acknowledged: Yes

Decision to publish in: 3 months

Accepted manuscript published in: 3 months

Rejected manuscript returned: Yes, with return postage paid by publication.

Rejected manuscript criticized: Yes

Submit to:

Robert A. Day

Managing Editor

(See address above)

APPLIED RADIOLOGY   [2284]

The Journal of Radiologic Technique
825 South Barrington Avenue
Los Angeles, California 90049
(213) 826-8388

First published in 1972

SUBSCRIPTION DATA

Issues and rates: Published bi-monthly.

Average paid circulation: 254; 16,174 controlled

Annual rate(s): $20; Foreign $40

Managing Editor: Hal Spector;
Martin H. Waldman

EDITORIAL DESCRIPTION

Articles cover the entire gamut of professional interests: technical advances, case histories, facilities reports, equipment, supplies, etc. Directed to both radiologists and radiologic technologists in diagnostic radiology, radiation therapy and nuclear medicine.

Manuscripts accepted in English

Medicine (general)

MANUSCRIPT INFORMATION
Subject field(s): Techniques, problems and solutions, hospital care, facility reports
Manuscript requirements: Style sheet sent on request.
  Preferred length: 3000-5000 words
  Number of copies to be submitted: Two
Author information and reprints: Payment: None.
  Is simultaneous submission of article to other journals permitted: No
  Exclusive manuscript rights between acceptance and publication: Yes
  Copyright: Held by author.
  Reprints: Available at cost
Additional information: Desire reproducible artwork.
Disposition of manuscript:
  Receipt of manuscript acknowledged: Yes
  Decision to publish in: Varies
  Accepted manuscript published in: Varies
  Rejected manuscript returned: Yes
  Rejected manuscript criticized: No
Submit to:
  Roberta Atchison
  Editorial Coordinator
  (See address above)

ARCHIVES OF PHYSICAL MEDICINE AND REHABILITATION   [2285]
Suite 922
30 North Michigan Avenue
Chicago, Illinois 60602
(312) 236-9512

Previously entitled *Journal of Radiology*

First published in 1920

SUBSCRIPTION DATA
Issues and rates: Published monthly.
  Average paid circulation: 5400
  Annual rate(s): $20.00
Publisher or Sponsor: American Congress of Rehabilitation Medicine
Managing Editor: Marvin Schroder

EDITORIAL DESCRIPTION
  Contains scientific articles of interest to persons working in the field of physical medicine and rehabilitation.
  Manuscripts accepted in English

MANUSCRIPT INFORMATION
Subject field(s): Physiology, physical therapy, occupational therapy, vocational counseling, rehabilitation nursing, speech therapy, prosthetics, orthotics
Manuscript requirements: Style sheet sent on request.
  Preferred length: None
  Number of copies to be submitted: 4
  Abstract: Yes
Author information and reprints: Payment: None.
  Is simultaneous submission of article to other journals permitted: No
  Exclusive manuscript rights between acceptance and publication: Yes
  Copyright: Held by publication.
  Reprints: Available at cost.

Disposition of manuscript:
  Query letter: No
  Receipt of manuscript acknowledged: Yes
  Decision to publish in: 6 months
  Accepted manuscript published in: 6-12 months
  Rejected manuscript returned: Yes
  Rejected manuscript criticized: Yes
Submit to:
  Chairman, Editorial Board
  (See address above)

ARCHIVES OF TOXICOLOGY   [2286]
Archiv für Toxikologie
Springer-Verlag
175 Fifth Avenue
New York, New York 10010

First published in 1930

SUBSCRIPTION DATA
  Annual rate(s): DM 108 per volume

EDITORIAL DESCRIPTION
  Reviews, original papers and short communications concerned with the observation, description, and experimental investigation of the toxic effects of substances on humans and animals.
Audience: Toxicologists
  Manuscripts accepted in English

MANUSCRIPT INFORMATION
Subject field(s): Toxicology, including methods of treatment or attempted treatment and detection methods in forensic toxicology.
Manuscript requirements: Style sheet sent on request.
  Preferred length: As required
  Number of copies to be submitted: 2
  Abstract: Yes. An abstract in both English and German
Author information and reprints: Payment: Reprints only. 50 offprints
  Is simultaneous submission of article to other journals permitted: Not permitted.
  Exclusive manuscript rights between acceptance and publication: Yes
  Copyright: Held by publication.
  Reprints: Available at cost.
Additional information: Papers should be typewritten, double-spaced with divisions into the following sections: Introduction, Materials and Methods, Results, Discussion, References
Submit to:
  Professor Dr. William B. Deichmann
  Member, Editorial Board
  Research and Training Center of Toxicology, P. O. Box 8216
  University of Miami School of Medicine
  Coral Gables, Florida 33124

ARTHRITIS AND RHEUMATISM   [2287]
Journal of the American Rheumatism Association
The Arthritis Foundation
1212 Avenue of the Americas
New York, New York 10036
(212) 757-7600

First published in 1958

SUBSCRIPTION DATA
Issues and rates: Published bi-monthly.
  Average paid circulation: 5,400; 100 controlled
  Annual rate(s): $23.00; Foreign $24.00; Institutions $23.00
Publisher or Sponsor: American Rheumatism Association;
  The Arthritis Foundation

Managing Editor: Barbara Conover

EDITORIAL DESCRIPTION
  Publishes original work, progress reports, clinical rounds and review articles to provide a clear exposition of clinical experience and advances made in the treatment of rheumatoid arthritis, rheumatic fever, osteoarthritis, gout, nonarticular rheumatism and the field of connective tissue diseases.
Articles per average issue: 18
Audience: Professional, medical, general as well as the specialist
  Manuscripts accepted in English

MANUSCRIPT INFORMATION
Subject field(s): Case reports only if they include controlled observations of an exceptionally revealing nature.
Manuscript requirements: See latest issue for style requirements. IM
  Preferred length: 6-12 pages
  Number of copies to be submitted: 2
  Abstract: Yes. A synopsis of the article of not more than 75 words.
Author information and reprints: Payment: None.
  Is simultaneous submission of article to other journals permitted: Not permitted.
  Exclusive manuscript rights between acceptance and publication: Yes
  Copyright: Held by publication.
  Reprints: Available at cost.
Disposition of manuscript:
  Query letter: Not necessary.
  Receipt of manuscript acknowledged: Yes
  Decision to publish in: 4-6 weeks
  Accepted manuscript published in: 4 months
  Rejected manuscript returned: Yes, with return postage paid by publication.
  Rejected manuscript criticized: Yes
Submit to:
  Charles L. Christian, M.D.
  Editor
  Hospital for Special Surgery
  535 East 70th Street
  New York, New York 10021
  (212) 535-5500

AUDECIBEL   [2288]
The Official Journal of the National Hearing Aid Society
20361 Middlebelt
Livonia, Michigan 48152
(313) 537-2610

SUBSCRIPTION DATA
Issues and rates: Published quarterly.
  Average paid circulation: 3,500; 8,500 controlled

Annual rate(s): $3.00, Foreign $6.00

Publisher or Sponsor: National Hearing Aid Society

EDITORIAL DESCRIPTION

Contains technical articles dealing with hearing aids and their selection and fitting; technical articles dealing with sound, acoustics, noise; psychology of the hearing impaired; medical and physiological aspects of hearing loss; "opinion" articles dealing with professional standards, ethics, and the future of the hearing aid profession.

MANUSCRIPT INFORMATION

Manuscript requirements: No specific style guide.

Preferred length: 200-2000 words

Number of copies to be submitted: One

Author information and reprints: Payment: By publication to author. $.01-$.025 per word.

Is simultaneous submission of article to other journals permitted: No

Exclusive manuscript rights between acceptance and publication: Yes

Copyright: Held by publication.

Reprints: Sometimes available

Additional information: A "Fact Sheet for Writers" providing more information about submitting manuscripts will be sent on request.

Disposition of manuscript:

Receipt of manuscript acknowledged: Yes

Decision to publish in: 3 months

Rejected manuscript returned: Yes, if self-addressed, stamped envelope is sent with manuscript.

Rejected manuscript criticized: No

Submit to:

Anthony DiRocco

Editor and Executive Secretary

(See address above)

AUDIOLOGY [2289]

Journal of Auditory Communication

S. Karger AG

Arnold-Böcklin Strasse 25

CH-4011 Basel, Switzerland

061-390880

Previously entitled *International Audiology*

SUBSCRIPTION DATA

Issues and rates: Published bi-monthly.

Average paid circulation: 935; 72 controlled

Annual rate(s): SFr. 150.00; Foreign $60.00

Publisher or Sponsor: International Society of Audiology

EDITORIAL DESCRIPTION

Reflects the diverse international activities of this broad interdisciplinary field embracing the scientific, social and practical aspects of hearing.

Articles per average issue: 6-7

Audience: Professional

Manuscripts accepted in English, French, German

MANUSCRIPT INFORMATION

Subject field(s): Emphasizes cooperation between the varying fields of anatomy, histology, pathology, physiology, neurophysiology, physical acoustics, psychology, psychiatry, social sciences and lastly otology, which being the science of ear diseases, is the central and leading branch of this comprehensive teamwork.

Manuscript requirements: Style sheet sent on request.

Preferred length: No limitations

Number of copies to be submitted: 3

Abstract: Yes, including key words

Author information and reprints: Payment: Reprints only. 100 reprints

Is simultaneous submission of article to other journals permitted: No

Exclusive manuscript rights between acceptance and publication: Yes

Copyright: Held by the Society

Reprints: Available

Disposition of manuscript:

Query letter: No

Receipt of manuscript acknowledged: Yes

Decision to publish in: 1-2 months

Accepted manuscript published in: 6-7 months

Rejected manuscript returned: Yes

Rejected manuscript criticized: Yes

Submit to:

Prof. Ing. E. König

Editor-in-Chief

Audiologische Abteilung

Otolaryngologische Universitätsklinik

Hebelstrasse 10 CH-4004 Basel, Switzerland

AUSTRALIAN AND NEW ZEALAND JOURNAL OF MEDICINE [2290]

Royal Australasian College of Physicians

P.O. Box H 129

Sydney, N.S.W. 2000 Australia

27-3288

Previously entitled *Australasian Annals of Medicine*

First published in 1952

SUBSCRIPTION DATA

Issues and rates: Published bi-monthly.

Annual rate(s): $20.00

Publisher or Sponsor: Royal Australasian College of Physicians

EDITORIAL DESCRIPTION

Emphasis on maintaining high standards in internal medicine; encourages research, medical education and certain aspects of health care delivery.

Articles per average issue: 14

Manuscripts accepted in English

MANUSCRIPT INFORMATION

Subject field(s): Internal medicine (all specialties), pediatrics, clinical pathology, clinical chemistry, clinical physiology, clinical pharmacology

Manuscript requirements: Style sheet sent on request.

Number of copies to be submitted: Two

Abstract: No

Author information and reprints: Payment: None.

Is simultaneous submission of article to other journals permitted: No

Exclusive manuscript rights between acceptance and publication: Yes

Copyright: Held by publication.

Reprints: Available

Disposition of manuscript:

Query letter: No

Receipt of manuscript acknowledged: Yes

Decision to publish in: 1 months

Accepted manuscript published in: 6-8 months

Rejected manuscript returned: Yes

Rejected manuscript criticized: Yes

Submit to:

A.Z. Gyory

Honorary Editor

(See address above)

AUSTRALIAN AND NEW ZEALAND JOURNAL OF OBSTETRICS AND GYNAECOLOGY [2291]

8 Latrobe Street

Melbourne, Victoria 3000 Australia

347-1262

SUBSCRIPTION DATA

Issues and rates: Published quarterly.

Average paid circulation: 1050

Annual rate(s): $15.00; Foreign $18.00

Publisher or Sponsor: Royal College of Obstetrics and Gynaecology, Australia and New Zealand Councils

EDITORIAL DESCRIPTION

Publishes clinical and scientific research articles on obstetrics and gynaecology.

MANUSCRIPT INFORMATION

Manuscript requirements: See latest issue for style requirements.

Number of copies to be submitted: Two

Author information and reprints: Payment: None.

Is simultaneous submission of article to other journals permitted: No

Exclusive manuscript rights between acceptance and publication: Yes

Copyright: Held by publication.

Reprints: Available

Disposition of manuscript:

Receipt of manuscript acknowledged: Yes

Decision to publish in: 6-8 weeks

Accepted manuscript published in: 6-9 months

Rejected manuscript returned: Yes

Rejected manuscript criticized: Yes

Submit to:

E. V. Mackay

Queensland University

Department of Obstetrics and Gynaecology

Brisbane, Queensland, Australia

Medicine (general)

BIOLOGY OF THE NEONATE [2292]

Fetal and Neonatal Research
S. Karger AG
Arnold-Böcklin Strasse 25
CH-4011 Basel, Switzerland
061-390880

Previously entitled *Biologica Neonatorum*

First published in 1959

SUBSCRIPTION DATA

Issues and rates: Published monthly.
Average paid circulation: 953; 65
controlled
Annual rate(s): SFr. 165.00; Foreign
$66.00

EDITORIAL DESCRIPTION

Publishes papers on laboratory work and
clinical research, including physiological
and biochemical research work applicable
to the clinic. It contains in equal parts
fundamental research papers and articles
on applied research work, with the
exclusion of particular clinical
observations or reports.
Articles per average issue: 10-15
Audience: Professional, academic
Manuscripts accepted in English

MANUSCRIPT INFORMATION

Subject field(s): The majority of the papers
deal with findings of basic research and
even though they seem only remotely
connected with the clinician, their
contents provide indispensable
information which should be brought to
the attention of all pediatricians.
Manuscript requirements: See latest issue for
style requirements.
Preferred length: 12 pages
Number of copies to be submitted: 2
Abstract: Yes, with key words
Author information and reprints: Payment:
None. A charge of SFr. 150.00 for excess
pages.
Is simultaneous submission of article to
other journals permitted: No
Exclusive manuscript rights between
acceptance and publication: Yes
Copyright: Held by publication.
Reprints: Available at cost
Disposition of manuscript:
Query letter: No
Receipt of manuscript acknowledged: Yes
Decision to publish in: 1-3 months
Accepted manuscript published in:
5-7months
Rejected manuscript returned: Yes
Rejected manuscript criticized: Yes
Submit to:
Prof. A. Minkowski
Editor-in-Chief
Centre de Recherches Biologiques
Néonatales
123, Boulevard du Port-Royale
F-75674 Paris Cedex 14, France

BLOOD VESSELS [2293]

International Journal of Blood and
Lymphatic Vessels
S. Karger AG
Arnold-Böcklin Strasse 25
CH-4011 Basel, Switzerland
061-390880

Previously entitled *Angiologica*

SUBSCRIPTION DATA

Issues and rates: Published bi-monthly.
Average paid circulation: 642; 58
controlled
Annual rate(s): SFr. 132.00; Foreign
$54.00 per volume

EDITORIAL DESCRIPTION

The recent increase in vascular disease
has lent to angiology a dominant position
in medicine. The journal publishes both
clinical and basic research results to
further knowledge through the
co-ordination of research.
Manuscripts accepted in English

MANUSCRIPT INFORMATION

Subject field(s): Morphological, physical,
biochemical and functional character of
blood vessels, as well as vascular-tissular
relations and the nutritional aspects of
angiology.
Manuscript requirements: Style sheet sent
on request. See latest issue for style
requirements.
Preferred length: 10 pages
Number of copies to be submitted: 3
Abstract: Yes
Author information and reprints: Payment:
None.
Is simultaneous submission of article to
other journals permitted: No
Exclusive manuscript rights between
acceptance and publication: Yes, 6 key
words
Copyright: Held by publication.
Reprints: Available
Disposition of manuscript:
Query letter: No
Receipt of manuscript acknowledged: Yes
Decision to publish in: 1 month
Accepted manuscript published in: 6
months
Rejected manuscript returned: Yes
Rejected manuscript criticized: Yes
Submit to:
John A. Beran
Department of Pharmacology, School of
Medicine
Center for Health Sciences
University of California
Los Angeles, California 90024

BRAIN, BEHAVIOR AND EVOLUTION [2294]

S. Karger AG
Arnold-Böcklin Strasse 25
CH-4011 Basel, Switzerland
061-390880

First published in 1968

SUBSCRIPTION DATA

Issues and rates: Published monthly.
Average paid circulation: 600; 34
controlled
Annual rate(s): SFr. 132.00; Foreign
$54.00

EDITORIAL DESCRIPTION

The relationship between the anatomical
and physiological organization of the
nervous system and the natural units of
the organization of behavior are
discussed. The journal permits
meaningful interaction among the three
basic disciplines of neuroanatomy,
neurophysiology and behavioral sciences.
Articles per average issue: 4-5
Manuscripts accepted in English

MANUSCRIPT INFORMATION

Manuscript requirements: See latest issue for
style requirements.
Preferred length: 12 pages
Number of copies to be submitted: 3
Abstract: Yes, with keys words
Author information and reprints: Payment:
None.
Is simultaneous submission of article to
other journals permitted: No
Exclusive manuscript rights between
acceptance and publication: Yes
Copyright: Held by publication.
Reprints: Available at cost
Disposition of manuscript:
Query letter: No
Receipt of manuscript acknowledged: Yes
Decision to publish in: 1-2 months
Accepted manuscript published in: 5-6
months
Rejected manuscript returned: Yes
Rejected manuscript criticized: Yes
Submit to:
Dr. Walter Riss
Editor-in-Chief
Department of Anatomy
SUNY Downstate Medical Center
450 Clarckson Avenue
Brooklyn, New York 11203

BRAIN RESEARCH [2295]

International Multidisciplinary Journal of
Fundamental Research in the Brain Sciences
Elsevier Scientific Publishing Co.
Jan van Galenstraat 335
Amsterdam, The Netherlands
(020) 515-3200

First published in 1966

SUBSCRIPTION DATA

Issues and rates: Published weekly.
Annual rate(s): 1728 Dfl.
Managing Editor: Konrad Akert

EDITORIAL DESCRIPTION

To publish articles in the fields of
neuroanatomy, neurochemistry,
neuroendocrinology, neuropharmacology,
neurocommunication, behavioral sciences,
molecular neurology and biocybernetics.
Articles per average issue: 15
Audience: Neuroscientists

Manuscripts accepted in English, French, German

MANUSCRIPT INFORMATION

Manuscript requirements: See latest issue for style requirements. Style sheet sent on request.
Preferred length: 1,500 words; 16 pages
Abstract: A summary of about 200 words. Articles in French or German should be accompanied by a summary in English.
Author information and reprints: Payment: Reprints only. 50 reprints
Is simultaneous submission of article to other journals permitted: Not permitted.
Exclusive manuscript rights between acceptance and publication: Yes
Copyright: Held by publisher
Reprints: Available at no cost. 50
Disposition of manuscript:
Query letter: Not necessary.
Receipt of manuscript acknowledged: Yes
Decision to publish in: 1 month
Accepted manuscript published in: 5 months
Rejected manuscript returned: Yes, with return postage paid by publication.
Rejected manuscript criticized: Yes
Submit to:
For full-length papers:
Professor Konrad Akert
University of Zürich
August Forelstrasse 1
CH-8028 Zürich, Switzerland

Short communications to:
Professor D.P. Purpura
Kennedy Center for Research in Mental Retardation and Human Development
Albert Einstein College of Medicine
1410 Pelham Parkway South
Bronx, New York 10461

BRITISH JOURNAL OF EXPERIMENTAL PATHOLOGY [2296]
136 Gower Street
London WC1E 6BS, England
(01) 387-4282

SUBSCRIPTION DATA
Issues and rates: Published bi-monthly.
Annual rate(s): £12.00

EDITORIAL DESCRIPTION
Publishes original communications describing technique and the results of experimental research into causation, diagnosis and cure of diseases in man.

MANUSCRIPT INFORMATION
Subject field(s): Bacteriological, biochemical, pharmacological, physiological subjects
Manuscript requirements: No specific style guide. See latest issue for style requirements.
Preferred length: Not specified
Number of copies to be submitted: 2
Abstract: Yes. A short summary at the beginning of the article.

Author information and reprints: Payment: None.
Is simultaneous submission of article to other journals permitted: Not permitted.
Exclusive manuscript rights between acceptance and publication: Yes
Copyright: Held by publication.
Additional information: To be typewritten, double-spaced, one side only. Any illustrations should be camera-ready.
Disposition of manuscript:
Query letter: Not necessary, but advisable.
Receipt of manuscript acknowledged: Yes
Decision to publish in: 3-4 weeks
Accepted manuscript published in: 6 months
Rejected manuscript returned: Yes, if return postage is supplied by author.
Rejected manuscript criticized: No
Submit to:
Dr. R. E. M. Thompson
Editor
School of Pathology, Middlesex Hospital Medical School
Riding House Street
London W1P 7LD, England
(01) 636-8333, ext. 7373

BRITISH JOURNAL OF INDUSTRIAL MEDICINE [2297]
B.M.A. House
Tavistock Square
London WC1H 9JR, England
01-387-4499

First published in 1944

SUBSCRIPTION DATA
Issues and rates: Published quarterly.
Annual rate(s): $25.00
Publisher or Sponsor: British Medical Journal Group

EDITORIAL DESCRIPTION
Contains articles on industrial medicine.
Manuscripts accepted in English

MANUSCRIPT INFORMATION
Manuscript requirements: See latest issue for style requirements.
Number of copies to be submitted: Two
Abstract: Yes
Author information and reprints: Payment: None.
Is simultaneous submission of article to other journals permitted: No
Exclusive manuscript rights between acceptance and publication: Yes
Copyright: Held by publication.
Reprints: Available
Disposition of manuscript:
Query letter: No
Receipt of manuscript acknowledged: Yes
Decision to publish in: One month
Accepted manuscript published in: Six months
Rejected manuscript returned: Yes
Rejected manuscript criticized: No
Submit to:
Editor
(See address above)

BRITISH JOURNAL OF MEDICAL EDUCATION [2298]
The Journal of the Association for the Study of Medical Education
BMA House
Tavistock Square
London WC1H 9JR England
01-387-4499

First published in 1966

SUBSCRIPTION DATA
Issues and rates: Published quarterly.
Annual rate(s): $22.00
Publisher or Sponsor: Association for the Study of Medical Education
Managing Editor: Dr. John Ellis

EDITORIAL DESCRIPTION
Contains articles on all aspects of medical education.
Articles per average issue: 12
Manuscripts accepted in English

MANUSCRIPT INFORMATION
Manuscript requirements: See latest issue for style requirements.
Number of copies to be submitted: 3
Abstract: Yes
Author information and reprints: Payment: None.
Is simultaneous submission of article to other journals permitted: No
Exclusive manuscript rights between acceptance and publication: Yes
Copyright: Held by publication.
Reprints: Available, cost varies
Disposition of manuscript:
Receipt of manuscript acknowledged: Yes
Decision to publish in: One month
Accepted manuscript published in: Six months
Rejected manuscript returned: Yes, if return postage is supplied by author.
Rejected manuscript criticized: No
Submit to:
The Editor
(See address above)

BRITISH JOURNAL OF OBSTETRICS & GYNAECOLOGY [2299]
27 Sussex Place
Regent's Park
London NW1 4RG, England
(01) 262-5425

Previously entitled *The Journal of Obstetrics and Gynaecology of the British Commonwealth*

First published in 1902

SUBSCRIPTION DATA
Issues and rates: Published monthly.
Average paid circulation: 6000 controlled
Annual rate(s): £12.00; Foreign $22.00

Medicine (general)

Publisher or Sponsor: The Royal College of Obstetricians and Gynaecologists
Managing Editor: F. E. Loeffler

EDITORIAL DESCRIPTION
Contains articles on obstetrics, gynaecology and closely related subjects.

MANUSCRIPT INFORMATION
Manuscript requirements: See latest issue for style requirements.
Number of copies to be submitted: Two
Abstract: A summary
Author information and reprints: Payment: Reprints only. One copy of issue in which article appears.
Is simultaneous submission of article to other journals permitted: No
Exclusive manuscript rights between acceptance and publication: Yes
Copyright: Held by publication.
Reprints: Available, cost estimates supplied.
Disposition of manuscript:
Query letter: No
Receipt of manuscript acknowledged: Yes
Decision to publish in: One to two months
Accepted manuscript published in: Three months
Rejected manuscript returned: Yes
Rejected manuscript criticized: Sometimes
Submit to:
Frank E. Loeffler
Editor
(See address above)

BRITISH JOURNAL OF OPHTHALMOLOGY [2300]
B.M.A. House
Tavistock Square
London WC1H 9JR England
01-387 4499

First published in 1917

SUBSCRIPTION DATA
Issues and rates: Published monthly.
Average paid circulation: Not available.
Annual rate(s): $46.50
Publisher or Sponsor: British Medical Journal Group

EDITORIAL DESCRIPTION
Contains medical research on the eye.
Articles per average issue: 12
Audience: Specialist
Manuscripts accepted in English

MANUSCRIPT INFORMATION
Manuscript requirements: See latest issue for style requirements.
Preferred length: None
Number of copies to be submitted: Two
Abstract: Yes
Author information and reprints: Payment: None.
Is simultaneous submission of article to other journals permitted: No
Exclusive manuscript rights between acceptance and publication: Yes

Copyright: Held by publication.
Reprints: Available
Disposition of manuscript:
Query letter: No
Receipt of manuscript acknowledged: Yes
Decision to publish in: One month
Accepted manuscript published in: Six months
Rejected manuscript returned: Yes
Rejected manuscript criticized: No
Submit to:
The Editor
(See address above)

BRITISH JOURNAL OF PREVENTIVE AND SOCIAL MEDICINE [2301]
B.M.A. House
Tavistock Square
London WC1H 9JR England
01-387 4499

First published in 1947

SUBSCRIPTION DATA
Issues and rates: Published quarterly.
Average paid circulation: Not available.
Annual rate(s): $19.50
Publisher or Sponsor: British Medical Journal Group

EDITORIAL DESCRIPTION
Contains articles on medical research.
Manuscripts accepted in English

MANUSCRIPT INFORMATION
Manuscript requirements: See latest issue for style requirements.
Preferred length: None
Number of copies to be submitted: Two
Abstract: Yes
Author information and reprints: Payment: None.
Is simultaneous submission of article to other journals permitted: No
Exclusive manuscript rights between acceptance and publication: Yes
Copyright: Held by publication.
Reprints: Available
Disposition of manuscript:
Query letter: No
Receipt of manuscript acknowledged: Yes
Decision to publish in: One month
Accepted manuscript published in: Six months
Rejected manuscript returned: Yes
Rejected manuscript criticized: No
Submit to:
The Editor
(See address above)

BRITISH JOURNAL OF VENEREAL DISEASES [2302]
Journal of the Medical Society for the Study of Veneral Diseases
B.M.A. House
Tavistock Square
London WC1H 9JR, England
(01) 387-4499

First published in 1925

SUBSCRIPTION DATA
Issues and rates: Published bi-monthly.
Average paid circulation: Not available.
Annual rate(s): $32.00
Publisher or Sponsor: Medical Society for the Study of Veneral Diseases

EDITORIAL DESCRIPTION
Contains medical research on venereal disease.
Articles per average issue: 15
Audience: Specialists, consultants
Manuscripts accepted in English

MANUSCRIPT INFORMATION
Manuscript requirements: See latest issue for style requirements.
Preferred length: None
Number of copies to be submitted: Two
Abstract: Yes
Author information and reprints: Payment: None.
Is simultaneous submission of article to other journals permitted: No
Exclusive manuscript rights between acceptance and publication: Yes
Copyright: Held by publication.
Reprints: Available
Additional information: Full information on inside front cover of each issue.
Disposition of manuscript:
Query letter: No
Receipt of manuscript acknowledged: Yes
Decision to publish in: One month
Accepted manuscript published in: Six months
Rejected manuscript returned: Yes
Rejected manuscript criticized: No
Submit to:
The Editor
(See address above)

BRITISH MEDICAL JOURNAL [2303]
B.M.A. House
Tavistock Square
London WC1H 9JR, England
(01) 387-4499

First published in 1832

SUBSCRIPTION DATA
Issues and rates: Published weekly.
Average paid circulation: 85,948
Annual rate(s): $44.00
Publisher or Sponsor: British Medical Journal Group
Managing Editor: Dr. Martin Ware

EDITORIAL DESCRIPTION
Contains articles on general medical research.
Articles per average issue: 15-20
Audience: Practitioners, researchers
Manuscripts accepted in English

MANUSCRIPT INFORMATION
Manuscript requirements: See latest issue for style requirements.
Preferred length: None

Number of copies to be submitted: Two
Abstract: No
Author information and reprints: Payment:
None.
Is simultaneous submission of article to
other journals permitted: No
Exclusive manuscript rights between
acceptance and publication: Yes
Copyright: Held by publication.
Reprints: Available
Disposition of manuscript:
Query letter: No
Receipt of manuscript acknowledged: Yes
Decision to publish in: One month
Accepted manuscript published in: 3-4
months
Rejected manuscript returned: Yes
Rejected manuscript criticized: No
Submit to:
The Editor
(See address above)

BULLETIN OF
PROSTHETICS RESEARCH [2304]
Research Center for Prosthetics
Veterans Administration
252 Seventh Avenue
New York, New York 10001
(212) 620-6671

SUBSCRIPTION DATA
Issues and rates: Published semi-annually.
Average paid circulation: 2,500; 3,000
controlled
Publisher or Sponsor: Veterans
Administration, Research Center
for Prosthetics
Managing Editor: Rhoda Beiser

EDITORIAL DESCRIPTION
Contains technical articles on research
and development in the fields of
prosthetics, orthotics, sensory aids, etc.
Articles per average issue: 10
Audience: Professional
Manuscripts accepted in English

MANUSCRIPT INFORMATION
Subject field(s): Prosthetics, orthotics,
sensory aids, maxillofacial restorations
(excluding dentistry)
Manuscript requirements: See latest issue for
style requirements.
Number of copies to be submitted: Two
Author information and reprints: Payment:
None.
Is simultaneous submission of article to
other journals permitted: No
Exclusive manuscript rights between
acceptance and publication: No
Copyright: None held
Reprints: Available occasionally at no
cost.
Additional information: Would like a credit
line whenever reprinted or quoted from
the bulletin.
Disposition of manuscript:
Query letter: No
Receipt of manuscript acknowledged: Yes
Decision to publish in: 2 to 4 months
Accepted manuscript published in: 6
months
Rejected manuscript returned: Yes

Rejected manuscript criticized: No
Submit to:
Earl A. Lewis
Editor
(See address above)

CA: A CANCER JOURNAL
FOR CLINICIANS [2305]
219 East 42nd Street
New York, New York 10017
(212) 867-3700

Previously entitled *CA: Bulletin of Cancer
Progress*

First published in 1950

SUBSCRIPTION DATA
Issues and rates: Published bi-monthly.
Publisher or Sponsor: American Cancer
Society, Inc.
Managing Editor: John Aschemeier

EDITORIAL DESCRIPTION
Articles, special features and abstracts of
interest to the medical and related
professions on the diagnosis, treatment
and prevention of cancer(examination,
surgery, radiation, chemotherapy, etc.).
Articles per average issue: 10
Audience: Professional, academic
Manuscripts accepted in English

MANUSCRIPT INFORMATION
Manuscript requirements: No specific style
guide.
Preferred length: No restriction
Number of copies to be submitted: 1
original
Abstract: Not necessary.
Author information and reprints: Payment:
Reprints only. Up to 300 copies
Is simultaneous submission of article to
other journals permitted: Not permitted.
Exclusive manuscript rights between
acceptance and publication: Yes
Copyright: Held by American Cancer
Society; permission to reprint is usually
given freely and gladly.
Reprints: Not available.
Additional information: Articles are
sometimes reprinted by the ACS as
Professional Education Publications for
distribution to the medical professions
through ACS local divisions. Copies of
these publications are also available gratis
to authors.
Disposition of manuscript:
Query letter: Not necessary.
Receipt of manuscript acknowledged: Yes
Decision to publish in: 1-2 weeks
Accepted manuscript published in: 2-6
months
Rejected manuscript returned: Yes, if
return postage is supplied by author.
Rejected manuscript criticized: Reasons
for rejections only
Submit to:
Arthur I. Holleb, M.D.
Editor-in-Chief
(See address above)

CALCIFIED TISSUE
RESEARCH [2306]
Springer-Verlag
175 Fifth Avenue
New York, New York 10010

SUBSCRIPTION DATA
Annual rate(s): DM 108 per volume

EDITORIAL DESCRIPTION
Publishes research into the structure and
function of bone and other mineralized
systems in living organisms.
Manuscripts accepted in English

MANUSCRIPT INFORMATION
Subject field(s): Reports and reviews of
connective tissues and cells, ion
metabolism and transport, hormones,
nutrition, ultrastructure and molecular
biology.
Manuscript requirements: Style sheet sent
on request.
Preferred length: As required
Number of copies to be submitted: 3
Abstract: Yes. A summary, in English, of
not more than 250 words.
Author information and reprints: Payment:
Reprints only. 75 reprints of paper
Is simultaneous submission of article to
other journals permitted: Not permitted.
Exclusive manuscript rights between
acceptance and publication: Yes
Copyright: Held by publication.
Reprints: Available at cost.
Additional information: Manuscripts should
be submitted typewritten, double-spaced
and conform to standard practice by
arrangement into Introduction, Methods,
Results and Discussion.
Submit to:
D. B. Scott;
B. A. Friedman
Editorial Secretaries
Case Western Reserve University, School
of Dentistry
2123 Abington Road
Cleveland, Ohio 44106

CANADIAN
ANAESTHETISTS'
SOCIETY JOURNAL [2307]
Journal de la Société Canadienne des
Anesthetistes
178 St. George Street
Toronto, Ontario M5R 2M7 Canada
(416) 923-1154

SUBSCRIPTION DATA
Issues and rates: Published bi-monthly.
Average paid circulation: 3700; 50
controlled
Annual rate(s): $15.00
Publisher or Sponsor: Canadian
Anaesthetists' Society
Managing Editor: R. A. Gordon

EDITORIAL DESCRIPTION
Contains original papers on
anaesthesiology and related fields.
Articles per average issue: 14
Audience: Anaesthesiologists
Manuscripts accepted in English, French

Medicine (general)

MANUSCRIPT INFORMATION

Manuscript requirements: Style sheet sent on request.
  Number of copies to be submitted: Two
  Abstract: Yes
Author information and reprints: Payment: None.
  Is simultaneous submission of article to other journals permitted: No
  Exclusive manuscript rights between acceptance and publication: Yes
  Copyright: Held jointly by author and publication.
  Reprints: Available, consult journal office
Additional information: Typewritten double-spaced, illustrations India ink or glossy prints. Captions on separate list.
Disposition of manuscript:
  Query letter: No
  Receipt of manuscript acknowledged: Yes
  Decision to publish in: Up to 3 months
  Accepted manuscript published in: 4-6 months
  Rejected manuscript returned: Yes
  Rejected manuscript criticized: Yes
Submit to:
  R. A. Gordon
  Editor
  (See address above)

CANADIAN JOURNAL OF COMPARATIVE MEDICINE [2308]

Revue Canadienne de Médecine Comparée
360 Bronson Avenue
Ottawa, Ontario K1R 6J3, Canada
(613) 236-1162

Previously entitled *Canadian Journal of Comparative Medicine and Veterinary Science*

First published in 1937

SUBSCRIPTION DATA

Issues and rates: Published quarterly.
  Average paid circulation: 3,600
  Annual rate(s): $10.00, Foreign $12.00
Publisher or Sponsor: Canadian Veterinary Medical Association
Managing Editor: Nella McKellar

EDITORIAL DESCRIPTION

Contains research articles pertaining to comparative medicine.
Articles per average issue: 16
Audience: Professional
  Manuscripts accepted in English, French

MANUSCRIPT INFORMATION

Manuscript requirements: Style sheet sent on request.
  Preferred length: No preference
  Number of copies to be submitted: Three
  Abstract: No
Author information and reprints: Payment: By author to publication. $15.00 per page. Engravings extra.
  Is simultaneous submission of article to other journals permitted: No
  Exclusive manuscript rights between acceptance and publication: Yes

Copyright: Held by publication.
Reprints: Available
Disposition of manuscript:
  Query letter: No
  Receipt of manuscript acknowledged: Yes
  Decision to publish in: 5-6 months
  Accepted manuscript published in: 3-4 months
  Rejected manuscript returned: Yes
  Rejected manuscript criticized: Yes
Submit to:
  R. G. Thomson
  Editor
  (See address above)

SPECIAL STIPULATIONS

All manuscripts are subjected to editorial action and to review for adequacy of scientific content.

CANADIAN JOURNAL OF MEDICAL TECHNOLOGY [2309]

P.O. Box 830
Hamilton, Ontario L8N 3N8 Canada
(416) 528-8642

First published in 1937

SUBSCRIPTION DATA

Issues and rates: Published bi-monthly.
  Average paid circulation: 15,500
  Annual rate(s): $11.00; Foreign $13.00
Publisher or Sponsor: Canadian Society of Laboratory Technologists
Managing Editor: L. Seibel

EDITORIAL DESCRIPTION

Contains scientific and general articles of interest to medical technologists.
Articles per average issue: 2-4
Audience: Medical Technologists
  Manuscripts accepted in English, French

MANUSCRIPT INFORMATION

Subject field(s): Chemistry, hematology, histology, clinical microbiology, cytology, immunology, immunohematology, serology, virology, electron microscopy, cytogenetics, administration
Manuscript requirements: Style sheet sent on request.
  Preferred length: On request
  Number of copies to be submitted: Two
  Abstract: Not necessary
Author information and reprints: Payment: None.
  Is simultaneous submission of article to other journals permitted: No
  Exclusive manuscript rights between acceptance and publication: Yes
  Copyright: Held by publication.
  Reprints: Available
Additional information: Manuscript must be submitted in proper style. Author's name and affiliation should appear only on a separate page.
Disposition of manuscript:
  Query letter: No
  Receipt of manuscript acknowledged: Yes
  Decision to publish in: 4-6 weeks
  Accepted manuscript published in: 4-6 months

Rejected manuscript returned: Yes
Rejected manuscript criticized: Yes
Submit to:
  L. D. Mellor
  Editor
  (See address above)

CANADIAN JOURNAL OF NEUROLOGICAL SCIENCES [2310]

1516-233 Kennedy Street
Winnipeg, Manitoba R3C 3J5, Canada
(204) 942-3341

First published in 1974

SUBSCRIPTION DATA

Average paid circulation: 500
Annual rate(s): $20.00; Foreign $20.00;
Institutions $20.00; Students $10.00;
Foreign institutions $20.00
Managing Editor: R. T. Ross

EDITORIAL DESCRIPTION

Clinical and basic neuroscience, medicine and surgery.
Articles per average issue: 40
Audience: Neurologists, neurosurgeons, basic neuroscientists
  Manuscripts accepted in English, French

MANUSCRIPT INFORMATION

Subject field(s): Neurology, neurosurgery, neuroanatomy, chemistry, physiology, and pathology
Manuscript requirements: See latest issue for style requirements. Style sheet sent on request.
  Preferred length: As required
  Number of copies to be submitted: 2
  Abstract: Yes. 150-200 words
Author information and reprints: Payment: Reprints only. 50 reprints
  Is simultaneous submission of article to other journals permitted: Not permitted.
  Exclusive manuscript rights between acceptance and publication: Yes
  Copyright: Held by publication.
  Reprints: Available at cost.
Disposition of manuscript:
  Query letter: Not necessary.
  Receipt of manuscript acknowledged: Yes
  Decision to publish in: 30 days
  Accepted manuscript published in: 3-4 months
  Rejected manuscript returned: Yes, with return postage paid by publication.
  Rejected manuscript criticized: Yes
Submit to:
  R. T. Ross
  Editor
  (See address above)

CANADIAN JOURNAL OF PHARMACEUTICAL SCIENCES [2311]

175 College Street
Toronto, Ontario M5T 1P8, Canada
(416) 962-3431

First published in 1966

SUBSCRIPTION DATA

Issues and rates: Published quarterly.
Average paid circulation: 900
Annual rate(s): $15.00; Foreign $15.00;
Institutions $15.00
Publisher or Sponsor: Canadian
Pharmaceutical Association
Managing Editor: Arnold V. Raison

EDITORIAL DESCRIPTION

Original pharmaceutical research in
industry, government, and universities.
Articles per average issue: 9
Audience: Those involved in research
relative to drugs
Manuscripts accepted in English, French

MANUSCRIPT INFORMATION

Subject field(s): Pharmaceutical chemistry,
biochemistry, pharmacology,
biopharmaceutics, toxicology, and related
areas.
Manuscript requirements: See latest issue for
style requirements.
Preferred length: 10,000 words; 8 pages
Number of copies to be submitted: 2
Abstract: Yes. Not more than 100 words
Author information and reprints: Payment:
None.
Is simultaneous submission of article to
other journals permitted: Not permitted.
Exclusive manuscript rights between
acceptance and publication: Yes
Copyright: Held by publication.
Reprints: Available at cost.
Disposition of manuscript:
Query letter: Not necessary.
Receipt of manuscript acknowledged: Yes
Decision to publish in: 1-3 months
Accepted manuscript published in: 6
months
Rejected manuscript returned: Yes, with
return postage paid by publication.
Rejected manuscript criticized: Yes
Submit to:
Dr. Donald A. Zuck
Scientific Editor
College of Pharmacy
University of Saskatchewan
Saskatoon, Saskatchewan, Canada
(306) 343-3707

CANADIAN JOURNAL OF PHYSIOLOGY AND PHARMACOLOGY [2312]

National Research Council of Canada
100 Sussex Drive
Ottawa, Ontario K1A 0R6, Canada
(613) 992-5411

Previously entitled *Can. Journal of
Research,* 1929-1949; *Can. Journal of
Biochemistry and Physiology,* 1951-1962

First published in 1929

SUBSCRIPTION DATA

Issues and rates: Published monthly.
Average paid circulation: 1600
Annual rate(s): Individuals $10.00;
Institutions $20.00

Publisher or Sponsor: National Research
Council of Canada
Managing Editor: H. Williamson

EDITORIAL DESCRIPTION

Publishes results of original scientific
research in all branches of physiology
and pharmacology.
Articles per average issue: 25
Audience: Researchers
Manuscripts accepted in English, French

MANUSCRIPT INFORMATION

Manuscript requirements: Style sheet sent
on request.
Preferred length: Under 25 pages
Number of copies to be submitted: Two
Abstract: Yes
Author information and reprints: Payment:
None.
Is simultaneous submission of article to
other journals permitted: No
Exclusive manuscript rights between
acceptance and publication: Yes
Copyright: Held by publication.
Reprints: Available only at time of
publication
Disposition of manuscript:
Query letter: No
Receipt of manuscript acknowledged: Yes
Decision to publish in: 4 months
Accepted manuscript published in: 3
months
Rejected manuscript returned: Yes
Rejected manuscript criticized: Yes
Submit to:
K. Krnjevic
Editor
Department of Research in Anaesthesia
McGill University, Room 1209
Montreal 109, Quebec, Canada
(514) 392-4879

CANADIAN JOURNAL OF PUBLIC HEALTH [2313]

55 Parkdale Avenue
Ottawa, Ontario K1Y 1E5, Canada
(613) 725-3769

First published in 1929

SUBSCRIPTION DATA

Issues and rates: Published bi-monthly.
Average paid circulation: 4,000
Annual rate(s): $12.00; Foreign $15.00
Publisher or Sponsor: Canadian Public
Health Association
Managing Editor: Gerald H. Dafoe

EDITORIAL DESCRIPTION

Covers public health subjects in Canada
and abroad.
Articles per average issue: 8-10
Audience: Public health professionals
Manuscripts accepted in English, French

MANUSCRIPT INFORMATION

Subject field(s): areas

EDITORIAL DESCRIPTION

Covers public health subjects in Canada
and abroad.
Articles per average issue: 8-10
Audience: Public health professionals
Manuscripts accepted in English, French

MANUSCRIPT INFORMATION

Subject field(s): All areas of public health
Manuscript requirements: See latest issue for
style requirements. Style sheet sent on
request.
Preferred length: 15 pages or less
Number of copies to be submitted: 1
Abstract: Not necessary.
Author information and reprints: Payment:
By publication to author.
Is simultaneous submission of article to
other journals permitted: Not permitted.
Exclusive manuscript rights between
acceptance and publication: Yes
Copyright: Held by publication.
Reprints: Available at cost.
Disposition of manuscript:
Query letter: Not necessary, but
advisable.
Receipt of manuscript acknowledged: Yes
Decision to publish in: 6 weeks
Accepted manuscript published in: 3
months
Rejected manuscript returned: Yes, with
return postage paid by publication.
Rejected manuscript criticized: No
Submit to:
Eileen McGovern
Editorial Assistant
(See address above)

CANADIAN PHARMACEUTICAL JOURNAL [2314]

175 College Street
Toronto, Ontario M5T 1P8, Canada
(416) 962-3431

First published in 1868

SUBSCRIPTION DATA

Issues and rates: Published monthly.
Average paid circulation: 1,000; 11,000
controlled
Annual rate(s): $12.00; Foreign $12.00;
Institutions $12.00; Students $2.00;
Foreign individuals $12.00; Foreign
institutions $12.00
Publisher or Sponsor: Canadian
Pharmaceutical Association
Managing Editor: Arnold V. Raison

EDITORIAL DESCRIPTION

A medium for continuing education,
current trends in pharmacy practice,
legislative changes affecting the
profession and other items of current
interest.
Articles per average issue: 5
Audience: Pharmacists in all areas
Manuscripts accepted in English

Medicine (general)

MANUSCRIPT INFORMATION

Subject field(s): Prescription services, professional practice, modernization, clinical pharmacy, continuing education

Manuscript requirements: No specific style guide.

Preferred length: 2,000 to 3,000 words; 3-4 pages

Number of copies to be submitted: 2

Abstract: Not necessary.

Author information and reprints: Payment: By publication to author. $40.00 per page.

Is simultaneous submission of article to other journals permitted: Not permitted.

Exclusive manuscript rights between acceptance and publication: Yes

Copyright: Held by publication.

Reprints: Available at cost.

Disposition of manuscript:

Query letter: Not necessary, but advisable.

Receipt of manuscript acknowledged: Yes

Decision to publish in: 1-2 months

Accepted manuscript published in: 2 months

Rejected manuscript returned: Yes, with return postage paid by publication.

Rejected manuscript criticized: Reasons for rejections only

Submit to:

Arnold V. Raison

Editor

(See address above)

CANCER RESEARCH [2315]

Editorial Office

Fels Research Institute

Temple University School of Medicine

Philadelphia, Pennsylvania 19140

(215) 221-4720

SUBSCRIPTION DATA

Issues and rates: Published monthly.

Average paid circulation: 4,300

Annual rate(s): $75.00

Publisher or Sponsor: American Association for Cancer Research

Managing Editor: Margaret Foti

EDITORIAL DESCRIPTION

Contains articles in the fields of cancer research and cancer-related biomedical science.

Articles per average issue: 40

Audience: Scientific and medical communities

Manuscripts accepted in English

MANUSCRIPT INFORMATION

Subject field(s): Subfields of cancer research including biochemistry, virology, and immunology

Manuscript requirements: See January or July issue.

Preferred length: 30 pages (maximum)

Number of copies to be submitted: Three

Abstract: Yes.

Author information and reprints: Payment: None.

Is simultaneous submission of article to other journals permitted: Not permitted.

Exclusive manuscript rights between acceptance and publication: Yes.

Copyright: Held by publication.

Reprints: Available at cost.

Disposition of manuscript:

Query letter:

Receipt of manuscript acknowledged: Yes

Decision to publish in: 6-7 weeks

Accepted manuscript published in: 3 months

Rejected manuscript returned: Yes

Rejected manuscript criticized: Yes

Submit to:

Sidney Weinhouse

Editor

(See address above)

CARDIOLOGY [2316]

International Archives of Cardiology

S. Karger AG

Arnold-Böocklin-Strasse 25

CH-4011 Basel, Switzerland

061/39 08 80

Previously entitled *Cardiologia*

SUBSCRIPTION DATA

Issues and rates: Published bi-monthly.

Average paid circulation: 861; 42 controlled

Annual rate(s): SFr. 132.00; Foreign $54.00

EDITORIAL DESCRIPTION

Contains research reports pertaining to cardiovascular function in health or disease, case reports describing new entities or new features of familiar conditions in the cardiovascular area.

Articles per average issue: 5

Audience: Primarily aimed at the practicing cardiologist.

Manuscripts accepted in English

MANUSCRIPT INFORMATION

Subject field(s): Clinical cardiology, cardiovascular research

Manuscript requirements: Style sheet sent on request.

Preferred length: 10 pages maximum

Number of copies to be submitted: Three

Abstract: Yes, with 6 key words.

Author information and reprints: Payment: None.

Is simultaneous submission of article to other journals permitted: No

Exclusive manuscript rights between acceptance and publication: Yes

Copyright: Held by publication.

Reprints: Available

Additional information: Papers must be written in English.

Disposition of manuscript:

Query letter: No

Receipt of manuscript acknowledged: Yes

Decision to publish in: 6-8 weeks

Accepted manuscript published in: 3-6 months

Rejected manuscript returned: Yes

Rejected manuscript criticized: Yes

Submit to:

Pierre M. Galletti

Director of Biological and Medical Sciences

Brown University

Providence, Rhode Island 02912

CELLULAR IMMUNOLOGY [2317]

Academic Press, Inc.

111 Fifth Avenue

New York, New York 10003

(212) 741-6821

First published in 1970

SUBSCRIPTION DATA

Issues and rates: Published monthly.

Annual rate(s): $83.00; Foreign $201.00

EDITORIAL DESCRIPTION

Contains articles on original research and study in the fields of cellular biology and immunology.

Audience: Research community

Manuscripts accepted in English

MANUSCRIPT INFORMATION

Manuscript requirements: See latest issue for style requirements.

Number of copies to be submitted: 3

Abstract: Yes.

Author information and reprints: Payment: None.

Is simultaneous submission of article to other journals permitted: Not permitted.

Exclusive manuscript rights between acceptance and publication: Yes

Copyright: Held by publication.

Disposition of manuscript:

Query letter: Not necessary.

Receipt of manuscript acknowledged: Yes

Decision to publish in: 3-5 weeks

Rejected manuscript returned: Yes, with return postage paid by publication.

Rejected manuscript criticized: Yes

Submit to:

Dr. H. Sherwood Lawrence

Editor-in-Chief

Infectious Disease and Immunology Division, New York University Medical Center

550 First Avenue

New York, New York 10016

(212) 679-3200 ext. 2522

CENTRAL AFRICAN JOURNAL OF MEDICINE [2318]

P.O. Box 2073

11 Lawson Avenue

Salisbury, Rhodesia

29033

First published in 1955

SUBSCRIPTION DATA

Issues and rates: Published monthly.

Average paid circulation: 1500

EDITORIAL DESCRIPTION

A medical journal dealing with medicine in Africa.

Articles per average issue: 5

Audience: Professional, medical, academic

Manuscripts accepted in English

MANUSCRIPT INFORMATION

Subject field(s): Medicine, African diseases, diseases occuring in the tropics
Manuscript requirements: No specific style guide.
　Preferred length: 3000-4000 words
　Number of copies to be submitted: One
　Abstract: No
Author information and reprints: Payment: None.
　Is simultaneous submission of article to other journals permitted: No
　Exclusive manuscript rights between acceptance and publication: Yes
　Copyright: Held jointly by author and publication.
　Reprints: Available, cost varies
Disposition of manuscript:
　Query letter: No
　Receipt of manuscript acknowledged: Yes
　Decision to publish in: 2-3 weeks
　Accepted manuscript published in: 9-12 months unless original research, then much sooner.
　Rejected manuscript returned: Yes
　Rejected manuscript criticized: No
Submit to:
　M. Gelfand
　Editor
　(See address above)

CHEMOTHERAPY [2319]

International Journal of Experimental and Clinical Chemotherapy
S. Karger AG
Arnold-Boecklin Strasse 25
CH-4011 Basel, Switzerland
061-390880

Previously entitled *Chemotherapia*

SUBSCRIPTION DATA

Issues and rates: Published bi-monthly.
　Average paid circulation: 752; 71 controlled
　Annual rate(s): SFr. 132.00; Foreign $54.00

EDITORIAL DESCRIPTION

　Reports on the essential results of experimental and clinical research in this important branch of medicine through the publication of representative papers from the fields of bacteriology, virology, oncology and pharmacokinetics. In particular, reports on the clinical results of new antibiotics, chemotherapeutics and cytostatics are characteristic of the journal.
Articles per average issue: 5
　Manuscripts accepted in English only

MANUSCRIPT INFORMATION

Manuscript requirements: Style sheet sent on request. See latest issue for style requirements.
　Preferred length: 8 printed pages maximum
　Number of copies to be submitted: 2
　Abstract: Yes, with 6 key words

Author information and reprints: Payment: None.
　Is simultaneous submission of article to other journals permitted: No
　Exclusive manuscript rights between acceptance and publication: Yes
　Copyright: Held by publication.
　Reprints: Available
Disposition of manuscript:
　Query letter: No
　Receipt of manuscript acknowledged: Yes
　Decision to publish in: 1 week
　Accepted manuscript published in: 5 months
　Rejected manuscript returned: Yes
　Rejected manuscript criticized: Yes
Submit to:
　Editor
　(See address above)

CHEST [2320]

The Journal of Circulation, Respiration and Related Systems
911 Busse Highway
Park Ridge, Illinois 60068
(312) 698-2200

Previously entitled *Diseases of the chest*

First published in 1935

SUBSCRIPTION DATA

Issues and rates: Published monthly.
　Average paid circulation: 17,000; 300 controlled
　Annual rate(s): $21, Foreign $25
Publisher or Sponsor: American College of Chest Physicians

EDITORIAL DESCRIPTION

　Contains original articles dealing with diseases of the heart and lungs and their treatment. Major categories: clinical investigations; experimental approaches; critical review; selected reports; clinical conferences in pulmonary disease; roentgenogram of the month; electrocardiogram of the month; therapeutic guidelines.
Articles per average issue: 40
Audience: Physicians
　Manuscripts accepted in English

MANUSCRIPT INFORMATION

Subject field(s): Medicine, heart disease, pulmonary disease
Manuscript requirements: Style sheet sent on request.
　Preferred length: Not available.
　Number of copies to be submitted: Two
　Abstract: Yes
Author information and reprints: Payment: None.
　Is simultaneous submission of article to other journals permitted: No
　Exclusive manuscript rights between acceptance and publication: Yes
　Copyright: Held by publication.
　Reprints: Available, cost depends on number of pages.
Disposition of manuscript:
　Query letter: No
　Receipt of manuscript acknowledged: Yes

Decision to publish in: 3-4 weeks
Accepted manuscript published in: Six months
Rejected manuscript returned: Yes
Rejected manuscript criticized: Yes
Submit to:
　Alfred Soffer
　Editor-in-Chief
　(See address above)

CIRCULATION [2321]

An Official Journal of the American Heart Association
44 East 23rd Street
New York, New York 10010
(212) 477-9170

First published in 1950

SUBSCRIPTION DATA

Issues and rates: Published monthly.
　Average paid circulation: 17,000
　Annual rate(s): $25.00; Foreign $30.00
Publisher or Sponsor: American Heart Association

EDITORIAL DESCRIPTION

　Contents include clinical research and advances in the cardiovascular field: original articles, symposia, and editorials.
Articles per average issue: 28
Audience: Physicians
　Manuscripts accepted in English

MANUSCRIPT INFORMATION

Subject field(s): Cardiovascular medicine
Manuscript requirements: See latest issue for style requirements.
　Preferred length: No preference
　Number of copies to be submitted: 3
　Abstract: Yes
Author information and reprints: Payment: None.
　Is simultaneous submission of article to other journals permitted: No
　Exclusive manuscript rights between acceptance and publication: No
　Copyright: Held by publication.
　Reprints: Available
Disposition of manuscript:
　Receipt of manuscript acknowledged: Yes
　Rejected manuscript returned: Yes
Submit to:
　Editor
　Box 2912, Duke Hospital
　Durham, North Carolina 27710

SPECIAL STIPULATIONS

　Publication accepts manuscripts only from physicians or research workers in the cardiovascular field.

THE CLEFT PALATE JOURNAL* [2322]

An International Journal of Craniofacial Anomalies
2201 North Second Street
Harrisburg, Pennsylvania 17110
(717) 233-4691

Medicine (general)

SUBSCRIPTION DATA
Issues and rates: Published quarterly.
Average paid circulation: 3,000
Annual rate(s): $20.00
Publisher or Sponsor: The American Cleft
Palate Association

EDITORIAL DESCRIPTION
Designed to reflect, on an international
basis, clinical and research activities in
the fields of plastic surgery, dentistry,
speech pathology and other specialties
concerned with cleft lip and cleft palate
and related problems.

MANUSCRIPT INFORMATION
Manuscript requirements: See latest issue for
style requirements.
Number of copies to be submitted: Two
Is simultaneous submission of article to
other journals permitted: No
Copyright: Held by publication.
Reprints: Available
Disposition of manuscript:
Receipt of manuscript acknowledged: Yes
Decision to publish in: Four months
Accepted manuscript published in: Six
months
Rejected manuscript returned: Yes
Rejected manuscript criticized: Yes
Submit to:
Robert L. Harding
Editor
(See address above)

CLINICAL IMMUNOLOGY AND IMMUNOPATHOLOGY [2323]

An International Journal
Academic Press, Inc.
111 Fifth Avenue
New York, New York 10003

First published in 1972

SUBSCRIPTION DATA
Issues and rates: Published bi-monthly.
Annual rate(s): $76.00; Foreign $80.00

EDITORIAL DESCRIPTION
Covers all areas of clinical immunology
and immunopathology.
Articles per average issue: 16
Manuscripts accepted in English

MANUSCRIPT INFORMATION
Manuscript requirements: See latest issue for
style requirements.
Preferred length: 6-10 pages
Number of copies to be submitted: 3
Abstract: Yes.
Author information and reprints: Payment:
None.
Is simultaneous submission of article to
other journals permitted: Not permitted.
Exclusive manuscript rights between
acceptance and publication: Yes
Copyright: Held by publisher
Reprints: Available at no cost. 50
Disposition of manuscript:
Query letter: Not necessary.
Receipt of manuscript acknowledged: Yes

Decision to publish in: 6 weeks
Accepted manuscript published in: 6
months
Rejected manuscript returned: Yes, with
return postage paid by publication.
Rejected manuscript criticized: Yes
Submit to:
Hugh Fudenky
University of California
School of Medicine
San Francisco, California 94134

Robert McCluskey
Massachusetts General Hospital
Boston, Massachusetts
(415) 666-1711
Editors

CLINICAL PHARMACOLOGY AND THERAPEUTICS [2324]

The C.V. Mosby Company
11830 Westline Industrial Drive
St. Louis, Missouri 63141
(314) 872-8370

First published in 1960

SUBSCRIPTION DATA
Issues and rates: Published monthly.
Average paid circulation: 5,137
Annual rate(s): $20.00, Foreign $22.50
Publisher or Sponsor: American Society for
Clinical Pharmacology and Therapeutics

EDITORIAL DESCRIPTION
Published for the clinical pharmacologist,
internists, family physicians, and medical
specialists who prescribe modern
pharmaceuticals as a prime function of
their daily practice. By presenting
manuscripts illustrating the proper and
enduring use of drugs in man, it serves
those physicians concerned about the
pharmacological basis of their therapy.
Articles per average issue: 15
Audience: Professional
Manuscripts accepted in English

MANUSCRIPT INFORMATION
Manuscript requirements: Style sheet sent
on request.
Preferred length: 10 pages
Number of copies to be submitted: 1
original, 1 copy
Abstract: Yes, of 250 words or less
Author information and reprints: Payment:
By author to publication. $25.00 per
page. For each page over 8 pages, $40.00
per page.
Is simultaneous submission of article to
other journals permitted: No
Exclusive manuscript rights between
acceptance and publication: Yes
Copyright: Held by publication.
Reprints: Available at cost
Disposition of manuscript:
Query letter: No
Receipt of manuscript acknowledged: Yes
Decision to publish in: 1-2 months
Accepted manuscript published in: 2-3
months

Rejected manuscript returned: Yes
Rejected manuscript criticized: No
Submit to:
Walter Modell, M.D.
Editor
Box 119
Larchmont, New York 10538
(914) 834-5979

CLINICAL TOXICOLOGY [2325]

Official Journal of the American Academy
of Clinical Toxicology
Marcel Dekker, Inc.
270 Madison Avenue
New York, New York 10016
(212) 490-7700

SUBSCRIPTION DATA
Issues and rates: 6 issues per year
Average paid circulation: 1,000
Annual rate(s): $60.00; Foreign $66.30
Publisher or Sponsor: American Academy
of Clinical Toxicology

EDITORIAL DESCRIPTION
Contains articles on acute, chronic
intoxications in humans; means of
identifying toxic agents, antidotes and
treatments; all scientific and medical
aspects of toxicology.

MANUSCRIPT INFORMATION
Subject field(s): Toxic case histories,
laboratory procedures, drug studies,
allergic problems
Manuscript requirements: See latest issue for
style requirements.
Preferred length: None
Number of copies to be submitted: Two
Abstract: Optional
Author information and reprints: Payment:
None.
Is simultaneous submission of article to
other journals permitted: No
Exclusive manuscript rights between
acceptance and publication: Yes
Copyright: Held by publication.
Reprints: Available, first 25 free
Disposition of manuscript:
Query letter: No
Receipt of manuscript acknowledged: Yes
Decision to publish in: 30 days
Accepted manuscript published in: 9
months
Rejected manuscript returned: Yes
Rejected manuscript criticized: Yes
Submit to:
Richard T. Rappolt, M.D.
Executive Editor
4141 Geary Boulevard, Suite 403
San Francisco, California 94118
(415) 387-4613

CONFINIA NEUROLOGICA [2326]

Borderlands of Neurology
S. Karger AG
Arnold-Boecklin Strasse 25
CH-4011 Basel, Switzerland
061-390880

SUBSCRIPTION DATA

Issues and rates: Published bi-monthly.
Average paid circulation: 796; 54
controlled
Annual rate(s): SFr. 110.00; Foreign
$44.00

Publisher or Sponsor: International Society
for Research in Stereoencephalotomy

EDITORIAL DESCRIPTION

Concerns itself with the relationship of
the discipline of neurology with allied
specialties such as psychiatry, internal
medicine, surgery, endocrinology,
radiology, otology and ophthalmology.
The journal is composed of complete and
preliminary original articles, reviews,
society transactions and book reviews.

Articles per average issue: 4-6
Manuscripts accepted in English

MANUSCRIPT INFORMATION

Manuscript requirements: Style sheet sent
on request.
Preferred length: 12 pages
Number of copies to be submitted: 2
Abstract: Yes, with a list of key words

Author information and reprints: Payment:
By author to publication. for excess pages
only.
Is simultaneous submission of article to
other journals permitted: No
Exclusive manuscript rights between
acceptance and publication: Yes
Copyright: Held by publication.
Reprints: Available at cost

Disposition of manuscript:
Query letter: No
Receipt of manuscript acknowledged: Yes
Decision to publish in: 2-3 months
Accepted manuscript published in: 6-7
months
Rejected manuscript returned: Yes
Rejected manuscript criticized: Yes

Submit to:
Prof. Dr. L. Gildenberg
Editor
Division of Neurosurgery
University of Arizona Medical Center
Tuscon, Arizona 85724

CRC CRITICAL REVIEWS IN CLINICAL LABORATORY SCIENCES [2327]

The Chemical Rubber Company
18901 Cranwood Parkway
Cleveland, Ohio 44128
(216) 475-9000

First published in 1970

SUBSCRIPTION DATA

Issues and rates: Published quarterly.
Average paid circulation: 1,000
Annual rate(s): $56.00, Foreign $64.00

EDITORIAL DESCRIPTION

Provides a qualitative approach to the
total mass of scientific literature
published throughout the world in this
discipline. This is accomplished by
utilizing outstanding experts in each field
to select and critically evaluate the most

significant papers published in their
particular specialties.

Articles per average issue: 3

Audience: Professional
Manuscripts accepted in English

MANUSCRIPT INFORMATION

Subject field(s): Clinical science, clinical
chemistry

Manuscript requirements: Style sheet sent
on request.
Preferred length: 75 to 150 pages
Number of copies to be submitted: Three
Abstract: Yes

Author information and reprints: Payment:
By publication to author.
Is simultaneous submission of article to
other journals permitted: No
Exclusive manuscript rights between
acceptance and publication: Yes
Copyright: Held by publication.
Reprints: Available, 25 free to author

Disposition of manuscript:
Query letter: No
Receipt of manuscript acknowledged: Yes
Decision to publish in: 3 weeks
Accepted manuscript published in: 3
months
Rejected manuscript returned: Yes
Rejected manuscript criticized: Yes

Submit to:
Gerald A. Becker
Director, Editorial Operations
(See address above)

CRC CRITICAL REVIEWS IN CLINICAL RADIOLOGY AND NUCLEAR MEDICINE [2328]

CRC Press, Inc.
18901 Cranwood Parkway
Cleveland, Ohio 44128
(216) 475-9000

Previously entitled *CRC Critical Reviews in
Radiological Sciences*

First published in 1970

SUBSCRIPTION DATA

Issues and rates: Published quarterly.
Average paid circulation: 1,000
Annual rate(s): $56.00, Foreign $64.00

EDITORIAL DESCRIPTION

The basic concept of this program is to
provide a qualitative approach to the
total mass of scientific literature
published throughout the world in this
discipline. This is accomplished by
utilizing outstanding experts in each field
to select and critically evaluate the most
significant papers published in their
particular specialties. To insure accuracy
and objectivity, each review is refereed
prior to publication.

Articles per average issue: 4

Audience: Research Laboratories
Manuscripts accepted in English

MANUSCRIPT INFORMATION

Subject field(s): Nuclear medicine,
radiological science

Manuscript requirements: Style sheet sent
on request.
Preferred length: 75-150 pages
Number of copies to be submitted: Three
Abstract: Yes.

Author information and reprints: Payment:
By publication to author.
Is simultaneous submission of article to
other journals permitted: No
Exclusive manuscript rights between
acceptance and publication: Yes
Copyright: Held by publication.
Reprints: Available, 25 free to author

Disposition of manuscript:
Query letter:
Receipt of manuscript acknowledged: Yes
Decision to publish in: 3 weeks
Accepted manuscript published in: 3
months
Rejected manuscript returned: Yes
Rejected manuscript criticized: Yes

Submit to:
Gerald A. Becker
Director, Editorial Operations
(See address above)

CVP [2329]

The Journal of Cardiovascular and
Pulmonary Technology
825 South Barrington Avenue
Los Angeles, California 90049
(213) 826-8388

First published in 1973

SUBSCRIPTION DATA

Issues and rates: Published bi-monthly.
Average paid circulation: 13,711
Annual rate(s): $20; Foreign $40

Managing Editor: Hal Spector;
Martin H. Waldman

EDITORIAL DESCRIPTION

Articles serve as a constant up-date on
developments in the field, concentrating
on solutions to problems, technical
advances, case histories, facilities reports,
equipment, supplies, etc. Serving the
medium for both technical papers and
individual opinions of cardiovascular and
cardiopulmonary technologists; heads of
catheterization, stress, pulmonary
function and cardiovascular/pulmonary
research laboratories.
Manuscripts accepted in English

MANUSCRIPT INFORMATION

Manuscript requirements: Style sheet sent
on request.
Preferred length: 3000-5000 words
Number of copies to be submitted: Two

Author information and reprints: Payment:
None.
Is simultaneous submission of article to
other journals permitted: No
Exclusive manuscript rights between
acceptance and publication: Yes
Copyright: Held by author.
Reprints: Available at cost

Additional information: Desire reproducible
artwork.

Disposition of manuscript:
Receipt of manuscript acknowledged: Yes

Medicine (general)

Decision to publish in: Varies
Accepted manuscript published in: Varies
Rejected manuscript returned: Yes
Rejected manuscript criticized: No
Submit to:
Roberta Atchison
Editorial Coordinator
(See address above)

DANISH MEDICAL
BULLETIN [2330]
Danish Medical Association
Domus Medica
Copenhagen, Denmark
01 TR 4828

First published in 1953

SUBSCRIPTION DATA
Issues and rates: 10 issues per year
Average paid circulation: 16,500
controlled
Publisher or Sponsor: Danish Medical
Association
Managing Editor: John Philip

EDITORIAL DESCRIPTION
Contains general medical articles.
Articles per average issue: 10
Audience: Physicians
Manuscripts accepted in English

MANUSCRIPT INFORMATION
Subject field(s): Medicine
Manuscript requirements: Style sheet sent
on request.
Preferred length: 20-22 pages maximum
Number of copies to be submitted: Two
Abstract: Yes
Author information and reprints: Payment:
None.
Is simultaneous submission of article to
other journals permitted: No
Exclusive manuscript rights between
acceptance and publication: Yes
Copyright: Held by publication.
Reprints: Available, cost on request
Additional information: Color figures must
be paid for by author. Foreign authors
must pay printing costs.
Disposition of manuscript:
Query letter: No
Receipt of manuscript acknowledged: Yes
Decision to publish in: 8-10 weeks
Accepted manuscript published in: 3-6
months
Rejected manuscript returned: Yes
Rejected manuscript criticized: Yes
Submit to:
Editor
(See address above)

DERMATOLOGICA [2331]
Official Organ of the Society for
Dermatology and Venereology of
Switzerland
S. Karger AG
Arnold-Boecklin Strasse 25
CH-4011 Basel, Switzerland
061-390880

Previously entitled *Dermatologische
Zeitschrift*

First published in 1893

SUBSCRIPTION DATA
Issues and rates: Published monthly.
Average paid circulation: 1242; 31
controlled
Annual rate(s): SFr. 110.00; Foreign
$44.00 per volume
Publisher or Sponsor: Society for
Dermatology and Venereology of
Switzerland, Netherlands Society
of Dermatologists

EDITORIAL DESCRIPTION
Provides a survey of dermatological
research activity concerned with clinical
dermatology and therapy throughout the
world, informing the general
dermatologist of the implications of
recent research; also editorials and
reviews, short communications, book
reviews, symposia, etc.
Articles per average issue: 8
Manuscripts accepted in English (French,
German)

MANUSCRIPT INFORMATION
Manuscript requirements: See latest issue for
style requirements.
Preferred length: 8 printed pages
(including figures)
Number of copies to be submitted: 2
Abstract: Yes, with 3-9 key words
Author information and reprints: Payment:
Reprints only.
Is simultaneous submission of article to
other journals permitted: No
Exclusive manuscript rights between
acceptance and publication: Yes
Copyright: Held by publication.
Disposition of manuscript:
Query letter: No
Receipt of manuscript acknowledged: Yes
Decision to publish in: 1 month
Accepted manuscript published in: 5
months
Rejected manuscript returned: Yes
Rejected manuscript criticized: Yes
Submit to:
Editors
(See address above)

DIABETES [2332]
The Journal of the American Diabetes
Association
1 West 48th Street
New York, New York 10020
(212) 541-4310

SUBSCRIPTION DATA
Issues and rates: Published monthly.
Average paid circulation: 6,699
Annual rate(s): $28.00; Students $14.00
Publisher or Sponsor: American Diabetes
Association, Inc.
Managing Editor: Edward W. Sanderson

EDITORIAL DESCRIPTION
The official journal of the American
Diabetes Association, it is published to

furnish the medical and allied professions
with information concerning diabetes and
related fields of medicine.

MANUSCRIPT INFORMATION
Subject field(s): Diabetes, related metabolic
problems
Manuscript requirements: See latest issue for
style requirements.
Preferred length: 5,000 words
Number of copies to be submitted: Three
Author information and reprints: Payment:
None.
Is simultaneous submission of article to
other journals permitted: No
Exclusive manuscript rights between
acceptance and publication: Yes
Copyright: Held by publication.
Reprints: Available, cost depends on
length
Disposition of manuscript:
Receipt of manuscript acknowledged: Yes
Decision to publish in: 3 months
Accepted manuscript published in: 3-4
months
Rejected manuscript returned: Yes
Rejected manuscript criticized: Yes
Submit to:
David M. Kipnis
Editor
(See address above)

DIABETOLOGIA [2333]
Springer-Verlag
175 Fifth Avenue
New York, New York 10010

SUBSCRIPTION DATA
Issues and rates: 6 times per year
Annual rate(s): DM 154 per volume;
Students DM 123.20 per volume;
Members DM 103 per volume
Managing Editor: Professor Dr. W.
Creutzfeldt

EDITORIAL DESCRIPTION
Publishes reports of clinical and
experimental work on all aspects of
diabetes research and related subjects,
provided they have scientific merit and
present important new facts or new data.
Manuscripts accepted in English

MANUSCRIPT INFORMATION
Manuscript requirements: Style sheet sent
on request.
Preferred length: 5,000 words maximum
Number of copies to be submitted: 3
Abstract: Yes. A summary of not more
than 150 words; a list of from 5 to 15
key words to facilitate indexing
Author information and reprints: Payment:
Reprints only.
Is simultaneous submission of article to
other journals permitted: Not permitted.
Exclusive manuscript rights between
acceptance and publication: Yes
Copyright: Held by publication.
Submit to:
Professor Dr. W. Creutzfeldt
Editor-in-Chief
Medizinische Klinik, Universitäts Klinik
Humboldtallee 1

D-34 Göttingen, Federal Republic of Germany

DIGESTION [2334]

International Journal of Gastroenterology
S. Karger AG
Arnold-Boecklin Strasse 25
CH-4011 Basel, Switzerland
061-390880

Previously entitled *Gastroenterologia*

First published in 1895

SUBSCRIPTION DATA

Issues and rates: Published monthly.
Average paid circulation: 862; 82 controlled
Annual rate(s): SFr. 110.00; Foreign $44.00

EDITORIAL DESCRIPTION

Devoted to the diseases of the gastrointestinal tract, liver and pancreas and to their pathophysiology. The papers, written in English, may concern investigative physiology in humans and animals, metabolic studies, and the etiology, geographic distribution symptoms, evolution and therapeutics of human diseases.

Articles per average issue: 6-7
Audience: Professional
Manuscripts accepted in English

MANUSCRIPT INFORMATION

Subject field(s): The content of the journal is divided into various sections: original articles, case reports, editorials, progress reports summarizing the recent knowledge in any particular field of gastroenterology and abstracts of the medical literature commented upon by specialists.
Manuscript requirements: Style sheet sent on request.
Preferred length: No limits
Number of copies to be submitted: 3
Abstract: Yes
Author information and reprints: Payment: Reprints only.
Is simultaneous submission of article to other journals permitted: No
Exclusive manuscript rights between acceptance and publication: Yes
Copyright: Held by publication.
Reprints: Available at cost
Disposition of manuscript:
Query letter: No
Receipt of manuscript acknowledged: Yes
Rejected manuscript returned: Yes
Submit to:
Prof. Dr. R. Lambert
Editor
Hôpital E. Herriot
Pavillon H
F-69003 Lyons, France

DRUG INTELLIGENCE AND CLINICAL PHARMACY [2335]

For the Clinical Pharmacist, Physician and Nurse
234 Goodman Street
University of Cincinnati Medical Center
Cincinnati, Ohio 45267
(513) 281-7737

Previously entitled *Drug Intelligence*

First published in 1967

SUBSCRIPTION DATA

Issues and rates: Published monthly.
Average paid circulation: 6500; 1000 controlled
Annual rate(s): $12
Managing Editor: Donald E. Francke
Publisher or Sponsor: University of Cincinnati Medical Center

EDITORIAL DESCRIPTION

Interdisciplinary journal for clinical pharmacists, physicians, nurses and other members of the health professions who prescribe, select, procure, dispense, administer, evaluate or otherwise work with drugs in hospitals and related health institutions.
Articles per average issue: 5
Manuscripts accepted in English, French, Spanish, German

MANUSCRIPT INFORMATION

Subject field(s): Drug therapy, drug interactions, adverse reactions, drug evaluations, drug abuse, drug bioavailability, drug administration, intravenous therapy, clinical studies, clinical reviews, health care sociology
Manuscript requirements: AIBS
Preferred length: 2000-3000 words; 8-12 pages
Number of copies to be submitted: Original and two copies
Abstract: Preferred, of about 200 words
Author information and reprints: Payment: None.
Is simultaneous submission of article to other journals permitted: No
Exclusive manuscript rights between acceptance and publication: Yes
Copyright: Held by publication.
Reprints: Available, cost on request
Additional information: Refer to "Instructions to Authors" section in front of current issue. All manuscripts are sent to outside referees.
Disposition of manuscript:
Query letter: No
Receipt of manuscript acknowledged: Yes
Decision to publish in: 8-12 weeks
Accepted manuscript published in: 6 or more months
Rejected manuscript returned: Yes
Rejected manuscript criticized: Yes
Submit to:
Harvey A. K. Whitney, Jr.
Associate Editor

Donald E. Francke

Editor
(See address above)

DRUG METABOLISM AND DISPOSITION [2336]

The Biological Fate of Chemicals
428 East Preston Street
Baltimore, Maryland 21202
(301) 528-4116

First published in 1973

SUBSCRIPTION DATA

Issues and rates: Published bi-monthly.
Average paid circulation: 500
Publisher or Sponsor: American Society for Pharmacology and Experimental Therapeutics

EDITORIAL DESCRIPTION

Contains original papers in the area of metabolism and disposition of foreign compounds in biological systems.
Articles per average issue: 12
Manuscripts accepted in English

MANUSCRIPT INFORMATION

Manuscript requirements: See latest issue for style requirements.
Preferred length: None
Number of copies to be submitted: 2
Abstract: Yes
Author information and reprints: Payment: By author to publication. $15.00 per page.
Is simultaneous submission of article to other journals permitted: No
Exclusive manuscript rights between acceptance and publication: Yes
Copyright: Held by publication.
Reprints: Available, cost depends on length
Disposition of manuscript:
Query letter: No
Receipt of manuscript acknowledged: Yes
Decision to publish in: 6-8 weeks
Accepted manuscript published in: 3-4 months
Rejected manuscript returned: Yes
Rejected manuscript criticized: Yes, Sometimes
Submit to:
Kenneth C. Leibman
Editor
Box 728, College of Medicine
University of Florida
Gainesville, Florida 32601
(904) 392-3547

ENVIRONMENTAL HEALTH [2337]

Association of Public Health Inspectors
19 Grosvenor Square
London SW1, England
(01) 235-5152

Previously entitled *Public Health Inspector*

SUBSCRIPTION DATA

Issues and rates: Published monthly.

Average paid circulation: 7,000
controlled
Annual rate(s): £3.25
Publisher or Sponsor: Association of Public
Health Inspectors
Managing Editor: Reginald Johnson

EDITORIAL DESCRIPTION

Contains papers and articles on
environmental health connected with the
work of public health inspectors.
Articles per average issue: 3
Audience: Professional, governmental
Manuscripts accepted in English

MANUSCRIPT INFORMATION

Subject field(s): Food hygiene, housing, clear
air, public cleansing, noise control,
leisure, legislation
Manuscript requirements: No specific style
guide.
Preferred length: 1,5000-2,000 words
Number of copies to be submitted: 2
Abstract: Not necessary.
Author information and reprints: Payment:
None.
Reprints: Available at cost.
Disposition of manuscript:
Query letter: Necessary.
Receipt of manuscript acknowledged: Yes
Decision to publish in: 2 weeks
Accepted manuscript published in: 2-3
months
Rejected manuscript returned: Yes, if
return postage is supplied by author.
Rejected manuscript criticized: Reasons
for rejections only
Submit to:
Victoria Finlay
Editor
(See address above)

EUROPEAN JOURNAL OF APPLIED PHYSIOLOGY   [2338]

Springer-Verlag
175 Fifth Avenue
NewYork, New York 10010

SUBSCRIPTION DATA

Annual rate(s): DM 144 per volume
Managing Editor: Professor Dr. H. G.
Wenzel

EDITORIAL DESCRIPTION

Publishes articles on all aspects of
experimental and clinical physiology.
Manuscript requirements: Style sheet sent
on request.
Manuscript requirements: Style sheet sent
on request.
Preferred length: As required
Number of copies to be submitted: 3
Abstract: Yes. Papers not written in
English should have an abstract in
English followed by a list of five or more
key words for indexing purposes.
Author information and reprints: Payment:
Reprints only. 40 offprints
Is simultaneous submission of article to
other journals permitted: Not permitted.
Exclusive manuscript rights between
acceptance and publication: Yes
Copyright: Held by publication.
Submit to:
Professor Dr. H. G. Wenzel

Editor
Institut für Arbeitsphysiologie
Universität Dortmund
D-4600 Dortmund, Federal Republic of
Germany

EUROPEAN JOURNAL OF CANCER RESEARCH   [2339]

Pergamon Press, Inc.
Fairview Park
Elmsford, New York 10523
(914) 592-7700

First published in 1965

SUBSCRIPTION DATA

Issues and rates: Published monthly.
Annual rate(s): Individuals $25.00;
Institutions $100.00

EDITORIAL DESCRIPTION

Encourages the collaboration among
scientists and clinical investigators in the
broad field of cancer research.
Articles per average issue: 7-10
Audience: Researchers, professional,
academic
Manuscripts accepted in English

MANUSCRIPT INFORMATION

Subject field(s): Oncology in its broadest
sense: Including chemistry, biochemistry,
biology, clinical medicine, pathology,
virology, genetics, pharmacology, in so
far as these disciplines study normal and
abnormal growth.
Manuscript requirements: See latest issue for
style requirements.
Preferred length: None
Number of copies to be submitted:
Original and 2 copies
Abstract: Yes. A summary in English.
Author information and reprints: Payment:
Reprints only.
Is simultaneous submission of article to
other journals permitted: Not permitted.
Exclusive manuscript rights between
acceptance and publication: Yes
Copyright: Held by publication.
Reprints: Available at cost.
Disposition of manuscript:
Query letter: Not necessary.
Receipt of manuscript acknowledged: Yes
Decision to publish in: 4 weeks
Accepted manuscript published in: 5
months
Rejected manuscript returned: Yes, if
return postage is supplied by author.
Rejected manuscript criticized: Reasons
for rejections only
Submit to:
Dr. H. J. Tagnon, FACP
Editor
Institut Jules Bordet
1, rue Héger-Bordet
B-1000 Bruxelles, Belgium

EUROPEAN JOURNAL OF CLINICAL INVESTIGATION   [2340]

Springer-Verlag
175 Fifth Avenue
New York, New York 10010

First published in 1865

SUBSCRIPTION DATA

Annual rate(s): DM 120 per volume
Publisher or Sponsor: The European Society
for Clinical Investigation

EDITORIAL DESCRIPTION

Publishes original papers on research
pertinent to human biology and disease.
Manuscripts accepted in English

MANUSCRIPT INFORMATION

Manuscript requirements: Style sheet sent
on request.
Preferred length: As required
Number of copies to be submitted: 3
Abstract: Yes. The Abstract should be of
about 300 words followed by a list of
about 5 to 15 key words appearing in the
article to facilitate indexing.
Author information and reprints: Payment:
Reprints only. 75 offprints
Is simultaneous submission of article to
other journals permitted: Not permitted.
Exclusive manuscript rights between
acceptance and publication: Yes
Copyright: Held by the European Society
for Clinical Investigation
Reprints: Available at cost.
Submit to:
Editorial Board
1224 Chêne-Bougeries
Case Postale 21
Geneva, Switzerland

EUROPEAN JOURNAL OF CLINICAL PHARMACOLOGY   [2341]

Pharmacologia Clinica
Springer-Verlag
175 Fifth Avenue
New York, New York 10010

SUBSCRIPTION DATA

Annual rate(s): DM 150 per volume

EDITORIAL DESCRIPTION

Publishes original papers on all aspects of
pharmacology and therapeutics in man.
Manuscripts accepted in English

MANUSCRIPT INFORMATION

Manuscript requirements: See latest issue for
style requirements. Style sheet sent on
request.
Preferred length: As required
Number of copies to be submitted: 2
Abstract: Yes. Summary should be
informative, understandable without
reference to the text.
Author information and reprints: Payment:
Reprints only. 75 offprints
Is simultaneous submission of article to
other journals permitted: Not permitted.
Exclusive manuscript rights between
acceptance and publication: Yes
Copyright: Held by publication.
Reprints: Available at cost.

Submit to:
Professor Dr. H. J. Dengler
Editor
Medizinische Universitätsklinik
D-5300 Bonn-Venusberg, Federal
Republic of Germany

EUROPEAN JOURNAL OF PHARMACOLOGY [2342]

Rudolf Magnus Institute for Pharmacology
Faculty of Medicine University of Utrecht
Vondellaan 6
Utrecht, The Netherlands
030-880521

SUBSCRIPTION DATA
Issues and rates: Published monthly.
Average paid circulation: 1150
Annual rate(s): Dfl. 344
Managing Editor: D. de Wied

EDITORIAL DESCRIPTION
Publishes original articles and notes concerning pharmacology, taken in the broadest sense. The journal will cover: general pharmacology and pharmacodynamics; animal and human pharmacology; pharmacology of the nervous system, including behavioral pharmacology; pharmacology of the uro-genital, the gastrointestinal and the respiratory tract; pharmacology of the cardiovascular system. Articles on original methods and techniques in pharmacology will also be considered.
Articles per average issue: 18; 5 short communications
Manuscripts accepted in English only

MANUSCRIPT INFORMATION
Manuscript requirements: AIBS
Preferred length: Average of 6 printed pages
Number of copies to be submitted: Original and one carbon copy
Abstract: Yes
Author information and reprints: Payment: None.
Is simultaneous submission of article to other journals permitted: No
Exclusive manuscript rights between acceptance and publication: No
Copyright: Held by publication.
Reprints: Available, cost depends upon length of article
Additional information: Two referees are asked to evaluate the manuscripts. Acceptance depends on their rating.
Disposition of manuscript:
Query letter: No
Receipt of manuscript acknowledged: Yes
Decision to publish in: 4 months
Accepted manuscript published in: 3-4 months
Rejected manuscript returned: Yes
Rejected manuscript criticized: Yes
Submit to:
The Editorial Office
(See address above)

EUROPEAN NEUROLOGY [2343]

S. Karger
Arnold Böcklin Strasse 25
CH-4011 Basel, Switzerland
061-39 08 80

SUBSCRIPTION DATA
Issues and rates: Published bi-monthly.
Average paid circulation: 579; 33 controlled
Annual rate(s): SFr. 198.00; Foreign $80.00

EDITORIAL DESCRIPTION
Contains articles on clinical neurology and research in neurology, neurochemistry, neuropathology, neuroanatomy.
Articles per average issue: 6
Manuscripts accepted in English

MANUSCRIPT INFORMATION
Subject field(s): Neurology, neuropathology, epidemiology, EEG, EMG, echoencephalography, neurochemistry
Manuscript requirements: Style sheet sent on request.
Preferred length: 12 printed pages maximum
Number of copies to be submitted: Two
Abstract: Yes, with 6 key words
Author information and reprints: Payment. None.
Is simultaneous submission of article to other journals permitted: No
Exclusive manuscript rights between acceptance and publication: Yes
Copyright: Held by publication.
Reprints: Available
Disposition of manuscript:
Query letter: No
Receipt of manuscript acknowledged: Yes
Decision to publish in: 4 weeks
Accepted manuscript published in: 3-6 months
Rejected manuscript returned: Yes
Rejected manuscript criticized: Yes
Submit to:
Henry E. Kaeser
Neurological Clinic
Socinstr. 55
CH-4000 Basel, Switzerland

EXPERIMENTAL GERONTOLOGY [2344]

Pergamon Press, Inc.
Fairview Park
Elmsford, New York 10523
(914) 592-7700

First published in 1965

SUBSCRIPTION DATA
Issues and rates: Published bi-monthly.
Annual rate(s): $25.00; Institutions $60.00

EDITORIAL DESCRIPTION
Promotes the experimental study of the mechanisms of senescence in organisms.
Articles per average issue: 4-5

Audience: Professional, academic
Manuscripts accepted in English

MANUSCRIPT INFORMATION
Subject field(s): Age-dependent processes at the cellular or molecular level; review articles; theoretical or critical articles; book reviews
Manuscript requirements: See latest issue for style requirements.
Preferred length: None
Number of copies to be submitted: Original and 1 copy
Abstract: Yes. A concise summary not to exceed 300 words designed to give a picture of the results without reference to the text.
Author information and reprints: Payment: Reprints only. 50 reprints
Is simultaneous submission of article to other journals permitted: Not permitted.
Exclusive manuscript rights between acceptance and publication: Yes
Copyright: Held by publication.
Reprints: Available at cost.
Disposition of manuscript:
Query letter: Not necessary.
Receipt of manuscript acknowledged: Yes
Decision to publish in: 4 weeks
Accepted manuscript published in: 5 months
Rejected manuscript returned: Yes, if return postage is supplied by author.
Rejected manuscript criticized: Reasons for rejections only
Submit to:
Dr. A. Comfort
Editor-in-Chief
P. O. Box 4068
Santa Barbara, California 93103

Or any regional board member.

FERTILITY AND STERILITY* [2345]

428 East Preston Street
Baltimore, Maryland 21202
(301) 528-4116

SUBSCRIPTION DATA
Issues and rates. Published monthly.
Average paid circulation: 7100
Annual rate(s): $25.00, Foreign $27.40
Publisher or Sponsor: American Fertility Society

EDITORIAL DESCRIPTION
Contains original papers in the fields of fertility, sterility, and physiology of reproduction.

MANUSCRIPT INFORMATION
Manuscript requirements: Style sheet sent on request.
Preferred length: None
Author information and reprints: Payment: None.
Is simultaneous submission of article to other journals permitted: No
Exclusive manuscript rights between acceptance and publication: Yes
Copyright: Held by publication.

Medicine (general)

Reprints: Available
Disposition of manuscript:
  Receipt of manuscript acknowledged: Yes
  Decision to publish in: 6-8 weeks
  Accepted manuscript published in: 3-4 months
  Rejected manuscript returned: Yes
  Rejected manuscript criticized: Sometimes
Submit to:
  Luigi Mastroianni
  Editor
  106 Dulles Building
  3400 Spruce Street
  Philadelphia, Pennsylvania 19104
  (215) 662-2970

FORENSIC SCIENCE [2346]
Incorporating the Journal of Forensic Medicine
Elsevier Sequoia SA
P.O. Box 851
1001 Lausanne 1, Switzerland
(021) 20 73 81

First published in 1972

SUBSCRIPTION DATA
Issues and rates: Published semi-monthly.
  Average paid circulation: 1,150
  Annual rate(s): SFr. 160.00
Managing Editor: H. A. Shapiro

EDITORIAL DESCRIPTION
  Contains articles which pertain to knowledge in the many scientific disciplines that bear upon forensic problems. Types of articles: reports of original research, case reports, review articles, book reviews, letters to the correspondence columns.
Articles per average issue: 11
Audience: Professional, academic
  Manuscripts accepted in English, French, German

MANUSCRIPT INFORMATION
Subject field(s): Forensic pathology, histochemistry, chemistry, biochemistry, toxicology, biology, serology, odontology, psychiatry; law
Manuscript requirements: Style sheet sent on request.
  Preferred length: 2 pages: case histories
  Number of copies to be submitted: Three
  Abstract: Yes. Papers in French and German a summary in English.
Author information and reprints: Payment: Reprints only. 50 reprints
  Is simultaneous submission of article to other journals permitted: No
  Exclusive manuscript rights between acceptance and publication: Yes
  Copyright: Held by publication.
  Reprints: Available, cost quoted upon publication
Disposition of manuscript:
  Receipt of manuscript acknowledged: Yes
  Rejected manuscript returned: Yes
Submit to:
  Editor-in-Chief
  P.O. Box 330
  Amsterdam, The Netherlands
  (020) 12 99 12

GASTROENTEROLOGY [2347]
428 East Preston Street
Baltimore, Maryland 21202
(301) 528-4116

First published in 1943

SUBSCRIPTION DATA
Issues and rates: Published monthly.
  Average paid circulation: 9,500
  Annual rate(s): $35.00; Foreign $38.25

EDITORIAL DESCRIPTION
  Contains original papers on all aspects of the digestive tract and liver.
Articles per average issue: 20
Audience: Professional
  Manuscripts accepted in English

MANUSCRIPT INFORMATION
Manuscript requirements: Style sheet sent on request.
  Preferred length: None
  Number of copies to be submitted: Two
  Abstract: Yes
Author information and reprints: Payment: None.
  Is simultaneous submission of article to other journals permitted: No
  Exclusive manuscript rights between acceptance and publication: Yes
  Copyright: Held by publication.
  Reprints: Available
Disposition of manuscript:
  Query letter: No
  Receipt of manuscript acknowledged: Yes
  Decision to publish in: 2-3 months
  Accepted manuscript published in: 6 months
  Rejected manuscript returned: Yes
  Rejected manuscript criticized: Sometimes
Submit to:
  Robert M. Donaldson, Jr.
  Editor
  VA Hospital
  West Spring Street
  West Haven, Connecticut 06516
  (203) 933-2561

GASTROINTESTINAL ENDOSCOPY [2348]
476 Prospect Street
La Jolla, California 92037
(714) 459-2390 ext. 593

Previously entitled *Bulletin of Gastrointestinal Endoscopy*

First published in 1957

SUBSCRIPTION DATA
Issues and rates: Published quarterly.
  Average paid circulation: 1,750
  Annual rate(s): $10.00, Foreign $12.00

Publisher or Sponsor: American Society for Gastrointestinal Endoscopy
Managing Editor: William S. Haubrich

EDITORIAL DESCRIPTION
  Contains original observations and investigations in the field of gastrointestinal endoscopy or relating to conditions within the gastrointestinal tract of interest to endoscopists; descriptions of new endoscopic or related techniques; instructive case reports; selected abstracts from the world literature pertaining to gastrointestinal endoscopy; news and notices of events of concern to gastrointestinal endoscopists.
Articles per average issue: 12
Audience: Professional
  Manuscripts accepted in English

MANUSCRIPT INFORMATION
Manuscript requirements: See latest issue for style requirements.
  Preferred length: 4-8 pages
  Number of copies to be submitted: Two
  Abstract: Yes
Author information and reprints: Payment: None.
  Is simultaneous submission of article to other journals permitted: No
  Exclusive manuscript rights between acceptance and publication: Yes
  Copyright: Not copyrighted
  Reprints: Available, $25.00 for 2 pages, $10.00 each additional page.
Disposition of manuscript:
  Query letter: No
  Receipt of manuscript acknowledged: Yes
  Decision to publish in: 2 months
  Accepted manuscript published in: 2 to 6 months
  Rejected manuscript returned: Yes
  Rejected manuscript criticized: Sometimes
Submit to:
  William S. Haubrich
  Editor
  (See address above)

GERONTOLOGIA [2349]
International Journal of Gerontological Research
S. Karger AG
Arnold-Boecklin Strasse 25
CH-4011 Basel, Switzerland
061-390880

SUBSCRIPTION DATA
Issues and rates: Published quarterly.
  Average paid circulation: 670; 50 controlled
  Annual rate(s): SFr.110.00; Foreign $44.00

EDITORIAL DESCRIPTION
  The three fields of research covered are the following: molecular and cellular ageing, including connective tissue research; systemic and organismic ageing, including comparative physiology, experimental pathology, and experimental pharmacology; the behavioral sciences, including experimental psychology and psychopharmacology.

Articles per average issue: 6
Manuscripts accepted in English, German, French

MANUSCRIPT INFORMATION

Manuscript requirements: Style sheet sent on request.
Preferred length: 8 printed pages
Number of copies to be submitted: 2
Abstract: Yes
Author information and reprints: Payment: Reprints only. 25 reprints
Is simultaneous submission of article to other journals permitted: No
Exclusive manuscript rights between acceptance and publication: Yes
Copyright: Held by publication.
Reprints: Available
Disposition of manuscript:
Query letter: No
Receipt of manuscript acknowledged: Yes
Decision to publish in: 1 month
Accepted manuscript published in: 4-5 months
Rejected manuscript returned: Yes
Rejected manuscript criticized: Yes
Submit to:
F. Bouliere
Editor
(See address above)

GERONTOLOGIA CLINICA [2350]

S. Karger AG
Arnold-Boecklin Strasse 25
CH-4011 Basel, Switzerland
061-390880

SUBSCRIPTION DATA

Issues and rates: Published quarterly.
Average paid circulation: 627; 40 controlled
Annual rate(s): SFr. 88.00; Foreign $36.00

EDITORIAL DESCRIPTION

An international journal publishing original articles on new trends in various countries on the clinical aspects of ageing. The journal also acts as a liaison between doctors in various countries in Europe and throughout the world who are carrying out similar work to promote original scientific research into the problems of old age.
Articles per average issue: 5
Manuscripts accepted in English, French, German

MANUSCRIPT INFORMATION

Manuscript requirements: Style sheet sent on request.
Preferred length: 8 printed pages
Number of copies to be submitted: 2
Abstract: Yes
Author information and reprints: Payment: Reprints only. 25 reprints
Is simultaneous submission of article to other journals permitted: No
Exclusive manuscript rights between acceptance and publication: Yes
Copyright: Held by publication.
Reprints: Available

Disposition of manuscript:
Query letter: No
Receipt of manuscript acknowledged: Yes
Rejected manuscript returned: Yes
Submit to:
E. Woodford-Williams
Editor
Department of Geriatric Medicine
Sunderland Co. General Hospital
Durham, England

GYNECOLOGIC INVESTIGATION [2351]

International Journal of the Science of Reproduction
S. Karger AG
Arnold-Boecklin Strasse 25
CH-4011 Basel, Switzerland
061-390880

Previously entitled *Monatsschrift für Geburtshilfe und Gynaekologie* until 1946; *Gynaecologia* until 1969

First published in 1895

SUBSCRIPTION DATA

Issues and rates: Published bi-monthly.
Average paid circulation: 961; 29 controlled
Annual rate(s): SFr. 132.00; Foreign $54.00
Publisher or Sponsor: Society for Gynecologic Investigation

EDITORIAL DESCRIPTION

This journal has over the years become a working tool and source of reference for scientists and research workers in countries all over the world. With all due respect for the clinical practice of gynecology and the usefulness of statistical clinical studies, case reports, applied pharmacology, etc., the editors recognize that experimentation is the key to progress.
Articles per average issue: 4-6
Manuscripts accepted in English

MANUSCRIPT INFORMATION

Manuscript requirements: Style sheet sent on request.
Preferred length: 8 printed pages
Number of copies to be submitted: 3
Abstract: Yes, with 3-9 key words
Author information and reprints: Payment: Reprints only.
Is simultaneous submission of article to other journals permitted: No
Exclusive manuscript rights between acceptance and publication: Yes
Copyright: Held by publication.
Reprints: Available
Disposition of manuscript:
Query letter: No
Receipt of manuscript acknowledged: Yes
Decision to publish in: 1 month
Accepted manuscript published in: 4 months
Rejected manuscript returned: Yes
Rejected manuscript criticized: Yes

Submit to:
Dr. Walter Hermann
Department of Obstetrics and Gynecology
University of Washington
Seattle, Washington 98195

Manuscripts from Europe to:
Prof. Dr. O. Käser
Universitäts-Frauenklinik
CH-4000 Basel, Switzerland
Editors

HAEMOSTASIS [2352]

International Journal on Haemostasis and Thrombosis Research
S. Karger AG
Arnold-Boecklin Strasse 25
CH-4011 Basel, Switzerland
061-3900880

First published in 1973

SUBSCRIPTION DATA

Issues and rates: Published quarterly.
Average paid circulation: 563; 47 controlled
Annual rate(s): SFr. 88.00; Foreign $36.00

EDITORIAL DESCRIPTION

Contains original papers concerning haemostasis and coagulation, their physiological and experimental aspects, clinical facts concerning hemorrhage and thrombosis, biological tests and examinations, and therapy. Each issue will contain a bibliographical index of similar articles published in other international medical journals.
Articles per average issue: 6
Manuscripts accepted in English (French, German)

MANUSCRIPT INFORMATION

Manuscript requirements: Style sheet sent on request.
Preferred length: 10 printed pages
Number of copies to be submitted: 3
Abstract: Yes, with 6 key words
Author information and reprints: Payment: None.
Is simultaneous submission of article to other journals permitted: No
Exclusive manuscript rights between acceptance and publication: Yes
Copyright: Held by publication.
Reprints: Available
Disposition of manuscript:
Query letter: No
Receipt of manuscript acknowledged: Yes
Rejected manuscript returned: Yes
Submit to:
E. F. Lüscher
Editor
Theodor Kocher Institut
Freiestrasse 1
CH-3012 Bern, Switzerland

Medicine (general)

THE HAND [2353]

Longman Group Ltd., Journals Division
Burnt Mill
Harlow, Essex, England
26721

SUBSCRIPTION DATA
Issues and rates: Published three times per year.
  Annual rate(s): £6.00, Foreign $18.00
Publisher or Sponsor: British Society for Surgery of the Hand
Managing Editor: H. Graham Stack

EDITORIAL DESCRIPTION
  Devoted to surgery on the hand.

Submit to:
  H. Graham Stack
  Editor
  (See address above)

SPECIAL STIPULATIONS
  Request additional information from editor.

HEADACHE [2354]

621 South New Ballas Road
St. Louis, Missouri 63141
(714) 459-2390

SUBSCRIPTION DATA
Issues and rates: Published quarterly.
  Average paid circulation: 1500; 5000 controlled
  Annual rate(s): $10.00
Publisher or Sponsor: American Association for the Study of Headache

EDITORIAL DESCRIPTION
  Publishes clinical and experimental studies on headache, headpain, or the nature of pain itself.

MANUSCRIPT INFORMATION
Subject field(s): Headache, head pain, study of pain, neurological diseases
Manuscript requirements: Style sheet sent on request.
  Number of copies to be submitted: Two
Author information and reprints: Payment: None.
  Is simultaneous submission of article to other journals permitted: No
  Exclusive manuscript rights between acceptance and publication: No
  Copyright: Held by publication.
  Reprints: Available at cost
Disposition of manuscript:
  Receipt of manuscript acknowledged: Yes
  Decision to publish in: 4 weeks
  Accepted manuscript published in: 2 to 6 months or longer
  Rejected manuscript returned: Yes
  Rejected manuscript criticized: Yes
Submit to:
  Donald John Dalessio
  Head, Division of Neurology
  Scripps Clinic
  476 Prospect Street
  La Jolla, California 92037

HEALTH TEAM [2355]

P. O. Box 845
Bellevue, Washington 98009
(206) 747-5500

First published in January 1974

SUBSCRIPTION DATA
Issues and rates: Published monthly.
  Average paid circulation: 100; 19,000 controlled
  Annual rate(s): $20.00; Foreign $36.00
Managing Editor: James A. Nelson

EDITORIAL DESCRIPTION
  Trans-professional communications concerning all health care subjects.
Articles per average issue: 3-5
Audience: Health professionals
  Manuscripts accepted in English

MANUSCRIPT INFORMATION
Subject field(s): Any topic in the field of health care: team approach, delivery
Manuscript requirements: No specific style guide.
  Preferred length: 3-5 pages
  Number of copies to be submitted: 3
  Abstract: Not necessary.
Author information and reprints: Payment: None.
  Is simultaneous submission of article to other journals permitted: Not permitted.
  Exclusive manuscript rights between acceptance and publication: Yes
  Copyright: Held by publication.
  Reprints: Available at cost.
Additional information: Layout is returned for author's approval in page form.
Disposition of manuscript:
  Query letter: Not necessary.
  Receipt of manuscript acknowledged: Yes
  Decision to publish in: 1 month
  Accepted manuscript published in: 3 months
  Rejected manuscript returned: Yes, with return postage paid by publication.
  Rejected manuscript criticized: Reasons for rejections only
Submit to:
  James A. Nelson
  Publisher
  (See address above)

HORMONE RESEARCH [2356]

Internatinal Journal of Experimental and Clinical Endocrinology
S. Karger AG
Arnold-Boecklin Strasse 25
CH-4011 Basel, Switzerland
061-390880

Previously entitled *Hormones*

First published in 1970

SUBSCRIPTION DATA
Issues and rates: Published bi-monthly.
  Average paid circulation: 401; 39 controlled
  Annual rate(s): SFr. 132.00; Foreign $54.00

Publisher or Sponsor: The European Association of Endocrinology

EDITORIAL DESCRIPTION
  Reports upon the essential results of experimental and clinical research in the important branch of endocrinology. Its scope covers every aspect of physiology and pathology and it refers to a great variety of disciplines from the most classical to the most modern ones. The aim of this journal is to follow closely every phase in the development of endocrinology and it hopes to serve the scientific community of Europe and the world.
Articles per average issue: 5-6
  Manuscripts accepted in English

MANUSCRIPT INFORMATION
Manuscript requirements: Style sheet sent on request.
  Preferred length: 12 pages
  Number of copies to be submitted: 3
  Abstract: Yes, with key words
Author information and reprints: Payment: None.
  Is simultaneous submission of article to other journals permitted: No
  Exclusive manuscript rights between acceptance and publication: Yes
  Copyright: Held by publication.
  Reprints: Available at cost
Disposition of manuscript:
  Query letter: No
  Receipt of manuscript acknowledged: Yes
  Decision to publish in: 2-3 months
  Accepted manuscript published in: 6-7 months
  Rejected manuscript returned: Yes
  Rejected manuscript criticized: Yes
Submit to:
  Dr. J. Girard
  Editor
  Kinderspital
  Römergasse
  CH-4000 Basel, Switzerland

HOSPITAL ADMINISTRATION [2357]

840 North Lake Shore Drive
Chicago, Illinois 60611
(312) 943-0544

First published in 1956

SUBSCRIPTION DATA
Issues and rates: Published quarterly.
  Average paid circulation: 1,200; 10,000 controlled
  Annual rate(s): $5.00
Publisher or Sponsor: American College of Hospital Administrators
Managing Editor: Carol McCune

EDITORIAL DESCRIPTION
  To keep the hospital administrator abreast and informed of new developments and thinking in the broad fields of management that have implications for hospital administration. Emphasis is given to the scholarly and

professional rather than to descriptive and operational material.

Articles per average issue: 5

Audience: Executive officers of health care delivery

Manuscripts accepted in English only

MANUSCRIPT INFORMATION

Subject field(s): Administration, organization, planning, evaluation, communication, public relations, human relations

Manuscript requirements: Chicago

Preferred length: 3,500 words; 16-30 pages

Number of copies to be submitted: Three

Abstract: No

Author information and reprints: Payment: None.

Is simultaneous submission of article to other journals permitted: No

Exclusive manuscript rights between acceptance and publication: Yes

Copyright: Held by publication.

Reprints: Available, 10 free

Additional information: Charts, graphs and illustrations that supplement text are accepted.

Disposition of manuscript:

Query letter: Not necessary, but advisable.

Receipt of manuscript acknowledged: Yes

Decision to publish in: 3 months

Accepted manuscript published in: 6-12 months

Rejected manuscript returned: Yes

Rejected manuscript criticized: Sometimes

Submit to:

Lynn C. Wimmer

Editor

(See address above)

HOSPITAL HOUSEKEEPING [2358]

The Journal of Health Care Facility Housekeeping

825 South Barrington Avenue

Los Angeles, California 90049

(213) 826-8388

First published in 1972

SUBSCRIPTION DATA

Issues and rates: Published bi-monthly.

Average paid circulation: 217; 15,745 controlled

Annual rate(s): $20; Foreign £40

Managing Editor: Hal Spector;

Martin H. Waldman

EDITORIAL DESCRIPTION

Articles cover the entire gamut of professional interests: technical advances, case histories, facilities reports, equipment, supplies, etc. A "how-to" publication directed to the executive housekeeper in hospitals and other health care facilities throughout the U.S. and the World.

MANUSCRIPT INFORMATION

Subject field(s): Techniques, problems and solutions, hospital care, facility reports

Manuscript requirements: Style sheet sent on request.

Preferred length: 3000-5000 words

Number of copies to be submitted: Two

Author information and reprints: Payment: None.

Is simultaneous submission of article to other journals permitted: No

Exclusive manuscript rights between acceptance and publication: Yes

Copyright: Held by author.

Reprints: Available, cost varies with length

Additional information: Desire reproducible artwork.

Disposition of manuscript:

Receipt of manuscript acknowledged: Yes

Decision to publish in: Varies

Accepted manuscript published in: Varies

Rejected manuscript returned: Yes

Rejected manuscript criticized: No

Submit to:

Roberta Atchison

Editorial Coordinator

(See address above)

HOSPITAL PROGRESS [2359]

Journal of the Catholic Hospital Association

1438 South Grand

St. Louis, Missouri 63104

(314) 773-0646

First published in 1920

SUBSCRIPTION DATA

Issues and rates: Published monthly.

Average paid circulation: 12,692; 1,295 controlled

Annual rate(s): $7.00, Foreign $8.00

Publisher or Sponsor: The Catholic Hospital Association

Managing Editor: Anne M. Stephens

EDITORIAL DESCRIPTION

Publishes articles concerning the management of Catholic health care institutions.

Articles per average issue: 10

Audience: Professional

Manuscripts accepted in English

MANUSCRIPT INFORMATION

Subject field(s): Management, hospital administration, Catholic theology, economics, personnel administration, hospital departments

Manuscript requirements: See latest issue for style requirements.

Preferred length: 2,500 words

Number of copies to be submitted: Two

Abstract: Yes

Author information and reprints: Payment: By publication to author. Amount varies.

Is simultaneous submission of article to other journals permitted: No

Exclusive manuscript rights between acceptance and publication: Yes

Copyright: Held by publication.

Reprints: Available at cost

Disposition of manuscript:

Query letter: No

Receipt of manuscript acknowledged: Yes

Decision to publish in: 2 to 3 months

Accepted manuscript published in: 3 to 6 months

Rejected manuscript returned: Yes

Rejected manuscript criticized: No

Submit to:

Robert J. Stephens

Editor

(See address above)

HOSPITALS [2360]

Journal of the American Hospital Association

840 North Lake Shore Drive

Chicago, Illinois 60611

(312) 645-9400

SUBSCRIPTION DATA

Issues and rates: Published semi-monthly.

Annual rate(s): $15.00; Foreign $17.00

Publisher or Sponsor: American Hospital Association

EDITORIAL DESCRIPTION

Contains articles, features, and news of interest to the administrative heads of hospitals and other health care institutions. Emphasis on "how-to" type of editorial material, designed to aid administrators improve the quality of care provided in their institutions.

Articles per average issue: 12

Audience: Professional

Manuscripts accepted in English

MANUSCRIPT INFORMATION

Subject field(s): Health planning, finance, nursing, pharmacy, food service, laundry, purchasing, engineering, surgery, medical staff, trusteeship, general administration

Manuscript requirements: Style sheet sent on request.

Preferred length: 8-12 pages

Number of copies to be submitted: Two

Abstract: No

Author information and reprints: Payment: None.

Is simultaneous submission of article to other journals permitted: No

Exclusive manuscript rights between acceptance and publication: Yes

Copyright: Held by publication.

Reprints: Available, cost varies with length

Disposition of manuscript:

Query letter: Not necessary, but advisable.

Receipt of manuscript acknowledged: Yes

Decision to publish in: 3-5 months

Accepted manuscript published in: 12-15 months

Rejected manuscript returned: Yes

Rejected manuscript criticized: No

Submit to:

Wesley Curry

Managing Editor

(See address above)

(312) 645-9479

Medicine (general)

ILLINOIS MEDICAL JOURNAL [2361]

55 East Monroe Street, Suite 3510
Chicago, Illinois 60603
(312) 782-1654

First published in 1899

SUBSCRIPTION DATA

Issues and rates: Published monthly.
    Annual rate(s): $8.00; Foreign $10.00
Publisher or Sponsor: Illinois State Medical Society
Managing Editor: R. A. Ott

EDITORIAL DESCRIPTION

    Publishes articles on the clinical, socio-economic, and legal aspects of the medical profession.
Articles per average issue: 6-7
Audience: Professional
    Manuscripts accepted in English

MANUSCRIPT INFORMATION

Subject field(s): Medical case reports, recent advances in medicine, etc.
Manuscript requirements: No specific style guide.
    Preferred length: 12-15 pages
    Number of copies to be submitted: 2
    Abstract: Not necessary.
Author information and reprints: Payment: None.
    Is simultaneous submission of article to other journals permitted: Not permitted.
    Exclusive manuscript rights between acceptance and publication: Yes
    Copyright: Held by publication.
    Reprints: Available at cost.
Disposition of manuscript:
    Query letter: Not necessary.
    Receipt of manuscript acknowledged: Yes
    Decision to publish in: 3 months
    Accepted manuscript published in: 6-12 months
    Rejected manuscript returned: Yes, with return postage paid by publication.
    Rejected manuscript criticized: Reasons for rejections only
Submit to:
    Theodore R. Van Dellen, M. D.
    Editor
    (See address above)

IMMUNOLOGICAL COMMUNICATIONS [2362]

Marcel Dekker, Inc.
270 Madison Avenue
New York, New York 10016
(212) 490-7700

SUBSCRIPTION DATA

Issues and rates: Published bi-monthly.
    Annual rate(s): Individuals $15.00; Students $15.00; Foreign individuals $19.50; Foreign institutions $19.50

Publisher or Sponsor: State University of New York at Buffalo, The Center for Immunology
Managing Editor: Carel J. van Oss

EDITORIAL DESCRIPTION

    For the rapid communication of immunological information.
Articles per average issue: 6-8
Audience: Immunologists
    Manuscripts accepted in English

MANUSCRIPT INFORMATION

Subject field(s): All aspects of immunology and related sciences
Manuscript requirements: See latest issue for style requirements. Style sheet sent on request.
    Preferred length: As required
    Number of copies to be submitted: 3
    Abstract: Yes.
Author information and reprints: Payment: None.
    Is simultaneous submission of article to other journals permitted: Not permitted.
    Exclusive manuscript rights between acceptance and publication: Yes
    Copyright: Held by publication.
    Reprints: Available at cost.
Additional information: Typewritten, double-spaced, on standard sized paper. It is essential to use a black typewriter ribbon.
Disposition of manuscript:
    Query letter: Not necessary.
    Receipt of manuscript acknowledged: Yes
    Decision to publish in: 1-2 months
    Accepted manuscript published in: 2-4 months
    Rejected manuscript returned: Yes, with return postage paid by publication.
    Rejected manuscript criticized: Yes
Submit to:
    Editorial Committee
    The Center of Immunology
    School of Medicine, State University of New York at Buffalo
    Buffalo, New York 14214
    (716) 831-2900

INDIAN JOURNAL OF MEDICAL RESEARCH [2363]

Ansari Nagar
New Delhi-16, India
621736

First published in 1913

SUBSCRIPTION DATA

Issues and rates: Published monthly.
    Average paid circulation: 700; 300 controlled
    Annual rate(s): Rs. 108, Foreign $15.00
Publisher or Sponsor: Indian Council of Medical Research
Managing Editor: S.V. Apte

EDITORIAL DESCRIPTION

    Contains articles on basic medical research.
Articles per average issue: 20-25
Audience: Professional
    Manuscripts accepted in English

MANUSCRIPT INFORMATION

Subject field(s): Microbiology, pathology, hematology, surgery, physiology, phamacology, biochemistry, nutrition
Manuscript requirements: See latest issue for style requirements.
    Preferred length: 10 pages
    Number of copies to be submitted: Two
    Abstract: Yes, not to exceed 300 words.
Author information and reprints: Payment: None.
    Is simultaneous submission of article to other journals permitted: No
    Exclusive manuscript rights between acceptance and publication: Yes
    Copyright: Held by publication.
    Reprints: Available
Disposition of manuscript:
    Query letter: No
    Receipt of manuscript acknowledged: Yes
    Decision to publish in: 4-5 months
    Accepted manuscript published in: 5-6 months
    Rejected manuscript returned: Yes
    Rejected manuscript criticized: No
Submit to:
    Editorial Board
    (See address above)

INDIANA STATE MEDICAL ASSOCIATION JOURNAL [2364]

3935 North Meridian Street
Indianapolis, Indiana 46151
(317) 925-7545

First published in 1907

SUBSCRIPTION DATA

Issues and rates: Published monthly.
    Average paid circulation: 4,575
    Annual rate(s): $14.00; Foreign $17.00; Institutions $12.00; Students $14.00; Foreign institutions $17.00
Publisher or Sponsor: Indiana State Medical Association
Managing Editor: Frank B. Ramsey, M. D.

EDITORIAL DESCRIPTION

    Scientific medical articles of interest to members as well as socio-economic articles and official membership activities.
Articles per average issue: 5
Audience: Indiana medical profession
    Manuscripts accepted in English

MANUSCRIPT INFORMATION

Subject field(s): All areas of medicine
Manuscript requirements: See latest issue for style requirements.
    Preferred length: As required
    Number of copies to be submitted: 2
    Abstract: Not necessary.
Author information and reprints: Payment: None.
    Is simultaneous submission of article to other journals permitted: Permitted, but not encouraged.
    Exclusive manuscript rights between acceptance and publication: Yes
    Copyright: Held by publication.
    Reprints: Available at cost.

Disposition of manuscript:
Query letter: Necessary.
Receipt of manuscript acknowledged: Yes
Decision to publish in: 1 month
Accepted manuscript published in: 8-10 months
Rejected manuscript returned: Yes, with return postage paid by publication.
Rejected manuscript criticized: No
Submit to:
Frank B. Ramsey, M. D.
Editor
(See address above)

SPECIAL STIPULATIONS
At this time, manuscripts are being accepted from Indiana physicians only.

INFECTION AND IMMUNITY [2365]
1913 I Street, N. W.
Washington, D.C. 20006
(202) 833-9416

First published in 1970

SUBSCRIPTION DATA
Issues and rates: Published monthly.
Average paid circulation: 5,400
Annual rate(s): $50.00; Foreign $51.00
Publisher or Sponsor: American Society for Microbiology
Managing Editor: Robert A. Day

EDITORIAL DESCRIPTION
Devoted to the advancement and dissemination of fundamental knowledge concerning pathogenic microorganisms and infections, and the ecology, epidemiology and host factors, as well as immunology.
Articles per average issue: 30
Audience: Medical microbiologists
Manuscripts accepted in English

MANUSCRIPT INFORMATION
Manuscript requirements: See latest issue for style requirements.
Preferred length: None
Number of copies to be submitted: 2
Abstract: Yes.
Author information and reprints: Payment: None.
Is simultaneous submission of article to other journals permitted: Not permitted.
Exclusive manuscript rights between acceptance and publication: Yes
Copyright: Held by the Society
Reprints: Available at cost.
Disposition of manuscript:
Query letter: Not necessary.
Receipt of manuscript acknowledged: Yes
Decision to publish in: 2 months
Accepted manuscript published in: 2 months
Rejected manuscript returned: Yes, with return postage paid by publication.
Rejected manuscript criticized: Yes
Submit to:
Robert A. Day
Managing Editor
(See address above)

INQUIRY [2366]
A Journal of Medical Care Organization, Provision and Financing
Blue Cross Association
840 North Lake Shore Drive
Chicago, Illinois 60611
(312) 329-5769

First published in 1963

SUBSCRIPTION DATA
Issues and rates: Published quarterly.
Average paid circulation: 3600; 87 controlled
Annual rate(s): $4.00
Publisher or Sponsor: Blue Cross Association
Managing Editor: Valeda Slade

EDITORIAL DESCRIPTION
Publishes articles concerned with the financing of medical care; the organization and delivery of health care services; various forms of medical care practice, and the cultural and social aspects of health care. Concerned with original research, demonstrations, or the concepts and philosophy surrounding the organization, provision and financing of medical care. Discussions of innovative programs particularly desired
Articles per average issue: 8
Audience: Professional, academic
Manuscripts accepted in English

MANUSCRIPT INFORMATION
Subject field(s): Medical economics, health care organization, delivery of health care services, health insurance, cultural and social aspects of health care
Manuscript requirements: See latest issue for style requirements.
Preferred length: 5,000 to 7,500 words; 20-30 pages
Number of copies to be submitted: Three
Abstract: Yes
Author information and reprints: Payment: Reprints only. 50 tearsheets
Is simultaneous submission of article to other journals permitted: No
Exclusive manuscript rights between acceptance and publication: Yes
Copyright: Held by publication.
Reprints: Available at cost
Additional information: Author's name and affiliation should appear only on a separate cover page.
Disposition of manuscript:
Query letter: No
Receipt of manuscript acknowledged: Yes
Decision to publish in: 6-8 weeks
Accepted manuscript published in: 6-9 months
Rejected manuscript returned: Yes
Rejected manuscript criticized: Yes
Submit to:
Valeda Slade
Managing Editor
Blue Cross Association
370 Bassett Road
North Haven, Connecticut 06473
(203) 239-7835

INTERNATIONAL ARCHIVES OF ALLERGY AND APPLIED IMMUNOLOGY [2367]
S. Karger AG
Arnold-Boecklin Strasse 25
CH-4011 Basel, Switzerland
061-390880

First published in 1950

SUBSCRIPTION DATA
Issues and rates: Published monthly.
Average paid circulation: 1,205; 25 controlled
Annual rate(s): SFr. 242.00; Foreign $98.00

EDITORIAL DESCRIPTION
An international journal that not only deals in allergic and related diseases, but also covers research work done in their experimental and theoretical background.
Articles per average issue: 10
Manuscripts accepted in English

MANUSCRIPT INFORMATION
Manuscript requirements: Style sheet sent on request.
Preferred length: 16 printed pages maximum
Number of copies to be submitted: 2
Abstract: Yes
Author information and reprints: Payment: None.
Is simultaneous submission of article to other journals permitted: No
Exclusive manuscript rights between acceptance and publication: Yes
Copyright: Held by publication.
Reprints: Available
Disposition of manuscript:
Query letter: No
Receipt of manuscript acknowledged: Yes
Decision to publish in: 1 month
Accepted manuscript published in: 5 months
Rejected manuscript returned: Yes
Rejected manuscript criticized: Yes
Submit to:
P. Kallos
Editor
Villatomsvagen 12
S-25234 Helsingborg, Sweden

INTERNATIONAL ARCHIVES OF OCCUPATIONAL HEALTH [2368]
Springer-Verlag
175 Fifth Avenue
New York, New York 10010

SUBSCRIPTION DATA
Annual rate(s): DM 168 per volume
Managing Editor: Professor Dr. G. Lehnert

EDITORIAL DESCRIPTION
Review articles, original investigations, short communications, and documents of international meetings pertinent to the field of occupational health
Manuscripts accepted in English, French, German

Medicine (general)

MANUSCRIPT INFORMATION

Manuscript requirements: See latest issue for style requirements. Style sheet sent on request.
    Preferred length: As required
    Number of copies to be submitted: 3
    Abstract: Yes. A short summary of the main points of the article. Papers not written in English should include a summary in English with a translation of the title.
Author information and reprints: Payment: Reprints only. 75 offprints
    Is simultaneous submission of article to other journals permitted: Not permitted.
    Exclusive manuscript rights between acceptance and publication: Yes
    Copyright: Held by publication.
    Reprints: Available at cost.
Submit to:
    Professor Dr. B.D. Dinman
    Medical Director
    Aluminium Company of America
    Alcoa Building
    Pittsburgh, Pennsylvania 12519

INTERNATIONAL JOURNAL OF HEALTH SCIENCES [2368-1]

43 Central Drive
Farmingdale, New York 11735
(516) 293-7130

First published in 1971

SUBSCRIPTION DATA

Issues and rates: Published quarterly.
    Average paid circulation: 2,000
    Annual rate(s): $35.00; Foreign $37.00

EDITORIAL DESCRIPTION

    Provides a vehicle for the exchange of information among health professionals in a variety of political, social and economic environments.
Articles per average issue: 14
Audience: Health professionals
    Manuscripts accepted in English

MANUSCRIPT INFORMATION

Subject field(s): New thinking on the policies, concepts, problems and techniques in planning, administration, and evaluation of health services.
Manuscript requirements: See latest issue for style requirements. Style sheet sent on request.
    Preferred length: 20-30 pages
    Number of copies to be submitted: 3
    Abstract: Yes. 200 words or less.
Author information and reprints: Payment: Reprints only. 20 copies
    Is simultaneous submission of article to other journals permitted: Not permitted.
    Exclusive manuscript rights between acceptance and publication: Yes
    Copyright: Held by publication.
    Reprints: Available at cost.

Disposition of manuscript:
    Query letter: Not necessary, but advisable.
    Receipt of manuscript acknowledged: Yes
    Decision to publish in: 4-6 weeks
    Accepted manuscript published in: 6 months
    Rejected manuscript returned: Yes, with return postage paid by publication.
    Rejected manuscript criticized: Sometimes
Submit to:
    Dr. Vincents Navarro
    Editor-in-Chief
    School of Hygiene and Public Health
    The Johns Hopkins University
    Baltimore, Maryland 21205

INTERNATIONAL JOURNAL OF LEPROSY [2369]

P. O. Box G, Madison Square Station
New York, New York 10010

First published in 1933

SUBSCRIPTION DATA

Issues and rates: Published quarterly.
    Average paid circulation: 950; 1,100 controlled
    Annual rate(s): $25.00; Foreign $25.00
Publisher or Sponsor: International Leprosy Association
Managing Editor: Olaf K. Skinsnes, M.D., Ph. D.

EDITORIAL DESCRIPTION

    Any medical or social contribution to the understanding, prevention and treatment of leprosy and other mycobacterial diseases
Articles per average issue: 8-10
Audience: Persons engaged in leprosy work and research
    Manuscripts accepted in English, French, Spanish

MANUSCRIPT INFORMATION

Manuscript requirements: See latest issue for style requirements.
    Preferred length: 4,000 to 5,000
    Number of copies to be submitted: 2
    Abstract: Yes. A brief explanatory summary which is also translated into French and Spanish
Author information and reprints: Payment: None.
    Exclusive manuscript rights between acceptance and publication: Yes
    Copyright: None
    Reprints: Available at cost.
Additional information: See inside back cover of latest issue for instructions to authors.
Disposition of manuscript:
    Query letter: Not necessary.

Receipt of manuscript acknowledged: Yes
Decision to publish in: 3 months
Accepted manuscript published in: 6 months
Rejected manuscript returned: Yes, with return postage paid by publication.
Rejected manuscript criticized: Yes
Submit to:
    Olaf K. Skinsnes, M.D.
    Editor
    Leahi Hospital
    3675 Kilauea Avenue
    Honolulu, Hawaii 96816
    734-0221

INTERNATIONAL JOURNAL OF PSYCHIATRY IN MEDICINE [2370]

Baywood Publishing Company, Inc.
43 Central Drive
Farmingdale, New York 11735
(516) 293-7130

First published in 1970

SUBSCRIPTION DATA

Issues and rates: Published quarterly.
    Annual rate(s): $30.00; Foreign $32.00

EDITORIAL DESCRIPTION

    Publishes papers on the problems and issues of psychological medicine as it is practiced, taught and investigated. Covers all aspects of general hospital medicine, community health programs and the examination of preventive medicine.
Articles per average issue: 13
Audience: Professional, academic
    Manuscripts accepted in English

MANUSCRIPT INFORMATION

Subject field(s): Definitions of psychosomatic, including psychological aspects of all illness; patient-doctor relationships; social and familial factors in the development and treatment of illness.
Manuscript requirements: See latest issue for style requirements. Style sheet sent on request.
    Preferred length: 5,000 words maximum
    Number of copies to be submitted: 3
    Abstract: Yes. 250 words or less
Author information and reprints: Payment: Reprints only. 20 copies
    Is simultaneous submission of article to other journals permitted: Not permitted.
    Exclusive manuscript rights between acceptance and publication: Yes
    Copyright: Held by publication.
    Reprints: Available at cost.
Disposition of manuscript:
    Query letter: Not necessary, but advisable.
    Receipt of manuscript acknowledged: Yes
    Decision to publish in: 4-6 weeks
    Accepted manuscript published in: 6 months
    Rejected manuscript returned: Yes, with return postage paid by publication.
    Rejected manuscript criticized: Sometimes

Submit to:
Dr. Don R. Lipsitt
Editor
Department of Psychiatry, Mount Auburn Hospital
330 Mount Auburn Street
Cambridge, Massachusetts 02138

INTERVIROLOGY [2371]
The Journal of the Virology Section
S. Karger AG
Arnold-Boecklin Strasse 25
CH-4011 Basel, Switzerland
061-390880

SUBSCRIPTION DATA
Issues and rates: Published monthly.
Average paid circulation: 422; 52 controlled
Publisher or Sponsor: International Association of Microbiological Societies

EDITORIAL DESCRIPTION
Initiated in order to encourage the relatively rapid publication of concisely presented studies in the field of virology and presents articles from all branches of the science.
Articles per average issue: 6
Manuscripts accepted in English

MANUSCRIPT INFORMATION
Subject field(s): Major subject areas include structure of viruses, plant virology, invertebrate virology, bacteriophage, replication of animal viruses, genetics, epidemiology, oncology, immunology and classification and nomenclature.
Manuscript requirements: See latest issue for style requirements.
Preferred length: 6 pages maximum
Number of copies to be submitted: 2
Abstract: Yes, with 6 key words
Author information and reprints: Payment: None.
Is simultaneous submission of article to other journals permitted: No
Exclusive manuscript rights between acceptance and publication: Yes
Copyright: Held by publication.
Reprints: Available
Disposition of manuscript:
Query letter: No
Receipt of manuscript acknowledged: Yes
Decision to publish in: 1 month
Accepted manuscript published in: 4 months
Rejected manuscript returned: Yes
Rejected manuscript criticized: Yes
Submit to:
J. L. Melnick
Editor-in-Chief
Department of Virology and Epidemiology
Baylor College of Medicine
Houston, Texas 77025

INVESTIGATIVE OPHTHALMOLOGY* [2372]
The C.V. Mosby Company
11830 Westline Industrial Drive
St. Louis, Missouri 63141
(314) 873-8370

SUBSCRIPTION DATA
Issues and rates: Published monthly.
Average paid circulation: 2,035
Annual rate(s): $30.00, Foreign $33.75
Publisher or Sponsor: Association for Research in Vision and Ophthalmology, Inc.

EDITORIAL DESCRIPTION
Bridges the gap between progress in eye research and communication of resulting applications of clinical ophthalmology.
Audience: University/hospital affiliated professors of ophthalmology, chiefs of services, and heads of departments

MANUSCRIPT INFORMATION
Subject field(s): Original and scientific articles concerning diagnosis, treatment and management of diseases of the ocular complex.
Manuscript requirements: See latest issue for style requirements.
Preferred length: 2,000 words; 8 pages
Number of copies to be submitted: Three
Author information and reprints: Payment: None.
Is simultaneous submission of article to other journals permitted: No
Exclusive manuscript rights between acceptance and publication: Yes
Copyright: Held by the Association
Reprints: Available at cost
Disposition of manuscript:
Receipt of manuscript acknowledged: Yes
Rejected manuscript returned: Yes
Rejected manuscript criticized: Yes
Submit to:
Herbert E. Kaufman
Editor
College of Medicine
University of Florida
Gainesville, Florida 32601

INVESTIGATIVE UROLOGY [2373]
428 East Preston Street
Baltimore, Maryland 21202
(301) 528-4116

First published in 1963

SUBSCRIPTION DATA
Issues and rates: Published bi-monthly.
Average paid circulation: 1,600
Annual rate(s): $25.00, Foreign $26.50

EDITORIAL DESCRIPTION
Contains original papers based on clinical or laboratory research of a fundamental nature in genito-urinary systems.
Articles per average issue: 15
Audience: Professional
Manuscripts accepted in English

MANUSCRIPT INFORMATION
Manuscript requirements: Style sheet sent on request.
Preferred length: None
Number of copies to be submitted: 2
Abstract: Yes
Author information and reprints: Payment: None.
Is simultaneous submission of article to other journals permitted: No
Exclusive manuscript rights between acceptance and publication: Yes
Copyright: Held by publication.
Reprints: Available
Disposition of manuscript:
Query letter: No
Receipt of manuscript acknowledged: Yes
Decision to publish in: 3 months
Accepted manuscript published in: 7-8 months
Rejected manuscript returned: Yes
Rejected manuscript criticized: Sometimes
Submit to:
William W. Scott
Editor
Brady Urological Institute
Johns Hopkins Hospital
Baltimore, Maryland 21205
(301) 955-6769

IOWA MEDICAL SOCIETY JOURNAL [2374]
1001 Grand Avenue
West Des Moines, Iowa 50265
(515) 255-2105 ext. 46

First published in 1910

SUBSCRIPTION DATA
Issues and rates: Published monthly.
Average paid circulation: 2500
Annual rate(s): $5.00
Publisher or Sponsor: Iowa Medical Society

EDITORIAL DESCRIPTION
Contains scientific articles in the medical field; socio-economic material relating to medical care.
Articles per average issue: 3
Audience: Professional, physicians
Manuscripts accepted in English

MANUSCRIPT INFORMATION
Subject field(s): Medicine, medical education, medical economics
Manuscript requirements: No specific style guide.
Preferred length: 8-10 pages
Number of copies to be submitted: Two
Abstract: No
Author information and reprints: Payment: None.
Is simultaneous submission of article to other journals permitted: Yes
Exclusive manuscript rights between acceptance and publication: No
Copyright: Held by publication.
Reprints: Available

Medicine (general)

Additional information: Double-space typescript; include a separate title-page.
Disposition of manuscript:
  Query letter: No
  Receipt of manuscript acknowledged: Yes
  Decision to publish in: 6-8 weeks
  Accepted manuscript published in: 6-12 months
  Rejected manuscript returned: Yes
  Rejected manuscript criticized: No
Submit to:
  Donald L. Neumann
  Managing Editor
  (See address above)

ISRAEL JOURNAL OF MEDICAL SCIENCES [2375]

P. O. Box 1435
Jerusalem, Israel
(02) 222 739

First published in 1965

SUBSCRIPTION DATA
Issues and rates: Published monthly.
  Annual rate(s): 35.00 Israeli pounds; Foreign $25.00; Institutions $40.00
Publisher or Sponsor: Israel Medical Association; Israel National Council for Research and Development
Managing Editor: Moshe Pyrwes

EDITORIAL DESCRIPTION
  Broad coverage of the medical sciences, both preclinical and clinical.
Articles per average issue: 16
Audience: International medical and scientific
  Manuscripts accepted in English

MANUSCRIPT INFORMATION
Subject field(s): Experimental and clinical medicine
Manuscript requirements: See latest issue for style requirements.
  Number of copies to be submitted: 2
  Abstract: Yes. Of about 150 words indicating the nature of the problem, the significant data, and the conclusions.
Author information and reprints: Payment: None. Special costs for the publication of figures
  Is simultaneous submission of article to other journals permitted: Not permitted.
  Exclusive manuscript rights between acceptance and publication: Yes
  Copyright: Held jointly by author and publication.
  Reprints: Available at cost.
Disposition of manuscript:
  Query letter: Not necessary.
  Receipt of manuscript acknowledged: Yes
  Decision to publish in: 4-6 months
  Accepted manuscript published in: 4 months
  Rejected manuscript returned: Yes, with return postage paid by publication.
  Rejected manuscript criticized: Sometimes
Submit to:
  Moshe Pyrwes
  Editor-in-Chief
  (See address above)

JAPANESE HEART JOURNAL [2376]

Second Department of Internal Medicine
University of Tokyo
Hongo, Bunkyo-ku
Tokyo, Japan
(03) 815-5411, Ext. 8239

First published in 1960

SUBSCRIPTION DATA
Issues and rates: Published bi-monthly.
  Average paid circulation: 357; 210 controlled
  Annual rate(s): 7,000 Yen
Publisher or Sponsor: Japanese Heart Association
Managing Editor: Hideo Ueda

EDITORIAL DESCRIPTION
  Contains articles of basic and clinical studies in the field of cardiology. All articles are written in English.
Articles per average issue: 10
Audience: Professional
  Manuscripts accepted in English

MANUSCRIPT INFORMATION
Subject field(s): Cardiology
Manuscript requirements: See latest issue for style requirements.
  Preferred length: 5,000 words; 10 pages
  Number of copies to be submitted: Two
  Abstract: Yes
Author information and reprints: Payment: By author to publication. For pages in excess of 8 printed pages
  Is simultaneous submission of article to other journals permitted: No
  Exclusive manuscript rights between acceptance and publication: Yes
  Copyright: Held by author.
  Reprints: Available
Disposition of manuscript:
  Query letter: No
  Receipt of manuscript acknowledged: Yes
  Decision to publish in: Within 6 months
  Accepted manuscript published in: 4-12 months
  Rejected manuscript returned: Yes
  Rejected manuscript criticized: Yes
Submit to:
  Hideo Ueda
  Editor-in-Chief
  (See address above)

JOURNAL OF ANATOMY [2377]

Cambridge University Press
32 East 57th Street
New York, New York 10022

Managing Editor: Professor J. J. Pritchard

EDITORIAL DESCRIPTION
  All discussions cover the field of anatomy and related areas.
Audience: Anatomists, physicians, researchers
  Manuscripts accepted in English

MANUSCRIPT INFORMATION
Manuscript requirements: See latest issue for style requirements.
  Preferred length: As required
  Number of copies to be submitted: 1
  Abstract: Yes. Each article must terminate with a brief summary in English of the chief observations and any conclusions drawn there from.
Author information and reprints: Payment: None.
  Is simultaneous submission of article to other journals permitted: Not permitted.
  Exclusive manuscript rights between acceptance and publication: Yes
  Copyright: Held by publication.
  Reprints: Available at no cost. 25
Submit to:
  Mrs. R. Davies
  Editorial Assistant
  Cotswold
  66 Cole Park Road
  Twickenham, Middlesex TW1 1HU, England

JOURNAL OF ANATOMY AND EMBRYOLOGY [2378]

Springer-Verlag
175 Fifth Avenue
New York, New York 10010

SUBSCRIPTION DATA
  Annual rate(s): DM 180 per volume
Managing Editor: Professor Dr. R. Ortmann

EDITORIAL DESCRIPTION
  Publishes papers on gross anatomy, histology, embryology, and experimental morphology in vertebrates
  Manuscripts accepted in French, German, preferably English

MANUSCRIPT INFORMATION
Manuscript requirements: See latest issue for style requirements. Style sheet sent on request.
  Preferred length: As required
  Number of copies to be submitted: 3
  Abstract: Yes. Paper should be preceded by a short summary. French and German papers should include in addition a more detailed summary in English.
Author information and reprints: Payment: Reprints only. 75 offprints
  Is simultaneous submission of article to other journals permitted: Not permitted.
  Exclusive manuscript rights between acceptance and publication: Yes
  Copyright: Held by publication.
  Reprints: Available at cost.
Submit to:
  Professor S. L. Palay, M. D.
  Editorial Board
  Department of Anatomy, Harvard Medical School
  25 Shattuck Street
  Boston, Massachusetts 02115

JOURNAL OF APPLIED NUTRITION [2379]

Box 386
La Habra, California 90631
(312) 697-4576

First published in 1949

SUBSCRIPTION DATA

Issues and rates: Published semi-annually.
Average paid circulation: 2,500
Annual rate(s): $10.00, Foreign $12.00
Publisher or Sponsor: International College
of Applied Nutrition

EDITORIAL DESCRIPTION

Provides current, factual, scientific
information on the inter-relationship of
food, health and life. Presents the highest
standards in nutritional education:
medical, dental, and nutritional practice,
and research in nutrition.
Articles per average issue: 4-7
Audience: Professional, general
Manuscripts accepted in English only

MANUSCRIPT INFORMATION

Subject field(s): All phases of nutritional
research
Manuscript requirements: See latest issue for
style requirements.
Preferred length: Helpful
Number of copies to be submitted: Two
Abstract: No preference
Author information and reprints: Payment:
None.
Is simultaneous submission of article to
other journals permitted: No
Exclusive manuscript rights between
acceptance and publication: Yes
Copyright: Held by publication.
Reprints: Available, cost upon request
Additional information: Typewritten,
double-spaced
Disposition of manuscript:
Query letter: Not necessary
Receipt of manuscript acknowledged: Yes
Decision to publish in: 1 month
Accepted manuscript published in: Varies
Rejected manuscript returned: Yes, if
return postage is supplied by author.
Rejected manuscript criticized: Upon
request
Submit to:
Harold Stone
Editor-in-Chief
(See address above)

JOURNAL OF BIOMECHANICS [2380]

Pergamon Press, Inc.
Fairview Park
Elmsford, New York 10523
(914) 592-7700

First published in 1968

SUBSCRIPTION DATA

Issues and rates: Published bi-monthly.
Annual rate(s): $60.00; Individuals
$25.00

EDITORIAL DESCRIPTION

Provides the researcher with an effective
means of presenting his material from the
medical, dental and basic sciences as well
as engineering related to the field of
biomechanics.
Articles per average issue: 10

Audience: Professional, academic
Manuscripts accepted in English

MANUSCRIPT INFORMATION

Subject field(s): Fluids, materials, prosthetics
and orthotics, solid mechanics, stress
analysis of various parts of the body,
etiology of trauma, design and study of
dental materials involved in chewing
process, etc.
Manuscript requirements: See latest issue for
style requirements.
Preferred length: Surveys: 4,000-6,000
words; papers: 1,000-4,000 words
Number of copies to be submitted: 2 or 3
Abstract: Yes. A short abstract, not
exceeding 150 words to precede the
article.
Author information and reprints: Payment:
Reprints only. 50 reprints
Is simultaneous submission of article to
other journals permitted: Not permitted.
Exclusive manuscript rights between
acceptance and publication: Yes
Copyright: Held by publication.
Reprints: Available at cost.
Disposition of manuscript:
Query letter: Not necessary.
Receipt of manuscript acknowledged: Yes
Decision to publish in: 4 weeks
Accepted manuscript published in: 5
months
Rejected manuscript returned: Yes, if
return postage is supplied by author.
Rejected manuscript criticized: Reasons
for rejections only
Submit to:
Prof. Verne L. Roberts
Department of Engineering Mechanics
Duke University
Durham, North Carolina 27706

Dr. F. Gaynor Evans
Department of Anatomy
University of Michigan
Ann Arbor, Michigan 48104
Editors-in-Chief

JOURNAL OF CHRONIC DISEASES [2381]

Pergamon Press, Inc.
Fairview Park
Elmsford, New York 10523
(914) 592-7700

First published in 1955

SUBSCRIPTION DATA

Issues and rates: Published monthly.
Annual rate(s): $25.00; Institutions
$55.00

EDITORIAL DESCRIPTION

Publishes significant original articles
dealing with various phases of chronic
illness of all age groups.
Articles per average issue: 5-7
Audience: Professional, academic
Manuscripts accepted in English

MANUSCRIPT INFORMATION

Subject field(s): Natural history of chronic
disease, early diagnosis, treatment, the
impact of the chronically ill on the
community, long-term medical and
nursing care, rehabilitation, preventive
medicine
Manuscript requirements: See latest issue for
style requirements.
Preferred length: None
Number of copies to be submitted:
Original and 1 copy double-spaced
Abstract: Yes
Author information and reprints: Payment:
None.
Is simultaneous submission of article to
other journals permitted: Not permitted.
Exclusive manuscript rights between
acceptance and publication: Yes
Copyright: Held by publication.
Reprints: Available at cost.
Disposition of manuscript:
Query letter: Not necessary.
Receipt of manuscript acknowledged: Yes
Decision to publish in: 4 weeks
Accepted manuscript published in: 5
months
Rejected manuscript returned: Yes, if
return postage is supplied by author.
Rejected manuscript criticized: Reasons
for rejections only
Submit to:
Prof. David P. Earle, M.D.,
Prof. Martin Brandfonbrenner, M.D
Editor and Associate Editor
Department of Medicine, Northwestern
Medical School
303 East Chicago Ave
Chicago, Illinois 60611

THE JOURNAL OF CLINICAL INVESTIGATION [2382]

The Rockefeller University Press
1230 York Avenue
New York, New York 10021
(212) 360-1565

First published in 1924

SUBSCRIPTION DATA

Issues and rates: Published monthly.
Average paid circulation: 6489; 29
controlled
Annual rate(s): $60.00; Foreign $70.00
Publisher or Sponsor: The American Society
for Clinical Investigation, Inc.

EDITORIAL DESCRIPTION

Publishes original papers on research
pertinent to human biology and disease.
Work using animals or in vitro
techniques is acceptable if it is relevant to
human normal or abnormal biology. It is
assumed that all clinical investigation
described in manuscripts submitted to
this Journal shall have been conducted
according to the principles expressed in
the Declaration of Helsinki.

MANUSCRIPT INFORMATION

Manuscript requirements: AIBS
Preferred length: 8 printed pages or less

Number of copies to be submitted: Two
Abstract: Yes
Author information and reprints: Payment:
By author to publication. Page charges
on request
Is simultaneous submission of article to
other journals permitted: No
Exclusive manuscript rights between
acceptance and publication: Yes
Copyright: Held by the American Society
for Clinical Investigation, Inc.
Reprints: Available; cost to author on
sliding scale
Disposition of manuscript:
Query letter: No
Receipt of manuscript acknowledged: Yes
Rejected manuscript returned: Yes
Submit to:
Jean D. Wilson
Editor
University of Texas Health Science
Center
5323 Harry Hines Boulevard
Dallas, Texas 75235
(214) 631-3220 ext. 2025

THE JOURNAL OF CLINICAL PHARMACOLOGY [2383]

Hall Associates
Stamford, Connecticut 06904

Previously entitled *The Journal of New Drugs*

First published in 1961

SUBSCRIPTION DATA
Issues and rates: 8 times per year
Annual rate(s): $20.00; Foreign $23.00
Publisher or Sponsor: College of Clinical
Pharmacology
Managing Editor: McKeen Cattell, M. D.

EDITORIAL DESCRIPTION
Contains articles on clinical
pharmacology.
Articles per average issue: 12
Audience: Clinical pharmacologists,
physicians
Manuscripts accepted in English

MANUSCRIPT INFORMATION
Subject field(s): All areas of clinical
pharmacology
Manuscript requirements: See latest issue for
style requirements.
Number of copies to be submitted: 2
Abstract: Yes.
Author information and reprints: Payment:
Reprints only. 100 reprints
Is simultaneous submission of article to
other journals permitted: Not permitted.
Exclusive manuscript rights between
acceptance and publication: Yes
Copyright: Held by publication.
Reprints: Available at cost.
Disposition of manuscript:
Query letter: Not necessary.
Receipt of manuscript acknowledged: Yes
Decision to publish in: 2-4 weeks

Accepted manuscript published in: 4-6
months
Rejected manuscript returned: Yes, with
return postage paid by publication.
Rejected manuscript criticized: Yes
Submit to:
Dr. McKeen Cattell
Editor
1300 York Avenue
New York, New York 10021
(212) 734-1832

JOURNAL OF COMPARATIVE PHYSIOLOGY-A [2384]

Sensory, Neural and Behavioral Physiology
Springer-Verlag
175 Fifth Avenue
New York, New York 10010

First published in 1924

SUBSCRIPTION DATA
Annual rate(s): DM 160 per volume
Managing Editor: K. von Frisch

EDITORIAL DESCRIPTION
For speedy publication of articles in the
field of animal physiology
Manuscripts accepted in German,
preferably English

MANUSCRIPT INFORMATION
Subject field(s): Physiological basis of
behavior, sensory physiology, neural
physiology, orientation, communication,
locomotion, hormonal control of behavior
Manuscript requirements: See latest issue for
style requirements.
Preferred length: As required
Number of copies to be submitted: 3
Abstract: Yes. A summary of the main
results written in clear and correct
English.
Author information and reprints: Payment:
Reprints only. 50 offprints
Is simultaneous submission of article to
other journals permitted: Not permitted.
Exclusive manuscript rights between
acceptance and publication: Yes
Copyright: Held by publication.
Submit to:
Professor D. Kennedy
Editorial Board
Department of Biological Sciences
Stanford University
Stanford, California 94305

JOURNAL OF COMPARATIVE PHYSIOLOGY-B [2385]

Metabolic and Transport Functions
Springer-Verlag
175 Fifth Avenue
New York, New York 10010

First published in 1924

SUBSCRIPTION DATA
Annual rate(s): DM 160 per volume
Managing Editor: A. Kühn

EDITORIAL DESCRIPTION
Publishes original articles in the field of
animal physiology

Manuscripts accepted in English, German

MANUSCRIPT INFORMATION
Subject field(s): Comparative aspects of
metabolism and enzymology, metabolic
regulation, respiration and gas transport,
physiology of body fluids, circulation,
temperature relations, muscular
physiology
Manuscript requirements: See latest issue for
style requirements.
Preferred length: As required
Number of copies to be submitted: 3
Abstract: Yes. Articles written in
German must be accompanied by a
summary in English.
Author information and reprints: Payment:
Reprints only. 75 offprints
Is simultaneous submission of article to
other journals permitted: Not permitted.
Exclusive manuscript rights between
acceptance and publication: Yes
Copyright: Held by publication.
Submit to:
Professor C. Ladd Prosser
Editorial Board
Department of Physiology and Biophysics
University of Illinois, 524 Burill Hall
Urbana, Illinois 61801

JOURNAL OF ELECTROCARDIOLOGY [2386]

P.O. Box 923-B
San Diego, California 92109
(714) 270-1241

First published in 1968

SUBSCRIPTION DATA
Issues and rates: Published quarterly.
Average paid circulation: 2131; 50
controlled
Annual rate(s): Individuals $20.00;
Foreign individuals $22.00; Institutions
$25.00; Foreign institutions $28.00
Publisher or Sponsor: Research in
Electrocardiology, Inc.

EDITORIAL DESCRIPTION
Scientific publication concerned
exclusively with electrical activity of the
heart. Designed to meet the needs of the
internist, cardiologist, thoracic surgeon,
general practitioner, and researchers.
Articles per average issue: 12-14
Audience: Professional
Manuscripts accepted in English

MANUSCRIPT INFORMATION
Subject field(s): Electrocardiology,
vectorcardiography, cardiac
instrumentation, cardiac pacing,
monitoring, computer technology, drug
effects, electrophysiology, cardiac
biophysics, arrhythmias
Manuscript requirements: See latest issue for
style requirements.
Preferred length: None
Number of copies to be submitted: Two
Abstract: Yes, at the beginning
Author information and reprints: Payment:
By author to publication.
Is simultaneous submission of article to
other journals permitted: No

Exclusive manuscript rights between acceptance and publication: Yes
Copyright: Held by publication.
Reprints: Available, cost given at time of publication
Disposition of manuscript:
Query letter: No
Receipt of manuscript acknowledged: Yes
Decision to publish in: 8-10 weeks
Accepted manuscript published in: 6-9 months
Rejected manuscript returned: Yes
Rejected manuscript criticized: Usually
Submit to:
Zang Z. Zao, M.D.
Editor
(See address above)

THE JOURNAL OF ENDOCRINOLOGY [2387]

The Official Journal of the Society for Endocrinology
Department of Pharmacology
The Medical School
Bristol BS8 1TD, England
(0276) 24161

First published in 1939

SUBSCRIPTION DATA
Issues and rates: Published monthly.
Average paid circulation: 2,500
Annual rate(s): £40.00; Foreign $110.00 (U.S.)

EDITORIAL DESCRIPTION
Contains papers reporting results of research; invited reviews; short communications (reporting small completed investigations, new techniques etc); proceedings of the Society
Articles per average issue: 24
Audience: Professional
Manuscripts accepted in English only

MANUSCRIPT INFORMATION
Subject field(s): Nature and functions of the endocrine organs in vertebrates and invertebrates; the anatomy, physiology and biochemistry of reproduction; endocrine chemistry; clinical endocrinology; the influence of hormones on behaviour
Manuscript requirements: See latest issue for style requirements.
Preferred length: 5,000 words
Number of copies to be submitted: Two
Abstract: Yes, concise
Author information and reprints: Payment: Reprints only. 25
Is simultaneous submission of article to other journals permitted: No
Exclusive manuscript rights between acceptance and publication: No
Copyright: Held by publication.
Reprints: Available at cost.
Additional information: Manuscripts must be typewritten, double-spaced. Include also a short title for the running heading.
Disposition of manuscript:
Query letter: No
Receipt of manuscript acknowledged: Yes
Decision to publish in: 2-3 months

Accepted manuscript published in: 4-5 months
Rejected manuscript returned: Yes, if return postage is supplied by author.
Rejected manuscript criticized: Yes
Submit to:
Professor B. T. Donovan
(See address above)

THE JOURNAL OF GENERAL PHYSIOLOGY [2388]

Rockefeller University Press
New York, New York 10021
(212) 360-1278

SUBSCRIPTION DATA
Issues and rates: Published monthly.
Average paid circulation: 2375; 60 controlled
Annual rate(s): $50.00; Foreign $56.00
Publisher or Sponsor: Society of General Physiologists

EDITORIAL DESCRIPTION
Publishes papers on general physiology.

MANUSCRIPT INFORMATION
Manuscript requirements: CBE
Preferred length: 20 printed pages
Number of copies to be submitted: Original and one copy
Author information and reprints: Payment: By author to publication. $20 per page.
Is simultaneous submission of article to other journals permitted: No
Exclusive manuscript rights between acceptance and publication: Yes
Copyright: Held by publication.
Reprints: Available from author
Disposition of manuscript:
Receipt of manuscript acknowledged: Yes
Rejected manuscript returned: Yes
Submit to:
Paul F. Cranefield
Editor
The Rockefeller University
1230 York Avenue
New York, New York 10021
(212) 360-1695

JOURNAL OF GENERAL VIROLOGY [2389]

Cambridge University Press
32 East 57th Street
New York, New York 10022

EDITORIAL DESCRIPTION
Original work in general virology
Manuscripts accepted in English

MANUSCRIPT INFORMATION
Subject field(s): Study of bacterial, plant and animal viruses, including structure, genetics, systematics and interactions with host cells; investigations of pathogenesis will be considered, but predominantly clinical or epidemiological content will generally not be included.

Manuscript requirements: See latest issue for style requirements. Style sheet sent on request.
Preferred length: As required
Number of copies to be submitted: 3, double-spaced with adequate margins
Abstract: Yes.
Author information and reprints: Payment: None.
Is simultaneous submission of article to other journals permitted: Not permitted.
Exclusive manuscript rights between acceptance and publication: Yes
Copyright: Held by publication.
Reprints: Available at no cost.
Additional information: Submission of manuscript implies that it has not been published previously or is being considered elsewhere. Papers should be divided: a) Summary, b) Introduction, c) Methods, d) Results, e) Discussion, f) Acknowledgements, and g) References.
Disposition of manuscript:
Query letter: Not necessary, but advisable.
Receipt of manuscript acknowledged: Yes
Rejected manuscript returned: Yes, if return postage is supplied by author.
Rejected manuscript criticized: Sometimes
Submit to:
Editorial Office
Harvest House
62 London Road
Reading RG1 5AS, England

JOURNAL OF THE HISTORY OF MEDICINE AND ALLIED SCIENCES [2390]

Owen H. Wangensteen Historical Library
Biomedical Library, University of Minnesota
Minneapolis, Minnesota 55455
(612) 373-5946

SUBSCRIPTION DATA
Issues and rates: Published quarterly.
Average paid circulation: 1000
Annual rate(s): $20.00
Managing Editor: Leonard G. Wilson

EDITORIAL DESCRIPTION
Publishes work relating to all aspects of the history of medicine and of the various sciences impinging on it.
Articles per average issue: 4
Audience: Historians of medicine and science, physicians, historians.
Manuscripts accepted in English

MANUSCRIPT INFORMATION
Subject field(s): History of medicine, history of public health, history of biological sciences
Manuscript requirements: Style sheet sent on request.
Preferred length: 6,000-8000 words; 25-30 pages
Number of copies to be submitted: One
Abstract: No

Medicine (general)

Author information and reprints: Payment: None.
Is simultaneous submission of article to other journals permitted: No
Exclusive manuscript rights between acceptance and publication: Yes
Copyright: Held by publication.
Reprints: Available
Disposition of manuscript:
Query letter: No
Receipt of manuscript acknowledged: Yes
Decision to publish in: 3 months
Accepted manuscript published in: One year
Rejected manuscript returned: Yes
Rejected manuscript criticized: Sometimes
Submit to:
Leonard G. Wilson
Editor
(See address above)

JOURNAL OF HYGIENE [2391]

Cambridge University Press
32 East 57th Street
New York, New York 10022

SUBSCRIPTION DATA
Issues and rates: Published semi-monthly.
Annual rate(s): £3.50; Foreign $11.50

EDITORIAL DESCRIPTION
Concerned with bacterial and virus diseases of man and animals as well as the identification of pathogens, epidemiology, and immunology.
Audience: Those involved in experimental and applied biology, public health and pathology
Manuscripts accepted in English

MANUSCRIPT INFORMATION
Manuscript requirements: See latest issue for style requirements.
Preferred length: No preference
Number of copies to be submitted: 2
Author information and reprints: Payment: Reprints only. 25
Is simultaneous submission of article to other journals permitted: Not permitted.
Exclusive manuscript rights between acceptance and publication: Yes
Copyright: Held by publication.
Reprints: Available at no cost. 25
Disposition of manuscript:
Query letter: Not necessary, but advisable.
Submit to:
Dr. R. M. Fry
Editor
Department of Pathology
Tennis Court Road
Cambridge CB2 1QP, England

JOURNAL OF IMMUNOLOGY [2392]

428 East Preston Street
Baltimore, Maryland 21202
(301) 528-4116

First published in 1916

SUBSCRIPTION DATA
Issues and rates: Published monthly.
Average paid circulation: 6,000
Annual rate(s): $60.00; Foreign $63.25
Publisher or Sponsor: American Association of Immunologists

EDITORIAL DESCRIPTION
Covers all areas of immunology including cellular, tumor, viral and microbial immunology, immunochemistry, immunogenetics and transplantation.
Articles per average issue: 48
Manuscripts accepted in English

MANUSCRIPT INFORMATION
Manuscript requirements: See latest issue for style requirements.
Preferred length: None
Number of copies to be submitted: Three
Abstract: Yes
Author information and reprints: Payment: By author to publication. $70.00 per page. For pages in excess of 6 per article.
Is simultaneous submission of article to other journals permitted: No
Exclusive manuscript rights between acceptance and publication: Yes
Copyright: Held by publication.
Reprints: Available
Disposition of manuscript:
Query letter: No
Receipt of manuscript acknowledged: Yes
Decision to publish in: 2-3 months
Accepted manuscript published in: 4-5 months
Rejected manuscript returned: Yes
Rejected manuscript criticized: Sometimes
Submit to:
Joseph D. Feldman, M.D.
Editor-in-Chief
Department of Experimental Pathology
Scripps Clinic and Research Foundation
La Jolla, California 92037
(714) 459-2390

THE JOURNAL OF INFECTIOUS DISEASES [2393]

University of Chicago Press
5801 Ellis Avenue
Chicago, Illinois 60637
(312) 753-3347

SUBSCRIPTION DATA
Issues and rates: Published monthly.
Average paid circulation: 3300
Annual rate(s): $25.00, Foreign $30.00
Managing Editor: Julie McCoy Spaulding

EDITORIAL DESCRIPTION
Contains articles on medical microbiology, epidemiology, immunology.
Articles per average issue: 15-18
Audience: Researchers, clinicians
Manuscripts accepted in English

MANUSCRIPT INFORMATION
Subject field(s): Virology, immunology, bacterial disease, epidemiology, biology of microorganisms, techniques in microbiology
Manuscript requirements: See latest issue for style requirements.
Preferred length: 5000 words or less
Number of copies to be submitted: Three
Abstract: Yes, of less than 150 words
Author information and reprints: Payment: None.
Is simultaneous submission of article to other journals permitted: No
Exclusive manuscript rights between acceptance and publication: Yes
Copyright: Held by publication.
Reprints: Available
Disposition of manuscript:
Query letter: No
Receipt of manuscript acknowledged: Yes
Decision to publish in: 1-3 months
Accepted manuscript published in: 2-5 months
Rejected manuscript returned: Yes
Rejected manuscript criticized: Yes
Submit to:
Edward H. Kass
Editor
(See address above)
(617) 247-2530

JOURNAL OF INVESTIGATIVE DERMATOLOGY [2394]

428 East Preston Street
Baltimore, Maryland 21202
(301) 528-4116

First published in 1938

SUBSCRIPTION DATA
Issues and rates: Published monthly.
Average paid circulation: 3,800
Annual rate(s): $40.00, Foreign $42.60
Publisher or Sponsor: Society for Investigative Dermatology

EDITORIAL DESCRIPTION
Contains original papers and reviews pertinent to the normal and abnormal function of the skin.
Articles per average issue: 10
Manuscripts accepted in English

MANUSCRIPT INFORMATION
Manuscript requirements: Style sheet sent on request.
Preferred length: None
Number of copies to be submitted: Three
Abstract: No
Author information and reprints: Payment: By author to publication. $40.00 per page. Illustrations in excess of 1-3 pages.
Is simultaneous submission of article to other journals permitted: No
Exclusive manuscript rights between acceptance and publication: Yes
Copyright: Held by publication.
Reprints: Available
Disposition of manuscript:
Query letter: No
Receipt of manuscript acknowledged: Yes
Decision to publish in: 3 months

Accepted manuscript published in: 4 months

Rejected manuscript returned: Yes

Rejected manuscript criticized: Sometimes

Submit to:

Irwin M. Freedberg, M.D.

Editor

Beth Israel Hospital

300 Brookline Avenue

Boston, Massachusetts 02215

(617) 734-4400 ext. 769

JOURNAL OF LONG TERM CARE ADMINISTRATION [2395]

American College of Nursing Home Administrators

8641 Colesville Road, Suite 409

Silver Spring, Maryland 20910

(301) 589-3230

Previously entitled *Journal of the American College of Nursing Home Administrators*

First published in 1972

SUBSCRIPTION DATA

Issues and rates: Published quarterly.

Average paid circulation: 75; 5,000 controlled

Annual rate(s): $9.00; Foreign $12.00; Institutions $9.00

Publisher or Sponsor: The American College of Nursing Home Administrators

EDITORIAL DESCRIPTION

Welcomes articles concerning long term care, nursing homes, administrative techniques which will be of interest to nursing home administrators as well as significant to the existing literature of the field.

Articles per average issue: 5

Audience: Professional

Manuscripts accepted in English

MANUSCRIPT INFORMATION

Subject field(s): The practice of nursing home administration, health care education, management theories, legislation, philosophy, trends in the field, labor unions, etc.

Manuscript requirements: Style sheet sent on request.

Preferred length: 15 pages or less

Number of copies to be submitted: 1

Abstract: Not necessary.

Author information and reprints: Payment: None.

Is simultaneous submission of article to other journals permitted: Not permitted.

Exclusive manuscript rights between acceptance and publication: Yes

Copyright: Held by publication.

Reprints: Not available.

Additional information: Typewritten, double-spaced, on one side of standard-sized paper, with liberal margins. Author identification on cover letter only.

Disposition of manuscript:

Query letter: Not necessary, but advisable.

Receipt of manuscript acknowledged: Yes

Decision to publish in: 3 months

Accepted manuscript published in: 6 months

Rejected manuscript returned: Yes, with return postage paid by publication.

Rejected manuscript criticized: Reasons for rejections only

Submit to:

Michael J. Stotts

Managing Editor

(See address above)

JOURNAL OF MEDICAL EDUCATION [2396]

One Dupont Circle, N.W.

Washington, D.C. 20036

(202) 466-5180

SUBSCRIPTION DATA

Issues and rates: Published monthly.

Average paid circulation: 6500

Annual rate(s): $15.00, Foreign $18.00

Publisher or Sponsor: Association of American Medical Colleges

Managing Editor: Merrill T. McCord

EDITORIAL DESCRIPTION

Contains articles on medical education, health planning, health services administration, etc.

Articles per average issue: 16

Manuscripts accepted in English

MANUSCRIPT INFORMATION

Manuscript requirements: See latest issue for style requirements.

Preferred length: 15-18 pages

Number of copies to be submitted: Two

Abstract: Yes

Author information and reprints: Payment: None.

Is simultaneous submission of article to other journals permitted: No

Exclusive manuscript rights between acceptance and publication: Yes

Copyright: Held jointly by both author and publication

Reprints: Available

Disposition of manuscript:

Query letter: No

Receipt of manuscript acknowledged: Yes

Decision to publish in: 4-6 weeks

Accepted manuscript published in: 5-6 months

Rejected manuscript returned: Yes

Rejected manuscript criticized: Sometimes

Submit to:

Editor

(See address above)

JOURNAL OF MEDICAL GENETICS [2397]

B.M.A. House

Tavistock Square

London WC1H 9JR, England

01-387 4499

First published in 1964

SUBSCRIPTION DATA

Issues and rates: Published quarterly.

Average paid circulation: Not available.

Annual rate(s): $22.00

Publisher or Sponsor: British Medical Association

EDITORIAL DESCRIPTION

Contains medical research on genetics.

Articles per average issue: Varies

Manuscripts accepted in English only

MANUSCRIPT INFORMATION

Manuscript requirements: See latest issue for style requirements.

Preferred length: None

Number of copies to be submitted: Two

Abstract: Yes

Author information and reprints: Payment: None.

Is simultaneous submission of article to other journals permitted: No

Exclusive manuscript rights between acceptance and publication: Yes

Copyright: Held by publication.

Reprints: Available.

Disposition of manuscript:

Receipt of manuscript acknowledged: Yes

Decision to publish in: One month

Accepted manuscript published in: Six months

Rejected manuscript returned: Yes

Rejected manuscript criticized: No

Submit to:

The Editor

Sir Cyril Clarke

Editor

Cedric Carter;

D. G. Harnden

Assistant Editors

(See address above)

JOURNAL OF MEDICAL MICROBIOLOGY [2398]

Longman Group, Ltd., Journals Division

Burnt Mill

Harlow, Essex, England

26721

SUBSCRIPTION DATA

Issues and rates: Published quarterly.

Annual rate(s): £10.00; Foreign $30.00

Publisher or Sponsor: The Pathological Society of Great Britain and Ireland

EDITORIAL DESCRIPTION

Publishes papers on all aspects of microbiology, bacteriology, protozoology, virology, mycology and immunology as applicable to human and veterinary medicine.

Articles per average issue: 10
Manuscripts accepted in English

MANUSCRIPT INFORMATION
Manuscript requirements: See latest issue for
style requirements.
Preferred length: None
Number of copies to be submitted: 2
Abstract: Yes
Submit to:
M. T. Parker
Editor
(See address above)

SPECIAL STIPULATIONS
Request additional information from
editor.

JOURNAL OF MEDICAL
PRIMATOLOGY   [2399]
S. Karger AG
Arnold-Boecklin Strasse 25
CH-4011 Basel, Switzerland
061-390-880

First published in 1972

SUBSCRIPTION DATA
Issues and rates: Published bi-monthly.
Average paid circulation: 261; 58
controlled
Annual rate(s): SFr. 132.00; Foreign
$54.00

EDITORIAL DESCRIPTION
A forum for medical scientists and
biologists interested in approximating the
health and disease conditions of man in
his phylogenetically closest relatives, the
apes and monkeys. Because medical
investigations require a thorough
knowledge of the experimental subject,
the journal also publishes material
pertaining to simian biology per se.
Medical primatology is a new discipline
and new techniques are of particular
interest. Therefore, papers on problems of
simian husbandry are particularly
welcomed.
Articles per average issue: 5-6
Audience: English

MANUSCRIPT INFORMATION
Manuscript requirements: Style sheet sent
on request.
Preferred length: 12 pages
Number of copies to be submitted: 3
Abstract: Yes, with key words
Author information and reprints: Payment:
None.
Is simultaneous submission of article to
other journals permitted: No
Exclusive manuscript rights between
acceptance and publication: Yes
Copyright: Held by publication.
Reprints: Available at cost
Disposition of manuscript:
Query letter: No
Receipt of manuscript acknowledged: Yes
Decision to publish in: 1-2 months
Accepted manuscript published in: 6-7
months
Rejected manuscript returned: Yes

Rejected manuscript criticized: Yes
Submit to:
J. Moor-Jankowski
Editor
Laboratory for Experimental Medicine
and Surgery in Primates
New York University Medical Center
550 First Avenue
New York, New York 10011

JOURNAL OF NERVOUS
AND MENTAL DISEASE   [2400]
428 East Preston Street
Baltimore, Maryland 21202
(301) 528-4116

First published in 1874

SUBSCRIPTION DATA
Issues and rates: Published monthly.
Average paid circulation: 2,600
Annual rate(s): $30.00; Foreign $32.60

EDITORIAL DESCRIPTION
Contains original articles on all aspects of
nervous and mental disease and
behavioral sciences.
Articles per average issue: 8
Manuscripts accepted in English

MANUSCRIPT INFORMATION
Manuscript requirements: Style sheet sent
on request.
Preferred length: None
Number of copies to be submitted: Two
Abstract: No
Author information and reprints: Payment:
None.
Is simultaneous submission of article to
other journals permitted: No
Exclusive manuscript rights between
acceptance and publication: Yes
Copyright: Held by publication.
Reprints: Available
Disposition of manuscript:
Query letter: No
Receipt of manuscript acknowledged: Yes
Decision to publish in: 6-8 weeks
Accepted manuscript published in: 4-6
months
Rejected manuscript returned: Yes
Rejected manuscript criticized:
Sometimes
Submit to:
Eugene B. Brody, M.D.
Editor
Institute of Psychiatry and Human
Behavior
University of Maryland School of
Medicine
Baltimore, Maryland 20201

JOURNAL OF
NEUROCYTOLOGY   [2401]
Periodicals Department, Associated Book
Publishers
North Way
Andover, Hampshire SP10 5BE, England
(0264) 62141

First published in 1972

SUBSCRIPTION DATA
Issues and rates: Published bi-monthly.
Annual rate(s): £24.00; Foreign £27.00;
$62.90; Individuals £4.80; $11.08
Managing Editor: E. George Gray;
A. Robert Lieberman

EDITORIAL DESCRIPTION
Devoted to fine structural and associated
cytochemical, biochemical, physiological
and pharmacological studies of neurons,
receptors, synapses, neuro-effector
junctions, and other elements of the
peripheral and central nervous systems of
vertebrates and invertebrates under
normal and experimental conditions.
Articles per average issue: 9
Audience: Neurobiologists
Manuscripts accepted in English only

MANUSCRIPT INFORMATION
Manuscript requirements: See latest issue for
style requirements. Style sheet sent on
request.
Preferred length: As required
Number of copies to be submitted:
Original and 2 copies
Abstract: Yes. Clearly written, factual
and comprehensible without reference to
the text, it should normally not exceed
200 words
Author information and reprints: Payment:
None. Minimal charges for more than
three plates.
Is simultaneous submission of article to
other journals permitted: Not permitted.
Exclusive manuscript rights between
acceptance and publication: Yes
Copyright: Held by publication.
Reprints: Available at no cost. 25
Additional information: Manuscript to be
typewritten, double-spaced on one side of
standard sized paper. Send for author's
instructions.
Disposition of manuscript:
Query letter: Not necessary.
Receipt of manuscript acknowledged: Yes
Decision to publish in: 2-6 weeks
Accepted manuscript published in: 3-5
months
Rejected manuscript returned: Yes, with
return postage paid by publication.
Rejected manuscript criticized: Yes
Submit to:
The Editors
Department of Neuroanatomy, University
College London
Gower Street
London WC1E 6BT, England
387-7050 ext. 630

JOURNAL OF THE
NEUROLOGICAL
SCIENCES   [2402]
Official Bulletin of the World Federation of
Neurology
Elsevier Scientific Publishing Company
P. O. Box 152B
Amsterdam, The Netherlands
(020) 515-9111

SUBSCRIPTION DATA
Issues and rates: Published monthly.

Average paid circulation: 1000
Annual rate(s): 285 Dfl. plus postage
Publisher or Sponsor: World Federation of Neurology

EDITORIAL DESCRIPTION

Publishes papers on neurological subjects with an emphasis on clinical research although papers concerning basic research are also accepted.
Articles per average issue: 10-15
Audience: Professional
Manuscripts accepted in English, French, German, Spanish

MANUSCRIPT INFORMATION

Manuscript requirements: Style sheet sent on request.
    Number of copies to be submitted: Three
    Abstract: Yes
Author information and reprints: Payment: Reprints only. 50 reprints
    Is simultaneous submission of article to other journals permitted: No
    Exclusive manuscript rights between acceptance and publication: Yes
    Copyright: Held by Publisher
    Reprints: Available; 50 free
Disposition of manuscript:
    Query letter: Preferrable
    Receipt of manuscript acknowledged: Yes
    Decision to publish in: 6-8 weeks
    Accepted manuscript published in: 5-7 months
    Rejected manuscript returned: Yes
    Rejected manuscript criticized: Sometimes
Submit to:
    Prof. John N. Walton
    Editor
    Regional Neurological Centre
    General Hospital, Westgate Road
    Newcastle upon Tyne NE4 6BE, England
    0944 632-38811

JOURNAL OF NEUROLOGY [2403]

Springer-Verlag
175 Fifth Avenue
New York, New York 10010
    Annual rate(s): DM 148 per volume
Publisher or Sponsor: German Neurological Society,
German Society for Neurosurgery

EDITORIAL DESCRIPTION

Surveys of progress, original investigations and short communications dealing with the field of neurology
Manuscripts accepted in English

MANUSCRIPT INFORMATION

Manuscript requirements: See latest issue for style requirements. Style sheet sent on request.
    Preferred length: As required
    Number of copies to be submitted: 2
    Abstract: Yes. Articles in English should include a summary in German; articles in German should include a more detailed summary in English

Author information and reprints: Payment: Reprints only. 75 offprints
    Is simultaneous submission of article to other journals permitted: Not permitted.
    Exclusive manuscript rights between acceptance and publication: Yes
    Copyright: Held by publication.
Submit to:
    Professor Dr. M. Alter
    Chief, Neurology Services
    Veterans Administration Hospital
    54th Street and 48th Avenue South
    Minneapolis, Minnesota 55417

JOURNAL OF NEUROLOGY, NEUROSURGERY AND PSYCHIATRY [2404]

B.M.A. House
Tavistock Square
London WC1H 9JR, England
01-387 4499

First published in 1944

SUBSCRIPTION DATA

Issues and rates: Published monthly.
    Average paid circulation: Not available.
    Annual rate(s): $46.50
Publisher or Sponsor: British Medical Journal Group

EDITORIAL DESCRIPTION

Contains medical research on the brain.
Manuscripts accepted in English

MANUSCRIPT INFORMATION

Manuscript requirements: See latest issue for style requirements.
    Preferred length: None
    Number of copies to be submitted: Two
    Abstract: Yes
Author information and reprints: Payment: None.
    Is simultaneous submission of article to other journals permitted: No
    Exclusive manuscript rights between acceptance and publication: Yes
    Copyright: Held by publication.
    Reprints: Available
Disposition of manuscript:
    Query letter: No
    Receipt of manuscript acknowledged: Yes
    Decision to publish in: One month
    Accepted manuscript published in: Six months
    Rejected manuscript returned: Yes
    Rejected manuscript criticized: No
Submit to:
    The Editor
    (See address above)

JOURNAL OF NUTRITION [2405]

9650 Rockville Pike
Bethesda, Maryland 20014
(301) 530-7080

SUBSCRIPTION DATA

Issues and rates: Published monthly.
    Average paid circulation: 4,082

Annual rate(s): $35.00; Pan-Am $37.00; Foreign $39.00
Publisher or Sponsor: American Institute of Nutrition
Managing Editor: Fredric W. Hill

EDITORIAL DESCRIPTION

All phases of experimental nutrition are included in the papers published. Edited for the investigator in experimental nutrition, the journal serves an audience composed of nutritional scientists, dietitians, home economists, faculty of state universities, federal researchers, etc.
Articles per average issue: 20
Audience: Professional
Manuscripts accepted in English

MANUSCRIPT INFORMATION

Subject field(s): Nutrition
Manuscript requirements: January issue contains Instructions for Authors.
    Preferred length: None
    Number of copies to be submitted: Two
    Abstract: Yes, of 200 words or less, giving a concise description of the plan or design and giving the results and conclusions.
Author information and reprints: Payment: None.
    Is simultaneous submission of article to other journals permitted: No
    Exclusive manuscript rights between acceptance and publication: Yes
    Copyright: Held by publication.
    Reprints: Available, rates supplied with proofs.
Disposition of manuscript:
    Receipt of manuscript acknowledged: Yes
    Decision to publish in: 1 month
    Accepted manuscript published in: three months
    Rejected manuscript returned: Yes
    Rejected manuscript criticized: Yes
Submit to:
    Editor
    (See address above)
    (301) 530-7100

THE JOURNAL OF PEDIATRICS* [2406]

The C.V. Mosby Company
11830 Westline Industrial Drive
St. Louis, Missouri 63141
(314) 872-8370

SUBSCRIPTION DATA

Issues and rates: Published monthly.
    Average paid circulation: 18,461
    Annual rate(s): $17.50, Foreign $22.25

EDITORIAL DESCRIPTION

An independent clinical publication devoted to the diseases of infants and children. Edited to serve the pediatric specialist and resident, it additionally reaches those in allied medical practice. Its original articles encompass various phases of pediatric therapy.

Medicine (general)

MANUSCRIPT INFORMATION

Manuscript requirements: See latest issue for style requirements.
Number of copies to be submitted: 1 original, 1 copy

Author information and reprints: Payment: None.
Is simultaneous submission of article to other journals permitted: No
Exclusive manuscript rights between acceptance and publication: Yes
Copyright: Held by publication.
Reprints: Available at cost

Disposition of manuscript:
Receipt of manuscript acknowledged: Yes
Rejected manuscript returned: Yes

Submit to:
Waldo E. Nelson
Editor
3300 Henry Avenue
Philadelphia, Pennsylvania 19129

JOURNAL OF PEDIATRICS [2407]

Springer-Verlag
175 Fifth Avenue
New York, New York 10010

First published in 1910

SUBSCRIPTION DATA
Annual rate(s): DM 128 per volume
Managing Editor: Professor Dr. H. Ewerbeck

EDITORIAL DESCRIPTION
Publishes papers on all aspects of the field of pediatrics and related fields
Manuscripts accepted in English

MANUSCRIPT INFORMATION
Manuscript requirements: See latest issue for style requirements.
Preferred length: As required
Number of copies to be submitted: 3
Abstract: Yes. A short summary emphasizing the main points covered as well as a summary in English for articles written in German.
Author information and reprints: Payment: Reprints only. 50 offprints
Is simultaneous submission of article to other journals permitted: Not permitted.
Exclusive manuscript rights between acceptance and publication: Yes
Copyright: Held by publication.
Reprints: Available at cost.
Submit to:
Professor Dr. H. Ewerbeck
Editor
Kinderkrankenhaus der Stadt Köln
Amsterdamerstrasse 59
D-5000 Köln-Riehl, Federal Republic of Germany

JOURNAL OF PHARMACEUTICAL SCIENCES [2408]

2215 Constitution Avenue, N.W.
Washington, D.C. 20037
(202) 628-4410

SUBSCRIPTION DATA
Issues and rates: Published monthly.
Average paid circulation: 12,384
Annual rate(s): Institutions $50; Individuals $30.00
Publisher or Sponsor: American Pharmaceutical Association
Managing Editor: Edward G. Feldmann

EDITORIAL DESCRIPTION
Contains review articles, original research articles, articles on product and method development, communications, book reviews, and an editorial.
Articles per average issue: 45-50
Audience: Professional
Manuscripts accepted in English

MANUSCRIPT INFORMATION
Subject field(s): Pharmacy, pharmacology, pharmacognosy, pharmaceutical chemistry, pharmaceutical analysis, pharmacokinetics, pharmaceutical technology, biopharmaceutics
Manuscript requirements: Style sheet sent on request.
Preferred length: 10-15 pages
Number of copies to be submitted: Two
Abstract: Yes
Author information and reprints: Payment: By author to publication. $50.00 per page.
Is simultaneous submission of article to other journals permitted: No
Exclusive manuscript rights between acceptance and publication: Yes
Copyright: Held by publication.
Reprints: Available to author
Disposition of manuscript:
Query letter: No
Receipt of manuscript acknowledged: Yes
Decision to publish in: 1-3 months
Accepted manuscript published in: 3-4 months
Rejected manuscript returned: Yes
Rejected manuscript criticized: Yes
Submit to:
Mary H. Ferguson
Editor
(See address above)

JOURNAL OF PHARMACOLOGY AND EXPERIMENTAL THERAPEUTICS [2409]

428 East Preston Street
Baltimore, Maryland 21202
(301) 528-4116

First published in 1909

SUBSCRIPTION DATA
Issues and rates: Published monthly.
Average paid circulation: 3000
Annual rate(s): $70.00; Foreign $73.25
Publisher or Sponsor: American Society for Pharmacology and Experimental Therapeutics

EDITORIAL DESCRIPTION
Contains original papers dealing with any aspect of interaction of chemicals with biological systems.

Articles per average issue: 25
Manuscripts accepted in English

MANUSCRIPT INFORMATION
Manuscript requirements: Style sheet sent on request.
Preferred length: None
Number of copies to be submitted: Two
Abstract: Yes
Author information and reprints: Payment: By author to publication. $15.00 per page.
Is simultaneous submission of article to other journals permitted: No
Exclusive manuscript rights between acceptance and publication: Yes
Copyright: Held by publication.
Reprints: Available
Disposition of manuscript:
Receipt of manuscript acknowledged: Yes
Decision to publish in: 6-8 weeks
Accepted manuscript published in: 4 months
Rejected manuscript returned: Yes
Rejected manuscript criticized: Sometimes
Submit to:
Marion deV. Cotten
Editor
Route 3, Box 229
Sylvania, Georgia 30467
(912) 863-4343

JOURNAL OF PSYCHOSOMATIC RESEARCH [2410]

Pergamon Press, Inc.
Fairview Park
Elmsford, New York 10523
(914) 592-7700

First published in 1956

SUBSCRIPTION DATA
Issues and rates: Published bi-monthly.
Annual rate(s): $25.00; Institutions $50.00

EDITORIAL DESCRIPTION
Contains original papers of work in the field of psychosomatic medicine and related disciplines.
Articles per average issue: 5-7
Audience: Professional, academic
Manuscripts accepted in English, French, German

MANUSCRIPT INFORMATION
Manuscript requirements: See latest issue for style requirements.
Preferred length: None
Number of copies to be submitted: 2, double-spaced
Abstract: Yes. In English for all papers.
Author information and reprints: Payment: Reprints only. 50 reprints
Is simultaneous submission of article to other journals permitted: Not permitted.
Exclusive manuscript rights between acceptance and publication: Yes
Copyright: Held by publication.
Reprints: Available at cost.

Disposition of manuscript:
  Query letter: Not necessary.
  Receipt of manuscript acknowledged: Yes
  Decision to publish in: 4 weeks
  Accepted manuscript published in: 5 months
  Rejected manuscript returned: Yes, if return postage is supplied by author.
  Rejected manuscript criticized: Reasons for rejections only
Submit to:
  Dr. Denis Leigh
  Editor-in-Chief
  The Maudsley Hospital
  Denmark Hill
  London SE5, England

THE JOURNAL OF SCHOOL HEALTH   [2411]

American School Health Association
7263 State Road 43, P. O. Box 708
Kent, Ohio 44240
(216) 678-1601

First published in 1931

SUBSCRIPTION DATA
Issues and rates: Published monthly.
  Average paid circulation: 12,000
  Annual rate(s): $20.00, Foreign $22.00;
  Institutions $20.00; Students $15.00;
  Foreign institutions $22.00
Publisher or Sponsor: American School Health Association

EDITORIAL DESCRIPTION
  Publishes articles on timely subjects of interest to school health professionals, school physicians, school nurses, health educators, psychologists and other members of the school health team.
Articles per average issue: 10
Audience: Professional, academic
  Manuscripts accepted in English

MANUSCRIPT INFORMATION
Subject field(s): Alcohol, health careers, college health, community health, dental education, drug education, environmental health, exceptional children, family life, sex education, first aid and society, growth and development, learning disabilities, mental health, nutrition, philosophy, smoking, vision, etc.
Manuscript requirements: Style sheet sent on request. AMA
  Preferred length: 10 pages
  Number of copies to be submitted: 2
  Abstract: Not necessary.
Author information and reprints: Payment:
  Reprints only. 2 copies of issue
  Is simultaneous submission of article to other journals permitted: Not permitted.
  Exclusive manuscript rights between acceptance and publication: Yes
  Copyright: Held by publication.
Disposition of manuscript:
  Query letter: Not necessary, but advisable.
  Receipt of manuscript acknowledged: Yes
  Decision to publish in: 1 month

Accepted manuscript published in: 3 months
  Rejected manuscript returned: Yes, if return postage is supplied by author.
  Rejected manuscript criticized: Reasons for rejections only
Submit to:
  Glenn R. Knotts
  Editor
  (See address above)

JOURNAL OF SPEECH AND HEARING DISORDERS   [2412]

9030 Old Georgetown Road
Washington, D.C. 20014
(301) 530-3400

Previously entitled *Journal of Speech Disorders*

SUBSCRIPTION DATA
Issues and rates: Published quarterly.
  Average paid circulation: 28,000
  Annual rate(s): $28.00; Foreign $31.00
Publisher or Sponsor: American Speech and Hearing Association

EDITORIAL DESCRIPTION
  Publishes case studies of disorders of speech, language and hearing.
Audience: Professional
  Manuscripts accepted in English

MANUSCRIPT INFORMATION
Manuscript requirements: Chicago; see also latest issue of publication
  Preferred length: 10 to 20 pages
  Number of copies to be submitted: Three
  Abstract: Yes
Author information and reprints: Payment:
  By author to publication. $50.00 per page.
  Is simultaneous submission of article to other journals permitted: No
  Exclusive manuscript rights between acceptance and publication: Yes
  Copyright: Held by author.
  Reprints: Available
Disposition of manuscript:
  Query letter: No
  Receipt of manuscript acknowledged: Yes
  Decision to publish in: Varies
  Accepted manuscript published in: Varies
  Rejected manuscript returned: Yes
  Rejected manuscript criticized: Yes
Submit to:
  Ralph L. Shelton, Jr.
  Editor
  Department of Speech and Hearing Sciences
  Building 25
  University of Arizona
  Tucson, Arizona 84721

JOURNAL OF SPEECH AND HEARING RESEARCH   [2413]

9030 Old Georgetown Road
Washington, D.C. 20014
(301) 530-3400

SUBSCRIPTION DATA
Issues and rates: Published quarterly.
  Average paid circulation: 25,000
  Annual rate(s): $28.00; Foreign $31.00
Publisher or Sponsor: American Speech and Hearing Association

EDITORIAL DESCRIPTION
  Publishes research in the field of speech and hearing.
Articles per average issue: Varies
Audience: Professional
  Manuscripts accepted in English

MANUSCRIPT INFORMATION
Manuscript requirements: Chicago
  Preferred length: 10-20 pages
  Number of copies to be submitted: Three
  Abstract: Yes
Author information and reprints: Payment:
  By author to publication. $50.00 per page.
  Is simultaneous submission of article to other journals permitted: No
  Exclusive manuscript rights between acceptance and publication: Yes
  Copyright: Held by author.
  Reprints: Available
Disposition of manuscript:
  Query letter: No
  Receipt of manuscript acknowledged: Yes
  Decision to publish in: Varies
  Accepted manuscript published in: Varies
  Rejected manuscript returned: Yes
  Rejected manuscript criticized: Yes
Submit to:
  Thomas J. Hixson
  Editor
  Department of Communicative Disorders
  1975 Willow Drive
  University of Wisconsin
  Madison, Wisconsin 53706

JOURNAL OF TRAUMA   [2414]

428 East Preston Street
Baltimore, Maryland 21202
(301) 528-4116

First published in 1961

SUBSCRIPTION DATA
Issues and rates: Published monthly.
  Average paid circulation: 4,500
  Annual rate(s): $30.00; Foreign $32.60
Publisher or Sponsor: American Association for the Study of Trauma

EDITORIAL DESCRIPTION
  Contains articles on all aspects of trauma, clinical and experimental, case reports.
Articles per average issue: 12
Audience: Medical, professional
  Manuscripts accepted in English

MANUSCRIPT INFORMATION
Manuscript requirements: See latest issue for style requirements.
  Preferred length: None
  Number of copies to be submitted: Three
  Abstract: No

Medicine (general)

Author information and reprints: Payment: None.
Is simultaneous submission of article to other journals permitted: No
Exclusive manuscript rights between acceptance and publication: Yes
Copyright: Held by publication.
Reprints: Available at cost
Disposition of manuscript:
Query letter: No
Receipt of manuscript acknowledged: Yes
Decision to publish in: 6 weeks
Accepted manuscript published in: 4-6 months
Rejected manuscript returned: Yes
Rejected manuscript criticized: Sometimes
Submit to:
William T. Fitts, Jr.
Editor
Hospital of the University of Pennsylvania
3400 Spruce Street
Philadelphia, Pennsylvania 19104
(215) 662-2030

JOURNAL OF UROLOGY   [2415]
428 East Preston Street
Baltimore, Maryland 21202
(301) 528-4116

First published in 1917

SUBSCRIPTION DATA
Issues and rates: Published monthly.
Average paid circulation: 12,800
Annual rate(s): $40.00; Foreign $43.75
Publisher or Sponsor: American Urological Association

EDITORIAL DESCRIPTION
Contains articles on all aspects of urology and genito-urinary diseases.
Articles per average issue: 38
Manuscripts accepted in English

MANUSCRIPT INFORMATION
Manuscript requirements: Style sheet sent on request.
Preferred length: None
Number of copies to be submitted: Two
Abstract: No
Author information and reprints: Payment: None.
Is simultaneous submission of article to other journals permitted: No
Exclusive manuscript rights between acceptance and publication: Yes
Copyright: Held by publication.
Reprints: Available
Disposition of manuscript:
Query letter: No
Receipt of manuscript acknowledged: Yes
Decision to publish in: 6-8 weeks
Accepted manuscript published in: 4-5 months
Rejected manuscript returned: Yes
Rejected manuscript criticized: Sometimes
Submit to:
Hugh J. Jewett, M.D.
Editor

1120 North Charles Street
Baltimore, Maryland 21201
(301) 539-8138

JOURNAL OF VIROLOGY   [2416]
1913 I Street, N. W.
Washington, D. C. 20006
(202) 833-9416

First published in 1967

SUBSCRIPTION DATA
Issues and rates: Published monthly.
Average paid circulation: 5,500
Annual rate(s): $60.00; Foreign $61.00; Institutions $60.00
Publisher or Sponsor: American Society for Microbiology
Managing Editor: Robert A. Day

EDITORIAL DESCRIPTION
Devoted to the dissemination of fundamental knowledge concerning viruses of bacteria, plants and animals, it contains reports of original research in all areas of basic virology.
Articles per average issue: 33
Audience: Virologists
Manuscripts accepted in English

MANUSCRIPT INFORMATION
Subject field(s): Virology, biochemistry, biophysics, genetics, immunology, morphology, and physiology
Manuscript requirements: See latest issue for style requirements.
Preferred length: None
Number of copies to be submitted: 2
Abstract: Yes.
Author information and reprints: Payment: None.
Is simultaneous submission of article to other journals permitted: Not permitted.
Exclusive manuscript rights between acceptance and publication: Yes
Copyright: Held by the Society
Reprints: Available at cost.
Disposition of manuscript:
Query letter: Not necessary.
Receipt of manuscript acknowledged: Yes
Decision to publish in: 3 months
Accepted manuscript published in: 4 months
Rejected manuscript returned: Yes, with return postage paid by publication.
Rejected manuscript criticized: Yes
Submit to:
Robert A. Day
Managing Editor
(See address above)

KOBE JOURNAL OF MEDICAL SCIENCES   [2417]
Kobe University School of Medicine
Kusunoki-cho, Ikuta-ku
Kobe, Japan
(078) 341-7451 Ext. 240

First published in 1955

SUBSCRIPTION DATA
Issues and rates: Published quarterly.
Average paid circulation: 650 controlled
Publisher or Sponsor: Kobe University School of Medicine
Managing Editor: Shosuke Okamoto

EDITORIAL DESCRIPTION
Contains original papers in medical sciences. Edited to facilitate the rapid information exchange of medical sciences beyond disciplines, and to open the door for the younger workers to participate in the global medical activities.
Articles per average issue: 3-5
Audience: Medical researchers, practitioners, students
Manuscripts accepted in English, German, French, Japanese

MANUSCRIPT INFORMATION
Subject field(s): Medical sciences
Manuscript requirements: See latest issue for style requirements.
Preferred length: 14 pages
Number of copies to be submitted: One
Author information and reprints: Payment: By author to publication. Page charge over 14 pages. 4,000 yen per page.
Is simultaneous submission of article to other journals permitted: No
Exclusive manuscript rights between acceptance and publication: Yes
Copyright: Held by publication.
Reprints: Available, 2.50 Yen per page
Disposition of manuscript:
Query letter: No
Receipt of manuscript acknowledged: Yes
Decision to publish in: One month
Accepted manuscript published in: Three months
Rejected manuscript returned: No
Rejected manuscript criticized: No
Submit to:
Shosuke Okamoto
Executive Editor
(See address above)

LA VIE MEDICALE AU CANADA FRANÇAIS   [2418]
Faculty of Medicine
Laval University
Quebec G1K 7P4, Canada
(418) 656-2944

Previously entitled *Laval médicale*

First published in 1972

SUBSCRIPTION DATA
Issues and rates: Published monthly.
Average paid circulation: 7,500
Annual rate(s): $20.00
Managing Editor: George A. Bergeron

EDITORIAL DESCRIPTION
Contains medical papers, review, analysis, medical news. The journal is oriented toward the medical practitioners, either general or specialized. It also deals with social aspects of medicine as well as that of medical education.
Articles per average issue: 14

Audience: Professional
Manuscripts accepted in French

MANUSCRIPT INFORMATION
Subject field(s): Medicine, surgery, obstetrics, gynecology, paediatrics, psychiatry, social medicine, medical education, history of medicine
Manuscript requirements: See latest issue for style requirements.
  Preferred length: 2,500 to 8000 words; 3 to 9 pages
  Number of copies to be submitted: Two
  Abstract: Yes
Author information and reprints: Payment: Reprints only. 25 reprints supplied to author.
  Is simultaneous submission of article to other journals permitted: No
  Exclusive manuscript rights between acceptance and publication: Yes
  Copyright: Held by publication.
  Reprints: Available, cost quotation upon request only.
Additional information: A reasonable number of figures and tables are published free of charge to the author.
Disposition of manuscript:
  Query letter: No
  Receipt of manuscript acknowledged: Yes
  Decision to publish in: 1 to 2 months
  Accepted manuscript published in: 2 to 3 months
  Rejected manuscript returned: No
  Rejected manuscript criticized: Yes
Submit to:
  George A. Bergeron
  Editor-in-Chief
  (See address above)
  (418) 656-2400

LABORATORY INVESTIGATION [2419]
A Journal of Pathology
428 East Preston Street
Baltimore, Maryland 21202
(301) 528-4116

First published in 1952

SUBSCRIPTION DATA
Issues and rates: Published monthly.
  Average paid circulation: 4,500
  Annual rate(s): $40.00, Foreign $43.75
Publisher or Sponsor: International Academy of Pathology, U.S.-Canada Division

EDITORIAL DESCRIPTION
  Features prompt publication of significant advances in research in pathology. Contains original research, brief communications, review articles.
Articles per average issue: 14
  Manuscripts accepted in English

MANUSCRIPT INFORMATION
Manuscript requirements: Style sheet sent on request.
  Preferred length: None
  Number of copies to be submitted: Two
  Abstract: Yes

Author information and reprints: Payment: By author to publication. $80.00 per page. Illustrations in excess of 1 page.
  Is simultaneous submission of article to other journals permitted: No
  Exclusive manuscript rights between acceptance and publication: Yes
  Copyright: Held by publication.
  Reprints: Available
Disposition of manuscript:
  Query letter: No
  Receipt of manuscript acknowledged: Yes
  Decision to publish in: 6 weeks
  Accepted manuscript published in: 3-5 months
  Rejected manuscript returned: Yes
  Rejected manuscript criticized: Sometimes
Submit to:
  Nathan Kaufman, M.D.
  Editor
  Richardson Laboratory
  Queen's University
  Kingston, Ontario Canada
  (613) 547-6923

LABORATORY MANAGEMENT [2420]
750 Third Avenue
New York, New York 10017
(212) 697-8300 ext. 250, 251

First published in 1962

SUBSCRIPTION DATA
Issues and rates: Published monthly.
  Average paid circulation: 30,000 controlled
  Annual rate(s): $8.00; Foreign $11.50
Managing Editor: Bennett Zucker

EDITORIAL DESCRIPTION
  Serves directors and department supervisors of clinical laboratories. Subject matter encompasses a broad range of management topics, including personnel and fiscal management, new clinical methodologies, laboratory design, marketing information.
Articles per average issue: 6-8
Audience: Directors and department supervisors in hospital and independent clinical laboratories.
  Manuscripts accepted in English

MANUSCRIPT INFORMATION
Manuscript requirements: No specific style guide.
  Preferred length: 8-12 pages
  Number of copies to be submitted: Two
  Abstract: Not necessary.
Author information and reprints: Payment: Honorarium of $100.00 per article
  Is simultaneous submission of article to other journals permitted: Not permitted.
  Exclusive manuscript rights between acceptance and publication: Yes
  Copyright: Held by publication.
  Reprints: Available at cost. Depends on length
Disposition of manuscript:
  Query letter: Not necessary.

  Receipt of manuscript acknowledged: Yes
  Decision to publish in: 1-2 weeks
  Accepted manuscript published in: 3 months
  Rejected manuscript returned: Yes, if return postage is supplied by author.
  Rejected manuscript criticized: No
Submit to:
  Bennett Zucker
  Associate Editor
  (See address above)

LABORATORY MEDICINE [2421]
2100 West Harrison Street
Chicago, Illinois 60612
(312) 738-1336 ext. 124

First published in 1960

SUBSCRIPTION DATA
Issues and rates: Published monthly.
  Average paid circulation: 93,000
  Annual rate(s): $2.40, Foreign $10.00
Publisher or Sponsor: American Society of Clinical Pathologists
Managing Editor: John L. Normoyle

EDITORIAL DESCRIPTION
  Covers trends, new developments, personalities, new techniques, equipment and practices in the clinical laboratory, news of major Society meetings, continuing educational materials. Emphasis is on practical material to help readers do better job in their profession, rather than theoretical or research. Stresses the practical that will help readers in their day-to-day professional activities, trends, new techniques, etc.
Articles per average issue: 7
  Manuscripts accepted in English only

MANUSCRIPT INFORMATION
Subject field(s): New techniques, new developments, trends, outstanding personalities, continuing education, laboratory management, laboratory design, outstanding cases in forensic medicine.
Manuscript requirements: Style sheet sent on request.
  Preferred length: 1000-5,000 words
  Number of copies to be submitted: Two
  Abstract: No
Author information and reprints: Payment: No payment for technical papers. Payment for general articles, usually on assignment, depending on nature and length of article.
  Is simultaneous submission of article to other journals permitted: No
  Exclusive manuscript rights between acceptance and publication: Yes
  Copyright: Held by publication.
  Reprints: Available; cost negotiated with publisher.
Additional information: Typewritten, double-spaced.
Disposition of manuscript:
  Query letter: No
  Receipt of manuscript acknowledged: Yes
  Decision to publish in: 4-6 weeks
  Accepted manuscript published in: 3-4 months

Medicine (general)

Rejected manuscript returned: Yes
Rejected manuscript criticized: No
Submit to:
Managing Editor
(See address above)

SPECIAL STIPULATIONS
Technical articles generally accepted only from pathologists, medical technologists and technicians. General articles occasionally purchased from free-lance writers, but are ordinarily assigned.

THE LANCET*   [2422]
7 Adam Street
London WC2N 6AD, England
(01) 836-7228

SUBSCRIPTION DATA
Issues and rates: Published weekly.
Average paid circulation: 50,000
Annual rate(s): £8.00, Foreign $18.50

EDITORIAL DESCRIPTION
Contains signed articles on medical research, hypotheses, methods and devices, preliminary communications, general articles and book reviews.

MANUSCRIPT INFORMATION
Subject field(s): Medicine in all its aspects, scientific and social
Manuscript requirements: Style sheet sent on request.
Preferred length: Varies
Number of copies to be submitted: One
Author information and reprints: Payment: None.
Is simultaneous submission of article to other journals permitted: No
Exclusive manuscript rights between acceptance and publication: Yes
Copyright: Held by publication.
Reprints: Available, cost estimates supplied
Disposition of manuscript:
Receipt of manuscript acknowledged: Yes
Decision to publish in: 1-2 weeks
Accepted manuscript published in: 4-6 weeks
Rejected manuscript returned: Yes
Rejected manuscript criticized: Occasionally
Submit to:
The Editor
(See address above)

THE LARYNGOSCOPE*   [2423]
222 Pine Lake Road
Collinsville, Illinois 62234
(618) 344-8383

SUBSCRIPTION DATA
Issues and rates: Published monthly.
Annual rate(s): $28.00, Foreign $30.00

EDITORIAL DESCRIPTION
Contains clinical and research contributions in otolaryngology, broncho-esophagology, communicative disorders, maxillofacial surgery, head and

neck surgery and facial and plastic reconstructive surgery.

MANUSCRIPT INFORMATION
Manuscript requirements: See latest issue for style requirements.
Preferred length: 16 pages
Number of copies to be submitted: Three
Author information and reprints: Payment: By author to publication. For extra illustrations and extra bibliographical references.
Is simultaneous submission of article to other journals permitted: No
Exclusive manuscript rights between acceptance and publication: Yes
Copyright: Held by publication.
Reprints: Available
Disposition of manuscript:
Receipt of manuscript acknowledged: Yes
Decision to publish in: 30-60 days
Accepted manuscript published in: 6-9 months
Rejected manuscript returned: Yes
Rejected manuscript criticized: Yes
Submit to:
Pearl E. Lutz
Managing Editor
(See address above)

MARYLAND STATE
MEDICAL JOURNAL   [2424]
1211 Cathedral Street
Baltimore, Maryland 21201
(301) 539-0872

SUBSCRIPTION DATA
Issues and rates: Published monthly.
Average paid circulation: 5,400
Annual rate(s): $8, Foreign $10
Publisher or Sponsor: Medical and Chirurgical Faculty of the State of Maryland

EDITORIAL DESCRIPTION
Official organ of the state medical society; socioeconomic, society news, scientific and general medical interest articles.
Articles per average issue: 8-10
Audience: Professional
Manuscripts accepted in English

MANUSCRIPT INFORMATION
Subject field(s): Medical scientific, medical general/local
Manuscript requirements: AMA
Preferred length: 500 to 2500 words
Number of copies to be submitted: Two
Abstract: Yes
Author information and reprints: Payment: Reprints only. 100 Reprints and 1 copy of journal
Is simultaneous submission of article to other journals permitted: No
Exclusive manuscript rights between acceptance and publication: Yes
Copyright: Held by author and publication
Reprints: Few available at cost
Disposition of manuscript:
Query letter: No
Receipt of manuscript acknowledged: Yes

Decision to publish in: 1 month
Accepted manuscript published in: 6 months
Rejected manuscript returned: Yes
Rejected manuscript criticized: No
Submit to:
Blaine Taylor
Managing Editor
(See address above)

MEDICAL ASSOCIATION
OF GEORGIA. JOURNAL   [2425]
938 Peachtree Street, N. E.
Atlanta, Georgia 30309
(404) 876-7535

First published in 1911

SUBSCRIPTION DATA
Issues and rates: Published monthly.
Average paid circulation: 4,200
Annual rate(s): $7.00; Foreign $8.00
Publisher or Sponsor: The Medical Association of Georgia
Managing Editor: Kathy Morse

EDITORIAL DESCRIPTION
Scientific and special articles on the practice of medicine.
Articles per average issue: 3-4
Audience: Member physicians in the state of Georgia
Manuscripts accepted in English only

MANUSCRIPT INFORMATION
Subject field(s): Medicine: office practice, research, government interference, activities of the association and its members
Manuscript requirements: See latest issue for style requirements. Style sheet sent on request.
Preferred length: Under 3,000 words
Number of copies to be submitted: 2
Abstract: Not necessary.
Author information and reprints: Payment: None.
Is simultaneous submission of article to other journals permitted: Permitted, but not encouraged.
Exclusive manuscript rights between acceptance and publication: Yes
Copyright: Held by publication.
Reprints: Available at cost. Rates available upon publication
Disposition of manuscript:
Query letter: Not necessary.
Receipt of manuscript acknowledged: Yes
Decision to publish in: 1-3 months
Accepted manuscript published in: 6-12 months
Rejected manuscript returned: Yes, with return postage paid by publication.
Rejected manuscript criticized: Sometimes
Submit to:
Edgar Woody, Jr., M. D.
Editor
(See address above)

MEDICAL BIOLOGY [2426]

Runeberginkatu 47 A
00260 Helsinki 26, Finland

Previously entitled *Annales Medicinae Experimentalis et Biologiae Fenniae*

SUBSCRIPTION DATA

Issues and rates: Published semi-monthly.
Average paid circulation: 1,100
Annual rate(s): $25.00
Publisher or Sponsor: Finnish Medical Society Duodecim
Managing Editor: T. Hovi

EDITORIAL DESCRIPTION

Publishes original articles and reviews on experimental medicine.
Articles per average issue: 10
Manuscripts accepted in English

MANUSCRIPT INFORMATION

Subject field(s): Pharmacology, immunology, bacteriology, virology, endocrinology, anatomy, experimental pathology
Manuscript requirements: See latest issue for style requirements.
Preferred length: 3-8 pages
Number of copies to be submitted: 3
Author information and reprints: Payment: None.
Is simultaneous submission of article to other journals permitted: No
Exclusive manuscript rights between acceptance and publication: Yes
Copyright: Held by author.
Reprints: Available
Disposition of manuscript:
Receipt of manuscript acknowledged: Yes
Decision to publish in: 1-2 months
Accepted manuscript published in: 3-8 months
Rejected manuscript returned: Yes
Rejected manuscript criticized: Yes
Submit to:
K. Penttinen
Editor-in-Chief
(See address above)

MEDICAL HISTORY [2427]

Wellcome Institute for the History of Medicine
183 Euston Road
London NW1 2BP, England
01-387-4477

First published in 1956

SUBSCRIPTION DATA

Issues and rates: Published quarterly.
Average paid circulation: 1300
Annual rate(s): £7.00; Foreign $20.00
Publisher or Sponsor: Wellcome Institute for the History of Medicine

EDITORIAL DESCRIPTION

Contains articles devoted to the history and bibliography of medicine and the related sciences.
Articles per average issue: 7
Audience: Physicians, scientists, historians
Manuscripts accepted in English

MANUSCRIPT INFORMATION

Manuscript requirements: No specific style guide.
Number of copies to be submitted: 2
Abstract: No
Is simultaneous submission of article to other journals permitted: No
Exclusive manuscript rights between acceptance and publication: Yes
Copyright: Held by publication.
Reprints: Available
Disposition of manuscript:
Query letter: No
Receipt of manuscript acknowledged: Yes
Decision to publish in: 6 weeks
Accepted manuscript published in: 1-2 years
Rejected manuscript returned: Yes
Rejected manuscript criticized: No
Submit to:
Edwin Clarke, M.D.
Editor
(See address above)

MEDICAL MICROBIOLOGY AND IMMUNOLOGY [2428]

Springer-Verlag
175 Fifth Avenue
New York, New York 10010

SUBSCRIPTION DATA

Annual rate(s): DM 120 per volume
Managing Editor: Professor Dr. R. Rott

EDITORIAL DESCRIPTION

Publishes original papers in the field of virology, bacteriology, immunology and epidemiology.
Manuscripts accepted in English, German

MANUSCRIPT INFORMATION

Subject field(s): Pathogenic mechanisms as underlying causes of origin, treatment, and prophylaxis of infectious diseases. Commitment to problems of basic research in biology is secondary.
Manuscript requirements: See latest issue for style requirements. Style sheet sent on request.
Preferred length: As required
Number of copies to be submitted: 2
Abstract: Yes. An informative abstract in English
Author information and reprints: Payment: Reprints only. 50 offprints
Is simultaneous submission of article to other journals permitted: Not permitted.
Exclusive manuscript rights between acceptance and publication: Yes
Copyright: Held by publication.
Submit to:
Professor Dr. R. Rott
Editor
Institut für Virologie der Justus-Liebig Universität
Schubertstrasse 1
D-6300 Giessen, Federal Republic of Germany

MEDICAL OPINION [2429]

575 Madison Avenue
New York, New York 10010
(212) 751-2350

Previously entitled *Medical Opinion & Review*

SUBSCRIPTION DATA

Issues and rates: Published monthly.
Average paid circulation: 165,000 controlled
Annual rate(s): $14.00

EDITORIAL DESCRIPTION

Contains articles of interest to practicing physicians on medical issues, clinical and social.
Articles per average issue: 5
Audience: Primary care physicians
Manuscripts accepted in English

MANUSCRIPT INFORMATION

Subject field(s): Medicine
Manuscript requirements: See latest issue for style requirements.
Preferred length: 2000-3000 words; 8-12 pages
Number of copies to be submitted: Two
Abstract:
Author information and reprints: Payment: By publication to author. $100-$350 per article.
Is simultaneous submission of article to other journals permitted: No
Exclusive manuscript rights between acceptance and publication: Yes
Copyright: Held by publication.
Reprints: Not available.
Disposition of manuscript:
Query letter: Not necessary, but advisable.
Receipt of manuscript acknowledged: Yes
Decision to publish in: 4-6 weeks
Accepted manuscript published in: 1-3 months
Rejected manuscript returned: Yes, if return postage is supplied by author.
Rejected manuscript criticized: No
Submit to:
Richard E. Luna
Managing Editor
(See address above)

MEDICAL PROGRESS THROUGH TECHNOLOGY [2430]

Springer-Verlag
175 Fifth Avenue
New York, New York 10010
Annual rate(s): DM 120 per volume
Managing Editor: C. D. Ray

EDITORIAL DESCRIPTION

Papers dealing with the practical applications of advanced technology and modern methods of management and systems analysis important to problem areas of health care.
Manuscripts accepted in English, German

Medicine (general)

MANUSCRIPT INFORMATION

Subject field(s): Reviews of activites in major clinics and hospitals, instructional material, bibliographical listings, reviews of international meetings, use of the latest technical advances in teaching methods for medical instruction

Preferred length: As required

Number of copies to be submitted: 2

Abstract: Yes. Articles must be accompanied by an abstract of between 75 and 150 words followed by a list of about ten key words for indexing.

Author information and reprints: Payment: Reprints only. 75 offprints

Is simultaneous submission of article to other journals permitted: Not permitted.

Exclusive manuscript rights between acceptance and publication: Yes

Copyright: Held by publication.

Submit to:
Charles D. Ray
Co-Editor-in-Chief
Medtronic, Inc.
3055 Old Highway Eight
Minneapolis, Minnesota 55418

MEDICAL RESEARCH ENGINEERING [2431]

P.O. Box 542, Ramapo College
Mahwah, New Jersey 07430
(201) 256-8698

Previously entitled *American Journal of Medical Electronics*

First published in 1961

SUBSCRIPTION DATA

Issues and rates: Published semi-monthly.
Average paid circulation: 2,000; 15,000 controlled
Annual rate(s): $30.00; Foreign $33.00
Managing Editor: Carl Berkley

EDITORIAL DESCRIPTION

Contains articles on scientific techniques applied to medicine, research and engineering,
Articles per average issue: 6
Audience: Professional
Manuscripts accepted in English

MANUSCRIPT INFORMATION

Subject field(s): Medicine, research engineering, diagnosis, therapy, instrumentation, computers, prognosis, surgery, artificial organs

Manuscript requirements: Style sheet sent on request.
Preferred length: None
Number of copies to be submitted: Three
Abstract: Yes, of about 100 words

Author information and reprints: Payment: None. Six copies of issue in which articles appears.
Is simultaneous submission of article to other journals permitted: No
Exclusive manuscript rights between acceptance and publication: Yes
Copyright: Held by publication.
Reprints: Available

Disposition of manuscript:
Query letter: No
Receipt of manuscript acknowledged: Yes
Decision to publish in: 4 weeks
Accepted manuscript published in: 2 months
Rejected manuscript returned: Yes
Rejected manuscript criticized: Yes

Submit to:
Carl Berkley
Editor
(See address above)

MEDICAL SOCIETY OF NEW JERSEY. JOURNAL [2432]

P. O. Box 904
Trenton, New Jersey 08605
(609) 394-3154

First published in 1904

SUBSCRIPTION DATA

Issues and rates: Published monthly.
Average paid circulation: 9,000
Annual rate(s): $10.00; Pan-Am $12.50; Foreign $12.50
Publisher or Sponsor: The Medical Society of New Jersey
Managing Editor: Marjorie D. Treptow

EDITORIAL DESCRIPTION

Scientific and socio-economic items geared to the medical profession; includes information on Society activities
Articles per average issue: 6-8
Audience: Medical professional
Manuscripts accepted in English

MANUSCRIPT INFORMATION

Manuscript requirements: See latest issue for style requirements.
Preferred length: As required
Number of copies to be submitted: Original and 1 copy
Abstract: Yes. Of approximately 50 words

Author information and reprints: Payment: None.
Is simultaneous submission of article to other journals permitted: Not permitted.
Exclusive manuscript rights between acceptance and publication: Yes
Copyright: Held by publication.
Reprints: Available at no cost. 250

Disposition of manuscript:
Query letter: Not necessary.
Receipt of manuscript acknowledged: Yes
Decision to publish in: 1 month
Accepted manuscript published in: 3-6 months
Rejected manuscript returned: Reasons for rejections only

Submit to:
Arthur Krosnick, M. D.;
Marjorie D. Treptow
Editors
(See address above)

MEDICINE [2433]

Analytical Reviews of Internal Medicine, Dermatology, Neurology, Pediatrics and Psychiatry
428 East Preston Street
Baltimore, Maryland 21202
(301) 528-4116

First published in 1922

SUBSCRIPTION DATA

Issues and rates: Published bi-monthly.
Average paid circulation: 6,800
Annual rate(s): $12.00, Foreign $13.20
Managing Editor: A. McGehee Harvey

EDITORIAL DESCRIPTION

Contains review articles with more complete development than in most journals.
Articles per average issue: 3
Manuscripts accepted in English

MANUSCRIPT INFORMATION

Manuscript requirements: Style sheet sent on request.
Preferred length: None
Number of copies to be submitted: Two
Abstract: No

Author information and reprints: Payment: None.
Is simultaneous submission of article to other journals permitted: No
Exclusive manuscript rights between acceptance and publication: Yes
Copyright: Held by publication.
Reprints: Available

Disposition of manuscript:
Query letter: No
Receipt of manuscript acknowledged: Yes
Decision to publish in: 6-8 weeks
Accepted manuscript published in: 5-6 months
Rejected manuscript returned: Yes
Rejected manuscript criticized: Sometimes

Submit to:
A. McGehee Harvey, M.D.
Editor
Johns Hopkins Hospital
Baltimore, Maryland 21205
(301) 955-3896

MEDICINE, SCIENCE AND THE LAW [2434]

The Official Journal of the British Academy of Forensic Sciences
42-44 Triangle West
Bristol BS8 1EX, England
0272-23237

First published in 1960

SUBSCRIPTION DATA

Issues and rates: Published quarterly.
Average paid circulation: 1,700
Annual rate(s): £7.50

Publisher or Sponsor: British Academy of Forensio Sciences
Managing Editor: J. Malcolm Cameron

EDITORIAL DESCRIPTION

Contains articles of a medico-legal and forensic nature; proceedings of scientific meetings of British Academy of Forensic Sciences; proceedings of British Association in Forensic Medicine.
Articles per average issue: 11
Audience: Professional
Manuscripts accepted in English

MANUSCRIPT INFORMATION

Subject field(s): Forensic medicine, forensic science, medico-legal
Manuscript requirements: HLRA; Journal abbreviations as in *World List of Scientific Periodicals*
Preferred length: As required
Number of copies to be submitted: Two
Abstract: Yes
Author information and reprints: Payment: None.
Is simultaneous submission of article to other journals permitted: No
Exclusive manuscript rights between acceptance and publication: No
Copyright: Held by the Academy
Reprints: Available, cost depends on length
Additional information: Manuscripts should be typewritten with double spacing and wide margins. References, tables, and charts should be on separate pages.
Disposition of manuscript:
Query letter: Not necessary
Receipt of manuscript acknowledged: Yes
Decision to publish in: 1-2 months
Accepted manuscript published in: 6-9 months
Rejected manuscript returned: Yes
Rejected manuscript criticized: Sometimes
Submit to:
J. Malcolm Cameron
Department of Forensic Medicine
The London Hospital Medical College
Turner Street
London E1 2AD, England
(01) 638-0368

MEDICO-LEGAL BULLETIN [2435]
9 North 14th Street
Richmond, Virginia 23219
(804) 770-3174

First published in 1952

SUBSCRIPTION DATA
Issues and rates: Published monthly.
Average paid circulation: 1300 controlled
Publisher or Sponsor: Commonwealth of Virginia, Office of the Chief Medical Examiner
Managing Editor: David K. Wiecking

EDITORIAL DESCRIPTION

Contains articles on medical jurisprudence, toxicology, forensic pathology, and other matters relating to

forensic science; matters of interest to medical examiners and forensic pathologists and the law affecting the practice of medicine and hospital patient care and treatment.
Articles per average issue: 1
Audience: Professional
Manuscripts accepted in English

MANUSCRIPT INFORMATION
Subject field(s): Forensic pathology, toxicology, medical jurisprudence, hospital law, police science, serology, forensic psychiatry, law-medicine topics
Manuscript requirements: See latest issue for style requirements.
Preferred length: 1000-1500 words; 4-6 pages
Number of copies to be submitted: Two
Abstract: No
Author information and reprints: Payment: None.
Is simultaneous submission of article to other journals permitted: No
Exclusive manuscript rights between acceptance and publication: Yes
Copyright: Held by publication.
Reprints: Available at no cost
Disposition of manuscript:
Query letter: No
Receipt of manuscript acknowledged: Yes
Decision to publish in: Two months
Accepted manuscript published in: Three months
Rejected manuscript returned: Yes
Rejected manuscript criticized: Yes
Submit to:
David K. Wiecking
Chief Medical Examiner
(See address above)

SPECIAL STIPULATIONS
Include *curriculum vitae* of the author.

MICHIGAN MEDICINE [2436]
Journal of the Michigan State Medical Society
120 West Saginaw Street
East Lansing, Michigan 48823
(517) 337-1351 ext. 65

First published in 1902

SUBSCRIPTION DATA
Issues and rates: Published monthly.
Average paid circulation: 7,215; 7,952 controlled
Annual rate(s): $9.00, Pan-Am $10.00, Foreign $11.50
Publisher or Sponsor: Michigan State Medical Society
Managing Editor: Judith Marr

EDITORIAL DESCRIPTION
Contains original scientific manuscripts, state medical society activities and policy stands, new state medical achievements, news of state's three medical schools and related health organizations, by-lined articles on medical socio-economic issues, reports of medical legislation.
Articles per average issue: 4
Audience: Physicians

Manuscripts accepted in English

MANUSCRIPT INFORMATION
Subject field(s): Medicine, medical socio-economics
Manuscript requirements: See latest issue for style requirements.
Preferred length: 8-10 pages
Number of copies to be submitted: Two
Abstract: No
Author information and reprints: Payment: None.
Is simultaneous submission of article to other journals permitted: No
Exclusive manuscript rights between acceptance and publication: Yes
Copyright: Held by publication.
Reprints: Available, cost on request
Additional information: On page one, include title, authors, degrees, academic titles, institutional credits. Illustrations should be in form of glossy prints or original sketches. References should conform to cumulative *Index Medicus*. Everything typewritten, double-spaced.
Disposition of manuscript:
Receipt of manuscript acknowledged: Yes
Decision to publish in: 2-3 months
Accepted manuscript published in: 4-6 months
Rejected manuscript returned: Yes
Rejected manuscript criticized: No
Submit to:
Publication Committee, Michigan State Medical Society
(See address above)

SPECIAL STIPULATIONS
Authors are responsible for all statements, methods and conclusions. These may or may not be in harmony with the views of the editorial staff. The Publication Committee expressly reserves the right to alter or reject any manuscript, whether solicited or not.

MILBANK MEMORIAL FUND QUARTERLY [2437]
Health and Society
Cornell Medical College
Department of Public Health
1300 York Avenue
New York, New York 10021
(212) 472-5220

First published in 1923

SUBSCRIPTION DATA
Issues and rates: Published quarterly.
Average paid circulation: 2500
Annual rate(s): Individuals $10, Institutions $15, Foreign individuals $11, Foreign institutions $15
Managing Editor: George G. Reader

EDITORIAL DESCRIPTION
A multidisciplinary journal in the field of health devoted to original research or discussion of problems and issues of interest to a broad audience of scholars and professionals.
Articles per average issue: 4
Audience: Professionals

Medicine (general)

Manuscripts accepted in English

MANUSCRIPT INFORMATION

Subject field(s): Any topic relevant to issues and problems of health

Manuscript requirements: See latest issue for style requirements.

Preferred length: 10,000 words; 40 pages maximum

Number of copies to be submitted: Three

Abstract: Yes

Author information and reprints: Payment: None.

Is simultaneous submission of article to other journals permitted: No

Exclusive manuscript rights between acceptance and publication: Yes

Copyright: Held by publication.

Reprints: Available at no cost. To Authors only

Additional information: Author identification on cover page only. Observe specific format rules published in each issue.

Disposition of manuscript:

Query letter: No

Receipt of manuscript acknowledged: Yes

Decision to publish in: 6 weeks

Accepted manuscript published in: 3 months

Rejected manuscript returned: Yes, on request

Rejected manuscript criticized: Yes

Submit to:

George G. Reader

Editor

(See address above)

MOLECULAR PHARMACOLOGY [2438]

An International Journal

Academic Press, Inc.

111 Fifth Avenue

New York, New York 10003

SUBSCRIPTION DATA

Issues and rates: 7 times per year

Annual rate(s): Institutions $58.50

EDITORIAL DESCRIPTION

Contains results of investigations that shed light on drug action or selective toxicity at the molecular level. Term "drug" defined to include chemical agents that selectively modify biological function.

MANUSCRIPT INFORMATION

Subject field(s): Biochemisty, biophysics, genetics, molecular biology to problems in pharmacology or toxicology.

Manuscript requirements:

Number of copies to be submitted: Three

Author information and reprints: Payment: By author to publication. $10.00 per page.

Is simultaneous submission of article to other journals permitted: No

Exclusive manuscript rights between acceptance and publication: Yes

Copyright: Held by publication.

Reprints: First 25 free

Additional information: "Short Communications" may be scheduled for rapid publication if subject matter is within scope of journal, and is considered of immediate importance to work of other investigators.

Disposition of manuscript:

Receipt of manuscript acknowledged: Yes

Submit to:

Steven E. Mayer

Editor

Department of Medicine

Basic Science Building

University of California

La Jolla, California 92037

NEPHRON [2439]

Arnold-Boecklin Strasse 25

CH-4011 Basel, Switzerland

061-390880

SUBSCRIPTION DATA

Issues and rates: Monthly, in 2 volumes

Average paid circulation: 1,657; 125 controlled

Annual rate(s): SFr.132.00, Foreign $54.00

EDITORIAL DESCRIPTION

Primary concern is clinical nephrology, extensive information being offered on dialysis, transplantation and new techniques. In order to be accepted for publication, all articles must be approved by at least two referees of international repute so as to assure a high standard of contents. Among the regular features offered are letters to the editors, review articles and editorials of contemporary interest.

Articles per average issue: 5

Manuscripts accepted in English

MANUSCRIPT INFORMATION

Manuscript requirements: Style sheet sent on request.

Preferred length: 8 printed pages maximum

Number of copies to be submitted: 3

Abstract: Yes, with 6 key words

Author information and reprints: Payment: None.

Is simultaneous submission of article to other journals permitted: No

Exclusive manuscript rights between acceptance and publication: Yes

Copyright: Held by publication.

Reprints: Available

Disposition of manuscript:

Query letter: No

Receipt of manuscript acknowledged: Yes

Decision to publish in: 2 months

Accepted manuscript published in: 6 months

Rejected manuscript returned: Yes

Rejected manuscript criticized: Yes

Submit to:

Editors

(See address above)

NEUROENDOCRINOLOGY [2440]

International Journal for Basic and Clinical Studies on Neuroendocrine Relationships

S. Karger AG

Arnold-Boecklin Strasse 25

CH-4011 Basel, Switzerland

061-390880

First published in 1965

SUBSCRIPTION DATA

Issues and rates: Published monthly.

Average paid circulation: 944; 42 controlled

Annual rate(s): SFr. 132.00; Foreign $54.00

Publisher or Sponsor: International Society of Neuroendocrinology

EDITORIAL DESCRIPTION

Publishes original and brief review papers on experimental and clinical studies of neuroendocrine relationships, which serve to keep clinicians and research workers informed of the latest developments in the field

Articles per average issue: 6

Manuscripts accepted in English

MANUSCRIPT INFORMATION

Manuscript requirements: Style sheet sent on request.

Preferred length: 9 printed pages including figures

Number of copies to be submitted: 2

Abstract: Yes, with a short title and 9 key words.

Author information and reprints: Payment: Reprints only.

Is simultaneous submission of article to other journals permitted: No

Exclusive manuscript rights between acceptance and publication: Yes

Copyright: Held by publication.

Reprints: Available

Additional information: Short communications should not exceed 5 double-spaced typescript pages.

Disposition of manuscript:

Query letter: No

Receipt of manuscript acknowledged: Yes

Decision to publish in: 1 month

Accepted manuscript published in: 5 months

Rejected manuscript returned: Yes

Rejected manuscript criticized: No

Submit to:

Dr. K. M. Knigge

Editor

Department of Anatomy

University of Rochester

School of Medicine and Dentistry

Rochester, New York 14620

NEUROLOGY [2441]

4015 West 65th Street

Minneapolis, Minnesota 55435

(612) 927-4471

First published in 1951

SUBSCRIPTION DATA

Issues and rates: Published monthly.

Average paid circulation: 9,393
Annual rate(s): $24.00; Pan-Am $24.00;
Foreign $27.00
Publisher or Sponsor: American Academy
of Neurology
Managing Editor: Harold J. Quarfoth

EDITORIAL DESCRIPTION

Contains articles about the diagnosis and
treatment of neurological diseases and
conditions and research in the field of
neurology.
Articles per average issue: 15-18
Audience: Neurologists and other physicians
interested in neurology.
Manuscripts accepted in English

MANUSCRIPT INFORMATION

Subject field(s): Neurology, neurosurgery,
neurophysiology, anatomy of the brain;
psychology as related to neurological
diagnosis and treatment.
Manuscript requirements: See latest issue for
style requirements.
Preferred length: None
Number of copies to be submitted: 2
Abstract: Yes. Abstract should be 100
words or less.
Author information and reprints: Payment:
None.
Is simultaneous submission of article to
other journals permitted: Not permitted.
Exclusive manuscript rights between
acceptance and publication: Yes
Copyright: Held by publication.
Reprints: Available at cost. Based on
length
Disposition of manuscript:
Query letter: Not necessary.
Receipt of manuscript acknowledged: Yes
Decision to publish in: 1 to 2 months
Accepted manuscript published in: 5 to 7
months
Rejected manuscript returned: Yes, with
return postage paid by publication.
Rejected manuscript criticized:
Sometimes
Submit to:
Dr. Russell N. DeJong
Editor-in-Chief
University Hospital
Ann Arbor, Michigan 48104
(313) 764-4183

NEUROPHARMACOLOGY [2442]

Pergamon Press, Inc.
Fairview Park
Elmsford, New York 10523
(914) 592-7700

Previously entitled *International Journal of
Neuropharmacology*

First published in 1962

SUBSCRIPTION DATA

Issues and rates: Published monthly.
Annual rate(s): $25.00; Institutions
$90.00

EDITORIAL DESCRIPTION

Publishes original papers on studies of
the actions of drugs and biologically

active substances on the central and
peripheral nervous systems in animals
and man; the aim is to further the
understanding of the mechanisms of drug
action on the nervous system as well as
to facilitate the communication between
basic science and clinical investigation.
Articles per average issue: 4-6
Audience: Professional, academic
Manuscripts accepted in English

MANUSCRIPT INFORMATION

Subject field(s): Molecular pharmacology,
eletrophysiological pharmacology,
cytochemical and neuropharmacology,
behavioral and psychopharmacology
Manuscript requirements: See latest issue for
style requirements.
Preferred length: None
Number of copies to be submitted: 2,
double-spaced
Abstract: Yes. In English
Author information and reprints: Payment:
None.
Is simultaneous submission of article to
other journals permitted: Not permitted.
Exclusive manuscript rights between
acceptance and publication: Yes
Copyright: Held by publication.
Reprints: Available at cost.
Disposition of manuscript:
Query letter: Not necessary.
Receipt of manuscript acknowledged: Yes
Decision to publish in: 4 weeks
Accepted manuscript published in: 5
months
Rejected manuscript returned: Yes, if
return postage is supplied by author.
Rejected manuscript criticized: Reasons
for rejections only
Submit to:
P. B. Bradley
Department of Pharmacology
(Preclinical)
Medical School
Birmingham B15 2TJ, England

E. Costa
National Institute of Mental Health
Laboratory of Preclinical Pharmacology
St. Elizabeth's Hospital, William A.
White Building
Washington, D. C. 20032
Chief Editors

NEUROPSYCHOLOGIA [2443]

An International Journal
Pergamon Press, Inc.
Fairview Park
Elmsford, New York 10523
(914) 592-7700

First published in 1963

SUBSCRIPTION DATA

Issues and rates: Published quarterly.
Annual rate(s): $25.00; Institutions
$45.00

Managing Editor: Dr. H. Hécaen, Paris

EDITORIAL DESCRIPTION

Contains original research in the broad
field of neurology and its allied
disciplines.
Articles per average issue: 10-12
Audience: Professional, academic
Manuscripts accepted in English, French,
German

MANUSCRIPT INFORMATION

Manuscript requirements: See latest issue for
style requirements.
Preferred length: None
Number of copies to be submitted: 2
double-spaced
Abstract: Yes. One in each of the three
languages, English, German and French;
none to be more than 100 words
supplementing the title giving the
essentials of the paper.
Author information and reprints: Payment:
Reprints only. 50 reprints
Is simultaneous submission of article to
other journals permitted: Not permitted.
Exclusive manuscript rights between
acceptance and publication: Yes
Copyright: Held by publication.
Reprints: Available at cost.
Disposition of manuscript:
Query letter: Not necessary.
Receipt of manuscript acknowledged: Yes
Decision to publish in: 4 weeks
Accepted manuscript published in: 5
months
Rejected manuscript returned: Yes, if
return postage is supplied by author.
Rejected manuscript criticized: Reasons
for rejections only
Submit to:
Prof. K. A. Pribram
Stanford University
Jordan Hall
Stanford, California 94305

Prof. H. L. Teuber
Department of Psychology and Brain
Sciences
Massachusetts Institute of Technology
Cambridge, Massachusetts 02139
Board of Editors

NEURORADIOLOGY [2444]

Springer-Verlag
175 Fifth Avenue
New York, New York 10010

SUBSCRIPTION DATA

Issues and rates: Published monthly.
Annual rate(s): DM 96 per volume
Publisher or Sponsor: The European Society
of Neuroradiology

EDITORIAL DESCRIPTION

To make the results of scientific research
and modern clinical practice more readily
available to medical practitioners with an
interest in the subject.
Manuscripts accepted in English

Medicine (general)

MANUSCRIPT INFORMATION

Subject field(s): The whole field of neuroradiologically based diagnosis, including neuroradiological investigations with contrast media and the use of radioisotopes in the diagnosis of cerebral and spinal diseases

Manuscript requirements: See latest issue for style requirements. Style sheet sent on request.
Preferred length: As required
Number of copies to be submitted: 2
Abstract: Yes. Short summaries in English, French and German of a maximum of 30 lines.

Author information and reprints: Payment: Reprints only. 75 offprints
Is simultaneous submission of article to other journals permitted: Not permitted.
Exclusive manuscript rights between acceptance and publication: Yes
Copyright: Held by publication.

Submit to:
Professor M. M. Schechter
Editorial Secretary
Department of Radiology, Albert Einstein College of Medicine
1300 Morris Park Avenue
Bronx, New York 10461

NEW ENGLAND JOURNAL OF MEDICINE [2445]

Massachusetts Medical Society
10 Shattuck Street
Boston, Massachusetts 02115
(617) 734-9800

First published in 1812

SUBSCRIPTION DATA

Issues and rates: Published weekly.
Average paid circulation: 150,000
Annual rate(s): $22.00

Publisher or Sponsor: Massachusetts Medical Society

EDITORIAL DESCRIPTION

Contains original research papers, review papers, short case studies, and case records of the Massachusetts General Hospital.

Articles per average issue: 8

Audience: Professional
Manuscripts accepted in English

MANUSCRIPT INFORMATION

Subject field(s): Medicine: research and practice

Manuscript requirements: See first issue of the year for contributors' information
Preferred length: None specified
Number of copies to be submitted: Two
Abstract: Yes factual not descriptive, of less than 150 words stating the reason for study, main findings and conclusions.

Author information and reprints: Payment: None.
Is simultaneous submission of article to other journals permitted: No
Exclusive manuscript rights between acceptance and publication: Yes
Copyright: Held by the Massachusetts Medical Society

Reprints: Available at cost.

Disposition of manuscript:
Query letter: No
Receipt of manuscript acknowledged: Yes
Decision to publish in: One month
Accepted manuscript published in: Time required for editorial revision plus 7 weeks
Rejected manuscript returned: Yes
Rejected manuscript criticized: Yes

Submit to:
Franz J. Ingelfinger
Editor
(See address above)

THE NEW PHYSICIAN [2446]

Student American Medical Association
1400 Hicks Road
Rolling Meadows, Illinois 60008
(312) 259-7450

First published in 1951

SUBSCRIPTION DATA

Issues and rates: Published monthly.
Average paid circulation: 78,000
Annual rate(s): $10.00, Foreign $15.00

Publisher or Sponsor: Student American Medical Association

Managing Editor: Patricia Sanberg

EDITORIAL DESCRIPTION

Examines issues of critical concern to young health professionals. Also publishes a comprehensive series of basic clinical features on electrocardiography, surgical, medical and radiologic topics, and forensic and social medicine.

Articles per average issue: 2

Audience: Medical students, interns, residents
Manuscripts accepted in English

MANUSCRIPT INFORMATION

Subject field(s): Student health projects, health care delivery, medical education, social and political issues in medicine

Manuscript requirements: See latest issue for style requirements.
Preferred length: 3,000 words
Number of copies to be submitted: Two
Abstract: No

Author information and reprints: Payment: By publication to author. Only solicited manuscripts.
Is simultaneous submission of article to other journals permitted: Yes
Exclusive manuscript rights between acceptance and publication: No
Copyright: Held by publication.
Reprints: Available, charge for any number above 100

Disposition of manuscript:
Query letter: No
Receipt of manuscript acknowledged: Yes
Decision to publish in: 4-6 weeks
Accepted manuscript published in: 3-6 months
Rejected manuscript returned: Yes
Rejected manuscript criticized: Occasionally

Submit to:
Terrence S. Carden, Jr.

Editor
(See address above)

NEW YORK STATE JOURNAL OF MEDICINE [2447]

420 Lakeville Road
Lake Success, New York 11040
(516) 488-6100 ext. 219

First published in 1901

SUBSCRIPTION DATA

Issues and rates: Published monthly.
Average paid circulation: 1,083; 28,603 controlled
Annual rate(s): $3.50

Publisher or Sponsor: Medical Society of the State of New York

Managing Editor: Elizabeth C. Smith

EDITORIAL DESCRIPTION

Contains articles of medical interest: general, clinical, and scientific.

MANUSCRIPT INFORMATION

Manuscript requirements: See latest issue for style requirements.
Preferred length: None
Number of copies to be submitted: Two
Abstract: Yes

Author information and reprints: Payment: None.
Is simultaneous submission of article to other journals permitted: No
Exclusive manuscript rights between acceptance and publication: Yes
Copyright: Held by publication.
Reprints: Available

Disposition of manuscript:
Query letter: No
Receipt of manuscript acknowledged: Yes
Decision to publish in: Varies
Accepted manuscript published in: Varies
Rejected manuscript returned: Yes
Rejected manuscript criticized: Yes

Submit to:
Alfred A. Angrist
Editor
(See address above)

SPECIAL STIPULATIONS

There is a backlog of case reports.

NORTH CAROLINA MEDICAL JOURNAL [2448]

300 South Hawthorne Road
Winston-Salem, North Carolina 27103
(919) 727-4382

SUBSCRIPTION DATA

Issues and rates: Published monthly.
Average paid circulation: 5,000
Annual rate(s): $5.00

Publisher or Sponsor: North Carolina Medical Society

EDITORIAL DESCRIPTION

Contains original articles; editorials; bulletin board; book reviews; obituaries; classified ads; advertisers' index; month in Washington report; emergency medical services report (abstracts from AMA reports).

MANUSCRIPT INFORMATION

Subject field(s): Medicine (any field)

Manuscript requirements: See latest issue for style requirements.

Preferred length: 6 to 8 pages

Number of copies to be submitted: Two

Author information and reprints: Payment: None.

Is simultaneous submission of article to other journals permitted: No

Exclusive manuscript rights between acceptance and publication: Yes

Copyright: Held by publication.

Reprints: Available through printer

Disposition of manuscript:

Receipt of manuscript acknowledged: Yes

Decision to publish in: 4 to 6 weeks

Accepted manuscript published in: 6 months

Rejected manuscript returned: Yes

Rejected manuscript criticized: Yes

Submit to:

John H. Felts

Editor

(See address above)

NUTRITION AND METABOLISM [2449]

Journal of Nutrition, Metabolic Diseases and Dietetics

S. Karger AG

Arnold-Boecklin Strasse 25

CH-4011 Basel, Switzerland

061-390880

Previously entitled *Nutritio et Dieta*

SUBSCRIPTION DATA

Issues and rates: Published monthly.

Average paid circulation: 635; 55 controlled

Annual rate(s): SFr. 110.00; Foreign $44.00

EDITORIAL DESCRIPTION

Publishes research data on human nutrition, accepting works on animals only when these are applicable to the human problem. Guidelines for the selection of foodstuffs from bountiful choices has become an even more important research goal, and the progress of clinical medicine, notably in genetics and epidemiology, has posed new questions.

Articles per average issue: 5

Manuscripts accepted in English

MANUSCRIPT INFORMATION

Manuscript requirements: Style sheet sent on request.

Preferred length: 8 printed pages maximum

Number of copies to be submitted: 2

Abstract: Yes, with 6 key words

Author information and reprints: Payment: None.

Is simultaneous submission of article to other journals permitted: No

Exclusive manuscript rights between acceptance and publication: Yes

Copyright: Held by publication.

Reprints: Available

Disposition of manuscript:

Query letter: No

Receipt of manuscript acknowledged: Yes

Decision to publish in: 2 months

Accepted manuscript published in: 4-6 months

Rejected manuscript returned: Yes

Rejected manuscript criticized: Yes

Submit to:

N. Zoellner

Main Editor

Medizinische-Poliklinik der Universität

Pettenkoferstrasse 8a

D-8 München 2, Federal Republic of Germany

NUTRITION TODAY [2450]

P. O. Box 465

101 Ridgley Avenue

Annapolis, Maryland 21404

(301) 267-8616

First published in 1966

SUBSCRIPTION DATA

Issues and rates: Published bi-monthly.

Annual rate(s): $12.50; Institutions $13.50; Students $6.25; Foreign individuals $14.50; Foreign institutions $15.50

EDITORIAL DESCRIPTION

Professional level articles on all fields relating to nutrition.

Articles per average issue: 3

Audience: Professional, academic

Manuscripts accepted in English

MANUSCRIPT INFORMATION

Subject field(s): Nutrition and allied fields: agriculture, technology, home economics, medicine, nursing, paramedicine, food service, biochemistry, dentistry, dietetics

Manuscript requirements: GPO, NYT

Preferred length: None

Number of copies to be submitted: 1

Abstract: Not necessary.

Author information and reprints: Payment: By publication to author.

Is simultaneous submission of article to other journals permitted: Not permitted.

Exclusive manuscript rights between acceptance and publication: Yes

Copyright: Held by publication.

Reprints: Not available.

Disposition of manuscript:

Query letter: Necessary.

Receipt of manuscript acknowledged: Yes

Decision to publish in: 60 days

Accepted manuscript published in: 3-6 months

Rejected manuscript returned: Yes, with return postage paid by publication.

Rejected manuscript criticized: Reasons for rejections only

Submit to:

Cortez F. Enloe, Jr., M.D.

Editor and Publisher

(See address above)

THE OHIO STATE MEDICAL JOURNAL [2451]

600 South High Street

Columbus, Ohio 43215

(416) 228-6971

First published in 1905

SUBSCRIPTION DATA

Issues and rates: Published monthly.

Average paid circulation: 10,850 controlled

Annual rate(s): $5.00; Foreign $6.50; Institutions $5.00; Students $2.00; Foreign institutions $6.50

Publisher or Sponsor: Ohio State Medical Association

Managing Editor: Janis H. Tanner

EDITORIAL DESCRIPTION

Original scientific articles (medical case reports, research, etc.) and organizational news from the Ohio State Medical Association, the American Medical Association, and county medical societies in Ohio; also reports on the medical colleges in Ohio

Articles per average issue: 3-4

Audience: Physicians in Ohio primarily

Manuscripts accepted in English

MANUSCRIPT INFORMATION

Subject field(s): Any subject pertinent to physicians either professionally, scientifically; socio-economic subjects; subjects related to the medical field today such as federal or state legislation, insurance, nationalized health care, etc. No geographical limitations

Manuscript requirements: Style sheet sent on request.

Preferred length: Maximum of 10 double-spaced pages

Number of copies to be submitted: Original and one copy

Abstract: Not necessary.

Author information and reprints: Payment: None.

Is simultaneous submission of article to other journals permitted: Not permitted.

Exclusive manuscript rights between acceptance and publication: Yes

Copyright: Held by author and publication

Reprints: Available at cost.

Disposition of manuscript:

Query letter: Not necessary, but advisable.

Receipt of manuscript acknowledged: Yes

Decision to publish in: 1-2 weeks

Accepted manuscript published in: 3 months

Rejected manuscript returned: Yes, if return postage is supplied by author.

Rejected manuscript criticized: Reasons for rejections only

Submit to:

Janis H. Tanner

News Editor

(See address above)

Medicine (general)

OKLAHOMA STATE MEDICAL ASSOCIATION JOURNAL [2452]
601 N.W. Expressway
Oklahoma City, Oklahoma 73118
(405) 842-3361

First published in 1908

SUBSCRIPTION DATA
Issues and rates: Published monthly.
  Average paid circulation: 2,750
  Annual rate(s): $6.50, Foreign $8.50
Publisher or Sponsor: Oklahoma State
  Medical Association
Managing Editor: Don Blair

EDITORIAL DESCRIPTION
  Contains medical, scientific articles and
  news.
Articles per average issue: 3
Audience: Medical
  Manuscripts accepted in English

MANUSCRIPT INFORMATION
Subject field(s): Medical, scientific
Manuscript requirements: See latest issue for
  style requirements.
  Preferred length: 10-14 pages
  Number of copies to be submitted:
  Original and one copy
  Abstract: Yes
Author information and reprints: Payment:
  None.
  Is simultaneous submission of article to
  other journals permitted: No
  Exclusive manuscript rights between
  acceptance and publication: Yes
  Copyright: Held by publication.
  Reprints: Available, 100 four-page for
  $55.40
Additional information: Everything
  typewritten, double-spaced, wide margins;
  illustrations should be glossy prints.
Disposition of manuscript:
  Query letter: No
  Receipt of manuscript acknowledged: Yes
  Decision to publish in: Three months
  Accepted manuscript published in: 3-4
  months
  Rejected manuscript returned: Yes
Submit to:
  Mark R. Johnson
  Editor-in-Chief
  (See address above)

ONCOLOGY [2453]
Journal of Clinical and Experimental Cancer
Research
S. Karger AG
Arnold-Boecklin Strasse 25
CH-4011 Basel, Switzerland
061-390880

Previously entitled *Oncologia*

First published in 1948

SUBSCRIPTION DATA
Issues and rates: Published monthly.
  Average paid circulation: 751; 59
  controlled
  Annual rate(s): SFr. 132.00; Foreign
  $54.00

EDITORIAL DESCRIPTION
  Designed to cope with the information
  explosion in the field of cancer. Publishes
  papers of clinical significance, reviews
  basic scientific progress in the ancillary
  disciplines bearing on cancer, and
  contains a section on abnormal and
  normal tissue growth entitled
  "Oncogenesis-Morphogenesis". One or
  two symposia on important topics are
  published yearly. The journal is designed
  to keep the ordinary physician abreast of
  current knowledge in clinical cancer and
  in cancer research.
Articles per average issue: 6-7
  Manuscripts accepted in English

MANUSCRIPT INFORMATION
Manuscript requirements: See latest issue for
  style requirements.
  Preferred length: 12 pages
  Number of copies to be submitted: 2
  Abstract: Yes, with key words
Author information and reprints: Payment:
  None. There is a page charge for excess
  pages.
  Is simultaneous submission of article to
  other journals permitted: No
  Exclusive manuscript rights between
  acceptance and publication: Yes
  Copyright: Held by publication.
  Reprints: Available at cost
Disposition of manuscript:
  Receipt of manuscript acknowledged: Yes
  Rejected manuscript returned: Yes
Submit to:
  Dr. V. Richards
  Editor
  2714 Broadway
  San Francisco, California 94115

  For the Oncogenesis-Morphogenesis
  Section:
  Dr. Alexander Wolsky
  Department of Radiology
  New York University Medical Center
  550 First Avenue
  New York, New York 10016

OPHTHALMIC RESEARCH [2454]
S. Karger, A. G.
Arnold Boecklinstrasse 25
CH-4011 Basel, Switzerland

First published in 1970

SUBSCRIPTION DATA
Issues and rates: Published bi-monthly.
  Annual rate(s): $40.00; Foreign SFr. 108;
  DM 103; £16.20

EDITORIAL DESCRIPTION
  Founded as a vehicle for rapid
  presentation of important original articles
  in the fields of experimental and clinical
  ophthalmology.
Articles per average issue: Varies
Audience: Professional, research, academic
  Manuscripts accepted in English only

MANUSCRIPT INFORMATION
Subject field(s): Anatomy, physiology,
  biochemistry, biophysics, and the use of
  statistical methods in ophthalmic
  research and applications to the daily
  clinical work of the eye specialist.
Manuscript requirements: Style sheet sent
  on request.
  Preferred length: 8 printed pages
  maximum
  Number of copies to be submitted: 2
  Abstract: Yes. Of not more than 10 lines;
  include 3-9 key words for indexing
  purposes.
Author information and reprints: Payment:
  Reprints only. 100 reprints
  Is simultaneous submission of article to
  other journals permitted: Not permitted.
  Exclusive manuscript rights between
  acceptance and publication: Yes
  Copyright: Held by publication.
  Reprints: Available at cost.
Disposition of manuscript:
  Query letter: Not necessary.
  Receipt of manuscript acknowledged: Yes
Submit to:
  Prof. O. Hockwin
  Editor
  Klinisches Institut für experimentalle
  Ophthalmologie der Universität
  Abbestrasse 2
  D-53 Bonn-Venusberg, Federal Republic
  of Germany

OPHTHALMOLOGICA [2455]
International Journal of Ophthalmology
S. Karger AG
Arnold-Boecklin Strasse 25
CH-4011 Basel, Switzerland
061-390880

First published in 1899

SUBSCRIPTION DATA
Issues and rates: Published monthly.
  Average paid circulation: 1309; 41
  controlled
  Annual rate(s): SFr. 132.00; Foreign
  $54.00

EDITORIAL DESCRIPTION
  As the official organ of a number of
  European professional societies,
  publication has been serving the
  international ophthalmological
  community.
Articles per average issue: 8
  Manuscripts accepted in English,
  German, French

MANUSCRIPT INFORMATION
Manuscript requirements: See latest issue for
  style requirements.
  Preferred length: 8 printed pages
  maximum
  Number of copies to be submitted: 2
  Abstract: Yes
Author information and reprints: Payment:
  None.
  Is simultaneous submission of article to
  other journals permitted: No

Exclusive manuscript rights between acceptance and publication: Yes
Copyright: Held by publication.
Reprints: Available
Disposition of manuscript:
  Query letter: No
  Receipt of manuscript acknowledged: Yes
  Decision to publish in: 2 months
  Accepted manuscript published in: 6-12 months
  Rejected manuscript returned: Yes
  Rejected manuscript criticized: Yes
Submit to:
  E. B. Streiff
  Editor
  (See address above)

ORL   [2456]

Journal for Oto-Rhino-Laryngology and its Borderlands
S. Karger AG
Arnold-Boecklin Strasse 25
CH-4011 Basel, Switzerland
061-390880

Previously entitled *Practica Oto-Rhino Laryngolica*

SUBSCRIPTION DATA
Issues and rates: Published bi-monthly.
  Average paid circulation: 944; 43 controlled
  Annual rate(s): SFr. 132.00; Foreign $54.00

EDITORIAL DESCRIPTION
  Publishes papers on the following subjects: clinical studies of ENT diseases, allergy in ORL, anesthesia in ORL, broncho-oesophagology, hearing and speech disorders, head and neck surgery, plastic and reconstructive surgery in ORL, neuro-otology, and oncology and traumatology in ORL; basic research in audiology and otology as well as in rhino-laryngology (morphology, experimental pathology, physiology and pathophysiology, biochemistry).
Articles per average issue: 6
  Manuscripts accepted in English

MANUSCRIPT INFORMATION
Manuscript requirements: See latest issue for style requirements.
  Preferred length: 8 pages maximum
  Number of copies to be submitted: 2
  Abstract: Yes
Author information and reprints: Payment: None.
  Is simultaneous submission of article to other journals permitted: No
  Exclusive manuscript rights between acceptance and publication: Yes
  Copyright: Held by publication.
  Reprints: Available
Disposition of manuscript:
  Query letter: No
  Receipt of manuscript acknowledged: Yes
  Decision to publish in: 2 months
  Accepted manuscript published in: 4-5 months
  Rejected manuscript returned: Yes
  Rejected manuscript criticized: Yes

Submit to:
  C. R. Pfaltz
  ORL-Klinik
  CH-4000 Basel, Switzerland
  Managing Editor

PAEDIATRICIAN   [2457]

International Journal for the Pediatrician in Practice
S. Karger AG
Arnold-Boecklin Strasse 25
CH-4011 Basel, Switzerland
061-390880

First published in 1972

SUBSCRIPTION DATA
Issues and rates: Published bi-monthly.
  Average paid circulation: Not available.
  Annual rate(s): SFr. 132.00; Foreign $54.00
Publisher or Sponsor: The International College of Pediatrics

EDITORIAL DESCRIPTION
  An international journal on current pediatric practice. It is organized in seminar fashion by acknowledged experts and all contributions are reviewed by an international panel of editors.
Articles per average issue: 7
Audience: Urban and rural, academic and practising as well as governmental and private physicians.
  Manuscripts accepted in English

MANUSCRIPT INFORMATION
Manuscript requirements: See latest issue for style requirements.
  Preferred length: 10 printed pages
  Number of copies to be submitted: 2
  Abstract: Yes, with 10 key words
Author information and reprints: Payment: Reprints only.
  Is simultaneous submission of article to other journals permitted: No
  Exclusive manuscript rights between acceptance and publication: Yes
  Copyright: Held by publication.
  Reprints: Available
Disposition of manuscript:
  Query letter: No
  Receipt of manuscript acknowledged: Yes
  Decision to publish in: 1-2 months
  Accepted manuscript published in: 6 months
  Rejected manuscript returned: Yes
  Rejected manuscript criticized: No
Submit to:
  G. D. Maragos
  Department of Pediatrics
  Creighton University School of Medicine
  Omaha, Nebraska 68108

  Ch. A. Greene
  141 Washington Avenue
  Endicott, New York 13760
  Editors

PEDIATRIC RADIOLOGY   [2458]

Springer-Verlag
175 Fifth Avenue
New York, New York 10010

SUBSCRIPTION DATA
Issues and rates: Published quarterly.
  Annual rate(s): DM 120 per volume

EDITORIAL DESCRIPTION
  An independent, lively, and extensive specialist in the fields of work and research in pediatric radiology.
Audience: Experienced pediatric radiologists
  Manuscripts accepted in English, German

MANUSCRIPT INFORMATION
Subject field(s): Original papers, continuing education, technology, methodology, new apparatus and auxiliary equipment, case histories, journal summaries, bibliographies, book reviews, announcements and reviews
Manuscript requirements: See latest issue for style requirements.
  Preferred length: As required
  Number of copies to be submitted: 2
  Abstract: Yes. An abstract of 10 to 15 lines followed by a list of about 6 key words for indexing purposes
Author information and reprints: Payment: Reprints only. 75 offprints
  Is simultaneous submission of article to other journals permitted: Not permitted.
  Exclusive manuscript rights between acceptance and publication: Yes
  Copyright: Held by publication.
Submit to:
  Dr. W. E. Berdon
  Editorial Secretary
  Babies Hospital, Columbia Medical Center
  622 West 168th Street
  New York, New York 10032

PEDIATRIC RESEARCH   [2459]

International Journal of Clinical, Laboratory and Developmental Investigation
428 East Preston Street
Baltimore, Maryland 21202
(301) 528-4116

First published in 1967

SUBSCRIPTION DATA
Issues and rates: Published monthly.
  Average paid circulation: 1,900
  Annual rate(s): $30.00, Foreign $32.00
Publisher or Sponsor: International Pediatric Research Foundation

EDITORIAL DESCRIPTION
  Contains clinical research dealing with behavioral, biochemical, physiological and structural aspects of human development.
Articles per average issue: 10
  Manuscripts accepted in English

MANUSCRIPT INFORMATION
Manuscript requirements: Style sheet sent on request.
  Preferred length: 15-20 pages

Medicine (general)

Number of copies to be submitted: Two
Abstract: Yes
Author information and reprints: Payment: None.
Is simultaneous submission of article to other journals permitted: No
Exclusive manuscript rights between acceptance and publication: Yes
Copyright: Held by publication.
Reprints: Available
Disposition of manuscript:
Query letter: No
Receipt of manuscript acknowledged: Yes
Decision to publish in: 6 weeks
Accepted manuscript published in: 4 months
Rejected manuscript returned: Yes
Rejected manuscript criticized: Sometimes
Submit to:
Charles U. Lowe M.D.
Editor
National Institutes of Health
Building 31, Room 2A-50
Bethesda, Maryland 20014
(301) 496-5410

PEDIATRICS* [2460]

Official Publication of The American Academy of Pediatrics Inc.
1801 Hinman
Evanston, Illinois 60201
(312) 869-4255

SUBSCRIPTION DATA
Issues and rates: Published monthly.
Average paid circulation: 22,000
Annual rate(s): $17.00, Foreign $24.00
Publisher or Sponsor: American Academy of Pediatrics, Inc.
Managing Editor: Robert G. Frazier

EDITORIAL DESCRIPTION
Edited for the pediatrician and those concerned with child health and development. Each issue contains papers on original research and special feature or review articles in the field of pediatrics as broadly defined.

MANUSCRIPT INFORMATION
Subject field(s): Premature and newborn, infant diseases and immunology, nutrition, metabolism, pediatric practice, heart and blood vessel, endocrinology, neurology and psychiatry, respiratory tract, surgery, genito-urinary tract, orthopedics, allergy, tumors, drugs
Manuscript requirements: See latest issue for style requirements.
Preferred length: None
Number of copies to be submitted: Two
Is simultaneous submission of article to other journals permitted: No
Exclusive manuscript rights between acceptance and publication: Yes
Copyright: Held by publication.
Reprints: Available
Disposition of manuscript:
Receipt of manuscript acknowledged: Yes
Decision to publish in: 30 days
Accepted manuscript published in: 90 to 180 days

Rejected manuscript returned: Yes
Rejected manuscript criticized: Yes
Submit to:
Clement A. Smith
Editor
300 Longwood Avenue
Boston, Massachusetts 02115
(617) 734-6000 ext. 2681

PERSPECTIVES IN BIOLOGY AND MEDICINE [2461]

University of Chicago Press
5801 Ellis Avenue
Chicago, Illinois 60637
(312) 753-2592

First published in 1957

SUBSCRIPTION DATA
Issues and rates: Published quarterly.
Average paid circulation: 5,000
Annual rate(s): $10.00, Foreign $11.00
Managing Editor: Claire Landau

EDITORIAL DESCRIPTION
Contains new ideas and original thought in biological and medical sciences; brief proposals of new research problems representing informed thinking; interpretive essays on recent and current research; heuristic ideas not yet tested; autobiographical sketches; book reviews; letters to the editor; relief verse.
Articles per average issue: 12
Audience: Professional
Manuscripts accepted in English

MANUSCRIPT INFORMATION
Subject field(s): All disciplines within the biological and medical fields
Manuscript requirements: Chicago
Preferred length: 10-12 pages
Number of copies to be submitted: Three
Abstract: No
Author information and reprints: Payment: By author to publication. $50.00 per page. Voluntary contribution.
Is simultaneous submission of article to other journals permitted: No
Exclusive manuscript rights between acceptance and publication: Yes
Copyright: Held by publication.
Reprints: Available, cost per page and quantity
Disposition of manuscript:
Query letter: Helpful, not necessary
Receipt of manuscript acknowledged: Yes
Decision to publish in: 3 weeks
Accepted manuscript published in: 6-9 months
Rejected manuscript returned: Yes
Rejected manuscript criticized: Yes
Submit to:
Editorial Office
Culver 403
1025 East 57th Street
Chicago, Illinois 60637
(312) 753-4083

PHARMACOLOGICAL REVIEWS [2462]

428 East Preston Street
Baltimore, Maryland 21202
(301) 528-4116

First published in 1949

SUBSCRIPTION DATA
Issues and rates: Published quarterly.
Average paid circulation: 3,600
Annual rate(s): $12.00; Foreign $18.50
Publisher or Sponsor: American Society for Pharmacology and Experimental Therapeutics

EDITORIAL DESCRIPTION
Contains original review articles in pharmacology, experimental therapeutics, and chemotherapy.
Articles per average issue: 3
Manuscripts accepted in English

MANUSCRIPT INFORMATION
Manuscript requirements: See latest issue for style requirements.
Preferred length: Not specified
Number of copies to be submitted: Two
Abstract: Yes
Author information and reprints: Payment: None.
Is simultaneous submission of article to other journals permitted: No
Exclusive manuscript rights between acceptance and publication: Yes
Copyright: Held by publication.
Reprints: Available at cost
Disposition of manuscript:
Query letter: No
Receipt of manuscript acknowledged: Yes
Decision to publish in: 3-4 weeks
Accepted manuscript published in: 6 months
Rejected manuscript returned: Yes
Rejected manuscript criticized: Sometimes
Submit to:
Marion DeV. Cotten
Editor
Route 3, Box 229
Sylvania, Georgia 30469
(912) 863-4343

PHARMACOLOGY [2463]

International Journal of Experimental and Clinical Pharmacology
S. Karger AG
Arnold-Boecklin Strasse 25
CH-4011 Basel, Switzerland
061-390880

Previously entitled *Medicina Experimentalis*

First published in 1959

SUBSCRIPTION DATA
Issues and rates: Published bi-monthly.
Average paid circulation: 643; 57 controlled
Annual rate(s): SFr. 198.00; Foreign $80.00

EDITORIAL DESCRIPTION

Publishes valuable information from the vast range of pharmacological studies and drug research. Relevant contributions from both experimental and clinical research, as well as papers on classical pharmacology, are regularly published. Articles concerned with a number of specialised areas are also featured.

Articles per average issue: 6-10

Manuscripts accepted in English

MANUSCRIPT INFORMATION

Subject field(s): Molecular pharmacology, biochemical pharmacology, neuropsychopharmacology, toxicology, pharmacogenetics and clinical pharmacology.

Manuscript requirements: See latest issue for style requirements.

Preferred length: 12 pages

Number of copies to be submitted: 2

Abstract: Yes, with key words

Author information and reprints: Payment: None. A page charge for excess pages.

Is simultaneous submission of article to other journals permitted: No

Exclusive manuscript rights between acceptance and publication: Yes

Copyright: Held by publication.

Reprints: Available

Disposition of manuscript:

Query letter: No

Receipt of manuscript acknowledged: Yes

Decision to publish in: 1-2 months

Accepted manuscript published in: 4-5 months

Rejected manuscript returned: Yes

Rejected manuscript criticized: Yes

Submit to:

From U.S. to:

Dr. E. S. Vesell

Milton S. Hershey Medical Center

Department of Pharmacology

Pennsylvania State University

Hershey, Pennsylvania 17033

From all other countries to:

Dr. R. Domenjoz

Pharmacologisches Institut der Universität

Reuterstrasse 26

D-5300 Bonn, Federal Republic of Germany

Editors

PHYSICAL THERAPY* [2464]

Journal of the American Physical Therapy Association

1156 15th Street, N.W.

Washington, D.C. 20005

(202) 466-2070

SUBSCRIPTION DATA

Issues and rates: Published monthly.

Average paid circulation: 21,800

Annual rate(s): $12.00, Foreign $15.00

Publisher or Sponsor: American Physical Therapy Association

Managing Editor: Jean K. Sherier

EDITORIAL DESCRIPTION

Contains scientific and professional articles on clinical and testing procedures, the basic sciences, research, administration, education, and association activities.

MANUSCRIPT INFORMATION

Subject field(s): Physical therapy, basic sciences related to physical therapy, education

Manuscript requirements: See latest issue for style requirements.

Preferred length: Not over 12 pages

Number of copies to be submitted: Two

Author information and reprints: Payment: None.

Is simultaneous submission of article to other journals permitted: No

Exclusive manuscript rights between acceptance and publication: Yes

Copyright: Held by publication.

Reprints: Available at nominal cost

Disposition of manuscript:

Receipt of manuscript acknowledged: Yes

Decision to publish in: Four to six weeks

Accepted manuscript published in: Three to six months

Rejected manuscript returned: Yes

Rejected manuscript criticized: Yes

Submit to:

Elizabeth J. Davies

Editor

(See address above)

THE PHYSIOLOGIST [2465]

The American Physiological Society

9650 Rockville Pike

Bethesda, Maryland 20795

(301) 530-7164

First published in 1958

SUBSCRIPTION DATA

Issues and rates: Published quarterly.

Average paid circulation: 5,000

Annual rate(s): $4.00 (and Canada); Foreign $5.00; Individuals $4.00; Institutions $4.00; Members Free; Foreign individuals $5.00; Foreign institutions $5.00

Publisher or Sponsor: American Physiological Society

Managing Editor: Orr E. Reynolds

EDITORIAL DESCRIPTION

Information of interest to members, fiscal reports, reports of council, scientific articles, new members elected, etc.

Articles per average issue: 4-5

Audience: Departmental staff

Manuscripts accepted in English

Author information and reprints: Payment: None.

Exclusive manuscript rights between acceptance and publication: No

Reprints: Available at cost.

Submit to:

Editor

(See address above)

PNEUMONOLOGY [2466]

Springer-Verlag

175 Fifth Avenue

New York, New York 10010

First published in 1903

Annual rate(s): DM 128 per volume

Publisher or Sponsor: German Society for Lung Diseases and Tuberculosis; Society for Lung and Respiration Research

Managing Editor: E. Gaubatz

EDITORIAL DESCRIPTION

Publishes original papers on all aspects of diseases of the bronchi and lungs and cognate subjects.

Manuscripts accepted in English, German

MANUSCRIPT INFORMATION

Subject field(s): Clinical, physiopathological and epidemiological studies; case reports, short communications and technical notes. Review articles are solicited by the editors.

Manuscript requirements: See latest issue for style requirements. Style sheet sent on request.

Preferred length: As required

Number of copies to be submitted: 2

Abstract: Yes. Each paper should be preceded by a brief abstract of the essential results and a list of up to five key words for indexing purposes.

Author information and reprints: Payment: Reprints only. 40 offprints

Is simultaneous submission of article to other journals permitted: Not permitted.

Exclusive manuscript rights between acceptance and publication: Yes

Copyright: Held by publication.

Submit to:

Dr. Marvin Kuschner

Editorial Secretary

Department of Pathology

State University of New York at Stony Brook

Stony Brook, New York 11790

POSTGRADUATE MEDICINE [2467]

The Journal of Applied Medicine

4015 West 65th Street

Minneapolis, Minnesota 55435

(612) 927-5461

SUBSCRIPTION DATA

Issues and rates: Published monthly.

Average paid circulation: 51,000

Annual rate(s): $10, Foreign $20

Managing Editor: Beth Grendahl

EDITORIAL DESCRIPTION

Contains practical clinical articles and current material that the general physician can apply in his daily practice.

MANUSCRIPT INFORMATION

Subject field(s): Any medical subject that applies to medical practice

Medicine (general)

Manuscript requirements: Style sheet sent on request.
  Preferred length: 2000 words; 8 pages
  Number of copies to be submitted: Two
Author information and reprints: Payment: None.
  Is simultaneous submission of article to other journals permitted: No
  Exclusive manuscript rights between acceptance and publication: Yes
  Copyright: Held by publication.
  Reprints: Available, schedule submitted
Disposition of manuscript:
  Receipt of manuscript acknowledged: Yes
  Decision to publish in: 4-6 weeks
  Accepted manuscript published in: 6-12 months
  Rejected manuscript returned: Yes
  Rejected manuscript criticized: Sometimes
Submit to:
  John P. Connors
  Executive Editor
  (See address above)

PSYCHOPHARMACOLOGY BULLETIN [2468]

National Institute of Mental Health
5600 Fishers Lane
Rockville, Maryland 20852
(301) 443-3549

SUBSCRIPTION DATA

Issues and rates: Published quarterly.
  Average paid circulation: 1200; 3500 controlled
  Annual rate(s): $3.70
Publisher or Sponsor: National Institute of Mental Health, Division of Extramural Research Programs

EDITORIAL DESCRIPTION

Purpose is to facilitate the dissemination and exchange of information among scientists in the field of psychopharmacology. The emphasis is on rapid, informal reporting of work which has not appeared in the scientific literature.
Articles per average issue: 3
Audience: Psychiatrists, psychologists, chemists, pharmacists
  Manuscripts accepted in English

MANUSCRIPT INFORMATION

Subject field(s): Methodology of psychotropic drug trials, description and results of drug trials, summaries of research under NIMH grants, bibliography, letters
Manuscript requirements: See latest issue for style requirements.
  Preferred length: None
  Number of copies to be submitted: Two
Author information and reprints: Payment: None.
  Is simultaneous submission of article to other journals permitted: Yes
  Exclusive manuscript rights between acceptance and publication: No
  Copyright: No copyright
  Reprints. Available

Disposition of manuscript:
  Receipt of manuscript acknowledged: Yes
  Decision to publish in: 2 weeks
  Accepted manuscript published in: 2-3 months
  Rejected manuscript returned: Yes
  Rejected manuscript criticized: Yes
Submit to:
  Alice A. Leeds, M.D.
  Scientific Editor
  (See address above)

PUBLIC HEALTH REPORTS [2469]

5600 Fishers Lane
Parklawn Building, Room 10A-41
Rockville, Maryland 20852
(301) 443-2525

Previously entitled *Health Services Reports*

First published in 1878

SUBSCRIPTION DATA

Issues and rates: Published bi-monthly.
  Average paid circulation· 4,106; 14,000 controlled
  Annual rate(s): $10.10; Foreign $12.65
Publisher or Sponsor: Health Resources Administration

EDITORIAL DESCRIPTION

Contains scientific papers concerned with the delivery of health services and health care, research pertinent to public health, health education of the public, descriptions of new projects, services, and experiments pertinent to health care.
Articles per average issue: 14
Audience: Professional
  Manuscripts accepted in English only

MANUSCRIPT INFORMATION

Subject field(s): Health care delivery, health economics, community medicine, health policy, preventive medicine, training health care personnel, health education, organization of health and medical care
Manuscript requirements: Style sheet sent on request.
  Preferred length: 3,000 words
  Number of copies to be submitted: Four
  Abstract: Yes
Author information and reprints: Payment: None.
  Is simultaneous submission of article to other journals permitted: No
  Exclusive manuscript rights between acceptance and publication: Yes
  Copyright: Not copyrighted
  Reprints: Available, 100 to authors
Additional information: Tables, charts and references on separate pages; no footnotes in text.
Disposition of manuscript:
  Query letter: No
  Receipt of manuscript acknowledged: Yes
  Decision to publish in: 3 months
  Accepted manuscript published in: 6-10 months
  Rejected manuscript returned: Yes
  Rejected manuscript criticized: Yes

Submit to:
  Marian Priest Tebben
  Acting Executive Editor
  (See address above)

RADIOLOGIA CLINICA [2470]

S. Karger AG
Arnold-Boecklin Strasse 25
CH-4011 Basel, Switzerland
061-390880

Previously entitled *Radiologia Clinica et Biologica*

First published in 1933

SUBSCRIPTION DATA

Issues and rates: Published bi-monthly.
  Average paid circulation: 1,102; 25 controlled
  Annual rate(s): SFr. 198.00; Foreign $80.00
Publisher or Sponsor: Schweizerischen Vereinigung für Radiologie

EDITORIAL DESCRIPTION

Publishes experimental investigations in radiology of interest to those involved in practical clinical medicine. Occasional special issues are specifically concerned with the subject of radiological therapy.
Articles per average issue: 5-6
  Manuscripts accepted in English, French, German

MANUSCRIPT INFORMATION

Manuscript requirements: See latest issue for style requirements.
  Preferred length: 12 pages
  Number of copies to be submitted: 2
  Abstract: Yes, with key words
Author information and reprints: Payment: None. Excess page charges
  Is simultaneous submission of article to other journals permitted: No
  Exclusive manuscript rights between acceptance and publication: Yes
  Copyright: Held by publication.
  Reprints: Available at cost
Disposition of manuscript:
  Query letter: No
  Receipt of manuscript acknowledged: Yes
  Decision to publish in: 1-3 months
  Accepted manuscript published in: 6-7 months
  Rejected manuscript returned: Yes
  Rejected manuscript criticized: Yes
Submit to:
  Paper on radiodiagnostics to:
  Prof. William Penn
  University Clinics
  Nijmegen, The Netherlands

  Papers on radiotherapy to:
  Prof. P. Veraguth
  Klinik für Strahlentherapie
  Inselspital
  CH-3000 Bern, Switzerland

RADIOLOGIC TECHNOLOGY [2471]

428 East Preston Street
Baltimore, Maryland 21202
(301) 528-4116

Previously entitled *X-Ray Technician*

First published in 1929

SUBSCRIPTION DATA
Issues and rates: Published bi-monthly.
   Average paid circulation: $15,700
   Annual rate(s): $12.50; Foreign $14.00
Publisher or Sponsor: American Society of
   Radiologic Technologists

EDITORIAL DESCRIPTION
Contains scientific articles by and for
radiologic technologists, society news.
Articles per average issue: 5
   Manuscripts accepted in English

MANUSCRIPT INFORMATION
Manuscript requirements: No specific style
   guide.
   Number of copies to be submitted: Two
   Abstract: No
Author information and reprints: Payment:
   None.
   Is simultaneous submission of article to
   other journals permitted: No
   Exclusive manuscript rights between
   acceptance and publication: Yes
   Copyright: Held by publication.
   Reprints: Available, cost depends on
   length
Disposition of manuscript:
   Query letter: No
   Receipt of manuscript acknowledged: Yes
   Decision to publish in: 6 weeks
   Accepted manuscript published in: 4-6
   months
   Rejected manuscript returned: Yes
   Rejected manuscript criticized: No
Submit to:
   Jean I Widger
   Editor
   Alden Park Manor, 408D
   8100 East Jefferson Street
   Detroit, Michigan 48214
   (313) 577-1958

RADIOLOGY [2472]

1 Mony Plaza, Suite 1505
Syracuse, New York 13202
(315) 476-5318

SUBSCRIPTION DATA
Issues and rates: Published monthly.
   Average paid circulation: 18,000
   Annual rate(s): $35.00, Foreign $42.50
Publisher or Sponsor: The Radiological
   Society of America, Inc.

EDITORIAL DESCRIPTION
Contains scientific articles, diagnostic
radiology, nuclear medicine, radiation
biology, radiation physics,
neuroradiology, pediatric radiology,
ultrasound; work in progress.

MANUSCRIPT INFORMATION
Subject field(s): Radiology
Manuscript requirements: See latest issue for
   style requirements.
   Number of copies to be submitted: Two
Author information and reprints: Payment:
   None.
   Is simultaneous submission of article to
   other journals permitted: No
   Exclusive manuscript rights between
   acceptance and publication: Yes
   Copyright: Held by publication.
   Reprints: Available
Disposition of manuscript:
   Receipt of manuscript acknowledged: Yes
   Rejected manuscript returned: Yes
Submit to:
   William R. Eyler
   Editor
   Tower 14
   21700 Northwestern Highway
   Southfield, Michigan 48075
   (313) 873-0902

RESPIRATION [2473]

International Review of Thoracic Diseases
S. Karger AG
Arnold-Boecklin Strasse 25
CH-4011 Basel, Switzerland
061-390880

Previously entitled *Medicina Thoracalis*

First published in 1944

SUBSCRIPTION DATA
Issues and rates: Published bi-monthly.
   Average paid circulation: 764; 42
   controlled
   Annual rate(s): SFr. 165.00; Foreign
   $66.00

EDITORIAL DESCRIPTION
Publishes papers from the fields of
experimental and clinical physiology and
pathophysiology.
Articles per average issue: 7-8
   Manuscripts accepted in English,
   German, French

MANUSCRIPT INFORMATION
Manuscript requirements: See latest issue for
   style requirements.
   Preferred length: 15 pages
   Number of copies to be submitted: 2
   Abstract: Yes, with key words
Author information and reprints: Payment:

None.
   Is simultaneous submission of article to
   other journals permitted: No
   Exclusive manuscript rights between
   acceptance and publication: Yes
   Copyright: Held by publication.
   Reprints: Available at cost
Disposition of manuscript:
   Query letter: Yes
   Receipt of manuscript acknowledged: Yes
   Decision to publish in: 2-3 months
   Accepted manuscript published in: 6-7
   months
   Rejected manuscript returned: Yes
   Rejected manuscript criticized: Yes
Submit to:
   Prof. Dr. H. Herzog
   Editor
   Medizinische Universitätsklinik
   Cantonspital
   CH-4004 Basel, Switzerland

RESPIRATORY THERAPY [2474]

The Journal of Inhalation Technology
825 South Barrington Avenue
Los Angeles, California 90049
(213) 826-8388

First published in 1971

SUBSCRIPTION DATA
Issues and rates: Published bi-monthly.
   Average paid circulation: 1,053; 15,408
   controlled
   Annual rate(s): $20; Foreign $40
Managing Editor: Hal Spector;
Martin H. Waldman

EDITORIAL DESCRIPTION
Articles report on medical advances,
department management, training,
licensing, equipment, supplies, etc.
Directed to inhalation and
cardiopulmonary therapists, medical
directors, technicians and paramedical
personnel.

MANUSCRIPT INFORMATION
Subject field(s): Techniques, problems and
   solutions, hospital care, facility reports,
   home care
Manuscript requirements: Style sheet sent
   on request.
   Preferred length: 3000-5000 words
   Number of copies to be submitted: Two
Author information and reprints: Payment:
   None.
   Is simultaneous submission of article to
   other journals permitted: No
   Exclusive manuscript rights between
   acceptance and publication: Yes
   Copyright: Held by author.
   Reprints: Available at cost

Medicine (general)

Additional information: Desire reproducible artwork.
Disposition of manuscript:
 Receipt of manuscript acknowledged: Yes
 Decision to publish in: Varies
 Accepted manuscript published in: Varies
 Rejected manuscript returned: Yes
 Rejected manuscript criticized: No
Submit to:
 Roberta Atchison
 Editorial Coordinator
 (See address above)

RHODE ISLAND MEDICAL JOURNAL [2476]

106 Francis Street
Providence, Rhode Island 02903
(401) 331-3208

First published in 1917

SUBSCRIPTION DATA
Issues and rates: Published monthly.
 Average paid circulation: 1,532
 Annual rate(s): $5.00
Publisher or Sponsor: Rhode Island Medical Society
Managing Editor: Timothy B. Novbeck

EDITORIAL DESCRIPTION
 Contains medical-scientific articles, items of interest to the physician on medical socio-economic matters.
Articles per average issue: 4
Audience: Professional
 Manuscripts accepted in English

MANUSCRIPT INFORMATION
Subject field(s): Medical science, socio-economic aspects of medicine
Manuscript requirements: Style sheet sent on request.
 Preferred length: 10 pages
 Number of copies to be submitted: Two
Author information and reprints: Payment: None.
 Is simultaneous submission of article to other journals permitted: NO
 Copyright: Held by publication.
 Reprints: Available
Disposition of manuscript:
 Query letter: No
 Receipt of manuscript acknowledged: Yes
 Decision to publish in: Three weeks
 Accepted manuscript published in: Two to three months
 Rejected manuscript returned: Yes, if self-addressed, stamped envelope is sent with manuscript.
 Rejected manuscript criticized: No
Submit to:
 Seebert J. Goldowsky
 Editor-in-Chief
 (See address above)

SCANDINAVIAN JOURNAL OF HAEMATOLOGY [2477]

Medical Department C, Amtssygehuset
Copenhagen, Denmark
GE-1200 Ext. 531

First published in 1964

SUBSCRIPTION DATA
Issues and rates: 10 per year
 Annual rate(s): $25.95

EDITORIAL DESCRIPTION
 Contains articles on hematology, clinical and experimental.
Articles per average issue: 11
Audience: Hematologists and coagulationists
 Manuscripts accepted in English only.

MANUSCRIPT INFORMATION
Manuscript requirements: See latest issue for style requirements.
 Preferred length: 14 printed pages
 Number of copies to be submitted: Two
 Abstract: Yes.
Author information and reprints: Payment: None.
 Is simultaneous submission of article to other journals permitted: No
 Exclusive manuscript rights between acceptance and publication: Yes
 Copyright: Held by publication.
 Reprints: Available, 50 free
Additional information: Papers exceeding 20 printed pages may be published as supplements. The full cost will be paid by the author.
Disposition of manuscript:
 Query letter:
 Receipt of manuscript acknowledged: Yes
 Decision to publish in: 4-6 weeks
 Accepted manuscript published in: 4-6 months
 Rejected manuscript returned: Yes, if return postage is supplied by author.
 Rejected manuscript criticized: Yes
Submit to:
 Aage Videbaek
 Editor-in-Chief
 (See address above)

SPECIAL STIPULATIONS
 Concise style and clear disposition; explanation (short) why the article should be published.

SCANDINAVIAN JOURNAL OF INFECTIOUS DISEASES [2478]

Almqvist & Wiksell Periodical Company
P. O. Box 62
S-101 20 Stockholm 1, Sweden
08/23 79 90

First published in 1968

SUBSCRIPTION DATA
Issues and rates: Published quarterly.
 Average paid circulation: 1,000
 Annual rate(s): Sw.Kr. 110; Foreign $28.75

EDITORIAL DESCRIPTION
 Publishes papers on clinical aspects of infectious diseases, including therapy and prophylaxis, laboratory investigations of clinical significance (bacteriological, virological, parasitological, mycological, immunological, pathological, physiological, chemical and pharmacological), epidemiology and epizoology of human infections, as well as papers on hospital infections. All papers are published in English.

MANUSCRIPT INFORMATION
Subject field(s): Research on infectious diseases with clinical application
Manuscript requirements: See latest issue for style requirements.
 Preferred length: See latest issue of publication
Author information and reprints: Payment: None.
 Exclusive manuscript rights between acceptance and publication: Yes
 Copyright: Held by publication.
Submit to:
 Folke Nordbring
 Managing Editor
 Department of Infectious Diseases
 Akademiska Sjukhuset
 S-750 14 Uppsala, Sweden

SCANDINAVIAN JOURNAL OF REHABILITATION MEDICINE [2479]

Almqvist & Wiksell Periodical Company
Box 62
S-101 20 Stockholm 1, Sweden
08/23 79 90

First published in 1968

SUBSCRIPTION DATA
Issues and rates: Published quarterly.
 Average paid circulation: Not available.
 Annual rate(s): Sw.Kr. 90.00; Foreign $23.75

EDITORIAL DESCRIPTION

Publishes original articles, editorials and invited reviews on rehabilitation medicine. Short preliminary reports and important case-reports are published promptly. All papers are published in English.

MANUSCRIPT INFORMATION

Subject field(s): Rehabilitation medicine
Manuscript requirements: Style sheet sent on request.
Additional information: All instructions will be sent to author on request
Submit to:
Olle Höök
Chief Editor
Institute of Medical Rehabilitation
Ö. Husargatan 36
S-413 14 Gothenburg, Sweden

SCANDINAVIAN JOURNAL OF RHEUMATOLOGY [2480]

Almqvist & Wiksell Periodical Company
Box 62
S-101 20 Stockholm 1, Sweden
08/23 79 90

First published in 1970

SUBSCRIPTION DATA

Issues and rates: Published quarterly.
Average paid circulation: 1,000
Annual rate(s): Sw.Kr. 100.00; Foreign $26.25
Publisher or Sponsor: The Scandinavian Society of Rheumatologists

EDITORIAL DESCRIPTION

Publishes papers on clinical aspects of rheumatic disorders including therapy, prophylaxis and surgical treatment; laboratory investigations, including biochemistry, immunology, microbiology, pathology, pathophysiology; radiological investigations; epidemiological and social aspects of rheumatic disorders. All articles published in English.

MANUSCRIPT INFORMATION

Manuscript requirements: Style sheet sent on request.
Preferred length: 30 pages maximum
Number of copies to be submitted: Original and one copy
Author information and reprints: Payment: By author to publication. Cost for printed pages over 12.
Is simultaneous submission of article to other journals permitted: No
Exclusive manuscript rights between acceptance and publication: Yes
Copyright: Held by The Scandinavian Society of Rheumatologists
Reprints: Available on order
Disposition of manuscript:
Rejected manuscript returned: Yes
Submit to:
Olle Lovgren
Managing Editor
St. Eriks Sjukhus, P.O. Box 12600
S-112 82 Stockholm, Sweden

SCANDINAVIAN JOURNAL OF SOCIAL MEDICINE [2481]

Almqvist & Wiksell Periodical Company
Box 62
S-101 20 Stockholm 1, Sweden
08/23 79 90

Previously entitled *Acta Socio-Medica Scandinavica*

SUBSCRIPTION DATA

Issues and rates: Published three times per year.
Average paid circulation: Not available.
Annual rate(s): Sw.kr. 90, Foreign $20.50
Publisher or Sponsor: The Scandinavian Association for Social Medicine

EDITORIAL DESCRIPTION

Publishes articles from all spheres of social-medical research. The main emphasis is upon prevention of disease and behavioural deviations.
Articles per average issue: Varies
Manuscripts accepted in English

MANUSCRIPT INFORMATION

Subject field(s): Epidemiological research, studies on the need and demand for care, as well as the organization of the medical services and social welfare are other important areas. Disease-producing conditions in the family, working life and the rest of the community, social-medical studies on various diseases, the clinical work and treatment of individual patients.
Manuscript requirements: Style sheet sent on request.
Preferred length: None
Number of copies to be submitted: Original and one copy
Author information and reprints: Payment: Reprints only. 50 offprints of article
Is simultaneous submission of article to other journals permitted: No
Exclusive manuscript rights between acceptance and publication: Yes
Copyright: Held by publication.
Reprints: Additional may be ordered.
Disposition of manuscript:
Receipt of manuscript acknowledged: Yes
Submit to:
Gunnar Inghe
Editor
Socialmedicinska Institutionen
Karolinska Inst., Industriv. 13
S-104 01 Stockholm 60, Sweden

SCANDINAVIAN JOURNAL OF UROLOGY AND NEPHROLOGY [2482]

Almqvist & Wiksell Periodical Company
P. O. Box 62
S-101 20 Stockholm 1, Sweden
08/23 79 90

SUBSCRIPTION DATA

Issues and rates: Published three times per year.
Average paid circulation: Not available.
Annual rate(s): Sw.Kr. 100.00; Foreign $26.25
Publisher or Sponsor: Society for the Publication of *Acta Chirurgica Scandinavica*

EDITORIAL DESCRIPTION

Publishes urological papers from Denmark, Finland, Iceland, Norway, and Sweden, as well as nephrologic papers when of special interest to operative urology. Short preliminary reports and important case-reports are published promptly. As basic research work is of increasing importance to surgery, papers of this kind are also accepted. All papers printed in English.

MANUSCRIPT INFORMATION

Subject field(s): Urology, case reports, nephrology when of special interest to operative urology, basic research work
Manuscript requirements: Style sheet sent on request.
Is simultaneous submission of article to other journals permitted: No
Exclusive manuscript rights between acceptance and publication: Yes
Copyright: Held by publication.
Reprints: Available
Additional information: Instructions to authors sent upon request. Write to Chief Editor.
Submit to:
Gustav Giertz
Chief Editor
Karolinska Sjukhuset
S-104 01 Stockholm 60, Sweden

THE SIGHT-SAVING REVIEW [2483]

79 Madison Avenue
New York, New York 10016
(212) 684-3505 ext. 40

First published in 1931

SUBSCRIPTION DATA

Issues and rates: Published quarterly.
Average paid circulation: 5,638; 538 controlled
Annual rate(s): $7.00, Foreign $7.20
Publisher or Sponsor: National Society for the Prevention of Blindness, Inc.
Managing Editor: Joseph J. Kerstein

EDITORIAL DESCRIPTION

Publishes medical and medically oriented review articles on the diseases and conditions which cause blindness and how they may be prevented, including general presentations of new and important clinical data; extensions of existing studies; fresh approaches to traditional subjects; reports of outstanding work; matters of extreme timeliness; new concepts of special interest; and subjects of pertinence

Medicine (general)

relating to law, government, health legislation, and finance.
Articles per average issue: 5
Audience: Professional
Manuscripts accepted in English

MANUSCRIPT INFORMATION
Subject field(s): Causes of blindness, advances in treatment of blinding eye diseases, trends in blindness, use of new drugs, pediatric eye care, nurse and eye health, safety eye legislation, prevention of eye injuries, illumination standards, government and voluntary programs, genetic and nutritional counseling, recommendations for screening techniques
Manuscript requirements: Chicago
  Preferred length: 6-18 pages
  Number of copies to be submitted: Two
  Abstract: No
Author information and reprints: Payment: Reprints only. 25
  Is simultaneous submission of article to other journals permitted: No
  Exclusive manuscript rights between acceptance and publication: Yes
  Copyright: Held by publication.
  Reprints: Available at cost.
Additional information: Black and white figures may be included.
Disposition of manuscript:
  Query letter: No
  Receipt of manuscript acknowledged: Yes
  Decision to publish in: 4 weeks
  Accepted manuscript published in: 6-9 weeks
  Rejected manuscript returned: Yes
  Rejected manuscript criticized: Sometimes
Submit to:
  Joseph J. Kerstein
  Editor-in-Chief
  (See address above)

SPECIAL STIPULATIONS
  Articles printed upon the authority of the writers.

SOUTH AFRICAN JOURNAL OF MEDICAL SCIENCES   [2484]
Witwatersrand University Press
1 Jan Smuts Avenue
Johannesburg 2001, South Africa
724-1311 Ext. 794

SUBSCRIPTION DATA
Issues and rates: Published quarterly.
  Average paid circulation: 1,900
Publisher or Sponsor: South African Institute for Medical Research

EDITORIAL DESCRIPTION
  Contains original research and investigation in any science represented in the curriculum of the medical schools. The journal is devoted to the basic medical sciences and not to clinical medicine.
Articles per average issue: 5
Audience: Researchers
  Manuscripts accepted in English

MANUSCRIPT INFORMATION
Manuscript requirements: Style sheet sent on request.
  Preferred length: None
  Number of copies to be submitted: One original
  Abstract: Yes
Author information and reprints: Payment: Reprints only. 25 offprints
  Is simultaneous submission of article to other journals permitted: No
  Exclusive manuscript rights between acceptance and publication: Yes
  Copyright: Held by publication.
Additional information: Double-spaced typescript; footnotes in full at end
Disposition of manuscript:
  Query letter: No
  Receipt of manuscript acknowledged: Yes
  Decision to publish in: 3 weeks to 3 months
  Accepted manuscript published in: 6-9 months
  Rejected manuscript returned: Yes
  Rejected manuscript criticized: Yes
Submit to:
  G. R. Beaton
  Editor
  (See address above)

SOUTH DAKOTA JOURNAL OF MEDICINE   [2485]
608 West Avenue, North
Sioux Falls, South Dakota 57104
(605) 366-1965

First published in 1948

SUBSCRIPTION DATA
Issues and rates: Published monthly.
  Average paid circulation: 1100 controlled
  Annual rate(s): $5.00
Publisher or Sponsor: South Dakota State Medical Association
Managing Editor: Robert D. Johnson

EDITORIAL DESCRIPTION
  Contains articles of a scientific nature of interest to practicing doctors of medicine.
Articles per average issue: 2
  Manuscripts accepted in English

MANUSCRIPT INFORMATION
Subject field(s): Case reports, research, advances in medicine and surgery
Manuscript requirements: See latest issue for style requirements.
  Preferred length: 4 pages typewritten, double-spaced
  Number of copies to be submitted: One
  Abstract: No
Author information and reprints: Payment: None.
  Is simultaneous submission of article to other journals permitted: No
  Exclusive manuscript rights between acceptance and publication: Yes
  Copyright: Not copyrighted
  Reprints: Available; author advised after publication
Additional information: Manuscripts accepted are not returned. Every effort

will be made to return manuscripts not accepted.
Disposition of manuscript:
  Query letter: No
  Receipt of manuscript acknowledged: Yes
  Decision to publish in: One month
  Accepted manuscript published in: Six months
  Rejected manuscript returned: Yes
  Rejected manuscript criticized: No
Submit to:
  Robert E. VanDemark
  Editor
  (See address above)

THORAX   [2486]
The Official Journal of the Thoracic Society
B.M.A. House
Tavistock Square
London WC1H 9JR England
01-387 4499

First published in 1946

SUBSCRIPTION DATA
Issues and rates: Published bi-monthly.
  Average paid circulation: Not available.
  Annual rate(s): $32.00
Publisher or Sponsor: The Thoracic Society

EDITORIAL DESCRIPTION
  Contains medical research on the chest.
  Manuscripts accepted in English

MANUSCRIPT INFORMATION
Manuscript requirements: See latest issue for style requirements.
  Preferred length: None
  Number of copies to be submitted: Two
  Abstract: Yes
Author information and reprints: Payment: None.
  Is simultaneous submission of article to other journals permitted: No
  Exclusive manuscript rights between acceptance and publication: Yes
  Copyright: Held by publication.
  Reprints: Available
Disposition of manuscript:
  Query letter: No
  Receipt of manuscript acknowledged: Yes
  Decision to publish in: One month
  Accepted manuscript published in: Six months
  Rejected manuscript returned: Yes
  Rejected manuscript criticized: No
Submit to:
  The Editor
  (See address above)

THROMBOSIS RESEARCH   [2487]
An International Journal on Vascular Obstruction, Hemorrhage and Hemostasis
Pergamon Press, Inc.
Fairview Park
Elmsford, New York 10523
(914) 592-7700

First published in 1972

SUBSCRIPTION DATA
Issues and rates: Published monthly.
Annual rate(s): $25.00; Institutions
$70.00

EDITORIAL DESCRIPTION
Contains original papers, short
communications and letters in the area of
thrombosis research and related studies.
Articles per average issue: 10-15
Audience: Professional, academic
Manuscripts accepted in English, French,
German, Russian

MANUSCRIPT INFORMATION
Manuscript requirements: See latest issue for
style requirements. Style sheet sent on
request.
Preferred length: None
Number of copies to be submitted:
Original and 2 copies, double-spaced
Abstract: Yes. For full-length papers
only. In English for papers in other
languages.
Author information and reprints: Payment:
None.
Is simultaneous submission of article to
other journals permitted: Not permitted.
Exclusive manuscript rights between
acceptance and publication: Yes
Copyright: Held by publication.
Reprints: Available at cost.
Additional information: Because all
communications are reproduced
photographically, it is essential that the
MSS. conform accurately to the
specifications given in each issue.
Disposition of manuscript:
Query letter: Not necessary.
Receipt of manuscript acknowledged: Yes
Decision to publish in: 4 weeks
Accepted manuscript published in: 5
months
Rejected manuscript returned: Yes, if
return postage is supplied by author.
Rejected manuscript criticized: Reasons
for rejections only
Submit to:
Alfred L. Copley
Co-Editor-in-Chief
(See address above)

TOXICOLOGY AND APPLIED PHARMACOLOGY [2488]
Official Organ of the Society of Toxicology
Academic Press, Inc.
111 Fifth Avenue
New York, New York 10003

SUBSCRIPTION DATA
Issues and rates: Published monthly.
Average paid circulation: Not available.
Annual rate(s): $138.00
Publisher or Sponsor: Society of Toxicology

EDITORIAL DESCRIPTION
Publishes papers containing original
scientific research pertaining to
alterations in tissue structure or function
resulting from the administration of
chemicals, drugs or natural products to
animals or man.

MANUSCRIPT INFORMATION
Manuscript requirements: See latest issue for
style requirements.
Preferred length: None
Number of copies to be submitted: Two
Author information and reprints: Payment:
Reprints only. 50 free
Is simultaneous submission of article to
other journals permitted: No
Exclusive manuscript rights between
acceptance and publication: Yes
Copyright: Held by publication.
Reprints: Available at no cost.
Additional information: Detailed
information for authors may be found on
back pages of publication.
Disposition of manuscript:
Receipt of manuscript acknowledged: Yes
Rejected manuscript returned: Yes, if
return postage is supplied by author.
Rejected manuscript criticized: No
Submit to:
Gabriel L. Plaa
Editor
Department of Pharmacology
Université de Montreal, P.O. Box 6128
Montreal 101, Canada

TRANSPLANTATION [2489]
428 East Preston Street
Baltimore, Maryland 21202
(301) 528-4116

Previously entitled *Transplantation Bulletin*

First published in 1963

SUBSCRIPTION DATA
Issues and rates: Published monthly.
Average paid circulation: 2,500
Annual rate(s): $40.00, Foreign $42.60
Managing Editor: E. J. Eichwald

EDITORIAL DESCRIPTION
Contains original completed research and
brief communications in pathology and
immunology.

MANUSCRIPT INFORMATION
Manuscript requirements: See latest issue
for style requirements.
Preferred length: None
Number of copies to be submitted: Three
Abstract: Yes, not to exceed 250 words
Author information and reprints: Payment:
By author to publication. $55.00 per
page. All pages over 6.
Is simultaneous submission of article to
other journals permitted: Yes
Exclusive manuscript rights between
acceptance and publication: No
Copyright: Held by publication.
Reprints: Available, cost depends on
length
Disposition of manuscript:
Query letter: No
Receipt of manuscript acknowledged: Yes
Decision to publish in: 1-3 months
Accepted manuscript published in: 4-6
months
Rejected manuscript returned: Yes

Rejected manuscript criticized:
Sometimes
Submit to:
E. J. Eichwald, M.D.
Editor
University of Utah Medical Center
Salt Lake City, Utah 84132
(801) 581-7480

ULTRASOUND IN MEDICINE AND BIOLOGY [2490]
Pergamon Press, Inc.
Fairview Park
Elmsford, New York 10523
(914) 592-7700

First published in 1974

SUBSCRIPTION DATA
Issues and rates: Published quarterly.
Annual rate(s): $25.00; Institutions
$40.00
Publisher or Sponsor: World Federation for
Ultrasound in Medicine and Biology

EDITORIAL DESCRIPTION
Contains original articles dealing with the
interaction of ultrasonic energy with
living systems; this can emcompass a
broad range of subjects, however, the
majority deal with ultrasound
applications to medicine.
Articles per average issue: 3-4
Audience: Professional, academic
Manuscripts accepted in English (French,
German)

MANUSCRIPT INFORMATION
Manuscript requirements: See latest issue for
style requirements.
Preferred length: 1,000-2,000 technical
articles; 300-1,000 words for letters
Number of copies to be submitted: 2
Abstract: Yes. Of about 100 words
summarizing the main facts and
conclusions of the paper. Include also a
list of up to 20 key words for indexing
purposes.
Author information and reprints: Payment:
Reprints only. 50 reprints
Is simultaneous submission of article to
other journals permitted: Not permitted.
Exclusive manuscript rights between
acceptance and publication: Yes
Copyright: Held by publication.
Reprints: Available at cost.
Disposition of manuscript:
Query letter: Not necessary.
Receipt of manuscript acknowledged: Yes
Decision to publish in: 4 weeks
Accepted manuscript published in: 5
months
Rejected manuscript returned: Yes, if
return postage is supplied by author.
Rejected manuscript criticized: Reasons
for rejections only
Submit to:
Prof. Denis N. White
Editor
Queen's University
Etherington Hall
Kingston, Ontario, Canada

Medicine (general)

UROLOGIA INTERNATIONALIS [2491]

S. Karger AG
Arnold-Boecklin Strasse 25
CH-4011 Basel, Switzerland
061-390880

First published in 1955

SUBSCRIPTION DATA

Issues and rates: Published bi-monthly.
Average paid circulation: 1,002; 65 controlled
Annual rate(s): SFr. 165.00; Foreign $66.00

EDITORIAL DESCRIPTION

Publishes original articles concerned with urological surgery and related areas of study. The primary objective is to provide the practitioner as well as the researcher with the results of original research in urological surgery, in addition to information on new techniques and methods. Case histories are rarely accepted. Included are book reviews, summaries of congresses, and meeting schedules.

Articles per average issue: 6-7
Manuscripts accepted in English, German, French

MANUSCRIPT INFORMATION

Manuscript requirements: See latest issue for style requirements.
Preferred length: 12 pages
Number of copies to be submitted: 2
Abstract: Yes, with key words
Author information and reprints: Payment: None. Excess page charges
Is simultaneous submission of article to other journals permitted: No
Exclusive manuscript rights between acceptance and publication: Yes
Copyright: Held by publication.
Reprints: Available at cost
Disposition of manuscript:
Query letter: No
Receipt of manuscript acknowledged: Yes
Decision to publish in: 1-2 months
Accepted manuscript published in: 6-8 months
Rejected manuscript returned: Yes
Rejected manuscript criticized: Yes
Submit to:
Prof. Dr. G. Mayor
Urologische Universitätsklinik
Rämerstrasse 100
CH-8006 Zürich, Switzerland

VIRCHOWS ARCHIV-A [2492]

Pathological Anatomy and Histology
Springer-Verlag
175 Fifth Avenue
New York, New York 10010
Annual rate(s): DM 148 per volume

Managing Editor: Dr. W. Doerr

EDITORIAL DESCRIPTION

Publishes research on disease in the widest sense and on human pathological anatomy and histology in particular.
Manuscripts accepted in English, German

MANUSCRIPT INFORMATION

Subject field(s): Experimental morphology, ultrastructural research, teratology, nosology, comparative pathology, statistical and geomedical investigations and studies in the history of medicine.
Manuscript requirements: See latest issue for style requirements.
Preferred length: As required
Number of copies to be submitted: 3
Abstract: Yes.
Author information and reprints: Payment: Reprints only. 75 offprints
Is simultaneous submission of article to other journals permitted: Not permitted.
Exclusive manuscript rights between acceptance and publication: Yes
Copyright: Held by publication.
Reprints: Available at cost.
Submit to:
Dr. A. A. Liebow
Editorial Board
Department of Pathology, School of Medicine
University of California at San Diego
La Jolla, California 92037

VISION RESEARCH [2493]

An International Journal
Pergamon Press, Inc.
Fairview Park
Elmsford, New York 10523
(914) 592-7700

First published in 1961

SUBSCRIPTION DATA

Issues and rates: Published monthly.
Annual rate(s): $25.00; Institutions $115.00

EDITORIAL DESCRIPTION

Accepts experimental and observational studies, reviews and theoretical papers based upon the current facts of visual science.
Articles per average issue: 10-15
Audience: Professional, academic
Manuscripts accepted in English, French, German, Russian

MANUSCRIPT INFORMATION

Subject field(s): Theoretical, observational, new techniques, history of the visual sciences, etc.
Manuscript requirements: See latest issue for style requirements.
Preferred length: None
Number of copies to be submitted: 2, double-spaced
Abstract: Yes. Not to exceed 100 words in all four languages, if possible.

Author information and reprints: Payment: Reprints only. 50 reprints
Is simultaneous submission of article to other journals permitted: Not permitted
Exclusive manuscript rights between acceptance and publication: Yes
Copyright: Held by publication.
Reprints: Available at cost.
Disposition of manuscript:
Query letter: Not necessary.
Receipt of manuscript acknowledged: Yes
Decision to publish in: 4 weeks
Accepted manuscript published in: 5 months
Rejected manuscript returned: Yes, if return postage is supplied by author.
Rejected manuscript criticized: Reasons for rejections only
Submit to:
T. Shipley
Editorial Board
Bascom Palmer Eye Institute, Vision Laboratories
University of Miami School of Medicine
Miami, Florida 33152

Or to an appropriate regional editor.

VOX SANGUINIS [2494]

Journal of Blood Transfusion, Immunohaematology and Immunopathology
S. Karger AG
Arnold-Boecklin Strasse 25
CH-4011 Basel, Switzerland
061-390880

SUBSCRIPTION DATA

Issues and rates: Published monthly.
Average paid circulation: 1,273; 108 controlled
Annual rate(s): SFr. 132.00; Foreign $54.00 per volume
Publisher or Sponsor: International Society of Blood Transfusion

EDITORIAL DESCRIPTION

Publishes papers on all aspects of blood transfusion and immunohaematology.
Articles per average issue: 12
Audience: English

MANUSCRIPT INFORMATION

Manuscript requirements: See latest issue for style requirements.
Preferred length: 8 printed pages maximum
Number of copies to be submitted: 2
Abstract: Yes
Author information and reprints: Payment: None.
Is simultaneous submission of article to other journals permitted: No
Exclusive manuscript rights between acceptance and publication: Yes
Copyright: Held by publication.
Reprints: Available
Disposition of manuscript:
Query letter: No
Receipt of manuscript acknowledged: Yes
Decision to publish in: 1 month
Accepted manuscript published in: 5 months

Rejected manuscript returned: Yes

Rejected manuscript criticized: Yes

Submit to:

L. P. Holländer

Editor

Blutspendezentrum

Kantonsspital

CH-4004 Basel, Switzerland

YALE JOURNAL OF BIOLOGY AND MEDICINE [2495]

L220 SHM

Yale University School of Medicine

New Haven, Connecticut 06510

(203) 436-4800

SUBSCRIPTION DATA

Issues and rates: Published bi-monthly.

Average paid circulation: 660

Annual rate(s): Institutions $24.00, Individuals $15.00, Foreign $28.00

Managing Editor: Jean T. Brunjes

EDITORIAL DESCRIPTION

Articles range from descriptions of experimental data obtained through superspecialized laboratory research through articles on the history of medicine and historical scientists to philosophical discussions on the state of laboratory and clinical medicine.

Articles per average issue: 8-10

Manuscripts accepted in English

MANUSCRIPT INFORMATION

Subject field(s): Biology, medicine, history of science and medicine

Manuscript requirements: See latest issue for style requirements.

Preferred length: None

Number of copies to be submitted: Two

Abstract: Yes

Author information and reprints: Payment: None.

Is simultaneous submission of article to other journals permitted: No

Exclusive manuscript rights between acceptance and publication: Yes

Copyright: Held by publication.

Reprints: Available, $28 per 100 copies for up to 4 pages

Disposition of manuscript:

Receipt of manuscript acknowledged: Yes

Decision to publish in: 6-8 weeks

Accepted manuscript published in: 6 months

Rejected manuscript returned: Yes

Rejected manuscript criticized: Yes

Submit to:

Lawrence R. Freedman

Editor

(See address above)

Dentistry

ACADEMY OF GENERAL DENTISTRY. JOURNAL [2496]

211 East Chicago Avenue

Chicago, Illinois 60611

Previously entitled *Bulletin of the Academy of General Dentistry*

First published in 1952

SUBSCRIPTION DATA

Issues and rates: Published bi-monthly.

Average paid circulation: 12,500; 55,000 controlled

Annual rate(s): $5.00; Members $5.00 (part of dues)

Publisher or Sponsor: Academy of General Dentistry

Managing Editor: Joanna A. Carey

EDITORIAL DESCRIPTION

Publishes articles on dental practice, especially those which provide useful information to the general practitioner in his practice. Also publishes articles in areas affecting dentistry, e.g. national legislation, psychology, economics, etc.

Articles per average issue: Four to six

Audience: General dental practitioners

Manuscripts accepted in English

MANUSCRIPT INFORMATION

Subject field(s): Dental practice (clinical), new techniques and technology (research), feature articles on dentistry (travel, missionary work), behavioral sciences (how to motivate patients), politics affecting or interesting dentists, economics affecting practice.

Manuscript requirements: Style sheet sent on request.

Preferred length: 2,000-5,000 words; 4-10 (double-spaced) pages

Number of copies to be submitted: Two

Abstract: Not necessary.

Author information and reprints: Payment: None. Reprints only. 100

Is simultaneous submission of article to other journals permitted: Not permitted.

Exclusive manuscript rights between acceptance and publication: Yes

Copyright: Held by publication.

Reprints: Available at no cost. 100

Disposition of manuscript:

Query letter: Not necessary.

Receipt of manuscript acknowledged: Yes

Decision to publish in: 2-6 months

Accepted manuscript published in: 2-6 months

Rejected manuscript returned: Yes, with return postage paid by publication.

Rejected manuscript criticized: Sometimes

Submit to:

J. A. Carey

Managing Editor

(See address above)

SPECIAL STIPULATIONS

If using photos of patients, patient must sign waiver forms, or photos must be disguised so the patient is unidentifiable.

AMERICAN JOURNAL OF ORTHODONTICS* [2497]

The C.V. Mosby Company

11830 Westline Industrial Drive

St. Louis, Missouri 63141

(314) 872-8370

SUBSCRIPTION DATA

Issues and rates: Published monthly.

Average paid circulation: 10,175

Annual rate(s): $18.00, Foreign $21.75

Publisher or Sponsor: American Association of Orthodontists

EDITORIAL DESCRIPTION

Edited for orthodontists and those general dental practitioners who include orthodontics as a major portion of their practice.

MANUSCRIPT INFORMATION

Subject field(s): Orthodontic treatment, including light wire, labio-lingual, edgewise, twin arch and removable appliance techniques.

Manuscript requirements: See latest issue for style requirements.

Number of copies to be submitted: Two

Author information and reprints: Payment: None.

Is simultaneous submission of article to other journals permitted: No

Exclusive manuscript rights between acceptance and publication: Yes

Copyright: Held by publisher

Reprints: Available at cost

Disposition of manuscript:

Receipt of manuscript acknowledged: Yes

Rejected manuscript returned: Yes

Rejected manuscript criticized: Yes

Submit to:

B. F. Dewel

Editor-in-Chief

708 Church Street

Evanston, Illinois 60201

AMERICAN SOCIETY FOR GERIATRIC DENTISTRY. JOURNAL [2498]

431 Oakdale-9B

Chicago, Illinois 60657

(312) 477-2729

First published in 1966 - as a newsletter

SUBSCRIPTION DATA

Issues and rates: Published quarterly.

Average paid circulation: 600

Annual rate(s): Members $25.00

Managing Editor: Arthur Elfenbaum, D.D.S.

EDITORIAL DESCRIPTION

To encourage the dental practitioner to approach every oral problem from the biologic as well as from the mechanical

Dentistry

and cosmetic point of view. The mouth is an integral part of the body, and any disorder in it may be the cause or effect of a disturbance in any other part of the body or of the mind.

Articles per average issue: One

Audience: Practicing dentists and all who are concerned about the oral health of the elderly. They may be scientific organizations interested in human development or in the general welfare of older individuals.
Manuscripts accepted in English

MANUSCRIPT INFORMATION

Subject field(s): Dental and oral subjects in light of the whole individual are given precedence.

Manuscript requirements: No specific style guide.
Preferred length: 4 pages
Number of copies to be submitted: One
Abstract: Not necessary.

Author information and reprints: Payment: None.
Is simultaneous submission of article to other journals permitted: Permitted.
Exclusive manuscript rights between acceptance and publication: No
Reprints: Available at no cost.

Additional information: Manuscript should be submitted typewritten and double spaced.

Disposition of manuscript:
Query letter: Not necessary.
Receipt of manuscript acknowledged: Yes
Decision to publish in: Varies
Accepted manuscript published in: 3 to 6 months
Rejected manuscript returned: Yes, with return postage paid by publication.
Rejected manuscript criticized: Yes

Submit to:
Dr. Arthur Elfenbaum
Editor
(See address above)

SPECIAL STIPULATIONS
Must apply to geriatric dentistry

ARCHIVES OF ORAL BIOLOGY [2499]

An International Journal
Pergamon Press, Inc.
Fairview Park
Elmsford, New York 10523
(914) 592-7700

First published in 1959

SUBSCRIPTION DATA
Issues and rates: Published monthly.
Annual rate(s): $25.00; Institutions $30.00

EDITORIAL DESCRIPTION
Publishes papers concerned with every aspect of the oral and dental tissues and bone, their environment and functions, whether from the standpoint of anatomy, physiology, chemistry, physics, pathology, bacteriology, epidemiology, or genetics, etc.

Articles per average issue: 15
Audience: Professional, academic
Manuscripts accepted in English preferred, French, German

MANUSCRIPT INFORMATION
Manuscript requirements: See latest issue for style requirements. AIBS
Preferred length: None
Number of copies to be submitted: 2, double-spaced
Abstract: Yes
Submit to:
Prof. A. E. W. Miles
Executive Editor
Department of Oral Pathology
London Hospital Medical College
Turner Street
London E1, England

For current Papers:
Dr. J. P. Waterhouse
Department of Oral Pathology
University of Illinois
808 South Wood Street
Chicago, Illinois 60680

BRITISH DENTAL JOURNAL [2500]

64, Wimpole Street
London, W1M 8AL, England
(01)-935-3963

First published in 1880

SUBSCRIPTION DATA
Issues and rates: Published semi-monthly.
Average paid circulation: 17,000
Annual rate(s): Foreign $38.50
Publisher or Sponsor: British Dental Association

EDITORIAL DESCRIPTION
Contains scientific articles, news, and opinion about and of interest to dentists

MANUSCRIPT INFORMATION
Subject field(s): Dentistry and cognate subjects.
Manuscript requirements: Style sheet sent on request.
Author information and reprints: Payment: None.
Is simultaneous submission of article to other journals permitted: No
Exclusive manuscript rights between acceptance and publication: Yes
Copyright: Held by publication.
Reprints: Available
Disposition of manuscript:
Receipt of manuscript acknowledged: Yes
Decision to publish in: 2-4 weeks
Accepted manuscript published in: 4-6 months
Rejected manuscript returned: Yes
Rejected manuscript criticized: No
Submit to:
J. A. Donaldson, F.D.S.
Editor
(See address above)

BULLETIN OF THE HISTORY OF DENTISTRY [2501]

4 Bank Street
Batavia, New York 14020
(716) 343-3406

First published in 1953

SUBSCRIPTION DATA
Issues and rates: Published semi-annually.
Average paid circulation: 500
Annual rate(s): $10.00
Publisher or Sponsor: American Academy of the History of Dentistry

EDITORIAL DESCRIPTION
Contains articles on the history and bibliography of dentistry; biographical material; book reviews.
Articles per average issue: 6
Audience: Dental and medical
Manuscripts accepted in English

MANUSCRIPT INFORMATION
Subject field(s): History of dentistry
Manuscript requirements: No specific style guide.
Preferred length: Maximum of 5,000 words
Number of copies to be submitted: One
Abstract: No
Author information and reprints: Payment: None.
Is simultaneous submission of article to other journals permitted: No
Exclusive manuscript rights between acceptance and publication: Yes
Copyright: Held by publication.
Reprints: Available at cost
Disposition of manuscript:
Query letter: No
Receipt of manuscript acknowledged: Yes
Decision to publish in: 2 weeks
Accepted manuscript published in: 3-6 months
Rejected manuscript returned: Yes
Rejected manuscript criticized: Yes
Submit to:
Malvin E. Ring
Editor
(See address above)

CANADIAN DENTAL ASSOCIATION. JOURNAL [2502]

Dental Journal Dentaire
234 St. George Street
Toronto, Ontario M5R 2P2, Canada
(416) 962-3261

SUBSCRIPTION DATA
Issues and rates: Published monthly.
Average paid circulation: 10,000
Annual rate(s): $15.00; Foreign $17.00 (Canadian)
Publisher or Sponsor: Canadian Dental Association

EDITORIAL DESCRIPTION
Reflects the aims and purposes of the Association and encompasses the highest standards of ethical practice; provides a vehicle through which Canadian dentists

can communicate; includes articles, features, news, reports of councils, original research, case histories of interest to the profession.

Articles per average issue: 2
Audience: Professional, academic
Manuscripts accepted in English, French

MANUSCRIPT INFORMATION

Subject field(s): Dentistry and the sciences related to dental practice
Manuscript requirements: Style sheet sent on request.
Preferred length: None
Number of copies to be submitted: 3
Abstract: Yes
Author information and reprints: Payment: None.
Is simultaneous submission of article to other journals permitted: Permitted, but not encouraged.
Exclusive manuscript rights between acceptance and publication: Yes
Copyright: Held by publication.
Reprints: Available at cost.
Additional information: From time to time issues are devoted to subjects arranged in advance. Enquire of the editor about future topics.
Disposition of manuscript:
Query letter: Not necessary, but advisable.
Receipt of manuscript acknowledged: Yes
Decision to publish in: 3-4 months
Accepted manuscript published in: 1 year
Rejected manuscript returned: Yes, with return postage paid by publication.
Rejected manuscript criticized: Yes
Submit to:
Dr. Frank Compton
Scientific Editor
(See address above)

CARIES RESEARCH [2503]

Journal of the European Organization for Caries Research
S. Karger AG
Arnold-Boecklin Strasse 25
CH-4011 Basel, Switzerland
061-390880

SUBSCRIPTION DATA

Issues and rates: Published bi-monthly.
Average paid circulation: 818; 62 controlled
Annual rate(s): SFr. 132.00; Foreign $54.00

EDITORIAL DESCRIPTION

Offers a variety of articles ranging from the fundamental properties of dental tissues to late sequelae of those diseases affecting them.
Articles per average issue: 5
Manuscripts accepted in English

MANUSCRIPT INFORMATION

Subject field(s): Tooth formation, mineralization, histology, and histopathology; post-eruptive biophysics, biochemistry and physiology of dental tissues; environmental factors such as saliva and gingival secretion; fluorides

and other substances with a specific action to these tissues; direct studies on caries resistance and susceptibility; and general diseases and medications of importance to the dental hard tissues.
Manuscript requirements: AIBS
Preferred length: 5 pages maximum
Number of copies to be submitted: Two
Abstract: Yes, with 6 key words
Author information and reprints: Payment: None.
Is simultaneous submission of article to other journals permitted: No
Exclusive manuscript rights between acceptance and publication: Yes Held by publication.
Reprints: Available at cost
Disposition of manuscript:
Query letter: No
Receipt of manuscript acknowledged: Yes
Decision to publish in: 2 months
Accepted manuscript published in: 9-12 months
Rejected manuscript returned: Yes
Rejected manuscript criticized: Yes
Submit to:
K. G. Koenig
Editor
University of Nijmegen
Heyendael
Nijmegen, The Netherlands
80-55 85 85 ext. 1043

THE DENTAL ASSISTANT [2504]

Journal of the American Dental Assistants Association
Suite 1224
211 East Chicago Avenue
Chicago, Illinois 60611
(312) 664-3376

First published in 1931

SUBSCRIPTION DATA

Issues and rates: Published monthly.
Average paid circulation: 22,000; 25,000 controlled
Annual rate(s): $12.00; Foreign $15.00
Publisher or Sponsor: American Dental Assistants Association

EDITORIAL DESCRIPTION

An educational, professional journal for those employed as dental assistants or office managers in dental offices.
Articles per average issue: 3-4
Manuscripts accepted in English

MANUSCRIPT INFORMATION

Subject field(s): Technical dental, philosophy of dental practice, allied health fields, dental theory, business practice administration, psychology
Manuscript requirements: No specific style guide.
Preferred length: 1,800 to 2,400 words
Number of copies to be submitted: Two
Abstract: No
Author information and reprints: Payment: None.
Is simultaneous submission of article to other journals permitted: No

Exclusive manuscript rights between acceptance and publication: Yes
Copyright: Held by publication.
Reprints: Available
Disposition of manuscript:
Query letter: No
Receipt of manuscript acknowledged: Yes
Decision to publish in: 3 weeks
Accepted manuscript published in: 2-6 months
Rejected manuscript returned: Yes, if self-addressed, stamped envelope is sent with manuscript.
Rejected manuscript criticized: No
Submit to:
Bee Helgeson
Editor
(See address above)

DENTAL ECONOMICS [2505]

P.O. Box 1260
Tulsa, Oklahoma 74101
(918) 582-0065

Previously entitled *Oral Hygiene*

First published in 1911

SUBSCRIPTION DATA

Issues and rates: Published monthly.
Average paid circulation: 103,000 controlled

EDITORIAL DESCRIPTION

Serves the non-clinical aspects of dental practice administration, including the human aspects of patient and employee relations, recruiting, training, motivating auxiliaries, accounting, fees, credit, taxes, investments.
Articles per average issue: 7
Audience: Professional, staff
Manuscripts accepted in English only

MANUSCRIPT INFORMATION

Subject field(s): Patient relations, employee relations, recruiting, motivating, office management, accounting, taxes, investments, estate planning, fees and collections
Manuscript requirements: See latest issue for style requirements.
Preferred length: 1500 to 2500 words
Number of copies to be submitted: One
Abstract: Optional
Author information and reprints: Payment: By publication to author. $100 to $300 per feature
Is simultaneous submission of article to other journals permitted: No
Exclusive manuscript rights between acceptance and publication: Yes
Copyright: Held by publication.
Reprints: Not available.
Disposition of manuscript:
Query letter: No, but helpful
Receipt of manuscript acknowledged: Yes
Decision to publish in: 2-4 weeks
Accepted manuscript published in: 3 months
Rejected manuscript returned: Yes
Rejected manuscript criticized: Yes

Dentistry

Submit to:
Richard L. Henn, Jr.
Editor
(See address above)

GEORGIA DENTAL ASSOCIATION. JOURNAL [2506]

813 American Federal Building
544 Mulberry Street
Macon, Georgia 31201
(912) 742-2730

First published in 1937

SUBSCRIPTION DATA

Issues and rates: Published quarterly.
Average paid circulation: 1,545
Annual rate(s): $6.00; Institutions $4.00;
Members $2.00; Foreign individuals
$10.00; Foreign institutions $8.00
Managing Editor: Fay M. Wood

EDITORIAL DESCRIPTION

The Journal is informational in nature;
keeping the membership informed on
proceedings of the House of Delegates,
committee meetings, forthcoming
continuing education programs,
presenting clinical reports and news on
state and national levels.
Articles per average issue: 2
Audience: Practicing dentists
Manuscripts accepted in English

MANUSCRIPT INFORMATION

Subject field(s): Dentistry - dental education,
all phases of dental science and related
topics concerning dental health, care and
treatment.
Manuscript requirements: No specific style
guide.
Preferred length: 1500-2500 words
Number of copies to be submitted: One
Abstract: Not necessary.
Author information and reprints: Payment:
None.
Is simultaneous submission of article to
other journals permitted: Permitted, but
not encouraged.
Exclusive manuscript rights between
acceptance and publication: No
Copyright: Held by publisher-reprints
with approval of Editor or Managing
Editor
Reprints: Available at no cost. One
Available at cost.
Disposition of manuscript:
Query letter: Necessary.
Receipt of manuscript acknowledged: No
Decision to publish in: 4 Months
Accepted manuscript published in: 1 year
Rejected manuscript returned: No
Submit to:
Fay M. Wood
Managing Editor
(See address above)

SPECIAL STIPULATIONS

Must have scientific value in field of
dentistry.

INTERNATIONAL JOURNAL OF ORTHODONTICS [2507]

Suite 104
5678 North Palm
Fresno, California 93704
(209) 431-2792

First published in 1962
Average paid circulation: 3,000
Annual rate(s): $14.00; Pan-Am $15.00;
Foreign $16.00
Publisher or Sponsor: The Federation of
Orthodontic Associations
Managing Editor: Dr. Godfrey A. Muller

EDITORIAL DESCRIPTION

Subjects oriented toward orthodontics
and news of component organizations.
Articles per average issue: 3
Audience: Practicing dentists and
universities
Manuscripts accepted in English, Spanish

MANUSCRIPT INFORMATION

Subject field(s): Any article dealing with the
prevention or rehabilitation of the facial
complexities.
Manuscript requirements: No specific style
guide.
Preferred length: 1,200 to 5,000 words;
4-8 pages
Number of copies to be submitted: 1
Abstract: Not necessary.
Author information and reprints: Payment:
Reprints only. 50 reprints
Is simultaneous submission of article to
other journals permitted: Permitted, but
not encouraged.
Exclusive manuscript rights between
acceptance and publication: Yes
Copyright: Held by publication.
Reprints: Available at cost.
Additional information: Supplementary
illustrations are welcomed as long as they
are clear and sharp.
Disposition of manuscript:
Query letter: Not necessary.
Receipt of manuscript acknowledged: Yes
Decision to publish in: 1 month
Accepted manuscript published in: 3-6
months
Rejected manuscript returned: Yes, with
return postage paid by publication.
Rejected manuscript criticized:
Sometimes
Submit to:
Dr. Godfrey A. Muller
Editor
6451 Whittier Boulevard
Los Angeles, California 90022
(213) 721-7614

JOURNAL OF DENTAL EDUCATION [2508]

Department of Dental Research
University of Rochester School of Medicine
and Dentistry
Rochester, New York 14642

SUBSCRIPTION DATA

Issues and rates: Published monthly.

Average paid circulation: 3,200
Annual rate(s): $15.00, Foreign $20.00
Publisher or Sponsor: American Association
of Dental Schools

EDITORIAL DESCRIPTION

Publishes articles concerning dental
education. Both philosophical and
practical (new methods of teaching
courses, administration, admissions
procedures, etc.) articles are acceptable.
Articles per average issue: 8
Audience: Dental educators
Manuscripts accepted in English

MANUSCRIPT INFORMATION

Subject field(s): Dental education, auxiliary
education, accreditation, aptitude tests,
delivery health care, dentist-patient
relations, educational measurement,
health manpower, dental licensure,
practice management
Manuscript requirements: AMA
Preferred length: None
Number of copies to be submitted:
Original and 2 copies
Abstract: No
Author information and reprints: Payment:
None.
Is simultaneous submission of article to
other journals permitted: Possibly in a
special case if permission is requested
Exclusive manuscript rights between
acceptance and publication: Yes
Copyright: Held by publication.
Reprints: Available
Disposition of manuscript:
Query letter: No
Receipt of manuscript acknowledged: Yes
Decision to publish in: 3-4 months
Accepted manuscript published in: 3-4
months
Rejected manuscript returned: Yes
Rejected manuscript criticized: Yes
Submit to:
Erling Johansen
Editor
(See address above)

JOURNAL OF DENTAL RESEARCH [2509]

410 Beauty Avenue
Indianapolis, Indiana 46202
(317) 264-8822 ext. 27

First published in 1919

SUBSCRIPTION DATA

Issues and rates: Published bi-monthly.
Average paid circulation: 4300
Publisher or Sponsor: International
Association for Dental Research, North
American Division
Managing Editor: John B. Goetz

EDITORIAL DESCRIPTION

Dedicated to the dissemination of
knowledge pertaining to the oral cavity,
its contents and contiguous parts, and its
relation to and effect on the total human
organism.
Articles per average issue: 30 articles; 10
annotations

Manuscripts accepted in English

MANUSCRIPT INFORMATION
Manuscript requirements: See
January-February and July-August issues.
Number of copies to be submitted: 3
Author information and reprints: Payment:
By author to publication. $60 per page.
In excess of four pages.
Is simultaneous submission of article to
other journals permitted: No
Exclusive manuscript rights between
acceptance and publication: Yes
Copyright: Held by publication.
Reprints: Available by order to author
only
Additional information: A one page
annotation format is used for more rapid
processing of research reports not
exceeding 500 words.
Disposition of manuscript:
Query letter: No
Receipt of manuscript acknowledged: Yes
Accepted manuscript published in: Four
months
Rejected manuscript returned: Yes
Rejected manuscript criticized: Yes
Submit to:
David F. Mitchell
Editor
(See address above)

JOURNAL OF DENTISTRY [2510]
42-44 Triangle West
Bristol BS8 1EX, England
0272 23237

Previously entitled *Dental Practitioner and
Dental Record*

First published in 1972

SUBSCRIPTION DATA
Issues and rates: Published bi-monthly.
Average paid circulation: 1,400
Annual rate(s): £6.00; Students £3.00

EDITORIAL DESCRIPTION
Advances science and the practice of
dentistry by publishing articles of the
highest scientific stature in all fields of
dentistry and associated fields.
Articles per average issue: 5-10
Audience: Professional, academic
Manuscripts accepted in English

MANUSCRIPT INFORMATION
Subject field(s): Prosthetics, orthodontics,
periodontics, endodontics, dental
materials and related subjects
Manuscript requirements: No specific style
guide.
Preferred length: None
Number of copies to be submitted: 1
Abstract: Yes. A short abstract of about
100-250 words summarizing the aims,
results and conclusions.
Author information and reprints: Payment:
None.
Is simultaneous submission of article to
other journals permitted: Not permitted.
Exclusive manuscript rights between
acceptance and publication: Yes

Copyright: Held by publication.
Reprints: Available at cost.
Disposition of manuscript:
Query letter: Not necessary.
Receipt of manuscript acknowledged: Yes
Decision to publish in: 1-3 months
Accepted manuscript published in: 3-9
months
Rejected manuscript returned: Yes, with
return postage paid by publication.
Rejected manuscript criticized: Yes
Submit to:
Robert I. Nairn
Editor
(See address above)

JOURNAL OF HOSPITAL DENTAL PRACTICE [2511]
1371 Poinciani Road
Venice, Florida 33595
(813) 488-5354

SUBSCRIPTION DATA
Issues and rates: Published quarterly.
Annual rate(s): $10.00; Foreign $10.00;
Students $5.00
Publisher or Sponsor: American Association
of Hospital Dentists
Managing Editor: Raymond F. Zambito

EDITORIAL DESCRIPTION
Seeks to fulfill the objectives of the
AAHD and to further the involvement of
dentists in patient care, education and
research in the hospital.
Articles per average issue: 2-5
Audience: Professional, academic,
administrative
Manuscripts accepted in English

MANUSCRIPT INFORMATION
Subject field(s): Anything relating to
hospital dentistry: post-doctoral hospital
programming, clerkships, administration
of hospital dental departments, case
reports of unusual interest and teaching
value
Manuscript requirements: No specific style
guide.
Preferred length: 6-12 pages
Number of copies to be submitted: 2
Abstract: Not necessary.
Author information and reprints: Payment:
None.
Is simultaneous submission of article to
other journals permitted: Not permitted.
Exclusive manuscript rights between
acceptance and publication: Yes
Copyright: Held by publication.
Reprints: Available at cost.
Disposition of manuscript:
Query letter: Not necessary.
Receipt of manuscript acknowledged: Yes
Decision to publish in: 2 months
Accepted manuscript published in: 1 year
Rejected manuscript returned: Yes, with
return postage paid by publication.
Rejected manuscript criticized:
Sometimes
Submit to:
Raymond F. Zambito, D.D.S.
Editor
88-25 153rd Street, 2S

Jamaica, New York 11432
(212) 291-3300

JOURNAL OF ORAL MEDICINE [2512]
Attention Joyce Guithues
829 Hanamoor Court
Glendale, Missouri 63122
(314) 821-2446

Previously entitled *Journal of Dental
Medicine*

First published in 1946

SUBSCRIPTION DATA
Issues and rates: Published quarterly.
Average paid circulation: 1,600; 200
controlled
Annual rate(s): $10.00; Individuals
$10.00; Institutions $10.00; Students
$10.00; Foreign individuals $11.00 plus
postage; Foreign institutions $11.00 plus
postage
Publisher or Sponsor: American Academy
of Oral Medicine
Managing Editor: Sheldon J. Ross

EDITORIAL DESCRIPTION
Interested in well thought-out articles in
any field of dentistry or medicine relating
to oral and systemic disease, in which
clinical application is evident. Research
material is presented as well.
Articles per average issue: 6
Audience: Dental and medical practitioners,
paramedical persons interested in the
field
Manuscripts accepted in English

MANUSCRIPT INFORMATION
Subject field(s): Oral medicine, pathology,
all related dental fields, all areas of
general medicine relating to oral
manifestations, pharmacology, research,
oral surgery
Manuscript requirements: See latest issue for
style requirements.
Preferred length: Open
Number of copies to be submitted: 2
Abstract: Not necessary.
Author information and reprints: Payment:
None.
Is simultaneous submission of article to
other journals permitted: Not permitted.
Exclusive manuscript rights between
acceptance and publication: Yes
Copyright: Held by publication, but will
permit reproduction as long as credit is
acknowledged.
Reprints: Available at cost. Varies
Additional information: Two black and
white photographs printed free; others
printed at author's expense.
Disposition of manuscript:
Query letter: Not necessary.
Receipt of manuscript acknowledged: Yes
Decision to publish in: 1-3 months
Accepted manuscript published in: 3-9
months
Rejected manuscript returned: Yes, with
return postage paid by publication.
Rejected manuscript criticized: Yes

Dentistry

Submit to:
Dr. Sheldon J. Ross
Editor
136 East 36th Street
New York, New York 10016
(212) MUrray Hill 3-3337

JOURNAL OF PERIODONTAL RESEARCH [2513]

Munksgaard International Publishers Ltd.
35 Norre Sogade
D-1370 Copenhagen K, Denmark
45 112 70 30

SUBSCRIPTION DATA

Issues and rates: Published bi-monthly.
Average paid circulation: 900
Annual rate(s): $33.00

EDITORIAL DESCRIPTION

To publish original investigations concerned with every aspect of periodontology and related sciences. Review articles, reports of scientific meetings, and other short communications may also be accepted.

MANUSCRIPT INFORMATION

Manuscript requirements: Style sheet sent on request.
Preferred length: 20 pages maximum
Number of copies to be submitted: Two
Author information and reprints: Payment: None.
Is simultaneous submission of article to other journals permitted: No
Exclusive manuscript rights between acceptance and publication: Yes
Copyright: Held by publication.
Reprints: Available, first 100 free, additional at cost
Disposition of manuscript:
Receipt of manuscript acknowledged: Yes
Decision to publish in: 30 days
Accepted manuscript published in: 6 to 9 months
Rejected manuscript returned: Yes
Rejected manuscript criticized: Yes
Submit to:
Harald Löoe
Editor
Dental Research Institute
University of Michigan
Ann Arbor, Michigan 48104
(313) 763-3391

THE JOURNAL OF PUBLIC HEALTH DENTISTRY [2514]

2918 Barmettler Street
Raleigh, North Carolina 27607

Previously entitled *Public Health Dentistry*

SUBSCRIPTION DATA

Issues and rates: Published quarterly.
Average paid circulation: 900
Annual rate(s): $10.00

Publisher or Sponsor: American Association of Public Health Dentists

EDITORIAL DESCRIPTION

Seeks to promote improved practice of dental public health and maintain capability of the practitioners.
Articles per average issue: 7
Manuscripts accepted in English

MANUSCRIPT INFORMATION

Subject field(s): Research programs, papers of annual meetings, social sciences, epidemiological surveys, fluoridation, prepayment, group-practice, preventive practice, dental auxiliaires, dental health education
Manuscript requirements: Style sheet sent on request.
Number of copies to be submitted: Two
Abstract: No
Author information and reprints: Payment: None.
Is simultaneous submission of article to other journals permitted: No
Exclusive manuscript rights between acceptance and publication: Yes
Copyright: Held by publication.
Reprints: Available, cost upon request
Disposition of manuscript:
Receipt of manuscript acknowledged: Yes
Decision to publish in: One week
Accepted manuscript published in: 3-6 months
Rejected manuscript returned: Yes
Rejected manuscript criticized: Yes
Submit to:
Kenneth A. Easlick
Editor
School of Public Health
University of Michigan
Ann Arbor, Michigan 48104
(313) 764-5477

MARYLAND STATE DENTAL ASSOCIATION JOURNAL [2515]

1924 Wilkens Avenue
Baltimore, Maryland 21223
(301) 233-1754

First published in 1958

SUBSCRIPTION DATA

Issues and rates: Published three times per year.
Average paid circulation: 2100; 100 controlled
Annual rate(s): $3.00
Publisher or Sponsor: Maryland State Dental Association
Managing Editor: Robert P. Fleishman

EDITORIAL DESCRIPTION

Seeks to elevate the dental profession by keeping members of the Association informed of the scientific, social, and economic developments which affect the health and welfare of the public. It contains research and practical articles, abstracts of current literature, book reviews, editorials, news of dentistry and

allied groups and reports of the Association's official actions.
Articles per average issue: 2-3
Audience: Professional
Manuscripts accepted in English

MANUSCRIPT INFORMATION

Manuscript requirements: See latest issue for style requirements.
Preferred length: 1500-4400 words; 4-8 pages
Number of copies to be submitted: One
Abstract: No
Author information and reprints: Payment: None.
Is simultaneous submission of article to other journals permitted: Yes
Exclusive manuscript rights between acceptance and publication: No
Copyright: Held by publication.
Reprints: Available at cost.
Additional information: Typewritten, double-spaced on standard bond paper.
Disposition of manuscript:
Query letter: No
Receipt of manuscript acknowledged: Yes
Decision to publish in: 1-3 months
Accepted manuscript published in: 1-3 months
Rejected manuscript returned: Yes
Rejected manuscript criticized: Sometimes
Submit to:
Bernard Gordon
Editor
(See address above)

ORAL SURGERY, ORAL MEDICINE AND ORAL PATHOLOGY* [2516]

The C.V. Mosby Company
11830 Westline Industrial Drive
St. Louis, Missouri 63141
(314) 872-8370

SUBSCRIPTION DATA

Issues and rates: Published monthly.
Average paid circulation: 10,780
Annual rate(s): $18.50, Foreign $22.25
Publisher or Sponsor: American Association of Endodontists, American Academy of Oral Pathology, Southern Academy of Oral Pathologists, American Academy of Dental Radiology, New York Institute of Clinical Oral Pathology

EDITORIAL DESCRIPTION

Editorially dedicated to the medical aspects of dentistry. The content is concerned with the diagnostic aids, medical treatment and surgical techniques of dental practice as it is correlated with significant developments in medicine as apply to the practice of dentistry.
Audience: Oral surgeon, periodontist, endodontist, oral pathologist, and dental student.

757

MANUSCRIPT INFORMATION

Manuscript requirements: See latest issue for style requirements.

Number of copies to be submitted: Two

Author information and reprints: Payment: None.

Is simultaneous submission of article to other journals permitted: No

Exclusive manuscript rights between acceptance and publication: Yes

Copyright: Held by publication.

Reprints: Available at cost

Disposition of manuscript:

Receipt of manuscript acknowledged: Yes

Rejected manuscript returned: Yes

Submit to:

Robert B. Shira
Editor-in-Chief
School of Dental Medicine
Tufts University
136 Harrison Avenue
Boston, Massachusetts 02111

OREGON DENTAL ASSOCIATION. JOURNAL [2517]

Room 810
620 S. W. Fifth Avenue
Portland, Oregon 97204
(503) 227-5421

Previously entitled *Journal of the Oregon State Dental Association*

First published in 1930

SUBSCRIPTION DATA

Issues and rates: Published quarterly.

Average paid circulation: 1,500; 1,600 controlled

Annual rate(s): $7.00

Publisher or Sponsor: The Oregon Dental Association

Managing Editor: Dr. Niclaus L. Marineau, D.M.D.

EDITORIAL DESCRIPTION

Features articles geared toward the profession of dentistry, news of individual component societies and related organizations.

Articles per average issue: 1-3

Audience: Professional

Manuscripts accepted in English

MANUSCRIPT INFORMATION

Subject field(s): Dentistry and all related fields

Manuscript requirements: Style sheet sent on request.

Preferred length: 1,500 words or less

Number of copies to be submitted: 1

Abstract: Not necessary.

Author information and reprints: Payment: By author to publication.

Is simultaneous submission of article to other journals permitted: Permitted.

Exclusive manuscript rights between acceptance and publication: No

Copyright: Held by author.

Reprints: Available at no cost.

Additional information: If illustrations are to be included, they should be black and white glossies suitable for reduction.

Disposition of manuscript:

Receipt of manuscript acknowledged: No

Decision to publish in: 1-2 months

Accepted manuscript published in: 1-2 months

Rejected manuscript returned: Yes, if return postage is supplied by author.

Rejected manuscript criticized: Reasons for rejections only

Submit to:

Dr. Niclaus H. Marineau, D.M.D.
Editor
12755 S. W. 2nd Avenue
Beaverton, Oregon 97005
(503) 646-8191

THE TEXAS DENTAL JOURNAL [2518]

Box 109
4920 North Interregional
Austin, Texas 78751
(512) 454-7624

SUBSCRIPTION DATA

Issues and rates: Published monthly.

Average paid circulation: 4,500

Annual rate(s): $8.00; Individuals $8.00; Institutions $8.00; Students $8.00; Members $4.00; Foreign individuals $8.00; Foreign institutions $8.00

Publisher or Sponsor: Texas Dental Association

Managing Editor: Billy B. Howard

EDITORIAL DESCRIPTION

Contains science, news, editorials and features pertaining to the dental profession in Texas

Audience: Practicing dentists

Manuscripts accepted in English

MANUSCRIPT INFORMATION

Subject field(s): Dentistry as an ethically organized profession; from continuing education to legislation; from programs to personalities

Manuscript requirements: No specific style guide.

Preferred length: No preference

Number of copies to be submitted: 2

Abstract: Not necessary.

Author information and reprints: Payment: None.

Is simultaneous submission of article to other journals permitted: Permitted, but not encouraged.

Exclusive manuscript rights between acceptance and publication: No

Copyright: None

Reprints: Not available.

Additional information: Manuscripts should be typewritten and double-spaced.

Disposition of manuscript:

Query letter: Not necessary.

Rejected manuscript criticized: Reasons for rejections only

Submit to:

Billy B. Howard
Editor
(See address above)

TIC [2519]

P. O. Box 407
North Chatham, New York 12132
(518) 766-3047

First published in 1942

SUBSCRIPTION DATA

Issues and rates: Published monthly.

Annual rate(s): $5.00

EDITORIAL DESCRIPTION

Publishes interesting, helpful, and informative material for dentists, dental hygienists, and dental assistants. All material must be based on dental themes or subjects of interest to dentists and written in a simple, direct style.

Articles per average issue: 7

Manuscripts accepted in English

MANUSCRIPT INFORMATION

Preferred length: 600-2000 words

Number of copies to be submitted: One

Author information and reprints: Payment: By publication to author. Amount varies; payment upon acceptance of article.

Is simultaneous submission of article to other journals permitted: No

Exclusive manuscript rights between acceptance and publication: Yes

Copyright: Held by publication.

Reprints: Not available.

Disposition of manuscript:

Receipt of manuscript acknowledged: No

Decision to publish in: 2 weeks

Accepted manuscript published in: 3 to 4 months

Rejected manuscript returned: Yes, if return postage is supplied by author.

Submit to: Joseph Strack
Editor
(See address above)

Nursing

AMERICAN JOURNAL OF NURSING [2520]

10 Columbus Circle
New York, New York 10019
(212) 582-8820

First published in 1900

SUBSCRIPTION DATA

Issues and rates: Published monthly.

Average paid circulation: 312,000

Annual rate(s): $10.00

Publisher or Sponsor: American Nurses' Association

Managing Editor: Gretchen Gerds

EDITORIAL DESCRIPTION

Includes contributions by nursing and allied medical and health specialists on new techniques, equipment, professionalism, case studies, clinical reports.

Articles per average issue: 16-20

Audience: Professional

Nursing

Manuscripts accepted in English

MANUSCRIPT INFORMATION

Subject field(s): Clinical nursing practice, nursing and medical economics, nursing in other countries, related fields

Manuscript requirements: Chicago; style is adjusted by editor.
   Preferred length: 1500 words
   Number of copies to be submitted: One original, one copy
   Abstract: No

Author information and reprints: Payment: By publication to author. $20.00 per page.
   Is simultaneous submission of article to other journals permitted: No
   Exclusive manuscript rights between acceptance and publication: Yes
   Copyright: Held by publication.
   Reprints: Available in minimum orders of 25

Additional information: Double-space typescript

Disposition of manuscript:
   Query letter: Yes
   Receipt of manuscript acknowledged: Yes
   Decision to publish in: 1-6 months
   Accepted manuscript published in: 3-12 months
   Rejected manuscript returned: Yes
   Rejected manuscript criticized: No

Submit to:
   Thelma M. Schorr
   Chief Editor
   (See address above)

THE CANADIAN NURSE [2521]

50 The Driveway
Ottawa, Ontario K2P 1E2, Canada
(613) 237-2133 ext. 45

First published in 1904

SUBSCRIPTION DATA

Issues and rates: Published monthly.
   Average paid circulation: 82,419 controlled
   Annual rate(s): $6.50

Publisher or Sponsor: Canadian Nurses' Association

EDITORIAL DESCRIPTION

Contains technical articles, trends, research, opinions, human interest in nursing, medicine, psychiatry and psychology as they relate to patients, nurses, nurse-patient interaction.

Articles per average issue: 7
Audience: Registered Nurses
   Manuscripts accepted in French and English

MANUSCRIPT INFORMATION

Subject field(s): Nursing, medicine, behavioral sciences

Manuscript requirements: Chicago
   Preferred length: 2500 words; 7-15 pages
   Number of copies to be submitted: Two
   Abstract: Not necessary.

Author information and reprints: Payment: By publication to author. $25.00 per

article. 3 copies of issue in which article appears.
   Is simultaneous submission of article to other journals permitted: No
   Exclusive manuscript rights between acceptance and publication: Yes
   Copyright: Held by publication.
   Reprints: Available at cost

Additional information: Include curriculum vitae.

Disposition of manuscript:
   Query letter: Not necessary, but advisable.
   Receipt of manuscript acknowledged: Yes
   Decision to publish in: 2 months
   Accepted manuscript published in: 4-6 months
   Rejected manuscript returned: Yes
   Rejected manuscript criticized: No

Submit to:
   Virginia A. Lindabury
   Editor
   (See address above)

GEORGIA NURSING [2522]

269 Tenth Street, N. E.
Atlanta, Georgia 30309
(404) 875-9766

First published in 1931

SUBSCRIPTION DATA

Issues and rates: Published quarterly.
   Average paid circulation: 2500; 100 controlled
   Annual rate(s): $3.00

Publisher or Sponsor: Georgia Nurses' Association

Managing Editor: Barbara DeSha Dowl

EDITORIAL DESCRIPTION

Medical information as it pertains to Registered Nurses

Articles per average issue: 1-2
Audience: Registered Nurses
   Manuscripts accepted in English

MANUSCRIPT INFORMATION

Subject field(s): Nursing practice, medicine as it pertains to nursing, human interest stories involving nurses, research by nurses

Manuscript requirements: No specific style guide.
   Preferred length: 5 pages maximum
   Number of copies to be submitted: 2
   Abstract: Not necessary.

Author information and reprints: Payment: Reprints only. 3 issues to each author
   Is simultaneous submission of article to other journals permitted: Permitted.
   Exclusive manuscript rights between acceptance and publication: No
   Copyright: Held by author.
   Reprints: Not available.

Disposition of manuscript:
   Query letter: Not necessary, but advisable.
   Receipt of manuscript acknowledged: Yes
   Decision to publish in: 1 month
   Accepted manuscript published in: 1 quarter

Rejected manuscript returned: Yes, if return postage is supplied by author.
Rejected manuscript criticized: Sometimes

Submit to:
   Barbara DeSha Dowl;
   Faye Gamel
   Editor and Managing Editor
   (See address above)

INTERNATIONAL JOURNAL OF NURSING STUDIES [2523]

Pergamon Press, Inc.
Fairview Park
Elmsford, New York 10523
(914) 592-7700

First published in 1964

SUBSCRIPTION DATA

Issues and rates: Published quarterly.
   Annual rate(s): $25.00; Institutions $35.00

EDITORIAL DESCRIPTION

Publishes papers on all aspects of nursing and allied professions throughout the world.

Articles per average issue: 4-8
Audience: Professional, academic
   Manuscripts accepted in English, French, German

MANUSCRIPT INFORMATION

Subject field(s): Emphasis is on three main points: Meeting the community's needs for all types of nursing care; preparing young people for assuming nursing duties; encouragement of all types of nursing research.

Manuscript requirements: See latest issue for style requirements.
   Preferred length: None
   Number of copies to be submitted: 1
   Abstract: Yes. A Summary of 200-300 words which will be translated into French, Spanish and Russian.

Author information and reprints: Payment: Reprints only. 50 reprints
   Is simultaneous submission of article to other journals permitted: Not permitted.
   Exclusive manuscript rights between acceptance and publication: Yes
   Copyright: Held by publication.
   Reprints: Available at cost.

Additional information: Include also a *curriculum vitae* of the author of not more than 75 words.

Disposition of manuscript:
   Query letter: Not necessary.
   Receipt of manuscript acknowledged: Yes
   Decision to publish in: 4 weeks
   Accepted manuscript published in: 5 months
   Rejected manuscript returned: Yes, if return postage is supplied by author.
   Rejected manuscript criticized: Reasons for rejections only

Submit to:
   Dr. Kathleen J. W. Wison
   Editor
   The Health Services Research Centre

University of Birmingham Medical School

Edgbaston, Birmingham B15 2TJ, England

INTERNATIONAL NURSING REVIEW [2524]

Official Journal of the International Council of Nurses

P.O. Box 42

CH-1211 Geneva 20, Switzerland

(022) 336400

Previously entitled *The ICN*

First published in 1926

SUBSCRIPTION DATA

Issues and rates: Published bi-monthly.
Average paid circulation: 3,500
Annual rate(s): Swiss francs 30.00, Foreign $10.00

Publisher or Sponsor: International Council of Nurses

Managing Editor: Merren Tardivelle

EDITORIAL DESCRIPTION

Carries articles about nursing in various countries and about trends and developments in nursing education, practice and service, social and economic welfare of nurses, nursing research and legislation affecting nursing.

Articles per average issue: 4

Audience: Nurses and health institutions
Manuscripts accepted in English, French and Spanish.

MANUSCRIPT INFORMATION

Subject field(s): All areas of nursing (with the exception of clinical articles)

Manuscript requirements: See latest issue for style requirements.
Preferred length: 2,000-3,000 words
Number of copies to be submitted: Two
Abstract:

Author information and reprints: Payment: None. 50 reprints sent free of charge
Is simultaneous submission of article to other journals permitted: No
Exclusive manuscript rights between acceptance and publication: Yes.
Copyright: Held by publication.
Reprints: Available

Disposition of manuscript:
Query letter:
Receipt of manuscript acknowledged: Yes
Decision to publish in: 2-3 months
Accepted manuscript published in: Within a year
Rejected manuscript returned: Yes

Submit to:
The Editor
(See address above)

THE JOURNAL OF NURSING EDUCATION [2525]

Charles B. Slack, Inc.

6900 Grove Road

Thorofare, New Jersey 08086

SUBSCRIPTION DATA

Issues and rates: Published quarterly.
Average paid circulation: 5000
Annual rate(s): $6.00, Foreign $8.00

EDITORIAL DESCRIPTION

Provides nurse educators with a forum in which they can discuss the major trends in nursing education, describe new programs and courses, including their evaluation. Special theme issues deal with contemporary matters such as continuing education in nursing, etc.

Articles per average issue: 20

Audience: Nursing educators

MANUSCRIPT INFORMATION

Subject field(s): Nursing education

Manuscript requirements: Style sheet sent on request.
Preferred length: 10-12 pages
Number of copies to be submitted: Two

Author information and reprints: Payment: None.
Is simultaneous submission of article to other journals permitted: No
Exclusive manuscript rights between acceptance and publication: Yes
Copyright: Held by publication.
Reprints: Not available.

Disposition of manuscript:
Receipt of manuscript acknowledged: Yes
Decision to publish in: 6-8 weeks
Accepted manuscript published in: 1-1½ years
Rejected manuscript returned: Yes, if return postage is supplied by author.
Rejected manuscript criticized: Yes

Submit to:
Cathy L. Dilworth
Publisher
(See address above)

THE JOURNAL OF PRACTICAL NURSING [2526]

122 East 42nd Street

New York, New York 10017

(212) 682-3400

First published in 1951

SUBSCRIPTION DATA

Issues and rates: Published monthly.
Average paid circulation: 40,000
Annual rate(s): $7.00, Foreign $8.00

Publisher or Sponsor: National Association for Practical Nurse Education and Service, Inc.

EDITORIAL DESCRIPTION

Contains articles relating to clinical, educational, legislative and medical developments of interest to practical nursing.

Articles per average issue: 7
Manuscripts accepted in English

MANUSCRIPT INFORMATION

Subject field(s): Medical/surgical, geriatrics, pediatrics, all medical specializations, nursing education, research in medicine, personal nursing experiences

Manuscript requirements: See latest issue for style requirements.
Preferred length: 1,500-2,500 words
Number of copies to be submitted: Two
Abstract:

Author information and reprints: Payment: None. Complimentary copies of the issue
Is simultaneous submission of article to other journals permitted: No
Exclusive manuscript rights between acceptance and publication: Yes
Copyright: Held by publication.
Reprints: Available, cost varies

Additional information: Photos, illustrations and charts supplementing the article are always desirable.

Disposition of manuscript:
Query letter: Not necessary, but advisable.
Receipt of manuscript acknowledged: Yes
Decision to publish in: 4-6 weeks
Accepted manuscript published in: 2 to 6 months
Rejected manuscript returned: Yes
Rejected manuscript criticized: No

Submit to:
Candace S. Gulko
Editor
(See address above)

NEW YORK STATE NURSES ASSOCIATION. JOURNAL [2527]

Executive Park East

Stuyvesant Plaza

Albany, New York 12203

(518) 489-2569

Previously entitled *New York State Nurse*

First published in 1929

SUBSCRIPTION DATA

Issues and rates: Published quarterly.
Average paid circulation: 22,500
Annual rate(s): $5.00; Foreign $5.00; Institutions $5.00; Students $4.50

Publisher or Sponsor: New York State Nurses Association

Managing Editor: Catherine Leach

EDITORIAL DESCRIPTION

Offers a variety of articles focusing on clinical, educational, and research aspects of the independent and interdependent practice of professional nursing; social, political, ethical and economic issues as related to the profession of nursing and the total health care delivery system.

Articles per average issue: 5

Audience: Professional, academic
Manuscripts accepted in English

MANUSCRIPT INFORMATION

Manuscript requirements: See latest issue for style requirements. Style sheet sent on request.
Preferred length: 2,500 words

Nursing

Number of copies to be submitted: 2
Abstract: Not necessary.
Author information and reprints: Payment:
Reprints only. 1 copy of issue
Is simultaneous submission of article to
other journals permitted: Not permitted.
Exclusive manuscript rights between
acceptance and publication: Yes
Copyright: Held by author.
Reprints: Available at cost.
Additional information: Please include some
biographical information on the author.
Disposition of manuscript:
Query letter: Not necessary.
Receipt of manuscript acknowledged: Yes
Decision to publish in: 3-6 months
Accepted manuscript published in: 3-6
months
Rejected manuscript returned: Yes, with
return postage paid by publication.
Rejected manuscript criticized:
Sometimes
Submit to:
Veronica M. Driscoll
Editor
(See address above)

NURSING CARE [2528]

75 East 55th Street
New York, New York 10022
(212) 688-7110

Previously entitled *Bedside Nurse*

First published in 1968

SUBSCRIPTION DATA
Issues and rates: Published monthly.
Average paid circulation: 65,000; 3,000
controlled
Annual rate(s): $7.00, Foreign $9.00
Publisher or Sponsor: National Federation
of Licensed Practical Nurses

EDITORIAL DESCRIPTION
Contains articles on clinical nursing;
national health news; news of National
Federation of Licensed Practical Nurses
Articles per average issue: 5
Audience: Licensed practical and vocational
nurses
Manuscripts accepted in English

MANUSCRIPT INFORMATION
Subject field(s): Clinical nursing, disease
summary, nursing research, nursing
education, health information
Manuscript requirements: No specific style
guide.
Preferred length: 1,500-2,500 words
Number of copies to be submitted: Two
Abstract: Yes.
Author information and reprints: Payment:
By publication to author. $15-$20 per
page.
Is simultaneous submission of article to
other journals permitted: No
Exclusive manuscript rights between
acceptance and publication: Yes
Copyright: Held by publication.
Reprints: Available at cost.

Additional information: Photographs and
diagrams can be submitted with
manuscript.
Disposition of manuscript:
Query letter: Necessary.
Receipt of manuscript acknowledged: Yes
Decision to publish in: 2 weeks
Accepted manuscript published in:
Variable
Rejected manuscript returned: Yes, if
return postage is supplied by author.
Rejected manuscript criticized: No
Submit to:
Fyat Raines
Editor
(See address above)

NURSING OUTLOOK [2529]

10 Columbus Circle
New York, New York 10019
(212) 582-8820 ext. 230

First published in 1953

SUBSCRIPTION DATA
Issues and rates: Published monthly.
Average paid circulation: 32,000
Annual rate(s). $12.00, Foreign $16.00
Publisher or Sponsor: National League for
Nursing

EDITORIAL DESCRIPTION
Primarily concerned with trends and
issues in modern professional nursing,
with content directed toward nurses in
leadership positions in nursing education,
service, and community health.
Articles per average issue: 8
Manuscripts accepted in English

MANUSCRIPT INFORMATION
Subject field(s): Nursing, education,
behavioral and physical sciences,
philosophy
Manuscript requirements: See latest issue for
style requirements.
Preferred length: Maximum of 4,000
words
Number of copies to be submitted: Two
Abstract:
Author information and reprints: Payment:
By publication to author. $20.00 per
page. 100 free reprints in lieu of cash
payment.
Is simultaneous submission of article to
other journals permitted: No
Exclusive manuscript rights between
acceptance and publication: Yes
Copyright: Held by publication.
Reprints: Available, cost varies with
length
Disposition of manuscript:
Query letter: Not necessary.
Receipt of manuscript acknowledged: Yes
Decision to publish in: 6 weeks
Accepted manuscript published in: 6
months
Rejected manuscript returned: Yes
Rejected manuscript criticized: Yes
Submit to:
Edith P. Lewis
Editor
(See address above)

NURSING '75 [2530]

Benjamin Fox Pavillon
Jenkintown, Pennsylvania 19046
(215) TU 6-0616

First published in 1971

SUBSCRIPTION DATA
Issues and rates: Published monthly.
Average paid circulation: 202,000
Annual rate(s): $12.00; Students $6.00

EDITORIAL DESCRIPTION
Articles on nursing problems encountered
in everyday practice.
Articles per average issue: 15
Audience: Professional nurses
Manuscripts accepted in English

MANUSCRIPT INFORMATION
Manuscript requirements: Chicago
Preferred length: 30 pages
Number of copies to be submitted: 3
Abstract: Not necessary.
Author information and reprints: Payment:
None.
Is simultaneous submission of article to
other journals permitted: Not permitted.
Exclusive manuscript rights between
acceptance and publication: Yes
Copyright: Held by author.
Reprints: Not available.
Disposition of manuscript:
Query letter: Not necessary.
Receipt of manuscript acknowledged: Yes
Decision to publish in: Varies
Accepted manuscript published in: Varies
Rejected manuscript returned: Yes, with
return postage paid by publication.
Rejected manuscript criticized:
Sometimes
Submit to:
Francis I. Villemain
Executive Editor
(See address above)

RN-THE NATIONAL MAGAZINE FOR NURSES [2531]

496 Kinderkamack Road
Oradell, New Jersey 07649
(201) 262-3030

SUBSCRIPTION DATA
Issues and rates: Published monthly.
Average paid circulation: 206,000
Annual rate(s): $8.00; Students $1.00
Managing Editor: Rhea Felknor

EDITORIAL DESCRIPTION
To keep nurses, particularly those based
in hospitals, abreast of the significant
clinical and professional developments in
their field.
Articles per average issue: 10-12
Audience: Registered professional nurses
Manuscripts accepted in English only

MANUSCRIPT INFORMATION
Subject field(s): Anything that may be of
interest to registered nurses.

Manuscript requirements: See latest issue for style requirements. Style sheet sent on request.
Preferred length: 2,000 words; 6-8 pages
Number of copies to be submitted: Not necessary.
Author information and reprints: Payment: By publication to author. Up to 10 cents per word.
Is simultaneous submission of article to other journals permitted: Not permitted.
Exclusive manuscript rights between acceptance and publication: Yes
Copyright: Held by publication.
Reprints: Available at cost.
Additional information: Almost all articles published are written by registered nurses.
Disposition of manuscript:
Query letter: Not necessary.
Receipt of manuscript acknowledged: Yes
Decision to publish in: 2-3 weeks
Accepted manuscript published in: 6 months
Rejected manuscript returned: Yes, if return postage is supplied by author.
Rejected manuscript criticized: Sometimes
Submit to:
John H. Lavin
Editor
(See address above)

Surgery

ACTA CHIRURGICA SCANDINAVICA [2532]

Almqvist & Wiksell Periodical Company
Box 62
S-101 20 Stockholm 1, Sweden
08/23 79 90

SUBSCRIPTION DATA
Issues and rates: 8 issues per year
Average paid circulation: 2,500
Annual rate(s): Sw.Kr 250; Foreign $63.75
Publisher or Sponsor: Society for the Publication of *Acta Chirurgica Scandinavica*

EDITORIAL DESCRIPTION
Publishes papers on general surgery from Denmark, Finland, Iceland, Norway and Sweden. Papers are published in English. (French and German on special request)

MANUSCRIPT INFORMATION
Subject field(s): General surgery
Manuscript requirements: Style sheet sent on request.
Is simultaneous submission of article to other journals permitted: No
Exclusive manuscript rights between acceptance and publication: Yes
Copyright: Held by publication.
Additional information: All instructions for authors will be sent on request.
Submit to:
Bengt Fries
Assistant Editor

Sabbatsbergs Sjukhus
Dalagatan 9-11
S-113 24 Stockholm, Sweden

CHILD'S BRAIN [2533]

S. Karger, A.G.
Arnold Boecklin-Strasse 25
CH-4011 Basel, Switzerland

First published in 1975

SUBSCRIPTION DATA
Issues and rates: Published bi-monthly.
Annual rate(s): $48.00; Foreign SFr. 132.00; DM 125.00
Publisher or Sponsor: International Society for Pediatric Neurosurgery

EDITORIAL DESCRIPTION
Provides for the transfer of new information and observations in pediatric neurosurgery and its allied sciences of neurology, neuroradiology, and neuropathology.
Audience: Professional, academic
Manuscripts accepted in English only

MANUSCRIPT INFORMATION
Subject field(s): Basic science, clinical observations, and technical procedures
Manuscript requirements: Style sheet sent on request.
Preferred length: 8 printed pages maximum
Number of copies to be submitted: 2
Abstract: Yes. Of not more than 10 lines, with about 5 key words for indexing purposes.
Author information and reprints: Payment: None.
Is simultaneous submission of article to other journals permitted: Not permitted.
Exclusive manuscript rights between acceptance and publication: Yes
Copyright: Held by publication.
Additional information: Contact editor for further information regarding editorial refereeing.
Disposition of manuscript:
Query letter: Not necessary.
Receipt of manuscript acknowledged: Yes
Accepted manuscript published in: 4-6 months
Rejected manuscript returned: Yes, if return postage is supplied by author.
Rejected manuscript criticized: Yes
Submit to:
Dr. Anthony J. Raimondi
Main Editor
2300 Children's Plaza
Chicago, Illinois 60614

CHIRURGIA PLASTICA [2534]

Springer-Verlag
175 Fifth Avenue
New York, New York 10010

SUBSCRIPTION DATA
Annual rate(s): DM 132 per volume

Managing Editor: D. Buck-Gramcko

EDITORIAL DESCRIPTION
To publish recent research in all fields pertaining to plastic surgery.
Audience: Surgeons
Manuscripts accepted in English

MANUSCRIPT INFORMATION
Manuscript requirements: Style sheet sent on request.
Preferred length: As required
Number of copies to be submitted: 3
Abstract: Yes.
Author information and reprints: Payment: Reprints only. 50 offprints
Is simultaneous submission of article to other journals permitted: Not permitted.
Exclusive manuscript rights between acceptance and publication: Yes
Copyright: Held by publication.
Reprints: Available at cost.
Submit to:
G. Lister, F.R.C.S.
Editorial Board Member
1001 Doctors Office Building
East Liberty Street
Louisville, Kentucky 40202

EUROPEAN SURGICAL RESEARCH [2535]

S. Karger AG
Arnold-Boecklin Strasse 25
CH-4011 Basel, Switzerland
061-390880

First published in 1969

SUBSCRIPTION DATA
Issues and rates: Published bi-monthly.
Average paid circulation: 692; 83 controlled
Annual rate(s): SFr. 132.00; Foreign $54.00
Publisher or Sponsor: The European Society for Experimental Surgery

EDITORIAL DESCRIPTION
Grants prompt publication of the latest results of clinical and laboratory investigations in surgery, including original manuscripts dealing with clinical and experimental research. An aid to the transmission of the principals, techniques and knowledge of the basic sciences into clinical practice.
Articles per average issue: 7
Manuscripts accepted in English, German, French

MANUSCRIPT INFORMATION
Manuscript requirements: Style sheet sent on request.
Preferred length: 8 printed pages
Number of copies to be submitted: 3
Abstract: Yes, including an English title and 3-9 key words.
Author information and reprints: Payment: Reprints only.
Is simultaneous submission of article to other journals permitted: No
Exclusive manuscript rights between acceptance and publication: Yes

Surgery

Copyright: Held by publication.
Reprints: Available
Disposition of manuscript:
Query letter: No
Receipt of manuscript acknowledged: Yes
Decision to publish in: 1 month
Accepted manuscript published in: 6 months
Rejected manuscript returned: Yes
Rejected manuscript criticized: No
Submit to:
Editorial Board
(See address above)

THE JOURNAL OF BONE AND JOINT SURGERY [2536]

Longman Group Ltd., Journals Division
Burnt Mill
Harlow, Essex, England
26721

SUBSCRIPTION DATA
Issues and rates: Published quarterly.
Annual rate(s): £6.00; Foreign £7.50

EDITORIAL DESCRIPTION
Contains articles on progress, new ideas and techniques in orthopaedic surgery and in the sciences on which it is based.
Submit to:
R.C.F. Catterall
Editor
(See address above)

SPECIAL STIPULATIONS
Request additional information from editor.

JOURNAL OF SURGICAL RESEARCH [2537]

Academic Press, Inc.
111 Fifth Avenue
New York, New York 10003

First published in 1959

SUBSCRIPTION DATA
Issues and rates: Published monthly.
Average paid circulation: 2,000
Publisher or Sponsor: Association for Academic Surgery
Managing Editor: David B. Skinner

EDITORIAL DESCRIPTION
Publishes original scientific manuscripts describing clinical and laboratory research problems related to surgery.
Articles per average issue: 15
Audience: Surgeons and biomedical scientists
Manuscripts accepted in English

MANUSCRIPT INFORMATION
Manuscript requirements: See latest issue for style requirements. Style sheet sent on request.
Preferred length: 10 pages
Number of copies to be submitted: 3
Abstract: Not necessary.

Author information and reprints: Payment: Reprints only. 50 reprints
Is simultaneous submission of article to other journals permitted: Not permitted.
Exclusive manuscript rights between acceptance and publication: Yes
Copyright: Held by publication.
Reprints: Available at cost.
Disposition of manuscript:
Query letter: Not necessary.
Receipt of manuscript acknowledged: Yes
Decision to publish in: 4-6 weeks
Accepted manuscript published in: 4 months
Rejected manuscript returned: Yes, with return postage paid by publication.
Rejected manuscript criticized: Reasons for rejections only
Submit to:
David B. Skinner
Editor
Department of Surgery, University of Chicago Hospital
950 East 59th Street
Chicago, Illinois 60637
(312) 947-6031

THE JOURNAL OF THORACIC AND CARDIOVASCULAR SURGERY* [2538]

The C.V. Mosby Company
11830 Westline Industrial Drive
St. Louis, Missouri 63141
(314) 872-8370

SUBSCRIPTION DATA
Issues and rates: Published monthly.
Average paid circulation: 7,653
Annual rate(s): $32.50, Foreign $36.25
Publisher or Sponsor: Society for Thoracic Surgeons of Great Britain and Ireland, American Association for Thoracic Surgery

EDITORIAL DESCRIPTION
Published for physicians specializing in diseases of the chest, heart, lungs and great vessels where surgical intervention is indicated. Also directed to physicians in training programs leading to certification in the specialty of thoracic surgery.

MANUSCRIPT INFORMATION
Manuscript requirements: See latest issue for style requirements.
Number of copies to be submitted: Two
Author information and reprints: Payment: None.
Is simultaneous submission of article to other journals permitted: No
Exclusive manuscript rights between acceptance and publication: Yes
Copyright: Held by publication.
Reprints: Available at cost
Disposition of manuscript:
Receipt of manuscript acknowledged: Yes
Rejected manuscript returned: Yes
Submit to:
Brian Blades
Editor
50 Irving Street, N.W.
Washington, D.C. 20422

PLASTIC AND RECONSTRUCTIVE SURGERY [2539]

428 East Preston Street
Baltimore, Maryland 21202
(301) 528-4116

First published in 1946

SUBSCRIPTION DATA
Issues and rates: Published monthly.
Average paid circulation: 7,300
Annual rate(s): $30.00; Foreign $32.60
Publisher or Sponsor: American Society of Plastic and Reconstructive Surgeons

EDITORIAL DESCRIPTION
Contains original papers on any phase of plastic surgery: operative procedures, research, case reports.

MANUSCRIPT INFORMATION
Manuscript requirements: See latest issue for style requirements.
Preferred length: 4000 words maximum
Number of copies to be submitted: Two
Abstract: No
Author information and reprints: Payment: By author to publication. $50.00 per page. In excess of 10 pages per article.
Is simultaneous submission of article to other journals permitted: No
Exclusive manuscript rights between acceptance and publication: Yes
Copyright: Held by publication.
Reprints: Available, cost depends on length
Disposition of manuscript:
Query letter: No
Receipt of manuscript acknowledged: Yes
Decision to publish in: 6-8 weeks
Accepted manuscript published in: 6 months
Rejected manuscript returned: Yes
Rejected manuscript criticized: Sometimes
Submit to:
Frank McDowell
Editor
Alexander Young Building
Honolulu, Hawaii 96813

SCANDINAVIAN JOURNAL OF PLASTIC AND RECONSTRUCTIVE SURGERY [2540]

Almqvist & Wiksell Periodical Company
P.O. Box 62
S-101 20 Stockholm 1, Sweden
08/23 79 90

First published in 1964

SUBSCRIPTION DATA
Issues and rates: Published semi-annually.
Average paid circulation: Not available.
Annual rate(s): Sw.Kr. 100; Foreign $26.25

Publisher or Sponsor: Society for the Publication of *Acta Chirurgica Scandinavica*

EDITORIAL DESCRIPTION

Publishes papers in the field of plastic and reconstructive surgery from Denmark, Finland, Iceland, Norway, and Sweden. All papers printed in English.

MANUSCRIPT INFORMATION

Subject field(s): Plastic and reconstructive surgery

Manuscript requirements: Style sheet sent on request.

Additional information: All instructions will be sent to authors on request.

Submit to:
Bengt Johanson
Chief Editor
Plastikkirurgiska Kliniken
Sahlgrenska Sjukhuset
413 45 Göteborg, Sweden

SCANDINAVIAN JOURNAL OF THORACIC AND CARDIOVASCULAR SURGERY   [2541]

Almqvist & Wiksell Periodical Company
P.O. Box 62
S-101 20 Stockholm 1, Sweden
08/23 79 90

SUBSCRIPTION DATA

Issues and rates: Published three times per year.
Average paid circulation: Not available.
Annual rate(s): Sw.Kr. 100.00; Foreign $26.25

Publisher or Sponsor: Society for the Publication of *Acta Chirurgica Scandinavica*

EDITORIAL DESCRIPTION

Publishes papers in the field of thoracic and cardiovascular surgery from Denmark, Finland, Iceland, Norway, and Sweden. All papers published in English

MANUSCRIPT INFORMATION

Subject field(s): Thoracic and cardiovascular surgery

Manuscript requirements: Style sheet sent on request.

Author information and reprints: Payment: None.
Is simultaneous submission of article to other journals permitted: No
Exclusive manuscript rights between acceptance and publication: Yes
Copyright: Held by publication.

Additional information: All instructions will be sent to authors on request

Submit to:
Viking Olov Björk
Chief Editor
Thoraxkirurgiska Kliniken
Karolinska Sjukhuset
S-104 01 Stockholm 60, Sweden

Veterinary

AMERICAN JOURNAL OF VETERINARY RESEARCH   [2542]

American Veterinary Medical Association
600 South Michigan Avenue
Chicago, Illinois 60605
(312) 922-7930

First published in 1940

SUBSCRIPTION DATA

Issues and rates: Published monthly.
Average paid circulation: 5,077; 38 controlled
Annual rate(s): $33.00, Foreign $38.00

EDITORIAL DESCRIPTION

Contains scientific reports of research involving animals.

Articles per average issue: 25

Audience: Veterinarians and researchers working on animals
Manuscripts accepted in English

MANUSCRIPT INFORMATION

Subject field(s): Veterinary medicine, biomedical research

Manuscript requirements: See latest issue for style requirements.
Preferred length: None
Number of copies to be submitted: Two

Author information and reprints: Payment: None.
Is simultaneous submission of article to other journals permitted: No
Exclusive manuscript rights between acceptance and publication: Yes
Copyright: Held by publication.
Reprints: Available, first 200 free

Disposition of manuscript:
Query letter:
Receipt of manuscript acknowledged: Yes
Decision to publish in: 6 months
Accepted manuscript published in: 9-12 months
Rejected manuscript returned: Yes
Rejected manuscript criticized: Yes

Submit to:
Arthur Freeman
Editor
(See address above)

AMERICAN VETERINARY MEDICAL ASSOCIATION JOURNAL   [2543]

600 South Michigan Avenue
Chicago, Illinois 60605
(312) 922-7930 ext. 32

Previously entitled *American Veterinary Review*

First published in 1877

SUBSCRIPTION DATA

Issues and rates: Published semi-monthly.
Average paid circulation: 29,319; 114 controlled

Annual rate(s): $33.00, Foreign $38.00

Managing Editor: Arthur Freeman

EDITORIAL DESCRIPTION

To report original contributions to veterinary science and medicine; and to disseminate news to the veterinary community; including announcements of coming meetings.

Articles per average issue: 8

Audience: Veterinarians and animal researchers
Manuscripts accepted in English

MANUSCRIPT INFORMATION

Subject field(s): Large and small animal medicine; public health; zoo, wildlife and laboratory animals; other animals; veterinary education

Manuscript requirements: Style sheet sent on request.
Preferred length: 500-800 words; 5-8 Pages
Number of copies to be submitted: Two

Author information and reprints: Payment: None. Small honorarium for specific features
Is simultaneous submission of article to other journals permitted: No
Exclusive manuscript rights between acceptance and publication: Yes
Copyright: Held by publication.
Reprints: Available, Price list on request

Disposition of manuscript:
Query letter:
Receipt of manuscript acknowledged: Yes
Decision to publish in: 3 months
Accepted manuscript published in: 4-6 months
Rejected manuscript returned: Yes
Rejected manuscript criticized: Yes

Submit to:
Albert J. Koltveit
Associate Editor
(See address above)

AVIAN DISEASES   [2544]

Department of Veterinary Microbiology
Texas A & M University
College Station, Texas 77843
(713) 845-5941

First published in 1957

SUBSCRIPTION DATA

Issues and rates: Published quarterly.
Average paid circulation: 1725
Annual rate(s): $15.00, Foreign $18.00

Publisher or Sponsor: American Association of Avian Pathologists

Managing Editor: C. F. Hall

EDITORIAL DESCRIPTION

Contains research reports and case reports involving avian diseases, particularly those of the domestic chicken and turkey.

Articles per average issue: 24

Audience: Poultry pathologists and researchers in poultry diseases.
Manuscripts accepted in English

Veterinary

MANUSCRIPT INFORMATION
Subject field(s): Avian only
Manuscript requirements: See latest issue for style requirements.
    Preferred length: None
    Number of copies to be submitted: Two
Author information and reprints: Payment: By author to publication. $10.00 per page.
    Is simultaneous submission of article to other journals permitted: No
    Exclusive manuscript rights between acceptance and publication: Yes
    Copyright: Held by publication.
    Reprints: Available at cost
Disposition of manuscript:
    Receipt of manuscript acknowledged: Yes
    Decision to publish in: 30-45 days
    Accepted manuscript published in: 6 months
    Rejected manuscript returned: Yes
    Rejected manuscript criticized: Yes
Submit to:
    David Anderson
    Editor
    College of Veterinary Medicine
    University of Georgia
    Athens, Georgia 30601
    (404) 542-1904

THE CANADIAN VETERINARY JOURNAL [2545]

La Revue Vétérinaire Canadienne
360 Bronson Avenue
Ottawa, Ontario K1R 6J3, Canada
(613) 236-1162

First published in 1960

SUBSCRIPTION DATA
Issues and rates: Published monthly.
    Average paid circulation: 4,000
    Annual rate(s): $10.00
Publisher or Sponsor: Canadian Veterinary Medical Association
Managing Editor: Nella McKellar

EDITORIAL DESCRIPTION
    Contains papers dealing with an aspect of applied veterinary medicine; case reports, clinical notes, etc.
Articles per average issue: 6-7
Audience: Veterinarians
    Manuscripts accepted in English and French

MANUSCRIPT INFORMATION
Manuscript requirements: Style sheet sent on request.
    Number of copies to be submitted: 3
    Abstract: Yes.
Author information and reprints: Payment: None.
    Is simultaneous submission of article to other journals permitted: No
    Exclusive manuscript rights between acceptance and publication: Yes
    Copyright: Held by publication.
    Reprints: Available
Disposition of manuscript:
    Query letter:
    Receipt of manuscript acknowledged: Yes

Decision to publish in: 5-6 months
Accepted manuscript published in: 2-3 months
Rejected manuscript returned: Yes
Rejected manuscript criticized: Yes
Submit to:
    O. M. Radostits
    Editor
    (See address above)

THE CORNELL VETERINARIAN [2546]

New York State Veterinary College
Cornell University
Ithaca, New York 14853
(607) 256-5409

First published in 1911

SUBSCRIPTION DATA
Issues and rates: Published quarterly.
    Annual rate(s): $10.00; Foreign $12.00

EDITORIAL DESCRIPTION
    Publishes papers on veterinary medicine including anatomy, histology, physiology, pharmacology, microbiology, pathology, surgery, obstetrics, ophthalmology, laboratory animal medicine, electron microscopy, etc.
Articles per average issue: 10-12
Audience: Professional, academic
    Manuscripts accepted in English

MANUSCRIPT INFORMATION
Manuscript requirements: See latest issue for style requirements. AIBS
    Preferred length: Up to 30 pages
    Number of copies to be submitted: 2
    Abstract: Yes. Not to exceed 200 words. Include a list of key words used.
Author information and reprints: Payment: None. There is a page charge of $12.00 per photographic engraving and $6.00 per table.
    Is simultaneous submission of article to other journals permitted: Not permitted.
    Exclusive manuscript rights between acceptance and publication: Yes
    Copyright: Held by publication.
    Reprints: Available at cost.
Disposition of manuscript:
    Query letter: Not necessary.
    Receipt of manuscript acknowledged: Yes
    Decision to publish in: 1 month
    Accepted manuscript published in: 6-9 months
Submit to:
    Lennert Krook
    Editor
    (See address above)

JOURNAL OF COMPARATIVE PATHOLOGY [2547]

Quarterly Journal of Veterinary Research
Academic Press, Ltd.
24-28 Oval Road
London NW1 7DX, England
(01) 267-4466

Previously entitled *Journal of Comparative Pathology and Therapeutics*

First published in 1888

SUBSCRIPTION DATA
Issues and rates: Published quarterly.
    Average paid circulation: 900
    Annual rate(s): £14.50, Foreign £16.55

EDITORIAL DESCRIPTION
    contains results of research and original scientific findings relevant to the diseases of domesticated and other vertebrate animals. Articles on diseases of man are also appropriate if they present features of special interest when viewed against the general background of vertebrate pathology.
Articles per average issue: 16
Audience: Veterinary research workers
    Manuscripts accepted in English

MANUSCRIPT INFORMATION
Subject field(s): Pathology, microbiology, and parasitology
Manuscript requirements: See latest issue for style requirements.
    Preferred length: 3-23 pages
    Number of copies to be submitted: Two
    Abstract:
Author information and reprints: Payment: By author to publication. For colour plate depending on size.
    Is simultaneous submission of article to other journals permitted: No
    Exclusive manuscript rights between acceptance and publication: Yes
    Copyright: Held by publication.
    Reprints: Available, cost on request.
Additional information: See inside front cover of Journal
Disposition of manuscript:
    Query letter: See latest issue for style requirements.
    Receipt of manuscript acknowledged: Yes
    Decision to publish in: Four weeks
    Accepted manuscript published in: Six to twelve months
    Rejected manuscript returned: Yes
    Rejected manuscript criticized: Yes
Submit to:
    Dr. M.J. Clarkson
    Editor
    Department of Veterinary Parasitology
    School of Tropical Medicine
    Liverpool L3 5QA, England

JOURNAL OF WILDLIFE DISEASES [2548]

P.O. Box 886
Ames, Iowa 50010

Previously entitled *Bulletin of the Wildlife Disease Association*

First published in 1965

SUBSCRIPTION DATA
Issues and rates: Published quarterly.
    Average paid circulation: 1300
    Annual rate(s): $15.00

Publisher or Sponsor: Wildlife Disease Association
Managing Editor: John H. Bryner

EDITORIAL DESCRIPTION

Published quarterly for the recording of reports of wildlife disease investigators, research papers, brief research notes, case and epizootic reports, and information concerning WDA activities.
Articles per average issue: 20
Audience: Epidemiologists, environmentalists, and medical community
Manuscripts accepted in English

MANUSCRIPT INFORMATION

Subject field(s): Wildlife diseases and effects of environmental pollutants
Manuscript requirements: See latest issue for style requirements.
Preferred length: 4 printed pages
Number of copies to be submitted: 3
Abstract: Yes.
Author information and reprints: Payment: By author to publication.
Is simultaneous submission of article to other journals permitted: No
Exclusive manuscript rights between acceptance and publication: Yes
Reprints: Available
Disposition of manuscript:
Query letter:
Receipt of manuscript acknowledged: Yes
Decision to publish in: 6 weeks
Accepted manuscript published in: 4-6 Months
Rejected manuscript returned: Yes
Rejected manuscript criticized: Yes
Submit to:
Lars Karstad
Editor
Ontario Veterinary College
University of Guelph
Guelph, Ontario, Canada

POULTRY SCIENCE [2549]

Texas A & M University
College Station, Texas 77843
(713) 845-1931

SUBSCRIPTION DATA

Issues and rates: Published bi-monthly.
Average paid circulation: 3700
Annual rate(s): $45.00
Publisher or Sponsor: The Poultry Science Association, Inc.

EDITORIAL DESCRIPTION

Contains scientific research findings in the various areas of avian science, instruction, and extension work. Areas covered are nutrition, breeding, physiology, pathology, environment, management, product technology, marketing, general, and teaching.

MANUSCRIPT INFORMATION

Manuscript requirements: Style sheet sent on request.
Number of copies to be submitted: Three

Author information and reprints: Payment: By publication to author. $30.00 per page.
Is simultaneous submission of article to other journals permitted: No
Exclusive manuscript rights between acceptance and publication: Yes
Copyright: Held by the Association
Reprints: Available at cost
Disposition of manuscript:
Receipt of manuscript acknowledged: Yes
Decision to publish in: 6 weeks
Accepted manuscript published in: 8-12 months
Rejected manuscript returned: Yes
Rejected manuscript criticized: Yes
Submit to:
H. D. Branion
Editor
The University of Guelph
Guelph, Ontario N1G 2W1 Canada
(519)824-4120 ext. 3880

TROPICAL ANIMAL HEALTH AND PRODUCTION [2550]

Journal Division, Longman Group Ltd.
Burnt Mill
Harlow, Essex, England
26721

SUBSCRIPTION DATA

Issues and rates: Published quarterly.
Annual rate(s): £8.00, Foreign $24.00
Managing Editor: W. G. Beaton

EDITORIAL DESCRIPTION

Publishes the results of original research, investigations of technology in the field of veterinary medicine and animal production.
Submit to:
W. G. Beaton
Editor
(See address above)

VETERINARY MEDICINE/SMALL ANIMAL CLINICIAN [2551]

144 North Nettleton
Bonner Springs, Kansas 66012
(913) 422-5010

Previously entitled *Veterinary Medicine*

First published in 1905

SUBSCRIPTION DATA

Issues and rates: Published monthly.
Average paid circulation: 13,044; 1,518 controlled
Annual rate(s): $15.00, Foreign $20.00
Managing Editor: Ray E. Ottinger, Jr.

EDITORIAL DESCRIPTION

Contains information of special interest to the practicing veterinarian; covers pet animals, farm animals and zoo species. Emphasis is on diagnosis, therapy, surgical procedures, laboratory

techniques, and practice management. Presents practical approaches to familiar problems encountered in the practice of veterinary medicine, documented to as great an extent as possible with illustrations.
Articles per average issue: 17
Audience: Practicing veterinarians
Manuscripts accepted in English

MANUSCRIPT INFORMATION

Subject field(s): New surgical techniques, uses of new products, diagnostic techniques, case histories, practice management
Manuscript requirements: Style sheet sent on request.
Preferred length: 1,500-4,000 words; 8-12 pages
Number of copies to be submitted: Two
Abstract: Not necessary, but advisable.
Author information and reprints: Payment: By publication to author. $10-$15 per page.
Is simultaneous submission of article to other journals permitted: No
Exclusive manuscript rights between acceptance and publication: Yes
Copyright: Held by publication.
Reprints: Available, cost based on number of printed pages, color, etc.
Additional information: Color transparencies and color prints accepted as illustrative matter.
Disposition of manuscript:
Query letter:
Receipt of manuscript acknowledged: Yes
Decision to publish in: 2 to 4 weeks
Accepted manuscript published in: 6 to 10 months, but varies depending on editorial needs
Rejected manuscript returned: Yes, if return postage is supplied by author.
Rejected manuscript criticized: Sometimes
Submit to:
Carlos M. Cooper, D.V.M.
Publisher/Editor
(See address above)

VETERINARY PARASITOLOGY [2552]

An International Scientific Journal
Elsevier Scientific Publishing Company
P. O. Box 211, Jan van Galenstraat 335
Amsterdam, The Netherlands

First published in 1975

SUBSCRIPTION DATA

Issues and rates: Published quarterly.
Annual rate(s): Dfl. 90.00
Managing Editor: S. M. Gaafar

EDITORIAL DESCRIPTION

Concerned with those aspects of helminthology, protozoology, and entomology which are of interest to animal health investigators, veterinary practitioners and others with an interest in parasitology.
Articles per average issue: Varies
Audience: Professional, academic, research

Veterinary

Manuscripts accepted in English

MANUSCRIPT INFORMATION
Subject field(s): Disease prevention, pathology, treatment, epidemiology and control of parasites of veterinary importance
Manuscript requirements: See latest issue for style requirements. Style sheet sent on request.
Preferred length: None
Number of copies to be submitted: 3
Abstract: Yes. Not to exceed 500 words
Author information and reprints: Payment: Reprints only. 50 reprints
Is simultaneous submission of article to other journals permitted: Not permitted.
Exclusive manuscript rights between acceptance and publication: Yes
Copyright: Held by publication.
Reprints: Available at cost.
Additional information: Typewritten, double-spaced, with ample margins. Organize paper in the following manner: a. Title; b. Name of author and his affiliation; c. Abstract; d. Introduction
Disposition of manuscript:
Query letter: Not necessary.
Receipt of manuscript acknowledged: Yes
Decision to publish in: 2 months
Accepted manuscript published in: 4-6 months
Rejected manuscript returned: Yes, with return postage paid by publication.
Rejected manuscript criticized: Yes
Submit to:
Editorial Office
P. O. Box 330
Jan van Galenstraat 335
Amsterdam, The Netherlands

VETERINARY PATHOLOGY [2553]
S. Karger AG
Arnold-Boecklin Strasse 25
CH-4011 Basel, Switzerland
061-390880

SUBSCRIPTION DATA
Issues and rates: Published bi-monthly.
Average paid circulation: 951; 17 controlled
Annual rate(s): SFr. 165.00; Foreign $66.00
Publisher or Sponsor: American College of Veterinary Pathologists

EDITORIAL DESCRIPTION
Open to all papers dealing with the pathology of diseases of animals other than man; in general this applies to vertebrate species. Pathology is defined in as broad a sense as possible. Thus, papers that deal with either naturally occurring or experimentally induced disease, are acceptable.
Articles per average issue: 6
Manuscripts accepted in English, German

MANUSCRIPT INFORMATION
Manuscript requirements: See latest issue for style requirements.
Preferred length: 12 pages

Number of copies to be submitted: 2
Abstract: Yes
Author information and reprints: Payment: None.
Is simultaneous submission of article to other journals permitted: No
Exclusive manuscript rights between acceptance and publication: Yes
Copyright: Held by publication.
Reprints: Available
Disposition of manuscript:
Query letter: No
Receipt of manuscript acknowledged: Yes
Decision to publish in: 1 month
Accepted manuscript published in: 6 months
Rejected manuscript returned: Yes
Rejected manuscript criticized: Yes
Submit to:
D. C. Dodd
Editor
University of Pennsylvania
School of Veterinary Medicine
New Bolton Center, R.D. 1
Kenneth Square, Pennsylvania 19348

WILDLIFE DISEASE [2554]
(Microfiche)
P.O. Box 886
Ames, Iowa 50010

First published in 1959

SUBSCRIPTION DATA
Issues and rates: Irregular
Average paid circulation: 1600
Publisher or Sponsor: Wildlife Disease Association
Managing Editor: John H. Bryner

EDITORIAL DESCRIPTION
Published in microfiche for the recording primarily of extensive bibliographies, reviews, tabulations, theses, and monographic works.
Articles per average issue: 1-2
Audience: Wildlife scientists, veterinarians, parasitologists
Manuscripts accepted in English

MANUSCRIPT INFORMATION
Subject field(s): All areas of diseases of wild animals, both vertebrate and invertebrate.
Manuscript requirements: Style sheet sent on request.
Preferred length: 59 pages, maximum or multiples of 59 pages to fit 60 frames of microfiche.
Number of copies to be submitted: 3
Abstract: Yes.
Exclusive manuscript rights between acceptance and publication: Yes
Reprints: Available
Disposition of manuscript:
Query letter: Yes.
Receipt of manuscript acknowledged: Yes.
Decision to publish in: 2-6 months
Accepted manuscript published in: 6-10 months
Rejected manuscript returned: Yes
Rejected manuscript criticized: Yes

Submit to:
Harry W. Huizinga
Editor
Department of Biological Sciences
Illinois State University
Normal, Illinois 61761

Trades, manufacturing and industry

Trades, manufacturing and industry

Trades, manufacturing and industry

ABRASIVE ENGINEERING [2555]
Hitchcock Building
Wheaton, Illinois 60187
(312) 665-1000 ext. 304

SUBSCRIPTION DATA
Issues and rates: Published bi-monthly.
Average paid circulation: 37,000
controlled
Annual rate(s): $7.50

EDITORIAL DESCRIPTION
Contains articles on the use and
applications of abrasive processes in the
metalworking industry.

MANUSCRIPT INFORMATION
Subject field(s): Grinding, abrasive
machining, mechanical finishing,
toolroom
Manuscript requirements: See latest issue for
style requirements.
Number of copies to be submitted: Two
Author information and reprints: Payment:
None.
Is simultaneous submission of article to
other journals permitted: No
Exclusive manuscript rights between
acceptance and publication: Yes
Copyright: Held by publication.
Reprints: Available
Disposition of manuscript:
Receipt of manuscript acknowledged: Yes
Decision to publish in: Varies
Accepted manuscript published in: Varies
Rejected manuscript returned: Yes
Rejected manuscript criticized: Yes
Submit to:
M. M. Patterson
Editor
(See address above)

ADHESIVES AGE [2556]
461 Eighth Avenue
New York, New York 10001
(212) 239-6200

First published in 1958

SUBSCRIPTION DATA
Issues and rates: Published monthly.
Average paid circulation: 1,912; 15,291
controlled
Annual rate(s): $10.00, Foreign $20.00
Managing Editor: Mary McMurrer

EDITORIAL DESCRIPTION
Contains articles, news and departmental
coverage of the manufacture, application,
research and sale of industrial adhesives.
Articles per average issue: 4

Audience: Users and manufacturers of
industrial adhesives
Manuscripts accepted in English

MANUSCRIPT INFORMATION
Subject field(s): Adhesive manufacture,
adhesive technology, adhesive marketing,
management, general interest
Manuscript requirements: Style sheet sent
on request.
Preferred length: None
Number of copies to be submitted: Two
Abstract: Yes.
Author information and reprints: Payment:
By publication to author. $10.00 per
page. Occasional, primarily when article
is commissioned.
Is simultaneous submission of article to
other journals permitted: No
Exclusive manuscript rights between
acceptance and publication: Yes
Copyright: Held by publication.
Reprints: Available, cost to be
determined
Disposition of manuscript:
Query letter: Yes.
Receipt of manuscript acknowledged: Yes
Decision to publish in: 1 to 2 weeks
Accepted manuscript published in: Three
months
Rejected manuscript returned: Yes
Rejected manuscript criticized: Yes
Submit to:
B. J. Kotsher
Editorial Director
(See address above)

A.G.A. MONTHLY [2557]
1515 Wilson Boulevard
Arlington, Virginia 22209
(703) 524-2000 ext. 264

SUBSCRIPTION DATA
Issues and rates: Published monthly.
Average paid circulation: 7,000
Annual rate(s): $5.00, Foreign $6.00
Publisher or Sponsor: American Gas
Association

EDITORIAL DESCRIPTION
Articles cover gas company, industry
research, merchandising, public relations,
cost control, etc. Natural gas industry
(investor-owned) oriented.
Audience: Primary readership is industry
executives and management-level
personnel.
Manuscripts accepted in English

MANUSCRIPT INFORMATION
Subject field(s): Gas technology, public
utility management, public utility
accounting, public utility regulation, gas
research, gas transmission and pipelining,
gas production (limited)
Manuscript requirements: See latest issue for
style requirements.
Preferred length: 8-12 pages
Number of copies to be submitted: Two
Abstract: Yes.

Author information and reprints: Payment:
None.
Is simultaneous submission of article to
other journals permitted: Yes
Exclusive manuscript rights between
acceptance and publication: No
Copyright: Case-by-case consideration
Reprints: Available, cost must be
requested
Additional information: All illustrations
must be in original form, and suitable for
reproduction and fully identified
including any necessary clearances.
Disposition of manuscript:
Receipt of manuscript acknowledged: Yes
Decision to publish in: Two months
Accepted manuscript published in: Three
to four months
Rejected manuscript returned: Yes
Rejected manuscript criticized: Yes
Submit to:
William J. Nickel
Editor-in-Chief
(See address above)

AMERICAN CERAMIC SOCIETY BULLETIN [2558]
65 Ceramic Drive
Columbus, Ohio 43214
(614) 268-8645

First published in 1922

SUBSCRIPTION DATA
Issues and rates: Published monthly.
Average paid circulation: 10,500
Annual rate(s): $20.00, Foreign $22.00
Managing Editor: Donald C. Snyder

EDITORIAL DESCRIPTION
Publishes applications of scientific and
engineering information to the daily
operation of ceramic plants. Also carries
articles of general ceramics interest; news
of the activities of the Society and
programs for the Society's meeting.
Articles per average issue: 8
Audience: Engineers, plant managers, and
sales managers
Manuscripts accepted in English

MANUSCRIPT INFORMATION
Subject field(s): Raw materials, processes,
equipment, instrumentation, quality and
production control, electronic ceramics,
glass, refractories, coatings, whitewares,
nuclear ceramics, structural clay products
Manuscript requirements: Style sheet sent
on request.
Preferred length: 10 pages (Maximum)
Number of copies to be submitted: Three
Abstract: Yes.
Author information and reprints: Payment:
None.
Is simultaneous submission of article to
other journals permitted: No
Exclusive manuscript rights between
acceptance and publication: Yes
Copyright: Held by publication.
Reprints: Available, rates on publication

Additional information: Manuscripts receive at least two reviews for technical evaluation.

Disposition of manuscript:
Query letter:
Receipt of manuscript acknowledged: Yes
Decision to publish in: Three to four months
Accepted manuscript published in: Three to four months
Rejected manuscript returned: Yes
Rejected manuscript criticized: Yes
Submit to:
Margie K. Reser
Technical Editor
(See address above)

AMERICAN GLASS REVIEW [2559]

1115 Clifton Avenue
Clifton, New Jersey 07013
(201) 779-1600

First published in 1882

SUBSCRIPTION DATA
Issues and rates: Published monthly.
Average paid circulation: 1600
Annual rate(s): $10, Foreign $15

EDITORIAL DESCRIPTION
Covers the manufacture, distribution, and processing of flat glass, glass containers, glass tableware, fiber glass, industrial glass, scientific and optical glass.
Articles per average issue: 2-3
Audience: Members of top management, researchers, buying executives of glass manufacturers and distributors
Manuscripts accepted in English

MANUSCRIPT INFORMATION
Subject field(s): Any and all aspects of glass manufacture and application
Manuscript requirements: No specific style guide.
Preferred length: 1,000 to 1,500 words
Number of copies to be submitted: One
Author information and reprints: Payment: By publication to author. $25 per page.
Is simultaneous submission of article to other journals permitted: No
Exclusive manuscript rights between acceptance and publication: Yes
Copyright: Held by publication.
Reprints: Available, cost varies according to quantity
Additional information: Good illustrations are required.
Disposition of manuscript:
Query letter: Not necessary, but advisable.
Receipt of manuscript acknowledged: No
Decision to publish in: 3-4 weeks
Accepted manuscript published in: 60 days
Rejected manuscript returned: Yes, if return postage is supplied by author.
Rejected manuscript criticized: No
Submit to:
Donald Doctorow
Editor and Co-Publisher
(See address above)

AMERICAN INK MAKER [2560]

101 West 31st Street
New York, New York 10001
(212) 279-4456

SUBSCRIPTION DATA
Issues and rates: Published monthly.
Average paid circulation: 3200
Annual rate(s): $7.50

EDITORIAL DESCRIPTION
Contains articles on letterpress, offset, gravure, flexographic, screen process, wood grain and metal decorating inks, chemical coatings, colors, carbon paper, marking, stamping, duplicating and office machine inks, ball pen and writing inks, artist's colors, dye solutions, graphic arts chemicals and allied products.
Articles per average issue: 3

MANUSCRIPT INFORMATION
Manuscript requirements: See latest issue for style requirements.
Preferred length: 1500 words; 6-8 pages
Number of copies to be submitted: One
Abstract:
Author information and reprints: Payment: By publication to author. $80-$90 per article.
Is simultaneous submission of article to other journals permitted: Yes
Exclusive manuscript rights between acceptance and publication: No
Copyright: Held by either author or publication
Reprints: Not available.
Disposition of manuscript:
Query letter:
Receipt of manuscript acknowledged: Yes
Decision to publish in: Immediate
Accepted manuscript published in: Within 3 months
Rejected manuscript returned: Yes
Rejected manuscript criticized: No
Submit to:
John Vollmuth
Editor
(See address above)

AMERICAN LEATHER CHEMISTS ASSOCIATION JOURNAL [2561]

c/o Campus Station, Location 14
Cincinnati, Ohio 45221
(513) 475-2643

First published in 1906

SUBSCRIPTION DATA
Issues and rates: Published monthly.
Average paid circulation: 1,317; 106 controlled
Annual rate(s): $29.00; Foreign $31.50

Publisher or Sponsor: The American Leather Chemists Association
Managing Editor: Clara L. Deasy

EDITORIAL DESCRIPTION
Published for the benefit of technologists and management of the leather industry. The articles are original research reports in the field of leather chemistry and technology. Relevant patents issued are covered in abstract form, as well as foreign research articles.
Articles per average issue: 2-3
Manuscripts accepted in English

MANUSCRIPT INFORMATION
Subject field(s): Leather chemistry, wastewater effluent handling, collagen chemistry, mineral, vegetable and synthetic tannins, coloring and fatliquoring, protein and polymeric finishes
Manuscript requirements: Instructions in the January issue.
Number of copies to be submitted: Three
Abstract: Yes
Author information and reprints: Payment: None.
Is simultaneous submission of article to other journals permitted: No
Exclusive manuscript rights between acceptance and publication: Yes
Copyright: Held by publication.
Reprints: Available, 25 free to author
Disposition of manuscript:
Receipt of manuscript acknowledged: Yes
Decision to publish in: Two months
Accepted manuscript published in: Four months
Rejected manuscript returned: Yes
Submit to:
Robert M. Lollar
Editor-in-Chief
216 Eastern Avenue
Clarendon Hills, Illinois 60514

AMERICAN ROOFER AND BUILDING IMPROVEMENT CONTRACTOR [2562]

ABC Magazine
221 Lake Street
Oak Park, Illinois 60302
(312) 386-4984

First published in 1911

SUBSCRIPTION DATA
Issues and rates: Published monthly.
Average paid circulation: 17,500; 2,000 controlled
Annual rate(s): $8.00

EDITORIAL DESCRIPTION
Contains technical research data, application data and methods, new products, industry news.
Articles per average issue: 3
Audience: Roofing contractors, engineers, and architects
Manuscripts accepted in English

Trades, manufacturing and industry

MANUSCRIPT INFORMATION

Subject field(s): Technical research, applications, management, news pertaining to the roofing and improvement industry

Manuscript requirements: Style sheet sent on request.

Preferred length: 1,000-2,500 words

Number of copies to be submitted: One

Author information and reprints: Payment: By publication to author. $.03 per word. No payment for material supplied by manufacturers.

Is simultaneous submission of article to other journals permitted: No

Exclusive manuscript rights between acceptance and publication: Yes

Copyright: Held by publication.

Reprints: Available at cost

Disposition of manuscript:

Query letter: Not necessary, but advisable.

Receipt of manuscript acknowledged: No

Decision to publish in: One week

Accepted manuscript published in: 2-6 months

Rejected manuscript returned: Yes, if self-addressed, stamped envelope is sent with manuscript.

Rejected manuscript criticized: No

Submit to:

J. C. Gudas

Editor-Publisher

(See address above)

ANIMAL SHELTER SHOPTALK [2563]

The Trade Magazine for Animal Care Personnel

P.O. Box 1266

Denver, Colorado 80201

(303) 771-1300

Previously entitled *National Humane Shoptalk*

First published in 1952

SUBSCRIPTION DATA

Issues and rates: Published monthly.

Average paid circulation: 4000 controlled

Annual rate(s): $2.50

Publisher or Sponsor: The American Humane Association

EDITORIAL DESCRIPTION

Contains information for animal shelter operation, including how-to, publicity, personnel news, fund raising, general professional improvement, local agency activity reports from both humane society and government animal facilities.

Articles per average issue: 3-6

Audience: Animal shelter management

Manuscripts accepted in English

MANUSCRIPT INFORMATION

Subject field(s): Activity reports, product application, shelter operation

Manuscript requirements: No specific style guide.

Preferred length: 1000-2000 words

Number of copies to be submitted: One

Author information and reprints: Payment: None.

Is simultaneous submission of article to other journals permitted: Yes

Exclusive manuscript rights between acceptance and publication: No

Copyright: Not copyrighted

Reprints: Not available.

Disposition of manuscript:

Query letter:

Receipt of manuscript acknowledged: No

Decision to publish in: Varies

Accepted manuscript published in: Two months or less

Rejected manuscript returned: Yes.

Rejected manuscript criticized: No

Submit to:

Eileen F. Schoen

Periodicals Editor

(See address above)

AREA DEVELOPMENT MAGAZINE [2564]

Sites & Facility Planning

114 East 32nd Street

New York, New York 10016

(212) 532-4360

First published in 1965

SUBSCRIPTION DATA

Issues and rates: Published monthly.

Average paid circulation: 32,000 controlled

Annual rate(s): $12.00 (and Canada); Foreign $20.00

EDITORIAL DESCRIPTION

Covers every subject matter pertaining to site selection and facility planning.

Articles per average issue: 8-10

Audience: Chief executives of major corporations

Manuscripts accepted in English

MANUSCRIPT INFORMATION

Subject field(s): Case histories, site selection, community relations, financing, construction and design, site preparations, education and training, legal aspects, security and protection

Manuscript requirements: See latest issue for style requirements.

Preferred length: None

Number of copies to be submitted: One

Abstract:

Author information and reprints: Payment: By publication to author.

Is simultaneous submission of article to other journals permitted: No

Exclusive manuscript rights between acceptance and publication: Yes

Copyright: Held by publication.

Reprints: Available on request

Disposition of manuscript:

Query letter: Yes.

Receipt of manuscript acknowledged: Yes

Decision to publish in: Varies

Accepted manuscript published in: Varies

Rejected manuscript returned: Yes, if return postage is supplied by author.

Rejected manuscript criticized: Sometimes

Submit to:

Albert H. Jaeggin

Editor

(See address above)

SPECIAL STIPULATIONS

Check with editor before sending any material.

ASCAP TODAY [2565]

One Lincoln Plaza

New York, New York 10023

(212) 595-3050 ext. 381

First published in 1967

SUBSCRIPTION DATA

Issues and rates: Published three times per year.

Average paid circulation: 33,000 controlled

Publisher or Sponsor: American Society of Composers, Authors, Publishers

EDITORIAL DESCRIPTION

Contains news and articles about achievements, activities and prospects of writers (lyricists or composers) or publishers (music) in ASCAP.

Articles per average issue: 3-4

Audience: Composers, lyricists, musicians, media, educators

Manuscripts accepted in English

MANUSCRIPT INFORMATION

Manuscript requirements: See latest issue for style requirements.

Preferred length: 500-1,200 words; 3-6 pages

Number of copies to be submitted: One

Abstract: Not necessary.

Author information and reprints: Payment: By publication to author. $75-$150 per article.

Is simultaneous submission of article to other journals permitted: No

Exclusive manuscript rights between acceptance and publication: Yes

Copyright: Held by author.

Reprints: Available, 10-30 free

Disposition of manuscript:

Query letter: Not necessary.

Receipt of manuscript acknowledged: Yes

Decision to publish in: 1 month

Accepted manuscript published in: 3-5 months

Rejected manuscript returned: Yes

Rejected manuscript criticized: Yes

Submit to:

Walter Wager

Editor

(See address above)

ASHRAE JOURNAL [2566]

345 East 47th Street

New York, New York 10017

(212) 752-6800 ext. 377

First published in 1959

SUBSCRIPTION DATA

Issues and rates: Published monthly.
Average paid circulation: 33,000
Annual rate(s): $9.00, Foreign $11.00
Publisher or Sponsor: American Society of
Heating, Refrigerating, and
Air-Conditioning Engineers, Inc.

EDITORIAL DESCRIPTION

Publishes papers concerning the practical
uses of heating, refrigeration, and
air-conditioning equipment.
Articles per average issue: 6-8
Audience: Engineers, architects, contractors,
educators and students
Manuscripts accepted in English

MANUSCRIPT INFORMATION

Subject field(s): Air-conditioning, heating,
food-preservation, refrigeration,
ventilation, domestic water, cooling
towers, air pollution, energy costs, odor
control, noise control, filtration (air)
Manuscript requirements: See latest issue for
style requirements.
Preferred length: 16 pages
Number of copies to be submitted: Three
Abstract: Yes.
Author information and reprints: Payment:
None.
Is simultaneous submission of article to
other journals permitted: No
Exclusive manuscript rights between
acceptance and publication: Yes
Copyright: Held by publication.
Reprints: Available
Disposition of manuscript:
Query letter:
Receipt of manuscript acknowledged: Yes
Decision to publish in: 3 months
Accepted manuscript published in: 3
months
Rejected manuscript returned: Yes
Rejected manuscript criticized:
Submit to:
James H. Cansdale
Editor
(See address above)

ASSEMBLY ENGINEERING [2567]

For Better Design and Manufacture of
Assembled Products
Geneva Road
Wheaton, Illinois 60187
(312) 665-1000

Previously entitled *Assembly & Fastener
Engineering*

First published in 1958

SUBSCRIPTION DATA

Issues and rates: Published monthly.
Average paid circulation: 817; 71,106
controlled
Annual rate(s): $15.00, Foreign $35.00
Managing Editor: Hank Stein

EDITORIAL DESCRIPTION

Published for better design and
manufacture of assembled products. Each

month, feature editorial covers four
major areas of interest: management,
fastening and joining,
electrical/electronic, and assembly
systems. Short items cover areas of
interest under these headings.
Audience: Design and management
engineers, corporate management, and
purchasing.
Manuscripts accepted in English

MANUSCRIPT INFORMATION

Subject field(s): Fastening technology,
joining processes, electronic assembly,
assembly improvement, automatic
assembly, adhesive bonding, management
methods, computer systems
Manuscript requirements: Style sheet sent
on request.
Preferred length: 2500-3000 words
Number of copies to be submitted: 2
Abstract: Not necessary.
Author information and reprints: Payment:
By publication to author. $20 to $35 per
page.
Is simultaneous submission of article to
other journals permitted: No
Exclusive manuscript rights between
acceptance and publication: Yes
Copyright: Held by publication.
Reprints: Available, cost depends on
quantity
Disposition of manuscript:
Query letter: Not necessary.
Receipt of manuscript acknowledged: Yes
Decision to publish in: 2-5 weeks
Accepted manuscript published in: Varies
from 2 to 6 months
Rejected manuscript returned: Yes
Rejected manuscript criticized: No
Submit to:
Robert T. Kelly
Editor
(See address above)

AUSTRALIAN FISHERIES [2568]

Fisheries Division
Australian Department of Agriculture
Canberra, A.C.T. 2600, Australia
062 476144 ext. 46

First published in 1942

SUBSCRIPTION DATA

Issues and rates: Published monthly.
Average paid circulation: 1,200; 13,000
controlled
Annual rate(s): $A9.95
Publisher or Sponsor: Commonwealth
Department of Primary Industry

EDITORIAL DESCRIPTION

Provides technical advice and information
to the commercial fishing industry,
summarizes local and overseas research
in fisheries, also local and export fish
marketing information.
Articles per average issue: 4
Manuscripts accepted in English

MANUSCRIPT INFORMATION

Manuscript requirements: See latest issue for
style requirements.
Preferred length: 1,500 to 3,000 words
Number of copies to be submitted: One
Abstract: Preferable
Author information and reprints: Payment:
By publication to author. By
arrangement
Is simultaneous submission of article to
other journals permitted: Yes
Exclusive manuscript rights between
acceptance and publication: No
Copyright: Held by author.
Reprints: Available at cost
Disposition of manuscript:
Query letter: Yes
Receipt of manuscript acknowledged: Yes
Accepted manuscript published in: 2
months
Rejected manuscript returned: Yes
Rejected manuscript criticized: No
Submit to:
Peter C. Pownall
Editor
(See address above)

AUTOMATIC MACHINING [2569]

65 Broad Street
Rochester, New York 14614
(716) 454-3763

First published in 1939

SUBSCRIPTION DATA

Issues and rates: Published monthly.
Average paid circulation: 14,000
controlled
Annual rate(s): $5.00

EDITORIAL DESCRIPTION

Contains technical articles for users of
automatic screw machines, lathes, cold
heading machines; also, news of
materials, tools, equipment and
techniques.
Articles per average issue: 5
Audience: Metal working production
personnel
Manuscripts accepted in English

MANUSCRIPT INFORMATION

Subject field(s): Machining case studies, new
theoretical developments in
metalworking, simplified (shop level)
explanation of applicable math concepts.
Manuscript requirements: No specific style
guide.
Preferred length: Open
Number of copies to be submitted: One
Abstract: Not necessary.
Author information and reprints: Payment:
By publication to author. $25.00 per
page.
Is simultaneous submission of article to
other journals permitted: Yes, if so
informed.
Exclusive manuscript rights between
acceptance and publication: Yes
Copyright: Held by publication.
Reprints: Available, cost quoted on
request

Trades, manufacturing and industry

Additional information: Author should know specialized metalworking field. Not a market for broad scope general articles.

Disposition of manuscript:
Query letter: Yes.
Receipt of manuscript acknowledged: Yes
Decision to publish in: Two weeks
Accepted manuscript published in: Three months.
Rejected manuscript returned: Yes, if return postage is supplied by author.
Rejected manuscript criticized: Yes

Submit to:
Donald E. Wood
Editor and Publisher
(See address above)

THE BRITISH STEELMAKER [2570]

Review of the Steel Industry
886 High Road
Finchley, London N12 9SB, England
01-445 6870

First published in 1935

SUBSCRIPTION DATA
Issues and rates: Published bi-monthly.
Average paid circulation: 1,000; 2,000 controlled
Annual rate(s): £5.00
Publisher or Sponsor: British Steelmaker Ltd.
Managing Editor: J. F. S. Russell

EDITORIAL DESCRIPTION
Contains short articles and features on all aspects of steel production, from ore preparation through ironmaking and steelmaking to rolling, forging and finishing.
Audience: Top and middle managers, both line and functional, and technologists who are actually employed in the steel industry.
Manuscripts accepted in English

MANUSCRIPT INFORMATION
Subject field(s): Steelmaking, forging, case histories, ironmaking, finishing, inspection, rolling, coating, etc.
Manuscript requirements: No specific style guide.
Preferred length: 2,500 words maximum
Number of copies to be submitted: One
Abstract:
Author information and reprints: Payment: By publication to author. Paid for by arrangement.
Is simultaneous submission of article to other journals permitted: Author should state whether material is offered exclusively or not.
Exclusive manuscript rights between acceptance and publication: No
Reprints: Available
Disposition of manuscript:
Query letter:
Receipt of manuscript acknowledged: Yes
Decision to publish in: Two months
Accepted manuscript published in: 4 months

Rejected manuscript returned: Yes, if return postage is supplied by author.
Rejected manuscript criticized: No

Submit to:
The Editor
(See address above)

BUILDING SERVICES ENGINEER [2571]

Journal of the Institution of Heating and Ventilating Engineers
49 Cadogan Square
London SW1X 0JB, England
01-235-7671

SUBSCRIPTION DATA
Issues and rates: Published monthly.
Average paid circulation: 7000
Annual rate(s): £6.50
Managing Editor: Henry Swinburne

EDITORIAL DESCRIPTION
Contains articles on all engineering services in buildings (heating, air conditioning, lighting, plumbing, water services, lifts, controls, etc.).
Manuscripts accepted in English

MANUSCRIPT INFORMATION
Manuscript requirements: Style sheet sent on request.
Preferred length: 5000 words maximum
Number of copies to be submitted: Two
Abstract: Yes.
Author information and reprints: Payment: None.
Is simultaneous submission of article to other journals permitted: No
Exclusive manuscript rights between acceptance and publication: Yes
Copyright: Held by publication.
Reprints: Available
Disposition of manuscript:
Receipt of manuscript acknowledged: Yes
Decision to publish in: 6 weeks
Accepted manuscript published in: 3 months
Rejected manuscript returned: Yes
Rejected manuscript criticized: Yes
Submit to:
The Editor
(See address above)

CANADIAN MACHINERY AND METALWORKING [2572]

481 University Avenue
Toronto, Ontario M5W 1A7, Canada
(416) 595-1811 ext. 440

SUBSCRIPTION DATA
Issues and rates: Published monthly.
Average paid circulation: 1,000; 10,000 controlled
Annual rate(s): $10.00, Foreign $12.00

EDITORIAL DESCRIPTION
Publication covers the metalworking manufacturing field and includes automotive, appliance, aerospace and other industries with accent on the production sector.

Articles per average issue: 6-8
Audience: Production management
Manuscripts accepted in English

MANUSCRIPT INFORMATION
Subject field(s): Production facilities, staff training, management, new developments, new products
Manuscript requirements: See latest issue for style requirements.
Preferred length: 2 to 3 pages
Number of copies to be submitted: Two
Author information and reprints: Payment: By publication to author. $0.07 per word.
Is simultaneous submission of article to other journals permitted: No
Exclusive manuscript rights between acceptance and publication: No
Copyright: Held by publication.
Reprints: Available at cost.
Additional information: All articles should be accompanied by suitable pictures and/or charts, diagrams etc.
Disposition of manuscript:
Query letter: Yes.
Receipt of manuscript acknowledged: Yes
Decision to publish in: 2 to 3 weeks
Accepted manuscript published in: One to two months
Rejected manuscript returned: Yes
Rejected manuscript criticized: Yes
Submit to:
Antony Whitney
Editor
(See address above)

COLLEGE STORE EXECUTIVE [2573]

P.O. Box 788
Lynbrook, New York 11563
(516) 887-1800

First published in 1970

SUBSCRIPTION DATA
Issues and rates: Published monthly.
Average paid circulation: 10,000 controlled
Annual rate(s): $8.50

EDITORIAL DESCRIPTION
Contains news articles, features, products and advertisements pertinent to and directed to college book store managers across the country. Completely open to all opinions as well as occurences at stores.
Articles per average issue: 5
Audience: Buyers and managers of college stores
Manuscripts accepted in English

MANUSCRIPT INFORMATION
Subject field(s): Particular book stores, college store managers, interesting promotions, merchandising techniques, architectural design, student-store relation, student comment, faculty comment, novel methods of sale, shoplifting prevention, lines of merchandise

Manuscript requirements: No specific style guide.
  Preferred length: 1,500 words typewritten, double-spaced
  Number of copies to be submitted: One
  Abstract: No
Author information and reprints: Payment: By publication to author. $.05 per word. $5.00 per photo.
  Is simultaneous submission of article to other journals permitted: No
  Exclusive manuscript rights between acceptance and publication: No
  Copyright: Held by publication.
  Reprints: Available at cost per issue
Additional information: Publication seeks clear, concise, factual data rather than generalizations.
Disposition of manuscript:
  Query letter: Yes
  Receipt of manuscript acknowledged: Yes
  Decision to publish in: Two weeks
  Accepted manuscript published in: Depends upon editorial needs
  Rejected manuscript returned: Yes, if self-addressed, stamped envelope is sent with manuscript.
  Rejected manuscript criticized: No
Submit to:
  Robert Zeig
  Editor
  (See address above)

COMPRESSED AIR [2574]

A Review of the Capabilities and Economies of Air and Gases
942 Memorial Parkway
Phillipsburg, New Jersey 08865
(201) 859-2770

First published in 1896

SUBSCRIPTION DATA
Issues and rates: Published monthly.
  Average paid circulation: 143; 150,000 controlled
  Annual rate(s): $5.00, Foreign $7.00

EDITORIAL DESCRIPTION
  Contains case histories of pneumatic applications; in-depth articles about companies using pneumatics; construction and mining projects; unusual and unique applications of air power.
Articles per average issue: 3-4
Audience: Management and upper management personnel concerned with the production, distribution, and utilization of compressed air and other gases in all industries.
  Manuscripts accepted in English

MANUSCRIPT INFORMATION
Subject field(s): Pneumatic applications, technical applications, historical
Manuscript requirements: Style sheet sent on request.
  Preferred length: None
  Number of copies to be submitted: One
  Abstract:
Author information and reprints: Payment: By publication to author. $35 per page.

Payment varies according to quality and amount of editorial work needed.
  Is simultaneous submission of article to other journals permitted: No
  Exclusive manuscript rights between acceptance and publication: Yes
  Copyright: Held by publication.
Additional information: Copy must be factually and technically accurate, but in a quasi-technical style. Articles should be accompanied by illustrations, either black-and-white prints or carefully drawn diagrams, curves, etc. These should be captioned clearly.
Disposition of manuscript:
  Query letter: Yes.
  Receipt of manuscript acknowledged: Yes
  Decision to publish in: 2-3 weeks
  Accepted manuscript published in: 4-5 months
  Rejected manuscript returned: Yes
  Rejected manuscript criticized: Sometimes
Submit to:
  S. M. Parkhill
  Editor
  (See address above)

CUTTING TOOL ENGINEERING [2575]

120½ North Hale Street
P.O. Box 937
Wheaton, Illinois 60187
(312) 653-3210

Previously entitled *Carbide Engineering*

First published in 1955

SUBSCRIPTION DATA
Issues and rates: Published bi-monthly.
  Average paid circulation: 280; 25,500 controlled
  Annual rate(s): $6.00, Foreign $12.00

EDITORIAL DESCRIPTION
  Contains articles on new products, updated methods, applications and new developments in the metal-cutting and metal-removal areas of metalworking.
Audience: Operating management and engineering personnel who are responsible for metal cutting and metal removal
  Manuscripts accepted in English

MANUSCRIPT INFORMATION
Subject field(s): Metal cutting and metal removal
Manuscript requirements: No specific style guide.
  Preferred length: Depends on subject
  Number of copies to be submitted: One
  Abstract:
Author information and reprints: Payment: By publication to author. $35 per page.
  Is simultaneous submission of article to other journals permitted: No
  Exclusive manuscript rights between acceptance and publication: Yes
  Copyright: Held by publication.
  Reprints: Available, cost depends on quantity

Disposition of manuscript:
  Query letter:
  Receipt of manuscript acknowledged: Yes
  Decision to publish in: 3 weeks
  Accepted manuscript published in: 3-6 months
  Rejected manuscript returned: Held by publication.
  Rejected manuscript criticized: No
Submit to:
  Noel D. O'Daniell
  Publisher and Editorial Director
  (See address above)

DIE CASTING ENGINEER [2576]

16007 West Eight Mile Road
Detroit, Michigan 48235
(313) 273-2180

SUBSCRIPTION DATA
Issues and rates: Published bi-monthly.
  Average paid circulation: 3,000; 2,000 controlled
  Annual rate(s): $8.00, Foreign $10.00
Publisher or Sponsor: Society of Die Casting Engineers, Inc.
Managing Editor: Burton L. Stern

EDITORIAL DESCRIPTION
  Contains practical articles of interest to die casting companies, machine and die builders, heat treaters, news of die casting industry.

MANUSCRIPT INFORMATION
Subject field(s): Die casting, process control, plant management, metallurgy, design of die castings, education of engineers, machine design, marketing, safety
Manuscript requirements: See latest issue for style requirements.
  Number of copies to be submitted: One
Author information and reprints: Payment: None.
  Is simultaneous submission of article to other journals permitted: Yes
  Exclusive manuscript rights between acceptance and publication: No
  Copyright: Held jointly by author and publication.
  Reprints: Available
Disposition of manuscript:
  Receipt of manuscript acknowledged: Yes
  Decision to publish in: Two weeks
  Accepted manuscript published in: 2 to 6 months
  Rejected manuscript returned: Yes
  Rejected manuscript criticized: If requested
Submit to:
  Robert E. Green
  Editor
  (See address above)

EL ARTE TIPOGRAFICO [2577]

134 North Thirteenth Street
Philadelphia, Pennsylvania 19107
(215) 564-5170 ext. 259

SUBSCRIPTION DATA
Issues and rates: 6 times per year

Trades, manufacturing and industry

Average paid circulation: 15,735
controlled
Annual rate(s): $15.00; Foreign $18.00

EDITORIAL DESCRIPTION
Written for the Latin American
countries, Spain and Portugal, the
publication emphasizes new
developments, new equipment, technology
and production methods in the graphic
arts and converting. All articles and
editorial material are written in Castillian
Spanish.

MANUSCRIPT INFORMATION
Subject field(s): Commercial printing,
package printing, newspaper printing,
magazine printing, converting letterpress,
offset, gravure, flexography, color
process, screen process, photomechanics,
binding
Manuscript requirements: Style sheet sent
on request.
Preferred length: Not to exceed 2000
words
Number of copies to be submitted: Two
Author information and reprints: Payment:
By publication to author. Negotiable
Is simultaneous submission of article to
other journals permitted: No
Exclusive manuscript rights between
acceptance and publication: Yes
Copyright: Held by publication.
Reprints: Available; 3 free
Disposition of manuscript:
Query letter: Best to submit outline first.
Receipt of manuscript acknowledged: Yes
Decision to publish in: 2 to 6 weeks
Accepted manuscript published in: Up to
6 months
Rejected manuscript returned: Yes, if
self-addressed, stamped envelope is sent
with manuscript.
Rejected manuscript criticized:
Sometimes
Submit to:
Guillermo Boehme-Vargas
Editor and Publisher
41 East 42nd Street
New York, New York 10017

ENGINEERING AND CONTRACT RECORD   [2578]
Incorporating Canadian Pit and Quarry
1450 Don Mills Road
Don Mills, Ontario M3B 2X7, Canada
(416) 445-6641

First published in 1888

SUBSCRIPTION DATA
Issues and rates: Published monthly.
Average paid circulation: 17,300
controlled
Annual rate(s): $13.00, Foreign $39.00

EDITORIAL DESCRIPTION
Publishes the latest ideas in construction
methods and design, technology and
equipment; the latest in aggregates
production; provides informed analysis of
economic, financial, legal, and political
trends that affect construction in Canada.
Articles per average issue: 10

Audience: Construction executives,
engineers, public works officials, field and
shop personnel
Manuscripts accepted in English

MANUSCRIPT INFORMATION
Subject field(s): Heavy construction, bridges
and dams, foundation work, roads and
streets, sewer and waterworks
construction, new methods
Manuscript requirements: Canadian Press or
AP
Preferred length: 1,000 to 1500 words
Number of copies to be submitted: One
Abstract: No
Author information and reprints: Payment:
By publication to author. $50.00 per
page. $.07 per word. $5.00 per
photograph
Is simultaneous submission of article to
other journals permitted: No
Exclusive manuscript rights between
acceptance and publication: Yes
Copyright: First and second Canadian
rights held by publisher.
Reprints: Available; cost varies
Disposition of manuscript:
Query letter: No
Receipt of manuscript acknowledged: Yes
Decision to publish in: Within one week
Accepted manuscript published in: 1 to 2
months
Rejected manuscript returned: Yes
Rejected manuscript criticized: No
Submit to:
Al Scott
Associate Editor
(See address above)

FACTORY   [2579]
Plant Operating Management
16 West 61st Street
New York, New York 10023
(212) 765-7290

First published in 1889

SUBSCRIPTION DATA
Issues and rates: Published monthly.

EDITORIAL DESCRIPTION
Serves those who are responsible for
providing support to manufacturing
activities
Articles per average issue: 8
Manuscripts accepted in English

MANUSCRIPT INFORMATION
Subject field(s): Plant facilities, power
transmission, fluid power, electrical, plant
services, material handling, plant safety,
pollution control, tools, and operating
supplies
Manuscript requirements: See latest issue for
style requirements.
Preferred length: None
Number of copies to be submitted: 2
Abstract: Not necessary.
Author information and reprints: Payment:
None.
Is simultaneous submission of article to
other journals permitted: Not permitted.

Exclusive manuscript rights between
acceptance and publication: Yes
Copyright: Held by publication.
Reprints: Available at cost.
Additional information: An objective, clear
copy, with complete details is imperative.
Disposition of manuscript:
Query letter: Not necessary, but
advisable.
Receipt of manuscript acknowledged: Yes
Decision to publish in: 1-2 months
Accepted manuscript published in: 3-6
months
Rejected manuscript returned: Yes, if
return postage is supplied by author.
Rejected manuscript criticized: Reasons
for rejections only
Submit to:
Richard A. Coccola
Editor
(See address above)

FOOD TECHNOLOGY   [2580]
221 North LaSalle Street
Chicago, Illinois 60601
(312) 782-8425

First published in 1947

SUBSCRIPTION DATA
Issues and rates: Published monthly.
Average paid circulation: 15,000
Annual rate(s): $30.00, Foreign $35.00
Publisher or Sponsor: Institute of Food
Technologists

EDITORIAL DESCRIPTION
Features articles that are designed to aid
professional food technologists, scientists,
engineers, executives and educators solve
their technological and management
problems in the entire chain of producing
wholesome foods. News departments
cover the food industry and news of the
Institute of Food Technologists.
Articles per average issue: 10
Audience: Professional
Manuscripts accepted in English only

MANUSCRIPT INFORMATION
Subject field(s): Product development,
processing and engineering, nutrition,
packaging, pollution control, quality
assurance, food safety, marketing, food
laws and regulations, advertising,
distribution, laboratory methods
Manuscript requirements: Style sheet sent
on request.
Preferred length: Maximum of 15 pages
Number of copies to be submitted: Three
Author information and reprints: Payment:
None.
Is simultaneous submission of article to
other journals permitted: No
Exclusive manuscript rights between
acceptance and publication: Yes
Copyright: Held by publication.
Reprints: Available at cost.
Disposition of manuscript:
Query letter: No
Receipt of manuscript acknowledged: Yes
Decision to publish in: One month

Accepted manuscript published in: Three months
Rejected manuscript returned: Yes
Rejected manuscript criticized: Yes
Submit to:
John B. Klis
Editor and Director of Publications
(See address above)

THE FOREMAN'S LETTER [2581]
24 Rope Ferry Road
Waterford, Connecticut 06385
(203) 442-4365

First published in 1943

SUBSCRIPTION DATA
Issues and rates: Published semi-monthly.
Average paid circulation: 36,000
Annual rate(s): $16.20
Publisher or Sponsor: National Foremen's Institute

EDITORIAL DESCRIPTION
Contains interviews with first-line industrial supervisors, concerning their effective interpersonal job relationships, in which they are quoted without editorial comment. Seeks to supply managements and their supervisors with a regular stream of reminders that workers can be won over to cooperation by intelligent utilization of human relations techniques.
Articles per average issue: 5
Audience: Industiral Supervisors
Manuscripts accepted in English

MANUSCRIPT INFORMATION
Subject field(s): First-line industrial supervision
Manuscript requirements: Style sheet sent on request.
Preferred length: 300-600 words
Number of copies to be submitted: One
Abstract: No
Author information and reprints: Payment: By publication to author. $.07 per word.
Is simultaneous submission of article to other journals permitted: No
Exclusive manuscript rights between acceptance and publication: Yes
Copyright: Held by publication.
Reprints: Not available.
Additional information: Typewritten, double- or triple-spaced, on standard, unlined paper. Photographs welcomed
Disposition of manuscript:
Query letter: Yes, for first-time authors
Receipt of manuscript acknowledged: Yes
Decision to publish in: 2-3 weeks
Accepted manuscript published in: Within one year
Rejected manuscript returned: Yes, if return postage is supplied by author.
Rejected manuscript criticized: No
Submit to:
Frank Berkowitz
Supervisory Editor
(See address above)

FUELOIL & OIL HEAT [2582]
200 Commerce Road
Cedar Grove, New Jersey 07009
(201) 239-5800

First published in 1922

SUBSCRIPTION DATA
Issues and rates: Published monthly.
Average paid circulation: 12,000
Annual rate(s): $7.00, Foreign $17.00

EDITORIAL DESCRIPTION
Contains articles on marketing and management of fueloil retail business; selling and service of oil heating equipment.
Articles per average issue: 1
Audience: Retailers
Manuscripts accepted in English

MANUSCRIPT INFORMATION
Manuscript requirements: See latest issue for style requirements.
Preferred length: 1,500 words
Number of copies to be submitted: 1
Abstract: No
Author information and reprints: Payment: By publication to author. $100 per article.
Is simultaneous submission of article to other journals permitted: No
Exclusive manuscript rights between acceptance and publication: Yes
Copyright: Held by publication.
Reprints: Not available.
Disposition of manuscript:
Query letter: Preferred
Receipt of manuscript acknowledged: Yes
Decision to publish in: 2 weeks
Accepted manuscript published in: 2 months
Rejected manuscript returned: Yes, if return postage is supplied by author.
Rejected manuscript criticized: No
Submit to:
Paul Geiger
Editor
(See address above)

GAS WORLD [2583]
25 New Street Square
London EC4A 3JA, England
01-353-3212

SUBSCRIPTION DATA
Issues and rates: Published weekly.
Average paid circulation: 2,743; 420 controlled
Annual rate(s): £9.00; Foreign $20.40

EDITORIAL DESCRIPTION
Contains technical information on gas transmission, distribution and storage.

MANUSCRIPT INFORMATION
Subject field(s): Gas engineering, transmission, distribution, storage
Manuscript requirements: Style sheet sent on request.
Preferred length: 2000 words; 3 pages
Number of copies to be submitted: One

Author information and reprints: Payment: By publication to author. To be negotiated.
Is simultaneous submission of article to other journals permitted: Yes
Exclusive manuscript rights between acceptance and publication: Yes
Copyright: Held by publication.
Reprints: Available at cost
Disposition of manuscript:
Receipt of manuscript acknowledged: Yes
Decision to publish in: 1 month
Accepted manuscript published in: 1 month
Rejected manuscript returned: Yes, if self-addressed, stamped envelope is sent with manuscript.
Rejected manuscript criticized: No
Submit to:
Geoffrey W. Battison
Editor-in-Chief
(See address above)

GLASS DIGEST [2584]
15 East 40th Street
New York, New York 10016
(212) 685-0785

SUBSCRIPTION DATA
Issues and rates: Published monthly.
Average paid circulation: 8,000; 600 controlled
Annual rate(s): $8.00, Foreign $10.00

EDITORIAL DESCRIPTION
Contents include merchandising feature articles; case history articles on distributors, dealers, and major building projects; and departments dealing with flat glass, architectural metal, and related products. Provides merchandising ideas for management.
Articles per average issue: 8
Audience: Distributors, dealers, contractors
Manuscripts accepted in English only

MANUSCRIPT INFORMATION
Subject field(s): Case histories, merchandising, building jobs, storefront remodeling
Manuscript requirements: See latest issue for style requirements.
Preferred length: 1,200-1,400 words
Number of copies to be submitted: Original and carbon
Abstract: No
Author information and reprints: Payment: By publication to author. $.04 per word, often more, based upon subject, scope, and length
Is simultaneous submission of article to other journals permitted: No
Exclusive manuscript rights between acceptance and publication: Yes
Copyright: Held by publication.
Reprints: Available, cost varies
Additional information: All manuscripts should be double-spaced.
Disposition of manuscript:
Query letter: Yes
Receipt of manuscript acknowledged: Yes
Decision to publish in: One week

Trades, manufacturing and industry

Accepted manuscript published in: Four to six months

Rejected manuscript returned: Yes, if self-addressed, stamped envelope is sent with manuscript.

Rejected manuscript criticized: No

Submit to:
Oscar S. Glasberg
Publisher and Editor
(See address above)

GRAPHIC ARTS SUPPLIER NEWS [2585]

134 North Thirteenth Street
Philadelphia, Pennsylvania 19107
(215) 564-5170 ext. 313

SUBSCRIPTION DATA

Issues and rates: Published bi-monthly.
Average paid circulation: 4760 controlled
Annual rate(s): $6.00, Foreign $8.00

EDITORIAL DESCRIPTION

Written to help manufacturers and distributors increase sales and profits. Edited for owners, executives and salesmen, manufacturers, dealers and distributors of graphic arts equipment and supplies.

MANUSCRIPT INFORMATION

Subject field(s): Sales management, sales cost analysis, supplier relationship, salesmen's profiles, "how-to" articles on selling graphic arts equipment for dealers

Manuscript requirements: Will send upon request; suggest that outline be submitted first

Preferred length: Not to exceed 2000 words

Number of copies to be submitted: Two

Author information and reprints: Payment: By publication to author. Amount varies.

Is simultaneous submission of article to other journals permitted: No

Exclusive manuscript rights between acceptance and publication: Yes

Copyright: Held by publication.

Reprints: Available; 3 free

Disposition of manuscript:
Receipt of manuscript acknowledged: Yes
Decision to publish in: 6 to 8 weeks
Accepted manuscript published in: 2 to 6 months
Rejected manuscript returned: Yes, if self-addressed, stamped envelope is sent with manuscript.
Rejected manuscript criticized: No

Submit to:
Peggy Bicknell
Editor

HEATING/PIPING/AIR CONDITIONING [2586]

The Reinhold Publication for Mechanical Systems Engineering
600 Summer Street
Stamford, Connecticut 06904
(203) 348-7531

First published in 1929

SUBSCRIPTION DATA

Issues and rates: Published monthly.
Average paid circulation: 23,000
Annual rate(s): $9.00; Foreign $19.00

EDITORIAL DESCRIPTION

Contains articles on the design, installation, operation, and maintenance of heating, piping, air conditioning, and ventilation systems in commercial, public and institutional buildings and in industrial plants.

Articles per average issue: 8-10

MANUSCRIPT INFORMATION

Manuscript requirements: No specific style guide.

Preferred length: 6 to 10 pages

Number of copies to be submitted: Two

Author information and reprints: Payment: By publication to author.

Is simultaneous submission of article to other journals permitted: No

Exclusive manuscript rights between acceptance and publication: Yes

Copyright: Held by publication.

Reprints: Available, cost upon request

Disposition of manuscript:
Receipt of manuscript acknowledged: Yes
Decision to publish in: Three to six weeks
Accepted manuscript published in: Two to four months
Rejected manuscript returned: Yes, if self-addressed, stamped envelope is sent with manuscript.
Rejected manuscript criticized: No

Submit to:
Robert T. Korte
Editor
(See address above)

I.A.T.S.E. OFFICIAL BULLETIN [2587]

1270 Avenue of the Americas
New York, New York 10020
(212) 245-4369 ext. 15

First published in 1910

SUBSCRIPTION DATA

Issues and rates: Published quarterly.
Average paid circulation: 61,000 controlled
Annual rate(s): $2.00, Members $1.00

Publisher or Sponsor: International Alliance of Theatrical Stage Employes and Moving Picture Machine Operators of the United States and Canada

EDITORIAL DESCRIPTION

Contains articles on behind the scene of motion picture production; technical articles on film projection, operation of television, new equipment articles pertaining to the production of films; labor news, union local news, and AFL-CIO coverage.

Articles per average issue: Varies

Audience: Theatrical
Manuscripts accepted in English

MANUSCRIPT INFORMATION

Subject field(s): Projection, making of films, making of TV films, film editing

Manuscript requirements: No specific style guide.

Preferred length: Unlimited

Number of copies to be submitted: One original

Abstract: No

Author information and reprints: Payment: None.

Is simultaneous submission of article to other journals permitted: No

Exclusive manuscript rights between acceptance and publication: Yes

Copyright: Held by publication.

Reprints: Available at no cost.

Disposition of manuscript:
Query letter: No
Receipt of manuscript acknowledged: Yes
Decision to publish in: Two weeks
Accepted manuscript published in: Two to four months
Rejected manuscript returned: Yes, if self-addressed, stamped envelope is sent with manuscript.
Rejected manuscript criticized: No

Submit to:
Rene L. Ash
Editor
(See address above)

INDUSTRIAL AND COMMERCIAL PHOTOGRAPHER [2588]

Davis House, 69-77 High Street
Croydon CR9 1QH, England
01-688-7788

SUBSCRIPTION DATA

Issues and rates: Published monthly.
Average paid circulation: 4,950; 1,095 controlled
Annual rate(s): £5.00; Foreign £6.00

EDITORIAL DESCRIPTION

Contains articles describing how photography is used in business; the work of leading studios and inplant departments; business methods for photographers; commercial, scientific, industrial, wedding and social photography; graphic arts uses; microfilm usage; test reports of equipment; editorial articles on professional matters. The readership is world-wide and articles have been commissioned from photographers in many countries.

Articles per average issue: 6

Audience: Professional
Manuscripts accepted in English

MANUSCRIPT INFORMATION

Manuscript requirements: Style sheet sent on request.

Preferred length: None

Number of copies to be submitted: One

Author information and reprints: Payment: By publication to author.

Is simultaneous submission of article to other journals permitted: Not in same fields.

Exclusive manuscript rights between acceptance and publication: Yes
Copyright: Held by publication.
Reprints: Available, cost depends on length.
Additional information: Include glossy photographs. Manuscript should be typewritten, double-spaced.
Disposition of manuscript:
Receipt of manuscript acknowledged: Yes
Decision to publish in: 3 weeks
Accepted manuscript published in: 2-4 months
Rejected manuscript returned: Yes
Rejected manuscript criticized: No
Submit to:
J. Charles Hall
Editor
(See address above)

INDUSTRIAL DESIGN [2589]
One Astor Plaza
New York, New York 10036
(212) 764-7525

First published in 1954

SUBSCRIPTION DATA
Issues and rates: 10 per year
Average paid circulation: 13,000
Annual rate(s): $20.00; Foreign $40.00
Managing Editor: George T. Finley

EDITORIAL DESCRIPTION
Contains articles on design trends and ideas, materials technology with the emphasis on the applied arts.
Manuscripts accepted in English

MANUSCRIPT INFORMATION
Subject field(s): Product planning, product design, environmental planning, modular construction, packaging, design personalities, design offices, design trends, design conferences
Manuscript requirements: NYT
Preferred length: 3000-6000 words
Number of copies to be submitted: 2
Abstract: No
Author information and reprints: Payment: None.
Is simultaneous submission of article to other journals permitted: No
Exclusive manuscript rights between acceptance and publication: Yes
Copyright: Held by publication.
Reprints: Available at cost.
Additional information: All manuscripts should be accompanied by author's biography as well as any illustrations, drawings, photographs necessary to the understanding of the article.
Disposition of manuscript:
Query letter: Preferred
Receipt of manuscript acknowledged: Yes
Decision to publish in: 3 months
Accepted manuscript published in: 4-5 months
Rejected manuscript returned: Yes
Rejected manuscript criticized: No
Submit to:
J. Roger Guilfoyle
Editor-in-Chief
(See address above)

INDUSTRIAL DEVELOPMENT [2590]
Peachtree Air Terminal
1954 Airport Road
Atlanta, Georgia 30341
(404) 458-6026

First published in 1925

SUBSCRIPTION DATA
Issues and rates: Published bi-monthly.
Average paid circulation: 2,000
Annual rate(s): $25.00; Foreign $33.00; Individuals $25.00
Publisher or Sponsor: Industrial Development Research Council
Managing Editor: Linda L. Liston

EDITORIAL DESCRIPTION
All articles pertinent to industrial development, laws governing or limiting development, ecology, environment, site selection, facility planning.
Articles per average issue: 4-6
Audience: Industrial developers, realtors, investors.
Manuscripts accepted in English

MANUSCRIPT INFORMATION
Subject field(s): New plant concepts, OSHA, new legislation and how it affects developers, twin plants (Mexican-American border plants), environmental developments, land management, facility planning, site selection, revenue bonds, economic considerations for development.
Manuscript requirements: See latest issue for style requirements.
Preferred length: Varies
Number of copies to be submitted: 1
Abstract: Not necessary.
Author information and reprints: Payment: Reprints only. 6-10
Copyright: Held by publication.
Reprints: Not available.
Disposition of manuscript:
Query letter: Not necessary.
Receipt of manuscript acknowledged: Yes
Decision to publish in: Varies
Accepted manuscript published in: Varies
Rejected manuscript returned: Yes, with return postage paid by publication.
Rejected manuscript criticized: Reasons for rejections only
Submit to:
Linda L. Liston
Editor
(See address above)

INDUSTRIAL DISTRIBUTION [2591]
16 West 61st Street
New York, New York 10023
(212) 765-7290

Previously entitled *Mill Supplies*

First published in 1910

SUBSCRIPTION DATA
Issues and rates: Published monthly.
Average paid circulation: 4,900; 28,000 controlled
Annual rate(s): $15.00; Foreign $35.00
Managing Editor: George J. Berkwitt

EDITORIAL DESCRIPTION
Provides industrial distributors with helpful operating, financial, administrative, sales, promotional and marketing material; includes personals, job changes, etc.
Articles per average issue: 6
Audience: Managers and sales personnel in individual distribution firms

MANUSCRIPT INFORMATION
Subject field(s): Fields of interest to distributor sales, management and operating personnel
Manuscript requirements: See latest issue for style requirements.
Preferred length: 1,500 to 2,000 words; 6-8 pages
Abstract: Not necessary.
Author information and reprints: Payment: None.
Is simultaneous submission of article to other journals permitted: Permitted, but not encouraged.
Exclusive manuscript rights between acceptance and publication: Yes
Copyright: Held by publication but permission to reprint generally granted with credit to the publication
Disposition of manuscript:
Query letter: Not necessary, but advisable.
Receipt of manuscript acknowledged: No
Decision to publish in: 1 month
Accepted manuscript published in: 2 to 6 months
Rejected manuscript returned: Yes, if return postage is supplied by author.
Rejected manuscript criticized: Sometimes
Submit to:
George J. Berkwitt
Chief Editor
(See address above)

INDUSTRIAL FINISHING [2592]
The Management and Engineering Magazine for Better Finishing Systems
Hitchcock Building
Wheaton, Illinois 60187
(312) 665-1000

First published in 1924

SUBSCRIPTION DATA
Issues and rates: Published monthly.
Average paid circulation: 40,000 controlled

EDITORIAL DESCRIPTION
Covers surface preparation, painting, plating, porcelain enameling, vacuum metallizing, laminating, in plants finishing metal, plastics or wood products on a highproduction basis.
Articles per average issue: 6-9
Audience: Professional
Manuscripts accepted in English

Trades, manufacturing and industry

MANUSCRIPT INFORMATION

Subject field(s): Finishing, cleaning/pretreatment, post-treatment, finishing management

Manuscript requirements: No specific style guide.

Preferred length: 8 to 10 pages

Number of copies to be submitted: One

Author information and reprints: Payment: By publication to author. $15 to $20 per published page.

Is simultaneous submission of article to other journals permitted: No

Exclusive manuscript rights between acceptance and publication: Yes

Copyright: Held by publication.

Reprints: Available on order

Disposition of manuscript:

Receipt of manuscript acknowledged: Yes

Decision to publish in: Two weeks

Accepted manuscript published in: Two to three months

Rejected manuscript returned: Yes, if self-addressed, stamped envelope is sent with manuscript.

Rejected manuscript criticized: Sometimes

Submit to:

Matt Heuertz

Editor

(See address above)

INDUSTRIAL MARKETING [2593]

The Newsletter of Advertising and Selling to Business, Industry and the Professions

740 Rush Street

Chicago, Illinois 60614

(312) 649-5260

First published in 1936

SUBSCRIPTION DATA

Issues and rates: Published monthly.

Average paid circulation: 23,000

Annual rate(s): $10.00; Foreign $13.00; Institutions $10.00; Students $10.00; Members $10.00; Foreign institutions $13.00

Managing Editor: Sally R. Strong

EDITORIAL DESCRIPTION

Covers advertising, marketing, and selling of products and services from business to business. Not directed to the consumer.

Articles per average issue: 1-5

Audience: Advertising, marketing and sales managers, directors and coporate marketing executives.

Manuscripts accepted in English

MANUSCRIPT INFORMATION

Subject field(s): Business-to-business advertising, marketing and sales as it is related to advertising and promotion.

Manuscript requirements: Chicago

Preferred length: As necessary to cover subject

Number of copies to be submitted: Two

Abstract: Not necessary.

Author information and reprints: Payment: By publication to author. $50.00 per article.

Is simultaneous submission of article to other journals permitted: Not permitted.

Exclusive manuscript rights between acceptance and publication: Yes

Copyright: Held by publisher: Crain Communications, Inc., Chicago, Illinois

Reprints: Available at cost.

Disposition of manuscript:

Query letter: Necessary.

Receipt of manuscript acknowledged: Yes

Decision to publish in: 6 Weeks

Accepted manuscript published in: 3 Months

Rejected manuscript returned: Yes, if return postage is supplied by author.

Rejected manuscript criticized: Reasons for rejections only

Submit to:

George B. Young

Editor

708 Third Avenue

New York, New York 10017

(212) 406-5050

INDUSTRIAL PHOTOGRAPHY* [2594]

750 Third Avenue

New York, New York 10017

(212) 697-8300 ext. 261

SUBSCRIPTION DATA

Issues and rates: Published monthly.

Average paid circulation: Not available.

Managing Editor: Frances H. Lee

EDITORIAL DESCRIPTION

Features material on professional-level photographic techniques, ideas, new approaches and applications; motion picture production, audio-visuals, TV, instrumentation, management and administration of department, industry news.

Audience: Staff photographers in business, industrial, government, military, educational, scientific and research organizations and company management.

MANUSCRIPT INFORMATION

Manuscript requirements: Style sheet sent on request.

Preferred length: Varies according to subject

Number of copies to be submitted: Two

Author information and reprints: Payment: By publication to author. Determined by agreement with author.

Is simultaneous submission of article to other journals permitted: Yes, by agreement with author

Exclusive manuscript rights between acceptance and publication: No

Copyright: Held by publication.

Reprints: Available, cost depends on request

Additional information: Publication does not want amateur-level material. Author should query first for professional orientation.

Disposition of manuscript:

Receipt of manuscript acknowledged: Yes

Decision to publish in: About 3 weeks

Accepted manuscript published in: 2-3 months

Rejected manuscript returned: Yes

Rejected manuscript criticized: Yes

Submit to:

Natalie Canavor

Editor

(See address above)

INSULATION/CIRCUITS [2595]

P.O. Box 159

700 Peterson Road

Libertyville, Illinois 60048

(312) 362-8711

Previously entitled *Insulation*

First published in 1955

SUBSCRIPTION DATA

Issues and rates: Published monthly.

Average paid circulation: 28,348 controlled

Annual rate(s): $30.00; Foreign $45.00

EDITORIAL DESCRIPTION

Devoted to reaching and informing the production men, designers, engineers, and others who buy and specify the materials, parts and basic components used in manufacturing all types of electrical/electronic products and systems.

Articles per average issue: 8

Audience: Manufacturers

Manuscripts accepted in English

MANUSCRIPT INFORMATION

Subject field(s): Concerned with everything in the circuit system or package: insulation, conductors, structural parts, shielding, components, etc.

Manuscript requirements: See latest issue for style requirements.

Preferred length: None

Number of copies to be submitted: Two

Abstract: No

Author information and reprints: Payment: None. in most cases.

Is simultaneous submission of article to other journals permitted: No

Exclusive manuscript rights between acceptance and publication: Yes

Copyright: Held by publication.

Reprints: Available, cost depends on length and quantity

Additional information: Everything typewritten, double-spaced. Illustrations 8 x 10 glossy prints.

Disposition of manuscript:

Receipt of manuscript acknowledged: Yes

Decision to publish in: Two months

Accepted manuscript published in: Four to six months

Rejected manuscript returned: Yes

Rejected manuscript criticized: No

Submit to:

Donald E. Swanson

Executive Editor

(See address above)

INTERNATIONAL PHOTOGRAPHER [2596]

7715 Sunset Boulevard
Hollywood, California 90046
(213) 876-0160

First published in 1928

SUBSCRIPTION DATA

Issues and rates: Published monthly.
Average paid circulation: 2,000; 2,200 controlled
Annual rate(s): $2.50; Foreign $3.00; Institutions $2.00; Foreign institutions $3.00

Publisher or Sponsor: International Alliance of Theatrical Stage Employes and Moving Picture Machine Operators of the U.S. and Canada

EDITORIAL DESCRIPTION

Features articles by professional cameramen on equipment and techniques on various phases of production and newsreel.
Audience: Professional
Manuscripts accepted in English

MANUSCRIPT INFORMATION

Subject field(s): Photography of all types; matters regarding television, movies, theater and broadcasting
Manuscript requirements: No specific style guide.
Preferred length: None
Number of copies to be submitted: 2
Abstract: Not necessary.
Author information and reprints: Payment: Reprints only. Unlimited
Is simultaneous submission of article to other journals permitted: Permitted.
Exclusive manuscript rights between acceptance and publication: No
Reprints: Available at cost.
Disposition of manuscript:
Query letter: Not necessary, but advisable.
Receipt of manuscript acknowledged: No
Accepted manuscript published in: 2-4 months
Rejected manuscript returned: Yes, with return postage paid by publication.
Rejected manuscript criticized: Sometimes
Submit to:
Mrs. Terry M. Burley
Business Manager
(See address above)

THE IRON WORKER [2597]

Drawer 411
Lynchburg, Virginia 24505
(703) 847-4411 ext. 325

First published in 1919

SUBSCRIPTION DATA

Issues and rates: Published quarterly.
Average paid circulation: 10,000 controlled

EDITORIAL DESCRIPTION

Contains historical articles about Virginia with national significance, technical articles about iron manufacturing, customer profiles, stories about geographical locales (not necessarily Virginia).
Articles per average issue: 4
Audience: Community, customers
Manuscripts accepted in English

MANUSCRIPT INFORMATION

Subject field(s): Virginia history, iron manufacturing
Manuscript requirements: See latest issue for style requirements.
Preferred length: 3500-5000 words; 14-20 pages
Number of copies to be submitted: One
Abstract: Yes. Outline of proposed article should follow query letter
Author information and reprints: Payment: By publication to author. From $100 to $350 upon acceptance per article.
Is simultaneous submission of article to other journals permitted: Yes
Exclusive manuscript rights between acceptance and publication: Yes
Copyright: Held by publication.
Reprints: Available at cost
Disposition of manuscript:
Query letter: Yes
Receipt of manuscript acknowledged: Yes
Decision to publish in: 6 months
Accepted manuscript published in: 1 year
Rejected manuscript returned: Yes, if return postage is supplied by author.
Rejected manuscript criticized: Yes
Submit to:
F.T. Hausman
Editor
(See address above)

THE LOGISTICS AND TRANSPORTATION REVIEW [2598]

Faculty of Commerce and Business Administration
University of British Columbia
Vancouver, British Columbia V6T 1W5, Canada
(604) 228-4510

Previously entitled *The Logistics Review*

First published in 1964

SUBSCRIPTION DATA

Issues and rates: Published quarterly.
Annual rate(s): $15.00
Publisher or Sponsor: The University of British Columbia
Managing Editor: Karl M. Ruppenthal

EDITORIAL DESCRIPTION

Contains articles dealing with various aspects of transportation and logistics. Articles may be managerial or quantitative in nature, or may deal with economic questions.
Articles per average issue: 10
Audience: Academic, research, government,
Manuscripts accepted in English, French

MANUSCRIPT INFORMATION

Subject field(s): Transportation, logistics, transportation management, transportation problems, economics and planning
Manuscript requirements: Style sheet sent on request.
Preferred length: 5 to 30 pages
Number of copies to be submitted: Two
Abstract: Yes
Author information and reprints: Payment: None.
Is simultaneous submission of article to other journals permitted: No
Exclusive manuscript rights between acceptance and publication: Yes
Copyright: Held by publication.
Permission to reprint normally given.
Reprints: Available, schedule furnished to author
Disposition of manuscript:
Query letter: No
Receipt of manuscript acknowledged: Yes
Decision to publish in: 45 days
Accepted manuscript published in: 3 to 6 months
Rejected manuscript returned: Yes, if return postage is supplied by author.
Rejected manuscript criticized: Yes
Submit to:
Karl M. Ruppenthal
Editor
(See address above)

MACHINE AND TOOL BLUE BOOK [2599]

America's Leading Magazine for Profitable Metalworking Manufacturing
Hitchcock Building
Wheaton, Illinois 60187
(312) 665-1000 ext. 310

First published in 1905

SUBSCRIPTION DATA

Issues and rates: Published monthly.
Average paid circulation: 92,000 controlled
Annual rate(s): $20.00
Managing Editor: Walter J. Reed

EDITORIAL DESCRIPTION

Dedicated to the continuing technical education of the men responsible for the operation of plants engaged in metalworking manufacturing. Content is directed to all persons involved in executive, managerial, engineering and supervisory functions who have a direct interest in plant modernization and the engineering and manufacture of products from metal or plastics.
Articles per average issue: 8
Manuscripts accepted in English

MANUSCRIPT INFORMATION

Subject field(s): Manufacturing, engineering, management, metal fabricating, tooling/tool design, metals/plastics, quality control, abrasive engineering cost reduction applications

Trades, manufacturing and industry

Manuscript requirements: See latest issue for style requirements.
Preferred length: 1,000 to 2,000 words; 3-7 pages
Number of copies to be submitted: One
Abstract: No
Author information and reprints: Payment: By publication to author. $25 per page.
Is simultaneous submission of article to other journals permitted: No
Exclusive manuscript rights between acceptance and publication: Yes
Copyright: Held by publication.
Reprints: Available at no cost
Additional information: Manuscripts should be in proper style and include title, subtitle and subheads in copy where needed. Suitable camera-ready drawings, charts and/or photographs must accompany article.
Disposition of manuscript:
Query letter: No
Receipt of manuscript acknowledged: Yes
Decision to publish in: 2 to 4 weeks
Accepted manuscript published in: 2 to 6 months
Rejected manuscript returned: Yes
Rejected manuscript criticized: Occasionally
Submit to:
Raymond H. Spiotta
Editor
(See address above)

METAL TREATING [2600]

19 Church Street
Berea, Ohio 44017
(216) 243-8250

First published in 1950

SUBSCRIPTION DATA
Issues and rates: Published semi-monthly.
Average paid circulation: 14,000 controlled
Annual rate(s): $9.00, Foreign $15.00

EDITORIAL DESCRIPTION
Contains articles on all phases, techniques, materials and processes dealing with heat treating industry.
Articles per average issue: 4
Audience: Professional
Manuscripts accepted in English

MANUSCRIPT INFORMATION
Subject field(s): Heat treating
Manuscript requirements: See latest issue for style requirements.
Preferred length: 8 to 10 pages
Number of copies to be submitted: Two
Abstract: No
Author information and reprints: Payment: None.
Is simultaneous submission of article to other journals permitted: No
Exclusive manuscript rights between acceptance and publication: Yes
Copyright: Held by publication.
Reprints: Available, cost on request

Additional information: Typewritten, double-spaced
Disposition of manuscript:
Query letter: Helpful
Receipt of manuscript acknowledged: Yes
Decision to publish in: 4 weeks or less
Accepted manuscript published in: Within 7 weeks
Rejected manuscript returned: Yes
Submit to:
James Toedtman
Publisher
(See address above)

PACKAGE PRINTING AND DIECUTTING [2601]

Flexography Section
134 North Thirteenth Street
Philadelphia, Pennsylvania 19107
(215) 564-5170 ext. 302

Previously entitled *Flexography*

SUBSCRIPTION DATA
Issues and rates: Published monthly.
Average paid circulation: 9,100
Annual rate(s): $14.00 Foreign $17.00

EDITORIAL DESCRIPTION
Articles deal with management, production, new techniques, new products and industry news within the field of rubber and flexible plate printing and related converting fields.

MANUSCRIPT INFORMATION
Manuscript requirements: Style sheet sent on request.
Preferred length: Not to exceed 2000 words
Number of copies to be submitted: Three
Author information and reprints: Payment: By publication to author. Amount varies.
Is simultaneous submission of article to other journals permitted: No
Exclusive manuscript rights between acceptance and publication: Yes
Copyright: Held by publication.
Reprints: Available; 3 free
Disposition of manuscript:
Query letter: Best to submit outline first.
Receipt of manuscript acknowledged: Yes
Decision to publish in: 2 to 6 weeks
Accepted manuscript published in: 2 to 8 months
Rejected manuscript returned: Yes, if self-addressed, stamped envelope is sent with manuscript.
Rejected manuscript criticized: No
Submit to:
Daniel Flanigan
Editor
(See address above)

PAPERBOARD PACKAGING [2602]

777 Third Avenue
New York, New York 10017
(212) 838-7778

Previously entitled *Fiber Containers*

SUBSCRIPTION DATA
Issues and rates: Published monthly.
Average paid circulation: 8,500
Annual rate(s): $9.00

EDITORIAL DESCRIPTION
Serves the entire spectrum of the paperboard converting industry with balanced coverage of the corrugated container, folding carton, paperboard mill, fibre can and tube, and converted board products fields.
Audience: corporate management, production management, engineers
Manuscripts accepted in English only

MANUSCRIPT INFORMATION
Subject field(s): Technical development, products in use
Manuscript requirements: Style is prescribed upon inquiry to editor.
Preferred length: 1500-2500 words
Number of copies to be submitted: One
Abstract: No
Author information and reprints: Payment: By publication to author. $50.00 per page.
Is simultaneous submission of article to other journals permitted: No
Exclusive manuscript rights between acceptance and publication: Yes
Copyright: Held by publication.
Reprints: Not available.
Additional information: No manuscripts accepted without query by author or verbal acceptance by editor.
Disposition of manuscript:
Query letter: Yes
Receipt of manuscript acknowledged: Yes
Decision to publish in: Several days
Accepted manuscript published in: Less than 1 month
Rejected manuscript returned: Yes
Rejected manuscript criticized: Sometimes
Submit to:
Joel J. Shulman
Editor
(See address above)

PHOTOMETHODS [2603]

One Park Avenue
New York, New York 10016

Previously entitled *PMI, Photomethods for Industry*

First published in 1957

SUBSCRIPTION DATA
Issues and rates: Published monthly.
Average paid circulation: 50,000 controlled
Managing Editor: Rosalie Mancini

EDITORIAL DESCRIPTION
Contains news, how-to articles, theoretical articles on photographic subjects, analyses of photographic departments, news and articles on video, graphic arts, cinema, anything else dealing with imaging.
Articles per average issue: 5

Audience: Professional

Manuscripts accepted in English

MANUSCRIPT INFORMATION

Subject field(s): Photography (still), motion pictures, video, photographic lighting, photochemistry, equipment application, graphic reproduction

Manuscript requirements: See latest issue for style requirements.

Preferred length: 2500-3000 words limit

Number of copies to be submitted: One

Abstract: Helpful

Author information and reprints: Payment: By publication to author. $75.00 per page. By arrangement.

Is simultaneous submission of article to other journals permitted: No

Exclusive manuscript rights between acceptance and publication: Yes

Copyright: Held by publication.

Reprints: Available

Additional information: As an adjunct to the article, photographs should tell a story

Disposition of manuscript:

Query letter: Yes

Receipt of manuscript acknowledged: Yes

Decision to publish in: 2-4 weeks

Accepted manuscript published in: 3-6 months

Rejected manuscript returned: Yes

Rejected manuscript criticized: No

Submit to:

Editor

(See address above)

PIPELINE & GAS JOURNAL [2604]

Energy Supply, Transportation and Distribution

Box 1589

Dallas, Texas 75221

(214) 748-4403

Previously entitled *American Gas Journal,* 1859; *Pipeline Engineer,* 1949

SUBSCRIPTION DATA

Issues and rates: Monthly, plus extra issues March 15 to July 15

Average paid circulation: 23,500

Annual rate(s): $6.00; Foreign $8.00

EDITORIAL DESCRIPTION

Contents include energy supply, transportation and distribution (pipelines, utilities, etc.) including management, economics, engineering.

Articles per average issue: 10

Manuscripts accepted in English

MANUSCRIPT INFORMATION

Subject field(s): Economics, engineering, management sciences, petroleum (oil and gas), petrochemistry, research and development, hydraulics, materials development, utility regulation

Manuscript requirements: See latest issue for style requirements.

Preferred length: 1000-2000 words

Number of copies to be submitted: One

Abstract: No

Author information and reprints: Payment: By publication to author. $25 and up per page.

Is simultaneous submission of article to other journals permitted: Yes, only if in another non-related field

Exclusive manuscript rights between acceptance and publication: Yes

Copyright: Held by publication.

Reprints: Available, cost varies

Disposition of manuscript:

Query letter: Not necessary, but advisable

Receipt of manuscript acknowledged: Yes

Decision to publish in: 1-6 weeks

Accepted manuscript published in: 1-6 months

Rejected manuscript returned: Yes

Rejected manuscript criticized: No

Submit to:

Dean Hale

Editor

(See address above)

PLASTICS DESIGN & PROCESSING [2605]

P.O. Box 159

700 Peterson Road

Libertyville, Illinois 60048

(312) 362-8711

First published in 1961

SUBSCRIPTION DATA

Issues and rates: Published monthly.

Average paid circulation: 42,880 controlled

Annual rate(s): $20, Foreign $30

EDITORIAL DESCRIPTION

Concentrates on serving the interests of those who use, specify, and buy plastics materials, products, processing equipment, and related supplies. This coverage includes both the custom, proprietary, or independent plastic companies as well as the "captive" plastics operations in other manufacturing companies.

Articles per average issue: 5

Manuscripts accepted in English

MANUSCRIPT INFORMATION

Subject field(s): Plastics

Manuscript requirements: See latest issue for style requirements.

Preferred length: None

Number of copies to be submitted: Two

Abstract: No

Author information and reprints: Payment: None.

Is simultaneous submission of article to other journals permitted: No

Exclusive manuscript rights between acceptance and publication: Yes

Copyright: Held by publication.

Reprints: Available; cost depends on length and quantity.

Additional information: Typewritten, double-spaced, with illustrations being glossy 8 x 10 photographs.

Disposition of manuscript:

Receipt of manuscript acknowledged: Yes

Decision to publish in: Two months

Accepted manuscript published in: Four to six months

Rejected manuscript returned: Yes

Rejected manuscript criticized: No

Submit to:

Donald Swanson

Editor

(See address above)

PLASTICS ENGINEERING [2606]

Official Publication of The Society of Plastics Engineers, Inc.

656 West Putnam Avenue

Greenwich, Connecticut 06830

(203) 661-4770

Previously entitled *SPE Journal*

SUBSCRIPTION DATA

Issues and rates: Published monthly.

Average paid circulation: 18,500

Annual rate(s): $12.00, Foreign $17.00

Publisher or Sponsor: The Society of Plastics Engineers, Inc.

EDITORIAL DESCRIPTION

Contains articles on machinery, materials, processing, applications, management, R & D, marketing, as related to the plastics industry.

Articles per average issue: 6

Audience: Professional

Manuscripts accepted in English

MANUSCRIPT INFORMATION

Subject field(s): Plastics industry and technology, related fields

Manuscript requirements: Style sheet sent on request.

Preferred length: 2500 words typewritten, double-spaced

Number of copies to be submitted: 3-5 copies

Abstract: Yes

Author information and reprints: Payment: None.

Is simultaneous submission of article to other journals permitted: No

Exclusive manuscript rights between acceptance and publication: Yes

Copyright: Held by publication.

Reprints: Available, single copy free; request price list

Additional information: Author's Style Guide available on request.

Disposition of manuscript:

Query letter: Not necessary, but helpful

Receipt of manuscript acknowledged: Yes

Decision to publish in: 1-2 months

Accepted manuscript published in: 3-6 months

Rejected manuscript returned: Yes

Rejected manuscript criticized: Usually

Submit to:

A.A. Schoengood

Editor

(See address above)

Trades, manufacturing and industry

PLASTICS IN BUILDING CONSTRUCTION [2607]

P. O. Box 42
Georgetown, Connecticut 06829
(203) 438-7068

First published in 1974

SUBSCRIPTION DATA
Issues and rates: Published monthly.
Average paid circulation: 5,000
Annual rate(s): $28.00; Pan-Am $31.00;
Foreign $33.00
Managing Editor: Richard L. Dunn

EDITORIAL DESCRIPTION
Technology, product development, and
marketing of plastics for use in building
construction
Articles per average issue: 2
Audience: Plastics industry, building
products manufacturers, architects,
builders, contractors
Manuscripts accepted in English,
German, Spanish

MANUSCRIPT INFORMATION
Subject field(s): Use of plastics in building
construction
Manuscript requirements: Style sheet sent
on request.
Preferred length: 5-20 pages
Number of copies to be submitted: 2
Abstract: Not necessary.
Author information and reprints: Payment:
Reprints only. 100 reprints
Is simultaneous submission of article to
other journals permitted: Permitted, but
not encouraged.
Exclusive manuscript rights between
acceptance and publication: No
Copyright: Held by author.
Reprints: Available at no cost. 100
Additional information: Author must have
technical or professional competence in
this field
Disposition of manuscript:
Query letter: Not necessary, but
advisable.
Receipt of manuscript acknowledged: Yes
Decision to publish in: 10 days
Accepted manuscript published in: 2
months
Rejected manuscript returned: Yes, with
return postage paid by publication.
Rejected manuscript criticized: Reasons
for rejections only
Submit to:
Richard L. Dunn
Managing Editor and Publisher
(See address above)

SPECIAL STIPULATIONS
Photographs and other illustrations
recommended

PLATING [2608]

Journal of the American Electroplaters'
Society
56 Melmore Gardens
East Orange, New Jersey 07017
(201) 678-4100

Previously entitled *Monthly Review*

First published in 1913

SUBSCRIPTION DATA
Issues and rates: Published monthly.
Average paid circulation: 10,000
Annual rate(s): $14.00, Foreign $16.00
Publisher or Sponsor: American
Electroplaters' Society, Inc.
Managing Editor: William K. Brush

EDITORIAL DESCRIPTION
Contains articles on electroplating,
finishing of metals, organic finishing,
allied finishing processes.
Articles per average issue: 5
Manuscripts accepted in English

MANUSCRIPT INFORMATION
Subject field(s): Deposition of metals, metal
cleaning, painting of metals, powder
coatings
Manuscript requirements: Style sheet sent
on request.
Preferred length: 10-15 pages
Number of copies to be submitted: Three
Abstract: Yes, of about 100 words stating
the scope of the paper and summarizing
the results.
Author information and reprints: Payment:
None.
Is simultaneous submission of article to
other journals permitted: No
Exclusive manuscript rights between
acceptance and publication: Yes
Copyright: Held by publication.
Reprints: Available at cost
Disposition of manuscript:
Query letter: No
Receipt of manuscript acknowledged: Yes
Decision to publish in: 3 weeks
Accepted manuscript published in: 4
months
Rejected manuscript returned: Yes
Rejected manuscript criticized:
Sometimes
Submit to:
James H. Lindsay
Technical Editor
P.O. Box 3
Fenton, Michigan 48430

POLYMER AGE [2609]

Tenterden, Kent TN30 6UT, England
Tenterden (058 06) 2184

First published in 1970

SUBSCRIPTION DATA
Issues and rates: Published monthly.
Average paid circulation: 4,484
Annual rate(s): £12.00

EDITORIAL DESCRIPTION
Primarily aimed at the rubber and
plastics industries and for specifiers in
the main user industries. In-depth
analysis is given of case histories, cost
effectiveness comparison and the selection
of materials, processes and equipment.
Manuscripts accepted in English only

MANUSCRIPT INFORMATION
Subject field(s): Plastics and rubbers in:
building, packaging, reinforced polymers,
composites, product design, equipment,
furniture/furnishing, instrumentation,
chemicals, automobiles, electrical,
engineering
Manuscript requirements: See latest issue for
style requirements.
Preferred length: 800-2,000 words
Number of copies to be submitted: Two
Abstract: No
Author information and reprints: Payment:
By publication to author. Negotiable.
Is simultaneous submission of article to
other journals permitted: Yes, if within
Europa-Plastics group of journals.
Exclusive manuscript rights between
acceptance and publication: Yes
Copyright: Held by publication.
Reprints: Available, charge dependent on
number of pages
Disposition of manuscript:
Query letter: No
Receipt of manuscript acknowledged: Yes
Decision to publish in: One month
Accepted manuscript published in: Varies
Rejected manuscript returned: Yes, if
self-addressed, stamped envelope is sent
with manuscript
Rejected manuscript criticized: No
Submit to:
Peter Welham Grange
Editor
(See address above)

POWER TRANSMISSION DESIGN [2610]

614 Superior Avenue West
Cleveland, Ohio 44113
(216) 696-0300

First published in 1959

SUBSCRIPTION DATA
Issues and rates: Published monthly.
Average paid circulation: 46,000
Annual rate(s): $18.00; Foreign $36.00

EDITORIAL DESCRIPTION
Contains news and application articles
about motors, drives, bearings, and
controls of industrial mechanical
power-transmission systems, the use of
components in the field to help readers
use them better. Does not advocate the
use of any particular group of
components or of any method of
purchase.
Articles per average issue: 4
Audience: Production manufacture,
engineering
Manuscripts accepted in English

MANUSCRIPT INFORMATION
Subject field(s): Industrial gear drives, belt
drives, chain drives, bearings,
motor-speed controls, clutches and
brakes, shaft coupling, lubrication,
rotary-shaft seals, vibration-measurement
equipment, linear actuators, electric
motors

Manuscript requirements: See latest issue for style requirements.
Preferred length: No preference
Number of copies to be submitted: One
Abstract: Optional
Author information and reprints: Payment: By publication to author. $25 per page.
Is simultaneous submission of article to other journals permitted: Not to competitive publications.
Exclusive manuscript rights between acceptance and publication: Yes
Copyright: Held by publication.
Reprints: Available, cost quoted individually
Additional information: Typewritten, double-spaced
Disposition of manuscript:
Query letter: No
Receipt of manuscript acknowledged: Yes
Decision to publish in: 2 weeks
Accepted manuscript published in: 2-8 months
Rejected manuscript returned: Yes
Submit to:
Tom Hughes
Editor
(See address above)

PRINTING IMPRESSIONS [2611]

134 North Thirteenth Street
Philadelphia, Pennsylvania 19107
(215) 564-5170 ext. 230

SUBSCRIPTION DATA
Issues and rates: Published monthly.
Average paid circulation: 2,982; 59,900 controlled
Annual rate(s): $15.00; Foreign $20.00

EDITORIAL DESCRIPTION
Written for supervisory management, the journal points to new developments and new opportunities for profit in graphic arts.
Articles per average issue: 20
Audience: Commercial
Manuscripts accepted in English

MANUSCRIPT INFORMATION
Subject field(s): Management methods, production how-to, financial management, specification of equipment, industry trends or background for equipment, layout typography, stock market reports, graphic arts
Manuscript requirements: See latest issue; suggest that outline be sent first.
Preferred length: Not to exceed 2000 typewritten, double-spaced words
Number of copies to be submitted: Two
Abstract: Good idea for speculative articles
Author information and reprints: Payment: By publication to author. $0.04 per word.
Is simultaneous submission of article to other journals permitted: No
Exclusive manuscript rights between acceptance and publication: Yes
Copyright: Held by publication.
Reprints: Available; 3 free tear sheets
Disposition of manuscript:
Receipt of manuscript acknowledged: Yes

Decision to publish in: 2-6 weeks
Accepted manuscript published in: 2-8 months
Rejected manuscript returned: Yes, if self-addressed, stamped envelope is sent with manuscript.
Rejected manuscript criticized: Sometimes
Submit to:
Jim Bukus
Editor
(See address above)

THE PROFESSIONAL PHOTOGRAPHER [2612]

1090 Executive Way
Des Plaines, Illinois 60018
(312) 298-4680

First published in 1907

SUBSCRIPTION DATA
Issues and rates: Published monthly.
Average paid circulation: 25,000; 5,000 controlled
Annual rate(s): $12.00; Foreign $15.00
Publisher or Sponsor: Professional Photographers of America, Inc.

EDITORIAL DESCRIPTION
Contains feature articles for the person who earns his living in photography, plus regular columns and departments.
Articles per average issue: 10-12
Manuscripts accepted in English only

MANUSCRIPT INFORMATION
Subject field(s): Small business management, photographic technique, photography as a tool, new avenues of business, corporate use of photography, audio-visual production, photoinstrumentation; areas related to photography, such as microfilm, photofabrication, in-plant video production.
Manuscript requirements: Style sheet sent on request.
Preferred length: 1,000-2,000 words; 3-8 pages
Number of copies to be submitted: One
Author information and reprints: Payment: None. Achievement Merits awarded by Professional Photographers of America, Inc.
Is simultaneous submission of article to other journals permitted: No
Exclusive manuscript rights between acceptance and publication: Yes
Copyright: Held by author.
Reprints: Available, cost quote on request
Additional information: Prefer query first. Send for Information for Contributors sheet. Four special emphasis issues per year; send for current list. Illustrations must be of excellent quality for reproduction.
Disposition of manuscript:
Query letter: No, but recommended
Receipt of manuscript acknowledged: Yes
Decision to publish in: 2-4 weeks
Accepted manuscript published in: 8-12 months

Rejected manuscript returned: Yes, if self-addressed, stamped envelope is sent with manuscript.
Rejected manuscript criticized: Sometimes
Submit to:
Donald L. Wiley
Managing Editor
(See address above)

PULSE [2613]

The Film and TV Newsmagazine
Box 5268, Terminal
Toronto, Ontario M5W 1N5, Canada
(416)661-5449

First published in 1974

SUBSCRIPTION DATA
Issues and rates: Published monthly.
Average paid circulation: 3,000; 225 controlled
Annual rate(s): $5.00; Foreign $7.00 (U.S.); Students $4.00

EDITORIAL DESCRIPTION
The emphasis is on information, marketing, and the technical end of the film and TV industries; includes information of major foreign markets, e.g. New York, Hollywood, London, etc. as well as feature articles.
Articles per average issue: 2
Audience: Professional, academic, students, researchers
Manuscripts accepted in English only

MANUSCRIPT INFORMATION
Subject field(s): Motion pictures, television, cable television, film history, aesthetics, film criticism, reviews, educational television, television engineering
Manuscript requirements: No specific style guide.
Preferred length: 1,000-1,200 words; 3-4 pages
Number of copies to be submitted: 1
Abstract: Yes. If technical or scholarly.
Author information and reprints: Payment: Reprints only. 15-25 reprints
Is simultaneous submission of article to other journals permitted: Permitted, but not encouraged.
Exclusive manuscript rights between acceptance and publication: No
Copyright: Held by author.
Reprints: Available at no cost.
Additional information: Articles dealing with the Canadian film and television interface are preferred.
Disposition of manuscript:
Query letter: Not necessary, but advisable.
Receipt of manuscript acknowledged: Yes
Decision to publish in: 1 month
Accepted manuscript published in: 2-3 months
Rejected manuscript returned: Yes, if return postage is supplied by author.
Rejected manuscript criticized: Sometimes
Submit to:
Rick J. Harris

Trades, manufacturing and industry

Editor-Publisher
(See address above)

RAIL INTERNATIONAL [2614]
Rue de Louvrain 17-21
Brussels 1000, Belgium
(02) 513 72 13

First published in 1970

SUBSCRIPTION DATA
Issues and rates: Published monthly.
   Average paid circulation: 3500
   Annual rate(s): 1500 Belgian francs
Publisher or Sponsor: International Railway
   Congress Association; International
   Union of Railways
Managing Editor: R. Squilbin

EDITORIAL DESCRIPTION
   Contains articles on general railway
   policy and technical papers dealing with
   all branches of railway activity, including
   economic, finanical and social problems.
Articles per average issue: Varies
   Manuscripts accepted in English, French,
   German, Russian, Italian, Dutch

MANUSCRIPT INFORMATION
Subject field(s): Railway activity, transport
   policy
Manuscript requirements: See latest issue for
   style requirements.
   Preferred length: None
   Number of copies to be submitted: Three
   Abstract: Yes
Author information and reprints: Payment:
   By publication to author. 1250 Belgian
   francs per printed page.
   Is simultaneous submission of article to
   other journals permitted: No
   Exclusive manuscript rights between
   acceptance and publication: Yes
   Copyright: Held by publication.
   Reprints: Available, 30 free
Additional information: Figures and
   drawings should be supplied on canvas or
   thick paper, sufficiently clear to allow
   good quality blocks to be prepared.
Disposition of manuscript:
   Query letter: No
   Receipt of manuscript acknowledged: Yes
   Decision to publish in: Three weeks
   Accepted manuscript published in: Varies
   Rejected manuscript returned: Yes
   Rejected manuscript criticized: No
Submit to:
   R. Squilbin
   Secretary General
   (See address above)

THE RANGEFINDER [2615]
3511 Centinela Avenue
P.O. Box 66925
Los Angeles, California 90066
(213) 390-3688

First published in 1952

SUBSCRIPTION DATA
Issues and rates: Published monthly.

Average paid circulation: 13,500; 26,500
   controlled
   Annual rate(s): $8.00; Foreign $13.00
Managing Editor: Janet Marshall Victor

EDITORIAL DESCRIPTION
   Features encompass all phases of
   professional photography: solutions to
   technical problems, business practices,
   handling of assignments, equipment test
   reports, processing techniques, readers'
   open forum, future trends.

MANUSCRIPT INFORMATION
Subject field(s): New techniques,
   merchandising, profitable sidelines, latest
   devices, pricing methods, inspirational
Manuscript requirements: See latest issue for
   style requirements.
   Preferred length: 1000 to 2000
   typewritten words
   Number of copies to be submitted: One
   Abstract: No
Author information and reprints: Payment:
   By publication to author. $18-$24 per
   page. Much material is either
   staff-written or reader contributed.
   Is simultaneous submission of article to
   other journals permitted: No
   Exclusive manuscript rights between
   acceptance and publication: Yes
   Copyright: Held by author.
   Reprints: Available at publication cost
Additional information: Prepare article in
   concise and objective form in duplicate
   retaining a copy for author's file.
   Emphasize new and/or novel aspects of
   the subject. Trade names may be
   mentioned. No biographies.
Disposition of manuscript:
   Query letter: No
   Receipt of manuscript acknowledged: Yes
   Decision to publish in: Two weeks
   Accepted manuscript published in: Up to
   four months
   Rejected manuscript returned: Yes, if
   return postage is supplied by author.
   Rejected manuscript criticized: Yes
Submit to:
   Janet Marshall Victor
   Editor
   (See address above)

THE REFRACTORIES JOURNAL [2616]
Official Organ of the Refractories
Association of Great Britain
886 High Road
Finchley, London, England
(01) 445-6870

First published in 1925

SUBSCRIPTION DATA
Issues and rates: Published monthly.
   Average paid circulation: 2,500
   Annual rate(s): £6.00

Managing Editor: J. F. S. Russell
Publisher or Sponsor: Refractories
   Association of Great Britain

EDITORIAL DESCRIPTION
   Contains news of the refractories industry
   and articles on manufacture and
   application of refractories in such
   industries as iron, steel, glass, cement,
   chemicals.
Articles per average issue: 2
   Manuscripts accepted in English

MANUSCRIPT INFORMATION
Subject field(s): Manufacture of refractories,
   testing of refractories, application of
   refractories, refractories raw materials
Manuscript requirements: No specific style
   guide.
   Preferred length: 3000 words maximum
   Number of copies to be submitted: One
Author information and reprints: Payment:
   By publication to author. By
   arrangement.
   Is simultaneous submission of article to
   other journals permitted: Yes
   Exclusive manuscript rights between
   acceptance and publication: Yes
   Copyright: Held by publication.
   Reprints: Available, cost on request
Disposition of manuscript:
   Query letter: No
   Receipt of manuscript acknowledged: Yes
   Decision to publish in: Three months
   Accepted manuscript published in: Three
   months
   Rejected manuscript returned: Yes, if
   self-addressed, stamped envelope is sent
   with manuscript.
   Rejected manuscript criticized: No
Submit to:
   The Editor
   (See address above)

REPRODUCTIONS REVIEW & METHODS [2617]
134 North 13th Street
Philadelphia, Pennsylvania 19107
(215) 564-5170 ext. 290

SUBSCRIPTION DATA
Issues and rates: Published monthly.
   Average paid circulation: 2,650; 40,592
   controlled
   Annual rate(s): $15.00, Foreign $20.00

EDITORIAL DESCRIPTION
   Subjects covered include offset,
   letterpress, diazo, spirit, stencil,
   microfilming, electrostatics and diffusion
   transfer reproduction process. Edited for
   management and technical personnel
   concerned with graphic arts techniques.
Articles per average issue: 3-4
Audience: Inplant management
   Manuscripts accepted in English

MANUSCRIPT INFORMATION
Manuscript requirements: Style sheet sent
   on request.
   Preferred length: Up to 2,000 words
   Number of copies to be submitted: One
   Abstract: No

Author information and reprints: Payment:
By publication to author. Negotiable
Is simultaneous submission of article to
other journals permitted: No
Exclusive manuscript rights between
acceptance and publication: Yes
Copyright: Held by publication.
Reprints: Available, 3 free
Additional information: Best to send outline
of paper first. Author's name and
affiliation should appear only on a
separate cover page.
Disposition of manuscript:
Query letter: No
Receipt of manuscript acknowledged: Yes
Decision to publish in: 2-6 weeks
Accepted manuscript published in: 2-8
months
Rejected manuscript returned: Yes, if
self-addressed, stamped envelope is sent
with manuscript.
Rejected manuscript criticized:
Sometimes
Submit to:
William B. Leonard, Jr.
Editor
(See address above)

ROCK PRODUCTS [2618]

300 West Adams Street
Chicago, Illinois 60606
(312) 726-2802

SUBSCRIPTION DATA
Issues and rates: Published monthly.
Annual rate(s): $10.00, Foreign $35.00

EDITORIAL DESCRIPTION
Contains articles on mining and
processing operations pertaining to
production of the construction minerals:
cement, lime, gypsum, sand and gravel,
crushed stone, slag, and the lightweight
aggregates (expanded clay and shale,
exfoliated vermiculite, expanded perlite,
pumice).
Manuscripts accepted in English

MANUSCRIPT INFORMATION
Manuscript requirements: No specific style
guide.
Preferred length: None
Number of copies to be submitted: One
Abstract: No
Author information and reprints: Payment:
By publication to author.
Is simultaneous submission of article to
other journals permitted: No
Exclusive manuscript rights between
acceptance and publication: Yes
Copyright: Held by publication.
Reprints: Not available.
Disposition of manuscript:
Query letter: No
Receipt of manuscript acknowledged: Yes
Decision to publish in: Varies
Rejected manuscript returned: Yes
Rejected manuscript criticized: No
Submit to:
Sidney Levine
Editor
(See address above)

ROLLSIGN [2619]

P. O. Box 102
Cambridge, Massachusetts 02138

SUBSCRIPTION DATA
Issues and rates: 10 times per year
Annual rate(s): $3.00; Pan-Am $3.00;
Members $5.00
Publisher or Sponsor: The Boston Street
Railway Association, Inc.
Managing Editor: Daniel T. Lenihan

EDITORIAL DESCRIPTION
To publish articles dealing with
electrified and non-electrified
transportation, current news, stories and
histories.
Audience: Those interested in mass
transportation
Manuscripts accepted in English

MANUSCRIPT INFORMATION
Subject field(s): Mass transportation, current
and historical; area, primarily New
England;
Manuscript requirements: No specific style
guide.
Preferred length: As required
Number of copies to be submitted: 1
Abstract: Not necessary.
Author information and reprints: Payment:
None.
Is simultaneous submission of article to
other journals permitted: Permitted.
Exclusive manuscript rights between
acceptance and publication: No
Copyright: Held by publication.
Reprints: Available at cost.
Disposition of manuscript:
Query letter: Not necessary, but
advisable.
Receipt of manuscript acknowledged: Yes
Decision to publish in: 1 month
Accepted manuscript published in: 2-4
months
Rejected manuscript returned: Yes, with
return postage paid by publication.
Rejected manuscript criticized:
Sometimes
Submit to:
Daniel T. Lenihan
Editor
(See address above)

RUBBER AGE [2620]

461 Eighth Avenue
New York, New York 10001
(212) 239-6200

First published in 1917

SUBSCRIPTION DATA
Issues and rates: Published monthly.
Average paid circulation: 5,398; 1,738
controlled
Annual rate(s): $10.00; Foreign $20.00
Managing Editor: John Graham

EDITORIAL DESCRIPTION
Edited for administrative, scientific and
technical personnel of rubber goods
manufacturing installations, through

feature articles, news and market
coverage.
Articles per average issue: 4
Manuscripts accepted in English

MANUSCRIPT INFORMATION
Subject field(s): Technology, case history,
plant visit, interview
Manuscript requirements: Style sheet sent
on request.
Number of copies to be submitted: Two
Abstract: Yes
Author information and reprints: Payment:
By publication to author. $10.00 per
page. Commissioned articles.
Is simultaneous submission of article to
other journals permitted: No
Exclusive manuscript rights between
acceptance and publication: Yes
Copyright: Held by publication.
Reprints: Available, cost to be
determined
Disposition of manuscript:
Query letter: Yes
Receipt of manuscript acknowledged: Yes
Decision to publish in: Two weeks
Accepted manuscript published in: Three
months
Rejected manuscript returned: Yes
Rejected manuscript criticized: Yes
Submit to:
B. J. Kotsher
Editorial Director
(See address above)

SURGICAL BUSINESS [2621]

2009 Morris Avenue
Union, New Jersey 07083
(201) 687-8282

First published in 1935

SUBSCRIPTION DATA
Issues and rates: Published monthly.
Average paid circulation: 6,800
Annual rate(s): $8.50

EDITORIAL DESCRIPTION
Contains articles of interest to the
medical-surgical supply trade; product,
laboratory, personnel and industry news.
Articles per average issue: 3-4
Manuscripts accepted in English

MANUSCRIPT INFORMATION
Subject field(s): Health care, innovations in
industry, government activities affecting
trade
Manuscript requirements: Style sheet sent
on request.
Preferred length: Varies
Number of copies to be submitted: One
Author information and reprints: Payment:
By publication to author. Varies
Is simultaneous submission of article to
other journals permitted: No
Exclusive manuscript rights between
acceptance and publication: Yes
Copyright: Held by publication.
Reprints: Available
Disposition of manuscript:
Query letter: No

Trades, manufacturing and industry

Receipt of manuscript acknowledged: No
Decision to publish in: 2 to 6 months
Accepted manuscript published in: 2 to 12 months
Rejected manuscript returned: Yes, if self-addressed, stamped envelope is sent with manuscript.
Rejected manuscript criticized: No
Submit to:
Albert L. Cassak
Publisher
(See address above)

TAPPI [2622]

Journal of the Technical Association of the Pulp and Paper Industry
1 Dunwood Park
Atlanta, Georgia 30341
(404) 457-6352

First published in 1949

SUBSCRIPTION DATA
Issues and rates: Published monthly.
Average paid circulation: 13,000
Publisher or Sponsor: Technical Association of the Pulp and Paper Industry
Managing Editor: Michael Kouris

EDITORIAL DESCRIPTION
Contains articles on technical advances in the pulp and paper industry and in allied disciplines.
Articles per average issue: 20
Audience: Engineering, scientific
Manuscripts accepted in English

MANUSCRIPT INFORMATION
Subject field(s): Pulping, papermaking, converting, allied sciences and technology
Manuscript requirements: Chicago; Skillin
Preferred length: 3000 words
Number of copies to be submitted: Three
Abstract: Yes
Author information and reprints: Payment: None.
Is simultaneous submission of article to other journals permitted: No
Exclusive manuscript rights between acceptance and publication: Yes
Copyright: Held by publication.
Reprints: Available
Disposition of manuscript:
Query letter: No
Receipt of manuscript acknowledged: Yes
Decision to publish in: 4 weeks
Accepted manuscript published in: 6-8 months
Rejected manuscript returned: Yes
Rejected manuscript criticized: Sometimes
Submit to:
Bengt Leopold
Editor
(See address above)

TRANSPORTATION USA [2623]

Superintendent of Documents
U.S. Government Printing Office
Washington, D. C. 20402

First published in 1974

SUBSCRIPTION DATA
Issues and rates: Published quarterly.
Annual rate(s): $3.00; Foreign $3.75

EDITORIAL DESCRIPTION
Covers all aspects of transportation; i.e., diversity of America's transportation mechanism, noteworthy happenings in transportation, strengths and weaknesses of America's transportation system, transportation developments in other countries, etc.
Articles per average issue: 4
Audience: Leaders in transportation, government, and industry, and others interested in transportation.
Manuscripts accepted in English

MANUSCRIPT INFORMATION
Subject field(s): Any transportation-related field.
Manuscript requirements: GPO
Preferred length: 2,000
Number of copies to be submitted: 1
Abstract: Not necessary.
Author information and reprints: Payment: By publication to author. Up to $.25 per word.
Is simultaneous submission of article to other journals permitted: Permitted.
Exclusive manuscript rights between acceptance and publication: No
Copyright: Held by author.
Reprints: Not available.
Disposition of manuscript:
Query letter: Not necessary.
Receipt of manuscript acknowledged: No
Decision to publish in: 4 weeks
Accepted manuscript published in: 6-12 months
Rejected manuscript returned: Yes, with return postage paid by publication.
Rejected manuscript criticized: Sometimes
Submit to:
Editor
Room 9421 (S-81)
400 Seventh Street, S.W.
Washington, D.C. 20590
(202) 426-4321

WATER SERVICES [2624]

Queensway House
2 Queensway
Redhill, Surrey RH1 1QS, England
68611

Previously entitled *Water and Water Engineering*

First published in 1899

SUBSCRIPTION DATA
Issues and rates: Published monthly.
Average paid circulation: 3,979

..ual rate(s): £10.00; Foreign £12.00

EDITORIAL DESCRIPTION
Provides technical articles and news dealing with all aspects of the water cycle
Articles per average issue: 3-4
Audience: Water industry
Manuscripts accepted in English

MANUSCRIPT INFORMATION
Subject field(s): Water resources location and exploitation, planning, development of surface and ground water supplies, treatment, distribution and use for public supply, industrial purposes, irrigation and the generation of electrical power; water pollution control, treatment of sewage and trade waste waters or effluents for disposal or recycling, hydrology, hydraulics, river training and flood control.
Manuscript requirements: Style sheet sent on request.
Preferred length: 1,500-5,000 words
Number of copies to be submitted: One
Abstract: Yes
Author information and reprints: Payment: By publication to author. By arrangement
Is simultaneous submission of article to other journals permitted: Yes
Exclusive manuscript rights between acceptance and publication: No
Copyright: Held by author.
Reprints: Available, cost depends on length
Disposition of manuscript:
Query letter: No
Receipt of manuscript acknowledged: Yes
Decision to publish in: 2 weeks
Accepted manuscript published in: 3-12 months
Rejected manuscript returned: Yes
Rejected manuscript criticized: No
Submit to:
V. H. French
Editor
(See address above)

THE WELDING DISTRIBUTOR [2625]

5811 Dempster Avenue, Box 128
Morton Grove, Illinois 60053
(312) 965-5130 ext. 101

First published in 1956

SUBSCRIPTION DATA
Issues and rates: Published bi-monthly.
Average paid circulation: 1600; 4400 controlled
Annual rate(s): $2.00, Foreign $5.00

EDITORIAL DESCRIPTION
A merchandising magazine of the welding industry for those engaged in the sales and distribution of welding equipment and supplies.
Articles per average issue: 5-7
Manuscripts accepted in English

MANUSCRIPT INFORMATION

Subject field(s): Management, sales, merchandising

Manuscript requirements: See latest issue for style requirements.
Preferred length: 1500-2000 words; 4 to 6 pages
Number of copies to be submitted: One

Author information and reprints: Payment: By publication to author. Amount depends on uniqueness and quality.
Is simultaneous submission of article to other journals permitted: Yes, if not competitive
Exclusive manuscript rights between acceptance and publication: Yes
Copyright: Held by publication.
Reprints: Available, cost depends on length

Disposition of manuscript:
Receipt of manuscript acknowledged: Yes
Decision to publish in: 1 month
Accepted manuscript published in: 4-6 months
Rejected manuscript returned: Yes, if self-addressed, stamped envelope is sent with manuscript.
Rejected manuscript criticized: No

Submit to:
Donald T. Jefferson
Editor
(See address above)

THE WELDING ENGINEER [2626]
5811 Dempster Avenue, Box 128
Morton Grove, Illinois 60053
(312) 965-5130

First published in 1916

SUBSCRIPTION DATA

Issues and rates: Published monthly.
Average paid circulation: Not available.
Annual rate(s): $5.00, Foreign $15.00

Managing Editor: Jeffery D. Weber

EDITORIAL DESCRIPTION
The consumer magazine of the welding field.

Articles per average issue: 5
Manuscripts accepted in English

MANUSCRIPT INFORMATION

Subject field(s): Engineering, metal working, construction, pipe lining, ship building, quality assurance, training

Manuscript requirements: See latest issue for style requirements.
Preferred length: 2000-2500 words; 6-8 pages
Number of copies to be submitted: One

Author information and reprints: Payment: By publication to author. Depending on quality of material.
Is simultaneous submission of article to other journals permitted: Yes, if so advised and not to competitive magazines in field.
Exclusive manuscript rights between acceptance and publication: Yes
Copyright: Held by publication.
Reprints: Available, cost depends on length

Additional information: Manuscripts should deal with practical aspects of welding and cutting in production or maintenance in the metal working industry.

Disposition of manuscript:
Query letter: Desirable
Receipt of manuscript acknowledged: Yes
Decision to publish in: One month
Accepted manuscript published in: Varies, depending on theme issue schedule.
Rejected manuscript returned: Yes, if return postage is supplied by author.

Submit to:
T.B. Jefferson
Editor
(See address above)

WIRE [2627]
The Technical Journal for the Wire Industry
P.O. Box 691
Uferstrasse 11
D-8630 Coburg, Federal Republic of Germany
09561 ext. 1295

First published in 1952

SUBSCRIPTION DATA

Issues and rates: Published bi-monthly.
Average paid circulation: 4,000
Annual rate(s): DM 40.00

Managing Editor: Hans Meiner

EDITORIAL DESCRIPTION
Contains articles on the manufacture and fabrication of wire including wire products such as fasteners, cables, wire rope, springs etc.

MANUSCRIPT INFORMATION

Subject field(s): Wire manufacture, wire fabrication, wire surface and heat treatment etc.

Articles per average issue: 10

Audience: Professional
Manuscripts accepted in English, German, Spanish, French, Italian

Manuscript requirements: See latest issue for style requirements.
Preferred length: None
Number of copies to be submitted: Two

Author information and reprints: Payment: By publication to author.
Is simultaneous submission of article to other journals permitted: No
Exclusive manuscript rights between acceptance and publication: Yes
Copyright: Held by publication.
Reprints: Available

Additional information: Authors are requested to contact the editor specifying length and subject before submitting articles.

Disposition of manuscript:
Query letter: Yes
Receipt of manuscript acknowledged: Yes
Decision to publish in: 1-2 months
Accepted manuscript published in: 2-6 months
Rejected manuscript returned: Yes
Rejected manuscript criticized: No

Submit to:
The Editor
(See address above)

WIRE JOURNAL [2628]
Official Publication of The Wire Association
209 Montowese Street
Branford, Connecticut 06405
(203) 488-6321

First published in 1968

SUBSCRIPTION DATA

Issues and rates: Published monthly.
Average paid circulation: 11,000
Annual rate(s): $25, Foreign $30

Publisher or Sponsor: The Wire Association

EDITORIAL DESCRIPTION
Publishes articles on the technology of steel wire, electrical wire and cable, communications wire and cable, control cable, electronic wire and cable, manufacturing and fabrication of wire products. Bulk of material is transactions of the technical sessions of The Wire Association.

Articles per average issue: 5
Manuscripts accepted in English

MANUSCRIPT INFORMATION

Subject field(s): Wire and cable, insulation, alloys for wire, rolling mill practice, inspection techniques, plant procedures, fabrication techniques, shop practices, lubricants, laws that affect the industry

Manuscript requirements: ANSI
Preferred length: 2500 words; 10 typewritten, double-spaced pages
Number of copies to be submitted: Four
Abstract: Yes

Author information and reprints: Payment: None.
Is simultaneous submission of article to other journals permitted: No
Exclusive manuscript rights between acceptance and publication: Yes
Copyright: Held by publication.
Reprints: Available, cost depends on length

Additional information: Graphics must be black and white, 8x10 contact prints or larger, professional quality.

Disposition of manuscript:
Receipt of manuscript acknowledged: Yes
Decision to publish in: 2 weeks
Accepted manuscript published in: 6 months
Rejected manuscript returned: Yes, if return postage is supplied by author.
Rejected manuscript criticized: Yes

Submit to:
Laurence W. Collins, Jr.
Editorial Director
(See address above)

WOOD AND FIBER [2629]
P.O. Box 5062
Madison, Wisconsin 53711
(608) 257-2211

First published in 1969

SUBSCRIPTION DATA

Issues and rates: Published quarterly.
Average paid circulation: 800; 800
controlled
Annual rate(s): $20.00; Institutions
$20.00; Members Included in
membership
Publisher or Sponsor: Society of Wood
Science and Technology
Managing Editor: Robert W. Meyer

EDITORIAL DESCRIPTION

Contains articles on wood and paper
science and technology. Goal is to ensure
that papers are brought to the attention
of researchers and institutions throughout
the world. Original, unpublished papers
contributed in the area of wood and
paper science or technology are reviewed
for content, accuracy and clarity.
Articles per average issue: 10
Audience: Professional, business, academic
Manuscripts accepted in English

MANUSCRIPT INFORMATION

Subject field(s): Wood science, paper
science, wood and paper technology,
wood and paper processing, wood and
paper manufacture and professional
issues
Manuscript requirements: See latest issue for
style requirements.
Preferred length: None
Number of copies to be submitted: Four
Abstract: Yes
Author information and reprints: Payment:
By author to publication. $40 per page.
Is simultaneous submission of article to
other journals permitted: No
Exclusive manuscript rights between
acceptance and publication: Yes
Copyright: Held by Society
Reprints: Available, cost based on length
Disposition of manuscript:
Query letter: No
Receipt of manuscript acknowledged: Yes
Decision to publish in: 6-8 weeks
Accepted manuscript published in: 3-6
months after revised manuscript is
received.
Rejected manuscript returned: Yes
Rejected manuscript criticized: Yes
Submit to:
Robert W. Meyer
Editor
Forest Products Laboratory
6620 Northwest Marine Drive
Vancouver 8, British Columbia, Canada
(604) 224-3221

SPECIAL STIPULATIONS

A brief statement to the editor submitted
with the manuscript will suffice as
application for waiver of page charges.

WORLD FISHING [2630]

Riverside House
Hough Street
Woolwich, London SE18 6LR, England
(01) 855-7001

First published in 1952

SUBSCRIPTION DATA

Issues and rates: Published monthly.
Average paid circulation: 2,000; 7,500
controlled
Annual rate(s): $20.00 worldwide

EDITORIAL DESCRIPTION

An international journal serving the
commercial fishing industry and
concerned with the location, catching,
and processing of fish at sea.
Articles per average issue: 6
Audience: Professional, academic, scientific,
governmental, manufacturers, etc.
Manuscripts accepted in English, French,
Spanish, German

MANUSCRIPT INFORMATION

Subject field(s): Vessel design and
construction; developments in catching
methods and gear; on-the-spot reports of
operations in developing countries;
illustrated reports of operations at sea;
news items of international interest
Manuscript requirements: No specific style
guide.
Preferred length: 750-1,000 words
Number of copies to be submitted: 1
Abstract: Not necessary.
Author information and reprints: Payment:
By publication to author. $35.00 per
page.
Is simultaneous submission of article to
other journals permitted: Not permitted.
Exclusive manuscript rights between
acceptance and publication: Yes
Copyright: First serial rights only
Reprints: Available at cost.
Additional information: Copy should be
factual, in a straightforward style,
readable also by persons not fluent in
English. Photos, when possible, with
captions.
Disposition of manuscript:
Query letter: Not necessary, but
advisable.
Receipt of manuscript acknowledged: Yes
Decision to publish in: 14 days
Accepted manuscript published in: 30
days
Rejected manuscript returned: Yes, with
return postage paid by publication.
Rejected manuscript criticized: Yes
Submit to:
H. S. Noel
Managing Editor
(See address above)

Indexes

Periodical title index

A

AACSB Bulletin: 829
AB Bookman's Weekly: 849
ABCA Bulletin: 850
Aberdeen University Review: 1
Abrasive Engineering: 2555
The Academic Reviewer: 67
Academic Therapy: 901
Academy of General Dentistry. Journal: 2496
Academy of Management Journal: 830
Acadiensis: 1112
Accountancy: 729
The ACES Bulletin: 742
ACM Communications: 2226
Acta Anatomica: 2249
Acta Astronautica: 2047
Acta Chirurgica Scandinavica: 2532
Acta Cytologica: 2250
Acta Haematologica: 2251
Acta Metallurgica: 1701
Acta Zoologica: 1977
The Activist: 1330
ADE Bulletin: 902
Adhesives Age: 2556
Administrative Science Quarterly: 743
Adolescence: 697
Adolescent Psychiatry: 1361
ADRIS Newsletter: 526
Advances in Applied Probability: 2186
Advances in Mathematics: 2187
AEDS Journal: 903
AEDS Monitor: 2227
The Aeronautical Quarterly: 2048
Aerospace Historian: 1113
AFB Research Bulletin: 1492
Africa Report: 627
Africa Today: 628
African Affairs: 629
African Arts: 127
African Music: 128
African Progress: 630
African Studies: 631
African Studies Review: 632
Afro-American Studies*: 678
AFS Cast Metals Research Journal: 1702
AGA Monthly: 2557
Agenda: 470
Agents and Actions: 2252
Agricultural History: 1875
Agricultural History Review: 1876
Agricultural Meteorology: 2021
Agro-Ecosystems: 1802
Agrologist: 1877
AIA Journal: 129
AIAA Journal: 2049
AICHE Journal: 1703
Air Force Law Review: 1316
Air University Review: 1317
Akwesasne Notes: 679
Alabama Business: 744
Alberta Historical Review: 1114
Alberta Journal of Educational Research: 904
Alberta Law Review: 1191
The Alberta School Trustee: 905
The Alcoholism Digest: 1493
Alpha Psi Omega Playbill: 130
Alternatives: 1803
Ambix: 2065
America: 527
American Academy of Psychoanalysis. Journal: 1362
American Academy of Religion. Journal: 528

American Annals of the Deaf: 906, 2253
American Anthropologist: 1530
American Antiquity*: 1630
American Archives of Rehabilitation Therapy: 1494
The American Archivist: 250
The American Art Journal: 131
American Association of Petroleum Geologists Bulletin: 1667
American Association of Teacher Educators in Agriculture. Journal: 907
American Aviation Historical Society. Journal: 1115
American Bar Association Journal: 1192
The American Benedictine Review: 529
The American Biology Teacher: 908
American Birds: 1978
American Business Law Journal: 1193
American Ceramic Society Bulletin: 2558
The American Ceramic Society Journal: 1704, 1585
American Chemical Society. Journal*: 2066
American City Magazine: 1194
American College of Emergency Physicians. Journal: 2254
American Concrete Institute Journal: 1586
American Corrective Therapy Journal: 2255
American Dietetic Association Journal: 2256
American Economic Review: 745
The American Economist: 746
American Education: 909
American Educational Research Journal: 910
American Ethnologist: 1531
American Family Physician: 2257
American Forensic Association Journal: 896
American Forests*: 1804
The American Genealogist: 1116
American Geriatrics Society Journal: 2258
American Glass Review: 2559
American Heart Journal*: 2259
American Heritage: 1117
The American Historical Review: 1118
American Imago: 1363
American Indian Culture and Research Journal: 680
American Indian Quarterly: 681
American Industrial Development Council. Journal: 747
American Ink Maker: 2560
American Jewish Historical Quarterly: 530
American Journal of Archaeology: 1631
American Journal of Art Therapy: 1364
American Journal of Botany: 1947
The American Journal of Chinese Medicine: 2260
American Journal of Clinical Hypnosis: 1365
The American Journal of Clinical Nutrition: 2261
American Journal of Comparative Law: 1195
American Journal of Criminal Law: 1196
American Journal of Diseases of Children: 2262
American Journal of Enology and Viticulture: 1948
American Journal of Epidemiology: 2263
American Journal of Gastroenterology: 2264
American Journal of Hospital Pharmacy: 2265
The American Journal of Human Genetics: 1887
American Journal of International Law: 1197
American Journal of Jurisprudence: 1198
American Journal of Nursing: 2520
American Journal of Obstetrics and Gynecology*: 2267
American Journal of Ophthalmology: 2268
American Journal of Optometry and Physiological Optics: 2269
American Journal of Orthodontics*: 2497
American Journal of Orthopsychiatry: 1366
American Journal of Pharmacy and the Sciences Supporting Public Health: 2270
American Journal of Physical Medicine: 2271
American Journal of Physics: 911
American Journal of Political Science: 1331
The American Journal of Psychiatry: 1367
The American Journal of Psychology: 1368

References in Index refer to entry numbers

American Journal of Sociology: 1532
American Journal of Veterinary Research: 2542
American Journal of the Medical Sciences: 2266
American Leather Chemists Association Journal: 2561
American Libraries: 251
American Literary Realism, 1870-1910: 322
American Literature: 323
The American Mathematical Monthly: 2188
American Mathematical Society Bulletin: 2189
American Mathematical Society Proceedings: 2190
American Mathematical Society Transactions: 2191
American Medical Association. Journal (JAMA): 2272
American Medical Technologists Journal: 2273
American Meteorological Society Bulletin: 1644
The American Mineralogist: 1678
American Musicological Society. Journal: 132
The American Naturalist*: 1862
The American Neptune: 1119
American Notes & Queries: 68
American Oil Chemists Society Journal: 2067
American Opinion: 1332
American Osteopathic Association Journal: 2274
American Philological Association Transactions and Proceedings*: 69
American Podiatry Association Journal: 2275
The American Political Science Review: 1333
American Politics Quarterly: 1334
American Psychoanalytic Association Journal: 1369
American Psychologist: 1370
American Quarterly: 682
The American Rationalist: 2
American Review of Respiratory Disease: 2276
American Roofer and Building Improvement Contractor: 2562
The American Scholar: 3
American School and University: 913
The American School Board Journal: 912
American Scientific Affiliation Journal: 531
American Scientist: 1587
American Secondary Education: 914
The American Sephardi: 532
American Society for Geriatric Dentistry. Journal: 2498
American Society for Information Science. Journal: 252
American Society of Psychosomatic Dentistry and Medicine Journal: 2277
American Sociological Review: 1533
The American Sociologist: 1534
American Speech: 196
American Studies*: 683
American Teacher: 915
American Veterinary Medical Association Journal: 2543
American Water Works Association Journal: 1805
The American West: 684
Analytical Chemistry: 2068
Angewandte Chemie: 2069
Anglican Theological Review: 533
Animal Production: 1878
Animal Shelter Shoptalk: 2563
Annales Chirurgiae et Gynaecologiae Fenniae: 2278
Annals of Clinical Research: 2279
Annals of Human Biology: 1888
Annals of Human Genetics: 1889
Annals of Internal Medicine: 2280
Annals of Iowa: 1120
Annals of Mathematics: 2192
Annals of Mathematics: 2193
Annals of Nuclear Science and Engineering: 2174
Annals of Otology, Rhinology and Laryngology: 2281
Annals of Physics: 2132 , 2133
Annals of Tropical Medicine and Parasitology: 2282
Annals of Wyoming: 1121
Annuale Mediaevale: 70
Antaeus: 471

Antarctic Journal of the United States: 606
Anthropological Journal of Canada: 1535
Anthropological Linguistics: 197
Anthropological Quarterly: 1536
The Antigonish Review: 472
Antimicrobial Agents and Chemotherapy: 2283
The Antitrust Bulletin: 748
APA Monitor: 1371
Applied Acoustics: 2022
Applied Animal Ethology: 1979
Applied Christianity: 534
Applied Microbiology: 1890
Applied Optics: 2023
Applied Physics: 2134
Applied Radiology: 2284
Applied Spectroscopy: 2024
Aquaculture: 1690
Aquasphere: 1806
Aquatic Botany: 1949
The Arbitration Journal: 1199
Archaeological Society of Virginia. Quarterly Bulletin: 1632
Archaeology: 1633
Architectural Design: 1640
Archive for History of Exact Sciences: 1588
Archive for Rational Mechanics and Analysis: 2194
Archives of Biochemistry and Biophysics: 1891
Archives of Microbiology: 1892
Archives of Oral Biology: 2499
Archives of Physical Medicine and Rehabilitation: 2285
Archives of Sexual Behavior: 1372
Archives of Toxicology: 2286
Archives: 253
Arctic and Alpine Research: 607
Arctic Anthropology: 1537
Arctic Bulletin: 608
Area Development Magazine: 2564
Ariel: 71
Arion: 72
The Arithmetic Teacher: 916
Arizona and the West: 1122
Arizona English Bulletin: 917
Arizona Quarterly: 324
The Ark River Review: 473
The Arkansas Historical Quarterly: 1123
Arkansas Libraries: 254
The Arlington Historical Magazine: 1124
Army: 1318
Art and Archaeology Newsletter: 1634
Art Education: 918
Arthritis and Rheumatism: 2287
Artibus Asiae: 133
Arts in Society: 73, 134
Arts Magazine: 135
ASCAP Today: 2565
ASHA: 1495
ASHRAE Journal: 1705, 2566
Asian Perspectives: 1635
Asian Survey: 636
ASLE Transactions: 1706
ASLIB Proceedings: 255
Assembly Engineering: 2567
The Assistant Librarian: 256
Association & Society Manager: 831
The Association of American Geographers Annals: 1099
Association of Collegiate Schools of Planning Bulletin: 919
Association of Engineering Geologists. Bulletin: 1668
Association of Lunar and Planetary Observers. Journal: 2056
Association of Official Analytical Chemists Journal: 2070
ASTM Standardization News: 1707
Astronautics & Aeronautics: 2050
Astronomical Society of the Pacific. Publications: 2057

References in Index refer to entry numbers

Periodical title index

Astronomy and Astrophysics: 2058
The Astrophysical Journal, Supplement Series: 2060
The Astrophysical Journal: 2059
Astrophysical Letters: 2135
ATE Newsletter: 920
Athletic Journal: 921
Atlanta Economic Review: 749
The Atlantic Monthly: 4
Atlantic Naturalist: 1807
Atmospheric Environment: 1808
Atomic Absorption Newsletter: 2175
Atomic Energy Review: 2176
Audecibel: 2288
Audience: 870
Audiology: 2289
Audiovisual Instruction: 866
AUMLA: 198
Australasian Corrosion Engineering: 1708
Australasian Journal of Philosophy: 442
Australian and New Zealand Journal of Medicine: 2290
Australian and New Zealand Journal of Obstetrics and Gynaecology: 2291
Australian Chemical Engineering: 1709
Australian Fisheries: 2568
Australian Journal of Botany: 1950
Australian Journal of Experimental Biology and Medical Science: 1893
Australian Psychologist: 1373
Austrian History Yearbook: 646
Authorship: 879
Automatic Machining: 2569
Automatica: 1710
Automation: 1711
A V Communication Review: 867
Avian Diseases: 2544
Aztlán: 5

B

Bacteriological Reviews: 1894
Baileya: 1951
Ball Bearing Journal: 1712
Ball State University Forum: 6
The Bankers Magazine: 808
The Banking Law Journal: 1200
Bardic Echoes: 474
The Bay State Librarian: 257
Baylor Business Studies: 750
Baylor Law Review: 1201
Behavior Genetics: 1895
Behavior Research and Therapy: 1375
Behavior Research Methods & Instrumentation: 1374
Behavior Science Research: 698
Behavior Therapy: 1376
Behavioral & Social Science Teacher: 922
Behavioral Sciences and Community Development: 699
Beloit Poetry Journal: 475
Berkshire Review: 74
Beyond Time: 1202
Biblical Theology Bulletin: 535
Bibliographical Society of America. Papers: 258, 325
Bijdragen: 536
The Bilingual Review/la Revista Bilingüe: 199
Biochemical and Biophysical Research Communications: 1896
Biochemical Genetics: 1897
Biochemical Journal: 2071
Biochemical Pharmacology: 2072
Biochemical Systematics and Ecology: 1898
Biochemistry: 2073
Biological Conservation: 1809
Biological Psychiatry*: 1377
Biology of the Neonate: 2292
Biology of Reproduction*: 1899
Biomedical Engineering: 1713

Biometrics: 2195
Bio-organic chemistry: 2074
Biophysical Journal: 1863
Biophysics of Structure and Mechanism: 1900
Biorheology: 1901
Bios: 1902
Biotropica: 1903
The Black Scholar: 609
Black Times: 7
Blackwood's Magazine: 75
Blake Newsletter: 326
Blake Studies: 327
Blood Vessels: 2293
Bodleian Library Record: 259
Book Forum: 8
Books Abroad: 328
Boston College Industrial and Commercial Law Review: 1203
Boston University Journal: 9
Boundary 2: 476
Brain, Behavior and Evolution: 2294
Brain Research: 2295
Brigham Young University Studies: 537
Brio: 260
British Astronomical Association Journal: 2061
British Columbia Library Quarterly: 261
British Dental Journal: 2500
British Interplanetary Society Journal: 1589
British Journal of Addiction: 1496
The British Journal of Aesthetics: 76
The British Journal of Disorders of Communication: 200
British Journal of Educational Psychology: 923
British Journal of Experimental Pathology: 2296
British Journal of Industrial Medicine: 2297
British Journal of Medical Education: 2298
The British Journal of Non-destructive Testing: 2025
British Journal of Obstetrics & Gynaecology: 2299
British Journal of Ophthalmology: 2300
British Journal of Preventive and Social Medicine: 2301
The British Journal of Psychiatry: 1378
British Journal of Venereal Diseases: 2302
British Medical Journal: 2303
British Phycological Journal: 1952
British Polymer Journal: 2075
British Society of Rheology Bulletin: 2026
The British Steelmaker: 2570
The Bryologist: 1953
Buffalo Law Review: 1204
Building Science: 1714
Building Services Engineer: 2571
Bulletin Baudelairien: 329
Bulletin of Bibliography and Magazine Notes: 262
Bulletin of Concerned Asian Scholars: 637
Bulletin of Entomological Research: 1980
Bulletin of Hispanic Studies: 201
Bulletin of Marine Science: 1691
Bulletin of Prosthetics Research: 2304
Bulletin of the Atomic Scientists: 1590
Bulletin of the Comediantes: 330
Bulletin of the History of Dentistry: 2501
Bulletin of the History of Dentistry: 2501
The Burroughs Bulletin: 331
Burroughs Clearing House: 809
Business and Economic Dimensions: 751
Business and Society Review: 755
Business Education World: 924
Business History 752
Business History Review: 753
Business Horizons: 754
Business Today: 756
The Byron Journal: 332

References in Index refer to entry numbers

C

C.A.S.I. Transactions: 2052
CA: A Cancer Journal for Clinicians: 2305
The CABE Journal: 925
Calcified Tissue Research: 2306
California Academy of Sciences. Occasional Papers: 1591
California Academy of Sciences. Proceedings: 1592
The California CPA Quarterly: 730
California Engineer: 1715
California Fish and Game: 1810
California Geology: 1669
California Historical Quarterly: 1125
California Journal: 1335
California Law Review: 1205
California Management Review: 757
California Quarterly: 477
California School Law Digest: 1206
California School Libraries: 263
California State Bar Journal: 1207
California Vector Views: 1811
California Western Law Review: 1208
Cambridge Philosophical Society Biological Reviews: 1904
The Canadian Administrator: 926
Canadian Aeronautics and Space Journal: 2051
Canadian-American Review of Hungarian Studies: 648
Canadian Anaesthetists' Society Journal: 2307
Canadian and International Education: 927
The Canadian Composer: 136
Canadian Constitutional Journal: 1209
Canadian Counsellor/Conseiller Canadien: 1379
Canadian Dental Association. Journal: 2502
The Canadian Field-Naturalist: 1864
The Canadian Forum: 10
Canadian Frontier: 1126
Canadian Geotechnical Journal: 1645
Canadian Historical Review: 1127
Canadian Home Economics Journal: 11
Canadian Institute of Food Science and Technology Journal: 1865
Canadian Journal of Animal Science: 1879
Canadian Journal of Behavioural Science: 1380
Canadian Journal of Biochemistry: 2076
Canadian Journal of Botany: 1954
Canadian Journal of Chemistry: 2077
Canadian Journal of Civil Engineering: 1716
Canadian Journal of Comparative Medicine: 2308
Canadian Journal of Earth Sciences: 1646
Canadian Journal of Economics: 758
Canadian Journal of Forest Research: 1812
Canadian Journal of Genetics and Cytology: 1905
Canadian Journal of History: 1128
Canadian Journal of Mathematics: 2196
Canadian Journal of Medical Technology: 2309
Canadian Journal of Microbiology: 1906
Canadian Journal of Neurological Sciences: 2310
Canadian Journal of Occupational Therapy: 1497
Canadian Journal of Pharmaceutical Sciences: 2311
Canadian Journal of Physics: 2136
Canadian Journal of Physiology and Pharmacology: 2312
Canadian Journal of Plant Science: 1955
Canadian Journal of Public Health: 2313
Canadian Journal of Soil Science: 1880
Canadian Journal of Zoology: 1981
Canadian Library Journal: 264
Canadian Literature: 333
Canadian Machinery and Metalworking: 2572
Canadian Metallurgical Quarterly: 1717
The Canadian Mining and Metallurgical Bulletin: 1680
Canadian Mining Journal: 1679
Canadian Modern Language Review: 202
Canadian Newsletter of Research on Women: 1575
Canadian Notes and Queries: 685

The Canadian Nurse: 2521
Canadian Pharmaceutical Journal: 2314
Canadian Public Administration: 1210
The Canadian Review of American Studies: 686
The Canadian Review of Sociology and Anthropology: 1538
Canadian Short Story Magazine: 478
Canadian Slavonic Papers: 647
The Canadian Veterinary Journal: 2545
Canadian Welfare: 1498
Cancer Research: 2315
Caravel Magazine: 479
Carbohydrate Research: 2078
Carbon: 2079
Cardiology: 2316
Caries Research: 2503
The Carleton Miscellany: 480
Carolina Quarterly: 481
Case Western Reserve Journal of International Law: 1211
Catalogue & Index: 265
Catalyst: 700
Catechist: 928
Cathedral Age: 1641
The Catholic Biblical Quarterly: 538
Catholic Historical Review: 539
Catholic Library World: 266
Catholic University Law Review: 1212
The CEA Critic: 929
The CEA Forum: 930
Cell and Tissue Kinetics: 1907
Cell and Tissue Research: 1908
Cellular Immunology: 2317
Cement and Concrete Research: 1718
Centaurus: 1129
The Centennial Review: 77
Central African Journal of Medicine: 2318
Central European History: 1130
Challenge: 759
Change: 931
Changing Education: 932
Character Potential: 1381
Chelonia: 1982
Chemica Scripta: 2080
Chemical Engineering: 1719
Chemical Engineering Communications: 1720
The Chemical Engineering Journal: 1721
Chemical Engineering Science: 1722
Chemical Technology*: 2081
Chemico-Biological Interactions: 2082
Chemistry: 2083
Chemistry and Industry: 2084
Chemosphere: 1813
Chemotherapy: 2319
Chesapeake Science: 1814
The Chesopiean*: 1636
Chest: 2320
Chicago Journalism Review: 880
Chicago Review: 482
Chicago Studies: 540
Child Care Quarterly: 1499
Child Development: 1382
Child Psychiatry and Human Development: 1383
Child Study Journal: 1384
Child Welfare: 1500
Child's Brain: 2533
Childhood Education: 933
Children's Theatre Review: 137
China Notes: 541
Chirurgia Plastica: 2534
The Choral Journal: 138
Christian Century: 542
Christianity Today: 543

References in Index refer to entry numbers

Periodical title index

Chromatographia: 1723
Chromosoma: 1909
The Chronicle of ABA: 1131
The Chronicle of Higher Education: 934
Church and State: 546
The Church Herald: 544
Church History: 545
Church Music: 139
The Churchman: 547
Cinema Journal: 871
Circulation: 2321
Civil Engineering: 1724
Civil War History: 1132
CLA Journal*: 203
Classical Philology: 78
The Classical World: 79
Claudel Studies: 334
Clavier: 140
Clays and Clay Minerals: 1681
The Cleft Palate Journal*: 2322
Clinica Chimica Acta: 2085
Clinical Chemistry: 2086
Clinical Immunology and Immunopathology: 2323
Clinical Pharmacology and Therapeutics: 2324
Clinical Social Work Journal: 1501
Clinical Toxicology: 2325
CMA/AMC Gazette: 141
The Coaching Clinic: 935
Coast Magazine: 12
Coastal Research: 1593
Coda: 142
Cognitive Psychology: 1385
Colby Library Quarterly: 335
The Coleopterists Bulletin: 1983
College & Research Libraries: 267
College and University: 939
College Composition and Communication: 936
College English: 937
College Literature: 336
College Press Review: 881
College Store Executive: 2573
College Student Journal: 938
Collegiate Journalist: 882
Colorado Business Review: 760
The Colorado Magazine: 1133
The Colorado Quarterly: 13
Colorado School of Mines Quarterly: 1647
The Columbia Forum: 14
Columbia Journal of Transnational Law: 1213
The Columbia Law Review: 1214
Combustion and Flame: 1594
Commentationes Physico-mathematicae: 2027
Commodities: 761
Common Market Law Review: 1215
Commonweal: 548
Communication: 851
Communication Arts International: 868
Communications in Mathematical Physics: 2137
Community Education Journal: 940
Community Mental Health Journal: 1386
Comparative Biochemistry and Physiology. Parts A, B, and C: 2087
Comparative Drama: 143
Comparative Education Review: 941
Comparative Literature Studies: 337
Comparative Politics: 1336
Comparative Studies in Society and History: 80
Compressed Air: 2574
The Computer Educator: 942
The Computer Journal: 2228
Computer Law Service: 1216

Computer Magazine: 2229
Computers and Electrical Engineering: 2230
Computers and Fluids: 2231
Computers and the Humanities: 2232
Computers in Biology and Medicine: 2233
Computing Surveys: 2234
Concerning Poetry: 483
The Conch: 633
The Conch Review of Books: 634
Concordia Historical Institute Quarterly: 549
The Condor: 1984
Confinia Neurologica: 2326
Confinia Psychiatrica: 1387
Connecticut Law Review: 1217
Conradiana: 338
The Conservationist: 1815
Conservative Judaism: 550
The Consort: 144
Consumers Digest: 15
Contemporary Drug Problems: 1502
Contemporary Education: 943
Contemporary Literature: 339
Contemporary Psychology*: 1388
Continuing Higher Education: 944
Contributions To Asian Studies: 638
Control Engineering: 1725
Coordination Chemistry Reviews: 2088
Copeia· 1985
The Cord: 551
The Core Teacher: 945
The Cornell Engineer: 1726
Cornell Journal of Social Relations: 701
Cornell Law Review: 1218
The Cornell Plantations: 1956
The Cornell Veterinarian: 2546
Corrective and Social Psychiatry: 1389
Corrosion: 1727
Corrosion Science: 1728
Cost and Management: 731
The Counseling Psychologist: 1390
Court Review: 1219
The CPA Journal: 732
CRC Critical Reviews in Analytical Chemistry: 2089
CRC Critical Reviews in Clinical Laboratory Sciences: 2327
CRC Critical Reviews in Clinical Radiology and Nuclear Medicine: 2328
CRC Critical Reviews in Environmental Control: 1816
CRC Critical Reviews in Solid State Sciences: 2138
Credit and Financial Management: 810
The Credit World: 811
Creighton Law Review: 1220
The Cresset: 16
Crime and Delinquency: 1539
Criminal Law Bulletin: 1221
The Criminal Law Review: 1222
The Crisis: 17
Critical Quarterly: 340
The Critical Review: 341
Critical Reviews in Bioengineering: 1910
Critical Reviews in Microbiology: 1911
Critique: 342
Cross and Crown: 552
Crustaceana: 1986
Crux: 553
Cryobiology: 1912
Cryogenics: 1729
Crystal Lattice Defects: 2028
Curator: 145
Current Anthropology: 1540
Current Musicology: 146
Current Sociology/la Sociologie Contemporaine: 1541

References in Index refer to entry numbers

Cutting Tool Engineering: 2575
CVP: 2329
Cytobiologie: 1913
Cytobios: 1914
Cytogenetics and Cell Genetics: 1915

D

The Dalhousie Review: 81, 18
Dance Magazine: 147
Dance Perspectives: 148
Dance Scope: 149
Danish Medical Bulletin: 2330
Dante Studies: 344
Data Processing: 2235
DB: the Sound Engineering Magazine: 869
The DECA Distributor: 946
December: 484
Deep-Sea Research: 1692
Defense Law Journal: 1223
Defense Management Journal: 1319
Dekalb Literary Arts Journal: 485
Delaware History: 1134
The Dental Assistant: 2504
Dental Economics: 2505
Denver Law Journal: 1224
DePaul Law Review: 1225
Dermatologica: 2331
Desalination: 1595
Descant: 486
Design: 150
Detroit Institute of Arts. Bulletin: 151
Detroit Society for Genealogical Research Magazine: 1135
Developmental Biology: 1916
Developmental Psychology: 1391
The D.H. Lawrence Review: 343
Diabetes: 2332
Diabetologia: 2333
Dialogue: 443
Dialogue: A Journal of Mormon Thought: 554
Dickens Studies Newsletter: 345
The Dickensian: 346
Die Casting Engineer: 2576
Digestion: 2334
Dimension: 204
Directions: 1100
The Director: 762
Drama & Theatre: 152
The Drama Review: 153
Dramatics: 154
Dramatika: 155
The Drew Gateway: 555
Drexel Library Quarterly: 268
Driftwood East Quarterly: 487
Drug Forum: 1503
Drug Intelligence and Clinical Pharmacy: 2335
Drug Metabolism and Disposition: 2336
Durham University Journal: 82

E

Early American Literature: 347
Earth Law Journal: 1226
Earth Science Bulletin: 1648
Earth-Science Reviews: 1649
East European Quarterly: 649
Eastern Churches Review: 556
Eastman Organic Chemical Bulletin: 2090
EBU Review: 887
Eco-Logos: 1818
Ecological Modelling: 1817
Economic Inquiry: 763
Economic Notes: 764

EdCentric Magazine: 947
Education: 948
Education and Training: 950
Education Canada: 949
Educational & Industrial Television: 888
Educational Broadcasting: 889
Educational Courier: 951
Educational Horizons: 952
Educational Record: 953
Educational Researcher: 954
Educational Review: 955
Educational Signpost: 956
Educational Studies: 957
Educational Theatre Journal: 156
Educational Theory: 958
Educators Guide To Media and Methods: 959
Educom: 960
Effluent and Water Treatment Journal: 1819
Eighteenth-Century Studies: 83
Eire-Ireland: 650
Ekistics: 702
El Arte Tipografico: 2577
El Grito: 19
Electrochimica Acta: 2091
Electrodeposition and Surface Treatment: 2029
Electromechanical Design: 1730
Electronics & Power: 1731
Electronics Letters: 1732
Electro-Optical Systems Design: 1733
Elementary English: 961
Elementary School Guidance and Counseling: 962
Elementary School Journal: 963
The Elepaio: 1820
ELH: 348
Emily Dickenson Bulletin: 349
Emory Law Journal: 1227
Encore: 488
Encounter: 557
Energy Conversion: 2139
Engineering and Contract Record: 2578
Engineering Digest: 1734
Engineering Fracture Mechanics: 1735
Engineering Geology: 1670
English Education: 964
English Journal: 965
English Language Notes: 350
English Language Teaching Journal: 205
English Literary Renaissance: 351
English Literature in Transition: 352
English Record: 966
English Studies: 353
English Studies in Africa: 84
Entomological Society of America Annals: 1987
Environment: 1821
Environment and Behavior: 1822
Environment and Planning-A: 1823
Environment and Planning-B 1824
Environmental Conservation: 1825
Environmental Health: 2337
Environmental Letters: 1826
Environmental Pollution: 1827
Environmental Research*: 1828
Environmental Science & Technology: 1829
Enzyme: 1917
Epoch: 489
ESQ: A Journal of the American Renaissance: 354
Essays in Criticism: 355
Essence: 490
Estate Planning: 812
Ethnology: 1542
Ethnomusicology: 157

References in Index refer to entry numbers

Periodical title index

Euromoney: 813
European Journal of Applied Physiology: 2338
European Journal of Biochemistry: 2092
European Journal of Cancer Research: 2339
European Journal of Clinical Investigation: 2340
European Journal of Clinical Pharmacology: 2341
European Journal of Pharmacology: 2342
European Journal of Political Research: 1337
European Neurology: 2343
European Surgical Research: 2535
Evangelical Missions Quarterly: 558
The Evangelical Quarterly: 559
Evelyn Waugh Newsletter: 356
Evolution: 1918
Experientia: 1866
Experimental Gerontology: 2344
Experimental Mechanics: 1736
Experimental Parasitology: 1988
The Explicator: 357
Explorations in Economic History: 765
Explosives and Pyrotechnics: 1596
Extrapolation: 358

F
Factory: 2579
The Family Coordinator: 1504
Family Planning Perspectives: 1505
Family Process: 1506
Federal Bar News: 1228
Federation Proceedings: 1919
Feedback: 890
The Feminist Art Journal: 1576
Fertility and Sterility*: 2345
FID News Bulletin: 269
Fieldiana: Botany: 1957
Fieldiana: Zoology: 1989
Fields and Quanta*: 2140
Fifth Estate: 20
Film Culture: 872
Film Heritage: 873
The Film Journal: 874
Film Library Quarterly: 270
Film Quarterly: 875
Filmmakers Newsletter: 876
Filmograph: 877
The Filson Club History Quarterly: 1136
Financial Analysts Journal: 814
Fire Technology: 1737
The Florida Naturalist: 1830
Florida Scientist: 1597
Fluidics Quarterly: 1738
Focus/Midwest 21
Focus on Indiana Libraries: 271
Folia Phoniatrica: 897
Folia Primatologica: 1990
Food Technology: 2580
Foreign Affairs*: 1338
Foreign Language Annals: 967
Foreign Service Journal: 1339
The Foreman's Letter: 2581
Forensic Science: 2346
Forest Science: 1831
Forest-Conservation: 1832
Forum: 968
Forum Italicum: 206
Foundations: 560
Four Quarters: 85
The Free Lance: 491
The Freeman: 766, 22
French Historical Studies: 1137
The French Review: 207

Friday Letter: 1507
Fueloil & Oil Heat: 2582
The Futurist: 23

G
Gastroenterology: 2347
Gastrointestinal Endoscopy: 2348
Gas World: 2583
General Linguistics: 208
General Relativity and Gravitation: 2141
General Systems: 2197
Genetic Psychology Monographs: 1392
Genetical Research: 1920
Geochimica et Cosmochimica Acta: 2093
Geoderma: 1881
Geoforum: 1101
Geographical Analysis: 1102
The Geographical Journal: 1103
The Geographical Magazine: 1104
The Geographical Review: 1105
Geophysical Prospecting: 1650
Geophysics: 1651
The George Washington Law Review: 1229
Georgia Academy of Science Bulletin: 1598
Georgia Dental Association. Journal: 2506
Georgia Entomological Society. Journal: 1991
The Georgia Historical Quarterly: 1138
Georgia Nursing: 2522
The Georgia Review: 359
Georgia State Bar Journal: 1230
Geothermics: 1671
German-American Studies: 360
The Germanic Review: 209
Gerontologia: 2349
Gerontologia Clinica: 2350
The Gerontologist: 610
Gesta: 86
Ghost Dance: 492
The Gifted Child Quarterly: 969
Glass Digest: 2584
Global Dialogue: 1340
Glossa: 210
GP Newsletter: 891
Graphic Arts Supplier News: 2585
The Great Lakes Entomologist: 1992
Great Plains Journal: 687
Green River Review: 87
Group Process: 1393
Group Psychotherapy and Psychodrama: 1394
Growth: 1921
Growth and Change: 1833
The Guidance Clinic: 970
Gynecologic Investigation: 2351
The Gypsy Scholar: 361

H
Haemostasis: 2352
Ham Radio Magazine: 892
The Hand: 2353
The Harpsichord: 158
Hartford Studies in Literature: 362
Harvard Business Review: 767
Harvard Civil Rights-Civil Liberties Law Review: 1231
Harvard Educational Review: 971
Harvard International Law Journal: 1232
Harvard Journal of Asiatic Studies: 639
Harvard Journal on Legislation: 1233
Harvard Law Review: 1234
Harvard Library Bulletin: 272
Harvard Theological Review*: 561

References in Index refer to entry numbers

Headache: 2354
Health Physics: 2177
Health Team: 2355
Heating/Piping/Air Conditioning: 2586
Herpetologica: 1993
Hesperia: 88
The Heythrop Journal: 562
High Speed Ground Transportation Journal: 1599
High Temperature Science: 1600
High Temperatures-High Pressures: 2142
Higher Education: 972
Higher Education Bulletin: 973
The Hiram Poetry Review: 493
Hispania: 211
Hispanic American Historical Review*: 665
Hispanic Review: 212
Hispanófila: 213
Histochemistry: 2094
The Historian: 1139
Historic Preservation: 24
The Historical Journal: 1140
Historical Magazine of the Protestant Episcopal Church: 563
Historical Methods Newsletter: 703
Historical Reflections: 1141
Historiographia Linguistica: 214
History and Theory: 1143
History of Childhood Quarterly: 1395
History of Education Quarterly: 1142
History of Religion*: 564
The History Teacher: 974
Horizon Magazine: 25
Hormone Research: 2356
Horn Book Magazine: 363
Hospital Administration: 2357
Hospital Engineering: 1739
Hospital Housekeeping: 2358
Hospital Progress: 2359
Hospitals: 2360
Hovering Craft & Hydrofoil: 1740
Human Biology: 1922
Human Development: 1396
Human Genetics: 1923
Human Heredity: 1924
Human Relations*: 704
Human Rights: 1235
The Humanist: 89
Humanities Association Review: 90
Hydrocarbon Processing: 1652

I
IAPPW Journal: 975
IATSE Offical Bulletin 2587
IAVA Journal: 976
Ideas Magazine: 26
IEEE Proceedings: 1741
IEEE Transactions on Magnetics: 1742
IEEE Transactions on Systems, Man and Cybernetics: 1743
The Iliff Review: 565
Illinois Geographical Society Bulletin: 1106
Illinois Libraries: 273
Illinois Medical Journal: 2361
Illinois State Historical Society Journal: 1144
Illuminating Engineering Society. Journal: 1744
Immunochemistry: 2095
Immunological Communications: 2362
Improving College and University Teaching: 977
Improving Human Performance: 978
The Incorporated Linguist: 215
The Independent School Bulletin: 979
The Indian Historian: 688
Indian Journal of Medical Research: 2363

Indian Truth: 689
Indiana Law Journal: 1236
Indiana Magazine of History: 1145
Indiana State Medical Association Journal: 2364
Individual Psychologist: 1397
Individual Psychology Newsletter: 1398
Industrial and Commercial Photographer: 2588
Industrial and Labor Relations Review: 821
Industrial Design: 2589
Industrial Development: 2590
Industrial Distribution: 2591
Industrial Engineering: 1745
Industrial Finishing: 2592
Industrial Gerontology: 1508
Industrial Marketing: 2593
Industrial Mathematics: 2198
Industrial Photography*: 2594
Industrial Relations: 822
Infantry Magazine: 1320
Infection and Immunity: 2365
The Info Journal: 1601
Information News and Sources: 274
The Information Scientist: 275
Information Storage and Retrieval: 276
Infrared Physics: 2143
Inorganic and Nuclear Chemistry Letters: 2097
Inorganic Chemistry*: 2096
Inquiry: 444, 2366
Inspection News: 768
Instant Research on Peace and Violence: 1341
Institution of Electrical Engineers. Proceedings: 1746
Institution of Nuclear Engineers. Journal: 2178
Instructor: 980
The Instrumentalist: 159
Instrumentation Technology: 2236
Insulation/Circuits: 2595
Integrated Education: 981
Interamerican Journal of Psychology: 1399
Interceptor: 1321
Interchange: 982
The Intercollegiate Review: 27
The Internal Auditor: 733
International Affairs: 611
International Archives of Allergy and Applied Immunology: 2367
International Archives of Occupational Health: 2368
International Arthurian Society. Biographical Bulletin: 364
International Development Review: 705
International Educational and Cultural Exchange: 983
International Forum on Information and Documentation: 2237
International Insurance Monitor: 769
International Journal: 612
International Journal for Numerical Methods in Engineering: 1747
International Journal for Parasitology: 1994
International Journal for Radiation Physics and Chemistry: 2144
The International Journal of Accounting Education and Research: 734
International Journal of Aging and Human Development: 1400
International Journal of American Linguistics: 216
International Journal of Bio-medical Computing: 2238
International Journal of Clinical and Experimental Hypnosis: 1401
International Journal of Comparative Sociology: 1543
International Journal of Computer Mathematics Section A*: 2239
International Journal of Computer Mathematics Section B*: 2240
International Journal of Contemporary Sociology: 1544
International Journal of Engineering Science: 1748
The International Journal of Environmental Studies: 1834
International Journal of Fracture: 2030
International Journal of Group Psychotherapy: 1402
International Journal of Health Sciences: 2368-1
International Journal of Heat and Mass Transfer: 1749
International Journal of Insect Morphology and Embryology: 1995

References in Index refer to entry numbers

Periodical title index

International Journal of Instructional Media: 984
International Journal of Leprosy: 2369
International Journal of Machine Tool Design and Research: 1750
International Journal of Mass Spectrometry and Ion Physics: 2145
International Journal of Mechanical Science: 1751
International Journal of Middle East Studies: 671
International Journal of Multiphase Flow: 1752
International Journal of Non-linear Mechanics: 1753
International Journal of Nursing Studies: 2523
International Journal of Orthodontics: 2507
International Journal of Peptide and Protein Research: 2098
International Journal of Powder Metallurgy and Powder Technology: 1653
International Journal of Psychiatry in Medicine: 2370
International Journal of Rock Mechanics and Mining Sciences: 1682
International Journal of Sociology of the Family: 1545
International Journal of Symbology: 91
International Journal of Systematic Bacteriology: 1925
International Journal of Theoretical Physics: 2146
International Labour Review: 823
International Legal Materials: 1237
International Migration Review: 1546
International Musician: 160
International Nursing Review: 2524
International Organization: 1238
International Pharmacopsychiatry: 1403
International Philosophical Quarterly: 445
International Photographer: 2596
International Pollution Control Magazine: 1835
International Problems: 613
The International Psychologist: 1404
International Review of Community Development: 706
International Review of Education: 985
International Review of Mission: 566
International Review of Social History: 1146
International Social Science Journal: 707
International Social Work: 1509
International Socialist Review: 1342
International Studies Quarterly: 614
The International Sugar Journal: 1882
International Understanding: 1405
Interpersonal Development: 1406
Interracial Books for Children: 365
Intervirology: 2371
Inventiones Mathematicae: 2199
Investigative Ophthalmology*: 2372
Investigative Urology: 2373
Iowa Medical Society Journal: 2374
The Iowa Review: 494
The Iron Worker: 2597
ISA Transactions: 1754
Isis: 1147
Israel Exploration Journal: 1637
Israel Journal of Botany: 1958
Israel Journal of Chemistry: 2099
Israel Journal of Earth Sciences: 1654
Israel Journal of Mathematics: 2200
Israel Journal of Medical Sciences: 2375
Israel Journal of Technology: 1602
Israel Journal of Zoology: 1996
Issues in Radical Therapy: 1407
Italian Quarterly: 651
Italica: 217
Iustitia: 1239

J

Jack London Newsletter: 366
James Joyce Quarterly: 367
Japanese Heart Journal: 2376
Japanese Journal of Applied Physics: 2147
Japanese Journal of Microbiology: 1926

Jazz Magazine: 161
JEMF Quarterly: 162
JGE: The Journal of General Education: 986
John Marshall Journal of Practice and Procedure: 1240
Johnsonian Newsletter: 368
Journal for the Scientific Study of Religion: 567
Journal of Abnormal Child Psychology: 1408
Journal of Abnormal Psychology: 1409
The Journal of Academic Librarianship: 277
The Journal of Accountancy: 735
Journal of Accounting Research: 736
Journal of Advertising Research: 847
Journal of Advertising: 846
Journal of Aerosol Science: 2031
The Journal of Aesthetic Education: 987
The Journal of Aesthetics and Art Criticism: 163
Journal of African History: 1148
Journal of Agricultural Science: 1883
Journal of Air Law and Commerce: 1241
Journal of Aircraft: 2053
Journal of American Folklore: 1547
Journal of American History: 1149
Journal of American Indian Education: 988
Journal of American Studies: 690
The Journal of Analytical Psychology: 1410
Journal of Anatomy: 2377
Journal of Anatomy and Embryology: 2378
Journal of Animal Morphology: 1997
Journal of Anthropological Research: 1548
Journal of Applied Behavior Analysis: 1411
Journal of Applied Chemistry and Biotechnology: 2100
Journal of Applied Meteorology: 1655
Journal of Applied Nutrition: 2379
Journal of Applied Physics*: 2148
Journal of Applied Probability: 2201
Journal of Applied Psychology*: 1412
Journal of Asian and African Studies: 640
Journal of Asian History: 1150
Journal of Asian Studies: 641
Journal of Bacteriology: 1927
Journal of Baltic Studies: 652
Journal of Band Research: 164
Journal of Basic Engineering*: 1755
Journal of Behavior Therapy and Experimental Psychiatry: 1413
Journal of Biochemistry: 2101
Journal of Biogeography: 1107
Journal of Biological Chemistry: 2102
Journal of Biological Education: 989
Journal of Biomechanics: 2380
Journal of Biosocial Science: 1867
Journal of Black Studies: 615
The Journal of Bone and Joint Surgery: 2536
Journal of Broadcasting: 893
Journal of Business: 770
Journal of Business Administration: 771
The Journal of Business Communication: 852
The Journal of Business Education: 990
The Journal of Canadian Petroleum Technology: 1656
Journal of Canadian Studies/Revue d'Études Canadiennes: 691
Journal of Carbohydrates-Nucleosides-& Nucleotides: 2103
The Journal of Cell Biology: 1928
Journal of Cellular Plastics: 2104
Journal of Chemical Education: 2105
The Journal of Chemical Physics: 2149
Journal of Child Psychology and Psychiatry: 1414
Journal of Chromatography: 2033
Journal of Chronic Diseases: 2381
Journal of Church and State: 568
Journal of Church Music: 165
The Journal of Clinical Investigation: 2382
The Journal of Clinical Pharmacology: 2383

References in Index refer to entry numbers

Journal of Clinical Psychology: 1415
Journal of Coated Fabrics: 1756
Journal of Collective Negotiations in the Public Sector: 824
Journal of College Radio: 894
Journal of College Science Teaching: 991
Journal of Combinatorial Theory: 2202
The Journal of Commercial Bank Lending: 815
The Journal of Commonwealth Literature: 369
Journal of Communication: 853
Journal of Community Psychology: 1416
Journal of Comparative and Physiological Psychology: 1417
Journal of Comparative Administration*: 1242
Journal of Comparative Family Studies: 1549
Journal of Comparative Pathology: 2547
Journal of Comparative Physiology-A: 2384
Journal of Comparative Physiology-B: 2385
Journal of Composite Materials: 1757
Journal of Computational Physics: 2150
The Journal of Conchology: 1998
Journal of Conflict Resolution: 1343
Journal of Consulting and Clinical Psychology*: 1418
Journal of Consumer Affairs: 28, 772
Journal of Contemporary History: 1151
Journal of Coordination Chemistry*: 2106
Journal of Counseling Psychology*: 1419
Journal of Creative Behavior: 992
Journal of Criminal Law and Criminology: 1243
The Journal of Critical Analysis: 446
Journal of Cross-Cultural Psychology: 1420
Journal of Dental Education: 2508
Journal of Dental Research: 2509
Journal of Dentistry: 2510
The Journal of Developing Areas: 616
Journal of Development Studies: 773
Journal of Differential Geometry: 2203
Journal of Drug Education: 1510
Journal of Drug Issues: 1511
The Journal of Economic Education: 993
Journal of Economic Entomology: 1999
Journal of Economic History: 774
Journal of Economic Issues: 775
Journal of Economics and Business: 776
Journal of Ecumenical Studies: 569
Journal of Education: 994
Journal of Education: 995
Journal of Education for Librarianship: 278
Journal of Educational Measurement: 996
Journal of Educational Psychology*: 1421
Journal of Educational Technology Systems: 997
The Journal of Educational Thought: 998
Journal of Elasticity: 1603
The Journal of Elastomers and Plastics: 2107
Journal of Electroanalytical Chemistry and Interfacial Electro-chemistry: 2108
Journal of Electrocardiology: 2386
Journal of Electron Spectroscopy and Related Phenomena: 2034
The Journal of Endocrinology: 2387
Journal of Engineering for Industry*: 1758
Journal of Engineering for Power*: 1759
Journal of Engineering Mathematics: 2204
The Journal of English and Germanic Philology: 218
Journal of English Teaching Techniques: 999
Journal of Environmental Health: 1836
Journal of Environmental Sciences: 1837
Journal of Environmental Systems: 1838
Journal of Experimental Biology: 1929
Journal of Experimental Botany: 1959
The Journal of Experimental Child Psychology: 1423
Journal of Experimental Psychology*: 1424
Journal of Extension: 1000
Journal of Family Counseling: 1425

Journal of Family Law: 1244
Journal of Finance: 816
Journal of Financial Education: 1001
Journal of Fire and Flammability: 1760
Journal of Fluid Mechanics: 2035
Journal of Fluorine Chemistry: 2109
Journal of Food Science: 1604
Journal of Forensic Sciences: 1605
Journal of Forest History: 1839
Journal of General Microbiology: 1930
The Journal of General Physiology: 2388
The Journal of General Psychology: 1426
Journal of General Virology: 2389
The Journal of Genetic Psychology: 1427
The Journal of Geography: 1002
Journal of Geological Education: 1003
Journal of Geology: 1672
Journal of Geophysical Research: 2151
Journal of Geriatric Psychiatry: 1428
Journal of Gerontology: 617
Journal of Graphoanalysis: 1429
Journal of Health and Social Behavior: 1550
Journal of Heat Transfer*: 1761
Journal of Helminthology: 2000
Journal of Heredity: 1931
Journal of Herpetology: 2001
Journal of Heterocyclic Chemistry: 2110
The Journal of Higher Education: 1004
Journal of Histochemistry and Cytochemistry: 2111
Journal of Homosexuality: 1430
Journal of Hospital Dental Practice: 2511
Journal of Human Evolution: 2002
The Journal of Human Resources: 777
Journal of Humanistic Psychology: 1431
Journal of Hydronautics: 1693
Journal of Hygiene: 2391
Journal of Immunology: 2392
Journal of Imperial and Commonwealth History: 1152
Journal of Individual Psychology: 1432
Journal of Indo-European Studies: 653
Journal of Industrial Relations: 825
The Journal of Infectious Diseases: 2393
Journal of Inorganic and Nuclear Chemistry: 2112
Journal of Insect Physiology: 2003
The Journal of Insurance: 778
Journal of Interamerican Studies and World Affairs*: 666
Journal of International Law and Economics: 1245
Journal of International Law and Politics: 1246
Journal of Investigative Dermatology: 2394
Journal of Jazz Studies: 166
Journal of Latin American Studies: 667
Journal of Learning Disabilities: 1006
Journal of Leisurability: 1512
Journal of Librarianship: 279
Journal of Library Automation: 280
Journal of Library History, Philosophy, and Comparative Librari-anship: 281
Journal of Linguistics: 219
Journal of Long Term Care Administration: 2395
Journal of Low Temperature Physics: 2152
Journal of Lubrication Technology*: 1762
Journal of Macromolecular Science, Part A: 2113
Journal of Macromolecular Science, Part B: 2153
Journal of Mammalogy: 2004
Journal of Marine Research: 1694
Journal of Marketing: 779
Journal of Marketing Research: 780
Journal of Marriage and the Family: 1513
Journal of Materials Science: 1606
Journal of Mathematical Analysis and Applications*: 2205

References in Index refer to entry numbers

Periodical title index

Journal of Mathematical Geology: 1673
Journal of Medical Education: 2396
Journal of Medical Entomology: 2005
Journal of Medical Genetics: 2397
Journal of Medical Microbiology: 2398
Journal of Medical Primatology: 2399
Journal of Medicinal Chemistry*: 2114
Journal of Medieval History: 1153
Journal of Mental Health: 1433
Journal of Mexican-American History: 1154
Journal of Microwave Power: 1764
Journal of Milk and Food Technology: 1868
The Journal of Mississippi History: 1155
Journal of Modern African Studies: 635
The Journal of Modern History: 1156
Journal of Modern Literature: 370
Journal of Molecular Evolution: 1932
Journal of Molecular Structure: 2154
Journal of Money, Credit, and Banking: 817
Journal of Motor Behavior: 1434
Journal of Multivariate Analysis: 2206
Journal of Music Theory: 167
Journal of Music Therapy: 1435
The Journal of Narrative Technique: 371
Journal of Near Eastern Studies: 672
The Journal of Negro Education: 1007
The Journal of Negro History*: 692
Journal of Nematology: 2006
Journal of Nervous and Mental Disease: 2400
Journal of Neurocytology: 2401
Journal of Neurology: 2403
Journal of Neurology; Neurosurgery and Psychiatry: 2404
The Journal of Nursing Education: 2525
Journal of Nutrition Education: 1008
Journal of Optimization Theory and Applications: 2207
Journal of Oral Medicine: 2512
The Journal of Organic Chemistry*: 2115
Journal of Organometallic Chemistry: 2116
The Journal of Pacific History: 642
Journal of Paint Technology: 1607
Journal of Palestine Studies: 673
Journal of Parapsychology: 1436
Journal of Parasitology: 2007
Journal of Pastoral Care*: 570
Journal of Peasant Studies: 709
The Journal of Pediatrics*: 2406
Journal of Pediatrics: 2407
Journal of Periodontal Research: 2513
Journal of Personality and Social Psychology: 1438
Journal of Personality Assessment: 1437
Journal of Pharmaceutical Sciences: 2408
Journal of Pharmacology and Experimental Therapeutics: 2409
Journal of Phenomenological Psychology: 1439
The Journal of Philosophy: 447
Journal of Photochemistry: 2117
Journal of Phycology: 1960
Journal of Physical Chemistry*: 2118
Journal of Physical Education*: 1009
Journal of Physical Oceanography: 1695
Journal of Physics A: 2155
Journal of Physics B: 2156
Journal of Physics C: 2157
Journal of Physics D: 2158
Journal of Physics E: 2159
Journal of Physics F: 2160
Journal of Physics G: 2179
Journal of Plasma Physics: 2161
Journal of Police Science and Administration: 1247
Journal of Political Economy*: 781
Journal of Popular Culture: 1551

Journal of Popular Film: 878
The Journal of Practical Nursing: 2526
Journal of Psychedelic Drugs: 1514
Journal of Psychiatry and Law: 1248; 1440
Journal of Psycholinguistic Research: 854
The Journal of Psychology: 1441
Journal of Psychosomatic Research: 2410
The Journal of Public Health Dentistry: 2514
Journal of Purchasing and Materials Management: 782
Journal of Raman Spectroscopy: 2162
Journal of Reading: 1010
Journal of Reading Behavior: 1011
Journal of Recreational Mathematics: 2208
Journal of Rehabilitation: 1515
Journal of Rehabilitation of the Deaf: 1516
Journal of Religion: 571
Journal of Religion and Health: 572
Journal of Religious Thought: 573
Journal of Research in Crime and Delinquency: 710
Journal of Research in Music Education: 1012
Journal of Retailing: 783
Journal of Risk and Insurance: 784
Journal of Roman Studies: 93
Journal of Safety Research: 618, 1840
The Journal of School Health: 2411
Journal of School Psychology: 1442
Journal of Sex and Marital Therapy: 1443
Journal of Sex Research: 711
Journal of Small Business Management: 832
Journal of Social History: 1157
The Journal of Social Psychology: 1444
Journal of Soil and Water Conservation: 1841
Journal of Solution Chemistry: 2119
Journal of Sound and Vibration: 2037
Journal of South Asian Literature: 372
Journal of Southeast Asian Studies: 643
Journal of Southern History: 1158
Journal of Space Craft and Rockets: 2054
Journal of Spanish Studies: Twentieth Century: 373
The Journal of Special Education: 1013
Journal of Speech and Hearing Disorders: 2412
Journal of Speech and Hearing Research: 2413
Journal of Statistical Computation and Simulation*: 2241
Journal of Statistical Physics: 2209
The Journal of Steroid Biochemistry: 2120
Journal of Structural Mechanics: 1765
Journal of Studies on Alcohol: 1517
Journal of Surgical Research: 2537
The Journal of Symbolic Logic: 449, 2210
Journal of Systems Engineering: 1766
Journal of Systems Management: 2242
The Journal of Taxation: 737
Journal of Teacher Education: 1014
Journal of Technical Writing and Communication: 855
Journal of Terramechanics: 1767
Journal of Testing and Evaluation: 1608
Journal of Theoretical Biology: 1933
The Journal of Thoracic and Cardiovascular Surgery*: 2538
Journal of Traffic Safety Education: 1015
Journal of Trauma: 2414
Journal of Travel Research: 785
Journal of Urban Law: 1249
Journal of Urology: 2415
Journal of Verbal Learning and Verbal Behavior: 220, 1016
Journal of Virology: 2416
Journal of Vocational Behavior: 1445
Journal of Wildlife Diseases: 2548
The Journal of Wildlife Management: 1842
Journal of the Atmospheric Sciences: 2032
Journal of the Experimental Analysis of Behavior: 1422
Journal of the History of the Behavioral Sciences: 708

References in Index refer to entry numbers

Journal of the History of Ideas: 92
Journal of the History of Medicine and Allied Sciences: 2390
Journal of the Less-common Metals: 2036
Journal of the Mechanics and Physics of Solids: 1763
Journal of the Neurological Sciences: 2402
Journal of the Science of Food & Agriculture: 1884
Journal of the West: 1159
Journalism Educator: 1017
Journalism Quarterly: 883
JUCO Review: 1018
Judaism: 574
Judicature: 1250
Juvenile Justice: 1251

K

Kalki: 374
Kansas (Central States) Entomological Society. Journal: 2008
Kansas Quarterly: 495
Kansas School Board Journal: 1019
Karamu: 496
K-Eight: 1020
The Kentucky English Bulletin: 1021
Kentucky Folklore Record: 1552
Kentucky Historical Society Register: 1160
Keynote: 1518
The Kipling Journal: 375
The Kiva: 1638
Kobe Journal of Medical Sciences: 2417
Kyklos: 712

L

Labor-Management Alcoholism Journal: 1519
Labor Today 826
Laboratory Animal Science: 1609
Laboratory Animals: 2009
Laboratory Investigation: 2419
Laboratory Management: 2420
Laboratory Medicine: 2421
La Coronica: 221
Lancaster County Historical Society Journal: 1161
The Lancet*: 2422
Landscape Planning: 1843
Language: 222
Language and Style: 94
Language Learning: 223
Language Sciences: 224
The Laryngoscope*: 2423
Latin American Research Review: 668
La Vie Medicale au Canada Français: 2418
Law & Society Review: 1252
Law and Contemporary Problems: 1253
Law Office Economics and Management: 1254
Lawyer of the Americas: 1255
Learning: 1023
Learning & Motivation: 1446
Learning Today: 282
Leeds Philosophical and Literary Society Proceedings: 95
Le Magister: 1022
Leonardo: 168
L'Esprit Créateur: 376
Letters in Applied and Engineering Sciences: 1768
Lexington Theological Quarterly: 575
Liberation: 29
The Libertarian Forum: 30
Library Association of Alberta. Bulletin: 283
Library History: 284
Library Journal: 285
Library Occurrent: 286

Library Quarterly: 287
Library Resources & Technical Services: 288
Life Sciences*: 1869
Linear and Multilinear Algebra*: 2211
The Linguistic Reporter: 225
Linguistics: 226
Linnean Society Biological Journal: 1934
Linnean Society Botanical Journal: 1961
Lipids: 2121
The Literary Review: 377
Literary Sketches: 378
Literature/Film Quarterly: 379
The Little Magazine: 497
Lituanus: 654
Livestock Production Science: 1885
The Living Light: 576
The Living Wilderness: 1844
The Log Analyst: 1657
The Logistics and Transportation Review: 2598
The London Collector: 380
Louisiana Business Review: 786
Louisiana Law Review: 1256
Louisiana Schools: 1024
Louvain Studies: 577
Luso-Brazilian Review: 669
Lutheran Education: 1025
Lyrica Germanica: 227

M

Machine and Tool Blue Book: 2599
Machine Design: 1769
Madroño: 1962
The Magazine of Bank Administration: 818
Main Currents in Modern Thought: 450
Maitreya: 578
Malacologia: 2010
Malacological Review: 2011
The Malahat Review: 498
Man: 1553
Man and World: 451
Man-Environment Systems: 1845
Man/Society/Technology: 1027
Management Science: 833
Management Today: 834
Management World: 835
Manitoba Pageant: 1162
The Manitoba Teacher: 1026
Mankind: 1163
Manuscripta: 96
Manuscripts: 97
Margins: 856
Marine Biology: 1696
Marine Chemistry: 1697
Marine Geology: 1698
Marine Geotechnology: 1699
Mariners Weather Log: 1658
Mark Twain Journal: 381
Marketing: 787
The Markham Review: 98
Marquette Business Review: 788
Maryland Herpetological Society Bulletin: 2012
The Maryland Historian: 1164
Maryland Law Review: 1257
Maryland State Dental Association Journal: 2515
Maryland State Medical Journal: 2424
Massachusetts Journal of Mental Health: 1447
Massachusetts Music News: 1028
Massachusetts Studies in English: 382
Master Drawings: 169
The Masterkey: 693

References in Index refer to entry numbers

Periodical title index

Matchbox: 1344
Materials and Structures: 1772
Materials Engineering: 1770
Materials Science and Engineering: 1771
Mathematics of Computation: 2212
The Mathematics Teacher: 1029
May Trends: 789
McGill Law Journal: 1258
Meanjin Quarterly: 31
Measurement and Evaluation in Guidance: 1030
Mechanical Engineering*: 1773
Mechanics Research Communications: 1774
Mechanism and Machine Theory: 1775
Mechanisms of Ageing and Development: 1870
Media & Consumer: 32
Media: Library Services Journal: 289
Medical Association of Georgia. Journal: 2425
Medical Biology: 2426
Medical Group Management: 836
Medical History: 2427
Medical Library Association Bulletin: 290
Medical Microbiology and Immunology: 2428
Medical Opinion: 2429
Medical Progress Through Technology: 2430
Medical Research Engineering: 2431
Medical Society of New Jersey. Journal: 2432
Medicine: 2433
Medicine, Science and the Law: 2434
Medico-legal Bulletin: 2435
Medievalia et Humanistica: 99
Mélanges Malraux Miscellany 387
Memory and Cognition: 1448
Menninger Clinic Bulletin: 1449
The Mennonite: 579
Mental Health and Society: 1450
Mental Retardation: 1451
Mental Retardation/Déficience Mentale: 1520
Merip Reports: 674
Merrill-Palmer Quarterly of Behavior and Development: 1452
Metal Treating: 2600
Metals Engineering Quarterly: 1776
Metanoia: 580
Meteoritics: 1659
Methodist History: 581
Metrologia: 2213
The Michigan Botanist: 1963
Michigan History: 1165
Michigan Law Review: 1259
The Michigan Librarian: 291
Michigan Mathematical Journal: 2214
Michigan Medicine: 2436
Michigan Quarterly Review: 33
Microbios: 1935
Microchemical Journal*: 2122
Microform Review: 292
Micropaleontology: 1871
The Microscope: 1610
Mid-America: 1166
The Middle East Journal: 675
Middle East Studies Association Bulletin: 676
Middle Eastern Studies: 677
Middle School Journal: 1031
Midstream Magazine: 34
Midwest Modern Language Association Bulletin: 228
The Midwest Quarterly: 100
The Migrant: 2013
Milbank Memorial Fund Quarterly: 2437
Military Affairs: 1322
Military Law Review: 1323
Military Police Journal: 1324
Military Review: 1325

Milton Quarterly: 383
Mind: 452
Mineral Industries Bulletin: 1683
Mineralium Deposita: 1684
The Mineralogical Record: 1685
Mineralogy and Petrology: 1686
Minerals Science and Engineering: 1687
Minnesota History: 1167
Minnesota Reading Quarterly: 1032
The Mississippi Folklore Register: 1554
Mississippi Law Journal: 1260
Mississippi Music Educator: 170
Mississippi Quarterly: 694
Mississippi Review: 499
Missouri Botanical Garden Annals: 1964
Missouri Engineer: 1777
Missouri Library Association Newsletter: 293
Missouri Mineral News: 1688
Modern Asian Studies: 644
Modern Drama: 171
Modern Fiction Studies: 384
Modern Geology: 1674
The Modern Language Journal: 229
Modern Language Review: 230
Modern Language Studies: 231
Modern Languages: 232
Modern Packaging: 1778
Modern Philology: 385
Molecular & General Genetics: 1936
Molecular Pharmacology: 2438
Momentum: 1033
Monarchy Canada: 695
Monastic Studies: 582
Monatshefte für Deutschen Unterricht, Deutsche Sprache und Literatur: 233
The Monist: 453
Montana Business Quarterly: 790
Montana Law Review: 1261
Montana: The Magazine of Western History: 1168
The Month: 583
Monthly Labor Review: 827
Monthly Review: 1345
Monument in Cantos and Essays: 500
Morehead State University Bulletin of Applied Linguistics: 234
Mosaic: 386
Mountain-Plains Library Quarterly: 294
MSHA: 1521
MSU Business Topics: 791
Museums Journal: 172
Music Educators Journal: 1034
Music Journal: 173
Music Ministry: 174
Musical Analysis: 175
The Musical Times: 176
Mustang Review: 501
Mutation Research: 1937

N

NACWPI Journal: 177
NALLD Journal: 235
Names: 101
Nassau Review: 502
National Academy of Sciences of the United States Proceedings*: 1611
National Association for Women Deans, Administrators, and Counselors. Journal: 1577
National Association of Colleges and Teachers of Agriculture. Journal: 1035
National Business Woman: 1578
National Defense: 1326
National Elementary Principal: 1036

References in Index refer to entry numbers

National Geographic: 1108
The National Guardsman: 1327
The National Humane Review: 35
The National Public Accountant: 738
National Review: 36
The NATS Bulletin: 178
Natural History Magazine: 1612
Natural Resources Journal: 1846
Nature: 1613
Nature Study: 1037
The Nautilus: 2014
Naval Engineers Journal: 1779
NCAA News: 1038
Nebraska History: 1169
Nebraska Library Association Quarterly: 295
Negro American Literature Forum: 388
The Negro Educational Review: 1039
Negro Heritage: 37
Nephron: 2439
Netherlands International Law Review: 1262
Network International Communications in Library Automation: 296
Neuroendocrinology: 2440
Neurology: 2441
Neuropharmacology: 2442
Neuropsychobiology: 1453
Neuropsychologia: 2443
Neuroradiology: 2444
Neuva Narrativa Hispanoamerica: 389
New Blackfriars: 584
New England Journal of Medicine: 2445
New England Journal on Prison Law: 1263
The New England Quarterly*: 390
The New Englander: 792
New Humanist: 38
New Jersey History: 1170
New Jersey Music & Arts Magazine: 179
New Jersey School Leader: 1040
New Jersey State Bar Journal: 1264
The New Leader: 39
New Letters: 503
New Literary History: 391
New Mexico Historical Review: 1171
New Orleans Review: 102
The New Outlook for the Blind: 1522
The New Physician: 2446
The New Renaissance: 103
The New Scholar: 713
The New Scholasticism: 454
New Statesman: 40
New World Review: 655
New Writers: 504
New York Entomological Society. Journal: 2015
The New York Historical Society Quarterly: 1172
New York History: 1173
New York Law Forum: 1265
New York Public Library. Bulletin: 297
New York State Bar Journal: 1266
New York State Journal of Medicine: 2447
New York State Nurses Association. Journal: 2527
New York State School Boards Association. Journal: 1041
New York University Law Review: 1267
The Newberry Library Bulletin: 104
The Newsboy: 392
Newsletter on Intellectual Freedom: 298; 857
Nineteenth-Century Fiction: 393
Nineteenth-Century French Studies: 394
NJEA Review: 1042
Noûs: 455
Nolpe School Law Journal: 1268
The North American Review: 505

The North Carolina Historical Review: 1174
North Carolina Law Review: 1269
North Carolina Medical Journal: 2448
North Carolina Review of Business and Economics: 793
The North Country Librarian: 299
North Dakota Law Review: 1270
North-Nord: 619
The Northern Engineer: 1780
Northern Light: 506
Northwest Anthropological Research Notes: 1555
Northwest Passage: 41
Northwest Review: 507
Northwest Science: 1614
Northwestern University Law Review: 1271
Not Man Apart: 1847
Notes: 301
Notes on Mississippi Writers: 395
Notre Dame Journal of Formal Logic: 2215
Nottingham French Studies: 396
Nottingham Mediaeval Studies: 105
Novel: A Forum on Fiction: 397
NSPI Newsletter: 1043
Nuclear Fusion: 2180
Nuclear Materials Management: 2181
Nuclear Science and Engineering Journal: 2182
Nuclear Technology: 2183
Nursing '75: 2530
Nursing Care: 2528
Nursing Outlook: 2529
Nusa: 236
Nutrition and Metabolism: 2449
Nutrition Today: 2450
N.Y.S. Journal of H.Y.P.E.R. 1044

O
The Observatory: 2062
Occasional Papers: 302
The Occasional Review: 42
Oceania: 1556
Oceanic Linguistics: 237
Oecologia: 1872
Of Sea and Shore: 2016
Offshore: 1660
Ohio History: 1175
Ohio Journal of Religious Studies: 585
The Ohio Journal of Science: 1615
Ohio Library Association Bulletin: 303
The Ohio State Medical Journal: 2451
Oklahoma Geological Survey Bulletin: 1675
Oklahoma Geology Notes: 1676
Oklahoma Law Review: 1272
Oklahoma State Medical Association Journal: 2452
Old English Newsletter: 238
Omega: 837
Omega-The Journal of Death and Dying: 1454
Omega: 837
Oncology: 2453
Ontario Mathematics Gazette: 2216
The Ontario Psychologist: 1455
The Opera Journal: 180
Operational Research Quarterly: 838
Operations Research: 2217
Ophthalmic Research: 2454
Ophthalmologica: 2455
Opinion: 106
Optical Engineering: 1781
Optical Society of America. Journal*: 2038
Optical Spectra: 2039
Oral Surgery, Oral Medicine and Oral Pathology*: 2516
Orbis: 620
Oregon ASCD Curriculum Bulletin: 1045

References in Index refer to entry numbers

Periodical title index

Oregon Dental Association. Journal: 2517
Oregon Historical Quarterly: 1176
Oriental Art: 181
ORL: 2456
Ottawa Law Review: 1273
Otto Rank Association Journal: 1456
Outposts: 508
Oxidation of Metals: 2040

P

Pacific Discovery: 1616
The Pacific Historian: 1177
Pacific Historical Review: 1178
Pacific Science: 1617
Package Printing and Diecutting: 2601
Paediatrician: 2457
Paleobios: 1661
Palimpsest: 1179
The Pan-Pacific Entomologist: 2017
Paperboard Packaging: 2602
Papers on Language and Literature: 398
Parameters: 1328
Parapsychology Review: 1457
Parks and Recreation Magazine: 1848
Particulate Matter: 1782
Pastoral Counseling: 586
Pastoral Life Magazine: 587
Pathologia et Microbiologia: 1938
Pattern Recognition: 2243
Paunch: 399
Peabody Journal of Education: 1046
Pediatric Radiology: 2458
Pediatric Research: 2459
Pediatrics*: 2460
Penmen's Newsletter: 1047
People's World: 43
Perception: 621
Perception & Psychophysics: 1458
Percussionist: 182
Percussive Notes: 1048
Performing Arts in Canada Magazine: 183
Perkins Journal: 588
The Personalist: 456
Personnel: 839
The Personnel and Guidance Journal: 1049
The Personnel Administrator: 840
Personnel Journal: 841
Personnel News for School Systems: 1050
Personnel Psychology: 1459
Perspective: 509
Perspectives in Biology and Medicine: 2461
Perspectives of New Music: 184
Pesticide Science: 2041
Petroleum Engineer International: 1662
Pharmacological Reviews: 2462
Pharmacology: 2463
Phi Sigma Iota Newsletter: 239
Philological Quarterly: 240
Philosophia: 457
The Philosophical Quarterly: 458
The Philosophical Review: 459
Philosophy and Rhetoric: 464
Philosophy East and West: 461
Philosophy in Context: 462
Philosophy & Public Affairs: 460
Philosophy of Science: 463
Philosophy Today: 465
Phonetica: 241
Photochemistry and Photobiology: 1939
Photogrammetric Engineering & Remote Sensing: 2042
Photomethods: 2603

Physica Scripta: 2163
Physical Review Letters: 2164
Physical Society of Japan Journal: 2165
Physical Therapy*: 2464
Physics Bulletin: 2166
Physics Education: 1051
The Physics Teacher: 1052
Physics in Canada/la Physique au Canada: 2167
Physics in Medicine and Biology: 2168
Physics of Condensed Matter: 2169
Physiological Chemistry and Physics: 1940
The Physiologist: 2465
Physiology and Behavior: 1873
Phytochemistry: 1965
Phytologia: 1966
The Piano Quarterly: 185
Pipeline & Gas Journal: 2604
Pittsburgh Business Review: 794
PLA Bulletin: 304
The Planetarian: 2063
Planning: 1274
Planning for Higher Education: 1053
Planning Review: 795
Plant and Soil: 1970
Plant Physiology: 1967
Plant Science Bulletin: 1968
Plant Science Letters: 1969
Planta: 1971
Plasma Physics: 2170
Plastic and Reconstructive Surgery: 2539
Plastics Design & Processing: 2605
Plastics Engineering: 1783, 2606
Plastics in Building Construction: 2607
Plateau: 696
Plating: 2608
PMLA: 400
Pneumonology: 2466
PNLA Quarterly: 305
Poe Studies: 401
Poet and Critic: 510
Poetry Venture: 511
The Police Chief: 1275
Policy Studies Journal: 1346
The Political Quarterly: 1347
Political Science Quarterly: 1348
Pollution Equipment News: 1849
Polymer Age: 2609
Population Studies: 714
Postgraduate Medicine: 2467
The Potomac Review: 715
Poultry Science: 2549
Powder Technology: 1618
Power: 1784
Power Transmission Design: 2610
The Practical Lawyer: 1276
Practical Papers for the Bible Translator: 589
Preparative Biochemistry: 1941
Present Tense: 44
Press Woman: 1579
The Priest: 590
Principes: 1972
Printing Impressions: 2611
Prism International: 512
The Private Library: 306
Process Studies: 466
Production Engineer: 1785
The Professional Geographer: 1109
The Professional Photographer: 2612
Professional Psychology*: 1460
Professional Sanitation Management: 1850
Progress in Organic Coatings: 2043

References in Index refer to entry numbers

Progressive Architecture: 1642
Progressive World: 107
Prologue: The Journal of the National Archives: 1180
Proof: 307
Prose: 1580
PS 1349
PSBA Bulletin: 1054
Psychiatria Clinica: 1461
The Psychiatric Forum: 1462
Psychiatric Quarterly: 1463
Psychiatry: 1464
Psychic: 1465
The Psychoanalytic Quarterly: 1466
The Psychoanalytic Review: 1467
Psychoenergetic Systems: 1468
Psychological Bulletin*: 1469
Psychological Issues: 1470
Psychological Medicine: 1471
The Psychological Record: 1472
Psychological Reports: 1473
Psychological Research: 1474
Psychological Review: 1475
Psychology: 1476
Psychology in the Schools: 1477
Psychology Today: 1478
Psychopharmacologia: 1479
Psychopharmacology Bulletin: 2468
Psychosomatics: 1480
Psychotherapy and Psychosomatics: 1481
Psychotherapy and Social Science Review: 1482
Psychotherapy: Theory, Research and Practice*: 1483
Public Administration Review: 1277
Public Finance Quarterly*: 819
Public Health Reports: 2469
The Public Interest: 716
Public Management: 1278
Public Policy: 1350
Public Power: 1279
Public Relations Journal: 848
Public Welfare: 1523
Public Works: 1786
Publishers Weekly: 858
Pulse: 2613
Purdue Engineer Magazine: 1787

Q

Quality Assurance News: 1788
Quality Progress: 1789
Quarterly Journal of Economics: 796
Quarterly Journal of Speech: 898
The Quarterly Review of Biology: 1942
Quarterly Review of Economics and Business: 797
Quarterly Review of Literature: 402
Quarterly Reviews of Biophysics: 1943
Quaternary Research: 1663
Queen's Quarterly: 45
Quest: 1055
Quill & Quire: 859

R

Race Today: 46
Radiation Data and Reports: 2184
Radiation Research: 2185
The Radio and Electronic Engineer: 1790
Radio-Electronics: 1791
Radiologia Clinica: 2470
Radiologic Technology: 2471
Radiology: 2472
Rail International: 2614
The Rangefinder: 2615
RCDA: Religion in Communist Dominated Areas: 591

Reading Horizons: 1056
Reading Improvement: 1057
Reading Research Quarterly: 1058
The Reading Teacher: 1059
Real Estate Review: 820
Re: Artes Liberales: 47
Reclamation Era: 1851
Reformed Review: 592
The Refractories Journal: 2616
Regional Studies: 1852
The Rehabilitation Teacher: 1524
Relations Industrielles: 828
Religion and Society: 593
Religious Education: 1060
Religious Humanism: 594
Renaissance Quarterly: 108
Renaissance Review: 48
Rendezvous: 49
Report and Historical Collections: 1181
Representative Research in Social Psychology: 1484
Reproductions Review & Methods: 2617
Research Communications in Chemical Pathology and Pharmacology: 1874
Research/Development: 1620
Research in African Literatures: 403
Research in Phenomenology: 467
Research in the Teaching of English: 1061
Research Management: 1619
Research Quarterly*: 1062
Research Studies: 109
Researches in Population Ecology: 1557
Respiration: 2473
Respiratory Therapy: 2474
Restoration and Eighteenth Century Theatre Research: 186
The Review of Black Political Economy: 798
The Review of Books and Religion: 595
The Review of Economic Studies: 799
The Review of Economics and Statistics: 800
Review of Educational Research: 1063
The Review of English Studies: 404
Review of Metaphysics: 468
Review of Paleobotany and Palynology: 1973
The Review of Politics: 1351
Review of Religious Research: 596
Review of Social Economy: 801
The Review of Socialist Law: 1280
Reviews of Modern Physics*: 2171
Revista de Estudios Hispánicos: 405
Revista Iberoamericana: 406
Revue de Geographie de Montreal: 1110
Rhode Island Medical Journal: 2476
Rising Up Angry: 1352
RN-The National Magazine for Nurses: 2531
Rock Products: 2618
Rocky Mountain Journal of Mathematics: 2218
Rocky Mountain Review of Language and Literature: 407
Rollsign: 2619
Romance Notes: 242
Romance Philology: 243
Romanic Review: 408
Royal Astronomical Society of Canada Journal: 2064
Royal United Services Institute for Defence Studies Journal: 1329
RQ: 308
Rubber Age: 2620
Rubber Chemistry and Technology: 2123
Rundschau: 656
Rural Sociology: 1558
Russell: The Journal of the Bertrand Russell Archives: 469
Russian Literature Triquarterly: 409
The Russian Review: 657
Rutgers Journal of Computers and the Law: 1281

References in Index refer to entry numbers

Periodical title index

Rutgers Law Review: 1282
Rutgers-Camden Law Journal: 1283

S

Sacred Music: 187
Sage Professional Papers in Administrative and Policy Studies*: 1284
Sage Professional Papers in American Politics: 1353
Sage Professional Papers in Comparative Politics*: 1354
Sage Professional Papers in International Studies: 1355
Saint Louis University Law Journal: 1285
Salary and Merit: 1064
Sales Management: 842
Salmagundi: 50
Salt Lick: 513
SAMPE Journal: 1792
SAMPE Quarterly: 1793
San Francisco Business Magazine: 802
San José Studies: 51
Saturday Review: 110
Scandinavian Journal of Haematology: 2477
Scandinavian Journal of Infectious Diseases: 2478
Scandinavian Journal of Plastic and Reconstructive Surgery: 2540
Scandinavian Journal of Psychology: 1485
Scandinavian Journal of Rehabilitation Medicine: 2479
Scandinavian Journal of Rheumatology: 2480
Scandinavian Journal of Social Medicine: 2481
Scandinavian Journal of Thoracic and Cardiovascular Surgery: 2541
Scandinavian Journal of Urology and Nephrology: 2482
Scandinavian Review: 658
Scholarly Publishing: 860
Scholastic Editor-Graphics/Communications: 884
School and Community: 1066
School Business Affairs: 1065
The School Counselor: 1067
The School Guidance Worker: 1068
The School Librarian: 309
School Library Journal: 310
School Media Quarterly*: 311
School Science and Mathematics: 1069
School Shop: 1070
The School Trustee: 1071
Science: 1621
Science and Children: 1072
Science and Society: 52
Science Education: 1073
Science for the People: 1622
Science Forum: 1623
The Science Teacher: 1074
Science of the Total Environment: 1853
Scientia Horticulturae: 1974
Scottish Journal of Political Economy: 803
The Scriblerian and the Kit-Cats: 410
Scripta Metallurgica: 1794
Sea Frontiers: 1700
Second City Political and Literary Review: 53
Securities Regulation Law Journal: 1286
Seismological Society of America Bulletin: 1664
Seminar: 244
Sephardic Scholar: 597
Seventeenth-Century News: 111
The Sewanee Review: 411
The Shakespeare Newsletter: 412
Shakespeare Quarterly: 413
The Shavian: 414
The Shaw Review: 415
SIAM Journal on Applied Mathematics: 2219
SIAM Journal on Computing: 2244
SIAM Journal on Control: 2220
SIAM Journal on Mathematical Analysis: 2221

SIAM Journal on Numerical Analysis: 2222
SIAM News: 2223
SIAM Review: 2224
SIDA: 1975
The Sight-Saving Review: 2483
Simulation: 2245
Simulation and Games*: 1559
Simulation Councils Proceedings: 2246
Sipapu: 861
Sisters Today: 598
The Sixteenth Century Journal: 112, 1182
Slavic and East European Journal: 245
Slavic Review: 659
Sloan Management Review: 843
Slow Learner Workshop: 1075
The Slow Learning Child: 1076
The Small Pond Magazine of Literature: 514
Small Press Review: 862
Smith College Studies in Social Work: 1525
Snowy Egret: 54
Social and Economic Studies: 670
The Social and Rehabilitation Record: 1526
Social Behavior and Personality: 1486
Social Biology: 717
Social Change: Ideas and Applications: 718
Social Forces: 1560
Social Psychiatry: 1487
Social Science: 719
Social Science and Medicine: 720
Social Science Quarterly: 721
Social Service Review: 1527
The Social Studies: 1077
Social Theory and Practice: 722
Socialist Revolution: 1356
Society: 723
Society for Research in Child Development. Monographs: 724
Society of Architectural Historians. Journal: 1643
Society of Motion Picture and Television Engineers Journal: 895
Society of Professional Investigators. Bulletin: 1287
Sociological Analysis: 599
Sociological Inquiry: 1561
Sociological Methods and Research: 1562
The Sociological Quarterly: 1563
The Sociological Review: 1564
Sociological Symposium: 1565
Sociology: 1566
Sociology and Social Research: 1568
Sociology of Education: 1567
Sociometry: 1569
Software, Practice and Experience: 2247
Soil Science: 1886
Solar Energy: 2044
Solid State Technology: 1795
Sound and Vibration: 1796
Soundings: 113
Source: Music of the Avant Garde: 188
South African Institute of Mining and Metallurgy Journal: 1689
South African Journal of Medical Sciences: 2484
South Asian Studies: 645
The South Atlantic Quarterly: 55
South Carolina Librarian: 312
The South Carolina Review: 416
South Dakota History: 1183
South Dakota Journal of Medicine: 2485
South Dakota Law Review: 1288
South Dakota Review: 515
The South Magazine: 804
Southeastern Geographer: 1111
Southeastern Geology: 1677
The Southeastern Librarian: 313
Southern Association of Colleges and Schools. Proceedings: 1078

References in Index refer to entry numbers

Southern California Law Review: 1289
Southern Economic Journal: 805
Southern Humanities Review: 56
Southern Literary Journal: 516
Southern Poetry Review: 517
The Southern Review: 518
Southern Speech Communication Journal: 899
Southwest Review: 57
Southwestern American Literature: 417
Southwestern Lore: 1639
Southwestern Musician and Texas Music Educator: 189
Soviet Studies: 660
Spaceflight: 2055
The Sparrow Magazine: 519
Special Education: Forward Trends: 1079
Special Libraries: 314
Specialia: 58
Spectrochimica Acta, Part A: 2045
Spectrochimica Acta, Part B: 2045-1
Spectroscopia Molecular: 2172
Spectroscopy Letters: 2173
Speech Monographs: 900
Spelling Progress Bulletin: 1080
Spiritual Life: 600
Spring Rain: 520
The Springfielder: 601
St. Louis Journalism Review: 885
Stain Technology: 2124
Star West of America: 521
State Government: 1290
Staten Island Institute of Arts & Sciences. Proceedings: 1624
Steinbeck Quarterly: 418
Steroids: 2125
Steward Anthropological Society. Journal: 1570
Strain: 1797
Student Lawyer: 1291
Student Personnel Association for Teacher Education. Journal: 1081
Studies in African Linguistics: 246
Studies in Art Education: 1082
Studies in Black Literature: 419
Studies in Browning and His Circle: 420
Studies in Burke and His Time: 1357
Studies in Comparative Communism: 1358
Studies in Comparative International Development: 725
Studies in English Literature 1500-1900: 421
Studies in Linguistics: 247
Studies in Philology*: 423
Studies in Philosophy and Education: 1083
Studies in Romanticism: 115
Studies in Scottish Literature: 424
Studies in Short Fiction: 425
Studies in the Humanities: 114
Studies in the Novel: 422
Studies in the Twentieth Century: 116
Studio International: 190
Style: 426
Suicide: 1488
Sulphur Institute Journal: 2126
Surgical Business: 2621
Survey: 661
Survive: 59
Symposium: 427
Synthesis: 1625
Synthetic Communications: 2127

T
Tactics: 1359
Talanta: 2128
Tall Windows: 60
TAPPI: 2622

The Tax Adviser: 739
Taxation for Accountants: 740
Taxation for Lawyers: 1292
Teacher: 1084
The Teacher of the Deaf: 1085
The Teacher Paper: 1086
Teacher's Voice: 1087
Teaching Political Science: 1088
Technical Communication: 863
Technical Papers for the Bible Translator: 602
Technology and Culture: 1184
Technology Review: 1626
Tectonophysics: 1665
The Teilhard Review: 117
Telecommunications: 1798
Tellus: 1666
Telos: 118
The Tennessee Conservationist: 1854
Tennessee Folklore Society Bulletin: 1571
Tennessee Librarian: 315
Tennessee Public Welfare Record: 1528
Tetrahedron: 2129
Tetrahedron Letters: 2130
Texas Bar Journal: 1293
The Texas Dental Journal: 2518
The Texas Elementary Principals and Supervisors Association. Journal: 1089
Texas International Law Journal: 1294
Texas Journal of Science: 1627
Texas Library Journal: 316
The Texas Quarterly: 119
Texas Studies in Literature and Language: 428
Theatre Crafts: 191
Theatre Design and Technology: 192
Theatre Notebook: 193
Theatre Quarterly: 194
Theological Education: 1090
Theological Studies: 603
Theoretica Chimica Acta: 2131
Theoretical and Applied Genetics: 1944
Thin Solid Films: 1628
The Third World Review: 622
Thorax: 2486
Thoreau Journal: 429
The Thoreau Society Bulletin: 430
Thought: 61
Thrombosis Research: 2487
Tic: 2519
Today in France: 662
Today's Catholic Teacher: 1091
Today's Education: 1092
Today's Speech: 864
Top of the News: 317
Topology: 2225
Toxicology and Applied Pharmacology: 2488
Toxicomanies: 1529
The Tracker: 195
Traditio: 120
Traffic Engineering & Control: 1799
Traffic Quarterly: 1295
Training: 844
Training and Development Journal: 845
The Training School Bulletin: 1489
Transactional Analysis Journal: 1490
Transcultural Psychiatric Research Review: 1491
Transmission and Distribution: 1800
Transplantation: 2489
Transportation Journal: 1296
Transportation Research: 1855
Transportation USA: 2623
Trial Magazine: 1297

References in Index refer to entry numbers

Periodical title index

TriQuarterly: 43[1]
Trivium: 121
Tropical Animal Health and Production: 2550
Tulsa: 62
Twentieth Century Literature: 432

U

The Ukrainian Historian: 663
Ultrasound in Medicine and Biology: 2490
Unauthorized Practice News: 1298
Understanding: 63
Uniform Commercial Code Law Journal: 1299
Union Seminary Quarterly Review: 604
United States Track and Field Quarterly Review: 1093
University of Chicago Law Review: 1300
University of Chicago School Review*: 1094
University of Cincinnati Law Review: 1301
University of Colorado Law Review: 1302
University of Illinois Law Forum: 1303
University of Michigan Business Review: 806
University of Michigan Journal of Law Reform: 1304
University of Pennsylvania Law Review: 1305
University of Portland Review: 64
University of San Francisco Law Review: 1306
University of Toronto Law Journal: 1307
University of Toronto Quarterly: 122
University of Windsor Review: 65
Urban and Social Change Review: 1573
Urban Affairs Quarterly*: 1308
Urban Education: 1095
Urban Land: 1856
Urban Life: 1572
Urban Studies: 726
Urologia Internationalis: 2491
Utah Law Review: 1309
Utah Libraries: 318

V

Vacuum: 2046
The Veliger: 2018
Vergilius: 433
Vermont History: 1185
Vermont Libraries: 319
Veterinary Medicine/Small Animal Clinician: 2551
Veterinary Parasitology: 2552
Veterinary Pathology: 2553
Victorian Periodicals Newsletter: 123
Victorian Poetry: 434
Victorian Studies: 124
Virchows Archiv-A: 2492
Virchows Archiv-B: 1945
The Virginia Accountant: 741
Virginia Cavalcade: 1186
The Virginia Magazine of History and Biography: 1187
Virginia Municipal Review: 1310
The Virginia Quarterly Review: 66
Virology: 1946
Visible Language: 248
Vision Research: 2493
The Vocational Guidance Quarterly: 1096
Voices International: 522
The Volta Review: 1097
Vortice: 435
Vox Sanguinis: 2494

W

Wake Forest Law Review: 1311
Walt Whitman Review: 436
War/Peace Report: 623
Wascana Review: 664
Washington and Lee Law Review: 1313

Washington Academy of Sciences. Journal: 1629
Washington Law Review: 1312
Waste Age: 1857
Water & Sewage Works: 1858
Water Pollution Control Federation Journal: 1859
Water Research: 1860
Water Resources Research: 1861
Water Services: 2624
Wear: 1801
Webster Review: 523
Weid: 524
The Welding Distributor: 2625
The Welding Engineer: 2626
Wellsiana: 437
West Virginia University Philological Papers: 249
Western American Literature: 438
Western Birds: 2019
Western Folklore: 1574
The Western Historical Quarterly: 1188
Western Humanities Review: 125
Western Political Quarterly: 1360
Western States Jewish Historical Quarterly: 1189
The Wharton Quarterly: 807
Wildlife Disease: 2554
The William and Mary Quarterly: 1190
Wilson Library Bulletin: 320
Wire: 2627
Wire Journal: 2628
Wisconsin Law Review: 1314
Wisconsin Library Bulletin: 321
Women: 1581
Women in Business: 1582
Women Studies Abstracts: 1583
Women's Studies: 1584
Wood and Fiber: 2629
Wood Science and Technology: 1976
The Wordsworth Circle: 439
Working Papers for A New Society: 727
World Affairs Report: 624
World Fishing: 2630
World Politics: 625
The World Today: 626
The Writer: 865
Writer's Digest: 886

Y

Yale French Studies: 440
Yale Journal of Biology and Medicine: 2495
Yale Law Journal: 1315
Yale Lit: 525
The Yale Review: 126
Young Children: 1098
Youth and Society*: 728

Z

Zeitschrift für Deutschamerikanische Literatur: 441
Zygon: 605

References in Index refer to entry numbers

A

Abnormal Psychology. See Psychology, Pathological.

Accounting: 729, 730, 731, 732, 734, 735, 736, 738, 739, 740, 741, 815 (See Also: Auditing; Taxation)

Acoustics. See Hearing; Sound.

Acquisitions (Libraries): 306

Adhesives: 2556

Administration. See Management.

Adolescence: 697, 728, 1361, 1383, 1384 (See Also: Youth–Culture and Development)

Adult Education. See Education, Adult.

Advertising: 810, 846, 847 (See Also: Marketing; Packaging; Public Relations; Salesmen and Salesmanship)

Aeronautics and Space Flight: 1113, 1115, 1321, 1589, 2047, 2048, 2049, 2050, 2051, 2052, 2053, 2054, 2055

Aerosols: 2031

Aesthetics: 73, 76, 163, 491, 987 (See Also: Art; Art Criticism; Criticism; Poetry)

African Studies: 84, 127, 128, 246, 403, 419, 627, 628, 629, 630, 631, 632, 633, 634, 635, 640, 1148

Afro-American Studies. See Black Studies.

Aged and Aging: 610, 617; 1400; 1428, 1508, 1870, 2258, 2344; 2349, 2350; 2498

Agricultural Chemicals See soil science.

Agriculture: 1802, 1875, 1876, 1877, 1879, 1880, 1883, 1884, 1885, 1974, 2021

Agriculture–Study and Teaching: 907, 1035, 1875

Air Pollution: 1816, 1835, 1836, 1849

Air Purification: 2566

Alabama: 744

Alcoholism: 1493, 1496, 1507, 1517, 1519, 1529 (See Also: Drugs and Drug Abuse)

Alger, Horatio–Life and Works: 392

Allergy: 2367 (See Also: Immunology)

Alternative Life Styles: 2, 20, 41, 727, 861

Amateur Radio: 892

American Civilization: 690

American History. See U.S.–History.

American Indian Studies: 216, 679, 680, 681, 688, 689, 693, 988, 1632

American Literature: 57, 98, 218, 297, 322, 323, 335, 347, 348, 350, 354, 371, 382, 388, 390, 417, 419, 428, 431, 441, 515, 516, 1547 (See Also: English Language and Literature; also names of individual authors)

Analytical Chemistry. See Chemistry, Analytic.

Anatomy: 1921, 2249, 2377, 2378, 2426, 2492 (See Also: Nervous System; Physiology; also names of organs and regions of the body)

Anesthesiology: 2307

Animals: 35, 1609, 1878, 1879, 1885, 2543, 2548, 2551, 2554, 2563 (See Also: Domestic Animals; Natural History; Zoology; also names of classes of the animal kingdom)

Animals–Laboratory Use. See Laboratory Animals.

Anthropology: 197, 698, 702, 717, 1491, 1530, 1532, 1535, 1536, 1537, 1538, 1540, 1548, 1551, 1553, 1555, 1556, 1566, 1570, 1612, 1633, 1636, 1663 (See Also: American Indian Studies; Archaeology; Ethnology; Language and Languages; Sociology)

Anticorrosive Paint. See Corrosion and Anticorrosives; Paint.

Applied Psychology. See Psychology, Applied.

Archaeology: 88, 93, 133, 433, 538, 1108, 1535, 1548, 1553, 1555, 1630, 1631, 1632, 1633, 1634, 1635, 1636, 1637, 1638, 1639, 1663 (See Also: Biblical Studies; Ethnology)

Architecture: 129, 1640, 1641, 1642, 1643, 1714, 1824 (See Also: Building and Construction; Building Materials; Material–Testing)

Archives: 97, 250, 253, 306

Arctic: 607, 619, 1537, 1780

Arizona: 324, 696, 1638

Arkansas: 254, 1123

Art: 86, 131, 133, 135, 150, 153, 168, 179, 181, 190, 1082, 1576 (See Also: Aesthetics; Archaeology; Architecture; Bookplates; Graphic Arts)

Art–Galleries and Museums: 141, 151

Art–History: 115, 131, 135, 169, 1633

Art–Study and Teaching: 73, 135, 150, 918, 1082

Art Criticism: 76, 135, 525

Arts: 10, 65, 103, 134

Art Therapy. See Expressive Therapy.

Arthritis and Rheumatism: 2287

Asian Studies: 133, 237, 372, 461, 636, 637, 638, 639, 640, 641, 643, 644, 645, 699, 1150, 1556, 1635 (See Also: Communist Countries; India; Middle Eastern Studies; Pacific Islands; Russian Studies)

Astronomy: 2027, 2057, 2058, 2059, 2060, 2061, 2062, 2063, 2064, 2135 (See Also: Aeronautics and Space Flight; Spectrum)

Astrophysics: 2058, 2059, 2060, 2135

Athletics: 921, 1018, 1038, 1093 (See Also: Physical Education)

Atmospheric Sciences: 1655, 1808, 2032, 2046, 2151 (See Also: Air Pollution; Meteorology)

Atomic Energy: 1759, 2139, 2174, 2178, 2182, 2183 (See Also: Nuclear Physics)

Audiology: 200

Audio-Visual Education: 235, 270, 866, 867, 868, 888, 889, 891, 959, 960, 976, 1020 (See Also: Computers in Education)

Auditing: 732, 733, 735, 736, 738, 741 (See Also: Accounting)

Australia: 2568

Austria: 646

Automation: 1711, 1746, 1754, 2567, 2569 (See Also: Systems Engineering)

Aviation: 1241

B

Bacteriology: 1894, 1925, 1926, 1927, 1935, 1938, 2393 (See Also: Immunology; Virology)

Balkan Studies: 654 (See Also: Eastern Europe)

Baltic Studies: 652

Bands (Music): 159, 164

Banks and Banking: 808, 809, 810, 815, 817, 818, 1200 (See Also: Credit; Investments)

Baptists and Baptist Church: 560

Baudelaire–Life and Works: 329

Behavior: 220, 718, 743, 992, 1375, 1393, 1411, 1413, 1420, 1422, 1434, 1445, 1446, 1464, 1467, 1476, 1486, 1551, 1559, 1822, 1895, 2294 (See Also: Character; Ethics; Family; Human Relations)

Behavioral Sciences–Study and Teaching (See Also: Psychology)

Biblical Studies: 535, 538, 552, 553, 555, 557, 559, 561, 562, 565, 571, 577, 589, 602, 1637 (See Also: Theology)

Bibliography: 238, 258, 262, 269, 285, 294, 307, 322, 325, 849 (See Also: Archives; Information Storage and Retrieval; Library Science and Library Services; Printing)

Biochemistry: 1697, 1866, 1869, 1870, 1891, 1896, 1897, 1898, 1901, 1921, 1926, 1929, 1935, 1940, 1941, 1965, 2071, 2072, 2073, 2074, 2076, 2082, 2085, 2087, 2092, 2101, 2102, 2113, 2120

Biology: 1107, 1422, 1591, 1592, 1809, 1813, 1862, 1867, 1869, 1872, 1874, 1888, 1893, 1901, 1902, 1904, 1909, 1910, 1916, 1919, 1922, 1929, 1932, 1933, 1934, 1942, 1971, 1993, 1997, 2195, 2340, 2380, 2382, 2393, 2461, 2490, 2495 (See Also: Anatomy; Botany; Cells; Ecology; Evolution; Genetics; Marine Biology; Microbioloby; Natural History; Parasitology; Physiology; Reproduction; Sex; Zoology)

Biology–Study and Teaching: 908, 989

Biophysics: 1863, 1891, 1896, 1900, 1914, 1940, 1943, 2131, 2168 (See Also: Cells)

Birds: 1820, 2019

Black Studies: 7, 37, 228, 388, 419, 609, 615, 678, 692, 798, 1007, 1039 (See Also: Minorities–Education; Race Relations)

Blake, William–Life and Works: 326, 327

Blind and Blindness: 1492, 1522, 1524, 2483 (See Also: Eye; Handicapped–Education and Rehabilitation; Ophthalmology)

Blood and Circulation: 2251, 2352, 2477, 2494 (See Also: Cardiovascular Research; Heart)

Book Reviews: 8, 34, 45, 56, 67, 122, 328, 365, 425, 472, 482, 498, 524, 548, 592, 595, 634, 713, 849, 957 (See Also: Acquisitions–Libraries; Criticism)

Bookplates: 306

References in Index refer to entry numbers

Subject index

Botany: 1947, 1949, 1950, 1951, 1952, 1954, 1955, 1957, 1958, 1959, 1960, 1961, 1962, 1963, 1966, 1968, 1969, 1970, 1971, 1973, 1974 (See Also: Bryology; Ecology; Gardening; Plants)

Botany–Classification: 1951, 1964, 1975

Brain Research: 2295

British Columbia: 261

British Law. See Law–Great Britian.

Broadcasting. See Radio and Television Broadcasting.

Browning, Robert–Life and Works: 420

Bryology: 1953

Building and Construction: 1642, 1714, 1718, 1780, 2562, 2564, 2578, 2607 (See Also: Architecture; Engineering)

Building Materials: 1586, 1642, 1772, 2584, 2607, 2618 (See Also: Ceramics–Industrial; Glass; Materials–Testing; Metals and Metallurgy; Steel Industry and Trade; Wood)

Building Services: 1705, 2566, 2571, 2586

Burke, Edmund–Life and Works: 1357

Burr, Aaron–Life: 1131

Burroughs, Edgar Rice–Life and Works: 331

Business: 743, 744, 748, 749, 750, 751, 754, 755, 756, 757, 760, 767, 770, 776, 786, 788, 790, 791, 792, 793, 794, 795, 797, 802, 806, 807, 829, 833, 850, 924, 1578 (See Also: Advertising; Banks and Banking; Commercial Law; Credit; Economic Conditions; Industrial Management; Marketing; Real Estate; Salesmen and Salemanship)

Business Education: 850, 990

Business History: 753

Business Law. See Commercial La.

Buying. See Purchasing

Byron, Lord–Life and Works: 332

C

Cabell, James Branch–Life and Works: 374

California: 12, 263, 757, 802, 1125, 1206, 1207, 1289, 1335, 1591, 1592, 1616, 1669, 1715

Canada: 202, 264, 283, 333, 478, 685, 687, 691, 695, 730, 758, 859, 904, 905, 927, 949, 1022, 1026, 1112, 1114, 1126, 1127, 1128, 1162, 1209, 1258, 1379, 1380, 1455, 1498, 1623, 1645, 1646, 1679, 1716, 1734, 1864, 1955, 2051, 2136, 2167, 2307, 2308, 2309, 2312, 2314, 2418, 2502

Cancer Research: 1914, 1935, 2305, 2315, 2339, 2453 (See Also: Research)

Cardiovascular Research: 2259, 2293, 2316, 2321, 2329, 2376, 2386, 2541 (See Also: Blood and Circulation; Heart; Research)

Catholicism: 539, 551, 576, 583, 590, 928, 1091 (See Also: Church and State; Monasticism and Religious Orders)

Caves and Speleology: 1114

Cells: 1743, 1907, 1908, 1913, 1914, 1915, 1928, 1945, 2076, 2111, 2124, 2154, 2250

Censorship and Freedom of Information: 298, 857

Ceramics (Industrial): 1585, 1704, 2558 (See Also: Glass)

Character: 1381, 1486 (See Also: Behavior)

Chemical Engineering: 1687, 1703, 1719, 1720, 1721, 1722 (See Also: Chemistry, Technical; Metals and Metallurgy)

Chemical Geology. See Geochemistry.

Chemistry: 1771, 1897, 2020, 2045, 2065, 2066, 2069, 2075, 2077, 2078, 2079, 2080, 2083, 2084, 2088, 2094, 2099, 2100, 2103, 2105, 2106, 2110, 2113, 2118, 2119, 2122, 2131 (See Also: Agricultural Chemicals; Biochemistry; Geochemistry; Pharmacy and Pharmacology; Photochemistry; Spectrum)

Chemistry, Analytic: 1628, 2067, 2068, 2070, 2089, 2128

Chemistry, Biological. See Biochemistry.

Chemistry, Inorganic: 1600, 2028, 2096, 2097, 2109, 2112, 2142, 2149 (See Also: Metals and Metallurgy)

Chemistry, Medical and Pharmaceutical: 1874, 2086, 2114, 2327 (See Also: Drugs and Drug Abuse; Pharmacy and Pharmacology; Toxicology)

Chemistry, Organic: 2043, 2074, 2076, 2090, 2098, 2111, 2115, 2116, 2125, 2127, 2129, 2130 (See Also: Plastics and Polymers)

Chemistry, Technical: 2081, 2084, 2100 (See Also: Ceramics–Industrial; Chemical Engineering; Corrosion and Anticorrosives; Electrochemistry; also names of specific industries)

Chemotherapy: 2283, 2319, 2324, 2462

Chest Diseases: 2276, 2320, 2329, 2473, 2474, 2486, 2538, 2541 (See Also: Heart)

Chicano Studies: 5, 19, 1154

Child Study: 724, 933, 1098, 1382, 1383, 1384, 1408, 1414, 1423, 1452 (See Also: Adolescence; Educational Psychology; Family; Youth–Culture and Development)

Child Welfare: 975, 1499, 1500

Children's Literature: 309, 310, 363, 365, 961

China: 2260 (See Also: People's Republic of China)

Chirpody: 2275

Choral Music: 138, 187

Christian Education: 576

Christian Ethics: 16, 48, 534, 542, 547, 553, 577, 580

Christian Unity: 556, 569, 604

Church and State: 546, 568

Church History: 539, 545, 551, 556, 557, 561, 562, 563, 577, 604 (See Also: Baptists and Baptist Church; Jews–History; Methodist Church; Monasticism and Religious Orders)

Church Music: 139, 165, 174, 176, 187 (See Also: Choral Music; Organs and Organ Music)

Circus: 191

City Government. See Municipal Government.

City Planning: 1274, 1834 (See Also: Regional Planning; Urban Development)

Civil Engineering: 1645, 1716, 1724, 1799, 2578 (See Also: Hydroelectric Power; Materials–Testing; Mechanical Engineering; Sanitation; Water Resources and Conservation)

Civil Law: 22, 1223, 1228, 1231, 1249, 1258

Civil Rights: 17, 1344

Civil War. See U.S.–History–Civil War.

Civilization, Medieval: 70, 86, 99, 105, 120, 228, 238

Classical Languages and Literature: 69, 72, 78, 79, 93, 423, 433, 435

Claudel, Paul–Life and Works: 334

Clergy: 540, 570, 576, 587, 590 (See Also: Monasticism and Religious Orders)

Clinical Psychology See Psychology, Clinical; Mental Health.

Collective Bargaining; Negotiations: 824 (See Also: Labor)

Colorado: 13, 760, 1133

Combustion Science; Flame Study: 1594

Commerce: 748, 1197, 1213, 1245 (See Also: Banks and Banking; Business; Transportation)

Commercial Law: 730, 737, 748, 825, 1196, 1200, 1203, 1281, 1286, 1292, 1294, 1299

Common Market: 1215

Communication: 200, 248, 464, 850, 851, 852, 853, 854, 855, 859, 863, 864, 883, 884, 890, 898, 899, 900, 1743, 1818 (See Also: Language and Languages; Speech; Telecommunication; Transportation; Writing)

Communist Countries: 591, 1358 (See Also: Eastern Europe; Marxism and Related Philosophies; Russian Studies)

Composers: 136, 138, 144, 184, 2565

Compressed Air. See Pneumatics.

Computers: 269, 275, 942, 1281, 2226, 2227, 2229, 2230, 2231, 2232, 2233, 2243, 2244, 2247 (See Also: Electronic Data Processing)

Computers–Legal and Social Aspects: 1216

Computers in Education: 903, 960, 2226, 2227

Conrad, Joseph–Life and Works: 338

Conservation: 35, 1807, 1809, 1815, 1820, 1830, 1832, 1842, 1844, 1847, 1851 (See Also: Forests and Forestry; Natural Resources; Water Resources and Conservation; Wildlife Conservation)

Construction. See Building and Construction.

Consumer Affairs: 15, 28, 32, 772, 811

Contemporary Literature: 9, 416, 500, 523

Control Engineering: 1710, 1732

Copyright: 879

Corrosion and Anticorrosives: 1607, 1708, 1727, 1728

Counseling: 943, 962, 970, 1030, 1067, 1068, 1096, 1379, 1390, 1397, 1419, 1504 (See Also: Educational Psychology; Social Work)

Credit: 809, 810, 811, 1200 (See Also: Banks and Banking)

Crime and Criminals: 710, 1202, 1221, 1243, 1539 (See Also: Justice, Administration of; Police Science)

Criminal Law: 1196, 1202, 1222, 1243 (See Also: Forensic Science and Forensic Medicine)

Criticism: 9, 94, 163, 307 (See Also: Art Criticism; Book Reviews; Dramatic Criticism; Literature–History and Criticism; Music–History and Criticism)

Crustacea: 1986

Cryogenics: 1729, 1912, 2152

Crystallography: 1678, 2028, 2142 (See Also: Mineralogy)

Curricula. See Education, Curricula

Cytology. See Cells.

D

Dance: 73, 147, 148, 149, 153, 154, 179, 183

Dante–Life and Works: 344

Data Processing. See Computers: Electronic Data Processing.

Deaf and Deafness: 906, 1085, 1097, 1495, 1516, 1521, 2253, 2288, 2412 (See Also: Otolaryngology; Handicapped–Education and Rehabilitation; Hearing)

Death and Dying: 1454

Delaware: 1134

Demography: 714, 1102, 1505, 1546, 1557, 1895

Dentistry–Study and Teaching: 2508

Dentists and Dentistry: 2496, 2497, 2498, 2499, 2500, 2501, 2502, 2503, 2504; 2505, 2506, 2507, 2509, 2510, 2511, 2512, 2513, 2514, 2515, 2516, 2517, 2518, 2519 (See Also: Oral Surgery)

Dermatology: 2331, 2394, 2433

Desalination; Water Technology. See Water Resources.

Design, Industrial: 1730, 1745, 1750 1758, 1769, 2159, 2576, 2589 (See Also: Systems Engineering)

Development. See Growth.

Developmental Psychology. See Psychology, Developmental.

Diabetes: 2332, 2333

Dickens, Charles–Life and Works: 345, 346

Dickenson, Emily–Life and Works: 349

Diet. See Nutrition and Diet.

Disability: 1512

Diseases: 2085, 2262, 2263, 2301, 2340, 2369, 2381, 2428, 2478, 2481 (See Also: Cancer Research; Chest Diseases; Diabetes; Immunology; Medicine–Practice; Pathology; Rheumatic Diseases; Tropics–Diseases and Hygiene)

Domestic Animals: 1914, 2125, 2544 (See Also: Poultry)

Drama–History and Criticism: 143, 155, 171, 330, 664, 898 (See Also: Film–History and Criticism)

Dramatic Criticism: 53, 152, 527

Drawing; Draughtsmanship: 169

Drugs and Drug Abuse: 1493, 1496, 1502, 1503, 1510, 1511, 1514, 1529, 2252, 2265, 2335, 2336, 2468 (See Also: Pharmacy and Parmacology; Toxicology)

E

Earth Sciences: 1647, 1649, 1665

Eastern Europe: 245, 648, 649, 654, 659, 660, 661, 663 (See Also: Baltic Studies; Communist Countries; Hungarian Studies; Russian Studies; Slavic Languages and Literature)

Ecology: 41, 1802, 1816, 1818, 1820, 1846, 1847, 1862, 1872, 1898, 1956, 1958, 1961, 1981, 1996 (See Also: Environmental Studies)

Economic Development: 613, 616, 626, 670, 705, 706, 725, 742, 765, 766, 773, 819, 1213, 1238, 1255, 1340 (See Also: Demography; Natural Resources)

Economic Policy: 30, 716, 725, 801, 817, 819, 1284, 1350

Economics: 10, 734, 742, 745, 746, 747, 749, 750, 751, 758, 759, 763, 766, 767, 775, 776, 777, 781, 786, 788, 790, 793, 796, 797, 798, 799, 800, 803, 804, 805, 806, 807, 814, 827, 1340, 1345 (See Also: Business; Commerce; Credit; Economic Policy; Finance; Labor)

Economics–History: 752, 753, 765, 774 (See Also: Marxism and Related Philosophies)

Economics—Study and Teaching: 993

Education: 904, 909, 911, 915, 918, 925, 932, 934, 940, 943, 946, 947, 948, 952, 955, 956, 957, 968, 969, 971, 978, 982, 984, 985, 986, 987, 988, 989, 990, 992, 994, 995, 998, 1007, 1013, 1014, 1017, 1022, 1024, 1026, 1031, 1036, 1041, 1043, 1046, 1054, 1071, 1077, 1082, 1083, 1087, 1092, 1094, 1095, 1110, 1381, 1396, 1567, 2411 (See Also: Audio-Visual Education; Child Study; Learning and Learning Disabilities; Minorities–Education; Physical Education; Religious Education; Teaching; also references beginning with the word School and subjects with the subdivision Study and Teaching)

Education, Adult: 944, 950, 1000

Education, Curricula: 939, 945, 1045, 1098

Education, Elementary: 137, 916, 949, 951, 961, 963, 979, 980, 1020, 1072, 1084, 1086 (See Also: Public Schools)

Education, Higher: 902, 931, 934, 936, 937, 938, 939, 944, 953, 972, 973, 977, 991, 1004, 1046, 1053, 1081, 2487

Education, History: 1142

Education, Preschool: 933, 1098

Education, Secondary: 914, 917, 949, 965, 979, 1021, 1031, 1074, 1086

Education, Theory, Aims and Objectives: 450, 923, 927, 941, 957, 958, 972

Education, Vocational: 355, 664, 777, 823, 845, 924, 946, 1027, 1070, 1096, 1526 (See Also: Handicapped–Education and Rehabilitation; also names of professions with the subdivision Study and Teaching)

Educational Exchange: 983

Educational Law and Legislation (See Also: School Administration and Organization)

Educational Psychology: 1005, 1079, 1384, 1446

Educational Research: 904, 910, 954, 955, 958, 1053, 1063

Educational Technology: 997

Educational Tests and Measurements: 910, 955, 996, 1030, 1445, 1992, 2017

Eighteenth Century: 83, 186, 368, 410

Ekistics: 702

Electrical Engineering: 1741, 1746, 1791, 1800, 2139, 2230 (See Also: Magnetism; Radio and Television Broadcasting; Solid State Physics and Technology; Telecommunications)

Electrochemistry: 2033, 2091

Electronic Components See Solid State Physics and Technology.)

Electronic Data Processing: 1040, 1054 (See Also: Computers)

Electronics: 1731, 1732, 1741, 1790

Elementary Education. See Education, Elementary.

Employment. See Labor.

Endocrinology: 2356, 2387, 2440

Engineering: 1709, 1710, 1722, 1723, 1735, 1747, 1748, 1749, 1752, 1763, 1768, 1776, 1780, 1786, 1797, 1910, 2046, 2204 (See Also: Aeronautics and Space Flight; Chemical Engineering; Civil Engineering; Electrical Engineering; Mechanical Engineering; Systems Engineering)

England–History. See Great Britain–History.

English as a Foreign Language: 205, 224

English Language and Literature: 70, 84, 124, 218, 228, 230, 238, 348, 350, 351, 352, 353, 364, 368, 369, 371, 382, 393, 404, 421, 424, 428, 434, 923, 966, 1016 (See Also: names of individual authors)

English Language and Literature—Study and Teaching: 196, 902, 917, 929, 936, 937, 966, 999, 1061

Entomology. See Insects.

Environmental Sciences: 1786, 1802, 1808, 1813, 1823, 1824, 1827, 1837, 1841, 1843, 1853, 1859, 1868

Environmental Studies: 1037, 1226, 1612, 1803, 1813, 1815, 1817, 1821, 1822, 1825, 1826, 1828, 1829, 1833, 1834, 1836, 1838, 1843, 1844, 1847, 1848, 1850, 1853 (See Also: Air Pollution; Conservation; Ecology; Forests and Forestry; Natural Resources; Sanitation; Transportation; Water Pollution; Water Resources and Conservation; Wildlife Conservation

Enzymes: 1190, 1917

Ethics: 38, 89, 557, 593 (See Also: Behavior; Character; Christian Ethics)

Ethology: 1979

Ethnology: 698, 1531, 1542, 1546, 1547, 1548, 1556, 1572, 1638, 1639, 1895 (See Also: Anthropology; Archaeology; Black Studies; Chicano Studies; Folklore; Language and Languages; Race Relations)

Ethnomusicology: 157, 166 (See Also: Folk Music; Jazz)

Subject index

Europe–History: 658, 1130, 1151 (See Also; Civilization, Medieval; Great Britain–History; Renaissance)

Evangelism: 544, 558, 559, 566, 1764

Evolution: 1918, 1932, 2002 (See Also: Biology; Genetics; Psychology, Developmental; Religion and Science)

Experimental Psychology. See Psychology, Physiological

Expressive Therapy: 1435, 1862, 2029, 2108

Eye: 1596, 2493, 2595 (See Also: Blind and Blindness; Ophthalmology)

F

Family: 903, 1244, 1545, 1549, 1725, 1754, 2226, 2228, 2234, 2236, 2239, 2240, 2241, 2245, 2246, 2372, 2431, 2483

Family. 701, 1504, 1505, 1506, 1513

Farm Animals. See Domestic Animals.

Farm Management: 1600, 1602, 1670, 1715, 1726, 1734, 1777, 1779, 1787, 1792, 1793, 2236, 2431

Farming. See Agriculture; Farm Management.

Fibrous Technology: 1756

Fiction: 9, 60, 397, 422, 471, 473, 476, 477, 480, 489, 497, 499, 500, 503, 505, 512, 523 (See Also: Folklore; Romanticism; Science Fiction; Short Stories)

Film—History and Criticism: 53, 379, 484, 870, 871, 872, 873, 874, 875, 877, 878, 2613

Film—Production and Direction: 872, 873, 874, 875, 876, 877, 2587, 2613 (See Also: Photography; Sound–Recording and Reproducing

Film Coefficients (Physics): 1628

Finance: 776, 788, 808, 809, 812, 813, 814, 816, 818, 843, 1001 (See Also: Banks and Banking; Commerce; Credit; Insurance; Investments; Taxation)

Finishes and Finishing: 1770, 2555, 2592, 2608 (See Also: Corrosion and Anticorrosives; Paint)

Fire Prevention: 1737, 1760

Fish and Fisheries: 1810, 2568, 2630

Florida: 1597, 1830

Fluid Mechanics: 1693, 1738, 1755, 1861, 2026, 2035

Fluorine: 2109

Folk Music: 157, 162 (See Also: Ethnology; Ethnomusicology)

Folklore: 57, 68, 417, 694, 1547, 1552, 1554, 1571, 1574 (See Also: Ehtnology)

Food: 1604, 1690

Food Industry: 1868, 2580, 2630 (See Also: Nutrition and Diet; Poultry; Sugar)

Food Science: 1604, 1865, 1884 (See Also: Agriculture; Economics; Nutrition and Diet)

Foot Care. See Chiropody.

Foreign Relations. See International Relations; U.S.–Foreign Relations.

Forensic Science and Forensic Medicine: 1447, 1605, 2346, 2421, 2434, 2435, 2446 (See Also: Medicine–Laws and Regulations)

Forests and Forestry: 1614, 1804, 1812, 1831, 1832, 1839, 1956 (See Also: Wood)

Fossils. See Paleontology.

Fracture (Mechanics): 1736, 1755, 2030 (See Also: Materials–Testing)

Freedom of Information. See Censorship and Freedom of Information

French History: 1137

French Language and Literature: 122, 207, 329, 334, 376, 387, 394, 396, 440

Friction: 1762, 1801, 2555 (See Also: Lubrication and Lubricants)

Future: 23

G

Gardening: 1956 (See Also: Botany; Plants)

Gas, Natural: 2557, 2583

Gastroenterology: 2264, 2334, 2347, 2348

Genealogy: 1116, 1135, 1136, 1155

Genetics: 1862, 1887, 1889, 1895, 1897, 1905, 1908, 1909, 1915, 1920, 1922, 1923, 1924, 1931, 1932, 1936, 1937, 1944, 2397 (See Also: Biology; Evolution; Psychology, Developmental; Reproduction)

Genito-urinary Organs: 2302, 2373, 2415, 2439, 2491 (See Also: Gynecology; Sex; Urology)

Geochemistry: 1659, 1667, 1677, 1678, 2093

Geography: 686, 1099, 1100, 1101, 1102, 1103, 1104, 1105, 1106, 1107, 1108, 1109, 1110, 1111, 1676, 1823 (See Also: Demography; Ethnology)

Geography–Study and Teaching: 1002, 1100

Geology: 607, 1003, 1591, 1592, 1593, 1645, 1646, 1647, 1648, 1649, 1654, 1664, 1665, 1667, 1668, 1669, 1670, 1671, 1672, 1673, 1674, 1675, 1676, 1677, 1680, 1682, 1684, 1686, 1687, 1688, 2027 (See Also: Gas, Natural; Mineralogy; Mines and Mineral Resources; Oceanography; Paleontology; Petroleum Industry and Trade; Soil Science; Wells)

Geometry: 2203

Geophysics: 1648, 1650, 1651, 1654, 1666, 1667, 1675, 1676, 1677, 2151 (See Also: Meteorology; Oceanography)

Georgia: 1138, 1230, 1598, 2425, 2506, 2522

German Language and Literature: 204, 209, 218, 227, 230, 233, 244, 360, 441

German Studies: 244, 656

Germs. See Bacteriology.

Gerontology. See Aged and Aging.

Gifted Child Education: 969

Glands, Ductless. See Endocrinology.

Glass: 2559, 2584

Government: 22, 1228

Graphic Arts: 2560, 2577, 2585, 2611, 2617 (See Also: Printing)

Great Britain–History: 364, 1152

Great Britain–Nineteenth Century: 123, 124, 345

Great Plains (North America): 687, 1169 (See Also: The West)

Greek Language and Literature. See Classical Languages and Literature.

Growth: 1382, 1391, 1396, 1870, 1916, 1921, 2459 (See Also: Psychology, Developmental)

Guidance. See Counseling.

Gynecology: 2267, 2278, 2291, 2299, 2351 (See Also: Genito-urinary Organs; Obstetrics; Reproduction; Sex)

H

Handicapped–Education and Rehabilitation: 906, 1079, 1085, 1492, 1494, 1515, 1522, 1524, 1526, 2285, 2304, 2479 (See Also: Blind and Blindness; Deaf and Deafness; Education, Vocational; Physical Therapy)

Hawaii: 1820

Health Care: 2248, 2355, 2395, 2411, 2469, 2621

Hearing: 1097, 1495, 2253, 2281, 2288, 2289, 2413 (See Also: Deaf and Deafness; Otolaryngology)

Heart: 2259, 2293, 2320, 2376, 2538 (See Also: Blood and Circulation)

Heating and Cooling. See Building Services.

Herpetology: 1982, 1985, 2001 (See Also: Reptiles; Zoology)

High School. See Education, Secondary

Higher Education. See Education, Higher.

Histology: 2492

History and Historiography: 25, 27, 80, 214, 284, 530, 646, 663, 703, 1112, 1118, 1120, 1124, 1128, 1139, 1140, 1141, 1143, 1148, 1153, 1156, 1157, 1161, 1163, 1164, 1170, 1172, 1178, 1180, 1185, 1588, 1641, 1643, 1876, 1880 (See Also: Archaeology; Church History; Ethnology; Maritime History; Military History; Political Science; also names of countries and subjects with the subdivision History)

History, Ancient: 69, 93, 96, 1634, 1637 (See Also: Archaeology; Biblical Studies; Classical Languages and Literature)

History, Medieval and Modern: 104, 686, 1151, 1153 (See Also: Civilization, Medieval; Eighteenth Century; Nineteenth Century; Renaissance; Seventeenth Century)

History–Philosophy: 92

History–Study and Teaching: 974

Home Economics: 11

Homosexuals and Homosexuality: 1430

Horticulture. See Botany; Gardening.

References in Index refer to entry numbers

Hospitals and Clinics: 836, 1739, 2357, 2358, 2359, 2360, 2511 (See Also: Nurses and Nursing)

Human Body. See Anatomy; Physiology.

Human Relations: 623, 701, 704, 718, 1343, 1405, 1551, 1568 (See Also: Behavior; Family; Personnel Management; Psychology, Applied)

Humanism: 107

Humanities: 1, 2, 3, 4, 12, 13, 14, 18, 23, 25, 26, 27, 31, 40, 42, 47, 48, 49, 50, 51, 55, 56, 60, 61, 66, 67, 72, 74, 75, 77, 80, 82, 83, 84, 86, 87, 89, 90, 95, 100, 103, 107, 108, 109, 110, 112, 113, 114, 116, 117, 119, 121, 122, 125, 126, 359, 386, 428, 451, 513, 548, 633, 1387, 2232 (See Also: subjects such as Art; Literature; Music; Philosophy, etc.)

Hungarian Studies: 648

Hydroelectric Power: 1668, 2624 (See Also: Fluid Dynamics; Water Resources and Conservation)

Hygiene: 2391

Hypnosis: 1365, 1401, 2277 (See Also: Medicine, Psychsomatic; Psychoanalysis; Psychotherapy)

I

Ichthyology: 1985 (See Also: Zoology)

Illinois: 53, 273, 540, 1106, 1144, 2361

Illumination Engineering: 1744

Immunology: 2095, 2317, 2323, 2362, 2365, 2392, 2393, 2398, 2428, 2489 (See Also: Diseases)

India: 699, 2363

Indiana: 271, 286, 1145, 2364

Indians of North America. See American Indian Studies.

Industrial Chemistry. See Chemical Engineering; Chemistry, Technical.

Indo-European Studies: 653

Indonesia: 236

Industrial Design. See Design, Industrial.

Industrial Development: 747, 2590

Industrial Engineering: 1785, 1788

Industrial Management: 1711, 1745, 1746, 1758, 1778, 1785, 2236, 2567, 2576, 2599 (See Also: Business; Industrial Relations; Marketing; Personnel Management; Purchasing)

Industrial Medicine. See Medicine, Industrial: 2368

Industrial Relations: 803, 821, 822, 823, 824, 825, 828, 839, 840, 841, 843, 915, 1199, 2581 (See Also: Labor; Personnel Management)

Information Storage and Retrieval: 252, 265, 269, 274, 275, 276, 280, 285, 314, 526, 2235, 2237 (See Also: Computers; Electronic Data Processing)

Inhalation Therapy and Technology: 2475 (See Also: Respiratory Disease and Therapy)

Inorganic Chemistry. See Chemistry, Inorganic.

Insects: 1980, 1983, 1987, 1991, 1992, 1995, 1999, 2003, 2005, 2006, 2008, 2015, 2017, 2282

Insurance: 768, 769, 778, 784, 810

International Development: 622, 705 (See Also: International Relations)

International Law: 1197, 1209, 1211, 1213, 1215, 1222, 1226, 1232, 1237, 1245, 1246, 1258, 1262, 1280, 1294 (See Also: International Relations; Military Law)

International Relations: 39, 611, 612, 613, 614, 620, 623, 624, 625, 626, 661, 662, 1197, 1238, 1329, 1339, 1340, 1341, 1343, 1355 (See Also: International Law; U. S.–Foreign Relations)

Interpersonal Relations. See Human Relations.

Invertebrates: 1929, 2006 (See Also: Insects; Mollusks; Zoology)

Investments: 814, 1286 (See Also: Banks and Banking; Stocks and Bonds)

Iowa: 1120, 1179, 2374

Irish in America: 650

Israel: 71, 457, 1958, 2375 (See Also: Jews and Judaism; Jews-History)

Italian Language and Literature: 206, 217

Italian Studies: 651

J

Japan: 2376, 2417

Jazz: 142, 161, 166

Jews and Judaism: 26, 34, 44, 71, 532, 550, 574 (See Also: Biblical Studies; Israel)

Jews–History: 530, 1189

Journalism: 862, 880, 881, 882, 883, 884, 885, 886, 1017, 1579 (See Also: Censorship and Freedom of Information; Graphic Arts; Photography; Writing)

Johnson, Samuel–Life and Works: 367, 368

Joyce, James–Life and Works

Justice, Administration of: 1198, 1208, 1219, 1221, 1250, 1251, 1539 (See Also: Crime and Criminals; Law)

K

Kansas: 1019, 2008

Kentucky: 1021, 1136, 1160, 1552

Keyboard Instruments: 158

Kidney: See Genito-urinary Organs.

Kipling, Rudyard–Life and Works: 375

L

Labor: 43, 764, 777, 821, 822, 823, 824, 826, 827, 828, 840, 915, 1146, 1352 (See Also: Industrial Relations; Marxism and Related Philosophies; Labor Laws and Legislation; Women—Employment)

Labor Laws and Legislation: 1199

Labor Relations. See Industrial Relations; Labor.

Laboratory Animals: 2009, 2543

Language and Linguistics: 101, 121, 197, 198, 199, 200, 203, 208, 210, 214, 215, 216, 217, 220, 222, 223, 224, 225, 226, 231, 232, 234, 237, 240, 241, 244, 245, 246, 247, 248, 249, 398, 400, 538, 589, 854, 1548 (See Also: Linguistics; Literature; Speech; Writing; also names of languages or groups of cognate languages)

Languages–Study and Teaching: 202, 207, 223, 228, 229, 235, 242, 244, 967, 1057 (See Also: names of languages or groups of cognate languages)

Latin American Studies: 201, 212, 389, 405, 406, 665, 666, 667, 668, 669, 670, 1255 (See Also: Portuguese Language and Literature; Spanish Language and Literature)

Latin Language and Literature. See Classical Languages and Literature.

Law: 768, 1191, 1192, 1195, 1201, 1204, 1205, 1206, 1207, 1208, 1211, 1212, 1214, 1215, 1217, 1218, 1220, 1224, 1225, 1226, 1227, 1228, 1229, 1230, 1234, 1235, 1236, 1237, 1239, 1240, 1241, 1244, 1248, 1249, 1253, 1255, 1256, 1257, 1259, 1260, 1261, 1263, 1264, 1265, 1266, 1267, 1268, 1269, 1270, 1271, 1272, 1273, 1276, 1280, 1282, 1283, 1285, 1288, 1289, 1291, 1293, 1297, 1298, 1300, 1301, 1302, 1303, 1304, 1305, 1306, 1307, 1309, 1311, 1312, 1313, 1314, 1315, 1440, 1580 (See Also: Civil Law; Commercial Law; Criminal Law; Educational Law and Legislation; Forensic Science and Forensic Medicine; International Law; Justice, Administration of; Labor Laws and Legislation; Legislation; Medicine–Laws and Regulations; Military Law; Natural Law

Law, Civil. See Civil Law.

Law, Commercial. See Commercial Law.

Law, Criminal. See Criminal Law.

Law Enforcement: 1287

Law–Great Britain: 1222

Law, International. See International Law.

Law, Military. See Military Law.

Law, Natural. See Natural Law.

Law–Social and Political Aspects: 1235, 1248, 1252

Law as a Profession: 1254

Lawrence, D. H.–Life and Works: 343

Learning and Learning Disabilities: 901, 1006, 1013, 1016, 1056, 1075, 1076, 1366, 1434, 1446, 1477 (See Also: Education; Educational Psychology; Mental Retardation)

Leather Industry and Trade: 2561

References in Index refer to entry numbers

Subject index

U.S.–History: 57, 68, 98, 297, 390, 687, 1117, 1121, 1122, 1123, 1125, 1133, 1134, 1136, 1144, 1145, 1149, 1155, 1159, 1160, 1161, 1165, 1166, 1167, 1168, 1169, 1171, 1173, 1174, 1175, 1176, 1177, 1178, 1178, 1179, 1180, 1181, 1183, 1186, 1187, 1188, 1190, 1632, 2597 (See Also: Individual states)
U.S.–History–Civil War: 1132, 1138, 1158
U.S.–Literature. See American Literature.
Urban Development: 62, 706, 726, 749, 919, 1194, 1274, 1308, 1573, 1823, 1833, 1856, 2619 (See Also: City Planning; Regional Planning)
Urology: 2415, 2482 (See Also: Genito-urinary Organs)
Utah: 318
Utilities. See Public Utilities.

V

Vector Control: 1811
Vermont: 1185
Veterinary Medicine: 2398, 2542, 2543, 2544, 2545, 2546, 2547, 2548, 2550, 2551, 2553, 2554
Virginia: 741, 1124, 1186, 1187, 1632, 2597
Virology: 1926, 1946, 2371, 2389, 2398, 2416, 2426 (See Also: Bacteriology; Immunology)
Vocational Education. See Education, Vocational.

W

Wales–Life and Culture
Water Pollution: 1816, 1835, 1849, 1859, 1860, 2624
Water Power. See Hydroelectric Power.
Water Resources and Conservation: 1595, 1805, 1806, 1819, 1851, 1858, 1860, 1861, 2624 (See Also: Hydroelectric Power; Wells)
Waugh, Evelyn–Life and Works: 356
Welding: 2625, 2626
Wells: 1657 (See Also: Gas, Natural; Petroleum Industry and Trade; Water Resources and Conservation)
Wells, H.G.–Life and Works: 437
The West: 438, 507, 515, 684, 1122, 1125, 1159, 1168, 1177, 1188, 1360, 1555, 1574, 1614 (See Also: names of individual states)
West Virginia: 249
Whitman, Walt–Life and Works: 436
Wildlife Conservation: 1614, 1804, 1810, 1842, 1851, 1854 (See Also: Birds; Fish and Fisheries; Forests and Forestry; Natural Resources)
Wine and Wine Making: 1948
Wire and Cable Technology: 2627, 2628
Wisconsin: 321
Women–Employment: 1577, 1578, 1579
Women's Studies: 29, 1575, 1576, 1577, 1579, 1580, 1581, 1582, 1583, 1584
Wood: 1976, 2629 (See Also: Forests and Forestry)
Wordsworth, William–Life and Works: 439
Writing: 850, 852, 855, 858, 860, 863, 865, 879, 886, 1047
Wyoming: 1121, 1648

Y

Youth–Culture and Development: 728 (See Also: Adolescence; Child Study)

Z

Zoology: 1977, 1981, 1989, 1996, 1997, 2004 (See Also: Animals; Evolution; Invertebrates; Natural History; Paleontology; Primates; Reptiles; also names of classes in the animal kingdom)

References in Index refer to entry numbers

A

The Aaron Burr Association: 1131
Aberdeen University Alumnus Association: 1
Academy of General Dentistry: 2496
Academy of Management: 830
The Academy of Political Science: 1348
Academy of Psychosomatic Medicine: 1480
The Academy of Sciences and Literature of Mainz: 2131
Administrative Management Society: 835
Advertising Research Foundation, Inc.: 847
AEIS: 1073
The African Music Society: 128
African Studies Association: 403, 632
African Studies Center, UCLA: 246
African-American Institute: 627
Agricultural History Society: 1875
Agricultural Institute of Canada: 1877, 1879, 1955
Air Force Historical Foundation: 1113
Aktiebolagel Svenska Kullagerfabriken: 1712
Alberta School Trustees Association: 905
The Alexander Graham Bell Association for the Deaf: 1097
Alfred University: 1357
Alpha Kappa Delta: 1561
Alpha Phi Gamma, National Honorary Journalism Fraternity: 882
Alpha Psi Omega National Honorary in Theatre: 130
The American Academy of Advertising: 846
American Academy of Clinical Toxicology: 2325
American Academy of Dental Radiology: 2516
American Academy of Family Physicians: 2257
American Academy of Neurology: 2441
American Academy of Optometry: 2269
American Academy of Oral Medicine: 2512
American Academy of Oral Pathology: 2516
American Academy of Pediatrics, Inc.: 2460
American Academy of Psychoanalysis: 1362
American Academy of Religion: 528
American Academy of the History of Dentistry: 2501
American Anthropological Association: 216, 1530, 1531
American Arbitration Association: 1199
American Assembly of Collegiate Schools of Business: 829
American Association for Cancer Research: 2315
American Association for Health, Physical Education, and Recreation: 1062
American Association for Higher Education: 1004
American Association for Laboratory Animal Science: 1609
American Association for Rehabilitation Therapy, Inc: 1494
American Association for Thoracic Surgery: 2538
American Association for the Advancement of Science: 1621
American Association for the Advancement of Slavic Studies: 659
American Association for the Comparative Study of Law: 1195
American Association for the Study of Headache: 2354
American Association for the Study of Trauma: 2414
American Association of Avian Pathologists: 2544
American Association of Colleges for Teacher Education: 1014
American Association of Collegiate Registrars and Admissions Officers (AACRAO): 939
American Association of Dental Schools: 2508
American Association of Hospital Dentists: 2511
American Association of Immunologists: 2392
American Association of Orthodontists: 2497
American Association of Pastoral Counselors: 570
The American Association of Petroleum Geologists: 1667
American Association of Physicists in Medicine: 2168
American Association of Physics Teachers: 911, 1052
American Association of Public Health Dentists: 2514
American Association of School Librarians: 311
American Association of Teacher Educators in Agriculture: 907
American Association of Teachers of French: 207
American Association of Teachers of Italian: 217
American Association of Teachers of Slavic and East European Languages: 245
American Association of Teachers of Spanish and Portugese: 211

American Association on Mental Deficiency: 1451
American Astronomical Society: 2059, 2060
American Aviation Historical Society: 1115
American Bandmasters Association: 164
American Baptist Historical Society: 560
American Bar Association: 1192, 1298
American Bar Association, Committee on Continuing Education: 1276
American Bar Association, Law Student Division: 1291
American Bar Association, Section on Individual Rights and Responsibilities: 1235
American Benedictine Review: 529
The American Blake Foundation: 327
American Broncho-Esophagological Association: 2281
American Bryological and Lichenological Society, Inc.: 1953
American Business Communication Association: 850, 852
American Business Law Association: 1193
American Business Women's Association: 1582
American Cancer Society, Inc.: 2305
American Carbon Committee: 2079
American Catholic Philosophical Association: 454
American Ceramic Society, Inc.: 1585
American Chemical Society: 1829, 2066, 2068, 2073, 2081, 2083, 2096, 2114, 2115, 2118
American Chemical Society, Division of Chemical Education: 2105
American Chemical Society, Rubber Division: 2123
The American Choral Directors Association: 138
The American Cleft Palate Association: 2322
American College of Chest Physicians: 2320
American College of Emergency Physicians: 2254
American College of Gastroenterology: 2264
American College of Hospital Administrators: 2357
The American College of Nursing Home Administrators: 2395
American College of Obstetricians and Gynecologists: 2267
American College of Physicians: 2280
American College of Veterinary Pathologists: 2553
American Concrete Institute: 1586, 1718
American Congress of Rehabilitation Medicine: 2285
American Corrective Therapy Association, Inc.: 2255
American Council on Consumer Interests: 28, 772
American Council on Education: 953
American Council on the Teaching of Foreign Languages: 967
The American Dance Guild: 149
The American Defence Preparedness Association: 1326
American Dental Assistants Association: 2504
American Diabetes Association, Inc.: 2332
American Dialect Society: 196
The American Dietetic Association: 2256
American Economic Association: 745
American Education Association: 956
American Educational Research Association: 910, 954, 1063
The American Educational Studies Association: 957
American Electroplaters' Society, Inc.: 2608
American Ethical Union: 89
American Federation of Musicians: 160
American Federation of Teachers, AFL-CIO: 915, 932
American Fertility Society: 2345
American Finance Association: 816
American Folklore Society: 1547
American Foreign Service Association: 1339
American Forensic Association: 896
The American Forestry Association: 1804
American Foundation for the Blind, Inc.: 1492, 1522
American Foundrymen's Society: 1702
American Gas Association: 2557
American Genetic Association: 1931
The American Geographical Society: 1105
American Geophysical Union: 1861, 2151
American Geriatrics Society: 2258
American Group Psychotherapy Association: 1402
American Gynecological Society: 2267

References in Index refer to entry numbers

Publisher and sponsoring organization index

American Heart Association: 2321
American Historical Association: 1118
American Historical Association, Conference Group for Central European History: 1130
American Historical Association, Conference on Latin American History: 665
American Historical Association, Modern European History Section: 1156
American Historical Association, Pacific Coast Branch: 1178
American Hospital Association: 2360
The American Humane Association: 35, 2563
American Humanist Association: 89
American Indian Historical Society: 688
American Industrial Arts Association: 1027
American Industrial Development Council, Inc.: 747
American Institute for Mental Studies, Training School Unit: 1489
American Institute of Aeronautics and Astronautics: 1693, 2049, 2050, 2053, 2054
American Institute of Architects: 129
American Institute of Certified Public Accountants: 735, 739
American Institute of Chemical Engineers: 1703
American Institute of Industrial Engineers: 1745
American Institute of Mining, Metallurgical and Petroleum Engineers: 1701, 1794
American Institute of Nutrition: 2405
American Institute of Physics: 2038, 2148, 2149, 2171
American Instructors of the Deaf: 2253
The American Jewish Committee: 44
American Jewish Congress: 574
American Jewish Historical Society: 530
American Judges Association: 1219
The American Judicature Society: 1250
American Labor Conference on International Affairs, Inc.: 39
American Laryngological Association: 2281
The American Law Institute: 1276
The American Leather Chemists Association: 2561
American Library Association: 251, 285, 298
The American Library Association, Children's and Young Adult's Services Division: 317
American Library Association, Information Science and Automation Division: 280
American Library Association, Intellectual Freedom Committee: 857
American Library Association, Reference and Adult Services: 308
American Library Association, Resources and Technical Services Division: 288
American Management Associations, Inc.: 839
American Marketing Association: 779, 780
American Mathematical Society: 2189, 2190, 2191, 2212
American Medical Association: 2262, 2272
American Medical Technologists: 2273
American Meteorological Society: 1644, 1655, 1695, 2032
American Microchemical Society: 2122
American Military Institute: 1322
American Museum of Natural History: 145, 1612
American Musicological Society, Inc.: 132
American Name Society: 101
American Nature Study Society: 1037
American Nuclear Society: 2182, 2183
American Nurses' Association: 2520
American Oil Chemists' Society: 2121
American Orthopsychiatric Association, Inc.: 1366
American Osteopathic Association: 2274
American Otological Society, Inc.: 2281
The American Personnel and Guidance Association: 1049
American Pharmaceutical Association: 2408
The American Philological Association, Inc.: 69
American Physical Society: 2164
American Physical Therapy Association: 2464
American Physiological Society: 2465
The American Podiatry Association: 2275
The American Political Science Association: 1333, 1349

American Powder Metallurgy Institute: 1653
American Psychiatric Association: 1367
American Psychoanalytic Association: 1369
American Psychological Association: 1370, 1371, 1388, 1391, 1409, 1412, 1417, 1418, 1419, 1421, 1424, 1438, 1460, 1469, 1475
American Psychological Association, Division 17: 1390
American Psychological Association, Psychotherapy Division: 1483
American Public Power Association: 1279
The American Public Welfare Association: 1523
American Rheumatism Association: 2287
American Risk and Insurance Association: 784
The American-Scandinavian Foundation: 658
American School Counselor Association: 962, 1067
American School Health Association: 2411
American Schools for the Deaf: 2253
American Scientific Affiliation: 531
American Society for Adolescent Psychiatry: 1361
American Society for Aesthetics: 163
The American Society for Cell Biology: 1928
The American Society for Clinical Investigation, Inc.: 2382
The American Society for Clinical Nutrition: 2261
American Society for Clinical Pharmacology and Therapeutics: 2324
American Society for Eighteenth-Century Studies: 83
American Society for Gastrointestinal Endoscopy: 2348
American Society for Information Science: 252
American Society for Metals: 1701, 1776, 1794
American Society for Microbiology: 1890, 1894, 1927, 2283, 2365, 2416
The American Society for Personnel Administration: 840
American Society for Pharmacology and Experimental Therapeutics: 2336, 2409, 2462
The American Society for Photobiology: 1939
American Society for Public Administration: 1277
American Society for Public Administration, Comparative Administration Group: 1242
American Society for Quality Control: 1789
American Society for Testing and Materials: 1605, 1608, 1707, 1794
American Society for Training and Development, Inc.: 845
American Society of Adlerian Psychology: 1397, 1432
American Society of Biological Chemists, Inc.: 2102
American Society of Church History: 545
American Society of Civil Engineers: 1724
American Society of Clinical Hypnosis: 1365
American Society of Clinical Pathologists: 2421
American Society of Composers, Authors, Publishers: 2565
American Society of Enologists: 1948
American Society of Heating, Refrigerating, and Air-Conditioning Engineers, Inc. 1705, 2566
American Society of Hospital Pharmacists: 2265
American Society of Human Genetics: 1887
American Society of Ichthyologists and Herpetologists: 1985
American Society of International Law: 1197, 1237
American Society of Lubrication Engineers: 1706
American Society of Mammalogists: 2004
American Society of Mechanical Engineers: 1755, 1758, 1759, 1761, 1762, 1773
American Society of Naturalists: 1862
The American Society of Naval Engineers: 1779
American Society of Photogrammetry: 2042
American Society of Planning Officials: 1274
American Society of Plant Physiologists: 1967
American Society of Plastic and Reconstructive Surgeons: 2539
American Society of Psychosomatic Dentistry and Medicine: 2277
American Society of Radiologic Technologists: 2471
American Society of Traffic and Transportation Inc: 1296
American Sociological Association: 1533, 1534, 1550, 1567, 1569
American Speech and Hearing Association: 1495, 2412, 2413
American Studies Association: 682

References in Index refer to entry numbers

American Theatre Association: 156
American Thoracic Society: 2276
American Urological Association: 2415
American Water Works Association: 1805
Americans United for the Separation of Church and State: 546
Amnesty International of the U.S.A.: 1344
Annenberg School of Communications: 853
Anthropological Association of Canada: 1535
Antiquarian Booksellers Association of Canada: 685
Applied Probability Trust: 2186, 2201
Archaeological Institute of America: 1631, 1633
Archaeological Society of Virginia: 1632
Archives of Languages of the World: 197
Arizona Archaeological and Historical Society, Inc.: 1638
Arizona English Teachers Association: 917
Arizona State University: 1659
Arizona State University, Bureau of Educational Research and Services: 988
Arkansas Historical Association: 1123
Arkansas Library Association: 254
Arkansas Library Commission: 254
The Arlington Historical Society: 1124
Armstrong Browning Library,: 420
Ars Moriendi: 1454
The Arthritis Foundation: 2287
ASLIB: 255
Associated Collegiate Press: 884
Association for Academic Surgery: 2537
Association for Asian Studies, Inc.: 641
Association for Child Psychology and Psychiatry: 1414
Association for Childhood Education International: 933
Association for Clinical Pastoral Education, Inc.: 570
Association for Community-Wide Protection from Nuclear Attack: 59
Association for Comparative Economic Studies: 742
Association for Computing Machinery: 2226, 2234
Association for Continuing Higher Education: 944
Association for Education in Journalism: 883, 1017
Association for Educational Communications and Technology, Inc.: 866, 867
Association for Educational Data Systems: 903, 2227
Association for Evolutionary Economics: 775
Association for Humanistic Psychology: 1431
The Association for Library Automation Research Communications (LARC): 296
Association for Measurement and Evaluation in Guidance: 1030
Association for Professional Broadcasting Education: 893
Association for Research in Vision and Ophthalmology, Inc.: 2372
Association for Social Economics: 801
Association for Symbolic Logic: 449, 2210
Association for Systems Management: 2242
Association for the Advancement of Ageing Research: 1870
Association for the Advancement of Baltic Studies, Inc (AABS): 652
Association for The Development of Religious Information Systems (ADRIS): 526
Association for the Sociology of Religion: 599
Association for the Study of Man-Environment Relations, Inc.: 1845
Association for the Study of Medical Education: 2298
The Association for the Study of Negro Life and History, Inc.: 692
The Association for Tropical Biology, Inc.: 1903
Association of American Geographers: 1099, 1109
Association of American Geographers, Southeastern Division: 1111
Association of American Library Schools: 278
Association of American Medical Colleges: 2396
Association of Assistant Librarians: 256
Association of College and Research Libraries: 267
Association of Collegiate Schools of Planning: 919
Association of Departments of English: 902

Association of Engineering Geologists: 1668
Association of German Chemists: 2069
The Association of German-Speaking Authors in America: 441
Association of Lunar and Planetary Observers: 2056
Association of Official Analytical Chemists: 2070
Association of Public Health Inspectors: 2337
Association of School Business Officials: 1065
Association of Teacher Educators: 920
The Association of the U.S. Army: 1318
Association of Theological Schools in the U.S. and Canada: 1090
The Association of Trial Lawyers of America: 1297
Association of Working Press, Inc.: 880
Astronomical Society of the Pacific: 2057
Auburn University: 56
Audubon Naturalist Society of the Central Atlantic States, Inc.: 1807
Australasian Association of Philosophy: 442
Australasian Corrosion Association: 1708
Australasian Universities Language and Literature Association: 244
Australian Psychological Society: 1373
Australian Universities Language and Literature Association: 198

B
Bailey Hortorium: 1951
Ball State University: 6
Bank Administration Institute: 818
The Bards of Grand Rapids: 474
Baylor University: 420, 750
Bernice P. Bishop Museum: 2005
The Bertrand Russell Society: 469
Beta Beta Beta Biological Society: 1902
The Bibliographical Society of America: 258
The Biochemical Society: 2071
Biological Stain Commission: 2124
The Biometric Society: 2195
The Biophysical Society: 1863
Black Economic Research Center: 798
Black World Foundation: 609
Blue Cross Association: 2366
Bodleian Library: 259
Boston College, Graduate School of Social Work: 1573
Boston College Law School: 1203
The Boston Society for Gerontologic Psychiatry, Inc.: 1428
The Boston Street Railway Association, Inc.: 2619
Boston University: 9, 115
Boston University, Department of University Professors: 72
Boston University, School of Education: 995
Botanical Society of America, Inc.: 1947, 1968
Boys' Clubs of America: 1518
Brigham Young University: 537
British Academy of Forensic Sciences: 2434
British Agricultural History Society: 1876
British Association for American Studies: 690
British Columbia Library Association: 261
The British Computer Society: 2228
British Dental Association: 2500
British Institute of International and Comparative Law, London: 1215
British Interplanetary Society: 1589, 2055
British Medical Association: 2397
British Medical Journal Group: 1471, 2297, 2300, 2301, 2303, 2404
British Psychological Society: 923, 1952
British Records Association: 253
British Society for Surgery of the Hand: 2353
The British Society of Aesthetics: 76
British Society of Animal Production: 1878
British Society of Rheology: 2026
British Sociological Association: 1566
British Steelmaker Ltd.: 2570
British Theatre Institute: 194

References in Index refer to entry numbers

Publisher and sponsoring organization index

British Vacuum Council: 2046
Broadcast Education Association: 890
Bureau of Economic and Business Research: 751
The Burroughs Bibliophiles: 331
Burroughs Corporation, Detroit: 809
The Byron Society: 332

C

California Academy of Sciences: 1591, 1592, 1616
California Association of School Librarians: 263
California Botanical Society: 1962
California Bureau of Vector Control and Solid Waste
   Management: 1811
California Center for Research and Education in Government:
   1335
California Department of Fish and Game: 1810
California Division of Mines and Geology: 1669
California Driver Education Association: 1015
California Field Ornithologists: 2019
California Folklore Society: 1574
California Historical Society: 1125
California Institute of International Studies: 624
California Malacozoological Society, Inc.: 2018
The California Society of Certified Public Accountants: 730
Cambridge Historical Society: 1140
Cambridge Philosophical Society: 1904
The Cambridge Policy Studies Institute, Inc.: 727
The Canada Council: 512, 1491
Canadian Aeronautics and Space Institute: 2051, 2052
Canadian Anaesthetists' Society: 2307
Canadian Association for South Asian Studies: 638
Canadian Association for the Mentally Retarded: 1520
Canadian Association of American Studies: 686
The Canadian Association of Occupational Therapists: 1497
Canadian Association of Psysicists: 2167
Canadian Association of Physicists, Medical & Biological Section:
   2168
Canadian Association of Slavists: 647
Canadian Association of University Teachers of German,: 244
The Canadian Council on Social Development: 1498
Canadian Dental Association: 2502
Canadian Economics Association: 758
Canadian Education Association: 949
Canadian Guidance and Counselling Association: 1379
Canadian Home Economics Association: 11
Canadian Industrial Relations Research Institute: 828
Canadian Institute of Food Science and Technology: 1865
Canadian Institute of International Affairs: 612
The Canadian Institute of Mining and Metallurgy: 1656, 1680
Canadian Library Association: 264
The Canadian Mathematical Congress: 2196
Canadian Museums Association: 141
Canadian Nurses' Association: 2521
Canadian Pharmaceutical Association: 2311, 2314
Canadian Philosophical Association: 443
Canadian Psychological Association: 1380
Canadian Public Health Association: 2313, 2313
Canadian Society of Animal Science: 1879
Canadian Society of Horticultural Science: 1955
Canadian Society of Laboratory Technologists: 2309
Canadian Society of Soil Science: 1880
Canadian Sociology and Anthropology Association: 1538
Canadian Veterinary Medical Association: 2308, 2545
Case Western Reserve University: 1211
The Catholic Biblical Association of America: 538
The Catholic Hospital Association: 2359
Catholic Library Association: 266
The Catholic University of America: 539
Catholic University of Louvain, Faculty of Theology: 577
Center for Advanced Study in Religion and Science: 605
Center for Applied Linguistics: 225
Center for Christian Studies: 48

The Center for Integrative Education: 450
Center for International Education and Research in Accounting:
   734
Center for Migration Studies of New York, Inc.: 1546
Center for Reformation Research: 1182
Center for Reformation Research, Central Renaissance
   Conference: 112
Center for War/Peace Studies: 623
Center of Alcohol Studies: 1517
Centre Belge d'Etude de la Corrosion: 1728
The Chesopiean Archaeological Association: 1636
Chicano Studies Center, UCLA: 5
Child Welfare League of America, Inc.: 1500
Christ Catholic Church, Diocese of Boston: 586
Christian Century Foundation: 542
Christian Freedom Foundation, Inc.: 534
Christian Theological Seminary: 557
Church Historical Society: 563
Church Music Association of America: 187
City College, CUNY, School of Education: 922
City University of New York: 199, 1336
The Classical Association of the Atlantic States: 79
Clay Minerals Society: 1681
Clemson University, College of Liberal Arts: 416
The Coleopterists Society: 1983
College Art Association: 1576
The College English Association, Inc.: 929, 930
The College Language Association: 203
College of Clinical Pharmacology: 2383
College of Speech Therapists, London: 200
The Colonial Society of Massachusetts: 390
Colorado Archaeological Society: 1639
Colorado School of Mines: 1647
Colorado School of Mines Research Institute: 1683
Columbia University: 14
Columbia University, Department of Germanic Languages: 209
Columbia University, Graduate School of Music: 146
The Combustion Institute: 1594
Committee of Concerned Asian Scholars: 637
Commonwealth of Virginia, Office of the Chief Medical Examiner:
   2435
Commonwealth Department of Primary Industry: 2568
Commonwealth Institute of Entomology: 1980
Commonwealth Scientific and Industrial Research Organization:
   1950
Company of Biologists, Ltd.: 1929
Comparative and International Education Society: 941
The Comparative and International Education Society of Canada:
   927
Composers, Authors and Publishers Association of Canada,
   Limited: 136
Concordia Historical Institute: 549
Concordia Theological Seminary: 601
Conference Group for Central European History: 646
Conference of Executives of American Schools for the Deaf and:
   906
Connecticut Association of Boards of Education, Inc.: 925
Conseil National de Recherches du Canada: 1110
Convention of American Instructors of the Deaf: 906
Cooper Ornithological Society: 1984
The Cornell Plantations: 1956
Cornell Society of Engineers: 1726
Cornell University: 489, 821, 1951, 1956
Cornell University, Graduate School of Business and Public
   Administration: 743
Cornell University, Sage School of Philosophy: 459
Corrosion and Protection Association: 1728
COSMEP; CCLM: 155, 507
The Council of State Governments: 1290
Council on Interracial Books for Children, Inc.: 365
Creative Education Foundation, Inc.: 992

References in Index refer to entry numbers

Creighton University School of Law: 1220

D
Dalhousie University: 81
Danish Medical Association: 2330
Dante Society of America, Inc.: 344
DeKalb College: 485
Department of Commerce: 1658
Department of HEW: 1526
Detroit Institute of Arts, Founders Society: 151
The Detroit Society for Genealogical Research, Inc.: 1135
Dialogue Foundation: 554
The Dickens Fellowship: 346
The Dickens Society: 345
Distributive Education Clubs of America: 946
Documentation Office for East European Law, Leiden: 1280
Dolmetsch Foundation: 144
The Drew University Theological School: 555
Drexel University, Graduate School of Library Science: 268
Duke University, School of Law: 1253

E
Eastern Churches Review Trust: 556
Eastern Communication Association: 864
Economic History Association: 774
EDICOM, The Hague: 226
Educational Facilities Laboratories: 1053
Educational Foundation for Nuclear Science, Inc.: 1590
Educational Service Bureau, Inc.: 1050, 1064
Emory University, School of Law: 1227
English Dominicans: 584
Eno Foundation for Transportation, Inc.: 1295
Entomological Society of America: 1987, 1999
Environmental Data Service: 1658
Environmental Law Institute, Washington:: 1226
Environmental Management Association: 1850
The Europa Institute: 1215
European Association for Animal Production: 1885
The European Association of Endocrinology: 2356
European Association of Exploration Geophysicists: 1650
European Broadcasting Union: 887
The European Consortium for Political Research: 1337
The European Society for Clinical Investigation: 2340
The European Society for Experimental Surgery: 2535
The European Society of Neuroradiology: 2444
European Southern Observatory (ESO): 2058
Evangelical Missions Information Service: 558
The Explicator Literary Foundation, Inc.: 357

F
The Faculty Press: 1935
Family Institute, New York: 1506
The Federal Bar Association: 1228
Federal Legal Publications, Inc.: 748
Federation of American Societies for Experimental Biology: 1919
The Federation of European Biochemical Societies: 2092
The Federation of Orthodontic Associations: 2507
Federation of Societies for Paint Technology: 1607
Federation of Women Teachers of Ontario: 951
Fellowship of Religious Humanists: 594
Field Museum of Natural History: 1957, 1989
Film Library Information Council: 270
The Filson Club, Inc.: 1136
Financial Analysts Federation: 814
Finnish Medical Society Duodecim: 2278, 2279, 2426
Florida Academy of Sciences: 1597
The Florida Audubon Society: 1830
Florida State University, Department of Philosophy: 722
Florida State University, Geology Department: 1593
Florida State University, School of Library Science: 281
Folger Shakespeare Library: 413

Fordham University: 120
Foreign Policy Research Institute: 620
Forest History Society: 1839
Fort Worth Museum of Science and History: 681
Foundation for Economic Education, Inc.: 22, 766
Foundation for International Philosophical Exchange: 445
Foundation for Research on the Nature of Man: 1436
Foundation for Student Communication: 756
The Franciscan Institute: 551
Franklin Institute Research Laboratories: 1596
Franklin Thomas Backus School of Law: 1211
Fred and Eleanor Schonell Educational Research Centre: 1076
Friends of the Earth: 1847

G
The Galton Foundation: 1867
The Genetics Society of Canada: 1905
Genossenschaftliche Zentralbank, Basel: 712
The Geochemical Society: 2093
George Peabody College for Teachers: 1046
George S. May International Company: 789
George Washington University, National Law Center: 1245
Georgia Academy of Science: 1598
Georgia Entomological Society: 1991
Georgia Historical Society: 1138
Georgia Nurses' Association: 2522
Georgia State University, School of Business Administration: 749
German Neurological Society: 2403
German Society for Electronmicroscopy: 1913
German Society for Lung Diseases and Tuberculosis: 2466
German Society for Neurosurgery: 2403
Gerontological Society: 610, 617
Gesellschaft Deutscher Chemiker: 2069
Glossa Society: 210
Graduate Christian Fellowship: 553
Great Plains National Instructional Television Library: 891
Greater San Francisco Chamber of Commerce: 802
Guild Cooperative Fellowship: 53

H
H. G. Wells Society International: 437
Hall Psychiatric Institute of the South Carolina Department of Mental Health: 1462
Hankamer School of Business: 750
Harvard College: 800
Harvard Divinity School: 561
Harvard Graduate School of Business Administration: 753, 767
Harvard Graduate School of Education: 971
Harvard Law Review Association: 1234
Harvard Legislative Research Bureau: 1233
Harvard-Yenching Institute: 639
Hawaii Audubon Society: 1820
Health Physics Society: 2177
Health Resources Administration: 2469
Herpetologists' League: 1993
Hiram College, Department of English: 493
Histochemical Society, Inc.: 2111
Historical Society of Alberta: 1114
Historical Society of Delaware: 1134
History of Education Society: 1142
History of Science Society, Inc.: 1147
The Hoover Institution: 657
Horatio Alger Society: 392
Hospital Physicists' Association: 2168
Howard University: 1007
Human Relations Area Files, Inc.: 698
The Humanities Association of Canada: 90

I
IEEE Computer Society: 2229
Illinois Audiovisual Association: 976

References in Index refer to entry numbers

Publisher and sponsoring organization index

Illinois Geographical Society: 1106
Illinois State Historical Society: 1144
Illinois State Library: 273
Illinois State Medical Society: 2361
Illuminating Engineering Society: 1744
Indian Council of Medical Research: 2363
The Indian Rights Association: 689
Indiana Historical Society: 1145
Indiana Library Association: 271
Indiana State Library: 286
Indiana State Medical Association: 2364
Indiana State University, School of Education: 943
Indiana University: 455
Indiana University, Anthropology Department: 197
Indiana University, Graduate School of Business: 754
Indiana University, School of Law: 1239
Industrial Development Research Council: 2590
Industrial Management Review Association: 843
Industrial Mathematics Society: 2198
Industrial Relations Society of New South Wales: 825
The Industrial Research Institute: 1619
Information Planning Associates, Inc.: 1493
Institute for Inter-American Legal Studies: 1255
Institute for Palestine Studies: 673
Institute for the Study of Drug Addiction: 1503
Institute of Biology, London: 989
The Institute of Chartered Accountants in England and Wales: 729
Institute of Community Development: 699
Institute of Directors: 762
Institute of Early American History and Culture: 1190
Institute of Electrical and Electronics Engineers, Inc.: 1741, 1742, 1743
Institute of Environmental Sciences: 1837
Institute of Fine Arts: 133
Institute of Food Technologists: 1604, 2580
Institute of Industrial Relations: 822
The Institute of Information Scientists: 275
The Institute of Internal Auditors, Inc.: 733
Institute of Malacology: 2010
Institute of Management Sciences: 833
Institute of Marketing: 787
The Institute of Nuclear Materials Management, Inc.: 2181
The Institute of Physics: 1051, 2155, 2156, 2157, 2158, 2159, 2160, 2166, 2179
The Institute of Public Administration of Canada: 1210
The Institute of Quality Assurance: 1788
Institute on Religion in an Age of Science: 605
Institutes of Latin American Studies at the Universities of Cambridge, Glasgow, and Oxford:
Institutes of Religion and Health: 572
Institution of Electrical Engineers: 1731, 1732, 1746
Institution of Electronic and Radio Engineers: 1790
Institution of Production Engineers: 1785
Instituto Internacional de Literatura Iberoamericana: 406
Instrument Society of America: 1754, 2236
Insurance Information Institute: 778
Integrated Education Associates: 981
Intercollegiate Broadcasting System: 894
The Intercollegiate Studies Institute: 27, 67
Internationaal Instituut voor Sociale Geschiedenis: 1146
International Academy of Astronautics: 2047
International Academy of Cytology: 2250
International Academy of Pathology, U.S.-Canada Division: 2419
International Arthurian Society: 364
International Association for Cultural Freedom: 661
International Association for Dental Research, North American Division: 2509
International Association for Ecology (Intecol): 1802, 1872
International Association for Mathematical Geology: 1673
International Association for Psychotronic Research: 1468
International Association of Chiefs of Police: 1247, 1275

International Association of Cross-Cultural Psychology: 1420
International Association of Independent Producers: 868
International Association of Individual Psychology: 1398
International Association of Master Penmen and Teachers of Handwriting: 1047
International Association of Microbiological Societies: 1925, 2371
International Association of Milk, Food and Environmental Sanitarians, Inc.: 1868
International Association of Music Libraries: 260
International Association of Pupil Personnel Workers: 975
International Association of Schools of Social Work: 1509
International Association on Water Pollution Research: 1860
International Atomic Energy Agency: 2176, 2180
International Center of Medieval Art: 86
International Centre for Mechanical Sciences: 1774
International City Management Association: 1278
International College of Applied Nutrition: 2379
The International College of Pediatrics: 2457
International Committee on General Relativity and Gravitation: 2141
International Committee on Weights and Measures: 2213
International Communication Association: 853
International Conferences on Environmental Future (ICEF): 1825
International Consumer Credit Association: 811
International Council of Nurses: 2524
International Council of Psychologists, Inc.: 1404, 1405
International Council on Social Welfare: 1509
International Federation for Documentation: 269
International Federation for Medical Psychotherapy: 1481
International Federation for the Theory of Machines and Mechanisms: 1775
International Federation of Automatic Control: 1710
International Federation of Social Workers: 1509
The International Fortean Organization (INFO): 1601
International Graphoanalysis Society: 1429
International Harpsichord Society: 158
International Institute for Geothermal Research, Pisa: 1671
International Institute for Social History: 1146
International Labour Office: 823
International Leprosy Association: 2369
International Microwave Power Institute: 1764
International Oceanographic Foundation: 1700
International Organization for Medical Physics: 2168
International Pediatric Research Foundation: 2459
International Radiation Protection Association: 2177
International Railway Congress Association: 2614
International Reading Association: 1010, 1058, 1059
International Society for Horticultural Science: 1974
International Society for Pediatric Neurosurgery: 2533
International Society for Research in Stereoencephalotomy: 2326
International Society for Terrain Vehicle Systems: 1767
International Society for the Study of Symbols: 91
The International Society of Art and Psychopathology: 1387
International Society of Audiology: 2289
International Society of Biorheology: 1901
International Society of Blood Transfusion: 2494
International Society of Electrochemistry: 2091
The International Society of Geographical Pathology: 1938
International Society of Haematology: 2251
International Society of Neuroendocrinology: 2440
International Society of Phonetic Sciences: 241
International Society of Planetarium Educators: 2063
The International Sociological Association: 1541
International Solar Energy Society: 2044
International Studies Association: 614
International Team of Scripture Scholars: 535
International Thespian Society: 154
International Transactional Analysis Association: 1490
International Union for Conservation of Nature and Natural Resources (IUCN): 1825
International Union for Pure and Applied Biophysics: 1943
International Union of Railways: 2614

References in Index refer to entry numbers

International Union of Testing and Research: 1772
Interuniversity Communications Council: 960
Interuniversity Research Center of International Law: 1262
Iowa Historical Department: 1120
Iowa Medical Society: 2374
Iowa State University: 510
Irish American Cultural Institute: 650
IRT Collective: 1407
Israel Exploration Society: 1637
Israel Medical Association: 2375
Israel National Council for Research and Development: 2375
The Israeli Institute for the Study of International Affairs: 613
Israeli Ministry for Foreign Affairs, Cultural and Scientific Relations Division 71
Italian National Research Council: 1671
I.U.C.N., Morges, Switzerland: 1226 1407

J
The James Branch Cabell Society: 374
Japan Society of Applied Physics: 2147
Japanese Biochemical Society: 2101
Japanese Heart Association: 2376
Japanese Society for Bacteriology: 1926
Jewish Theological Seminary: 550
John Dewey Society: 958 017
John Edwards Memorial Foundation: 162
John Steinbeck Society of America: 418
Johns Hopkins University, School of Hygiene: 2263
The Joint Council on Economic Education: 993
Judge Advocate General's Department: 1316

K
Kansas Arts Commission: 473
Kansas Association of School Boards: 1019
Kansas State College of Pittsburg: 100
Kennedy Galleries, Inc.: 131
Kennedy School of Government: 1350
Kentucky Council of Teachers of English: 1021
Kentucky Folklore Society: 1552
The Kentucky Historical Society: 1160
The Kipling Society: 375
Kobe University School of Medicine: 2417
Kuwait University: 673

L
Labor Research Association: 764
Labor Today Association: 826
Laboratory Animals Limited: 2009
Lancaster County Historical Society: 1161
La Salle College: 85
Latin American Studies Association: 668
Law and Society Association: 1252
Leeds Philosophical and Literary Society: 95
Lehigh University: 2203
Leisure and Disability Publications Steering Committee: 1512
Lexington Theological Seminary: 575
The Library Association: 279
Library Association, Library History Group: 284
Library Association of Alberta: 283
Library-College Associates, Inc.: 282
Linguistic Society of America: 216, 222
Linguistics Association of Great Britain: 219
Linnean Society of London: 1934, 1961
List Gesellschaft, Dülsseldorf: 712
Liverpool School of Tropical Medicine: 2282
Liverpool University Press: 201
London School of Hygiene and Tropical Medicine: 2000
Louisiana State University: 518
Louisiana State University, Division of Research, College of Business Administration: 786
Louisiana Teachers' Association: 1024
Loyola University, Chicago: 1166

Loyola University, Chicago; Department of English: 186
Loyola University, New Orleans: 102
Lutheran Church in America: 165
The Lutheran Church Missouri Synod: 549

M
Magyar Lektoratus, Inc.: 648
The Malraux Society: 387
Manitoba Historical Society: 1162
The Manitoba Teachers' Society: 1026
The Manuscript Society: 97
Marquette University, College of Business Administration: 788
Martin Psychiatric Research Foundation, Inc.: 1389
Maryland State Dental Association: 2515
Massachusetts Department of Mental Health: 1447
Massachusetts Institute of Technology, Alumni Association: 1626
Massachusetts Library Association: 257
Massachusetts Medical Society: 2445
Massachusetts Music Educators Association: 1028
The Mathematical Association of America: 2188
McMaster University: 469
Media & Consumer Foundation: 32
Medical and Chirurgical Faculty of the State of Maryland: 2424
The Medical Association of Georgia: 2425
Medical Group Management Association: 836
Medical Library Association: 290
Medical Society for the Study of Veneral Diseases: 2302
The Medical Society of New Jersey: 2432
Medical Society of the State of New York: 2447
The Menninger Foundation: 1449
Mennonite Church, General Conference: 579
Mental Research Institute, Palo Alto: 1506
The Merrill-Palmer Institute: 1452
The Metallurgical Society of C.I.M.: 1717
The Meteoritic Society: 1659, 2093
Metropolitan Tulsa Chamber of Commerce: 62
Miami School of Law: 1255
Michigan Botanical Club: 1963
Michigan Education Association: 1087
Michigan Entomological Society: 1992
Michigan Law Review Association: 1259
Michigan Library Association: 291
Michigan Speech and Hearing Association: 1521
Michigan State Medical Society: 2436
Michigan State University: 775
Michigan State University, Division of Research, Graduate School of Business Administration: 791
Midcontinent American Studies Association: 683
The Middle East Institute: 675
Middle East Research and Information Project: 674
Middle East Studies Association: 671, 676
Midwest Modern Language Association: 228
Midwest Political Science Association: 1331
Midwest Sociological Society: 1563
Military Police Association: 1324
The Mind Association: 452
The Mineralogical Society of America: 1678
Ministere de L'Education du Quebec: 1110
Minnesota Historical Society: 1167
Minnesota Library Association: 299
Minnesota Reading Association, Inc.: 1032
The Mississippi Folklore Society: 1554
Mississippi Department of Archives and History: 1155
Mississippi Historical Society: 1155
Mississippi Music Educators Association: 170
Mississippi State Bar: 1260
Missouri Department of Natural Resources: 1688
Missouri Library Association: 293
Missouri Society of Professional Engineers: 1777
Missouri State Teachers Association: 1066
Modern Humanities Research Association: 230

References in Index refer to entry numbers

Publisher and sponsoring organization index

Modern Language Association of America: 99, 232, 400, 403
Modern Language Association of America, American Literature Section: 323
Modern Language Association of America, Conference of Learned Editors: 349
Modern Language Association of America, Early American Literature Group: 347
Modern Language Association of America, Group I, Old English: 238
Modern Language Association of America, Seminar on Science Fiction: 358
Modern Language Association of America, Sp. I: 221
Monarchist League of Canada: 695, 1209
The Montana Historical Society: 1168
Mountain Plains Library Association: 294
Museum of the Great Plains: 687
The Museums Association: 172
Music Educators National Conference: 1012, 1034
Music Library Association, Inc.: 301

N

Nassau Community College: 502
National Academy of Sciences: 1611
National Affairs Inc.: 716
National Alliance for Family Life, Inc.: 1425
National Archives and Records Service: 1180
National Art Education Association: 918, 1082
National Association for Core Curriculum, Inc.: 945
The National Association for Gifted Children: 969
National Association for Music Therapy, Inc.: 1435
National Association for Physical Education of College Women: 1055
National Association for Practical Nurse Education and Service, Inc.: 2526
National Association for the Advancement of Colored People: 17
National Association for the Education of Young Children: 1098
National Association for Women Deans, Administrators, and Counselors: 1577
The National Association of Bank Loan and Credit: 815
National Association of Biology Teachers, Inc.: 908
National Association of College Wind and Percussion Instructors: 177
National Association of Colleges and Teachers of Agriculture: 1035
The National Association of Corrosion Engineers: 1727
National Association of Credit Management: 810
National Association of Elementary School Principals: 1036
National Association of Geology Teachers: 1003
National Association of Independent Schools: 979
National Association of Language Laboratory Directors: 235
National Association of Purchasing Management, Inc.: 782
National Association of Teachers of Singing, Inc.: 178
National Audubon Society: 1978
National Carl Schurz Association: 656
National Catholic Educational Association: 1033
National Children's Theatre Association: 137
National College of Teachers of the Deaf: 1085
National College Physical Education for Men: 1055
National Collegiate Athletic Association: 1038
The National Council for Critical Analysis: 446
National Council for Geographic Education: 1002
National Council for Small Business Management: 832
National Council for Special Education: 1079
The National Council of Churches, USA: 541
National Council of College Publications Advisers: 881
National Council of Juvenile Court Judges: 1251
National Council of Teachers of English: 936, 937, 961, 964, 965, 1061
National Council of Teachers of Mathematics: 916, 1029
National Council on Alcoholism, Inc.: 1507
National Council on Alcoholism, Inc., Labor-Management Division: 1519
National Council on Crime and Delinquency: 710, 1539

National Council on Family Relations: 1504, 1513
National Council on Measurement in Education: 996
National Council on the Aging: 1508
National Education Association of the U.S.: 1092
National Environmental Health Association: 1836
The National Federation of Business and Professional Women's Clubs, Inc.: 1578
National Federation of Licensed Practical Nurses: 2528
National Federation of Modern Language Teachers Associations: 229
National Federation of Press Women, Inc.: 1579
National Federation of Societies for Clinical Social Work: 1501
National Fire Protection Association: 1737
National Foremen's Institute: 2581
National Geographic Society: 1108
National Guard Association of the United States: 1327
National Hearing Aid Society: 2288
National Institute for Metallurgy: 1687
National Institute of Mental Health, Division of Extramural Research Programs: 2468
National Junior College Athletic Association: 1018
National League for Nursing: 2529
National Middle School Association: 1031
The National Opera Association: 180
National Organization on Legal Problems of Education: 1268
The National Physical Education Society: 1009
National Psychological Association for Psychoanalysis: 1467
National Reading Conference, Inc.: 1011
National Recreation and Park Association: 1848
National Rehabilitation Association: 1515
National Research Council of Canada: 1645, 1646, 1716, 1812, 2076, 2136, 2312
The National Safety Council: 618, 1840
National Scholastic Press Association: 884
National School Boards Association: 912
National Science Foundation: 606
National Science Foundation, Interagency Arctic Research Coordinating Committee: 608
National Science Teachers Association: 991, 1072, 1074
National Society for Performance and Instruction: 978, 1043
National Society for the Prevention of Blindness, Inc:
National Society of Public Accountants: 738
National Trust for Historic Preservation: 24
National Vocational Guidance Association: 1096
The National Writers Club: 879
Natural Law Forum, Inc.: 1198
Nebraska Library Association: 295
Nebraska State Historical Society: 1169
Netherlands Society of Dermatologists: 2331
Neurotics Anonymous International Liaison, Inc.: 1433
New England Aquarium: 1806
New Jersey Council for Geographic Education: 1100
New Jersey Education Association: 1042
The New Jersey Historical Society: 1170
New Jersey School Boards Association: 1040
New Jersey State Bar Association: 1264
New York Entomological Society: 2015
New York Institute of Clinical Oral Pathology: 2516
New York Law School: 1265
New York Public Library: 297
New York State Association for Health, Physical Education and Recreation: 1044
New York State Bar Association: 1266
New York State Department of Mental Hygiene: 1463
New York State English Council: 966
New York State Historical Association: 1173
New York State Nurses Association: 2527
New York State School Boards Association, Inc.: 1041
New York State Society of Certified Public Accountants: 732
New York University: 133
New York University, Institute of Retail Management: 783
New York University, School of Law: 1246

References in Index refer to entry numbers

New York University, School of the Arts: 153
Newberry College: 425
The Newberry Library: 104
The Non-Destructive Testing Society of Great Britain: 2025
North American Society for Corporate Planning, Inc.: 795
North Carolina Division of Archives and History: 1174
North Carolina Law Review Association: 1269
North Carolina Medical Society: 2448
North Dakota State Bar Association: 1270
North Texas State University: 99, 422
Northeast Modern Language Association of America: 231
Northern Arizona Society of Science and Art, Inc.: 696
Northwest Scientific Association: 1614
Northwestern University: 431, 1247
Northwestern University School of Law: 1243
Nova Scotia Department of Education: 994
The NTL Institute for Applied Behavioral Science: 718

O

Office de la Prévention l'Alcoolisme et des Autres Toxicomanies: 1529
Office of the Secretary of Defense: 1319
Ohio Academy of Religion: 585
Ohio Academy of Science: 1615
Ohio Association of Secondary School Principals: 914
Ohio Historical Society: 1175
Ohio Library Association: 303
Ohio State Medical Association: 2451
Oklahoma Geological Survey: 1675, 1676
Oklahoma State Medical Association: 2452
Oklahoma University College of Law: 1272
Omicron Delta Epsilon, International Honor Society in Economics: 746
Ontario Association for Mathematics Education: 2216
The Ontario Institute for Studies in Education: 982
Ontario Modern Language Teachers' Association: 202
Ontario Psychological Association: 1455
Ontario Public School Men Teachers Federation: 951
Operational Research Society, Ltd.: 838
Operations Research Society of America: 2217
Optical Society of America: 2023
Oregon Association for Supervision and Curriculum Development: 1045
The Oregon Dental Association: 2517
Oregon Historical Society: 1176
Oregon State University, Graduate School: 977
Organ Historical Society, Inc.: 195
Organization of American Historians: 1149
The Ottawa Field-Naturalist's Club: 1864
The Otto Rank Association: 1456

P

The Pacific Coast Entomological Society: 2017
Pacific Northwest Library Association: 305
The Palm Society: 1972
Parapsychology Foundation: 1457
The Pathological Society of Great Britain and Ireland: 2398
Pattern Recognition Society: 2243
Peabody Museum of Salem: 1119
Pennsylvania Library Association: 304
Pennsylvania School Boards Association: 1054
The Percussive Arts Society: 182, 1048
The Perkin-Elmer Corporation: 2175
Phi Alpha Theta: 1139
Phi Sigma Iota Romance Language Honor Society: 239
Philadelphia College of Pharmacy and Science: 2270
Philosophy of Education Society: 958, 1083
Philosophy of Science Association: 463
Philosophy Education Society, Inc.: 468
Phonemic Spelling Council: 1080
Phycological Society of America: 1960
Physical Society of Japan: 2147

Pi Gamma Mu: 719
Pi Lambda Theta: 952
Planned Parenthood Federation of America, Inc.: 1505
Planning Transport Associates, Inc.: 1599
Policy Studies Organization: 1346
The Poultry Science Association, Inc.: 2549
Powder Advisory Centre: 1782
Princeton University, Center of International Studies: 625
Princeton University Press: 460
The Private Libraries Association: 306
Professional Photographers of America, Inc.: 2612
Professional Productivity Associates: 58
Professional Rehabilitation Workers with the Adult Deaf, Inc.: 1516
Program in American Indian Studies: 679
Project Innovation: 938, 948, 1057
Protestant Episcopal Cathedral Foundation: 1641
Province St. Albert the Great: 552
Psychiatry and Social Science Book Club: 1482
The Psychological Association of Scandinavia: 1485
Psychonomic Society, Inc.: 1374, 1448, 1458
Public Relations Society of America, Inc.: 848

Q
Queen's University: 45

R
The Rabbinical Assembly,: 550
Radiation Research Society: 2185
The Radiological Society of America, Inc.: 2472
The Rationalist Press Association: 38
The Reformed Church in America: 544
The Reformed Church in America, Theological Seminaries: 592
Refractories Association of Great Britain: 2616
The Regional Studies Association: 1852
Religion and Society, Inc.: 593
The Religious Education Association: 1060
The Religious Research Association, Inc.: 596
Renaissance Society of America: 108
Research in Electrocardiology, Inc.: 2386
Research Center for Prosthetics: 2304
Research Center for Religion and Human Rights in Closed Societies, Ltd.: 591
Research Council of Israel: 1602
Research Society for Victorian Periodicals: 123
Retail Credit Company: 768
Rhode Island Medical Society: 2476
Rice University: 646
Rocky Mountain Mathematics Consortium: 2218
Rocky Mountain Modern Language Association: 407
Rosenstiel School of Marine and Atmospheric Science: 1691
Royal Aeronautical Society: 2048
Royal African Society: 629
Royal Anthropological Institute: 1553
Royal Australasian College of Physicians: 2290
The Royal College of Obstetricians and Gynaecologists: 2299
Royal College of Obstetrics and Gynaecology, Australia and New Zealand Councils: 2291
The Royal College of Psychiatrists: 1378
The Royal Geographical Society: 1103
Royal Geographical Society: 1104
Royal Institute of International Affairs: 611, 626
The Royal Swedish Academy of Sciences: 2080, 2163
Royal United Services Institute for Defence Studies: 1329
Rural Sociological Society: 1558
Rutgers Institute of Jazz Studies: 166
Rutgers University: 798, 1517, 1886
Rutgers-Camden School of Law: 1283

S
St. Francis Xavier University: 472
St. John's Abbey, Collegeville, Minnesota: 598

References in Index refer to entry numbers

Publisher and sponsoring organization index

San José State University: 51
Saskatchewan School Trustees Association: 1071
The Scandinavian Association for Social Medicine: 2481
The Scandinavian Society of Rheumatologists: 2480
School Library Association: 309
School Science and Mathematics Association, Inc.: 1069
Schweizerischen Vereinigung für Radiologie: 2470
Science Associates/International, Inc.: 274
Science Fiction Research Association, Inc.: 358
The Scientific Research Company of North America, Inc.: 1587
Scientists and Engineers for Social and Political Action: 1622
Scientists' Institute for Public Information: 1821
Scots Philosophical Club: 458
Sears Foundation for Marine Research: 1694
Seismological Society of America: 1664
The Shaw Society: 414
The Sixteenth Century Studies Conference: 112, 1182
Smith College School for Social Work: 1525
Social and Rehabilitation Service: 1526
Societas Scientiarum Fennica: 2027
Society for American Archaeology: 1630
Society for Applied Learning Technology: 997
Society for Applied Spectroscopy: 2024
Society for Cinema Studies: 871
Society for Clinical and Experimental Hypnosis, Inc.: 1401
Society for College and University Planning: 1053
The Society for Computer Simulation: 2245, 2246
Society for Cryobiology: 1912
Society for Dermatology and Venereology of Switzerland: 2331
Society for Developmental Biology: 1916
Society for Economic Analysis, Ltd.: 799
Society for Ethnomusicology, Inc.: 157
Society for Experimental and Descriptive Malacology: 2011
Society for Experimental Biology: 1959
Society for Experimental Stress Analysis: 1736
Society for French-American Affairs: 662
Society for French Historical Studies: 1137
Society for General Microbiology: 1930
Society for General Systems Research: 2197
The Society for Geology Applied to Mineral Deposits: 1684
The Society for German-American Studies: 360
Society for Gynecologic Investigation: 2351
Society for History Education: 974
Society for Industrial and Applied Mathematics: 2219, 2220, 2221, 2222, 2223, 2224, 2244
Society for International Development: 705
Society for Investigative Dermatology: 2394
Society for Lung and Respiration Research: 2466
Society for Nutrition Education: 1008
Society for Personality Assessment, Inc.: 1437
Society for Personality Research Incorporated: 1486
The Society for Religion in Higher Education: 113
Society for Research in Child Development: 724
Society for Research in Music Education of the Music Educators National Conference: 1012
Society for Technical Communication: 863
Society for the Advancement of Material and Process Engineering (SAMPE): 1792, 1793
Society for the Experimental Analysis of Behavior, Inc.: 1411, 1422
Society for the History of Alchemy and Chemistry: 2065
Society for the History of Technology: 1184
Society for the Promotion of Roman Studies: 93
Society for the Publication of Acta Chirurgica Scandinavica: 2482, 2532, 2540, 2541
Society for the Scientific Study of Religion: 567
Society for the Scientific Study of Sex: 711
Society for the Study of Addiction: 1496
Society for the Study of Amphibians and Reptiles: 2001
The Society for the Study of Evolution: 1918
Society for the Study of Human Biology: 1888
The Society for the Study of Reproduction: 1899

Society for the Study of Social Biology: 717
The Society for Theatre Research: 193
Society for Thoracic Surgeons of Great Britain and Ireland: 2538
Society of American Archivists: 250
Society of American Foresters: 1831
The Society of Analytical Psychology, Ltd.: 1410
Society of Architectural Historians: 1643
Society of Biological Psychiatry: 1377
Society of Chemical Industry: 1884, 2041, 2075, 2084, 2100
Society of Die Casting Engineers, Inc.: 2576
Society of Exploration Geophysicists: 1651
Society of General Physiologists: 2388
Society of Industrial Accountants of Canada: 731
Society of Japanese Virologists: 1926
Society of Motion Picture and Television Engineers: 895
Society of Nematologists: 2006
Society of Photo-optical Instrumentation Engineers: 1781
Society of Plastics Engineers, Inc.: 1783, 2606
The Society of Population Ecology: 1557
The Society of Professional Investigators: 1287
Society of Professional Well Log Analysts, Inc.: 1657
Society of St. Paul: 587
The Society of the Sigma XI: 1587
Society of Toxicology: 2488
Society of Wood Science and Technology: 2629
Soil Conservation Society of America: 1841
South and West, Inc.: 522
South African Institute for Medical Research: 2484
South African Institute of Mining and Metallurgy: 1689
South Carolina Library Association: 312
South Dakota State Historical Society: 1181
South Dakota State Medical Association: 2485
Southeast Minnesota State College, Literature and American Language Program: 999
The Southeastern Library Association: 313
Southern Academy of Oral Pathologists: 2516
Southern Association of Colleges and Schools, Inc.: 1078
Southern Baptist Convention, Sunday School Board: 289
Southern California Jewish Historical Society: 1189
Southern Economic Association: 805
Southern Historical Association: 1158
Southern Illinois University, Edwardsville: 398
Southern Methodist University: 57, 1235
Southern Methodist University, School of Law: 1241
Southern Speech Communication Association: 899
Southwest Museum: 693
Southwestern American Indian Society,: 681
Southwestern American Literature Association: 417
Southwestern Social Science Association: 721
Special Libraries Association: 314
Speech Communication Association: 898, 900
Stanford University: 435, 661
State Bar Association of California: 1207
State Bar of Georgia: 1230
State Bar of Texas: 1293
State Historical Society of Colorado: 1133
State Historical Society of Iowa: 1179
State University of New York, Buffalo: 679
State University of New York at Buffalo, The Center for Immunology: 2362
State University of New York, Buffalo, Child Study Center: 1384
State University of New York, Fredonia: 152
Staten Island Institute of Arts and Sciences: 1624
Stephen F. Austin State University, School of Liberal Arts: 47
Steward Anthropological Society: 1570
The Stony Brook Foundation, Inc.: 1942
Student American Medical Association: 2446
Student Association for the Study of Hallucinogens, Inc.: 1514
Student Personnel Association for Teacher Education: 1081
The Sulphur Institute: 2126
Swedish Geophysical Society: 1666
The Swedish Natural Science Research Council (NFR): 1977

References in Index refer to entry numbers

T

T. M. C. Asser Institute,: 1262
Tampere Peace Research Institute: 1341
Tavistock Institute of Human Relations: 704
Tax Research Group Ltd.: 1292
Technical Association of the Pulp and Paper Industry: 2622
The Teilhard Centre for the Future of Man: 117
Tennessee Department of Conservation and Fish Commission: 1854
Tennessee Department of Public Welfare: 1528
Tennessee Folklore Society: 1571
Tennessee Library Association: 315
The Tennessee Ornithological Society: 2013
Texas Academy of Science: 1627
Texas Christian University: 486
Texas Dental Association: 2518
Texas Elementary Principals and Supervisors Association: 1089
Texas Library Association: 316
Texas Music Educators Association: 189
Texas Technological University, Textual Studies Institute,
  Department of English 338
Theodor Herzl Foundation: 34
The Thoracic Society: 2486
The Thoreau Fellowship, Inc.: 429
The Thoreau Society Inc.: 430
Topeka Public Library: 60
Towards Racial Justice: 46
Transaction, Inc.: 725
The Travel Research Association: 785
Trent University: 691

U 1093

Ukrainian Historical Association, Inc.: 663
Union College Character Research Project: 1381
Union Theological Seminary: 604
United Bible Societies: 589, 602
The United Chapters of Phi Beta Kappa: 3
United Methodist Church: 174
United Methodist Church, Commission on Archives and History:
  581
United Nations Educational, Scientific and Cultural Organization
  (UNESCO): 707
United States Advisory Committee on
  International Educational and Cultural Affairs: 983
United States Air Force: 1316, 1317
United States Army Command and General Staff College: 1325
United States Army Infantry School: 1320
United States Army War College: 1328
United States Catholic Conference: 576
United States Department of Labor: 1508
United States Department of the Army: 1323
United States Department of the Interior, Bureau of Reclamation:
  1851
United States Environmental Protection Agency, Office of
  Radiation Programs: 2184
United States International University: 1208
United States Institute for Theatre Technology: 192
United States National Student Association: 947
United States Office of Education: 909
United States Track Coaches Association: 1093
Università di Roma, Centro Educazione Professionale Assistenti
  Società: 706
University and College Theatre Association: 156
University of Adelaide, South Australia: 1893
The University of Alabama: 744
University of Alaska-Fairbanks, Geophysical Institute: 1780
University of Alberta, Faculty of Education: 904
University of Arizona: 324, 1122
University of Arkansas, Department of English: 426
University of Birmingham School of Education: 955
University of British Columbia: 512, 2598
University of British Columbia, Faculty of Commerce: 771
The University of Calgary, Faculty of Education: 998

University of California: 243
University of California at Berkeley, Los Angeles, and Irvine;
  Schools of Business Administration: 757
University of California, Berkeley: 636, 822
University of California, Engineers Joint Council: 1715
University of California, Los Angeles: 680
University of California, Los Angeles, African Studies Center: 127
University of California, Museum of Paleontology: 1661
University of Chicago, Department of Education: 1094
University of Chicago, Department of Education, and Graduate
  School of Education 963
University of Chicago, Department of Near Eastern Languages
  and Civilizations: 672
University of Chicago, Divinity School: 571
University of Chicago, Division of Humanities: 385
University of Chicago, Law School: 1300
University of Chicago, School of Social Service Administration:
  1527
University of Cincinnati: 1301
University of Cincinnati Medical Center: 2335
University of Colorado, Business Research Division: 760
University of Colorado, Institute of Arctic and Alpine Research:
  607
University of Detroit, School of Law: 1249
University of Durham: 82
University of Florida,: 751
University of Georgia: 359
University of Glasgow: 660
University of Hartford: 362
University of Hawaii: 237, 461, 1617
University of Illinois: 337, 958, 987, 1368
University of Illinois, Bureau of Economic and Business Research:
  797
University of Illinois, College of Law: 1303
University of Illinois, Graduate College: 218
University of Illinois, Graduate School of Library Science: 302
University of Iowa: 240
University of Iowa, Graduate College, School of Letters: 494
University of Kentucky, College of Business and Economics: 1833
University of Leeds: 369
University of Leiden: 1215
University of Manitoba: 506
University of Maryland: 1814
University of Maryland School of Law: 1257
University of Massachusetts, Graduate English Program: 382
University of Melbourne: 31
University of Miami: 1691
University of Miami, Center for Advanced International Studies:
  666
University of Michigan: 33, 2214
University of Michigan, Graduate School of Business
  Administration: 806
University of Michigan, Law School: 1304
University of Mississippi Law School: 1260
University of Missouri, Kansas City: 503
University of Montana, Bureau of Business and Economic
  Research: 790
University of New Mexico: 1171, 1548
University of New Mexico, School of Law: 1846
University of New South Wales Chemical Engineering
  Association: 1709
University of North Carolina at Greensboro: 793
University of North Carolina, Department of Romance
  Languages: 242
University of North Dakota School of Law,: 1270
University of Notre Dame: 1351, 2215
The University of Nottingham: 105, 396
University of Oregon: 507
University of Pennsylvania: 682, 807
University of Pennsylvania, Department of Romance Languages:
  212
University of Pittsburgh: 1542

Publisher and sponsoring organization index

University of Pittsburgh, Bureau of Business Research, Graduate
    School of Busine 794
University of Rajasthan, South Asia Studies Centre: 645
University of St. Andrews: 458
University of San Francisco, School of Law: 1306
University of Singapore, History Department: 643
University of South Dakota: 515
University of Southern California: 456, 1568
University of Southern California, School of International
    Relations: 1358
University of Southern Mississippi: 499
University of Sydney: 1556
University of Texas, Department of Germanic Languages: 204
University of Texas at Arlington, Department of English: 322
The University of Texas at Houston: 119
University of Texas School of Law: 1294
University of the Pacific: 1177
University of the South: 411
University of Toronto, Graduate Center for the Study of Drama:
    171
University of Tulsa: 367
University of Utah: 125
University of Victoria: 498
The University of Washington: 1663
University of Windsor: 65
University of Wisconsin: 73, 134, 777
University of Wisconsin Press: 1238
Urban Land Institute: 1856
Utah Law Review Society: 1309
Utah Library Association: 318

V

Valparaiso University: 16
Vanderbilt University: 113
Verband deutschsprachiger Autoren in Amerika: 441
Vergilian Society Inc.: 433
Vermont Department of Libraries: 319
Vermont Historical Society: 1185
Vermont Library Association: 319
Vermont Library Trustees Association: 319
Veterans Administration: 2304
Viniti: 2237
The Virginia Historical Society: 1187
Virginia Society of Certified Public Accountants: 741
Virginia State Library: 1186

W

W. T. Bandy Center for Baudelaire Studies: 329
Wagner College, Horrmann Library: 98
Washington Academy of Sciences: 1629
Washington Province of Discalced Carmelite Fathers, Inc.: 600
Washington State University: 354, 401
Water Pollution Control Federation: 1859
Webster College: 523
Wellcome Institute for the History of Medicine: 2427
Wenner-Gren Foundation for Anthropological Research: 1540
West Virginia University: 249
West Virginia University, Bureau of Business Research: 832
Western Economic Association: 763
Western History Association: 1188
Western Literature Association: 438
Western Political Science Association: 1360
Western Washington State College: 1420
The Wharton School: 807
The Wilderness Society: 1844
Wildlife Disease Association: 2548, 2554
The Wildlife Society, Inc.: 1842
William Alanson White Psychiatric Foundation, Inc.: 1464
Williams College: 74
The Wire Association: 2628
Wisconsin Department of Public Instruction, Division for Library
    Services: 321

Witwatersrand University: 84
World Council of Churches, Commission on World Mission and
    Evangelism: 566
World Federation for Ultrasound in Medicine and Biology: 2490
World Federation of Neurology: 2402
The World Future Society: 23
World Peace Foundation, Boston, Massachusetts: 1238
World Research, Inc.: 42
World Wildlife Fund: 1825
Wright State University: 873
Wyoming Geological Association: 1648
Wyoming State Archives and Historical Department: 1121

Y

Yale University: 126, 167
Yeshiva University, Sephardic Studies Program: 532, 597
York College: 199

References in Index refer to entry numbers

A

Aaboe, A.: 1588
Abbott, R. Tucker: 2014
Abelson, Philip H.: 1621
Abercromby, Alison: 2282
Ablin, Fred: 759
Abplanalp, H.: 1944
Abt, Helmut A.: 2059, 2060
Acheson, T. William: 1112
Ackermann, Paul Kurt: 9
Adams, Eleanor B.: 1171
Adams, George M.: 1042
Addison, Max: 1196
Adler, Claire: 2197
Adler, Marjorie: 610, 617
Adler, Wendy J.: 24
Agras, Dr. Stewart: 1411
Ahart, Alan: 1204
Akert, Konrad: 2295
Albert, Barbara L.: 150
Albert, Robert H.: 842
Alberts, Mark E.: 1229
Albright, Paul: 1290
Alder, Berni J.: 2150
Alderdice, Dr. D. F.: 1690
Aldridge, A. Owen: 337
Alexander, Jaclyn J.: 1049
Alexander, Rosemary: 980
Algeo, John: 196
Allard, R. W.: 1944
Allen, Richard B.: 1192
Allen, Robert L.: 609
Allen, Victor H.: 895
Allio, Robert J.: 795
Alrich, William M.: 807
Altbach, Philip G.: 972
Alter, Professor Dr. M.: 2403
Altmann, Dr. H. W.: 1945
Amabile, George: 506
Amidei, Rosemary: 991
Ammons, Carol H.: 1473
Anders, Don: 733
Anderson, David: 2544
Anderson, Dole A.: 791
Anderson, Hilton: 395
Anderson, Mary J.: 317
Anderson, Paul J.: 2111
Anderson, Dr. Stuart: 1914, 1935
Andover, James J.: 810
Andrews, A. James: 2242
Andrews, Colman: 12
Andrews, John F.: 413
Andrews, Dr. Robert J.: 1076
Andrews, Valerie: 1482
Anglin, Betty: 1520
Angoff, Charles: 377
Angrist, Alfred A.: 2447
Annis, Susan J.: 1451
Anozie, Lynda S.: 633, 634
Anozie, Dr. Sunday O.: 633, 634
Ansbacher, H. L.: 1432
Antonson, Rick: 1126
Appling, Gregory B.: 701
Apte, S.V.: 2363
Araoz, Dr. Daniel L.: 1425
Arbib, Robert: 1978
Archer, Dr. Margaret S.: 1541
Arena, John I.: 901
Arguello, Michael: 713
Ariek, Bess E.: 2281
Arieti, Silvano: 1362
Aris, Prof. R.: 1722, 2194

Arlow, Jacob A.: 1466
Arnold, Alvin L.: 820
Arnold, Brian C.: 256
Aronson, Leonard: 880
Aschemeier, John: 2305
Ash, Lee: 68
Ash, Marian Neal: 68
Ash, Rene L.: 2587
Ashenhurst, Robert L.: 2226
Asquith, Peter D.: 463
Atchison, Roberta: 831, 889, 2284, 2329, 2358, 2474, 2475
Atkins, Russell: 491
Atkins, Thomas R.: 874
Atmore, A.E.: 629
Aumann, Jordan: 590
Aviram, Joseph: 1637
Ax, Professor Dr. Peter: 1997
Axelby, George S.: 1710

B

Bach, Martin: 975
Bach, Robert: 869
Bach-y-Rita, P.: 621 876
Bahn, Catherine I.: 1124
Bailey, Harold Whitney: 876
Bailey, Janet Dee: 314
Bain, Roy B.: 804
Bakalinsky, Eric L.: 7
Baker, James M.: 167
Baker, John F.: 858
Baker, Karl: 1283
Baker, Robert J.: 2004
Baker, William C.: 1024
Balaban, Miriam: 1595
Balcerak, Carl: 1033
Baldwin, A. R.: 2067
Baler, Lenin A.: 1386
Bales, Jack: 392
Ballard, Stanley: 160
Bamborough, John B.: 404
Bandy, W. T.: 329
Bardis, Dr. Panos D.: 719
Barham, Thomas J.: 1320
Barker, Dr. K. R.: 2006
Barker, Thomas A.: 154
Barlow, H.: 621
Barnes, Ian M.: 2025
Barnes, L. W.: 234
Barr, William R.: 575
Barron, David W.: 2247
Barry, H.: 1479
Bartlett, Carol: 1218
Bartlett, Clifford: 260
Basehart, Harry: 1548
Bass, Frank M.: 780
Bass, I. Scott: 1304
Bassey, Linus A.: 630
Batchelor, Prof. G. K.: 2035
Bateman, J.: 69
Batley, Edward M.: 232
Batten, Earl L.: 1648
Battison, Geoffrey W.: 2583
Batts, M. S.: 244
Baughman, M. Dale: 943
Bauke, Joseph Padur: 209
Baxter, Glenn W.: 639
Baxter, Richard R.: 1197
Bayldon, Margaret C.: 1336
Ba-Yunus, Ilgas: 622
Bazett, D. J.: 1645

Beach, Walter E.: 1349
Beadles, William T.: 784
Bealer, Robert C.: 1558
Beales, D. E. D.: 1140
Beament, Professor J. W. L.: 1883
Beardsley, Charles W.: 1744
Beaton, G. R.: 2484
Beaton, W. G.: 2550
Beaumont, S. D.: 215
Beck, Rochelle: 971
Becker, Gerald A.:
    1816, 1910, 1911, 2089,
    2138, 2327, 2328
Becker, Walter E.: 2104
Bedal, Carl L.: 1068
Bedell, Laureen: 1267
Bedworth, Albert E.: 1510
Beebe, Maurice: 370
Behague, Gerard: 157
Behm, Tom F.: 137
Beigel, Hugo G.: 711
Beilin, Harry: 1423
Beiser, Rhoda: 2304
Beker, Jerome: 1499
Beless, Rosemary: 407
Bell, Albert R. H.: 1311
Bell, D. R.: 2282
Bell, Gwen K.: 702
Bell, Tom: 102
Bellman, Richard: 2205
Belshaw, Cyril S.: 1540
Benario, Dr. Janice M.: 433
Bender, Byron W.: 237
Bennett, James R.: 426
Benninghoff, Hanns: 2029
Benton, W. Duane: 1315
Beran, John A.: 2293
Bercholz, Samuel: 578
Berdon, Dr. W. E.: 2458
Berezin, Martin A.: 1428
Bergbusch, Martin L. T.: 664
Bergeron, George A.: 2418
Berkley, Carl: 2431
Berkowitz, Frank: 2581
Berkwitt, George J.: 2591
Berner, Prof. Dr. P.: 1461
Bernstein, Lawrence F.: 132
Bernstein, Professor H. J.: 2162
Berry, John N.: 285
Berry, Dr. Margaret C.: 1577
Bershader, Prof. D.: 2161
Berton, Peter A.: 1358
Bessom, Malcolm E.: 1034
Betchkal, James: 912
Bethge, W.: 241
Beutler, Frederick J.: 2219
Bevan, Allan R.: 18, 81
Bianchi, Jan: 1236
Biblarz, Dora: 861
Bicknell, Peggy: 2585
Bidnead, Margaret J.: 255
Bidwell, Charles E.: 1532
Bidwell, R.G.S.: 1329
Biegert, Prof. Dr. J.: 1990
Bigelow, Robert P.: 1216, 1254
Biggers, John D.: 1899
Biggs, Robert D.: 672
Biles, Robert: 722
Binder, L. James: 1318
Bingham, N. E.: 1073
Biondi, Angelo M.: 992

References in Index refer to entry numbers

Editorial staff index

Birdsall, Stephen S.: 1111
Bisbee, Margaret K.: 1524
Björk, Viking Olov: 2541
Blackburn, Jean: 922, 1383, 1386, 1442, 1443, 1488, 1501
Blackman, Margaret: 77
Blackwell, Kenneth: 469
Blackwood, A. Clark: 1906
Blackwood, Douglas: 75
Blades, Brian: 2538
Blair, Don: 2452
Blake, William Henry: 811
Blazer, John A.: 1476
Bleznick, Donald W.: 211
Blissett, W. F.: 122
Bloch, Donald A.: 1506
Block, Bradford E.: 1225
Bloice, Carl: 43
Bloom, Martin H.: 2231
Bloss, Dr. F. Donald: 1678
Blum, Harold P.: 1369
Bodey, Donald: 507
Boehme-Vargas, Guillermo: 2577
Bohrnstedt, George W.: 1562
Bolen, James Grayson: 1465
Boley, Prof. Bruno A.: 1774
Bolin, Bert: 1666
Bond, Jean Carey: 365
Bonjean, Charles M.: 721
Bookhout, Theodore A.: 1842
Boolden, Larry L.: 1711
Borel, Prof. Armand: 2193
Boretz, Benjamin: 184
Borgatta, Edgar F.: 1562
Borgers, Alfons: 449, 2210
Borich, Patrick J.: 1000
Bork, Albert W.: 58
Bors, Eleanore M.: 2273
Borts, George H.: 745
Borysewicz, Mary L.: 2268
Boshkov, Stefan R.: 1213
Bostian, Irma R.: 273
Bott, Prof. R.: 2225
Bouliere, F.: 2349
Bouman, H. D.: 2271
Bourg, Carroll J.: 599
Bourgea, Ron: 1526
Bouxsein, Peter: 1308
Bower, Catherine: 840
Bower, Donald E.: 879
Boyce, W. E.: 2224
Boyd, George A.: 1659
Boydston, Grover: 1433
Boyer, Paul D.: 1896
Boyers, Robert: 50
Brace, Michele J.: 1012
Braceland, Francis J.: 1367
Bradfisch, Jean: 1700
Bradley, Bert E.: 899
Bradley, Derek: 950
Bradley, P. B.: 2442
Bradley, R. C.: 1089
Bradtke, Joel H.: 845
Brady, Michael: 1218
Bragg, David: 1201
Bramble, James H.: 2212
Brand, C. P.: 230
Brandfonbrenner, Prof. Martin: 2381
Brandt, Carol: 1113, 1322
Branion, H. D.: 2549
Braun, H. Myron: 174
Brennan, Joseph Payne: 490

Breton, Raymond: 1538
Breul, Frank R.: 1527
Brewer, John I.: 2267
Bricker, Victoria: 1531
Briggs, Miss G. M.: 259
Bright, William: 222
Briley, Alice S.: 488
Brittin, Norman A.: 56
Brock, William H.: 2065
Broderick, Carlfred B.: 1513
Brodie, Deborah: 550
Brody, Eugene B.: 2400
Brody, Dr. Harold: 617
Brooks, Robert J.: 1202
Brossman, Donald G.: 1041
Brother Peter: 582
Brown, Andrew H.: 1108
Brown, Betty Byers: 200
Brown, Dr. Elizabeth A. R.: 120
Brown, Gina: 1780
Brown, H. Douglas: 223
Brown, Herbert Ross: 390
Brown, Lawrence D.: 1350
Brown, Lawrence L.: 563
Brown, Marice C.: 1554
Brown, Robert: 442
Brown, Spencer H.: 616
Brown, Walter L.: 1123
Browne, Ray B.: 1551
Bruce, Carol: 866
Bruce, F. F.: 559
Brundle, Dr. C. R.: 2034
Brune, K.: 2252
Brunjes, Jean T.: 2495
Bruno, James N.: 835
Bruns, Gerald L.: 228
Brush, William K.: 2608
Bryan, Bruce: 693
Bryan, Miriam M.: 952
Bryant, Christopher: 458
Bryner, John H.: 2548, 2554
Bube, Richard H.: 531
Buck-Gramcko, D.: 2534
Buckley, Priscilla L.: 36
Buffham, B. A.: 1721
Bukus, Jim: 2611
Bull, George: 762
Buller, Melvin C.: 920
Bullock, Michael: 512
Bumbarger, C.S.: 926
Burack, A. S.: 865
Burch, George E.: 2259
Burdin, Joel L.: 1014
Burger, Alfred: 2114
Burghardt, Walter J.: 603
Burhoe, Ralph Wendell: 605
Burke, Louis: 478
Burke, Robert G.: 1660
Burley, Mrs. Terry M.: 2596
Burnett, Joe R.: 958
Burnett, Norman: 1064
Burnham, Donald L.: 1464
Burns, Kenneth: 1233
Burr, Samuel Engle: 1131
Busch, Professor Dr. G.: 2169
Bush, Louise: 1902
Buttell, Louis G.: 2275
Buttenheim, Curtis R.: 1194
Button, Warren: 1095

C

Cabrera, Vincente: 373

Cain, Glen G.: 777
Calcraft, M.: 2168
Calkins, Jacqueline W.: 1399
Callenbach, Ernest: 875
Callihan, Dixon: 2182
Camburn, Robert A.: 165
Cameron, J. Malcolm: 2434
Cameron, Rondo: 774
Campbell, Joyce M.: 848
Campbell, Prof. Dan H.: 2095
Campbell, Robert W.: 742
Campion, Donald R.: 527
Canaday, Dayton W.: 1181
Canavor, Natalie: 2594
Cansdale, James H.: 1705, 2566
Cantrall, Irving J.: 1992
Canty, Donald: 129
Capon, Edmund: 181
Caraley, Demetrios: 1348
Carden, Terrence S.: 2446
Cardona-Hine, Alvaro: 1163
Carette, Nicole: 1110
Carey, J. A.: 2496
Carey, Joanna A.: 2496
Carles, Philippe: 161
Carley, Kenneth A.: 1167
Carlson, Dr. T. A.: 2034
Carmony, Donald F.: 1145
Carney, Mary Margaret: 952
Carrier, Prof. G. F.: 2035
Carroll, Anne: 1436
Carroll, Marguerite R.: 1067
Carter, Donald E.: 1384
Carter, Jack L.: 908
Carter, Patricia: 1575
Carter, Paul: 13
Carter, Ross: 261
Carver, Wayne M.: 480
Cary, Richard: 335
Case, John: 727
Casini, Barbara P.: 268
Cassak, Albert L.: 2621
Cassel, Lan M.: 938, 948, 1057
Cassel, Russell N.: 938, 948, 1057
Cassidy, Robert: 1274
Castañeda, Hector-Neri: 455
Castle, Raymond N.: 2110
Cate, Jean M.: 2018
Cattell, McKeen: 2383
Catterall, R.C.F.: 2536
Cauman, Leigh S.: 447
Cavalier, Elwood A.: 1494
Cayer, David: 166
Cayton, Robert F.: 303
Chabot, Rénald: 1529
Chalmers, Prof. Bruce: 1701, 1794
Chambers, Bradford: 365
Chance, Paul B.: 1478
Chang, Prof. T. S.: 2170
Chapman, Mary Lewis: 378
Chartier, Armand B.: 231
Cheadle, B. D.: 84
Chernofsky, Jacob L.: 849
Chiarelli, Prof. A. B.: 2002
Chrisman, Robert: 609
Christ, John M.: 294
Christensen, Richard M.: 1982
Christian, Charles L.: 2287
Christiansen, Marie D.: 1243, 1271
Church, Margaret: 384
Ciferri, Orio: 1969
Clabault, James M.: 748

References in Index refer to entry numbers

Claesson, Stig: 2080
Clareson, Thomas D.: 358
Clark, James W.: 1677
Clark, Leslie L.: 1492
Clarke, Sir Cyril: 2397
Clarke, Edwin: 2427
Clarke, Norris: 445
Clarke, Robert L.: 2167
Clarkson, Dr. M.J.: 2547
Clauser, H. R.: 1619
Clayton, Howard: 282
Clemens, Cyril: 381
Cleveland, Forrest F.: 2172
Click, Professor J. W.: 882
Clifford, G. D.: 1790
Clifford, James L.: 368
Clogan, Prof. Paul: 99
Clower, Robert W.: 763
Coakley, William L.: 297
Cobbett, Peter Albert:
    2051, 2052
Coccola, Richard A.: 2579
Codrea, John E.: 1211
Coffey, John J.: 789
Coffey, Timothy G.: 1517
Cogan, Neil H.: 1235
Cohan, Professor A.: 816
Cohen, Fred: 1221
Cohen, Dr. Monroe D.: 933
Cohen, Norm: 162
Cohen, Ralph: 391
Cohen, Selma Jeanne: 148
Cohn, Emma: 270
Cohn, Gunther: 1596
Coker, Fred W.: 250
Cole, D. T.: 631
Cole, Martin: 1115
Cole, Professor Jonathan O.: 1479
Coleman, James: 1559
Collins, D. Jean: 73, 134
Collins, Laurence W.: 2628
Collins, Mary Frances: 267
Collins, R.A.: 1810
Collins, R.G.: 386
Collins, Raymond F.: 577
Colman, Bruce E.: 1847
Colquitt, Betsy Feagan: 486
Comfort, Dr. A.: 2344
Comfort, W. Wistar: 2190
Como, William: 147
Compton, Dr. Frank: 2502
Compton, Robert D.: 1733
Connolly, P. H.: 283
Connor, Timothy: 639
Connors, John P.: 2467
Conover, Barbara: 2287
Cook-Radmore, D.: 215
Cookson, William: 470
Cooper, Carlos M.: 2551
Cooper, Dr. Cary L.: 1406
Cooper, John Christopher: 1731
Cooper, Prof. E. H.: 1907
Copley, Alfred L.: 1901, 2487
Coppola, Carlo: 372
Corbett, Edward P. J.: 936
Coriell, Vern W.: 331
Cornell, F. J.: 279
Cornish, Edward S.: 23
Cornish, Sally W.: 23
Corrigan, John T.: 266, 287
Corsini, Raymond J.: 1432
Costa, E.: 2442

Costantino, Josephine: 963
Cotten, Marion deV.: 2409, 2462
Cotton, John: 306
Courtney, Charles: 555
Coviello, Roselle: 220
Cowan, James C.: 343
Cox, Anthony J.: 2156
Cox, C. B.: 340
Craddick, I. H.: 91
Craddick, Ray A.: 91
Craig, Alan M.: 2019
Craig, James B.: 1804
Craig, Richard A.: 2032
Cramer, Curtis: 746
Cranefield, Paul F.: 2388
Cranfill, Thomas M.: 119
Cravitz, Susan: 1455
Crawford, Bryce: 2118
Creager, Joe S.: 1663
Creutzfeldt, Professor Dr. W.: 2333
Croft, Arthur C.: 841
Crone, W. R.: 1741
Cross, Michael S.: 10, 1127
Crowl, John: 934
Cullen, Donald E.: 821
Cully, Iris V.: 595
Cully, Kendig Brubaker: 595
Culp, William H.: 1397
Cumming, Robert: 173
Cundiff, Edward W.: 779
Current-Garcia, Eugene: 56
Currier, Susan: 382
Curry, Wesley: 2360
Curtis, Marcia S.: 382
Curwen, C. A.: 709

D

Dafoe, Gerald H.: 2313
Dahl, Norman: 1498
Dale, Peter: 470
Dales, G. G.: 1093
Dalessio, Donald John: 2354
Dalton, Harriet: 1283
Dalven, Dr. Rachel: 597
Daly, Lowrie J.: 96
Dane, Chase: 263
Daniel, Dave R.: 1038
Daniel, George B.: 242
Danielli, James F.: 1933
Darack, Arthur: 15
Das, Man Singh: 1545
Daunt, John G.: 2152
Davenport, Alan G.: 1716
Davidse, Gerritt: 1964
Davidson, Clifford: 143
Davidson, Park O.: 1380
Davies, Dr. David: 1613
Davies, Elizabeth J.: 2464
Davies, Ernest: 1799
Davies, Mrs. R.: 2377
Davis, Beverly Jeanne: 918, 1082
Davis, Douglas F.: 1839
Davis, George H.: 1861
Davis, George M.: 2010
Davis, Julie S.: 99
Davis, Ronald J.: 1227
Davis, Sharon: 137
Davis, Vincent: 1355
Dawson, George G.: 993
Day, Robert A.: 1890, 1894, 1925, 1927,
    2283, 2365, 2416
Deans, Robert H.: 776

Deasy, Clara L.: 2561
de Boer, H.: 1885
DeCicco, Paul R.: 1838
Deedy, John: 548
Deese, James: 1469
de Groot, S. J.: 1690
Deichmann, Professor Dr. William B.: 2286
D'Elia, Joseph A.: 1510
D'Iorio, Antoine: 2076
DeJong, Russell N.: 2441
de Levie, R.: 2108
Delmas, A.: 2249
Deman, J. M.: 1865
De Marco, Joseph P.: 462
de Mause, Lloyd: 1395
Dembo, L. S.: 339
Dempsey, Hugh A.: 1114
Denerstein, Robert L.: 627
Dengler, Professor Dr. H. J.: 2341
Dennis, Barbara D.: 777
Denton, Dr. J.: 2139
Derolez, Prof. R.: 353
Déry, André: 141
de Serres, F. J.: 1937
Deutsch, Eliot: 461
DeVelis, John B.: 1781
DeVivo, Anita: 1391, 1409,
    1417, 1475
Dewel, B. F.: 2497
de Wied, D.: 2342
Diamond, Gerald X.: 1702
Dicke, Karen P.: 785
Dickenson, F. E.: 1976
Dickinson, James C.: 1081
Diercks, Louis: 138
Dietz, Janet: 208
Di Giore, J. Anthony: 1028
Dilworth, Cathy L.: 2525
Dinman, Professor Dr. B.D.: 2368
Dion, Gérard: 828
Di Scala, Spencer: 651
Distad, N. Merrill: 123
Divine, Thomas F.: 788
Dixon, Frank C.: 2090
Dixon, John Morris: 1642
Dixon, Joyce A.: 1220
Dixon, Rob: 989
Doak, P. E.: 2037
Dobrinsky, Herbert: 532
Doctorow, Donald: 2559
Dodd, D. C.: 2553
Dodge, Frederick A.: 1863
Doerr, Edd: 546
Doerr, Dr. W.: 2492
Doherty, William O.: 735
Doll, Paul N.: 1777
Dombrower, Ralph L.: 1310
Domenjoz, Dr. R.: 2463
Domning, Daryl P.: 1661
Donaldson, J. A.: 2500
Donaldson, Robert M.: 2347
Donelson, Kenneth L.: 917
Donlan, Walter: 79
Donnell, John D.: 1193
Donno, Elizabeth Story: 108
Donohue, E. Dolores: 1542
Donohue, Judge Michael J.: 1219
Donovan, Professor B. T.: 2387
Dopuch, Nicholas: 736
Dorfman, Wilfred: 1480
Dorney, Cathryn Laurentia: 956
Dougherty, Dr. J. P.: 2161

References in Index refer to entry numbers

Editorial staff index

Dougherty, Jude P.: 468
Dougherty, Percy H.: 1100
Dougherty, Dr. Richard M.: 277
Doughtie, Edward: 421
Douglas, George H.: 850, 852
Douglas, Norman E.: 809
Douglass, D. L.: 2040
Dowl, Barbara DeSha: 2522
Downs, Colonel Eldon W.: 1317
Doyen, John I.: 2017
Doyle, Paul A.: 356, 502
Doyle, Sandra: 1124
Drake, Marjorie Look: 487
Dreiling, David A.: 2264
Dreisziger, Nandor F.: 648
Driscoll, Veronica M.: 2527
Duchesneau, Dr. Francois: 443
Duffey, Dr. Eric: 1809
Duffy, John C.: 1383
Duncan, Lester E.: 312
Dunkin, William S.: 1519
Dunkley, Bernard: 1732, 1746
Dunn, Richard L.: 2607
Dunn, Robert W.: 764
Dunne, Gerald T.: 1200
Dunworth, J. V.: 2174
Dupree, Robert S.: 334
Durken, Daniel: 598
Dykshorn, Janice M.: 1183
Dyne, Prof. P. J.: 2144
Dyson, A. E.: 340
Dziekonski, Chester B.: 2273

E

Eaborn, C.: 2116
Eagleton, Rosemary: 584
Eames, William: 2216
Earle, Prof. David P.: 2381
Early, Stephen B.: 1241
Easlick, Kenneth A.: 2514
Easson, Kay Parkhurst: 327
East, Maurice: 1355
Easton, Miriam: 504
Eaves, Morris: 326
Eayrs, James: 612
Ebersole, A. V.: 213
Eckenfelder, W. W.: 1860
Eckhardt, Caroline D.: 986
Eckhardt, Robert B.: 986
Eckstein, Harry: 1354
Edd, Karl: 501
Edinborough, Arnold: 183
Edmonston, Dr. William E.: 1365
Edwards, John Nelson: 1565
Edwards, Keith J.: 1559
Effrat, Andrew: 982, 1561
Efron, Arthur: 399
Ehmann, Janet: 1837
Ehrlich, Arnold W.: 858
Eichelberger, Clayton L.: 322
Eichler, Margrit: 1575
Eicholtz, Virginia T.: 1449
Eichwald, E. J.: 2489
Eilon, Prof. Samuel: 837
Einstein, Dr. Stanley: 1503
Eisenberg, Prof. Leon: 1414
Ekker, Charles: 58
Elfenbaum, Arthur: 2498
Elias, Arthur W.: 252
Elkin, A. P.: 1556
Ellingworth, P.: 602
Elliott, Norman John: 1071

Ellis, Dr. John: 2298
Ellsworth, S. George: 1188
Elsila, David A.: 915, 932
Elwood, R. Carter: 647
Emeléus, H. J.: 2109
Emerson, Everett: 347
Emmons, Terence: 657
Emsley, Michael G.: 1903
Engstrom, Georgiana: 1098
Enloe, Cortez F.: 2450
Enticknap, Nicholas: 2235
Entwistle, Prof. Noel J.: 923
Epstein, Edmund L.: 94
Epstein, Joseph: 3
Erades, L.: 1262
Erdman, David V.: 297
Ericksen, Charles W.: 1458
Erickson, John D.: 376
Erickson, Richard J: 1316
Eringen, Prof. A. C.: 1748, 1768
Ernst, Dr. Eldon: 560
Eron, Leonard: 1409
Erskine, Thomas L.: 379
Esau, Dwight B.: 1065
Eshelman, William R.: 320
Esser, Ada R.: 1845
Esser, Aristide H.: 1845
Etris, Samuel F.: 1605, 1608, 1707
Ettling, Bruce V.: 1614
Ettre, L. S.: 1723
Eugster, H. P.: 1686
Evans, Dr. F. Gaynor: 2380
Evans, Frank L.: 1652
Evans, Les: 1342
Everly, Dr. Jack C.: 1035
Ewerbeck, Professor Dr. H.: 2407
Eyler, William R.: 2472
Eysenck, Prof. H. J.: 1375

F

Faatz, Anita J.: 1456
Fair, Clifford B.: 953
Fairbrother, Prof. F.: 2036
Faison, S. Lane: 74
Fales, Virginia B.: 767
Faller, Thompson M.: 64
Fallon, Pedraic: 813
Fanning, Thomas J.: 1489
Fantham, P. H. H.: 2196
Farber, Saul J.: 2266
Farner, Professor Dr. D. S.: 1908
Farr, Dr. Roger: 1058
Farrar, J. L.: 1812
Fateley, William B.: 2024
Fearon, Harold: 782
Feder, James L.: 1289
Feinberg, Charles E.: 436
Feinstein, Karen Wolk: 1573
Feinstein, Sherman C.: 1361
Feldbrugge, Prof. F. J. M.: 1280
Feldman, Joseph D.: 2392
Feldman, Robert P.: 1214
Feldmann, Edward G.: 2408
Feldmann, Kurt L.: 2184
Felknor, Rhea: 2531
Fellendorf, Dr. George W.: 1097
Felts, John H.: 2448
Fenner, Mildred S.: 1092
Fenton, Kathleen M.: 224
Ferguson, Arthlyn: 1052
Ferguson, Gerard A.: 1273
Ferguson, Mary H.: 2408

Ferguson, Oliver W.: 55
Ferguson, Sharon: 1368
Fernbach, Sidney: 2150
Ferrara, V. Peter: 1429
Ferrazzarra, Doreen: 723
Ferris, J. M.: 2006
Fickelson, M.: 1772
Finlay, Victoria: 2337
Finley, George T.: 2589
Finn, Bernard S.: 1147
Finson, Bruce: 1616
Fischer-Galati, Stephen: 649
Fish, Richard H.: 1679
Fisher, D. G.: 2155, 2156, 2157, 2158, 2160, 2168
Fisher, Franklin: 407
Fisher, John: 163
Fisher, Prof. Harwood: 922
Fisher, Robert W.: 827
Fisk, James R.: 892
Fitts, William T.: 2414
Fitzer, E.: 2142
Flanigan, Daniel: 2601
Fleck, Dr. Richard: 429
Fleck, Dr. Stephen: 1487
Fleishman, Robert P.: 2515
Fleming, John G.: 1195
Fletcher, H. G.: 120
Flohil, Richard: 136
Florence, Leah: 668
Fluegel, Neal L.: 182
Foecke, J.: 2227
Folger, Robert G.: 1484
Fonss-Bech, Peter: 2098
Foote, Richard H.: 1629
Forbes, Gilbert B.: 2262
Ford, Eric F. J.: 414, 437
Ford, Dr. J. A.: 1728
Ford, Lewis S.: 466
Forrest, Hugh S.: 1897
Forth, Sally: 7
Fortner, E. N.: 524
Foti, Margaret: 2315
Fourdrinier, Sylvia: 1703
Fouts, Dr. J. R.: 2082
Fowler, Natalie: 2245, 2246
Fox, Hugh Bernard: 492
Fox, Leland S.: 180
Fox, René C.: 720
Francis, H. J.: 2128
Francke, Donald E.: 2335
Frank, Jerome P.: 1778
Frank, R. Van: 1376
Frank, William A.: 468
Frankenberg, Ronald: 1564
Franklin, Carl W.: 313
Franklin, Inks: 1066
Franks, Cyril M.: 1376
Fransen, P.: 536
Franzen, J.: 2145
Fraser, Andrew F.: 1979
Fraser, W.J.: 1162
Fratus, David: 493
Frazer, S. C.: 2085
Frazier, Robert G.: 2460
Frederickson, H. George: 1284
Freedberg, Irwin M.: 2394
Freedheim, Donald: 1460
Freedman, Lawrence R.: 2495
Freeman, Ann: 453
Freeman, Arthur: 2542, 2543
Freeman, Prof. Eugene: 453

References in Index refer to entry numbers

Frei, Dr. J.: 1917
French, Roberts: 351
French, V. H.: 2624
Freshwater, D. C.: 1721
Freund, John R.: 114
Frey, Bruno S.: 712
Frey, René: 712
Friedlander, Prof. S. K.: 2031
Friedman, B. A.: 2306
Friedman, Shelly Scott: 1204
Friedrich, R.: 1696
Fries, Bengt: 2532
Friis, Erik J.: 658
Fritz, Nancy J.: 983
Fritz, Prof. J. S.: 2128
Fry, Bernard: 276
Fry, Daniel W.: 63
Fry, Rev. E. McG.: 589
Fry, Morris: 72
Fry, Dr. R. M.: 2391
Fry, Timothy P.: 529
Frye, Ronald P.: 695, 1209
Fudenky, Hugh: 2323
Fuller, Gerald B.: 1477
Fulton, Len: 862
Funke, W.: 2043
Furlong, Norman: 309

G

Gaafar, S. M.: 2552
Gaines, Stanley J.: 552
Galambos, Louis: 774
Galanter, Marc: 1252
Galbraith, Leslie R.: 557
Galletti, Pierre M.: 2316
Gamel, Faye: 2522
Gani, J.: 2186, 2201
Gannett, Elwood K.: 1743
Gardner, Cynthia: 721
Garlington, Jack: 125
Garner, Donald P.: 130
Garrett, Dr. James L.: 568
Garrett, Ronald W.: 1787
Gary, Joe: 976
Gaston, Edwin W.: 47
Gates, D. M.: 1872
Gatewood, Thomas E.: 1031
Gatland, K. W.: 2055
Gaubatz, E.: 2466
Gaull, Marilyn S.: 439
Gebhardt, R. Bruce: 1264
Geiger, Paul: 2582
Geir, Phillip H.: 2153
Gelfand, M.: 2318
Gendlin, Eugene T.: 1483
Gengler, Charles: 1045
Genoways, Hugh H.: 2004
George, Warren E.: 164
Gerber, Helmut E.: 352
Gerbner, George: 853
Gerdis, Tom: 2181
Gerds, Gretchen: 2520
Gerhardt, Lillian N.: 310
Gerhart, Eugene C.: 1266
Germeles, Patricia A.: 1415
Gervais, Albert: 1022
Giacoman, Helmy F.: 389
Gibbs, Martin: 1967
Gibson, George H.: 1134
Giertz, Gustav: 2482
Gifford, Dr. Ernest M.: 1947
Gilbert, Elliot L.: 477

Gilchrist, A.D.B.: 275
Gildenberg, Prof. Dr. L.: 2326
Gildner, Judith A.: 1120
Gill, George A.: 988
Gilleland, LaRue W.: 1017
Gilliss, Thomas P.: 1212
Giorgi, Amedeo P.: 1439
Girard, J.: 2356
Gladney, Frank Y.: 245
Glanville, Charles Richard: 1657
Glasberg, Oscar S.: 2584
Glaser, Dr. Peter E.: 2044
Glass, Prof. David V.: 714
Glatt, M. M.: 1496
Glickman, Constance: 504
Goble, Nicholas L.: 1054
Godfrey, Kneeland A.: 1724
Godshalk, William Leigh: 374
Godwin, Shelagh M.: 144
Goeldner, Charles R.: 760, 785
Goerlich, Robert F.: 1319
Goetz, John B.: 2509
Goetz, Thomas H.: 394
Gokhale, S. D.: 1509
Goldammer, Vance R.: 1288
Goldberg, Abraham S.: 1782
Goldberg, S. L.: 341
Golden, Herbert: 239
Goldhor, Herbert: 302
Goldin, George J.: 1494
Goldman, Leo: 1049
Goldowsky, Seebert J.: 2476
Goldsborough, Harriett: 949
Goldschmidt, Carl: 919
Goldstein, Harold: 281
Golledge, R.G.: 1102
Gonzales, John E.: 1155
González-del-Valle, Luis T.: 373
González-Gerth, Miguel: 119
Gooch, P. W.: 553
Goode, Delmer M.: 977
Goode, Stephen: 116
Goodin, Gayle: 485
Goodman, J: 1269
Goodman, Leroy V.: 909
Gordon, Basil: 2202
Gordon, Bernard: 2515
Gordon, R. A.: 2307
Gorsuch, Richard: 567
Gottesfeld, Mary L.: 1501
Gottlieb, Nancy: 1514
Gould, Jay R.: 855
Gould, John: 695
Grünewald, Dr. Helmut: 2069
Grace, George W.: 237
Graham, Fergus: 93
Graham, Fred E.: 836
Graham, John: 2620
Grange, Peter Welham: 2609
Granquist, W. T.: 1681
Grant, David: 1424
Grant, Mary Margaret: 1278
Grant, Dr. William F.: 1905
Grauert, H.: 2192
Graves, Clara: 489
Graves, Walter: 1092
Gray, E. George: 2401
Graybill, Franklin A.: 2195
Green, Richard: 1372
Green, Robert E.: 2576
Green, Roger Lancelyn: 375
Greenberg, Martin: 748

Greene, Ch. A.: 2457
Greene, Frederick D.: 2115
Greene, John: 1265
Greengard, Dr. O.: W. Eugene: 1917
Greening, Thomas C.: 1431
Gregg, Earl C.: 2123
Gregg, Karl C.: 330
Gregory, Richard L.: 621
Grendahl, Beth: 2467
Grenig, Jay E.: 1206
Griffith, John L.: 921
Griffith, Prof. W. C.: 2035
Griffiths, Raymond B.: 1928
Grodhaus, Gail: 1811
Grogg, Sam L.: 878
Grognet, Allene Guss: 225
Grosshans, Henry: 109
Grosvenor, Gilbert M.: 1108
Groves, G. V.: 1589
Gudas, J. C.: 2562
Guenther, Charles: 524
Guilfoil, John D.: 746
Guilfoyle, J. Roger: 2589
Gulko, Candace S.: 2526
Gupta, Prof. A. P.: 1995
Gustafson, John A.: 1037
Gustafson, Richard: 510
Guthals, Joel E.: 1261
Guthridge, Guy G.: 606
Guthrie, Charles Snow: 1552
Guttentag, Professor J.: 816
Gyory, A.Z.: 2290

H

Haas, Walter H.: 2056
Hagglund, Ben: 479
Haig, Stirling: 207
Haight, Frank A.: 1855
Haining, James: 513
Hakel, Dr. Milton D.: 1459
Hale, Dean: 2604
Hale, William S.: 847
Haley, Prof. K. B.: 838
Halinan, Conn: 43
Hall, Blaine H.: 318
Hall, C. F.: 2544
Hall, Cary H.: 1233
Hall, Elizabeth: 1478
Hall, J. Charles: 2588
Hall, Joseph G.: 1909
Hall, Peter: 1852
Hall, Robert F.: 1815
Halliday, E. M.: 1117
Halliday, Ian: 2064
Halling, Gary: 1306
Halpern, Daniel: 471
Halpern, Joseph H.: 440
Halverson, Katherine: 1121
Ham, George E.: 2113
Hamilton, William T.: 54
Hamlyn, David W.: 452
Hamm, Kenneth R.: 1263
Hammersley, Peter: 2228
Hammond, Jeffrey A.: 1257
Hammond-Tooke, W. D.: 631
Hand, Robert G.: 1754
Handley, John W.: 1231
Haney, Harold L.: 158
Hanh, Harlan: 1334
Hankins, I.W.: 1269
Hanle, Eve: 184
Hannay, Alastair: 444

References in Index refer to entry numbers

Editorial staff index

Hanson, Donald W.: 1360
Harborne, Dr. J. B.: 1965
Harding, Robert L.: 2322
Harding, Walter: 430
Hardt, John P.: 742
Hare, Edward H.: 1378
Harman, Eleanor: 860
Harmison, Eva Murell: 1135
Harmon, Dr. Robert E.: 2103
Harnden, D. G.: 2397
Harnett, Rosalind: 2171
Harootunian, H. D.: 641
Harper, J. L.: 1802
Harrar, H. Joanne: 313
Harris, Herbert S.: 2012
Harris, Rick J.: 2613
Harrison, John P.: 666
Harrod, Karen G.: 1830
Hart, John Fraser: 1099
Hart, Ray L.: 528
Hartley, Margaret L.: 57
Hartmann, Hermann: 2131
Hartnett, J. P.: 1749
Harvey, A. McGehee: 2433
Harvey, Ellen D.: 756
Harwood, Grace L.: 1344
Hatcher, Danny R.: 315
Hatfield, Cmdr. H. H.: 2061
Hathaway, Baxter: 489
Haubrich, William S.: 2348
Hauck, Jack E.: 1770
Hauge, Carl J.: 1669
Hauge, M.: 1924
Hausman, F.T.: 2597
Hausner, Henry H.: 1653
Hawking, Robert J.: 928
Hawkins, Mary E.: 1074
Hawkins, W. W.: 2076
Hawks, Tod W.: 60
Hawley, Edward A.: 628
Hawthorne, M. Frederick: 2096
Hay, Elizabeth D.: 1916
Hayashi, Dr. Tetsumaro: 418
Hayden, J. Michael: 1128
Hayes, Marshall: 8
Hayes, Phil: 946
Haynes, Jim: 802
Head, Christopher R.: 1191
Heal, G. M.: 799
Heaney, Ronnie: 1755, 1758, 1759, 1761,
    1762, 1773
Hécaen, H.: 2443
Hedrick, Hannah: 388
Hedrick, Phillip W.: 1918
Hedstrom, Kristi: 884
Heidmann, Dr. J.: 2058
Heimann, H.: 1387
Heinich, Robert: 867
Heinrichs, Dr. D. H.: 1955
Heins, Ethel: 363
Heister, Peter B.: 1241
Helbig, K.: 1650
Helbock, Lucy: 456
Held, A.: 2141
Helgeson, Bee: 2504
Heller, Robert: 834
Helmer, James B.: 1301
Henderson, Wesley E.: 1877
Hendry, D. F.: 799
Hendry, Prof. A. W.: 1714
Henn, Richard L.: 2505
Henry, Jeannette: 688

Henry, Jerry W.: 1651
Henry, Mary: 1230
Henzel, Hans W.: 656
Hepp, K.: 2137
Herber, Robert C.: 620
Hering, H.: 2144
Herman, Ernest: 1366
Herman, Robert H.: 2261
Hermann, Dr. Walter: 2351
Hermes, John N: 1272
Herring, Jack W.: 420
Hersch, Paul: 1805
Herzog, Prof. Dr. H.: 2473
Hester, James J.: 1639
Hetsroni, G.: 1752
Hetzel, Theodore B.: 689
Heuertz, Matt: 2592
Heumann, Karl F.: 1919
Heynen, Delaine: 228
Heynen, Jim: 507
Hickerson, P.J.: 999
Hicks, Dan R.: 731
Higdon, David L.: 338
Higginbotham, S. W.: 1158
Higgins, A. Stanley: 863
Higham, Robin: 1113, 1322
Hilado, Carlos J.: 1760
Hill, Charles R.: 1516
Hill, Fredric W.: 2405
Hill, Jane M.: 916
Hill, Richard J.: 1569
Hillman, John: 700
Hilton, Ronald: 624
Himmelfarb, Martin: 1730
Hinde, Wendy: 611
Hinnebusch, Thomas J.: 246
Hinton, Harwood P.: 1122
Hinton, Prof. H. E.: 2003
Hirano, Marshall J.: 971
Hirsch, Monroe J.: 2269
Hitchens, H. B.: 866
Hixson, Thomas J.: 2413
Hoagland, Robert S.: 594
Hoar, W. S.: 1981
Hoare, Peter A.: 284
Hobbs, J. Michael: 2026
Hockwin, Prof. O.: 2454
Hodges, Dr. Alton: 2255
Hodges, Richard E.: 963
Hodges, Trevor: 841
Hoefs, J.: 1686
Hoffman, Martin L.: 1452
Hoffmann, John: 1165
Hogan, Lloyd: 798
Hoke, Thomas T.: 1727
Holck, Dr. Frederick: 585
Holländer, L. P.: 2494
Holleb, Arthur I.: 2305
Holliman, Mary C.: 1678
Holm, Ed: 684
Holman, C. Hugh: 516
Holman, R. T.: 2121
Holmberg, Kaj: 1977
Holmes, Geoffrey A.: 729
Holmes, Robert S.: 1295
Honigberg, Professor B. M.: 2007
Hoogstraten, H. W.: 2204
Höök, Olle: 2479
Hoover, John E.: 2270
Hopcroft, John: 2244
Hope, Jane C.: 11
Hopkins, H. Garth: 1411, 1422, 1763

Horn, William A.: 909
Horobin, Gordon: 1566
Horowitz, Frances D.: 724
Horowitz, Irving Louis: 723, 725
Horowitz, Lin: 1580
Horrocks, Norman: 278
Horton, D.: 2078
Hoskins, Frank L.: 425
Hospers, John: 456
Hough, Mary Lu: 791
Hounsell, D. J.: 973
Houthakker, Hendrik S.: 800
Houts, Paul L.: 1036
Hovi, T.: 2426
Howard, Anthony: 40
Howard, Billy B.: 2518
Howard, John N.: 2023, 2038
Howarth, David: 1260
Howe, Charles W.: 1861
Howe, Darlus: 46
Howe, J. P.: 2174
Howe, John S.: 461
Howe, John: 1635
Howe, Leroy T.: 588
Howell, G. D.: 1667
Hoyt, Beryl E.: 321
Hrubéy, Blahoslav: 591
Hsiung, Chuan C.: 2203
Hubbell, John T.: 1132
Hubbs, Dr. Clark: 1985
Hudson, Richard: 623
Huff, Robert: 483
Hughes, Anthony J.: 627
Hughes, B. Noel: 1606
Hughes, J.T.: 726
Hughes, Tom: 2610
Hugoboom, R. Wayne: 138
Huizinga, Harry W.: 2554
Hulthén, Lamek: 2163
Humphreys, Lloyd G.: 1368
Hundley, Norris C.: 1178
Hunt, Sally: 271
Hunter, Edward: 1359
Hunter, L. C.: 803
Huth, Anne: 1693, 2049, 2053, 2054
Huth, Edward J.: 2280
Hutton, Robert W.: 466
Hyde, F. E.: 752
Hyde, Ralph W.: 1571
Hynas, Edward: 951

I

Inbau, Fred E.: 1247
Ingelfinger, Franz J.: 2445
Inghe, Gunnar: 2481
Ingram, John W.: 1951
Irvine, E. E.: 1509
Irwin, John: 1572
Isaacs, Ann Fabe: 969
Ishwaran, K.: 638, 640, 1543
Itzin, Catherine: 194
Iutte, W. I.: 2202
Ivask, Ivar: 328
Iwao, Shun'iti: 1557

J

Jackson, Crawford G.: 1993
Jackson, Jacquelyne J.: 1550
Jackson, John: 1538
Jackson, Michael R.: 1766
Jacques, March L.: 1789
Jaeger, Richard: 996

References in Index refer to entry numbers

Jaeggin, Albert H.: 2564
Jagger, Dr. John: 1939
Jakiela, Charles S.: 708, 1416
Jaklitsch, J. J.: 1755, 1758, 1759, 1761, 1762, 1773
James, M. E.: 82
James, Thomas M.: 1778
Janeway, Michael C.: 4
Jeanloz, R. W.: R. Stuart: 2078
Jefferson, Donald T.: 2625
Jefferson, T.B.: 2626
Jeffrey, David K.: 56
Jeffrey, W. E.: 1382
Jenkins, G. M.: 1766
Jenkins, Dr. S. H.: 1860
Jenness, S. E.: 1646
Jensen, Oliver: 1117
Jento, Mona L.: 2167
Jettner, Frank C.: 2063
Jewett, Hugh J.: 2415
Jhirad, Elijah E: 1299
Johansen, Erling: 2508
Johanson, Bengt: 2540
John, F.: 2192
Johnson, Cathryne Christine: 1133
Johnson, Clarence M.: 1493
Johnson, Curt: 484
Johnson, Edna Ruth: 547
Johnson, Dr. Gordon: 644
Johnson, Mark R.: 2452
Johnson, Peter K.: 1653
Johnson, Phillip: 407
Johnson, Reginald: 2337
Johnson, Richard D.: 267
Johnson, Robert D.: 2485
Johnson, W.: 1751
Johnstone, Henry W.: 464
Jones, Eleanor Cavanaugh: 262
Jones, Malinda: 1528
Jones, Rhys S.: 121
Jordan, Casper: 491
Jorgensen, S. E.: 1817
Joseph, 2519
Joyce, Thomas: 482
Jud, G. Donald: 793
Judy, Stephen N.: 965
June, David J.: 534
Justice, Harry: 7

K

Kaapcke, Bernard: 778
Kaeser, Henry E.: 2343
Kaganoff, Nathan M.: 530
Kahn, Howard: 1070
Kahrl, Stanley J.: 238
Kailin, John: 826
Kalerghi, Juanita: 1740
Kallos, P.: 2367
Kamarck, Edward L.: 73, 134
Kaminski, Richard K.: 2236
Kane, Gertrude: 6
Kao, Frederick: 2260
Kao, John J.: 2260
Kaplan, Gerald: 1286
Kaplan, Helen S.: 1443
Kaplan, Jerome: 610
Kapteyn, Prof. Paul J. G.: 1215
Karpman, Stephen B.: 1490
Karstad, Lars: 2548
Karush, Prof. Fred: 2095
Käser, O.: 2351
Kasher, Dr. Asa: 457

Kass, Edward H.: 2393
Kastenbaum, Dr. Robert J.: 1400, 1454
Kathan, Boardman W.: 1060
Katz, Joseph J.: 307, 2097, 2112
Katz, Phyllis Pollak: 1633
Katz, Robert N.: 757
Kaufman, Herbert E.: 2372
Kaufman, Nathan: 2419
Kay, E. Alison: 1617
Kay, Robert L.: 2119
Kaywood, Richard: 1015
Kazamias, Andreas M.: 941
Kearney, George E.: 1373
Keating, Karl M.: 42
Kebbon, Lars: 1485
Kedourie, Elie: 677
Keefer, Don: 1050
Keenan, John J.: 85
Kehler, Larry: 579
Keley, Michael C.: 1305
Keller, Eugenia: 2083
Keller, Gary D.: 199
Keller, Mary M.: 199
Kelley, John L.: 2189
Kellington, Myrtle R.: 2226
Kelly, Robert T.: 2567
Kelsall, , D. F.: A.: 1618
Kemp, Walter H.: 2257
Kennedy, D.: 2384
Kennedy, Francis Edward: 1708, 1709
Kennedy, J. P.: 2001
Kennedy, Jon R.: 48
Kennedy, Paul: 405
Kenny, Dr. Michael: 1536
Keohane, Robert O.: 1238
Kerby, Merle D.: 1632
Kerkut, Prof. G.A.: 2087
Kershen, Dr. Harry: 824
Kerstein, Joseph J.: 2483
Kessel, John H. C.: 1331
Kesten, Harry: 2191
Ketchum, Bradford W.: 792
Kiekhoefer, Kay: 1321
Kieren, Thomas E.: 904
Killeen, John: 2150
Killian, George E.: 1018
Killip, John David: 2071
Kimble, Prof. David: 635
Kimura, Hiroshi: 1771
King, Charles L.: 229
King, Glen D.: 1247
King, J. Stanton: 2086
King, Dr. L.: 1932
King, D.: 2116
Kingdon, Robert M.: 1182
Kinney, Arthur F.: 351
Kipnis, David M.: 2332
Kirkman, Ralph E.: 1046
Kirsten, Professor Dr. W.: 1945
Kirwan, Sir Laurence: 1103
Kitsuse, John I.: 1567
Kivett, Marvin F.: 1169
Kivilaakso, E.: 2278
Kjonegaard, Vernon H.: 713
Kleffner, Frank R.: 1495
Klein, Arthur: 1725
Klein, M. J.: 1588
Klein, Richard K.: 811
Kline, Lloyd W.: 1010, 1059
Klinger, H. P.: 1915
Klis, John B.: 2580
Kloc, Stanley J.: 832

Klopfer, Walter: 1437
Klotzer, Charles L.: 21, 885
Knigge, Dr. K. M.: 2440
Knotts, Glenn R.: 2411
Knudson, Richard L.: 966
Knudten, Richard D.: 596
Knuth, P.: 1176
Koch, Mitchell: 2149
Koch-Weser, Suzanne: 1625
Kocis, Thomas A.: 1607
Koenig, K. G.: 2503
Koepke, John William: 1019
Koerner, Dr. E.F.K.: 214
Kogan, Michael S.: 26
Kohler, Charlotte: 66
Kojima, U.: 1820
Kolatch, Myron: 39
Kolb, Gwin J.: 385
Kolb, Robert A.: 112
Kollmann, F. F. P.: 1976
Koltveit, Albert J.: 2543
Kompass, Edward J.: 1725
König, Prof. Ing. E.: 2289
Koon, William: 416
Koontz, Patricia P.: 741
Koprowski, Richard: 146
Korby, Kenneth F.: 16
Korte, Robert T.: 2586
Kotkin, Minna J.: 1283
Kotsher, B. J.: 2556, 2620
Kouris, Michael: 2622
Kramer, Dale: 218
Kramer, Lawrence F.: 1053
Kranzberg, Melvin: 1184
Kreitman, N.: 1487
Kretzmann, Norman: 459
Krishnaiah, P. R.: 2206
Krislov, Samuel: 1088
Krnjevic, K.: 2312
Kroetsch, Robert: 476
Kroll, William: 697
Krook, Lennert: 2546
Krosnick, Arthur: 2432
Krug, Judith F.: 298, 857
Krumhansl, J.A.: 2164
Krutchkoff, Richard G.: 2241
Kucharsky, David E.: 543
Kühn, A.: 2385
Kuhn, Barbara C.: 1931
Kuhn, Dr. Marylou: 1082
Kukla, Jon: 1186
Kuklick, Bruce: 682
Kupfer-Halstuck, Rosalie: 1497
Kupfersmith, William: 240
Kurian, Dr. George: 1549
Kurland, Jon H.: 1263
Kurtz, Paul: 89
Kuschner, Dr. Marvin: 2466
Kutschke, K. O.: 2077

L

Labedz, Leopold: 661
Labor, Earle: 929, 930
Lacy, Susana B.: 1255
Ladebz, Leopold: 661
Laffer, Kingsley: 825
Laitinen, Herbert A.: 2068
Lake, Marilyn H.: 293
Lambert, Prof. Dr. R.: 2334
Landau, Claire: 2461
Landell, Penny: 1251
Landis, Carolyn: 960

Editorial staff index

Landis, Elwood W.: 1087
Lane, Nancy: 1118
Lane, Patricia E.: 1006
Lang, Charles A.: 2247
Lang, Professor Anton: 1971
Lange, Eunice K.: 829
Langlois, Walter G.: 387
Lanzetta, John: 1438
Laqueur, Walter: 1151
Larsen, Otto N.: 1533, 1534, 1550, 1567, 1569
Larson, Dr. Albert J.: 1106
Laska, John A.: 957
Lasker, Gabriel W.: 1922
Lass, Jack: 252
Laties, Victor G.: 1422
Latimer, Christopher: 600
Laurin, Teddi C.: 2039
Lavelle, Gregory J.: 1211
Laverdiere, Camille: 1110
Lavin, John H.: 2531
Law, Frank G.: 1779
Lawrence, Dr. H. Sherwood: 2317
Leach, Catherine: 2527
Leahy, Virginia W.: 800
Lear, Harold A.: 1443
Leash, Aaron M.: 1609
Leath, Helen Lang: 417
Lebowitz, Professor J. L.: 2137
Lechner, Robert F.: 465
Leder, Charles P: 1224
Ledley, Robert S.: 2233, 2243
Lee, Dr. Fitzhugh T.: 1668
Lee, Frances H.: 2594
Lee, James W.: 422
Lee, Jeanine: 978, 1043
Lee, L. L.: 483
Lee, Thomas E.: 1535
Lee, W. R.: 205
Leedale, Gordon Frank: 1952
Leeds, Alice A.: 2468
Lees, J.: 2142
Lehmann, Irvin J.: 996
Lehnert, Professor Dr. G.: 2368
Leib, Clyde E.: 1040
Leibman, Kenneth C.: 2336
Leibowitz, Professor H. W.: 1474
Leigh, Dr. Denis: 2410
Leighton, D.: 1882
Lengyel, Peter: 707
Lenihan, Daniel T.: 2619
Lenzo, J. F.: 189
Leo, Mia: 14
Leonard, William B.: 2617
Leopold, Bengt: 2622
Lepson, Ruth R.: 9
Lessler, M.A.: 1615
Lester, Larry: 1602, 1654, 1958, 1996, 2099, 2200
Lever, Dr. A. B. P.: 2088
Levi, Anna Maria: 706
Levin, Ronald M.: 1300
Levin, Sidney: 1428
Levine, Jonathan: 703
Levine, Prof. Robert L.: 2072
Levine, Sidney: 2618
Levine, Stuart: 683
Levinson, Kenneth S.: 1245
Levitt, Judith: 1204
Lewin, Elsbeth G.: 625
Lewis, Earl A.: 2304
Lewis, Edith P.: 2529

Lewis, R. E.: 1326
Lewis, Richard S.: 1590
Lewis, Robert: 290
Lewis, Stuart M.: 1800
Lewis, Thomas J.: 769
L'Hermite, R.: 1772
Liao, Dr. Thomas T.: 997
Lieb, Judith: 1506
Lieb, Roslyn Corenzwit: 1225
Liébecq, Claude: 2092
Lieberman, A. Robert: 2401
Liebow, Dr. A. A.: 2492
Liebowitz, Prof. Harold: 1735
Lightner, Jerry P.: 908
Lima, Darlene L.: 1207
Lincicome, David R.: 1988
Lincoln, Richard: 1505
Lindabury, Virginia A.: 2521
Lindfors, Bernth O.: 403
Lindsay, George E.: 1616
Lindsay, James H.: 2608
Lindsell, Harold: 543
Lindsey, Jonathan A.: 1214
Lineberry, Wanda C.: 289
Linett, E. S.: 739
Lippincott, W. T.: 2105
Lippmann, Prof. Horst: 1774
Lipsitt, Dr. Don R.: 2370
Lipton, Michael: 773
Liska, Bernard J.: 1604
Lister, Dr. E. E.: 1879
Lister, G.: 2534
Liston, Linda L.: 2590
Little, Kenneth B.: 1370
Littledale, Harold: 844
Livingston, Jon: 637
Lloyd, Glenn T.: 1516
Lloyd, Markland G.: 383
Lloyd, R. Grann: 1039
Locke, Leslie: 1218
Lodge, Dr. L. P.: 1808
Loebell, Prof. Dr. E.: 897
Loeffler, Frank E.: 2299
Lofton, Edgar K.: 761
Lollar, Robert M.: 2561
London, Paul: 755
London, Roberta: 1502
Long, D. A.: 2162
Long, Melvin E.: 1769
Long, Robert W.: 1968
Long, William G.: 1793
Longley, J. B.: 2124
Lonner, Walter J.: 1420
Löoe, Harald: 2513
Loose, John Ward Willson: 1161
Lopes, Jane: 257
Lorber, Richard: 149
Lord, Marian G.: 1078
Lord, Peter: 2022
LoSasso, John S.: 290
Lotan, Yael: 71
Lotsch, Helmut K. V.: 2134
Love, Dorothy J.: 2266
Loveless, Kathy Wood: 1851
Lovell, Ernest J.: 428
Lovgren, Olle: 2480
Low, W. Augustus: 692
Lowe, Charles U.: 2459
Lowe, George E.: 1041
Luberoff, B. J.: 2081
Luborsky, F. E.: 1742
Lüdin, H.: 2251

Luhrs, Kathleen: 1172
Luna, Richard E.: 2429
Lund, Horace O.: 1991
Lunetta, Stanley G.: 188
Lüscher, E. F.: 2352
Luther, Ardi: 1854
Lutz, Paul V.: 97
Lutz, Pearl E.: 2423
Lyght, Charles E.: 2258
Lyon, James: 2067, 2121
Lyon, Thomas J.: 438
Lyons, Nancy: 727
Lyphart, Arend: 1337

M

MacAdam, David L.: 2038
MacCann, Richard Dyer: 871
Macduff, I. B.: 1797
Macéas, Reynaldo: 5
MacInnis, Donald: 541
Mackay, E. V.: 2291
MacKay, Patricia J.: 191
Mackin, David: 1739
Macklin, F. Anthony: 873
MacRae, Pamela Lee: 264
MacRae, Scotia W.: 460
MacSween, R. J.: 472
Madachy, Joseph S.: 2208
Maddin, Robert: 1771
Magdoff, Harry: 1345
Mahler, William F.: 1975
Mahn, Robert E.: 939
Mahoney, Joseph F.: 1170
Majum Dar, M. K.: 799
Malina, Frank J.: 168
Maliszewski, Michael: 1468
Malkiel, Yakov: 243
Malkofsky, Morton: 1023
Mallinson, George G.: 1069
Malone, Robert A.: 1096
Mancini, Rosalie: 2603
Mandler, George: 1475
Manheim, Leonard F.: 362
Manley, D. F.: 2158
Manley, Robert L.: 1270
Mann, Lester: 1013
Manning, Robert: 4
Manoski, Paul A.: 590
Mansfield, Steven: 925
Maragos, G. D.: 2457
Maramorosch, Karl: 2015
March, L.: 1824
March, Rev. Ralph S.: 187
Marcuccio, Phyllis R.: 1072
Marcus, Marvin: 2211
Marcy, Henry O.: 319
Marder, Louis: 412
Margrave, John L.: 1600
Marineau, Niclaus: 2517
Marini, Frank: 1277
Marion, Mushkat: 613
Mark, Russell: 1850
Marker, Frederick: 171
Marr, Judith: 2436
Marr, Warren: 17
Marrs, Craig: 894
Marshall, James A.: 2127
Marshall, Samuel L.: 1795
Martell, Arthur E.: 2106
Marth, Elmer H.: 1868
Marthaler, Berard L.: 576
Martin, Charles A.: 1007

References in Index refer to entry numbers

Martin, David: 912, 1291
Martin, Edwin: 220, 1016
Martin, Hal: 905
Martin, Lucy Prete: 933
Martin, Richard: 135
Martin, Susan K.: 280
Martin, Wendy: 1584
Martinau, Duarte J.: 868
Martz, John D.: 668
Massarik, Dr. F.: 1406
Massarsky, Ellen: 970
Mastroianni, Luigi: 2345
Masur, E. F.: 1765
Matheny, Ruth A.: 1091
Mathieu, Pierre: 1832
Matlin, Matthew: 1539
Matsumoto, Charles: 1869
Matthews, J. H.: 427
Mattill, John I.: 1626
Mattingly, Paul H.: 1142
Mattson, Judith: 1081
Mattsson, Jan-Erik: 1712
Maucher, Professor Dr.-Ing. A.: 1684
Maxwell, Alan: 2135
Mayer, Steven E.: 2438
Mayhew, Leon: 1534
Maylone, Theresa: 431
Maynard, Charles: 1294
Maynard, Glenn: 1031
Mayo, Bernard: 458
Mayo, Robert W.: 2262, 2272
Mayor, Prof. Dr. G.: 2491
McAllister, Dr. Marian H.: 88
McBrien, William: 432
McCabe, Frank G.: 818
McCabe, Herbert: 584
McCahill, Ed: 1274
McCall, Joan M.: 1577
McCamman, Carol V.: 1029
McCartney, James L.: 1563
McCartney, Kenneth H.: 1525
McClanahan, Randy: 1256
McClellan, Catherine: 1537
McClintock, David: 1934, 1961
McCloskey, Michael: 596
McCluskey, Robert: 2323
McCord, Merrill T.: 2396
McCormick, Marilyn G.: 274
McCracken, George E.: 1116
McCrone, W. C.: 1610
McCune, Carol: 2357
McDaniels, Theodore C.: 815
McDonald, Angus: 593
McDonald, Janet H.: 1879, 1880, 1955
McDonald, John J.: 552
McDonald, Robert C.: 1325
McDowell, Frank: 2539
McDowell, Robert E.: 1136
McEachern, Alex W.: 728
McElroy, Blair: 979
McEwen, John: 190
McFadyen, Donald J.: 1311
McGhehey, M. A.: 1019, 1268
McGiffert, Michael: 1190
McGill, Richard: 1281
McGinnis, Dorothy J.: 1056
McGlamry, E. Dalton: 2275
McGovern, Eileen: 2313
McGuire, James: 1203
McIntyre, Alister: 670
McKee, Richard A.: 817, 1004, 1102
McKellar, Nella: 2308, 2545

McKiernan, Eoin: 650
McKinnon, Russell F.: 1228
McLaughlin, Diane I.: 1940
McLaughlin, Frank: 959
McLoughlin, K.: 2179
McMurrer, Mary: 2556
McNamara, D. Harold: 2057
McNamara, Eugene J.: 65
McNeill, William H.: 1156
McQuade, H. A.: 768
McRainey, John H.: 1711
McSweeney, Kerry: 45
Mead, C. David: 77
Meckler, Alan M.: 292
Mee, Fiona: 859
Meek, Margaret: 309
Mehrens, Dr. William A.: 1030
Meier, Elizabeth L.: 1508
Meilach, Michael D.: 551
Meiner, Hans: 2627
Mekas, Jonas: 872
Melchers, Georg: 1936
Mellanby, Prof. Kenneth: 1827
Mellor, L. D.: 2309
Melman, Leslie E.: 1285
Melnick, J. L.: 2371
Meltzer, Daniel J: 1234
Mendlewicz, J.: 1453
Menendez, Albert J.: 546
Mentag, John V.: 1166
Meredith, Dennis: 1626
Merker, Kim: 494
Merriam, D. F.: 1673
Meserole, Harrison T.: 111
Meserve, Harry C.: 572
Messick, Samuel J.: 1063
Metcalfe, John R.: 1980
Meyer, Michael J.: 1240
Meyer, Robert W.: 2629
Meyer, Sue: 106
Meyfarth, Werner H.: 1734
Middendorf, John H.: 368
Miele, Angelo: 2207
Mikhailov, Professor A. I.: 2237
Milburn, Patrick: 450
Miles, Prof. A. E. W.: 2499
Millar, Burtholme: 93
Millar, James R.: 659
Miller, Dr. David C.: 997
Miller, Ernest C.: 839
Miller, Harvey A.: 1597
Miller, J.: 660
Miller, Larry E.: 907
Miller, Louis: 1450
Miller, Randolph Crump: 1060
Miller, Richard B.: 808
Miller, Roger R.: 1525
Miller, Stanton S.: 1829
Miller, Stuart: 1020
Miller, William E.: 1831
Milligan, Charles S.: 565
Milton, John R.: 515
Miner, John B.: 830
Miner, Michael: 880
Mingay, Prof. G. E.: 1876
Minkowski, Prof. A.: 2292
Minkowycz, W. J.: 1749
Miser, Hugh J.: 2217
Mislin, Professor Hans: 1866
Mitchell, David F.: 2509
Mitchell, Memory F.: 1174
Mitchell, P. M.: 218

Mitchell, R. J.: 2125
Mitchell, Timothy A.: 956
Moberg, David O.: 526
Mock, Col. Alfred J.: 1328
Mock, John A.: 1770
Modell, Walter: 2324
Moffatt, Dr. H. K.: 2035
Mohan, Raj P.: 1544
Mojzes, Paul: 569
Moldenke, Alma L.: 1966
Moldenke, Harold N.: 1966
Mole, Chris D.: 1819
Moler, C. B.: 2222
Mollica, Anthony S.: 202
Momberger, William: 2024
Moment, Gairdner B.: 1921
Monkman, J. L.: 1853
Montag, Tom: 856
Montague, George T.: 538
Montgomery, Nancy S.: 1641
Mooney, Jack H.: 1317
Moore, Carleton B.: 1659
Moore, Harold E.: 1951, 1972
Moore, James L.: 1048
Moore, Richard E.: 305
Moor-Jankowski, J.: 2399
Mordus, Joanne H.: 1582
Moreno, Zerka T.: 1394, 1425
Morewhite, Margaret: 1430
Morey, Dr. Frederick L.: 349
Morgan, Clifford T.: 1374, 1458
Morgan, K. Z.: 2177
Morgan, Kathleen: 370
Morley, William F. E.: 685
Morris, Celia: 931
Morrison, Eric Elmslie: 1
Morrison, Lorrin L.: 1159
Morrissey, Charles T.: 1185
Morse, John D.: 131
Morse, Kathy: 2425
Morse, Philip M.: 2133
Morton, Herbert C.: 827
Morton, Terry B.: 24
Mosbacher, C. J.: 1620
Moser, Robert H.: 2272
Moss, T. S.: 2143
Mosse, George L.: 1151
Mossotti, Prof. V. G.: 2020
Motulsky, Arno G.: 1887, 1923
Mountjoy, Paul T.: 1472
Mowry, Jack K.: 1796
Mrozowski, S.: 2079
Mueller, Dale M.J.: 1953
Mullen, Frances A.: 1405
Muller, Dr. Godfrey A.: 2507
Muller, R. L.: 2000
Multhauf, Robert P.: 1147
Murchison, Powell: 1392, 1426, 1427, 1441, 1444
Murphey, Walter: 59
Murphy, Aniela: 1198
Murphy, James A.: 1642
Murray, James J.: 1599
Murray, John F.: 2276
Murray, R. G. E.: 1894
Murray, Dr. Robert: 562
Musgrave, Professor Richard A.: 796
Mustakallio, K. K.: 2279
Myer, William Edwin: 975
Myers, Evelyn S.: 1367
Myers, Dr. Sarah K.: 1105
Myers, Victor C.: 500

References in Index refer to entry numbers

Editorial staff index

Myrick, Robert D.: 962

N

Nachbar, John G.: 878
Naess, Arne: 444
Nagel, Stuart S.: 1346
Nagy, Moses M.: 334
Naim, C. M.: 372
Nairn, Robert I.: 2510
Nanry, Charles: 166
Nash, Dr. Gerald: 1139
Nash, William A.: 1753
Nashel, Dianne: 1248, 1440
Natalicio, Luiz F.S.: 1399
Nathanson, Neal: 2263
Navarro, Joseph P.: 1154
Navarro, Dr. Vincents: 2248
Neale, E. R. W.: 1646
Nebergall, Roger E.: 900
Neff, Allen: 496
Neidig, Kenneth L.: 159
Nelms, Ben F.: 964
Nelson, Dr. Constance: 1404
Nelson, James A.: 2355
Nelson, Klayton E.: 1948
Nelson, Larry A.: 2195
Nelson, Ronald E.: 1002
Nelson, Waldo E.: 2406
Nemser, Charles S.: 1576
Nemser, Cindy: 1576
Ness, John H.: 581
Neumann, Donald L.: 2374
Neurath, Hans: 2073
Nevison, Myrne B.: 1379
New, John F. H.: 1141
Newbauer, John: 2050
Newbrough, J.R.: 1416
Newell, Frank W.: 2268
Newhall, Shirley R.: 1339
Newman, Bernarr A.: 1726
Newman, J. E.: 2021
Newson, Dr. John D.: 117
Nichols, William C.: 1504
Nickel, William J.: 2557
Nielsen, M. C.: 1992
Niimi, Tatsuya: 2147
Nilsson, Nils Robert: 2163
Nollendorfs, Valters: 233
Nordbring, Folke: 2478
Norden, Robert B.: 1719
Normoyle, John L.: 2421
Norris, John W.: 142
Northart, Leo J.: 737, 1292
Northup, George W.: 2274
Novak, Zdenek: 1729
Novbeck, Timothy B.: 2476
Novick, Sheldon: 1821
Nuttli, Otto W.: 1664
Nyberg, Ben: 495
Nygaard, Oddvar F.: 2185

O

Oberman, Michael A.: 1857
O'Brien, George E.: 1217
O'Bryon, Martha Seffer: 1177
O'Connor, Audrey H.: 1956
O'Connor, James J.: 1784
O'Daniel, Therman B.: 203
O'Daniell, Noel D.: 2575
Odom, Richard D.: 1391
Oesterle, John A.: 454
O'Donoghue, P. N.: 2009

O'Gara, James: 548
Oguchi, T.: 2165
O'Higgins, Peggy A.: 50
Ohmann, Richard: 937
Okamoto, Shosuke: 2417
Okerlund, Arlene N.: 51
Oldsey, Dr. Bernard: 336
Oliver, Daniel: 36
Olsen, Humphrey A.: 54
Olson, Jane V.: 1587
Olson, Richard C.: 1844
Olsson, Ragnar: 1977
Olver, F. W. J.: 2221
O'Neill, Joseph Eugene: 61
Ongkeko, Lourdes A.: 1568
Oppenheim, Prof. A. K.: 2047
Ormes, Robert V.: 1621
Orne, Martin T.: 1401
Ortmann, Professor Dr. R.: 2378
Orville-Thomas, W. J.: 2154
Osborn, Ben O.: 1807
Osborne, H.: 76
Osborne, Richard H.: 717
Osipow, Samuel H.: 1419, 1445
Osterhaven, M. Eugene: 592
Ostrander, Gilman M.: 1141
Ott, R. A.: 2361
Ottinger, Ray E.: 2551
Otto, Christian F.: 1643
Overmier, J. Bruce: 1446
Overmier, Judith: 299
Owen, A.E.B.: 253
Owen, Guy: 517
Owen, John W.: 1518

P

Packard, Dorothy R.: 140
Packer, James S.: 1987, 1999,
Padykula, Professor Dr. Helen A.: 2094
Paehlke, Robert C.: 1803
Painter, Floyd: 1636
Paist, Donald: 1683
Paladin, Vivian A.: 1168
Palay, Professor S. L.: 2378
Palex, Morton D.: 326
Palmer, F. R.: 219
Palmer, Howard B.: 1594
Palmer, John J. E.: 126
Palmer, R.: 2157
Paramahamsa, V.R.K.: 699
Pariente, Vita: 867
Parker, Jane K.: 1143
Parker, M. T.: 2398
Parkes, Sir Alan: 1867
Parkhill, S. M.: 2574
Parloff, Gloria H.: 1464
Parsons, Burke A.: 750
Parsons, R.: 2108
Partlow, Robert B.: 345
Parton, Virginia: 1293
Pasqualini, J. R.: 2120
Passman, S. P.: 2143
Patterson, C. M.: 2011
Patterson, M. M.: 2555
Patterson, Penelope: 1785, 1788
Patterson, Rebecca: 100
Patton, Donald J.: 1109
Paul, C. R. C.: 1998
Paulus, Kurt: 2166
Payne, Prof. A. R.: 1756
Pearse, J. S.: 1696
Pearson, Professor Dr. Ralph G.: 2131

Pearson, Dr. Roger: 653
Peattie, Noel R.: 861
Peavy, Nancy C.: 1508
Peck, Thomas D.: 1811
Pedersen, Olaf: 1129
Pell, William: 400
Pellegrini, Anthony L.: 344
Pendell, Richard C.: 940
Penn, Prof. William: 2470
Penston, M. V.: 2062
Penttinen, K.: 2426
Perabo, George W.: 361
Perkins, George: 371
Perlow, Gilbert J.: 2148
Perry, Daniel R.: 1324
Peskin, R. L.: 1752
Peter, Margaret: 1079
Peters, Stanley T.: 1792
Peterson, B. L.: 1837
Petit, Herbert H.: 70
Pettman, Mary E.: 172
Petzold, Robert G.: 1012
Pfaltz, C. R.: 2456
Philip, John: 2330
Phillips, Beeman N.: 1442
Phillips, Janet: 278
Phillips, Joseph D.: 797
Phillips, Steven R.: 1357
Philp, Richard: 147
Pichois, Claude: 329
Pidgeon, Monica: 1640
Piecuch, Peter J.: 1859
Pihl, Mogens: 1129
Pike, E. C.: 2048
Pilgrim, Lily: 1221
Pines, David: 2171
Pings, Cornelius J.: 1720
Pinkney, David H.: 1137
Piranian, George: 2214
Pishkin, Vladimir: 1415
Pitcher, Alice C.: 1275
Plaa, Gabriel L.: 2488
Planek, Thomas W.: 618
Platou, J.: 2126
Plattner, Marc F.: 716
Plaut, A.: 1410
Pletz, Frances H.: 291
Plotnik, Arthur: 251
Pohlit, Nicholas: 1836
Poirot, Paul L.: 22, 766, 766
Pokrass, Gregory S.: 1314
Polakoff, Keith Ian: 974
Pollard, Carolyn R.: 749
Pollitt, Jerome J.: 1631
Pollock, Francis X.: 32
Polner, Murray: 44
Polsby, Nelson W.: 1333
Polunin, Prof. Dr. Nicholas: 1825
Pomeroy, Morris: 1854
Pope, Dorothy H.: 1436
Porianda, Alex: 869
Porter, Barbara: 822
Porter, Lawrence: 718
Post, Roy G.: 2183
Postgate, J. R.: 1930
Pottasch, Dr. S. R.: 2058
Pound, Mary: 316
Povey, John F.: 127
Powell, Dr. Douglas R.: 1452
Pownall, Peter C.: 2568
Pratt, Allen: 296
Pressley, Lucius C.: 1462

References in Index refer to entry numbers

Preston-Thomas, H.: 2213
Pribram, Prof. K. A.: 2443
Price, Cyril A.: 2100
Price, Mary: 126
Pritchard, Professor J. J.: 2377
Proffer, Carl R.: 409
Proffer, Ellendea: 409
Prosser, Professor C. Ladd: 2385
Protter, Benjamin: 662
Proudfit, Charles L.: 350
Pruett, James W.: 301
Pruter, Karl: 586
Purcell, L. Edward: 1179
Purpura, Professor D.P.: 2295
Purves, Alan C.: 1061
Pyros, John: 155
Pyrwes, Moshe: 2375

Q

Quain, Dr. Edwin A.: 120
Quarfoth, Harold J.: 2441
Quay, Dr. Herbert C.: 1408
Quintrelle, Nixon: 1660

R

Raben, Joseph: 2232
Rachal, William M. E.: 1187
Rachin, Richard L.: 1511
Rachman, Dr. S.: 1375
Rackauskas, John A.: 654
Radcliffe, Dr. David J.: 927
Radforth, N. W.: 1767
Radke, Merle Louis: 1025
Radostits, O. M.: 2545
Radovsky, Frank J.: 2005
Raese, Jon W.: 1647, 1683
Raffelock, David: 879
Ragsdale, John W.: 1818
Ragusa, Olga: 217
Raimondi, A.A.: 1706
Raimondi, Dr. Anthony J.: 2533
Raines, Fyat: 2528
Raison, Arnold V.: 2311, 2314, 2314
Rakow, Joel: 995
Ramsay, J. A.: 1929
Ramseier, H.: 1938
Ramsey, Frank B.: 2364
Randel, Don M.: 132
Rankin, Lois: 1547
Rapoport, Anatol: 2197
Rapoport, Robert: 704
Rapp, R. Robert: 1655
Rappolt, Richard T.: 2325
Rash, Jack D.: 1389
Rath, Prof. R. John: 646
Raun, Gerald G.: 1627
Ravenscroft, Arthur: 369
Ray, Charles D.: 2430
Ray, David: 503
Reader, George G.: 2437
Reapsome, James W.: 558
Rector, Theresa A.: 1007
Reed, Walter J.: 2599
Rees, Robert A.: 554
Reese, Trevor: 1152
Reeve, Dr. E. C. R.: 1920
Reeves, John Kenneth: 1085
Regenbogen, Susan R.: 1856
Regueiro, José M.: 212
Reid, Anthony: 156
Reid, Frank: 1858
Reid, George C.: 2151

Reid, Robert C.: 1703
Reid, Robert O.: 1695
Reiss, H.: 2209
Reiss, Otto F.: 1634
Remmert, H.: 1872
Remmert, Dr. Reinhold: 2199
Renold, Evelyn: 12
Reser, Margie K.: 1585, 1704, 2558
Resnikoff, Arthur: 1390
Revens, Lee: 2234
Revill, J. A.: 2155
Reynolds, Helen L.: 2070
Reynolds, Louise T.: 103
Reynolds, Orr E.: 2465
Rhodes, Dr. Eric F.: 1050
Ribbans, Geoffrey: 201
Ribbens, Dennis N.: 308
Ricciardelli, Michael: 206
Rice, Andrew E.: 705
Rice, Clovita: 522
Rice, Robert S.: 1745
Rice, Thomas C.: 2016
Richards, Dr. Adrian F.: 1699
Richards, Prof. Francis A.: 1692
Richards, Jeff: 481
Richards, Dr. V.: 2453
Richards, William J.: 1691
Richardson, Charles P.: 235
Richardson, Eileen: 1047
Richter, Gustav: 2132
Ricks, James M.: 1455
Rider, Jeff: 525
Ridge, Martin: 1149
Rieber, R. W.: 854
Riegel, Klaus F.: 1396
Riffaterre, Michael: 408
Righini, Marilou M.: 1237
Rimbach, Richard: 1849
Rines, Michael: 787
Ring, J.: 2159
Ring, Malvin E.: 2501
Ringel, Harvey: 178
Ripley, Randall B.: 1353
Ripley, William: 2242
Risk, R.C.B.: 1307
Riss, Dr. Walter: 2294
Rittenberg, Professor Dr. S. C.: 1892
Rivière, P. G.: 1553
Roat, Evelyn C.: 696
Roberts, Dr. A.: 1682
Roberts, Betty Winkler: 1515
Roberts, J. Deotis: 573
Roberts, Jean A.: 1806
Roberts, Millard L.: 1044
Roberts, Prof. Verne L.: 2380
Robinson, Albert F.: 195
Robinson, G. de B.: 2196
Robinson, James William: 1826, 2173
Robinson, Nicholas A.: 1226
Robinson, Virginia P.: 1456
Robinson, William J.: 1638
Robinson, William P.: 1203
Rodie, Edward B.: 1786
Roemer, Kenneth M.: 322
Roepke, Dr. Howard G.: 747
Rogers, Phillip W.: 90
Rogers, Stanley: 2246
Roggiano, Alfredo A.: 406
Rom, Paul: 1398
Romano-V., Octavio I.: 19
Ronan, Colin A.: 2061
Ronca, Luciano B.: 1674

Rooney, P. G.: 2196
Rose, J.: 1834
Rose, John: 2238
Rose, Leo E.: 636
Rose, William D.: 1675, 1676
Rosen, Charlotte Z.: 1483
Rosen, Edward: 92
Rosenbaum, Dr. Max: 1393
Rosenberg, Alex Z.: 2188
Rosenblatt, Stephen W.: 1260
Rosenblum, Gail S.: 471
Rosenbluth, Gideon: 758
Rosenfeld, Sybil: 193
Rosenheim, Edward W.: 385
Rosewarren, Leonard: 1009
Rosin, Gary: 1294
Ross, Alec M.: 972
Ross, David F.: 1833
Ross, Jack: 26
Ross, R. T.: 2310
Ross, Ron: 1279
Ross, Sheldon J.: 2512
Ross, Stanley R.: 665
Rossen, Susan F.: 151
Rossi, B. E.: 1736
Rota, Gian-Carlo: 2187
Roth, L. E.: 1913
Rothbard, Murray N.: 30
Rothkirch, Dr. Edward J.: 868
Rothkopf, Sally: 1507
Rothrauff, Conrad M.: 101
Rothschild, Bruce: 2202
Rotolo, Louis S.: 2243
Rott, Professor Dr. R.: 2428
Rowe, Dr. Arthur W.: 1912
Rowe, W.: 20
Rowley, Derrick: 1893
Roy, Prof. Della M.: 1718
Roy, G. Ross: 424
Rubin, Louis D.: 516
Rubin, Dr. M.: 2085
Ruck, Daniel C.: 761
Ruettner, J. R.: 1938
Ruiz-Fornells, Enrique: 405
Rumbarger, John J.: 1180
Rumsey, Alma Dean: 216
Rupp, Ralph R.: 1521
Ruppenthal, Karl M.: 2598
Russell, J. F. S.: 2570, 2616
Russett, Bruce M.: 1343
Russo, James R.: 913
Rustin, Randall: 2239, 2240
Ryan, Frank M.: 2236
Ryan, Paul R.: 153
Ryan, William G.: 754

S

Sabourin, Leopold: 535
Sadie, Stanley: 176
Sadofsky, Michael D.: 1798
Sage, Andrew P.: 1743
St. Cyr, Napoleon: 514
Saito, T.: 1871
Salerno, Henry F.: 152
Sallis, John: 467
Salomon, Dr. Herman P.: 532
Salti, Danielle: 725
Salzberg, Kathleen A.: 607
Salzman, Ed: 1335
Sams, Carol: 986
Samuels, Warren J.: 775
Sanberg, Patricia: 2446

References in Index refer to entry numbers

Editorial staff index

Sanderson, Edward W.: 2332
Sanderson, Dr. George R.: 1001
Sanderson, George R.: 1001
Sands, William: 675
Sanford, Ann L.: 1448
Sanford, Jonathan E.: 715
Sankar, D. Barbara: 1874
Sankey, Harriet E.: 2256
San Pietro, A.: 1900
Sartorelli, Prof. Alan C.: 2072
Sato, Ryo: 2101
Sauer, F.: 1900
Savage, Peter: 1242
Scaer, David P.: 601
Scalapino, Robert A.: 636
Scalf, Robert Alan: 1223
Scebold, C. Edward: 967
Schadler, Robert A.: 27, 67
Schaefer, William D.: 400
Schalk, Carl: 139
Schaum, Jack H.: 1702
Schechter, Professor M. M.: 2444
Scheidlinger, Saul: 1402
Schiebler, Professor Dr. T. H.: 2094
Schievella, P. S.: 446
Schlegel, Professor H. G.: 1892
Schlegel, Ronald J.: 549
Schlesinger, Herbert J.: 1470
Schmalstieg, William Riegel: 208
Schmidt, Richard A.: 1434
Schmidt, Robert: 2198
Schneider, C. K.: 1624
Schneider, Harold: 495
Schnepf, Max Owen: 1841
Schnucker, Robert V.: 112, 1182
Schoen, Eileen F.: 35, 2563
Schoenberg, Carl: 1500
Schoengood, A.A.: 1783, 2606
Schoffeniels, E.: 1898
Scholler, R.: 2120
Schorr, Thelma M.: 2520
Schroder, Marvin: 2285
Schrumpf, Susan S.: 924
Schubert, Leo: 991
Schuck, Marjorie: 511
Schukraft, Bernard: 1604
Schulert, Barbara R.: 1250
Schultz, Dr. Rudolph: 1448
Schutz, Richard E.: 954
Schwab, Elena Laborde: 435
Schwartz, Donald E.: 1286
Schwartz, Katherine B.: 743
Schwartz, Lucille J.: 1330
Schweiger, Irving: 770
Scofield, Norma C.: 1560
Scott, Al: 2578
Scott, D. B.: 2306
Scott, Douglas: 1801, 2029
Scott, Ian: 1713
Scott, John: 1662
Scott, Loren C.: 786
Scott, Jr., Nathan A.: 571
Scott, Robert L.: 898
Scott, Virginia: 156
Scott, William R.: 2218
Scott, William W.: 2373
Seaborn, H. T.: 2229
Sears, Margaret: 1435
Sears, Robert R.: 724
Seavey, Ormond A.: 497
Seeliger, Ronald: 316
Seever, Claudine: 13

Segal, A.: 613
Segaloff, Albert: 2125
Seibel, L.: 2309
Seidel, Linda: 86
Seinfeld, John H.: 1720
Self, J. Teague: 1902
Sellon, Emily: 450
Senturia, Ben H.: 2281
Sergeant, Howard: 508
Sergent, Dr. F.: 1813
Series, Professor G. W.: 2156
Serrin, J.: 2194
Sewell, Sallie W.: 783
Shafer, Dale M.: 1069
Shaffer, Jay C.: 1903
Shanin, Teodor: 709
Shannon, Dianne M.: 1084
Shannon, Robert F. J.: 619
Shapin, Betty: 1457
Shapiro, H. A.: 2346
Shapiro, Karl: 477
Shapiro, Nancy: 523
Sharabi, Hisham B.: 673
Sharp, Frank W.: 1790
Sharpe, Myron E.: 759
Sharrer, Harvey L.: 221
Shaw, Prof. D. M.: 2093
Shaw, Prof. M. C.: 1750
Shaw, Michael: 1954
Shaw, Stanford J.: 671
Shea, James H.: 1003
Shea, John S.: 186
Shelledy, Louise B.: 295
Shelton, Ralph L.: 2412
Shemer, Dr. Jack E.: 2229
Sherier, Jean K.: 2464
Sherman, Murray H.: 1467
Sherrington, Andrew M.: 1875
Sherwood, Mary P.: 429
Shideler, James H.: 1875, 1880
Shipley, Grant: 1236
Shipley, T.: 2493
Shira, Robert B.: 2516
Shneidman, Edwin S.: 1488
Shokoff, James: 152
Shontz, Patricia J.: 806
Shulman, Joel J.: 2602
Shumate, Paul W.: 1742
Siddall, George: 1628
Siddons, James: 175
Sidowski, Joseph B.: 1374
Sifneos, Peter E.: 1481
Signorelli, Peggy J.: 1202
Silber, Hazel: 578
Silverman, Robert J.: 185, 1004
Silverstein, Charles: 1430
Silvey, Larry: 62
Simberloff, Daniel: 1107
Simon, Brian: 968
Simons, Lennart: 2027
Simonton, Wesley: 288
Simpson, H. C.: 1595
Simpson, Lewis P.: 518
Simpson, Raymond A.: 994
Singer, Armand E.: 249
Singh, Raman K.: 419
Single, J. T.: 2071
Sinick, Daniel: 1096
Sinor, Prof. Denis: 1150
Sirocky, Gerald J.: 730
Sisterson, William D.: 531
Sitzer, William: 1285

Skaer, Dr. R. J.: 1929
Skeen, Matthew D.: 1302
Skelton, Robin: 498
Skinner, David B.: 2537
Skinsnes, Olaf K.: 2369
Slade, Joseph W.: 98
Slade, Valeda: 2366
Slater, Jane: 1222
Slater, Michael: 346
Slaughter, John B.: 2230
Slavin, Sabina: 2175
Sleeman, Dr. Phillip J.: 984
Sloan, James J.: 1115
Sloan, William: 270
Slochower, Harry: 1363
Smiley, Douglas V.: 1210
Smith, Alan K.: 632
Smith, Arthur L.: 615
Smith, Austin C.: 1463
Smith, Clement A.: 2460
Smith, D. V.: 524
Smith, Denis: 691
Smith, Elizabeth C.: 2447
Smith, F. May: 1700
Smith, J. B.: 1994
Smith, Jesse M.: 829
Smith, Jessica: 655
Smith, Dr. Lorraine C.: 1864
Smith, M. Geraldine: 1585, 1704
Smith, Marcus: 102
Smith, Margaret F.: 1848
Smith, Mary Jeanette: 286
Smith, Patricia Scherf: 1522
Smith, Philip C.F.: 1119
Smith, Ralph A.: 987
Smith, Robert R.: 890
Smith, Robin C.: 903
Smith, Sydney R.: 1449
Smolker, Rosemary G.: 1942
Smoluchowski, R.: 2028
Sneddon, I. N.: 1748
Snell, Esmond E.: 1896
Snyder, Donald C.: 2558
Sobels, Frits H.: 1937
Sobocinski, Boleslaw: 2215
Soffer, Alfred: 2320
Sokal, Robert R.: 1862
Sokoloff, Boris: 1921
Solheim, Wilhelm G.: 1635
Sollid, John: 520
Sollid, Karen: 520
Sonstegard, Manford A.: 1397
Soper, Prof. Alexander C.: 133
Sovik, Ruth: 566
Spadafora, Jo-Una: 1246
Spahr, Frederick T.: 1495
Spanos, William V.: 476
Spaulding, Julie McCoy: 2393
Spaulding, Phinizy: 1138
Spears, Dr. Betty: 1055
Spector, Hal: 831, 889, 2284, 2329, 2358, 2474
Spence, Janet: 1388
Spence, Richard L.: 891
Spencer, Paul: 374
Spencer, Robert: 612
Spengler, Kenneth C.: 1644, 1655, 1695, 2032
Spera, Diane: 836
Sperry, John B.: 741
Spiess, Eliot B.: 1918
Spilhaus, A.F.: 1861, 2151

References in Index refer to entry numbers

Spilka, Mark: 397
Spiotta, Raymond H.: 2599
Spiro, Leon: 521
Sprague, Roderick: 1555
Springborn, R.K.: 1620
Spurgeon, David C.: 1623
Squilbin, R.: 2614
Staab, Fred L.: 1086
Staab, Robin B.: 1086
Stack, H. Graham: 2353
Staehle, Roger W.: 1727
Stafford, William T.: 384
Stahel, Thomas H.: 527
Stahl, Arthur: 2
Stahl, Charles J.: 1605
Staley, Thomas F.: 367
Stamm, Colleen P.: 1027
Stampfle, Felice: 169
Stanford, Donald E.: 518
Stange, Douglas C.: 580
Stanick, Katherine C.: 254
Stanley, Scott: 1332
Stapert, John A.: 544
Starr, Gary S.: 1217
Starr, M. K.: 833
Stasny, John F.: 434
Stearns, Peter N.: 1157
Steckler, Larry: 1791
Steeves, Edna L.: 231
Stefanile, Felix: 519
Stefanile, Selma: 519
Stein, Arnold: 348
Stein, Hank: 2567
Stein, Janet: 1960
Steinberg, Florence: 135
Steingiser, Samuel: 2107
Stelzner, Hermann G.: 864
Stempel, Randall: 883
Stephen, Dr. T.: 2129, 2130
Stephens, Anne M.: 2359
Stephens, Robert J.: 2359
Stephenson, Jean T.: 618, 1840
Sterling, Christopher H.: 893
Stern, Burton L.: 2576
Stern, Norton B.: 1189
Stettenheim, Dr. Peter R.: 1984
Stevenson, W. Taylor: 533
Stevermark, Al: 2122
Stewart, Charlotte C.: 367
Stewart, Daniel K.: 846
Stewart, Dr. Robert A. C.: 1486
Stewart, Virginia E.: 2068
Stillman, Dr. Mary E.: 304
Stippes, Marvin: 1603
Stivers, Patricia E.: 910, 954, 1063
Stock, Dr. Jan H.: 1986
Stoeckle, John: 720
Stohler, R.: 2018
Stone, Charles F.: 115
Stone, Evelyn M.: 1447
Stone, Harold: 2379
Stone, Morris: 1199
Storch, Raymond: 1281
Stotts, Michael J.: 2395
Stout, J. W.: 2149
Straschnov, J.: 887
Strässler, S.: 2169
Strauss, Sheldon D.: 1784
Strehler, B. L.: 1870
Streiff, E. B.: 2455
Strelow, Michael H.: 507
Stringer, Jerry R.: 608

Stritch, Thomas: 1351
Strong, John W.: 647
Strong, Sally R.: 2593
Strother, John L.: 1962
Stroupe, C. J.: 143
Styles, Martin: 2066
Sudarshan, E.C.G.: 2140
Sullivan, Alvin: 398
Sullivan, Barbara E.: 1297
Summers, Murray: 877
Sussex, R.T.: 198
Svec, A.: 2145
Swain, T.: 1898, 1965
Swallow, Mrs. J. C.: 1692
Swanson, Donald E.: 2595, 2605
Swartz, Clifford: 1052
Sweeney, Russell: 265
Sweezy, Paul: 1345
Swidler, Leonard: 569
Swift, Elizabeth P.: 698
Swinburne, Henry: 2571
Swinney, Donald: 192

T
Taff, Charles A.: 1296
Tagnon, Dr. H. J.: 2339
Tanner, Janis H.: 2451
Tanner, Prof. James M.: 1888
Tanner, W. F.: 1593
Tapp, E. Gordon: 1656, 1680
Tapp, Hambleton: 1160
Tarascio, Vincent J.: 805
Tardivelle, Merren: 2524
Tarumoto, D. H.: 1738
Tate, Charles D.: 537
Tatlow, J. C.: 2109
Taxis, Linda A.: 738
Taylor, Blaine: 2424
Taylor, Edwin F.: 911
Taylor, John: 95
Tebben, Marian Priest: 2469
Tedrow, J.C.F.: 1886
Ternes, Alan: 1612
Terrell, Jennifer A. K.: 642
Terry, Michael O.: 1309
Terry, Robbyelee: 53
TeSeller, Sallie: 113
Teuber, Prof. H. L.: 2443
Tewinkel, G. C.: 2042
Theobald, Budd: 1075
Thériault, Michel: 685
Thirsk, Prof. H. R.: 2091
Thomas, Garth J.: 1417
Thomas, Geraldine R.: 1459
Thomas, Kogee: 680
Thomas, Marc E.: 1249
Thompson, Clarence H.: 944
Thompson, G. R.: 354, 401
Thompson, James H.: 832
Thompson, Dr. R. E. M.: 2296
Thompson, Ralph B.: 751
Thompson, Robert C.: 2211
Thompson, W. B.: 2161
Thomson, R. G.: 2308
Thorne, Eleanor C.: 1477
Thorpe, Lewis: 105, 364, 364, 396
Thurston, Helen M.: 1175
Thurston, Jarvis: 509
Tice, Linwood F.: 2270
Tiedt, Dr. Iris M.: 961
Tiefenbrun, Susan: 408
Tietze, Dr. Wolf: 1101

Tilden, Lola S.: 1578
Tillett, Susan C.: 1268
Timell, T. E.: 1976
Timman, R.: 2204
Tobias, Prof. S. A.: 1750
Todd, Wayne E.: 289
Todd, William B.: 258, 325
Toedtman, James: 2600
Toelken, J. Barre: 1547
Toguri, J. M.: 1717
Tokes, Rudolf L.: 1358
Tolzmann, Don H.: 441
Tomasi, S. M.: 1546
Tomkievicz, Shirley: 25
Tomlinson, T. B.: 341
Tongiorgi, Ezio: 1671
Tonne, Dr. Elizabeth V.: 990
Towns, Fred B.: 2254
Townsend, Peter: 190
Trabasso, Tom: 1385
Tracey, Andrew T. N.: 128
Trager, George L.: 247
Trent, Richard D.: 678
Treptow, Marjorie D.: 2432
Trethaway, Robert C.: 990
Treynor, Jack L.: 814
Trigg, George L.: 2164
Tripp, Wendell: 1173
Trisco, Robert: 539
Trist, Eric: 704
Trotter, Sharland: 1371
Truesdell, C.: 1588, 2194
Trussler, Simon: 194
Tsai, Dr. Stephen W.: 1757
Tuck, Charles A.: 1737
Tuinman, J. Jaap: 1011
Tuley, Robert J.: 170
Tummons, Patricia: 118
Tune, Newell W.: 1080
Turano, Jane V.: 131
Turekian, Karl K.: Edward A.: 2151
Turnbull, William L.: 681
Turner, Arlin: 323
Turner, Dorothea F.: 2256
Turner, Tom: 1847
Turunen, M. I.: 2278
Tuzi, Yutaka: 2147
Twaddle, Michael: 629
Twersky, Dorianna: 2176, 2180
Tylenda, Joseph N.: 603
Tyler, Tracy F.: 1032
Tyner, Raymond: 87

U
Ueda, Hideo: 2376
Uetake, Hisao: 1926
Uhl, Joseph N.: 28, 772, 772
Uhlig, Dr. George E.: 1005
Uiker, Prof. John J.: 1775
Ullrich, Helen D.: 1008
Ulman, Elinor: 1364
Unfug, Douglas A.: 1130
Urquhart, Effie B.: 719
Usher, Newell E.: 942
Uslaner, Selma: 1795
Utton, Albert E.: 1846

V
Valtonen, V.: 2279
Van Ausdall, Gay: 843
Van Cott, Harold P.: 1438
Van Dellen, Theodore R.: 2361

References in Index refer to entry numbers

Editorial staff index

Van den Berg, Ger P.: 1280
Vandenberg, Steven G.: 1895
Van Demark, Robert E.: 2485
van der Brugghen, W.: 269
Van Duyn, Mona: 509
van Luijk, H.: 536
Vann, Richard T.: 1143
van Oss, Carel J.: 1941, 2362
van Raalte, Mrs. Miep: 1026
Van Stone, James W.: 1957, 1989
van Tamelen, Eugene F.: 2074
van Woerden, A. V. N.: 1146
Varma, Shanti Prasad: 645
Vars, Gordon F.: 945
Vasquez, Alma G.: 1005
Vaughan, Alan: 1465
Vaughan, Prof. Richard: 1153
Veaner, Allen B.: 292
Veraguth, Prof. P.: 2470
Verhaar, John W. M.: 236
Vernon, McCay: 906, 2253
Veronis, George: 1694
Vertinsky, Ilan: 771
Vesa, Unto: 1341
Vesell, Dr. E. S.: 2463
Viberti, Victor L.: 587
Vicinus, Martha: 124
Victor, Janet Marshall: 2615
Videbaek, Aage: 2477
Villemain, Francis I.: 1083, 2530
Vineyard, Jerry D.: 1688
Voegelin, C. F.: 216
Voegelin, Florence M.: 197
Vogelsang, Arthur: 473
Vollmuth, John: 2560
Vollono, Ralph: 1287
von Frisch, K.: 2384
Vorwerk, Elsa L.: 1531
Voss, Edward G.: 1963
Voss, W. A. Geoffrey: 1764

W

Wade, C.B.: 955
Wager, Walter: 2565
Wagner, Robert P.: 1897
Wainwright, E. H.: 1687
Wakeling, P. R.: 2023
Walby, Basil: 1950
Walcher, Wilhelm: 2132
Waldman, Martin H.: 831, 889, 2284, 2329,
    2358, 2474
Walker, M.T.: 1318
Wall, James M.: 542
Wall, Stephen: 355
Wallace, Gary O.: 2013
Wallace, P. R.: 2136
Wallin, Einar: 1712
Walsh, Margaret M.: 794
Walsh, Michael J.: 583
Walter, Nicholas: 38
Walton, Gary: 765
Walton, Prof. John N.: 2402
Walwin-Jones, Dennis: 332
Ward, Dr. Robert E.: 360
Wardell, Dwight: 935
Ware, Kallistos Timothy: 556
Ware, Dr. Martin: 2303
Warga, J.: 2220
Warick, G. P.: 2082
Warner, Dr. Lee: 281
Warnock-Smith, Neil: 1051, 2159

Warren, Sue Allen: 1451
Washburn, A. L.: 1663
Washburn, Brian H.: 1468
Wassenaar, Dirk: 51
Wasserman, Clifford: 1265
Wasserman, Prof. H. H.: 2129, 2130
Waszink, Paul M.: 226
Waterhouse, Dr. J. P.: 2499
Waters, William R.: 801
Watkins, Sylvestre C.: 37
Watson, H. Lee: 1205
Watson, Robert I.: 708
Watson, Thomas S.: 192
Watts, Dr. David: 1107
Wax, Bernard: 530
Waxman, Ruth B.: 574
Wayne, Richard P.: 2117
Wayner, Matthew J.: 1873
Weaver, Clarence L.: 474
Weaver, Gordon: 499
Webb, Robert K.: 1118
Webb, Stewart: 1257
Weber, Derek: 1104
Weber, Jeffery D.: 2626
Weddle, A. E.: 1843
Weerts, Richard Kenneth: 177
Weidel, Ruth Ann: 1281
Weiderman, Richard L.: 380
Weidlein, Edward R.: 934
Weiland, Paula: 33
Weinberg, Meyer: 981
Weinberger, Hans F.: 2189
Weiner, Gerald: 1878
Weiner, Skip: 886
Weinfeld, E.: 1340
Weinhouse, Sidney: 2315
Weintraub, Samuel: 1058
Weintraub, Stanley: 415
Weisenborn, Eleanor: 2193
Weiss, Allen: 732
Weiss, Daniel: 2264
Weiss, George H.: 1855
Weiss, René: 402
Weiss, T.: 402
Wellensiek, S.J.: 1974
Wells, James M.: 104
Welsh, Alexander: 393
Wensberg, Erik: 14
Wenzel, Professor Dr. H. G.: 2338
Wertheim, Lee Hilles: 1282
West, Tristram F.: 1884, 2041, 2075, 2084,
    2100
Weymueller, Carl R.: 1776
Whaley, Sara S.: 1583
Wheeler, Harriette M: 1135
Whitaker, Thomas: 494
White, Prof. Denis N.: 2490
White, John S.: 1685
White, Robert L.: 686
White, Prof. S. H.: 1414
White, William: 436
Whitehead, Marvin D.: 1598
Whiteleather, Alan K.: 751
Whitesell, J. Edwin: 357
Whitney, Antony: 2572
Whitney, Ellen M.: 1144
Whitney, Harvey A. K.: 2335
Whittingham, Dr. C. P.: 1959
Widger, Jean I: 2471
Wiecking, David K.: 2435
Wied, George L.: 2250
Wieder, Samuel: 2184

Wiedyke, Robert G.: 1586
Wiener, Philip P.: 92
Wigginton, Waller E: 49
Wigglesworth, V. B.: 1929
Wikoff, Wally: 884
Wilcox, Marilyn M.: 372
Wilder, Warren: 239
Wiley, Donald L.: 2612
Wiley, Martin L.: 1814
Wilfong, W. Thomas: 657
Wilgus, D. K.: 1574
Wilkenfield, Jonathan: 614
Williams, Mrs. Carol: 838
Williams, Edwin E.: 272
Williams, Herman J.: 1381
Williams, J. C.: 1618
Williams, Jim: 826
Williams, Joanna: 1421
Williams, M.L.: 2030
Williams, Mary C.: 517
Williams, Patricia M.: 1989
Williams, Peyton W.: 694
Williams, Ruthann: 179
Williams, W. M.: 1564
Williamson, Clark M.: 557
Williamson, H. W.: 1645
Williamson, H.: 1716, 1812, 1906, 1954,
    1981, 2312
Willis, Paul J.: 1601
Willmer, Prof. E. N.: 1904
Willson, A. Leslie: 204
Wilmsen, Edwin N.: 1630
Wilson, Alan G.: 1823
Wilson, C. B.: 1714
Wilson, Elwyn E.: 1658
Wilson, Everett K.: 1560
Wilson, Jean D.: 2382
Wilson, Leonard G.: 2390
Wilson, M. Kent: 2045
Wilson, Mrs. N. H.: 84, 631
Wilson, Robert A.: 870
Wilson, Robley: 505
Wilson, Steve: 687
Wilson, Wayne D.: 1208
Wimmer, Lynn C.: 2357
Windhauser, John: 881
Windriech, Lee: 261
Windsor, Robert K.: 2223
Winger, Howard W.: 266, 287
Winkel, Gary H.: 1822
Wise, David A.: 1350
Wison, Dr. Kathleen J. W.: 2523
Witt, Dr. Peter A.: 1512
Wittkower, Eric D.: 1491
Wittman, Gerald P.: 1251
Wittusen, Robin: 1097
Wolf, Dr. Irvin S.: 1472
Wolf-Heidegger, G.: 2249
Wolfe, David E.: 1435
Wolfe, Lois Lauer: 1579
Wolkin, Paul A.: 1276
Wollman, Leo: 2277
Wolpe, Prof. Joseph: 1413
Wolpert, Professor L.: 1933
Wolsky, Dr. Alexander: 2453
Wonderley, A. Wayne: 227
Wonn, David E.: 1787
Wood, Charles L.: 914
Wood, Donald E.: 2569
Wood, Fay M.: 2506
Woodard, G. D.: 1610
Woodbridge, Hensley Charles: 366

References in Index refer to entry numbers

Woodcock, George: 333
Woodcock, Prof. C. L. F.: 1969
Woodford-Williams, E.: 2350
Woodruff, Laurence: 2008
Woodruff, Robert Eugene: 1983
Woods, John: 443
Woody, Edgar: 2425
Woolf, Mary M.: 888
Wooten, Elizabeth: 902
Wortis, Joseph: 1377
Wortley, John: 386
Wortman, Philip W.: 1009
Wosk, Julie: 339
Wright, Benjamin D.: 1094
Wright, Earl O.: 1868
Wrolstad, Merald E.: 248
Wylder, Delbert: 999
Wyllie, Peter J.: 1672
Wynar, Dr. L. R.: 663

Y
Yamamoto, Kaoru: 910
Yarwood, J.: 2046
Yates, John: 2146
Yaver, Joseph: 1781
Ybarra, Andres: 19
Young, Diana R.: 1591, 1592
Young, George B.: 2593
Young, James Dean: 342
Young, Peter: 110
Youngman, Bruce: 2178

Z
Zacek, Joyce D.: 790
Zambito, Raymond F.: 2511
Zao, Zang Z.: 2386
Zaretsky, Eli: 1356
Zartman, I. William: 676
Zeig, Robert: 2573
Zelditch, Morris: 1533
Zellmer, William A.: 2265
Zemel, Jay N.: 1628
Ziebarth, Marilyn: 1125
Ziedonis, Arvids: 652
Ziegelmueller, George W.: 896
Ziegler, Jesse H.: 1090
Ziemba, Joseph: 1835, 1858
Zienkiewicz, Olgierd C.: 1747
Zier, Mark A.: 604
Zimmerman, V. K.: 734
Zoellner, N.: 2449
Zuck, Dr. Donald A.: 2311
Zucker, Bennett: 2420
Zucker, Sydney A.: 107
Zuckerkandl, Dr. E.: 1932

References in Index refer to entry numbers

N
6944
S3
D57
1975